PRESENTED TO

Caroline Summar

BY:

ON:

Then he said to me,
"These words are faithful and true."

—Revelation 22:6a

CSB Restoration Bible

CSB Restoration Bible

Embracing God's Word in Difficult Seasons

Stephen Arterburn, General Editor

J. D. Green, Associate Editor

David Veerman, Managing Editor

HOLMAN BIBLE PUBLISHERS
NASHVILLE, TENNESSEE

Life Restoration Bible

Produced with the assistance of Livingstone, the Publishing Services Division of Barton-Veerman Co. (www.livingstonecorp.com). Project Staff include David Veerman, Bruce Barton, Linda Taylor, Ross DeLong, Larry Taylor, Ashley Taylor, Tom Shumaker.

Proofreading was provided by Peachtree Editorial Services, Peachtree City, Georgia.

Topical index used by permission of the Barton-Veerman Company © 2018.

Binding	***ISBN***
Paperback	978-1-4627-9690-8
Brown LeatherTouch	978-1-4627-9691-5
Brown LeatherTouch Indexed	978-1-4627-9692-2

Printed in China

1 2 3 4 5 — 20 19 18

RRD

Contents

Books of the Bible (arranged alphabetically)

Preface to the | CSB Restoration Bible

By Stephen Arterburn

You are holding in your hands the culmination of a dream that was birthed over ten years ago. That's when the hope for the *CSB Restoration Bible* was birthed, a Bible for those who are in difficult seasons of life. If you are like me, those seasons seem to be more frequent than the easy ones. For some of us, struggle seems to be more of a reality than times without it. But in the struggle of those difficult seasons, we can come to know God better and experience his presence in a deeper and richer way. When we turn to him, we grow into a finer, more meaningful way of life full with a new sense of purpose and promise. The path and the process to a new life of purpose and promise is found in God's Word where his truth can transform us.

Isaiah 40:8 says that the grass withers and flowers fade but the Word of God remains forever. Hebrews 4:12 states that God's Word is "living and effective and sharper than any double-edged sword, penetrating as far as the separation of soul and spirit, joints and marrow. It is able to judge the thoughts and intentions of the heart." God's Word is powerful like nothing else on this earth, and it is at all times right at our fingertips. In all of my struggles, I have never found it lacking in what I needed as long as I was willing to do what it instructed me to do. Sadly, just reading Scripture in older translations with little to help me fully understand it made it difficult to determine the real meaning or the "true truth" as I call it. I needed help in knowing what God intended each passage to mean for me and the struggle I was facing. The *CSB Restoration Bible* is designed to make the path and process that God intends for you easy to find and follow. It can become your most valuable tool in doing the work that is needed to restore what is broken or shore up what needs to be strengthened.

To help you the most, this Bible utilizes the Christian Standard Bible translation. It is accurate, easy to read, and a great tool in clearly understanding the intent of any verse or passage. Added to this powerful translation is the result of thousands of hours of work to develop notes, devotional themes, explanations of key passages, the seven Restoration Principles, and rich insights on how to RESTORE your soul and repair redemptive relationships.

Throughout the *CSB Restoration Bible*, I highlight the need and benefits of rest and reflection, the value of support from others, the results of exercising our faith, and so many more areas that will impact you directly at the point of your greatest need. If you will not just read this Bible but study it daily, you will find new hope within its covers and countless innovative and powerful ways to access and experience that hope. I invite you to open up this collection of God's Word, read it, study it, and then do what it challenges you to do. If you accept this invitation, it is my sincere belief and intense desire that you will experience a restoration—a complete life restoration—and your life will be transformed forever.

Overview of Restoration Principles

R - Rest and Reflection

This Restoration Principle focuses on taking the time to slow down—to rest and reflect on the life issue, circumstance, or difficult season we face. Through rest and reflection, we gain new insights and perspectives that help foster honesty, admission, responsibility, and a right attitude as we begin our journey toward life restoration.

"Come to me, all of you who are weary and burdened, and I will give you rest"
(Matthew 11:28).

E - Eternal Perspective

This Restoration Principle focuses on developing an eternal perspective toward the life issue, circumstance, or difficult season. When we begin to understand who God is, and when we accept and stand on the promises and truths found in God's Word, we are empowered to walk forward with confidence and hope in our restoration journey.

"For I know the plans I have for you" — this is the LORD's declaration — "plans for your well-being, not for disaster, to give you a future and a hope"
(Jeremiah 29:11).

S - Support

This Restoration Principle focuses on having the humility and strength to ask for help and support as we continue on the path toward life restoration. We were never meant to do life alone. Hope, joy, and peace come when we humble ourselves before God, fully surrender our lives to Jesus Christ, and invite others to come alongside us to help us in our journey.

"So I say to you, ask, and it will be given to you. Seek, and you will find. Knock, and the door will be opened to you"
(Luke 11:9).

T - Thanksgiving and Contentment

This Restoration Principle focuses on being thankful and content with God's blessings so that we remove any obstacles that may prevent us from being good stewards of those blessings. Thankfulness and contentment bring us joy and peace as we continue this journey of restoration and grow in our relationship with Jesus.

Give thanks in everything; for this is God's will for you in Christ Jesus
(1 Thessalonians 5:18).

O - Other-centeredness

We all have a tendency to be self-centered, particularly in difficult seasons of life. This Restoration Principle focuses on exhibiting the love of Jesus to family, friends, coworkers, and others in need. Letting go of selfish desires and earthly security and choosing instead to focus on others and the truth of God's Word bring us freedom and joy.

"This is my command: Love one another as I have loved you"
(John 15:12).

R - Relationships

This Restoration Principle focuses on restoring relationships, resolving relational conflicts, and accepting forgiveness from those we may have wronged or giving forgiveness to those who may have wronged us. Life restoration comes through living in community and right relationship with others, so that we may encourage one another, serve one another, keep one another accountable, and experience the harmony and reward of restored relationships.

Two are better than one because they have a
good reward for their efforts
(Ecclesiastes 4:9).

E - Exercise of Faith

This Restoration Principle focuses on exercising and living out our faith through service to others. This includes trusting God, applying Scripture in our everyday life, helping other Christians grow in their faith, and sharing the good news of the gospel with those who may not know Jesus. Lasting life restoration is found and sustained when we are able to share our restoration story and the hope, joy, and peace we found in God's Word and a personal relationship with Jesus Christ.

Just as each one has received a gift, use it to serve others,
as good stewards of the varied grace of God
(1 Peter 4:10).

How to Use the | CSB Restoration Bible

The *CSB Restoration Bible* is designed with an easy-to-follow format that includes over 450 Guided and devotional style RESTORE notes placed throughout the Bible that expound upon the seven Restoration Principles through related topics and verses via an easy-to-remember R.E.S.T.O.R.E acrostic.

Rest and Reflection
Eternal Perspective
Support
Thanksgiving and Contentment
Other-centeredness
Relationships
Exercise of Faith

The RESTORE notes are where the "rubber meets the road" in the restoration process and are permeated with the hope, joy, and peace found in the good news of the gospel and through a personal relationship with Jesus Christ.

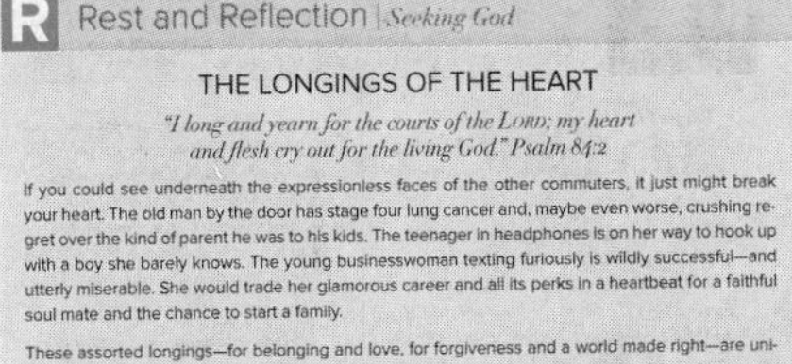

R Rest and Reflection | *Seeking God*

THE LONGINGS OF THE HEART

"I long and yearn for the courts of the LORD; my heart and flesh cry out for the living God." Psalm 84:2

If you could see underneath the expressionless faces of the other commuters, it just might break your heart. The old man by the door has stage four lung cancer and, maybe even worse, crushing regret over the kind of parent he was to his kids. The teenager in headphones is on her way to hook up with a boy she barely knows. The young businesswoman texting furiously is wildly successful—and utterly miserable. She would trade her glamorous career and all its perks in a heartbeat for a faithful soul mate and the chance to start a family.

These assorted longings—for belonging and love, for forgiveness and a world made right—are universal. We see glimpses of them in songs and movies. We sometimes get a taste of them in our own human interactions. The psalmist, however, understood that all these deep yearnings are satisfied ultimately only in the Lord. Saint Augustine put it well, "You have made us for yourself, O God, and our hearts are restless till they rest in you."

When do you sense your earthly longings pointing to something deeper?

For the next note on *Rest and Reflection*, see Psalm 104:24.

R Rest and Reflection | *Reflecting*

ONE EYE ON THE FUTURE

"Look, I am coming soon, and my reward is with me to repay each person according to his work." Revelation 22:12

Socrates famously said, "The unexamined life is not worth living."

Anyone who has been around a while has experienced this truth. Life has a way of sucking us in and turning us into hamsters on a wheel. Soon we are running furiously, but we have no idea why. Some people spend an entire lifetime never asking important questions such as, *Where am I going? Why am I doing what I'm doing? Am I spending my life in ways that matter?*

Thus the value of an examined life! Of regularly calling time out. Of routinely unplugging from all the trivial froth and bubble of life. Of rigorously reflecting on what's true—like this promise of the Lord.

Do you see it? Jesus will return! And when he does, John says we will each have a face-to-face audience with him. It will be like an annual job review—only this one will encompass our entire lives!

Because this great eternal reality is true, we must take time to examine and reflect. Healthy souls do this—they live fully and wisely in the present, but always with one eye on this great day still to come.

For the first note on *Eternal Perspective*, see Genesis 1:1.

Each RESTORE note always makes the next step in your restoration journey easy to find, engage, and apply by providing the Scripture reference for the next note in that Restoration Principle at the end of the entry.

Once you have worked through all the RESTORE notes for a particular Restoration Principle, the last note will point you to the first note for the next Restoration Principle. For example, on the last note for "Rest and Reflection," you will be pointed to the first note for "Eternal Perspective."

Each book introduction also includes a list of the RESTORE notes for each Restoration Principle found in that book.

RESTORATION THEMES

R	Rest and Reflection	*Resting and Recharging—26:17-18*
E	Eternal Perspective	*God's Grace/Kindness—15:11* *God's Plans—16:6-7*
S	Support	*Prayer—6:4*
T	Thanksgiving and Contentment	*For the next note, see Roman 3:23-24.*
O	Other-centeredness	*Giving Generously—4:32* *Praying for Others—9:3-4* *Encouraging—9:26-27*
R	Relationships	*Being Impartial—10:34-35* *Resolving Arguments/Disagreements/Conflicts—15:37-39*
E	Exercise of Faith	*Sharing Faith/Gospel—1:8; 4:19-20; 16:14* *Being Involved in Church—2:42* *Reflecting Christ—4:13* *Setting a Good Example—7:59-60* *Rejecting False Teaching—20:30* *Sharing Story—22:3*

In addition to the over 500 extensive and guided RESTORE notes, there are many other restoration-focused features and study helps to encourage you on your journey. A short description of each feature is below (an index of all RESTORE notes and the additional features listed below can be found starting on page XLV).

- Thirty Restoration Devotions—daily devotionals focused on the parables of Jesus and the story of the Prodigal Son in Luke 15.
- Sixty-six Restoration profiles of biblical people and My Story notes from real-life people who found true and lasting life restoration through the power of Christ and the truths found in God's Word.

My Story | Marvin

Life was good. My kids, grown and on their own, were flourishing. My wife and I were enjoying the empty nest—no grandkids yet, but plenty to keep us busy, especially at church. Relationships and responsibilities were on track at work. And I felt fine physically. But I suffered from a severe case of the blahs.

As I sat in worship, settling in for the sermon, I heard the pastor read the Bible text on which the message would be based. It was familiar—Psalm 51—so I listened only half paying attention. But when he came to verse 12, "Restore the joy of your salvation to me, and sustain me by giving me a willing spirit," I began to tear up. My reaction was surprising because I don't cry much. But that phrase, "restore the joy of your salvation," got to me. And I realized what was missing—I had lost the jo... Life was good, but I was going through the motions with my living ... I want to know you, to love you with all ... significant

Joseph | Restoration Profile

GENESIS 37–50; HEBREWS 11:22

One of the ways of picturing restoration is to describe it as keeping up to date on our relationship with God. Joseph is a prime biblical example of this practice. He did not let the setbacks and disappointments in his life pile up; each one was firmly put behind him as yet another reminder, not that life was unfair, but that God was in control.

In his youth, God gave Joseph amazing dreams and their interpretation that Joseph didn't manage well. This, combined with the handicap of being his father's favorite, set into motion events that severely tested Joseph's willingness to trust God. Joseph experienced firsthand the betrayal of brothers, a boss's wife, and someone he had helped. Each disappointment seemed to take Joseph further from the possibility of his early dreams coming true. Yet he continued on, doggedly and cheerfully, rising from each blow to make the best of his circumstances.

Later we learn the thought and prayer process that Joseph used to restore his equilibrium with each setback. When his brothers revealed that they still lived in abject fear of their little brother's possible reprisals, Joseph explained that their guilt and anxiety had been wasted: "You planned evil against me; God planned it for good to bring about the present result—the survival of many people" (Gn 50:20). He could have said the same thing to Potiphar's wife and the forgetful cupbearer.

We can benefit from Joseph's wise approach to life. When we learn to recognize God's hand in everything, even in those experiences we can't understand and when we can't actually see his hand, we are traveling in the way of restoration.

- Ten Embracing God's Word charts with multiple Scripture references for important faith and restoration topics.
- Over one hundred Joyful Noise designed callouts embedded within the biblical text of Scripture passages that offer hope, encouragement, and joy to accompany you on your journey.
- A Topical Index structured in a "When you need . . ." and "When you feel . . ." format pointing you to applicable RESTORE notes, other restoration features, and Scripture references. This also includes a "What the Bible Says about . . ." section.
- Bible Reading Plans to read through the entire Bible in one year or three years.
- A 52-Week Scripture Memory Plan based on fifty-two biblical topics and associated biblical concepts.

We recommend that you begin your restoration journey with the thirty days of Restoration Devotions (page XIII). Beginning with this daily devotional will help you to prayerfully evaluate where you are in your personal journey as you prepare to explore, engage, embrace, and apply the truths found in God's Word and the restoration-focused features and study helps included in the *CSB Restoration Bible*.

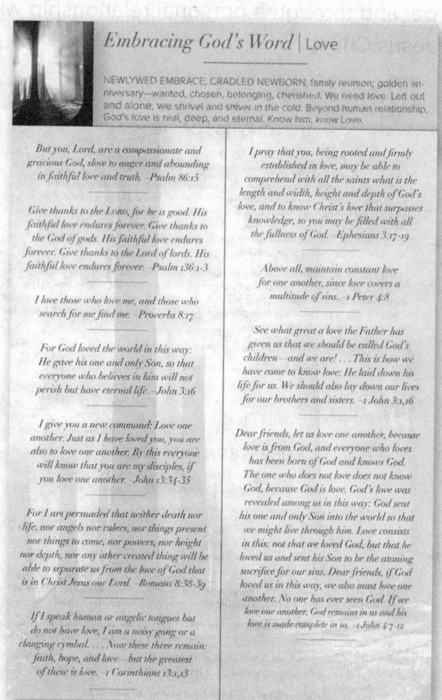

Embracing God's Word | Love

NEWLYWED EMBRACE, CRADLED NEWBORN, family reunion; golden anniversary—wanted, chosen, belonging, cherished. We need love. Left out and alone, we shrivel and shiver in the cold. Beyond human relationship, God's love is real, deep, and eternal. Know him; know Love.

But you, Lord, are a compassionate and gracious God, slow to anger and abounding in faithful love and truth. –Psalm 86:15

Give thanks to the LORD, for he is good. His faithful love endures forever. Give thanks to the God of gods. His faithful love endures forever. Give thanks to the Lord of lords. His faithful love endures forever. –Psalm 136:1-3

I love those who love me, and those who search for me find me. –Proverbs 8:17

For God loved the world in this way: He gave his one and only Son, so that everyone who believes in him will not perish but have eternal life. –John 3:16

I give you a new command: Love one another. Just as I have loved you, you are also to love one another. By this everyone will know that you are my disciples, if you love one another. –John 13:34-35

For I am persuaded that neither death nor life, nor angels nor rulers, nor things present nor things to come, nor powers, nor height nor depth, nor any other created thing will be able to separate us from the love of God that is in Christ Jesus our Lord. –Romans 8:38-39

If I speak human or angelic tongues but do not have love, I am a noisy gong or a clanging cymbal. . . . Now these three remain: faith, hope, and love—but the greatest of these is love. –1 Corinthians 13:1,13

I pray that you, being rooted and firmly established in love, may be able to comprehend with all the saints what is the length and width, height and depth of God's love, and to know Christ's love that surpasses knowledge, so you may be filled with all the fullness of God. –Ephesians 3:17-19

Above all, maintain constant love for one another, since love covers a multitude of sins. –1 Peter 4:8

See what great a love the Father has given us that we should be called God's children—and we are! . . . This is how we have come to know love: He laid down his life for us. We should also lay down our lives for our brothers and sisters. –1 John 3:1,16

Dear friends, let us love one another, because love is from God, and everyone who loves has been born of God and knows God. The one who does not love does not know God, because God is love. God's love was revealed among us in this way: God sent his one and only Son into the world so that we might live through him. Love consists in this: not that we loved God, but that he loved us and sent his Son to be the atoning sacrifice for our sins. Dear friends, if God loved us in this way, we also must love one another. No one has ever seen God. If we love one another, God remains in us and his love is made complete in us. –1 John 4:7-12

Restoration Devotions

Introduction

Workers restoring a historic building use wrecking bars and sledge hammers. Painters rescuing a mural on canvas or plaster from the ravages of time use swabs, soft brushes, and solvent. Jesus restores lives with stories. His parables still have delight and intrigue many, while at the same time they transfix and transform the few who see in his short narratives something of their own lives. These find comfort that Jesus understands them and, in that realization, comes the hope of restoration.

Jesus's stories have suffered heavy-handed analysis, harebrained allegorizing, and inattentive interpretations, yet they bear fruit long after the abuse of generations should have consigned them to the junkyard of clichés and outmoded tales. But while familiarity may have lessened their uniquenesses, the incisive, surgical effects of the parables on those who study them point to the compelling identity of the storyteller. Jesus knew his audience. And he knows us.

Meditating for thirty days on a single story of Jesus seems out of place in our sound-bite, instant-explanation world to remind us that some truths dawn slowly and grow gradually. Like the restoration of a painting, approaching the parables requires us to clear away the rubble of misunderstanding in order to place ourselves in the world of those who first heard the stories. Jesus *does* speak to us today, but we often hear him more clearly when we identify the culture, era, and setting in which he first spoke. That will guard against reading our culture into his and help us hear how clearly his parables speak into our culture. Allow Jesus's story of the Prodigal Son to seep into the furthest corners of your soul in the weeks to come.

Note that the first week of reflections sets the stage for the parable and provides some understanding of Jesus's teaching style, beginning with why he used parables and setting the historical and biblical context. We will dive directly into the story of the Prodigal Son on Day 8.

DAY 1

He Taught in Parables

He taught them many things in parables (Mark 4:2).

Setting the Scene

Jesus didn't use parables as a way to teach a lesson; each parable *was* the lesson. A comparison of story telling and story teaching reveals a significant difference between the way truth is learned by the Western mind and the way it is grasped in the Middle Eastern mind. In the West, stories illustrate and provide examples of the stated truth. In the Middle East, a story presents the lesson-in-life from which one or more conclusions may be drawn, much like life itself.

What, then, is a parable? The term is used throughout the Bible to indicate a variety of narrative approaches that expect the hearer to understand by careful reflection. These include metaphors, similes, and even brief case studies. Parables require attention. The stories may appear at first glance to be simplistic, but they carry deep meaning. Parables don't hide truth; they present truth in a subtle and elegant way to those willing to think.

By using parables, Jesus fit right in with the long history of teachers and prophets in Israel. The people who heard him didn't remark that he had invented a new form of teaching. They were accustomed to storytelling teachers. But Jesus's stories had an added quality. "They were astonished at his teaching because he was teaching them as one who had authority, and not like the scribes" (Mk 1:22). For those willing to listen, Jesus's stories had a convicting, life-changing quality that communicated to those who heard them. The same is true today. He still teaches us many truths through parables.

Getting Personal

Like the prophet Nathan's approach with King David centuries before (2Sm 12), Jesus got inside his audience's defenses with stories that made their point before listeners realized they were being singled out.

- Which of Jesus's parables have had that effect on you? Why?
- In what way(s) has your life changed because of this specific teaching of Jesus?

Talking to God

Lord, open my heart and mind to respond to what you have to teach me as I think about this amazing story of restoration that Jesus told when he talked about the prodigal son. Please help me see my place in the parable. Amen.

Accusation

"This man welcomes sinners and eats with them" (Luke 15:2).

Setting the Scene

In the eyes of the watchful Pharisees and scribes, so many unsavory people were flocking to be with Jesus that "all" of them seemed to be coming (Lk 15:1). Their complaint stemmed from their strict view of personal ritual cleanliness that went to great lengths to avoid contact with "sinners." They abhorred the idea of being close to and even sharing a table with the despised tax collectors (whom they saw as traitors) and assorted other sinners.

Thus, the Pharisees and scribes complained, not to a higher authority, but to one another. They were working themselves into a righteous rage. The focus of their reaction is expressed in the word *welcomes*. The same term is used positively in Romans 16:2 and Philippians 2:29 with the added phrase "in the Lord," to express an openhearted acceptance of someone who reflects Jesus's way with others. The Pharisees and scribes rejected the people whom Jesus was receiving because they saw them as unfit for hospitality or any opportunity to have their condition changed. Judging sinners is an effective way to avoid offering them help. Unkindness, motivated by superior moral assumptions, continues to keep people from experiencing God's love.

Jesus never denied that those who were drawn to him were sinners. On another occasion, he responded to a similar accusation with the blistering comment, "It is not those who are well who need a doctor, but those who are sick. Go and learn what this means: *I desire mercy and not sacrifice*. For I didn't come to call the righteous, but sinners" (Mt 9:12-13, italics added). In this situation, Jesus told three stories to demolish a dangerous misunderstanding.

Getting Personal

Rejecting people along with their sins is easier than accepting people while not affirming their sinfulness. Yet, since we are all sinful enough in some way to be unfit as flawless examples, why wouldn't we want to treat others in the same way that we long to be treated?

- When have you been critical of someone for associating with "sinners"? Why?
- What would have been a better way to respond?

Talking to God

Thank you, Father, for the reminders that I need to learn humility from your Son in order that I might exercise the proper balance between justice and mercy toward others. Help me in this way to be more like Jesus. I pray in his name, amen.

DAY 3

Big Picture

He answered, "Because the secrets of the kingdom of heaven have been given for you to know, but it has not been given to them" (Matthew 13:11).

Setting the Scene

All of Jesus's parables have in common the perspective he had as the eternal heir of the kingdom of heaven. His stories reveal ordinary, everyday interactions as the places where God is at work bringing about the restoration of a ruined creation. In the Sermon on the Mount, when Jesus said, "But seek first the kingdom of God and his righteousness" (Mt 6:33), he wasn't just giving an instruction for living; he was also describing his own way of life. Jesus's thinking and acting offer the ultimate model for us. The parables showed the kingdom's perspective. They didn't shut people out; they presented glimpses of the kingdom of heaven for those ready to see and hear. Jesus welcomed those ready to enter, people like the tax collectors and sinners. Those who were hostile, vaguely interested, or distracted remained unaffected and outside the kingdom.

When Jesus referred to the "kingdom," what did he mean? When he eventually informed Pilate "My kingdom is not of this world" (Jn 18:36), he didn't say, "My kingdom is not *in* this world." For Jesus, kingdom wasn't about territory but about relationship and authority. Whenever God's sovereignty and direction are acknowledged, the kingdom *is* operating. Perhaps a better way of understanding Jesus's words is to think in terms of "kingship" rather than "kingdom."

Citizenship in Jesus's kingdom means having a relationship with him. If we recognize Christ as Lord and King of our lives, we are under his kingship. Salvation is a change of citizenship. Colossians 1:13-14 describes how this change occurs: "He has rescued us from the domain of darkness and transferred us into the kingdom of the Son he loves. In him we have redemption, the forgiveness of sins."

Getting Personal

The key to understanding Jesus and his message is to look at life from his point of view, to see the big picture. Christ's kingdom is not of this world but in the lives of all who trust in him as Savior and Lord.

- What is the status of your eternal citizenship today?
- How does Colossians 1:13-14 describe your experience with Jesus?
- Before you claim citizenship in Christ's kingdom, consider this: In what ways are you living as someone who has been rescued and transferred into his kingdom?

Talking to God

Thank you for rescuing me, Father. Thank you for making me part of your family and a citizen of your kingdom. Forgive me when I fail to show those around me a life of freedom and genuine love that ought to flow from all you have done for me. I ask this in Jesus's name, amen.

Participants

All the tax collectors and sinners were approaching to listen to him. And the Pharisees and scribes were complaining (Luke 15:1-2).

Setting the Scene

We find at least six groups in the audience of Luke 15. The tax collectors were a hated minority of Jews who cooperated with the Romans by gathering the taxes from a subjugated people and skimming from the proceeds for themselves. "Sinners" refers to the ragtag lower rung of society made up of prostitutes, beggars, and those considered unfit to mingle with common folk. The Pharisees were the spiritual conservatives, proud defenders of God's Word and secure in their righteousness. The scribes were preservers of the written law, carefully reproducing the documents that represented and commented on God's law. A few people from ordinary walks of life, curious about Jesus, probably were present as well. The disciples rounded out the crowd that day.

Determining a pecking order does the same thing in religion as it does in henhouses. The process puts someone at the bottom. Was the complaint of the Pharisees and scribes against Jesus or against the unsavory people showing up to hear him? They said, "This man welcomes sinners and eats with them" (Lk 15:2). Their complaint allowed them to dismiss both Jesus and the rest of his audience. The tax collectors and sinners were unacceptable; and because Jesus welcomed them, he was also unacceptable. Even as they rejected both Jesus and others in his audience, Jesus graciously invited all to come home to his Father.

This interaction provides a vivid example of the description in John 1:11-12, "He came to his own, and his own people did not receive him. But to all who did receive him, he gave them the right to be children of God, to those who believe in his name."

Getting Personal

Complaining is one of the easiest holes to fall into; and once we land in its depths, we quickly make ourselves at home. Griping tends to multiply and spread through life until every circumstance triggers more fault finding and anger. Complaining usually indicates that we've made a choice not to respond to life in a healthy way.

- How readily do you engage in negative criticism?
- In what places and situations do you tend to be most critical of people and institutions?
- Why, do you think?

Talking to God

Lord, I realize that when I complain, I am often finding fault with you. In rejecting immediate circumstances or even other people, I am also rejecting your role in my life. Forgive my tendency to consider my comfort, interests, and preferences to be of chief importance. Teach me to desire your will first even when it forces me to accept inconvenience and to change my attitudes. I know this is part of what it actually means to call you Lord, Lord Jesus. Amen.

DAY 5

One Answer; Three Stories

So he told them this parable (Luke 15:3).

Setting the Scene

On our way to the parable of the Prodigal Son in Luke 15, we pass through two other stories. Luke introduces the trilogy as a single parable. The similarities between the stories are striking. They seem to indicate that part of Jesus's purpose was to drive home at least one point with increasing intensity. Yet, as we will see next time, these three short accounts also have significant differences.

All three stories begin with a painful loss. One sheep among a hundred wanders away unnoticed; one coin becomes misplaced; a son leaves. Jesus was using a common experience of loss to awaken compassion in his critics and show compassion to his audience. Attentive listeners would see themselves as the valued sheep, coin, and son. Jesus may have wanted his hardened opponents to see themselves as possible shepherds, caring housewives, or loving fathers. They would have to repent over the way they had been looking at others. To do so would require a big change.

Each parable also includes a moment of finding: the stray sheep rescued, the coin located, and the son suddenly finding himself. The sheep and coin cannot participate in their rescue; they merely wait to be found. The son must recognize his lost-ness as the first step to being found.

All three stories end with a celebration. The joy of return eclipses the pain of loss. The repeated punchline of gladness must not have interested most of Jesus's critics. But always possible was that one or two of them might suddenly find themselves and come home.

Getting Personal

Our experiences of losing, finding, and celebrating form a familiar pattern we see in life. But thinking of the things we've lost is always easier than acknowledging that *we* are lost. These escalating similarities that Jesus used have a way of getting behind our defenses and confronting us.

- What was needed for you to realize and admit that you were lost?

- How and when did God find you?

Talking to God

Lord, thank you for your patience in showing me my proneness to wander and the times I have been lost. Thank you for welcoming me home when I did not deserve your forgiveness. Please keep my eyes open to see all you want to show me. In Jesus's name, amen.

When Difference Matters

Now when he heard this, he said, "It is not those who are well who need a doctor, but those who are sick. Go and learn what this means: I desire mercy and not sacrifice. For I didn't come to call the righteous, but sinners" (Matthew 9:12-13).

Setting the Scene

While the three parables Jesus told in Luke 15 share significant similarities, the differences in the stories are also meaningful. The lost objects are not only different from each other, but they also fall into very different categories. The first is a mindless animal; the second, an inanimate coin; the third, an intelligent, though immature, human being. The sheep and coin represent value lost; the son represents value wasted. The sheep was helpless, the coin, clueless, and the son, hopeless. In the first story, the wandering is incidental; in the second, it's accidental; in the third, it is stubborn and intentional.

The first two stories focus on the simple relationship between an object and its owner. The last story unfolds a complex family structure with multiple relationships that need to be made right. Three relationships are featured: father and younger son, father and older son, and younger and older sons. The third story is unique in that no searching takes place. The shepherd scours the countryside until he finds the sheep, and the woman dismantles her house in search of the coin. But the father waits for the son to come to his senses.

The differences in the stories reveal Jesus's hierarchy of values. Objects and animals are worth looking for, but people are worth waiting for. With objects, no free will is involved. With personal relationships, however, a free will is in play. As we move into the story of the lost son in the days to come, we will clearly see that Jesus wanted his third story to make an indelible impression. He made it decisively different from the other two. The people he wanted to reach were not objects to be found; they were lost persons to be rescued and restored. When we read it, we join his audience.

Getting Personal

- When you read these three stories in a row, how do they impact you?
- In what ways do you sense Jesus moving closer to you as he describes, with increasing intensity and feeling, the longing that he has for you to come home?

Talking to God

Thank you, God, for all you have done to reach my heart and mind. You are unpredictably persistent in all your ways. Thank you for even using simple stories to change my life. Amen.

DAY 7

Life Lessons

These things happened to them as examples, and they were written for our instruction, on whom the ends of the ages have come (1 Corinthians 10:11).

Setting the Scene

Each of the three parables Jesus told in Luke 15 includes at least one person, but the third parable showcases a collection of personal dynamics that display God at work. One of the best ways to grasp the lessons and truth God has for us in his Word is to identify the people in Scripture and reflect on their responses to life and to God.

The parable of the prodigal features three main characters: a father and two sons. Perhaps a minor fourth character is the farmer who hired the younger son in the far country, who is worth mentioning because Jesus points out that no one else there was willing to give him anything. The father's servants back home have a small supporting role. Doubtless the younger son had numerous people willing to assist him in squandering his newfound wealth.

As we read this story, we can give special attention to the way various people impacted the life of the younger son. The central storyline revolves around the son's choices, but others influenced the outcome of his journey away from home and back again. Each person, to some degree, helped or hindered the young man's progress, sometimes unintentionally. For example, the friends in the far country were happy to join him in wasting his inheritance, but they also made his moment of truth come more quickly when they deserted him. The pig farmer needed a field hand; the young man needed to get to the end of his rope. God brought people across his path that provided the best opportunities for him to see how very far he was from where he really wanted to be. He had taken his home for granted and assumed that escaping it was the answer. His real need, however, the same need of his older brother, was to *want* to be home. But a painful journey was necessary to bring him full circle.

Getting Personal

Every day various people help or hinder us on our way to experiencing all God has for us. We do the same for them. The question is, are we actively seeking to do good or simply wandering through life, not paying attention to how we influence people? Pray regularly that God would use you to positively affect others.

- With whom do you plan on interacting today?
- How do you think you might be able to be a positive influence on each one?

Talking to God

Spirit of God, I am not wise enough to always know how to help others, but teach me not to avoid doing what I do know and guide me to learn how I may do better in assisting others on their way. Thank you for the way you've used others in my life. In Jesus's name I pray, amen.

DAY 8

The Son's Preparation

He also said: "A man had two sons. The younger of them said to his father, 'Father, give me the share of the estate I have coming to me.' So he distributed the assets to them" (Luke 15:11-12).

Setting the Scene

As we have seen, this is a "parable," a teaching story. As far as we know, Jesus was not talking about an actual family he knew, with a father and two sons, and he gave no backstory, family history, or other details. We can use our imaginations, however. In a situation like this, we can be pretty sure that the son wouldn't suddenly decide to ask for his inheritance and skip town. He must have been thinking and planning for days and even months. Perhaps the lure of the "distant country" and the pleasures it offered drew him away. Or, chafing under his father's restrictions and the continual reminder of his model older sibling, he wanted freedom to make his own decisions about life. Or, maybe as an older adolescent, he wanted to break free, find himself, and make his own way in the world. He may have often thought or even voiced to his father or brother, "Stop telling me what to do!"

Whatever the motivation, the younger son planned, probably chose the right words to say and time to say them, and made his move. Pride took him away. He wanted to be on his own, the master of his own fate.

In addition to rehearsing his speech, how else would this young man have prepared? He knew the direction he wanted to go—away from home and to the other place he had heard so much about. But how would he get there, and what would he take—the substance of most normal preparations. The story hints that he probably thought all he needed was the money and that he would be able to buy everything he needed on his journey and at his destination. He doesn't seem to have given much thought to anything else about his adventure.

Getting Personal

Self-reliance and independence are highly valued in society, and we certainly don't appreciate living under tight rules and other restrictions. Thus, we can understand this young man wanting to leave home and make his own way in the world. But, if we're honest, we can also sense the draw of temptations offered in the attractive destination. So, whether during adolescent rebellion, midlife crisis, or alluring enticement, we can be tempted to cash in and take off, leaving family and faith in the dust.

- When have you felt hemmed in and have wanted to break free?
- What "distant countries" seem exciting and tempting?
- How have you dealt with those fantasies of leaving home?

Talking to God

Father, I admit that sometimes I fantasize about going where I shouldn't go and doing what I shouldn't do. I know that at these times I am being "drawn away and enticed by [my] own evil desire" (Jms 1:14). Please change my desires and keep me focused on living for you. In Christ's name, amen.

DAY 9

The Son's Demand

"The younger of them said to his father, 'Father, give me the share of the estate I have coming to me'" (Luke 15:12).

Setting the Scene

Here, again, we need to use our imaginations, especially because we have no audio of Jesus telling the story to hear the son's tone of voice. But in the phrase "Father, give me the share of the estate I have coming to me," we sense not a request, but a demand. No softening preamble, "I've been thinking . . ." or "What would you think about . . ." or "I would like to try ______. What do you think?"

Also, this was not a teenager asking for a bigger allowance or a young man wanting a loan for a business venture. This son was saying, in effect, "I know that when you die, I'll inherit half the estate. I can't wait. Give it to me now, and I'm gone—I'm out of here!" He didn't even hint about how he would use the money. Total disrespect.

For those listening to Jesus, the demand made by the younger son was an insult worthy of death. The Pharisees knew the command to "Honor your father and your mother" (Ex 20:12) and that the death penalty was prescribed for extremely rebellious children (Lv 20:9; Dt 18:18-21). So this was a religious/theological issue. The son's demand also violated cultural norms: In Jewish society, the father was the authority in the home, and children were expected to humbly submit and obey. The son's actions would have been humiliating for the father and scandalous for the family.

We can also wonder how the boy expected his father to respond. With anger? Frustration? Sadness? Certainly not indifference. Whatever the supposed response, he expected to be given his inheritance. Maybe he was taking advantage of his father's love for him. The son certainly was taking him for granted.

Getting Personal

God is our Father, and we often talk with him about what we need or want. He loves us and says we can come to him as a beloved child, "with boldness" (Heb 4:16). Too often, however, we approach him carelessly with our self-centered requests. Even if we aren't planning a sinful trip, we do well to consider how we relate to our loving Father.

- When do you tend to take God for granted: when you are content and life is going well; when you have a need; or when you are experiencing pain, loss, or fear and feel desperate? Why?
- The Lord's Prayer begins, "Your name be honored as holy" (Mt 6:9). How can you honor God in your prayers, especially with your requests?

Talking to God

Dear Father, I am so grateful that you are my Father. Forgive me for taking you for granted and for treating you as merely a dispenser to grant my every wish, even if it would be harmful to me. Thank you for loving me and for giving me the freedom to make choices on life's journey. Please give me the strength to do what honors you. In Jesus's name, amen.

DAY 10

The Son's Journey

"Not many days later, the younger son gathered together all he had and traveled to a distant country" (Luke 15:13).

Setting the Scene

Again, the story gives few details, but this sentence provides three short phrases that are telling.

- "Not many days later" implies that the boy left as soon as he could. We may wonder what could have compelled him to want to get away. What was he leaving? A loving father, a brother, comfort, security, a stable environment—but at this point all those positive features meant nothing to him. He was determined to leave, to strike out on his own down the road away from home, even though he didn't know for certain what awaited him at his destination.
- "Gathered together all he had" implies finality—the young man was leaving for good. This wasn't a trip or a fling; it was a life change. Not only was this son moving out, he was moving on. He didn't plan on returning anytime soon. We don't know the amount of his "share of the estate" (15:12)—evidently a substantial financial resource—but *everything* he gathered had come from his father.
- "Distant country" reveals that this son wanted significant separation from his past and everything associated with it. His new address wouldn't be nearby but "distant." At this point, he didn't know where he would be living except that it was far from home, where no one would know him.

The boy "traveled," but we don't know how. He must have walked much of the way, but perhaps he used a first-century version of hitchhiking. Because his destination was "distant," the journey probably took several days. During that time, what was he thinking and feeling? Probably relief and exhilaration for finally doing what he had been dreaming about and excitement as he anticipated all the thrills the new place would offer. He probably wasn't feeling regret or guilt or planning very far into the future.

Whatever the son's reasons for leaving, he wanted to get as far away as possible as soon as possible, and he was on his way.

Getting Personal

Daily we are confronted with difficult people, frustrating situations, resource needs, conflicts, and pain. When those build, we can imagine ditching it all and starting over. At other times, we can fantacize about traveling miles from home where we can be anonymous. After all, what happens in the distant country stays in the distant country!

- When recently have you imagined escaping from your present problems and starting over? What stopped you?
- What can you do to take advantage of the resources and relationships that God has given you here and now, instead of wishing for something better or more exciting?

Talking to God

Jesus, I confess that I have thought, especially during times of struggle and pain, about leaving and traveling far away. And while still physically present, at times I am distant emotionally from those I love. Help me, Savior, to focus on what you have given me instead of imagining a better life somewhere else. Amen.

DAY 11

The Son's New Life

"Not many days later, the younger son gathered together all he had and traveled to a distant country, where he squandered his estate in foolish living. After he had spent everything, a severe famine struck that country, and he had nothing. Then he went to work for one of the citizens of that country, who sent him into his fields to feed pigs" (Luke 15:13-15).

Setting the Scene

Eventually, the young man reached his destination—the "distant country." His activities in that place are described only with the statement, "squandered his estate in foolish living." Other Bible translations use "wild" or "reckless" to describe the son's lifestyle. In other words, having no restraints and giving in to all his impulses, he exhausted all his resources. We can imagine the younger son spending freely, going from party to party. Perhaps he had an entourage, people who flattered him, pretending to enjoy his company as long as he was buying the drinks and more. Later we read the older son's conclusion that his formerly flush brother had "devoured [his] assets with prostitutes" (15:30)—a real possibility.

Whether all this happened quickly or over several years, eventually the boy was broke. That's when the famine hit. The timing couldn't have been worse. His pretend friends left, and everyone was scrounging for food. He was free, on his own, just as he had planned! But with no family or other safety net, the young man was destitute—"he had nothing"—and desperate. He needed some way to support himself. He needed some place to live. He needed to eat. So, we find him hired out to a farmer.

What a life reversal! Previously, this young man had a secure and comfortable home, warm bed, and plenty to eat; now, he was vulnerable, cold, and hungry. Not long ago, he had sat at the table with a father and brother who loved him; now he was alone. Before beginning this adventure, "hired workers" (15:17) would do the dirty work at his home; now he was slopping the pigs.

Getting Personal

A profound biblical principle is that "whatever a person sows he will also reap" (Gl 6:7). In other words, thoughts, attitudes, and actions have consequences. When we make poor decisions, God often allows us to experience the results. Usually our self-centeredness gets us in trouble. In this story, we can see several bad decisions: disrespecting the father, asking for the inheritance, traveling far from home, mismanaging money, and, certainly, leading a destructive lifestyle.

- Divide your life into thirds. In each third, think about one or two bad decisions you made. What were the consequences for each? What happened to get you back on track?
- Today, in what situations do you think you might be tempted to make poor or even self-destructive choices? What can you do to make sure you do what is right instead?

Talking to God

Holy Spirit, I know that you are working in me, helping me want to do what is right (Php 2:13). Day by day, moment by moment, I want to submit to your leading and live God's way. Through Christ I pray, amen.

DAY 12

The Son's Desperation

"He longed to eat his fill from the pods that the pigs were eating, but no one would give him anything. When he came to his senses, he said, 'How many of my father's hired workers have more than enough food, and here I am dying of hunger!'" (Luke 15:16-17).

Setting the Scene

Remember, Jesus was talking to a Jewish audience. So, when he spoke about the young man feeding pigs and even longing for the "pods," the listeners would have understood the depth of the boy's desperation. For Jews, pigs were unclean, and pious Jews (especially Pharisees) would have nothing to do with anything associated with those animals. "Pigs, though they have divided hooves, do not chew the cud—they are unclean for you. Do not eat any of their meat or touch their carcasses—they are unclean for you" (Lv 11:7-8).

This boy was in the pen, feeding the pigs and trying to eat their fare. The story hasn't told us anything about the young man's religious background, but we can assume that he was a Jew. There he was, so far from home in every aspect of life: physical, social, moral, emotional, and spiritual.

Jesus said, "When he came to his senses." This means the young man understood his condition, that he was totally bankrupt. Jesus didn't say that the boy decided on a course of action to get out of his mess, another self-centered plan. No—he had stopped running and was ready to be rescued and restored.

What causes people to come to their senses? How much time is needed? How many life reversals? This desperate situation didn't happen suddenly. Along the way, in stages, the son lost all his money and friends and, probably, his health. But his hunger and time in the pigsty finally got his attention. Then his mind drifted to home, the place from which he had run so far. Starvation caused him to remember the meals he had enjoyed at the family table and the realization that "many of [his] father's hired workers have more than enough food." He knew what he had to do.

Getting Personal

Some of the most difficult people to reach with the gospel are those who seem to have it all: fame, fortune, friends. They are healthy, wealthy, and influential, with no apparent or felt needs—until an addiction, divorce, poor investments, reckless spending, business failure, doctor's diagnosis, natural disaster, death of a loved one, or just the aging process causes them to reevaluate their life's trajectory, values, and relationship with God. That's when they "come to their senses."

Solomon wrote, "So remember your Creator in the days of your youth: Before the days of adversity come, and the years approach when you will say, 'I have no delight in them'" (Ec 12:1).

- When you wandered (or ran) away from God, what caused you to come to your senses?
- Who do you know who needs a wake-up call? What can you do to help them see that they are headed in the wrong direction and need to turn for home?

"My brothers and sisters, if any among you strays from the truth, and someone turns him back, let that person know that whoever turns a sinner from the error of his way will save his soul from death and cover a multitude of sins" (Jms 5:19-20).

Talking to God

O dear Father, right now I'm thinking of ____ and ____ who need you desperately but don't know it. Please convict them of sin, and help them come to their senses and turn to you. Show me how I can be part of this restoration process. Amen.

DAY 13

The Son's Repentance

"'I'll get up, go to my father, and say to him, "Father, I have sinned against heaven and in your sight. I'm no longer worthy to be called your son. Make me like one of your hired workers"'" (Luke 15:18-19).

Setting the Scene

Having finally realized his true condition, the desperate young man must have been filled with disgust for himself and with sorrow and regret. He knew he had wronged and hurt his father deeply. We know he was sincere because of his admission that he had "sinned against heaven." He didn't rationalize his condition or the behavior that had put him there. His intended words to his father didn't include statements such as, "I made a mistake" or "People took advantage of me" or even, "I was immature, and I've learned." He understood the gravity and reality of his situation: he had *sinned* with his thoughts, words, and actions.

Repentance is the first word of the gospel message, the first step. It means admitting our offense and turning away from sin. But we must also turn *toward* God: "repent" and "believe." In preparing the way for Jesus, John the Baptist preached "Repent, because the kingdom of heaven has come near!" (Mt 3:2). Then he pointed people to the Savior: "Here is the Lamb of God, who takes away the sin of the world!" (Jn 1:29). Jesus proclaimed, "The time is fulfilled, and the kingdom of God has come near. Repent and believe the good news!" (Mk 1:15). Being sorry for our sins is the first step, but it is incomplete. We must also believe.

So, the son decided to return to his home and his father. He knew what he had to say, and his short speech has three parts, three sentences:

- I have sinned against heaven and in your sight.
- I'm no longer worthy to be called your son.
- Make me like one of your hired workers.

The last time we heard the younger son speak to his father, he had said, with the attitude of prideful entitlement, "Give me the share of the estate I have coming to me" (Lk 15:12). Now his speech sounds much different—humble and contrite. In the first, he asserted his *right* as a son. Here he planned to say, "I'm no longer worthy to be called your son."

Getting Personal

Repentance is not simply feeling bad about what has happened. And it's not merely saying, "I'm sorry." Many who use those words mean, "I'm sorry that what I did made you feel bad" or "I'm sorry that I got caught." True repentance is deep and genuine sorrow for what we have done, taking full responsibility for our actions and admitting our wrong. The son knew he had to "get up" (turn away from his current situation), "go" (travel home to his loving father), and "say" (confess).

- When did you first realize that you were a lost sinner in need of the Savior?
- How did you come to put your faith in Christ?
- What role does repentance play in your life today?

Talking to God

My Savior, I admit that my repentance is not always sincere. Often, I'm just saying the words. Sometimes I'm just sorry that my sin was discovered. Forgive me. I want to be your person, to live your way. I want people to know that I am your child. In your name, amen.

DAY 14

The Son's Return

"So he got up and went to his father" (Luke 15:20).

Setting the Scene

In this story, we see the son deciding to go home and then actually making the trip. This was his first step of faith.

The trip home must have seemed to take forever. On his previous journey, he had been filled with anticipation about what he would do in his new surroundings. Now, feeling remorseful and guilty, he slowly made his way back, not knowing what to expect but hoping for the best, at least to be accepted as a hired worker. He was ready to accept anything—perhaps expecting rejection or punishment for his shameful behavior—just as long as he was accepted back into the house.

This is the essence of saving faith. The son admitted his sin and expressed his deep sorrow for it ("I have sinned against heaven and in your sight"—15:18); acknowledged his unworthiness ("I'm no longer worthy to be called your son"—15:19); left that sinful way of life behind ("he got up"), and moved forward, toward love and forgiveness ("went to his father"), submitting himself to his father with no conditions. Note that he had said, "I'll get up, go to my father" (15:18); he was trusting that his father would be there when he arrived.

Scripture continually affirms that believing facts about God is important but not enough: "You believe that God is one. Good! Even the demons believe—and they shudder" (Jms 2:19). We must trust him fully, forsaking anything that would stand in his place, and commit our lives to him.

Getting Personal

Our natural tendency—consciously or unconsciously—is to place conditions in our relationship with God. We may pray something like,"Get me out of this mess, and I'll do what you want." We may donate time or money to the church expecting some sort of earthly or heavenly reward. Or we may assume that following Christ will lead to health and prosperity. But God wants us to trust him completely, no strings attached, fully accepting his decisions and plans.

- When have you felt far from your heavenly Father?
- What drew you back to him?
- What steps do you need to take to be restored in your relationship with God?

Talking to God

Lord, forgive me for putting conditions in my prayers, in my relationship with you. I love you; I trust you; I fully submit to you, no strings attached. In Christ's name, amen.

DAY 15

The Father

He also said, "A man had two sons" (Luke 15:11).

Setting the Scene

Now that we have followed the younger son's adventure for a few days, let's go back to the beginning and catch up with the father in this story. Before we can compare this father to our own fathers, or even think about other fathers we've known, we need to consider how Jesus and his audience used the term *father*.

As we saw earlier, in Jesus's day, a father held the life of his family and their future in his hands. His word and authority were not to be challenged. If they were, swift and harsh punishment was expected to follow, including the possibility of death. The people in Jesus's audience would have been expecting similar responses from the father in the story, based on the general view of fathers (in many ways still prevalent) in the Middle East.

But the father in Jesus's story was a different sort, and he repeatedly challenged their expectations. As we look at the father of the prodigal, we will see a very remarkable parent. Jesus will also provide a definition of what the term *father* meant to him in speaking about his own heavenly Father. The central character trait embodied in the father of the story is love. It is the underlying answer that explains every action by the father in dealing with his two boys. (The fact that he has two children is a simple way of saying God has many.) But, as we will see, the father treated each child with love.

While the Old Testament includes references to God as Father (for example, Dt 32:6; Ps 2:7), those uses tended to be formal rather than personal and intimate. Jesus departed from the norm, referring to God as his Father in a way that was noticed by his audiences as a claim about his own identity. Clearly, to describe God as having qualities of a father is one thing; it is quite another to address him as "Father." But loving the Father and being loved by him are two sides of the greatest relationship anyone can have.

Getting Personal

Many struggle with feelings of disappointment, fear, and even anger when hearing the word *father*. The startling responses of the father in Jesus's parable are in different ways as countercultural and politically incorrect now as they were in Jesus's time.

- What positive memories do you have of your father? What negative ones?
- In what ways have those memories and feelings affected your view of God as Father?
- How willing are you to meet the Father in Jesus's story on *his* terms and let him treat you as another of his children?

Talking to God

Dear God, I am grateful to be able to call you Father. As I have seen myself repeatedly in the story of the prodigal, I now see myself before a Father who loves me as you do. Thank you for the joy and freedom of returning again and again to the thought that you are my Father in heaven, who has the very best plans for me in mind and has made them possible through your Son, Jesus. In his name I pray, amen.

The Father's Releasing Love

"The younger of them said to his father, 'Father, give me the share of the estate I have coming to me.' So he distributed the assets to them" (Luke 15:12).

Setting the Scene

As highlighted on Day 9, to those listening to Jesus, the son's request was a capital offense. It was the son's way of declaring that he considered his own father dead and the estate open for disbursement. No hint is given about the father's feelings, only that he proceeded to split up his estate between his sons.

The father released his resources and then released his son. The son's success in liquidating his newly acquired assets assumes the permission of the father. The fabric of a father-son relationship was being torn, but the father's responses were already laying the groundwork for restoration. He didn't return hurt when hurt was received. The audience would have expected retaliation and rejection; instead, they were shown a loving father painfully allowing his son to hurt him and then walk away.

A relationship between two people always involves more than one will. Either party can love the other with unreturned love, but a loving relationship requires shared love, willingly offered by each person. God's love is the unconditional constant in our relationship with him. The conditional and intermittent aspect that allows or prevents a loving relationship is *our* love for God.

Clearly, the father in Jesus's story loved his son, but the son had decided that he did not love his father. He loved his freedom, his funds, and his future prospects more, and they provided a temptation he couldn't resist. The father recognized the son's determination and let him go on his way, risking permanent loss in exchange for the possibility of a future reconciliation if the son were to change his mind. The father's love remained; the son's love remained to be seen.

Getting Personal

How often do we wander away from our Father's love, fully aware that he loves us but drawn away by the world, the flesh, and the devil? Our love proves conditional and intermittent. We prove again the words of 1 John 4:10, "Love consists in this: not that we loved God, but that he loved us and sent his Son to be the atoning sacrifice for our sins."

- How do you know your heavenly Father loves you?
- What does God's love mean to you?
- At what times do you tend to take his love for granted?

Talking to God

Father, thank you for loving me first and always. Thank you for always leaving the door open and the lights on, even as I walk out the door in forgetfulness or disobedience. Thank you for remaining faithful even when I am not. Please guard me against callously taking your love for granted and thereby putting myself farther from you. Teach me the benefits of an ever-repentant spirit. In Jesus's name I pray, amen.

DAY 17

God's Pursuing-Waiting Love

"Not many days later, the younger son gathered together all he had and traveled to a distant country" (Luke 15:13).

Setting the Scene

Love pursues, but it doesn't chase. Love understands that chasing simply causes the one loved to run away faster. Love pursues with a vacuum, a powerful, lingering effect in the escapee's life that something significant has been left behind. Love offers freedom, even when that freedom leads to separation.

The younger son wasted little time before carrying out phase two of his plan. First, he had to convince his father to give him access to his share of the estate so he could liquidate it. Then he had the assets in a form he could take with him. The father may have been weeping, but he wasn't following his son down the road pleading for him to stay. Clinging isn't loving. The toughest part of love is saying no to the impulse to hold the one loved against his or her will.

Waiting isn't easy. It is fertile ground for growing impatience and resentment. For those who love and are left behind, the questions become: "When will he return?" and "Why can't she see what her absence is doing to me?" Waiting that loves ignores those impulses and focuses instead on prayer for the wandering one and planning, in hope, for their return.

The witness of prodigals leads us to believe that few of them are entirely oblivious to the pull of genuine love in their past. They resent it and resist it. They anticipated that distance would diminish the bonds of love, but they often find the bonds are stronger. The elasticity that allowed them to leave becomes a constant, subtle pull to bring them home. The father has stayed at home, waiting, but his love pursues like the bloodhound of heaven.

Getting Personal

Fortunately, we don't have to limit our roles in life to being prodigals. We can also find (and should find) ourselves in the father's role sometimes, loving others. The father's responses become valuable lessons to us in the way love acts and responds.

- What have you discovered about the quality of waiting in the way that you love?
- How do you resist impatience and resentment when love is not returned or is rejected?

Your responses say a lot about your personal development in the area of love.

Talking to God

Father, your love overwhelms and humbles me. I long to love others the way you love, but I recognize that such love is not in me, except as you provide it. Lord, I ask you to pour your love not only into my life but through my living, so that others benefit. Never let me forget that when I love best, I am simply giving to others what was first given to me. In Jesus's name, amen.

DAY 20

God's Open-Armed Love

"His father . . . ran, threw his arms around his neck, and kissed him" (Luke 15:20).

Setting the Scene

We can hardly imagine a more loving, open, and welcoming reception than the prodigal received from his father. No hint of an angry and sullen parent waiting ominously at the gate while the son approaches for his well-deserved punishment. Instead, we hear sandals hitting the road as the father, with arms opened wide, rushed to the son, crushed him in a joyful embrace, and smothered him with kisses.

This is not a generous father meeting his son halfway to negotiate his return under careful conditions. It is an absolutely loving father going beyond halfway to envelop his filthy, shamed, and reticent son with a welcome beyond words. Neither son nor father had said anything yet, but each had made his statement. The son had returned; the father had welcomed. The son said little. He was empty-handed and devoid of pride, confidence, or assumptions. But the father's actions speak profoundly about the love he had held inside during the time his son had been away.

The wordless moment is so sweet that words seem like an intrusion, yet they must be said. We know the son had prepared a confession and a request for re-admittance to the household as a servant. But the father only allowed his son to verbalize his confession before he rejected the son's self-designation as "no longer worthy to be called your son" (15:21) and announced a party. He made a point to call him "this son of mine" (15:24).

The father still hadn't said anything to his wayward son. His only words had been instructions for the servants. He had already expressed what he really wanted his son to know by the actions he had taken outside the gate. He was a father who loved so much that he didn't speak but he gave. He said more by his actions than he could have put into words. In fact, he reminds us perfectly of God, "For God loved the world in this way: He gave his one and only Son, so that everyone who believes in him will not perish but have eternal life" (Jn 3:16).

Getting Personal

The son brought back nothing but himself. The father accepted him as he was. What a stunning picture of our encounter with our heavenly Father. We bring nothing but our sorry selves; he covers us with his embrace and kisses. He's the God worth coming home to.

- When have you felt the Father's loving embrace?
- In what ways has his forgiveness changed your life?

Talking to God

I, too, am not worthy to be called your child, Father, yet you use that term to describe me. Thank you, not only for loving me but for doing all you had to do to make being in your family possible for me. Thank you for coming all the way to welcome me. In Jesus's name, who made it possible, amen.

DAY 21

God's Honoring Love

"But the father told his servants, 'Quick! Bring out the best robe and put it on him; put a ring on his finger and sandals on his feet'" (Luke 15:22).

Setting the Scene

The son returned disheveled but was welcomed like a prince. Anything of value he had already sold in order to survive. He approached home barefoot and bankrupt and probably smelling like pigs. In a manner of moments, his father had greeted him with love and instructed the servants to dress him befitting the son that he was. The needed bathing went without saying.

The son who had dishonored the father as he walked out the door with his inheritance, the father now honored as he returned with nothing. The honor given by the father restored their relationship. It also restored the son's position within the household.

The servants were ordered to move quickly. The "best" robe would be the father's own finery. When others would see the father's robe on the son, they would know immediately that reconciliation had occurred. Putting a ring on his finger combines the idea of trust and reinstatement of access to the household wealth. The sandals are simple symbols of dignity and self-respect. In a walking culture, sandals are the essential possession that indicates a person is free to travel, to carry himself where he wants to go. In all this, the father was placing the wayward son in a social and household position next to his own. In that culture, a greater demonstration of honor could hardly be given.

Back in the pigsty, the prodigal son had rehearsed a speech of repentance that included the hope that if the father would give him a lowly position, he might earn his way back to a position of trust in the father's eyes. But the father's welcome was so lavish that the son no longer dared to insult his father's grace and generosity by suggesting that he should be made a servant.

Getting Personal

One of the mistakes we make when we repent to our heavenly Father is to think now we will live in a way that demonstrates we actually deserve the grace he has freely given to us. Nothing we can do makes that possible. God has already given us all that we need; we can never deserve it but only live in gratitude for it.

- *Grace* means "undeserved favor." When did you realize God's grace for you?
- How has his grace changed your life?
- What can you do to live in the light of God's grace for you?

Talking to God

O Father, thank you for the unspeakable honor of being accepted as your child. Your grace is amazing, overwhelming. Please help me learn to live in such a way that both my words and actions are saturated with gratitude for all you have done for me. Thank you for giving up your only Son that he might bring home many sons and daughters to the kingdom. In his name I pray, amen.

God's Celebrating Love

"'Then bring the fattened calf and slaughter it, and let's celebrate with a feast, because this son of mine was dead and is alive again, he was lost and is found!'" (Luke 15:23-24).

Setting the Scene

Earlier Jesus had ended the first parable, in which a wandering sheep was found and the shepherd threw a party, by declaring, "I tell you, in the same way, there will be more joy in heaven over one sinner who repents than over ninety-nine righteous people who don't need repentance" (Lk 15:7).

Several verses later, the second parable concludes with similar words, "I tell you, in the same way, there is joy in the presence of God's angels over one sinner who repents" (15:10). In the first conclusion, Jesus locates the joy "in heaven"; in the second, "in the presence of God's angels." So, if the joy is in heaven but not being expressed *by* the angels but in their presence, then who is expressing the joy? The implication is that *God* joyfully celebrates each sinner's repentance.

The servants in this parable and the angels in heaven arrange the details of the celebration, but the chief celebrator was the father; this is God himself. The father's declaration of the reason for the celebration expresses the essence of restoration. First, the son "was dead and is alive again." In that culture, the behavior of the son would have been treated as a death in the family. Had he tried to contact anyone in his family or village, they would have been bound to tell him, "You are dead to me." But since the offended party, the father himself, had declared the son alive, everyone else could welcome him home.

Second, the father said his son "was lost and is found." The father had never accepted his son's death, but he knew he was truly lost. He didn't find himself; the father's love found him. At the end of his rope, knee-deep in slop with nowhere else to turn, the reality of his father's love and his home had come crashing in with hope. Repentance had gotten him moving toward home. The same father's love that had reached him in the far country was there to welcome him on the road to bring him the rest of the way home.

Getting Personal

The idea that God's love for each person is so great that he would celebrate our repentance ought to be continually humbling and awe-inspiring. Perhaps the prophet Zephaniah said it as well as anyone: "The LORD your God is among you, a warrior who saves. He will rejoice over you with gladness. He will be quiet in his love. He will delight in you with singing" (Zph 3:17).

- What can you do to help yourself remember how much God loves you?
- How can you express your gratitude to God for his profound love for you?

Talking to God

Father, faced with the fact of your celebrating after rescuing me, I can only respond with the apostle John's stunned words, "See what great love the Father has given us that we should be called God's children—and we are!" (1Jn 3:1). With heartfelt gratitude, I want to join you in celebrating not only my own rescue but also the rescue of countless others. You are the great and good Father. I praise you in Jesus's name, amen.

DAY 23

The Older Brother's Attitude

"Now his older son was in the field; as he came near the house, he heard music and dancing. So he summoned one of the servants, questioning what these things meant. 'Your brother is here,' he told him, 'and your father has slaughtered the fattened calf because he has him back safe and sound.' Then he became angry and didn't want to go in" (Luke 15:25-28).

Setting the Scene

Now the story takes a turn, especially in tone. The prodigal has returned! Rejoicing has ensued! Enter the older son.

Again, the narrative provides few details, only that the son was "older" and "in the field." We can guess the age gap between the two boys was probably at least five years because the brothers don't seem to have been close. As firstborn, the older son would have had many responsibilities around the house. The mother may have died several years earlier, adding more pressure on him to help his father and care for his young brother. The fact that he came from the field indicates that he had been working or supervising the workers.

During the time between the younger son's dramatic prideful departure and his humble return, the older son probably had grown increasingly resentful for his brother's impudence and disrespect and that even more responsibility and work had fallen on him. So, upon hearing of his rebellious and reprobate brother's return, he wanted nothing to do with him.

This older one had *not* run off and run wild. He had stayed with his father. While his father had been looking and hoping, he had been laboring—hard. A happy reunion was the last thing on his mind.

When considering the main characters in this parable, we think first of the younger boy. Then we think of the father. But the older son is important, for he represents the Pharisees and scribes in the crowd. Remember their critical comments about Jesus eating with "sinners" (Lk 15:2)? As Jesus explained the older son's attitude and actions, we can imagine him looking right at those critics.

Getting Personal

In the older son's response to his father, count the number of times he refers to himself—"I," "me," and "my" (15:29). Certainly, his brother had been selfish in asking for his share of the estate and running off. But this older son was self-absorbed. Some prodigals never leave home.

We are like the older brother when we are quick to judge. We are like him when we excuse our sins by comparing ourselves to others who are "worse." We are like him when we think God owes us because we've been good.

- In what ways do attitudes similar to those of the older brother hinder a person's spiritual restoration?
- How do you feel when someone with a dramatic conversion story gets the spotlight at church?
- At what times do you find yourself thinking that you are more spiritual and devoted to God and his work than others?

Talking to God

Dear Lord, I should know better, but I often find myself judging people for their sins while overlooking my own. I confess my sins of pride and self-absorption. Help me to remember that I am a sinner saved by grace. In Jesus's name, amen.

DAY 24

The Older Brother's Spirituality

"Then he became angry and didn't want to go in. So his father came out and pleaded with him. But he replied to his father, 'Look, I have been slaving many years for you, and I have never disobeyed your orders, yet you never gave me a goat so that I could celebrate with my friends. But when this son of yours came, who has devoured your assets with prostitutes, you slaughtered the fattened calf for him'" (Luke 15:28-30).

Setting the Scene

Not only was the older son self-absorbed, but he also was self-righteous. After refusing to join the joyous reunion and celebration for his long-lost brother and rejecting his father's pleas, he vented. Notice, in the son's minispeech to his father, the emphasis on his good works: "I have been slaving many years for you" and "I have never disobeyed your orders."

He sounds like a decent and upright young man—at least outwardly. Contrast the older son's words with these that his sibling had planned to say: "I have sinned against heaven and in your sight. I'm no longer worthy to be called your son. Make me like one of your hired workers" (15:18-19). The younger son came in humility, admitting his sinful attitudes and acts and unworthiness, while the older son came in pride, asserting his goodness and merit, his words dripping with self-righteousness. He was saying, in effect, "I have worked hard and *earned* your favor and accolades, and I *deserve* a party in my honor!"

This sure sounds a lot like the Pharisees. Careful to observe the letter of the law, they epitomized a "holier than thou" attitude. Focusing on their righteous acts, they were quick to judge those who fell short; in doing so, they missed the heart of God's Word. In other confrontations, Jesus had harsh words for them: "Woe to you, scribes and Pharisees, hypocrites! You shut the door of the kingdom of heaven in people's faces. For you don't go in, and you don't allow those entering to go in" (Mt 23:13).

"Older sons"—Pharisees—expect a payoff for their goodness. When they don't see the reward, they get angry. They become blind to their sins and God's grace. The older son was missing the whole point of the music, dancing, and feasting. The party was not thrown to reward the younger son for *anything*. It was purely to celebrate his return.

Getting Personal

The easiest way to justify ourselves (in our own minds) is to compare our actions to someone who seems worse. Instead of looking honestly at ourselves and admitting our foibles and failures, we think we're all right, especially in comparison to those other folks. But God's Word is clear: "There is no one righteous, not even one. . . . For all have sinned and fall short of the glory of God" (Rm 3:10,23). Regardless of how bad anyone else is, we are sinners and stand guilty before our holy God. Salvation is by grace—undeserved favor—not by works (Eph 2:8-9).

- Which of your sins do you tend to overlook, minimize, or rationalize? Why?
- When are you tempted to think you deserve God's favor more than others?

Talking to God

Jesus, I confess my self-righteous attitude and my tendency to think that somehow I can earn your favor. I know you are my Savior, that you have forgiven me and saved me from the penalty and power of my sins. Please help me to always remember that I do not deserve your love, mercy, and eternal life. Amen.

DAY 25

The Older Brother's Character

"Now his older son was in the field; as he came near the house, he heard music and dancing. . . . But he replied to his father, 'Look, I have been slaving many years for you, and I have never disobeyed your orders, yet you never gave me a goat so that I could celebrate with my friends. But when this son of yours came, who has devoured your assets with prostitutes, you slaughtered the fattened calf for him'" (Luke 15:25,29-30).

Setting the Scene

Notice the contrasts in the story: working in the field vs. celebrating in the house; clean and orderly vs. filthy and ragged; contributing vs. wasting; not even a goat vs. fattened calf. Those differences were not lost on the older son.

He "heard music and dancing" and asked what was happening. All he knew at that point was that his brother was home, "safe and sound" (15:27), and that his father was throwing a party. He knew nothing about his brother's life in the pigsty, his humility, or his repentance—and he didn't want to know. He didn't even call his younger sibling his "brother," instead saying to his father, "this son of yours."

At some time in the older son's life, he must have felt love for his brother, but at this point in the story he had no compassion and no joy. He also seems to have been questioning his father's love for him: "You never threw a party for me!" If pressed, this son probably would have said that he loved his father; yet he was quick to condemn his father's actions and was, in effect, dictating those to whom his father could show mercy and grace. He was usurping his father's place—disrespecting him as much as his brother had when he had demanded what was his and had left home.

The Pharisees and scribes listening to this story would have identified with the older son's attitude and words. They, too, would have seen the unfairness, the injustice, of it all. Like the son, they claimed to be devoted to God (the "father"), but they easily condemned "sinful people" (15:2). In so doing, they were disrespecting the God whom they claimed to love and serve.

Getting Personal

For all elder brothers, in addition to thinking their good works earns them status and reward, their self-righteous attitude creates a judgmental and unforgiving spirit. They can become oblivious to the desperate needs of those they deem unworthy, even in their own families. They, too, are lost and must be found. Jesus left the story open-ended, leaving us to wonder if this older son ever came around.

- When have you questioned God's mercy for and restoration of a "notorious sinner"?
- In what ways would an attitude like this affect your relationship with God?
- What keeps you from trusting your heavenly Father fully in all his actions?

Talking to God

Father, forgive me for my condescending and judgmental attitudes toward people who are notorious for their sinful actions and for questioning your love, mercy, and perfect plan. I know you love me and that you love others as well, even those who have wandered far from you. In Jesus's name I pray, amen.

DAY 26

God the Father

"So his father came out and pleaded with him. . . . 'Son,' he said to him, 'you are always with me, and everything I have is yours. But we had to celebrate and rejoice, because this brother of yours was dead and is alive again; he was lost and is found'" (Luke 15:28,31-32).

Setting the Scene

We have already realized that the father in Jesus's story represents God. So, we can learn much about God and our relationship with him by considering how the father in the parable related to both of his sons.

First, we see that the father *rejoices*. The return of the younger son was cause for celebration. We have discussed this several times over the past couple of weeks of devotions, but it bears highlighting again. God yearns for his children to come home, and he rejoices in their return.

Next, the joyful reunion included a feast—the father *feeds*. Simply being filled with joy wasn't enough, the father "slaughtered the fattened calf" (15:30), making sure that everyone had plenty to eat. This is God's plan for all his sons and daughters—he provides for us abundantly, generously, "above and beyond all that we ask or think" (Eph 3:20).

Then, we find that he *welcomes*. This celebration would have been a community event, including all those who knew the family, their turmoil, and the father's longing to be reunited with his son. His joy would have been incomplete in isolation—he needed to share it with others. He wanted the friends and neighbors to welcome and affirm his wayward boy. God wants restoration to be a community event—the whole family of faith should be involved.

Finally, we see that the father *includes*. He also invited his angry and pouting older son to the party. God invites people of every type and station in life (even those who say they aren't interested) to come home: those who are down and out, hungry and desperate, and those who are up and out, satisfied and self-righteous.

Getting Personal

Unfortunately, many churches are filled with "older sons," Pharisee-like people who would struggle with welcoming any flagrant and public miscreant into their building, let alone their fellowship. For them, church is more like a club than a hospital. Instead, we should welcome all sinners home and throw a party!

- Who do you know who needs to hear about God's love, mercy, and grace?
- What can you do to rejoice, feed, welcome, and include those who are new or have been restored to God's family?

Talking to God

I praise you, Lord, that you rejoice at my presence, provide for my needs, welcome me and all who believe to your banquet table, and invite even your most stubborn and strong-willed children to the party. Your love is amazing. Thank you, Lord. Amen.

DAY 27

Pharisees and Scribes

All the tax collectors and sinners were approaching to listen to him. And the Pharisees and scribes were complaining, "This man welcomes sinners and eats with them!" So he told them this parable" (Luke 15:1-3).

Setting the Scene

We see in the text at the beginning of Luke 15, that in addition to the disciples, Jesus's audience included "tax collectors," "sinners," "Pharisees," and "scribes." We can imagine the crowd gathered around Jesus to hear him teach, with his critics at the outside fringes, shaking their heads and grumbling. The pious, religious leaders (Pharisees and scribes) didn't appreciate the fact that Jesus was associating himself with notorious sinners, and they voiced their judgment. Jesus's parable was a direct response to their critical comments.

How did the people who heard these lost-and-found stories react? We'll first look at the Pharisees and scribes.

At the end of the story of the Prodigal Son, Luke doesn't say how anyone responded or what happened next. Instead, he moves directly into another teaching of Jesus, the parable of the Dishonest Manager. Then he writes this: "The Pharisees, who were lovers of money, were listening to all these things and scoffing at him" (16:14). We can probably assume, therefore, that these men didn't appreciate being identified as the older son in the message of the earlier parable.

We know that their hatred of Jesus grew over the following days and weeks, so much so that after he raised Lazarus from the dead, "from that day on they plotted to kill him" (Jn 11:53).

Jesus's teachings and actions threatened their power, position, and purpose for living. So rather than seriously consider what he was saying about God and his Word, they moved to silence him. Not all the religious leaders felt this way; Nicodemus, for example, became his follower (Jn 3:1-21; 7:50-52; 19:39).

Getting Personal

The Pharisees and scribes were attempting to prevent people—ordinary, sinful men and women—from following the Savior and being restored. Their self-righteous and judgmental attitudes also hindered their own restoration.

Today we easily identify our "Pharisees and scribes" as bishops, pastors, elders, deacons, and other denominational and local church leaders. And that may be the case. But *anyone* can harbor similar thoughts and feelings.

- Why might a pharisaical outlook on life keep a person from knowing Jesus?
- How do you deal with similar thoughts and feelings?
- How welcoming is your church to those considered misfits, outcasts, or notorious sinners?

Talking to God

Holy Spirit, sensitize me to the self-righteous and judgmental attitudes in me, and remove any barrier that I have put in my relationship with God. Please empower me to help others be restored to the Savior. Amen.

DAY 28

Disciples and Sinners

Now great crowds were traveling with him (Luke 14:25).

All the tax collectors and sinners were approaching to listen to him. And the Pharisees and scribes were complaining, "This man welcomes sinners and eats with them." (Luke 15:1-2).

Now he said to the disciples (Luke 16:1).

Setting the Scene

The "great crowds" with Jesus must have included the curious, those just wanting to see what all the fuss was about. Others probably followed to witness a miracle or two. Many may have been intrigued by Jesus's teachings and wanted to learn more. We know that the Jewish religious leaders were watching and listening to find fault with Jesus or trap him into heresy. Some in the multitude were desperate, needing healing, comfort, or forgiveness—restoration. Into that category, we can assume, fall the "tax collectors and sinners." Rejected by the Pharisees and shunned by "good" people, these men and women knew their sins and their reputations . . . and their need. So, they saw themselves in the story when Jesus told about the lost son coming to his senses and turning homeward, engulfed in his father's loving embrace, and restored to the family. They heard the message of hope.

The disciples were with Jesus most of the time. A motley crew—one, Matthew, had been a tax collector, and the group included several fishermen and a revolutionary. They were eye- and ear-witnesses to all that Jesus said and did. With each teaching, confrontation, and miracle, they were learning more and more about him. They had questions, doubts, and stumbles along the way (and wouldn't put it all together until after the resurrection), but they had left everything to follow Jesus (Mt 19:27; Jn 6:68). The disciples would have had a variety of reactions to the lost-and-found stories and probably quizzed Jesus about them later. Every experience with Jesus deepened the disciples' understanding of his identity and mission.

Getting Personal

These two groups would have listened intently to the parable for different reasons, but they would have responded positively. The "sinners" deeply understood their sin and need for a Savior. The disciples knew much about Jesus, the Messiah, and wanted to learn more. Both were open and receptive to his message of truth and eternal life.

- In what ways can you identify with the "sinners"? What drew you to Jesus? When did you realize that he was your Savior?
- With what aspect of being a "disciple" do you most identify? What can you do to learn more about Christ?
- What might your church do to help restored sinners become disciples?

Talking to God

I know I'm a sinner in desperate need of the Savior. Now, saved by grace, I want to know more of you, to learn more of your Word, to follow you fully as a disciple. In Christ's name, amen.

DAY 29

In the Crowd

Now great crowds were traveling with him (Luke 14:25).

All the tax collectors and sinners were approaching to listen to him. And the Pharisees and scribes were complaining, "This man welcomes sinners and eats with them." (Luke 15:1-2).

Now he said to the disciples (Luke 16:1).

Setting the Scene

We have seen, especially the last two days, that Jesus's audience that day included "tax collectors," "sinners," "Pharisees," "scribes," and "disciples." Certainly the gathered crowd also included those who wouldn't have fit neatly into those categories—they were sinners ("all have sinned"), but they avoided that label because their sins were not obvious and known.

We can read the Bible and find the stories interesting, engaging. But if we only see Scripture as a retelling of historical events and teachings or a book of religious doctrine, we haven't gone far enough. We need to study and apply the principles in God's Word.

One of the most important steps in Bible study that leads to application is to see ourselves in the story and to determine where these people would be today, in our world.

- Who might those people (tax collectors, sinners, Pharisees, scribes, disciples) be in your community?
- How about in your church?

Getting Personal

Now let's take it a step deeper.

- With which type of person do you most identify? Where do you see yourself in the crowd—curious onlooker, legalistic and judgmental critic, notorious sinner, typical sinner, or disciple?
- Imagine sitting or standing near Jesus and hearing him tell the three stories. What do these stories tell you about Jesus?
- What are you thinking and feeling after he speaks these final words: "'Son,' he said to him, 'you are always with me, and everything I have is yours. But we had to celebrate and rejoice, because this brother of yours was dead and is alive again; he was lost and is found'" (15:31-32)?

Talking to God

Jesus, I want to know you more. I need you. I want to be a seeker, not a Pharisee. I was lost in my sins, and you found me and welcomed me home. Now, I want to be your faithful disciple, ever learning and growing. Please help me, I pray. Amen.

DAY 30

In the Story

He also said: "A man had two sons" (Luke 15:11).

For I am persuaded that neither death nor life, nor angels nor rulers, nor things present nor things to come, nor powers, nor height nor depth, nor any other created thing will be able to separate us from the love of God that is in Christ Jesus our Lord (Romans 8:38-39).

Setting the Scene

Let's look at the parable again, this time noting the *places*.

The story begins in the home of a father and two brothers. Soon after the younger son asks for his share of the estate, he leaves home and travels far away. Eventually he arrives in the "distant country." There, after squandering all his resources, he finds work with a farmer and ends up feeding the pigs. Realizing his physical, moral, and spiritual bankruptcy, the repentant son begins his homeward journey. As he gets close, his father runs and embraces him on the road; then they complete the trip together. Finally, we see him at the party thrown to celebrate his return.

Home—road away—distant country—pigsty—road home—father's embrace—home again: We can imagine hurting and needy men and women listening intently, seeing themselves in that story.

Getting Personal

So, where are you? Perhaps you're still home. To all outward appearances you are doing well, but you've been fantasizing about—perhaps even planning—another life in another place.

But you may be on the road away from home, going in the wrong direction.

Or you may be in that "distant country," anonymous and doing what you know you shouldn't (others can't see it, but you know you're there).

You may be in the farmer's field, famished, desperate, and longing for home.

Or you could be on your way back.

Wherever you are *in the story*, know this: You can never be lost to God's love. The Father knows where you are, and he is waiting and watching, ready to embrace you, take you to his house, meet your needs, and celebrate your presence.

Come home—be restored!

Talking to God

O Father, I confess that I am not where I need to be. I have sinned against you and want to come home. Thank you, Lord, for your open-armed welcome, love, and joy. Amen.

Index of Restore Notes

The RESTORE notes are where the rubber meets the road in the restoration process. Each of the seven Restoration Principles are expounded upon and fully realized through topics and issues that directly relate to the corresponding Restoration Principle and related Scriptures. The RESTORE notes are permeated with the hope, joy, and peace found in the good news of the gospel and enjoyed through a personal relationship with Jesus Christ.

R — *Rest and Reflection*

E — *Eternal Perspective*

- ○ Biblical Hope (Psalm 27:14; Isaiah 61:1-2; Jeremiah 29:11; Ezekiel 37:2-3; Romans 15:13; Titus 2:13)
- ○ Biblical Joy (Proverbs 17:22; John 2:2-3; Philippians 4:4)
- ○ Biblical Peace (John 16:33; 2 Thessalonians 3:16)
- ○ Christ Focus (2 Corinthians 11:3)
- ○ Death's Defeat/Resurrection (Job 19:25-27; John 11:35)
- ○ Fear Overcome (Psalm 56:3; 118:5-6; 2 Timothy 1:7)
- ○ Forward Look (Haggai 2:9; 2 Corinthians 4:17-18; Philippians 3:13-14)
- ○ God Never Changing (Malachi 3:6)
- ○ God the Creator (Genesis 1:1; Nehemiah 9:6)
- ○ God's Character (Psalm 22:1)
- ○ God's Children (Mark 14:36; Galatians 4:4-5)
- ○ God's Compassion (Psalm 103:7-8; 145:8-9; Isaiah 30:18; Lamentations 3:22-23; Luke 15:20)
- ○ God's Faithfulness (Deuteronomy 7:9; Psalm 31:7; 89:1-2)
- ○ God's Family (Romans 16:14)
- ○ God's Forgiveness (Psalm 24:3-4; 32:1-2; Zephaniah 3:15)
- ○ God's Goodness (Psalm 86:15; Nahum 1:7; Zechariah 12:8)
- ○ God's Grace/Kindness (Joel 2:12-13; Acts 15:11)
- ○ God's Holiness (Isaiah 6:3)
- ○ God's Inside View (1 Samuel 16:7; Luke 16:14-15)
- ○ God's Justice (Psalm 5:6)
- ○ God's Knowledge/Omniscience (Psalm 33:13-15; 139:1-3; 144:3; Jeremiah 1:5)
- ○ God's Love (Isaiah 49:15-16; Zephaniah 3:17; John 3:16; Romans 5:8; 8:38-39; Ephesians 3:17-19)
- ○ God's Majesty (Psalm 93:4)
- ○ God's Memory (Leviticus 26:45)
- ○ God's Mercy (Isaiah 42:3; Micah 7:8; Luke 1:49-50; Ephesians 2:4-5)
- ○ God's Plans (Psalm 40:5; Micah 5:2; Matthew 6:33; Acts 16:6-7; Revelation 21:4-5)
- ○ God's Power (2 Samuel 7:22; 2 Kings 6:16-17; Job 42:2; Isaiah 46:10; Jeremiah 32:26-27; Matthew 19:25-26; Luke 1:37)
- ○ God's Presence (Joshua 1:9)
- ○ God's Promises (Numbers 23:19)
- ○ God's Protection (Psalm 121:5-8)
- ○ God's Purposes (Jonah 4:6-8; Ephesians 3:1; Philippians 1:6; Revelation 21:1)
- ○ God's Strengthening (Deuteronomy 20:3-4)
- ○ God's Timing (Esther 4:13-14; Romans 5:6)
- ○ God's View of Sin (Psalm 5:4; Romans 6:23)
- ○ God's Work in Us (Jeremiah 31:33; Mark 7:32-33; 8:24-25; John 17:3; Philippians 2:12-13)
- ○ Heaven and Hell (John 14:1-3)
- ○ Identity in Christ (Ephesians 4:1)
- ○ Personal Limitations (Isaiah 55:8-9)
- ○ Personal Value/Worth (Genesis 1:27; Psalm 8:3-5; 100:1-3; Matthew 10:29-31; Luke 2:25-26; Ephesians 2:10)
- ○ Positive Focus (Philippians 2:14)
- ○ Redemption/Salvation (Isaiah 43:1; Ephesians 1:7)
- ○ Stewardship (Matthew 25:21)
- ○ Supremacy of Christ (Colossians 1:15-17)

S — *Support*

T — *Thanksgiving and Contentment*

- O Shortcomings/Weaknesses (2 Corinthians 5:21; 12:9)
- O Thanksgiving (1 Chronicles 16:8; Psalm 118:24; 1 Thessalonians 5:18)

O — *Other-centeredness*

- O Assuming the Best (Joshua 9:14; 1 Corinthians 13:6-7)
- O Avoiding Jealousy/Coveting (Exodus 20:17; James 3:15-16)
- O Being Compassionate (Jeremiah 9:1; Matthew 9:35-36)
- O Being Honest (Psalm 25:21; James 5:12)
- O Being Humble (Obadiah 3-4; Luke 14:11)
- O Being Patient (2 Timothy 2:24-25)
- O Being Unselfish (John 15:12-13; Philippians 2:3-4; Hebrews 13:16)
- O Caring (Hebrews 13:1)
- O Dealing with Difficult People (Luke 6:8; 2 Corinthians 10:3; 3 John 10)
- O Encouraging (Deuteronomy 31:6; Proverbs 12:25; Isaiah 35:3-4; Acts 9:26-27)
- O Giving Generously (Isaiah 32:8; Acts 4:32; 2 Corinthians 9:7)
- O Helping People in Need (Leviticus 19:10; Psalm 41:1; Amos 5:24; Matthew 25:40; 1 John 3:17)
- O Helping Widows and Orphans (Job 29:12-13; Psalm 68:5; Isaiah 1:17)
- O Identifying Those We Have Wronged (Leviticus 25:17; Numbers 5:6-7; Mark 11:25)
- O Learning Other People's Stories (1 Samuel 25:24; Ecclesiastes 3:7)
- O Living Peacefully (Hebrews 12:14)
- O Loving God (Deuteronomy 6:4-5; 10:12; Joshua 23:11; Psalm 18:1)
- O Loving Others (Philemon 4-5; 1 John 3:18)
- O Loving the Unlovable (2 Peter 3:9)
- O Not Being Judgmental (Matthew 7:1; Mark 2:17; Luke 6:37; Romans 2:1)
- O Not Holding Resentment/Grudges (Leviticus 19:18)
- O Praying for Others (1 Samuel 12:23; Ezekiel 33:11; Acts 9:3-4; Colossians 1:9-11; 4:12; 1 Timothy 2:1-2)
- O Showing Mercy (Jude 22)

R — *Relationships*

- O Admitting Weakness (Ephesians 6:19)
- O Admitting Wrongs (Proverbs 28:13; James 5:16)
- O Avoiding Harmful Relationships (2 Corinthians 6:14)
- O Being Impartial (Acts 10:34-35; Galatians 3:28; James 2:1)
- O Building Healthy Friendships (Proverbs 18:24; 1 Corinthians 15:33)
- O Building Positive Relationships (Proverbs 13:20; Ephesians 4:31; Hebrews 10:24)
- O Celebrating Diversity (Revelation 5:9)
- O Communicating (2 John 12)
- O Confronting in Love (Leviticus 19:17; Luke 17:4)
- O Controlling Speech (Psalm 19:14; 141:3; Colossians 4:5-6; 2 Timothy 2:16)
- O Dealing with Anger and Hatred (James 1:19-20; 1 John 2:10-11)

- O Dealing with Persecution (2 Timothy 3:12)
- O Encouraging Each Other (Psalm 88:9; 2 Peter 3:18)
- O Helping Weaker Believers (1 Corinthians 8:13)
- O Loving Our Neighbors (Matthew 22:39-40)
- O Making Amends (Leviticus 6:2-5; Proverbs 14:9)
- O Making Peace (Micah 5:5)
- O Mentoring (Psalm 71:18; Proverbs 9:9)
- O Offering Forgiveness (Jeremiah 15:21)
- O Relating to Children (Proverbs 22:6; Matthew 18:2,5; Ephesians 6:4)
- O Relating to Church Family (John 13:34-35; Romans 1:16; 12:15-18; 1 Corinthians 6:1; Hebrews 6:10; 1 Peter 4:8)
- O Relating to Coworkers (Proverbs 12:24; Ecclesiastes 2:18,20)
- O Relating to Family (Luke 4:28-29)
- O Relating to Friends (1 Samuel 18:1-3; Proverbs 27:6; Ecclesiastes 4:9-10,12)
- O Relating to Parents (Exodus 20:12)
- O Relating to Spiritual Leaders (1 Corinthians 3:5-6; Hebrews 13:17)
- O Relating to Spouse/Marriage (Genesis 2:24; Song of Songs 2:15; Matthew 19:4-6; Ephesians 5:33)
- O Resolving Arguments/Disagreements/Conflicts (Acts 15:37-39; 2 Corinthians 2:14)
- O Restoring Damaged Relationships (1 Peter 3:8-9)
- O Submitting to Others (Ephesians 5:21)
- O Taking Personal Inventory (Psalm 26:2)
- O Telling the Truth (Exodus 20:16; 23:1; 1 Chronicles 29:17; Luke 6:26-27)
- O Treating Others Fairly (Psalm 106:3)
- O Working for Unity in the Church (John 17:23)

E — *Exercise of Faith*

- O Applying God's Word (Psalm 19:7-8; Hosea 4:6; 2 Timothy 3:16-17)
- O Being Involved in Church (Acts 2:42)
- O Continuing to Do Good (Galatians 6:9)
- O Dealing with Doubt (1 Corinthians 15:6)
- O Discipling Others (Galatians 6:1)
- O Enduring Suffering (John 9:1-2; Philippians 1:29)
- O Experiencing New Life in Christ (2 Corinthians 5:17)
- O Finishing Strong (1 Corinthians 9:24-25; 2 Timothy 4:7-8)
- O Following God's Lead (Isaiah 6:8; Galatians 5:25)
- O Guarding the Heart (1 Kings 11:4; Job 31:7-8; Proverbs 4:23; Zephaniah 1:12; Romans 13:14)
- O Honoring/Glorifying God (1 Corinthians 10:31)
- O Increasing Faith (Luke 7:9; 17:5)
- O Knowing Christ (Philippians 3:7-8)
- O Living by Faith (2 Corinthians 5:7; Galatians 2:20; Colossians 2:6; 2 Thessalonians 1:3)
- O Making Right Choices/Priorities/Values (Joshua 24:15; Matthew 16:25-26; Luke 10:41-42; 12:31; 18:22; Ephesians 5:15; 1 John 2:15)
- O Making the Most of Time on Earth (Psalm 103:15-16; Haggai 1:5; 1 Thessalonians 5:6)
- O Managing Money (1 Timothy 6:9-10)

Index of Restoration Profiles

Index of My Story Notes

- ○ Bonnie—Infertility (Genesis 30)
- ○ Cathy—Importance of rest (Leviticus 23)
- ○ Judith—Worry (Joshua 21)
- ○ Dawn—Sexual abuse (Judges 16)
- ○ Joey—Forgiveness (2 Samuel 12)
- ○ Lucy—Suicidal feelings (1 Kings 15)
- ○ Steve—Finding joy (2 Kings 11)
- ○ Shayleen—Hurt and harassment (1 Chronicles 4)
- ○ Mia—Death of spouse (Job 9)
- ○ Ian—Thankfulness (Psalm 11)
- ○ Marvin—Boredom with faith (Psalm 48)
- ○ Jill—Fear and doubt (Psalm 79)
- ○ Tim—Alcoholism (Proverbs 23)
- ○ Ed—Finding faith (Ecclesiastes 12)
- ○ Casey—Pornography (Isaiah 24)
- ○ Christine—Facing cancer (Isaiah 41)
- ○ Jason—Brokenness (Jeremiah 23)
- ○ Cord—Doubt (Jeremiah 36)
- ○ Franklyn—Emotional healing (Lamentations 2)
- ○ Jordan—Hurt and anger (Ezekiel 3)
- ○ Sherry—Searching for faith (Ezekiel 18)
- ○ Rita—Online affairs (Daniel 6)
- ○ Javier—Faith (Hosea 11)
- ○ Mandy—Commitment and compassion (Micah 2)
- ○ Morris—Stress (Matthew 15)
- ○ Colin—Seeking faith and purpose (Luke 15)
- ○ Marcus—Seeking God's love (Luke 23)
- ○ Mickey—Dealing with depression (John 3)
- ○ Sabrina—Doubt vs. faith (Romans 9)
- ○ Josh—Marriage reconciliation (1 Corinthians 16)
- ○ Rhonda—Peace in relationships (2 Corinthians 6)
- ○ Cara—Healing from addiction (Philippians 1)
- ○ Cliff—Self-worth and priorities (Colossians 2)
- ○ Neil—Marriage relationship (1 Peter 3)

Index of Embracing God's Word Charts

- O Comfort (Revelation 9)
- O Courage (1 Chronicles 28)
- O Forgiveness (Matthew 27)
- O Hope (Romans 14)
- O Joy (Philippians 3)
- O Love (1 Corinthians 13)
- O Peace (Psalm 29)
- O Provision (Psalm 111)
- O Renewal (Hebrews 5)
- O Victory (2 Corinthians 1)

Index of Joyful Noise Callouts

- Genesis 5:24; 15:1; 18:14; 21:22; 39:2; 50:20
- Exodus 3:12; 13:14; 18:18,23; 29:46; 31:2-6; 33:13; 34:6-7
- Leviticus 9:23-24; 16:30; 17:11; 22:32
- Numbers 9:23; 10:35; 13:30; 14:9; 21:9
- Deuteronomy 1:21; 2:7; 30:14; 32:3-4; 32:46-47; 33:27
- Joshua 4:6-7; 5:9; 10:8; 11:15; 14:14
- Judges 2:7; 5:31; 10:15-16
- Ruth 4:14
- 1 Samuel 3:10; 14:6; 20:42; 30:6
- 2 Samuel 5:12
- 1 Kings 2:2-3; 8:23
- 2 Kings 2:11; 12:15; 14:26-27; 17:28; 18:5-6; 23:2-3
- 1 Chronicles 19:13; 22:19
- 2 Chronicles 1:10; 5:13-14; 6:21; 15:2; 16:9; 20:15; 32:7
- Ezra 1:1-2; 6:21
- Nehemiah 1:11; 4:14; 6:15-16; 12:43
- Esther 9:21-22
- Job 1:20-22; 12:10; 14:14,17; 23:10; 28:28
- Psalms 58:11; 130:5; 148:1
- Proverbs 8:17; 25:11
- Ecclesiastes 7:11; 8:15
- Song of Songs 7:10
- Isaiah 12:2; 16:5; 26:3; 58:11; 64:8; 65:17
- Jeremiah 6:16; 17:14; 50:34; 51:15
- Lamentations 5:19
- Ezekiel 12:20; 34:26; 36:26; 48:35
- Daniel 2:22; 3:17-18; 9:9; 12:3
- Hosea 1:7; 13:14; 14:9
- Joel 2:32
- Amos 3:3; 9:14
- Jonah 2:7
- Micah 4:5
- Habakkuk 2:14
- Zephaniah 2:3
- Zechariah 2:11; 7:10; 8:13; 9:10
- Matthew 1:21; 17:20
- Mark 5:19; 16:6
- Acts 13:38
- 1 Thessalonians 2:13
- 2 Thessalonians 2:13
- Revelation 11:15; 15:3

Writers & Contributors for the CSB Restoration Bible

Writers

Nancy Taylor   Neil Wilson

David Veerman   Len Woods

Contributors

Dave Barber   Karlea Jones

Cathy Bartelt   Donald Limmer

Brenda Bonn   Faith Limmer

Bob Chandler   Dave McChristian

Benjamin Case   Judith VanCooney

Sherrie Clark   Dave Veerman

Laura DeVries   Josh White

Steve Doro   Lee Wilson

J.D. Green   Neil Wilson

Introduction to the Christian Standard Bible®

The Bible is God's revelation to humanity. It is our only source for completely reliable information about God, what happens when we die, and where history is headed. The Bible does these things because it is God's inspired Word, inerrant in the original manuscripts. Bible translation brings God's Word from the ancient languages (Hebrew, Greek, and Aramaic) into today's world. In dependence on God's Spirit to accomplish this sacred task, the CSB Translation Oversight Committee and Holman Bible Publishers present the Christian Standard Bible.

Textual Base of the CSB

The textual base for the New Testament (NT) is the Nestle-Aland *Novum Testamentum Graece*, 28th edition, and the United Bible Societies' *Greek New Testament*, 5th corrected edition. The text for the Old Testament (OT) is the *Biblia Hebraica Stuttgartensia,* 5th edition. Where there are significant differences among Hebrew, Aramaic, or Greek manuscripts, the translators follow what they believe is the original reading and indicate the main alternative(s) in footnotes.

Goals of This Translation

- Provide English-speaking people worldwide with an accurate translation in contemporary English.
- Provide an accurate translation for personal study, sermon preparation, private devotions, and memorization.
- Provide a text that is clear and understandable, suitable for public reading, and shareable so that all may access its life-giving message.
- Affirm the authority of Scripture and champion its absolute truth against skeptical viewpoints.

Translation Philosophy of the Christian Standard Bible

Most discussions of Bible translations speak of two opposite approaches: formal equivalence and dynamic equivalence. However, Bible translations cannot be neatly sorted into these categories. Optimal equivalence capitalizes on the strengths of both approaches.

Optimal equivalence balances contemporary English readability with linguistic precision to the original languages.

In the many places throughout the Bible where a word-for-word rendering is understandable, a literal translation is used. When a word-for-word rendering might obscure the meaning for a modern audience, a more dynamic translation is used. This process assures that both the words and the thoughts contained in the original text are conveyed accurately for today's readers. The Christian Standard Bible places equal value on fidelity to the original and readability for a modern audience, resulting in a translation that achieves both goals.

History of the CSB

Holman Bible Publishers assembled an interdenominational team of one hundred scholars, editors, stylists, and proofreaders, all of whom were committed to biblical inerrancy. Working from the original languages, the translation team edited and polished the manuscript, which was first published as the Holman Christian Standard Bible in 2004.

A standing committee maintained the translation, while also seeking ways to improve both readability and accuracy. As with the original translation, the committee that prepared this revision, renamed the Christian Standard Bible, is international and interdenominational, comprising evangelical scholars who honor the inspiration and authority of God's written Word.

Footnotes

Footnotes are used to show readers how the original biblical language has been understood in the CSB.

1. Old Testament (OT) Textual Footnotes

OT textual notes show important differences among Hebrew (Hb) manuscripts and ancient OT versions, such as the Septuagint and the Vulgate. See the list of abbreviations that follows for a list of other ancient versions used.

Some OT textual notes (like NT textual notes) give only an alternate textual reading. However, other OT textual notes also give the support for the reading chosen by the editors as well as for the alternate textual reading. For example, the CSB text of Psalm 12:7 reads,

> You, LORD, will guard us;
> you will protect us[A] from this generation forever.

The textual footnote for this verse reads,

[A]12:7 Some Hb mss, LXX; other Hb mss read *him*

The textual note in this example means that there are two different readings found in the Hebrew manuscripts: some manuscripts read *us* and others read *him*. The CSB translators chose the reading *us*, which is also found in the Septuagint (LXX), and placed the other Hebrew reading *him* in the footnote.

Two other kinds of OT textual notes are

Alt Hb tradition reads ____	a variation given by scribes in the Hebrew manuscript tradition (known as *Kethiv/Qere* and *Tiqqune Sopherim* readings)
Hb uncertain	when it is unclear what the original Hebrew text was

2. New Testament (NT) Textual Footnotes

NT textual notes indicate significant differences among Greek manuscripts (mss) and are normally indicated in one of three ways:

Other mss read ____
Other mss add ____
Other mss omit ____

In the NT, some textual footnotes that use the word "add" or "omit" also have square brackets before and after the corresponding verses in the biblical text. Examples of this use of square brackets are Mark 16:9-20 and John 7:53–8:11.

3. Other Kinds of Footnotes

Lit ____	a more literal rendering in English of the Hebrew, Aramaic, or Greek text
Or ____	an alternate or less likely English translation of the same Hebrew, Aramaic, or Greek text
=	an abbreviation for "it means" or "it is equivalent to"

Hb, Aramaic, Gk	the actual Hebrew, Aramaic, or Greek word is given using equivalent English letters
Hb obscure	the existing Hebrew text is especially difficult to translate
emend[ed] to ____	the original Hebrew text is so difficult to translate that competent scholars have conjectured or inferred a restoration of the original text based on the context, probable root meanings of the words, and uses in comparative languages

In some editions of the CSB, additional footnotes clarify the meaning of certain biblical texts or explain biblical history, persons, customs, places, activities, and measurements. Cross references are given for parallel passages or passages with similar wording, and in the NT, for passages quoted from the OT.

Abbreviations in | CSB Bibles

AD	In the year of our Lord
aka	also known as
Akk	Akkadian
alt	alternate
a.m.	from midnight until noon
ANET	Ancient Near Eastern Texts, 3rd ed., James B. Pritchard, ed. (Princeton, 1969)
Ant.	Antiquities—a history of the Jewish people by Josephus
Aq	Aquila
BC	before Christ
c.	century
ca	circa
chap(s).	chapter(s)
cp.	compare
DSS	Dead Sea Scrolls
e.g.	for example
Eng	English
esp.	especially
etc.	et cetera
ff.	following
Gk	Greek
Hb	Hebrew
i.e.	that is
Jer	Latin translation of Psalms by Jerome
Lat	Latin
Lit/lit	Literally/literally
LXX	Septuagint—an ancient translation of the Old Testament into Greek
MT	Masoretic Text
NT	New Testament
ms(s)	manuscript(s)
OT	Old Testament
p., pp.	page, pages
p.m.	from noon until midnight
pl.	plural
Ps(s)	Psalm(s)
Sam	Samaritan Pentateuch
sg.	singular
Sir	Sirach
Sym	Symmachus
Syr	Syriac
Tg	Targum
Theod	Theodotian
v., vv.	verse, verses
Vg	Vulgate—an ancient translation of the Bible into Latin
vol(s).	volume(s)
vs.	versus
x	times

Notes

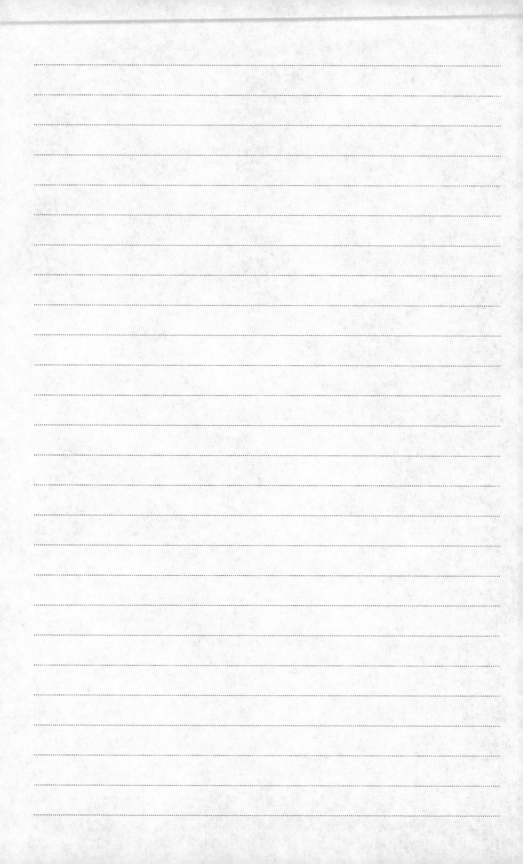

The Old Testament

Genesis—Any new venture can go better than we dare to hope or worse than we could predict. Genesis has that familiar tension and blend—a perfect creation with an open relationship between God and humankind, and terror when Adam and Eve's tragic choice makes everything go horribly wrong. Here we see the darkness of humanity that lurks in our souls as well as the hope of God's promise that he will one day restore and redeem fallen humanity.

From the beginning, God's love and holiness shine through. Everything was good as he walked with Adam and Eve. But their rebellion broke that relationship. Yet he still loved humanity, the pinnacle of creation. So, God promised to make a people for himself who, eventually, would be able to live in his presence forever.

God had a solution to the consequences of the fall and the curse: God would redeem his broken and sinful people and make a way for them to have peace with him, to restore their relationship.

The promise to bless all nations through Abraham reaches to us, for through the promised descendant of Abraham, Jesus Christ, we are able to come before the throne of our loving and holy Creator and be declared righteous in his sight.

GENESIS

AUTHOR: Moses

DATE WRITTEN: 1446–1406 BC

ORIGINAL AUDIENCE: The Israelites

SETTING: Moses penned Genesis, as well as the rest of the Pentateuch (the first five books of the OT (Old Testament) during the forty years the Israelites wandered in the wilderness. The nation had been miraculously rescued from slavery in Egypt, but then they had failed to trust God to continue to lead and protect them. Their punishment was that they would spend forty years wandering through the wilderness while they waited for the entire adult population to die. At this crucial juncture in the early history of the nation, they needed to understand where they had come from and what they were working toward.

PURPOSE FOR WRITING: Genesis sets up the key theological truths that God is the Creator of all that is, and that he is making for himself a people who will love and serve him forever. It establishes both the beginnings of the world and humanity, as well as the beginnings of their relationship with God, the origin and pervasiveness of sin, and God's redemptive solution that would come through one particular descendant of Abraham—the Messiah.

OUTLINE:

1. Prologue (1:1–11:32)

Creation (1:1–2:25)

The fall (3:1-24)

The consequences (4:1–5:32)

The flood and its aftermath (6:1–9:29)

Early nations and the tower of Babel (10:1–11:32)

2. The Covenant (12:1–50:26)

Abraham and Sarah (12:1–25:34)

Isaac and Rebekah (26:1–27:45)

Jacob and Esau (27:46–36:43)

Joseph (37:1–50:26)

KEY VERSE:

"Is anything impossible for the LORD?" —Genesis 18:14

24 Then God said, "Let the earth produce
living creatures according to their kinds:
livestock, creatures that crawl, and the wildlife of the earth according to their kinds."
And it was so. 25 So God made the wildlife
of the earth according to their kinds, the
livestock according to their kinds, and all
the creatures that crawl on the ground according to their kinds. And God saw that
it was good.
26 Then God said, "Let us make man[A] in[B] our
image, according to our likeness. They will
rule the fish of the sea, the birds of the sky, the
livestock, the whole earth,[C] and the creatures
that crawl[D] on the earth."
27 So God created man in his own image;
he created him in[E] the image of God;
he created them male and female.
28 God blessed them, and God said to them,
"Be fruitful, multiply, fill the earth, and subdue it. Rule the fish of the sea, the birds of
the sky, and every creature that crawls[F] on
the earth." 29 God also said, "Look, I have
given you every seed-bearing plant on the
surface of the entire earth and every tree
whose fruit contains seed. This will be food
for you, 30 for all the wildlife of the earth, for
every bird of the sky, and for every creature
that crawls on the earth — everything having the breath of life in it — I have given[G]
every green plant for food." And it was so.
31 God saw all that he had made, and it was
very good indeed. Evening came and then
morning: the sixth day.

2 So the heavens and the earth and everything in them were completed. 2 On the
seventh[H] day God had completed his work
that he had done, and he rested[I] on the seventh day from all his work that he had done.
3 God blessed the seventh day and declared
it holy, for on it he rested from all his work
of creation.[J]

MAN AND WOMAN IN THE GARDEN

4 These are the records of the heavens and
the earth, concerning their creation. At the
time[K] that the LORD God made the earth and
the heavens, 5 no shrub of the field had yet
grown on the land,[L] and no plant of the field
had yet sprouted, for the LORD God had not
made it rain on the land, and there was no man
to work the ground. 6 But mist would come
up from the earth and water all the ground.
7 Then the LORD God formed the man out of

Eternal Perspective | *Personal Value/Worth*

WHY WE MATTER

"So God created man in his own image; he created him in the image of God; he created them male and female." Genesis 1:27

Genesis depicts humanity as the crowning touch, the best work of God's creation. God called all his previous handiwork "good." But when the triune God completed his creative efforts with a man and a woman, Scripture shows the Almighty studying his work admiringly and concluding that it "was very good indeed" (Gn 1:31).

Genesis describes humanity by the short phrase "the image of God." What does this mean? Theologians have written thick tomes trying to answer this question. At the very least, the idea seems to be that we were made to resemble God. Though not divine, we reflect God in important ways. We are wired for relationship and marvelously creative—just as the One who made us. We can reason and feel deeply (love!). What's more, we have the capacity to make moral decisions.

Consistently and consciously remembering that the One who is the essence of love (1Jn 4:8) purposefully created us would do wonders for our self-worth.

For the next note on *Eternal Perspective*, see Leviticus 26:45.

[A] **1:26** Or *human beings*; Hb *'adam*, also in v. 27 [B] **1:26** Or *as* [C] **1:26** Syr reads *sky, and over every animal of the land* [D] **1:26** Or *scurry* [E] **1:27** Or *man as his own image; he created him as* [F] **1:28** Or *and all scurrying animals* [G] **1:30** *I have given* added for clarity [H] **2:2** Sam, LXX, Syr read *sixth* [I] **2:2** Or *ceased*, also in v. 3 [J] **2:3** Lit *work that God created to make* [K] **2:4** Lit *creation on the day* [L] **2:5** Or *earth*

the dust from the ground and breathed the
breath of life into his nostrils, and the man
became a living being.
8 The LORD God planted a garden in Eden,
in the east, and there he placed the man he
had formed. 9 The LORD God caused to grow
out of the ground every tree pleasing in appearance and good for food, including the
tree of life in the middle of the garden, as
well as the tree of the knowledge of good
and evil.
10 A river went[A] out from Eden to water the
garden. From there it divided and became the
source of four rivers.[B] 11 The name of the first
is Pishon, which flows through the entire
land of Havilah,[C] where there is gold. 12 Gold
from that land is pure;[D] bdellium[E] and onyx[F]
are also there. 13 The name of the second river is Gihon, which flows through the entire
land of Cush. 14 The name of the third river
is Tigris, which runs east of Assyria. And the
fourth river is the Euphrates.
15 The LORD God took the man and placed
him in the garden of Eden to work it and
watch over it. 16 And the LORD God commanded the man, "You are free to eat from
any tree of the garden, 17 but you must not
eat from the tree of the knowledge of good
and evil, for on the day you eat from it, you
will certainly die." 18 Then the LORD God said,
"It is not good for the man to be alone. I
will make a helper corresponding to him."
19 The LORD God formed out of the ground
every wild animal and every bird of the sky,
and brought each to the man to see what he
would call it. And whatever the man called
a living creature, that was its name. 20 The
man gave names to all the livestock, to the
birds of the sky, and to every wild animal;
but for the man[G] no helper was found corresponding to him. 21 So the LORD God caused
a deep sleep to come over the man, and he
slept. God took one of his ribs and closed
the flesh at that place. 22 Then the LORD God
made the rib he had taken from the man
into a woman and brought her to the man.
23 And the man said:

This one, at last, is bone of my bone
and flesh of my flesh;
this one will be called "woman,"
for she was taken from man.

24 This is why a man leaves his father and
mother and bonds with his wife, and they
become one flesh. 25 Both the man and his
wife were naked, yet felt no shame.

Rest and Reflection | *Observing Sabbath*

BEING VS. DOING

"On the seventh day God had completed his work that he had done, and he rested on the seventh day from all his work that he had done. God blessed the seventh day and declared it holy, for on it he rested from all his work of creation." Genesis 2:2-3

Long before Moses descended Mount Sinai with a commandment requiring the Jewish people to take a day off each week (Ex 20:8-10), God wove the idea of "rest" into the very fabric of his new creation.

After all his creative labors, God "rested." Or we could say, he refrained from any more *doing* and devoted himself to *being*. He did this, of course, not because he was tired and needed a nap, but, ostensibly, to enjoy the fruit of his labors. Remember, too, he did this before sin entered the world.

Because we live in a culture that places so much worth on what a person accomplishes, we can easily fall into the trap of *never* resting. We assume that if doing some work is good, then doing more is better. But just as farmland needs to rest to replenish its nutrients, so must we find rest to rebuild ourselves. Take a break and *rest*.

For the next note on *Rest and Reflection*, see Exodus 20:8-10.

[A] **2:10** Or *goes* [B] **2:10** Lit *became four heads* [C] **2:11** Or *of the Havilah* [D] **2:12** Lit *good* [E] **2:12** A yellowish, transparent gum resin [F] **2:12** Identity of this precious stone uncertain [G] **2:20** Or *for Adam*

THE TEMPTATION AND THE FALL

3 Now the serpent was the most cunning of
all the wild animals that the LORD God had
made. He said to the woman, "Did God really
say, 'You can't eat from any tree in the garden'?"
2 The woman said to the serpent, "We may
eat the fruit from the trees in the garden. 3 But
about the fruit of the tree in the middle of the
garden, God said, 'You must not eat it or touch
it, or you will die.'"
4 "No! You will not die," the serpent said to
the woman. 5 "In fact, God knows that when[A]
you eat it your eyes will be opened and you
will be like God,[B] knowing good and evil."
6 The woman saw that the tree was good for
food and delightful to look at, and that it was
desirable for obtaining wisdom. So she took
some of its fruit and ate it; she also gave some
to her husband, who was with her, and he
ate it. 7 Then the eyes of both of them were
opened, and they knew they were naked;
so they sewed fig leaves together and made
coverings for themselves.

SIN'S CONSEQUENCES

8 Then the man and his wife heard the sound
of the LORD God walking in the garden at the
time of the evening breeze,[C] and they hid from
the LORD God among the trees of the garden.
9 So the LORD God called out to the man and
said to him, "Where are you?"
10 And he said, "I heard you[D] in the garden,
and I was afraid because I was naked, so I hid."
11 Then he asked, "Who told you that you
were naked? Did you eat from the tree that I
commanded you not to eat from?"
12 The man replied, "The woman you gave
to be with me — she gave me some fruit from
the tree, and I ate."
13 So the LORD God asked the woman, "What
is this you have done?"
And the woman said, "The serpent deceived
me, and I ate."
14 So the LORD God said to the serpent:
Because you have done this,
you are cursed more than any
livestock
and more than any wild animal.
You will move on your belly
and eat dust all the days of your life.
15 I will put hostility between you
and the woman,
and between your offspring
and her offspring.

Relationships | *Relating to Spouse/Marriage*

MARRIAGE AS GOD INTENDED

"This is why a man leaves his father and mother and bonds with his wife, and they become one flesh." Genesis 2:24

The Bible's marital ideal requires leaving, cleaving, and weaving.

First, a man and his soon-to-be wife willingly agree to *leave* behind their past lives, which requires them to redefine and reconfigure old relationships. Then the couple "bonds." This is the Hebrew "glue" word, meaning to join or cling tightly. It suggests an abiding commitment. (The old-fashioned word is *cleave*.) Third, they "become one flesh." This is the *weaving* aspect of marriage: two disparate lives becoming one, morphing into something new and beautiful. The couple's coming together physically/sexually is meant to mirror a deeper co-mingling of souls, hopes, and dreams. This process continues throughout married life.

Biblical marriage then, has no place for superficial, short-term commitment. It is a far cry from the common contemporary version of marriage—two people who fiercely want to maintain their separate lives and only want to share a name (perhaps), an address, and a bed.

When modern marriages skip these three steps, they desperately need restoration. By emphasizing them, they can begin to find it.

For the next note on *Relationships*, see Exodus 20:12.

[A] **3:5** Lit *on the day* [B] **3:5** Or *gods*, or *divine beings* [C] **3:8** Lit *at the wind of the day* [D] **3:10** Lit *the sound of you*

He will strike your head,
and you will strike his heel.

16 He said to the woman:
I will intensify your labor pains;
you will bear children with painful
effort.
Your desire will be for your
husband,
yet he will rule over you.

17 And he said to the man, "Because you listened to your wife and ate from the tree about
which I commanded you, 'Do not eat from it':
The ground is cursed because of you.
You will eat from it by means of
painful labor[A]
all the days of your life.
18 It will produce thorns and thistles
for you,
and you will eat the plants of the field.
19 You will eat bread[B] by the sweat
of your brow
until you return to the ground,
since you were taken from it.
For you are dust,
and you will return to dust."

20 The man named his wife Eve[C] because she
was the mother of all the living. 21 The LORD
God made clothing from skins for the man
and his wife, and he clothed them.
22 The LORD God said, "Since the man has become like one of us, knowing good and evil, he
must not reach out, take from the tree of life,
eat, and live forever." 23 So the LORD God sent
him away from the garden of Eden to work the
ground from which he was taken. 24 He drove
the man out and stationed the cherubim and
the flaming, whirling sword east of the garden
of Eden to guard the way to the tree of life.

CAIN MURDERS ABEL

4 The man was intimate with his wife Eve,
and she conceived and gave birth to Cain.
She said, "I have had a male child with the
LORD's help."[D] 2 She also gave birth to his
brother Abel. Now Abel became a shepherd
of flocks, but Cain worked the ground. 3 In
the course of time Cain presented some of
the land's produce as an offering to the LORD.
4 And Abel also presented an offering — some
of the firstborn of his flock and their fat portions. The LORD had regard for Abel and his
offering, 5 but he did not have regard for Cain
and his offering. Cain was furious, and he
looked despondent.[E]
6 Then the LORD said to Cain, "Why are you
furious? And why do you look despondent?[F]
7 If you do what is right, won't you be accepted? But if you do not do what is right, sin is
crouching at the door. Its desire is for you,
but you must rule over it."
8 Cain said to his brother Abel, "Let's go
out to the field."[G] And while they were in
the field, Cain attacked his brother Abel and
killed him.
9 Then the LORD said to Cain, "Where is your
brother Abel?"
"I don't know," he replied. "Am I my brother's guardian?"
10 Then he said, "What have you done? Your
brother's blood cries out to me from the
ground! 11 So now you are cursed, alienated
from the ground that opened its mouth to
receive your brother's blood you have shed.[H]
12 If you work the ground, it will never again
give you its yield. You will be a restless wanderer on the earth."
13 But Cain answered the LORD, "My punishment[I] is too great to bear! 14 Since you are
banishing me today from the face of the earth,
and I must hide from your presence and become a restless wanderer on the earth, whoever finds me will kill me."
15 Then the LORD replied to him, "In that
case,[J] whoever kills Cain will suffer vengeance
seven times over."[K] And he placed a mark
on Cain so that whoever found him would
not kill him. 16 Then Cain went out from the
LORD's presence and lived in the land of Nod,
east of Eden.

THE LINE OF CAIN

17 Cain was intimate with his wife, and she
conceived and gave birth to Enoch. Then Cain
became the builder of a city, and he named
the city Enoch after his son. 18 Irad was born
to Enoch, Irad fathered Mehujael, Mehujael
fathered Methushael, and Methushael fathered
Lamech. 19 Lamech took two wives for himself, one named Adah and the other named
Zillah. 20 Adah bore Jabal; he was the father
of the nomadic herdsmen.[L] 21 His brother was

[A] **3:17** Lit *it through pain* [B] **3:19** Or *food* [C] **3:20** Lit *Living*, or *Life* [D] **4:1** Lit *the LORD* [E] **4:5** Lit *and his face fell* [F] **4:6** Lit *why has your face fallen* [G] **4:8** Sam, LXX, Syr, Vg; MT omits *"Let's go out to the field."* [H] **4:11** Lit *blood from your hand* [I] **4:13** Or *sin* [J] **4:15** LXX, Syr, Vg read *"Not so!"* [K] **4:15** Or *suffer severely* [L] **4:20** Lit *the dweller of tent and livestock*

named Jubal; he was the father of all who play
the lyre and the flute. 22 Zillah bore Tubal-cain,
who made all kinds of bronze and iron tools.
Tubal-cain's sister was Naamah.

23 Lamech said to his wives:
Adah and Zillah, hear my voice;
wives of Lamech, pay attention
to my words.
For I killed a man for wounding me,
a young man for striking me.
24 If Cain is to be avenged
seven times over,
then for Lamech it will be
seventy-seven times!

25 Adam was intimate with his wife again,
and she gave birth to a son and named him
Seth, for she said, "God has given[A] me another
child[B] in place of Abel, since Cain killed him."
26 A son was born to Seth also, and he named
him Enosh. At that time people began to call
on the name of the LORD.

THE LINE OF SETH

5 This is the document containing the family[C] records of Adam.[D] On the day that God
created man,[E] he made him in the likeness of
God; 2 he created them male and female. When
they were created, he blessed them and called
them mankind.[F]
3 Adam was 130 years old when he fathered
a son in his likeness, according to his image,
and named him Seth. 4 Adam lived 800 years
after he fathered Seth, and he fathered other
sons and daughters. 5 So Adam's life lasted
930 years; then he died.
6 Seth was 105 years old when he fathered
Enosh. 7 Seth lived 807 years after he fathered
Enosh, and he fathered other sons and daughters. 8 So Seth's life lasted 912 years; then he
died.
9 Enosh was 90 years old when he fathered
Kenan. 10 Enosh lived 815 years after he fathered Kenan, and he fathered other sons and
daughters. 11 So Enosh's life lasted 905 years;
then he died.
12 Kenan was 70 years old when he fathered
Mahalalel. 13 Kenan lived 840 years after he
fathered Mahalalel, and he fathered other
sons and daughters. 14 So Kenan's life lasted
910 years; then he died.
15 Mahalalel was 65 years old when he
fathered Jared. 16 Mahalalel lived 830 years
after he fathered Jared, and he fathered other sons and daughters. 17 So Mahalalel's life
lasted 895 years; then he died.
18 Jared was 162 years old when he fathered
Enoch. 19 Jared lived 800 years after he fathered
Enoch, and he fathered other sons and daughters. 20 So Jared's life lasted 962 years; then
he died.
21 Enoch was 65 years old when he fathered
Methuselah. 22 And after he fathered Methuselah, Enoch walked with God 300 years and fathered other sons and daughters. 23 So Enoch's
life lasted 365 years. 24 Enoch walked with God;
then he was not there because God took him.

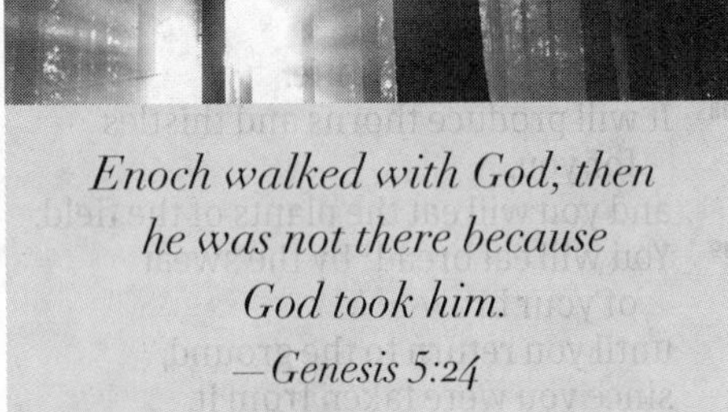
*Enoch walked with God; then
he was not there because
God took him.*
—Genesis 5:24

25 Methuselah was 187 years old when he
fathered Lamech. 26 Methuselah lived 782 years
after he fathered Lamech, and he fathered
other sons and daughters. 27 So Methuselah's
life lasted 969 years; then he died.
28 Lamech was 182 years old when he fathered a son. 29 And he named him Noah,[G]
saying, "This one will bring us relief from
the agonizing labor of our hands, caused by
the ground the LORD has cursed." 30 Lamech
lived 595 years after he fathered Noah, and
he fathered other sons and daughters. 31 So
Lamech's life lasted 777 years; then he died.
32 Noah was 500 years old, and he fathered
Shem, Ham, and Japheth.

SONS OF GOD AND DAUGHTERS OF MANKIND

6 When mankind began to multiply on the
earth and daughters were born to them,
2 the sons of God saw that the daughters of
mankind were beautiful, and they took any
they chose as wives[H] for themselves. 3 And the
LORD said, "My Spirit will not remain[I] with[J]
mankind forever, because they are corrupt.[K]
Their days will be 120 years." 4 The Nephilim[L] were on the earth both in those days and

[A] **4:25** The Hb word for *given* sounds like the name "Seth." [B] **4:25** Lit *seed* [C] **5:1** Lit *written family* [D] **5:1** Or *mankind* [E] **5:1** Or *Adam, human beings* [F] **5:2** Hb *'adam* [G] **5:29** In Hb, the name *Noah* sounds like "bring us relief." [H] **6:2** Or *women* [I] **6:3** Or *strive* [J] **6:3** Or *in* [K] **6:3** Lit *flesh* [L] **6:4** Possibly means "fallen ones"; traditionally, "giants"; Nm 13:31-33

afterward, when the sons of God came to the daughters of mankind, who bore children to them. They were the powerful men of old, the famous men.

JUDGMENT DECREED

5 When the LORD saw that human wickedness was widespread on the earth and that every inclination of the human mind was nothing but evil all the time, 6 the LORD regretted that he had made man on the earth, and he was deeply grieved.[A] 7 Then the LORD said, "I will wipe mankind, whom I created, off the face of the earth, together with the animals, creatures that crawl, and birds of the sky — for I regret that I made them." 8 Noah, however, found favor with the LORD.

GOD WARNS NOAH

9 These are the family records of Noah. Noah was a righteous man, blameless among his contemporaries; Noah walked with God. 10 And Noah fathered three sons: Shem, Ham, and Japheth.

11 Now the earth was corrupt in God's sight, and the earth was filled with wickedness.[B] 12 God saw how corrupt the earth was, for every creature had corrupted its way on the earth. 13 Then God said to Noah, "I have decided to put an end to every creature, for the earth is filled with wickedness because of them; therefore I am going to destroy them along with the earth.

14 "Make yourself an ark of gopher[C] wood. Make rooms in the ark, and cover it with pitch inside and outside. 15 This is how you are to make it: The ark will be 450 feet long, 75 feet wide, and 45 feet high.[D] 16 You are to make a roof,[E] finishing the sides of the ark to within eighteen inches[F] of the roof. You are to put a door in the side of the ark. Make it with lower, middle, and upper decks.

17 "Understand that I am bringing a flood — floodwaters on the earth to destroy every creature under heaven with the breath of life in it. Everything on earth will perish. 18 But I will establish my covenant with you, and you will enter the ark with your sons, your wife, and your sons' wives. 19 You are also to bring into the ark two of all the living creatures, male and female, to keep them alive with you. 20 Two of everything — from the birds according to their kinds, from the livestock according to their kinds, and from the animals that crawl on the ground according to their kinds — will come to you so that you can keep them alive. 21 Take with you every kind of food that is eaten; gather it as food for you and for them." 22 And Noah did this. He did everything that God had commanded him.

ENTERING THE ARK

7 Then the LORD said to Noah, "Enter the ark, you and all your household, for I have seen that you alone are righteous before me in this generation. 2 You are to take with you seven pairs, a male and its female, of all the clean animals, and two of the animals that are not clean, a male and its female, 3 and seven pairs, male and female, of the birds of the sky — in order to keep offspring alive throughout the earth. 4 Seven days from now I will make it rain on the earth forty days and forty nights, and every living thing I have made I will wipe off the face of the earth." 5 And Noah did everything that the LORD commanded him.

6 Noah was six hundred years old when the flood came and water covered the earth. 7 So Noah, his sons, his wife, and his sons' wives entered the ark because of the floodwaters. 8 From the clean animals, unclean animals, birds, and every creature that crawls on the ground, 9 two of each, male and female, came to Noah and entered the ark, just as God had commanded him. 10 Seven days later the floodwaters came on the earth.

THE FLOOD

11 In the six hundredth year of Noah's life, in the second month, on the seventeenth day of the month, on that day all the sources of the vast watery depths burst open, the floodgates of the sky were opened, 12 and the rain fell on the earth forty days and forty nights. 13 On that same day Noah along with his sons Shem, Ham, and Japheth, Noah's wife, and his three sons' wives entered the ark with him. 14 They entered it with all the wildlife according to their kinds, all livestock according to their kinds, all the creatures that crawl on the earth according to their kinds, every flying creature — all the birds and every winged creature — according to their kinds. 15 Two of every creature that has the breath of life in it came to Noah and entered the ark. 16 Those that entered, male and female of every creature, entered just

[A] **6:6** Lit *was grieved to his heart* [B] **6:11** Or *injustice*, also in v. 13 [C] **6:14** Unknown species of tree; perhaps pine or cypress
[D] **6:15** Or *300 cubits long, 50 cubits wide, and 30 cubits high* [E] **6:16** Or *window*, or *hatch*; Hb uncertain [F] **6:16** Lit *to a cubit*

as God had commanded him. Then the LORD shut him in.

17 The flood continued for forty days on the earth; the water increased and lifted up the ark so that it rose above the earth. 18 The water surged and increased greatly on the earth, and the ark floated on the surface of the water. 19 Then the water surged even higher on the earth, and all the high mountains under the whole sky were covered. 20 The mountains were covered as the water surged above them more than twenty feet.[A] 21 Every creature perished — those that crawl on the earth, birds, livestock, wildlife, and those that swarm[B] on the earth, as well as all mankind. 22 Everything with the breath of the spirit of life in its nostrils — everything on dry land died. 23 He wiped out every living thing that was on the face of the earth, from mankind to livestock, to creatures that crawl, to the birds of the sky, and they were wiped off the earth. Only Noah was left, and those that were with him in the ark. 24 And the water surged on the earth 150 days.

THE FLOOD RECEDES

8 God remembered Noah, as well as all the wildlife and all the livestock that were with him in the ark. God caused a wind[C] to pass over the earth, and the water began to subside. 2 The sources of the watery depths and the floodgates of the sky were closed, and the rain from the sky stopped. 3 The water steadily receded from the earth, and by the end of 150 days the water had decreased significantly. 4 The ark came to rest in the seventh month, on the seventeenth day of the month, on the mountains of Ararat.

5 The water continued to recede until the tenth month; in the tenth month, on the first day of the month, the tops of the mountains were visible. 6 After forty days Noah opened the window of the ark that he had made, 7 and he sent out a raven. It went back and forth until the water had dried up from the earth. 8 Then he sent out a dove to see whether the water on the earth's surface had gone down, 9 but the dove found no resting place for its foot. It returned to him in the ark because water covered the surface of the whole earth. He reached out and brought it into the ark to himself. 10 So Noah waited seven more days and sent out the dove from the ark again. 11 When the dove came to him at evening, there was a plucked olive leaf in its beak. So Noah knew that the water on the earth's surface had gone down. 12 After he had waited another seven days, he sent out the dove, but it did not return to him again. 13 In the six hundred and first year,[D] in the first month, on the first day of the month, the water that had covered the earth was dried up. Then Noah removed the ark's cover and saw that the surface of the ground was drying. 14 By the twenty-seventh day of the second month, the earth was dry.

THE LORD'S PROMISE

15 Then God spoke to Noah, 16 "Come out of the ark, you, your wife, your sons, and your sons' wives with you. 17 Bring out all the living creatures[E] that are with you — birds, livestock, those that crawl on the earth — and they will spread over the earth and be fruitful and multiply on the earth." 18 So Noah, along with his sons, his wife, and his sons' wives, came out. 19 All the animals, all the creatures that crawl, and all the flying creatures — everything that moves on the earth — came out of the ark by their families.

20 Then Noah built an altar to the LORD. He took some of every kind of clean animal and every kind of clean bird and offered burnt offerings on the altar. 21 When the LORD smelled the pleasing aroma, he said to himself, "I will never again curse the ground because of human beings, even though the inclination of the human heart is evil from youth onward. And I will never again strike down every living thing as I have done.

22 As long as the earth endures,
seedtime and harvest, cold and heat,
summer and winter, and day and night
will not cease."

GOD'S COVENANT WITH NOAH

9 God blessed Noah and his sons and said to them, "Be fruitful and multiply and fill the earth. 2 The fear and terror of you will be in every living creature on the earth, every bird of the sky, every creature that crawls on the ground, and all the fish of the sea. They are placed under your authority.[F] 3 Every creature that lives and moves will be food for you; as I gave the green plants, I have given you everything. 4 However, you must not eat meat with its lifeblood in it. 5 And I will require a

[A] **7:20** Lit *surged 15 cubits* [B] **7:21** Lit *all the swarming swarms* [C] **8:1** Or *spirit*; Gn 1:2 [D] **8:13** = of Noah's life [E] **8:17** Lit *creatures of all flesh* [F] **9:2** Lit *are given in your hand*

penalty for your lifeblood;[A] I will require it
from any animal and from any human; if someone murders a fellow human, I will require
that person's life.[B]

6 Whoever sheds human blood,
by humans his blood will be shed,
for God made humans in his image.

7 But you, be fruitful and multiply; spread out
over the earth and multiply on it."

8 Then God said to Noah and his sons with
him, 9 "Understand that I am establishing my
covenant with you and your descendants after
you, 10 and with every living creature that is
with you — birds, livestock, and all wildlife
of the earth that are with you — all the animals of the earth that came out of the ark.
11 I establish my covenant with you that never again will every creature be wiped out by
floodwaters; there will never again be a flood
to destroy the earth."

12 And God said, "This is the sign of the covenant I am making between me and you and
every living creature with you, a covenant
for all future generations: 13 I have placed my
bow in the clouds, and it will be a sign of the
covenant between me and the earth. 14 Whenever I form clouds over the earth and the bow
appears in the clouds, 15 I will remember my
covenant between me and you and all the living creatures:[C] water will never again become
a flood to destroy every creature. 16 The bow
will be in the clouds, and I will look at it and
remember the permanent covenant between
God and all the living creatures[D] on earth."
17 God said to Noah, "This is the sign of the
covenant that I have established between me
and every creature on earth."

PROPHECIES ABOUT NOAH'S FAMILY

18 Noah's sons who came out of the ark were
Shem, Ham, and Japheth. Ham was the father
of Canaan. 19 These three were Noah's sons,
and from them the whole earth was populated.

20 Noah, as a man of the soil, began by planting[E] a vineyard. 21 He drank some of the wine,
became drunk, and uncovered himself inside
his tent. 22 Ham, the father of Canaan, saw his
father naked and told his two brothers outside. 23 Then Shem and Japheth took a cloak
and placed it over both their shoulders, and
walking backward, they covered their father's
nakedness. Their faces were turned away, and
they did not see their father naked.

24 When Noah awoke from his drinking and
learned what his youngest son had done to
him, 25 he said:

Canaan is cursed.
He will be the lowest of slaves
to his brothers.

26 He also said:

Blessed be the LORD, the God of Shem;
Let Canaan be[F] Shem's slave.
27 Let God extend Japheth;[G]
let Japheth dwell in the tents of Shem;
let Canaan be Shem's slave.

28 Now Noah lived 350 years after the flood.
29 So Noah's life lasted 950 years; then he died.

THE TABLE OF NATIONS

10 These are the family records of Noah's
sons, Shem, Ham, and Japheth. They also
had sons after the flood.

2 Japheth's sons: Gomer, Magog, Madai,
Javan, Tubal, Meshech, and Tiras. 3 Gomer's
sons: Ashkenaz, Riphath, and Togarmah. 4 And
Javan's sons: Elishah, Tarshish, Kittim, and
Dodanim.[H] 5 From these descendants, the peoples of the coasts and islands spread out into
their lands according to their clans in their
nations, each with its own language.

6 Ham's sons: Cush, Mizraim, Put, and Ca-
naan. 7 Cush's sons: Seba, Havilah, Sabtah,
Raamah, and Sabteca. And Raamah's sons:
Sheba and Dedan.

8 Cush fathered Nimrod, who began to be
powerful in the land. 9 He was a powerful
hunter in the sight of the LORD. That is why
it is said, "Like Nimrod, a powerful hunter in
the sight of the LORD." 10 His kingdom started
with Babylon, Erech,[I] Accad,[J] and Calneh,[K] in
the land of Shinar.[L] 11 From that land he went
to Assyria and built Nineveh, Rehoboth-ir,
Calah, 12 and Resen, between Nineveh and the
great city Calah.

13 Mizraim[M] fathered the people of Lud,
Anam, Lehab, Naphtuh, 14 Pathrus, Casluh
(the Philistines came from them), and Caphtor.

15 Canaan fathered Sidon his firstborn and
Heth, 16 as well as the Jebusites, the Amorites,

[A] **9:5** Lit *And your blood belonging to your life I will seek* [B] **9:5** Lit *any human; from the hand of a man his brother I will seek the life of the human.* [C] **9:15** Lit *and creatures of all flesh* [D] **9:16** Lit *creatures of all flesh* [E] **9:20** Or *Noah began to be a farmer and planted* [F] **9:26** As a wish or prayer; others interpret the verbs in vv. 26-27 as prophecy: *Canaan will be . . .* [G] **9:27** In Hb, the name *Japheth* sounds like the word "extend." [H] **10:4** Some Hb mss, Sam, LXX read *Rodanim*; 1Ch 1:7 [I] **10:10** Or *Uruk* [J] **10:10** Or *Akkad* [K] **10:10** Or *and all of them* [L] **10:10** Or *in Babylonia* [M] **10:13** = Egypt

the Girgashites, 17 the Hivites, the Arkites, the Sinites, 18 the Arvadites, the Zemarites, and the Hamathites. Afterward the Canaanite clans scattered. 19 The Canaanite border went from Sidon going toward Gerar as far as Gaza, and going toward Sodom, Gomorrah, Admah, and Zeboiim as far as Lasha.

20 These are Ham's sons by their clans, according to their languages, in their lands and their nations.

21 And Shem, Japheth's older brother, also had sons. Shem was the father of all the sons of Eber. 22 Shem's sons were Elam, Asshur, Arpachshad, Lud, and Aram.

23 Aram's sons: Uz, Hul, Gether, and Mash.

24 Arpachshad fathered[A] Shelah, and Shelah fathered Eber. 25 Eber had two sons. One was named Peleg,[B] for during his days the earth was divided; his brother was named Joktan. 26 And Joktan fathered Almodad, Sheleph, Hazarmaveth, Jerah, 27 Hadoram, Uzal, Diklah, 28 Obal, Abimael, Sheba, 29 Ophir, Havilah, and Jobab. All these were Joktan's sons. 30 Their settlements extended from Mesha to Sephar, the eastern hill country.

31 These are Shem's sons by their clans, according to their languages, in their lands and their nations.

32 These are the clans of Noah's sons, according to their family records, in their nations. The nations on earth spread out from these after the flood.

THE TOWER OF BABYLON

11 The whole earth had the same language and vocabulary.[C] 2 As people[D] migrated from the east,[E] they found a valley in the land of Shinar and settled there. 3 They said to each other, "Come, let us make oven-fired bricks." (They used brick for stone and asphalt for mortar.) 4 And they said, "Come, let us build ourselves a city and a tower with its top in the sky. Let us make a name for ourselves; otherwise, we will be scattered throughout the earth."

5 Then the LORD came down to look over the city and the tower that the humans[F] were building. 6 The LORD said, "If they have begun to do this as one people all having the same language, then nothing they plan to do will be impossible for them. 7 Come, let's go down there and confuse their language so that they will not understand one another's speech." 8 So from there the LORD scattered them throughout the earth, and they stopped building the city. 9 Therefore it is called Babylon,[G,H] for there the LORD confused the language of the whole earth, and from there the LORD scattered them throughout the earth.

FROM SHEM TO ABRAM

10 These are the family records of Shem. Shem lived 100 years and fathered Arpachshad two years after the flood. 11 After he fathered Arpachshad, Shem lived 500 years and fathered other sons and daughters. 12 Arpachshad lived 35 years[I] and fathered Shelah. 13 After he fathered Shelah, Arpachshad lived 403 years and fathered other sons and daughters. 14 Shelah lived 30 years and fathered Eber. 15 After he fathered Eber, Shelah lived 403 years and fathered other sons and daughters. 16 Eber lived 34 years and fathered Peleg. 17 After he fathered Peleg, Eber lived 430 years and fathered other sons and daughters. 18 Peleg lived 30 years and fathered Reu. 19 After he fathered Reu, Peleg lived 209 years and fathered other sons and daughters. 20 Reu lived 32 years and fathered Serug. 21 After he fathered Serug, Reu lived 207 years and fathered other sons and daughters. 22 Serug lived 30 years and fathered Nahor. 23 After he fathered Nahor, Serug lived 200 years and fathered other sons and daughters. 24 Nahor lived 29 years and fathered Terah. 25 After he fathered Terah, Nahor lived 119 years and fathered other sons and daughters. 26 Terah lived 70 years and fathered Abram, Nahor, and Haran.

27 These are the family records of Terah. Terah fathered Abram, Nahor, and Haran, and Haran fathered Lot. 28 Haran died in his native land, in Ur of the Chaldeans, during his father Terah's lifetime. 29 Abram and Nahor took wives: Abram's wife was named Sarai, and Nahor's wife was named Milcah. She was the daughter of Haran, the father of both Milcah and Iscah. 30 Sarai was unable to conceive; she did not have a child.

[A] **10:24** LXX reads *fathered Cainan, and Cainan fathered*; Gn 11:12-13; Lk 3:35-36 [B] **10:25** = Division [C] **11:1** Lit *one lip and the same words* [D] **11:2** Lit *they* [E] **11:2** Or *migrated eastward* [F] **11:5** Or *the descendants of Adam* [G] **11:9** Hb *Babel* [H] **11:9** In Hb, the name for "Babylon," *babel* sounds like the word for "confuse," *balal*. [I] **11:12-13** LXX reads *years and fathered Cainan.* 13*After he fathered Cainan, Arpachshad lived 430 years and fathered other sons and daughters, and he died. Cainan lived 130 years and fathered Shelah. After he fathered Shelah, Cainan lived 330 years and fathered other sons and daughters, and he died*; Gn 10:24; Lk 3:35-36

31 Terah took his son Abram, his grandson Lot (Haran's son), and his daughter-in-law Sarai, his son Abram's wife, and they set out together from Ur of the Chaldeans to go to the land of Canaan. But when they came to Haran, they settled there. 32 Terah lived 205 years and died in Haran.

THE CALL OF ABRAM

12 The LORD said to Abram:
Go out from your land,
your relatives,
and your father's house
to the land that I will show you.
2 I will make you into a great nation,
I will bless you,
I will make your name great,
and you will be a blessing.
3 I will bless those who bless you,
I will curse anyone who treats you
with contempt,
and all the peoples[A] on earth
will be blessed[B] through you.[C]

4 So Abram went, as the LORD had told him, and Lot went with him. Abram was seventy-five years old when he left Haran. 5 He took his wife Sarai, his nephew Lot, all the possessions they had accumulated, and the people they had acquired in Haran, and they set out for the land of Canaan. When they came to the land of Canaan, 6 Abram passed through the land to the site of Shechem, at the oak of Moreh. (At that time the Canaanites were in the land.) 7 The LORD appeared to Abram and said, "To your offspring I will give this land." So he built an altar there to the LORD who had appeared to him. 8 From there he moved on to the hill country east of Bethel and pitched his tent, with Bethel on the west and Ai on the east. He built an altar to the LORD there, and he called on the name of the LORD. 9 Then Abram journeyed by stages to the Negev.

ABRAM IN EGYPT

10 There was a famine in the land, so Abram went down to Egypt to stay there for a while because the famine in the land was severe. 11 When he was about to enter Egypt, he said to his wife Sarai, "Look, I know what a beautiful woman you are. 12 When the Egyptians see you, they will say, 'This is his wife.' They will kill me but let you live. 13 Please say you're my sister so it will go well for me because of you, and my life will be spared on your account." 14 When Abram entered Egypt, the Egyptians saw that the woman was very beautiful. 15 Pharaoh's officials saw her and praised her to Pharaoh, so the woman was taken to Pharaoh's household. 16 He treated Abram well because of her, and Abram acquired flocks and herds, male and female donkeys, male and female slaves, and camels.

17 But the LORD struck Pharaoh and his household with severe plagues because of Abram's wife Sarai. 18 So Pharaoh sent for Abram and said, "What have you done to me? Why didn't you tell me she was your wife? 19 Why did you say, 'She's my sister,' so that I took her as my wife? Now, here is your wife. Take her and go!" 20 Then Pharaoh gave his men orders about him, and they sent him away with his wife and all he had.

ABRAM AND LOT SEPARATE

13 Abram went up from Egypt to the Negev — he, his wife, and all he had, and Lot with him. 2 Abram was very rich in livestock, silver, and gold. 3 He went by stages from the Negev to Bethel, to the place between Bethel and Ai where his tent had formerly been, 4 to the site where he had built the altar. And Abram called on the name of the LORD there.

5 Now Lot, who was traveling with Abram, also had flocks, herds, and tents. 6 But the land was unable to support them as long as they stayed together, for they had so many possessions that they could not stay together, 7 and there was quarreling between the herdsmen of Abram's livestock and the herdsmen of Lot's livestock. (At that time the Canaanites and the Perizzites were living in the land.)

8 So Abram said to Lot, "Please, let's not have quarreling between you and me, or between your herdsmen and my herdsmen, since we are relatives.[D] 9 Isn't the whole land before you? Separate from me: if you go to the left, I will go to the right; if you go to the right, I will go to the left."

10 Lot looked out and saw that the entire plain[E] of the Jordan as far as[F] Zoar was well watered everywhere like the LORD's garden and the land of Egypt. (This was before the LORD destroyed Sodom and Gomorrah.) 11 So Lot chose the entire plain of the Jordan for himself. Then Lot journeyed eastward, and they

[A] **12:3** Lit *clans* [B] **12:3** Or *will find blessing* [C] **12:3** Or *will bless themselves by you* [D] **13:8** Lit *brothers* [E] **13:10** Lit *circle*; i.e., probably the large round plain where the Jordan River empties into the Dead Sea, also in v. 11 [F] **13:10** Lit *Jordan as you go to*

17 When the sun had set and it was dark, a smoking fire pot and a flaming torch appeared and passed between the divided animals. 18 On that day the LORD made a covenant with Abram, saying, "I give this land to your offspring, from the Brook of Egypt to the great river, the Euphrates River: 19 the land of the Kenites, Kenizzites, Kadmonites, 20 Hethites, Perizzites, Rephaim, 21 Amorites, Canaanites, Girgashites, and Jebusites."

HAGAR AND ISHMAEL

16 Abram's wife Sarai had not borne any children for him, but she owned an Egyptian slave named Hagar. 2 Sarai said to Abram, "Since the LORD has prevented me from bearing children, go to my slave; perhaps through her I can build a family." And Abram agreed to what Sarai said.[A] 3 So Abram's wife Sarai took Hagar, her Egyptian slave, and gave her to her husband Abram as a wife for him. This happened after Abram had lived in the land of Canaan ten years. 4 He slept with[B] Hagar, and she became pregnant. When she saw that she was pregnant, her mistress became contemptible to her. 5 Then Sarai said to Abram, "You are responsible for my suffering![C] I put my slave in your arms,[D] and when she saw that she was pregnant, I became contemptible to her. May the LORD judge between me and you."

6 Abram replied to Sarai, "Here, your slave is in your hands; do whatever you want with her." Then Sarai mistreated her so much that she ran away from her.

7 The angel of the LORD found her by a spring in the wilderness, the spring on the way to Shur. 8 He said, "Hagar, slave of Sarai, where have you come from and where are you going?"

She replied, "I'm running away from my mistress Sarai."

9 The angel of the LORD said to her, "Go back to your mistress and submit to her authority." 10 The angel of the LORD said to her, "I will greatly multiply your offspring, and they will be too many to count."

11 The angel of the LORD said to her, "You have conceived and will have a son. You will name him Ishmael,[E] for the LORD has heard your cry of affliction. 12 This man will be like a wild donkey. His hand will be against everyone, and everyone's hand will be against him; he will settle near all his relatives."

13 So she named the LORD who spoke to her: "You are El-roi,"[F] for she said, "In this place, have I actually seen the one who sees me?"[G] 14 That is why the well is called Beer-lahai-roi.[H] It is between Kadesh and Bered.

15 So Hagar gave birth to Abram's son, and Abram named his son (whom Hagar bore) Ishmael. 16 Abram was eighty-six years old when Hagar bore Ishmael to him.

COVENANT CIRCUMCISION

17 When Abram was ninety-nine years old, the LORD appeared to him, saying, "I am God Almighty. Live[I] in my presence and be blameless. 2 I will set up my covenant between me and you, and I will multiply you greatly."

3 Then Abram fell facedown and God spoke with him: 4 "As for me, here is my covenant with you: You will become the father of many nations. 5 Your name will no longer be Abram;[J] your name will be Abraham,[K] for I will make you the father of many nations. 6 I will make you extremely fruitful and will make nations and kings come from you. 7 I will confirm my covenant that is between me and you and your future offspring throughout their generations. It is a permanent covenant to be your God and the God of your offspring after you. 8 And to you and your future offspring I will give the land where you are residing — all the land of Canaan — as a permanent possession, and I will be their God."

9 God also said to Abraham, "As for you, you and your offspring after you throughout their generations are to keep my covenant. 10 This is my covenant between me and you and your offspring after you, which you are to keep: Every one of your males must be circumcised. 11 You must circumcise the flesh of your foreskin to serve as a sign of the covenant between me and you.[L] 12 Throughout your generations, every male among you is to be circumcised at eight days old — every male born in your household or purchased from any foreigner and not your offspring. 13 Whether born in your household or purchased, he must be circumcised. My covenant will be marked in your flesh as a permanent covenant. 14 If any male is not circumcised in the flesh of his foreskin, that man will be cut off from his people; he has broken my covenant."

15 God said to Abraham, "As for your wife

[A] **16:2** Lit *Abram listened to the voice of Sarai* [B] **16:4** Lit *He came to* [C] **16:5** Or *"May my suffering be on you!* [D] **16:5** Lit *bosom* [E] **16:11** = God Hears [F] **16:13** = God Sees Me [G] **16:13** Hb obscure [H] **16:14** = Well of the Living One Who Sees Me [I] **17:1** Or *Walk* [J] **17:5** = The Father Is Exalted [K] **17:5** = Father of a Multitude [L] **17:11** *You* in v. 11 is pl.

Sarai, do not call her Sarai, for Sarah[A] will
be her name. 16 I will bless her; indeed, I will
give you a son by her. I will bless her, and she
will produce nations; kings of peoples will
come from her."
17 Abraham fell facedown. Then he laughed
and said to himself, "Can a child be born to a
hundred-year-old man? Can Sarah, a ninety-
year-old woman, give birth?" 18 So Abraham
said to God, "If only Ishmael were acceptable[B]
to you!"
19 But God said, "No. Your wife Sarah will bear
you a son, and you will name him Isaac.[C] I will
confirm my covenant with him as a permanent covenant for his future offspring. 20 As
for Ishmael, I have heard you. I will certainly
bless him; I will make him fruitful and will
multiply him greatly. He will father twelve
tribal leaders, and I will make him into a great
nation. 21 But I will confirm my covenant with
Isaac, whom Sarah will bear to you at this time
next year." 22 When he finished talking with
him, God withdrew[D] from Abraham.
23 So Abraham took his son Ishmael and
those born in his household or purchased
— every male among the members of Abraham's household — and he circumcised the
flesh of their foreskin on that very day, just
as God had said to him. 24 Abraham was
ninety-nine years old when the flesh of his
foreskin was circumcised, 25 and his son
Ishmael was thirteen years old when the
flesh of his foreskin was circumcised. 26 On
that same day Abraham and his son Ishmael
were circumcised. 27 And all the men of his
household — whether born in his household
or purchased from a foreigner — were circumcised with him.

ABRAHAM'S THREE VISITORS

18 The LORD appeared to Abraham at the
oaks of Mamre while he was sitting at
the entrance of his tent during the heat of
the day. 2 He looked up, and he saw three men
standing near him. When he saw them, he ran
from the entrance of the tent to meet them,
bowed to the ground, 3 and said, "My lord, if
I have found favor with you, please do not go
on past your servant. 4 Let a little water be
brought, that you may wash your feet and rest
yourselves under the tree. 5 I will bring a bit of
bread so that you may strengthen yourselves.[E]
This is why you have passed your servant's
way. Later, you can continue on."
"Yes," they replied, "do as you have said."
6 So Abraham hurried into the tent and said
to Sarah, "Quick! Knead three measures[F] of
fine flour and make bread."[G] 7 Abraham ran
to the herd and got a tender, choice calf. He
gave it to a young man, who hurried to prepare it. 8 Then Abraham took curds[H] and milk,
as well as the calf that he had prepared, and
set them before the men. He served[I] them as
they ate under the tree.

SARAH LAUGHS

9 "Where is your wife Sarah?" they asked him.
"There, in the tent," he answered.
10 The LORD said, "I will certainly come back
to you in about a year's time, and your wife
Sarah will have a son!" Now Sarah was listening at the entrance of the tent behind him.
11 Abraham and Sarah were old and getting on in years.[J] Sarah had passed the age
of childbearing.[K] 12 So she laughed to herself:
"After I am worn out and my lord is old, will
I have delight?"
13 But the LORD asked Abraham, "Why did
Sarah laugh, saying, 'Can I really have a baby
when I'm old?' 14 Is anything impossible for the
LORD? At the appointed time I will come back
to you, and in about a year she will have a son."

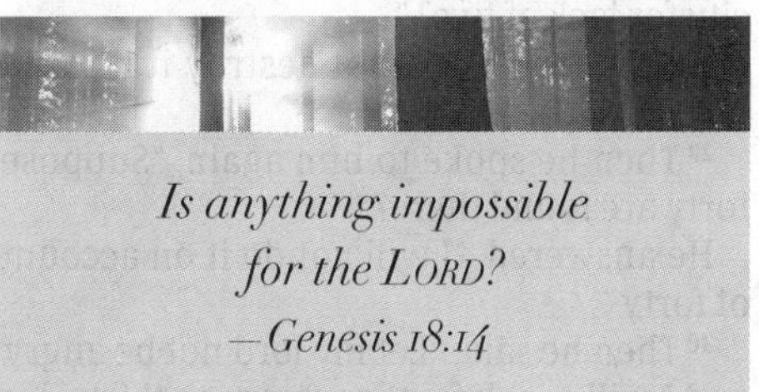
Is anything impossible
for the LORD?
—Genesis 18:14

15 Sarah denied it. "I did not laugh," she said,
because she was afraid.
But he replied, "No, you did laugh."

ABRAHAM'S PLEA FOR SODOM

16 The men got up from there and looked out
over Sodom, and Abraham was walking with
them to see them off. 17 Then the LORD said,
"Should I hide what I am about to do from
Abraham? 18 Abraham is to become a great
and powerful nation, and all the nations of
the earth will be blessed through him. 19 For
I have chosen[L] him so that he will command

[A] **17:15** = Princess [B] **17:18** Lit *alive* [C] **17:19** = He Laughs [D] **17:22** Lit *went up*, or *ascended* [E] **18:5** Lit *may sustain your heart* [F] **18:6** Lit *three seahs*; about 21 quarts [G] **18:6** A round, thin, unleavened bread [H] **18:8** Or *butter* [I] **18:8** Lit *was standing by* [J] **18:11** Lit *days* [K] **18:11** Lit *The way of women had ceased for Sarah* [L] **18:19** Lit *known*

his children and his house after him to keep
the way of the LORD by doing what is right
and just. This is how the LORD will fulfill to
Abraham what he promised him." 20 Then the
LORD said, "The outcry against Sodom and Gomorrah is immense, and their sin is extremely
serious. 21 I will go down to see if what they
have done justifies the cry that has come up
to me. If not, I will find out."

22 The men turned from there and went toward Sodom while Abraham remained standing before the LORD.[A] 23 Abraham stepped
forward and said, "Will you really sweep away
the righteous with the wicked? 24 What if there
are fifty righteous people in the city? Will
you really sweep it away instead of sparing
the place for the sake of the fifty righteous
people who are in it? 25 You could not possibly do such a thing: to kill the righteous
with the wicked, treating the righteous and
the wicked alike. You could not possibly do
that! Won't the Judge of the whole earth do
what is just?"

26 The LORD said, "If I find fifty righteous
people in the city of Sodom, I will spare the
whole place for their sake."

27 Then Abraham answered, "Since I have
ventured to speak to my lord — even though
I am dust and ashes — 28 suppose the fifty
righteous lack five. Will you destroy the whole
city for lack of five?"

He replied, "I will not destroy it if I find
forty-five there."

29 Then he spoke to him again, "Suppose
forty are found there?"

He answered, "I will not do it on account
of forty."

30 Then he said, "Let my lord not be angry,
and I will speak further. Suppose thirty are
found there?"

He answered, "I will not do it if I find thirty
there."

31 Then he said, "Since I have ventured to
speak to my lord, suppose twenty are found
there?"

He replied, "I will not destroy it on account
of twenty."

32 Then he said, "Let my lord not be angry,
and I will speak one more time. Suppose ten
are found there?"

He answered, "I will not destroy it on account of ten." 33 When the LORD had finished
speaking with Abraham, he departed, and
Abraham returned to his place.

THE DESTRUCTION OF SODOM AND GOMORRAH

19 The two angels entered Sodom in the
evening as Lot was sitting in Sodom's
gateway. When Lot saw them, he got up to meet
them. He bowed with his face to the ground
2 and said, "My lords, turn aside to your servant's house, wash your feet, and spend the
night. Then you can get up early and go on
your way."

"No," they said. "We would rather spend
the night in the square." 3 But he urged them
so strongly that they followed him and went
into his house. He prepared a feast and baked
unleavened bread for them, and they ate.

4 Before they went to bed, the men of the city
of Sodom, both young and old, the whole population, surrounded the house. 5 They called
out to Lot and said, "Where are the men who
came to you tonight? Send them out to us so
we can have sex with them!"

6 Lot went out to them at the entrance and
shut the door behind him. 7 He said, "Don't
do this evil, my brothers. 8 Look, I've got two
daughters who haven't been intimate with a
man. I'll bring them out to you, and you can
do whatever you want[B] to them. However,
don't do anything to these men, because they
have come under the protection of my roof."

9 "Get out of the way!" they said, adding, "This
one came here as an alien, but he's acting like
a judge! Now we'll do more harm to you than
to them." They put pressure on Lot and came
up to break down the door. 10 But the angels[C]
reached out, brought Lot into the house with
them, and shut the door. 11 They struck the men
who were at the entrance of the house, both
young and old, with blindness[D] so that they
were unable to find the entrance.

12 Then the angels said to Lot, "Do you have
anyone else here: a son-in-law, your sons and
daughters, or anyone else in the city who
belongs to you? Get them out of this place,
13 for we are about to destroy this place because the outcry against its people is so great
before the LORD, that the LORD has sent us to
destroy it."

14 So Lot went out and spoke to his sons-in-
law, who were going to marry[E] his daughters.

[A] **18:22** Alt Hb tradition reads *while the LORD remained standing before Abraham* [B] **19:8** Lit *do what is good in your eyes* [C] **19:10** Lit *men*, also in v. 12 [D] **19:11** Or *a blinding light* [E] **19:14** Lit *take*

Get up," he said. "Get out of this place, for the LORD is about to destroy the city!" But his sons-in-law thought he was joking.

15 At daybreak the angels urged Lot on: "Get up! Take your wife and your two daughters who are here, or you will be swept away in the punishment[A] of the city." 16 But he hesitated. Because of the LORD's compassion for him, the men grabbed his hand, his wife's hand, and the hands of his two daughters. They brought him out and left him outside the city.

17 As soon as the angels got them outside, one of them[B] said, "Run for your lives! Don't look back and don't stop anywhere on the plain! Run to the mountains, or you will be swept away!"

18 But Lot said to them, "No, my lords[C] — please. 19 Your servant has indeed found favor with you, and you have shown me great kindness by saving my life. But I can't run to the mountains; the disaster will overtake me, and I will die. 20 Look, this town is close enough for me to flee to. It is a small place. Please let me run to it — it's only a small place, isn't it? — so that I can survive."

21 And he said to him, "All right,[D] I'll grant your request[E] about this matter too and will not demolish the town you mentioned. 22 Hurry up! Run to it, for I cannot do anything until you get there." Therefore the name of the city is Zoar.[F]

23 The sun had risen over the land when Lot reached Zoar. 24 Then out of the sky the LORD rained on Sodom and Gomorrah burning sulfur from the LORD. 25 He demolished these cities, the entire plain, all the inhabitants of the cities, and whatever grew on the ground. 26 But Lot's wife looked back and became a pillar of salt.

27 Early in the morning Abraham went to the place where he had stood before the LORD. 28 He looked down toward Sodom and Gomorrah and all the land of the plain, and he saw that smoke was going up from the land like the smoke of a furnace. 29 So it was, when God destroyed the cities of the plain, he remembered Abraham and brought Lot out of the middle of the upheaval when he demolished the cities where Lot had lived.

THE ORIGIN OF MOAB AND AMMON

30 Lot departed from Zoar and lived in the mountains along with his two daughters, because he was afraid to live in Zoar. Instead, he and his two daughters lived in a cave. 31 Then the firstborn said to the younger, "Our father is old, and there is no man in the land to sleep with us as is the custom of all the land. 32 Come, let's get our father to drink wine so that we can sleep with him and preserve our father's line." 33 So they got their father to drink wine that night, and the firstborn came and slept with her father; he did not know when she lay down or when she got up.

34 The next day the firstborn said to the younger, "Look, I slept with my father last night. Let's get him to drink wine again tonight so you can go sleep with him and we can preserve our father's line." 35 That night they again got their father to drink wine, and the younger went and slept with him; he did not know when she lay down or when she got up.

36 So both of Lot's daughters became pregnant by their father. 37 The firstborn gave birth to a son and named him Moab.[G] He is the father of the Moabites of today. 38 The younger also gave birth to a son, and she named him Ben-ammi.[H] He is the father of the Ammonites of today.

SARAH RESCUED FROM ABIMELECH

20 From there Abraham traveled to the region of the Negev and settled between Kadesh and Shur. While he was staying in Gerar, 2 Abraham said about his wife Sarah, "She is my sister." So King Abimelech of Gerar had Sarah brought to him.

3 But God came to Abimelech in a dream by night and said to him, "You are about to die because of the woman you have taken, for she is a married woman."[I]

4 Now Abimelech had not approached her, so he said, "Lord, would you destroy a nation even though it is innocent? 5 Didn't he himself say to me, 'She is my sister'? And she herself said, 'He is my brother.' I did this with a clear conscience[J] and clean[K] hands."

6 Then God said to him in the dream, "Yes, I know that you did this with a clear conscience.[L] I have also kept you from sinning against me. Therefore I have not let you touch her. 7 Now return the man's wife, for he is a prophet, and he will pray for you and you will live. But if you

---

[A] **19:15** Or *iniquity*, or *guilt* [B] **19:17** LXX, Syr, Vg read *outside, they* [C] **19:18** Or *my Lord*, or *my lord* [D] **19:21** Or *"Look!* [E] **19:21** Lit *I will lift up your face* [F] **19:22** In Hb, the name *Zoar* is related to "small" in v. 20; its previous name was "Bela"; Gn 14:2. [G] **19:37** = From My Father [H] **19:38** = Son of My People [I] **20:3** Lit *is possessed by a husband* [J] **20:5** Lit *with integrity of my heart* [K] **20:5** Lit *cleanness of my* [L] **20:6** Lit *with integrity of your heart*

do not return her, know that you will certainly
die, you and all who are yours."
8 Early in the morning Abimelech got up,
called all his servants together, and personally[A] told them all these things, and the men
were terrified.
9 Then Abimelech called Abraham in and said
to him, "What have you done to us? How did
I sin against you that you have brought such
enormous guilt on me and on my kingdom?
You have done things to me that should never
be done." 10 Abimelech also asked Abraham,
"What made you do this?"
11 Abraham replied, "I thought, 'There is absolutely no fear of God in this place. They will
kill me because of my wife.' 12 Besides, she
really is my sister, the daughter of my father
though not the daughter of my mother, and
she became my wife. 13 So when God had me
wander from my father's house, I said to her:
Show your loyalty to me wherever we go and
say about me: 'He's my brother.'"
14 Then Abimelech took flocks and herds and
male and female slaves, gave them to Abraham,
and returned his wife Sarah to him. 15 Abimelech
said, "Look, my land is before you. Settle wherever you want."[B] 16 And he said to Sarah, "Look,
I am giving your brother one thousand pieces
of silver. It is a verification of your honor[C] to
all who are with you. You are fully vindicated."
17 Then Abraham prayed to God, and God
healed Abimelech, his wife, and his female
slaves so that they could bear children, 18 for
the LORD had completely closed all the wombs
in Abimelech's household on account of Sarah, Abraham's wife.

THE BIRTH OF ISAAC

21 The LORD came to Sarah as he had said,
and the LORD did for Sarah what he had
promised. 2 Sarah became pregnant and bore
a son to Abraham in his old age, at the appointed time God had told him. 3 Abraham
named his son who was born to him — the
one Sarah bore to him — Isaac. 4 When his
son Isaac was eight days old, Abraham circumcised him, as God had commanded him.
5 Abraham was a hundred years old when his
son Isaac was born to him.
6 Sarah said, "God has made me laugh, and
everyone who hears will laugh with me."[D] 7 She
also said, "Who would have told Abraham that
Sarah would nurse children? Yet I have borne
a son for him[E] in his old age."

HAGAR AND ISHMAEL SENT AWAY

8 The child grew and was weaned, and Abraham held a great feast on the day Isaac was
weaned. 9 But Sarah saw the son mocking
— the one Hagar the Egyptian had borne to
Abraham. 10 So she said to Abraham, "Drive
out this slave with her son, for the son of this
slave will not be a coheir with my son Isaac!"
11 This was very distressing to[F] Abraham
because of his son. 12 But God said to Abraham, "Do not be distressed[G] about the boy
and about your slave. Whatever Sarah says
to you, listen to her, because your offspring
will be traced through Isaac, 13 and I will also
make a nation of the slave's son because he
is your offspring."
14 Early in the morning Abraham got up, took
bread and a waterskin, put them on Hagar's
shoulders, and sent her and the boy away.
She left and wandered in the Wilderness of
Beer-sheba. 15 When the water in the skin was
gone, she left the boy under one of the bushes
16 and went and sat at a distance, about a bow-
shot away, for she said, "I can't bear to watch
the boy die!" While she sat at a distance, she[H]
wept loudly.
17 God heard the boy crying, and the[I] angel
of God called to Hagar from heaven and said
to her, "What's wrong, Hagar? Don't be afraid,
for God has heard the boy crying from the
place where he is. 18 Get up, help the boy up,
and grasp his hand, for I will make him a great
nation." 19 Then God opened her eyes, and she
saw a well. So she went and filled the waterskin
and gave the boy a drink. 20 God was with the
boy, and he grew; he settled in the wilderness
and became an archer. 21 He settled in the Wilderness of Paran, and his mother got a wife
for him from the land of Egypt.

ABRAHAM'S COVENANT WITH ABIMELECH

22 At that time Abimelech, accompanied by
Phicol the commander of his army, said to
Abraham, "God is with you in everything you
do. 23 Swear to me by God here and now, that
you will not break an agreement with me or
with my children and descendants. As I have
been loyal to you, so you will be loyal to me and
to the country where you are a resident alien."

[A] **20:8** Lit *in their ears* [B] **20:15** Lit *Settle in the good in your eyes* [C] **20:16** Lit *a covering of the eyes* [D] **21:6** Isaac = He Laughs; Gn 17:19 [E] **21:7** Sam, Tg Jonathan; MT omits *him* [F] **21:11** Lit *was very bad in the eyes of* [G] **21:12** Lit *"Let it not be bad in your eyes* [H] **21:16** LXX reads *the boy* [I] **21:17** Or *an*

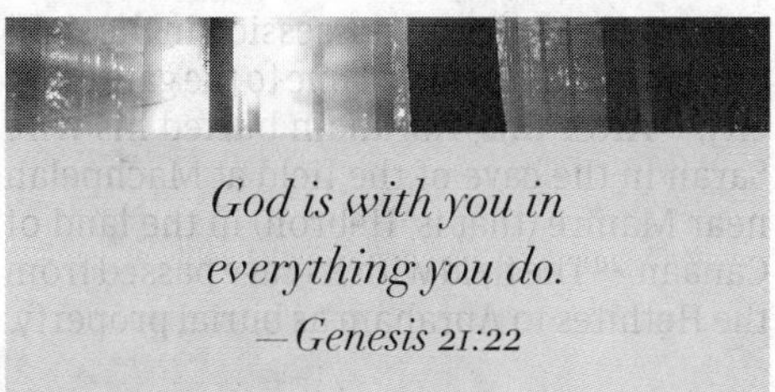
God is with you in
everything you do.
—Genesis 21:22

24 And Abraham said, "I swear it." 25 But Abraham complained to Abimelech because of the
well that Abimelech's servants had seized.
26 Abimelech replied, "I don't know who did
this thing. You didn't report anything to me,
so I hadn't heard about it until today."
27 Abraham took flocks and herds and gave
them to Abimelech, and the two of them made
a covenant. 28 Abraham separated seven ewe
lambs from the flock. 29 And Abimelech said
to Abraham, "Why have you separated these
seven ewe lambs?"
30 He replied, "You are to accept the seven
ewe lambs from me so that this act[A] will serve
as my witness that I dug this well." 31 Therefore
that place was called Beer-sheba[B] because
it was there that the two of them swore an
oath. 32 After they had made a covenant at
Beer-sheba, Abimelech and Phicol, the commander of his army, left and returned to the
land of the Philistines.
33 Abraham planted a tamarisk tree in Beer-
sheba, and there he called on the name of the
LORD, the Everlasting God. 34 And Abraham
lived as an alien in the land of the Philistines
for many days.

THE SACRIFICE OF ISAAC

22 After these things God tested Abraham
and said to him, "Abraham!"
"Here I am," he answered.
2 "Take your son," he said, "your only son
Isaac, whom you love, go to the land of Moriah, and offer him there as a burnt offering
on one of the mountains I will tell you about."
3 So Abraham got up early in the morning,
saddled his donkey, and took with him two of
his young men and his son Isaac. He split wood
for a burnt offering and set out to go to the
place God had told him about. 4 On the third
day Abraham looked up and saw the place
in the distance. 5 Then Abraham said to his
young men, "Stay here with the donkey. The
boy and I will go over there to worship; then
we'll come back to you." 6 Abraham took the
wood for the burnt offering and laid it on his
son Isaac. In his hand he took the fire and the
knife, and the two of them walked on together.
7 Then Isaac spoke to his father Abraham
and said, "My father."
And he replied, "Here I am, my son."
Isaac said, "The fire and the wood are here,
but where is the lamb for the burnt offering?"
8 Abraham answered, "God himself will provide[C] the lamb for the burnt offering, my son."
Then the two of them walked on together.
9 When they arrived at the place that God
had told him about, Abraham built the altar
there and arranged the wood. He bound his
son Isaac[D] and placed him on the altar on top
of the wood. 10 Then Abraham reached out and
took the knife to slaughter his son.
11 But the angel of the LORD called to him
from heaven and said, "Abraham, Abraham!"
He replied, "Here I am."
12 Then he said, "Do not lay a hand on the boy
or do anything to him. For now I know that
you fear God, since you have not withheld
your only son from me." 13 Abraham looked
up and saw a ram[E] caught in the thicket by
its horns. So Abraham went and took the ram
and offered it as a burnt offering in place of
his son. 14 And Abraham named that place
The LORD Will Provide,[F] so today it is said: "It
will be provided[G] on the LORD's mountain."
15 Then the angel of the LORD called to Abraham a second time from heaven 16 and said,
"By myself I have sworn," this is the LORD's
declaration: "Because you have done this thing
and have not withheld your only son, 17 I will
indeed bless you and make your offspring as
numerous as the stars of the sky and the sand
on the seashore. Your offspring will possess the
city gates of their enemies. 18 And all the nations
of the earth will be blessed[H] by your offspring
because you have obeyed my command."
19 Abraham went back to his young men, and
they got up and went together to Beer-sheba.
And Abraham settled in Beer-sheba.

REBEKAH'S FAMILY

20 Now after these things Abraham was told,
"Milcah also has borne sons to your broth-
er Nahor: 21 Uz his firstborn, his brother Buz,
Kemuel the father of Aram, 22 Chesed, Hazo,

[A] **21:30** Lit *that it* [B] **21:31** = Well of the Oath, or Seven Wells [C] **22:8** Lit *see* [D] **22:9** Or *Isaac hand and foot* [E] **22:13** Some Hb mss, Sam, LXX, Syr, Tg; other Hb mss read *saw behind him a ram* [F] **22:14** = *Yahweh-yireh* [G] **22:14** Or *"He will be seen* [H] **22:18** Or *will bless themselves*, or *will find blessing*

Pildash, Jidlaph, and Bethuel." 23 And Bethuel
fathered Rebekah. Milcah bore these eight to
Nahor, Abraham's brother. 24 His concubine,
whose name was Reumah, also bore Tebah,
Gaham, Tahash, and Maacah.

SARAH'S BURIAL

23 Now Sarah lived 127 years; these were
all the years of her life. 2 Sarah died
in Kiriath-arba (that is, Hebron) in the land
of Canaan, and Abraham went to mourn for
Sarah and to weep for her.
3 Then Abraham got up from beside his dead
wife and spoke to the Hethites: 4 "I am an alien
residing among you. Give me burial property
among you so that I can bury my dead."[A]
5 The Hethites replied to Abraham,[B] 6 "Listen
to us, my lord. You are a prince of God[C] among
us. Bury your dead in our finest burial place.[D]
None of us will withhold from you his burial
place for burying your dead."
7 Then Abraham rose and bowed down to
the Hethites, the people of the land. 8 He said
to them, "If you are willing for me to bury
my dead, listen to me and ask Ephron son of
Zohar on my behalf 9 to give me the cave of
Machpelah that belongs to him; it is at the
end of his field. Let him give it to me in your
presence, for the full price, as burial property."
10 Ephron was sitting among the Hethites. So
in the hearing[E] of all the Hethites who came
to the gate of his city, Ephron the Hethite answered Abraham: 11 "No, my lord. Listen to
me. I give you the field, and I give you the cave
that is in it. I give it to you in the sight[F] of my
people. Bury your dead."
12 Abraham bowed down to the people of
the land 13 and said to Ephron in the hearing
of the people of the land, "Listen to me, if you
please. Let me pay the price of the field. Accept
it from me, and let me bury my dead there."
14 Ephron answered Abraham and said
to him, 15 "My lord, listen to me. Land worth
four hundred shekels of silver — what is
that between you and me? Bury your dead."
16 Abraham agreed with Ephron, and Abraham weighed out to Ephron the silver that
he had agreed to in the hearing of the Hethites: four hundred standard shekels[G] of silver.
17 So Ephron's field at Machpelah near Mamre
— the field with its cave and all the trees anywhere within the boundaries of the field —
became 18 Abraham's possession in the sight
of all the Hethites who came to the gate of his
city. 19 After this, Abraham buried his wife
Sarah in the cave of the field at Machpelah
near Mamre (that is, Hebron) in the land of
Canaan. 20 The field with its cave passed from
the Hethites to Abraham as burial property.

A WIFE FOR ISAAC

24 Abraham was now old, getting on in
years,[H] and the LORD had blessed him
in everything. 2 Abraham said to his servant,
the elder of his household who managed all
he owned, "Place your hand under my thigh,
3 and I will have you swear by the LORD, God
of heaven and God of earth, that you will not
take a wife for my son from the daughters of
the Canaanites among whom I live, 4 but will
go to my land and my family to take a wife for
my son Isaac."
5 The servant said to him, "Suppose the
woman is unwilling to follow me to this land?
Should I have your son go back to the land
you came from?"
6 Abraham answered him, "Make sure that
you don't take my son back there. 7 The LORD,
the God of heaven, who took me from my father's house and from my native land, who
spoke to me and swore to me, 'I will give this
land to your offspring' — he will send his angel before you, and you can take a wife for my
son from there. 8 If the woman is unwilling to
follow you, then you are free from this oath
to me, but don't let my son go back there." 9 So
the servant placed his hand under his master
Abraham's thigh and swore an oath to him
concerning this matter.
10 The servant took ten of his master's camels, and with all kinds of his master's goods in
hand, he went to Aram-naharaim, to Nahor's
town. 11 At evening, the time when women
went out to draw water, he made the camels
kneel beside a well outside the town.
12 "LORD, God of my master Abraham," he
prayed, "make this happen for me today, and
show kindness to my master Abraham. 13 I am
standing here at the spring where the daughters of the men of the town are coming out to
draw water. 14 Let the girl to whom I say, 'Please
lower your water jug so that I may drink,' and
who responds, 'Drink, and I'll water your camels
also' — let her be the one you have appointed

[A] **23:4** Lit *dead from before me* [B] **23:5** Lit *Abraham, saying to him* [C] **23:6** Or *a mighty prince* [D] **23:6** Or *finest graves*
[E] **23:10** Lit *ears*, also in vv. 13,16 [F] **23:11** Lit *in the eyes of the sons* [G] **23:16** Lit *400 shekels passing to the merchant*
[H] **24:1** Lit *days*

for your servant Isaac. By this I will know that
you have shown kindness to my master."
15 Before he had finished speaking, there
was Rebekah — daughter of Bethuel son of
Milcah, the wife of Abraham's brother Nahor
— coming with a jug on her shoulder. 16 Now
the girl was very beautiful, a virgin — no man
had been intimate with her. She went down to
the spring, filled her jug, and came up. 17 Then
the servant ran to meet her and said, "Please
let me have a little water from your jug."
18 She replied, "Drink, my lord." She quickly
lowered her jug to her hand and gave him a
drink. 19 When she had finished giving him a
drink, she said, "I'll also draw water for your
camels until they have had enough to drink."[A]
20 She quickly emptied her jug into the trough
and hurried to the well again to draw water.
She drew water for all his camels 21 while the
man silently watched her to see whether or
not the LORD had made his journey a success.
22 As the camels finished drinking, the man
took a gold ring weighing half a shekel, and for
her wrists two bracelets weighing ten shekels
of gold. 23 "Whose daughter are you?" he asked.
"Please tell me, is there room in your father's
house for us to spend the night?"
24 She answered him, "I am the daughter of
Bethuel son of Milcah, whom she bore to Nahor." 25 She also said to him, "We have plenty of
straw and feed and a place to spend the night."
26 Then the man knelt low, worshiped the
LORD, 27 and said, "Blessed be the LORD, the God
of my master Abraham, who has not withheld
his kindness and faithfulness from my master.
As for me, the LORD has led me on the journey
to the house of my master's relatives."
28 The girl ran and told her mother's household about these things. 29 Now Rebekah had
a brother named Laban, and Laban ran out
to the man at the spring. 30 As soon as he had
seen the ring and the bracelets on his sister's
wrists, and when he had heard his sister Rebekah's words — "The man said this to me!"
— he went to the man. He was standing there
by the camels at the spring.
31 Laban said, "Come, you who are blessed
by the LORD. Why are you standing out here?
I have prepared the house and a place for the
camels." 32 So the man came to the house, and
the camels were unloaded. Straw and feed were
given to the camels, and water was brought to
wash his feet and the feet of the men with him.
33 A meal was set before him, but he said, "I
will not eat until I have said what I have to say."
So Laban said, "Please speak."
34 "I am Abraham's servant," he said. 35 "The
LORD has greatly blessed my master, and he
has become rich. He has given him flocks and
herds, silver and gold, male and female slaves,
and camels and donkeys. 36 Sarah, my master's wife, bore a son to my master in her[B]
old age, and he has given him everything he
owns. 37 My master put me under this oath:
'You will not take a wife for my son from the
daughters of the Canaanites in whose land I
live 38 but will go to my father's family and to
my clan to take a wife for my son.' 39 But I said
to my master, 'Suppose the woman will not
come back with me?' 40 He said to me, 'The
LORD before whom I have walked will send
his angel with you and make your journey a
success, and you will take a wife for my son
from my clan and from my father's family.
41 Then you will be free from my oath if you
go to my family and they do not give her to
you — you will be free from my oath.'
42 "Today when I came to the spring, I prayed:
LORD, God of my master Abraham, if only you
will make my journey successful! 43 I am standing here at a spring. Let the young woman[C]
who comes out to draw water, and I say to her,
'Please let me drink a little water from your
jug,' 44 and who responds to me, 'Drink, and
I'll draw water for your camels also' — let
her be the woman the LORD has appointed
for my master's son.
45 "Before I had finished praying silently,
there was Rebekah coming with her jug on
her shoulder, and she went down to the spring
and drew water. So I said to her, 'Please let me
have a drink.' 46 She quickly lowered her jug
from her shoulder and said, 'Drink, and I'll
water your camels also.' So I drank, and she
also watered the camels. 47 Then I asked her,
'Whose daughter are you?' She responded,
'The daughter of Bethuel son of Nahor, whom
Milcah bore to him.' So I put the ring on her
nose and the bracelets on her wrists. 48 Then
I knelt low, worshiped the LORD, and blessed
the LORD, the God of my master Abraham,
who guided me on the right way to take the
granddaughter of my master's brother for his
son. 49 Now, if you are going to show kindness
and faithfulness to my master, tell me; if not,
tell me, and I will go elsewhere."[D]

[A] **24:19** Lit *they are finished drinking* [B] **24:36** Sam, LXX read *his* [C] **24:43** Or *the virgin* [D] **24:49** Lit *go to the right or to the left*

50 Laban and Bethuel answered, "This is from
the LORD; we have no choice in the matter.[A]
51 Rebekah is here in front of you. Take her and
go, and let her be a wife for your master's son,
just as the LORD has spoken."
52 When Abraham's servant heard their
words, he bowed to the ground before the
LORD. 53 Then he brought out objects of silver and gold, and garments, and gave them
to Rebekah. He also gave precious gifts to
her brother and her mother. 54 Then he and
the men with him ate and drank and spent
the night.
When they got up in the morning, he said,
"Send me to my master."
55 But her brother and mother said, "Let the
girl stay with us for about ten days.[B] Then
she[C] can go."
56 But he responded to them, "Do not delay
me, since the LORD has made my journey a
success. Send me away so that I may go to
my master."
57 So they said, "Let's call the girl and ask
her opinion."[D]
58 They called Rebekah and said to her, "Will
you go with this man?"
She replied, "I will go." 59 So they sent away
their sister Rebekah with the one who had
nursed and raised her,[E] and Abraham's servant and his men.
60 They blessed Rebekah, saying to her:

Our sister, may you become
thousands upon ten thousands.
May your offspring possess
the city gates of their[F] enemies.

61 Then Rebekah and her female servants
got up, mounted the camels, and followed the
man. So the servant took Rebekah and left.
62 Now Isaac was returning from Beer-lahai-roi,[G] for he was living in the Negev region. 63 In the early evening Isaac went out
to walk[H] in the field, and looking up he saw
camels coming. 64 Rebekah looked up, and
when she saw Isaac, she got down from her
camel 65 and asked the servant, "Who is that
man in the field coming to meet us?"
The servant answered, "It is my master." So
she took her veil and covered herself. 66 Then
the servant told Isaac everything he had done.
67 And Isaac brought her into the tent of his
mother Sarah and took Rebekah to be his wife.
Isaac loved her, and he was comforted after
his mother's death.

ABRAHAM'S OTHER WIFE AND SONS

25 Abraham had taken[I] another wife,
whose name was Keturah, 2 and she
bore him Zimran, Jokshan, Medan, Midian,
Ishbak, and Shuah. 3 Jokshan fathered Sheba
and Dedan. Dedan's sons were the Asshu-
rim, Letushim, and Leummim. 4 And Midian's sons were Ephah, Epher, Hanoch, Abida,
and Eldaah. All these were sons of Keturah.
5 Abraham gave everything he owned to Isaac.
6 But Abraham gave gifts to the sons of his
concubines, and while he was still alive he
sent them eastward, away from his son Isaac,
to the land of the East.

ABRAHAM'S DEATH

7 This is the length of Abraham's life:[J] 175
years. 8 He took his last breath and died at a
good old age, old and contented,[K] and he was
gathered to his people. 9 His sons Isaac and
Ishmael buried him in the cave of Machpelah near Mamre, in the field of Ephron son
of Zohar the Hethite. 10 This was the field that
Abraham bought from the Hethites. Abraham
was buried there with his wife Sarah. 11 After
Abraham's death, God blessed his son Isaac,
who lived near Beer-lahai-roi.

ISHMAEL'S FAMILY RECORDS

12 These are the family records of Abraham's
son Ishmael, whom Hagar the Egyptian, Sarah's
slave, bore to Abraham. 13 These are the names
of Ishmael's sons; their names according to the
family records are Nebaioth, Ishmael's firstborn, then Kedar, Adbeel, Mibsam, 14 Mishma,
Dumah, Massa, 15 Hadad, Tema, Jetur, Naphish,
and Kedemah. 16 These are Ishmael's sons, and
these are their names by their settlements
and encampments: twelve leaders[L] of their
clans.[M] 17 This is the length[N] of Ishmael's life:
137 years. He took his last breath and died,
and was gathered to his people. 18 And they[O]
settled from Havilah to Shur, which is opposite
Egypt as you go toward Asshur.[P] He[Q] stayed
near[R] all his relatives.

[A] **24:50** Lit *we cannot say to you anything bad or good* [B] **24:55** Lit *us days or tenth* [C] **24:55** Or *you* [D] **24:57** Lit *mouth* [E] **24:59** Lit *with her wet nurse*; Gn 35:8 [F] **24:60** Lit *his* [G] **24:62** = A Well of the Living One Who Sees Me [H] **24:63** Or *pray*, or *meditate*; Hb obscure [I] **25:1** Or *Abraham took* [J] **25:7** Lit *And these are the days of the years of the life of Abraham that he lived* [K] **25:8** Sam, LXX, Syr read *full of days* [L] **25:16** Or *chieftains* [M] **25:16** Or *peoples* [N] **25:17** Lit *And these are the years* [O] **25:18** LXX, Vg read *he* [P] **25:18** Or *Assyria* [Q] **25:18** = Ishmael and his descendants [R] **25:18** Or *He settled down alongside of*

THE BIRTH OF JACOB AND ESAU

19 These are the family records of Isaac son of
Abraham. Abraham fathered Isaac. 20 Isaac
was forty years old when he took as his wife
Rebekah daughter of Bethuel the Aramean
from Paddan-aram and sister of Laban the
Aramean. 21 Isaac prayed to the LORD on behalf
of his wife because she was childless.
The LORD was receptive to his prayer, and his
wife Rebekah conceived. 22 But the children
inside her struggled with each other, and she
said, "Why is this happening to me?"[A] So she
went to inquire of the LORD. 23 And the LORD
said to her:

Two nations are in your
womb;
two peoples will come from you
and be separated.
One people will be stronger
than the other,
and the older will serve
the younger.

24 When her time came to give birth, there
were indeed twins in her womb. 25 The first
one came out red-looking,[B] covered with hair[C]
like a fur coat, and they named him Esau.
26 After this, his brother came out grasping
Esau's heel with his hand. So he was named
Jacob.[D] Isaac was sixty years old when they
were born.

ESAU SELLS HIS BIRTHRIGHT

27 When the boys grew up, Esau became an
expert hunter, an outdoorsman,[E] but Jacob
was a quiet man who stayed at home.[F] 28 Isaac
loved Esau because he had a taste for wild
game, but Rebekah loved Jacob.

29 Once when Jacob was cooking a stew, Esau
came in from the field exhausted. 30 He said
to Jacob, "Let me eat some of that red stuff,
because I'm exhausted." That is why he was
also named Edom.[G]

31 Jacob replied, "First sell me your birthright."

32 "Look," said Esau, "I'm about to die, so
what good is a birthright to me?"

33 Jacob said, "Swear to me first." So he swore
to Jacob and sold his birthright to him. 34 Then
Jacob gave bread and lentil stew to Esau; he
ate, drank, got up, and went away. So Esau
despised his birthright.

THE PROMISE REAFFIRMED TO ISAAC

26 There was another famine in the land
in addition to the one that had occurred
in Abraham's time. And Isaac went to Abimelech,
king of the Philistines, at Gerar. 2 The
LORD appeared to him and said, "Do not go
down to Egypt. Live in the land that I tell you
about; 3 stay in this land as an alien, and I will
be with you and bless you. For I will give all
these lands to you and your offspring, and I
will confirm the oath that I swore to your father
Abraham. 4 I will make your offspring as
numerous as the stars of the sky, I will give your
offspring all these lands, and all the nations of
the earth will be blessed[H] by your offspring,
5 because Abraham listened to me and kept
my mandate, my commands, my statutes, and
my instructions." 6 So Isaac settled in Gerar.

ISAAC'S DECEPTION

7 When the men of the place asked about his
wife, he said, "She is my sister," for he was
afraid to say "my wife," thinking, "The men of
the place will kill me on account of Rebekah,
for she is a beautiful woman." 8 When Isaac had
been there for some time, Abimelech king of
the Philistines looked down from the window
and was surprised to see[I] Isaac caressing his
wife Rebekah.

9 Abimelech sent for Isaac and said, "So she
is really your wife! How could you say, 'She is
my sister'?"

Isaac answered him, "Because I thought I
might die on account of her."

10 Then Abimelech said, "What is this you've
done to us? One of the people could easily
have slept with your wife, and you would have
brought guilt on us." 11 So Abimelech warned
all the people, "Whoever harms this man or
his wife will certainly be put to death."

CONFLICTS OVER WELLS

12 Isaac sowed seed in that land, and in that
year he reaped[J] a hundred times what was
sown. The LORD blessed him, 13 and the man
became rich and kept getting richer until he
was very wealthy. 14 He had flocks of sheep,
herds of cattle, and many slaves, and the Philistines
were envious of him. 15 Philistines
stopped up all the wells that his father's servants
had dug in the days of his father Abraham,
filling them with dirt. 16 And Abimelech

[A] **25:22** Lit *said, "If thus, why this I?"* [B] **25:25** In Hb, *red-looking* sounds like "Edom"; Gn 32:3. [C] **25:25** In Hb, *hair* sounds like "Seir"; Gn 32:3. [D] **25:26** = He Grasps the Heel [E] **25:27** Lit *a man of the field* [F] **25:27** Lit *man living in tents* [G] **25:30** = Red [H] **26:4** Or *will bless themselves* [I] **26:8** Or *and he looked and behold—* [J] **26:12** Lit *found*

said to Isaac, "Leave us, for you are much too powerful for us."[A]

17 So Isaac left there, camped in the Gerar Valley, and lived there. 18 Isaac reopened the wells that had been dug in the days of his father Abraham and that the Philistines had stopped up after Abraham died. He gave them the same names his father had given them. 19 Then Isaac's servants dug in the valley and found a well of spring[B] water there. 20 But the herdsmen of Gerar quarreled with Isaac's herdsmen and said, "The water is ours!" So he named the well Esek[C] because they argued with him. 21 Then they dug another well and quarreled over that one also, so he named it Sitnah.[D] 22 He moved from there and dug another, and they did not quarrel over it. He named it Rehoboth[E] and said, "For now the LORD has made space for us, and we will be fruitful in the land."

THE LORD APPEARS TO ISAAC

23 From there he went up to Beer-sheba, 24 and the LORD appeared to him that night and said, "I am the God of your father Abraham. Do not be afraid, for I am with you. I will bless you and multiply your offspring because of my servant Abraham."

25 So he built an altar there, called on the name of the LORD, and pitched his tent there. Isaac's servants also dug a well there.

COVENANT WITH ABIMELECH

26 Now Abimelech came to him from Gerar with Ahuzzath his adviser and Phicol the commander of his army. 27 Isaac said to them, "Why have you come to me? You hated me and sent me away from you."

28 They replied, "We have clearly seen how the LORD has been with you. We think there should be an oath between two parties — between us and you. Let us make a covenant with you: 29 You will not harm us, just as we have not harmed you but have done only what was good to you, sending you away in peace. You are now blessed by the LORD."

30 So he prepared a banquet for them, and they ate and drank. 31 They got up early in the morning and swore an oath to each other.[F] Isaac sent them on their way, and they left him in peace. 32 On that same day Isaac's servants came to tell him about the well they had dug, saying to him, "We have found water!" 33 He called it Sheba.[G] Therefore the name of the city is still Beer-sheba[H] today.

ESAU'S WIVES

34 When Esau was forty years old, he took as his wives Judith daughter of Beeri the Hethite, and Basemath daughter of Elon the Hethite. 35 They made life bitter[I] for Isaac and Rebekah.

THE STOLEN BLESSING

27 When Isaac was old and his eyes were so weak that he could not see, he called his older son Esau and said to him, "My son."

And he answered, "Here I am."

2 He said, "Look, I am old and do not know the day of my death. 3 So now take your hunting gear, your quiver and bow, and go out in the field to hunt some game for me. 4 Then make me a delicious meal that I love and bring it to me to eat, so that I can bless you before I die."

5 Now Rebekah was listening to what Isaac said to his son Esau. So while Esau went to the field to hunt some game to bring in, 6 Rebekah said to her son Jacob, "Listen! I heard your father talking with your brother Esau. He said, 7 'Bring me game and make a delicious meal for me to eat so that I can bless you in the LORD's presence before I die.' 8 Now, my son, listen to me and do what I tell you. 9 Go to the flock and bring me two choice young goats, and I will make them into a delicious meal for your father — the kind he loves. 10 Then take it to your father to eat so that he may bless you before he dies."

11 Jacob answered Rebekah his mother, "Look, my brother Esau is a hairy man, but I am a man with smooth skin. 12 Suppose my father touches me. Then I will be revealed to him as a deceiver and bring a curse rather than a blessing on myself."

13 His mother said to him, "Your curse be on me, my son. Just obey me and go get them for me."

14 So he went and got the goats and brought them to his mother, and his mother made the delicious food his father loved. 15 Then Rebekah took the best clothes of her older son Esau, which were in the house, and had her younger son Jacob wear them. 16 She put the skins of the young goats on his hands and the smooth part of his neck. 17 Then she handed the delicious food and the bread she had made to her son Jacob.

[A] **26:16** Or *are more numerous than we are* [B] **26:19** Lit *living* [C] **26:20** = Argument [D] **26:21** = Hostility [E] **26:22** = Open Spaces [F] **26:31** Lit *swore, each man to his brother* [G] **26:33** Or *Shibah* [H] **26:33** = Well of the Oath [I] **26:35** Lit *And they became bitterness of spirit*

Jacob | Restoration Profile

GENESIS 25–50

God's work in people's lives seldom involves instantaneous restoration. His perspective is long-term. He has invested in us for life and for eternity. In Jacob's case, God's restoring efforts can be traced for decades.

Almost from conception, Jacob's personality asserted itself. He wrestled with his twin brother, Esau, in his mother's womb, and God informed Rebekah that she was carrying two nations. Jacob was born trying to trip his brother, so the name they gave him means "grabber." Later, when giving Jacob a new name, God simply expanded the original to Israel, which means "struggled with God" (Gn 32:28).

Jacob was a consummate conniver. No matter where he was, his priority was figuring the angles to get an advantage. Whether dealing with his parents, brother, or father-in-law, Jacob couldn't keep from guarding his own interests. Fortunately for Jacob, God's plan included him but was a lot larger than his own often dysfunctional life strategy. God was committed to working through Jacob to create a nation he would call his chosen people. For Jacob, God's restoring work involved divine encounters at Bethel (Gn 28; 35), Haran (Gn 31), and Mahanaim (Gn 32).

The book of Hebrews lists Jacob among the heroes of faith. The summary of his life hints at God's persevering grace: "By faith Jacob, when he was dying, blessed each of the sons of Joseph, and he worshiped, leaning on the top of his staff" (Heb 11:21). When the patriarch took his last breath, God was still working on his struggling, wrestling character. With God's patient, restoring touches, everyone is a work in progress.

18 When he came to his father, he said, "My
father."

And he answered, "Here I am. Who are you, my son?"

19 Jacob replied to his father, "I am Esau, your
firstborn. I have done as you told me. Please sit up and eat some of my game so that you may bless me."

20 But Isaac said to his son, "How did you
ever find it so quickly, my son?"

He replied, "Because the LORD your God made it happen for me."

21 Then Isaac said to Jacob, "Please come
closer so I can touch you, my son. Are you really my son Esau or not?"

22 So Jacob came closer to his father Isaac.
When he touched him, he said, "The voice is the voice of Jacob, but the hands are the hands
of Esau." 23 He did not recognize him, because
his hands were hairy like those of his brother
Esau; so he blessed him. 24 Again he asked,
"Are you really my son Esau?"

And he replied, "I am."

25 Then he said, "Bring it closer to me, and
let me eat some of my son's game so that I can bless you." Jacob brought it closer to him, and he ate; he brought him wine, and he drank.

26 Then his father Isaac said to him, "Please
come closer and kiss me, my son." 27 So he came
closer and kissed him. When Isaac smelled[A] his clothes, he blessed him and said:

Ah, the smell of my son
is like the smell of a field
that the LORD has blessed.

28 May God give to you —
from the dew of the sky
and from the richness of the land —
an abundance of grain
and new wine.

29 May peoples serve you
and nations bow in worship to you.
Be master over your relatives;
may your mother's sons bow
in worship to you.
Those who curse you will be cursed,
and those who bless you
will be blessed.

30 As soon as Isaac had finished blessing
Jacob and Jacob had left the presence of his father Isaac, his brother Esau arrived from
his hunting. 31 He had also made some deli-
cious food and brought it to his father. He said to his father, "Let my father get up and

[A] **27:27** Lit *smelled the smell of*

eat some of his son's game, so that you may
bless me."
32 But his father Isaac said to him, "Who
are you?"
He answered, "I am Esau your firstborn son."
33 Isaac began to tremble uncontrollably.
"Who was it then," he said, "who hunted game
and brought it to me? I ate it all before you
came in, and I blessed him. Indeed, he will
be blessed!"
34 When Esau heard his father's words, he
cried out with a loud and bitter cry and said
to his father, "Bless me too, my father!"
35 But he replied, "Your brother came deceitfully and took your blessing."
36 So he said, "Isn't he rightly named Jacob?[A]
For he has cheated me twice now. He took my
birthright, and look, now he has taken my
blessing." Then he asked, "Haven't you saved
a blessing for me?"
37 But Isaac answered Esau, "Look, I have
made him a master over you, have given him
all of his relatives as his servants, and have
sustained him with grain and new wine. What
then can I do for you, my son?"
38 Esau said to his father, "Do you have only
one blessing, my father? Bless me too, my father!" And Esau wept loudly.[B]
39 His father Isaac answered him,
Look, your dwelling place will be
away from the richness of the land,
away from the dew of the sky above.
40 You will live by your sword,
and you will serve your brother.
But when you rebel,[C]
you will break his yoke from your neck.

ESAU'S ANGER

41 Esau held a grudge against Jacob because
of the blessing his father had given him. And
Esau determined in his heart: "The days of
mourning for my father are approaching; then
I will kill my brother Jacob."
42 When the words of her older son Esau
were reported to Rebekah, she summoned her
younger son Jacob and said to him, "Listen,
your brother Esau is consoling himself by
planning to kill you. 43 So now, my son, listen
to me. Flee at once to my brother Laban in
Haran, 44 and stay with him for a few days
until your brother's anger subsides — 45 until
your brother's rage turns away from you and
he forgets what you have done to him. Then
I will send for you and bring you back from
there. Why should I lose you both in one day?"
46 So Rebekah said to Isaac, "I'm sick of my
life because of these Hethite girls. If Jacob marries someone from around here,[D] like these
Hethite girls, what good is my life?"

JACOB'S DEPARTURE

28 So Isaac summoned Jacob, blessed him,
and commanded him, "Do not marry a
Canaanite girl. 2 Go at once to Paddan-aram,
to the house of Bethuel, your mother's father.
Marry one of the daughters of Laban, your
mother's brother. 3 May God Almighty bless
you and make you fruitful and multiply you
so that you become an assembly of peoples.
4 May God give you and your offspring the
blessing of Abraham so that you may possess
the land where you live as a foreigner, the land
God gave to Abraham." 5 So Isaac sent Jacob
to Paddan-aram, to Laban son of Bethuel the
Aramean, the brother of Rebekah, the mother
of Jacob and Esau.
6 Esau noticed that Isaac blessed Jacob and
sent him to Paddan-aram to get a wife there.
When he blessed him, Isaac commanded Jacob,
"Do not marry a Canaanite girl." 7 And Jacob
listened to his father and mother and went to
Paddan-aram. 8 Esau realized that his father
Isaac disapproved of the Canaanite women,
9 so Esau went to Ishmael and married, in addition to his other wives, Mahalath daughter
of Ishmael, Abraham's son. She was the sister
of Nebaioth.

JACOB AT BETHEL

10 Jacob left Beer-sheba and went toward Haran. 11 He reached a certain place and spent the
night there because the sun had set. He took
one of the stones from the place, put it there
at his head, and lay down in that place. 12 And
he dreamed: A stairway was set on the ground
with its top reaching the sky, and God's angels
were going up and down on it. 13 The LORD was
standing there beside him,[E] saying, "I am the
LORD, the God of your father Abraham and
the God of Isaac. I will give you and your offspring the land on which you are lying. 14 Your
offspring will be like the dust of the earth, and
you will spread out toward the west, the east,
the north, and the south. All the peoples on
earth will be blessed through you and your
offspring. 15 Look, I am with you and will watch

[A] **27:36** = He Grasps the Heel [B] **27:38** Lit *Esau lifted up his voice and wept* [C] **27:40** Hb obscure [D] **27:46** Lit *someone like these daughters of the land* [E] **28:13** Or *there above it*

over you wherever you go. I will bring you back
to this land, for I will not leave you until I have
done what I have promised you."
16 When Jacob awoke from his sleep, he said,
"Surely the LORD is in this place, and I did not
know it." 17 He was afraid and said, "What an
awesome place this is! This is none other than
the house of God. This is the gate of heaven."
18 Early in the morning Jacob took the stone
that was near his head and set it up as a marker. He poured oil on top of it 19 and named the
place Bethel,[A] though previously the city was
named Luz. 20 Then Jacob made a vow: "If God
will be with me and watch over me during
this journey I'm making, if he provides me
with food to eat and clothing to wear, 21 and if
I return safely to my father's family, then the
LORD will be my God. 22 This stone that I have
set up as a marker will be God's house, and I
will give to you a tenth of all that you give me."

JACOB MEETS RACHEL

29 Jacob resumed his journey[B] and went
to the eastern country.[C] 2 He looked and
saw a well in a field. Three flocks of sheep were
lying there beside it because the sheep were
watered from this well. But a large stone covered the opening of the well. 3 The shepherds
would roll the stone from the opening of the
well and water the sheep when all the flocks[D]
were gathered there. Then they would return
the stone to its place over the well's opening.
4 Jacob asked the men at the well, "My brothers! Where are you from?"
"We're from Haran," they answered.
5 "Do you know Laban grandson of Nahor?"
Jacob asked them.
They answered, "We know him."
6 "Is he well?" Jacob asked.
"Yes," they said, "and here is his daughter
Rachel, coming with his sheep."
7 Then Jacob said, "Look, it is still broad
daylight. It's not time for the animals to be
gathered. Water the flock, then go out and
let them graze."
8 But they replied, "We can't until all the
flocks have been gathered and the stone is
rolled from the well's opening. Then we will
water the sheep."
9 While he was still speaking with them, Rachel came with her father's sheep, for she was a
shepherdess. 10 As soon as Jacob saw his uncle
Laban's daughter Rachel with his sheep,[E] he
went up and rolled the stone from the opening
and watered his uncle Laban's sheep. 11 Then
Jacob kissed Rachel and wept loudly.[F] 12 He
told Rachel that he was her father's relative,
Rebekah's son. She ran and told her father.

JACOB DECEIVED

13 When Laban heard the news about his sister's
son Jacob, he ran to meet him, hugged him,
and kissed him. Then he took him to his house,
and Jacob told him all that had happened.
14 Laban said to him, "Yes, you are my own
flesh and blood."[G]
After Jacob had stayed with him a month,
15 Laban said to him, "Just because you're my
relative, should you work for me for nothing?
Tell me what your wages should be."
16 Now Laban had two daughters: the older
was named Leah, and the younger was named
Rachel. 17 Leah had tender eyes, but Rachel was
shapely and beautiful. 18 Jacob loved Rachel,
so he answered Laban, "I'll work for you sev-
en years for your younger daughter Rachel."
19 Laban replied, "Better that I give her to
you than to some other man. Stay with me."
20 So Jacob worked seven years for Rachel,
and they seemed like only a few days to him
because of his love for her.
21 Then Jacob said to Laban, "Since my time
is complete, give me my wife, so I can sleep
with[H] her." 22 So Laban invited all the men of the
place and sponsored a feast. 23 That evening,
Laban took his daughter Leah and gave her
to Jacob, and he slept with her. 24 And Laban
gave his slave Zilpah to his daughter Leah as
her slave.
25 When morning came, there was Leah! So
he said to Laban, "What is this you have done
to me? Wasn't it for Rachel that I worked for
you? Why have you deceived me?"
26 Laban answered, "It is not the custom in
this place to give the younger daughter in
marriage before the firstborn. 27 Complete
this week of wedding celebration, and we
will also give you this younger one in return
for working yet another seven years for me."
28 And Jacob did just that. He finished the
week of celebration, and Laban gave him his
daughter Rachel as his wife. 29 And Laban
gave his slave Bilhah to his daughter Rachel
as her slave. 30 Jacob slept with Rachel also,

[A] **28:19** = House of God [B] **29:1** Lit *Jacob picked up his feet* [C] **29:1** Lit *the land of the children of the east* [D] **29:3** Sam, some LXX mss read *flocks and the shepherds* [E] **29:10** Lit *with the sheep of Laban his mother's brother* [F] **29:11** Lit *and he lifted his voice and wept* [G] **29:14** Lit *my bone and my flesh* [H] **29:21** Lit *can go to*

and indeed, he loved Rachel more than Leah.
And he worked for Laban another seven years.

JACOB'S SONS

31 When the LORD saw that Leah was unloved,
he opened her womb; but Rachel was unable
to conceive. 32 Leah conceived, gave birth to
a son, and named him Reuben,[A] for she said,
"The LORD has seen my affliction; surely my
husband will love me now."

33 She conceived again, gave birth to a son,
and said, "The LORD heard that I am unloved
and has given me this son also." So she named
him Simeon.[B]

34 She conceived again, gave birth to a son,
and said, "At last, my husband will become
attached to me because I have borne three
sons for him." Therefore he was named Levi.[C]

35 And she conceived again, gave birth to a
son, and said, "This time I will praise the LORD."
Therefore she named him Judah.[D] Then Leah
stopped having children.

30 When Rachel saw that she was not
bearing Jacob any children, she envied her sister. "Give me sons, or I will die!"
she said to Jacob.

2 Jacob became angry with Rachel and said,
"Am I in God's place, who has withheld offspring[E] from you?"

3 Then she said, "Here is my maid Bilhah.
Go sleep with her, and she'll bear children
for me[F] so that through her I too can build a
family." 4 So Rachel gave her slave Bilhah to
Jacob as a wife, and he slept with her. 5 Bilhah
conceived and bore Jacob a son. 6 Rachel said,
"God has vindicated me; yes, he has heard me
and given me a son," so she named him Dan.[G]

7 Rachel's slave Bilhah conceived again and
bore Jacob a second son. 8 Rachel said, "In my
wrestlings with God,[H] I have wrestled with my
sister and won," and she named him Naphtali.[I]

9 When Leah saw that she had stopped having
children, she took her slave Zilpah and gave
her to Jacob as a wife. 10 Leah's slave Zilpah
bore Jacob a son. 11 Then Leah said, "What good
fortune!"[J] and she named him Gad.[K]

12 When Leah's slave Zilpah bore Jacob a second son, 13 Leah said, "I am happy that the wom-
en call me happy," so she named him Asher.[L]

14 Reuben went out during the wheat harvest and found some mandrakes in the field.
When he brought them to his mother Leah,
Rachel asked, "Please give me some of your
son's mandrakes."

15 But Leah replied to her, "Isn't it enough
that you have taken my husband? Now you
also want to take my son's mandrakes?"

"Well then," Rachel said, "he can sleep with
you tonight in exchange for your son's mandrakes."

16 When Jacob came in from the field that
evening, Leah went out to meet him and said,
"You must come with me, for I have hired you
with my son's mandrakes." So Jacob slept with
her that night.

17 God listened to Leah, and she conceived
and bore Jacob a fifth son. 18 Leah said, "God
has rewarded me for giving my slave to my
husband," and she named him Issachar.[M]

19 Then Leah conceived again and bore Jacob a sixth son. 20 "God has given me a good
gift," Leah said. "This time my husband will
honor me because I have borne six sons for
him," and she named him Zebulun.[N] 21 Later,
Leah bore a daughter and named her Dinah.

22 Then God remembered Rachel. He listened
to her and opened her womb. 23 She conceived
and bore a son, and she said, "God has taken
away my disgrace." 24 She named him Joseph[O]
and said, "May the LORD add another son to me."

JACOB'S FLOCKS MULTIPLY

25 After Rachel gave birth to Joseph, Jacob said
to Laban, "Send me on my way so that I can return to my homeland. 26 Give me my wives and
my children that I have worked for, and let me
go. You know how hard I have worked for you."

27 But Laban said to him, "If I have found
favor with you, stay. I have learned by divination that the LORD has blessed me because of
you." 28 Then Laban said, "Name your wages,
and I will pay them."

29 So Jacob said to him, "You know how I have
served you and how your herds have fared with
me. 30 For you had very little before I came, but
now your wealth has increased. The LORD has
blessed you because of me. And now, when
will I also do something for my own family?"

A **29:32** = See, a Son; in Hb, the name *Reuben* sounds like "has seen my affliction." B **29:33** In Hb, the name *Simeon* sounds like "has heard." C **29:34** In Hb, the name *Levi* sounds like "attached to." D **29:35** In Hb, the name *Judah* sounds like "praise." E **30:2** Lit *the fruit of the womb* F **30:3** Lit *bear on my knees* G **30:6** In Hb, the name *Dan* sounds like "has vindicated," or "has judged." H **30:8** Or *"With mighty wrestlings* I **30:8** In Hb, the name *Naphtali* sounds like "my wrestling." J **30:11** Alt Hb tradition, LXX, Vg read *"Good fortune has come!"* K **30:11** = Good Fortune L **30:13** = Happy M **30:18** In Hb, the name *Issachar* sounds like "reward." N **30:20** In Hb, the name *Zebulun* sounds like "honored." O **30:24** = He Adds

My Story | Bonnie

Inviting Jesus into my heart as a child at a backyard Bible school was the easy part for me. Living for him, in his will, was the hard part. Life routinely went according to my plan: graduated college, married a great guy, worked in downtown Chicago, and started a family right on schedule. The challenges and responsibilities of motherhood brought me again to Christ, and I made profession of faith. I casually assumed God's blessing over our plans for an expanded family. However, secondary infertility brought me to my knees and into a deeper and more intimate relationship with my Lord and Savior.

Infertility is a tool God frequently used in the lives of Bible people that succeeds in getting a woman's attention (and often, her husband's). Rachel, Hannah, Sarai and many more learned that a closed womb can lead to your own private heartache, especially when you try to resolve the issue yourself.

We spent a year trying to conceive on our own, another year with a specialist, and many years being forever hopeful that child number two would come along. But God's plan prevailed, and my heartache instead gave birth to deeper empathy for others. My "infertility theme song" was a familiar lyric that assured me God always does make all things beautiful at just the right time. The Lord knew better, and he had given me a son.

When the years go by and "no" becomes your answer, somehow hope remains – your Savior fills your heart with what his plan and purpose is for you. Christ has filled that hole in my life with himself. He has continued to give me the strength, ability, and courage to make his plan my blessing.

31 Laban asked, "What should I give you?"
And Jacob said, "You don't need to give me
anything. If you do this one thing for me, I will
continue to shepherd and keep your flock.
32 Let me go through all your sheep today and
remove every sheep that is speckled or spotted,
every dark-colored sheep among the lambs,
and the spotted and speckled among the female goats. Such will be my wages. 33 In the
future when you come to check on my wages,
my honesty will testify for me. If I have any
female goats that are not speckled or spotted,
or any lambs that are not black, they will be
considered stolen."
34 "Good," said Laban. "Let it be as you have
said."
35 That day Laban removed the streaked and
spotted male goats and all the speckled and
spotted female goats — every one that had
any white on it — and every dark-colored one
among the lambs, and he placed his sons in
charge of them. 36 He put a three-day journey
between himself and Jacob. Jacob, meanwhile,
was shepherding the rest of Laban's flock.
37 Jacob then took branches of fresh poplar,
almond, and plane wood, and peeled the bark,
exposing white stripes on the branches. 38 He
set the peeled branches in the troughs in front
of the sheep — in the water channels where
the sheep came to drink. And the sheep bred
when they came to drink. 39 The flocks bred
in front of the branches and bore streaked,
speckled, and spotted young. 40 Jacob separated the lambs and made the flocks face the
streaked sheep and the completely dark sheep
in Laban's flocks. Then he set his own stock
apart and didn't put them with Laban's sheep.
41 Whenever the stronger of the flock were
breeding, Jacob placed the branches in the
troughs, in full view of the flocks, and they
would breed in front of the branches. 42 As for
the weaklings of the flocks, he did not put out
the branches. So it turned out that the weak
sheep belonged to Laban and the stronger
ones to Jacob. 43 And the man became very
rich.[A] He had many flocks, female and male
slaves, and camels and donkeys.

JACOB SEPARATES FROM LABAN

31 Now Jacob heard what Laban's sons
were saying: "Jacob has taken all that
was our father's and has built this wealth from
what belonged to our father." 2 And Jacob saw
from Laban's face that his attitude toward him
was not the same as before.
3 The LORD said to him, "Go back to the land
of your fathers and to your family, and I will
be with you."

[A] **30:43** Lit *The man spread out very much, very much*

4 Jacob had Rachel and Leah called to the
field where his flocks were. 5 He said to them,
"I can see from your father's face that his attitude toward me is not the same as before,
but the God of my father has been with me.
6 You know that with all my strength I have
served your father 7 and that he has cheated
me and changed my wages ten times. But
God has not let him harm me. 8 If he said,
'The spotted sheep will be your wages,' then
all the sheep were born spotted. If he said,
'The streaked sheep will be your wages,' then
all the sheep were born streaked. 9 God has
taken away your father's herds and given
them to me.

10 "When the flocks were breeding, I saw in a
dream that the streaked, spotted, and speckled
males were mating with the females. 11 In that
dream the angel of God said to me, 'Jacob!'
and I said, 'Here I am.' 12 And he said, 'Look
up and see: all the males that are mating with
the flocks are streaked, spotted, and speckled,
for I have seen all that Laban has been doing
to you. 13 I am the God of Bethel, where you
poured oil on the stone marker and made a
solemn vow to me. Get up, leave this land, and
return to your native land.'"

14 Then Rachel and Leah answered him,
"Do we have any portion or inheritance in
our father's family? 15 Are we not regarded by
him as outsiders? For he has sold us and has
certainly spent our purchase price. 16 In fact,
all the wealth that God has taken away from
our father belongs to us and to our children.
So do whatever God has said to you."

17 So Jacob got up and put his children and
wives on the camels. 18 He took all the livestock
and possessions he had acquired in Paddan-
aram, and he drove his herds to go to the land
of Canaan, to his father Isaac. 19 When Laban
had gone to shear his sheep, Rachel stole her father's household idols. 20 And Jacob deceived[A]
Laban the Aramean, not telling him that he
was fleeing. 21 He fled with all his possessions,
crossed the Euphrates, and headed for[B] the
hill country of Gilead.

LABAN OVERTAKES JACOB

22 On the third day Laban was told that Jacob
had fled. 23 So he took his relatives with him,
pursued Jacob for seven days, and overtook
him in the hill country of Gilead. 24 But God
came to Laban the Aramean in a dream at night.
"Watch yourself!" God warned him. "Don't
say anything to Jacob, either good or bad."

25 When Laban overtook Jacob, Jacob had
pitched his tent in the hill country, and Laban
and his relatives also pitched their tents in the
hill country of Gilead. 26 Laban said to Jacob,
"What have you done? You have deceived me
and taken my daughters away like prisoners
of war! 27 Why did you secretly flee from me,
deceive me, and not tell me? I would have sent
you away with joy and singing, with tambourines and lyres, 28 but you didn't even let me
kiss my grandchildren and my daughters. You
have acted foolishly. 29 I could do you great
harm, but last night the God of your father
said to me: 'Watch yourself! Don't say anything
to Jacob, either good or bad.' 30 Now you have
gone off because you long for your father's
family — but why have you stolen my gods?"

31 Jacob answered, "I was afraid, for I thought
you would take your daughters from me by
force. 32 If you find your gods with anyone here,
he will not live! Before our relatives, point out
anything that is yours and take it." Jacob did
not know that Rachel had stolen the idols.

33 So Laban went into Jacob's tent, Leah's
tent, and the tents of the two concubines,[C]
but he found nothing. When he left Leah's
tent, he went into Rachel's tent. 34 Now Rachel had taken Laban's household idols, put
them in the saddlebag of the camel, and sat
on them. Laban searched the whole tent but
found nothing.

35 She said to her father, "Don't be angry, my
lord, that I cannot stand up in your presence;
I am having my period." So Laban searched,
but could not find the household idols.

JACOB'S COVENANT WITH LABAN

36 Then Jacob became incensed and brought
charges against Laban. "What is my crime?" he
said to Laban. "What is my sin, that you have
pursued me? 37 You've searched all my possessions! Have you found anything of yours?[D]
Put it here before my relatives and yours, and
let them decide between the two of us. 38 I've
been with you these twenty years. Your ewes
and female goats have not miscarried, and I
have not eaten the rams from your flock. 39 I
did not bring you any of the flock torn by wild
beasts; I myself bore the loss. You demanded
payment from me for what was stolen by day or
by night. 40 There I was — the heat consumed

[A] **31:20** Lit *And he stole the heart of* [B] **31:21** Lit *and set his face to* [C] **31:33** Lit *servants* [D] **31:37** Lit *What have you found from all of the possessions of your house?*

me by day and the frost by night, and sleep
fled from my eyes. 41 For twenty years in your
household I served you — fourteen years for
your two daughters and six years for your
flocks — and you have changed my wages
ten times! 42 If the God of my father, the God
of Abraham, the Fear of Isaac, had not been
with me, certainly now you would have sent
me off empty-handed. But God has seen my
affliction and my hard work,[A] and he issued
his verdict last night."

43 Then Laban answered Jacob, "The daughters are my daughters; the sons, my sons; and
the flocks, my flocks! Everything you see is
mine! But what can I do today for these daughters of mine or for the children they have borne?
44 Come now, let's make a covenant, you and
I. Let it be a witness between the two of us."

45 So Jacob picked out a stone and set it up
as a marker. 46 Then Jacob said to his relatives,
"Gather stones." And they took stones and
made a mound, then ate there by the mound.
47 Laban named the mound Jegar-sahadutha,
but Jacob named it Galeed.[B]

48 Then Laban said, "This mound is a witness
between you and me today." Therefore the place
was called Galeed 49 and also Mizpah,[C] for he
said, "May the LORD watch between you and
me when we are out of each other's sight. 50 If
you mistreat my daughters or take other wives,
though no one is with us, understand that God
will be a witness between you and me." 51 Laban
also said to Jacob, "Look at this mound and the
marker I have set up between you and me. 52 This
mound is a witness and the marker is a witness
that I will not pass beyond this mound to you,
and you will not pass beyond this mound and
this marker to do me harm. 53 The God of Abraham, and the gods of Nahor — the gods of their
father[D] — will judge between us." And Jacob
swore by the Fear of his father Isaac. 54 Then
Jacob offered a sacrifice on the mountain and
invited his relatives to eat a meal. So they ate
a meal and spent the night on the mountain.
55 Laban got up early in the morning, kissed
his grandchildren and daughters, and blessed
them. Then Laban left to return home.

PREPARING TO MEET ESAU

32 Jacob went on his way, and God's angels
met him. 2 When he saw them, Jacob
said, "This is God's camp." So he called that
place Mahanaim.[E]

3 Jacob sent messengers ahead of him to
his brother Esau in the land of Seir, the territory of Edom. 4 He commanded them, "You
are to say to my lord Esau, 'This is what your
servant Jacob says. I have been staying with
Laban and have been delayed until now. 5 I have
oxen, donkeys, flocks, and male and female
slaves. I have sent this message to inform my
lord, in order to seek your favor.'"

6 When the messengers returned to Jacob,
they said, "We went to your brother Esau; he
is coming to meet you — and he has four hundred men with him." 7 Jacob was greatly afraid
and distressed; he divided the people with him
into two camps, along with the flocks, herds,
and camels. 8 He thought, "If Esau comes to
one camp and attacks it, the remaining one
can escape."

9 Then Jacob said, "God of my father Abraham and God of my father Isaac, the LORD
who said to me, 'Go back to your land and to
your family, and I will cause you to prosper,'
10 I am unworthy of all the kindness and faithfulness you have shown your servant. Indeed,
I crossed over the Jordan with my staff, and
now I have become two camps. 11 Please rescue
me from my brother Esau, for I am afraid of
him; otherwise, he may come and attack me,
the mothers, and their children. 12 You have
said, 'I will cause you to prosper, and I will
make your offspring like the sand of the sea,
too numerous to be counted.'"

13 He spent the night there and took part of
what he had brought with him as a gift for his
brother Esau: 14 two hundred female goats,
twenty male goats, two hundred ewes, twenty
rams, 15 thirty milk camels with their young,
forty cows, ten bulls, twenty female donkeys,
and ten male donkeys. 16 He entrusted them to
his slaves as separate herds and said to them,
"Go on ahead of me, and leave some distance
between the herds."

17 And he told the first one: "When my brother
Esau meets you and asks, 'Who do you belong to? Where are you going? And whose
animals are these ahead of you?' 18 then tell
him, 'They belong to your servant Jacob. They
are a gift sent to my lord Esau. And look, he
is behind us.'"

19 He also told the second one, the third, and
everyone who was walking behind the animals,
"Say the same thing to Esau when you find
him. 20 You are also to say, 'Look, your servant

[A] **31:42** Lit *and the work of my hands* [B] **31:47** *Jegar-sahadutha* is Aramaic, and *Galeed* is Hb; both names = Mound of Witness [C] **31:49** = Watchtower [D] **31:53** Two Hb mss, LXX omit *the gods of their father* [E] **32:2** = Two Camps

Jacob is right behind us.' " For he thought,
"I want to appease Esau with the gift that is
going ahead of me. After that, I can face him,
and perhaps he will forgive me."
21 So the gift was sent on ahead of him while
he remained in the camp that night. 22 During
the night Jacob got up and took his two wives,
his two slave women, and his eleven sons, and
crossed the ford of Jabbok. 23 He took them
and sent them across the stream, along with
all his possessions.

JACOB WRESTLES WITH GOD

24 Jacob was left alone, and a man wrestled
with him until daybreak. 25 When the man saw
that he could not defeat him, he struck Jacob's
hip socket as they wrestled and dislocated his
hip. 26 Then he said to Jacob, "Let me go, for
it is daybreak."
But Jacob said, "I will not let you go unless
you bless me."
27 "What is your name?" the man asked.
"Jacob," he replied.
28 "Your name will no longer be Jacob,"
he said. "It will be Israel[A] because you have
struggled with God and with men and have
prevailed."
29 Then Jacob asked him, "Please tell me your
name."
But he answered, "Why do you ask my
name?" And he blessed him there.
30 Jacob then named the place Peniel,[B] "For
I have seen God face to face," he said, "yet my
life has been spared." 31 The sun shone on him
as he passed by Penuel[C]—limping because of
his hip. 32 That is why, still today, the Israelites
don't eat the thigh muscle that is at the hip
socket: because he struck Jacob's hip socket
at the thigh muscle.[D]

JACOB MEETS ESAU

33 Now Jacob looked up and saw Esau coming toward him with four hundred men.
So he divided the children among Leah, Rachel,
and the two slave women. 2 He put the slaves
and their children first, Leah and her children
next, and Rachel and Joseph last. 3 He himself
went on ahead and bowed to the ground seven
times until he approached his brother.
4 But Esau ran to meet him, hugged him,
threw his arms around him, and kissed him.
Then they wept. 5 When Esau looked up and
saw the women and children, he asked, "Who
are these with you?"
He answered, "The children God has graciously given your servant." 6 Then the slaves
and their children approached him and bowed
down. 7 Leah and her children also approached
and bowed down, and then Joseph and Rachel
approached and bowed down.
8 So Esau said, "What do you mean by this
whole procession[E] I met?"
"To find favor with you, my lord," he answered.
9 "I have enough, my brother," Esau replied.
"Keep what you have."
10 But Jacob said, "No, please! If I have found
favor with you, take this gift from me. For
indeed, I have seen your face, and it is like
seeing God's face, since you have accepted
me. 11 Please take my present that was brought
to you, because God has been gracious to me
and I have everything I need." So Jacob urged
him until he accepted.
12 Then Esau said, "Let's move on, and I'll go
ahead of you."
13 Jacob replied, "My lord knows that the
children are weak, and I have nursing flocks
and herds. If they are driven hard for one day,
the whole herd will die. 14 Let my lord go ahead
of his servant. I will continue on slowly, at a
pace suited to the livestock and the children,
until I come to my lord at Seir."
15 Esau said, "Let me leave some of my people with you."
But he replied, "Why do that? Please indulge
me,[F] my lord."
16 That day Esau started on his way back to
Seir, 17 but Jacob went to Succoth. He built a
house for himself and shelters for his livestock;
that is why the place was called Succoth.[G]
18 After Jacob came from Paddan-aram, he
arrived safely at Shechem in the land of Canaan
and camped in front of the city. 19 He purchased
a section of the field where he had pitched
his tent from the sons of Hamor, Shechem's
father, for a hundred pieces of silver.[H] 20 And
he set up an altar there and called it God, the
God of Israel.[I]

DINAH DEFILED

34 Leah's daughter Dinah, whom Leah bore
to Jacob, went out to see some of the
young women of the area. 2 When Shechem

[A] 32:28 In Hb, the name *Israel* sounds like "he struggled (with) God." [B] 32:30 = Face of God [C] 32:31 Variant of *Peniel* [D] 32:32 Or *tendon* [E] 33:8 Lit *camp* [F] 33:15 Lit *May I find favor in your eyes* [G] 33:17 = Stalls or Huts [H] 33:19 Lit *100 qesitahs*; the value of this currency is unknown [I] 33:20 = *El-Elohe-Israel*

— son of Hamor the Hivite, who was the region's chieftain — saw her, he took her and
raped her. 3 He became infatuated with Jacob's
daughter Dinah. He loved the young girl and
spoke tenderly to her.[A] 4 "Get me this girl as
a wife," he told his father.

5 Jacob heard that Shechem had defiled his
daughter Dinah, but since his sons were with
his livestock in the field, he remained silent
until they returned. 6 Meanwhile, Shechem's father Hamor came to speak with Jacob. 7 Jacob's
sons returned from the field when they heard
about the incident and were deeply grieved
and very angry. For Shechem had committed
an outrage against Israel by raping Jacob's
daughter, and such a thing should not be done.

8 Hamor said to Jacob's sons, "My son Shechem has his heart set on your[B] daughter.
Please give her to him as a wife. 9 Intermarry
with us; give your daughters to us, and take
our daughters for yourselves. 10 Live with us.
The land is before you. Settle here, move about,
and acquire property in it."

11 Then Shechem said to Dinah's father and
brothers, "Grant me this favor,[C] and I'll give
you whatever you say. 12 Demand of me a high
compensation[D] and gift; I'll give you whatever
you ask me. Just give the girl to be my wife!"

13 But Jacob's sons answered Shechem and
his father Hamor deceitfully because he had
defiled their sister Dinah. 14 "We cannot do this
thing," they said to them. "Giving our sister
to an uncircumcised man is a disgrace to us.
15 We will agree with you only on this condition: if all your males are circumcised as we
are. 16 Then we will give you our daughters,
take your daughters for ourselves, live with
you, and become one people. 17 But if you will
not listen to us and be circumcised, then we
will take our daughter and go."

18 Their words seemed good to Hamor and
his son Shechem. 19 The young man did not
delay doing this, because he was delighted
with Jacob's daughter. Now he was the most
important in all his father's family. 20 So Hamor and his son Shechem went to the gate of
their city and spoke to the men of their city.

21 "These men are peaceful toward us," they
said. "Let them live in our land and move about
in it, for indeed, the region is large enough
for them. Let us take their daughters as our
wives and give our daughters to them. 22 But
the men will agree to live with us and be one
people only on this condition: if all our men
are circumcised as they are. 23 Won't their livestock, their possessions, and all their animals
become ours? Only let us agree with them,
and they will live with us."

24 All the men who had come to the city gates
listened to Hamor and his son Shechem, and
all those men were circumcised. 25 On the third
day, when they were still in pain, two of Jacob's sons, Simeon and Levi, Dinah's brothers,
took their swords, went into the unsuspecting
city, and killed every male. 26 They killed Hamor and his son Shechem with their swords,
took Dinah from Shechem's house, and went
away. 27 Jacob's sons came to the slaughter and
plundered the city because their sister had
been defiled. 28 They took their flocks, herds,
donkeys, and whatever was in the city and in
the field. 29 They captured all their possessions, dependents, and wives and plundered
everything in the houses.

30 Then Jacob said to Simeon and Levi, "You
have brought trouble on me, making me odious
to the inhabitants of the land, the Canaanites
and the Perizzites. We are few in number; if
they unite against me and attack me, I and
my household will be destroyed."

31 But they answered, "Should he treat our
sister like a prostitute?"

RETURN TO BETHEL

35 God said to Jacob, "Get up! Go to Bethel
and settle there. Build an altar there to
the God who appeared to you when you fled
from your brother Esau."

2 So Jacob said to his family and all who
were with him, "Get rid of the foreign gods
that are among you. Purify yourselves and
change your clothes. 3 We must get up and go
to Bethel. I will build an altar there to the God
who answered me in my day of distress. He
has been with me everywhere I have gone."

4 Then they gave Jacob all their foreign gods
and their earrings, and Jacob hid them under
the oak near Shechem. 5 When they set out, a
terror from God came over the cities around
them, and they did not pursue Jacob's sons.
6 So Jacob and all who were with him came
to Luz (that is, Bethel) in the land of Canaan.
7 Jacob built an altar there and called the place
El-bethel[E] because it was there that God had
revealed himself to him when he was fleeing
from his brother.

[A] **34:3** Lit *spoke to her heart* [B] **34:8** The Hb word for *your* is pl, showing that Hamor is speaking to Jacob and his sons.
[C] **34:11** Lit *"May I find favor in your eyes* [D] **34:12** Or *bride-price*, or *betrothal present* [E] **35:7** = God of Bethel

8 Deborah, the one who had nursed and
raised Rebekah,[A] died and was buried under
the oak south of Bethel. So Jacob named it
Allon-bacuth.[B]

9 God appeared to Jacob again after he returned from Paddan-aram, and he blessed
him. 10 God said to him, "Your name is Jacob;
you will no longer be named Jacob, but your
name will be Israel." So he named him Israel.
11 God also said to him, "I am God Almighty.
Be fruitful and multiply. A nation, indeed an
assembly of nations, will come from you, and
kings will descend from you.[C] 12 I will give
to you the land that I gave to Abraham and
Isaac. And I will give the land to your future
descendants." 13 Then God withdrew[D] from
him at the place where he had spoken to him.
14 Jacob set up a marker at the place where
he had spoken to him — a stone marker. He
poured a drink offering on it and anointed it
with oil. 15 Jacob named the place where God
had spoken with him Bethel.

RACHEL'S DEATH

16 They set out from Bethel. When they were
still some distance from Ephrath, Rachel began to give birth, and her labor was difficult.
17 During her difficult labor, the midwife said
to her, "Don't be afraid, for you have another
son." 18 With her last breath — for she was
dying — she named him Ben-oni,[E] but his father called him Benjamin.[F] 19 So Rachel died
and was buried on the way to Ephrath (that
is, Bethlehem). 20 Jacob set up a marker on
her grave; it is the marker at Rachel's grave
still today.

ISRAEL'S SONS

21 Israel set out again and pitched his tent beyond the Tower of Eder.[G] 22 While Israel was
living in that region, Reuben went in and slept
with his father's concubine Bilhah, and Israel
heard about it.

Jacob had twelve sons:

23 Leah's sons were Reuben
(Jacob's firstborn),
Simeon, Levi, Judah,
Issachar, and Zebulun.
24 Rachel's sons were
Joseph and Benjamin.
25 The sons of Rachel's slave Bilhah
were Dan and Naphtali.
26 The sons of Leah's slave Zilpah
were Gad and Asher.

These are the sons of Jacob, who were born
to him in Paddan-aram.

ISAAC'S DEATH

27 Jacob came to his father Isaac at Mamre in
Kiriath-arba (that is, Hebron), where Abraham
and Isaac had stayed. 28 Isaac lived 180 years.
29 He took his last breath and died, and was
gathered to his people, old and full of days.
His sons Esau and Jacob buried him.

ESAU'S FAMILY

36 These are the family records of Esau
(that is, Edom). 2 Esau took his wives
from the Canaanite women: Adah daughter
of Elon the Hethite, Oholibamah daughter of
Anah and granddaughter[H] of Zibeon the Hivite, 3 and Basemath daughter of Ishmael and
sister of Nebaioth. 4 Adah bore Eliphaz to Esau,
Basemath bore Reuel, 5 and Oholibamah bore Jeush, Jalam, and Korah. These were Esau's sons,
who were born to him in the land of Canaan.
6 Esau took his wives, sons, daughters, and
all the people of his household, as well as his
herds, all his livestock, and all the property he
had acquired in Canaan; he went to a land away
from his brother Jacob. 7 For their possessions
were too many for them to live together, and
because of their herds, the land where they
stayed could not support them. 8 So Esau (that
is, Edom) lived in the mountains of Seir.
9 These are the family records of Esau, father of the Edomites in the mountains of Seir.

10 These are the names of Esau's sons:
Eliphaz son of Esau's wife Adah,
and Reuel son of Esau's wife Basemath.
11 The sons of Eliphaz were
Teman, Omar, Zepho, Gatam, and Kenaz.
12 Timna, a concubine of Esau's son
Eliphaz,
bore Amalek to Eliphaz.
These are the sons of Esau's wife Adah.

13 These are Reuel's sons:
Nahath, Zerah, Shammah, and Mizzah.
These are the sons of Esau's wife
Basemath.

14 These are the sons of Esau's wife
Oholibamah

[A] 35:8 Lit *Deborah, Rebekah's wet nurse*; Gn 24:59 [B] 35:8 = Oak of Weeping [C] 35:11 Lit *will come from your loins* [D] 35:13 Lit *went up* [E] 35:18 = Son of My Sorrow [F] 35:18 = Son of the Right Hand [G] 35:21 Or *beyond Migdal-eder* [H] 36:2 Sam, LXX read *Anah son*

daughter of Anah and granddaughter[A]
of Zibeon:
She bore Jeush, Jalam, and Korah
to Edom.
15 These are the chiefs among Esau's sons:
the sons of Eliphaz, Esau's firstborn:
chief Teman, chief Omar, chief Zepho,
chief Kenaz,
16 chief Korah,[B] chief Gatam, and chief
Amalek.
These are the chiefs descended
from Eliphaz
in the land of Edom.
These are the sons of Adah.
17 These are the sons of Reuel, Esau's son:
chief Nahath, chief Zerah, chief
Shammah, and chief Mizzah.
These are the chiefs descended
from Reuel
in the land of Edom.
These are the sons of Esau's wife
Basemath.
18 These are the sons of Esau's wife
Oholibamah:
chief Jeush, chief Jalam, and chief
Korah.
These are the chiefs descended
from Esau's wife Oholibamah
daughter of Anah.
19 These are the sons of Esau
(that is, Edom),
and these are their chiefs.

SEIR'S FAMILY

20 These are the sons of Seir the Horite,
the inhabitants of the land:
Lotan, Shobal, Zibeon, Anah,
21 Dishon, Ezer, and Dishan.
These are the chiefs among the Horites,
the sons of Seir, in the land of Edom.
22 The sons of Lotan were Hori
and Heman.
Timna was Lotan's sister.
23 These are Shobal's sons:
Alvan, Manahath, Ebal, Shepho,
and Onam.
24 These are Zibeon's sons:
Aiah and Anah.
This was the Anah who found
the hot springs[C] in the wilderness
while he was pasturing the donkeys
of his father Zibeon.
25 These are the children of Anah:
Dishon and Oholibamah
daughter of Anah.
26 These are Dishon's sons:
Hemdan, Eshban, Ithran, and Cheran.
27 These are Ezer's sons:
Bilhan, Zaavan, and Akan.
28 These are Dishan's sons: Uz and Aran.

29 These are the chiefs among the Horites:
chief Lotan, chief Shobal, chief Zibeon,
chief Anah,
30 chief Dishon, chief Ezer, and chief
Dishan.
These are the chiefs among the Horites,
clan by clan,[D] in the land of Seir.

RULERS OF EDOM

31 These are the kings who reigned
in the land of Edom
before any king reigned
over the Israelites:
32 Bela son of Beor reigned in Edom;
the name of his city was Dinhabah.
33 When Bela died, Jobab son of Zerah
from Bozrah reigned in his place.
34 When Jobab died, Husham
from the land of the Temanites
reigned in his place.
35 When Husham died, Hadad
son of Bedad reigned in his place.
He defeated Midian in the field
of Moab;
the name of his city was Avith.
36 When Hadad died, Samlah
from Masrekah reigned in his place.
37 When Samlah died, Shaul
from Rehoboth on the
Euphrates River reigned in his place.
38 When Shaul died, Baal-hanan
son of Achbor reigned in his place.
39 When Baal-hanan son of Achbor died,
Hadar[E] reigned in his place.
His city was Pau, and his wife's name
was Mehetabel
daughter of Matred daughter
of Me-zahab.

40 These are the names of Esau's chiefs,
according to their families
and their localities,

[A] **36:14** Sam, LXX read *Anah son* [B] **36:16** Sam omits *Korah* [C] **36:24** Syr, Vg; Tg reads *the mules*; Hb obscure [D] **36:30** Lit *Horites, for their chiefs* [E] **36:39** Many Hb mss, Sam, Syr read *Hadad*

by their names:
chief Timna, chief Alvah, chief Jetheth,
41 chief Oholibamah, chief Elah, chief Pinon,
42 chief Kenaz, chief Teman, chief Mibzar,
43 chief Magdiel, and chief Iram.
These are Edom's chiefs,
according to their settlements
in the land they possessed.
Esau[A] was father of the Edomites.

JOSEPH'S DREAMS

37 Jacob lived in the land where his father
had stayed, the land of Canaan. 2 These
are the family records of Jacob.
At seventeen years of age, Joseph tended
sheep with his brothers. The young man was
working with the sons of Bilhah and Zilpah,
his father's wives, and he brought a bad report
about them to their father.
3 Now Israel loved Joseph more than his
other sons because Joseph was a son born
to him in his old age, and he made a robe of
many colors[B] for him. 4 When his brothers
saw that their father loved him more than all
his brothers, they hated him and could not
bring themselves to speak peaceably to him.
5 Then Joseph had a dream. When he told
it to his brothers, they hated him even more.
6 He said to them, "Listen to this dream I had:
7 There we were, binding sheaves of grain in
the field. Suddenly my sheaf stood up, and
your sheaves gathered around it and bowed
down to my sheaf."
8 "Are you really going to reign over us?" his
brothers asked him. "Are you really going to
rule us?" So they hated him even more because
of his dream and what he had said.
9 Then he had another dream and told it to
his brothers. "Look," he said, "I had another
dream, and this time the sun, moon, and eleven
stars were bowing down to me."
10 He told his father and brothers, and his
father rebuked him. "What kind of dream is
this that you have had?" he said. "Am I and
your mother and your brothers really going
to come and bow down to the ground before
you?" 11 His brothers were jealous of him, but
his father kept the matter in mind.

JOSEPH SOLD INTO SLAVERY

12 His brothers had gone to pasture their father's flocks at Shechem. 13 Israel said to Joseph, "Your brothers, you know, are pasturing
the flocks at Shechem. Get ready. I'm sending
you to them."
"I'm ready," Joseph replied.
14 Then Israel said to him, "Go and see how
your brothers and the flocks are doing, and
bring word back to me." So he sent him from
the Hebron Valley, and he went to Shechem.
15 A man found him there, wandering in the
field, and asked him, "What are you looking
for?"
16 "I'm looking for my brothers," Joseph said.
"Can you tell me where they are pasturing
their flocks?"
17 "They've moved on from here," the man
said. "I heard them say, 'Let's go to Dothan.'"
So Joseph set out after his brothers and found
them at Dothan.
18 They saw him in the distance, and before
he had reached them, they plotted to kill him.
19 They said to one another, "Oh, look, here
comes that dream expert![C] 20 So now, come
on, let's kill him and throw him into one of the
pits.[D] We can say that a vicious animal ate him.
Then we'll see what becomes of his dreams!"
21 When Reuben heard this, he tried to save
him from them.[E] He said, "Let's not take his life."
22 Reuben also said to them, "Don't shed blood.
Throw him into this pit in the wilderness, but
don't lay a hand on him" — intending to rescue
him from them and return him to his father.
23 When Joseph came to his brothers, they
stripped off Joseph's robe, the robe of many
colors that he had on. 24 Then they took him
and threw him into the pit. The pit was empty,
without water.
25 They sat down to eat a meal, and when
they looked up, there was a caravan of Ishmaelites coming from Gilead. Their camels
were carrying aromatic gum, balsam, and
resin, going down to Egypt.
26 Judah said to his brothers, "What do we
gain if we kill our brother and cover up his
blood? 27 Come on, let's sell him to the Ishmaelites and not lay a hand on him, for he is
our brother, our own flesh," and his brothers
agreed. 28 When Midianite traders passed by,
his brothers pulled Joseph out of the pit and
sold him for twenty pieces of silver to the Ishmaelites, who took Joseph to Egypt.
29 When Reuben returned to the pit and saw
that Joseph was not there, he tore his clothes.
30 He went back to his brothers and said, "The
boy is gone! What am I going to do?"[F] 31 So

[A] **36:43** Lit *He Esau* [B] **37:3** Or *robe with long sleeves*; see 2Sm 13:18,19 [C] **37:19** Lit *comes the lord of the dreams* [D] **37:20** Or *cisterns* [E] **37:21** Lit *their hands* [F] **37:30** Lit *And I, where am I going?*

Joseph | Restoration Profile

GENESIS 37–50; HEBREWS 11:22

One of the ways of picturing restoration is to describe it as keeping up to date on our relationship with God. Joseph is a prime biblical example of this practice. He did not let the setbacks and disappointments in his life pile up; each one was firmly put behind him as yet another reminder, not that life was unfair, but that God was in control.

In his youth, God gave Joseph amazing dreams and their interpretations that Joseph didn't manage well. This, combined with the handicap of being his father's favorite, set into motion events that severely tested Joseph's willingness to trust God. Joseph experienced firsthand the betrayal of brothers, a boss's wife, and someone he had helped. Each disappointment seemed to take Joseph further from the possibility of his early dreams coming true. Yet he continued on, doggedly and cheerfully, rising from each blow to make the best of his circumstances.

Later we learn the thought and prayer process that Joseph used to restore his equilibrium with each setback. When his brothers revealed that they still lived in abject fear of their little brother's possible reprisals, Joseph explained that their guilt and anxiety had been wasted: "You planned evil against me; God planned it for good to bring about the present result—the survival of many people" (Gn 50:20). He could have said the same thing to Potiphar's wife and the forgetful cupbearer.

We can benefit from Joseph's wise approach to life. When we learn to recognize God's hand in everything, even in those experiences we can't understand and when we can't actually see his hand, we are traveling in the way of restoration.

they took Joseph's robe, slaughtered a male
goat, and dipped the robe in its blood. 32 They
sent the robe of many colors to their father
and said, "We found this. Examine it. Is it your
son's robe or not?"
33 His father recognized it. "It is my son's
robe," he said. "A vicious animal has devoured
him. Joseph has been torn to pieces!" 34 Then
Jacob tore his clothes, put sackcloth around
his waist, and mourned for his son many days.
35 All his sons and daughters tried to comfort
him, but he refused to be comforted. "No,"
he said. "I will go down to Sheol to my son,
mourning." And his father wept for him.
36 Meanwhile, the Midianites sold Joseph in
Egypt to Potiphar, an officer of Pharaoh and
the captain of the guards.

JUDAH AND TAMAR

38 At that time Judah left his brothers and
settled near an Adullamite named Hirah.
2 There Judah saw the daughter of a Canaanite
named Shua; he took her as a wife and slept with
her. 3 She conceived and gave birth to a son, and
he named him Er. 4 She conceived again, gave
birth to a son, and named him Onan. 5 She gave
birth to another son and named him Shelah.
It was at Chezib that[A,B] she gave birth to him.
6 Judah got a wife for Er, his firstborn, and her
name was Tamar. 7 Now Er, Judah's firstborn,
was evil in the LORD's sight, and the LORD put
him to death. 8 Then Judah said to Onan, "Sleep
with your brother's wife. Perform your duty as
her brother-in-law and produce offspring for
your brother." 9 But Onan knew that the offspring would not be his, so whenever he slept
with his brother's wife, he released his semen
on the ground so that he would not produce
offspring for his brother. 10 What he did was evil
in the LORD's sight, so he put him to death also.
11 Then Judah said to his daughter-in-law
Tamar, "Remain a widow in your father's house
until my son Shelah grows up." For he thought,
"He might die too, like his brothers." So Tamar
went to live in her father's house.
12 After a long time[C] Judah's wife, the daughter of Shua, died. When Judah had finished
mourning, he and his friend Hirah the Adullamite went up to Timnah to his sheepshearers. 13 Tamar was told, "Your father-in-law is
going up to Timnah to shear his sheep." 14 So
she took off her widow's clothes, veiled her

[A] **38:5** LXX reads *She was at Chezib when* [B] **38:5** Or *He was at Chezib when* [C] **38:12** Lit *And there were many days, and*

face, covered herself, and sat at the entrance
to Enaim,[A] which is on the way to Timnah.
For she saw that, though Shelah had grown
up, she had not been given to him as a wife.
15 When Judah saw her, he thought she was a
prostitute, for she had covered her face.
16 He went over to her and said, "Come, let
me sleep with you," for he did not know that
she was his daughter-in-law.
She said, "What will you give me for sleeping with me?"
17 "I will send you a young goat from my
flock," he replied.
But she said, "Only if you leave something
with me until you send it."
18 "What should I give you?" he asked.
She answered, "Your signet ring, your cord,
and the staff in your hand." So he gave them to
her and slept with her, and she became pregnant by him. 19 She got up and left, then removed
her veil and put her widow's clothes back on.
20 When Judah sent the young goat by his
friend the Adullamite in order to get back the
items he had left with the woman, he could
not find her. 21 He asked the men of the place,
"Where is the cult prostitute who was beside
the road at Enaim?"
"There has been no cult prostitute here,"
they answered.
22 So the Adullamite returned to Judah,
saying, "I couldn't find her, and besides, the
men of the place said, 'There has been no cult
prostitute here.'"
23 Judah replied, "Let her keep the items for
herself; otherwise we will become a laughingstock. After all, I did send this young goat, but
you couldn't find her."
24 About three months later Judah was told,
"Your daughter-in-law, Tamar, has been acting
like a prostitute, and now she is pregnant."
"Bring her out," Judah said, "and let her be
burned to death!"
25 As she was being brought out, she sent her
father-in-law this message: "I am pregnant by
the man to whom these items belong." And
she added, "Examine them. Whose signet ring,
cord, and staff are these?"
26 Judah recognized them and said, "She is
more in the right[B] than I, since I did not give
her to my son Shelah." And he did not know
her intimately again.
27 When the time came for her to give birth,
there were twins in her womb. 28 As she was
giving birth, one of them put out his hand, and
the midwife took it and tied a scarlet thread
around it, announcing, "This one came out
first." 29 But then he pulled his hand back,
out came his brother, and she said, "What a
breakout you have made for yourself!" So he
was named Perez.[C] 30 Then his brother, who
had the scarlet thread tied to his hand, came
out, and was named Zerah.[D]

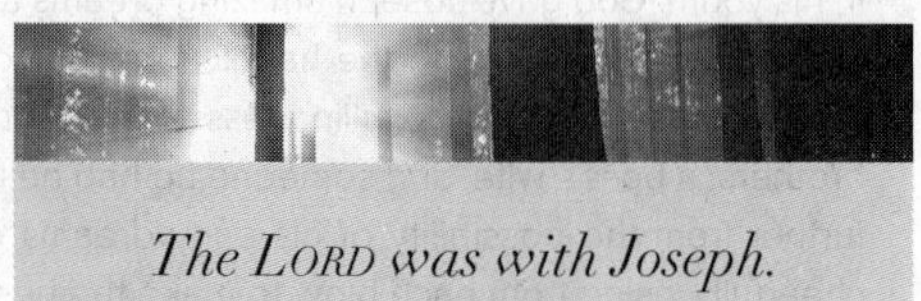

The LORD was with Joseph.
—Genesis 39:2

JOSEPH IN POTIPHAR'S HOUSE

39 Now Joseph had been taken to Egypt. An
Egyptian named Potiphar, an officer of
Pharaoh and the captain of the guards, bought
him from the Ishmaelites who had brought
him there. 2 The LORD was with Joseph, and
he became a successful man, serving[E] in the
household of his Egyptian master. 3 When his
master saw that the LORD was with him and
that the LORD made everything he did successful, 4 Joseph found favor with his master
and became his personal attendant. Potiphar
also put him in charge of his household and
placed all that he owned under his authority.[F]
5 From the time that he put him in charge of
his household and of all that he owned, the
LORD blessed the Egyptian's house because of
Joseph. The LORD's blessing was on all that he
owned, in his house and in his fields. 6 He left
all that he owned under Joseph's authority;[G]
he did not concern himself with anything except the food he ate.
Now Joseph was well-built and handsome.
7 After some time[H] his master's wife looked
longingly at Joseph and said, "Sleep with me."
8 But he refused. "Look," he said to his master's
wife, "with me here my master does not concern
himself with anything in his house, and he has
put all that he owns under my authority.[I] 9 No
one in this house is greater than I am. He has
withheld nothing from me except you, because
you are his wife. So how could I do this immense
evil, and how could I sin against God?"

[A] **38:14** Or *sat by the mouth of the springs* [B] **38:26** Or *more righteous* [C] **38:29** = Breaking Out [D] **38:30** = Brightness of Sunrise; perhaps related to the scarlet thread [E] **39:2** Lit *and he was* [F] **39:4** Lit *owned in his hand* [G] **39:6** Lit *owned in Joseph's hand* [H] **39:7** Lit *And after these things* [I] **39:8** Lit *owns in my hand*

10 Although she spoke to Joseph day after day,
he refused to go to bed with her.[A] 11 Now one
day he went into the house to do his work, and
none of the household servants were there.[B]
12 She grabbed him by his garment and said,
"Sleep with me!" But leaving his garment in
her hand, he escaped and ran outside. 13 When
she saw that he had left his garment with her
and had run outside, 14 she called her household servants. "Look," she said to them, "my
husband brought a Hebrew man to make fools
of us. He came to me so he could sleep with
me, and I screamed as loud as I could. 15 When
he heard me screaming for help,[C] he left his
garment beside me and ran outside."

16 She put Joseph's garment beside her until
his master came home. 17 Then she told him the
same story: "The Hebrew slave you brought
to us came to make a fool of me, 18 but when I
screamed for help,[D] he left his garment beside
me and ran outside."

19 When his master heard the story his wife
told him — "These are the things your slave
did to me" — he was furious 20 and had him
thrown into prison, where the king's prisoners
were confined. So Joseph was there in prison.

JOSEPH IN PRISON

21 But the LORD was with Joseph and extended
kindness to him. He granted him favor with
the prison warden. 22 The warden put all the
prisoners who were in the prison under Joseph's authority,[E] and he was responsible for
everything that was done there. 23 The warden
did not bother with anything under Joseph's
authority,[F] because the LORD was with him,
and the LORD made everything that he did
successful.

JOSEPH INTERPRETS TWO PRISONERS' DREAMS

40 After this, the king of Egypt's cupbearer and baker offended their master,
the king of Egypt. 2 Pharaoh was angry with
his two officers, the chief cupbearer and the
chief baker, 3 and put them in custody in the
house of the captain of the guards in the prison
where Joseph was confined. 4 The captain of
the guards assigned Joseph to them as their
personal attendant, and they were in custody
for some time.[G]

5 The king of Egypt's cupbearer and baker,
who were confined in the prison, each had a
dream. Both had a dream on the same night,
and each dream had its own meaning. 6 When
Joseph came to them in the morning, he saw
that they looked distraught. 7 So he asked Pharaoh's officers who were in custody with him
in his master's house, "Why do you look so
sad today?"

8 "We had dreams," they said to him, "but
there is no one to interpret them."

Then Joseph said to them, "Don't interpretations belong to God? Tell me your dreams."

9 So the chief cupbearer told his dream to
Joseph: "In my dream there was a vine in front
of me. 10 On the vine were three branches. As
soon as it budded, its blossoms came out and
its clusters ripened into grapes. 11 Pharaoh's
cup was in my hand, and I took the grapes,
squeezed them into Pharaoh's cup, and placed
the cup in Pharaoh's hand."

12 "This is its interpretation," Joseph said
to him. "The three branches are three days.
13 In just three days Pharaoh will lift up your
head and restore you to your position. You
will put Pharaoh's cup in his hand the way
you used to when you were his cupbearer.
14 But when all goes well for you, remember
that I was with you. Please show kindness to
me by mentioning me to Pharaoh, and get
me out of this prison. 15 For I was kidnapped
from the land of the Hebrews, and even here
I have done nothing that they should put me
in the dungeon."[H]

16 When the chief baker saw that the interpretation was positive, he said to Joseph,
"I also had a dream. Three baskets of white
bread were on my head. 17 In the top basket
were all sorts of baked goods for Pharaoh, but
the birds were eating them out of the basket
on my head."

18 "This is its interpretation," Joseph replied.
"The three baskets are three days. 19 In just three
days Pharaoh will lift up your head — from
off you — and hang you on a tree.[I] Then the
birds will eat the flesh from your body."[J]

20 On the third day, which was Pharaoh's
birthday, he gave a feast for all his servants.
He elevated[K] the chief cupbearer and the chief
baker among his servants. 21 Pharaoh restored
the chief cupbearer to his position as cupbearer,
and he placed the cup in Pharaoh's hand. 22 But

[A] **39:10** Lit *he did not listen to her to lie beside her, to be with her* [B] **39:11** Lit *there in the house* [C] **39:15** Lit *he heard that I raised my voice and I screamed* [D] **39:18** Lit *I raised my voice and screamed* [E] **39:22** Lit *prison in the hand of Joseph* [F] **39:23** Lit *anything in his hand* [G] **40:4** Lit *custody days* [H] **40:15** Or *pit*, or *cistern* [I] **40:19** Or *and impale you on a pole* [J] **40:19** Lit *eat your flesh from upon you* [K] **40:20** Lit *He lifted up the head of*

Pharaoh hanged[A] the chief baker, just as Joseph
had explained to them. 23 Yet the chief cupbearer did not remember Joseph; he forgot him.

JOSEPH INTERPRETS PHARAOH'S DREAMS

41 At the end of two years Pharaoh had a
dream: He was standing beside the Nile,
2 when seven healthy-looking, well-fed cows
came up from the Nile and began to graze
among the reeds. 3 After them, seven other
cows, sickly and thin, came up from the Nile
and stood beside those cows along the bank of
the Nile. 4 The sickly, thin cows ate the healthy,
well-fed cows. Then Pharaoh woke up. 5 He
fell asleep and dreamed a second time: Seven
heads of grain, plump and good, came up on
one stalk. 6 After them, seven heads of grain,
thin and scorched by the east wind, sprouted
up. 7 The thin heads of grain swallowed up the
seven plump, full ones. Then Pharaoh woke
up, and it was only a dream.

8 When morning came, he was troubled, so
he summoned all the magicians of Egypt and
all its wise men. Pharaoh told them his dreams,
but no one could interpret them for him.

9 Then the chief cupbearer said to Pharaoh,
"Today I remember my faults. 10 Pharaoh was
angry with his servants, and he put me and
the chief baker in the custody of the captain
of the guards. 11 He and I had dreams on the
same night; each dream had its own meaning.
12 Now a young Hebrew, a slave of the captain
of the guards, was with us there. We told him
our dreams, he interpreted our dreams for
us, and each had its own interpretation. 13 It
turned out just the way he interpreted them
to us: I was restored to my position, and the
other man was hanged."

14 Then Pharaoh sent for Joseph, and they
quickly brought him from the dungeon.[B] He
shaved, changed his clothes, and went to Pharaoh.

15 Pharaoh said to Joseph, "I have had a
dream, and no one can interpret it. But I have
heard it said about you that you can hear a
dream and interpret it."

16 "I am not able to," Joseph answered Pharaoh. "It is God who will give Pharaoh a favorable answer."[C]

17 So Pharaoh said to Joseph: "In my dream I
was standing on the bank of the Nile, 18 when
seven well-fed, healthy-looking cows came
up from the Nile and grazed among the reeds.
19 After them, seven other cows — weak, very
sickly, and thin — came up. I've never seen
such sickly ones as these in all the land of
Egypt. 20 Then the thin, sickly cows ate the
first seven well-fed cows. 21 When they had
devoured them, you could not tell that they
had devoured them; their appearance was
as bad as it had been before. Then I woke up.
22 In my dream I also saw seven heads of grain,
full and good, coming up on one stalk. 23 After
them, seven heads of grain — withered, thin,
and scorched by the east wind — sprouted
up. 24 The thin heads of grain swallowed the
seven good ones. I told this to the magicians,
but no one can tell me what it means."

25 Then Joseph said to Pharaoh, "Pharaoh's
dreams mean the same thing. God has revealed
to Pharaoh what he is about to do. 26 The sev-
en good cows are seven years, and the seven
good heads are seven years. The dreams mean
the same thing. 27 The seven thin, sickly cows
that came up after them are seven years, and
the seven worthless, scorched heads of grain
are seven years of famine.

28 "It is just as I told Pharaoh: God has shown
Pharaoh what he is about to do. 29 Seven years
of great abundance are coming throughout
the land of Egypt. 30 After them, seven years of
famine will take place, and all the abundance in
the land of Egypt will be forgotten. The famine
will devastate the land. 31 The abundance in the
land will not be remembered because of the
famine that follows it, for the famine will be
very severe. 32 Since the dream was given twice
to Pharaoh, it means that the matter has been
determined by God, and he will carry it out soon.

33 "So now, let Pharaoh look for a discerning
and wise man and set him over the land of
Egypt. 34 Let Pharaoh do this: Let him appoint
overseers over the land and take a fifth of the
harvest of the land of Egypt during the seven
years of abundance. 35 Let them gather all the
excess food during these good years that are
coming. Under Pharaoh's authority, store the
grain in the cities, so they may preserve it as
food. 36 The food will be a reserve for the land
during the seven years of famine that will take
place in the land of Egypt. Then the country
will not be wiped out by the famine."

JOSEPH EXALTED

37 The proposal pleased Pharaoh and all his
servants, 38 and he said to them, "Can we find

[A] **40:22** Or *impaled* [B] **41:14** Or *pit*, or *cistern* [C] **41:16** Or *"God will answer Pharaoh with peace of mind."*

anyone like this, a man who has God's spirit[A]
in him?" 39 So Pharaoh said to Joseph, "Since
God has made all this known to you, there
is no one as discerning and wise as you are.
40 You will be over my house, and all my people
will obey your commands.[B] Only I, as king,[C]
will be greater than you." 41 Pharaoh also
said to Joseph, "See, I am placing you over
all the land of Egypt." 42 Pharaoh removed
his signet ring from his hand and put it on
Joseph's hand, clothed him with fine linen
garments, and placed a gold chain around
his neck. 43 He had Joseph ride in his second
chariot, and servants called out before him,
"Make way!"[D] So he placed him over all the
land of Egypt. 44 Pharaoh said to Joseph, "I
am Pharaoh and no one will be able to raise
his hand or foot in all the land of Egypt without your permission." 45 Pharaoh gave Joseph
the name Zaphenath-paneah and gave him a
wife, Asenath daughter of Potiphera, priest at
On.[E] And Joseph went throughout[F] the land
of Egypt.

JOSEPH'S ADMINISTRATION

46 Joseph was thirty years old when he entered the service of Pharaoh king of Egypt.
Joseph left Pharaoh's presence and traveled
throughout the land of Egypt.

47 During the seven years of abundance the
land produced outstanding harvests. 48 Joseph
gathered all the excess food in the land of
Egypt during the seven years and put it in the
cities. He put the food in every city from the
fields around it. 49 So Joseph stored up grain
in such abundance — like the sand of the sea
— that he stopped measuring it because it
was beyond measure.

50 Two sons were born to Joseph before the
years of famine arrived. Asenath daughter
of Potiphera, priest at On, bore them to him.
51 Joseph named the firstborn Manasseh[G]
and said, "God has made me forget all my
hardship and my whole family." 52 And the
second son he named Ephraim[H] and said,
"God has made me fruitful in the land of my
affliction."

53 Then the seven years of abundance in the
land of Egypt came to an end, 54 and the seven
years of famine began, just as Joseph had said.
There was famine in every land, but in the
whole land of Egypt there was food. 55 When
the whole land of Egypt was stricken with
famine, the people cried out to Pharaoh for
food. Pharaoh told all Egypt, "Go to Joseph and
do whatever he tells you." 56 Now the famine
had spread across the whole region, so Joseph
opened all the storehouses and sold grain to
the Egyptians, for the famine was severe in the
land of Egypt. 57 Every land came to Joseph in
Egypt to buy grain, for the famine was severe
in every land.

JOSEPH'S BROTHERS IN EGYPT

42 When Jacob learned that there was
grain in Egypt, he said to his sons, "Why
do you keep looking at each other? 2 Listen,"
he went on, "I have heard there is grain in
Egypt. Go down there and buy some for us
so that we will live and not die." 3 So ten of
Joseph's brothers went down to buy grain
from Egypt. 4 But Jacob did not send Joseph's
brother Benjamin with his brothers, for he
thought, "Something might happen to him."

5 The sons of Israel were among those who
came to buy grain, for the famine was in the
land of Canaan. 6 Joseph was in charge of the
country; he sold grain to all its people. His
brothers came and bowed down before him
with their faces to the ground. 7 When Joseph
saw his brothers, he recognized them, but he
treated them like strangers and spoke harshly to them.

"Where do you come from?" he asked.

"From the land of Canaan to buy food," they
replied.

8 Although Joseph recognized his brothers, they did not recognize him. 9 Joseph remembered his dreams about them and said
to them, "You are spies. You have come to see
the weakness[I] of the land."

10 "No, my lord. Your servants have come
to buy food," they said. 11 "We are all sons of
one man. We are honest; your servants are
not spies."

12 "No," he said to them. "You have come to
see the weakness of the land."

13 But they replied, "We, your servants, were
twelve brothers, the sons of one man in the
land of Canaan. The youngest is now[J] with our
father, and one is no longer living."

14 Then Joseph said to them, "I have spoken:[K]

[A] **41:38** Or *the spirit of the gods*, or *a god's spirit* [B] **41:40** Lit *will kiss your mouth* [C] **41:40** Lit *Only the throne I* [D] **41:43** Or *"Kneel!"* [E] **41:45** Or *Heliopolis*, also in v. 50 [F] **41:45** Or *Joseph gained authority over* [G] **41:51** In Hb, the name *Manasseh* sounds like the verb "forget." [H] **41:52** In Hb, the name *Ephraim* sounds like the word for "fruitful." [I] **42:9** Lit *nakedness*, also in v. 12 [J] **42:13** Or *today*, also in v. 32 [K] **42:14** Lit *"That which I spoke to you saying:*

'You are spies!' 15 This is how you will be tested:
As surely as Pharaoh lives, you will not leave
this place unless your youngest brother comes
here. 16 Send one from among you to get your
brother. The rest of you will be imprisoned so
that your words can be tested to see if they are
true. If they are not, then as surely as Pharaoh
lives, you are spies!" 17 So Joseph imprisoned
them together for three days.

18 On the third day Joseph said to them, "I
fear God — do this and you will live. 19 If you
are honest, let one of you[A] be confined to the
guardhouse, while the rest of you go and take
grain to relieve the hunger of your households.
20 Bring your youngest brother to me so that
your words can be confirmed; then you won't
die." And they consented to this.

21 Then they said to each other, "Obviously,
we are being punished for what we did to our
brother. We saw his deep distress when he
pleaded with us, but we would not listen. That
is why this trouble has come to us."

22 But Reuben replied: "Didn't I tell you not
to harm the boy? But you wouldn't listen. Now
we must account for his blood!"[B]

23 They did not realize that Joseph understood them, since there was an interpreter
between them. 24 He turned away from them
and wept. When he turned back and spoke
to them, he took Simeon from them and had
him bound before their eyes. 25 Joseph then
gave orders to fill their containers with grain,
return each man's silver to his sack, and give
them provisions for their journey. This order
was carried out. 26 They loaded the grain on
their donkeys and left there.

THE BROTHERS RETURN HOME

27 At the place where they lodged for the night,
one of them opened his sack to get feed for
his donkey, and he saw his silver there at the
top of his bag. 28 He said to his brothers, "My
silver has been returned! It's here in my bag."
Their hearts sank. Trembling, they turned to
one another and said, "What is this that God
has done to us?"

29 When they reached their father Jacob in
the land of Canaan, they told him all that had
happened to them: 30 "The man who is the lord
of the country spoke harshly to us and accused
us of spying on the country. 31 But we told him:
We are honest and not spies. 32 We were twelve
brothers, sons of the same[C] father. One is no
longer living, and the youngest is now with
our father in the land of Canaan. 33 The man
who is the lord of the country said to us, 'This
is how I will know if you are honest: Leave
one brother with me, take food to relieve the
hunger of your households, and go. 34 Bring
back your youngest brother to me, and I will
know that you are not spies but honest men.
I will then give your brother back to you, and
you can trade in the country.'"

35 As they began emptying their sacks, there
in each man's sack was his bag of silver! When
they and their father saw their bags of silver,
they were afraid.

36 Their father Jacob said to them, "It's me
that you make childless. Joseph is gone, and
Simeon is gone. Now you want to take Benjamin. Everything happens to me!"

37 Then Reuben said to his father, "You can
kill my two sons if I don't bring him back to
you. Put him in my care,[D] and I will return
him to you."

38 But Jacob answered, "My son will not go
down with you, for his brother is dead and
he alone is left. If anything happens to him
on your journey, you will bring my gray hairs
down to Sheol in sorrow."

DECISION TO RETURN TO EGYPT

43 Now the famine in the land was severe.
2 When they had used up the grain they
had brought back from Egypt, their father said
to them, "Go back and buy us a little food."

3 But Judah said to him, "The man specifically
warned us: 'You will not see me again unless
your brother is with you.' 4 If you will send our
brother with us, we will go down and buy food
for you. 5 But if you will not send him, we will
not go, for the man said to us, 'You will not see
me again unless your brother is with you.'"

6 "Why have you caused me so much trouble?" Israel asked. "Why did you tell the man
that you had another brother?"

7 They answered, "The man kept asking about
us and our family: 'Is your father still alive? Do
you have another brother?' And we answered
him accordingly. How could we know that he
would say, 'Bring your brother here'?"

8 Then Judah said to his father Israel, "Send
the boy with me. We will be on our way so that
we may live and not die — neither we, nor you,
nor our dependents. 9 I will be responsible for
him. You can hold me personally accountable![E]

[A] **42:19** Lit *your brothers* [B] **42:22** Lit *Even his blood is being sought!* [C] **42:32** Lit *of our* [D] **42:37** Lit *hand* [E] **43:9** Lit *can seek him from my hand*

Jacob blessed Pharaoh and departed from
Pharaoh's presence.
11 Then Joseph settled his father and brothers in the land of Egypt and gave them property in the best part of the land, the land of
Rameses, as Pharaoh had commanded. 12 And
Joseph provided his father, his brothers, and
all his father's family with food for their dependents.

THE LAND BECOMES PHARAOH'S

13 But there was no food in the entire region,
for the famine was very severe. The land of
Egypt and the land of Canaan were exhausted
by the famine. 14 Joseph collected all the silver to be found in the land of Egypt and the
land of Canaan in exchange for the grain they
were purchasing, and he brought the silver
to Pharaoh's palace. 15 When the silver from
the land of Egypt and the land of Canaan was
gone, all the Egyptians came to Joseph and
said, "Give us food. Why should we die here
in front of you? The silver is gone!"
16 But Joseph said, "Give me your livestock.
Since the silver is gone, I will give you food in
exchange for your livestock." 17 So they brought
their livestock to Joseph, and he gave them
food in exchange for the horses, the flocks of
sheep, the herds of cattle, and the donkeys.
That year he provided them with food in exchange for all their livestock.
18 When that year was over, they came the
next year and said to him, "We cannot hide
from our lord that the silver is gone and that
all our livestock belongs to our lord. There
is nothing left for our lord except our bodies
and our land. 19 Why should we die here in
front of you — both us and our land? Buy us
and our land in exchange for food. Then we
with our land will become Pharaoh's slaves.
Give us seed so that we can live and not die,
and so that the land won't become desolate."
20 In this way, Joseph acquired all the land
in Egypt for Pharaoh, because every Egyptian
sold his field since the famine was so severe
for them. The land became Pharaoh's, 21 and
Joseph moved the people to the cities[A] from
one end of Egypt to the other. 22 The only land
he did not acquire belonged to the priests, for
they had an allowance from Pharaoh. They
ate from their allowance that Pharaoh gave
them; therefore they did not sell their land.
23 Joseph said to the people, "Understand
today that I have acquired you and your land
for Pharaoh. Here is seed for you. Sow it in the
land. 24 At harvest, you are to give a fifth of it
to Pharaoh, and four-fifths will be yours as
seed for the field and as food for yourselves,
your households, and your dependents."
25 "You have saved our lives," they said. "We
have found favor with our lord and will be
Pharaoh's slaves." 26 So Joseph made it a law,
still in effect today in the land of Egypt, that a
fifth of the produce belongs to Pharaoh. Only
the priests' land does not belong to Pharaoh.

ISRAEL SETTLES IN GOSHEN

27 Israel settled in the land of Egypt, in the
region of Goshen. They acquired property
in it and became fruitful and very numerous.
28 Now Jacob lived in the land of Egypt 17 years,
and his life span was 147 years. 29 When the
time approached for him to die, he called his
son Joseph and said to him, "If I have found
favor with you, put your hand under my thigh
and promise me that you will deal with me in
kindness and faithfulness. Do not bury me in
Egypt. 30 When I rest with my fathers, carry
me away from Egypt and bury me in their
burial place."
Joseph answered, "I will do what you have
asked."
31 And Jacob said, "Swear to me." So Joseph
swore to him. Then Israel bowed in thanks at
the head of his bed.[B]

JACOB BLESSES EPHRAIM AND MANASSEH

48 Some time after this, Joseph was told,
"Your father is weaker." So he set out
with his two sons, Manasseh and Ephraim.
2 When Jacob was told, "Your son Joseph has
come to you," Israel summoned his strength
and sat up in bed.
3 Jacob said to Joseph, "God Almighty appeared to me at Luz in the land of Canaan and
blessed me. 4 He said to me, 'I will make you
fruitful and numerous; I will make many nations come from you, and I will give this land
as a permanent possession to your future descendants.' 5 Your two sons born to you in the
land of Egypt before I came to you in Egypt are
now mine. Ephraim and Manasseh belong to
me just as Reuben and Simeon do. 6 Children
born to you after them will be yours and will
be recorded under the names of their brothers
with regard to their inheritance. 7 When I was

[A] **47:21** Sam, LXX, Vg read *and he made the people servants* [B] **47:31** Or *Israel worshiped while leaning on the top of his staff*

returning from Paddan, to my sorrow Rachel
died along the way, some distance from Ephrath in the land of Canaan. I buried her there
along the way to Ephrath" (that is, Bethlehem).
8 When Israel saw Joseph's sons, he said,
"Who are these?"
9 And Joseph said to his father, "They are
my sons God has given me here."
So Israel said, "Bring them to me and I will
bless them." 10 Now his eyesight was poor because of old age; he could hardly[A] see. Joseph
brought them to him, and he kissed and embraced them. 11 Israel said to Joseph, "I never
expected to see your face again, but now God
has even let me see your offspring." 12 Then
Joseph took them from his father's knees and
bowed with his face to the ground.

EPHRAIM'S GREATER BLESSING

13 Then Joseph took them both — with his right
hand Ephraim toward Israel's left, and with
his left hand Manasseh toward Israel's right
— and brought them to Israel. 14 But Israel
stretched out his right hand and put it on the
head of Ephraim, the younger, and crossing
his hands, put his left on Manasseh's head,
although Manasseh was the firstborn. 15 Then
he blessed Joseph and said:

The God before whom my fathers
Abraham and Isaac walked,
the God who has been my shepherd
all my life to this day,
16 the angel who has redeemed me
from all harm —
may he bless these boys.
And may they be called by my name
and the names of my fathers Abraham
and Isaac,
and may they grow to be numerous
within the land.

17 When Joseph saw that his father had placed
his right hand on Ephraim's head, he thought
it was a mistake[B] and took his father's hand to
move it from Ephraim's head to Manasseh's.
18 Joseph said to his father, "Not that way, my
father! This one is the firstborn. Put your right
hand on his head."
19 But his father refused and said, "I know, my
son, I know! He too will become a tribe,[C] and
he too will be great; nevertheless, his younger brother will be greater than he, and his
offspring will become a populous nation."[D]
20 So he blessed them that day, putting Ephraim
before Manasseh when he said, "The nation
Israel will invoke blessings by you, saying, 'May
God make you like Ephraim and Manasseh.'"
21 Israel said to Joseph, "Look, I am about to
die, but God will be with you and will bring
you back to the land of your fathers. 22 Over
and above what I am giving your brothers, I
am giving you the one mountain slope[E] that
I took from the Amorites with my sword and
bow."

JACOB'S LAST WORDS

49 Then Jacob called his sons and said,
"Gather around, and I will tell you what
will happen to you in the days to come.[F]
2 Come together and listen, sons of Jacob;
listen to your father Israel:

3 Reuben, you are my firstborn,
my strength and the firstfruits
of my virility,
excelling in prominence,
excelling in power.
4 Turbulent as water, you will not excel,
because you got into your father's bed
and you defiled it — he[G] got
into my bed.

5 Simeon and Levi are brothers;
their knives are vicious weapons.
6 May I never enter their council;
may I never join their assembly.
For in their anger they kill men,
and on a whim they hamstring oxen.
7 Their anger is cursed, for it is strong,
and their fury, for it is cruel!
I will disperse them throughout Jacob
and scatter them throughout Israel.

8 Judah, your brothers will praise you.
Your hand will be on the necks
of your enemies;
your father's sons will bow down to you.
9 Judah is a young lion —
my son, you return from the kill.
He crouches; he lies down like a lion
or a lioness — who dares to rouse him?
10 The scepter will not depart from Judah
or the staff from between his feet
until he whose right it is comes[H]

[A] **48:10** Lit *he was not able to* [B] **48:17** Or *he was displeased*; lit *head, it was bad in his eyes* [C] **48:19** Lit *people* [D] **48:19** Or *a multitude of nations*; lit *a fullness of nations* [E] **48:22** Or *Shechem*, Joseph's burial place; lit *one shoulder* [F] **49:1** Or *in the last days* [G] **49:4** LXX, Syr, Tg read *you* [H] **49:10** Or *until tribute comes to him*, or *until Shiloh comes*, or *until he comes to Shiloh*

and the obedience of the peoples
belongs to him.
11 He ties his donkey to a vine,
and the colt of his donkey
to the choice vine.
He washes his clothes in wine
and his robes in the blood of grapes.
12 His eyes are darker than wine,
and his teeth are whiter than milk.

13 Zebulun will live by the seashore
and will be a harbor for ships,
and his territory will be next to Sidon.

14 Issachar is a strong donkey
lying down between the saddlebags.[A]
15 He saw that his resting place was good
and that the land was pleasant,
so he leaned his shoulder to bear a load
and became a forced laborer.

16 Dan will judge his people
as one of the tribes of Israel.
17 Dan will be a snake by the road,
a viper beside the path,
that bites the horse's heels
so that its rider falls backward.
18 I wait for your salvation, LORD.

19 Gad will be attacked by raiders,
but he will attack their heels.

20 Asher's[B] food will be rich,
and he will produce royal delicacies.

21 Naphtali is a doe set free
that bears beautiful fawns.

22 Joseph is a fruitful vine,
a fruitful vine beside a spring;
its branches[C] climb over the wall.[D]
23 The archers attacked him,
shot at him, and were hostile
toward him.
24 Yet his bow remained steady,
and his strong arms were made agile
by the hands of the Mighty One
of Jacob,
by the name of[E] the Shepherd, the Rock
of Israel,
25 by the God of your father who helps you,
and by the Almighty who blesses you
with blessings of the heavens above,
blessings of the deep that lies below,
and blessings of the breasts
and the womb.
26 The blessings of your father excel
the blessings of my ancestors[F]
and[G] the bounty of the ancient hills.[D]
May they rest on the head of Joseph,
on the brow of the prince
of his brothers.

27 Benjamin is a wolf; he tears his prey.
In the morning he devours the prey,
and in the evening he divides
the plunder."

28 These are the tribes of Israel, twelve in all,
and this is what their father said to them. He
blessed them, and he blessed each one with
a suitable blessing.

JACOB'S BURIAL INSTRUCTIONS

29 Then he commanded them: "I am about to
be gathered to my people. Bury me with my
fathers in the cave in the field of Ephron the
Hethite. 30 The cave is in the field of Machpelah near Mamre, in the land of Canaan. This
is the field Abraham purchased from Ephron
the Hethite as burial property. 31 Abraham and
his wife Sarah are buried there, Isaac and his
wife Rebekah are buried there, and I buried
Leah there. 32 The field and the cave in it were
purchased from the Hethites." 33 When Jacob
had finished giving charges to his sons, he
drew his feet into the bed, took his last breath,
and was gathered to his people.

JACOB'S BURIAL

50 Then Joseph, leaning over his father's
face, wept and kissed him. 2 He commanded his servants who were physicians to
embalm his father. So they embalmed Israel.
3 They took forty days to complete this, for
embalming takes that long, and the Egyptians
mourned for him seventy days.

4 When the days of mourning were over,
Joseph said to Pharaoh's household, "If I have
found favor with you, please tell[H] Pharaoh that
5 my father made me take an oath, saying, 'I
am about to die. You must bury me there in
the tomb that I made for myself in the land of

[A] **49:14** Or *sheep pens* [B] **49:19-20** LXX, Syr, Vg; MT reads *their heel.* [20]*From Asher* [C] **49:22** Lit *daughters* [D] **49:22,26** Hb obscure [E] **49:24** Syr, Tg; MT reads *Jacob, from there* [F] **49:26** Or *of the mountains* [G] **49:26** Lit *to* [H] **50:4** Lit *please speak in the ears of*

Canaan.' Now let me go and bury my father.
Then I will return."
6 So Pharaoh said, "Go and bury your father
in keeping with your oath."
7 Then Joseph went to bury his father, and all
Pharaoh's servants, the elders of his household,
and all the elders of the land of Egypt went
with him, 8 along with all Joseph's family, his
brothers, and his father's family. Only their
dependents, their flocks, and their herds were
left in the land of Goshen. 9 Horses and chariots went up with him; it was a very impressive
procession. 10 When they reached the threshing floor of Atad, which is across the Jordan,
they lamented and wept loudly, and Joseph
mourned seven days for his father. 11 When
the Canaanite inhabitants of the land saw the
mourning at the threshing floor of Atad, they
said, "This is a solemn mourning on the part of
the Egyptians." Therefore the place is named
Abel-mizraim.[A] It is across the Jordan.
12 So Jacob's sons did for him what he had
commanded them. 13 They carried him to the
land of Canaan and buried him in the cave at
Machpelah in the field near Mamre, which
Abraham had purchased as burial property from Ephron the Hethite. 14 After Joseph
buried his father, he returned to Egypt with
his brothers and all who had gone with him
to bury his father.

JOSEPH'S KINDNESS

15 When Joseph's brothers saw that their father
was dead, they said to one another, "If Joseph
is holding a grudge against us, he will certainly
repay us for all the suffering we caused him."
16 So they sent this message to Joseph, "Before
he died your father gave a command: 17 'Say
this to Joseph: Please forgive your brothers'
transgression and their sin — the suffering
they caused you.' Therefore, please forgive
the transgression of the servants of the God
of your father." Joseph wept when their message came to him. 18 His brothers also came to
him, bowed down before him, and said, "We
are your slaves!"
19 But Joseph said to them, "Don't be afraid.
Am I in the place of God? 20 You planned evil
against me; God planned it for good to bring
about the present result — the survival of
many people. 21 Therefore don't be afraid. I will
take care of you and your children." And he
comforted them and spoke kindly to them.[B]

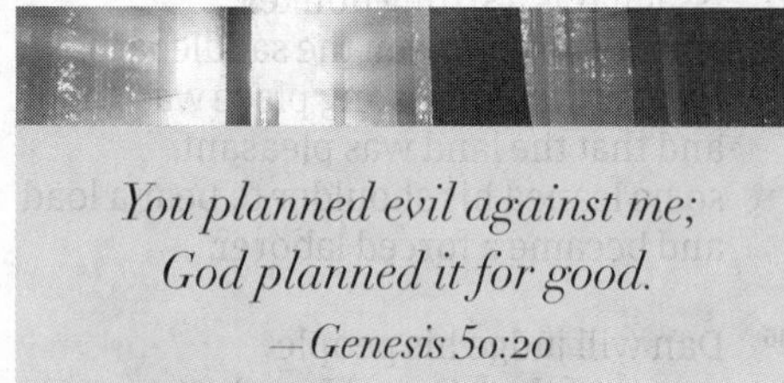
You planned evil against me;
God planned it for good.
—*Genesis 50:20*

JOSEPH'S DEATH

22 Joseph and his father's family remained
in Egypt. Joseph lived 110 years. 23 He saw
Ephraim's sons to the third generation; the
sons of Manasseh's son Machir were recognized by[C,D] Joseph.
24 Joseph said to his brothers, "I am about
to die, but God will certainly come to your aid
and bring you up from this land to the land he
swore to give to Abraham, Isaac, and Jacob."
25 So Joseph made the sons of Israel take an
oath: "When God comes to your aid, you are
to carry my bones up from here."
26 Joseph died at the age of 110. They embalmed him and placed him in a coffin in Egypt.

[A] **50:11** = Mourning of Egypt [B] **50:21** Lit *spoke to their hearts* [C] **50:23** Lit *were born on the knees of* [D] **50:23** Referring to a ritual of adoption or of legitimation; Gn 30:3

Exodus—The Israelites were oppressed for four hundred years, and God seemed to have forgotten his covenant promises. But God had not abandoned his people, and he chose Moses to lead them out of captivity. God's rescue involved the faith of a Hebrew mother, providential circumstances in an Egyptian court, the rise of an unlikely deliverer, and divine intervention.

Exodus reveals God's covenant name—Yahweh, "I AM." He is the eternal and almighty God. Yahweh is not distant, however; he hears the cries of his people and defends them. He speaks through a burning bush, miraculously intervenes to rescue his people, gives the law, and provides a way for them to draw near to him in worship, restoring a close relationship with him.

Exodus serves as a perspective-altering corrective to us as well as to the Israelites who heard these words as they were poised to enter the promised land after forty years of wilderness wandering.

Every person, at some point, goes through a "wilderness of the soul"—part of our human experience is to occasionally feel lonely and discouraged. At those times, we can remember God's faithfulness in the wilderness, to his people in Egypt, and to us. Allow that faithfulness to give courage and hope for the future.

EXODUS

AUTHOR: Moses

DATE WRITTEN: 1446–1406 BC (during the wilderness wanderings)

ORIGINAL AUDIENCE: The Israelites

SETTING: Moses penned Exodus, as well as the rest of the Pentateuch (Genesis through Deuteronomy) during the forty years the Israelites wandered in the wilderness. Exodus tells the story of how the nation was miraculously rescued from slavery in Egypt, God's covenant law and promises, and the nation's rebellion against his rule. These words served an important purpose in giving the nation their identity as the people of God and reminding them of his faithfulness.

PURPOSE FOR WRITING: Exodus is structured as a historical narrative about the life of Moses and the Israelite nation he was charged to lead. The events recounted serve as an encouragement to the Israelites that God will be with them in the future as he had been in the past. It is both a record of God's redemption of the people out of slavery in Egypt and a symbolic portrait of the redemption we have through Christ. In addition, it records the law and the establishment of worship through the tabernacle.

OUTLINE:

1. Oppression of Israel in Egypt (1:1–11:10)

   Slavery in Egypt (1:1-22)

   The birth of the deliverer (2:1–4:31)

   The Plagues (5:1–11:10)

2. God Rescues His People (12:1–14:31)

   Redemption through blood (12:1-51)

   Redemption by divine miracles (13:1–14:31)

3. Wilderness Teaching (15:1–18:27)

   Song of Victory (15:1-21)

   Testing and Trials (15:22–17:16)

   Leadership of the nation (18:1-27)

4. Consecration and Covenant (19:1–34:35)

   Acceptance of the law (19:1–31:18)

   Breaking of the law (32:1-35)

   Restoration (33:1–34:35)

5. Tabernacle Worship (35:1–40:38)

   Gifting for the tabernacle (35:1-35)

   Construction and furnishings of the tabernacle (36:1–39:43)

   God's glory filling the tabernacle (40:1-38)

KEY VERSE:

"The LORD is my strength and my song; he has become my salvation." —Exodus 15:2

RESTORATION THEMES

R	Rest and Reflection	*Observing Sabbath—20:8-10*
E	Eternal Perspective	*For the next note, see Leviticus 26:45.*
S	Support	*For the next note, see Numbers 14:9.*
T	Thanksgiving and Contentment	*Praise for Salvation—Exodus 15:2* *Praise—15:13*
O	Other-centeredness	*Avoiding Jealousy/Coveting—20:17*
R	Relationships	*Relating to Parents—20:12* *Telling the Truth—20:16; 23:1*
E	Exercise of Faith	*Standing Firm—14:13-14*

ISRAEL OPPRESSED IN EGYPT

1 These are the names of the sons of Israel
who came to Egypt with Jacob; each came
with his family:
2 Reuben, Simeon, Levi, and Judah;
3 Issachar, Zebulun, and Benjamin;
4 Dan and Naphtali; Gad and Asher.
5 The total number of Jacob's descendants[A]
was seventy;[B] Joseph was already in Egypt.
6 Joseph and all his brothers and all that
generation eventually died. 7 But the Israelites
were fruitful, increased rapidly, multiplied,
and became extremely numerous so that the
land was filled with them.
8 A new king, who did not know about Joseph, came to power in Egypt. 9 He said to
his people, "Look, the Israelite people are
more numerous and powerful than we are.
10 Come, let's deal shrewdly with them; otherwise they will multiply further, and when
war breaks out, they will join our enemies,
fight against us, and leave the country." 11 So
the Egyptians assigned taskmasters over the
Israelites to oppress them with forced labor.
They built Pithom and Rameses as supply
cities for Pharaoh. 12 But the more they oppressed them, the more they multiplied and
spread so that the Egyptians came to dread[C]
the Israelites. 13 They worked the Israelites
ruthlessly 14 and made their lives bitter with
difficult labor in brick and mortar and in all
kinds of fieldwork. They ruthlessly imposed
all this work on them.
15 The king of Egypt said to the Hebrew midwives — the first whose name was Shiph-
rah and the second whose name was Puah
— 16 "When you help the Hebrew women
give birth, observe them as they deliver. If
the child is a son, kill him, but if it's a daughter, she may live." 17 The midwives, however,
feared God and did not do as the king of Egypt
had told them; they let the boys live. 18 So the
king of Egypt summoned the midwives and
asked them, "Why have you done this and let
the boys live?"
19 The midwives said to Pharaoh, "The Hebrew women are not like the Egyptian women,
for they are vigorous and give birth before
the midwife can get to them."
20 So God was good to the midwives, and
the people multiplied and became very numerous. 21 Since the midwives feared God,
he gave them families. 22 Pharaoh then commanded all his people: "You must throw every
son born to the Hebrews into the Nile, but let
every daughter live."

MOSES'S BIRTH AND ADOPTION

2 Now a man from the family of Levi married a Levite woman. 2 The woman became
pregnant and gave birth to a son; when she
saw that he was beautiful,[D] she hid him for
three months. 3 But when she could no longer
hide him, she got a papyrus basket for him and
coated it with asphalt and pitch. She placed
the child in it and set it among the reeds by
the bank of the Nile. 4 Then his sister stood at
a distance in order to see what would happen to him.
5 Pharaoh's daughter went down to bathe at
the Nile while her servant girls walked along
the riverbank. She saw the basket among the
reeds, sent her slave girl, took it, 6 opened it,
and saw him, the child — and there he was,
a little boy, crying. She felt sorry for him and
said, "This is one of the Hebrew boys."
7 Then his sister said to Pharaoh's daughter,
"Should I go and call a Hebrew woman who is
nursing to nurse the boy for you?"
8 "Go," Pharaoh's daughter told her. So the
girl went and called the boy's mother. 9 Then
Pharaoh's daughter said to her, "Take this child
and nurse him for me, and I will pay your wages." So the woman took the boy and nursed
him. 10 When the child grew older, she brought
him to Pharaoh's daughter, and he became her
son. She named him Moses,[E] "Because," she
said, "I drew him out of the water."

MOSES IN MIDIAN

11 Years later,[F] after Moses had grown up, he
went out to his own people[G] and observed
their forced labor. He saw an Egyptian striking a Hebrew, one of his people. 12 Looking
all around and seeing no one, he struck the
Egyptian dead and hid him in the sand. 13 The
next day he went out and saw two Hebrews
fighting. He asked the one in the wrong, "Why
are you attacking your neighbor?"[H]
14 "Who made you a commander and judge
over us?" the man replied. "Are you planning
to kill me as you killed the Egyptian?"
Then Moses became afraid and thought,
"What I did is certainly known."

[A] **1:5** Lit *of people issuing from Jacob's loins* [B] **1:5** LXX, DSS read *75*; Gn 46:27; Ac 7:14 [C] **1:12** Or *Egyptians loathed* [D] **2:2** Or *healthy* [E] **2:10** The name *Moses* sounds like "drawing out" in Hb and "born" in Egyptian. [F] **2:11** Lit *And it was in those days* [G] **2:11** Lit *his brothers* [H] **2:13** Or *fellow Hebrew*

the rest of his skin. 8 "If they will not believe you and will not respond to the evidence of the first sign, they may believe the evidence of the second sign. 9 And if they don't believe even these two signs or listen to what you say, take some water from the Nile and pour it on the dry ground. The water you take from the Nile will become blood on the ground."

10 But Moses replied to the LORD, "Please, Lord, I have never been eloquent — either in the past or recently or since you have been speaking to your servant — because my mouth and my tongue are sluggish."[A]

11 The LORD said to him, "Who placed a mouth on humans? Who makes a person mute or deaf, seeing or blind? Is it not I, the LORD? 12 Now go! I will help you speak[B] and I will teach you what to say."

13 Moses said, "Please, Lord, send someone else."[C]

14 Then the LORD's anger burned against Moses, and he said, "Isn't Aaron the Levite your brother? I know that he can speak well. And also, he is on his way now to meet you. He will rejoice when he sees you. 15 You will speak with him and tell him what to say. I will help both you and him to speak[D] and will teach you both what to do. 16 He will speak to the people for you. He will serve as a mouth for you, and you will serve as God to him. 17 And take this staff in your hand that you will perform the signs with."

MOSES'S RETURN TO EGYPT

18 Then Moses went back to his father-in-law Jethro and said to him, "Please let me return to my relatives in Egypt and see if they are still living."

Jethro said to Moses, "Go in peace."

19 Now in Midian the LORD told Moses, "Return to Egypt, for all the men who wanted to kill you are dead." 20 So Moses took his wife and sons, put them on a donkey, and returned to the land of Egypt. And Moses took God's staff in his hand.

21 The LORD instructed Moses, "When you go back to Egypt, make sure you do before Pharaoh all the wonders that I have put within your power. But I will harden his heart[E] so that he won't let the people go. 22 And you will say to Pharaoh: This is what the LORD says: Israel is my firstborn son. 23 I told you: Let my son go so that he may worship me, but you refused to let him go. Look, I am about to kill your firstborn son!"

24 On the trip, at an overnight campsite, it happened that the LORD confronted him and intended to put him to death. 25 So Zipporah took a flint, cut off her son's foreskin, threw it at Moses's feet, and said, "You are a bridegroom of blood to me!" 26 So he let him alone. At that time she said, "You are a bridegroom of blood," referring to the circumcision.

REUNION OF MOSES AND AARON

27 Now the LORD had said to Aaron, "Go and meet Moses in the wilderness." So he went and met him at the mountain of God and kissed him. 28 Moses told Aaron everything the LORD had sent him to say, and about all the signs he had commanded him to do. 29 Then Moses and Aaron went and assembled all the elders of the Israelites. 30 Aaron repeated everything the LORD had said to Moses and performed the signs before the people. 31 The people believed, and when they heard that the LORD had paid attention to them and that he had seen their misery, they knelt low and worshiped.

MOSES CONFRONTS PHARAOH

5 Later, Moses and Aaron went in and said to Pharaoh, "This is what the LORD, the God of Israel, says: Let my people go, so that they may hold a festival for me in the wilderness."

2 But Pharaoh responded, "Who is the LORD that I should obey him by letting Israel go? I don't know[F] the LORD, and besides, I will not let Israel go."

3 They answered, "The God of the Hebrews has met with us. Please let us go on a three-day trip into the wilderness so that we may sacrifice to the LORD our God, or else he may strike us with plague or sword."

4 The king of Egypt said to them, "Moses and Aaron, why are you causing the people to neglect their work? Get to your labor!" 5 Pharaoh also said, "Look, the people of the land are so numerous, and you would stop them from their labor."

FURTHER OPPRESSION OF ISRAEL

6 That day Pharaoh commanded the overseers of the people as well as their foremen: 7 "Don't continue to supply the people with straw for making bricks, as before. They must go and gather straw for themselves. 8 But require the

[A] 4:10 Lit *heavy of mouth and heavy of tongue* [B] 4:12 Lit *will be with your mouth* [C] 4:13 Lit *send by the hand of whom you will send* [D] 4:15 Lit *will be with your mouth and with his mouth* [E] 4:21 Or *will make him stubborn* [F] 5:2 Or *recognize*

same quota of bricks from them as they were
making before; do not reduce it. For they are
slackers — that is why they are crying out,
'Let us go and sacrifice to our God.' 9 Impose
heavier work on the men. Then they will be
occupied with it and not pay attention to deceptive words."
10 So the overseers and foremen of the people went out and said to them, "This is what
Pharaoh says: 'I am not giving you straw. 11 Go
get straw yourselves wherever you can find
it, but there will be no reduction at all in your
workload.' " 12 So the people scattered throughout the land of Egypt to gather stubble for
straw. 13 The overseers insisted, "Finish your
assigned work each day, just as you did when
straw was provided." 14 Then the Israelite foremen, whom Pharaoh's slave drivers had set
over the people, were beaten and asked, "Why
haven't you finished making your prescribed
number of bricks yesterday or today, as you
did before?"
15 So the Israelite foremen went in and cried
for help to Pharaoh: "Why are you treating
your servants this way? 16 No straw has been
given to your servants, yet they say to us, 'Make
bricks!' Look, your servants are being beaten,
but it is your own people who are at fault."
17 But he said, "You are slackers. Slackers!
That is why you are saying, 'Let us go sacrifice
to the LORD.' 18 Now get to work. No straw will
be given to you, but you must produce the
same quantity of bricks."
19 The Israelite foremen saw that they were
in trouble when they were told, "You cannot
reduce your daily quota of bricks." 20 When
they left Pharaoh, they confronted Moses
and Aaron, who stood waiting to meet them.
21 "May the LORD take note of you and judge,"
they said to them, "because you have made us
reek to Pharaoh and his officials — putting a
sword in their hand to kill us!"
22 So Moses went back to the LORD and asked,
"Lord, why have you caused trouble for this
people? And why did you ever send me? 23 Ever
since I went in to Pharaoh to speak in your
name he has caused trouble for this people,
and you haven't rescued your people at all."
6 But the LORD replied to Moses, "Now you
will see what I will do to Pharaoh: because
of a strong hand he will let them go, and because of a strong hand he will drive them from
his land."

GOD PROMISES FREEDOM

2 Then God spoke to Moses, telling him, "I am
the LORD. 3 I appeared to Abraham, Isaac, and
Jacob as God Almighty, but I was not known to
them by my name 'the LORD.'[A] 4 I also established
my covenant with them to give them the land
of Canaan, the land they lived in as aliens. 5 Furthermore, I have heard the groaning of the Israelites, whom the Egyptians are forcing to work
as slaves, and I have remembered my covenant.
6 "Therefore tell the Israelites: I am the LORD,
and I will bring you out from the forced labor
of the Egyptians and rescue you from slavery
to them. I will redeem you with an outstretched
arm and great acts of judgment. 7 I will take
you as my people, and I will be your God. You
will know that I am the LORD your God, who
brought you out from the forced labor of the
Egyptians. 8 I will bring you to the land that I
swore[B] to give to Abraham, Isaac, and Jacob,
and I will give it to you as a possession. I am
the LORD." 9 Moses told this to the Israelites,
but they did not listen to him because of their
broken spirit and hard labor.
10 Then the LORD spoke to Moses, 11 "Go and
tell Pharaoh king of Egypt to let the Israelites
go from his land."
12 But Moses said in the LORD's presence: "If
the Israelites will not listen to me, then how
will Pharaoh listen to me, since I am such a
poor speaker?"[C] 13 Then the LORD spoke to
Moses and Aaron and gave them commands
concerning both the Israelites and Pharaoh
king of Egypt to bring the Israelites out of the
land of Egypt.

GENEALOGY OF MOSES AND AARON

14 These are the heads of their fathers' families:
The sons of Reuben, the firstborn
of Israel:
Hanoch and Pallu, Hezron and Carmi.
These are the clans of Reuben.

15 The sons of Simeon:
Jemuel, Jamin, Ohad, Jachin,
Zohar, and Shaul, the son
of a Canaanite woman.
These are the clans of Simeon.

16 These are the names of the sons of Levi
according to their family records;
Gershon, Kohath, and Merari.
Levi lived 137 years.

[A] 6:3 *LORD* (in small capitals) stands for the personal name of God, which in Hb is *Yahweh*. There is a long tradition of substituting "LORD" for "Yahweh" out of reverence. [B] 6:8 Lit *raised my hand* [C] 6:12 Lit *I have uncircumcised lips*, also in v. 30

17 The sons of Gershon:
Libni and Shimei, by their clans.
18 The sons of Kohath:
Amram, Izhar, Hebron, and Uzziel.
Kohath lived 133 years.
19 The sons of Merari:
Mahli and Mushi.
These are the clans of the Levites
according to their family records.

20 Amram married his father's sister
Jochebed,
and she bore him Aaron and Moses.
Amram lived 137 years.
21 The sons of Izhar:
Korah, Nepheg, and Zichri.
22 The sons of Uzziel:
Mishael, Elzaphan, and Sithri.
23 Aaron married Elisheba,
daughter of Amminadab and sister
of Nahshon.
She bore him Nadab and Abihu, Eleazar
and Ithamar.
24 The sons of Korah:
Assir, Elkanah, and Abiasaph.
These are the clans of the Korahites.
25 Aaron's son Eleazar married
one of the daughters of Putiel,
and she bore him Phinehas.
These are the heads of the Levite
families by their clans.

26 It was this Aaron and Moses whom the
LORD told, "Bring the Israelites out of the land
of Egypt according to their military divisions."
27 Moses and Aaron were the ones who spoke
to Pharaoh king of Egypt in order to bring the
Israelites out of Egypt.

MOSES AND AARON BEFORE PHARAOH

28 On the day the LORD spoke to Moses in the
land of Egypt, 29 he said to him, "I am the LORD;
tell Pharaoh king of Egypt everything I am
telling you."
30 But Moses replied in the LORD's presence,
"Since I am such a poor speaker, how will Pharaoh listen to me?"

7 The LORD answered Moses, "See, I have made
you like God to Pharaoh, and Aaron your
brother will be your prophet. 2 You must say
whatever I command you; then Aaron your
brother must declare it to Pharaoh so that he
will let the Israelites go from his land. 3 But
I will harden Pharaoh's heart and multiply
my signs and wonders in the land of Egypt.
4 Pharaoh will not listen to you, but I will put
my hand into Egypt and bring the military
divisions of my people the Israelites out of
the land of Egypt by great acts of judgment.
5 The Egyptians will know that I am the LORD
when I stretch out my hand against Egypt and
bring out the Israelites from among them."
6 So Moses and Aaron did this; they did just
as the LORD commanded them. 7 Moses was
eighty years old and Aaron eighty-three when
they spoke to Pharaoh.
8 The LORD said to Moses and Aaron, 9 "When
Pharaoh tells you, 'Perform a miracle,' tell
Aaron, 'Take your staff and throw it down
before Pharaoh. It will become a serpent.'"
10 So Moses and Aaron went in to Pharaoh and
did just as the LORD had commanded. Aaron
threw down his staff before Pharaoh and his
officials, and it became a serpent. 11 But then
Pharaoh called the wise men and sorcerers
— the magicians of Egypt, and they also did
the same thing by their occult practices. 12 Each
one threw down his staff, and it became a serpent. But Aaron's staff swallowed their staffs.
13 However, Pharaoh's heart was hard, and he
did not listen to them, as the LORD had said.

THE FIRST PLAGUE: WATER TURNED TO BLOOD

14 Then the LORD said to Moses, "Pharaoh's
heart is hard: He refuses to let the people go.
15 Go to Pharaoh in the morning. When you see
him walking out to the water, stand ready to
meet him by the bank of the Nile. Take in your
hand the staff that turned into a snake. 16 Tell
him: The LORD, the God of the Hebrews, has
sent me to tell you: Let my people go, so that
they may worship[A] me in the wilderness, but
so far you have not listened. 17 This is what the
LORD says: Here is how you will know that I
am the LORD. Watch. I am about to strike the
water in the Nile with the staff in my hand,
and it will turn to blood. 18 The fish in the Nile
will die, the river will stink, and the Egyptians
will be unable to drink water from it."
19 So the LORD said to Moses, "Tell Aaron: Take
your staff and stretch out your hand over the
waters of Egypt — over their rivers, canals,
ponds, and all their water reservoirs — and
they will become blood. There will be blood
throughout the land of Egypt, even in wooden
and stone containers."

[A] 7:16 Or *serve*; Ex 4:23

20 Moses and Aaron did just as the LORD had
commanded; in the sight of Pharaoh and his
officials, he raised the staff and struck the
water in the Nile, and all the water in the Nile
was turned to blood. 21 The fish in the Nile died,
and the river smelled so bad the Egyptians
could not drink water from it. There was blood
throughout the land of Egypt.
22 But the magicians of Egypt did the same
thing by their occult practices. So Pharaoh's
heart was hard, and he would not listen to
them, as the LORD had said. 23 Pharaoh turned
around, went into his palace, and didn't take
even this to heart. 24 All the Egyptians dug
around the Nile for water to drink because
they could not drink the water from the river. 25 Seven days passed after the LORD struck
the Nile.

THE SECOND PLAGUE: FROGS

8 Then the LORD said to Moses, "Go in to
Pharaoh and tell him: This is what the LORD
says: Let my people go, so that they may worship me. 2 But if you refuse to let them go, then
I will plague all your territory with frogs. 3 The
Nile will swarm with frogs; they will come up
and go into your palace, into your bedroom
and on your bed, into the houses of your officials and your people, and into your ovens
and kneading bowls. 4 The frogs will come up
on you, your people, and all your officials."
5 The LORD then said to Moses, "Tell Aaron:
Stretch out your hand with your staff over the
rivers, canals, and ponds, and cause the frogs
to come up onto the land of Egypt." 6 When
Aaron stretched out his hand over the waters
of Egypt, the frogs came up and covered the
land of Egypt. 7 But the magicians did the same
thing by their occult practices and brought
frogs up onto the land of Egypt.
8 Pharaoh summoned Moses and Aaron and
said, "Appeal to the LORD to remove the frogs
from me and my people. Then I will let the
people go and they can sacrifice to the LORD."
9 Moses said to Pharaoh, "You may have the
honor of choosing. When should I appeal on
behalf of you, your officials, and your people,
that the frogs be taken away from you and
your houses, and remain only in the Nile?"
10 "Tomorrow," he answered.
Moses replied, "As you have said, so that you
may know there is no one like the LORD our
God, 11 the frogs will go away from you, your
houses, your officials, and your people. The
frogs will remain only in the Nile." 12 After Moses and Aaron went out from Pharaoh, Moses
cried out to the LORD for help concerning the
frogs that he had brought against Pharaoh.
13 The LORD did as Moses had said: the frogs in
the houses, courtyards, and fields died. 14 They
piled them in countless heaps, and there was a
terrible odor in the land. 15 But when Pharaoh
saw there was relief, he hardened his heart and
would not listen to them, as the LORD had said.

THE THIRD PLAGUE: GNATS

16 Then the LORD said to Moses, "Tell Aaron:
Stretch out your staff and strike the dust of
the land, and it will become gnats[A] throughout
the land of Egypt." 17 And they did this. Aaron
stretched out his hand with his staff, and when
he struck the dust of the land, gnats were on
people and animals. All the dust of the land
became gnats throughout the land of Egypt.
18 The magicians tried to produce gnats using
their occult practices, but they could not. The
gnats remained on people and animals.
19 "This is the finger of God," the magicians
said to Pharaoh. But Pharaoh's heart was hard,
and he would not listen to them, as the LORD
had said.

THE FOURTH PLAGUE: SWARMS OF FLIES

20 The LORD said to Moses, "Get up early in
the morning and present yourself to Pharaoh
when you see him going out to the water. Tell
him: This is what the LORD says: Let my people go, so that they may worship[B] me. 21 But if
you will not let my people go, then I will send
swarms of flies[C] against you, your officials,
your people, and your houses. The Egyptians'
houses will swarm with flies, and so will the
land where they live.[D] 22 But on that day I will
give special treatment to the land of Goshen,
where my people are living; no flies will be
there. This way you will know that I, the LORD,
am in the land. 23 I will make a distinction[E] between my people and your people. This sign
will take place tomorrow."
24 And the LORD did this. Thick swarms of
flies went into Pharaoh's palace and his officials' houses. Throughout Egypt the land was
ruined because of the swarms of flies. 25 Then
Pharaoh summoned Moses and Aaron and said,
"Go sacrifice to your God within the country."
26 But Moses said, "It would not be right[F] to

[A] **8:16** Perhaps sand fleas or mosquitoes [B] **8:20** Or *serve* [C] **8:21** Or *insects* [D] **8:21** Lit *are* [E] **8:23** LXX, Syr, Vg; MT reads *will place redemption* [F] **8:26** Or *allowable*

do that, because what we will sacrifice to the LORD our God is detestable to the Egyptians. If we sacrifice what the Egyptians detest in front of them, won't they stone us? 27 We must go a distance of three days into the wilderness and sacrifice to the LORD our God as he instructs us."

28 Pharaoh responded, "I will let you go and sacrifice to the LORD your God in the wilderness, but don't go very far. Make an appeal for me."

29 "As soon as I leave you," Moses said, "I will appeal to the LORD, and tomorrow the swarms of flies will depart from Pharaoh, his officials, and his people. But Pharaoh must not act deceptively again by refusing to let the people go and sacrifice to the LORD." 30 Then Moses left Pharaoh's presence and appealed to the LORD. 31 The LORD did as Moses had said: He removed the swarms of flies from Pharaoh, his officials, and his people; not one was left. 32 But Pharaoh hardened his heart this time also and did not let the people go.

THE FIFTH PLAGUE: DEATH OF LIVESTOCK

9 Then the LORD said to Moses, "Go in to Pharaoh and say to him: This is what the LORD, the God of the Hebrews, says: Let my people go, so that they may worship me. 2 But if you refuse to let them go and keep holding them, 3 then the LORD's hand will bring a severe plague against your livestock in the field — the horses, donkeys, camels, herds, and flocks. 4 But the LORD will make a distinction between the livestock of Israel and the livestock of Egypt, so that nothing of all that the Israelites own will die." 5 And the LORD set a time, saying, "Tomorrow the LORD will do this thing in the land." 6 The LORD did this the next day. All the Egyptian livestock died, but none among the Israelite livestock died. 7 Pharaoh sent messengers who saw that not a single one of the Israelite livestock was dead. But Pharaoh's heart was hard, and he did not let the people go.

THE SIXTH PLAGUE: BOILS

8 Then the LORD said to Moses and Aaron, "Take handfuls of furnace soot, and Moses is to throw it toward heaven in the sight of Pharaoh. 9 It will become fine dust over the entire land of Egypt. It will become festering boils on people and animals throughout the land of Egypt." 10 So they took furnace soot and stood before Pharaoh. Moses threw it toward heaven, and it became festering boils on people and animals. 11 The magicians could not stand before Moses because of the boils, for the boils were on the magicians as well as on all the Egyptians. 12 But the LORD hardened Pharaoh's heart and he did not listen to them, as the LORD had told Moses.

THE SEVENTH PLAGUE: HAIL

13 Then the LORD said to Moses, "Get up early in the morning and present yourself to Pharaoh. Tell him: This is what the LORD, the God of the Hebrews says: Let my people go, so that they may worship me. 14 For this time I am about to send all my plagues against you,[A] your officials, and your people. Then you will know there is no one like me on the whole earth. 15 By now I could have stretched out my hand and struck you and your people with a plague, and you would have been obliterated from the earth. 16 However, I have let you live for this purpose: to show you my power and to make my name known on the whole earth. 17 You are still acting arrogantly against[B] my people by not letting them go. 18 Tomorrow at this time I will rain down the worst hail that has ever occurred in Egypt from the day it was founded until now. 19 Therefore give orders to bring your livestock and all that you have in the field into shelters. Every person and animal that is in the field and not brought inside will die when the hail falls on them." 20 Those among Pharaoh's officials who feared the word of the LORD made their servants and livestock flee to shelters, 21 but those who didn't take to heart the LORD's word left their servants and livestock in the field.

22 Then the LORD said to Moses, "Stretch out your hand toward heaven and let there be hail throughout the land of Egypt — on people and animals and every plant of the field in the land of Egypt." 23 So Moses stretched out his staff toward heaven, and the LORD sent thunder and hail. Lightning struck the land, and the LORD rained hail on the land of Egypt. 24 The hail, with lightning flashing through it, was so severe that nothing like it had occurred in the land of Egypt since it had become a nation. 25 Throughout the land of Egypt, the hail struck down everything in the field, both people and animals. The hail beat down every plant of the field and shattered every tree in the field. 26 The only

[A] 9:14 Lit *plagues to your heart* [B] 9:17 Or *still obstructing*

place it didn't hail was in the land of Goshen,
where the Israelites were.
27 Pharaoh sent for Moses and Aaron. "I have
sinned this time," he said to them. "The LORD
is the righteous one, and I and my people are
the guilty ones. 28 Make an appeal to the LORD.
There has been enough of God's thunder and
hail. I will let you go; you don't need to stay
any longer."
29 Moses said to him, "When I have left the
city, I will spread out my hands to the LORD.
The thunder will cease, and there will be no
more hail, so that you may know the earth[A]
belongs to the LORD. 30 But as for you and your
officials, I know that you still do not fear the
LORD God."
31 The flax and the barley were destroyed
because the barley was ripe[B] and the flax was
budding, 32 but the wheat and the spelt were
not destroyed since they are later crops.[C]
33 Moses left Pharaoh and the city, and spread
out his hands to the LORD. Then the thunder and
hail ceased, and rain no longer poured down
on the land. 34 When Pharaoh saw that the rain,
hail, and thunder had ceased, he sinned again
and hardened his heart, he and his officials.
35 So Pharaoh's heart was hard, and he did
not let the Israelites go, as the LORD had said
through Moses.

THE EIGHTH PLAGUE: LOCUSTS

10 Then the LORD said to Moses, "Go to Pharaoh, for I have hardened his heart and
the hearts of his officials so that I may do these
miraculous signs of mine among them,[D] 2 and
so that you may tell[E] your son and grandson
how severely I dealt with the Egyptians and
performed miraculous signs among them,
and you will know that I am the LORD."
3 So Moses and Aaron went in to Pharaoh
and told him, "This is what the LORD, the God
of the Hebrews, says: How long will you refuse to humble yourself before me? Let my
people go, that they may worship me. 4 But if
you refuse to let my people go, then tomorrow
I will bring locusts into your territory. 5 They
will cover the surface of the land so that no
one will be able to see the land. They will eat
the remainder left to you that escaped the
hail; they will eat every tree you have growing in the fields. 6 They will fill your houses,
all your officials' houses, and the houses of
all the Egyptians — something your fathers
and grandfathers never saw since the time
they occupied the land until today." Then he
turned and left Pharaoh's presence.
7 Pharaoh's officials asked him, "How long
must this man be a snare to us? Let the men go,
so that they may worship the LORD their God.
Don't you realize yet that Egypt is devastated?"
8 So Moses and Aaron were brought back
to Pharaoh. "Go, worship the LORD your God,"
Pharaoh said. "But exactly who will be going?"
9 Moses replied, "We will go with our young
and with our old; we will go with our sons and
with our daughters, with our flocks and with
our herds because we must hold the LORD's
festival."
10 He said to them, "The Lord would have to be
with you if I would ever let you and your families go! Look out — you're heading for trouble.
11 No, go — just able-bodied men — worship
the LORD, since that's what you want." And
they were driven from Pharaoh's presence.
12 The LORD then said to Moses, "Stretch out
your hand over the land of Egypt, and the
locusts will come up over it and eat every
plant in the land, everything that the hail
left." 13 So Moses stretched out his staff over
the land of Egypt, and the LORD sent an east
wind over the land all that day and through
the night. By morning the east wind had
brought in the locusts. 14 The locusts went up
over the entire land of Egypt and settled on
the whole territory of Egypt. Never before
had there been such a large number of locusts, and there never will be again. 15 They
covered the surface of the whole land so
that the land was black, and they consumed
all the plants on the ground and all the fruit
on the trees that the hail had left. Nothing
green was left on the trees or the plants in
the field throughout the land of Egypt.
16 Pharaoh urgently sent for Moses and Aaron and said, "I have sinned against the LORD
your God and against you. 17 Please forgive
my sin once more and make an appeal to the
LORD your God, so that he will just take this
death away from me." 18 Moses left Pharaoh's
presence and appealed to the LORD. 19 Then
the LORD changed the wind to a strong west[F]
wind, and it carried off the locusts and blew
them into the Red Sea. Not a single locust was
left in all the territory of Egypt. 20 But the LORD
hardened Pharaoh's heart, and he did not let
the Israelites go.

[A] **9:29** Or *land* [B] **9:31** Lit *was ears of grain* [C] **9:32** Lit *are late* [D] **10:1** Lit *mine in his midst* [E] **10:2** Lit *tell in the ears of* [F] **10:19** Lit *sea*

THE NINTH PLAGUE: DARKNESS

21 Then the LORD said to Moses, "Stretch out your hand toward heaven, and there will be darkness over the land of Egypt, a darkness that can be felt." 22 So Moses stretched out his hand toward heaven, and there was thick darkness throughout the land of Egypt for three days. 23 One person could not see another, and for three days they did not move from where they were. Yet all the Israelites had light where they lived.

24 Pharaoh summoned Moses and said, "Go, worship the LORD. Even your families may go with you; only your flocks and herds must stay behind."

25 Moses responded, "You must also let us have[A] sacrifices and burnt offerings to prepare for the LORD our God. 26 Even our livestock must go with us; not a hoof will be left behind because we will take some of them to worship the LORD our God. We will not know what we will use to worship the LORD until we get there."

27 But the LORD hardened Pharaoh's heart, and he was unwilling to let them go. 28 Pharaoh said to him, "Leave me! Make sure you never see my face again, for on the day you see my face, you will die."

29 "As you have said," Moses replied, "I will never see your face again."

THE TENTH PLAGUE: DEATH OF THE FIRSTBORN

11 The LORD said[B] to Moses, "I will bring one more plague on Pharaoh and on Egypt. After that, he will let you go from here. When he lets you go,[C] he will drive you out of here. 2 Now announce to the people that both men and women should ask their neighbors for silver and gold items." 3 The LORD gave[D] the people favor with the Egyptians. In addition, Moses himself was very highly regarded[E] in the land of Egypt by[F] Pharaoh's officials and the people.

4 So Moses said, "This is what the LORD says: About midnight I will go throughout Egypt, 5 and every firstborn male in the land of Egypt will die, from the firstborn of Pharaoh who sits on his throne to the firstborn of the servant girl who is at the grindstones, as well as every firstborn of the livestock. 6 Then there will be a great cry of anguish through all the land of Egypt such as never was before or ever will be again. 7 But against all the Israelites, whether people or animals, not even a dog will snarl,[G] so that you may know that the LORD makes a distinction between Egypt and Israel. 8 All these officials of yours will come down to me and bow before me, saying: Get out, you and all the people who follow you.[H] After that, I will get out." And he went out from Pharaoh's presence fiercely angry.

9 The LORD said to Moses, "Pharaoh will not listen to you, so that my wonders may be multiplied in the land of Egypt." 10 Moses and Aaron did all these wonders before Pharaoh, but the LORD hardened Pharaoh's heart, and he would not let the Israelites go out of his land.

INSTRUCTIONS FOR THE PASSOVER

12 The LORD said to Moses and Aaron in the land of Egypt: 2 "This month is to be the beginning of months for you; it is the first month of your year. 3 Tell the whole community of Israel that on the tenth day of this month they must each select an animal of the flock according to their fathers' families, one animal per family. 4 If the household is too small for a whole animal, that person and the neighbor nearest his house are to select one based on the combined number of people; you should apportion the animal according to what each will eat. 5 You must have an unblemished animal, a year-old male; you may take it from either the sheep or the goats. 6 You are to keep it until the fourteenth day of this month; then the whole assembly of the community of Israel will slaughter the animals at twilight. 7 They must take some of the blood and put it on the two doorposts and the lintel of the houses where they eat them. 8 They are to eat the meat that night; they should eat it, roasted over the fire along with unleavened bread and bitter herbs. 9 Do not eat any of it raw or cooked in boiling[I] water, but only roasted over fire — its head as well as its legs and inner organs. 10 You must not leave any of it until morning; any part of it left until morning you must burn. 11 Here is how you must eat it: You must be dressed for travel,[J] your sandals on your feet, and your staff in your hand. You are to eat it in a hurry; it is the LORD's Passover.

12 "I will pass through the land of Egypt on that night and strike every firstborn male in the land of Egypt, both people and animals. I

[A] **10:25** Lit *also give in our hand* [B] **11:1** Or *had said* [C] **11:1** Or *go, it will be finished —* [D] **11:3** Or *had given* [E] **11:3** Lit *was very great* [F] **11:3** Or *in the eyes of* [G] **11:7** Lit *point its tongue* [H] **11:8** Lit *people at your feet* [I] **12:9** Or *or boiled at all in* [J] **12:11** Lit *must have your waist girded*

am the LORD; I will execute judgments against all the gods of Egypt. 13 The blood on the houses where you are staying will be a distinguishing mark for you; when I see the blood, I will pass over you. No plague will be among you to destroy you when I strike the land of Egypt.

14 "This day is to be a memorial for you, and you must celebrate it as a festival to the LORD. You are to celebrate it throughout your generations as a permanent statute. 15 You must eat unleavened bread for seven days. On the first day you must remove yeast from your houses. Whoever eats what is leavened from the first day through the seventh day must be cut off from Israel. 16 You are to hold a sacred assembly on the first day and another sacred assembly on the seventh day. No work may be done on those days except for preparing what people need to eat — you may do only that.

17 "You are to observe the Festival of Unleavened Bread because on this very day I brought your military divisions out of the land of Egypt. You must observe this day throughout your generations as a permanent statute. 18 You are to eat unleavened bread in the first month, from the evening of the fourteenth day of the month until the evening of the twenty-first day. 19 Yeast must not be found in your houses for seven days. If anyone eats something leavened, that person, whether a resident alien or native of the land, must be cut off from the community of Israel. 20 Do not eat anything leavened; eat unleavened bread in all your homes."[A]

21 Then Moses summoned all the elders of Israel and said to them, "Go, select an animal from the flock according to your families, and slaughter the Passover animal. 22 Take a cluster of hyssop, dip it in the blood that is in the basin, and brush the lintel and the two doorposts with some of the blood in the basin. None of you may go out the door of his house until morning. 23 When the LORD passes through to strike Egypt and sees the blood on the lintel and the two doorposts, he will pass over the door and not let the destroyer enter your houses to strike you.

24 "Keep this command permanently as a statute for you and your descendants. 25 When you enter the land that the LORD will give you as he promised, you are to observe this ceremony. 26 When your children ask you, 'What does this ceremony mean to you?' 27 you are to reply, 'It is the Passover sacrifice to the LORD, for he passed over the houses of the Israelites in Egypt when he struck the Egyptians and spared our homes.'" So the people knelt low and worshiped. 28 Then the Israelites went and did this; they did just as the LORD had commanded Moses and Aaron.

THE EXODUS

29 Now at midnight the LORD struck every firstborn male in the land of Egypt, from the firstborn of Pharaoh who sat on his throne to the firstborn of the prisoner who was in the dungeon, and every firstborn of the livestock. 30 During the night Pharaoh got up, he along with all his officials and all the Egyptians, and there was a loud wailing throughout Egypt because there wasn't a house without someone dead. 31 He summoned Moses and Aaron during the night and said, "Get out immediately from among my people, both you and the Israelites, and go, worship the LORD as you have said. 32 Take even your flocks and your herds as you asked and leave, and also bless me."

33 Now the Egyptians pressured the people in order to send them quickly out of the country, for they said, "We're all going to die!" 34 So the people took their dough before it was leavened, with their kneading bowls wrapped up in their clothes on their shoulders.

35 The Israelites acted on Moses's word and asked the Egyptians for silver and gold items and for clothing. 36 And the LORD gave the people such favor with the Egyptians that they gave them what they requested. In this way they plundered the Egyptians.

37 The Israelites traveled from Rameses to Succoth, about six hundred thousand able-bodied men on foot, besides their families. 38 A mixed crowd also went up with them, along with a huge number of livestock, both flocks and herds. 39 The people baked the dough they had brought out of Egypt into unleavened loaves, since it had no yeast; for when they were driven out of Egypt, they could not delay and had not prepared provisions for themselves.

40 The time that the Israelites lived in Egypt[B] was 430 years. 41 At the end of 430 years, on that same day, all the LORD's military divisions went out from the land of Egypt. 42 It was a night of vigil in honor of the LORD, because he would bring them out of the land of Egypt. This same night is in honor of the LORD, a night

[A] **12:20** Or *settlements* [B] **12:40** LXX, Sam add *and in Canaan*

ESCAPE THROUGH THE RED SEA

15 The LORD said to Moses, "Why are you crying out to me? Tell the Israelites to break
camp. 16 As for you, lift up your staff, stretch
out your hand over the sea, and divide it so
that the Israelites can go through the sea
on dry ground. 17 As for me, I am going to
harden the hearts of the Egyptians so that
they will go in after them, and I will receive
glory by means of Pharaoh, all his army, and
his chariots and horsemen. 18 The Egyptians
will know that I am the LORD when I receive
glory through Pharaoh, his chariots, and his
horsemen."

19 Then the angel of God, who was going in
front of the Israelite forces, moved and went
behind them. The pillar of cloud moved from
in front of them and stood behind them. 20 It
came between the Egyptian and Israelite forces. There was cloud and darkness, it lit up the
night, and neither group came near the other
all night long.

21 Then Moses stretched out his hand over
the sea. The LORD drove the sea back with a
powerful east wind all that night and turned
the sea into dry land. So the waters were divided, 22 and the Israelites went through the
sea on dry ground, with the waters like a wall
to them on their right and their left.

23 The Egyptians set out in pursuit — all Pharaoh's horses, his chariots, and his horsemen
— and went into the sea after them. 24 During
the morning watch, the LORD looked down at the
Egyptian forces from the pillar of fire and cloud,
and threw the Egyptian forces into confusion.
25 He caused their chariot wheels to swerve[A,B]
and made them drive[C] with difficulty. "Let's get
away from Israel," the Egyptians said, "because
the LORD is fighting for them against Egypt!"

26 Then the LORD said to Moses, "Stretch out
your hand over the sea so that the water may
come back on the Egyptians, on their chariots and horsemen." 27 So Moses stretched
out his hand over the sea, and at daybreak
the sea returned to its normal depth. While
the Egyptians were trying to escape from
it, the LORD threw them into the sea. 28 The
water came back and covered the chariots
and horsemen, plus the entire army of Pharaoh that had gone after them into the sea.
Not even one of them survived.

29 But the Israelites had walked through the
sea on dry ground, with the waters like a wall
to them on their right and their left. 30 That

Thanksgiving and Contentment | *Praise for Salvation*

SO GREAT A SALVATION

"The LORD is my strength and my song; he has become my salvation. This is my God, and I will praise him, my father's God, and I will exalt him." Exodus 15:2

When people of faith hear (or read) the word *salvation*, they think almost invariably in spiritual terms: forgiveness, spiritual pardon, reconciliation with God. Yet as wonderful as all those blessings are, biblical salvation is even bigger and better.

The Hebrew word (from which we get the names Joshua and Jesus) broadly means "deliverance." In the Bible, such rescue often involves being plucked or snatched from much more than sin and its consequences. In this passage, for example, Moses and the people of God were celebrating in song how the Lord had powerfully delivered or saved them from physical death at the hands of the Egyptian army.

"Our God is a God of salvation," the psalm writer declares (Ps 68:20). This is great news for anyone who is caught in the trap of addiction, mired in depression, or stuck in the woes of financial trouble.

Where in your life do you need rescue? Call on the God who is able to save—in every way we need saving!

For the next note on *Thanksgiving and Contentment*, see Exodus 15:13.

[A] **14:25** Sam, LXX, Syr read *He bound their chariot wheels* [B] **14:25** Or *fall off* [C] **14:25** Or *and they drove them*

day the LORD saved Israel from the power of
the Egyptians, and Israel saw the Egyptians
dead on the seashore. 31 When Israel saw the
great power that the LORD used against the
Egyptians, the people feared the LORD and
believed in him and in his servant Moses.

ISRAEL'S SONG

15 Then Moses and the Israelites sang this song to the LORD. They said:

I will sing to the LORD,
for he is highly exalted;
he has thrown the horse
and its rider into the sea.
2 The LORD is my strength and my song;[A]
he has become my salvation.
This is my God, and I will praise him,
my father's God, and I will exalt him.
3 The LORD is a warrior;
the LORD is his name.

4 He threw Pharaoh's chariots
and his army into the sea;
the elite of his officers
were drowned in the Red Sea.
5 The floods covered them;
they sank to the depths like a stone.
6 LORD, your right hand is glorious
in power.
LORD, your right hand shattered
the enemy.
7 You overthrew your adversaries
by your great majesty.
You unleashed your burning wrath;
it consumed them like stubble.
8 The water heaped up at the blast
from your nostrils;
the currents stood firm like a dam.
The watery depths congealed
in the heart of the sea.
9 The enemy said:
"I will pursue, I will overtake,
I will divide the spoil.
My desire will be gratified
at their expense.
I will draw my sword;
my hand will destroy[B] them."
10 But you blew with your breath,
and the sea covered them.
They sank like lead
in the mighty waters.

11 LORD, who is like you among the gods?
Who is like you, glorious in holiness,

Thanksgiving and Contentment | *Praise*

THE POWER OF PRAISE

"With your faithful love, you will lead the people you have redeemed; you will guide them to your holy dwelling with your strength." Exodus 15:13

The Red Sea incident was a defining moment in Jewish history, a breathtaking, unforgettable demonstration of God's faithful love. Look at the aftermath: "When Israel saw the great power that the LORD used against the Egyptians, the people feared the LORD and believed in him and in his servant Moses" (Ex 14:31).

They "feared the LORD," which is to say they were in awe. But they were not merely overcome by a sense of reverence; they were also filled with faith. What did they do as a result? Someone (perhaps Moses) wrote a song of celebration. Then the entire nation joined together in singing this new song of praise.

Realize that we don't praise God because he's insecure and needs his ego stroked. We do it because it's fitting. And praising God has a way of changing us. Sometimes we praise God because we are feeling thankful; other times by praising God we come to feel more thankful. In other words, praise is both the result of joy and the catalyst for more joy!

Lift your heart and voice in praise to your loving Father.

For the next note on *Thanksgiving and Contentment*, see Numbers 32:23.

[A] **15:2** Or *might* [B] **15:9** Or *conquer*

revered with praises,
performing wonders?
12 You stretched out your right hand,
and the earth swallowed them.
13 With your faithful love,
you will lead the people
you have redeemed;
you will guide them
to your holy dwelling
with your strength.

14 When the peoples hear,
they will shudder;
anguish will seize the inhabitants
of Philistia.
15 Then the chiefs of Edom will be
terrified;
trembling will seize the leaders of Moab;
all the inhabitants of Canaan will panic;
16 terror and dread will fall on them.
They will be as still[A] as a stone
because of your powerful arm
until your people pass by, LORD,
until the people whom you purchased[B]
pass by.

17 You will bring them in and plant them
on the mountain of your possession;
LORD, you have prepared the place
for your dwelling;
Lord,[C] your hands have established
the sanctuary.
18 The LORD will reign forever and ever!

19 When Pharaoh's horses with his chariots
and horsemen went into the sea, the LORD
brought the water of the sea back over them.
But the Israelites walked through the sea on
dry ground. 20 Then the prophetess Miriam,
Aaron's sister, took a tambourine in her hand,
and all the women came out following her
with tambourines and dancing. 21 Miriam
sang to them:

Sing to the LORD,
for he is highly exalted;
he has thrown the horse
and its rider into the sea.

WATER PROVIDED

22 Then Moses led Israel on from the Red Sea,
and they went out to the Wilderness of Shur.
They journeyed for three days in the wilderness without finding water. 23 They came to
Marah, but they could not drink the water at
Marah because it was bitter — that is why it
was named Marah.[D] 24 The people grumbled
to Moses, "What are we going to drink?" 25 So
he cried out to the LORD, and the LORD showed
him a tree. When he threw it into the water,
the water became drinkable.

The LORD made a statute and ordinance for
them at Marah, and he tested them there. 26 He
said, "If you will carefully obey the LORD your
God, do what is right in his sight, pay attention
to his commands, and keep all his statutes,
I will not inflict any illnesses on you that I
inflicted on the Egyptians. For I am the LORD
who heals you."

27 Then they came to Elim, where there were
twelve springs and seventy date palms, and
they camped there by the water.

MANNA AND QUAIL PROVIDED

16 The entire Israelite community departed
from Elim and came to the Wilderness of
Sin, which is between Elim and Sinai, on the
fifteenth day of the second month after they
had left the land of Egypt. 2 The entire Israelite community grumbled against Moses and
Aaron in the wilderness. 3 The Israelites said
to them, "If only we had died by the LORD's
hand in the land of Egypt, when we sat by
pots of meat and ate all the bread we wanted.
Instead, you brought us into this wilderness
to make this whole assembly die of hunger!"

4 Then the LORD said to Moses, "I am going
to rain bread from heaven for you. The people are to go out each day and gather enough
for that day. This way I will test them to see
whether or not they will follow my instructions. 5 On the sixth day, when they prepare
what they bring in, it will be twice as much
as they gather on other days."[E]

6 So Moses and Aaron said to all the Israelites: "This evening you will know that it was
the LORD who brought you out of the land of
Egypt, 7 and in the morning you will see the
LORD's glory because he has heard your complaints about him. For who are we that you
complain about us?" 8 Moses continued, "The
LORD will give you meat to eat this evening and
all the bread you want in the morning, for he
has heard the complaints that you are raising
against him. Who are we? Your complaints are
not against us but against the LORD."

9 Then Moses told Aaron, "Say to the entire

[A] **15:16** Or *silent* [B] **15:16** Or *created* [C] **15:17** Some Hb mss, DSS, Sam, Tg read *LORD* [D] **15:23** = Bitter or Bitterness [E] **16:5** Lit *as gathering day to day*

Israelite community, 'Come before the LORD, for he has heard your complaints.' " 10 As Aaron was speaking to the entire Israelite community, they turned toward the wilderness, and there in a cloud the LORD's glory appeared.

11 The LORD spoke to Moses, 12 "I have heard the complaints of the Israelites. Tell them: At twilight you will eat meat, and in the morning you will eat bread until you are full. Then you will know that I am the LORD your God."

13 So at evening quail came and covered the camp. In the morning there was a layer of dew all around the camp. 14 When the layer of dew evaporated, there were fine flakes on the desert surface, as fine as frost on the ground. 15 When the Israelites saw it, they asked one another, "What is it?" because they didn't know what it was.

Moses told them, "It is the bread the LORD has given you to eat. 16 This is what the LORD has commanded: 'Gather as much of it as each person needs to eat. You may take two quarts[A] per individual, according to the number of people each of you has in his tent.' "

17 So the Israelites did this. Some gathered a lot, some a little. 18 When they measured it by quarts,[B] the person who gathered a lot had no surplus, and the person who gathered a little had no shortage. Each gathered as much as he needed to eat. 19 Moses said to them, "No one is to let any of it remain until morning." 20 But they didn't listen to Moses; some people left part of it until morning, and it bred worms and stank. Therefore Moses was angry with them.

21 They gathered it every morning. Each gathered as much as he needed to eat, but when the sun grew hot, it melted. 22 On the sixth day they gathered twice as much food, four quarts[C] apiece, and all the leaders of the community came and reported this to Moses. 23 He told them, "This is what the LORD has said: 'Tomorrow is a day of complete rest, a holy Sabbath to the LORD. Bake what you want to bake, and boil what you want to boil, and set aside everything left over to be kept until morning.' "

24 So they set it aside until morning as Moses commanded, and it didn't stink or have maggots in it. 25 "Eat it today," Moses said, "because today is a Sabbath to the LORD. Today you won't find any in the field. 26 For six days you will gather it, but on the seventh day, the Sabbath, there will be none."

27 Yet on the seventh day some of the people went out to gather, but they did not find any. 28 Then the LORD said to Moses, "How long will you[D] refuse to keep my commands and instructions? 29 Understand that the LORD has given you the Sabbath; therefore on the sixth day he will give you two days' worth of bread. Each of you stay where you are; no one is to leave his place on the seventh day." 30 So the people rested on the seventh day.

31 The house of Israel named the substance manna.[E] It resembled coriander seed, was white, and tasted like wafers made with honey. 32 Moses said, "This is what the LORD has commanded: 'Two quarts[F] of it are to be preserved throughout your generations, so that they may see the bread I fed you in the wilderness when I brought you out of the land of Egypt.' "

33 Moses told Aaron, "Take a container and put two quarts[G] of manna in it. Then place it before the LORD to be preserved throughout your generations." 34 As the LORD commanded Moses, Aaron placed it before the testimony to be preserved.

35 The Israelites ate manna for forty years, until they came to an inhabited land. They ate manna until they reached the border of the land of Canaan. 36 (They used a measure called an omer, which held two quarts.[H])

WATER FROM THE ROCK

17 The entire Israelite community left the Wilderness of Sin, moving from one place to the next according to the LORD's command. They camped at Rephidim, but there was no water for the people to drink. 2 So the people complained to Moses, "Give us water to drink."

"Why are you complaining to me?" Moses replied to them. "Why are you testing the LORD?"

3 But the people thirsted there for water and grumbled against Moses. They said, "Why did you ever bring us up from Egypt to kill us and our children and our livestock with thirst?"

4 Then Moses cried out to the LORD, "What should I do with these people? In a little while they will stone me!"

5 The LORD answered Moses, "Go on ahead of the people and take some of the elders of Israel with you. Take the staff you struck the Nile with in your hand and go. 6 I am going to

[A] **16:16** Lit *an omer* [B] **16:18** Lit *by an omer* [C] **16:22** Lit *two omers* [D] **16:28** The Hb word for *you* is pl, referring to the whole nation. [E] **16:31** = what?; Ex 16:15 [F] **16:32** Lit *'A full omer* [G] **16:33** Lit *a full omer* [H] **16:36** Lit *(The omer is a tenth of an ephah.)*

stand there in front of you on the rock at Horeb;
when you hit the rock, water will come out of
it and the people will drink." Moses did this
in the sight of the elders of Israel. 7 He named
the place Massah[A] and Meribah[B] because the
Israelites complained, and because they tested
the LORD, saying, "Is the LORD among us or not?"

THE AMALEKITES ATTACK

8 At Rephidim, Amalek[C] came and fought
against Israel. 9 Moses said to Joshua, "Select
some men for us and go fight against Amalek. Tomorrow I will stand on the hilltop with
God's staff in my hand."

10 Joshua did as Moses had told him, and
fought against Amalek, while Moses, Aaron,
and Hur went up to the top of the hill. 11 While
Moses held up his hand,[D] Israel prevailed, but
whenever he put his hand[D] down, Amalek
prevailed. 12 When Moses's hands grew heavy,
they took a stone and put it under him, and
he sat down on it. Then Aaron and Hur supported his hands, one on one side and one on
the other so that his hands remained steady
until the sun went down. 13 So Joshua defeated
Amalek and his army[E] with the sword.

14 The LORD then said to Moses, "Write this
down on a scroll as a reminder and recite it to
Joshua: I will completely blot out the memory
of Amalek under heaven."

15 And Moses built an altar and named it, "The
LORD Is My Banner."[F] 16 He said, "Indeed, my
hand is lifted up toward[G] the LORD's throne.
The LORD will be at war with Amalek from
generation to generation."

JETHRO'S VISIT

18 Moses's father-in-law Jethro, the priest
of Midian, heard about everything that
God had done for Moses and for God's people Israel when the LORD brought Israel out
of Egypt.

2 Now Jethro, Moses's father-in-law, had
taken in Zipporah, Moses's wife, after he had
sent her back, 3 along with her two sons, one
of whom was named Gershom[H] (because Moses had said, "I have been a resident alien in
a foreign land") 4 and the other Eliezer (because he had said, "The God of my father was
my helper and rescued me from Pharaoh's
sword").[I]

5 Moses's father-in-law Jethro, along with
Moses's wife and sons, came to him in the
wilderness where he was camped at the mountain of God. 6 He sent word to Moses, "I, your
father-in-law Jethro, am coming to you with
your wife and her two sons."

7 So Moses went out to meet his father-in-
law, bowed down, and then kissed him. They
asked each other how they had been[J] and
went into the tent. 8 Moses recounted to his
father-in-law all that the LORD had done to
Pharaoh and the Egyptians for Israel's sake,
all the hardships that confronted them on the
way, and how the LORD rescued them.

9 Jethro rejoiced over all the good things the
LORD had done for Israel when he rescued them
from the power of the Egyptians. 10 "Blessed
be the LORD," Jethro exclaimed, "who rescued
you from the power of Egypt and from the
power of Pharaoh. He has rescued the people from under the power of Egypt! 11 Now I
know that the LORD is greater than all gods,
because he did wonders when the Egyptians
acted arrogantly against Israel."[K]

12 Then Jethro, Moses's father-in-law, brought
a burnt offering and sacrifices to God, and
Aaron came with all the elders of Israel to eat
a meal with Moses's father-in-law in God's
presence.

13 The next day Moses sat down to judge the
people, and they stood around Moses from
morning until evening. 14 When Moses's father-in-law saw everything he was doing for
them he asked, "What is this thing you're doing
for the people? Why are you alone sitting as
judge, while all the people stand around you
from morning until evening?"

15 Moses replied to his father-in-law, "Because the people come to me to inquire of God.
16 Whenever they have a dispute, it comes to me,
and I make a decision between one man and
another. I teach them God's statutes and laws."

17 "What you're doing is not good," Moses's
father-in-law said to him. 18 "You will certainly
wear out both yourself and these people who
are with you, because the task is too heavy
for you. You can't do it alone. 19 Now listen
to me; I will give you some advice, and God
be with you. You be the one to represent the
people before God and bring their cases to
him. 20 Instruct them about the statutes and

[A] **17:7** = Testing [B] **17:7** = Quarreling [C] **17:8** A seminomadic people descended from *Amalek*, a grandson of Esau; Gn 36:12 [D] **17:11** Sam, LXX, Syr, Tg, Vg read *hands* [E] **17:13** Or *people* [F] **17:15** = *Yahweh-nissi* [G] **17:16** Or *hand was on*, or *hand was against*; Hb obscure [H] **18:3** In Hb the name *Gershom* sounds like the phrase "a stranger there." [I] **18:4** = My God Is Help [J] **18:7** Lit *other about well-being* [K] **18:11** Hb obscure

> *You will certainly wear out both yourself and these people who are with you, because the task is too heavy for you. You can't do it alone. . . . In this way you will lighten your load, and they will bear it with you. If you do this, and God so directs you, you will be able to endure, and also all these people will be able to go home satisfied.*
>
> *—Exodus 18:18, 22-23*

laws, and teach them the way to live and what they must do. 21 But you should select from all the people able men, God-fearing, trustworthy, and hating dishonest profit. Place them over the people as commanders of thousands, hundreds, fifties, and tens. 22 They should judge the people at all times. Then they can bring you every major case but judge every minor case themselves. In this way you will lighten your load,[A] and they will bear it with you. 23 If you do this, and God so directs you, you will be able to endure, and also all these people will be able to go home satisfied."[B]

24 Moses listened to his father-in-law and did everything he said. 25 So Moses chose able men from all Israel and made them leaders over the people as commanders of thousands, hundreds, fifties, and tens. 26 They judged the people at all times; they would bring the hard cases to Moses, but they would judge every minor case themselves.

27 Moses let his father-in-law go, and he journeyed to his own land.

ISRAEL AT SINAI

19 In the third month from the very day the Israelites left the land of Egypt, they came to the Sinai Wilderness. 2 They traveled from Rephidim, came to the Sinai Wilderness, and camped in the wilderness. Israel camped there in front of the mountain.

3 Moses went up the mountain to God, and the LORD called to him from the mountain: "This is what you must say to the house of Jacob and explain to the Israelites: 4 'You have seen what I did to the Egyptians and how I carried you on eagles' wings and brought you to myself. 5 Now if you will carefully listen to me and keep my covenant, you will be my own possession out of all the peoples, although the whole earth is mine, 6 and you will be my kingdom of priests and my holy nation.' These are the words that you are to say to the Israelites."

7 After Moses came back, he summoned the elders of the people and set before them all these words that the LORD had commanded him. 8 Then all the people responded together, "We will do all that the LORD has spoken." So Moses brought the people's words back to the LORD.

9 The LORD said to Moses, "I am going to come to you in a dense cloud, so that the people will hear when I speak with you and will always believe you." Moses reported the people's words to the LORD, 10 and the LORD told Moses, "Go to the people and consecrate them today and tomorrow. They must wash their clothes 11 and be prepared by the third day, for on the third day the LORD will come down on Mount Sinai in the sight of all the people. 12 Put boundaries for the people all around the mountain and say: Be careful that you don't go up on the mountain or touch its base. Anyone who touches the mountain must be put to death. 13 No hand may touch him;[C] instead he will be stoned or shot with arrows and not live, whether animal or human. When the ram's horn sounds a long blast, they may go up the mountain."

14 Then Moses came down from the mountain to the people and consecrated them, and they washed their clothes. 15 He said to the people, "Be prepared by the third day. Do not have sexual relations with women."

16 On the third day, when morning came, there was thunder and lightning, a thick cloud on the mountain, and a very loud trumpet sound, so that all the people in the camp shuddered. 17 Then Moses brought the people out of the camp to meet God, and they stood at the foot of the mountain. 18 Mount Sinai was completely enveloped in smoke because the LORD came down on it in fire. Its smoke went up like the smoke of a furnace, and the whole

[A] **18:22** Lit *lighten from on you* [B] **18:23** Lit *go to their place in peace* [C] **19:13** Or *it*

mountain shook violently. 19 As the sound of
the trumpet grew louder and louder, Moses
spoke and God answered him in the thunder.
20 The LORD came down on Mount Sinai at the
top of the mountain. Then the LORD summoned
Moses to the top of the mountain, and he went
up. 21 The LORD directed Moses, "Go down and
warn the people not to break through to see
the LORD; otherwise many of them will die.
22 Even the priests who come near the LORD
must consecrate themselves, or the LORD will
break out in anger against them."
23 Moses responded to the LORD, "The people
cannot come up Mount Sinai, since you warned
us: Put a boundary around the mountain and
consecrate it." 24 And the LORD replied to him,
"Go down and come back with Aaron. But the
priests and the people must not break through
to come up to the LORD, or he will break out in
anger against them." 25 So Moses went down
to the people and told them.

THE TEN COMMANDMENTS

20 Then God spoke all these words:
2 I am the LORD your God, who
brought you out of the land of Egypt,
out of the place of slavery.
3 Do not have other gods besides me.
4 Do not make an idol for yourself,
whether in the shape of anything in the
heavens above or on the earth below
or in the waters under the earth. 5 Do
not bow in worship to them, and do
not serve them; for I, the LORD your
God, am a jealous God, punishing the
children for the fathers' iniquity, to the
third and fourth generations of those
who hate me, 6 but showing faithful
love to a thousand generations of those
who love me and keep my commands.
7 Do not misuse the name of the LORD
your God, because the LORD will not
leave anyone unpunished who misuses
his name.
8 Remember the Sabbath day, to keep it
holy: 9 You are to labor six days and do
all your work, 10 but the seventh day is
a Sabbath to the LORD your God. You
must not do any work — you, your
son or daughter, your male or female
servant, your livestock, or the resident
alien who is within your city gates.
11 For the LORD made the heavens and
the earth, the sea, and everything in
them in six days; then he rested on
the seventh day. Therefore the LORD
blessed the Sabbath day and declared it
holy.
12 Honor your father and your mother so
that you may have a long life in the land
that the LORD your God is giving you.
13 Do not murder.

Rest and Reflection | *Observing Sabbath*

HOLY DAY

"Remember the Sabbath day, to keep it holy: You are to labor six days and do all your work, but the seventh day is a Sabbath to the LORD your God. You must not do any work." Exodus 20:8-10

The physical reason for practicing Sabbath would seem to be this: We are finite and have limits. We weren't designed to grind 24/7/365, year after year. If we don't rest, we will eventually wear out and burn out.

The spiritual reason for observing Sabbath would seem to be this: Human nature is prideful. We can become self-important. If we are not vigilant and don't resist, we will buy the lie that life (success, sustenance, security, and so forth) is utterly contingent on our efforts. Therefore, we need the jarring peace of Sabbath—knowing that even when we go off duty, God is still in control. The world won't end, and God's grace and provision won't stop just because we take a needed break.

Experiment with the spiritual discipline of Sabbath this week. But be forewarned: stopping and resisting the compulsion to *do* takes as much faith as any other habit in the Christian life.

For the next note on *Rest and Reflection*, see Numbers 6:24-26.

14 Do not commit adultery.
15 Do not steal.
16 Do not give false testimony against
your neighbor.
17 Do not covet your neighbor's house. Do
not covet your neighbor's wife, his male
or female servant, his ox or donkey, or
anything that belongs to your neighbor.

THE PEOPLE'S REACTION

18 All the people witnessed[A] the thunder and
lightning, the sound of the trumpet, and the
mountain surrounded by smoke. When the
people saw it[B] they trembled and stood at a
distance. 19 "You speak to us, and we will listen," they said to Moses, "but don't let God
speak to us, or we will die."
20 Moses responded to the people, "Don't be
afraid, for God has come to test you, so that you
will fear him and will not[C] sin." 21 And the people remained standing at a distance as Moses
approached the total darkness where God was.

MOSES RECEIVES ADDITIONAL LAWS

22 Then the LORD told Moses, "This is what you
are to say to the Israelites: You have seen that
I have spoken to you from heaven. 23 Do not
make gods of silver to rival me; do not make
gods of gold for yourselves.
24 "Make an earthen altar for me, and sacrifice on it your burnt offerings and fellowship
offerings, your flocks and herds. I will come to
you and bless you in every place where I cause
my name to be remembered. 25 If you make a
stone altar for me, do not build it out of cut
stones. If you use your chisel on it, you will
defile it. 26 Do not go up to my altar on steps,
so that your nakedness is not exposed on it.

21 "These are the ordinances that you are
to set before them:

LAWS ABOUT SLAVES

2 "When you buy a Hebrew slave, he is to serve
for six years; then in the seventh he is to leave
as a free man[D] without paying anything. 3 If
he arrives alone, he is to leave alone; if he
arrives with[E] a wife, his wife is to leave with
him. 4 If his master gives him a wife and she
bears him sons or daughters, the wife and her
children belong to her master, and the man
must leave alone.
5 "But if the slave declares, 'I love my master,
my wife, and my children; I do not want to
leave as a free man,' 6 his master is to bring

Relationships | *Relating to Parents*

MOM AND DAD

"Honor your father and your mother so that you may have a long life in the land that the LORD your God is giving you." Exodus 20:12

Say the words "mom" or "dad" to some folks, and they light up with joy. Mention the subject of "parents" to others, and they sigh and hang their heads.

Are any realities as mysterious or tricky as parent-child relationships? One day our parents are putting diapers on us and trying to make sense of our gibberish. In no time at all, the situation is exactly reversed. The kids have become the caretakers.

Because we don't get to choose our parents and since we can't change them—no matter how hard we try—and because few relationships can cause as much joy or trigger as much pain, this command is especially critical.

"Honor your father and your mother." The verb *honor* conveys the sense of "being heavy." The idea is to respect one's parents, to treat them as weighty, significant, and important—in short, to value them.

To respect someone is far easier, of course, when that person is acting respectably. But God can give us the grace to show respect regardless of how a parent is acting.

For the next note on *Relationships*, see Exodus 23:1.

[A] **20:18** Lit *saw* [B] **20:18** Sam, LXX, Syr, Tg, Vg read *smoke. The people* (or *they*) *were afraid,* [C] **20:20** Lit *that the fear of him may be in you, and you do not* [D] **21:2** Lit *to go forth* [E] **21:3** Lit *he is the husband of*

him to the judges[A] and then bring him to the
door or doorpost. His master will pierce his
ear with an awl, and he will serve his master for life.
7 "When a man sells his daughter as a concubine,[B] she is not to leave as the male slaves
do. 8 If she is displeasing to her master, who
chose her for himself, then he must let her
be redeemed. He has no right to sell her to
foreigners because he has acted treacherously toward her. 9 Or if he chooses her for
his son, he must deal with her according to
the customary treatment of daughters. 10 If he
takes an additional wife, he must not reduce
the food, clothing, or marital rights of the
first wife. 11 And if he does not do these three
things for her, she may leave free of charge,
without any payment.[C]

LAWS ABOUT PERSONAL INJURY

12 "Whoever strikes a person so that he dies
must be put to death. 13 But if he did not intend any harm,[D] and yet God allowed it to
happen, I will appoint a place for you where
he may flee. 14 If a person schemes and willfully[E] acts against his neighbor to murder
him, you must take him from my altar to be
put to death.
15 "Whoever strikes his father or his mother
must be put to death.
16 "Whoever kidnaps a person must be put
to death, whether he sells him or the person
is found in his possession.
17 "Whoever curses his father or his mother
must be put to death.
18 "When men quarrel and one strikes the
other with a stone or his fist, and the injured
man does not die but is confined to bed, 19 if
he can later get up and walk around outside
leaning on his staff, then the one who struck
him will be exempt from punishment. Nevertheless, he must pay for his lost work time[F]
and provide for his complete recovery.
20 "When a man strikes his male or female
slave with a rod, and the slave dies under his
abuse,[G] the owner must be punished.[H] 21 However, if the slave can stand up after a day or
two, the owner should not be punished[I] because he is his owner's property.[J]
22 "When men get in a fight and hit a pregnant
woman so that her children are born prematurely but there is no injury, the one who hit
her must be fined as the woman's husband demands from him, and he must pay according to
judicial assessment. 23 If there is an injury, then
you must give life for life, 24 eye for eye, tooth

Other-centeredness | *Avoiding Jealousy/Coveting*

CONTENTMENT

"Do not covet your neighbor's house. Do not covet your neighbor's wife, his male or female servant, his ox or donkey, or anything that belongs to your neighbor." Exodus 20:17

Covet isn't a word we use much anymore in daily conversation; however, it is an action we're tempted to do all the time! To covet means "to strongly desire" or even to lust after (and not just in a sexual way). The idea is that we see something attractive and delightful—a neighbor's new house (or spouse), a friend's lifestyle or summer vacation plans, someone's great new job or luxurious new car—and we begin daydreaming and fantasizing about having that thing for ourselves. It's not enough to appreciate it—we have to *acquire* it.

Obviously one way to tamp down the tendency to covet is to resist the deadly lure of comparing one's life with others. Another way is to practice contentment. Instead of listening to advertisers, whose objective is to get us to fixate on all the things we don't have, we flip the script. We focus on the gifts God has given us and give thanks. Instead of lusting, we spend time "listing" (our blessings). Instead of resentment, we rejoice.

For the next note on *Other-centeredness*, see Leviticus 19:10.

[A] **21:6** Or *to God*; that is, to his sanctuary or court [B] **21:7** Or *servant* [C] **21:11** She doesn't have to pay any redemption price. [D] **21:13** Lit *he was not lying in wait* [E] **21:14** Or *maliciously* [F] **21:19** Lit *his inactivity* [G] **21:20** Lit *hand* [H] **21:20** Or *must suffer vengeance* [I] **21:21** Or *not suffer vengeance* [J] **21:21** Lit *silver*

for tooth, hand for hand, foot for foot, 25 burn
for burn, bruise for bruise, wound for wound.
26 "When a man strikes the eye of his male
or female slave and destroys it, he must let
the slave go free in compensation for his eye.
27 If he knocks out the tooth of his male or
female slave, he must let the slave go free in
compensation for his tooth.
28 "When an ox[A] gores a man or a woman to death, the ox must be stoned, and its
meat may not be eaten, but the ox's owner is innocent. 29 However, if the ox was in
the habit of goring, and its owner has been
warned yet does not restrain it, and it kills
a man or a woman, the ox must be stoned,
and its owner must also be put to death. 30 If
instead a ransom is demanded of him, he
can pay a redemption price for his life in
the full amount demanded from him. 31 If it
gores a son or a daughter, he is to be dealt
with according to this same law. 32 If the ox
gores a male or female slave, he must give
thirty shekels of silver[B] to the slave's master,
and the ox must be stoned.
33 "When a man uncovers a pit or digs a pit,
and does not cover it, and an ox or a donkey
falls into it, 34 the owner of the pit must give
compensation; he must pay to its owner, but
the dead animal will become his.
35 "When a man's ox injures his neighbor's
ox and it dies, they must sell the live ox and
divide its proceeds; they must also divide
the dead animal. 36 If, however, it is known
that the ox was in the habit of goring, yet its
owner has not restrained it, he must compensate fully, ox for ox; the dead animal will
become his.

LAWS ABOUT THEFT

22 "When a man steals an ox or a sheep and
butchers it or sells it, he must repay five
cattle for the ox or four sheep for the sheep.
2 If a thief is caught in the act of breaking in,
and he is beaten to death, no one is guilty of
bloodshed. 3 But if this happens after sunrise,
the householder is guilty of bloodshed. A thief
must make full restitution. If he is unable,
he is to be sold because of his theft. 4 If what
was stolen — whether ox, donkey, or sheep
— is actually found alive in his possession,
he must repay double.

LAWS ABOUT CROP PROTECTION

5 "When a man lets a field or vineyard be grazed
in, and then allows his animals to go and graze
in someone else's field, he must repay[C] with
the best of his own field or vineyard.
6 "When a fire gets out of control, spreads
to thornbushes, and consumes stacks of cut
grain, standing grain, or a field, the one who
started the fire must make full restitution for
what was burned.

LAWS ABOUT PERSONAL PROPERTY

7 "When a man gives his neighbor valuables[D]
or goods to keep, but they are stolen from
that person's house, the thief, if caught, must
repay double. 8 If the thief is not caught, the
owner of the house must present himself to
the judges[E] to determine[F] whether or not he
has taken his neighbor's property. 9 In any
case of wrongdoing involving an ox, a donkey, a sheep, a garment, or anything else lost,
and someone claims, 'That's mine,'[G] the case
between the two parties is to come before the
judges.[H] The one the judges condemn[I] must
repay double to his neighbor.
10 "When a man gives his neighbor a donkey,
an ox, a sheep, or any other animal to care
for, but it dies, is injured, or is stolen, while
no one is watching, 11 there must be an oath
before the LORD between the two of them to
determine whether or not he has taken his
neighbor's property. Its owner must accept
the oath, and the other man does not have to
make restitution. 12 But if, in fact, the animal
was stolen from his custody, he must make
restitution to its owner. 13 If it was actually
torn apart by a wild animal, he is to bring it
as evidence; he does not have to make restitution for the torn carcass.
14 "When a man borrows an animal from his
neighbor, and it is injured or dies while its owner is not there with it, the man must make full
restitution. 15 If its owner is there with it, the
man does not have to make restitution. If it was
rented, the loss is covered by[J] its rental price.

LAWS ABOUT SEDUCTION

16 "If a man seduces a virgin who is not engaged,
and he sleeps with her, he must certainly pay
the bridal price for her to be his wife. 17 If her
father absolutely refuses to give her to him,

[A] **21:28** Or *a bull*, or *a steer* [B] **21:32** About one pound of silver [C] **22:5** LXX adds *from his field according to its produce. But if someone lets his animals graze an entire field, he must repay*; DSS, Sam also support this reading. [D] **22:7** Lit *silver* [E] **22:8** Or *to God* [F] **22:8** LXX, Tg, Vg read *swear* [G] **22:9** Lit *That is it* [H] **22:9** Or *before God* [I] **22:9** Or *one whom God condemns* [J] **22:15** Lit *rented, it comes with*

he must pay an amount in silver equal to the bridal price for virgins.

CAPITAL OFFENSES

18 "Do not allow a sorceress to live.

19 "Whoever has sexual intercourse with an animal must be put to death.

20 "Whoever sacrifices to any gods, except the LORD alone, is to be set apart for destruction.

LAWS PROTECTING THE VULNERABLE

21 "You must not exploit a resident alien or oppress him, since you were resident aliens in the land of Egypt.

22 "You must not mistreat any widow or fatherless child. 23 If you do mistreat them, they will no doubt cry to me, and I will certainly hear their cry. 24 My anger will burn, and I will kill you with the sword; then your wives will be widows and your children fatherless.

25 "If you lend silver to my people, to the poor person among you, you must not be like a creditor to him; you must not charge him interest.

26 "If you ever take your neighbor's cloak as collateral, return it to him before sunset. 27 For it is his only covering; it is the clothing for his body.[A] What will he sleep in? And if he cries out to me, I will listen because I am gracious.

RESPECT FOR GOD

28 "You must not blaspheme God[B] or curse a leader among your people.

29 "You must not hold back offerings from your harvest or your vats. Give me the firstborn of your sons. 30 Do the same with your cattle and your flock. Let them stay with their mothers for seven days, but on the eighth day you are to give them to me.

31 "Be my holy people. You must not eat the meat of a mauled animal found in the field; throw it to the dogs.

LAWS ABOUT HONESTY AND JUSTICE

23 "You must not spread a false report. Do not join[C] the wicked to be a malicious witness.

2 "You must not follow a crowd in wrongdoing. Do not testify in a lawsuit and go along with a crowd to pervert justice. 3 Do not show favoritism to a poor person in his lawsuit.

4 "If you come across your enemy's stray ox or donkey, you must return it to him.

5 "If you see the donkey of someone who hates you lying helpless under its load, and

Relationships | *Telling the Truth*

TRUTH-TELLERS

"Do not give false testimony against your neighbor." Exodus 20:16

"You must not spread a false report. Do not join the wicked to be a malicious witness." Exodus 23:1

To be mostly honest is easy. For example, a situation can involve one hundred facts, and we can tell ninety-eight of them. We haven't actually lied. But by conveniently omitting two small but relevant details, we have created a narrative that conveys the wrong impression. Perhaps in so doing, we have made someone else appear slightly less honorable and cast ourselves in a better light. In effect, we have been untruthful without technically telling a lie. We have conveyed a "false report."

The Bible declares that the Lord is the "God of truth" (Is 65:16) who is "abounding in" truth (Ex 34:6), and who—in love—"rejoices in the truth" (1Co 13:6). We should not be surprised then to read here that God calls his people to be truthful.

How are you in this regard? Ask God for help in developing a relentless commitment to truth telling—even when it costs you. Having a bruised ego is far better than a guilty conscience and a reputation as a liar.

For the next note on *Relationships*, see Leviticus 6:2-5.

[A] **22:27** Lit *skin* [B] **22:28** Or *judges* [C] **23:1** Lit *join hands with*

you want to refrain from helping it, you must
help with it.[A]
6 "You must not deny justice to a poor person
among you in his lawsuit. 7 Stay far away from
a false accusation. Do not kill the innocent and
the just, because I will not justify the guilty.
8 You must not take a bribe, for a bribe blinds
the clear-sighted and corrupts the words[B] of
the righteous. 9 You must not oppress a resident
alien; you yourselves know how it feels to be
a resident alien because you were resident
aliens in the land of Egypt.

SABBATHS AND FESTIVALS

10 "Sow your land for six years and gather its
produce. 11 But during the seventh year you
are to let it rest and leave it uncultivated, so
that the poor among your people may eat from
it and the wild animals may consume what
they leave. Do the same with your vineyard
and your olive grove.
12 "Do your work for six days but rest on the
seventh day so that your ox and your donkey
may rest, and the son of your female slave as
well as the resident alien may be refreshed.
13 "Pay strict attention to everything I have
said to you. You must not invoke the names
of other gods; they must not be heard on your
lips.[C]
14 "Celebrate a festival in my honor three times
a year. 15 Observe the Festival of Unleavened
Bread. As I commanded you, you are to eat unleavened bread for seven days at the appointed
time in the month of Abib,[D] because you came
out of Egypt in that month. No one is to appear
before me empty-handed. 16 Also observe the
Festival of Harvest[E] with the firstfruits of your
produce from what you sow in the field, and
observe the Festival of Ingathering[F] at the end
of the year, when you gather your produce[G]
from the field. 17 Three times a year all your
males are to appear before the Lord GOD.
18 "You must not offer the blood of my sacrifices with anything leavened. The fat of my festival offering must not remain until morning.
19 "Bring the best of the firstfruits of your
land to the house of the LORD your God.
"You must not boil a young goat in its mother's milk.

PROMISES AND WARNINGS

20 "I am going to send an angel before you to
protect you on the way and bring you to the
place I have prepared. 21 Be attentive to him
and listen to him. Do not defy him, because
he will not forgive your acts of rebellion, for
my name is in him. 22 But if you will carefully
obey him and do everything I say, then I will
be an enemy to your enemies and a foe to
your foes. 23 For my angel will go before you
and bring you to the land of the Amorites,
Hethites, Perizzites, Canaanites, Hivites, and
Jebusites, and I will wipe them out. 24 Do not
bow in worship to their gods, and do not
serve them. Do not imitate their practices.
Instead, demolish them[H] and smash their
sacred pillars to pieces. 25 Serve the LORD
your God, and he[I] will bless your bread and
your water. I will remove illnesses from you.
26 No woman will miscarry or be childless
in your land. I will give you the full number
of your days.
27 "I will cause the people ahead of you to
feel terror[J] and will throw into confusion all
the nations you come to. I will make all your
enemies turn their backs to you in retreat.[K]
28 I will send hornets[L] in front of you, and they
will drive the Hivites, Canaanites, and Hethites
away from you. 29 I will not drive them out
ahead of you in a single year; otherwise, the
land would become desolate, and wild animals
would multiply against you. 30 I will drive them
out little by little ahead of you until you have
become numerous[M] and take possession of
the land. 31 I will set your borders from the Red
Sea to the Mediterranean Sea,[N] and from the
wilderness to the Euphrates River.[O] For I will
place the inhabitants of the land under your
control, and you will drive them out ahead
of you. 32 You must not make a covenant with
them or their gods. 33 They must not remain
in your land, or else they will make you sin
against me. If you serve their gods, it will be
a snare for you."

THE COVENANT CEREMONY

24 Then he said to Moses, "Go up to the
LORD, you and Aaron, Nadab, and Abihu, and seventy of Israel's elders, and bow

[A] 23:5 Or *load, you must refrain from leaving it to him; you must set it free with him* [B] 23:8 Or *and subverts the cause* [C] 23:13 Lit *mouth* [D] 23:15 March–April; called Nisan in the post-exilic period; Neh 2:1; Est 3:7 [E] 23:16 The *Festival of Harvest* is called Festival of Weeks elsewhere; Ex 34:22. In the NT it is called Pentecost; Ac 2:1. [F] 23:16 The *Festival of Ingathering* is called Festival of Shelters elsewhere; Lv 23:34-36. [G] 23:16 Lit *labors* [H] 23:24 Probably the idols [I] 23:25 LXX, Vg read *I* [J] 23:27 Lit *will send terror of me ahead of you* [K] 23:27 Or *I will give your enemies to you by the neck* [L] 23:28 Or *send panic* [M] 23:30 Lit *fruitful* [N] 23:31 Lit *the Sea of the Philistines* [O] 23:31 Lit *the River*

gold rings and attach them to the bottom of the ephod's two shoulder pieces on its front, close to its seam,[A] and above the ephod's woven waistband. 28 The artisans are to tie the breastpiece from its rings to the rings of the ephod with a cord of blue yarn, so that the breastpiece is above the ephod's waistband and does not come loose from the ephod.

29 "Whenever he enters the sanctuary, Aaron is to carry the names of Israel's sons over his heart on the breastpiece for decisions, as a continual reminder before the LORD. 30 Place the Urim and Thummim in the breastpiece for decisions, so that they will also be over Aaron's heart whenever he comes before the LORD. Aaron will continually carry the means of decisions for the Israelites over his heart before the LORD.

THE ROBE

31 "You are to make the robe of the ephod entirely of blue yarn. 32 There should be an opening at its top in the center of it. Around the opening, there should be a woven collar with an opening like that of body armor[B] so that it does not tear. 33 Make pomegranates of blue, purple, and scarlet yarn on its lower hem and all around it. Put gold bells between them all the way around, 34 so that gold bells and pomegranates alternate around the lower hem of the robe. 35 The robe will be worn by Aaron whenever he ministers, and its sound will be heard when he enters the sanctuary before the LORD and when he exits, so that he does not die.

THE TURBAN

36 "You are to make a pure gold medallion and engrave it, like the engraving of a seal: HOLY TO THE LORD. 37 Fasten it to a cord of blue yarn so it can be placed on the turban; the medallion is to be on the front of the turban. 38 It will be on Aaron's forehead so that Aaron may bear the guilt connected with the holy offerings that the Israelites consecrate as all their holy gifts. It is always to be on his forehead, so that they may find acceptance with the LORD.

OTHER PRIESTLY GARMENTS

39 "You are to weave the tunic from fine linen, make a turban of fine linen, and make an embroidered sash. 40 Make tunics, sashes, and headbands for Aaron's sons to give them glory and beauty. 41 Put these on your brother Aaron and his sons; then anoint, ordain,[C] and consecrate them, so that they may serve me as priests. 42 Make them linen undergarments to cover their naked bodies; they must extend from the waist to the thighs. 43 These must be worn by Aaron and his sons whenever they enter the tent of meeting or approach the altar to minister in the sanctuary area, so that they do not incur guilt and die. This is to be a permanent statute for Aaron and for his future descendants.

INSTRUCTIONS ABOUT CONSECRATION

29 "This is what you are to do for them to consecrate them to serve me as priests. Take a young bull and two unblemished rams, 2 with unleavened bread, unleavened cakes mixed with oil, and unleavened wafers coated with oil. Make them out of fine wheat flour, 3 put them in a basket, and bring them in the basket, along with the bull and two rams. 4 Bring Aaron and his sons to the entrance to the tent of meeting and wash them with water. 5 Then take the garments and clothe Aaron with the tunic, the robe for the ephod, the ephod itself, and the breastpiece; fasten the ephod on him with its woven waistband. 6 Put the turban on his head and place the holy diadem on the turban. 7 Take the anointing oil, pour it on his head, and anoint him. 8 You must also bring his sons and clothe them with tunics. 9 Tie the sashes on Aaron and his sons and fasten headbands on them. The priesthood is to be theirs by a permanent statute. This is the way you will ordain Aaron and[D] his sons.

10 "You are to bring the bull to the front of the tent of meeting, and Aaron and his sons must lay their hands on the bull's head. 11 Slaughter the bull before the LORD at the entrance to the tent of meeting. 12 Take some of the bull's blood and apply it to the horns of the altar with your finger; then pour out all the rest of the blood at the base of the altar. 13 Take all the fat that covers the entrails, the fatty lobe of the liver, and the two kidneys with the fat on them, and burn them on the altar. 14 But burn the bull's flesh, its hide, and its waste outside the camp; it is a sin offering.

15 "Take one ram, and Aaron and his sons are to lay their hands on the ram's head. 16 You are to slaughter the ram, take its blood, and splatter it on all sides of the altar. 17 Cut

---

[A] **28:27** The place where the *shoulder pieces* join the front of the ephod [B] **28:32** Hb obscure [C] **28:41** Lit *anoint them, fill their hand* [D] **29:9** Lit *you will fill the hand of Aaron and the hand of*; Ex 29:23-24

the ram into pieces. Wash its entrails and
legs, and place them with its head and its
pieces on the altar. 18 Then burn the whole
ram on the altar; it is a burnt offering to the
LORD. It is a pleasing aroma, a fire offering
to the LORD.
19 "You are to take the second ram, and Aaron and his sons must lay their hands on the
ram's head. 20 Slaughter the ram, take some of
its blood, and put it on Aaron's right earlobe,
on his sons' right earlobes, on the thumbs of
their right hands, and on the big toes of their
right feet. Splatter the remaining blood on all
sides of the altar. 21 Take some of the blood that
is on the altar and some of the anointing oil,
and sprinkle them on Aaron and his garments,
as well as on his sons and their garments. So
he and his garments will be holy, as well as
his sons and their garments.
22 "Take the fat from the ram, the fat tail,
the fat covering the entrails, the fatty lobe
of the liver, the two kidneys and the fat on
them, and the right thigh (since this is a ram
for ordination[A]); 23 take one loaf of bread, one
cake of bread made with oil, and one wafer
from the basket of unleavened bread that is
before the LORD; 24 and put all of them in the
hands of Aaron and his[B] sons and present
them as a presentation offering before the
LORD. 25 Take them from their hands and burn
them on the altar on top of the burnt offering,
as a pleasing aroma before the LORD; it is a
fire offering to the LORD.
26 "Take the breast from the ram of Aaron's
ordination and present it as a presentation
offering before the LORD; it is to be your portion. 27 Consecrate for Aaron and his sons
the breast of the presentation offering that
is presented and the thigh of the contribution
that is lifted up from the ram of ordination.
28 This will belong to Aaron and his sons as a
regular portion from the Israelites, for it is a
contribution. It will be the Israelites' contribution from their fellowship sacrifices, their
contribution to the LORD.
29 "The holy garments that belong to Aaron
are to belong to his sons after him, so that
they can be anointed and ordained[C] in them.
30 Any priest who is one of his sons and who
succeeds him and enters the tent of meeting
to minister in the sanctuary must wear them
for seven days.
31 "You are to take the ram of ordination and
boil its flesh in a holy place. 32 Aaron and his
sons are to eat the meat of the ram and the
bread that is in the basket at the entrance to
the tent of meeting. 33 They must eat those
things by which atonement was made at the
time of their ordination[D] and consecration.
An unauthorized person must not eat them,
for these things are holy. 34 If any of the meat
of ordination or any of the bread is left until
morning, burn what is left over. It must not
be eaten because it is holy.
35 "This is what you are to do for Aaron and
his sons based on all I have commanded you.
Take seven days to ordain them. 36 Sacrifice a
bull as a sin offering each day for atonement.
Purify[E] the altar when you make atonement
for it, and anoint it in order to consecrate it.
37 For seven days you must make atonement
for the altar and consecrate it. The altar will
be especially holy. Whatever touches the altar
will be consecrated.
38 "This is what you are to offer regularly on
the altar every day: two year-old lambs. 39 In the
morning offer one lamb, and at twilight offer
the other lamb. 40 With the first lamb offer two
quarts[F] of fine flour mixed with one quart[G] of
oil from crushed olives, and a drink offering of
one quart of wine. 41 You are to offer the second
lamb at twilight. Offer a grain offering and a
drink offering with it, like the one in the morning, as a pleasing aroma, a fire offering to the
LORD. 42 This will be a regular burnt offering
throughout your generations at the entrance
to the tent of meeting before the LORD, where
I will meet you[H] to speak with you. 43 I will also
meet with the Israelites there, and that place

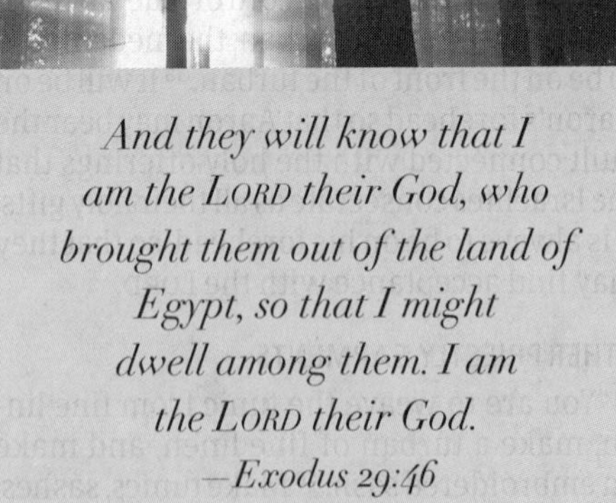
And they will know that I am the LORD their God, who brought them out of the land of Egypt, so that I might dwell among them. I am the LORD their God.
—*Exodus 29:46*

[A] **29:22** The priest would normally receive the right thigh to be eaten, but here it is burned; Lv 7:32-34. [B] **29:24** Lit *in the hands of his* [C] **29:29** Lit *him for anointing in them and for filling their hand* [D] **29:33** Lit *made to fill their hand* [E] **29:36** Or *Make a sin offering on* [F] **29:40** Lit *offer a tenth* [G] **29:40** Lit *a fourth of a hin* [H] **29:42** = Moses

will be consecrated by my glory. 44 I will consecrate the tent of meeting and the altar; I will
also consecrate Aaron and his sons to serve me
as priests. 45 I will dwell among the Israelites
and be their God. 46 And they will know that
I am the LORD their God, who brought them
out of the land of Egypt, so that I might dwell
among them. I am the LORD their God.

THE INCENSE ALTAR

30 "You are to make an altar for the burning of incense; make it of acacia wood.
2 It must be square, eighteen inches long and
eighteen inches wide;[A] it must be thirty-six
inches high.[B] Its horns must be of one piece
with it. 3 Overlay its top, all around its sides,
and its horns with pure gold; make a gold
molding all around it. 4 Make two gold rings
for it under the molding on two of its sides;
put these on opposite sides of it to be holders
for the poles to carry it with. 5 Make the poles
of acacia wood and overlay them with gold.
6 "You are to place the altar in front of the
curtain by the ark of the testimony — in front
of the mercy seat that is over the testimony
— where I will meet with you. 7 Aaron must
burn fragrant incense on it; he must burn it every morning when he tends the lamps. 8 When
Aaron sets up the lamps at twilight, he must
burn incense. There is to be an incense offering
before the LORD throughout your generations.
9 You must not offer unauthorized incense on
it, or a burnt or grain offering; you are not to
pour a drink offering on it.
10 "Once a year Aaron is to perform the atonement ceremony for the altar. Throughout your
generations he is to perform the atonement
ceremony for[C] it once a year, with the blood of
the sin offering for atonement on the horns.
The altar is especially holy to the LORD."

THE ATONEMENT MONEY

11 The LORD spoke to Moses: 12 "When you take
a census of the Israelites to register them,
each of the men must pay a ransom for his
life to the LORD as they are registered. Then
no plague will come on them as they are registered. 13 Everyone who is registered must
pay half a shekel[D] according to the sanctuary
shekel (twenty gerahs to the shekel). This half
shekel is a contribution to the LORD. 14 Each
man who is registered, twenty years old or
more, must give this contribution to the LORD.
15 The wealthy may not give more and the poor
may not give less than half a shekel when giving the contribution to the LORD to atone for[E]
your lives. 16 Take the atonement price[F] from
the Israelites and use it for the service of the
tent of meeting. It will serve as a reminder
for the Israelites before the LORD to atone
for your lives."

THE BRONZE BASIN

17 The LORD spoke to Moses: 18 "Make a bronze
basin for washing and a bronze stand for it. Set
it between the tent of meeting and the altar,
and put water in it. 19 Aaron and his sons must
wash their hands and feet from the basin.
20 Whenever they enter the tent of meeting
or approach the altar to minister by burning
an offering to the LORD, they must wash with
water so that they will not die. 21 They must
wash their hands and feet so that they will not
die; this is to be a permanent statute for them,
for Aaron and his descendants throughout
their generations."

THE ANOINTING OIL

22 The LORD spoke to Moses: 23 "Take for yourself the finest spices: 12 ½ pounds[G] of liquid
myrrh, half as much (6 ¼ pounds[H]) of fragrant
cinnamon, 6 ¼ pounds of fragrant cane, 24 12 ½
pounds of cassia (by the sanctuary shekel), and
a gallon[I] of olive oil. 25 Prepare from these a
holy anointing oil, a scented blend, the work
of a perfumer; it will be holy anointing oil.
26 "With it you are to anoint the tent of meeting, the ark of the testimony, 27 the table with
all its utensils, the lampstand with its utensils,
the altar of incense, 28 the altar of burnt offering with all its utensils, and the basin with its
stand. 29 Consecrate them and they will be
especially holy. Whatever touches them will
be consecrated. 30 Anoint Aaron and his sons
and consecrate them to serve me as priests.
31 "Tell the Israelites: This will be my holy
anointing oil throughout your generations.
32 It must not be used for ordinary anointing
on a person's body, and you must not make
anything like it using its formula. It is holy,
and it must be holy to you. 33 Anyone who
blends something like it or puts some of it
on an unauthorized person must be cut off
from his people."

[A] **30:2** Lit *one cubit its length and one cubit its width* [B] **30:2** Lit *wide; and two cubits its height* [C] **30:10** Or *on* [D] **30:13** A shekel is about two-fifths of an ounce of silver [E] **30:15** Or *to ransom*, also in v. 16 [F] **30:16** Lit *the silver of the atonement* [G] **30:23** Lit *500* (shekels), also in v. 24 [H] **30:23** Lit *250* (shekels) [I] **30:24** Lit *a hin*

THE SACRED INCENSE

34 The LORD said to Moses: "Take fragrant spices: stacte, onycha, and galbanum; the spices
and pure frankincense are to be in equal measures. 35 Prepare expertly blended incense from
these; it is to be seasoned with salt, pure and
holy. 36 Grind some of it into a fine powder
and put some in front of the testimony in the
tent of meeting, where I will meet with you.
It must be especially holy to you. 37 As for the
incense you are making, you must not make
any for yourselves using its formula. It is to
be regarded by you as holy — belonging to
the LORD. 38 Anyone who makes something
like it to smell its fragrance must be cut off
from his people."

GOD'S PROVISION OF THE SKILLED WORKERS

31 The LORD also spoke to Moses: 2 "Look, I
have appointed by name Bezalel son of
Uri, son of Hur, of the tribe of Judah. 3 I have
filled him with God's Spirit, with wisdom, understanding, and ability in every craft 4 to design artistic works in gold, silver, and bronze,
5 to cut gemstones for mounting, and to carve
wood for work in every craft. 6 I have also selected Oholiab[A] son of Ahisamach, of the tribe

I have appointed by name Bezalel son of Uri, son of Hur, of the tribe of Judah. I have filled him with God's Spirit, with wisdom, understanding, and ability in every craft to design artistic works in gold, silver, and bronze, to cut gemstones for mounting, and to carve wood for work in every craft. . . . I have put wisdom in the heart of every skilled artisan in order to make all that I have commanded you.

—Exodus 31:2-6

of Dan, to be with him. I have put wisdom in
the heart of every skilled artisan[B] in order
to make all that I have commanded you: 7 the
tent of meeting, the ark of the testimony, the
mercy seat that is on top of it, and all the other
furnishings of the tent — 8 the table with its
utensils, the pure gold lampstand with all its
utensils, the altar of incense, 9 the altar of burnt
offering with all its utensils, the basin with its
stand — 10 the specially woven[C] garments, both
the holy garments for the priest Aaron and
the garments for his sons to serve as priests,
11 the anointing oil, and the fragrant incense
for the sanctuary. They must make them according to all that I have commanded you."

OBSERVING THE SABBATH

12 The LORD said to Moses: 13 "Tell the Israelites: You must observe my Sabbaths, for it is
a sign between me and you throughout your
generations, so that you will know that I am
the LORD who consecrates you. 14 Observe the
Sabbath, for it is holy to you. Whoever profanes
it must be put to death. If anyone does work
on it, that person must be cut off from his
people. 15 Work may be done for six days, but
on the seventh day there must be a Sabbath
of complete rest, holy to the LORD. Anyone
who does work on the Sabbath day must be
put to death. 16 The Israelites must observe
the Sabbath, celebrating it throughout their
generations as a permanent covenant. 17 It is
a sign forever between me and the Israelites,
for in six days the LORD made the heavens and
the earth, but on the seventh day he rested
and was refreshed."

THE TWO STONE TABLETS

18 When he finished speaking with Moses on
Mount Sinai, he gave him the two tablets of
the testimony, stone tablets inscribed by the
finger of God.

THE GOLD CALF

32 When the people saw that Moses delayed in coming down from the mountain, they gathered around Aaron and said to
him, "Come, make gods[D] for us who will go
before us because this Moses, the man who
brought us up from the land of Egypt — we
don't know what has happened to him!"
2 Aaron replied to them, "Take off the gold
rings that are on the ears of your wives, your

[A] **31:6** LXX, Syr read *Eliab* [B] **31:6** Lit *everyone wise of heart* [C] **31:10** Hb obscure [D] **32:1** Or *make a god*, also in v. 23

sons, and your daughters and bring them to
me." 3 So all the people took off the gold rings
that were on their ears and brought them to
Aaron. 4 He took the gold from them, fashioned it with an engraving tool, and made it
into an image of a calf.

Then they said, "Israel, these are your gods,[A]
who brought you up from the land of Egypt!"
5 When Aaron saw this, he built an altar in
front of it and made an announcement: "There
will be a festival to the LORD tomorrow." 6 Early
the next morning they arose, offered burnt
offerings, and presented fellowship offerings. The people sat down to eat and drink,
and got up to party.

7 The LORD spoke to Moses: "Go down at
once! For your people you brought up from
the land of Egypt have acted corruptly. 8 They
have quickly turned from the way I commanded them; they have made for themselves an
image of a calf. They have bowed down to
it, sacrificed to it, and said, 'Israel, these are
your gods, who brought you up from the land
of Egypt.'" 9 The LORD also said to Moses: "I
have seen this people, and they are indeed a
stiff-necked people. 10 Now leave me alone,
so that my anger can burn against them and
I can destroy them. Then I will make you into
a great nation."

11 But Moses sought the favor of the LORD his
God: "LORD, why does your anger burn against
your people you brought out of the land of
Egypt with great power and a strong hand?
12 Why should the Egyptians say, 'He brought
them out with an evil intent to kill them in the
mountains and eliminate them from the face
of the earth'? Turn from your fierce anger
and relent concerning this disaster planned
for your people. 13 Remember your servants
Abraham, Isaac, and Israel — you swore to
them by yourself and declared, 'I will make
your offspring as numerous as the stars of the
sky and will give your offspring all this land
that I have promised, and they will inherit it
forever.'" 14 So the LORD relented concerning
the disaster he had said he would bring on
his people.

15 Then Moses turned and went down the
mountain with the two tablets of the testimony in his hands. They were inscribed on
both sides — inscribed front and back. 16 The
tablets were the work of God, and the writing
was God's writing, engraved on the tablets.

17 When Joshua heard the sound of the people as they shouted, he said to Moses, "There
is a sound of war in the camp."

18 But Moses replied:

It's not the sound of a victory cry
and not the sound of a cry of defeat;
I hear the sound of singing!

19 As he approached the camp and saw the calf
and the dancing, Moses became enraged and
threw the tablets out of his hands, smashing
them at the base of the mountain. 20 He took the
calf they had made, burned it up, and ground
it to powder. He scattered the powder over the
surface of the water and forced the Israelites
to drink the water.

21 Then Moses asked Aaron, "What did these
people do to you that you have led them into
such a grave sin?"

22 "Don't be enraged, my lord," Aaron replied.
"You yourself know that the people are intent
on evil. 23 They said to me, 'Make gods for us
who will go before us because this Moses, the
man who brought us up from the land of Egypt
— we don't know what has happened to him!'
24 So I said to them, 'Whoever has gold, take
it off,' and they gave it to me. When I threw it
into the fire, out came this calf!"

25 Moses saw that the people were out of
control, for Aaron had let them get out of
control, making them a laughingstock to
their enemies.[B] 26 And Moses stood at the
camp's entrance and said, "Whoever is for
the LORD, come to me." And all the Levites
gathered around him. 27 He told them, "This
is what the LORD, the God of Israel, says, 'Every man fasten his sword to his side; go back
and forth through the camp from entrance
to entrance, and each of you kill his brother,
his friend, and his neighbor.'" 28 The Levites
did as Moses commanded, and about three
thousand men fell dead that day among the
people. 29 Afterward Moses said, "Today you
have been dedicated[C] to the LORD, since each
man went against his son and his brother.
Therefore you have brought a blessing on
yourselves today."

30 The following day Moses said to the people, "You have committed a grave sin. Now I
will go up to the LORD; perhaps I will be able
to atone for your sin."

31 So Moses returned to the LORD and said,
"Oh, these people have committed a grave sin;
they have made a god of gold for themselves.

[A] **32:4** Or *"Israel, this is your god* or *"Israel, this is your God*, also in v. 8 [B] **32:25** Hb obscure [C] **32:29** Text emended; MT reads *"Today dedicate yourselves*; LXX, Vg read *"Today you have dedicated yourselves*

32 Now if you would only forgive their sin.
But if not, please erase me from the book you
have written."
33 The LORD replied to Moses: "Whoever
has sinned against me I will erase from my
book. 34 Now go, lead the people to the place
I told you about; see, my angel will go before
you. But on the day I settle accounts, I will
hold them accountable for their sin." 35 And
the LORD inflicted a plague on the people for
what they did with the calf Aaron had made.

THE TENT OUTSIDE THE CAMP

33 The LORD spoke to Moses: "Go up from
here, you and the people you brought
up from the land of Egypt, to the land I promised to Abraham, Isaac, and Jacob, saying:
I will give it to your offspring. 2 I will send
an angel ahead of you and will drive out the
Canaanites, Amorites, Hethites, Perizzites,[A]
Hivites, and Jebusites. 3 Go up to a land flowing with milk and honey. But I will not go
up with you because you are a stiff-necked
people; otherwise, I might destroy you on
the way." 4 When the people heard this bad
news, they mourned and didn't put on their
jewelry.
5 For the LORD said to Moses: "Tell the Israelites: You are a stiff-necked people. If I went up
with you for a single moment, I would destroy
you. Now take off your jewelry, and I will decide what to do with you." 6 So the Israelites
remained stripped of their jewelry from Mount
Horeb onward.
7 Now Moses took a tent and pitched it outside the camp, at a distance from the camp;
he called it the tent of meeting. Anyone who
wanted to consult the LORD would go to the
tent of meeting that was outside the camp.
8 Whenever Moses went out to the tent, all
the people would stand up, each one at the
door of his tent, and they would watch Moses until he entered the tent. 9 When Moses
entered the tent, the pillar of cloud would
come down and remain at the entrance to
the tent, and the LORD would speak with Moses. 10 As all the people saw the pillar of cloud
remaining at the entrance to the tent, they
would stand up, then bow in worship, each
one at the door of his tent. 11 The LORD would
speak with Moses face to face, just as a man
speaks with his friend, then Moses would
return to the camp. His assistant, the young
man Joshua son of Nun, would not leave the
inside of the tent.

THE LORD'S GLORY

12 Moses said to the LORD, "Look, you have told
me, 'Lead this people up,' but you have not let
me know whom you will send with me. You
said, 'I know you by name, and you have also
found favor with me.' 13 Now if I have indeed
found favor with you, please teach me your
ways, and I will know you, so that I may find
favor with you. Now consider that this nation
is your people."

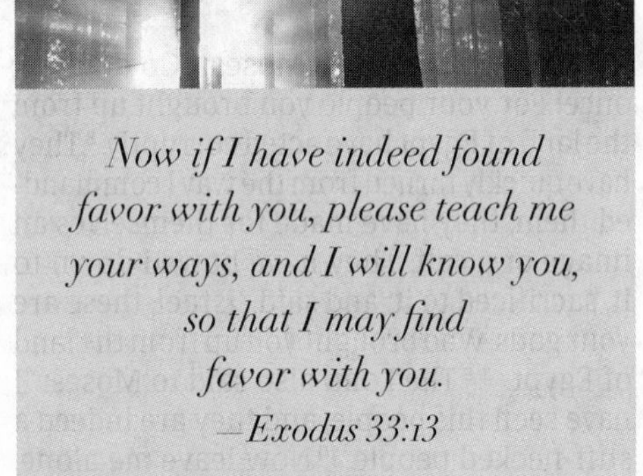
*Now if I have indeed found
favor with you, please teach me
your ways, and I will know you,
so that I may find
favor with you.*
—Exodus 33:13

14 And he replied, "My presence will go with
you, and I will give you rest."
15 "If your presence does not go," Moses responded to him, "don't make us go up from
here. 16 How will it be known that I and your
people have found favor with you unless you
go with us? I and your people will be distinguished by this from all the other people on
the face of the earth."
17 The LORD answered Moses, "I will do this
very thing you have asked, for you have found
favor with me, and I know you by name."
18 Then Moses said, "Please, let me see your
glory."
19 He said, "I will cause all my goodness to
pass in front of you, and I will proclaim the
name 'the LORD' before you. I will be gracious
to whom I will be gracious, and I will have
compassion on whom I will have compassion." 20 But he added, "You cannot see my
face, for humans cannot see me and live."
21 The LORD said, "Here is a place near me.
You are to stand on the rock, 22 and when my
glory passes by, I will put you in the crevice
of the rock and cover you with my hand until
I have passed by. 23 Then I will take my hand

[A] **33:2** Sam, LXX add *Girgashites*

away, and you will see my back, but my face
will not be seen."

NEW STONE TABLETS

34 The LORD said to Moses, "Cut two stone
tablets like the first ones, and I will
write on them the words that were on the
first tablets, which you broke. 2 Be prepared by
morning. Come up Mount Sinai in the morning and stand before me on the mountaintop.
3 No one may go up with you; in fact, no one
should be seen anywhere on the mountain.
Even the flocks and herds are not to graze in
front of that mountain."

4 Moses cut two stone tablets like the first
ones. He got up early in the morning, and
taking the two stone tablets in his hand, he
climbed Mount Sinai, just as the LORD had
commanded him.

5 The LORD came down in a cloud, stood
with him there, and proclaimed his name,
"the LORD." 6 The LORD passed in front of him
and proclaimed:

The LORD — the LORD is a compassionate and gracious God, slow to anger and
abounding in faithful love and truth,
7 maintaining faithful love to a thousand
generations, forgiving iniquity, rebellion,
and sin. But he will not leave the guilty
unpunished, bringing the fathers' iniquity on the children and grandchildren to
the third and fourth generation.

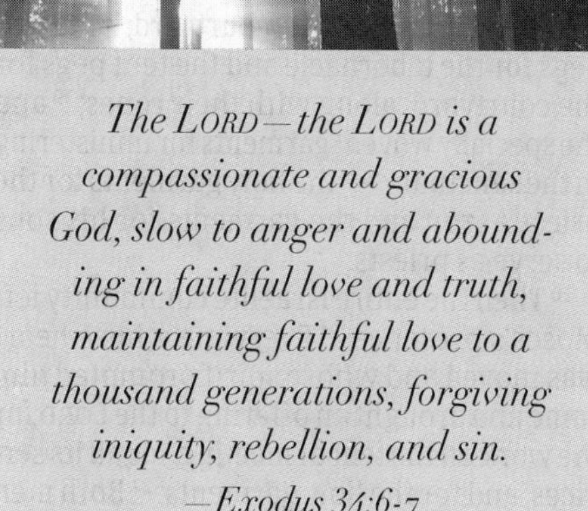
The LORD — the LORD is a compassionate and gracious God, slow to anger and abounding in faithful love and truth, maintaining faithful love to a thousand generations, forgiving iniquity, rebellion, and sin.
—Exodus 34:6-7

8 Moses immediately knelt low on the ground
and worshiped. 9 Then he said, "My Lord, if I
have indeed found favor with you, my Lord,
please go with us (even though this is a stiff-
necked people), forgive our iniquity and our
sin, and accept us as your own possession."

COVENANT OBLIGATIONS

10 And the LORD responded: "Look, I am making a covenant. I will perform wonders in the
presence of all your people that have never
been done[A] in the whole earth or in any nation. All the people you live among will see
the LORD's work, for what I am doing with you
is awe-inspiring. 11 Observe what I command
you today. I am going to drive out before you
the Amorites, Canaanites, Hethites, Perizzites,
Hivites,[B] and Jebusites. 12 Be careful not to make
a treaty with the inhabitants of the land that
you are going to enter; otherwise, they will
become a snare among you. 13 Instead, you
must tear down their altars, smash their sacred
pillars, and chop down their Asherah poles.
14 Because the LORD is jealous for his reputation, you are never to bow down to another
god.[C] He is a jealous God.

15 "Do not make a treaty with the inhabitants of the land, or else when they prostitute
themselves with their gods and sacrifice to
their gods, they will invite you, and you will
eat their sacrifices. 16 Then you will take some
of their daughters as brides for your sons.
Their daughters will prostitute themselves
with their gods and cause your sons to prostitute themselves with their gods.

17 "Do not make cast images of gods for
yourselves.

18 "Observe the Festival of Unleavened Bread.
You are to eat unleavened bread for seven
days at the appointed time in the month of
Abib,[D] as I commanded you, for you came out
of Egypt in the month of Abib.

19 "The firstborn male from every womb
belongs to me, including all your male[E,F] livestock, the firstborn of cattle or sheep. 20 You
may redeem the firstborn of a donkey with
a sheep, but if you do not redeem it, break
its neck. You must redeem all the firstborn
of your sons. No one is to appear before me
empty-handed.

21 "You are to labor six days but you must
rest on the seventh day; you must even rest
during plowing and harvesting times.

22 "Observe the Festival of Weeks with the
firstfruits of the wheat harvest, and the Festival

[A] **34:10** Lit *created* [B] **34:11** DSS, Sam, LXX add *Girgashites* [C] **34:14** Or *the LORD — his name is Jealous* or *the LORD, being jealous by nature* [D] **34:18** March–April; called Nisan in the post-exilic period; Neh 2:1; Est 3:7 [E] **34:19** LXX, Theod, Vg, Tg read *males* [F] **34:19** Hb obscure

of Ingathering[A] at the turn of the agricultural
year. 23 Three times a year all your males are
to appear before the Lord GOD, the God of
Israel. 24 For I will drive out nations before
you and enlarge your territory. No one will
covet your land when you go up three times
a year to appear before the LORD your God.

25 "Do not present[B] the blood for my sacrifice with anything leavened. The sacrifice of
the Passover Festival must not remain until
morning.

26 "Bring the best firstfruits of your land to
the house of the LORD your God.

"You must not boil a young goat in its mother's milk."

27 The LORD also said to Moses, "Write down
these words, for I have made a covenant with
you and with Israel based on these words."

28 Moses was there with the LORD forty days
and forty nights; he did not eat food or drink
water. He wrote the Ten Commandments, the
words of the covenant, on the tablets.

MOSES'S RADIANT FACE

29 As Moses descended from Mount Sinai —
with the two tablets of the testimony in his
hands as he descended the mountain — he did
not realize that the skin of his face shone as a
result of his speaking with the LORD.[C] 30 When
Aaron and all the Israelites saw Moses, the skin
of his face shone! They were afraid to come
near him. 31 But Moses called out to them, so
Aaron and all the leaders of the community
returned to him, and Moses spoke to them.
32 Afterward all the Israelites came near, and
he commanded them to do everything the
LORD had told him on Mount Sinai. 33 When
Moses had finished speaking with them, he
put a veil over his face. 34 But whenever Moses
went before the LORD to speak with him, he
would remove the veil until he came out. After
he came out, he would tell the Israelites what
he had been commanded, 35 and the Israelites
would see that Moses's face[D] was radiant. Then
Moses would put the veil over his face again
until he went to speak with the LORD.

THE SABBATH COMMAND

35 Moses assembled the entire Israelite
community and said to them, "These
are the things that the LORD has commanded
you to do: 2 For six days work is to be done, but
on the seventh day you are to have a holy day,
a Sabbath of complete rest to the LORD. Anyone who does work on it must be executed.
3 Do not light a fire in any of your homes on
the Sabbath day."

BUILDING THE TABERNACLE

4 Then Moses said to the entire Israelite community, "This is what the LORD has commanded:
5 Take up an offering among you for the LORD.
Let everyone whose heart is willing bring this
as the LORD's offering: gold, silver, and bronze;
6 blue, purple, and scarlet yarn; fine linen and
goat hair; 7 ram skins dyed red and fine leather;[E] acacia wood; 8 oil for the light; spices for
the anointing oil and for the fragrant incense;
9 and onyx with gemstones to mount on the
ephod and breastpiece.

10 "Let all the skilled artisans[F] among you
come and make everything that the LORD has
commanded: 11 the tabernacle — its tent and
covering, its clasps and supports, its crossbars,
its pillars and bases; 12 the ark with its poles,
the mercy seat, and the curtain for the screen;
13 the table with its poles, all its utensils, and
the Bread of the Presence; 14 the lampstand
for light with its utensils and lamps as well as
the oil for the light; 15 the altar of incense with
its poles; the anointing oil and the fragrant
incense; the entryway screen for the entrance
to the tabernacle; 16 the altar of burnt offering
with its bronze grate, its poles, and all its utensils; the basin with its stand; 17 the hangings
of the courtyard, its posts and bases, and the
screen for the gate of the courtyard; 18 the tent
pegs for the tabernacle and the tent pegs for
the courtyard, along with their ropes; 19 and
the specially woven[E] garments for ministering
in the sanctuary — the holy garments for the
priest Aaron and the garments for his sons
to serve as priests."

20 Then the entire Israelite community left
Moses's presence. 21 Everyone whose heart
was moved and whose spirit prompted him
came and brought an offering to the LORD for
the work on the tent of meeting, for all its services, and for the holy garments. 22 Both men
and women came; all who had willing hearts
brought brooches, earrings, rings, necklaces,
and all kinds of gold jewelry — everyone who
presented a presentation offering of gold to
the LORD. 23 Everyone who possessed blue,

[A] **34:22** The *Festival of Ingathering* is called Festival of Shelters elsewhere; Lv 23:34-36. [B] **34:25** Lit *slaughter*
[C] **34:29** Lit *with him* [D] **34:35** Lit *see Moses's face, that the skin of his face* [E] **35:7,19** Hb obscure [F] **35:10** Lit *the wise of heart*

purple, or scarlet yarn, fine linen or goat hair,
ram skins dyed red or fine leather,[A] brought
them. 24 Everyone making an offering of silver or bronze brought it as a contribution to
the LORD. Everyone who possessed acacia
wood useful for any task in the work brought
it. 25 Every skilled[B] woman spun yarn with
her hands and brought it: blue, purple, and
scarlet yarn, and fine linen. 26 And all the
women whose hearts were moved spun the
goat hair by virtue of their skill. 27 The leaders
brought onyx and gemstones to mount on
the ephod and breastpiece, 28 as well as the
spice and oil for the light, for the anointing
oil, and for the fragrant incense. 29 So the
Israelites brought a freewill offering to the
LORD, all the men and women whose hearts
prompted them to bring something for all
the work that the LORD, through Moses, had
commanded to be done.

BEZALEL AND OHOLIAB

30 Moses then said to the Israelites: "Look,
the LORD has appointed by name Bezalel son
of Uri, son of Hur, of the tribe of Judah. 31 He
has filled him with God's Spirit, with wisdom,
understanding, and ability in every kind of
craft 32 to design artistic works in gold, silver,
and bronze, 33 to cut gemstones for mounting,
and to carve wood for work in every kind of
artistic craft. 34 He has also given[C] both him
and Oholiab son of Ahisamach, of the tribe of
Dan, the ability to teach others. 35 He has filled
them with skill[D] to do all the work of a gem
cutter; a designer; an embroiderer[E] in blue,
purple, and scarlet yarn and fine linen; and
a weaver. They can do every kind of craft and
36 design artistic designs. 1 Bezalel, Oholiab, and all the skilled[F] people are to
work based on everything the LORD has commanded. The LORD has given them wisdom
and understanding to know how to do all the
work of constructing the sanctuary."
2 So Moses summoned Bezalel, Oholiab, and
every skilled person in whose heart the LORD
had placed wisdom, all whose hearts moved
them, to come to the work and do it. 3 They
took from Moses's presence all the contributions that the Israelites had brought for the
task of making the sanctuary. Meanwhile, the
people continued to bring freewill offerings
morning after morning.
4 Then all the artisans who were doing all
the work for the sanctuary came one by one
from the work they were doing 5 and said to
Moses, "The people are bringing more than is
needed for the construction of the work the
LORD commanded to be done."
6 After Moses gave an order, they sent a proclamation throughout the camp: "Let no man
or woman make anything else as an offering
for the sanctuary." So the people stopped. 7 The
materials were sufficient for them to do all the
work. There was more than enough.

BUILDING THE TABERNACLE

8 All the skilled artisans[G] among those doing
the work made the tabernacle with ten curtains. Bezalel made them of finely spun linen,
as well as blue, purple, and scarlet yarn, with a
design of cherubim worked into them. 9 Each
curtain was forty-two feet[H] long and six feet[I]
wide; all the curtains had the same measurements. 10 He joined five of the curtains to each
other, and the other five curtains he joined to
each other. 11 He made loops of blue yarn on the
edge of the last curtain in the first set and did
the same on the edge of the outermost curtain
in the second set. 12 He made fifty loops on the
one curtain and fifty loops on the edge of the
curtain in the second set, so that the loops lined
up with each other. 13 He also made fifty gold
clasps and joined the curtains to each other,
so that the tabernacle became a single unit.
14 He made curtains of goat hair for a tent
over the tabernacle; he made eleven of them.
15 Each curtain was forty-five feet[J] long and
six feet wide. All eleven curtains had the same
measurements. 16 He joined five of the curtains
together, and the other six together. 17 He made
fifty loops on the edge of the outermost curtain in the first set and fifty loops on the edge
of the corresponding curtain in the second
set. 18 He made fifty bronze clasps to join the
tent together as a single unit. 19 He also made
a covering for the tent from ram skins dyed
red and a covering of fine leather[A] on top of it.
20 He made upright supports[K] of acacia wood
for the tabernacle. 21 Each support was fifteen
feet[L] long and twenty-seven inches[M] wide.
22 Each support had two tenons for joining one
to another. He did the same for all the supports
of the tabernacle. 23 He made supports for the
tabernacle as follows: twenty for the south

[A] **35:23; 36:19** Hb obscure [B] **35:25** Lit *wise of heart* [C] **35:34** Lit *also put in his heart* [D] **35:35** Lit *with wisdom of heart*
[E] **35:35** Or *weaver* [F] **36:1** Lit *wise of heart*, also in v. 2 [G] **36:8** Lit *the wise of heart* [H] **36:9** Lit *28 cubits* [I] **36:9** Lit *four cubits*, also in v. 15 [J] **36:15** Lit *30 cubits* [K] **36:20** Or *made frames* [L] **36:21** Lit *10 cubits* [M] **36:21** Lit *a cubit and a half*

side, 24 and he made forty silver bases to put
under the twenty supports, two bases under
the first support for its two tenons, and two
bases under each of the following supports
for their two tenons; 25 for the second side of
the tabernacle, the north side, he made twenty
supports, 26 with their forty silver bases, two
bases under the first support and two bases
under each of the following ones; 27 and for
the back of the tabernacle, on the west side,
he made six supports. 28 He also made two
additional supports for the two back corners
of the tabernacle. 29 They were paired at the
bottom and joined together[A] at the[B] top in a
single ring. This is what he did with both of
them for the two corners. 30 So there were
eight supports with their sixteen silver bases,
two bases under each one.

31 He made five crossbars of acacia wood
for the supports on one side of the tabernacle,
32 five crossbars for the supports on the other
side of the tabernacle, and five crossbars for
those at the back of the tabernacle on the west.
33 He made the central crossbar run through
the middle of the supports from one end to
the other. 34 He overlaid them with gold and
made their rings out of gold as holders for
the crossbars. He also overlaid the crossbars
with gold.

35 Then he made the curtain with blue, purple, and scarlet yarn, and finely spun linen. He
made it with a design of cherubim worked into
it. 36 He made four pillars of acacia wood for
it and overlaid them with gold; their hooks
were of gold. And he cast four silver bases
for the pillars.

37 He made a screen embroidered[C] with blue,
purple, and scarlet yarn, and finely spun linen
for the entrance to the tent, 38 together with
its five pillars and their hooks. He overlaid the
tops of the pillars and their bands with gold,
but their five bases were bronze.

MAKING THE ARK

37 Bezalel made the ark of acacia wood,
forty-five inches long, twenty-seven
inches wide, and twenty-seven inches high.[D]
2 He overlaid it with pure gold inside and out
and made a gold molding all around it. 3 He
cast four gold rings for it, for its four feet,
two rings on one side and two rings on the
other side. 4 He made poles of acacia wood
and overlaid them with gold. 5 He inserted
the poles into the rings on the sides of the
ark for carrying the ark.

6 He made a mercy seat of pure gold, forty-five inches long and twenty-seven inches
wide.[E] 7 He made two cherubim of gold; he
made them of hammered work at the two ends
of the mercy seat, 8 one cherub at one end and
one cherub at the other end. At each end, he
made a cherub of one piece with the mercy
seat. 9 They had wings spread out. They faced
each other and covered the mercy seat with
their wings. The faces of the cherubim were
looking toward the mercy seat.

MAKING THE TABLE

10 He constructed the table of acacia wood, thirty-six inches long, eighteen inches wide, and
twenty-seven inches high.[F] 11 He overlaid it with
pure gold and made a gold molding all around
it. 12 He made a three-inch[G] frame all around it
and made a gold molding all around its frame.
13 He cast four gold rings for it and attached the
rings to the four corners at its four legs. 14 The
rings were next to the frame as holders for the
poles to carry the table. 15 He made the poles
for carrying the table from acacia wood and
overlaid them with gold. 16 He also made the
utensils that would be on the table out of pure
gold: its plates and cups, as well as its bowls and
pitchers for pouring drink offerings.

MAKING THE LAMPSTAND

17 Then he made the lampstand out of pure hammered gold. He made it all of one piece: its base
and shaft, its ornamental cups, and its buds and
petals. 18 Six branches extended from its sides,
three branches of the lampstand from one side
and three branches of the lampstand from the
other side. 19 There were three cups shaped like
almond blossoms, each with a bud and petals,
on one branch, and three cups shaped like almond blossoms, each with a bud and petals,
on the next branch. It was this way for the six
branches that extended from the lampstand.
20 There were four cups shaped like almond
blossoms on the lampstand shaft along with
its buds and petals. 21 For the six branches that
extended from it, a bud was under the first pair
of branches from it, a bud under the second

[A] **36:29** Lit *and together they are to be complete* [B] **36:29** Lit *its* [C] **36:37** Or *woven* [D] **37:1** Lit *two and a half cubits its length, one and a half cubits its width, and one and a half cubits its height* [E] **37:6** Lit *two and a half cubits its length and one and a half cubits its width* [F] **37:10** Lit *two cubits its length, one cubit its width, and one and a half cubits its height* [G] **37:12** Lit *a handbreadth*

pair of branches from it, and a bud under the third pair of branches from it. 22 Their buds and branches were of one piece with it. All of it was a single hammered piece of pure gold. 23 He also made its seven lamps, snuffers, and firepans of pure gold. 24 He made it and all its utensils of seventy-five pounds[A] of pure gold.

MAKING THE ALTAR OF INCENSE

25 He made the altar of incense out of acacia wood. It was square, eighteen inches long and eighteen inches wide; it was thirty-six inches high.[B] Its horns were of one piece with it. 26 He overlaid it, its top, all around its sides, and its horns with pure gold. Then he made a gold molding all around it. 27 He made two gold rings for it under the molding on two of its sides; he put these on opposite sides of it to be holders for the poles to carry it with. 28 He made the poles of acacia wood and overlaid them with gold.

29 He also made the holy anointing oil and the pure, fragrant, and expertly blended incense.

MAKING THE ALTAR OF BURNT OFFERING

38 Bezalel constructed the altar of burnt offering from acacia wood. It was square, 7 1/2 feet long and 7 1/2 feet wide,[C] and was 4 1/2 feet[D] high. 2 He made horns for it on its four corners; the horns were of one piece with it. Then he overlaid it with bronze.

3 He made all the altar's utensils: the pots, shovels, basins, meat forks, and firepans; he made all its utensils of bronze. 4 He constructed for the altar a grate of bronze mesh under its ledge,[E] halfway up from the bottom. 5 He cast four rings at the four corners of the bronze grate as holders for the poles. 6 He made the poles of acacia wood and overlaid them with bronze. 7 Then he inserted the poles into the rings on the sides of the altar in order to carry it with them. He constructed the altar with boards so that it was hollow.

MAKING THE BRONZE BASIN

8 He made the bronze basin and its stand from the bronze mirrors of the women who served at the entrance to the tent of meeting.

MAKING THE COURTYARD

9 Then he made the courtyard. The hangings on the south side of the courtyard were of finely spun linen, 150 feet[F] long, 10 including their twenty posts and their twenty bronze bases, with silver hooks and silver bands[G] for the posts. 11 The hangings on the north side were also 150 feet long, including their twenty posts and twenty bronze bases. The hooks and bands of the posts were silver. 12 The hangings on the west side were 75 feet[H] long, including their ten posts and their ten bases, with silver hooks and silver bands for the posts. 13 And for the east side toward the sunrise, 75 feet long, 14 the hangings on one side of the gate were 22 1/2 feet,[I] including their three posts and their three bases. 15 It was the same for the other side of the courtyard gate. The hangings were 22 1/2 feet, including their three posts and their three bases. 16 All the hangings around the courtyard were of finely spun linen. 17 The bases for the posts were bronze; the hooks and bands of the posts were silver; and the plating for the tops of the posts was silver. All the posts of the courtyard were banded with silver.

18 The screen for the gate of the courtyard was made of finely spun linen, expertly embroidered[J] with blue, purple, and scarlet yarn. It was 30 feet[K] long, and like the hangings of the courtyard, 7 1/2 feet[L] high.[M] 19 It had four posts with their four bronze bases. Their hooks were silver, and their top plating and their bands were silver. 20 All the tent pegs for the tabernacle and for the surrounding courtyard were bronze.

INVENTORY OF MATERIALS

21 This is the inventory for the tabernacle, the tabernacle of the testimony, that was recorded at Moses's command. It was the work of the Levites under the direction of[N] Ithamar son of Aaron the priest. 22 Bezalel son of Uri, son of Hur, of the tribe of Judah, made everything that the LORD commanded Moses. 23 With him was Oholiab son of Ahisamach, of the tribe of Dan, a gem cutter, a designer, and an embroiderer with blue, purple, and scarlet yarn, and fine linen.

24 All the gold of the presentation offering that was used for the project in all the work on the sanctuary, was 2,193 pounds,[O] according to the sanctuary shekel. 25 The silver from those of the community who were registered

[A] **37:24** Lit *a talent* [B] **37:25** Lit *a cubit its length, a cubit its width, and two cubits its height* [C] **38:1** Lit *five cubits its length and five cubits its width* [D] **38:1** Lit *three cubits* [E] **38:4** Or *rim* [F] **38:9** Lit *100 cubits*, also in v. 11 [G] **38:10** Or *connecting rods*, also in vv. 11,17,19,28 [H] **38:12** Lit *50 cubits*, also in v. 13 [I] **38:14** Lit *15 cubits*, also in v. 15 [J] **38:18** Or *woven* [K] **38:18** Lit *20 cubits* [L] **38:18** Lit *five cubits* [M] **38:18** Lit *high in width* [N] **38:21** Lit *Levites by the hand of* [O] **38:24** Lit *29 talents and 730 shekels*

was 7,544 pounds,[A] according to the sanctuary
shekel — 26 one-fifth of an ounce[B] per man,
that is, half a shekel according to the sanctuary shekel, from everyone twenty years old
or more who had crossed over to the registered group, 603,550 men. 27 There were 7,500
pounds[C] of silver used to cast the bases of the
sanctuary and the bases of the curtain — one
hundred bases from 7,500 pounds, 75 pounds[D]
for each base. 28 With the remaining 44 pounds[E]
he made the hooks for the posts, overlaid their
tops, and supplied bands for them.

29 The bronze of the presentation offering
totaled 5,310 pounds.[F] 30 He made with it the
bases for the entrance to the tent of meeting,
the bronze altar and its bronze grate, all the
utensils for the altar, 31 the bases for the surrounding courtyard, the bases for the gate of
the courtyard, all the tent pegs for the tabernacle, and all the tent pegs for the surrounding
courtyard.

MAKING THE PRIESTLY GARMENTS

39 They made specially woven[G] garments
for ministry in the sanctuary, and the
holy garments for Aaron from the blue, purple,
and scarlet yarn, just as the LORD had commanded Moses.

MAKING THE EPHOD

2 Bezalel made the ephod of gold, of blue, purple, and scarlet yarn, and of finely spun linen.
3 They hammered out thin sheets of gold, and
he[H] cut threads from them to interweave with
the blue, purple, and scarlet yarn, and the fine
linen in a skillful design. 4 They made shoulder
pieces for attaching it; it was joined together at its two edges. 5 The artistically woven
waistband that was on the ephod was of one
piece with the ephod, according to the same
workmanship of gold, of blue, purple, and
scarlet yarn, and of finely spun linen, just as
the LORD had commanded Moses.

6 Then they mounted the onyx stones surrounded with gold filigree settings, engraved
with the names of Israel's sons as a gem cutter
engraves a seal. 7 He fastened them on the
shoulder pieces of the ephod as memorial
stones for the Israelites, just as the LORD had
commanded Moses.

MAKING THE BREASTPIECE

8 He also made the embroidered[I] breastpiece
with the same workmanship as the ephod of
gold, of blue, purple, and scarlet yarn, and of
finely spun linen. 9 They made the breastpiece
square and folded double, nine inches long
and nine inches wide.[J] 10 They mounted four
rows of gemstones[K] on it.

The first row was
a row of carnelian, topaz, and
emerald;[L]
11 the second row,
a turquoise,[M] a lapis lazuli, and a
diamond;[N]
12 the third row,
a jacinth,[G] an agate, and an amethyst;
13 and the fourth row,
a beryl, an onyx, and a jasper.

They were surrounded with gold filigree in
their settings.

14 The twelve stones corresponded to the
names of Israel's sons. Each stone was engraved like a seal with one of the names of
the twelve tribes.

15 They made braided chains of pure gold
cord for the breastpiece. 16 They also fashioned
two gold filigree settings and two gold rings
and attached the two rings to its two corners.
17 Then they attached the two gold cords to the
two gold rings on the corners of the breastpiece.
18 They attached the other ends of the two cords
to the two filigree settings, and in this way
they attached them to the ephod's shoulder
pieces in front. 19 They made two other gold
rings and put them at the two other corners
of the breastpiece on the edge that is next to
the inner border of the ephod. 20 They made
two more gold rings and attached them to the
bottom of the ephod's two shoulder pieces on
its front, close to its seam,[O] above the ephod's
woven waistband. 21 Then they tied the breastpiece from its rings to the rings of the ephod
with a cord of blue yarn, so that the breastpiece
was above the ephod's waistband and did not
come loose from the ephod. They did just as
the LORD had commanded Moses.

MAKING THE ROBE

22 They made the woven robe of the ephod
entirely of blue yarn. 23 There was an opening

[A] **38:25** Lit *100 talents and 1,775 shekels* [B] **38:26** Lit *a beka* [C] **38:27** Lit *100 talents* [D] **38:27** Lit *one talent* [E] **38:28** Lit *1,775* (shekels) [F] **38:29** Lit *70 talents and 2,400 shekels* [G] **39:1,12** Hb obscure [H] **39:3** Sam, Syr, Tg read *they* [I] **39:8** Or *woven* [J] **39:9** Lit *a span its length and a span its width* [K] **39:10** Many of these stones cannot be identified with certainty. [L] **39:10** Or *beryl* [M] **39:11** Or *malachite*, or *garnet* [N] **39:11** Hb uncertain; LXX, Vg read *jasper* [O] **39:20** The place where the *shoulder pieces* join the front of the ephod

Many assume *Leviticus* is boring and irrelevant. But this law book presents a multifaceted portrait of our holy God and standards for the way he wants to be worshiped.

In Leviticus, God may seem remote, but that is intentional. God gave these words to his people to remind them of his holiness. He is pure and powerful; thus, we must approach him on his terms. He is worthy of our worship, and we should stand in awe of him.

God also invites us to draw near. He made possible for rebellious sinners to be clean through purification rituals and to be forgiven through sacrifices for sin. He also provided a mediator, the priest who could enter into the holy place to intercede for them.

Christ perfectly fulfilled these requirements. Reading Leviticus through the New Testament lens, we see God making a way for sinful people to come to him, holy and dearly loved. In fact, the writer of Hebrews drew heavily on Leviticus in describing the person and role of Jesus Christ.

He daily intercedes before the Father for us. He is the once-for-all sacrifice, the Great High Priest, and the fulfillment of all the law who makes possible for us to approach the holy God. Behold, the Lamb of God.

LEVITICUS

AUTHOR: Moses

DATE WRITTEN: 1446–1406 BC (during the wilderness wanderings)

ORIGINAL AUDIENCE: The Israelites

SETTING: The book of Leviticus records the words of God to Moses at Mount Sinai. After leaving Egypt, Israel camped at the base of the mountain for about a year. During that time, Moses received the covenant and constructed the tabernacle, and those events are recorded in Exodus 19 through Numbers 10. In other words, the entire book of Leviticus plus the end of Exodus and the beginning of Numbers are divinely given instructions for appropriate worship of Almighty God.

PURPOSE FOR WRITING: Leviticus must be placed in the context of redemption history. God made a covenant with Israel (Ex 20–24) and gave specific instructions for the tabernacle where he would dwell among his people (Ex 25–40). In order for the holy God to live among them, they needed to be holy in character and behavior, and the book of Leviticus outlines these requirements for God's people. The ceremonial laws found in this book demonstrate God's holiness and the holiness he requires of his people. Even though we now live as new covenant believers saved by the blood of Christ, we must take God's holiness seriously and strive to live worthy of bearing the name "Christian."

OUTLINE:

1. Laws for Sacrifices and the Priesthood (1:1–7:38)

   Instructions for offerings (1:1–6:7)

   Regulations for priests (6:8–7:38)

2. Ordination and Services of the Priests (8:1–10:20)

   Consecration of Aaron (8:1-36)

   Dedication of the tabernacle (9:1-24)

   Warning against immoral priests (10:1-20)

3. Laws of Purification (11:1–16:34)

   Clean and unclean animals (11:1-47)

   Purification rituals (12:1–15:33)

   The Day of Atonement (16:1-34)

4. Requirements for Holiness (17:1–27:34)

   Reverence for blood (17:1-16)

   Obedience to God's laws (18:1–22:33)

   True worship (23:1–26:46)

   Making and keeping vows (27:1-34)

KEY VERSE:

"I am the LORD who sets you apart."
—Leviticus 22:32

RESTORATION THEMES

R	Rest and Reflection	*For the next note, see Numbers 6:24-26.*
E	Eternal Perspective	*God's Memory—Leviticus 26:45*
S	Support	*For the next note, see Numbers 14:9.*
T	Thanksgiving and Contentment	*For the next note, see Numbers 32:23.*
O	Other-centeredness	*Helping People in Need—Leviticus 19:10* *Not Holding Resentment/Grudges—19:18* *Identifying Those We Have Wronged—25:17*
R	Relationships	*Making Amends—6:2-5* *Confronting in Love—19:17*
E	Exercise of Faith	*Tithing—27:30*

THE BURNT OFFERING

1 Then the LORD summoned Moses and spoke to him from the tent of meeting: 2 "Speak to the Israelites and tell them: When any of you brings an offering to the LORD from the livestock, you may bring your offering from the herd or the flock.

3 "If his offering is a burnt offering from the herd, he is to bring an unblemished male. He will bring it to the entrance to the tent of meeting so that he[A] may be accepted by the LORD. 4 He is to lay his hand on the head of the burnt offering so it can be accepted on his behalf to make atonement for him. 5 He is to slaughter the bull before the LORD; Aaron's sons the priests are to present the blood and splatter it on all sides of the altar that is at the entrance to the tent of meeting. 6 Then he is to skin the burnt offering and cut it into pieces.[B] 7 The sons of Aaron the priest will prepare a fire on the altar and arrange wood on the fire. 8 Aaron's sons the priests are to arrange the pieces, the head, and the fat on top of the burning wood on the altar. 9 The offerer is to wash its entrails and legs with water. Then the priest will burn all of it on the altar as a burnt offering, a fire offering of a pleasing aroma to the LORD.

10 "But if his offering for a burnt offering is from the flock, from sheep or goats, he is to present an unblemished male. 11 He will slaughter it on the north side of the altar before the LORD. Aaron's sons the priests will splatter its blood against the altar on all sides. 12 He will cut the animal into pieces with its head and its fat, and the priest will arrange them on top of the burning wood on the altar. 13 But he is to wash the entrails and legs with water. The priest will then present all of it and burn it on the altar; it is a burnt offering, a fire offering of a pleasing aroma to the LORD.

14 "If his offering to the LORD is a burnt offering of birds, he is to present his offering from the turtledoves or young pigeons.[C] 15 Then the priest is to bring it to the altar, and will twist off its head and burn it on the altar; its blood should be drained at the side of the altar. 16 He will remove its digestive tract,[D] cutting off the tail feathers, and throw it on the east side of the altar at the place for ashes. 17 He will tear it open by its wings without dividing the bird. Then the priest is to burn it on the altar on top of the burning wood. It is a burnt offering, a fire offering of a pleasing aroma to the LORD.

THE GRAIN OFFERING

2 "When anyone presents a grain offering as an offering to the LORD, it is to consist of fine flour. He is to pour olive oil on it, put frankincense on it, 2 and bring it to Aaron's sons the priests. The priest will take a handful of fine flour and oil from it, along with all its frankincense, and will burn this memorial portion of it on the altar, a fire offering of a pleasing aroma to the LORD. 3 But the rest of the grain offering will belong to Aaron and his sons; it is the holiest part of the fire offerings to the LORD.

4 "When you present a grain offering baked in an oven, it is to be made of fine flour, either unleavened cakes mixed with oil or unleavened wafers coated with oil. 5 If your offering is a grain offering prepared on a griddle, it is to be unleavened bread made of fine flour mixed with oil. 6 Break it into pieces and pour oil on it; it is a grain offering. 7 If your offering is a grain offering prepared in a pan, it is to be made of fine flour with oil. 8 When you bring to the LORD the grain offering made in any of these ways, it is to be presented to the priest, and he will take it to the altar. 9 The priest will remove the memorial portion[E] from the grain offering and burn it on the altar, a fire offering of a pleasing aroma to the LORD. 10 But the rest of the grain offering will belong to Aaron and his sons; it is the holiest part of the fire offerings to the LORD.

11 "No grain offering that you present to the LORD is to be made with yeast, for you are not to burn[F] any yeast or honey as a fire offering to the LORD. 12 You may present them to the LORD as an offering of firstfruits, but they are not to be offered on the altar as a pleasing aroma. 13 You are to season each of your grain offerings with salt; you must not omit from your grain offering the salt of the covenant with your God. You are to present salt with each of your offerings.

14 "If you present a grain offering of firstfruits to the LORD, you are to present fresh heads of grain, crushed kernels, roasted on the fire, for your grain offering of firstfruits. 15 You are to put oil and frankincense on it; it is a grain offering. 16 The priest will then burn some of its crushed kernels and oil

[A] **1:3** Or *it* [B] **1:6** Lit *its pieces*, also in v. 12 [C] **1:14** Or *or pigeons* [D] **1:16** Or *its crop*, or *its crissum* [E] **2:9** Lit *portion of it*
[F] **2:11** Some Hb mss, Sam, LXX, Tg read *present*

with all its frankincense as a fire offering to the LORD.

THE FELLOWSHIP OFFERING

3 "If his offering is a fellowship sacrifice, and he is presenting an animal from the herd, whether male or female, he is to present one without blemish before the LORD. 2 He is to lay his hand on the head of his offering and slaughter it at the entrance to the tent of meeting. Then Aaron's sons the priests will splatter the blood on all sides of the altar. 3 He will present part of the fellowship sacrifice as a fire offering to the LORD: the fat surrounding the entrails, all the fat that is on the entrails, 4 and the two kidneys with the fat on them at the loins; he will also remove the fatty lobe of the liver with the kidneys. 5 Aaron's sons will burn it on the altar along with the burnt offering that is on the burning wood, a fire offering of a pleasing aroma to the LORD.

6 "If his offering as a fellowship sacrifice to the LORD is from the flock, he is to present a male or female without blemish. 7 If he is presenting a lamb for his offering, he is to present it before the LORD. 8 He must lay his hand on the head of his offering, then slaughter it before the tent of meeting. Aaron's sons will splatter its blood on all sides of the altar. 9 He will then present part of the fellowship sacrifice as a fire offering to the LORD consisting of its fat and the entire fat tail, which he is to remove close to the backbone. He will also remove the fat surrounding the entrails, all the fat on the entrails, 10 the two kidneys with the fat on them at the loins, and the fatty lobe of the liver above the kidneys. 11 Then the priest will burn the food on the altar, as a fire offering to the LORD.

12 "If his offering is a goat, he is to present it before the LORD. 13 He must lay his hand on its head and slaughter it before the tent of meeting. Aaron's sons will splatter[A] its blood on all sides of the altar. 14 He will present part of his offering as a fire offering to the LORD: the fat surrounding the entrails, all the fat that is on the entrails, 15 and the two kidneys with the fat on them at the loins; he will also remove the fatty lobe of the liver with the kidneys. 16 Then the priest will burn the food on the altar, as a fire offering for a pleasing aroma.[B]

"All fat belongs to the LORD. 17 This is a permanent statute throughout your generations, wherever you live: you must not eat any fat or any blood."

THE SIN OFFERING

4 Then the LORD spoke to Moses: 2 "Tell the Israelites: When someone sins unintentionally against any of the LORD's commands and does anything prohibited by them —

3 "If the anointed priest sins, bringing guilt on the people, he is to present to the LORD a young, unblemished bull as a sin[C] offering for the sin he has committed. 4 He is to bring the bull to the entrance to the tent of meeting before the LORD, lay his hand on the bull's head, and slaughter it before the LORD. 5 The anointed priest will then take some of the bull's blood and bring it into the tent of meeting. 6 The priest is to dip his finger in the blood and sprinkle some of it seven times before the LORD in front of the curtain of the sanctuary. 7 The priest is to apply some of the blood to the horns of the altar of fragrant incense that is before the LORD in the tent of meeting. He must pour out the rest of the bull's blood at the base of the altar of burnt offering that is at the entrance to the tent of meeting. 8 He is to remove all the fat from the bull of the sin offering: the fat surrounding the entrails, all the fat that is on the entrails, 9 and the two kidneys with the fat on them at the loins. He will also remove the fatty lobe of the liver with the kidneys, 10 just as the fat is removed from the ox of the fellowship sacrifice. The priest is to burn them on the altar of burnt offering. 11 But the hide of the bull and all its flesh, with its head and legs, and its entrails and waste — 12 all the rest of the bull — he must bring to a ceremonially clean place outside the camp to the ash heap, and must burn it on a wood fire. It is to be burned at the ash heap.

13 "Now if the whole community of Israel errs, and the matter escapes the notice of the assembly, so that they violate any of the LORD's commands and incur guilt by doing what is prohibited, 14 then the assembly must present a young bull as a sin offering. They are to bring it before the tent of meeting when the sin they have committed in regard to the command becomes known. 15 The elders of the community are to lay their hands on the bull's head before the LORD and it is to be slaughtered before the LORD. 16 The anointed priest will bring some of the bull's blood into

---

[A] **3:13** Or *dash* [B] **3:16** Sam, LXX add *to the LORD* [C] **4:3** Or *purification*

the tent of meeting. 17 The priest is to dip his finger in the blood and sprinkle it seven times before the LORD in front of the curtain. 18 He is to apply some of the blood to the horns of the altar that is before the LORD in the tent of meeting. He will pour out the rest of the blood at the base of the altar of burnt offering that is at the entrance to the tent of meeting. 19 He is to remove all the fat from it and burn it on the altar. 20 He is to offer this bull just as he did with the bull in the sin offering; he will offer it the same way. So the priest will make atonement on their behalf, and they will be forgiven. 21 Then he will bring the bull outside the camp and burn it just as he burned the first bull. It is the sin offering for the assembly.

22 "When a leader[A] sins and unintentionally violates any of the commands of the LORD his God by doing what is prohibited, and incurs guilt, 23 or someone informs him about the sin he has committed, he is to bring an unblemished male goat as his offering. 24 He is to lay his hand on the head of the goat and slaughter it at the place where the burnt offering is slaughtered before the LORD. It is a sin offering. 25 Then the priest is to take some of the blood from the sin offering with his finger and apply it to the horns of the altar of burnt offering. The rest of its blood he is to pour out at the base of the altar of burnt offering. 26 He must burn all its fat on the altar, like the fat of the fellowship sacrifice. In this way the priest will make atonement on his behalf for that person's sin, and he will be forgiven.

27 "Now if any of the common people[B] sins unintentionally by violating one of the LORD's commands, does what is prohibited, and incurs guilt, 28 or if someone informs him about the sin he has committed, then he is to bring an unblemished female goat as his offering for the sin that he has committed. 29 He is to lay his hand on the head of the sin offering and slaughter it at the place of the burnt offering. 30 Then the priest is to take some of its blood with his finger and apply it to the horns of the altar of burnt offering. He is to pour out the rest of its blood at the base of the altar. 31 He is to remove all its fat just as the fat is removed from the fellowship sacrifice. The priest is to burn it on the altar as a pleasing aroma to the LORD. In this way the priest will make atonement on his behalf, and he will be forgiven.

32 "Or if the offering that he brings as a sin offering is a lamb, he is to bring an unblemished female. 33 He is to lay his hand on the head of the sin offering and slaughter it as a sin offering at the place where the burnt offering is slaughtered. 34 Then the priest is to take some of the blood of the sin offering with his finger and apply it to the horns of the altar of burnt offering. He is to pour out the rest of its blood at the base of the altar. 35 He is to remove all its fat just as the fat of the lamb is removed from the fellowship sacrifice. The priest will burn it on the altar along with the fire offerings to the LORD. In this way the priest will make atonement on his behalf for the sin he has committed, and he will be forgiven.

CASES REQUIRING SIN OFFERINGS

5 "When someone sins in any of these ways:
If he has seen, heard, or known about
something he has witnessed, and did not
respond to a public call to testify, he will
bear his iniquity.

2 Or if someone touches anything unclean
— a carcass of an unclean wild animal,
or unclean livestock, or an unclean
swarming creature — without being
aware of it, he is unclean and incurs guilt.

3 Or if he touches human uncleanness
— any uncleanness by which one can become defiled — without being aware of
it, but later recognizes it, he incurs guilt.

4 Or if someone swears rashly to do what
is good or evil — concerning anything
a person may speak rashly in an oath
— without being aware of it, but later
recognizes it, he incurs guilt in such an
instance.

5 If someone incurs guilt in one of these cases, he is to confess he has committed that sin. 6 He must bring his penalty for guilt for the sin he has committed to the LORD: a female lamb or goat from the flock as a sin offering. In this way the priest will make atonement on his behalf for his sin.

7 "But if he cannot afford an animal from the flock, then he may bring to the LORD two turtledoves or two young pigeons as penalty for guilt for his sin — one as a sin offering and the other as a burnt offering. 8 He is to bring them to the priest, who will first present the one for the sin offering. He is to twist its head at the back of the neck without severing it. 9 Then

[A] **4:22** Or *ruler* [B] **4:27** Lit *the people of the land*

he will sprinkle some of the blood of the sin
offering on the side of the altar, while the rest
of the blood is to be drained out at the base of
the altar; it is a sin offering. 10 He will prepare
the second bird as a burnt offering according
to the regulation. In this way the priest will
make atonement on his behalf for the sin he
has committed, and he will be forgiven.
11 "But if he cannot afford two turtledoves or
two young pigeons, he may bring two quarts[A]
of fine flour[B] as an offering for his sin. He
must not put olive oil or frankincense on it,
for it is a sin offering. 12 He is to bring it to the
priest, who will take a handful from it as its
memorial portion and burn it on the altar
along with the fire offerings to the LORD; it
is a sin offering. 13 In this way the priest will
make atonement on his behalf concerning the
sin he has committed in any of these cases,
and he will be forgiven. The rest will belong
to the priest, like the grain offering."

THE GUILT OFFERING

14 Then the LORD spoke to Moses: 15 "If someone offends by sinning unintentionally in
regard to any of the LORD's holy things,[C] he
must bring his penalty for guilt to the LORD:
an unblemished ram from the flock (based on
your assessment of its value in silver shekels,
according to the sanctuary shekel) as a guilt
offering. 16 He is to make restitution for his
sin regarding any holy thing, adding a fifth
of its value to it, and give it to the priest. Then
the priest will make atonement on his behalf
with the ram of the guilt offering, and he will
be forgiven.
17 "If someone sins and without knowing
it violates any of the LORD's commands concerning anything prohibited, he is guilty, and
he will bear his iniquity. 18 He must bring an
unblemished ram from the flock according
to your assessment of its value as a guilt offering to the priest. Then the priest will make
atonement on his behalf for the error he has
committed unintentionally, and he will be
forgiven. 19 It is a guilt offering; he is indeed
guilty before the LORD."
6 The LORD spoke to Moses: 2 "When someone sins and offends the LORD by deceiving
his neighbor in regard to a deposit, a security,[D] or a robbery; or defrauds his neighbor;
3 or finds something lost and lies about it; or
swears falsely about any of the sinful things
a person may do — 4 once he has sinned and
acknowledged his guilt — he must return what
he stole or defrauded, or the deposit entrusted

Relationships | *Making Amends*

ACTIONS SPEAK LOUDER

"When someone sins and offends the LORD by deceiving his neighbor in regard to a deposit, a security, or a robbery; or defrauds his neighbor; or finds something lost and lies about it; or swears falsely about any of the sinful things a person may do—once he has sinned and acknowledged his guilt—he must return what he stole or defrauded, or the deposit entrusted to him, or the lost item he found, or anything else about which he swore falsely. He will make full restitution for it and add a fifth of its value to it." Leviticus 6:2-5

Every parent knows the frustration of listening to a child offer a half-hearted apology. Mere words—and insincere ones at that—can't possibly take away the sting of a grievous offense.

This is why the Bible requires "restitution." Much more than a quick, glib effort to smooth things over, restitution does whatever is needed to make things right. When an offender does that—all the parties involved *feel* right about it. And this goes a long way to rebuilding broken trust.

For what unresolved instances of wrongdoing do you still need to make amends? Ask God for the courage and strength to heal that relationship.

For the next note on *Relationships*, see Leviticus 19:17.

[A] **5:11** Lit *one-tenth of an ephah* [B] **5:11** Lit *flour as a sin offering* [C] **5:15** Things dedicated to the LORD [D] **6:2** Or *an investment*

to him, or the lost item he found, 5 or anything else about which he swore falsely. He
will make full restitution for it and add a fifth
of its value to it. He is to pay it to its owner
on the day he acknowledges his guilt. 6 Then
he is to bring his guilt offering to the LORD:
an unblemished ram from the flock according to your assessment of its value as a guilt
offering to the priest. 7 In this way the priest
will make atonement on his behalf before the
LORD, and he will be forgiven for anything he
may have done to incur guilt."

THE BURNT OFFERING

8 The LORD spoke to Moses: 9 "Command Aaron
and his sons: This is the law of the burnt offering; the burnt offering itself must remain on
the altar's hearth all night until morning, while
the fire of the altar is kept burning on it. 10 The
priest is to put on his linen robe and linen undergarments.[A] He is to remove the ashes of the
burnt offering the fire has consumed on the
altar, and place them beside the altar. 11 Then he
will take off his garments, put on other clothes,
and bring the ashes outside the camp to a ceremonially clean place. 12 The fire on the altar
is to be kept burning; it must not go out. Every
morning the priest will burn wood on the fire.
He is to arrange the burnt offering on the fire
and burn the fat portions from the fellowship
offerings on it. 13 Fire must be kept burning on
the altar continually; it must not go out.

THE GRAIN OFFERING

14 "Now this is the law of the grain offering:
Aaron's sons will present it before the LORD
in front of the altar. 15 The priest is to remove
a handful of fine flour and olive oil from the
grain offering, with all the frankincense that
is on the offering, and burn its memorial portion on the altar as a pleasing aroma to the
LORD. 16 Aaron and his sons may eat the rest of
it. It is to be eaten in the form of unleavened
bread in a holy place; they are to eat it in the
courtyard of the tent of meeting. 17 It must not
be baked with yeast; I have assigned it as their
portion from my fire offerings. It is especially
holy, like the sin offering and the guilt offering.
18 Any male among Aaron's descendants may
eat it. It is a permanent portion[B] throughout
your generations from the fire offerings to
the LORD. Anything that touches the offerings
will become holy."

19 The LORD spoke to Moses: 20 "This is the
offering that Aaron and his sons are to present to the LORD on the day that he is anointed:
two quarts[C] of fine flour as a regular grain
offering, half of it in the morning and half in
the evening. 21 It is to be prepared with oil on
a griddle; you are to bring it well-kneaded. You
are to present it as a grain offering of baked
pieces,[D] a pleasing aroma to the LORD. 22 The
priest, who is one of Aaron's sons and will be
anointed to take his place, is to prepare it. It
must be completely burned as a permanent
portion for the LORD. 23 Every grain offering
for a priest will be a whole burnt offering; it
is not to be eaten."

THE SIN OFFERING

24 The LORD spoke to Moses: 25 "Tell Aaron and
his sons: This is the law of the sin offering. The
sin offering is most holy and must be slaughtered before the LORD at the place where the
burnt offering is slaughtered. 26 The priest
who offers it as a sin offering will eat it. It is
to be eaten in a holy place, in the courtyard of
the tent of meeting. 27 Anything that touches
its flesh will become holy, and if any of its
blood spatters on a garment, then you must
wash that garment[E] in a holy place. 28 A clay
pot in which the sin offering is boiled is to be
broken; if it is boiled in a bronze vessel, it is
to be scoured and rinsed with water. 29 Any
male among the priests may eat it; it is especially holy. 30 But no sin offering may be eaten
if its blood has been brought into the tent of
meeting to make atonement in the holy place;
it must be burned.

THE GUILT OFFERING

7 "Now this is the law of the guilt[F] offering;
it is especially holy. 2 The guilt offering is
to be slaughtered at the place where the burnt
offering is slaughtered, and the priest is to
splatter its blood on all sides of the altar. 3 The
offerer is to present all the fat from it: the fat
tail, the fat surrounding the entrails,[G] 4 and the
two kidneys with the fat on them at the loins;
he will also remove the fatty lobe of the liver
with the kidneys. 5 The priest will burn them
on the altar as a fire offering to the LORD; it is
a guilt offering. 6 Any male among the priests
may eat it. It is to be eaten in a holy place; it
is especially holy.
7 "The guilt offering is like the sin offering;

[A] **6:10** Lit *undergarments on his flesh* [B] **6:18** Or *statute* [C] **6:20** Lit *a tenth of an ephah* [D] **6:21** Hb obscure [E] **6:27** Lit *wash what it spattered on* [F] **7:1** Or *restitution* [G] **7:3** LXX, Sam add *and all the fat that is on the entrails*; Lv 3:3,9,14; 4:8

the law is the same for both. It belongs to the priest who makes atonement with it. [8] As for the priest who presents someone's burnt offering, the hide of the burnt offering he has presented belongs to him; it is the priest's. [9] Any grain offering that is baked in an oven or prepared in a pan or on a griddle belongs to the priest who presents it; it is his. [10] But any grain offering, whether dry or mixed with oil, belongs equally to all of Aaron's sons.

THE FELLOWSHIP SACRIFICE

[11] "Now this is the law of the fellowship sacrifice that someone may present to the LORD: [12] If he presents it for thanksgiving, in addition to the thanksgiving sacrifice, he is to present unleavened cakes mixed with olive oil, unleavened wafers coated with oil, and well-kneaded cakes of fine flour mixed with oil. [13] He is to present as his offering cakes of leavened bread with his thanksgiving sacrifice of fellowship. [14] From the cakes he is to present one portion of each offering as a contribution to the LORD. It will belong to the priest who splatters the blood of the fellowship offering; it is his. [15] The meat of his thanksgiving sacrifice of fellowship must be eaten on the day he offers it; he may not leave any of it until morning.

[16] "If the sacrifice he offers is a vow or a freewill offering, it is to be eaten on the day he presents his sacrifice, and what is left over may be eaten on the next day. [17] But what remains of the sacrificial meat by the third day must be burned. [18] If any of the meat of his fellowship sacrifice is eaten on the third day, it will not be accepted. It will not be credited to the one who presents it; it is repulsive. The person who eats any of it will bear his iniquity.[A]

[19] "Meat that touches anything unclean must not be eaten; it is to be burned. Everyone who is clean may eat any other meat. [20] But the one who eats meat from the LORD's fellowship sacrifice while he is unclean, that person must be cut off from his people. [21] If someone touches anything unclean, whether human uncleanness, an unclean animal, or any unclean, abhorrent[B] creature, and eats meat from the LORD's fellowship sacrifice, that person is to be cut off from his people."

FAT AND BLOOD PROHIBITED

[22] The LORD spoke to Moses: [23] "Tell the Israelites: You are not to eat any fat of an ox, a sheep, or a goat. [24] The fat of an animal that dies naturally or is mauled by wild beasts[C] may be used for any other purpose, but you must not eat it. [25] If anyone eats animal fat from a fire offering presented to the LORD, the person who eats it is to be cut off from his people. [26] Wherever you live, you must not eat the blood of any bird or animal. [27] Whoever eats any blood is to be cut off from his people."

THE PORTION FOR THE PRIESTS

[28] The LORD spoke to Moses: [29] "Tell the Israelites: The one who presents a fellowship sacrifice to the LORD is to bring an offering to the LORD from his sacrifice. [30] His own hands will bring the fire offerings to the LORD. He will bring the fat together with the breast. The breast is to be presented as a presentation offering before the LORD. [31] The priest is to burn the fat on the altar, but the breast belongs to Aaron and his sons. [32] You are to give the right thigh to the priest as a contribution from your fellowship sacrifices. [33] The son of Aaron who presents the blood of the fellowship offering and the fat will have the right thigh as a portion. [34] I have taken from the Israelites the breast of the presentation offering and the thigh of the contribution from their fellowship sacrifices, and have assigned them to the priest Aaron and to his sons as a permanent portion[D] from the Israelites."

[35] This is the portion from the fire offerings to the LORD for Aaron and his sons since the day they were presented to serve the LORD as priests. [36] The LORD commanded this to be given to them by the Israelites on the day he anointed them. It is a permanent portion throughout their generations.

[37] This is the law for the burnt offering, the grain offering, the sin offering, the guilt offering, the ordination offering, and the fellowship sacrifice, [38] which the LORD commanded Moses on Mount Sinai on the day he commanded the Israelites to present their offerings to the LORD in the Wilderness of Sinai.

ORDINATION OF AARON AND HIS SONS

8 The LORD spoke to Moses: [2] "Take Aaron, his sons with him, the garments, the anointing oil, the bull of the sin[E] offering, the two rams, and the basket of unleavened bread, [3] and assemble the whole community at the entrance to the tent of meeting." [4] So Moses did as the

[A] **7:18** Or *will bear his guilt* [B] **7:21** Some Hb mss, Sam, Syr, Tg read *swarming* [C] **7:24** Lit *fat of a carcass or the fat of a mauled beast* [D] **7:34** Or *statute*, also in v. 36 [E] **8:2** Or *purification*

LORD commanded him, and the community assembled at the entrance to the tent of meeting. 5 Moses said to them, "This is what the LORD has commanded to be done."

6 Then Moses presented Aaron and his sons and washed them with water. 7 He put the tunic on Aaron, wrapped the sash around him, clothed him with the robe, and put the ephod on him. He put the woven band of the ephod around him and fastened it to him. 8 Then he put the breastpiece on him and placed the Urim and Thummim into the breastpiece. 9 He also put the turban on his head and placed the gold medallion, the holy diadem, on the front of the turban, as the LORD had commanded Moses.

10 Then Moses took the anointing oil and anointed the tabernacle and everything in it to consecrate them. 11 He sprinkled some of the oil on the altar seven times, anointing the altar with all its utensils, and the basin with its stand, to consecrate them. 12 He poured some of the anointing oil on Aaron's head and anointed and consecrated him. 13 Then Moses presented Aaron's sons, clothed them with tunics, wrapped sashes around them, and fastened headbands on them, as the LORD had commanded Moses.

14 Then he brought the bull near for the sin offering, and Aaron and his sons laid their hands on the head of the bull for the sin offering. 15 Then Moses slaughtered it,[A] took the blood, and applied it with his finger to the horns of the altar on all sides, purifying the altar. He poured out the blood at the base of the altar and consecrated it so that atonement can be made on it.[B] 16 Moses took all the fat that was on the entrails, the fatty lobe of the liver, and the two kidneys with their fat, and he burned them on the altar. 17 He burned the bull with its hide, flesh, and waste outside the camp, as the LORD had commanded Moses.

18 Then he presented the ram for the burnt offering, and Aaron and his sons laid their hands on the head of the ram. 19 Moses slaughtered it and[C] splattered the blood on all sides of the altar. 20 Moses cut the ram into pieces and burned the head, the pieces, and the fat, 21 but he washed the entrails and legs with water. He then burned the entire ram on the altar. It was a burnt offering for a pleasing aroma, a fire offering to the LORD as he had commanded Moses.

22 Next he presented the second ram, the ram of ordination, and Aaron and his sons laid their hands on the head of the ram. 23 Moses slaughtered it,[D] took some of its blood, and put it on Aaron's right earlobe, on the thumb of his right hand, and on the big toe of his right foot. 24 Moses also presented Aaron's sons and put some of the blood on their right earlobes, on the thumbs of their right hands, and on the big toes of their right feet. Then Moses splattered the blood on all sides of the altar. 25 He took the fat — the fat tail, all the fat that was on the entrails, the fatty lobe of the liver, and the two kidneys with their fat — as well as the right thigh. 26 From the basket of unleavened bread that was before the LORD he took one cake of unleavened bread, one cake of bread made with oil, and one wafer, and placed them on the fat portions and the right thigh. 27 He put all these in the hands of Aaron and his sons and presented them before the LORD as a presentation offering. 28 Then Moses took them from their hands and burned them on the altar with the burnt offering. This was an ordination offering for a pleasing aroma, a fire offering to the LORD. 29 He also took the breast and presented it before the LORD as a presentation offering; it was Moses's portion of the ordination ram as the LORD had commanded him.

30 Then Moses took some of the anointing oil and some of the blood that was on the altar and sprinkled them on Aaron and his garments, as well as on his sons and their garments. In this way he consecrated Aaron and his garments, as well as his sons and their garments.

31 Moses said to Aaron and his sons, "Boil the meat at the entrance to the tent of meeting and eat it there with the bread that is in the basket for the ordination offering as I commanded:[E] Aaron and his sons are to eat it. 32 Burn up what remains of the meat and bread. 33 Do not go outside the entrance to the tent of meeting for seven days, until the time your days of ordination are completed, because it will take seven days to ordain you.[F] 34 The LORD commanded what has been done today in order to make atonement for you. 35 You must remain at the entrance to the tent of meeting day and night for seven days and keep the LORD's charge so that you will not die, for this is what I was commanded." 36 So

[A] **8:14-15** Or *offering, and he slaughtered it.* 15*Then Moses* [B] **8:15** Or *it by making atonement for it* [C] **8:18-19** Or *ram,* 19*and he slaughtered it. Moses* [D] **8:22-23** Or *ram,* 23*and he slaughtered it. Moses* [E] **8:31** LXX, Syr, Tg read *was commanded*; Ex 29:31-32 [F] **8:33** Lit *because he will fill your hands for seven days*

Aaron and his sons did everything the LORD
had commanded through Moses.

THE PRIESTLY MINISTRY INAUGURATED

9 On the eighth day Moses summoned Aaron,
his sons, and the elders of Israel. 2 He said
to Aaron, "Take a young bull for a sin[A] offering
and a ram for a burnt offering, both without
blemish, and present them before the LORD.
3 And tell the Israelites:[B] Take a male goat for
a sin offering; a calf and a lamb, male year-
lings without blemish, for a burnt offering;
4 an ox and a ram for a fellowship offering to
sacrifice before the LORD; and a grain offering
mixed with oil. For today the LORD is going to
appear to you."

5 They brought what Moses had commanded to the front of the tent of meeting, and the
whole community came forward and stood
before the LORD. 6 Moses said, "This is what
the LORD commanded you to do, that the glory
of the LORD may appear to you." 7 Then Moses said to Aaron, "Approach the altar and
sacrifice your sin offering and your burnt
offering; make atonement for yourself and
the people.[C] Sacrifice the people's offering
and make atonement for them, as the LORD
commanded."

8 So Aaron approached the altar and slaughtered the calf as a sin offering for himself.
9 Aaron's sons brought the blood to him, and
he dipped his finger in the blood and applied
it to the horns of the altar. He poured out the
blood at the base of the altar. 10 He burned the
fat, the kidneys, and the fatty lobe of the liver
from the sin offering on the altar, as the LORD
had commanded Moses. 11 He burned the flesh
and the hide outside the camp.

12 Then he slaughtered the burnt offering.
Aaron's sons brought him the blood, and he
splattered it on all sides of the altar. 13 They
brought him the burnt offering piece by piece,
along with the head, and he burned them on
the altar. 14 He washed the entrails and the
legs and burned them with the burnt offering on the altar.

15 Aaron presented the people's offering. He
took the male goat for the people's sin offering, slaughtered it, and made a sin offering
with it as he did before. 16 He presented the
burnt offering and sacrificed it according to
the regulation. 17 Next he presented the grain
offering, took a handful of it, and burned it
on the altar in addition to the morning burnt
offering.

18 Finally, he slaughtered the ox and the ram
as the people's fellowship sacrifice. Aaron's
sons brought him the blood, and he splattered
it on all sides of the altar. 19 They also brought
the fat portions from the ox and the ram — the
fat tail, the fat surrounding the entrails, the
kidneys, and the fatty lobe of the liver — 20 and
placed these on the breasts. Aaron burned the
fat portions on the altar, 21 but he presented
the breasts and the right thigh as a presentation offering before the LORD, as Moses had
commanded.[D]

22 Aaron lifted up his hands toward the
people and blessed them. He came down after sacrificing the sin offering, the burnt offering, and the fellowship offering. 23 Moses
and Aaron then entered the tent of meeting.
When they came out, they blessed the people,
and the glory of the LORD appeared to all the
people. 24 Fire came from the LORD and consumed the burnt offering and the fat portions
on the altar. And when all the people saw it,
they shouted and fell facedown.

Moses and Aaron then entered the tent of meeting. When they came out, they blessed the people, and the glory of the LORD appeared to all the people. Fire came from the LORD and consumed the burnt offering and the fat portions on the altar. And when all the people saw it, they shouted and fell facedown.

—Leviticus 9:23-24

NADAB AND ABIHU

10 Aaron's sons Nadab and Abihu each took
his own firepan, put fire in it, placed
incense on it, and presented unauthorized
fire before the LORD, which he had not commanded them to do. 2 Then fire came from
the LORD and consumed them, and they died

[A] 9:2 Or *purification* [B] 9:3 Sam, LXX read *elders of Israel* [C] 9:7 LXX reads *and your household* [D] 9:21 Some Hb mss, LXX, Sam read *as the LORD commanded Moses*

before the LORD. 3 Moses said to Aaron, "This
is what the LORD has spoken:
I will demonstrate my holiness[A]
to those who are near me,
and I will reveal my glory[B]
before all the people."
And Aaron remained silent.
4 Moses summoned Mishael and Elzaphan,
sons of Aaron's uncle Uzziel, and said to them,
"Come here and carry your relatives away from
the front of the sanctuary to a place outside
the camp." 5 So they came forward and carried them in their tunics outside the camp,
as Moses had said.
6 Then Moses said to Aaron and his sons Eleazar and Ithamar, "Do not let your hair hang
loose and do not tear your clothes, or else you
will die, and the LORD will become angry with
the whole community. However, your brothers,
the whole house of Israel, may weep over the
conflagration the LORD ignited. 7 You must not
go outside the entrance to the tent of meeting
or you will die, for the LORD's anointing oil is
on you." So they did as Moses said.

REGULATIONS FOR PRIESTS

8 The LORD spoke to Aaron: 9 "You and your
sons are not to drink wine or beer when you
enter the tent of meeting, or else you will
die; this is a permanent statute throughout
your generations. 10 You must distinguish between the holy and the common, and the clean
and the unclean, 11 and teach the Israelites all
the statutes that the LORD has given to them
through Moses."
12 Moses spoke to Aaron and his remaining
sons, Eleazar and Ithamar: "Take the grain
offering that is left over from the fire offerings to the LORD, and eat it prepared without
yeast beside the altar, because it is especially
holy. 13 You must eat it in a holy place because
it is your portion[C] and your sons' from the
fire offerings to the LORD, for this is what I
was commanded. 14 But you and your sons
and your daughters may eat the breast of the
presentation offering and the thigh of the
contribution in any ceremonially clean place,
because these portions have been assigned
to you and your children from the Israelites'
fellowship sacrifices. 15 They are to bring the
thigh of the contribution and the breast of the
presentation offering, together with the offerings of fat portions made by fire, to present
as a presentation offering before the LORD.
It will belong permanently to you and your
children, as the LORD commanded."
16 Then Moses inquired carefully about the
male goat of the sin offering, but it had already
been burned up. He was angry with Eleazar and
Ithamar, Aaron's surviving sons, and asked,
17 "Why didn't you eat the sin offering in the
sanctuary area? For it is especially holy, and
he has assigned it to you to take away the
guilt of the community and make atonement
for them before the LORD. 18 Since its blood
was not brought inside the sanctuary, you
should have eaten it in the sanctuary area,
as I commanded."
19 But Aaron replied to Moses, "See, today
they presented their sin offering and their
burnt offering before the LORD. Since these
things have happened to me, if I had eaten
the sin offering today, would it have been acceptable in the LORD's sight?" 20 When Moses
heard this, it was acceptable to him.[D]

CLEAN AND UNCLEAN LAND ANIMALS

11 The LORD spoke to Moses and Aaron: 2 "Tell
the Israelites: You may eat all these kinds
of land animals. 3 You may eat any animal with
divided hooves and that chews the cud. 4 But
among the ones that chew the cud or have
divided hooves you are not to eat these:
camels, though they chew the cud,
do not have divided hooves — they are
unclean for you;
5 hyraxes, though they chew the cud,
do not have hooves — they are unclean
for you;
6 hares, though they chew the cud,
do not have hooves — they are unclean
for you;
7 pigs, though they have divided hooves,
do not chew the cud — they are
unclean for you.
8 Do not eat any of their meat or touch their
carcasses — they are unclean for you.

CLEAN AND UNCLEAN AQUATIC ANIMALS

9 "This is what you may eat from all that is
in the water: You may eat everything in the
water that has fins and scales, whether in
the seas or streams. 10 But these are to be
abhorrent to you: everything in the seas or
streams that does not have fins and scales
among all the swarming things and other

[A] 10:3 Or *will be treated as holy* [B] 10:3 Or *will be glorified* [C] 10:13 Or *statute* [D] 10:20 Lit *acceptable in his sight*

living creatures in the water. 11 They are to
remain abhorrent to you; you must not eat
any of their meat, and you must abhor their
carcasses. 12 Everything in the water that
does not have fins and scales will be abhorrent to you.

UNCLEAN BIRDS

13 "You are to abhor these birds. They must not
be eaten because they are abhorrent:
eagles,[A] bearded vultures,
Egyptian vultures,[B] 14 kites,[C]
any kind of falcon,[D]
15 every kind of raven, 16 ostriches,[E]
short-eared owls, gulls,[F]
any kind of hawk,
17 little[G] owls, cormorants,[H]
long-eared owls,[I]
18 barn[J] owls, eagle owls,[K]
ospreys, 19 storks,[L]
any kind of heron,[M]
hoopoes, and bats.

CLEAN AND UNCLEAN FLYING INSECTS

20 "All winged insects that walk on all fours
are to be abhorrent to you. 21 But you may
eat these kinds of all the winged insects that
walk on all fours: those that have jointed legs
above their feet for hopping on the ground.
22 You may eat these:
any kind of locust, katydid, cricket,
and grasshopper.
23 All other winged insects that have four feet
are to be abhorrent to you.

PURIFICATION AFTER TOUCHING DEAD ANIMALS

24 "These will make you unclean. Whoever
touches their carcasses will be unclean until
evening, 25 and whoever carries any of their
carcasses is to wash his clothes and will be
unclean until evening. 26 All animals that have
hooves but do not have a divided hoof and do
not chew the cud are unclean for you. Whoever touches them becomes unclean. 27 All
the four-footed animals that walk on their
paws are unclean for you. Whoever touches
their carcasses will be unclean until evening,
28 and anyone who carries their carcasses is
to wash his clothes and will be unclean until
evening. They are unclean for you.

29 "These creatures that swarm on the ground
are unclean for you:
weasels,[N] mice,
any kind of large lizard,[O]
30 geckos, monitor lizards,[P]
common lizards,[Q] skinks,[R]
and chameleons.[S]
31 These are unclean for you among all the
swarming creatures. Whoever touches them
when they are dead will be unclean until evening. 32 When any one of them dies and falls
on anything it becomes unclean — any item
of wood, clothing, leather, sackcloth, or any
implement used for work. It is to be rinsed with
water and will remain unclean until evening;
then it will be clean. 33 If any of them falls into
any clay pot, everything in it will become unclean; you are to break it. 34 Any edible food
coming into contact with that unclean water
will become unclean, and any drinkable liquid in any container will become unclean.
35 Anything one of their carcasses falls on will
become unclean. If it is an oven or stove, it is
to be smashed; it is unclean and will remain
unclean for you. 36 A spring or cistern containing water will remain clean, but someone who touches a carcass in it will become
unclean. 37 If one of their carcasses falls on
any seed that is to be sown, it is clean; 38 but
if water has been put on the seed and one of
their carcasses falls on it, it is unclean for you.

39 "If one of the animals that you use for food
dies, anyone who touches its carcass will be
unclean until evening. 40 Anyone who eats
some of its carcass is to wash his clothes and
will be unclean until evening. Anyone who
carries its carcass must wash his clothes and
will be unclean until evening.

UNCLEAN SWARMING CREATURES

41 "All the creatures that swarm on the earth
are abhorrent; they must not be eaten. 42 Do
not eat any of the creatures that swarm on
the earth, anything that moves on its belly or
walks on all fours or on many feet,[T] for they
are abhorrent. 43 Do not become contaminated
by any creature that swarms; do not become

[A] **11:13** Or *griffon-vultures* [B] **11:13** Or *ospreys*, or *bearded vultures* [C] **11:14** Or *hawks* [D] **11:14** Or *buzzards*, or *hawks* [E] **11:16** Or *eagle owls* [F] **11:16** Or *long-eared owls* [G] **11:17** Or *tawny* [H] **11:17** Or *pelicans* [I] **11:17** Or *ibis* [J] **11:18** Or *little* [K] **11:18** Or *pelicans*, or *horned owls* [L] **11:19** Or *herons* [M] **11:19** Or *cormorants*, or *hawks* [N] **11:29** Or *mole rats*, or *rats* [O] **11:29** Or *of thorn-tailed*, or *dabb lizard*, or *of crocodile* [P] **11:30** Or *spotted lizards*, or *chameleons* [Q] **11:30** Or *geckos*, or *newts*, or *salamanders* [R] **11:30** Or *sand lizards*, or *newts*, or *snails* [S] **11:30** Or *salamanders*, or *moles* [T] **11:42** Lit *fours, to anything multiplying pairs of feet*

unclean or defiled by them. 44 For I am the LORD your God, so you must consecrate yourselves and be holy because I am holy. Do not defile yourselves by any swarming creature that crawls on the ground. 45 For I am the LORD, who brought you up from the land of Egypt to be your God, so you must be holy because I am holy.

46 "This is the law concerning animals, birds, all living creatures that move in the water, and all creatures that swarm on the ground, 47 in order to distinguish between the unclean and the clean, between the animals that may be eaten and those that may not be eaten."

PURIFICATION AFTER CHILDBIRTH

12 The LORD spoke to Moses: 2 "Tell the Israelites: When a woman becomes pregnant and gives birth to a male child, she will be unclean seven days, as she is during the days of her menstrual impurity. 3 The flesh of his foreskin must be circumcised on the eighth day. 4 She will continue in purification from her bleeding for thirty-three days. She must not touch any holy thing or go into the sanctuary until completing her days of purification. 5 But if she gives birth to a female child, she will be unclean for two weeks as she is during her menstrual impurity. She will continue in purification from her bleeding for sixty-six days.

6 "When her days of purification are complete, whether for a son or daughter, she is to bring to the priest at the entrance to the tent of meeting a year-old male lamb for a burnt offering, and a young pigeon or a turtledove for a sin[A] offering. 7 He will present them before the LORD and make atonement on her behalf; she will be clean from her discharge of blood. This is the law for a woman giving birth, whether to a male or female. 8 But if she doesn't have sufficient means[B] for a sheep, she may take two turtledoves or two young pigeons, one for a burnt offering and the other for a sin offering. Then the priest will make atonement on her behalf, and she will be clean."

SKIN DISEASES

13 The LORD spoke to Moses and Aaron: 2 "When a person has a swelling,[C] scab,[D] or spot on the skin of his body, and it may be a serious disease on the skin of his body, he is to be brought to the priest Aaron or to one of his sons, the priests. 3 The priest will examine the sore on the skin of his body. If the hair in the sore has turned white and the sore appears to be deeper than the skin of his body, it is in fact a serious skin disease. After the priest examines him, he must pronounce him unclean. 4 But if the spot on the skin of his body is white and does not appear to be deeper than the skin, and the hair in it has not turned white, the priest will quarantine the stricken person for seven days. 5 The priest will then reexamine him on the seventh day. If he sees that the sore remains unchanged and has not spread on the skin, the priest will quarantine him for another seven days. 6 The priest will examine him again on the seventh day. If the sore has faded and has not spread on the skin, the priest is to pronounce him clean; it is a scab. The person is to wash his clothes and will become clean. 7 But if the scab spreads further on his skin after he has presented himself to the priest for his cleansing, he is to present himself again to the priest. 8 The priest will examine him, and if the scab has spread on the skin, then the priest must pronounce him unclean; he has a serious skin disease.

9 "When a case of serious skin disease may have developed on a person, he is to be brought to the priest. 10 The priest will examine him. If there is a white swelling on the skin that has turned the hair white, and there is a patch of raw flesh in the swelling, 11 it is a chronic serious disease on the skin of his body, and the priest must pronounce him unclean. He need not quarantine him, for he is unclean. 12 But if the skin disease breaks out all over the skin so that it covers all the skin of the stricken person from his head to his feet so far as the priest can see, 13 the priest will look, and if the skin disease has covered his entire body, he is to pronounce the stricken person clean. Since he has turned totally white, he is clean. 14 But whenever raw flesh appears on him, he will be unclean. 15 When the priest examines the raw flesh, he must pronounce him unclean. Raw flesh is unclean; this is a serious skin disease. 16 But if the raw flesh changes[E] and[F] turns white, he is to go to the priest. 17 The priest will examine him, and if the sore has turned white, the priest must pronounce the stricken person clean; he is clean.

18 "When a boil appears on the skin of someone's body and it heals, 19 and a white swelling

---

[A] **12:6** Or *purification*, also in v. 8 [B] **12:8** Lit *if her hand cannot obtain what is sufficient* [C] **13:2** Or *discoloration* [D] **13:2** Or *rash*, or *eruption* [E] **13:16** Or *recedes* [F] **13:16** Or *flesh again*

or a reddish-white spot develops where the
boil was, the person is to present himself to
the priest. 20 The priest will make an examination, and if the spot seems to be beneath
the skin and the hair in it has turned white,
the priest must pronounce him unclean; it is
a case of serious skin disease that has broken
out in the boil. 21 But when the priest examines
it, if there is no white hair in it, and it is not
beneath the skin but is faded, the priest will
quarantine him seven days. 22 If it spreads further on the skin, the priest must pronounce
him unclean; it is in fact a disease. 23 But if the
spot remains where it is and does not spread,
it is only the scar from the boil. The priest is
to pronounce him clean.

24 "When there is a burn on the skin of one's
body produced by fire, and the patch made raw
by the burn becomes reddish-white or white,
25 the priest is to examine it. If the hair in the
spot has turned white and the spot appears
to be deeper than the skin, it is a serious skin
disease that has broken out in the burn. The
priest must pronounce him unclean; it is a
serious skin disease. 26 But when the priest
examines it, if there is no white hair in the
spot and it is not beneath the skin but is faded, the priest will quarantine him seven days.
27 The priest will reexamine him on the seventh day. If it has spread further on the skin,
the priest must pronounce him unclean; it is
in fact a case of serious skin disease. 28 But
if the spot has remained where it was and
has not spread on the skin but is faded, it is
the swelling from the burn. The priest is to
pronounce him clean, for it is only the scar
from the burn.

29 "When a man or woman has a condition
on the head or chin, 30 the priest is to examine the condition. If it appears to be deeper
than the skin, and the hair in it is yellow and
sparse, the priest must pronounce the person
unclean. It is a scaly outbreak, a serious skin
disease of the head or chin. 31 When the priest
examines the scaly condition, if it does not
appear to be deeper than the skin, and there
is no black hair in it, the priest will quarantine the person with the scaly condition for
seven days. 32 The priest will reexamine the
condition on the seventh day. If the scaly outbreak has not spread and there is no yellow
hair in it and it does not appear to be deeper
than the skin, 33 the person is to shave himself
but not shave the scaly area. Then the priest
will quarantine the person who has the scaly
outbreak for another seven days. 34 The priest
will examine the scaly outbreak on the seventh
day, and if it has not spread on the skin and
does not appear to be deeper than the skin,
the priest is to pronounce the person clean.
He is to wash his clothes, and he will be clean.
35 But if the scaly outbreak spreads further on
the skin after his cleansing, 36 the priest is to
examine the person. If the scaly outbreak has
spread on the skin, the priest does not need
to look for yellow hair; the person is unclean.
37 But if as far as he can see, the scaly outbreak
remains unchanged and black hair has grown
in it, then it has healed; he is clean. The priest
is to pronounce the person clean.

38 "When a man or a woman has white spots
on the skin of the body, 39 the priest is to make
an examination. If the spots on the skin of the
body are dull white, it is only a rash[A] that has
broken out on the skin; the person is clean.

40 "If a man loses the hair of his head, he is
bald, but he is clean. 41 Or if he loses the hair
at his hairline, he is bald on his forehead, but
he is clean. 42 But if there is a reddish-white
condition on the bald head or forehead, it is
a serious skin disease breaking out on his
head or forehead. 43 The priest is to examine
him, and if the swelling of the condition on
his bald head or forehead is reddish-white,
like the appearance of a serious skin disease
on his body, 44 the man is afflicted with a serious skin disease; he is unclean. The priest
must pronounce him unclean; the infection
is on his head.

45 "The person who has a case of serious
skin disease is to have his clothes torn and
his hair hanging loose, and he must cover
his mouth and cry out, 'Unclean, unclean!'
46 He will remain unclean as long as he has
the disease; he is unclean. He must live alone
in a place outside the camp.

CONTAMINATED FABRICS

47 "If a fabric is contaminated with mildew
— in wool or linen fabric, 48 in the warp or
weft of linen or wool, or in leather or anything
made of leather — 49 and if the contamination
is green or red in the fabric, the leather, the
warp, the weft, or any leather article, it is a
mildew contamination and is to be shown
to the priest. 50 The priest is to examine the

[A] **13:39** Hb obscure

contamination and quarantine the contaminated fabric for seven days. 51 The priest is to
reexamine the contamination on the seventh
day. If it has spread in the fabric, the warp, the
weft, or the leather, regardless of how it is
used, the contamination is harmful mildew;
it is unclean. 52 He is to burn the fabric, the
warp or weft in wool or linen, or any leather article, which is contaminated. Since it is
harmful mildew it must be burned.

53 "When the priest examines it, if the contamination has not spread in the fabric, the
warp or weft, or any leather article, 54 the
priest is to order whatever is contaminated
to be washed and quarantined for another
seven days. 55 After it has been washed, the
priest is to reexamine the contamination. If
the appearance of the contaminated article
has not changed, it is unclean. Even though
the contamination has not spread, you must
burn the fabric. It is a fungus[A] on the front or
back of the fabric.

56 "If the priest examines it, and the contamination has faded after it has been washed, he
is to cut the contaminated section out of the
fabric, the leather, or the warp or weft. 57 But
if it reappears in the fabric, the warp or weft,
or any leather article, it has broken out again.
You must burn whatever is contaminated.
58 But if the contamination disappears from
the fabric, the warp or weft, or any leather
article, which have been washed, it is to be
washed again, and it will be clean.

59 "This is the law concerning a mildew contamination in wool or linen fabric, warp or
weft, or any leather article, in order to pronounce it clean or unclean."

CLEANSING OF SKIN DISEASES

14 The LORD spoke to Moses: 2 "This is the
law concerning the person afflicted
with a skin disease on the day of his cleansing. He is to be brought to the priest, 3 who
will go outside the camp and examine him.
If the skin disease has disappeared from the
afflicted person,[B] 4 the priest will order that
two live clean birds, cedar wood, scarlet yarn,
and hyssop be brought for the one who is to
be cleansed. 5 Then the priest will order that
one of the birds be slaughtered over fresh
water in a clay pot. 6 He is to take the live bird
together with the cedar wood, scarlet yarn,
and hyssop, and dip them all into the blood of
the bird that was slaughtered over the fresh
water. 7 He will then sprinkle the blood sev-
en times on the one who is to be cleansed
from the skin disease. He is to pronounce him
clean and release the live bird over the open
countryside. 8 The one who is to be cleansed
must wash his clothes, shave off all his hair,
and bathe with water; he is clean. Afterward
he may enter the camp, but he must remain
outside his tent for seven days. 9 He is to shave
off all his hair again on the seventh day: his
head, his beard, his eyebrows, and the rest of
his hair. He is to wash his clothes and bathe
himself with water; he is clean.

10 "On the eighth day he must take two unblemished male lambs, an unblemished year-
old ewe lamb, a grain offering of six quarts[C] of
fine flour mixed with olive oil, and one-third of
a quart[D] of olive oil. 11 The priest who performs
the cleansing will place the person who is to
be cleansed, together with these offerings,
before the LORD at the entrance to the tent
of meeting. 12 The priest is to take one male
lamb and present it as a guilt offering, along
with the one-third quart of olive oil, and he
will present them as a presentation offering before the LORD. 13 He is to slaughter the
male lamb at the place in the sanctuary area
where the sin offering and burnt offering are
slaughtered, for like the sin offering, the guilt
offering belongs to the priest; it is especially
holy. 14 The priest is to take some of the blood
from the guilt offering and put it on the lobe
of the right ear of the one to be cleansed, on
the thumb of his right hand, and on the big
toe of his right foot. 15 Then the priest will
take some of the one-third quart of olive oil
and pour it into his left palm. 16 The priest
will dip his right finger into the oil in his left
palm and sprinkle some of the oil with his
finger seven times before the LORD. 17 From
the oil remaining in his palm the priest will
put some on the lobe of the right ear of the
one to be cleansed, on the thumb of his right
hand, and on the big toe of his right foot, on
top of the blood of the guilt offering. 18 What
is left of the oil in the priest's palm he is to put
on the head of the one to be cleansed. In this
way the priest will make atonement for him
before the LORD. 19 The priest is to sacrifice
the sin offering and make atonement for the
one to be cleansed from his uncleanness. Afterward he will slaughter the burnt offering.

[A] **13:55** Hb obscure [B] **14:3** Lit *the person afflicted with skin disease* [C] **14:10** Lit *three-tenths*; probably three-tenths of an ephah [D] **14:10** Lit *one log*, also in vv. 12,15,21,24

20 The priest is to offer the burnt offering and the grain offering on the altar. The priest will make atonement for him, and he will be clean.

21 "But if he is poor and cannot afford these, he is to take one male lamb for a guilt offering to be presented in order to make atonement for him, along with two quarts[A] of fine flour mixed with olive oil for a grain offering, one-third of a quart of olive oil, 22 and two turtledoves or two young pigeons, whatever he can afford, one to be a sin offering and the other a burnt offering. 23 On the eighth day he is to bring these things for his cleansing to the priest at the entrance to the tent of meeting before the LORD. 24 The priest will take the male lamb for the guilt offering and the one-third quart of olive oil, and present them as a presentation offering before the LORD. 25 After he slaughters the male lamb for the guilt offering, the priest is to take some of the blood of the guilt offering and put it on the right earlobe of the one to be cleansed, on the thumb of his right hand, and on the big toe of his right foot. 26 Then the priest will pour some of the oil into his left palm. 27 With his right finger the priest will sprinkle some of the oil in his left palm seven times before the LORD. 28 The priest will also put some of the oil in his palm on the right earlobe of the one to be cleansed, on the thumb of his right hand, and on the big toe of his right foot, on the same place as the blood of the guilt offering. 29 What is left of the oil in the priest's palm he is to put on the head of the one to be cleansed to make atonement for him before the LORD. 30 He is to then sacrifice one type of what he can afford, either the turtledoves or young pigeons, 31 one as a sin offering and the other as a burnt offering, sacrificing what he can afford together with the grain offering. In this way the priest will make atonement before the LORD for the one to be cleansed. 32 This is the law for someone who has[B] a skin disease and cannot afford the cost of his cleansing."

CLEANSING OF CONTAMINATED OBJECTS

33 The LORD spoke to Moses and Aaron: 34 "When you enter the land of Canaan that I am giving you as a possession, and I place a mildew contamination in a house in the land you possess,[C] 35 the owner of the house is to come and tell the priest: Something like mildew contamination has appeared[D] in my house. 36 The priest must order them to clear the house before he enters to examine the contamination, so that nothing in the house becomes unclean. Afterward the priest will come to examine the house. 37 He will examine it, and if the contamination in the walls of the house consists of green or red indentations[E] that appear to be beneath the surface of the wall, 38 the priest is to go outside the house to its doorway and quarantine the house for seven days. 39 The priest is to return on the seventh day and examine it. If the contamination has spread on the walls of the house, 40 the priest must order that the stones with the contamination be pulled out and thrown into an unclean place outside the city. 41 He is to have the inside of the house completely scraped, and have the plaster[F] that is scraped off dumped in an unclean place outside the city. 42 Then they are to take different stones to replace the former ones and take additional plaster to replaster the house.

43 "If the contamination reappears in the house after the stones have been pulled out, and after the house has been scraped and replastered, 44 the priest is to come and examine it. If the contamination has spread in the house, it is harmful mildew; the house is unclean. 45 It must be torn down with its stones, its beams, and all its plaster, and taken outside the city to an unclean place. 46 Whoever enters the house during any of the days the priest quarantines it will be unclean until evening. 47 Whoever lies down in the house is to wash his clothes, and whoever eats in it is to wash his clothes.

48 "But when the priest comes and examines it, if the contamination has not spread in the house after it was replastered, he is to pronounce the house clean because the contamination has disappeared.[G] 49 He is to take two birds, cedar wood, scarlet yarn, and hyssop to purify the house, 50 and he is to slaughter one of the birds over a clay pot containing fresh water. 51 He will take the cedar wood, the hyssop, the scarlet yarn, and the live bird, dip them in the blood of the slaughtered bird and the fresh water, and sprinkle the house seven times. 52 He will purify the house with the blood of the bird, the fresh water, the live bird, the cedar wood, the hyssop, and the scarlet yarn. 53 Then he is to release the live bird

[A] **14:21** Lit *him, and one-tenth*; probably one-tenth of an ephah [B] **14:32** Lit *someone on whom there is* [C] **14:34** Lit *land of your possession* [D] **14:35** Lit *appeared to me* [E] **14:37** Or *eruptions*; Hb obscure [F] **14:41** Lit *dust*, also in v. 42 [G] **14:48** Lit *healed*

into the open countryside outside the city.
In this way he will make atonement for the
house, and it will be clean.
54 "This is the law for any skin disease or
mildew, for a scaly outbreak, 55 for mildew in
clothing or on a house, 56 and for a swelling,
scab, or spot, 57 to determine when something
is unclean or clean. This is the law regarding
skin disease and mildew."

BODILY DISCHARGES

15 The LORD spoke to Moses and Aaron:
2 "Speak to the Israelites and tell them:
When any man has a discharge from his member, he is unclean. 3 This is uncleanness of his
discharge: Whether his member secretes the
discharge or retains it, he is unclean. All the
days that his member secretes or retains anything because of his discharge,[A] he is unclean.
4 Any bed the man with the discharge lies on
will be unclean, and any furniture he sits on
will be unclean. 5 Anyone who touches his bed
is to wash his clothes and bathe with water,
and he will remain unclean until evening.
6 Whoever sits on furniture that the man with
the discharge was sitting on is to wash his
clothes and bathe with water, and he will remain unclean until evening. 7 Whoever touches
the body[B] of the man with a discharge is to
wash his clothes and bathe with water, and
he will remain unclean until evening. 8 If the
man with the discharge spits on anyone who
is clean, he is to wash his clothes and bathe
with water, and he will remain unclean until
evening. 9 Any saddle the man with the discharge rides on will be unclean. 10 Whoever
touches anything that was under him will be
unclean until evening, and whoever carries
such things is to wash his clothes and bathe
with water, and he will remain unclean until
evening. 11 If the man with the discharge touches anyone without first rinsing his hands in
water, the person who was touched is to wash
his clothes and bathe with water, and he will
remain unclean until evening. 12 Any clay pot
that the man with the discharge touches must
be broken, while any wooden utensil is to be
rinsed with water.
13 "When the man with the discharge has
been cured of it, he is to count seven days for
his cleansing, wash his clothes, and bathe his
body in fresh water; he will be clean. 14 He must
take two turtledoves or two young pigeons on
the eighth day, come before the LORD at the
entrance to the tent of meeting, and give them
to the priest. 15 The priest is to sacrifice them,
one as a sin offering and the other as a burnt
offering. In this way the priest will make atonement for him before the LORD because of his
discharge.
16 "When a man has an emission of semen, he
is to bathe himself completely with water, and
he will remain unclean until evening. 17 Any
clothing or leather on which there is an emission of semen is to be washed with water, and
it will remain unclean until evening. 18 If a man
sleeps with a woman and has an emission of
semen, both of them are to bathe with water,
and they will remain unclean until evening.
19 "When a woman has a discharge, and it
consists of blood from her body, she will be
unclean because of her menstruation for sev-
en days. Everyone who touches her will be
unclean until evening. 20 Anything she lies on
during her menstruation will become unclean,
and anything she sits on will become unclean.
21 Everyone who touches her bed is to wash
his clothes and bathe with water, and he will
remain unclean until evening. 22 Everyone
who touches any furniture she was sitting on
is to wash his clothes and bathe with water,
and he will remain unclean until evening. 23 If
discharge is on the bed or the furniture she
was sitting on, when he touches it he will be
unclean until evening. 24 If a man sleeps with
her, and blood from her menstruation gets
on him, he will be unclean for seven days,
and every bed he lies on will become unclean.
25 "When a woman has a discharge of her
blood for many days, though it is not the time
of her menstruation, or if she has a discharge
beyond her period, she will be unclean all the
days of her unclean discharge, as she is during the days of her menstruation. 26 Any bed
she lies on during the days of her discharge
will be like her bed during menstrual impurity; any furniture she sits on will be unclean
as in her menstrual period. 27 Everyone who
touches them will be unclean; he must wash
his clothes and bathe with water, and he will
remain unclean until evening. 28 When she is
cured of her discharge, she is to count seven
days, and after that she will be clean. 29 On
the eighth day she must take two turtledoves
or two young pigeons and bring them to the
priest at the entrance to the tent of meeting.

[A] **15:3** DSS, Sam, LXX; MT omits *he is unclean. All the days that his member secretes or retains anything because of his discharge* [B] **15:7** Or *member*, also in v. 13

30 The priest is to sacrifice one as a sin offering and the other as a burnt offering. In this way the priest will make atonement for her before the LORD because of her unclean discharge.

31 "You must keep the Israelites from their uncleanness, so that they do not die by defiling my tabernacle that is among them. 32 This is the law for someone with a discharge: a man who has an emission of semen, becoming unclean by it; 33 a woman who is in her menstrual period; anyone who has a discharge, whether male or female; and a man who sleeps with a woman who is unclean."

THE DAY OF ATONEMENT

16 The LORD spoke to Moses after the death of two of Aaron's sons when they approached the presence of[A] the LORD and died. 2 The LORD said to Moses: "Tell your brother Aaron that he may not come whenever he wants into the holy place behind the curtain in front of the mercy seat on the ark or else he will die, because I appear in the cloud above the mercy seat.

3 "Aaron is to enter the most holy place in this way: with a young bull for a sin offering and a ram for a burnt offering. 4 He is to wear a holy linen tunic, and linen undergarments are to be on his body. He is to tie a linen sash around him and wrap his head with a linen turban. These are holy garments; he must bathe his body with water before he wears them. 5 He is to take from the Israelite community two male goats for a sin offering and one ram for a burnt offering.

6 "Aaron will present the bull for his sin offering and make atonement for himself and his household. 7 Next he will take the two goats and place them before the LORD at the entrance to the tent of meeting. 8 After Aaron casts lots for the two goats, one lot for the LORD and the other for an uninhabitable place,[B,C] 9 he is to present the goat chosen by lot for the LORD and sacrifice it as a sin offering. 10 But the goat chosen by lot for an uninhabitable place is to be presented alive before the LORD to make atonement with it by sending it into the wilderness for an uninhabitable place.

11 "When Aaron presents the bull for his sin offering and makes atonement for himself and his household, he will slaughter the bull for his sin offering. 12 Then he is to take a firepan full of blazing coals from the altar before the LORD and two handfuls of finely ground fragrant incense, and bring them inside the curtain. 13 He is to put the incense on the fire before the LORD, so that the cloud of incense covers the mercy seat that is over the testimony, or else he will die. 14 He is to take some of the bull's blood and sprinkle it with his finger against the east side of the mercy seat; then he will sprinkle some of the blood with his finger before the mercy seat seven times.

15 "When he slaughters the male goat for the people's sin offering and brings its blood inside the curtain, he will do the same with its blood as he did with the bull's blood: He is to sprinkle it against the mercy seat and in front of it. 16 He will make atonement for the most holy place in this way for all their sins because of the Israelites' impurities and rebellious acts. He will do the same for the tent of meeting that remains among them, because it is surrounded by their impurities. 17 No one may be in the tent of meeting from the time he enters to make atonement in the most holy place until he leaves after he has made atonement for himself, his household, and the whole assembly of Israel. 18 Then he will go out to the altar that is before the LORD and make atonement for it. He is to take some of the bull's blood and some of the goat's blood and put it on the horns on all sides of the altar. 19 He is to sprinkle some of the blood on it with his finger seven times to cleanse and set it apart from the Israelites' impurities.

20 "When he has finished making atonement for the most holy place, the tent of meeting, and the altar, he is to present the live male goat. 21 Aaron will lay both his hands on the head of the live goat and confess over it all the Israelites' iniquities and rebellious acts — all their sins. He is to put them on the goat's head and send it away into the wilderness by the man appointed for the task.[D] 22 The goat will carry all their iniquities into a desolate land, and the man will release it there.

23 "Then Aaron is to enter the tent of meeting, take off the linen garments he wore when he entered the most holy place, and leave them there. 24 He will bathe his body with water in a holy place and put on his clothes. Then he must go out and sacrifice his burnt offering and the people's burnt offering; he will make

[A] **16:1** LXX, Tg, Syr, Vg read *they brought strange fire before*; Nm 3:4 [B] **16:8** Lit *for Azazel*, also in vv. 10 (2x), 26 [C] **16:8** Perhaps a term that means "for the goat that departs," or "for removal," or "for a rough, difficult place," or "for a goat demon"; Hb obscure, also in vv. 10, 26 [D] **16:21** Lit *wilderness in the hand of a ready man*

atonement for himself and for the people. 25 He is to burn the fat of the sin offering on the altar. 26 The man who released the goat for an uninhabitable place is to wash his clothes and bathe his body with water; afterward he may reenter the camp. 27 The bull for the sin offering and the goat for the sin offering, whose blood was brought into the most holy place to make atonement, must be brought outside the camp and their hide, flesh, and waste burned. 28 The one who burns them is to wash his clothes and bathe himself with water; afterward he may reenter the camp.

Atonement will be made for you on this day to cleanse you, and you will be clean from all your sins before the LORD.
—Leviticus 16:30

29 "This is to be a permanent statute for you: In the seventh month, on the tenth day of the month you are to practice self-denial and do no work, both the native and the alien who resides among you. 30 Atonement will be made for you on this day to cleanse you, and you will be clean from all your sins before the LORD. 31 It is a Sabbath of complete rest for you, and you must practice self-denial; it is a permanent statute. 32 The priest who is anointed and ordained[A] to serve as high priest in place of his father will make atonement. He will put on the linen garments, the holy garments, 33 and make atonement for the most holy place. He will make atonement for the tent of meeting and the altar and will make atonement for the priests and all the people of the assembly. 34 This is to be a permanent statute for you, to make atonement for the Israelites once a year because of all their sins." And all this was done as the LORD commanded Moses.

FORBIDDEN SACRIFICES

17 The LORD spoke to Moses: 2 "Speak to Aaron, his sons, and all the Israelites and tell them: This is what the LORD has commanded: 3 Anyone from the house of Israel who slaughters an ox, sheep, or goat in the camp, or slaughters it outside the camp, 4 instead of bringing it to the entrance to the tent of meeting to present it as an offering to the LORD before his tabernacle — that person will be considered guilty.[B] He has shed blood and is to be cut off from his people. 5 This is so the Israelites will bring to the LORD the sacrifices they have been offering in the open country. They are to bring them to the priest at the entrance to the tent of meeting and offer them as fellowship sacrifices to the LORD. 6 The priest will then splatter the blood on the LORD's altar at the entrance to the tent of meeting and burn the fat as a pleasing aroma to the LORD. 7 They must no longer offer their sacrifices to the goat-demons that they have prostituted themselves with. This will be a permanent statute for them throughout their generations.

8 "Say to them: Anyone from the house of Israel or from the aliens who reside among them who offers a burnt offering or a sacrifice 9 but does not bring it to the entrance to the tent of meeting to sacrifice it to the LORD, that person is to be cut off from his people.

EATING BLOOD AND CARCASSES PROHIBITED

10 "Anyone from the house of Israel or from the aliens who reside among them who eats any blood, I will turn[C] against that person who eats blood and cut him off from his people. 11 For the life of a creature is in the blood, and I have appointed it to you to make atonement on the altar for[D] your lives, since it is the lifeblood that makes atonement. 12 Therefore I say to the Israelites: None of you and no alien who resides among you may eat blood.

13 "Any Israelite or alien residing among them, who hunts down a wild animal or bird

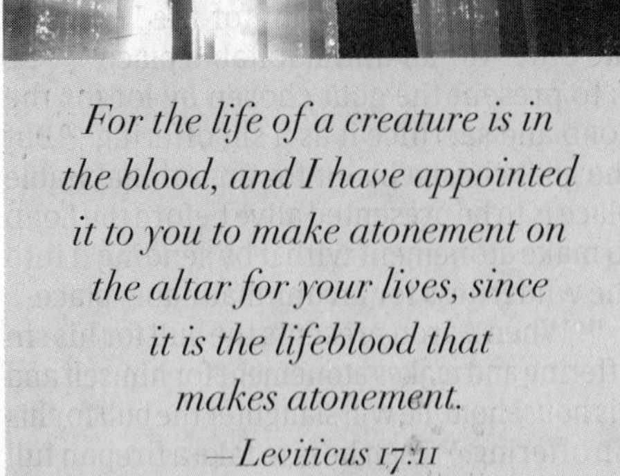
For the life of a creature is in the blood, and I have appointed it to you to make atonement on the altar for your lives, since it is the lifeblood that makes atonement.
—Leviticus 17:11

[A] 16:32 Lit *and will fill his hand* [B] 17:4 Lit *tabernacle — blood will be charged against that person* [C] 17:10 Lit *will set my face* [D] 17:11 Or *to ransom*

that may be eaten must drain its blood and cover it with dirt. 14 Since the life of every creature is its blood, I have told the Israelites: You are not to eat the blood of any creature, because the life of every creature is its blood; whoever eats it must be cut off.

15 "Every person, whether the native or the resident alien, who eats an animal that died a natural death or was mauled by wild beasts is to wash his clothes and bathe with water, and he will remain unclean until evening; then he will be clean. 16 But if he does not wash his clothes and bathe himself, he will bear his iniquity."

PROHIBITED PAGAN PRACTICES

18 The LORD spoke to Moses: 2 "Speak to the Israelites and tell them: I am the LORD your God. 3 Do not follow the practices of the land of Egypt, where you used to live, or follow the practices of the land of Canaan, where I am bringing you. You must not follow their customs. 4 You are to practice my ordinances and you are to keep my statutes by following them; I am the LORD your God. 5 Keep my statutes and ordinances; a person will live if he does them. I am the LORD.

6 "You are not to come near any close relative[A] for sexual intercourse; I am the LORD. 7 You are not to violate the intimacy that belongs to your father and mother.[B] She is your mother; you must not have sexual intercourse with her. 8 You are not to have sex with your father's wife; she is your father's family. 9 You are not to have sexual intercourse with your sister, either your father's daughter or your mother's, whether born at home or born elsewhere. You are not to have sex with her. 10 You are not to have sexual intercourse with your son's daughter or your daughter's daughter, for they are your family.[C] 11 You are not to have sexual intercourse with your father's wife's daughter, who is adopted by[D] your father; she is your sister. 12 You are not to have sexual intercourse with your father's sister; she is your father's close relative. 13 You are not to have sexual intercourse with your mother's sister, for she is your mother's close relative. 14 You are not to violate the intimacy that belongs to[E] your father's brother by approaching his wife to have sexual intercourse; she is your aunt. 15 You are not to have sexual intercourse with your daughter-in-law. She is your son's wife; you are not to have sex with her. 16 You are not to have sexual intercourse with your brother's wife; she is your brother's family. 17 You are not to have sexual intercourse with a woman and her daughter. You are not to marry her son's daughter or her daughter's daughter and have sex with her. They are close relatives; it is depraved. 18 You are not to marry a woman as a rival to her sister and have sexual intercourse with her during her sister's lifetime.

19 "You are not to approach a woman during her menstrual impurity to have sexual intercourse with her. 20 You are not to have sexual intercourse with[F] your neighbor's wife, defiling yourself with her.

21 "You are not to sacrifice any of your children in the fire[G] to Molech. Do not profane the name of your God; I am the LORD. 22 You are not to sleep with a man as with a woman; it is detestable. 23 You are not to have sexual intercourse with[H] any animal, defiling yourself with it; a woman is not to present herself to an animal to mate with it; it is a perversion.

24 "Do not defile yourselves by any of these practices, for the nations I am driving out before you have defiled themselves by all these things. 25 The land has become defiled, so I am punishing it for its iniquity, and the land will vomit out its inhabitants. 26 But you are to keep my statutes and ordinances. You must not commit any of these detestable acts — not the native or the alien who resides among you. 27 For the people who were in the land prior to you have committed all these detestable acts, and the land has become defiled. 28 If you defile the land, it will vomit you out as it has vomited out the nations that were before you. 29 Any person who does any of these detestable practices is to be cut off from his people. 30 You must keep my instruction to not do any of the detestable customs that were practiced before you, so that you do not defile yourselves by them; I am the LORD your God."

LAWS OF HOLINESS

19 The LORD spoke to Moses: 2 "Speak to the entire Israelite community and tell them: Be holy because I, the LORD your God, am holy.

3 "Each of you is to respect his mother and

[A] 18:6 Lit *any flesh of his flesh* [B] 18:7 Lit *Do not uncover your father's nakedness and your mother's nakedness* [C] 18:10 Lit *because they are your nakedness* [D] 18:11 Lit *daughter, a relative of* [E] 18:14 Lit *Do not uncover the nakedness of* [F] 18:20 Lit *to give your emission of semen to* [G] 18:21 Lit *to make any of your children pass through the fire* [H] 18:23 Lit *to give your emission to*

father. You are to keep my Sabbaths; I am the
LORD your God. 4 Do not turn to idols or make
cast images of gods for yourselves; I am the
LORD your God.
5 "When you offer a fellowship sacrifice to
the LORD, sacrifice it so that you may be accepted. 6 It is to be eaten on the day you sacrifice it or on the next day, but what remains
on the third day must be burned. 7 If any is
eaten on the third day, it is a repulsive thing; it
will not be accepted. 8 Anyone who eats it will
bear his iniquity, for he has profaned what is
holy to the LORD. That person is to be cut off
from his people.
9 "When you reap the harvest of your land,
you are not to reap to the very edge of your
field or gather the gleanings of your harvest.
10 Do not strip your vineyard bare or gather
its fallen grapes. Leave them for the poor and
the resident alien; I am the LORD your God.
11 "Do not steal. Do not act deceptively or
lie to one another. 12 Do not swear falsely by
my name, profaning the name of your God;
I am the LORD.
13 "Do not oppress your neighbor or rob
him. The wages due a hired worker must not
remain with you until morning. 14 Do not curse
the deaf or put a stumbling block in front
of the blind, but you are to fear your God; I
am the LORD.
15 "Do not act unjustly when deciding a case.
Do not be partial to the poor or give preference
to the rich; judge your neighbor fairly. 16 Do
not go about spreading slander among your
people; do not jeopardize[A] your neighbor's
life; I am the LORD.
17 "Do not harbor hatred against your brother.[B] Rebuke your neighbor directly, and you will
not incur guilt because of him. 18 Do not take
revenge or bear a grudge against members
of your community, but love your neighbor
as yourself; I am the LORD.
19 "You are to keep my statutes. Do not cross-
breed two different kinds of your livestock,
sow your fields with two kinds of seed, or put
on a garment made of two kinds of material.
20 "If a man has sexual intercourse with a
woman who is a slave designated for another
man, but she has not been redeemed or giv-
en her freedom, there must be punishment.[C]
They are not to be put to death, because she
had not been freed. 21 However, he must bring
a ram as his guilt[D] offering to the LORD at the
entrance to the tent of meeting. 22 The priest
will make atonement on his behalf before
the LORD with the ram of the guilt offering
for the sin he has committed, and he will be
forgiven for the sin he committed.
23 "When you come into the land and plant
any kind of tree for food, you are to consider

Other-centeredness | *Helping People in Need*

POOR PROVISION

"Do not strip your vineyard bare or gather its fallen grapes. Leave them for the poor and the resident alien; I am the LORD your God." Leviticus 19:10

Ancient Israel had no government programs to take care of those in need. Instead, God called on his people to be generous and share with the poor. One plan involved the Israelites purposefully leaving sections of their fields or portions of a particular crop unharvested. The disadvantaged were then allowed, even encouraged, to come into the fields and vineyards and help themselves to these leftovers. This ingenious welfare system involved generosity on the part of the donor and a bit of effort on the part of the recipient.

Modern versions of this practice are many. One family throws all their coins each day into a jar and uses this money monthly to support an international student who's working her way through school. Habitat for Humanity provides human assistance and material resources to help homeless families construct their own homes. In each case, all the parties find great blessing!

What creative steps can you take to free up some of your resources to help those in need?

For the next note on *Other-centeredness*, see Leviticus 19:18.

[A] **19:16** Lit *not stand against* [B] **19:17** Or *your fellow Israelite* [C] **19:20** Or *compensation* [D] **19:21** Or *restitution*

the fruit forbidden.[A] It will be forbidden to
you for three years; it is not to be eaten. **24** In
the fourth year all its fruit is to be consecrated as a praise offering to the LORD. **25** But in
the fifth year you may eat its fruit. In this
way its yield will increase for you; I am the
LORD your God.
26 "You are not to eat anything with blood
in it.[B] You are not to practice divination or
witchcraft. **27** You are not to cut off the hair
at the sides of your head or mar the edge of
your beard. **28** You are not to make gashes on
your bodies for the dead or put tattoo marks
on yourselves; I am the LORD.
29 "Do not debase[C] your daughter by making
her a prostitute, or the land will be prostituted and filled with depravity. **30** Keep my
Sabbaths and revere my sanctuary; I am the
LORD.
31 "Do not turn to mediums[D] or consult spiritists,[E] or you will be defiled by them; I am the
LORD your God.
32 "You are to rise in the presence of the elderly and honor the old. Fear your God; I am
the LORD.
33 "When an alien resides with you in your
land, you must not oppress him. **34** You will
regard the alien who resides with you as the
native-born among you. You are to love him
as yourself, for you were aliens in the land of
Egypt; I am the LORD your God.
35 "Do not be unfair in measurements of
length, weight, or volume. **36** You are to have
honest balances, honest weights, an honest
dry measure,[F] and an honest liquid measure;[G]
I am the LORD your God, who brought you
out of the land of Egypt. **37** Keep all my statutes and all my ordinances and do them; I
am the LORD."

MOLECH WORSHIP AND SPIRITISM

20 The LORD spoke to Moses: **2** "Say to the
Israelites: Any Israelite or alien residing
in Israel who gives any of his children to Molech must be put to death; the people of the
country are to stone him. **3** I will turn[H] against
that man and cut him off from his people,
because he gave his offspring to Molech, defiling my sanctuary and profaning my holy
name. **4** But if the people of the country look
the other way when that man[I] gives any of
his children to Molech, and do not put him to
death, **5** then I will turn against that man and
his family, and cut off from their people both
him and all who follow[J] him in prostituting
themselves with Molech.

Relationships | *Confronting in Love*

SPEAK UP

"Do not harbor hatred against your brother. Rebuke your neighbor directly, and you will not incur guilt because of him." Leviticus 19:17

Almost every day, a spouse, child, parent, sibling, or friend says or does something hurtful. For a few brief moments, we consider addressing the person's misbehavior. Then we talk ourselves out of it: "Aw, that would just get them all worked up." Consequently *we* stay worked up—at least internally—battling a host of bad attitudes, resentment, maybe even bitterness!

God offers a better way. Rather than tip-toeing around conflict situations, we are called to boldly enter them. We speak up. "Rebuke your neighbor directly" doesn't mean ranting or berating. It means firmly but gently telling the truth—and talking directly to the person and not complaining to all the other neighbors! The goal is to address behavior, not attack a person.

If we do it right, our efforts at confrontation may result in an apology and a better relationship. We have no guarantee of that, of course. We have to remember that the response of the other person is not our responsibility. All we are called to do is our part. If you are wronged, say something, and say it in the right spirit. Trust the outcome to God.

For the next note on *Relationships*, see 1 Samuel 18:1-3.

[A] **19:23** Lit *uncircumcised* [B] **19:26** Or *anything over its blood* [C] **19:29** Lit *profane* [D] **19:31** Or *spirits of the dead* [E] **19:31** Or *familiar spirits* [F] **19:36** Lit *honest ephah* [G] **19:36** Lit *honest hin* [H] **20:3** Lit *will set my face*, also in vv. 5,6 [I] **20:4** Lit *country ever close their eyes from that man when he* [J] **20:5** Lit *prostitute themselves with*

[6] "Whoever turns to mediums[A] or spiritists[B]
and prostitutes himself with them, I will turn
against that person and cut him off from his
people. [7] Consecrate yourselves and be holy,
for I am the LORD your God. [8] Keep my statutes
and do them; I am the LORD who sets you apart.

FAMILY AND SEXUAL OFFENSES

[9] "If anyone curses his father or mother, he
must be put to death. He has cursed his father
or mother; his death is his own fault.[C]
[10] "If a man commits adultery with a married woman — if he commits adultery with
his neighbor's wife — both the adulterer and
the adulteress must be put to death. [11] If a man
sleeps with his father's wife, he has violated
the intimacy that belongs to his father.[D] Both
of them must be put to death; their death is
their own fault.[E] [12] If a man sleeps with his
daughter-in-law, both of them must be put to
death. They have acted perversely; their death
is their own fault. [13] If a man sleeps with a man
as with a woman, they have both committed a
detestable act. They must be put to death; their
death is their own fault. [14] If a man marries[F] a
woman and her mother, it is depraved. Both he
and they must be burned, so that there will be
no depravity among you. [15] If a man has sexual
intercourse with[G] an animal, he must be put
to death; you are also to kill the animal. [16] If
a woman approaches any animal and mates
with it, you are to kill the woman and the animal. They must be put to death; their death is
their own fault. [17] If a man marries his sister,
whether his father's daughter or his mother's
daughter, and they have sexual relations,[H] it is
a disgrace. They are to be cut off publicly from
their people. He has had sexual intercourse
with his sister; he will bear his iniquity. [18] If
a man sleeps with a menstruating woman
and has sexual intercourse with her, he has
exposed the source of her flow, and she has
uncovered the source of her blood. Both of
them are to be cut off from their people. [19] You
must not have sexual intercourse with your
mother's sister or your father's sister, for it is
exposing one's own blood relative; both people will bear their iniquity. [20] If a man sleeps
with his aunt, he has violated the intimacy
that belongs to his uncle;[I] they will bear their
guilt and die childless. [21] If a man marries his
brother's wife, it is impurity. He has violated
the intimacy that belongs to his brother;[J] they
will be childless.

Other-centeredness | *Not Holding Resentment/Grudges*

LET IT GO

"Do not take revenge or bear a grudge against members of your community, but love your neighbor as yourself; I am the LORD." Leviticus 19:18

What are our options when someone wrongs us? One possibility is to take revenge. We pay the person back in kind: insult for insult, rumor for rumor, blow for blow. This is the way of children and foolish nations. It solves nothing and only escalates the tensions.

Another possibility is to bear a grudge. By this internal act, we replay and rehearse in our minds the damage done. In time, we are full of *resentment*. Such harbored bitterness mostly hurts us—not our offenders—as medical science increasingly shows.

The third way is the rare, noble response of love. "Love your neighbor as yourself," God says. This doesn't mean we minimize an offense, much less pretend no wrong occurred. It simply means we don't keep a record of wrongs (see 1Co 13:5). In other words, we forgive.

If you are lugging around any grudges, those may be at least part of the reason your soul is so exhausted.

For the next note on *Other-centeredness*, see Leviticus 25:17.

[A] **20:6** Or *spirits of the dead* [B] **20:6** Or *familiar spirits* [C] **20:9** Lit *his blood on him* [D] **20:11** Lit *has uncovered his father's nakedness* [E] **20:11** Lit *their blood on them*, also in vv. 12,13,16,27 [F] **20:14** Lit *takes*, also in vv. 17,21 [G] **20:15** Lit *man gives his emission to* [H] **20:17** Lit *and he sees her nakedness and she sees his nakedness* [I] **20:20** Lit *has uncovered his uncle's nakedness* [J] **20:21** Lit *has uncovered his brother's nakedness*

HOLINESS IN THE LAND

22 "You are to keep all my statutes and all my ordinances, and do them, so that the land where I am bringing you to live will not vomit you out. 23 You must not follow the statutes of the nations I am driving out before you, for they did all these things, and I abhorred them. 24 And I promised you: You will inherit their land, since I will give it to you to possess, a land flowing with milk and honey. I am the LORD your God who set you apart from the peoples. 25 Therefore you are to distinguish the clean animal from the unclean one, and the unclean bird from the clean one. Do not become contaminated by any land animal, bird, or whatever crawls on the ground; I have set these apart as unclean for you. 26 You are to be holy to me because I, the LORD, am holy, and I have set you apart from the nations to be mine.

27 "A man or a woman who is[A] a medium or a spiritist must be put to death. They are to be stoned; their death is their own fault."

THE HOLINESS OF THE PRIESTS

21 The LORD said to Moses: "Speak to Aaron's sons, the priests, and tell them: A priest is not to make himself ceremonially unclean for a dead person among his relatives, 2 except for his immediate family: his mother, father, son, daughter, or brother. 3 He may make himself unclean for his unmarried virgin sister in his immediate family. 4 He is not to make himself unclean for those related to him by marriage[B] and so defile himself.

5 "Priests may not make bald spots on their heads, shave the edge of their beards, or make gashes on their bodies. 6 They are to be holy to their God and not profane the name of their God. For they present the fire offerings to the LORD, the food of their God, and they must be holy. 7 They are not to marry a woman defiled by prostitution.[C] They are not to marry one divorced by her husband, for the priest is holy to his God. 8 You are to consider him holy since he presents the food of your God. He will be holy to you because I, the LORD who sets you apart, am holy. 9 If a priest's daughter defiles herself by promiscuity,[D] she defiles her father; she must be burned to death.

10 "The priest who is highest among his brothers, who has had the anointing oil poured on his head and has been ordained[E] to wear the clothes, must not dishevel his hair[F] or tear his clothes. 11 He must not go near any dead person or make himself unclean even for his father or mother. 12 He must not leave the sanctuary or he will desecrate the sanctuary of his God, for the consecration of the anointing oil of his God is on him; I am the LORD.

13 "He is to marry a woman who is a virgin. 14 He is not to marry a widow, a divorced woman, or one defiled by prostitution. He is to marry a virgin from his own people, 15 so that he does not corrupt his bloodline[G] among his people, for I am the LORD who sets him apart."

PHYSICAL DEFECTS AND PRIESTS

16 The LORD spoke to Moses: 17 "Tell Aaron: None of your descendants throughout your generations who has a physical defect is to come near to present the food of his God. 18 No man who has any defect is to come near: no man who is blind, lame, facially disfigured, or deformed; 19 no man who has a broken foot or hand, 20 or who is a hunchback or a dwarf,[H] or who has an eye defect, a festering rash, scabs, or a crushed testicle. 21 No descendant of the priest Aaron who has a defect is to come near to present the fire offerings to the LORD. He has a defect and is not to come near to present the food of his God. 22 He may eat the food of his God from what is especially holy as well as from what is holy. 23 But because he has a defect, he must not go near the curtain or approach the altar. He is not to desecrate my holy places, for I am the LORD who sets them apart." 24 Moses said this to Aaron and his sons and to all the Israelites.

PRIESTS AND THEIR FOOD

22 The LORD spoke to Moses: 2 "Tell Aaron and his sons to deal respectfully with the holy offerings of the Israelites that they have consecrated to me, so they do not profane my holy name; I am the LORD. 3 Say to them: If any man from any of your descendants throughout your generations is in a state of uncleanness yet approaches the holy offerings that the Israelites consecrate to the LORD, that person will be cut off from my presence; I am the LORD. 4 No man of Aaron's descendants who has a skin disease[I] or a discharge is to eat from the holy offerings until he is clean. Whoever touches anything made unclean by a

[A] **20:27** Lit *is in them* [B] **21:4** Lit *unclean a husband among his people* [C] **21:7** Or *a prostitute*, or *a defiled woman* [D] **21:9** Or *prostitution* [E] **21:10** Lit *and one has filled his hand* [F] **21:10** Or *not uncover his head* [G] **21:15** Lit *not profane his seed* [H] **21:20** Or *or emaciated* [I] **22:4** Or *has leprosy* or *scale disease*

dead person or by a man who has an emission of semen, 5 or whoever touches any swarming creature that makes him unclean or any person who makes him unclean — whatever his uncleanness — 6 the man who touches any of these will remain unclean until evening and is not to eat from the holy offerings unless he has bathed his body with water. 7 When the sun has set, he will become clean, and then he may eat from the holy offerings, for that is his food. 8 He must not eat an animal that died naturally or was mauled by wild beasts,[A] making himself unclean by it; I am the LORD. 9 They must keep my instruction, or they will be guilty and die because they profane it; I am the LORD who sets them apart.

10 "No one outside a priest's family[B] is to eat the holy offering. A foreigner staying with a priest or a hired worker is not to eat the holy offering. 11 But if a priest purchases someone with his own silver, that person may eat it, and those born in his house may eat his food. 12 If the priest's daughter is married to a man outside a priest's family,[C] she is not to eat from the holy contributions.[D] 13 But if the priest's daughter becomes widowed or divorced, has no children, and returns to her father's house as in her youth, she may share her father's food. But no outsider may share it. 14 If anyone eats a holy offering in error, he is to add a fifth to its value and give the holy offering to the priest. 15 The priests must not profane the holy offerings the Israelites give to the LORD 16 by letting the people eat their holy offerings and having them bear the penalty of restitution. For I am the LORD who sets them apart."

ACCEPTABLE SACRIFICES

17 The LORD spoke to Moses: 18 "Speak to Aaron, his sons, and all the Israelites and tell them: Any man of the house of Israel or of the resident aliens in Israel who presents his offering — whether they present payment of vows or freewill gifts to the LORD as burnt offerings — 19 must offer an unblemished male from the cattle, sheep, or goats in order for you to be accepted. 20 You are not to present anything that has a defect, because it will not be accepted on your behalf.

21 "When a man presents a fellowship sacrifice to the LORD to fulfill a vow or as a freewill offering from the herd or flock, it has to be unblemished to be acceptable; there must be no defect in it. 22 You are not to present any animal to the LORD that is blind, injured, maimed, or has a running sore, festering rash, or scabs; you may not put any of them on the altar as a fire offering to the LORD. 23 You may sacrifice as a freewill offering any animal from the herd or flock that has an elongated or stunted limb, but it is not acceptable as a vow offering. 24 You are not to present to the LORD anything that has bruised, crushed, torn, or severed testicles; you must not sacrifice them in your land. 25 Neither you nor[E] a foreigner are to present food to your God from any of these animals. They will not be accepted for you because they are deformed and have a defect."

26 The LORD spoke to Moses: 27 "When an ox, sheep, or goat is born, it is to remain with[F] its mother for seven days; from the eighth day on, it will be acceptable as an offering, a fire offering to the LORD. 28 But you are not to slaughter an animal from the herd or flock on the same day as its young. 29 When you sacrifice a thank offering to the LORD, sacrifice it so that you may be accepted. 30 It is to be eaten on the same day. Do not let any of it remain until morning; I am the LORD.

31 "You are to keep my commands and do them; I am the LORD. 32 You must not profane my holy name; I must be treated as holy among the Israelites. I am the LORD who sets you apart, 33 the one who brought you out of the land of Egypt to be your God; I am the LORD."

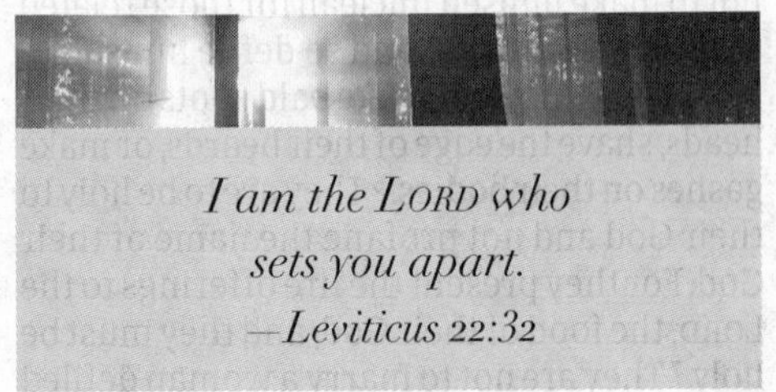

I am the LORD who sets you apart.
—Leviticus 22:32

HOLY DAYS

23 The LORD spoke to Moses: 2 "Speak to the Israelites and tell them: These are my appointed times, the times of the LORD that you will proclaim as sacred assemblies.

3 "Work may be done for six days, but on the seventh day there is to be a Sabbath of complete rest, a sacred assembly. You are not to do any work; it is a Sabbath to the LORD wherever you live.

4 "These are the LORD's appointed times, the

[A] 22:8 Lit *eat a carcass or a mauled beast* [B] 22:10 Lit *"No stranger* [C] 22:12 Lit *to a stranger* [D] 22:12 Lit *the contribution of holy offerings* [E] 22:25 Lit *nor from the hand of* [F] 22:27 Lit *under*

My Story | Cathy

Some of my earliest life lessons from home were about working hard. Part of it was taught but most caught. My dad was a grocer, and Mom was a teacher. Both those jobs were service oriented and had a way of taking up much of each day. But Mom was off during the summers, and my sisters and I had wonderful months with her. Tending the garden and canning was playful work. I was the kid on the block who started the lemonade stand and then hired other kids to run it for me. When I was old enough to work in the grocery store, I had a job waiting for me. And by the time I graduated from high school, I knew I wanted to follow my mom's example and become a teacher. At that point, my life was about work.

Along the way, our family was nominally religious, but it wasn't until I got married that I started taking seriously a faith that was modelled and taught to me. I discovered Christ's love and accepted him as my Savior. But, like the other parts of my life, trusting God was mostly about working hard.

Until one day I heard the curious word *Sabbath*. At first, I thought it was just another word for "Sunday." But gradually I learned that it was actually a word about rest and restoration. Those concepts didn't get much attention in my working-hard world. But the older I got, the more I became aware of a growing restlessness, a tiredness that was deeper and different than simply lacking physical energy. I knew I was missing something, and I decided to think again about the Sabbath. If God worked as hard as God ever worked for six days in creation and then took a day off, who was I to think I could keep up a harder or faster pace?

The experience of Sabbath rest was relief for me. I have discovered that God built into life a do-over for me in my relationship with him. It became a weekly time of renewal and refreshment. The drive to work has been tempered by grace, and I look forward to a regular seventh day of rest so I can hear God speak to me.

sacred assemblies you are to proclaim at their
appointed times. 5 The Passover to the LORD
comes in the first month, at twilight on the
fourteenth day of the month. 6 The Festival
of Unleavened Bread to the LORD is on the
fifteenth day of the same month. For seven
days you must eat unleavened bread. 7 On the
first day you are to hold a sacred assembly;
you are not to do any daily work. 8 You are to
present a fire offering to the LORD for seven
days. On the seventh day there will be a sacred
assembly; do not do any daily work."
9 The LORD spoke to Moses: 10 "Speak to the
Israelites and tell them: When you enter the
land I am giving you and reap its harvest,[A]
you are to bring the first sheaf of your harvest to the priest. 11 He will present the sheaf
before the LORD so that you may be accepted;
the priest is to present it on the day after the
Sabbath. 12 On the day you present the sheaf,
you are to offer a year-old male lamb[B] without blemish as a burnt offering to the LORD.
13 Its grain offering is to be four quarts[C] of fine
flour mixed with oil as a fire offering to the
LORD, a pleasing aroma, and its drink offering
will be one quart[D] of wine. 14 You must not eat
bread, roasted grain, or any new grain[E] until
this very day, and until you have brought the
offering to your God. This is to be a permanent
statute throughout your generations wherever you live.
15 "You are to count seven[F] complete weeks[G]
starting from the day after the Sabbath, the
day you brought the sheaf of the presentation offering. 16 You are to count fifty days
until the day after the seventh Sabbath and
then present an offering of new grain to
the LORD. 17 Bring two loaves of bread from
your settlements as a presentation offering,
each of them made from four quarts of fine
flour, baked with yeast, as firstfruits to the
LORD. 18 You are to present with the bread
seven unblemished male lambs a year old,
one young bull, and two rams. They will be
a burnt offering to the LORD, with their grain
offerings and drink offerings, a fire offering
of a pleasing aroma to the LORD. 19 You are also
to prepare one male goat as a sin offering,
and two male lambs a year old as a fellowship
sacrifice. 20 The priest will present the lambs

[A] **23:10** = the barley harvest [B] **23:12** Or *a male lamb in its first year* [C] **23:13** Lit *two-tenths of an ephah*, also in v. 17 [D] **23:13** Lit *one-fourth of a hin* [E] **23:14** Grain or bread from the new harvest [F] **23:15** Lit *count; they will be seven* [G] **23:15** Or *Sabbaths*

with the bread of firstfruits as a presentation
offering before the LORD; the bread and the
two lambs will be holy to the LORD for the
priest. 21 On that same day you are to make
a proclamation and hold a sacred assembly.
You are not to do any daily work. This is to
be a permanent statute wherever you live
throughout your generations. 22 When you
reap the harvest of your land, you are not to
reap all the way to the edge of your field or
gather the gleanings of your harvest. Leave
them for the poor and the resident alien; I
am the LORD your God."

23 The LORD spoke to Moses: 24 "Tell the Israelites: In the seventh month, on the first
day of the month, you are to have a day of
complete rest, commemoration, and trumpet blasts — a sacred assembly. 25 You must
not do any daily work, but you must present
a fire offering to the LORD."

26 The LORD again spoke to Moses: 27 "The
tenth day of this seventh month is the Day of
Atonement. You are to hold a sacred assembly
and practice self-denial; you are to present a
fire offering to the LORD. 28 On this particular
day you are not to do any work, for it is a Day of
Atonement to make atonement for yourselves
before the LORD your God. 29 If any person does
not practice self-denial on this particular day,
he is to be cut off from his people. 30 I will destroy among his people anyone who does any
work on this same day. 31 You are not to do any
work. This is a permanent statute throughout
your generations wherever you live. 32 It will
be a Sabbath of complete rest for you, and you
must practice self-denial. You are to observe
your Sabbath from the evening of the ninth
day of the month until the following evening."

33 The LORD spoke to Moses: 34 "Tell the Israelites: The Festival of Shelters[A] to the LORD
begins on the fifteenth day of this seventh
month and continues for seven days. 35 There
is to be a sacred assembly on the first day;
you are not to do any daily work. 36 You are
to present a fire offering to the LORD for sev-
en days. On the eighth day you are to hold a
sacred assembly and present a fire offering
to the LORD. It is a solemn gathering; you are
not to do any daily work.

37 "These are the LORD's appointed times that
you are to proclaim as sacred assemblies for
presenting fire offerings to the LORD, burnt
offerings and grain offerings, sacrifices and
drink offerings, each on its designated day.
38 These are in addition to the offerings for
the LORD's Sabbaths, your gifts, all your vow
offerings, and all your freewill offerings that
you give to the LORD.

39 "You are to celebrate the LORD's festival
on the fifteenth day of the seventh month
for seven days after you have gathered the
produce of the land. There will be complete
rest on the first day and complete rest on the
eighth day. 40 On the first day you are to take
the product of majestic trees — palm fronds,
boughs of leafy trees, and willows of the brook
— and rejoice before the LORD your God for
seven days. 41 You are to celebrate it as a festival to the LORD seven days each year. This
is a permanent statute for you throughout
your generations; celebrate it in the seventh
month. 42 You are to live in shelters for seven
days. All the native-born of Israel must live
in shelters, 43 so that your generations may
know that I made the Israelites live in shelters when I brought them out of the land of
Egypt; I am the LORD your God." 44 So Moses
declared the LORD's appointed times to the
Israelites.

TABERNACLE OIL AND BREAD

24 The LORD spoke to Moses: 2 "Command
the Israelites to bring you pure oil
from crushed olives for the light, in order
to keep the lamp burning regularly. 3 Aaron
is to tend it continually from evening until
morning before the LORD outside the curtain of the testimony in the tent of meeting.
This is a permanent statute throughout your
generations. 4 He must continually tend the
lamps on the pure gold lampstand in the
LORD's presence.

5 "Take fine flour and bake it into twelve
loaves; each loaf is to be made with four
quarts.[B] 6 Arrange them in two rows, six to a
row, on the pure gold table before the LORD.
7 Place pure frankincense near each row, so
that it may serve as a memorial portion for
the bread and a fire offering to the LORD. 8 The
bread is to be set out before the LORD every
Sabbath day as a permanent covenant obligation on the part of the Israelites. 9 It belongs
to Aaron and his sons, who are to eat it in a
holy place, for it is the holiest portion for him
from the fire offerings to the LORD; this is a
permanent rule."

[A] **23:34** Or *Tabernacles, or Booths* [B] **24:5** Lit *two-tenths of an ephah*

A CASE OF BLASPHEMY

10 Now the son of an Israelite mother and an
Egyptian father was[A] among the Israelites.
A fight broke out in the camp between the
Israelite woman's son and an Israelite man.
11 Her son cursed and blasphemed the Name,
and they brought him to Moses. (His mother's
name was Shelomith, a daughter of Dibri of
the tribe of Dan.) 12 They put him in custody
until the LORD's decision could be made clear
to them.

13 Then the LORD spoke to Moses: 14 "Bring the
one who has cursed to the outside of the camp
and have all who heard him lay their hands
on his head; then have the whole community
stone him. 15 And tell the Israelites: If anyone
curses his God, he will bear the consequences
of his sin. 16 Whoever blasphemes the name
of the LORD must be put to death; the whole
community is to stone him. If he blasphemes
the Name, he is to be put to death, whether
the resident alien or the native.

17 "If a man kills anyone, he must be put to
death. 18 Whoever kills an animal is to make
restitution for it, life for life. 19 If any man inflicts a permanent injury on his neighbor,
whatever he has done is to be done to him:
20 fracture for fracture, eye for eye, tooth for
tooth. Whatever injury he inflicted on the
person, the same is to be inflicted on him.
21 Whoever kills an animal is to make restitution for it, but whoever kills a person is to be
put to death. 22 You are to have the same law
for the resident alien and the native, because
I am the LORD your God."

23 After Moses spoke to the Israelites, they
brought the one who had cursed to the outside
of the camp and stoned him. So the Israelites
did as the LORD had commanded Moses.

SABBATH YEARS AND JUBILEE

25 The LORD spoke to Moses on Mount
Sinai: 2 "Speak to the Israelites and tell
them: When you enter the land I am giving
you, the land will observe a Sabbath to the
LORD. 3 You may sow your field for six years,
and you may prune your vineyard and gather
its produce for six years. 4 But there will be a
Sabbath of complete rest for the land in the
seventh year, a Sabbath to the LORD: you are not
to sow your field or prune your vineyard. 5 You
are not to reap what grows by itself from your
crop, or harvest the grapes of your untended
vines. It is to be a year of complete rest for the
land. 6 Whatever the land produces during
the Sabbath year can be food for you — for
yourself, your male or female slave, and the
hired worker or alien who resides with you.

Other-centeredness | *Identifying Those We Have Wronged*

MAKE IT RIGHT

"You are not to cheat one another, but fear your God, for I am the LORD your God." Leviticus 25:17

This verse has two important commands—one negative and one positive. The command—"You are not to cheat one another" forbids everything from merely taking advantage of someone to cruelly and violently oppressing another.

The positive command to "fear your God" suggests a reverent mind-set. Fearing the Lord means living with an awareness of his holiness and power. It's realizing that he is both the awesome King and the righteous Judge of the universe. In truth, only this kind of perpetual, deep respect for God will deter us from mistreating others.

Think over your relationships. Reflect on your interactions with family members, neighbors, and co-workers over the last few days. Are you guilty of "cheating" anyone? Can you recall any instances in which you've taken advantage of others or treated someone harshly? When God-fearing people become aware of such sins, they immediately seek forgiveness from God and from the one(s) wronged. This is restorative relationally, emotionally, and spiritually.

For the next note on *Other-centeredness*, see Numbers 5:6-7.

[A] **24:10** Lit *went out*

7 All of its growth may serve as food for your livestock and the wild animals in your land.

8 "You are to count seven sabbatical years, seven times seven years, so that the time period of the seven sabbatical years amounts to forty-nine. 9 Then you are to sound a trumpet loudly in the seventh month, on the tenth day of the month; you will sound it throughout your land on the Day of Atonement. 10 You are to consecrate the fiftieth year and proclaim freedom in the land for all its inhabitants. It will be your Jubilee, when each of you is to return to his property and each of you to his clan. 11 The fiftieth year will be your Jubilee; you are not to sow, reap what grows by itself, or harvest its untended vines. 12 It is to be holy to you because it is the Jubilee; you may only eat its produce directly from the field.

13 "In this Year of Jubilee, each of you will return to his property. 14 If you make a sale to your neighbor or a purchase from him, do not cheat one another. 15 You are to make the purchase from your neighbor based on the number of years since the last Jubilee. He is to sell to you based on the number of remaining harvest years. 16 You are to increase its price in proportion to a greater amount of years, and decrease its price in proportion to a lesser amount of years, because what he is selling to you is a number of harvests. 17 You are not to cheat one another, but fear your God, for I am the LORD your God.

18 "You are to keep my statutes and ordinances and carefully observe them, so that you may live securely in the land. 19 Then the land will yield its fruit, so that you can eat, be satisfied, and live securely in the land. 20 If you wonder: 'What will we eat in the seventh year if we don't sow or gather our produce?' 21 I will appoint my blessing for you in the sixth year, so that it will produce a crop sufficient for three years. 22 When you sow in the eighth year, you will be eating from the previous harvest. You will be eating this until the ninth year when its harvest comes in.

23 "The land is not to be permanently sold because it is mine, and you are only aliens and temporary residents on my land.[A] 24 You are to allow the redemption of any land you occupy. 25 If your brother becomes destitute and sells part of his property, his nearest relative may come and redeem what his brother has sold. 26 If a man has no family redeemer, but he prospers[B] and obtains enough to redeem his land, 27 he may calculate the years since its sale, repay the balance to the man he sold it to, and return to his property. 28 But if he cannot obtain enough to repay him, what he sold will remain in the possession of its purchaser until the Year of Jubilee. It is to be released at the Jubilee, so that he may return to his property.

29 "If a man sells a residence in a walled city, his right of redemption will last until a year has passed after its sale; his right of redemption will last a year. 30 If it is not redeemed by the end of a full year, then the house in the walled city is permanently transferred to its purchaser throughout his generations. It is not to be released on the Jubilee. 31 But houses in settlements that have no walls around them are to be classified as open fields. The right to redeem such houses stays in effect, and they are to be released at the Jubilee.

32 "Concerning the Levitical cities, the Levites always have the right to redeem houses in the cities they possess. 33 Whatever property one of the Levites can redeem[C] — a house sold in a city they possess — is to be released at the Jubilee, because the houses in the Levitical cities are their possession among the Israelites. 34 The open pastureland around their cities may not be sold, for it is their permanent possession.

35 "If your brother becomes destitute and cannot sustain himself among[D] you, you are to support him as an alien or temporary resident, so that he can continue to live among you. 36 Do not profit or take interest from him, but fear your God and let your brother live among you. 37 You are not to lend him your silver with interest or sell him your food for profit. 38 I am the LORD your God, who brought you out of the land of Egypt to give you the land of Canaan and to be your God.

39 "If your brother among you becomes destitute and sells himself to you, you must not force him to do slave labor. 40 Let him stay with you as a hired worker or temporary resident; he may work for you until the Year of Jubilee. 41 Then he and his children are to be released from you, and he may return to his clan and his ancestral property. 42 They are not to be sold as slaves,[E] because they are my servants[F] that I brought out of the land of Egypt. 43 You are not to rule over them harshly but fear your

[A] **25:23** Lit *residents with me* [B] **25:26** Lit *but his hand reaches* [C] **25:33** Hb obscure [D] **25:35** Lit *and his hand falters with* [E] **25:42** Lit *sold with a sale of a slave* [F] **25:42** Or *slaves*

God. 44 Your male and female slaves are to be
from the nations around you; you may purchase male and female slaves. 45 You may also
purchase them from the aliens residing with
you, or from their families living among you
— those born in your land. These may become
your property. 46 You may leave them to your
sons after you to inherit as property; you can
make them slaves for life. But concerning your
brothers, the Israelites, you must not rule over
one another harshly.

47 "If an alien or temporary resident living
among you prospers, but your brother living
near him becomes destitute and sells himself
to the alien living among you, or to a member
of the resident alien's clan, 48 he has the right
of redemption after he has been sold. One of
his brothers may redeem him. 49 His uncle or
cousin may redeem him, or any of his close
relatives from his clan may redeem him. If he
prospers, he may redeem himself. 50 The one
who purchased him is to calculate the time
from the year he sold himself to him until
the Year of Jubilee. The price of his sale will
be determined by the number of years. It will
be set for him like the daily wages of a hired
worker. 51 If many years are still left, he must
pay his redemption price in proportion to them
based on his purchase price. 52 If only a few
years remain until the Year of Jubilee, he will
calculate and pay the price of his redemption
in proportion to his remaining years. 53 He
will stay with him like a man hired year by
year. A resident alien is not to rule over him
harshly in your sight. 54 If he is not redeemed
in any of these ways, he and his children are
to be released at the Year of Jubilee. 55 For the
Israelites are my servants. They are my servants that I brought out of the land of Egypt;
I am the LORD your God.

COVENANT BLESSINGS AND DISCIPLINE

26 "Do not make idols for yourselves, set
up a carved image or sacred pillar for
yourselves, or place a sculpted stone in your
land to bow down to it, for I am the LORD your
God. 2 Keep my Sabbaths and revere my sanctuary; I am the LORD.

3 "If you follow my statutes and faithfully
observe my commands, 4 I will give you rain
at the right time, and the land will yield its
produce, and the trees of the field will bear
their fruit. 5 Your threshing will continue until
grape harvest, and the grape harvest will continue until sowing time; you will have plenty
of food to eat and live securely in your land.
6 I will give peace to the land, and you will lie
down with nothing to frighten you. I will remove dangerous animals from the land, and
no sword will pass through your land. 7 You
will pursue your enemies, and they will fall
before you by the sword. 8 Five of you will
pursue a hundred, and a hundred of you will
pursue ten thousand; your enemies will fall
before you by the sword.

9 "I will turn to you, make you fruitful and
multiply you, and confirm my covenant with
you. 10 You will eat the old grain of the previous year and will clear out the old to make
room for the new. 11 I will place my residence[A]
among you, and I will not reject you. 12 I will
walk among you and be your God, and you
will be my people. 13 I am the LORD your God,
who brought you out of the land of Egypt, so
that you would no longer be their slaves. I
broke the bars of your yoke and enabled you
to live in freedom.[B]

14 "But if you do not obey me and observe
all these commands — 15 if you reject my statutes and despise my ordinances, and do not
observe all my commands — and break my
covenant, 16 then I will do this to you: I will
bring terror on you — wasting disease and
fever that will cause your eyes to fail and your
life to ebb away. You will sow your seed in vain
because your enemies will eat it. 17 I will turn[C]
against you, so that you will be defeated by
your enemies. Those who hate you will rule
over you, and you will flee even though no
one is pursuing you.

18 "But if after these things you will not obey
me, I will proceed to discipline you seven times
for your sins. 19 I will break down your strong
pride. I will make your sky like iron and your
land like bronze, 20 and your strength will be
used up for nothing. Your land will not yield
its produce, and the trees of the land will not
bear their fruit.

21 "If you act with hostility toward me and
are unwilling to obey me, I will multiply your
plagues seven times for your sins. 22 I will send
wild animals against you that will deprive
you of your children, ravage your livestock,
and reduce your numbers until your roads
are deserted.

23 "If in spite of these things you do not accept

[A] **26:11** Or *tabernacle* [B] **26:13** Lit *to walk uprightly* [C] **26:17** Lit *will set my face*

my discipline, but act with hostility toward me, 24 then I will act with hostility toward you; I also will strike you seven times for your sins. 25 I will bring a sword against you to execute the vengeance of the covenant. Though you withdraw into your cities, I will send a pestilence among you, and you will be delivered into enemy hands. 26 When I cut off your supply of bread, ten women will bake your bread in a single oven and ration out your bread by weight, so that you will eat but not be satisfied.

27 "And if in spite of this you do not obey me but act with hostility toward me, 28 I will act with furious hostility toward you; I will also discipline you seven times for your sins. 29 You will eat the flesh of your sons; you will eat the flesh of your daughters. 30 I will destroy your high places, cut down your shrines,[A] and heap your lifeless bodies on the lifeless bodies of your idols; I will reject you. 31 I will reduce your cities to ruins and devastate your sanctuaries. I will not smell the pleasing aroma of your sacrifices. 32 I also will devastate the land, so that your enemies who come to live there will be appalled by it. 33 But I will scatter you among the nations, and I will draw a sword to chase after you. So your land will become desolate, and your cities will become ruins.

34 "Then the land will make up for its Sabbath years during the time it lies desolate, while you are in the land of your enemies. At that time the land will rest and make up for its Sabbaths. 35 As long as it lies desolate, it will have the rest it did not have during your Sabbaths when you lived there.

36 "I will put anxiety in the hearts of those of you who survive in the lands of their enemies. The sound of a wind-driven leaf will put them to flight, and they will flee as one flees from a sword, and fall though no one is pursuing them. 37 They will stumble over one another as if fleeing from a sword though no one is pursuing them. You will not be able to stand against your enemies. 38 You will perish among the nations; the land of your enemies will devour you. 39 Those[B] who survive in the lands of your enemies will waste away because of their iniquity; they will also waste away because of their fathers' iniquities along with theirs.

40 "But when they confess their iniquity and the iniquity of their fathers — their unfaithfulness that they practiced against me, and how they acted with hostility toward me, 41 and I acted with hostility toward them and brought them into the land of their enemies — and when their uncircumcised hearts are humbled and they make amends for their iniquity, 42 then I will remember my covenant with Jacob. I will also remember my covenant with Isaac and my covenant with Abraham,

Eternal Perspective | *God's Memory*

GOD'S REMEMBERS HIS PROMISES

"For their sake I will remember the covenant with their fathers, whom I brought out of the land of Egypt in the sight of the nations to be their God; I am the LORD." Leviticus 26:45

Careful readers of the Old Testament often express surprise at how blunt God is when talking to the Israelites. In passages like this one and many others throughout the Prophetic Books, God essentially tells his chosen people, "If you would only remain faithful to me, you would enjoy untold blessings. But of course you won't. You will rebel. You will turn away from me and pay a terrible price."

Even more stunning than such sobering warnings are the assurances that always accompany them. Notice the one here: "I will remember the covenant." God repeats this same idea to his people over and over again. In other words, he is faithful. We might turn away ten thousand times, but he never will. He will never abandon us, never renege on his promises.

How encouraging this is to people with wayward hearts—people like us! Such amazing grace! We may be, in the words of the old hymn, "prone to wander," but our God never will forget or forsake us.

For the next note on *Eternal Perspective*, see Numbers 23:19.

[A] **26:30** Or *incense altars* [B] **26:39** Lit *Those of you*

and I will remember the land. 43 For the land
abandoned by them will make up for its Sabbaths by lying desolate without the people,
while they make amends for their iniquity,
because they rejected my ordinances and
abhorred my statutes. 44 Yet in spite of this,
while they are in the land of their enemies, I
will not reject or abhor them so as to destroy
them and break my covenant with them, since
I am the LORD their God. 45 For their sake I will
remember the covenant with their fathers,
whom I brought out of the land of Egypt in
the sight of the nations to be their God; I am
the LORD."

46 These are the statutes, ordinances, and
laws the LORD established between himself and
the Israelites through Moses on Mount Sinai.

FUNDING THE SANCTUARY

27 The LORD spoke to Moses: 2 "Speak to the
Israelites and tell them: When someone
makes a special vow to the LORD that involves
the assessment of people, 3 if the assessment
concerns a male from twenty to sixty years
old, your assessment is fifty silver shekels
measured by the standard sanctuary shekel.
4 If the person is a female, your assessment is
thirty shekels. 5 If the person is from five to
twenty years old, your assessment for a male
is twenty shekels and for a female ten shekels.
6 If the person is from one month to five years
old, your assessment for a male is five silver
shekels, and for a female your assessment is
three shekels of silver. 7 If the person is sixty
years or more, your assessment is fifteen shekels for a male and ten shekels for a female. 8 But
if one is too poor to pay the assessment, he is
to present the person before the priest and
the priest will set a value for him. The priest
will set a value for him according to what the
one making the vow can afford.

9 "If the vow involves one of the animals that
may be brought as an offering to the LORD, any
of these he gives to the LORD will be holy. 10 He
may not replace it or make a substitution for
it, either good for bad, or bad for good. But if
he does substitute one animal for another,
both that animal and its substitute will be holy.

11 "If the vow involves any of the unclean
animals that may not be brought as an offering to the LORD, the animal must be presented
before the priest. 12 The priest will set its value,
whether high or low; the price will be set as
the priest makes the assessment for you. 13 If
the one who brought it decides to redeem it,
he must add a fifth to the[A] assessed value.

14 "When a man consecrates his house as
holy to the LORD, the priest will assess its value,
whether high or low. The price will stand just
as the priest assesses it. 15 But if the one who
consecrated his house redeems it, he must add
a fifth to the assessed value, and it will be his.

16 "If a man consecrates to the LORD any part
of a field that he possesses, your assessment
of value will be proportional to the seed needed to sow it, at the rate of fifty silver shekels
for every five bushels[B] of barley seed.[C] 17 If he
consecrates his field during the Year of Jubilee,
the price will stand according to your assessment. 18 But if he consecrates his field after the
Jubilee, the priest will calculate the price for
him in proportion to the years left until the
next Year of Jubilee, so that your assessment
will be reduced. 19 If the one who consecrated
the field decides to redeem it, he must add a
fifth to the assessed value, and the field will
transfer back to him. 20 But if he does not redeem the field or if he has sold it to another
man, it is no longer redeemable. 21 When the
field is released in the Jubilee, it will be holy
to the LORD like a field permanently set apart;
it becomes the priest's property.

22 "If a person consecrates to the LORD a field
he has purchased that is not part of his inherited landholding, 23 then the priest will calculate
for him the amount of the assessment up to
the Year of Jubilee, and the person will pay the
assessed value on that day as a holy offering
to the LORD. 24 In the Year of Jubilee the field
will return to the one he bought it from, the
original owner. 25 All your assessed values
will be measured by the standard sanctuary
shekel,[D] twenty gerahs to the shekel.

26 "But no one can consecrate a firstborn
of the livestock, whether an animal from the
herd or flock, to the LORD, because a firstborn
already belongs to the LORD. 27 If it is one of
the unclean livestock, it can be ransomed according to your assessment by adding a fifth
of its value to it. If it is not redeemed, it can be
sold according to your assessment.

28 "Nothing that a man permanently sets
apart to the LORD from all he owns, whether
a person, an animal, or his inherited landholding, can be sold or redeemed; everything
set apart is especially holy to the LORD. 29 No

[A] **27:13** Lit *your*, also in vv. 15,19,23 [B] **27:16** Lit *for a homer* [C] **27:16** Or *grain* [D] **27:25** A *shekel* is about two-fifths of an ounce of silver

person who has been set apart for destruction
is to be ransomed; he must be put to death.
30 "Every tenth of the land's produce, grain
from the soil or fruit from the trees, belongs
to the LORD; it is holy to the LORD. 31 If a man
decides to redeem any part of this tenth, he
must add a fifth to its value. 32 Every tenth
animal from the herd or flock, which passes
under the shepherd's rod, will be holy to the
LORD. 33 He is not to inspect whether it is good
or bad, and he is not to make a substitution
for it. But if he does make a substitution, both
the animal and its substitute will be holy; they
cannot be redeemed."
34 These are the commands the LORD gave
Moses for the Israelites on Mount Sinai.

Exercise of Faith | *Tithing*

GIVING TO THE LORD

"Every tenth of the land's produce, grain from the soil or fruit from the trees, belongs to the LORD; it is holy to the LORD." Leviticus 27:30

God didn't command his people to tithe because he was hurting for cash. This requirement was for his people's benefit, not his own. Just like the stipulation to observe the Sabbath (to set aside one day out of seven), the requirement to give back one-tenth was designed primarily to serve as a reminder. Remember the Giver and Sustainer of life—the true Owner of all things (Ps 24:1)! Remember the One who "richly provides us with all things to enjoy" (1Tm 6:17). Taken to heart, such reminders can stimulate even deeper trust and greater love and generosity.

Three and half millennia later, nothing has changed. Earning, saving, spending, giving—our financial habits continue to reveal, like nothing else, our priorities and values. And our giving or not giving shows what we really believe.

If you find you are reluctant to give, ask yourself why. What's behind that hesitation? If you already give a tenth—don't stop there. See if you can free up even more resources for spreading the love of Christ.

For the next note on *Exercise of Faith*, see Deuteronomy 12:5-6.

Numbers—Believers can be discouraged when they face their failures and rebellion against God. We may think we are obeying his Word but then get hit with a circumstance that reveals our inward disobedience. We wonder if we will ever progress in the Christian life. Numbers speaks to our discouragement in these moments.

The Israelites had been miraculously rescued from Egypt and promised a land "flowing with milk and honey" (Ex 33:3). Repeatedly, God had proven to be faithful as he had led and provided for them. Despite this, however, the nation responded with unbelief, complaining, and rebellion. What hope did these hard-hearted people have?

Their hope, as well as ours, is founded on God's character. Despite the people's rebellion, God would keep his promises. He would continue to lead them day and night, and his presence would dwell among them in the ark of the covenant. God's holiness and faithfulness will endure forever.

As we read Numbers, our frustration with the rebellious Israelites—and with ourselves as we recognize our own rebellion—can deepen our love for and faith in the unchanging God who keeps his promises despite our sin. He redeemed Sabbath-breaking, idol-worshiping rebels like us at the cross.

NUMBERS

AUTHOR: Moses

DATE WRITTEN: 1446–1406 BC (during the wilderness wanderings)

ORIGINAL AUDIENCE: The Israelites

SETTING: The book of Numbers, like the rest of the Pentateuch (Genesis through Deuteronomy) was written during the forty years of wilderness wandering. Its Hebrew name, *Bemadbar*, means "in the wilderness," and that barren habitat serves as the book's geographical setting. The Israelites were wandering from the Wilderness of Sinai to the arid plains of Moab as they waited for an entire generation to die so the faithful could take possession of the promised land and establish the nation of Israel under God's rule.

PURPOSE FOR WRITING: Moses wrote the book of Numbers as a continuation of Exodus, and it picks up the historical narrative found in that book. Though the action centers on Moses and the nation of Israel, God is really the principal character as he speaks words to Moses and directs the affairs of peoples and nations. The book presents God in his holiness but also highlights God's presence among his people, leading them with the pillar of fire by night and the pillar of cloud by day and filling the tabernacle with his glory.

OUTLINE:

1. First Census and Consecration of Israel (1:1–6:27)

   Numbering of the people (1:1–2:34)

   Choosing Levites (3:1–4:49)

   Purifying and blessing the people (5:1–6:27)

2. Departing for the Promised Land (7:1–10:36)

   Gifts of the people (7:1-89)

   Consecration of the Levites (8:1-26)

   Observance of the Passover (9:1-14)

   Departing of the people (9:15–10:36)

3. Disobedience and Rebellion (11:1–25:18)

   Complaints, fear, and defeat (11:1–14:45)

   Instructions and laws (15:1-41)

   Rebellion against the priesthood (16:1–19:22)

   Rebellion against Moses and judgment by snakes (20:1–21:35)

   Balaam's blessing (22:1–24:25)

   Phinehas campaigns against idolatry (25:1-18)

4. Second Census and the New Generation (26:1–30:16)

   Counting of Israel (26:1-65)

   The inheritance of Zelophehad's daughters (27:1-23)

   Instructions for the new generation (28:1–30:16)

5. Entering the Promised Land (31:1–36:13)

   Vengeance against the Midianites (31:1-54)

   Settlement beyond the Jordan (32:1-42)

   Summary of the exodus (33:1-49)

   Division of Canaan (33:50–34:29)

   Levitical cities and cities of refuge (35:1-34)

   Laws of female inheritance (36:1-13)

KEY VERSES:

"May the LORD bless you and protect you; may the LORD make his face shine on you and be gracious to you; may the LORD look with favor on you and give you peace." —Numbers 6:24-26

RESTORATION THEMES

R	Rest and Reflection	*Receiving God's Peace—6:24-26*
E	Eternal Perspective	*God's Promises—23:19*
S	Support	*God's Support—14:9*
T	Thanksgiving and Contentment	*Confession—32:23*
O	Other-centeredness	*Identifying Those We Have Wronged—5:6-7*
R	Relationships	*For the next note, see 1 Samuel 18:1-3.*
E	Exercise of Faith	*For the next note, see Deuteronomy 12:5-6.*

THE CENSUS OF ISRAEL

1 The LORD spoke to Moses in the tent of
meeting in the Wilderness of Sinai, on the
first day of the second month of the second
year after Israel's departure from the land of
Egypt: 2 "Take a census of the entire Israelite
community by their clans and their fathers'
families,[A] counting the names of every male
one by one. 3 You and Aaron are to register
those who are twenty years old or more by
their military divisions — everyone who can
serve in Israel's army.[B] 4 A man from each tribe
is to be with you, each one the head of his
ancestral family.[C] 5 These are the names of the
men who are to assist you:
Elizur son of Shedeur from Reuben;
6 Shelumiel son of Zurishaddai
from Simeon;
7 Nahshon son of Amminadab
from Judah;
8 Nethanel son of Zuar from Issachar;
9 Eliab son of Helon from Zebulun;
10 from the sons of Joseph:
Elishama son of Ammihud
from Ephraim,
Gamaliel son of Pedahzur
from Manasseh;
11 Abidan son of Gideoni from Benjamin;
12 Ahiezer son of Ammishaddai
from Dan;
13 Pagiel son of Ochran from Asher;
14 Eliasaph son of Deuel[D] from Gad;
15 Ahira son of Enan from Naphtali.
16 These are the men called from the community; they are leaders of their ancestral tribes,
the heads of Israel's clans."
17 So Moses and Aaron took these men who
had been designated by name, 18 and they assembled the whole community on the first
day of the second month. They recorded their
ancestry by their clans and their ancestral
families, counting one by one the names of
those twenty years old or more, 19 just as the
LORD commanded Moses. He registered them
in the Wilderness of Sinai:

20 The descendants of Reuben, the firstborn of Israel: according to their family
records by their clans and their ancestral
families, counting one by one the names
of every male twenty years old or more,
everyone who could serve in the army,
21 those registered for the tribe of Reuben
numbered 46,500.

22 The descendants of Simeon: according to
their family records by their clans and their
ancestral families, those registered counting one by one the names of every male
twenty years old or more, everyone who
could serve in the army, 23 those registered
for the tribe of Simeon numbered 59,300.

24 The descendants of Gad: according to
their family records by their clans and
their ancestral families, counting the
names of those twenty years old or more,
everyone who could serve in the army,
25 those registered for the tribe of Gad
numbered 45,650.

26 The descendants of Judah: according
to their family records by their clans and
their ancestral families, counting the
names of those twenty years old or more,
everyone who could serve in the army,
27 those registered for the tribe of Judah
numbered 74,600.

28 The descendants of Issachar: according to their family records by their clans
and their ancestral families, counting
the names of those twenty years old or
more, everyone who could serve in the
army, 29 those registered for the tribe of
Issachar numbered 54,400.

30 The descendants of Zebulun: according
to their family records by their clans
and their ancestral families, counting
the names of those twenty years old or
more, everyone who could serve in the
army, 31 those registered for the tribe of
Zebulun numbered 57,400.

32 The descendants of Joseph:

The descendants of Ephraim: according
to their family records by their clans
and their ancestral families, counting
the names of those twenty years old or
more, everyone who could serve in the
army, 33 those registered for the tribe of
Ephraim numbered 40,500.

34 The descendants of Manasseh: according to their family records by their clans
and their ancestral families, counting

[A] **1:2** Lit *the house of their fathers*, also in vv. 18,20,22,24,26,28,30,32,34,36,38,40,42,45 [B] **1:3** Lit *everyone going out to war in Israel* [C] **1:4** Lit *the house of his fathers*, also in v. 44 [D] **1:14** LXX, Syr read *Reuel*

CENSUS OF THE LEVITES

34 So Moses, Aaron, and the leaders of the community registered the Kohathites by their clans
and their ancestral families, 35 men from thirty
years old to fifty years old, everyone who was
qualified for work at the tent of meeting. 36 The
men registered by their clans numbered 2,750.
37 These were the registered men of the Kohathite clans, everyone who could serve at the
tent of meeting. Moses and Aaron registered
them at the LORD's command through Moses.

38 The Gershonites were registered by their
clans and their ancestral families, 39 men from
thirty years old to fifty years old, everyone who
was qualified for work at the tent of meeting.
40 The men registered by their clans and their
ancestral families numbered 2,630. 41 These
were the registered men of the Gershonite
clans. At the LORD's command Moses and
Aaron registered everyone who could serve
at the tent of meeting.

42 The men of the Merarite clans were registered by their clans and their ancestral families,
43 those from thirty years old to fifty years
old, everyone who was qualified for work
at the tent of meeting. 44 The men registered
by their clans numbered 3,200. 45 These were
the registered men of the Merarite clans; Moses and Aaron registered them at the LORD's
command through Moses.

46 Moses, Aaron, and the leaders of Israel
registered all the Levites by their clans and
their ancestral families, 47 from thirty years old
to fifty years old, everyone who was qualified
to do the work of serving at the tent of meeting
and transporting it. 48 Their registered men
numbered 8,580. 49 At the LORD's command
they were registered under the direction of
Moses, each one according to his work and
transportation duty, and his assignment was
as the LORD commanded Moses.

ISOLATION OF THE UNCLEAN

5 The LORD instructed Moses: 2 "Command
the Israelites to send away anyone from
the camp who is afflicted with a skin disease,
anyone who has a discharge, or anyone who
is defiled because of a corpse. 3 Send away
both male or female; send them outside the
camp, so that they will not defile their camps
where I dwell among them." 4 The Israelites
did this, sending them outside the camp. The
Israelites did as the LORD instructed Moses.

COMPENSATION FOR WRONGDOING

5 The LORD spoke to Moses: 6 "Tell the Israelites: When a man or woman commits any sin
against another, that person acts unfaithfully
toward the LORD and is guilty. 7 The person is to
confess the sin he has committed. He is to pay

Other-centeredness | *Identifying Those We Have Wronged*

COMING CLEAN

"Tell the Israelites: When a man or woman commits any sin against another, that person acts unfaithfully toward the LORD and is guilty. The person is to confess the sin he has committed. He is to pay full compensation, add a fifth of its value to it, and give it to the individual he has wronged." Numbers 5:6-7

Every week we hear tortured political and celebrity "apologies" (no doubt crafted by PR teams and law firms) that sound like this: "To anyone who misunderstood my true intentions and may have been offended, I want to say I'm sorry. I take full responsibility." Responsibility for what? For someone else misinterpreting your actions?

Statements like that aren't helpful to anyone! Because they're not admissions of guilt, because they're not sincere confessions, they don't clear the air—they only pollute it!

God's command is to "confess the sin." That means to call it what it is—no minimizing, excusing, rationalizing, or blame-shifting. It also means to take ownership, to accept responsibility to make it right.

We can't do any of this without humility; however, if we can bring ourselves to humble ourselves, God promises to meet us with grace (1Pt 5:5).

For the next note on *Other-centeredness*, see Deuteronomy 6:4-5.

full compensation, add a fifth of its value to it,
and give it to the individual he has wronged.
8 But if that individual has no relative to receive
compensation, the compensation goes to the
LORD for the priest, along with the atonement
ram by which the priest will make atonement
for the guilty person. 9 Every holy contribution
the Israelites present to the priest will be his.
10 Each one's holy contribution is his to give;
what each one gives to the priest will be his."

THE JEALOUSY RITUAL

11 The LORD spoke to Moses: 12 "Speak to the
Israelites and tell them: If any man's wife goes
astray, is unfaithful to him, 13 and sleeps with
another,[A] but it is concealed from her husband, and she is undetected, even though she
has defiled herself, since there is no witness
against her, and she wasn't caught in the act;
14 and if a feeling of jealousy comes over the
husband and he becomes jealous because of his
wife who has defiled herself — or if a feeling
of jealousy comes over him and he becomes
jealous of her though she has not defiled herself — 15 then the man is to bring his wife to
the priest. He is also to bring an offering for
her of two quarts[B] of barley flour. He is not
to pour oil over it or put frankincense on it
because it is a grain offering of jealousy, a
grain offering for remembrance to draw attention to guilt.

16 "The priest is to bring her forward and
have her stand before the LORD. 17 Then the
priest is to take holy water in a clay bowl, take
some of the dust from the tabernacle floor,
and put it in the water. 18 After the priest has
the woman stand before the LORD, he is to let
down her hair[C] and place in her hands the grain
offering for remembrance, which is the grain
offering of jealousy. The priest is to hold the
bitter water that brings a curse. 19 The priest
will require the woman to take an oath and
will say to her, 'If no man has slept with you,
if you have not gone astray and become defiled while under your husband's authority,
be unaffected by this bitter water that brings
a curse. 20 But if you have gone astray while
under your husband's authority, if you have
defiled yourself and a man other than your
husband has slept with you' — 21 at this point
the priest will make the woman take the oath
with the sworn curse, and he is to say to her
— 'May the LORD make you into an object of
your people's cursing and swearing when
he makes your womb[D] shrivel and your belly
swell. 22 May this water that brings a curse enter your stomach, causing your belly to swell
and your womb to shrivel.'

"And the woman will reply, 'Amen, Amen.'

23 "Then the priest is to write these curses
on a scroll and wash them off into the bitter
water. 24 He will require the woman to drink
the bitter water that brings a curse, and it will
enter her to cause bitter suffering. 25 The priest
is to take the grain offering of jealousy from the
woman, present the offering before the LORD,
and bring it to the altar. 26 The priest is to take
a handful of the grain offering as a memorial
portion and burn it on the altar. Afterward,
he will require the woman to drink the water.

27 "When he makes her drink the water, if
she has defiled herself and been unfaithful
to her husband, the water that brings a curse
will enter her to cause bitter suffering; her
belly will swell, and her womb will shrivel.
She will become a curse among her people.
28 But if the woman has not defiled herself
and is pure, she will be unaffected and will
be able to conceive children.

29 "This is the law regarding jealousy when
a wife goes astray and defiles herself while
under her husband's authority, 30 or when
a feeling of jealousy comes over a husband
and he becomes jealous of his wife. He is to
have the woman stand before the LORD, and
the priest will carry out all these instructions
for her. 31 The husband will be free of guilt, but
that woman will bear her iniquity."

THE NAZIRITE VOW

6 The LORD instructed Moses: 2 "Speak to
the Israelites and tell them: When a man
or woman makes a special vow, a Nazirite
vow, to consecrate himself to the LORD, 3 he
is to abstain from wine and beer. He must not
drink vinegar made from wine or from beer.
He must not drink any grape juice or eat fresh
grapes or raisins. 4 He is not to eat anything
produced by the grapevine, from seeds to skin,
during the period of his consecration.

5 "You must not cut his hair[E] throughout the
time of his vow of consecration. He may be
holy until the time is completed during which
he consecrates himself to the LORD; he is to
let the hair of his head grow long. 6 He must
not go near a dead body during the time he

[A] **5:13** Lit *and man lies with her and has an emission of semen* [B] **5:15** Lit *a tenth of an ephah* [C] **5:18** Or *to uncover her head*
[D] **5:21** Lit *thigh*, also in vv. 22,27 [E] **6:5** Lit *"A razor is not to pass over his head*

consecrates himself to the LORD. 7 He is not to defile himself for his father or mother, or his brother or sister, when they die, while the mark of consecration to his God is on his head. 8 He is holy to the LORD during the time of consecration.

9 "If someone suddenly dies near him, defiling his consecrated head, he must shave his head on the day of his purification; he is to shave it on the seventh day. 10 On the eighth day he is to bring two turtledoves or two young pigeons to the priest at the entrance to the tent of meeting. 11 The priest is to offer one as a sin offering and the other as a burnt offering to make atonement on behalf of the Nazirite, since he incurred guilt because of the corpse. On that day he is to consecrate his head again. 12 He is to rededicate his time of consecration to the LORD and to bring a year-old male lamb as a guilt offering. But do not count the initial period of consecration because it became defiled.

13 "This is the law of the Nazirite: On the day his time of consecration is completed, he is to be brought to the entrance to the tent of meeting. 14 He is to present an offering to the LORD of one unblemished year-old male lamb as a burnt offering, one unblemished year-old female lamb as a sin offering, one unblemished ram as a fellowship offering, 15 along with their grain offerings and drink offerings, and a basket of unleavened cakes made from fine flour mixed with oil, and unleavened wafers coated with oil.

16 "The priest is to present these before the LORD and sacrifice the Nazirite's sin offering and burnt offering. 17 He will also offer the ram as a fellowship sacrifice to the LORD, together with the basket of unleavened bread. Then the priest will offer the accompanying grain offering and drink offering.

18 "The Nazirite is to shave his consecrated head at the entrance to the tent of meeting, take the hair from his head, and put it on the fire under the fellowship sacrifice. 19 The priest is to take the boiled shoulder from the ram, one unleavened cake from the basket, and one unleavened wafer, and put them into the hands of the Nazirite after he has shaved his consecrated head. 20 The priest is to present them as a presentation offering before the LORD. It is a holy portion for the priest, in addition to the breast of the presentation offering and the thigh of the contribution. After that, the Nazirite may drink wine.

21 "These are the instructions about the Nazirite who vows his offering to the LORD for his consecration, in addition to whatever else he

Rest and Reflection | *Receiving God's Peace*

THE BLESSING

"May the LORD bless you and protect you; may the LORD make his face shine on you and be gracious to you; may the LORD look with favor on you and give you peace." Numbers 6:24-26

This famous, beloved Hebrew blessing was given to Moses. He, in turn, was instructed to teach it to Aaron and the priests. God's desire was for them to use it to "pronounce my name over the Israelites" (6:27).

What does that mean? Simply this: In ancient times, a person's name represented everything he or she was, had, and did. One's name called to mind that person's character, power, and authority. So invoking a person's name (in this case, God's, by repeating this beautiful blessing) was like calling to mind that person's presence. Here then was a practical way of asking God to live among his people and bring blessing.

What if you and your family could be marked by divine blessing? Protection? Grace? Favor? Peace? According to this passage, it can. Here, in just a few words, is a capsule summary of the desire of God for his people—in ancient times and modern. Ask God to "make his face shine" on you and your loved ones.

For the next note on *Rest and Reflection*, see Deuteronomy 4:29.

can afford; he must fulfill whatever vow he
makes in keeping with the instructions for
his consecration."

THE PRIESTLY BLESSING

22 The LORD spoke to Moses: 23 "Tell Aaron and
his sons, 'This is how you are to bless the Israelites. You should say to them,

24 "May the LORD bless you
and protect you;
25 may the LORD make his face shine
on you
and be gracious to you;
26 may the LORD look with favor on you[A]
and give you peace."'

27 In this way they will pronounce my name
over[B] the Israelites, and I will bless them."

OFFERINGS FROM THE LEADERS

7 On the day Moses finished setting up the
tabernacle, he anointed and consecrated it
and all its furnishings, along with the altar and
all its utensils. After he anointed and consecrated these things, 2 the leaders of Israel, the
heads of their ancestral families,[C] presented
an offering. They were the tribal leaders who
supervised the registration. 3 They brought
as their offering before the LORD six covered
carts and twelve oxen, a cart from every two
leaders and an ox from each one, and presented them in front of the tabernacle.

4 The LORD said to Moses, 5 "Accept these
from them to be used in the work of the tent of
meeting, and give this offering to the Levites,
to each division according to their service."

6 So Moses took the carts and oxen and gave
them to the Levites. 7 He gave the Gershonites
two carts and four oxen corresponding to
their service, 8 and gave the Merarites four
carts and eight oxen corresponding to their
service, under the direction of Ithamar son of
Aaron the priest. 9 But he did not give any to
the Kohathites, since their responsibility was
service related to the holy objects carried on
their shoulders.

10 The leaders also presented the dedication
gift for the altar when it was anointed. The
leaders presented their offerings in front of
the altar. 11 The LORD told Moses, "Each day
have one leader present his offering for the
dedication of the altar."

12 The one who presented his offering on
the first day was Nahshon son of Amminadab from the tribe of Judah. 13 His
offering was one silver dish weighing 3 1/4
pounds[D] and one silver basin weighing
1 3/4 pounds,[E] measured by the standard
sanctuary shekel, both of them full of fine
flour mixed with oil for a grain offering;
14 one gold bowl weighing four ounces,[F]
full of incense; 15 one young bull, one ram,
and one male lamb a year old, for a burnt
offering; 16 one male goat for a sin offering; 17 and two bulls, five rams, five male
goats, and five male lambs a year old,
for the fellowship sacrifice. This was the
offering of Nahshon son of Amminadab.

18 On the second day Nethanel son of Zuar,
leader of Issachar, presented an offering.
19 As his offering, he presented one silver
dish weighing 3 1/4 pounds and one silver
basin weighing 1 3/4 pounds, measured by
the standard sanctuary shekel, both of
them full of fine flour mixed with oil for a
grain offering; 20 one gold bowl weighing
four ounces, full of incense; 21 one young
bull, one ram, and one male lamb a year
old, for a burnt offering; 22 one male
goat for a sin offering; 23 and two bulls,
five rams, five male goats, and five male
lambs a year old, for the fellowship sacrifice. This was the offering of Nethanel
son of Zuar.

24 On the third day Eliab son of Helon,
leader of the Zebulunites, presented an
offering. 25 His offering was one silver
dish weighing 3 1/4 pounds and one silver
basin weighing 1 3/4 pounds, measured by
the standard sanctuary shekel, both of
them full of fine flour mixed with oil for
a grain offering; 26 one gold bowl weighing four ounces, full of incense; 27 one
young bull, one ram, and one male lamb
a year old, for a burnt offering; 28 one
male goat for a sin offering; 29 and two
bulls, five rams, five male goats, and five
male lambs a year old, for the fellowship
sacrifice. This was the offering of Eliab
son of Helon.

30 On the fourth day Elizur son of Shedeur,
leader of the Reubenites, presented an

[A] **6:26** Lit *LORD lift his face to you* [B] **6:27** Or *put my name on* [C] **7:2** Lit *the house of their fathers* [D] **7:13** Lit *dish, 130 its shekel-weight*, also in vv. 19,25,31,37,43,49,55,61,67,73,79 [E] **7:13** Lit *70 shekels*, also in vv. 19,25,31,37,43,49,55,61,67,73,79 [F] **7:14** Lit *10* (shekels), also in vv. 20,26,32,38,44,50,56,62,68,74,80,86

offering. 31 His offering was one silver
dish weighing 3 1/4 pounds and one silver
basin weighing 1 3/4 pounds, measured by
the standard sanctuary shekel, both of
them full of fine flour mixed with oil for
a grain offering; 32 one gold bowl weighing four ounces, full of incense; 33 one
young bull, one ram, and one male lamb
a year old, for a burnt offering; 34 one
male goat for a sin offering; 35 and two
bulls, five rams, five male goats, and five
male lambs a year old, for the fellowship
sacrifice. This was the offering of Elizur
son of Shedeur.

36 On the fifth day Shelumiel son of
Zurishaddai, leader of the Simeonites,
presented an offering. 37 His offering was
one silver dish weighing 3 1/4 pounds and
one silver basin weighing 1 3/4 pounds,
measured by the standard sanctuary
shekel, both of them full of fine flour
mixed with oil for a grain offering; 38 one
gold bowl weighing four ounces, full of
incense; 39 one young bull, one ram, and
one male lamb a year old, for a burnt
offering; 40 one male goat for a sin offering; 41 and two bulls, five rams, five male
goats, and five male lambs a year old,
for the fellowship sacrifice. This was the
offering of Shelumiel son of Zurishaddai.

42 On the sixth day Eliasaph son of Deuel,[A]
leader of the Gadites, presented an
offering. 43 His offering was one silver
dish weighing 3 1/4 pounds and one silver
basin weighing 1 3/4 pounds, measured by
the standard sanctuary shekel, both of
them full of fine flour mixed with oil for a
grain offering; 44 one gold bowl weighing
four ounces full of incense; 45 one young
bull, one ram, and one male lamb a year
old, for a burnt offering; 46 one male
goat for a sin offering; 47 and two bulls,
five rams, five male goats, and five male
lambs a year old, for the fellowship sacrifice. This was the offering of Eliasaph son
of Deuel.[A]

48 On the seventh day Elishama son of
Ammihud, leader of the Ephraimites,
presented an offering. 49 His offering was one silver dish weighing 3 1/4
pounds and one silver basin weighing
1 3/4 pounds, measured by the standard
sanctuary shekel, both of them full of
fine flour mixed with oil for a grain
offering; 50 one gold bowl weighing four
ounces, full of incense; 51 one young bull,
one ram, and one male lamb a year old,
for a burnt offering; 52 one male goat for
a sin offering; 53 and two bulls, five rams,
five male goats, and five male lambs a
year old, for the fellowship sacrifice.
This was the offering of Elishama son of
Ammihud.

54 On the eighth day Gamaliel son of
Pedahzur, leader of the Manassites,
presented an offering. 55 His offering was one silver dish weighing 3 1/4
pounds and one silver basin weighing
1 3/4 pounds, measured by the standard
sanctuary shekel, both of them full of
fine flour mixed with oil for a grain
offering; 56 one gold bowl weighing four
ounces, full of incense; 57 one young bull,
one ram, and one male lamb a year old,
for a burnt offering; 58 one male goat for
a sin offering; 59 and two bulls, five rams,
five male goats, and five male lambs a
year old, for the fellowship sacrifice.
This was the offering of Gamaliel son of
Pedahzur.

60 On the ninth day Abidan son of Gideoni, leader of the Benjaminites, presented
an offering. 61 His offering was one silver
dish weighing 3 1/4 pounds and one silver
basin weighing 1 3/4 pounds, measured by
the standard sanctuary shekel, both of
them full of fine flour mixed with oil for
a grain offering; 62 one gold bowl weighing four ounces, full of incense; 63 one
young bull, one ram, and one male lamb
a year old, for a burnt offering; 64 one
male goat for a sin offering; 65 and two
bulls, five rams, five male goats, and five
male lambs a year old, for the fellowship
sacrifice. This was the offering of Abidan
son of Gideoni.

66 On the tenth day Ahiezer son of Ammishaddai, leader of the Danites, presented
an offering. 67 His offering was one silver
dish weighing 3 1/4 pounds and one silver

[A] **7:42, 47** LXX, Syr read *Reuel*

basin weighing 1 3/4 pounds, measured by the standard sanctuary shekel, both of them full of fine flour mixed with oil for a grain offering; 68 one gold bowl weighing four ounces, full of incense; 69 one young bull, one ram, and one male lamb a year old, for a burnt offering; 70 one male goat for a sin offering; 71 and two bulls, five rams, five male goats, and five male lambs a year old, for the fellowship sacrifice. This was the offering of Ahiezer son of Ammishaddai.

72 On the eleventh day Pagiel son of Ochran, leader of the Asherites, presented an offering. 73 His offering was one silver dish weighing 3 1/4 pounds and one silver basin weighing 1 3/4 pounds, measured by the standard sanctuary shekel, both of them full of fine flour mixed with oil for a grain offering; 74 one gold bowl weighing four ounces, full of incense; 75 one young bull, one ram, and one male lamb a year old, for a burnt offering; 76 one male goat for a sin offering; 77 and two bulls, five rams, five male goats, and five male lambs a year old, for the fellowship sacrifice. This was the offering of Pagiel son of Ochran.

78 On the twelfth day Ahira son of Enan, leader of the Naphtalites, presented an offering. 79 His offering was one silver dish weighing 3 1/4 pounds and one silver basin weighing 1 3/4 pounds, measured by the standard sanctuary shekel, both of them full of fine flour mixed with oil for a grain offering; 80 one gold bowl weighing four ounces, full of incense; 81 one young bull, one ram, and one male lamb a year old, for a burnt offering; 82 one male goat for a sin offering; 83 and two bulls, five rams, five male goats, and five male lambs a year old, for the fellowship sacrifice. This was the offering of Ahira son of Enan.

84 This was the dedication gift from the leaders of Israel for the altar when it was anointed: twelve silver dishes, twelve silver basins, and twelve gold bowls. 85 Each silver dish weighed 3 1/4 pounds,[A] and each basin 1 3/4 pounds.[B] The total weight of the silver articles was 60 pounds[C] measured by the standard sanctuary shekel. 86 The twelve gold bowls full of incense each weighed four ounces measured by the standard sanctuary shekel. The total weight of the gold bowls was 3 pounds.[D] 87 All the livestock for the burnt offering totaled twelve bulls, twelve rams, and twelve male lambs a year old, with their grain offerings, and twelve male goats for the sin offering. 88 All the livestock for the fellowship sacrifice totaled twenty-four bulls, sixty rams, sixty male goats, and sixty male lambs a year old. This was the dedication gift for the altar after it was anointed.

89 When Moses entered the tent of meeting to speak with the LORD, he heard the voice speaking to him from above the mercy seat that was on the ark of the testimony, from between the two cherubim. He spoke to him that way.

THE LIGHTING IN THE TABERNACLE

8 The LORD spoke to Moses: 2 "Speak to Aaron and tell him: When you set up the lamps, the seven lamps are to give light in front of the lampstand." 3 So Aaron did this; he set up its lamps to give light in front of the lampstand just as the LORD had commanded Moses. 4 This is the way the lampstand was made: it was a hammered work of gold, hammered from its base to its flower petals. The lampstand was made according to the pattern the LORD had shown Moses.

CONSECRATION OF THE LEVITES

5 The LORD spoke to Moses: 6 "Take the Levites from among the Israelites and ceremonially cleanse them. 7 Do this to them for their purification: Sprinkle them with the purification water. Have them shave their entire bodies and wash their clothes, and so purify themselves.

8 "They are to take a young bull and its grain offering of fine flour mixed with oil, and you are to take a second young bull for a sin offering. 9 Bring the Levites before the tent of meeting and assemble the entire Israelite community. 10 Then present the Levites before the LORD, and have the Israelites lay their hands on them. 11 Aaron is to present the Levites before the LORD as a presentation offering from the Israelites, so that they may perform the LORD's work. 12 Next the Levites are to lay their hands on the heads of the bulls. Sacrifice one as a sin

[A] 7:85 Lit *130* (shekels) [B] 7:85 Lit *70* (shekels) [C] 7:85 Lit *2,400* (shekels) [D] 7:86 Lit *120* (shekels)

offering and the other as a burnt offering to the LORD, to make atonement for the Levites.

13 "You are to have the Levites stand before Aaron and his sons, and you are to present them before the LORD as a presentation offering. 14 In this way you are to separate the Levites from the rest of the Israelites so that the Levites will belong to me. 15 After that the Levites may come to serve at the tent of meeting, once you have ceremonially cleansed them and presented them as a presentation offering. 16 For they have been exclusively assigned to me from the Israelites. I have taken them for myself in place of all who come first from the womb, every Israelite firstborn. 17 For every firstborn among the Israelites is mine, both man and animal. I consecrated them to myself on the day I struck down every firstborn in the land of Egypt. 18 But I have taken the Levites in place of every firstborn among the Israelites. 19 From the Israelites, I have given the Levites exclusively to Aaron and his sons to perform the work for the Israelites at the tent of meeting and to make atonement on their behalf, so that no plague will come against the Israelites when they approach the sanctuary."

20 Moses, Aaron, and the entire Israelite community did this to the Levites. The Israelites did everything to them the LORD commanded Moses regarding the Levites. 21 The Levites purified themselves and washed their clothes; then Aaron presented[A] them before the LORD as a presentation offering. Aaron also made atonement for them to cleanse them ceremonially. 22 After that, the Levites came to do their work at the tent of meeting in the presence of Aaron and his sons. So they did to them as the LORD had commanded Moses concerning the Levites.

23 The LORD spoke to Moses: 24 "In regard to the Levites: From twenty-five years old or more, a man enters the service in the work at the tent of meeting. 25 But at fifty years old he is to retire from his service in the work and no longer serve. 26 He may assist his brothers to fulfill responsibilities[B] at the tent of meeting, but he must not do the work. This is how you are to deal with the Levites regarding their duties."

THE SECOND PASSOVER

9 In the first month of the second year after their departure from the land of Egypt, the LORD told Moses in the Wilderness of Sinai: 2 "The Israelites are to observe the Passover at its appointed time. 3 You must observe it at its appointed time on the fourteenth day of this month at twilight; you are to observe it according to all its statutes and ordinances." 4 So Moses told the Israelites to observe the Passover, 5 and they observed it in the first month on the fourteenth day at twilight in the Wilderness of Sinai. The Israelites did everything as the LORD had commanded Moses.

6 But there were some men who were unclean because of a human corpse, so they could not observe the Passover on that day. These men came before Moses and Aaron the same day 7 and said to him, "We are unclean because of a human corpse. Why should we be excluded from presenting the LORD's offering at its appointed time with the other Israelites?"

8 Moses replied to them, "Wait here until I hear what the LORD commands for you."

9 Then the LORD spoke to Moses: 10 "Tell the Israelites: When any one of you or your descendants is unclean because of a corpse or is on a distant journey, he may still observe the Passover to the LORD. 11 Such people are to observe it in the second month, on the fourteenth day at twilight. They are to eat the animal with unleavened bread and bitter herbs; 12 they may not leave any of it until morning or break any of its bones. They must observe the Passover according to all its statutes.

13 "But the man who is ceremonially clean, is not on a journey, and yet fails to observe the Passover is to be cut off from his people, because he did not present the LORD's offering at its appointed time. That man will bear the consequences of his sin.

14 "If an alien resides with you and wants to observe the Passover to the LORD, he is to do it according to the Passover statute and its ordinances. You are to apply the same statute to both the resident alien and the native of the land."

GUIDANCE BY THE CLOUD

15 On the day the tabernacle was set up, the cloud covered the tabernacle, the tent of the testimony, and it appeared like fire above the tabernacle from evening until morning. 16 It remained that way continuously: the cloud would cover it,[C] appearing like fire at night. 17 Whenever the cloud was lifted up above the

[A] **8:21** Lit *waved* [B] **8:26** Or *to keep guard* [C] **9:16** LXX, Vg, Syr, Tg read *it by day*

tent, the Israelites would set out; at the place where the cloud stopped, there the Israelites camped. 18 At the LORD's command the Israelites set out, and at the LORD's command they camped. As long as the cloud stayed over the tabernacle, they camped.

19 Even when the cloud stayed over the tabernacle many days, the Israelites carried out the LORD's requirement and did not set out. 20 Sometimes the cloud remained over the tabernacle for only a few days. They would camp at the LORD's command and set out at the LORD's command. 21 Sometimes the cloud remained only from evening until morning; when the cloud lifted in the morning, they set out. Or if it remained a day and a night, they moved out when the cloud lifted. 22 Whether it was two days, a month, or longer,[A] the Israelites camped and did not set out as long as the cloud stayed over the tabernacle. But when it was lifted, they set out. 23 They camped at the LORD's command, and they set out at the LORD's command. They carried out the LORD's requirement according to his command through Moses.

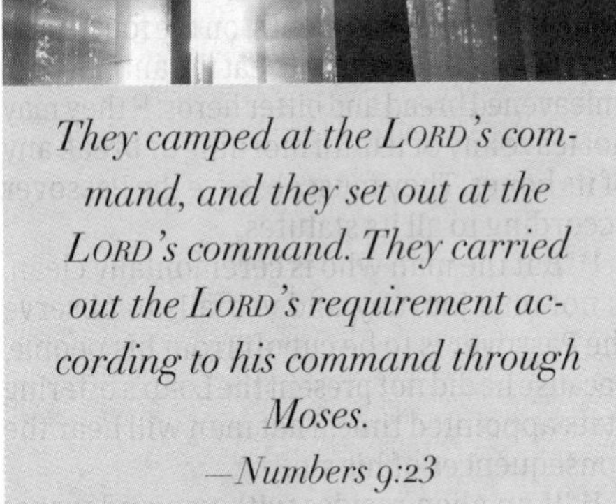

They camped at the LORD's command, and they set out at the LORD's command. They carried out the LORD's requirement according to his command through Moses.

—Numbers 9:23

TWO SILVER TRUMPETS

10 The LORD spoke to Moses: 2 "Make two trumpets of hammered silver to summon the community and have the camps set out. 3 When both are sounded in long blasts, the entire community is to gather before you at the entrance to the tent of meeting. 4 However, if one is sounded, only the leaders, the heads of Israel's clans, are to gather before you.

5 "When you sound short blasts, the camps pitched on the east are to set out. 6 When you sound short blasts a second time, the camps pitched on the south are to set out. Short blasts are to be sounded for them to set out. 7 When calling the assembly together, you are to sound long blasts, not short ones. 8 The sons of Aaron, the priests, are to sound the trumpets. Your use of these is a permanent statute throughout your generations.

9 "When you enter into battle in your land against an adversary who is attacking you, sound short blasts on the trumpets, and you will be remembered before the LORD your God and be saved from your enemies. 10 You are to sound the trumpets over your burnt offerings and your fellowship sacrifices and on your joyous occasions, your appointed festivals, and the beginning of each of your months. They will serve as a reminder for you before your God: I am the LORD your God."

FROM SINAI TO PARAN

11 During the second year, in the second month on the twentieth day of the month, the cloud was lifted up above the tabernacle of the testimony. 12 The Israelites traveled on from the Wilderness of Sinai, moving from one place to the next until the cloud stopped in the Wilderness of Paran. 13 They set out for the first time according to the LORD's command through Moses.

14 The military divisions of the camp of Judah's descendants with their banner set out first, and Nahshon son of Amminadab was over their divisions. 15 Nethanel son of Zuar was over the division of the tribe of Issachar's descendants, 16 and Eliab son of Helon was over the division of the tribe of Zebulun's descendants. 17 The tabernacle was then taken down, and the Gershonites and the Merarites set out, transporting the tabernacle.

18 The military divisions of the camp of Reuben with their banner set out, and Elizur son of Shedeur was over their divisions. 19 Shelumiel son of Zurishaddai was over the division of the tribe of Simeon's descendants, 20 and Eliasaph son of Deuel[B] was over the division of the tribe of Gad's descendants. 21 The Kohathites then set out, transporting the holy objects; the tabernacle was to be set up before their arrival.

22 Next the military divisions of the camp of Ephraim's descendants with their banner set out, and Elishama son of Ammihud was over their divisions. 23 Gamaliel son of Pedahzur was over the division of the tribe of Manasseh's descendants, 24 and Abidan son

[A] **9:22** Or *a year* [B] **10:20** LXX, Syr read *Reuel*

of Gideoni was over the division of the tribe
of Benjamin's descendants.
[25] The military divisions of the camp of Dan's
descendants with their banner set out, serving
as rear guard for all the camps, and Ahiezer
son of Ammishaddai was over their divisions.
[26] Pagiel son of Ochran was over the division
of the tribe of Asher's descendants, [27] and Ahira son of Enan was over the division of the
tribe of Naphtali's descendants. [28] This was
the order of march for the Israelites by their
military divisions as they set out.
[29] Moses said to Hobab, descendant of Reuel
the Midianite and Moses's relative by marriage: "We're setting out for the place the LORD
promised: 'I will give it to you.' Come with us,
and we will treat you well, for the LORD has
promised good things to Israel."
[30] But he replied to him, "I don't want to
go. Instead, I will go to my own land and my
relatives."
[31] "Please don't leave us," Moses said, "since
you know where we should camp in the wilderness, and you can serve as our eyes. [32] If
you come with us, whatever good the LORD
does for us we will do for you."
[33] They set out from the mountain of the
LORD on a three-day journey with the ark of
the LORD's covenant traveling ahead of them
for those three days to seek a resting place
for them. [34] Meanwhile, the cloud of the LORD
was over them by day when they set out from
the camp.
[35] Whenever the ark set out, Moses would
say:

Arise, LORD!
Let your enemies be scattered,
and those who hate you flee
from your presence.

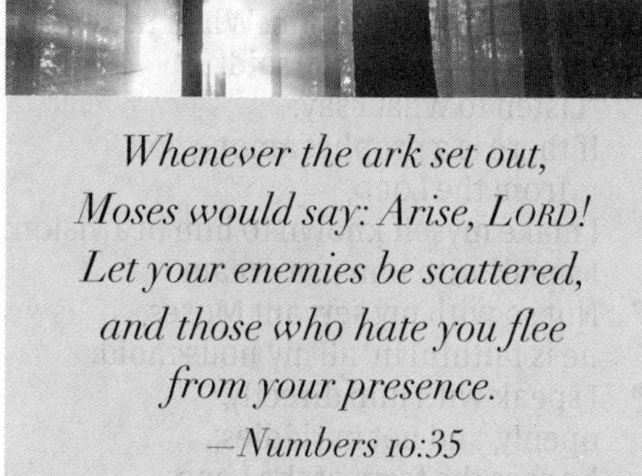

Whenever the ark set out,
Moses would say: Arise, LORD!
Let your enemies be scattered,
and those who hate you flee
from your presence.
—Numbers 10:35

[36] When it came to rest, he would say:
Return, LORD,
to the countless thousands of
Israel.

COMPLAINTS ABOUT HARDSHIP

11 Now the people began complaining openly
before[A] the LORD about hardship. When
the LORD heard, his anger burned, and fire
from the LORD blazed among them and consumed the outskirts of the camp. [2] Then the
people cried out to Moses, and he prayed to
the LORD, and the fire died down. [3] So that place
was named Taberah,[B] because the LORD's fire
had blazed among them.

COMPLAINTS ABOUT FOOD

[4] The riffraff[C] among them had a strong craving
for other food. The Israelites wept again and
said, "Who will feed us meat? [5] We remember
the free fish we ate in Egypt, along with the
cucumbers, melons, leeks, onions, and garlic.
[6] But now our appetite is gone;[D] there's nothing to look at but this manna!"
[7] The manna resembled coriander seed,
and its appearance was like that of bdellium.[E] [8] The people walked around and gathered it. They ground it on a pair of grinding
stones or crushed it in a mortar, then boiled
it in a cooking pot and shaped it into cakes.
It tasted like a pastry cooked with the finest
oil. [9] When the dew fell on the camp at night,
the manna would fall with it.
[10] Moses heard the people, family after
family, weeping at the entrance of their
tents. The LORD was very angry; Moses was
also provoked.[F] [11] So Moses asked the LORD,
"Why have you brought such trouble on your
servant? Why are you angry with me,[G] and
why do you burden me with all these people? [12] Did I conceive all these people? Did I
give them birth so you should tell me, 'Carry them at your breast, as a nanny carries
a baby,' to the land that you swore to give
their fathers? [13] Where can I get meat to give
all these people? For they are weeping to
me, 'Give us meat to eat!' [14] I can't carry all
these people by myself. They are too much
for me. [15] If you are going to treat me like this,
please kill me right now if I have found favor
with you, and don't let me see my misery[H]
anymore."

[A] **11:1** Lit *in the ears of* [B] **11:3** = Blaze [C] **11:4** Or *The mixed multitude*; Hb obscure [D] **11:6** Or *our lives are wasting away*, or *our throat is dry* [E] **11:7** A yellowish, transparent gum resin [F] **11:10** Lit *and it was evil in the eyes of Moses* [G] **11:11** Lit *Why have I not found favor in your eyes* [H] **11:15** Alt Hb tradition reads *your misery*

SEVENTY ELDERS ANOINTED

16 The LORD answered Moses, "Bring me seventy men from Israel known to you as elders
and officers of the people. Take them to the
tent of meeting and have them stand there
with you. 17 Then I will come down and speak
with you there. I will take some of the Spirit
who is on you and put the Spirit on them.
They will help you bear the burden of the
people, so that you do not have to bear it
by yourself.
18 "Tell the people: Consecrate yourselves
in readiness for tomorrow, and you will eat
meat because you wept in the LORD's hearing,
'Who will feed us meat? We were better off in
Egypt.' The LORD will give you meat and you
will eat. 19 You will eat, not for one day, or two
days, or five days, or ten days, or twenty days,
20 but for a whole month — until it comes out
of your nostrils and becomes nauseating to
you — because you have rejected the LORD
who is among you, and wept before him: 'Why
did we ever leave Egypt?' "
21 But Moses replied, "I'm in the middle of a
people with six hundred thousand foot soldiers, yet you say, 'I will give them meat, and
they will eat for a month.' 22 If flocks and herds
were slaughtered for them, would they have
enough? Or if all the fish in the sea were caught
for them, would they have enough?"
23 The LORD answered Moses, "Is the LORD's
arm weak?[A] Now you will see whether or not
what I have promised will happen to you."
24 Moses went out and told the people the
words of the LORD. He brought seventy men
from the elders of the people and had them
stand around the tent. 25 Then the LORD descended in the cloud and spoke to him. He
took some of the Spirit that was on Moses
and placed the Spirit on the seventy elders.
As the Spirit rested on them, they prophesied,
but they never did it again. 26 Two men had
remained in the camp, one named Eldad and
the other Medad; the Spirit rested on them
— they were among those listed, but had not
gone out to the tent — and they prophesied
in the camp. 27 A young man ran and reported
to Moses, "Eldad and Medad are prophesying
in the camp."
28 Joshua son of Nun, assistant to Moses
since his youth,[B] responded, "Moses, my lord,
stop them!"
29 But Moses asked him, "Are you jealous
on my account? If only all the LORD's people
were prophets and the LORD would place his
Spirit on them!" 30 Then Moses returned to the
camp along with the elders of Israel.

QUAIL IN THE CAMP

31 A wind sent by the LORD came up and blew
quail in from the sea; it dropped them all
around the camp. They were flying three feet[C]
off[D] the ground for about a day's journey in
every direction. 32 The people were up all that
day and night and all the next day gathering
the quail — the one who took the least gathered fifty bushels[E] — and they spread them
out all around the camp.[F]
33 While the meat was still between their
teeth, before it was chewed, the LORD's anger burned against the people, and the LORD
struck them with a very severe plague. 34 So
they named that place Kibroth-hattaavah,[G]
because there they buried the people who
had craved the meat.
35 From Kibroth-hattaavah the people moved
on to Hazeroth[H] and remained there.

MIRIAM AND AARON REBEL

12 Miriam and Aaron criticized Moses because of the Cushite woman he married
(for he had married a Cushite woman). 2 They
said, "Does the LORD speak only through Moses? Does he not also speak through us?" And
the LORD heard it. 3 Moses was a very humble
man, more so than anyone on the face of the
earth.
4 Suddenly the LORD said to Moses, Aaron,
and Miriam, "You three come out to the tent
of meeting." So the three of them went out.
5 Then the LORD descended in a pillar of cloud,
stood at the entrance to the tent, and summoned Aaron and Miriam. When the two of
them came forward, 6 he said:

"Listen to what I say:
If there is a prophet among you
from the LORD,
I make myself known to him in a vision;
I speak with him in a dream.
7 Not so with my servant Moses;
he is faithful in[I] all my household.
8 I speak with him directly,[J]
openly, and not in riddles;
he sees the form of the LORD.

[A] **11:23** Lit *the LORD's arm too short* [B] **11:28** Or *Moses, from his elite young men* [C] **11:31** Lit *two cubits* [D] **11:31** Or *They were three feet deep on* [E] **11:32** Lit *10 homers* [F] **11:32** To dry or cure the meat; 2Sm 17:19; Ezk 26:5,14 [G] **11:34** = Graves of Craving [H] **11:35** = Settlements; Nm 12:16; 33:16-17 [I] **12:7** Or *is entrusted with* [J] **12:8** Lit *mouth to mouth*

So why were you not afraid to speak against
my servant Moses?" [9] The LORD's anger burned
against them, and he left.
[10] As the cloud moved away from the tent,
Miriam's skin suddenly became diseased,
resembling snow.[A] When Aaron turned toward her, he saw that she was diseased [11] and
said to Moses, "My lord, please don't hold
against us this sin we have so foolishly committed. [12] Please don't let her be like a dead
baby[B] whose flesh is half eaten away when
he comes out of his mother's womb."
[13] Then Moses cried out to the LORD, "God,
please heal her!"
[14] The LORD answered Moses, "If her father
had merely spit in her face, wouldn't she remain in disgrace for seven days? Let her be
confined outside the camp for seven days;
after that she may be brought back in." [15] So
Miriam was confined outside the camp for
seven days, and the people did not move on
until Miriam was brought back in. [16] After
that, the people set out from Hazeroth and
camped in the Wilderness of Paran.

SCOUTING OUT CANAAN

13 The LORD spoke to Moses: [2] "Send men
to scout out the land of Canaan I am
giving to the Israelites. Send one man who
is a leader among them from each of their
ancestral tribes." [3] Moses sent them from the
Wilderness of Paran at the LORD's command.
All the men were leaders in Israel. [4] These
were their names:

Shammua son of Zaccur from the tribe of Reuben;
[5] Shaphat son of Hori from the tribe of Simeon;
[6] Caleb son of Jephunneh from the tribe of Judah;
[7] Igal son of Joseph from the tribe of Issachar;
[8] Hoshea son of Nun from the tribe of Ephraim;
[9] Palti son of Raphu from the tribe of Benjamin;
[10] Gaddiel son of Sodi from the tribe of Zebulun;
[11] Gaddi son of Susi from the tribe of Manasseh (from the tribe of Joseph);
[12] Ammiel son of Gemalli from the tribe of Dan;
[13] Sethur son of Michael from the tribe of Asher;
[14] Nahbi son of Vophsi from the tribe of Naphtali;
[15] Geuel son of Machi from the tribe of Gad.

[16] These were the names of the men Moses
sent to scout out the land, and Moses renamed
Hoshea son of Nun, Joshua.
[17] When Moses sent them to scout out the
land of Canaan, he told them, "Go up this way
to the Negev, then go up into the hill country.
[18] See what the land is like, and whether the
people who live there are strong or weak,
few or many. [19] Is the land they live in good
or bad? Are the cities they live in encampments or fortifications? [20] Is the land fertile
or unproductive? Are there trees in it or not?
Be courageous. Bring back some fruit from
the land." It was the season for the first ripe
grapes.
[21] So they went up and scouted out the land
from the Wilderness of Zin[C] as far as Rehob
near the entrance to Hamath.[D] [22] They went
up through the Negev and came to Hebron,
where Ahiman, Sheshai, and Talmai, the descendants of Anak, were living. Hebron was
built seven years before Zoan in Egypt. [23] When
they came to the Valley of Eshcol, they cut
down a branch with a single cluster of grapes,
which was carried on a pole by two men. They
also took some pomegranates and figs. [24] That
place was called the Valley of Eshcol[E] because
of the cluster of grapes the Israelites cut there.
[25] At the end of forty days they returned from
scouting out the land.

REPORT ABOUT CANAAN

[26] The men went back to Moses, Aaron, and
the entire Israelite community in the Wilderness of Paran at Kadesh. They brought back
a report for them and the whole community,
and they showed them the fruit of the land.
[27] They reported to Moses: "We went into the
land where you sent us. Indeed it is flowing with milk and honey, and here is some
of its fruit. [28] However, the people living in
the land are strong, and the cities are large
and fortified. We also saw the descendants
of Anak there. [29] The Amalekites are living
in the land of the Negev; the Hethites, Jebusites, and Amorites live in the hill country;

[A] **12:10** A reference to whiteness or flakiness of the skin [B] **12:12** Alt Hb tradition reads *baby who comes out of our mother's womb and our flesh is half eaten away.* [C] **13:21** Southern border of the promised land [D] **13:21** Or *near Lebo-hamath* [E] **13:24** = Cluster

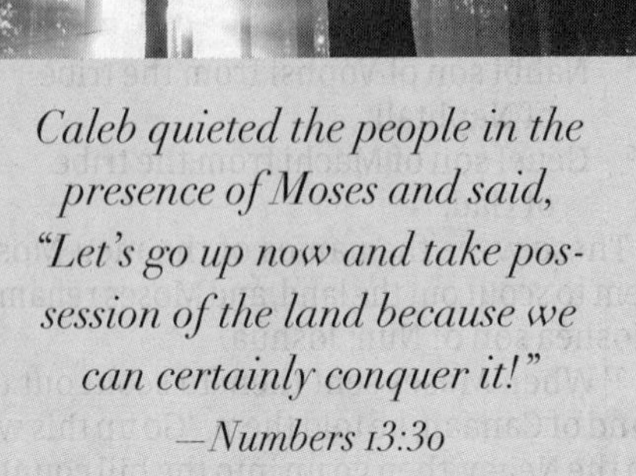

Caleb quieted the people in the presence of Moses and said, "Let's go up now and take possession of the land because we can certainly conquer it!"

—Numbers 13:30

and the Canaanites live by the sea and along
the Jordan."
30 Then Caleb quieted the people in the presence of Moses and said, "Let's go up now and
take possession of the land because we can
certainly conquer it!"
31 But the men who had gone up with him
responded, "We can't attack the people because they are stronger than we are!" 32 So
they gave a negative report to the Israelites
about the land they had scouted: "The land we
passed through to explore is one that devours
its inhabitants, and all the people we saw in it
are men of great size. 33 We even saw the Nephilim there — the descendants of Anak come
from the Nephilim! To ourselves we seemed
like grasshoppers, and we must have seemed
the same to them."

ISRAEL'S REFUSAL TO ENTER CANAAN

14 Then the whole community broke into
loud cries, and the people wept that night.
2 All the Israelites complained about Moses and
Aaron, and the whole community told them,
"If only we had died in the land of Egypt, or if
only we had died in this wilderness! 3 Why is
the LORD bringing us into this land to die by
the sword? Our wives and children will become plunder. Wouldn't it be better for us to go
back to Egypt?" 4 So they said to one another,
"Let's appoint a leader and go back to Egypt."
5 Then Moses and Aaron fell facedown in
front of the whole assembly of the Israelite
community. 6 Joshua son of Nun and Caleb son
of Jephunneh, who were among those who
scouted out the land, tore their clothes 7 and
said to the entire Israelite community: "The
land we passed through and explored is an
extremely good land. 8 If the LORD is pleased
with us, he will bring us into this land, a land

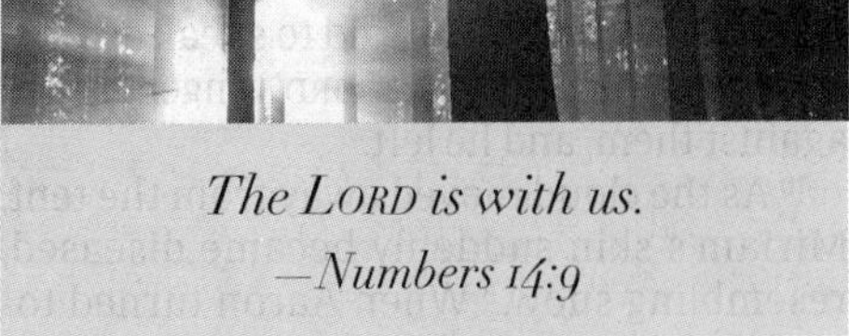

The LORD is with us.

—Numbers 14:9

flowing with milk and honey, and give it to
us. 9 Only don't rebel against the LORD, and
don't be afraid of the people of the land, for
we will devour them. Their protection has
been removed from them, and the LORD is
with us. Don't be afraid of them!"
10 While the whole community threatened
to stone them, the glory of the LORD appeared
to all the Israelites at the tent of meeting.

GOD'S JUDGMENT OF ISRAEL'S REBELLION

11 The LORD said to Moses, "How long will these
people despise me? How long will they not trust
in me despite all the signs I have performed
among them? 12 I will strike them with a plague
and destroy them. Then I will make you into
a greater and mightier nation than they are."
13 But Moses replied to the LORD, "The Egyptians will hear about it, for by your strength
you brought up this people from them. 14 They
will tell it to the inhabitants of this land. They
have heard that you, LORD, are among these
people, how you, LORD, are seen face to face,
how your cloud stands over them, and how
you go before them in a pillar of cloud by day
and in a pillar of fire by night. 15 If you kill this
people with a single blow,[A] the nations that
have heard of your fame will declare, 16 'Since
the LORD wasn't able to bring this people into
the land he swore to give them, he has slaughtered them in the wilderness.'
17 "So now, may my Lord's power be magnified just as you have spoken: 18 The LORD is
slow to anger and abounding in faithful love,
forgiving iniquity and rebellion. But he will
not leave the guilty unpunished, bringing the
consequences of the fathers' iniquity on the
children to the third and fourth generation.
19 Please pardon the iniquity of this people,
in keeping with the greatness of your faithful love, just as you have forgiven them from
Egypt until now."
20 The LORD responded, "I have pardoned
them as you requested. 21 Yet as surely as I
live and as the whole earth is filled with the
LORD's glory, 22 none of the men who have

[A] **14:15** Lit *people as one man*

seen my glory and the signs I performed in
Egypt and in the wilderness, and have tested me these ten times and did not obey me,
23 will ever see the land I swore to give their
fathers. None of those who have despised me
will see it. 24 But since my servant Caleb has
a different spirit and has remained loyal to
me, I will bring him into the land where he
has gone, and his descendants will inherit it.
25 Since the Amalekites and Canaanites are
living in the lowlands,[A] turn back tomorrow
and head for the wilderness in the direction
of the Red Sea."

26 Then the LORD spoke to Moses and Aaron: 27 "How long must I endure this evil community that keeps complaining about me? I
have heard the Israelites' complaints that they
make against me. 28 Tell them: As surely as I
live — this is the LORD's declaration — I will
do to you exactly as I heard you say. 29 Your
corpses will fall in this wilderness — all of
you who were registered in the census, the
entire number of you twenty years old or more
— because you have complained about me.
30 I swear that none of you will enter the land
I promised[B] to settle you in, except Caleb son
of Jephunneh and Joshua son of Nun. 31 I will
bring your children whom you said would
become plunder into the land you rejected,
and they will enjoy it. 32 But as for you, your
corpses will fall in this wilderness. 33 Your
children will be shepherds in the wilderness
for forty years and bear the penalty for your
acts of unfaithfulness until all your corpses
lie scattered in the wilderness. 34 You will bear
the consequences of your iniquities forty years
based on the number of the forty days that
you scouted the land, a year for each day.[C] You
will know my displeasure.[D] 35 I, the LORD, have
spoken. I swear that I will do this to the entire
evil community that has conspired against me.
They will come to an end in the wilderness,
and there they will die."

36 So the men Moses sent to scout out the
land, and who returned and incited the entire
community to complain about him by spreading a negative report about the land — 37 those
men who spread the negative report about the
land were struck down by the LORD. 38 Only
Joshua son of Nun and Caleb son of Jephunneh remained alive of those men who went
to scout out the land.

Support | *God's Support*

FOR US

"Only don't rebel against the LORD, and don't be afraid of the people of the land, for we will devour them. Their protection has been removed from them, and the LORD is with us. Don't be afraid of them!" Numbers 14:9

The Bible says God is both *with* his people and *in* them. And anyone with the faith to take these big claims to heart knows how life-changing they are. The apostle Paul also reveals one more bit of comfort: "God is *for* us." Therefore, "If God is for us, who is against us? He did not even spare his own Son but offered him up for us all. How will he not also with him grant us everything?" (Rm 8:31-32).

To say "God is for us" means he's tracking with us, in our corner, cheering us on. It means he wants our best. How can we be so sure of this? Easy. We know God is "for us" because he offered up Jesus "for us."

Let that soak in. Because Christ died in our place, we experience forgiveness instead of punishment. Instead of remaining God's enemies, we become his children. The implication? If God "did not even spare his own Son . . . how will he not also with him grant us everything?"

Maybe you feel as though the whole world is against you today. And maybe those feelings aren't too far from the truth. Good news. The maker of the entire world is *with* you, *in* you, and *for* you. Remember and rejoice.

For the next note on *Support*, see Joshua 1:5.

[A] **14:25** Lit *valley* [B] **14:30** Lit *I raised my hand* [C] **14:34** Lit *a day for the year, a day for the year* [D] **14:34** Or *my opposition*

ISRAEL ROUTED

39 When Moses reported these words to all the Israelites, the people were overcome with grief. 40 They got up early the next morning and went up the ridge of the hill country, saying, "Let's go to the place the LORD promised, for we were wrong."

41 But Moses responded, "Why are you going against the LORD's command? It won't succeed. 42 Don't go, because the LORD is not among you and you will be defeated by your enemies. 43 The Amalekites and Canaanites are right in front of you, and you will fall by the sword. The LORD won't be with you, since you have turned from following him."

44 But they dared to go up the ridge of the hill country, even though the ark of the LORD's covenant and Moses did not leave the camp. 45 Then the Amalekites and Canaanites who lived in that part of the hill country came down, attacked them, and routed them as far as Hormah.

LAWS ABOUT OFFERINGS

15 The LORD instructed Moses: 2 "Speak to the Israelites and tell them: When you enter the land I am giving you to settle in, 3 and you make a fire offering to the LORD from the herd or flock — either a burnt offering or a sacrifice, to fulfill a vow, or as a freewill offering, or at your appointed festivals — to produce a pleasing aroma for the LORD, 4 the one presenting his offering to the LORD is also to present a grain offering of two quarts[A] of fine flour mixed with a quart[B] of oil. 5 Prepare a quart of wine as a drink offering with the burnt offering or sacrifice of each lamb.

6 "If you prepare a grain offering with a ram, it is to be four quarts[C] of fine flour mixed with a third of a gallon[D] of oil. 7 Also present a third of a gallon of wine for a drink offering as a pleasing aroma to the LORD.

8 "If you prepare a young bull as a burnt offering or as a sacrifice, to fulfill a vow, or as a fellowship offering to the LORD, 9 a grain offering of six quarts[E] of fine flour mixed with two quarts[F] of oil is to be presented with the bull. 10 Also present two quarts of wine as a drink offering. It is a fire offering of pleasing aroma to the LORD. 11 This is to be done for each ox, ram, lamb, or goat. 12 This is how you are to prepare each of them, no matter how many.

13 "Every Israelite is to prepare these things in this way when he presents a fire offering as a pleasing aroma to the LORD. 14 When an alien resides with you or someone else is among you and wants to prepare a fire offering as a pleasing aroma to the LORD, he is to do exactly as you do throughout your generations. 15 The assembly is to have the same statute for both you and the resident alien as a permanent statute throughout your generations. You and the alien will be alike before the LORD. 16 The same law and the same ordinance will apply to both you and the alien who resides with you."

17 The LORD instructed Moses: 18 "Speak to the Israelites and tell them: After you enter the land where I am bringing you, 19 you are to offer a contribution to the LORD when you eat from the food of the land. 20 You are to offer a loaf from your first batch of dough as a contribution; offer it just like a contribution from the threshing floor. 21 Throughout your generations, you are to give the LORD a contribution from the first batch of your dough.

22 "When you sin unintentionally and do not obey all these commands that the LORD spoke to Moses — 23 all that the LORD has commanded you through Moses, from the day the LORD issued the commands and onward throughout your generations — 24 and if it was done unintentionally without the community's awareness, the entire community is to prepare one young bull for a burnt offering as a pleasing aroma to the LORD, with its grain offering and drink offering according to the regulation, and one male goat as a sin offering. 25 The priest will then make atonement for the entire Israelite community so that they may be forgiven, for the sin was unintentional. They are to bring their offering, one made by fire to the LORD, and their sin offering before the LORD for their unintentional sin. 26 The entire Israelite community and the alien who resides among them will be forgiven, since it happened to all the people unintentionally.

27 "If one person sins unintentionally, he is to present a year-old female goat as a sin offering. 28 The priest will then make atonement before the LORD on behalf of the person who acts in error sinning unintentionally, and when he makes atonement for him, he will be forgiven. 29 You are to have the same law for the person who acts in error, whether he is an Israelite or an alien who resides among you.

[A] **15:4** Lit *a tenth* (of an ephah) [B] **15:4** Lit *a fourth hin*, also in v. 5 [C] **15:6** Lit *two-tenths* (of an ephah) [D] **15:6** Lit *a third hin*, also in v. 7 [E] **15:9** Lit *three-tenths* (of an ephah) [F] **15:9** Lit *a half hin*, also in v. 10

30 "But the person who acts defiantly,[A] whether native or resident alien, blasphemes the LORD. That person is to be cut off from his people. 31 He will certainly be cut off, because he has despised the LORD's word and broken his command; his guilt remains on him."

SABBATH VIOLATION

32 While the Israelites were in the wilderness, they found a man gathering wood on the Sabbath day. 33 Those who found him gathering wood brought him to Moses, Aaron, and the entire community. 34 They placed him in custody because it had not been decided what should be done to him. 35 Then the LORD told Moses, "The man is to be put to death. The entire community is to stone him outside the camp." 36 So the entire community brought him outside the camp and stoned him to death, as the LORD had commanded Moses.

TASSELS FOR REMEMBRANCE

37 The LORD said to Moses, 38 "Speak to the Israelites and tell them that throughout their generations they are to make tassels for the corners of their garments, and put a blue cord on the tassel at each corner. 39 These will serve as tassels for you to look at, so that you may remember all the LORD's commands and obey them and not prostitute yourselves by following your own heart and your own eyes. 40 This way you will remember and obey all my commands and be holy to your God. 41 I am the LORD your God who brought you out of the land of Egypt to be your God; I am the LORD your God."

KORAH INCITES REBELLION

16 Now Korah son of Izhar, son of Kohath, son of Levi, with Dathan and Abiram, sons of Eliab, and On son of Peleth, sons of Reuben, took 2 two hundred and fifty prominent Israelite men who were leaders of the community and representatives in the assembly, and they rebelled against Moses. 3 They came together against Moses and Aaron and told them, "You have gone too far! Everyone in the entire community is holy, and the LORD is among them. Why then do you exalt yourselves above the LORD's assembly?"

4 When Moses heard this, he fell facedown. 5 Then he said to Korah and all his followers, "Tomorrow morning the LORD will reveal who belongs to him, who is set apart, and the one he will let come near him. He will let the one he chooses come near him. 6 Korah, you and all your followers are to do this: take firepans, and tomorrow 7 place fire in them and put incense on them before the LORD. Then the man the LORD chooses will be the one who is set apart. It is you Levites who have gone too far!"

8 Moses also told Korah, "Now listen, Levites! 9 Isn't it enough for you that the God of Israel has separated you from the Israelite community to bring you near to himself, to perform the work at the LORD's tabernacle, and to stand before the community to minister to them? 10 He has brought you near, and all your fellow Levites who are with you, but you are pursuing the priesthood as well. 11 Therefore, it is you and all your followers who have conspired against the LORD! As for Aaron, who is he[B] that you should complain about him?"

12 Moses sent for Dathan and Abiram, the sons of Eliab, but they said, "We will not come! 13 Is it not enough that you brought us up from a land flowing with milk and honey to kill us in the wilderness? Do you also have to appoint yourself as ruler over us? 14 Furthermore, you didn't bring us to a land flowing with milk and honey or give us an inheritance of fields and vineyards. Will you gouge out the eyes of these men? We will not come!"

15 Then Moses became angry and said to the LORD, "Don't respect their offering. I have not taken one donkey from them or mistreated a single one of them." 16 So Moses told Korah, "You and all your followers are to appear before the LORD tomorrow — you, they, and Aaron. 17 Each of you is to take his firepan, place incense on it, and present his firepan before the LORD — 250 firepans. You and Aaron are each to present your firepan also."

18 Each man took his firepan, placed fire in it, put incense on it, and stood at the entrance to the tent of meeting along with Moses and Aaron. 19 After Korah assembled the whole community against them at the entrance to the tent of meeting, the glory of the LORD appeared to the whole community. 20 The LORD spoke to Moses and Aaron, 21 "Separate yourselves from this community so I may consume them instantly."

22 But Moses and Aaron fell facedown and

[A] **15:30** Lit *with a high hand* [B] **16:11** Or *Aaron, what has he done* said, "God, God who gives breath to all,[A] when one man sins, will you vent your wrath on the whole community?"

23 The LORD replied to Moses, 24 "Tell the community: Get away from the dwellings of Korah, Dathan, and Abiram."

25 Moses got up and went to Dathan and Abiram, and the elders of Israel followed him. 26 He warned the community, "Get away now from the tents of these wicked men. Don't touch anything that belongs to them, or you will be swept away because of all their sins." 27 So they got away from the dwellings of Korah, Dathan, and Abiram. Meanwhile, Dathan and Abiram came out and stood at the entrance of their tents with their wives, children, and infants.

28 Then Moses said, "This is how you will know that the LORD sent me to do all these things and that it was not of my own will: 29 If these men die naturally as all people would, and suffer the fate of all, then the LORD has not sent me. 30 But if the LORD brings about something unprecedented, and the ground opens its mouth and swallows them along with all that belongs to them so that they go down alive into Sheol, then you will know that these men have despised the LORD."

31 Just as he finished speaking all these words, the ground beneath them split open. 32 The earth opened its mouth and swallowed them and their households, all Korah's people, and all their possessions. 33 They went down alive into Sheol with all that belonged to them. The earth closed over them, and they vanished from the assembly. 34 At their cries, all the people of Israel who were around them fled because they thought, "The earth may swallow us too!" 35 Fire also came out from the LORD and consumed the 250 men who were presenting the incense.

36 Then the LORD spoke to Moses: 37 "Tell Eleazar son of Aaron the priest to remove the firepans from the burning debris, because they are holy, and scatter the fire far away. 38 As for the firepans of those who sinned at the cost of their own lives, make them into hammered sheets as plating for the altar, for they presented them before the LORD, and the firepans are holy. They will be a sign to the Israelites."

39 So the priest Eleazar took the bronze firepans that those who were burned had presented, and they were hammered into plating for the altar, 40 just as the LORD commanded him through Moses. It was to be a reminder for the Israelites that no unauthorized person outside the lineage of Aaron should approach to offer incense before the LORD and become like Korah and his followers.

41 The next day the entire Israelite community complained about Moses and Aaron, saying, "You have killed the LORD's people!" 42 When the community assembled against them, Moses and Aaron turned toward the tent of meeting, and suddenly the cloud covered it, and the LORD's glory appeared.

43 Moses and Aaron went to the front of the tent of meeting, 44 and the LORD said to Moses, 45 "Get away from this community so that I may consume them instantly." But they fell facedown.

46 Then Moses told Aaron, "Take your firepan, place fire from the altar in it, and add incense. Go quickly to the community and make atonement for them, because wrath has come from the LORD; the plague has begun." 47 So Aaron took his firepan as Moses had ordered, ran into the middle of the assembly, and saw that the plague had begun among the people. After he added incense, he made atonement for the people. 48 He stood between the dead and the living, and the plague was halted. 49 But those who died from the plague numbered 14,700, in addition to those who died because of the Korah incident. 50 Aaron then returned to Moses at the entrance to the tent of meeting, since the plague had been halted.

AARON'S STAFF CHOSEN

17 The LORD instructed Moses: 2 "Speak to the Israelites and take one staff from them for each ancestral tribe,[B] twelve staffs from all the leaders of their tribes.[C] Write each man's name on his staff. 3 Write Aaron's name on Levi's staff, because there is to be one staff for the head of each tribe. 4 Then place them in the tent of meeting in front of the testimony where I meet with you. 5 The staff of the man I choose will sprout, and I will rid myself of the Israelites' complaints that they have been making about you."

6 So Moses spoke to the Israelites, and each of their leaders gave him a staff, one for each of the leaders of their tribes, twelve staffs in all. Aaron's staff was among them. 7 Moses placed the staffs before the LORD in the tent of the testimony.

[A] **16:22** Or *God of the spirits of all flesh* [B] **17:2** Lit *father's house* [C] **17:2** Lit *the house of their fathers*, also in vv. 3,6

8 The next day Moses entered the tent of the testimony and saw that Aaron's staff, representing the house of Levi, had sprouted, formed buds, blossomed, and produced almonds! 9 Moses then brought out all the staffs from the LORD's presence to all the Israelites. They saw them, and each man took his own staff. 10 The LORD told Moses, "Put Aaron's staff back in front of the testimony to be kept as a sign for the rebels, so that you may put an end to their complaints before me, or else they will die." 11 So Moses did as the LORD commanded him.

12 Then the Israelites declared to Moses, "Look, we're perishing! We're lost; we're all lost! 13 Anyone who comes near the LORD's tabernacle will die. Will we all perish?"

PROVISION FOR THE PRIESTHOOD

18 The LORD said to Aaron, "You, your sons, and your ancestral family[A] will be responsible for iniquity against the sanctuary. You and your sons will be responsible for iniquity involving your priesthood. 2 But also bring your relatives with you from the tribe of Levi, your ancestral tribe, so they may join you and assist you and your sons in front of the tent of the testimony. 3 They are to perform duties for you and for the whole tent. They must not come near the sanctuary equipment or the altar; otherwise, both they and you will die. 4 They are to join you and guard the tent of meeting, doing all the work at the tent, but no unauthorized person may come near you.

5 "You are to guard the sanctuary and the altar so that wrath may not fall on the Israelites again. 6 Look, I have selected your fellow Levites from the Israelites as a gift for you, assigned by the LORD to work at the tent of meeting. 7 But you and your sons will carry out your priestly responsibilities for everything concerning the altar and for what is inside the curtain, and you will do that work. I am giving you the work of the priesthood as a gift,[B] but an unauthorized person who comes near the sanctuary will be put to death."

SUPPORT FOR THE PRIESTS AND LEVITES

8 Then the LORD spoke to Aaron, "Look, I have put you in charge of the contributions brought to me. As for all the holy offerings of the Israelites, I have given them to you and your sons as a portion and a permanent statute. 9 A portion of the holiest offerings kept from the fire will be yours; every one of their offerings that they give me, whether the grain offering, sin offering, or guilt offering will be most holy for you and your sons. 10 You are to eat it as a most holy offering.[C] Every male may eat it; it is to be holy to you.

11 "The contribution of their gifts also belongs to you. I have given all the Israelites' presentation offerings to you and to your sons and daughters as a permanent statute. Every ceremonially clean person in your house may eat it. 12 I am giving you all the best of the fresh oil, new wine, and grain, which the Israelites give to the LORD as their firstfruits. 13 The firstfruits of all that is in their land, which they bring to the LORD, belong to you. Every clean person in your house may eat them.

14 "Everything in Israel that is permanently dedicated to the LORD belongs to you. 15 The firstborn of every living thing, human or animal, presented to the LORD belongs to you. But you must certainly redeem a human firstborn, and redeem the firstborn of an unclean animal. 16 You will pay the redemption price for a month-old male according to your assessment: five shekels[D] of silver by the standard sanctuary shekel, which is twenty gerahs.

17 "However, you must not redeem the firstborn of an ox, a sheep, or a goat; they are holy. You are to splatter their blood on the altar and burn their fat as a fire offering for a pleasing aroma to the LORD. 18 But their meat belongs to you. It belongs to you like the breast of the presentation offering and the right thigh.

19 "I give to you and to your sons and daughters all the holy contributions that the Israelites present to the LORD as a permanent statute. It is a permanent covenant of salt before the LORD for you as well as your offspring."

20 The LORD told Aaron, "You will not have an inheritance in their land; there will be no portion among them for you. I am your portion and your inheritance among the Israelites.

21 "Look, I have given the Levites every tenth in Israel as an inheritance in return for the work they do, the work of the tent of meeting. 22 The Israelites must never again come near the tent of meeting, or they will incur guilt and die. 23 The Levites will do the work of the tent of meeting, and they will bear the consequences of their iniquity. The Levites will not receive an inheritance among the Israelites; this is a permanent statute throughout

[A] **18:1** Lit *the house of your father* [B] **18:7** Or *curtain. So you are to perform the service; a gift of your priesthood I grant* [C] **18:10** Or *it in a most holy place* [D] **18:16** A shekel is about two-fifths of an ounce

your generations. 24 For I have given them the
tenth that the Israelites present to the LORD
as a contribution for their inheritance. That
is why I told them that they would not receive
an inheritance among the Israelites."
25 The LORD instructed Moses, 26 "Speak to
the Levites and tell them: When you receive
from the Israelites the tenth that I have given
you as your inheritance, you are to present
part of it as an offering to the LORD — a tenth
of the tenth. 27 Your offering will be credited to
you as if it were your grain from the threshing
floor or the full harvest from the winepress.
28 You are to present an offering to the LORD
from every tenth you receive from the Israelites. Give some of it to the priest Aaron as an
offering to the LORD. 29 You must present the
entire offering due the LORD from all your gifts.
The best part of the tenth is to be consecrated.
30 "Tell them further: Once you have presented the best part of the tenth, and it is credited
to you Levites as the produce of the threshing
floor or the winepress, 31 then you and your
household may eat it anywhere. It is your wage
in return for your work at the tent of meeting.
32 You will not incur guilt because of it once
you have presented the best part of it, but you
must not defile the Israelites' holy offerings,
so that you will not die."

PURIFICATION RITUAL

19 The LORD spoke to Moses and Aaron,
2 "This is the legal statute that the LORD
has commanded: Instruct the Israelites to bring
you an unblemished red cow that has no defect
and has never been yoked. 3 Give it to the priest
Eleazar, and he will have it brought outside the
camp and slaughtered in his presence. 4 The
priest Eleazar is to take some of its blood with
his finger and sprinkle it seven times toward
the front of the tent of meeting. 5 The cow is
to be burned in his sight. Its hide, flesh, and
blood, are to be burned along with its waste.
6 The priest is to take cedar wood, hyssop, and
crimson yarn, and throw them onto the fire
where the cow is burning. 7 Then the priest
must wash his clothes and bathe his body in
water; after that he may enter the camp, but
he will remain ceremonially unclean until evening. 8 The one who burned the cow must also
wash his clothes and bathe his body in water,
and he will remain unclean until evening.
9 "A man who is clean is to gather up the cow's
ashes and deposit them outside the camp in
a ceremonially clean place. The ashes will be
kept by the Israelite community for preparing the water to remove impurity; it is a sin
offering. 10 Then the one who gathers up the
cow's ashes must wash his clothes, and he
will remain unclean until evening. This is a
permanent statute for the Israelites and for
the alien who resides among them.
11 "The person who touches any human
corpse will be unclean for seven days. 12 He
is to purify himself with the water[A] on the
third day and the seventh day; then he will be
clean. But if he does not purify himself on the
third and seventh days, he will not be clean.
13 Anyone who touches a body of a person
who has died, and does not purify himself,
defiles the tabernacle of the LORD. That person will be cut off from Israel. He remains
unclean because the water for impurity has
not been sprinkled on him, and his uncleanness is still on him.
14 "This is the law when a person dies in a tent:
everyone who enters the tent and everyone
who is already in the tent will be unclean for
seven days, 15 and any open container without
a lid tied on it is unclean. 16 Anyone in the open
field who touches a person who has been killed
by the sword or has died, or who even touches a human bone, or a grave, will be unclean
for seven days. 17 For the purification of the
unclean person, they are to take some of the
ashes of the burnt sin offering, put them in a
jar, and add fresh water to them. 18 A person
who is clean is to take hyssop, dip it in the water, and sprinkle the tent, all the furnishings,
and the people who were there. He is also to
sprinkle the one who touched a bone, a grave,
a corpse, or a person who had been killed.
19 "The one who is clean is to sprinkle the unclean person on the third day and the seventh
day. After he purifies the unclean person on
the seventh day, the one being purified must
wash his clothes and bathe in water, and he
will be clean by evening. 20 But a person who
is unclean and does not purify himself, that
person will be cut off from the assembly because he has defiled the sanctuary of the LORD.
The water for impurity has not been sprinkled
on him; he is unclean. 21 This is a permanent
statute for them. The person who sprinkles
the water for impurity is to wash his clothes,
and whoever touches the water for impurity

[A] **19:12** Or *ashes*; lit *with it*

will be unclean until evening. 22 Anything the unclean person touches will become unclean, and anyone who touches it will be unclean until evening."

WATER FROM THE ROCK

20 The entire Israelite community entered the Wilderness of Zin in the first month, and they[A] settled in Kadesh. Miriam died and was buried there.

2 There was no water for the community, so they assembled against Moses and Aaron. 3 The people quarreled with Moses and said, "If only we had perished when our brothers perished before the LORD. 4 Why have you brought the LORD's assembly into this wilderness for us and our livestock to die here? 5 Why have you led us up from Egypt to bring us to this evil place? It's not a place of grain, figs, vines, and pomegranates, and there is no water to drink!"

6 Then Moses and Aaron went from the presence of the assembly to the doorway of the tent of meeting. They fell facedown, and the glory of the LORD appeared to them. 7 The LORD spoke to Moses, 8 "Take the staff and assemble the community. You and your brother Aaron are to speak to the rock while they watch, and it will yield its water. You will bring out water for them from the rock and provide drink for the community and their livestock."

9 So Moses took the staff from the LORD's presence just as he had commanded him. 10 Moses and Aaron summoned the assembly in front of the rock, and Moses said to them, "Listen, you rebels! Must we bring water out of this rock for you?" 11 Then Moses raised his hand and struck the rock twice with his staff, so that abundant water gushed out, and the community and their livestock drank.

12 But the LORD said to Moses and Aaron, "Because you did not trust me to demonstrate my holiness in the sight of the Israelites, you will not bring this assembly into the land I have given them." 13 These are the Waters of Meribah,[B] where the Israelites quarreled with the LORD, and he demonstrated his holiness to them.

EDOM DENIES PASSAGE

14 Moses sent messengers from Kadesh to the king of Edom, "This is what your brother Israel says, 'You know all the hardships that have overtaken us. 15 Our fathers went down to Egypt, and we lived in Egypt many years, but the Egyptians treated us and our fathers badly. 16 When we cried out to the LORD, he heard our plea,[C] and sent an angel,[D] and brought us out of Egypt. Now look, we are in Kadesh, a city on the border of your territory. 17 Please let us travel through your land. We won't travel through any field or vineyard, or drink any well water. We will travel the King's Highway; we won't turn to the right or the left until we have traveled through your territory.'"

18 But Edom answered him, "You will not travel through our land, or we will come out and confront you with the sword."

19 "We will go on the main road," the Israelites replied to them, "and if we or our herds drink your water, we will pay its price. There will be no problem; only let us travel through on foot."

20 Yet Edom insisted, "You may not travel through." And they came out to confront them with a large force of heavily-armed people.[E] 21 Edom refused to allow Israel to travel through their territory, and Israel turned away from them.

AARON'S DEATH

22 After they set out from Kadesh, the entire Israelite community came to Mount Hor. 23 The LORD said to Moses and Aaron at Mount Hor on the border of the land of Edom, 24 "Aaron will be gathered to his people; he will not enter the land I have given the Israelites, because you both rebelled against my command at the Waters of Meribah. 25 Take Aaron and his son Eleazar and bring them up Mount Hor. 26 Remove Aaron's garments and put them on his son Eleazar. Aaron will be gathered to his people and die there."

27 So Moses did as the LORD commanded, and they climbed Mount Hor in the sight of the whole community. 28 After Moses removed Aaron's garments and put them on his son Eleazar, Aaron died there on top of the mountain. Then Moses and Eleazar came down from the mountain. 29 When the whole community saw that Aaron had passed away, the entire house of Israel mourned for him thirty days.

CANAANITE KING DEFEATED

21 When the Canaanite king of Arad, who lived in the Negev, heard that Israel was coming on the Atharim road, he fought against Israel and captured some prisoners. 2 Then

---

[A] **20:1** Lit *the people* [B] **20:13** = Quarreling [C] **20:16** Lit *voice* [D] **20:16** Or *a messenger* [E] **20:20** Lit *with numerous people and a strong hand*

Israel made a vow to the LORD, "If you will hand this people over to us, we will completely destroy their cities." 3 The LORD listened to Israel's request and handed the Canaanites over to them, and Israel completely destroyed them and their cities. So they named the place Hormah.[A]

THE BRONZE SNAKE

4 Then they set out from Mount Hor by way of the Red Sea to bypass the land of Edom, but the people became impatient because of the journey. 5 The people spoke against God and Moses: "Why have you led us up from Egypt to die in the wilderness? There is no bread or water, and we detest this wretched food!" 6 Then the LORD sent poisonous[B] snakes among the people, and they bit them so that many Israelites died.

7 The people then came to Moses and said, "We have sinned by speaking against the LORD and against you. Intercede with the LORD so that he will take the snakes away from us." And Moses interceded for the people.

8 Then the LORD said to Moses, "Make a snake image and mount it on a pole. When anyone who is bitten looks at it, he will recover." 9 So Moses made a bronze snake and mounted it on a pole. Whenever someone was bitten, and he looked at the bronze snake, he recovered.

> *Moses made a bronze snake and mounted it on a pole. Whenever someone was bitten, and he looked at the bronze snake, he recovered.*
> *—Numbers 21:9*

JOURNEY AROUND MOAB

10 The Israelites set out and camped at Oboth. 11 They set out from Oboth and camped at Iye-abarim in the wilderness that borders Moab on the east. 12 From there they went and camped at Zered Valley. 13 They set out from there and camped on the other side of the Arnon River, in the wilderness that extends from the Amorite border, because the Arnon was the Moabite border between Moab and the Amorites. 14 Therefore it is stated in the Book of the LORD's Wars:

Waheb in Suphah
and the ravines of the Arnon,
15 even the slopes of the ravines
that extend to the site of Ar
and lie along the border of Moab.

16 From there they went to Beer,[C] the well the LORD told Moses about, "Gather the people so I may give them water." 17 Then Israel sang this song:

Spring up, well — sing to it!
18 The princes dug the well;
the nobles of the people hollowed it out
with a scepter and with their staffs.

They went from the wilderness to Mattanah, 19 from Mattanah to Nahaliel, from Nahaliel to Bamoth, 20 from Bamoth to the valley in the territory of Moab near the Pisgah highlands that overlook the wasteland.[D]

AMORITE KINGS DEFEATED

21 Israel sent messengers to say to King Sihon of the Amorites: 22 "Let us travel through your land. We won't go into the fields or vineyards. We won't drink any well water. We will travel the King's Highway until we have traveled through your territory." 23 But Sihon would not let Israel travel through his territory. Instead, he gathered his whole army and went out to confront Israel in the wilderness. When he came to Jahaz, he fought against Israel. 24 Israel struck him with the sword and took possession of his land from the Arnon to the Jabbok, but only up to the Ammonite border, because it was fortified.[E]

25 Israel took all the cities and lived in all these Amorite cities, including Heshbon and all its surrounding villages. 26 Heshbon was the city of King Sihon of the Amorites, who had fought against the former king of Moab and had taken control of all his land as far as the Arnon. 27 Therefore the poets[F] say:

Come to Heshbon, let it be rebuilt;
let the city of Sihon be restored.[G]
28 For fire came out of Heshbon,
a flame from the city of Sihon.
It consumed Ar of Moab,
the citizens of Arnon's heights.
29 Woe to you, Moab!
You have been destroyed,
people of Chemosh!

[A] **21:3** = Destruction [B] **21:6** Lit *Burning* [C] **21:16** = Well [D] **21:20** Or *overlook Jeshimon* [E] **21:24** LXX reads *because the Ammonite border was Jazer* [F] **21:27** Lit *ones who speak proverbs* [G] **21:27** Or *firmly founded*

He gave up his sons as refugees,
and his daughters into captivity
to Sihon the Amorite king.
30 We threw them down;
Heshbon has been destroyed
as far as Dibon.
We caused desolation as far as Nophah,
which reaches as far as Medeba.
31 So Israel lived in the Amorites' land. 32 After
Moses sent spies to Jazer, Israel captured its
surrounding villages and drove out the Amorites who were there.
33 Then they turned and went up the road
to Bashan, and King Og of Bashan came out
against them with his whole army to do battle
at Edrei. 34 But the LORD said to Moses, "Do
not fear him, for I have handed him over to
you along with his whole army and his land.
Do to him as you did to King Sihon of the
Amorites, who lived in Heshbon." 35 So they
struck him, his sons, and his whole army
until no one was left,[A] and they took possession of his land.

BALAK HIRES BALAAM

22 The Israelites traveled on and camped
in the plains of Moab near the Jordan
across from Jericho. 2 Now Balak son of Zippor
saw all that Israel had done to the Amorites.
3 Moab was terrified of the people because
they were numerous, and Moab dreaded the
Israelites. 4 So the Moabites said to the elders
of Midian, "This horde will devour everything
around us like an ox eats up the green plants
in the field."
Since Balak son of Zippor was Moab's king at
that time, 5 he sent messengers to Balaam son
of Beor at Pethor, which is by the Euphrates
in the land of his people.[B,C] Balak said to him:
"Look, a people has come out of Egypt; they
cover the surface of the land and are living
right across from me. 6 Please come and put
a curse on these people for me because they
are more powerful than I am. I may be able to
defeat them and drive them out of the land,
for I know that those you bless are blessed
and those you curse are cursed."
7 The elders of Moab and Midian departed
with fees for divination in hand. They came
to Balaam and reported Balak's words to him.
8 He said to them, "Spend the night here, and
I will give you the answer the LORD tells me."
So the officials of Moab stayed with Balaam.
9 Then God came to Balaam and asked, "Who
are these men with you?"
10 Balaam replied to God, "Balak son of Zippor, king of Moab, sent this message to me:
11 'Look, a people has come out of Egypt, and
they cover the surface of the land. Now come
and put a curse on them for me. I may be able
to fight against them and drive them away.'"
12 Then God said to Balaam, "You are not to
go with them. You are not to curse this people,
for they are blessed."
13 So Balaam got up the next morning and
said to Balak's officials, "Go back to your land,
because the LORD has refused to let me go
with you."
14 The officials of Moab arose, returned to
Balak, and reported, "Balaam refused to come
with us."
15 Balak sent officials again who were more
numerous and higher in rank than the others. 16 They came to Balaam and said to him,
"This is what Balak son of Zippor says: 'Let
nothing keep you from coming to me, 17 for I
will greatly honor you and do whatever you
ask me. So please come and put a curse on
these people for me!'"
18 But Balaam responded to the servants of
Balak, "If Balak were to give me his house full
of silver and gold, I could not go against the
command of the LORD my God to do anything
small or great. 19 Please stay here overnight
as the others did, so that I may find out what
else the LORD has to tell me."
20 God came to Balaam at night and said to
him, "Since these men have come to summon
you, get up and go with them, but you must
only do what I tell you." 21 When he got up in
the morning, Balaam saddled his donkey and
went with the officials of Moab.

BALAAM'S DONKEY AND THE ANGEL

22 But God was incensed that Balaam was going, and the angel of the LORD took his stand
on the path to oppose him. Balaam was riding
his donkey, and his two servants were with
him. 23 When the donkey saw the angel of the
LORD standing on the path with a drawn sword
in his hand, she turned off the path and went
into the field. So Balaam hit her to return her
to the path. 24 Then the angel of the LORD stood
in a narrow passage between the vineyards,
with a stone wall on either side. 25 The donkey saw the angel of the LORD and pressed

[A] **21:35** Lit *left to him* [B] **22:5** Sam, Vg, Syr read *of the Ammonites* [C] **22:5** Or *of the Amawites*

herself against the wall, squeezing Balaam's foot against it. So he hit her once again. 26 The angel of the LORD went ahead and stood in a narrow place where there was no room to turn to the right or the left. 27 When the donkey saw the angel of the LORD, she crouched down under Balaam. So he became furious and beat the donkey with his stick.

28 Then the LORD opened the donkey's mouth, and she asked Balaam, "What have I done to you that you have beaten me these three times?"

29 Balaam answered the donkey, "You made me look like a fool. If I had a sword in my hand, I'd kill you now!"

30 But the donkey said, "Am I not the donkey you've ridden all your life until today? Have I ever treated you this way before?"

"No," he replied.

31 Then the LORD opened Balaam's eyes, and he saw the angel of the LORD standing in the path with a drawn sword in his hand. Balaam knelt low and bowed in worship on his face. 32 The angel of the LORD asked him, "Why have you beaten your donkey these three times? Look, I came out to oppose you, because I consider what you are doing to be evil.[A] 33 The donkey saw me and turned away from me these three times. If she had not turned away from me, I would have killed you by now and let her live."

34 Balaam said to the angel of the LORD, "I have sinned, for I did not know that you were standing in the path to confront me. And now, if it is evil in your sight, I will go back."

35 Then the angel of the LORD said to Balaam, "Go with the men, but you are to say only what I tell you." So Balaam went with Balak's officials.

36 When Balak heard that Balaam was coming, he went out to meet him at the Moabite city[B] on the Arnon border at the edge of his territory. 37 Balak asked Balaam, "Did I not send you an urgent summons? Why didn't you come to me? Am I really not able to reward you?"

38 Balaam said to him, "Look, I have come to you, but can I say anything I want? I must speak only the message God puts in my mouth." 39 So Balaam went with Balak, and they came to Kiriath-huzoth.[C] 40 Balak sacrificed cattle, sheep, and goats and sent for Balaam and the officials who were with him.

41 In the morning, Balak took Balaam and brought him to Bamoth-baal.[D] From there he saw the outskirts of the people's camp.

BALAAM'S ORACLES

23 Then Balaam said to Balak, "Build me seven altars here and prepare seven bulls and seven rams for me." 2 So Balak did as Balaam directed, and they offered a bull and a ram on each altar. 3 Balaam said to Balak, "Stay here by your burnt offering while I am gone. Maybe the LORD will meet with me. I will tell you whatever he reveals to me." So he went to a barren hill.

4 God met with him and Balaam said to him, "I have arranged seven altars and offered a bull and a ram on each altar." 5 Then the LORD put a message in Balaam's mouth and said, "Return to Balak and say what I tell you."

6 So he returned to Balak, who was standing there by his burnt offering with all the officials of Moab.

BALAAM'S FIRST ORACLE

7 Balaam proclaimed his poem:

Balak brought me from Aram;
the king of Moab,
from the eastern mountains:
"Come, put a curse on Jacob for me;
come, denounce Israel!"
8 How can I curse someone
God has not cursed?
How can I denounce someone the LORD
has not denounced?
9 I see them from the top of rocky cliffs,
and I watch them from the hills.
There is a people living alone;
it does not consider itself
among the nations.
10 Who has counted the dust of Jacob
or numbered even one-fourth of
Israel?
Let me die the death of the upright;
let the end of my life be like theirs.

11 "What have you done to me?" Balak asked Balaam. "I brought you to curse my enemies, but look, you have only blessed them!"

12 He answered, "Shouldn't I say exactly what the LORD puts in my mouth?"

BALAAM'S SECOND ORACLE

13 Then Balak said to him, "Please come with me to another place where you can see them. You will only see the outskirts of their camp; you won't see all of them. From there, put a curse on them for me." 14 So Balak took him to

---

A 22:32 Lit *because your way is perverse before me* B 22:36 Or *at Ir-moab*, or *at Ar of Moab* C 22:39 = The City of Streets
D 22:41 = The High Places of Baal

Lookout Field[A] on top of Pisgah, built seven altars, and offered a bull and a ram on each altar.
15 Balaam said to Balak, "Stay here by your burnt offering while I seek the LORD over there."
16 The LORD met with Balaam and put a message in his mouth. Then he said, "Return to Balak and say what I tell you."
17 So he returned to Balak, who was standing there by his burnt offering with the officials of Moab. Balak asked him, "What did the LORD say?"
18 Balaam proclaimed his poem:

Balak, get up and listen;
son of Zippor, pay attention to what
  I say!
19 God is not a man, that he might lie,
or a son of man, that he might change
  his mind.
Does he speak and not act,
or promise and not fulfill?
20 I have indeed received a command
  to bless;
since he has blessed,[B]
  I cannot change it.
21 He considers no disaster for Jacob;
he sees no trouble for Israel.[C]
The LORD their God is with them,
and there is rejoicing over the King
  among them.
22 God brought them out of Egypt;
he is like the horns of a wild ox
  for them.[D]
23 There is no magic curse against
  Jacob
and no divination against Israel.
It will now be said about Jacob
  and Israel,
"What great things God has done!"
24 A people rise up like a lioness;
they rouse themselves like a lion.
They will not lie down
  until they devour the prey
and drink the blood of the slain.

25 Then Balak told Balaam, "Don't curse them and don't bless them!"
26 But Balaam answered him, "Didn't I tell you: Whatever the LORD says, I must do?"

BALAAM'S THIRD ORACLE

27 Again Balak said to Balaam, "Please come.
I will take you to another place. Maybe it will
be agreeable to God that you can put a curse
on them for me there." 28 So Balak took Balaam to the top of Peor, which overlooks the
wasteland.[E]
29 Balaam told Balak, "Build me seven altars
here and prepare seven bulls and seven rams

Eternal Perspective | *God's Promises*

REMEMBER AND WAIT

"God is not a man, that he might lie, or a son of man, that he might change his mind. Does he speak and not act, or promise and not fulfill?" Numbers 23:19

For many people—perhaps even for you today—W-A-I-T is the foulest of all four-letter words. Waiting for your opportunity. Waiting for a much-needed break. Waiting for a job offer. Waiting for the tide to turn. You've likely been there—you were trusting God to come through in some way, counting on him to meet a pressing need, to show himself strong on your behalf. You prayed fervently and faithfully. But the days turned into weeks, then into months, perhaps even into years.

How do we continue to trust our God when the waiting seems endless? By remembering his character. We must cling to the truth that he's not arbitrary or moody. He's never inconsistent or wishy-washy. He doesn't jerk his people around by making lavish promises and then going back on his word. People do that all the time. God's never been guilty of that once.

Ask for the grace to keep believing in the dependability of the Lord.

For the next note on *Eternal Perspective*, see Deuteronomy 7:9.

[A] **23:14** Or *to the field of Zophim* [B] **23:20** Sam, LXX read *since I will bless* [C] **23:21** Or *He does not observe sin in Jacob; he does not see wrongdoing in Israel* [D] **23:22** Or *Egypt; they have the horns of a wild ox* [E] **23:28** Or *overlooks Jeshimon*

for me." 30 So Balak did as Balaam said and
offered a bull and a ram on each altar.

24 Since Balaam saw that it pleased the
LORD to bless Israel, he did not go to seek
omens as on previous occasions, but turned[A]
toward the wilderness. 2 When Balaam looked
up and saw Israel encamped tribe by tribe,
the Spirit of God came on him, 3 and he proclaimed his poem:

The oracle of Balaam son of Beor,
the oracle of the man whose eyes
are opened,
4 the oracle of one who hears the sayings
of God,
who sees a vision from the Almighty,
who falls into a trance with his eyes
uncovered:
5 How beautiful are your tents, Jacob,
your dwellings, Israel.
6 They stretch out like river valleys,[B]
like gardens beside a stream,
like aloes the LORD has planted,
like cedars beside the water.
7 Water will flow from his buckets,
and his seed will be by abundant water.
His king will be greater than Agag,
and his kingdom will be exalted.
8 God brought him out of Egypt;
he is like[C] the horns of a wild ox for them.
He will feed on enemy nations
and gnaw their bones;
he will strike them with his arrows.
9 He crouches, he lies down like a lion
or a lioness — who dares to rouse him?
Those who bless you will be blessed,
and those who curse you will be cursed.

10 Then Balak became furious with Balaam,
struck his hands together, and said to him, "I
summoned you to put a curse on my enemies,
but instead, you have blessed them these three
times. 11 Now go to your home! I said I would
reward you richly, but look, the LORD has denied you a reward."
12 Balaam answered Balak, "Didn't I previously tell the messengers you sent me: 13 If
Balak were to give me his house full of silver
and gold, I could not go against the LORD's
command, to do anything good or bad of my
own will? I will say whatever the LORD says.
14 Now I am going back to my people, but first,
let me warn you what these people will do to
your people in the future."

BALAAM'S FOURTH ORACLE

15 Then he proclaimed his poem:

The oracle of Balaam son of Beor,
the oracle of the man whose eyes
are opened;
16 the oracle of one who hears the sayings
of God
and has knowledge
from the Most High,
who sees a vision from the Almighty,
who falls into a trance with his
eyes uncovered:
17 I see him, but not now;
I perceive him, but not near.
A star will come from Jacob,
and a scepter will arise from Israel.
He will smash the forehead[D] of Moab
and strike down[E] all the Shethites.[F]
18 Edom will become a possession;
Seir will become a possession
of its enemies,
but Israel will be triumphant.
19 One who comes from Jacob will rule;
he will destroy the city's survivors.

20 Then Balaam saw Amalek and proclaimed
his poem:

Amalek was first among the nations,
but his future is destruction.

21 Next he saw the Kenites and proclaimed
his poem:

Your dwelling place is enduring;
your nest is set in the cliffs.
22 Kain will be destroyed
when Asshur takes you captive.

23 Once more he proclaimed his poem:

Ah, who can live when God does this?
24 Ships will come from the coast of Kittim;
they will carry out raids against Asshur
and Eber,
but they too will come to destruction.

25 Balaam then arose and went back to his
homeland, and Balak also went his way.

ISRAEL WORSHIPS BAAL

25 While Israel was staying in the Acacia
Grove,[G] the people began to prostitute
themselves with the women of Moab. 2 The
women invited them to the sacrifices for their
gods, and the people ate and bowed in worship
to their gods. 3 So Israel aligned itself with Baal

[A] 24:1 Lit *set his face* [B] 24:6 Or *like date palms* [C] 24:8 Or *he has* [D] 24:17 Or *frontiers* [E] 24:17 Sam reads *and the skulls of*; Jr 48:45 [F] 24:17 Or *Sethites* [G] 25:1 Or *in Shittim*

of Peor, and the LORD's anger burned against
Israel. 4 The LORD said to Moses, "Take all the
leaders of the people and execute[A] them in
broad daylight before the LORD so that his
burning anger may turn away from Israel."
5 So Moses told Israel's judges, "Kill each of
the men who aligned themselves with Baal
of Peor."

PHINEHAS INTERVENES

6 An Israelite man came bringing a Midianite
woman to his relatives in the sight of Moses
and the whole Israelite community while they
were weeping at the entrance to the tent of
meeting. 7 When Phinehas son of Eleazar, son of
Aaron the priest, saw this, he got up from the
assembly, took a spear in his hand, 8 followed
the Israelite man into the tent,[B] and drove it
through both the Israelite man and the woman
— through her belly. Then the plague on the
Israelites was stopped, 9 but those who died in
the plague numbered twenty-four thousand.
10 The LORD spoke to Moses, 11 "Phinehas
son of Eleazar, son of Aaron the priest, has
turned back my wrath from the Israelites because he was zealous among them with my
zeal,[C] so that I did not destroy the Israelites in
my zeal. 12 Therefore declare: I grant him my
covenant of peace. 13 It will be a covenant of
perpetual priesthood for him and his future
descendants, because he was zealous for his
God and made atonement for the Israelites."
14 The name of the slain Israelite man, who
was struck dead with the Midianite woman,
was Zimri son of Salu, the leader of a Simeonite family.[D] 15 The name of the slain Midianite
woman was Cozbi, the daughter of Zur, a tribal
head of a family in Midian.

VENGEANCE AGAINST THE MIDIANITES

16 The LORD told Moses: 17 "Attack the Midianites
and strike them dead. 18 For they attacked you
with the treachery that they used against you
in the Peor incident. They did the same in the
case involving their sister Cozbi, daughter of
the Midianite leader who was killed the day
the plague came at Peor."

THE SECOND CENSUS

26 After the plague, the LORD said to Moses
and Eleazar son of Aaron the priest,
2 "Take a census of the entire Israelite community by their ancestral families[E] of those
twenty years old or more who can serve in
Israel's army."
3 So Moses and the priest Eleazar said to them
in the plains of Moab by the Jordan across
from Jericho, 4 "Take a census of those twenty
years old or more, as the LORD had commanded Moses and the Israelites who came out of
the land of Egypt."

5 Reuben was the firstborn of Israel.
Reuben's descendants:
the Hanochite clan from Hanoch;
the Palluite clan from Pallu;
6 the Hezronite clan from Hezron;
the Carmite clan from Carmi.
7 These were the Reubenite clans,
and their registered men
numbered 43,730.
8 The son of Pallu was Eliab.
9 The sons of Eliab were Nemuel, Dathan,
and Abiram.
(It was Dathan and Abiram, chosen by
the community, who fought against
Moses and Aaron; they and Korah's
followers fought against the LORD. 10 The
earth opened its mouth and swallowed
them with Korah, when his followers
died and the fire consumed 250 men.
They serve as a warning sign. 11 The sons
of Korah, however, did not die.)

12 Simeon's descendants by their clans:
the Nemuelite clan from Nemuel;
the Jaminite clan from Jamin;
the Jachinite clan from Jachin;
13 the Zerahite clan from Zerah;
the Shaulite clan from Shaul.
14 These were the Simeonite clans,
numbering 22,200 men.

15 Gad's descendants by their clans:
the Zephonite clan from Zephon;
the Haggite clan from Haggi;
the Shunite clan from Shuni;
16 the Oznite clan from Ozni;
the Erite clan from Eri;
17 the Arodite clan from Arod;
the Arelite clan from Areli.
18 These were the Gadite clans numbered
by their registered men: 40,500.

19 Judah's sons included Er and Onan,
but they died in the land of Canaan.
20 Judah's descendants by their clans:

[A] **25:4** Or *impale*, or *hang*, or *expose*; Hb obscure [B] **25:8** Perhaps a tent shrine or bridal tent [C] **25:11** Or *jealousy* [D] **25:14** Lit *a father's house*, also in v. 15 [E] **26:2** Lit *the house of their fathers*

the Shelanite clan from Shelah;
the Perezite clan from Perez;
the Zerahite clan from Zerah.
21 The descendants of Perez:
the Hezronite clan from Hezron;
the Hamulite clan from Hamul.
22 These were Judah's clans numbered
by their registered men: 76,500.

23 Issachar's descendants by their clans:
the Tolaite clan from Tola;
the Punite clan from Puvah;[A]
24 the Jashubite clan from Jashub;
the Shimronite clan from Shimron.
25 These were Issachar's clans numbered
by their registered men: 64,300.

26 Zebulun's descendants by their clans:
the Seredite clan from Sered;
the Elonite clan from Elon;
the Jahleelite clan from Jahleel.
27 These were the Zebulunite
clans numbered by their
registered men: 60,500.

28 Joseph's descendants by their clans
from Manasseh and Ephraim:
29 Manasseh's descendants:
the Machirite clan from Machir.
Machir fathered Gilead;
the Gileadite clan from Gilead.
30 These were Gilead's descendants:
the Iezerite clan from Iezer;
the Helekite clan from Helek;
31 the Asrielite clan from Asriel;
the Shechemite clan from Shechem;
32 the Shemidaite clan from Shemida;
the Hepherite clan from Hepher;
33 Zelophehad son of Hepher had no
sons — only daughters. The names of
Zelophehad's daughters were Mahlah,
Noah, Hoglah, Milcah, and Tirzah.
34 These were Manasseh's
clans, numbered by their
registered men: 52,700.
35 These were Ephraim's descendants
by their clans:
the Shuthelahite clan from Shuthelah;
the Becherite clan from Becher;
the Tahanite clan from Tahan.
36 These were Shuthelah's descendants:
the Eranite clan from Eran.
37 These were the Ephraimite
clans numbered by their
registered men: 32,500.
These were Joseph's descendants
by their clans.

38 Benjamin's descendants
by their clans:
the Belaite clan from Bela;
the Ashbelite clan from Ashbel;
the Ahiramite clan from Ahiram;
39 the Shuphamite clan from Shupham;[B]
the Huphamite clan from Hupham.
40 Bela's descendants from Ard
and Naaman:
the Ardite clan from Ard;
the Naamite clan from Naaman.
41 These were the Benjaminite
clans numbered by their
registered men: 45,600.

42 These were Dan's descendants
by their clans:
the Shuhamite clan from Shuham.
These were the clans of Dan
by their clans.
43 All the Shuhamite clans numbered
by their registered men: 64,400.

44 Asher's descendants by their clans:
the Imnite clan from Imnah;
the Ishvite clan from Ishvi;
the Beriite clan from Beriah.
45 From Beriah's descendants:
the Heberite clan from Heber;
the Malchielite clan from Malchiel.
46 And the name of Asher's daughter
was Serah.
47 These were the Asherite
clans numbered by their
registered men: 53,400.

48 Naphtali's descendants
by their clans:
the Jahzeelite clan from Jahzeel;
the Gunite clan from Guni;
49 the Jezerite clan from Jezer;
the Shillemite clan from Shillem.
50 These were the Naphtali
clans numbered by their
registered men: 45,400.

51 These registered Israelite men
numbered 601,730.

[A] **26:23** Sam, LXX, Vg, Syr read *Puite clan from Puah*; 1Ch 7:1 [B] **26:39** Some Hb mss, Sam, LXX, Syr, Tg, Vg; other Hb mss read *Shephupham*

52 The LORD spoke to Moses, 53 "The land is
to be divided among them as an inheritance
based on the number of names. 54 Increase the
inheritance for a large tribe and decrease it for
a small one. Each is to be given its inheritance
according to those who were registered in it.
55 The land is to be divided by lot; they will receive an inheritance according to the names
of their ancestral tribes. 56 Each inheritance
will be divided by lot among the larger and
smaller tribes."

57 These were the Levites registered
by their clans:
the Gershonite clan from Gershon;
the Kohathite clan from Kohath;
the Merarite clan from Merari.
58 These were the Levite family groups:
the Libnite clan,
the Hebronite clan,
the Mahlite clan,
the Mushite clan,
and the Korahite clan.

Kohath was the ancestor of Amram. 59 The
name of Amram's wife was Jochebed, a descendant of Levi, born to Levi in Egypt. She
bore to Amram: Aaron, Moses, and their sister
Miriam. 60 Nadab, Abihu, Eleazar, and Ithamar
were born to Aaron, 61 but Nadab and Abihu died when they presented unauthorized
fire before the LORD. 62 Those registered were
23,000, every male one month old or more;
they were not registered among the other
Israelites, because no inheritance was given
to them among the Israelites.

63 These were the ones registered by Moses
and the priest Eleazar when they registered the
Israelites on the plains of Moab by the Jordan
across from Jericho. 64 But among them there
was not one of those who had been registered
by Moses and the priest Aaron when they
registered the Israelites in the Wilderness
of Sinai. 65 For the LORD had said to them that
they would all die in the wilderness. None of
them was left except Caleb son of Jephunneh
and Joshua son of Nun.

A CASE OF DAUGHTERS' INHERITANCE

27 The daughters of Zelophehad approached; Zelophehad was the son of
Hepher, son of Gilead, son of Machir, son of
Manasseh from the clans of Manasseh, the
son of Joseph. These were the names of his
daughters: Mahlah, Noah, Hoglah, Milcah, and
Tirzah. 2 They stood before Moses, the priest
Eleazar, the leaders, and the entire community
at the entrance to the tent of meeting and said,
3 "Our father died in the wilderness, but he was
not among Korah's followers, who gathered
together against the LORD. Instead, he died
because of his own sin, and he had no sons.
4 Why should the name of our father be taken
away from his clan? Since he had no son, give
us property among our father's brothers."

5 Moses brought their case before the LORD,
6 and the LORD answered him, 7 "What Zelophehad's daughters say is correct. You are
to give them hereditary property among
their father's brothers and transfer their
father's inheritance to them. 8 Tell the Israelites: When a man dies without having a
son, transfer his inheritance to his daughter.
9 If he has no daughter, give his inheritance
to his brothers. 10 If he has no brothers, give
his inheritance to his father's brothers. 11 If
his father has no brothers, give his inheritance to the nearest relative of his clan, and
he will take possession of it. This is to be a
statutory ordinance for the Israelites as the
LORD commanded Moses."

JOSHUA COMMISSIONED TO SUCCEED MOSES

12 Then the LORD said to Moses, "Go up this
mountain of the Abarim range[A] and see the
land that I have given the Israelites. 13 After
you have seen it, you will also be gathered
to your people, as Aaron your brother was.
14 When the community quarreled in the Wilderness of Zin, both of you rebelled against
my command to demonstrate my holiness
in their sight at the waters." Those were the
Waters of Meribah-kadesh[B] in the Wilderness of Zin.

15 So Moses appealed to the LORD, 16 "May
the LORD, the God who gives breath to all,[C]
appoint a man over the community 17 who will
go out before them and come back in before
them, and who will bring them out and bring
them in, so that the LORD's community won't
be like sheep without a shepherd."

18 The LORD replied to Moses, "Take Joshua
son of Nun, a man who has the Spirit in him,
and lay your hands on him. 19 Have him stand
before the priest Eleazar and the whole community, and commission him in their sight.
20 Confer some of your authority on him so

[A] **27:12** = Mount Nebo; Nm 33:47-48; Dt 32:49; Jr 22:20 [B] **27:14** = Quarreling [C] **27:16** Or *God of the spirits of all flesh*

that the entire Israelite community will obey him. 21 He will stand before the priest Eleazar who will consult the LORD for him with the decision of the Urim. He and all the Israelites with him, even the entire community, will go out and come back in at his command."

22 Moses did as the LORD commanded him. He took Joshua, had him stand before the priest Eleazar and the entire community, 23 laid his hands on him, and commissioned him, as the LORD had spoken through Moses.

PRESCRIBED OFFERINGS

28 The LORD spoke to Moses, 2 "Command the Israelites and say to them: Be sure to present to me at its appointed time my offering and my food as my fire offering, a pleasing aroma to me. 3 And say to them: This is the fire offering you are to present to the LORD:

DAILY OFFERINGS

"Each day present two unblemished year-old male lambs as a regular burnt offering. 4 Offer one lamb in the morning and the other lamb at twilight, 5 along with two quarts[A] of fine flour for a grain offering mixed with a quart[B] of olive oil from crushed olives. 6 It is a regular burnt offering established at Mount Sinai for a pleasing aroma, a fire offering to the LORD. 7 The drink offering is to be a quart with each lamb. Pour out the offering of beer to the LORD in the sanctuary area. 8 Offer the second lamb at twilight, along with the same kind of grain offering and drink offering as in the morning. It is a fire offering, a pleasing aroma to the LORD.

SABBATH OFFERINGS

9 "On the Sabbath day present two unblemished year-old male lambs, four quarts[C] of fine flour mixed with oil as a grain offering, and its drink offering. 10 It is the burnt offering for every Sabbath, in addition to the regular burnt offering and its drink offering.

MONTHLY OFFERINGS

11 "At the beginning of each of your months present a burnt offering to the LORD: two young bulls, one ram, seven male lambs a year old — all unblemished — 12 with six quarts[D] of fine flour mixed with oil as a grain offering for each bull, four quarts of fine flour mixed with oil as a grain offering for the ram, 13 and two quarts[E] of fine flour mixed with oil as a grain offering for each lamb. It is a burnt offering, a pleasing aroma, a fire offering to the LORD. 14 Their drink offerings are to be two quarts[F] of wine with each bull, one and a third quarts[G] with the ram, and one quart[H] with each male lamb. This is the monthly burnt offering for all the months of the year. 15 And one male goat is to be offered as a sin offering to the LORD, in addition to the regular burnt offering with its drink offering.

OFFERINGS FOR PASSOVER

16 "The Passover to the LORD comes in the first month, on the fourteenth day of the month. 17 On the fifteenth day of this month there will be a festival; unleavened bread is to be eaten for seven days. 18 On the first day there is to be a sacred assembly; you are not to do any daily work. 19 Present a fire offering, a burnt offering to the LORD: two young bulls, one ram, and seven male lambs a year old. Your animals are to be unblemished. 20 The grain offering with them is to be of fine flour mixed with oil; offer six quarts with each bull and four quarts with the ram. 21 Offer two quarts with each of the seven lambs 22 and one male goat for a sin offering to make atonement for yourselves. 23 Offer these with the morning burnt offering that is part of the regular burnt offering. 24 You are to offer the same food each day for seven days as a fire offering, a pleasing aroma to the LORD. It is to be offered with its drink offering and the regular burnt offering. 25 On the seventh day you are to hold a sacred assembly; you are not to do any daily work.

OFFERINGS FOR THE FESTIVAL OF WEEKS

26 "On the day of firstfruits, you are to hold a sacred assembly when you present an offering of new grain to the LORD at your Festival of Weeks; you are not to do any daily work. 27 Present a burnt offering for a pleasing aroma to the LORD: two young bulls, one ram, and seven male lambs a year old, 28 with their grain offering of fine flour mixed with oil, six quarts with each bull, four quarts with the ram, 29 and two quarts with each of the seven lambs, 30 and one male goat to make atonement for yourselves. 31 Offer them with

[A] **28:5** Lit *one-tenth of an ephah* [B] **28:5** Lit *a fourth of a hin*, also in v. 7 [C] **28:9** Lit *two-tenths* (of an ephah), also in vv. 12,20,28 [D] **28:12** Lit *three-tenths* (of an ephah), also in vv. 20,28 [E] **28:13** Lit *one-tenth* (of an ephah), also in vv. 21,29 [F] **28:14** Lit *a half hin* [G] **28:14** Lit *bull, a third hin* [H] **28:14** Lit *a fourth hin*

their drink offerings in addition to the regular burnt offering and its grain offering. Your animals are to be unblemished.

FESTIVAL OF TRUMPETS OFFERINGS

29 "You are to hold a sacred assembly in the seventh month, on the first day of the month, and you are not to do any daily work. This will be a day of trumpet blasts for you. 2 Offer a burnt offering as a pleasing aroma to the LORD: one young bull, one ram, seven male lambs a year old — all unblemished — 3 with their grain offering of fine flour mixed with oil, six quarts[A] with the bull, four quarts[B] with the ram, 4 and two quarts[C] with each of the seven male lambs. 5 Also offer one male goat as a sin offering to make atonement for yourselves. 6 These are in addition to the monthly and regular burnt offerings with their prescribed grain offerings and drink offerings. They are a pleasing aroma, a fire offering to the LORD.

OFFERINGS FOR THE DAY OF ATONEMENT

7 "You are to hold a sacred assembly on the tenth day of this seventh month and practice self-denial; do not do any work. 8 Present a burnt offering to the LORD, a pleasing aroma: one young bull, one ram, and seven male lambs a year old. All your animals are to be unblemished. 9 Their grain offering is to be of fine flour mixed with oil, six quarts with the bull, four quarts with the ram, 10 and two quarts with each of the seven lambs. 11 Offer one male goat for a sin offering. The regular burnt offering with its grain offering and drink offerings are in addition to the sin offering of atonement.

OFFERINGS FOR THE FESTIVAL OF SHELTERS

12 "You are to hold a sacred assembly on the fifteenth day of the seventh month; you do not do any daily work. You are to celebrate a seven-day festival for the LORD. 13 Present a burnt offering, a fire offering as a pleasing aroma to the LORD: thirteen young bulls, two rams, and fourteen male lambs a year old. They are to be unblemished. 14 Their grain offering is to be of fine flour mixed with oil, six quarts with each of the thirteen bulls, four quarts with each of the two rams, 15 and two quarts with each of the fourteen lambs. 16 Also offer one male goat as a sin offering. These are in addition to the regular burnt offering with its grain and drink offerings.

17 "On the second day present twelve young bulls, two rams, and fourteen male lambs a year old — all unblemished — 18 with their grain and drink offerings for the bulls, rams, and lambs, in proportion to their number. 19 Also offer one male goat as a sin offering. These are in addition to the regular burnt offering with its grain and drink and their drink offerings.

20 "On the third day present eleven bulls, two rams, fourteen male lambs a year old — all unblemished — 21 with their grain and drink offerings for the bulls, rams, and lambs, in proportion to their number. 22 Also offer one male goat as a sin offering. These are in addition to the regular burnt offering with its grain and drink offerings.

23 "On the fourth day present ten bulls, two rams, fourteen male lambs a year old — all unblemished — 24 with their grain and drink offerings for the bulls, rams, and lambs, in proportion to their number. 25 Also offer one male goat as a sin offering. These are in addition to the regular burnt offering with its grain and drink offerings.

26 "On the fifth day present nine bulls, two rams, fourteen male lambs a year old — all unblemished — 27 with their grain and drink offerings for the bulls, rams, and lambs, in proportion to their number. 28 Also offer one male goat as a sin offering. These are in addition to the regular burnt offering with its grain and drink offerings.

29 "On the sixth day present eight bulls, two rams, fourteen male lambs a year old — all unblemished — 30 with their grain and drink offerings for the bulls, rams, and lambs, in proportion to their number. 31 Also offer one male goat as a sin offering. These are in addition to the regular burnt offering with its grain and drink offerings.

32 "On the seventh day present seven bulls, two rams, and fourteen male lambs a year old — all unblemished — 33 with their grain and drink offerings for the bulls, rams, and lambs, in proportion to their number. 34 Also offer one male goat as a sin offering. These are in addition to the regular burnt offering with its grain and drink offerings.

35 "On the eighth day you are to hold a solemn assembly; you are not to do any daily work. 36 Present a burnt offering, a fire offering as a pleasing aroma to the LORD: one bull, one ram, seven male lambs a year old

[A] **29:3** Lit *three-tenths* (of an ephah), also in vv. 9,14 [B] **29:3** Lit *two-tenths* (of an ephah), also in vv. 9,14 [C] **29:4** Lit *one-tenth* (of an ephah), also in vv. 10,15

—all unblemished—37 with their grain and drink offerings for the bulls, rams, and lambs, in proportion to their number. 38 Also offer one male goat as a sin offering. These are in addition to the regular burnt offering with its grain and drink offerings.

39 "Offer these to the LORD at your appointed times in addition to your vow and freewill offerings, whether burnt, grain, drink, or fellowship offerings." 40 So Moses told the Israelites everything the LORD had commanded him.

REGULATIONS ABOUT VOWS

30 Moses told the leaders of the Israelite tribes, "This is what the LORD has commanded: 2 When a man makes a vow to the LORD or swears an oath to put himself under an obligation, he must not break his word; he must do whatever he has promised.

3 "When a woman in her father's house during her youth makes a vow to the LORD or puts herself under an obligation, 4 and her father hears about her vow or the obligation she put herself under, and he says nothing to her, all her vows and every obligation she put herself under are binding. 5 But if her father prohibits her on the day he hears about it, none of her vows and none of the obligations she put herself under are binding. The LORD will release her because her father has prohibited her.

6 "If a woman marries while her vows or the rash commitment she herself made are binding, 7 and her husband hears about it and says nothing to her when he finds out, her vows are binding, and the obligations she put herself under are binding. 8 But if her husband prohibits her when he hears about it, he will cancel her vow that is binding or the rash commitment she herself made, and the LORD will release her.

9 "Every vow a widow or divorced woman puts herself under is binding on her.

10 "If a woman in her husband's house has made a vow or put herself under an obligation with an oath, 11 and her husband hears about it, says nothing to her, and does not prohibit her, all her vows are binding, and every obligation she put herself under is binding. 12 But if her husband cancels them on the day he hears about it, nothing that came from her lips, whether her vows or her obligation, is binding. Her husband has canceled them, and the LORD will release her. 13 Her husband may confirm or cancel any vow or any sworn obligation to deny herself. 14 If her husband says nothing at all to her from day to day, he confirms all her vows and obligations, which are binding. He has confirmed them because he said nothing to her when he heard about them. 15 But if he cancels them after he hears about them, he will be responsible for her commitment."[A]

16 These are the statutes that the LORD commanded Moses concerning the relationship between a man and his wife, or between a father and his daughter in his house during her youth.

WAR WITH MIDIAN

31 The LORD spoke to Moses, 2 "Execute vengeance for the Israelites against the Midianites. After that, you will be gathered to your people."

3 So Moses spoke to the people, "Equip some of your men for war. They will go against Midian to inflict the LORD's vengeance on them. 4 Send one thousand men to war from each Israelite tribe." 5 So one thousand were recruited from each Israelite tribe out of the thousands[B] in Israel—twelve thousand equipped for war. 6 Moses sent one thousand from each tribe to war. They went with Phinehas son of Eleazar the priest, in whose care were the holy objects and signal trumpets.

7 They waged war against Midian, as the LORD had commanded Moses, and killed every male. 8 Along with the others slain by them, they killed the Midianite kings—Evi, Rekem, Zur, Hur, and Reba, the five kings of Midian. They also killed Balaam son of Beor with the sword. 9 The Israelites took the Midianite women and their dependents captive, and they plundered all their cattle, flocks, and property. 10 Then they burned all the cities where the Midianites lived, as well as all their encampments, 11 and took away all the spoils of war and the captives, both people and animals. 12 They brought the prisoners, animals, and spoils of war to Moses, the priest Eleazar, and the Israelite community at the camp on the plains of Moab by the Jordan across from Jericho.

13 Moses, the priest Eleazar, and all the leaders of the community went to meet them outside the camp. 14 But Moses became furious with the officers, the commanders of thousands and commanders of hundreds, who were returning from the military campaign. 15 "Have you let every female live?" he asked

[A] **30:15** Or *will bear her guilt* [B] **31:5** Or *clans*

them. 16 "Yet they are the ones who, at Balaam's
advice, incited the Israelites to unfaithfulness against the LORD in the Peor incident,
so that the plague came against the LORD's
community. 17 So now, kill every male among
the dependents and kill every woman who
has gone to bed with a man, 18 but keep alive
for yourselves all the young females who have
not gone to bed with a man.
19 "You are to remain outside the camp for
seven days. All of you and your prisoners who
have killed a person or touched the dead are
to purify yourselves on the third day and the
seventh day. 20 Also purify everything: garments, leather goods, things made of goat
hair, and every article of wood."
21 Then the priest Eleazar said to the soldiers who had gone to battle, "This is the legal
statute the LORD commanded Moses: 22 The
gold, silver, bronze, iron, tin, and lead — 23 everything that can withstand fire — you are
to pass through fire, and it will be clean. It
must still be purified with the purification
water. Anything that cannot withstand fire,
pass through the water. 24 On the seventh day
wash your clothes, and you will be clean. After
that you may enter the camp."
25 The LORD told Moses, 26 "You, the priest
Eleazar, and the family heads of the community are to take a count of what was captured, people and animals. 27 Then divide
the captives between the troops who went
out to war and the entire community. 28 Set
aside a tribute for the LORD from what belongs to the fighting men who went out to
war: one out of every five hundred people,
cattle, donkeys, sheep, and goats. 29 Take
the tribute from their half and give it to the
priest Eleazar as a contribution to the LORD.
30 From the Israelites' half, take one out of
every fifty from the people, cattle, donkeys,
sheep, and goats, all the livestock, and give
them to the Levites who perform the duties
of[A] the LORD's tabernacle."
31 So Moses and the priest Eleazar did as
the LORD commanded Moses. 32 The captives
remaining from the plunder the army had
taken totaled:

675,000 sheep and goats,
33 72,000 cattle,
34 61,000 donkeys,
35 and 32,000 people, all the females
who had not gone to bed with a man.

36 The half portion for those who went out
to war numbered:

337,500 sheep and goats,
37 and the tribute to the LORD was 675
from the sheep and goats;
38 from the 36,000 cattle,
the tribute to the LORD was 72;
39 from the 30,500 donkeys,
the tribute to the LORD was 61;
40 and from the 16,000 people,
the tribute to the LORD was 32 people.

41 Moses gave the tribute to the priest Eleazar
as a contribution for the LORD, as the LORD
had commanded Moses.
42 From the Israelites' half, which Moses
separated from the men who fought, 43 the
community's half was:

337,500 sheep and goats,
44 36,000 cattle,
45 30,500 donkeys,
46 and 16,000 people.

47 Moses took one out of every fifty, selected
from the people and the livestock of the Israelites' half. He gave them to the Levites who
perform the duties of the LORD's tabernacle,
as the LORD had commanded him.
48 The officers who were over the thousands
of the army, the commanders of thousands
and of hundreds, approached Moses 49 and
told him, "Your servants have taken a census
of the fighting men under our command, and
not one of us is missing. 50 So we have presented to the LORD an offering of the gold articles
each man found — armlets, bracelets, rings,
earrings, and necklaces — to make atonement
for ourselves before the LORD."
51 Moses and the priest Eleazar received from
them all the articles made out of gold. 52 All
the gold of the contribution they offered to
the LORD, from the commanders of thousands
and of hundreds, was 420 pounds.[B] 53 Each of
the soldiers had taken plunder for himself.
54 Moses and the priest Eleazar received the
gold from the commanders of thousands and
of hundreds and brought it into the tent of
meeting as a memorial for the Israelites before the LORD.

TRANSJORDAN SETTLEMENTS

32 The Reubenites and Gadites had a
very large number of livestock. When
they surveyed the lands of Jazer and Gilead,
they saw that the region was a good one for

[A] **31:30** Or *who protect* [B] **31:52** Lit *16,750 shekels*

livestock. 2 So the Gadites and Reubenites came
to Moses, the priest Eleazar, and the leaders
of the community and said: 3 "The territory
of Ataroth, Dibon, Jazer, Nimrah, Heshbon,
Elealeh, Sebam,[A] Nebo, and Beon, 4 which the
LORD struck down before the community of
Israel, is good land for livestock, and your
servants own livestock." 5 They said, "If we
have found favor with you, let this land be
given to your servants as a possession. Don't
make us cross the Jordan."

6 But Moses asked the Gadites and Reubenites, "Should your brothers go to war while
you stay here? 7 Why are you discouraging the
Israelites from crossing into the land the LORD
has given them? 8 That's what your fathers did
when I sent them from Kadesh-barnea to see
the land. 9 After they went up as far as Eshcol
Valley and saw the land, they discouraged the
Israelites from entering the land the LORD had
given them. 10 So the LORD's anger burned that
day, and he swore an oath: 11 'Because they did
not remain loyal to me, none of the men twenty
years old or more who came up from Egypt
will see the land I swore to give Abraham,
Isaac, and Jacob — 12 none except Caleb son
of Jephunneh the Kenizzite and Joshua son of
Nun, because they did remain loyal to the LORD.'
13 The LORD's anger burned against Israel, and
he made them wander in the wilderness forty
years until the whole generation that had done
what was evil in the LORD's sight was gone.
14 And here you, a brood of sinners, stand in
your fathers' place adding even more to the
LORD's burning anger against Israel. 15 If you
turn back from following him, he will once
again leave this people in the wilderness, and
you will destroy all of them."

16 Then they approached him and said, "We
want to build sheep pens here for our livestock
and cities for our dependents. 17 But we will
arm ourselves and be ready to go ahead of
the Israelites until we have brought them into
their place. Meanwhile, our dependents will
remain in the fortified cities because of the
inhabitants of the land. 18 We will not return
to our homes until each of the Israelites has
taken possession of his inheritance. 19 Yet we
will not have an inheritance with them across
the Jordan and beyond, because our inheritance will be across the Jordan to the east."

20 Moses replied to them, "If you do this — if
you arm yourselves for battle before the LORD,
21 and every one of your armed men crosses
the Jordan before the LORD until he has driven
his enemies from his presence, 22 and the land

Thanksgiving and Contentment | *Confession*

BEING A TEAM PLAYER

"But if you don't do this, you will certainly sin against the LORD; be sure your sin will catch up with you." Numbers 32:23

At God's command, the tribes of Israel were preparing to cross the Jordan River and take possession of the promised land. That's when the Reubenites and Gadites stepped forward and expressed their desire to settle the lush pasturelands where they were already camped. What they actually meant was, "We want to come back and settle here *after* Canaan is completely subdued." Moses, however, thought they were chickening out and walking back on their earlier promise to join the other tribes in capturing the land.

Deeply concerned about national morale, Moses gave a stern history lesson-lecture to the leaders of these two tribes. Only then did they realize how their intentions had been misunderstood. When they were able to assure Moses they would certainly help fight till the task was complete, a potential crisis was averted.

This incident underscores a couple realities: the importance of clear communication and the necessity of camaraderie. Communities, churches, teams, and families are healthier and happier when everyone is committed till the very end.

For the next note on *Thanksgiving and Contentment*, see Deuteronomy 7:13.

[A] **32:3** Sam, LXX read *Sibmah* (v. 38); Syr reads *Sebah*

is subdued before the LORD — afterward you
may return and be free from obligation to the
LORD and to Israel. And this land will belong to
you as a possession before the LORD. 23 But if
you don't do this, you will certainly sin against
the LORD; be sure your sin will catch up with
you. 24 Build cities for your dependents and
pens for your flocks, but do what you have
promised."

25 The Gadites and Reubenites answered
Moses, "Your servants will do just as my lord
commands. 26 Our dependents, wives, livestock, and all our animals will remain here
in the cities of Gilead, 27 but your servants are
equipped for war before the LORD and will go
across to the battle as my lord orders."

28 So Moses gave orders about them to the
priest Eleazar, Joshua son of Nun, and the family heads of the Israelite tribes. 29 Moses told
them, "If the Gadites and Reubenites cross the
Jordan with you, every man in battle formation before the LORD, and the land is subdued
before you, you are to give them the land of
Gilead as a possession. 30 But if they don't go
across with you in battle formation, they must
accept land in Canaan with you."

31 The Gadites and Reubenites replied, "What
the LORD has spoken to your servants is what
we will do. 32 We will cross over in battle formation before the LORD into the land of Canaan,
but we will keep our hereditary possession
across the Jordan."

33 So Moses gave them — the Gadites, Reubenites, and half the tribe of Manasseh son
of Joseph — the kingdom of King Sihon of
the Amorites and the kingdom of King Og of
Bashan, the land including its cities with the
territories surrounding them. 34 The Gadites rebuilt Dibon, Ataroth, Aroer, 35 Atroth-shophan,
Jazer, Jogbehah, 36 Beth-nimrah, and Beth-ha-
ran as fortified cities, and built sheep pens.
37 The Reubenites rebuilt Heshbon, Elealeh,
Kiriathaim, 38 as well as Nebo and Baal-meon
(whose names were changed), and Sibmah.
They gave names to the cities they rebuilt.

39 The descendants of Machir son of Manasseh went to Gilead, captured it, and drove
out the Amorites who were there. 40 So Moses
gave Gilead to the clan of Machir son of Manasseh, and they settled in it. 41 Jair, a descendant of Manasseh, went and captured their
villages, which he renamed Jair's Villages.[A]
42 Nobah went and captured Kenath with its
surrounding villages and called it Nobah after
his own name.

WILDERNESS TRAVELS REVIEWED

33 These were the stages of the Israelites' journey when they went out of
the land of Egypt by their military divisions
under the leadership of Moses and Aaron.
2 At the LORD's command, Moses wrote down
the starting points for the stages of their
journey; these are the stages listed by their
starting points:

3 They traveled from Rameses in the
first month, on the fifteenth day of the
month. On the day after the Passover
the Israelites went out defiantly[B] in the
sight of all the Egyptians. 4 Meanwhile,
the Egyptians were burying every
firstborn male the LORD had struck down
among them, for the LORD had executed
judgment against their gods. 5 The
Israelites traveled from Rameses and
camped at Succoth.
6 They traveled from Succoth and camped
at Etham, which is on the edge of the
wilderness.
7 They traveled from Etham and turned
back to Pi-hahiroth, which faces Baal-ze-
phon, and they camped before Migdol.
8 They traveled from Pi-hahiroth[C] and
crossed through the middle of the
sea into the wilderness. They took a
three-day journey into the Wilderness of
Etham and camped at Marah.
9 They traveled from Marah and came
to Elim. There were twelve springs and
seventy date palms at Elim, so they
camped there.
10 They traveled from Elim and camped by
the Red Sea.
11 They traveled from the Red Sea and
camped in the Wilderness of Sin.
12 They traveled from the Wilderness of
Sin and camped in Dophkah.
13 They traveled from Dophkah and
camped at Alush.
14 They traveled from Alush and camped
at Rephidim, where there was no water
for the people to drink.
15 They traveled from Rephidim and
camped in the Wilderness of Sinai.
16 They traveled from the Wilderness of
Sinai and camped at Kibroth-hattaavah.

[A] **32:41** Or *renamed Havvoth-jair* [B] **33:3** Lit *with a raised hand*; Ex 14:8 [C] **33:8** Some Hb mss, Sam, Syr, Vg; other Hb mss read *from before Hahiroth*

17 They traveled from Kibroth-hattaavah
and camped at Hazeroth.
18 They traveled from Hazeroth and
camped at Rithmah.
19 They traveled from Rithmah and
camped at Rimmon-perez.
20 They traveled from Rimmon-perez and
camped at Libnah.
21 They traveled from Libnah and camped
at Rissah.
22 They traveled from Rissah and camped
at Kehelathah.
23 They traveled from Kehelathah and
camped at Mount Shepher.
24 They traveled from Mount Shepher and
camped at Haradah.
25 They traveled from Haradah and
camped at Makheloth.
26 They traveled from Makheloth and
camped at Tahath.
27 They traveled from Tahath and camped
at Terah.
28 They traveled from Terah and camped
at Mithkah.
29 They traveled from Mithkah and
camped at Hashmonah.
30 They traveled from Hashmonah and
camped at Moseroth.
31 They traveled from Moseroth and
camped at Bene-jaakan.
32 They traveled from Bene-jaakan and
camped at Hor-haggidgad.
33 They traveled from Hor-haggidgad and
camped at Jotbathah.
34 They traveled from Jotbathah and
camped at Abronah.
35 They traveled from Abronah and
camped at Ezion-geber.
36 They traveled from Ezion-geber and
camped in the Wilderness of Zin (that is,
Kadesh).
37 They traveled from Kadesh and camped
at Mount Hor on the edge of the land of
Edom. 38 At the LORD's command, the
priest Aaron climbed Mount Hor and died
there on the first day of the fifth month
in the fortieth year after the Israelites
went out of the land of Egypt. 39 Aaron
was 123 years old when he died on Mount
Hor. 40 At that time the Canaanite king
of Arad, who lived in the Negev in the
land of Canaan, heard the Israelites were
coming.
41 They traveled from Mount Hor and
camped at Zalmonah.
42 They traveled from Zalmonah and
camped at Punon.
43 They traveled from Punon and camped
at Oboth.
44 They traveled from Oboth and camped
at Iye-abarim on the border of Moab.
45 They traveled from Iyim[A] and camped
at Dibon-gad.
46 They traveled from Dibon-gad and
camped at Almon-diblathaim.
47 They traveled from Almon-diblathaim
and camped in the Abarim range facing
Nebo.
48 They traveled from the Abarim range
and camped on the plains of Moab
by the Jordan across from Jericho.
49 They camped by the Jordan from
Beth-jeshimoth to the Acacia Meadow[B]
on the plains of Moab.

INSTRUCTIONS FOR OCCUPYING CANAAN

50 The LORD spoke to Moses in the plains of
Moab by the Jordan across from Jericho, 51 "Tell
the Israelites: When you cross the Jordan
into the land of Canaan, 52 you must drive
out all the inhabitants of the land before
you, destroy all their stone images and cast
images, and demolish all their high places.
53 You are to take possession of the land and
settle in it because I have given you the land
to possess. 54 You are to receive the land as
an inheritance by lot according to your clans.
Increase the inheritance for a large clan and
decrease it for a small one. Whatever place
the lot indicates for someone will be his. You
will receive an inheritance according to your
ancestral tribes. 55 But if you don't drive out
the inhabitants of the land before you, those
you allow to remain will become barbs for
your eyes and thorns for your sides; they will
harass you in the land where you will live.
56 And what I had planned to do to them, I
will do to you."

BOUNDARIES OF THE PROMISED LAND

34 The LORD spoke to Moses, 2 "Command
the Israelites and say to them: When
you enter the land of Canaan, it will be allotted
to you as an inheritance[C] with these borders:
3 Your southern side will be from the
Wilderness of Zin along the boundary

[A] 33:45 A shortened form of Iye-abarim [B] 33:49 Or *to Abel-shittim* [C] 34:2 Lit *inheritance — the land of Canaan*

of Edom. Your southern border on the east will begin at the east end of the Dead Sea. 4 Your border will turn south of the Scorpions' Ascent,[A] proceed to Zin, and end south of Kadesh-barnea. It will go to Hazar-addar and proceed to Azmon. 5 The border will turn from Azmon to the Brook of Egypt, where it will end at the Mediterranean Sea.

6 Your western border will be the coastline of the Mediterranean Sea; this will be your western border.

7 This will be your northern border: From the Mediterranean Sea draw a line to Mount Hor; 8 from Mount Hor draw a line to the entrance of Hamath,[B] and the border will reach Zedad. 9 Then the border will go to Ziphron and end at Hazar-enan. This will be your northern border.

10 For your eastern border, draw a line from Hazar-enan to Shepham. 11 The border will go down from Shepham to Riblah east of Ain. It will continue down and reach the eastern slope of the Sea of Chinnereth.[C] 12 Then the border will go down to the Jordan and end at the Dead Sea. This will be your land defined by its borders on all sides."

13 So Moses commanded the Israelites, "This is the land you are to receive by lot as an inheritance, which the LORD commanded to be given to the nine and a half tribes. 14 For the tribe of Reuben's descendants and the tribe of Gad's descendants have received their inheritance according to their ancestral families,[D] and half the tribe of Manasseh has received its inheritance. 15 The two and a half tribes have received their inheritance across the Jordan east of Jericho, toward the sunrise."

LEADERS FOR DISTRIBUTING THE LAND

16 The LORD spoke to Moses, 17 "These are the names of the men who are to distribute the land as an inheritance for you: the priest Eleazar and Joshua son of Nun. 18 Take one leader from each tribe to distribute the land. 19 These are the names of the men:

Caleb son of Jephunneh from the tribe of Judah;
20 Shemuel son of Ammihud from the tribe of Simeon's descendants;
21 Elidad son of Chislon from the tribe of Benjamin;
22 Bukki son of Jogli, a leader from the tribe of Dan's descendants;
23 from the sons of Joseph:
Hanniel son of Ephod, a leader from the tribe of Manasseh's descendants,
24 Kemuel son of Shiphtan, a leader from the tribe of Ephraim's descendants;
25 Eli-zaphan son of Parnach, a leader from the tribe of Zebulun's descendants;
26 Paltiel son of Azzan, a leader from the tribe of Issachar's descendants;
27 Ahihud son of Shelomi, a leader from the tribe of Asher's descendants;
28 Pedahel son of Ammihud, a leader from the tribe of Naphtali's descendants."

29 These are the ones the LORD commanded to distribute the inheritance to the Israelites in the land of Canaan.

CITIES FOR THE LEVITES

35 The LORD again spoke to Moses in the plains of Moab by the Jordan across from Jericho: 2 "Command the Israelites to give cities out of their hereditary property for the Levites to live in and pastureland around the cities. 3 The cities will be for them to live in, and their pasturelands will be for their herds, flocks, and all their other animals. 4 The pasturelands of the cities you are to give the Levites will extend from the city wall five hundred yards[E] on every side. 5 Measure a thousand yards[F] outside the city for the east side, a thousand yards for the south side, a thousand yards for the west side, and a thousand yards for the north side, with the city in the center. This will belong to them as pasturelands for the cities.

6 "The cities you give the Levites will include six cities of refuge, which you will provide so that the one who kills someone may flee there; in addition to these, give forty-two other cities. 7 The total number of cities you give the Levites will be forty-eight, along with their pasturelands. 8 Of the cities that you give from the Israelites' territory, you should take more from a larger tribe and less from a smaller one. Each tribe is to give some of its cities to the Levites in proportion to the inheritance it receives."

[A] **34:4** Lit *of Scorpions*; Jos 15:3; Jdg 1:36 [B] **34:8** Or *to Lebo-hamath* [C] **34:11** = the Sea of Galilee; Jos 12:3; 13:27; Lk 5:1
[D] **34:14** Lit *the house of their fathers* [E] **35:4** Lit *1,000 cubits* [F] **35:5** Lit *2,000 cubits*

CITIES OF REFUGE

9 The LORD said to Moses, 10 "Speak to the Israelites and tell them: When you cross the Jordan into the land of Canaan, 11 designate cities to serve as cities of refuge for you, so that a person who kills someone unintentionally may flee there. 12 You will have the cities as a refuge from the avenger, so that the one who kills someone will not die until he stands trial before the assembly. 13 The cities you select will be your six cities of refuge. 14 Select three cities across the Jordan and three cities in the land of Canaan to be cities of refuge. 15 These six cities will serve as a refuge for the Israelites and for the alien or temporary resident among them, so that anyone who kills a person unintentionally may flee there.

16 "If anyone strikes a person with an iron object and death results, he is a murderer; the murderer must be put to death. 17 If anyone has in his hand a stone capable of causing death and strikes another person and he dies, the murderer must be put to death. 18 If anyone has in his hand a wooden object capable of causing death and strikes another person and he dies, the murderer must be put to death. 19 The avenger of blood himself is to kill the murderer; when he finds him, he is to kill him. 20 Likewise, if anyone in hatred pushes a person or throws an object at him with malicious intent and he dies, 21 or if in hostility he strikes him with his hand and he dies, the one who struck him must be put to death; he is a murderer. The avenger of blood is to kill the murderer when he finds him.

22 "But if anyone suddenly pushes a person without hostility or throws any object at him without malicious intent 23 or without looking drops a stone that could kill a person and he dies, but he was not his enemy and didn't intend to harm him, 24 the assembly is to judge between the person who kills someone and the avenger of blood according to these ordinances. 25 The assembly is to protect the one who kills someone from the avenger of blood. Then the assembly will return him to the city of refuge he fled to, and he must live there until the death of the high priest who was anointed with the holy oil.

26 "If the one who kills someone ever goes outside the border of the city of refuge he fled to, 27 and the avenger of blood finds him outside the border of his city of refuge and kills him, the avenger will not be guilty of bloodshed, 28 for the one who killed a person was supposed to live in his city of refuge until the death of the high priest. Only after the death of the high priest may the one who has killed a person return to the land he possesses. 29 These instructions will be a statutory ordinance for you throughout your generations wherever you live.

30 "If anyone kills a person, the murderer is to be put to death based on the word of witnesses. But no one is to be put to death based on the testimony of one witness. 31 You are not to accept a ransom for the life of someone who is guilty of murder; he must be put to death. 32 Neither should you accept a ransom for the person who flees to his city of refuge, allowing him to return and live in the land before the death of the high priest.

33 "Do not defile the land where you live, for bloodshed defiles the land, and there can be no atonement for the land because of the blood that is shed on it, except by the blood of the person who shed it. 34 Do not make the land unclean where you live and where I dwell; for I, the LORD, reside among the Israelites."

THE INHERITANCE OF ZELOPHEHAD'S DAUGHTERS

36 The family heads from the clan of the descendants of Gilead — the son of Machir, son of Manasseh — who were from the clans of the sons of Joseph, approached and addressed Moses and the leaders who were heads of the Israelite families. 2 They said, "The LORD commanded my lord to give the land as an inheritance by lot to the Israelites. My lord was further commanded by the LORD to give our brother Zelophehad's inheritance to his daughters. 3 If they marry any of the men from the other Israelite tribes, their inheritance will be taken away from our fathers' inheritance and added to that of the tribe into which they marry. Therefore, part of our allotted inheritance would be taken away. 4 When the Jubilee comes for the Israelites, their inheritance will be added to that of the tribe into which they marry, and their inheritance will be taken away from the inheritance of our ancestral tribe."

5 So Moses commanded the Israelites at the word of the LORD, "What the tribe of Joseph's descendants says is right. 6 This is what the LORD has commanded concerning Zelophehad's daughters: They may marry anyone they like provided they marry within a clan of their ancestral tribe. 7 No inheritance belonging

great nation is there that has a god near to it
as the LORD our God is to us whenever we call
to him? 8 And what great nation has righteous
statutes and ordinances like this entire law I
set before you today?
9 "Only be on your guard and diligently
watch yourselves, so that you don't forget
the things your eyes have seen and so that
they don't slip from your mind[A] as long as
you live. Teach them to your children and your
grandchildren. 10 The day you stood before the
LORD your God at Horeb, the LORD said to me,
'Assemble the people before me, and I will let
them hear my words, so that they may learn
to fear me all the days they live on the earth
and may instruct their children.' 11 You came
near and stood at the base of the mountain, a
mountain blazing with fire into the heavens
and enveloped in a totally black cloud. 12 Then
the LORD spoke to you from the fire. You kept
hearing the sound of the words, but didn't see
a form; there was only a voice. 13 He declared
his covenant to you. He commanded you to
follow the Ten Commandments, which he
wrote on two stone tablets. 14 At that time
the LORD commanded me to teach you statutes and ordinances for you to follow in the
land you are about to cross into and possess.

WORSHIPING THE TRUE GOD

15 "Diligently watch yourselves — because
you did not see any form on the day the LORD
spoke to you out of the fire at Horeb — 16 so
you don't act corruptly and make an idol for
yourselves in the shape of any figure: a male
or female form, 17 or the form of any animal
on the earth, any winged creature that flies
in the sky, 18 any creature that crawls on the
ground, or any fish in the waters under the
earth. 19 When you look to the heavens and
see the sun, moon, and stars — all the stars
in the sky — do not be led astray to bow in
worship to them and serve them. The LORD
your God has provided them for all people
everywhere under heaven. 20 But the LORD
selected you and brought you out of Egypt's
iron furnace to be a people for his inheritance,
as you are today.
21 "The LORD was angry with me on your
account. He swore that I would not cross
the Jordan and enter the good land the LORD
your God is giving you as an inheritance.
22 I won't be crossing the Jordan because
I am going to die in this land. But you are
about to cross over and take possession of
this good land. 23 Be careful not to forget the
covenant of the LORD your God that he made
with you, and make an idol for yourselves
in the shape of anything he has forbidden
you. 24 For the LORD your God is a consuming
fire, a jealous God.
25 "When you have children and grandchildren and have been in the land a long time,
and if you act corruptly, make an idol in the

Rest and Reflection | *Seeking God*

SEARCHING FOR GOD

"But from there, you will search for the LORD your God, and you will find him when you seek him with all your heart and all your soul." Deuteronomy 4:29

Realizing his days were numbered (Ps 90:12), Moses poured out his heart to the stubborn people he loved so much. These messages known collectively as Deuteronomy are his last words. Moses gave heartfelt pleas, pointed warnings, valuable lessons, and encouraging reminders—such as this one.

"Search for the LORD your God . . . seek him with all your heart and all your soul." In other words, guard against spiritual complacency. Pray *against* apathy and indifference and pray *for* a greater zeal for God. Ask God to give you a relentless hunger to know him. Then read his Word with ears to hear. Long for the Lord. Look for him the way a thirsty person hunts for water.

A promise of Jesus in the New Testament echoes this same idea: "Blessed are those who hunger and thirst for righteousness, for they will be filled" (Mt 5:6). The upside of having nothing is that God delights in giving his children everything! And he always does when we ask him.

For the next note on *Rest and Reflection*, see 1 Samuel 2:26.

[A] **4:9** Or *don't depart from your heart*

form of anything, and do what is evil in the
sight of the LORD your God, angering him, 26 I
call heaven and earth as witnesses against
you today that you will quickly perish from
the land you are about to cross the Jordan to
possess. You will not live long there, but you
will certainly be destroyed. 27 The LORD will
scatter you among the peoples, and you will
be reduced to a few survivors[A] among the
nations where the LORD your God will drive
you. 28 There you will worship man-made
gods of wood and stone, which cannot see,
hear, eat, or smell. 29 But from there, you will
search for the LORD your God, and you will
find him when you seek him with all your
heart and all your soul. 30 When you are in
distress and all these things have happened
to you, in the future you will return to the
LORD your God and obey him. 31 He will not
leave you, destroy you, or forget the covenant
with your fathers that he swore to them by
oath, because the LORD your God is a compassionate God.

32 "Indeed, ask about the earlier days that
preceded you, from the day God created mankind[B] on the earth and from one end of the
heavens to the other: Has anything like this
great event ever happened, or has anything
like it been heard of? 33 Has a people heard
God's voice speaking from the fire as you
have, and lived? 34 Or has a god attempted to
go and take a nation as his own out of another
nation, by trials, signs, wonders, and war, by
a strong hand and an outstretched arm, by
great terrors, as the LORD your God did for
you in Egypt before your eyes? 35 You were
shown these things so that you would know
that the LORD is God; there is no other besides
him. 36 He let you hear his voice from heaven
to instruct you. He showed you his great fire
on earth, and you heard his words from the
fire. 37 Because he loved your fathers, he chose
their descendants after them and brought you
out of Egypt by his presence and great power, 38 to drive out before you nations greater
and stronger than you and to bring you in
and give you their land as an inheritance, as
is now taking place. 39 Today, recognize and
keep in mind that the LORD is God in heaven
above and on earth below; there is no other.
40 Keep his statutes and commands, which
I am giving you today, so that you and your
children after you may prosper and so that
you may live long in the land the LORD your
God is giving you for all time."

CITIES OF REFUGE

41 Then Moses set apart three cities across
the Jordan to the east. 42 Someone could flee
there who committed manslaughter, killing
his neighbor accidentally without previously hating him. He could flee to one of these
cities and stay alive: 43 Bezer in the wilderness on the plateau land, belonging to the
Reubenites; Ramoth in Gilead, belonging to
the Gadites; or Golan in Bashan, belonging
to the Manassites.

INTRODUCTION TO THE LAW

44 This is the law Moses gave the Israelites.
45 These are the decrees, statutes, and ordinances Moses proclaimed to them after they
came out of Egypt, 46 across the Jordan in the
valley facing Beth-peor in the land of King Sihon of the Amorites. He lived in Heshbon, and
Moses and the Israelites defeated him after
they came out of Egypt. 47 They took possession
of his land and the land of Og king of Bashan,
the two Amorite kings who were across the
Jordan to the east, 48 from Aroer on the rim
of the Arnon Valley as far as Mount Sion (that
is, Hermon) 49 and all the Arabah on the east
side of the Jordan as far as the Dead Sea below
the slopes of Pisgah.

THE TEN COMMANDMENTS

5 Moses summoned all Israel and said to
them, "Israel, listen to the statutes and ordinances I am proclaiming as you hear them
today. Learn and follow them carefully. 2 The
LORD our God made a covenant with us at
Horeb. 3 He did not make this covenant with
our fathers, but with all of us who are alive
here today. 4 The LORD spoke to you face to face
from the fire on the mountain. 5 At that time
I was standing between the LORD and you to
report the word[C] of the LORD to you, because
you were afraid of the fire and did not go up
the mountain. And he said:

6 I am the LORD your God, who brought
you out of the land of Egypt, out of the
place of slavery.
7 Do not have other gods besides me.
8 Do not make an idol for yourself in
the shape of anything in the heavens
above or on the earth below or in the

[A] **4:27** Lit *be left few in number* [B] **4:32** Or *Adam* [C] **5:5** One Hb ms, DSS, Sam, LXX, Syr, Vg read *words*

waters under the earth. 9 Do not bow
in worship to them, and do not serve
them, because I, the LORD your God, am
a jealous God, punishing the children
for the fathers' iniquity to the third
and fourth generations of those who
hate me, 10 but showing faithful love to
a thousand generations of those who
love me and keep my commands.
11 Do not misuse the name of the LORD
your God, because the LORD will not
leave anyone unpunished who misuses
his name.
12 Be careful to remember the Sabbath
day, to keep it holy as the LORD your
God has commanded you. 13 You are
to labor six days and do all your work,
14 but the seventh day is a Sabbath
to the LORD your God. Do not do any
work — you, your son or daughter,
your male or female slave, your ox or
donkey, any of your livestock, or the
resident alien who lives within your
city gates, so that your male and female
slaves may rest as you do.
15 Remember that you were a slave in the
land of Egypt, and the LORD your God
brought you out of there with a strong
hand and an outstretched arm. That is
why the LORD your God has commanded you to keep the Sabbath day.
16 Honor your father and your mother,
as the LORD your God has commanded
you, so that you may live long and so
that you may prosper in the land the
LORD your God is giving you.
17 Do not murder.
18 Do not commit adultery.
19 Do not steal.
20 Do not give dishonest testimony
against your neighbor.
21 Do not covet your neighbor's wife or
desire your neighbor's house, his field,
his male or female slave, his ox or donkey, or anything that belongs to your
neighbor.

THE PEOPLE'S RESPONSE

22 "The LORD spoke these commands in a loud
voice to your entire assembly from the fire,
cloud, and total darkness on the mountain; he
added nothing more. He wrote them on two
stone tablets and gave them to me. 23 All of
you approached me with your tribal leaders
and elders when you heard the voice from the
darkness and while the mountain was blazing
with fire. 24 You said, 'Look, the LORD our God
has shown us his glory and greatness, and we
have heard his voice from the fire. Today we
have seen that God speaks with a person, yet
he still lives. 25 But now, why should we die?
This great fire will consume us and we will
die if we hear the voice of the LORD our God
any longer. 26 For who out of all mankind has
heard the voice of the living God speaking from
the fire, as we have, and lived? 27 Go near and
listen to everything the LORD our God says.
Then you can tell us everything the LORD our
God tells you; we will listen and obey.'
28 "The LORD heard your[A] words when you
spoke to me. He said to me, 'I have heard the
words that these people have spoken to you.
Everything they have said is right. 29 If only
they had such a heart to fear me and keep all
my commands always, so that they and their
children would prosper forever. 30 Go and tell
them: Return to your tents. 31 But you stand here
with me, and I will tell you every command
— the statutes and ordinances — you are to
teach them, so that they may follow them in
the land I am giving them to possess.'
32 "Be careful to do as the LORD your God has
commanded you; you are not to turn aside to
the right or the left. 33 Follow the whole instruction the LORD your God has commanded
you, so that you may live, prosper, and have a
long life in the land you will possess.

THE GREATEST COMMAND

6 "This is the command — the statutes and
ordinances — the LORD your God has commanded me to teach you, so that you may
follow them in the land you are about to enter
and possess. 2 Do this so that you may fear
the LORD your God all the days of your life
by keeping all his statutes and commands I
am giving you, your son, and your grandson,
and so that you may have a long life. 3 Listen,
Israel, and be careful to follow them, so that
you may prosper and multiply greatly, because
the LORD, the God of your fathers, has promised you a land flowing with milk and honey.
4 "Listen, Israel: The LORD our God, the LORD
is one.[B] 5 Love the LORD your God with all your
heart, with all your soul, and with all your
strength. 6 These words that I am giving you

[A] **5:28** Lit *the sound of your* [B] **6:4** Or *the LORD is our God; the LORD is one*, or *The LORD is our God, the LORD alone*, or *The LORD our God is one LORD*

today are to be in your heart. [7] Repeat them to
your children. Talk about them when you sit
in your house and when you walk along the
road, when you lie down and when you get
up. [8] Bind them as a sign on your hand and let
them be a symbol[A] on your forehead.[B] [9] Write
them on the doorposts of your house and on
your city gates.

REMEMBERING GOD THROUGH OBEDIENCE

[10] "When the LORD your God brings you into
the land he swore to your fathers Abraham,
Isaac, and Jacob that he would give you — a
land with large and beautiful cities that you
did not build, [11] houses full of every good thing
that you did not fill them with, cisterns that
you did not dig, and vineyards and olive groves
that you did not plant — and when you eat
and are satisfied, [12] be careful not to forget
the LORD who brought you out of the land of
Egypt, out of the place of slavery. [13] Fear the
LORD your God, worship him, and take your
oaths in his name. [14] Do not follow other gods,
the gods of the peoples around you, [15] for the
LORD your God, who is among you, is a jealous
God. Otherwise, the LORD your God will become
angry with you and obliterate you from the
face of the earth. [16] Do not test the LORD your
God as you tested him at Massah. [17] Carefully
observe the commands of the LORD your God,
the decrees and statutes he has commanded
you. [18] Do what is right and good in the LORD's
sight, so that you may prosper and so that
you may enter and possess the good land the
LORD your God swore to give your fathers,
[19] by driving out all your enemies before you,
as the LORD has said.

[20] "When your son asks you in the future,
'What is the meaning of the decrees, statutes,
and ordinances that the LORD our God has
commanded you?' [21] tell him, 'We were slaves
of Pharaoh in Egypt, but the LORD brought us
out of Egypt with a strong hand. [22] Before our
eyes the LORD inflicted great and devastating
signs and wonders on Egypt, on Pharaoh, and
on all his household, [23] but he brought us from
there in order to lead us in and give us the
land that he swore to our fathers. [24] The LORD
commanded us to follow all these statutes and
to fear the LORD our God for our prosperity
always and for our preservation, as it is today.
[25] Righteousness will be ours if we are careful

Other-centeredness | *Loving God*

EXCLUSIVE ALLEGIANCE

"Listen, Israel: The LORD our God, the LORD is one. Love the LORD your God with all your heart, with all your soul, and with all your strength." Deuteronomy 6:4-5

Here is Israel's famous *Shema* (from the Hebrew verb that means "listen" or "hear"). This concise statement is the Jewish people's great confession of faith, its revered call to worship. Unlike their neighbors who believed in an assortment of deities (each god with its own agenda), the Jews were monotheistic. They served "one" God, "the LORD" (or Yahweh).

In this passage (and countless others), we see that the one true God, the God of the Bible, demands absolute and exclusive allegiance. Nothing less than wholehearted, all-encompassing love will suffice.

In the New Testament, Jesus explains what this kind of love for the Lord looks like: "The one who has my commands and keeps them is the one who loves me" (Jn 14:21). In other words, love for the Lord is never measured by warm feelings or goose bumps during a church service. It's measured by obedience.

The more we grasp the deep love God has for us, the more we find ourselves loving him. When love fills our hearts, obedience is a delight, not a duty.

For the next note on *Other-centeredness*, see Deuteronomy 10:12.

[A] **6:8** Or *phylactery*; Mt 23:5 [B] **6:8** Lit *symbol between your eyes*

to follow every one of these commands before
the LORD our God, as he has commanded us.'

ISRAEL TO DESTROY IDOLATROUS NATIONS

7 "When the LORD your God brings you into
the land you are entering to possess, and
he drives out many nations before you — the
Hethites, Girgashites, Amorites, Canaanites,
Perizzites, Hivites and Jebusites, seven nations
more numerous and powerful than you —
2 and when the LORD your God delivers them
over to you and you defeat them, you must
completely destroy them. Make no treaty
with them and show them no mercy. 3 You
must not intermarry with them, and you must
not give your daughters to their sons or take
their daughters for your sons, 4 because they
will turn your sons away from me to worship
other gods. Then the LORD's anger will burn
against you, and he will swiftly destroy you.
5 Instead, this is what you are to do to them:
tear down their altars, smash their sacred
pillars, cut down their Asherah poles, and
burn their carved images. 6 For you are a holy
people belonging to the LORD your God. The
LORD your God has chosen you to be his own
possession out of all the peoples on the face
of the earth.
7 "The LORD had his heart set on you and chose
you, not because you were more numerous
than all peoples, for you were the fewest of
all peoples. 8 But because the LORD loved you
and kept the oath he swore to your fathers,
he brought you out with a strong hand and
redeemed you from the place of slavery, from
the power of Pharaoh king of Egypt. 9 Know
that the LORD your God is God, the faithful God
who keeps his gracious covenant loyalty for
a thousand generations with those who love
him and keep his commands. 10 But he directly
pays back[A] and destroys those who hate him.
He will not hesitate to pay back directly[B] the
one who hates him. 11 So keep the command
— the statutes and ordinances — that I am
giving you to follow today.
12 "If you listen to and are careful to keep
these ordinances, the LORD your God will keep
his covenant loyalty with you, as he swore to
your fathers. 13 He will love you, bless you, and
multiply you. He will bless your offspring,[C] and
the produce of your land — your grain, new
wine, and fresh oil — the young of your herds,
and the newborn of your flocks, in the land he
swore to your fathers that he would give you.
14 You will be blessed above all peoples; there
will be no infertile male or female among you
or your livestock. 15 The LORD will remove all
sickness from you; he will not put on you all
the terrible diseases of Egypt that you know
about, but he will inflict them on all who hate

Eternal Perspective | *God's Faithfulness*

COVENANT-KEEPER

"Know that the LORD your God is God, the faithful God who keeps his gracious covenant loyalty for a thousand generations with those who love him and keep his commands." Deuteronomy 7:9

Look in any direction and you'll see disappointments to the horizon and beyond: the deadbeat dad, the lying politician, the spouse who cheated, the friend who bailed, and the boss who hung his employees out to dry. Be careful. If you keep looking for too long, you might get jaded. Reviewing all the broken promises, all the brokenhearted people, we can easily conclude that the world has not a speck of reliability or dependability.

While that may *feel* true, it isn't, of course. As Moses reminded the children of Israel here, God is "the faithful God." This doesn't mean that he always gives us exactly what we want, right when we want it. It does mean that he'll never lie to us or do wrong by us. He is greater than all the disappointments.

The Lord has pledged to change us and to bring us safely home. Sometimes the journey will unnerve us. But we can count on the reality of our future home.

For the next note on *Eternal Perspective*, see Deuteronomy 20:3-4.

[A] 7:10 Lit *He pays back to their faces* [B] 7:10 Lit *to pay back to their faces* [C] 7:13 Lit *bless the fruit of your womb*

you. 16 You must destroy all the peoples the
LORD your God is delivering over to you and
not look on them with pity. Do not worship
their gods, for that will be a snare to you.
17 "If you say to yourself, 'These nations are
greater than I; how can I drive them out?' 18 do
not be afraid of them. Be sure to remember
what the LORD your God did to Pharaoh and
all Egypt: 19 the great trials that you saw, the
signs and wonders, the strong hand and outstretched arm, by which the LORD your God
brought you out. The LORD your God will do
the same to all the peoples you fear. 20 The
LORD your God will also send hornets against
them until all the survivors and those hiding
from you perish. 21 Don't be terrified of them,
for the LORD your God, a great and awesome
God, is among you. 22 The LORD your God will
drive out these nations before you little by little. You will not be able to destroy them all at
once; otherwise, the wild animals will become
too numerous for you. 23 The LORD your God
will give them over to you and throw them
into great confusion until they are destroyed.
24 He will hand their kings over to you, and
you will wipe out their names under heaven.
No one will be able to stand against you; you
will annihilate them. 25 Burn up the carved
images of their gods. Don't covet the silver
and gold on the images and take it for yourself, or else you will be ensnared by it, for it
is detestable to the LORD your God. 26 Do not
bring any detestable thing into your house,
or you will be set apart for destruction like it.
You are to abhor and detest it utterly because
it is set apart for destruction.

REMEMBER THE LORD

8 "Carefully follow every command I am
giving you today, so that you may live and
increase, and may enter and take possession
of the land the LORD swore to your fathers.
2 Remember that the LORD your God led you
on the entire journey these forty years in
the wilderness, so that he might humble you
and test you to know what was in your heart,
whether or not you would keep his commands.
3 He humbled you by letting you go hungry;
then he gave you manna to eat, which you and
your fathers had not known, so that you might
learn that man does not live on bread alone
but on every word that comes from the mouth
of the LORD. 4 Your clothing did not wear out,
and your feet did not swell these forty years.
5 Keep in mind that the LORD your God has been
disciplining you just as a man disciplines his
son. 6 So keep the commands of the LORD your
God by walking in his ways and fearing him.
7 For the LORD your God is bringing you into a
good land, a land with streams, springs, and
deep water sources, flowing in both valleys
and hills; 8 a land of wheat, barley, vines, figs,

Thanksgiving and Contentment | *Blessings*

BLESSINGS

"He will love you, bless you, and multiply you. He will bless your offspring, and the produce of your land—your grain, new wine, and fresh oil—the young of your herds, and the newborn of your flocks, in the land he swore to your fathers that he would give you." Deuteronomy 7:13

At times, we just feel cursed. The pay cut, the marital fight, the trip to the ER, the scuttled vacation—nothing seems to goes right. The whole world seems to be conspiring against us.

While this often seems true, verses like this one remind us of a *truer* truth. God's heart is good. He loves to shower blessings on his people. This prompts the question: Why then so many setbacks in life?

Look at it this way: Some things that seem like curses at the time end up being blessings in disguise. Or at least they lead to greater blessing in the end.

The trick in pushing through "cursed" times is not to deny what's unpleasant but to ask God to help us bring to mind previous blessings and rejoice in current blessings. This may not change our situation. It will, however, change us.

For the next note on *Thanksgiving and Contentment*, see Judges 3:7-9.

and pomegranates; a land of olive oil and honey; 9 a land where you will eat food without
shortage, where you will lack nothing; a land
whose rocks are iron and from whose hills
you will mine copper. 10 When you eat and are
full, you will bless the LORD your God for the
good land he has given you.

11 "Be careful that you don't forget the LORD
your God by failing to keep his commands,
ordinances, and statutes that I am giving
you today. 12 When you eat and are full, and
build beautiful houses to live in, 13 and your
herds and flocks grow large, and your silver
and gold multiply, and everything else you
have increases, 14 be careful that your heart
doesn't become proud and you forget the LORD
your God who brought you out of the land
of Egypt, out of the place of slavery. 15 He led
you through the great and terrible wilderness
with its poisonous[A] snakes and scorpions, a
thirsty land where there was no water. He
brought water out of the flint rock for you.
16 He fed you in the wilderness with manna,
which your fathers had not known, in order
to humble and test you, so that in the end he
might cause you to prosper. 17 You may say to
yourself, 'My power and my own ability have
gained this wealth for me,' 18 but remember
that the LORD your God gives you the power
to gain wealth, in order to confirm his covenant he swore to your fathers, as it is today.
19 If you ever forget the LORD your God and
follow other gods to serve them and bow in
worship to them, I testify against you today
that you will perish. 20 Like the nations the
LORD is about to destroy before you, you will
perish if you do not obey the LORD your God.

WARNING AGAINST SELF-RIGHTEOUSNESS

9 "Listen, Israel: Today you are about to cross
the Jordan to enter and drive out nations
greater and stronger than you, with large cities fortified to the heavens. 2 The people are
strong and tall, the descendants of the Anakim.
You know about them and you have heard it
said about them, 'Who can stand up to the
sons of Anak?' 3 But understand that today
the LORD your God will cross over ahead of
you as a consuming fire; he will devastate and
subdue them before you. You will drive them
out and destroy them swiftly, as the LORD has
told you. 4 When the LORD your God drives
them out before you, do not say to yourself,
'The LORD brought me in to take possession
of this land because of my righteousness.'
Instead, the LORD will drive out these nations
before you because of their wickedness. 5 You
are not going to take possession of their land
because of your righteousness or your integrity. Instead, the LORD your God will drive
out these nations before you because of their
wickedness, in order to fulfill the promise he
swore to your fathers, Abraham, Isaac, and
Jacob. 6 Understand that the LORD your God
is not giving you this good land to possess
because of your righteousness, for you are a
stiff-necked people.

ISRAEL'S REBELLION AND MOSES'S INTERCESSION

7 "Remember and do not forget how you provoked the LORD your God in the wilderness.
You have been rebelling against the LORD from
the day you left the land of Egypt until you
reached this place. 8 You provoked the LORD at
Horeb, and he was angry enough with you to
destroy you. 9 When I went up the mountain
to receive the stone tablets, the tablets of the
covenant the LORD made with you, I stayed
on the mountain forty days and forty nights.
I did not eat food or drink water. 10 On the day
of the assembly the LORD gave me the two
stone tablets, inscribed by God's finger. The
exact words were on them, which the LORD
spoke to you from the fire on the mountain.
11 The LORD gave me the two stone tablets, the
tablets of the covenant, at the end of the forty
days and forty nights.

12 "The LORD said to me, 'Get up and go down
immediately from here. For your people whom
you brought out of Egypt have acted corruptly.
They have quickly turned from the way that
I commanded them; they have made a cast
image for themselves.' 13 The LORD also said
to me, 'I have seen this people, and indeed,
they are a stiff-necked people. 14 Leave me
alone, and I will destroy them and blot out
their name under heaven. Then I will make
you into a nation stronger and more numerous than they.'

15 "So I went back down the mountain, while
it was blazing with fire, and the two tablets of
the covenant were in my hands. 16 I saw how
you had sinned against the LORD your God;
you had made a calf image for yourselves. You
had quickly turned from the way the LORD

[A] **8:15** Lit *burning*

had commanded for you. 17 So I took hold
of the two tablets and threw them from my
hands, shattering them before your eyes. 18 I
fell down like the first time in the presence
of the LORD for forty days and forty nights;
I did not eat food or drink water because of
all the sin you committed, doing what was
evil in the LORD's sight and angering him. 19 I
was afraid of the fierce anger the LORD had
directed against you, because he was about
to destroy you. But again the LORD listened
to me on that occasion. 20 The LORD was angry enough with Aaron to destroy him. But
I prayed for Aaron at that time also. 21 I took
the sinful calf you had made and burned it. I
crushed it, thoroughly grinding it to powder
as fine as dust, and threw its dust into the
stream that came down from the mountain.

22 "You continued to provoke the LORD at Taberah, Massah, and Kibroth-hattaavah. 23 When
the LORD sent you from Kadesh-barnea, he
said, 'Go up and possess the land I have given
you'; you rebelled against the command of the
LORD your God. You did not believe or obey
him. 24 You have been rebelling against the
LORD ever since I have[A] known you.

25 "I fell down in the presence of the LORD
forty days and forty nights because the LORD
had threatened to destroy you. 26 I prayed to
the LORD:
Lord GOD, do not annihilate your people,
your inheritance, whom you redeemed
through your greatness and brought out
of Egypt with a strong hand. 27 Remember
your servants Abraham, Isaac, and Jacob.
Disregard this people's stubbornness,
and their wickedness and sin. 28 Otherwise, those in the land you brought us
from will say, 'Because the LORD wasn't
able to bring them into the land he had
promised them, and because he hated
them, he brought them out to kill them
in the wilderness.' 29 But they are your
people, your inheritance, whom you
brought out by your great power and
outstretched arm.

THE COVENANT RENEWED

10 "The LORD said to me at that time, 'Cut
two stone tablets like the first ones and
come to me on the mountain and make a
wooden ark. 2 I will write on the tablets the
words that were on the first tablets you broke,
and you are to place them in the ark.' 3 So I
made an ark of acacia wood, cut two stone
tablets like the first ones, and climbed the
mountain with the two tablets in my hand.
4 Then on the day of the assembly, the LORD
wrote on the tablets what had been written
previously, the Ten Commandments that he

Other-centeredness | *Loving God*

SIMPLIFIED RELIGION

"And now, Israel, what does the LORD your God ask of you except to fear the LORD your God by walking in all his ways, to love him, and to worship the LORD your God with all your heart and all your soul?" Deuteronomy 10:12

For some people, the spiritual life feels like the drudgery of doing taxes: hours of combing through reams of fine print, struggling to understand puzzling rules, and trying to abide by obscure stipulations.

The result? Some throw up their hands. Others grimly settle in for a dreary life of trying not to screw up.

Contrast this religious mess with the simplified spirituality prescribed here: "love . . . and . . . worship the LORD your God."

How can we do this? How do we cultivate a deeper love for God? The simplest way is to spend time with him and in a loving Christian community. Worshiping alone can be difficult, but by loving and helping others, we discover the One who is perfectly loving, merciful, and kind.

For the next note on *Other-centeredness*, see Deuteronomy 31:6.

[A] **9:24** Sam, LXX read *since he has*

had spoken to you on the mountain from
the fire. The LORD gave them to me, 5 and I
went back down the mountain and placed the
tablets in the ark I had made. And they have
remained there, as the LORD commanded me."
6 The Israelites traveled from Beeroth Bene-
jaakan[A] to Moserah. Aaron died and was buried
there, and Eleazar his son became priest in his
place. 7 They traveled from there to Gudgodah,
and from Gudgodah to Jotbathah, a land with
flowing streams.
8 "At that time the LORD set apart the tribe of
Levi to carry the ark of the LORD's covenant,
to stand before the LORD to serve him, and to
pronounce blessings in his name, as it is today.
9 For this reason, Levi does not have a portion
or inheritance like his brothers; the LORD is his
inheritance, as the LORD your God told him.
10 "I stayed on the mountain forty days and
forty nights like the first time. The LORD also
listened to me on this occasion; he agreed not
to annihilate you. 11 Then the LORD said to me,
'Get up. Continue your journey ahead of the
people, so that they may enter and possess
the land I swore to give their fathers.'

WHAT GOD REQUIRES

12 "And now, Israel, what does the LORD your
God ask of you except to fear the LORD your
God by walking in all his ways, to love him,
and to worship the LORD your God with all
your heart and all your soul? 13 Keep the LORD's
commands and statutes I am giving you today,
for your own good. 14 The heavens, indeed the
highest heavens, belong to the LORD your God,
as does the earth and everything in it. 15 Yet
the LORD had his heart set on your fathers and
loved them. He chose their descendants after
them — he chose you out of all the peoples, as
it is today. 16 Therefore, circumcise your hearts
and don't be stiff-necked any longer. 17 For the
LORD your God is the God of gods and Lord of
lords, the great, mighty, and awe-inspiring God,
showing no partiality and taking no bribe.
18 He executes justice for the fatherless and
the widow, and loves the resident alien, giving
him food and clothing. 19 You are also to love
the resident alien, since you were resident
aliens in the land of Egypt. 20 You are to fear
the LORD your God and worship him. Remain
faithful[B] to him and take oaths in his name.
21 He is your praise and he is your God, who
has done for you these great and awe-inspiring
works your eyes have seen. 22 Your fathers
went down to Egypt, seventy people in all,
and now the LORD your God has made you
numerous, like the stars of the sky.

REMEMBER AND OBEY

11 "Therefore, love the LORD your God and
always keep his mandate and his statutes, ordinances, and commands. 2 Understand today that it is not your children who
experienced or saw the discipline of the LORD
your God:

His greatness, strong hand, and outstretched arm; 3 his signs and the works
he did in Egypt to Pharaoh king of Egypt
and all his land; 4 what he did to Egypt's
army, its horses and chariots, when
he made the water of the Red Sea flow
over them as they pursued you, and he
destroyed them completely;[C] 5 what he did
to you in the wilderness until you reached
this place; 6 and what he did to Dathan and
Abiram, the sons of Eliab the Reubenite,
when in the middle of the whole Israelite
camp the earth opened its mouth and
swallowed them, their households, their
tents, and every living thing with them.

7 Your own eyes have seen every great work
the LORD has done.
8 "Keep every command I am giving you today, so that you may have the strength to cross
into and possess the land you are to inherit,
9 and so that you may live long in the land the
LORD swore to your fathers to give them and
their descendants, a land flowing with milk and
honey. 10 For the land you are entering to possess is not like the land of Egypt, from which
you have come, where you sowed your seed
and irrigated by hand[D] as in a vegetable garden.
11 But the land you are entering to possess is
a land of mountains and valleys, watered by
rain from the sky. 12 It is a land the LORD your
God cares for. He is always watching over it
from the beginning to the end of the year.
13 "If you carefully obey my commands I am
giving you today, to love the LORD your God
and worship him with all your heart and all
your soul, 14 I[E] will provide rain for your land
in the proper time, the autumn and spring
rains, and you will harvest your grain, new
wine, and fresh oil. 15 I[F] will provide grass in
your fields for your livestock. You will eat
and be satisfied. 16 Be careful that you are not

[A] **10:6** Or *from the wells of Bene-jaakan*, or *from the wells of the Jaakanites* [B] **10:20** Lit *Hold on* [C] **11:4** Lit *to this day* [D] **11:10** Lit *foot* [E] **11:14** DSS, Sam, LXX read *he* [F] **11:15** DSS, Sam, LXX read *He*

enticed to turn aside, serve, and bow in worship to other gods. 17 Then the LORD's anger
will burn against you. He will shut the sky,
and there will be no rain; the land will not
yield its produce, and you will perish quickly
from the good land the LORD is giving you.
18 "Imprint these words of mine on your
hearts and minds, bind them as a sign on your
hands, and let them be a symbol[A] on your foreheads.[B] 19 Teach them to your children, talking
about them when you sit in your house and
when you walk along the road, when you lie
down and when you get up. 20 Write them
on the doorposts of your house and on your
city gates, 21 so that as long as the heavens are
above the earth, your days and those of your
children may be many in the land the LORD
swore to give your fathers. 22 For if you carefully observe every one of these commands
I am giving you to follow — to love the LORD
your God, walk in all his ways, and remain
faithful[C] to him — 23 the LORD will drive out
all these nations before you, and you will
drive out nations greater and stronger than
you are. 24 Every place the sole of your foot
treads will be yours. Your territory will extend
from the wilderness to Lebanon and from the
Euphrates River[D] to the Mediterranean Sea.
25 No one will be able to stand against you;
the LORD your God will put fear and dread of
you in all the land where you set foot, as he
has promised you.

A BLESSING AND A CURSE

26 "Look, today I set before you a blessing and a
curse: 27 there will be a blessing, if you obey the
commands of the LORD your God I am giving
you today, 28 and a curse, if you do not obey
the commands of the LORD your God and you
turn aside from the path I command you today
by following other gods you have not known.
29 When the LORD your God brings you into the
land you are entering to possess, you are to
proclaim the blessing at Mount Gerizim and
the curse at Mount Ebal. 30 Aren't these mountains across the Jordan, beyond the western
road in the land of the Canaanites, who live
in the Arabah, opposite Gilgal, near the oaks[E]
of Moreh? 31 For you are about to cross the
Jordan to enter and take possession of the
land the LORD your God is giving you. When
you possess it and settle in it, 32 be careful to
follow all the statutes and ordinances I set
before you today.

Exercise of Faith | *Tithing*

GIVING BABY STEPS

"Instead, turn to the place the LORD your God chooses from all your tribes to put his name for his dwelling and go there. You are to bring there your burnt offerings and sacrifices, your tenths and personal contributions, your vow offerings and freewill offerings, and the firstborn of your herds and flocks." Deuteronomy 12:5-6

A wise person once said, "If you have something you can't give away, you don't own it; it owns you." This reveals the dark side of wealth and possessions. When we begin to clutch money and things too tightly, we soon find that they have taken hold of us.

This is why God mandated tithing for his people. Giving back a percentage of one's income was a way to bush back against the temptation to trust in worldly wealth.

Some scholars believe the Old Testament actually prescribes *two* annual tithes (see Lv 27:30 and Dt 14:22), and an additional tithe every three years (Dt 14:28). This would mean faithful Jews would end up giving about 23 percent of their income back to God, not counting freewill gifts.

Establishing the practice of being generous can free you from money's grip.

For the next note on *Exercise of Faith*, see Joshua 24:15.

[A] **11:18** Or *phylactery*; Mt 23:5 [B] **11:18** Lit *symbol between your eyes*; Ex 13:16; Dt 6:8 [C] **11:22** Lit *and hold on* [D] **11:24** Some Hb mss, LXX, Tg, Vg read *the great river, the river Euphrates* [E] **11:30** Sam, LXX, Syr, Aq, Sym read *oak*; Gn 12:6

THE CHOSEN PLACE OF WORSHIP

12 "Be careful to follow these statutes and
ordinances in the land that the LORD, the
God of your fathers, has given you to possess
all the days you live on the earth. 2 Destroy
completely all the places where the nations
that you are driving out worship their gods
— on the high mountains, on the hills, and
under every green tree. 3 Tear down their altars, smash their sacred pillars, burn their
Asherah poles, cut down the carved images
of their gods, and wipe out their names from
every[A] place. 4 Don't worship the LORD your
God this way. 5 Instead, turn to the place the
LORD your God chooses from all your tribes
to put his name for his dwelling and go there.
6 You are to bring there your burnt offerings
and sacrifices, your tenths and personal contributions,[B] your vow offerings and freewill
offerings, and the firstborn of your herds and
flocks. 7 You will eat there in the presence of the
LORD your God and rejoice with your household in everything you do,[C] because the LORD
your God has blessed you.

8 "You are not to do as we are doing here today; everyone is doing whatever seems right
in his own sight. 9 Indeed, you have not yet
come into the resting place and the inheritance the LORD your God is giving you. 10 When
you cross the Jordan and live in the land the
LORD your God is giving you to inherit, and he
gives you rest from all the enemies around you
and you live in security, 11 then the LORD your
God will choose the place to have his name
dwell. Bring there everything I command you:
your burnt offerings, sacrifices, offerings of
the tenth, personal contributions,[D] and all
your choice offerings you vow to the LORD.
12 You will rejoice before the LORD your God
— you, your sons and daughters, your male
and female slaves, and the Levite who is within your city gates, since he has no portion or
inheritance among you. 13 Be careful not to
offer your burnt offerings in all the sacred
places you see. 14 You must offer your burnt
offerings only in the place the LORD chooses
in one of your tribes, and there you must do
everything I command you.

SLAUGHTERING ANIMALS TO EAT

15 "But whenever you want, you may slaughter
and eat meat within any of your city gates,
according to the blessing the LORD your God
has given you. Those who are clean or unclean may eat it, as they would a gazelle or
deer, 16 but you must not eat the blood; pour
it on the ground like water. 17 Within your city
gates you may not eat the tenth of your grain,
new wine, or fresh oil; the firstborn of your
herd or flock; any of your vow offerings that
you pledge; your freewill offerings; or your
personal contributions.[E] 18 You are to eat them
in the presence of the LORD your God at the
place the LORD your God chooses — you, your
son and daughter, your male and female slave,
and the Levite who is within your city gates.
Rejoice before the LORD your God in everything you do, 19 and be careful not to neglect
the Levite, as long as you live in your land.

20 "When the LORD your God enlarges your
territory as he has promised you, and you say,
'I want to eat meat' because you have a strong
desire to eat meat, you may eat it whenever
you want. 21 If the place where the LORD your
God chooses to put his name is too far from
you, you may slaughter any of your herd or
flock he has given you, as I have commanded
you, and you may eat it within your city gates
whenever you want. 22 Indeed, you may eat
it as the gazelle and deer are eaten; both the
clean and the unclean may eat it. 23 But don't
eat the blood, since the blood is the life, and
you must not eat the life with the meat. 24 Do
not eat blood; pour it on the ground like water.
25 Do not eat it, so that you and your children
after you will prosper, because you will be
doing what is right in the LORD's sight.

26 "But you are to take the holy offerings you
have and your vow offerings and go to the
place the LORD chooses. 27 Present the meat
and blood of your burnt offerings on the altar of the LORD your God. The blood of your
other sacrifices is to be poured out beside the
altar of the LORD your God, but you may eat
the meat. 28 Be careful to obey all these things
I command you, so that you and your children
after you may prosper forever, because you
will be doing what is good and right in the
sight of the LORD your God.

29 "When the LORD your God annihilates the
nations before you, which you are entering
to take possession of, and you drive them out
and live in their land, 30 be careful not to be
ensnared by their ways after they have been
destroyed before you. Do not inquire about
their gods, asking, 'How did these nations

[A] **12:3** Lit *that* [B] **12:6** Lit *and the contributions from your hands* [C] **12:7** Lit *you put your hand to,* also in v. 18 [D] **12:11** Lit *tenth, the contributions from your hands* [E] **12:17** Lit *or the contributions from your hands*

worship their gods? I'll also do the same.'
31 You must not do the same to the LORD your
God, because they practice every detestable
act, which the LORD hates, for their gods. They
even burn their sons and daughters in the fire
to their gods. 32 Be careful to do everything I
command you; do not add anything to it or
take anything away from it.

THE FALSE PROPHET

13 "If a prophet or someone who has dreams
arises among you and proclaims a sign
or wonder to you, 2 and that sign or wonder he
has promised you comes about, but he says,
'Let us follow other gods,' which you have
not known, 'and let us worship them,' 3 do
not listen to that prophet's words or to that
dreamer. For the LORD your God is testing you
to know whether you love the LORD your God
with all your heart and all your soul. 4 You must
follow the LORD your God and fear him. You
must keep his commands and listen to him;
you must worship him and remain faithful[A]
to him. 5 That prophet or dreamer must be
put to death, because he has urged rebellion
against the LORD your God who brought you
out of the land of Egypt and redeemed you
from the place of slavery, to turn you from
the way the LORD your God has commanded
you to walk. You must purge the evil from you.

DON'T TOLERATE IDOLATRY

6 "If your brother, the son of your mother,[B] or
your son or daughter, or the wife you embrace,
or your closest friend secretly entices you,
saying, 'Let us go and worship other gods'
— which neither you nor your fathers have
known, 7 any of the gods of the peoples around
you, near you or far from you, from one end of
the earth to the other — 8 do not yield to him
or listen to him. Show him no pity,[C] and do not
spare him or shield him. 9 Instead, you must
kill him. Your hand is to be the first against
him to put him to death, and then the hands of
all the people. 10 Stone him to death for trying
to turn you away from the LORD your God who
brought you out of the land of Egypt, out of
the place of slavery. 11 All Israel will hear and
be afraid, and they will no longer do anything
evil like this among you.

12 "If you hear it said about one of your cities
the LORD your God is giving you to live in, 13 that
wicked men have sprung up among you, led
the inhabitants of their city astray, and said,
'Let us go and worship other gods,' which you
have not known, 14 you are to inquire, investigate, and interrogate thoroughly. If the report
turns out to be true that this detestable act
has been done among you, 15 you must strike
down the inhabitants of that city with the
sword. Completely destroy everyone in it as
well as its livestock with the sword. 16 You are
to gather all its spoil in the middle of the city
square and completely burn the city and all
its spoil for the LORD your God. The city is to
remain a mound of ruins forever; it is not to
be rebuilt. 17 Nothing set apart for destruction
is to remain in your hand, so that the LORD will
turn from his burning anger and grant you
mercy, show you compassion, and multiply
you as he swore to your fathers. 18 This will
occur if you obey the LORD your God, keeping
all his commands I am giving you today, doing
what is right in the sight of the LORD your God.

FORBIDDEN PRACTICES

14 "You are sons of the LORD your God; do
not cut yourselves or make a bald spot
on your head[D] on behalf of the dead, 2 for you
are a holy people belonging to the LORD your
God. The LORD has chosen you to be his own
possession out of all the peoples on the face
of the earth.

CLEAN AND UNCLEAN FOODS

3 "You must not eat any detestable thing. 4 These
are the animals you may eat:

oxen, sheep, goats,
5 deer, gazelles, roe deer,
wild goats, ibexes, antelopes,
and mountain sheep.

6 You may eat any animal that has hooves divided in two and chews the cud.[E] 7 But among
the ones that chew the cud or have divided
hooves, you are not to eat these:

camels, hares, and hyraxes,
though they chew the cud, they do not
have hooves —
they are unclean for you;
8 and pigs, though they have hooves,
they do not chew the cud —
they are unclean for you.

Do not eat their meat or touch their carcasses.
9 "You may eat everything from the water

[A] 13:4 Lit *and hold on* [B] 13:6 DSS, Sam, LXX read *If the son of your father or the son of your mother* [C] 13:8 Lit *Your eye must not pity him* [D] 14:1 Or *forehead* [E] 14:6 The Hb does not specify chewing the cud, but bringing up partially digested food and swallowing it again.

that has fins and scales, 10 but you may not eat
anything that does not have fins and scales
— it is unclean for you.
11 "You may eat every clean bird, 12 but these
are the ones you may not eat:
eagles, bearded vultures,
black vultures, 13 the kites,
any kind of falcon,[A]
14 every kind of raven, 15 ostriches,
short-eared owls, gulls,
any kind of hawk,
16 little owls, long-eared owls,
barn owls, 17 eagle owls,
ospreys, cormorants, 18 storks,
any kind of heron,
hoopoes, and bats.[B]
19 All winged insects are unclean for you; they
may not be eaten. 20 But you may eat every
clean flying creature.
21 "You are not to eat any carcass; you may
give it to a resident alien within your city gates,
and he may eat it, or you may sell it to a foreigner. For you are a holy people belonging to
the LORD your God. Do not boil a young goat
in its mother's milk.

A TENTH FOR THE LORD

22 "Each year you are to set aside a tenth of all
the produce grown in your fields. 23 You are
to eat a tenth of your grain, new wine, and
fresh oil, and the firstborn of your herd and
flock, in the presence of the LORD your God at
the place where he chooses to have his name
dwell, so that you will always learn to fear the
LORD your God. 24 But if the distance is too
great for you to carry it, since the place where
the LORD your God chooses to put his name
is too far away from you and since the LORD
your God has blessed you, 25 then exchange
it for silver, take the silver in your hand, and
go to the place the LORD your God chooses.
26 You may spend the silver on anything you
want: cattle, sheep, goats, wine, beer, or anything you desire. You are to feast there in the
presence of the LORD your God and rejoice
with your family. 27 Do not neglect the Levite
within your city gates, since he has no portion
or inheritance among you.
28 "At the end of every three years, bring a
tenth of all your produce for that year and
store it within your city gates. 29 Then the Levite, who has no portion or inheritance among
you, the resident alien, the fatherless, and
the widow within your city gates may come,
eat, and be satisfied. And the LORD your God
will bless you in all the work of your hands
that you do.

DEBTS CANCELED

15 "At the end of every seven years you
must cancel debts. 2 This is how to cancel
debt: Every creditor[C] is to cancel what he has
lent his neighbor. He is not to collect anything
from his neighbor or brother, because the
LORD's release of debts has been proclaimed.
3 You may collect something from a foreigner,
but you must forgive whatever your brother
owes you.
4 "There will be no poor among you, however, because the LORD is certain to bless you
in the land the LORD your God is giving you to
possess as an inheritance — 5 if only you obey
the LORD your God and are careful to follow
every one of these commands I am giving you
today. 6 When the LORD your God blesses you
as he has promised you, you will lend to many
nations but not borrow; you will rule many
nations, but they will not rule you.

LENDING TO THE POOR

7 "If there is a poor person among you, one of
your brothers within any of your city gates in
the land the LORD your God is giving you, do
not be hardhearted or tightfisted toward your
poor brother. 8 Instead, you are to open your
hand to him and freely loan him enough for
whatever need he has. 9 Be careful that there
isn't this wicked thought in your heart, 'The
seventh year, the year of canceling debts, is
near,' and you are stingy toward your poor
brother and give him nothing. He will cry out
to the LORD against you, and you will be guilty.
10 Give to him, and don't have a stingy heart[D]
when you give, and because of this the LORD
your God will bless you in all your work and
in everything you do.[E] 11 For there will never
cease to be poor people in the land; that is
why I am commanding you, 'Open your hand
willingly to your poor and needy brother in
your land.'

RELEASE OF SLAVES

12 "If your fellow Hebrew, a man or woman, is
sold to you and serves you six years, you must

[A] 14:13 Some Hb mss, Sam, LXX; other Hb mss, Vg read *the falcon, the various kinds of kite* [B] 14:5-18 The identification of some of these animals is uncertain. [C] 15:2 Lit *owner of a loan of his hand* [D] 15:10 Lit *and let not your heart be grudging* [E] 15:10 Lit *you put your hand to*

set him free in the seventh year. 13 When you set
him free, do not send him away empty-handed.
14 Give generously to him from your flock, your
threshing floor, and your winepress. You are
to give him whatever the LORD your God has
blessed you with. 15 Remember that you were
a slave in the land of Egypt and the LORD your
God redeemed you; that is why I am giving you
this command today. 16 But if your slave says
to you, 'I don't want to leave you,' because he
loves you and your family, and is well off with
you, 17 take an awl and pierce through his ear
into the door, and he will become your slave
for life. Also treat your female slave the same
way. 18 Do not regard it as a hardship[A] when
you set him free, because he worked for you
six years — worth twice the wages of a hired
worker. Then the LORD your God will bless you
in everything you do.

CONSECRATION OF FIRSTBORN ANIMALS

19 "Consecrate to the LORD your God every firstborn male produced by your herd and flock.
You are not to put the firstborn of your oxen
to work or shear the firstborn of your flock.
20 Each year you and your family are to eat it
before the LORD your God in the place the LORD
chooses. 21 But if there is a defect in the animal,
if it is lame or blind or has any serious defect,
you may not sacrifice it to the LORD your God.
22 Eat it within your city gates; both the unclean
person and the clean may eat it, as though
it were a gazelle or deer. 23 But you must not
eat its blood; pour it on the ground like water.

THE FESTIVAL OF PASSOVER

16 "Set aside the month of Abib[B] and observe
the Passover to the LORD your God, because the LORD your God brought you out of
Egypt by night in the month of Abib. 2 Sacrifice
to the LORD your God a Passover animal from
the herd or flock in the place where the LORD
chooses to have his name dwell. 3 Do not eat
leavened bread with it. For seven days you are
to eat unleavened bread with it, the bread of
hardship — because you left the land of Egypt
in a hurry — so that you may remember for
the rest of your life the day you left the land
of Egypt. 4 No yeast is to be found anywhere
in your territory for seven days, and none of
the meat you sacrifice in the evening of the
first day is to remain until morning. 5 You are
not to sacrifice the Passover animal in any of
the towns the LORD your God is giving you.
6 Sacrifice the Passover animal only at the place
where the LORD your God chooses to have
his name dwell. Do this in the evening as the
sun sets at the same time of day you departed
from Egypt. 7 You are to cook and eat it in the
place the LORD your God chooses, and you are
to return to your tents in the morning. 8 Eat
unleavened bread for six days. On the seventh
day there is to be a solemn assembly to the
LORD your God; do not do any work.

THE FESTIVAL OF WEEKS

9 "You are to count seven weeks, counting the
weeks from the time the sickle is first put to
the standing grain. 10 You are to celebrate the
Festival of Weeks to the LORD your God with
a freewill offering that you give in proportion to how the LORD your God has blessed
you. 11 Rejoice before the LORD your God in
the place where he chooses to have his name
dwell — you, your son and daughter, your male
and female slave, the Levite within your city
gates, as well as the resident alien, the fatherless, and the widow among you. 12 Remember
that you were slaves in Egypt; carefully follow
these statutes.

THE FESTIVAL OF SHELTERS

13 "You are to celebrate the Festival of Shelters for seven days when you have gathered
in everything from your threshing floor and
winepress. 14 Rejoice during your festival —
you, your son and daughter, your male and
female slave, as well as the Levite, the resident
alien, the fatherless, and the widow within
your city gates. 15 You are to hold a seven-day
festival for the LORD your God in the place he
chooses, because the LORD your God will bless
you in all your produce and in all the work of
your hands, and you will have abundant joy.
16 "All your males are to appear three times
a year before the LORD your God in the place
he chooses: at the Festival of Unleavened
Bread, the Festival of Weeks, and the Festival of Shelters. No one is to appear before the
LORD empty-handed. 17 Everyone must appear
with a gift suited to his means, according to
the blessing the LORD your God has given you.

APPOINTING JUDGES AND OFFICIALS

18 "Appoint judges and officials for your tribes
in all your towns the LORD your God is giving

[A] **15:18** Lit *Let it not be hard in your sight* [B] **16:1** March–April; called Nisan in the post-exilic period; Neh 2:1; Est 3:7

you. They are to judge the people with righteous judgment. 19 Do not deny justice or show
partiality to anyone. Do not accept a bribe, for
it blinds the eyes of the wise and twists the
words of the righteous. 20 Pursue justice and
justice alone, so that you will live and possess
the land the LORD your God is giving you.

FORBIDDEN WORSHIP

21 "Do not set up an Asherah of any kind of
wood next to the altar you will build for the
LORD your God, 22 and do not set up a sacred
pillar; the LORD your God hates them.

17 "Do not sacrifice to the LORD your God an
ox or sheep with a defect or any serious
flaw, for that is detestable to the LORD your God.

THE JUDICIAL PROCEDURE FOR IDOLATRY

2 "If a man or woman among you in one of your
towns that the LORD your God will give you is
discovered doing evil in the sight of the LORD
your God and violating his covenant 3 and has
gone to serve other gods by bowing in worship to the sun, moon, or all the stars in the
sky — which I have forbidden — 4 and if you
are told or hear about it, then investigate it
thoroughly. If the report turns out to be true
that this detestable act has been done in Israel,
5 you are to bring out to your city gates that
man or woman who has done this evil thing
and stone them to death. 6 The one condemned
to die is to be executed on the testimony of
two or three witnesses. No one is to be executed on the testimony of a single witness. 7 The
witnesses' hands are to be the first in putting
him to death, and after that, the hands of all
the people. You must purge the evil from you.

DIFFICULT CASES

8 "If a case is too difficult for you — concerning bloodshed, lawsuits, or assaults — cases
disputed at your city gates, then go up to the
place the LORD your God chooses. 9 You are to
go to the Levitical priests and to the judge who
presides at that time. Ask, and they will give
you a verdict in the case. 10 You must abide by
the verdict they give you at the place the LORD
chooses. Be careful to do exactly as they instruct you. 11 You must abide by the instruction
they give you and the verdict they announce
to you. Do not turn to the right or the left from
the decision they declare to you. 12 The person
who acts arrogantly, refusing to listen either
to the priest who stands there serving the
LORD your God or to the judge, must die. You
must purge the evil from Israel. 13 Then all
the people will hear about it, be afraid, and
no longer behave arrogantly.

APPOINTING A KING

14 "When you enter the land the LORD your God
is giving you, take possession of it, live in it, and
say, 'I will set a king over me like all the nations
around me,' 15 you are to appoint over you the
king the LORD your God chooses. Appoint a
king from your brothers. You are not to set a
foreigner over you, or one who is not of your
people. 16 However, he must not acquire many
horses for himself or send the people back to
Egypt to acquire many horses, for the LORD has
told you, 'You are never to go back that way
again.' 17 He must not acquire many wives for
himself so that his heart won't go astray. He
must not acquire very large amounts of silver
and gold for himself. 18 When he is seated on
his royal throne, he is to write a copy of this
instruction for himself on a scroll in the presence of the Levitical priests. 19 It is to remain
with him, and he is to read from it all the days
of his life, so that he may learn to fear the LORD
his God, to observe all the words of this instruction, and to do these statutes. 20 Then his heart
will not be exalted above his countrymen, he
will not turn from this command to the right
or the left, and he and his sons will continue
reigning many years[A] in Israel.

PROVISIONS FOR THE LEVITES

18 "The Levitical priests, the whole tribe of
Levi, will have no portion or inheritance
with Israel. They will eat the LORD's fire offerings; that is their[B,C] inheritance. 2 Although
Levi has no inheritance among his brothers,
the LORD is his inheritance, as he promised
him. 3 This is the priests' share from the people who offer a sacrifice, whether it is an ox,
a sheep, or a goat; the priests are to be given
the shoulder, jaws, and stomach. 4 You are to
give him the firstfruits of your grain, new
wine, and fresh oil, and the first sheared wool
of your flock. 5 For the LORD your God has
chosen him and his sons from all your tribes
to stand and minister in his name from now
on.[D] 6 When a Levite leaves one of your towns
in Israel where he was staying and wants to
go to the place the LORD chooses, 7 he may

[A] **17:20** Lit *will lengthen days on his kingdom* [B] **18:1** LXX; MT reads *his* [C] **18:1** Or *his* [D] **18:5** Lit *name all the days*

serve in the name of the LORD his God like all
his fellow Levites who minister there in the
presence of the LORD. 8 They will eat equal
portions besides what he has received from
the sale of the family estate.[A]

OCCULT PRACTICES VERSUS PROPHETIC REVELATION

9 "When you enter the land the LORD your God
is giving you, do not imitate the detestable
customs of those nations. 10 No one among you
is to sacrifice his son or daughter in the fire,[B]
practice divination, tell fortunes, interpret
omens, practice sorcery, 11 cast spells, consult
a medium or a spiritist, or inquire of the dead.
12 Everyone who does these acts is detestable
to the LORD, and the LORD your God is driving
out the nations before you because of these
detestable acts. 13 You must be blameless before
the LORD your God. 14 Though these nations you
are about to drive out listen to fortune-tellers
and diviners, the LORD your God has not permitted you to do this.

15 "The LORD your God will raise up for you a
prophet like me from among your own brothers. You must listen to him. 16 This is what you
requested from the LORD your God at Horeb
on the day of the assembly when you said, 'Let
us not continue to hear the voice of the LORD
our God or see this great fire any longer, so
that we will not die!' 17 Then the LORD said to
me, 'They have spoken well. 18 I will raise up
for them a prophet like you from among their
brothers. I will put my words in his mouth,
and he will tell them everything I command
him. 19 I will hold accountable whoever does
not listen to my words that he speaks in my
name. 20 But the prophet who presumes to
speak a message in my name that I have not
commanded him to speak, or who speaks in
the name of other gods — that prophet must
die.' 21 You may say to yourself, 'How can we
recognize a message the LORD has not spoken?'
22 When a prophet speaks in the LORD's name,
and the message does not come true or is not
fulfilled, that is a message the LORD has not
spoken. The prophet has spoken it presumptuously. Do not be afraid of him.

CITIES OF REFUGE

19 "When the LORD your God annihilates
the nations whose land he is giving you,
so that you drive them out and live in their
cities and houses, 2 you are to set apart three
cities for yourselves within the land the LORD
your God is giving you to possess. 3 You are
to determine the distances[C] and divide the
land the LORD your God is granting you as an
inheritance into three regions, so that anyone who commits manslaughter can flee to
these cities.[D]

4 "Here is the law concerning a case of someone who kills a person and flees there to save
his life, having killed his neighbor accidentally
without previously hating him: 5 If, for example,
he goes into the forest with his neighbor to cut
timber, and his hand swings the ax to chop
down a tree, but the blade flies off the handle
and strikes his neighbor so that he dies, that
person may flee to one of these cities and live.
6 Otherwise, the avenger of blood in the heat of
his anger[E] might pursue the one who committed manslaughter, overtake him because the
distance is great, and strike him dead. Yet he did
not deserve to die,[F] since he did not previously
hate his neighbor. 7 This is why I am commanding you to set apart three cities for yourselves.
8 If the LORD your God enlarges your territory as
he swore to your fathers, and gives you all the
land he promised to give them — 9 provided
you keep every one of these commands I am
giving you today and follow them, loving the
LORD your God and walking in his ways at all
times — you are to add three more cities to
these three. 10 In this way, innocent blood will
not be shed, and you will not become guilty
of bloodshed in the land the LORD your God is
giving you as an inheritance. 11 But if someone
hates his neighbor, lies in ambush for him, attacks him, and strikes him fatally, and flees to
one of these cities, 12 the elders of his city are
to send for him, take him from there, and hand
him over to the avenger of blood and he will
die. 13 Do not look on him with pity but purge
from Israel the guilt of shedding innocent blood,
and you will prosper.

BOUNDARY MARKERS

14 "Do not move your neighbor's boundary
marker, established at the start in the inheritance you will receive in the land the LORD
your God is giving you to possess.

WITNESSES IN COURT

15 "One witness cannot establish any iniquity
or sin against a person, whatever that person

[A] **18:8** Hb obscure [B] **18:10** Lit *to make his son or daughter pass through the fire* [C] **19:3** Or *to prepare the roads* [D] **19:3** Lit *flee there* [E] **19:6** Lit *heart* [F] **19:6** Lit *did not have a judgment of death*

has done. A fact must be established by the
testimony of two or three witnesses.
16 "If a malicious witness testifies against
someone accusing him of a crime, 17 the two
people in the dispute are to stand in the presence of the LORD before the priests and judges
in authority at that time. 18 The judges are to
make a careful investigation, and if the witness turns out to be a liar who has falsely accused his brother, 19 you must do to him as he
intended to do to his brother. You must purge
the evil from you. 20 Then everyone else will
hear and be afraid, and they will never again
do anything evil like this among you. 21 Do not
show pity: life for life, eye for eye, tooth for
tooth, hand for hand, and foot for foot.

RULES FOR WAR

20 "When you go out to war against your
enemies and see horses, chariots, and
an army larger than yours, do not be afraid of
them, for the LORD your God, who brought you
out of the land of Egypt, is with you. 2 When
you are about to engage in battle, the priest is
to come forward and address the army. 3 He
is to say to them: 'Listen, Israel: Today you
are about to engage in battle with your enemies. Do not be cowardly. Do not be afraid,
alarmed, or terrified because of them. 4 For
the LORD your God is the one who goes with
you to fight for you against your enemies to
give you victory.'
5 "The officers are to address the army, 'Has
any man built a new house and not dedicated
it? Let him leave and return home. Otherwise,
he may die in battle and another man dedicate
it. 6 Has any man planted a vineyard and not
begun to enjoy its fruit?[A] Let him leave and
return home. Otherwise he may die in battle
and another man enjoy its fruit.[B] 7 Has any
man become engaged to a woman and not
married her? Let him leave and return home.
Otherwise he may die in battle and another
man marry her.' 8 The officers will continue
to address the army and say, 'Is there any man
who is afraid or cowardly? Let him leave and
return home, so that his brothers won't lose
heart as he did.'[C] 9 When the officers have finished addressing the army, they will appoint
military commanders to lead it.
10 "When you approach a city to fight against
it, make an offer of peace. 11 If it accepts your
offer of peace and opens its gates to you, all
the people found in it will become forced laborers for you and serve you. 12 However, if
it does not make peace with you but wages
war against you, lay siege to it. 13 When the
LORD your God hands it over to you, strike
down all its males with the sword. 14 But you
may take the women, dependents, animals,

Eternal Perspective | *God's Strengthening*

PRIESTLY REMINDERS

"He is to say to them: 'Listen, Israel: Today you are about to engage in battle with your enemies. Do not be cowardly. Do not be afraid, alarmed, or terrified because of them. For the LORD your God is the one who goes with you to fight for you against your enemies to give you victory.'" Deuteronomy 20:3-4

Before the ancient Israelites engaged in battle, God stipulated that a priest should step forward and encourage the people. He would give them two reminders: God was with them, and God would give them success. These realities were a tonic against cowardice, fear, and terror.

The battles we fight may not be with armies, but daily we face a host of "enemies"—doubt, anxiety, the pull toward depression, and more. When we feel like running and hiding from life, we need the same kind of encouraging reminders our ancient brothers and sisters needed.

Ask God for a "priest"—someone who will come alongside and speak truth to you. Also, tell God you would like to be a "priest" in the life of another today. Then keep your eyes open for folks who look scared and discouraged!

For the next note on *Eternal Perspective*, see Joshua 1:9.

[A] **20:6** Lit *not put it to use* [B] **20:6** Lit *man put it to use* [C] **20:8** Lit *brothers' hearts won't melt like his own*

and whatever else is in the city — all its spoil — as plunder. You may enjoy the spoil of your enemies that the LORD your God has given you. 15 This is how you are to treat all the cities that are far away from you and are not among the cities of these nations. 16 However, you must not let any living thing survive among the cities of these people the LORD your God is giving you as an inheritance. 17 You must completely destroy them — the Hethite, Amorite, Canaanite, Perizzite, Hivite, and Jebusite — as the LORD your God has commanded you, 18 so that they won't teach you to do all the detestable acts they do for their gods, and you sin against the LORD your God.

19 "When you lay siege to a city for a long time, fighting against it in order to capture it, do not destroy its trees by putting an ax to them, because you can get food from them. Do not cut them down. Are trees of the field human, to come under siege by you? 20 But you may destroy the trees that you know do not produce food. You may cut them down to build siege works against the city that is waging war against you, until it falls.

UNSOLVED MURDERS

21 "If a murder victim is found lying in a field in the land the LORD your God is giving you to possess, and it is not known who killed him, 2 your elders and judges are to come out and measure the distance from the victim to the nearby cities. 3 The elders of the city nearest to the victim are to get a young cow that has not been yoked or used for work. 4 The elders of that city will bring the cow down to a continually flowing stream, to a place not tilled or sown, and they will break its neck there by the stream. 5 Then the priests, the sons of Levi, will come forward, for the LORD your God has chosen them to serve him and pronounce blessings in his name, and they are to give a ruling in[A] every dispute and case of assault. 6 All the elders of the city nearest to the victim will wash their hands by the stream over the young cow whose neck has been broken. 7 They will declare, 'Our hands did not shed this blood; our eyes did not see it. 8 LORD, wipe away the guilt of your people Israel whom you redeemed, and do not hold the shedding of innocent blood against them.' Then the responsibility for bloodshed will be wiped away from them. 9 You must purge from yourselves the guilt of shedding innocent blood, for you will be doing what is right in the LORD's sight.

FAIR TREATMENT OF CAPTURED WOMEN

10 "When you go to war against your enemies and the LORD your God hands them over to you and you take some of them prisoner, and 11 if you see a beautiful woman among the captives, desire her, and want to take her as your wife, 12 you are to bring her into your house. She is to shave her head, trim her nails, 13 remove the clothes she was wearing when she was taken prisoner, live in your house, and mourn for her father and mother a full month. After that, you may have sexual relations with her and be her husband, and she will be your wife. 14 Then if you are not satisfied with her, you are to let her go where she wants, but you must not sell her or treat her as merchandise,[B] because you have humiliated her.

THE RIGHT OF THE FIRSTBORN

15 "If a man has two wives, one loved and the other unloved, and both the loved and the unloved bear him sons, and if the unloved wife has the firstborn son, 16 when that man gives what he has to his sons as an inheritance, he is not to show favoritism to the son of the loved wife as his firstborn over the firstborn of the unloved wife. 17 He must acknowledge the firstborn, the son of the unloved wife, by giving him two shares[C,D] of his estate, for he is the firstfruits of his virility; he has the rights of the firstborn.

A REBELLIOUS SON

18 "If a man has a stubborn and rebellious son who does not obey his father or mother and doesn't listen to them even after they discipline him, 19 his father and mother are to take hold of him and bring him to the elders of his city, to the gate of his hometown. 20 They will say to the elders of his city, 'This son of ours is stubborn and rebellious; he doesn't obey us. He's a glutton and a drunkard.' 21 Then all the men of his city will stone him to death. You must purge the evil from you, and all Israel will hear and be afraid.

DISPLAY OF EXECUTED PEOPLE

22 "If anyone is found guilty of an offense deserving the death penalty and is executed,

[A] **21:5** Lit *and according to their mouth will be* [B] **21:14** Hb obscure [C] **21:17** Lit *him mouth of two*, or *two mouthfuls* [D] **21:17** Or *two-thirds*

and you hang his body on a tree, 23 you are
not to leave his corpse on the tree overnight
but are to bury him that day, for anyone hung
on a tree is under God's curse. You must not
defile the land the LORD your God is giving
you as an inheritance.

CARING FOR YOUR BROTHER'S PROPERTY

22 "If you see your brother Israelite's ox or
sheep straying, do not ignore it; make
sure you return it to your brother. 2 If your
brother does not live near you or you don't
know him, you are to bring the animal to your
home to remain with you until your brother
comes looking for it; then you can return it
to him. 3 Do the same for his donkey, his garment, or anything your brother has lost and
you have found. You must not ignore it. 4 If you
see your brother's donkey or ox fallen down
on the road, do not ignore it; help him lift it up.

PRESERVING NATURAL DISTINCTIONS

5 "A woman is not to wear male clothing, and
a man is not to put on a woman's garment, for
everyone who does these things is detestable
to the LORD your God.

6 "If you come across a bird's nest with
chicks or eggs, either in a tree or on the
ground along the road, and the mother is
sitting on the chicks or eggs, do not take the
mother along with the young. 7 You may take
the young for yourself, but be sure to let the
mother go free, so that you may prosper and
live long. 8 If you build a new house, make a
railing around your roof, so that you don't
bring bloodguilt on your house if someone
falls from it. 9 Do not plant your vineyard
with two types of seed; otherwise, the entire harvest, both the crop you plant and the
produce of the vineyard, will be defiled. 10 Do
not plow with an ox and a donkey together.
11 Do not wear clothes made of both wool and
linen. 12 Make tassels on the four corners of
the outer garment you wear.

VIOLATIONS OF PROPER SEXUAL CONDUCT

13 "If a man marries a woman, has sexual relations with her, and comes to hate her, 14 and
accuses her of shameful conduct, and gives
her a bad name, saying, 'I married this woman
and was intimate with her, but I didn't find any
evidence of her virginity,' 15 the young woman's
father and mother will take the evidence of her
virginity and bring it to the city elders at the
city gate. 16 The young woman's father will say
to the elders, 'I gave my daughter to this man
as a wife, but he hates her. 17 He has accused
her of shameful conduct, saying: "I didn't find
any evidence of your daughter's virginity," but
here is the evidence of my daughter's virginity.'
They will spread out the cloth before the city
elders. 18 Then the elders of that city will take
the man and punish him. 19 They will also fine
him a hundred silver shekels and give them
to the young woman's father, because that
man gave an Israelite virgin a bad name. She
will remain his wife; he cannot divorce her
as long as he lives. 20 But if this accusation is
true and no evidence of the young woman's
virginity is found, 21 they will bring the woman
to the door of her father's house, and the men
of her city will stone her to death. For she has
committed an outrage in Israel by being promiscuous while living in her father's house.
You must purge the evil from you.

22 "If a man is discovered having sexual
relations with another man's wife, both the
man who had sex with the woman and the
woman must die. You must purge the evil from
Israel. 23 If there is a young woman who is a
virgin engaged to a man, and another man
encounters her in the city and sleeps with
her, 24 take the two of them out to the gate
of that city and stone them to death — the
young woman because she did not cry out
in the city and the man because he has violated his neighbor's fiancée. You must purge
the evil from you. 25 But if the man encounters an engaged woman in the open country,
and he seizes and rapes her, only the man
who raped her must die. 26 Do nothing to the
young woman, because she is not guilty of
an offense deserving death. This case is just
like one in which a man attacks his neighbor
and murders him. 27 When he found her in
the field, the engaged woman cried out, but
there was no one to rescue her. 28 If a man
encounters a young woman, a virgin who is
not engaged, takes hold of her and rapes her,
and they are discovered, 29 the man who raped
her is to give the young woman's father fifty
silver shekels, and she will become his wife
because he violated her. He cannot divorce
her as long as he lives.

30 "A man is not to marry his father's wife;
he must not violate his father's marriage bed.[A]

[A] **22:30** Lit *not uncover the edge of his father's garment*; Ru 3:9; Ezk 16:8

EXCLUSION AND INCLUSION

23 "No man whose testicles have been crushed[A] or whose penis has been cut off may enter the LORD's assembly. 2 No one of illegitimate birth may enter the LORD's assembly; none of his descendants, even to the tenth generation, may enter the LORD's assembly. 3 No Ammonite or Moabite may enter the LORD's assembly; none of their descendants, even to the tenth generation, may ever enter the LORD's assembly. 4 This is because they did not meet you with food and water on the journey after you came out of Egypt, and because Balaam son of Beor from Pethor in Aram-naharaim was hired to curse you. 5 Yet the LORD your God would not listen to Balaam, but he turned the curse into a blessing for you because the LORD your God loves you. 6 Never pursue their welfare or prosperity as long as you live. 7 Do not despise an Edomite, because he is your brother. Do not despise an Egyptian, because you were a resident alien in his land. 8 The children born to them in the third generation may enter the LORD's assembly.

CLEANLINESS OF THE CAMP

9 "When you are encamped against your enemies, be careful to avoid anything offensive. 10 If there is a man among you who is unclean because of a bodily emission during the night, he must go outside the camp; he may not come anywhere inside the camp. 11 When evening approaches, he is to wash with water, and when the sun sets he may come inside the camp. 12 You are to have a place outside the camp and go there to relieve yourself. 13 You are to have a digging tool in your equipment; when you relieve yourself, dig a hole with it and cover up your excrement. 14 For the LORD your God walks throughout your camp to protect you and deliver your enemies to you; so your encampments must be holy. He must not see anything indecent among you or he will turn away from you.

FUGITIVE SLAVES

15 "Do not return a slave to his master when he has escaped from his master to you. 16 Let him live among you wherever he wants within your city gates. Do not mistreat him.

CULT PROSTITUTION FORBIDDEN

17 "No Israelite woman is to be a cult prostitute, and no Israelite man is to be a cult prostitute. 18 Do not bring a female prostitute's wages or a male prostitute's[B] earnings into the house of the LORD your God to fulfill any vow, because both are detestable to the LORD your God.

INTEREST ON LOANS

19 "Do not charge your brother interest on silver, food, or anything that can earn interest. 20 You may charge a foreigner interest, but you must not charge your brother Israelite interest, so that the LORD your God may bless you in everything you do[C] in the land you are entering to possess.

KEEPING VOWS

21 "If you make a vow to the LORD your God, do not be slow to keep it, because he will require it of you, and it will be counted against you as sin. 22 But if you refrain from making a vow, it will not be counted against you as sin. 23 Be careful to do whatever comes from your lips, because you have freely vowed what you promised[D] to the LORD your God.

NEIGHBOR'S CROPS

24 "When you enter your neighbor's vineyard, you may eat as many grapes as you want until you are full, but do not put any in your container. 25 When you enter your neighbor's standing grain, you may pluck heads of grain with your hand, but do not put a sickle to your neighbor's grain.

MARRIAGE AND DIVORCE LAWS

24 "If a man marries a woman, but she becomes displeasing to him[E] because he finds something indecent about her, he may write her a divorce certificate, hand it to her, and send her away from his house. 2 If after leaving his house she goes and becomes another man's wife, 3 and the second man hates her, writes her a divorce certificate, hands it to her, and sends her away from his house or if he dies, 4 the first husband who sent her away may not marry her again after she has been defiled, because that would be detestable to the LORD. You must not bring guilt on the land the LORD your God is giving you as an inheritance.

5 "When a man takes a bride, he must not go out with the army or be liable for any duty. He is free to stay at home for one year, so that he can bring joy to the wife he has married.

[A] **23:1** Lit *man bruised by crushing* [B] **23:18** Lit *a dog's* [C] **23:20** Lit *you put your hand to* [D] **23:23** Lit *promised with your mouth* [E] **24:1** Lit *she does not find favor in his eyes*

SAFEGUARDING LIFE

6 "Do not take a pair of grindstones or even the upper millstone as security for a debt, because that is like taking a life as security.

7 "If a man is discovered kidnapping one of his Israelite brothers, whether he treats him as a slave or sells him, the kidnapper must die. You must purge the evil from you.

8 "Be careful with a person who has a case of serious skin disease, following carefully everything the Levitical priests instruct you to do. Be careful to do as I have commanded them. 9 Remember what the LORD your God did to Miriam on the journey after you left Egypt.

CONSIDERATION FOR PEOPLE IN NEED

10 "When you make a loan of any kind to your neighbor, do not enter his house to collect what he offers as security. 11 Stand outside while the man you are making the loan to brings the security out to you. 12 If he is a poor man, do not sleep with the garment he has given as security. 13 Be sure to return it[A] to him at sunset. Then he will sleep in it and bless you, and this will be counted as righteousness to you before the LORD your God.

14 "Do not oppress a hired worker who is poor and needy, whether one of your Israelite brothers or one of the resident aliens in a town[B] in your land. 15 You are to pay him his wages each day before the sun sets, because he is poor and depends on them. Otherwise he will cry out to the LORD against you, and you will be held guilty.

16 "Fathers are not to be put to death for their children, and children are not to be put to death for their fathers; each person will be put to death for his own sin. 17 Do not deny justice to a resident alien or fatherless child, and do not take a widow's garment as security. 18 Remember that you were a slave in Egypt, and the LORD your God redeemed you from there. Therefore I am commanding you to do this.

19 "When you reap the harvest in your field, and you forget a sheaf in the field, do not go back to get it. It is to be left for the resident alien, the fatherless, and the widow, so that the LORD your God may bless you in all the work of your hands. 20 When you knock down the fruit from your olive tree, do not go over the branches again. What remains will be for the resident alien, the fatherless, and the widow. 21 When you gather the grapes of your vineyard, do not glean what is left. What remains will be for the resident alien, the fatherless, and the widow. 22 Remember that you were a slave in the land of Egypt. Therefore I am commanding you to do this.

FAIRNESS AND MERCY

25 "If there is a dispute between men, they are to go to court, and the judges will hear their case. They will clear the innocent and condemn the guilty. 2 If the guilty party deserves to be flogged, the judge will make him lie down and be flogged in his presence with the number of lashes appropriate for his crime. 3 He may be flogged with forty lashes, but no more. Otherwise, if he is flogged with more lashes than these, your brother will be degraded in your sight.

4 "Do not muzzle an ox while it treads out grain.

PRESERVING THE FAMILY LINE

5 "When brothers live on the same property[C] and one of them dies without a son, the wife of the dead man may not marry a stranger outside the family. Her brother-in-law is to take her as his wife, have sexual relations with her, and perform the duty of a brother-in-law for her. 6 The first son she bears will carry on the name of the dead brother, so his name will not be blotted out from Israel. 7 But if the man doesn't want to marry his sister-in-law, she is to go to the elders at the city gate and say, 'My brother-in-law refuses to preserve his brother's name in Israel. He isn't willing to perform the duty of a brother-in-law for me.' 8 The elders of his city will summon him and speak with him. If he persists and says, 'I don't want to marry her,' 9 then his sister-in-law will go up to him in the sight of the elders, remove his sandal from his foot, and spit in his face. Then she will declare, 'This is what is done to a man who will not build up his brother's house.' 10 And his family name in Israel will be 'The house of the man whose sandal was removed.'

11 "If two men are fighting with each other, and the wife of one steps in to rescue her husband from the one striking him, and she puts out her hand and grabs his genitals, 12 you are to cut off her hand. Do not show pity.

[A] **24:13** Lit *return what he has given as security* [B] **24:14** Lit *within the city gates* [C] **25:5** Lit *live together*

HONEST WEIGHTS AND MEASURES

13 "Do not have differing weights[A] in your bag,
one heavy and one light. 14 Do not have differing dry measures in your house, a larger and
a smaller. 15 You must have a full and honest
weight, a full and honest dry measure, so that
you may live long in the land the LORD your
God is giving you. 16 For everyone who does
such things and acts unfairly is detestable to
the LORD your God.

REVENGE ON THE AMALEKITES

17 "Remember what the Amalekites did to you
on the journey after you left Egypt. 18 They
met you along the way and attacked all your
stragglers from behind when you were tired
and weary. They did not fear God. 19 When the
LORD your God gives you rest from all the enemies around you in the land the LORD your
God is giving you to possess as an inheritance,
blot out the memory of Amalek under heaven.
Do not forget.

GIVING THE FIRSTFRUITS

26 "When you enter the land the LORD your
God is giving you as an inheritance, and
you take possession of it and live in it, 2 take
some of the first of all the land's produce that
you harvest from the land the LORD your God
is giving you and put it in a basket. Then go to
the place where the LORD your God chooses to
have his name dwell. 3 When you come before
the priest who is serving at that time, say to
him, 'Today I declare to the LORD your[B] God
that I have entered the land the LORD swore
to our fathers to give us.'
4 "Then the priest will take the basket from
you and place it before the altar of the LORD
your God. 5 You are to respond by saying in
the presence of the LORD your God:

> My father was a wandering Aramean. He
> went down to Egypt with a few people
> and resided there as an alien. There he
> became a great, powerful, and populous
> nation. 6 But the Egyptians mistreated and
> oppressed us, and forced us to do hard
> labor. 7 So we called out to the LORD, the
> God of our fathers, and the LORD heard
> our cry and saw our misery, hardship, and
> oppression. 8 Then the LORD brought us
> out of Egypt with a strong hand and an
> outstretched arm, with terrifying power,
> and with signs and wonders. 9 He led us
> to this place and gave us this land, a land
> flowing with milk and honey. 10 I have
> now brought the first of the land's pro-
> duce that you, LORD, have given me.

You will then place the container before the
LORD your God and bow down to him. 11 You,
the Levites, and the resident aliens among
you will rejoice in all the good things the LORD
your God has given you and your household.

THE TENTH IN THE THIRD YEAR

12 "When you have finished paying all the tenth
of your produce in the third year, the year of
the tenth, you are to give it to the Levites, resident aliens, fatherless children and widows,
so that they may eat in your towns and be
satisfied. 13 Then you will say in the presence
of the LORD your God:

> I have taken the consecrated portion
> out of my house; I have also given it to
> the Levites, resident aliens, fatherless
> children, and widows, according to all
> the commands you gave me. I have not
> violated or forgotten your commands. 14 I
> have not eaten any of it while in mourn-
> ing, or removed any of it while unclean,
> or offered any of it for the dead. I have
> obeyed the LORD my God; I have done all
> you commanded me. 15 Look down from
> your holy dwelling, from heaven, and
> bless your people Israel and the land you
> have given us as you swore to our fathers,
> a land flowing with milk and honey.

COVENANT SUMMARY

16 "The LORD your God is commanding you this
day to follow these statutes and ordinances.
Follow them carefully with all your heart and
all your soul. 17 Today you have affirmed that
the LORD is your God and that you will walk
in his ways, keep his statutes, commands, and
ordinances, and obey him. 18 And today the
LORD has affirmed that you are his own possession as he promised you, that you are to
keep all his commands, 19 that he will elevate
you to praise, fame, and glory above all the nations he has made, and that you will be a holy
people to the LORD your God as he promised."

THE LAW WRITTEN ON STONES

27 Moses and the elders of Israel commanded the people, "Keep every command I am
giving you today. 2 When you cross the Jordan

[A] 25:13 Lit *have a stone and a stone* [B] 26:3 LXX reads *my*

into the land the LORD your God is giving you,
set up large stones and cover them with plaster.
3 Write all the words of this law on the stones
after you cross to enter the land the LORD your
God is giving you, a land flowing with milk and
honey, as the LORD, the God of your fathers,
has promised you. 4 When you have crossed
the Jordan, you are to set up these stones on
Mount Ebal, as I am commanding you today,
and you are to cover them with plaster. 5 Build
an altar of stones there to the LORD your God
— do not use any iron tool on them. 6 Use uncut
stones to build the altar of the LORD your God
and offer burnt offerings to the LORD your God
on it. 7 There you are to sacrifice fellowship offerings, eat, and rejoice in the presence of the
LORD your God. 8 Write clearly all the words of
this law on the plastered stones."

THE COVENANT CURSES

9 Moses and the Levitical priests spoke to all
Israel, "Be silent, Israel, and listen! This day
you have become the people of the LORD your
God. 10 Obey the LORD your God and follow his
commands and statutes I am giving you today."
11 On that day Moses commanded the people,
12 "When you have crossed the Jordan, these
tribes will stand on Mount Gerizim to bless the
people: Simeon, Levi, Judah, Issachar, Joseph,
and Benjamin. 13 And these tribes will stand
on Mount Ebal to deliver the curse: Reuben,
Gad, Asher, Zebulun, Dan, and Naphtali. 14 The
Levites will proclaim in a loud voice to every
Israelite:

15 'The person who makes a carved idol
or cast image, which is detestable to the
LORD, the work of a craftsman, and sets it
up in secret is cursed.'
And all the people will reply, 'Amen!'
16 'The one who dishonors his father or
mother is cursed.'
And all the people will say, 'Amen!'
17 'The one who moves his neighbor's
boundary marker is cursed.'
And all the people will say, 'Amen!'
18 'The one who leads a blind person
astray on the road is cursed.'
And all the people will say, 'Amen!'
19 'The one who denies justice to a
resident alien, a fatherless child, or a
widow is cursed.'
And all the people will say, 'Amen!'
20 'The one who sleeps with his father's
wife is cursed, for he has violated his
father's marriage bed.'[A]
And all the people will say, 'Amen!'
21 'The one who has sexual intercourse
with any animal is cursed.'
And all the people will say, 'Amen!'
22 'The one who sleeps with his sister,
whether his father's daughter or his
mother's daughter is cursed.'
And all the people will say, 'Amen!'
23 'The one who sleeps with his
mother-in-law is cursed.'
And all the people will say, 'Amen!'
24 'The one who secretly kills his neighbor
is cursed.'
And all the people will say, 'Amen!'
25 'The one who accepts a bribe to kill an
innocent person is cursed.'
And all the people will say, 'Amen!'
26 'Anyone who does not put the words of
this law into practice is cursed.'
And all the people will say, 'Amen!'

BLESSINGS FOR OBEDIENCE

28 "Now if you faithfully obey the LORD
your God and are careful to follow
all his commands I am giving you today, the
LORD your God will put you far above all the
nations of the earth. 2 All these blessings will
come and overtake you, because you obey the
LORD your God:

3 You will be blessed in the city
and blessed in the country.
4 Your offspring[B] will be blessed,
and your land's produce,
and the offspring of your livestock,
including the young of your herds
and the newborn of your flocks.
5 Your basket and kneading bowl
will be blessed.
6 You will be blessed when you come in
and blessed when you go out.

7 "The LORD will cause the enemies who rise
up against you to be defeated before you. They
will march out against you from one direction
but flee from you in seven directions. 8 The
LORD will grant you a blessing on your barns
and on everything you do;[C] he will bless you in
the land the LORD your God is giving you. 9 The
LORD will establish you as his holy people, as
he swore to you, if you obey the commands of
the LORD your God and walk in his ways. 10 Then

[A] **27:20** Lit *has uncovered the edge of his father's garment*; Ru 3:9; Ezk 16:8 [B] **28:4** Lit *The fruit of your womb*, also in v. 18 [C] **28:8** Lit *you put your hand to*, also in v. 20

all the peoples of the earth will see that you
bear the LORD's name, and they will stand in
awe of you. 11 The LORD will make you prosper
abundantly with offspring,[A] the offspring of
your livestock, and your land's produce in the
land the LORD swore to your fathers to give
you. 12 The LORD will open for you his abundant
storehouse, the sky, to give your land rain in its
season and to bless all the work of your hands.
You will lend to many nations, but you will not
borrow. 13 The LORD will make you the head
and not the tail; you will only move upward
and never downward if you listen to the LORD
your God's commands I am giving you today
and are careful to follow them. 14 Do not turn
aside to the right or the left from all the things
I am commanding you today, and do not follow
other gods to worship them.

CURSES FOR DISOBEDIENCE

15 "But if you do not obey the LORD your God
by carefully following all his commands and
statutes I am giving you today, all these curses
will come and overtake you:

16 You will be cursed in the city
and cursed in the country.
17 Your basket and kneading bowl
will be cursed.
18 Your offspring will be cursed,
and your land's produce,
the young of your herds,
and the newborn of your flocks.
19 You will be cursed when you come in
and cursed when you go out.

20 The LORD will send against you curses,
confusion, and rebuke in everything you do
until you are destroyed and quickly perish,
because of the wickedness of your actions in
abandoning me. 21 The LORD will make pestilence cling to you until he has exterminated
you from the land you are entering to possess. 22 The LORD will afflict you with wasting
disease, fever, inflammation, burning heat,
drought,[B] blight, and mildew; these will pursue you until you perish. 23 The sky above you
will be bronze, and the earth beneath you
iron. 24 The LORD will turn the rain of your
land into falling[C] dust; it will descend on you
from the sky until you are destroyed. 25 The
LORD will cause you to be defeated before
your enemies. You will march out against
them from one direction but flee from them
in seven directions. You will be an object
of horror to all the kingdoms of the earth.
26 Your corpses will be food for all the birds
of the sky and the wild animals of the earth,
with no one to scare them away.

27 "The LORD will afflict you with the boils of
Egypt, tumors, a festering rash, and scabies,
from which you cannot be cured. 28 The LORD
will afflict you with madness, blindness, and
mental confusion, 29 so that at noon you will
grope as a blind person gropes in the dark. You
will not be successful in anything you do. You
will only be oppressed and robbed continually,
and no one will help you. 30 You will become
engaged to a woman, but another man will
rape her. You will build a house but not live
in it. You will plant a vineyard but not enjoy
its fruit. 31 Your ox will be slaughtered before
your eyes, but you will not eat any of it. Your
donkey will be taken away from you and not
returned to you. Your flock will be given to
your enemies, and no one will help you. 32 Your
sons and daughters will be given to another
people, while your eyes grow weary looking
for them every day. But you will be powerless
to do anything.[D] 33 A people you don't know will
eat your land's produce and everything you
have labored for. You will only be oppressed
and crushed continually. 34 You will be driven
mad by what you see. 35 The LORD will afflict
you with painful and incurable boils on your
knees and thighs — from the sole of your foot
to the top of your head.

36 "The LORD will bring you and your king
that you have appointed to a nation neither you
nor your fathers have known, and there you
will worship other gods, of wood and stone.
37 You will become an object of horror, scorn,
and ridicule among all the peoples where the
LORD will drive you.

38 "You will sow much seed in the field but
harvest little, because locusts will devour it.
39 You will plant and cultivate vineyards but
not drink the wine or gather the grapes, because worms will eat them. 40 You will have
olive trees throughout your territory but not
moisten your skin with oil, because your olives will drop off. 41 You will father sons and
daughters, but they will not remain yours,
because they will be taken prisoner. 42 Buzzing
insects will take possession of all your trees
and your land's produce. 43 The resident alien
among you will rise higher and higher above
you, while you sink lower and lower. 44 He will

[A] **28:11** Lit *abundantly in the fruit of your womb* [B] **28:22** Or *sword* [C] **28:24** Lit *powder and* [D] **28:32** Lit *day, and not for power your hand*

lend to you, but you won't lend to him. He will be the head, and you will be the tail.

45 "All these curses will come, pursue, and overtake you until you are destroyed, since you did not obey the LORD your God and keep the commands and statutes he gave you. 46 These curses will be a sign and a wonder against you and your descendants forever. 47 Because you didn't serve the LORD your God with joy and a cheerful heart, even though you had an abundance of everything, 48 you will serve your enemies the LORD will send against you, in famine, thirst, nakedness, and a lack of everything. He will place an iron yoke on your neck until he has destroyed you. 49 The LORD will bring a nation from far away, from the ends of the earth, to swoop down on you like an eagle, a nation whose language you won't understand, 50 a ruthless nation,[A] showing no respect for the old and not sparing the young. 51 They will eat the offspring of your livestock and your land's produce until you are destroyed. They will leave you no grain, new wine, fresh oil, young of your herds, or newborn of your flocks until they cause you to perish. 52 They will besiege you within all your city gates until your high and fortified walls, that you trust in, come down throughout your land. They will besiege you within all your city gates throughout the land the LORD your God has given you.

53 "You will eat your offspring,[B] the flesh of your sons and daughters the LORD your God has given you during the siege and hardship your enemy imposes on you. 54 The most sensitive and refined man among you will look grudgingly[C] at his brother, the wife he embraces,[D] and the rest of his children, 55 refusing to share with any of them his children's flesh that he will eat because he has nothing left during the siege and hardship your enemy imposes on you in all your towns. 56 The most sensitive and refined woman among you, who would not venture to set the sole of her foot on the ground because of her refinement and sensitivity, will begrudge the husband she embraces, her son, and her daughter, 57 the afterbirth that comes out from between her legs and the children she bears, because she will secretly eat them for lack of anything else during the siege and hardship your enemy imposes on you within your city gates.

58 "If you are not careful to obey all the words of this law, which are written in this scroll, by fearing this glorious and awe-inspiring name — the LORD, your God — 59 he will bring wondrous plagues on you and your descendants, severe and lasting plagues, and terrible and chronic sicknesses. 60 He will afflict you again with all the diseases of Egypt, which you dreaded, and they will cling to you. 61 The LORD will also afflict you with every sickness and plague not recorded in the book of this law, until you are destroyed. 62 Though you were as numerous as the stars of the sky, you will be left with only a few people, because you did not obey the LORD your God. 63 Just as the LORD was glad to cause you to prosper and to multiply you, so he will also be glad to cause you to perish and to destroy you. You will be ripped out of the land you are entering to possess. 64 Then the LORD will scatter you among all peoples from one end of the earth to the other, and there you will worship other gods, of wood and stone, which neither you nor your fathers have known. 65 You will find no peace among those nations, and there will be no resting place for the sole of your foot. There the LORD will give you a trembling heart, failing eyes, and a despondent spirit. 66 Your life will hang in doubt before you. You will be in dread night and day, never certain of survival. 67 In the morning you will say, 'If only it were evening!' and in the evening you will say, 'If only it were morning!' — because of the dread you will have in your heart and because of what you will see. 68 The LORD will take you back in ships to Egypt by a route that I said you would never see again. There you will sell yourselves to your enemies as male and female slaves, but no one will buy you."

RENEWING THE COVENANT

29 These are the words of the covenant the LORD commanded Moses to make with the Israelites in the land of Moab, in addition to the covenant he had made with them at Horeb. 2 Moses summoned all Israel and said to them, "You have seen with your own eyes everything the LORD did in Egypt to Pharaoh, to all his officials, and to his entire land. 3 You saw with your own eyes the great trials and those great signs and wonders. 4 Yet to this day the LORD has not given you a mind to understand, eyes to see, or ears to hear. 5 I led you forty years in the wilderness; your

[A] 28:50 Lit *a nation strong of face* [B] 28:53 Lit *eat the fruit of your womb* [C] 28:54 Lit *you his eye will be evil* [D] 28:54 Lit *wife of his bosom*

clothes and the sandals on your feet did not
wear out; 6 you did not eat food or drink wine
or beer — so that you might know that I am
the LORD your God. 7 When you reached this
place, King Sihon of Heshbon and King Og
of Bashan came out against us in battle, but
we defeated them. 8 We took their land and
gave it as an inheritance to the Reubenites,
the Gadites, and half the tribe of Manasseh.
9 Therefore, observe the words of this covenant
and follow them, so that you will succeed in
everything you do.

10 "All of you are standing today before the
LORD your God — your leaders, tribes, elders,
officials, all the men of Israel, 11 your dependents, your wives, and the resident aliens in
your camps who cut your wood and draw your
water — 12 so that you may enter into the covenant of the LORD your God, which he is making
with you today, so that you may enter into his
oath 13 and so that he may establish you today
as his people and he may be your God as he
promised you and as he swore to your fathers
Abraham, Isaac, and Jacob. 14 I am making this
covenant and this oath not only with you, 15 but
also with those who are standing here with us
today in the presence of the LORD our God and
with those who are not here today.

ABANDONING THE COVENANT

16 "Indeed, you know how we lived in the land
of Egypt and passed through the nations where
you traveled. 17 You saw their abhorrent images and idols made of wood, stone, silver, and
gold, which were among them. 18 Be sure there
is no man, woman, clan, or tribe among you
today whose heart turns away from the LORD
our God to go and worship the gods of those
nations. Be sure there is no root among you
bearing poisonous and bitter fruit. 19 When
someone hears the words of this oath, he may
consider himself exempt,[A] thinking, 'I will have
peace even though I follow my own stubborn
heart.' This will lead to the destruction of the
well-watered land as well as the dry land. 20 The
LORD will not be willing to forgive him. Instead,
his anger and jealousy will burn against that
person, and every curse written in this scroll
will descend on him. The LORD will blot out his
name under heaven, 21 and single him out for
harm from all the tribes of Israel, according
to all the curses of the covenant written in
this book of the law.

22 "Future generations of your children who
follow you and the foreigner who comes from
a distant country will see the plagues of that
land and the sicknesses the LORD has inflicted
on it. 23 All its soil will be a burning waste of
sulfur and salt, unsown, producing nothing,
with no plant growing on it, just like the fall
of Sodom and Gomorrah, Admah and Zeboiim, which the LORD demolished in his fierce
anger. 24 All the nations will ask, 'Why has the
LORD done this to this land? Why this intense
outburst of anger?' 25 Then people will answer,
'It is because they abandoned the covenant of
the LORD, the God of their fathers, which he
had made with them when he brought them
out of the land of Egypt. 26 They began to serve
other gods, bowing in worship to gods they
had not known — gods that the LORD had not
permitted them to worship. 27 Therefore the
LORD's anger burned against this land, and he
brought every curse written in this book on it.
28 The LORD uprooted them from their land in
his anger, rage, and intense wrath, and threw
them into another land where they are today.'
29 The hidden things belong to the LORD our
God, but the revealed things belong to us and
our children forever, so that we may follow
all the words of this law.

RETURNING TO THE LORD

30 "When all these things happen to you
— the blessings and curses I have set
before you — and you come to your senses
while you are in all the nations where the
LORD your God has driven you, 2 and you and
your children return to the LORD your God and
obey him with all your heart and all your soul
by doing[B] everything I am commanding you
today, 3 then he will restore your fortunes,[C]
have compassion on you, and gather you again
from all the peoples where the LORD your God
has scattered you. 4 Even if your exiles are at
the farthest horizon,[D] he will gather you and
bring you back from there. 5 The LORD your
God will bring you into the land your fathers
possessed, and you will take possession of
it. He will cause you to prosper and multiply
you more than he did your fathers. 6 The LORD
your God will circumcise your heart and the
hearts of your descendants, and you will love
him with all your heart and all your soul so
that you will live. 7 The LORD your God will put
all these curses on your enemies who hate

[A] **29:19** Lit *may bless himself in his heart* [B] **30:2** Lit *soul according to* [C] **30:3** Or *will end your captivity* [D] **30:4** Lit *skies*

and persecute you. 8 Then you will again obey
him and follow all his commands I am commanding you today. 9 The LORD your God will
make you prosper abundantly in all the work
of your hands, your offspring,[A] the offspring
of your livestock, and the produce of your
land. Indeed, the LORD will again delight in
your prosperity, as he delighted in that of your
fathers, 10 when you obey the LORD your God
by keeping his commands and statutes that
are written in this book of the law and return
to him with all your heart and all your soul.

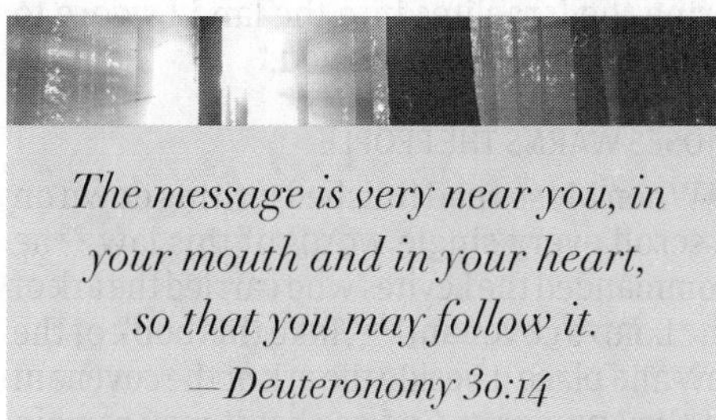
The message is very near you, in
your mouth and in your heart,
so that you may follow it.
—Deuteronomy 30:14

CHOOSE LIFE

11 "This command that I give you today is certainly not too difficult or beyond your reach.
12 It is not in heaven so that you have to ask,
'Who will go up to heaven, get it for us, and
proclaim it to us so that we may follow it?'
13 And it is not across the sea so that you have
to ask, 'Who will cross the sea, get it for us,
and proclaim it to us so that we may follow
it?' 14 But the message is very near you, in
your mouth and in your heart, so that you
may follow it. 15 See, today I have set before
you life and prosperity, death and adversity.
16 For[B] I am commanding you today to love
the LORD your God, to walk in his ways, and
to keep his commands, statutes, and ordinances, so that you may live[C] and multiply,
and the LORD your God may bless you in the
land you are entering to possess. 17 But if your
heart turns away and you do not listen and
you are led astray to bow in worship to other
gods and serve them, 18 I tell you today that
you will certainly perish and will not prolong your days in the land you are entering
to possess across the Jordan. 19 I call heaven
and earth as witnesses against you today that
I have set before you life and death, blessing
and curse. Choose life so that you and your
descendants may live, 20 love the LORD your
God, obey him, and remain faithful[D] to him.
For he is your life, and he will prolong your
days as you live in the land the LORD swore
to give to your fathers Abraham, Isaac, and
Jacob."

JOSHUA TAKES MOSES'S PLACE

31 Then Moses continued to speak these[E]
words to all Israel, 2 saying, "I am now
120 years old; I can no longer act as your leader.[F] The LORD has told me, 'You will not cross
the Jordan.' 3 The LORD your God is the one who
will cross ahead of you. He will destroy these
nations before you, and you will drive them
out. Joshua is the one who will cross ahead
of you, as the LORD has said. 4 The LORD will
deal with them as he did Sihon and Og, the
kings of the Amorites, and their land when
he destroyed them. 5 The LORD will deliver
them over to you, and you must do to them
exactly as I have commanded you. 6 Be strong
and courageous; don't be terrified or afraid
of them. For the LORD your God is the one
who will go with you; he will not leave you
or abandon you."

7 Moses then summoned Joshua and said to
him in the sight of all Israel, "Be strong and
courageous, for you will go with[G] this people
into the land the LORD swore to give to their
fathers. You will enable them to take possession of it. 8 The LORD is the one who will go
before you. He will be with you; he will not
leave you or abandon you. Do not be afraid
or discouraged."

9 Moses wrote down this law and gave it to
the priests, the sons of Levi, who carried the ark
of the LORD's covenant, and to all the elders of
Israel. 10 Moses commanded them, "At the end
of every seven years, at the appointed time in
the year of debt cancellation, during the Festival of Shelters, 11 when all Israel assembles[H]
in the presence of the LORD your God at the
place he chooses, you are to read this law aloud
before all Israel. 12 Gather the people — men,
women, dependents, and the resident aliens
within your city gates — so that they may
listen and learn to fear the LORD your God
and be careful to follow all the words of this
law. 13 Then their children who do not know
the law will listen and learn to fear the LORD
your God as long as you live in the land you
are crossing the Jordan to possess."

[A] **30:9** Lit *hands in the fruit of your womb* [B] **30:16** LXX reads *If you obey the commands of the LORD your God that* [C] **30:16** LXX reads *ordinances, then you will live* [D] **30:20** Lit *and hold on* [E] **31:1** Some Hb mss, DSS, LXX, Syr, Vg read *all these* [F] **31:2** Lit *no longer go out or come in* [G] **31:7** Some Hb mss, Sam, Syr, Vg read *you will bring* [H] **31:11** Lit *comes to appear*

14 The LORD said to Moses, "The time of your
death is now approaching. Call Joshua and
present yourselves at the tent of meeting so
that I may commission him." When Moses
and Joshua went and presented themselves
at the tent of meeting, 15 the LORD appeared
at the tent in a pillar of cloud, and the cloud
stood at the entrance to the tent.

16 The LORD said to Moses, "You are about to
rest with your fathers, and these people will
soon prostitute themselves with the foreign
gods of the land they are entering. They will
abandon me and break the covenant I have
made with them. 17 My anger will burn against
them on that day; I will abandon them and
hide my face from them so that they will become easy prey.[A] Many troubles and afflictions
will come to them. On that day they will say,
'Haven't these troubles come to us because
our God is no longer with us?' 18 I will certainly
hide my face on that day because of all the
evil they have done by turning to other gods.
19 Therefore write down this song for yourselves and teach it to the Israelites; have them
sing it,[B] so that this song may be a witness
for me against the Israelites. 20 When I bring
them into the land I swore to give their fathers, a land flowing with milk and honey, they
will eat their fill and prosper.[C] They will turn
to other gods and worship them, despising
me and breaking my covenant. 21 And when
many troubles and afflictions come to them,
this song will testify against them, because[D]
their descendants will not have forgotten it.
For I know what they are prone to do,[E] even
before I bring them into the land I swore to
give them." 22 So Moses wrote down this song
on that day and taught it to the Israelites.

23 The LORD commissioned Joshua son of
Nun, "Be strong and courageous, for you will
bring the Israelites into the land I swore to
them, and I will be with you."

MOSES WARNS THE PEOPLE

24 When Moses had finished writing down on
a scroll every single word[F] of this law, 25 he
commanded the Levites who carried the ark of
the LORD's covenant, 26 "Take this book of the
law and place it beside the ark of the covenant
of the LORD your God so that it may remain
there as a witness against you. 27 For I know
how rebellious and stiff-necked you are. If you
are rebelling against the LORD now, while I am
still alive, how much more will you rebel after
I am dead! 28 Assemble all your tribal elders
and officers before me so that I may speak

Other-centeredness | *Encouraging*

ENCOURAGEMENT

"Be strong and courageous; don't be terrified or afraid of them. For the LORD your God is the one who will go with you; he will not leave you or abandon you." Deuteronomy 31:6

As the time drew near for the Jews to enter the promised land, the tension in the air must have been palpable. They were losing their leader and facing fierce enemies. Perhaps this explains why Moses made a final effort to encourage the people staring at him with knocking knees.

Our English word *encourage* comes from the Old French word *corage*, which means "heart" or "inner strength" and the prefix *en*, which means "to put in." Encouragement, then, is literally, the act of putting your heart into another.

Encouragement can take a thousand forms: verbal reminders, written notes, thoughtful texts, stirring stories, personal testimonies, undeniable facts, real-life examples. All these things reassure and restore confidence. Coming alongside another without saying a word can revive the deflated heart of an overwhelmed soul. How so? It lets the person know that he is not alone.

Think of someone you could encourage today. How specifically will you go about it?

For the next note on *Other-centeredness*, see Joshua 9:14.

[A] **31:17** Lit *will be for devouring* [B] **31:19** Lit *Israelites; put it in their mouths* [C] **31:20** Lit *be fat* [D] **31:21** Lit *because the mouths of* [E] **31:21** Or *know the plans they are devising* [F] **31:24** Lit *scroll the words to their completion*

these words directly to them and call heaven
and earth as witnesses against them. 29 For I
know that after my death you will become
completely corrupt and turn from the path I
have commanded you. Disaster will come to
you in the future, because you will do what
is evil in the LORD's sight, angering him with
what your hands have made." 30 Then Moses
recited aloud every single word[A] of this song
to the entire assembly of Israel:

SONG OF MOSES

32 Pay attention, heavens, and I
will speak;
listen, earth, to the words
from my mouth.
2 Let my teaching fall like rain
and my word settle like dew,
like gentle rain on new grass
and showers on tender plants.
3 For I will proclaim the LORD's name.
Declare the greatness of our God!
4 The Rock — his work is perfect;
all his ways are just.
A faithful God, without bias,
he is righteous and true.

For I will proclaim the LORD's name. Declare the greatness of our God! The Rock—his work is perfect; all his ways are just. A faithful God, without bias, he is righteous and true.
—Deuteronomy 32:3-4

5 His people have acted corruptly
toward him;
this is their defect[B] — they are not
his children
but a devious and crooked generation.
6 Is this how you repay the LORD,
you foolish and senseless people?
Isn't he your Father and Creator?[C]
Didn't he make you and sustain you?
7 Remember the days of old;
consider the years of past generations.
Ask your father, and he will tell you,
your elders, and they will teach you.
8 When the Most High gave the nations
their inheritance[D]
and divided the human race,
he set the boundaries of the peoples
according to the number of the people
of Israel.[E]
9 But the LORD's portion is his people,
Jacob, his own inheritance.

10 He found him in a desolate land,
in a barren, howling wilderness;
he surrounded him, cared for him,
and protected him as the pupil
of his eye.
11 He watches over[F] his nest like an eagle
and hovers over his young;
he spreads his wings, catches him,
and carries him on his feathers.
12 The LORD alone led him,
with no help from a foreign god.[G]
13 He made him ride on the heights
of the land
and eat the produce of the field.
He nourished him with honey
from the rock
and oil from flinty rock,
14 curds from the herd and milk
from the flock,
with the fat of lambs,
rams from Bashan, and goats,
with the choicest grains of wheat;
you drank wine from the finest grapes.[H]

15 Then[I] Jeshurun[J] became fat
and rebelled —
you became fat, bloated, and gorged.
He abandoned the God who made him
and scorned the Rock of his salvation.
16 They provoked his jealousy
with different gods;
they enraged him
with detestable practices.
17 They sacrificed to demons, not God,
to gods they had not known,
new gods that had just arrived,
which your fathers did not fear.
18 You ignored the Rock
who gave you birth;

[A] 31:30 Lit *recited the words to their completion* [B] 32:5 Or *him; through their fault*; Hb obscure [C] 32:6 Or *Possessor* [D] 32:8 Or *Most High divided the nations* [E] 32:8 One DSS reads *number of the sons of God*; LXX reads *number of the angels of God* [F] 32:11 Or *He stirs up* [G] 32:12 Lit *him, and no foreign god with him* [H] 32:14 Lit *drank the blood of grapes, fermenting wine* [I] 32:15 DSS, Sam, LXX add *Jacob ate his fill;* [J] 32:15 = Upright One, referring to Israel

you forgot the God who gave birth
to you.
19 When the LORD saw this,
he despised them,
angered by his sons and daughters.
20 He said: "I will hide my face from them;
I will see what will become of them,
for they are a perverse generation —
unfaithful children.
21 They have provoked my jealousy
with what is not a god;[A]
they have enraged me
with their worthless idols.
So I will provoke their jealousy
with what is not a people;[B]
I will enrage them
with a foolish nation.
22 For fire has been kindled because of
my anger
and burns to the depths of Sheol;
it devours the land and its produce,
and scorches the foundations
of the mountains.

23 "I will pile disasters on them;
I will use up my arrows against them.
24 They will be weak from hunger,
ravaged by pestilence
and bitter plague;
I will unleash on them wild beasts
with fangs,
as well as venomous snakes that slither
in the dust.
25 Outside, the sword will take
their children,
and inside, there will be terror;
the young man and the young woman
will be killed,
the infant and the gray-haired man.

26 "I would have said: I will cut them
to pieces[C]
and blot out the memory of them
from mankind,
27 if I had not feared provocation
from the enemy,
or feared that these foes
might misunderstand
and say: 'Our own hand
has prevailed;
it wasn't the LORD who did all this.' "
28 Israel is a nation lacking sense
with no understanding at all.[D]
29 If only they were wise,
they would comprehend this;
they would understand their fate.
30 How could one pursue a thousand,
or two put ten thousand to flight,
unless their Rock had sold them,
unless the LORD had given them up?
31 But their "rock" is not like our Rock,
as even our enemies concede.
32 For their vine is from the vine
of Sodom
and from the fields of Gomorrah.
Their grapes are poisonous;
their clusters are bitter.
33 Their wine is serpents' venom,
the deadly poison of cobras.

34 "Is it not stored up with me,
sealed up in my vaults?
35 Vengeance[E] belongs to me; I will repay.[F]
In time their foot will slip,
for their day of disaster is near,
and their doom is coming quickly."
36 The LORD will indeed vindicate
his people
and have compassion on his servants
when he sees that their strength is gone
and no one is left — slave or free.[G]
37 He will say: "Where are their gods,
the 'rock' they found refuge in?
38 Who ate the fat of their sacrifices
and drank the wine
of their drink offerings?
Let them rise up and help you;
let it[H] be a shelter for you.
39 See now that I alone am he;
there is no God but me.
I bring death and I give life;
I wound and I heal.
No one can rescue anyone
from my power.
40 I raise my hand to heaven and declare:
As surely as I live forever,
41 when I sharpen my flashing sword,
and my hand takes hold of judgment,
I will take vengeance
on my adversaries
and repay those who hate me.
42 I will make my arrows drunk
with blood

[A] 32:21 Lit *with no gods* [B] 32:21 Lit *with no people* [C] 32:26 LXX reads *will scatter them* [D] 32:28 Lit *understanding in them* [E] 32:35 Sam, LXX read *On a day of vengeance* [F] 32:35 LXX, Tg, Vg read *me; and recompense I will recompense* [G] 32:36 Or *left—even the weak and impaired*; Hb obscure [H] 32:38 Sam, LXX, Tg, Vg read *them*

while my sword devours flesh —
the blood of the slain and the captives,
the heads of the enemy leaders."[A]

43 Rejoice, you nations,
concerning his people,[B]
for he will avenge the blood
of his servants.[C]
He will take vengeance
on his adversaries;[D]
he will purify his land and his people.[E]

44 Moses came with Joshua[F] son of Nun and
recited all the words of this song in the presence of the people. 45 After Moses finished
reciting all these words to all Israel, 46 he said
to them, "Take to heart all these words I am
giving as a warning to you today, so that you
may command your children to follow all the
words of this law carefully. 47 For they are not
meaningless words to you but they are your
life, and by them you will live long in the land
you are crossing the Jordan to possess."

Take to heart all these words I am giving as a warning to you today, so that you may command your children to follow all the words of this law carefully. For they are not meaningless words to you but they are your life.
—Deuteronomy 32:46-47

MOSES'S IMPENDING DEATH

48 On that same day the LORD spoke to Moses,
49 "Go up Mount Nebo in the Abarim range in
the land of Moab, across from Jericho, and
view the land of Canaan I am giving the Israelites as a possession. 50 Then you will die on
the mountain that you go up, and you will be
gathered to your people, just as your brother
Aaron died on Mount Hor and was gathered
to his people. 51 For both of you broke faith
with me among the Israelites at the Waters of
Meribath-kadesh in the Wilderness of Zin by
failing to treat me as holy in their presence.
52 Although from a distance you will view the
land that I am giving the Israelites, you will
not go there."

MOSES'S BLESSINGS

33 This is the blessing that Moses, the man
of God, gave the Israelites before his
death. 2 He said:

The LORD came from Sinai
and appeared to them from Seir;
he shone on them from Mount Paran
and came with ten thousand
holy ones,[G]
with lightning[H] from his right hand[I]
for them.

3 Indeed he loves the people.[J]
All your[K] holy ones are in your hand,
and they assemble[L] at your feet.
Each receives your words.

4 Moses gave us instruction,
a possession for the assembly of Jacob.

5 So he became King in Jeshurun[M]
when the leaders of the people
gathered
with the tribes of Israel.

6 Let Reuben live and not die
though his people become few.

7 He said this about Judah:
LORD, hear Judah's cry and bring him
to his people.
He fights for his cause[N]
with his own hands,
but may you be a help against his foes.

8 He said about Levi:
Your Thummim and Urim belong to
your faithful one;[O]
you tested him at Massah
and contended with him at the Waters
of Meribah.

9 He said about his father and mother,
"I do not regard them."
He disregarded his brothers

[A] **32:42** Or *the long-haired heads of the enemy* [B] **32:43** LXX reads *Rejoice, you heavens, along with him, and let all the sons of God worship him; rejoice, you nations, with his people, and let all the angels of God strengthen themselves in him*; DSS read *Rejoice, you heavens, along with him, and let all the angels worship him*; Heb 1:6 [C] **32:43** DSS, LXX read *sons* [D] **32:43** DSS, LXX add *and he will recompense those who hate him*; v. 41 [E] **32:43** Syr, Tg; DSS, Sam, LXX, Vg read *his people's land* [F] **32:44** LXX, Syr, Vg; MT reads *Hoshea*; Nm 13:8,16 [G] **33:2** LXX reads *Mount Paran with ten thousands from Kadesh* [H] **33:2** Or *fiery law*; Hb obscure [I] **33:2** Or *ones, from his southland to the mountain slopes* [J] **33:3** Or *peoples* [K] **33:3** Lit *his*, or *its* [L] **33:3** Hb obscure [M] **33:5** = Upright One, referring to Israel, also in v. 26 [N] **33:7** Or *He contends for them* [O] **33:8** DSS, LXX read *Give to Levi your Thummim, your Urim to your favored one*

and didn't acknowledge his sons,
for they kept your word
and maintained your covenant.
10 They will teach your ordinances
to Jacob
and your instruction to Israel;
they will set incense before you
and whole burnt offerings
on your altar.
11 LORD, bless his possessions,[A]
and accept the work of his hands.
Break the back[B] of his adversaries
and enemies,
so that they cannot rise again.
12 He said about Benjamin:
The LORD's beloved rests[C] securely
on him.
He[D] shields him all day long,
and he rests on his shoulders.[E]
13 He said about Joseph:
May his land be blessed by the LORD
with the dew of heaven's bounty
and the watery depths that lie beneath;
14 with the bountiful harvest from the sun
and the abundant yield of the seasons;
15 with the best products
of the ancient mountains
and the bounty of the eternal hills;
16 with the choice gifts of the land
and everything in it;
and with the favor of him
who appeared[F] in the burning bush.
May these rest on the head of Joseph,
on the brow of the prince
of his brothers.
17 His firstborn bull has[G] splendor,
and horns like[H] those of a wild ox;
he gores all the peoples with them
to the ends of the earth.
Such are the ten thousands of Ephraim,
and such are the thousands
of Manasseh.
18 He said about Zebulun:
Rejoice, Zebulun, in your journeys,
and Issachar, in your tents.
19 They summon the peoples
to a mountain;
there they offer acceptable sacrifices.
For they draw from the wealth
of the seas
and the hidden treasures of the sand.
20 He said about Gad:
The one who enlarges Gad's territory
will be blessed.
He lies down like a lion
and tears off an arm or even a head.
21 He chose the best part for himself,
because a ruler's portion was assigned
there for him.
He came with the leaders
of the people;
he carried out the LORD's justice
and his ordinances for Israel.
22 He said about Dan:
Dan is a young lion,
leaping out of Bashan.
23 He said about Naphtali:
Naphtali, enjoying approval,
full of the LORD's blessing,
take[I] possession to the west
and the south.
24 He said about Asher:
May Asher[J] be the most blessed
of the sons;
may he be the most favored
among his brothers
and dip his foot in olive oil.
25 May the bolts of your gate be iron
and bronze,
and your strength last as long as
you live.

26 There is none like the God of Jeshurun,
who rides the heavens to your aid,
the clouds in his majesty.
27 The God of old is your dwelling place,
and underneath are
the everlasting arms.
He drives out the enemy before you
and commands, "Destroy!"

There is none like the God of Jeshurun, who rides the heavens to your aid, the clouds in his majesty. The God of old is your dwelling place, and underneath are the everlasting arms.
—Deuteronomy 33:26-27

[A] **33:11** Or *abilities* [B] **33:11** Or *waist* [C] **33:12** Or *Let the LORD's beloved rest* [D] **33:12** LXX reads *The Most High* [E] **33:12** Or *and he dwells among his mountain slopes* [F] **33:16** Lit *dwelt* [G] **33:17** Some DSS, Sam, LXX, Syr, Vg read *A firstborn bull — he has* [H] **33:17** Lit *and his horns are* [I] **33:23** Sam, LXX, Syr, Vg, Tg read *he will take* [J] **33:24** = Happy or Blessed; Gn 30:13

28 So Israel dwells securely;
Jacob lives untroubled[A]
in a land of grain and new wine;
even his skies drip with dew.
29 How happy you are, Israel!
Who is like you,
a people saved by the LORD?
He is the shield that protects you,
the sword you boast in.
Your enemies will cringe before you,
and you will tread on their backs.[B]

MOSES'S DEATH

34 Then Moses went up from the plains of
Moab to Mount Nebo, to the top of Pisgah, which faces Jericho, and the LORD showed
him all the land: Gilead as far as Dan, 2 all of
Naphtali, the land of Ephraim and Manasseh,
all the land of Judah as far as the Mediterranean[C] Sea, 3 the Negev, and the plain in the
Valley of Jericho, the City of Palms, as far as
Zoar. 4 The LORD then said to him, "This is the
land I promised Abraham, Isaac, and Jacob,
'I will give it to your descendants.' I have let
you see it with your own eyes, but you will
not cross into it."
5 So Moses the servant of the LORD died there
in the land of Moab, according to the LORD's
word. 6 He buried him[D] in the valley in the land
of Moab facing Beth-peor, and no one to this
day knows where his grave is. 7 Moses was one
hundred twenty years old when he died; his
eyes were not weak, and his vitality had not left
him. 8 The Israelites wept for Moses in the plains
of Moab thirty days. Then the days of weeping
and mourning for Moses came to an end.
9 Joshua son of Nun was filled with the
spirit of wisdom because Moses had laid his
hands on him. So the Israelites obeyed him
and did as the LORD had commanded Moses.
10 No prophet has arisen again in Israel like
Moses, whom the LORD knew face to face. 11 He
was unparalleled for all the signs and wonders
the LORD sent him to do against the land of
Egypt — to Pharaoh, to all his officials, and
to all his land, 12 and for all the mighty acts
of power[E] and terrifying deeds that Moses
performed in the sight of all Israel.

[A] **33:28** Text emended; MT reads *Jacob's fountain is alone* [B] **33:29** Or *high places* [C] **34:2** Lit *Western* [D] **34:6** Or *he was buried* [E] **34:12** Lit *the strong hand*

Joshua—The themes of work and rest play throughout the book of Joshua. The years of wandering over, God had proven true to his word, and the new generation of Israelites was finally receiving the land they had yearned for. This was a time of hopes fulfilled and promises kept.

The Israelites still had to possess what was theirs, battling mighty armies—sometimes using unorthodox methods—as they followed God's commands and relied on his strength.

We, too, are called to rest in God's care as we trust in him to guide us and provide for us. But it also means battling against spiritual enemies. In this book, we also sense a foreshadowing of gloom as we read that various tribes failed to obey God and drive out all their enemies. We, too, are called to full obedience; when we fail to root out sin as God convicts us, we reap the consequences.

In Joshua, we see the constant comfort of God's presence. He does not call us to battle alone; instead, he promises to be with us always. Just like Joshua, the key to receiving God's strength and encouragement is to keep his Word in our minds and hearts (1:6-9).

JOSHUA

AUTHOR: Though the book is named for its central character, Joshua, the leader of Israel, the author is not identified. Scholars suggest that Joshua himself may have written much of it. If not penned by Joshua, the book was at least written by someone close to him because the account is personal and specific. Numerous references in the book, including the death of Joshua and memorials that were "still there today" (e.g. 4:9) suggest that the book was completed after his death.

DATE WRITTEN: 1400–1370 BC

ORIGINAL AUDIENCE: The Israelites

SETTING: In the book of Joshua, a new generation of Israelites enter the promised land and begin to take hold of God's promise to give the land to them. The action takes place in the land they had hoped for and waited for, "a land flowing with milk and honey" (Ex 3:8), but also a land full of giants and enemies. In this new place, God's people would have to trust God as they battled danger and discouragement.

PURPOSE FOR WRITING: The book of Joshua tells the history of God's people as they conquer and settle in the promised land. God promised to be with them always and to fight for them, but the people of Israel had to fight to take control of the land. It is a book of battles, courage, and triumph. In the leader Joshua, whose name literally means "the Lord saves," we see a prototype of Christ. He is their deliverer and warrior, as well as the spiritual leader who keeps God's covenant before the people's vision.

OUTLINE:

1. Entering the Promised Land (1:1–12:24)

    Joshua assumes leadership (1:1-18)

    Rahab expresses faith (2:1-24)

    The Jordan River is crossed (3:1–4:24)

    Passover is observed (5:1-12)

    Jericho is defeated (5:13–6:27)

    Achan's sin is discovered and punished (7:1-26)

    Ai is defeated (8:1-29)

    The covenant is renewed (8:30-35)

    Gibeon's deception (9:1-27)

    Miraculous victories (10:1–12:24)

2. Dividing the Promised Land (13:1–22:34)

    Geographical divisions by tribe (13:1–19:51)

    Cities of refuge (20:1-9)

    Levitical allotments (21:1-42)

    Summary of God's promises fulfilled (21:43-45)

    Controversy at the Transjordan (22:1-34)

3. Joshua's Farewell (23:1–24:33)

KEY VERSE:

"Haven't I commanded you: be strong and courageous? Do not be afraid or discouraged, for the LORD your God is with you wherever you go." —Joshua 1:9

RESTORATION THEMES

R	Rest and Reflection	*For the next note, see 1 Samuel 2:26.*
E	Eternal Perspective	*God's Presence—Joshua 1:9*
S	Support	*God's Support—1:5*
T	Thanksgiving and Contentment	*For the next note, see Judges 3:7-9.*
O	Other-centeredness	*Assuming the Best—Joshua 9:14* *Loving God—23:11*
R	Relationships	*For the next note, see 1 Samuel 18:1-3.*
E	Exercise of Faith	*Making Right Choices/Priorities/Values—Joshua 24:15*

ENCOURAGEMENT OF JOSHUA

1 After the death of Moses the LORD's servant, the LORD spoke to Joshua son of Nun,
Moses's assistant: 2 "Moses my servant is
dead. Now you and all the people prepare to
cross over the Jordan to the land I am giving
the Israelites. 3 I have given you every place
where the sole of your foot treads, just as I
promised Moses. 4 Your territory will be from
the wilderness and Lebanon to the great river, the Euphrates River — all the land of the
Hittites — and west to the Mediterranean
Sea.[A] 5 No one will be able to stand against
you as long as you live. I will be with you,
just as I was with Moses. I will not leave you
or abandon you.

6 "Be strong and courageous, for you will
distribute the land I swore to their fathers to
give them as an inheritance. 7 Above all, be
strong and very courageous to observe carefully the whole instruction my servant Moses
commanded you. Do not turn from it to the
right or the left, so that you will have success
wherever you go. 8 This book of instruction
must not depart from your mouth; you are
to meditate on[B] it day and night so that you
may carefully observe everything written in
it. For then you will prosper and succeed in
whatever you do. 9 Haven't I commanded you:
be strong and courageous? Do not be afraid
or discouraged, for the LORD your God is with
you wherever you go."

JOSHUA PREPARES THE PEOPLE

10 Then Joshua commanded the officers of the
people: 11 "Go through the camp and tell the
people, 'Get provisions ready for yourselves,
for within three days you will be crossing the
Jordan to go in and take possession of the land
the LORD your God is giving you to inherit.' "

12 Joshua said to the Reubenites, the Gadites,
and half the tribe of Manasseh: 13 "Remember
what Moses the LORD's servant commanded
you when he said, 'The LORD your God will
give you rest, and he will give you this land.'
14 Your wives, dependents, and livestock may
remain in the land Moses gave you on this
side of the Jordan. But your best soldiers must
cross over in battle formation[C] ahead of your
brothers and help them 15 until the LORD gives
your brothers rest, as he has given you, and
they too possess the land the LORD your God
is giving them. You may then return to the
land of your inheritance and take possession
of what Moses the LORD's servant gave you on
the east side of the Jordan."

16 They answered Joshua, "Everything you
have commanded us we will do, and everywhere you send us we will go. 17 We will obey
you, just as we obeyed Moses in everything.

Support | *God's Support*

GOD'S SURE PRESENCE

"No one will be able to stand against you as long as you live.
I will be with you, just as I was with Moses.
I will not leave you or abandon you." Joshua 1:5

Often in prayer we plead, "God, please be with us." If someone wanted to get picky and technical, they could pull us aside and say, "Such a prayer request is unnecessary because God is *always* with his people. We might as well pray, "God, please be holy." We are asking for something that's already true, something we already have.

We might frown at such a rebuke, but the point is well taken. Just as God pledged in this moment to be continually with Joshua, Jesus pledged to be with his followers always (Mt 28:20). We find this teaching of God's presence throughout the Bible. Even the psalm writer marveled at the truth that he could not evade God's presence (Ps 139:1-12).

Instead of merely asking God to be with us, let us also pray, "Lord, give me eyes to see that you are with me. Help me rest in your presence."

For the next note on *Support*, see Judges 8:22-23.

[A] **1:4** Lit *and to the Great Sea, the going down of the sun* [B] **1:8** Or *to recite* [C] **1:14** Or *over armed*

Certainly the LORD your God will be with you,
as he was with Moses. 18 Anyone who rebels
against your order and does not obey your
words in all that you command him, will be
put to death. Above all, be strong and courageous!"

SPIES SENT TO JERICHO

2 Joshua son of Nun secretly sent two men
as spies from the Acacia Grove,[A] saying,
"Go and scout the land, especially Jericho."
So they left, and they came to the house of
a prostitute named Rahab, and stayed there.
2 The king of Jericho was told, "Look, some
of the Israelite men have come here tonight to
investigate the land." 3 Then the king of Jericho
sent word to Rahab and said, "Bring out the
men who came to you and entered your house,
for they came to investigate the entire land."
4 But the woman had taken the two men
and hidden them. So she said, "Yes, the men
did come to me, but I didn't know where they
were from. 5 At nightfall, when the city gate
was about to close, the men went out, and I
don't know where they were going. Chase
after them quickly, and you can catch up with
them!" 6 But she had taken them up to the roof
and hidden them among the stalks of flax
that she had arranged on the roof. 7 The men
pursued them along the road to the fords of
the Jordan, and as soon as they left to pursue
them, the city gate was shut.

THE PROMISE TO RAHAB

8 Before the men fell asleep, she went up on
the roof 9 and said to them, "I know that the
LORD has given you this land and that the
terror of you has fallen on us, and everyone
who lives in the land is panicking because
of you.[B] 10 For we have heard how the LORD
dried up the water of the Red Sea before you
when you came out of Egypt, and what you
did to Sihon and Og, the two Amorite kings
you completely destroyed across the Jordan.
11 When we heard this, we lost heart, and everyone's courage failed[C] because of you, for
the LORD your God is God in heaven above
and on earth below. 12 Now please swear to
me by the LORD that you will also show kindness to my father's family,[D] because I showed
kindness to you. Give me a sure sign[E] 13 that
you will spare the lives of my father, mother,
brothers, sisters, and all who belong to them,
and save us from death."
14 The men answered her, "We will give our
lives for yours. If you don't report our mission,
we will show kindness and faithfulness to you
when the LORD gives us the land."

Eternal Perspective | *God's Presence*

BEING STRONG

"Haven't I commanded you: be strong and courageous? Do not be afraid or discouraged, for the LORD your God is with you wherever you go." Joshua 1:9

Have you ever noticed how the Bible emphasizes actions much more than feelings? God doesn't tell Joshua to *feel* courageous. He tells him to *be* courageous. That is a huge difference.

Almost every day we face situations that make us anxious or make us want to run. Let's be honest—who *feels* like wading into a conversation that might very well go south? Who gets fired up at the prospect of painful rejection? Who feels giddy when embarking on a daunting project that could very likely end in failure and embarrassment?

Our emotions matter and are valid. But we can't afford to be controlled by our feelings. World War I ace pilot Eddie Rickenbacker put it well, "Courage is doing what you're afraid to do. There can be no courage unless you are scared." In other words, courage isn't a feeling, it's taking necessary action. And being uneasy is a fact of life.

Pick out a task you've been avoiding. Today, take a risk. Live by faith, not by feelings.

For the next note on *Eternal Perspective*, see 1 Samuel 16:7.

[A] **2:1** Or *from Shittim* [B] **2:9** Or *land panics at your approach* [C] **2:11** Lit *and spirit no longer remained in anyone* [D] **2:12** Lit *my father's house* [E] **2:12** Or *a sign of truth*

15 Then she let them down by a rope through
the window, since she lived in a house that was
built into the wall of the city. 16 "Go to the hill
country so that the men pursuing you won't
find you," she said to them. "Hide there for
three days until they return; afterward, go
on your way."
17 The men said to her, "We will be free from
this oath you made us swear, 18 unless, when
we enter the land, you tie this scarlet cord to
the window through which you let us down.
Bring your father, mother, brothers, and all
your father's family into your house. 19 If anyone goes out the doors of your house, his death
will be his own fault,[A] and we will be innocent.
But if anyone with you in the house should be
harmed,[B] his death will be our fault.[C] 20 And if
you report our mission, we are free from the
oath you made us swear."
21 "Let it be as you say," she replied, and she
sent them away. After they had gone, she tied
the scarlet cord to the window.
22 So the two men went into the hill country
and stayed there three days until the pursuers had returned. They searched all along the
way, but did not find them. 23 Then the men
returned, came down from the hill country,
and crossed the Jordan. They went to Joshua son of Nun and reported everything that
had happened to them. 24 They told Joshua,
"The LORD has handed over the entire land
to us. Everyone who lives in the land is also
panicking because of us."[D]

CROSSING THE JORDAN

3 Joshua started early the next morning and
left the Acacia Grove[E] with all the Israelites. They went as far as the Jordan and stayed
there before crossing. 2 After three days the
officers went through the camp 3 and commanded the people: "When you see the ark of
the covenant of the LORD your God carried by
the Levitical priests, you are to break camp
and follow it. 4 But keep a distance of about
a thousand yards[F] between yourselves and
the ark. Don't go near it, so that you can see
the way to go, for you haven't traveled this
way before."[G]
5 Joshua told the people, "Consecrate yourselves, because the LORD will do wonders
among you tomorrow." 6 Then he said to the
priests, "Carry the ark of the covenant and go
on ahead of the people." So they carried the
ark of the covenant and went ahead of them.
7 The LORD spoke to Joshua: "Today I will
begin to exalt you in the sight of all Israel, so
they will know that I will be with you just as I
was with Moses. 8 Command the priests carrying the ark of the covenant: When you reach
the edge of the water,[H] stand in the Jordan."
9 Then Joshua told the Israelites, "Come closer and listen to the words of the LORD your
God." 10 He said: "You will know that the living
God is among you and that he will certainly
dispossess before you the Canaanites, Hethites,
Hivites, Perizzites, Girgashites, Amorites, and
Jebusites 11 when the ark of the covenant of the
Lord of the whole earth goes ahead of you into
the Jordan. 12 Now choose twelve men from
the tribes of Israel, one man for each tribe.
13 When the feet[I] of the priests who carry the
ark of the LORD, the Lord of the whole earth,
come to rest in the Jordan's water, its water
will be cut off. The water flowing downstream
will stand up in a mass."
14 When the people broke camp to cross the
Jordan, the priests carried the ark of the covenant ahead of the people. 15 Now the Jordan
overflows its banks throughout the harvest
season. But as soon as the priests carrying
the ark reached the Jordan, their feet touched
the water at its edge 16 and the water flowing
downstream stood still, rising up in a mass
that extended as far as[J] Adam, a city next to
Zarethan. The water flowing downstream into
the Sea of the Arabah — the Dead Sea — was
completely cut off, and the people crossed
opposite Jericho. 17 The priests carrying the
ark of the LORD's covenant stood firmly on
dry ground in the middle of the Jordan, while
all Israel crossed on dry ground until the entire nation had finished crossing the Jordan.

THE MEMORIAL STONES

4 After the entire nation had finished crossing the Jordan, the LORD spoke to Joshua:
2 "Choose twelve men from the people, one
man for each tribe, 3 and command them: Take
twelve stones from this place in the middle of
the Jordan where the priests[K] are standing,
carry them with you, and set them down at
the place where you spend the night."
4 So Joshua summoned the twelve men he
had selected from the Israelites, one man for

[A] **2:19** Lit *his blood on his head* [B] **2:19** Lit *if a hand should be on him* [C] **2:19** Lit *his blood on our heads* [D] **2:24** Or *land also panics at our approach* [E] **3:1** Or *left Shittim* [F] **3:4** Lit *2,000 cubits* [G] **3:4** Lit *yesterday and the day before* [H] **3:8** Lit *waters of the Jordan* [I] **3:13** Lit *soles of the feet* [J] **3:16** Alt Hb tradition reads *mass at* [K] **4:3** Lit *feet of the priests*, also in v. 9

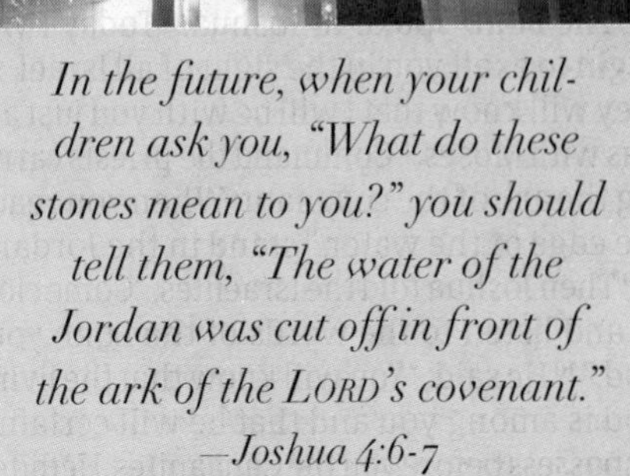
In the future, when your children ask you, "What do these stones mean to you?" you should tell them, "The water of the Jordan was cut off in front of the ark of the LORD's covenant."
—Joshua 4:6-7

each tribe, 5 and said to them, "Go across to
the ark of the LORD your God in the middle of
the Jordan. Each of you lift a stone onto his
shoulder, one for each[A] of the Israelite tribes,
6 so that this will be a sign among you. In the
future, when your children ask you, 'What do
these stones mean to you?' 7 you should tell
them, 'The water of the Jordan was cut off in
front of the ark of the LORD's covenant. When
it crossed the Jordan, the Jordan's water was
cut off.' Therefore these stones will always be
a memorial for the Israelites."

8 The Israelites did just as Joshua had commanded them. The twelve men took stones
from the middle of the Jordan, one for each[B]
of the Israelite tribes, just as the LORD had
told Joshua. They carried them to the camp
and set them down there. 9 Joshua also set
up twelve stones in the middle[C] of the Jordan
where the priests who carried the ark of the
covenant were standing. The stones are still
there today.

10 The priests carrying the ark continued
standing in the middle of the Jordan until
everything was completed that the LORD
had commanded Joshua to tell the people, in
keeping with all that Moses had commanded
Joshua. The people hurried across, 11 and after
everyone had finished crossing, the priests
with the ark of the LORD crossed in the sight
of the people. 12 The Reubenites, Gadites, and
half the tribe of Manasseh went in battle formation in front of the Israelites, as Moses
had instructed them. 13 About forty thousand
equipped for war crossed to the plains of Jericho in the LORD's presence.

14 On that day the LORD exalted Joshua in
the sight of all Israel, and they revered him
throughout his life, as they had revered Moses. 15 The LORD told Joshua, 16 "Command the
priests who carry the ark of the testimony to
come up from the Jordan."

17 So Joshua commanded the priests, "Come
up from the Jordan." 18 When the priests carrying the ark of the LORD's covenant came up
from the middle of the Jordan, and their feet[D]
stepped out on solid ground, the water of the
Jordan resumed its course, flowing over all
the banks as before.

19 The people came up from the Jordan on
the tenth day of the first month, and camped at
Gilgal on the eastern limits of Jericho. 20 Then
Joshua set up in Gilgal the twelve stones they
had taken from the Jordan, 21 and he said to
the Israelites, "In the future, when your children ask their fathers, 'What is the meaning
of these stones?' 22 you should tell your children, 'Israel crossed the Jordan on dry ground.'
23 For the LORD your God dried up the water of
the Jordan before you until you had crossed
over, just as the LORD your God did to the Red
Sea, which he dried up before us until we had
crossed over. 24 This is so that all the peoples
of the earth may know that the LORD's hand
is mighty, and so that you may always fear
the LORD your God."

CIRCUMCISION OF THE ISRAELITES

5 When all the Amorite kings across the
Jordan to the west and all the Canaanite
kings near the sea heard how the LORD had
dried up the water of the Jordan before the
Israelites until they had crossed over, they
lost heart and their courage failed[E] because
of the Israelites.

2 At that time the LORD said to Joshua,
"Make flint knives and circumcise the Israelite men again." 3 So Joshua made flint
knives and circumcised the Israelite men at
Gibeath-haaraloth.[F] 4 This is the reason Joshua
circumcised them: All the people who came
out of Egypt who were males — all the men
of war — had died in the wilderness along
the way after they had come out of Egypt.
5 Though all the people who came out were
circumcised, none of the people born in the
wilderness along the way were circumcised
after they had come out of Egypt. 6 For the
Israelites wandered in the wilderness forty
years until all the nation's men of war who

[A] 4:5 Lit *shoulder according to the number* [B] 4:8 Lit *Jordan according to the number* [C] 4:9 Or *Now Joshua set up the twelve stones that had been in the middle* [D] 4:18 Lit *and the soles of the feet of the priests* [E] 5:1 Lit *and they did not have spirit in them any more* [F] 5:3 Or *The Hill of Foreskins*

came out of Egypt had died off because they did not obey the LORD. So the LORD vowed never to let them see the land he had sworn to their fathers to give us, a land flowing with milk and honey. 7 He raised up their sons in their place; it was these Joshua circumcised. They were still uncircumcised, since they had not been circumcised along the way. 8 After the entire nation had been circumcised, they stayed where they were in the camp until they recovered. 9 The LORD then said to Joshua, "Today I have rolled away the disgrace of Egypt from you." Therefore, that place is still called Gilgal today.

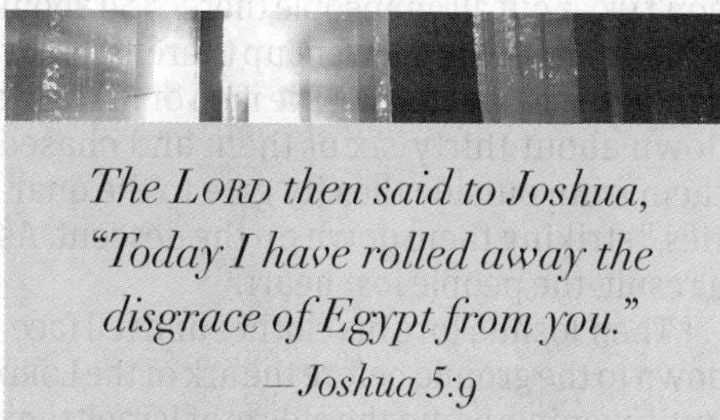
The LORD then said to Joshua,
"Today I have rolled away the
disgrace of Egypt from you."
—Joshua 5:9

FOOD FROM THE LAND

10 While the Israelites camped at Gilgal on the plains of Jericho, they observed the Passover on the evening of the fourteenth day of the month. 11 The day after Passover they ate unleavened bread and roasted grain from the produce of the land. 12 And the day after they ate from the produce of the land, the manna ceased. Since there was no more manna for the Israelites, they ate from the crops of the land of Canaan that year.

COMMANDER OF THE LORD'S ARMY

13 When Joshua was near Jericho, he looked up and saw a man standing in front of him with a drawn sword in his hand. Joshua approached him and asked, "Are you for us or for our enemies?"

14 "Neither," he replied. "I have now come as commander of the LORD's army."

Then Joshua bowed with his face to the ground in worship and asked him, "What does my lord want to say to his servant?"

15 The commander of the LORD's army said to Joshua, "Remove the sandals from your feet, for the place where you are standing is holy." And Joshua did that.

THE CONQUEST OF JERICHO

6 Now Jericho was strongly fortified because of the Israelites — no one leaving or entering. 2 The LORD said to Joshua, "Look, I have handed Jericho, its king, and its best soldiers over to you. 3 March around the city with all the men of war, circling the city one time. Do this for six days. 4 Have seven priests carry seven ram's-horn trumpets in front of the ark. But on the seventh day, march around the city seven times, while the priests blow the trumpets. 5 When there is a prolonged blast of the horn and you hear its sound, have all the troops give a mighty shout. Then the city wall will collapse, and the troops will advance, each man straight ahead."

6 So Joshua son of Nun summoned the priests and said to them, "Take up the ark of the covenant and have seven priests carry seven trumpets in front of the ark of the LORD." 7 He said to the troops, "Move forward, march around the city, and have the armed men go ahead of the ark of the LORD."

8 After Joshua had spoken to the troops, seven priests carrying seven trumpets before the LORD moved forward and blew the trumpets; the ark of the LORD's covenant followed them. 9 While the trumpets were blowing, the armed men went in front of the priests who blew the trumpets, and the rear guard went behind the ark. 10 But Joshua had commanded the troops: "Do not shout or let your voice be heard. Don't let one word come out of your mouth until the time I say, 'Shout!' Then you are to shout." 11 So the ark of the LORD was carried around the city, circling it once. They returned to the camp and spent the night there.[A]

12 Joshua got up early the next morning. The priests took the ark of the LORD, 13 and the seven priests carrying seven trumpets marched in front of the ark of the LORD. While the trumpets were blowing, the armed men went in front of them, and the rear guard went behind the ark of the LORD. 14 On the second day they marched around the city once and returned to the camp. They did this for six days.

15 Early on the seventh day, they started at dawn and marched around the city seven times in the same way. That was the only day they marched around the city seven times. 16 After the seventh time, the priests blew

[A] **6:11** Lit *at the camp*

the trumpets, and Joshua said to the troops,
"Shout! For the LORD has given you the city.
17 But the city and everything in it are set apart
to the LORD for destruction. Only Rahab the
prostitute and everyone with her in the house
will live, because she hid the messengers we
sent. 18 But keep yourselves from the things set
apart, or you will be set apart for destruction.
If you[A] take any of those things, you will set
apart the camp of Israel for destruction and
make trouble for it. 19 For all the silver and
gold, and the articles of bronze and iron, are
dedicated to the LORD and must go into the
LORD's treasury."
20 So the troops shouted, and the trumpets
sounded. When they heard the blast of the
trumpet, the troops gave a great shout, and
the wall collapsed. The troops advanced into
the city, each man straight ahead, and they
captured the city. 21 They completely destroyed
everything in the city with the sword — every
man and woman, both young and old, and
every ox, sheep, and donkey.

RAHAB AND HER FAMILY SPARED

22 Joshua said to the two men who had scouted
the land, "Go to the prostitute's house and bring
the woman out of there, and all who are with
her, just as you swore to her." 23 So the young
men who had scouted went in and brought
out Rahab and her father, mother, brothers,
and all who belonged to her. They brought out
her whole family and settled them outside the
camp of Israel.
24 They burned the city and everything in
it, but they put the silver and gold and the articles of bronze and iron into the treasury of
the LORD's house. 25 However, Joshua spared
Rahab the prostitute, her father's family, and
all who belonged to her, because she hid the
messengers Joshua had sent to spy on Jericho,
and she still lives in Israel today.
26 At that time Joshua imposed this curse:

The man who undertakes
the rebuilding of this city, Jericho,
is cursed before the LORD.
He will lay its foundation
at the cost of his firstborn;
he will finish its gates
at the cost of his youngest.

27 And the LORD was with Joshua, and his
fame spread throughout the land.

DEFEAT AT AI

7 The Israelites, however, were unfaithful
regarding the things set apart for destruction. Achan son of Carmi, son of Zabdi, son of
Zerah, of the tribe of Judah, took some of what
was set apart, and the LORD's anger burned
against the Israelites.
2 Joshua sent men from Jericho to Ai, which
is near Beth-aven, east of Bethel, and told them,
"Go up and scout the land." So the men went
up and scouted Ai.
3 After returning to Joshua they reported
to him, "Don't send all the people, but send
about two thousand or three thousand[B] men
to attack Ai. Since the people of Ai are so few,
don't wear out all our people there." 4 So about
three thousand men[C] went up there, but they
fled from the men of Ai. 5 The men of Ai struck
down about thirty-six of them and chased
them from outside the city gate to the quarries,[D] striking them down on the descent. As
a result, the people lost heart.[E]
6 Then Joshua tore his clothes and fell facedown to the ground before the ark of the LORD
until evening, as did the elders of Israel; they
all put dust on their heads. 7 "Oh, Lord GOD,"
Joshua said, "why did you ever bring these
people across the Jordan to hand us over to the
Amorites for our destruction? If only we had
been content to remain on the other side of the
Jordan! 8 What can I say, Lord, now that Israel
has turned its back and run from its enemies?
9 When the Canaanites and all who live in the
land hear about this, they will surround us
and wipe out our name from the earth. Then
what will you do about your great name?"
10 The LORD then said to Joshua, "Stand up!
Why have you fallen facedown? 11 Israel has
sinned. They have violated my covenant that
I appointed for them. They have taken some
of what was set apart. They have stolen, deceived, and put those things with their own
belongings. 12 This is why the Israelites cannot
stand against their enemies. They will turn
their backs and run from their enemies, because they have been set apart for destruction.
I will no longer be with you unless you remove
from among you what is set apart.
13 "Go and consecrate the people. Tell them
to consecrate themselves for tomorrow, for
this is what the LORD, the God of Israel, says:
There are things that are set apart among you,
Israel. You will not be able to stand against

[A] **6:18** LXX reads *you covet and*; Jos 7:21 [B] **7:3** Or *send two or three military units of* [C] **7:4** Lit *men from the people*
[D] **7:5** Or *to Shebarim* [E] **7:5** Lit *people's hearts melted and became like water*

Rahab | Restoration Profile

JOSHUA 2:1-3; 6:17-25; MATTHEW 1:5; HEBREWS 11:31; JAMES 2:25

Rahab enters the Bible narrative as a prostitute, rescues the spies of Israel in Jericho, becomes part of the lineage of Jesus, and is listed among the enduring examples of faith in Hebrews 11. Both she and her reputation were unexpectedly restored. Interestingly, the writer of Hebrews makes no effort to hide her former history, highlighting the miraculous transformation that can come to a person through faith. The scarlet cord Rahab hung from the window of her house as a sign to Israel's army represents the recurring message that God keeps his promises to anyone who trusts him.

Security was tight in Jericho when Joshua sent two spies to scout their first military objective. Alerted to their presence and last-known location, the king expected Rahab to hand them over. Instead, she hid the spies and misdirected the search party. Several phrases stand out in her explanation to the spies: "I know that the LORD has given you this land and that the terror of you has fallen on us. . . . The LORD your God is God in heaven above and on earth below" (Jos 2:8-11). That's about as clear an expression of the fear of the Lord that a person can make.

After Jericho fell, Rahab became part of God's people. Despite her past, she married and raised a family. At some point in the conquering of the promised land, Rahab settled in Bethlehem, the place of her lineage, which included the Savior, and called it home.

Rahab's role in the taking of Jericho highlights God's willingness to use humble people despite their checkered past. And the rest of Scripture bears witness to the truth that Rahab's faith was genuine.

your enemies until you remove what is set
apart. 14 In the morning, present yourselves
tribe by tribe. The tribe the LORD selects is to
come forward clan by clan. The clan the LORD
selects is to come forward family by family.
The family the LORD selects is to come forward
man by man. 15 The one who is caught with
the things set apart must be burned, along
with everything he has, because he has violated the LORD's covenant and committed an
outrage in Israel."

ACHAN JUDGED

16 Joshua got up early the next morning. He
had Israel come forward tribe by tribe, and the
tribe of Judah was selected. 17 He had the clans
of Judah come forward, and the Zerahite clan
was selected. He had the Zerahite clan come
forward by heads of families,[A] and Zabdi was
selected. 18 He then had Zabdi's family come
forward man by man, and Achan son of Carmi, son of Zabdi, son of Zerah, of the tribe of
Judah, was selected.

19 So Joshua said to Achan, "My son, give
glory to the LORD, the God of Israel, and make
a confession to him.[B] I urge you, tell me what
you have done. Don't hide anything from me."
20 Achan replied to Joshua, "It is true. I have
sinned against the LORD, the God of Israel.
This is what I did: 21 When I saw among the
spoils a beautiful cloak from Babylon,[C] five
pounds[D] of silver, and a bar of gold weighing
a pound and a quarter,[E] I coveted them and
took them. You can see for yourself. They
are concealed in the ground inside my tent,
with the silver under the cloak." 22 So Joshua
sent messengers who ran to the tent, and
there was the cloak, concealed in his tent,
with the silver underneath. 23 They took the
things from inside the tent, brought them
to Joshua and all the Israelites, and spread
them out in the LORD's presence.

24 Then Joshua and all Israel with him took
Achan son of Zerah, the silver, the cloak,
and the bar of gold, his sons and daughters,
his ox, donkey, and sheep, his tent, and all
that he had, and brought them up to the
Valley of Achor. 25 Joshua said, "Why have
you brought us trouble? Today the LORD will
bring you trouble!" So all Israel stoned them[F]
to death. They burned their bodies, threw
stones on them, 26 and raised over him a
large pile of rocks that remains still today.
Then the LORD turned from his burning anger. Therefore that place is called the Valley
of Achor[G] still today.

[A] **7:17** Lit *forward man by man* [B] **7:19** Or *and praise him* [C] **7:21** Lit *Shinar* [D] **7:21** Lit *200 shekels* [E] **7:21** Lit *50 shekels* [F] **7:25** Lit *him* [G] **7:26** Or *of Trouble*

CONQUEST OF AI

8 The LORD said to Joshua, "Do not be afraid or discouraged. Take all the troops with you and go attack Ai. Look, I have handed over to you the king of Ai, his people, city, and land. 2 Treat Ai and its king as you did Jericho and its king, except that you may plunder its spoil and livestock for yourselves. Set an ambush behind the city."

3 So Joshua and all the troops set out to attack Ai. Joshua selected thirty thousand of his best soldiers and sent them out at night. 4 He commanded them: "Pay attention. Lie in ambush behind the city, not too far from it, and all of you be ready. 5 Then I and all the people who are with me will approach the city. When they come out against us as they did the first time, we will flee from them. 6 They will come after us until we have drawn them away from the city, for they will say, 'They are fleeing from us as before.' While we are fleeing from them, 7 you are to come out of your ambush and seize the city. The LORD your God will hand it over to you. 8 After taking the city, set it on fire. Follow the LORD's command — see that you do as I have ordered you." 9 So Joshua sent them out, and they went to the ambush site and waited between Bethel and Ai, to the west of Ai. But he spent that night with the troops.

10 Joshua started early the next morning and mobilized them. Then he and the elders of Israel led the troops up to Ai. 11 All those[A] who were with him went up and approached the city, arriving opposite Ai, and camped to the north of it, with a valley between them and the city. 12 Now Joshua had taken about five thousand men and set them in ambush between Bethel and Ai, to the west of the city. 13 The troops were stationed in this way: the main[B] camp to the north of the city and its rear guard to the west of the city. And that night Joshua went into the valley.

14 When the king of Ai saw the Israelites, the men of the city hurried and went out early in the morning so that he and all his people could engage Israel in battle at a suitable place facing the Arabah. But he did not know there was an ambush waiting for him behind the city. 15 Joshua and all Israel pretended to be beaten back by them and fled toward the wilderness. 16 Then all the troops of Ai were summoned to pursue them, and they pursued Joshua and were drawn away from the city. 17 Not a man was left in Ai or Bethel who did not go out after Israel, leaving the city exposed while they pursued Israel.

18 Then the LORD said to Joshua, "Hold out the javelin in your hand toward Ai, for I will hand the city over to you." So Joshua held out his javelin toward it. 19 When he held out his hand, the men in ambush rose quickly from their position. They ran, entered the city, captured it, and immediately set it on fire.

20 The men of Ai turned and looked back, and smoke from the city was rising to the sky! They could not escape in any direction, and the troops who had fled to the wilderness now became the pursuers. 21 When Joshua and all Israel saw that the men in ambush had captured the city and that smoke was rising from it, they turned back and struck down the men of Ai. 22 Then men in ambush came out of the city against them, and the men of Ai were trapped between the Israelite forces, some on one side and some on the other. They struck them down until no survivor or fugitive remained, 23 but they captured the king of Ai alive and brought him to Joshua.

24 When Israel had finished killing everyone living in Ai who had pursued them into the open country, and when every last one of them had fallen by the sword, all Israel returned to Ai and struck it down with the sword. 25 The total of those who fell that day, both men and women, was twelve thousand — all the people of Ai. 26 Joshua did not draw back his hand that was holding the javelin until all the inhabitants of Ai were completely destroyed. 27 Israel plundered only the cattle and spoil of that city for themselves, according to the LORD's command that he had given Joshua.

28 Joshua burned Ai and left it a permanent ruin, still desolate today. 29 He hung[C] the body of the king of Ai on a tree[D] until evening, and at sunset Joshua commanded that they take his body down from the tree. They threw it down at the entrance of the city gate and put a large pile of rocks over it, which still remains today.

RENEWED COMMITMENT TO THE LAW

30 At that time Joshua built an altar on Mount Ebal to the LORD, the God of Israel, 31 just as Moses the LORD's servant had commanded the Israelites. He built it according to what is written in the book of the law of Moses: an altar

[A] **8:11** Lit *the people of war* [B] **8:13** Lit *way: all the* [C] **8:29** Or *impaled* [D] **8:29** Or *wooden stake*

of uncut stones on which no iron tool has been
used. Then they offered burnt offerings to the
LORD and sacrificed fellowship offerings on it.
32 There on the stones, Joshua copied the law of
Moses, which he had written in the presence
of the Israelites. 33 All Israel — resident alien
and citizen alike — with their elders, officers,
and judges, stood on either side of the ark of
the LORD's covenant facing the Levitical priests
who carried it. Half of them were in front of
Mount Gerizim and half in front of Mount Ebal,
as Moses the LORD's servant had commanded
earlier concerning blessing the people of Israel.
34 Afterward, Joshua read aloud all the words
of the law — the blessings as well as the curses
— according to all that is written in the book
of the law. 35 There was not a word of all that
Moses had commanded that Joshua did not
read before the entire assembly of Israel, including the women, the dependents, and the
resident aliens who lived[A] among them.

DECEPTION BY GIBEON

9 When all the kings heard about Jericho and
Ai, those who were west of the Jordan in
the hill country, in the Judean foothills,[B] and
all along the coast of the Mediterranean Sea
toward Lebanon — the Hethites, Amorites,
Canaanites, Perizzites, Hivites, and Jebusites —
2 they formed a unified alliance to fight against
Joshua and Israel.

3 When the inhabitants of Gibeon heard what
Joshua had done to Jericho and Ai, 4 they acted
deceptively. They gathered provisions[C] and
took worn-out sacks on their donkeys and
old wineskins, cracked and mended. 5 They
wore old, patched sandals on their feet and
threadbare clothing on their bodies. Their entire provision of bread was dry and crumbly.
6 They went to Joshua in the camp at Gilgal
and said to him and the men of Israel, "We
have come from a distant land. Please make
a treaty with us."

7 The men of Israel replied to the Hivites,
"Perhaps you live among us. How can we make
a treaty with you?"

8 They said to Joshua, "We are your servants."
Then Joshua asked them, "Who are you and
where do you come from?"

9 They replied to him, "Your servants have
come from a faraway land because of the reputation of the LORD your God. For we have
heard of his fame, and all that he did in Egypt,
10 and all that he did to the two Amorite kings

Other-centeredness | *Assuming the Best*

TRUST BUT VERIFY

"Then the men of Israel took some of their provisions, but did not seek the LORD's decision." Joshua 9:14

During the Cold War of the 1970s and 80s, the U.S. embraced the famous Russian proverb "Trust but verify." In other words, even as America pursued better relations with the Soviet Union, our leaders vowed to keep their eyes wide open for any violations of various signed nuclear agreements. Joshua and his leaders would have benefitted from such a strategy.

"Trust but verify" is actually a good guideline for all relationships. We want healthy marriages, mutually beneficial friendships, and functional—not dysfunctional—work partnerships. This means we can't be foolish. Solomon wrote, "The inexperienced one believes anything, but the sensible one watches his steps" (Pr 14:15). We have to be sensible and watch our steps.

Practically this means we don't ignore relational danger signs. When we have legitimate concerns, we talk about them. When a relationship becomes unsafe, we exit—returning only if and when the danger has passed.

In relationships, are you more naïve and trusting, or more wary? Why do you think? What are the beliefs in your heart, or experiences from your past, that make you the way you are?

For the next note on *Other-centeredness*, see Joshua 23:11.

[A] **8:35** Lit *walked* [B] **9:1** Or *the Shephelah* [C] **9:4** Some Hb mss, LXX, Syr, Vg; other Hb mss read *They went disguised as ambassadors*

beyond the Jordan — King Sihon of Heshbon
and King Og of Bashan, who was in Ashtaroth.
11 So our elders and all the inhabitants of our
land told us, 'Take provisions with you for
the journey; go and meet them and say, "We
are your servants. Please make a treaty with
us."' 12 This bread of ours was warm when we
took it from our houses as food on the day we
left to come to you; but see, it is now dry and
crumbly. 13 These wineskins were new when
we filled them; but see, they are cracked. And
these clothes and sandals of ours are worn out
from the extremely long journey." 14 Then the
men of Israel took some of their provisions,
but did not seek the LORD's decision. 15 So Joshua established peace with them and made a
treaty to let them live, and the leaders of the
community swore an oath to them.

GIBEON'S DECEPTION DISCOVERED

16 Three days after making the treaty with
them, they heard that the Gibeonites were
their neighbors, living among them. 17 So the Israelites set out and reached the Gibeonite cities
on the third day. Now their cities were Gibeon,
Chephirah, Beeroth, and Kiriath-jearim. 18 But
the Israelites did not attack them, because
the leaders of the community had sworn an
oath to them by the LORD, the God of Israel.
Then the whole community grumbled against
the leaders.

19 All the leaders answered them, "We have
sworn an oath to them by the LORD, the God of
Israel, and now we cannot touch them. 20 This
is how we will treat them: we will let them
live, so that no wrath will fall on us because
of the oath we swore to them." 21 They also
said, "Let them live." So the Gibeonites became
woodcutters and water carriers for the whole
community, as the leaders had promised them.

22 Joshua summoned the Gibeonites and said
to them, "Why did you deceive us by telling us
you live far away from us, when in fact you
live among us? 23 Therefore you are cursed
and will always be slaves — woodcutters and
water carriers for the house of my God."

24 The Gibeonites answered him, "It was
clearly communicated to your servants that
the LORD your God had commanded his servant
Moses to give you all the land and to destroy
all the inhabitants of the land before you. We
greatly feared for our lives because of you, and
that is why we did this. 25 Now we are in your
hands. Do to us whatever you think is right."[A]
26 This is what Joshua did to them: he rescued
them from the Israelites, and they did not kill
them. 27 On that day he made them woodcutters and water carriers — as they are today
— for the community and for the LORD's altar
at the place he would choose.

THE DAY THE SUN STOOD STILL

10 Now King Adoni-zedek of Jerusalem
heard that Joshua had captured Ai and
completely destroyed it, treating Ai and its king
as he had Jericho and its king, and that the inhabitants of Gibeon had made peace with Israel
and were living among them. 2 So Adoni-zedek
and his people were[B] greatly alarmed because
Gibeon was a large city like one of the royal
cities; it was larger than Ai, and all its men were
warriors. 3 Therefore King Adoni-zedek of Jerusalem sent word to King Hoham of Hebron,
King Piram of Jarmuth, King Japhia of Lachish,
and King Debir of Eglon, saying, 4 "Come up and
help me. We will attack Gibeon, because they
have made peace with Joshua and the Israelites." 5 So the five Amorite kings — the kings
of Jerusalem, Hebron, Jarmuth, Lachish, and
Eglon — joined forces, advanced with all their
armies, besieged Gibeon, and fought against it.

6 Then the men of Gibeon sent word to Joshua in the camp at Gilgal: "Don't give up on[C]
your servants. Come quickly and save us! Help
us, for all the Amorite kings living in the hill
country have joined forces against us." 7 So
Joshua and all his troops, including all his
best soldiers, came from Gilgal.

8 The LORD said to Joshua, "Do not be afraid of
them, for I have handed them over to you. Not
one of them will be able to stand against you."

9 So Joshua caught them by surprise, after
marching all night from Gilgal. 10 The LORD

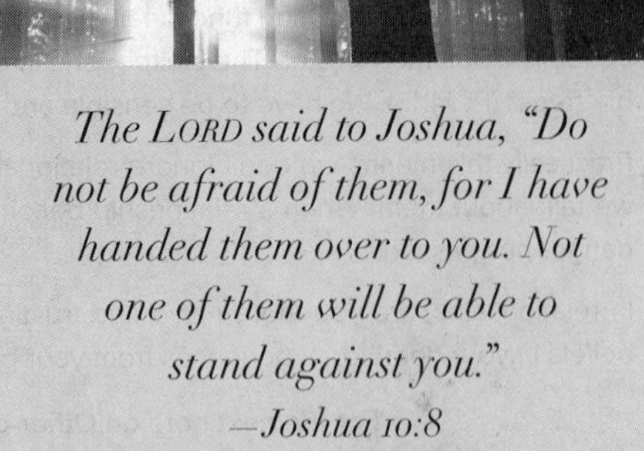
*The LORD said to Joshua, "Do
not be afraid of them, for I have
handed them over to you. Not
one of them will be able to
stand against you."
—Joshua 10:8*

[A] **9:25** Lit *us as is good and as is right in your eyes do your hands from* [B] **10:2** One Hb ms, Syr, Vg read *So he was* [C] **10:6** Lit *Don't withdraw*

threw them into confusion before Israel. He
defeated them in a great slaughter at Gibeon,
chased them through the ascent of Beth-horon,
and struck them down as far as Azekah and
Makkedah. 11 As they fled before Israel, the
LORD threw large hailstones on them from
the sky along the descent of Beth-horon all
the way to Azekah, and they died. More of
them died from the hail than the Israelites
killed with the sword.

12 On the day the LORD gave the Amorites
over to the Israelites, Joshua spoke to the LORD
in the presence of Israel:

"Sun, stand still over Gibeon,
and moon, over the Valley of Aijalon."
13 And the sun stood still
and the moon stopped
until the nation took vengeance
on its enemies.

Isn't this written in the Book of Jashar?[A]

So the sun stopped
in the middle of the sky
and delayed its setting
almost a full day.

14 There has been no day like it before or since,
when the LORD listened to a man, because the
LORD fought for Israel. 15 Then Joshua and all
Israel with him returned to the camp at Gilgal.

EXECUTION OF THE FIVE KINGS

16 Now the five defeated kings had fled and hidden in the cave at Makkedah. 17 It was reported
to Joshua: "The five kings have been found;
they are hiding in the cave at Makkedah."

18 Joshua said, "Roll large stones against the
mouth of the cave, and station men by it to
guard the kings. 19 But as for the rest of you,
don't stay there. Pursue your enemies and attack them from behind. Don't let them enter
their cities, for the LORD your God has handed
them over to you." 20 So Joshua and the Israelites finished inflicting a terrible slaughter
on them until they were destroyed, although
a few survivors ran away to the fortified cities. 21 The people returned safely to Joshua in
the camp at Makkedah. And no one dared to
threaten[B] the Israelites.

22 Then Joshua said, "Open the mouth of the
cave, and bring those five kings to me out of
there." 23 That is what they did. They brought
the five kings of Jerusalem, Hebron, Jarmuth,
Lachish, and Eglon to Joshua out of the cave.
24 When they had brought the kings to him,
Joshua summoned all the men of Israel and said
to the military commanders who had accompanied him, "Come here and put your feet on
the necks of these kings." So the commanders
came forward and put their feet on their necks.
25 Joshua said to them, "Do not be afraid or discouraged. Be strong and courageous, for the
LORD will do this to all the enemies you fight."

26 After this, Joshua struck them down and
executed them. He hung[C] their bodies on five
trees[D] and they were there until evening. 27 At
sunset Joshua commanded that they be taken
down from the trees and thrown into the cave
where they had hidden. Then large stones
were placed against the mouth of the cave,
and the stones are still there today.

CONQUEST OF SOUTHERN CITIES

28 On that day Joshua captured Makkedah and
struck it down with the sword, including its
king. He completely destroyed it[E] and everyone in it, leaving no survivors. So he treated
the king of Makkedah as he had the king of
Jericho.

29 Joshua and all Israel with him crossed
from Makkedah to Libnah and fought against
Libnah. 30 The LORD also handed it and its king
over to Israel. He struck it down, putting everyone in it to the sword, and left no survivors
in it. He treated Libnah's king as he had the
king of Jericho.

31 From Libnah, Joshua and all Israel with
him crossed to Lachish. They laid siege to it and
attacked it. 32 The LORD handed Lachish over
to Israel, and Joshua captured it on the second
day. He struck it down, putting everyone in it
to the sword, just as he had done to Libnah.
33 At that time King Horam of Gezer went to
help Lachish, but Joshua struck him down
along with his people, leaving no survivors.

34 Then Joshua crossed from Lachish to Eglon and all Israel with him. They laid siege to
it and attacked it. 35 On that day they captured
it and struck it down, putting everyone in it
to the sword. He completely destroyed it that
day, just as he had done to Lachish.

36 Next, Joshua and all Israel with him went
up from Eglon to Hebron and attacked it. 37 They
captured it and struck down its king, all its
villages, and everyone in it with the sword.
He left no survivors, just as he had done at
Eglon. He completely destroyed Hebron and
everyone in it.

[A] **10:13** Or *of the Upright* [B] **10:21** Lit *No one sharpened his tongue against* [C] **10:26** Or *impaled* [D] **10:26** Or *wooden stakes,* also in v. 27 [E] **10:28** Some Hb mss read *them*

38 Finally, Joshua turned toward Debir and
attacked it. And all Israel was with him. 39 He
captured it — its king and all its villages. They
struck them down with the sword and completely destroyed everyone in it, leaving no
survivors. He treated Debir and its king as
he had treated Hebron and as he had treated
Libnah and its king.
40 So Joshua conquered the whole region
— the hill country, the Negev, the Judean
foothills,[A] and the slopes — with all their
kings, leaving no survivors. He completely
destroyed every living being, as the LORD,
the God of Israel, had commanded. 41 Joshua
conquered everyone from Kadesh-barnea
to Gaza, and all the land of Goshen as far as
Gibeon. 42 Joshua captured all these kings
and their land in one campaign,[B] because
the LORD, the God of Israel, fought for Israel.
43 Then Joshua returned with all Israel to the
camp at Gilgal.

CONQUEST OF NORTHERN CITIES

11 When King Jabin of Hazor heard this
news, he sent a message to: King Jobab
of Madon, the kings of Shimron and Achshaph,
2 and the kings of the north in the hill country,
the Arabah south of Chinnereth, the Judean
foothills,[C] and the Slopes of Dor[D] to the west,
3 the Canaanites in the east and west, the Amorites, Hethites, Perizzites, and Jebusites in
the hill country, and the Hivites at the foot of
Hermon in the land of Mizpah. 4 They went
out with all their armies — a multitude as numerous as the sand on the seashore — along
with a vast number of horses and chariots.
5 All these kings joined forces; they came and
camped together at the Waters of Merom to
attack Israel.
6 The LORD said to Joshua, "Do not be afraid
of them, for at this time tomorrow I will cause
all of them to be killed before Israel. You are to
hamstring their horses and burn their chariots."
7 So Joshua and all his troops surprised them at
the Waters of Merom and attacked them. 8 The
LORD handed them over to Israel, and they struck
them down, pursuing them as far as greater Sidon and Misrephoth-maim, and to the east as
far as the Valley of Mizpeh. They struck them
down, leaving no survivors. 9 Joshua treated
them as the LORD had told him; he hamstrung
their horses and burned their chariots.
10 At that time Joshua turned back, captured
Hazor, and struck down its king with the sword,
because Hazor had formerly been the leader
of all these kingdoms. 11 They struck down
everyone in it with the sword, completely
destroying them; he left no one alive. Then
he burned Hazor.
12 Joshua captured all these kings and their
cities and struck them down with the sword.
He completely destroyed them, as Moses the
LORD's servant had commanded. 13 However, Israel did not burn any of the cities that
stood on their mounds except Hazor, which
Joshua burned. 14 The Israelites plundered all
the spoils and cattle of these cities for themselves. But they struck down every person
with the sword until they had annihilated
them, leaving no one alive. 15 Just as the LORD
had commanded his servant Moses, Moses
commanded Joshua. That is what Joshua did,
leaving nothing undone of all that the LORD
had commanded Moses.

Just as the LORD had commanded his servant Moses, Moses commanded Joshua. That is what Joshua did, leaving nothing undone of all that the LORD had commanded Moses.

— Joshua 11:15

SUMMARY OF CONQUESTS

16 So Joshua took all this land — the hill country, all the Negev, all the land of Goshen, the
foothills, the Arabah, and the hill country of
Israel with its foothills — 17 from Mount Halak, which ascends to Seir, as far as Baal-gad
in the Valley of Lebanon at the foot of Mount
Hermon. He captured all their kings and struck
them down, putting them to death. 18 Joshua
waged war with all these kings for a long time.
19 No city made peace with the Israelites except
the Hivites who inhabited Gibeon; all of them
were taken in battle. 20 For it was the LORD's
intention to harden their hearts, so that they
would engage Israel in battle, be completely
destroyed without mercy, and be annihilated, just as the LORD had commanded Moses.

[A] **10:40** Or *the Shephelah* [B] **10:42** Lit *land at one time* [C] **11:2** Or *Shephelah*, also in v. 16 [D] **11:2** Or *and in Naphoth-dor*

21 At that time Joshua proceeded to exter-
minate the Anakim from the hill country
— Hebron, Debir, Anab — all the hill country of Judah and of Israel. Joshua completely
destroyed them with their cities. 22 No Anakim
were left in the land of the Israelites, except for
some remaining in Gaza, Gath, and Ashdod.
23 So Joshua took the entire land, in keeping
with all that the LORD had told Moses. Joshua
then gave it as an inheritance to Israel according to their tribal allotments. After this, the
land had rest from war.

TERRITORY EAST OF THE JORDAN

12 The Israelites struck down the following
kings of the land and took possession
of their land beyond the Jordan to the east
and from the Arnon River to Mount Hermon,
including all the Arabah eastward:
2 King Sihon of the Amorites lived in Heshbon. He ruled from Aroer on the rim of the
Arnon River, along the middle of the valley,
and half of Gilead up to the Jabbok River (the
border of the Ammonites), 3 the Arabah east
of the Sea of Chinnereth to the Sea of Arabah (that is, the Dead Sea), eastward through
Beth-jeshimoth and southward[A] below the
slopes of Pisgah.
4 King Og[B] of Bashan, of the remnant of the
Rephaim, lived in Ashtaroth and Edrei. 5 He
ruled over Mount Hermon, Salecah, all Bashan
up to the Geshurite and Maacathite border,
and half of Gilead to the border of King Sihon
of Heshbon. 6 Moses the LORD's servant and
the Israelites struck them down. And Moses
the LORD's servant gave their land as an inheritance to the Reubenites, Gadites, and half
the tribe of Manasseh.

TERRITORY WEST OF THE JORDAN

7 Joshua and the Israelites struck down the
following kings of the land beyond the Jordan
to the west, from Baal-gad in the Valley of Lebanon to Mount Halak, which ascends toward
Seir (Joshua gave their land as an inheritance
to the tribes of Israel according to their allotments: 8 the hill country, the Judean foothills,[C]
the Arabah, the slopes, the wilderness, and the
Negev — the lands of the Hethites, Amorites,
Canaanites, Perizzites, Hivites, and Jebusites):

9 the king of Jericho — one
the king of Ai, which is next to Bethel — one
10 the king of Jerusalem — one
the king of Hebron — one
11 the king of Jarmuth — one
the king of Lachish — one
12 the king of Eglon — one
the king of Gezer — one
13 the king of Debir — one
the king of Geder — one
14 the king of Hormah — one
the king of Arad — one
15 the king of Libnah — one
the king of Adullam — one
16 the king of Makkedah — one
the king of Bethel — one
17 the king of Tappuah — one
the king of Hepher — one
18 the king of Aphek — one
the king of Lasharon — one
19 the king of Madon — one
the king of Hazor — one
20 the king of Shimron-meron — one
the king of Achshaph — one
21 the king of Taanach — one
the king of Megiddo — one
22 the king of Kedesh — one
the king of Jokneam in Carmel — one
23 the king of Dor in Naphath-dor[D] — one
the king of Goiim in Gilgal[E] — one
24 the king of Tirzah — one
the total number of all kings: thirty-one.

UNCONQUERED LANDS

13 Joshua was now old, advanced in age,
and the LORD said to him, "You have become old, advanced in age, but a great deal of
the land remains to be possessed. 2 This is the
land that remains:

All the districts of the Philistines and
the Geshurites: 3 from the Shihor east
of Egypt to the border of Ekron on the
north (considered to be Canaanite territory) — the five Philistine rulers of Gaza,
Ashdod, Ashkelon, Gath, and Ekron,
as well as the Avvites 4 in the south; all
the land of the Canaanites, from Arah
of the Sidonians to Aphek and as far as
the border of the Amorites; 5 the land of
the Gebalites; and all Lebanon east from
Baal-gad below Mount Hermon to the
entrance of Hamath[F] — 6 all the inhabitants of the hill country from Lebanon to
Misrephoth-maim, all the Sidonians.

I will drive them out before the Israelites, only

[A] **12:3** Or *and from Teman* [B] **12:4** LXX; MT reads *The territory of Og* [C] **12:8** Or *the Shephelah* [D] **12:23** Or *in the Slopes of Dor* [E] **12:23** LXX reads *Galilee* [F] **13:5** Or *to Lebo-hamath*

distribute the land as an inheritance for Israel,
as I have commanded you. 7 Therefore, divide
this land as an inheritance to the nine tribes
and half the tribe of Manasseh."

THE INHERITANCE EAST OF THE JORDAN

8 With the other half of the tribe of Manasseh, the Reubenites and Gadites had received
the inheritance Moses gave them beyond the
Jordan to the east, just as Moses the LORD's
servant had given them:
9 From Aroer on the rim of the Arnon
Valley, along with the city in the middle
of the valley, all the Medeba plateau as far
as Dibon, 10 and all the cities of King Sihon
of the Amorites, who reigned in Heshbon,
to the border of the Ammonites; 11 also
Gilead and the territory of the Geshurites
and Maacathites, all Mount Hermon,
and all Bashan to Salecah — 12 the whole
kingdom of Og in Bashan, who reigned in
Ashtaroth and Edrei; he was one of the
remaining Rephaim.
Moses struck them down and drove them
out, 13 but the Israelites did not drive out the
Geshurites and Maacathites. So Geshur and
Maacath still live in Israel today.
14 He did not, however, give any inheritance
to the tribe of Levi. This was their inheritance,
just as he had promised: the offerings made
by fire to the LORD, the God of Israel.

REUBEN'S INHERITANCE

15 To the tribe of Reuben's descendants by their
clans, Moses gave 16 this as their territory:
From Aroer on the rim of the Arnon
Valley, along with the city in the middle
of the valley, the whole plateau as far as[A]
Medeba, 17 with Heshbon and all its cities
on the plateau — Dibon, Bamoth-baal,
Beth-baal-meon, 18 Jahaz, Kedemoth,
Mephaath, 19 Kiriathaim, Sibmah,
Zereth-shahar on the hill in the valley,
20 Beth-peor, the slopes of Pisgah, and Beth-
jeshimoth — 21 all the cities of the plateau,
and all the kingdom of King Sihon of
the Amorites, who reigned in Heshbon.
Moses had killed him and the chiefs of
Midian — Evi, Rekem, Zur, Hur, and Reba
— the princes of Sihon who lived in the
land. 22 Along with those the Israelites
put to death, they also killed the diviner,
Balaam son of Beor, with the sword.
23 The border of the Reubenites was the Jordan
and its plain. This was the inheritance of the
Reubenites by their clans, with the cities and
their settlements.

GAD'S INHERITANCE

24 To the tribe of the Gadites by their clans,
Moses gave 25 this as their territory:
Jazer and all the cities of Gilead, and half
the land of the Ammonites to Aroer, near
Rabbah; 26 from Heshbon to Ramath-miz-
peh and Betonim, and from Mahanaim
to the border of Debir;[B] 27 in the valley:
Beth-haram, Beth-nimrah, Succoth, and
Zaphon — the rest of the kingdom of
King Sihon of Heshbon. Their land also
included the Jordan and its territory as
far as the edge of the Sea of Chinnereth
on the east side of the Jordan.[C]
28 This was the inheritance of the Gadites by
their clans, with the cities and their settlements.

EAST MANASSEH'S INHERITANCE

29 And to half the tribe of Manasseh (that is, to
half the tribe of Manasseh's descendants by
their clans) Moses gave 30 this as their territory:
From Mahanaim through all Bashan
— all the kingdom of King Og of Bashan,
including all of Jair's Villages[D] that are
in Bashan — sixty cities. 31 But half of
Gilead, and Og's royal cities in Bashan
— Ashtaroth and Edrei — are for the
descendants of Machir son of Manasseh
(that is, half the descendants of Machir by
their clans).
32 These were the portions Moses gave them
on the plains of Moab beyond the Jordan east
of Jericho. 33 But Moses did not give a portion to the tribe of Levi. The LORD, the God of
Israel, was their inheritance, just as he had
promised them.

ISRAEL'S INHERITANCE IN CANAAN

14 The Israelites received these portions
that the priest Eleazar, Joshua son of
Nun, and the family heads of the Israelite
tribes gave them in the land of Canaan.
2 Their inheritance was by lot as the LORD
commanded through Moses for the nine
and a half tribes, 3 because Moses had given
the inheritance to the two and a half tribes

[A] **13:16** Some Hb mss read *plateau near* [B] **13:26** Or *Lidbir*, or *Lo-debar* [C] **13:27** Lit *Chinnereth beyond the Jordan to the east*
[D] **13:30** Or *all of Havvoth-jair*

beyond the Jordan. But he gave no inheritance among them to the Levites. 4 The descendants of Joseph became two tribes, Manasseh and Ephraim. No portion of the land was given to the Levites except cities to live in, along with pasturelands for their cattle and livestock. 5 So the Israelites did as the LORD commanded Moses, and they divided the land.

CALEB'S INHERITANCE

6 The descendants of Judah approached Joshua at Gilgal, and Caleb son of Jephunneh the Kenizzite said to him, "You know what the LORD promised Moses the man of God at Kadesh-barnea about you and me. 7 I was forty years old when Moses the LORD's servant sent me from Kadesh-barnea to scout the land, and I brought back an honest report. 8 My brothers who went with me caused the people to lose heart,[A] but I followed the LORD my God completely. 9 On that day Moses swore to me: 'The land where you have set foot will be an inheritance for you and your descendants forever, because you have followed the LORD my God completely.'

10 "As you see, the LORD has kept me alive these forty-five years as he promised, since the LORD spoke this word to Moses while Israel was journeying in the wilderness. Here I am today, eighty-five years old. 11 I am still as strong today as I was the day Moses sent me out. My strength for battle and for daily tasks[B] is now as it was then. 12 Now give me this hill country the LORD promised me on that day, because you heard then that the Anakim are there, as well as large fortified cities. Perhaps the LORD will be with me and I will drive them out as the LORD promised."

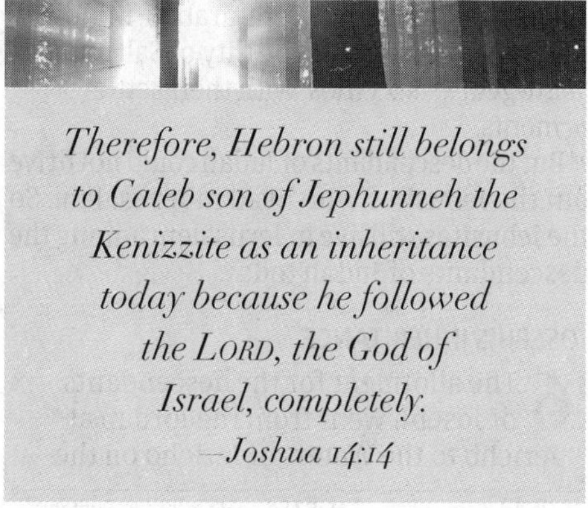
Therefore, Hebron still belongs to Caleb son of Jephunneh the Kenizzite as an inheritance today because he followed the LORD, the God of Israel, completely.
—*Joshua 14:14*

13 Then Joshua blessed Caleb son of Jephunneh and gave him Hebron as an inheritance. 14 Therefore, Hebron still belongs to Caleb son of Jephunneh the Kenizzite as an inheritance today because he followed the LORD, the God of Israel, completely. 15 Hebron's name used to be Kiriath-arba; Arba was the greatest man among the Anakim. After this, the land had rest from war.

JUDAH'S INHERITANCE

15 Now the allotment for the tribe of the descendants of Judah by their clans was in the southernmost region, south to the Wilderness of Zin and over to the border of Edom.

2 Their southern border began at the tip
of the Dead Sea on the south bay[C] 3 and
went south of the Scorpions' Ascent,[D]
proceeded to Zin, ascended to the south
of Kadesh-barnea, passed Hezron,
ascended to Addar, and turned to Karka.
4 It proceeded to Azmon and to the Brook
of Egypt and so the border ended at the
Mediterranean Sea. This is your[E] southern border.

5 Now the eastern border was along the
Dead Sea to the mouth of the Jordan.

The border on the north side was from
the bay of the sea at the mouth of the
Jordan. 6 It ascended to Beth-hoglah,
proceeded north of Beth-arabah, and
ascended to the Stone of Bohan son of
Reuben. 7 Then the border ascended to
Debir from the Valley of Achor, turning
north to the Gilgal that is opposite the
Ascent of Adummim, which is south
of the ravine. The border proceeded to
the Waters of En-shemesh and ended at
En-rogel. 8 From there the border ascended Ben Hinnom Valley to the southern
Jebusite slope (that is, Jerusalem) and
ascended to the top of the hill that
faces Hinnom Valley on the west, at the
northern end of Rephaim Valley. 9 From
the top of the hill the border curved to
the spring of the Waters of Nephtoah,
went to the cities of Mount Ephron, and
then curved to Baalah (that is, Kiriath-jearim). 10 The border turned westward
from Baalah to Mount Seir, went to the
northern slope of Mount Jearim (that is,

[A] **14:8** Lit *people's hearts to melt with fear* [B] **14:11** Lit *for going out and coming in* [C] **15:2** Lit *Sea at the tongue that turns southward* [D] **15:3** Lit *of scorpions* [E] **15:4** LXX reads *their*

Chesalon), descended to Beth-shemesh,
and proceeded to Timnah. 11 Then the border reached to the slope north of Ekron,
curved to Shikkeron, proceeded to Mount
Baalah, went to Jabneel, and ended at the
Mediterranean Sea.

12 Now the western border was the coastline of the Mediterranean Sea.

This was the boundary of the descendants
of Judah around their clans.

CALEB AND OTHNIEL

13 He gave Caleb son of Jephunneh the following portion among the descendants of Judah
based on the LORD's instruction to Joshua:
Kiriath-arba (that is, Hebron; Arba was the
father of Anak). 14 Caleb drove out from there
the three sons of Anak: Sheshai, Ahiman, and
Talmai, descendants of Anak. 15 From there
he marched against the inhabitants of Debir,
which used to be called Kiriath-sepher, 16 and
Caleb said, "Whoever attacks and captures
Kiriath-sepher, I will give my daughter Achsah
to him as a wife." 17 So Othniel son of Caleb's
brother, Kenaz, captured it, and Caleb gave his
daughter Achsah to him as a wife. 18 When she
arrived, she persuaded Othniel to ask her father for a field. As she got off her donkey, Caleb
asked her, "What can I do for you?" 19 She replied,
"Give me a blessing. Since you have given me
land in the Negev, give me the springs also."
So he gave her the upper and lower springs.

JUDAH'S CITIES

20 This was the inheritance of the tribe of the
descendants of Judah by their clans.

21 These were the outermost cities of the
tribe of the descendants of Judah toward
the border of Edom in the Negev: Kabzeel,
Eder, Jagur, 22 Kinah, Dimonah, Adadah,
23 Kedesh, Hazor, Ithnan, 24 Ziph, Telem,
Bealoth, 25 Hazor-hadattah, Kerioth-hez-
ron (that is, Hazor), 26 Amam, Shema,
Moladah, 27 Hazar-gaddah, Heshmon,
Beth-pelet, 28 Hazar-shual, Beer-sheba,
Biziothiah, 29 Baalah, Iim, Ezem, 30 Eltolad,
Chesil, Hormah, 31 Ziklag, Madmannah,
Sansannah, 32 Lebaoth, Shilhim, Ain, and
Rimmon — twenty-nine cities in all, with
their settlements.

33 In the Judean foothills:[A] Eshtaol, Zorah,
Ashnah, 34 Zanoah, En-gannim, Tappuah,[B]
Enam, 35 Jarmuth, Adullam, Socoh,[C]
Azekah, 36 Shaaraim, Adithaim, Gederah,
and Gederothaim — fourteen cities, with
their settlements; 37 Zenan, Hadashah,
Migdal-gad, 38 Dilan, Mizpeh, Jokthe-el,
39 Lachish, Bozkath, Eglon, 40 Cabbon, Lah-
mam, Chitlish, 41 Gederoth, Beth-dagon,
Naamah, and Makkedah — sixteen cities,
with their settlements; 42 Libnah, Ether,
Ashan, 43 Iphtah, Ashnah, Nezib, 44 Keilah,
Achzib, and Mareshah — nine cities,
with their settlements; 45 Ekron, with its
surrounding villages and settlements;
46 from Ekron to the sea, all the cities near
Ashdod, with their settlements; 47 Ashdod,
with its surrounding villages and settlements; Gaza, with its surrounding villages
and settlements, to the Brook of Egypt and
the coastline of the Mediterranean Sea.

48 In the hill country: Shamir, Jattir,
Socoh, 49 Dannah, Kiriath-sannah (that is,
Debir), 50 Anab, Eshtemoh, Anim, 51 Goshen, Holon, and Giloh — eleven cities,
with their settlements; 52 Arab, Dumah,[D]
Eshan, 53 Janim, Beth-tappuah, Aphekah,
54 Humtah, Kiriath-arba (that is, Hebron),
and Zior — nine cities, with their settlements; 55 Maon, Carmel, Ziph, Juttah,
56 Jezreel, Jokdeam, Zanoah, 57 Kain, Gibeah, and Timnah — ten cities, with their
settlements; 58 Halhul, Beth-zur, Gedor,
59 Maarath, Beth-anoth, and Eltekon — six
cities, with their settlements;[E] 60 Kiriath-
baal (that is, Kiriath-jearim), and Rabbah
— two cities, with their settlements.

61 In the wilderness: Beth-arabah, Middin,
Secacah, 62 Nibshan, the City of Salt,[F] and
En-gedi — six cities, with their settle-
ments.

63 But the descendants of Judah could not drive
out the Jebusites who lived in Jerusalem. So
the Jebusites still live in Jerusalem among the
descendants of Judah today.

JOSEPH'S INHERITANCE

16 The allotment for the descendants
of Joseph went from the Jordan at
Jericho to the Waters of Jericho on the

[A] **15:33** Or *the Shephelah* [B] **15:34** Or *En-gannim-tappuah* [C] **15:35** Or *Adullam-socoh* [D] **15:52** Some Hb mss read *Rumah* [E] **15:59** LXX adds *Tekoa, Ephrathah (that is, Bethlehem), Peor, Etam, Culom, Tatam, Sores, Carem, Gallim, Baither, and Manach — eleven cities, with their settlements* [F] **15:62** Or *Ir-hamelach*

east, through the wilderness ascending from Jericho into the hill country of Bethel. 2 From Bethel it went to Luz and proceeded to the border of the Archites by Ataroth. 3 It then descended westward to the border of the Japhletites as far as the border of lower Beth-horon, then to Gezer, and ended at the Mediterranean Sea. 4 So Ephraim and Manasseh, the sons of Joseph, received their inheritance.

EPHRAIM'S INHERITANCE

5 This was the territory of the descendants of Ephraim by their clans:

The border of their inheritance went from Ataroth-addar on the east to Upper Beth-horon. 6 In the north the border went westward from Michmethath; it turned eastward from Taanath-shiloh and passed it east of Janoah. 7 From Janoah it descended to Ataroth and Naarah, and then reached Jericho and went to the Jordan. 8 From Tappuah the border went westward along the Brook of Kanah and ended at the Mediterranean Sea.

This was the inheritance of the tribe of the descendants of Ephraim by their clans, together with 9 the cities set apart for the descendants of Ephraim within the inheritance of the descendants of Manasseh — all these cities with their settlements. 10 However, they did not drive out the Canaanites who lived in Gezer. So the Canaanites still live in Ephraim today, but they are forced laborers.

WEST MANASSEH'S INHERITANCE

17 This was the allotment for the tribe of Manasseh as Joseph's firstborn. Gilead and Bashan were given to Machir, the firstborn of Manasseh and the father of Gilead, because he was a man of war. 2 So the allotment was for the rest of Manasseh's descendants by their clans, for the sons of Abiezer, Helek, Asriel, Shechem, Hepher, and Shemida. These are the male descendants of Manasseh son of Joseph, by their clans.

3 Now Zelophehad son of Hepher, son of Gilead, son of Machir, son of Manasseh, had no sons, only daughters. These are the names of his daughters: Mahlah, Noah, Hoglah, Milcah, and Tirzah. 4 They came before the priest Eleazar, Joshua son of Nun, and the leaders, saying, "The LORD commanded Moses to give us an inheritance among our male relatives." So they gave them an inheritance among their father's brothers, in keeping with the LORD's instruction. 5 As a result, ten tracts fell to Manasseh, besides the land of Gilead and Bashan, which are beyond the Jordan,[A] 6 because Manasseh's daughters received an inheritance among his sons. The land of Gilead belonged to the rest of Manasseh's sons.

7 The border of Manasseh went from Asher to Michmethath near Shechem. It then went southward toward the inhabitants of En-tappuah. 8 The region of Tappuah belonged to Manasseh, but Tappuah itself on Manasseh's border belonged to the descendants of Ephraim. 9 From there the border descended to the Brook of Kanah; south of the brook, cities belonged to Ephraim among Manasseh's cities. Manasseh's border was on the north side of the brook and ended at the Mediterranean Sea. 10 Ephraim's territory was to the south and Manasseh's to the north, with the Sea as its border. They reached Asher on the north and Issachar on the east. 11 Within Issachar and Asher, Manasseh had Beth-shean, Ibleam, and the inhabitants of Dor with their surrounding villages; the inhabitants of En-dor, Taanach, and Megiddo — the three cities of[B] Naphath — with their surrounding villages.

12 The descendants of Manasseh could not possess these cities, because the Canaanites were determined to stay in this land. 13 However, when the Israelites grew stronger, they imposed forced labor on the Canaanites but did not drive them out completely.

JOSEPH'S ADDITIONAL INHERITANCE

14 Joseph's descendants said to Joshua, "Why did you give us only one tribal allotment[C] as an inheritance? We have many people, because the LORD has been blessing us greatly."

15 "If you have so many people," Joshua replied to them, "go to the forest and clear an area for yourselves there in the land of the Perizzites and the Rephaim, because Ephraim's hill country is too small for you."

16 But the descendants of Joseph said, "The hill country is not enough for us, and all the Canaanites who inhabit the valley area have iron chariots, both at Beth-shean with its surrounding villages and in the Jezreel Valley."

[A] **17:5** = east of the Jordan River [B] **17:11** LXX, Vg read *the third is* [C] **17:14** Lit *one lot and one territory*, also in v. 17

17 So Joshua replied to Joseph's family (that
is, Ephraim and Manasseh), "You have many
people and great strength. You will not have
just one allotment, 18 because the hill country
will be yours also. It is a forest; clear it and
its outlying areas will be yours. You can also
drive out the Canaanites, even though they
have iron chariots and are strong."

LAND DISTRIBUTION AT SHILOH

18 The entire Israelite community assembled at Shiloh and set up the tent of meeting there. The land had been subdued before
them, 2 but seven tribes among the Israelites
were left who had not divided up their inheritance. 3 So Joshua asked the Israelites,
"How long will you delay going out to take
possession of the land that the LORD, the God
of your fathers, gave you? 4 Appoint for yourselves three men from each tribe, and I will
send them out. They are to go and survey the
land, write a description of it for the purpose
of their inheritance, and return to me. 5 Then
they are to divide it into seven portions. Judah
is to remain in its territory in the south and
Joseph's family in their territory in the north.
6 When you have written a description of the
seven portions of land and brought it to me, I
will cast lots for you here in the presence of the
LORD our God. 7 But the Levites among you do
not get a portion, because their inheritance is
the priesthood of the LORD. Gad, Reuben, and
half the tribe of Manasseh have taken their
inheritance beyond the Jordan to the east,
which Moses the LORD's servant gave them."
8 As the men prepared to go, Joshua commanded them[A] to write down a description
of the land, saying, "Go and survey the land,
write a description of it, and return to me. I
will then cast lots for you here in Shiloh in the
presence of the LORD." 9 So the men left, went
through the land, and described it by towns in
a document of seven sections. They returned
to Joshua at the camp in Shiloh. 10 Joshua cast
lots for them at Shiloh in the presence of the
LORD where he distributed the land to the
Israelites according to their divisions.

BENJAMIN'S INHERITANCE

11 The lot came up for the tribe of Benjamin's
descendants by their clans, and their allotted
territory lay between Judah's descendants
and Joseph's descendants.

12 Their border on the north side began
at the Jordan, ascended to the slope of
Jericho on the north, through the hill
country westward, and ended at the
wilderness around Beth-aven. 13 From
there the border went toward Luz, to the
southern slope of Luz (that is, Bethel); it
then went down by Ataroth-addar, over
the hill south of Lower Beth-horon.

14 On the west side, from the hill facing
Beth-horon on the south, the border
curved, turning southward, and ended at
Kiriath-baal (that is, Kiriath-jearim), a city
of the descendants of Judah. This was the
west side of their border.

15 The south side began at the edge of
Kiriath-jearim, and the border extended westward; it went to the spring at
the Waters of Nephtoah. 16 The border
descended to the foot of the hill that faces
Ben Hinnom Valley at the northern end of
Rephaim Valley. It ran down Hinnom Valley toward the south Jebusite slope and
downward to En-rogel. 17 It curved northward and went to En-shemesh and on to
Geliloth, which is opposite the Ascent of
Adummim, and continued down to the
Stone of Bohan son of Reuben. 18 Then
it went north to the slope opposite the
Arabah[B] and proceeded into the plains.[C]
19 The border continued to the north slope
of Beth-hoglah and ended at the northern
bay of the Dead Sea, at the southern end of
the Jordan. This was the southern border.

20 The Jordan formed the border on the
east side.
This was the inheritance of Benjamin's descendants, by their clans, according to its
surrounding borders.

BENJAMIN'S CITIES

21 These were the cities of the tribe of Benjamin's descendants by their clans:
Jericho, Beth-hoglah, Emek-keziz,
22 Beth-arabah, Zemaraim, Bethel, 23 Avvim,
Parah, Ophrah, 24 Chephar-ammoni, Ophni,
and Geba — twelve cities, with their
settlements; 25 Gibeon, Ramah, Beeroth,
26 Mizpeh, Chephirah, Mozah, 27 Rekem,
Irpeel, Taralah, 28 Zela, Haeleph, Jebus[D]

[A] **18:8** Lit *the ones going around* [B] **18:18** LXX reads *went northward to Beth-arabah* [C] **18:18** Or *the Arabah* [D] **18:28** Lit *Jebusite*

(that is, Jerusalem), Gibeah, and Kiriath[A] —
fourteen cities, with their settlements.
This was the inheritance for Benjamin's descendants by their clans.

SIMEON'S INHERITANCE

19 The second lot came out for Simeon,
for the tribe of his descendants by their
clans, but their inheritance was within the
inheritance given to Judah's descendants.
2 Their inheritance included
Beer-sheba (or Sheba), Moladah, 3 Hazar-
shual, Balah, Ezem, 4 Eltolad, Bethul,
Hormah, 5 Ziklag, Beth-marcaboth, Hazar-
susah, 6 Beth-lebaoth, and Sharuhen
— thirteen cities, with their settlements;
7 Ain, Rimmon, Ether, and Ashan — four
cities, with their settlements; 8 and all the
settlements surrounding these cities as
far as Baalath-beer (Ramah in the south[B]).
This was the inheritance of the tribe of Simeon's descendants by their clans. 9 The inheritance of Simeon's descendants was within the
territory of Judah's descendants, because the
share for Judah's descendants was too large.
So Simeon's descendants received an inheritance within Judah's portion.

ZEBULUN'S INHERITANCE

10 The third lot came up for Zebulun's descendants by their clans.
The territory of their inheritance
stretched as far as Sarid; 11 their border
went up westward to Maralah, reached
Dabbesheth, and met the brook east of
Jokneam. 12 From Sarid, it turned due
east along the border of Chisloth-ta-
bor, went to Daberath, and went up to
Japhia. 13 From there, it went due east to
Gath-hepher and to Eth-kazin; it extended to Rimmon, curving around to Neah.
14 The border then circled around Neah
on the north to Hannathon and ended
at Iphtah-el Valley, 15 along with Kattath,
Nahalal, Shimron, Idalah, and Bethlehem
— twelve cities, with their settlements.
16 This was the inheritance of Zebulun's descendants by their clans, these cities, with
their settlements.

ISSACHAR'S INHERITANCE

17 The fourth lot came out for the tribe of Issachar's descendants by their clans.
18 Their territory went to Jezreel, and
included Chesulloth, Shunem, 19 Haphara-
im, Shion, Anaharath, 20 Rabbith, Kishion,
Ebez, 21 Remeth, En-gannim, En-haddah,
and Beth-pazzez. 22 The border reached
Tabor, Shahazumah, and Beth-shemesh,
and ended at the Jordan — sixteen cities,
with their settlements.
23 This was the inheritance of the tribe of Issachar's descendants by their clans, the cities,
with their settlements.

ASHER'S INHERITANCE

24 The fifth lot came out for the tribe of Asher's
descendants by their clans.
25 Their boundary included Helkath, Hali,
Beten, Achshaph, 26 Allammelech, Amad,
and Mishal and reached westward to
Carmel and Shihor-libnath. 27 It turned
eastward to Beth-dagon, reached Zebulun and Iphtah-el Valley, north toward
Beth-emek and Neiel, and went north
to Cabul, 28 Ebron, Rehob, Hammon, and
Kanah, as far as greater Sidon. 29 The
boundary then turned to Ramah as far as
the fortified city of Tyre; it turned back to
Hosah and ended at the Mediterranean
Sea, including Mahalab, Achzib,[C] 30 Um-
mah, Aphek, and Rehob — twenty-two
cities, with their settlements.
31 This was the inheritance of the tribe of Asher's descendants by their clans, these cities
with their settlements.

NAPHTALI'S INHERITANCE

32 The sixth lot came out for Naphtali's descendants by their clans.
33 Their boundary went from Heleph
and from the oak in Zaanannim, including Adami-nekeb and Jabneel, as far
as Lakkum, and ended at the Jordan.
34 To the west, the boundary turned to
Aznoth-tabor and went from there to
Hukkok, reaching Zebulun on the south,
Asher on the west, and Judah[D] at the
Jordan on the east. 35 The fortified cities
were Ziddim, Zer, Hammath, Rakkath,
Chinnereth, 36 Adamah, Ramah, Hazor,
37 Kedesh, Edrei, En-hazor, 38 Iron,
Migdal-el, Horem, Beth-anath, and Beth-
shemesh — nineteen cities, with their
settlements.
39 This was the inheritance of the tribe of

[A] **18:28** LXX, Syr read *Kiriath-jearim* [B] **19:8** Or *the Negev* [C] **19:29** Or *Sea, in the region of Achzib* [D] **19:34** LXX omits *Judah*

Naphtali's descendants by their clans, the cities with their settlements.

DAN'S INHERITANCE

40 The seventh lot came out for the tribe of Dan's descendants by their clans.

41 The territory of their inheritance
included Zorah, Eshtaol, Ir-shemesh,
42 Shaalabbin, Aijalon, Ithlah, 43 Elon,
Timnah, Ekron, 44 Eltekeh, Gibbethon,
Baalath, 45 Jehud, Bene-berak, Gath-rimmon, 46 Me-jarkon, and Rakkon, with the
territory facing Joppa.

47 When the territory of the descendants of Dan slipped out of their control, they went up and fought against Leshem, captured it, and struck it down with the sword. So they took possession of it, lived there, and renamed Leshem after their ancestor Dan. 48 This was the inheritance of the tribe of Dan's descendants by their clans, these cities with their settlements.

JOSHUA'S INHERITANCE

49 When they had finished distributing the land into its territories, the Israelites gave Joshua son of Nun an inheritance among them. 50 By the LORD's command, they gave him the city Timnath-serah in the hill country of Ephraim, which he requested. He rebuilt the city and lived in it.

51 These were the portions that the priest Eleazar, Joshua son of Nun, and the family heads distributed to the Israelite tribes by lot at Shiloh in the LORD's presence at the entrance to the tent of meeting. So they finished dividing up the land.

CITIES OF REFUGE

20 Then the LORD spoke to Joshua, 2 "Tell the Israelites: Select your cities of refuge, as I instructed you through Moses, 3 so that a person who kills someone unintentionally or accidentally may flee there. These will be your refuge from the avenger of blood. 4 When someone flees to one of these cities, stands at the entrance of the city gate, and states his case before[A] the elders of that city, they are to bring him into the city and give him a place to live among them. 5 And if the avenger of blood pursues him, they must not hand the one who committed manslaughter over to him, for he killed his neighbor accidentally and did not hate him beforehand. 6 He is to stay in that city until he stands trial before the assembly and until the death of the high priest serving at that time. Then the one who committed manslaughter may return home to his own city from which he fled."

7 So they designated Kedesh in the hill country of Naphtali in Galilee, Shechem in the hill country of Ephraim, and Kiriath-arba (that is, Hebron) in the hill country of Judah. 8 Across the Jordan east of Jericho, they selected Bezer on the wilderness plateau from Reuben's tribe, Ramoth in Gilead from Gad's tribe, and Golan in Bashan from Manasseh's tribe.

9 These are the cities appointed for all the Israelites and the aliens residing among them, so that anyone who kills a person unintentionally may flee there and not die at the hand of the avenger of blood until he stands before the assembly.

CITIES OF THE LEVITES

21 The Levite family heads approached the priest Eleazar, Joshua son of Nun, and the family heads of the Israelite tribes. 2 At Shiloh, in the land of Canaan, they told them, "The LORD commanded through Moses that we be given cities to live in, with their pasturelands for our livestock." 3 So the Israelites, by the LORD's command, gave the Levites these cities with their pasturelands from their inheritance.

4 The lot came out for the Kohathite clans:
The Levites who were the descendants of
the priest Aaron received thirteen cities
by lot from the tribes of Judah, Simeon,
and Benjamin. 5 The remaining descendants of Kohath received ten cities by lot
from the clans of the tribes of Ephraim,
Dan, and half the tribe of Manasseh.

6 Gershon's descendants received thirteen cities by lot from the clans of the
tribes of Issachar, Asher, Naphtali, and
half the tribe of Manasseh in Bashan.

7 Merari's descendants received twelve
cities for their clans from the tribes of
Reuben, Gad, and Zebulun.

8 The Israelites gave these cities with their pasturelands around them to the Levites by lot, as the LORD had commanded through Moses.

A 20:4 Lit *in the ears of*

My Story | Judith

Without warning, my husband informed me he wasn't happy, so he was leaving us. Heartbroken, I knew this would change everything. I had no money, no job. How could I provide for the family? What was I going to do? I cried to God for help, but I didn't know how because worry and anxious thoughts dominated my mind. I prayed over and over, "God help me, Lord help, help me, help me." It became my mantra.

I prayed Scripture: "Don't worry about anything, but in everything, through prayer and petition with thanksgiving, present your requests to God. And the peace of God, which surpasses all understanding, will guard your hearts and minds in Christ Jesus" (Php 4:6-7); "casting all your cares on him, because he cares about you" (1Pt 5:7). But it felt like he didn't hear; maybe he didn't care for me after all.

God *did* hear and answer my heart's cry. I got a job, my mother cared for the children, and though not without trials, we managed. God continues to teach me to trust Him and to face trials by taking every thought captive making them obedient to Christ. (2Co 10:5) I'm still learning that ability to read and quote scripture is not enough, I must believe it, do it, and live it. Most of the time, I can now say, " Lord, you hear my voice...I plead my case to you and watch expectantly" (Ps. 5:3).

When I'm tempted to revert to my former anxious ways, I know being "strong and courageous" does not mean without fear but that "the LORD your God is with you wherever you go" (Jos 1:9). I also know I will always need his continual grace. With Joshua, I have to "be very strong and continue obeying" (Jos 23:6).

CITIES OF AARON'S DESCENDANTS

9 The Israelites gave these cities by name from the tribes of the descendants of Judah and Simeon 10 to the descendants of Aaron from the Kohathite clans of the Levites, because they received the first lot. 11 They gave them Kiriath-arba (that is, Hebron; Arba was the father of Anak) with its surrounding pasturelands in the hill country of Judah. 12 But they gave the fields and settlements of the city to Caleb son of Jephunneh as his possession.

13 They gave to the descendants of the priest Aaron:

Hebron, the city of refuge for the one who commits manslaughter, with its pasturelands, Libnah with its pasturelands, 14 Jattir with its pasturelands, Eshtemoa with its pasturelands, 15 Holon with its pasturelands, Debir with its pasturelands, 16 Ain with its pasturelands, Juttah with its pasturelands, and Beth-shemesh with its pasturelands — nine cities from these two tribes.

17 From the tribe of Benjamin they gave:

Gibeon with its pasturelands, Geba with its pasturelands, 18 Anathoth with its pasturelands, and Almon with its pasturelands — four cities. 19 All thirteen cities with their pasturelands were for the priests, the descendants of Aaron.

CITIES OF KOHATH'S OTHER DESCENDANTS

20 The allotted cities to the remaining clans of Kohath's descendants, who were Levites, came from the tribe of Ephraim. 21 The Israelites gave them:

Shechem, the city of refuge for the one who commits manslaughter, with its pasturelands in the hill country of Ephraim, Gezer with its pasturelands, 22 Kibzaim with its pasturelands, and Beth-horon with its pasturelands — four cities.

23 From the tribe of Dan they gave:

Elteke with its pasturelands, Gibbethon with its pasturelands, 24 Aijalon with its pasturelands, and Gath-rimmon with its pasturelands — four cities.

25 From half the tribe of Manasseh they gave:

Taanach with its pasturelands and Gath-rimmon[A] with its pasturelands — two cities.

26 All ten cities with their pasturelands were for the clans of Kohath's other descendants.

CITIES OF GERSHON'S DESCENDANTS

27 From half the tribe of Manasseh, they gave to the descendants of Gershon, who were one of the Levite clans:

Golan, the city of refuge for the one who commits manslaughter, with its

[A] **21:25** Or *Ibleam*

pasturelands in Bashan, and Beeshterah
with its pasturelands — two cities.

28 From the tribe of Issachar they gave:
Kishion with its pasturelands, Daberath
with its pasturelands, 29 Jarmuth with its
pasturelands, and En-gannim with its
pasturelands — four cities.

30 From the tribe of Asher they gave:
Mishal with its pasturelands, Abdon with
its pasturelands, 31 Helkath with its pasturelands, and Rehob with its pasturelands — four cities.

32 From the tribe of Naphtali they gave:
Kedesh in Galilee, the city of refuge for
the one who commits manslaughter,
with its pasturelands, Hammoth-dor
with its pasturelands, and Kartan with its
pasturelands — three cities.
33 All thirteen cities with their pasturelands
were for the Gershonites by their clans.

CITIES OF MERARI'S DESCENDANTS

34 From the tribe of Zebulun, they gave to the
clans of the descendants of Merari, who were
the remaining Levites:
Jokneam with its pasturelands, Kartah
with its pasturelands, 35 Dimnah with
its pasturelands, and Nahalal with its
pasturelands — four cities.

36 From the tribe of Reuben they gave:
Bezer with its pasturelands, Jahzah[A]
with its pasturelands, 37 Kedemoth with
its pasturelands, and Mephaath with its
pasturelands — four cities.[B]

38 From the tribe of Gad they gave:
Ramoth in Gilead, the city of refuge
for the one who commits manslaughter, with its pasturelands, Mahanaim
with its pasturelands, 39 Heshbon with
its pasturelands, and Jazer with its
pasturelands — four cities in all. 40 All
twelve cities were allotted to the clans
of Merari's descendants, the remaining
Levite clans.

41 Within the Israelite possession there were
forty-eight cities in all with their pasturelands
for the Levites. 42 Each of these cities had its
own surrounding pasturelands; this was true
for all the cities.

THE LORD'S PROMISES FULFILLED

43 So the LORD gave Israel all the land he had
sworn to give their fathers, and they took
possession of it and settled there. 44 The LORD
gave them rest on every side according to all
he had sworn to their fathers. None of their
enemies were able to stand against them,
for the LORD handed over all their enemies
to them. 45 None of the good promises the
LORD had made to the house of Israel failed.
Everything was fulfilled.

EASTERN TRIBES RETURN HOME

22 Joshua summoned the Reubenites, Gadites, and half the tribe of Manasseh 2 and
told them, "You have done everything Moses
the LORD's servant commanded you and have
obeyed me in everything I commanded you.
3 You have not deserted your brothers even
once this whole time but have carried out the
requirement of the command of the LORD your
God. 4 Now that he has given your brothers
rest, just as he promised them, return to your
homes in your own land that Moses the LORD's
servant gave you across the Jordan. 5 Only carefully obey the command and instruction that
Moses the LORD's servant gave you: to love the
LORD your God, walk in all his ways, keep his
commands, be loyal to him, and serve him
with all your heart and all your soul."
6 Joshua blessed them and sent them on their
way, and they went to their homes. 7 Moses had
given territory to half the tribe of Manasseh in
Bashan, but Joshua had given territory to the
other half,[C] with their brothers, on the west
side of the Jordan. When Joshua sent them
to their homes and blessed them, 8 he said,
"Return to your homes with great wealth: a
huge number of cattle, and silver, gold, bronze,
iron, and a large quantity of clothing. Share
the spoil of your enemies with your brothers."

EASTERN TRIBES BUILD AN ALTAR

9 The Reubenites, Gadites, and half the tribe
of Manasseh left the Israelites at Shiloh in the
land of Canaan to return to their own land of
Gilead, which they took possession of according to the LORD's command through Moses.
10 When they came to the region of[D] the Jordan
in the land of Canaan, the Reubenites, Gadites,

[A] **21:36** Or *Jahaz* [B] **21:36-37** Some Hb mss omit these vv. [C] **22:7** Lit *to his half* [D] **22:10** Or *to Geliloth by*

and half the tribe of Manasseh built a large, impressive altar there by the Jordan.

11 Then the Israelites heard it said, "Look, the Reubenites, Gadites, and half the tribe of Manasseh have built an altar on the frontier of the land of Canaan at the region of[A] the Jordan, on the Israelite side." 12 When the Israelites heard this, the entire Israelite community assembled at Shiloh to go to war against them.

EXPLANATION OF THE ALTAR

13 The Israelites sent Phinehas son of Eleazar the priest to the Reubenites, Gadites, and half the tribe of Manasseh, in the land of Gilead. 14 They sent ten leaders with him — one family leader for each tribe of Israel. All of them were heads of their ancestral families[B] among the clans of Israel. 15 They went to the Reubenites, Gadites, and half the tribe of Manasseh, in the land of Gilead, and told them, 16 "This is what the LORD's entire community says: 'What is this treachery you have committed today against the God of Israel by turning away from the LORD and building an altar for yourselves, so that you are in rebellion against the LORD today? 17 Wasn't the iniquity of Peor, which brought a plague on the LORD's community, enough for us? We have not cleansed ourselves from it even to this day, 18 and now would you turn away from the LORD? If you rebel against the LORD today, tomorrow he will be angry with the entire community of Israel. 19 But if the land you possess is defiled, cross over to the land the LORD possesses where the LORD's tabernacle stands, and take possession of it among us. But don't rebel against the LORD or against us by building for yourselves an altar other than the altar of the LORD our God. 20 Wasn't Achan son of Zerah unfaithful regarding what was set apart for destruction, bringing wrath on the entire community of Israel? He was not the only one who perished because of his iniquity.' "

21 The Reubenites, Gadites, and half the tribe of Manasseh answered the heads of the Israelite clans, 22 "The Mighty One, God, the LORD! The Mighty One, God, the LORD![C] He knows, and may Israel also know. Do not spare us today, if it was in rebellion or treachery against the LORD 23 that we have built for ourselves an altar to turn away from him. May the LORD himself hold us accountable if we intended to offer burnt offerings and grain offerings on it, or to sacrifice fellowship offerings on it. 24 We actually did this from a specific concern that in the future your descendants might say to our descendants, 'What relationship do you have with the LORD, the God of Israel? 25 For the LORD has made the Jordan a border between us and you descendants of Reuben and Gad. You have no share in the LORD!' So your descendants may cause our descendants to stop fearing the LORD.

26 "Therefore we said: Let us take action and build an altar for ourselves, but not for burnt offering or sacrifice. 27 Instead, it is to be a witness between us and you, and between the generations after us, so that we may carry out the worship of the LORD in his presence with our burnt offerings, sacrifices, and fellowship offerings. Then in the future, your descendants will not be able to say to our descendants, 'You have no share in the LORD!' 28 We thought that if they said this to us or to our generations in the future, we would reply: Look at the replica of the LORD's altar that our fathers made, not for burnt offering or sacrifice, but as a witness between us and you. 29 We would never ever rebel against the LORD or turn away from him today by building an altar for burnt offering, grain offering, or sacrifice, other than the altar of the LORD our God, which is in front of his tabernacle."

CONFLICT RESOLVED

30 When the priest Phinehas and the community leaders, the heads of Israel's clans who were with him, heard what the descendants of Reuben, Gad, and Manasseh had to say, they were pleased. 31 Phinehas son of Eleazar the priest said to the descendants of Reuben, Gad, and Manasseh, "Today we know that the LORD is among us, because you have not committed this treachery against him. As a result, you have rescued the Israelites from the LORD's power."

32 Then the priest Phinehas son of Eleazar and the leaders returned from the Reubenites and Gadites in the land of Gilead to the Israelites in the land of Canaan and brought back a report to them. 33 The Israelites were pleased with the report, and they blessed God. They spoke no more about going to war against them to ravage the land where the Reubenites and Gadites lived. 34 So the Reubenites and Gadites named the altar: It[D] is a witness between us that the LORD is God.

[A] **22:11** Or *at Geliloth by* [B] **22:14** Lit *the house of their fathers* [C] **22:22** Or *The LORD is the God of gods! The LORD is the God of gods!* [D] **22:34** Some Hb mss, Syr, Tg read *altar Witness because it*

JOSHUA'S FAREWELL ADDRESS

23 A long time after the LORD had given
Israel rest from all the enemies around
them, Joshua was old, advanced in age. 2 So
Joshua summoned all Israel, including its elders, leaders, judges, and officers, and said to
them, "I am old, advanced in age, 3 and you have
seen for yourselves everything the LORD your
God did to all these nations on your account,
because it was the LORD your God who was
fighting for you. 4 See, I have allotted these
remaining nations to you as an inheritance
for your tribes, including all the nations I have
destroyed, from the Jordan westward to the
Mediterranean Sea. 5 The LORD your God will
force them back on your account and drive
them out before you so that you can take possession of their land, as the LORD your God
promised you.

6 "Be very strong and continue obeying all
that is written in the book of the law of Moses,
so that you do not turn from it to the right or
left 7 and so that you do not associate with these
nations remaining among you. Do not call on
the names of their gods or make an oath to
them; do not serve them or bow in worship
to them. 8 Instead, be loyal to the LORD your
God, as you have been to this day.

9 "The LORD has driven out great and
powerful nations before you, and no one is
able to stand against you to this day. 10 One
of you routed a thousand because the LORD
your God was fighting for you, as he promised.[A] 11 So diligently watch yourselves! Love
the LORD your God! 12 If you ever turn away
and become loyal to the rest of these nations
remaining among you, and if you intermarry
or associate with them and they with you,
13 know for certain that the LORD your God
will not continue to drive these nations out
before you. They will become a snare and
a trap for you, a sharp stick[B] for your sides
and thorns in your eyes, until you disappear
from this good land the LORD your God has
given you.

14 "I am now going the way of the whole
earth, and you know with all your heart and
all your soul that none of the good promises
the LORD your God made to you has failed. Everything was fulfilled for you; not one promise
has failed. 15 Since every good thing the LORD
your God promised you has come about, so
he will bring on you every bad thing until he
has annihilated you from this good land the
LORD your God has given you. 16 If you break
the covenant of the LORD your God, which he
commanded you, and go and serve other gods,
and bow in worship to them, the LORD's anger

Other-centeredness | *Loving God*

ENTROPY

"So diligently watch yourselves! Love the LORD your God!" Joshua 23:11

Scientists like to talk about "entropy," that tendency of material things in the physical world to break down and fall apart. We see it all around us, all the time. The stove breaks, and the paint peels. Our muscles sag underneath our wrinkling skin. In six weeks, that closet that was clean and re-organized is once again a dusty mess.

Guess what? Things fail and fall apart *everywhere* in our fallen world. Entropy chips away at our souls, our character, our relationships—even the way we relate to God.

This explains why Joshua gathered the Israelites near the end of his life. "Diligently watch yourselves!" he thundered. In other words, "Guard your heart" (Pr 4:23).

The old man had obviously lived long enough to know that we must fan the flames of spiritual devotion or decline sets in. Spiritual carelessness leads to spiritual coldness.

Assess yourself. Where are you strong? Where is your spiritual life springing a leak? Who can you call to help you get back on track?

For the next note on *Other-centeredness*, see 1 Samuel 12:23.

[A] **23:10** Lit *promised you* [B] **23:13** Or *a whip*; Hb obscure

will burn against you, and you will quickly disappear from this good land he has given you."

REVIEW OF ISRAEL'S HISTORY

24 Joshua assembled all the tribes of Israel at Shechem and summoned Israel's
elders, leaders, judges, and officers, and they
presented themselves before God. 2 Joshua
said to all the people, "This is what the LORD,
the God of Israel, says: 'Long ago your ancestors, including Terah, the father of Abraham
and Nahor, lived beyond the Euphrates River
and worshiped other gods. 3 But I took your
father Abraham from the region beyond the
Euphrates River, led him throughout the land
of Canaan, and multiplied his descendants. I
gave him Isaac, 4 and to Isaac I gave Jacob and
Esau. I gave the hill country of Seir to Esau as
a possession.
"'Jacob and his sons, however, went
down to Egypt. 5 I sent Moses and Aaron,
and I defeated Egypt by what I did within
it, and afterward I brought you out. 6 When
I brought your fathers out of Egypt and you
reached the Red Sea, the Egyptians pursued
your fathers with chariots and horsemen
as far as the sea. 7 Your fathers cried out to
the LORD, so he put darkness between you
and the Egyptians, and brought the sea over
them, engulfing them. Your own eyes saw
what I did to Egypt. After that, you lived in
the wilderness a long time.
8 "'Later, I brought you to the land of the
Amorites who lived beyond the Jordan. They
fought against you, but I handed them over to
you. You possessed their land, and I annihilated
them before you. 9 Balak son of Zippor, king of
Moab, set out to fight against Israel. He sent
for Balaam son of Beor to curse you, 10 but I
would not listen to Balaam. Instead, he repeatedly blessed you, and I rescued you from him.
11 "'You then crossed the Jordan and came
to Jericho. Jericho's citizens — as well as the
Amorites, Perizzites, Canaanites, Hethites,
Girgashites, Hivites, and Jebusites — fought
against you, but I handed them over to you. 12 I
sent hornets[A] ahead of you, and they drove out
the two Amorite kings before you. It was not
by your sword or bow. 13 I gave you a land you
did not labor for, and cities you did not build,
though you live in them; you are eating from
vineyards and olive groves you did not plant.'

THE COVENANT RENEWAL

14 "Therefore, fear the LORD and worship him
in sincerity and truth. Get rid of the gods your
fathers worshiped beyond the Euphrates River and in Egypt, and worship the LORD. 15 But
if it doesn't please you to worship the LORD,
choose for yourselves today: Which will you

Exercise of Faith | *Making Right Choices/Priorities/Values*

THE QUESTION AND THE CHOICE

"But if it doesn't please you to worship the LORD, choose for yourselves today: Which will you worship — the gods your fathers worshiped beyond the Euphrates River or the gods of the Amorites in whose land you are living? As for me and my family, we will worship the LORD." Joshua 24:15

No generation in history has ever had as many choices as citizens in the first world do today. From running shoes to breakfast cereals, from entertainment options to vacation destinations, the possibilities are dizzying. It's gotten so overwhelming that some counselors now make a handsome living treating patients who suffer from "decision anxiety."

This passage reveals Joshua cutting through the clutter and pinpointing *the* choice that looms above all other choices in life. (It's even more significant than "What are we going to watch tonight?"). It's this: Will you worship and serve the Lord—or not?

We have to ask ourselves this question because putting it off or ignoring the decision is actually making a choice. So we should revisit this profound question each day and reaffirm our choice.

For the next note on *Exercise of Faith*, see 1 Kings 11:4.

[A] **24:12** Or *sent terror*

worship — the gods your fathers worshiped beyond the Euphrates River or the gods of the Amorites in whose land you are living? As for me and my family, we will worship the LORD."

16 The people replied, "We will certainly not abandon the LORD to worship other gods! 17 For the LORD our God brought us and our fathers out of the land of Egypt, out of the place of slavery, and performed these great signs before our eyes. He also protected us all along the way we went and among all the peoples whose lands we traveled through. 18 The LORD drove out before us all the peoples, including the Amorites who lived in the land. We too will worship the LORD, because he is our God."

19 But Joshua told the people, "You will not be able to worship the LORD, because he is a holy God. He is a jealous God; he will not forgive your transgressions and sins. 20 If you abandon the LORD and worship foreign gods, he will turn against you, harm you, and completely destroy you, after he has been good to you."

21 "No! " the people answered Joshua. "We will worship the LORD."

22 Joshua then told the people, "You are witnesses against yourselves that you yourselves have chosen to worship the LORD."

"We are witnesses," they said.

23 "Then get rid of the foreign gods that are among you and turn your hearts to the LORD, the God of Israel."

24 So the people said to Joshua, "We will worship the LORD our God and obey him."

25 On that day Joshua made a covenant for the people at Shechem and established a statute and ordinance for them. 26 Joshua recorded these things in the book of the law of God; he also took a large stone and set it up there under the oak at the sanctuary of the LORD. 27 And Joshua said to all the people, "You see this stone — it will be a witness against us, for it has heard all the words the LORD said to us, and it will be a witness against you, so that you will not deny your God." 28 Then Joshua sent the people away, each to his own inheritance.

BURIAL OF THREE LEADERS

29 After these things, the LORD's servant, Joshua son of Nun, died at the age of 110. 30 They buried him in his allotted territory at Timnath-serah, in the hill country of Ephraim north of Mount Gaash. 31 Israel worshiped the LORD throughout Joshua's lifetime and during the lifetimes of the elders who outlived Joshua and who had experienced all the works the LORD had done for Israel.

32 Joseph's bones, which the Israelites had brought up from Egypt, were buried at Shechem in the parcel of land Jacob had purchased from the sons of Hamor, Shechem's father, for a hundred pieces of silver.[A] It was an inheritance for Joseph's descendants.

33 And Eleazar son of Aaron died, and they buried him at Gibeah,[B] which had been given to his son Phinehas in the hill country of Ephraim.

[A] **24:32** Lit *a hundred qesitahs* [B] **24:33** = the Hill

RESTORATION THEMES

R	Rest and Reflection	*For the next note, see 1 Samuel 2:26.*
E	Eternal Perspective	*For the next note, see 1 Samuel 16:7.*
S	Support	*Knowing Your Role—Judges 8:22-23*
T	Thanksgiving and Contentment	*Confession—3:7-9*
O	Other-centeredness	*For the next note, see 1 Samuel 12:23.*
R	Relationships	*For the next note, see 1 Samuel 18:1-3.*
E	Exercise of Faith	*For the next note, see 1 Kings 11:4.*

JUDAH'S LEADERSHIP AGAINST THE CANAANITES

1 After the death of Joshua, the Israelites inquired of the LORD, "Who will be the first to fight for us against the Canaanites?"

2 The LORD answered, "Judah is to go. I have handed the land over to him."

3 Judah said to his brother Simeon, "Come with me to my allotted territory, and let us fight against the Canaanites. I will also go with you to your allotted territory." So Simeon went with him.

4 When Judah attacked, the LORD handed the Canaanites and Perizzites over to them. They struck down ten thousand men in Bezek. 5 They found Adoni-bezek in Bezek, fought against him, and struck down the Canaanites and Perizzites.

6 When Adoni-bezek fled, they pursued him, caught him, and cut off his thumbs and big toes. 7 Adoni-bezek said, "Seventy kings with their thumbs and big toes cut off used to pick up scraps[A] under my table. God has repaid me for what I have done." They brought him to Jerusalem, and he died there.

8 The men of Judah fought against Jerusalem, captured it, put it to the sword, and set the city on fire. 9 Afterward, the men of Judah marched down to fight against the Canaanites who were living in the hill country, the Negev, and the Judean foothills.[B] 10 Judah also marched against the Canaanites who were living in Hebron (Hebron was formerly named Kiriath-arba). They struck down Sheshai, Ahiman, and Talmai. 11 From there they marched against the residents of Debir (Debir was formerly named Kiriath-sepher).

12 Caleb said, "Whoever attacks and captures Kiriath-sepher, I will give my daughter Achsah to him as a wife." 13 So Othniel son of Kenaz, Caleb's youngest brother, captured it, and Caleb gave his daughter Achsah to him as his wife.

14 When she arrived, she persuaded Othniel to ask her father for a field. As she got off her donkey, Caleb asked her, "What do you want?" 15 She answered him, "Give me a blessing. Since you have given me land in the Negev, give me springs also." So Caleb gave her both the upper and lower springs.

16 The descendants of the Kenite, Moses's father-in-law, had gone up with the men of Judah from the City of Palms[C] to the Wilderness of Judah, which was in the Negev of Arad. They went to live among the people.

17 Judah went with his brother Simeon, struck the Canaanites who were living in Zephath, and completely destroyed the town. So they named the town Hormah. 18 Judah captured Gaza and its territory, Ashkelon and its territory, and Ekron and its territory. 19 The LORD was with Judah and enabled them to take possession of the hill country, but they could not drive out the people who were living in the valley because those people had iron chariots.

20 Judah gave Hebron to Caleb, just as Moses had promised. Then Caleb drove out the three sons of Anak who lived there.

BENJAMIN'S FAILURE

21 At the same time the Benjaminites did not drive out the Jebusites who were living in Jerusalem. The Jebusites have lived among the Benjaminites in Jerusalem to this day.

SUCCESS OF THE HOUSE OF JOSEPH

22 The house of Joseph also attacked Bethel, and the LORD was with them. 23 They sent spies to Bethel (the town was formerly named Luz). 24 The spies saw a man coming out of the town and said to him, "Please show us how to get into town, and we will show you kindness." 25 When he showed them the way into the town, they put the town to the sword but released the man and his entire family. 26 Then the man went to the land of the Hittites, built a town, and named it Luz. That is its name still today.

FAILURE OF THE OTHER TRIBES

27 At that time Manasseh failed to take possession of Beth-shean and Taanach and their surrounding villages, or the residents of Dor, Ibleam, and Megiddo and their surrounding villages; the Canaanites were determined to stay in this land. 28 When Israel became stronger, they made the Canaanites serve as forced labor but never drove them out completely.

29 At that time Ephraim failed to drive out the Canaanites who were living in Gezer, so the Canaanites have lived among them in Gezer.

30 Zebulun failed to drive out the residents of Kitron or the residents of Nahalol, so the Canaanites lived among them and served as forced labor.

31 Asher failed to drive out the residents of

[A] **1:7** Lit *toes cut off are gathering* [B] **1:9** Or *the Shephelah* [C] **1:16** = Jericho; Dt 34:3; Jdg 3:13; 2Ch 28:15

Acco or of Sidon, or Ahlab, Achzib, Helbah,
Aphik, or Rehob. 32 The Asherites lived among
the Canaanites who were living in the land,
because they failed to drive them out.
33 Naphtali did not drive out the residents
of Beth-shemesh or the residents of Beth-
anath. They lived among the Canaanites who
were living in the land, but the residents of
Beth-shemesh and Beth-anath served as their
forced labor.
34 The Amorites forced the Danites into
the hill country and did not allow them to
go down into the valley. 35 The Amorites were
determined to stay in[A] Har-heres, Aijalon, and
Shaalbim. When the house of Joseph got the
upper hand,[B] the Amorites[C] were made to
serve as forced labor. 36 The territory of the
Amorites extended from the Scorpions' Ascent, that is from Sela upward.

PATTERN OF SIN AND JUDGMENT

2 The angel of the LORD went up from Gilgal
to Bochim and said, "I brought you out of
Egypt and led you into the land I had promised to your fathers. I also said: I will never
break my covenant with you. 2 You are not
to make a covenant with the inhabitants of
this land. You are to tear down their altars.
But you have not obeyed me. What is this you
have done? 3 Therefore, I now say: I will not
drive out these people before you. They will be
thorns[D,E] in your sides, and their gods will be
a trap for you." 4 When the angel of the LORD
had spoken these words to all the Israelites,
the people wept loudly. 5 So they named that
place Bochim[F] and offered sacrifices there
to the LORD.

JOSHUA'S DEATH

6 Previously, when Joshua had sent the people
away, the Israelites had gone to take possession of the land, each to his own inheritance.
7 The people worshiped the LORD throughout
Joshua's lifetime and during the lifetimes of
the elders who outlived[G] Joshua. They had
seen all the LORD's great works he had done
for Israel.
8 Joshua son of Nun, the servant of the LORD,
died at the age of 110. 9 They buried him in the
territory of his inheritance, in Timnath-her-
es, in the hill country of Ephraim, north of
Mount Gaash. 10 That whole generation was

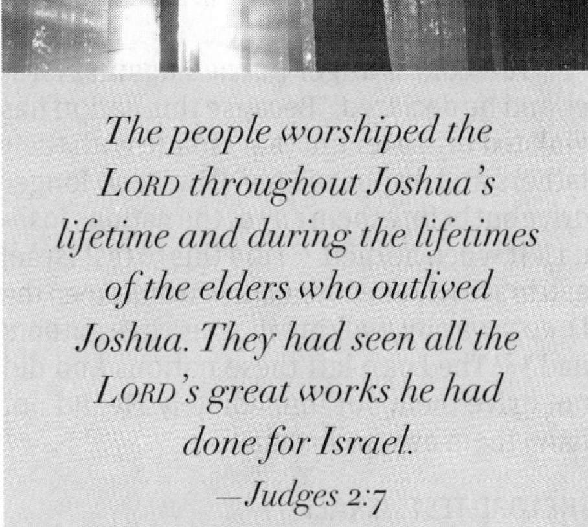
The people worshiped the LORD throughout Joshua's lifetime and during the lifetimes of the elders who outlived Joshua. They had seen all the LORD's great works he had done for Israel.
—*Judges 2:7*

also gathered to their ancestors. After them
another generation rose up who did not know
the LORD or the works he had done for Israel.
11 The Israelites did what was evil in the
LORD's sight. They worshiped the Baals 12 and
abandoned the LORD, the God of their fathers,
who had brought them out of Egypt. They
followed other gods from the surrounding
peoples and bowed down to them. They angered the LORD, 13 for they abandoned him and
worshiped Baal and the Ashtoreths.
14 The LORD's anger burned against Israel,
and he handed them over to marauders who
raided them. He sold them to[H] the enemies
around them, and they could no longer resist
their enemies. 15 Whenever the Israelites went
out, the LORD[I] was against them and brought
disaster on them, just as he had promised
and sworn to them. So they suffered greatly.
16 The LORD raised up judges, who saved them
from the power of their marauders, 17 but they
did not listen to their judges. Instead, they prostituted themselves with other gods, bowing
down to them. They quickly turned from the
way of their fathers, who had walked in obedience to the LORD's commands. They did not
do as their fathers did. 18 Whenever the LORD
raised up a judge for the Israelites, the LORD
was with him and saved the people from the
power of their enemies while the judge was
still alive.[J] The LORD was moved to pity whenever they groaned because of those who were
oppressing and afflicting them. 19 Whenever
the judge died, the Israelites would act even
more corruptly than their fathers, following
other gods to serve them and bow in worship

[A] **1:35** Or *Amorites determined to live in* [B] **1:35** Lit *When the hand of the house of Joseph was heavy* [C] **1:35** LXX reads *Joseph became strong on the Amorites, they* [D] **2:3** LXX reads *affliction* [E] **2:3** Lit *traps* [F] **2:5** Or *Weeping* [G] **2:7** Lit *extended their days after* [H] **2:14** Lit *into the hand of* [I] **2:15** Lit *the hand of the LORD* [J] **2:18** Lit *enemies all the days of the judge*

to them. They did not turn from their evil practices or their obstinate ways.
20 The LORD's anger burned against Israel, and he declared, "Because this nation has
violated my covenant that I made with their
fathers and disobeyed me, 21 I will no longer
drive out before them any of the nations Joshua left when he died. 22 I did this to test Israel
and to see whether or not they would keep the
LORD's way by walking in it, as their fathers
had." 23 The LORD left these nations and did
not drive them out immediately. He did not
hand them over to Joshua.

THE LORD TESTS ISRAEL

3 These are the nations the LORD left in order
to test all those in Israel who had experienced[A] none of the wars in Canaan. 2 This was
to teach the future generations of the Israelites
how to fight in battle, especially those who had
not fought before.[B] 3 These nations included
the five rulers of the Philistines and all of the
Canaanites, the Sidonians, and the Hivites who
lived in the Lebanese mountains from Mount
Baal-hermon as far as the entrance to Hamath.[C]
4 The LORD left them to test Israel, to determine
if they would keep the LORD's commands he
had given their fathers through[D] Moses. 5 But
they settled among the Canaanites, Hethites,
Amorites, Perizzites, Hivites, and Jebusites.
6 The Israelites took their daughters as wives
for themselves, gave their own daughters to
their sons, and worshiped their gods.

OTHNIEL, THE FIRST JUDGE

7 The Israelites did what was evil in the LORD's
sight; they forgot the LORD their God and worshiped the Baals and the Asherahs. 8 The LORD's
anger burned against Israel, and he sold them
to[E] King Cushan-rishathaim[F] of Aram-naharaim,[G] and the Israelites served him eight years.
9 The Israelites cried out to the LORD. So the
LORD raised up Othniel son of Kenaz, Caleb's
youngest brother, as a deliverer to save the Israelites. 10 The Spirit of the LORD came on him, and
he judged Israel. Othniel went out to battle, and
the LORD handed over King Cushan-rishathaim
of Aram to him, so that Othniel overpowered
him. 11 Then the land had peace for forty years,
and Othniel son of Kenaz died.

EHUD

12 The Israelites again did what was evil in
the LORD's sight. He gave King Eglon of Moab

Thanksgiving and Contentment | *Confession*

THE POWER IN CONFESSION

"The Israelites did what was evil . . . they forgot the LORD their God. . . . The LORD's anger burned against Israel. . . . The Israelites cried out to the LORD. So the LORD raised up Othniel . . . as a deliverer to save the Israelites." Judges 3:7-9

This passage tells the story of the entire book of Judges in miniature. For almost four hundred years, the Israelites repeatedly turned away from God. In each of these sad, dysfunctional episodes, God raised up a nearby nation to afflict his people. He did this in order to capture their wandering attention and pierce their hard hearts. And it worked. God's people would finally admit their sin to God and beg for help. He would forgive and rescue. In each case, he would then send a deliverer or "judge."

The obvious lesson from this dark period in Israel's history is: Don't turn away from God! But, of course, that's easier said than done. We all turn away from him, in big ways and small, every day. And so the next best lesson is to admit your wrongdoing, confess your sin. The example of the Israelites and the eternal promise of God (1Jn 1:9) teaches us that when we humbly acknowledge our rebelliousness, God forgives.

Confession is the all-important first step in spiritual restoration.

For the next note on *Thanksgiving and Contentment*, see Ruth 1:20-21.

[A] **3:1** Lit *had known* [B] **3:2** Lit *not known it* [C] **3:3** Or *as Lebo-hamath* [D] **3:4** Lit *by the hand of* [E] **3:8** Lit *into the hand of*
[F] **3:8** Lit *Doubly-Evil* [G] **3:8** = Mesopotamia

power over Israel, because they had done what was evil in the LORD's sight. 13 After Eglon convinced the Ammonites and the Amalekites to join forces with him, he attacked and defeated Israel and took possession of the City of Palms.[A] 14 The Israelites served King Eglon of Moab eighteen years.

15 Then the Israelites cried out to the LORD, and he raised up Ehud son of Gera, a left-handed Benjaminite,[B] as a deliverer for them. The Israelites sent him with the tribute for King Eglon of Moab.

16 Ehud made himself a double-edged sword eighteen inches long.[C] He strapped it to his right thigh under his clothes 17 and brought the tribute to King Eglon of Moab, who was an extremely fat man. 18 When Ehud had finished presenting the tribute, he dismissed the people who had carried it. 19 At the carved images near Gilgal he returned and said, "King Eglon, I have a secret message for you." The king said, "Silence!" and all his attendants left him. 20 Then Ehud approached him while he was sitting alone in his upstairs room where it was cool. Ehud said, "I have a message from God for you," and the king stood up from his throne. 21 Ehud reached with his left hand, took the sword from his right thigh, and plunged it into Eglon's belly. 22 Even the handle went in after the blade, and Eglon's fat closed in over it, so that Ehud did not withdraw the sword from his belly. And the waste came out.[D] 23 Ehud escaped by way of the porch, closing and locking the doors of the upstairs room behind him.

24 Ehud was gone when Eglon's servants came in. They looked and found the doors of the upstairs room locked and thought he was relieving himself[E] in the cool room. 25 The servants waited until they became embarrassed and saw that he had still not opened the doors of the upstairs room. So they took the key and opened the doors — and there was their lord lying dead on the floor!

26 Ehud escaped while the servants waited. He passed the Jordan near the carved images and reached Seirah. 27 After he arrived, he sounded the ram's horn throughout the hill country of Ephraim. The Israelites came down with him from the hill country, and he became their leader. 28 He told them, "Follow me, because the LORD has handed over your enemies, the Moabites, to you." So they followed him, captured the fords of the Jordan leading to Moab, and did not allow anyone to cross over. 29 At that time they struck down about ten thousand Moabites, all stout and able-bodied men. Not one of them escaped. 30 Moab became subject to Israel that day, and the land had peace for eighty years.

SHAMGAR

31 After Ehud, Shamgar son of Anath became judge. He also delivered Israel, striking down six hundred Philistines with a cattle prod.

DEBORAH AND BARAK

4 The Israelites again did what was evil in the sight of the LORD after Ehud had died. 2 So the LORD sold them to King Jabin of Canaan, who reigned in Hazor. The commander of his army was Sisera who lived in Harosheth of the Nations.[F] 3 Then the Israelites cried out to the LORD, because Jabin had nine hundred iron chariots, and he harshly oppressed them twenty years.

4 Deborah, a prophetess and the wife of Lappidoth, was judging Israel at that time. 5 She would sit under the palm tree of Deborah between Ramah and Bethel in the hill country of Ephraim, and the Israelites went up to her to settle disputes.

6 She summoned Barak son of Abinoam from Kedesh in Naphtali and said to him, "Hasn't the LORD, the God of Israel, commanded you: 'Go, deploy the troops on Mount Tabor, and take with you ten thousand men from the Naphtalites and Zebulunites? 7 Then I will lure Sisera commander of Jabin's army, his chariots, and his infantry at the Wadi Kishon to fight against you, and I will hand him over to you.' "

8 Barak said to her, "If you will go with me, I will go. But if you will not go with me, I will not go."

9 "I will gladly go with you," she said, "but you will receive no honor on the road you are about to take, because the LORD will sell Sisera to a woman." So Deborah got up and went with Barak to Kedesh. 10 Barak summoned Zebulun and Naphtali to Kedesh; ten thousand men followed him, and Deborah also went with him.

11 Now Heber the Kenite had moved away from the Kenites, the sons of Hobab, Moses's

[A] **3:13** = Jericho; Dt 34:3; Jdg 1:16; 2Ch 28:15 [B] **3:15** = son of the right hand [C] **3:16** Lit *sword a gomed in length* [D] **3:22** Or *And Eglon's bowels discharged* [E] **3:24** Lit *was covering his feet* [F] **4:2** Or *Harosheth-ha-goiim*, also in vv. 13,16

father-in-law, and pitched his tent beside the
oak tree of Zaanannim, which was near Kedesh.
12 It was reported to Sisera that Barak son of
Abinoam had gone up Mount Tabor. 13 Sisera
summoned all his nine hundred iron chariots
and all the troops who were with him from
Harosheth of the Nations to the Wadi Kishon.
14 Then Deborah said to Barak, "Go! This is the
day the LORD has handed Sisera over to you.
Hasn't the LORD gone before you?" So Barak
came down from Mount Tabor with ten thousand men following him.

15 The LORD threw Sisera, all his charioteers,
and all his army into a panic before Barak's
assault. Sisera left his chariot and fled on foot.
16 Barak pursued the chariots and the army
as far as Harosheth of the Nations, and the
whole army of Sisera fell by the sword; not a
single man was left.

17 Meanwhile, Sisera had fled on foot to
the tent of Jael, the wife of Heber the Kenite,
because there was peace between King Jabin
of Hazor and the family of Heber the Kenite.
18 Jael went out to greet Sisera and said to
him, "Come in, my lord. Come in with me.
Don't be afraid." So he went into her tent,
and she covered him with a blanket. 19 He
said to her, "Please give me a little water to
drink for I am thirsty." She opened a container
of milk, gave him a drink, and covered him
again. 20 Then he said to her, "Stand at the
entrance to the tent. If a man comes and asks
you, 'Is there a man here?' say, 'No.'" 21 While
he was sleeping from exhaustion, Heber's
wife Jael took a tent peg, grabbed a hammer,
and went silently to Sisera. She hammered
the peg into his temple and drove it into the
ground, and he died.

22 When Barak arrived in pursuit of Sisera,
Jael went out to greet him and said to him,
"Come and I will show you the man you are
looking for." So he went in with her, and there
was Sisera lying dead with a tent peg through
his temple!

23 That day God subdued King Jabin of Ca-
naan before the Israelites. 24 The power of the
Israelites continued to increase against King
Jabin of Canaan until they destroyed him.

DEBORAH'S SONG

5 On that day Deborah and Barak son of
Abinoam sang:

2 When the leaders lead[A] in Israel,
when the people volunteer,
blessed be the LORD.
3 Listen, kings! Pay attention, princes!
I will sing to the LORD;
I will sing praise to the LORD God
of Israel.
4 LORD, when you came from Seir,
when you marched from the fields
of Edom,
the earth trembled,
the skies poured rain,
and the clouds poured water.
5 The mountains melted before the LORD,
even Sinai,[B] before the LORD, the God
of Israel.

6 In the days of Shamgar son of Anath,
in the days of Jael,
the main roads were deserted
because travelers kept
to the side roads.
7 Villages were deserted,[C]
they were deserted in Israel,
until I,[D] Deborah, arose,
a mother in Israel.
8 Israel chose new gods,
then there was war in the city gates.
Not a shield or spear was seen
among forty thousand in Israel.
9 My heart is with the leaders of Israel,
with the volunteers of the people.
Blessed be the LORD!
10 You who ride on white[C] donkeys,
who sit on saddle blankets,
and who travel on the road, give praise!
11 Let them tell the righteous acts
of the LORD,
the righteous deeds of his warriors
in Israel,
with the voices of the singers
at the watering places.[C]

Then the LORD's people went down
to the city gates.
12 "Awake! Awake, Deborah!
Awake! Awake, sing a song!
Arise, Barak,
and take your prisoners,
son of Abinoam!"
13 Then the survivors came down
to the nobles;
the LORD's people came down to me[E]
with the warriors.

[A] 5:2 Or *the locks of hair are loose* [B] 5:5 Or *LORD, this one of Sinai* [C] 5:7,10,11 Hb obscure [D] 5:7 Or *you* [E] 5:13 LXX reads *down for him*

14 Those with their roots in Amalek[A]
came from Ephraim;
Benjamin came with your people
after you.
The leaders came down from Machir,
and those who carry a marshal's staff
came from Zebulun.
15 The princes of Issachar were
with Deborah;
Issachar was with Barak;
they were under his leadership[B]
in the valley.
There was great searching[C] of heart
among the clans of Reuben.
16 Why did you sit among the sheep
pens[D]
listening to the playing of pipes
for the flocks?
There was great searching of heart
among the clans of Reuben.
17 Gilead remained beyond the Jordan.
Dan, why did you linger at the ships?
Asher remained at the seashore
and stayed in his harbors.
18 The people of Zebulun defied death,
Naphtali also, on the heights
of the battlefield.

19 Kings came and fought.
Then the kings of Canaan fought
at Taanach by the Waters of Megiddo,
but they did not plunder the silver.
20 The stars fought from the heavens;
the stars fought with Sisera
from their paths.
21 The river Kishon swept them away,
the ancient river, the river Kishon.
March on, my soul, in strength!
22 The horses' hooves then hammered —
the galloping, galloping
of his[E] stallions.
23 "Curse Meroz," says the angel
of the LORD,
"Bitterly curse her inhabitants,
for they did not come to help the
LORD,
to help the LORD with the warriors."

24 Jael is most blessed of women,
the wife of Heber the Kenite;
she is most blessed among
tent-dwelling women.
25 He asked for water; she gave him milk.
She brought him cream
in a majestic bowl.
26 She reached for a tent peg,
her right hand,
for a workman's hammer.
Then she hammered Sisera —
she crushed his head;
she shattered and pierced his temple.
27 He collapsed, he fell, he lay down
between her feet;
he collapsed, he fell between her feet;
where he collapsed, there he fell —
dead.

28 Sisera's mother looked
through the window;
she peered through the lattice,
crying out:
"Why is his chariot so long
in coming?
Why don't I hear the hoofbeats
of his horses?"[F]
29 Her wisest princesses answer her;
she even answers herself:[G]
30 "Are they not finding and dividing
the spoil —
a girl or two[H] for each warrior,
the spoil of colored garments
for Sisera,
the spoil of an embroidered garment
or two for my neck?"[I]

31 LORD, may all your enemies perish
as Sisera did.[J]
But may those who love him
be like the rising of the sun
in its strength.

And the land had peace for forty years.

LORD, may all your enemies perish as Sisera did. But may those who love him be like the rising of the sun in its strength.
—Judges 5:31

[A] 5:14 LXX reads *in the valley* [B] 5:15 Lit *they set out as his feet* [C] 5:15 Some Hb mss, Syr read *There were great resolves* [D] 5:16 Or *the campfires* [E] 5:22 = Sisera's [F] 5:28 Lit *Why have the hoofbeats of his chariots delayed* [G] 5:29 Lit *answers her words* [H] 5:30 Lit *a womb or two wombs* [I] 5:30 Hb obscure [J] 5:31 Lit *perish in this way*

MIDIAN OPPRESSES ISRAEL

6 The Israelites did what was evil in the sight of the LORD. So the LORD handed them over to Midian seven years, 2 and they oppressed Israel. Because of Midian, the Israelites made hiding places for themselves in the mountains, caves, and strongholds. 3 Whenever the Israelites planted crops, the Midianites, Amalekites, and the Qedemites came and attacked them. 4 They encamped against them and destroyed the produce of the land, even as far as Gaza. They left nothing for Israel to eat, as well as no sheep, ox, or donkey. 5 For the Midianites came with their cattle and their tents like a great swarm of locusts. They and their camels were without number, and they entered the land to lay waste to it. 6 So Israel became poverty-stricken because of Midian, and the Israelites cried out to the LORD.

7 When the Israelites cried out to him because of Midian, 8 the LORD sent a prophet to them. He said to them, "This is what the LORD God of Israel says: 'I brought you out of Egypt and out of the place of slavery. 9 I rescued you from the power of Egypt and the power of all who oppressed you. I drove them out before you and gave you their land. 10 I said to you: I am the LORD your God. Do not fear the gods of the Amorites whose land you live in. But you did not obey me.' "

THE LORD CALLS GIDEON

11 The angel of the LORD came, and he sat under the oak that was in Ophrah, which belonged to Joash, the Abiezrite. His son Gideon was threshing wheat in the winepress in order to hide it from the Midianites. 12 Then the angel of the LORD appeared to him and said: "The LORD is with you, valiant warrior."

13 Gideon said to him, "Please, my lord, if the LORD is with us, why has all this happened? And where are all his wonders that our fathers told us about? They said, 'Hasn't the LORD brought us out of Egypt?' But now the LORD has abandoned us and handed us over to Midian."

14 The LORD turned to him and said, "Go in the strength you have and deliver Israel from the grasp of Midian. I am sending you!"

15 He said to him, "Please, Lord, how can I deliver Israel? Look, my family is the weakest in Manasseh, and I am the youngest in my father's family."

16 "But I will be with you," the LORD said to him. "You will strike Midian down as if it were one man."

17 Then he said to him, "If I have found favor with you, give me a sign that you are speaking with me. 18 Please do not leave this place until I return to you. Let me bring my gift and set it before you."

And he said, "I will stay until you return."

19 So Gideon went and prepared a young goat and unleavened bread from a half bushel[A] of flour. He placed the meat in a basket and the broth in a pot. He brought them out and offered them to him under the oak.

20 The angel of God said to him, "Take the meat with the unleavened bread, put it on this stone, and pour the broth on it." So he did that. 21 The angel of the LORD extended the tip of the staff that was in his hand and touched the meat and the unleavened bread. Fire came up from the rock and consumed the meat and the unleavened bread. Then the angel of the LORD vanished from his sight.

22 When Gideon realized that he was the angel of the LORD, he said, "Oh no, Lord GOD! I have seen the angel of the LORD face to face!"

23 But the LORD said to him, "Peace to you. Don't be afraid, for you will not die." 24 So Gideon built an altar to the LORD there and called it The LORD Is Peace.[B] It is still in Ophrah of the Abiezrites today.

GIDEON TEARS DOWN A BAAL ALTAR

25 On that very night the LORD said to him, "Take your father's young bull and a second bull seven years old. Then tear down the altar of Baal that belongs to your father and cut down the Asherah pole beside it. 26 Build a well-constructed altar to the LORD your God on the top of this mound. Take the second bull and offer it as a burnt offering with the wood of the Asherah pole you cut down." 27 So Gideon took ten of his male servants and did as the LORD had told him. But because he was too afraid of his father's family and the men of the city to do it in the daytime, he did it at night.

28 When the men of the city got up in the morning, they found Baal's altar torn down, the Asherah pole beside it cut down, and the second bull offered up on the altar that had been built. 29 They said to each other, "Who did this?" After they made a thorough investigation, they said, "Gideon son of Joash did it."

30 Then the men of the city said to Joash,

[A] **6:19** Lit *an ephah* [B] **6:24** = *Yahweh-shalom*

"Bring out your son. He must die, because he
tore down Baal's altar and cut down the Asherah pole beside it."
31 But Joash said to all who stood against
him, "Would you plead Baal's case for him?
Would you save him? Whoever pleads his
case will be put to death by morning! If he
is a god, let him plead his own case because
someone tore down his altar." 32 That day
he was called Jerubbaal, since Joash said,
"Let Baal contend with him," because he tore
down his altar.

THE SIGN OF THE FLEECE

33 All the Midianites, Amalekites, and Qedemites gathered together, crossed over the
Jordan, and camped in the Jezreel Valley.
34 The Spirit of the LORD enveloped[A] Gideon,
and he blew the ram's horn and the Abiezrites rallied behind him. 35 He sent messengers
throughout all of Manasseh, who rallied behind him. He also sent messengers throughout
Asher, Zebulun, and Naphtali, who also came
to meet him.
36 Then Gideon said to God, "If you will deliver Israel by my hand, as you said, 37 I will
put a wool fleece here on the threshing floor.
If dew is only on the fleece, and all the ground
is dry, I will know that you will deliver Israel
by my strength, as you said." 38 And that is
what happened. When he got up early in the
morning, he squeezed the fleece and wrung
dew out of it, filling a bowl with water.
39 Gideon then said to God, "Don't be angry
with me; let me speak one more time. Please
allow me to make one more test with the fleece.
Let it remain dry, and the dew be all over the
ground." 40 That night God did as Gideon requested: only the fleece was dry, and dew was
all over the ground.

GOD SELECTS GIDEON'S ARMY

7 Jerubbaal (that is, Gideon) and all the
troops who were with him, got up early
and camped beside the spring of Harod. The
camp of Midian was north of them, below the
hill of Moreh, in the valley. 2 The LORD said to
Gideon, "You have too many troops for me to
hand the Midianites over to them, or else Israel
might elevate themselves over me and say,[B] 'My
own strength saved me.' 3 Now announce to
the troops: 'Whoever is fearful and trembling
may turn back and leave Mount Gilead.'" So
twenty-two thousand of the troops turned
back, but ten thousand remained.
4 Then the LORD said to Gideon, "There are
still too many troops. Take them down to the
water, and I will test them for you there. If I
say to you, 'This one can go with you,' he can
go. But if I say about anyone, 'This one cannot
go with you,' he cannot go." 5 So he brought
the troops down to the water, and the LORD
said to Gideon, "Separate everyone who laps
water with his tongue like a dog. Do the same
with everyone who kneels to drink." 6 The
number of those who lapped with their hands
to their mouths was three hundred men, and
all the rest of the troops knelt to drink water.
7 The LORD said to Gideon, "I will deliver you
with the three hundred men who lapped and
hand the Midianites over to you. But everyone else is to go home." 8 So Gideon sent all
the Israelites to their tents but kept the three
hundred troops, who took the provisions and
their trumpets. The camp of Midian was below
him in the valley.

GIDEON SPIES ON THE MIDIANITE CAMP

9 That night the LORD said to him, "Get up and
attack the camp, for I have handed it over to
you. 10 But if you are afraid to attack the camp,
go down with Purah your servant. 11 Listen to
what they say, and then you will be encouraged[C] to attack the camp." So he went down
with Purah his servant to the outpost of the
troops[D] who were in the camp.
12 Now the Midianites, Amalekites, and all
the Qedemites had settled down in the valley
like a swarm of locusts, and their camels were
as innumerable as the sand on the seashore.
13 When Gideon arrived, there was a man telling his friend about a dream. He said, "Listen,
I had a dream: a loaf of barley bread came
tumbling into the Midianite camp, struck a
tent, and it fell. The loaf turned the tent upside
down so that it collapsed."
14 His friend answered: "This is nothing less
than the sword of Gideon son of Joash, the Israelite. God has handed the entire Midianite
camp over to him."

GIDEON ATTACKS THE MIDIANITES

15 When Gideon heard the account of the dream
and its interpretation, he bowed in worship. He
returned to Israel's camp and said, "Get up, for
the LORD has handed the Midianite camp over

[A] **6:34** Lit *clothed;* 1Ch 12:18; 2Ch 24:20 [B] **7:2** Lit *brag against me* [C] **7:11** Lit *then your hands will be strengthened* [D] **7:11** Lit *of those who were arranged in companies of 50*

to you." 16 Then he divided the three hundred
men into three companies and gave each of
the men a trumpet in one hand and an empty
pitcher with a torch inside it in the other hand.
17 "Watch me," he said to them, "and do what
I do. When I come to the outpost of the camp,
do as I do. 18 When I and everyone with me
blow our trumpets, you are also to blow your
trumpets all around the camp. Then you will
say, 'For the LORD and for Gideon!'"
19 Gideon and the hundred men who were
with him went to the outpost of the camp at
the beginning of the middle watch after the
sentries had been stationed. They blew their
trumpets and broke the pitchers that were in
their hands. 20 The three companies blew their
trumpets and shattered their pitchers. They
held their torches in their left hands, their
trumpets[A] in their right hands, and shouted,
"A sword for the LORD and for Gideon!" 21 Each
Israelite took his position around the camp,
and the entire Midianite army began to run,
and they cried out as they fled. 22 When Gideon's men blew their three hundred trumpets,
the LORD caused the men in the whole army
to turn on each other with their swords. They
fled to Acacia House[B] in the direction of Zer-
erah as far as the border of Abel-meholah
near Tabbath. 23 Then the men of Israel were
called from Naphtali, Asher, and Manasseh,
and they pursued the Midianites.

THE MEN OF EPHRAIM JOIN THE BATTLE

24 Gideon sent messengers throughout the
hill country of Ephraim with this message:
"Come down to intercept the Midianites and
take control of the watercourses ahead of
them as far as Beth-barah and the Jordan."
So all the men of Ephraim were called out,
and they took control of the watercourses
as far as Beth-barah and the Jordan. 25 They
captured Oreb and Zeeb, the two princes of
Midian; they killed Oreb at the rock of Oreb
and Zeeb at the winepress of Zeeb, while they
were pursuing the Midianites. They brought
the heads of Oreb and Zeeb to Gideon across
the Jordan.

8 The men of Ephraim said to him, "Why
have you done this to us, not calling us
when you went to fight against the Midianites?" And they argued with him violently.
2 So he said to them, "What have I done
now compared to you? Is not the gleaning
of Ephraim better than the grape harvest of
Abiezer? 3 God handed over to you Oreb and
Zeeb, the two princes of Midian. What was I
able to do compared to you?" When he said
this, their anger against him subsided.

GIDEON PURSUES THE KINGS OF MIDIAN

4 Gideon and the three hundred men came to
the Jordan and crossed it. They were exhausted but still in pursuit. 5 He said to the men of
Succoth, "Please give some loaves of bread
to the troops under my command,[C] because
they are exhausted, for I am pursuing Zebah
and Zalmunna, the kings of Midian."
6 But the princes of Succoth asked, "Are[D]
Zebah and Zalmunna now in your hands that
we should give bread to your army?"
7 Gideon replied, "Very well, when the LORD
has handed Zebah and Zalmunna over to me,
I will tear[E] your flesh with thorns and briers
from the wilderness!" 8 He went from there to
Penuel and asked the same thing from them.
The men of Penuel answered just as the men
of Succoth had answered. 9 He also told the
men of Penuel, "When I return safely, I will
tear down this tower!"
10 Now Zebah and Zalmunna were in Karkor,
and with them was their army of about fifteen
thousand men, who were all those left of the
entire army of the Qedemites. Those who had
been killed were one hundred twenty thousand armed men.[F] 11 Gideon traveled on the
caravan route[G] east of Nobah and Jogbehah
and attacked their army while the army felt
secure. 12 Zebah and Zalmunna fled, and he
pursued them. He captured these two kings
of Midian and routed the entire army.
13 Gideon son of Joash returned from the
battle by the Ascent of Heres. 14 He captured
a youth from the men of Succoth and interrogated him. The youth wrote down for him
the names of the seventy-seven leaders and
elders of Succoth. 15 Then he went to the men
of Succoth and said, "Here are Zebah and Zalmunna. You taunted me about them, saying,
'Are Zebah and Zalmunna now in your power
that we should give bread to your exhausted
men?'" 16 So he took the elders of the city,
and he took some thorns and briers from
the wilderness, and he disciplined the men
of Succoth with them. 17 He also tore down
the tower of Penuel and killed the men of
the city.

[A] 7:20 Lit *trumpets to blow* [B] 7:22 Or *Beth-shittah* [C] 8:5 Lit *troops at my feet* [D] 8:6 Lit *Are the hands of*, also in v. 15
[E] 8:7 Lit *thresh* [F] 8:10 Lit *men who drew the sword* [G] 8:11 Lit *on the route of those who live in tents*

18 He asked Zebah and Zalmunna, "What kind
of men did you kill at Tabor?"
"They were like you," they said. "Each resembled the son of a king."
19 So he said, "They were my brothers, the
sons of my mother! As the LORD lives, if you
had let them live, I would not kill you." 20 Then
he said to Jether, his firstborn, "Get up and kill
them." The youth did not draw his sword, for
he was afraid because he was still a youth.
21 Zebah and Zalmunna said, "Get up and
strike us down yourself, for a man is judged
by his strength." So Gideon got up, killed
Zebah and Zalmunna, and took the crescent
ornaments that were on the necks of their
camels.

GIDEON'S LEGACY

22 Then the Israelites said to Gideon, "Rule
over us, you as well as your sons and your
grandsons, for you delivered us from the power of Midian."
23 But Gideon said to them, "I will not rule
over you, and my son will not rule over you;
the LORD will rule over you." 24 Then he said
to them, "Let me make a request of you: Everyone give me an earring from his plunder."
Now the enemy had gold earrings because
they were Ishmaelites.
25 They said, "We agree to give them." So they
spread out a cloak, and everyone threw an
earring from his plunder on it. 26 The weight of
the gold earrings he requested was forty-three
pounds[A] of gold, in addition to the crescent
ornaments and ear pendants, the purple garments on the kings of Midian, and the chains
on the necks of their camels. 27 Gideon made
an ephod from all this and put it in Ophrah, his
hometown. Then all Israel prostituted themselves by worshiping it there, and it became a
snare to Gideon and his household.
28 So Midian was subdued before the Israelites, and they were no longer a threat.[B] The
land had peace for forty years during the days
of Gideon. 29 Jerubbaal (that is, Gideon) son of
Joash went back to live at his house.
30 Gideon had seventy sons, his own offspring, since he had many wives. 31 His concubine who was in Shechem also bore him a
son, and he named him Abimelech. 32 Then
Gideon son of Joash died at a good old age and
was buried in the tomb of his father Joash in
Ophrah of the Abiezrites.
33 When Gideon died, the Israelites turned
and prostituted themselves by worshiping the
Baals and made Baal-berith[C] their god. 34 The
Israelites did not remember the LORD their God
who had rescued them from the hand of the

Support | *Knowing Your Role*

SERVING GOD VS. PLAYING GOD

"Then the Israelites said to Gideon, 'Rule over us, you as well as your sons and your grandsons, for you delivered us from the power of Midian.' But Gideon said to them, 'I will not rule over you, and my son will not rule over you; the LORD will rule over you.'" Judges 8:22-23

After years of foreign oppression, the Israelites cried out to God for help, and he provided it in the form of Gideon. So remarkable was Gideon's victory with an army of just three hundred men over Midian that the Israelites asked him to be their king. Gideon wisely refused, saying, "The LORD will rule over you."

Here is a great lesson. To be used by God to bless others is wonderful, but to try to take the place of God in the lives of others is wrong.

By all means, help others. Offer support and encouragement. Use your gifts. Fulfill whatever role or ministry God has given you: parent, friend, sibling, mentor, employer, pastor, small group leader, and more. But stay in your lane. Don't exceed the limits of your calling. Only one Lord exists. No one is qualified to play God's role in someone else's life.

For the next note on *Support*, see 2 Samuel 22:28.

[A] **8:26** Lit *1,700 shekels* [B] **8:28** Lit *they no longer raised their head* [C] **8:33** Lit *Baal of the Covenant*, or *Lord of the Covenant*

enemies around them. 35 They did not show
kindness to the house of Jerubbaal (that is,
Gideon) for all the good he had done for Israel.

ABIMELECH BECOMES KING

9 Abimelech son of Jerubbaal went to Shechem and spoke to his uncles and to his
mother's whole clan, saying, 2 "Please speak
in the hearing of all the citizens of Shechem,
'Is it better for you that seventy men, all the
sons of Jerubbaal, rule over you or that one
man rule over you?' Remember that I am your
own flesh and blood."[A]
3 His mother's relatives spoke all these
words about him in the hearing of all the
citizens of Shechem, and they were favorable
to Abimelech, for they said, "He is our brother." 4 So they gave him seventy pieces of silver
from the temple of Baal-berith.[B] Abimelech
used it to hire worthless and reckless men,
and they followed him. 5 He went to his father's house in Ophrah and killed his seventy
brothers, the sons of Jerubbaal, on top of a
large stone. But Jotham, the youngest son of
Jerubbaal, survived, because he hid. 6 Then
all the citizens of Shechem and of Beth-millo
gathered together and proceeded to make
Abimelech king at the oak of the pillar in
Shechem.

JOTHAM'S PARABLE

7 When they told Jotham, he climbed to the
top of Mount Gerizim, raised his voice, and
called to them:

Listen to me, citizens of Shechem,
and may God listen to you:

8 The trees decided
to anoint a king over themselves.
They said to the olive tree,
"Reign over us."
9 But the olive tree said to them,
"Should I stop giving my oil
that people use to honor both God
and men,
and rule[C] over the trees?"

10 Then the trees said to the fig tree,
"Come and reign over us."
11 But the fig tree said to them,
"Should I stop giving
my sweetness and my good fruit,
and rule over trees?"
12 Later, the trees said to the grapevine,
"Come and reign over us."
13 But the grapevine said to them,
"Should I stop giving my wine
that cheers both God and man,
and rule over trees?"
14 Finally, all the trees said to the bramble,
"Come and reign over us."
15 The bramble said to the trees,
"If you really are anointing me
as king over you,
come and find refuge in my shade.
But if not,
may fire come out from the bramble
and consume the cedars of Lebanon."

16 "Now if you have acted faithfully and honestly in making Abimelech king, if you have
done well by Jerubbaal and his family, and
if you have rewarded him appropriately for
what he did — 17 for my father fought for you,
risked his life, and rescued you from Midian,
18 and now you have attacked my father's family
today, killed his seventy sons on top of a large
stone, and made Abimelech, the son of his slave
woman, king over the citizens of Shechem 'because he is your brother' — 19 so if you have
acted faithfully and honestly with Jerubbaal
and his house this day, rejoice in Abimelech
and may he also rejoice in you. 20 But if not, may
fire come from Abimelech and consume the
citizens of Shechem and Beth-millo, and may
fire come from the citizens of Shechem and
Beth-millo and consume Abimelech." 21 Then
Jotham fled, escaping to Beer, and lived there
because of his brother Abimelech.

ABIMELECH'S PUNISHMENT

22 When Abimelech had ruled over Israel
three years, 23 God sent an evil spirit between
Abimelech and the citizens of Shechem. They
treated Abimelech deceitfully, 24 so that the
crime against the seventy sons of Jerubbaal
might come to justice and their blood would
be avenged on their brother Abimelech, who
killed them, and on the citizens of Shechem,
who had helped him[D] kill his brothers. 25 The
citizens of Shechem rebelled against him by
putting men in ambush on the tops of the
mountains, and they robbed everyone who
passed by them on the road. So this was reported to Abimelech.

[A] **9:2** Lit *your bone and your flesh* [B] **9:4** Lit *Baal of the Covenant*, or *Lord of the Covenant* [C] **9:9** Lit *and go to sway*, also in vv. 11,13 [D] **9:24** Lit *had strengthened his hands*

26 Gaal son of Ebed came with his brothers and crossed into Shechem, and the citizens of Shechem trusted him. 27 So they went out to the countryside and harvested grapes from their vineyards. They trampled the grapes and held a celebration. Then they went to the house of their god, and as they ate and drank, they cursed Abimelech. 28 Gaal son of Ebed said, "Who is Abimelech and who is Shechem that we should serve him? Isn't he the son of Jerubbaal, and isn't Zebul his officer? You are to serve the men of Hamor, the father of Shechem. Why should we serve Abimelech? 29 If only these people were in my power, I would remove Abimelech." So he said[A] to Abimelech, "Gather your army and come out."

30 When Zebul, the ruler of the city, heard the words of Gaal son of Ebed, he was angry. 31 So he secretly sent messengers to Abimelech, saying, "Beware! Gaal son of Ebed, with his brothers, have come to Shechem and are turning the city against you.[B] 32 Now tonight, you and the troops with you, come and wait in ambush in the countryside. 33 Then get up early, and at sunrise attack the city. When he and the troops who are with him come out against you, do to him whatever you can." 34 So Abimelech and all the troops with him got up at night and waited in ambush for Shechem in four units.

35 Gaal son of Ebed went out and stood at the entrance of the city gate. Then Abimelech and the troops who were with him got up from their ambush. 36 When Gaal saw the troops, he said to Zebul, "Look, troops are coming down from the mountaintops!" But Zebul said to him, "The shadows of the mountains look like men to you."

37 Then Gaal spoke again, "Look, troops are coming down from the central part of the land, and one unit is coming from the direction of the Diviners' Oak." 38 Zebul replied, "What do you have to say now? You said, 'Who is Abimelech that we should serve him?' Aren't these the troops you despised? Now go and fight them!"

39 So Gaal went out leading the citizens of Shechem and fought against Abimelech, 40 but Abimelech pursued him, and Gaal fled before him. Numerous bodies were strewn as far as the entrance of the city gate. 41 Abimelech stayed in Arumah, and Zebul drove Gaal and his brothers from Shechem.

42 The next day when the people of Shechem[C] went into the countryside, this was reported to Abimelech. 43 He took the troops, divided them into three companies, and waited in ambush in the countryside. He looked, and the people were coming out of the city, so he arose against them and struck them down. 44 Then Abimelech and the units that were with him rushed forward and took their stand at the entrance of the city gate. The other two units rushed against all who were in the countryside and struck them down. 45 So Abimelech fought against the city that entire day, captured it, and killed the people who were in it. Then he tore down the city and sowed it with salt.

46 When all the citizens of the Tower of Shechem heard, they entered the inner chamber[D] of the temple of El-berith.[E] 47 Then it was reported to Abimelech that all the citizens of the Tower of Shechem had gathered. 48 So Abimelech and all the troops who were with him went up to Mount Zalmon. Abimelech took his ax in his hand and cut a branch from the trees. He picked up the branch, put it on his shoulder, and said to the troops who were with him, "Hurry and do what you have seen me do." 49 Each of the troops also cut his own branch and followed Abimelech. They put the branches against the inner chamber and set it on fire; about a thousand men and women died, including all the men of the Tower of Shechem.

50 Abimelech went to Thebez, camped against it, and captured it. 51 There was a strong tower inside the city, and all the men, women, and citizens of the city fled there. They locked themselves in and went up to the roof of the tower. 52 When Abimelech came to attack the tower, he approached its entrance to set it on fire. 53 But a woman threw the upper portion of a millstone on Abimelech's head and fractured his skull. 54 He quickly called his armor-bearer and said to him, "Draw your sword and kill me, or they'll say about me, 'A woman killed him.'" So his armor-bearer ran him through, and he died. 55 When the Israelites saw that Abimelech was dead, they all went home.

56 In this way, God brought back Abimelech's evil—the evil that Abimelech had done to his father when he killed his seventy brothers. 57 God also brought back to the men of Shechem all their evil. So the curse of Jotham son of Jerubbaal came upon them.

[A] **9:29** DSS read *They said*; LXX reads *I would say* [B] **9:31** Hb obscure [C] **9:42** *of Shechem* supplied for clarity [D] **9:46** Or *the crypt*, or *the vault* [E] **9:46** = God of the Covenant

TOLA AND JAIR

10 After Abimelech, Tola son of Puah, son
of Dodo became judge and began to deliver Israel. He was from Issachar and lived in
Shamir in the hill country of Ephraim. 2 Tola
judged Israel twenty-three years and when
he died, was buried in Shamir.
3 After him came Jair the Gileadite, who
judged Israel twenty-two years. 4 He had thirty
sons who rode on thirty donkeys. They had
thirty towns[A] in Gilead, which are still called
Jair's Villages[B] today. 5 When Jair died, he was
buried in Kamon.

ISRAEL'S REBELLION AND REPENTANCE

6 Then the Israelites again did what was evil
in the sight of the LORD. They worshiped the
Baals and the Ashtoreths, the gods of Aram,
Sidon, and Moab, and the gods of the Ammonites and the Philistines. They abandoned the
LORD and did not worship him. 7 So the LORD's
anger burned against Israel, and he sold them
to[C] the Philistines and the Ammonites. 8 They
shattered and crushed the Israelites that year,
and for eighteen years they did the same to all
the Israelites who were on the other side of the
Jordan in the land of the Amorites in Gilead.
9 The Ammonites also crossed the Jordan to
fight against Judah, Benjamin, and the house
of Ephraim. Israel was greatly oppressed, 10 so
they cried out to the LORD, saying, "We have
sinned against you. We have abandoned our
God and worshiped the Baals."
11 The LORD said to the Israelites, "When the
Egyptians, Amorites, Ammonites, Philistines,
12 Sidonians, Amalekites, and Maonites[D] oppressed you, and you cried out to me, did I
not deliver you from them? 13 But you have
abandoned me and worshiped other gods.
Therefore, I will not deliver you again. 14 Go and
cry out to the gods you have chosen. Let them
deliver you whenever you are oppressed."
15 But the Israelites said, "We have sinned.
Deal with us as you see fit;[E] only rescue us
today!" 16 So they got rid of the foreign gods
among them and worshiped the LORD, and he
became weary of Israel's misery.
17 The Ammonites were called together, and
they camped in Gilead. So the Israelites assembled and camped at Mizpah. 18 The rulers[F] of
Gilead said to one another, "Which man will
begin the fight against the Ammonites? He will
be the leader of all the inhabitants of Gilead."

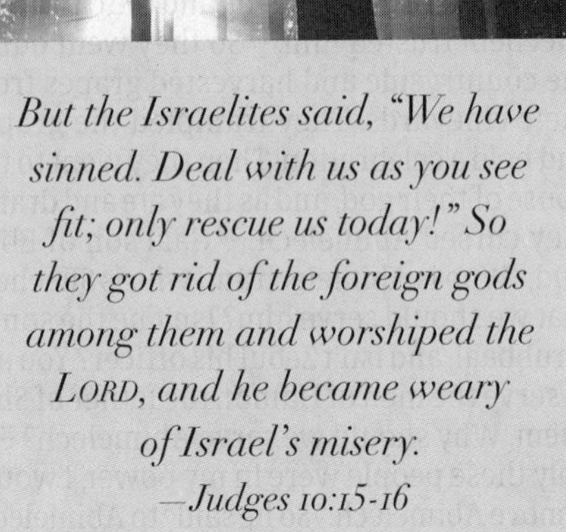
But the Israelites said, "We have sinned. Deal with us as you see fit; only rescue us today!" So they got rid of the foreign gods among them and worshiped the LORD, and he became weary of Israel's misery.
—*Judges 10:15-16*

JEPHTHAH BECOMES ISRAEL'S LEADER

11 Jephthah the Gileadite was a valiant
warrior, but he was the son of a prostitute, and Gilead was his father. 2 Gilead's
wife bore him sons, and when they grew
up, they drove Jephthah out and said to him,
"You will have no inheritance in our father's
family, because you are the son of another
woman." 3 So Jephthah fled from his brothers and lived in the land of Tob. Then some
worthless men joined Jephthah and went
on raids with him.
4 Some time later, the Ammonites fought
against Israel. 5 When the Ammonites made
war with Israel, the elders of Gilead went to
get Jephthah from the land of Tob. 6 They said
to him, "Come, be our commander, and let's
fight the Ammonites."
7 Jephthah replied to the elders of Gilead,
"Didn't you hate me and drive me out of my
father's family? Why then have you come to
me now when you're in trouble?"
8 They answered Jephthah, "That's true. But
now we turn to you. Come with us, fight the
Ammonites, and you will become leader of
all the inhabitants of Gilead."
9 So Jephthah said to them, "If you are bringing me back to fight the Ammonites and the
LORD gives them to me, I will be your leader."
10 The elders of Gilead said to Jephthah,
"The LORD is our witness if we don't do as
you say." 11 So Jephthah went with the elders
of Gilead. The people made him their leader and commander, and Jephthah repeated
all his terms in the presence of the LORD at
Mizpah.

[A] **10:4** LXX; MT reads *donkeys* [B] **10:4** Or *called Havvoth-jair* [C] **10:7** Lit *into the hand of* [D] **10:12** LXX reads *Midianites*
[E] **10:15** Lit *Do to us what is good in your eyes* [F] **10:18** Lit *The people, rulers*

JEPHTHAH REJECTS AMMONITE CLAIMS

12 Jephthah sent messengers to the king of the Ammonites, asking, "What do you have against me that you have come to fight me in my land?"

13 The king of the Ammonites said to Jephthah's messengers, "When Israel came from Egypt, they seized my land from the Arnon to the Jabbok and the Jordan. Now restore it peaceably."

14 Jephthah again sent messengers to the king of the Ammonites 15 to tell him, "This is what Jephthah says: Israel did not take away the land of Moab or the land of the Ammonites. 16 But when they came from Egypt, Israel traveled through the wilderness to the Red Sea and came to Kadesh. 17 Israel sent messengers to the king of Edom, saying, 'Please let us travel through your land,' but the king of Edom would not listen. They also sent messengers to the king of Moab, but he refused. So Israel stayed in Kadesh.

18 "Then they traveled through the wilderness and around the lands of Edom and Moab. They came to the east side of the land of Moab and camped on the other side of the Arnon but did not enter into the territory of Moab, for the Arnon was the boundary of Moab.

19 "Then Israel sent messengers to Sihon king of the Amorites, king of Heshbon. Israel said to him, 'Please let us travel through your land to our country,' 20 but Sihon would not trust Israel to pass through his territory. Instead, Sihon gathered all his troops, camped at Jahaz, and fought with Israel. 21 Then the LORD God of Israel handed over Sihon and all his troops to Israel, and they defeated them. So Israel took possession of the entire land of the Amorites who lived in that country. 22 They took possession of all the territory of the Amorites from the Arnon to the Jabbok and from the wilderness to the Jordan.

23 "The LORD God of Israel has now driven out the Amorites before his people Israel, and will you now force us out? 24 Isn't it true that you can have whatever your god Chemosh conquers for you, and we can have whatever the LORD our God conquers for us? 25 Now are you any better than Balak son of Zippor, king of Moab? Did he ever contend with Israel or fight against them? 26 While Israel lived three hundred years in Heshbon and Aroer and their surrounding villages, and in all the cities that are on the banks of the Arnon, why didn't you take them back at that time? 27 I have not sinned against you, but you are doing me wrong by fighting against me. Let the LORD who is the judge decide today between the Israelites and the Ammonites." 28 But the king of the Ammonites would not listen to Jephthah's message that he sent him.

JEPHTHAH'S VOW AND SACRIFICE

29 The Spirit of the LORD came on Jephthah, who traveled through Gilead and Manasseh, and then through Mizpah of Gilead. He crossed over to the Ammonites from Mizpah of Gilead. 30 Jephthah made this vow to the LORD: "If you in fact hand over the Ammonites to me, 31 whoever comes out the doors of my house to greet me when I return safely from the Ammonites will belong to the LORD, and I will offer that person as a burnt offering."

32 Jephthah crossed over to the Ammonites to fight against them, and the LORD handed them over to him. 33 He defeated twenty of their cities with a great slaughter from Aroer all the way to the entrance of Minnith and to Abel-keramim. So the Ammonites were subdued before the Israelites.

34 When Jephthah went to his home in Mizpah, there was his daughter, coming out to meet him with tambourines and dancing! She was his only child; he had no other son or daughter besides her. 35 When he saw her, he tore his clothes and said, "No! Not my daughter! You have devastated me! You have brought great misery on me.[A] I have given my word to the LORD and cannot take it back."

36 Then she said to him, "My father, you have given your word to the LORD. Do to me as you have said, for the LORD brought vengeance on your enemies, the Ammonites." 37 She also said to her father, "Let me do this one thing: Let me wander two months through the mountains with my friends and mourn my virginity."

38 "Go," he said. And he sent her away two months. So she left with her friends and mourned her virginity as she wandered through the mountains. 39 At the end of two months, she returned to her father, and he kept the vow he had made about her. And she had never been intimate with a man. Now it became a custom in Israel 40 that four days each year the young women of Israel would commemorate the daughter of Jephthah the Gileadite.

[A] **11:35** Lit *have been among those who trouble me*

CONFLICT WITH EPHRAIM

12 The men of Ephraim were called together
and crossed the Jordan to Zaphon. They
said to Jephthah, "Why have you crossed over
to fight against the Ammonites but didn't call
us to go with you? We will burn your house
with you in it!"
2 Then Jephthah said to them, "My people
and I had a bitter conflict with the Ammonites. So I called for you, but you didn't deliver
me from their power. 3 When I saw that you
weren't going to deliver me, I took my life in
my own hands and crossed over to the Ammonites, and the LORD handed them over to
me. Why then have you come today to fight
against me?"
4 Then Jephthah gathered all of the men of
Gilead. They fought and defeated Ephraim,
because Ephraim had said, "You Gileadites
are Ephraimite fugitives in the territories
of Ephraim and Manasseh." 5 The Gileadites
captured the fords of the Jordan leading to
Ephraim. Whenever a fugitive from Ephraim
said, "Let me cross over," the Gileadites asked
him, "Are you an Ephraimite?" If he answered,
"No," 6 they told him, "Please say Shibboleth."
If he said, "Sibboleth," because he could not
pronounce it correctly, they seized him and
executed him at the fords of the Jordan. At that
time forty-two thousand from Ephraim died.
7 Jephthah judged Israel six years, and when
he died, he was buried in one of the cities of
Gilead.[A]

IBZAN, ELON, AND ABDON

8 Ibzan, who was from Bethlehem, judged
Israel after Jephthah 9 and had thirty sons.
He gave his thirty daughters in marriage to
men outside the tribe and brought back thirty wives for his sons from outside the tribe.
Ibzan judged Israel seven years, 10 and when
he died, he was buried in Bethlehem.
11 Elon, who was from Zebulun, judged Israel
after Ibzan. He judged Israel ten years, 12 and
when he died, he was buried in Aijalon in the
land of Zebulun.
13 After Elon, Abdon son of Hillel, who was
from Pirathon, judged Israel. 14 He had forty sons and thirty grandsons, who rode on
seventy donkeys. Abdon judged Israel eight
years, 15 and when he died, he was buried in
Pirathon in the land of Ephraim, in the hill
country of the Amalekites.

BIRTH OF SAMSON

13 The Israelites again did what was evil
in the LORD's sight, so the LORD handed them over to the Philistines forty years.
2 There was a certain man from Zorah, from
the family of Dan, whose name was Manoah;
his wife was unable to conceive and had no
children. 3 The angel of the LORD appeared to
the woman and said to her, "It is true that you
are unable to conceive and have no children,
but you will conceive and give birth to a son.
4 Now please be careful not to drink wine or
beer, or to eat anything unclean; 5 for indeed,
you will conceive and give birth to a son. You
must never cut his hair,[B] because the boy will
be a Nazirite to God from birth, and he will
begin to save Israel from the power of the
Philistines."
6 Then the woman went and told her husband, "A man of God came to me. He looked
like the awe-inspiring angel of God. I didn't
ask him where he came from, and he didn't
tell me his name. 7 He said to me, 'You will conceive and give birth to a son. Therefore, do not
drink wine or beer, and do not eat anything
unclean, because the boy will be a Nazirite to
God from birth until the day of his death.'"
8 Manoah prayed to the LORD and said,
"Please, Lord, let the man of God you sent come
again to us and teach us what we should do
for the boy who will be born."
9 God listened to[C] Manoah, and the angel
of God came again to the woman. She was
sitting in the field, and her husband Manoah
was not with her. 10 The woman ran quickly
to her husband and told him, "The man who
came to me the other day has just come back!"
11 So Manoah got up and followed his wife.
When he came to the man, he asked, "Are you
the man who spoke to my wife?"
"I am," he said.
12 Then Manoah asked, "When your words
come true, what will be the boy's responsibilities and work?"
13 The angel of the LORD answered Manoah,
"Your wife needs to do everything I told her.
14 She must not eat anything that comes from
the grapevine or drink wine or beer. And she
must not eat anything unclean. Your wife must
do everything I have commanded her."
15 "Please stay here," Manoah told him, "and
we will prepare a young goat for you."
16 The angel of the LORD said to him, "If I

[A] **12:7** LXX reads *in his city in Gilead* [B] **13:5** Lit *And a razor is not to go up on his head* [C] **13:9** Lit *to the voice of*

Samson | Restoration Profile

JUDGES 13–16

Samson's story shows the unravelling of a person. By the time he came along, the pattern of judges functioning as Israel's leaders was well established; so was the cyclical pattern of idolatry leading to national humiliation and captivity, followed by repentance and crying out to God for relief, followed by God's provision of another rescuing leader. But God's restoration was always tempered by the character of his judges and the persistence of rebelliousness by his people.

Samson was born after a forty-year stint of Philistine control over Israel. His parents were a previously infertile couple from Zorah. His birth was announced to his mother with instructions about his upbringing and a promise that he would "begin to save Israel from the power of the Philistines" (Jdg 13:5).

Samson grew with an unusual spiritual gift that translated into physical strength, but he had little control over his appetites. He seems to have taken God's instruction of no spirits or haircuts in stride but showed little interest in God's direction for the other areas of life. Many of his clashes with the Philistines were caused as much by his personal conflicts with them as by his actions in defense of Israel. And Samson's lack of control or discernment with women was his undoing. Delilah was the last in a string of liaisons that demonstrated Samson's vulnerability.

Delilah succeeded in getting Samson to betray himself. He was captured, humiliated, blinded, and put on display. His unravelling was complete. But in the months that followed, God worked a restoration in Samson that led to his death while finally accomplishing what God had gifted him to do.

stay, I won't eat your food. But if you want to
prepare a burnt offering, offer it to the LORD."
(Manoah did not know he was the angel of
the LORD.)
17 Then Manoah said to him, "What is your
name, so that we may honor you when your
words come true?"
18 "Why do you ask my name," the angel of
the LORD asked him, "since it is beyond understanding."
19 Manoah took a young goat and a grain offering and offered them on a rock to the LORD,
who did something miraculous[A] while Manoah
and his wife were watching. 20 When the flame
went up from the altar to the sky, the angel of
the LORD went up in its flame. When Manoah
and his wife saw this, they fell facedown on the
ground. 21 The angel of the LORD did not appear
again to Manoah and his wife. Then Manoah
realized that it was the angel of the LORD.
22 "We're certainly going to die," he said to
his wife, "because we have seen God!"
23 But his wife said to him, "If the LORD had
intended to kill us, he wouldn't have accepted
the burnt offering and the grain offering from
us, and he would not have shown us all these
things or spoken to us like this."
24 So the woman gave birth to a son and
named him Samson. The boy grew, and the
LORD blessed him. 25 Then the Spirit of the
LORD began to stir him in the Camp of Dan,[B]
between Zorah and Eshtaol.

SAMSON'S RIDDLE

14 Samson went down to Timnah and saw
a young Philistine woman there. 2 He
went back and told his father and his mother: "I have seen a young Philistine woman in
Timnah. Now get her for me as a wife."
3 But his father and mother said to him, "Can't
you find a young woman among your relatives
or among any of our people? Must you go to
the uncircumcised Philistines for a wife?"
But Samson told his father, "Get her for me.
She's the right one for me." 4 Now his father
and mother did not know this was from the
LORD, who wanted the Philistines to provide
an opportunity for a confrontation.[C] At that
time, the Philistines were ruling Israel.
5 Samson went down to Timnah with his father and mother and came to the vineyards of
Timnah. Suddenly a young lion came roaring
at him, 6 the Spirit of the LORD came powerfully on him, and he tore the lion apart with his

[A] **13:19** LXX reads *to the LORD, to the one who works wonders* [B] **13:25** Or *in Mahaneh-dan* [C] **14:4** *for a confrontation* supplied for clarity

bare hands as he might have torn a young goat.
But he did not tell his father or mother what
he had done. 7 Then he went and spoke to the
woman, because she seemed right to Samson.
8 After some time, when he returned to marry
her, he left the road to see the lion's carcass,
and there was a swarm of bees with honey
in the carcass. 9 He scooped some honey into
his hands and ate it as he went along. When
he came to his father and mother, he gave
some to them and they ate it. But he did not
tell them that he had scooped the honey from
the lion's carcass.
10 His father went to visit the woman, and
Samson prepared a feast there, as young men
were accustomed to do. 11 When the Philistines saw him, they brought thirty men to
accompany him.
12 "Let me tell you a riddle," Samson said
to them. "If you can explain it to me during
the seven days of the feast and figure it out, I
will give you thirty linen garments and thirty
changes of clothes. 13 But if you can't explain it
to me, you must give me thirty linen garments
and thirty changes of clothes."
"Tell us your riddle," they replied.[A] "Let's
hear it."
14 So he said to them:

Out of the eater came something to eat,
and out of the strong came something
sweet.

After three days, they were unable to explain
the riddle. 15 On the fourth[B] day they said to
Samson's wife, "Persuade your husband to
explain the riddle to us, or we will burn you
and your father's family to death. Did you invite us here to rob us?"
16 So Samson's wife came to him, weeping,
and said, "You hate me and don't love me! You
told my people the riddle, but haven't explained
it to me."
"Look," he said,[C] "I haven't even explained
it to my father or mother, so why should I explain it to you?"
17 She wept the whole seven days of the feast,
and at last, on the seventh day, he explained it
to her, because she had nagged him so much.
Then she explained it to her people. 18 On the
seventh day, before sunset, the men of the
city said to him:

What is sweeter than honey?
What is stronger than a lion?

So he said to them:

If you hadn't plowed with
my young cow,
you wouldn't know my riddle now!

19 The Spirit of the LORD came powerfully
on him, and he went down to Ashkelon and
killed thirty of their men. He stripped them
and gave their clothes to those who had explained the riddle. In a rage, Samson returned
to his father's house, 20 and his wife was given
to one of the men who had accompanied him.

SAMSON'S REVENGE

15 Later on, during the wheat harvest, Samson took a young goat as a gift and visited
his wife. "I want to go to my wife in her room,"
he said. But her father would not let him enter.
2 "I was sure you hated her," her father said,
"so I gave her to one of the men who accompanied you. Isn't her younger sister more beautiful than she is? Why not take her instead?"
3 Samson said to them, "This time I will be
blameless when I harm the Philistines." 4 So he
went out and caught three hundred foxes. He
took torches, turned the foxes tail-to-tail, and
put a torch between each pair of tails. 5 Then
he ignited the torches and released the foxes
into the standing grain of the Philistines. He
burned the piles of grain and the standing
grain as well as the vineyards and olive groves.
6 Then the Philistines asked, "Who did this?"
They were told, "It was Samson, the Tim-
nite's son-in-law, because he took Samson's
wife and gave her to his companion." So the
Philistines went to her and her father and
burned them to death.
7 Then Samson told them, "Because you did
this, I swear that I won't rest until I have taken
vengeance on you." 8 He tore them limb from
limb[D] and then went down and stayed in the
cave at the rock of Etam.
9 The Philistines went up, camped in Judah,
and raided Lehi. 10 So the men of Judah said,
"Why have you attacked us?"
They replied, "We have come to tie Samson
up and pay him back for what he did to us."
11 Then three thousand men of Judah went
to the cave at the rock of Etam, and they asked
Samson, "Don't you realize that the Philistines
rule us? What have you done to us?"
"I have done to them what they did to me,"
he answered.[E]

[A] **14:13** Lit *replied to him* [B] **14:15** LXX, Syr; MT reads *seventh* [C] **14:16** Lit *said to her* [D] **15:8** Lit *He struck them hip and thigh with a great slaughter* [E] **15:11** Lit *answered them*

My Story | Dawn

I was raised in church all my young life, mostly by choice. My stepfather was sexually abusive, and my mother was never home. I remember going to church as young as six years old, just to get away from home if only for a little while. God was intervening for me. I could have been out getting into trouble or worse—but God kept me.

As a young adult, at fifteen, I began doing drugs and alcohol. I was sexually active and became pregnant. Three kids and five marriages later, after being beaten and raped, in and out of rehab centers, and three serious car wrecks that should have claimed my life, I finally realized that Someone was watching out for me in spite of myself. God had kept me alive.

At that point, someone told me about Jesus, and I was ready to listen. They walked me through the Bible until I understood that Jesus could not only rescue me but also guide my life every day. I could trust him rather than my own understanding. And believe me, by then I was ready not to trust myself any longer. I turned my past, my future, and my life over to God.

I am so grateful to Jesus, my Lord, for saving me and giving me another chance at a good life with my kids. As of now, I have been involved in church almost two years. My children are thriving in God's house and in his Word. I've noticed my children tend to think of others first. They talk to their friends about what God can do for them. I am so fortunate to have such wonderful children, especially after all they have been through. I realize God has kept them as he kept me.

Now I am involved with the jail ministry, women's ministry, nursing home ministry, and the food bank. We try to be active in everything that concerns spreading God's Word. It's great to see what God does in other people's lives. My only regret is that I wasted so much time on the devil. Yet, my life is proof that no matter what you have done, who you are, or where you've been, God will forgive you and provide for you.

God kept me until I was ready to let him restore me.

12 They said to him, "We've come to tie you
up and hand you over to the Philistines."
Then Samson told them, "Swear to me that
you yourselves won't kill me."
13 "No," they said,[A] "we won't kill you, but we
will tie you up securely and hand you over to
them." So they tied him up with two new ropes
and led him away from the rock.
14 When he came to Lehi, the Philistines
came to meet him shouting. The Spirit of the
LORD came powerfully on him, and the ropes
that were on his arms and wrists became like
burnt flax and fell off. 15 He found a fresh jawbone of a donkey, reached out his hand, took
it, and killed a thousand men with it. 16 Then
Samson said:

With the jawbone of a donkey
I have piled them in heaps.
With the jawbone of a donkey
I have killed a thousand men.

17 When he finished speaking, he threw away
the jawbone and named that place Ramath-
lehi.[B] 18 He became very thirsty and called out
to the LORD: "You have accomplished this great
victory through your servant. Must I now die
of thirst and fall into the hands of the uncircumcised?" 19 So God split a hollow place in
the ground at Lehi, and water came out of it.
After Samson drank, his strength returned,
and he revived. That is why he named it En-
hakkore,[C] which is still in Lehi today. 20 And
he judged Israel twenty years in the days of
the Philistines.

SAMSON AND DELILAH

16 Samson went to Gaza, where he saw
a prostitute and went to bed with her.
2 When the Gazites heard that Samson was
there, they surrounded the place and waited
in ambush for him all that night at the city
gate. They kept quiet all night, saying, "Let's
wait until dawn; then we will kill him." 3 But
Samson stayed in bed only until midnight.
Then he got up, took hold of the doors of the
city gate along with the two gateposts, and
pulled them out, bar and all. He put them on

[A] **15:13** Lit *said to him* [B] **15:17** = High Place of the Jawbone [C] **15:19** = Spring of the One Who Cried Out

his shoulders and took them to the top of the
mountain overlooking Hebron.
4 Some time later, he fell in love with a woman
named Delilah, who lived in the Sorek Valley.
5 The Philistine leaders went to her and said,
"Persuade him to tell you[A] where his great
strength comes from, so we can overpower
him, tie him up, and make him helpless. Each
of us will then give you 1,100 pieces of silver."
6 So Delilah said to Samson, "Please tell me,
where does your great strength come from?
How could someone tie you up and make you
helpless?"
7 Samson told her, "If they tie me up with sev-
en fresh bowstrings that have not been dried, I
will become weak and be like any other man."
8 The Philistine leaders brought her seven
fresh bowstrings that had not been dried, and
she tied him up with them. 9 While the men in
ambush were waiting in her room, she called
out to him, "Samson, the Philistines are here!"[B]
But he snapped the bowstrings as a strand of
yarn snaps when it touches fire. The secret of
his strength remained unknown.
10 Then Delilah said to Samson, "You have
mocked me and told me lies! Won't you please
tell me how you can be tied up?"
11 He told her, "If they tie me up with new
ropes that have never been used, I will become
weak and be like any other man."
12 Delilah took new ropes, tied him up with
them, and shouted, "Samson, the Philistines
are here!" But while the men in ambush were
waiting in her room, he snapped the ropes off
his arms like a thread.
13 Then Delilah said to Samson, "You have
mocked me all along and told me lies! Tell me
how you can be tied up."
He told her, "If you weave the seven braids
on my head into the fabric on a loom —"[C]
14 She fastened the braids with a pin and
called to him, "Samson, the Philistines are
here!" He awoke from his sleep and pulled
out the pin, with the loom and the web.
15 "How can you say, 'I love you,'" she told
him, "when your heart is not with me? This is
the third time you have mocked me and not
told me what makes your strength so great!"
16 Because she nagged him day after day and
pleaded with him until she wore him out,[D]
17 he told her the whole truth and said to her,
"My hair has never been cut,[E] because I am
a Nazirite to God from birth. If I am shaved,
my strength will leave me, and I will become
weak and be like any other man."
18 When Delilah realized that he had told
her the whole truth, she sent this message to
the Philistine leaders: "Come one more time,
for he has told me the whole truth." The Philistine leaders came to her and brought the
silver with them.
19 Then she let him fall asleep on her lap and
called a man to shave off the seven braids on
his head. In this way, she made him helpless,
and his strength left him. 20 Then she cried,
"Samson, the Philistines are here!" When he
awoke from his sleep, he said, "I will escape
as I did before and shake myself free." But
he did not know that the LORD had left him.

SAMSON'S DEFEAT AND DEATH

21 The Philistines seized him and gouged out
his eyes. They brought him down to Gaza and
bound him with bronze shackles, and he was
forced to grind grain in the prison. 22 But his hair
began to grow back after it had been shaved.
23 Now the Philistine leaders gathered together to offer a great sacrifice to their god
Dagon. They rejoiced and said:

Our god has handed over
our enemy Samson to us.

24 When the people saw him, they praised their
god and said:

Our god has handed over to us
our enemy who destroyed our land
and who multiplied our dead.

25 When they were in good spirits,[F] they said,
"Bring Samson here to entertain us." So they
brought Samson from prison, and he entertained them. They had him stand between
the pillars.
26 Samson said to the young man who was
leading him by the hand, "Lead me where I can
feel the pillars supporting the temple, so I can
lean against them." 27 The temple was full of men
and women; all the leaders of the Philistines
were there, and about three thousand men and
women were on the roof watching Samson
entertain them. 28 He called out to the LORD:
"Lord GOD, please remember me. Strengthen
me, God, just once more. With one act of vengeance, let me pay back the Philistines for my

[A] **16:5** Lit *him and see* [B] **16:9** Lit *are on you*, also in vv. 12,14,20 [C] **16:13-14** LXX reads *loom and fasten them with a pin into the wall and I will become weak and be like any other man." 14And while he was sleeping, Delilah wove the seven braids on his head into the loom.* [D] **16:16** Lit *him and he became short to death* [E] **16:17** Lit *A razor has not gone up on my head* [F] **16:25** Or *When they were feeling good*

two eyes." 29 Samson took hold of the two middle pillars supporting the temple and leaned against them, one on his right hand and the other on his left. 30 Samson said, "Let me die with the Philistines." He pushed with all his might, and the temple fell on the leaders and all the people in it. And those he killed at his death were more than those he had killed in his life.

31 Then his brothers and all his father's family came down, carried him back, and buried him between Zorah and Eshtaol in the tomb of his father Manoah. So he judged Israel twenty years.

MICAH'S PRIEST

17 There was a man from the hill country of Ephraim named Micah. 2 He said to his mother, "The 1,100 pieces of silver taken from you, and that I heard you place a curse on—here's the silver. I took it."

Then his mother said, "My son, may you be blessed by the LORD!"

3 He returned the 1,100 pieces of silver to his mother, and his mother said, "I personally consecrate the silver to the LORD for my son's benefit to make a carved image and a silver idol.[A] I will give it back to you." 4 So he returned the silver to his mother, and she took five pounds of silver and gave it to a silversmith. He made it into a carved image and a silver idol, and it was in Micah's house.

5 This man Micah had a shrine, and he made an ephod and household idols, and installed one of his sons to be his priest. 6 In those days there was no king in Israel; everyone did whatever seemed right to him.

7 There was a young man, a Levite from Bethlehem in Judah, who was staying within the clan of Judah. 8 The man left the town of Bethlehem in Judah to stay wherever he could find a place. On his way he came to Micah's home in the hill country of Ephraim.

9 "Where do you come from?" Micah asked him.

He answered him, "I am a Levite from Bethlehem in Judah, and I'm going to stay wherever I can find a place."

10 Micah replied,[B] "Stay with me and be my father and priest, and I will give you four ounces of silver a year, along with your clothing and provisions." So the Levite went in 11 and agreed to stay with the man, and the young man became like one of his sons. 12 Micah consecrated the Levite, and the young man became his priest and lived in Micah's house. 13 Then Micah said, "Now I know that the LORD will be good to me, because a Levite has become my priest."

DAN'S INVASION AND IDOLATRY

18 In those days, there was no king in Israel, and the Danite tribe was looking for territory to occupy. Up to that time no territory had been captured by them among the tribes of Israel. 2 So the Danites sent out five brave men from all their clans, from Zorah and Eshtaol, to scout out the land and explore it. They told them, "Go and explore the land."

They came to the hill country of Ephraim as far as the home of Micah and spent the night there. 3 While they were near Micah's home, they recognized the accent of the young Levite. So they went over to him and asked, "Who brought you here? What are you doing in this place? What is keeping you here?" 4 He told them, "This is what Micah has done for me: He has hired me, and I became his priest."

5 Then they said to him, "Please inquire of God for us to determine if we will have a successful journey."

6 The priest told them, "Go in peace. The LORD is watching over the journey you are going on."

7 The five men left and came to Laish. They saw that the people who were there were living securely, in the same way as the Sidonians, quiet and unsuspecting. There was nothing lacking[C] in the land and no oppressive ruler. They were far from the Sidonians, having no alliance with anyone.[D]

8 When the men went back to their relatives at Zorah and Eshtaol, their relatives asked them, "What did you find out?"

9 They answered, "Come on, let's attack them, for we have seen the land, and it is very good. Why wait? Don't hesitate to go and invade and take possession of the land! 10 When you get there, you will come to an unsuspecting people and a spacious land, for God has handed it over to you. It is a place where nothing on earth is lacking." 11 Six hundred Danites departed from Zorah and Eshtaol armed with weapons of war. 12 They went up and camped at Kiriath-jearim in Judah. This is why the place is still called the Camp of Dan[E] today; it is west of Kiriath-jearim. 13 From there they traveled to the hill country of Ephraim and arrived at Micah's house.

[A] **17:3** Or *image and a cast image*, also in v. 4 [B] **17:10** Lit *replied to him* [C] **18:7** Hb obscure [D] **18:7** MT; some LXX mss, Sym, Old Lat, Syr read *Aram* [E] **18:12** Or *called Mahaneh-dan*

14 The five men who had gone to scout out
the land of Laish told their brothers, "Did you
know that there are an ephod, household gods,
and a carved image and a silver idol[A] in these
houses? Now think about what you should do."
15 So they detoured there and went to the house
of the young Levite at the home of Micah and
greeted him. 16 The six hundred Danite men
were standing by the entrance of the city gate,
armed with their weapons of war. 17 Then the
five men who had gone to scout out the land
went in and took the carved image, the ephod,
the household idols, and the silver idol,[B] while
the priest was standing by the entrance of the
city gate with the six hundred men armed
with weapons of war.
18 When they entered Micah's house and
took the carved image, the ephod, the household idols, and the silver idol, the priest said
to them, "What are you doing?"
19 They told him, "Be quiet. Keep your mouth
shut.[C] Come with us and be a father and a
priest to us. Is it better for you to be a priest
for the house of one person or for you to be a
priest for a tribe and family in Israel?" 20 So the
priest was pleased and took his ephod, household idols, and carved image, and went with
the people. 21 They prepared to leave, putting
their dependents, livestock, and possessions
in front of them.
22 After they were some distance from Micah's
house, the men who were in the houses near
it were mustered and caught up with the Danites. 23 They called to the Danites, who turned
to face them, and said to Micah, "What's the
matter with you that you mustered the men?"
24 He said, "You took the gods I had made
and the priest, and went away. What do I have
left? How can you say to me, 'What's the matter with you?'"
25 The Danites said to him, "Don't raise your
voice against us, or angry men will attack you,
and you and your family will lose your lives."
26 The Danites went on their way, and Micah
turned to go back home, because he saw that
they were stronger than he was.
27 After they had taken the gods Micah had
made and the priest that belonged to him, they
went to Laish, to a quiet and unsuspecting
people. They killed them with their swords
and burned the city. 28 There was no one to
rescue them because it was far from Sidon
and they had no alliance with anyone. It was
in a valley that belonged to Beth-rehob. They
rebuilt the city and lived in it. 29 They named
the city Dan, after the name of their ancestor
Dan, who was born to Israel. The city was formerly named Laish.
30 The Danites set up the carved image for
themselves. Jonathan son of Gershom, son
of Moses,[D] and his sons were priests for the
Danite tribe until the time of the exile from the
land. 31 So they set up for themselves Micah's
carved image that he had made, and it was
there as long as the house of God was in Shiloh.

OUTRAGE IN BENJAMIN

19 In those days, when there was no king
in Israel, a Levite staying in a remote
part of the hill country of Ephraim acquired
a woman from Bethlehem in Judah as his
concubine. 2 But she was unfaithful to[E] him
and left him for her father's house in Bethlehem in Judah. She was there for four months.
3 Then her husband got up and followed her
to speak kindly to her[F] and bring her back.
He had his servant with him and a pair of
donkeys. So she brought him to her father's
house, and when the girl's father saw him,
he gladly welcomed him. 4 His father-in-law,
the girl's father, detained him, and he stayed
with him for three days. They ate, drank, and
spent the nights there.
5 On the fourth day, they got up early in the
morning and prepared to go, but the girl's father
said to his son-in-law, "Have something to eat
to keep up your strength and then you can go."
6 So they sat down and the two of them ate and
drank together. Then the girl's father said to
the man, "Please agree to stay overnight and
enjoy yourself." 7 The man got up to go, but his
father-in-law persuaded him, so he stayed and
spent the night there again. 8 He got up early
in the morning of the fifth day to leave, but the
girl's father said to him, "Please keep up your
strength." So they waited until late afternoon
and the two of them ate. 9 The man got up to
go with his concubine and his servant, when
his father-in-law, the girl's father, said to him,
"Look, night is coming. Please spend the night.
See, the day is almost over. Spend the night
here, enjoy yourself, then you can get up early
tomorrow for your journey and go home."
10 But the man was unwilling to spend the
night. He got up, departed, and arrived opposite Jebus (that is, Jerusalem). The man had

[A] **18:14** Or *image, the cast image* [B] **18:17** Or *the cast image*, also in v. 18 [C] **18:19** Lit *Put your hand on your mouth*
[D] **18:30** Some Hb mss, LXX, Vg; other Hb mss read *Manasseh* [E] **19:2** LXX reads *was angry with* [F] **19:3** Lit *speak to her heart*

his two saddled donkeys and his concubine
with him. 11 When they were near Jebus and
the day was almost gone, the servant said
to his master, "Please, why not let us stop at
this Jebusite city and spend the night here?"
12 But his master replied to him, "We will not
stop at a foreign city where there are no Israelites. Let's move on to Gibeah." 13 "Come on,"
he said,[A] "let's try to reach one of these places
and spend the night in Gibeah or Ramah."
14 So they continued on their journey, and the
sun set as they neared Gibeah in Benjamin.
15 They stopped[B] to go in and spend the night
in Gibeah. The Levite went in and sat down
in the city square, but no one took them into
their home to spend the night.
16 In the evening, an old man came in from
his work in the field. He was from the hill
country of Ephraim, but he was residing in
Gibeah where the people were Benjaminites.
17 When he looked up and saw the traveler in
the city square, the old man asked, "Where
are you going, and where do you come from?"
18 He answered him, "We're traveling from
Bethlehem in Judah to the remote hill country of Ephraim, where I am from. I went to
Bethlehem in Judah, and now I'm going to the
house of the LORD.[C] No one has taken me into
his home, 19 although there's straw and feed
for the donkeys, and I have bread and wine
for me, my concubine, and the servant[D] with
us. There is nothing we lack."
20 "Welcome!" said the old man. "I'll take
care of everything you need. Only don't spend
the night in the square." 21 So he brought him
to his house and fed the donkeys. Then they
washed their feet and ate and drank. 22 While
they were enjoying themselves, all of a sudden,
wicked men of the city surrounded the house
and beat on the door. They said to the old man
who was the owner of the house, "Bring out
the man who came to your house so we can
have sex with him!"
23 The owner of the house went out and said
to them, "Please don't do this evil, my brothers.
After all, this man has come into my house.
Don't commit this horrible outrage. 24 Here,
let me bring out my virgin daughter and the
man's concubine now. Abuse them and do
whatever you want[E] to them. But don't commit this outrageous thing against this man."
25 But the men would not listen to him, so
the man seized his concubine and took her
outside to them. They raped[F] her and abused
her all night until morning. At daybreak they
let her go. 26 Early that morning, the woman
made her way back, and as it was getting light,
she collapsed at the doorway of the man's
house where her master was.
27 When her master got up in the morning,
opened the doors of the house, and went out
to leave on his journey, there was the woman,
his concubine, collapsed near the doorway of
the house with her hands on the threshold.
28 "Get up," he told her. "Let's go." But there
was no response. So the man put her on his
donkey and set out for home.
29 When he entered his house, he picked up a
knife, took hold of his concubine, cut her into
twelve pieces, limb by limb, and then sent her
throughout the territory of Israel. 30 Everyone
who saw it said, "Nothing like this has ever
happened or has been seen since the day the
Israelites came out of the land of Egypt until
now.[G] Think it over, discuss it, and speak up!"

WAR AGAINST BENJAMIN

20 All the Israelites from Dan to Beer-sheba
and from the land of Gilead came out,
and the community assembled as one body
before the LORD at Mizpah. 2 The leaders of all
the people and of all the tribes of Israel presented themselves in the assembly of God's
people: four hundred thousand armed[H] foot
soldiers. 3 The Benjaminites heard that the
Israelites had gone up to Mizpah.
The Israelites asked, "Tell us, how did this
evil act happen?"
4 The Levite, the husband of the murdered
woman, answered: "I went to Gibeah in Benjamin with my concubine to spend the night.
5 Citizens of Gibeah came to attack me and surrounded the house at night. They intended to
kill me, but they raped my concubine, and she
died. 6 Then I took my concubine and cut her
in pieces, and sent her throughout Israel's territory, because they have committed a wicked
outrage in Israel. 7 Look, all of you are Israelites.
Give your judgment and verdict here and now."
8 Then all the people stood united and said,
"None of us will go to his tent or return to his
house. 9 Now this is what we will do to Gibeah:

[A] **19:13** Lit *said to his servant* [B] **19:15** Lit *stopped there* [C] **19:18** LXX reads *to my house* [D] **19:19** Some Hb mss, Syr, Tg, Vg; other Hb mss read *servants* [E] **19:24** Lit *do what is good in your eyes* [F] **19:25** Lit *knew* [G] **19:30** LXX reads *until now." He commanded the men he sent out, saying, "You will say this to all the men of Israel: Has anything like this happened since the day the Israelites came out of Egypt until this day?* [H] **20:2** Lit *drawing the sword*

we will attack it. By lot 10 we will take ten men out of every hundred from all the tribes of Israel, and one hundred out of every thousand, and one thousand out of every ten thousand to get provisions for the troops when they go to Gibeah in Benjamin to punish them for all the outrage they committed in Israel."

11 So all the men of Israel gathered united against the city. 12 Then the tribes of Israel sent men throughout the tribe of Benjamin, saying, "What is this evil act that has happened among you? 13 Hand over the wicked men in Gibeah so we can put them to death and eradicate evil from Israel." But the Benjaminites would not listen to their fellow Israelites. 14 Instead, the Benjaminites gathered together from their cities to Gibeah to go out and fight against the Israelites. 15 On that day the Benjaminites mobilized twenty-six thousand armed men[A] from their cities, besides seven hundred fit young men rallied by the inhabitants of Gibeah. 16 There were seven hundred fit young men who were left-handed among all these troops; all could sling a stone at a hair and not miss.

17 The Israelites, apart from Benjamin, mobilized four hundred thousand armed men, every one an experienced warrior. 18 They set out, went to Bethel, and inquired of God. The Israelites asked, "Who is to go first to fight for us against the Benjaminites?"

And the LORD answered, "Judah will be first." 19 In the morning, the Israelites set out and camped near Gibeah. 20 The men of Israel went out to fight against Benjamin and took their battle positions against Gibeah. 21 The Benjaminites came out of Gibeah and slaughtered twenty-two thousand men of Israel on the field that day. 22 But the Israelite troops rallied and again took their battle positions in the same place where they positioned themselves on the first day. 23 They went up, wept before the LORD until evening, and inquired of him: "Should we again attack our brothers the Benjaminites?"

And the LORD answered: "Fight against them."

24 On the second day the Israelites advanced against the Benjaminites. 25 That same day the Benjaminites came out from Gibeah to meet them and slaughtered an additional eighteen thousand Israelites on the field; all were armed.[B]

26 The whole Israelite army went to Bethel where they wept and sat before the LORD. They fasted that day until evening and offered burnt offerings and fellowship offerings to the LORD. 27 Then the Israelites inquired of the LORD. In those days, the ark of the covenant of God was there, 28 and Phinehas son of Eleazar, son of Aaron, was serving before it. The Israelites asked: "Should we again fight against our brothers the Benjaminites or should we stop?"

The LORD answered: "Fight, because I will hand them over to you tomorrow." 29 So Israel set up an ambush around Gibeah. 30 On the third day the Israelites fought against the Benjaminites and took their battle positions against Gibeah as before. 31 Then the Benjaminites came out against the troops and were drawn away from the city. They began to attack the troops as before, killing about thirty men of Israel on the highways, one of which goes up to Bethel and the other to Gibeah through the open country. 32 The Benjaminites said, "We are defeating them as before."

But the Israelites said, "Let's flee and draw them away from the city to the highways." 33 So all the men of Israel got up from their places and took their battle positions at Baal-tamar, while the Israelites in ambush charged out of their places west of[C] Geba. 34 Then ten thousand fit young men from all Israel made a frontal assault against Gibeah, and the battle was fierce, but the Benjaminites did not know that disaster was about to strike them. 35 The LORD defeated Benjamin in the presence of Israel, and on that day the Israelites slaughtered 25,100 men of Benjamin; all were armed. 36 Then the Benjaminites realized they had been defeated.

The men of Israel had retreated before Benjamin, because they were confident in the ambush they had set against Gibeah. 37 The men in ambush had rushed quickly against Gibeah; they advanced and put the whole city to the sword. 38 The men of Israel had a prearranged signal with the men in ambush: when they sent up a great cloud of smoke from the city, 39 the men of Israel would return to the battle. When Benjamin had begun to strike them down, killing about thirty men of Israel, they said, "They're defeated before us, just as they were in the first battle." 40 But when the column of smoke began to go up from the city, Benjamin looked behind them, and the whole city was going up in smoke.[D] 41 Then the men of Israel returned,

[A] **20:15** Lit *men drawing the sword*, also in vv. 17,46 [B] **20:25** Lit *were drawing the sword*, also in v. 35 [C] **20:33** LXX, Syr, Vg; MT reads *places in the plain of*, or *places in the cave of* [D] **20:40** Lit *up to the sky*

and the men of Benjamin were terrified when they realized that disaster had struck them. 42 They retreated before the men of Israel toward the wilderness, but the battle overtook them, and those who came out of the cities[A] slaughtered those between them. 43 They surrounded the Benjaminites, pursued them, and easily overtook them near Gibeah toward the east. 44 There were eighteen thousand men who died from Benjamin; all were warriors. 45 Then Benjamin turned and fled toward the wilderness to Rimmon Rock, and Israel killed five thousand men on the highways. They overtook them at Gidom and struck two thousand more dead.

46 All the Benjaminites who died that day were twenty-five thousand armed men; all were warriors. 47 But six hundred men escaped into the wilderness to Rimmon Rock and stayed there four months. 48 The men of Israel turned back against the other Benjaminites and killed them with their swords — the entire city, the animals, and everything that remained. They also burned all the cities that remained.

BRIDES FOR BENJAMIN

21 The men of Israel had sworn an oath at Mizpah: "None of us will give his daughter to a Benjaminite in marriage." 2 So the people went to Bethel and sat there before God until evening. They wept loudly and bitterly, 3 and cried out, "Why, LORD God of Israel, has it occurred[B] that one tribe is missing in Israel today?" 4 The next day the people got up early, built an altar there, and offered burnt offerings and fellowship offerings. 5 The Israelites asked, "Who of all the tribes of Israel didn't come to the LORD with the assembly?" For a great oath had been taken that anyone who had not come to the LORD at Mizpah would certainly be put to death.

6 But the Israelites had compassion on their brothers, the Benjaminites, and said, "Today a tribe has been cut off from Israel. 7 What should we do about wives for the survivors? We've sworn to the LORD not to give them any of our daughters as wives." 8 They asked, "Which city among the tribes of Israel didn't come to the LORD at Mizpah?" It turned out that no one from Jabesh-gilead had come to the camp and the assembly. 9 For when the roll was called, no men were there from the inhabitants of Jabesh-gilead.

10 The congregation sent twelve thousand brave warriors[C] there and commanded them: "Go and kill the inhabitants of Jabesh-gilead with the sword, including women and dependents. 11 This is what you should do: Completely destroy every male, as well as every woman who has gone to bed with a man." 12 They found among the inhabitants of Jabesh-gilead four hundred young virgins, who had not gone to bed with a man, and they brought them to the camp at Shiloh in the land of Canaan.

13 The whole congregation sent a message of peace to the Benjaminites who were at Rimmon Rock. 14 Benjamin returned at that time, and Israel gave them the women they had kept alive from Jabesh-gilead. But there were not enough for them.

15 The people had compassion on Benjamin, because the LORD had made this gap in the tribes of Israel. 16 The elders of the congregation said, "What should we do about wives for those who are left, since the women of Benjamin have been destroyed?" 17 They said, "There must be heirs for the survivors of Benjamin, so that a tribe of Israel will not be wiped out. 18 But we can't give them our daughters as wives." For the Israelites had sworn, "Anyone who gives a wife to a Benjaminite is cursed." 19 They also said, "Look, there's an annual festival to the LORD in Shiloh, which is north of Bethel, east of the highway that goes up from Bethel to Shechem, and south of Lebonah."

20 Then they commanded the Benjaminites: "Go and hide in the vineyards. 21 Watch, and when you see the young women of Shiloh come out to perform the dances, each of you leave the vineyards and catch a wife for yourself from the young women of Shiloh, and go to the land of Benjamin. 22 When their fathers or brothers come to us and protest, we will tell them, 'Show favor to them, since we did not get enough wives for each of them in the battle. You didn't actually give the women to them, so[D] you are not guilty of breaking your oath.' "

23 The Benjaminites did this and took the number of women they needed from the dancers they caught. They went back to their own inheritance, rebuilt their cities, and lived in them. 24 At that time, each of the Israelites returned from there to his own tribe and family. Each returned from there to his own inheritance.

25 In those days there was no king in Israel; everyone did whatever seemed right to him.

[A] **20:42** LXX, Vg read *city* [B] **21:3** Lit *has this occurred in Israel at this time* [C] **21:10** Lit *twelve thousand of their sons of valor* [D] **21:22** Lit

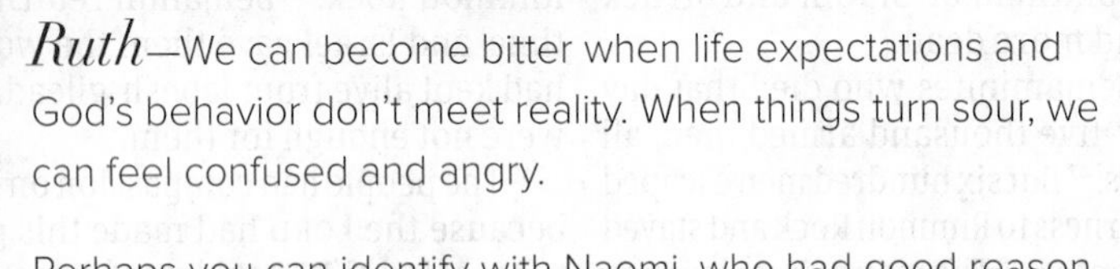

Ruth—We can become bitter when life expectations and God's behavior don't meet reality. When things turn sour, we can feel confused and angry.

Perhaps you can identify with Naomi, who had good reason to say, "The Almighty has made me very bitter" (1:20). But God had more chapters to write in Naomi's story.

First, he gave her a daughter-in-law, Ruth, who was loyal both to Naomi and to the God of Israel. Then he provided for them a kind kinsman, Boaz, who ensured that Ruth could get enough grain to keep them alive. In his rich grace, God gave Naomi even more. Ruth found a loving husband, a family redeemer, and through their union Naomi became a grandmother.

Whatever your story, God is writing more chapters in your life. He is your Redeemer. The redemption God offers is complete and eternal. Let Naomi and Ruth's story of loyalty, miraculous providence, and restoration encourage you as you trust in Christ your Redeemer.

RUTH

AUTHOR: The Talmud names Samuel as the author of the book of Ruth, but the book itself does not name an author.

DATE WRITTEN: An exact date cannot be determined, but the book was likely written during or later than the reign of King David (1011–971 BC), possibly as late as after the exile.

ORIGINAL AUDIENCE: The Israelites

SETTING: The beautiful love story of Ruth and Boaz, centered around the life of one Moabite woman who claims Israel's God as her own, is a bright spot during the time of the judges. The nation was in upheaval, with spiritual and moral decay prevalent throughout, but God was still at work calling people to himself.

PURPOSE FOR WRITING: Up to this point, the Old Testament has centered around one nation arising from Abraham. The Israelites understood that the descendants of Abraham were God's chosen people and heirs of the promises of God. But even when the covenant was first communicated in Genesis, God included in his promise that all the nations of the world would be blessed. The book of Ruth is the first glimpse we have of how that would be fulfilled. Here God calls a Moabite woman into the family of God, showing that salvation is by faith and that it is available to everyone—from every nation.

OUTLINE:

1. Scene 1: Moab (1:1-22)

   Elimelech flees the famine (1:1-5)

   Naomi is bereft (1:6-13)

   Ruth chooses the God of Israel (1:14-22)

2. Scene 2: A Farm in Bethlehem (2:1-23)

   Ruth meets Boaz (2:1-14)

   Boaz shows mercy (2:15-23)

3. Scene 3: The Threshing Floor of Boaz (3:1-18)

   Boaz pledges marriage to Ruth (3:1-11)

   Marriage is delayed (3:12-18)

4. Scene 4: The City Gate of Bethlehem (4:1-22)

   Boaz marries Ruth (4:1-12)

   Ruth gives birth to Obed (4:13-15)

   A family is restored to Naomi (4:16)

   Ruth is an ancestor of David (4:17-22)

KEY VERSE:

"May you receive a full reward from the LORD God of Israel, under whose wings you have come for refuge." —Ruth 2:12

RESTORATION THEMES

R	Rest and Reflection	*For the next note, see 1 Samuel 2:26.*
E	Eternal Perspective	*For the next note, see 1 Samuel 16:7.*
S	Support	*For the next note, see 2 Samuel 22:28.*
T	Thanksgiving and Contentment	*Gratitude—Ruth 1:20-21*
O	Other-centeredness	*For the next note, see 1 Samuel 12:23.*
R	Relationships	*For the next note, see 1 Samuel 18:1-3.*
E	Exercise of Faith	*For the next note, see 1 Kings 11:4.*

NAOMI'S FAMILY IN MOAB

1 During the time[A] of the judges, there was a
famine in the land. A man left Bethlehem[B]
in Judah with his wife and two sons to stay in
the territory of Moab for a while. 2 The man's
name was Elimelech,[C] and his wife's name
was Naomi.[D] The names of his two sons were
Mahlon[E] and Chilion.[F] They were Ephrathites
from Bethlehem in Judah. They entered the
fields of Moab and settled there. 3 Naomi's
husband Elimelech died, and she was left with
her two sons. 4 Her sons took Moabite wom-
en as their wives: one was named Orpah and
the second was named Ruth. After they lived
in Moab about ten years, 5 both Mahlon and
Chilion also died, and Naomi was left without
her two children and without her husband.

RUTH'S LOYALTY TO NAOMI

6 She and her daughters-in-law set out to return
from the territory of Moab, because she had
heard in Moab that the LORD had paid attention to his people's need by providing them
food. 7 She left the place where she had been
living, accompanied by her two daughters-
in-law, and traveled along the road leading
back to the land of Judah.
8 Naomi said to them, "Each of you go back
to your mother's home. May the LORD show
kindness to you as you have shown to the
dead and to me. 9 May the LORD grant each of
you rest in the house of a new husband." She
kissed them, and they wept loudly.
10 They said to her, "We insist on returning
with you to your people."
11 But Naomi replied, "Return home, my
daughters. Why do you want to go with me?
Am I able to have any more sons who could
become your husbands? 12 Return home, my
daughters. Go on, for I am too old to have another husband. Even if I thought there was still
hope for me to have a husband tonight and to
bear sons, 13 would you be willing to wait for
them to grow up? Would you restrain yourselves from remarrying?[G] No, my daughters,
my life is much too bitter for you to share,[H]

Thanksgiving and Contentment | *Gratitude*

WHEN GRATITUDE IS LACKING

"'Don't call me Naomi. Call me Mara,' she answered, 'for the Almighty has made me very bitter. I went away full, but the LORD has brought me back empty. Why do you call me Naomi, since the LORD has opposed me, and the Almighty has afflicted me?'" Ruth 1:20-21

Naomi certainly experienced terrible tragedy in Moab, burying a husband and two grown sons during her stay. But her gloomy statement that "the LORD has brought me back empty" didn't reflect her real situation.

Just before this scene, Naomi's daughter-in-law (and fellow widow) Ruth had made a breathtaking, lifelong pledge of devotion to her mother-in-law. Waving goodbye to her homeland of Moab, with Naomi, Ruth set out for the older woman's ancestral home in Israel. There, the two widows intended to scratch out a life together.

This was a massive sacrifice on Ruth's part—a brave, generous, and rare act. Naomi thanked her by greeting her once and future neighbors with this lament, "No longer call me Naomi (which means sweet). Call me Mara (which means bitter). There's nothing good left in my life!"

We can almost hear Ruth mumbling, "What am I—chopped liver?"

We've all been in Naomi's shoes—and Ruth's. In bleak situations, be careful not to casually dismiss all the good things (or people) in your life. And when others seem ungrateful, remember that pain is often blinding and consuming in its effect.

For the next note on *Thanksgiving and Contentment*, see 2 Samuel 22:2-4.

[A] **1:1** Lit *In the days of the judging* [B] **1:1** = House of Bread [C] **1:2** = My God Is King [D] **1:2** = Pleasant [E] **1:2** = Sickly [F] **1:2** = Weak or Failing [G] **1:13** Lit *marrying a man* [H] **1:13** Lit *daughters, for more bitter to me than you*

because the LORD's hand has turned against
me." 14 Again they wept loudly, and Orpah
kissed her mother-in-law, but Ruth clung to
her. 15 Naomi said, "Look, your sister-in-law
has gone back to her people and to her gods.
Follow your sister-in-law."
16 But Ruth replied:

Don't plead with me to abandon you
or to return and not follow you.
For wherever you go, I will go,
and wherever you live, I will live;
your people will be my people,
and your God will be my God.
17 Where you die, I will die,
and there I will be buried.
May the LORD punish me,[A]
and do so severely,
if anything but death separates you
and me.

18 When Naomi saw that Ruth was determined
to go with her, she stopped talking to her.
19 The two of them traveled until they came
to Bethlehem. When they entered Bethlehem,
the whole town was excited about their arrival[B] and the local women exclaimed, "Can
this be Naomi?"
20 "Don't call me Naomi. Call me Mara,"[C] she
answered, "for the Almighty has made me
very bitter. 21 I went away full, but the LORD
has brought me back empty. Why do you call
me Naomi, since the LORD has opposed[D] me,
and the Almighty has afflicted me?"
22 So Naomi came back from the territory
of Moab with her daughter-in-law Ruth the
Moabitess. They arrived in Bethlehem at the
beginning of the barley harvest.

RUTH AND BOAZ MEET

2 Now Naomi had a relative on her husband's side. He was a prominent man of
noble character from Elimelech's family. His
name was Boaz.
2 Ruth the Moabitess asked Naomi, "Will you
let me go into the fields and gather fallen grain
behind someone with whom I find favor?"
Naomi answered her, "Go ahead, my daughter." 3 So Ruth left and entered the field to gather
grain behind the harvesters. She happened to
be in the portion of the field belonging to Boaz,
who was from Elimelech's family.
4 Later, when Boaz arrived from Bethlehem,
he said to the harvesters, "The LORD be with
you."
"The LORD bless you," they replied.
5 Boaz asked his servant who was in charge of
the harvesters, "Whose young woman is this?"
6 The servant answered, "She is the young
Moabite woman who returned with Naomi
from the territory of Moab. 7 She asked, 'Will
you let me gather fallen grain among the bundles behind the harvesters?' She came and has
been on her feet since early morning, except
that she rested a little in the shelter."[E]
8 Then Boaz said to Ruth, "Listen, my daughter.[F] Don't go and gather grain in another field,
and don't leave this one, but stay here close
to my female servants. 9 See which field they
are harvesting, and follow them. Haven't I
ordered the young men not to touch you?[G]
When you are thirsty, go and drink from the
jars the young men have filled."
10 She fell facedown, bowed to the ground,
and said to him, "Why have I found favor with
you, so that you notice me, although I am a
foreigner?"
11 Boaz answered her, "Everything you have
done for your mother-in-law since your husband's death has been fully reported to me:
how you left your father and mother and your
native land, and how you came to a people
you didn't previously know. 12 May the LORD
reward you for what you have done, and may
you receive a full reward from the LORD God
of Israel, under whose wings you have come
for refuge."
13 "My lord," she said, "I have found favor with
you, for you have comforted and encouraged[H]
your servant, although I am not like one of
your female servants."
14 At mealtime Boaz told her, "Come over here
and have some bread and dip it in the vinegar
sauce." So she sat beside the harvesters, and
he offered her roasted grain. She ate and was
satisfied and had some left over.
15 When she got up to gather grain, Boaz
ordered his young men, "Let her even gather
grain among the bundles, and don't humiliate
her. 16 Pull out some stalks from the bundles
for her and leave them for her to gather. Don't
rebuke her." 17 So Ruth gathered grain in the
field until evening. She beat out what she had
gathered, and it was about twenty-six quarts[I]

[A] **1:17** A solemn oath formula; 1Sm 3:17; 2Sm 3:9,35; 1Kg 2:23; 2Kg 6:31 [B] **1:19** Lit *excited because of them* [C] **1:20** = Bitter
[D] **1:21** LXX, Syr, Vg read *has humiliated* [E] **2:7** LXX reads *morning, and until evening she has not rested in the field a little*; Vg reads *morning until now and she did not return to the house*; Hb uncertain [F] **2:8** Lit *"Haven't you heard, my daughter?*
[G] **2:9** Either sexual or physical harassment [H] **2:13** Lit *and spoken to the heart of* [I] **2:17** Lit *about an ephah*

Naomi | Restoration Profile

RUTH 1–4

Behind the story of Ruth is the restoration of Naomi. The account is set in the time of the judges when neither God nor king was a recognized authority and "everyone did whatever seemed right to him" (Jdg 21:25). Naomi's experience began with disaster and led to tragedy. Because of a devastating famine, she left Bethlehem with her husband and two sons and relocated in Moab, the traditional enemy of Israel, but where survival might be possible.

Soon, Naomi's husband died. Her growing sons married local girls, but before either one started a family, they also died, leaving three women stranded without support. Naomi decided to return to Bethlehem and sent her two daughters-in-law back to their families. One of them, Ruth, refused to leave. In fact, she accompanied Naomi, who at this point in the story was angry with God: "'Don't call me Naomi. Call me Mara,' she answered, 'for the Almighty has made me very bitter'" (Ru 1:20). Naomi means "pleasant"; Mara means "bitter." She was a woman in desperate need of restoration.

God began his work by injecting hope into the situation. Ruth met someone who turned out to be a relative of Naomi and capable of offering her and her mother-in-law safety. Caught up in the matchmaking for Ruth, Naomi was distracted from her bitterness. Naomi may not have been in a position to initiate the redemption process, which required another member in the family to intervene, but she advised Ruth in her courtship with Boaz.

Soon Boaz devised a plan of action, and he secured his position as Ruth's husband and caretaker of Naomi's inheritance. God provided security for Naomi through Boaz's purchase of her husband and sons' property. And shortly, Ruth delivered her a grandson, to bring about Naomi's restoration from bitterness.

of barley. 18 She picked up the grain and went
into the town, where her mother-in-law saw
what she had gleaned. She brought out what
she had left over from her meal and gave it
to her.
19 Her mother-in-law said to her, "Where
did you gather barley today, and where did
you work? May the LORD bless the man who
noticed you."
Ruth told her mother-in-law whom she had
worked with and said, "The name of the man
I worked with today is Boaz."
20 Then Naomi said to her daughter-in-law,
"May the LORD bless him because he has not
abandoned his kindness to the living or the
dead." Naomi continued, "The man is a close
relative. He is one of our family redeemers."
21 Ruth the Moabitess said, "He also told me,
'Stay with my young men until they have finished all of my harvest.'"
22 So Naomi said to her daughter-in-law Ruth,
"My daughter, it is good for you to work[A] with
his female servants, so that nothing will happen to you in another field." 23 Ruth stayed
close to Boaz's female servants and gathered
grain until the barley and the wheat harvests
were finished. And she lived with[B] her mother-in-law.

RUTH'S APPEAL TO BOAZ

3 Ruth's mother-in-law Naomi said to her,
"My daughter, shouldn't I find rest for you,
so that you will be taken care of? 2 Now isn't
Boaz our relative? Haven't you been working
with his female servants? This evening he will
be winnowing barley on the threshing floor.
3 Wash, put on perfumed oil, and wear your
best clothes. Go down to the threshing floor,
but don't let the man know you are there until
he has finished eating and drinking. 4 When he
lies down, notice the place where he's lying,
go in and uncover his feet, and lie down. Then
he will explain to you what you should do."
5 So Ruth said to her, "I will do everything
you say."[C] 6 She went down to the threshing
floor and did everything her mother-in-law
had charged her to do. 7 After Boaz ate, drank,
and was in good spirits,[D] he went to lie down

[A] **2:22** Lit *go out* [B] **2:23** Some Hb mss, Vg read *she returned to* [C] **3:5** Alt Hb tradition reads *say to me* [D] **3:7** Lit *and his heart was glad*

at the end of the pile of barley, and she came secretly, uncovered his feet, and lay down.

8 At midnight, Boaz was startled, turned over, and there lying at his feet was a woman! 9 So he asked, "Who are you?"

"I am Ruth, your servant," she replied. "Take me under your wing,[A] for you are a family redeemer."

10 Then he said, "May the LORD bless you, my daughter. You have shown more kindness now than before,[B] because you have not pursued younger men, whether rich or poor. 11 Now don't be afraid, my daughter. I will do for you whatever you say,[C] since all the people in my town[D] know that you are a woman of noble character. 12 Yes, it is true that I am a family redeemer, but there is a redeemer closer than I am. 13 Stay here tonight, and in the morning, if he wants to redeem you, that's good. Let him redeem you. But if he doesn't want to redeem you, as the LORD lives, I will. Now lie down until morning."

14 So she lay down at his feet until morning but got up while it was still dark.[E] Then Boaz said, "Don't let it be known that a[F] woman came to the threshing floor." 15 And he told Ruth, "Bring the shawl you're wearing and hold it out." When she held it out, he shoveled six measures of barley into her shawl, and she[G] went into the town.

16 She went to her mother-in-law, Naomi, who asked her, "What happened,[H] my daughter?"

Then Ruth told her everything the man had done for her. 17 She said, "He gave me these six measures of barley, because he said,[I] 'Don't go back to your mother-in-law empty-handed.'"

18 Naomi said, "My daughter, wait until you find out how things go, for he won't rest unless he resolves this today."

RUTH AND BOAZ MARRY

4 Boaz went to the gate of the town and sat down there. Soon the family redeemer Boaz had spoken about came by. Boaz said, "Come over here[J] and sit down." So he went over and sat down. 2 Then Boaz took ten men of the town's elders and said, "Sit here." And they sat down. 3 He said to the redeemer, "Naomi, who has returned from the territory of Moab, is selling the portion of the field that belonged to our brother Elimelech. 4 I thought I should inform you:[K] Buy it back in the presence of those seated here and in the presence of the elders of my people. If you want to redeem it, do it. But if you do[L] not want to redeem it, tell me so that I will know, because there isn't anyone other than you to redeem it, and I am next after you."

"I want to redeem it," he answered.

5 Then Boaz said, "On the day you buy the field from Naomi, you will acquire[M] Ruth the Moabitess, the wife of the deceased man, to perpetuate the man's name on his property."[N]

6 The redeemer replied, "I can't redeem it myself, or I will ruin my own inheritance. Take my right of redemption, because I can't redeem it."

7 At an earlier period in Israel, a man removed his sandal and gave it to the other party in order to make any matter legally binding concerning the right of redemption or the exchange of property. This was the method of legally binding a transaction in Israel.

8 So the redeemer removed his sandal and said to Boaz, "Buy back the property yourself."

9 Boaz said to the elders and all the people, "You are witnesses today that I am buying from Naomi everything that belonged to Elimelech, Chilion, and Mahlon. 10 I have also acquired Ruth the Moabitess, Mahlon's widow, as my wife, to perpetuate the deceased man's name on his property, so that his name will not disappear among his relatives or from the gate of his hometown. You are witnesses today."

11 All the people who were at the city gate, including the elders, said, "We are witnesses. May the LORD make the woman who is entering your house like Rachel and Leah, who together built the house of Israel. May you be powerful in Ephrathah and your name well known in Bethlehem. 12 May your house become like the house of Perez, the son Tamar bore to Judah, because of the offspring the LORD will give you by this young woman."

13 Boaz took Ruth and she became his wife. He slept with her, and the LORD granted conception to her, and she gave birth to a son.

[A] **3:9** Or *"Spread the edge of your garment*; lit *"Spread the wing of your garment*; Ru 2:12 [B] **3:10** Lit *kindness at the last than at the first* [C] **3:11** Some Hb mss, Orig, Syr, Tg, Vg read *say to me* [D] **3:11** Lit *all the gate of my people* [E] **3:14** Lit *up before a man could recognize his companion* [F] **3:14** LXX; MT reads *the* [G] **3:15** Some Hb mss, Aramaic, Syr, Vg; other Hb mss read *he* [H] **3:16** Lit *"Who are you* [I] **3:17** Alt Hb tradition, LXX, Syr, Tg read *said to me* [J] **4:1** Or *said, "Come here Mr. So-and-so* [K] **4:4** Lit *should uncover your ear, saying* [L] **4:4** Some Hb mss, LXX, Syr, Vg; other Hb mss read *if he does* [M] **4:5** Lit *Naomi and from* [N] **4:5** Alt Hb tradition reads *Naomi, I will have already acquired from Ruth the Moabitess, the wife of the dead man, the privilege of raising up the name of the dead man on his property*

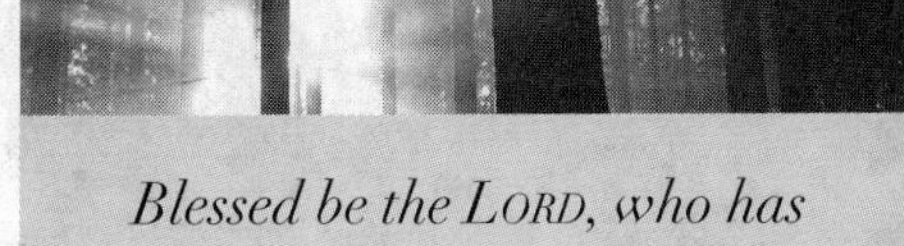

Blessed be the Lord, who has not left you without a family redeemer today. May his name become well known in Israel.
—Ruth 4:14

14 The women said to Naomi, "Blessed be the
Lord, who has not left you without a family redeemer today. May his name become
well known in Israel. 15 He will renew your
life and sustain you in your old age. Indeed,
your daughter-in-law, who loves you and is
better to you than seven sons, has given birth
to him." 16 Naomi took the child, placed him on
her lap, and became his nanny. 17 The neighbor
women said, "A son has been born to Naomi,"
and they named him Obed.[A] He was the father
of Jesse, the father of David.

DAVID'S GENEALOGY FROM JUDAH'S SON

18 Now these are the family records of Perez:
Perez fathered Hezron,
19 Hezron fathered Ram,[B]
Ram fathered Amminadab,
20 Amminadab fathered Nahshon,
Nahshon fathered Salmon,
21 Salmon fathered Boaz,
Boaz fathered Obed,
22 Obed fathered Jesse,
and Jesse fathered David.

[A] **4:17** = Servant [B] **4:19** LXX reads *Aram*; Mt 1:3-4

1 Samuel provides us with stories we know and love: Hannah's longing and God's provision, Samuel hearing God's voice, Saul rising from obscurity to the throne, David confronting Goliath, and Saul pursuing of David borne out of a jealous rage that cost him the throne.

The Israelites' longing for a king had been a rejection of God's rule. He had proven himself both faithful and powerful as they conquered the promised land, and had tenderly forgiven them repeatedly during the period of the judges. Their King was all-powerful and all-loving, but they were not content.

Fearing the surrounding nations, they wanted to feel secure and didn't trust God to save them. God gave them a king, and the results were as bad as predicted (Dt. 17:14-20). Choosing our way over God's way leads to unintended consequences that don't match our hopes.

In 1 Samuel, we find portraits of kings who follow God's law and kings who fail miserably, great triumph through trusting in God, and the misery of being unjustly hunted down by a powerful king. Yet, the faithful God restores and renews his people as they trust in him through life's ups and downs.

He does the same for us.

1 SAMUEL

AUTHOR: No author is specifically named for 1 or 2 Samuel, which were likely originally written as one book. Scholars speculate that 1 Samuel 1–25 was written by Samuel, then the rest of 1 and 2 Samuel was completed by Nathan and Gad (1Ch 29:29), but we have no proof of authorship.

DATE WRITTEN: Based on 1 Samuel 27:6, the book likely was not completed until a few generations after the division of the kingdom in 930 BC. The reference to "kings of Judah" places the writing of 1 and 2 Samuel after the division of Israel into northern and southern kingdoms.

ORIGINAL AUDIENCE: The Israelites

SETTING: First Samuel picks up where Judges left off. God's people are living in apostasy, and as a final rejection of God's rule, they demand that he give them a king. Though Samuel knows a monarchy will draw the people further away from the covenant relationship they were designed to have with him, God provides them with a king. This lies at the root of many prayers. Fearing the future or the dangers around us, we ask God for quick fixes rather than trust him to take care of us. We want him to act the way we want and give us what will make us feel secure, when the only true security comes from trusting him. Unfortunately, when we reject God's rule, we can find ourselves in a situation similar to Israel's.

PURPOSE FOR WRITING: In the history of the world, often a nation will move from tribal leadership to a monarchy. But in Israel's case, this was not a natural progression—they were God's covenant people, and God was their King. Asking for a king "like all the other the nations" (8:20) was an act of rebellion against the true King, their Lord and Deliverer. This portion of Israel's history serves as a warning against rejecting God's rule and an encouragement that no matter how often we reject him, God continues to love us.

OUTLINE:

1. Samuel's ministry (1:1–12:25)

   Samuel's birth and call (1:1–3:21)

   Ark of the covenant, captured and restored (4:1–7:17)

   Request for a king and God's provision of Saul (8:1–12:25)

2. Saul's reign (13:1–31:13)

   Saul's victory over the Philistines (13:1–14:52)

   Saul's failure against the Amalekites (15:1–35)

   Choice of David as Saul's successor (16:1–23)

   David's triumph over Goliath (17:1-58)

   Saul's pursuit of David (18:1–26:25)

   The end of Saul's reign (27:1–31:13)

KEY VERSE:

"There is no one holy like the LORD. There is no one besides you! And there is no rock like our God." —1 Samuel 2:2

RESTORATION THEMES

R	Rest and Reflection	*Watching Health—2:26*
E	Eternal Perspective	*God's Inside View—16:7*
S	Support	*For the next note, see 2 Samuel 22:28.*
T	Thanksgiving and Contentment	*For the next note, see 2 Samuel 22:2-4.*
O	Other-centeredness	*Praying for Others—1 Samuel 12:23* *Learning Other People's Stories—25:24*
R	Relationships	*Relating to Friends—18:1-3*
E	Exercise of Faith	*For the next note, see 1 Kings 11:4.*

HANNAH'S VOW

1 There was a man from Ramathaim-zophim in[A] the hill country of Ephraim. His name was Elkanah son of Jeroham, son of Elihu, son of Tohu, son of Zuph, an Ephraimite. 2 He had two wives, the first named Hannah and the second Peninnah. Peninnah had children, but Hannah was childless. 3 This man would go up from his town every year to worship and to sacrifice to the LORD of Armies at Shiloh, where Eli's two sons, Hophni and Phinehas, were the LORD's priests.

4 Whenever Elkanah offered a sacrifice, he always gave portions of the meat to his wife Peninnah and to each of her sons and daughters. 5 But he gave a double[B] portion to Hannah, for he loved her even though the LORD had kept her from conceiving. 6 Her rival would taunt her severely just to provoke her, because the LORD had kept Hannah from conceiving. 7 Year after year, when she went up to the LORD's house, her rival taunted her in this way. Hannah would weep and would not eat. 8 "Hannah, why are you crying?" her husband Elkanah would ask. "Why won't you eat? Why are you troubled? Am I not better to you than ten sons?"

9 On one occasion, Hannah got up after they ate and drank at Shiloh.[C] The priest Eli was sitting on a chair by the doorpost of the LORD's temple. 10 Deeply hurt, Hannah prayed to the LORD and wept with many tears. 11 Making a vow, she pleaded, "LORD of Armies, if you will take notice of your servant's affliction, remember and not forget me, and give your servant a son,[D] I will give him to the LORD all the days of his life, and his hair will never be cut."[E]

12 While she continued praying in the LORD's presence, Eli watched her mouth. 13 Hannah was praying silently,[F] and though her lips were moving, her voice could not be heard. Eli thought she was drunk 14 and said to her, "How long are you going to be drunk? Get rid of your wine!"

15 "No, my lord," Hannah replied. "I am a woman with a broken heart. I haven't had any wine or beer; I've been pouring out my heart before the LORD. 16 Don't think of me as a wicked woman; I've been praying from the depth of my anguish and resentment."

17 Eli responded, "Go in peace, and may the God of Israel grant the request you've made of him."

18 "May your servant find favor with you," she replied. Then Hannah went on her way; she ate and no longer looked despondent.[G]

SAMUEL'S BIRTH AND DEDICATION

19 The next morning Elkanah and Hannah got up early to worship before the LORD. Afterward, they returned home to Ramah. Then Elkanah was intimate with his wife Hannah, and the LORD remembered her. 20 After some time,[H] Hannah conceived and gave birth to a son. She named him Samuel,[I] because she said, "I requested him from the LORD."

21 When Elkanah and all his household went up to make the annual sacrifice and his vow offering to the LORD, 22 Hannah did not go and explained to her husband, "After the child is weaned, I'll take him to appear in the LORD's presence and to stay there permanently."

23 Her husband Elkanah replied, "Do what you think is best,[J] and stay here until you've weaned him. May the LORD confirm your[K] word." So Hannah stayed there and nursed her son until she weaned him. 24 When she had weaned him, she took him with her to Shiloh, as well as a three-year-old bull,[L] half a bushel[M] of flour, and a clay jar of wine. Though the boy was still young,[N] she took him to the LORD's house at Shiloh. 25 Then they slaughtered the bull and brought the boy to Eli.

26 "Please, my lord," she said, "as surely as you live, my lord, I am the woman who stood here beside you praying to the LORD. 27 I prayed for this boy, and since the LORD gave me what I asked him for, 28 I now give the boy to the LORD. For as long as he lives, he is given to the LORD." Then he[O] worshiped the LORD there.[P]

HANNAH'S TRIUMPHANT PRAYER

2 Hannah prayed:
My heart rejoices in the LORD;
my horn is lifted up by the LORD.
My mouth boasts over my enemies,
because I rejoice in your salvation.
2 There is no one holy like the LORD.
There is no one besides you!
And there is no rock like our God.

[A] 1:1 Or *from Ramathaim, a Zuphite from* [B] 1:5 Or *gave only one*; Hb obscure [C] 1:9 LXX adds *and presented herself before the LORD* [D] 1:11 Lit *a seed of men* [E] 1:11 Lit *and no razor will go up on his head* [F] 1:13 Lit *praying to her heart* [G] 1:18 Lit *and her face was not to her again* [H] 1:20 Lit *In the turning of the days* [I] 1:20 In Hb, the name *Samuel* sounds like the phrase "requested from God." [J] 1:23 Lit *what is good in your eyes* [K] 1:23 DSS, LXX, Syr; MT reads *his* [L] 1:24 DSS, LXX, Syr; MT reads *Shiloh with three bulls* [M] 1:24 Lit *bull and an ephah* [N] 1:24 Lit *And the youth was a youth* [O] 1:28 DSS read *she*; some Hb mss, Syr, Vg read *they* [P] 1:28 LXX reads *Then she left him there before the LORD*

3 Do not boast so proudly,
or let arrogant words come out of
your mouth,
for the LORD is a God of knowledge,
and actions are weighed by him.
4 The bows of the warriors are broken,
but the feeble are clothed
with strength.
5 Those who are full hire themselves out
for food,
but those who are starving hunger
no more.
The woman who is childless gives birth
to seven,
but the woman with many sons
pines away.
6 The LORD brings death and gives life;
he sends some down to Sheol,
and he raises others up.
7 The LORD brings poverty and gives
wealth;
he humbles and he exalts.
8 He raises the poor from the dust
and lifts the needy from the trash heap.
He seats them with noblemen
and gives them a throne of honor.[A]
For the foundations of the earth are the
LORD's;
he has set the world on them.
9 He guards the steps[B]
of his faithful ones,
but the wicked perish in darkness,
for a person does not prevail by
his own strength.
10 Those who oppose the LORD
will be shattered;[C]
he will thunder in the heavens
against them.
The LORD will judge the ends
of the earth.
He will give power to his king;
he will lift up the horn of his anointed.[D]

11 Elkanah went home to Ramah, but the
boy served the LORD in the presence of the
priest Eli.

ELI'S FAMILY JUDGED

12 Eli's sons were wicked men; they did not respect the LORD 13 or the priests' share of the
sacrifices from the people. When anyone offered a sacrifice, the priest's servant would
come with a three-pronged meat fork while
the meat was boiling 14 and plunge it into the
container, kettle, cauldron, or cooking pot. The
priest would claim for himself whatever the
meat fork brought up. This is the way they treated all the Israelites who came there to Shiloh.

Rest and Reflection | *Watching Health*

ARE YOU GROWING?

"By contrast, the boy Samuel grew in stature and in favor with the LORD and with people." 1 Samuel 2:26

Have you ever noticed how some people are motivated to get better, smarter, and healthier? Restless to improve their lives, they learn and practice new skills. They work at becoming more capable. In time, sure enough, they see their lives improve and influence increase.

Meanwhile, others settle for mediocrity. They pack it in. Slide. Coast. Eventually they stagnate and even regress. Their impact is minimal—if not downright negative!

That was the story playing out near the end of Eli's life. Eli was the priest of Israel. He had two sons who were far more interested in making a killing than making a difference. But Eli also was mentoring a boy named Samuel who was eager to learn, grow, and serve. Maybe you know the rest of this story? The sons of Eli ended in shame. Samuel became one of Israel's greatest leaders.

This cautionary tale prompts a question worth pondering: What steps are you taking to become healthier and better—spiritually, socially, physically, and intellectually?

For the next note on *Rest and Reflection*, see 1 Kings 3:9-10.

[A] **2:8** DSS, LXX add *He gives the vow of the one who makes a vow and he blesses the years of the just.* [B] **2:9** Lit *feet*
[C] **2:10** DSS, LXX read *The LORD shatters those who dispute with him* [D] **2:10** Or *Messiah*

Hannah | Restoration Profile

1 SAMUEL 1–2

The entire nation of Israel began with an infertile couple. Sarah was unable to conceive until old age. The often unexplainable heartache of infertility has echoed through history in every generation. Hannah was a loved wife who couldn't get pregnant. Her rival, husband Elkanah's other wife Peninnah, took glee in displaying her fruitfulness, much to Hannah's shame.

Her husband's helplessness, her own hopelessness, and Eli the priest's dismissiveness were three obstacles Hannah had to overcome on her way to restoration. Her story is not a prescription for overcoming infertility; it is a pathway for healthy restoration in any setback in life. First, she was hurt but not embittered by her husband's kind but clumsy love: "Am I not better to you than ten sons?" (1Sm 1:8). Second, she put her request to God with an open hand, recognizing that even if God answered her prayer, the result would not be her possession. She did what every mother must eventually do—released the child she hoped to receive. Third, she responded graciously to Eli's false observation, explaining what she was doing but not sharing the content of her prayer. His chastised blessing had no specifics in mind, so he had no opportunity to weigh in on the appropriateness of her request. His own life was a mess, but in his role as God's priest, his blessing carried weight.

Hannah accepted Eli's blessing as a renewal of hope; "Then Hannah went on her way; she ate and no longer looked despondent" (1Sm 1:18). Her new attitude was no doubt much to the delight of her husband. And when God answered her prayer, she thoughtfully followed through on her promise. She received further blessing from God, in this case in the form of more children. Genuine restoration isn't so much about getting what we want; it's about getting something better from God.

15 Even before the fat was burned, the priest's
servant would come and say to the one who
was sacrificing, "Give the priest some meat to
roast, because he won't accept boiled meat from
you — only raw." 16 If that person said to him,
"The fat must be burned first; then you can take
whatever you want for yourself," the servant
would reply, "No, I insist that you hand it over
right now. If you don't, I'll take it by force!"
17 So the servants' sin was very severe in the
presence of the LORD, because the men treated
the LORD's offering with contempt.
18 Samuel served in the LORD's presence—
this mere boy was dressed in the linen ephod.
19 Each year his mother made him a little robe
and took it to him when she went with her
husband to offer the annual sacrifice. 20 Eli
would bless Elkanah and his wife: "May the
LORD give you children by this woman in place
of the one she[A] has given to the LORD." Then
they would go home.
21 The LORD paid attention to Hannah's
need, and she conceived and gave birth to
three sons and two daughters. Meanwhile,
the boy Samuel grew up in the presence of the
LORD.
22 Now Eli was very old. He heard about everything his sons were doing to all Israel and
how they were sleeping with the women who
served at the entrance to the tent of meeting.
23 He said to them, "Why are you doing these
things? I have heard about your evil actions
from all these people. 24 No, my sons, the news
I hear the LORD's people spreading is not good.
25 If one person sins against another, God can
intercede for him, but if a person sins against
the LORD, who can intercede for him?" But
they would not listen to their father, since the
LORD intended to kill them. 26 By contrast, the
boy Samuel grew in stature and in favor with
the LORD and with people.
27 A man of God came to Eli and said to him,
"This is what the LORD says: 'Didn't I reveal
myself to your forefather's family[B] when they
were in Egypt and belonged to Pharaoh's palace? 28 Out of all the tribes of Israel, I chose
your house[C] to be my priests, to offer sacrifices on my altar, to burn incense, and to
wear an ephod in my presence. I also gave
your forefather's family all the Israelite fire
offerings. 29 Why, then, do all of you despise
my sacrifices and offerings that I require at

[A] **2:20** DSS; MT reads *he* [B] **2:27** Lit *the palace of your father* [C] **2:28** Lit *selected him*

the place of worship? You have honored your
sons more than me, by making yourselves fat
with the best part of all of the offerings of my
people Israel.'
30 "Therefore, this is the declaration of the
LORD, the God of Israel: 'I did say that your
family and your forefather's family would
walk before me forever. But now,' this is the
LORD's declaration, 'no longer! For those who
honor me I will honor, but those who despise
me will be disgraced. 31 Look, the days are
coming when I will cut off your strength and
the strength of your forefather's house, so
that none in your family will reach old age.
32 You will see distress in the place of worship, in spite of all that is good in Israel, and
no one in your family will ever again reach
old age. 33 Any man from your family I do not
cut off from my altar will bring grief[A] and
sadness to you. All your descendants will
die violently.[B,C] 34 This will be the sign that
will come to you concerning your two sons
Hophni and Phinehas: both of them will die
on the same day.
35 " 'Then I will raise up a faithful priest for
myself. He will do whatever is in my heart
and mind. I will establish a lasting dynasty
for him, and he will walk before my anointed
one for all time. 36 Anyone who is left in your
family will come and bow down to him for a
piece of silver or a loaf of bread. He will say:
Please appoint me to some priestly office so
I can have a piece of bread to eat.' "

SAMUEL'S CALL

3 The boy Samuel served the LORD in Eli's
presence. In those days the word of the
LORD was rare and prophetic visions were
not widespread.
2 One day Eli, whose eyesight was failing,
was lying in his usual place. 3 Before the lamp
of God had gone out, Samuel was lying down
in the temple of the LORD, where the ark of
God was located.
4 Then the LORD called Samuel,[D] and he answered, "Here I am." 5 He ran to Eli and said,
"Here I am; you called me."
"I didn't call," Eli replied. "Go back and lie
down." So he went and lay down.
6 Once again the LORD called, "Samuel!"
Samuel got up, went to Eli, and said, "Here
I am; you called me."
"I didn't call, my son," he replied. "Go back
and lie down."
7 Now Samuel did not yet know the LORD,
because the word of the LORD had not yet been
revealed to him. 8 Once again, for the third
time, the LORD called Samuel. He got up, went
to Eli, and said, "Here I am; you called me."
Then Eli understood that the LORD was
calling the boy. 9 He told Samuel, "Go and lie
down. If he calls you, say, 'Speak, LORD, for
your servant is listening.' " So Samuel went
and lay down in his place.
10 The LORD came, stood there, and called
as before, "Samuel, Samuel!"
Samuel responded, "Speak, for your servant
is listening."

The LORD came, stood there, and called as before, "Samuel, Samuel!" Samuel responded, "Speak, for your servant is listening."

—1 Samuel 3:10

11 The LORD said to Samuel, "I am about to do
something in Israel that everyone who hears
about it will shudder.[E] 12 On that day I will carry out against Eli everything I said about his
family, from beginning to end. 13 I told him that
I am going to judge his family forever because
of the iniquity he knows about: his sons are
cursing God,[F] and he has not stopped them.
14 Therefore, I have sworn to Eli's family: The
iniquity of Eli's family will never be wiped
out by either sacrifice or offering."
15 Samuel lay down until the morning; then
he opened the doors of the LORD's house. He
was afraid to tell Eli the vision, 16 but Eli called
him and said, "Samuel, my son."
"Here I am," answered Samuel.
17 "What was the message he gave you?" Eli
asked. "Don't hide it from me. May God punish
you and do so severely if you hide anything
from me that he told you." 18 So Samuel told
him everything and did not hide anything
from him. Eli responded, "He is the LORD. Let
him do what he thinks is good."[G]

[A] **2:33** Lit *grief to your eyes* [B] **2:33** DSS, LXX read *die by the sword of men* [C] **2:33** Lit *die men* [D] **3:4** DSS, LXX read *called, "Samuel! Samuel!"* [E] **3:11** Lit *about it, his two ears will tingle*; Hb obscure [F] **3:13** LXX, Old Lat; MT reads *them* [G] **3:18** Lit *what is good in his eyes*

19 Samuel grew, and the LORD was with him, and he fulfilled everything Samuel prophesied.[A] 20 All Israel from Dan to Beer-sheba knew that Samuel was a confirmed prophet of the LORD. 21 The LORD continued to appear in Shiloh, because there he revealed himself to
4 Samuel by his word. 1 And Samuel's words came to all Israel.

THE ARK CAPTURED BY THE PHILISTINES

Israel went out to meet the Philistines in battle and[B] camped at Ebenezer while the Philistines camped at Aphek. 2 The Philistines lined up in battle formation against Israel, and as the battle intensified, Israel was defeated by the Philistines, who struck down about four thousand men on the battlefield.

3 When the troops returned to the camp, the elders of Israel asked, "Why did the LORD defeat us today before the Philistines? Let's bring the ark of the LORD's covenant from Shiloh. Then it[C] will go with us and save us from our enemies." 4 So the people sent men to Shiloh to bring back the ark of the covenant of the LORD of Armies, who is enthroned between the cherubim. Eli's two sons, Hophni and Phinehas, were there with the ark of the covenant of God. 5 When the ark of the covenant of the LORD entered the camp, all the Israelites raised such a loud shout that the ground shook.

6 The Philistines heard the sound of the war cry and asked, "What's this loud shout in the Hebrews' camp?" When the Philistines discovered that the ark of the LORD had entered the camp, 7 they panicked. "A god has entered their camp!" they said. "Woe to us, nothing like this has happened before.[D] 8 Woe to us, who will rescue us from these magnificent gods? These are the gods that slaughtered the Egyptians with all kinds of plagues in the wilderness. 9 Show some courage and be men, Philistines! Otherwise, you'll serve the Hebrews just as they served you. Now be men and fight!"

10 So the Philistines fought, and Israel was defeated, and each man fled to his tent. The slaughter was severe — thirty thousand of the Israelite foot soldiers fell. 11 The ark of God was captured, and Eli's two sons, Hophni and Phinehas, died.

ELI'S DEATH AND ICHABOD'S BIRTH

12 That same day, a Benjaminite man ran from the battle and came to Shiloh. His clothes were torn, and there was dirt on his head. 13 When he arrived, there was Eli sitting on his chair beside the road watching, because he was anxious about the ark of God. When the man entered the city to give a report, the entire city cried out.

14 Eli heard the outcry and asked, "Why this commotion?" The man quickly came and reported to Eli. 15 At that time Eli was ninety-eight years old, and his eyes didn't move[E] because he couldn't see.

16 The man said to Eli, "I'm the one who came from the battle.[F] I fled from there today."

"What happened, my son?" Eli asked.

17 The messenger answered, "Israel has fled from the Philistines, and also there was a great slaughter among the people. Your two sons, Hophni and Phinehas, are both dead, and the ark of God has been captured." 18 When he mentioned the ark of God, Eli fell backward off the chair by the city gate, and since he was old and heavy, his neck broke and he died. Eli had judged Israel forty years.

19 Eli's daughter-in-law, the wife of Phinehas, was pregnant and about to give birth. When she heard the news about the capture of God's ark and the deaths of her father-in-law and her husband, she collapsed and gave birth because her labor pains came on her. 20 As she was dying,[G] the women taking care of her said, "Don't be afraid. You've given birth to a son!" But she did not respond or pay attention. 21 She named the boy Ichabod,[H] saying, "The glory has departed from Israel," referring to the capture of the ark of God and to the deaths of her father-in-law and her husband. 22 "The glory has departed from Israel," she said, "because the ark of God has been captured."

THE ARK IN PHILISTINE HANDS

5 After the Philistines had captured the ark of God, they took it from Ebenezer to Ashdod, 2 brought it into the temple of Dagon[I] and placed it next to his statue.[J] 3 When the people of Ashdod got up early the next morning, there was Dagon, fallen with his face to the ground before the ark of the LORD. So they took Dagon and returned him to his place. 4 But when they got up early the next

---

[A] **3:19** Lit *he let none of his words fall to the ground* [B] **4:1** LXX reads *In those days the Philistines gathered together to fight against Israel, and Israel went out to engage them in battle. They* [C] **4:3** Or *he* [D] **4:7** Lit *yesterday or the day before* [E] **4:15** Lit *his eyes stood*; 1Kg 14:4 [F] **4:16** LXX reads *camp* [G] **4:20** LXX reads *And in her time of delivery, she was about to die* [H] **4:21** = Where Is Glory? [I] **5:2** A Philistine god of the sea, grain, or storm [J] **5:2** Lit *to Dagon*

morning, there was Dagon, fallen with his face to the ground before the ark of the LORD. This time, Dagon's head and both of his hands were broken off and lying on the threshold. Only Dagon's torso remained.[A] 5 That is why, still today, the priests of Dagon and everyone who enters the temple of Dagon in Ashdod do not step on Dagon's threshold.

6 The LORD's hand was heavy on the people of Ashdod. He terrified the people of Ashdod and its territory and afflicted them with tumors.[B,C] 7 When the people of Ashdod saw what was happening, they said, "The ark of Israel's God must not stay here with us, because his hand is strongly against us and our god Dagon." 8 So they called all the Philistine rulers together and asked, "What should we do with the ark of Israel's God?"

"The ark of Israel's God should be moved to Gath," they replied. So they moved the ark of Israel's God. 9 After they had moved it, the LORD's hand was against the city of Gath, causing a great panic. He afflicted the people of the city, from the youngest to the oldest, with an outbreak of tumors.

10 The people of Gath then sent the ark of God to Ekron, but when it got there, the Ekronites cried out, "They've moved the ark of Israel's God to us to kill us and our people!"[D]

11 The Ekronites called all the Philistine rulers together. They said, "Send the ark of Israel's God away. Let it return to its place so it won't kill us and our people!"[E] For the fear of death pervaded the city; God's hand was oppressing them. 12 Those who did not die were afflicted with tumors, and the outcry of the city went up to heaven.

THE RETURN OF THE ARK

6 When the ark of the LORD had been in Philistine territory for seven months, 2 the Philistines summoned the priests and the diviners and pleaded, "What should we do with the ark of the LORD? Tell us how we can send it back to its place."

3 They replied, "If you send the ark of Israel's God away, do not send it without an offering. Send back a guilt offering to him, and you will be healed. Then the reason his hand hasn't been removed from you will be revealed."[F]

4 They asked, "What guilt offering should we send back to him?"

And they answered, "Five gold tumors and five gold mice corresponding to the number of Philistine rulers, since there was one plague for both you[G] and your rulers. 5 Make images of your tumors and of your mice that are destroying the land. Give glory to Israel's God, and perhaps he will stop oppressing you,[H] your gods, and your land. 6 Why harden your hearts as the Egyptians and Pharaoh hardened theirs? When he afflicted them, didn't they send Israel away, and Israel left?

7 "Now then, prepare one new cart and two milk cows that have never been yoked. Hitch the cows to the cart, but take their calves away and pen them up. 8 Take the ark of the LORD, place it on the cart, and put the gold objects that you're sending him as a guilt offering in a box beside the ark. Send it off and let it go its way. 9 Then watch: If it goes up the road to its homeland toward Beth-shemesh, it is the LORD who has made this terrible trouble for us. However, if it doesn't, we will know that it was not his hand that punished us — it was just something that happened to us by chance."

10 The men did this: They took two milk cows, hitched them to the cart, and confined their calves in the pen. 11 Then they put the ark of the LORD on the cart, along with the box containing the gold mice and the images of their tumors. 12 The cows went straight up the road to Beth-shemesh. They stayed on that one highway, lowing as they went; they never strayed to the right or to the left. The Philistine rulers were walking behind them to the territory of Beth-shemesh.

13 The people of Beth-shemesh were harvesting wheat in the valley, and when they looked up and saw the ark, they were overjoyed to see it. 14 The cart came to the field of Joshua of Beth-shemesh and stopped there near a large rock. The people of the city chopped up the cart and offered the cows as a burnt offering to the LORD. 15 The Levites removed the ark of the LORD, along with the box containing the gold objects, and placed them on the large rock. That day the people of Beth-shemesh offered burnt offerings and made sacrifices to the LORD. 16 When the five Philistine rulers

[A] **5:4** LXX; Hb reads *Only Dagon remained on it* [B] **5:6** LXX adds *He brought up mice against them, and they swarmed in their ships. Then mice went up into the land and there was a mortal panic in the city.* [C] **5:6** Perhaps bubonic plague [D] **5:10** DSS, LXX read *"Why have you moved . . . people?"* [E] **5:11** DSS, LXX read *"Why don't you return it to . . . people?"* [F] **6:3** DSS, LXX read *healed, and an atonement shall be made for you. Shouldn't his hand be removed from you?"* [G] **6:4** Some Hb mss, LXX; other Hb mss read *them* [H] **6:5** Lit *will lighten the heaviness of his hand from you*

observed this, they returned to Ekron that same day.

17 As a guilt offering to the LORD, the Philistines had sent back one gold tumor for each city: Ashdod, Gaza, Ashkelon, Gath, and Ekron. 18 The number of gold mice also corresponded to the number of Philistine cities of the five rulers, the fortified cities and the outlying villages. The large rock[A] on which the ark of the LORD was placed is still in the field of Joshua of Beth-shemesh today.

19 God struck down the people of Beth-shemesh because they looked inside the ark of the LORD.[B] He struck down seventy persons.[C] The people mourned because the LORD struck them with a great slaughter. 20 The people of Beth-shemesh asked, "Who is able to stand in the presence of the LORD this holy God? To whom should the ark go from here?"

21 They sent messengers to the residents of Kiriath-jearim, saying, "The Philistines have returned the ark of the LORD. Come down and get it."[D]

7 So the people of Kiriath-jearim came for the ark of the LORD and took it to Abinadab's house on the hill. They consecrated his son Eleazar to take care of it.

VICTORY AT MIZPAH

2 Time went by until twenty years had passed since the ark had been taken to Kiriath-jearim. Then the whole house of Israel longed for the LORD. 3 Samuel told them, "If you are returning to the LORD with all your heart, get rid of the foreign gods and the Ashtoreths that are among you, dedicate yourselves to[E] the LORD, and worship only him. Then he will rescue you from the Philistines." 4 So the Israelites removed the Baals and the Ashtoreths and only worshiped the LORD.

5 Samuel said, "Gather all Israel at Mizpah, and I will pray to the LORD on your behalf." 6 When they gathered at Mizpah, they drew water and poured it out in the LORD's presence. They fasted that day, and there they confessed, "We have sinned against the LORD." And Samuel judged the Israelites at Mizpah.

7 When the Philistines heard that the Israelites had gathered at Mizpah, their rulers marched up toward Israel. When the Israelites heard about it, they were afraid because of the Philistines. 8 The Israelites said to Samuel, "Don't stop crying out to the LORD our God for us, so that he will save us from the Philistines."

9 Then Samuel took a young lamb and offered it as a whole burnt offering to the LORD. He cried out to the LORD on behalf of Israel, and the LORD answered him. 10 Samuel was offering the burnt offering as the Philistines approached to fight against Israel. The LORD thundered loudly against the Philistines that day and threw them into such confusion that they were defeated by Israel. 11 Then the men of Israel charged out of Mizpah and pursued the Philistines striking them down all the way to a place below Beth-car.

12 Afterward, Samuel took a stone and set it upright between Mizpah and Shen. He named it Ebenezer,[F] explaining, "The LORD has helped us to this point." 13 So the Philistines were subdued and[G] did not invade Israel's territory again. The LORD's hand was against the Philistines all of Samuel's life. 14 The cities from Ekron to Gath, which they had taken from Israel, were restored; Israel even rescued their surrounding territories from Philistine control. There was also peace between Israel and the Amorites.

15 Samuel judged Israel throughout his life. 16 Every year he would go on a circuit to Bethel, Gilgal, and Mizpah and would judge Israel at all these locations. 17 Then he would return to Ramah because his home was there, he judged Israel there, and he built an altar to the LORD there.

ISRAEL'S DEMAND FOR A KING

8 When Samuel grew old, he appointed his sons as judges over Israel. 2 His firstborn son's name was Joel and his second was Abijah. They were judges in Beer-sheba. 3 However, his sons did not walk in his ways — they turned toward dishonest profit, took bribes, and perverted justice.

4 So all the elders of Israel gathered together and went to Samuel at Ramah. 5 They said to him, "Look, you are old, and your sons do not walk in your ways. Therefore, appoint a king to judge us the same as all the other nations have."

6 When they said, "Give us a king to judge us," Samuel considered their demand wrong, so he prayed to the LORD. 7 But the LORD told him, "Listen to the people and everything they

---

[A] **6:18** Some Hb mss, DSS, LXX, Tg; other Hb mss read *meadow* [B] **6:19** LXX reads *But the sons of Jeconiah did not rejoice with the men of Beth-shemesh when they saw the ark of the LORD.* [C] **6:19** Some Hb mss, Josephus; other Hb mss read *70 men, 50,000 men* [D] **6:21** Lit *and bring it up to you* [E] **7:3** Lit *you and set your hearts on* [F] **7:12** = Stone of Help [G] **7:13** LXX reads *The LORD humbled the Philistines and they*

say to you. They have not rejected you; they
have rejected me as their king. 8 They are doing
the same thing to you that they have done to
me,[A] since the day I brought them out of Egypt
until this day, abandoning me and worshiping other gods. 9 Listen to them, but solemnly
warn them and tell them about the customary
rights of the king who will reign over them."
10 Samuel told all the LORD's words to the people who were asking him for a king. 11 He said,
"These are the rights of the king who will reign
over you: He will take your sons and put them
to his use in his chariots, on his horses, or running in front of his chariots. 12 He can appoint
them for his use as commanders of thousands
or commanders of fifties, to plow his ground
and reap his harvest, or to make his weapons
of war and the equipment for his chariots. 13 He
can take your daughters to become perfumers,
cooks, and bakers. 14 He can take your best fields,
vineyards, and olive orchards and give them to
his servants. 15 He can take a tenth of your grain
and your vineyards and give them to his officials
and servants. 16 He can take your male servants,
your female servants, your best young men,[B]
and your donkeys and use them for his work.
17 He can take a tenth of your flocks, and you
yourselves can become his servants. 18 When
that day comes, you will cry out because of
the king you've chosen for yourselves, but the
LORD won't answer you on that day."
19 The people refused to listen to Samuel.
"No!" they said. "We must have a king over
us. 20 Then we'll be like all the other nations:
our king will judge us, go out before us, and
fight our battles."
21 Samuel listened to all the people's words
and then repeated them to the LORD.[C] 22 "Listen to them," the LORD told Samuel. "Appoint
a king for them."
Then Samuel told the men of Israel, "Each
of you, go back to your city."

SAUL ANOINTED KING

9 There was a prominent man of Benjamin
named Kish son of Abiel, son of Zeror, son
of Becorath, son of Aphiah, son of a Benjaminite. 2 He had a son named Saul, an impressive
young man. There was no one more impressive
among the Israelites than he. He stood a head
taller than anyone else.[D]
3 One day the donkeys of Saul's father
Kish wandered off. Kish said to his son Saul,
"Take one of the servants with you and go
look for the donkeys." 4 Saul and his servant
went through the hill country of Ephraim
and then through the region of Shalishah,
but they didn't find them. They went through
the region of Shaalim — nothing. Then they
went through the Benjaminite region but still
didn't find them.
5 When they came to the land of Zuph, Saul
said to the servant who was with him, "Come
on, let's go back, or my father will stop worrying about the donkeys and start worrying
about us."
6 "Look," the servant said, "there's a man
of God in this city who is highly respected;
everything he says is sure to come true. Let's
go there now. Maybe he'll tell us which way
we should go."
7 "Suppose we do go," Saul said to his servant,
"what do we take the man? The food from our
packs is gone, and there's no gift to take to the
man of God. What do we have?"
8 The servant answered Saul: "Here, I have
a little[E] silver. I'll give it to the man of God,
and he will tell us which way we should go."
9 Formerly in Israel, a man who was going
to inquire of God would say, "Come, let's go
to the seer," for the prophet of today was formerly called the seer.
10 "Good," Saul replied to his servant. "Come
on, let's go." So they went to the city where the
man of God was. 11 As they were climbing the
hill to the city, they found some young wom-
en coming out to draw water and asked, "Is
the seer here?"
12 The women answered, "Yes, he is ahead
of you. Hurry, he just now entered the city,
because there's a sacrifice for the people at
the high place today. 13 As soon as you enter
the city, you will find him before he goes to the
high place to eat. The people won't eat until
he comes because he must bless the sacrifice;
after that, the guests can eat. Go up immediately — you can find him now." 14 So they went
up toward the city.
Saul and his servant were entering the city
when they saw Samuel coming toward them
on his way to the high place. 15 Now the day
before Saul's arrival, the LORD had informed
Samuel,[F] 16 "At this time tomorrow I will send
you a man from the land of Benjamin. Anoint

[A] 8:8 LXX; MT omits *to me* [B] 8:16 LXX reads *best cattle* [C] 8:21 Lit *them in the LORD's ears* [D] 9:2 Lit *From his shoulder and up higher than any of the people* [E] 9:8 Lit *a quarter of a shekel* (about a tenth of an ounce) [F] 9:15 Lit *had uncovered Samuel's ear, saying*

him ruler over my people Israel. He will save
them from the Philistines because I have seen
the affliction of my people, for their cry has
come to me." 17 When Samuel saw Saul, the
LORD told him, "Here is the man I told you
about; he will govern my people."

18 Saul approached Samuel in the city gate
and asked, "Would you please tell me where
the seer's house is?"

19 "I am the seer," Samuel answered.[A] "Go up
ahead of me to the high place and eat with me
today. When I send you off in the morning, I'll
tell you everything that's in your heart. 20 As
for the donkeys that wandered away from
you three days ago, don't worry about them
because they've been found. And who does
all Israel desire but you and all your father's
family?"

21 Saul responded, "Am I not a Benjaminite
from the smallest of Israel's tribes and isn't
my clan the least important of all the clans of
the Benjaminite tribe? So why have you said
something like this to me?"

22 Samuel took Saul and his servant, brought
them to the banquet hall, and gave them a
place at the head of the thirty[B] or so men who
had been invited. 23 Then Samuel said to the
cook, "Get the portion of meat that I gave you
and told you to set aside."

24 The cook picked up the thigh and what
was attached to it and set it before Saul. Then
Samuel said, "Notice that the reserved piece is
set before you. Eat it because it was saved for
you for this solemn event at the time I said, 'I've
invited the people.'" So Saul ate with Samuel
that day. 25 Afterward, they went down from
the high place to the city, and Samuel spoke
with Saul on the roof.[C]

26 They got up early, and just before dawn,
Samuel called to Saul on the roof, "Get up, and
I'll send you on your way!" Saul got up, and
both he and Samuel went outside. 27 As they
were going down to the edge of the city, Samuel
said to Saul, "Tell the servant to go on ahead of
us, but you stay for a while, and I'll reveal the
word of God to you." So the servant went on.

10 Samuel took the flask of oil, poured it
out on Saul's head, kissed him, and said,
"Hasn't the LORD anointed you ruler over his
inheritance?[D] 2 Today when you leave me, you'll
find two men at Rachel's Grave at Zelzah in
the territory of Benjamin. They will say to
you, 'The donkeys you went looking for have
been found, and now your father has stopped
being concerned about the donkeys and is
worried about you, asking: What should I do
about my son?'

3 "You will proceed from there until you come
to the oak of Tabor. Three men going up to God
at Bethel will meet you there, one bringing
three goats, one bringing three loaves of bread,
and one bringing a clay jar of wine. 4 They will
ask how you are and give you two loaves[E] of
bread, which you will accept from them.

5 "After that you will come to Gibeah of God
where there are Philistine garrisons.[F] When
you arrive at the city, you will meet a group of
prophets coming down from the high place
prophesying. They will be preceded by harps,
tambourines, flutes, and lyres. 6 The Spirit of
the LORD will come powerfully on you, you will
prophesy with them, and you will be transformed. 7 When these signs have happened
to you, do whatever your circumstances require[G] because God is with you. 8 Afterward,
go ahead of me to Gilgal. I will come to you to
offer burnt offerings and to sacrifice fellowship offerings. Wait seven days until I come
to you and show you what to do."

9 When Saul turned around[H] to leave Samuel,
God changed his heart,[I] and all the signs came
about that day. 10 When Saul and his servant
arrived at Gibeah, a group of prophets met
him. Then the Spirit of God came powerfully
on him, and he prophesied along with them.

11 Everyone who knew him previously and
saw him prophesy with the prophets asked
each other, "What has happened to the son
of Kish? Is Saul also among the prophets?"

12 Then a man who was from there asked,
"And who is their father?"

As a result, "Is Saul also among the prophets?" became a popular saying. 13 Then Saul
finished prophesying and went to the high
place.

14 Saul's uncle asked him and his servant,
"Where did you go?"

"To look for the donkeys," Saul answered.
"When we saw they weren't there, we went
to Samuel."

[A] **9:19** Lit *answered Saul* [B] **9:22** LXX reads *70* [C] **9:25** LXX reads *city. They prepared a bed for Saul on the roof, and he slept.*
[D] **10:1** LXX adds *And you will reign over the LORD's people, and you will save them from the hand of their enemies all around. And this is the sign to you that the LORD has anointed you ruler over his inheritance.* [E] **10:4** DSS, LXX read *wave offerings*
[F] **10:5** Or *governors* [G] **10:7** Lit *do for yourself whatever your hand finds* [H] **10:9** Lit *turned his shoulder* [I] **10:9** Lit *God turned to him another heart*

15 "Tell me," Saul's uncle asked, "what did
Samuel say to you?"
16 Saul told him, "He assured us the donkeys
had been found." However, Saul did not tell
him what Samuel had said about the matter
of kingship.

SAUL RECEIVED AS KING

17 Samuel summoned the people to the LORD
at Mizpah 18 and said to the Israelites, "This
is what the LORD, the God of Israel, says: 'I
brought Israel out of Egypt, and I rescued you
from the power of the Egyptians and all the
kingdoms that were oppressing you.' 19 But
today you have rejected your God, who saves
you from all your troubles and afflictions. You
said to him, 'You[A] must set a king over us.' Now
therefore present yourselves before the LORD
by your tribes and clans."
20 Samuel had all the tribes of Israel come
forward, and the tribe of Benjamin was selected. 21 Then he had the tribe of Benjamin
come forward by its clans, and the Matrite
clan was selected.[B] Finally, Saul son of Kish
was selected. But when they searched for
him, they could not find him. 22 They again
inquired of the LORD, "Has the man come
here yet?"

The LORD replied, "There he is, hidden among
the supplies."
23 They ran and got him from there. When
he stood among the people, he stood a head
taller than anyone else.[C] 24 Samuel said to all
the people, "Do you see the one the LORD has
chosen? There is no one like him among the
entire population."

And all the people shouted,[D] "Long live the
king!"
25 Samuel proclaimed to the people the rights
of kingship. He wrote them on a scroll, which
he placed in the presence of the LORD. Then
Samuel sent all the people home.
26 Saul also went to his home in Gibeah, and
brave men whose hearts God had touched
went with him. 27 But some wicked men said,
"How can this guy save us?" They despised
him and did not bring him a gift, but Saul said
nothing.[E,F]

SAUL'S DELIVERANCE OF JABESH-GILEAD

11 Nahash[G] the Ammonite came up and laid
siege to Jabesh-gilead. All the men of Jabesh said to him, "Make a treaty with us, and
we will serve you."
2 Nahash the Ammonite replied, "I'll make
one with you on this condition: that I gouge out
everyone's right eye and humiliate all Israel."
3 "Don't do anything to us for seven days,"
the elders of Jabesh said to him, "and let us
send messengers throughout the territory
of Israel. If no one saves us, we will surrender to you."
4 When the messengers came to Gibeah,
Saul's hometown, and told the terms to[H] the
people, all wept aloud. 5 Just then Saul was
coming in from the field behind his oxen.
"What's the matter with the people? Why
are they weeping?" Saul inquired, and they
repeated to him the words of the men from
Jabesh.
6 When Saul heard these words, the Spirit
of God suddenly came powerfully on him,
and his anger burned furiously. 7 He took a
team of oxen, cut them in pieces, and sent
them throughout the territory of Israel by
messengers who said, "This is what will be
done to the ox of anyone who doesn't march
behind Saul and Samuel." As a result, the terror of the LORD fell on the people, and they
went out united.
8 Saul counted them at Bezek. There were
three hundred thousand[I] Israelites and thirty thousand[J] men from Judah. 9 He told the
messengers who had come, "Tell this to the
men of Jabesh-gilead: 'Deliverance will be
yours tomorrow by the time the sun is hot.'"
So the messengers told the men of Jabesh,
and they rejoiced.
10 Then the men of Jabesh said to Nahash,
"Tomorrow we will come out, and you can do
whatever you want[K] to us."
11 The next day Saul organized the troops into
three divisions. During the morning watch,
they invaded the Ammonite camp and slaughtered them until the heat of the day. There were
survivors, but they were so scattered that no
two of them were left together.

[A] **10:19** Some Hb mss, LXX, Syr, Vg read *You said, 'No, you* [B] **10:21** LXX adds *And he had the Matrite clan come forward, man by man.* [C] **10:23** Lit *people, and he was higher than any of the people from his shoulder and up* [D] **10:24** LXX reads *acknowledged and said* [E] **10:27** DSS add *Nahash king of the Ammonites had been severely oppressing the Gadites and Reubenites. He gouged out the right eye of each of them and brought fear and trembling on Israel. Of the Israelites beyond the Jordan none remained whose right eye Nahash, king of the Ammonites, had not gouged out. But there were seven thousand men who had escaped from the Ammonites and entered Jabesh-gilead.* [F] **10:27** Lit *gift, and he was like a mute person* [G] **11:1** DSS, LXX read *About a month later, Nahash* [H] **11:4** Lit *in the ears of* [I] **11:8** LXX reads *600,000* [J] **11:8** DSS, LXX read *70,000* [K] **11:10** Lit *do what is good in your eyes*

SAUL'S CONFIRMATION AS KING

12 Afterward, the people said to Samuel, "Who
said that Saul should not[A] reign over us? Give
us those men so we can kill them!"
13 But Saul ordered, "No one will be executed this day, for today the LORD has provided
deliverance in Israel."
14 Then Samuel said to the people, "Come,
let's go to Gilgal, so we can renew the kingship
there." 15 So all the people went to Gilgal, and
there in the LORD's presence they made Saul
king. There they sacrificed fellowship offerings in the LORD's presence, and Saul and all
the men of Israel rejoiced greatly.

SAMUEL'S FINAL PUBLIC SPEECH

12 Then Samuel said to all Israel, "I have
carefully listened to everything you said
to me and placed a king over you. 2 Now you
can see that the king is leading you. As for me,
I'm old and gray, and my sons are here with
you. I have led you from my youth until now.
3 Here I am. Bring charges against me before
the LORD and his anointed: Whose ox or donkey have I taken? Whom have I wronged or
mistreated? From whom have I accepted a
bribe to overlook something?[B,C] I will return
it to you."
4 "You haven't wronged us, you haven't mistreated us, and you haven't taken anything
from anyone," they responded.
5 He said to them, "The LORD is a witness
against you, and his anointed is a witness today
that you haven't found anything in my hand."
"He is a witness," they said.
6 Then Samuel said to the people, "The LORD,
who appointed Moses and Aaron and who
brought your ancestors up from the land of
Egypt, is a witness.[D] 7 Now present yourselves,
so I may confront you before the LORD about
all the righteous acts he has done for you and
your ancestors.
8 "When Jacob went to Egypt,[E] your ancestors cried out to the LORD, and he sent them
Moses and Aaron, who led your ancestors out
of Egypt and settled them in this place. 9 But
they forgot the LORD their God, so he handed
them over to Sisera commander of the army
of Hazor, to the Philistines, and to the king of
Moab. These enemies fought against them.
10 Then they cried out to the LORD and said, 'We
have sinned, for we abandoned the LORD and
worshiped the Baals and the Ashtoreths. Now
rescue us from the power of our enemies, and
we will serve you.' 11 So the LORD sent Jerubbaal, Barak,[F] Jephthah, and Samuel. He rescued

Other-centeredness | *Praying for Others*

DAILY PRACTICE

"As for me, I vow that I will not sin against the LORD by ceasing to pray for you. I will teach you the good and right way." 1 Samuel 12:23

Christians may tell their hurting friends and loved ones, "I pray for you all the time—I only wish I could do *more* than pray!"

The Old Testament prophet Samuel would likely cringe at such a statement. Not that he would dismiss the importance of emotional support, financial help, or physical assistance—but the suggestion that we can do something more vital than prayer? Unthinkable. "Prayer," as one old saint has reminded us, "is not preparation for battle, it is the battle."

When Israel clamored for a human king (and then realized that was a terrible mistake), they asked the aged Samuel to pray for them. He vowed to lift them up to the Lord continually.

Is part of your daily plan to pray for others? If not, you can start right now. Begin with your immediate family and then move on to friends and neighbors. Prayer makes a difference—for us and those for whom we pray.

For the next note on *Other-centeredness*, see 1 Samuel 25:24.

[A] **11:12** Some Hb mss, LXX; other Hb mss omit *not* [B] **12:3** LXX reads *bribe or a pair of shoes? Testify against me*. [C] **12:3** Lit *bribe and will hide my eyes with it?* [D] **12:6** LXX; MT omits *is a witness* [E] **12:8** LXX reads *"When Jacob and his sons went to Egypt and Egypt humbled them* [F] **12:11** LXX, Syr; MT reads *Bedan*; Jdg 4:6; Heb 11:32

you from the power of the enemies around you, and you lived securely. 12 But when you saw that Nahash king of the Ammonites was coming against you, you said to me, 'No, we must have a king reign over us' — even though the LORD your God is your king.

13 "Now here is the king you've chosen, the one you requested. Look, this is the king the LORD has placed over you. 14 If you fear the LORD, worship and obey him, and if you don't rebel against the LORD's command, then both you and the king who reigns over you will follow the LORD your God. 15 However, if you disobey the LORD and rebel against his command, the LORD's hand will be against you as it was against your ancestors.[A]

16 "Now, therefore, present yourselves and see this great thing that the LORD will do before your eyes. 17 Isn't the wheat harvest today? I will call on the LORD, and he will send thunder and rain so that you will recognize[B] what an immense evil you committed in the LORD's sight by requesting a king for yourselves." 18 Samuel called on the LORD, and on that day the LORD sent thunder and rain. As a result, all the people greatly feared the LORD and Samuel.

19 They pleaded with Samuel, "Pray to the LORD your God for your servants so we won't die! For we have added to all our sins the evil of requesting a king for ourselves."

20 Samuel replied, "Don't be afraid. Even though you have committed all this evil, don't turn away from following the LORD. Instead, worship the LORD with all your heart. 21 Don't turn away to follow worthless[C] things that can't profit or rescue you; they are worthless. 22 The LORD will not abandon his people, because of his great name and because he has determined to make you his own people.

23 "As for me, I vow that I will not sin against the LORD by ceasing to pray for you. I will teach you the good and right way. 24 Above all, fear the LORD and worship him faithfully with all your heart; consider the great things he has done for you. 25 However, if you continue to do what is evil, both you and your king will be swept away."

SAUL'S FAILURE

13 Saul was thirty years[D] old when he became king, and he reigned forty-two years[E] over Israel.[F] 2 He chose three thousand men from Israel for himself: two thousand were with Saul at Michmash and in Bethel's hill country, and one thousand were with Jonathan in Gibeah of Benjamin. He sent the rest of the troops away, each to his own tent.

3 Jonathan attacked the Philistine garrison[G] that was in Geba, and the Philistines heard about it. So Saul blew the ram's horn throughout the land saying, "Let the Hebrews hear!"[H] 4 And all Israel heard the news, "Saul has attacked the Philistine garrison, and Israel is now repulsive to the Philistines." Then the troops were summoned to join Saul at Gilgal.

5 The Philistines also gathered to fight against Israel: three thousand[I] chariots, six thousand horsemen, and troops as numerous as the sand on the seashore. They went up and camped at Michmash, east of Beth-aven.[J] 6 The men of Israel saw that they were in trouble because the troops were in a difficult situation. They hid in caves, in thickets, among rocks, and in holes and cisterns. 7 Some Hebrews even crossed the Jordan to the land of Gad and Gilead.

Saul, however, was still at Gilgal, and all his troops were gripped with fear. 8 He waited seven days for the appointed time that Samuel had set, but Samuel didn't come to Gilgal, and the troops were deserting him. 9 So Saul said, "Bring me the burnt offering and the fellowship offerings." Then he offered the burnt offering.

10 Just as he finished offering the burnt offering, Samuel arrived. So Saul went out to greet him, 11 and Samuel asked, "What have you done?"

Saul answered, "When I saw that the troops were deserting me and you didn't come within the appointed days and the Philistines were gathering at Michmash, 12 I thought, 'The Philistines will now descend on me at Gilgal, and I haven't sought the LORD's favor.' So I forced myself to offer the burnt offering."

13 Samuel said to Saul, "You have been foolish. You have not kept the command the LORD your God gave you. It was at this time that the LORD would have permanently established your reign over Israel, 14 but now your reign will not endure. The LORD has found a man after his own heart,[K] and the LORD has appointed him as ruler over his people, because you have

[A] 12:15 LXX *against you and against your king* [B] 12:17 Lit *know and see* [C] 12:21 LXX reads *away after empty* [D] 13:1 Some LXX mss; MT reads *was one year* [E] 13:1 Text emended; MT reads *two years* [F] 13:1 Some LXX mss omit v. 1 [G] 13:3 Or *governor*, also in v. 4 [H] 13:3 LXX reads *"The slaves have revolted"* [I] 13:5 One LXX ms, Syr; MT reads *30,000* [J] 13:5 LXX reads *Michmash, opposite Beth-horon to the south* [K] 13:14 Lit *man according to his heart*

not done what the LORD commanded." 15 Then
Samuel went[A] from Gilgal to Gibeah in Benjamin. Saul registered the troops who were
with him, about six hundred men.
16 Saul, his son Jonathan, and the troops who
were with them were staying in Geba of Benjamin, and the Philistines were camped at
Michmash. 17 Raiding parties went out from
the Philistine camp in three divisions. One
division headed toward the Ophrah road leading to the land of Shual. 18 The next division
headed toward the Beth-horon road, and the
last division headed down the border road
that looks out over the Zeboim Valley toward
the wilderness.
19 No blacksmith could be found in all the
land of Israel because the Philistines had said,
"Otherwise, the Hebrews will make swords
or spears." 20 So all the Israelites went to the
Philistines to sharpen their plows, mattocks,
axes, and sickles.[B] 21 The price was two-thirds
of a shekel[C] for plows and mattocks, and one-
third of a shekel for pitchforks and axes, and
for putting a point on a cattle prod. 22 So on
the day of battle not a sword or spear could
be found in the hand of any of the troops who
were with Saul and Jonathan; only Saul and
his son Jonathan had weapons.

JONATHAN'S VICTORY OVER THE PHILISTINES

23 Now a Philistine garrison took control of the
14 pass at Michmash. 1 That same day Saul's
son Jonathan said to the attendant who
carried his weapons, "Come on, let's cross over
to the Philistine garrison on the other side."
However, he did not tell his father.
2 Saul was staying under the pomegranate
tree in Migron on the outskirts of Gibeah.[D] The
troops with him numbered about six hundred.
3 Ahijah, who was wearing an ephod, was also
there. He was the son of Ahitub, the brother of
Ichabod son of Phinehas, son of Eli the LORD's
priest at Shiloh. But the troops did not know
that Jonathan had left.
4 There were sharp columns[E] of rock on
both sides of the pass that Jonathan intended
to cross to reach the Philistine garrison. One
was named Bozez and the other Seneh; 5 one
stood to the north in front of Michmash and the
other to the south in front of Geba. 6 Jonathan
said to the attendant who carried his weapons,
"Come on, let's cross over to the garrison of

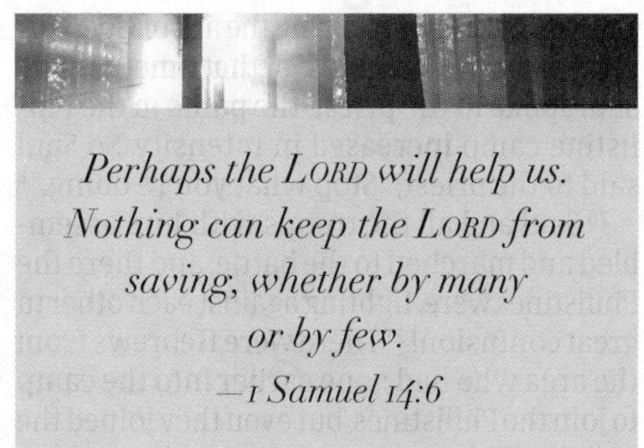
Perhaps the LORD will help us.
Nothing can keep the LORD from
saving, whether by many
or by few.
—1 Samuel 14:6

these uncircumcised men. Perhaps the LORD
will help us. Nothing can keep the LORD from
saving, whether by many or by few."
7 His armor-bearer responded, "Do what is
in your heart. You choose. I'm right here with
you whatever you decide."
8 "All right," Jonathan replied, "we'll cross
over to the men and then let them see us. 9 If
they say, 'Wait until we reach you,' then we
will stay where we are and not go up to them.
10 But if they say, 'Come on up,' then we'll go
up, because the LORD has handed them over
to us — that will be our sign."
11 They let themselves be seen by the Philistine garrison, and the Philistines said, "Look,
the Hebrews are coming out of the holes where
they've been hiding!" 12 The men of the garrison called to Jonathan and his armor-bearer.
"Come on up, and we'll teach you a lesson!"
they said.
"Follow me," Jonathan told his armor-bearer,
"for the LORD has handed them over to Israel."
13 Jonathan climbed up using his hands and
feet, with his armor-bearer behind him. Jonathan cut them down, and his armor-bearer
followed and finished them off. 14 In that first
assault Jonathan and his armor-bearer struck
down about twenty men in a half-acre field.

A DEFEAT FOR THE PHILISTINES

15 Terror spread through the Philistine camp
and the open fields to all the troops. Even the
garrison and the raiding parties were terrified.
The earth shook, and terror spread from God.[F]
16 When Saul's watchmen in Gibeah of Benjamin
looked, they saw the panicking troops scattering in every direction. 17 So Saul said to the
troops with him, "Call the roll and determine
who has left us." They called the roll and saw
that Jonathan and his armor-bearer were gone.

[A] **13:15** LXX reads *Samuel left Gilgal and went on his way, and the rest of the people followed Saul to join the people in his army. They went* [B] **13:20** LXX; MT reads *plowshares* [C] **13:21** Lit *of a pim*; about one-fourth ounce of silver [D] **14:2** LXX reads *on top of the hill* [E] **14:4** Lit *There was a tooth* [F] **14:15** Or *and a great terror spread*

18 Saul told Ahijah, "Bring the ark of God," for it was with the Israelites[A] at that time. 19 While Saul spoke to the priest, the panic in the Philistine camp increased in intensity. So Saul said to the priest, "Stop what you're doing."[B]

20 Saul and all the troops with him assembled and marched to the battle, and there the Philistines were, fighting against each other in great confusion! 21 There were Hebrews from the area who had gone earlier into the camp to join the Philistines, but even they joined the Israelites who were with Saul and Jonathan. 22 When all the Israelite men who had been hiding in the hill country of Ephraim heard that the Philistines were fleeing, they also joined Saul and Jonathan in the battle. 23 So the LORD saved Israel that day.

SAUL'S RASH OATH

The battle extended beyond Beth-aven, 24 and the men of Israel were worn out that day, for Saul had[C] placed the troops under an oath: "The man who eats food before evening, before I have taken vengeance on my enemies is cursed." So none of the troops tasted any food.

25 Everyone[D] went into the forest, and there was honey on the ground. 26 When the troops entered the forest, they saw the flow of honey, but none of them ate any of it[E] because they feared the oath. 27 However, Jonathan had not heard his father make the troops swear the oath. He reached out with the end of the staff he was carrying and dipped it into the honeycomb. When he ate the honey,[F] he had renewed energy.[G] 28 Then one of the troops said, "Your father made the troops solemnly swear, 'The man who eats food today is cursed,' and the troops are exhausted."

29 Jonathan replied, "My father has brought trouble to the land. Just look at how I have renewed energy[H] because I tasted a little of this honey. 30 How much better if the troops had eaten freely today from the plunder they took from their enemies! Then the slaughter of the Philistines would have been much greater."

31 The Israelites struck down the Philistines that day from Michmash all the way to Aijalon. Since the Israelites were completely exhausted, 32 they rushed to the plunder, took sheep, goats, cattle, and calves, slaughtered them on the ground, and ate meat with the blood still in it. 33 Some reported to Saul: "Look, the troops are sinning against the LORD by eating meat with the blood still in it."

Saul said, "You have been unfaithful. Roll a large stone over here at once." 34 He then said, "Go among the troops and say to them, 'Let each man bring me his ox or his sheep. Do the slaughtering here and then you can eat. Don't sin against the LORD by eating meat with the blood in it.' " So every one of the troops brought his ox that night and slaughtered it there. 35 Then Saul built an altar to the LORD; it was the first time he had built an altar to the LORD.

36 Saul said, "Let's go down after the Philistines tonight and plunder them until morning. Don't let even one remain!"

"Do whatever you want,"[I] the troops replied.

But the priest said, "Let's approach God here."

37 So Saul inquired of God, "Should I go after the Philistines? Will you hand them over to Israel?" But God did not answer him that day.

38 Saul said, "All you leaders of the troops, come here. Let us investigate[J] how this sin has occurred today. 39 As surely as the LORD lives who saves Israel, even if it is because of my son Jonathan, he must die!" Not one of the troops answered him.

40 So he said to all Israel, "You will be on one side, and I and my son Jonathan will be on the other side."

And the troops replied, "Do whatever you want."

41 So Saul said to the LORD, "God of Israel, why have you not answered your servant today? If the unrighteousness is in me or in my son Jonathan, LORD God of Israel, give Urim; but if the fault is in your people Israel, give Thummim."[K] Jonathan and Saul were selected, and the troops were cleared of the charge.

42 Then Saul said, "Cast the lot between me and my son Jonathan," and Jonathan was selected. 43 Saul commanded him, "Tell me what you did."

Jonathan told him, "I tasted a little honey with the end of the staff I was carrying. I am ready to die!"

44 Saul declared to him, "May God punish me and do so severely if you do not die, Jonathan!"

[A] **14:18** LXX reads *"Bring the ephod." For he wore the ephod before Israel* [B] **14:19** Lit *"Withdraw your hand"* [C] **14:24** LXX adds *committed a great act of ignorance and* [D] **14:25** Lit *All the land* [E] **14:26** Lit *but there was none who raised his hand to his mouth* [F] **14:27** Lit *he returned his hand to his mouth* [G] **14:27** Lit *his eyes became bright* [H] **14:29** Lit *how my eyes became bright* [I] **14:36** Lit *Do what is good in your eyes,* also in v. 40 [J] **14:38** Lit *know and see* [K] **14:41** LXX; MT reads *said to the LORD, "God of Israel, give us the right decision."*

45 But the people said to Saul, "Must Jonathan die, who accomplished such a great
deliverance for Israel? No, as the LORD lives,
not a hair of his head will fall to the ground,
for he worked with God's help today." So the
people redeemed Jonathan, and he did not
die. 46 Then Saul gave up the pursuit of the
Philistines, and the Philistines returned to
their own territory.

SUMMARY OF SAUL'S KINGSHIP

47 When Saul assumed the kingship over Israel, he fought against all his enemies in every direction: against Moab, the Ammonites,
Edom, the kings of Zobah, and the Philistines.
Wherever he turned, he caused havoc.[A] 48 He
fought bravely, defeated the Amalekites, and
rescued Israel from those who plundered them.
49 Saul's sons were Jonathan, Ishvi, and
Malchishua. The names of his two daughters were Merab, his firstborn, and Michal,
the younger. 50 The name of Saul's wife was
Ahinoam daughter of Ahimaaz. The name of
the commander of his army was Abner son
of Saul's uncle Ner. 51 Saul's father was Kish.
Abner's father was Ner son of Abiel.
52 The conflict with the Philistines was fierce
all of Saul's days, so whenever Saul noticed
any strong or valiant man, he enlisted him.

SAUL REJECTED AS KING

15 Samuel told Saul, "The LORD sent me to
anoint you as king over his people Israel.
Now, listen to the words of the LORD. 2 This is
what the LORD of Armies says: 'I witnessed[B]
what the Amalekites did to the Israelites when
they opposed them along the way as they were
coming out of Egypt. 3 Now go and attack the
Amalekites and completely destroy everything they have. Do not spare them. Kill men
and women, infants and nursing babies, oxen
and sheep, camels and donkeys.'"
4 Then Saul summoned the troops and counted them at Telaim: two hundred thousand foot
soldiers and ten thousand men from Judah.
5 Saul came to the city of Amalek and set up
an ambush in the wadi. 6 He warned the Kenites, "Since you showed kindness to all the
Israelites when they came out of Egypt, go on
and leave! Get away from the Amalekites, or
I'll sweep you away with them." So the Kenites
withdrew from the Amalekites.
7 Then Saul struck down the Amalekites from
Havilah all the way to Shur, which is next to
Egypt. 8 He captured King Agag of Amalek alive,
but he completely destroyed all the rest of the
people with the sword. 9 Saul and the troops
spared Agag, and the best of the sheep, goats,
cattle, and choice animals,[C] as well as the young
rams and the best of everything else. They were
not willing to destroy them, but they did destroy all the worthless and unwanted things.
10 Then the word of the LORD came to Samuel, 11 "I regret that I made Saul king, for he has
turned away from following me and has not
carried out my instructions." So Samuel became angry and cried out to the LORD all night.
12 Early in the morning Samuel got up to
confront Saul, but it was reported to Samuel,
"Saul went to Carmel where he set up a monument for himself. Then he turned around and
went down to Gilgal." 13 When Samuel came
to him, Saul said, "May the LORD bless you.
I have carried out the LORD's instructions."
14 Samuel replied, "Then what is this sound
of sheep, goats,[D] and cattle I hear?"
15 Saul answered, "The troops brought
them from the Amalekites and spared the
best sheep, goats, and cattle in order to offer
a sacrifice to the LORD your God, but the rest
we destroyed."
16 "Stop!" exclaimed Samuel. "Let me tell you
what the LORD said to me last night."
"Tell me," he replied.
17 Samuel continued, "Although you once
considered yourself unimportant, have you
not become the leader of the tribes of Israel?
The LORD anointed you king over Israel 18 and
then sent you on a mission and said: 'Go and
completely destroy the sinful Amalekites. Fight
against them until you have annihilated them.'
19 So why didn't you obey the LORD? Why did
you rush on the plunder and do what was evil
in the LORD's sight?"
20 "But I did obey the LORD!" Saul answered.[E]
"I went on the mission the LORD gave me: I
brought back King Agag of Amalek, and I
completely destroyed the Amalekites. 21 The
troops took sheep, goats, and cattle from the
plunder — the best of what was set apart for
destruction — to sacrifice to the LORD your
God at Gilgal."
22 Then Samuel said:

Does the LORD take pleasure
in burnt offerings and sacrifices
as much as in obeying the LORD?

[A] **14:47** LXX reads *he was victorious* [B] **15:2** LXX reads *I will avenge* [C] **15:9** Lit *and the second ones* [D] **15:14** Lit *sheep in my ears* [E] **15:20** Lit *answered Samuel*

Look: to obey is better than sacrifice,
to pay attention is better than the fat
of rams.
23 For rebellion is like the sin
of divination,
and defiance is like wickedness
and idolatry.
Because you have rejected the word
of the LORD,
he has rejected you as king.

24 Saul answered Samuel, "I have sinned. I
have transgressed the LORD's command and
your words. Because I was afraid of the people, I obeyed them. 25 Now therefore, please
forgive my sin and return with me so I can
worship the LORD."
26 Samuel replied to Saul, "I will not return
with you. Because you rejected the word of the
LORD, the LORD has rejected you from being
king over Israel." 27 When Samuel turned to go,
Saul grabbed the corner of his robe, and it tore.
28 Samuel said to him, "The LORD has torn the
kingship of Israel away from you today and
has given it to your neighbor who is better
than you. 29 Furthermore, the Eternal One of
Israel does not lie or change his mind, for he
is not man who changes his mind."
30 Saul said, "I have sinned. Please honor
me now before the elders of my people and
before Israel. Come back with me so I can
bow in worship to the LORD your God." 31 Then
Samuel went back, following Saul, and Saul
bowed down to the LORD.
32 Samuel said, "Bring me King Agag of Amalek."
Agag came to him trembling,[A] for he thought,
"Certainly the bitterness of death has come."[B,C]
33 Samuel declared:

As your sword has made women
childless,
so your mother will be childless
among women.

Then he hacked Agag to pieces before the
LORD at Gilgal.
34 Samuel went to Ramah, and Saul went
up to his home in Gibeah of Saul. 35 Even to
the day of his death, Samuel never saw Saul
again. Samuel mourned for Saul, and the LORD
regretted he had made Saul king over Israel.

SAMUEL ANOINTS DAVID

16 The LORD said to Samuel, "How long
are you going to mourn for Saul, since
I have rejected him as king over Israel? Fill
your horn with oil and go. I am sending you
to Jesse of Bethlehem because I have selected
a king from his sons."
2 Samuel asked, "How can I go? Saul will
hear about it and kill me!"

Eternal Perspective | *God's Inside View*

THE HEART OF THE MATTER

"But the LORD said to Samuel, 'Do not look at his appearance or his stature because I have rejected him. Humans do not see what the LORD sees, for humans see what is visible, but the LORD sees the heart.'" 1 Samuel 16:7

The reign of Saul was a disaster almost from the start. His shocking disobedience prompted God to instruct the prophet Samuel to go to Bethlehem and select a replacement king from among the sons of Jesse.

As soon as he saw Eliab, Jesse's strapping, good-looking oldest, the prophet started reaching for his anointing oil. That's when God had to remind Samuel that internal character is far more important than external appearance or credentials. God's royal choice was David, Jesse's less-impressive and youngest son. David's flaws eventually became known, but he had this going for him: He was a person with a heart for God's heart (13:14).

Our appearance-obsessed culture desperately needs this teaching. Rather than striving to improve your looks, take steps to strengthen your heart.

For the next note on *Eternal Perspective*, see 2 Samuel 7:22.

[A] **15:32** Hb obscure [B] **15:32** LXX reads *"Is death bitter in this way?"* [C] **15:32** Lit *turned*

The LORD answered, "Take a young cow with you and say, 'I have come to sacrifice to the LORD.' 3 Then invite Jesse to the sacrifice, and I will let you know what you are to do. You are to anoint for me the one I indicate to you."

4 Samuel did what the LORD directed and went to Bethlehem. When the elders of the town met him, they trembled[A] and asked, "Do[B] you come in peace?"

5 "In peace," he replied. "I've come to sacrifice to the LORD. Consecrate yourselves and come with me to the sacrifice."[C] Then he consecrated Jesse and his sons and invited them to the sacrifice. 6 When they arrived, Samuel saw Eliab and said, "Certainly the LORD's anointed one is here before him."

7 But the LORD said to Samuel, "Do not look at his appearance or his stature because I have rejected him. Humans do not see what the LORD sees,[D] for humans see what is visible,[E] but the LORD sees the heart."

8 Jesse called Abinadab and presented him to Samuel. "The LORD hasn't chosen this one either," Samuel said. 9 Then Jesse presented Shammah, but Samuel said, "The LORD hasn't chosen this one either." 10 After Jesse presented seven of his sons to him, Samuel told Jesse, "The LORD hasn't chosen any of these." 11 Samuel asked him, "Are these all the sons you have?"

"There is still the youngest," he answered, "but right now he's tending the sheep." Samuel told Jesse, "Send for him. We won't sit down to eat until he gets here." 12 So Jesse sent for him. He had beautiful eyes and a healthy,[F] handsome appearance.

Then the LORD said, "Anoint him, for he is the one." 13 So Samuel took the horn of oil and anointed him in the presence of his brothers, and the Spirit of the LORD came powerfully on David from that day forward. Then Samuel set out and went to Ramah.

DAVID IN SAUL'S COURT

14 Now the Spirit of the LORD had left Saul, and an evil spirit sent from the LORD began to torment him, 15 so Saul's servants said to him, "You see that an evil spirit from God is tormenting you. 16 Let our lord command your servants here in your presence to look for someone who knows how to play the lyre. Whenever the evil spirit from God comes on you, that person can play the lyre, and you will feel better."

17 Then Saul commanded his servants, "Find me someone who plays well and bring him to me."

18 One of the young men answered, "I have seen a son of Jesse of Bethlehem who knows how to play the lyre. He is also a valiant man, a warrior, eloquent, handsome, and the LORD is with him."

19 Then Saul dispatched messengers to Jesse and said, "Send me your son David, who is with the sheep." 20 So Jesse took a donkey loaded with bread, a wineskin, and one young goat and sent them by his son David to Saul. 21 When David came to Saul and entered his service, Saul loved him very much, and David became his armor-bearer. 22 Then Saul sent word to Jesse: "Let David remain in my service, for he has found favor with me." 23 Whenever the spirit from God came on Saul, David would pick up his lyre and play, and Saul would then be relieved, feel better, and the evil spirit would leave him.

DAVID VERSUS GOLIATH

17 The Philistines gathered their forces for war at Socoh in Judah and camped between Socoh and Azekah in Ephes-dammim. 2 Saul and the men of Israel gathered and camped in the Valley of Elah; then they lined up in battle formation to face the Philistines.

3 The Philistines were standing on one hill, and the Israelites were standing on another hill with a ravine between them. 4 Then a champion named Goliath, from Gath, came out from the Philistine camp. He was nine feet, nine inches[G,H] tall 5 and wore a bronze helmet[I] and bronze scale armor that weighed one hundred twenty-five pounds.[J] 6 There was bronze armor on his shins, and a bronze javelin was slung between his shoulders. 7 His spear shaft was like a weaver's beam, and the iron point of his spear weighed fifteen pounds.[K] In addition, a shield-bearer was walking in front of him.

8 He stood and shouted to the Israelite battle formations: "Why do you come out to line up in battle formation?" He asked them, "Am I not a Philistine and are you not servants of

[A] **16:4** LXX reads *were astonished* [B] **16:4** DSS, LXX read *"Seer, do* [C] **16:5** LXX reads *and rejoice with me today* [D] **16:7** LXX reads *God does not see as a man sees* [E] **16:7** Lit *for the man sees according to the eyes* [F] **16:12** Or *ruddy* [G] **17:4** DSS, LXX read *four cubits and a span* [H] **17:4** Lit *was six cubits and a span* [I] **17:5** Lit *helmet on his head* [J] **17:5** Lit *5,000 shekels* [K] **17:7** Lit *600 shekels*

Saul? Choose one of your men and have him
come down against me. 9 If he wins in a fight
against me and kills me, we will be your servants. But if I win against him and kill him,
then you will be our servants and serve us."
10 Then the Philistine said, "I defy the ranks of
Israel today. Send me a man so we can fight
each other!" 11 When Saul and all Israel heard
these words from the Philistine, they lost their
courage and were terrified.

12 Now David was the son of the Ephrathite
from Bethlehem of Judah named Jesse. Jesse
had eight sons and during Saul's reign was
already an old man. 13 Jesse's three oldest
sons had followed Saul to the war, and their
names were Eliab, the firstborn, Abinadab,
the next, and Shammah, the third, 14 and David was the youngest. The three oldest had
followed Saul, 15 but David kept going back
and forth from Saul to tend his father's flock
in Bethlehem.

16 Every morning and evening for forty days
the Philistine came forward and took his stand.
17 One day Jesse had told his son David: "Take
this half-bushel[A] of roasted grain along with
these ten loaves of bread for your brothers
and hurry to their camp. 18 Also take these
ten portions of cheese to the field commander.[B] Check on the well-being of your brothers
and bring a confirmation from them. 19 They
are with Saul and all the men of Israel in the
Valley of Elah fighting with the Philistines."

20 So David got up early in the morning, left
the flock with someone to keep it, loaded up,
and set out as Jesse had charged him.

He arrived at the perimeter of the camp as
the army was marching out to its battle formation shouting their battle cry. 21 Israel and the
Philistines lined up in battle formation facing
each other. 22 David left his supplies in the care
of the quartermaster and ran to the battle
line. When he arrived, he asked his brothers
how they were. 23 While he was speaking with
them, suddenly the champion named Goliath, the Philistine from Gath, came forward
from the Philistine battle line and shouted his
usual words, which David heard. 24 When all
the Israelite men saw Goliath, they retreated
from him terrified.

25 Previously, an Israelite man had declared:
"Do you see this man who keeps coming out?
He comes to defy Israel. The king will make
the man who kills him very rich and will give
him his daughter. The king will also make
the family of that man's father exempt from
paying taxes in Israel."

26 David spoke to the men who were standing
with him: "What will be done for the man who
kills that Philistine and removes this disgrace
from Israel? Just who is this uncircumcised
Philistine that he should defy the armies of
the living God?"

27 The troops told him about the offer, concluding, "That is what will be done for the man
who kills him."

28 David's oldest brother Eliab listened as he
spoke to the men, and he became angry with
him. "Why did you come down here?" he asked.
"Who did you leave those few sheep with in the
wilderness? I know your arrogance and your
evil heart — you came down to see the battle!"

29 "What have I done now?" protested David.
"It was just a question." 30 Then he turned from
those beside him to others in front of him and
asked about the offer. The people gave him
the same answer as before.

31 What David said was overheard and reported to Saul, so he had David brought to
him. 32 David said to Saul, "Don't let anyone
be discouraged by[C] him; your servant will go
and fight this Philistine!"

33 But Saul replied, "You can't go fight this
Philistine. You're just a youth, and he's been
a warrior since he was young."

34 David answered Saul: "Your servant has
been tending his father's sheep. Whenever a
lion or a bear came and carried off a lamb from
the flock, 35 I went after it, struck it down, and
rescued the lamb from its mouth. If it reared
up against me, I would grab it by its fur,[D] strike
it down, and kill it. 36 Your servant has killed
lions and bears; this uncircumcised Philistine
will be like one of them, for he has defied the
armies of the living God." 37 Then David said,
"The LORD who rescued me from the paw of
the lion and the paw of the bear will rescue
me from the hand of this Philistine."

Saul said to David, "Go, and may the LORD
be with you."

38 Then Saul had his own military clothes
put on David. He put a bronze helmet on David's head and had him put on armor. 39 David strapped his sword on over the military
clothes and tried to walk, but he was not used
to them. "I can't walk in these," David said to
Saul, "I'm not used to them." So David took

[A] **17:17** Lit *this ephah* [B] **17:18** Lit *the leader of 1,000* [C] **17:32** Lit *let a man's heart fall over* [D] **17:35** LXX reads *throat*; lit *beard*

them off. 40 Instead, he took his staff in his
hand and chose five smooth stones from the
wadi and put them in the pouch, in his shepherd's bag. Then, with his sling in his hand,
he approached the Philistine.

41 The Philistine came closer and closer to
David, with the shield-bearer in front of him.
42 When the Philistine looked and saw David,
he despised him because he was just a youth,
healthy[A] and handsome. 43 He said to David,
"Am I a dog that you come against me with
sticks?"[B] Then he cursed David by his gods.
44 "Come here," the Philistine called to David,
"and I'll give your flesh to the birds of the sky
and the wild beasts!"

45 David said to the Philistine: "You come
against me with a sword, spear, and javelin, but
I come against you in the name of the LORD of
Armies, the God of the ranks of Israel — you
have defied him. 46 Today, the LORD will hand
you over to me. Today, I'll strike you down,
remove your head, and give the corpses[C] of
the Philistine camp to the birds of the sky and
the wild creatures of the earth. Then all the
world will know that Israel has a God, 47 and
this whole assembly will know that it is not by
sword or by spear that the LORD saves, for the
battle is the LORD's. He will hand you over to us."

48 When the Philistine started forward to attack him, David ran quickly to the battle line to
meet the Philistine. 49 David put his hand in the
bag, took out a stone, slung it, and hit the Philistine on his forehead. The stone sank into his
forehead, and he fell facedown to the ground.
50 David defeated the Philistine with a sling and
a stone. David overpowered the Philistine and
killed him without having a sword. 51 David ran
and stood over him. He grabbed the Philistine's
sword, pulled it from its sheath, and used it to
kill him. Then he cut off his head. When the Philistines saw that their hero was dead, they fled.
52 The men of Israel and Judah rallied, shouting
their battle cry, and chased the Philistines to
the entrance of the valley and to the gates of
Ekron.[D] Philistine bodies were strewn all along
the Shaaraim road to Gath and Ekron.

53 When the Israelites returned from the
pursuit of the Philistines, they plundered
their camps. 54 David took Goliath's[E] head and
brought it to Jerusalem, but he put Goliath's
weapons in his own tent.

55[F] When Saul had seen David going out to
confront the Philistine, he asked Abner the
commander of the army, "Whose son is this
youth, Abner?"

"Your Majesty, as surely as you live, I don't
know," Abner replied.

56 The king said, "Find out whose son this
young man is!"

57 When David returned from killing the
Philistine, Abner took him and brought him
before Saul with the Philistine's head still in
his hand. 58 Saul said to him, "Whose son are
you, young man?"

"The son of your servant Jesse of Bethlehem," David answered.

DAVID'S SUCCESS

18 When David had finished speaking with
Saul, Jonathan was bound to David in
close friendship,[G] and loved him as much as
he loved himself. 2 Saul kept David with him
from that day on and did not let him return
to his father's house.

3 Jonathan made a covenant with David because he loved him as much as himself. 4 Then
Jonathan removed the robe he was wearing
and gave it to David, along with his military
tunic, his sword, his bow, and his belt.

5 David marched out with the army and was
successful in everything Saul sent him to do.
Saul put him in command of the fighting men,
which pleased all the people and Saul's servants as well.

6 As the troops were coming back, when
David was returning from killing the Philistine, the women came out from all the cities of
Israel to meet King Saul, singing and dancing
with tambourines, with shouts of joy, and with
three-stringed instruments. 7 As they danced,
the women sang:

> Saul has killed his thousands,
> but David his tens of thousands.

8 Saul was furious and resented this song.[H]
"They credited tens of thousands to David," he
complained, "but they only credited me with
thousands. What more can he have but the
kingdom?" 9 So Saul watched David jealously
from that day forward.

SAUL ATTEMPTS TO KILL DAVID

10 The next day an evil spirit sent from God
came powerfully on Saul, and he began to

[A] **17:42** Or *ruddy* [B] **17:43** Some LXX mss add *and stones?" And David said, "No! Worse than a dog!"* [C] **17:46** LXX reads *give your limbs and the limbs* [D] **17:52** LXX reads *Ashkelon* [E] **17:54** Lit *the Philistine's* [F] **17:55** LXX omits 1Sm 17:55–18:5
[G] **18:1** Lit *the life of Jonathan was bound to the life of David* [H] **18:8** Lit *furious; this saying was evil in his eyes*

rave[A] inside the palace. David was playing
the lyre as usual, but Saul was holding a spear,
11 and he threw it, thinking, "I'll pin David to
the wall." But David got away from him twice.
12 Saul was afraid of David, because the LORD
was with David but had left Saul. 13 Therefore,
Saul sent David away from him and made him
commander over a thousand men. David led
the troops 14 and continued to be successful in all his activities because the LORD was
with him. 15 When Saul observed that David
was very successful, he dreaded him. 16 But
all Israel and Judah loved David because he
was leading their troops. 17 Saul told David,
"Here is my oldest daughter Merab. I'll give
her to you as a wife, if you will be a warrior
for me and fight the LORD's battles." But Saul
was thinking, "I don't need to raise a hand
against him; let the hand of the Philistines
be against him."
18 Then David responded, "Who am I, and
what is my family or my father's clan in Israel
that I should become the king's son-in-law?"
19 When it was time to give Saul's daughter
Merab to David, she was given to Adriel the
Meholathite as a wife.

DAVID'S MARRIAGE TO MICHAL

20 Now Saul's daughter Michal loved David,
and when it was reported to Saul, it pleased
him.[B] 21 "I'll give her to him," Saul thought.
"She'll be a trap for him, and the hand of the
Philistines will be against him." So Saul said
to David a second time, "You can now be my
son-in-law."
22 Saul then ordered his servants, "Speak to
David in private and tell him, 'Look, the king
is pleased with you, and all his servants love
you. Therefore, you should become the king's
son-in-law.'"
23 Saul's servants reported these words directly to David,[C] but he replied, "Is it trivial in
your sight to become the king's son-in-law? I
am a poor commoner."
24 The servants reported back to Saul, "These
are the words David spoke."
25 Then Saul replied, "Say this to David: 'The
king desires no other bride-price except a hundred Philistine foreskins, to take revenge on
his enemies.'" Actually, Saul intended to cause
David's death at the hands of the Philistines.
26 When the servants reported these terms
to David, he was pleased[D] to become the king's

Relationships | *Relating to Friends*

CONNECTING

"When David had finished speaking with Saul, Jonathan was bound to David in close friendship, and loved him as much as he loved himself. Saul kept David with him from that day on and did not let him return to his father's house. Jonathan made a covenant with David because he loved him as much as himself." 1 Samuel 18:1-3

The average person now spends hours every week scrolling through various social media feeds, "liking:" the pictures and responding to the comments and posts of hundreds (or even thousands) of "friends" and "followers." We're supposedly the most connected generation in history; yet many people admit to deep loneliness. Why do you suppose that is?

Many who lack a close friendship could learn a lot from observing the relationship of Jonathan and David. It's exactly what you might expect. Notice their selflessness and fierce commitment to each other in hard times. Consider the time they spent interacting face-to-face and their numerous acts of love and concern.

Friendships don't magically happen. The old saying is true: To have a friend, you have to be a friend. Do this experiment. Instead of connecting online, call. Better yet, drop by and see an old friend in person. That connection will encourage you both.

For the next note on *Relationships*, see 1 Chronicles 29:17.

[A] **18:10** Or *prophesy* [B] **18:20** Lit *Saul, the thing was right in his eyes* [C] **18:23** Lit *words in David's ears* [D] **18:26** Lit *David, it was right in David's eyes*

son-in-law. Before the wedding day arrived,[A]
27 David and his men went out and killed two
hundred[B] Philistines. He brought their foreskins and presented them as full payment
to the king to become his son-in-law. Then
Saul gave his daughter Michal to David as his
wife. 28 Saul realized[C] that the LORD was with
David and that his daughter Michal loved
him, 29 and he became even more afraid of
David. As a result, Saul was David's enemy
from then on.

30 Every time the Philistine commanders
came out to fight, David was more successful
than all of Saul's officers. So his name became
well known.

DAVID DELIVERED FROM SAUL

19 Saul ordered his son Jonathan and all
his servants to kill David. But Saul's son
Jonathan liked David very much, 2 so he told
him: "My father Saul intends to kill you. Be on
your guard in the morning and hide in a secret
place and stay there. 3 I'll go out and stand
beside my father in the field where you are
and talk to him about you. When I see what
he says, I'll tell you."

4 Jonathan spoke well of David to his father
Saul. He said to him: "The king should not sin
against his servant David. He hasn't sinned
against you; in fact, his actions have been a
great advantage to you. 5 He took his life in his
hands when he struck down the Philistine,
and the LORD brought about a great victory
for all Israel. You saw it and rejoiced, so why
would you sin against innocent blood by killing David for no reason?"

6 Saul listened to Jonathan's advice and swore
an oath: "As surely as the LORD lives, David will
not be killed." 7 So Jonathan summoned David
and told him all these words. Then Jonathan
brought David to Saul, and he served him as
he did before.

8 When war broke out again, David went
out and fought against the Philistines. He defeated them with such great force that they
fled from him.

9 Now an evil spirit sent from the LORD came
on Saul as he was sitting in his palace holding
a spear. David was playing the lyre, 10 and Saul
tried to pin David to the wall with the spear. As
the spear struck the wall, David eluded Saul, ran
away, and escaped that night. 11 Saul sent agents
to David's house to watch for him and kill him
in the morning. But his wife Michal warned
David, "If you don't escape tonight, you will be
dead tomorrow!" 12 So she lowered David from
the window, and he fled and escaped. 13 Then
Michal took the household idol and put it on
the bed, placed some goat hair on its head, and
covered it with a garment. 14 When Saul sent
agents to seize David, Michal said, "He's sick."

15 Saul sent the agents back to see David and
said, "Bring him on his bed so I can kill him."
16 When the agents arrived, to their surprise,
the household idol was on the bed with some
goat hair on its head.

17 Saul asked Michal, "Why did you deceive
me like this? You sent my enemy away, and he
has escaped!"

She answered him, "He said to me, 'Let me
go! Why should I kill you?'"

18 So David fled and escaped and went to
Samuel at Ramah and told him everything
Saul had done to him. Then he and Samuel
left and stayed at Naioth.

19 When it was reported to Saul that David
was at Naioth in Ramah, 20 he sent agents to
seize David. However, when they saw the group
of prophets prophesying with Samuel leading
them, the Spirit of God came on Saul's agents,
and they also started prophesying. 21 When
they reported to Saul, he sent other agents,
and they also began prophesying. So Saul
tried again and sent a third group of agents,
and even they began prophesying. 22 Then
Saul himself went to Ramah. He came to the
large cistern at Secu and asked, "Where are
Samuel and David?"

"At Naioth in Ramah," someone said.

23 So he went to Naioth in Ramah. The Spirit
of God also came on him, and as he walked
along, he prophesied until he entered Naioth
in Ramah. 24 Saul then removed his clothes and
also prophesied before Samuel; he collapsed
and lay naked all that day and all that night.
That is why they say, "Is Saul also among the
prophets?"

JONATHAN PROTECTS DAVID

20 David fled from Naioth in Ramah and
came to Jonathan and asked, "What
have I done? What did I do wrong? How have
I sinned against your father so that he wants
to take my life?"

2 Jonathan said to him, "No, you won't die.
Listen, my father doesn't do anything, great or

[A] **18:26** Lit *And the days were not full* [B] **18:27** LXX reads *100* [C] **18:28** Lit *saw and knew*

small, without telling me.[A] So why would he hide this matter from me? This can't be true."

3 But David said, "Your father certainly knows that I have found favor with you. He has said, 'Jonathan must not know of this, or else he will be grieved.' " David also swore, "As surely as the LORD lives and as you yourself live, there is but a step between me and death."

4 Jonathan said to David, "Whatever you say, I will do for you."

5 So David told him, "Look, tomorrow is the New Moon, and I'm supposed to sit down and eat with the king. Instead, let me go, and I'll hide in the countryside for the next two nights.[B] 6 If your father misses me at all, say, 'David urgently requested my permission to go quickly to his hometown Bethlehem for an annual sacrifice there involving the whole clan.' 7 If he says, 'Good,' then your servant is safe, but if he becomes angry, you will know he has evil intentions. 8 Deal kindly with[C] your servant, for you have brought me into a covenant with you before the LORD. If I have done anything wrong, then kill me yourself; why take me to your father?"

9 "No!" Jonathan responded. "If I ever find out my father has evil intentions against you, wouldn't I tell you about it?"

10 So David asked Jonathan, "Who will tell me if your father answers you harshly?"

11 He answered David, "Come on, let's go out to the countryside." So both of them went out to the countryside. 12 "By the LORD, the God of Israel, I will sound out my father by this time tomorrow or the next day. If I find out that he is favorable toward you, will I not send for you and tell you?[D] 13 If my father intends to bring evil on you, may the LORD punish Jonathan and do so severely if I do not tell you[E] and send you away so you may leave safely. May the LORD be with you, just as he was with my father. 14 If I continue to live, show me kindness[F] from the LORD, but if I die, 15 don't ever withdraw your kindness from my household — not even when the LORD cuts off every one of David's enemies from the face of the earth." 16 Then Jonathan made a covenant with the house of David, saying, "May the LORD hold David's enemies accountable."[G] 17 Jonathan once again swore to David[H] in his love for him, because he loved him as he loved himself.

18 Then Jonathan said to him, "Tomorrow is the New Moon; you'll be missed because your seat will be empty. 19 The following day hurry down and go to the place where you hid on the day this incident began and stay beside the rock Ezel. 20 I will shoot three arrows beside it as if I'm aiming at a target. 21 Then I will send a servant and say, 'Go and find the arrows!' Now, if I expressly say to the servant, 'Look, the arrows are on this side of you — get them,' then come, because as the LORD lives, it is safe for you and there is no problem. 22 But if I say this to the youth, 'Look, the arrows are beyond you!' then go, for the LORD is sending you away. 23 As for the matter you and I have spoken about, the LORD will be a witness[I] between you and me forever." 24 So David hid in the countryside.

At the New Moon, the king sat down to eat the meal. 25 He sat at his usual place on the seat by the wall. Jonathan sat facing him[J] and Abner took his place beside Saul, but David's place was empty. 26 Saul did not say anything that day because he thought, "Something unexpected has happened; he must be ceremonially unclean — yes, that's it, he is unclean."

27 However, the day after the New Moon, the second day, David's place was still empty, and Saul asked his son Jonathan, "Why didn't Jesse's son come to the meal either yesterday or today?"

28 Jonathan answered, "David asked for my permission to go to Bethlehem. 29 He said, 'Please let me go because our clan is holding a sacrifice in the town, and my brother has told me to be there. So now, if I have found favor with you, let me go so I can see my brothers.' That's why he didn't come to the king's table."

30 Then Saul became angry with Jonathan and shouted, "You son of a perverse and rebellious woman! Don't I know that you are siding with Jesse's son to your own shame and to the disgrace of your mother?[K] 31 Every day Jesse's son lives on earth you and your kingship are not secure. Now send for him and bring him to me — he must die!"

32 Jonathan answered his father back: "Why is he to be killed? What has he done?"

33 Then Saul threw his spear at Jonathan to kill him, so he knew that his father was determined to kill David. 34 He got up from the table fiercely angry and did not eat any

[A] **20:2** Lit *without uncovering my ear* [B] **20:5** Lit *countryside until the third night* [C] **20:8** Or *Show loyalty to* [D] **20:12** Lit *and uncover your ear* [E] **20:13** Lit *severely — I will uncover your ear* [F] **20:14** Or *loyalty*, also in v. 15 [G] **20:16** Lit *LORD require it from the hand of David's enemies* [H] **20:17** LXX; MT reads *Jonathan once again made David swear* [I] **20:23** LXX; MT omits *a witness* [J] **20:25** Text emended; MT reads *Jonathan got up* [K] **20:30** Lit *your mother's nakedness*

food that second day of the New Moon, for he
was grieved because of his father's shameful
behavior toward David.

35 In the morning Jonathan went out to
the countryside for the appointed meeting
with David. A young servant was with him.
36 He said to the servant, "Run and find the
arrows I'm shooting." As the servant ran,
Jonathan shot an arrow beyond him. 37 He
came to the location of the arrow that Jonathan had shot, but Jonathan called to him
and said, "The arrow is beyond you, isn't it?"
38 Then Jonathan called to him, "Hurry up and
don't stop!" Jonathan's servant picked up the
arrow and returned to his master. 39 He did
not know anything; only Jonathan and David
knew the arrangement. 40 Then Jonathan gave
his equipment to the servant who was with
him and said, "Go, take it back to the city."

41 When the servant had gone, David got
up from the south side of the stone Ezel, fell
facedown to the ground, and paid homage
three times. Then he and Jonathan kissed each
other and wept with each other, though David
wept more.

42 Jonathan then said to David, "Go in the
assurance the two of us pledged in the name
of the LORD when we said: The LORD will be a
witness between you and me and between my
offspring and your offspring forever." Then
David left, and Jonathan went into the city.

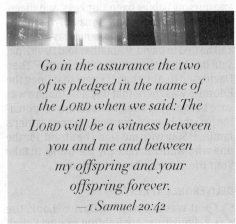

Go in the assurance the two of us pledged in the name of the LORD when we said: The LORD will be a witness between you and me and between my offspring and your offspring forever.

—1 Samuel 20:42

DAVID FLEES TO NOB

21 David went to the priest Ahimelech at
Nob. Ahimelech was afraid to meet David, so he said to him, "Why are you alone and
no one is with you?"

2 David answered the priest Ahimelech, "The
king gave me a mission, but he told me, 'Don't
let anyone know anything about the mission
I'm sending you on or what I have ordered
you to do.' I have stationed my young men at
a certain place. 3 Now what do you have on
hand? Give me five loaves of bread or whatever can be found."

4 The priest told him, "There is no ordinary
bread on hand. However, there is consecrated bread, but the young men may eat it[A] only
if they have kept themselves from women."

5 David answered him, "I swear that women
are being kept from us, as always when I go
out to battle. The young men's bodies[B] are
consecrated even on an ordinary mission,
so of course their bodies are consecrated today." 6 So the priest gave him the consecrated
bread, for there was no bread there except
the Bread of the Presence that had been removed from the presence of the LORD. When
the bread was removed, it had been replaced
with warm bread.

7 One of Saul's servants, detained before the
LORD, was there that day. His name was Doeg
the Edomite, chief of Saul's shepherds.

8 David said to Ahimelech, "Do you have a
spear or sword on hand? I didn't even bring
my sword or my weapons since the king's
mission was urgent."

9 The priest replied, "The sword of Goliath
the Philistine, whom you killed in the Valley
of Elah, is here, wrapped in a cloth behind
the ephod. If you want to take it for yourself,
then take it, for there isn't another one here."

"There's none like it!" David said. "Give it
to me."

DAVID FLEES TO GATH

10 David fled that day from Saul's presence and
went to King Achish of Gath. 11 But Achish's
servants said to him, "Isn't this David, the king
of the land? Don't they sing about him during
their dances:

> Saul has killed his thousands,
> but David his tens of thousands?"

12 David took this to heart[C] and became very
afraid of King Achish of Gath, 13 so he pretended
to be insane in their presence. He acted like
a madman around them,[D] scribbling[E] on the
doors of the city gate and letting saliva run
down his beard.

[A] **21:4** DSS; MT omits *may eat it* [B] **21:5** Lit *vessels* [C] **21:12** Lit *David placed these words in his heart* [D] **21:13** Lit *madman in their hand* [E] **21:13** LXX reads *drumming*

14 "Look! You can see the man is crazy," Achish
said to his servants. "Why did you bring him to
me? 15 Do I have such a shortage of crazy people
that you brought this one to act crazy around
me? Is this one going to come into my house?"

SAUL'S INCREASING PARANOIA

22 So David left Gath and took refuge in the
cave of Adullam. When David's brothers and his father's whole family heard, they
went down and joined him there. 2 In addition, every man who was desperate, in debt,
or discontented rallied around him, and he
became their leader. About four hundred men
were with him.
3 From there David went to Mizpeh of Moab
where he said to the king of Moab, "Please
let my father and mother stay with you until
I know what God will do for me." 4 So he left
them in the care of the king of Moab, and they
stayed with him the whole time David was in
the stronghold.
5 Then the prophet Gad said to David, "Don't
stay in the stronghold. Leave and return to
the land of Judah." So David left and went to
the forest of Hereth.
6 Saul heard that David and his men had
been discovered. At that time Saul was in
Gibeah, sitting under the tamarisk tree at
the high place. His spear was in his hand,
and all his servants were standing around
him. 7 Saul said to his servants, "Listen, men
of Benjamin: Is Jesse's son going to give all of
you fields and vineyards? Do you think he'll
make all of you commanders of thousands
and commanders of hundreds? 8 That's why
all of you have conspired against me! Nobody
tells me[A] when my own son makes a covenant
with Jesse's son. None of you cares about me
or tells me[B] that my son has stirred up my
own servant to wait in ambush for me, as is
the case today."
9 Then Doeg the Edomite, who was in charge
of Saul's servants, answered: "I saw Jesse's
son come to Ahimelech son of Ahitub at Nob.
10 Ahimelech inquired of the LORD for him
and gave him provisions. He also gave him
the sword of Goliath the Philistine."

SLAUGHTER OF THE PRIESTS

11 The king sent messengers to summon the
priest Ahimelech son of Ahitub, and his father's whole family, who were priests in Nob.
All of them came to the king. 12 Then Saul said,
"Listen, son of Ahitub!"
"I'm at your service, my lord," he said.
13 Saul asked him, "Why did you and Jesse's
son conspire against me? You gave him bread
and a sword and inquired of God for him, so
he could rise up against me and wait in ambush, as is the case today."
14 Ahimelech replied to the king: "Who
among all your servants is as faithful as David? He is the king's son-in-law, captain of
your bodyguard, and honored in your house.
15 Was today the first time I inquired of God for
him? Of course not! Please don't let the king
make an accusation against your servant or
any of my father's family, for your servant
didn't have any idea[C] about all this."
16 But the king said, "You will die, Ahimelech — you and your father's whole family!"
17 Then the king ordered the guards standing by him, "Turn and kill the priests of the
LORD because they sided with David. For they
knew he was fleeing, but they didn't tell me."[D]
But the king's servants would not lift a hand
to execute the priests of the LORD.
18 So the king said to Doeg, "Go and execute
the priests!" So Doeg the Edomite went and executed the priests himself. On that day, he killed
eighty-five men who wore linen ephods. 19 He
also struck down Nob, the city of the priests,
with the sword — both men and women, infants
and nursing babies, oxen, donkeys, and sheep.
20 However, one of the sons of Ahimelech
son of Ahitub escaped. His name was Abiathar,
and he fled to David. 21 Abiathar told David that
Saul had killed the priests of the LORD. 22 Then
David said to Abiathar, "I knew that Doeg the
Edomite was there that day and that he was
sure to report to Saul. I myself am responsible for[E] the lives of everyone in your father's
family. 23 Stay with me. Don't be afraid, for the
one who wants to take my life wants to take
your life. You will be safe with me."

DELIVERANCE AT KEILAH

23 It was reported to David: "Look, the
Philistines are fighting against Keilah
and raiding the threshing floors."
2 So David inquired of the LORD: "Should I
launch an attack against these Philistines?"
The LORD answered David, "Launch an attack
against the Philistines and rescue Keilah."
3 But David's men said to him, "Look, we're

[A] **22:8** Lit *No one uncovers my ear* [B] **22:8** Lit *or uncovers my ear* [C] **22:15** Lit *didn't know a thing, small or large* [D] **22:17** Lit *didn't uncover my ear* [E] **22:22** LXX, Syr, Vg; MT reads *I myself turn in*

afraid here in Judah; how much more if we
go to Keilah against the Philistine forces!"
4 Once again, David inquired of the LORD,
and the LORD answered him: "Go at once to
Keilah, for I will hand the Philistines over to
you." 5 Then David and his men went to Keilah, fought against the Philistines, drove their
livestock away, and inflicted heavy losses
on them. So David rescued the inhabitants
of Keilah. 6 Abiathar son of Ahimelech fled
to David at Keilah, and he brought an ephod
with him.
7 When it was reported to Saul that David
had gone to Keilah, he said, "God has handed
him over to me, for he has trapped himself by
entering a town with barred gates." 8 Then
Saul summoned all the troops to go to war at
Keilah and besiege David and his men.
9 When David learned that Saul was plotting
evil against him, he said to the priest Abiathar,
"Bring the ephod."
10 Then David said, "LORD God of Israel, your
servant has reliable information that Saul intends to come to Keilah and destroy the town
because of me. 11 Will the citizens of Keilah
hand me over to him? Will Saul come down
as your servant has heard? LORD God of Israel,
please tell your servant."
The LORD answered, "He will come down."
12 Then David asked, "Will the citizens of
Keilah hand me and my men over to Saul?"
"They will," the LORD responded.
13 So David and his men, numbering about six
hundred, left Keilah at once and moved from
place to place. When it was reported to Saul
that David had escaped from Keilah, he called
off the expedition. 14 David then stayed in the
wilderness strongholds and in the hill country
of the Wilderness of Ziph. Saul searched for
him every day, but God did not hand David
over to him.

A RENEWED COVENANT

15 David was in the Wilderness of Ziph in Horesh when he saw that Saul had come out to
take his life. 16 Then Saul's son Jonathan came
to David in Horesh and encouraged him in his
faith[A] in God, 17 saying, "Don't be afraid, for
my father Saul will never lay a hand on you.
You yourself will be king over Israel, and I'll
be your second-in-command. Even my father Saul knows it is true." 18 Then the two of
them made a covenant in the LORD's presence.
Afterward, David remained in Horesh, while
Jonathan went home.

DAVID'S NARROW ESCAPE

19 Some Ziphites came up to Saul at Gibeah
and said, "David is[B] hiding among us in the
strongholds in Horesh on the hill of Hachilah
south of Jeshimon. 20 Now, whenever the king
wants to come down, let him come down. Our
part will be to hand him over to the king."
21 "May you be blessed by the LORD," replied
Saul, "for you have shown concern for me.
22 Go and check again. Investigate[C] where he
goes[D] and who has seen him there; they tell
me he is extremely cunning. 23 Investigate[E] all
the places where he hides. Then come back to
me with accurate information, and I'll go with
you. If it turns out he really is in the region, I'll
search for him among all the clans[F] of Judah."
24 So they went to Ziph ahead of Saul.
Now David and his men were in the wilderness near Maon in the Arabah south of
Jeshimon, 25 and Saul and his men went to
look for him. When David was told about it,
he went down to the rock and stayed in the
Wilderness of Maon. Saul heard of this and
pursued David there.
26 Saul went along one side of the mountain and David and his men went along the
other side. Even though David was hurrying
to get away from Saul, Saul and his men were
closing in on David and his men to capture
them. 27 Then a messenger came to Saul saying, "Come quickly, because the Philistines
have raided the land!" 28 So Saul broke off his
pursuit of David and went to engage the Philistines. Therefore, that place was named the
Rock of Separation. 29 From there David went
up and stayed in the strongholds of En-gedi.

DAVID SPARES SAUL

24 When Saul returned from pursuing the
Philistines, he was told, "David is in the
wilderness near En-gedi." 2 So Saul took three
thousand of Israel's fit young men and went
to look for David and his men in front of the
Rocks of the Wild Goats. 3 When Saul came
to the sheep pens along the road, a cave was
there, and he went in to relieve himself.[G] David
and his men were staying in the recesses of
the cave, 4 so they said to him, "Look, this is
the day the LORD told you about: 'I will hand
your enemy over to you so you can do to him

[A] **23:16** Lit *and strengthened his hand* [B] **23:19** Lit *"Is David not . . . Jeshimon?* [C] **23:22** Lit *Know and see* [D] **23:22** Lit *watch his place where his foot will be* [E] **23:23** Lit *See and know* [F] **23:23** Or *thousands* [G] **24:3** Lit *to cover his feet*

whatever you desire.'" Then David got up and secretly cut off the corner of Saul's robe.

5 Afterward, David's conscience bothered[A] him because he had cut off the corner of Saul's robe.[B] 6 He said to his men, "I swear before the LORD: I would never do such a thing to my lord, the LORD's anointed. I will never lift my hand against him, since he is the LORD's anointed." 7 With these words David persuaded[C] his men, and he did not let them rise up against Saul.

Then Saul left the cave and went on his way. 8 After that, David got up, went out of the cave, and called to Saul, "My lord the king!" When Saul looked behind him, David knelt low with his face to the ground and paid homage. 9 David said to Saul, "Why do you listen to the words of people who say, 'Look, David intends to harm you'? 10 You can see with your own eyes that the LORD handed you over to me today in the cave. Someone advised me to kill you, but I[D,E] took pity on you and said: I won't lift my hand against my lord, since he is the LORD's anointed. 11 Look, my father! Look at the corner of your robe in my hand, for I cut it off, but I didn't kill you. Recognize[F] that I've committed no crime or rebellion. I haven't sinned against you even though you are hunting me down to take my life.

12 "May the LORD judge between me and you, and may the LORD take vengeance on you for me, but my hand will never be against you. 13 As the old proverb says, 'Wickedness comes from wicked people.' My hand will never be against you. 14 Who has the king of Israel come after? What are you chasing after? A dead dog? A single flea? 15 May the LORD be judge and decide between you and me. May he take notice and plead my case and deliver[G] me from you."

16 When David finished saying these things to him, Saul replied, "Is that your voice, David my son?" Then Saul wept aloud 17 and said to David, "You are more righteous than I, for you have done what is good to me though I have done what is evil to you. 18 You yourself have told me today what good you did for me: when the LORD handed me over to you, you didn't kill me. 19 When a man finds his enemy, does he let him go unharmed?[H] May the LORD repay you with good for what you've done for me today.

20 "Now I know for certain you will be king, and the kingdom of Israel will be established[I] in your hand. 21 Therefore swear to me by the LORD that you will not cut off my descendants or wipe out my name from my father's family." 22 So David swore to Saul. Then Saul went back home, and David and his men went up to the stronghold.

DAVID, NABAL, AND ABIGAIL

25 Samuel died, and all Israel assembled to mourn for him, and they buried him by his home in Ramah. David then went down to the Wilderness of Paran.[J]

2 A man in Maon had a business in Carmel; he was a very rich man with three thousand sheep and one thousand goats and was shearing his sheep in Carmel. 3 The man's name was Nabal, and his wife's name, Abigail. The woman was intelligent and beautiful, but the man, a Calebite, was harsh and evil in his dealings.

4 While David was in the wilderness, he heard that Nabal was shearing sheep, 5 so David sent ten young men instructing them, "Go up to Carmel, and when you come to Nabal, greet him[K] in my name. 6 Then say this: 'Long life to you,[L] and peace to you, peace to your family, and peace to all that is yours. 7 I hear that you are shearing.[M] When your shepherds were with us, we did not harass them, and nothing of theirs was missing the whole time they were in Carmel. 8 Ask your young men, and they will tell you. So let my young men find favor with you, for we have come on a feast[N] day. Please give whatever you have on hand to your servants and to your son David.'"

9 David's young men went and said all these things to Nabal on David's behalf,[O] and they waited.[P] 10 Nabal asked them, "Who is David? Who is Jesse's son? Many slaves these days are running away from their masters. 11 Am I supposed to take my bread, my water, and my meat that I butchered for my shearers and give them to these men? I don't know where they are from."

12 David's young men retraced their steps. When they returned to him, they reported all these words. 13 He said to his men, "All of you, put on your swords!" So each man put on his sword, and David also put on his sword. About

[A] **24:5** Lit *David's heart struck* [B] **24:5** Some Hb mss, LXX, Syr, Vg; other Hb mss omit *robe* [C] **24:7** Or *restrained* [D] **24:10** LXX, Syr, Tg; MT reads *she* or *it* [E] **24:10** Or *my eye* [F] **24:11** Lit *Know and see* [G] **24:15** Lit *render a verdict for* [H] **24:19** Lit *go on a good way* [I] **24:20** Or *will flourish* [J] **25:1** LXX reads *to Maon* [K] **25:5** Or *Nabal, ask him for peace* [L] **25:6** Lit *'To life* [M] **25:7** Lit *you have shearers* [N] **25:8** Lit *good* [O] **25:9** Lit *name* [P] **25:9** LXX reads *and he became arrogant*

four hundred men followed David while two hundred stayed with the supplies.

14 One of Nabal's young men informed Abigail, Nabal's wife: "Look, David sent messengers from the wilderness to greet our master, but he screamed at them. 15 The men treated us very well. When we were in the field, we weren't harassed and nothing of ours was missing the whole time we were living among them. 16 They were a wall around us, both day and night, the entire time we were with them herding the sheep. 17 Now consider carefully[A] what you should do, because there is certain to be trouble for our master and his entire family. He is such a worthless fool nobody can talk to him!"

18 Abigail hurried, taking two hundred loaves of bread, two clay jars of wine, five butchered sheep, a bushel[B] of roasted grain, one hundred clusters of raisins, and two hundred cakes of pressed figs, and loaded them on donkeys. 19 Then she said to her male servants, "Go ahead of me. I will be right behind you." But she did not tell her husband Nabal.

20 As she rode the donkey down a mountain pass hidden from view, she saw David and his men coming toward her and met them. 21 David had just said, "I guarded everything that belonged to this man in the wilderness for nothing. He was not missing anything, yet he paid me back evil for good. 22 May God punish me[C] and do so severely if I let any of his males[D] survive until morning."

23 When Abigail saw David, she quickly got off the donkey and knelt down with her face to the ground and paid homage to David. 24 She knelt at his feet and said, "The guilt is mine, my lord, but please let your servant speak to you directly. Listen to the words of your servant. 25 My lord should pay no attention to this worthless fool Nabal, for he lives up to his name:[E] His name means 'stupid,' and stupidity is all he knows.[F] I, your servant, didn't see my lord's young men whom you sent. 26 Now my lord, as surely as the LORD lives and as you yourself live— it is the LORD who kept you from participating in bloodshed and avenging yourself by your own hand—may your enemies and those who intend to harm my lord be like Nabal. 27 Let this gift your servant has brought to my lord be given to the young men who follow my lord. 28 Please forgive your servant's offense, for the LORD is certain to make a lasting dynasty for my lord

Other-centeredness | *Learning Other People's Stories*

LISTEN AND LEARN

"She knelt at his feet and said, 'The guilt is mine, my lord, but please let your servant speak to you directly. Listen to the words of your servant.'" 1 Samuel 25:24

One of the greatest gifts we can give others is to give them our full attention. Think of how rare this has become. We are forever glancing over at the TV, laser focused on our computer monitors, looking down at our smart phones, impatiently interrupting and tossing out advice, or changing the subject altogether.

Hopefully you've had this experience: You needed to process some things swirling in your mind. A friend or family members picked up on these nonverbal cues. They stopped whatever they were doing, turned, faced you, and fully engaged. They leaned in. They listened intently, nodding, maybe asking a few clarifying questions. They didn't look at the clock on the wall once. They never made you feel rushed. You felt heard. And that did something amazing for your soul.

You can do this for another person every day of your life. It doesn't have to take hours. You'd be amazed at what a difference it makes to give someone even fifteen minutes of active listening and genuine concern.

For the next note on *Other-centeredness*, see Job 29:12-13.

[A] **25:17** Lit *Now know and see* [B] **25:18** Lit *sheep, five seahs* [C] **25:22** LXX; MT reads *David's enemies* [D] **25:22** Lit *of those of his who are urinating against the wall* [E] **25:25** Lit *for as is his name is, so he is* [F] **25:25** Lit *and foolishness is with him*

because he fights the LORD's battles. Throughout your life, may evil[A] not be found in you.

29 "Someone is pursuing you and intends to take your life. My lord's life is tucked safely in the place[B] where the LORD your God protects the living, but he is flinging away your enemies' lives like stones from a sling. 30 When the LORD does for my lord all the good he promised you and appoints you ruler over Israel, 31 there will not be remorse or a troubled conscience for my lord because of needless bloodshed or my lord's revenge. And when the LORD does good things for my lord, may you remember me your servant."

32 Then David said to Abigail, "Blessed be the LORD God of Israel, who sent you to meet me today! 33 May your discernment be blessed, and may you be blessed. Today you kept me from participating in bloodshed and avenging myself by my own hand. 34 Otherwise, as surely as the LORD God of Israel lives, who prevented me from harming you, if you had not come quickly to meet me, Nabal wouldn't have had any males[C] left by morning light." 35 Then David accepted what she had brought him and said, "Go home in peace. See, I have heard what you said and have granted your request."

36 Then Abigail went to Nabal, and there he was in his house, holding a feast fit for a king. Nabal's heart was cheerful,[D] and he was very drunk, so she didn't say anything[E] to him until morning light.

37 In the morning when Nabal sobered up,[F] his wife told him about these events. His heart died[G] and he became a stone. 38 About ten days later, the LORD struck Nabal dead.

39 When David heard that Nabal was dead, he said, "Blessed be the LORD who championed my cause against Nabal's insults and restrained his servant from doing evil. The LORD brought Nabal's evil deeds back on his own head."

Then David sent messengers to speak to Abigail about marrying him. 40 When David's servants came to Abigail at Carmel, they said to her, "David sent us to bring you to him as a wife."

41 She stood up, paid homage with her face to the ground, and said, "Here I am, your servant, a slave to wash the feet of my lord's servants." 42 Then Abigail got up quickly, and with her five female servants accompanying her, rode on the donkey following David's messengers. And so she became his wife.

43 David also married Ahinoam of Jezreel, and the two of them became his wives. 44 But Saul gave his daughter Michal, David's wife, to Palti son of Laish, who was from Gallim.

DAVID AGAIN SPARES SAUL

26 Then the Ziphites came to Saul at Gibeah saying, "David is hiding on the hill of Hachilah opposite Jeshimon." 2 So Saul, accompanied by three thousand of the fit young men of Israel, went immediately to the Wilderness of Ziph to search for David there. 3 Saul camped beside the road at the hill of Hachilah opposite Jeshimon. David was living in the wilderness and discovered Saul had come there after him. 4 So David sent out spies and knew for certain that Saul had come. 5 Immediately, David went to the place where Saul had camped. He saw the place where Saul and Abner son of Ner, the commander of his army, were lying down. Saul was lying inside the inner circle of the camp with the troops camped around him. 6 Then David asked Ahimelech the Hethite and Joab's brother Abishai son of Zeruiah, "Who will go with me into the camp to Saul?"

"I'll go with you," answered Abishai.

7 That night, David and Abishai came to the troops, and Saul was lying there asleep in the inner circle of the camp with his spear stuck in the ground by his head. Abner and the troops were lying around him. 8 Then Abishai said to David, "Today God has delivered your enemy to you. Let me thrust the spear through him into the ground just once. I won't have to strike him twice!"

9 But David said to Abishai, "Don't destroy him, for who can lift a hand against the LORD's anointed and be innocent?" 10 David added, "As the LORD lives, the LORD will certainly strike him down: either his day will come and he will die, or he will go into battle and perish. 11 However, because of the LORD, I will never lift my hand against the LORD's anointed. Instead, take the spear and the water jug by his head, and let's go."

12 So David took the spear and the water jug by Saul's head, and they went their way. No one saw them, no one knew, and no one woke up; they all remained asleep because a deep sleep from the LORD came over them.

[A] **25:28** Or *trouble* [B] **25:29** Lit *bundle* [C] **25:34** Lit *had anyone urinating against a wall* [D] **25:36** Lit *Nabal's heart was good on him* [E] **25:36** Lit *anything at all* [F] **25:37** Lit *when the wine had gone out of Nabal* [G] **25:37** Lit *Then his heart died within him*

13 David crossed to the other side and stood on top of the mountain at a distance; there was a considerable space between them. 14 Then David shouted to the troops and to Abner son of Ner: "Aren't you going to answer, Abner?"

"Who are you who calls to the king?" Abner asked.

15 David called to Abner, "You're a man, aren't you? Who in Israel is your equal? So why didn't you protect your lord the king when one of the people came to destroy him? 16 What you have done is not good. As the LORD lives, all of you deserve to die[A] since you didn't protect your lord, the LORD's anointed. Now look around; where are the king's spear and water jug that were by his head?"

17 Saul recognized David's voice and asked, "Is that your voice, my son David?"

"It is my voice, my lord and king," David said. 18 Then he continued, "Why is my lord pursuing his servant? What have I done? What crime have I committed? 19 Now, may my lord the king please hear the words of his servant: If it is the LORD who has incited you against me, then may he accept an offering. But if it is people, may they be cursed in the presence of the LORD, for today they have banished me from sharing in the inheritance of the LORD saying, 'Go and worship other gods.' 20 So don't let my blood fall to the ground far from the LORD's presence, for the king of Israel has come out to search for a single flea, like one who pursues a partridge in the mountains."

21 Saul responded, "I have sinned. Come back, my son David, I will never harm you again because today you considered my life precious. I have been a fool! I've committed a grave error."

22 David answered, "Here is the king's spear; have one of the young men come over and get it. 23 The LORD will repay every man for his righteousness and his loyalty. I wasn't willing to lift my hand against the LORD's anointed, even though the LORD handed you over to me today. 24 Just as I considered your life valuable today, so may the LORD consider my life valuable and rescue me from all trouble."

25 Saul said to him, "You are blessed, my son David. You will certainly do great things and will also prevail." Then David went on his way, and Saul returned home.

DAVID FLEES TO ZIKLAG

27 David said to himself, "One of these days I'll be swept away by Saul. There is nothing better for me than to escape immediately to the land of the Philistines. Then Saul will give up searching for me everywhere in Israel, and I'll escape from him." 2 So David set out with his six hundred men and went over to Achish son of Maoch, the king of Gath. 3 David and his men stayed with Achish in Gath. Each man had his family with him, and David had his two wives: Ahinoam of Jezreel and Abigail of Carmel, Nabal's widow. 4 When it was reported to Saul that David had fled to Gath, he no longer searched for him.

5 Now David said to Achish, "If I have found favor with you, let me be given a place in one of the outlying towns, so I can live there. Why should your servant live in the royal city with you?" 6 That day Achish gave Ziklag to him, and it still belongs to the kings of Judah today. 7 The length of time that David stayed in Philistine territory amounted to a year and four months.

8 David and his men went up and raided the Geshurites, the Girzites,[B] and the Amalekites. From ancient times they had been the inhabitants of the region through Shur as far as the land of Egypt. 9 Whenever David attacked the land, he did not leave a single person alive, either man or woman, but he took flocks, herds, donkeys, camels, and clothing. Then he came back to Achish, 10 who inquired, "Where did you raid today?"[C]

David replied, "The south country of Judah," "The south country of the Jerahmeelites," or "The south country of the Kenites."

11 David did not let a man or woman live to be brought to Gath, for he said, "Or they will inform on us and say, 'This is what David did.'" This was David's custom during the whole time he stayed in the Philistine territory. 12 So Achish trusted David, thinking, "Since he has made himself repulsive to his people Israel, he will be my servant forever."

SAUL AND THE MEDIUM

28 At that time, the Philistines gathered their military units into one army to fight against Israel. So Achish said to David, "You know, of course, that you and your men must march out in the army[D] with me."

2 David replied to Achish, "Good, you will find out what your servant can do."

[A] **26:16** Lit *you are sons of death* [B] **27:8** Alt Hb tradition reads *Gezerites* [C] **27:10** Some Hb mss, Syr, Tg; LXX, Vg, DSS read *"Against whom did you raid today?"* [D] **28:1** DSS, LXX read *battle*

So Achish said to David, "Very well, I will
appoint you as my permanent bodyguard."
3 By this time Samuel had died, all Israel had
mourned for him and buried him in Ramah,
his city, and Saul had removed the mediums
and spiritists from the land. 4 The Philistines
gathered and camped at Shunem. So Saul gathered all Israel, and they camped at Gilboa.
5 When Saul saw the Philistine camp, he was
afraid and his heart pounded. 6 He inquired of
the LORD, but the LORD did not answer him in
dreams or by the Urim or by the prophets. 7 Saul
then said to his servants, "Find me a woman
who is a medium, so I can go and consult her."

His servants replied, "There is a woman at
En-dor who is a medium."

8 Saul disguised himself by putting on different clothes and set out with two of his men.
They came to the woman at night, and Saul
said, "Consult a spirit for me. Bring up for me
the one I tell you."

9 But the woman said to him, "You surely
know what Saul has done, how he has cut off
the mediums and spiritists from the land. Why
are you setting a trap for me to get me killed?"
10 Then Saul swore to her by the LORD: "As
surely as the LORD lives, no punishment will
come to you[A] from this."

11 "Who is it that you want me to bring up
for you?" the woman asked.

"Bring up Samuel for me," he answered.

12 When the woman saw Samuel, she
screamed, and then she asked Saul, "Why
did you deceive me? You are Saul!"

13 But the king said to her, "Don't be afraid.
What do you see?"

"I see a spirit form[B] coming up out of the
earth," the woman answered.

14 Then Saul asked her, "What does he look
like?"

"An old man is coming up," she replied. "He's
wearing a robe." Then Saul knew that it was
Samuel, and he knelt low with his face to the
ground and paid homage.

15 "Why have you disturbed me by bringing
me up?" Samuel asked Saul.

"I'm in serious trouble," replied Saul. "The
Philistines are fighting against me and God
has turned away from me. He doesn't answer
me anymore, either through the prophets or
in dreams. So I've called on you to tell me what
I should do."

16 Samuel answered, "Since the LORD has
turned away from you and has become your
enemy, why are you asking me? 17 The LORD
has done[C] exactly what he said through me:
The LORD has torn the kingship out of your
hand and given it to your neighbor David.
18 You did not obey the LORD and did not carry out his burning anger against Amalek;
therefore the LORD has done this to you today.
19 The LORD will also hand Israel over to the
Philistines along with you. Tomorrow you and
your sons will be with me,[D] and the LORD will
hand Israel's army over to the Philistines."

20 Immediately, Saul fell flat on the ground.
He was terrified by Samuel's words and was
also weak because he had not eaten anything
all day and all night. 21 The woman came over
to Saul, and she saw that he was terrified and
said to him, "Look, your servant has obeyed
you. I took my life in my hands and did what
you told me to do. 22 Now please listen to your
servant. Let me set some food in front of you.
Eat and it will give you strength so you can
go on your way."

23 He refused, saying, "I won't eat," but when
his servants and the woman urged him, he
listened to them. He got up off the ground
and sat on the bed.

24 The woman had a fattened calf at her
house, and she quickly slaughtered it. She
also took flour, kneaded it, and baked unleavened bread. 25 She served it to Saul and his
servants, and they ate. Afterward, they got
up and left that night.

PHILISTINES REJECT DAVID

29 The Philistines brought all their military units together at Aphek while
Israel was camped by the spring in Jezreel. 2 As the Philistine leaders were passing
in review with their units of hundreds and
thousands, David and his men were passing
in review behind them with Achish. 3 Then
the Philistine commanders asked, "What are
these Hebrews doing here?"

Achish answered the Philistine command-
ers, "That is David, servant of King Saul of Israel.
He has been with me a considerable period of
time.[E] From the day he defected until today,
I've found no fault with him."

4 The Philistine commanders, however, were
enraged with Achish and told him, "Send that
man back and let him return to the place you
assigned him. He must not go down with us

[A] 28:10 Or *lives, you will not incur guilt* [B] 28:13 Or *a god*, or *a divine being* [C] 28:17 Some Hb, some LXX mss, Vg read *done to you* [D] 28:19 LXX reads *sons will fall* [E] 29:3 Hb obscure

into battle only to become our adversary during
the battle. What better way could he ingratiate
himself with his master than with the heads
of our men? 5 Isn't this the David they sing
about during their dances:

Saul has killed his thousands,
but David his tens of thousands?"

6 So Achish summoned David and told him,
"As the LORD lives, you are an honorable man.
I think it is good[A] to have you fighting[B] in
this unit with me, because I have found no
fault in you from the day you came to me
until today. But the leaders don't think you
are reliable. 7 Now go back quietly and you
won't be doing anything the Philistine leaders think is wrong."

8 "But what have I done?" David replied to
Achish. "From the first day I entered your service until today, what have you found against
your servant to keep me from going to fight
against the enemies of my lord the king?"

9 Achish answered David, "I'm convinced
that you are as reliable as an angel of God. But
the Philistine commanders have said, 'He must
not go into battle with us.' 10 So get up early in
the morning, you and your masters' servants
who came with you.[C] When you've all gotten
up early, go as soon as it's light." 11 So David
and his men got up early in the morning to
return to the land of the Philistines. And the
Philistines went up to Jezreel.

DAVID'S DEFEAT OF THE AMALEKITES

30 David and his men arrived in Ziklag
on the third day. The Amalekites had
raided the Negev and attacked and burned
Ziklag. 2 They also had kidnapped the women
and everyone[D] in it from youngest to oldest.
They had killed no one but had carried them
off as they went on their way.

3 When David and his men arrived at the
town, they found it burned. Their wives, sons,
and daughters had been kidnapped. 4 David
and the troops with him wept loudly until
they had no strength left to weep. 5 David's
two wives, Ahinoam the Jezreelite and Abigail
the widow of Nabal the Carmelite, had also
been kidnapped. 6 David was in an extremely
difficult position because the troops talked
about stoning him, for they were all very bitter over the loss of their sons and daughters.
But David found strength in the LORD his God.

David found strength in
the LORD his God.
—1 Samuel 30:6

7 David said to the priest Abiathar son of
Ahimelech, "Bring me the ephod." So Abiathar brought it to him, 8 and David asked the
LORD: "Should I pursue these raiders? Will I
overtake them?"

The LORD replied to him, "Pursue them, for
you will certainly overtake them and rescue
the people."

9 So David and the six hundred men with
him went. They came to the Wadi Besor, where
some stayed behind. 10 David and four hundred
of the men continued the pursuit, while two
hundred stopped because they were too exhausted to cross the Wadi Besor.

11 David's men found an Egyptian in the open
country and brought him to David. They gave
him some bread to eat and water to drink.
12 Then they gave him some pressed figs and
two clusters of raisins. After he ate he revived,
for he hadn't eaten food or drunk water for
three days and three nights.

13 Then David said to him, "Who do you belong to? Where are you from?"

"I'm an Egyptian, the slave of an Amalekite man," he said. "My master abandoned me
when I got sick three days ago. 14 We raided the
south country of the Cherethites, the territory
of Judah, and the south country of Caleb, and
we burned Ziklag."

15 David then asked him, "Will you lead me
to these raiders?"

He said, "Swear to me by God that you won't
kill me or turn me over to my master, and I
will lead you to them."

16 So he led him, and there were the Amalekites, spread out over the entire area, eating,
drinking, and celebrating because of the great
amount of plunder they had taken from the
land of the Philistines and the land of Judah.
17 David slaughtered them from twilight until
the evening of the next day. None of them escaped, except four hundred young men who
got on camels and fled.

18 David recovered everything the Amalekites

[A] **29:6** Lit *It was good in my eyes* [B] **29:6** Lit *you going out and coming in* [C] **29:10** LXX adds *and go to the place I appointed you to. Don't take this evil matter to heart, for you are good before me.* [D] **30:2** LXX; MT omits *and everyone*

had taken; he also rescued his two wives. 19 Nothing of theirs was missing from the youngest to the oldest, including the sons and daughters, and all the plunder the Amalekites had taken. David got everything back. 20 He took all the flocks and herds, which were driven ahead of the other livestock, and the people shouted, "This is David's plunder!"

21 When David came to the two hundred men who had been too exhausted to go with him and had been left at the Wadi Besor, they came out to meet him and to meet the troops with him. When David approached the men, he greeted them, 22 but all the corrupt and worthless men among those who had gone with David argued, "Because they didn't go with us, we will not give any of the plunder we recovered to them except for each man's wife and children. They may take them and go."

23 But David said, "My brothers, you must not do this with what the LORD has given us. He protected us and handed over to us the raiders who came against us. 24 Who can agree to your proposal? The share of the one who goes into battle is to be the same as the share of the one who remains with the supplies. They will share equally." 25 And it has been so from that day forward. David established this policy[A] as a law and an ordinance for Israel and it still continues today.

26 When David came to Ziklag, he sent some of the plunder to his friends, the elders of Judah, saying, "Here is a gift for you from the plunder of the LORD's enemies." 27 He sent gifts[B] to those in Bethel, in Ramoth of the Negev, and in Jattir; 28 to those in Aroer, in Siphmoth, and in Eshtemoa; 29 to those in Racal, in the towns of the Jerahmeelites, and in the towns of the Kenites; 30 to those in Hormah, in Bor-ashan, and in Athach; 31 to those in Hebron, and to those in all the places where David and his men had roamed.

THE DEATH OF SAUL AND HIS SONS

31 The Philistines fought against Israel, and Israel's men fled from them and were killed on Mount Gilboa. 2 The Philistines pursued Saul and his sons and killed his sons, Jonathan, Abinadab, and Malchishua. 3 When the battle intensified against Saul, the archers found him and severely wounded him.[C] 4 Then Saul said to his armor-bearer, "Draw your sword and run me through with it, or these uncircumcised men will come and run me through and torture me!" But his armor-bearer would not do it because he was terrified. Then Saul took his sword and fell on it. 5 When his armor-bearer saw that Saul was dead, he also fell on his own sword and died with him. 6 So on that day, Saul died together with his three sons, his armor-bearer, and all his men.

7 When the men of Israel on the other side of the valley and on the other side of the Jordan saw that Israel's men had fled and that Saul and his sons were dead, they abandoned the cities and fled. So the Philistines came and settled in them.

8 The next day when the Philistines came to strip the slain, they found Saul and his three sons dead on Mount Gilboa. 9 They cut off Saul's head, stripped off his armor, and sent messengers throughout the land of the Philistines to spread the good news in the temples of their idols and among the people. 10 Then they put his armor in the temple of the Ashtoreths and hung his body on the wall of Beth-shan.

11 When the residents of Jabesh-gilead heard what the Philistines had done to Saul, 12 all their brave men set out, journeyed all night, and retrieved the body of Saul and the bodies of his sons from the wall of Beth-shan. When they arrived at Jabesh, they burned the bodies there. 13 Afterward, they took their bones and buried them under the tamarisk tree in Jabesh and fasted seven days.

[A] **30:25** *this policy* supplied for clarity [B] **30:27** *He sent gifts* supplied for clarity [C] **31:3** LXX reads *and he was wounded under the ribs*

2 Samuel—David's rise to the throne is legendary. He was anointed by God and, through God's power, killed lions and a giant. Shortly thereafter, however, he spent years fleeing King Saul. During that time, David wrote many psalms, questioning if God would keep his promises. Any outsider would conclude that God had abandoned him, but David kept faith.

Second Samuel begins with David mourning over the death of his maniacal enemy, Saul, even honoring him because Saul had been God's anointed. David's example of faith in God's sovereign goodness and respect for flawed leaders offers needed correction when we are tempted to doubt that God knows what he's doing.

Despite a promising beginning, later David struggled. He committed adultery with Bathsheba, had her husband killed, and failed as a father. Yet he is called God's friend, a "man after his own heart" (1Sm 13:14).

If God can use such a man, he can use us—despite our failures and defeats. David's story, with all its twists and turns, gives us hope that God can redeem any life for his good purposes. No one is beyond the reach of his restorative power.

2 SAMUEL

AUTHOR: No author is specifically named for 1 or 2 Samuel, which were likely originally written as one book. Scholars speculate that 2 Samuel was written by Nathan and Gad (1Ch 29:29), but we have no proof of authorship.

DATE WRITTEN: The reference to "kings of Judah" in 1 Samuel 27:6 places the writing of 1 and 2 Samuel after the division of Israel into northern and southern kingdoms. It was likely composed between 931 and 722 BC.

ORIGINAL AUDIENCE: The Israelites

SETTING: Continuing the account of 1 Samuel, 2 Samuel narrates the life of Israel's second and most famous king, David. He was the promised covenant king and the ancestor of the true King, Jesus Christ.

PURPOSE FOR WRITING: David had been anointed many years before (1Sm 16:1-13), and here (recorded in 2Sm) the promises God made to him finally came to fruition. God made a covenant with David—really an expansion on the covenant given to Abraham—promising him fame, rest from his enemies, and an expanding empire. This book shows the place of David in covenant history and his role as prefiguring Christ the eternal King.

OUTLINE:

1. The Rule of King David (1:1–15:6)

   Grief for Saul (1:1-27)

   King of Judah (2:1–4:12)

   Military successes (5:1–10:19)

   Sin with Bathsheba and its consequences (11:1–13:39)

   Problems with Absalom (14:1–15:6)

2. Absalom's Rebellion and David's Final Days (15:7–24:25)

   Insurrection and death of Absalom (15:7–19:8)

   David's return to Jerusalem as king (19:9–20:26)

   The latter days of David's reign (21:1–24:25)

KEY VERSES:

"He reached down from on high and took hold of me; he pulled me out of deep water. . . . He brought me out to a spacious place; he rescued me because he delighted in me."
—2 Samuel 22:17-20

RESTORATION THEMES

R	Rest and Reflection	*For the next note, see 1 Kings 3:9-10.*
E	Eternal Perspective	*God's Power—2 Samuel 7:22*
S	Support	*Humility—22:28*
T	Thanksgiving and Contentment	*Praise for God's Security—22:2-4; 23:5* *Praise for Salvation—22:47*
O	Other-centeredness	*For the next note, see Job 29:12-13.*
R	Relationships	*For the next note, see 1 Chronicles 29:17.*
E	Exercise of Faith	*For the next note, see 1 Kings 11:4.*

RESPONSES TO SAUL'S DEATH

1 After the death of Saul, David returned from
defeating the Amalekites and stayed at Ziklag two days. 2 On the third day a man with
torn clothes and dust on his head came from
Saul's camp. When he came to David, he fell
to the ground and paid homage. 3 David asked
him, "Where have you come from?"
He replied to him, "I've escaped from the
Israelite camp."
4 "What was the outcome? Tell me," David
asked him.
"The troops fled from the battle," he answered. "Many of the troops have fallen and
are dead. Also, Saul and his son Jonathan are
dead."
5 David asked the young man who had
brought him the report, "How do you know
Saul and his son Jonathan are dead?"
6 "I happened to be on Mount Gilboa," he
replied, "and there was Saul, leaning on his
spear. At that very moment the chariots and
the cavalry were closing in on him. 7 When
he turned around and saw me, he called out
to me, so I answered: I'm at your service. 8 He
asked me, 'Who are you?' I told him: I'm an
Amalekite. 9 Then he begged me, 'Stand over
me and kill me, for I'm mortally wounded,[A] but
my life still lingers.' 10 So I stood over him and
killed him because I knew that after he had
fallen he couldn't survive. I took the crown
that was on his head and the armband that
was on his arm, and I've brought them here
to my lord."
11 Then David took hold of his clothes and
tore them, and all the men with him did the
same. 12 They mourned, wept, and fasted until
the evening for those who died by the sword
— for Saul, his son Jonathan, the LORD's people, and the house of Israel.
13 David inquired of the young man who had
brought him the report, "Where are you from?"
"I'm the son of a resident alien," he said.
"I'm an Amalekite."
14 David questioned him, "How is it that you
were not afraid to lift your hand to destroy the
LORD's anointed?" 15 Then David summoned
one of his servants and said, "Come here and
kill him!" The servant struck him, and he died.
16 For David had said to the Amalekite, "Your
blood is on your own head because your own
mouth testified against you by saying, 'I killed
the LORD's anointed.'"
17 David sang the following lament for Saul
and his son Jonathan, 18 and he ordered that
the Judahites be taught The Song of the Bow.
It is written in the Book of Jashar:[B]

19 The splendor of Israel lies slain
on your heights.
How the mighty have fallen!
20 Do not tell it in Gath,
don't announce it in the marketplaces
of Ashkelon,
or the daughters of the Philistines
will rejoice,
and the daughters
of the uncircumcised will celebrate.
21 Mountains of Gilboa,
let no dew or rain be on you,
or fields of offerings,[C]
for there the shield of the mighty
was defiled —
the shield of Saul, no longer anointed
with oil.
22 Jonathan's bow never retreated,
Saul's sword never returned
unstained,[D]
from the blood of the slain,
from the flesh[E] of the mighty.
23 Saul and Jonathan,
loved and delightful,
they were not parted in life or in death.
They were swifter than eagles,
stronger than lions.
24 Daughters of Israel, weep for Saul,
who clothed you in scarlet,
with luxurious things,
who decked your garments
with gold ornaments.
25 How the mighty have fallen in the thick
of battle!
Jonathan lies slain on your heights.
26 I grieve for you, Jonathan, my brother.
You were such a friend to me.
Your love for me was more wondrous
than the love of women.
27 How the mighty have fallen
and the weapons of war
have perished!

DAVID, KING OF JUDAH

2 Some time later, David inquired of the LORD:
"Should I go to one of the towns of Judah?"
The LORD answered him, "Go."
Then David asked, "Where should I go?"
"To Hebron," the LORD replied.

[A] **1:9** LXX reads *for terrible darkness has taken hold of me* [B] **1:18** Or *of the Upright* [C] **1:21** LXX reads *firstfruits*
[D] **1:22** Lit *empty* [E] **1:22** Lit *fat*

David | Restoration Profile

RUTH; 1 SAMUEL; 2 SAMUEL; 1 CHRONICLES; PSALMS; FREQUENT NEW TESTAMENT REFERENCES

How does an eighth son get noticed? He doesn't. As the runt in the clan, David was given the chores no one else wanted. In his case, that meant days in the hills around Bethlehem tending sheep. He must have done a good job because he was all but forgotten. Whatever else being on his own at a young age taught David, it also developed a rock-solid relationship with God. By the time the prophet Samuel came along to anoint David as the king to replace Saul, God described the young man as someone "after his own heart" (1Sm 13:14). And when he applied for the mission to face the giant Goliath in a battle to the death, David gave God credit for his past survival in dangerous situations and was confident in God as he faced an apparently superior foe.

David's life is a case study in the dynamics of restoration. God continually worked on David, and David continually required restoration. The low point for David was a year-long episode of boredom, adultery, betrayal, and murder involving Bathsheba and her husband Uriah (2Sm 11). Before he could restore, God had to confront David, and David had to repent (Ps 51). Tragic consequences followed. But a broken and humbled David experienced the restoration of the joy of his salvation in his relationship with God.

Restoration never means everything is back to where it was before. Some damages are permanent, but God's restoration brings a person to a better place, not only a truthful place where sin is left behind but also a forgiven place where there is genuine hope in the future with God. Even at his very worst, David always knew he could trust God.

2 So David went there with his two wives,
Ahinoam the Jezreelite and Abigail, the widow of Nabal the Carmelite. 3 In addition, David
brought the men who were with him, each one
with his family, and they settled in the towns
near Hebron. 4 Then the men of Judah came,
and there they anointed David king over the
house of Judah. They told David: "It was the
men of Jabesh-gilead who buried Saul."
5 David sent messengers to the men of
Jabesh-gilead and said to them, "The LORD
bless you, because you have shown this kindness to Saul your lord when you buried him.
6 Now, may the LORD show kindness and faithfulness to you, and I will also show the same
goodness to you because you have done this
deed. 7 Therefore, be strong[A] and valiant, for
though Saul your lord is dead, the house of
Judah has anointed me king over them."
8 Abner son of Ner, commander of Saul's
army, took Saul's son Ish-bosheth[B,C] and moved
him to Mahanaim. 9 He made him king over Gilead, Asher, Jezreel, Ephraim, Benjamin — over
all Israel. 10 Saul's son Ish-bosheth was forty
years old when he became king over Israel;
he reigned for two years. The house of Judah,
however, followed David. 11 The length of time
that David was king in Hebron over the house
of Judah was seven years and six months.
12 Abner son of Ner and soldiers of Ish-
bosheth son of Saul marched out from Mahanaim to Gibeon. 13 So Joab son of Zeruiah and
David's soldiers marched out and met them
by the pool of Gibeon. The two groups took
up positions on opposite sides of the pool.
14 Then Abner said to Joab, "Let's have the
young men get up and compete in front of us."
"Let them get up," Joab replied.
15 So they got up and were counted off —
twelve for Benjamin and Ish-bosheth son
of Saul, and twelve from David's soldiers.
16 Then each man grabbed his opponent by
the head and thrust his sword into his opponent's side so that they all died together.
So this place, which is in Gibeon, is named
Field of Blades.[D]
17 The battle that day was extremely fierce,
and Abner and the men of Israel were defeated
by David's soldiers. 18 The three sons of Zeruiah
were there: Joab, Abishai, and Asahel. Asahel
was a fast runner, like one of the wild gazelles.
19 He chased Abner and did not turn to the

[A] **2:7** Lit *Therefore, strengthen your hands* [B] **2:8** Some LXX mss read *Ishbaal*; 1Ch 8:33; 9:39 [C] **2:8** = Man of Shame
[D] **2:16** Or *Helkath-hazzurim*

right or the left in his pursuit of him. 20 Abner glanced back and said, "Is that you, Asahel?"

"Yes it is," Asahel replied.

21 Abner said to him, "Turn to your right or left, seize one of the young soldiers, and take whatever you can get from him." But Asahel would not stop chasing him. 22 Once again, Abner warned Asahel, "Stop chasing me. Why should I strike you to the ground? How could I ever look your brother Joab in the face?"

23 But Asahel refused to turn away, so Abner hit him in the stomach with the butt of his spear. The spear went through his body, and he fell and died right there. As they all came to the place where Asahel had fallen and died, they stopped, 24 but Joab and Abishai pursued Abner. By sunset, they had gone as far as the hill of Ammah, which is opposite Giah on the way to the wilderness of Gibeon.

25 The Benjaminites rallied to Abner; they formed a unit and took their stand on top of a hill. 26 Then Abner called out to Joab: "Must the sword devour forever? Don't you realize this will only end in bitterness? How long before you tell the troops to stop pursuing their brothers?"

27 "As God lives," Joab replied, "if you had not spoken up, the troops wouldn't have stopped pursuing their brothers until morning." 28 Then Joab blew the ram's horn, and all the troops stopped; they no longer pursued Israel or continued to fight. 29 So Abner and his men marched through the Arabah all that night. They crossed the Jordan, marched all morning,[A] and arrived at Mahanaim.

30 When Joab had turned back from pursuing Abner, he gathered all the troops. In addition to Asahel, nineteen of David's soldiers were missing, 31 but they had killed 360 of the Benjaminites and Abner's men. 32 Afterward, they carried Asahel to his father's tomb in Bethlehem and buried him. Then Joab and his men marched all night and reached Hebron at dawn.

CIVIL WAR

3 During the long war between the house of Saul and the house of David, David was growing stronger and the house of Saul was becoming weaker.

2 Sons were born to David in Hebron:

His firstborn was Amnon,
by Ahinoam the Jezreelite;
3 his second was Chileab,
by Abigail, the widow of Nabal
the Carmelite;
the third was Absalom,
son of Maacah the daughter
of King Talmai of Geshur;
4 the fourth was Adonijah,
son of Haggith;
the fifth was Shephatiah,
son of Abital;
5 the sixth was Ithream,
by David's wife Eglah.

These were born to David in Hebron.

6 During the war between the house of Saul and the house of David, Abner kept acquiring more power in the house of Saul. 7 Now Saul had a concubine whose name was Rizpah daughter of Aiah, and Ish-bosheth questioned Abner, "Why did you sleep with my father's concubine?"

8 Abner was very angry about Ish-bosheth's accusation. "Am I a dog's head[B] who belongs to Judah?" he asked. "All this time I've been loyal to the family of your father Saul, to his brothers, and to his friends and haven't betrayed you to David, but now you accuse me of wrongdoing with this woman! 9 May God punish Abner and do so severely if I don't do for David what the LORD swore to him: 10 to transfer the kingdom from the house of Saul and establish the throne of David over Israel and Judah from Dan to Beer-sheba." 11 Ish-bosheth did not dare respond to Abner because he was afraid of him.

12 Abner sent messengers as his representatives to say to David, "Whose land is it? Make your covenant with me, and you can be certain I am on your side to turn all Israel over to you."

13 David replied, "Good, I will make a covenant with you. However, there's one thing I require of you: You will not see my face unless you first bring Saul's daughter Michal when you come to see me."

14 Then David sent messengers to say to Ish-bosheth son of Saul, "Give me back my wife, Michal. I was engaged to her for the price of a hundred Philistine foreskins."

15 So Ish-bosheth sent someone to take her away from her husband, Paltiel son of Laish. 16 Her husband followed her, weeping all the way to Bahurim. Abner said to him, "Go back." So he went back.

[A] **2:29** Or *marched through the Bithron* [B] **3:8** = a despised person

THE ASSASSINATION OF ABNER

17 Abner conferred with the elders of Israel:
"In the past you wanted David to be king over
you. 18 Now take action, because the LORD has
spoken concerning David: 'Through my servant David I will save my people Israel from
the power of the Philistines and the power of
all Israel's enemies.' "

19 Abner also informed the Benjaminites and
went to Hebron to inform David about all that
was agreed on by Israel and the whole house
of Benjamin. 20 When Abner and twenty men
came to David at Hebron, David held a banquet
for him and his men.

21 Abner said to David, "Let me now go and I
will gather all Israel to my lord the king. They
will make a covenant with you, and you will
reign over all you desire." So David dismissed
Abner, and he went in peace.

22 Just then David's soldiers and Joab returned from a raid and brought a large amount
of plundered goods with them. Abner was not
with David in Hebron because David had dismissed him, and he had gone in peace. 23 When
Joab and his whole army arrived, Joab was
informed, "Abner son of Ner came to see the
king, the king dismissed him, and he went
in peace."

24 Joab went to the king and said, "What have
you done? Look here, Abner came to you. Why
did you dismiss him? Now he's getting away.
25 You know that Abner son of Ner came to
deceive you and to find out about your military activities[A] and everything you're doing."
26 Then Joab left David and sent messengers
after Abner. They brought him back from
the well[B] of Sirah, but David was unaware of
it. 27 When Abner returned to Hebron, Joab
pulled him aside to the middle of the city gate,
as if to speak to him privately, and there Joab
stabbed him in the stomach. So Abner died
in revenge for the death of Asahel,[C] Joab's
brother.

28 David heard about it later and said: "I and
my kingdom are forever innocent before the
LORD concerning the blood of Abner son of
Ner. 29 May it hang over Joab's head and his
father's whole family, and may the house of
Joab never be without someone who has a
discharge or a skin disease, or a man who
can only work a spindle,[D] or someone who
falls by the sword or starves." 30 Joab and his
brother Abishai killed Abner because he had
put their brother Asahel to death in the battle
at Gibeon.

31 David then ordered Joab and all the people
who were with him, "Tear your clothes, put on
sackcloth, and mourn over Abner." And King
David walked behind the coffin.[E]

32 When they buried Abner in Hebron, the
king wept aloud at Abner's tomb. All the people
wept, 33 and the king sang a lament for Abner:

Should Abner die as a fool dies?
34 Your hands were not bound,
your feet not placed in bronze shackles.
You fell like one who falls victim
to criminals.

And all the people wept over him even more.

35 Then they came to urge David to eat food
while it was still day, but David took an oath:
"May God punish me and do so severely if I
taste bread or anything else before sunset!"
36 All the people took note of this, and it pleased
them. In fact, everything the king did pleased
them. 37 On that day all the troops and all Israel
were convinced that the king had no part in
the killing of Abner son of Ner.

38 Then the king said to his soldiers, "You
must know that a great leader has fallen in
Israel today. 39 As for me, even though I am
the anointed king, I have little power today.
These men, the sons of Zeruiah, are too fierce
for me. May the LORD repay the evildoer according to his evil!"

THE ASSASSINATION OF ISH-BOSHETH

4 When Saul's son Ish-bosheth heard that
Abner had died in Hebron, he gave up,[F] and
all Israel was dismayed. 2 Saul's son had two
men who were leaders of raiding parties: one
named Baanah and the other Rechab, sons of
Rimmon the Beerothite of the Benjaminites.
Beeroth is also considered part of Benjamin,
3 and the Beerothites fled to Gittaim and still
reside there as aliens today.

4 Saul's son Jonathan had a son whose feet
were crippled. He was five years old when the
report about Saul and Jonathan came from
Jezreel. His nanny[G] picked him up and fled,
but as she was hurrying to flee, he fell and
became lame. His name was Mephibosheth.

5 Rechab and Baanah, the sons of Rimmon
the Beerothite, set out and arrived at Ish-
bosheth's house during the heat of the day
while the king was taking his midday nap.
6 They entered the interior of the house as if

[A] **3:25** Lit *your going out and your coming in* [B] **3:26** Or *cistern* [C] **3:27** Lit *And he died for the blood of Asahel*
[D] **3:29** LXX reads *who uses a crutch* [E] **3:31** Or *the bier*; lit *the bed* [F] **4:1** Lit *his hands dropped* [G] **4:4** Lit *His nurse*

to get wheat and stabbed him in the stomach. Then Rechab and his brother Baanah escaped. 7 They had entered the house while Ish-bosheth was lying on his bed in his bedroom and stabbed and killed him. They removed his head, took it, and traveled by way of the Arabah all night. 8 They brought Ish-bosheth's head to David at Hebron and said to the king, "Here's the head of Ish-bosheth son of Saul, your enemy who intended to take your life. Today the LORD has granted vengeance to my lord the king against Saul and his offspring."

9 But David answered Rechab and his brother Baanah, sons of Rimmon the Beerothite, "As the LORD lives, the one who has redeemed my life from every distress, 10 when the person told me, 'Look, Saul is dead,' he thought he was a bearer of good news, but I seized him and put him to death at Ziklag. That was my reward to him for his news! 11 How much more when wicked men kill a righteous man in his own house on his own bed! So now, should I not require his blood from you and purge you from the earth?"

12 So David gave orders to the young men, and they killed Rechab and Baanah. They cut off their hands and feet and hung their bodies by the pool in Hebron, but they took Ish-bosheth's head and buried it in Abner's tomb in Hebron.

DAVID, KING OF ISRAEL

5 All the tribes of Israel came to David at Hebron and said, "Here we are, your own flesh and blood.[A] 2 Even while Saul was king over us, you were the one who led us out to battle and brought us back. The LORD also said to you, 'You will shepherd my people Israel, and you will be ruler over Israel.'"

3 So all the elders of Israel came to the king at Hebron. King David made a covenant with them at Hebron in the LORD's presence, and they anointed David king over Israel.

4 David was thirty years old when he began his reign; he reigned forty years. 5 In Hebron he reigned over Judah seven years and six months, and in Jerusalem he reigned thirty-three years over all Israel and Judah.

6 The king and his men marched to Jerusalem against the Jebusites who inhabited the land. The Jebusites had said to David: "You will never get in here. Even the blind and lame can repel you" thinking, "David can't get in here."

7 Yet David did capture the stronghold of Zion, that is, the city of David. 8 He said that day, "Whoever attacks the Jebusites must go through the water shaft to reach the lame and the blind who are despised by David."[B] For this reason it is said, "The blind and the lame will never enter the house."[C]

9 David took up residence in the stronghold, which he named the city of David. He built it up all the way around from the supporting terraces inward. 10 David became more and more powerful, and the LORD God of Armies was with him. 11 King Hiram of Tyre sent envoys to David; he also sent cedar logs, carpenters, and stonemasons, and they built a palace for David. 12 Then David knew that the LORD had established him as king over Israel and had exalted his kingdom for the sake of his people Israel.

13 After he arrived from Hebron, David took more concubines and wives from Jerusalem,

David knew that the LORD had established him as king over Israel and had exalted his kingdom for the sake of his people Israel.

—2 Samuel 5:12

and more sons and daughters were born to him. 14 These are the names of those born to him in Jerusalem: Shammua, Shobab, Nathan, Solomon, 15 Ibhar, Elishua, Nepheg, Japhia, 16 Elishama, Eliada, and Eliphelet.

17 When the Philistines heard that David had been anointed king over Israel, they all went in search of David, but he heard about it and went down to the stronghold. 18 So the Philistines came and spread out in the Valley of Rephaim.

19 Then David inquired of the LORD: "Should I attack the Philistines? Will you hand them over to me?"

The LORD replied to David, "Attack, for I will certainly hand the Philistines over to you."

20 So David went to Baal-perazim and defeated them there and said, "Like a bursting flood, the LORD has burst out against my enemies

[A] **5:1** Lit *your bone and your flesh* [B] **5:8** Alt Hb tradition, LXX, Tg, Syr read *who despise David* [C] **5:8** Or *temple*, or *palace*

before me." Therefore, he named that place The Lord Bursts Out.[A] 21 The Philistines abandoned their idols there, and David and his men carried them off.

22 The Philistines came up again and spread out in the Valley of Rephaim. 23 So David inquired of the LORD, and he answered, "Do not attack directly, but circle around behind them and come at them opposite the balsam trees. 24 When you hear the sound of marching in the tops of the balsam trees, act decisively, for then the LORD will have gone out ahead of you to strike down the army of the Philistines." 25 So David did exactly as the LORD commanded him, and he struck down the Philistines all the way from Geba to Gezer.

DAVID MOVES THE ARK

6 David again assembled all the fit young men in Israel: thirty thousand. 2 He and all his troops set out to bring the ark of God from Baale-judah.[B] The ark bears the Name, the name of the LORD of Armies who is enthroned between the cherubim. 3 They set the ark of God on a new cart and transported it from Abinadab's house, which was on the hill. Uzzah and Ahio,[C] sons of Abinadab, were guiding the cart 4 and brought it with the ark of God from Abinadab's house on the hill. Ahio walked in front of the ark. 5 David and the whole house of Israel were dancing before the LORD with all kinds of fir wood instruments,[D] lyres, harps, tambourines, sistrums,[E] and cymbals.

6 When they came to Nacon's threshing floor, Uzzah reached out to the ark of God and took hold of it because the oxen had stumbled. 7 Then the LORD's anger burned against Uzzah, and God struck him dead on the spot for his irreverence, and he died there next to the ark of God. 8 David was angry because of the LORD's outburst against Uzzah, so he named that place Outburst Against Uzzah,[F] as it is today. 9 David feared the LORD that day and said, "How can the ark of the LORD ever come to me?" 10 So he was not willing to bring the ark of the LORD to the city of David; instead, he diverted it to the house of Obed-edom of Gath. 11 The ark of the LORD remained in his house three months, and the LORD blessed Obed-edom and his whole family.

12 It was reported to King David: "The LORD has blessed Obed-edom's family and all that belongs to him because of the ark of God." So David went and had the ark of God brought up from Obed-edom's house to the city of David with rejoicing. 13 When those carrying the ark of the LORD advanced six steps, he sacrificed an ox and a fattened calf. 14 David was dancing[G] with all his might before the LORD wearing a linen ephod. 15 He and the whole house of Israel were bringing up the ark of the LORD with shouts and the sound of the ram's horn. 16 As the ark of the LORD was entering the city of David, Saul's daughter Michal looked down from the window and saw King David leaping and dancing before the LORD, and she despised him in her heart.

17 They brought the ark of the LORD and set it in its place inside the tent David had pitched for it. Then David offered burnt offerings and fellowship offerings in the LORD's presence. 18 When David had finished offering the burnt offering and the fellowship offerings, he blessed the people in the name of the LORD of Armies. 19 Then he distributed a loaf of bread, a date cake, and a raisin cake to each one in the entire Israelite community, both men and women. Then all the people went home.

20 When David returned home to bless his household, Saul's daughter Michal came out to meet him. "How the king of Israel honored himself today!" she said. "He exposed himself today in the sight of the slave girls of his subjects like a vulgar person would expose himself."

21 David replied to Michal, "It was before the LORD who chose me over your father and his whole family to appoint me ruler over the LORD's people Israel. I will dance before the LORD, 22 and I will dishonor myself and humble myself even more.[H,I] However, by the slave girls you spoke about, I will be honored." 23 And Saul's daughter Michal had no child to the day of her death.

THE LORD'S COVENANT WITH DAVID

7 When the king had settled into his palace and the LORD had given him rest on every side from all his enemies, 2 the king said to the prophet Nathan, "Look, I am living in a cedar house while the ark of God sits inside tent curtains."

[A] **5:20** Or *Baal-perazim*; 2Sm 6:8; 1Ch 13:11 [B] **6:2** = Kiriath-jearim in 1Sm 7:1; 1Ch 13:6; 2Ch 1:4 [C] **6:3** Or *And his brothers*
[D] **6:5** DSS, LXX read *with tuned instruments with strength, with songs*; 1Ch 13:8 [E] **6:5** = an Egyptian percussion instrument
[F] **6:8** Or *Perez-uzzah*; 2Sm 5:20 [G] **6:14** Or *whirling* [H] **6:22** LXX reads *more and I will be humble in your eyes* [I] **6:22** Lit *more and I will be humble in my own eyes*

[3] So Nathan told the king, "Go and do all that
is on your mind, for the LORD is with you."
[4] But that night the word of the LORD came
to Nathan: [5] "Go to my servant David and say,
'This is what the LORD says: Are you to build me
a house to dwell in? [6] From the time I brought
the Israelites out of Egypt until today I have
not dwelt in a house; instead, I have been moving around with a tent as my dwelling. [7] In
all my journeys with all the Israelites, have
I ever spoken a word to one of the tribes of
Israel, whom I commanded to shepherd my
people Israel, asking: Why haven't you built
me a house of cedar?'
[8] "So now this is what you are to say to my
servant David: 'This is what the LORD of Armies says: I took you from the pasture, from
tending the flock, to be ruler over my people
Israel. [9] I have been with you wherever you
have gone, and I have destroyed all your enemies before you. I will make a great name
for you like that of the greatest on the earth.
[10] I will designate a place for my people Israel
and plant them, so that they may live there
and not be disturbed again. Evildoers will
not continue to oppress them as they have
done [11] ever since the day I ordered judges to
be over my people Israel. I will give you rest
from all your enemies.
"'The LORD declares to you: The LORD himself will make a house for you. [12] When your
time comes and you rest with your fathers, I
will raise up after you your descendant, who
will come from your body, and I will establish
his kingdom. [13] He is the one who will build a
house for my name, and I will establish the
throne of his kingdom forever. [14] I will be his
father, and he will be my son. When he does
wrong, I will discipline him with a rod of men
and blows from mortals. [15] But my faithful love
will never leave him as it did when I removed
it from Saul, whom I removed from before
you. [16] Your house and kingdom will endure
before me[A] forever, and your throne will be
established forever.'"
[17] Nathan reported all these words and this
entire vision to David.

DAVID'S PRAYER OF THANKSGIVING

[18] Then King David went in, sat in the LORD's
presence, and said,

Who am I, Lord GOD, and what is my
house that you have brought me this far?
[19] What you have done so far[B] was a little
thing to you, Lord GOD, for you have also
spoken about your servant's house in the
distant future. And this is a revelation[C]
for mankind, Lord GOD. [20] What more can
David say to you? You know your servant,
Lord GOD. [21] Because of your word and
according to your will, you have revealed
all these great things to your servant.

Eternal Perspective | *God's Power*

GOD THE ONE AND ONLY

"This is why you are great, Lord GOD. There is no one like you, and there is no God besides you, as all we have heard confirms." 2 Samuel 7:22

When people are sad or fearful, stressed or confused, they tend to run in many different directions. Some seek comfort in food or shopping, sex or chemicals. Others look for escape in entertainment or porn. Even good gifts like vacations, exercise, work, and other people can be used as pain relievers or escapes from reality.

Imagine the swirling feelings inside David when he was assuming the kingship of Israel. Surely he was bombarded by a thousand whispering voices. No question he felt immense pressure. Given his position, he could have gone any number of ways. Thankfully he recognized that God is "great," like no one and nothing else. And if he is the one, true God, it means everything else is a substitute savior.

Follow David's convictions: finite possessions, people, and experiences can numb us and distract us temporarily, but only the love of our infinite God can meet the deep needs of our hearts.

For the next note on *Eternal Perspective*, see 2 Kings 6:16-17.

[A] **7:16** Some Hb mss, LXX, Syr; other Hb mss read *you* [B] **7:19** Lit *Yet this* [C] **7:19** Or *custom*, or *instruction*

22 This is why you are great, Lord God.
There is no one like you, and there is no
God besides you, as all we have heard
confirms. 23 And who is like your people
Israel? God came to one nation on earth
in order to redeem a people for himself,
to make a name for himself, and to perform for them[A] great and awesome acts,[B]
driving out nations and their gods before
your people you redeemed for yourself
from Egypt. 24 You established your people Israel to be your own people forever,
and you, LORD, have become their God.

25 Now, LORD God, fulfill the promise forever that you have made to your servant
and his house. Do as you have promised,
26 so that your name will be exalted forever, when it is said, "The LORD of Armies is
God over Israel." The house of your servant David will be established before you
27 since you, LORD of Armies, God of Israel,
have revealed this to your servant when
you said, "I will build a house for you."
Therefore, your servant has found the
courage to pray this prayer to you. 28 Lord
GOD, you are God; your words are true,
and you have promised this good thing
to your servant. 29 Now, please bless your
servant's house so that it will continue
before you forever. For you, Lord GOD,
have spoken, and with your blessing your
servant's house will be blessed forever.

DAVID'S VICTORIES

8 After this, David defeated the Philistines,
subdued them, and took Metheg-ammah[C]
from Philistine control.[D] 2 He also defeated the
Moabites, and after making them lie down
on the ground, he measured them off with a
cord. He measured every two cord lengths of
those to be put to death and one full length of
those to be kept alive. So the Moabites became
David's subjects and brought tribute.
3 David also defeated Hadadezer son of Rehob, king of Zobah, when he went to restore his
control at the Euphrates River. 4 David captured
seventeen hundred horsemen[E] and twenty thousand foot soldiers from him, and he hamstrung
all the horses and kept a hundred chariots.[F]
5 When the Arameans of Damascus came to
assist King Hadadezer of Zobah, David struck
down twenty-two thousand Aramean men.
6 Then he placed garrisons in Aram of Damascus, and the Arameans became David's
subjects and brought tribute. The LORD made
David victorious wherever he went.
7 David took the gold shields of Hadadezer's
officers and brought them to Jerusalem. 8 King
David also took huge quantities of bronze from
Betah[G] and Berothai, Hadadezer's cities.
9 When King Toi of Hamath heard that David
had defeated the entire army of Hadadezer, 10 he
sent his son Joram to King David to greet him
and to congratulate him because David had
fought against Hadadezer and defeated him,
for Toi and Hadadezer had fought many wars.
Joram had items of silver, gold, and bronze
with him. 11 King David also dedicated these
to the LORD, along with the silver and gold he
had dedicated from all the nations he had subdued — 12 from Edom,[H] Moab, the Ammonites,
the Philistines, the Amalekites, and the spoil
of Hadadezer son of Rehob, king of Zobah.
13 David made a reputation for himself
when he returned from striking down eighteen thousand Edomites[I] in Salt Valley.[J] 14 He
placed garrisons throughout Edom, and all
the Edomites were subject to David. The LORD
made David victorious wherever he went.
15 So David reigned over all Israel, administering justice and righteousness for all his
people.

16 Joab son of Zeruiah was over the army;
Jehoshaphat son of Ahilud was
court historian;
17 Zadok son of Ahitub and Ahimelech
son of Abiathar were priests;
Seraiah was court secretary;
18 Benaiah son of Jehoiada was over the
Cherethites and the Pelethites;
and David's sons were chief officials.[K]

DAVID'S KINDNESS TO MEPHIBOSHETH

9 David asked, "Is there anyone remaining
from the family of Saul I can show kindness
to for Jonathan's sake?" 2 There was a servant
of Saul's family named Ziba. They summoned
him to David, and the king said to him, "Are
you Ziba?"

[A] **7:23** Some Hb mss, Tg, Vg, Syr; other Hb mss read *you* [B] **7:23** LXX; MT reads *acts for your land* [C] **8:1** Or *took control of the mother city*; Hb obscure [D] **8:1** LXX reads *them, and David took tribute out of the hand of the Philistines* [E] **8:4** LXX, DSS read *1,000 chariots and 7,000 horsemen* [F] **8:4** Or *chariot horses* [G] **8:8** Some LXX mss, Syr read *Tebah* [H] **8:12** Some Hb mss, LXX, Syr; other Hb mss read *Aram*; 1Ch 18:11 [I] **8:13** Some Hb mss, LXX, Syr; other Hb mss read *Arameans*; 1Ch 18:12 [J] **8:13** = the Dead Sea region [K] **8:18** LXX; MT reads *were priests*; 1Ch 18:17

"I am your servant," he replied.

3 So the king asked, "Is there anyone left of Saul's family that I can show the kindness of God to?"

Ziba said to the king, "There is still Jonathan's son who was injured in both feet."

4 The king asked him, "Where is he?"

Ziba answered the king, "You'll find him in Lo-debar at the house of Machir son of Ammiel." 5 So King David had him brought from the house of Machir son of Ammiel in Lo-debar.

6 Mephibosheth son of Jonathan son of Saul came to David, fell facedown, and paid homage. David said, "Mephibosheth!"

"I am your servant," he replied.

7 "Don't be afraid," David said to him, "since I intend to show you kindness for the sake of your father Jonathan. I will restore to you all your grandfather Saul's fields, and you will always eat meals at my table."

8 Mephibosheth paid homage and said, "What is your servant that you take an interest in a dead dog like me?"

9 Then the king summoned Saul's attendant Ziba and said to him, "I have given to your master's grandson all that belonged to Saul and his family. 10 You, your sons, and your servants are to work the ground for him, and you are to bring in the crops so your master's grandson will have food to eat. But Mephibosheth, your master's grandson, is always to eat at my table." Now Ziba had fifteen sons and twenty servants.

11 Ziba said to the king, "Your servant will do all my lord the king commands."

So Mephibosheth ate at David's[A] table just like one of the king's sons. 12 Mephibosheth had a young son whose name was Mica. All those living in Ziba's house were Mephibosheth's servants. 13 However, Mephibosheth lived in Jerusalem because he always ate at the king's table. His feet had been injured.

WAR WITH THE AMMONITES

10 Some time later, the king of the Ammonites died, and his son Hanun became king in his place. 2 Then David said, "I'll show kindness to Hanun son of Nahash, just as his father showed kindness to me."

So David sent his emissaries to console Hanun concerning his father. However, when they arrived in the land of the Ammonites, 3 the Ammonite leaders said to Hanun their lord, "Just because David has sent men with condolences for you, do you really believe he's showing respect for your father? Instead, hasn't David sent his emissaries in order to scout out the city, spy on it, and demolish it?" 4 So Hanun took David's emissaries, shaved off half their beards, cut their clothes in half at the hips, and sent them away.

5 When this was reported to David, he sent someone to meet them, since they were deeply humiliated. The king said, "Stay in Jericho until your beards grow back; then return."

6 When the Ammonites realized they had become repulsive to David, they hired twenty thousand foot soldiers from the Arameans of Beth-rehob and Zobah, one thousand men from the king of Maacah, and twelve thousand men from Tob.

7 David heard about it and sent Joab and all the elite troops. 8 The Ammonites marched out and lined up in battle formation at the entrance to the city gate while the Arameans of Zobah and Rehob and the men of Tob and Maacah were in the field by themselves. 9 When Joab saw that there was a battle line in front of him and another behind him, he chose some of Israel's finest young men and lined up in formation to engage the Arameans. 10 He placed the rest of the forces under the command of his brother Abishai. They lined up in formation to engage the Ammonites.

11 "If the Arameans are too strong for me," Joab said, "then you will be my help. However, if the Ammonites are too strong for you, I'll come to help you. 12 Be strong! Let's prove ourselves strong for our people and for the cities of our God. May the LORD's will be done."[B]

13 Joab and his troops advanced to fight against the Arameans, and they fled before him. 14 When the Ammonites saw that the Arameans had fled, they too fled before Abishai and entered the city. So Joab withdrew from the attack against the Ammonites and went to Jerusalem.

15 When the Arameans saw that they had been defeated by Israel, they regrouped. 16 Hadadezer sent messengers to bring the Arameans who were beyond the Euphrates River, and they came to Helam with Shobach, commander of Hadadezer's army, leading them.

17 When this was reported to David, he gathered all Israel, crossed the Jordan, and went to Helam. Then the Arameans lined up to engage David in battle and fought against him.

[A] **9:11** LXX; Syr reads *the king's*; Vg reads *your*; MT reads *my* [B] **10:12** Lit *the LORD do what is good in his eyes*

18 But the Arameans fled before Israel, and David killed seven hundred of their charioteers and forty thousand foot soldiers.[A] He also struck down Shobach commander of their army, who died there. 19 When all the kings who were Hadadezer's subjects saw that they had been defeated by Israel, they made peace with Israel and became their subjects. After this, the Arameans were afraid to ever help the Ammonites again.

DAVID'S ADULTERY WITH BATHSHEBA

11 In the spring when kings march out to war, David sent Joab with his officers and all Israel. They destroyed the Ammonites and besieged Rabbah, but David remained in Jerusalem.

2 One evening David got up from his bed and strolled around on the roof of the palace. From the roof he saw a woman bathing — a very beautiful woman. 3 So David sent someone to inquire about her, and he said, "Isn't this Bathsheba, daughter of Eliam and wife of Uriah the Hethite?"[B]

4 David sent messengers to get her, and when she came to him, he slept with her. Now she had just been purifying herself from her uncleanness. Afterward, she returned home. 5 The woman conceived and sent word to inform David: "I am pregnant."

6 David sent orders to Joab: "Send me Uriah the Hethite." So Joab sent Uriah to David. 7 When Uriah came to him, David asked how Joab and the troops were doing and how the war was going. 8 Then he said to Uriah, "Go down to your house and wash your feet." So Uriah left the palace, and a gift from the king followed him. 9 But Uriah slept at the door of the palace with all his master's servants; he did not go down to his house.

10 When it was reported to David, "Uriah didn't go home," David questioned Uriah, "Haven't you just come from a journey? Why didn't you go home?"

11 Uriah answered David, "The ark, Israel, and Judah are dwelling in tents, and my master Joab and his soldiers[C] are camping in the open field. How can I enter my house to eat and drink and sleep with my wife? As surely as you live and by your life, I will not do this!"

12 "Stay here today also," David said to Uriah, "and tomorrow I will send you back." So Uriah stayed in Jerusalem that day and the next. 13 Then David invited Uriah to eat and drink with him, and David got him drunk. He went out in the evening to lie down on his cot with his master's servants, but he did not go home.

URIAH'S DEATH ARRANGED

14 The next morning David wrote a letter to Joab and sent it with Uriah. 15 In the letter he wrote:

> Put Uriah at the front of the fiercest fighting, then withdraw from him so that he is struck down and dies.

16 When Joab was besieging the city, he put Uriah in the place where he knew the best enemy soldiers were. 17 Then the men of the city came out and attacked Joab, and some of the men from David's soldiers fell in battle; Uriah the Hethite also died.

18 Joab sent someone to report to David all the details of the battle. 19 He commanded the messenger, "When you've finished telling the king all the details of the battle — 20 if the king's anger gets stirred up and he asks you, 'Why did you get so close to the city to fight? Didn't you realize they would shoot from the top of the wall? 21 At Thebez, who struck Abimelech son of Jerubbesheth?[D,E] Didn't a woman drop an upper millstone on him from the top of the wall so that he died? Why did you get so close to the wall?' — then say, 'Your servant Uriah the Hethite is dead also.'" 22 Then the messenger left.

When he arrived, he reported to David all that Joab had sent him to tell. 23 The messenger reported to David, "The men gained the advantage over us and came out against us in the field, but we counterattacked right up to the entrance of the city gate. 24 However, the archers shot down on your servants from the top of the wall, and some of the king's servants died. Your servant Uriah the Hethite is also dead."

25 David told the messenger, "Say this to Joab: 'Don't let this matter upset you because the sword devours all alike. Intensify your fight against the city and demolish it.' Encourage him."

26 When Uriah's wife heard that her husband Uriah had died, she mourned for him.[F] 27 When the time of mourning ended, David had her brought to his house. She became his wife and bore him a son. However, the LORD considered what David had done to be evil.

[A] **10:18** Some LXX mss; MT reads *horsemen*; 1Ch 19:18 [B] **11:3** DSS add *Joab's armor-bearer* [C] **11:11** Lit *servants*
[D] **11:21** LXX reads *Jerubbaal* [E] **11:21** = Gideon [F] **11:26** Lit *her husband*

NATHAN'S PARABLE AND DAVID'S REPENTANCE

12 So the LORD sent Nathan to David. When he arrived, he said to him:

There were two men in a certain city, one rich and the other poor. 2 The rich man had very large flocks and herds, 3 but the poor man had nothing except one small ewe lamb that he had bought. He raised her, and she grew up with him and with his children. From his meager food she would eat, from his cup she would drink, and in his arms she would sleep. She was like a daughter to him. 4 Now a traveler came to the rich man, but the rich man could not bring himself to take one of his own sheep or cattle to prepare for the traveler who had come to him. Instead, he took the poor man's lamb and prepared it for his guest.[A]

5 David was infuriated with the man and said to Nathan: "As the LORD lives, the man who did this deserves to die! 6 Because he has done this thing and shown no pity, he must pay four lambs for that lamb."

7 Nathan replied to David, "You are the man! This is what the LORD God of Israel says: 'I anointed you king over Israel, and I rescued you from Saul. 8 I gave your master's house to you and your master's wives into your arms,[B] and I gave you the house of Israel and Judah, and if that was not enough, I would have given you even more. 9 Why then have you despised the LORD's command by doing what I consider[C] evil? You struck down Uriah the Hethite with the sword and took his wife as your own wife — you murdered him with the Ammonite's sword. 10 Now therefore, the sword will never leave your house because you despised me and took the wife of Uriah the Hethite to be your own wife.'

11 "This is what the LORD says, 'I am going to bring disaster on you from your own family: I will take your wives and give them to another[D] before your very eyes, and he will sleep with them in broad daylight.[E] 12 You acted in secret, but I will do this before all Israel and in broad daylight.'"[F]

13 David responded to Nathan, "I have sinned against the LORD."

Then Nathan replied to David, "And the LORD has taken away your sin; you will not die. 14 However, because you treated[G] the LORD with such contempt in this matter, the son born to you will die." 15 Then Nathan went home.

THE DEATH OF BATHSHEBA'S SON

The LORD struck the baby that Uriah's wife had borne to David, and he became deathly ill. 16 David pleaded with God for the boy. He fasted, went home, and spent the night lying on the ground. 17 The elders of his house stood beside him to get him up from the ground, but he was unwilling and would not eat anything with them.

18 On the seventh day the baby died. But David's servants were afraid to tell him the baby was dead. They said, "Look, while the baby was alive, we spoke to him, and he wouldn't listen to us. So how can we tell him the baby is dead? He may do something desperate."

19 When David saw that his servants were whispering to each other, he guessed that the baby was dead. So he asked his servants, "Is the baby dead?"

"He is dead," they replied.

20 Then David got up from the ground. He washed, anointed himself, changed his clothes, went to the LORD's house, and worshiped. Then he went home and requested something to eat. So they served him food, and he ate.

21 His servants asked him, "Why have you done this? While the baby was alive, you fasted and wept, but when he died, you got up and ate food."

22 He answered, "While the baby was alive, I fasted and wept because I thought, 'Who knows? The LORD may be gracious to me and let him live.' 23 But now that he is dead, why should I fast? Can I bring him back again? I'll go to him, but he will never return to me."

THE BIRTH OF SOLOMON

24 Then David comforted his wife Bathsheba; he went to her and slept with her. She gave birth to a son and named[H] him Solomon.[I] The LORD loved him, 25 and he sent a message through the prophet Nathan, who named[J] him Jedidiah,[K] because of the LORD.

CAPTURE OF THE CITY OF RABBAH

26 Joab fought against Rabbah of the Ammonites and captured the royal fortress. 27 Then Joab

[A] 12:4 Lit *for the man who had come to him* [B] 12:8 Lit *bosom* [C] 12:9 Alt Hb tradition reads *what he considers* [D] 12:11 Or *to your neighbor* [E] 12:11 Lit *in the eyes of this sun* [F] 12:12 Lit *and before the sun* [G] 12:14 Alt Hb tradition, one LXX ms; MT reads *treated the enemies of*; DSS read *treated the word of* [H] 12:24 Alt Hb tradition reads *he named* [I] 12:24 In Hb, the name *Solomon* sounds like "peace." [J] 12:25 Or *prophet to name* [K] 12:25 = Beloved of the LORD

My Story | Joey

Childhood sins become haunting memories. The deeds done in secret with others remain like axes about to fall or a continually eroding at the foundations of life. The discovery of God's forgiveness sets things right with the universe, but what about the unsettled matters of lingering guilt toward others? I knew God had forgiven me for past sins that had violated others, but doubts remained about the possibility of forgiveness at the human level. Could those I hurt forgive me? Could I summon the courage to confess to them; could I ask for forgiveness and bear the vulnerability of waiting to hear if they would or not?

These questions hindered my spiritual growth and often made my efforts to share my faith with others seem hypocritical. When I told an older believer about these misgivings, his answer set me on a course that would change my life. He told me that recurrent guilt has basically two sources: the Holy Spirit or the devil. The Holy Spirit confronts us with unconfessed sin that we might be free; the devil reminds us of past sin in order to keep us in bondage. When the Bible urges us to confess to one another, the point is not to obtain forgiveness that comes from God but to offer one another *assurance* of forgiveness. He went on to deal with my loss of contact with the person with whom I most wanted to reconcile, advising me, "God knows where this person is and whether it's important for you to ask her for forgiveness. If you've settled things with God, let him decide about finding that person. Be ready to seek forgiveness from her should the opportunity arise. Until that happens, refuse to think of recurring guilt as nothing more than your enemy trying to bring up settled matters to unsettle you."

I took his advice and settled in for a wait. I had no idea how to even begin tracing this person's whereabouts. Three days later, *she* called *me*. She had found me because she wanted to ask a favor. I interrupted with almost a rude insistence that I had to ask her something first. I briefly referred to our childhood and told her I had carried guilt for mistreating her many years before. I knew I had been wrong and wanted to ask her to forgive me.

The silence on the other end of the phone almost killed me. After what seemed like too long, she said, "I didn't answer immediately because I was trying to remember what you could possibly have in mind. I gladly forgive you, but I have to say I don't remember anything you ever did that hurt me." Her forgiveness was an unexpected double restoration. I was not only set free from my own memories, I was freed from thinking she had been weighed down with the same guilt that had haunted me. I also realized God really takes seriously every aspect of forgiveness.

sent messengers to David to say, "I have fought
against Rabbah and have also captured its water supply. 28 Now therefore, assemble the rest
of the troops, lay siege to the city, and capture
it. Otherwise I will be the one to capture the
city, and it will be named after me." 29 So David
assembled all the troops and went to Rabbah;
he fought against it and captured it. 30 He took
the crown from the head of their king,[A] and it
was placed on David's head. The crown weighed
seventy-five pounds[B] of gold, and it had a precious stone in it. In addition, David took away
a large quantity of plunder from the city. 31 He
removed the people who were in the city and
put them to work with saws, iron picks, and
iron axes, and to labor at brickmaking. He did
the same to all the Ammonite cities. Then he
and all his troops returned to Jerusalem.

AMNON RAPES TAMAR

13 Some time passed. David's son Absalom
had a beautiful sister named Tamar,
and David's son Amnon was infatuated with
her. 2 Amnon was frustrated to the point of
making himself sick over his sister Tamar
because she was a virgin, but it seemed impossible to do anything to her. 3 Amnon had
a friend named Jonadab, a son of David's
brother Shimeah. Jonadab was a very shrewd
man, 4 and he asked Amnon, "Why are you,
the king's son, so miserable every morning?
Won't you tell me?"

Amnon replied, "I'm in love with Tamar, my
brother Absalom's sister."

5 Jonadab said to him, "Lie down on your
bed and pretend you're sick. When your father
comes to see you, say to him, 'Please let my

[A] **12:30** LXX reads *of Milcom*; some emend to *Molech*; 1Kg 11:5,33 [B] **12:30** Lit *a talent*

sister Tamar come and give me something to
eat. Let her prepare a meal in my presence so
I can watch and eat from her hand.' "
6 So Amnon lay down and pretended to be
sick. When the king came to see him, Amnon
said to him, "Please let my sister Tamar come
and make a couple of cakes in my presence
so I can eat from her hand."
7 David sent word to Tamar at the palace:
"Please go to your brother Amnon's house
and prepare a meal for him."
8 Then Tamar went to his house while Amnon was lying down. She took dough, kneaded
it, made cakes in his presence, and baked
them. 9 She brought the pan and set it down
in front of him, but he refused to eat. Amnon
said, "Everyone leave me! " And everyone
left him. 10 "Bring the meal to the bedroom,"
Amnon told Tamar, "so I can eat from your
hand." Tamar took the cakes she had made
and went to her brother Amnon's bedroom.
11 When she brought them to him to eat, he
grabbed her and said,[A] "Come sleep with me,
my sister! "
12 "Don't, my brother! " she cried. "Don't disgrace me, for such a thing should never be done
in Israel. Don't commit this outrage! 13 Where
could I ever go with my humiliation? And you
— you would be like one of the outrageous
fools in Israel! Please, speak to the king, for
he won't keep me from you." 14 But he refused
to listen to her, and because he was stronger
than she was, he disgraced her by raping her.
15 So Amnon hated Tamar with such intensity
that the hatred he hated her with was greater
than the love he had loved her with. "Get out
of here! " he said.
16 "No," she cried,[B] "sending me away is much
worse than the great wrong you've already
done to me! "
But he refused to listen to her. 17 Instead,
he called to the servant who waited on him:
"Get this away from me, throw her out, and
bolt the door behind her! " 18 Amnon's servant
threw her out and bolted the door behind her.
Now Tamar was wearing a long-sleeved[C] garment, because this is what the king's virgin
daughters wore. 19 Tamar put ashes on her
head and tore the long-sleeved garment she
was wearing. She put her hand on her head
and went away crying out.
20 Her brother Absalom said to her: "Has
your brother Amnon been with you? Be quiet
for now, my sister. He is your brother. Don't
take this thing to heart." So Tamar lived as a
desolate woman in the house of her brother
Absalom.

ABSALOM MURDERS AMNON

21 When King David heard about all these
things, he was furious.[D] 22 Absalom didn't
say anything to Amnon, either good or bad,
because he hated Amnon since he disgraced
his sister Tamar.
23 Two years later, Absalom's sheepshearers
were at Baal-hazor near Ephraim, and Absalom
invited all the king's sons. 24 Then he went to
the king and said, "Your servant has just hired
sheepshearers. Will the king and his servants
please come with your servant? "
25 The king replied to Absalom, "No, my son,
we should not all go, or we would be a burden to you." Although Absalom urged him, he
wasn't willing to go, though he did bless him.
26 "If not," Absalom said, "please let my brother Amnon go with us."
The king asked him, "Why should he go with
you? " 27 But Absalom urged him, so he sent
Amnon and all the king's sons.[E]
28 Now Absalom commanded his young men,
"Watch Amnon until he is in a good mood
from the wine. When I order you to strike
Amnon, then kill him. Don't be afraid. Am I not
the one who has commanded you? Be strong
and valiant! " 29 So Absalom's young men did
to Amnon just as Absalom had commanded.
Then all the rest of the king's sons got up, and
each fled on his mule.
30 While they were on the way, a report
reached David: "Absalom struck down all
the king's sons; not even one of them survived! " 31 In response the king stood up, tore
his clothes, and lay down on the ground, and all
his servants stood by with their clothes torn.
32 But Jonadab, son of David's brother Shimeah, spoke up: "My lord must not think they
have killed all the young men, the king's sons,
because only Amnon is dead. In fact, Absalom
has planned this[F] ever since the day Amnon
disgraced his sister Tamar. 33 So now, my lord
the king, don't take seriously the report that
says all the king's sons are dead. Only Amnon
is dead."
34 Meanwhile, Absalom had fled. When the

[A] **13:11** Lit *said to her* [B] **13:16** Lit *she said to him* [C] **13:18** Or *an ornamented*; Gn 37:3 [D] **13:21** LXX, DSS add *but he did not grieve the spirit of Amnon his son, for he loved him because he was his firstborn*; 1Kg 1:6 [E] **13:27** LXX adds *And Absalom prepared a feast like a royal feast.* [F] **13:32** Lit *In fact, it was established on the mouth of Absalom*

young man who was standing watch looked up, there were many people coming from the road west of him from the side of the mountain.[A] 35 Jonadab said to the king, "Look, the king's sons have come! It's exactly like your servant said." 36 Just as he finished speaking, the king's sons entered and wept loudly. Then the king and all his servants also wept very bitterly. 37 But Absalom fled and went to Talmai son of Ammihud, king of Geshur. And David mourned for his son[B] every day.

38 After Absalom had fled to Geshur and had been there three years, 39 King David[C] longed to go to Absalom, for David had finished grieving over Amnon's death.

ABSALOM RESTORED TO DAVID

14 Joab son of Zeruiah realized that the king's mind was on Absalom. 2 So Joab sent someone to Tekoa to bring a wise woman from there. He told her, "Pretend to be in mourning: dress in mourning clothes and don't put on any oil. Act like a woman who has been mourning for the dead for a long time. 3 Go to the king and speak these words to him." Then Joab told her exactly what to say.[D]

4 When the woman from Tekoa came[E] to the king, she fell facedown to the ground, paid homage, and said, "Help me, Your Majesty!"

5 "What's the matter?" the king asked her.

"Sadly, I am a widow; my husband died," she said. 6 "Your servant had two sons. They were fighting in the field with no one to separate them, and one struck the other and killed him. 7 Now the whole clan has risen up against your servant and said, 'Hand over the one who killed his brother so we may put him to death for the life of the brother he murdered. We will eliminate the heir!' They would extinguish my one remaining ember by not preserving my husband's name or posterity on earth."

8 The king told the woman, "Go home. I will issue a command on your behalf."

9 Then the woman of Tekoa said to the king, "My lord the king, may any blame be on me and my father's family, and may the king and his throne be innocent."

10 "Whoever speaks to you," the king said, "bring him to me. He will not trouble you again!"

11 She replied, "Please, may the king invoke the LORD your God, so that the avenger of blood will not increase the loss, and they will not eliminate my son!"

"As the LORD lives," he vowed, "not a hair of your son will fall to the ground."

12 Then the woman said, "Please, may your servant speak a word to my lord the king?"

"Speak," he replied.

13 The woman asked, "Why have you devised something similar against the people of God? When the king spoke as he did about this matter, he has pronounced his own guilt. The king has not brought back his own banished one. 14 We will certainly die and be like water poured out on the ground, which can't be recovered. But God would not take away a life; he would devise plans so that the one banished from him does not remain banished.

15 "Now therefore, I've come to present this matter to my lord the king because the people have made me afraid. Your servant thought: I must speak to the king. Perhaps the king will grant his servant's request. 16 The king will surely listen in order to keep his servant from the grasp of this man who would eliminate both me and my son from God's inheritance. 17 Your servant thought: May the word of my lord the king bring relief, for my lord the king is able to discern the good and the bad like the angel of God. May the LORD your God be with you."

18 Then the king answered the woman, "I'm going to ask you something; don't conceal it from me!"

"Let my lord the king speak," the woman replied.

19 The king asked, "Did Joab put you up to[F] all this?"

The woman answered. "As you live, my lord the king, no one can turn to the right or left from all my lord the king says. Yes, your servant Joab is the one who gave orders to me; he told your servant exactly what to say.[G] 20 Joab your servant has done this to address the issue indirectly,[H] but my lord has wisdom like the wisdom of the angel of God, knowing everything on earth."

21 Then the king said to Joab, "I hereby grant this request. Go, bring back the young man Absalom."

22 Joab fell with his face to the ground in

[A] **13:34** LXX adds *And the watchman came and reported to the king saying, "I see men on the Horonaim road on the side of the mountain."* [B] **13:37** Probably Amnon [C] **13:39** DSS, LXX, Tg read *David's spirit* [D] **14:3** Lit *Joab put the words into her mouth* [E] **14:4** Some Hb mss, LXX, Syr, Tg, Vg; other Hb mss read *spoke* [F] **14:19** Lit *"Is the hand of Joab in* [G] **14:19** Lit *he put all these words into the mouth of your servant* [H] **14:20** Lit *to go around the face of the matter*

homage and blessed the king. "Today," Joab
said, "your servant knows I have found favor
with you, my lord the king, because the king
has granted the request of your servant."
23 So Joab got up, went to Geshur, and brought
Absalom to Jerusalem. 24 However, the king
added, "He may return to his house, but he may
not see my face." So Absalom returned to his
house, but he did not see the king.[A]
25 No man in all Israel was as handsome and
highly praised as Absalom. From the sole of
his foot to the top of his head, he did not have
a single flaw. 26 When he shaved his head — he
shaved it at the end of every year because his
hair got so heavy for him that he had to shave
it off — he would weigh the hair from his head
and it would be five pounds[B] according to the
royal standard.
27 Three sons were born to Absalom, and a
daughter named Tamar, who was a beautiful
woman. 28 Absalom resided in Jerusalem two
years but never saw the king. 29 Then Absalom
sent for Joab in order to send him to the king,
but Joab was unwilling to come to him. So he
sent again, a second time, but he still would
not come. 30 Then Absalom said to his servants,
"See, Joab has a field right next to mine, and
he has barley there. Go and set fire to it!" So
Absalom's servants set the field on fire.[C]
31 Then Joab came to Absalom's house and
demanded, "Why did your servants set my
field on fire?"
32 "Look," Absalom explained to Joab, "I sent
for you and said, 'Come here. I want to send
you to the king to ask: Why have I come back
from Geshur? I'd be better off if I were still
there.' So now, let me see the king. If I am guilty,
let him kill me."
33 Joab went to the king and told him. So David summoned Absalom, who came to the king
and paid homage with his face to the ground
before him. Then the king kissed Absalom.

ABSALOM'S REVOLT

15 After this, Absalom got himself a chariot,
horses, and fifty men to run before him.
2 He would get up early and stand beside the
road leading to the city gate. Whenever anyone had a grievance to bring before the king
for settlement, Absalom called out to him and
asked, "What city are you from?" If he replied,
"Your servant is from one of the tribes of Israel,"
3 Absalom said to him, "Look, your claims are
good and right, but the king does not have
anyone to listen to you." 4 He added, "If only
someone would appoint me judge in the land.
Then anyone who had a grievance or dispute
could come to me, and I would make sure he
received justice." 5 When a person approached
to pay homage to him, Absalom reached out
his hand, took hold of him, and kissed him.
6 Absalom did this to all the Israelites who
came to the king for a settlement. So Absalom
stole the hearts of the men of Israel.
7 When four[D] years had passed, Absalom
said to the king, "Please let me go to Hebron
to fulfill a vow I made to the LORD. 8 For your
servant made a vow when I lived in Geshur
of Aram, saying: If the LORD really brings me
back to Jerusalem, I will worship the LORD
in Hebron."[E]
9 "Go in peace," the king said to him. So he
went to Hebron.
10 Then Absalom sent agents throughout the
tribes of Israel with this message: "When you
hear the sound of the ram's horn, you are to
say, 'Absalom has become king in Hebron!'"
11 Two hundred men from Jerusalem went
with Absalom. They had been invited and were
going innocently, for they did not know the
whole situation. 12 While he was offering the
sacrifices, Absalom sent for David's adviser
Ahithophel the Gilonite, from his city of Giloh.
So the conspiracy grew strong, and the people
supporting Absalom continued to increase.
13 Then an informer came to David and reported, "The hearts of the men of Israel are
with Absalom."
14 David said to all the servants with him in
Jerusalem, "Get up. We have to flee, or we will
not escape from Absalom! Leave quickly, or he
will overtake us quickly, heap disaster on us,
and strike the city with the edge of the sword."
15 The king's servants said to the king, "Whatever my lord the king decides, we are your servants." 16 Then the king set out, and his entire
household followed him. But he left behind
ten concubines to take care of the palace. 17 So
the king set out, and all the people followed
him. They stopped at the last house 18 while all
his servants marched past him. Then all the
Cherethites, the Pelethites, and the people of
Gath — six hundred men who came with him
from there — marched past the king.

[A] 14:24 Lit *king's face* [B] 14:26 Lit *200 shekels* [C] 14:30 DSS, LXX add *So Joab's servants came to him with their clothes torn and said, "Absalom's servants have set the field on fire!"* [D] 15:7 Some LXX mss, Syr, Vg; other LXX mss, MT read *40*
[E] 15:8 Some LXX mss; MT omits *in Hebron*

19 The king said to Ittai of Gath, "Why are you
also going with us? Go back and stay with the
new king since you're both a foreigner and an
exile from your homeland. 20 Besides, you only
arrived yesterday; should I make you wander
around with us today while I go wherever I
can? Go back and take your brothers with
you. May the LORD show you[A] kindness and
faithfulness."

21 But in response, Ittai vowed to the king,
"As the LORD lives and as my lord the king
lives, wherever my lord the king is, whether it
means life or death, your servant will be there!"

22 "March on," David replied to Ittai. So Ittai
of Gath marched past with all his men and the
dependents who were with him. 23 Everyone
in the countryside was weeping loudly while
all the people were marching out of the city.
As the king was crossing the Kidron Valley, all
the people were marching past on the road
that leads to the wilderness.

24 Zadok was also there, and all the Levites
with him were carrying the ark of the covenant
of God. They set the ark of God down, and
Abiathar offered sacrifices[B] until the people
had finished marching past. 25 Then the king
instructed Zadok, "Return the ark of God to
the city. If I find favor with the LORD, he will
bring me back and allow me to see both it and
its[C] dwelling place. 26 However, if he should
say, 'I do not delight in you,' then here I am
—he can do with me whatever pleases him."[D]

27 The king also said to the priest Zadok,
"Look,[E] return to the city in peace and your
two sons with you: your son Ahimaaz and Abiathar's son Jonathan. 28 Remember, I'll wait at
the fords[F] of the wilderness until word comes
from you to inform me." 29 So Zadok and Abiathar returned the ark of God to Jerusalem
and stayed there.

30 David was climbing the slope of the Mount
of Olives, weeping as he ascended. His head
was covered, and he was walking barefoot.
All of the people with him covered their heads
and went up, weeping as they ascended.

31 Then someone reported to David: "Ahithophel is among the conspirators with Absalom."

"LORD," David pleaded, "please turn the counsel of Ahithophel into foolishness!"

32 When David came to the summit where he
used to worship God, Hushai the Archite was
there to meet him with his robe torn and dust
on his head. 33 David said to him, "If you go away
with me, you'll be a burden to me, 34 but if you
return to the city and tell Absalom, 'I will be
your servant, Your Majesty! Previously, I was
your father's servant, but now I will be your
servant,' then you can counteract Ahithophel's
counsel for me. 35 Won't the priests Zadok and
Abiathar be there with you? Report everything
you hear from the palace to the priests Zadok
and Abiathar. 36 Take note: their two sons are
there with them—Zadok's son Ahimaaz and
Abiathar's son Jonathan. Send them to tell me
everything you hear." 37 So Hushai, David's
personal adviser, entered Jerusalem just as
Absalom was entering the city.

ZIBA HELPS DAVID

16 When David had gone a little beyond the
summit,[G] Ziba, Mephibosheth's servant,
was right there to meet him. He had a pair of
saddled donkeys loaded with two hundred
loaves of bread, one hundred clusters of raisins, one hundred bunches of summer fruit,
and a clay jar of wine. 2 The king said to Ziba,
"Why do you have these?"

Ziba answered, "The donkeys are for the
king's household to ride, the bread and summer fruit are for the young men to eat, and
the wine is for those to drink who become
exhausted in the wilderness."

3 "Where is your master's grandson?" the
king asked.

"Why, he's staying in Jerusalem," Ziba replied
to the king, "for he said, 'Today, the house of
Israel will restore my grandfather's kingdom
to me.'"

4 The king said to Ziba, "All that belongs to
Mephibosheth is now yours!"

"I bow before you," Ziba said. "May I find
favor with you, my lord the king!"

SHIMEI CURSES DAVID

5 When King David got to Bahurim, a man
belonging to the family of the house of Saul
was just coming out. His name was Shimei
son of Gera, and he was yelling curses as he
approached. 6 He threw stones at David and
at all the royal[H] servants, the people and the
warriors on David's right and left. 7 Shimei
said as he cursed: "Get out, get out, you man
of bloodshed, you wicked man! 8 The LORD has
paid you back for all the blood of the house

[A] **15:20** LXX; MT omits Lit *May the LORD show you* [B] **15:24** Or *Abiathar went up* [C] **15:25** Or *his* [D] **15:26** Lit *me what is good in his eyes* [E] **15:27** LXX; MT reads *"Are you a seer?* [F] **15:28** Alt Hb tradition reads *plains* [G] **16:1** = Mount of Olives [H] **16:6** Lit *all King David's*

of Saul in whose place you became king, and
the LORD has handed the kingdom over to
your son Absalom. Look, you are in trouble
because you're a man of bloodshed!"
9 Then Abishai son of Zeruiah said to the king,
"Why should this dead dog curse my lord the
king? Let me go over and remove his head!"
10 The king replied, "Sons of Zeruiah, do we
agree on anything? He curses me this way because the LORD[A] told him, 'Curse David!' Therefore, who can say, 'Why did you do that?'" 11 Then
David said to Abishai and all his servants, "Look,
my own son, my own flesh and blood,[B] intends
to take my life — how much more now this
Benjaminite! Leave him alone and let him curse
me; the LORD has told him to. 12 Perhaps the LORD
will see my affliction[C] and restore goodness
to me instead of Shimei's curses today." 13 So
David and his men proceeded along the road
as Shimei was going along the ridge of the hill
opposite him. As Shimei went, he cursed David, threw stones at him, and kicked up dust.
14 Finally, the king and all the people with him
arrived[D] exhausted, so they rested there.

ABSALOM'S ADVISERS

15 Now Absalom and all the Israelites came
to Jerusalem. Ahithophel was also with him.
16 When David's friend Hushai the Archite came
to Absalom, Hushai said to Absalom, "Long
live the king! Long live the king!"
17 "Is this your loyalty to your friend?" Absalom asked Hushai. "Why didn't you go with
your friend?"
18 "Not at all," Hushai answered Absalom. "I
am on the side of the one that the LORD, this
people, and all the men of Israel have chosen.
I will stay with him. 19 Furthermore, whom
will I serve if not his son? As I served in your
father's presence, I will also serve in yours."
20 Then Absalom said to Ahithophel, "Give
me your advice. What should we do?"
21 Ahithophel replied to Absalom, "Sleep
with your father's concubines whom he left to
take care of the palace. When all Israel hears
that you have become repulsive to your father,
everyone with you will be encouraged."[E] 22 So
they pitched a tent for Absalom on the roof,
and he slept with his father's concubines in
the sight of all Israel.
23 Now the advice Ahithophel gave in those
days was like someone asking about a word
from God — such was the regard that both
David and Absalom had for Ahithophel's
17 advice. 1 Ahithophel said to Absalom,
"Let me choose twelve thousand men,
and I will set out in pursuit of David tonight.
2 I will attack him while he is weary and discouraged,[F] throw him into a panic, and all
the people with him will scatter. I will strike
down only the king 3 and bring all the people
back to you. When everyone returns except
the man you're looking for, all[G] the people will
be at peace." 4 This proposal seemed right to
Absalom and all the elders of Israel.
5 Then Absalom said, "Summon Hushai the
Archite also. Let's hear what he has to say
as well."
6 So Hushai came to Absalom, and Absalom
told him: "Ahithophel offered this proposal.
Should we carry out his proposal? If not, what
do you say?"
7 Hushai replied to Absalom, "The advice
Ahithophel has given this time is not good."
8 Hushai continued, "You know your father and
his men. They are warriors and are desperate
like a wild bear robbed of her cubs. Your father
is an experienced soldier who won't spend the
night with the people. 9 He's probably already
hiding in one of the caves[H] or some other place.
If some of our troops fall[I] first, someone is
sure to hear and say, 'There's been a slaughter among the people who follow Absalom.'
10 Then, even a brave man with the heart of a
lion will lose heart[J] because all Israel knows
that your father and the valiant men with him
are warriors. 11 Instead, I advise that all Israel
from Dan to Beer-sheba — as numerous as the
sand by the sea — be gathered to you and that
you personally go into battle. 12 Then we will
attack David wherever we find him, and we
will descend on him like dew on the ground.
Not even one will be left—neither he nor any
of the men with him. 13 If he retreats to some
city, all Israel will bring ropes to that city, and
we will drag its stones[K] into the valley until
not even a pebble can be found there." 14 Since
the LORD had decreed that Ahithophel's good
advice be undermined in order to bring about
Absalom's ruin, Absalom and all the men of

[A] **16:10** Alt Hb tradition reads *If he curses, and if the LORD* [B] **16:11** Lit *son who came from my belly* [C] **16:12** Some Hb mss, LXX, Syr, Vg; one Hb tradition reads *iniquity*; alt Hb tradition reads *eyes*; another Hb tradition reads *will look with his eye* [D] **16:14** LXX adds *at the Jordan* [E] **16:21** Lit *father, the hands of everyone with you will be strong* [F] **17:2** Lit *and weak of hands* [G] **17:3** LXX reads *to you as a bride returns to her husband. You seek the life of only one man, and all* [H] **17:9** Or *pits*, or *ravines* [I] **17:9** Lit *And it will be when a falling on them at* [J] **17:10** Lit *melt* [K] **17:13** Lit *drag it*

Israel said, "The advice of Hushai the Archite is better than Ahithophel's advice."

DAVID INFORMED OF ABSALOM'S PLANS

15 Hushai then told the priests Zadok and Abiathar, "This is what[A] Ahithophel advised Absalom and the elders of Israel, and this is what[B] I advised. 16 Now send someone quickly and tell David, 'Don't spend the night at the wilderness ford,[C] but be sure to cross over the Jordan,[D] or the king and all the people with him will be devoured.' "

17 Jonathan and Ahimaaz were staying at En-rogel, where a servant girl would come and pass along information to them. They in turn would go and inform King David, because they dared not be seen entering the city. 18 However, a young man did see them and informed Absalom. So the two left quickly and came to the house of a man in Bahurim. He had a well in his courtyard, and they climbed down into it. 19 Then his wife took the cover, placed it over the mouth of the well, and scattered grain on it so nobody would know anything.

20 Absalom's servants came to the woman at the house and asked, "Where are Ahimaaz and Jonathan?"

"They passed by toward the water,"[E] the woman replied to them. The men searched but did not find them, so they returned to Jerusalem.

21 After they had gone, Ahimaaz and Jonathan climbed out of the well and went and informed King David. They told him, "Get up and immediately ford the river, for Ahithophel has given this advice against you." 22 So David and all the people with him got up and crossed the Jordan. By daybreak, there was no one who had not crossed the Jordan. 23 When Ahithophel realized that his advice had not been followed, he saddled his donkey and set out for his house in his hometown. He set his house in order and hanged himself. So he died and was buried in his father's tomb.

24 David had arrived at Mahanaim by the time Absalom crossed the Jordan with all the men of Israel. 25 Now Absalom had appointed Amasa over the army in Joab's place. Amasa was the son of a man named Ithra[F] the Israelite;[G] Ithra had married Abigail daughter of Nahash.[H] Abigail was a sister to Zeruiah, Joab's mother. 26 And Israel and Absalom camped in the land of Gilead. 27 When David came to Mahanaim, Shobi son of Nahash from Rabbah of the Ammonites, Machir son of Ammiel from Lo-debar, and Barzillai the Gileadite from Rogelim 28 brought beds, basins,[I] and pottery items. They also brought wheat, barley, flour, roasted grain, beans, lentils,[J] 29 honey, curds, sheep, goats, and cheese[K] from the herd for David and the people with him to eat. They had reasoned, "The people must be hungry, exhausted, and thirsty in the wilderness."

ABSALOM'S DEFEAT

18 David reviewed his troops and appointed commanders of thousands and of hundreds over them. 2 He then sent out the troops, a third under Joab, a third under Joab's brother Abishai son of Zeruiah, and a third under Ittai of Gath. The king said to the troops, "I must also march out with you."

3 "You must not go!" the people pleaded. "If we have to flee, they will not pay any attention to us. Even if half of us die, they will not pay any attention to us because you are worth[L] ten thousand of us. Therefore, it is better if you support us from the city."

4 "I will do whatever you think is best," the king replied to them. So he stood beside the city gate while all the troops marched out by hundreds and thousands. 5 The king commanded Joab, Abishai, and Ittai, "Treat the young man Absalom gently for my sake." All the people heard the king's orders to all the commanders about Absalom.

6 Then David's forces marched into the field to engage Israel in battle, which took place in the forest of Ephraim. 7 Israel's army was defeated by David's soldiers, and the slaughter there was vast that day — twenty thousand dead. 8 The battle spread over the entire area, and that day the forest claimed more people than the sword.

ABSALOM'S DEATH

9 Absalom was riding on his mule when he happened to meet David's soldiers. When the mule went under the tangled branches of a large oak tree, Absalom's head was caught fast

---

[A] **17:15** Lit *"Like this and like this* [B] **17:15** Lit *and like this and like this* [C] **17:16** Some Hb mss; MT reads *plains* [D] **17:16** *the Jordan* supplied for clarity [E] **17:20** Or *brook*; Hb obscure [F] **17:25** Or *Jether* [G] **17:25** Some LXX mss read *Ishmaelite*
[H] **17:25** Some LXX mss read *Jesse* [I] **17:28** LXX reads *brought 10 embroidered beds with double coverings, 10 vessels*
[J] **17:28** LXX, Syr; MT adds *roasted grain* [K] **17:29** Hb obscure [L] **18:3** Some Hb mss, LXX, Vg; other Hb mss read *because there would now be about*

in the tree. The mule under him kept going, so he was suspended in midair.[A] 10 One of the men saw him and informed Joab. He said, "I just saw Absalom hanging in an oak tree!"

11 "You just saw him!" Joab exclaimed.[B] "Why didn't you strike him to the ground right there? I would have given you ten silver pieces[C] and a belt!"

12 The man replied to Joab, "Even if I had the weight of a thousand pieces of silver[D] in my hand, I would not raise my hand against the king's son. For we heard the king command you, Abishai, and Ittai, 'Protect the young man Absalom for me.'[E] 13 If I had jeopardized my own[F] life — and nothing is hidden from the king — you would have abandoned me."

14 Joab said, "I'm not going to waste time with you!" He then took three spears in his hand and thrust them into Absalom's chest. While Absalom was still alive in the oak tree, 15 ten young men who were Joab's armor-bearers surrounded Absalom, struck him, and killed him. 16 Joab blew the ram's horn, and the troops broke off their pursuit of Israel because Joab restrained them. 17 They took Absalom, threw him into a large pit in the forest, and raised up a huge mound of stones over him. And all Israel fled, each to his tent.

18 When he was alive, Absalom had taken a pillar and raised it up for himself in the King's Valley, since he thought, "I have no son to preserve the memory of my name." So he named the pillar after himself. It is still called Absalom's Monument today.

19 Ahimaaz son of Zadok said, "Please let me run and tell the king the good news that the LORD has vindicated him by freeing him from his enemies."

20 Joab replied to him, "You are not the man to take good news today. You may do it another day, but today you aren't taking good news, because the king's son is dead." 21 Joab then said to a Cushite, "Go tell the king what you have seen." The Cushite bowed to Joab and took off running.

22 However, Ahimaaz son of Zadok persisted and said to Joab, "No matter what, please let me also run behind the Cushite!"

Joab replied, "My son, why do you want to run since you won't get a reward?"[G]

23 "No matter what, I want to run!"

"Then run!" Joab said to him. So Ahimaaz ran by way of the plain and outran the Cushite.

24 David was sitting between the city gates when the watchman went up to the roof of the city gate and over to the wall. The watchman looked out and saw a man running alone. 25 He called out and told the king.

The king said, "If he's alone, he bears good news."

As the first runner came closer, 26 the watchman saw another man running. He called out to the gatekeeper, "Look! Another man is running alone!"

"This one is also bringing good news," said the king.

27 The watchman said, "The way the first man runs looks to me like the way Ahimaaz son of Zadok runs."

"This is a good man; he comes with good news," the king commented.

28 Ahimaaz called out to the king, "All is well," and paid homage to the king with his face to the ground. He continued, "Blessed be the LORD your God! He delivered up the men who rebelled against my lord the king."

29 The king asked, "Is the young man Absalom all right?"

Ahimaaz replied, "When Joab sent the king's servant and your servant, I saw a big disturbance, but I don't know what it was."

30 The king said, "Move aside and stand here." So he stood to one side.

31 Just then the Cushite came and said, "May my lord the king hear the good news: The LORD has vindicated you today by freeing you from all who rise against you!"

32 The king asked the Cushite, "Is the young man Absalom all right?"

The Cushite replied, "I wish that the enemies of my lord the king, along with all who rise up against you with evil intent, would become like that young man."

33 The king was deeply moved and went up to the chamber above the city gate and wept. As he walked, he cried, "My son Absalom! My son, my son Absalom! If only I had died instead of you, Absalom, my son, my son!"

DAVID'S KINGDOM RESTORED

19 It was reported to Joab, "The king is weeping. He's mourning over Absalom." 2 That day's victory was turned into mourning for all the troops because on that day the troops heard, "The king is grieving over his son." 3 So

---

[A] **18:9** Lit *was between heaven and earth* [B] **18:11** Lit *Joab said to the man who told him* [C] **18:11** About four ounces of silver [D] **18:12** About 25 pounds of silver [E] **18:12** Some Hb mss, LXX, Tg, Vg; other Hb mss read *'Protect, whoever, the young man Absalom'*; Hb obscure [F] **18:13** Alt Hb tradition reads *jeopardized his* [G] **18:22** Or *you have no good news?*

they returned to the city quietly that day like troops come in when they are humiliated after fleeing in battle. 4 But the king covered his face and cried loudly, "My son Absalom! Absalom, my son, my son!"

5 Then Joab went into the house to the king and said, "Today you have shamed all your soldiers — those who saved your life as well as your sons, your wives, and your concubines — 6 by loving your enemies and hating those who love you! Today you have made it clear that the commanders and soldiers mean nothing to you. In fact, today I know that if Absalom were alive and all of us were dead, it would be fine with you![A]

7 "Now get up! Go out and encourage[B] your soldiers, for I swear by the LORD that if you don't go out, not a man will remain with you tonight. This will be worse for you than all the trouble that has come to you from your youth until now!"

8 So the king got up and sat in the city gate, and all the people were told: "Look, the king is sitting in the city gate." Then they all came into the king's presence.

Meanwhile, each Israelite had fled to his tent. 9 People throughout all the tribes of Israel were arguing among themselves, saying, "The king rescued us from the grasp of our enemies, and he saved us from the grasp of the Philistines, but now he has fled from the land because of Absalom. 10 But Absalom, the man we anointed over us, has died in battle. So why do you say nothing about restoring the king?"

11 King David sent word to the priests Zadok and Abiathar: "Say to the elders of Judah, 'Why should you be the last to restore the king to his palace? The talk of all Israel has reached the king at his house. 12 You are my brothers, my flesh and blood.[C] So why should you be the last to restore the king?' 13 And tell Amasa, 'Aren't you my flesh and blood?[D] May God punish me and do so severely if you don't become commander of my army from now on instead of Joab!'"

14 So he won over[E] all the men of Judah, and they unanimously sent word to the king: "Come back, you and all your servants." 15 Then the king returned. When he arrived at the Jordan, Judah came to Gilgal to meet the king and escort him across the Jordan.

16 Shimei son of Gera, the Benjaminite from Bahurim, hurried down with the men of Judah to meet King David. 17 There were a thousand men from Benjamin with him. Ziba, an attendant from the house of Saul, with his fifteen sons and twenty servants also rushed down to the Jordan ahead of the king. 18 They forded the Jordan to bring the king's household across and do whatever the king desired.[F]

When Shimei son of Gera crossed the Jordan, he fell facedown before the king 19 and said to him, "My lord, don't hold me guilty, and don't remember your servant's wrongdoing on the day my lord the king left Jerusalem. May the king not take it to heart. 20 For your servant knows that I have sinned. But look! Today I am the first one of the entire house of Joseph to come down to meet my lord the king."

21 Abishai son of Zeruiah asked, "Shouldn't Shimei be put to death for this, because he cursed the LORD's anointed?"

22 David answered, "Sons of Zeruiah, do we agree on anything? Have you become my adversary today? Should any man be killed in Israel today? Am I not aware that today I'm king over Israel?" 23 So the king said to Shimei, "You will not die." Then the king gave him his oath.

24 Mephibosheth, Saul's grandson, also went down to meet the king. He had not taken care of his feet, trimmed his mustache, or washed his clothes from the day the king left until the day he returned safely. 25 When he came from Jerusalem to meet the king, the king asked him, "Mephibosheth, why didn't you come with me?"

26 "My lord the king," he replied, "my servant Ziba betrayed me. Actually your servant said: 'I'll saddle the donkey for myself[G] so that I may ride it and go with the king' — for your servant is lame. 27 Ziba slandered your servant to my lord the king. But my lord the king is like the angel of God, so do whatever you think best.[H] 28 For my grandfather's entire family deserves death from my lord the king, but you set your servant among those who eat at your table. So what further right do I have to keep on making appeals to the king?"

29 The king said to him, "Why keep on speaking about these matters of yours? I hereby declare: you and Ziba are to divide the land."

[A] **19:6** Lit *be right in your eyes* [B] **19:7** Lit *speak to the heart of* [C] **19:12** Lit *my bone and my flesh* [D] **19:13** Lit *my bone and my flesh?* [E] **19:14** Lit *he turned the heart of* [F] **19:18** Lit *do what is good in his eyes* [G] **19:26** LXX, Syr, Vg read *said to him, 'Saddle the donkey for me* [H] **19:27** Lit *do what is good in your eyes*

30 Mephibosheth said to the king, "Instead,
since my lord the king has come to his palace
safely, let Ziba take it all!"
31 Barzillai the Gileadite had come down
from Rogelim and accompanied the king to
the Jordan River to see him off at the Jordan.
32 Barzillai was a very old man — eighty years
old — and since he was a very wealthy man, he
had provided for the needs of the king while
he stayed in Mahanaim.
33 The king said to Barzillai, "Cross over
with me, and I'll provide for you[A] at my side
in Jerusalem."
34 Barzillai replied to the king, "How many
years of my life are left that I should go up to
Jerusalem with the king? 35 I'm now eighty
years old. Can I discern what is pleasant and
what is not? Can your servant taste what he
eats or drinks? Can I still hear the voice of
male and female singers? Why should your
servant be an added burden to my lord the
king? 36 Since your servant is only going with
the king a little way across the Jordan, why
should the king repay me with such a reward?
37 Please let your servant return so that I may
die in my own city near the tomb of my father
and mother. But here is your servant Chimham:
let him cross over with my lord the king. Do
for him what seems good to you."[B]
38 The king replied, "Chimham will cross
over with me, and I will do for him what seems
good to you, and whatever you desire from me
I will do for you." 39 So all the people crossed
the Jordan, and then the king crossed. The
king kissed Barzillai and blessed him, and
Barzillai returned to his home.
40 The king went on to Gilgal, and Chimham
went with him. All the troops of Judah and
half of Israel's escorted the king. 41 Suddenly,
all the men of Israel came to the king. They
asked him, "Why did our brothers, the men of
Judah, take you away secretly and transport
the king and his household across the Jordan,
along with all of David's men?"
42 All the men of Judah responded to the
men of Israel, "Because the king is our relative. Why does this make you angry? Have
we ever eaten anything of the king's or been
honored at all?"[C]
43 The men of Israel answered the men of
Judah: "We have ten shares in the king, so we
have a greater claim to David than you. Why
then do you despise us? Weren't we the first
to speak of restoring our king?" But the words
of the men of Judah were harsher than those
of the men of Israel.

SHEBA'S REVOLT

20 Now a wicked man, a Benjaminite
named Sheba son of Bichri, happened to
be there. He blew the ram's horn and shouted:

We have no portion in David,
no inheritance in Jesse's son.
Each man to his tent,[D] Israel!

2 So all the men of Israel deserted David and
followed Sheba son of Bichri, but the men of
Judah from the Jordan all the way to Jerusalem remained loyal to their king.
3 When David came to his palace in Jerusalem, he took the ten concubines he had
left to take care of the palace and placed
them under guard. He provided for them,
but he was not intimate with them. They
were confined until the day of their death,
living as widows.
4 The king said to Amasa, "Summon the men
of Judah to me within three days and be here
yourself." 5 Amasa went to summon Judah, but
he took longer than the time allotted him. 6 So
David said to Abishai, "Sheba son of Bichri will
do more harm to us than Absalom. Take your
lord's soldiers and pursue him, or he will find
fortified cities and elude us."[E]
7 So Joab's men, the Cherethites, the Pelethites, and all the warriors marched out under Abishai's command;[F] they left Jerusalem
to pursue Sheba son of Bichri. 8 They were
at the great stone in Gibeon when Amasa
joined them. Joab was wearing his uniform
and over it was a belt around his waist with
a sword in its sheath. As he approached, the
sword fell out. 9 Joab asked Amasa, "Are you
well, my brother?" Then with his right hand
Joab grabbed Amasa by the beard to kiss him.
10 Amasa was not on guard against the sword
in Joab's hand, and Joab stabbed him in the
stomach with it and spilled his intestines out
on the ground. Joab did not stab him again,
and Amasa died.
Joab and his brother Abishai pursued Sheba son of Bichri. 11 One of Joab's young men
had stood over Amasa saying, "Whoever
favors Joab and whoever is for David, follow Joab!" 12 Now Amasa had been writhing

---

[A] 19:33 LXX reads *for your old age*; Ru 4:15 [B] 19:37 Lit *what is good in your eyes*, also in v. 38 [C] 19:42 LXX reads *king's or has he given us a gift or granted us a portion* [D] 20:1 Alt Hb tradition reads *gods* [E] 20:6 Lit *and snatch away our eyes* [F] 20:7 Lit *out following him*

in his blood in the middle of the highway,
and the man had seen that all the troops
stopped. So he moved Amasa from the highway to the field and threw a garment over
him because he realized that all those who
encountered Amasa were stopping. 13 When
he was removed from the highway, all the
men passed by and followed Joab to pursue
Sheba son of Bichri.
14 Sheba passed through all the tribes of Israel to Abel of Beth-maacah. All the Berites[A]
came together and followed him. 15 Joab's
troops came and besieged Sheba in Abel of
Beth-maacah. They built a siege ramp against
the outer wall of the city. While all the troops
with Joab were battering the wall to make it
collapse, 16 a wise woman called out from the
city, "Listen! Listen! Please tell Joab to come
here and let me speak with him."
17 When he had come near her, the woman
asked, "Are you Joab?"

"I am," he replied.

"Listen to the words of your servant," she
said to him.

He answered, "I'm listening."
18 She said, "In the past they used to say, 'Seek
counsel in Abel,' and that's how they settled
disputes. 19 I am one of the peaceful and faithful in Israel, but you're trying to destroy a city
that is like a mother in Israel. Why would you
devour the LORD's inheritance?"
20 Joab protested: "Never! I would never devour or demolish! 21 That is not the case. There
is a man named Sheba son of Bichri, from the
hill country of Ephraim, who has rebelled
against King David. Deliver this one man, and
I will withdraw from the city."

The woman replied to Joab, "Watch! His head
will be thrown over the wall to you." 22 The
woman went to all the people with her wise
counsel, and they cut off the head of Sheba
son of Bichri and threw it to Joab. So he blew
the ram's horn, and they dispersed from the
city, each to his own tent. Joab returned to
the king in Jerusalem.

23 Joab commanded the whole army of
Israel;
Benaiah son of Jehoiada was over the
Cherethites and Pelethites;
24 Adoram[B] was over forced labor;
Jehoshaphat son of Ahilud was court
historian;
25 Sheva was court secretary;
Zadok and Abiathar were priests;
26 and in addition, Ira the Jairite was
David's priest.

JUSTICE FOR THE GIBEONITES

21 During David's reign there was a famine
for three successive years, so David inquired[C] of the LORD. The LORD answered, "It is
due to Saul and to his bloody family, because
he killed the Gibeonites."
2 The Gibeonites were not Israelites but
rather a remnant of the Amorites. The Israelites had taken an oath concerning them,
but Saul had tried to kill them in his zeal
for the Israelites and Judah. So David summoned the Gibeonites and spoke to them.
3 He asked the Gibeonites, "What should I
do for you? How can I make atonement so
that you will bring a blessing on[D] the LORD's
inheritance?"
4 The Gibeonites said to him, "We are not
asking for silver and gold from Saul or his
family, and we cannot put anyone to death
in Israel."

"Whatever you say, I will do for you," he said.
5 They replied to the king, "As for the man
who annihilated us and plotted to destroy us so
we would not exist within the whole territory
of Israel, 6 let seven of his male descendants
be handed over to us so we may hang[E] them
in the presence of the LORD at Gibeah of Saul,
the LORD's chosen."

The king answered, "I will hand them over."
7 David spared Mephibosheth, the son of
Saul's son Jonathan, because of the oath of
the LORD that was between David and Jonathan, Saul's son. 8 But the king took Armoni
and Mephibosheth, who were the two sons
whom Rizpah daughter of Aiah had borne to
Saul, and the five sons whom Merab[F] daughter of Saul had borne to Adriel son of Barzillai
the Meholathite 9 and handed them over to
the Gibeonites. They hanged[G] them on the
hill in the presence of the LORD; the seven of
them died together. They were executed in
the first days of the harvest at the beginning
of the barley harvest.[H]

THE BURIAL OF SAUL'S FAMILY

10 Rizpah, Aiah's daughter, took sackcloth and
spread it out for herself on the rock from the

[A] **20:14** LXX, Vg read *Bichrites* [B] **20:24** Some Hb mss, LXX, Syr read *Adoniram*; 1Kg 4:6; 5:14 [C] **21:1** Lit *sought the face of*
[D] **21:3** Lit *will bless* [E] **21:6** Or *impale*, or *expose* [F] **21:8** Some Hb mss, LXX, Syr, Tg; other Hb mss read *Michal*
[G] **21:9** Or *impaled*, or *exposed*, also in v. 13 [H] **21:9** = March–April

beginning of the harvest[A] until the rain poured
down from heaven on the bodies. She kept
the birds of the sky from them by day and
the wild animals by night.
11 When it was reported to David what Saul's
concubine Rizpah daughter of Aiah had done,
12 he went and got the bones of Saul and his
son Jonathan from the citizens of Jabesh-
gilead. They had stolen them from the public
square of Beth-shan where the Philistines
had hung the bodies the day the Philistines
killed Saul at Gilboa. 13 David had the bones
brought from there. They gathered up the
bones of Saul's family who had been hanged
14 and buried the bones of Saul and his son
Jonathan at Zela in the land of Benjamin in
the tomb of Saul's father Kish. They did everything the king commanded. After this,
God was receptive to prayer for the land.

THE PHILISTINE GIANTS

15 The Philistines again waged war against
Israel. David went down with his soldiers,
and they fought the Philistines, but David became exhausted. 16 Then Ishbi-benob, one of
the descendants of the giant,[B] whose bronze
spear weighed about eight pounds[C] and who
wore new armor, intended to kill David. 17 But
Abishai son of Zeruiah came to his aid, struck
the Philistine, and killed him. Then David's
men swore to him: "You must never again go
out with us to battle. You must not extinguish
the lamp of Israel."
18 After this, there was another battle with
the Philistines at Gob. At that time Sibbecai
the Hushathite killed Saph, who was one of the
descendants of the giant.
19 Once again there was a battle with the Philistines at Gob, and Elhanan son of Jaare-oregim
the Bethlehemite killed[D] Goliath of Gath. The
shaft of his spear was like a weaver's beam.
20 At Gath there was still another battle. A
huge man was there with six fingers on each
hand and six toes on each foot — twenty-four
in all. He, too, was descended from the giant.
21 When he taunted Israel, Jonathan, son of
David's brother Shimei, killed him.
22 These four were descended from the giant in Gath and were killed by David and his
soldiers.

DAVID'S SONG OF THANKSGIVING

22 David spoke the words of this song to
the LORD on the day the LORD rescued
him from the grasp of all his enemies and
from the grasp of Saul. 2 He said:

Thanksgiving and Contentment | *Praise for God's Security*

INDESCRIBABLE

"The LORD is my rock, my fortress, and my deliverer, my God, my rock where I seek refuge. My shield, the horn of my salvation, my stronghold, my refuge, and my Savior, you save me from violence. I called to the LORD, who is worthy of praise, and I was saved from my enemies." 2 Samuel 22:2-4

In this beautiful hymn of praise, David used many words to describe the matchless character and one-of-a-kind works of God.

It's an avalanche of word pictures! God is a rock (solid formation). He's also a shield (protection), a horn of salvation (power), a stronghold (defense), a refuge (shelter), and a Savior. But more significant than all these rich descriptions is another tiny word. Do you see it? It's the possessive pronoun "my." David uses it eleven times in these verses!

In other words, God does not merely have these wonderful attributes; he was all of them *to* and *for* David, just as he is for us.

When you pray, thank God that he is your rock, shield, horn of salvation, stronghold, refuge, and Savior.

For the next note on *Thanksgiving and Contentment*, see 2 Samuel 22:47.

[A] **21:10** = April to October [B] **21:16** Or *Raphah*, also in vv. 18,20,22 [C] **21:16** Lit *300* (shekels) [D] **21:19** 1Ch 20:5 adds *the brother of*

The LORD is my rock, my fortress,
and my deliverer,
3 my God,[A] my rock where I seek refuge.
My shield, the horn of my salvation,
my stronghold, my refuge,
and my Savior, you save me
from violence.
4 I called to the LORD, who is worthy
of praise,
and I was saved from my enemies.
5 For the waves of death engulfed me;
the torrents of destruction terrified me.
6 The ropes of Sheol entangled me;
the snares of death confronted me.

7 I called to the LORD in my distress;
I called to my God.
From his temple he heard my voice,
and my cry for help reached his ears.
8 Then the earth shook and quaked;
the foundations of the heavens[B]
trembled;
they shook because he burned
with anger.
9 Smoke rose from his nostrils,
and consuming fire came
from his mouth;
coals were set ablaze by it.[C]
10 He bent the heavens and came down,
total darkness beneath his feet.
11 He rode on a cherub and flew,
soaring[D] on the wings of the wind.
12 He made darkness a canopy
around him,
a gathering[E] of water and thick clouds.
13 From the radiance of his presence,
blazing coals were ignited.
14 The LORD thundered from heaven;
the Most High made his voice heard.
15 He shot arrows and scattered them;
he hurled lightning bolts
and routed them.
16 The depths of the sea became visible,
the foundations of the world
were exposed
at the rebuke of the LORD,
at the blast of the breath
of his nostrils.

17 He reached down from on high
and took hold of me;
he pulled me out of deep water.
18 He rescued me
from my powerful enemy
and from those who hated me,
for they were too strong for me.
19 They confronted me in the day
of my calamity,
but the LORD was my support.
20 He brought me out to a spacious place;
he rescued me because he delighted
in me.

Support | *Humility*

THE GREAT SIN

"You rescue an oppressed people, but your eyes are set against the proud—you humble them." 2 Samuel 22:28

Correctly noting that "it was through Pride that the devil became the devil," C. S. Lewis labeled pride "the great sin." What is pride? The Hebrew word conveys the idea of self-exaltation. A proud man elevates himself above others. A prideful business owner, from her lofty perch, looks with scorn on all her low-wage employees, seeing them as beneath her.

When we are looking down on others, we cannot see the One who is above us. No wonder God hates pride (Pr 6:16-17). It blinds us to the true perspective of the universe—that God alone is high and exalted.

Today, remember David' song of humility. Resist the urge to look down on others in a haughty way. Instead, look up in humility to the One who opposes the proud but gives grace to the humble.

For the next note on *Support*, see 1 Chronicles 16:11.

[A] **22:3** LXX, Ps 18:2 read *my God*; MT reads *God of* [B] **22:8** Some Hb mss, Syr, Vg read *mountains*; Ps 18:7 [C] **22:9** Or *him*
[D] **22:11** Some Hb mss; other Hb mss, Syr, Tg read *he was seen* [E] **22:12** Or *sieve*, or *mass*; Hb obscure

21 The LORD rewarded me
according to my righteousness;
he repaid me
according to the cleanness
of my hands.
22 For I have kept the ways of the LORD
and have not turned from my God
to wickedness.
23 Indeed, I let all his ordinances
guide me[A]
and have not disregarded his statutes.
24 I was blameless before him
and kept myself from my iniquity.
25 So the LORD repaid me
according to my righteousness,
according to my cleanness[B]
in his sight.

26 With the faithful
you prove yourself faithful,
with the blameless
you prove yourself blameless,
27 with the pure
you prove yourself pure;
but with the crooked
you prove yourself shrewd.
28 You rescue an oppressed people,
but your eyes are set
against the proud —
you humble them.
29 LORD, you are my lamp;
the LORD illuminates my darkness.
30 With you I can attack a barricade,[C]
and with my God I can leap over a wall.
31 God — his way is perfect;
the word of the LORD is pure.
He is a shield to all who take refuge
in him.

32 For who is God besides the LORD?
And who is a rock? Only our God.
33 God is my strong refuge;[D]
he makes my way perfect.[E]
34 He makes my feet like the feet of a deer
and sets me securely on the[F] heights.[G]
35 He trains my hands for war;
my arms can bend a bow of bronze.
36 You have given me the shield
of your salvation;
your help[H] exalts me.
37 You make a spacious place beneath me
for my steps,
and my ankles do not give way.
38 I pursue my enemies and destroy them;

Thanksgiving and Contentment | *Praise for Salvation*

GOD OUR ROCK

"The LORD lives—blessed be my rock! God, the rock of my salvation, is exalted." 2 Samuel 22:47

The weary hiker pauses in the shadow of a boulder next to the path. Rubbing his hand across its smooth surface, he marvels at how massive it is—so solid and enduring. It is so heavy that a hundred pro football players couldn't budge it! What a picture of strength.

No wonder the Bible repeatedly pictures God as a rock!

The difference of course, is that, as David points out in this verse, "the LORD lives." In other words, he is a *living* rock. He is responsive to those who cry out to him. And he does much more than offer a bit of shade from time to time. He is "the rock of my salvation," which is to say, he rescues those who are in trouble! "Rock" also means "foundation" and "fortress." This "rock" is solid: Our salvation is secure in him. For all these reasons and more, we bless and exalt God.

Do this. Find a small stone and carry it around with you for the next few days. As you feel it in your pocket or see it on your desk or dashboard, let it remind you to trust God as your sure strength.

For the next note on *Thanksgiving and Contentment*, see 2 Samuel 23:5.

[A] **22:23** Lit *Indeed, all his ordinances have been in front of me* [B] **22:25** LXX, Syr, Vg read *to the cleanness of my hands*; Ps 18:24 [C] **22:30** Or *a ridge*, or *raiders* [D] **22:33** DSS, some LXX mss, Syr, Vg read *God clothes me with strength*; Ps 18:32 [E] **22:33** Some LXX mss, Syr; MT reads *he sets free the blameless his way*; Hb obscure [F] **22:34** LXX; some Hb mss read *my*; other Hb mss read *his* [G] **22:34** Or *on my high places* [H] **22:36** LXX reads *humility*; Ps 18:35

I do not turn back until they are
wiped out.
39 I wipe them out and crush them,
and they do not rise;
they fall beneath my feet.
40 You have clothed me with strength
for battle;
you subdue my adversaries
beneath me.
41 You have made my enemies retreat
before me;[A]
I annihilate those who hate me.
42 They look, but there is no one
to save them —
they look to the LORD, but he does not
answer them.
43 I pulverize them like dust of the earth;
I crush them and trample them
like mud in the streets.

44 You have freed me from the feuds
among my people;
you have preserved me as head
of nations;
a people I had not known serve me.
45 Foreigners submit to me cringing;
as soon as they hear, they obey me.
46 Foreigners lose heart
and come trembling
from their fortifications.

47 The LORD lives — blessed be my rock!
God, the rock of my salvation,
is exalted.
48 God — he grants me vengeance
and casts down peoples under me.
49 He frees me from my enemies.
You exalt me above my adversaries;
you rescue me from violent men.

50 Therefore I will give thanks to you
among the nations, LORD;
I will sing praises about your name.
51 He is a tower of salvation for[B] his king;
he shows loyalty to his anointed,
to David and his descendants forever.

DAVID'S LAST WORDS

23 These are the last words of David:
The declaration of David
son of Jesse,
the declaration of the man
raised on high,[C]
the one anointed by the God of Jacob.
This is the most delightful
of Israel's songs.

Thanksgiving and Contentment | *Praise for God's Security*

THE GIVER OF ALL GOOD THINGS

"Is it not true my house is with God? For he has established a permanent covenant with me, ordered and secured in every detail. Will he not bring about my whole salvation and my every desire?" 2 Samuel 23:5

In the New Testament, the apostle Paul asks a profound question: "What do you have that you didn't receive?" (1Co 4:7). Here, in David's last words, he essentially replied, "Nothing!"

This is a humble summary of God's marvelous faithfulness to Israel's king. Because of the promise God made to David ("permanent covenant with me"), the Spirit of the Lord spoke through him. What's more, God gave David the capacity to rule "in the fear of God" (2Sm 23:3). In every detail, God "ordered and secured" David's life and rule.

We are not kings like David, nor are we under the Davidic covenant. However, we are the beloved children of God through faith in Christ, and we are reconciled to him by the new covenant. This means that in countless ways we experience God's faithful care and provision.

You are loved! You are secure in him!

For the next note on *Thanksgiving and Contentment*, see 1 Chronicles 16:8.

[A] **22:41** Lit *you gave me the neck of my enemies* [B] **22:51** DSS read *he gives great victory to* [C] **23:1** Or *raised up by the high God*

2 The Spirit of the LORD spoke
through me,
his word was on my tongue.
3 The God of Israel spoke;
the Rock of Israel said to me,
"The one who rules the people
with justice,
who rules in the fear of God,
4 is like the morning light when the sun
rises
on a cloudless morning,
the glisten of rain on sprouting grass."

5 Is it not true my house is with God?
For he has established
a permanent covenant with me,
ordered and secured in every detail.
Will he not bring about
my whole salvation
and my every desire?
6 But all the wicked are like thorns
raked aside;
they can never be picked up by hand.
7 The man who touches them
must be armed with iron and the shaft
of a spear.
They will be completely burned up
on the spot.

EXPLOITS OF DAVID'S WARRIORS

8 These are the names of David's warriors:
Josheb-basshebeth the Tahchemonite was
chief of the officers.[A] He wielded his spear[B]
against eight hundred men that he killed at
one time.
9 After him, Eleazar son of Dodo son of an
Ahohite was among the three warriors with
David when they defied the Philistines. The men
of Israel retreated in the place they had gathered for battle, 10 but Eleazar stood his ground
and attacked the Philistines until his hand was
tired and stuck to his sword. The LORD brought
about a great victory that day. Then the troops
came back to him, but only to plunder the dead.
11 After him was Shammah son of Agee
the Hararite. The Philistines had assembled
in formation where there was a field full of
lentils. The troops fled from the Philistines,
12 but Shammah took his stand in the middle of the field, defended it, and struck down
the Philistines. So the LORD brought about a
great victory.
13 Three of the thirty leading warriors went
down at harvest time and came to David at the
cave of Adullam, while a company of Philistines was camping in the Valley of Rephaim.
14 At that time David was in the stronghold,
and a Philistine garrison was at Bethlehem.
15 David was extremely thirsty[C] and said, "If
only someone would bring me water to drink
from the well at the city gate of Bethlehem!"
16 So three of the warriors broke through the
Philistine camp and drew water from the well
at the gate of Bethlehem. They brought it back
to David, but he refused to drink it. Instead, he
poured it out to the LORD. 17 David said, "LORD,
I would never do such a thing! Is this not the
blood of men who risked their lives?" So he
refused to drink it. Such were the exploits of
the three warriors.
18 Abishai, Joab's brother and son of Zeruiah, was leader of the Three.[D] He wielded his
spear against three hundred men and killed
them, gaining a reputation among the Three.
19 Was he not more honored than the Three?
He became their commander even though he
did not become one of the Three.
20 Benaiah son of Jehoiada was the son of
a brave man from Kabzeel, a man of many
exploits. Benaiah killed two sons[E] of Ariel[F]
of Moab, and he went down into a pit on a
snowy day and killed a lion. 21 He also killed
an Egyptian, an impressive man. Even though
the Egyptian had a spear in his hand, Benaiah
went down to him with a club, snatched the
spear out of the Egyptian's hand, and then
killed him with his own spear. 22 These were
the exploits of Benaiah son of Jehoiada, who
had a reputation among the three warriors.
23 He was the most honored of the Thirty, but
he did not become one of the Three. David put
him in charge of his bodyguard.

24 Among the Thirty were
Joab's brother Asahel,
Elhanan son of Dodo of Bethlehem,
25 Shammah the Harodite,
Elika the Harodite,
26 Helez the Paltite,
Ira son of Ikkesh the Tekoite,
27 Abiezer the Anathothite,
Mebunnai the Hushathite,
28 Zalmon the Ahohite,
Maharai the Netophathite,
29 Heleb son of Baanah the Netophathite,
Ittai son of Ribai from Gibeah
of the Benjaminites,

[A] **23:8** Some Hb mss, LXX read *Three* [B] **23:8** Some Hb mss; other Hb mss, LXX read *He was Adino the Eznite* [C] **23:15** Lit *And David craved* [D] **23:18** Some Hb mss, Syr read *the Thirty* [E] **23:20** LXX; MT omits *sons* [F] **23:20** Or *two warriors*

30 Benaiah the Pirathonite,
Hiddai from the wadis of Gaash,[A]
31 Abi-albon the Arbathite,
Azmaveth the Barhumite,
32 Eliahba the Shaalbonite,
the sons of Jashen,
Jonathan son of[B] 33 Shammah
the Hararite,
Ahiam son of Sharar the Hararite,
34 Eliphelet son of Ahasbai
son of the Maacathite,
Eliam son of Ahithophel the Gilonite,
35 Hezro the Carmelite,
Paarai the Arbite,
36 Igal son of Nathan from Zobah,
Bani the Gadite,
37 Zelek the Ammonite,
Naharai the Beerothite,
the armor-bearer for Joab
son of Zeruiah,
38 Ira the Ithrite,
Gareb the Ithrite,
39 and Uriah the Hethite.
There were thirty-seven in all.

DAVID'S MILITARY CENSUS

24 The LORD's anger burned against Israel
again, and he stirred up David against
them to say: "Go, count the people of Israel
and Judah."
2 So the king said to Joab, the commander
of his army, "Go through all the tribes of Israel from Dan to Beer-sheba and register the
troops so I can know their number."
3 Joab replied to the king, "May the LORD
your God multiply the troops a hundred times
more than they are — while my lord the king
looks on! But why does my lord the king want
to do this?"
4 Yet the king's order prevailed over Joab
and the commanders of the army. So Joab and
the commanders of the army left the king's
presence to register the troops of Israel.
5 They crossed the Jordan and camped in
Aroer, south of the town in the middle of the
valley, and then proceeded toward Gad and
Jazer. 6 They went to Gilead and to the land of
the Hittites[C] and continued on to Dan-jaan
and around to Sidon. 7 They went to the fortress of Tyre and all the cities of the Hivites
and Canaanites. Afterward, they went to the
Negev of Judah at Beer-sheba.
8 When they had gone through the whole
land, they returned to Jerusalem at the end of
nine months and twenty days. 9 Joab gave the
king the total of the registration of the troops.
There were eight hundred thousand valiant
armed men[D] from Israel and five hundred
thousand men from Judah.
10 David's conscience troubled him after he
had taken a census of the troops. He said to
the LORD, "I have sinned greatly in what I've
done. Now, LORD, because I've been very foolish, please take away your servant's guilt."

DAVID'S PUNISHMENT

11 When David got up in the morning, the word
of the LORD had come to the prophet Gad, David's seer: 12 "Go and say to David, 'This is what
the LORD says: I am offering you three choices.
Choose one of them, and I will do it to you.'"
13 So Gad went to David, told him the choices,
and asked him, "Do you want three[E] years of
famine to come on your land, to flee from
your foes three months while they pursue
you, or to have a plague in your land three
days? Now, consider carefully[F] what answer
I should take back to the one who sent me."
14 David answered Gad, "I have great anxiety. Please, let us fall into the LORD's hands
because his mercies are great, but don't let
me fall into human hands."
15 So the LORD sent a plague on Israel from
that morning until the appointed time, and
from Dan to Beer-sheba seventy thousand
men died. 16 Then the angel extended his hand
toward Jerusalem to destroy it, but the LORD
relented concerning the destruction and said
to the angel who was destroying the people,
"Enough, withdraw your hand now!" The angel
of the LORD was then at the threshing floor of
Araunah[G] the Jebusite.
17 When David saw the angel striking the
people, he said to the LORD, "Look, I am the
one who has sinned; I am the one[H] who has
done wrong. But these sheep, what have they
done? Please, let your hand be against me and
my father's family."

DAVID'S ALTAR

18 Gad came to David that day and said to him,
"Go up and set up an altar to the LORD on the
threshing floor of Araunah the Jebusite." 19 David went up in obedience to Gad's command,

[A] **23:30** Or *from Nahale-gaash* [B] **23:32** Some LXX mss; MT omits *son of*; 1Ch 11:34 [C] **24:6** LXX; MT reads *of Tahtim-hodshi*; Hb obscure [D] **24:9** Lit *men of valor drawing the sword* [E] **24:13** LXX; MT reads *seven*; 1Ch 21:12 [F] **24:13** Lit *Now, know and see* [G] **24:16** = Ornan in 1Ch 21:15-28; 2Ch 3:1 [H] **24:17** LXX reads *shepherd*

just as the LORD had commanded. 20 Araunah
looked down and saw the king and his servants coming toward him, so he went out
and paid homage to the king with his face
to the ground.
21 Araunah said, "Why has my lord the king
come to his servant?"
David replied, "To buy the threshing floor
from you in order to build an altar to the LORD,
so the plague on the people may be halted."
22 Araunah said to David, "My lord the king
may take whatever he wants[A] and offer it.
Here are the oxen for a burnt offering and the
threshing sledges and ox yokes for the wood.
23 Your Majesty, Araunah gives everything
here to the king." Then he said to the king,
"May the LORD your God accept you."
24 The king answered Araunah, "No, I insist
on buying it from you for a price, for I will not
offer to the LORD my God burnt offerings that
cost me nothing." David bought the threshing
floor and the oxen for twenty ounces[B] of silver. 25 He built an altar to the LORD there and
offered burnt offerings and fellowship offerings. Then the LORD was receptive to prayer
for the land, and the plague on Israel ended.

[A] **24:22** Lit *take what is good in his eyes* [B] **24:24** Lit *50 shekels*

1 Kings—King Solomon was a blessed man. God gave him wisdom beyond that of anyone before or since (3:5-15). He wrote most of the book of Proverbs and was awarded the task of building the temple.

Solomon's wealth was renowned, and many nations sought alliances with him. But this led to his marrying foreign wives, drift into idolatry, and tragic decline. Even great wisdom cannot protect us from spiritual compromise.

Solomon's flawed leadership led to Israel's eventual downfall. First the kingdom divided (11:9-13). Both kingdoms' history after Solomon was often marked by instability, idolatry, and apostasy. King Ahab's confrontation with the prophet Elijah on Mount Carmel revealed God's supreme power through it all (18:1-40).

First Kings shows how quickly we can slide away from following God. But we find hope. God faithfully sends his prophets—Elijah in the book of 1 Kings, and preachers and teachers of God's Word today—to keep us on the path that leads to life. We are not doomed to perpetuate the cycle of sin that our forefathers committed or to repeat our own failures.

Reflect on the stories of 1 Kings to help you guard your heart as you focus on God and his holy love.

1 KINGS

AUTHOR: The books of 1 and 2 Kings were originally one book, but the author cannot be identified. Possibilities include Samuel and Jeremiah. The books seem to be constructed from several early documents, perhaps written by many different authors under the inspiration of the Holy Spirit.

DATE WRITTEN: The books of 1 and 2 Kings were completed after the release of Jehoiachin from Babylonian imprisonment (562 BC).

ORIGINAL AUDIENCE: The Israelites

SETTING: The books of 1 and 2 Kings cover a period of about 410 years, beginning in 970 BC when King David died. The narrative covers the division of Israel into two kingdoms and the exile of both kingdoms (Israel in 722 BC and Judah in 587 BC).

PURPOSE FOR WRITING: The repeating theme throughout 1 and 2 Kings is the sinful failure of the kings who ruled over God's people. Israel and Judah both failed to keep their side of the covenant to obey and serve God alone, so they suffered at the hands of surrounding nations and were eventually carried into exile. Themes explored include sin and judgment, personal faithfulness in the face of social pressure, and the conflict between worshiping the Lord and worshiping other gods.

OUTLINE:

1. Final Days of King David (1:1–2:12)

   Adonijah's attempt to unseat David (1:1-40)

   Solomon's anointing as king of Israel (1:41-53)

   David's charge to Solomon (2:1-12)

2. Solomon's Reign over the United Kingdom (2:13–11:43)

   Solomon's overcoming of his opponents (2:13-46)

   Solomon's wisdom (3:1-28)

   Solomon's kingdom (4:1-34)

   Construction of the temple (5:1–8:66)

   Solomon's fame and reputation (9:1–10:29)

   Solomon's sin and death (11:1-43)

3. Kings of Judah and Israel (12:1–22:53)

   King Rehoboam—Judah (12:1-24)

   King Jeroboam—Israel (12:25–14:20)

   King Rehoboam—Judah, continued (14:21-31)

   Kings Abijam and Asa—Judah (15:1-24)

   Kings Nadab and Baasha—Israel (15:25–16:7)

   Kings Elah, Zimri, Tibni, and Omri—Israel (16:8-28)

   King Ahab—Israel, and the prophet Elijah (16:29–22:40)

   King Jehoshaphat—Judah (22:41-50)

   King Ahaziah—Israel (22:51-53)

KEY VERSE:

"LORD God of Israel, there is no God like you in heaven above or on earth below, who keeps the gracious covenant with your servants who walk before you with all their heart." —1 Kings 8:23

RESTORATION THEMES

R	Rest and Reflection	*Asking for Wisdom—3:9-10* *Sitting Silent—19:11-12*
E	Eternal Perspective	*For the next note, see 2 Kings 6:16-17.*
S	Support	*For the next note, see 1 Chronicles 16:11.*
T	Thanksgiving and Contentment	*For the next note, see 1 Chronicles 16:8.*
O	Other-centeredness	*For the next note, see Job 29:12-13.*
R	Relationships	*For the next note, see 1 Chronicles 29:17.*
E	Exercise of Faith	*Guarding the Heart—1 Kings 11:4*

DAVID'S LAST DAYS

1 Now King David was old and advanced
in age. Although they covered him with
bedclothes, he could not get warm. 2 So his
servants said to him: "Let us[A] search for a
young virgin for my lord the king. She is to
attend the king and be his caregiver. She is to
lie by your side so that my lord the king will
get warm." 3 They searched for a beautiful
girl throughout the territory of Israel; they
found Abishag the Shunammite[B] and brought
her to the king. 4 The girl was of unsurpassed
beauty, and she became the king's caregiver.
She attended to him, but he was not intimate
with[C] her.

ADONIJAH'S BID FOR POWER

5 Adonijah son of Haggith kept exalting himself,
saying, "I will be king!" He prepared chariots,
cavalry, and fifty men to run ahead of him.[D]
6 But his father had never once infuriated him
by asking, "Why did you do that?" In addition,
he was quite handsome and was born after
Absalom. 7 He conspired[E] with Joab son of
Zeruiah and with the priest Abiathar. They
supported Adonijah, 8 but the priest Zadok,
Benaiah son of Jehoiada, the prophet Nathan,
Shimei, Rei, and David's royal guard[F] did not
side with Adonijah.

9 Adonijah sacrificed sheep, goats, cattle,
and fattened cattle near the stone of Zoheleth,
which is next to En-rogel. He invited all his
royal brothers and all the men of Judah, the
servants of the king, 10 but he did not invite
the prophet Nathan, Benaiah, the royal guard,
or his brother Solomon.

NATHAN'S AND BATHSHEBA'S APPEALS

11 Then Nathan said to Bathsheba, Solomon's
mother, "Have you not heard that Adonijah
son of Haggith has become king and our lord
David does not know it? 12 Now please come
and let me advise you. Save your life and the
life of your son Solomon. 13 Go, approach King
David and say to him, 'My lord the king, did you
not swear to your servant: Your son Solomon
is to become king after me, and he is the one
who is to sit on my throne? So why has Adonijah become king?' 14 At that moment, while
you are still there speaking with the king, I'll
come in after you and confirm your words."

15 So Bathsheba went to the king in his
bedroom. Since the king was very old, Abishag the Shunammite was attending to him.
16 Bathsheba knelt low and paid homage to
the king, and he asked, "What do you want?"

17 She replied, "My lord, you swore to your
servant by the LORD your God, 'Your son Solomon is to become king after me, and he is the
one who is to sit on my throne.' 18 Now look,
Adonijah has become king. And,[G] my lord
the king, you didn't know it. 19 He has lavishly
sacrificed oxen, fattened cattle, and sheep. He
invited all the king's sons, the priest Abiathar,
and Joab the commander of the army, but he
did not invite your servant Solomon. 20 Now,
my lord the king, the eyes of all Israel are on
you to tell them who will sit on the throne
of my lord the king after him. 21 Otherwise,
when my lord the king rests with his fathers,
I and my son Solomon will be regarded as
criminals."

22 At that moment, while she was still
speaking with the king, the prophet Nathan
arrived, 23 and it was announced to the king,
"The prophet Nathan is here." He came into
the king's presence and paid homage to him
with his face to the ground.

24 "My lord the king," Nathan said, "did you
say, 'Adonijah is to become king after me, and
he is the one who is to sit on my throne'? 25 For
today he went down and lavishly sacrificed
oxen, fattened cattle, and sheep. He invited
all the sons of the king, the commanders of
the army, and the priest Abiathar. And look!
They're eating and drinking in his presence,
and they're saying, 'Long live King Adonijah!'
26 But he did not invite me — me, your servant — or the priest Zadok or Benaiah son
of Jehoiada or your servant Solomon. 27 I'm
certain my lord the king would not have let
this happen without letting your servant[H]
know who will sit on my lord the king's throne
after him."

SOLOMON CONFIRMED KING

28 King David responded by saying, "Call in
Bathsheba for me." So she came into the king's
presence and stood before him. 29 The king
swore an oath and said, "As the LORD lives,
who has redeemed my life from every difficulty, 30 just as I swore to you by the LORD God
of Israel: Your son Solomon is to become king
after me, and he is the one who is to sit on my

[A] **1:2** Lit *them* [B] **1:3** Shunem was a town in the hill country of Issachar at the foot of Mt. Moreh; Jos 19:17-18. [C] **1:4** Lit *he did not know* [D] **1:5** Heralds announcing his procession [E] **1:7** Lit *His words were* [F] **1:8** Lit *David's warriors* [G] **1:18** Some Hb mss, LXX, Vg, Syr; other Hb mss read *And now* [H] **1:27** Some Hb mss, LXX; alt Hb tradition reads *servants*

throne in my place, that is exactly what I will do this very day."

31 Bathsheba knelt low with her face to the ground, paying homage to the king, and said, "May my lord King David live forever!"

32 King David then said, "Call in the priest Zadok, the prophet Nathan, and Benaiah son of Jehoiada for me." So they came into the king's presence. 33 The king said to them, "Take my servants with you, have my son Solomon ride on my own mule, and take him down to Gihon. 34 There, the priest Zadok and the prophet Nathan are to anoint him as king over Israel. You are to blow the ram's horn and say, 'Long live King Solomon!' 35 You are to come up after him, and he is to come in and sit on my throne. He is the one who is to become king in my place; he is the one I have commanded to be ruler over Israel and Judah."

36 "Amen," Benaiah son of Jehoiada replied to the king. "May the LORD, the God of my lord the king, so affirm it. 37 Just as the LORD was with my lord the king, so may he[A] be with Solomon and make his throne greater than the throne of my lord King David."

38 Then the priest Zadok, the prophet Nathan, Benaiah son of Jehoiada, the Cherethites, and the Pelethites went down, had Solomon ride on King David's mule, and took him to Gihon. 39 The priest Zadok took the horn of oil from the tabernacle and anointed Solomon. Then they blew the ram's horn, and all the people proclaimed, "Long live King Solomon!" 40 All the people went up after him, playing flutes and rejoicing with such a great joy that the earth split open from the sound.[B]

ADONIJAH HEARS OF SOLOMON'S CORONATION

41 Adonijah and all the invited guests who were with him heard the noise as they finished eating. Joab heard the sound of the ram's horn and said, "Why is the town in such an uproar?" 42 He was still speaking when Jonathan son of Abiathar the priest, suddenly arrived. Adonijah said, "Come in, for you are an important man, and you must be bringing good news."

43 "Unfortunately not," Jonathan answered him. "Our lord King David has made Solomon king. 44 And with Solomon, the king has sent the priest Zadok, the prophet Nathan, Benaiah son of Jehoiada, the Cherethites, and the Pelethites, and they have had him ride on the king's mule. 45 The priest Zadok and the prophet Nathan have anointed him king in Gihon. They have gone up from there rejoicing. The town has been in an uproar; that's the noise you heard. 46 Solomon has even taken his seat on the royal throne.

47 "The king's servants have also gone to congratulate our lord King David, saying, 'May your God make the name of Solomon more well known than your name, and may he make his throne greater than your throne.' Then the king bowed in worship on his bed. 48 And the king went on to say this: 'Blessed be the LORD God of Israel! Today he has provided one to sit on my throne, and I am a witness.'"[C]

49 Then all of Adonijah's guests got up trembling and went their separate ways. 50 Adonijah was afraid of Solomon, so he got up and went to take hold of the horns of the altar.

51 It was reported to Solomon: "Look, Adonijah fears King Solomon, and he has taken hold of the horns of the altar, saying, 'Let King Solomon first[D] swear to me that he will not kill his servant with the sword.'"

52 Then Solomon said, "If he is a man of character, not a single hair of his will fall to the ground, but if evil is found in him, he dies." 53 So King Solomon sent for him, and they took him down from the altar. He came and paid homage to King Solomon, and Solomon said to him, "Go to your home."

DAVID'S DYING INSTRUCTIONS TO SOLOMON

2 As the time approached for David to die, he ordered his son Solomon, 2 "As for me, I am going the way of all of the earth. Be strong and be a man, 3 and keep your obligation to the LORD your God to walk in his ways and to keep his statutes, commands, ordinances, and decrees. This is written in the law of Moses, so that you will have success in everything you do and wherever you turn, 4 and so that the LORD will fulfill his promise that he made to me: 'If your sons guard their way to walk faithfully before me with all their heart and all their soul, you will never fail to have a man on the throne of Israel.'

5 "You also know what Joab son of Zeruiah did to me and what he did to the two commanders of Israel's army, Abner son of Ner and Amasa son of Jether. He murdered them in a time of peace to avenge blood shed in war. He spilled that blood on his own waistband

[A] **1:37** Alt Hb tradition reads *so he will* [B] **1:40** LXX reads *the land resounded with their noise* [C] **1:48** Lit *and my eyes are seeing* [D] **1:51** Some Hb mss, LXX, Syr, Vg read *today*

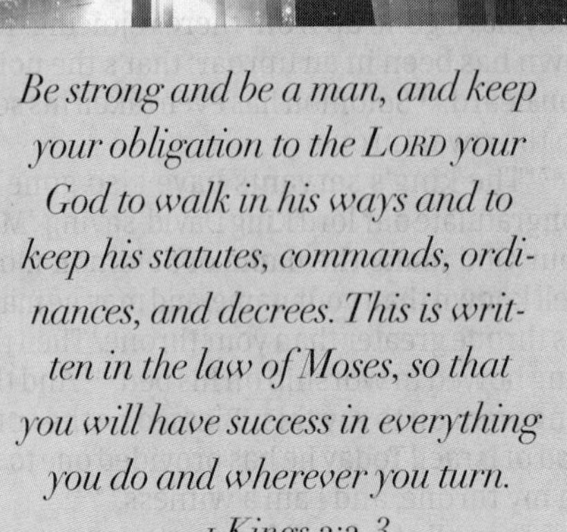
Be strong and be a man, and keep
your obligation to the LORD your
God to walk in his ways and to
keep his statutes, commands, ordinances, and decrees. This is written in the law of Moses, so that
you will have success in everything
you do and wherever you turn.
—1 Kings 2:2-3

and on the sandals of his feet.[A] 6 Act according
to your wisdom, and do not let his gray head
descend to Sheol in peace.
7 "Show kindness to the sons of Barzillai the
Gileadite and let them be among those who
eat at your table because they supported me
when I fled from your brother Absalom.
8 "Keep an eye on Shimei son of Gera, the
Benjaminite from Bahurim who is with you. He
uttered malicious curses against me the day I
went to Mahanaim. But he came down to meet
me at the Jordan River, and I swore to him by
the LORD: 'I will never kill you with the sword.'
9 So don't let him go unpunished, for you are a
wise man. You know how to deal with him to
bring his gray head down to Sheol with blood."
10 Then David rested with his fathers and
was buried in the city of David. 11 The length
of time David reigned over Israel was forty
years: he reigned seven years in Hebron and
thirty-three years in Jerusalem. 12 Solomon
sat on the throne of his father David, and his
kingship was firmly established.

ADONIJAH'S FOOLISH REQUEST

13 Now Adonijah son of Haggith came to Bathsheba, Solomon's mother. She asked, "Do you
come peacefully?"
"Peacefully," he replied, 14 and then asked,
"May I talk with you?"[B]
"Go ahead," she answered.
15 "You know the kingship was mine," he said.
"All Israel expected me to be king, but then the
kingship was turned over to my brother, for
the LORD gave it to him. 16 So now I have just
one request of you; don't turn me down."[C]
She said to him, "Go on."
17 He replied, "Please speak to King Solomon
since he won't turn you down. Let him give me
Abishag the Shunammite as a wife."
18 "Very well," Bathsheba replied. "I will speak
to the king for you."
19 So Bathsheba went to King Solomon to
speak to him about Adonijah. The king stood
up to greet her, bowed to her, sat down on his
throne, and had a throne placed for the king's
mother. So she sat down at his right hand.
20 Then she said, "I have just one small request of you. Don't turn me down."
"Go ahead and ask, mother," the king replied,
"for I won't turn you down."
21 So she said, "Let Abishag the Shunammite
be given to your brother Adonijah as a wife."
22 King Solomon answered his mother, "Why
are you requesting Abishag the Shunammite
for Adonijah? Since he is my elder brother, you
might as well ask the kingship for him, for
the priest Abiathar, and for Joab son of Zeruiah."[D] 23 Then King Solomon took an oath by the
LORD: "May God punish me and do so severely
if Adonijah has not made this request at the
cost of his life. 24 And now, as the LORD lives
— the one who established me, seated me on
the throne of my father David, and made me a
dynasty as he promised — I swear Adonijah
will be put to death today!" 25 Then King Solomon dispatched Benaiah son of Jehoiada, who
struck down Adonijah, and he died.

ABIATHAR'S BANISHMENT

26 The king said to the priest Abiathar, "Go
to your fields in Anathoth. Even though you
deserve to die, I will not put you to death today, since you carried the ark of the Lord GOD
in the presence of my father David and you
suffered through all that my father suffered."
27 So Solomon banished Abiathar from being
the LORD's priest, and it fulfilled the LORD's
prophecy he had spoken at Shiloh against
Eli's family.

JOAB'S EXECUTION

28 The news reached Joab. Since he had supported Adonijah but not Absalom, Joab fled
to the LORD's tabernacle and took hold of the
horns of the altar.

[A] **2:5** LXX, Old Lat read *on my waistband and . . . my feet*; v. 31 [B] **2:14** Lit *then said, "I have a word for you."* [C] **2:16** Lit *don't make me turn my face* [D] **2:22** LXX, Vg, Syr read *kingship for him, and on his side are Abiathar the priest and Joab son of Zeruiah*

29 It was reported to King Solomon: "Joab has
fled to the LORD's tabernacle and is now beside
the altar." Then Solomon sent[A] Benaiah son of Jehoiada and told him, "Go and strike him down!"
30 So Benaiah went to the tabernacle and said
to Joab, "This is what the king says: 'Come out!'"
But Joab said, "No, for I will die here."
So Benaiah took a message back to the king,
"This is what Joab said, and this is how he
answered me."
31 The king said to him, "Do just as he says.
Strike him down and bury him in order to
remove from me and from my father's family
the blood that Joab shed without just cause.
32 The LORD will bring back his own blood on
his head because he struck down two men
more righteous and better than he, without
my father David's knowledge. With his sword,
Joab murdered Abner son of Ner, commander
of Israel's army, and Amasa son of Jether, commander of Judah's army. 33 The responsibility
for their deaths will come back to Joab and
to his descendants[B] forever, but for David,
his descendants, his dynasty, and his throne,
there will be peace from the LORD forever."
34 Benaiah son of Jehoiada went up, struck
down Joab, and put him to death. He was buried at his house in the wilderness. 35 Then the
king appointed Benaiah son of Jehoiada in
Joab's place over the army, and he appointed
the priest Zadok in Abiathar's place.

SHIMEI'S BANISHMENT AND EXECUTION

36 Then the king summoned Shimei and said
to him, "Build a house for yourself in Jerusalem and live there, but don't leave there and
go anywhere else. 37 On the day you do leave
and cross the Kidron Valley, know for sure
that you will certainly die. Your blood will be
on your own head."
38 Shimei said to the king, "The sentence is
fair; your servant will do as my lord the king
has spoken." And Shimei lived in Jerusalem
for a long time.
39 But then, at the end of three years, two
of Shimei's slaves ran away to Achish son of
Maacah, king of Gath. Shimei was informed,
"Look, your slaves are in Gath." 40 So Shimei
saddled his donkey and set out to Achish at
Gath to search for his slaves. He went and
brought them back from Gath.
41 It was reported to Solomon that Shimei
had gone from Jerusalem to Gath and had
returned. 42 So the king summoned Shimei
and said to him, "Didn't I make you swear
by the LORD and warn you, saying, 'On the
day you leave and go anywhere else, know
for sure that you will certainly die'? And you
said to me, 'The sentence is fair; I will obey.'
43 So why have you not kept the LORD's oath
and the command that I gave you?" 44 The
king also said, "You yourself know all the evil
that you did to my father David. Therefore,
the LORD has brought back your evil on your
head, 45 but King Solomon will be blessed, and
David's throne will remain established before
the LORD forever."
46 Then the king commanded Benaiah son of
Jehoiada, and he went out and struck Shimei
down, and he died. So the kingdom was established in Solomon's hand.

THE LORD APPEARS TO SOLOMON

3 Solomon made an alliance[C] with Pharaoh
king of Egypt by marrying Pharaoh's
daughter. Solomon brought her to the city
of David until he finished building his palace,
the LORD's temple, and the wall surrounding Jerusalem. 2 However, the people were
sacrificing on the high places, because until
that time a temple for the LORD's name had
not been built. 3 Solomon loved the LORD by
walking in the statutes of his father David,
but he also sacrificed and burned incense on
the high places.
4 The king went to Gibeon to sacrifice there
because it was the most famous high place.
He offered a thousand burnt offerings on that
altar. 5 At Gibeon the LORD appeared to Solomon in a dream at night. God said, "Ask. What
should I give you?"
6 And Solomon replied, "You have shown
great and faithful love to your servant, my
father David, because he walked before you
in faithfulness, righteousness, and integrity.[D]
You have continued this great and faithful
love for him by giving him a son to sit on his
throne, as it is today.
7 "LORD my God, you have now made your
servant king in my father David's place. Yet I
am just a youth with no experience in leadership.[E] 8 Your servant is among your people

[A] **2:29** LXX adds *Joab a message: "What is the matter with you, that you have fled to the altar?" And Joab replied, "Because I feared you, I have fled to the Lord." And Solomon the king sent* [B] **2:33** Lit *Their blood will return on the head of Joab and on the head of his seed* [C] **3:1** Lit *Solomon made himself a son-in-law* [D] **3:6** Lit *and uprightness of heart with you* [E] **3:7** Lit *am a little youth and do not know to go out or come in*

you have chosen, a people too many to be
numbered or counted. 9 So give your servant
a receptive heart to judge your people and
to discern between good and evil. For who
is able to judge this great people of yours?"
10 Now it pleased the Lord that Solomon had
requested this. 11 So God said to him, "Because
you have requested this and did not ask for
long life[A] or riches for yourself, or the death[B]
of your enemies, but you asked discernment
for yourself to administer justice, 12 I will therefore do what you have asked. I will give you a
wise and understanding heart, so that there
has never been anyone like you before and
never will be again. 13 In addition, I will give
you what you did not ask for: both riches and
honor, so that no king will be your equal during
your entire life. 14 If you walk in my ways and
keep my statutes and commands just as your
father David did, I will give you a long life."
15 Then Solomon woke up and realized it had
been a dream. He went to Jerusalem, stood
before the ark of the Lord's covenant, and
offered burnt offerings and fellowship offerings. Then he held a feast for all his servants.

SOLOMON'S WISDOM

16 Then two women who were prostitutes came
to the king and stood before him. 17 One woman
said, "Please, my lord, this woman and I live
in the same house, and I had a baby while
she was in the house. 18 On the third day after I gave birth, she also had a baby and we
were alone. No one else[C] was with us in the
house; just the two of us were there. 19 During
the night this woman's son died because she
lay on him. 20 She got up in the middle of the
night and took my son from my side while
your servant was asleep. She laid him in her
arms, and she put her dead son in my arms.
21 When I got up in the morning to nurse my
son, I discovered he was dead. That morning,
when I looked closely at him I realized that he
was not the son I gave birth to."
22 "No," the other woman said. "My son is the
living one; your son is the dead one."

The first woman said, "No, your son is the
dead one; my son is the living one." So they
argued before the king.
23 The king replied, "This woman says, 'This
is my son who is alive, and your son is dead,'
but that woman says, 'No, your son is dead, and
my son is alive.' " 24 The king continued, "Bring
me a sword." So they brought the sword to the
king. 25 And the king said, "Cut the living boy in
two and give half to one and half to the other."
26 The woman whose son was alive spoke to
the king because she felt great compassion[D]

Rest and Reflection | *Asking for Wisdom*

GOD'S BLANK CHECK

"So give your servant a receptive heart to judge your people and to discern between good and evil. For who is able to judge this great people of yours?' Now it pleased the Lord that Solomon had requested this." 1 Kings 3:9-10

Imagine God coming to you and saying, "Ask whatever you wish, and I'll give it to you."

That was Solomon's experience. As he waited to be installed as Israel's third king, he must have been intimidated. Although very young and untested, he was being called to follow in the footsteps of his legendary father, David.

So when God offered him a blank check, Solomon didn't hesitate. He asked for a "receptive" (teachable, understanding) heart. He asked for the ability to "discern between good and evil." In short, he asked for wisdom to make right choices.

Wisdom isn't the same thing as book smarts. It's more than a high IQ. It's skill in living. Ask God for wisdom to navigate sticky situations in a way that honors him and blesses others.

For the record, God still loves to give wisdom to those who seek it—see Proverbs 2:1-7.

For the next note on *Rest and Reflection*, see 1 Kings 19:11-12.

[A] **3:11** Lit *for many days* [B] **3:11** Lit *life* [C] **3:18** Lit *No stranger* [D] **3:26** Lit *because her compassion grew hot*

for her son. "My lord, give her the living baby,"
she said, "but please don't have him killed!"
But the other one said, "He will not be mine
or yours. Cut him in two!"
27 The king responded, "Give the living baby
to the first woman, and don't kill him. She is his
mother." 28 All Israel heard about the judgment
the king had given, and they stood in awe of
the king because they saw that God's wisdom
was in him to carry out justice.

SOLOMON'S OFFICIALS

4 King Solomon reigned over all Israel, 2 and
these were his officials:
Azariah son of Zadok, priest;
3 Elihoreph and Ahijah the sons of Shisha,
secretaries;
Jehoshaphat son of Ahilud, court
historian;
4 Benaiah son of Jehoiada, in charge of
the army;
Zadok and Abiathar, priests;
5 Azariah son of Nathan, in charge of the
deputies;
Zabud son of Nathan, a priest and adviser
to the king;
6 Ahishar, in charge of the palace;
and Adoniram son of Abda, in charge of
forced labor.

7 Solomon had twelve deputies for all Israel.
They provided food for the king and his household; each one made provision for one month
out of the year. 8 These were their names:
Ben-hur, in the hill country of Ephraim;
9 Ben-deker, in Makaz, Shaalbim,
Beth-shemesh, and Elon-beth-hanan;
10 Ben-hesed, in Arubboth (he had Socoh
and the whole land of Hepher);
11 Ben-abinadab, in all Naphath-dor
(Taphath daughter of Solomon was his
wife);
12 Baana son of Ahilud, in Taanach,
Megiddo, and all Beth-shean which is
beside Zarethan below Jezreel, from
Beth-shean to Abel-meholah, as far as the
other side of Jokmeam;
13 Ben-geber, in Ramoth-gilead (he had
the villages of Jair son of Manasseh,
which are in Gilead, and he had the
region of Argob, which is in Bashan, sixty
great cities with walls and bronze bars);
14 Ahinadab son of Iddo, in Mahanaim;
15 Ahimaaz, in Naphtali (he also had
married a daughter of Solomon —
Basemath);
16 Baana son of Hushai, in Asher and
Bealoth;
17 Jehoshaphat son of Paruah, in Issachar;
18 Shimei son of Ela, in Benjamin;
19 Geber son of Uri, in the land of Gilead,
the country of King Sihon of the Amorites
and of King Og of Bashan.
There was one deputy in the land of Judah.[A]

SOLOMON'S PROVISIONS

20 Judah and Israel were as numerous as the
sand by the sea; they were eating, drinking, and
rejoicing. 21 Solomon ruled all the kingdoms
from the Euphrates River to the land of the
Philistines and as far as the border of Egypt.
They offered tribute and served Solomon all
the days of his life.
22 Solomon's provisions for one day were
150 bushels[B] of fine flour and 300 bushels[C]
of meal, 23 ten fattened cattle, twenty range
cattle, and a hundred sheep and goats, besides
deer, gazelles, roebucks, and pen-fed poultry,[D]
24 for he had dominion over everything west
of the Euphrates from Tiphsah to Gaza and
over all the kings west of the Euphrates. He
had peace on all his surrounding borders.
25 Throughout Solomon's reign, Judah and
Israel lived in safety from Dan to Beer-sheba,
each person under his own vine and his own
fig tree. 26 Solomon had forty thousand[E] stalls
of horses for his chariots, and twelve thousand horsemen. 27 Each of those deputies for
a month in turn provided food for King Solomon and for everyone who came to King Solomon's table. They neglected nothing. 28 Each
man brought the barley and the straw for the
chariot teams and the other horses to the required place according to his assignment.[F]

SOLOMON'S WISDOM AND LITERARY GIFTS

29 God gave Solomon wisdom, very great insight, and understanding as vast as the sand
on the seashore. 30 Solomon's wisdom was
greater than the wisdom of all the people of
the East, greater than all the wisdom of Egypt.
31 He was wiser than anyone — wiser than
Ethan the Ezrahite, and Heman, Calcol, and
Darda, sons of Mahol. His reputation extended
to all the surrounding nations.
32 Solomon spoke 3,000 proverbs, and his

[A] 4:19 LXX; MT omits *of Judah* [B] 4:22 Lit *30 cors* [C] 4:22 Lit *60 cors* [D] 4:23 Hb obscure [E] 4:26 2Ch 9:25 reads *4,000 stalls*
[F] 4:28 Lit *judgment*

songs numbered 1,005. 33 He spoke about trees, from the cedar in Lebanon to the hyssop growing out of the wall. He also spoke about animals, birds, reptiles, and fish. 34 Emissaries of all peoples, sent by every king on earth who had heard of his wisdom, came to listen to Solomon's wisdom.

HIRAM'S BUILDING MATERIALS

5 King Hiram of Tyre sent his emissaries to Solomon when he heard that he had been anointed king in his father's place, for Hiram had always been friends with David.

2 Solomon sent this message to Hiram: 3 "You know my father David was not able to build a temple for the name of the LORD his God. This was because of the warfare all around him until the LORD put his enemies under his feet. 4 The LORD my God has now given me rest on every side; there is no enemy or crisis. 5 So I plan to build a temple for the name of the LORD my God, according to what the LORD promised my father David: 'I will put your son on your throne in your place, and he will build the temple for my name.'

6 "Therefore, command that cedars from Lebanon be cut down for me. My servants will be with your servants, and I will pay your servants' wages according to whatever you say, for you know that not a man among us knows how to cut timber like the Sidonians."

7 When Hiram heard Solomon's words, he rejoiced greatly and said, "Blessed be the LORD today! He has given David a wise son to be over this great people!" 8 Then Hiram sent a reply to Solomon, saying, "I have heard your message; I will do everything you want regarding the cedar and cypress timber. 9 My servants will bring the logs down from Lebanon to the sea, and I will make them into rafts to go by sea to the place you indicate. I will break them apart there, and you can take them away. You then can meet my needs by providing my household with food."

10 So Hiram provided Solomon with all the cedar and cypress timber he wanted, 11 and Solomon provided Hiram with one hundred thousand bushels[A] of wheat as food for his household and one hundred ten thousand gallons[B] of oil from crushed olives. Solomon did this for Hiram year after year.

12 The LORD gave Solomon wisdom, as he had promised him. There was peace between Hiram and Solomon, and the two of them made a treaty.

SOLOMON'S WORKFORCE

13 Then King Solomon drafted forced laborers from all Israel; the labor force numbered thirty thousand men. 14 He sent ten thousand to Lebanon each month in shifts; one month they were in Lebanon, two months they were at home. Adoniram was in charge of the forced labor. 15 Solomon had seventy thousand porters and eighty thousand stonecutters in the mountains, 16 not including his thirty-three hundred[C] deputies in charge of the work. They supervised the people doing the work. 17 The king commanded them to quarry large, costly stones to lay the foundation of the temple with dressed stones. 18 So Solomon's builders and Hiram's builders, along with the Gebalites, quarried the stone and prepared the timber and stone for the temple's construction.

BUILDING THE TEMPLE

6 Solomon began to build the temple for the LORD in the four hundred eightieth year after the Israelites came out of the land of Egypt, in the fourth year of his reign over Israel, in the month of Ziv, which is the second month.[D] 2 The temple that King Solomon built for the LORD was ninety feet[E] long, thirty feet[F] wide, and forty-five feet[G] high. 3 The portico in front of the temple sanctuary was thirty feet long extending across the temple's width, and fifteen feet deep[H] in front of the temple. 4 He also made windows with beveled frames[I] for the temple.

5 He then built a chambered structure[J] along the temple wall, encircling the walls of the temple, that is, the sanctuary and the inner sanctuary. And he made side chambers[K] all around. 6 The lowest chamber was 7½ feet[L] wide, the middle was 9 feet[M] wide, and the third was 10½ feet[N] wide. He also provided offset ledges for the temple all around the outside so that nothing would be inserted into the temple walls. 7 The temple's construction used finished stones cut at the quarry so that no hammer, chisel, or any iron tool was heard in the temple while it was being built.

[A] **5:11** Lit *20,000 cors* [B] **5:11** LXX reads *20,000 baths*; MT reads *20 cors* [C] **5:16** Some LXX mss read *3,600*; 2Ch 2:2,18
[D] **6:1** April–May [E] **6:2** Lit *60 cubits* [F] **6:2** Lit *20 cubits*, also in vv. 3,16,20 [G] **6:2** Lit *30 cubits* [H] **6:3** Lit *10 cubits wide*
[I] **6:4** Hb obscure [J] **6:5** Lit *built the temple of chamber* [K] **6:5** Lit *made ribs* or *sides* [L] **6:6** Lit *five cubits*, also in vv. 10,24
[M] **6:6** Lit *six cubits* [N] **6:6** Lit *seven cubits*

8 The door for the lowest[A] side chamber was on the right side of the temple. They[B] went up a stairway[C] to the middle chamber, and from the middle to the third. 9 When he finished building the temple, he paneled it with boards and planks of cedar. 10 He built the chambers along the entire temple, joined to the temple with cedar beams; each story was 7 ½ feet high.

11 The word of the LORD came to Solomon: 12 "As for this temple you are building — if you walk in my statutes, observe my ordinances, and keep all my commands by walking in them, I will fulfill my promise to you, which I made to your father David. 13 I will dwell among the Israelites and not abandon my people Israel."

14 When Solomon finished building the temple,[D] 15 he paneled the interior temple walls with cedar boards; from the temple floor to the surface of the ceiling he overlaid the interior with wood. He also overlaid the floor with cypress boards. 16 Then he lined thirty feet of the rear of the temple with cedar boards from the floor to the surface of the ceiling,[E] and he built the interior as an inner sanctuary, the most holy place. 17 The temple, that is, the sanctuary in front of the most holy place,[F] was sixty feet[G] long. 18 The cedar paneling inside the temple was carved with ornamental gourds and flower blossoms. Everything was cedar; not a stone could be seen.

19 He prepared the inner sanctuary inside the temple to put the ark of the LORD's covenant there. 20 The interior of the sanctuary was thirty feet long, thirty feet wide, and thirty feet high; he overlaid it with pure gold. He also overlaid the cedar altar. 21 Next, Solomon overlaid the interior of the temple with pure gold, and he hung[H] gold chains across the front of the inner sanctuary and overlaid it with gold. 22 So he added the gold overlay to the entire temple until everything was completely finished, including the entire altar that belongs to the inner sanctuary.

23 In the inner sanctuary he made two cherubim 15 feet[I] high out of olive wood. 24 One wing of the first cherub was 7 ½ feet long, and the other wing was 7 ½ feet long. The wingspan was 15 feet from tip to tip. 25 The second cherub also was 15 feet; both cherubim had the same size and shape. 26 The first cherub's height was 15 feet and so was the second cherub's. 27 Then he put the cherubim inside the inner temple. Since their wings were spread out, the first one's wing touched one wall while the second cherub's wing touched the other[J] wall, and in the middle of the temple their wings were touching wing to wing. 28 He also overlaid the cherubim with gold.

29 He carved all the surrounding temple walls with carved engravings — cherubim, palm trees, and flower blossoms — in the inner and outer sanctuaries. 30 He overlaid the temple floor with gold in both the inner and the outer sanctuaries.

31 For the entrance of the inner sanctuary, he made olive wood doors. The pillars of the doorposts were five-sided.[C] 32 The two doors were made of olive wood. He carved cherubim, palm trees, and flower blossoms on them and overlaid them with gold, hammering gold over the cherubim and palm trees. 33 In the same way, he made four-sided[C] olive wood doorposts for the sanctuary entrance. 34 The two doors were made of cypress wood; the first door had two folding sides, and the second door had two folding panels. 35 He carved cherubim, palm trees, and flower blossoms on them and overlaid them with gold applied evenly over the carving. 36 He built the inner courtyard with three rows of dressed stone and a row of trimmed cedar beams.

37 The foundation of the LORD's temple was laid in Solomon's fourth year in the month of Ziv. 38 In his eleventh year in the month of Bul, which is the eighth month,[K] the temple was completed in every detail and according to every specification. So he built it in seven years.

SOLOMON'S PALACE COMPLEX

7 Solomon completed his entire palace complex after thirteen years of construction. 2 He built the House of the Forest of Lebanon. It was one hundred fifty feet[L] long, seventy-five feet[M] wide, and forty-five feet[N] high on four rows of cedar pillars, with cedar beams on top of the pillars. 3 It was paneled above with cedar at the top of the chambers that rested on forty-five pillars, fifteen per row. 4 There were three rows of window frames, facing

[A] **6:8** LXX, Tg; MT reads *middle* [B] **6:8** = People [C] **6:8,31,33** Hb obscure [D] **6:11-14** LXX omits these vv. [E] **6:16** LXX; MT omits *of the ceiling*; 1Kg 6:15 [F] **6:17** Lit *front of me*; Hb obscure [G] **6:17** Lit *40 cubits* [H] **6:21** Lit *he caused to pass across* [I] **6:23** Lit *10 cubits*, also in vv. 24,25,26 [J] **6:27** Lit *the second* [K] **6:38** = October–November [L] **7:2** Lit *100 cubits* [M] **7:2** Lit *50 cubits*, also in v. 6 [N] **7:2** Lit *30 cubits*, also in vv. 6,23

each other[A] in three tiers.[B] 5 All the doors
and doorposts had rectangular frames, the
openings facing each other[C] in three tiers.
6 He made the hall of pillars seventy-five feet
long and forty-five feet wide. A portico was in
front of the pillars, and a canopy with pillars[D]
was in front of them. 7 He made the Hall of the
Throne where he would judge — the Hall of
Judgment. It was paneled with cedar from the
floor to the rafters.[E] 8 Solomon's own palace
where he would live, in the other courtyard
behind the hall, was of similar construction.
And he made a house like this hall for Pharaoh's daughter, his wife.[F]

9 All of these buildings were of costly stones,
cut to size and sawed with saws on the inner
and outer surfaces, from foundation to coping
and from the outside to the great courtyard.
10 The foundation was made of large, costly
stones twelve and fifteen feet[G] long. 11 Above
were also costly stones, cut to size, as well as
cedar wood. 12 Around the great courtyard, as
well as the inner courtyard of the LORD's temple and the portico of the temple, were three
rows of dressed stone and a row of trimmed
cedar beams.

13 King Solomon had Hiram[H] brought from
Tyre. 14 He was a widow's son from the tribe of
Naphtali, and his father was a man of Tyre, a
bronze craftsman. Hiram had great skill, understanding, and knowledge to do every kind
of bronze work. So he came to King Solomon
and carried out all his work.

THE BRONZE PILLARS

15 He cast two bronze pillars, each 27 feet[I] high
and 18 feet[J] in circumference.[K] 16 He also made
two capitals of cast bronze to set on top of the
pillars; 7 ½ feet[L] was the height of the first
capital, and 7 ½ feet was also the height of
the second capital. 17 The capitals on top of the
pillars had gratings of latticework, wreaths[M]
made of chainwork — seven for the first capital and seven for the second.

18 He made the pillars with two encircling
rows of pomegranates on the one grating to
cover the capital on top; he did the same for
the second capital. 19 And the capitals on top
of the pillars in the portico were shaped like
lilies, six feet[N] high. 20 The capitals on the two
pillars were also immediately above the rounded surface next to the grating, and two hundred
pomegranates were in rows encircling each[O]
capital. 21 He set up the pillars at the portico
of the sanctuary: he set up the right pillar and
named it Jachin;[P] then he set up the left pillar
and named it Boaz.[Q] 22 The tops of the pillars
were shaped like lilies. Then the work of the
pillars was completed.

THE BASIN

23 He made the cast metal basin,[R] 15 feet[S] from
brim to brim, perfectly round. It was 7 ½ feet
high and 45 feet in circumference. 24 Ornamental gourds encircled it below the brim,
ten every half yard,[T] completely encircling the
basin. The gourds were cast in two rows when
the basin was cast. 25 It stood on twelve oxen,
three facing north, three facing west, three
facing south, and three facing east. The basin
was on top of them and all their hindquarters
were toward the center. 26 The basin was three
inches[U] thick, and its rim was fashioned like
the brim of a cup or of a lily blossom. It held
eleven thousand gallons.[V]

THE BRONZE WATER CARTS

27 Then he made ten bronze water carts.[W] Each
water cart was 6 feet long, 6 feet wide, and
4 ½ feet[X] high. 28 This was the design of the
carts: They had frames; the frames were between the cross-pieces, 29 and on the frames
between the cross-pieces were lions, oxen,
and cherubim. On the cross-pieces there was a
pedestal above, and below the lions and oxen
were wreaths of hanging[Y] work. 30 Each cart
had four bronze wheels with bronze axles.
Underneath the four corners of the basin
were cast supports, each next to a wreath.
31 And the water cart's opening inside the
crown on top was eighteen inches[Z] wide.
The opening was round, made as a pedestal
twenty-seven inches[AA] wide. On it were carvings, but their frames were square, not round.
32 There were four wheels under the frames,
and the wheel axles were part of the water
cart; each wheel was twenty-seven inches[AB]
tall. 33 The wheels' design was similar to that of

[A] **7:4** Lit *frames, window to window* [B] **7:4** Lit *three times*; = at 3 different places, also in v. 5 [C] **7:5** Lit *frames, opposing window to window* [D] **7:6** Hb obscure [E] **7:7** Syr, Vg; MT reads *floor* [F] **7:8** Lit *daughter he had taken* [G] **7:10** Lit *ten cubits and eight cubits* [H] **7:13** = Huram in 2Ch 4:11 [I] **7:15** Lit *18 cubits* [J] **7:15** Lit *12 cubits* [K] **7:15** LXX adds *and the thickness of the pillar was four fingers hollowed and similarly the second pillar* [L] **7:16** Lit *five cubits*, also in v. 23 [M] **7:17** Lit *tassels* [N] **7:19** Lit *four cubits*, also in vv. 27,38 [O] **7:20** Lit *encircling the second* [P] **7:21** = He Will Establish [Q] **7:21** = In Him Is Strength [R] **7:23** Lit *sea* [S] **7:23** Lit *10 cubits* [T] **7:24** Lit *10 per cubit* [U] **7:26** Lit *a handbreadth* [V] **7:26** Lit *2,000 baths* [W] **7:27** Lit *bronze stands* [X] **7:27** Lit *three cubits* [Y] **7:29** Or *hammered-down* [Z] **7:31** Lit *a cubit* [AA] **7:31** Lit *one and a half cubits* [AB] **7:32** Lit *was one and a half cubits*

chariot wheels: their axles, rims, spokes, and hubs were all of cast metal. 34 Four supports were at the four corners of each water cart; each support was one piece with the water cart. 35 At the top of the cart was a band nine inches[A] high encircling it; also, at the top of the cart, its braces and its frames were one piece with it. 36 He engraved cherubim, lions, and palm trees on the plates of its braces and on its frames, wherever each had space, with encircling wreaths. 37 In this way he made the ten water carts using the same casting, dimensions, and shape for all of them.

BRONZE BASINS AND OTHER UTENSILS

38 Then he made ten bronze basins — each basin held 220 gallons[B] and each was six feet wide — one basin for each of the ten water carts. 39 He set five water carts on the right side of the temple and five on the left side. He put the basin near the right side of the temple toward the southeast. 40 Then Hiram made the basins, the shovels, and the sprinkling basins.

COMPLETION OF THE BRONZE WORKS

So Hiram finished all the work that he was doing for King Solomon on the LORD's temple: 41 two pillars; bowls for the capitals that were on top of the two pillars; the two gratings for covering both bowls of the capitals that were on top of the pillars; 42 the four hundred pomegranates for the two gratings (two rows of pomegranates for each grating covering both capitals' bowls on top of the pillars); 43 the ten water carts; the ten basins on the water carts; 44 the basin; the twelve oxen underneath the basin; 45 and the pots, shovels, and sprinkling basins. All the utensils that Hiram made for King Solomon at the LORD's temple were made of burnished bronze. 46 The king had them cast in clay molds in the Jordan Valley between Succoth and Zarethan. 47 Solomon left all the utensils unweighed because there were so many; the weight of the bronze was not determined.

COMPLETION OF THE GOLD FURNISHINGS

48 Solomon also made all the equipment in the LORD's temple: the gold altar; the gold table that the Bread of the Presence was placed on; 49 the pure gold lampstands in front of the inner sanctuary, five on the right and five on the left; the gold flowers, lamps, and tongs; 50 the pure gold ceremonial bowls, wick trimmers, sprinkling basins, ladles,[C] and firepans; and the gold hinges for the doors of the inner temple (that is, the most holy place) and for the doors of the temple sanctuary.

51 So all the work King Solomon did in the LORD's temple was completed. Then Solomon brought in the consecrated things of his father David — the silver, the gold, and the utensils — and put them in the treasuries of the LORD's temple.

SOLOMON'S DEDICATION OF THE TEMPLE

8 At that time Solomon assembled the elders of Israel, all the tribal heads and the ancestral leaders of the Israelites before him at Jerusalem in order to bring the ark of the LORD's covenant from the city of David, that is Zion. 2 So all the men of Israel were assembled in the presence of King Solomon in the month of Ethanim, which is the seventh month,[D] at the festival.

3 All the elders of Israel came, and the priests picked up the ark. 4 The priests and the Levites brought the ark of the LORD, the tent of meeting, and the holy utensils that were in the tent. 5 King Solomon and the entire congregation of Israel, who had gathered around him and were with him in front of the ark, were sacrificing sheep, goats, and cattle that could not be counted or numbered, because there were so many. 6 The priests brought the ark of the LORD's covenant to its place, into the inner sanctuary of the temple, to the most holy place beneath the wings of the cherubim. 7 For the cherubim were spreading their wings over[E] the place of the ark, so that the cherubim covered the ark and its poles from above. 8 The poles were so long that their ends were seen from the holy place in front of the inner sanctuary, but they were not seen from outside the sanctuary; they are still there today. 9 Nothing was in the ark except the two stone tablets that Moses had put there at Horeb,[F] where the LORD made a covenant with the Israelites when they came out of the land of Egypt.

10 When the priests came out of the holy place, the cloud filled the LORD's temple, 11 and because of the cloud, the priests were not able to continue ministering, for the glory of the LORD filled the temple.

[A] **7:35** Lit *half a cubit* [B] **7:38** Lit *40 baths* [C] **7:50** Or *dishes*, or *spoons*; lit *palms* [D] **8:2** = September–October [E] **8:7** LXX; MT reads *toward* [F] **8:9** = Sinai

[12] Then Solomon said:
The LORD said that he would dwell
in total darkness.
[13] I have indeed built an exalted temple
for you,
a place for your dwelling forever.
[14] The king turned around and blessed the
entire congregation of Israel while they were
standing. [15] He said:
Blessed be the LORD God of Israel!
He spoke directly to my father David,
and he has fulfilled the promise
by his power.
He said,
[16] "Since the day I brought
my people Israel out of Egypt,
I have not chosen a city to build
a temple in
among any of the tribes of Israel,
so that my name would be there.
But I have chosen David to rule
my people Israel."
[17] My father David had his heart set
on building a temple for the name
of the LORD, the God of Israel.
[18] But the LORD said to my father David,
"Since your heart was set on building
a temple for my name,
you have done well to have this desire.[A]
[19] Yet you are not the one to build it;
instead, your son, your own offspring,
will build it for my name."
[20] The LORD has fulfilled what he promised.
I have taken the place
of my father David,
and I sit on the throne of Israel,
as the LORD promised.
I have built the temple for the name
of the LORD, the God of Israel.
[21] I have provided a place there for the ark,
where the LORD's covenant is
that he made with our ancestors
when he brought them out of the land
of Egypt.

SOLOMON'S PRAYER

[22] Then Solomon stood before the altar of the
LORD in front of the entire congregation of
Israel and spread out his hands toward heav-
en. [23] He said:
LORD God of Israel,
there is no God like you
in heaven above or on earth below,

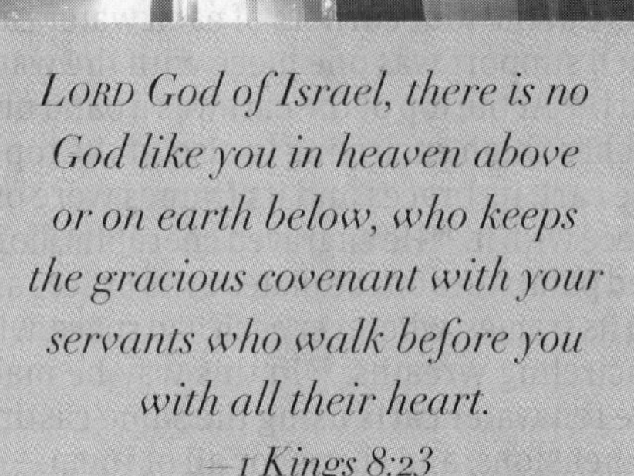

LORD God of Israel, there is no God like you in heaven above or on earth below, who keeps the gracious covenant with your servants who walk before you with all their heart.

—1 Kings 8:23

who keeps the gracious covenant
with your servants who walk
before you
with all their heart.
[24] You have kept what you promised
to your servant, my father David.
You spoke directly to him
and you fulfilled your promise
by your power
as it is today.
[25] Therefore, LORD God of Israel,
keep what you promised
to your servant, my father David:
You will never fail to have a man
to sit before me on the throne of Israel,
if only your sons take care to walk
before me
as you have walked before me.
[26] Now LORD[B] God of Israel,
please confirm what you promised
to your servant, my father David.
[27] But will God indeed live on earth?
Even heaven, the highest heaven,
cannot contain you,
much less this temple I have built.
[28] Listen[C] to your servant's prayer
and his petition,
LORD my God,
so that you may hear the cry
and the prayer
that your servant prays
before you today,
[29] so that your eyes may watch over
this temple night and day,
toward the place where you said,
"My name will be there,"
and so that you may hear the prayer

[A] **8:18** Lit *well because it was with your heart* [B] **8:26** Some Hb mss, LXX, Syr, Tg, Vg, 2Ch 6:16; other Hb mss omit *LORD*
[C] **8:28** Lit *Turn*

that your servant prays
toward this place.
30 Hear the petition of your servant
and your people Israel,
which they pray toward this place.
May you hear in your dwelling place
in heaven.
May you hear and forgive.

31 When a man sins against his neighbor
and is forced to take an oath,[A]
and he comes to take an oath
before your altar in this temple,
32 may you hear in heaven and act.
May you judge your servants,
condemning the wicked man by bringing
what he has done on his own head
and providing justice for the righteous
by rewarding him according to
his righteousness.

33 When your people Israel are defeated
before an enemy,
because they have sinned against you,
and they return to you and praise
your name,
and they pray and plead with you
for mercy in this temple,
34 may you hear in heaven
and forgive the sin
of your people Israel.
May you restore them to the land
you gave their ancestors.

35 When the skies are shut and there is
no rain,
because they have sinned against you,
and they pray toward this place
and praise your name,
and they turn from their sins
because you are afflicting them,
36 may you hear in heaven
and forgive the sin of your servants
and your people Israel,
so that you may teach them
the good way
they should walk in.
May you send rain on your land
that you gave your people
for an inheritance.

37 When there is famine in the land,
when there is pestilence,
when there is blight or mildew, locust
or grasshopper,
when their enemy besieges them
in the land and its cities,[B]
when there is any plague or illness,
38 every prayer or petition
that any person or that all
your people Israel may have —
they each know their own affliction[C] —
as they spread out their hands
toward this temple,
39 may you hear in heaven,
your dwelling place,
and may you forgive, act, and give to
everyone
according to all their ways,
since you know each heart,
for you alone know every
human heart,
40 so that they may fear you
all the days they live on the land
you gave our ancestors.

41 Even for the foreigner who is not
of your people Israel
but has come from a distant land
because of your name —
42 for they will hear of your great name,
strong hand, and outstretched arm,
and will come and pray
toward this temple —
43 may you hear in heaven,
your dwelling place,
and do according to all
the foreigner asks.
Then all peoples of earth will know
your name,
to fear you as your people Israel do
and to know that this temple
I have built
bears your name.

44 When your people go out to fight
against their enemies,[D]
wherever you send them,
and they pray to the LORD
in the direction of the city
you have chosen
and the temple I have built
for your name,
45 may you hear their prayer and petition
in heaven
and uphold their cause.

[A] **8:31** Lit *and he lifts a curse against him to curse him* [B] **8:37** Lit *land of its gates* [C] **8:38** Lit *know in his heart of a plague*
[D] **8:44** Some Hb mss, some ancient versions, 2Ch 6:34; other Hb mss read *enemy*

46 When they sin against you —
for there is no one who does not sin —
and you are angry with them
and hand them over to the enemy,
and their captors deport them
to the enemy's country —
whether distant or nearby —
47 and when they come
to their senses[A]
in the land where they were deported
and repent and petition you
in their captors' land:
"We have sinned and done wrong;
we have been wicked,"
48 and when they return to you
with all their heart and all their soul
in the land of their enemies
who took them captive,
and when they pray to you
in the direction of their land
that you gave their ancestors,
the city you have chosen,
and the temple I have built
for your name,
49 may you hear in heaven,
your dwelling place,
their prayer and petition and uphold
their cause.
50 May you forgive your people
who sinned against you
and all their rebellions[B] against you,
and may you grant them compassion
before their captors,
so that they may treat them
compassionately.
51 For they are your people
and your inheritance;
you brought them out of Egypt,
out of the middle of an iron furnace.
52 May your eyes be open
to your servant's petition
and to the petition
of your people Israel,
listening to them whenever they call
to you.
53 For you, Lord GOD, have set them apart
as your inheritance
from all peoples of the earth,
as you spoke
through your servant Moses
when you brought our ancestors
out of Egypt.

SOLOMON'S BLESSING

54 When Solomon finished praying this entire
prayer and petition to the LORD, he got up from
kneeling before the altar of the LORD, with
his hands spread out toward heaven, 55 and
he stood and blessed the whole congregation
of Israel with a loud voice: 56 "Blessed be the
LORD! He has given rest to his people Israel
according to all he has said. Not one of all the
good promises he made through his servant
Moses has failed. 57 May the LORD our God be
with us as he was with our ancestors. May
he not abandon us or leave us 58 so that he
causes us to be devoted[C] to him, to walk in
all his ways, and to keep his commands, statutes, and ordinances, which he commanded
our ancestors. 59 May my words with which
I have made my petition before the LORD be
near the LORD our God day and night. May he
uphold his servant's cause and the cause of his
people Israel, as each day requires. 60 May all
the peoples of the earth know that the LORD
is God. There is no other! 61 Be wholeheartedly devoted to the LORD our God to walk in
his statutes and to keep his commands, as
it is today."

62 The king and all Israel with him were
offering sacrifices in the LORD's presence.
63 Solomon offered a sacrifice of fellowship
offerings to the LORD: twenty-two thousand
cattle and one hundred twenty thousand sheep
and goats. In this manner the king and all the
Israelites dedicated the LORD's temple.

64 On the same day, the king consecrated
the middle of the courtyard that was in front
of the LORD's temple because that was where
he offered the burnt offering, the grain offering, and the fat of the fellowship offerings
since the bronze altar before the LORD was
too small to accommodate the burnt offerings, the grain offerings, and the fat of the
fellowship offerings.

65 Solomon and all Israel with him — a great
assembly, from the entrance of Hamath[D] to
the Brook of Egypt — observed the festival at
that time in the presence of the LORD our God,
seven days, and seven more days — fourteen
days.[E] 66 On the fifteenth day[F] he sent the people away. So they blessed the king and went to
their homes[G] rejoicing and with happy hearts
for all the goodness that the LORD had done
for his servant David and for his people Israel.

[A] **8:47** Lit *they return to their heart* [B] **8:50** Lit *rebellions that they have rebelled* [C] **8:58** Lit *causes our hearts to be inclined*
[D] **8:65** Or *from Lebo-hamath* [E] **8:65** Temple dedication lasted seven days, and the Festival of Shelters lasted seven days.
[F] **8:66** Lit *the eighth day* [G] **8:66** Lit *tents*

THE LORD'S RESPONSE

9 When Solomon finished building the temple of the LORD, the royal palace, and all
that Solomon desired to do, 2 the LORD appeared to Solomon a second time just as he
had appeared to him at Gibeon. 3 The LORD
said to him:

I have heard your prayer and petition
you have made before me. I have consecrated this temple you have built, to put[A]
my name there forever; my eyes and my
heart will be there at all times.

4 As for you, if you walk before me as
your father David walked, with a heart
of integrity and in what is right, doing
everything I have commanded you, and
if you keep my statutes and ordinances,
5 I will establish your royal throne over
Israel forever, as I promised your father
David: You will never fail to have a man
on the throne of Israel.

6 If you or your sons turn away from following me and do not keep my commands
— my statutes that I have set before you
— and if you go and serve other gods and
bow in worship to them, 7 I will cut off
Israel from the land I gave them, and I will
reject[B] the temple I have sanctified for
my name. Israel will become an object of
scorn and ridicule among all the peoples.
8 Though this temple is now exalted,[C] everyone who passes by will be appalled and
will scoff.[D] They will say: Why did the LORD
do this to this land and this temple? 9 Then
they will say: Because they abandoned
the LORD their God who brought their ancestors out of the land of Egypt. They held
on to other gods and bowed in worship
to them and served them. Because of this,
the LORD brought all this ruin on them.

KING HIRAM'S TWENTY TOWNS

10 At the end of twenty years during which
Solomon had built the two houses, the LORD's
temple and the royal palace — 11 King Hiram
of Tyre having supplied him with cedar and
cypress logs and gold for his every wish —
King Solomon gave Hiram twenty towns in
the land of Galilee. 12 So Hiram went out from
Tyre to look over the towns that Solomon had
given him, but he was not pleased with them.
13 So he said, "What are these towns you've
given me, my brother?" So he called them the
Land of Cabul,[E] as they are still called today.
14 Now Hiram had sent the king nine thousand
pounds[F] of gold.

SOLOMON'S FORCED LABOR

15 This is the account of the forced labor that
King Solomon had imposed to build the LORD's
temple, his own palace, the supporting terraces, the wall of Jerusalem, and Hazor, Megiddo,
and Gezer. 16 Pharaoh king of Egypt had attacked and captured Gezer. He then burned it,
killed the Canaanites who lived in the city, and
gave it as a dowry to his daughter, Solomon's
wife. 17 Then Solomon rebuilt Gezer, Lower
Beth-horon, 18 Baalath, Tamar[G,H] in the Wilderness of Judah, 19 all the storage cities that
belonged to Solomon, the chariot cities, the
cavalry cities, and whatever Solomon desired
to build in Jerusalem, Lebanon, or anywhere
else in the land of his dominion.
20 As for all the peoples who remained of
the Amorites, Hethites, Perizzites, Hivites, and
Jebusites, who were not Israelites — 21 their
descendants who remained in the land after
them, those whom the Israelites were unable
to destroy completely — Solomon imposed
forced labor on them; it is still this way today.
22 But Solomon did not consign the Israelites
to slavery; they were soldiers, his servants, his
commanders, his captains, and commanders
of his chariots and his cavalry. 23 These were
the deputies who were over Solomon's work:
550 who supervised the people doing the work.

SOLOMON'S OTHER ACTIVITIES

24 Pharaoh's daughter moved from the city of
David to the house that Solomon had built for
her; he then built the terraces.
25 Three times a year Solomon offered burnt
offerings and fellowship offerings on the altar he had built for the LORD, and he burned
incense with them in the LORD's presence. So
he completed the temple.
26 King Solomon put together a fleet of
ships at Ezion-geber, which is near Eloth on
the shore of the Red Sea in the land of Edom.
27 With the fleet, Hiram sent his servants, experienced seamen, along with Solomon's servants. 28 They went to Ophir and acquired gold

[A] 9:3 Or *by putting* [B] 9:7 Lit *send from my presence* [C] 9:8 Some ancient versions read *temple will become a ruin* [D] 9:8 Lit *hiss* [E] 9:13 = Like Nothing [F] 9:14 Lit *120 talents* [G] 9:18 Alt Hb traditions, LXX, Syr, Tg, Vg read *Tadmor*; 2Ch 8:4 [H] 9:18 Tamar was a city in southern Judah; Ezk 47:19; 48:28.

there — sixteen tons[A] — and delivered it to Solomon.

THE QUEEN OF SHEBA

10 The queen of Sheba heard about Solomon's fame connected with the name of the LORD and came to test him with riddles. 2 She came to Jerusalem with a very large entourage, with camels bearing spices, gold in great abundance, and precious stones. She came to Solomon and spoke to him about everything that was on her mind. 3 So Solomon answered all her questions; nothing was too difficult for the king to explain to her. 4 When the queen of Sheba observed all of Solomon's wisdom, the palace he had built, 5 the food at his table, his servants' residence, his attendants' service and their attire, his cupbearers, and the burnt offerings he offered at the LORD's temple, it took her breath away.

6 She said to the king, "The report I heard in my own country about your words and about your wisdom is true. 7 But I didn't believe the reports until I came and saw with my own eyes. Indeed, I was not even told half. Your wisdom and prosperity far exceed the report I heard. 8 How happy are your men.[B] How happy are these servants of yours, who always stand in your presence hearing your wisdom. 9 Blessed be the LORD your God! He delighted in you and put you on the throne of Israel, because of the LORD's eternal love for Israel. He has made you king to carry out justice and righteousness."

10 Then she gave the king four and a half tons[C] of gold, a great quantity of spices, and precious stones. Never again did such a quantity of spices arrive as those the queen of Sheba gave to King Solomon.

11 In addition, Hiram's fleet that carried gold from Ophir brought from Ophir a large quantity of almug[D] wood and precious stones. 12 The king made the almug wood into steps for the LORD's temple and the king's palace and into lyres and harps for the singers. Never before did such almug wood arrive, and the like has not been seen again.

13 King Solomon gave the queen of Sheba her every desire — whatever she asked — besides what he had given her out of his royal bounty. Then she, along with her servants, returned to her own country.

SOLOMON'S WEALTH

14 The weight of gold that came to Solomon annually was twenty-five tons,[E] 15 besides what came from merchants, traders' merchandise, and all the Arabian kings and governors of the land.

16 King Solomon made two hundred large shields of hammered gold; fifteen pounds[F] of gold went into each shield. 17 He made three hundred small shields of hammered gold; nearly four pounds[G] of gold went into each shield. The king put them in the House of the Forest of Lebanon.

18 The king also made a large ivory throne and overlaid it with fine gold. 19 The throne had six steps; there was a rounded top at the back of the throne, armrests on either side of the seat, and two lions standing beside the armrests. 20 Twelve lions were standing there on the six steps, one at each end. Nothing like it had ever been made in any other kingdom.

21 All of King Solomon's drinking cups were gold, and all the utensils of the House of the Forest of Lebanon were pure gold. There was no silver, since it was considered as nothing in Solomon's time, 22 for the king had ships of Tarshish at sea with Hiram's fleet, and once every three years the ships of Tarshish would arrive bearing gold, silver, ivory, apes, and peacocks.[H]

23 King Solomon surpassed all the kings of the world in riches and in wisdom. 24 The whole world wanted an audience with Solomon to hear the wisdom that God had put in his heart. 25 Every man would bring his annual tribute: items[I] of silver and gold, clothing, weapons,[J] spices, and horses and mules.

26 Solomon accumulated 1,400 chariots and 12,000 horsemen and stationed them in the chariot cities and with the king in Jerusalem. 27 The king made silver as common in Jerusalem as stones, and he made cedar as abundant as sycamore in the Judean foothills. 28 Solomon's horses were imported from Egypt and Kue.[K] The king's traders bought them from Kue at the going price. 29 A chariot was imported from Egypt for fifteen pounds[L] of silver, and a horse for nearly four pounds.[M] In the same way, they exported them to all the kings of the Hittites and to the kings of Aram through their agents.

[A] **9:28** Lit *420 talents* [B] **10:8** LXX, Syr read *your wives* [C] **10:10** Lit *120 talents* [D] **10:11** = algum in 2Ch 2:8; 9:10-11 [E] **10:14** Lit *666 talents* [F] **10:16** Lit *600* (shekels) [G] **10:17** Lit *three minas* [H] **10:22** Or *baboons* [I] **10:25** Or *vessels*, or *weapons* [J] **10:25** Or *fragrant balsam* [K] **10:28** = Cilicia [L] **10:29** Lit *600 shekels* [M] **10:29** Lit *150 shekels*

SOLOMON'S UNFAITHFULNESS TO GOD

11 King Solomon loved many foreign wom-
en in addition to Pharaoh's daughter:
Moabite, Ammonite, Edomite, Sidonian,
and Hittite women 2 from the nations about
which the LORD had told the Israelites, "You
must not intermarry with them, and they
must not intermarry with you, because they
will turn your heart away to follow their
gods." To these women Solomon was deeply
attached[A] in love. 3 He had seven hundred
wives who were princesses and three hundred who were concubines, and they turned
his heart away.
4 When Solomon was old, his wives turned
his heart away to follow other gods. He was
not wholeheartedly devoted to the LORD his
God, as his father David had been. 5 Solomon
followed Ashtoreth, the goddess of the Sidonians, and Milcom, the abhorrent idol
of the Ammonites. 6 Solomon did what was
evil in the LORD's sight, and unlike his father
David, he did not remain loyal to the LORD.
7 At that time, Solomon built a high place for
Chemosh, the abhorrent idol of Moab, and for
Milcom,[B] the abhorrent idol of the Ammonites, on the hill across from Jerusalem. 8 He
did the same for all his foreign wives, who
were burning incense and offering sacrifices
to their gods.
9 The LORD was angry with Solomon, because his heart had turned away from the
LORD, the God of Israel, who had appeared to
him twice. 10 He had commanded him about
this, so that he would not follow other gods,
but Solomon did not do what the LORD had
commanded.
11 Then the LORD said to Solomon, "Since you
have done this[C] and did not keep my covenant
and my statutes, which I commanded you,
I will tear the kingdom away from you and
give it to your servant. 12 However, I will not
do it during your lifetime for the sake of your
father David; I will tear it out of your son's
hand. 13 Yet I will not tear the entire kingdom
away from him. I will give one tribe to your
son for the sake of my servant David and for
the sake of Jerusalem that I chose."

Exercise of Faith | *Guarding the Heart*

SLIP SLIDING AWAY

"When Solomon was old, his wives turned his heart away to follow other gods. He was not wholeheartedly devoted to the LORD his God, as his father David had been." 1 Kings 11:4

Has any ruler ever stepped into a better situation than Solomon? His father handed him a kingdom at peace. Then God blessed him with supernatural wisdom. With no enemies to fight, Solomon ruled over Israel's golden age. He built Israel's first temple, entertained a stream of foreign dignitaries, and wrote the book of Proverbs, one of which warned, "Guard your heart above all else, for it is the source of life" (Pr 4:23).

Too bad Solomon didn't practice what he preached. Defying the law of God (Dt 17:17), which prohibited Israel's kings from practicing polygamy, Solomon married seven hundred women, and he had another three hundred concubines. Making matters worse, many of these women were non-Israelites, meaning they worshiped pagan gods.

A junior high kid could guess the ending of this story—even without reading the verse above. Solomon didn't do the one thing he said people should do "above all else." He didn't guard his heart. His wives led him astray.

Solomon's sad saga clearly warns us that knowing the truth and living out the truth are two entirely different matters. Also, the people we get close to *do* affect us.

Soften, do not harden, your heart to the clear-cut commands of God.

For the next note on *Exercise of Faith*, see Nehemiah 8:10.

[A] **11:2** Lit *Solomon clung* [B] **11:7** Lit *Molech* [C] **11:11** Lit *"Since this was with you*

SOLOMON'S ENEMIES

14 So the LORD raised up Hadad the Edomite as
an enemy against Solomon. He was of the royal
family in Edom. 15 Earlier, when David was in
Edom, Joab, the commander of the army, had
gone to bury the dead and had struck down
every male in Edom. 16 For Joab and all Israel
had remained there six months, until he had
killed every male in Edom. 17 Hadad fled to
Egypt, along with some Edomites from his
father's servants. At the time Hadad was a
small boy. 18 Hadad and his men set out from
Midian and went to Paran. They took men
with them from Paran and went to Egypt,
to Pharaoh king of Egypt, who gave Hadad
a house, ordered that he be given food, and
gave him land. 19 Pharaoh liked Hadad so
much[A] that he gave him a wife, the sister of
his own wife, Queen Tahpenes. 20 Tahpenes's
sister gave birth to Hadad's son Genubath.
Tahpenes herself weaned him in Pharaoh's
palace, and Genubath lived there along with
Pharaoh's sons.

21 When Hadad heard in Egypt that David
rested with his fathers and that Joab, the commander of the army, was dead, Hadad said
to Pharaoh, "Let me leave, so I may go to my
own country."

22 But Pharaoh asked him, "What do you
lack here with me for you to want to go back
to your own country?"

"Nothing," he replied, "but please let me
leave."

23 God raised up Rezon son of Eliada as an
enemy against Solomon. Rezon had fled from
his master King Hadadezer of Zobah 24 and
gathered men to himself. He became leader of a raiding party when David killed the
Zobaites. He[B] went to Damascus, lived there,
and became king in Damascus. 25 Rezon was
Israel's enemy throughout Solomon's reign,
adding to the trouble Hadad had caused. He
reigned over Aram[C] and loathed Israel.

26 Now Solomon's servant, Jeroboam son of
Nebat, was an Ephraimite from Zeredah. His
widowed mother's name was Zeruah. Jeroboam rebelled against Solomon, 27 and this is
the reason he rebelled against the king: Solomon had built the supporting terraces and
repaired the opening in the wall of the city
of his father David. 28 Now the man Jeroboam
was capable, and Solomon noticed the young
man because he was getting things done. So
he appointed him over the entire labor force
of the house of Joseph.

29 During that time, the prophet Ahijah the
Shilonite met Jeroboam on the road as Jeroboam came out of Jerusalem. Now Ahijah
had wrapped himself with a new cloak, and
the two of them were alone in the open field.
30 Then Ahijah took hold of the new cloak he
had on, tore it into twelve pieces, 31 and said
to Jeroboam, "Take ten pieces for yourself,
for this is what the LORD God of Israel says:
'I am about to tear the kingdom out of Solomon's hand. I will give you ten tribes, 32 but
one tribe will remain his for the sake of my
servant David and for the sake of Jerusalem,
the city I chose out of all the tribes of Israel.
33 For they have abandoned me; they have
bowed down to Ashtoreth, the goddess of the
Sidonians, to Chemosh, the god of Moab, and
to Milcom, the god of the Ammonites. They
have not walked in my ways to do what is
right in my sight and to carry out my statutes
and my judgments as his father David did.

34 " 'However, I will not take the whole kingdom from him but will let him be ruler all the
days of his life for the sake of my servant David,
whom I chose and who kept my commands
and my statutes. 35 I will take ten tribes of the
kingdom from his son and give them to you.
36 I will give one tribe to his son, so that my
servant David will always have a lamp before
me in Jerusalem, the city I chose for myself to
put my name there. 37 I will appoint you, and
you will reign as king over all you want, and
you will be king over Israel.

38 " 'After that, if you obey all I command
you, walk in my ways, and do what is right in
my sight in order to keep my statutes and my
commands as my servant David did, I will be
with you. I will build you a lasting dynasty just
as I built for David, and I will give you Israel.
39 I will humble David's descendants, because
of their unfaithfulness, but not forever.' "[D]

40 Therefore, Solomon tried to kill Jeroboam, but he fled to Egypt, to King Shishak of
Egypt, where he remained until Solomon's
death.

SOLOMON'S DEATH

41 The rest of the events of Solomon's reign,
along with all his accomplishments and his
wisdom, are written in the Book of Solomon's
Events. 42 The length of Solomon's reign in

[A] **11:19** Lit *Hadad found much favor in Pharaoh's eyes* [B] **11:24** LXX; Hb reads *They* [C] **11:25** Some Hb mss, LXX, Syr read *Edom*
[D] **11:38-39** LXX omits *and I will give . . . but not forever*

Jerusalem over all Israel totaled forty years.
43 Solomon rested with his fathers and was
buried in the city of his father David. His son
Rehoboam became king in his place.

THE KINGDOM DIVIDED

12 Then Rehoboam went to Shechem, for
all Israel had gone to Shechem to make
him king. 2 When Jeroboam son of Nebat heard
about it, he stayed in Egypt, where he had fled
from King Solomon's presence. Jeroboam
stayed in Egypt.[A] 3 But they summoned him,
and Jeroboam and the whole assembly of
Israel came and spoke to Rehoboam: 4 "Your
father made our yoke harsh. You, therefore,
lighten your father's harsh service and the
heavy yoke he put on us, and we will serve
you."

5 Rehoboam replied, "Go away for three days
and then return to me." So the people left.
6 Then King Rehoboam consulted with the
elders who had served his father Solomon
when he was alive, asking, "How do you advise me to respond to this people?"

7 They replied, "Today if you will be a servant to this people and serve them, and if you
respond to them by speaking kind words to
them, they will be your servants forever."

8 But he rejected the advice of the elders
who had advised him and consulted with the
young men who had grown up with him and
attended him. 9 He asked them, "What message do you advise that we send back to this
people who said to me, 'Lighten the yoke your
father put on us'?"
10 Then the young men who had grown up
with him told him, "This is what you should
say to this people who said to you, 'Your father
made our yoke heavy, but you, make it lighter
on us!' This is what you should tell them: 'My
little finger is thicker than my father's waist!
11 Although my father burdened you with a
heavy yoke, I will add to your yoke; my father
disciplined you with whips, but I will discipline you with barbed whips.'"[B]
12 So Jeroboam and all the people came to
Rehoboam on the third day, as the king had
ordered: "Return to me on the third day." 13 Then
the king answered the people harshly. He rejected the advice the elders had given him 14 and
spoke to them according to the young men's
advice: "My father made your yoke heavy, but
I will add to your yoke; my father disciplined
you with whips, but I will discipline you with
barbed whips."
15 The king did not listen to the people, because this turn of events came from the LORD
to carry out his word, which the LORD had
spoken through Ahijah the Shilonite to Jeroboam son of Nebat. 16 When all Israel saw that
the king had not listened to them, the people
answered him:

> What portion do we have in David?
> We have no inheritance in the son
> of Jesse.
> Israel, return to your tents;
> David, now look after your own house!

So Israel went to their tents, 17 but Rehoboam
reigned over the Israelites living in the cities
of Judah.
18 Then King Rehoboam sent Adoram,[C] who
was in charge of forced labor, but all Israel
stoned him to death. King Rehoboam managed
to get into the chariot and flee to Jerusalem.
19 Israel is still in rebellion against the house
of David today.

REHOBOAM IN JERUSALEM

20 When all Israel heard that Jeroboam had
come back, they summoned him to the assembly and made him king over all Israel. No one
followed the house of David except the tribe
of Judah alone. 21 When Rehoboam arrived in
Jerusalem, he mobilized one hundred eighty
thousand fit young soldiers from the entire
house of Judah and the tribe of Benjamin to
fight against the house of Israel to restore the
kingdom to Rehoboam son of Solomon. 22 But
the word of God came to Shemaiah, the man
of God: 23 "Say to Rehoboam son of Solomon,
king of Judah, to the whole house of Judah
and Benjamin, and to the rest of the people,
24 'This is what the LORD says: You are not to
march up and fight against your brothers,
the Israelites. Each of you return home, for
this situation is from me.'"

So they listened to the word of the LORD and
went back according to the word of the LORD.

JEROBOAM'S IDOLATRY

25 Jeroboam built Shechem in the hill country
of Ephraim and lived there. From there he
went out and built Penuel. 26 Jeroboam said
to himself, "The kingdom might now return to
the house of David. 27 If these people regularly
go to offer sacrifices in the LORD's temple in

[A] 12:2 LXX, Vg read *Jeroboam returned from Egypt*; 2Ch 10:2 [B] 12:11 Lit *with scorpions*, also in v. 14 [C] 12:18 LXX reads *Adoniram*; 1Kg 4:6; 5:14

Jerusalem, the heart of these people will return to their lord, King Rehoboam of Judah.
They will kill me and go back to the king of
Judah." 28 So the king sought advice.
Then he made two golden calves, and he
said to the people, "Going to Jerusalem is too
difficult for you. Israel, here are your gods[A]
who brought you up from the land of Egypt."
29 He set up one in Bethel, and put the other
in Dan. 30 This led to sin; the people walked
in procession before one of the calves all the
way to Dan.[B]
31 Jeroboam also made shrines[C] on the high
places and made priests from the ranks of
the people who were not Levites. 32 Jeroboam
made a festival in the eighth month on the
fifteenth day of the month, like the festival
in Judah. He offered sacrifices on the altar;
he made this offering in Bethel to sacrifice
to the calves he had made. He also stationed
the priests in Bethel for the high places he had
made. 33 He offered sacrifices on[D] the altar he
had set up in Bethel on the fifteenth day of the
eighth month. He chose this month on his own.
He made a festival for the Israelites, offered
sacrifices on the altar, and burned incense.

JUDGMENT ON JEROBOAM

13 A man of God came, however, from Judah to Bethel by the word of the LORD
while Jeroboam was standing beside the altar
to burn incense. 2 The man of God cried out
against the altar by the word of the LORD: "Altar, altar, this is what the LORD says, 'A son will
be born to the house of David, named Josiah,
and he will sacrifice on you the priests of the
high places who are burning incense on you.
Human bones will be burned on you.' " 3 He
gave a sign that day. He said, "This is the sign
that the LORD has spoken: 'The altar will now
be ripped apart, and the ashes that are on it
will be poured out.' "
4 When the king heard the message that the
man of God had cried out against the altar at
Bethel, Jeroboam stretched out his hand from
the altar and said, "Arrest him!" But the hand
he stretched out against him withered, and
he could not pull it back to himself. 5 The altar
was ripped apart, and the ashes poured from
the altar, according to the sign that the man
of God had given by the word of the LORD.
6 Then the king responded to the man of
God, "Plead for the favor of the LORD your
God and pray for me so that my hand may
be restored to me." So the man of God pleaded for the favor of the LORD, and the king's
hand was restored to him and became as it
had been at first.
7 Then the king declared to the man of God,
"Come home with me, refresh yourself, and
I'll give you a reward."
8 But the man of God replied, "If you were
to give me half your house, I still wouldn't
go with you, and I wouldn't eat food or drink
water in this place, 9 for this is what I was
commanded by the word of the LORD: 'You
must not eat food or drink water or go back
the way you came.' " 10 So he went another
way; he did not go back by the way he had
come to Bethel.

THE OLD PROPHET AND THE MAN OF GOD

11 Now a certain old prophet was living in Bethel. His son[E] came and told him all the deeds that
the man of God had done that day in Bethel.
His sons also told their father the words that
he had spoken to the king. 12 Then their father
asked them, "Which way did he go?" His sons
had seen[F] the way taken by the man of God
who had come from Judah. 13 Then he said to
his sons, "Saddle the donkey for me." So they
saddled the donkey for him, and he got on it.
14 He followed the man of God and found him
sitting under an oak tree. He asked him, "Are
you the man of God who came from Judah?"
"I am," he said.
15 Then he said to him, "Come home with
me and eat some food."
16 But he answered, "I cannot go back with
you or accompany you; I will not eat food or
drink water with you in this place. 17 For a
message came to me by the word of the LORD:
'You must not eat food or drink water there
or go back by the way you came.' "
18 He said to him, "I am also a prophet like
you. An angel spoke to me by the word of the
LORD: 'Bring him back with you to your house
so that he may eat food and drink water.' " The
old prophet deceived him, 19 and the man of
God went back with him, ate food in his house,
and drank water.
20 While they were sitting at the table, the
word of the LORD came to the prophet who
had brought him back, 21 and the prophet cried
out to the man of God who had come from
Judah, "This is what the LORD says: 'Because

[A] **12:28** Or *here is your God*, or *here is your god* [B] **12:30** Some LXX mss read *calves to Bethel and the other to Dan* [C] **12:31** Lit *a house* [D] **12:33** Or *He went up to* [E] **13:11** Some Hb mss, LXX, Syr, Vg read *sons* [F] **13:12** LXX, Syr, Tg, Vg read *sons showed him*

you rebelled against the LORD's command
and did not keep the command that the LORD
your God commanded you — 22 but you went
back and ate food and drank water in the place
that he said to you, "Do not eat food and do
not drink water" — your corpse will never
reach the grave of your fathers.' "
23 So after he had eaten food and after he had
drunk, the old prophet saddled the donkey
for the prophet he had brought back. 24 When
he left,[A] a lion attacked[B] him along the way
and killed him. His corpse was thrown on the
road, and the donkey was standing beside it;
the lion was standing beside the corpse too.
25 There were men passing by who saw the
corpse thrown on the road and the lion standing beside it, and they went and spoke about it
in the city where the old prophet lived. 26 When
the prophet who had brought him back from
his way heard about it, he said, "He is the man
of God who disobeyed the LORD's command.
The LORD has given him to the lion, and it has
mauled and killed him, according to the word
of the LORD that he spoke to him."
27 Then the old prophet instructed his sons,
"Saddle the donkey for me." They saddled it,
28 and he went and found the corpse thrown on
the road with the donkey and the lion standing beside the corpse. The lion had not eaten
the corpse or mauled the donkey. 29 So the
prophet lifted the corpse of the man of God
and laid it on the donkey and brought it back.
The old prophet came into the city to mourn
and to bury him. 30 Then he laid the corpse in
his own grave, and they mourned over him:
"Oh, my brother!"
31 After he had buried him, he said to his
sons, "When I die, bury me in the grave where
the man of God is buried; lay my bones beside
his bones, 32 for the message that he cried out
by the word of the LORD against the altar in
Bethel and against all the shrines of the high
places in the cities of Samaria is certain to
happen."
33 Even after this, Jeroboam did not repent
of his evil way but again made priests for the
high places from the ranks of the people. He
ordained whoever so desired it, and they became priests of the high places. 34 This was
the sin that caused the house of Jeroboam
to be cut off and obliterated from the face
of the earth.

DISASTER ON THE HOUSE OF JEROBOAM

14 At that time Abijah son of Jeroboam became sick. 2 Jeroboam said to his wife,
"Go disguise yourself, so they won't know
that you're Jeroboam's wife, and go to Shiloh. The prophet Ahijah is there; it was he
who told about me becoming king over this
people. 3 Take with you ten loaves of bread,
some cakes, and a jar of honey, and go to him.
He will tell you what will happen to the boy."
4 Jeroboam's wife did that: she went to Shiloh
and arrived at Ahijah's house. Ahijah could
not see; he was blind[C] due to his age. 5 But the
LORD had said to Ahijah, "Jeroboam's wife is
coming soon to ask you about her son, for
he is sick. You are to say such and such to
her. When she arrives, she will be disguised."
6 When Ahijah heard the sound of her feet
entering the door, he said, "Come in, wife of
Jeroboam! Why are you disguised? I have bad
news for you. 7 Go tell Jeroboam, 'This is what
the LORD God of Israel says: I raised you up
from among the people, appointed you ruler over my people Israel, 8 tore the kingdom
away from the house of David, and gave it to
you. But you were not like my servant David,
who kept my commands and followed me
with all his heart, doing only what is right in
my sight. 9 You behaved more wickedly than
all who were before you. In order to anger
me, you have proceeded to make for yourself other gods and cast images, but you have
flung me behind your back. 10 Because of all
this, I am about to bring disaster on the house
of Jeroboam:

I will wipe out all of Jeroboam's males,[D]
both slave and free,[E] in Israel;
I will sweep away the house
of Jeroboam
as one sweeps away dung until it is
all gone!
11 Anyone who belongs to Jeroboam
and dies in the city,
the dogs will eat,
and anyone who dies in the field,
the birds[F] will eat,
for the LORD has spoken!'

12 "As for you, get up and go to your house.
When your feet enter the city, the boy will die.
13 All Israel will mourn for him and bury him.
He alone out of Jeroboam's house will be given

[A] **13:23-24** LXX reads *donkey, and he turned* [24]*and left, and* [B] **13:24** Lit *met* [C] **14:4** Lit *see, for his eyes stood*; 1Sm 4:15 [D] **14:10** Lit *eliminate Jeroboam's one who urinates against the wall* [E] **14:10** Or *males, even the weak and impaired*; Hb obscure [F] **14:11** Lit *birds of the sky*

a proper burial because out of the house of
Jeroboam something favorable to the LORD
God of Israel was found in him. 14 The LORD
will raise up for himself a king over Israel, who
will wipe out the house of Jeroboam. This is
the day, yes,[A] even today! 15 For the LORD will
strike Israel so that they will[B] shake as a reed
shakes in water. He will uproot Israel from this
good soil that he gave to their ancestors. He will
scatter them beyond the Euphrates because
they made their Asherah poles, angering the
LORD. 16 He will give up Israel because of Jeroboam's sins that he committed and caused
Israel to commit."

17 Then Jeroboam's wife got up and left and
went to Tirzah. As she was crossing the threshold of the house, the boy died. 18 He was buried,
and all Israel mourned for him, according to
the word of the LORD he had spoken through
his servant the prophet Ahijah.

19 As for the rest of the events of Jeroboam's
reign, how he waged war and how he reigned,
note that they are written in the Historical
Record of Israel's Kings. 20 The length of Jeroboam's reign was twenty-two years. He rested
with his fathers, and his son Nadab became
king in his place.

JUDAH'S KING REHOBOAM

21 Now Rehoboam, Solomon's son, reigned
in Judah. Rehoboam was forty-one years old
when he became king; he reigned seventeen
years in Jerusalem, the city where the LORD
had chosen from all the tribes of Israel to put
his name. Rehoboam's mother's name was
Naamah the Ammonite.

22 Judah did what was evil in the LORD's sight.
They provoked him to jealous anger more
than all that their ancestors had done with
the sins they committed. 23 They also built for
themselves high places, sacred pillars, and
Asherah poles on every high hill and under
every green tree; 24 there were even male cult
prostitutes in the land. They imitated all the
detestable practices of the nations the LORD
had dispossessed before the Israelites.

25 In the fifth year of King Rehoboam,
King Shishak of Egypt went to war against
Jerusalem. 26 He seized the treasuries of the
LORD's temple and the treasuries of the royal
palace. He took everything. He took all the
gold shields that Solomon had made. 27 King
Rehoboam made bronze shields to replace
them and committed them into the care of
the captains of the guards[C] who protected the
entrance to the king's palace. 28 Whenever the
king entered the LORD's temple, the guards
would carry the shields, then they would take
them back to the armory.[D]

29 The rest of the events of Rehoboam's
reign, along with all his accomplishments,
are written about in the Historical Record
of Judah's Kings. 30 There was war between
Rehoboam and Jeroboam throughout their
reigns. 31 Rehoboam rested with his fathers
and was buried with his fathers in the city
of David. His mother's name was Naamah
the Ammonite. His son Abijam[E] became king
in his place.

JUDAH'S KING ABIJAM

15 In the eighteenth year of Israel's King
Jeroboam son of Nebat, Abijam became
king over Judah, 2 and he reigned three years
in Jerusalem. His mother's name was Maacah
daughter[F] of Abishalom.

3 Abijam walked in all the sins his father
before him had committed, and he was not
wholeheartedly devoted to the LORD his God
as his ancestor David had been. 4 But for the
sake of David, the LORD his God gave him a
lamp in Jerusalem by raising up his son after
him and by preserving Jerusalem. 5 For David
did what was right in the LORD's sight, and
he did not turn aside from anything he had
commanded him all the days of his life, except
in the matter of Uriah the Hethite.

6 There had been war between Rehoboam
and Jeroboam all the days of Rehoboam's life.
7 The rest of the events of Abijam's reign, along
with all his accomplishments, are written in
the Historical Record of Judah's Kings. There
was also war between Abijam and Jeroboam.
8 Abijam rested with his fathers and was buried in the city of David. His son Asa became
king in his place.

JUDAH'S KING ASA

9 In the twentieth year of Israel's King Jeroboam, Asa became king of Judah, 10 and he
reigned forty-one years in Jerusalem. His
grandmother's[G] name was Maacah daughter of Abishalom.

11 Asa did what was right in the LORD's sight,
as his ancestor David had done. 12 He banished
the male cult prostitutes from the land and

[A] **14:14** Hb obscure [B] **14:15** *so that they will* supplied for clarity [C] **14:27** Lit *the runners* [D] **14:28** Lit *the chamber of the runners* [E] **14:31** = Abijah in 2Ch 13 [F] **15:2** Possibly granddaughter, also in v. 10; 2Ch 13:2 [G] **15:10** Lit *mother's*

My Story | Lucy

Growing up in a traditional mainline church, I learned a lot about God but missed the personal, intimate invitation to walk with him. As my teenage years rolled through, I remember feeling a deep ache inside. Seeking to fill the void, I fell hard and fast for a boy. After three years of emotional abuse, I found myself isolated, afraid, and without hope. As I expressed my desire to break free from the relationship, my small frame crumbled under his last words as he waved a rifle, laughed, and violently spewed that no one would ever love me as much he did. If what he was offering was love, I wanted death.

Suicidal thoughts overwhelmed my mind. Soon I could see no other solution than to take my own life. But as I reached my lowest point of hopelessness and helplessness, I was suddenly aware I was not alone. The "still small voice" that was a curious remembered phrase from my childhood suddenly became an almost audible reality in my heart. That quiet voice offered me a way out that would require me to simply trust the One who made me. As I knelt, convicted and tear-soaked, a soft and tender warmth filled my cold, stone heart.

In that moment, I knew that the God I had heard so much about was in the room. Weak and bruised, I spoke into the heavens, asking him to take the pain away. As I lay curled like a fetus in the womb, something miraculous began to happen. From head to toe, Light gradually moved in. In that moment, I knew that I had been found by the Maker of heaven and earth.

Wooed and filled with joy, my eyes opened as my renewed heart heard, "No one will ever love you as much as I do!" The Lord himself, my Savior, the One who had already demonstrated that love on the cross, had just restored and reclaimed what was only his to give. Love!

removed all of the idols that his fathers had
made. 13 He also removed his grandmother[A]
Maacah from being queen mother because
she had made an obscene image of Asherah.
Asa chopped down her obscene image and
burned it in the Kidron Valley. 14 The high places
were not taken away, but Asa was wholeheartedly devoted to the LORD his entire life. 15 He
brought his father's consecrated gifts and his
own consecrated gifts into the LORD's temple:
silver, gold, and utensils.

16 There was war between Asa and King Baasha of Israel throughout their reigns. 17 Israel's
King Baasha went to war against Judah. He
built Ramah in order to keep anyone from
leaving or coming to King Asa of Judah. 18 So
Asa withdrew all the silver and gold that remained in the treasuries of the LORD's temple
and the treasuries of the royal palace and gave
it to his servants. Then King Asa sent them to
Ben-hadad son of Tabrimmon son of Hezion
king of Aram who lived in Damascus, saying,
19 "There is a treaty between me and you, between my father and your father. Look, I have
sent you a gift of silver and gold. Go and break
your treaty with King Baasha of Israel so that
he will withdraw from me."

20 Ben-hadad listened to King Asa and sent
the commanders of his armies against the
cities of Israel. He attacked Ijon, Dan, Abel-
beth-maacah, all Chinnereth, and the whole
land of Naphtali. 21 When Baasha heard about
it, he quit building Ramah and stayed in Tirzah.
22 Then King Asa gave a command to everyone
without exception in Judah, and they carried
away the stones of Ramah and the timbers
Baasha had built it with. Then King Asa built
Geba of Benjamin and Mizpah with them.

23 The rest of all the events of Asa's reign,
along with all his might, all his accomplishments, and the cities he built, are written in
the Historical Record of Judah's Kings. But in
his old age he developed a disease in his feet.
24 Then Asa rested with his fathers and was
buried in the city of his ancestor David. His
son Jehoshaphat became king in his place.

ISRAEL'S KING NADAB

25 Nadab son of Jeroboam became king over
Israel in the second year of Judah's King Asa;
he reigned over Israel two years. 26 Nadab did
what was evil in the LORD's sight and walked
in the ways of his father and the sin he had
caused Israel to commit.

27 Then Baasha son of Ahijah of the house
of Issachar conspired against Nadab, and

[A] **15:13** Lit *mother*

Baasha struck him down at Gibbethon of the Philistines while Nadab and all Israel were besieging Gibbethon. 28 In the third year of Judah's King Asa, Baasha killed Nadab and reigned in his place.

29 When Baasha became king, he struck down the entire house of Jeroboam. He did not leave Jeroboam any survivors but[A] destroyed his family according to the word of the LORD he had spoken through his servant Ahijah the Shilonite. 30 This was because Jeroboam had angered[B] the LORD God of Israel by the sins he had committed and had caused Israel to commit.

31 The rest of the events of Nadab's reign, along with all his accomplishments, are written in the Historical Record of Israel's Kings. 32 There was war between Asa and King Baasha of Israel throughout their reigns.

ISRAEL'S KING BAASHA

33 In the third year of Judah's King Asa, Baasha son of Ahijah became king over all Israel, and he reigned in Tirzah twenty-four years. 34 He did what was evil in the LORD's sight and walked in the ways of Jeroboam and the sin he had caused Israel to commit.

16 Now the word of the LORD came to Jehu son of Hanani against Baasha: 2 "Because I raised you up from the dust and made you ruler over my people Israel, but you have walked in the ways of Jeroboam and have caused my people Israel to sin, angering me with their sins, 3 take note: I will eradicate Baasha and his house, and I will make your house like the house of Jeroboam son of Nebat:

4 Anyone who belongs to Baasha
and dies in the city,
the dogs will eat,
and anyone who is his and dies
in the field,
the birds[C] will eat."

5 The rest of the events of Baasha's reign, along with all his accomplishments and might, are written in the Historical Record of Israel's Kings. 6 Baasha rested with his fathers and was buried in Tirzah. His son Elah became king in his place. 7 But through the prophet Jehu son of Hanani the word of the LORD also had come against Baasha and against his house because of all the evil he had done in the LORD's sight. His actions angered the LORD, and Baasha's house became like the house of Jeroboam, because he had struck it down.

ISRAEL'S KING ELAH

8 In the twenty-sixth year of Judah's King Asa, Elah son of Baasha became king over Israel, and he reigned in Tirzah two years.

9 His servant Zimri, commander of half his chariots, conspired against him while Elah was in Tirzah getting drunk in the house of Arza, who was in charge of the household at Tirzah. 10 In the twenty-seventh year of Judah's King Asa, Zimri went in, struck Elah down, killing him. Then Zimri became king in his place.

11 When he became king, as soon as he was seated on his throne, Zimri struck down the entire house of Baasha. He did not leave a single male,[D] including his kinsmen and his friends. 12 So Zimri destroyed the entire house of Baasha, according to the word of the LORD he had spoken against Baasha through the prophet Jehu. 13 This happened because of all the sins of Baasha and those of his son Elah, which they committed and caused Israel to commit, angering the LORD God of Israel with their worthless idols.

14 The rest of the events of Elah's reign, along with all his accomplishments, are written in the Historical Record of Israel's Kings.

ISRAEL'S KING ZIMRI

15 In the twenty-seventh year of Judah's King Asa, Zimri became king for seven days in Tirzah. Now the troops were encamped against Gibbethon of the Philistines. 16 When these troops heard that Zimri had not only conspired but had also struck down the king, then all Israel made Omri, the army commander, king over Israel that very day in the camp. 17 Omri along with all Israel marched up from Gibbethon and besieged Tirzah. 18 When Zimri saw that the city was captured, he entered the citadel of the royal palace and burned it down over himself. He died 19 because of the sin he committed by doing what was evil in the LORD's sight and by walking in the ways of Jeroboam and the sin he caused Israel to commit.

20 The rest of the events of Zimri's reign, along with the conspiracy that he instigated, are written in the Historical Record of Israel's Kings. 21 At that time the people of Israel were divided: half the people followed Tibni son of Ginath, to make him king, and half followed Omri. 22 However, the people who followed Omri proved

[A] **15:29** Lit *Jeroboam anyone breathing until he* [B] **15:30** Lit *provoked in the provocation of* [C] **16:4** Lit *birds of the sky*
[D] **16:11** Lit *leave him one who urinates against the wall*

Elijah | Restoration Profile

1 KINGS 17—2 KINGS 2; 2 CHRONICLES 21:12-15

When God sent two Old Testament figures to meet with Jesus on the Mount of Transfiguration, one of those he chose was Elijah (Mt 17:1-13). There he was, brought back from eternal serenity to have a conversation with the Son of God. The three disciples with Jesus were certainly impressed. Elijah was the prophet's prophet, the servant of God whom everyone else emulated. His successor Elisha had simply asked, "I want to be like you, Elijah." Elijah's stellar reputation would not lead us to expect that part of his history was a desperate time of fear and depression during which he asked God to take his life. How could such a man of God prove so weak?

Following the great showdown with the priests of Baal and the end of a long drought by the prayer of Elijah, the prophet was served with a death notice by Queen Jezebel. Elijah fled. He was fearful and emotionally spent. Sitting under a broom tree, he said to God, "I have had enough! LORD, take my life" (1Kg 19:4). Then he fell asleep.

God initiated Elijah's restoration. He let Elijah sleep and then fed and hydrated him. Sometimes the key to restoration is simply healthy living. Rest and nourishment restored Elijah physically, but he was still emotionally off balance. After his forty-day hike and a night in the cave, God confronted his underlying attitude of hopeless uselessness. God gave Elijah an amazing display of his power and presence. When that didn't break through Elijah's self-centeredness, God simply reminded him that his assumption of being the lone faithful one was off by seven thousand. Then he told Elijah to get back to work! Restoration is ultimately God's way of helping us go on.

stronger than those who followed Tibni son of Ginath. So Tibni died and Omri became king.

ISRAEL'S KING OMRI

23 In the thirty-first year of Judah's King Asa,
Omri became king over Israel, and he reigned
twelve years. He reigned six years in Tirzah,
24 then he bought the hill of Samaria from Shemer for 150 pounds[A] of silver, and he built up
the hill. He named the city he built Samaria[B]
based on the name Shemer, the owner of the hill.
25 Omri did what was evil in the LORD's sight;
he did more evil than all who were before him.
26 He walked in all the ways of Jeroboam son of
Nebat in every respect and continued in his sins
that he caused Israel to commit, angering the
LORD God of Israel with their worthless idols.
27 The rest of the events of Omri's reign, along
with his accomplishments and the might he
exercised, are written in the Historical Record of Israel's Kings.
28 Omri rested with his
fathers and was buried in Samaria. His son
Ahab became king in his place.

ISRAEL'S KING AHAB

29 Ahab son of Omri became king over Israel
in the thirty-eighth year of Judah's King Asa;
Ahab son of Omri reigned over Israel in Samaria
twenty-two years.
30 But Ahab son of Omri did
what was evil in the LORD's sight more than all
who were before him.
31 Then, as if following
the sin of Jeroboam son of Nebat were not
enough, he married Jezebel, the daughter of
Ethbaal king of the Sidonians, and then proceeded to serve Baal and bow in worship to
him.
32 He set up an altar for Baal in the temple
of Baal that he had built in Samaria.
33 Ahab
also made an Asherah pole. Ahab did more to
anger the LORD God of Israel than all the kings
of Israel who were before him.
34 During his reign, Hiel the Bethelite built
Jericho. At the cost of Abiram his firstborn, he
laid its foundation, and at the cost of Segub his
youngest, he finished its gates, according to
the word of the LORD he had spoken through
Joshua son of Nun.

ELIJAH ANNOUNCES FAMINE

17 Now Elijah the Tishbite, from the Gilead
settlers,[C] said to Ahab, "As the LORD God
of Israel lives, in whose presence I stand, there
will be no dew or rain during these years except by my command!"
2 Then the word of the LORD came to him:

[A] 16:24 Lit *for two talents* [B] 16:24 = Belonging to Shemer's Clan [C] 17:1 LXX reads *from Tishbe of Gilead*

3 "Leave here, turn eastward, and hide at the
Wadi Cherith where it enters the Jordan. 4 You
are to drink from the wadi. I have commanded
the ravens to provide for you there."

5 So he proceeded to do what the LORD commanded. Elijah left and lived at the Wadi Cherith where it enters the Jordan. 6 The ravens
kept bringing him bread and meat in the morning and in the evening, and he would drink
from the wadi. 7 After a while, the wadi dried
up because there had been no rain in the land.

ELIJAH AND THE WIDOW

8 Then the word of the LORD came to him: 9 "Get
up, go to Zarephath that belongs to Sidon and
stay there. Look, I have commanded a woman
who is a widow to provide for you there." 10 So
Elijah got up and went to Zarephath. When
he arrived at the city gate, there was a widow
gathering wood. Elijah called to her and said,
"Please bring me a little water in a cup and let
me drink." 11 As she went to get it, he called
to her and said, "Please bring me a piece of
bread in your hand."

12 But she said, "As the LORD your God lives,
I don't have anything baked — only a handful
of flour in the jar and a bit of oil in the jug.
Just now, I am gathering a couple of sticks in
order to go prepare it for myself and my son
so we can eat it and die."

13 Then Elijah said to her, "Don't be afraid;
go and do as you have said. But first make
me a small loaf from it and bring it out to me.
Afterward, you may make some for yourself
and your son, 14 for this is what the LORD God
of Israel says, 'The flour jar will not become
empty and the oil jug will not run dry until
the day the LORD sends rain on the surface
of the land.'"

15 So she proceeded to do according to the
word of Elijah. Then the woman, Elijah, and
her household ate for many days. 16 The flour
jar did not become empty, and the oil jug did
not run dry, according to the word of the LORD
he had spoken through[A] Elijah.

THE WIDOW'S SON RAISED

17 After this, the son of the woman who owned
the house became ill. His illness got worse
until he stopped breathing. 18 She said to Elijah, "Man of God, why are you here? Have you
come to call attention to my iniquity so that
my son is put to death?"

19 But Elijah said to her, "Give me your son."
So he took him from her arms, brought him
up to the upstairs room where he was staying, and laid him on his own bed. 20 Then he
cried out to the LORD and said, "LORD my God,
have you also brought tragedy on the widow
I am staying with by killing her son?" 21 Then
he stretched himself out over the boy three
times. He cried out to the LORD and said,
"LORD my God, please let this boy's life come
into him again!"

22 So the LORD listened to Elijah, and the
boy's life came into him again, and he lived.
23 Then Elijah took the boy, brought him down
from the upstairs room into the house, and
gave him to his mother. Elijah said, "Look,
your son is alive."

24 Then the woman said to Elijah, "Now I
know you are a man of God and the LORD's
word from your mouth is true."

ELIJAH'S MESSAGE TO AHAB

18 After a long time, the word of the LORD
came to Elijah in the third year: "Go and
present yourself to Ahab. I will send rain on
the surface of the land." 2 So Elijah went to
present himself to Ahab.

The famine was severe in Samaria. 3 Ahab
called for Obadiah, who was in charge of the
palace. Obadiah was a man who greatly feared
the LORD 4 and took a hundred prophets and hid
them, fifty men to a cave, and provided them
with food and water when Jezebel slaughtered
the LORD's prophets. 5 Ahab said to Obadiah,
"Go throughout the land to every spring and
to every wadi. Perhaps we'll find grass so we
can keep the horses and mules alive and not
have to destroy any cattle." 6 They divided the
land between them in order to cover it. Ahab
went one way by himself, and Obadiah went
the other way by himself.

7 While Obadiah was walking along the road,
Elijah suddenly met him. When Obadiah recognized him, he fell facedown and said, "Is it
you, my lord Elijah?"

8 "It is I," he replied. "Go tell your lord, 'Elijah is here!'"[B]

9 But Obadiah said, "What sin have I committed, that you are handing your servant over
to Ahab to put me to death? 10 As the LORD
your God lives, there is no nation or kingdom
where my lord has not sent someone to search
for you. When they said, 'He is not here,' he

[A] **17:16** Lit *by the hand of* [B] **18:8** The Hb words translated *'Elijah is here'* also mean *'Look, my God is the LORD'*

made that kingdom or nation swear they had
not found you.
11 "Now you say, 'Go tell your lord, "Elijah is
here!" ' 12 But when I leave you, the Spirit of the
LORD may carry you off to some place I don't
know. Then when I go report to Ahab and he
doesn't find you, he will kill me. But I, your
servant, have feared the LORD from my youth.
13 Wasn't it reported to my lord what I did when
Jezebel slaughtered the LORD's prophets? I hid
a hundred of the prophets of the LORD, fifty
men to a cave, and I provided them with food
and water. 14 Now you say, 'Go tell your lord,
"Elijah is here!" ' He will kill me!"
15 Then Elijah said, "As the LORD of Armies
lives, in whose presence I stand, today I will
present myself to Ahab."
16 Obadiah went to meet Ahab and told him.
Then Ahab went to meet Elijah. 17 When Ahab
saw Elijah, Ahab said to him, "Is that you, the
one ruining Israel?"
18 He replied, "I have not ruined Israel, but
you and your father's family have, because you
have abandoned the LORD's commands and
followed the Baals. 19 Now summon all Israel
to meet me at Mount Carmel, along with the
450 prophets of Baal and the 400 prophets of
Asherah who eat at Jezebel's table."

ELIJAH AT MOUNT CARMEL

20 So Ahab summoned all the Israelites and
gathered the prophets at Mount Carmel.
21 Then Elijah approached all the people and
said, "How long will you waver between two
opinions?[A] If the LORD is God, follow him. But
if Baal, follow him." But the people didn't answer him a word.
22 Then Elijah said to the people, "I am the
only remaining prophet of the LORD, but Baal's
prophets are 450 men. 23 Let two bulls be given
to us. They are to choose one bull for themselves, cut it in pieces, and place it on the wood
but not light the fire. I will prepare the other
bull and place it on the wood but not light
the fire. 24 Then you call on the name of your
god, and I will call on the name of the LORD.
The God who answers with fire, he is God."
All the people answered, "That's fine."
25 Then Elijah said to the prophets of Baal,
"Since you are so numerous, choose for yourselves one bull and prepare it first. Then call on
the name of your god but don't light the fire."
26 So they took the bull that he gave them,
prepared it, and called on the name of Baal
from morning until noon, saying, "Baal, answer us!" But there was no sound; no one answered. Then they danced[B] around the altar
they had made.
27 At noon Elijah mocked them. He said, "Shout
loudly, for he's a god! Maybe he's thinking it
over; maybe he has wandered away;[C] or maybe he's on the road. Perhaps he's sleeping and
will wake up!" 28 They shouted loudly, and cut
themselves with knives and spears, according
to their custom, until blood gushed over them.
29 All afternoon they kept on raving until the offering of the evening sacrifice, but there was no
sound; no one answered, no one paid attention.
30 Then Elijah said to all the people, "Come
near me." So all the people approached him.
Then he repaired the LORD's altar that had
been torn down: 31 Elijah took twelve stones
— according to the number of the tribes of
the sons of Jacob, to whom the word of the
LORD had come, saying, "Israel will be your
name" — 32 and he built an altar with the stones
in the name of the LORD. Then he made a trench
around the altar large enough to hold about
four gallons.[D,E] 33 Next, he arranged the wood,
cut up the bull, and placed it on the wood.
He said, "Fill four water pots with water and
pour it on the offering to be burned and on
the wood." 34 Then he said, "A second time!"
and they did it a second time. And then he
said, "A third time!" and they did it a third
time. 35 So the water ran all around the altar;
he even filled the trench with water.
36 At the time for offering the evening sacrifice, the prophet Elijah approached the altar
and said, "LORD, the God of Abraham, Isaac,
and Israel, today let it be known that you are
God in Israel and I am your servant, and that at
your word I have done all these things. 37 Answer me, LORD! Answer me so that this people
will know that you, the LORD, are God and that
you have turned their hearts back."
38 Then the LORD's fire fell and consumed
the burnt offering, the wood, the stones, and
the dust, and it licked up the water that was
in the trench. 39 When all the people saw it,
they fell facedown and said, "The LORD, he is
God! The LORD, he is God!"
40 Then Elijah ordered them, "Seize the prophets of Baal! Do not let even one of them escape."
So they seized them, and Elijah brought them
down to the Wadi Kishon and slaughtered them

[A] **18:21** Lit *you hobble on two crutches?* [B] **18:26** Or *hobbled* [C] **18:27** Or *has turned aside*; possibly to relieve himself
[D] **18:32** LXX reads *trench containing two measures of seed* [E] **18:32** Lit *altar corresponding to a house of two seahs of seed*

there. 41 Elijah said to Ahab, "Go up, eat and
drink, for there is the sound of a rainstorm."
42 So Ahab went to eat and drink, but Elijah
went up to the summit of Carmel. He bent
down on the ground and put his face between
his knees. 43 Then he said to his servant, "Go
up and look toward the sea."

So he went up, looked, and said, "There's
nothing."

Seven times Elijah said, "Go back."

44 On the seventh time, he reported, "There's
a cloud as small as a man's hand coming up
from the sea."

Then Elijah said, "Go and tell Ahab, 'Get
your chariot ready and go down so the rain
doesn't stop you.'"

45 In a little while, the sky grew dark with
clouds and wind, and there was a downpour.
So Ahab got in his chariot and went to Jezreel.
46 The power of the LORD was on Elijah, and
he tucked his mantle under his belt and ran
ahead of Ahab to the entrance of Jezreel.

ELIJAH'S JOURNEY TO HOREB

19 Ahab told Jezebel everything that Elijah
had done and how he had killed all the
prophets with the sword. 2 So Jezebel sent a
messenger to Elijah, saying, "May the gods
punish me and do so severely if I don't make
your life like the life of one of them by this
time tomorrow!"

3 Then Elijah became afraid[A] and immediately ran for his life. When he came
to Beer-sheba that belonged to Judah, he
left his servant there, 4 but he went on a
day's journey into the wilderness. He sat
down under a broom tree and prayed that
he might die. He said, "I have had enough!
LORD, take my life, for I'm no better than
my fathers." 5 Then he lay down and slept
under the broom tree.

Suddenly, an angel touched him. The angel
told him, "Get up and eat." 6 Then he looked,
and there at his head was a loaf of bread
baked over hot stones, and a jug of water.
So he ate and drank and lay down again.
7 Then the angel of the LORD returned for a
second time and touched him. He said, "Get
up and eat, or the journey will be too much
for you." 8 So he got up, ate, and drank. Then
on the strength from that food, he walked
forty days and forty nights to Horeb, the
mountain of God. 9 He entered a cave there
and spent the night.

Rest and Reflection | *Sitting Silent*

THE VOICE OF GOD

"A great and mighty wind was tearing at the mountains and was shattering cliffs before the LORD, but the LORD was not in the wind. After the wind there was an earthquake, but the LORD was not in the earthquake. After the earthquake there was a fire, but the LORD was not in the fire. And after the fire there was a voice, a soft whisper." 1 Kings 19:11-12

Elijah was fried. Done. Running on empty.

Following a spiritually and emotionally draining duel with the false prophets of Baal on Mount Carmel—and then after fleeing more than a hundred miles south to escape the death threats of Queen Jezebel—the prophet had nothing left in his tank. He was depressed, even suicidal.

Part one of God's restoration process was physical: Eat. Sleep. Repeat.

Then, following this time of rest and nourishment, God spoke—but not in big, loud, dramatic ways. Instead, God whispered to Elijah in the silence.

Perhaps you need a time of R&R. A weekend break—some good food and long naps away from the struggle. A place of solitude and a time of silence can restore our souls. Perhaps then we can hear God's soft whisper.

For the next note on *Rest and Reflection*, see Job 42:6.

[A] **19:3** Some Hb mss, LXX, Syr, Vg; other Hb mss read *He saw*

ELIJAH'S ENCOUNTER WITH THE LORD

Suddenly, the word of the LORD came to him,
and he said to him, "What are you doing here,
Elijah?"
10 He replied, "I have been very zealous for
the LORD God of Armies, but the Israelites
have abandoned your covenant, torn down
your altars, and killed your prophets with the
sword. I alone am left, and they are looking
for me to take my life."
11 Then he said, "Go out and stand on the
mountain in the LORD's presence."
At that moment, the LORD passed by. A great
and mighty wind was tearing at the mountains
and was shattering cliffs before the LORD, but
the LORD was not in the wind. After the wind
there was an earthquake, but the LORD was
not in the earthquake. 12 After the earthquake
there was a fire, but the LORD was not in the
fire. And after the fire there was a voice, a soft
whisper. 13 When Elijah heard it, he wrapped
his face in his mantle and went out and stood
at the entrance of the cave.
Suddenly, a voice came to him and said,
"What are you doing here, Elijah?"
14 "I have been very zealous for the LORD
God of Armies," he replied, "but the Israelites
have abandoned your covenant, torn down
your altars, and killed your prophets with the
sword. I alone am left, and they're looking for
me to take my life."
15 Then the LORD said to him, "Go and return by the way you came to the Wilderness
of Damascus. When you arrive, you are to
anoint Hazael as king over Aram. 16 You are to
anoint Jehu son of Nimshi as king over Israel
and Elisha son of Shaphat from Abel-meholah as prophet in your place. 17 Then Jehu will
put to death whoever escapes the sword of
Hazael, and Elisha will put to death whoever
escapes the sword of Jehu. 18 But I will leave
seven thousand in Israel — every knee that
has not bowed to Baal and every mouth that
has not kissed him."

ELISHA'S APPOINTMENT AS ELIJAH'S SUCCESSOR

19 Elijah left there and found Elisha son of
Shaphat as he was plowing. Twelve teams of
oxen were in front of him, and he was with
the twelfth team. Elijah walked by him and
threw his mantle over him. 20 Elisha left the
oxen, ran to follow Elijah, and said, "Please
let me kiss my father and mother, and then I
will follow you."
"Go on back," he replied, "for what have I
done to you?"
21 So he turned back from following him,
took the team of oxen, and slaughtered[A] them.
With the oxen's wooden yoke and plow, he
cooked the meat and gave it to the people,
and they ate. Then he left, followed Elijah,
and served him.

VICTORY OVER BEN-HADAD

20 Now King Ben-hadad of Aram assembled his entire army. Thirty-two kings,
along with horses and chariots, were with
him. He marched up, besieged Samaria, and
fought against it. 2 He sent messengers into
the city to King Ahab of Israel and said to him,
"This is what Ben-hadad says: 3 'Your silver and
your gold are mine! And your best wives and
children are mine as well!'"
4 Then the king of Israel answered, "Just as
you say, my lord the king: I am yours, along
with all that I have."
5 The messengers then returned and said,
"This is what Ben-hadad says: 'I have sent
messengers to you, saying: You are to give
me your silver, your gold, your wives, and
your children. 6 But at this time tomorrow I
will send my servants to you,[B] and they will
search your palace and your servants' houses.
They will lay their hands on and take away
whatever is precious to you.'"
7 Then the king of Israel called for all the
elders of the land and said, "Recognize[C] that
this one is only looking for trouble, for he
demanded my wives, my children, my silver,
and my gold, and I didn't turn him down."
8 All the elders and all the people said to
him, "Don't listen or agree."
9 So he said to Ben-hadad's messengers, "Say
to my lord the king, 'Everything you demanded of your servant the first time, I will do, but
this thing I cannot do.'" So the messengers left
and took word back to him.
10 Then Ben-hadad sent messengers to him
and said, "May the gods punish me and do so
severely if Samaria's dust amounts to a handful for each of the people who follow me."
11 The king of Israel answered, "Say this:
'Don't let the one who puts on his armor boast
like the one who takes it off.'"
12 When Ben-hadad heard this response,

[A] **19:21** Or *sacrificed* [B] **20:6** Lit *take all the delight of your eyes* [C] **20:7** Lit *"Know and see*

while he and the kings were drinking in their quarters,[A] he said to his servants, "Take your positions." So they took their positions against the city.

13 A prophet approached King Ahab of Israel and said, "This is what the LORD says: 'Do you see this whole huge army? Watch, I am handing it over to you today so that you may know that I am the LORD.'"

14 Ahab asked, "By whom?"

And the prophet said, "This is what the LORD says: 'By the young men of the provincial leaders.'"

Then he asked, "Who is to start the battle?"

He said, "You."

15 So Ahab mobilized the young men of the provincial leaders, and there were 232. After them he mobilized all the Israelite troops: 7,000. 16 They marched out at noon while Ben-hadad and the thirty-two kings who were helping him were getting drunk in their quarters. 17 The young men of the provincial leaders marched out first. Then Ben-hadad sent out scouts, and they reported to him, saying, "Men are marching out of Samaria."

18 So he said, "If they have marched out in peace, take them alive, and if they have marched out for battle, take them alive."

19 The young men of the provincial leaders and the army behind them marched out from the city, 20 and each one struck down his opponent. So the Arameans fled and Israel pursued them, but King Ben-hadad of Aram escaped on a horse with the cavalry. 21 Then the king of Israel marched out and attacked the cavalry and the chariots. He inflicted a severe slaughter on Aram.

22 The prophet approached the king of Israel and said to him, "Go and strengthen yourself, then consider carefully[B] what you should do, for in the spring the king of Aram will attack you."

23 Now the king of Aram's servants said to him, "Their gods are gods of the hill country. That's why they were stronger than we were. Instead, we should fight with them on the plain; then we will certainly be stronger than they are. 24 Also do this: remove each king from his position and appoint captains in their place. 25 Raise another army for yourself like the army you lost — horse for horse, chariot for chariot — and let's fight with them on the plain; and we will certainly be stronger than they are." The king listened to them and did it.

26 In the spring, Ben-hadad mobilized the Arameans and went up to Aphek to battle Israel. 27 The Israelites mobilized, gathered supplies, and went to fight them. The Israelites camped in front of them like two little flocks of goats, while the Arameans filled the landscape.

28 Then the man of God approached and said to the king of Israel, "This is what the LORD says: 'Because the Arameans have said: The LORD is a god of the mountains and not a god of the valleys, I will hand over all this whole huge army to you. Then you will know that I am the LORD.'"

29 They camped opposite each other for seven days. On the seventh day, the battle took place, and the Israelites struck down the Arameans — one hundred thousand foot soldiers in one day. 30 The ones who remained fled into the city of Aphek, and the wall fell on those twenty-seven thousand remaining men.

Ben-hadad also fled and went into an inner room in the city. 31 His servants said to him, "Consider this: we have heard that the kings of the house of Israel are merciful kings. So let's put sackcloth around our waists and ropes around our heads, and let's go out to the king of Israel. Perhaps he will spare your life."

32 So they dressed with sackcloth around their waists and ropes around their heads, went to the king of Israel, and said, "Your servant Ben-hadad says, 'Please spare my life.'"

So he said, "Is he still alive? He is my brother."

33 Now the men were looking for a sign of hope, so they quickly picked up on this[C] and responded, "Yes, it is your brother Ben-hadad."

Then he said, "Go and bring him."

So Ben-hadad came out to him, and Ahab had him come up into the chariot. 34 Then Ben-hadad said to him, "I restore to you the cities that my father took from your father, and you may set up marketplaces for yourself in Damascus, like my father set up in Samaria."

Ahab responded, "On the basis of this treaty, I release you." So he made a treaty with him and released him.

AHAB REBUKED BY THE LORD

35 One of the sons of the prophets said to his fellow prophet by the word of the LORD, "Strike me!" But the man refused to strike him.

[A] **20:12** Lit *booths*, also in v. 16 [B] **20:22** Lit *then know and see* [C] **20:33** Some Hb mss, alt Hb tradition, LXX; other Hb mss read *they hastened and caught hold; "Is this it?"*

36 He told him, "Because you did not listen to the LORD, mark my words: When you leave me, a lion will kill you." When he left him, a lion attacked and killed him.

37 The prophet found another man and said to him, "Strike me!" So the man struck him, inflicting a wound. 38 Then the prophet went and waited for the king on the road. He disguised himself with a bandage over his eyes. 39 As the king was passing by, he cried out to the king and said, "Your servant marched out into the middle of the battle. Suddenly, a man turned aside and brought someone to me and said, 'Guard this man! If he is ever missing, it will be your life in place of his life, or you will weigh out seventy-five pounds[A] of silver.' 40 But while your servant was busy here and there, he disappeared."

The king of Israel said to him, "That will be your sentence; you yourself have decided it."

41 He quickly removed the bandage from his eyes. The king of Israel recognized that he was one of the prophets. 42 The prophet said to him, "This is what the LORD says: 'Because you released from your hand the man I had set apart for destruction, it will be your life in place of his life and your people in place of his people.'" 43 The king of Israel left for home resentful and angry, and he entered Samaria.

AHAB AND NABOTH'S VINEYARD

21 Some time passed after these events. Naboth the Jezreelite had a vineyard; it was in Jezreel next to the palace of King Ahab of Samaria. 2 So Ahab spoke to Naboth, saying, "Give me your vineyard so I can have it for a vegetable garden, since it is right next to my palace. I will give you a better vineyard in its place, or if you prefer, I will give you its value in silver."

3 But Naboth said to Ahab, "I will never give my fathers' inheritance to you."

4 So Ahab went to his palace resentful and angry because of what Naboth the Jezreelite had told him. He had said, "I will not give you my fathers' inheritance." He lay down on his bed, turned his face away, and didn't eat any food.

5 Then his wife Jezebel came to him and said to him, "Why are you so upset that you refuse to eat?"

6 "Because I spoke to Naboth the Jezreelite," he replied. "I told him: Give me your vineyard for silver, or if you wish, I will give you a vineyard in its place. But he said, 'I won't give you my vineyard!'"

7 Then his wife Jezebel said to him, "Now, exercise your royal power over Israel. Get up, eat some food, and be happy. For I will give you the vineyard of Naboth the Jezreelite." 8 So she wrote letters in Ahab's name and sealed them with his seal. She sent the letters to the elders and nobles who lived with Naboth in his city. 9 In the letters, she wrote:

> Proclaim a fast and seat Naboth at the head of the people. 10 Then seat two wicked men opposite him and have them testify against him, saying, "You have cursed God and the king!" Then take him out and stone him to death.

11 The men of his city, the elders and nobles who lived in his city, did as Jezebel had sent word to them, just as it was written in the letters she had sent them. 12 They proclaimed a fast and seated Naboth at the head of the people. 13 The two wicked men came in and sat opposite him. Then the wicked men testified against Naboth in the presence of the people, saying, "Naboth has cursed God and the king!" So they took him outside the city and stoned him to death with stones. 14 Then they sent word to Jezebel: "Naboth has been stoned to death."

15 When Jezebel heard that Naboth had been stoned to death, she said to Ahab, "Get up and take possession of the vineyard of Naboth the Jezreelite who refused to give it to you for silver, since Naboth isn't alive, but dead." 16 When Ahab heard that Naboth was dead, he got up to go down to the vineyard of Naboth the Jezreelite to take possession of it.

THE LORD'S JUDGMENT ON AHAB

17 Then the word of the LORD came to Elijah the Tishbite: 18 "Get up and go to meet King Ahab of Israel, who is in Samaria. He's in Naboth's vineyard, where he has gone to take possession of it. 19 Tell him, 'This is what the LORD says: Have you murdered and also taken possession?' Then tell him, 'This is what the LORD says: In the place where the dogs licked up Naboth's blood, the dogs will also lick up your blood!'"

20 Ahab said to Elijah, "So, my enemy, you've found me, have you?"

[A] **20:39** Lit *a talent*

He replied, "I have found you because you
devoted yourself to do what is evil in the LORD's
sight. 21 This is what the LORD says:[A] 'I am about
to bring disaster on you and will eradicate
your descendants:

I will wipe out all of Ahab's males,[B]
both slave and free,[C] in Israel;

22 I will make your house like the house of
Jeroboam son of Nebat and like the house
of Baasha son of Ahijah, because you have
angered me and caused Israel to sin.' 23 The
LORD also speaks of Jezebel: 'The dogs will eat
Jezebel in the plot of land[D] at Jezreel:

24 Anyone who belongs to Ahab and dies
in the city, the dogs will eat,
and anyone who dies in the field,
the birds[E] will eat.'"

25 Still, there was no one like Ahab, who
devoted himself to do what was evil in the
LORD's sight, because his wife Jezebel incited him. 26 He committed the most detestable
acts by following idols as the Amorites had,
whom the LORD had dispossessed before the
Israelites.

27 When Ahab heard these words, he tore
his clothes, put sackcloth over his body, and
fasted. He lay down in sackcloth and walked
around subdued. 28 Then the word of the LORD
came to Elijah the Tishbite: 29 "Have you seen
how Ahab has humbled himself before me? I
will not bring the disaster during his lifetime,
because he has humbled himself before me.
I will bring the disaster on his house during
his son's lifetime."

JEHOSHAPHAT'S ALLIANCE WITH AHAB

22 There was a lull of three years without
war between Aram and Israel. 2 Howev-
er, in the third year, King Jehoshaphat of Judah
went to visit the king of Israel. 3 The king of
Israel had said to his servants, "Don't you know
that Ramoth-gilead is ours, but we're doing
nothing to take it from the king of Aram?"
4 So he asked Jehoshaphat, "Will you go with
me to fight Ramoth-gilead?"

Jehoshaphat replied to the king of Israel, "I
am as you are, my people as your people, my
horses as your horses." 5 But Jehoshaphat said
to the king of Israel, "First, please ask what
the LORD's will is."

6 So the king of Israel gathered the prophets,
about four hundred men, and asked them,
"Should I go against Ramoth-gilead for war
or should I refrain?"

They replied, "March up, and the Lord will
hand it over to the king."

7 But Jehoshaphat asked, "Isn't there a prophet of the LORD here anymore? Let's ask him."

8 The king of Israel said to Jehoshaphat,
"There is still one man who can inquire of
the LORD, but I hate him because he never
prophesies good about me, but only disaster.
He is Micaiah son of Imlah."

"The king shouldn't say that!" Jehoshaphat
replied.

9 So the king of Israel called an officer and
said, "Hurry and get Micaiah son of Imlah!"

10 Now the king of Israel and King Jehoshaphat of Judah, clothed in royal attire, were
each sitting on his own throne. They were
on the threshing floor at the entrance to the
gate of Samaria, and all the prophets were
prophesying in front of them. 11 Then Zedekiah
son of Chenaanah made iron horns and said,
"This is what the LORD says: 'You will gore the
Arameans with these until they are finished
off.'" 12 And all the prophets were prophesying the same: "March up to Ramoth-gilead
and succeed, for the LORD will hand it over
to the king."

MICAIAH'S MESSAGE OF DEFEAT

13 The messenger who went to call Micaiah
instructed him, "Look, the words of the prophets are unanimously favorable for the king.
So let your words be like theirs, and speak
favorably."

14 But Micaiah said, "As the LORD lives, I will
say whatever the LORD says to me."

15 So he went to the king, and the king asked
him, "Micaiah, should we go to Ramoth-gilead
for war, or should we refrain?"

Micaiah told him, "March up and succeed.
The LORD will hand it over to the king."

16 But the king said to him, "How many times
must I make you swear not to tell me anything
but the truth in the name of the LORD?"

17 So Micaiah said:

I saw all Israel scattered on the hills
like sheep without a shepherd.
And the LORD said,
"They have no master;
let everyone return home in peace."

[A] 21:21 LXX; MT omits *This is what the LORD says* [B] 21:21 Lit *eliminate Ahab's one who urinates against the wall*
[C] 21:21 Or *males, even the weak and impaired*; Hb obscure [D] 21:23 Some Hb mss, Syr, Tg, Vg, 2Kg 9:36; other Hb mss,
LXX read *the rampart* [E] 21:24 Lit *birds of the sky*

18 So the king of Israel said to Jehoshaphat,
"Didn't I tell you he never prophesies good
about me, but only disaster?"
19 Then Micaiah said, "Therefore, hear the
word of the LORD: I saw the LORD sitting on
his throne, and the whole heavenly army was
standing by him at his right hand and at his
left hand. 20 And the LORD said, 'Who will entice
Ahab to march up and fall at Ramoth-gilead?'
So one was saying this and another was saying that.
21 "Then a spirit came forward, stood in the
LORD's presence, and said, 'I will entice him.'
22 "The LORD asked him, 'How?'
"He said, 'I will go and become a lying spirit
in the mouth of all his prophets.'
"Then he said, 'You will certainly entice him
and prevail. Go and do that.'
23 "You see, the LORD has put a lying spirit
into the mouth of all these prophets of yours,
and the LORD has pronounced disaster against
you."
24 Then Zedekiah son of Chenaanah came
up, hit Micaiah on the cheek, and demanded, "Did[A] the Spirit of the LORD leave me to
speak to you?"
25 Micaiah replied, "You will soon see when
you go to hide in an inner chamber on that
day."
26 Then the king of Israel ordered, "Take Micaiah and return him to Amon, the governor
of the city, and to Joash, the king's son, 27 and
say, 'This is what the king says: Put this guy
in prison and feed him only a little bread and
water[B] until I come back safely.'"
28 But Micaiah said, "If you ever return safely,
the LORD has not spoken through me." Then
he said, "Listen, all you people!"[C]

AHAB'S DEATH

29 Then the king of Israel and Judah's King Jehoshaphat went up to Ramoth-gilead. 30 But
the king of Israel said to Jehoshaphat, "I will
disguise myself and go into battle, but you
wear your royal attire." So the king of Israel
disguised himself and went into battle.
31 Now the king of Aram had ordered his
thirty-two chariot commanders, "Do not fight
with anyone at all[D] except the king of Israel."
32 When the chariot commanders saw Jehoshaphat, they shouted, "He must be the
king of Israel!" So they turned to fight against
him, but Jehoshaphat cried out. 33 When the
chariot commanders saw that he was not
the king of Israel, they turned back from
pursuing him.
34 But a man drew his bow without taking special aim and struck the king of Israel
through the joints of his armor. So he said
to his charioteer, "Turn around and take me
out of the battle,[E] for I am badly wounded!"
35 The battle raged throughout that day, and
the king was propped up in his chariot facing the Arameans. He died that evening, and
blood from his wound flowed into the bottom
of the chariot. 36 Then the cry rang out in the
army as the sun set, declaring:

Each man to his own city,
and each man to his own land!

37 So the king died and was brought to Samaria. They buried the king in Samaria. 38 Then
someone washed the chariot at the pool of
Samaria. The dogs licked up his blood, and
the prostitutes bathed in it, according to the
word of the LORD that he had spoken.
39 The rest of the events of Ahab's reign,
along with all his accomplishments, including
the ivory palace he built, and all the cities
he built, are written in the Historical Record of Israel's Kings. 40 Ahab rested with his
fathers, and his son Ahaziah became king
in his place.

JUDAH'S KING JEHOSHAPHAT

41 Jehoshaphat son of Asa became king over
Judah in the fourth year of Israel's King Ahab.
42 Jehoshaphat was thirty-five years old when
he became king; he reigned twenty-five years
in Jerusalem. His mother's name was Azubah daughter of Shilhi. 43 He walked in all
the ways of his father Asa; he did not turn
away from them but did what was right in
the LORD's sight. However, the high places
were not taken away;[F] the people still sacrificed and burned incense on the high places. 44 Jehoshaphat also made peace with the
king of Israel.
45 The rest of the events of Jehoshaphat's
reign, along with the might he exercised and
how he waged war, are written in the Historical Record of Judah's Kings. 46 He eradicated
from the land the rest of the male cult prostitutes who were left from the days of his father

[A] **22:24** Lit *"Which way did* [B] **22:27** Lit *him on bread of oppression and water of oppression* [C] **22:28** LXX omits *Then he said, "Listen, all you people!"* [D] **22:31** Lit *with small or with great* [E] **22:34** LXX; MT reads *camp* [F] **22:43** LXX, Syr, Vg read *he did not remove the high places*

Asa. 47 There was no king in Edom; a deputy
served as king. 48 Jehoshaphat made ships of
Tarshish to go to Ophir for gold, but they did
not go because the ships were wrecked at
Ezion-geber. 49 At that time, Ahaziah son of
Ahab said to Jehoshaphat, "Let my servants
go with your servants in the ships," but Jehoshaphat was not willing. 50 Jehoshaphat
rested with his fathers and was buried with
them in the city of his ancestor David. His son
Jehoram became king in his place.

ISRAEL'S KING AHAZIAH

51 Ahaziah son of Ahab became king over Israel
in Samaria in the seventeenth year of Judah's
King Jehoshaphat, and he reigned over Israel
two years. 52 He did what was evil in the LORD's
sight. He walked in the ways of his father, in
the ways of his mother, and in the ways of Jeroboam son of Nebat, who had caused Israel to
sin. 53 He served Baal and bowed in worship
to him. He angered the LORD God of Israel just
as his father had done.

2 Kings—The kings whose history is narrated in 2 Kings can be summed up with one of two sets of words: either the king "did what was evil in the LORD's sight" (3:2) or "did what was right in the LORD's sight" (14:3).

Actually, that sums up every life. Either we submit to God's rule or reject him. The results in the lives of the kings of Judah and Israel reveal the importance of that choice. So, will we submit to the sovereign God, or will we reject his offer of salvation and live in bondage to sin?

Second Kings shows that even during national spiritual and moral decay, God was working. He saved a poor widow with miraculous provision of olive oil (4:1-7). He helped a barren woman in Shunem (4:8-37). He healed an enemy commander of leprosy (5:1-19). Surely countless other unnamed individuals followed God even when the prevailing culture did not—and were blessed.

The people around us may ignore God, and our leaders may even discourage our faith, but we can choose to follow God anyway. If we do, he will make us conduits of his peace, restoration, healing, and redemption.

2 KINGS

AUTHOR: The books of 1 and 2 Kings were originally one book, but the author cannot be identified. Possibilities include Samuel and Jeremiah. The books seem to be constructed from several early documents, perhaps written by many different authors under the inspiration of the Holy Spirit.

DATE WRITTEN: The books of 1 and 2 Kings were completed after the release of Jehoiachin from Babylonian imprisonment (562 BC).

ORIGINAL AUDIENCE: The Israelites

SETTING: The books of 1 and 2 Kings cover a period of about 410 years, beginning in 970 BC when King David died. The narrative covers the division of Israel into two kingdoms and the exile of both kingdoms (Israel in 722 BC and Judah in 587 BC).

PURPOSE FOR WRITING: The repeating theme throughout 1 and 2 Kings is the sinful failure of the kings who ruled over God's people. Israel and Judah both failed to keep their side of the covenant to obey and serve God alone, so they suffered at the hands of surrounding nations and were eventually carried into exile. Themes explored include sin and judgment, personal faithfulness in the face of social pressure, and the conflict between worshiping the Lord and worshiping other gods.

OUTLINE:

1. The Divided Kingdom from Israel's Ahaziah to the Fall of Israel (1:1–17:41)

   King Ahaziah—Israel and the prophet Elijah (1:1-18)

   Elisha and Elijah (2:1-25)

   King Joram—Israel (3:1-27)

   Elisha's miracles (4:1–8:15)

   King Jehoram—Judah (8:16-24)

   King Ahaziah—Judah (8:25-29)

   King Jehu—Israel, and the prophet Elisha (9:1–10:36)

   Queen Athaliah—Judah (11:1-16)

   King Joash—Judah (11:17–12:21)

   Kings Jehoahaz and Jehoash—Israel (13:1-25)

   Kings Amaziah and Azariah—Judah (14:1–15:7)

   Five bad kings: Zechariah, Shallum, Menahem, Pekahiah, and Pekah—Israel (15:8-31)

   King Jotham—Judah (15:32-38)

   King Ahaz—Judah (16:1-20)

   King Hoshea and the fall of Israel (17:1-41)

2. The Kingdom of Judah from King Hezekiah to Captivity (18:1–25:30)

   Revival under King Hezekiah and apostasy (18:1–21:26)

   Revival under Josiah and apostasy (22:1–25:7)

   Jerusalem falls to the Babylonians (25:8-30)

KEY VERSE:

"Don't be afraid, for those who are with us outnumber those who are with them."
—2 Kings 6:16

RESTORATION THEMES

R	Rest and Reflection	*For the next note, see Job 42:6.*
E	Eternal Perspective	*God's Power—2 Kings 6:16-17*
S	Support	*For the next note, see 1 Chronicles 16:11.*
T	Thanksgiving and Contentment	*For the next note, see 1 Chronicles 16:8.*
O	Other-centeredness	*For the next note, see Job 29:12-13.*
R	Relationships	*For the next note, see 1 Chronicles 29:17.*
E	Exercise of Faith	*For the next note, see Nehemiah 8:10.*

AHAZIAH'S SICKNESS AND DEATH

1 After Ahab's death, Moab rebelled against Israel. 2 Ahaziah had fallen through the latticed window of his upstairs room in Samaria and was injured. So he sent messengers, instructing them, "Go inquire of Baal-zebub,[A] the god of Ekron, whether I will recover from this injury."

3 But the angel of the LORD said to Elijah the Tishbite, "Go and meet the messengers of the king of Samaria and say to them, 'Is it because there is no God in Israel that you are going to inquire of Baal-zebub, the god of Ekron? 4 Therefore, this is what the LORD says: You will not get up from your sickbed; you will certainly die.' " Then Elijah left.

5 The messengers returned to the king, who asked them, "Why have you come back?"

6 They replied, "A man came to meet us and said, 'Go back to the king who sent you and declare to him: This is what the LORD says: Is it because there is no God in Israel that you're sending these men to inquire of Baal-zebub, the god of Ekron? Therefore, you will not get up from your sickbed; you will certainly die.' "

7 The king asked them, "What sort of man came up to meet you and spoke those words to you?"

8 They replied, "A hairy man with a leather belt around his waist."

He said, "It's Elijah the Tishbite."

9 So King Ahaziah sent a captain with his fifty men to Elijah. When the captain went up to him, he was sitting on top of the hill. He announced, "Man of God, the king declares, 'Come down!' "

10 Elijah responded to the captain, "If I am a man of God, may fire come down from heaven and consume you and your fifty men." Then fire came down from heaven and consumed him and his fifty men.

11 So the king sent another captain with his fifty men to Elijah. He took in the situation[B] and announced, "Man of God, this is what the king says: 'Come down immediately!' "

12 Elijah responded, "If I am a man of God, may fire come down from heaven and consume you and your fifty men." So a divine fire[C] came down from heaven and consumed him and his fifty men.

13 Then the king sent a third captain with his fifty men. The third captain went up and fell on his knees in front of Elijah and begged him, "Man of God, please let my life and the lives of these fifty servants of yours be precious to you. 14 Already fire has come down from heaven and consumed the first two captains with their companies, but this time let my life be precious to you."

15 The angel of the LORD said to Elijah, "Go down with him. Don't be afraid of him." So he got up and went down with him to the king.

16 Then Elijah said to King Ahaziah, "This is what the LORD says: 'Because you have sent messengers to inquire of Baal-zebub, the god of Ekron — is it because there is no God in Israel for you to inquire of his will? — you will not get up from your sickbed; you will certainly die.' "

17 Ahaziah died according to the word of the LORD that Elijah had spoken. Since he had no son, Joram[D] became king in his place. This happened in the second year of Judah's King Jehoram son of Jehoshaphat.[E] 18 The rest of the events of Ahaziah's reign, along with his accomplishments, are written in the Historical Record of Israel's Kings.[F]

ELIJAH IN THE WHIRLWIND

2 The time had come for the LORD to take Elijah up to heaven in a whirlwind. Elijah and Elisha were traveling from Gilgal, 2 and Elijah said to Elisha, "Stay here; the LORD is sending me on to Bethel."

But Elisha replied, "As the LORD lives and as you yourself live, I will not leave you." So they went down to Bethel.

3 Then the sons of the prophets who were at Bethel came out to Elisha and said, "Do you know that the LORD will take your master away from you today?"

He said, "Yes, I know. Be quiet."

4 Elijah said to him, "Elisha, stay here; the LORD is sending me to Jericho."

But Elisha said, "As the LORD lives and as you yourself live, I will not leave you." So they went to Jericho.

5 Then the sons of the prophets who were in Jericho came up to Elisha and said, "Do you know that the LORD will take your master away from you today?"

He said, "Yes, I know. Be quiet."

6 Elijah said to him, "Stay here; the LORD is sending me to the Jordan."

But Elisha said, "As the LORD lives and as

[A] **1:2** = Lord of the Flies [B] **1:11** Lit *He answered* [C] **1:12** Lit *a fire of God* [D] **1:17** Lit *Jehoram*; 2Kg 8:16 [E] **1:17** LXX omits *in the second year . . . Jehoshaphat* [F] **1:18** LXX adds 4 more vv. here similar to 2Kg 3:1-3.

you yourself live, I will not leave you." So the
two of them went on.
7 Fifty men from the sons of the prophets
came and stood observing them at a distance
while the two of them stood by the Jordan.
8 Elijah took his mantle, rolled it up, and struck
the water, which parted to the right and left.
Then the two of them crossed over on dry
ground. 9 When they had crossed over, Elijah
said to Elisha, "Tell me what I can do for you
before I am taken from you."
So Elisha answered, "Please, let me inherit
two shares of your spirit."
10 Elijah replied, "You have asked for something difficult. If you see me being taken from
you, you will have it. If not, you won't."

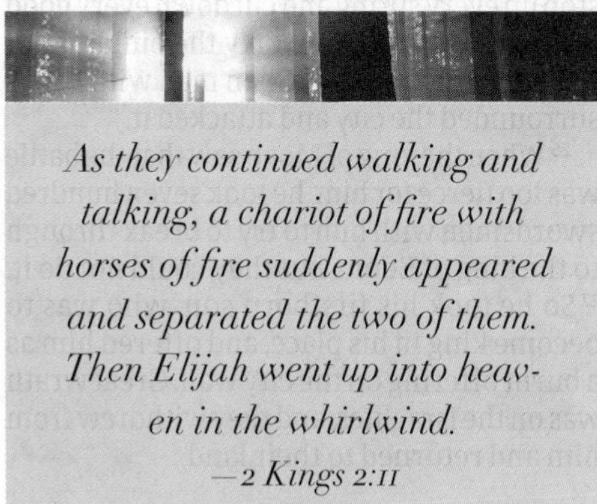
As they continued walking and
talking, a chariot of fire with
horses of fire suddenly appeared
and separated the two of them.
Then Elijah went up into heav-
en in the whirlwind.
—2 Kings 2:11

11 As they continued walking and talking,
a chariot of fire with horses of fire suddenly
appeared and separated the two of them. Then
Elijah went up into heaven in the whirlwind.
12 As Elisha watched, he kept crying out, "My
father, my father, the chariots and horsemen
of Israel!"

ELISHA SUCCEEDS ELIJAH

When he could see him no longer, he took hold
of his own clothes, tore them in two, 13 picked
up the mantle that had fallen off Elijah, and
went back and stood on the bank of the Jordan. 14 He took the mantle Elijah had dropped,
and he struck the water. "Where is the LORD
God of Elijah?" he asked. He struck the water
himself, and it parted to the right and the left,
and Elisha crossed over.
15 When the sons of the prophets from Jericho who were observing saw him, they said,
"The spirit of Elijah rests on Elisha." They came
to meet him and bowed down to the ground
in front of him.
16 Then the sons of the prophets said to
Elisha, "Since there are fifty strong men here
with your servants, please let them go and
search for your master. Maybe the Spirit of
the LORD has carried him away and put him
on one of the mountains or into one of the
valleys."
He answered, "Don't send them."
17 However, they urged him to the point of
embarrassment, so he said, "Send them." They
sent fifty men, who looked for three days but
did not find him. 18 When they returned to him
in Jericho where he was staying, he said to
them, "Didn't I tell you not to go?"
19 The men of the city said to Elisha, "My lord
can see that even though the city's location is
good, the water is bad and the land unfruitful."
20 He replied, "Bring me a new bowl and
put salt in it."
After they had brought him one, 21 Elisha
went out to the spring, threw salt in it, and said,
"This is what the LORD says: 'I have healed this
water. No longer will death or unfruitfulness
result from it.'" 22 Therefore, the water still
remains healthy today according to the word
that Elisha spoke.
23 From there Elisha went up to Bethel. As he
was walking up the path, some small boys came
out of the city and jeered at him, chanting, "Go
up, baldy! Go up, baldy!" 24 He turned around,
looked at them, and cursed them in the name
of the LORD. Then two female bears came out
of the woods and mauled forty-two of the
children. 25 From there Elisha went to Mount
Carmel, and then he returned to Samaria.

ISRAEL'S KING JORAM

3 Joram son of Ahab became king over Israel in Samaria during the eighteenth year
of Judah's King Jehoshaphat, and he reigned
twelve years. 2 He did what was evil in the
LORD's sight, but not like his father and mother, for he removed the sacred pillar of Baal
his father had made. 3 Nevertheless, Joram
clung to the sins that Jeroboam son of Nebat
had caused Israel to commit. He did not turn
away from them.

MOAB'S REBELLION AGAINST ISRAEL

4 King Mesha of Moab was a sheep breeder.
He used to pay the king of Israel one hundred thousand lambs and the wool of one
hundred thousand rams, 5 but when Ahab
died, the king of Moab rebelled against the
king of Israel. 6 So King Joram marched out
from Samaria at that time and mobilized all

Israel. 7 Then he sent a message to King Jehoshaphat of Judah: "The king of Moab has
rebelled against me. Will you go with me to
fight against Moab?"
Jehoshaphat said, "I will go. I am as you are,
my people as your people, my horses as your
horses."
8 He asked, "Which route should we take?"
He replied, "The route of the Wilderness
of Edom."
9 So the king of Israel, the king of Judah,
and the king of Edom set out. After they had
traveled their indirect route for seven days,
they had no water for the army or the animals
with them.
10 Then the king of Israel said, "Oh no, the
LORD has summoned these three kings, only
to hand them over to Moab."
11 But Jehoshaphat said, "Isn't there a prophet of the LORD here? Let's inquire of the LORD
through him."
One of the servants of the king of Israel answered, "Elisha son of Shaphat, who used to
pour water on Elijah's hands, is here."
12 Jehoshaphat affirmed, "The word of the
LORD is with him." So the king of Israel and
Jehoshaphat and the king of Edom went to him.
13 However, Elisha said to King Joram of Israel, "What do we have in common? Go to the
prophets of your father and your mother!"
But the king of Israel replied, "No, because
it is the LORD who has summoned these three
kings to hand them over to Moab."
14 Elisha responded, "By the life of the LORD
of Armies, before whom I stand: If I did not
have respect for King Jehoshaphat of Judah,
I wouldn't look at you; I would not take notice
of you. 15 Now, bring me a musician."
While the musician played, the LORD's hand
came on Elisha. 16 Then he said, "This is what
the LORD says: 'Dig ditch after ditch in this
wadi.' 17 For the LORD says, 'You will not see
wind or rain, but the wadi will be filled with
water, and you will drink — you and your
cattle and your animals.' 18 This is easy in the
LORD's sight. He will also hand Moab over to
you. 19 Then you will attack every fortified city
and every choice city. You will cut down every
good tree and stop up every spring. You will
ruin every good piece of land with stones."
20 About the time for the grain offering the
next morning, water suddenly came from the
direction of Edom and filled the land.
21 All Moab had heard that the kings had come
up to fight against them. So all who could bear
arms, from the youngest to the oldest, were
summoned and took their stand at the border.
22 When they got up early in the morning, the
sun was shining on the water, and the Moabites
saw that the water across from them was red
like blood. 23 "This is blood!" they exclaimed.
"The kings have crossed swords[A] and their men
have killed one another. So, to the spoil, Moab!"
24 However, when the Moabites came to Israel's camp, the Israelites attacked them, and
they fled from them. So Israel went into the land
attacking the Moabites. 25 They would destroy
the cities, and each of them would throw a stone
to cover every good piece of land. They would
stop up every spring and cut down every good
tree. This went on until only the buildings of
Kir-hareseth were left. Then men with slings
surrounded the city and attacked it.
26 When the king of Moab saw that the battle
was too fierce for him, he took seven hundred
swordsmen with him to try to break through
to the king of Edom, but they could not do it.
27 So he took his firstborn son, who was to
become king in his place, and offered him as
a burnt offering on the city wall. Great wrath
was on the Israelites, and they withdrew from
him and returned to their land.

THE WIDOW'S OIL MULTIPLIED

4 One of the wives of the sons of the prophets cried out to Elisha, "Your servant, my
husband, has died. You know that your servant
feared the LORD. Now the creditor is coming
to take my two children as his slaves."
2 Elisha asked her, "What can I do for you?
Tell me, what do you have in the house?"
She said, "Your servant has nothing in the
house except a jar of oil."
3 Then he said, "Go out and borrow empty
containers from all your neighbors. Do not
get just a few. 4 Then go in and shut the door
behind you and your sons, and pour oil into
all these containers. Set the full ones to one
side." 5 So she left.
After she had shut the door behind her and
her sons, they kept bringing her containers,
and she kept pouring. 6 When they were full,
she said to her son, "Bring me another container."
But he replied, "There aren't any more." Then
the oil stopped.

[A] 3:23 Or *have been laid waste*

7 She went and told the man of God, and he
said, "Go sell the oil and pay your debt; you
and your sons can live on the rest."

THE SHUNAMMITE WOMAN'S HOSPITALITY

8 One day Elisha went to Shunem. A prominent woman who lived there persuaded him
to eat some food. So whenever he passed by,
he stopped there to eat. 9 Then she said to her
husband, "I know that the one who often passes
by here is a holy man of God, 10 so let's make a
small, walled-in upper room and put a bed, a
table, a chair, and a lamp there for him. Whenever he comes, he can stay there."

THE SHUNAMMITE WOMAN'S SON

11 One day he came there and stopped at the
upstairs room to lie down. 12 He ordered his
attendant Gehazi, "Call this Shunammite
woman." So he called her and she stood before him.
13 Then he said to Gehazi, "Say to her, 'Look,
you've gone to all this trouble for us. What can
we do for you? Can we speak on your behalf to
the king or to the commander of the army?'"
She answered, "I am living among my own
people."
14 So he asked, "Then what should be done
for her?"
Gehazi answered, "Well, she has no son,
and her husband is old."
15 "Call her," Elisha said. So Gehazi called
her, and she stood in the doorway. 16 Elisha
said, "At this time next year you will have a
son in your arms."
Then she said, "No, my lord. Man of God, do
not lie to your servant."
17 The woman conceived and gave birth to
a son at the same time the following year, as
Elisha had promised her.

THE SHUNAMMITE'S SON RAISED

18 The child grew and one day went out to his
father and the harvesters. 19 Suddenly he complained to his father, "My head! My head!"
His father told his servant, "Carry him to
his mother." 20 So he picked him up and took
him to his mother. The child sat on her lap
until noon and then died. 21 She went up and
laid him on the bed of the man of God, shut
him in, and left.
22 She summoned her husband and said,
"Please send me one of the servants and one
of the donkeys, so I can hurry to the man of
God and come back again."
23 But he said, "Why go to him today? It's
not a New Moon or a Sabbath."
She replied, "Everything is all right."
24 Then she saddled the donkey and said
to her servant, "Go fast; don't slow the pace
for me unless I tell you." 25 So she came to the
man of God at Mount Carmel.
When the man of God saw her at a distance,
he said to his attendant Gehazi, "Look, there's
the Shunammite woman. 26 Run out to meet
her and ask, 'Are you all right? Is your husband
all right? Is your son all right?'"
And she answered, "Everything's all right."
27 When she came up to the man of God at
the mountain, she clung to his feet. Gehazi
came to push her away, but the man of God
said, "Leave her alone — she is in severe anguish, and the LORD has hidden it from me.
He hasn't told me."
28 Then she said, "Did I ask my lord for a son?
Didn't I say, 'Do not lie to me?'"
29 So Elisha said to Gehazi, "Tuck your mantle
under your belt, take my staff with you, and
go. If you meet anyone, don't stop to greet
him, and if a man greets you, don't answer
him. Then place my staff on the boy's face."
30 The boy's mother said to Elisha, "As the
LORD lives and as you yourself live, I will not
leave you." So he got up and followed her.
31 Gehazi went ahead of them and placed
the staff on the boy's face, but there was no
sound or sign of life, so he went back to meet
Elisha and told him, "The boy didn't wake up."
32 When Elisha got to the house, he discovered
the boy lying dead on his bed. 33 So he went in,
closed the door behind the two of them, and
prayed to the LORD. 34 Then he went up and lay
on the boy: he put mouth to mouth, eye to eye,
hand to hand. While he bent down over him, the
boy's flesh became warm. 35 Elisha got up, went
into the house, and paced back and forth. Then
he went up and bent down over him again. The
boy sneezed seven times and opened his eyes.
36 Elisha called Gehazi and said, "Call the
Shunammite woman." He called her and she
came. Then Elisha said, "Pick up your son."
37 She came, fell at his feet, and bowed to the
ground; she picked up her son and left.

THE DEADLY STEW

38 When Elisha returned to Gilgal, there was a
famine in the land. The sons of the prophets
were sitting before him. He said to his attendant, "Put on the large pot and make stew for
the sons of the prophets."

39 One went out to the field to gather herbs
and found a wild vine from which he gathered
as many wild gourds as his garment would
hold. Then he came back and cut them up
into the pot of stew, but they were unaware
of what they were.[A]

40 They served some for the men to eat, but
when they ate the stew they cried out, "There's
death in the pot, man of God!" And they were
unable to eat it.

41 Then Elisha said, "Get some flour." He
threw it into the pot and said, "Serve it for
the people to eat." And there was nothing bad
in the pot.

THE MULTIPLIED BREAD

42 A man from Baal-shalishah came to the man
of God with his sack full of[B] twenty loaves of
barley bread from the first bread of the harvest.
Elisha said, "Give it to the people to eat."

43 But Elisha's attendant asked, "What? Am
I to set this before a hundred men?"

"Give it to the people to eat," Elisha said, "for
this is what the LORD says: 'They will eat, and
they will have some left over.'" 44 So he set it
before them, and as the LORD had promised,
they ate and had some left over.

NAAMAN'S DISEASE HEALED

5 Naaman, commander of the army for the
king of Aram, was a man important to his
master and highly regarded because through
him, the LORD had given victory to Aram. The
man was a valiant warrior, but he had a skin
disease.

2 Aram had gone on raids and brought back
from the land of Israel a young girl who served
Naaman's wife. 3 She said to her mistress, "If
only my master were with the prophet who
is in Samaria, he would cure him of his skin
disease."

4 So Naaman went and told his master
what the girl from the land of Israel had said.
5 Therefore, the king of Aram said, "Go, and
I will send a letter with you to the king of
Israel."

So he went and took with him 750 pounds[C]
of silver, 150 pounds[D] of gold, and ten sets of
clothing. 6 He brought the letter to the king
of Israel, and it read:

When this letter comes to you, note that
I have sent you my servant Naaman for
you to cure him of his skin disease.

7 When the king of Israel read the letter, he
tore his clothes and asked, "Am I God, killing
and giving life that this man expects me to
cure a man of his skin disease? Recognize[E]
that he is only picking a fight with me."

8 When Elisha the man of God heard that
the king of Israel had torn his clothes, he sent
a message to the king, "Why have you torn
your clothes? Have him come to me, and he
will know there is a prophet in Israel." 9 So
Naaman came with his horses and chariots
and stood at the door of Elisha's house.

10 Then Elisha sent him a messenger, who
said, "Go wash seven times in the Jordan and
your skin will be restored and you will be
clean."

11 But Naaman got angry and left, saying,
"I was telling myself: He will surely come
out, stand and call on the name of the LORD
his God, and wave his hand over the place
and cure the skin disease. 12 Aren't Abana
and Pharpar, the rivers of Damascus, better
than all the waters of Israel? Couldn't I wash
in them and be clean?" So he turned and left
in a rage.

13 But his servants approached and said to
him, "My father, if the prophet had told you
to do some great thing, would you not have
done it? How much more should you do it
when he only tells you, 'Wash and be clean'?"
14 So Naaman went down and dipped himself
in the Jordan seven times, according to the
command of the man of God. Then his skin
was restored and became like the skin of a
small boy, and he was clean.

15 Then Naaman and his whole company
went back to the man of God, stood before
him, and declared, "I know there's no God in
the whole world except in Israel. Therefore,
please accept a gift from your servant."

16 But Elisha said, "As the LORD lives, in whose
presence I stand, I will not accept it." Naaman
urged him to accept it, but he refused.

17 Naaman responded, "If not, please let your
servant be given as much soil as a pair of mules
can carry, for your servant will no longer offer
a burnt offering or a sacrifice to any other god
but the LORD. 18 However, in a particular matter
may the LORD pardon your servant: When
my master, the king of Aram, goes into the
temple of Rimmon to bow in worship while
he is leaning on my arm,[F] and I have to bow
in the temple of Rimmon — when I bow[G] in

[A] 4:39 *of what they were* added for clarity [B] 4:42 Or *with some heads of fresh grain and* [C] 5:5 Lit *10 talents* [D] 5:5 Lit *6,000 shekels* [E] 5:7 Lit *Know and see* [F] 5:18 Lit *worship, and he leans on my hand* [G] 5:18 LXX, Vg read *when he bows himself*

Naaman | Restoration Profile

2 KINGS 5:1-27

Scattered throughout the Old Testament are reminders of God's sovereign plans for the world. He chose a man (Abram) from whom to birth a people (Israel). Through that nation, he would fulfill his promise given to Eve that a descendant of hers would deal a fatal blow to the curse of sin in the world (Gn 3:15). Along the way, men and women who were not part of the chosen people still received God's blessing. One such story of foreign restoration is Naaman.

Naaman was a Syrian general who had fought against Israel and had been victorious. However, he had leprosy. Part of his plunder was a young Jewish slave girl whose lowly station did not keep her from telling her master about God and his willingness to restore. She was apparently moved by compassion for Naaman who faced the dreaded disease. Often the news of possible restoration comes from an unlikely source.

When Naaman arrived at Elisha's home, laden with gifts, he was greeted with a twofold offense. Not only did Elisha not come out and greet him, the prophet also sent a servant with the curt instruction: "Go wash seven times in the Jordan and your skin will be restored and you will be clean" (2Kg 5:10). The message of restoration often comes to us in offensive ways, for God does not ingratiate himself to anyone.

Livid, Naaman initially turned to return home. Fortunately for him, those with him urged him to keep his eye on the main objective. Compared to the possibility of restoration, washing in the Jordan was a small requirement. We often need the help of others to persevere toward restoration.

Naaman was not only restored physically, but he also recognized the God of Israel as the true God and was set on a path of spiritual restoration. God restores in mysterious ways.

the temple of Rimmon, may the LORD pardon
your servant in this matter."
19 So he said to him, "Go in peace."

GEHAZI'S GREED PUNISHED

After Naaman had traveled a short distance
from Elisha, 20 Gehazi, the attendant of Elisha
the man of God, thought, "My master has let
this Aramean Naaman off lightly by not accepting from him what he brought. As the
LORD lives, I will run after him and get something from him."
21 So Gehazi pursued Naaman. When Naaman saw someone running after him, he got
down from the chariot to meet him and asked,
"Is everything all right?"
22 Gehazi said, "It's all right. My master has
sent me to say, 'I have just now discovered that
two young men from the sons of the prophets have come to me from the hill country
of Ephraim. Please give them seventy-five
pounds[A] of silver and two sets of clothing.'"
23 But Naaman insisted, "Please, accept one
hundred fifty pounds."[B] He urged Gehazi and
then packed one hundred fifty pounds of silver
in two bags with two sets of clothing. Naaman
gave them to two of his attendants who carried them ahead of Gehazi. 24 When Gehazi
came to the hill,[C] he took the gifts from them
and deposited them in the house. Then he
dismissed the men, and they left.
25 Gehazi came and stood by his master.
"Where did you go, Gehazi?" Elisha asked him.
He replied, "Your servant didn't go anywhere."
26 "And my heart didn't go[D] when the man
got down from his chariot to meet you," Elisha
said. "Is this a time to accept silver and clothing, olive orchards and vineyards, flocks and
herds, and male and female slaves? 27 Therefore,
Naaman's skin disease will cling to you and
your descendants forever." So Gehazi went out
from his presence diseased, resembling snow.[E]

THE FLOATING AX HEAD

6 The sons of the prophets said to Elisha,
"Please notice that the place where we
live under your supervision[F] is too small for
us. 2 Please let us go to the Jordan where we
can each get a log and can build ourselves a
place to live there."

[A] 5:22 Lit *a talent* [B] 5:23 Lit *two talents* [C] 5:24 Or *citadel* [D] 5:26 Or *"Did not my heart go* [E] 5:27 A reference to whiteness or flakiness of the skin [F] 6:1 Lit *we are living before you*

"Go," he said.
³ Then one said, "Please come with your
servants."
"I'll come," he answered.
⁴ So he went with them, and when they came
to the Jordan, they cut down trees. ⁵ As one
of them was cutting down a tree, the iron ax
head fell into the water, and he cried out, "Oh,
my master, it was borrowed!"
⁶ Then the man of God asked, "Where did
it fall?"

When he showed him the place, the man of
God cut a piece of wood, threw it there, and
made the iron float. ⁷ Then he said, "Pick it
up." So he reached out and took it.

THE ARAMEAN WAR

⁸ When the king of Aram was waging war
against Israel, he conferred with his servants,
"My camp will be at such and such a place."
⁹ But the man of God sent word to the king
of Israel: "Be careful passing by this place, for
the Arameans are going down there." ¹⁰ Consequently, the king of Israel sent word to the
place the man of God had told him about. The
man of God repeatedly[A] warned the king, so
the king would be on his guard.
¹¹ The king of Aram was enraged because
of this matter, and he called his servants and
demanded of them, "Tell me, which one of us
is for the king of Israel?"
¹² One of his servants said, "No one, my lord
the king. Elisha, the prophet in Israel, tells
the king of Israel even the words you speak
in your bedroom."
¹³ So the king said, "Go and see where he is,
so I can send men to capture him."

When he was told, "Elisha is in Dothan," ¹⁴ he
sent horses, chariots, and a massive army there.
They went by night and surrounded the city.
¹⁵ When the servant of the man of God got
up early and went out, he discovered an army
with horses and chariots surrounding the
city. So he asked Elisha, "Oh, my master, what
are we to do?"
¹⁶ Elisha said, "Don't be afraid, for those
who are with us outnumber those who are
with them."
¹⁷ Then Elisha prayed, "LORD, please open his
eyes and let him see." So the LORD opened the
servant's eyes, and he saw that the mountain
was covered with horses and chariots of fire
all around Elisha.
¹⁸ When the Arameans came against him,

Eternal Perspective | *God's Power*

EYES TO SEE

"Elisha said, 'Don't be afraid, for those who are with us outnumber those who are with them.' Then Elisha prayed, 'LORD, please open his eyes and let him see.' So the LORD opened the servant's eyes, and he saw that the mountain was covered with horses and chariots of fire all around Elisha." 2 Kings 6:16-17

If you look through a gap in a fence, you may see what is directly in front of you but precious little else. In the same way, when we view the world with just our physical eyes, we miss bigger, more important spiritual realities seen by faith.

Elijah's servant had this problem. Because he saw only the approaching Aramean army—and not the vast angelic host that encircled them—he was terrified. For this reason, the prophet prayed that the man's spiritual eyes might be opened—that he might be granted the ability to see the unseeable. In a very short time the servant was smiling, not shaking.

This is exactly what Paul prayed for the Ephesian Christians—"that the eyes of your heart may be enlightened" (Eph 1:18). Ask God to help you see his power at work and not the problems and enemies around you.

For the next note on *Eternal Perspective*, see Nehemiah 9:6.

[A] 6:10 Lit *not once and not twice*

Elisha prayed to the LORD, "Please strike this
nation with blindness."[A] So he struck them
with blindness, according to Elisha's word.
19 Then Elisha said to them, "This is not the way,
and this is not the city. Follow me, and I will
take you to the man you're looking for." And
he led them to Samaria. 20 When they entered
Samaria, Elisha said, "LORD, open these men's
eyes and let them see." So the LORD opened
their eyes, and they saw that they were in the
middle of Samaria.
21 When the king of Israel saw them, he said
to Elisha, "Should I kill them, should I kill them,
my father?"
22 Elisha replied, "Don't kill them. Do you
kill those you have captured with your sword
or your bow? Set food and water in front of
them so they can eat and drink and go to their
master."
23 So he prepared a big feast for them. When
they had eaten and drunk, he sent them away,
and they went to their master. The Aramean
raiders did not come into Israel's land again.

THE SIEGE OF SAMARIA

24 Some time later, King Ben-hadad of Aram
brought all his military units together and
marched up and laid siege to Samaria. 25 So
there was a severe famine in Samaria, and
they continued the siege against it until a
donkey's head sold for thirty-four ounces[B]
of silver, and a cup[C] of dove's dung[D] sold for
two ounces[E] of silver.
26 As the king of Israel was passing by on
the wall, a woman cried out to him, "My lord
the king, help!"
27 He answered, "If the LORD doesn't help
you, where can I get help for you? From the
threshing floor or the winepress?" 28 Then the
king asked her, "What's the matter?"
She said, "This woman said to me, 'Give up
your son, and we will eat him today. Then we
will eat my son tomorrow.' 29 So we boiled my
son and ate him, and I said to her the next day,
'Give up your son, and we will eat him,' but
she has hidden her son."
30 When the king heard the woman's words,
he tore his clothes. Then, as he was passing
by on the wall, the people saw that there was
sackcloth under his clothes next to his skin.
31 He announced, "May God punish me and do
so severely if the head of Elisha son of Shaphat
remains on his shoulders today."
32 Elisha was sitting in his house, and the
elders were sitting with him. The king sent a
man ahead of him, but before the messenger
got to him, Elisha said to the elders, "Do you
see how this murderer has sent someone to
remove my head? Look, when the messenger
comes, shut the door to keep him out. Isn't
the sound of his master's feet behind him?"
33 While Elisha was still speaking with them,
the messenger[F] came down to him. Then he
said, "This disaster is from the LORD. Why
should I wait for the LORD any longer?"
7 Elisha replied, "Hear the word of the LORD!
This is what the LORD says: 'About this time
tomorrow at Samaria's gate, six quarts[G] of
fine flour will sell for a half ounce of silver[H]
and twelve quarts[I] of barley will sell for a half
ounce of silver.'"
2 Then the captain, the king's right-hand
man,[J] responded to the man of God, "Look,
even if the LORD were to make windows in
heaven, could this really happen?"
Elisha announced, "You will in fact see it with
your own eyes, but you won't eat any of it."
3 Now four men with a skin disease were
at the entrance to the city gate. They said to
each other, "Why just sit here until we die? 4 If
we say, 'Let's go into the city,' we will die there
because the famine is in the city, but if we sit
here, we will also die. So now, come on. Let's
surrender to the Arameans' camp. If they let
us live, we will live; if they kill us, we will die."
5 So the diseased men got up at twilight to
go to the Arameans' camp. When they came
to the camp's edge, they discovered that no
one was there, 6 for the Lord[K] had caused the
Aramean camp to hear the sound of chariots,
horses, and a large army. The Arameans had
said to each other, "The king of Israel must have
hired the kings of the Hittites and the kings
of Egypt to attack us." 7 So they had gotten up
and fled at twilight, abandoning their tents,
horses, and donkeys. The camp was intact,
and they had fled for their lives.
8 When these diseased men came to the edge
of the camp, they went into a tent to eat and
drink. Then they picked up the silver, gold,
and clothing and went off and hid them. They
came back and entered another tent, picked

[A] **6:18** Or *a blinding light* [B] **6:25** Lit *for 80*; "shekels" is assumed [C] **6:25** Lit *a fourth of a kab* [D] **6:25** Or *seedpods*, or *wild onions* [E] **6:25** Lit *for five*; "shekels" is assumed [F] **6:33** Some emend to *king* [G] **7:1** Lit *a seah*, also in vv. 16,18 [H] **7:1** Lit *for a shekel*, also in vv. 16,18 [I] **7:1** Lit *two seahs*, also in vv. 16,18 [J] **7:2** Lit *captain, upon whose hand the king leaned*, also in v. 17 [K] **7:6** Some Hb mss read *LORD*

things up, and hid them. 9 Then they said to each other, "We're not doing what is right. Today is a day of good news. If we are silent and wait until morning light, our punishment will catch up with us. So let's go tell the king's household."

10 The diseased men came and called to the city's gatekeepers and told them, "We went to the Aramean camp and no one was there — no human sounds. There was nothing but tethered horses and donkeys, and the tents were intact." 11 The gatekeepers called out, and the news was reported to the king's household.

12 So the king got up in the night and said to his servants, "Let me tell you what the Arameans have done to us. They know we are starving, so they have left the camp to hide in the open country, thinking, 'When they come out of the city, we will take them alive and go into the city.'"

13 But one of his servants responded, "Please, let messengers take five of the horses that are left in the city. Their fate is like the entire Israelite community who will die,[A] so let's send them and see."

14 The messengers took two chariots with horses, and the king sent them after the Aramean army, saying, "Go and see." 15 So they followed them as far as the Jordan. They saw that the whole way was littered with clothes and equipment the Arameans had thrown off in their haste. The messengers returned and told the king.

16 Then the people went out and plundered the Aramean camp. It was then that six quarts of fine flour sold for a half ounce of silver and twelve quarts of barley sold for a half ounce of silver, according to the word of the LORD. 17 The king had appointed the captain, his right-hand man, to be in charge of the city gate, but the people trampled him in the gate. He died, just as the man of God had predicted when the king had come to him. 18 When the man of God had said to the king, "About this time tomorrow twelve quarts of barley will sell for a half ounce of silver and six quarts of fine flour will sell for a half ounce of silver at Samaria's gate," 19 this captain had answered the man of God, "Look, even if the LORD were to make windows in heaven, could this really happen?" Elisha had said, "You will in fact see it with your own eyes, but you won't eat any of it." 20 This is what happened to him: the people trampled him in the city gate, and he died.

THE SHUNAMMITE'S LAND RESTORED

8 Elisha said to the woman whose son he had restored to life, "Get ready, you and your household, and go live as a resident alien wherever you can. For the LORD has announced a seven-year famine, and it has already come to the land."

2 So the woman got ready and did what the man of God said. She and her household lived as resident aliens in the land of the Philistines for seven years. 3 When the woman returned from the land of the Philistines at the end of seven years, she went to appeal to the king for her house and field.

4 The king had been speaking to Gehazi, the attendant of the man of God, saying, "Tell me all the great things Elisha has done."

5 While he was telling the king how Elisha restored the dead son to life, the woman whose son he had restored to life came to appeal to the king for her house and field. So Gehazi said, "My lord the king, this is the woman and this is the son Elisha restored to life."

6 When the king asked the woman, she told him the story. So the king appointed a court official for her, saying, "Restore all that was hers, along with all the income from the field from the day she left the country until now."

ARAM'S KING HAZAEL

7 Elisha came to Damascus while King Ben-hadad of Aram was sick, and the king was told, "The man of God has come here." 8 So the king said to Hazael, "Take a gift with you and go meet the man of God. Inquire of the LORD through him, 'Will I recover from this sickness?'"

9 Hazael went to meet Elisha, taking with him a gift: forty camel-loads of all the finest products of Damascus. When he came and stood before him, he said, "Your son, King Ben-hadad of Aram, has sent me to ask you, 'Will I recover from this sickness?'"

10 Elisha told him, "Go say to him, 'You are sure to[B] recover.' But the LORD has shown me that he is sure to die." 11 Then he stared steadily at him until he was ashamed.

The man of God wept, 12 and Hazael asked, "Why is my lord weeping?"

He replied, "Because I know the evil you will do to the people of Israel. You will set their fortresses on fire. You will kill their young men with the sword. You will dash their children to pieces. You will rip open their pregnant women."

[A] **7:13** Some Hb mss, LXX, Syr, Vg; other Hb mss read *left in it. Indeed, they are like the whole multitude of Israel that are left in it; indeed, they are like the whole multitude of Israel who will die.* [B] **8:10** Alt Hb tradition reads *You will not*

13 Hazael said, "How could your servant, a
mere dog, do such a mighty deed?"
Elisha answered, "The LORD has shown me
that you will be king over Aram."
14 Hazael left Elisha and went to his master,
who asked him, "What did Elisha say to you?"
He responded, "He told me you are sure to
recover." 15 The next day Hazael took a heavy
cloth, dipped it in water, and spread it over
the king's face. Ben-hadad died, and Hazael
reigned in his place.

JUDAH'S KING JEHORAM

16 In the fifth year of Israel's King Joram son of
Ahab, Jehoram[A] son of Jehoshaphat became
king of Judah, replacing his father.[B] 17 He was
thirty-two years old when he became king,
and he reigned eight years in Jerusalem. 18 He
walked in the ways of the kings of Israel, as the
house of Ahab had done, for Ahab's daughter
was his wife. He did what was evil in the LORD's
sight. 19 For the sake of his servant David, the
LORD was unwilling to destroy Judah, since
he had promised to give a lamp to David and
his sons forever.
20 During Jehoram's reign, Edom rebelled
against Judah's control and appointed their
own king. 21 So Jehoram crossed over to Zair
with all his chariots. Then at night he set out
to attack the Edomites who had surrounded him and the chariot commanders, but his
troops fled to their tents. 22 So Edom is still in
rebellion against Judah's control today. Libnah
also rebelled at that time.
23 The rest of the events of Jehoram's reign,
along with all his accomplishments, are written in the Historical Record of Judah's Kings.
24 Jehoram rested with his fathers and was
buried with his fathers in the city of David,
and his son Ahaziah became king in his place.

JUDAH'S KING AHAZIAH

25 In the twelfth year of Israel's King Joram son
of Ahab, Ahaziah son of Jehoram became king
of Judah. 26 Ahaziah was twenty-two years
old when he became king, and he reigned
one year in Jerusalem. His mother's name
was Athaliah, granddaughter of Israel's King
Omri. 27 He walked in the ways of the house
of Ahab and did what was evil in the LORD's
sight like the house of Ahab, for his father had
married into[C] the house of Ahab.
28 Ahaziah went with Joram son of Ahab to
fight against King Hazael of Aram in Ramoth-gilead, and the Arameans wounded Joram. 29 So
King Joram returned to Jezreel to recover from
the wounds that the Arameans had inflicted on
him in Ramoth-gilead[D] when he fought against
Aram's King Hazael. Then Judah's King Ahaziah
son of Jehoram went down to Jezreel to visit
Joram son of Ahab since Joram was ill.

JEHU ANOINTED AS ISRAEL'S KING

9 The prophet Elisha called one of the sons
of the prophets and said, "Tuck your mantle under your belt, take this flask of oil with
you, and go to Ramoth-gilead. 2 When you get
there, look for Jehu son of Jehoshaphat, son
of Nimshi. Go in, get him away from his colleagues, and take him to an inner room. 3 Then
take the flask of oil, pour it on his head, and
say, 'This is what the LORD says: "I anoint you
king over Israel."' Open the door and escape.
Don't wait." 4 So the young prophet[E] went to
Ramoth-gilead.
5 When he arrived, the army commanders
were sitting there, so he said, "I have a message for you, commander."
Jehu asked, "For which one of us?"
He answered, "For you, commander."
6 So Jehu got up and went into the house.
The young prophet poured the oil on his head
and said, "This is what the LORD God of Israel
says: 'I anoint you king over the LORD's people, Israel. 7 You are to strike down the house
of your master Ahab so that I may avenge
the blood shed by the hand of Jezebel — the
blood of my servants the prophets and of all
the servants of the LORD. 8 The whole house
of Ahab will perish, and I will wipe out all of
Ahab's males,[F] both slave and free,[G] in Israel.
9 I will make the house of Ahab like the house
of Jeroboam son of Nebat and like the house
of Baasha son of Ahijah. 10 The dogs will eat
Jezebel in the plot of land at Jezreel — no one
will bury her.'" Then the young prophet opened
the door and escaped.
11 When Jehu came out to his master's servants, they asked, "Is everything all right? Why
did this crazy person come to you?"
Then he said to them, "You know the sort
and their ranting."
12 But they replied, "That's a lie! Tell us!"
So Jehu said, "He talked to me about this

[A] **8:16** = The LORD is Exalted [B] **8:16** Lit *Judah; Jehoshaphat had been king of Judah* [C] **8:27** Lit *for he was related by marriage to* [D] **8:29** Lit *Ramah* [E] **9:4** Or *the young man, the attendant of the prophet* [F] **9:8** Lit *wipe out Ahab's one who urinates against a wall* [G] **9:8** Or *males, even the weak and impaired*; Hb obscure

and that and said, 'This is what the LORD says:
I anoint you king over Israel.'"
13 Each man quickly took his garment and
put it under Jehu on the bare steps.[A] They blew
the ram's horn and proclaimed, "Jehu is king!"
14 Then Jehu son of Jehoshaphat, son of Nimshi, conspired against Joram. Joram and all
Israel had been at Ramoth-gilead on guard
against King Hazael of Aram. 15 But King Joram had returned to Jezreel to recover from
the wounds that the Arameans had inflicted
on him when he fought against Aram's King
Hazael. Jehu said, "If you commanders wish to
make me king,[B] then don't let anyone escape
from the city to go tell about it in Jezreel."

JEHU KILLS JORAM AND AHAZIAH

16 Jehu got into his chariot and went to Jezreel
since Joram was laid up there and King Ahaziah
of Judah had gone down to visit Joram. 17 Now
the watchman was standing on the tower in
Jezreel. He saw Jehu's mob approaching and
shouted, "I see a mob!"

Joram responded, "Choose a rider and send
him to meet them and have him ask, 'Do you
come in peace?'"
18 So a horseman went to meet Jehu and
said, "This is what the king asks: 'Do you come
in peace?'"

Jehu replied, "What do you have to do with
peace?[C] Fall in behind me."

The watchman reported, "The messenger
reached them but hasn't started back."
19 So he sent out a second horseman, who
went to them and said, "This is what the king
asks: 'Do you come in peace?'"

Jehu answered, "What do you have to do
with peace? Fall in behind me."
20 Again the watchman reported, "He
reached them but hasn't started back. Also,
the driving is like that of Jehu son of Nimshi
— he drives like a madman."
21 "Get the chariot ready!" Joram shouted,
and they got it ready. Then King Joram of Israel
and King Ahaziah of Judah set out, each in his
own chariot, and met Jehu at the plot of land
of Naboth the Jezreelite. 22 When Joram saw
Jehu he asked, "Do you come in peace, Jehu?"

He answered, "What peace can there be as
long as there is so much prostitution and sorcery from your mother Jezebel?"
23 Joram turned around and fled, shouting
to Ahaziah, "It's treachery, Ahaziah!"
24 Then Jehu drew his bow and shot Joram between the shoulders. The arrow went
through his heart, and he slumped down in
his chariot. 25 Jehu said to Bidkar his aide,
"Pick him up and throw him on the plot of
ground belonging to Naboth the Jezreelite.
For remember when you and I were riding
side by side behind his father Ahab, and the
LORD uttered this pronouncement against
him: 26 'As surely as I saw the blood of Naboth
and the blood of his sons yesterday' — this
is the LORD's declaration — 'so will I repay
you on this plot of land' — this is the LORD's
declaration. So now, according to the word
of the LORD, pick him up and throw him on
the plot of land."
27 When King Ahaziah of Judah saw what
was happening, he fled up the road toward
Beth-haggan. Jehu pursued him, shouting,
"Shoot him too!" So they shot him in his chariot[D] at Gur Pass near Ibleam, but he fled to
Megiddo and died there. 28 Then his servants
carried him to Jerusalem in a chariot and
buried him in his fathers' tomb in the city of
David. 29 It was in the eleventh year of Joram
son of Ahab that Ahaziah had become king
over Judah.

JEHU KILLS JEZEBEL

30 When Jehu came to Jezreel, Jezebel heard
about it, so she painted her eyes, fixed her
hair,[E] and looked down from the window. 31 As
Jehu entered the city gate, she said, "Do you
come in peace, Zimri, killer of your master?"
32 He looked up toward the window and
said, "Who is on my side? Who?" Two or three
eunuchs looked down at him, 33 and he said,
"Throw her down!" So they threw her down,
and some of her blood splattered on the wall
and on the horses, and Jehu rode over her.
34 Then he went in, ate and drank, and said,
"Take care of this cursed woman and bury her,
since she's a king's daughter." 35 But when
they went out to bury her, they did not find
anything but the skull, the feet, and the hands.
36 So they went back and told him, and he said,
"This fulfills the LORD's word that he spoke
through his servant Elijah the Tishbite: 'In
the plot of land at Jezreel, the dogs will eat
Jezebel's flesh. 37 Jezebel's corpse will be like
manure on the surface of the ground in the
plot of land at Jezreel so that no one will be
able to say: This is Jezebel.'"

[A] **9:13** Lit *on the bones of the steps* [B] **9:15** Lit *"If your desire exists* [C] **9:18** Lit *What to you and to peace*, also in v. 19
[D] **9:27** LXX, Syr, Vg; MT omits *So they shot him* [E] **9:30** Lit *made her head pleasing*

JEHU KILLS THE HOUSE OF AHAB

10 Since Ahab had seventy sons in Samaria, Jehu wrote letters and sent them to Samaria to the rulers of Jezreel, to the elders, and to the guardians of Ahab's sons,[A] saying:

> 2 Your master's sons are with you, and you have chariots, horses, a fortified city, and weaponry, so when this letter arrives 3 select the most qualified[B] of your master's sons, set him on his father's throne, and fight for your master's house.

4 However, they were terrified and reasoned, "Look, two kings couldn't stand against him; how can we?"

5 So the overseer of the palace, the overseer of the city, the elders, and the guardians sent a message to Jehu: "We are your servants, and we will do whatever you tell us. We will not make anyone king. Do whatever you think is right."[C]

6 Then Jehu wrote them a second letter, saying:

> If you are on my side, and if you will obey me, bring me the heads of your master's sons[D] at this time tomorrow at Jezreel.

All seventy of the king's sons were being cared for by the city's prominent men. 7 When the letter came to them, they took the king's sons and slaughtered all seventy, put their heads in baskets, and sent them to Jehu at Jezreel. 8 When the messenger came and told him, "They have brought the heads of the king's sons," the king said, "Pile them in two heaps at the entrance of the city gate until morning."

9 The next morning when he went out and stood at the gate, he said to all the people, "You are innocent. It was I who conspired against my master and killed him. But who struck down all these? 10 Know, then, that not a word the LORD spoke against the house of Ahab will fail, for the LORD has done what he promised through his servant Elijah." 11 So Jehu killed all who remained of the house of Ahab in Jezreel — all his great men, close friends, and priests — leaving him no survivors.

12 Then he set out and went to Samaria. On the way, while he was at Beth-eked of the Shepherds, 13 Jehu met the relatives of King Ahaziah of Judah and asked, "Who are you?"

They answered, "We're Ahaziah's relatives. We've come down to greet the king's sons and the queen mother's sons."

14 Then Jehu ordered, "Take them alive." So they took them alive and then slaughtered them at the pit of Beth-eked — forty-two men. He didn't spare any of them.

15 When he left there, he found Jehonadab son of Rechab coming to meet him. He greeted him and then asked, "Is your heart one with mine?"[E]

"It is," Jehonadab replied.

Jehu said, "If it is,[F] give me your hand."

So he gave him his hand, and Jehu pulled him up into the chariot with him. 16 Then he said, "Come with me and see my zeal for the LORD!" So he let him ride with him in his chariot. 17 When Jehu came to Samaria, he struck down all who remained from the house of Ahab in Samaria until he had annihilated his house, according to the word of the LORD spoken to Elijah.

JEHU KILLS THE BAAL WORSHIPERS

18 Then Jehu brought all the people together and said to them, "Ahab served Baal a little, but Jehu will serve him a lot. 19 Now, therefore, summon to me all the prophets of Baal, all his servants, and all his priests. None must be missing, for I have a great sacrifice for Baal. Whoever is missing will not live." However, Jehu was acting deceptively in order to destroy the servants of Baal. 20 Jehu commanded, "Consecrate a solemn assembly for Baal." So they called one.

21 Then Jehu sent messengers throughout all Israel, and all the servants of Baal[G] came; no one failed to come. They entered the temple of Baal, and it was filled from one end to the other. 22 Then he said to the custodian of the wardrobe, "Bring out the garments for all the servants of Baal." So he brought out their garments.

23 Then Jehu and Jehonadab son of Rechab entered the temple of Baal, and Jehu said to the servants of Baal, "Look carefully to see that there are no servants of the LORD here among you — only servants of Baal." 24 Then they went in to offer sacrifices and burnt offerings.

Now Jehu had stationed eighty men outside, and he warned them, "Whoever allows any of the men I am placing in your hands to escape

---

[A] **10:1** LXX; MT reads *of Ahab* [B] **10:3** Lit *the good and the upright* [C] **10:5** Lit *Do what is good in your eyes* [D] **10:6** Lit *heads of the men of the sons of your master* [E] **10:15** Lit *heart upright like my heart is with your heart* [F] **10:15** LXX, Syr, Vg; MT reads *mine?" Jehonadab said, "It is and it is* [G] **10:21** LXX adds — *all his priests and all his prophets* —

will forfeit his life for theirs." 25 When he finished offering the burnt offering, Jehu said to the guards and officers, "Go in and kill them. Don't let anyone out." So they struck them down with the sword. Then the guards and officers threw the bodies out and went into the inner room of the temple of Baal. 26 They brought out the pillar of the temple of Baal and burned it, 27 and they tore down the pillar of Baal. Then they tore down the temple of Baal and made it a latrine — which it still is today.

EVALUATION OF JEHU'S REIGN

28 Jehu eliminated Baal worship from Israel, 29 but he did not turn away from the sins that Jeroboam son of Nebat had caused Israel to commit — worshiping the gold calves that were in Bethel and Dan. 30 Nevertheless, the LORD said to Jehu, "Because you have done well in carrying out what is right in my sight and have done to the house of Ahab all that was in my heart, four generations of your sons will sit on the throne of Israel."

31 Yet Jehu was not careful to follow the instruction of the LORD God of Israel with all his heart. He did not turn from the sins that Jeroboam had caused Israel to commit.

32 In those days the LORD began to reduce the size of Israel. Hazael defeated the Israelites throughout their territory 33 from the Jordan eastward: the whole land of Gilead — the Gadites, the Reubenites, and the Manassites — from Aroer which is by the Arnon Valley through Gilead to Bashan.[A]

34 The rest of the events of Jehu's reign, along with all his accomplishments and all his might, are written in the Historical Record of Israel's Kings. 35 Jehu rested with his fathers and was buried in Samaria. His son Jehoahaz became king in his place. 36 The length of Jehu's reign over Israel in Samaria was twenty-eight years.

ATHALIAH USURPS THE THRONE

11 When Athaliah, Ahaziah's mother, saw that her son was dead, she proceeded to annihilate all the royal heirs. 2 Jehosheba, who was King Jehoram's daughter and Ahaziah's sister, secretly rescued Joash son of Ahaziah from among the king's sons who were being killed and put him and the one who nursed him in a bedroom. So he was hidden from Athaliah and was not killed. 3 Joash was in hiding with her in the LORD's temple six years while Athaliah reigned over the land.

ATHALIAH OVERTHROWN

4 In the seventh year, Jehoiada sent for the commanders of hundreds, the Carites, and the guards. He had them come to him in the LORD's temple, where he made a covenant with them and put them under oath. He showed them the king's son 5 and commanded them, "This is what you are to do: A third of you who come on duty on the Sabbath are to provide protection for the king's palace. 6 A third are to be at the Foundation[B] Gate and a third at the gate behind the guards. You are to take turns providing protection for the palace.[C]

7 "Your two divisions that go off duty on the Sabbath are to provide the king protection at the LORD's temple. 8 Completely surround the king with weapons in hand. Anyone who approaches the ranks is to be put to death. Be with the king in all his daily tasks."[D]

9 So the commanders of hundreds did everything the priest Jehoiada commanded. They each brought their men — those coming on duty on the Sabbath and those going off duty — and came to the priest Jehoiada. 10 The priest gave to the commanders of hundreds King David's spears and shields that were in the LORD's temple. 11 Then the guards stood with their weapons in hand surrounding the king — from the right side of the temple to the left side, by the altar and by the temple.

12 Jehoiada brought out the king's son, put the crown on him, gave him the testimony,[E] and made him king. They anointed him and clapped their hands and cried, "Long live the king!"

13 When Athaliah heard the noise from the guard and the crowd, she went out to the people at the LORD's temple. 14 She looked, and there was the king standing by the pillar according to the custom. The commanders and the trumpeters were by the king, and all the people of the land were rejoicing and blowing trumpets. Athaliah tore her clothes and screamed "Treason! Treason!"

15 Then the priest Jehoiada ordered the commanders of hundreds in charge of the army, "Take her out between the ranks, and put to death by the sword anyone who follows her," for the priest had said, "She is not to be put to death in the LORD's temple." 16 So they

[A] **10:33** Lit *Arnon Valley and Gilead and Bashan* [B] **11:6** See 2Ch 23:5; MT here reads *Sur* [C] **11:6** Hb obscure [D] **11:8** Lit *king when he goes out and when he comes in* [E] **11:12** Or *him the copy of the covenant*, or *him a diadem*, or *him jewels*

My Story | Steve

I'm a dairy farmer, the son and grandson of dairy farmers, and one of my children is well on his way to taking over my farm as the fourth-generation farmer in our family. Farming has changed a lot over the years: technology, health practices, herd management, and many other details. But some things haven't changed at all. Farming is still a lifestyle. Cattle are a 24/7 responsibility. The size of the animals and power of the equipment make for dangerous work. As I saw in my grandfather and father's lives, farming is wearing me out physically, but I can't imagine not doing it.

In the background of our family was a faith that we wore like a label, but it didn't have much impact on our daily lives. Attendance at church was a duty, and the rare prayers were by rote. And always in the back of my mind lurked a feeling of discontent and a whisper asking, *Isn't there more?*

Then my kids started attending a Vacation Bible School during the summer at a small country church nearby. Suddenly they were memorizing and quoting Bible verses while they did their chores. They got milking done early so they could attend the evening sessions. But what really got to me was the apparent joy that infected them. They came home humming catchy tunes, and their attitudes around the farm had a different tone. Over the course of several summers, each of my children talked about starting a personal relationship with Jesus. I saw my kids change in ways I wanted.

Everything they talked about I could find mentioned in some way in our family faith, but what we had seemed lifeless. Eventually, between their example and a health crisis, I decided to simply turn to Jesus and ask him to come into my life. I didn't know what exactly would happen, but his presence has made all the difference. As I watch my son take the reins of the farm and raise my grandchildren in the Christian life, I know I now have a life that had been missing in the past.

arrested her, and she went through the horse
entrance to the king's palace, where she was
put to death.

JEHOIADA'S REFORMS

17 Then Jehoiada made a covenant between the
LORD, the king, and the people that they would
be the LORD's people and another covenant
between the king and the people.[A] 18 So all the
people of the land went to the temple of Baal
and tore it down. They smashed its altars and
images to pieces, and they killed Mattan, the
priest of Baal, at the altars.

Then Jehoiada the priest appointed guards
for the LORD's temple. 19 He took the commanders of hundreds, the Carites, the guards, and
all the people of the land, and they brought the
king from the LORD's temple. They entered the
king's palace by way of the guards' gate. Then
Joash sat on the throne of the kings. 20 All the
people of the land rejoiced, and the city was
quiet, for they had put Athaliah to death by
the sword in the king's palace.

JUDAH'S KING JOASH

21 Joash[B] was seven years old when he became
king.
12 1 In the seventh year of Jehu, Joash
became king, and he reigned forty years
in Jerusalem. His mother's name was Zibiah;
she was from Beer-sheba. 2 Throughout the
time the priest Jehoiada instructed him, Joash
did what was right in the LORD's sight. 3 Yet the
high places were not taken away; the people
continued sacrificing and burning incense
on the high places.

REPAIRING THE TEMPLE

4 Then Joash said to the priests, "All the dedicated silver brought to the LORD's temple,
census silver, silver from vows, and all silver
voluntarily given for the LORD's temple —
5 each priest is to take it from his assessor[C]
and repair whatever damage is found in the
temple."[D]

6 But by the twenty-third year of the reign
of King Joash, the priests had not repaired the
damage[E] to the temple. 7 So King Joash called
the priest Jehoiada and the other priests and
asked, "Why haven't you repaired the temple's
damage? Since you haven't, don't take any silver from your assessors; instead, hand it over
for the repair of the temple." 8 So the priests

[A] **11:17** Some Gk versions, 2Ch 23:16 omit *and another covenant between the king and the people* [B] **11:21** = The LORD Has Bestowed [C] **12:5** Hb obscure [D] **12:5** Lit *repair the breach of the temple wherever there is found a breach* [E] **12:6** Lit *breach* in 2Kg 12:5-12

agreed that they would receive no silver from
the people and would not be the ones to repair
the temple's damage.
9 Then the priest Jehoiada took a chest, bored
a hole in its lid, and set it beside the altar on
the right side as one enters the LORD's temple;
the priests who guarded the threshold put
into the chest all the silver that was brought to
the LORD's temple. 10 Whenever they saw there
was a large amount of silver in the chest, the
king's secretary and the high priest would go
bag up and tally the silver found in the LORD's
temple. 11 Then they would give the weighed
silver to those doing the work — those who
oversaw the LORD's temple. They in turn would
pay it out to those working on the LORD's temple — the carpenters, the builders, 12 the masons, and the stonecutters — and would use
it to buy timber and quarried stone to repair
the damage to the LORD's temple and for all
expenses for temple repairs.
13 However, no silver bowls, wick trimmers,
sprinkling basins, trumpets, or any articles of
gold or silver were made for the LORD's temple from the contributions[A] brought to the
LORD's temple. 14 Instead, it was given to those
doing the work, and they repaired the LORD's
temple with it. 15 No accounting was required
from the men who received the silver to pay
those doing the work, since they worked with
integrity. 16 The silver from the guilt offering
and the sin offering was not brought to the
LORD's temple since it belonged to the priests.

No accounting was required from the men who received the silver to pay those doing the work, since they worked with integrity.

— 2 Kings 12:15

ARAMEAN INVASION OF JUDAH

17 At that time King Hazael of Aram marched up
and fought against Gath and captured it. Then
he planned to attack Jerusalem. 18 So King Joash of Judah took all the items consecrated by
himself and by his ancestors — Judah's kings
Jehoshaphat, Jehoram, and Ahaziah — as well
as all the gold found in the treasuries of the
LORD's temple and in the king's palace, and
he sent them to King Hazael of Aram. Then
Hazael withdrew from Jerusalem.

JOASH ASSASSINATED

19 The rest of the events of Joash's reign, along
with all his accomplishments, are written in
the Historical Record of Judah's Kings. 20 Joash's servants conspired against him and
attacked him at Beth-millo on the road that
goes down to Silla. 21 It was his servants Jozabad[B] son of Shimeath and Jehozabad son
of Shomer who attacked him. He died and
they buried him with his fathers in the city
of David, and his son Amaziah became king
in his place.

ISRAEL'S KING JEHOAHAZ

13 In the twenty-third year of Judah's King
Joash son of Ahaziah, Jehoahaz son of
Jehu became king over Israel in Samaria, and
he reigned seventeen years. 2 He did what
was evil in the LORD's sight and followed the
sins that Jeroboam son of Nebat had caused
Israel to commit; he did not turn away from
them. 3 So the LORD's anger burned against
Israel, and he handed them over to King Hazael of Aram and to his son Ben-hadad during
their reigns.
4 Then Jehoahaz sought the LORD's favor,
and the LORD heard him, for he saw the oppression the king of Aram inflicted on Israel.
5 Therefore, the LORD gave Israel a deliverer,
and they escaped from the power of the Arameans. Then the people of Israel returned
to their former way of life,[C] 6 but they didn't
turn away from the sins that the house of Jeroboam had caused Israel to commit. Jehoahaz
continued them, and the Asherah pole also
remained standing in Samaria. 7 Jehoahaz
did not have an army left, except for fifty
horsemen, ten chariots, and ten thousand
foot soldiers, because the king of Aram had
destroyed them, making them like dust at
threshing.
8 The rest of the events of Jehoahaz's reign,
along with all his accomplishments and his
might, are written in the Historical Record
of Israel's Kings. 9 Jehoahaz rested with his
fathers, and he was buried in Samaria. His son
Jehoash[D] became king in his place.

[A] **12:13** Lit *silver* [B] **12:21** Some Hb mss, LXX read *Jozacar*; 2Ch 24:26 reads *Zabad* [C] **13:5** Lit *Israel dwelt in their tents as formerly* [D] **13:9** Lit *Joash*

ISRAEL'S KING JEHOASH

10 In the thirty-seventh year of Judah's King Joash, Jehoash son of Jehoahaz became king over Israel in Samaria, and he reigned sixteen years. 11 He did what was evil in the LORD's sight. He did not turn away from all the sins that Jeroboam son of Nebat had caused Israel to commit, but he continued them.

12 The rest of the events of Jehoash's reign, along with all his accomplishments and the power he had to wage war against Judah's King Amaziah, are written in the Historical Record of Israel's Kings. 13 Jehoash rested with his fathers, and Jeroboam sat on his throne. Jehoash was buried in Samaria with the kings of Israel.

ELISHA'S DEATH

14 When Elisha became sick with the illness from which he died, King Jehoash of Israel went down and wept over him and said, "My father, my father, the chariots and horsemen of Israel!"

15 Elisha responded, "Get a bow and arrows." So he got a bow and arrows. 16 Then Elisha said to the king of Israel, "Grasp the bow." So the king grasped it, and Elisha put his hands on the king's hands. 17 Elisha said, "Open the east window." So he opened it. Elisha said, "Shoot!" So he shot. Then Elisha said, "The LORD's arrow of victory, yes, the arrow of victory over Aram. You are to strike down the Arameans in Aphek until you have put an end to them."

18 Then Elisha said, "Take the arrows!" So he took them. Then Elisha said to the king of Israel, "Strike the ground!" So he struck the ground three times and stopped. 19 The man of God was angry with him and said, "You should have struck the ground five or six times. Then you would have struck down Aram until you had put an end to them, but now you will strike down Aram only three times." 20 Then Elisha died and was buried.

Now Moabite raiders used to come into the land in the spring of the year. 21 Once, as the Israelites were burying a man, suddenly they saw a raiding party, so they threw the man into Elisha's tomb. When he touched Elisha's bones, the man revived and stood up!

GOD'S MERCY ON ISRAEL

22 King Hazael of Aram oppressed Israel throughout the reign of Jehoahaz, 23 but the LORD was gracious to them, had compassion on them, and turned toward them because of his covenant with Abraham, Isaac, and Jacob. He was not willing to destroy them. Even now he has not banished them from his presence.

24 King Hazael of Aram died, and his son Ben-hadad became king in his place. 25 Then Jehoash son of Jehoahaz took back from Ben-hadad son of Hazael the cities that Hazael had taken in war from Jehoash's father Jehoahaz. Jehoash defeated Ben-hadad three times and recovered the cities of Israel.

JUDAH'S KING AMAZIAH

14 In the second year of Israel's King Jehoash[A] son of Jehoahaz,[B] Amaziah son of Joash became king of Judah. 2 He was twenty-five years old when he became king, and he reigned twenty-nine years in Jerusalem. His mother's name was Jehoaddan;[C] she was from Jerusalem. 3 He did what was right in the LORD's sight, but not like his ancestor David. He did everything his father Joash had done. 4 Yet the high places were not taken away, and the people continued sacrificing and burning incense on the high places.

5 As soon as the kingdom was firmly in his grasp, Amaziah killed his servants who had killed his father the king. 6 However, he did not put the children of the killers to death, as it is written in the book of the law of Moses where the LORD commanded, "Fathers are not to be put to death because of children, and children are not to be put to death because of fathers; instead, each one will be put to death for his own sin."

7 Amaziah killed ten thousand Edomites in Salt Valley. He took Sela in battle and called it Joktheel, which is still its name today. 8 Amaziah then sent messengers to Jehoash son of Jehoahaz, son of Jehu, king of Israel, and challenged him: "Come, let's meet face to face."

9 King Jehoash of Israel sent word to King Amaziah of Judah, saying, "The thistle in Lebanon once sent a message to the cedar in Lebanon, saying, 'Give your daughter to my son as a wife.' Then a wild animal in Lebanon passed by and trampled the thistle. 10 You have indeed defeated Edom, and you have become overconfident.[D] Enjoy your glory and stay at home. Why should you stir up such trouble that you fall — you and Judah with you?"

11 But Amaziah would not listen, so King

[A] **14:1** Lit *Joash*, also in vv. 23,27 [B] **14:1** Lit *Joahaz* [C] **14:2** Alt Hb tradition, some Hb mss, Syr, Tg, Vg, 2Ch 25:1; other Hb mss, LXX read *Jehoaddin* [D] **14:10** Lit *and your heart has lifted you*

Jehoash of Israel advanced. He and King Amaziah of Judah met face to face at Beth-shemesh that belonged to Judah. 12 Judah was
routed before Israel, and each man fled to
his own tent. 13 King Jehoash of Israel captured Judah's King Amaziah son of Joash,[A]
son of Ahaziah, at Beth-shemesh. Then Jehoash went to Jerusalem and broke down two
hundred yards[B] of Jerusalem's wall from the
Ephraim Gate to the Corner Gate. 14 He took
all the gold and silver, all the articles found
in the LORD's temple and in the treasuries of
the king's palace, and some hostages. Then
he returned to Samaria.

JEHOASH'S DEATH

15 The rest of the events of Jehoash's reign,
along with his accomplishments, his might,
and how he waged war against King Amaziah
of Judah, are written in the Historical Record
of Israel's Kings. 16 Jehoash rested with his
fathers, and he was buried in Samaria with
the kings of Israel. His son Jeroboam became
king in his place.

AMAZIAH'S DEATH

17 Judah's King Amaziah son of Joash lived
fifteen years after the death of Israel's King
Jehoash son of Jehoahaz. 18 The rest of the
events of Amaziah's reign are written in the
Historical Record of Judah's Kings. 19 A conspiracy was formed against him in Jerusalem,
and he fled to Lachish. However, men were
sent after him to Lachish, and they put him
to death there. 20 They carried him back on
horses, and he was buried in Jerusalem with
his fathers in the city of David.

21 Then all the people of Judah took Azariah,[C] who was sixteen years old, and made him
king in place of his father Amaziah. 22 After
Amaziah the king rested with his fathers, Azariah rebuilt Elath[D] and restored it to Judah.

ISRAEL'S KING JEROBOAM

23 In the fifteenth year of Judah's King Amaziah son of Joash, Jeroboam son of Jehoash became king of Israel in Samaria, and he
reigned forty-one years. 24 He did what was
evil in the LORD's sight. He did not turn away
from all the sins Jeroboam son of Nebat had
caused Israel to commit.

25 He restored Israel's border from Lebo-

> *For the LORD saw that the affliction of Israel was very bitter for both slaves and free people. There was no one to help Israel. The LORD . . . delivered them.*
>
> *—2 Kings 14:26-27*

hamath as far as the Sea of the Arabah, according to the word the LORD, the God of
Israel, had spoken through his servant, the
prophet Jonah son of Amittai from Gath-
hepher. 26 For the LORD saw that the affliction
of Israel was very bitter for both slaves and
free people.[E] There was no one to help Israel.
27 The LORD had not said he would blot out the
name of Israel under heaven, so he delivered
them by the hand of Jeroboam son of Jehoash.
28 The rest of the events of Jeroboam's reign
— along with all his accomplishments, the
power he had to wage war, and how he recovered for Israel Damascus and Hamath, which
had belonged to Judah[F] — are written in the
Historical Record of Israel's Kings. 29 Jeroboam rested with his fathers, the kings of Israel.
His son Zechariah became king in his place.

JUDAH'S KING AZARIAH

15 In the twenty-seventh year of Israel's
King Jeroboam, Azariah[G] son of Amaziah
became king of Judah. 2 He was sixteen years
old when he became king, and he reigned
fifty-two years in Jerusalem. His mother's
name was Jecoliah; she was from Jerusalem.
3 Azariah did what was right in the LORD's sight
just as his father Amaziah had done. 4 Yet the
high places were not taken away; the people
continued sacrificing and burning incense
on the high places.

5 The LORD afflicted the king, and he had a
serious skin disease until the day of his death.
He lived in quarantine,[H] while Jotham, the
king's son, was over the household governing
the people of the land.

6 The rest of the events of Azariah's reign,
along with all his accomplishments, are written in the Historical Record of Judah's Kings.

[A] **14:13** Lit *Jehoash* [B] **14:13** Lit *400 cubits* [C] **14:21** = Uzziah in 2Ch 26:1 [D] **14:22** = Eloth in 2Ch 26:2 [E] **14:26** Hb obscure [F] **14:28** Lit *recovered Damascus and for Judah in Israel*; Hb obscure [G] **15:1** = Uzziah in 2Ch 26:3 [H] **15:5** Lit *in a house of exemption from duty*

7 Azariah rested with his fathers and was buried
with his fathers in the city of David. His son
Jotham became king in his place.

ISRAEL'S KING ZECHARIAH

8 In the thirty-eighth year of Judah's King Azariah, Zechariah son of Jeroboam reigned
over Israel in Samaria for six months. 9 He
did what was evil in the LORD's sight as his
fathers had done. He did not turn away from
the sins Jeroboam son of Nebat had caused
Israel to commit.
10 Shallum son of Jabesh conspired against
Zechariah. He struck him down publicly,[A]
killed him, and became king in his place. 11 As
for the rest of the events of Zechariah's reign,
they are written in the Historical Record of
Israel's Kings. 12 The word of the LORD that
he spoke to Jehu was, "Four generations of
your sons will sit on the throne of Israel,"
and it was so.

ISRAEL'S KING SHALLUM

13 In the thirty-ninth year of Judah's King Uzziah,[B] Shallum son of Jabesh became king;
he reigned in Samaria a full month. 14 Then
Menahem son of Gadi came up from Tirzah
to Samaria and struck down Shallum son of
Jabesh there. He killed him and became king
in his place. 15 As for the rest of the events of
Shallum's reign, along with the conspiracy
that he formed, they are written in the Historical Record of Israel's Kings.

ISRAEL'S KING MENAHEM

16 At that time, starting from Tirzah, Menahem
attacked Tiphsah, all who were in it, and its
territory because they wouldn't surrender. He
ripped open all the pregnant women.
17 In the thirty-ninth year of Judah's King
Azariah, Menahem son of Gadi became king
over Israel, and he reigned ten years in Samaria. 18 He did what was evil in the LORD's
sight. Throughout his reign, he did not turn
away from the sins Jeroboam son of Nebat
had caused Israel to commit.
19 King Pul[C] of Assyria invaded the land, so
Menahem gave Pul seventy-five thousand
pounds[D] of silver so that Pul would support
him to strengthen his grasp on the kingdom.
20 Then Menahem exacted twenty ounces[E]
of silver from each of the prominent men of
Israel to give to the king of Assyria. So the
king of Assyria withdrew and did not stay
there in the land.
21 The rest of the events of Menahem's reign,
along with all his accomplishments, are written in the Historical Record of Israel's Kings.
22 Menahem rested with his fathers, and his
son Pekahiah became king in his place.

ISRAEL'S KING PEKAHIAH

23 In the fiftieth year of Judah's King Azariah,
Pekahiah son of Menahem became king over
Israel in Samaria, and he reigned two years.
24 He did what was evil in the LORD's sight and
did not turn away from the sins Jeroboam son
of Nebat had caused Israel to commit.
25 Then his officer, Pekah son of Remaliah,
conspired against him and struck him down
in Samaria at the citadel of the king's palace
— with Argob and Arieh.[F] There were fifty
Gileadite men with Pekah. He killed Pekahiah
and became king in his place.
26 As for the rest of the events of Pekahiah's
reign, along with all his accomplishments,
they are written in the Historical Record of
Israel's Kings.

ISRAEL'S KING PEKAH

27 In the fifty-second year of Judah's King
Azariah, Pekah son of Remaliah became king
over Israel in Samaria, and he reigned twenty
years. 28 He did what was evil in the LORD's
sight. He did not turn away from the sins
Jeroboam son of Nebat had caused Israel to
commit.
29 In the days of King Pekah of Israel, King
Tiglath-pileser of Assyria came and captured
Ijon, Abel-beth-maacah, Janoah, Kedesh, Hazor,
Gilead, and Galilee — all the land of Naphtali
— and deported the people to Assyria.
30 Then Hoshea son of Elah organized a conspiracy against Pekah son of Remaliah. He
attacked him, killed him, and became king
in his place in the twentieth year of Jotham
son of Uzziah.
31 As for the rest of the events of Pekah's
reign, along with all his accomplishments,
they are written in the Historical Record of
Israel's Kings.

JUDAH'S KING JOTHAM

32 In the second year of Israel's King Pekah son
of Remaliah, Jotham son of Uzziah became
king of Judah. 33 He was twenty-five years

[A] **15:10** Some LXX mss read *down at Ibleam*; Hb uncertain [B] **15:13** = Azariah, also in vv. 30,32,34 [C] **15:19** = Tiglath-pileser
[D] **15:19** Lit *1,000 talents* [E] **15:20** Lit *50 shekels* [F] **15:25** Hb obscure

old when he became king, and he reigned sixteen years in Jerusalem. His mother's name was Jerusha daughter of Zadok. 34 He did what was right in the LORD's sight just as his father Uzziah had done. 35 Yet the high places were not taken away; the people continued sacrificing and burning incense on the high places.

Jotham built the Upper Gate of the LORD's temple. 36 The rest of the events of Jotham's reign, along with all his accomplishments, are written in the Historical Record of Judah's Kings. 37 In those days the LORD began sending Aram's King Rezin and Pekah son of Remaliah against Judah. 38 Jotham rested with his fathers and was buried with his fathers in the city of his ancestor David. His son Ahaz became king in his place.

JUDAH'S KING AHAZ

16 In the seventeenth year of Pekah son of Remaliah, Ahaz son of Jotham became king of Judah. 2 Ahaz was twenty years old when he became king, and he reigned sixteen years in Jerusalem. He did not do what was right in the sight of the LORD his God like his ancestor David 3 but walked in the ways of the kings of Israel. He even sacrificed his son in the fire,[A] imitating the detestable practices of the nations the LORD had dispossessed before the Israelites. 4 He sacrificed and burned incense on the high places, on the hills, and under every green tree.

5 Then Aram's King Rezin and Israel's King Pekah son of Remaliah came to wage war against Jerusalem. They besieged Ahaz but were not able to conquer him. 6 At that time Aram's King Rezin recovered Elath for Aram and expelled the Judahites from Elath. Then the Arameans came to Elath, and they still live there today.

7 So Ahaz sent messengers to King Tiglath-pileser of Assyria, saying, "I am your servant and your son. March up and save me from the grasp of the king of Aram and of the king of Israel, who are rising up against me." 8 Ahaz also took the silver and gold found in the LORD's temple and in the treasuries of the king's palace and sent them to the king of Assyria as a bribe. 9 So the king of Assyria listened to him and marched up to Damascus and captured it. He deported its people to Kir but put Rezin to death.

AHAZ'S IDOLATRY

10 King Ahaz went to Damascus to meet King Tiglath-pileser of Assyria. When he saw the altar that was in Damascus, King Ahaz sent a model of the altar and complete plans for its construction to the priest Uriah. 11 Uriah built the altar according to all the instructions King Ahaz sent from Damascus. Therefore, by the time King Ahaz came back from Damascus, the priest Uriah had completed it. 12 When the king came back from Damascus, he saw the altar. Then he approached the altar and ascended it.[B] 13 He offered his burnt offering and his grain offering, poured out his drink offering, and splattered the blood of his fellowship offerings on the altar. 14 He took the bronze altar that was before the LORD in front of the temple between his altar and the LORD's temple, and put it on the north side of his altar.

15 Then King Ahaz commanded the priest Uriah, "Offer on the great altar the morning burnt offering, the evening grain offering, and the king's burnt offering and his grain offering. Also offer the burnt offering of all the people of the land, their grain offering, and their drink offerings. Splatter on the altar all the blood of the burnt offering and all the blood of sacrifice. The bronze altar will be for me to seek guidance."[C] 16 The priest Uriah did everything King Ahaz commanded.

17 Then King Ahaz cut off the frames of the water carts[D] and removed the bronze basin from each of them. He took the basin[E] from the bronze oxen that were under it and put it on a stone pavement. 18 To satisfy the king of Assyria, he removed from the LORD's temple the Sabbath canopy they had built in the palace, and he closed the outer entrance for the king.

AHAZ'S DEATH

19 The rest of the events of Ahaz's reign, along with his accomplishments, are written in the Historical Record of Judah's Kings. 20 Ahaz rested with his fathers and was buried with his fathers in the city of David, and his son Hezekiah became king in his place.

ISRAEL'S KING HOSHEA

17 In the twelfth year of Judah's King Ahaz, Hoshea son of Elah became king over Israel in Samaria, and he reigned nine years. 2 He did what was evil in the LORD's sight, but not like the kings of Israel who preceded him.

[A] **16:3** Lit *even made his son pass through the fire* [B] **16:12** Or *and offered on it:* [C] **16:15** Hb obscure [D] **16:17** Lit *the stands* [E] **16:17** Lit *sea*

3 King Shalmaneser of Assyria attacked him,
and Hoshea became his vassal and paid him
tribute. 4 But the king of Assyria caught Hoshea in a conspiracy: He had sent envoys to So
king of Egypt and had not paid tribute to the
king of Assyria as in previous years.[A] Therefore the king of Assyria arrested him and put
him in prison. 5 The king of Assyria invaded
the whole land, marched up to Samaria, and
besieged it for three years.

THE FALL OF SAMARIA

6 In the ninth year of Hoshea, the king of Assyria captured Samaria. He deported the Israelites to Assyria and settled them in Halah,
along the Habor (Gozan's river), and in the
cities of the Medes.

WHY ISRAEL FELL

7 This disaster happened because the people of
Israel sinned against the LORD their God who
had brought them out of the land of Egypt
from the power of Pharaoh king of Egypt and
because they worshiped[B] other gods. 8 They
lived according to the customs of the nations
that the LORD had dispossessed before the
Israelites and according to what the kings of
Israel did. 9 The Israelites secretly did things[C]
against the LORD their God that were not right.
They built high places in all their towns from
watchtower to fortified city. 10 They set up for
themselves sacred pillars and Asherah poles
on every high hill and under every green tree.
11 They burned incense there on all the high
places just like the nations that the LORD had
driven out before them had done. They did evil
things, angering the LORD. 12 They served idols,
although the LORD had told them, "You must
not do this." 13 Still, the LORD warned Israel and
Judah through every prophet and every seer,
saying, "Turn from your evil ways and keep
my commands and statutes according to the
whole law I commanded your ancestors and
sent to you through my servants the prophets."

14 But they would not listen. Instead they
became obstinate like[D] their ancestors who
did not believe the LORD their God. 15 They
rejected his statutes and his covenant he had
made with their ancestors and the warnings
he had given them. They followed worthless
idols and became worthless themselves, following the surrounding nations the LORD had
commanded them not to imitate.

16 They abandoned all the commands of the
LORD their God. They made cast images for
themselves, two calves, and an Asherah pole.
They bowed in worship to all the stars in the
sky and served Baal. 17 They sacrificed their
sons and daughters in the fire[E] and practiced
divination and interpreted omens. They devoted themselves to do what was evil in the
LORD's sight and angered him.

18 Therefore, the LORD was very angry with
Israel, and he removed them from his presence. Only the tribe of Judah remained. 19 Even
Judah did not keep the commands of the LORD
their God but lived according to the customs
Israel had practiced. 20 So the LORD rejected
all the descendants of Israel, punished them,
and handed them over to plunderers until he
had banished them from his presence.

SUMMARY OF ISRAEL'S HISTORY

21 When the LORD tore Israel from the house
of David, Israel made Jeroboam son of Nebat
king. Then Jeroboam led Israel away from
following the LORD and caused them to commit immense sin. 22 The Israelites persisted
in all the sins that Jeroboam committed and
did not turn away from them. 23 Finally, the
LORD removed Israel from his presence just
as he had declared through all his servants
the prophets. So Israel has been exiled to Assyria from their homeland to this very day.

FOREIGN REFUGEES IN ISRAEL

24 Then the king of Assyria brought people
from Babylon, Cuthah, Avva, Hamath, and
Sepharvaim and settled them in place of the
Israelites in the cities of Samaria. The settlers
took possession of Samaria and lived in its cities. 25 When they first lived there, they did not
fear the LORD. So the LORD sent lions among
them, which killed some of them. 26 The settlers
said to the king of Assyria, "The nations that
you have deported and placed in the cities of
Samaria do not know the requirements of the
god of the land. Therefore he has sent lions
among them that are killing them because
the people don't know the requirements of
the god of the land."

27 Then the king of Assyria issued a command: "Send back one of the priests you deported. Have him go and live there so he can
teach them the requirements of the god of
the land." 28 So one of the priests they had

[A] **17:4** Lit *as year by year* [B] **17:7** Lit *feared* [C] **17:9** Or *Israelites spoke words* [D] **17:14** Lit *they stiffened their neck like the neck of* [E] **17:17** Lit *They made their sons and daughters pass through the fire*

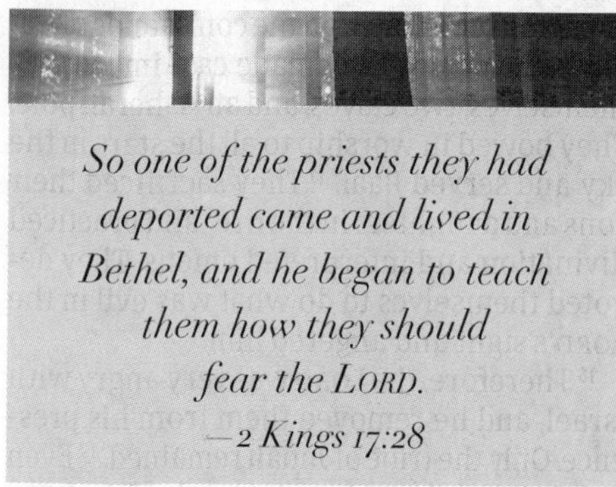
So one of the priests they had deported came and lived in Bethel, and he began to teach them how they should fear the LORD.
—2 Kings 17:28

deported came and lived in Bethel, and he
began to teach them how they should fear
the LORD.
29 But the people of each nation were still
making their own gods in the cities where
they lived and putting them in the shrines of
the high places that the people of Samaria had
made. 30 The men of Babylon made Succoth-
benoth, the men of Cuth made Nergal, the men
of Hamath made Ashima, 31 the Avvites made
Nibhaz and Tartak, and the Sepharvites burned
their children in the fire to Adrammelech and
Anammelech, the gods of Sepharvaim. 32 They
feared the LORD, but they also made from their
ranks priests for the high places, who were
working for them at the shrines of the high
places. 33 They feared the LORD, but they also
worshiped their own gods according to the
practice of the nations from which they had
been deported.
34 They are still observing the former practices to this day. None of them fear the LORD or
observe the statutes and ordinances, the law
and commandments that the LORD had commanded the descendants of Jacob, whom he
had given the name Israel. 35 The LORD made a
covenant with Jacob's descendants and commanded them, "Do not fear other gods; do not
bow in worship to them; do not serve them;
do not sacrifice to them. 36 Instead fear the
LORD, who brought you up from the land of
Egypt with great power and an outstretched
arm. You are to bow down to him, and you are
to sacrifice to him. 37 You are to be careful always to observe the statutes, the ordinances,
the law, and the commandments he wrote for
you; do not fear other gods. 38 Do not forget the
covenant that I have made with you. Do not
fear other gods, 39 but fear the LORD your God,
and he will rescue you from all your enemies."
40 However, these nations would not listen
but continued observing their former practices. 41 They feared the LORD but also served
their idols. Still today, their children and grandchildren continue doing as their fathers did.

JUDAH'S KING HEZEKIAH

18 In the third year of Israel's King Hoshea
son of Elah, Hezekiah son of Ahaz became
king of Judah. 2 He was twenty-five years old
when he became king, and he reigned twenty-nine years in Jerusalem. His mother's name
was Abi[A] daughter of Zechariah. 3 He did what
was right in the LORD's sight just as his ancestor David had done. 4 He removed the high
places, shattered the sacred pillars, and cut
down the Asherah poles. He broke into pieces
the bronze snake that Moses made, for until
then the Israelites were burning incense to
it. It was called Nehushtan.[B]
5 Hezekiah relied on the LORD God of Israel;
not one of the kings of Judah was like him,
either before him or after him. 6 He remained
faithful to the LORD and did not turn from following him but kept the commands the LORD
had commanded Moses.

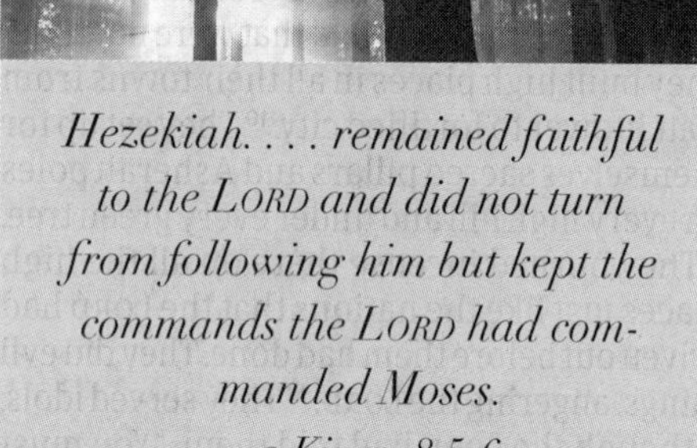
Hezekiah. . . remained faithful to the LORD and did not turn from following him but kept the commands the LORD had commanded Moses.
—2 Kings 18:5-6

7 The LORD was with him, and wherever he
went he prospered. He rebelled against the
king of Assyria and did not serve him. 8 He
defeated the Philistines as far as Gaza and
its borders, from watchtower to fortified city.

REVIEW OF ISRAEL'S FALL

9 In the fourth year of King Hezekiah, which was
the seventh year of Israel's King Hoshea son
of Elah, Assyria's King Shalmaneser marched
against Samaria and besieged it. 10 The Assyrians captured it at the end of three years.
In the sixth year of Hezekiah, which was the

[A] **18:2** = Abijah in 2Ch 29:1 [B] **18:4** = A Bronze Thing

ninth year of Israel's King Hoshea, Samaria was captured. 11 The king of Assyria deported the Israelites to Assyria and put them in Halah, along the Habor (Gozan's river), and in the cities of the Medes, 12 because they did not listen to the LORD their God but violated his covenant — all he had commanded Moses the servant of the LORD. They did not listen, and they did not obey.

SENNACHERIB'S INVASION

13 In the fourteenth year of King Hezekiah, Assyria's King Sennacherib attacked all the fortified cities of Judah and captured them. 14 So King Hezekiah of Judah sent word to the king of Assyria at Lachish: "I have done wrong; withdraw from me. Whatever you demand from me, I will pay." The king of Assyria demanded eleven tons[A] of silver and one ton[B] of gold from King Hezekiah of Judah. 15 So Hezekiah gave him all the silver found in the LORD's temple and in the treasuries of the king's palace.

16 At that time Hezekiah stripped the gold from the doors of the LORD's sanctuary and from the doorposts he had overlaid and gave it to the king of Assyria.

17 Then the king of Assyria sent the field marshal, the chief of staff, and his royal spokesman, along with a massive army, from Lachish to King Hezekiah at Jerusalem. They advanced and came to Jerusalem, and[C] they took their position by the aqueduct of the upper pool, by the road to the Launderer's Field. 18 They called for the king, but Eliakim son of Hilkiah, who was in charge of the palace, Shebnah the court secretary, and Joah son of Asaph, the court historian, came out to them.

THE ROYAL SPOKESMAN'S SPEECH

19 Then the royal spokesman said to them, "Tell Hezekiah this is what the great king, the king of Assyria, says: 'What are you relying on?[D] 20 You think mere words are strategy and strength for war. Who are you now relying on so that you have rebelled against me? 21 Now look, you are relying on Egypt, that splintered reed of a staff that will pierce the hand of anyone who grabs it and leans on it. This is what Pharaoh king of Egypt is to all who rely on him. 22 Suppose you say to me, "We rely on the LORD our God." Isn't he the one whose high places and altars Hezekiah has removed, saying to Judah and to Jerusalem, "You must worship at this altar in Jerusalem"?'

23 "So now, make a bargain with my master the king of Assyria. I'll give you two thousand horses if you're able to supply riders for them! 24 How then can you drive back a single officer among the least of my master's servants? How can you rely on Egypt for chariots and for horsemen? 25 Now, have I attacked this place to destroy it without the LORD's approval? The LORD said to me, 'Attack this land and destroy it.'"

26 Then Eliakim son of Hilkiah, Shebnah, and Joah said to the royal spokesman, "Please speak to your servants in Aramaic, since we understand it. Don't speak with us in Hebrew[E] within earshot of the people on the wall."

27 But the royal spokesman said to them, "Has my master sent me to speak these words only to your master and to you? Hasn't he also sent me to the men who sit on the wall, destined with you to eat their own excrement and drink their own urine?"

28 The royal spokesman stood and called out loudly in Hebrew: "Hear the word of the great king, the king of Assyria. 29 This is what the king says: 'Don't let Hezekiah deceive you; he can't rescue you from my power. 30 Don't let Hezekiah persuade you to rely on the LORD by saying, "Certainly the LORD will rescue us! This city will not be handed over to the king of Assyria."'

31 "Don't listen to Hezekiah, for this is what the king of Assyria says: 'Make peace[F] with me and surrender to me. Then each of you may eat from his own vine and his own fig tree, and each may drink water from his own cistern 32 until I come and take you away to a land like your own land — a land of grain and new wine, a land of bread and vineyards, a land of olive trees and honey — so that you may live and not die. But don't listen to Hezekiah when he misleads you, saying, "The LORD will rescue us." 33 Has any of the gods of the nations ever rescued his land from the power of the king of Assyria? 34 Where are the gods of Hamath and Arpad? Where are the gods of Sepharvaim, Hena, and Ivvah?[G] Have they rescued Samaria from my power? 35 Who among all the gods of the lands has rescued his land from my power? So will the LORD rescue Jerusalem from my power?'"

[A] **18:14** Lit *300 talents* [B] **18:14** Lit *30 talents* [C] **18:17** LXX, Syr, Vg; MT reads *and came and* [D] **18:19** Lit *'What is this trust which you trust* [E] **18:26** Lit *Judahite*, also in v. 28 [F] **18:31** Lit *a blessing* [G] **18:34** Some LXX mss, Old Lat read *Sepharvaim? Where are the gods of the land of Samaria?*

36 But the people kept silent; they did not
answer him at all, for the king's command
was, "Don't answer him." 37 Then Eliakim son
of Hilkiah, who was in charge of the palace,
Shebna the court secretary, and Joah son of
Asaph, the court historian, came to Hezekiah
with their clothes torn and reported to him
the words of the royal spokesman.

HEZEKIAH SEEKS ISAIAH'S COUNSEL

19 When King Hezekiah heard their report,
he tore his clothes, covered himself
with sackcloth, and went into the LORD's
temple. 2 He sent Eliakim, who was in charge
of the palace, Shebna the court secretary,
and the leading priests, who were wearing
sackcloth, to the prophet Isaiah son of Amoz.
3 They said to him, "This is what Hezekiah
says: 'Today is a day of distress, rebuke, and
disgrace, for children have come to the point
of birth, but there is no strength to deliver
them. 4 Perhaps the LORD your God will hear
all the words of the royal spokesman, whom
his master the king of Assyria sent to mock
the living God, and will rebuke him for the
words that the LORD your God has heard.
Therefore, offer a prayer for the surviving
remnant.' "
5 So the servants of King Hezekiah went to
Isaiah, 6 who said to them, "Tell your master,
'The LORD says this: Don't be afraid because
of the words you have heard, with which the
king of Assyria's attendants have blasphemed
me. 7 I am about to put a spirit in him, and he
will hear a rumor and return to his own land,
where I will cause him to fall by the sword.' "

SENNACHERIB'S DEPARTING THREAT

8 When the royal spokesman heard that the
king of Assyria had pulled out of Lachish, he
left and found him fighting against Libnah.
9 The king had heard concerning King Tirhakah of Cush, "Look, he has set out to fight
against you." So he again sent messengers
to Hezekiah, saying, 10 "Say this to King Hezekiah of Judah: 'Don't let your God, on whom
you rely, deceive you by promising that Jerusalem will not be handed over to the king
of Assyria. 11 Look, you have heard what the
kings of Assyria have done to all the countries: They completely destroyed them. Will
you be rescued? 12 Did the gods of the nations
that my predecessors destroyed rescue them
— nations such as Gozan, Haran, Rezeph, and
the Edenites in Telassar? 13 Where is the king
of Hamath, the king of Arpad, the king of the
city of[A] Sepharvaim, Hena, or Ivvah?' "

HEZEKIAH'S PRAYER

14 Hezekiah took the letter from the messengers' hands, read it, then went up to the LORD's
temple, and spread it out before the LORD.
15 Then Hezekiah prayed before the LORD:
LORD God of Israel, enthroned between
the cherubim, you are God — you alone
— of all the kingdoms of the earth. You
made the heavens and the earth. 16 Listen
closely, LORD, and hear; open your eyes,
LORD, and see. Hear the words that Sennacherib has sent to mock the living God.
17 LORD, it is true that the kings of Assyria
have devastated the nations and their
lands. 18 They have thrown their gods into
the fire, for they were not gods but made
by human hands — wood and stone. So
they have destroyed them. 19 Now, LORD
our God, please save us from his power
so that all the kingdoms of the earth may
know that you, LORD, are God — you
alone.

GOD'S ANSWER THROUGH ISAIAH

20 Then Isaiah son of Amoz sent a message to
Hezekiah: "The LORD, the God of Israel says,
'I have heard your prayer to me about King
Sennacherib of Assyria.' 21 This is the word
the LORD has spoken against him:

Virgin Daughter Zion
despises you and scorns you;
Daughter Jerusalem
shakes her head behind your back.
22 Who is it you mocked and blasphemed?
Against whom have you raised
your voice
and lifted your eyes in pride?
Against the Holy One of Israel!
23 You have mocked the Lord[B] through[C]
your messengers.
You have said, 'With my many chariots
I have gone up to the heights
of the mountains,
to the far recesses of Lebanon.
I cut down its tallest cedars,
its choice cypress trees.
I came to its farthest outpost,
its densest forest.

[A] 19:13 Or *king of Lair,* [B] 19:23 Many mss read *LORD* [C] 19:23 Lit *by the hand of*

24 I dug wells
and drank water in foreign lands.
I dried up all the streams of Egypt
with the soles of my feet.'
25 Have you not heard?
I designed it long ago;
I planned it in days gone by.
I have now brought it to pass,
and you have crushed fortified cities
into piles of rubble.
26 Their inhabitants have
become powerless,
dismayed, and ashamed.
They are plants of the field,
tender grass,
grass on the rooftops,
blasted by the east wind.[A]

27 But I know your sitting down,
your going out and your coming in,
and your raging against me.
28 Because your raging against me
and your arrogance have reached
my ears,
I will put my hook in your nose
and my bit in your mouth;
I will make you go back
the way you came.

29 "This will be the sign for you: This year
you will eat what grows on its own, and in the
second year what grows from that. But in the
third year sow and reap, plant vineyards and
eat their fruit. 30 The surviving remnant of the
house of Judah will again take root downward
and bear fruit upward. 31 For a remnant will
go out from Jerusalem, and survivors, from
Mount Zion. The zeal of the LORD of Armies
will accomplish this.
32 Therefore, this is what the LORD says
about the king of Assyria:
He will not enter this city,
shoot an arrow here,
come before it with a shield,
or build up a siege ramp against it.
33 He will go back
the way he came,
and he will not enter this city.
This is the LORD's declaration.
34 I will defend this city and rescue it
for my sake and for the sake of my
servant David."

DEFEAT AND DEATH OF SENNACHERIB

35 That night the angel of the LORD went out
and struck down one hundred eighty-five
thousand in the camp of the Assyrians. When
the people got up the next morning — there
were all the dead bodies! 36 So King Sennacherib
of Assyria broke camp and left. He returned
home and lived in Nineveh.
37 One day, while he was worshiping in the
temple of his god Nisroch, his sons Adrammelech and Sharezer struck him down with
the sword and escaped to the land of Ararat.
Then his son Esar-haddon became king in
his place.

HEZEKIAH'S ILLNESS AND RECOVERY

20 In those days Hezekiah became ter-
minally ill. The prophet Isaiah son of
Amoz came and said to him, "This is what the
LORD says: 'Set your house in order, for you are
about to die; you will not recover.'"
2 Then Hezekiah turned his face to the wall
and prayed to the LORD, 3 "Please, LORD, remember how I have walked before you faithfully and
wholeheartedly and have done what pleases
you."[B] And Hezekiah wept bitterly.
4 Isaiah had not yet gone out of the inner
courtyard when the word of the LORD came
to him: 5 "Go back and tell Hezekiah, the leader
of my people, 'This is what the LORD God of
your ancestor David says: I have heard your
prayer; I have seen your tears. Look, I will
heal you. On the third day from now you will
go up to the LORD's temple. 6 I will add fifteen
years to your life. I will rescue you and this
city from the grasp of the king of Assyria. I
will defend this city for my sake and for the
sake of my servant David.'"
7 Then Isaiah said, "Bring a lump of pressed
figs." So they brought it and applied it to his
infected skin, and he recovered.
8 Hezekiah had asked Isaiah, "What is the
sign that the LORD will heal me and that I
will go up to the LORD's temple on the third
day?"
9 Isaiah said, "This is the sign to you from the
LORD that he will do what he has promised:
Should the shadow go ahead ten steps or go
back ten steps?"
10 Then Hezekiah answered, "It's easy for
the shadow to lengthen ten steps. No, let the
shadow go back ten steps." 11 So the prophet
Isaiah called out to the LORD, and he brought

[A] **19:26** DSS; MT reads *blasted before standing grain*; Is 37:27 [B] **20:3** Lit *what is good in your eyes*

the shadow[A] back the ten steps it had descended on the stairway of Ahaz.[B]

HEZEKIAH'S FOLLY

12 At that time Merodach-baladan[C] son of Baladan, king of Babylon, sent letters and a gift
to Hezekiah since he heard that he had been
sick. 13 Hezekiah listened to the letters and
showed the envoys his whole treasure house
— the silver, the gold, the spices, and the precious oil — and his armory, and everything
that was found in his treasuries. There was
nothing in his palace and in all his realm that
Hezekiah did not show them.

14 Then the prophet Isaiah came to King Hezekiah and asked him, "Where did these men
come from and what did they say to you?"

Hezekiah replied, "They came from a distant
country, from Babylon."

15 Isaiah asked, "What have they seen in
your palace?"

Hezekiah answered, "They have seen everything in my palace. There isn't anything in my
treasuries that I didn't show them."

16 Then Isaiah said to Hezekiah, "Hear the
word of the LORD: 17 'Look, the days are coming
when everything in your palace and all that
your fathers have stored up until today will be
carried off to Babylon; nothing will be left,' says
the LORD. 18 'Some of your descendants — who
come from you, whom you father — will be
taken away, and they will become eunuchs[D]
in the palace of the king of Babylon.'"

19 Then Hezekiah said to Isaiah, "The word
of the LORD that you have spoken is good," for
he thought: Why not, if there will be peace
and security during my lifetime?

HEZEKIAH'S DEATH

20 The rest of the events of Hezekiah's reign,
along with all his might and how he made the
pool and the tunnel and brought water into
the city, are written in the Historical Record
of Judah's Kings. 21 Hezekiah rested with his
fathers, and his son Manasseh became king
in his place.

JUDAH'S KING MANASSEH

21 Manasseh was twelve years old when he
became king, and he reigned fifty-five
years in Jerusalem. His mother's name was
Hephzibah. 2 He did what was evil in the LORD's
sight, imitating the detestable practices of the
nations that the LORD had dispossessed before the Israelites. 3 He rebuilt the high places
that his father Hezekiah had destroyed and
reestablished the altars for Baal. He made an
Asherah, as King Ahab of Israel had done;
he also bowed in worship to all the stars in
the sky and served them. 4 He built altars in
the LORD's temple, where the LORD had said,
"Jerusalem is where I will put my name." 5 He
built altars to all the stars in the sky in both
courtyards of the LORD's temple. 6 He sacrificed his son in the fire,[E] practiced witchcraft
and divination, and consulted mediums and
spiritists. He did a huge amount of evil in the
LORD's sight, angering him.

7 Manasseh set up the carved image of Asherah, which he made, in the temple that the
LORD had spoken about to David and his son
Solomon: "I will establish my name forever
in this temple and in Jerusalem, which I have
chosen out of all the tribes of Israel. 8 I will
never again cause the feet of the Israelites to
wander from the land I gave to their ancestors if only they will be careful to do all I have
commanded them — the whole law that my
servant Moses commanded them." 9 But they
did not listen; Manasseh caused them to stray
so that they did worse evil than the nations
the LORD had destroyed before the Israelites.

10 The LORD said through his servants the
prophets, 11 "Since King Manasseh of Judah has
committed all these detestable acts — worse
evil than the Amorites who preceded him had
done — and by means of his idols has also
caused Judah to sin, 12 this is what the LORD
God of Israel says: 'I am about to bring such
disaster on Jerusalem and Judah that everyone who hears about it will shudder.[F] 13 I will
stretch over Jerusalem the measuring line used
on Samaria and the mason's level used on the
house of Ahab, and I will wipe Jerusalem clean
as one wipes a bowl — wiping it and turning
it upside down. 14 I will abandon the remnant
of my inheritance and hand them over to their
enemies. They will become plunder and spoil
to all their enemies, 15 because they have done
what is evil in my sight and have angered me
from the day their ancestors came out of Egypt
until today.'"

16 Manasseh also shed so much innocent
blood that he filled Jerusalem with it from

[A] **20:11** Lit *shadow on the steps* [B] **20:11** Tg, Vg; DSS read *on the steps of Ahaz's roof chamber*; Is 38:8 [C] **20:12** Some Hb mss, LXX, Syr, Tg, some Vg mss, Is 39:1; other Hb mss read *Berodach-baladan* [D] **20:18** Or *court officials* [E] **21:6** Lit *He made his son pass through the fire* [F] **21:12** Lit *about it, his two ears will tingle*; Hb obscure

one end to another. This was in addition to his sin that he caused Judah to commit, so that they did what was evil in the LORD's sight.

MANASSEH'S DEATH

17 The rest of the events of Manasseh's reign, along with all his accomplishments and the sin that he committed, are written in the Historical Record of Judah's Kings. 18 Manasseh rested with his fathers and was buried in the garden of his own house, the garden of Uzza. His son Amon became king in his place.

JUDAH'S KING AMON

19 Amon was twenty-two years old when he became king, and he reigned two years in Jerusalem. His mother's name was Meshullemeth daughter of Haruz; she was from Jotbah. 20 He did what was evil in the LORD's sight, just as his father Manasseh had done. 21 He walked in all the ways his father had walked; he served the idols his father had served, and he bowed in worship to them. 22 He abandoned the LORD God of his ancestors and did not walk in the ways of the LORD.

23 Amon's servants conspired against him and put the king to death in his own house. 24 The common people[A] killed all who had conspired against King Amon, and they made his son Josiah king in his place.

25 The rest of the events of Amon's reign, along with his accomplishments, are written in the Historical Record of Judah's Kings. 26 He was buried in his tomb in the garden of Uzza, and his son Josiah became king in his place.

JUDAH'S KING JOSIAH

22 Josiah was eight years old when he became king, and he reigned thirty-one years in Jerusalem. His mother's name was Jedidah the daughter of Adaiah; she was from Bozkath. 2 He did what was right in the LORD's sight and walked in all the ways of his ancestor David; he did not turn to the right or the left.

JOSIAH REPAIRS THE TEMPLE

3 In the eighteenth year of King Josiah, the king sent the court secretary Shaphan son of Azaliah, son of Meshullam, to the LORD's temple, saying, 4 "Go up to the high priest Hilkiah so that he may total up the silver brought into the LORD's temple — the silver the doorkeepers have collected from the people. 5 It is to be given to those doing the work — those who oversee the LORD's temple. They in turn are to give it to the workmen in the LORD's temple to repair the damage. 6 They are to give it to the carpenters, builders, and masons to buy timber and quarried stone to repair the temple. 7 But no accounting is to be required from them for the silver given to them since they work with integrity."

THE BOOK OF THE LAW FOUND

8 The high priest Hilkiah told the court secretary Shaphan, "I have found the book of the law in the LORD's temple," and he gave the book to Shaphan, who read it.

9 Then the court secretary Shaphan went to the king and reported,[B] "Your servants have emptied out the silver that was found in the temple and have given it to those doing the work — those who oversee the LORD's temple." 10 Then the court secretary Shaphan told the king, "The priest Hilkiah has given me a book," and Shaphan read it in the presence of the king.

11 When the king heard the words of the book of the law, he tore his clothes. 12 Then he commanded the priest Hilkiah, Ahikam son of Shaphan, Achbor son of Micaiah, the court secretary Shaphan, and the king's servant Asaiah: 13 "Go and inquire of the LORD for me, the people, and all Judah about the words in this book that has been found. For great is the LORD's wrath that is kindled against us because our ancestors have not obeyed the words of this book in order to do everything written about us."

HULDAH'S PROPHECY OF JUDGMENT

14 So the priest Hilkiah, Ahikam, Achbor, Shaphan, and Asaiah went to the prophetess Huldah, wife of Shallum son of Tikvah, son of Harhas, keeper of the wardrobe. She lived in Jerusalem in the Second District. They spoke with her.

15 She said to them, "This is what the LORD God of Israel says: Say to the man who sent you to me, 16 'This is what the LORD says: I am about to bring disaster on this place and on its inhabitants, fulfilling[C] all the words of the book that the king of Judah has read, 17 because they have abandoned me and burned incense to other gods in order to anger me with all the work of their hands. My wrath will be kindled

---

[A] **21:24** Lit *The people of the land* [B] **22:9** Lit *and returned a word to the king and said* [C] **22:16** *fulfilling* supplied for clarity

against this place, and it will not be quenched.'
18 Say this to the king of Judah who sent you
to inquire of the LORD: 'This is what the LORD
God of Israel says: As for the words that you
heard, 19 because your heart was tender and
you humbled yourself before the LORD when
you heard what I spoke against this place and
against its inhabitants, that they would become a desolation and a curse, and because
you have torn your clothes and wept before
me, I myself have heard' — this is the LORD's
declaration. 20 'Therefore, I will indeed gather
you to your fathers, and you will be gathered to
your grave in peace. Your eyes will not see all
the disaster that I am bringing on this place.' "
Then they reported[A] to the king.

COVENANT RENEWAL

23 So the king sent messengers, and they
gathered all the elders of Judah and
Jerusalem to him. 2 Then the king went to the
LORD's temple with all the men of Judah and
all the inhabitants of Jerusalem, as well as
the priests and the prophets — all the people
from the youngest to the oldest. He read in
their hearing all the words of the book of the
covenant that had been found in the LORD's
temple. 3 Next, the king stood by the pillar[B]
and made a covenant in the LORD's presence
to follow the LORD and to keep his commands,
his decrees, and his statutes with all his heart
and with all his soul in order to carry out the
words of this covenant that were written in this
book; all the people agreed to[C] the covenant.

The king stood by the pillar and made a covenant in the LORD's presence to follow the LORD and to keep his commands, his decrees, and his statutes with all his heart and with all his soul.

—2 Kings 23:3

JOSIAH'S REFORMS

4 Then the king commanded the high priest
Hilkiah and the priests of the second rank and
the doorkeepers to bring out of the LORD's
sanctuary all the articles made for Baal, Asherah, and all the stars in the sky. He burned them
outside Jerusalem in the fields of the Kidron
and carried their ashes to Bethel. 5 Then he
did away with the idolatrous priests the kings
of Judah had appointed to burn incense at
the high places in the cities of Judah and in
the areas surrounding Jerusalem. They had
burned incense to Baal, and to the sun, moon,
constellations, and all the stars in the sky. 6 He
brought out the Asherah pole from the LORD's
temple to the Kidron Valley outside Jerusalem. He burned it at the Kidron Valley, beat it
to dust, and threw its dust on the graves of
the common people.[D] 7 He also tore down the
houses of the male cult prostitutes that were in
the LORD's temple, in which the women were
weaving tapestries[E] for Asherah.
8 Then Josiah brought all the priests from
the cities of Judah, and he defiled the high
places from Geba to Beer-sheba, where the
priests had burned incense. He tore down
the high places of the city gates at the entrance of the gate of Joshua the governor
of the city (on the left at the city gate). 9 The
priests of the high places, however, did not
come up to the altar of the LORD in Jerusalem; instead, they ate unleavened bread with
their fellow priests.
10 He defiled Topheth, which is in Ben Hinnom Valley, so that no one could sacrifice his
son or daughter in the fire[F] to Molech. 11 He did
away with the horses that the kings of Judah
had dedicated to the sun. They had been at the
entrance of the LORD's temple in the precincts
by the chamber of Nathan-melech, the eunuch.
He also burned the chariots of the sun.
12 The king tore down the altars that the kings
of Judah had made on the roof of Ahaz's upper
chamber. He also tore down the altars that Manasseh had made in the two courtyards of the
LORD's temple. Then he smashed them[G] there
and threw their dust into the Kidron Valley.
13 The king also defiled the high places that
were across from Jerusalem, to the south of
the Mount of Destruction, which King Solomon
of Israel had built for Ashtoreth, the abhorrent idol of the Sidonians; for Chemosh, the
abhorrent idol of Moab; and for Milcom, the
detestable idol of the Ammonites. 14 He broke
the sacred pillars into pieces, cut down the
Asherah poles, then filled their places with
human bones.

[A] **22:20** Lit *returned a word* [B] **23:3** 2Ch 34:31 reads *platform* [C] **23:3** Lit *people took a stand in* [D] **23:6** Lit *the sons of the people* [E] **23:7** Or *clothing* [F] **23:10** Lit *could make his son or daughter pass through the fire* [G] **23:12** Text emended; MT reads *he ran from*

15 He even tore down the altar at Bethel and the high place that had been made by Jeroboam son of Nebat, who caused Israel to sin. He burned the high place, crushed it to dust, and burned the Asherah. 16 As Josiah turned, he saw the tombs there on the mountain. He sent someone to take the bones out of the tombs, and he burned them on the altar. He defiled it according to the word of the LORD proclaimed by the man of God[A] who proclaimed these things. 17 Then he said, "What is this monument I see?"

The men of the city told him, "It is the tomb of the man of God who came from Judah and proclaimed these things that you have done to the altar at Bethel."

18 So he said, "Let him rest. Don't let anyone disturb his bones." So they left his bones undisturbed with the bones of the prophet who came from Samaria.

19 Josiah also removed all the shrines of the high places that were in the cities of Samaria, which the kings of Israel had made to anger the LORD. Josiah did the same things to them that he had done at Bethel. 20 He slaughtered on the altars all the priests of those high places, and he burned human bones on the altars. Then he returned to Jerusalem.

PASSOVER OBSERVED

21 The king commanded all the people, "Observe the Passover of the LORD your God as written in the book of the covenant." 22 No such Passover had ever been observed from the time of the judges who judged Israel through the entire time of the kings of Israel and Judah. 23 But in the eighteenth year of King Josiah, the LORD's Passover was observed in Jerusalem.

FURTHER ZEAL FOR THE LORD

24 In addition, Josiah eradicated the mediums, the spiritists, household idols, images, and all the abhorrent things that were seen in the land of Judah and in Jerusalem. He did this in order to carry out the words of the law that were written in the book that the priest Hilkiah found in the LORD's temple. 25 Before him there was no king like him who turned to the LORD with all his heart and with all his soul and with all his strength according to all the law of Moses, and no one like him arose after him.

26 In spite of all that, the LORD did not turn from the fury of his intense burning anger, which burned against Judah because of all the affronts with which Manasseh had angered him. 27 For the LORD had said, "I will also remove Judah from my presence just as I have removed Israel. I will reject this city Jerusalem, that I have chosen, and the temple about which I said, 'My name will be there.'"

JOSIAH'S DEATH

28 The rest of the events of Josiah's reign, along with all his accomplishments, are written in the Historical Record of Judah's Kings. 29 During his reign, Pharaoh Neco king of Egypt marched up to help the king of Assyria at the Euphrates River. King Josiah went to confront him, and at Megiddo when Neco saw him he killed him. 30 From Megiddo his servants carried his dead body in a chariot, brought him into Jerusalem, and buried him in his own tomb. Then the common people[B] took Jehoahaz son of Josiah, anointed him, and made him king in place of his father.

JUDAH'S KING JEHOAHAZ

31 Jehoahaz was twenty-three years old when he became king, and he reigned three months in Jerusalem. His mother's name was Hamutal daughter of Jeremiah; she was from Libnah. 32 He did what was evil in the LORD's sight just as his ancestors had done. 33 Pharaoh Neco imprisoned him at Riblah in the land of Hamath to keep him from reigning in Jerusalem, and he imposed on the land a fine of seventy-five hundred pounds[C] of silver and seventy-five pounds[D] of gold.

JUDAH'S KING JEHOIAKIM

34 Then Pharaoh Neco made Eliakim son of Josiah king in place of his father Josiah and changed Eliakim's name to Jehoiakim. But Neco took Jehoahaz and went to Egypt, and he died there. 35 So Jehoiakim gave the silver and the gold to Pharaoh, but at Pharaoh's command he taxed the land to give it. He exacted the silver and the gold from the common people, each according to his assessment, to give it to Pharaoh Neco.

36 Jehoiakim was twenty-five years old when he became king, and he reigned eleven years in Jerusalem. His mother's name was Zebidah

---

[A] **23:16** LXX adds *when Jeroboam stood by the altar of the feast. And he turned and raised his eyes to the tomb of the man of God* [B] **23:30** Lit *the people of the land*, also in v. 35 [C] **23:33** Lit *100 talents* [D] **23:33** Lit *one talent*

daughter of Pedaiah; she was from Rumah. 37 He did what was evil in the LORD's sight just as his ancestors had done.

JEHOIAKIM'S REBELLION AND DEATH

24 During Jehoiakim's reign, King Nebuchadnezzar of Babylon attacked. Jehoiakim became his vassal for three years, and then he turned and rebelled against him. 2 The LORD sent Chaldean, Aramean, Moabite, and Ammonite raiders against Jehoiakim. He sent them against Judah to destroy it, according to the word of the LORD he had spoken through his servants the prophets. 3 Indeed, this happened to Judah at the LORD's command to remove them from his presence. It was because of the sins of Manasseh, according to all he had done, 4 and also because of all the innocent blood he had shed. He had filled Jerusalem with innocent blood, and the LORD was not willing to forgive.

5 The rest of the events of Jehoiakim's reign, along with all his accomplishments, are written in the Historical Record of Judah's Kings. 6 Jehoiakim rested with his fathers, and his son Jehoiachin became king in his place.

7 Now the king of Egypt did not march out of his land again, for the king of Babylon took everything that had belonged to the king of Egypt, from the Brook of Egypt to the Euphrates River.

JUDAH'S KING JEHOIACHIN

8 Jehoiachin was eighteen years old when he became king, and he reigned three months in Jerusalem. His mother's name was Nehushta daughter of Elnathan; she was from Jerusalem. 9 He did what was evil in the LORD's sight just as his father had done.

DEPORTATIONS TO BABYLON

10 At that time the servants of King Nebuchadnezzar of Babylon marched up to Jerusalem, and the city came under siege. 11 King Nebuchadnezzar of Babylon came to the city while his servants were besieging it. 12 King Jehoiachin of Judah, along with his mother, his servants, his commanders, and his officials,[A] surrendered to the king of Babylon.

So the king of Babylon took him captive in the eighth year of his reign. 13 He also carried off from there all the treasures of the LORD's temple and the treasures of the king's palace, and he cut into pieces all the gold articles that King Solomon of Israel had made for the LORD's sanctuary, just as the LORD had predicted. 14 He deported all Jerusalem and all the commanders and all the best soldiers — ten thousand captives including all the craftsmen and metalsmiths. Except for the poorest people of the land, no one remained.

15 Nebuchadnezzar deported Jehoiachin to Babylon. He took the king's mother, the king's wives, his officials, and the leading men of the land into exile from Jerusalem to Babylon. 16 The king of Babylon brought captive into Babylon all seven thousand of the best soldiers and one thousand craftsmen and metalsmiths — all strong and fit for war. 17 And the king of Babylon made Mattaniah, Jehoiachin's[B] uncle, king in his place and changed his name to Zedekiah.

JUDAH'S KING ZEDEKIAH

18 Zedekiah was twenty-one years old when he became king, and he reigned eleven years in Jerusalem. His mother's name was Hamutal daughter of Jeremiah; she was from Libnah. 19 Zedekiah did what was evil in the LORD's sight just as Jehoiakim had done. 20 Because of the LORD's anger, it came to the point in Jerusalem and Judah that he finally banished them from his presence. Then Zedekiah rebelled against the king of Babylon.

NEBUCHADNEZZAR'S SIEGE OF JERUSALEM

25 In the ninth year of Zedekiah's reign, on the tenth day of the tenth month, King Nebuchadnezzar of Babylon advanced against Jerusalem with his entire army. They laid siege to the city and built a siege wall against it all around. 2 The city was under siege until King Zedekiah's eleventh year.

3 By the ninth day of the fourth month the famine was so severe in the city that the common people had no food. 4 Then the city was broken into, and all the warriors fled at night by way of the city gate between the two walls near the king's garden, even though the Chaldeans surrounded the city. As the king made his way along the route to the Arabah, 5 the Chaldean army pursued him and overtook him in the plains of Jericho. Zedekiah's entire army left him and scattered. 6 The Chaldeans seized the king and brought him up to the king of Babylon at Riblah, and they passed sentence on him. 7 They slaughtered Zedekiah's sons before his eyes. Finally, the king of Babylon

---

[A] **24:12** Or *eunuchs* [B] **24:17** Lit *his*

blinded Zedekiah, bound him in bronze chains, and took him to Babylon.

JERUSALEM DESTROYED

8 On the seventh day of the fifth month — which was the nineteenth year of King Nebuchadnezzar of Babylon — Nebuzaradan, the captain of the guards, a servant of the king of Babylon, entered Jerusalem. 9 He burned the LORD's temple, the king's palace, and all the houses of Jerusalem; he burned down all the great houses. 10 The whole Chaldean army with the captain of the guards tore down the walls surrounding Jerusalem. 11 Nebuzaradan, the captain of the guards, deported the rest of the people who remained in the city, the deserters who had defected to the king of Babylon, and the rest of the population. 12 But the captain of the guards left some of the poorest of the land to be vinedressers and farmers.

13 Now the Chaldeans broke into pieces the bronze pillars of the LORD's temple, the water carts, and the bronze basin,[A] which were in the LORD's temple, and carried the bronze to Babylon. 14 They also took the pots, shovels, wick trimmers, dishes, and all the bronze articles used in the priests' service. 15 The captain of the guards took away the firepans and sprinkling basins — whatever was gold or silver.

16 As for the two pillars, the one basin, and the water carts that Solomon had made for the LORD's temple, the weight of the bronze of all these articles was beyond measure. 17 One pillar was twenty-seven feet[B] tall and had a bronze capital on top of it. The capital, encircled by a grating and pomegranates of bronze, stood five feet[C] high. The second pillar was the same, with its own grating.

18 The captain of the guards also took away Seraiah the chief priest, Zephaniah the priest of the second rank, and the three doorkeepers. 19 From the city he took a court official[D] who had been appointed over the warriors; five trusted royal aides[E] found in the city; the secretary of the commander of the army, who enlisted the people of the land for military duty; and sixty men from the common people[F] who were found within the city. 20 Nebuzaradan, the captain of the guards, took them and brought them to the king of Babylon at Riblah. 21 The king of Babylon put them to death at Riblah in the land of Hamath. So Judah went into exile from its land.

GEDALIAH MADE GOVERNOR

22 King Nebuchadnezzar of Babylon appointed Gedaliah son of Ahikam, son of Shaphan, over the rest of the people he left in the land of Judah. 23 When all the commanders of the armies — they and their men — heard that the king of Babylon had appointed Gedaliah, they came to Gedaliah at Mizpah. The commanders included Ishmael son of Nethaniah, Johanan son of Kareah, Seraiah son of Tanhumeth the Netophathite, and Jaazaniah son of the Maacathite — they and their men. 24 Gedaliah swore an oath to them and their men, assuring them, "Don't be afraid of the servants of the Chaldeans. Live in the land and serve the king of Babylon, and it will go well for you."

25 In the seventh month, however, Ishmael son of Nethaniah, son of Elishama, of the royal family, came with ten men and struck down Gedaliah, and he died. Also, they killed the Judeans and the Chaldeans who were with him at Mizpah. 26 Then all the people, from the youngest to the oldest, and the commanders of the army, left and went to Egypt, for they were afraid of the Chaldeans.

JEHOIACHIN PARDONED

27 On the twenty-seventh day of the twelfth month of the thirty-seventh year of the exile of Judah's King Jehoiachin, in the year Evil-merodach became king of Babylon, he pardoned King Jehoiachin of Judah and released him[G] from prison. 28 He spoke kindly to him and set his throne over the thrones of the kings who were with him in Babylon. 29 So Jehoiachin changed his prison clothes, and he dined regularly in the presence of the king of Babylon for the rest of his life. 30 As for his allowance, a regular allowance was given to him by the king, a portion for each day, for the rest of his life.

[A] **25:13** Lit *sea* [B] **25:17** Lit *18 cubits* [C] **25:17** Lit *three cubits* [D] **25:19** Or *eunuch* [E] **25:19** Lit *five men who look on the king's face* [F] **25:19** Lit *the people of the land* [G] **25:27** *and released him* supplied for clarity

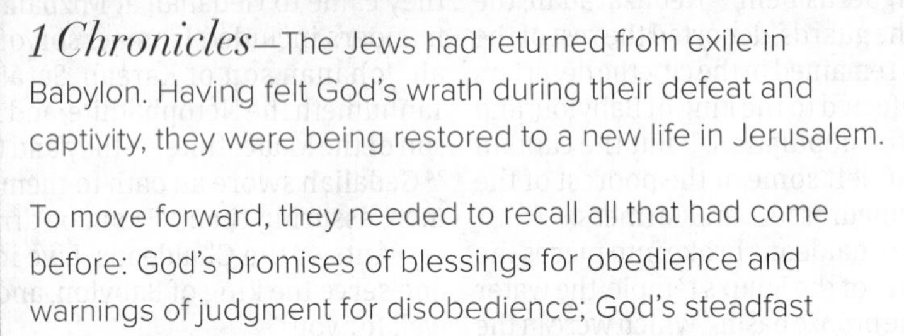

1 Chronicles—The Jews had returned from exile in Babylon. Having felt God's wrath during their defeat and captivity, they were being restored to a new life in Jerusalem.

To move forward, they needed to recall all that had come before: God's promises of blessings for obedience and warnings of judgment for disobedience; God's steadfast love and faithfulness; their propensity to sin and the dire consequences for not seeking God.

As with ancient Israel, an honest look at our past can prepare us embrace the future with hope. Knowing where we've been, we can face our failures and determine not to repeat them. We can trace God's merciful care even in our darkest days.

Whatever your past, 1 Chronicles offers hope. If the people of Israel—who had been carried into captivity because of their blatant rejection of God —were not beyond God's grace, neither are you. God will restore all who return to him. We just need to return, acknowledging our sin and submitting to him as Lord.

FROM ADAM TO ABRAHAM

1 Adam, Seth, Enosh,
2 Kenan, Mahalalel, Jared,
3 Enoch, Methuselah, Lamech,
4 Noah, Noah's sons:[A]
Shem, Ham, and Japheth.

5 Japheth's sons: Gomer, Magog, Madai,
Javan, Tubal, Meshech, and Tiras.
6 Gomer's sons: Ashkenaz, Riphath,[B] and
Togarmah.
7 Javan's sons: Elishah, Tarshish, Kittim,
and Rodanim.[C]

8 Ham's sons: Cush, Mizraim,[D] Put, and
Canaan.
9 Cush's sons: Seba, Havilah, Sabta,
Raama, and Sabteca.
Raama's sons: Sheba and Dedan.
10 Cush fathered Nimrod, who was the
first to become a great warrior on
earth.
11 Mizraim fathered the people of Lud,
Anam, Lehab, Naphtuh, 12 Pathrus, Casluh
(the Philistines came from them), and
Caphtor.
13 Canaan fathered Sidon as his firstborn
and Heth, 14 as well as the Jebusites,
Amorites, Girgashites, 15 Hivites, Arkites,
Sinites, 16 Arvadites, Zemarites, and
Hamathites.

17 Shem's sons: Elam, Asshur,
Arpachshad, Lud, Aram, Uz, Hul, Gether,
and Meshech.
18 Arpachshad fathered Shelah, and
Shelah fathered Eber. 19 Two sons were
born to Eber. One of them was named
Peleg[E] because the earth was divided
during his lifetime, and the name of his
brother was Joktan. 20 Joktan fathered
Almodad, Sheleph, Hazarmaveth, Jerah,
21 Hadoram, Uzal, Diklah, 22 Ebal, Abimael,
Sheba, 23 Ophir, Havilah, and Jobab. All of
these were Joktan's sons.

24 Shem, Arpachshad, Shelah,
25 Eber, Peleg, Reu,
26 Serug, Nahor, Terah,
27 and Abram (that is, Abraham).

ABRAHAM'S DESCENDANTS

28 Abraham's sons: Isaac and Ishmael.
29 These are their family records:
Nebaioth, Ishmael's firstborn, Kedar,
Adbeel, Mibsam, 30 Mishma, Dumah,
Massa, Hadad, Tema, 31 Jetur, Naphish,
and Kedemah.
These were Ishmael's sons.

32 The sons born to Keturah, Abraham's
concubine: Zimran, Jokshan, Medan,
Midian, Ishbak, and Shuah.
Jokshan's sons: Sheba and Dedan.
33 Midian's sons: Ephah, Epher, Hanoch,
Abida, and Eldaah.
All of these were Keturah's descendants.

34 Abraham fathered Isaac.
Isaac's sons: Esau and Israel.
35 Esau's sons: Eliphaz, Reuel, Jeush,
Jalam, and Korah.
36 Eliphaz's sons: Teman, Omar, Zephi,
Gatam, and Kenaz; and by Timna,
Amalek.[F]
37 Reuel's sons: Nahath, Zerah, Shammah,
and Mizzah.

THE EDOMITES

38 Seir's sons: Lotan, Shobal, Zibeon, Anah,
Dishon, Ezer, and Dishan.
39 Lotan's sons: Hori and Homam. Timna
was Lotan's sister.
40 Shobal's sons: Alian, Manahath, Ebal,
Shephi, and Onam.
Zibeon's sons: Aiah and Anah.
41 Anah's son: Dishon.
Dishon's sons: Hamran, Eshban, Ithran,
and Cheran.
42 Ezer's sons: Bilhan, Zaavan, and Jaakan.
Dishan's sons: Uz and Aran.

43 These were the kings who reigned
in the land of Edom
before any king reigned
over the Israelites:
Bela son of Beor.
Bela's town was named Dinhabah.
44 When Bela died, Jobab son of Zerah
from Bozrah reigned in his place.
45 When Jobab died, Husham
from the land of the Temanites
reigned in his place.
46 When Husham died, Hadad son of Bedad,
who defeated Midian in the territory
of Moab, reigned in his place.

[A] **1:4** LXX; MT omits *Noah's sons* [B] **1:6** Some Hb mss, LXX, Vg; other Hb mss read *Diphath*; Gn 10:3 [C] **1:7** Some Hb mss, Syr read *Dodanim*; Gn 10:4 [D] **1:8** = Egypt [E] **1:19** = Division [F] **1:36** LXX; MT reads *and Timna and Amalek*; Gn 36:12

Hadad's town was named Avith.
47 When Hadad died, Samlah
from Masrekah reigned
in his place.
48 When Samlah died, Shaul
from Rehoboth on the Euphrates
River reigned in his place.
49 When Shaul died, Baal-hanan
son of Achbor reigned in his place.
50 When Baal-hanan died, Hadad reigned
in his place.
Hadad's city was named Pai, and his
wife's name was Mehetabel
daughter of Matred, daughter
of Me-zahab.
51 Then Hadad died.

Edom's chiefs: Timna, Alvah,[A] Jetheth,
52 Oholibamah, Elah, Pinon, 53 Kenaz,
Teman, Mibzar, 54 Magdiel, and Iram.
These were Edom's chiefs.

ISRAEL'S SONS

2 These were Israel's sons:
Reuben, Simeon, Levi,
Judah, Issachar, Zebulun,
2 Dan, Joseph, Benjamin,
Naphtali, Gad, and Asher.

JUDAH'S DESCENDANTS

3 Judah's sons: Er, Onan, and Shelah.
These three were born to him by Bath-
shua the Canaanite woman. Er, Judah's
firstborn, was evil in the LORD's sight, so
he put him to death. 4 Judah's daughter-
in-law Tamar bore Perez and Zerah to
him. Judah had five sons in all.

5 Perez's sons: Hezron and Hamul.
6 Zerah's sons: Zimri, Ethan, Heman,
Calcol, and Dara[B] — five in all.
7 Carmi's son: Achar,[C] who brought
trouble on Israel when he was unfaithful
by taking the things set apart for
destruction.
8 Ethan's son: Azariah.
9 Hezron's sons, who were born to him:
Jerahmeel, Ram, and Chelubai.[D]

10 Ram fathered Amminadab, and
Amminadab fathered Nahshon, a leader
of Judah's descendants.
11 Nahshon fathered Salma, and Salma
fathered Boaz.
12 Boaz fathered Obed, and Obed fathered
Jesse.
13 Jesse fathered Eliab, his firstborn;
Abinadab was born second, Shimea third,
14 Nethanel fourth, Raddai fifth, 15 Ozem
sixth, and David seventh. 16 Their sisters
were Zeruiah and Abigail. Zeruiah's
three sons: Abishai, Joab, and Asahel.
17 Amasa's mother was Abigail, and his
father was Jether the Ishmaelite.

18 Caleb son of Hezron had children by his
wife Azubah and by Jerioth. These were
Azubah's sons: Jesher, Shobab, and Ardon.
19 When Azubah died, Caleb married
Ephrath, and she bore Hur to him. 20 Hur
fathered Uri, and Uri fathered Bezalel.
21 After this, Hezron slept with the daughter of Machir the father of Gilead. Hezron
had married her when he was sixty years
old, and she bore Segub to him. 22 Segub
fathered Jair, who possessed twenty-three
towns in the land of Gilead. 23 But Geshur
and Aram captured[E] Jair's Villages[F] along
with Kenath and its surrounding villages
— sixty towns. All these were the descendants of Machir father of Gilead. 24 After
Hezron's death in Caleb-ephrathah, his
wife Abijah bore[G] Ashhur to him. He was
the father of Tekoa.

25 The sons of Jerahmeel, Hezron's
firstborn: Ram, his firstborn, Bunah,
Oren, Ozem, and Ahijah. 26 Jerahmeel had
another wife named Atarah, who was the
mother of Onam.
27 The sons of Ram, Jerahmeel's firstborn:
Maaz, Jamin, and Eker.
28 Onam's sons: Shammai and Jada.
Shammai's sons: Nadab and Abishur.
29 Abishur's wife was named Abihail, who
bore Ahban and Molid to him.
30 Nadab's sons: Seled and Appaim. Seled
died without children.
31 Appaim's son: Ishi.
Ishi's son: Sheshan.
Sheshan's descendant: Ahlai.
32 The sons of Jada, brother of Shammai:
Jether and Jonathan. Jether died without
children.

[A] **1:51** Alt Hb tradition reads *Aliah* [B] **2:6** Some Hb mss, LXX, Syr, Tg, Vg read *Darda*; 1Kg 4:31 [C] **2:7** = Trouble; Achan in Jos 7:1,16–26 [D] **2:9** = Caleb [E] **2:23** Lit *took from them* [F] **2:23** Or *captured Havvoth-jair* [G] **2:24** LXX, Vg read *death, Caleb slept with Ephrath (Hezron's wife was Abijah) and she bore*

33 Jonathan's sons: Peleth and Zaza. These
were the descendants of Jerahmeel.
34 Sheshan had no sons, only daughters,
but he did have an Egyptian servant
whose name was Jarha. 35 Sheshan gave
his daughter in marriage to his servant
Jarha, and she bore Attai to him.

36 Attai fathered Nathan, and Nathan
fathered Zabad.
37 Zabad fathered Ephlal, and Ephlal
fathered Obed.
38 Obed fathered Jehu, and Jehu fathered
Azariah.
39 Azariah fathered Helez, and Helez
fathered Elasah.
40 Elasah fathered Sismai, and Sismai
fathered Shallum.
41 Shallum fathered Jekamiah, and
Jekamiah fathered Elishama.

42 The sons of Caleb brother of Jerahmeel:
Mesha, his firstborn, fathered Ziph, and
Mareshah, his second son,[A] fathered
Hebron.
43 Hebron's sons: Korah, Tappuah, Rekem,
and Shema.
44 Shema fathered Raham, who fathered
Jorkeam, and Rekem fathered Shammai.
45 Shammai's son was Maon, and Maon
fathered Beth-zur.
46 Caleb's concubine Ephah was the
mother of Haran, Moza, and Gazez. Haran
fathered Gazez.
47 Jahdai's sons: Regem, Jotham, Geshan,
Pelet, Ephah, and Shaaph.
48 Caleb's concubine Maacah was
the mother of Sheber and Tirhanah.
49 She was also the mother of Shaaph,
Madmannah's father, and of Sheva, the
father of Machbenah and Gibea. Caleb's
daughter was Achsah.
50 These were Caleb's descendants.

The sons of Hur, Ephrathah's firstborn:
Shobal fathered Kiriath-jearim;
51 Salma fathered Bethlehem,
and Hareph fathered Beth-gader.

52 These were the descendants of Shobal
the father of Kiriath-jearim: Haroeh,
half of the Manahathites,[B] 53 and the
families of Kiriath-jearim — the Ithrites,
Puthites, Shumathites, and Mishraites.
The Zorathites and Eshtaolites descended
from these.

54 Salma's descendants: Bethlehem, the
Netophathites, Atroth-beth-joab, and half
of the Manahathites, the Zorites, 55 and
the families of scribes who lived in Jabez
— the Tirathites, Shimeathites, and Su-
cathites. These are the Kenites who came
from Hammath, the father of Rechab's
family.

DAVID'S DESCENDANTS

3 These were David's sons who were born
to him in Hebron:
Amnon was the firstborn, by Ahinoam of
Jezreel;
Daniel was born second, by Abigail of
Carmel;
2 Absalom son of Maacah, daughter of
King Talmai of Geshur, was third;
Adonijah son of Haggith was fourth;
3 Shephatiah, by Abital, was fifth;
and Ithream, by David's wife Eglah, was
sixth.
4 Six sons were born to David in Hebron,
where he reigned seven years and six
months, and he reigned in Jerusalem
thirty-three years.
5 These sons were born to him in
Jerusalem:
Shimea, Shobab, Nathan, and Solomon.
These four were born to him by
Bath-shua daughter of Ammiel.
6 David's other sons: Ibhar, Elishua,[C]
Eliphelet, 7 Nogah, Nepheg, Japhia,
8 Elishama, Eliada, and Eliphelet — nine
sons.
9 These were all David's sons, with their
sister Tamar, in addition to the sons by
his concubines.

JUDAH'S KINGS

10 Solomon's son was Rehoboam;
his son was Abijah, his son Asa,
his son Jehoshaphat, 11 his son Jehoram,[D,E]
his son Ahaziah, his son Joash,
12 his son Amaziah, his son Azariah,
his son Jotham, 13 his son Ahaz,
his son Hezekiah, his son Manasseh,
14 his son Amon, and his son Josiah.
15 Josiah's sons:

[A] **2:42** Lit *and the sons of Mareshah* [B] **2:52** Lit *Manuhoth* [C] **3:6** Lit *Elishama*; 2Sm 5:15; 1Ch 14:5 [D] **3:11** Lit *Joram*
[E] **3:11** = The LORD is Exalted

Johanan was the firstborn, Jehoiakim
second,
Zedekiah third, and Shallum fourth.
16 Jehoiakim's sons:
his sons Jeconiah and Zedekiah.

DAVID'S LINE AFTER THE EXILE

17 The sons of Jeconiah the captive:
his sons Shealtiel, 18 Malchiram, Pedaiah,
Shenazzar, Jekamiah, Hoshama, and
Nedabiah.
19 Pedaiah's sons: Zerubbabel and Shimei.
Zerubbabel's sons: Meshullam and
Hananiah, with their sister Shelomith;
20 and five others — Hashubah, Ohel,
Berechiah, Hasadiah, and Jushab-hesed.
21 Hananiah's descendants: Pelatiah,
Jeshaiah, and the sons of Rephaiah,
Arnan, Obadiah, and Shecaniah.[A]
22 The son[B] of Shecaniah: Shemaiah.
Shemaiah's sons: Hattush, Igal, Bariah,
Neariah, and Shaphat — six.
23 Neariah's sons: Elioenai, Hizkiah, and
Azrikam — three.
24 Elioenai's sons: Hodaviah, Eliashib,
Pelaiah, Akkub, Johanan, Delaiah, and
Anani — seven.

JUDAH'S DESCENDANTS

4 Judah's sons: Perez, Hezron, Carmi, Hur,
and Shobal.
2 Reaiah son of Shobal fathered Jahath,
and Jahath fathered Ahumai and Lahad.
These were the families of the Zorathites.
3 These were Etam's sons:[C] Jezreel, Ishma,
and Idbash, and their sister was named
Hazzelelponi.
4 Penuel fathered Gedor, and Ezer
fathered Hushah.
These were the sons of Hur, Ephrathah's
firstborn and the father of Bethlehem:
5 Ashhur fathered Tekoa and had two
wives, Helah and Naarah.
6 Naarah bore Ahuzzam, Hepher, Temeni,
and Haahashtari to him. These were
Naarah's sons.
7 Helah's sons: Zereth, Zohar,[D] and Ethnan.
8 Koz fathered Anub, Zobebah,[E] and the
families of Aharhel son of Harum.

9 Jabez[F] was more honored than his brothers.
His mother named him Jabez and said, "I gave
birth to him in pain."
10 Jabez called out to the God of Israel: "If
only you would bless me, extend my border,
let your hand be with me, and keep me from
harm, so that I will not experience pain."[G] And
God granted his request.
11 Chelub brother of Shuhah fathered
Mehir, who was the father of Eshton.
12 Eshton fathered Beth-rapha, Paseah,
and Tehinnah the father of Irnahash.
These were the men of Recah.
13 Kenaz's sons: Othniel and Seraiah.
Othniel's sons: Hathath and
Meonothai.[H]
14 Meonothai fathered Ophrah,
and Seraiah fathered Joab, the ancestor
of those in the Craftsmen's Valley,[I] for
they were craftsmen.
15 The sons of Caleb son of Jephunneh:
Iru, Elah, and Naam.
Elah's son: Kenaz.
16 Jehallelel's sons: Ziph, Ziphah, Tiria, and
Asarel.
17 Ezrah's sons: Jether, Mered, Epher, and
Jalon. Mered's wife Bithiah gave birth to
Miriam, Shammai, and Ishbah the father
of Eshtemoa. 18 These were the sons of
Pharaoh's daughter Bithiah; Mered had
married her. His Judean wife gave birth
to Jered the father of Gedor, Heber the
father of Soco, and Jekuthiel the father of
Zanoah. 19 The sons of Hodiah's wife, the
sister of Naham: the father of Keilah the
Garmite and the father of Eshtemoa the
Maacathite.
20 Shimon's sons: Amnon, Rinnah,
Ben-hanan, and Tilon.
Ishi's sons: Zoheth and Ben-zoheth.

21 The sons of Shelah son of Judah: Er
the father of Lecah, Laadah the father
of Mareshah, the families of the guild[J]
of linen workers at Beth-ashbea, 22 Jo-
kim, the men of Cozeba; and Joash and
Saraph, who married Moabites[K] and
returned to Lehem.[L] These names are
from ancient records. 23 They were the
potters and residents of Netaim and
Gederah. They lived there in the service
of the king.

[A] **3:21** LXX reads *Jeshaiah, his son Rephaiah, his son Arnan, his son Obadiah, and his son Shecaniah* [B] **3:22** LXX; MT reads *sons* [C] **4:3** LXX; MT reads *father* [D] **4:7** Alt Hb tradition reads *Izhar* [E] **4:8** Or *Hazzobebah* [F] **4:9** In Hb, the name *Jabez* sounds like "he causes pain." [G] **4:10** Or *not cause any pain* [H] **4:13** LXX, Vg; MT omits *and Meonothai* [I] **4:14** Or *the Ge-harashim* [J] **4:21** Lit *house* [K] **4:22** Or *who ruled over Moab* [L] **4:22** Tg, Vg; MT reads *and Jashubi Lehem*

My Story | Shayleen

During eleven years of my childhood I was harassed daily. I could never understand why several people made it their goal to bully me. I feared going to school. The abuse left marks on me—mostly on my soul—but one on my arm still bears a reminder of what can happen when you go too far. I burned a cross into my arm hoping it would help ease my pain. It didn't.

My life wasn't always that bad. Although my parents divorced when I was young, my father would come around every summer to spend a week with us. That stopped in grade six, and I never saw him again. The last time he called, I yelled at him and said I never wanted to speak to him again. Man, I was stupid. My life got worse after that.

Every night I would ask God to let me die. I planned my death many times and took overdoses of medicine. I even ran out into traffic once. But something happened that gave me my hope back—God became real to me. Through him, I found hope in my life once more.

My life-changing encounter with God actually started on a bad day. I don't remember all that happened, but I do know that I had taken a knife with me to school to use in self-defense. I planned to hurt a girl who had bullied me the most. But I never brought the knife out. I don't think I saw that girl the entire day.

Later that night, I lay in bed awake with my eyes closed. I'm not sure if I had a dream or a vision, but I found myself standing in a field. A man walked up to me who I didn't recognize but whose words spoke into my heart. He said, "Shayleen, what you're planning to do—don't. God loves you and is always there for you." When I awoke, I found myself sitting up, huddled in a corner, overwhelmed that someone cared for me like that. Not long after, someone told me about Jesus, and I realized the words I had heard that day sounded like they had come from him. I turned to him and began a long journey of letting him restore my shattered life. Now I tell others about my battle and how God brought me hope.

SIMEON'S DESCENDANTS

24 Simeon's sons: Nemuel, Jamin, Jarib,
Zerah, and Shaul;
25 Shaul's sons: his son Shallum, his son
Mibsam, and his son Mishma.
26 Mishma's sons: his son Hammuel, his
son Zaccur, and his son Shimei.

27 Shimei had sixteen sons and six daughters, but his brothers did not have many
children, so their whole family did not become as numerous as the Judeans. 28 They
lived in Beer-sheba, Moladah, Hazar-
shual, 29 Bilhah, Ezem, Tolad, 30 Bethuel,
Hormah, Ziklag, 31 Beth-marcaboth, Hazar-
susim, Beth-biri, and Shaaraim. These
were their cities until David became king.
32 Their villages were Etam, Ain, Rimmon,
Tochen, and Ashan — five cities, 33 and all
their surrounding villages as far as Baal.
These were their settlements, and they
kept a genealogical record for themselves.

34 Meshobab, Jamlech, Joshah son of
Amaziah,
35 Joel, Jehu son of Joshibiah, son of
Seraiah, son of Asiel,
36 Elioenai, Jaakobah, Jeshohaiah, Asaiah,
Adiel, Jesimiel, Benaiah, 37 and Ziza son of
Shiphi, son of Allon, son of Jedaiah, son
of Shimri, son of Shemaiah —

38 these mentioned by name were leaders
in their families. Their ancestral houses
increased greatly. 39 They went to the
entrance of Gedor, to the east side of the
valley to seek pasture for their flocks.
40 They found rich, good pasture, and the
land was broad, peaceful, and quiet, for
some Hamites had lived there previously.

41 These who were recorded by name came
in the days of King Hezekiah of Judah, attacked the Hamites' tents and the Meunites
who were found there, and set them apart
for destruction, as they are today. Then they
settled in their place because there was pasture for their flocks. 42 Now five hundred
men from these sons of Simeon went with
Pelatiah, Neariah, Rephaiah, and Uzziel, the

descendants of Ishi, as their leaders to Mount
Seir. 43 They struck down the remnant of the
Amalekites who had escaped, and they still
live there today.

REUBEN'S DESCENDANTS

5 These were the sons of Reuben the firstborn of Israel. He was the firstborn, but
his birthright was given to the sons of Joseph
son of Israel, because Reuben defiled his father's bed. He is not listed in the genealogy
according to birthright. 2 Although Judah
became strong among his brothers and a
ruler came from him, the birthright was giv-
en to Joseph.

3 The sons of Reuben, Israel's firstborn:
Hanoch, Pallu, Hezron, and Carmi.
4 Joel's sons: his son Shemaiah,
his son Gog, his son Shimei,
5 his son Micah, his son Reaiah,
his son Baal, 6 and his son Beerah.

Beerah was a leader of the Reubenites, and
King Tiglath-pileser[A] of Assyria took him into
exile. 7 His relatives by their families as they
are recorded in their family records:
Jeiel the chief, Zechariah,
8 and Bela son of Azaz,
son of Shema, son of Joel.
They settled in Aroer as far as Nebo and
Baal-meon. 9 They also settled in the east as
far as the edge of the desert that extends to
the Euphrates River, because their herds had
increased in the land of Gilead. 10 During Saul's
reign they waged war against the Hagrites,
who were defeated by their power. And they
lived in their tents throughout the region east
of Gilead.

GAD'S DESCENDANTS

11 The sons of Gad lived next to them in
the land of Bashan as far as Salecah:
12 Joel the chief, Shapham the second in
command, Janai, and Shaphat in Bashan.
13 Their relatives according to their
ancestral houses: Michael, Meshullam,
Sheba, Jorai, Jacan, Zia, and Eber —
seven.
14 These were the sons of Abihail son of
Huri,
son of Jaroah, son of Gilead,
son of Michael, son of Jeshishai,
son of Jahdo, son of Buz.
15 Ahi son of Abdiel, son of Guni, was
head of their ancestral family.[B] 16 They
lived in Gilead, in Bashan and its
surrounding villages, and throughout
the pasturelands of Sharon. 17 All of
them were registered in the genealogies
during the reigns of Judah's King Jotham
and Israel's King Jeroboam.

18 The descendants of Reuben and Gad and
half the tribe of Manasseh had 44,760 warriors who could serve in the army — men
who carried shield and sword, drew the bow,
and were trained for war. 19 They waged war
against the Hagrites, Jetur, Naphish, and
Nodab. 20 They received help against these
enemies because they cried out to God in
battle, and the Hagrites and all their allies
were handed over to them. He was receptive
to their prayer because they trusted in him.
21 They captured the Hagrites' livestock — fifty
thousand of their camels, two hundred fifty
thousand sheep, and two thousand donkeys
— as well as one hundred thousand people.
22 Many of the Hagrites were killed because
it was God's battle. And they lived there in
the Hagrites' place until the exile.

HALF THE TRIBE OF MANASSEH

23 The descendants of half the tribe of Manasseh settled in the land from Bashan to
Baal-hermon (that is, Senir or Mount Hermon); they were numerous. 24 These were
the heads of their ancestral families: Epher,
Ishi, Eliel, Azriel, Jeremiah, Hodaviah, and
Jahdiel. They were valiant warriors, famous
men, and heads of their ancestral houses.
25 But they were unfaithful to the God of
their ancestors. They prostituted themselves with the gods of the nations[C] God
had destroyed before them. 26 So the God
of Israel roused the spirit of King Pul (that
is, Tiglath-pileser[D]) of Assyria, and he took
the Reubenites, Gadites, and half the tribe of
Manasseh into exile. He took them to Halah,
Habor, Hara, and Gozan's river, where they
are until today.

THE LEVITES

6 Levi's sons: Gershom,[E] Kohath,
and Merari.
2 Kohath's sons: Amram, Izhar, Hebron,
and Uzziel.

[A] 5:6 LXX; MT reads *Tilgath-pilneser* [B] 5:15 Lit *the house of their fathers*, also in v. 24 [C] 5:25 Lit *the peoples of the land*
[D] 5:26 LXX; MT reads *Tilgath-pilneser* [E] 6:1 In Hb Levi's son's name is spelled "Gershon" here and many other places

3 Amram's children: Aaron, Moses,
and Miriam.
Aaron's sons: Nadab, Abihu, Eleazar,
and Ithamar.
4 Eleazar fathered Phinehas;
Phinehas fathered Abishua;
5 Abishua fathered Bukki;
Bukki fathered Uzzi;
6 Uzzi fathered Zerahiah;
Zerahiah fathered Meraioth;
7 Meraioth fathered Amariah;
Amariah fathered Ahitub;
8 Ahitub fathered Zadok;
Zadok fathered Ahimaaz;
9 Ahimaaz fathered Azariah;
Azariah fathered Johanan;
10 Johanan fathered Azariah, who served
as priest in the temple that Solomon
built in Jerusalem;
11 Azariah fathered Amariah;
Amariah fathered Ahitub;
12 Ahitub fathered Zadok;
Zadok fathered Shallum;
13 Shallum fathered Hilkiah;
Hilkiah fathered Azariah;
14 Azariah fathered Seraiah;
and Seraiah fathered Jehozadak.
15 Jehozadak went into exile when the
LORD sent Judah and Jerusalem
into exile at the hands of
Nebuchadnezzar.

16 Levi's sons: Gershom, Kohath,
and Merari.
17 These are the names
of Gershom's sons: Libni and Shimei.
18 Kohath's sons: Amram, Izhar, Hebron
and Uzziel.
19 Merari's sons: Mahli and Mushi.
These are the Levites' families
according to their fathers:
20 Of Gershom: his son Libni,
his son Jahath, his son Zimmah,
21 his son Joah, his son Iddo,
his son Zerah, and his son Jeatherai.
22 Kohath's sons: his son Amminadab,
his son Korah, his son Assir,
23 his son Elkanah, his son Ebiasaph,
his son Assir, 24 his son Tahath,
his son Uriel, his son Uzziah,
and his son Shaul.
25 Elkanah's sons: Amasai and Ahimoth,
26 his son Elkanah, his son Zophai,
his son Nahath, 27 his son Eliab,
his son Jeroham, and his son Elkanah.
28 Samuel's sons: his firstborn Joel,[A]
and his second son Abijah.
29 Merari's sons: Mahli, his son Libni,
his son Shimei, his son Uzzah,
30 his son Shimea, his son Haggiah,
and his son Asaiah.

THE MUSICIANS

31 These are the men David put in charge of
the music in the LORD's temple after the ark
came to rest there. 32 They ministered with
song in front of the tabernacle, the tent of
meeting, until Solomon built the LORD's temple in Jerusalem, and they performed their
task according to the regulations given to
them. 33 These are the men who served with
their sons.
From the Kohathites:
Heman the singer,
son of Joel, son of Samuel,
34 son of Elkanah, son of Jeroham,
son of Eliel, son of Toah,
35 son of Zuph, son of Elkanah,
son of Mahath, son of Amasai,
36 son of Elkanah, son of Joel,
son of Azariah, son of Zephaniah,
37 son of Tahath, son of Assir,
son of Ebiasaph, son of Korah,
38 son of Izhar, son of Kohath,
son of Levi, son of Israel.

39 Heman's relative was Asaph,
who stood at his right hand:
Asaph son of Berechiah,
son of Shimea,
40 son of Michael, son of Baaseiah,
son of Malchijah, 41 son of Ethni,
son of Zerah, son of Adaiah,
42 son of Ethan, son of Zimmah,
son of Shimei, 43 son of Jahath,
son of Gershom, son of Levi.

44 On the left, their relatives were
Merari's sons:
Ethan son of Kishi, son of Abdi,
son of Malluch, 45 son of Hashabiah,
son of Amaziah, son of Hilkiah,
46 son of Amzi, son of Bani,
son of Shemer, 47 son of Mahli,
son of Mushi, son of Merari,
son of Levi.

[A] 6:28 Some LXX mss, Syr, Arabic; other Hb mss omit *Joel*; 1Sm 8:2

AARON'S DESCENDANTS

48 Their relatives, the Levites, were assigned to
all the service of the tabernacle, God's temple.
49 But Aaron and his sons did all the work of
the most holy place. They presented the offerings on the altar of burnt offerings and on
the altar of incense to make atonement for
Israel according to all that Moses the servant
of God had commanded.

50 These are Aaron's sons: his son Eleazar,
his son Phinehas, his son Abishua,
51 his son Bukki, his son Uzzi,
his son Zerahiah, 52 his son Meraioth,
his son Amariah, his son Ahitub,
53 his son Zadok, and his son Ahimaaz.

THE SETTLEMENTS OF THE LEVITES

54 These were the places assigned to Aaron's
descendants from the Kohathite family for
their settlements in their territory, because the
first lot was for them. 55 They were given Hebron in the land of Judah and its surrounding
pasturelands, 56 but the fields and settlements
around the city were given to Caleb son of Jephunneh. 57 Aaron's descendants were given:
Hebron (a city of refuge), Libnah and its
pasturelands, Jattir, Eshtemoa and its pasturelands, 58 Hilen[A] and its pasturelands,
Debir and its pasturelands, 59 Ashan and its
pasturelands, and Beth-shemesh and its
pasturelands. 60 From the tribe of Benjamin they were given Geba and its pasturelands, Alemeth and its pasturelands, and
Anathoth and its pasturelands. They had
thirteen towns in all among their families.

61 To the rest of the Kohathites, ten towns
from half the tribe of Manasseh were assigned
by lot.
62 The Gershomites were assigned thirteen
towns from the tribes of Issachar, Asher, Naphtali, and Manasseh in Bashan according to
their families.
63 The Merarites were assigned by lot twelve
towns from the tribes of Reuben, Gad, and
Zebulun according to their families. 64 So the
Israelites gave these towns and their pasturelands to the Levites. 65 They assigned by lot
the towns named above from the tribes of the
descendants of Judah, Simeon, and Benjamin.
66 Some of the families of the Kohathites
were given towns from the tribe of Ephraim
for their territory:
67 Shechem (a city of refuge) with its pasturelands in the hill country of Ephraim,
Gezer and its pasturelands, 68 Jokmeam
and its pasturelands, Beth-horon and its
pasturelands, 69 Aijalon and its pasturelands, and Gath-rimmon and its pasturelands. 70 From half the tribe of Manasseh,
Aner and its pasturelands, and Bileam
and its pasturelands were given to the
rest of the families of the Kohathites.

71 The Gershomites received:
Golan in Bashan and its pasturelands, and
Ashtaroth and its pasturelands from the
families of half the tribe of Manasseh.
72 From the tribe of Issachar they received
Kedesh and its pasturelands, Daberath
and its pasturelands, 73 Ramoth and its
pasturelands, and Anem and its pasturelands. 74 From the tribe of Asher they
received Mashal and its pasturelands, Abdon and its pasturelands, 75 Hukok and its
pasturelands, and Rehob and its pasturelands. 76 From the tribe of Naphtali they
received Kedesh in Galilee and its pasturelands, Hammon and its pasturelands,
and Kiriathaim and its pasturelands.

77 The rest of the Merarites received:
From the tribe of Zebulun they received
Rimmono and its pasturelands and Tabor
and its pasturelands. 78 From the tribe
of Reuben across the Jordan at Jericho,
to the east of the Jordan, they received
Bezer in the desert and its pasturelands,
Jahzah and its pasturelands, 79 Kedemoth
and its pasturelands, and Mephaath and
its pasturelands. 80 From the tribe of Gad
they received Ramoth in Gilead and its
pasturelands, Mahanaim and its pasturelands, 81 Heshbon and its pasturelands,
and Jazer and its pasturelands.

ISSACHAR'S DESCENDANTS

7 Issachar's sons: Tola, Puah, Jashub, and
Shimron — four.
2 Tola's sons: Uzzi, Rephaiah, Jeriel,
Jahmai, Ibsam, and Shemuel, the heads of
their ancestral families.[B] During David's
reign, 22,600 descendants of Tola were
recorded as valiant warriors in their
family records.
3 Uzzi's son: Izrahiah.

[A] 6:58 Some Hb mss, LXX; other Hb mss read *Hilez* [B] 7:2 Lit *the house of their fathers*, also in vv. 4,7,9,40

Izrahiah's sons: Michael, Obadiah, Joel,
Isshiah. All five of them were chiefs.
4 Along with them, they had 36,000
troops for battle according to the family
records of their ancestral families, for
they had many wives and children. 5 Their
tribesmen who were valiant warriors
belonging to all the families of Issachar
totaled 87,000 in their genealogies.

BENJAMIN'S DESCENDANTS

6 Three of Benjamin's sons: Bela, Becher,
and Jediael.
7 Bela's sons: Ezbon, Uzzi, Uzziel, Jerimoth,
and Iri — five. They were valiant warriors
and heads of their ancestral families;
22,034 were listed in their genealogies.
8 Becher's sons: Zemirah, Joash, Eliezer,
Elioenai, Omri, Jeremoth, Abijah,
Anathoth, and Alemeth; all these were
Becher's sons. 9 Their family records
were recorded according to the heads of
their ancestral families — 20,200 valiant
warriors.
10 Jediael's son: Bilhan.
Bilhan's sons: Jeush, Benjamin, Ehud,
Chenaanah, Zethan, Tarshish, and
Ahishahar. 11 All these sons of Jediael
listed by family heads were valiant
warriors; there were 17,200 who could
serve in the army. 12 Shuppim and
Huppim were sons of Ir, and the Hushim
were the sons of Aher.

NAPHTALI'S DESCENDANTS

13 Naphtali's sons: Jahziel, Guni, Jezer, and
Shallum — Bilhah's sons.

MANASSEH'S DESCENDANTS

14 Manasseh's sons through his Aramean
concubine: Asriel and Machir the father
of Gilead. 15 Machir took wives from
Huppim and Shuppim. The name of his
sister was Maacah. Another descendant
was named Zelophehad, but he had only
daughters.
16 Machir's wife Maacah gave birth to
a son, and she named him Peresh. His
brother was named Sheresh, and his sons
were Ulam and Rekem.
17 Ulam's son: Bedan. These were the
sons of Gilead son of Machir, son of
Manasseh. 18 His sister Hammolecheth
gave birth to Ishhod, Abiezer, and
Mahlah.
19 Shemida's sons: Ahian, Shechem, Likhi,
and Aniam.

EPHRAIM'S DESCENDANTS

20 Ephraim's sons: Shuthelah, and
his son Bered,
his son Tahath, his son Eleadah,
his son Tahath, 21 his son Zabad,
his son Shuthelah, also Ezer,
and Elead.

The men of Gath, born in the land, killed
them because they went down to raid
their cattle. 22 Their father Ephraim
mourned a long time, and his relatives[A]
came to comfort him. 23 He slept with
his wife, and she conceived and gave
birth to a son. So he named him Beriah,
because there had been misfortune in his
home.[B] 24 His daughter was Sheerah, who
built Lower and Upper Beth-horon and
Uzzen-sheerah,

25 his son Rephah,[C] his son Resheph,
his son Telah, his son Tahan,
26 his son Ladan, his son Ammihud,
his son Elishama, 27 his son Nun,
and his son Joshua.

28 Their holdings and settlements were
Bethel and its surrounding villages;
Naaran to the east, Gezer and its villages to the west, and Shechem and its
villages as far as Ayyah and its villages,
29 and along the borders of the descendants of Manasseh, Beth-shean, Taanach,
Megiddo, and Dor with their surrounding
villages. The sons of Joseph son of Israel
lived in these towns.

ASHER'S DESCENDANTS

30 Asher's sons: Imnah, Ishvah, Ishvi, and
Beriah, with their sister Serah.
31 Beriah's sons: Heber, and Malchiel, who
fathered Birzaith.
32 Heber fathered Japhlet, Shomer, and
Hotham, with their sister Shua.
33 Japhlet's sons: Pasach, Bimhal, and
Ashvath. These were Japhlet's sons.
34 Shemer's sons: Ahi, Rohgah, Hubbah,
and Aram.

[A] **7:22** Or *his brothers* [B] **7:23** In Hb, the name *Beriah* sounds like "in misfortune." [C] **7:25** Probably Ephraim's son

35 His brother Helem's sons: Zophah,
Imna, Shelesh, and Amal.
36 Zophah's sons: Suah, Harnepher, Shual,
Beri, Imrah, 37 Bezer, Hod, Shamma,
Shilshah, Ithran, and Beera.
38 Jether's sons: Jephunneh, Pispa, and Ara.
39 Ulla's sons: Arah, Hanniel, and Rizia.
40 All these were Asher's descendants.
They were the heads of their ancestral
families, chosen men, valiant warriors,
and chiefs among the leaders. The
number of men listed in their genealogies
for military service was 26,000.

BENJAMIN'S DESCENDANTS

8 Benjamin fathered Bela, his firstborn;
Ashbel was born second, Aharah third,
2 Nohah fourth, and Rapha fifth.
3 Bela's sons: Addar, Gera, Abihud,[A]
4 Abishua, Naaman, Ahoah, 5 Gera,
Shephuphan, and Huram.
6 These were Ehud's sons, who were
the heads of the families living in Geba
and who were deported to Manahath:
7 Naaman, Ahijah, and Gera. Gera
deported them and was the father of Uzza
and Ahihud.
8 Shaharaim had sons in the territory of
Moab after he had divorced his wives
Hushim and Baara. 9 His sons by his wife
Hodesh: Jobab, Zibia, Mesha, Malcam,
10 Jeuz, Sachia, and Mirmah. These were
his sons, family heads. 11 He also had sons
by Hushim: Abitub and Elpaal.
12 Elpaal's sons: Eber, Misham, and
Shemed who built Ono and Lod and its
surrounding villages, 13 Beriah and Shema,
who were the family heads of Aijalon's
residents and who drove out the residents
of Gath, 14 Ahio,[B] Shashak, and Jeremoth.
15 Zebadiah, Arad, Eder, 16 Michael, Ishpah,
and Joha were Beriah's sons.
17 Zebadiah, Meshullam, Hizki, Heber,
18 Ishmerai, Izliah, and Jobab were
Elpaal's sons.
19 Jakim, Zichri, Zabdi, 20 Elienai, Zillethai,
Eliel, 21 Adaiah, Beraiah, and Shimrath
were Shimei's sons.
22 Ishpan, Eber, Eliel, 23 Abdon, Zichri,
Hanan, 24 Hananiah, Elam, Anthothijah,
25 Iphdeiah, and Penuel were Shashak's
sons.
26 Shamsherai, Shehariah, Athaliah,
27 Jaareshiah, Elijah, and Zichri were
Jeroham's sons.
28 These were family heads, chiefs
according to their family records; they
lived in Jerusalem.

29 Jeiel[C] fathered Gibeon and lived in
Gibeon. His wife's name was Maacah.
30 Abdon was his firstborn son, then Zur,
Kish, Baal, Nadab, 31 Gedor, Ahio, Zecher,
32 and Mikloth who fathered Shimeah.
These also lived opposite their relatives
in Jerusalem, with their other relatives.
33 Ner fathered Kish, Kish fathered Saul,
and Saul fathered Jonathan, Malchishua,
Abinadab, and Esh-baal.[D]
34 Jonathan's son was Merib-baal,[E] and
Merib-baal fathered Micah.
35 Micah's sons: Pithon, Melech, Tarea,
and Ahaz.
36 Ahaz fathered Jehoaddah, Jehoaddah
fathered Alemeth, Azmaveth, and Zimri,
and Zimri fathered Moza.
37 Moza fathered Binea. His son was
Raphah, his son Elasah, and his son Azel.
38 Azel had six sons, and these were their
names: Azrikam, Bocheru, Ishmael,
Sheariah, Obadiah, and Hanan. All these
were Azel's sons.
39 His brother Eshek's sons: Ulam was his
firstborn, Jeush second, and Eliphelet third.
40 Ulam's sons were valiant warriors
and archers.[F] They had many sons and
grandsons — 150 of them.
All these were among Benjamin's sons.

AFTER THE EXILE

9 All Israel was registered in the genealogies
that are written in the Book of the Kings of
Israel. But Judah was exiled to Babylon because
of their unfaithfulness. 2 The first to live in their
towns on their own property again were Israelites, priests, Levites, and temple servants.
3 These people from the descendants
of Judah, Benjamin, Ephraim, and
Manasseh settled in Jerusalem:
4 Uthai son of Ammihud, son of Omri,
son of Imri, son of Bani, a descendant[G] of
Perez son of Judah;
5 from the Shilonites:
Asaiah the firstborn and his sons;
6 and from the descendants of Zerah:
Jeuel and their relatives — 690 in all.

[A] **8:3** Or *Gera father of Ehud*; Jdg 3:15 [B] **8:13-14** LXX reads *Gath* [14] *and their brother* [C] **8:29** LXX; MT omits *Jeiel*; 1Ch 9:35
[D] **8:33** = Man of Baal [E] **8:34** = Baal Contends [F] **8:40** Lit *valiant ones who string the bow* [G] **9:4** Lit *Bani, from the sons*

[7]The Benjaminites: Sallu son of
Meshullam, son of Hodaviah, son of
Hassenuah;
[8]Ibneiah son of Jeroham;
Elah son of Uzzi, son of Michri;
Meshullam son of Shephatiah, son of
Reuel, son of Ibnijah;
[9]and their relatives according to their
family records — 956 in all. All these men
were heads of their ancestral families.[A]

[10]The priests: Jedaiah; Jehoiarib; Jachin;
[11]Azariah son of Hilkiah, son of
Meshullam, son of Zadok, son of
Meraioth, son of Ahitub, the chief official
of God's temple;
[12]Adaiah son of Jeroham, son of Pashhur,
son of Malchijah;
Maasai son of Adiel, son of Jahzerah, son
of Meshullam, son of Meshillemith, son
of Immer;
[13]and their relatives, the heads of their
ancestral families — 1,760 in all. They
were capable men employed in the
ministry of God's temple.

[14]The Levites: Shemaiah son of Hasshub,
son of Azrikam, son of Hashabiah of the
Merarites;
[15]Bakbakkar, Heresh, Galal, and
Mattaniah, son of Mica, son of Zichri, son
of Asaph;
[16]Obadiah son of Shemaiah, son of Galal,
son of Jeduthun;
and Berechiah son of Asa, son of Elkanah
who lived in the settlements of the
Netophathites.

[17]The gatekeepers: Shallum, Akkub,
Talmon, Ahiman, and their relatives.
Shallum was their chief; [18]he was
previously stationed at the King's Gate on
the east side. These were the gatekeepers
from the camp of the Levites.
[19]Shallum son of Kore, son of Ebiasaph,
son of Korah and his relatives from his
father's family,[B] the Korahites, were
assigned to guard the thresholds of the
tent.[C] Their ancestors had been assigned
to the LORD's camp as guardians of the
entrance. [20]In earlier times Phinehas son
of Eleazar had been their leader, and the
LORD was with him. [21]Zechariah son of
Meshelemiah was the gatekeeper at the
entrance to the tent of meeting.

[22]The total number of those chosen to be
gatekeepers at the thresholds was 212. They
were registered by genealogy in their settlements. David and the seer Samuel had
appointed them to their trusted positions.
[23]So they and their sons were assigned as
guards to the gates of the LORD's temple,
which had been the tent-temple. [24]The gatekeepers were on the four sides: east, west,
north, and south. [25]Their relatives came from
their settlements at fixed times to be with
them seven days, [26]but the four chief gatekeepers, who were Levites, were entrusted
with the rooms and the treasuries of God's
temple. [27]They spent the night in the vicinity of God's temple, because they had guard
duty and were in charge of opening it every
morning.
[28]Some of them were in charge of the utensils used in worship. They would count them
when they brought them in and when they
took them out. [29]Others were put in charge
of the furnishings and all the utensils of the
sanctuary, as well as the fine flour, wine, oil,
incense, and spices. [30]Some of the priests'
sons mixed the spices. [31]A Levite called Mattithiah, the firstborn of Shallum the Korahite,
was entrusted with baking the bread.[D] [32]Some
of the Kohathites' relatives were responsible
for preparing the rows of the Bread of the
Presence every Sabbath.
[33]The singers, the heads of the Levite families, stayed in the temple chambers and were
exempt from other tasks because they were on
duty day and night. [34]These were the heads of
the Levite families, chiefs according to their
family records; they lived in Jerusalem.

SAUL'S FAMILY

[35]Jeiel fathered Gibeon and lived in
Gibeon. His wife's name was Maacah.
[36]Abdon was his firstborn son, then
Zur, Kish, Baal, Ner, Nadab, [37]Gedor,
Ahio, Zechariah, and Mikloth. [38]Mikloth
fathered Shimeam. These also lived
opposite their relatives in Jerusalem with
their other relatives.
[39]Ner fathered Kish, Kish fathered Saul,
and Saul fathered Jonathan, Malchishua,
Abinadab, and Esh-baal.

[A] **9:9** Lit *the house of their fathers*, also in v. 13 [B] **9:19** Lit *the house of his father* [C] **9:19** = the temple [D] **9:31** Lit *with things prepared in pans*

40 Jonathan's son was Merib-baal, and
Merib-baal fathered Micah.
41 Micah's sons: Pithon, Melech, Tahrea,
and Ahaz.[A]
42 Ahaz fathered Jarah;
Jarah fathered Alemeth, Azmaveth, and
Zimri;
Zimri fathered Moza.
43 Moza fathered Binea.
His son was Rephaiah, his son Elasah,
and his son Azel.
44 Azel had six sons, and these were their
names: Azrikam, Bocheru, Ishmael,
Sheariah, Obadiah, and Hanan. These
were Azel's sons.

THE DEATH OF SAUL AND HIS SONS

10 The Philistines fought against Israel, and Israel's men fled from them.
Many were killed on Mount Gilboa. 2 The
Philistines pursued Saul and his sons and
killed his sons Jonathan, Abinadab, and
Malchishua. 3 When the battle intensified
against Saul, the archers spotted him and
severely wounded him. 4 Then Saul said to
his armor-bearer, "Draw your sword and
run me through with it, or these uncircumcised men will come and torture me." But
his armor-bearer would not do it because
he was terrified. Then Saul took his sword
and fell on it. 5 When his armor-bearer saw
that Saul was dead, he also fell on his own
sword and died. 6 So Saul and his three sons
died — his whole house died together.
7 When all the men of Israel in the valley
saw that the army had fled and that Saul and
his sons were dead, they abandoned their
cities and fled. So the Philistines came and
settled in them.
8 The next day when the Philistines came to
strip the slain, they found Saul and his sons
dead on Mount Gilboa. 9 They stripped Saul,
cut off his head, took his armor, and sent messengers throughout the land of the Philistines
to spread the good news to their idols and
the people. 10 Then they put his armor in the
temple of their gods and hung his skull in the
temple of Dagon.
11 When all Jabesh-gilead heard of everything the Philistines had done to Saul, 12 all
their brave men set out and retrieved the
body of Saul and the bodies of his sons and
brought them to Jabesh. They buried their
bones under the oak[B] in Jabesh and fasted
seven days.
13 Saul died for his unfaithfulness to the LORD
because he did not keep the LORD's word. He
even consulted a medium for guidance, 14 but
he did not inquire of the LORD. So the LORD put
him to death and turned the kingdom over to
David son of Jesse.

DAVID'S ANOINTING AS KING

11 All Israel came together to David at Hebron and said, "Here we are, your own
flesh and blood.[C] 2 Even previously when
Saul was king, you were leading Israel out
to battle and bringing us back. The LORD your
God also said to you, 'You will shepherd my
people Israel, and you will be ruler over my
people Israel.' "
3 So all the elders of Israel came to the king
at Hebron. David made a covenant with them
at Hebron in the LORD's presence, and they
anointed David king over Israel, in keeping
with the LORD's word through Samuel.

DAVID'S CAPTURE OF JERUSALEM

4 David and all Israel marched to Jerusalem
(that is, Jebus); the Jebusites who inhabited
the land were there. 5 The inhabitants of Jebus
said to David, "You will never get in here." Yet
David did capture the stronghold of Zion, that
is, the city of David.
6 David said, "Whoever is the first to kill a
Jebusite will become chief commander." Joab
son of Zeruiah went up first, so he became
the chief.
7 Then David took up residence in the stronghold; therefore, it was called the city of David.
8 He built up the city all the way around, from
the supporting terraces to the surrounding
parts, and Joab restored the rest of the city.
9 David steadily grew more powerful, and the
LORD of Armies was with him.

EXPLOITS OF DAVID'S WARRIORS

10 The following were the chiefs of David's
warriors who, together with all Israel, strongly
supported him in his reign to make him king
according to the LORD's word about Israel.
11 This is the list of David's warriors:
Jashobeam son of Hachmoni was chief of
the Thirty;[D] he wielded his spear against three
hundred and killed them at one time.
12 After him, Eleazar son of Dodo the Ahohite

[A] **9:41** LXX, Syr, Tg, Vg, Arabic; MT omits *and Ahaz*; 1Ch 8:35 [B] **10:12** Or *terebinth*, or *large tree* [C] **11:1** Lit *your bone and your flesh* [D] **11:11** Alt Hb tradition reads *Three*

was one of the three warriors. 13 He was with
David at Pas-dammim when the Philistines had
gathered there for battle. There was a portion
of a field full of barley, where the troops had
fled from the Philistines. 14 But Eleazar and
David[A] took their stand in the middle of the
field and defended it. They killed the Philistines, and the LORD gave them a great victory.
15 Three of the thirty chief men went down
to David, to the rock at the cave of Adullam,
while the Philistine army was encamped in the
Valley of Rephaim. 16 At that time David was in
the stronghold, and a Philistine garrison was
at Bethlehem. 17 David was extremely thirsty[B]
and said, "If only someone would bring me
water to drink from the well at the city gate
of Bethlehem!" 18 So the Three broke through
the Philistine camp and drew water from the
well at the gate of Bethlehem. They brought
it back to David, but he refused to drink it.
Instead, he poured it out to the LORD. 19 David said, "I would never do such a thing in
the presence of my God! How can I drink the
blood of these men who risked their lives?"
For they brought it at the risk of their lives. So
he would not drink it. Such were the exploits
of the three warriors.
20 Abishai, Joab's brother, was the leader of
the Three.[C] He raised his spear against three
hundred men and killed them, gaining a reputation among the Three. 21 He was more honored
than the Three and became their commander
even though he did not become one of the Three.
22 Benaiah son of Jehoiada was the son of a
brave man[D] from Kabzeel, a man of many exploits. Benaiah killed two sons of Ariel of Moab,[E]
and he went down into a pit on a snowy day and
killed a lion. 23 He also killed an Egyptian who
was seven and a half feet tall.[F] Even though the
Egyptian had a spear in his hand like a weaver's
beam, Benaiah went down to him with a club,
snatched the spear out of the Egyptian's hand,
and then killed him with his own spear. 24 These
were the exploits of Benaiah son of Jehoiada,
who had a reputation among the three warriors.
25 He was the most honored of the Thirty, but
he did not become one of the Three. David put
him in charge of his bodyguard.

26 The best soldiers were
Joab's brother Asahel,
Elhanan son of Dodo of Bethlehem,
27 Shammoth the Harorite,
Helez the Pelonite,
28 Ira son of Ikkesh the Tekoite,
Abiezer the Anathothite,
29 Sibbecai the Hushathite,
Ilai the Ahohite,
30 Maharai the Netophathite,
Heled son of Baanah the Netophathite,
31 Ithai son of Ribai from Gibeah
of the Benjaminites,
Benaiah the Pirathonite,
32 Hurai from the wadis of Gaash,
Abiel the Arbathite,
33 Azmaveth the Baharumite,
Eliahba the Shaalbonite,
34 the sons of[G] Hashem the Gizonite,
Jonathan son of Shagee the Hararite,
35 Ahiam son of Sachar the Hararite,
Eliphal son of Ur,
36 Hepher the Mecherathite,
Ahijah the Pelonite,
37 Hezro the Carmelite,
Naarai son of Ezbai,
38 Joel the brother of Nathan,
Mibhar son of Hagri,
39 Zelek the Ammonite,
Naharai the Beerothite, the armor-bearer
for Joab son of Zeruiah,
40 Ira the Ithrite,
Gareb the Ithrite,
41 Uriah the Hethite,
Zabad son of Ahlai,
42 Adina son of Shiza the Reubenite,
chief of the Reubenites, and thirty
with him,
43 Hanan son of Maacah,
Joshaphat the Mithnite,
44 Uzzia the Ashterathite,
Shama and Jeiel the sons of Hotham
the Aroerite,
45 Jediael son of Shimri and his brother
Joha the Tizite,
46 Eliel the Mahavite,
Jeribai and Joshaviah, the sons
of Elnaam,
Ithmah the Moabite,
47 Eliel, Obed, and Jaasiel the Mezobaite.

DAVID'S FIRST SUPPORTERS

12 The following were the men who came to
David at Ziklag while he was still banned
from the presence of Saul son of Kish. They
were among the warriors who helped him in
battle. 2 They were archers who could use either the right or left hand, both to sling stones

[A] 11:14 Lit *But they* [B] 11:17 Lit *And David craved* [C] 11:20 Syr reads *Thirty* [D] 11:22 Or *was a valiant man* [E] 11:22 Or *He killed two Moabite warriors* [F] 11:23 Lit *who measured five cubits* [G] 11:34 LXX omits *the sons of*; 2Sm 23:32

and shoot arrows from a bow. They were Saul's
relatives from Benjamin:

3 Their chief was Ahiezer son of Shemaah
the Gibeathite.
Then there was his brother Joash;
Jeziel and Pelet sons of Azmaveth;
Beracah, Jehu the Anathothite;
4 Ishmaiah the Gibeonite, a warrior among
the Thirty and a leader over the Thirty;
Jeremiah, Jahaziel, Johanan, Jozabad the
Gederathite;
5 Eluzai, Jerimoth, Bealiah, Shemariah,
Shephatiah the Haruphite;
6 Elkanah, Isshiah, Azarel, Joezer, and
Jashobeam, the Korahites;
7 and Joelah and Zebadiah, the sons of
Jeroham from Gedor.

8 Some Gadites defected to David at his
stronghold in the desert. They were valiant
warriors, trained for battle, expert with shield
and spear. Their faces were like the faces of
lions, and they were as swift as gazelles on
the mountains.

9 Ezer was the chief, Obadiah second,
Eliab third,
10 Mishmannah fourth, Jeremiah fifth,
11 Attai sixth, Eliel seventh,
12 Johanan eighth, Elzabad ninth,
13 Jeremiah tenth, and
Machbannai eleventh.

14 These Gadites were army commanders; the
least of them was a match for a hundred, and
the greatest of them for a thousand. 15 These
are the men who crossed the Jordan in the
first month[A] when it was overflowing all its
banks, and put to flight all those in the valleys
to the east and to the west.

16 Other Benjaminites and men from Judah
also went to David at the stronghold. 17 David
went out to meet them and said to them, "If
you have come in peace to help me, my heart
will be united with you, but if you have come
to betray me to my enemies even though my
hands have done no wrong, may the God of
our ancestors look on it and judge."

18 Then the Spirit enveloped[B] Amasai, chief
of the Thirty, and he said:

We are yours, David,
we are with you, son of Jesse!
Peace, peace to you,
and peace to him who helps you,
for your God helps you.

So David received them and made them leaders of his troops.

19 Some Manassites defected to David when
he went with the Philistines to fight against
Saul. However, they did not help the Philistines
because the Philistine rulers sent David away
after a discussion. They said, "It will be our heads
if he defects to his master Saul." 20 When David
went to Ziklag, some men from Manasseh defected to him: Adnah, Jozabad, Jediael, Michael,
Jozabad, Elihu, and Zillethai, chiefs of thousands
in Manasseh. 21 They helped David against the
raiders, for they were all valiant warriors and
commanders in the army. 22 At that time, men
came day after day to help David until there
was a great army, like an army of God.[C]

DAVID'S SOLDIERS IN HEBRON

23 The numbers of the armed troops who came
to David at Hebron to turn Saul's kingdom
over to him, according to the LORD's word,
were as follows:

24 From the Judahites: 6,800 armed troops
bearing shields and spears.
25 From the Simeonites: 7,100 valiant
warriors ready for war.
26 From the Levites: 4,600 27 in addition
to Jehoiada, leader of the house of
Aaron, with 3,700 men; 28 and Zadok,
a young valiant warrior, with 22
commanders from his father's family.[D]
29 From the Benjaminites, the relatives
of Saul: 3,000 (up to that time
the majority of the Benjaminites
maintained their allegiance to
the house of Saul).
30 From the Ephraimites: 20,800 valiant
warriors who were famous men
in their ancestral families.[E]
31 From half the tribe of Manasseh:
18,000 designated by name to come
and make David king.
32 From the Issacharites, who understood
the times and knew what Israel
should do: 200 chiefs with all their
relatives under their command.
33 From Zebulun: 50,000 who could
serve in the army, trained for battle
with all kinds of weapons of war,
with one purpose to help David.[F]
34 From Naphtali: 1,000 commanders
accompanied by 37,000 men with
shield and spear.

[A] 12:15 = Nisan (March–April) [B] 12:18 Lit *clothed*; Jdg 6:34; 2Ch 24:20 [C] 12:22 Or *like the ultimate army* [D] 12:28 Lit *the house of his father* [E] 12:30 Lit *the house of their fathers* [F] 12:33 LXX; MT omits *David*

35 From the Danites: 28,600 trained for
battle.
36 From Asher: 40,000 who could serve in
the army, trained for battle.
37 From across the Jordan — from the
Reubenites, Gadites, and half the
tribe of Manasseh: 120,000 men
equipped with all the military
weapons of war.

38 All these warriors, lined up in battle formation, came to Hebron wholeheartedly determined to make David king over all Israel.
All the rest of Israel was also of one mind
to make David king. 39 They spent three days
there eating and drinking with David, for their
relatives had provided for them. 40 In addition,
their neighbors from as far away as Issachar,
Zebulun, and Naphtali came and brought food
on donkeys, camels, mules, and oxen — abundant provisions of flour, fig cakes, raisins,
wine and oil, herds, and flocks. Indeed, there
was joy in Israel.

DAVID AND THE ARK

13 David consulted with all his leaders, the
commanders of hundreds and of thousands. 2 Then he said to the whole assembly
of Israel, "If it seems good to you, and if this is
from the LORD our God, let us spread out and
send the message to the rest of our relatives in
all the districts of Israel, including the priests
and Levites in their cities with pasturelands,
that they should gather together with us. 3 Then
let us bring back the ark of our God, for we
did not inquire of him[A] in Saul's days." 4 Since
the proposal seemed right to all the people,
the whole assembly agreed to do it.
5 So David assembled all Israel, from the
Shihor of Egypt to the entrance of Hamath,[B]
to bring the ark of God from Kiriath-jearim.
6 David and all Israel went to Baalah (that is,
Kiriath-jearim that belongs to Judah) to take
from there the ark of God, which bears the
name of the LORD who is enthroned between
the cherubim. 7 At Abinadab's house they set
the ark of God on a new cart. Uzzah and Ahio[C]
were guiding the cart.
8 David and all Israel were dancing with all
their might before God with songs and with
lyres, harps, tambourines, cymbals, and trumpets. 9 When they came to Chidon's threshing floor, Uzzah reached out to hold the ark
because the oxen had stumbled. 10 Then the
LORD's anger burned against Uzzah, and he
struck him dead because he had reached out
to the ark. So he died there in the presence
of God.
11 David was angry because of the LORD's
outburst against Uzzah, so he named that place
Outburst Against Uzzah,[D] as it is still named
today. 12 David feared God that day and said,
"How can I ever bring the ark of God to me?"
13 So David did not bring the ark of God home[E]
to the city of David; instead, he diverted it to
the house of Obed-edom of Gath. 14 The ark
of God remained with Obed-edom's family
in his house for three months, and the LORD
blessed his family and all that he had.

GOD'S BLESSING ON DAVID

14 King Hiram of Tyre sent envoys to David,
along with cedar logs, stonemasons, and
carpenters to build a palace for him. 2 Then
David knew that the LORD had established him
as king over Israel and that his kingdom had
been exalted for the sake of his people Israel.
3 David took more wives in Jerusalem,
and he became the father of more sons and
daughters. 4 These are the names of the children born to him in Jerusalem: Shammua,
Shobab, Nathan, Solomon, 5 Ibhar, Elishua,
Elpelet, 6 Nogah, Nepheg, Japhia, 7 Elishama,
Beeliada, and Eliphelet.
8 When the Philistines heard that David had
been anointed king over all Israel, they all
went in search of David; when David heard
of this, he went out to face them. 9 Now the
Philistines had come and raided in the Valley of Rephaim, 10 so David inquired of God,
"Should I attack the Philistines? Will you hand
them over to me?"
The LORD replied, "Attack, and I will hand
them over to you."
11 So the Israelites went up to Baal-perazim,
and David defeated the Philistines there. Then
David said, "Like a bursting flood, God has
used me to burst out against my enemies."
Therefore, they named that place The Lord
Bursts Out.[F] 12 The Philistines abandoned their
idols there, and David ordered that they be
burned in the fire.
13 Once again the Philistines raided in the
valley. 14 So David again inquired of God, and
God answered him, "Do not pursue them directly. Circle around them and attack them

---

[A] **13:3** Or *did not seek it* [B] **13:5** Or *to Lebo-hamath* [C] **13:7** Or *And his brothers* [D] **13:11** Or *Perez-uzzah* [E] **13:13** Lit *to himself* [F] **14:11** Or *Baal-perazim*

opposite the balsam trees. 15 When you hear
the sound of marching in the tops of the balsam trees, then go out to battle, for God will
have gone out ahead of you to strike down the
army of the Philistines." 16 So David did as God
commanded him, and they struck down the
Philistine army from Gibeon to Gezer. 17 Then
David's fame spread throughout the lands,
and the LORD caused all the nations to be terrified of him.

THE ARK COMES TO JERUSALEM

15 David built houses for himself in the
city of David, and he prepared a place
for the ark of God and pitched a tent for it.
2 Then David said, "No one but the Levites may
carry the ark of God, because the LORD has
chosen them to carry the ark of the LORD and
to minister before him forever."

3 David assembled all Israel at Jerusalem to
bring the ark of the LORD to the place he had
prepared for it. 4 Then he gathered together
the descendants of Aaron and the Levites:

5 From the Kohathites, Uriel the leader and
120 of his relatives; 6 from the Merarites, Asaiah the leader and 220 of his relatives; 7 from
the Gershomites,[A] Joel the leader and 130 of
his relatives; 8 from the Elizaphanites, Shemaiah the leader and 200 of his relatives; 9 from
the Hebronites, Eliel the leader and 80 of his
relatives; 10 from the Uzzielites, Amminadab
the leader and 112 of his relatives.

11 David summoned the priests Zadok and
Abiathar and the Levites Uriel, Asaiah, Joel,
Shemaiah, Eliel, and Amminadab. 12 He said
to them, "You are the heads of the Levite families. You and your relatives must consecrate
yourselves so that you may bring the ark of
the LORD God of Israel to the place I have prepared for it. 13 For the LORD our God burst out
in anger against us because you Levites were
not with us the first time, for we didn't inquire of him about the proper procedures."
14 So the priests and the Levites consecrated
themselves to bring up the ark of the LORD
God of Israel. 15 Then the Levites carried the
ark of God the way Moses had commanded
according to the word of the LORD: on their
shoulders with the poles.

16 Then David told the leaders of the Levites to appoint their relatives as singers
and to have them raise their voices with
joy accompanied by musical instruments
— harps, lyres, and cymbals. 17 So the Levites
appointed Heman son of Joel; from his relatives, Asaph son of Berechiah; and from
their relatives the Merarites, Ethan son of
Kushaiah. 18 With them were their relatives
second in rank: Zechariah, Jaaziel,[B] Shemiramoth, Jehiel, Unni, Eliab, Benaiah, Maaseiah, Mattithiah, Eliphelehu, Mikneiah, and
the gatekeepers Obed-edom and Jeiel. 19 The
singers Heman, Asaph, and Ethan were to
sound the bronze cymbals; 20 Zechariah, Aziel,
Shemiramoth, Jehiel, Unni, Eliab, Maaseiah,
and Benaiah were to play harps according
to *Alamoth*[C] 21 and Mattithiah, Eliphelehu,
Mikneiah, Obed-edom, Jeiel, and Azaziah
were to lead the music with lyres according
to the *Sheminith*. 22 Chenaniah, the leader of
the Levites in music, was to direct the music because he was skillful. 23 Berechiah and
Elkanah were to be gatekeepers for the ark.
24 The priests, Shebaniah, Joshaphat, Nethanel, Amasai, Zechariah, Benaiah, and Eliezer,
were to blow trumpets before the ark of God.
Obed-edom and Jehiah were also to be gatekeepers for the ark.

25 David, the elders of Israel, and the commanders of thousands went with rejoicing
to bring the ark of the covenant of the LORD
from the house of Obed-edom. 26 Because God
helped the Levites who were carrying the ark
of the covenant of the LORD, with God's help,
they sacrificed seven bulls and seven rams.

27 Now David was dressed in a robe of fine
linen, as were all the Levites who were carrying
the ark, as well as the singers and Chenaniah,
the music leader of the singers. David also wore
a linen ephod. 28 So all Israel brought up the
ark of the covenant of the LORD with shouts,
the sound of the ram's horn, trumpets, and
cymbals, and the playing of harps and lyres.
29 As the ark of the covenant of the LORD was
entering the city of David, Saul's daughter
Michal looked down from the window and
saw King David leaping[D] and dancing, and
she despised him in her heart.

16 They brought the ark of God and placed
it inside the tent David had pitched for
it. Then they offered burnt offerings and fellowship offerings in God's presence. 2 When
David had finished offering the burnt offerings and the fellowship offerings, he blessed
the people in the name of the LORD. 3 Then he
distributed to each and every Israelite, both

[A] **15:7** = Gershonites [B] **15:18** Some Hb mss, LXX; other Hb mss read *Zechariah son and Jaaziel* [C] **15:20** This may refer to a high pitch, perhaps a tune sung by soprano voices; the Hb word means "young women"; Ps 46 title [D] **15:29** Or *whirling*

men and women, a loaf of bread, a date cake,
and a raisin cake.
[4] David appointed some of the Levites to be
ministers before the ark of the LORD, to celebrate the LORD God of Israel, and to give thanks
and praise to him. [5] Asaph was the chief and
Zechariah was second to him. Jeiel, Shemiramoth, Jehiel, Mattithiah, Eliab, Benaiah, Obed-
edom, and Jeiel played the harps and lyres, while
Asaph sounded the cymbals [6] and the priests
Benaiah and Jahaziel blew the trumpets regularly before the ark of the covenant of God.

DAVID'S PSALM OF THANKSGIVING

[7] On that day David decreed for the first time
that thanks be given to the LORD by Asaph
and his relatives:

8 Give thanks to the LORD; call on
his name;
proclaim his deeds among the peoples.
9 Sing to him; sing praise to him;
tell about all his wondrous works!
10 Honor his holy name;
let the hearts of those who seek the
LORD rejoice.
11 Seek the LORD and his strength;
seek his face always.
12 Remember the wondrous works
he has done,
his wonders, and the judgments
he has pronounced,[A]
13 you offspring of Israel his servant,
Jacob's descendants —
his chosen ones.
14 He is the LORD our God;
his judgments govern the whole earth.
15 Remember his covenant forever —
the promise he ordained
for a thousand generations,
16 the covenant he made with Abraham,
swore[B] to Isaac,
17 and confirmed to Jacob as a decree,
and to Israel as a permanent covenant:
18 "I will give the land of Canaan to you
as your inherited portion."
19 When they[C] were few in number,
very few indeed, and resident aliens
in Canaan
20 wandering from nation to nation
and from one kingdom to another,
21 he allowed no one to oppress them;
he rebuked kings on their behalf:
22 "Do not touch my anointed ones
or harm my prophets."

23 Let the whole earth sing to the LORD.
Proclaim his salvation from day to day.
24 Declare his glory among the nations,
his wondrous works
among all peoples.

Thanksgiving and Contentment | *Thanksgiving*

GRATITUDE LAUNCH

"Give thanks to the LORD; call on his name; proclaim his deeds among the peoples." 1 Chronicles 16:8

How many of the people you encounter in a typical day seem truly happy? You probably meet some, but here's guessing the majority of the people who cross your path feel blah at best and downright unhappy at worst. Why is this? Are we mere victims of our circumstances? Is our mood contingent on events around us?

The Bible suggests otherwise and recommends—as in this passage—that we practice gratitude. "Give thanks to the LORD." The verb used here literally means "to throw or to shoot a bow." It's a great word picture, people launching expressions of thankfulness to the skies like arrows!

Start each day thanking God for every gift and blessing. Discard the habit of grumbling and develop the habit of thankfulness. As the famed preacher Charles Spurgeon wisely observed, "It's not how much we have, but how much we enjoy, that makes happiness."

For the next note on *Thanksgiving and Contentment*, see 1 Chronicles 16:25.

[A] **16:12** Lit *judgments of his mouth* [B] **16:16** Lit *and his oath* [C] **16:19** One Hb ms, LXX, Vg; other Hb mss read *you*

25 For the LORD is great
and highly praised;
he is feared above all gods.
26 For all the gods of the peoples are idols,
but the LORD made the heavens.
27 Splendor and majesty are before him;
strength and joy are in his place.
28 Ascribe to the LORD, families
of the peoples,
ascribe to the LORD glory and strength.
29 Ascribe to the LORD the glory
of his name;
bring an offering and come before him.
Worship the LORD
in the splendor of his holiness;
30 let the whole earth tremble before him.

The world is firmly established;
it cannot be shaken.
31 Let the heavens be glad and the earth
rejoice,
and let them say among the nations,
"The LORD reigns!"
32 Let the sea and all that fills it resound;
let the fields and everything in them
exult.
33 Then the trees of the forest will shout
for joy before the LORD,
for he is coming to judge the earth.
34 Give thanks to the LORD, for he is good;
his faithful love endures forever.
35 And say: "Save us, God of our salvation;
gather us and rescue us from
the nations
so that we may give thanks to
your holy name
and rejoice in your praise.
36 Blessed be the LORD God of Israel
from everlasting to everlasting."
Then all the people said, "Amen" and "Praise
the LORD."
37 So David left Asaph and his relatives there
before the ark of the LORD's covenant to minister regularly before the ark according to the
daily requirements. 38 He assigned Obed-edom
and his[A] sixty-eight relatives. Obed-edom son
of Jeduthun and Hosah were to be gatekeepers.
39 David left the priest Zadok and his fellow
priests before the tabernacle of the LORD at
the high place in Gibeon 40 to offer burnt offerings regularly, morning and evening, to
the LORD on the altar of burnt offerings and
to do everything that was written in the law
of the LORD, which he had commanded Israel
to keep. 41 With them were Heman, Jeduthun,
and the rest who were chosen and designated by name to give thanks to the LORD — for
his faithful love endures forever. 42 Heman

S Support | *Honest Seeking*

NO TRIVIAL PURSUITS

"Seek the LORD and his strength; seek his face always." 1 Chronicles 16:11

We don't typically wake up and say, "Aha! My lifelong search continues!" but isn't that what each new day consists of?

Look around. Everybody's after something. Some are looking for love and meaning, validation or respect. Some are hunting for bargains and others for truth. Some seek a sign, while others seek satisfaction. Look within your soul. What motivates you? What are you pursuing? A better career? Better health? A bigger paycheck? Some lifelong dream?

Understand that nothing is wrong with any of these pursuits. Yet the Bible invites us to focus on Someone mightier and better than all. In this passage, David urges, "Seek the LORD." And the promise throughout Scripture is that in seeking him and his kingdom first, we'll find everything else (Mt 6:33).

Invite him to be present with you each moment of the day. Seek his counsel first, and absorb his teachings.

For the next note on *Support*, see 2 Chronicles 7:14.

[A] **16:38** LXX, Syr, Vg; Hb reads *their*

and Jeduthun had with them trumpets and
cymbals to play and musical instruments of
God. Jeduthun's sons were at the city gate.
43 Then all the people went home, and David
returned home to bless his household.

THE LORD'S COVENANT WITH DAVID

17 When David had settled into his palace,
he said to the prophet Nathan, "Look! I
am living in a cedar house while the ark of
the LORD's covenant is under tent curtains."
2 So Nathan told David, "Do all that is on
your mind, for God is with you."
3 But that night the word of God came to
Nathan: 4 "Go to David my servant and say,
'This is what the LORD says: You are not the
one to build me a house to dwell in. 5 From
the time I brought Israel out of Egypt until
today I have not dwelt in a house; instead, I
have moved from one tent site to another, and
from one tabernacle location to another.[A] 6 In
all my journeys throughout Israel, have I ever
spoken a word to even one of the judges of
Israel, whom I commanded to shepherd my
people, asking: Why haven't you built me a
house of cedar?'
7 "So now this is what you are to say to my
servant David: 'This is what the LORD of Armies
says: I took you from the pasture, from tending
the flock, to be ruler over my people Israel. 8 I
have been with you wherever you have gone,
and I have destroyed all your enemies before
you. I will make a name for you like that of
the greatest on the earth. 9 I will designate a
place for my people Israel and plant them, so
that they may live there and not be disturbed
again. Evildoers will not continue to oppress
them as they have done 10 ever since the day
I ordered judges to be over my people Israel.
I will also subdue all your enemies.
" 'Furthermore, I declare to you that the LORD
himself will build a house for you. 11 When your
time comes to be with your fathers, I will raise
up after you your descendant, who is one of
your own sons, and I will establish his kingdom. 12 He is the one who will build a house
for me, and I will establish his throne forever.
13 I will be his father, and he will be my son.
I will not remove my faithful love from him
as I removed it from the one who was before
you. 14 I will appoint him over my house and
my kingdom forever, and his throne will be
established forever.' "
15 Nathan reported all these words and this
entire vision to David.

DAVID'S PRAYER OF THANKSGIVING

16 Then King David went in, sat in the LORD's
presence, and said,
Who am I, LORD God, and what is my

Thanksgiving and Contentment | *Praise for God's Greatness*

AWESOME!

"For the LORD is great and highly praised; he is feared above all gods." 1 Chronicles 16:25

Are we too careless in the way we throw around our words? When a bacon cheeseburger is "fantastic," that new romantic comedy is "great," and our friend's new dress is "amazing," what superlatives are left for the truly extraordinary things of life? When the song about God is "totally incredible" and "absolutely awesome," what's left to say about the subject of the song?

Let's reserve our highest praise and deepest reverence for God.

One way to keep a proper perspective is to spend time in the psalms. Try this as a project: Read just five psalms a day; you can read all 150—the entire book—in just one month.

These honest and exuberant expressions point us again to the One who is truly worthy of our attention and praise. They remind us that God is worthy of the label of "awesome"—believe it or not, even more so than the "amazing" chocolate milkshake we had for lunch.

For the next note on *Thanksgiving and Contentment*, see Ezra 3:10-11.

[A] **17:5** Lit *I was from tent to tent and from tabernacle*

house that you have brought me this far?
17 This was a little thing to you,[A] God, for
you have spoken about your servant's
house in the distant future. You regard
me as a man of distinction,[B] LORD God.
18 What more can David say to you for
honoring your servant? You know your
servant. 19 LORD, you have done this whole
great thing, making known all these great
promises for the sake of your servant and
according to your will. 20 LORD, there is no
one like you, and there is no God besides
you, as all we have heard confirms. 21 And
who is like your people Israel? God, you
came to one nation on earth to redeem
a people for yourself, to make a name
for yourself through great and awesome
works by driving out nations before your
people you redeemed from Egypt. 22 You
made your people Israel your own people
forever, and you, LORD, have become
their God.

23 Now, LORD, let the word that you have
spoken concerning your servant and
his house be confirmed forever, and do
as you have promised. 24 Let your name
be confirmed and magnified forever in
the saying, "The LORD of Armies, the God
of Israel, is God over Israel." May the
house of your servant David be established before you. 25 Since you, my God,
have revealed to[C] your servant that you
will build him a house, your servant has
found courage to pray in your presence.
26 LORD, you indeed are God, and you have
promised this good thing to your servant.
27 So now, you have been pleased to bless
your servant's house that it may continue
before you forever. For you, LORD, have
blessed it, and it is blessed forever.

DAVID'S MILITARY CAMPAIGNS

18 After this, David defeated the Philistines,
subdued them, and took Gath and its
surrounding villages from Philistine control.
2 He also defeated the Moabites, and they became David's subjects and brought tribute.
3 David also defeated King Hadadezer of
Zobah at Hamath when he went to establish
his control at the Euphrates River. 4 David captured one thousand chariots, seven thousand
horsemen, and twenty thousand foot soldiers
from him, hamstrung all the horses, and kept
a hundred chariots.[D]
5 When the Arameans of Damascus came to
assist King Hadadezer of Zobah, David struck
down twenty-two thousand Aramean men.
6 Then he placed garrisons[E] in Aram of Damascus, and the Arameans became David's
subjects and brought tribute. The LORD made
David victorious wherever he went.
7 David took the gold shields carried by
Hadadezer's officers and brought them to
Jerusalem. 8 From Tibhath and Cun, Hadadezer's cities, David also took huge quantities of
bronze, from which Solomon made the bronze
basin,[F] the pillars, and the bronze articles.
9 When King Tou of Hamath heard that David
had defeated the entire army of King Hadadezer of Zobah, 10 he sent his son Hadoram
to King David to greet him and to congratulate him because David had fought against
Hadadezer and defeated him, for Tou and
Hadadezer had fought many wars. Hadoram
brought all kinds of gold, silver, and bronze
items. 11 King David also dedicated these to
the LORD, along with the silver and gold he
had carried off from all the nations — from
Edom, Moab, the Ammonites, the Philistines,
and the Amalekites.
12 Abishai son of Zeruiah struck down eighteen thousand Edomites in the Salt Valley. 13 He
put garrisons in Edom, and all the Edomites
were subject to David. The LORD made David
victorious wherever he went.
14 So David reigned over all Israel, administering justice and righteousness for all his
people.
15 Joab son of Zeruiah was over the army;
Jehoshaphat son of Ahilud was
court historian;
16 Zadok son of Ahitub and Ahimelech[G]
son of Abiathar were priests;
Shavsha was court secretary;
17 Benaiah son of Jehoiada was over the
Cherethites and the Pelethites;
and David's sons were
the chief officials at the king's side.

WAR WITH THE AMMONITES

19 Some time later, King Nahash of the Ammonites died, and his son became king in
his place. 2 Then David said, "I'll show kindness

[A] 17:17 Lit *thing in your eyes* [B] 17:17 Hb obscure [C] 17:25 Lit *have uncovered the ear of* [D] 18:4 Or *chariot horses*
[E] 18:6 Some Hb mss, LXX, Vg; other Hb mss omit *garrisons*; 2Sm 8:6 [F] 18:8 Lit *sea* [G] 18:16 Some Hb mss, LXX, Syr, Vg;
other Hb mss read *Abimelech*; 2Sm 8:17

to Hanun son of Nahash, because his father
showed kindness to me."
So David sent messengers to console him
concerning his father. However, when David's
emissaries arrived in the land of the Ammonites to console him, 3 the Ammonite leaders
said to Hanun, "Just because David has sent
men with condolences for you, do you really
believe he's showing respect for your father?
Instead, haven't his emissaries come in order
to scout out, overthrow, and spy on the land?"
4 So Hanun took David's emissaries, shaved
them, cut their clothes in half at the hips, and
sent them away.
5 It was reported to David about his men, so
he sent messengers to meet them, since the
men were deeply humiliated. The king said,
"Stay in Jericho until your beards grow back;
then return."
6 When the Ammonites realized they had
made themselves repulsive to David, Hanun
and the Ammonites sent thirty-eight tons[A]
of silver to hire chariots and horsemen from
Aram-naharaim, Aram-maacah, and Zobah.
7 They hired thirty-two thousand chariots and
the king of Maacah with his army, who came
and camped near Medeba. The Ammonites also
came together from their cities for the battle.
8 David heard about this and sent Joab and
all the elite troops. 9 The Ammonites marched
out and lined up in battle formation at the
entrance of the city while the kings who had
come were in the field by themselves. 10 When
Joab saw that there was a battle line in front of
him and another behind him, he chose some
of Israel's finest young men[B] and lined up in
formation to engage the Arameans. 11 He placed
the rest of the forces under the command of
his brother Abishai. They lined up in formation to engage the Ammonites.

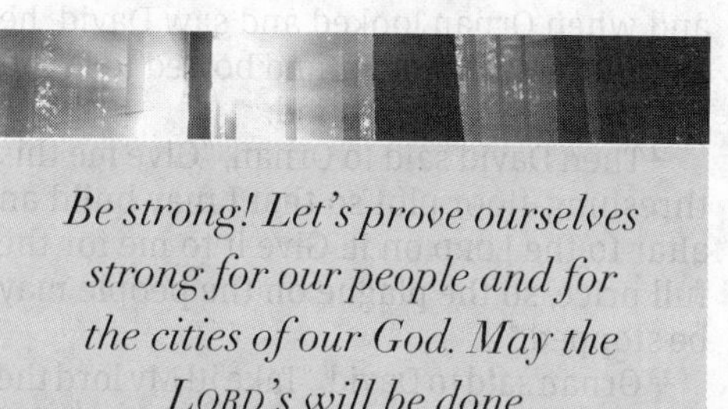
Be strong! Let's prove ourselves
strong for our people and for
the cities of our God. May the
LORD's will be done.
—1 Chronicles 19:13

12 "If the Arameans are too strong for me,"
Joab said, "then you'll be my help. However,
if the Ammonites are too strong for you, I'll
help you. 13 Be strong! Let's prove ourselves
strong for our people and for the cities of our
God. May the LORD's will be done."[C]
14 Joab and the people with him approached
the Arameans for battle, and they fled before
him. 15 When the Ammonites saw that the Arameans had fled, they likewise fled before
Joab's brother Abishai and entered the city.
Then Joab went to Jerusalem.
16 When the Arameans realized that they had
been defeated by Israel, they sent messengers
to summon the Arameans who were beyond
the Euphrates River. They were led by Shophach, the commander of Hadadezer's army.
17 When this was reported to David, he gathered all Israel and crossed the Jordan. He came
up to the Arameans and lined up against them.
When David lined up to engage them, they
fought against him. 18 But the Arameans fled
before Israel, and David killed seven thousand
of their charioteers and forty thousand foot
soldiers. He also killed Shophach, commander of the army. 19 When Hadadezer's subjects
saw that they had been defeated by Israel,
they made peace with David and became his
subjects. After this, the Arameans were never
willing to help the Ammonites again.

CAPTURE OF THE CITY OF RABBAH

20 In the spring[D] when kings march out to
war, Joab led the army and destroyed
the Ammonites' land. He came to Rabbah and
besieged it, but David remained in Jerusalem. Joab attacked Rabbah and demolished it.
2 Then David took the crown from the head of
their king,[E,F] and it was placed on David's head.
He found that the crown weighed seventy-five
pounds[G] of gold, and there was a precious
stone in it. In addition, David took away a
large quantity of plunder from the city. 3 He
brought out the people who were in it and
put them to work with saws,[H] iron picks, and
axes.[I] David did the same to all the Ammonite
cities. Then he and all his troops returned to
Jerusalem.

THE PHILISTINE GIANTS

4 After this, a war broke out with the Philistines
at Gezer. At that time Sibbecai the Hushathite

[A] **19:6** Lit *1,000 talents* [B] **19:10** Lit *Israel's choice ones* [C] **19:13** Lit *the LORD do what is good in his eyes* [D] **20:1** Lit *At the time of the return of the year* [E] **20:2** LXX, Vg read *of Milcom* [F] **20:2** = Molech; 1Kg 11:5,7 [G] **20:2** Lit *a talent* [H] **20:3** Text emended; MT reads *and sawed them with the saw*; 2Sm 12:31 [I] **20:3** Text emended; MT reads *saws*; 2Sm 12:31

killed Sippai, a descendant of the Rephaim,[A]
and the Philistines were subdued.
5 Once again there was a battle with the Philistines, and Elhanan son of Jair killed Lahmi
the brother of Goliath of Gath. The shaft of his
spear was like a weaver's beam.
6 There was still another battle at Gath where
there was a man of extraordinary stature
with six fingers on each hand and six toes
on each foot — twenty-four in all. He, too,
was descended from the giant.[B] 7 When he
taunted Israel, Jonathan son of David's brother
Shimei killed him.
8 These were the descendants of the giant in
Gath killed by David and his soldiers.

DAVID'S MILITARY CENSUS

21 Satan[C] rose up against Israel and incited
David to count the people of Israel. 2 So
David said to Joab and the commanders of the
troops, "Go and count Israel from Beer-sheba
to Dan and bring a report to me so I can know
their number."
3 Joab replied, "May the LORD multiply the
number of his people a hundred times over!
My lord the king, aren't they all my lord's servants? Why does my lord want to do this? Why
should he bring guilt on Israel?"
4 Yet the king's order prevailed over Joab. So
Joab left and traveled throughout Israel and
then returned to Jerusalem. 5 Joab gave the
total troop registration to David. In all Israel
there were one million one hundred thousand
armed men[D] and in Judah itself four hundred
seventy thousand armed men. 6 But he did
not include Levi and Benjamin in the count
because the king's command was detestable
to him. 7 This command was also evil in God's
sight, so he afflicted Israel.
8 David said to God, "I have sinned greatly
because I have done this thing. Now, please
take away your servant's guilt, for I've been
very foolish."

DAVID'S PUNISHMENT

9 Then the LORD instructed Gad, David's seer,
10 "Go and say to David, 'This is what the LORD
says: I am offering you three choices. Choose
one of them for yourself, and I will do it to you.'"
11 So Gad went to David and said to him, "This
is what the LORD says: 'Take your choice: 12 three
years of famine, or three months of devastation
by your foes with the sword of your enemy
overtaking you, or three days of the sword of
the LORD — a plague on the land, the angel of
the LORD bringing destruction to the whole
territory of Israel.' Now decide what answer
I should take back to the one who sent me."
13 David answered Gad, "I'm in anguish.
Please, let me fall into the LORD's hands because his mercies are very great, but don't let
me fall into human hands."
14 So the LORD sent a plague on Israel, and
seventy thousand Israelite men died. 15 Then
God sent an angel to Jerusalem to destroy it,
but when the angel was about to destroy the
city,[E] the LORD looked, relented concerning
the destruction, and said to the angel who
was destroying the people, "Enough, withdraw your hand now!" The angel of the LORD
was then standing at the threshing floor of
Ornan[F] the Jebusite.
16 When David looked up and saw the angel of
the LORD standing between earth and heaven,
with his drawn sword in his hand stretched out
over Jerusalem, David and the elders, clothed
in sackcloth, fell facedown. 17 David said to God,
"Wasn't I the one who gave the order to count
the people? I am the one who has sinned and
acted very wickedly. But these sheep, what have
they done? LORD my God, please let your hand
be against me and against my father's family,
but don't let the plague be against your people."

DAVID'S ALTAR

18 So the angel of the LORD ordered Gad to tell
David to go and set up an altar to the LORD
on the threshing floor of Ornan the Jebusite.
19 David went up at Gad's command spoken
in the name of the LORD.
20 Ornan was threshing wheat when he
turned and saw the angel. His four sons, who
were with him, hid. 21 David came to Ornan,
and when Ornan looked and saw David, he
left the threshing floor and bowed to David
with his face to the ground.
22 Then David said to Ornan, "Give me this
threshing-floor plot so that I may build an
altar to the LORD on it. Give it to me for the
full price, so the plague on the people may
be stopped."
23 Ornan said to David, "Take it! My lord the
king may do whatever he wants.[G] See, I give
the oxen for the burnt offerings, the threshing
sledges for the wood, and the wheat for the
grain offering — I give it all."

[A] **20:4** Or *the Rephaites* [B] **20:6** Or *Raphah*, also in v. 8 [C] **21:1** Or *An adversary*; Jb 1:6; Zch 3:1-2 [D] **21:5** Lit *men drawing the sword* [E] **21:15** Lit *but as he was destroying* [F] **21:15-28** = Araunah in 2Sm 24:16-24 [G] **21:23** Lit *do what is good in his eyes*

24 King David answered Ornan, "No, I insist on paying the full price, for I will not take for the LORD what belongs to you or offer burnt offerings that cost me nothing."

25 So David gave Ornan fifteen pounds of gold[A] for the plot. 26 He built an altar to the LORD there and offered burnt offerings and fellowship offerings. He called on the LORD, and he answered him with fire from heaven on the altar of burnt offering.

27 Then the LORD spoke to the angel, and he put his sword back into its sheath. 28 At that time, David offered sacrifices there when he saw that the LORD answered him at the threshing floor of Ornan the Jebusite. 29 The tabernacle of the LORD, which Moses made in the wilderness, and the altar of burnt offering were at the high place in Gibeon, 30 but David could not go before it to inquire of God, because he was terrified of the sword of the

22 LORD's angel. 1 Then David said, "This is the house of the LORD God, and this is the altar of burnt offering for Israel."

DAVID'S PREPARATIONS FOR THE TEMPLE

2 So David gave orders to gather the resident aliens that were in the land of Israel, and he appointed stonecutters to cut finished stones for building God's house. 3 David supplied a great deal of iron to make the nails for the doors of the gates and for the fittings, together with an immeasurable quantity of bronze, 4 and innumerable cedar logs because the Sidonians and Tyrians had brought a large quantity of cedar logs to David. 5 David said, "My son Solomon is young and inexperienced, and the house that is to be built for the LORD must be exceedingly great and famous and glorious in all the lands. Therefore, I will make provision for it." So David made lavish preparations for it before his death.

6 Then he summoned his son Solomon and charged him to build a house for the LORD God of Israel. 7 "My son," David said to Solomon, "It was in my heart to build a house for the name of the LORD my God, 8 but the word of the LORD came to me: 'You have shed much blood and waged great wars. You are not to build a house for my name because you have shed so much blood on the ground before me. 9 But a son will be born to you; he will be a man of rest. I will give him rest from all his surrounding enemies, for his name will be Solomon,[B] and I will give peace and quiet to Israel during his reign. 10 He is the one who will build a house for my name. He will be my son, and I will be his father. I will establish the throne of his kingdom over Israel forever.'

11 "Now, my son, may the LORD be with you, and may you succeed in building the house of the LORD your God, as he said about you. 12 Above all, may the LORD give you insight and understanding when he puts you in charge of Israel so that you may keep the law of the LORD your God. 13 Then you will succeed if you carefully follow the statutes and ordinances the LORD commanded Moses for Israel. Be strong and courageous. Don't be afraid or discouraged.

14 "Notice I have taken great pains to provide for the house of the LORD — 3,775 tons of gold, 37,750 tons of silver,[C] and bronze and iron that can't be weighed because there is so much of it. I have also provided timber and stone, but you will need to add more to them. 15 You also have many workers: stonecutters, masons, carpenters, and people skilled in every kind of work 16 in gold, silver, bronze, and iron — beyond number. Now begin the work, and may the LORD be with you."

17 Then David ordered all the leaders of Israel to help his son Solomon: 18 "The LORD your God is with you, isn't he? And hasn't he given you rest on every side? For he has handed the land's inhabitants over to me, and the land has been subdued before the LORD and his people. 19 Now determine in your mind and heart to seek the LORD your God. Get started building the LORD God's sanctuary so that you may bring the ark of the LORD's covenant and the holy articles of God to the temple that is to be built for the name of the LORD."

THE DIVISIONS OF THE LEVITES

23 When David was old and full of days, he installed his son Solomon as king over Israel. 2 Then he gathered all the leaders

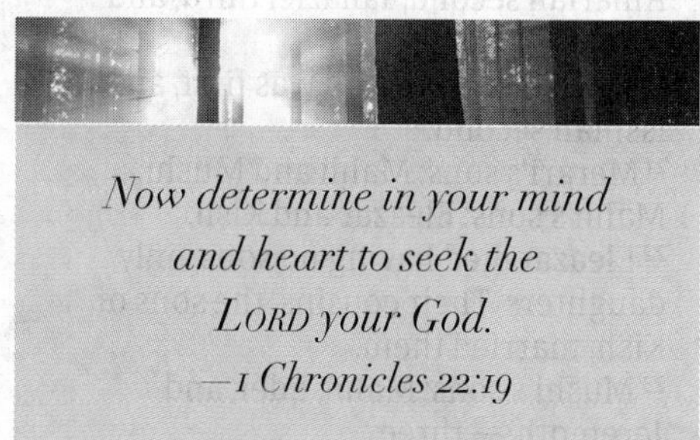
*Now determine in your mind
and heart to seek the
LORD your God.*
— 1 Chronicles 22:19

[A] 21:25 Lit *600 shekels of gold by weight* [B] 22:9 In Hb, the name *Solomon* sounds like "peace." [C] 22:14 Lit *100,000 talents of gold and 1,000,000 talents of silver*

of Israel, the priests, and the Levites. 3 The Levites thirty years old or more were counted; the total number of men was thirty-eight thousand by headcount. 4 "Of these," David said, "twenty-four thousand are to be in charge of the work on the LORD's temple, six thousand are to be officers and judges, 5 four thousand are to be gatekeepers, and four thousand are to praise the LORD with the instruments that I have made for worship."

6 Then David divided them into divisions according to Levi's sons: Gershom,[A] Kohath, and Merari.

7 The Gershonites: Ladan and Shimei.

8 Ladan's sons: Jehiel was the first, then Zetham, and Joel — three.

9 Shimei's sons: Shelomoth, Haziel, and Haran — three. Those were the heads of the families of Ladan.

10 Shimei's sons: Jahath, Zizah,[B] Jeush, and Beriah. Those were Shimei's sons — four.

11 Jahath was the first and Zizah was the second; however, Jeush and Beriah did not have many sons, so they became one family[C] and received a single assignment.

12 Kohath's sons: Amram, Izhar, Hebron, and Uzziel — four.

13 Amram's sons: Aaron and Moses.

Aaron, along with his descendants, was set apart forever to consecrate the most holy things, to burn incense in the presence of the LORD, to minister to him, and to pronounce blessings in his name forever. 14 As for Moses the man of God, his sons were named among the tribe of Levi.

15 Moses's sons: Gershom and Eliezer.

16 Gershom's sons: Shebuel was first.

17 Eliezer's sons were Rehabiah, first; Eliezer did not have any other sons, but Rehabiah's sons were very numerous.

18 Izhar's sons: Shelomith was first.

19 Hebron's sons: Jeriah was first, Amariah second, Jahaziel third, and Jekameam fourth.

20 Uzziel's sons: Micah was first, and Isshiah second.

21 Merari's sons: Mahli and Mushi. Mahli's sons: Eleazar and Kish.

22 Eleazar died having no sons, only daughters. Their cousins, the sons of Kish, married them.

23 Mushi's sons: Mahli, Eder, and Jeremoth — three.

24 These were the descendants of Levi by their ancestral families[D] — the family heads, according to their registration by name in the headcount — twenty years old or more, who worked in the service of the LORD's temple. 25 For David said, "The LORD God of Israel has given rest to his people, and he has come to stay in Jerusalem forever. 26 Also, the Levites no longer need to carry the tabernacle or any of the equipment for its service" — 27 for according to the last words of David, the Levites twenty years old or more were to be counted — 28 "but their duty will be to assist the descendants of Aaron with the service of the LORD's temple, being responsible for the courts and the chambers, the purification of all the holy things, and the work of the service of God's temple — 29 as well as the rows of the Bread of the Presence, the fine flour for the grain offering, the wafers of unleavened bread, the baking,[E] the mixing, and all measurements of volume and length. 30 They are also to stand every morning to give thanks and praise to the LORD, and likewise in the evening. 31 Whenever burnt offerings are offered to the LORD on the Sabbaths, New Moons, and appointed festivals, they are to offer them regularly in the LORD's presence according to the number prescribed for them. 32 They are to carry out their responsibilities for the tent of meeting, for the holy place, and for their relatives, the descendants of Aaron, in the service of the LORD's temple."

THE DIVISIONS OF THE PRIESTS

24 The divisions of the descendants of Aaron were as follows: Aaron's sons were Nadab, Abihu, Eleazar, and Ithamar. 2 But Nadab and Abihu died before their father, and they had no sons, so Eleazar and Ithamar served as priests. 3 Together with Zadok from the descendants of Eleazar and Ahimelech from the descendants of Ithamar, David divided them according to the assigned duties of their service. 4 Since more leaders were found among Eleazar's descendants than Ithamar's, they were divided accordingly: sixteen heads of ancestral families[F] were from Eleazar's descendants, and eight heads of ancestral families were from Ithamar's. 5 They were assigned by lot, for there were officers of the sanctuary and officers of God among both Eleazar's and Ithamar's descendants.

[A] **23:6** Lit *Gershon* [B] **23:10** LXX, Vg; MT reads *Zina* [C] **23:11** Lit *a father's house* [D] **23:24** Lit *the house of their fathers* [E] **23:29** Lit *the griddle* [F] **24:4** Lit *house of fathers*

6 The secretary, Shemaiah son of Nethanel,
a Levite, recorded them in the presence of
the king and the officers, the priest Zadok,
Ahimelech son of Abiathar, and the heads of
families of the priests and the Levites. One
ancestral family[A] was taken for Eleazar, and
then one for Ithamar.

7 The first lot fell to Jehoiarib, the second
to Jedaiah,
8 the third to Harim, the fourth
to Seorim,
9 the fifth to Malchijah, the sixth
to Mijamin,
10 the seventh to Hakkoz, the eighth
to Abijah,
11 the ninth to Jeshua, the tenth
to Shecaniah,
12 the eleventh to Eliashib, the twelfth
to Jakim,
13 the thirteenth to Huppah,
the fourteenth to Jeshebeab,
14 the fifteenth to Bilgah, the sixteenth
to Immer,
15 the seventeenth to Hezir,
the eighteenth to Happizzez,
16 the nineteenth to Pethahiah,
the twentieth to Jehezkel,
17 the twenty-first to Jachin,
the twenty-second to Gamul,
18 the twenty-third to Delaiah,
and the twenty-fourth to Maaziah.

19 These had their assigned duties for service
when they entered the LORD's temple, according
to their regulations, which they received
from their ancestor Aaron, as the LORD God
of Israel had commanded him.

THE REST OF THE LEVITES

20 As for the rest of Levi's sons:
from Amram's sons: Shubael;
from Shubael's sons: Jehdeiah.
21 From Rehabiah:
from Rehabiah's sons: Isshiah was the first.
22 From the Izharites: Shelomoth;
from Shelomoth's sons: Jahath.
23 Hebron's[B] sons:
Jeriah the first, Amariah the second,
Jahaziel the third, and Jekameam the
fourth.
24 From Uzziel's sons: Micah;
from Micah's sons: Shamir.
25 Micah's brother: Isshiah;
from Isshiah's sons: Zechariah.
26 Merari's sons: Mahli and Mushi,
and from his sons, Jaaziah his son.[C]
27 Merari's sons, by his son Jaaziah:[D]
Shoham, Zaccur, and Ibri.
28 From Mahli: Eleazar, who had no sons.
29 From Kish, from Kish's sons: Jerahmeel.
30 Mushi's sons: Mahli, Eder, and Jerimoth.

Those were the descendants of the Levites
according to their ancestral families.[E] 31 They
also cast lots the same way as their relatives
the descendants of Aaron did in the presence
of King David, Zadok, Ahimelech, and the heads
of the families of the priests and Levites — the
family heads and their younger brothers alike.

THE LEVITICAL MUSICIANS

25 David and the officers of the army also
set apart some of the sons of Asaph,
Heman, and Jeduthun, who were to prophesy
accompanied by lyres, harps, and cymbals.
This is the list of the men who performed
their service:
2 From Asaph's sons:
Zaccur, Joseph, Nethaniah, and Asarelah,
sons of Asaph, under Asaph's authority,
who prophesied under the authority of
the king.
3 From Jeduthun: Jeduthun's sons:
Gedaliah, Zeri, Jeshaiah, Shimei,[F]
Hashabiah, and Mattithiah — six — under
the authority of their father Jeduthun,
prophesying to the accompaniment of
lyres, giving thanks and praise to the LORD.
4 From Heman: Heman's sons:
Bukkiah, Mattaniah, Uzziel, Shebuel,
Jerimoth, Hananiah, Hanani, Eliathah,
Giddalti, Romamti-ezer, Joshbekashah,
Mallothi, Hothir, and Mahazioth. 5 All
these sons of Heman, the king's seer,
were given by the promises of God to
exalt him,[G] for God had given Heman
fourteen sons and three daughters.

6 All these men were under their own fathers' authority for the music in the LORD's
temple, with cymbals, harps, and lyres for
the service of God's temple. Asaph, Jeduthun,
and Heman were under the king's authority. 7 They numbered 288 together with their

[A] 24:6 Lit *father's house* [B] 24:23 Some Hb mss, some LXX mss; other Hb mss omit *Hebron's*; 1Ch 23:19 [C] 24:26 Or *Mushi; Jaaziah's sons: Beno.* [D] 24:27 Or *sons, Jaaziah: Beno,* [E] 24:30 Lit *the house of their fathers* [F] 25:3 One Hb ms, LXX; other Hb mss omit *Shimei* [G] 25:5 Lit *by the words of God to lift a horn*

relatives who were all trained and skillful
in music for the LORD. 8 They cast lots for
their duties, young and old alike, teacher as
well as pupil.

9 The first lot for Asaph fell to Joseph,
his sons, and his relatives— 12[A]
to Gedaliah the second: him,
his relatives, and his sons — 12
10 the third to Zaccur, his sons,
and his relatives — 12
11 the fourth to Izri,[B] his sons,
and his relatives — 12
12 the fifth to Nethaniah, his sons,
and his relatives — 12
13 the sixth to Bukkiah, his sons,
and his relatives — 12
14 the seventh to Jesarelah, his sons,
and his relatives — 12
15 the eighth to Jeshaiah, his sons,
and his relatives — 12
16 the ninth to Mattaniah, his sons,
and his relatives — 12
17 the tenth to Shimei, his sons,
and his relatives — 12
18 the eleventh to Azarel,[C] his sons,
and his relatives — 12
19 the twelfth to Hashabiah, his sons,
and his relatives — 12
20 the thirteenth to Shubael, his sons,
and his relatives — 12
21 the fourteenth to Mattithiah,
his sons, and his relatives — 12
22 the fifteenth to Jeremoth, his sons,
and his relatives — 12
23 the sixteenth to Hananiah, his sons,
and his relatives — 12
24 the seventeenth to Joshbekashah,
his sons, and his relatives — 12
25 the eighteenth to Hanani, his sons,
and his relatives — 12
26 the nineteenth to Mallothi, his sons,
and his relatives — 12
27 the twentieth to Eliathah, his sons,
and his relatives — 12
28 the twenty-first to Hothir, his sons,
and his relatives — 12
29 the twenty-second to Giddalti,
his sons, and his relatives — 12
30 the twenty-third to Mahazioth,
his sons, and his relatives — 12
31 and the twenty-fourth
to Romamti-ezer, his sons,
and his relatives — 12.

THE LEVITICAL GATEKEEPERS

26 The following were the divisions of
the gatekeepers:
From the Korahites: Meshelemiah son of
Kore, one of the sons of Asaph.
2 Meshelemiah had sons:
Zechariah the firstborn, Jediael the
second,
Zebadiah the third, Jathniel the fourth,
3 Elam the fifth, Jehohanan the sixth,
and Eliehoenai the seventh.
4 Obed-edom also had sons:
Shemaiah the firstborn, Jehozabad the
second,
Joah the third, Sachar the fourth,
Nethanel the fifth, 5 Ammiel the sixth,
Issachar the seventh, and Peullethai the
eighth,
for God blessed him.
6 Also, to his son Shemaiah were born
sons who ruled their ancestral families[D]
because they were strong, capable men.
7 Shemaiah's sons: Othni, Rephael,
Obed, and Elzabad; his relatives Elihu
and Semachiah were also capable men.
8 All of these were among the sons of
Obed-edom with their sons and relatives;
they were capable men with strength for
the work — sixty-two from Obed-edom.
9 Meshelemiah also had sons and
relatives who were capable men —
eighteen.
10 Hosah, from the Merarites, also had
sons: Shimri the first (although he
was not the firstborn, his father had
appointed him as the first), 11 Hilkiah the
second, Tebaliah the third, and Zechariah
the fourth. The sons and relatives of
Hosah were thirteen in all.

12 These divisions of the gatekeepers, under
their leading men, had duties for ministering
in the LORD's temple, just as their relatives did.
13 They cast lots for each temple gate according
to their ancestral families, young and old alike.
14 The lot for the east gate fell to Shelemiah.[E]
They also cast lots for his son Zechariah, an
insightful counselor, and his lot came out for
the north gate. 15 Obed-edom's was the south
gate, and his sons' lot was for the storehouses;
16 it was the west gate and the gate of Shalle-
cheth on the ascending highway for Shuppim
and Hosah.

[A] 25:9 LXX; MT lacks *his sons, and his relatives — 12* [B] 25:11 Variant of Zeri [C] 25:18 Variant of Uzziel [D] 26:6 Lit *the house of their fathers*, also in v. 13 [E] 26:14 Variant of Meshelemiah

There were guards stationed at every watch.
17 There were six Levites each day[A] on the east,
four each day on the north, four each day on
the south, and two pair at the storehouses.
18 As for the court on the west, there were four
at the highway and two at the court. 19 Those
were the divisions of the gatekeepers from the
descendants of the Korahites and Merarites.

THE LEVITICAL TREASURERS AND OTHER OFFICIALS

20 From the Levites, Ahijah was in charge of
the treasuries of God's temple and the treasuries of what had been dedicated. 21 From
the sons of Ladan, who were the descendants
of the Gershonites through Ladan and were
the family heads belonging to Ladan the Gershonite: Jehieli. 22 The sons of Jehieli, Zetham
and his brother Joel, were in charge of the
treasuries of the LORD's temple.
23 From the Amramites, the Izharites, the
Hebronites, and the Uzzielites: 24 Shebuel, a
descendant of Moses's son Gershom, was the
officer in charge of the treasuries. 25 His relatives through Eliezer: his son Rehabiah, his
son Jeshaiah, his son Joram, his son Zichri, and
his son Shelomith.[B] 26 This Shelomith and his
relatives were in charge of all the treasuries
of what had been dedicated by King David, by
the family heads who were the commanders of
thousands and of hundreds, and by the army
commanders. 27 They dedicated part of the
plunder from their battles for the repair of the
LORD's temple. 28 All that the seer Samuel, Saul
son of Kish, Abner son of Ner, and Joab son of
Zeruiah had dedicated, along with everything
else that had been dedicated, were in the care
of Shelomith and his relatives.
29 From the Izrahites: Chenaniah and his
sons had duties outside the temple[C] as officers
and judges over Israel. 30 From the Hebronites:
Hashabiah and his relatives, 1,700 capable
men, had assigned duties in Israel west of the
Jordan for all the work of the LORD and for
the service of the king. 31 From the Hebronites: Jerijah was the head of the Hebronites,
according to the family records of his ancestors. A search was made in the fortieth
year of David's reign and strong, capable men
were found among them at Jazer in Gilead.
32 There were among Jerijah's relatives 2,700
capable men who were family heads. King
David appointed them over the Reubenites,
the Gadites, and half the tribe of Manasseh
as overseers in every matter relating to God
and the king.

DAVID'S SECULAR OFFICIALS

27 This is the list of the Israelites, the family
heads, the commanders of thousands
and the commanders of hundreds, and their
officers who served the king in every matter
to do with the divisions that were on rotated
military duty each month throughout[D] the
year. There were 24,000 in each division:
2 Jashobeam son of Zabdiel was in charge
of the first division, for the first month;
24,000 were in his division. 3 He was a
descendant of Perez and chief of all the
army commanders for the first month.
4 Dodai the Ahohite was in charge of
the division for the second month, and
Mikloth was the leader; 24,000 were in
his division.
5 The third army commander, as chief
for the third month, was Benaiah son of
the priest Jehoiada; 24,000 were in his
division. 6 This Benaiah was a mighty
man among the Thirty and over the
Thirty, and his son Ammizabad was in
charge[E] of his division.
7 The fourth commander, for the fourth
month, was Joab's brother Asahel, and
his son Zebadiah was commander after
him; 24,000 were in his division.
8 The fifth, for the fifth month, was the
commander Shamhuth the Izrahite;
24,000 were in his division.
9 The sixth, for the sixth month, was Ira
son of Ikkesh the Tekoite; 24,000 were in
his division.
10 The seventh, for the seventh month,
was Helez the Pelonite from the
descendants of Ephraim; 24,000 were in
his division.
11 The eighth, for the eighth month, was
Sibbecai the Hushathite, a Zerahite;
24,000 were in his division.
12 The ninth, for the ninth month, was
Abiezer the Anathothite, a Benjaminite;
24,000 were in his division.
13 The tenth, for the tenth month, was
Maharai the Netophathite, a Zerahite;
24,000 were in his division.
14 The eleventh, for the eleventh month,
was Benaiah the Pirathonite from the

[A] **26:17** LXX; MT omits *each day* [B] **26:25** Or *Shelomoth*, also in vv. 26,28 [C] **26:29** *the temple* added for clarity [D] **27:1** Lit *that came in and went out month by month for all months of* [E] **27:6** LXX; MT omits *in charge*

descendants of Ephraim; 24,000 were in his division.

15 The twelfth, for the twelfth month, was Heldai the Netophathite, of Othniel's family;[A] 24,000 were in his division.

16 The following were in charge of the tribes of Israel:
For the Reubenites, Eliezer son of Zichri was the chief official;
for the Simeonites, Shephatiah son of Maacah;
17 for the Levites, Hashabiah son of Kemuel; for Aaron, Zadok;
18 for Judah, Elihu, one of David's brothers; for Issachar, Omri son of Michael;
19 for Zebulun, Ishmaiah son of Obadiah; for Naphtali, Jerimoth son of Azriel;
20 for the Ephraimites, Hoshea son of Azaziah;
for half the tribe of Manasseh, Joel son of Pedaiah;
21 for half the tribe of Manasseh in Gilead, Iddo son of Zechariah;
for Benjamin, Jaasiel son of Abner;
22 for Dan, Azarel son of Jeroham.
Those were the leaders of the tribes of Israel.

23 David didn't count the men aged twenty
or under, for the LORD had said he would make
Israel as numerous as the stars of the sky.
24 Joab son of Zeruiah began to count them,
but he didn't complete it. There was wrath against Israel because of this census, and the number was not entered in the Historical Record[B] of King David.

25 Azmaveth son of Adiel was in charge of the king's storehouses.
Jonathan son of Uzziah was in charge of the storehouses in the country, in the cities, in the villages, and in the fortresses.
26 Ezri son of Chelub was in charge of those who worked in the fields tilling the soil.
27 Shimei the Ramathite was in charge of the vineyards.
Zabdi the Shiphmite was in charge of the produce of the vineyards for the wine cellars.
28 Baal-hanan the Gederite was in charge of the olive and sycamore trees in the Judean foothills.[C]
Joash was in charge of the stores of olive oil.
29 Shitrai the Sharonite was in charge of the herds that grazed in Sharon, while Shaphat son of Adlai was in charge of the herds in the valleys.
30 Obil the Ishmaelite was in charge of the camels.
Jehdeiah the Meronothite was in charge of the donkeys.
31 Jaziz the Hagrite was in charge of the flocks.
All these were officials in charge of King David's property.

32 David's uncle Jonathan was a counselor;
he was a man of understanding and a scribe.
Jehiel son of Hachmoni attended[D] the king's
sons. 33 Ahithophel was the king's counselor.
Hushai the Archite was the king's friend. 34 After Ahithophel came Jehoiada son of Benaiah,
then Abiathar. Joab was the commander of
the king's army.

DAVID COMMISSIONS SOLOMON TO BUILD THE TEMPLE

28 David assembled all the leaders of Israel
in Jerusalem: the leaders of the tribes,
the leaders of the divisions in the king's service, the commanders of thousands and the
commanders of hundreds, and the officials in
charge of all the property and cattle of the king
and his sons, along with the court officials, the
fighting men, and all the best soldiers. 2 Then
King David rose to his feet and said, "Listen to
me, my brothers and my people. It was in my
heart to build a house as a resting place for
the ark of the LORD's covenant and as a footstool for our God. I had made preparations
to build, 3 but God said to me, 'You are not to
build a house for my name because you are
a man of war and have shed blood.'
4 "Yet the LORD God of Israel chose me out
of all my father's family to be king over Israel forever. For he chose Judah as leader, and
from the house of Judah, my father's family,
and from my father's sons, he was pleased to
make me king over all Israel. 5 And out of all
my sons — for the LORD has given me many
sons — he has chosen my son Solomon to
sit on the throne of the LORD's kingdom over
Israel. 6 He said to me, 'Your son Solomon is
the one who is to build my house and my

[A] 27:15 Lit *belonging to Othniel* [B] 27:24 LXX; MT reads *the number of the Historical Record* [C] 27:28 Or *the Shephelah*
[D] 27:32 Lit *was with*

Embracing God's Word | Courage

OPPRESSIVE DARKNESS. DOUBTS. SUSPICIONS. FEARS. Yet we can confidently advance, "strong and courageous," knowing "God is for us"!

Above all, be strong and very courageous to observe carefully the whole instruction my servant Moses commanded you. Do not turn from it to the right or the left, so that you will have success wherever you go. –Joshua 1:7

Elisha said, "Don't be afraid, for those who are with us outnumber those who are with them." –2 Kings 6:16

Then David said to his son Solomon, "Be strong and courageous, and do the work. Don't be afraid or discouraged, for the LORD God, my God, is with you." –1 Chronicles 28:20

The LORD will fulfill his purpose for me. LORD, your faithful love endures forever. –Psalm 138:8

When all has been heard, the conclusion of the matter is this: fear God and keep his commands, because this is for all humanity. For God will bring every act to judgment, including every hidden thing, whether good or evil. –Ecclesiastes 12:13-14

He will destroy death forever. The Lord GOD will wipe away the tears from every face and remove his people's disgrace from the whole earth, for the LORD has spoken. –Isaiah 25:8

For I am the LORD your God, who holds your right hand, who says to you, "Do not fear, I will help you." –Isaiah 41:13

What then are we to say about these things? If God is for us, who is against us? He did not even spare his own Son but offered him up for us all. How will he not also with him grant us everything? –Romans 8:31-32

So we are always confident and know that while we are at home in the body we are away from the Lord. For we walk by faith, not by sight. –2 Corinthians 5:6-7

This is according to his eternal purpose accomplished in Christ Jesus our Lord. In him we have boldness and confident access through faith in him. –Ephesians 3:11–12

I am sure of this, that he who started a good work in you will carry it on to completion until the day of Christ Jesus. –Philippians 1:6

For it is God who is working in you both to will and to work according to his good purpose. –Philippians 2:13

But I am not ashamed, because I know whom I have believed and am persuaded that he is able to guard what has been entrusted to me until that day. –2 Timothy 1:12

Now if any of you lacks wisdom, he should ask God—who gives to all generously and ungrudgingly—and it will be given to him. But let him ask in faith without doubting. For the doubter is like the surging sea, driven and tossed by the wind. –James 1:5-6

courts, for I have chosen him to be my son, and I will be his father. 7 I will establish his kingdom forever if he perseveres in keeping my commands and my ordinances as he is doing today.'

8 "So now in the sight of all Israel, the assembly of the LORD, and in the hearing of our God, observe and follow all the commands of the LORD your God so that you may possess this good land and leave it as an inheritance to your descendants forever.

9 "As for you, Solomon my son, know the God of your father, and serve him wholeheartedly and with a willing mind, for the LORD searches every heart and understands the intention of every thought. If you seek him, he will be found by you, but if you abandon him, he will reject you forever. 10 Realize now that the LORD has chosen you to build a house for the sanctuary. Be strong, and do it."

11 Then David gave his son Solomon the plans for the portico of the temple and its buildings, treasuries, upstairs rooms, inner rooms, and a room for the mercy seat. 12 The plans contained everything he had in mind[A] for the courts of the LORD's house, all the surrounding chambers, the treasuries of God's house, and the treasuries for what is dedicated. 13 Also included were plans for the divisions of the priests and the Levites; all the work of service in the LORD's house; all the articles of service of the LORD's house; 14 the weight of gold for all the articles for every kind of service; the weight of all the silver articles for every kind of service; 15 the weight of the gold lampstands and their gold lamps, including the weight of each lampstand and its lamps; the weight of each silver lampstand and its lamps, according to the service of each lampstand; 16 the weight of gold for each table for the rows of the Bread of the Presence and the silver for the silver tables; 17 the pure gold for the forks, sprinkling basins, and pitchers; the weight of each gold dish; the weight of each silver bowl; 18 the weight of refined gold for the altar of incense; and the plans for the chariot of[B] the gold cherubim that spread out their wings and cover the ark of the LORD's covenant.

19 David concluded, "By the LORD's hand on me, he enabled me to understand everything in writing, all the details of the plan."[C]

20 Then David said to his son Solomon, "Be strong and courageous, and do the work. Don't be afraid or discouraged, for the LORD God, my God, is with you. He won't leave you or abandon you until all the work for the service of the LORD's house is finished. 21 Here are the divisions of the priests and the Levites for all the service of God's house. Every willing person of any skill will be at your disposal for the work, and the leaders and all the people are at your every command."

CONTRIBUTIONS FOR BUILDING THE TEMPLE

29 Then King David said to all the assembly, "My son Solomon — God has chosen him alone — is young and inexperienced. The task is great because the building will not be built for a human but for the LORD God. 2 So to the best of my ability I've made provision for the house of my God: gold for the gold articles, silver for the silver, bronze for the bronze, iron for the iron, and wood for the wood, as well as onyx, stones for mounting,[D] antimony,[E] stones of various colors, all kinds of precious stones, and a great quantity of marble. 3 Moreover, because of my delight in the house of my God, I now give my personal treasures of gold and silver for the house of my God over and above all that I've provided for the holy house: 4 100 tons[F] of gold (gold of Ophir) and 250 tons[G] of refined silver for overlaying the walls of the buildings, 5 the gold for the gold work and the silver for the silver, for all the work to be done by the craftsmen. Now who will volunteer to consecrate himself to the LORD today?"

6 Then the leaders of the households, the leaders of the tribes of Israel, the commanders of thousands and of hundreds, and the officials in charge of the king's work gave willingly. 7 For the service of God's house they gave 185 tons[H] of gold and 10,000 gold coins,[I] 375 tons[J] of silver, 675 tons[K] of bronze, and 4,000 tons[L] of iron. 8 Whoever had precious stones gave them to the treasury of the LORD's house under the care of Jehiel the Gershonite. 9 Then the people rejoiced because of their leaders' willingness to give, for they had given to the LORD wholeheartedly. King David also rejoiced greatly.

DAVID'S PRAYER

10 Then David blessed the LORD in the sight of all the assembly. David said,

---

[A] **28:12** Or *he received from the Spirit* [B] **28:18** Or *chariot, that is*; Ps 18:10; Ezk 1:5,15 [C] **28:19** Hb obscure [D] **29:2** Or *mosaic* [E] **29:2** In Hb, the word *antimony* is similar to "turquoise"; Ex 28:18. [F] **29:4** Lit *3,000 talents* [G] **29:4** Lit *7,000 talents* [H] **29:7** Lit *5,000 talents* [I] **29:7** Or *drachmas*, or *darics* [J] **29:7** Lit *10,000 talents* [K] **29:7** Lit *18,000 talents* [L] **29:7** Lit *100,000 talents*

May you be blessed, LORD God of our
father Israel, from eternity to eternity.
11 Yours, LORD, is the greatness and the
power and the glory and the splendor
and the majesty, for everything in the
heavens and on earth belongs to you.
Yours, LORD, is the kingdom, and you are
exalted as head over all. 12 Riches and
honor come from you, and you are the
ruler of everything. Power and might
are in your hand, and it is in your hand
to make great and to give strength to all.
13 Now therefore, our God, we give you
thanks and praise your glorious name.

14 But who am I, and who are my people,
that we should be able to give as generously as this? For everything comes
from you, and we have given you only
what comes from your own hand.[A] 15 For
we are aliens and temporary residents
in your presence as were all our ancestors. Our days on earth are like a shadow,
without hope. 16 LORD our God, all this
wealth that we've provided for building
you a house for your holy name comes
from your hand; everything belongs
to you. 17 I know, my God, that you test
the heart and that you are pleased with
what is right. I have willingly given all
these things with an upright heart, and
now I have seen your people who are
present[B] here giving joyfully and[C] willingly to you. 18 LORD God of Abraham,
Isaac, and Israel, our ancestors, keep
this desire forever in the thoughts of
the hearts of your people, and confirm
their hearts toward you. 19 Give my son
Solomon an undivided heart to keep
and to carry out all your commands,
your decrees, and your statutes, and to
build the building for which I have made
provision.

20 Then David said to the whole assembly,
"Blessed be the LORD your God." So the whole
assembly praised the LORD God of their ancestors. They knelt low and paid homage to
the LORD and the king.
21 The following day they offered sacrifices
to the LORD and burnt offerings to the LORD:
a thousand bulls, a thousand rams, and a
thousand lambs, along with their drink offerings, and sacrifices in abundance for all
Israel. 22 They ate and drank with great joy
in the LORD's presence that day.

Relationships | *Telling the Truth*

X-RAY VISION

"I know, my God, that you test the heart and that you are pleased with what is right. I have willingly given all these things with an upright heart, and now I have seen your people who are present here giving joyfully and willingly to you." 1 Chronicles 29:17

X-rays, blood tests, cat scans, biopsies, MRIs, and more—doctors have a broad array of diagnostic tools to learn what is going on inside our bodies. Often a grim diagnosis—as discouraging as that can be—is the first step toward health.

As part of the great worship service connected to the coronation of Solomon, King David acknowledged the even more thorough and accurate way God is able to look into our souls. "You test the heart," David declared (from a lifetime of personal experiences). Or as Luke recorded in the New Testament, "You, Lord, know everyone's hearts" (Ac 1:24).

If God were malicious or unmerciful, this would be the worst of news. But because God is gracious and good, we can trust him to correct and heal what is wrong with our souls. All the more reason to let God X-ray your life!

For the next note on *Relationships*, see Psalm 19:14.

[A] **29:14** Lit *and from your hand we have given to you* [B] **29:17** Lit *found* [C] **29:17** Or *now with joy I've seen your people who are present here giving*

THE ENTHRONEMENT OF SOLOMON

Then, for a second time, they made David's
son Solomon king; they anointed him[A] as the
LORD's ruler, and Zadok as the priest. 23 Solomon sat on the LORD's throne as king in place
of his father David. He prospered, and all Israel obeyed him. 24 All the leaders and the
mighty men, and all of King David's sons as
well, pledged their allegiance to King Solomon. 25 The LORD highly exalted Solomon in
the sight of all Israel and bestowed on him
such royal majesty as had not been bestowed
on any king over Israel before him.

A SUMMARY OF DAVID'S LIFE

26 David son of Jesse was king over all Israel.
27 The length of his reign over Israel was forty
years; he reigned in Hebron for seven years
and in Jerusalem for thirty-three. 28 He died at
a good old age, full of days, riches, and honor,
and his son Solomon became king in his place.
29 As for the events of King David's reign, from
beginning to end, note that they are written
in the Events of the Seer Samuel, the Events
of the Prophet Nathan, and the Events of the
Seer Gad, 30 along with all his reign, his might,
and the incidents that affected him and Israel
and all the kingdoms of the surrounding lands.

[A] **29:22** LXX, Tg, Vg; MT omits *him*

2 Chronicles—The people of Judah faced an uncertain future. Having broken the covenant, they wondered if they could ever be restored to their former position as God's chosen people. The writer of 2 Chronicles promises that God's people who had been exiled could experience his blessing if they returned to a life of obedience.

At times you may feel exiled—perhaps separated from the family of God, or even your own family—through some bad decisions. Or maybe you feel lonely and apart, even when surrounded by people who love you.

If so, 2 Chronicles offers you the hope offered to Judah. God's promises are sure, regardless of our feelings or circumstances. We need to turn from our sins and turn to him (7:14). Humble repentance brings about God's plan to restore his people.

God is eternally the same, ever faithful to his Word. He fulfilled the promise he had made to send an everlasting King in the line of David—Jesus, the Messiah. In his name we can pray, repent, and be forgiven and restored.

No person is outside the reach of God's love, and no situation is beyond the reach of his redemption.

2 CHRONICLES

AUTHOR: Ancient sources ascribe the authorship of 1 and 2 Chronicles, which were originally one book, to the scribe Ezra, though that is uncertain. The author lived after the return of the Jews from Babylonian exile and was keenly interested in the reestablishment of the law and the temple.

DATE WRITTEN: No exact date for the writing of 1 and 2 Chronicles can be ascertained. Internal evidence points to a date sometime after the return from exile, perhaps around 400 BC.

ORIGINAL AUDIENCE: The Israelites

SETTING: The Jewish people have returned from exile in Babylon and need to be reminded of God's holy calling and faithful care for them through the generations.

PURPOSE FOR WRITING: The books of 1 and 2 Chronicles are just what the name suggests—an account of the religious history of Israel, specifically the tribe of Judah. They read almost like a journal of the highlights of Israel's relationship with God. Together with the books of Ezra and Nehemiah, they trace Israel's spiritual history from Adam to the rebuilding of the temple and walls of Jerusalem. The purpose was to remind the people of Judah of their identity as God's people and direct them back to worship and obedience.

OUTLINE:

1. The Reign of King Solomon (1:1–9:31)

   The building of the temple (1:1–7:22)

   The glory of the kingdom (8:1–9:31)

2. Solomon's Successors (10:1–36:23)

   Rehoboam (10:1–12:16)

   Abijah (13:1-22)

   Asa (14:1–16:14)

   Jehoshaphat (17:1–20:37)

   Jehoram (21:1-20)

   Ahaziah and Athaliah (22:1-12)

   Joash (23:1–24:27)

   Amaziah (25:1-28)

   Uzziah (26:1-23)

   Jotham (27:1-9)

   Ahaz (28:1-27)

   Hezekiah (29:1–32:33)

   Manasseh (33:1-20)

   Amon (33:21-25)

   Josiah (34:1–35:27)

   Last kings in Judah (36:1-23)

KEY VERSE:

"And my people, who bear my name, humble themselves, pray and seek my face, and turn from their evil ways, then I will hear from heaven, forgive their sin, and heal their land." —2 Chronicles 7:14

RESTORATION THEMES

R	Rest and Reflection	*For the next note, see Job 42:6.*
E	Eternal Perspective	*For the next note, see Nehemiah 9:6.*
S	Support	*Humility—2 Chronicles 7:14; 34:27*
T	Thanksgiving and Contentment	*For the next note, see Ezra 3:10-11.*
O	Other-centeredness	*For the next note, see Job 29:12-13.*
R	Relationships	*For the next note, see Psalm 19:14.*
E	Exercise of Faith	*For the next note, see Nehemiah 8:10.*

SOLOMON'S REQUEST FOR WISDOM

1 Solomon son of David strengthened his hold
on his kingdom. The LORD his God was with
him and highly exalted him. 2 Then Solomon
spoke to all Israel, to the commanders of thousands and of hundreds, to the judges, and to
every leader in all Israel — the family heads.
3 Solomon and the whole assembly with him
went to the high place that was in Gibeon because God's tent of meeting, which the LORD's
servant Moses had made in the wilderness,
was there. 4 Now David had brought the ark
of God from Kiriath-jearim to the place[A] he
had set up for it, because he had pitched a tent
for it in Jerusalem, 5 but he put[B] the bronze
altar, which Bezalel son of Uri, son of Hur,
had made, in front of the LORD's tabernacle.
Solomon and the assembly inquired of him[C]
there. 6 Solomon offered sacrifices there in
the LORD's presence on the bronze altar at the
tent of meeting; he offered a thousand burnt
offerings on it.
7 That night God appeared to Solomon and
said to him: "Ask. What should I give you?"
8 And Solomon said to God: "You have shown
great and faithful love to my father David, and
you have made me king in his place. 9 LORD
God, let your promise to my father David now
come true. For you have made me king over a
people as numerous as the dust of the earth.
10 Now grant me wisdom and knowledge so
that I may lead these people, for who can judge
this great people of yours?"

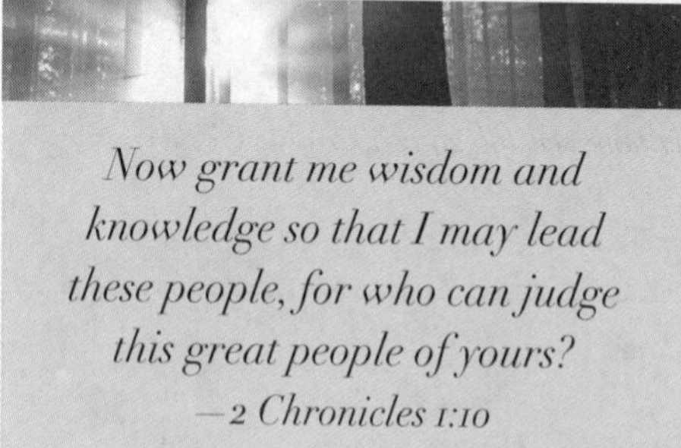
Now grant me wisdom and knowledge so that I may lead these people, for who can judge this great people of yours?
—2 Chronicles 1:10

11 God said to Solomon, "Since this was in
your heart, and you have not requested riches,
wealth, or glory, or for the life of those who
hate you, and you have not even requested
long life, but you have requested for yourself
wisdom and knowledge that you may judge
my people over whom I have made you king,
12 wisdom and knowledge are given to you. I
will also give you riches, wealth, and glory,
unlike what was given to the kings who were
before you, or will be given to those after you."
13 So Solomon went to Jerusalem from[D] the
high place that was in Gibeon in front of the
tent of meeting, and he reigned over Israel.

SOLOMON'S HORSES AND WEALTH

14 Solomon accumulated 1,400 chariots and
12,000 horsemen, which he stationed in the
chariot cities and with the king in Jerusalem.
15 The king made silver and gold as common
in Jerusalem as stones, and he made cedar
as abundant as sycamore in the Judean foothills. 16 Solomon's horses came from Egypt
and Kue.[E] The king's traders would get them
from Kue at the going price. 17 A chariot could
be imported from Egypt for fifteen pounds[F]
of silver and a horse for nearly four pounds.[G]
In the same way, they exported them to all the
kings of the Hittites and to the kings of Aram
through their agents.

SOLOMON'S LETTER TO HIRAM

2 Solomon decided to build a temple for the
name of the LORD and a royal palace for
himself, 2 so he assigned 70,000 men as porters,
80,000 men as stonecutters in the mountains,
and 3,600 as supervisors over them.
3 Then Solomon sent word to King Hiram[H]
of Tyre:

Do for me what you did for my father
David. You sent him cedars to build him
a house to live in. 4 Now I am building a
temple for the name of the LORD my God
in order to dedicate it to him for burning
fragrant incense before him, for displaying the rows of the Bread of the Presence
continuously, and for sacrificing burnt
offerings for the morning and the evening,
the Sabbaths and the New Moons, and the
appointed festivals of the LORD our God.
This is ordained for Israel permanently.
5 The temple that I am building will be
great, for our God is greater than any
of the gods. 6 But who is able to build a
temple for him, since even heaven and the
highest heaven cannot contain him? Who
am I then that I should build a temple for
him except as a place to burn incense before him? 7 Therefore, send me an artisan

---

[A] **1:4** Vg; MT omits *the place* [B] **1:5** Some Hb mss, Tg, Syr; other Hb mss, LXX, Vg read *but there was* [C] **1:5** Or *it* [D] **1:13** LXX, Vg; MT reads *to* [E] **1:16** = Cilicia [F] **1:17** Lit *600 shekels* [G] **1:17** Lit *150 shekels* [H] **2:3** Some Hb mss, LXX, Syr, Vg; other Hb mss read *Huram*; 2Sm 5:11; 1Kg 5:1-2

who is skilled in engraving to work with
gold, silver, bronze, and iron, and with
purple, crimson, and blue yarn. He will
work with the artisans who are with me in
Judah and Jerusalem, appointed by my father David. 8 Also, send me cedar, cypress,
and algum[A] logs from Lebanon, for I know
that your servants know how to cut the
trees of Lebanon. Note that my servants
will be with your servants 9 to prepare logs
for me in abundance because the temple
I am building will be great and wondrous.
10 I will give your servants, the woodcutters who cut the trees, one hundred thousand bushels[B] of wheat flour, one hundred
thousand bushels of barley, one hundred
ten thousand gallons[C] of wine, and one
hundred ten thousand gallons of oil.

HIRAM'S REPLY

11 Then King Hiram of Tyre wrote a letter[D] and
sent it to Solomon:
Because the LORD loves his people, he set
you over them as king.
12 Hiram also said:
Blessed be the LORD God of Israel, who
made the heavens and the earth! He gave
King David a wise son with insight and
understanding, who will build a temple for
the LORD and a royal palace for himself. 13 I
have now sent Huram-abi,[E] a skillful man
who has understanding. 14 He is the son of
a woman from the daughters of Dan. His
father is a man of Tyre. He knows how to
work with gold, silver, bronze, iron, stone,
and wood, with purple, blue, crimson yarn,
and fine linen. He knows how to do all
kinds of engraving and to execute any design that may be given him. I have sent him
to be with your artisans and the artisans
of my lord, your father David. 15 Now, let my
lord send the wheat, barley, oil, and wine to
his servants as promised. 16 We will cut logs
from Lebanon, as many as you need, and
bring them to you as rafts by sea to Joppa.
You can then take them up to Jerusalem.

SOLOMON'S WORKFORCE

17 Solomon took a census of all the resident alien
men in the land of Israel, after the census that
his father David had conducted, and the total
was 153,600. 18 Solomon made 70,000 of them
porters, 80,000 stonecutters in the mountains,
and 3,600 supervisors to make the people work.

BUILDING THE TEMPLE

3 Then Solomon began to build the LORD's
temple in Jerusalem on Mount Moriah
where the LORD[F] had appeared to his father
David, at the site David had prepared on the
threshing floor of Ornan[G] the Jebusite. 2 He
began to build on the second day of the second
month in the fourth year of his reign. 3 These
are Solomon's foundations[H] for building God's
temple: the length[I] was ninety feet,[J] and the
width thirty feet.[K] 4 The portico, which was
across the front extending across the width
of the temple, was thirty feet wide; its height
was thirty feet;[L] he overlaid its inner surface
with pure gold. 5 The larger room[M] he paneled
with cypress wood, overlaid with fine gold,
and decorated with palm trees and chains.
6 He adorned the temple with precious stones
for beauty, and the gold was the gold of Par-
vaim. 7 He overlaid the temple — the beams,
the thresholds, its walls and doors — with
gold, and he carved cherubim on the walls.

THE MOST HOLY PLACE

8 Then he made the most holy place; its length
corresponded to the width of the temple, 30
feet, and its width was 30 feet. He overlaid it
with forty-five thousand pounds[N] of fine gold.
9 The weight of the nails was twenty ounces[O]
of gold, and he overlaid the ceiling with gold.
10 He made two cherubim of sculptured work,
for the most holy place, and he overlaid them
with gold. 11 The overall length of the wings
of the cherubim was 30 feet: the wing of one
was 7 ½ feet,[P] touching the wall of the room;
its other wing was 7 ½ feet, touching the wing
of the other cherub. 12 The wing of the other[Q]
cherub was 7 ½ feet, touching the wall of the
room; its other wing was 7 ½ feet, reaching
the wing of the other cherub. 13 The wingspan
of these cherubim was 30 feet. They stood on
their feet and faced the larger room.[R]
14 He made the curtain of blue, purple, and
crimson yarn and fine linen, and he wove
cherubim into it.

[A] **2:8** = almug in 1Kg 10:11-12 [B] **2:10** Lit *20,000 cors* [C] **2:10** Lit *20,000 baths* [D] **2:11** Lit *Tyre said in writing* [E] **2:13** Lit *Huram my father* [F] **3:1** LXX; Tg reads *the angel of the LORD*; MT reads *he* [G] **3:1** = Araunah in 2Sm 24:16-24 [H] **3:3** Tg reads *The measurements which Solomon decreed* [I] **3:3** Lit *length — cubits in the former measure —* [J] **3:3** Lit *60 cubits* [K] **3:3** Lit *20 cubits*, also in vv. 4,8,11,13 [L] **3:4** LXX, Syr; MT reads *120 cubits* [M] **3:5** Lit *The house* [N] **3:8** Lit *600 talents* [O] **3:9** Lit *50 shekels* [P] **3:11** Lit *five cubits*, also in vv. 12,15 [Q] **3:12** Syr, Vg; MT reads *the one* [R] **3:13** Lit *the house*

THE BRONZE PILLARS

15 In front of the temple he made two pillars, each 27 feet[A] high. The capital on top of each was 7 ½ feet high. 16 He had made chainwork in the inner sanctuary and also put it on top of the pillars. He made a hundred pomegranates and fastened them into the chainwork. 17 Then he set up the pillars in front of the sanctuary, one on the right and one on the left. He named the one on the right Jachin[B] and the one on the left Boaz.[C]

THE ALTAR, RESERVOIR, AND BASINS

4 He made a bronze altar 30 feet[D] long, 30 feet wide, and 15 feet[E] high.

2 Then he made the cast metal basin,[F] 15 feet from brim to brim, perfectly round. It was 7 ½ feet[G] high and 45 feet[H] in circumference. 3 The likeness of oxen[I] was below it, completely encircling it, ten every half yard,[J] completely surrounding the basin. The oxen were cast in two rows when the basin was cast. 4 It stood on twelve oxen, three facing north, three facing west, three facing south, and three facing east. The basin was on top of them and all their hindquarters were toward the center. 5 The basin was three inches[K] thick, and its rim was fashioned like the brim of a cup or a lily blossom. It could hold eleven thousand gallons.[L]

6 He made ten basins for washing and he put five on the right and five on the left. The parts of the burnt offering were rinsed in them, but the basin was used by the priests for washing.

THE LAMPSTANDS, TABLES, AND COURTS

7 He made the ten gold lampstands according to their specifications and put them in the sanctuary, five on the right and five on the left. 8 He made ten tables and placed them in the sanctuary, five on the right and five on the left. He also made a hundred gold bowls.

9 He made the courtyard of the priests and the large court, and doors for the court. He overlaid the doors with bronze. 10 He put the basin on the right side, toward the southeast. 11 Then Huram[M] made the pots, the shovels, and the bowls.

COMPLETION OF THE BRONZE FURNISHINGS

So Huram finished doing the work that he was doing for King Solomon in God's temple: 12 two pillars; the bowls and the capitals on top of the two pillars; the two gratings for covering both bowls of the capitals that were on top of the pillars; 13 the four hundred pomegranates for the two gratings (two rows of pomegranates for each grating covering both capitals' bowls on top of the pillars). 14 He also made the water carts[N] and the basins on the water carts. 15 The one basin and the twelve oxen underneath it, 16 the pots, the shovels, the forks, and all their utensils — Huram-abi[O] made them for King Solomon for the LORD's temple. All these were made of polished bronze. 17 The king had them cast in clay molds in the Jordan Valley between Succoth and Zeredah. 18 Solomon made all these utensils in such great abundance that the weight of the bronze was not determined.

COMPLETION OF THE GOLD FURNISHINGS

19 Solomon also made all the equipment in God's temple: the gold altar; the tables on which to put the Bread of the Presence; 20 the lampstands and their lamps of pure gold to burn in front of the inner sanctuary according to specifications; 21 the flowers, lamps, and gold tongs — of purest gold; 22 the wick trimmers, sprinkling basins, ladles,[P] and firepans — of purest gold; and the entryway to the temple, its inner doors to the most holy place, and the doors of the temple sanctuary — of gold.

5 So all the work Solomon did for the LORD's temple was completed. Then Solomon brought the consecrated things of his father David — the silver, the gold, and all the utensils — and put them in the treasuries of God's temple.

PREPARATIONS FOR THE TEMPLE DEDICATION

2 At that time Solomon assembled at Jerusalem the elders of Israel — all the tribal heads, the ancestral chiefs of the Israelites — in order to bring the ark of the covenant of the LORD up from the city of David, that is, Zion. 3 So all the men of Israel were assembled in the king's presence at the festival; this was in the seventh month.[Q]

4 All the elders of Israel came, and the Levites picked up the ark. 5 They brought up the ark, the tent of meeting, and the holy utensils that

---

[A] **3:15** Syr reads *18 cubits* (27 feet); Hb reads *35 cubits* (52 ½ feet) [B] **3:17** = He Will Establish [C] **3:17** = Strength Is in Him [D] **4:1** Lit *20 cubits* [E] **4:1** Lit *10 cubits*, also in v. 2 [F] **4:2** Lit *sea* [G] **4:2** Lit *five cubits* [H] **4:2** Lit *30 cubits* [I] **4:3** = gourds in 1Kg 7:24 [J] **4:3** Lit *10 per cubit* [K] **4:5** Lit *a handbreadth* [L] **4:5** Text emended; MT reads *3,000 baths* in 1Kg 7:26 [M] **4:11** = Hiram in 1Kg 7:13,40,45 [N] **4:14** Lit *the stands* [O] **4:16** Lit *Huram my father* [P] **4:22** Or *dishes*, or *spoons*; lit *palms* [Q] **5:3** = Tishri (September–October)

were in the tent. The priests and the Levites
brought them up. 6 King Solomon and the entire congregation of Israel who had gathered
around him were in front of the ark sacrificing sheep, goats, and cattle that could not be
counted or numbered because there were so
many. 7 The priests brought the ark of the LORD's
covenant to its place, into the inner sanctuary
of the temple, to the most holy place, beneath
the wings of the cherubim. 8 And the cherubim
spread their wings over the place of the ark so
that the cherubim formed a cover above the
ark and its poles. 9 The poles were so long that
their ends were seen from the holy place[A] in
front of the inner sanctuary, but they were not
seen from outside; they are still there today.
10 Nothing was in the ark except the two tablets
that Moses had put in it at Horeb,[B] where the
LORD had made a covenant with the Israelites
when they came out of Egypt.
11 Now all the priests who were present had
consecrated themselves regardless of their
divisions. When the priests came out of the
holy place, 12 the Levitical singers dressed in
fine linen and carrying cymbals, harps, and
lyres were standing east of the altar, and with
them were 120 priests blowing trumpets. The
Levitical singers were descendants of Asaph,
Heman, and Jeduthun and their sons and relatives. 13 The trumpeters and singers joined
together to praise and thank the LORD with
one voice. They raised their voices, accompanied by trumpets, cymbals, and musical
instruments, in praise to the LORD:

They raised their voices . . . in praise to the LORD: "For he is good; his faithful love endures forever." The temple, the LORD's temple, was filled with a cloud. And because of the cloud, the priests were not able to continue ministering, for the glory of the LORD filled God's temple.
—2 Chronicles 5:13-14

For he is good;
his faithful love endures forever.
The temple, the LORD's temple, was filled with
a cloud. 14 And because of the cloud, the priests
were not able to continue ministering, for the
glory of the LORD filled God's temple.

SOLOMON'S DEDICATION OF THE TEMPLE

6 Then Solomon said:
The LORD said he would dwell
in total darkness,
2 but I have built an exalted temple
for you,
a place for your residence forever.

3 Then the king turned and blessed the entire congregation of Israel while they were
standing. 4 He said:

Blessed be the LORD God of Israel!
He spoke directly to my father David,
and he has fulfilled the promise
by his power.
He said,
5 "Since the day I brought
my people Israel
out of the land of Egypt,
I have not chosen a city to build
a temple in
among any of the tribes of Israel,
so that my name would be there,
and I have not chosen a man
to be ruler over my people Israel.
6 But I have chosen Jerusalem
so that my name will be there,
and I have chosen David
to be over my people Israel."

7 My father David had his heart set
on building a temple for the name
of the LORD, the God of Israel.
8 However, the LORD said
to my father David,
"Since it was your desire to build
a temple for my name,
you have done well to have this desire.
9 Yet, you are not the one to build
the temple,
but your son, your own offspring,
will build the temple for my name."
10 So the LORD has fulfilled
what he promised.
I have taken the place
of my father David

[A] **5:9** Some Hb mss, LXX; other Hb mss read *the ark*; 1Kg 8:8 [B] **5:10** = Sinai

and I sit on the throne of Israel, as the
LORD promised.
I have built the temple for the name
of the LORD, the God of Israel.
11 I have put the ark there,
where the LORD's covenant is
that he made with the Israelites.

SOLOMON'S PRAYER

12 Then Solomon stood before the altar of the
LORD in front of the entire congregation of Israel and spread out his hands. 13 For Solomon
had made a bronze platform 7 ½ feet[A] long, 7 ½
feet wide, and 4 ½ feet[B] high and put it in the
court. He stood on it, knelt down in front of
the entire congregation of Israel, and spread
out his hands toward heaven. 14 He said:

LORD God of Israel,
there is no God like you
in heaven or on earth,
who keeps his gracious covenant
with your servants who walk
before you
with all their heart.
15 You have kept what you promised
to your servant, my father David.
You spoke directly to him,
and you fulfilled your promise
by your power,
as it is today.
16 Therefore, LORD God of Israel,
keep what you promised
to your servant, my father David:
"You will never fail to have a man
to sit before me on the throne of Israel,
if only your sons guard their way
to walk in my Law
as you have walked before me."
17 Now, LORD God of Israel, please confirm
what you promised
to your servant David.

18 But will God indeed live on earth
with humans?
Even heaven, the highest heaven,
cannot contain you,
much less this temple I have built.
19 Listen[C] to your servant's prayer
and his petition,
LORD my God,
so that you may hear the cry
and the prayer
that your servant prays before you,
20 so that your eyes watch over this temple
day and night,
toward the place where you said
you would put your name;
and so that you may hear the prayer
your servant prays toward this place.
21 Hear the petitions of your servant
and your people Israel,
which they pray toward this place.
May you hear in your dwelling place
in heaven.
May you hear and forgive.

Hear the petitions of your servant and your people Israel, which they pray toward this place. May you hear in your dwelling place in heaven. May you hear and forgive.
—2 Chronicles 6:21

22 If a man sins against his neighbor
and is forced to take an oath[D]
and he comes to take an oath
before your altar in this temple,
23 may you hear in heaven and act.
May you judge your servants,
condemning the wicked man
by bringing
what he has done on his own head
and providing justice
for the righteous
by rewarding him according to
his righteousness.

24 If your people Israel are defeated
before an enemy,
because they have sinned against you,
and they return to you and praise
your name,
and they pray and plead for mercy
before you in this temple,
25 may you hear in heaven
and forgive the sin
of your people Israel.
May you restore them to the land
you gave them and their ancestors.

[A] **6:13** Lit *five cubits* [B] **6:13** Lit *three cubits* [C] **6:19** Lit *Turn* [D] **6:22** Lit *and he lifts a curse against him to curse him*

26 When the skies are shut and there is
no rain
because they have sinned against you,
and they pray toward this place
and praise your name,
and they turn from their sins
because you are afflicting[A] them,
27 may you hear in heaven
and forgive the sin of your servants
and your people Israel,
so that you may teach them the good way
they should walk in.
May you send rain on your land
that you gave your people
for an inheritance.

28 When there is famine in the land,
when there is pestilence,
when there is blight or mildew, locust
or grasshopper,
when their enemies besiege them
in the land and its cities,[B,C]
when there is any plague or illness,
29 every prayer or petition
that any person or that
all your people Israel may have —
they each know their own affliction[D]
and suffering —
as they spread out their hands
toward this temple,
30 may you hear in heaven,
your dwelling place,
and may you forgive
and give to everyone[E]
according to all their ways,
since you know each heart,
for you alone know the human heart,
31 so that they may fear you
and walk in your ways
all the days they live on the land
you gave our ancestors.

32 Even for the foreigner who is not of
your people Israel
but has come from a distant land
because of your great name
and your strong hand
and outstretched arm:
when he comes and prays
toward this temple,
33 may you hear in heaven in your
dwelling place,
and do all the foreigner asks you.
Then all the peoples of the earth
will know your name,
to fear you as your people Israel do
and know that this temple
I have built
bears your name.

34 When your people go out
to fight against their enemies,
wherever you send them,
and they pray to you
in the direction of this city
you have chosen
and the temple that I have built
for your name,
35 may you hear their prayer and petition
in heaven
and uphold their cause.

36 When they sin against you —
for there is no one who does not sin —
and you are angry with them
and hand them over to the enemy,
and their captors deport them
to a distant or nearby country,
37 and when they come to their senses
in the land where they were deported
and repent and petition you
in their captors' land,
saying: "We have sinned
and done wrong;
we have been wicked,"
38 and when they return to you with all
their mind and all their heart
in the land of their captivity
where they were taken captive,
and when they pray in the direction
of their land
that you gave their ancestors,
and the city you have chosen,
and toward the temple I have built
for your name,
39 may you hear their prayer
and petitions in heaven,
your dwelling place,
and uphold their cause.[F]
May you forgive your people
who sinned against you.

40 Now, my God,
please let your eyes be open
and your ears attentive
to the prayer of this place.

[A] **6:26** LXX, Vg; MT reads *answering*; 1Kg 8:35 [B] **6:28** Lit *land of its gates* [C] **6:28** Lit *if his* (Israel's) *enemies besiege him in the land of his gates*; Jos 2:7; Jdg 16:2-3 [D] **6:29** Lit *plague* [E] **6:30** Lit *give for the man* [F] **6:39** Lit *and do their judgment*, or *justice*

41 Now therefore:

Arise, LORD God, come
to your resting place,
you and your powerful ark.
May your priests, LORD God, be clothed
with salvation,
and may your faithful people rejoice
in goodness.
42 LORD God, do not reject
your anointed one;[A]
remember the promises
to your servant David.

THE DEDICATION CEREMONIES

When Solomon finished praying, fire
descended from heaven and consumed
the burnt offering and the sacrifices, and
the glory of the LORD filled the temple. 2 The
priests were not able to enter the LORD's temple because the glory of the LORD filled the
temple of the LORD. 3 All the Israelites were
watching when the fire descended and the
glory of the LORD came on the temple. They
bowed down on the pavement with their
faces to the ground. They worshiped and
praised the LORD:

For he is good,
for his faithful love endures forever.

4 The king and all the people were offering sacrifices in the LORD's presence. 5 King
Solomon offered a sacrifice of twenty-two
thousand cattle and one hundred twenty
thousand sheep and goats. In this manner
the king and all the people dedicated God's
temple. 6 The priests and the Levites were
standing at their stations. The Levites had
the musical instruments of the LORD, which
King David had made to give thanks to the
LORD — "for his faithful love endures forever" — when he offered praise with them.
Across from the Levites, the priests were
blowing trumpets, and all the people were
standing. 7 Since the bronze altar that Solomon had made could not accommodate the
burnt offering, the grain offering, and the
fat of the fellowship offerings, Solomon first
consecrated the middle of the courtyard that
was in front of the LORD's temple and then
offered the burnt offerings and the fat of the
fellowship offerings there.

8 So Solomon and all Israel with him — a
very great assembly, from the entrance to
Hamath[B] to the Brook of Egypt — observed
the festival at that time for seven days. 9 On the
eighth day[C] they held a sacred assembly, for the
dedication of the altar lasted seven days and
the festival seven days. 10 On the twenty-third

S Support | *Humility*

HIS HEALING

"And my people, who bear my name, humble themselves, pray and seek my face, and turn from their evil ways, then I will hear from heaven, forgive their sin, and heal their land." 2 Chronicles 7:14

Some Christians like to put this verse on billboards, bumper stickers, and yard signs in hopes of urging their neighbors to turn back to God. Others shake their heads and argue that this promise was given only to the ancient nation of Israel.

God does want his people (ancient and modern) to be humble, to have an honest view of ourselves. He also wants us to pray, to seek after him, and to turn from sin. And his nature is to forgive and heal.

Whether our obedience to these particular commands might trigger a wide-scale "revival" in contemporary culture, who can say? Such matters are totally up to God. We are not responsible for outcomes, only for our own attitudes and behavior and not for the actions and inactions of others.

At the very least we know this: Turning from sin, seeking after God, being humble, and praying fervently will bring great healing to us and our nation.

For the next note on *Support*, see 2 Chronicles 34:27.

[A] **6:42** Some Hb mss, LXX; other Hb mss read *ones*; Ps 132:10 [B] **7:8** Or *from Lebo-hamath* [C] **7:9** = the day after the festival, or the 15th day

day of the seventh month he sent the people home,[A] rejoicing and with happy hearts for the goodness the LORD had done for David, for Solomon, and for his people Israel.

11 So Solomon finished the LORD's temple and the royal palace. Everything that had entered Solomon's heart to do for the LORD's temple and for his own palace succeeded.

THE LORD'S RESPONSE

12 Then the LORD appeared to Solomon at night and said to him:

I have heard your prayer and have chosen this place for myself as a temple of sacrifice. 13 If I shut the sky so there is no rain, or if I command the grasshopper to consume the land, or if I send pestilence on my people, 14 and my people, who bear my name, humble themselves, pray and seek my face, and turn from their evil ways, then I will hear from heaven, forgive their sin, and heal their land. 15 My eyes will now be open and my ears attentive to prayer from this place. 16 And I have now chosen and consecrated this temple so that my name may be there forever; my eyes and my heart will be there at all times.

17 As for you, if you walk before me as your father David walked, doing everything I have commanded you, and if you keep my statutes and ordinances, 18 I will establish your royal throne, as I promised your father David: You will never fail to have a man ruling in Israel.

19 However, if you turn away and abandon my statutes and my commands that I have set before you and if you go and serve other gods and bow in worship to them, 20 then I will uproot Israel from the soil that I gave them, and this temple that I have sanctified for my name I will banish from my presence; I will make it an object of scorn and ridicule among all the peoples. 21 As for this temple, which was exalted, everyone who passes by will be appalled and will say: Why did the LORD do this to this land and this temple? 22 Then they will say: Because they abandoned the LORD God of their ancestors who brought them out of the land of Egypt. They clung to other gods and bowed in worship to them and served them. Because of this, he brought all this ruin on them.

SOLOMON'S LATER BUILDING PROJECTS

8 At the end of twenty years during which Solomon had built the LORD's temple and his own palace — 2 Solomon had rebuilt the cities Hiram[B] gave him and settled Israelites there — 3 Solomon went to Hamath-zobah and seized it. 4 He built Tadmor in the wilderness along with all the storage cities that he built in Hamath. 5 He built Upper Beth-horon and Lower Beth-horon — fortified cities with walls, gates, and bars — 6 Baalath, all the storage cities that belonged to Solomon, all the chariot cities, the cavalry cities, and everything Solomon desired to build in Jerusalem, Lebanon, or anywhere else in the land of his dominion.

7 As for all the peoples who remained of the Hethites, Amorites, Perizzites, Hivites, and Jebusites, who were not from Israel — 8 their descendants who remained in the land after them, those the Israelites had not completely destroyed — Solomon imposed forced labor on them; it is this way today. 9 But Solomon did not consign the Israelites to be slaves for his work; they were soldiers, commanders of his captains, and commanders of his chariots and his cavalry. 10 These were King Solomon's deputies: 250 who supervised the people.

11 Solomon brought the daughter of Pharaoh from the city of David to the house he had built for her, for he said, "My wife must not live in the house[C] of King David of Israel because the places the ark of the LORD has come into are holy."

PUBLIC WORSHIP ESTABLISHED AT THE TEMPLE

12 At that time Solomon offered burnt offerings to the LORD on the LORD's altar he had made in front of the portico. 13 He followed the daily requirement for offerings according to the commandment of Moses for Sabbaths, New Moons, and the three annual appointed festivals: the Festival of Unleavened Bread, the Festival of Weeks, and the Festival of Shelters. 14 According to the ordinances of his father David, he appointed the divisions of the priests over their service, of the Levites over their responsibilities to offer praise and to

[A] **7:10** Lit *people to their tents* [B] **8:2** = the king of Tyre [C] **8:11** LXX reads *city*

minister before the priests following the daily requirement, and of the gatekeepers by their divisions with respect to each temple gate, for this had been the command of David, the man of God. 15 They did not turn aside from the king's command regarding the priests and the Levites concerning any matter or concerning the treasuries. 16 All of Solomon's work was carried out from the day the foundation was laid for the LORD's temple until it was finished. So the LORD's temple was completed.

SOLOMON'S FLEET

17 At that time Solomon went to Ezion-geber and to Eloth on the seashore in the land of Edom. 18 So Hiram[A] sent ships to him by his servants along with crews of experienced seamen. They went with Solomon's servants to Ophir, took from there seventeen tons[B] of gold, and delivered it to King Solomon.

THE QUEEN OF SHEBA

9 The queen of Sheba heard of Solomon's fame, so she came to test Solomon with difficult questions at Jerusalem with a very large entourage, with camels bearing spices, gold in abundance, and precious stones. She came to Solomon and spoke with him about everything that was on her mind. 2 So Solomon answered all her questions; nothing was too difficult for Solomon to explain to her. 3 When the queen of Sheba observed Solomon's wisdom, the palace he had built, 4 the food at his table, his servants' residence, his attendants' service and their attire, his cupbearers and their attire, and the burnt offerings he offered at the LORD's temple, it took her breath away.

5 She said to the king, "The report I heard in my own country about your words and about your wisdom is true. 6 But I didn't believe their reports until I came and saw with my own eyes. Indeed, I was not even told half of your great wisdom! You far exceed the report I heard. 7 How happy are your men.[C] How happy are these servants of yours, who always stand in your presence hearing your wisdom. 8 Blessed be the LORD your God! He delighted in you and put you on his throne as king for the LORD your God. Because your God loved Israel enough to establish them forever, he has set you over them as king to carry out justice and righteousness."

9 Then she gave the king four and a half tons[D] of gold, a great quantity of spices, and precious stones. There never were such spices as those the queen of Sheba gave to King Solomon. 10 In addition, Hiram's servants and Solomon's servants who brought gold from Ophir also brought algum wood and precious stones. 11 The king made the algum wood into walkways for the LORD's temple and for the king's palace and into lyres and harps for the singers. Never before had anything like them been seen in the land of Judah.

12 King Solomon gave the queen of Sheba her every desire, whatever she asked — far more than she had brought the king. Then she, along with her servants, returned to her own country.

SOLOMON'S WEALTH

13 The weight of gold that came to Solomon annually was twenty-five tons,[E] 14 besides what was brought by the merchants and traders. All the Arabian kings and governors of the land also brought gold and silver to Solomon.

15 King Solomon made two hundred large shields of hammered gold; 15 pounds[F] of hammered gold went into each shield. 16 He made three hundred small shields of hammered gold; 7 1/2 pounds[G] of gold went into each shield. The king put them in the House of the Forest of Lebanon.

17 The king also made a large ivory throne and overlaid it with pure gold. 18 The throne had six steps; there was a footstool covered in gold for the throne, armrests on either side of the seat, and two lions standing beside the armrests. 19 Twelve lions were standing there on the six steps, one at each end. Nothing like it had ever been made in any other kingdom.

20 All of King Solomon's drinking cups were gold, and all the utensils of the House of the Forest of Lebanon were pure gold. There was no silver, since it was considered as nothing in Solomon's time, 21 for the king's ships kept going to Tarshish with Hiram's servants, and once every three years the ships of Tarshish would arrive bearing gold, silver, ivory, apes, and peacocks.[H]

22 King Solomon surpassed all the kings of the world in riches and wisdom. 23 All the kings of the world wanted an audience with Solomon to hear the wisdom God had put in his heart. 24 Each of them would bring his own gift — items[I] of silver and gold, clothing,

[A] **8:18** Lit *Huram* [B] **8:18** Lit *450 talents* [C] **9:7** LXX, Old Lat read *wives*; 1Kg 10:8 [D] **9:9** Lit *120 talents* [E] **9:13** Lit *666 talents* [F] **9:15** Lit *600* (shekels) [G] **9:16** Lit *300* (shekels) [H] **9:21** Or *baboons* [I] **9:24** Or *vessels*, or *weapons*

weapons,[A,B] spices, and horses and mules — as an annual tribute.

25 Solomon had four thousand stalls for horses and chariots, and twelve thousand horsemen. He stationed them in the chariot cities and with the king in Jerusalem. 26 He ruled over all the kings from the Euphrates River to the land of the Philistines and as far as the border of Egypt. 27 The king made silver as common in Jerusalem as stones, and he made cedar as abundant as sycamore in the Judean foothills. 28 They were bringing horses for Solomon from Egypt and from all the countries.

SOLOMON'S DEATH

29 The remaining events of Solomon's reign, from beginning to end, are written in the Events of the Prophet Nathan, the Prophecy of Ahijah the Shilonite, and the Visions of the Seer Iddo concerning Jeroboam son of Nebat. 30 Solomon reigned in Jerusalem over all Israel for forty years. 31 Solomon rested with his fathers and was buried in the city of his father David. His son Rehoboam became king in his place.

THE KINGDOM DIVIDED

10 Then Rehoboam went to Shechem, for all Israel had gone to Shechem to make him king. 2 When Jeroboam son of Nebat heard about it — for he was in Egypt where he had fled from King Solomon's presence — Jeroboam returned from Egypt. 3 So they summoned him. Then Jeroboam and all Israel came and spoke to Rehoboam: 4 "Your father made our yoke harsh. Therefore, lighten your father's harsh service and the heavy yoke he put on us, and we will serve you."

5 Rehoboam replied, "Return to me in three days." So the people left.

6 Then King Rehoboam consulted with the elders who had attended his father Solomon when he was alive, asking, "How do you advise me to respond to this people?"

7 They replied, "If you will be kind to this people and please them by speaking kind words to them, they will be your servants forever."

8 But he rejected the advice of the elders who had advised him, and he consulted with the young men who had grown up with him, the ones attending him. 9 He asked them, "What message do you advise we send back to this people who said to me, 'Lighten the yoke your father put on us'?"

10 Then the young men who had grown up with him told him, "This is what you should say to the people who said to you, 'Your father made our yoke heavy, but you, make it lighter on us!' This is what you should say to them: 'My little finger is thicker than my father's waist! 11 Now therefore, my father burdened you with a heavy yoke, but I will add to your yoke; my father disciplined you with whips, but I, with barbed whips.'"[C]

12 So Jeroboam and all the people came to Rehoboam on the third day, just as the king had ordered, saying, "Return to me on the third day." 13 Then the king answered them harshly. King Rehoboam rejected the elders' advice 14 and spoke to them according to the young men's advice, saying, "My father made your yoke heavy,[D] but I will add to it; my father disciplined you with whips, but I, with barbed whips."

15 The king did not listen to the people because the turn of events came from God, in order that the LORD might carry out his word that he had spoken through Ahijah the Shilonite to Jeroboam son of Nebat.

16 When all Israel saw[E] that the king had not listened to them, the people answered the king:

What portion do we have in David?
We have no inheritance in the son
of Jesse.
Israel, each to your tent;
David, look after your own house now!

So all Israel went to their tents. 17 But as for the Israelites living in the cities of Judah, Rehoboam reigned over them.

18 Then King Rehoboam sent Hadoram,[F] who was in charge of the forced labor, but the Israelites stoned him to death. However, King Rehoboam managed to get into his chariot to flee to Jerusalem. 19 Israel is in rebellion against the house of David until today.

REHOBOAM IN JERUSALEM

11 When Rehoboam arrived in Jerusalem, he mobilized the house of Judah and Benjamin — one hundred eighty thousand fit young soldiers — to fight against Israel to restore the reign to Rehoboam. 2 But the word of the LORD came to Shemaiah, the man of

[A] **9:24** LXX reads *resin* [B] **9:24** Or *fragrant balsam* [C] **10:11** Lit *with scorpions*, also in v. 14 [D] **10:14** Some Hb mss, LXX; other Hb mss read *I will make your yoke heavy*; 1Kg 12:14 [E] **10:16** Some Hb mss, LXX; other Hb mss omit *saw*; 1Kg 12:16
[F] **10:18** = Adoram in 1Kg 12:18

God: 3 "Say to Rehoboam son of Solomon, king of Judah, to all Israel in Judah and Benjamin, and to the rest of the people: 4 'This is what the LORD says: You are not to march up and fight against your brothers. Each of you return home, for this incident has come from me.' "

So they listened to what the LORD said and turned back from going against Jeroboam.

JUDAH'S KING REHOBOAM

5 Rehoboam stayed in Jerusalem, and he fortified cities[A] in Judah. 6 He built up Bethlehem, Etam, Tekoa, 7 Beth-zur, Soco, Adullam, 8 Gath, Mareshah, Ziph, 9 Adoraim, Lachish, Azekah, 10 Zorah, Aijalon, and Hebron, which are fortified cities in Judah and in Benjamin. 11 He strengthened their fortifications and put leaders in them with supplies of food, oil, and wine. 12 He also put large shields and spears in each and every city to make them very strong. So Judah and Benjamin were his.

13 The priests and Levites from all their regions throughout Israel took their stand with Rehoboam, 14 for the Levites left their pasturelands and their possessions and went to Judah and Jerusalem, because Jeroboam and his sons refused to let them serve as priests of the LORD. 15 Jeroboam appointed his own priests for the high places, the goat-demons, and the golden calves he had made. 16 Those from every tribe of Israel who had determined in their hearts to seek the LORD their God followed the Levites to Jerusalem to sacrifice to the LORD, the God of their ancestors. 17 So they strengthened the kingdom of Judah and supported Rehoboam son of Solomon for three years, because they walked in the ways of David and Solomon for three years.

18 Rehoboam married Mahalath, daughter of David's son Jerimoth and of Abihail daughter of Jesse's son Eliab. 19 She bore sons to him: Jeush, Shemariah, and Zaham. 20 After her, he married Maacah daughter[B] of Absalom. She bore Abijah, Attai, Ziza, and Shelomith to him. 21 Rehoboam loved Maacah daughter of Absalom more than all his wives and concubines. He acquired eighteen wives and sixty concubines and was the father of twenty-eight sons and sixty daughters.

22 Rehoboam appointed Abijah son of Maacah as chief, leader among his brothers, intending to make him king. 23 Rehoboam also showed discernment by dispersing some of his sons to all the regions of Judah and Benjamin and to all the fortified cities. He gave them plenty of provisions and sought many wives for them.

SHISHAK'S INVASION

12 When Rehoboam had established his sovereignty and royal power, he abandoned the law of the LORD — he and all Israel with him. 2 Because they were unfaithful to the LORD, in the fifth year of King Rehoboam, King Shishak of Egypt went to war against Jerusalem 3 with 1,200 chariots, 60,000 cavalrymen, and countless people who came with him from Egypt — Libyans, Sukkiim, and Cushites. 4 He captured the fortified cities of Judah and came as far as Jerusalem.

5 Then the prophet Shemaiah went to Rehoboam and the leaders of Judah who were gathered at Jerusalem because of Shishak. He said to them: "This is what the LORD says: 'You have abandoned me; therefore, I have abandoned you to Shishak.' "

6 So the leaders of Israel and the king humbled themselves and said, "The LORD is righteous."

7 When the LORD saw that they had humbled themselves, the LORD's message came to Shemaiah: "They have humbled themselves; I will not destroy them but will grant them a little deliverance. My wrath will not be poured out on Jerusalem through Shishak. 8 However, they will become his servants so that they may recognize the difference between serving me and serving the kingdoms of other lands."

9 So King Shishak of Egypt went to war against Jerusalem. He seized the treasuries of the LORD's temple and the treasuries of the royal palace. He took everything. He took the gold shields that Solomon had made. 10 King Rehoboam made bronze shields to replace them and committed them into the care of the captains of the guards[C] who protected the entrance to the king's palace. 11 Whenever the king entered the LORD's temple, the guards would carry the shields and take them back to the armory.[D] 12 When Rehoboam humbled himself, the LORD's anger turned away from him, and he did not destroy him completely. Besides that, conditions were good in Judah.

REHOBOAM'S LAST DAYS

13 King Rehoboam established his royal power in Jerusalem. Rehoboam was forty-one years

[A] **11:5** Lit *he built cities for a fortress* [B] **11:20** Possibly *granddaughter*, also in v. 21; 2Ch 13:2 [C] **12:10** Lit *the runners* [D] **12:11** Lit *the chamber of the runners*

old when he became king, and he reigned seventeen years in Jerusalem, the city the LORD had chosen from all the tribes of Israel to put his name. Rehoboam's mother's name was Naamah the Ammonite. 14 Rehoboam did what was evil, because he did not determine in his heart to seek the LORD.

15 The events of Rehoboam's reign, from beginning to end, are written in the Events of the Prophet Shemaiah and of the Seer Iddo concerning genealogies. There was war between Rehoboam and Jeroboam throughout their reigns. 16 Rehoboam rested with his fathers and was buried in the city of David. His son Abijah[A] became king in his place.

JUDAH'S KING ABIJAH

13 In the eighteenth year of Israel's King Jeroboam, Abijah[A] became king over Judah, 2 and he reigned three years in Jerusalem. His mother's name was Micaiah[B] daughter of Uriel; she was from Gibeah.

There was war between Abijah and Jeroboam. 3 Abijah set his army of warriors in order with four hundred thousand fit young men. Jeroboam arranged his mighty army of eight hundred thousand fit young men in battle formation against him. 4 Then Abijah stood on Mount Zemaraim, which is in the hill country of Ephraim, and said, "Jeroboam and all Israel, hear me. 5 Don't you know that the LORD God of Israel gave the kingship over Israel to David and his descendants forever by a covenant of salt? 6 But Jeroboam son of Nebat, a servant of Solomon son of David, rose up and rebelled against his lord. 7 Then worthless and wicked men gathered around him to resist Rehoboam son of Solomon when Rehoboam was young, inexperienced, and unable to assert himself against them.

8 "And now you are saying you can assert yourselves against the LORD's kingdom, which is in the hand of one of David's sons. You are a vast number and have with you the golden calves that Jeroboam made for you as gods.[C] 9 Didn't you banish the priests of the LORD, the descendants of Aaron and the Levites, and make your own priests like the peoples of other lands do? Whoever comes to ordain himself with a young bull and seven rams may become a priest of what are not gods.

10 "But as for us, the LORD is our God. We have not abandoned him; the priests ministering to the LORD are descendants of Aaron, and the Levites serve at their tasks. 11 They offer a burnt offering and fragrant incense to the LORD every morning and every evening, and they set the rows of the Bread of the Presence on the ceremonially clean table. They light the lamps of the gold lampstand every evening. We are carrying out the requirements of the LORD our God, while you have abandoned him. 12 Look, God and his priests are with us at our head. The trumpets are ready to sound the charge against you. Israelites, don't fight against the LORD God of your ancestors, for you will not succeed."

13 Now Jeroboam had sent an ambush around to advance from behind them. So they were in front of Judah, and the ambush was behind them. 14 Judah turned and discovered that the battle was in front of them and behind them, so they cried out to the LORD. Then the priests blew the trumpets, 15 and the men of Judah raised the battle cry. When the men of Judah raised the battle cry, God routed Jeroboam and all Israel before Abijah and Judah. 16 So the Israelites fled before Judah, and God handed them over to them. 17 Then Abijah and his people struck them with a mighty blow, and five hundred thousand fit young men of Israel were killed. 18 The Israelites were subdued at that time. The Judahites succeeded because they depended on the LORD, the God of their ancestors.

19 Abijah pursued Jeroboam and captured some cities from him: Bethel, Jeshanah, and Ephron,[D] along with their surrounding villages. 20 Jeroboam no longer retained his power[E] during Abijah's reign; ultimately, the LORD struck him and he died.

21 However, Abijah grew strong, acquired fourteen wives, and fathered twenty-two sons and sixteen daughters. 22 The rest of the events of Abijah's reign, along with his ways and his sayings, are written in the Writing of the

14 Prophet Iddo. 1 Abijah rested with his fathers and was buried in the city of David. His son Asa became king in his place. During his reign the land experienced peace for ten years.

JUDAH'S KING ASA

2 Asa did what was good and right in the sight of the LORD his God. 3 He removed the pagan

[A] **12:16; 13:1** = Abijam in 1Kg 14:31–15:8 [B] **13:2** LXX, Syr, Arabic read *Maacah*; 1Kg 15:2; 2Ch 11:22 [C] **13:8** Or *God*; 1Kg 12:28
[D] **13:19** Alt Hb tradition reads *Ephrain* [E] **13:20** Lit *He did not restrain the power of Jeroboam*

altars and the high places. He shattered their
sacred pillars and chopped down their Asherah poles. 4 He told the people of Judah to seek
the LORD God of their ancestors and to carry
out the instruction and the commands. 5 He
also removed the high places and the shrines[A]
from all the cities of Judah, and the kingdom
experienced peace under him.
6 Because the land experienced peace, Asa
built fortified cities in Judah. No one made
war with him in those days because the LORD
gave him rest. 7 So he said to the people of
Judah, "Let's build these cities and surround
them with walls and towers, with doors and
bars. The land is still ours because we sought
the LORD our God. We sought him and he
gave us rest on every side." So they built and
succeeded.

THE CUSHITE INVASION

8 Asa had an army of three hundred thousand
from Judah bearing large shields and spears,
and two hundred eighty thousand from Benjamin bearing regular shields and drawing the
bow. All these were valiant warriors. 9 Then
Zerah the Cushite came against them with an
army of one million men and three hundred[B]
chariots. They came as far as Mareshah. 10 So
Asa marched out against him and lined up
in battle formation in Zephathah Valley at
Mareshah.
11 Then Asa cried out to the LORD his God:
"LORD, there is no one besides you to help the
mighty and those without strength. Help us,
LORD our God, for we depend on you, and in
your name we have come against this large
army. LORD, you are our God. Do not let a mere
mortal hinder you."
12 So the LORD routed the Cushites before
Asa and before Judah, and the Cushites fled.
13 Then Asa and the people who were with
him pursued them as far as Gerar. The Cushites fell until they had no survivors, for they
were crushed before the LORD and his army.
So the people of Judah carried off a great
supply of loot. 14 Then they attacked all the
cities around Gerar because the terror of
the LORD was on them. They also plundered
all the cities, since there was a great deal of
plunder in them. 15 They also attacked the
tents of the herdsmen and captured many
sheep and camels. Then they returned to
Jerusalem.

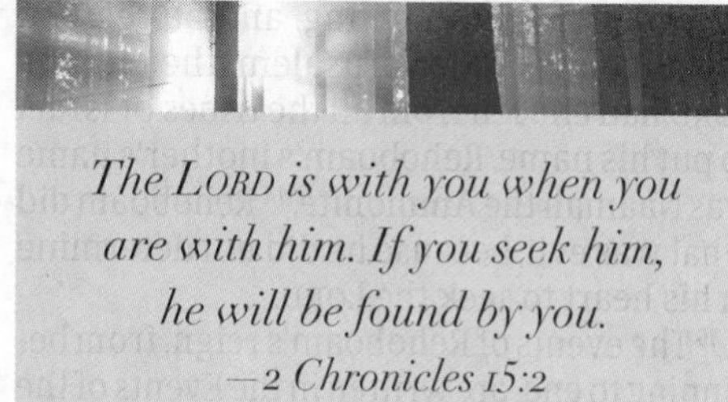
The LORD is with you when you
are with him. If you seek him,
he will be found by you.
—2 Chronicles 15:2

REVIVAL UNDER ASA

15 The Spirit of God came on Azariah son
of Oded. 2 So he went out to meet Asa
and said to him, "Asa and all Judah and Benjamin, hear me. The LORD is with you when
you are with him. If you seek him, he will
be found by you, but if you abandon him,
he will abandon you. 3 For many years Israel has been without the true God, without
a teaching priest, and without instruction,
4 but when they turned to the LORD God of
Israel in their distress and sought him, he was
found by them. 5 In those times there was no
peace for those who went about their daily
activities because the residents of the lands
had many conflicts. 6 Nation was crushed
by nation and city by city, for God troubled
them with every possible distress. 7 But as
for you, be strong; don't give up,[C] for your
work has a reward."
8 When Asa heard these words and the
prophecy of Azariah son of Oded the prophet, he took courage and removed the abhorrent idols from the whole land of Judah and
Benjamin and from the cities he had captured
in the hill country of Ephraim. He renovated
the altar of the LORD that was in front of the
portico of the LORD's temple. 9 Then he gathered all Judah and Benjamin, as well as those
from the tribes of Ephraim, Manasseh, and
Simeon who were residing among them, for
they had defected to him from Israel in great
numbers when they saw that the LORD his
God was with him.
10 They were gathered in Jerusalem in the
third month of the fifteenth year of Asa's reign.
11 At that time they sacrificed to the LORD seven
hundred cattle and seven thousand sheep and
goats from all the plunder they had brought.
12 Then they entered into a covenant to seek
the LORD God of their ancestors with all their
heart and all their soul. 13 Whoever would not

[A] **14:5** Or *incense altars* [B] **14:9** Syr, Arabic read *30,000* [C] **15:7** Lit *don't let your hands drop*

seek the LORD God of Israel would be put to
death, young or old,[A] man or woman. 14 They
took an oath to the LORD in a loud voice, with
shouting, with trumpets, and with rams' horns.
15 All Judah rejoiced over the oath, for they
had sworn it with all their mind. They had
sought him with all their heart, and he was
found by them. So the LORD gave them rest
on every side.

16 King Asa also removed Maacah, his grandmother,[B] from being queen mother because
she had made an obscene image of Asherah.
Asa chopped down her obscene image, then
crushed it and burned it in the Kidron Valley.
17 The high places were not taken away from
Israel; nevertheless, Asa was wholeheartedly devoted his entire life.[C] 18 He brought his
father's consecrated gifts and his own consecrated gifts into God's temple: silver, gold,
and utensils.

19 There was no war until the thirty-fifth
year of Asa's reign.

ASA'S TREATY WITH ARAM

16 In the thirty-sixth year of Asa, Israel's
King Baasha went to war against Judah.
He built Ramah in order to keep anyone from
leaving or coming to King Asa of Judah. 2 So
Asa brought out the silver and gold from the
treasuries of the LORD's temple and the royal
palace and sent it to Aram's King Ben-hadad,
who lived in Damascus, saying, 3 "There's a
treaty between me and you, between my father
and your father. Look, I have sent you silver
and gold. Go break your treaty with Israel's
King Baasha so that he will withdraw from me."

4 Ben-hadad listened to King Asa and sent
the commanders of his armies to the cities of
Israel. They attacked Ijon, Dan, Abel-maim,[D]
and all the storage cities[E] of Naphtali. 5 When
Baasha heard about it, he quit building Ramah and stopped his work. 6 Then King Asa
brought all Judah, and they carried away the
stones of Ramah and the timbers Baasha had
built it with. Then he built Geba and Mizpah
with them.

HANANI'S REBUKE OF ASA

7 At that time, the seer Hanani came to King
Asa of Judah and said to him, "Because you
depended on the king of Aram and have not
depended on the LORD your God, the army
of the king of Aram has escaped from you.
8 Were not the Cushites and Libyans a vast
army with many chariots and horsemen?
When you depended on the LORD, he handed them over to you. 9 For the eyes of the LORD
roam throughout the earth to show himself
strong for those who are wholeheartedly devoted to him. You have been foolish in this
matter. Therefore, you will have wars from
now on." 10 Asa was enraged with the seer
and put him in prison[F] because of his anger
over this. And Asa mistreated some of the
people at that time.

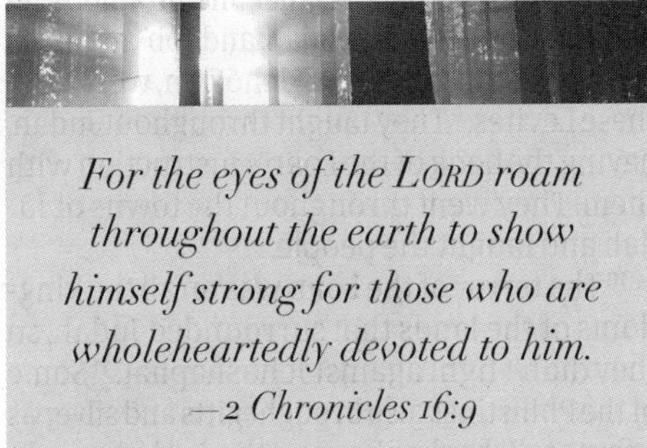
For the eyes of the LORD roam throughout the earth to show himself strong for those who are wholeheartedly devoted to him.
—2 Chronicles 16:9

ASA'S DEATH

11 Note that the events of Asa's reign, from beginning to end, are written in the Book of the
Kings of Judah and Israel. 12 In the thirty-ninth
year of his reign, Asa developed a disease in
his feet, and his disease became increasingly
severe. Yet even in his disease he didn't seek
the LORD but only the physicians. 13 Asa rested with his fathers; he died in the forty-first
year of his reign. 14 He was buried in his own
tomb that he had made for himself in the city
of David. They laid him out in a coffin that
was full of spices and various mixtures of
prepared ointments; then they made a great
fire in his honor.

JUDAH'S KING JEHOSHAPHAT

17 His son Jehoshaphat became king in his
place and strengthened himself against
Israel. 2 He stationed troops in every fortified
city of Judah and set garrisons in the land of
Judah and in the cities of Ephraim that his
father Asa had captured.

3 Now the LORD was with Jehoshaphat because he walked in the former ways of his
father David.[G] He did not seek the Baals 4 but
sought the God of his father and walked by his
commands, not according to the practices of

[A] **15:13** Or *insignificant or great* [B] **15:16** Lit *mother*; 1Kg 15:2; 2Ch 11:22 [C] **15:17** Lit *wholehearted all his days* [D] **16:4** *Abel-beth-maacah* in 1Kg 15:20 [E] **16:4** = all Chinnereth in 1Kg 15:20 [F] **16:10** Lit *the house of stocks* [G] **17:3** Some Hb mss, LXX omit *David*

Israel. 5 So the LORD established the kingdom in
his hand. Then all Judah brought him tribute,
and he had riches and honor in abundance.
6 His mind rejoiced in the LORD's ways, and he
again removed the high places and Asherah
poles from Judah.

JEHOSHAPHAT'S EDUCATIONAL PLAN

7 In the third year of his reign, Jehoshaphat sent
his officials — Ben-hail,[A] Obadiah, Zechariah,
Nethanel, and Micaiah — to teach in the cities of
Judah. 8 The Levites with them were Shemaiah,
Nethaniah, Zebadiah,[B] Asahel, Shemiramoth, Jehonathan, Adonijah, Tobijah, and Tob-adonijah;
the priests, Elishama and Jehoram, were with
these Levites. 9 They taught throughout Judah,
having the book of the LORD's instruction with
them. They went throughout the towns of Judah and taught the people.

10 The terror of the LORD was on all the kingdoms of the lands that surrounded Judah, so
they didn't fight against Jehoshaphat. 11 Some
of the Philistines also brought gifts and silver as
tribute to Jehoshaphat, and the Arabs brought
him flocks: 7,700 rams and 7,700 male goats.

JEHOSHAPHAT'S MILITARY MIGHT

12 Jehoshaphat grew stronger and stronger.
He built fortresses and storage cities in Judah
13 and carried out great works in the towns of
Judah. He had fighting men, valiant warriors,
in Jerusalem. 14 These are their numbers according to their ancestral families.[C] For Judah,
the commanders of thousands:

Adnah the commander and three
hundred thousand valiant warriors
with him;
15 next to him, Jehohanan the
commander and two hundred eighty
thousand with him;
16 next to him, Amasiah son of Zichri,
the volunteer of the LORD, and two
hundred thousand valiant warriors
with him;
17 from Benjamin, Eliada, a valiant
warrior, and two hundred thousand
with him armed with bow and shield;
18 next to him, Jehozabad and one
hundred eighty thousand with him
equipped for war.

19 These were the ones who served the king,
besides those he stationed in the fortified cities throughout all Judah.

JEHOSHAPHAT'S ALLIANCE WITH AHAB

18 Now Jehoshaphat had riches and honor
in abundance, and he made an alliance
with Ahab through marriage.[D] 2 Then after
some years, he went down to visit Ahab in
Samaria. Ahab sacrificed many sheep, goats,
and cattle for him and for the people who were
with him. Then he persuaded him to attack
Ramoth-gilead, 3 for Israel's King Ahab asked
Judah's King Jehoshaphat, "Will you go with
me to Ramoth-gilead?"

He replied to him, "I am as you are, my people as your people; we will be with you in the
battle." 4 But Jehoshaphat said to the king
of Israel, "First, please ask what the LORD's
will is."

5 So the king of Israel gathered the prophets,
four hundred men, and asked them, "Should
we go to Ramoth-gilead for war or should I
refrain?"

They replied, "March up, and God will hand
it over to the king."

6 But Jehoshaphat asked, "Isn't there a prophet of the LORD here anymore? Let's ask him."
7 The king of Israel said to Jehoshaphat,
"There is still one man who can inquire of
the LORD, but I hate him because he never
prophesies good about me, but only disaster.
He is Micaiah son of Imlah."

"The king shouldn't say that," Jehoshaphat
replied.

8 So the king of Israel called an officer and
said, "Hurry and get Micaiah son of Imlah!"

9 Now the king of Israel and King Jehoshaphat of Judah, clothed in royal attire, were
each sitting on his own throne. They were
sitting on the threshing floor at the entrance
to Samaria's gate, and all the prophets were
prophesying in front of them. 10 Then Zedekiah son of Chenaanah made iron horns and
said, "This is what the LORD says: 'You will
gore the Arameans with these until they are
finished off.'" 11 And all the prophets were
prophesying the same, saying, "March up to
Ramoth-gilead and succeed, for the LORD will
hand it over to the king."

MICAIAH'S MESSAGE OF DEFEAT

12 The messenger who went to call Micaiah
instructed him, "Look, the words of the prophets are unanimously favorable for the king.
So let your words be like theirs, and speak
favorably."

[A] **17:7** = Son of Power [B] **17:8** Some Hb mss, Syr, Tg, Arabic read *Zechariah* [C] **17:14** Lit *the house of their fathers* [D] **18:1** Lit *made himself a son-in-law to Ahab*; 1Kg 3:1; Ezr 9:14

13 But Micaiah said, "As the LORD lives, I will
say whatever my God says."[A]
14 So he went to the king, and the king asked
him, "Micaiah, should we go to Ramoth-gilead
for war, or should I[B] refrain?"
Micaiah said, "March up and succeed, for
they will be handed over to you."
15 But the king said to him, "How many times
must I make you swear not to tell me anything
but the truth in the name of the LORD?"
16 So Micaiah said:

I saw all Israel scattered on the hills
like sheep without a shepherd.
And the LORD said,
"They have no master;
let each return home in peace."

17 So the king of Israel said to Jehoshaphat,
"Didn't I tell you he never prophesies good
about me, but only disaster?"
18 Then Micaiah said, "Therefore, hear the
word of the LORD. I saw the LORD sitting on
his throne, and the whole heavenly army
was standing at his right hand and at his left
hand. 19 And the LORD said, 'Who will entice
King Ahab of Israel to march up and fall at
Ramoth-gilead?' So one was saying this and
another was saying that.
20 "Then a spirit came forward, stood before
the LORD, and said, 'I will entice him.'
"The LORD asked him, 'How?'
21 "So he said, 'I will go and become a lying
spirit in the mouth of all his prophets.'
"Then he said, 'You will entice him and also
prevail. Go and do that.'
22 "Now, you see, the LORD has put a lying
spirit into the mouth of[C] these prophets of
yours, and the LORD has pronounced disaster
against you."
23 Then Zedekiah son of Chenaanah came
up, hit Micaiah on the cheek, and demanded,
"Which way did the spirit from the LORD leave
me to speak to you?"
24 Micaiah replied, "You will soon see when
you go to hide in an inner chamber on that day."
25 Then the king of Israel ordered, "Take Micaiah and return him to Amon, the governor
of the city, and to Joash, the king's son, 26 and
say, 'This is what the king says: Put this guy
in prison and feed him only a little bread and
water[D] until I come back safely.'"
27 But Micaiah said, "If you ever return safely,
the LORD has not spoken through me." Then
he said, "Listen, all you people!"

AHAB'S DEATH

28 Then the king of Israel and Judah's King Jehoshaphat went up to Ramoth-gilead. 29 But
the king of Israel said to Jehoshaphat, "I will
disguise myself and go into battle, but you
wear your royal attire." So the king of Israel
disguised himself, and they went into battle.
30 Now the king of Aram had ordered his
chariot commanders, "Do not fight with anyone at all[E] except the king of Israel."
31 When the chariot commanders saw Jehoshaphat, they shouted, "He must be the king
of Israel!" So they turned to attack him, but
Jehoshaphat cried out and the LORD helped
him. God drew them away from him. 32 When
the chariot commanders saw that he was not
the king of Israel, they turned back from pursuing him.
33 But a man drew his bow without taking special aim and struck the king of Israel
through the joints of his armor. So he said
to the charioteer, "Turn around and take me
out of the battle,[F] for I am badly wounded!"
34 The battle raged throughout that day, and
the king of Israel propped himself up in his
chariot facing the Arameans until evening.
Then he died at sunset.

JEHU'S REBUKE OF JEHOSHAPHAT

19 King Jehoshaphat of Judah returned to
his home in Jerusalem in peace. 2 Then
Jehu son of the seer Hanani went out to confront him[G] and said to King Jehoshaphat, "Do
you help the wicked and love those who hate
the LORD? Because of this, the LORD's wrath is
on you. 3 However, some good is found in you,
for you have eradicated the Asherah poles
from the land and have decided to seek God."

JEHOSHAPHAT'S REFORMS

4 Jehoshaphat lived in Jerusalem, and once
again he went out among the people from
Beer-sheba to the hill country of Ephraim and
brought them back to the LORD, the God of
their ancestors. 5 He appointed judges in all
the fortified cities of the land of Judah, city
by city. 6 Then he said to the judges, "Consider
what you are doing, for you do not judge for
a mere mortal, but for the LORD, who is with

[A] 18:13 LXX, Vg add *to me*; 1Kg 22:14 [B] 18:14 LXX reads *we*; 1Kg 22:15 [C] 18:22 Some Hb mss, LXX, Syr, Vg add *all*; 1Kg 22:23
[D] 18:26 Lit *him on bread of oppression and water of oppression* [E] 18:30 Lit *with small or with great* [F] 18:33 LXX, Vg; MT reads *camp* [G] 19:2 Lit *to his face*

you in the matter of judgment. 7 And now, may
the terror of the LORD be on you. Watch what
you do, for there is no injustice or partiality or
taking bribes with the LORD our God."
8 Jehoshaphat also appointed in Jerusalem
some of the Levites and priests and some of
the Israelite family heads for deciding the
LORD's will and for settling disputes of the
residents of[A] Jerusalem. 9 He commanded
them, saying, "In the fear of the LORD, with
integrity, and wholeheartedly, you are to do
the following: 10 For every dispute that comes
to you from your brothers who dwell in their
cities — whether it regards differences of
bloodguilt, law, commandment, statutes, or
judgments — you are to warn them, so they
will not incur guilt before the LORD and wrath
will not come on you and your brothers. Do
this, and you will not incur guilt.
11 "Note that Amariah, the chief priest, is
over you in all matters related to the LORD,
and Zebadiah son of Ishmael, the ruler of the
house of Judah, in all matters related to the
king, and the Levites are officers in your presence. Be strong; may the LORD be with those
who do what is good."

WAR AGAINST EASTERN ENEMIES

20 After this, the Moabites and Ammonites,
together with some of the Meunites,[B]
came to fight against Jehoshaphat. 2 People
came and told Jehoshaphat, "A vast number
from beyond the Dead Sea and from Edom[C]
has come to fight against you; they are already
in Hazazon-tamar" (that is, En-gedi). 3 Jehoshaphat was afraid, and he resolved to seek the
LORD. Then he proclaimed a fast for all Judah,
4 who gathered to seek the LORD. They even
came from all the cities of Judah to seek him.

JEHOSHAPHAT'S PRAYER

5 Then Jehoshaphat stood in the assembly of
Judah and Jerusalem in the LORD's temple
before the new courtyard. 6 He said:

LORD, God of our ancestors, are you not
the God who is in heaven, and do you not
rule over all the kingdoms of the nations?
Power and might are in your hand, and
no one can stand against you. 7 Are you
not our God who drove out the inhabitants of this land before your people Israel and who gave it forever to the descendants of Abraham your friend? 8 They
have lived in the land and have built you
a sanctuary in it for your name and have
said, 9 "If disaster comes on us — sword
or judgment, pestilence or famine — we
will stand before this temple and before
you, for your name is in this temple. We
will cry out to you because of our distress, and you will hear and deliver."

10 Now here are the Ammonites,
Moabites, and the inhabitants of Mount
Seir. You did not let Israel invade them
when Israel came out of the land of
Egypt, but Israel turned away from them
and did not destroy them. 11 Look how
they repay us by coming to drive us out
of your possession that you gave us as an
inheritance. 12 Our God, will you not judge
them? For we are powerless before this
vast number that comes to fight against
us. We do not know what to do, but we
look to you.[D]

Do not be afraid or discouraged because of this vast number, for the battle is not yours, but God's.

— 2 Chronicles 20:15

GOD'S ANSWER

13 All Judah was standing before the LORD
with their dependents, their wives, and their
children. 14 In the middle of the congregation,
the Spirit of the LORD came on Jahaziel (son
of Zechariah, son of Benaiah, son of Jeiel,
son of Mattaniah, a Levite from Asaph's descendants), 15 and he said, "Listen carefully,
all Judah and you inhabitants of Jerusalem,
and King Jehoshaphat. This is what the LORD
says: 'Do not be afraid or discouraged because of this vast number, for the battle is
not yours, but God's. 16 Tomorrow, go down
against them. You will see them coming up
the Ascent of Ziz, and you will find them at
the end of the valley facing the Wilderness
of Jeruel. 17 You do not have to fight this battle. Position yourselves, stand still, and see
the salvation of the LORD. He is with you,
Judah and Jerusalem. Do not be afraid or

[A] 19:8 LXX, Vg; MT reads *disputes and they returned to* [B] 20:1 LXX; MT reads *Ammonites*; 2Ch 26:7 [C] 20:2 Some Hb mss, Old Lat; other Hb mss read *Aram* [D] 20:12 Lit *but on you our eyes*

discouraged. Tomorrow, go out to face them, for the LORD is with you.'"

18 Then Jehoshaphat knelt low with his face to the ground, and all Judah and the inhabitants of Jerusalem fell down before the LORD to worship him. 19 Then the Levites from the sons of the Kohathites and the Korahites stood up to praise the LORD God of Israel shouting loudly.

VICTORY AND PLUNDER

20 In the morning they got up early and went out to the wilderness of Tekoa. As they were about to go out, Jehoshaphat stood and said, "Hear me, Judah and you inhabitants of Jerusalem. Believe in the LORD your God, and you will be established; believe in his prophets, and you will succeed." 21 Then he consulted with the people and appointed some to sing for the LORD and some to praise the splendor of his holiness. When they went out in front of the armed forces, they kept singing:[A]

> Give thanks to the LORD,
> for his faithful love endures forever.

22 The moment they began their shouts and praises, the LORD set an ambush against the Ammonites, Moabites, and the inhabitants of Mount Seir who came to fight against Judah, and they were defeated. 23 The Ammonites and Moabites turned against the inhabitants of Mount Seir and completely annihilated them. When they had finished with the inhabitants of Seir, they helped destroy each other.

24 When Judah came to a place overlooking the wilderness, they looked for the large army, but there were only corpses lying on the ground; nobody had escaped. 25 Then Jehoshaphat and his people went to gather the plunder. They found among them[B] an abundance of goods on the bodies[C] and valuable items. So they stripped them until nobody could carry any more. They were gathering the plunder for three days because there was so much. 26 They assembled in the Valley of Beracah[D] on the fourth day, for there they blessed the LORD. Therefore, that place is still called the Valley of Beracah today.

27 Then all the men of Judah and Jerusalem turned back with Jehoshaphat their leader, returning joyfully to Jerusalem, for the LORD enabled them to rejoice over their enemies. 28 So they came into Jerusalem to the LORD's temple with harps, lyres, and trumpets.

29 The terror of God was on all the kingdoms of the lands when they heard that the LORD had fought against the enemies of Israel. 30 Then Jehoshaphat's kingdom was quiet, for his God gave him rest on every side.

SUMMARY OF JEHOSHAPHAT'S REIGN

31 Jehoshaphat became king over Judah. He was thirty-five years old when he became king, and he reigned twenty-five years in Jerusalem. His mother's name was Azubah daughter of Shilhi. 32 He walked in the ways of Asa his father; he did not turn away from it but did what was right in the LORD's sight. 33 However, the high places were not taken away; the people had not yet set their hearts on the God of their ancestors.

34 The rest of the events of Jehoshaphat's reign from beginning to end are written in the Events of Jehu son of Hanani, which is recorded in the Book of Israel's Kings.

JEHOSHAPHAT'S FLEET OF SHIPS

35 After this, Judah's King Jehoshaphat made an alliance with Israel's King Ahaziah, who was guilty of wrongdoing. 36 Jehoshaphat formed an alliance with him to make ships to go to Tarshish, and they made the ships in Ezion-geber. 37 Then Eliezer son of Dodavahu of Mareshah prophesied against Jehoshaphat, saying, "Because you formed an alliance with Ahaziah, the LORD has broken up what you have made." So the ships were wrecked and were not able to go to Tarshish.

JEHORAM BECOMES KING OVER JUDAH

21 Jehoshaphat rested with his fathers and was buried with his fathers in the city of David. His son Jehoram[E] became king in his place. 2 He had brothers, sons of Jehoshaphat: Azariah, Jehiel, Zechariah, Azariah, Michael, and Shephatiah; all these were the sons of King Jehoshaphat of Judah.[F] 3 Their father had given them many gifts of silver, gold, and valuable things, along with fortified cities in Judah, but he gave the kingdom to Jehoram because he was the firstborn. 4 When Jehoram had established himself over his father's kingdom, he strengthened his position by killing with the sword all his brothers as well as some of the princes of Israel.

[A] 20:21 Lit *saying* [B] 20:25 LXX reads *found cattle* [C] 20:25 Some Hb mss, Old Lat, Vg read *goods, garments* [D] 20:26 = Blessing [E] 21:1 = Joram [F] 21:2 Some Hb mss, LXX, Syr, Vg, Arabic; other Hb mss read *Israel*

JUDAH'S KING JEHORAM

5 Jehoram was thirty-two years old when he became king, and he reigned eight years in Jerusalem. 6 He walked in the ways of the kings of Israel, as the house of Ahab had done, for Ahab's daughter was his wife. He did what was evil in the LORD's sight, 7 but for the sake of the covenant the LORD had made with David, he was unwilling to destroy the house of David since the LORD had promised to give a lamp to David and to his sons forever.

8 During Jehoram's reign, Edom rebelled against Judah's control and appointed their own king. 9 So Jehoram crossed into Edom with his commanders and all his chariots. Then at night he set out to attack the Edomites who had surrounded him and the chariot commanders. 10 And now Edom is still in rebellion against Judah's control today. Libnah also rebelled at that time against his control because he had abandoned the LORD, the God of his ancestors. 11 Jehoram also built high places in the hills[A] of Judah, and he caused the inhabitants of Jerusalem to prostitute themselves, and he led Judah astray.

ELIJAH'S LETTER TO JEHORAM

12 Then a letter came to Jehoram from the prophet Elijah, saying:

This is what the LORD, the God of your ancestor David says: "Because you have not walked in the ways of your father Jehoshaphat or in the ways of King Asa of Judah 13 but have walked in the ways of the kings of Israel, have caused Judah and the inhabitants of Jerusalem to prostitute themselves like the house of Ahab prostituted itself, and also have killed your brothers, your father's family, who were better than you, 14 the LORD is now about to strike your people, your sons, your wives, and all your possessions with a horrible affliction. 15 You yourself will be struck with many illnesses, including a disease of the intestines, until your intestines come out day after day because of the disease."

JEHORAM'S LAST DAYS

16 The LORD roused the spirit of the Philistines and the Arabs who lived near the Cushites to attack Jehoram. 17 So they went to war against Judah and invaded it. They carried off all the possessions found in the king's palace and also his sons and wives; not a son was left to him except Jehoahaz,[B] his youngest son.

18 After all these things, the LORD afflicted him in his intestines with an incurable disease. 19 This continued day after day until two full years passed. Then his intestines came out because of his disease, and he died from severe[C] illnesses. But his people did not hold a fire in his honor like the fire in honor of his fathers.

20 Jehoram was thirty-two years old when he became king; he reigned eight years in Jerusalem. He died to no one's regret[D] and was buried in the city of David but not in the tombs of the kings.

JUDAH'S KING AHAZIAH

22 Then the inhabitants of Jerusalem made Ahaziah, his youngest son, king in his place, because the troops that had come with the Arabs to the camp had killed all the older sons.[E] So Ahaziah son of Jehoram became king of Judah. 2 Ahaziah was twenty-two[F] years old when he became king, and he reigned one year in Jerusalem. His mother's name was Athaliah, granddaughter[G] of Omri.

3 He walked in the ways of the house of Ahab, for his mother gave him evil advice. 4 So he did what was evil in the LORD's sight like the house of Ahab, for they were his advisers after the death of his father, to his destruction. 5 He also followed their advice and went with Joram[H] son of Israel's King Ahab to fight against King Hazael of Aram, in Ramoth-gilead. The Arameans[I] wounded Joram, 6 so he returned to Jezreel to recover from the wounds they inflicted on him in Ramoth-gilead[J] when he fought against King Hazael of Aram. Then Judah's King Ahaziah[K] son of Jehoram went down to Jezreel to visit Joram son of Ahab since Joram was ill.

7 Ahaziah's downfall came from God when he went to Joram. When Ahaziah arrived, he went out with Joram to meet Jehu son of Nimshi, whom the LORD had anointed to destroy the house of Ahab. 8 So when Jehu executed judgment on the house of Ahab, he found the rulers of Judah and the sons of Ahaziah's brothers who were serving Ahaziah, and he killed them. 9 Then Jehu looked for Ahaziah, and Jehu's soldiers captured him (he was hiding

---

[A] **21:11** Some Hb mss, LXX, Vg read *cities* [B] **21:17** LXX, Syr, Tg read *Ahaziah* [C] **21:19** Lit *evil* [D] **21:20** Lit *He walked in no desirability* [E] **22:1** Lit *the former ones* [F] **22:2** Some LXX mss, Syr; MT reads *42*; 2Kg 8:26 [G] **22:2** Lit *daughter* [H] **22:5** = Jehoram [I] **22:5** Lit *Rammites* [J] **22:6** Lit *in Ramah* [K] **22:6** Some Hb mss, LXX, Syr, Vg; other Hb mss read *Azariah*

in Samaria). So they brought Ahaziah to Jehu,
and they killed him. The soldiers buried him,
for they said, "He is the grandson of Jehoshaphat who sought the LORD with all his heart."
So no one from the house of Ahaziah had the
strength to rule the kingdom.

ATHALIAH USURPS THE THRONE

10 When Athaliah, Ahaziah's mother, saw that
her son was dead, she proceeded to annihilate all the royal heirs[A] of the house of Judah.
11 Jehoshabeath,[B] the king's daughter, rescued
Joash son of Ahaziah from the king's sons who
were being killed and put him and the one
who nursed him in a bedroom. Now Jehoshabeath was the daughter of King Jehoram and
the wife of the priest Jehoiada. Since she was
Ahaziah's sister, she hid Joash from Athaliah
so that she did not kill him. 12 While Athaliah
reigned over the land, he was hiding with
them in God's temple six years.

ATHALIAH OVERTHROWN

23 Then, in the seventh year, Jehoiada
summoned his courage and took the
commanders of hundreds into a covenant
with him: Azariah son of Jeroham, Ishmael
son of Jehohanan, Azariah son of Obed, Maaseiah son of Adaiah, and Elishaphat son of
Zichri. 2 They made a circuit throughout Judah.
They gathered the Levites from all the cities
of Judah and the family heads of Israel, and
they came to Jerusalem.

3 Then the whole assembly made a covenant
with the king in God's temple. Jehoiada said
to them, "Here is the king's son! He will reign,
just as the LORD promised concerning David's
sons. 4 This is what you are to do: a third of you,
priests and Levites who are coming on duty on
the Sabbath, are to be gatekeepers. 5 A third are
to be at the king's palace, and a third are to be
at the Foundation Gate, and all the troops will
be in the courtyards of the LORD's temple. 6 No
one is to enter the LORD's temple but the priests
and those Levites who serve; they may enter
because they are holy, but all the people are to
obey the requirement of the LORD. 7 Completely surround the king with weapons in hand.
Anyone who enters the temple is to be put to
death. Be with the king in all his daily tasks."[C]

8 So the commanders of hundreds did everything the priest Jehoiada commanded. They
each brought their men — those coming on
duty on the Sabbath and those going off duty
on the Sabbath — for the priest Jehoiada did
not release the divisions. 9 The priest Jehoiada
gave to the commanders of hundreds King David's spears, shields, and quivers[D] that were in
God's temple. 10 Then he stationed all the troops
with their weapons in hand surrounding the
king — from the right side of the temple to
the left side, by the altar and by the temple.

11 They brought out the king's son, put the
crown on him, gave him the testimony, and
made him king. Jehoiada and his sons anointed
him and cried, "Long live the king!"

12 When Athaliah heard the noise from the
troops, the guards, and those praising the king,
she went to the troops in the LORD's temple. 13 As
she looked, there was the king standing by his
pillar[E] at the entrance. The commanders and
the trumpeters were by the king, and all the
people of the land were rejoicing and blowing
trumpets while the singers with musical instruments were leading the praise. Athaliah tore
her clothes and screamed, "Treason! Treason!"

14 Then the priest Jehoiada sent out the commanders of hundreds, those in charge of the
army, saying, "Take her out between the ranks,
and put anyone who follows her to death by
the sword," for the priest had said, "Don't put
her to death in the LORD's temple." 15 So they
arrested her, and she went by the entrance
of the Horse Gate to the king's palace, where
they put her to death.

JEHOIADA'S REFORMS

16 Then Jehoiada made a covenant between
himself, the king, and the people that they
would be the LORD's people. 17 So all the people
went to the temple of Baal and tore it down.
They smashed its altars and images and killed
Mattan, the priest of Baal, at the altars.

18 Then Jehoiada put the oversight of the
LORD's temple into the hands of the Levitical priests, whom David had appointed over
the LORD's temple, to offer burnt offerings to
the LORD as it is written in the law of Moses,
with rejoicing and song ordained by[F] David.
19 He stationed gatekeepers at the gates of the
LORD's temple so that nothing unclean could
enter for any reason. 20 Then he took with him
the commanders of hundreds, the nobles, the
governors of the people, and all the people of
the land and brought the king down from the
LORD's temple. They entered the king's palace

[A] **22:10** Lit *seed* [B] **22:11** = Jehosheba; 2Kg 11:2 [C] **23:7** Lit *king when he comes in and when he goes out* [D] **23:9** Or *spears and large and small shields* [E] **23:13** LXX reads *post* [F] **23:18** Lit *song on the hands of*

through the Upper Gate and seated the king on the throne of the kingdom. 21 All the people of the land rejoiced, and the city was quiet, for they had put Athaliah to death by the sword.

JUDAH'S KING JOASH

24 Joash was seven years old when he became king, and he reigned forty years in Jerusalem. His mother's name was Zibiah; she was from Beer-sheba. 2 Throughout the time of the priest Jehoiada, Joash did what was right in the LORD's sight. 3 Jehoiada acquired two wives for him, and he was the father of sons and daughters.

REPAIRING THE TEMPLE

4 Afterward, Joash took it to heart to renovate the LORD's temple. 5 So he gathered the priests and Levites and said, "Go out to the cities of Judah and collect silver from all Israel to repair the temple of your God as needed year by year, and do it quickly."

However, the Levites did not hurry. 6 So the king called Jehoiada the high priest and said, "Why haven't you required the Levites to bring from Judah and Jerusalem the tax imposed by the LORD's servant Moses and the assembly of Israel for the tent of the testimony? 7 For the sons of that wicked Athaliah broke into the LORD's temple and even used the sacred things of the LORD's temple for the Baals."

8 At the king's command a chest was made and placed outside the gate of the LORD's temple. 9 Then a proclamation was issued in Judah and Jerusalem that the tax God's servant Moses imposed on Israel in the wilderness be brought to the LORD. 10 All the leaders and all the people rejoiced, brought the tax, and put it in the chest until it was full. 11 Whenever the chest was brought by the Levites to the king's overseers, and when they saw that there was a large amount of silver, the king's secretary and the high priest's deputy came and emptied the chest, picked it up, and returned it to its place. They did this daily and gathered the silver in abundance. 12 Then the king and Jehoiada gave it to those in charge of the labor on the LORD's temple, who were hiring stonecutters and carpenters to renovate the LORD's temple, also blacksmiths and coppersmiths to repair the LORD's temple.

13 The workmen did their work, and through them the repairs progressed. They restored God's temple to its specifications and reinforced it. 14 When they finished, they presented the rest of the silver to the king and Jehoiada, who made articles for the LORD's temple with it — articles for ministry and for making burnt offerings, and ladles[A] and articles of gold and silver. They regularly offered burnt offerings in the LORD's temple throughout Jehoiada's life.

JOASH'S APOSTASY

15 Jehoiada died when he was old and full of days; he was 130 years old at his death. 16 He was buried in the city of David with the kings because he had done what was good in Israel with respect to God and his temple.

17 However, after Jehoiada died, the rulers of Judah came and paid homage to the king. Then the king listened to them, 18 and they abandoned the temple of the LORD, the God of their ancestors, and served the Asherah poles and the idols. So there was wrath against Judah and Jerusalem for this guilt of theirs. 19 Nevertheless, he sent them prophets to bring them back to the LORD; they admonished them, but the people would not listen.

20 The Spirit of God enveloped[B] Zechariah son of Jehoiada the priest. He stood above the people and said to them, "This is what God says, 'Why are you transgressing the LORD's commands so that you do not prosper? Because you have abandoned the LORD, he has abandoned you.'" 21 But they conspired against him and stoned him at the king's command in the courtyard of the LORD's temple. 22 King Joash didn't remember the kindness that Zechariah's father Jehoiada had extended to him, but killed his son. While he was dying, he said, "May the LORD see and demand an account."

ARAMEAN INVASION OF JUDAH

23 At the turn of the year, an Aramean army attacked Joash. They entered Judah and Jerusalem and destroyed all the leaders of the people among them and sent all the plunder to the king of Damascus. 24 Although the Aramean army came with only a few men, the LORD handed over a vast army to them because the people of Judah had abandoned the LORD, the God of their ancestors. So they executed judgment on Joash.

[A] **24:14** Or *dishes*, or *spoons*; lit *palms* [B] **24:20** Lit *clothed*

JOASH ASSASSINATED

25 When the Arameans saw that Joash had
many wounds, they left him. His servants conspired against him, and killed him on his bed,
because he had shed the blood of the sons of
the priest Jehoiada. So he died, and they buried him in the city of David, but they did not
bury him in the tombs of the kings.
26 Those who conspired against him were
Zabad, son of the Ammonite woman Shimeath,
and Jehozabad, son of the Moabite woman
Shimrith.[A] 27 The accounts concerning his sons,
the many divine pronouncements about him,
and the restoration of God's temple are recorded in the Writing of the Book of the Kings.
His son Amaziah became king in his place.

JUDAH'S KING AMAZIAH

25 Amaziah became king when he was
twenty-five years old, and he reigned
twenty-nine years in Jerusalem. His mother's
name was Jehoaddan; she was from Jerusalem.
2 He did what was right in the LORD's sight but
not wholeheartedly.
3 As soon as the kingdom was firmly in his
grasp,[B] he executed his servants who had
killed his father the king. 4 However, he did
not put their children to death, because — as
it is written in the Law, in the book of Moses,
where the LORD commanded — "Fathers are
not to die because of children, and children
are not to die because of fathers, but each one
will die for his own sin."

AMAZIAH'S CAMPAIGN AGAINST EDOM

5 Then Amaziah gathered Judah and assembled
them according to ancestral families,[C] according
to commanders of thousands, and according
to commanders of hundreds. He numbered
those twenty years old or more for all Judah
and Benjamin. He found there to be three hundred thousand fit young men who could serve
in the army, bearing spear and shield. 6 Then for
7,500 pounds[D] of silver he hired one hundred
thousand valiant warriors from Israel.
7 However, a man of God came to him and
said, "King, do not let Israel's army go with
you, for the LORD is not with Israel — all the
Ephraimites. 8 But if you go with them, do it!
Be strong for battle! But God will make you
stumble before the enemy, for God has the
power to help or to make one stumble."
9 Then Amaziah said to the man of God,
"What should I do about the 7,500 pounds of
silver I gave to Israel's division?"
The man of God replied, "The LORD is able
to give you much more than this."
10 So Amaziah released the division that
came to him from Ephraim to go home. But
they got very angry with Judah and returned
home in a fierce rage.
11 Amaziah strengthened his position and led
his people to the Salt Valley. He struck down
ten thousand Seirites,[E] 12 and the Judahites
captured ten thousand alive. They took them
to the top of a cliff where they threw them off,
and all of them were dashed to pieces.
13 As for the men of the division that Amaziah sent back so they would not go with him
into battle, they raided the cities of Judah from
Samaria to Beth-horon, struck down three
thousand of their people, and took a great
deal of plunder.
14 After Amaziah came from the attack on the
Edomites, he brought the gods of the Seirites
and set them up as his gods. He worshiped
before them and burned incense to them. 15 So
the LORD's anger was against Amaziah, and he
sent a prophet to him, who said, "Why have
you sought a people's gods that could not rescue their own people from you?"
16 While he was still speaking to him, the king
asked, "Have we made you the king's counselor? Stop, why should you lose your life?"
So the prophet stopped, but he said, "I know
that God intends to destroy you, because you
have done this and have not listened to my
advice."

AMAZIAH'S WAR WITH ISRAEL'S KING JEHOASH

17 King Amaziah of Judah took counsel and
sent word to Jehoash[F] son of Jehoahaz, son
of Jehu, king of Israel, and challenged him:
"Come, let's meet face to face."
18 King Jehoash of Israel sent word to King
Amaziah of Judah, saying, "The thistle in Lebanon sent a message to the cedar in Lebanon,
saying, 'Give your daughter to my son as a
wife.' Then a wild animal in Lebanon passed
by and trampled the thistle. 19 You have said,
'Look, I[G] have defeated Edom,' and you have
become overconfident[H] that you will get glory.
Now stay at home. Why stir up such trouble
so that you fall and Judah with you?"

[A] **24:26** = Shomer in 2Kg 12:21 [B] **25:3** LXX, Syr; MT reads *was strong on him*; 1Kg 14:4 [C] **25:5** Lit *house of fathers* [D] **25:6** Lit *100 talents*, also in v. 9 [E] **25:11** = Edomites, also in v. 14 [F] **25:17** Lit *Joash* [G] **25:19** Some LXX mss, Old Lat, Tg, Vg; MT reads *you* [H] **25:19** Lit *and your heart has lifted you*

20 But Amaziah would not listen, for this turn of events was from God in order to hand them over to their enemies because they went after the gods of Edom. 21 So King Jehoash of Israel advanced. He and King Amaziah of Judah met face to face at Beth-shemesh that belonged to Judah. 22 Judah was routed before Israel, and each man fled to his own tent. 23 King Jehoash of Israel captured Judah's King Amaziah son of Joash, son of Jehoahaz,[A] at Beth-shemesh. Then Jehoash took him to Jerusalem and broke down two hundred yards[B] of Jerusalem's wall from the Ephraim Gate to the Corner Gate.[C] 24 He took all the gold, silver, all the utensils that were found with Obed-edom in God's temple, the treasures of the king's palace, and the hostages. Then he returned to Samaria.

AMAZIAH'S DEATH

25 Judah's King Amaziah son of Joash lived fifteen years after the death of Israel's King Jehoash son of Jehoahaz. 26 The rest of the events of Amaziah's reign, from beginning to end, are written in the Book of the Kings of Judah and Israel.

27 From the time Amaziah turned from following the LORD, a conspiracy was formed against him in Jerusalem, and he fled to Lachish. However, men were sent after him to Lachish, and they put him to death there. 28 They carried him back on horses and buried him with his fathers in the city of Judah.[D]

JUDAH'S KING UZZIAH

26 All the people of Judah took Uzziah,[E] who was sixteen years old, and made him king in place of his father Amaziah. 2 After Amaziah the king rested with his fathers, Uzziah rebuilt Eloth[F] and restored it to Judah.

3 Uzziah was sixteen years old when he became king, and he reigned fifty-two years in Jerusalem. His mother's name was Jecoliah; she was from Jerusalem. 4 He did what was right in the LORD's sight just as his father Amaziah had done. 5 He sought God throughout the lifetime of Zechariah, the teacher of the fear[G] of God. During the time that he sought the LORD, God gave him success.

UZZIAH'S EXPLOITS

6 Uzziah went out to wage war against the Philistines, and he tore down the wall of Gath, the wall of Jabneh, and the wall of Ashdod. Then he built cities in the vicinity of Ashdod and among the Philistines. 7 God helped him against the Philistines, the Arabs that live in Gur-baal, and the Meunites. 8 The Ammonites[H] paid tribute to Uzziah, and his fame spread as far as the entrance of Egypt, for God made him very powerful. 9 Uzziah built towers in Jerusalem at the Corner Gate, the Valley Gate, and the corner buttress, and he fortified them. 10 Since he had many cattle both in the Judean foothills[I] and the plain, he built towers in the desert and dug many wells. And since he was a lover of the soil, he had farmers and vinedressers in the hills and in the fertile lands.[J]

11 Uzziah had an army equipped for combat that went out to war by division according to their assignments, as recorded by Jeiel the court secretary and Maaseiah the officer under the authority of Hananiah, one of the king's commanders. 12 The total number of family heads was 2,600 valiant warriors. 13 Under their authority was an army of 307,500 equipped for combat, a powerful force to help the king against the enemy. 14 Uzziah provided the entire army with shields, spears, helmets, armor, bows, and slingstones. 15 He made skillfully designed devices in Jerusalem to shoot arrows and catapult large stones for use on the towers and on the corners. So his fame spread even to distant places, for he was wondrously helped until he became strong.

UZZIAH'S DISEASE

16 But when he became strong, he grew arrogant, and it led to his own destruction. He acted unfaithfully against the LORD his God by going into the LORD's sanctuary to burn incense on the incense altar. 17 The priest Azariah, along with eighty brave priests of the LORD, went in after him. 18 They took their stand against King Uzziah and said, "Uzziah, you have no right to offer incense to the LORD — only the consecrated priests, the descendants of Aaron, have the right to offer incense. Leave the sanctuary, for you have acted unfaithfully! You will not receive honor from the LORD God."

19 Uzziah, with a firepan in his hand to offer incense, was enraged. But when he became enraged with the priests, in the presence of the priests in the LORD's temple beside the altar of incense, a skin disease broke out on

[A] **25:23** = Ahaziah in 2Kg 14:13 [B] **25:23** Lit *400 cubits* [C] **25:23** Some Hb mss; other Hb mss read *to Happoneh* [D] **25:28** Some Hb mss read *city of David* [E] **26:1** = Azariah in 2Kg 14:21 [F] **26:2** LXX, Syr, Vg read *Elath* [G] **26:5** Some Hb mss, LXX, Syr, Tg, Arabic; other Hb mss, Vg read *visions* [H] **26:8** LXX reads *Meunites* [I] **26:10** Or *the Shephelah* [J] **26:10** Or *in Carmel*

his forehead. 20 Then Azariah the chief priest
and all the priests turned to him and saw that
he was diseased on his forehead. They rushed
him out of there. He himself also hurried to get
out because the LORD had afflicted him. 21 So
King Uzziah was diseased to the time of his
death. He lived in quarantine[A] with a serious
skin disease and was excluded from access
to the LORD's temple, while his son Jotham
was over the king's household governing the
people of the land.
22 Now the prophet Isaiah son of Amoz wrote
about the rest of the events of Uzziah's reign,
from beginning to end. 23 Uzziah rested with
his fathers, and he was buried with his fathers
in the burial ground of the kings' cemetery,
for they said, "He has a skin disease." His son
Jotham became king in his place.

JUDAH'S KING JOTHAM

27 Jotham was twenty-five years old when
he became king, and he reigned sixteen
years in Jerusalem. His mother's name was
Jerushah daughter of Zadok. 2 He did what
was right in the LORD's sight just as his father
Uzziah had done. In addition, he didn't enter
the LORD's sanctuary, but the people still behaved corruptly.
3 Jotham built the Upper Gate of the LORD's
temple, and he built extensively on the wall
of Ophel. 4 He also built cities in the hill country of Judah and fortresses and towers in the
forests. 5 He waged war against the king of
the Ammonites. He overpowered the Ammonites, and that year they gave him 7,500
pounds[B] of silver, 50,000 bushels[C] of wheat,
and 50,000 bushels of barley. They paid him
the same in the second and third years. 6 So
Jotham strengthened his position because he
did not waver in obeying[D] the LORD his God.
7 As for the rest of the events of Jotham's
reign, along with all his wars and his ways,
note that they are written in the Book of the
Kings of Israel and Judah. 8 He was twenty-five
years old when he became king, and he reigned
sixteen years in Jerusalem. 9 Jotham rested
with his fathers and was buried in the city of
David. His son Ahaz became king in his place.

JUDAH'S KING AHAZ

28 Ahaz was twenty years old when he
became king, and he reigned sixteen
years in Jerusalem. He did not do what was
right in the LORD's sight like his ancestor David, 2 for he walked in the ways of the kings
of Israel and made cast images of the Baals.
3 He burned incense in Ben Hinnom Valley and
burned his children in[E] the fire, imitating the
detestable practices of the nations the LORD
had dispossessed before the Israelites. 4 He
sacrificed and burned incense on the high
places, on the hills, and under every green tree.
5 So the LORD his God handed Ahaz over to
the king of Aram. He attacked him and took
many captives to Damascus.
Ahaz was also handed over to the king of
Israel, who struck him with great force: 6 Pekah
son of Remaliah killed one hundred twenty
thousand in Judah in one day — all brave men
— because they had abandoned the LORD God
of their ancestors. 7 An Ephraimite warrior
named Zichri killed the king's son Maaseiah,
Azrikam governor of the palace, and Elkanah
who was second to the king. 8 Then the Israelites took two hundred thousand captives from
their brothers — women, sons, and daughters.
They also took a great deal of plunder from
them and brought it to Samaria.
9 A prophet of the LORD named Oded was
there. He went out to meet the army that came
to Samaria and said to them, "Look, the LORD
God of your ancestors handed them over to
you because of his wrath against Judah, but
you slaughtered them in a rage that has
reached heaven. 10 Now you plan to reduce
the people of Judah and Jerusalem, male and
female, to slavery. Are you not also guilty before the LORD your God? 11 Listen to me and
return the captives you took from your brothers, for the LORD's burning anger is on you."
12 So some men who were leaders of the
Ephraimites — Azariah son of Jehohanan,
Berechiah son of Meshillemoth, Jehizkiah son
of Shallum, and Amasa son of Hadlai — stood
in opposition to those coming from the war.
13 They said to them, "You must not bring the
captives here, for you plan to bring guilt on
us from the LORD to add to our sins and our
guilt. For we have much guilt, and burning
anger is on Israel."
14 The army left the captives and the plunder
in the presence of the officers and the congregation. 15 Then the men who were designated by name took charge of the captives and
provided clothes for their naked ones from
the plunder. They clothed them, gave them

[A] **26:21** Lit *in a house of exemption from duty* [B] **27:5** Lit *100 talents* [C] **27:5** Lit *10,000 cors* [D] **27:6** Lit *he established his ways before* [E] **28:3** LXX, Syr, Tg read *and passed his children through*

sandals, food and drink, dressed their wounds,
and provided donkeys for all the feeble. The
Israelites brought them to Jericho, the City
of Palms, among their brothers. Then they
returned to Samaria.
16 At that time King Ahaz asked the king of
Assyria for help. 17 The Edomites came again,
attacked Judah, and took captives. 18 The Philistines also raided the cities of the Judean
foothills[A] and the Negev of Judah. They captured and occupied Beth-shemesh, Aijalon,
and Gederoth, as well as Soco, Timnah, and
Gimzo with their surrounding villages. 19 For
the LORD humbled Judah because of King Ahaz
of Judah,[B] who threw off restraint in Judah
and was unfaithful to the LORD. 20 Then King
Tiglath-pileser[C] of Assyria came against Ahaz;
he oppressed him and did not give him support. 21 Although Ahaz plundered the LORD's
temple and the palace of the king and of the
rulers and gave the plunder to the king of
Assyria, it did not help him.
22 At the time of his distress, King Ahaz
himself became more unfaithful to the LORD.
23 He sacrificed to the gods of Damascus which
had defeated him; he said, "Since the gods of
the kings of Aram are helping them, I will
sacrifice to them so that they will help me."
But they were the downfall of him and of
all Israel.
24 Then Ahaz gathered up the utensils of
God's temple, cut them into pieces, shut the
doors of the LORD's temple, and made himself
altars on every street corner in Jerusalem.
25 He made high places in every city of Judah
to offer incense to other gods, and he angered
the LORD, the God of his ancestors.

AHAZ'S DEATH

26 As for the rest of his deeds and all his ways,
from beginning to end, they are written in the
Book of the Kings of Judah and Israel. 27 Ahaz
rested with his fathers and was buried in the
city, in Jerusalem, but they did not bring him
into the tombs of the kings of Israel. His son
Hezekiah became king in his place.

JUDAH'S KING HEZEKIAH

29 Hezekiah was twenty-five years old
when he became king, and he reigned
twenty-nine years in Jerusalem. His mother's
name was Abijah[D] daughter of Zechariah. 2 He
did what was right in the LORD's sight just as
his ancestor David had done.
3 In the first year of his reign, in the first
month, he opened the doors of the LORD's
temple and repaired them. 4 Then he brought
in the priests and Levites and gathered them
in the eastern public square. 5 He said to them,
"Hear me, Levites. Consecrate yourselves now
and consecrate the temple of the LORD, the
God of your ancestors. Remove everything
impure from the holy place. 6 For our fathers
were unfaithful and did what is evil in the
sight of the LORD our God. They abandoned
him, turned their faces away from the LORD's
dwelling place, and turned their backs on him.[E]
7 They also closed the doors of the portico, extinguished the lamps, did not burn incense,
and did not offer burnt offerings in the holy
place of the God of Israel. 8 Therefore, the
wrath of the LORD was on Judah and Jerusalem, and he made them an object of terror,
horror, and mockery,[F] as you see with your
own eyes. 9 Our fathers fell by the sword, and
our sons, our daughters, and our wives are in
captivity because of this. 10 It is in my heart
now to make a covenant with the LORD, the
God of Israel so that his burning anger may
turn away from us. 11 My sons, don't be negligent now, for the LORD has chosen you to
stand in his presence, to serve him, and to be
his ministers and burners of incense."

CLEANSING THE TEMPLE

12 Then the Levites stood up:
Mahath son of Amasai and Joel son of
Azariah from the Kohathites;
Kish son of Abdi and Azariah son of
Jehallelel from the Merarites;
Joah son of Zimmah and Eden son of
Joah from the Gershonites;
13 Shimri and Jeuel from the
Elizaphanites;
Zechariah and Mattaniah from the
Asaphites;
14 Jehiel[G] and Shimei from the Hemanites;
Shemaiah and Uzziel from the
Jeduthunites.
15 They gathered their brothers together, con-
secrated themselves, and went according to
the king's command by the words of the LORD
to cleanse the LORD's temple.
16 The priests went to the entrance of the

[A] **28:18** Or *the Shephelah* [B] **28:19** Some Hb mss; other Hb mss read *Israel* [C] **28:20** Text emended; MT reads *Tilgath-pilneser*; 1Ch 5:6,26 [D] **29:1** = Abi in 2Kg 18:2 [E] **29:6** Lit *and they gave the back of the neck* [F] **29:8** Lit *hissing* [G] **29:14** Alt Hb tradition reads *Jehuel*

Hezekiah | Restoration Profile

2 KINGS 16:20–20:21; 2 CHRONICLES 28:27–32:33; ISAIAH 36:1–39:8

Hezekiah, king of Judah, ruled as a reformer. His kingdom had been overrun with pagan shrines and idols, which he proceeded to destroy. He even pulverized the much-revered bronze serpent that Moses had cast in the wilderness because rather than reminding people of their need for God's restoration, it had become a worshiped object. Hezekiah restored the land to a place where worshiping the God of Israel was the expected spiritual life of the people.

But even a king can only go so far.

Politically, Hezekiah stood up to the Assyrians who were the current world power. Then he found the Assyrians knocking on Jerusalem's door. Hezekiah tried to appease them with a payment of tribute, but the superpower wanted to teach the upstart kingdom a lesson. Jerusalem appeared doomed. Then the Assyrians made the mistake of thinking they were subduing both Judah and its God. Isaiah the prophet showed up to assure Hezekiah that God would deal with the Assyrians—and God did.

Despite his well-deserved reputation as a king who honored God, Hezekiah had his share of missteps along the way that required restoration. He had a recurring problem with pride. Following the miraculous reprieve from Assyria and multiplied blessings, he needed a terminal sickness to get his attention. Hezekiah humbled himself, and God gave him fifteen more years of life. But he promptly succumbed to pride again when visitors from Babylon arrived to wish him good health. His reckless display of his wealth to the Babylonians put Judah on the list of plum targets they would plunder when they came to power. God's grace was obvious in Hezekiah's life, but he took poor advantage of his restoration.

LORD's temple to cleanse it. They took all the
unclean things they found in the LORD's sanctuary to the courtyard of the LORD's temple.
Then the Levites received them and took them
outside to the Kidron Valley. 17 They began
the consecration on the first day of the first
month, and on the eighth day of the month
they came to the portico of the LORD's temple. They consecrated the LORD's temple for
eight days, and on the sixteenth day of the
first month they finished.
18 Then they went inside to King Hezekiah
and said, "We have cleansed the whole temple
of the LORD, the altar of burnt offering and all
its utensils, and the table for the rows of the
Bread of the Presence and all its utensils. 19 We
have set up and consecrated all the utensils
that King Ahaz rejected during his reign when
he became unfaithful. They are in front of the
altar of the LORD."

RENEWAL OF TEMPLE WORSHIP

20 King Hezekiah got up early, gathered the
city officials, and went to the LORD's temple.
21 They brought seven bulls, seven rams, seven
lambs, and seven male goats as a sin offering
for the kingdom, for the sanctuary, and for
Judah. Then he told the descendants of Aaron, the priests, to offer them on the altar of
the LORD. 22 So they slaughtered the bulls, and
the priests received the blood and splattered
it on the altar. They slaughtered the rams and
splattered the blood on the altar. They slaughtered the lambs and splattered the blood on
the altar. 23 Then they brought the goats for the
sin offering right into the presence of the king
and the congregation, who laid their hands on
them. 24 The priests slaughtered the goats and
put their blood on the altar for a sin offering,
to make atonement for all Israel, for the king
said that the burnt offering and sin offering
were for all Israel.
25 Hezekiah stationed the Levites in the
LORD's temple with cymbals, harps, and lyres
according to the command of David, Gad the
king's seer, and the prophet Nathan. For the
command was from the LORD through his
prophets. 26 The Levites stood with the instruments of David, and the priests with the
trumpets.
27 Then Hezekiah ordered that the burnt
offering be offered on the altar. When the
burnt offerings began, the song of the LORD
and the trumpets began, accompanied by the

instruments of King David of Israel. 28 The whole assembly was worshiping, singing the song, and blowing the trumpets — all this continued until the burnt offering was completed. 29 When the burnt offerings were completed, the king and all those present with him bowed down and worshiped. 30 Then King Hezekiah and the officials told the Levites to sing praise to the LORD in the words of David and of the seer Asaph. So they sang praises with rejoicing and knelt low and worshiped.

31 Hezekiah concluded, "Now you are consecrated[A] to the LORD. Come near and bring sacrifices and thank offerings to the LORD's temple." So the congregation brought sacrifices and thank offerings, and all those with willing hearts brought burnt offerings. 32 The number of burnt offerings the congregation brought was seventy bulls, one hundred rams, and two hundred lambs; all these were for a burnt offering to the LORD. 33 Six hundred bulls and three thousand sheep and goats were consecrated.

34 However, since there were not enough priests, they weren't able to skin all the burnt offerings, so their Levite brothers helped them until the work was finished and until the priests consecrated themselves. For the Levites were more conscientious[B] to consecrate themselves than the priests were. 35 Furthermore, the burnt offerings were abundant, along with the fat of the fellowship offerings and with the drink offerings for the burnt offering.

So the service of the LORD's temple was established. 36 Then Hezekiah and all the people rejoiced over how God had prepared the people, for it had come about suddenly.

CELEBRATION OF THE PASSOVER

30 Then Hezekiah sent word throughout all Israel and Judah, and he also wrote letters to Ephraim and Manasseh to come to the LORD's temple in Jerusalem to observe the Passover of the LORD, the God of Israel. 2 For the king and his officials and the entire congregation in Jerusalem decided to observe the Passover of the LORD in the second month, 3 because they were not able to observe it at the appropriate time. Not enough of the priests had consecrated themselves, and the people hadn't been gathered together in Jerusalem. 4 The proposal pleased the king and the congregation, 5 so they affirmed the proposal and spread the message throughout all Israel, from Beer-sheba to Dan, to come to observe the Passover of the LORD, the God of Israel in Jerusalem, for they hadn't observed it often,[C] as prescribed.[D]

6 So the couriers went throughout Israel and Judah with letters from the hand of the king and his officials, and according to the king's command, saying, "Israelites, return to the LORD, the God of Abraham, Isaac, and Israel so that he may return to those of you who remain, who have escaped the grasp of the kings of Assyria. 7 Don't be like your fathers and your brothers who were unfaithful to the LORD, the God of their ancestors so that he made them an object of horror as you yourselves see. 8 Don't become obstinate[E] now like your fathers did. Give your allegiance[F] to the LORD, and come to his sanctuary that he has consecrated forever. Serve the LORD your God so that he may turn his burning anger away from you, 9 for when you return to the LORD, your brothers and your sons will receive mercy in the presence of their captors and will return to this land. For the LORD your God is gracious and merciful; he will not turn his face away from you if you return to him."

10 The couriers traveled from city to city in the land of Ephraim and Manasseh as far as Zebulun, but the inhabitants[G] laughed at them and mocked them. 11 But some from Asher, Manasseh, and Zebulun humbled themselves and came to Jerusalem. 12 Also, the power of God was at work in Judah to unite them[H] to carry out the command of the king and his officials by the word of the LORD.

13 A very large assembly of people was gathered in Jerusalem to observe the Festival of Unleavened Bread in the second month. 14 They proceeded to take away the altars that were in Jerusalem, and they took away the incense altars and threw them into the Kidron Valley. 15 They slaughtered the Passover lamb on the fourteenth day of the second month. The priests and Levites were ashamed, and they consecrated themselves and brought burnt offerings to the LORD's temple. 16 They stood at their prescribed posts, according to the law of Moses, the man of God. The priests

---

[A] **29:31** Lit *Now you have filled your hands* [B] **29:34** Lit *upright of heart*; Ps 32:11; 64:10 [C] **30:5** Or *in great numbers* [D] **30:5** Lit *often, according to what is written* [E] **30:8** Lit *Don't stiffen your neck* [F] **30:8** Lit *hand* [G] **30:10** Lit *but they* [H] **30:12** Lit *to give them one heart*

splattered the blood received from the Levites,
17 for there were many in the assembly who
had not consecrated themselves, and so the
Levites were in charge of slaughtering the
Passover lambs for every unclean person to
consecrate the lambs to the LORD. 18 A large
number of the people — many from Ephraim,
Manasseh, Issachar, and Zebulun — were ritually unclean, yet they had eaten the Passover
contrary to what was written. But Hezekiah
had interceded for them, saying, "May the good
LORD provide atonement on behalf of 19 whoever sets his whole heart on seeking God, the
LORD, the God of his ancestors, even though
not according to the purification rules of the
sanctuary." 20 So the LORD heard Hezekiah and
healed the people. 21 The Israelites who were
present in Jerusalem observed the Festival of
Unleavened Bread seven days with great joy,
and the Levites and the priests praised the
LORD day after day with loud instruments.
22 Then Hezekiah encouraged[A] all the Levites
who performed skillfully before the LORD. They
ate at the appointed festival for seven days,
sacrificing fellowship offerings and giving
thanks to the LORD, the God of their ancestors.

23 The whole congregation decided to observe seven more days, so they observed seven
days with joy, 24 for King Hezekiah of Judah
contributed one thousand bulls and seven
thousand sheep for the congregation. Also,
the officials contributed one thousand bulls
and ten thousand sheep for the congregation,
and many priests consecrated themselves.
25 Then the whole assembly of Judah with the
priests and Levites, the whole assembly that
came from Israel, the resident aliens who came
from the land of Israel, and those who were
living in Judah, rejoiced. 26 There was great
rejoicing in Jerusalem, for nothing like this
was known since the days of Solomon son of
David, the king of Israel.

27 Then the priests and the Levites stood to
bless the people, and God heard them, and
their prayer came into his holy dwelling place
in heaven.

REMOVAL OF IDOLATRY

31 When all this was completed, all Israel
who had attended went out to the cities of Judah and broke up the sacred pillars,
chopped down the Asherah poles, and tore
down the high places and altars throughout
Judah and Benjamin, as well as in Ephraim
and Manasseh, to the last one.[B] Then all the
Israelites returned to their cities, each to his
own possession.

OFFERINGS FOR LEVITES

2 Hezekiah reestablished the divisions of the
priests and Levites for the burnt offerings and
fellowship offerings, for ministry, for giving
thanks, and for praise in the gates of the camp
of the LORD, each division corresponding to
his service among the priests and Levites. 3 The
king contributed[C] from his own possessions
for the regular morning and evening burnt
offerings, the burnt offerings of the Sabbaths,
of the New Moons, and of the appointed feasts,
as written in the law of the LORD. 4 He told the
people who lived in Jerusalem to give a contribution for the priests and Levites so that
they could devote their energy to the law of
the LORD. 5 When the word spread, the Israelites gave liberally of the best of the grain, new
wine, fresh oil, honey, and of all the produce of
the field, and they brought in an abundance, a
tenth of everything. 6 As for the Israelites and
Judahites who lived in the cities of Judah, they
also brought a tenth of the herds and flocks,
and a tenth of the dedicated things that were
consecrated to the LORD their God. They gathered them into large piles. 7 In the third month
they began building up the piles, and they finished in the seventh month. 8 When Hezekiah
and his officials came and viewed the piles,
they blessed the LORD and his people Israel.

9 Hezekiah asked the priests and Levites
about the piles. 10 The chief priest Azariah, of
the household of Zadok, answered him, "Since
they began bringing the offering to the LORD's
temple, we eat and are satisfied and there is
plenty left over because the LORD has blessed
his people; this abundance is what is left over."

11 Hezekiah told them to prepare chambers
in the LORD's temple, and they prepared them.
12 The offering, the tenth, and the dedicated
things were brought faithfully. Conaniah
the Levite was the officer in charge of them,
and his brother Shimei was second. 13 Jehiel,
Azaziah, Nahath, Asahel, Jerimoth, Jozabad,
Eliel, Ismachiah, Mahath, and Benaiah were
deputies under the authority of Conaniah and
his brother Shimei by appointment of King
Hezekiah and of Azariah the chief official of
God's temple.

[A] **30:22** Lit *spoke to the heart of* [B] **31:1** Lit *Manasseh, until finishing* [C] **31:3** Lit *The king's portion*

[14] Kore son of Imnah the Levite, the keeper
of the East Gate, was over the freewill offerings to God to distribute the contribution to
the LORD and the consecrated things. [15] Eden,
Miniamin, Jeshua, Shemaiah, Amariah, and
Shecaniah in the cities of the priests were to
distribute it faithfully under his authority to
their brothers by divisions, whether large or
small. [16] In addition, they distributed it to males
registered by genealogy three[A] years old and
above; to all who would enter the LORD's temple
for their daily duty, for their service in their
responsibilities according to their divisions.
[17] They distributed also to those recorded by
genealogy of the priests by their ancestral
families and the Levites twenty years old
and above, by their responsibilities in their
divisions; [18] to those registered by genealogy — with all their dependents, wives, sons,
and daughters — of the whole assembly (for
they had faithfully consecrated themselves as
holy); [19] and to the descendants of Aaron, the
priests, in the common fields of their cities,
in each and every city. There were men who
were registered by name to distribute a portion to every male among the priests and to
every Levite recorded by genealogy.

[20] Hezekiah did this throughout all Judah.
He did what was good and upright and true
before the LORD his God. [21] He was diligent in
every deed that he began in the service of God's
temple, in the instruction and the commands,
in order to seek his God, and he prospered.

SENNACHERIB'S INVASION

32 After these faithful deeds, King Sennacherib of Assyria came and entered Judah.
He laid siege to the fortified cities and intended[B] to break into them. [2] Hezekiah saw that
Sennacherib had come and that he planned[C]
war on Jerusalem, [3] so he consulted with his
officials and his warriors about stopping up
the water of the springs that were outside
the city, and they helped him. [4] Many people
gathered and stopped up all the springs and
the stream that flowed through the land; they
said, "Why should the kings of Assyria come
and find abundant water?" [5] Then Hezekiah
strengthened his position by rebuilding the
entire broken-down wall and heightening the
towers and the other outside wall. He repaired
the supporting terraces of the city of David, and
made an abundance of weapons and shields.

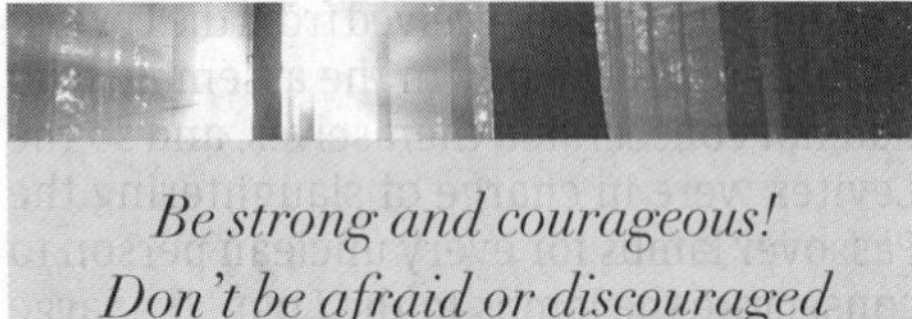

Be strong and courageous! Don't be afraid or discouraged before the king of Assyria or before the large army that is with him, for there are more with us than with him. He has only human strength, but we have the LORD our God to help us and to fight our battles.

—2 Chronicles 32:7-8

[6] He set military commanders over the people
and gathered the people in the square of the
city gate. Then he encouraged them,[D] saying,
[7] "Be strong and courageous! Don't be afraid or
discouraged before the king of Assyria or before the large army that is with him, for there
are more with us than with him. [8] He has only
human strength,[E] but we have the LORD our God
to help us and to fight our battles." So the people
relied on the words of King Hezekiah of Judah.

SENNACHERIB'S SERVANT'S SPEECH

[9] After this, while King Sennacherib of Assyria
with all his armed forces besieged[F] Lachish,
he sent his servants to Jerusalem against King
Hezekiah of Judah and against all those of Judah who were in Jerusalem, saying, [10] "This is
what King Sennacherib of Assyria says: 'What
are you relying on that you remain in Jerusalem under siege? [11] Isn't Hezekiah misleading
you to give you over to death by famine and
thirst when he says, "The LORD our God will
keep us from the grasp of the king of Assyria"?
[12] Didn't Hezekiah himself remove his high
places and his altars and say to Judah and Jerusalem, "You must worship before one altar,
and you must burn incense on it"?

[13] " 'Don't you know what I and my fathers
have done to all the peoples of the lands? Have
any of the national gods of the lands been able
to rescue their land from my power? [14] Who
among all the gods of these nations that my
predecessors completely destroyed was able
to rescue his people from my power, that your

[A] **31:16** Or *30*; 1Ch 23:3 [B] **32:1** Lit *said to himself* [C] **32:2** Lit *that his face was for* [D] **32:6** Lit *he spoke to their hearts*
[E] **32:8** Lit *With him an arm of flesh* [F] **32:9** Lit *with his dominion was against*

God should be able to deliver you from my
power? 15 So now, don't let Hezekiah deceive
you, and don't let him mislead you like this.
Don't believe him, for no god of any nation or
kingdom has been able to rescue his people
from my power or the power of my fathers.
How much less will your God rescue you from
my power!' "
16 His servants said more against the LORD
God and against his servant Hezekiah. 17 He
also wrote letters to mock the LORD, the God
of Israel, saying against him:

> Just like the national gods of the lands
> that did not rescue their people from my
> power, so Hezekiah's God will not rescue
> his people from my power.

18 Then they called out loudly in Hebrew[A]
to the people of Jerusalem, who were on the
wall, to frighten and discourage them in order
that he might capture the city. 19 They spoke
against the God of Jerusalem like they had
spoken against the gods of the peoples of the
earth, which were made by human hands.

DELIVERANCE FROM SENNACHERIB

20 King Hezekiah and the prophet Isaiah son
of Amoz prayed about this and cried out to
heaven, 21 and the LORD sent an angel who
annihilated every valiant warrior, leader, and
commander in the camp of the king of Assyria. So the king of Assyria returned in disgrace
to his land. He went to the temple of his god,
and there some of his own children struck
him down with the sword.
22 So the LORD saved Hezekiah and the inhabitants of Jerusalem from the power of King
Sennacherib of Assyria and from the power
of all others. He gave them rest[B] on every side.
23 Many were bringing an offering to the LORD
to Jerusalem and valuable gifts to King Hezekiah of Judah, and he was exalted in the eyes
of all the nations after that.

HEZEKIAH'S ILLNESS AND PRIDE

24 In those days Hezekiah became sick to the
point of death, so he prayed to the LORD, and he
spoke to him and gave him a miraculous sign.
25 However, because his heart was proud, Hezekiah didn't respond according to the benefit
that had come to him. So there was wrath on
him, Judah, and Jerusalem. 26 Then Hezekiah
humbled himself for the pride of his heart
— he and the inhabitants of Jerusalem — so
the LORD's wrath didn't come on them during
Hezekiah's lifetime.

HEZEKIAH'S WEALTH AND WORKS

27 Hezekiah had abundant riches and glory,
and he made himself treasuries for silver, gold,
precious stones, spices, shields, and every
desirable item. 28 He made warehouses for
the harvest of grain, new wine, and fresh oil,
and stalls for all kinds of cattle, and pens for
flocks. 29 He made cities for himself, and he
acquired vast numbers of flocks and herds,
for God gave him abundant possessions.
30 This same Hezekiah blocked the outlet of
the water of the Upper Gihon and channeled it
smoothly downward and westward to the city
of David. Hezekiah succeeded in everything
he did. 31 When the ambassadors of Babylon's
rulers were sent[C] to him to inquire about the
miraculous sign that happened in the land,
God left him to test him and discover what
was in his heart.

HEZEKIAH'S DEATH

32 As for the rest of the events of Hezekiah's
reign and his deeds of faithful love, note that
they are written in the Visions of the Prophet
Isaiah son of Amoz, and in the Book of the
Kings of Judah and Israel. 33 Hezekiah rested
with his fathers and was buried on the ascent
to the tombs of David's descendants. All Judah
and the inhabitants of Jerusalem paid him
honor at his death. His son Manasseh became
king in his place.

JUDAH'S KING MANASSEH

33 Manasseh was twelve years old when he
became king, and he reigned fifty-five
years in Jerusalem. 2 He did what was evil in the
LORD's sight, imitating the detestable practices
of the nations that the LORD had dispossessed
before the Israelites. 3 He rebuilt the high places
that his father Hezekiah had torn down and
reestablished the altars for the Baals. He made
Asherah poles, and he bowed in worship to
all the stars in the sky and served them. 4 He
built altars in the LORD's temple, where the
LORD had said, "Jerusalem is where my name
will remain forever." 5 He built altars to all the
stars in the sky in both courtyards of the LORD's
temple. 6 He passed his sons through the fire in
Ben Hinnom Valley. He practiced witchcraft,

[A] **32:18** Lit *Judahite* [B] **32:22** Lit *He led them*; Ps 23:2 [C] **32:31** LXX, Tg, Vg; MT reads *of Babylon sent*

divination, and sorcery, and consulted mediums and spiritists. He did a huge amount of evil in the LORD's sight, angering him.

7 Manasseh set up a carved image of the idol, which he had made, in God's temple that God had spoken about to David and his son Solomon: "I will establish my name forever[A] in this temple and in Jerusalem, which I have chosen out of all the tribes of Israel. 8 I will never again remove the feet of the Israelites from the land where I stationed your[B] ancestors, if only they will be careful to do all I have commanded them through Moses — all the law, statutes, and judgments." 9 So Manasseh caused Judah and the inhabitants of Jerusalem to stray so that they did worse evil than the nations the LORD had destroyed before the Israelites.

MANASSEH'S REPENTANCE

10 The LORD spoke to Manasseh and his people, but they didn't listen. 11 So he brought against them the military commanders of the king of Assyria. They captured Manasseh with hooks, bound him with bronze shackles, and took him to Babylon. 12 When he was in distress, he sought the favor of the LORD his God and earnestly humbled himself before the God of his ancestors. 13 He prayed to him, and the LORD was receptive to his prayer. He granted his request and brought him back to Jerusalem, to his kingdom. So Manasseh came to know that the LORD is God.

14 After this, he built the outer wall of the city of David from west of Gihon in the valley to the entrance of the Fish Gate; he brought it around the Ophel, and he heightened it considerably. He also placed military commanders in all the fortified cities of Judah.

15 He removed the foreign gods and the idol from the LORD's temple, along with all the altars that he had built on the mountain of the LORD's temple and in Jerusalem, and he threw them outside the city. 16 He built[C] the altar of the LORD and offered fellowship and thank offerings on it. Then he told Judah to serve the LORD, the God of Israel. 17 However, the people still sacrificed at the high places, but only to the LORD their God.

MANASSEH'S DEATH

18 The rest of the events of Manasseh's reign, along with his prayer to his God and the words of the seers who spoke to him in the name of the LORD, the God of Israel, are written in the Events of Israel's Kings. 19 His prayer and how God was receptive to his prayer, and all his sin and unfaithfulness and the sites where he built high places and set up Asherah poles and carved images before he humbled himself, they are written in the Events of Hozai. 20 Manasseh rested with his fathers, and he was buried in his own house. His son Amon became king in his place.

JUDAH'S KING AMON

21 Amon was twenty-two years old when he became king, and he reigned two years in Jerusalem. 22 He did what was evil in the LORD's sight, just as his father Manasseh had done. Amon sacrificed to all the carved images that his father Manasseh had made, and he served them. 23 But he did not humble himself before the LORD like his father Manasseh humbled himself; instead, Amon increased his guilt.

24 So his servants conspired against him and put him to death in his own house. 25 The common people[D] killed all who had conspired against King Amon, and they made his son Josiah king in his place.

JUDAH'S KING JOSIAH

34 Josiah was eight years old when he became king, and he reigned thirty-one years in Jerusalem. 2 He did what was right in the LORD's sight and walked in the ways of his ancestor David; he did not turn aside to the right or the left.

JOSIAH'S REFORM

3 In the eighth year of his reign, while he was still a youth, Josiah began to seek the God of his ancestor David, and in the twelfth year he began to cleanse Judah and Jerusalem of the high places, the Asherah poles, the carved images, and the cast images. 4 Then in his presence the altars of the Baals were torn down, and he chopped down the shrines[E] that were above them. He shattered the Asherah poles, the carved images, and the cast images, crushed them to dust, and scattered them over the graves of those who had sacrificed to them. 5 He burned the bones of the priests on their altars. So he cleansed Judah and Jerusalem. 6 He did the same in the cities of Manasseh, Ephraim, and Simeon, and as far as Naphtali

[A] **33:7** LXX, Syr, Tg, Vg; 2Kg 21:7; MT reads *name for Elom* [B] **33:8** LXX, Syr, Vg read *land I gave to their*; 2Kg 21:8 [C] **33:16** Some Hb mss, Syr, Tg, Arabic; other Hb mss, LXX, Vg read *restored* [D] **33:25** Lit *The people of the land* [E] **34:4** Lit *incense altars*, also in v. 7

and on their surrounding mountain shrines.[A]
7 He tore down the altars, and he smashed
the Asherah poles and the carved images to
powder. He chopped down all the shrines
throughout the land of Israel and returned
to Jerusalem.

JOSIAH'S REPAIR OF THE TEMPLE

8 In the eighteenth year of his reign, in order
to cleanse the land and the temple, Josiah sent
Shaphan son of Azaliah, along with Maaseiah
the governor of the city and the court historian
Joah son of Joahaz, to repair the temple of the
LORD his God.

9 So they went to the high priest Hilkiah
and gave him the silver brought into God's
temple. The Levites and the doorkeepers had
collected it from Manasseh, Ephraim, and
from the entire remnant of Israel, and from
all Judah, Benjamin, and the inhabitants of
Jerusalem. 10 They gave it to those doing the
work — those who oversaw the LORD's temple. They gave it to the workmen who were
working in the LORD's temple, to repair and
restore the temple; 11 they gave it to the carpenters and builders and also used it to buy
quarried stone and timbers — for joining and
making beams — for the buildings that Judah's
kings had destroyed.

12 The men were doing the work with integrity. Their overseers were Jahath and Obadiah,
Levites from the Merarites, and Zechariah
and Meshullam from the Kohathites as supervisors. The Levites were all skilled with
musical instruments. 13 They were also over
the porters and were supervising all those doing the work task by task. Some of the Levites
were secretaries, officers, and gatekeepers.

THE RECOVERY OF THE BOOK OF THE LAW

14 When they brought out the silver that had
been deposited in the LORD's temple, the priest
Hilkiah found the book of the law of the LORD
written by the hand of Moses. 15 Consequently,
Hilkiah told the court secretary Shaphan, "I
have found the book of the law in the LORD's
temple," and he gave the book to Shaphan.

16 Shaphan took the book to the king, and
also reported, "Your servants are doing all
that was placed in their hands. 17 They have
emptied out the silver that was found in the
LORD's temple and have given it to the overseers and to those doing the work." 18 Then the
court secretary Shaphan told the king, "The
priest Hilkiah gave me a book," and Shaphan
read from it in the presence of the king.

19 When the king heard the words of the law,
he tore his clothes. 20 Then he commanded
Hilkiah, Ahikam son of Shaphan, Abdon son
of Micah, the court secretary Shaphan, and
the king's servant Asaiah, 21 "Go and inquire
of the LORD for me and for those remaining
in Israel and Judah, concerning the words
of the book that was found. For great is the
LORD's wrath that is poured out on us because
our ancestors have not kept the word of the
LORD in order to do everything written in
this book."

HULDAH'S PROPHECY OF JUDGMENT

22 So Hilkiah and those the king had designated[B] went to the prophetess Huldah, the wife
of Shallum son of Tokhath, son of Hasrah,
keeper of the wardrobe. She lived in Jerusalem in the Second District. They spoke with
her about this.

23 She said to them, "This is what the LORD
God of Israel says: Say to the man who sent
you to me, 24 'This is what the LORD says: I am
about to bring disaster on this place and on its
inhabitants, fulfilling[C] all the curses written in
the book that they read in the presence of the
king of Judah, 25 because they have abandoned
me and burned incense to other gods so as to
anger me with all the works of their hands. My
wrath will be poured out on this place, and it
will not be quenched.' 26 Say this to the king
of Judah who sent you to inquire of the LORD:
'This is what the LORD God of Israel says: As for
the words that you heard, 27 because your heart
was tender and you humbled yourself before
God when you heard his words against this
place and against its inhabitants, and because
you humbled yourself before me, and you tore
your clothes and wept before me, I myself have
heard' — this is the LORD's declaration. 28 'I will
indeed gather you to your fathers, and you will
be gathered to your grave in peace. Your eyes
will not see all the disaster that I am bringing
on this place and on its inhabitants.'"

Then they reported to the king.

AFFIRMATION OF THE COVENANT BY JOSIAH AND THE PEOPLE

29 So the king sent messengers and gathered
all the elders of Judah and Jerusalem. 30 The

[A] **34:6** One Hb tradition reads *Naphtali with their swords*; alt Hb tradition, Syr, Vg read *Naphtali, the ruins all around*; Hb obscure [B] **34:22** LXX; MT omits *designated* [C] **34:24** *fulfilling* supplied for clarity

king went up to the LORD's temple with all the
men of Judah and the inhabitants of Jerusalem, as well as the priests and the Levites — all
the people from the oldest to the youngest.
He read in their hearing all the words of the
book of the covenant that had been found in
the LORD's temple. 31 Then the king stood at
his post and made a covenant in the LORD's
presence to follow the LORD and to keep his
commands, his decrees, and his statutes with
all his heart and with all his soul in order to
carry out the words of the covenant written
in this book.
32 He had all those present in Jerusalem and
Benjamin agree[A] to it. So all the inhabitants
of Jerusalem carried out the covenant of God,
the God of their ancestors.
33 So Josiah removed everything that was
detestable from all the lands belonging to the
Israelites, and he required all who were present
in Israel to serve the LORD their God. Throughout his reign they did not turn aside from following the LORD, the God of their ancestors.

JOSIAH'S PASSOVER OBSERVANCE

35 Josiah observed the LORD's Passover
and slaughtered the Passover lambs
on the fourteenth day of the first month. 2 He
appointed the priests to their responsibilities
and encouraged them to serve in the LORD's
temple. 3 He said to the Levites who taught
all Israel the holy things of the LORD, "Put the
holy ark in the temple built by Solomon son
of David king of Israel. Since you do not have
to carry it on your shoulders, now serve the
LORD your God and his people Israel.
4 "Organize your ancestral families[B] by your
divisions according to the written instruction of King David of Israel and that of his
son Solomon. 5 Serve in the holy place by the

Support | *Humility*

EXALTED PLACE

"'Because your heart was tender and you humbled yourself
before God when you heard his words against this place and against
its inhabitants, and because you humbled yourself before me,
and you tore your clothes and wept before me,
I myself have heard'—this is the LORD's declaration."
2 Chronicles 34:27

Everyone wants humility. And if we're honest, we would admit that it's also one of those undesirable habits nobody wants to practice.

Humility makes us think of nameless servants bowing, scraping, groveling, and being taken advantage of. We can't help but think of a related word: *humiliation*. So naturally when we read of King Josiah humbling himself, we wonder how that can be.

We consider the words of James: "Humble yourselves before the Lord," and we probably flinch. Humbling ourselves sounds so . . . humbling! But James adds, "and [God] will exalt you" (Jms 4:10). When we sink down or bow down before the Lord—the opposite of exalting ourselves—we can be sure that God will eventually exalt us.

While pride screams, "Promote yourself! Get others—including God—to serve your agenda!" humility whispers, "Lose yourself in fulfilling God's agenda. Trust that he will exalt you as he sees fit—either in this life or in the life to come."

Our calling is to make much of God, to live for *his* glory and fame. To do this consistently without the support of some likeminded souls is very difficult.

With whom you can pursue a life of humility?

For the next note on *Support*, see Job 6:24.

[A] **34:32** Lit *take a stand.* [B] **35:4** Lit *the house of your fathers*

groupings of the ancestral families[A] for your
brothers, the lay people,[B] and according to the
division of the Levites by family. 6 Slaughter
the Passover lambs, consecrate yourselves,
and make preparations for your brothers to
carry out the word of the LORD through Moses."
7 Then Josiah donated thirty thousand sheep,
lambs, and young goats, plus three thousand
cattle from his own possessions, for the Passover sacrifices for all the lay people who were
present.
8 His officials also donated willingly for the
people, the priests, and the Levites. Hilkiah,
Zechariah, and Jehiel, chief officials of God's
temple, gave twenty-six hundred Passover
sacrifices and three hundred cattle for the
priests. 9 Conaniah and his brothers Shemaiah and Nethanel, and Hashabiah, Jeiel, and
Jozabad, officers of the Levites, donated five
thousand Passover sacrifices for the Levites,
plus five hundred cattle.
10 So the service was established; the priests
stood at their posts and the Levites in their
divisions according to the king's command.
11 Then they slaughtered the Passover lambs,
and while the Levites were skinning the animals, the priests splattered the blood[C] they
had been given.[D] 12 They removed the burnt
offerings so that they might be given to the
groupings of the ancestral families[E] of the lay
people to offer to the LORD, according to what
is written in the book of Moses; they did the
same with the cattle. 13 They roasted the Passover lambs with fire according to regulation.
They boiled the holy sacrifices in pots, kettles,
and bowls; and they quickly brought them to
the lay people. 14 Afterward, they made preparations for themselves and for the priests,
since the priests, the descendants of Aaron,
were busy offering up burnt offerings and
fat until night. So the Levites made preparations for themselves and for the priests, the
descendants of Aaron.
15 The singers, the descendants of Asaph,
were at their stations according to the command of David, Asaph, Heman, and Jeduthun
the king's seer. Also, the gatekeepers were
at each temple gate. None of them left their
tasks because their Levite brothers had made
preparations for them.
16 So all the service of the LORD was established that day for observing the Passover and
for offering burnt offerings on the altar of
the LORD, according to the command of King
Josiah. 17 The Israelites who were present in
Judah also observed the Passover at that time
and the Festival of Unleavened Bread for seven
days. 18 No Passover had been observed like it
in Israel since the days of the prophet Samuel.
None of the kings of Israel ever observed a
Passover like the one that Josiah observed with
the priests, the Levites, all Judah, the Israelites
who were present in Judah, and the inhabitants of Jerusalem. 19 In the eighteenth year
of Josiah's reign, this Passover was observed.

JOSIAH'S LAST DEEDS AND DEATH

20 After all this that Josiah had prepared for
the temple, King Neco of Egypt marched up
to fight at Carchemish by the Euphrates, and
Josiah went out to confront him. 21 But Neco
sent messengers to him, saying, "What is the
issue between you and me, king of Judah? I
have not come against you today[F] but I am
fighting another dynasty.[G] God told me to hurry. Stop opposing God who is with me; don't
make him destroy you!"
22 But Josiah did not turn away from him;
instead, in order to fight with him he disguised
himself.[H] He did not listen to Neco's words
from the mouth of God, but went to the Valley of Megiddo to fight. 23 The archers shot
King Josiah, and he said to his servants, "Take
me away, for I am severely wounded!" 24 So
his servants took him out of the war chariot, carried him in his second chariot, and
brought him to Jerusalem. Then he died, and
they buried him in the tomb of his fathers.
All Judah and Jerusalem mourned for Josiah.
25 Jeremiah chanted a dirge over Josiah, and
all the male and female singers still speak of
Josiah in their dirges today. They established
them as a statute for Israel, and indeed they
are written in the Dirges.
26 The rest of the events of Josiah's reign,
along with his deeds of faithful love according
to what is written in the law of the LORD, 27 and
his words, from beginning to end, are written
in the Book of the Kings of Israel and Judah.

JUDAH'S KING JEHOAHAZ

36 Then the common people[I] took Jehoahaz son of Josiah and made him king
in Jerusalem in place of his father.

[A] 35:5 Lit *the house of the fathers* [B] 35:5 Lit *the sons of the people*, also in vv. 7,12,13 [C] 35:11 LXX, Vg, Tg; MT omits *blood* [D] 35:11 Lit *splattered from their hand* [E] 35:12 Lit *house of fathers* [F] 35:21 LXX, Syr, Tg, Vg; MT reads *Not against you, you today* [G] 35:21 Lit *house* [H] 35:22 LXX reads *he was determined* [I] 36:1 Lit *the people of the land*

2 Jehoahaz[A] was twenty-three years old when he became king, and he reigned three months in Jerusalem. 3 The king of Egypt deposed him in Jerusalem and fined the land seventy-five hundred pounds[B] of silver and seventy-five pounds[C] of gold.

JUDAH'S KING JEHOIAKIM

4 Then King Neco of Egypt made Jehoahaz's brother Eliakim king over Judah and Jerusalem and changed Eliakim's name to Jehoiakim. But Neco took his brother Jehoahaz and brought him to Egypt.

5 Jehoiakim was twenty-five years old when he became king, and he reigned eleven years in Jerusalem. He did what was evil in the sight of the LORD his God. 6 Now King Nebuchadnezzar of Babylon attacked him and bound him in bronze shackles to take him to Babylon. 7 Also Nebuchadnezzar took some of the articles of the LORD's temple to Babylon and put them in his temple in Babylon.

8 The rest of the deeds of Jehoiakim, the detestable actions he committed, and what was found against him, are written in the Book of Israel's Kings. His son Jehoiachin became king in his place.

JUDAH'S KING JEHOIACHIN

9 Jehoiachin was eighteen[D] years old when he became king, and he reigned three months and ten days in Jerusalem. He did what was evil in the LORD's sight. 10 In the spring[E] Nebuchadnezzar sent for him and brought him to Babylon along with the valuable articles of the LORD's temple. Then he made Jehoiachin's brother Zedekiah king over Judah and Jerusalem.

JUDAH'S KING ZEDEKIAH

11 Zedekiah was twenty-one years old when he became king, and he reigned eleven years in Jerusalem. 12 He did what was evil in the sight of the LORD his God and did not humble himself before the prophet Jeremiah at the LORD's command. 13 He also rebelled against King Nebuchadnezzar who had made him swear allegiance by God. He became obstinate[F] and hardened his heart against returning to the LORD, the God of Israel. 14 All the leaders of the priests and the people multiplied their unfaithful deeds, imitating all the detestable practices of the nations, and they defiled the LORD's temple that he had consecrated in Jerusalem.

THE DESTRUCTION OF JERUSALEM

15 But the LORD, the God of their ancestors sent word against them by the hand of his messengers, sending them time and time again, for he had compassion on his people and on his dwelling place. 16 But they kept ridiculing God's messengers, despising his words, and scoffing at his prophets, until the LORD's wrath was so stirred up against his people that there was no remedy. 17 So he brought up against them the king of the Chaldeans, who killed their fit young men with the sword in the house of their sanctuary. He had no pity on young men or young women, elderly or aged; he handed them all over to him. 18 He took everything to Babylon — all the articles of God's temple, large and small, the treasures of the LORD's temple, and the treasures of the king and his officials. 19 Then the Chaldeans burned God's temple. They tore down Jerusalem's wall, burned all its palaces, and destroyed all its valuable articles.

20 He deported those who escaped from the sword to Babylon, and they became servants to him and his sons until the rise of the Persian[G] kingdom. 21 This fulfilled the word of the LORD through Jeremiah, and the land enjoyed its Sabbath rest all the days of the desolation until seventy years were fulfilled.

THE DECREE OF CYRUS

22 In the first year of King Cyrus of Persia, in order to fulfill the word of the LORD spoken through[H] Jeremiah, the LORD roused the spirit of King Cyrus of Persia to issue a proclamation throughout his entire kingdom and also to put it in writing:

> 23 This is what King Cyrus of Persia says: The LORD, the God of the heavens, has given me all the kingdoms of the earth and has appointed me to build him a temple at Jerusalem in Judah. Any of his people among you may go up, and may the LORD his God be with him.

[A] **36:2** = Joahaz, also in v. 4 [B] **36:3** Lit *100 talents* [C] **36:3** Lit *one talent* [D] **36:9** Some Hb mss, LXX; 2Kg 24:8; other Hb mss read *eight* [E] **36:10** Lit *At the return of the year* [F] **36:13** Lit *He stiffened his neck* [G] **36:20** LXX reads *Median* [H] **36:22** Lit *LORD by the mouth of*

Ezra—The exiles returning from Babylon faced overwhelming obstacles. The trip was fraught with dangers and hardships, and they discovered that enemies had settled in their land. Hostile government policies and rulers made life difficult. How could they obey God and rebuild the temple under such circumstances?

The answer is that they needed to trust the One who had kept his promise to return them from exile—working through pagan rulers to do so—and would surely give them the strength to obey. God is sovereign and faithful. The people's job was to separate themselves from the world and follow God's laws even in a hostile environment when life was difficult.

We need to remember these principles when facing obstacles as to our faith. When people encourage us to make bad choices, we can trust God to help us obey. When the culture implies that following God's Word makes no sense, we can remember the truth that God is righteous and just and will fulfill his promises.

And when we can't find a way forward, we can follow Ezra's example of prayer, humbly seeking God's grace to restore and redeem us. This book reminds us that centering our lives around worshiping the one true God puts the rest of life into its proper place.

EZRA

AUTHOR: The book of Ezra, named after its principle character, is technically anonymous. Ancient Jewish sources, however, usually credit both Ezra and Nehemiah, which were originally a single book, to the scribe Ezra.

DATE WRITTEN: The book of Ezra is a continuation of 1 and 2 Chronicles and was likely written at the same time as those books, shortly after the completion of Nehemiah's ministry, around 400 BC. Ezra came to Jerusalem around 458 BC, and Nehemiah followed him approximately thirteen years later, in 445 BC.

ORIGINAL AUDIENCE: The Israelites

SETTING: Jerusalem, where a remnant of Israelites returned after seventy years of exile in Babylon. The people of God had been punished for their rebellion by being conquered by their enemies, but God had promised to return them to the promised land after seventy years (2Ch 36:21). When they returned, they found that the land had been settled by foreigners who did not worship God. At first they remained separated from the pagan culture, but in between when the first Israelites returned to Jerusalem and when Ezra returned to build the temple, the Jews had begun to marry foreigners and neglect their covenant responsibilities.

PURPOSE FOR WRITING: Ezra serves to connect the returning exiles with the pre-exilic community of Israel and the covenant promises of God. These people were part of God's redemptive plan—though they had been separated for a time from the land of promise—and they needed to live like it. Ezra called them to separate themselves from the pagan people who had settled the land and return to true worship of the living God. Themes of holiness, the centrality of the law to daily life, and a life of prayer and worship are prevalent in the book.

OUTLINE:

1. Return from Exile (1:1–6:22)

    Cyrus's decree (1:1-11)

    List of returning exiles (2:1-70)

    Restoration of worship restored (3:1-13)

    Opposition to rebuilding the temple (4:1-24)

    Resumption of construction (5:1—6:22)

2. Reform through Ezra (7:1–10:44)

    Ezra's arrival (7:1-10)

    Letter from Artaxerxes (7:11-28)

    List of exiles returning with Ezra (8:1-14)

    Search for Levites (8:15-20)

    Preparations for the return (8:21-30)

    Exiles' arrival in Jerusalem (8:31-36)

    Confession of intermarriage and repentance (9:1—10:44)

KEY VERSE:

"They sang with praise and thanksgiving to the LORD: 'For he is good; his faithful love to Israel endures forever.'" —Ezra 3:11

RESTORATION THEMES

R	Rest and Reflection	*For the next note, see Job 42:6.*
E	Eternal Perspective	*For the next note, see Nehemiah 9:6.*
S	Support	*For the next note, see Job 6:24.*
T	Thanksgiving and Contentment	*Gratitude—Ezra 3:10-11* *Repentance—10:1*
O	Other-centeredness	*For the next note, see Job 29:12-13.*
R	Relationships	*For the next note, see Psalm 19:14.*
E	Exercise of Faith	*For the next note, see Nehemiah 8:10.*

THE DECREE OF CYRUS

1 In the first year of King Cyrus of Persia, in
order to fulfill the word of the LORD spoken through Jeremiah, the LORD roused the
spirit of King Cyrus to issue a proclamation
throughout his entire kingdom and to put it
in writing:
2 This is what King Cyrus of Persia says:
"The LORD, the God of the heavens, has
given me all the kingdoms of the earth
and has appointed me to build him a
house at Jerusalem in Judah. 3 Any of
his people among you, may his God be
with him, and may he go to Jerusalem in
Judah and build the house of the LORD,
the God of Israel, the God who is in
Jerusalem. 4 Let every survivor, wherever he resides, be assisted by the men of
that region with silver, gold, goods, and
livestock, along with a freewill offering
for the house of God in Jerusalem."

The LORD roused the spirit of King Cyrus to issue a proclamation throughout his entire kingdom . . . "The LORD, the God of the heavens, has given me all the kingdoms of the earth and has appointed me to build him a house at Jerusalem in Judah."

—Ezra 1:1-2

RETURN FROM EXILE

5 So the family heads of Judah and Benjamin, along with the priests and Levites
— everyone whose spirit God had roused
— prepared to go up and rebuild the LORD's
house in Jerusalem. 6 All their neighbors
supported them[A] with silver articles, gold,
goods, livestock, and valuables, in addition
to all that was given as a freewill offering.
7 King Cyrus also brought out the articles of
the LORD's house that Nebuchadnezzar had
taken from Jerusalem and had placed in the
house of his gods. 8 King Cyrus of Persia had
them brought out under the supervision of
Mithredath the treasurer, who counted them
out to Sheshbazzar the prince of Judah. 9 This
was the inventory:
30 gold basins, 1,000 silver basins,
29 silver knives, 10 30 gold bowls,
410 various[B] silver bowls,
and 1,000 other articles.
11 The gold and silver articles totaled 5,400.
Sheshbazzar brought all of them when the
exiles went up from Babylon to Jerusalem.

THE EXILES WHO RETURNED

2 These now are the people of the province
who came from those captive exiles King
Nebuchadnezzar of Babylon[C] had deported
to Babylon. They returned to Jerusalem and
Judah, each to his own town. 2 They came
with Zerubbabel, Jeshua, Nehemiah, Seraiah,
Reelaiah, Mordecai, Bilshan, Mispar, Bigvai,
Rehum, and Baanah.
The number of the Israelite men included[D]

3	Parosh's descendants	2,172
4	Shephatiah's descendants	372
5	Arah's descendants	775
6	Pahath-moab's descendants: Jeshua's and Joab's descendants	2,812
7	Elam's descendants	1,254
8	Zattu's descendants	945
9	Zaccai's descendants	760
10	Bani's descendants	642
11	Bebai's descendants	623
12	Azgad's descendants	1,222
13	Adonikam's descendants	666
14	Bigvai's descendants	2,056
15	Adin's descendants	454
16	Ater's descendants: of Hezekiah	98
17	Bezai's descendants	323
18	Jorah's descendants	112
19	Hashum's descendants	223
20	Gibbar's descendants	95
21	Bethlehem's people	123
22	Netophah's men	56
23	Anathoth's men	128
24	Azmaveth's people	42
25	Kiriatharim's, Chephirah's, and Beeroth's people	743
26	Ramah's and Geba's people	621
27	Michmas's men	122
28	Bethel's and Ai's men	223
29	Nebo's people	52
30	Magbish's people	156
31	the other Elam's people	1,254
32	Harim's people	320

[A] **1:6** Lit *strengthened their hands* [B] **1:10** Or *similar* [C] **2:1** Nebuchadnezzar reigned 605–562 BC [D] **2:2** Lit *the men of the people of Israel*

33 Lod's, Hadid's, and Ono's people 725
34 Jericho's people 345
35 Senaah's people 3,630

36 The priests included
Jedaiah's descendants of
the house of Jeshua 973
37 Immer's descendants 1,052
38 Pashhur's descendants 1,247
39 and Harim's descendants 1,017

40 The Levites included
Jeshua's and Kadmiel's
descendants
from Hodaviah's descendants 74

41 The singers included
Asaph's descendants 128

42 The gatekeepers' descendants
included
Shallum's descendants,
Ater's descendants,
Talmon's descendants,
Akkub's descendants,
Hatita's descendants,
Shobai's descendants, in all 139

43 The temple servants included
Ziha's descendants,
Hasupha's descendants,
Tabbaoth's descendants,
44 Keros's descendants,
Siaha's descendants,
Padon's descendants,
45 Lebanah's descendants,
Hagabah's descendants,
Akkub's descendants,
46 Hagab's descendants,
Shalmai's[A] descendants,
Hanan's descendants,
47 Giddel's descendants,
Gahar's descendants,
Reaiah's descendants,
48 Rezin's descendants,
Nekoda's descendants,
Gazzam's descendants,
49 Uzza's descendants,
Paseah's descendants,
Besai's descendants,
50 Asnah's descendants,
Meunim's[B] descendants,
Nephusim's[C] descendants,
51 Bakbuk's descendants,
Hakupha's descendants,
Harhur's descendants,
52 Bazluth's descendants,
Mehida's descendants,
Harsha's descendants,
53 Barkos's descendants,
Sisera's descendants,
Temah's descendants,
54 Neziah's descendants,
and Hatipha's descendants.

55 The descendants of Solomon's
servants included
Sotai's descendants,
Hassophereth's descendants,
Peruda's descendants,
56 Jaalah's descendants,
Darkon's descendants,
Giddel's descendants,
57 Shephatiah's descendants,
Hattil's descendants,
Pochereth-hazzebaim's descendants,
and Ami's descendants.
58 All the temple servants
and the descendants
of Solomon's servants 392.

59 The following are those who came from
Tel-melah, Tel-harsha, Cherub, Addan, and Immer but were unable to prove that their ancestral families[D] and their lineage were Israelite:
60 Delaiah's descendants,
Tobiah's descendants,
Nekoda's descendants 652
61 and from the descendants of the priests: the
descendants of Hobaiah, the descendants of
Hakkoz, the descendants of Barzillai — who
had taken a wife from the daughters of Barzillai the Gileadite and who bore their name.
62 These searched for their entries in the genealogical records, but they could not be found,
so they were disqualified from the priesthood.
63 The governor ordered them not to eat the
most holy things until there was a priest who
could consult the Urim and Thummim.
64 The whole combined assembly
numbered 42,360
65 not including their 7,337 male
and female servants,
and their 200 male and female singers.
66 They had 736 horses, 245 mules,
67 435 camels, and 6,720 donkeys.

[A] **2:46** Alt Hb tradition reads *Shamlai's* [B] **2:50** Alt Hb tradition reads *Meinim's* [C] **2:50** Alt Hb tradition reads *Nephisim's*
[D] **2:59** Lit *that the house of their fathers*

GIFTS FOR THE WORK

68 After they arrived at the LORD's house in Jerusalem, some of the family heads gave freewill offerings for the house of God in order to have it rebuilt on its original site. 69 Based on what they could give, they gave 61,000 gold coins,[A] 6,250 pounds[B] of silver, and 100 priestly garments to the treasury for the project. 70 The priests, Levites, singers, gatekeepers, temple servants, and some of the people settled in their towns, and the rest of Israel settled in their towns.

SACRIFICE RESTORED

3 When the seventh month arrived, and the Israelites were in their towns, the people gathered as one in Jerusalem. 2 Jeshua son of Jozadak and his brothers the priests along with Zerubbabel son of Shealtiel and his brothers began to build the altar of Israel's God in order to offer burnt offerings on it, as it is written in the law of Moses, the man of God. 3 They set up the altar on its foundation and offered burnt offerings for the morning and evening on it to the LORD even though they feared the surrounding peoples. 4 They celebrated the Festival of Shelters as prescribed, and offered burnt offerings each day, based on the number specified by ordinance for each festival day. 5 After that, they offered the regular burnt offering and the offerings for the beginning of each month[C] and for all the LORD's appointed holy occasions, as well as the freewill offerings brought to[D] the LORD.

6 On the first day of the seventh month they began to offer burnt offerings to the LORD, even though the foundation of the LORD's temple had not yet been laid. 7 They gave money to the stonecutters and artisans, and gave food, drink, and oil to the people of Sidon and Tyre, so they would bring cedar wood from Lebanon to Joppa by sea, according to the authorization given them by King Cyrus of Persia.

REBUILDING THE TEMPLE

8 In the second month of the second year after they arrived at God's house in Jerusalem, Zerubbabel son of Shealtiel, Jeshua son of Jozadak, and the rest of their brothers, including the priests, the Levites, and all who

Thanksgiving and Contentment | *Gratitude*

A WAY OF LIFE

"When the builders had laid the foundation of the LORD's temple, the priests. . . . sang with praise and thanksgiving to the LORD: 'For he is good; his faithful love to Israel endures forever.' Then all the people gave a great shout of praise to the LORD because the foundation of the LORD's house had been laid." Ezra 3:10-11

Often gratitude is an afterthought. We give thanks—if we remember to do so at all—long after the fact, maybe when Thanksgiving rolls around.

This wasn't the case when Ezra led the people in rebuilding the temple. The entire project was permeated with praise and shows of appreciation. Priests and singers were constantly on site. So, for example, when the foundation was complete, everyone halted for a brief worship service.

This gives us a good model for living and working in the twenty-first century. Imagine the difference in your heart and mood if during your day you took prayer pauses and praise breaks. Finally got that report done? Why not walk down the hall to the break room, thanking God under your breath? Finished all the dishes and laundry? Lift your eyes to heaven and hum the doxology.

Restored people recognize that God is the power behind every accomplishment—and they pause to thank him.

For the next note on *Thanksgiving and Contentment*, see Ezra 10:1.

[A] **2:69** Or *drachmas*, or *darics* [B] **2:69** Lit *5,000 minas* [C] **3:5** Lit *for the new moons* [D] **3:5** Lit *well as those of everyone making a freewill offering to*

had returned to Jerusalem from the captivity,
began to build. They appointed the Levites who
were twenty years old or more to supervise
the work on the LORD'S house. 9 Jeshua with
his sons and brothers, Kadmiel with his sons,
and the sons of Judah[A] and of Henadad, with
their sons and brothers, the Levites, joined
together to supervise those working on the
house of God.

TEMPLE FOUNDATION COMPLETED

10 When the builders had laid the foundation of
the LORD'S temple, the priests, dressed in their
robes and holding trumpets, and the Levites
descended from Asaph, holding cymbals, took
their positions to praise the LORD, as King David of Israel had instructed. 11 They sang with
praise and thanksgiving to the LORD: "For he
is good; his faithful love to Israel endures forever." Then all the people gave a great shout
of praise to the LORD because the foundation
of the LORD'S house had been laid.
12 But many of the older priests, Levites, and
family heads, who had seen the first temple,
wept loudly when they saw the foundation
of this temple, but many others shouted joyfully. 13 The people could not distinguish the
sound of the joyful shouting from that of the[B]
weeping, because the people were shouting
so loudly. And the sound was heard far away.

OPPOSITION TO REBUILDING THE TEMPLE

4 When the enemies of Judah and Benjamin heard that the returned exiles[C]
were building a temple for the LORD, the
God of Israel, 2 they approached Zerubbabel and the family heads and said to them,
"Let us build with you, for we also worship
your God and have been sacrificing to him[D]
since the time King Esar-haddon of Assyria
brought us here."
3 But Zerubbabel, Jeshua, and the other heads
of Israel's families answered them, "You may
have no part with us in building a house for our
God, since we alone will build it for the LORD,
the God of Israel, as King Cyrus, the king of
Persia has commanded us." 4 Then the people
who were already in the land[E] discouraged[F]
the people of Judah and made them afraid to
build. 5 They also bribed officials to act against
them to frustrate their plans throughout the
reign of King Cyrus of Persia and until the
reign of King Darius of Persia.

OPPOSITION TO REBUILDING THE CITY

6 At the beginning of the reign of Ahasuerus,
the people who were already in the land wrote
an accusation against the residents of Judah
and Jerusalem. 7 During the time of King Artaxerxes of Persia, Bishlam, Mithredath, Tabeel
and the rest of his colleagues wrote to King
Artaxerxes. The letter was written in Aramaic
and translated.[G]
8 Rehum the chief deputy and Shimshai the
scribe wrote a letter to King Artaxerxes concerning Jerusalem as follows:

9 From Rehum[H] the chief deputy, Shimshai the scribe, and the rest of their
colleagues — the judges and magistrates[I]
from Tripolis, Persia, Erech, Babylon,
Susa (that is, the people of Elam),[J] 10 and
the rest of the peoples whom the great
and illustrious Ashurbanipal[K] deported
and settled in the cities of Samaria and
the region west of the Euphrates River.

11 This is the text of the letter they sent to him:

To King Artaxerxes from your servants,
the men from the region west of the
Euphrates River:

12 Let it be known to the king that the
Jews who came from you have returned
to us at Jerusalem. They are rebuilding
that rebellious and evil city, finishing its
walls, and repairing its foundations. 13 Let
it now be known to the king that if that
city is rebuilt and its walls are finished,
they will not pay tribute, duty, or land tax,
and the royal revenue[J] will suffer. 14 Since
we have taken an oath of loyalty to the
king,[L] and it is not right for us to witness
his dishonor, we have sent to inform
the king 15 that a search should be made
in your fathers' record books. In these
record books you will discover and verify
that the city is a rebellious city, harmful
to kings and provinces. There have been
revolts in it since ancient times. That is
why this city was destroyed. 16 We advise
the king that if this city is rebuilt and its
walls are finished, you will not have any
possession west of the Euphrates.

[A] 3:9 Or *Hodaviah*; Neh 7:43; 1 Esdras 5:58 [B] 3:13 Lit *the people* [C] 4:1 Lit *the sons of the exile* [D] 4:2 Alt Hb tradition reads *have not been sacrificing* [E] 4:4 Lit *people of the land*, also in v. 6 [F] 4:4 Lit *weakened the hands of* [G] 4:7 Ezr 4:8–6:18 is written in Aramaic. [H] 4:9 Lit *Then Rehum* [I] 4:9 Or *ambassadors* [J] 4:9,13 Aramaic obscure [K] 4:10 Lit *Osnappar* [L] 4:14 Lit *have eaten the salt of the palace*

ARTAXERXES'S REPLY

17 The king sent a reply to his chief deputy Rehum, Shimshai the scribe, and the rest of their colleagues living in Samaria and elsewhere in the region west of the Euphrates River:

Greetings.

18 The letter you sent us has been
translated and read[A] in my presence.
19 I issued a decree and a search was
conducted. It was discovered that this
city has had uprisings against kings
since ancient times, and there have been
rebellions and revolts in it. 20 Powerful
kings have also ruled over Jerusalem
and exercised authority over the whole
region west of the Euphrates River, and
tribute, duty, and land tax were paid to
them. 21 Therefore, issue an order for
these men to stop, so that this city will
not be rebuilt until a further decree
has been pronounced by me. 22 See that
you not neglect this matter. Otherwise,
the damage will increase and the royal
interests[B] will suffer.

23 As soon as the text of King Artaxerxes's letter was read to Rehum, Shimshai the scribe, and their colleagues, they immediately went to the Jews in Jerusalem and forcibly stopped them.

REBUILDING OF THE TEMPLE RESUMED

24 Now the construction of God's house in Jerusalem had stopped and remained at a standstill until the second year of the reign of King
5 Darius of Persia. 1 But when the prophets
Haggai and Zechariah son of Iddo prophesied to the Jews who were in Judah and Jerusalem, in the name of the God of Israel who
was over them, 2 Zerubbabel son of Shealtiel
and Jeshua son of Jozadak began to rebuild God's house in Jerusalem. The prophets of God were with them, helping them.
3 At that time Tattenai the governor of the region west of the Euphrates River, Shethar-bozenai, and their colleagues came to the Jews and asked, "Who gave you the order to rebuild this temple and finish this structure?"[C] 4 They also asked them, "What are the
names of the workers[D] who are constructing
this building?" 5 But God was watching[E] over
the Jewish elders. These men wouldn't stop them until a report was sent to Darius, so that they could receive written instructions about this matter.

THE LETTER TO DARIUS

6 This is the text of the letter that Tattenai the governor of the region west of the Euphrates River, Shethar-bozenai, and their colleagues, the officials in the region, sent to King Darius.
7 They sent him a report, written as follows:

To King Darius:

All greetings.

8 Let it be known to the king that we went
to the house of the great God in the province of Judah. It is being built with cut[F]
stones, and its beams are being set in the
walls. This work is being done diligently
and succeeding through the people's
efforts. 9 So we questioned the elders and
asked, "Who gave you the order to rebuild
this temple and finish this structure?"
10 We also asked them for their names, so
that we could write down the names of
their leaders for your information.

11 This is the reply they gave us:

We are the servants of the God of the
heavens and earth, and we are rebuilding
the temple that was built many years
ago, which a great king of Israel built and
finished. 12 But since our fathers angered
the God of the heavens, he handed them
over to King Nebuchadnezzar of Babylon,
the Chaldean, who destroyed this temple
and deported the people to Babylon.
13 However, in the first year of King Cyrus
of Babylon, he issued a decree to rebuild
the house of God. 14 He also took from the
temple in Babylon the gold and silver articles of God's house that Nebuchadnezzar
had taken from the temple in Jerusalem
and carried them to the temple in Babylon. He released them from the temple
in Babylon to a man named Sheshbazzar,
the governor by the appointment of King
Cyrus. 15 Cyrus told him, "Take these articles, put them in the temple in Jerusalem,
and let the house of God be rebuilt on its
original site." 16 Then this same Sheshbazzar came and laid the foundation of

---

[A] 4:18 Or *been read clearly* [B] 4:22 Lit *the kings* [C] 5:3 Or *finish its furnishings*, also in v. 9 [D] 5:4 One Aramaic ms, LXX, Syr; MT reads *Then we told them exactly what the names of the men were* [E] 5:5 Lit *But the eye of their God was* [F] 5:8 Or *huge*

God's house in Jerusalem. It has been under construction from that time until now, but it has not been completed.
17 So if it pleases the king, let a search of the royal archives[A] in Babylon be conducted to see if it is true that a decree was issued by King Cyrus to rebuild the house of God in Jerusalem. Let the king's decision regarding this matter be sent to us.

DARIUS'S SEARCH

6 King Darius gave the order, and they searched in the library of Babylon in the
archives.[B] 2 But it was in the fortress of Ecbat-
ana in the province of Media that a scroll was
found with this record written on it:
3 In the first year of King Cyrus, he issued a decree concerning the house of God in Jerusalem:

Let the house be rebuilt as a place for offering sacrifices, and let its original foundations be retained.[C] Its height is to be ninety feet[D] and its width ninety feet,
4 with three layers of cut[E] stones and one of timber. The cost is to be paid from the
royal treasury.[F] 5 The gold and silver articles of God's house that Nebuchadnezzar took from the temple in Jerusalem and carried to Babylon must also be returned. They are to be brought to the temple in Jerusalem where they belong[G] and put into the house of God.

DARIUS'S DECREE

6 Therefore, you must stay away from that place, Tattenai governor of the region west of the Euphrates River, Shethar-bozenai, and your[H] colleagues, the officials in the region. 7 Leave the construction of the house of God alone. Let the governor and elders of the Jews rebuild this house of God on its original site.

8 I hereby issue a decree concerning what you are to do, so that the elders of the Jews can rebuild the house of God:

The cost is to be paid in full to these men out of the royal revenues from the taxes of the region west of the Euphrates River,
so that the work will not stop. 9 Whatever
is needed — young bulls, rams, and lambs for burnt offerings to the God of the heavens, or wheat, salt, wine, and oil, as requested by the priests in Jerusalem — let it be given to them every day without
fail, 10 so that they can offer sacrifices of pleasing aroma to the God of the heavens and pray for the life of the king and his sons.

11 I also issue a decree concerning any man who interferes with this directive:

Let a beam be torn from his house and raised up; he will be impaled on it, and his house will be made into a garbage
dump because of this offense. 12 May the
God who caused his name to dwell there overthrow any king or people who dares[I] to harm or interfere with this house of God in Jerusalem. I, Darius, have issued the decree. Let it be carried out diligently.

13 Then Tattenai governor of the region west of the Euphrates River, Shethar-bozenai, and their colleagues diligently carried out what
King Darius had decreed. 14 So the Jewish el-
ders continued successfully with the building under the prophesying of Haggai the prophet and Zechariah son of Iddo. They finished the building according to the command of the God of Israel and the decrees of Cyrus,
Darius, and King Artaxerxes of Persia. 15 This
house was completed on the third day of the month of Adar in the sixth year of the reign of King Darius.

TEMPLE DEDICATION AND THE PASSOVER

16 Then the Israelites, including the priests, the Levites, and the rest of the exiles, celebrated the dedication of the house of God with joy.
17 For the dedication of God's house they offered one hundred bulls, two hundred rams, and four hundred lambs, as well as twelve male goats as a sin offering for all Israel — one
for each Israelite tribe. 18 They also appointed
the priests by their divisions and the Levites by their groups to the service of God in Jerusalem, according to what is written in the book of Moses.
19 The exiles observed the Passover on the
fourteenth day of the first month. 20 All of

[A] **5:17** Lit *treasure house* [B] **6:1** Lit *Babylon where the treasures were stored* [C] **6:3** Lit *be brought forth* [D] **6:3** Lit *60 cubits* [E] **6:4** Or *huge* [F] **6:4** Lit *the king's house* [G] **6:5** Lit *Jerusalem, to its place,* [H] **6:6** Lit *their* [I] **6:12** Lit *who stretches out its hand*

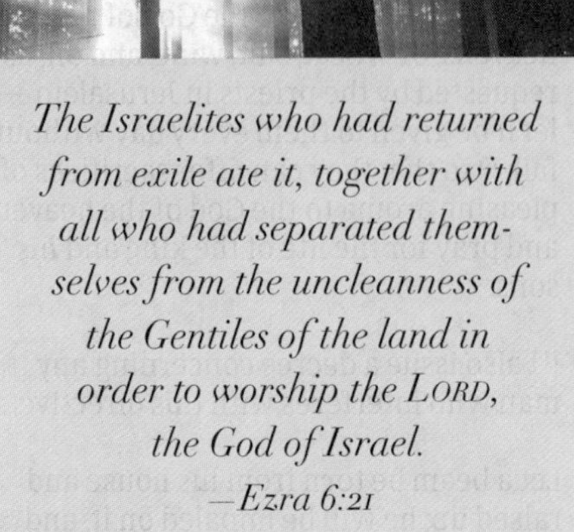
The Israelites who had returned from exile ate it, together with all who had separated themselves from the uncleanness of the Gentiles of the land in order to worship the LORD, the God of Israel.
—Ezra 6:21

the priests and Levites were ceremonially
clean, because they had purified themselves.
They killed the Passover lamb for themselves,
their priestly brothers, and all the exiles.
21 The Israelites who had returned from exile
ate it, together with all who had separated themselves from the uncleanness of the
Gentiles of the land[A] in order to worship
the LORD, the God of Israel. 22 They observed
the Festival of Unleavened Bread for seven
days with joy, because the LORD had made
them joyful, having changed the Assyrian
king's attitude toward them, so that he supported them[B] in the work on the house of
the God of Israel.

EZRA'S ARRIVAL

7 After these events, during the reign of King
Artaxerxes of Persia, Ezra—
Seraiah's son, Azariah's son,
Hilkiah's son, 2 Shallum's son,
Zadok's son, Ahitub's son,
3 Amariah's son, Azariah's son,
Meraioth's son, 4 Zerahiah's son,
Uzzi's son, Bukki's son,
5 Abishua's son, Phinehas's son,
Eleazar's son, the chief priest Aaron's
son
6 — came up from Babylon. He was a scribe
skilled in the law of Moses, which the LORD, the
God of Israel, had given. The king had granted
him everything he requested because the hand
of the LORD his God was on him. 7 Some of the
Israelites, priests, Levites, singers, gatekeepers,
and temple servants accompanied him to Jerusalem in the seventh year of King Artaxerxes.
8 Ezra[C] came to Jerusalem in the fifth month,
during the seventh year of the king. 9 He began the journey from Babylon on the first day
of the first month and arrived in Jerusalem
on the first day of the fifth month since the
gracious hand of his God was on him. 10 Now
Ezra had determined in his heart to study the
law of the LORD, obey it, and teach its statutes
and ordinances in Israel.

LETTER FROM ARTAXERXES

11 This is the text of the letter King Artaxerxes
gave to Ezra the priest and scribe, an expert
in matters of the LORD's commands and statutes for Israel:[D]

12 Artaxerxes, king of kings, to Ezra the
priest, an expert in the law of the God of
the heavens:

Greetings.

13 I issue a decree that any of the Israelites in my kingdom, including their
priests and Levites, who want to go to Jerusalem, may go with you. 14 You are sent
by the king and his seven counselors to
evaluate Judah and Jerusalem according
to the law of your God, which is in your
possession. 15 You are also to bring the
silver and gold the king and his counselors have willingly given to the God of
Israel, whose dwelling is in Jerusalem,
16 and all the silver and gold you receive
throughout the province of Babylon,
together with the freewill offerings
given by the people and the priests to
the house of their God in Jerusalem.
17 Then you are to be diligent to buy with
this money bulls, rams, and lambs, along
with their grain and drink offerings,
and offer them on the altar at the house
of your God in Jerusalem. 18 You may do
whatever seems best to you and your
brothers with the rest of the silver and
gold, according to the will of your God.
19 Deliver to the God of Jerusalem all the
articles given to you for the service of
the house of your God. 20 You may use
the royal treasury[E] to pay for anything
else needed for the house of your God.

21 I, King Artaxerxes, issue a decree to all
the treasurers in the region west of the
Euphrates River:

[A] **6:21** Lit *land to them* [B] **6:22** Lit *strengthened their hands* [C] **7:8** LXX, Syr, Vg read *They* [D] **7:11** Ezr 7:12-26 is written in Aramaic. [E] **7:20** Lit *the king's house*

Whatever Ezra the priest, an expert in the law of the God of the heavens, asks of you must be provided in full, 22 up to 7,500 pounds[A] of silver, 500 bushels[B] of wheat, 550 gallons[C] of wine, 550 gallons of oil, and salt without limit.[D] 23 Whatever is commanded by the God of heaven must be done diligently for the house of the God of the heavens, so that wrath will not fall on the realm of the king and his sons. 24 Be advised that you do not have authority to impose tribute, duty, and land tax on any priests, Levites, singers, doorkeepers, temple servants, or other servants of this house of God.

25 And you, Ezra, according to[E] God's wisdom that you possess, appoint magistrates and judges to judge all the people in the region west of the Euphrates who know the laws of your God and to teach anyone who does not know them. 26 Anyone who does not keep the law of your God and the law of the king, let the appropriate judgment be executed against him, whether death, banishment, confiscation of property, or imprisonment.

27 Blessed be the LORD, the God of our fathers, who has put it into the king's mind to glorify the house of the LORD in Jerusalem, 28 and who has shown favor to me before the king, his counselors, and all his powerful officers. So I took courage because I was strengthened by the hand of the LORD my God,[F] and I gathered Israelite leaders to return with me.

THOSE RETURNING WITH EZRA

8 These are the family heads and the genealogical records of those who returned with me from Babylon during the reign of King Artaxerxes:

2 Gershom,
from Phinehas's descendants;
Daniel, from Ithamar's descendants;
Hattush, from David's descendants,
3 who was of Shecaniah's descendants;
Zechariah, from Parosh's descendants,
and 150 men[G] with him
who were registered by genealogy;
4 Eliehoenai son of Zerahiah
from Pahath-moab's descendants,
and 200 men with him;
5 Shecaniah[H] son of Jahaziel
from Zattu's descendants,
and 300 men with him;
6 Ebed son of Jonathan
from Adin's descendants,
and 50 men with him;
7 Jeshaiah son of Athaliah
from Elam's descendants,
and 70 men with him;
8 Zebadiah son of Michael
from Shephatiah's descendants,
and 80 men with him;
9 Obadiah son of Jehiel
from Joab's descendants,
and 218 men with him;
10 Shelomith[I] son of Josiphiah
from Bani's descendants,
and 160 men with him;
11 Zechariah son of Bebai
from Bebai's descendants,
and 28 men with him;
12 Johanan son of Hakkatan
from Azgad's descendants,
and 110 men with him;
13 these are the last ones,
from Adonikam's descendants,
and their names are
Eliphelet, Jeuel, and Shemaiah,
and 60 men with them;
14 Uthai and Zaccur[J]
from Bigvai's descendants,
and 70 men with them.

15 I gathered them at the river[K] that flows to Ahava, and we camped there for three days. I searched among the people and priests, but found no Levites there. 16 Then I summoned the leaders: Eliezer, Ariel, Shemaiah, Elnathan, Jarib, Elnathan, Nathan, Zechariah, and Meshullam, as well as the teachers Joiarib and Elnathan. 17 I sent them to Iddo, the leader at Casiphia, with a message for[L] him and his brothers, the temple servants at Casiphia, that they should bring us ministers for the house of our God. 18 Since the gracious hand of our God was on us, they brought us Sherebiah—a man of insight from the descendants of Mahli, a descendant of Levi son of Israel

[A] 7:22 Lit *100 talents* [B] 7:22 Lit *100 cors* [C] 7:22 Lit *100 baths* [D] 7:22 Lit *without instruction* [E] 7:25 Lit *to your* [F] 7:28 Lit *because the hand of the LORD my God was on me* [G] 8:3 Or *males*; also in vv. 4-14 [H] 8:5 LXX, 1 Esdras 8:32; MT reads *the descendants of Shecaniah* [I] 8:10 Some LXX mss, 1 Esdras 8:36; MT reads *the descendants of Shelomith* [J] 8:14 Alt Hb tradition, some LXX mss read *Zabud* [K] 8:15 Or *canal* [L] 8:17 Lit *Casiphia, and I put in their mouth the words to speak to*

— along with his sons and brothers, 18 men,
19 plus Hashabiah, along with Jeshaiah, from
the descendants of Merari, and his brothers
and their sons, 20 men. 20 There were also 220 of
the temple servants, who had been appointed
by David and the leaders for the work of the
Levites. All were identified by name.

PREPARING TO RETURN

21 I proclaimed a fast by the Ahava River,[A] so
that we might humble ourselves before our
God and ask him for a safe journey for us, our
dependents, and all our possessions. 22 I did
this because I was ashamed to ask the king
for infantry and cavalry to protect us from
enemies during the journey, since we had told
him, "The hand of our God is gracious to all
who seek him, but his fierce anger is against
all who abandon him." 23 So we fasted and
pleaded with our God about this, and he was
receptive to our prayer.
24 I selected twelve of the leading priests,
along with Sherebiah, Hashabiah, and ten of
their brothers. 25 I weighed out to them the
silver, the gold, and the articles — the contribution for the house of our God that the
king, his counselors, his leaders, and all the
Israelites who were present had offered. 26 I
weighed out to them 24 tons[B] of silver, silver articles weighing 7,500 pounds,[C] 7,500
pounds of gold, 27 twenty gold bowls worth a
thousand gold coins,[D] and two articles of fine
gleaming bronze, as valuable as gold. 28 Then
I said to them, "You are holy to the LORD, and
the articles are holy. The silver and gold are a
freewill offering to the LORD God of your fathers. 29 Guard them carefully until you weigh
them out in the chambers of the LORD's house
before the leading priests, Levites, and heads
of the Israelite families in Jerusalem." 30 So
the priests and Levites took charge of the silver, the gold, and the articles that had been
weighed out, to bring them to the house of
our God in Jerusalem.

ARRIVAL IN JERUSALEM

31 We set out from the Ahava River on the
twelfth day of the first month to go to Jerusalem. We were strengthened by our God,[E] and
he kept us from the grasp of the enemy and
from ambush along the way. 32 So we arrived
at Jerusalem and rested there for three days.
33 On the fourth day the silver, the gold, and
the articles were weighed out in the house of
our God into the care of the priest Meremoth
son of Uriah. Eleazar son of Phinehas was with
him. The Levites Jozabad son of Jeshua and
Noadiah son of Binnui were also with them.
34 Everything was verified by number and
weight, and the total weight was recorded
at that time.
35 The exiles who had returned from the
captivity offered burnt offerings to the God
of Israel: twelve bulls for all Israel, ninety-six
rams, and seventy-seven lambs, along with
twelve male goats as a sin offering. All this
was a burnt offering for the LORD. 36 They
also delivered the king's edicts to the royal
satraps and governors of the region west of
the Euphrates, so that they would support the
people and the house of God.

ISRAEL'S INTERMARRIAGE

9 After these things had been done, the leaders approached me and said: "The people
of Israel, the priests, and the Levites have not
separated themselves from the surrounding
peoples whose detestable practices are like
those of the Canaanites, Hethites, Perizzites,
Jebusites, Ammonites, Moabites, Egyptians,
and Amorites. 2 Indeed, the Israelite men[F] have
taken some of their daughters as wives for
themselves and their sons, so that the holy
seed has become mixed with the surrounding peoples. The leaders[G] and officials have
taken the lead in this unfaithfulness!" 3 When
I heard this report, I tore my tunic and robe,
pulled out some of the hair from my head and
beard, and sat down devastated.

EZRA'S CONFESSION

4 Everyone who trembled at the words of the
God of Israel gathered around me, because
of the unfaithfulness of the exiles, while I sat
devastated until the evening offering. 5 At the
evening offering, I got up from my time of humiliation, with my tunic and robe torn. Then
I fell on my knees and spread out my hands
to the LORD my God. 6 And I said:

My God, I am ashamed and embarrassed
to lift my face toward you, my God,
because our iniquities are higher than
our heads and our guilt is as high as the
heavens. 7 Our guilt has been terrible
from the days of our fathers until the
present. Because of our iniquities we

[A] **8:21** Or *Canal*, also in v. 31 [B] **8:26** Lit *650 talents* [C] **8:26** Lit *100 talents* [D] **8:27** Or *1,000 drachmas*, or *1,000 darics*
[E] **8:31** Lit *The hand of our God was on us* [F] **9:2** Lit *they* [G] **9:2** Lit *hand of the leaders*

have been handed over, along with our
kings and priests, to the surrounding
kings, and to the sword, captivity, plundering, and open shame, as it is today.
8 But now, for a brief moment, grace has
come from the LORD our God to preserve
a remnant for us and give us a stake in
his holy place. Even in our slavery, God
has given us a little relief and light to our
eyes. 9 Though we are slaves, our God has
not abandoned us in our slavery. He has
extended grace to us in the presence of
the Persian kings, giving us relief, so that
we can rebuild the house of our God and
repair its ruins, to give us a wall in Judah
and Jerusalem.

10 Now, our God, what can we say in
light of[A] this? For we have abandoned
the commands 11 you gave through your
servants the prophets, saying: "The land
you are entering to possess is an impure
land. The surrounding peoples have filled
it from end to end with their uncleanness
by their impurity and detestable practices. 12 So do not give your daughters
to their sons in marriage or take their
daughters for your sons. Never pursue
their welfare or prosperity, so that you
will be strong, eat the good things of
the land, and leave it as an inheritance
to your sons forever." 13 After all that
has happened to us because of our evil
deeds and terrible guilt — though you,
our God, have punished us less than our
iniquities deserve and have allowed us
to survive[B] — 14 should we break your
commands again and intermarry with
the peoples who commit these detestable practices? Wouldn't you become so
angry with us that you would destroy us,
leaving neither remnant nor survivor?
15 LORD God of Israel, you are righteous,
for we survive as a remnant today. Here
we are before you with our guilt, though
no one can stand in your presence because of this.

SENDING AWAY FOREIGN WIVES

10 While Ezra prayed and confessed,
weeping and falling facedown before
the house of God, an extremely large assembly of Israelite men, women, and children
gathered around him. The people also wept
bitterly. 2 Then Shecaniah son of Jehiel, an
Elamite, responded to Ezra: "We have been

Thanksgiving and Contentment | *Repentance*

WEEPING

"While Ezra prayed and confessed, weeping and falling facedown before the house of God, an extremely large assembly of Israelite men, women, and children gathered around him. The people also wept bitterly." Ezra 10:1

Watching the bride come down the aisle. Hearing the doctor say, "I'm afraid the news is not good." Being told the relationship is over. Everyone, even the most stoic, has been blindsided by strong emotion.

Ezra and the people of Israel, however, weren't just trying to blink back tears. Facedown, on the floor weeping, they were overcome by a holy sorrow, the bitter sadness of realizing they had rebelled brazenly against a good and holy God who had blessed them abundantly and continually.

God doesn't mandate that we weep when we face up to our sin. And crying doesn't necessarily signify true repentance. But when the gravity of what we've done pulls tears from our eyes and drops us to the ground, that's a pretty good sign we're genuinely humbled. And humility opens the floodgates of grace.

When's the last time you were moved to tears because of your sin?

For the next note on *Thanksgiving and Contentment*, see Nehemiah 9:5.

[A] **9:10** Lit *say after* [B] **9:13** Lit *and gave us a remnant like this*

unfaithful to our God by marrying foreign
women from the surrounding peoples, but
there is still hope for Israel in spite of this.
3 Let us therefore make a covenant before
our God to send away all the foreign wives
and their children, according to the counsel
of my lord and of those who tremble at the
command of our God. Let it be done according to the law. 4 Get up, for this matter is your
responsibility, and we support you. Be strong
and take action!"

5 Then Ezra got up and made the leading
priests, Levites, and all Israel take an oath to
do what had been said; so they took the oath.
6 Ezra then went from the house of God and
walked to the chamber of Jehohanan son of
Eliashib, where he spent the night.[A] He did
not eat food or drink water, because he was
mourning over the unfaithfulness of the exiles.

7 They circulated a proclamation throughout Judah and Jerusalem that all the exiles
should gather at Jerusalem. 8 Whoever did
not come within three days would forfeit all
his possessions,[B] according to the decision of
the leaders and elders, and would be excluded
from the assembly of the exiles.

9 So all the men of Judah and Benjamin gathered in Jerusalem within the three days. On
the twentieth day of the ninth month, all the
people sat in the square at the house of God,
trembling because of this matter and because
of the heavy rain. 10 Then the priest Ezra stood
up and said to them, "You have been unfaithful
by marrying foreign women, adding to Israel's
guilt. 11 Therefore, make a confession to the
LORD, the God of your fathers, and do his will.
Separate yourselves from the surrounding
peoples and your foreign wives."

12 Then all the assembly responded loudly:
"Yes, we will do as you say! 13 But there are
many people, and it is the rainy season. We
don't have the stamina to stay out in the open.
This isn't something that can be done in a day
or two, for we have rebelled terribly in this
matter. 14 Let our leaders represent the entire assembly. Then let all those in our towns
who have married foreign women come at
appointed times, together with the elders
and judges of each town, in order to avert
the fierce anger of our God concerning[C] this
matter." 15 Only Jonathan son of Asahel and
Jahzeiah son of Tikvah opposed this, with
Meshullam and Shabbethai the Levite supporting them.

16 The exiles did what had been proposed.
The priest Ezra selected men[D] who were family heads, all identified by name, to represent[E]
their ancestral families.[F] They convened on
the first day of the tenth month to investigate
the matter, 17 and by the first day of the first
month they had dealt with all the men who
had married foreign women.

THOSE MARRIED TO FOREIGN WIVES

18 The following were found to have married
foreign women from the descendants of the
priests:

from the descendants of Jeshua son of
Jozadak and his brothers: Maaseiah,
Eliezer, Jarib, and Gedaliah. 19 They
pledged[G] to send their wives away, and
being guilty, they offered a ram from the
flock for their guilt;

20 Hanani and Zebadiah from Immer's
descendants;
21 Maaseiah, Elijah, Shemaiah,
Jehiel, and Uzziah
from Harim's descendants;
22 Elioenai, Maaseiah, Ishmael,
Nethanel, Jozabad, and Elasah
from Pashhur's descendants.

23 The Levites:
Jozabad, Shimei, Kelaiah (that is Kelita),
Pethahiah, Judah, and Eliezer.
24 The singers:
Eliashib.
The gatekeepers:
Shallum, Telem, and Uri.
25 The Israelites:
Parosh's descendants: Ramiah,
Izziah, Malchijah, Mijamin, Eleazar,
Malchijah,[H] and Benaiah;
26 Elam's descendants: Mattaniah,
Zechariah, Jehiel, Abdi, Jeremoth,
and Elijah;
27 Zattu's descendants: Elioenai, Eliashib,
Mattaniah, Jeremoth, Zabad,
and Aziza;
28 Bebai's descendants: Jehohanan,
Hananiah, Zabbai, and Athlai;
29 Bani's descendants: Meshullam,
Malluch, Adaiah, Jashub, Sheal,
and Jeremoth;

[A] **10:6** 1 Esdras 9:2, Syr; MT, Vg read *he went* [B] **10:8** Lit *would set apart all his possessions for destruction* [C] **10:14** Some Hb mss, LXX, Vg; other Hb mss read *until* [D] **10:16** 1 Esdras 9:16, Syr; MT, Vg read *priest and men were selected* [E] **10:16** Lit *name, for* [F] **10:16** Lit *the house of their fathers* [G] **10:19** Lit *gave their hand* [H] **10:25** Some LXX mss, 1 Esdras 9:26 read *Hashabiah*

30 Pahath-moab's descendants: Adna,
Chelal, Benaiah, Maaseiah,
Mattaniah, Bezalel, Binnui,
and Manasseh;
31 Harim's descendants: Eliezer,
Isshijah, Malchijah, Shemaiah,
Shimeon, 32 Benjamin, Malluch, and
Shemariah;
33 Hashum's descendants: Mattenai,
Mattattah, Zabad, Eliphelet, Jeremai,
Manasseh, and Shimei;

34 Bani's descendants: Maadai, Amram,
Uel, 35 Benaiah, Bedeiah, Cheluhi,
36 Vaniah, Meremoth, Eliashib,
37 Mattaniah, Mattenai, Jaasu, 38 Bani,
Binnui, Shimei, 39 Shelemiah, Nathan,
Adaiah, 40 Machnadebai, Shashai,
Sharai, 41 Azarel, Shelemiah, Shemariah,
42 Shallum, Amariah, and Joseph;
43 Nebo's descendants: Jeiel, Mattithiah,
Zabad, Zebina, Jaddai, Joel,
and Benaiah.

44 All of these had married foreign women, and
some of the wives had given birth to children.

Nehemiah was a strong and godly leader who became a trusted advisor to the king while maintaining his single-minded devotion to God. He was dedicated to God's Word and courageous in the face of opposition. But his successful leadership was not based on his abilities or ambition. Everything he did began and ended with prayer.

He prayed for God to rescue his people (1:1–2:8). He prayed for God to judge those who were opposing the Israelites from completing the task God had given them (4:4-5; 6:14). And he continually asked God to remember his people (5:19; 6:14; 13:14,22,29,31).

We also should pray in times of struggle. Asking God to remember us expresses our dependence on him, humbly seeking his grace, knowing we don't deserve it. That is where God wants us—in a state of humble dependence, trusting him for everything because we know we are nothing apart from him.

The first step in restoring a relationship with God is to submit to him, asking for his help in every situation because we know he cares for us. And then, gratefully receiving our good Father's unconditional love.

NEHEMIAH

AUTHOR: The book of Nehemiah, named after its principle character, is technically anonymous. However, ancient Jewish sources usually credit both Ezra and Nehemiah, which were originally a single book, to the scribe Ezra.

DATE WRITTEN: The book of Nehemiah picks up where Ezra left off and was likely written at the same time as 1 Chronicles, 2 Chronicles, and Ezra, shortly after the completion of Nehemiah's ministry, around 400 BC. Ezra came to Jerusalem around 458 BC, and Nehemiah followed him approximately thirteen years later, in 445 BC.

ORIGINAL AUDIENCE: The Israelites

SETTING: Jerusalem, where a remnant of Israelites has returned to rebuild the wall of Jerusalem.

PURPOSE FOR WRITING: Like the book of Ezra, Nehemiah serves to connect the returning exiles with the preexilic community of Israel. These people were part of God's redemptive plan, though they had been separated for a time from the land of promise. Themes of godly leadership, obedience in the face of opposition, the centrality of the law to daily life, and a life of prayer and worship are prevalent in the book.

OUTLINE:

1. Rebuilding the Walls (1:1–6:19)

   Nehemiah prays (1:1-11)

   Nehemiah surveys the damage (2:1-20)

   Rebuilding begins (3:1-32)

   Opposition and oppression come (4:1–6:19)

2. Restoring the Community (7:1–13:31)

   Exiles return (7:1-73)

   Covenant is renewed (8:1–10:39)

   Exiles resettle Jerusalem (11:1-21)

   Levites and priests are named (11:22–12:26)

   Wall is dedicated (12:27-47)

   Nehemiah's reforms are instituted (13:1-31)

KEY VERSE:

"The joy of the LORD is your strength."
—Nehemiah 8:10

RESTORATION THEMES

R	Rest and Reflection	*For the next note, see Job 42:6.*
E	Eternal Perspective	*God the Creator—Nehemiah 9:6*
S	Support	*For the next note, see Job 6:24.*
T	Thanksgiving and Contentment	*Praise—Nehemiah 9:5*
O	Other-centeredness	*For the next note, see Job 29:12-13.*
R	Relationships	*For the next note, see Psalm 19:14.*
E	Exercise of Faith	*Trusting God—Nehemiah 8:10*

1 The words of Nehemiah son of Hacaliah:

NEWS FROM JERUSALEM

During the month of Chislev in the twentieth year, when I was in the fortress city of
Susa, 2 Hanani, one of my brothers, arrived
with men from Judah, and I questioned them
about Jerusalem and the Jewish remnant that
had survived the exile. 3 They said to me, "The
remnant in the province, who survived the
exile, are in great trouble and disgrace. Jerusalem's wall has been broken down, and its
gates have been burned."

NEHEMIAH'S PRAYER

4 When I heard these words, I sat down and
wept. I mourned for a number of days, fasting
and praying before the God of the heavens.
5 I said,

LORD, the God of the heavens, the great
and awe-inspiring God who keeps his
gracious covenant with those who love
him and keep his commands, 6 let your
eyes be open and your ears be attentive to hear your servant's prayer that I
now pray to you day and night for your
servants, the Israelites. I confess the sins[A]
we have committed against you. Both I
and my father's family have sinned. 7 We
have acted corruptly toward you and
have not kept the commands, statutes,
and ordinances you gave your servant
Moses. 8 Please remember what you
commanded your servant Moses: "If you
are unfaithful, I will scatter you among
the peoples. 9 But if you return to me and
carefully observe my commands, even
though your exiles were banished to the
farthest horizon,[B] I will gather them from
there and bring them to the place where
I chose to have my name dwell." 10 They
are your servants and your people. You
redeemed them by your great power and
strong hand. 11 Please, Lord, let your ear
be attentive to the prayer of your servant
and to that of your servants who delight
to revere your name. Give your servant
success today, and grant him compassion
in the presence of this man.[C]

At the time, I was the king's cupbearer.

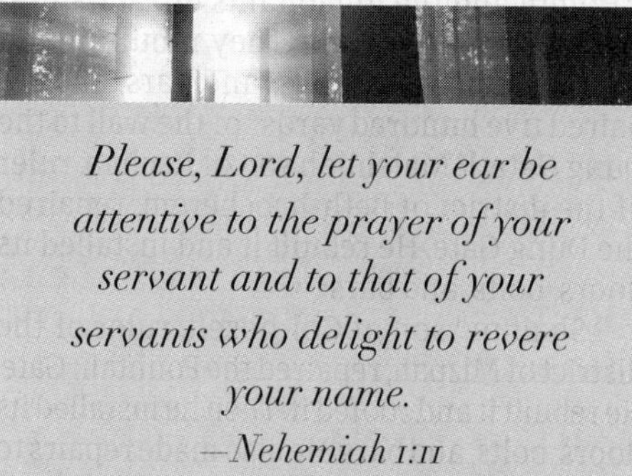
Please, Lord, let your ear be
attentive to the prayer of your
servant and to that of your
servants who delight to revere
your name.
—Nehemiah 1:11

NEHEMIAH SENT TO JERUSALEM

2 During the month of Nisan in the twentieth year of King Artaxerxes, when wine
was set before him, I took the wine and gave
it to the king. I had never been sad in his presence, 2 so the king said to me, "Why are you[D]
sad, when you aren't sick? This is nothing but
sadness of heart."

I was overwhelmed with fear 3 and replied
to the king, "May the king live forever! Why
should I[E] not be sad when the city where my
ancestors are buried lies in ruins and its gates
have been destroyed by fire?"

4 Then the king asked me, "What is your request?"

So I prayed to the God of the heavens 5 and
answered the king, "If it pleases the king, and
if your servant has found favor with you, send
me to Judah and to the city where my ancestors
are buried,[F] so that I may rebuild it."

6 The king, with the queen seated beside
him, asked me, "How long will your journey
take, and when will you return?" So I gave
him a definite time, and it pleased the king
to send me.

7 I also said to the king: "If it pleases the king,
let me have letters written to the governors
of the region west of the Euphrates River, so
that they will grant me safe passage until I
reach Judah. 8 And let me have a letter written
to Asaph, keeper of the king's forest, so that
he will give me timber to rebuild the gates of
the temple's fortress, the city wall, and the
home where I will live."[G] The king granted
my requests, for the gracious hand of my God
was on me.

9 I went to the governors of the region west
of the Euphrates and gave them the king's
letters. The king had also sent officers of the
infantry and cavalry with me. 10 When Sanballat the Horonite and Tobiah the Ammonite official heard that someone had come to

[A] **1:6** Lit *sins of the Israelites* [B] **1:9** Lit *skies* [C] **1:11** = the king [D] **2:2** Lit *"Why is your face* [E] **2:3** Lit *my face* [F] **2:5** Lit *city, the house of the graves of my fathers,* [G] **2:8** Lit *enter*

pursue the prosperity of the Israelites, they were greatly displeased.

PREPARING TO REBUILD THE WALLS

11 After I arrived in Jerusalem and had been there three days, 12 I got up at night and took a few men with me. I didn't tell anyone what my God had laid on my heart to do for Jerusalem. The only animal I took[A] was the one I was riding. 13 I went out at night through the Valley Gate toward the Serpent's[B] Well and the Dung Gate, and I inspected the walls of Jerusalem that had been broken down and its gates that had been destroyed by fire. 14 I went on to the Fountain Gate and the King's Pool, but farther down it became too narrow for my animal to go through. 15 So I went up at night by way of the valley and inspected the wall. Then heading back, I entered through the Valley Gate and returned. 16 The officials did not know where I had gone or what I was doing, for I had not yet told the Jews, priests, nobles, officials, or the rest of those who would be doing the work. 17 So I said to them, "You see the trouble we are in. Jerusalem lies in ruins and its gates have been burned. Come, let's rebuild Jerusalem's wall, so that we will no longer be a disgrace." 18 I told them how the gracious hand of my God had been on me, and what the king had said to me.

They said, "Let's start rebuilding," and their hands were strengthened[C] to do this good work.

19 When Sanballat the Horonite, Tobiah the Ammonite official, and Geshem the Arab heard about this, they mocked and despised us, and said, "What is this you're doing? Are you rebelling against the king?"

20 I gave them this reply, "The God of the heavens is the one who will grant us success. We, his servants, will start building, but you have no share, right, or historic claim in Jerusalem."

REBUILDING THE WALLS

3 The high priest Eliashib and his fellow priests began rebuilding the Sheep Gate. They dedicated it and installed its doors. After building the wall to the Tower of the Hundred and the Tower of Hananel, they dedicated it. 2 The men of Jericho built next to Eliashib, and next to them Zaccur son of Imri built.

FISH GATE

3 The sons of Hassenaah built the Fish Gate. They built it with beams and installed its doors, bolts, and bars. 4 Next to them Meremoth son of Uriah, son of Hakkoz, made repairs. Beside them Meshullam son of Berechiah, son of Meshezabel, made repairs. Next to them Zadok son of Baana made repairs. 5 Beside them the Tekoites made repairs, but their nobles did not lift a finger to help[D] their supervisors.

OLD GATE, BROAD WALL, AND TOWER OF THE OVENS

6 Joiada son of Paseah and Meshullam son of Besodeiah repaired the Old[E] Gate. They built it with beams and installed its doors, bolts, and bars. 7 Next to them the repairs were done by Melatiah the Gibeonite, Jadon the Meronothite, and the men of Gibeon and Mizpah, who were under the authority[F] of the governor of the region west of the Euphrates River. 8 After him Uzziel son of Harhaiah, the goldsmith, made repairs, and next to him Hananiah son of the perfumer made repairs. They restored Jerusalem as far as the Broad Wall.

9 Next to them Rephaiah son of Hur, ruler of half the district of Jerusalem, made repairs. 10 After them Jedaiah son of Harumaph made repairs across from his house. Next to him Hattush the son of Hashabneiah made repairs. 11 Malchijah son of Harim and Hasshub son of Pahath-moab made repairs to another section, as well as to the Tower of the Ovens. 12 Beside him Shallum son of Hallohesh, ruler of half the district of Jerusalem, made repairs — he and his daughters.

VALLEY GATE, DUNG GATE, AND FOUNTAIN GATE

13 Hanun and the inhabitants of Zanoah repaired the Valley Gate. They rebuilt it and installed its doors, bolts, and bars, and repaired five hundred yards[G] of the wall to the Dung Gate. 14 Malchijah son of Rechab, ruler of the district of Beth-haccherem, repaired the Dung Gate. He rebuilt it and installed its doors, bolts, and bars.

15 Shallun[H] son of Col-hozeh, ruler of the district of Mizpah, repaired the Fountain Gate. He rebuilt it and roofed it. Then he installed its doors, bolts, and bars. He also made repairs to the wall of the Pool of Shelah near the king's

[A] 2:12 Lit *animal with me* [B] 2:13 Or *Dragon's* [C] 2:18 Lit *they put their hands* [D] 3:5 Lit *not bring their neck to the work of* [E] 3:6 Or *Jeshanah* [F] 3:7 Or *Mizpah, the seat* [G] 3:13 Lit *1,000 cubits* [H] 3:15 Some Hb mss, Syr read *Shallum*

garden, as far as the stairs that descend from
the city of David.
16 After him Nehemiah son of Azbuk, ruler
of half the district of Beth-zur, made repairs
up to a point opposite the tombs of David,
as far as the artificial pool and the House of
the Warriors. 17 Next to him the Levites made
repairs under Rehum son of Bani. Beside
him Hashabiah, ruler of half the district of
Keilah, made repairs for his district. 18 After
him their fellow Levites made repairs under Binnui[A] son of Henadad, ruler of half
the district of Keilah. 19 Next to him Ezer son
of Jeshua, ruler of Mizpah, made repairs to
another section opposite the ascent to the
armory at the Angle.

THE ANGLE, WATER GATE, AND TOWER ON THE OPHEL

20 After him Baruch son of Zabbai[B] diligently
repaired another section, from the Angle to
the door of the house of the high priest Eliashib. 21 Beside him Meremoth son of Uriah, son
of Hakkoz, made repairs to another section,
from the door of Eliashib's house to the end of
his house. 22 And next to him the priests from
the surrounding area made repairs.
23 After them Benjamin and Hasshub made
repairs opposite their house. Beside them Azariah son of Maaseiah, son of Ananiah, made
repairs beside his house. 24 After him Binnui
son of Henadad made repairs to another section, from the house of Azariah to the Angle
and the corner. 25 Palal son of Uzai made repairs
opposite the Angle and tower that juts out
from the king's upper palace,[C] by the courtyard of the guard. Beside him Pedaiah son of
Parosh 26 and the temple servants living on
Ophel made repairs opposite the Water Gate
toward the east and the tower that juts out.
27 Next to him the Tekoites made repairs to another section from a point opposite the great
tower that juts out, as far as the wall of Ophel.

HORSE GATE, INSPECTION GATE, AND SHEEP GATE

28 Each of the priests made repairs above the
Horse Gate, each opposite his own house. 29 After them Zadok son of Immer made repairs
opposite his house. And beside him Shemaiah son of Shecaniah, guard of the East Gate,
made repairs. 30 Next to him Hananiah son of
Shelemiah and Hanun the sixth son of Zalaph
made repairs to another section.
After them Meshullam son of Berechiah
made repairs opposite his room. 31 Next to
him Malchijah, one of the goldsmiths, made
repairs to the house of the temple servants
and the merchants, opposite the Inspection[D]
Gate, and as far as the upstairs room on the
corner. 32 The goldsmiths and merchants made
repairs between the upstairs room on the corner and the Sheep Gate.

PROGRESS IN SPITE OF OPPOSITION

4 When Sanballat heard that we were rebuilding the wall, he became furious. He
mocked the Jews 2 before his colleagues and
the powerful men[E] of Samaria, and said, "What
are these pathetic Jews doing? Can they restore
it by themselves? Will they offer sacrifices?
Will they ever finish it? Can they bring these
burnt stones back to life from the mounds of
rubble?" 3 Then Tobiah the Ammonite, who
was beside him, said, "Indeed, even if a fox
climbed up what they are building, he would
break down their stone wall!"
4 Listen, our God, for we are despised. Make
their insults return on their own heads and
let them be taken as plunder to a land of captivity. 5 Do not cover their guilt or let their sin
be erased from your sight, because they have
angered[F] the builders.
6 So we rebuilt the wall until the entire wall
was joined together up to half its height, for
the people had the will to keep working.
7 When Sanballat, Tobiah, and the Arabs, Ammonites, and Ashdodites heard that the repair
to the walls of Jerusalem was progressing and
that the gaps were being closed, they became
furious. 8 They all plotted together to come
and fight against Jerusalem and throw it into
confusion. 9 So we prayed to our God and stationed a guard because of them day and night.
10 In Judah, it was said:[G]

The strength of the laborer fails,
since there is so much rubble.
We will never be able
to rebuild the wall.

11 And our enemies said, "They won't realize
it[H] until we're among them and can kill them
and stop the work." 12 When the Jews who
lived nearby arrived, they said to us time and

[A] **3:18** Some Hb mss, Syr, LXX; Neh 3:24; other Hb mss, Vg read *Bavvai* [B] **3:20** Alt Hb tradition, Vg read *Zaccai*; Ezr 2:9 [C] **3:25** Or *and the upper tower that juts out from the palace* [D] **3:31** Or *Muster* [E] **4:2** Or *the army* [F] **4:5** Or *provoked you in front of* [G] **4:10** Lit *Judah said* [H] **4:11** Lit *won't know or see*

again,[A] "Everywhere you turn, they attack[B]
us." 13 So I stationed people behind the lowest
sections of the wall, at the vulnerable areas. I
stationed them by families with their swords,
spears, and bows. 14 After I made an inspection,
I stood up and said to the nobles, the officials,
and the rest of the people, "Don't be afraid of
them. Remember the great and awe-inspiring
Lord, and fight for your countrymen, your
sons and daughters, your wives and homes."

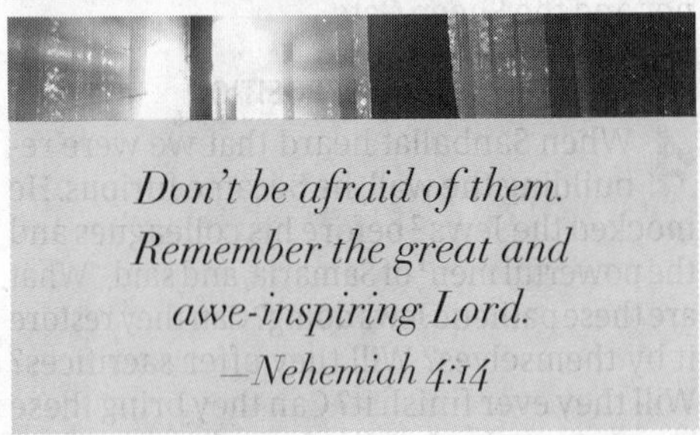
Don't be afraid of them.
Remember the great and
awe-inspiring Lord.
—*Nehemiah 4:14*

SWORD AND TROWEL

15 When our enemies heard that we knew their
scheme and that God had frustrated it, every
one of us returned to his own work on the wall.
16 From that day on, half of my men did the work
while the other half held spears, shields, bows,
and armor. The officers supported all the people
of Judah, 17 who were rebuilding the wall. The
laborers who carried the loads worked with
one hand and held a weapon with the other.
18 Each of the builders had his sword strapped
around his waist while he was building, and the
trumpeter was beside me. 19 Then I said to the
nobles, the officials, and the rest of the people:
"The work is enormous and spread out, and we
are separated far from one another along the
wall. 20 Wherever you hear the trumpet sound,
rally to us there. Our God will fight for us!" 21 So
we continued the work, while half of the men
were holding spears from daybreak until the
stars came out. 22 At that time, I also said to the
people, "Let everyone and his servant spend
the night inside Jerusalem, so that they can
stand guard by night and work by day." 23 And
I, my brothers, my servants, and the men of
the guard with me never took off our clothes.
Each carried his weapon, even when washing.[C]

SOCIAL INJUSTICE

5 There was a widespread outcry from the
people and their wives against their Jewish countrymen. 2 Some were saying, "We, our
sons, and our daughters are numerous. Let us
get grain so that we can eat and live." 3 Others
were saying, "We are mortgaging our fields,
vineyards, and homes to get grain during the
famine." 4 Still others were saying, "We have
borrowed money to pay the king's tax on our
fields and vineyards. 5 We and our children are
just like our countrymen and their children,
yet we are subjecting our sons and daughters
to slavery. Some of our daughters are already
enslaved, but we are powerless[D] because our
fields and vineyards belong to others."

6 I became extremely angry when I heard
their outcry and these complaints. 7 After seriously considering the matter, I accused the
nobles and officials, saying to them, "Each of
you is charging his countrymen interest." So
I called a large assembly against them 8 and
said, "We have done our best to buy back
our Jewish countrymen who were sold to
foreigners, but now you sell your own countrymen, and we have to buy them back." They
remained silent and could not say a word.
9 Then I said, "What you are doing isn't right.
Shouldn't you walk in the fear of our God and
not invite the reproach of our foreign enemies? 10 Even I, as well as my brothers and
my servants, have been lending them money
and grain. Please, let us stop charging this
interest.[E] 11 Return their fields, vineyards,
olive groves, and houses to them immediately, along with the percentage[F] of the money,
grain, new wine, and fresh oil that you have
been assessing them."

12 They responded: "We will return these
things and require nothing more from them.
We will do as you say."

So I summoned the priests and made everyone take an oath to do this. 13 I also shook the
folds of my robe and said, "May God likewise
shake from his house and property everyone
who doesn't keep this promise. May he be
shaken out and have nothing!"

The whole assembly said, "Amen," and they
praised the LORD. Then the people did as they
had promised.

GOOD AND BAD GOVERNORS

14 Furthermore, from the day King Artaxerxes
appointed me to be their governor in the land
of Judah — from the twentieth year until his
thirty-second year, twelve years — I and my
associates never ate from the food allotted to

[A] **4:12** Lit *us 10 times* [B] **4:12** Or *again from every place, "You must return to* [C] **4:23** Lit *Each his weapon the water* [D] **5:5** Lit *but there is not the power in our hand* [E] **5:10** Or *us forgive these debts* [F] **5:11** Lit *hundred*

the governor. 15 The governors who preceded me had heavily burdened the people, taking from them food and wine as well as a pound[A] of silver. Their subordinates also oppressed the people, but because of the fear of God, I didn't do this. 16 Instead, I devoted myself to the construction of this wall, and all my subordinates were gathered there for the work. We didn't buy any land.

17 There were 150 Jews and officials, as well as guests from the surrounding nations at my table. 18 Each[B] day, one ox, six choice sheep, and some fowl were prepared for me. An abundance of all kinds of wine was provided every ten days. But I didn't demand the food allotted to the governor, because the burden on the people was so heavy.

19 Remember me favorably, my God, for all that I have done for this people.

ATTEMPTS TO DISCOURAGE THE BUILDERS

6 When Sanballat, Tobiah, Geshem the Arab, and the rest of our enemies heard that I had rebuilt the wall and that no gap was left in it — though at that time I had not installed the doors in the city gates — 2 Sanballat and Geshem sent me a message: "Come, let's meet together in the villages of[C] the Ono Valley." They were planning to harm me.

3 So I sent messengers to them, saying, "I am doing important work and cannot come down. Why should the work cease while I leave it and go down to you?" 4 Four times they sent me the same proposal, and I gave them the same reply.

5 Sanballat sent me this same message a fifth time by his aide, who had an open letter in his hand. 6 In it was written:

> It is reported among the nations — and Geshem[D] agrees — that you and the Jews plan to rebel. This is the reason you are building the wall. According to these reports, you are to become their king 7 and have even set up the prophets in Jerusalem to proclaim on your behalf: "There is a king in Judah." These rumors will be heard by the king. So come, let's confer together.

8 Then I replied to him, "There is nothing to these rumors you are spreading; you are inventing them in your own mind." 9 For they were all trying to intimidate us, saying, "They will drop their hands from[E] the work, and it will never be finished."

But now, my God, strengthen my hands.

ATTEMPTS TO INTIMIDATE NEHEMIAH

10 I went to the house of Shemaiah son of Delaiah, son of Mehetabel, who was restricted to his house. He said:

> Let's meet at the house of God,
> inside the temple.
> Let's shut the temple doors
> because they're coming to kill you.
> They're coming to kill you tonight![F]

11 But I said, "Should a man like me run away? How can someone like me enter the temple and live? I will not go." 12 I realized that God had not sent him, because of the prophecy he spoke against me. Tobiah and Sanballat had hired him. 13 He was hired, so that I would be intimidated, do as he suggested, sin, and get a bad reputation, in order that they could discredit me.

14 My God, remember Tobiah and Sanballat for what they have done, and also the prophetess Noadiah and the other prophets who wanted to intimidate me.

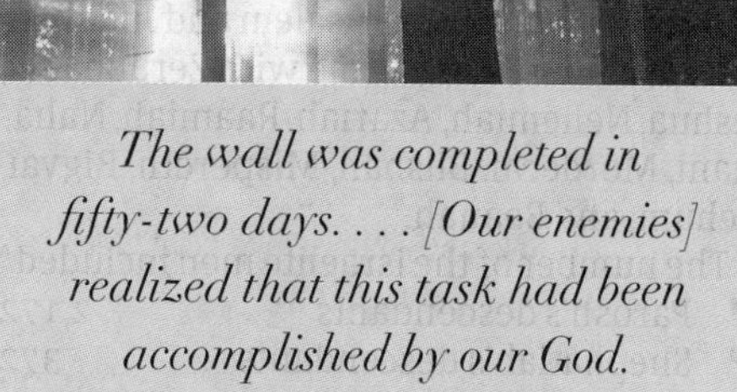

The wall was completed in fifty-two days. . . . [Our enemies] realized that this task had been accomplished by our God.

—Nehemiah 6:15-16

THE WALL COMPLETED

15 The wall was completed in fifty-two days, on the twenty-fifth day of the month Elul. 16 When all our enemies heard this, all the surrounding nations were intimidated and lost their confidence,[G] for they realized that this task had been accomplished by our God.

17 During those days, the nobles of Judah sent many letters to Tobiah, and Tobiah's letters came to them. 18 For many in Judah were bound by oath to him, since he was a son-in-law of Shecaniah son of Arah, and his son Jehohanan had married the daughter of Meshullam son of Berechiah. 19 These nobles kept mentioning Tobiah's good deeds to me, and they reported

---

[A] **5:15** Lit *40 shekels* [B] **5:18** Lit *And that which was prepared each* [C] **6:2** Or *together at Kephirim in* [D] **6:6** Lit *Gashmu* [E] **6:9** Or *will give up on* [F] **6:10** Or *by night* [G] **6:16** Lit *and fell greatly in their eyes*

my words to him. And Tobiah sent letters to intimidate me.

THE EXILES RETURN

7 When the wall had been rebuilt and I had the
doors installed, the gatekeepers, singers,
and Levites were appointed. 2 Then I put my
brother Hanani in charge of Jerusalem, along
with Hananiah, commander of the fortress,
because he was a faithful man who feared
God more than most. 3 I said to them, "Do not
open the gates of Jerusalem until the sun is
hot, and let the doors be shut and securely
fastened while the guards are on duty. Station
the citizens of Jerusalem as guards, some at
their posts and some at their homes."

4 The city was large and spacious, but there
were few people in it, and no houses had
been built yet. 5 Then my God put it into my
mind to assemble the nobles, the officials,
and the people to be registered by genealogy.
I found the genealogical record of those who
came back first, and I found the following
written in it:

6 These are the people of the province who
went up among the captive exiles deported
by King Nebuchadnezzar of Babylon. Each
of them returned to Jerusalem and Judah, to
his own town. 7 They came with Zerubbabel,
Jeshua, Nehemiah, Azariah, Raamiah, Nahamani, Mordecai, Bilshan, Mispereth, Bigvai,
Nehum, and Baanah.

The number of the Israelite men included[A]

8 Parosh's descendants 2,172
9 Shephatiah's descendants 372
10 Arah's descendants 652
11 Pahath-moab's descendants: Jeshua's and Joab's descendants 2,818
12 Elam's descendants 1,254
13 Zattu's descendants 845
14 Zaccai's descendants 760
15 Binnui's descendants 648
16 Bebai's descendants 628
17 Azgad's descendants 2,322
18 Adonikam's descendants 667
19 Bigvai's descendants 2,067
20 Adin's descendants 655
21 Ater's descendants: of Hezekiah 98
22 Hashum's descendants 328
23 Bezai's descendants 324
24 Hariph's descendants 112
25 Gibeon's[B] descendants 95
26 Bethlehem's and Netophah's men 188
27 Anathoth's men 128
28 Beth-azmaveth's men 42
29 Kiriath-jearim's, Chephirah's, and Beeroth's men 743
30 Ramah's and Geba's men 621
31 Michmas's men 122
32 Bethel's and Ai's men 123
33 the other Nebo's men 52
34 the other Elam's people 1,254
35 Harim's people 320
36 Jericho's people 345
37 Lod's, Hadid's, and Ono's people 721
38 Senaah's people 3,930.

39 The priests included
Jedaiah's descendants of the house of Jeshua 973
40 Immer's descendants 1,052
41 Pashhur's descendants 1,247
42 Harim's descendants 1,017.

43 The Levites included
Jeshua's descendants: of Kadmiel
Hodevah's descendants 74.

44 The singers included
Asaph's descendants 148.

45 The gatekeepers included
Shallum's descendants, Ater's descendants,
Talmon's descendants, Akkub's descendants,
Hatita's descendants, Shobai's descendants 138.

46 The temple servants included
Ziha's descendants, Hasupha's descendants,
Tabbaoth's descendants,
47 Keros's descendants,
Sia's descendants, Padon's descendants,
48 Lebanah's descendants, Hagabah's descendants,
Shalmai's descendants,
49 Hanan's descendants,
Giddel's descendants, Gahar's descendants,
50 Reaiah's descendants, Rezin's descendants,
Nekoda's descendants,
51 Gazzam's descendants,

[A] 7:7 Lit *the men of the people of Israel* [B] 7:25 = Gibbar's in Ezr 2:20

Uzza's descendants,
Paseah's descendants,
52 Besai's descendants,
Meunim's descendants,
Nephishesim's[A] descendants,
53 Bakbuk's descendants,
Hakupha's descendants,
Harhur's descendants,
54 Bazlith's descendants,
Mehida's descendants,
Harsha's descendants,
55 Barkos's descendants,
Sisera's descendants,
Temah's descendants,
56 Neziah's descendants,
Hatipha's descendants.

57 The descendants of Solomon's servants
included
Sotai's descendants,
Sophereth's descendants,
Perida's descendants,
58 Jaala's descendants,
Darkon's descendants,
Giddel's descendants,
59 Shephatiah's descendants,
Hattil's descendants,
Pochereth-hazzebaim's descendants,
Amon's descendants.

60 All the temple servants
and the descendants of Solomon's
servants 392.

61 The following are those who came from Tel-
melah, Tel-harsha, Cherub, Addon, and Immer,
but were unable to prove that their ancestral
families[B] and their lineage were Israelite:
62 Delaiah's descendants,
Tobiah's descendants,
and Nekoda's descendants 642
63 and from the priests: the descendants of
Hobaiah, the descendants of Hakkoz, and the
descendants of Barzillai — who had taken
a wife from the daughters of Barzillai the
Gileadite and who bore their name. 64 These
searched for their entries in the genealogical
records, but they could not be found, so they
were disqualified from the priesthood. 65 The
governor ordered them not to eat the most
holy things until there was a priest who could
consult the Urim and Thummim.

66 The whole combined assembly
numbered 42,360
67 not including their 7,337 male
and female servants,
as well as their 245 male
and female singers.
68 They had 736 horses, 245 mules,[C]
69 435 camels, and 6,720 donkeys.

70 Some of the family heads contributed
to the project. The governor gave 1,000 gold
coins,[D] 50 bowls, and 530 priestly garments
to the treasury. 71 Some of the family heads
gave 20,000 gold coins and 2,200 silver minas
to the treasury for the project. 72 The rest of
the people gave 20,000 gold coins, 2,000 silver minas, and 67 priestly garments. 73 The
priests, Levites, gatekeepers, temple singers,
some of the people, temple servants, and all
Israel settled in their towns.

PUBLIC READING OF THE LAW

When the seventh month came and the Is-
8 raelites had settled in their towns, 1 all the
people gathered together at the square in
front of the Water Gate. They asked the scribe
Ezra to bring the book of the law of Moses that
the LORD had given Israel. 2 On the first day
of the seventh month, the priest Ezra brought
the law before the assembly of men, women,
and all who could listen with understanding.
3 While he was facing the square in front of the
Water Gate, he read out of it from daybreak until noon before the men, the women, and those
who could understand. All the people listened
attentively[E] to the book of the law. 4 The scribe
Ezra stood on a high wooden platform made for
this purpose. Mattithiah, Shema, Anaiah, Uriah,
Hilkiah, and Maaseiah stood beside him on his
right; to his left were Pedaiah, Mishael, Malchijah, Hashum, Hash-baddanah, Zechariah, and
Meshullam. 5 Ezra opened the book in full view
of all the people, since he was elevated above
everyone. As he opened it, all the people stood
up. 6 Ezra blessed the LORD, the great God, and
with their hands uplifted all the people said,
"Amen, Amen!" Then they knelt low and worshiped the LORD with their faces to the ground.
7 Jeshua, Bani, Sherebiah, Jamin, Akkub,
Shabbethai, Hodiah, Maaseiah, Kelita, Azariah, Jozabad, Hanan, and Pelaiah, who were
Levites,[F] explained the law to the people as

[A] **7:52** Alt Hb tradition reads *Nephushesim's* [B] **7:61** Lit *the house of their fathers* [C] **7:68** Some Hb mss, LXX; Ezr 2:66; other Hb mss omit v. 68 [D] **7:70** Or *drachmas*, or *darics*; also in vv. 71,72 [E] **8:3** Lit *The ears of all the people listened* [F] **8:7** Vg, 1 Esdras 9:48; MT reads *Pelaiah and the Levites*

they stood in their places. [8] They read out of
the book of the law of God, translating and
giving the meaning so that the people could
understand what was read. [9] Nehemiah the
governor, Ezra the priest and scribe, and the
Levites who were instructing the people said
to all of them, "This day is holy to the LORD
your God. Do not mourn or weep." For all the
people were weeping as they heard the words
of the law. [10] Then he said to them, "Go and eat
what is rich, drink what is sweet, and send
portions to those who have nothing prepared,
since today is holy to our Lord. Do not grieve,
because the joy of the LORD is your strength."[A]
[11] And the Levites quieted all the people, saying, "Be still, since today is holy. Don't grieve."
[12] Then all the people began to eat and drink,
send portions, and have a great celebration,
because they had understood the words that
were explained to them.

FESTIVAL OF SHELTERS OBSERVED

[13] On the second day, the family heads of all
the people, along with the priests and Levites,
assembled before the scribe Ezra to study the
words of the law. [14] They found written in the
law how the LORD had commanded through
Moses that the Israelites should dwell in shelters during the festival of the seventh month.
[15] So they proclaimed and spread this news
throughout their towns and in Jerusalem, saying, "Go out to the hill country and bring back
branches of olive, wild olive, myrtle, palm, and
other leafy trees to make shelters, just as it is
written." [16] The people went out, brought back
branches, and made shelters for themselves
on each of their rooftops and courtyards, the
court of the house of God, the square by the
Water Gate, and the square by the Ephraim
Gate. [17] The whole community that had returned from exile made shelters and lived in
them. The Israelites had not celebrated like this
from the days of Joshua son of Nun until that
day. And there was tremendous joy. [18] Ezra[B]
read out of the book of the law of God every
day, from the first day to the last. The Israelites celebrated the festival for seven days,
and on the eighth day there was an assembly,
according to the ordinance.

NATIONAL CONFESSION OF SIN

9 On the twenty-fourth day of this month
the Israelites assembled; they were fasting, wearing sackcloth, and had put dust on
their heads. [2] Those of Israelite descent separated themselves from all foreigners, and
they stood and confessed their sins and the
iniquities of their fathers. [3] While they stood

Exercise of Faith | *Trusting God*

TRUE HOLINESS

"Then [Nehemiah] said to them, 'Go and eat what is rich, drink what is sweet, and send portions to those who have nothing prepared, since today is holy to our Lord. Do not grieve, because the joy of the LORD is your strength.'" Nehemiah 8:10

Many children grow up assuming that church and the spiritual life are always somber. Church mostly means prohibitions and correctives: "Shhh! Be quiet! Be still! This is serious! Stop goofing around!" No wonder many kids embrace the idea that God is grim and stern.

But notice this passage. After Nehemiah led the Jewish people in rebuilding the walls of Jerusalem, Ezra the priest led them in a kind of recommitment ceremony. They spent all day studying God's Word and worshiping. Then came the command to feast and celebrate lavishly.

"The joy of the LORD" means the joy that belongs to God or comes from God. In other words, our Creator is the source of true, eternal happiness. In fact, heaven is all about joy.

Focus on God—his goodness, love, grace, and empowerment—and rejoice!

For the next note on *Exercise of Faith*, see Job 23:12.

[A] **8:10** Or *stronghold* [B] **8:18** Some Hb mss, Syr read *They*

in their places, they read from the book of
the law of the LORD their God for a fourth of
the day and spent another fourth of the day
in confession and worship of the LORD their
God. 4 Jeshua, Bani, Kadmiel, Shebaniah, Bunni, Sherebiah, Bani, and Chenani stood on the
raised platform built for the Levites and cried
out loudly to the LORD their God. 5 Then the
Levites — Jeshua, Kadmiel, Bani, Hashabneiah,
Sherebiah, Hodiah, Shebaniah, and Pethahiah
— said, "Stand up. Blessed be the LORD your
God from everlasting to everlasting."

Blessed be your glorious name,
and may it be exalted above all blessing
and praise.
6 You,[A] LORD, are the only God.[B]
You created the heavens,
the highest heavens with all their stars,
the earth and all that is on it,
the seas and all that is in them.
You give life to all of them,
and all the stars of heaven worship you.
7 You, the LORD,
are the God who chose Abram
and brought him out of Ur
of the Chaldeans,
and changed his name to Abraham.
8 You found his heart faithful
in your sight,
and made a covenant with him
to give the land of the Canaanites,
Hethites, Amorites, Perizzites,
Jebusites, and Girgashites —
to give it to his descendants.
You have fulfilled your promise,
for you are righteous.

9 You saw the oppression
of our ancestors in Egypt
and heard their cry at the Red Sea.
10 You performed signs and wonders
against Pharaoh,
all his officials, and all the people
of his land,
for you knew how arrogantly
they treated our ancestors.
You made a name for yourself
that endures to this day.
11 You divided the sea before them,
and they crossed through it
on dry ground.
You hurled their pursuers into the depths
like a stone into raging water.
12 You led them with a pillar of cloud by day,
and with a pillar of fire by night,
to illuminate the way they should go.
13 You came down on Mount Sinai,
and spoke to them from heaven.

Thanksgiving and Contentment | *Praise*

THE RIGHT WAY TO WORSHIP

"Then the Levites . . . said, 'Stand up. Blessed be the LORD your God from everlasting to everlasting.' Blessed be your glorious name, and may it be exalted above all blessing and praise." Nehemiah 9:5

What's the right way to worship? Should we "stand up" all the time, as this passage seems to suggest, or can we sometimes sit still? (What about kneeling or lying prostrate?) Eyes shut or wide open? Laugh or weep? Be silent or shout? Clap, sway, or dance? Should we bow our heads or lift them? Fold our hands or raise them high?

Fixating on our body posture, we can easily miss the goal of worship: focusing on God. The truth is, Scripture commands or describes all these actions. Each one is a valid way to respond to God's character and works.

A celebrating fan at a football game doesn't obsess over, "Should I clap or high five the person in front of me if my team scores? Will people around me think I'm weird if I cheer?" He is simply in the moment and naturally responsive. In the same way, if we are turning worship celebrations into so much self-analyzing and people-pleasing, we've missed the point.

For the next note on *Thanksgiving and Contentment*, see Psalm 1:1-3.

[A] **9:6** LXX reads *And Ezra said: You* [B] **9:6** Lit *are alone*

You gave them impartial ordinances,
reliable instructions,
and good statutes and commands.
14 You revealed your holy Sabbath
to them,
and gave them commands, statutes,
and instruction
through your servant Moses.
15 You provided bread from heaven
for their hunger;
you brought them water from the rock
for their thirst.
You told them to go in and possess
the land
you had sworn[A] to give them.

16 But our ancestors acted arrogantly;
they became stiff-necked and did not
listen to your commands.
17 They refused to listen
and did not remember your wonders
you performed among them.
They became stiff-necked
and appointed a leader
to return to their slavery in Egypt.[B]
But you are a forgiving God,
gracious and compassionate,
slow to anger and abounding
in faithful love,
and you did not abandon them.
18 Even after they had cast an image
of a calf
for themselves and said,
"This is your god who brought you
out of Egypt,"
and they had committed
terrible blasphemies,
19 you did not abandon them
in the wilderness
because of your great compassion.
During the day the pillar of cloud
never turned away from them,
guiding them on their journey.
And during the night the pillar of fire
illuminated the way they should go.
20 You sent your good Spirit
to instruct them.
You did not withhold your manna
from their mouths,
and you gave them water
for their thirst.
21 You provided for them
in the wilderness forty years,
and they lacked nothing.
Their clothes did not wear out,
and their feet did not swell.

22 You gave them kingdoms and peoples
and established boundaries for them.
They took possession

Eternal Perspective | *God the Creator*

REASON FOR BEING

"You, LORD, are the only God. You created the heavens, the highest heavens with all their stars, the earth and all that is on it, the seas and all that is in them. You give life to all of them, and all the stars of heaven worship you." Nehemiah 9:6

Grateful for the rebuilt walls around them, and moved by all they had learned about God's faithfulness and mercy in their national Bible study (7:73–8:18), the Israelites called for a solemn day of fasting and prayer (9:1).

For "a fourth of the day" they read from "the book of the law of the LORD" (9:3). This was followed by hours more of confession and worship. As the Levites led the people in crying out to God, they acknowledged the first great truth of the Bible: God is our Creator. He gave (and still gives) us breath. He is the One to whom we owe our lives. He is our reason for being. This means self-made men or women do not exist. We're not as independent as we like to imagine.

Thank God for his creative work in you and for his protection and provision.

For the next note on *Eternal Perspective*, see Esther 4:13-14.

[A] **9:15** Lit *lifted your hand* [B] **9:17** Some Hb mss, LXX; other Hb mss read *in their rebellion*

of the land of King Sihon[A] of Heshbon
and of the land of King Og of Bashan.
23 You multiplied their descendants
like the stars of the sky
and brought them to the land
you told their ancestors to go in
and possess.
24 So their descendants went in
and possessed the land:
You subdued the Canaanites
who inhabited the land before them
and handed their kings
and the surrounding peoples
over to them,
to do as they pleased with them.
25 They captured fortified cities
and fertile land
and took possession of
well-supplied houses,
cisterns cut out of rock, vineyards,
olive groves, and fruit trees
in abundance.
They ate, were filled,
became prosperous, and delighted
in your great goodness.

26 But they were disobedient and rebelled
against you.
They flung your law behind their backs
and killed your prophets
who warned them
in order to turn them back to you.
They committed terrible blasphemies.
27 So you handed them over
to their enemies,
who oppressed them.
In their time of distress, they cried out
to you,
and you heard from heaven.
In your abundant compassion
you gave them deliverers,
who rescued them
from the power of their enemies.
28 But as soon as they had relief,
they again did what was evil
in your sight.
So you abandoned them to the power
of their enemies,
who dominated them.
When they cried out to you again,
you heard from heaven and rescued
them
many times in your compassion.
29 You warned them to turn back
to your law,
but they acted arrogantly
and would not obey your commands.
They sinned against your ordinances,
which a person will live by
if he does them.
They stubbornly resisted,[B]
stiffened their necks, and would not
obey.
30 You were patient with them
for many years,
and your Spirit warned them
through your prophets,
but they would not listen.
Therefore, you handed them over
to the surrounding peoples.
31 However,
in your abundant compassion,
you did not destroy them or abandon
them,
for you are a gracious
and compassionate God.

32 So now, our God — the great, mighty,
and awe-inspiring God who keeps
his gracious covenant —
do not view lightly all the hardships
that have afflicted us,
our kings and leaders,
our priests and prophets,
our ancestors and all your people,
from the days of the Assyrian kings
until today.
33 You are righteous concerning all
that has happened to us,
because you have acted faithfully,
while we have acted wickedly.
34 Our kings, leaders, priests,
and ancestors
did not obey your law
or listen to your commands
and warnings you gave them.
35 When they were in their kingdom,
with your abundant goodness that
you gave them,
and in the spacious and fertile land
you set before them,
they would not serve you or turn
from their wicked ways.

36 Here we are today,
slaves in the land you gave our ancestors

[A] **9:22** One Hb ms, LXX; other Hb mss, Vg read *of Sihon, even the land of the king* [B] **9:29** Lit *They gave a stubborn shoulder*

so that they could enjoy its fruit
and its goodness.
Here we are — slaves in it!
37 Its abundant harvest goes to the kings
you have set over us,
because of our sins.
They rule over our bodies
and our livestock as they please.
We are in great distress.

ISRAEL'S VOW OF FAITHFULNESS

38 In view of all this, we are making a binding
agreement in writing on a sealed document
containing the names of our leaders, Levites,
and priests.

10 Those whose seals were on the document were
the governor Nehemiah
son of Hacaliah, and Zedekiah,
2 Seraiah, Azariah, Jeremiah,
3 Pashhur, Amariah, Malchijah,
4 Hattush, Shebaniah, Malluch,
5 Harim, Meremoth, Obadiah,
6 Daniel, Ginnethon, Baruch,
7 Meshullam, Abijah, Mijamin,
8 Maaziah, Bilgai, and Shemaiah.
These were the priests.

9 The Levites were
Jeshua son of Azaniah,
Binnui of the sons of Henadad, Kadmiel,
10 and their brothers
Shebaniah, Hodiah, Kelita, Pelaiah,
Hanan,
11 Mica, Rehob, Hashabiah,
12 Zaccur, Sherebiah, Shebaniah,
13 Hodiah, Bani, and Beninu.

14 The heads of the people were
Parosh, Pahath-moab, Elam, Zattu, Bani,
15 Bunni, Azgad, Bebai,
16 Adonijah, Bigvai, Adin,
17 Ater, Hezekiah, Azzur,
18 Hodiah, Hashum, Bezai,
19 Hariph, Anathoth, Nebai,
20 Magpiash, Meshullam, Hezir,
21 Meshezabel, Zadok, Jaddua,
22 Pelatiah, Hanan, Anaiah,
23 Hoshea, Hananiah, Hasshub,
24 Hallohesh, Pilha, Shobek,
25 Rehum, Hashabnah, Maaseiah,
26 Ahijah, Hanan, Anan,
27 Malluch, Harim, Baanah.

28 The rest of the people — the priests,
Levites, gatekeepers, singers, and temple
servants, along with their wives, sons, and
daughters, everyone who is able to understand
and who has separated themselves from the
surrounding peoples to obey the law of God —
29 join with their noble brothers and commit
themselves with a sworn oath[A] to follow the
law of God given through God's servant Moses and to obey carefully all the commands,
ordinances, and statutes of the LORD our Lord.

DETAILS OF THE VOW

30 We will not give our daughters in
marriage to the surrounding peoples and
will not take their daughters as wives for
our sons.

31 When the surrounding peoples bring
merchandise or any kind of grain to sell
on the Sabbath day, we will not buy from
them on the Sabbath or a holy day. We will
also leave the land uncultivated in the
seventh year and will cancel every debt.

32 We will impose the following commands on ourselves:

To give an eighth of an ounce of silver[B]
yearly for the service of the house of our
God: 33 the bread displayed before the
LORD,[C] the daily grain offering, the regular burnt offering, the Sabbath and New
Moon offerings, the appointed festivals,
the holy things, the sin offerings to atone
for Israel, and for all the work of the
house of our God.

34 We have cast lots among the priests,
Levites, and people for the donation of
wood by our ancestral families[D] at the
appointed times each year. They are to
bring the wood to our God's house to
burn on the altar of the LORD our God, as
it is written in the law.

35 We will bring the firstfruits of our land
and of every fruit tree to the LORD's house
year by year. 36 We will also bring the
firstborn of our sons and our livestock,
as prescribed by the law, and will bring
the firstborn of our herds and flocks to
the house of our God, to the priests who

[A] **10:29** Lit *and enter in a curse and in an oath* [B] **10:32** Lit *give one-third of a shekel* [C] **10:33** Lit *rows of bread* [D] **10:34** Lit *the house of our fathers*

serve in our God's house. 37 We will bring
a loaf from our first batch of dough to the
priests at the storerooms of the house of
our God. We will also bring the firstfruits
of our grain offerings, of every fruit tree,
and of the new wine and fresh oil. A tenth
of our land's produce belongs to the
Levites, for the Levites are to collect the
one-tenth offering in all our agricultural
towns. 38 A priest from Aaron's descendants is to accompany the Levites when
they collect the tenth, and the Levites
are to take a tenth of this offering to the
storerooms of the treasury in the house
of our God. 39 For the Israelites and the
Levites are to bring the contributions
of grain, new wine, and fresh oil to the
storerooms where the articles of the sanctuary are kept and where the priests who
minister are, along with the gatekeepers
and singers. We will not neglect the house
of our God.

RESETTLING JERUSALEM

11 Now the leaders of the people stayed
in Jerusalem, and the rest of the people
cast lots for one out of ten to come and live
in Jerusalem, the holy city, while the other
nine-tenths remained in their towns. 2 The
people blessed all the men who volunteered
to live in Jerusalem.

3 These are the heads of the province who
stayed in Jerusalem (but in the villages of Judah each lived on his own property in their
towns — the Israelites, priests, Levites, temple servants, and descendants of Solomon's
servants — 4 while some of the descendants
of Judah and Benjamin settled in Jerusalem):
Judah's descendants:

Athaiah son of Uzziah, son of Zechariah,
son of Amariah, son of Shephatiah, son of
Mahalalel, of Perez's descendants; 5 and
Maaseiah son of Baruch, son of Col-
hozeh, son of Hazaiah, son of Adaiah, son
of Joiarib, son of Zechariah, a descendant
of the Shilonite. 6 The total number of
Perez's descendants, who settled in Jerusalem, was 468 capable men.

7 These were Benjamin's descendants:

Sallu son of Meshullam, son of Joed, son
of Pedaiah, son of Kolaiah, son of Maaseiah, son of Ithiel, son of Jeshaiah, 8 and
after him Gabbai and Sallai: 928. 9 Joel
son of Zichri was the officer over them,
and Judah son of Hassenuah was second
in command over the city.

10 The priests:

Jedaiah son of Joiarib, Jachin, and
11 Seraiah son of Hilkiah, son of Meshullam, son of Zadok, son of Meraioth, son
of Ahitub, the chief official of God's
temple, 12 and their relatives who did the
work at the temple: 822. Adaiah son of
Jeroham, son of Pelaliah, son of Amzi,
son of Zechariah, son of Pashhur, son of
Malchijah 13 and his relatives, the heads
of families: 242. Amashsai son of Azarel,
son of Ahzai, son of Meshillemoth, son
of Immer, 14 and their relatives, capable
men: 128. Zabdiel son of Haggedolim,
was their chief.

15 The Levites:

Shemaiah son of Hasshub, son of Azrikam, son of Hashabiah, son of Bunni;
16 and Shabbethai and Jozabad, from the
heads of the Levites, who supervised the
work outside the house of God; 17 Mattaniah son of Mica, son of Zabdi, son of
Asaph, the one[A] who began the thanksgiving in prayer; Bakbukiah, second
among his relatives; and Abda son of
Shammua, son of Galal, son of Jeduthun.
18 All the Levites in the holy city: 284.

19 The gatekeepers:

Akkub, Talmon, and their relatives, who
guarded the city gates: 172.

20 The rest of Israel, the priests, and the
Levites were in all the villages of Judah, each
on his own inherited property. 21 The temple
servants lived on Ophel; Ziha and Gishpa supervised the temple servants.

THE LEVITES AND PRIESTS

22 The leader of the Levites in Jerusalem was
Uzzi son of Bani, son of Hashabiah, son of
Mattaniah, son of Mica, of the descendants

[A] **11:17** Lit *the head*

of Asaph, who were singers for the service of
God's house. 23 There was, in fact, a command
of the king regarding them, and an ordinance
regulating the singers' daily tasks. 24 Pethahiah son of Meshezabel, of the descendants
of Zerah son of Judah, was the king's agent[A]
in every matter concerning the people.
25 As for the farming settlements with their
fields:

Some of Judah's descendants lived
in Kiriath-arba
and Dibon and their surrounding
villages, and Jekabzeel and
its settlements;
26 in Jeshua, Moladah, Beth-pelet,
27 Hazar-shual, and Beer-sheba
and its surrounding villages;
28 in Ziklag and Meconah
and its surrounding villages;
29 in En-rimmon, Zorah, Jarmuth, and
30 Zanoah and Adullam
with their settlements;
in Lachish with its fields and Azekah
and its surrounding villages.
So they settled from Beer-sheba
to Hinnom Valley.

31 Benjamin's descendants:
from Geba,[B] Michmash, Aija,
and Bethel
and its surrounding villages,
32 Anathoth, Nob, Ananiah,
33 Hazor, Ramah, Gittaim,
34 Hadid, Zeboim, Neballat,
35 Lod, and Ono, in Craftsmen's Valley.
36 Some of the Judean divisions of Levites
were in Benjamin.

12 These are the priests and Levites who
went up with Zerubbabel son of Shealtiel
and with Jeshua:

Seraiah, Jeremiah, Ezra,
2 Amariah, Malluch, Hattush,
3 Shecaniah, Rehum, Meremoth,
4 Iddo, Ginnethoi, Abijah,
5 Mijamin, Maadiah, Bilgah,
6 Shemaiah, Joiarib, Jedaiah,
7 Sallu, Amok, Hilkiah, Jedaiah.

These were the heads of the priests and their
relatives in the days of Jeshua.

8 The Levites:

Jeshua, Binnui, Kadmiel,
Sherebiah, Judah, and Mattaniah —
he and his relatives were in charge
of the songs of praise.
9 Bakbukiah, Unni,[C] and their relatives
stood opposite them
in the services.
10 Jeshua fathered Joiakim,
Joiakim fathered Eliashib,
Eliashib fathered Joiada,
11 Joiada fathered Jonathan,
and Jonathan fathered Jaddua.[D]

12 In the days of Joiakim, the heads of the
priestly families were

Meraiah of Seraiah,
Hananiah of Jeremiah,
13 Meshullam of Ezra,
Jehohanan of Amariah,
14 Jonathan of Malluchi,
Joseph of Shebaniah,
15 Adna of Harim,
Helkai of Meraioth,
16 Zechariah of Iddo,
Meshullam of Ginnethon,
17 Zichri of Abijah,
Piltai of Moadiah, of Miniamin,
18 Shammua of Bilgah,
Jehonathan of Shemaiah,
19 Mattenai of Joiarib,
Uzzi of Jedaiah,
20 Kallai of Sallai,
Eber of Amok,
21 Hashabiah of Hilkiah,
and Nethanel of Jedaiah.

22 In the days of Eliashib, Joiada, Johanan,
and Jaddua, the heads of the families of the
Levites and priests were recorded while Darius the Persian ruled. 23 Levi's descendants,
the family heads, were recorded in the Book
of the Historical Events during the days of
Johanan son of Eliashib. 24 The heads of the
Levites — Hashabiah, Sherebiah, and Jeshua
son of Kadmiel, along with their relatives
opposite them — gave praise and thanks,
division by division, as David the man of God
had prescribed. 25 This included Mattaniah,
Bakbukiah, and Obadiah. Meshullam, Talmon,
and Akkub were gatekeepers who guarded the storerooms at the city gates. 26 These
served in the days of Joiakim son of Jeshua,
son of Jozadak, and in the days of Nehemiah
the governor and Ezra the priest and scribe.

[A] **11:24** Lit *was at the king's hand* [B] **11:31** Or *descendants from Geba lived in* [C] **12:9** Alt Hb tradition reads *Unno*
[D] **12:10-11** These men were high priests.

DEDICATION OF THE WALL

27 At the dedication of the wall of Jerusalem,
they sent for the Levites wherever they lived
and brought them to Jerusalem to celebrate
the joyous dedication with thanksgiving and
singing accompanied by cymbals, harps, and
lyres. 28 The singers gathered from the region
around Jerusalem, from the settlements of the
Netophathites, 29 from Beth-gilgal, and from
the fields of Geba and Azmaveth, for they had
built settlements for themselves around Jerusalem. 30 After the priests and Levites had
purified themselves, they purified the people,
the city gates, and the wall.

31 Then I brought the leaders of Judah up
on top of the wall, and I appointed two large
processions that gave thanks. One went to
the right on the wall, toward the Dung Gate.
32 Hoshaiah and half the leaders of Judah followed, 33 along with Azariah, Ezra, Meshullam,
34 Judah, Benjamin, Shemaiah, Jeremiah, 35 and
some of the priests' sons with trumpets, and
Zechariah son of Jonathan, son of Shemaiah, son of Mattaniah, son of Micaiah, son
of Zaccur, son of Asaph followed 36 as well
as his relatives — Shemaiah, Azarel, Milalai,
Gilalai, Maai, Nethanel, Judah, and Hanani,
with the musical instruments of David, the
man of God. Ezra the scribe went in front of
them. 37 At the Fountain Gate they climbed
the steps of the city of David on the ascent of
the wall and went above the house of David
to the Water Gate on the east.

38 The second thanksgiving procession
went to the left, and I followed it with half
the people along the top of the wall, past
the Tower of the Ovens to the Broad Wall,
39 above the Ephraim Gate, and by the Old
Gate, the Fish Gate, the Tower of Hananel,
and the Tower of the Hundred, to the Sheep
Gate. They stopped at the Gate of the Guard.
40 The two thanksgiving processions stood
in the house of God. So did I and half of the
officials accompanying me, 41 as well as the
priests:

Eliakim, Maaseiah, Miniamin,
Micaiah, Elioenai, Zechariah,
and Hananiah, with trumpets;
42 and Maaseiah, Shemaiah, Eleazar,
Uzzi, Jehohanan, Malchijah, Elam,
and Ezer.

Then the singers sang, with Jezrahiah as
the leader. 43 On that day they offered great

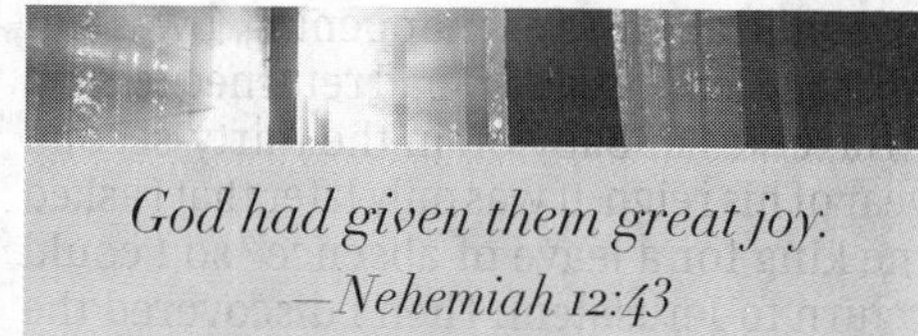

God had given them great joy.
—Nehemiah 12:43

sacrifices and rejoiced because God had giv-
en them great joy. The women and children
also celebrated, and Jerusalem's rejoicing was
heard far away.

SUPPORT OF THE LEVITES' MINISTRY

44 On that same day men were placed in charge
of the rooms that housed the supplies, contributions, firstfruits, and tenths. The legally
required portions for the priests and Levites
were gathered from the village fields, because Judah was grateful to the priests and
Levites who were serving. 45 They performed
the service of their God and the service of
purification, along with the singers and gatekeepers, as David and his son Solomon had
prescribed. 46 For long ago, in the days of David
and Asaph, there were heads[A] of the singers
and songs of praise and thanksgiving to God.
47 So in the days of Zerubbabel and Nehemiah,
all Israel contributed the daily portions for
the singers and gatekeepers. They also set
aside daily portions for the Levites, and the
Levites set aside daily portions for Aaron's
descendants.

NEHEMIAH'S FURTHER REFORMS

13 At that time the book of Moses was read
publicly to[B] the people. The command
was found written in it that no Ammonite or
Moabite should ever enter the assembly of
God, 2 because they did not meet the Israelites with food and water. Instead, they hired
Balaam against them to curse them, but our
God turned the curse into a blessing. 3 When
they heard the law, they separated all those
of mixed descent from Israel.

4 Now before this, the priest Eliashib had
been put in charge of the storerooms of the
house of our God. He was a relative[C] of Tobiah
5 and had prepared a large room for him where
they had previously stored the grain offerings,
the frankincense, the articles, and the tenths
of grain, new wine, and fresh oil prescribed
for the Levites, singers, and gatekeepers, along
with the contributions for the priests.

[A] **12:46** Alt Hb tradition reads *there was a head* [B] **13:1** Lit *read in the ears of* [C] **13:4** Or *an associate*

6 While all this was happening, I was not
in Jerusalem, because I had returned to King
Artaxerxes of Babylon in the thirty-second
year of his reign. It was only later that I asked
the king for a leave of absence 7 so I could
return to Jerusalem. Then I discovered the
evil that Eliashib had done on behalf of Tobiah by providing him a room in the courts
of God's house. 8 I was greatly displeased and
threw all of Tobiah's household possessions
out of the room. 9 I ordered that the rooms be
purified, and I had the articles of the house
of God restored there, along with the grain
offering and frankincense. 10 I also found out
that because the portions for the Levites had
not been given, each of the Levites and the
singers performing the service had gone back
to his own field. 11 Therefore, I rebuked the
officials, asking, "Why has the house of God
been neglected?" I gathered the Levites and
singers together and stationed them at their
posts. 12 Then all Judah brought a tenth of the
grain, new wine, and fresh oil into the storehouses. 13 I appointed as treasurers over the
storehouses the priest Shelemiah, the scribe
Zadok, and Pedaiah of the Levites, with Hanan
son of Zaccur, son of Mattaniah to assist them,
because they were considered trustworthy.
They were responsible for the distribution
to their colleagues.

14 Remember me for this, my God, and don't
erase the deeds of faithful love I have done
for the house of my God and for its services.

15 At that time I saw people in Judah treading winepresses on the Sabbath. They were
also bringing in stores of grain and loading
them on donkeys, along with wine, grapes, and
figs. All kinds of goods were being brought
to Jerusalem on the Sabbath day. So I warned
them against selling food on that day. 16 The
Tyrians living there were importing fish and all
kinds of merchandise and selling them on the
Sabbath to the people of Judah in Jerusalem.

17 I rebuked the nobles of Judah and said to
them: "What is this evil you are doing — profaning the Sabbath day? 18 Didn't your ancestors do the same, so that our God brought all
this disaster on us and on this city? And now
you are rekindling his anger against Israel by
profaning the Sabbath!"

19 When shadows began to fall on the city
gates of Jerusalem just before the Sabbath, I
gave orders that the city gates be closed and
not opened until after the Sabbath. I posted
some of my men at the gates, so that no goods
could enter during the Sabbath day. 20 Once
or twice the merchants and those who sell
all kinds of goods camped outside Jerusalem,
21 but I warned them, "Why are you camping in front of the wall? If you do it again,
I'll use force[A] against you." After that they
did not come again on the Sabbath. 22 Then I
instructed the Levites to purify themselves
and guard the city gates in order to keep the
Sabbath day holy.

Remember me for this also, my God, and
look on me with compassion according to
the abundance of your faithful love.

23 In those days I also saw Jews who had
married women from Ashdod, Ammon, and
Moab. 24 Half of their children spoke the language of Ashdod or the language of one of the
other peoples but could not speak Hebrew.[B]
25 I rebuked them, cursed them, beat some of
their men, and pulled out their hair. I forced
them to take an oath before God and said,
"You must not give your daughters in marriage to their sons or take their daughters as
wives for your sons or yourselves! 26 Didn't
King Solomon of Israel sin in matters like
this? There was not a king like him among
many nations. He was loved by his God, and
God made him king over all Israel, yet foreign women drew him into sin. 27 Why then
should we hear about you doing all this terrible evil and acting unfaithfully against our
God by marrying foreign women?" 28 Even
one of the sons of Jehoiada, son of the high
priest Eliashib, had become a son-in-law
to Sanballat the Horonite. So I drove him
away from me.

29 Remember them, my God, for defiling
the priesthood as well as the covenant of the
priesthood and the Levites.

30 So I purified them from everything foreign and assigned specific duties to each of
the priests and Levites. 31 I also arranged for
the donation of wood at the appointed times
and for the firstfruits.

Remember me, my God, with favor.

[A] **13:21** Lit *again, I will send a hand* [B] **13:24** Lit *Judahite*

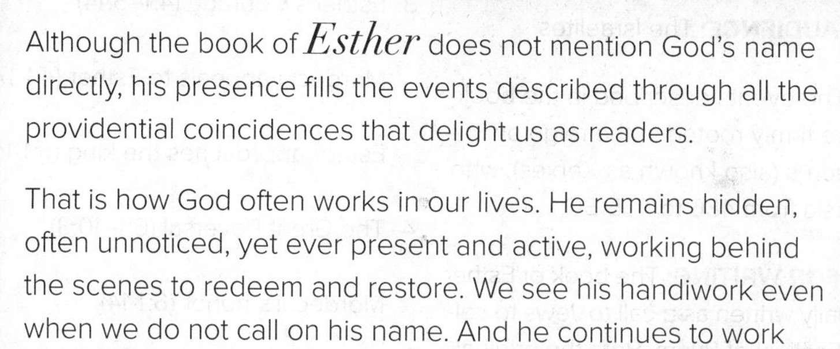

Although the book of *Esther* does not mention God's name directly, his presence fills the events described through all the providential coincidences that delight us as readers.

That is how God often works in our lives. He remains hidden, often unnoticed, yet ever present and active, working behind the scenes to redeem and restore. We see his handiwork even when we do not call on his name. And he continues to work for our good, even when we fail to give him credit. God is over all, through all, and in all, whether we acknowledge it or not.

Esther also shows that God uses even frightened, powerless people to accomplish his purposes. For Esther to reveal her ethnicity and speak up on behalf of the conquered Jews involved great risk. Yet she stepped out in faith to do her part in saving her people.

In God's hands, even the most unlikely individuals can accomplish much. We need to ask for God's help and then find ways to use our influence to speak up for truth and justice.

ESTHER

AUTHOR: Named after its principal character, the book of Esther does not state its author. Many early writers, both Jewish and Christian, suggested Mordecai as the author.

DATE WRITTEN: Based on the language of the book, Esther probably was written in the fourth century BC.

ORIGINAL AUDIENCE: The Israelites

SETTING: The events described in the book of Esther are firmly rooted in the reign of King Ahasuerus (also known as Xerxes), who ruled in Persia from 486 to 465 BC.

PURPOSE FOR WRITING: The book of Esther was principally written as a call to Jews to celebrate the Festival of Purim. Both the original audience of the book and modern-day readers can also glean theological truths about God's sovereignty over human events to work his redemptive purposes, and his tendency to use unlikely people to work out his plans.

OUTLINE:

1. A Replacement Queen (1:1–2:18)

   Vashti angers the king (1:1-12)

   The king issues a decree (1:13-22)

   Commissioners search for a new queen (2:1-14)

   Esther becomes queen (2:15-18)

2. Threat to the Jews (2:19–3:15)

   Mordecai saves the king (2:19-23)

   Mordecai takes a stand (3:1-4)

   Haman plots to kill the Jews (3:5-15)

3. Esther's Courage (4:1–5:14)

   Mordecai appeals to Esther (4:1-17)

   Esther approaches the king (5:1-14)

4. The Great Reversal (6:1–10:3)

   Mordecai's honor (6:1-14)

   Haman's execution (7:1-10)

   Esther's intervention for the Jews (8:1-17)

   The Jews' victories (9:1-32)

   Mordecai's legacy (10:1-3)

KEY VERSE:

"If you keep silent at this time, relief and deliverance will come to the Jewish people from another place. . . . Who knows, perhaps you have come to your royal position for such a time as this." —Esther 4:14

RESTORATION THEMES

R	Rest and Reflection	*For the next note, see Job 42:6.*
E	Eternal Perspective	*God's Timing—Esther 4:13-14*
S	Support	*For the next note, see Job 6:24.*
T	Thanksgiving and Contentment	*For the next note, see Psalm 1:1-3.*
O	Other-centeredness	*For the next note, see Job 29:12-13.*
R	Relationships	*For the next note, see Psalm 19:14.*
E	Exercise of Faith	*For the next note, see Job 23:12.*

VASHTI ANGERS THE KING

1 These events took place during the days of Ahasuerus, who ruled 127 provinces from India to Cush. 2 In those days King Ahasuerus reigned from his royal throne in the fortress at Susa. 3 He held a feast in the third year of his reign for all his officials and staff, the army of Persia and Media, the nobles, and the officials from the provinces. 4 He displayed the glorious wealth of his kingdom and the magnificent splendor of his greatness for a total of 180 days.

5 At the end of this time, the king held a week-long banquet in the garden courtyard of the royal palace for all the people, from the greatest to the least, who were present in the fortress of Susa. 6 White and violet linen hangings were fastened with fine white and purple linen cords to silver rods on marble[A] columns. Gold and silver couches were arranged on a mosaic pavement of red feldspar,[B] marble, mother-of-pearl, and precious stones.

7 Drinks were served in an array of gold goblets, each with a different design. Royal wine flowed freely, according to the king's bounty. 8 The drinking was according to royal decree: "There are no restrictions." The king had ordered every wine steward in his household to serve whatever each person wanted. 9 Queen Vashti also gave a feast for the women of King Ahasuerus's palace.

10 On the seventh day, when the king was feeling good from the wine, Ahasuerus commanded Mehuman, Biztha, Harbona, Bigtha, Abagtha, Zethar, and Carkas — the seven eunuchs who personally served him — 11 to bring Queen Vashti before him with her royal crown. He wanted to show off her beauty to the people and the officials, because she was very beautiful. 12 But Queen Vashti refused to come at the king's command that was delivered by his eunuchs. The king became furious and his anger burned within him.

THE KING'S DECREE

13 The king consulted the wise men who understood the times,[C] for it was his normal procedure to confer with experts in law and justice. 14 The most trusted ones[D] were Carshena, Shethar, Admatha, Tarshish, Meres, Marsena, and Memucan. They were the seven officials of Persia and Media who had personal access to the king and occupied the highest positions in the kingdom. 15 The king asked, "According to the law, what should be done with Queen Vashti, since she refused to obey King Ahasuerus's command that was delivered by the eunuchs?"

16 Memucan said in the presence of the king and his officials, "Queen Vashti has wronged not only the king, but all the officials and the peoples who are in every one of King Ahasuerus's provinces. 17 For the queen's action will become public knowledge to all the women and cause them to despise their husbands and say, 'King Ahasuerus ordered Queen Vashti brought before him, but she did not come.' 18 Before this day is over, the noble women of Persia and Media who hear about the queen's act will say the same thing to all the king's officials, resulting in more contempt and fury.

19 "If it meets the king's approval, he should personally issue a royal decree. Let it be recorded in the laws of Persia and Media, so that it cannot be revoked: Vashti is not to enter King Ahasuerus's presence, and her royal position is to be given to another woman who is more worthy than she. 20 The decree the king issues will be heard throughout his vast kingdom, so all women will honor their husbands, from the greatest to the least."

21 The king and his counselors approved the proposal, and he followed Memucan's advice. 22 He sent letters to all the royal provinces, to each province in its own script and to each ethnic group in its own language, that every man should be master of his own house and speak in the language of his own people.

THE SEARCH FOR A NEW QUEEN

2 Some time later, when King Ahasuerus's rage had cooled down, he remembered Vashti, what she had done, and what was decided against her. 2 The king's personal attendants suggested, "Let a search be made for beautiful young virgins for the king. 3 Let the king appoint commissioners in each province of his kingdom, so that they may gather all the beautiful young virgins to the harem at the fortress of Susa. Put them under the supervision of Hegai, the king's eunuch, keeper of the women, and give them the required beauty treatments. 4 Then the young woman who pleases the king will become queen instead of Vashti." This suggestion pleased the king, and he did accordingly.

5 In the fortress of Susa, there was a Jewish

[A] **1:6** Or *alabaster* [B] **1:6** Or *of porphyry* [C] **1:13** Or *understood propitious times* [D] **1:14** Lit *Those near him*

man named Mordecai son of Jair, son of Shimei,
son of Kish, a Benjaminite. 6 He had been taken
into exile from Jerusalem with the other captives when King Nebuchadnezzar of Babylon
took King Jeconiah of Judah into exile. 7 Mordecai was the legal guardian of his cousin[A]
Hadassah (that is, Esther), because she had no
father or mother. The young woman had a beautiful figure and was extremely good-looking.
When her father and mother died, Mordecai
had adopted her as his own daughter.

8 When the king's command and edict
became public knowledge and when many
young women were gathered at the fortress
of Susa under Hegai's supervision, Esther
was taken to the palace, into the supervision of Hegai, keeper of the women. 9 The
young woman pleased him and gained his
favor so that he accelerated the process of
the beauty treatments and the special diet
that she received. He assigned seven hand-
picked female servants to her from the palace
and transferred her and her servants to the
harem's best quarters.

10 Esther did not reveal her ethnicity or her
family background, because Mordecai had
ordered her not to make them known. 11 Every day Mordecai took a walk in front of the
harem's courtyard to learn how Esther was
doing and to see what was happening to her.

12 During the year before each young woman's turn to go to King Ahasuerus, the harem
regulation required her to receive beauty treatments with oil of myrrh for six months and
then with perfumes and cosmetics for another
six months. 13 When the young woman would
go to the king, she was given whatever she
requested to take with her from the harem to
the palace. 14 She would go in the evening, and
in the morning she would return to a second
harem under the supervision of the king's
eunuch Shaashgaz, keeper of the concubines.
She never went to the king again, unless he
desired her and summoned her by name.

ESTHER BECOMES QUEEN

15 Esther was the daughter of Abihail, the uncle of Mordecai who had adopted her as his
own daughter. When her turn came to go to
the king, she did not ask for anything except
what Hegai, the king's eunuch, keeper of the
women, suggested. Esther gained favor in the
eyes of everyone who saw her.
16 She was taken to King Ahasuerus in the
palace in the tenth month, the month Tebeth,
in the seventh year of his reign. 17 The king
loved Esther more than all the other women.
She won more favor and approval from him
than did any of the other virgins. He placed
the royal crown on her head and made her
queen in place of Vashti. 18 The king held a
great banquet for all his officials and staff. It
was Esther's banquet. He freed his provinces
from tax payments and gave gifts worthy of
the king's bounty.

MORDECAI SAVES THE KING

19 When the virgins were gathered a second
time, Mordecai was sitting at the King's Gate.
20 (Esther had not revealed her family background or her ethnicity, as Mordecai had directed. She obeyed Mordecai's orders, as she
always had while he raised her.)

21 During those days while Mordecai was
sitting at the King's Gate, Bigthan and Teresh,
two of the king's eunuchs who guarded the
entrance, became infuriated and planned to
assassinate[B] King Ahasuerus. 22 When Mordecai learned of the plot, he reported it to Queen
Esther, and she told the king on Mordecai's
behalf. 23 When the report was investigated
and verified, both men were hanged on the
gallows. This event was recorded in the Historical Record in the king's presence.

HAMAN'S PLAN TO KILL THE JEWS

3 After all this took place, King Ahasuerus
honored Haman, son of Hammedatha the
Agagite. He promoted him in rank and gave him
a higher position than all the other officials.
2 The entire royal staff at the King's Gate bowed
down and paid homage to Haman, because
the king had commanded this to be done for
him. But Mordecai would not bow down or
pay homage. 3 The members of the royal staff
at the King's Gate asked Mordecai, "Why are
you disobeying the king's command?" 4 When
they had warned him day after day and he still
would not listen to them, they told Haman in
order to see if Mordecai's actions would be
tolerated, since he had told them he was a Jew.

5 When Haman saw that Mordecai was not
bowing down or paying him homage, he was
filled with rage. 6 And when he learned of Mordecai's ethnic identity, it seemed repugnant to
Haman to do away with[C] Mordecai alone. He

[A] **2:7** Lit *uncle's daughter* [B] **2:21** Lit *and they sought to stretch out a hand against* [C] **3:6** Lit *to stretch out a hand against*

planned to destroy all of Mordecai's people, the Jews, throughout Ahasuerus's kingdom.

7 In the first month, the month of Nisan, in King Ahasuerus's twelfth year, the Pur — that is, the lot — was cast before Haman for each day in each month, and it fell on the twelfth month, the month Adar. 8 Then Haman informed King Ahasuerus, "There is one ethnic group, scattered throughout the peoples in every province of your kingdom, keeping themselves separate. Their laws are different from everyone else's and they do not obey the king's laws. It is not in the king's best interest to tolerate them. 9 If the king approves, let an order be drawn up authorizing their destruction, and I will pay 375 tons of silver to[A] the officials for deposit in the royal treasury."

10 The king removed his signet ring from his finger and gave it to Haman son of Hammedatha the Agagite, the enemy of the Jewish people. 11 Then the king told Haman, "The money and people are given to you to do with as you see fit."

12 The royal scribes were summoned on the thirteenth day of the first month, and the order was written exactly as Haman commanded. It was intended for the royal satraps, the governors of each of the provinces, and the officials of each ethnic group and written for each province in its own script and to each ethnic group in its own language. It was written in the name of King Ahasuerus and sealed with the royal signet ring. 13 Letters were sent by couriers to each of the royal provinces telling the officials to destroy, kill, and annihilate all the Jewish people — young and old, women and children — and plunder their possessions on a single day, the thirteenth day of Adar, the twelfth month.[B]

14 A copy of the text, issued as law throughout every province, was distributed to all the peoples so that they might get ready for that day. 15 The couriers left, spurred on by royal command, and the law was issued in the fortress of Susa. The king and Haman sat down to drink, while the city of Susa was in confusion.

MORDECAI APPEALS TO ESTHER

4 When Mordecai learned all that had occurred, he tore his clothes, put on sackcloth and ashes, went into the middle of the city, and cried loudly and bitterly. 2 He went only as far as the King's Gate, since the law prohibited anyone wearing sackcloth from entering the King's Gate. 3 There was great mourning among the Jewish people in every province where the king's command and edict came. They fasted, wept, and lamented, and many lay in sackcloth and ashes.

4 Esther's female servants and her eunuchs came and reported the news to her, and the queen was overcome with fear. She sent clothes for Mordecai to wear so that he would take off his sackcloth, but he did not accept them. 5 Esther summoned Hathach, one of the king's eunuchs who attended her, and dispatched him to Mordecai to learn what he was doing and why.[C] 6 So Hathach went out to Mordecai in the city square in front of the King's Gate. 7 Mordecai told him everything that had happened as well as the exact amount of money Haman had promised to pay the royal treasury for the slaughter of the Jews.

8 Mordecai also gave him a copy of the written decree issued in Susa ordering their destruction, so that Hathach might show it to Esther, explain it to her, and command her to approach the king, implore his favor, and plead with him personally for her people. 9 Hathach came and repeated Mordecai's response to Esther.

10 Esther spoke to Hathach and commanded him to tell Mordecai, 11 "All the royal officials and the people of the royal provinces know that one law applies to every man or woman who approaches the king in the inner courtyard and who has not been summoned — the death penalty — unless the king extends the gold scepter, allowing that person to live. I have not been summoned to appear before the king for the last[D] thirty days." 12 Esther's response was reported to Mordecai.

13 Mordecai told the messenger to reply to Esther, "Don't think that you will escape the fate of all the Jews because you are in the king's palace. 14 If you keep silent at this time, relief and deliverance will come to the Jewish people from another place, but you and your father's family will be destroyed. Who knows, perhaps you have come to your royal position for such a time as this."

15 Esther sent this reply to Mordecai: 16 "Go and assemble all the Jews who can be found in Susa and fast for me. Don't eat or drink for three days, night or day. I and my female

[A] **3:9** Lit *will weigh 10,000 silver talents on the hands of* [B] **3:13** LXX adds the text of Ahasuerus's letter here. [C] **4:5** Lit *what is this and why is this* [D] **4:11** Lit *king these*

servants will also fast in the same way. After
that, I will go to the king even if it is against
the law. If I perish, I perish." 17 So Mordecai
went and did everything Esther had commanded him.

ESTHER APPROACHES THE KING

5 On the third day, Esther dressed in her royal
clothing and stood in the inner courtyard
of the palace facing it. The king was sitting
on his royal throne in the royal courtroom,[A]
facing its entrance. 2 As soon as the king saw
Queen Esther standing in the courtyard, she
gained favor in his eyes. The king extended
the gold scepter in his hand toward Esther,
and she approached and touched the tip of
the scepter.
3 "What is it, Queen Esther?" the king asked
her. "Whatever you want, even to half the kingdom, will be given to you."
4 "If it pleases the king," Esther replied, "may
the king and Haman come today to the banquet I have prepared for them."
5 The king said, "Hurry, and get Haman so
we can do as Esther has requested." So the
king and Haman went to the banquet Esther
had prepared.
6 While drinking the[B] wine, the king asked
Esther, "Whatever you ask will be given to you.
Whatever you want, even to half the kingdom,
will be done."
7 Esther answered, "This is my petition and
my request: 8 If I have found favor in the eyes
of the king, and if it pleases the king to grant
my petition and perform my request, may the
king and Haman come to the banquet I will
prepare for them. Tomorrow I will do what
the king has asked."
9 That day Haman left full of joy and in good
spirits.[C] But when Haman saw Mordecai at
the King's Gate, and Mordecai didn't rise or
tremble in fear at his presence, Haman was
filled with rage toward Mordecai. 10 Yet Haman controlled himself and went home. He
sent for his friends and his wife Zeresh to join
him. 11 Then Haman described for them his
glorious wealth and his many sons. He told
them all how the king had honored him and
promoted him in rank over the other officials
and the royal staff. 12 "What's more," Haman
added, "Queen Esther invited no one but me
to join the king at the banquet she had prepared. I am invited again tomorrow to join
her with the king. 13 Still, none of this satisfies

Eternal Perspective | *God's Timing*

BEHIND THE SCENES

"Mordecai told the messenger to reply to Esther, 'Don't think that you will escape the fate of all the Jews because you are in the king's palace. If you keep silent at this time, relief and deliverance will come to the Jewish people from another place, but you and your father's family will be destroyed. Who knows, perhaps you have come to your royal position for such a time as this.'" Esther 4:13-14

The fascinating story of Esther tells of a Jewish girl who inexplicably became the queen of Persia. Later, when a genocidal plot emerged against the Jews who were in exile, Esther's relative Mordecai urged her to use her influence to save the day.

Without speaking directly about God, Mordecai highlighted the great truth that God is sovereign. Since he is the great orchestrator of life, nothing is random or accidental. Events really do happen for a reason.

What in your life seems unfair or hopeless? Where are you unable to see any way forward? Remember the story of Esther. God is always at work behind the scenes. Be encouraged. And be on the lookout for what he is arranging right now.

For the next note on *Eternal Perspective*, see Job 19:25-27.

[A] **5:1** Lit *house* [B] **5:6** Lit *During the banquet of* [C] **5:9** Lit *left rejoicing and good of heart*

me since I see Mordecai the Jew sitting at the King's Gate all the time."

14 His wife Zeresh and all his friends told him, "Have them build a gallows seventy-five feet[A] tall. Ask the king in the morning to hang Mordecai on it. Then go to the banquet with the king and enjoy yourself." The advice pleased Haman, so he had the gallows constructed.

MORDECAI HONORED BY THE KING

6 That night sleep escaped the king, so he ordered the book recording daily events to be brought and read to the king. 2 They found the written report of how Mordecai had informed on Bigthana and Teresh, two of the king's eunuchs who guarded the entrance, when they planned to assassinate King Ahasuerus. 3 The king inquired, "What honor and special recognition have been given to Mordecai for this act?"

The king's personal attendants replied, "Nothing has been done for him."

4 The king asked, "Who is in the court?" Now Haman was just entering the outer court of the palace to ask the king to hang Mordecai on the gallows he had prepared for him.

5 The king's attendants answered him, "Haman is there, standing in the court."

"Have him enter," the king ordered. 6 Haman entered, and the king asked him, "What should be done for the man the king wants to honor?"

Haman thought to himself, "Who is it the king would want to honor more than me?" 7 Haman told the king, "For the man the king wants to honor: 8 Have them bring a royal garment that the king himself has worn and a horse the king himself has ridden, which has a royal crown on its head. 9 Put the garment and the horse under the charge of one of the king's most noble officials. Have them clothe the man the king wants to honor, parade him on the horse through the city square, and proclaim before him, 'This is what is done for the man the king wants to honor.'"

10 The king told Haman, "Hurry, and do just as you proposed. Take a garment and a horse for Mordecai the Jew, who is sitting at the King's Gate. Do not leave out anything you have suggested."

11 So Haman took the garment and the horse. He clothed Mordecai and paraded him through the city square, crying out before him, "This is what is done for the man the king wants to honor."

12 Then Mordecai returned to the King's Gate, but Haman hurried off for home, mournful and with his head covered. 13 Haman told his wife Zeresh and all his friends everything that had happened. His advisers and his wife Zeresh said to him, "Since Mordecai is Jewish, and you have begun to fall before him, you won't overcome him, because your downfall is certain." 14 While they were still speaking with him, the king's eunuchs arrived and rushed Haman to the banquet Esther had prepared.

HAMAN IS EXECUTED

7 The king and Haman came to feast[B] with Esther the queen. 2 Once again, on the second day while drinking wine, the king asked Esther, "Queen Esther, whatever you ask will be given to you. Whatever you seek, even to half the kingdom, will be done."

3 Queen Esther answered, "If I have found favor in your eyes, Your Majesty, and if the king is pleased, spare my life; this is my request. And spare my people; this is my desire. 4 For my people and I have been sold to destruction, death, and extermination. If we had merely been sold as male and female slaves, I would have kept silent. Indeed, the trouble wouldn't be worth burdening the king."

5 King Ahasuerus spoke up and asked Queen Esther, "Who is this, and where is the one who would devise such a scheme?"[C]

6 Esther answered, "The adversary and enemy is this evil Haman."

Haman stood terrified before the king and queen. 7 The king arose in anger and went from where they were drinking wine to the palace garden.[D] Haman remained to beg Queen Esther for his life because he realized the king was planning something terrible for him. 8 Just as the king returned from the palace garden to the banquet hall,[E] Haman was falling on the couch where Esther was reclining. The king exclaimed, "Would he actually violate the queen while I am in the house?" As soon as the statement left the king's mouth, they covered Haman's face.

9 Harbona, one of the king's eunuchs, said: "There is a gallows seventy-five feet[A] tall at Haman's house that he made for Mordecai, who gave the report that saved[F] the king."

[A] **5:14; 7:9** Lit *50 cubits* [B] **7:1** Lit *drink* [C] **7:5** Lit *who would fill his heart to do this* [D] **7:7** Lit *the garden of the house*, also in v. 8 [E] **7:8** Or *the house of wine* [F] **7:9** Lit *who spoke good for*

The king said, "Hang him on it."
10 They hanged Haman on the gallows he
had prepared for Mordecai. Then the king's
anger subsided.

ESTHER INTERVENES FOR THE JEWS

8 That same day King Ahasuerus awarded
Queen Esther the estate of Haman, the enemy of the Jews. Mordecai entered the king's
presence because Esther had revealed her
relationship to Mordecai. 2 The king removed
his signet ring he had recovered from Haman
and gave it to Mordecai, and Esther put him
in charge of Haman's estate.
3 Then Esther addressed the king again. She
fell at his feet, wept, and begged him to revoke
the evil of Haman the Agagite and his plot
he had devised against the Jews. 4 The king
extended the gold scepter toward Esther, so
she got up and stood before the king.
5 She said, "If it pleases the king and I have
found favor before him, if the matter seems
right to the king and I am pleasing in his eyes,
let a royal edict be written. Let it revoke the
documents the scheming Haman son of Hammedatha the Agagite wrote to destroy the Jews
who are in all the king's provinces. 6 For how
could I bear to see the disaster that would
come on my people? How could I bear to see
the destruction of my relatives?"
7 King Ahasuerus said to Esther the queen
and to Mordecai the Jew, "Look, I have given
Haman's estate to Esther, and he was hanged
on the gallows because he attacked[A] the Jews.
8 Write in the king's name whatever pleases
you concerning the Jews, and seal it with the
royal signet ring. A document written in the
king's name and sealed with the royal signet
ring cannot be revoked."
9 On the twenty-third day of the third month
— that is, the month Sivan — the royal scribes
were summoned. Everything was written exactly as Mordecai commanded for the Jews,
to the satraps, the governors, and the officials of the 127 provinces from India to Cush.
The edict was written for each province in its
own script, for each ethnic group in its own
language, and to the Jews in their own script
and language.
10 Mordecai wrote in King Ahasuerus's name
and sealed the edicts with the royal signet ring.
He sent the documents by mounted couriers,
who rode fast horses bred in the royal stables.
11 The king's edict gave the Jews in each and
every city the right to assemble and defend
themselves, to destroy, kill, and annihilate
every ethnic and provincial army hostile to
them, including women and children, and to
take their possessions as spoils of war. 12 This
would take place on a single day throughout all the provinces of King Ahasuerus, on
the thirteenth day of the twelfth month, the
month Adar.
13 A copy of the text, issued as law throughout every province, was distributed to all the
peoples so the Jews could be ready to avenge
themselves against their enemies on that day.
14 The couriers rode out in haste on their royal horses at the king's urgent command. The
law was also issued in the fortress of Susa.
15 Mordecai went from the king's presence
clothed in royal purple and white, with a great
gold crown and a purple robe of fine linen. The
city of Susa shouted and rejoiced, 16 and the
Jews celebrated[B] with gladness, joy, and honor.
17 In every province and every city, wherever the king's command and his law reached,
joy and rejoicing took place among the Jews.
There was a celebration and a holiday.[C] And
many of the ethnic groups of the land pro-
fessed themselves to be Jews because fear of
the Jews had overcome them.

VICTORIES OF THE JEWS

9 The king's command and law went into
effect on the thirteenth day of the twelfth
month, the month Adar. On the day when the
Jews' enemies had hoped to overpower them,
just the opposite happened. The Jews overpowered those who hated them. 2 In each of
King Ahasuerus's provinces the Jews assembled in their cities to attack those who intended to harm them.[D] Not a single person
could withstand them; fear of them fell on
every nationality.
3 All the officials of the provinces, the satraps, the governors, and the royal civil administrators[E] aided the Jews because they
feared Mordecai. 4 For Mordecai exercised
great power in the palace, and his fame spread
throughout the provinces as he became more
and more powerful.
5 The Jews put all their enemies to the sword,
killing and destroying them. They did what
they pleased to those who hated them. 6 In the
fortress of Susa the Jews killed and destroyed

[A] 8:7 Lit *stretched out his hand against* [B] 8:16 Lit *had light* [C] 8:17 Lit *good day* [D] 9:2 Lit *cities to send out a hand against the seekers of their evil* [E] 9:3 Lit *and those who do the king's work*; Est 3:9

five hundred men, 7 including Parshandatha,
Dalphon, Aspatha, 8 Poratha, Adalia, Arida-
tha, 9 Parmashta, Arisai, Aridai, and Vaizatha.
10 They killed these ten sons of Haman son of
Hammedatha, the enemy of the Jews. However,
they did not seize[A] any plunder.

11 On that day the number of people killed in
the fortress of Susa was reported to the king.
12 The king said to Queen Esther, "In the fortress
of Susa the Jews have killed and destroyed five
hundred men, including Haman's ten sons.
What have they done in the rest of the royal
provinces? Whatever you ask will be given
to you. Whatever you seek will also be done."

13 Esther answered, "If it pleases the king,
may the Jews who are in Susa also have tomorrow to carry out today's law, and may the
bodies of Haman's ten sons be hung on the
gallows." 14 The king gave the orders for this
to be done, so a law was announced in Susa,
and they hung the bodies of Haman's ten sons.
15 The Jews in Susa assembled again on the
fourteenth day of the month of Adar and killed
three hundred men in Susa, but they did not
seize any plunder.

16 The rest of the Jews in the royal provinces
assembled, defended themselves, and gained
relief from their enemies. They killed seventy-five thousand[B] of those who hated them, but
they did not seize any plunder. 17 They fought
on the thirteenth day of the month of Adar
and rested on the fourteenth, and it became
a day of feasting and rejoicing.

18 But the Jews in Susa had assembled on
the thirteenth and the fourteenth days of the
month. They rested on the fifteenth day of the
month, and it became a day of feasting and
rejoicing. 19 This explains why the rural Jews
who live in villages observe the fourteenth
day of the month of Adar as a time of rejoicing
and feasting. It is a holiday when they send
gifts to one another.

20 Mordecai recorded these events and sent
letters to all the Jews in all of King Ahasuerus's
provinces, both near and far. 21 He ordered
them to celebrate the fourteenth and fifteenth
days of the month of Adar every year 22 because during those days the Jews gained relief
from their enemies. That was the month when
their sorrow was turned into rejoicing and
their mourning into a holiday. They were to
be days of feasting, rejoicing, and of sending
gifts to one another and to the poor.

[Mordecai] ordered them to celebrate. . . . That was the month when their sorrow was turned into rejoicing and their mourning into a holiday. They were to be days of feasting, rejoicing, and of sending gifts to one another and to the poor.

—Esther 9:21-22

23 So the Jews agreed to continue the practice they had begun, as Mordecai had written
them to do. 24 For Haman son of Hammedatha
the Agagite, the enemy of all the Jews, had
plotted against the Jews to destroy them. He
cast the Pur — that is, the lot — to crush and
destroy them. 25 But when the matter was
brought before the king, he commanded
by letter that the evil plan Haman had devised against the Jews return on his own
head and that he should be hanged with
his sons on the gallows. 26 For this reason
these days are called Purim, from the word
Pur. Because of all the instructions in this
letter as well as what they had witnessed
and what had happened to them, 27 the Jews
bound themselves, their descendants, and
all who joined with them to a commitment
that they would not fail to celebrate these
two days each and every year according to
the written instructions and according to
the time appointed. 28 These days are remembered and celebrated by every generation,
family, province, and city, so that these days
of Purim will not lose their significance in
Jewish life[C] and their memory will not fade
from their descendants.

29 Queen Esther, daughter of Abihail, along
with Mordecai the Jew, wrote this second letter
with full authority to confirm the letter about
Purim. 30 He sent letters with assurances of
peace and security[D] to all the Jews who were
in the 127 provinces of the kingdom of Ahasuerus, 31 in order to confirm these days of Purim at their proper time just as Mordecai the
Jew and Esther the queen had established them

[A] **9:10** Lit *not put their hands on*, also in vv. 15,16 [B] **9:16** Some LXX mss read *10,107*; other LXX mss read *15,000* [C] **9:28** LXX reads *will be celebrated into all times* [D] **9:30** Or *of peace and faithfulness*

and just as they had committed themselves
and their descendants to the practices of fasting and lamentation. 32 So Esther's command
confirmed these customs of Purim, which
were then written into the record.

MORDECAI'S FAME

10 King Ahasuerus imposed a tax throughout the land even to the farthest
shores.[A] 2 All of his powerful and magnificent
accomplishments and the detailed account of
Mordecai's great rank with which the king had
honored him, have they not been written in
the Book of the Historical Events of the Kings
of Media and Persia? 3 Mordecai the Jew was
second only to King Ahasuerus. He was famous among the Jews and highly esteemed by
many of his relatives. He continued to pursue
prosperity for his people and to speak for the
well-being of all his descendants.

[A] **10:1** Or *imposed forced labor on the land and the coasts of the sea*

Job—The universal human response to suffering is to look for reasons—why we are suffering, how a good God could allow such terrible events, and why God does not fix our situation on our timetable. The book of Job shows that we can ask God anything. God welcomes our honest struggles. He patiently dialogues with us even when we are misguided in our arguments.

At the end of all our questioning, however, we come to this bedrock truth: God is trustworthy. Even when we lose everything, as Job did, God is still in control, and everything he does is perfect. So even when we don't understand why God has chosen to allow evil to invade our lives, we can rest in God's unchanging character. He is righteous, faithful, and just. And that is enough for all our questions and enough for us to rest in.

The book of Job teaches that whatever our struggles, we can bow before God and trust in his sovereign goodness. If you are struggling against the hard things in life, rest in God's loving care. Let him restore your soul with the assurance of his sovereign power over all the forces of evil in the world.

JOB

AUTHOR: The author of Job is unknown. We can tell he was a learned man who knew about matters of science and anthropology as well as both spiritual and philosophical wisdom. The use of God's covenant name Yahweh suggests he was an Israelite. We can also see that he was a master storyteller, for the literary devices used in Job are artistically arranged. The story has a protagonist (Job), an antagonist (Satan), and literary foils who each represent a different type of traditional wisdom (Job's friends). Motifs of testing and courtroom dialogue are masterfully used to communicate the writer's message.

DATE WRITTEN: The story of Job takes place during the time of the patriarchs, but the date of writing is unknown. Traditionally it is dated to the time of Moses. Job may be the oldest book in the Bible.

ORIGINAL AUDIENCE: The Israelites

SETTING: The events depicted in Job occur during the time of the patriarchs, when wealth was measured in cattle and servants and the head of the household served as priest for the family. Job is the first of the Wisdom books, and as such it is not directed to a specific audience, but rather to Jewish people during the Old Testament era.

PURPOSE FOR WRITING: Job addresses the big questions of life: Why do good people suffer? Can we trust God even when we don't understand what is happening? Is God still in control, even when life seems to be out of control? Is it all right to question God when we are in pain? Job teaches how to rightly view suffering and gives examples of good and bad responses to the tragedies of life. Ultimately Job teaches that suffering is a part of life, but it is always under the sovereign control of a loving God. Our pain has a purpose; therefore, the right response to suffering is to revere God and submit to his power.

OUTLINE:

1. Prologue (1:1–2:13)

   Job's life before the test (1:1-5)

   Satan's accusation and test (1:6-12)

   Job's response to the first test (1:13-22)

   Satan's second accusation and test (2:1-7)

   Job's response to the second test (2:8-10)

   Job's comforters (2:11-13)

2. Dialogues on Suffering (3:1–37:24)

   Job gives his lament (3:1-26)

   Job and his friends debate his situation (4:1–27:23)

   Job declares innocence (28:1–31:40)

   Elihu responds (32:1–37:24)

3. Resolution: God's Greatness (38:1–42:17)

   God speaks of his power (38:1–40:2)

   Job responds in humility (40:3-5)

   God speaks of Job's impotence (40:6–41:34)

   Job repents (42:1-6)

   God restores Job's fortune (42:7-17)

KEY VERSE:

"Yet he knows the way I have taken; when he has tested me, I will emerge as pure gold."
—Job 23:10

RESTORATION THEMES

R	Rest and Reflection	*Being Willing to Change—42:6*
E	Eternal Perspective	*Death's Defeat/Resurrection—19:25-27* *God's Power—42:2*
S	Support	*Openness with God—6:24*
T	Thanksgiving and Contentment	*For the next note, see Psalm 1:1-3.*
O	Other-centeredness	*Helping Widows and Orphans—Job 29:12-13*
R	Relationships	*For the next note, see Psalm 19:14.*
E	Exercise of Faith	*Memorizing Scripture—Job 23:12* *Guarding the Heart—31:7-8*

JOB AND HIS FAMILY

1 There was a man in the country of Uz named
Job. He was a man of complete integrity, who
feared God and turned away from evil. 2 He had
seven sons and three daughters. 3 His estate
included seven thousand sheep and goats,
three thousand camels, five hundred yoke
of oxen, five hundred female donkeys, and
a very large number of servants. Job was the
greatest man among all the people of the east.
4 His sons used to take turns having banquets at their homes. They would send an invitation to their three sisters to eat and drink
with them. 5 Whenever a round of banqueting
was over, Job would send for his children and
purify them, rising early in the morning to
offer burnt offerings for[A] all of them. For Job
thought, "Perhaps my children have sinned,
having cursed God in their hearts." This was
Job's regular practice.

SATAN'S FIRST TEST OF JOB

6 One day the sons of God came to present themselves before the LORD, and Satan[B] also came
with them. 7 The LORD asked Satan, "Where
have you come from?"
"From roaming through the earth," Satan
answered him, "and walking around on it."
8 Then the LORD said to Satan, "Have you
considered my servant Job? No one else on
earth is like him, a man of perfect integrity,
who fears God and turns away from evil."
9 Satan answered the LORD, "Does Job fear
God for nothing? 10 Haven't you placed a hedge
around him, his household, and everything
he owns? You have blessed the work of his
hands, and his possessions have increased
in the land. 11 But stretch out your hand and
strike everything he owns, and he will surely
curse you to your face."
12 "Very well," the LORD told Satan, "everything he owns is in your power. However, do
not lay a hand on Job himself." So Satan left
the LORD's presence.
13 One day when Job's sons and daughters
were eating and drinking wine in their oldest
brother's house, 14 a messenger came to Job
and reported: "While the oxen were plowing
and the donkeys grazing nearby, 15 the Sabeans swooped down and took them away. They
struck down the servants with the sword, and
I alone have escaped to tell you!"
16 He was still speaking when another
messenger came and reported: "God's fire
fell from heaven. It burned the sheep and the
servants and devoured them, and I alone have
escaped to tell you!"
17 That messenger was still speaking when
yet another came and reported: "The Chaldeans formed three bands, made a raid on
the camels, and took them away. They struck
down the servants with the sword, and I alone
have escaped to tell you!"
18 He was still speaking when another messenger came and reported: "Your sons and
daughters were eating and drinking wine
in their oldest brother's house. 19 Suddenly
a powerful wind swept in from the desert
and struck the four corners of the house. It
collapsed on the young people so that they
died, and I alone have escaped to tell you!"
20 Then Job stood up, tore his robe, and
shaved his head. He fell to the ground and
worshiped, 21 saying:

Naked I came from my mother's womb,
and naked I will leave this life.[C]
The LORD gives, and the LORD
takes away.
Blessed be the name of the LORD.

22 Throughout all this Job did not sin or blame
God for anything.[D]

[Job] fell to the ground and worshiped, saying: "Naked I came from my mother's womb, and naked I will leave this life. The LORD gives, and the LORD takes away. Blessed be the name of the LORD." Throughout all this Job did not sin or blame God for anything.

—Job 1:20-22

SATAN'S SECOND TEST OF JOB

2 One day the sons of God came again to present themselves before the LORD, and Satan
also came with them to present himself before

[A] 1:5 Lit *for the number of* [B] 1:6 Or *the adversary* [C] 1:21 Lit *will return there*; Ps 139:13,15 [D] 1:22 Lit *or ascribe blame to God*

the LORD. 2 The LORD asked Satan, "Where have
you come from?"
"From roaming through the earth," Satan
answered him, "and walking around on it."
3 Then the LORD said to Satan, "Have you
considered my servant Job? No one else on
earth is like him, a man of perfect integrity,
who fears God and turns away from evil. He
still retains his integrity, even though you
incited me against him, to destroy him for
no good reason."
4 "Skin for skin!" Satan answered the LORD.
"A man will give up everything he owns in
exchange for his life. 5 But stretch out your
hand and strike his flesh and bones, and he
will surely curse you to your face."
6 "Very well," the LORD told Satan, "he is in your
power; only spare his life." 7 So Satan left the
LORD's presence and infected Job with terrible
boils from the soles of his feet to the top of his
head. 8 Then Job took a piece of broken pottery
to scrape himself while he sat among the ashes.
9 His wife said to him, "Are you still holding on to your integrity? Curse God and die!"
10 "You speak as a foolish woman speaks,"
he told her. "Should we accept only good from
God and not adversity?" Throughout all this
Job did not sin in what he said.[A]

JOB'S THREE FRIENDS

11 Now when Job's three friends — Eliphaz the
Temanite, Bildad the Shuhite, and Zophar the
Naamathite — heard about all this adversity
that had happened to him, each of them came
from his home. They met together to go and
sympathize with him and comfort him. 12 When
they looked from a distance, they could barely
recognize him. They wept aloud, and each man
tore his robe and threw dust into the air and
on his head. 13 Then they sat on the ground
with him seven days and nights, but no one
spoke a word to him because they saw that
his suffering was very intense.

JOB'S OPENING SPEECH

3 After this, Job began to speak and cursed
the day he was born. 2 He said:

3 May the day I was born perish,
and the night that said,
"A boy is conceived."
4 If only that day had turned to darkness!
May God above not care about it,
or light shine on it.
5 May darkness and gloom reclaim it,
and a cloud settle over it.
May what darkens the day terrify it.
6 If only darkness had taken
that night away!
May it not appear[B] among the days
of the year
or be listed in the calendar.[C]
7 Yes, may that night be barren;
may no joyful shout be heard in it.
8 Let those who curse days
condemn it,
those who are ready
to rouse Leviathan.
9 May its morning stars grow dark.
May it wait for daylight but have none;
may it not see the breaking[D] of dawn.
10 For that night did not shut
the doors of my mother's womb,
and hide sorrow from my eyes.

11 Why was I not stillborn;
why didn't I die as I came
from the womb?
12 Why did the knees receive me,
and why were there breasts for me
to nurse?
13 Now I would certainly be lying down
in peace;
I would be asleep.
Then I would be at rest
14 with the kings and counselors
of the earth,
who rebuilt ruined cities
for themselves,
15 or with princes who had gold,
who filled their houses with silver.
16 Or why was I not hidden
like a miscarried child,
like infants who never see daylight?
17 There the wicked cease
to make trouble,
and there the weary find rest.
18 The captives are completely at rest;
they do not hear a taskmaster's voice.
19 Both small and great are there,
and the slave is set free
from his master.

20 Why is light given to one burdened
with grief,
and life to those whose existence
is bitter,

[A] **2:10** Lit *sin with his lips* [B] **3:6** LXX, Syr, Tg, Vg; MT reads *rejoice* [C] **3:6** Lit *or enter the number of months* [D] **3:9** Lit *the eyelids*

Job | Restoration Profile

JOB; EZEKIEL 14:14,20; JAMES 5:11

When God included Job's story in his written revelation, he knew he was leaving himself open to various accusations from people like us: We would think him callous, unfaithful, arbitrary, and lacking compassion. Yet God authorized Job's experience and its record. And one reason for this is to help us understand restoration in the deepest possible way.

Job was a righteous man. Given his station in life when we meet him, we assume God had blessed him greatly. Job's life was rich in every way. We may even conclude (long before we hear Job's friends speak) that his good life was a reward for previous goodness and that loss or calamity could only be explained by some kind of sin on Job's part. We, like the friends, would be wrong.

Job's life became the collision point between earth and heaven, evil and good, human limitations and God's ways. On the plus side, Job endured (Jms 5:11); on the minus side, Job demonstrates the frustration of not knowing why we must endure. When we insist on knowing the reason for Job's suffering, we unwittingly put ourselves in Job's situation, without the personal suffering. We demand an explanation that God doesn't have to give. When Job gave up his right to know, his restoration began.

When questions are a form of resistance or rebellion, restoration is delayed. When questions are humble and recognize our limitations before Almighty God, restoration is underway. The depth of Job's repentance can be seen not so much in the replacement of what he lost but in his willingness to forgive those who misjudged his suffering.

21 who wait for death,
but it does not come,
and search for it more than
for hidden treasure,
22 who are filled with much joy
and are glad when they reach the grave?
23 Why is life given to a man whose path
is hidden,
whom God has hedged in?
24 I sigh when food is put before me,[A]
and my groans pour out like water.
25 For the thing I feared has overtaken me,
and what I dreaded has happened
to me.
26 I cannot relax or be calm;
I have no rest, for turmoil has come.

FIRST SERIES OF SPEECHES

ELIPHAZ SPEAKS

4 Then Eliphaz the Temanite replied:
2 Should anyone try to speak with you
when you are exhausted?
Yet who can keep from speaking?
3 Indeed, you have instructed many
and have strengthened weak hands.
4 Your words have steadied the one
who was stumbling
and braced the knees
that were buckling.
5 But now that this has happened to you,
you have become exhausted.
It strikes you, and you are dismayed.
6 Isn't your piety your confidence,
and the integrity of your life[B]
your hope?
7 Consider: Who has perished when he
was innocent?
Where have the honest[C]
been destroyed?
8 In my experience,
those who plow injustice
and those who sow trouble reap
the same.
9 They perish at a single blast from God
and come to an end by the breath
of his nostrils.
10 The lion may roar and the fierce
lion growl,
but the teeth of young lions are broken.
11 The strong lion dies if it catches
no prey,

[A] **3:24** Or *My sighing serves as my food* [B] **4:6** Lit *ways* [C] **4:7** Or *the upright,* or *those with integrity*

and the cubs of the lioness
are scattered.

12 A word was brought to me in secret;
my ears caught a whisper of it.
13 Among unsettling thoughts
from visions in the night,
when deep sleep comes over men,
14 fear and trembling came over me
and made all my bones shake.
15 I felt a draft[A] on my face,
and the hair on my body stood up.
16 A figure stood there,
but I could not recognize
its appearance;
a form loomed before my eyes.
I heard a whispering voice:
17 "Can a mortal be righteous before God?
Can a man be more pure
than his Maker?"
18 If God puts no trust in his servants
and he charges his angels
with foolishness,[B]
19 how much more those who dwell
in clay houses,
whose foundation is in the dust,
who are crushed like a moth!
20 They are smashed to pieces from dawn
to dusk;
they perish forever
while no one notices.
21 Are their tent cords not pulled up?
They die without wisdom.

5 Call out! Will anyone answer you?
Which of the holy ones will you
turn to?
2 For anger kills a fool,
and jealousy slays the gullible.
3 I have seen a fool taking root,
but I immediately pronounced a curse
on his home.
4 His children are far from safety.
They are crushed at the city gate,
with no one to rescue them.
5 The hungry consume his harvest,
even taking it out of the thorns.[C]
The thirsty[D] pant
for his children's wealth.
6 For distress does not grow
out of the soil,
and trouble does not sprout
from the ground.
7 But humans are born for trouble
as surely as sparks fly upward.

8 However, if I were you, I would appeal
to God
and would present my case to him.
9 He does great and unsearchable things,
wonders without number.
10 He gives rain to the earth
and sends water to the fields.
11 He sets the lowly on high,
and mourners are lifted to safety.
12 He frustrates the schemes of the crafty
so that they[E] achieve no success.
13 He traps the wise in their craftiness
so that the plans of the deceptive
are quickly brought to an end.
14 They encounter darkness by day,
and they grope at noon
as if it were night.
15 He saves the needy
from their sharp words[F]
and from the clutches of the powerful.
16 So the poor have hope,
and injustice shuts its mouth.
17 See how happy is the person whom
God corrects;
so do not reject the discipline
of the Almighty.
18 For he wounds but he also bandages;
he strikes, but his hands also heal.
19 He will rescue you from six calamities;
no harm will touch you in seven.
20 In famine he will redeem you from death,
and in battle, from the power
of the sword.
21 You will be safe from slander[G]
and not fear destruction
when it comes.
22 You will laugh at destruction
and hunger
and not fear the land's wild creatures.
23 For you will have a covenant
with the stones of the field,
and the wild animals will be at peace
with you.
24 You will know that your tent is secure,
and nothing will be missing
when you inspect your home.
25 You will also know that your offspring
will be many
and your descendants like the grass
of the earth.

[A] **4:15** Or *a spirit* [B] **4:18** Or *error*; Hb obscure [C] **5:5** Hb obscure [D] **5:5** Aq, Sym, Syr, Vg; MT reads *snares* [E] **5:12** Lit *their hands* [F] **5:15** Lit *from the sword of their mouth*; Ps 55:21; 59:7 [G] **5:21** Lit *be hidden from the whip of the tongue*

26 You will approach the grave
in full vigor,
as a stack of sheaves is gathered
in its season.

27 We have investigated this, and it is true!
Hear it and understand it for yourself.

JOB'S REPLY TO ELIPHAZ

6 Then Job answered:
2 If only my grief could be weighed
and my devastation placed with it
on the scales.
3 For then it would outweigh the sand
of the seas!
That is why my words are rash.
4 Surely the arrows of the Almighty
have pierced[A] me;
my spirit drinks their poison.
God's terrors are arrayed against me.
5 Does a wild donkey bray
over fresh grass
or an ox low over its fodder?
6 Is bland food eaten without salt?
Is there flavor in an egg white?[B]
7 I refuse to touch them;
they are like contaminated food.

8 If only my request would be granted
and God would provide what I hope for:
9 that he would decide to crush me,
to unleash his power and cut me off!
10 It would still bring me comfort,
and I would leap for joy
in unrelenting pain
that I have not denied[C] the words
of the Holy One.

11 What strength do I have, that I should
continue to hope?
What is my future, that I should
be patient?
12 Is my strength that of stone,
or my flesh made of bronze?
13 Since I cannot help myself,
the hope for success has been banished
from me.

14 A despairing man should receive
loyalty from his friends,[D]
even if he abandons the fear
of the Almighty.
15 My brothers are as treacherous
as a wadi,
as seasonal streams that overflow
16 and become darkened[E] because of ice,
and the snow melts into them.
17 The wadis evaporate in warm weather;
they disappear from their channels
in hot weather.

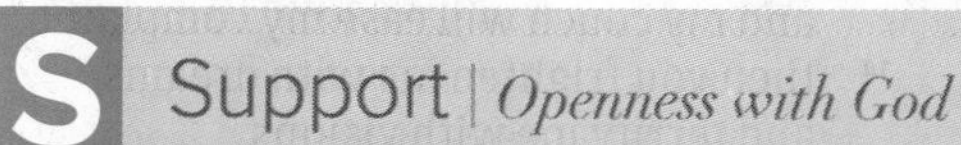

THE REASON FOR SUFFERING

"Teach me, and I will be silent. Help me understand what I did wrong." Job 6:24

Many of the difficulties we face in life are not our fault. In a fallen world with natural disasters and cruel people, the potential for being a victim is very high.

We are not always victims, however; sometimes we are agents. That is, we make choices—and not all of them are wise. This means that some of our troubles are self-caused.

So we need to do what Job did. As he mournfully assessed the smoldering ruins of his life, Job asked God to show him what part, if any, he had played in his trials. "Help me understand what I did wrong." This marks a humble and honest—not to mention brave—soul.

In the end, no definitive reason, certainly no sin on Job's part, was ever given for Job's suffering. His example helps us realize that we shouldn't ascribe all bad events in life to divine discipline. Help and healing begin only when we're willing to take an unflinching look in the mirror.

For the next note on *Support*, see Psalm 14:2.

[A] **6:4** Lit *Almighty are in* [B] **6:6** Hb obscure [C] **6:10** Lit *hidden* [D] **6:14** Lit *To the despairing his friend loyalty* [E] **6:16** Or *turbid*

18 Caravans turn away from their routes,
go up into the desert, and perish.
19 The caravans of Tema look
for these streams.
The traveling merchants of Sheba hope
for them.
20 They are ashamed because they
had been confident of finding water.
When they arrive there,
they are disappointed.
21 So this is what you have now become
to me.[A]
When you see something dreadful,
you are afraid.
22 Have I ever said: "Give me something"
or "Pay a bribe for me
from your wealth"
23 or "Deliver me from the enemy's hand"
or "Redeem me from the hand
of the ruthless"?

24 Teach me, and I will be silent.
Help me understand what I did wrong.
25 How painful honest words can be!
But what does your rebuke prove?
26 Do you think that you can disprove
my words
or that a despairing man's words are
mere wind?
27 No doubt you would cast lots
for a fatherless child
and negotiate a price to sell your friend.

28 But now, please look at me;
I will not lie to your face.
29 Reconsider; don't be unjust.
Reconsider; my righteousness is still
the issue.
30 Is there injustice on my tongue
or can my palate not taste disaster?

7 Isn't each person consigned
to forced labor on earth?
Are not his days like those
of a hired worker?
2 Like a slave he longs for shade;
like a hired worker he waits for his pay.
3 So I have been made to inherit months
of futility,
and troubled nights have been assigned
to me.
4 When I lie down I think,
"When will I get up?"
But the evening drags on endlessly,
and I toss and turn until dawn.
5 My flesh is clothed with maggots
and encrusted with dirt.[B]
My skin forms scabs[C] and then oozes.

6 My days pass more swiftly
than a weaver's shuttle;
they come to an end without hope.
7 Remember that my life is but a breath.
My eye will never again see
anything good.
8 The eye of anyone who looks on me
will no longer see me.
Your eyes will look for me, but I
will be gone.
9 As a cloud fades away and vanishes,
so the one who goes down to Sheol
will never rise again.
10 He will never return to his house;
his hometown will no longer
remember[D] him.

11 Therefore I will not restrain my mouth.
I will speak in the anguish of my spirit;
I will complain in the bitterness
of my soul.
12 Am I the sea[E] or a sea monster,
that you keep me under guard?
13 When I say, "My bed will comfort me,
and my couch will ease my complaint,"
14 then you frighten me with dreams,
and terrify me with visions,
15 so that I prefer strangling[F] —
death rather than life in this body.[G]
16 I give up! I will not live forever.
Leave me alone, for my days are
a breath.[H]

17 What is a mere human, that you think
so highly of him
and pay so much attention to him?
18 You inspect him every morning,
and put him to the test every moment.
19 Will you ever look away from me,
or leave me alone long enough
to swallow?[I]
20 If I have sinned, what have I done to you,
Watcher of humanity?
Why have you made me your target,
so that I have become a burden to you?[J]

[A] **6:21** Alt Hb tradition reads *So you have now become nothing* [B] **7:5** Or *and dirty scabs* [C] **7:5** Lit *skin hardens* [D] **7:10** Lit *know* [E] **7:12** Or *the sea god* [F] **7:15** Or *suffocation* [G] **7:15** Lit *than my bones* [H] **7:16** Or *are futile* [I] **7:19** Lit *swallow my saliva?* [J] **7:20** Alt Hb tradition, LXX; MT, Vg read *myself*

21 Why not forgive my sin
and pardon my iniquity?
For soon I will lie down in the grave.
You will eagerly seek me, but I
will be gone.

BILDAD SPEAKS

8 Then Bildad the Shuhite replied:
2 How long will you go on saying
these things?
Your words are a blast of wind.
3 Does God pervert justice?
Does the Almighty pervert what is right?
4 Since your children sinned against him,
he gave them over to their rebellion.
5 But if you earnestly seek God
and ask the Almighty for mercy,
6 if you are pure and upright,
then he will move even now
on your behalf
and restore the home where
your righteousness dwells.
7 Then, even if your beginnings
were modest,
your final days will be
full of prosperity.

8 For ask the previous generation,
and pay attention to what
their fathers discovered,
9 since we were born only yesterday
and know nothing.
Our days on earth are but a shadow.
10 Will they not teach you and tell you
and speak from their understanding?
11 Does papyrus grow where there is
no marsh?
Do reeds flourish without water?
12 While still uncut shoots,
they would dry up quicker than
any other plant.
13 Such is the destiny[A] of all
who forget God;
the hope of the godless will perish.
14 His source of confidence is fragile;[B]
what he trusts in is a spider's web.
15 He leans on his web, but it doesn't
stand firm.
He grabs it, but it does not hold up.
16 He is a well-watered plant
in the sunshine;
his shoots spread out over his garden.
17 His roots are intertwined around a pile
of rocks.
He looks for a home among the stones.
18 If he is uprooted[C] from his place,
it will deny knowing him, saying,
"I never saw you."
19 Surely this is the joy of his way of life;
yet others will sprout from the dust.
20 Look, God does not reject a person
of integrity,
and he will not support[D] evildoers.
21 He will yet fill your mouth
with laughter
and your lips with a shout of joy.
22 Your enemies will be clothed
with shame;
the tent of the wicked will no longer
exist.

JOB'S REPLY TO BILDAD

9 Then Job answered:
2 Yes, I know what you've said is true,
but how can a person be justified
before God?
3 If one wanted to take him to court,
he could not answer God[E] once
in a thousand times.
4 God is wise and all-powerful.
Who has opposed him
and come out unharmed?
5 He removes mountains
without their knowledge,
overturning them in his anger.
6 He shakes the earth from its place
so that its pillars tremble.
7 He commands the sun not to shine
and seals off the stars.
8 He alone stretches out the heavens
and treads on the waves of the sea.[F]
9 He makes the stars: the Bear,[G] Orion,
the Pleiades, and the constellations[H]
of the southern sky.
10 He does great and unsearchable things,
wonders without number.
11 If he passed by me, I wouldn't see him;
if he went by, I wouldn't recognize him.
12 If he snatches something,
who can stop[I] him?
Who can ask him, "What are you doing?"
13 God does not hold back his anger;
Rahab's assistants cringe in fear
beneath him!

[A] **8:13** Lit *Such are the ways* [B] **8:14** Or *cut off*; Hb obscure [C] **8:18** Or *destroyed* [D] **8:20** Lit *grasp the hand of* [E] **9:3** Or *court, God would not answer him* [F] **9:8** Or *and walks on the back of the sea god* [G] **9:9** Or *Aldebaran* [H] **9:9** Or *chambers* [I] **9:12** Or *dissuade*

14 How then can I answer him
or choose my arguments against him?
15 Even if I were in the right,
I could not answer.
I could only beg my Judge for mercy.
16 If I summoned him
and he answered me,
I do not believe he would
pay attention to what I said.
17 He batters me with a whirlwind
and multiplies my wounds
without cause.
18 He doesn't let me catch my breath
but fills me with bitter experiences.
19 If it is a matter of strength, look, he is
the powerful one!
If it is a matter of justice, who can
summon him?[A]
20 Even if I were in the right,
my own mouth would condemn me;
if I were blameless, my mouth would
declare me guilty.

21 Though I am blameless,
I no longer care about myself;
I renounce my life.
22 It is all the same. Therefore I say,
"He destroys both the blameless
and the wicked."
23 When catastrophe[B] brings sudden death,
he mocks the despair of the innocent.
24 The earth[C] is handed over
to the wicked;
he blindfolds[D] its judges.
If it isn't he, then who is it?

25 My days fly by faster than a runner;[E]
they flee without seeing any good.
26 They sweep by like boats made
of papyrus,
like an eagle swooping down
on its prey.
27 If I said, "I will forget my complaint,
change my expression, and smile,"
28 I would still live in terror of all
my pains.
I know you will not acquit me.
29 Since I will be found guilty,
why should I struggle in vain?
30 If I wash myself with snow,
and cleanse my hands with lye,
31 then you dip me in a pit of mud,
and my own clothes despise me!
32 For he is not a man like me, that I can
answer him,
that we can take each other to court.
33 There is no mediator between us,
to lay his hand on both of us.
34 Let him take his rod away from me
so his terror will no longer frighten me.
35 Then I would speak and not fear him.
But that is not the case; I am
on my own.

10 I am disgusted with my life.
I will give vent to my complaint
and speak in the bitterness of my soul.
2 I will say to God,
"Do not declare me guilty!
Let me know why you prosecute me.
3 Is it good for you to oppress,
to reject the work of your hands,
and favor[F] the plans of the wicked?
4 Do you have eyes of flesh,
or do you see as a human sees?
5 Are your days like those of a human,
or your years like those of a man,
6 that you look for my iniquity
and search for my sin,
7 even though you know that
I am not wicked
and that there is no one who can rescue
from your power?

8 "Your hands shaped me and formed me.
Will you now turn and destroy me?
9 Please remember that you formed me
like clay.
Will you now return me to dust?
10 Did you not pour me out like milk
and curdle me like cheese?
11 You clothed me with skin and flesh,
and wove me together with bones
and tendons.
12 You gave me life and faithful love,
and your care has guarded my life.

13 "Yet you concealed these thoughts
in your heart;
I know that this was your hidden plan:[G]
14 if I sin, you would notice,[H]
and would not acquit me of my iniquity.
15 If I am wicked, woe to me!
And even if I am righteous, I cannot
lift up my head.
I am filled with shame

[A] **9:19** LXX; MT reads *me* [B] **9:23** Or *whip*; Hb obscure [C] **9:24** Or *land* [D] **9:24** Lit *covers the faces of* [E] **9:25** = a royal messenger [F] **10:3** Lit *shine on* [G] **10:13** Lit *was with you* [H] **10:14** Lit *notice me*

My Story | Mia

A month or so had passed. The shock had worn off and the reality of my husband's death was an agony. The loneliness of that suffering was just awful. In the morning at the kitchen table, I depended on a book of prayers. Invariably as I then tried to take off on my own, the tears would come.

On one morning, my worst to that point, I simply had nothing of me left except grief.

I am not a visual person. I can't close my eyes and see anything that approaches what I see with my eyes. So, on two levels it's hard to explain what happened. First, I have to try to describe something that's not really visual, and, second, I try to describe something that God did not let me hold for very long—a day or two. For surely, had he let me keep the vision, I'd have worshiped the vision instead of the Giver of it.

As I sat sobbing, pleading for help, I saw . . . something. It took me a while to figure out what I was visualizing; but after a bit, I realized I was seeing my own heart. I don't recall what it looked like—or why I knew what I was seeing—but I knew beyond a doubt. It was my own broken heart, such a cracked-open mess. But then, I saw something else—the Spirit's presence coming down on that mangled mess. He did not flow over my heart; he filled up all the broken places with himself. And this was not once and done. I recall a sense of movement continuing. And warmth. Utter certainty of who was "speaking" to me, who was with me as never before.

I can't recreate the image—nor have I known before or since the extraordinary peace of those couple of days that the vision remained in my heart's eyes. I certainly don't wish upon myself the suffering of that time. But I long for the sweet intimacy that I knew with Jesus in the most painful time of my life.

I don't think that God means for me to not know that intimacy. For sure, in my rollercoaster swings spiritually and emotionally in the years following, I have often stopped and rested (and rejoiced) a while in the place of utter dependency on Jesus.

and have drunk deeply of[A]
my affliction.
16 If I am proud,[B] you hunt me like a lion
and again display
your miraculous power against me.
17 You produce new witnesses[C]
against me
and multiply your anger toward me.
Hardships assault me,
wave after wave.[D]

18 "Why did you bring me out of
the womb?
I should have died and never been seen.
19 I wish[E] I had never existed
but had been carried from the womb
to the grave.
20 Are my days not few? Stop it![F]
Leave me alone, so that I can smile
a little
21 before I go to a land of darkness
and gloom,
never to return.
22 It is a land of blackness
like the deepest darkness,
gloomy and chaotic,
where even the light is
like[G] the darkness."

ZOPHAR SPEAKS

11 Then Zophar the Naamathite replied:
2 Should this abundance of words
go unanswered
and such a talker[H] be acquitted?
3 Should your babbling put others
to silence,
so that you can keep on ridiculing
with no one to humiliate you?
4 You have said, "My teaching is sound,
and I am pure in your sight."
5 But if only God would speak
and open his lips against you!
6 He would show you the secrets of wisdom,
for true wisdom has two sides.
Know then that God has chosen
to overlook some of your iniquity.

[A] **10:15** Or *and look at me* [B] **10:16** Lit *If he lifts up* [C] **10:17** Or *You bring fresh troops* [D] **10:17** Lit *Changes and a host are with me* [E] **10:19** Lit *As if* [F] **10:20** Alt Hb tradition reads *Will he not leave my few days alone?* [G] **10:22** Lit *chaotic, and shines as* [H] **11:2** Lit *a man of lips*

7 Can you fathom the depths of God
or discover the limits of the Almighty?
8 They are higher than the heavens —
what can you do?
They are deeper than Sheol — what can
you know?
9 Their measure is longer than the earth
and wider than the sea.

10 If he passes by and throws
someone in prison
or convenes a court, who can stop him?
11 Surely he knows which people
are worthless.
If he sees iniquity, will he not take note
of it?
12 But a stupid person
will gain understanding
as soon as a wild donkey is born
a human!

13 As for you, if you redirect your heart
and spread out your hands to him
in prayer —
14 if there is iniquity in your hand, remove it,
and don't allow injustice to dwell
in your tents —
15 then you will hold your head high,
free from fault.
You will be firmly established
and unafraid.
16 For you will forget your suffering,
recalling it only as water
that has flowed by.
17 Your life will be brighter than noonday;
its darkness[A] will be like the morning.
18 You will be confident, because
there is hope.
You will look carefully about
and lie down in safety.

19 You will lie down with no one to
frighten you,
and many will seek your favor.
20 But the sight of the wicked will fail.
Their way of escape will be cut off,
and their only hope is their last breath.

JOB'S REPLY TO ZOPHAR

12 Then Job answered:
2 No doubt you are the people,
and wisdom will die with you!
3 But I also have a mind like you;
I am not inferior to you.
Who doesn't know the things you are
talking about?[B]

4 I am a laughingstock to my[C] friends,
by calling on God, who answers me.[D]
The righteous and upright man is
a laughingstock.
5 The one who is at ease holds calamity
in contempt
and thinks it is prepared for those
whose feet are slipping.
6 The tents of robbers are safe,
and those who trouble God
are secure;
God holds them in his hands.[E]

7 But ask the animals, and they will
instruct you;
ask the birds of the sky, and they will
tell you.
8 Or speak to the earth, and it will
instruct you;
let the fish of the sea inform you.
9 Which of all these does not know
that the hand of the LORD
has done this?
10 The life of every living thing is
in his hand,
as well as the breath of all mankind.

The life of every living thing is in his hand, as well as the breath of all mankind.
—Job 12:10

11 Doesn't the ear test words
as the palate tastes food?
12 Wisdom is found with the elderly,
and understanding comes
with long life.

13 Wisdom and strength belong to God;
counsel and understanding are his.
14 Whatever he tears down cannot
be rebuilt;
whoever he imprisons cannot
be released.

[A] **11:17** Text emended; MT reads *noonday; you are dark, you* [B] **12:3** Lit *With whom are not such things as these?* [C] **12:4** Lit *his* [D] **12:4** Lit *him* [E] **12:6** Or *secure; to those who bring their god in their hands*

15 When he withholds water, everything
dries up,
and when he releases it, it destroys
the land.
16 True wisdom and power belong to him.
The deceived and the deceiver are his.
17 He leads counselors away barefoot
and makes judges go mad.
18 He releases the bonds[A] put on by kings
and fastens a belt around their waists.
19 He leads priests away barefoot
and overthrows established leaders.
20 He deprives trusted advisers of speech
and takes away the elders'
good judgment.
21 He pours out contempt on nobles
and disarms[B] the strong.
22 He reveals mysteries
from the darkness
and brings the deepest darkness
into the light.
23 He makes nations great,
then destroys them;
he enlarges nations,
then leads them away.
24 He deprives the world's leaders
of reason,
and makes them wander
in a trackless wasteland.
25 They grope around in darkness
without light;
he makes them stagger like a drunkard.

13 Look, my eyes have seen all this;
my ears have heard and understood it.
2 Everything you know, I also know;
I am not inferior to you.
3 Yet I prefer to speak to the Almighty
and argue my case before God.
4 You use lies like plaster;
you are all worthless healers.
5 If only you would shut up
and let that be your wisdom!

6 Hear now my argument,
and listen to my defense.[C]
7 Would you testify unjustly
on God's behalf
or speak deceitfully for him?
8 Would you show partiality to him
or argue the case in his defense?
9 Would it go well if he examined you?
Could you deceive him
as you would deceive a man?
10 Surely he would rebuke you
if you secretly showed partiality.
11 Would God's majesty not terrify you?
Would his dread not fall on you?
12 Your memorable sayings are proverbs
of ash;
your defenses are made of clay.

13 Be quiet,[D] and I will speak.
Let whatever comes happen to me.
14 I will put[E] myself at risk[F]
and take my life in my own hands.
15 Even if he kills me, I will hope in him.[G]
I will still defend my ways before him.
16 Yes, this will result in my deliverance,
for no godless person can appear
before him.
17 Pay close attention to my words;
let my declaration ring in your ears.
18 Now then, I have prepared my case;
I know that I am right.
19 Can anyone indict me?
If so, I will be silent and die.

20 Only grant these two things
to me, God,
so that I will not have to hide
from your presence:
21 remove your hand from me,
and do not let your terror frighten me.
22 Then call, and I will answer,
or I will speak, and you can respond
to me.
23 How many iniquities and sins
have I committed?[H]
Reveal to me my transgression and sin.
24 Why do you hide your face
and consider me your enemy?
25 Will you frighten a wind-driven leaf?
Will you chase after dry straw?
26 For you record bitter accusations
against me
and make me inherit the iniquities
of my youth.
27 You put my feet in the stocks
and stand watch over all my paths,
setting a limit for the soles[I] of my feet.
28 A person wears out like something rotten,
like a moth-eaten garment.

[A] **12:18** Text emended; MT reads *discipline* [B] **12:21** Lit *and loosens the belt of* [C] **13:6** Lit *to the claims of my lips* [D] **13:13** Lit *quiet before me* [E] **13:14** LXX; MT reads *Why do I put* [F] **13:14** Lit *I take my flesh in my teeth* [G] **13:15** Some Hb mss read *I will be without hope* [H] **13:23** Lit *sins are to me* [I] **13:27** Lit *paths. You mark a line around the roots*

14 Anyone born of woman
is short of days and full of trouble.
2 He blossoms like a flower, then withers;
he flees like a shadow and does not last.
3 Do you really take notice of one like this?
Will you bring me into judgment
against you?[A]
4 Who can produce something pure
from what is impure?
No one!
5 Since a person's days are determined
and the number of his months depends
on you,
and since you have set[B] limits
he cannot pass,
6 look away from him and let him rest
so that he can enjoy his day
like a hired worker.

7 There is hope for a tree:
If it is cut down, it will sprout again,
and its shoots will not die.
8 If its roots grow old in the ground
and its stump starts to die in the soil,
9 the scent of water makes it thrive
and produce twigs like a sapling.
10 But a person dies and fades away;
he breathes his last — where is he?
11 As water disappears from a lake
and a river becomes parched and dry,
12 so people lie down never to rise again.
They will not wake up until the heavens
are no more;
they will not stir from their sleep.

13 If only you would hide me in Sheol
and conceal me
until your anger passes.
If only you would appoint a time for me
and then remember me.
14 When a person dies, will he come back
to life?
If so, I would wait all the days
of my struggle
until my relief comes.
15 You would call, and I would answer you.
You would long for the work
of your hands.
16 For then you would count my steps
but would not take note of my sin.
17 My rebellion would be sealed up
in a bag,
and you would cover over my iniquity.

When a person dies, will he come back to life? If so, I would wait all the days of my struggle until my relief comes. . . . My rebellion would be sealed up in a bag, and you would cover over my iniquity.

—Job 14:14,17

18 But as a mountain collapses
and crumbles
and a rock is dislodged from its place,
19 as water wears away stones
and torrents wash away the soil
from the land,
so you destroy a man's hope.
20 You completely overpower him, and he
passes on;
you change his appearance
and send him away.
21 If his sons receive honor, he does not
know it;
if they become insignificant,
he is unaware of it.
22 He feels only the pain
of his own body
and mourns only for himself.

SECOND SERIES OF SPEECHES

ELIPHAZ SPEAKS

15 Then Eliphaz the Temanite replied:
2 Does a wise man answer
with empty[C] counsel
or fill himself[D] with the hot east wind?
3 Should he argue with useless talk
or with words that serve
no good purpose?
4 But you even undermine the fear
of God
and hinder meditation before him.
5 Your iniquity teaches you what to say,
and you choose the language
of the crafty.
6 Your own mouth condemns you, not I;
your own lips testify against you.

[A] 14:3 LXX, Syr, Vg read *him* [B] 14:5 Lit *set his* [C] 15:2 Lit *windy*; Jb 16:3 [D] 15:2 Lit *his belly*

7 Were you the first human ever born,
or were you brought forth
before the hills?
8 Do you listen in on the council of God,
or have a monopoly on wisdom?
9 What do you know that we don't?
What do you understand that
is not clear to us?
10 Both the gray-haired and the elderly
are with us—
older than your father.
11 Are God's consolations not enough
for you,
even the words that deal gently with you?
12 Why has your heart misled you,
and why do your eyes flash
13 as you turn your anger[A] against God
and allow such words to leave
your mouth?

14 What is a mere human, that he
should be pure,
or one born of a woman, that he
should be righteous?
15 If God puts no trust in his holy ones
and the heavens are not pure
in his sight,
16 how much less one who is revolting
and corrupt,
who drinks injustice like water?

17 Listen to me and I will inform you.
I will describe what I have seen,
18 what the wise have declared and
not concealed,
that came from their ancestors,
19 to whom alone the land was given
when no foreigner passed
among them.
20 A wicked person writhes in pain
all his days,
throughout the number of
years reserved for the ruthless.
21 Dreadful sounds fill his ears;
when he is at peace, a robber
attacks him.
22 He doesn't believe he will return
from darkness;
he is destined for the sword.
23 He wanders about for food, asking,
"Where is it?"
He knows the day of darkness is
at hand.
24 Trouble and distress terrify him,
overwhelming him like a king
prepared for battle.
25 For he has stretched out his hand
against God
and has arrogantly opposed
the Almighty.
26 He rushes headlong at him
with his thick, studded shields.
27 Though his face is covered with fat[B]
and his waistline bulges with it,
28 he will dwell in ruined cities,
in abandoned houses destined
to become piles of rubble.
29 He will no longer be rich; his wealth
will not endure.
His possessions[C] will not increase
in the land.
30 He will not escape from the darkness;
flames will wither his shoots,
and by the breath of God's mouth,
he will depart.
31 Let him not put trust
in worthless things, being led astray,
for what he gets in exchange
will prove worthless.
32 It will be accomplished
before his time,
and his branch will not flourish.
33 He will be like a vine that drops
its unripe grapes
and like an olive tree that sheds
its blossoms.
34 For the company of the godless
will have no children,
and fire will consume the tents of those
who offer bribes.
35 They conceive trouble and give birth
to evil;
their womb prepares deception.

JOB'S REPLY TO ELIPHAZ

16 Then Job answered:
2 I have heard many things like these.
You are all miserable comforters.
3 Is there no end to your empty[D] words?
What provokes you that you
continue testifying?
4 If you were in my place I could also talk
like you.
I could string words together
against you
and shake my head at you.

[A] **15:13** Or *spirit* [B] **15:27** Lit *with his fat* [C] **15:29** Text emended; MT reads *Their gain* [D] **16:3** Lit *windy*; Jb 15:2

5 Instead, I would encourage you
with my mouth,
and the consolation from my lips
would bring relief.

6 If I speak, my suffering is not relieved,
and if I hold back, does any of it leave
me?
7 Surely he[A] has now exhausted me.
You have devastated my entire family.
8 You have shriveled me up[B]—
it has become a witness;
my frailty rises up against me
and testifies to my face.
9 His anger tears at me,
and he harasses me.
He gnashes his teeth at me.
My enemy pierces me with his eyes.
10 They open their mouths against me
and strike my cheeks with contempt;
they join themselves together against me.
11 God hands me over to the unjust;[C]
he throws me to the wicked.
12 I was at ease, but he shattered me;
he seized me by the scruff of the neck
and smashed me to pieces.
He set me up as his target;
13 his archers[D] surround me.
He pierces my kidneys without mercy
and pours my bile on the ground.
14 He breaks through my defenses again
and again;[E]
he charges at me like a warrior.

15 I have sewn sackcloth over my skin;
I have buried my strength[F] in the dust.
16 My face has grown red with weeping,
and darkness covers my eyes,
17 although my hands are free
from violence
and my prayer is pure.

18 Earth, do not cover my blood;
may my cry for help find
no resting place.
19 Even now my witness is in heaven,
and my advocate is in the heights!
20 My friends scoff at me
as I weep before God.
21 I wish that someone might argue
for a man with God
just as anyone[G] would for a friend.
22 For only a few years will pass
before I go the way of no return.

17 My spirit is broken.
My days are extinguished.
A graveyard awaits me.
2 Surely mockers surround[H] me,
and my eyes must gaze
at their rebellion.

3 Accept my pledge! Put up security
for me.
Who else will be my sponsor?[I]
4 You have closed their minds
to understanding,
therefore you will not honor them.
5 If a man denounces his friends
for a price,
the eyes of his children will fail.

6 He has made me an object of scorn
to the people;
I have become a man people spit at.[J]
7 My eyes have grown dim from grief,
and my whole body has become
but a shadow.
8 The upright are appalled at this,
and the innocent are roused
against the godless.
9 Yet the righteous person will hold
to his way,
and the one whose hands are clean
will grow stronger.
10 But come back and try again, all of you.[K]
I will not find a wise man among you.

11 My days have slipped by;
my plans have been ruined,
even the things dear to my heart.
12 They turned night into day
and made light seem near in the face
of darkness.
13 If I await Sheol as my home,
spread out my bed in darkness,
14 and say to corruption, "You are my father,"
and to the maggot, "My mother"
or "My sister,"
15 where then is my hope?
Who can see any hope for me?
16 Will it go down to the gates of Sheol,
or will we descend together
to the dust?

[A] **16:7** Or *it* [B] **16:8** Or *have seized me*; Hb obscure [C] **16:11** LXX, Vg; MT reads *to a boy* [D] **16:13** Or *arrows* [E] **16:14** Lit *through me, breach on breach* [F] **16:15** Lit *horn* [G] **16:21** Lit *a son of man* [H] **17:2** Lit *are with* [I] **17:3** Or *Who is there that will shake hands with me?* [J] **17:6** Lit *become a spitting to the faces* [K] **17:10** Some Hb mss, LXX, Vg; other Hb mss read *them*

BILDAD SPEAKS

18 Then Bildad the Shuhite replied:
2 How long until you stop talking?
Show some sense, and then we can talk.
3 Why are we regarded as cattle,
as stupid in your sight?
4 You who tear yourself in anger[A] —
should the earth be abandoned
on your account,
or a rock be removed from its place?

5 Yes, the light of the wicked
is extinguished;
the flame of his fire does not glow.
6 The light in his tent grows dark,
and the lamp beside him is put out.
7 His powerful stride is shortened,
and his own schemes trip him up.
8 For his own feet lead him into a net,
and he strays into its mesh.
9 A trap catches him by the heel;
a noose seizes him.
10 A rope lies hidden for him
on the ground,
and a snare waits for him
along the path.
11 Terrors frighten him on every side
and harass him at every step.
12 His strength is depleted;
disaster lies ready for him
to stumble.[B]
13 Parts of his skin are eaten away;
death's firstborn consumes his limbs.
14 He is ripped from the security
of his tent
and marched away to the king
of terrors.
15 Nothing he owned remains in his tent.
Burning sulfur is scattered
over his home.
16 His roots below dry up,
and his branches above wither away.
17 All memory of him perishes
from the earth;
he has no name anywhere.[C]
18 He is driven from light to darkness
and chased from the inhabited world.
19 He has no children or descendants
among his people,
no survivor where he used to live.
20 Those in the west are appalled
at his fate,
while those in the east tremble
in horror.
21 Indeed, such is the dwelling of the
unjust man,
and this is the place of the one
who does not know God.

JOB'S REPLY TO BILDAD

19 Then Job answered:
2 How long will you torment me
and crush me with words?
3 You have humiliated me ten times now,
and you mistreat[D] me without shame.
4 Even if it is true that I have sinned,
my mistake concerns only[E] me.
5 If you really want to appear superior
to me
and would use my disgrace as evidence
against me,
6 then understand that it is God
who has wronged me
and caught me in his net.

7 I cry out: "Violence!"
but get no response;
I call for help, but there is no justice.
8 He has blocked my way so that I cannot
pass through;
he has veiled my paths with darkness.
9 He has stripped me of my honor
and removed the crown from my head.
10 He tears me down on every side so that
I am ruined.[F]
He uproots my hope like a tree.
11 His anger burns against me,
and he regards me as one of his enemies.
12 His troops advance together;
they construct a ramp[G] against me
and camp around my tent.

13 He has removed my brothers from me;
my acquaintances
have abandoned me.
14 My relatives stop coming by,
and my close friends
have forgotten me.
15 My house guests[H] and female servants
regard me as a stranger;
I am a foreigner in their sight.
16 I call for my servant, but he
does not answer,
even if I beg him with my own mouth.

[A] **18:4** Lit *He who tears himself in his anger* [B] **18:12** Or *disaster hungers for him* [C] **18:17** Or *name in the streets* [D] **19:3** Hb obscure [E] **19:4** Lit *mistake lives with* [F] **19:10** Lit *gone* [G] **19:12** Lit *they raise up their way* [H] **19:15** Or *The resident aliens in my household*

17 My breath is offensive to my wife,
and my own family[A] finds me repulsive.
18 Even young boys scorn me.
When I stand up, they mock me.
19 All of my best friends[B] despise me,
and those I love have turned
against me.
20 My skin and my flesh cling
to my bones;
I have escaped with only the skin
of my teeth.

21 Have mercy on me, my friends,
have mercy,
for God's hand has struck me.
22 Why do you persecute me as God does?
Will you never get enough
of my flesh?

23 I wish that my words
were written down,
that they were recorded on a scroll
24 or were inscribed in stone forever
by an iron stylus and lead!
25 But I know that my Redeemer lives,[C]
and at the end he will stand on the dust.
26 Even after my skin
has been destroyed,[D]
yet I will see God in[E] my flesh.
27 I will see him myself;
my eyes will look at him, and not
as a stranger.[F]
My heart longs[G] within me.

28 If you say, "How will we pursue him,
since the root of the problem lies
with him?"[H]
29 then be afraid of the sword,
because wrath brings punishment
by the sword,
so that you may know there is
a judgment.

ZOPHAR SPEAKS

20 Then Zophar the Naamathite replied:
2 This is why my unsettling thoughts
compel me to answer,
because I am upset![I]
3 I have heard a rebuke
that insults me,
and my understanding[J]
makes me reply.

Eternal Perspective | *Death's Defeat/Resurrection*

FAITH'S EBB AND FLOW

"But I know that my Redeemer lives, and at the end he will stand on the dust. Even after my skin has been destroyed, yet I will see God in my flesh. I will see him myself; my eyes will look at him, and not as a stranger. My heart longs within me." Job 19:25-27

If the Bible demonstrates anything about faith it's this: Trust in God is fluid, not fixed. Study the characters of Scripture—like Job. Faith sometimes swells in them and sparks remarkable acts. It also shrivels at times in the boldest souls, leaving only deep doubt.

A man of great spiritual devotion, Job was wracked by physical pain, reeling from emotional grief, and awash in theological confusion. How had his life unraveled so dramatically and so completely?

Throughout the book that bears his name Job has low moments. Then, almost as if faith is as much a divine gift as it is a human decision, he has other moments—like this one—in which he is able to confess incredible hope.

If you are doubting, know that you're not alone. Remain diligent. Remember who God is and that he is well able to revive your flagging faith.

For the next note on *Eternal Perspective*, see Job 42:2.

[A] **19:17** Lit *and the sons of my belly* [B] **19:19** Lit *of the men of my council* [C] **19:25** Or *know my living Redeemer* [D] **19:26** Lit *skin which they destroyed*, or *skin they destroyed in this way* [E] **19:26** Or *apart from* [F] **19:27** Or *not a stranger* [G] **19:27** Lit *My kidneys grow faint* [H] **19:28** Some Hb mss, LXX, Vg; other Hb mss read *me* [I] **20:2** Lit *because of my feeling within me* [J] **20:3** Lit *and a spirit from my understanding*

4 Don't you know that ever since antiquity,
from the time a human was placed
on earth,
5 the joy of the wicked has been brief
and the happiness of the godless
has lasted only a moment?
6 Though his arrogance reaches heaven,
and his head touches the clouds,
7 he will vanish forever
like his own dung.
Those who know[A] him will ask,
"Where is he?"
8 He will fly away like a dream and never
be found;
he will be chased away like a vision
in the night.
9 The eye that saw him will see him
no more,
and his household will no longer
see him.
10 His children will beg from[B] the poor,
for his own hands must give back
his wealth.
11 His frame may be full of
youthful vigor,
but it will lie down with him in dust.

12 Though evil tastes sweet in his mouth
and he conceals it under his tongue,
13 though he cherishes it and will not
let it go
but keeps it in his mouth,
14 yet the food in his stomach turns
into cobras' venom inside him.
15 He swallows wealth but must
vomit it up;
God will force it from his stomach.
16 He will suck the poison of cobras;
a viper's fangs[C] will kill him.
17 He will not enjoy the streams,
the rivers flowing with honey
and curds.
18 He must return the fruit of his labor
without consuming it;
he doesn't enjoy the profits
from his trading.
19 For he oppressed and abandoned
the poor;
he seized a house he did not build.

20 Because his appetite is never satisfied,[D]
he does not let anything
he desires escape.
21 Nothing is left for him to consume;
therefore, his prosperity will not last.
22 At the height of his success[E]
distress will come to him;
the full weight of misery[F]
will crush him.
23 When he fills his stomach,
God will send his burning anger
against him,
raining it down on him
while he is eating.[G]
24 If he flees from an iron weapon,
an arrow from a bronze bow
will pierce him.
25 He pulls it out of his back,
the flashing tip out of his liver.[H]
Terrors come over him.
26 Total darkness is reserved
for his treasures.
A fire unfanned by human hands
will consume him;
it will feed on what is left in his tent.
27 The heavens will expose his iniquity,
and the earth will rise up against him.
28 The possessions in his house
will be removed,
flowing away on the day of God's anger.
29 This is the wicked person's lot from God,
the inheritance God ordained for him.

JOB'S REPLY TO ZOPHAR

21 Then Job answered:
2 Pay close attention to my words;
let this be the consolation you offer.
3 Bear with me while I speak;
then after I have spoken, you may
continue mocking.

4 As for me, is my complaint
against a human being?
Then why shouldn't I be impatient?
5 Look at me and shudder;
put your hand over your mouth.
6 When I think about it, I am terrified
and my body trembles in horror.
7 Why do the wicked continue to live,
growing old and becoming powerful?
8 Their children are established
while they are still alive,[I]

[A] **20:7** Lit *have seen* [B] **20:10** Or *children must compensate* [C] **20:16** Lit *tongue* [D] **20:20** Lit *Because he does not know ease in his stomach* [E] **20:22** Lit *In the fullness of his excess* [F] **20:22** Some Hb mss, LXX, Vg; other Hb mss read *the hand of everyone in misery* [G] **20:23** Text emended; MT reads *him, against his flesh* [H] **20:25** Or *gallbladder* [I] **21:8** Lit *established before them with them*

and their descendants,
before their eyes.
9 Their homes are secure and free of fear;
no rod from God strikes them.
10 Their bulls breed without fail;
their cows calve and do not miscarry.
11 They let their little ones run
around like lambs;
their children skip about,
12 singing to the tambourine and lyre
and rejoicing at the sound of the flute.
13 They spend[A] their days in prosperity
and go down to Sheol in peace.
14 Yet they say to God, "Leave us alone!
We don't want to know your ways.
15 Who is the Almighty, that we
should serve him,
and what will we gain by pleading
with him?"
16 But their prosperity is not
of their own doing.
The counsel of the wicked is far
from me!

17 How often is the lamp of the wicked
put out?
Does disaster[B] come on them?
Does he apportion destruction
in his anger?
18 Are they like straw before the wind,
like chaff a storm sweeps away?
19 God reserves a person's punishment
for his children.
Let God repay the person himself,
so that he may know it.
20 Let his own eyes see his demise;
let him drink from
the Almighty's wrath!
21 For what does he care about his family
once he is dead,
when the number of his months
has run out?

22 Can anyone teach God knowledge,
since he judges the exalted ones?[C]
23 One person dies in excellent health,[D]
completely secure[E] and at ease.
24 His body is[F] well fed,[G]
and his bones are full of marrow.[H]
25 Yet another person dies
with a bitter soul,
having never tasted prosperity.
26 But they both lie in the dust,
and worms cover them.

27 I know your thoughts very well,
the schemes by which you would
wrong me.
28 For you say, "Where now is
the nobleman's house?"
and "Where are the tents the wicked
lived in?"
29 Have you never consulted
those who travel the roads?
Don't you accept their reports?[I]
30 Indeed, the evil person is spared
from the day of disaster,
rescued from the day of wrath.
31 Who would denounce his behavior
to his face?
Who would repay him for what
he has done?
32 He is carried to the grave,
and someone keeps watch over
his tomb.
33 The dirt on his grave is[J] sweet to him.
Everyone follows behind him,
and those who go before him are
without number.

34 So how can you offer me
such futile comfort?
Your answers are deceptive.

THIRD SERIES OF SPEECHES

ELIPHAZ SPEAKS

22 Then Eliphaz the Temanite replied:
2 Can a man be of any use to God?
Can even a wise man be of use to him?
3 Does it delight the Almighty if you
are righteous?
Does he profit if you perfect
your behavior?

4 Does he correct you and take you
to court
because of your piety?
5 Isn't your wickedness abundant
and aren't your iniquities endless?
6 For you took collateral
from your brothers without cause,
stripping off their clothes
and leaving them naked.

[A] 21:13 Alt Hb tradition reads *fully enjoy* [B] 21:17 Lit *their disaster* [C] 21:22 Probably angels [D] 21:23 Lit *in bone of his perfection* [E] 21:23 Text emended; MT reads *health, all at ease* [F] 21:24 Or *His sides are*; Hb obscure [G] 21:24 Lit *is full of milk* [H] 21:24 Lit *and the marrow of his bones is watered* [I] 21:29 Lit *signs* [J] 21:33 Lit *The clods of the wadi are*

7 You gave no water to the thirsty
and withheld food from the famished,
8 while the land belonged
to a powerful man
and an influential man lived on it.
9 You sent widows away
empty-handed,
and the strength of the fatherless
was[A] crushed.
10 Therefore snares surround you,
and sudden dread terrifies you,
11 or darkness, so you cannot see,
and a flood of water covers you.

12 Isn't God as high as the heavens?
And look at the highest stars —
how lofty they are!
13 Yet you say, "What does God know?
Can he judge through total darkness?
14 Clouds veil him so that he cannot see,
as he walks on the circle of the sky."
15 Will you continue on the ancient path
that wicked men have walked?
16 They were snatched away
before their time,
and their foundations
were washed away by a river.
17 They were the ones who said to God,
"Leave us alone!"
and "What can the Almighty do
to us?"[B]
18 But it was he who filled their houses
with good things.
The counsel of the wicked is
far from me!
19 The righteous see this and rejoice;
the innocent mock them, saying,
20 "Surely our opponents are destroyed,
and fire has consumed
what they left behind."

21 Come to terms with God and be
at peace;
in this way[C] good will come to you.
22 Receive instruction from his mouth,
and place his sayings in your heart.
23 If you return to the Almighty, you will
be renewed.
If you banish injustice from your tent
24 and consign your gold to the dust,
the gold of Ophir to the stones
in the wadis,
25 the Almighty will be your gold
and your finest silver.
26 Then you will delight in the Almighty
and lift up your face to God.
27 You will pray to him, and he will hear you,
and you will fulfill your vows.
28 When you make a decision, it will be
carried out,[D]
and light will shine on your ways.
29 When others are humiliated
and you say, "Lift them up,"
God will save the humble.[E]
30 He will even rescue the guilty one,
who will be rescued by the purity
of your hands.

JOB'S REPLY TO ELIPHAZ

23 Then Job answered:
2 Today also my complaint is bitter.[F]
His[G] hand is heavy
despite my groaning.
3 If only I knew how to find him,
so that I could go to his throne.
4 I would plead my case before him
and fill my mouth with arguments.
5 I would learn how[H] he would
answer me;
and understand what he would say to me.
6 Would he prosecute me forcefully?
No, he would certainly pay attention
to me.
7 Then an upright man could reason
with him,
and I would escape
from my Judge[I] forever.

8 If I go east, he is not there,
and if I go west, I cannot perceive him.
9 When he is at work to the north,
I cannot see him;
when he turns south, I cannot find him.
10 Yet he knows the way I have taken;[J]

Yet he knows the way I have taken; when he has tested me, I will emerge as pure gold.
—*Job 23:10*

[A] 22:9 LXX, Syr, Vg, Tg read *you have* [B] 22:17 LXX, Syr; MT reads *them* [C] 22:21 Lit *peace; by them* [D] 22:28 Lit *out for you* [E] 22:29 Lit *bowed of eyes* [F] 23:2 Syr, Tg, Vg; MT reads *rebellion* [G] 23:2 LXX, Syr; MT reads *My* [H] 23:5 Lit *the words* [I] 23:7 Or *judgment* [J] 23:10 Lit *way with me*

when he has tested me, I will emerge
as pure gold.
11 My feet have followed
in his tracks;
I have kept to his way and not
turned aside.
12 I have not departed
from the commands from his lips;
I have treasured[A] the words
from his mouth
more than my daily food.

13 But he is unchangeable; who can
oppose him?
He does what he desires.
14 He will certainly accomplish
what he has decreed for me,
and he has many more things like these
in mind.[B]
15 Therefore I am terrified
in his presence;
when I consider this, I am afraid
of him.
16 God has made my heart faint;
the Almighty has terrified me.
17 Yet I am not destroyed[C]
by the darkness,
by the thick darkness that covers
my face.

24 Why does the Almighty not reserve
times for judgment?
Why do those who know him never see
his days?
2 The wicked displace
boundary markers.
They steal a flock and provide pasture
for it.
3 They drive away the donkeys owned
by the fatherless
and take the widow's ox as collateral.
4 They push the needy off the road;
the poor of the land are forced
into hiding.
5 Like wild donkeys in the wilderness,
the poor go out to their task of foraging
for food;
the desert provides nourishment
for their children.
6 They gather their fodder in the field
and glean the vineyards of the wicked.
7 Without clothing, they spend
the night naked,
having no covering against the cold.
8 Drenched by mountain rains,
they huddle against[D] the rocks,
shelterless.
9 The fatherless infant is snatched
from the breast;

Exercise of Faith | *Memorizing Scripture*

TREASURED WORDS

"I have not departed from the commands from his lips; I have treasured the words from his mouth more than my daily food." Job 23:12

Based on passages like this one, we might ask Job's counsel on how to survive unspeakable suffering. He would say, "Memorize lots of Scripture."

This practice is so valuable because when our minds depart from the truth and we say, "God has abandoned me . . . I can't survive this experience," divine truth holds us like an anchor. When suffering makes us shaky, God's Word gives us a solid foundation on which to stand. When we are tempted to seek relief from suffering by wandering down unhealthy paths, the Bible acts like a compass to put us back on track.

The Bible gives power in all these ways and more. Before we can call to mind "the words from [God's] mouth" in times of trouble, we first need to have those eternal truths memorized.

What biblical promises do you have tucked away in your memory? What passage would encourage you if only you could bring it to mind? Mark it in your Bible. Write the reference where you can find it.

For the next note on *Exercise of Faith*, see Job 31:7-8.

[A] **23:12** LXX, Vg read *treasured in my bosom* [B] **23:14** Lit *these with him* [C] **23:17** Or *silenced* [D] **24:8** Lit *they embrace*

the nursing child of the poor is seized
as collateral.[A]
10 Without clothing,
they wander about naked.
They carry sheaves but go hungry.
11 They crush olives in their presses;[B]
they tread the winepresses,
but go thirsty.
12 From the city, men[C] groan;
the mortally wounded cry for help,
yet God pays no attention to this crime.

13 The wicked are those who rebel
against the light.
They do not recognize its ways
or stay on its paths.
14 The murderer rises at dawn
to kill the poor and needy,
and by night he becomes a thief.
15 The adulterer's eye watches
for twilight,
thinking, "No eye will see me,"
and he covers his face.
16 In the dark they break[D] into houses;
by day they lock themselves in,[E]
never experiencing the light.
17 For the morning is like darkness
to them.
Surely they are familiar
with the terrors of darkness!

18 They float[F] on the surface of the water.
Their section of the land is cursed,
so that they never go to their vineyards.
19 As dry ground and heat snatch away
the melted snow,
so Sheol steals those who have sinned.
20 The womb forgets them;
worms feed on them;
they are remembered no more.
So injustice is broken like a tree.
21 They prey on[G] the childless woman
who is unable to conceive,
and do not deal kindly with the widow.
22 Yet God drags away[H] the mighty
by his power;
when he rises up, they have
no assurance of life.
23 He gives them a sense of security,
so they can rely on it,
but his eyes watch over their ways.
24 They are exalted for a moment,
then gone;
they are brought low and shrivel up
like everything else.[I]
They wither like heads of grain.

25 If this is not true, then who
can prove me a liar
and show that my speech is worthless?

BILDAD SPEAKS

25 Then Bildad the Shuhite replied:
2 Dominion and dread belong to him,
the one who establishes harmony
in his heights.
3 Can his troops be numbered?
Does his light not shine on everyone?
4 How can a human be justified
before God?
How can one born of woman be pure?
5 If even the moon does not shine
and the stars are not pure in his sight,
6 how much less a human, who is
a maggot,
a son of man,[J] who is a worm!

JOB'S REPLY TO BILDAD

26 Then Job answered:
2 How you have helped
the powerless
and delivered the arm that is weak!
3 How you have counseled the unwise
and abundantly provided insight!
4 With whom did you speak these words?
Whose breath came out of your mouth?

5 The departed spirits tremble
beneath the waters and all that
inhabit them.
6 Sheol is naked before God,
and Abaddon has no covering.
7 He stretches the northern skies
over empty space;
he hangs the earth on nothing.
8 He wraps up the water in his clouds,
yet the clouds do not burst
beneath its weight.
9 He obscures the view of his throne,
spreading his cloud over it.
10 He laid out the horizon on the surface
of the waters

[A] **24:9** Text emended; MT reads *breast; they seize collateral against the poor* [B] **24:11** Lit *olives between their rows* [C] **24:12** One Hb ms, Syr read *the dying* [D] **24:16** Lit *dig* [E] **24:16** Lit *they seal for themselves* [F] **24:18** Lit *are insignificant* [G] **24:21** LXX, Tg read *They harm* [H] **24:22** Or *God prolongs the life of* [I] **24:24** LXX reads *like a mallow plant in the heat* [J] **25:6** Or *a mere mortal*

at the boundary between light
and darkness.
11 The pillars that hold up
the sky tremble,
astounded at his rebuke.
12 By his power he stirred the sea,
and by his understanding
he crushed Rahab.
13 By his breath the heavens gained
their beauty;
his hand pierced
the fleeing serpent.[A]
14 These are but the fringes of his ways;
how faint is the word we hear of him!
Who can understand
his mighty thunder?

27 Job continued his discourse, saying:
2 As God lives, who has deprived me
of justice,
and the Almighty who has
made me bitter,
3 as long as my breath is still in me
and the breath from God remains
in my nostrils,
4 my lips will not speak unjustly,
and my tongue will not utter deceit.
5 I will never affirm that you are right.
I will maintain my integrity[B] until I die.
6 I will cling to my righteousness
and never let it go.
My conscience will not accuse me
as long as I live!
7 May my enemy be like the wicked
and my opponent like the unjust.
8 For what hope does
the godless person have when he is
cut off,
when God takes away his life?
9 Will God hear his cry
when distress comes on him?
10 Will he delight in the Almighty?
Will he call on God at all times?
11 I will teach you about God's power.
I will not conceal what the Almighty
has planned.[C]
12 All of you have seen this for yourselves,
why do you keep up this empty talk?
13 This is a wicked man's lot from God,
the inheritance the ruthless receive
from the Almighty.
14 Even if his children increase,
they are destined for the sword;
his descendants will never
have enough food.
15 Those who survive him will be buried
by the plague,
yet their widows will not weep
for them.
16 Though he piles up silver like dust
and heaps up fine clothing like clay —
17 he may heap it up, but the righteous
will wear it,
and the innocent will divide up
his silver.
18 The house he built is
like a moth's cocoon
or a shelter set up by a watchman.
19 He lies down wealthy, but will do so
no more;
when he opens his eyes, it is gone.
20 Terrors overtake him like a flood;
a storm wind sweeps him away
at night.
21 An east wind picks him up,
and he is gone;
it carries him away from his place.
22 It blasts at him without mercy,
while he flees desperately
from its force.
23 It claps its hands at him
and scoffs at him from its place.

A HYMN TO WISDOM

28 Surely there is a mine for silver
and a place where gold is refined.
2 Iron is taken from the ground,
and copper is smelted from ore.
3 A miner puts an end to the darkness;
he probes[D] the deepest recesses
for ore in the gloomy darkness.
4 He cuts a shaft far
from human habitation,
in places unknown to those who walk
above ground.
Suspended far away from people,
the miners swing back and forth.
5 Food may come from the earth,
but below the surface the earth
is transformed as by fire.
6 Its rocks are a source of lapis lazuli,
containing flecks of gold.
7 No bird of prey knows that path;
no falcon's eye has seen it.

[A] **26:13** = Leviathan [B] **27:5** Lit *will not remove my integrity from me* [C] **27:11** Lit *what is with the Almighty* [D] **28:3** Lit *probes all*

8 Proud beasts have never walked on it;
no lion has ever prowled over it.
9 The miner uses a flint tool
and turns up ore from the root
of the mountains.
10 He cuts out channels in the rocks,
and his eyes spot every treasure.
11 He dams up the streams from flowing[A]
so that he may bring to light
what is hidden.

12 But where can wisdom be found,
and where is understanding located?
13 No one can know its value,[B]
since it cannot be found in the land
of the living.
14 The ocean depths say, "It's not in me,"
while the sea declares, "I don't have it."
15 Gold cannot be exchanged for it,
and silver cannot be weighed out
for its price.
16 Wisdom cannot be valued in the gold
of Ophir,
in precious onyx or lapis lazuli.
17 Gold and glass do not compare with it,
and articles of fine gold
cannot be exchanged for it.
18 Coral and quartz are not
worth mentioning.
The price of wisdom is beyond pearls.
19 Topaz from Cush cannot compare
with it,
and it cannot be valued in pure gold.

20 Where then does wisdom come from,
and where is understanding located?
21 It is hidden from the eyes
of every living thing
and concealed from the birds
of the sky.
22 Abaddon and Death say,
"We have heard news of it
with our ears."
23 But God understands the way
to wisdom,
and he knows its location.
24 For he looks to the ends of the earth
and sees everything
under the heavens.
25 When God fixed the weight of the wind
and distributed the water by measure,
26 when he established a limit[C]
for the rain
and a path for the lightning,
27 he considered wisdom and evaluated it;
he established it and examined it.
28 He said to mankind,
"The fear of the Lord—that is wisdom.
And to turn from evil
is understanding."

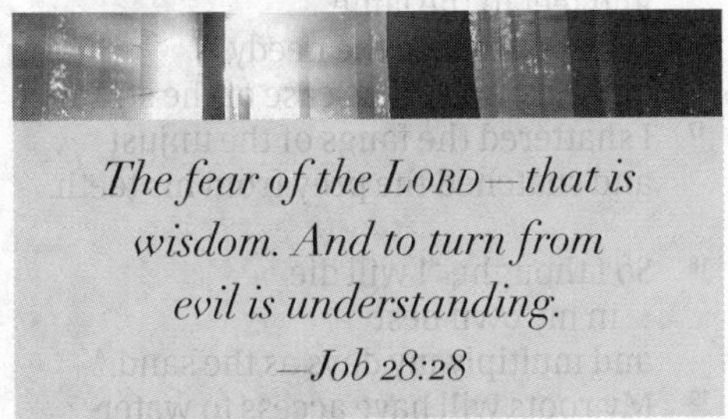

The fear of the LORD—that is wisdom. And to turn from evil is understanding.

—Job 28:28

JOB'S FINAL CLAIM OF INNOCENCE

29 Job continued his discourse, saying:
2 If only I could be as in months
gone by,
in the days when God watched over me,
3 when his lamp shone above my head,
and I walked through darkness
by his light!
4 I would be as I was in the days
of my youth
when God's friendship rested
on my tent,
5 when the Almighty was still with me
and my children were around me,
6 when my feet were bathed in curds
and the rock poured out streams of oil
for me!

7 When I went out to the city gate
and took my seat in the town square,
8 the young men saw me and withdrew,
while older men stood to their feet.
9 City officials stopped talking
and covered their mouths
with their hands.
10 The noblemen's voices were hushed,
and their tongues stuck to the roof
of their mouths.
11 When they heard me, they blessed me,
and when they saw me, they spoke well
of me.[D]
12 For I rescued the poor who cried out
for help,
and the fatherless child who had
no one to support him.

[A] **28:11** LXX, Vg read *He explores the sources of the streams* [B] **28:13** LXX reads *way* [C] **28:26** Or *decree* [D] **29:11** Lit *When an ear heard, it called me blessed, and when an eye saw, it testified for me*

13 The dying blessed me,
and I made the widow's heart rejoice.
14 I clothed myself in righteousness,
and it enveloped me;
my just decisions were like a robe
and a turban.
15 I was eyes to the blind
and feet to the lame.
16 I was a father to the needy,
and I examined the case of the stranger.
17 I shattered the fangs of the unjust
and snatched the prey from his teeth.

18 So I thought, "I will die
in my own nest
and multiply my days as the sand.[A]
19 My roots will have access to water,
and the dew will rest on my branches
all night.
20 My whole being will be refreshed
within me,
and my bow will be renewed
in my hand."
21 Men listened to me with expectation,
waiting silently for my advice.
22 After a word from me they did not
speak again;
my speech settled on them like dew.
23 They waited for me as for the rain
and opened their mouths as for
spring showers.
24 If I smiled at them, they couldn't believe it;
they were thrilled at[B] the light
of my countenance.
25 I directed their course and presided
as chief.
I lived as a king among his troops,
like one who comforts
those who mourn.

30 But now they mock me,
men younger than I am,
whose fathers I would have refused
to put
with my sheep dogs.
2 What use to me was the strength
of their hands?
Their vigor had left them.
3 Emaciated from poverty and hunger,
they gnawed the dry land,
the desolate wasteland by night.

Other-centeredness | *Helping Widows and Orphans*

MOVING OUTWARD

"For I rescued the poor who cried out for help, and the fatherless child who had no one to support him. The dying blessed me, and I made the widow's heart rejoice." Job 29:12-13

How can people believe in God, without knowing some things about God? Answer: They can't. This explains our great need for studying the Bible. Learning basic theology. Listening to sermons. Reading devotional literature. Gathering with other believers in small groups to wrestle with our faith.

But we can't stop there. Faith might begin with knowing, but it only grows by doing. Job had clearly helped others. According to James, faith can't just talk, it has to work: "Pure and undefiled religion before God the Father is this: to look after orphans and widows in their distress and to keep oneself unstained from the world" (Jms 1:27). Clearly, a faith that consists largely of concepts, conjecture, hypotheticals, and endless discussions isn't biblical faith at all. Job could tell you that.

God wants us to possess a faith that makes a difference. It should not only prompt us to live holy lives, but it should also propel us outward. When and where we see the poor, the fatherless child, the widow (that is, anyone in need, but especially those who are helpless and hopeless), we need to roll up our sleeves.

What person or group in the margins do you "look after"?

For the next note on *Other-centeredness*, see Psalm 18:1.

[A] **29:18** Or *as the phoenix* [B] **29:24** Lit *they did not cast down*

4 They plucked mallow[A]
among the shrubs,
and the roots of the broom tree were
their food.
5 They were banished
from human society;
people shouted at them
as if they were thieves.
6 They are living on the slopes
of the wadis,
among the rocks and in holes
in the ground.
7 They bray among the shrubs;
they huddle beneath the thistles.
8 Foolish men, without even a name.
They were forced to leave the land.

9 Now I am mocked by their songs;
I have become an object of scorn
to them.
10 They despise me and keep
their distance from me;
they do not hesitate to spit in my face.
11 Because God has loosened
my[B] bowstring and oppressed me,
they have cast off restraint
in my presence.
12 The rabble[C] rise up at my right;
they trap[D] my feet
and construct their siege ramp[E]
against me.
13 They tear up my path;
they contribute to my destruction,
without anyone to help them.
14 They advance as through
a gaping breach;
they keep rolling in through the ruins.
15 Terrors are turned loose against me;
they chase my dignity away
like the wind,
and my prosperity has passed by
like a cloud.

16 Now my life is poured out before me,
and days of suffering have seized me.
17 Night pierces my bones,
but my gnawing pains never rest.
18 My clothing is distorted with great force;
he chokes me by the neck
of my garment.[C]
19 He throws me into the mud,
and I have become like dust and ashes.
20 I cry out to you for help, but you do not
answer me;
when I stand up, you merely look at me.
21 You have turned against me
with cruelty;
you harass me with your strong hand.
22 You lift me up on the wind
and make me ride it;
you scatter me in the storm.
23 Yes, I know that you will lead me
to death —
the place appointed for all who live.

24 Yet no one would stretch out his hand
against a ruined person[F]
when he cries out to him for help
because of his distress.
25 Have I not wept for those
who have fallen on hard times?
Has my soul not grieved for the needy?
26 But when I hoped for good, evil came;
when I looked for light, darkness came.
27 I am churning within[G] and cannot rest;
days of suffering confront me.
28 I walk about blackened, but not
by the sun.[H]
I stood in the assembly and cried out
for help.
29 I have become a brother to jackals
and a companion of ostriches.
30 My skin blackens and flakes off,[I]
and my bones burn with fever.
31 My lyre is used for mourning
and my flute for the sound
of weeping.

31 I have made a covenant with my eyes.
How then could I look
at a young woman?[J]
2 For what portion would I have
from God above,
or what inheritance from the Almighty
on high?
3 Doesn't disaster come to the unjust
and misfortune to evildoers?
4 Does he not see my ways
and number all my steps?

5 If I have walked in falsehood
or my foot has rushed to deceit,
6 let God weigh me on accurate scales,
and he will recognize my integrity.

[A] **30:4** Or *saltwort* [B] **30:11** Alt Hb tradition, LXX, Vg read *his* [C] **30:12,18** Hb obscure [D] **30:12** Lit *stretch out* [E] **30:12** Lit *and raise up their destructive paths* [F] **30:24** Lit *a heap of ruins* [G] **30:27** Lit *My bowels boil* [H] **30:28** Or *walk in sunless gloom* [I] **30:30** Lit *blackens away from me* [J] **31:1** Or *a virgin*

7 If my step has turned from the way,
my heart has followed my eyes,
or impurity has stained my hands,
8 let someone else eat what I have sown,
and let my crops be uprooted.

9 If my heart has gone
astray over a woman
or I have lurked at my
neighbor's door,
10 let my own wife grind grain
for another man,
and let other men sleep with[A] her.
11 For that would be a disgrace;
it would be an iniquity
deserving punishment.
12 For it is a fire that consumes down
to Abaddon;
it would destroy my entire harvest.

13 If I have dismissed the case of my male
or female servants
when they made a complaint
against me,
14 what could I do when God stands up
to judge?
How should I answer him
when he calls me to account?
15 Did not the one who made me
in the womb also make them?
Did not the same God form us both
in the womb?

16 If I have refused the wishes of the poor
or let the widow's eyes go blind,
17 if I have eaten my few crumbs alone
without letting the fatherless
eat any of it —
18 for from my youth, I raised him
as his father,
and since the day I was born[B] I guided
the widow —
19 if I have seen anyone dying for lack
of clothing
or a needy person without a cloak,
20 if he[C] did not bless me
while warming himself with the fleece
from my sheep,
21 if I ever cast my vote[D]
against a fatherless child
when I saw that I had support
in the city gate,
22 then let my shoulder blade fall
from my back,
and my arm be pulled from its socket.
23 For disaster from God terrifies me,

Exercise of Faith | *Guarding the Heart*

WHERE'S YOUR FOCUS?

"If my step has turned from the way, my heart has followed my eyes, or impurity has stained my hands, let someone else eat what I have sown, and let my crops be uprooted." Job 31:7-8

Consider how many hours each day we spend staring at screens: smart phones, computers, tablets, and TVs. We have to admit that while some of what we watch is worthwhile, much of it is, at best, a waste of precious time.

No wonder the Job had been careful. In fact, the psalmist wrote, "Turn my eyes from looking at what is worthless; give me life in your ways" (Ps 119:37). Both of these ancient believers recognized that life is found in God's ways. The apostle Paul put it like this in the New Testament: "Whatever is true, whatever is honorable, whatever is just, whatever is pure, whatever is lovely, whatever is commendable—if there is any moral excellence and if there is anything praiseworthy—dwell on these things" (Php 4:8).

Your viewing habits are a big deal, because as author George MacDonald once observed, the eyes pull the heart. In other words, the things we continually focus on have a way of capturing our attention and stealing our affection. Let's let those things be the things of God.

For the next note on *Exercise of Faith*, see Psalm 19:7-8.

[A] **31:10** Lit *men kneel down over* [B] **31:18** Lit *and from my mother's womb* [C] **31:20** Lit *his loins* [D] **31:21** Lit *I raise my hand*

and because of his majesty
I could not do these things.

24 If I placed my confidence in gold
or called fine gold my trust,
25 if I have rejoiced because my wealth
is great
or because my own hand has acquired
so much,
26 if I have gazed at the sun
when it was shining
or at the moon moving in splendor,
27 so that my heart was secretly enticed
and I threw them a kiss,[A]
28 this would also be an iniquity
deserving punishment,
for I would have denied God above.

29 Have I rejoiced over
my enemy's distress,
or become excited when trouble came
his way?
30 I have not allowed my mouth to sin
by asking for his life with a curse.
31 Haven't the members
of my household said,
"Who is there who has not had enough
to eat at Job's table?"
32 No stranger had to spend the night
on the street,
for I opened my door to the traveler.
33 Have I covered my transgressions
as others do[B]
by hiding my iniquity in my heart
34 because I greatly feared the crowds
and because the contempt of the clans
terrified me,
so I grew silent and would not
go outside?

35 If only I had someone to hear my case!
Here is my signature; let the Almighty
answer me.
Let my Opponent compose
his indictment.
36 I would surely carry it on my shoulder
and wear it like a crown.
37 I would give him an account of all
my steps;
I would approach him like a prince.

38 If my land cries out against me
and its furrows join in weeping,
39 if I have consumed its produce
without payment
or shown contempt for its tenants,[C]
40 then let thorns grow instead of wheat
and stinkweed instead of barley.

The words of Job are concluded.

ELIHU'S ANGRY RESPONSE

32 So these three men quit answering Job,
because he was righteous in his own
eyes. 2 Then Elihu son of Barachel the Buzite
from the family of Ram became angry. He was
angry at Job because he had justified himself
rather than God. 3 He was also angry at Job's
three friends because they had failed to refute
him and yet had condemned him.[D]
4 Now Elihu had waited to speak to Job because they were all older than he. 5 But when
he saw that the three men could not answer
Job, he became angry.
6 So Elihu son of Barachel the Buzite replied:
I am young in years,
while you are old;
therefore I was timid and afraid
to tell you what I know.
7 I thought that age should speak
and maturity should teach wisdom.
8 But it is the spirit in a person—
the breath from the Almighty—
that gives anyone understanding.
9 It is not only the old who are wise
or the elderly who understand
how to judge.
10 Therefore I say, "Listen to me.
I too will declare what I know."
11 Look, I waited for your conclusions;
I listened to your insights
as you sought for words.
12 I paid close attention to you.
Yet no one proved Job wrong;
not one of you refuted his arguments.
13 So do not claim,
"We have found wisdom;
let God deal with him, not man."
14 But Job has not directed his argument
to me,
and I will not respond to him
with your arguments.

15 Job's friends are dismayed and can
no longer answer;
words have left them.

[A] 31:27 Lit *and my hand kissed my mouth* [B] 31:33 Or *as Adam* [C] 31:39 Lit *or caused the breath of its tenants to breathe out*
[D] 32:3 Alt Hb tradition reads *condemned God*

16 Should I continue to wait now that
they are silent,
now that they stand there
and no longer answer?
17 I too will answer;[A]
yes, I will tell what I know.
18 For I am full of words,
and my spirit[B] compels me to speak.
19 My heart[C] is like unvented wine;
it is about to burst
like new wineskins.
20 I must speak so that I can find relief;
I must open my lips and respond.
21 I will be partial to no one,
and I will not give anyone
an undeserved title.
22 For I do not know how to give
such titles;
otherwise, my Maker would remove me
in an instant.

ELIHU CONFRONTS JOB

33 But now, Job, pay attention
to my speech,
and listen to all my words.
2 I am going to open my mouth;
my tongue will form words on my palate.
3 My words come from my upright heart,
and my lips speak with sincerity
what they know.
4 The Spirit of God has made me,
and the breath of the Almighty
gives me life.
5 Refute me if you can.
Prepare your case against me;
take your stand.
6 I am just like you before God;
I was also pinched off
from a piece of clay.
7 Fear of me should not terrify you;
no pressure from me should weigh you
down.

8 Surely you have spoken in my hearing,
and I have heard these very[D] words:
9 "I am pure, without transgression;
I am clean and have no iniquity.
10 But he finds reasons to oppose me;
he regards me as his enemy.
11 He puts my feet in the stocks;
he stands watch over all my paths."
12 But I tell you that you are wrong
in this matter,
since God is greater than man.
13 Why do you take him to court
for not answering anything
a person asks?[E]
14 For God speaks time and again,
but a person may not notice it.
15 In a dream, a vision in the night,
when deep sleep comes over people
as they slumber on their beds,
16 he uncovers their ears
and terrifies them[F] with warnings,
17 in order to turn a person
from his actions
and suppress the pride of a person.
18 God spares his soul from the Pit,
his life from crossing the river
of death.[G]
19 A person may be disciplined on his bed
with pain
and constant distress in his bones,
20 so that he detests bread,
and his soul despises his favorite food.
21 His flesh wastes away to nothing,[H]
and his unseen bones stick out.
22 He draws near to the Pit,
and his life to the executioners.
23 If there is an angel on his side,
one mediator out of a thousand,
to tell a person what is right for him[I]
24 and to be gracious to him and say,
"Spare him from going down to the Pit;
I have found a ransom,"
25 then his flesh will be healthier[J] than
in his youth,
and he will return to the days
of his youthful vigor.
26 He will pray to God, and God
will delight in him.
That person will see his face
with a shout of joy,
and God will restore his righteousness
to him.
27 He will look at men and say,
"I have sinned and perverted
what was right;
yet I did not get what I deserved.[K]
28 He redeemed my soul from going down
to the Pit,
and I will continue to see the light."

[A] **32:17** Lit *answer my part* [B] **32:18** Lit *and the spirit of my belly* [C] **32:19** Lit *belly* [D] **33:8** Lit *heard a sound of* [E] **33:13** Lit *court, for he does not answer all his words* [F] **33:16** LXX; MT reads *and seals* [G] **33:18** Or *from perishing by the sword* [H] **33:21** Lit *away from sight* [I] **33:23** Or *to vouch for a person's uprightness* [J] **33:25** Hb obscure [K] **33:27** Lit *and the same was not to me*

29 God certainly does all these things
two or three times to a person
30 in order to turn him back from the Pit,
so he may shine with the light of life.
31 Pay attention, Job, and listen to me.
Be quiet, and I will speak.
32 But if you have something to say,[A]
answer me;
speak, for I would like to justify you.
33 If not, then listen to me;
be quiet, and I will teach you wisdom.

34 Then Elihu continued,[B] saying:
2 Hear my words, you wise ones,
and listen to me,
you knowledgeable ones.
3 Doesn't the ear test words
as the palate tastes food?
4 Let us judge for ourselves what is right;
let us decide together what is good.
5 For Job has declared, "I am righteous,
yet God has deprived me of justice.
6 Would I lie about my case?
My wound[C] is incurable,
though I am without transgression."
7 What man is like Job?
He drinks derision like water.
8 He keeps company with evildoers
and walks with wicked men.
9 For he has said, "A man gains nothing
when he becomes God's friend."

10 Therefore listen to me, you men
of understanding.
It is impossible for God to do wrong,
and for the Almighty to act unjustly.
11 For he repays a person according to
his deeds,
and he gives him what his conduct
deserves.[D]
12 Indeed, it is true that God does not
act wickedly
and the Almighty does not
pervert justice.
13 Who gave him authority over the earth?
Who put him in charge of
the entire world?
14 If he put his mind to it
and withdrew the spirit and breath
he gave,
15 every living thing
would perish together
and mankind would return to the dust.
16 If you have understanding, hear this;
listen to what I have to say.
17 Could one who hates justice
govern the world?
Will you condemn the mighty
Righteous One,
18 who says to a king, "Worthless man!"
and to nobles, "Wicked men!"?
19 God is not partial to princes
and does not favor the rich
over the poor,
for they are all the work of his hands.
20 They die suddenly in the middle
of the night;
people shudder, then pass away.
Even the mighty are removed
without effort.

21 For his eyes watch over a man's ways,
and he observes all his steps.
22 There is no darkness, no deep darkness,
where evildoers can hide.
23 God does not need to examine
a person further,
that one should[E] approach him in court.
24 He shatters the mighty
without an investigation
and sets others in their place.
25 Therefore, he recognizes their deeds
and overthrows them by night,
and they are crushed.
26 In full view of the public,[F]
he strikes them for their wickedness,
27 because they turned aside
from following him
and did not understand any of his ways
28 but caused the poor to cry out to him,
and he heard the outcry of the needy.
29 But when God is silent, who can declare
him guilty?
When he hides his face, who can
see him?
Yet he watches over both individuals
and nations,
30 so that godless men should not rule
or ensnare the people.

31 Suppose someone says to God,
"I have endured my punishment;
I will no longer act wickedly.
32 Teach me what I cannot see;
if I have done wrong, I won't
do it again."

[A] **33:32** Lit *If there are words* [B] **34:1** Lit *answered* [C] **34:6** Lit *arrow* [D] **34:11** Lit *and like a path of a man, he causes him to find* [E] **34:23** Some emend to *God has not appointed a time for man to* [F] **34:26** Lit *In a place of spectators*

33 Should God repay you on your terms
when you have rejected his?
You must choose, not I!
So declare what you know.
34 Reasonable men will say to me,
along with the wise men who hear me,
35 "Job speaks without knowledge;
his words are without insight."
36 If only Job were tested to the limit,
because his answers are like those
of wicked men.
37 For he adds rebellion to his sin;
he scornfully claps in our presence,
while multiplying his words against God.

35 Then Elihu continued, saying:
2 Do you think it is just when you say,
"I am righteous before God"?
3 For you ask, "What does it profit you,[A]
and what benefit comes to me,
if I do not sin?"
4 I will answer you
and your friends with you.
5 Look at the heavens and see;
gaze at the clouds high above you.
6 If you sin, how does it affect God?
If you multiply your transgressions,
what does it do to him?
7 If you are righteous, what do you
give him,
or what does he receive from your hand?
8 Your wickedness affects a person
like yourself,
and your righteousness, a son of man.[B]
9 People cry out because of
severe oppression;
they shout for help because of
the power of the mighty.
10 But no one asks, "Where is God
my Maker,
who provides us with songs in the night,
11 who gives us more understanding
than the animals of the earth
and makes us wiser than the birds
of the sky?"
12 There they cry out,
but he does not answer,
because of the pride of evil people.
13 Indeed, God does not listen
to empty cries,
and the Almighty does not take note
of it —
14 how much less when[C] you complain[D]
that you do not see him,
that your case is before him
and you are waiting for him.
15 But now, because God's anger
does not punish
and he does not pay attention
to transgression,[E]
16 Job opens his mouth in vain
and multiplies words
without knowledge.

36 Then Elihu continued, saying:
2 Be patient with me a little longer,
and I will inform you,
for there is still more to be said
on God's behalf.
3 I will get my knowledge from a
distant place
and ascribe justice to my Maker.
4 Indeed, my words are not false;
one who has complete knowledge is
with you.

5 Yes, God is mighty, but he despises
no one;
he understands all things.[F]
6 He does not keep the wicked alive,
but he gives justice to the oppressed.
7 He does not withdraw his gaze
from the righteous,
but he seats them forever
with enthroned kings,
and they are exalted.

8 If people are bound with chains
and trapped by the cords of affliction,
9 God tells them what they have done
and how arrogantly
they have transgressed.
10 He opens their ears to correction
and tells them to repent from iniquity.
11 If they listen and serve him,
they will end their days in prosperity
and their years in happiness.
12 But if they do not listen,
they will cross the river of death[G]
and die without knowledge.

13 Those who have a godless heart
harbor anger;
even when God binds them,
they do not cry for help.
14 They die in their youth;

[A] 35:3 Some emend to *me* [B] 35:8 Or *a mere mortal* [C] 35:14 Or *how then can* [D] 35:14 Lit *say* [E] 35:15 LXX, Vg; MT reads *folly*, or *arrogance*; Hb obscure [F] 36:5 Lit *he is mighty in strength of heart* [G] 36:12 Or *will perish by the sword*

their life ends among
male cult prostitutes.
15 God rescues the afflicted by
their affliction;
he instructs them by their torment.
16 Indeed, he lured you from the jaws[A]
of distress
to a spacious and unconfined place.
Your table was spread with choice food.
17 Yet now you are obsessed
with the judgment due the wicked;
judgment and justice have seized you.
18 Be careful that no one lures you
with riches;[B]
do not let a large ransom[C] lead you astray.
19 Can your wealth[D] or all
your physical exertion
keep you from distress?
20 Do not long for the night
when nations will disappear
from their places.
21 Be careful that you do not turn
to iniquity,
for that is why you have been tested
by[E] affliction.

22 Look, God shows himself exalted
by his power.
Who is a teacher like him?
23 Who has appointed his way for him,
and who has declared, "You have
done wrong"?
24 Remember that you should praise
his work,
which people have sung about.
25 All mankind has seen it;
people have looked at it from a distance.
26 Yes, God is exalted
beyond our knowledge;
the number of his years
cannot be counted.
27 For he makes waterdrops evaporate;[F]
they distill the rain into its[G] mist,
28 which the clouds pour out
and shower abundantly on mankind.
29 Can anyone understand how the clouds
spread out
or how the thunder roars
from God's pavilion?
30 See how he spreads his lightning
around him
and covers the depths
of the sea.
31 For he judges the nations with these;
he gives food in abundance.
32 He covers his hands with lightning
and commands it to hit its mark.
33 The[H] thunder declares his presence;[I]
the cattle also,
the approaching storm.

37 My heart pounds at this
and leaps from my chest.[J]
2 Just listen to his thunderous voice
and the rumbling that comes
from his mouth.
3 He lets it loose beneath the entire sky;
his lightning to the ends of the earth.
4 Then there comes a roaring sound;
God thunders with his majestic voice.
He does not restrain the lightning
when his rumbling voice is heard.
5 God thunders wondrously
with his voice;
he does great things that
we cannot comprehend.
6 For he says to the snow,
"Fall to the earth,"
and the torrential rains,
his mighty torrential rains,
7 serve as his sign to all mankind,
so that all men may know his work.
8 The wild animals enter their lairs
and stay in their dens.
9 The windstorm comes from its chamber,
and the cold
from the driving north winds.
10 Ice is formed by the breath of God,
and watery expanses are frozen.
11 He saturates clouds with moisture;
he scatters his lightning through them.
12 They swirl about,
turning round and round at his direction,
accomplishing everything
he commands them
over the surface of the inhabited world.
13 He causes this to happen
for punishment,
for his land, or for his faithful love.

14 Listen to this, Job.
Stop and consider God's wonders.

[A] 36:16 Lit *from a mouth of narrowness* [B] 36:18 Or *you into mockery* [C] 36:18 Or *bribe* [D] 36:19 Or *cry for help* [E] 36:21 Or *for you have preferred this to* [F] 36:27 Lit *he draws in waterdrops* [G] 36:27 Or *his* [H] 36:33 Lit *His*, or *Its* [I] 36:33 Lit *thunder announces concerning him* or *it* [J] 37:1 Lit *from its place*

15 Do you know how God directs
his clouds
or makes their lightning flash?
16 Do you understand
how the clouds float,
those wonderful works of him who has
perfect knowledge?
17 You whose clothes get hot
when the south wind brings calm
to the land,
18 can you help God spread out the skies
as hard as a cast metal mirror?
19 Teach us what we should say to him;
we cannot prepare our case because of
our darkness.
20 Should he be told that I want to speak?
Can a man speak
when he is confused?
21 Now no one can even look at the sun
when it is in the skies,
after a wind has swept through and
cleared the clouds away.[A]
22 Yet out of the north he comes,
shrouded in a golden glow;
awesome majesty surrounds him.
23 The Almighty — we cannot
reach him —
he is exalted in power!
He will not violate justice and
abundant righteousness,
24 therefore, men fear him.
He does not look favorably on any
who are wise in heart.

THE LORD SPEAKS

38 Then the LORD answered Job from the
whirlwind. He said:
2 Who is this who obscures my counsel
with ignorant words?
3 Get ready to answer me like a man;
when I question you,
you will inform me.
4 Where were you when I established
the earth?
Tell me, if you have[B] understanding.
5 Who fixed its dimensions?
Certainly you know!
Who stretched a measuring line
across it?
6 What supports its foundations?
Or who laid its cornerstone
7 while the morning stars sang together
and all the sons of God shouted for joy?
8 Who enclosed the sea behind doors
when it burst from the womb,
9 when I made the clouds its garment
and total darkness its blanket,[C]
10 when I determined its boundaries[D]
and put its bars and doors in place,
11 when I declared: "You may come
this far, but no farther;
your proud waves stop here"?

12 Have you ever in your life commanded
the morning
or assigned the dawn its place,
13 so it may seize the edges of the earth
and shake the wicked out of it?
14 The earth is changed as clay is by a seal;
its hills stand out like the folds of
a garment.
15 Light[E] is withheld from the wicked,
and the arm raised in violence
is broken.

16 Have you traveled to the sources
of the sea
or walked in the depths of the oceans?
17 Have the gates of death been revealed
to you?
Have you seen the gates
of deep darkness?
18 Have you comprehended the extent
of the earth?
Tell me, if you know all this.

19 Where is the road to the home
of light?
Do you know where darkness lives,
20 so you can lead it back to its border?
Are you familiar with the paths
to its home?
21 Don't you know? You were
already born;
you have lived so long![F]
22 Have you entered the place
where the snow is stored?
Or have you seen the storehouses
of hail,
23 which I hold in reserve for times
of trouble,
for the day of warfare and battle?
24 What road leads to the place
where light is dispersed?[G]
Where is the source of the east wind
that spreads across the earth?

[A] **37:21** Lit *and cleaned them* [B] **38:4** Lit *know* [C] **38:9** Lit *swaddling clothes* [D] **38:10** Lit *I broke my statute on it* [E] **38:15** Lit *Their light* [F] **38:21** Lit *born; the number of your days is great* [G] **38:24** Or *where lightning is distributed*

25 Who cuts a channel
for the flooding rain
or clears the way for lightning,
26 to bring rain on an uninhabited land,
on a desert with no human life,[A]
27 to satisfy the parched wasteland
and cause the grass to sprout?
28 Does the rain have a father?
Who fathered the drops of dew?
29 Whose womb did the ice come from?
Who gave birth to the frost of heaven
30 when water becomes as hard as stone,[B]
and the surface of the watery depths
is frozen?

31 Can you fasten the chains
of the Pleiades
or loosen the belt of Orion?
32 Can you bring out the constellations[C]
in their season
and lead the Bear[D] and her cubs?
33 Do you know the laws of heaven?
Can you impose its[E] authority on earth?
34 Can you command[F] the clouds
so that a flood of water covers you?
35 Can you send out lightning bolts,
and they go?
Do they report to you: "Here we are"?

36 Who put wisdom in the heart[G]
or gave the mind understanding?
37 Who has the wisdom to number
the clouds?
Or who can tilt the water jars of heaven
38 when the dust hardens like cast metal
and the clods of dirt stick together?

39 Can you hunt prey for a lioness
or satisfy the appetite of young lions
40 when they crouch in their dens
and lie in wait within their lairs?
41 Who provides the raven's food
when its young cry out to God
and wander about for lack of food?

39 Do you know when mountain goats
give birth?
Have you watched the deer in labor?
2 Can you count the months
they are pregnant[H]
so you can know the time
they give birth?
3 They crouch down to give birth
to their young;
they deliver their newborn.[I]
4 Their offspring are healthy
and grow up in the open field.
They leave and do not return.[J]

5 Who set the wild donkey free?
Who released the swift donkey
from its harness?
6 I made the desert its home,
and the salty wasteland its dwelling.
7 It scoffs at the noise of the village
and never hears the shouts of a driver.
8 It roams the mountains
for its pastureland,
searching for anything green.
9 Would the wild ox be willing
to serve you?
Would it spend the night
by your feeding trough?
10 Can you hold the wild ox to a furrow
by its harness?
Will it plow the valleys behind you?
11 Can you depend on it because
its strength is great?
Would you leave it to do
your hard work?
12 Can you trust the wild ox to harvest
your grain
and bring it to your threshing floor?

13 The wings of the ostrich flap joyfully,
but are her feathers and plumage
like the stork's?[K]
14 She abandons her eggs on the ground
and lets them be warmed in the sand.
15 She forgets that a foot may crush them
or that some wild animal
may trample them.
16 She treats her young harshly, as if
they were not her own,
with no fear that her labor
may have been in vain.
17 For God has deprived her of wisdo
he has not endowed her
with understanding.
18 When she proudly[K] spreads he
she laughs at the horse and its
e?
19 Do you give strength to the hane?[K]
Do you adorn his neck wit

[A] 38:26 Lit *no man in it* [B] 38:30 Lit *water hides itself as the stone* [C] 38:32 Or *Mazzaroth*; Hb obscure .32 Or lead Aldebaran [E] 38:33 Or *God's* [F] 38:34 Lit *lift up your voice to* [G] 38:36 Or *the inner self*; Ps 51:6 [H] 39:2 months they fulfill [I] 39:3 Or *they send away their labor pains* [J] 39:4 Lit *return to them* [K] 39:13,18,19 Hb obscure

20 Do you make him leap like a locust?
His proud snorting fills one with terror.
21 He paws[A] in the valley and rejoices
in his strength;
he charges into battle.[B]
22 He laughs at fear, since he is afraid
of nothing;
he does not run from the sword.
23 A quiver rattles at his side,
along with a flashing spear
and a javelin.
24 He charges ahead[C] with trembling rage;
he cannot stand still
at the trumpet's sound.
25 When the trumpet blasts,
he snorts defiantly.[D]
He smells the battle from a distance;
he hears the officers' shouts
and the battle cry.

26 Does the hawk take flight
by your understanding
and spread its wings to the south?
27 Does the eagle soar at your command
and make its nest on high?
28 It lives on a cliff where it spends
the night;
its stronghold is on a rocky crag.
29 From there it searches for prey;
its eyes penetrate the distance.
30 Its brood gulps down blood,
and where the slain are, it is there.

40 The LORD answered Job:
2 Will the one who contends
with the Almighty correct him?
Let him who argues with God
give an answer.[E]

3 Then Job answered the LORD:
4 I am so insignificant. How can I
answer you?
I place my hand over my mouth.
5 I have spoken once, and I will not reply;
twice, but now I can add nothing.

hen the LORD answered Job from the
wind:
t ready to answer me like a man;
n I question you, you will
8 Worm me.
you really challenge my justice?
Would you declare me guilty
to justify yourself?
9 Do you have an arm like God's?
Can you thunder with a voice like his?
10 Adorn yourself with majesty
and splendor,
and clothe yourself with honor
and glory.
11 Pour out your raging anger;
look on every proud person
and humiliate him.
12 Look on every proud person
and humble him;
trample the wicked where they stand.[F]
13 Hide them together in the dust;
imprison them in the grave.[G]
14 Then I will confess to you
that your own right hand
can deliver you.

15 Look at Behemoth,
which I made along with you.
He eats grass like cattle.
16 Look at the strength of his back[H]
and the power in the muscles
of his belly.
17 He stiffens his tail like a cedar tree;
the tendons of his thighs are woven
firmly together.
18 His bones are bronze tubes;
his limbs are like iron rods.
19 He is the foremost of God's works;
only his Maker can draw the sword
against him.
20 The hills yield food for him,
while all sorts of wild animals
play there.
21 He lies under the lotus plants,
hiding in the protection[I]
of marshy reeds.
22 Lotus plants cover him
with their shade;
the willows by the brook
surround him.
23 Though the river rages,
Behemoth is unafraid;
he remains confident, even if
the Jordan surges up to his mouth.
24 Can anyone capture him
while he looks on,
or pierce his nose with snares?

[A] 39:21 LXX, Syr, reads *They dig* [B] 39:21 Lit *he goes out to meet the weaponry* [C] 39:24 Lit *He swallows the ground* [D] 39:25 Lit *he says,* ha!" [E] 40:2 Lit *God respond to it* [F] 40:12 Lit *wicked in their place* [G] 40:13 Lit *together; bind their faces in the hidden* ce [H] 40:16 Or *waist* [I] 40:21 Lit *plants, in the hiding place* [J] 40:24 Lit *capture it in its eyes*

41 Can you pull in Leviathan
with a hook
or tie his tongue down with a rope?
2 Can you put a cord[A] through his nose
or pierce his jaw with a hook?
3 Will he beg you for mercy
or speak softly to you?
4 Will he make a covenant with you
so that you can take him
as a slave forever?
5 Can you play with him like a bird
or put him on a leash[B] for your girls?
6 Will traders bargain for him
or divide him among the merchants?
7 Can you fill his hide with harpoons
or his head with fishing spears?
8 Lay a[C] hand on him.
You will remember the battle
and never repeat it!
9 Any hope of capturing him
proves false.
Does a person not collapse
at the very sight of him?
10 No one is ferocious enough
to rouse Leviathan;
who then can stand against me?
11 Who confronted me, that I
should repay him?
Everything under heaven belongs
to me.
12 I cannot be silent about his limbs,
his power,
and his graceful proportions.
13 Who can strip off his outer covering?
Who can penetrate his double layer
of armor?[D]
14 Who can open his jaws,[E]
surrounded by those terrifying teeth?
15 His pride is in his rows of scales,
closely sealed together.
16 One scale is so close to another[F]
that no air can pass between them.
17 They are joined to one another,
so closely connected[G] they cannot
be separated.
18 His snorting[H] flashes with light,
while his eyes are like the rays[I]
of dawn.
19 Flaming torches shoot from his mouth;
fiery sparks fly out!
20 Smoke billows from his nostrils
as from a boiling pot
or burning reeds.
21 His breath sets coals ablaze,
and flames pour out of his mouth.

Eternal Perspective | *God's Power*

UNSTOPPABLE

"I know that you can do anything and no plan of yours can be thwarted." Job 42:2

When his life was shattered by one terrible disaster after another (chaps. 1–2), Job and his counselor-friends wrestled with one question, "How do we explain such suffering?"

Not until the last five chapters of the book do we find God finally joining the conversation. And does he ever! God fires more than sixty questions at the tongue-tied Job.

The gist of all these divine queries seems to be, "I don't have to explain myself to you. I am the Creator, and you are my creature."

God's response may seem harsh and insensitive, but far from being offended or angry at the Almighty, Job was humbled, and he reverently bowed in humility. Job realized that God was the ruler of the universe, not he.

God is in control. He doesn't need to run his plans by us before he acts.

For the next note on *Eternal Perspective*, see Psalm 5:4.

[A] **41:2** Lit *reed* [B] **41:5** Lit *or bind him* [C] **41:8** Lit *your* [D] **41:13** LXX; MT reads *double bridle* [E] **41:14** Lit *open the doors of his face* [F] **41:16** Lit *One by one they approach* [G] **41:17** Lit *another; they cling together and* [H] **41:18** Or *sneezing* [I] **41:18** Lit *eyelids*

22 Strength resides in his neck,
and dismay dances before him.
23 The folds of his flesh
are joined together,
solid as metal[A] and immovable.
24 His heart is as hard as a rock,
as hard as a lower millstone!
25 When Leviathan rises, the mighty[B]
are terrified;
they withdraw because of
his thrashing.
26 The sword that reaches him will have
no effect,
nor will a spear, dart, or arrow.
27 He regards iron as straw,
and bronze as rotten wood.
28 No arrow can make him flee;
slingstones become like stubble
to him.
29 A club is regarded as stubble,
and he laughs at the sound
of a javelin.
30 His undersides are jagged potsherds,
spreading the mud
like a threshing sledge.
31 He makes the depths seethe
like a cauldron;
he makes the sea like an ointment jar.
32 He leaves a shining wake behind him;[C]
one would think the deep had
gray hair!
33 He has no equal on earth—
a creature devoid of fear!
34 He surveys everything that is haughty;
he is king over all the proud beasts.[D]

JOB REPLIES TO THE LORD

42 Then Job replied to the LORD:
2 I[E] know that you can do anything
and no plan of yours can be thwarted.
3 You asked, "Who is this who conceals
my counsel with ignorance?"
Surely I spoke about things I did not
understand,
things too wondrous for me to[F] know.
4 You said, "Listen now, and I will speak.
When I question you, you will
inform me."
5 I had heard reports about you,
but now my eyes have seen you.
6 Therefore, I reject my words and am
sorry for them;
I am dust and ashes.[G,H]

7 After the LORD had finished speaking[I] to
Job, he said to Eliphaz the Temanite: "I am

Rest and Reflection | *Being Willing to Change*

DUST AND ASHES

"Therefore, I reject my words and am sorry for them; I am dust and ashes." Job 42:6

At key moments in life, the curtain between the seen and the unseen worlds parts. Temporal, mundane issues fade from view. Eternal, holy matters come into focus.

This was Job's experience. After a time of intense suffering, and after debating the Lord's intentions and questioning his ways, Job was stunned into silence by a revelation of God himself.

When he was able at last to speak again, Job stammered, "Surely I spoke about things I did not understand, things too wondrous for me to know" (42:3).

Job took back his hasty, ill-informed words, apologizing for the way he—mere "dust and ashes"—called into question the actions of a holy Creator. Being able to admit, "I was wrong" and being willing to change one's mind-set are the marks of a healthy soul.

Facing the reality of your past behavior can be the first step to restoration.

For the next note on *Rest and Reflection*, see Psalm 5:3.

[A] **41:23** Lit *together, hard on him* [B] **41:25** Or *the divine beings* [C] **41:32** Lit *a path* [D] **41:34** Lit *the children of pride* [E] **42:2** Alt Hb tradition reads *You* [F] **42:3** Lit *me, and I did not* [G] **42:6** LXX reads *I despise myself and melt; I consider myself dust and ashes* [H] **42:6** Lit *I reject and I relent, concerning dust and ashes* [I] **42:7** Lit *speaking these words*

angry with you and your two friends, for you have not spoken the truth about me, as my servant Job has. 8 Now take seven bulls and seven rams, go to my servant Job, and offer a burnt offering for yourselves. Then my servant Job will pray for you. I will surely accept his prayer and not deal with you as your folly deserves. For you have not spoken the truth about me, as my servant Job has." 9 Then Eliphaz the Temanite, Bildad the Shuhite, and Zophar the Naamathite went and did as the LORD had told them, and the LORD accepted Job's prayer.

GOD RESTORES JOB

10 After Job had prayed for his friends, the LORD restored his fortunes and doubled his previous possessions. 11 All his brothers, sisters, and former acquaintances came to him and dined with him in his house. They sympathized with him and comforted him concerning all the adversity the LORD had brought on him. Each one gave him a piece of silver[A] and a gold earring.

12 So the LORD blessed the last part of Job's life more than the first. He owned fourteen thousand sheep and goats, six thousand camels, one thousand yoke of oxen, and one thousand female donkeys. 13 He also had seven sons and three daughters. 14 He named his first daughter Jemimah, his second Keziah, and his third Keren-happuch. 15 No women as beautiful as Job's daughters could be found in all the land, and their father granted them an inheritance with their brothers.

16 Job lived 140 years after this and saw his children and their children to the fourth generation. 17 Then Job died, old and full of days.

[A] **42:11** Lit *a qesitah*; the value of this currency is unknown

The book of *Psalms* is really an entire book of restoration themes. Each psalm is a treasure trove of truths about God's character and ways, as well as the human response to the trials and triumphs of life. Here we find ways to voice the full range of our life experience in words of beauty and truth. The book has honest and desperate cries for help, formal hymns of praise, and everything in between. Undergirding it all is the truth that God is the Sovereign Ruler of the universe, worthy of all glory and honor, and that we are his subjects who should obey and worship him.

Interspersed throughout the psalms is the denotation *Selah*, which scholars interpret as a musical interlude. You can think of these as pauses for reflection and rest. In fact, all the psalms can be thought of that way. These are works of poetry, meant to be lingered over. Spend time with the imagery and metaphors. Unpack the parallel structures and see what each repetition adds to the meaning of the psalm. Enjoy the beauty of hyperbole and symbolism. Imagine these poems being used in worship, either sung or recited. The psalms can only do their restorative work in us if we will slow down, pause, and meditate.

PSALMS

AUTHOR: The book of Psalms is a collection of psalms written by many authors, including David, Solomon (72; 127), Asaph (50; 73—83), the sons of Korah (42; 44–49; 84–85; 87–88), Ethan the Ezrahite (89), Heman the Ezrahite (88), and Moses (90).

DATE WRITTEN: Because it is a collection of psalms written by many authors, the date of the writing of the psalms spans many years, from the fifteenth century BC (Moses) to after the exile (sixth century BC or later). Some psalms contain indications of historical setting although the actual writing could have occurred well after the events that inspired a specific psalm.

ORIGINAL AUDIENCE: The Israelites

SETTING: The word *psalms* literally means "praise" or "songs of praise," and that is what this book is. It is the book of songs and prayers that were used by the Israelites to worship God.

PURPOSE FOR WRITING: Each psalm is an individual poetic unit with its own purpose, but the overall theme of the book is how to approach God in prayer and worship, as well as how God's character affects our daily circumstances. God's steadfast love and faithfulness shines through nearly every psalm, as well as his eternal goodness and justice.

OUTLINE:

The book of Psalms can be organized in a variety of ways, including by author or use (psalms of David, psalms of Asaph, songs of ascent, etc.). Some people choose to group them according to genre (psalms of thanksgiving, lament, praise, etc.). The common grouping according to Jewish tradition is into five books that are based on the arrangement of the Pentateuch, as follows.

Book 1 (chaps. 1–41)

Book 2 (chaps. 42–72)

Book 3 (chaps. 73–89)

Book 4 (chaps. 90–106)

Book 5 (chaps. 107–150)

KEY VERSE:

"Restore us, God; make your face shine on us, so that we may be saved." —Psalm 80:3

RESTORATION THEMES

R	Rest and Reflection	*Waiting on God*—5:3; 27:4; 37:7; 62:1 *Enjoying Creation*—19:1-2; 104:24 *Sitting Silent*—46:10 *Honestly Evaluating Yourself*—51:3-4 *Being Willing to Change*—51:10 *Resting and Recharging*—55:6 *Remembering God's Truth*—62:5; 77:11 *Reflecting*—68:19 *Seeking God*—84:2 *Meditating on God and His Word*—119:15-16 *Avoiding Burnout*—127:2 *Identifying the Issue/Difficulty*—139:23-24
E	Eternal Perspective	*God's View of Sin*—5:4 *God's Justice*—5:6 *Personal Value/Worth*—8:3-5; 100:1-3 *God's Character*—22:1 *God's Forgiveness*—24:3-4; 32:1-2 *Biblical Hope*—27:14 *God's Faithfulness*—31:7; 89:1-2 *God's Knowledge/Omniscience*—33:13-15; 139:1-3; 144:3 *God's Plans*—40:5 *Fear Overcome*—56:3; 118:5-6 *God's Goodness*—86:15 *God's Majesty*—93:4 *God's Compassion*—103:7-8; 145:8-9 *God's Protection*—121:5-8
S	Support	*Honest Seeking*—14:2 *God's Counsel*—16:7-8; 32:8-9; 73:24 *Commitment to God*—37:5 *Prayer*—55:17; 116:1-2; 143:6-7 *Mentors*—145:4
T	Thanksgiving and Contentment	*Perspective*—1:1-3 *Comfort*—23:1-4; 56:8 *Confession*—32:5 *Thanksgiving*—118:24 *Gratitude*—136:1
O	Other-centeredness	*Loving God*—18:1 *Being Honest*—25:21 *Helping People in Need*—41:1 *Helping Widows and Orphans*—68:5

RESTORATION THEMES

R	Relationships	*Controlling Speech—19:14; 141:3* *Taking Personal Inventory—26:2* *Mentoring—71:18* *Encouraging Each Other—88:9* *Treating Others Fairly—106:3*
E	Exercise of Faith	*Applying God's Word—19:7-8* *Sharing Faith/Gospel—96:2-4* *Making the Most of Time on Earth—103:15-16* *Memorizing Scripture—119:11*

BOOK I (Psalms 1–41)

THE TWO WAYS

1 How happy is the one who does not
walk in the advice of the wicked
or stand in the pathway with sinners
or sit in the company of mockers!
2 Instead, his delight is in the
LORD's instruction,
and he meditates on it day and night.
3 He is like a tree planted beside flowing
streams[A]
that bears its fruit in its season
and whose leaf does not wither.
Whatever he does prospers.

4 The wicked are not like this;
instead, they are like chaff
that the wind blows away.
5 Therefore the wicked will not stand up
in the judgment,
nor sinners in the assembly
of the righteous.

6 For the LORD watches over the way
of the righteous,
but the way of the wicked
leads to ruin.

CORONATION OF THE SON

2 Why do the nations rage
and the peoples plot in vain?
2 The kings of the earth take their stand,
and the rulers conspire together
against the LORD
and his Anointed One:[B]
3 "Let's tear off their chains
and throw their ropes off of us."

4 The one enthroned[C] in heaven laughs;
the Lord ridicules them.
5 Then he speaks to them in his anger
and terrifies them in his wrath:
6 "I have installed my king
on Zion, my holy mountain."

7 I will declare the LORD's decree.
He said to me, "You are my Son;[D]
today I have become your Father.
8 Ask of me,
and I will make the nations
your inheritance
and the ends of the earth
your possession.
9 You will break them
with an iron scepter;
you will shatter them like pottery."

Thanksgiving and Contentment | *Perspective*

TWO KINDS OF PEOPLE

"How happy is the one who does not walk in the advice of the wicked or stand in the pathway with sinners or sit in the company of mockers! Instead, his delight is in the LORD's instruction, and he meditates on it day and night. He is like a tree planted beside flowing streams that bears its fruit in its season and whose leaf does not wither. Whatever he does prospers." Psalm 1:1-3

The first prayer-song in Israel's national worship manual contrasts two types of people: the righteous and the wicked.

The righteous (1:1-3) delight in "the LORD's instruction." God's Word—not the trendy ideas of a sinful world—forms their thoughts and guides their behavior. Rooted in truth, their lives resemble a flourishing fruit tree, planted by a flowing stream. Picture a life of rest, blessing, and refreshment.

The wicked (1:4-5), meanwhile, are like those dry husks that blow away in the breeze when grain is being threshed. Picture something lifeless, worthless, and insignificant.

We have a choice in the kind of life we want. We can be fruit trees or chaff. Prosperity and health begin with listening to the Lord's instruction.

For the next note on *Thanksgiving and Contentment*, see Psalm 23:1-4.

[A] **1:3** Or *beside irrigation channels* [B] **2:2** Or *anointed one* [C] **2:4** Lit *who sits* [D] **2:7** Or *son*, also in v. 12

10 So now, kings, be wise;
receive instruction, you judges
of the earth.
11 Serve the LORD with reverential awe
and rejoice with trembling.
12 Pay homage to[A] the Son or he
will be angry
and you will perish in your rebellion,[B]
for his anger may ignite
at any moment.
All who take refuge in him are happy.

CONFIDENCE IN TROUBLED TIMES

3 *A psalm of David when he fled from his son Absalom.*

1 LORD, how my foes increase!
There are many who attack me.
2 Many say about me,
"There is no help for him in God." *Selah*

3 But you, LORD, are a shield around me,
my glory, and the one who lifts up
my head.
4 I cry aloud to the LORD,
and he answers me
from his holy mountain. *Selah*

5 I lie down and sleep;
I wake again because the LORD
sustains me.
6 I will not be afraid of thousands
of people
who have taken their stand against me
on every side.

7 Rise up, LORD!
Save me, my God!
You strike all my enemies on the cheek;
you break the teeth of the wicked.
8 Salvation belongs to the LORD;
may your blessing be
on your people. *Selah*

A NIGHT PRAYER

4 *For the choir director: with stringed instruments. A psalm of David.*

1 Answer me when I call,
God, who vindicates me.[C]
You freed me from affliction;
be gracious to me and hear my prayer.

2 How long, exalted ones,[D] will my honor
be insulted?
How long will you love
what is worthless
and pursue a lie? *Selah*

Rest and Reflection | *Waiting on God*

MORNINGS WITH GOD

"In the morning, LORD, you hear my voice; in the morning I plead my case to you and watch expectantly." Psalm 5:3

To the question—"Which is better: reading my Bible in the morning or at night?" —the answer is simple: Do it whenever you are most alert!

Evenings are fine for having a "quiet time." But we also need *something* at the beginning of each new day to keep a healthy perspective. Just because we're out of bed and moving doesn't mean our souls are awake. Author George MacDonald expressed this truth well, writing, "Sometimes I wake and, lo, I have forgot, and drifted out upon an ebbing sea. My soul that was at rest, now resteth not. For I am with myself and not with thee."

This explains why so many Christians choose to spend a few minutes in the morning being still before the Lord, monitoring their hearts (Pr 4:23) and praying about the scheduled events of the day. Morning prayers were David's practice. (Of course, elsewhere he speaks of praying morning, noon, and night! See Ps 55:17.)

Even five minutes focused on God's presence and power will make a huge difference as you launch out into your day.

For the next note on *Rest and Reflection*, see Psalm 19:1-2.

[A] **2:12** Lit *Kiss* [B] **2:12** Lit *perish in the way* [C] **4:1** Or *God of my righteousness* [D] **4:2** Lit *long, sons of a man*

3 Know that the LORD has set apart
the faithful for himself;
the LORD will hear when I call to him.
4 Be angry[A] and do not sin;
on your bed, reflect in your heart
and be still. *Selah*
5 Offer sacrifices in righteousness[B]
and trust in the LORD.

6 Many are asking, "Who can show us
anything good?"
Let the light of your face shine
on us, LORD.

7 You have put more joy in my heart
than they have when their grain
and new wine abound.
8 I will both lie down and sleep in peace,
for you alone, LORD, make me live
in safety.

THE REFUGE OF THE RIGHTEOUS

For the choir director: with the flutes.
A psalm of David.
1 Listen to my words, LORD;
consider my sighing.
2 Pay attention to the sound of my cry,
my King and my God,
for I pray to you.
3 In the morning, LORD, you hear
my voice;
in the morning I plead my case to you
and watch expectantly.

4 For you are not a God who delights
in wickedness;
evil cannot dwell with you.
5 The boastful cannot stand in your sight;
you hate all evildoers.
6 You destroy those who tell lies;
the LORD abhors
violent and treacherous people.

7 But I enter your house
by the abundance of your faithful love;
I bow down toward your holy temple
in reverential awe of you.
8 LORD, lead me in your righteousness
because of my adversaries;
make your way straight before me.

9 For there is nothing reliable in what
they say;
destruction is within them;
their throat is an open grave;
they flatter with their tongues.
10 Punish them, God;
let them fall by their own schemes.

E Eternal Perspective | *God's View of Sin*

ABSOLUTELY PURE

"For you are not a God who delights in wickedness; evil cannot dwell with you." Psalm 5:4

A tablespoon of pure water added to a pitcher full of toxic waste leaves us with toxic waste. On the other hand, if we add a tablespoon of toxic waste to a pitcher full of pure water—we also get toxic waste. (Why would anyone drink from either pitcher?) Pure water has *no* impurities.

This illustrates holiness. When we speak of God being holy, we mean that he is morally pure. No part of his character is polluted by evil. Not one of his actions is ethically wrong; they're all perfect. It is not just that he is without sin; instead, by his nature, he hates it because it kills what he loves.

The good news of the gospel is that Jesus died to take away our unholiness and to give us his righteousness. Through Jesus, we get to become the children of a holy God!

This should make us less tolerant of sin in our lives. We should "pursue . . . holiness" (Heb 12:14), keeping in mind this amazing promise: "So if anyone purifies himself from anything dishonorable, he will be a special instrument, set apart, useful to the Master, prepared for every good work" (2Tm 2:21).

For the next note on *Eternal Perspective*, see Psalm 5:6.

[A] **4:4** Or *Tremble* [B] **4:5** Or *Offer right sacrifices*

Drive them out because of
their many crimes,
for they rebel against you.

11 But let all who take refuge in you
rejoice;
let them shout for joy forever.
May you shelter them,
and may those who love your name
boast about you.
12 For you, LORD, bless the righteous one;
you surround him with favor
like a shield.

A PRAYER FOR MERCY

6 *For the choir director: with stringed instruments, according to* Sheminith. *A psalm of David.*

1 LORD, do not rebuke me in your anger;
do not discipline me in your wrath.
2 Be gracious to me, LORD,
for I am weak;[A]
heal me, LORD, for my bones are shaking;
3 my whole being is shaken with terror.
And you, LORD — how long?

4 Turn, LORD! Rescue me;
save me because of your faithful love.
5 For there is no remembrance of you
in death;
who can thank you in Sheol?
6 I am weary from my groaning;
with my tears I dampen my bed
and drench my couch every night.
7 My eyes are swollen from grief;
they grow old because of all
my enemies.

8 Depart from me, all evildoers,
for the LORD has heard the sound
of my weeping.
9 The LORD has heard my plea for help;
the LORD accepts my prayer.
10 All my enemies will be ashamed
and shake with terror;
they will turn back and suddenly
be disgraced.

PRAYER FOR JUSTICE

7 A Shiggaion *of David, which he sang to the LORD concerning the words of Cush, a Benjaminite.*

1 LORD my God, I seek refuge in you;
save me from all my pursuers
and rescue me
2 or they[B] will tear me like a lion,

E Eternal Perspective | *God's Justice*

THE JUDGE OF ALL THE EARTH

"You destroy those who tell lies; the LORD abhors violent and treacherous people." Psalm 5:6

We find turmoil in our souls because we rightly hate injustice. People have wronged us (or others we love) and we want these culprits to be held accountable. We insist that allowing people to lie, steal, harm, or take advantage and avoid the consequences is not fair.

Nothing is wrong with any of those feelings. But when we refuse to entrust such matters to God, we become angry, resentful, and obsessed with payback.

Talk about backfiring! Such attitudes have no effect on the people who have wronged us. They only have a toxic effect on our own souls. Such bitterness, as someone has noted, is like drinking poison and waiting for the other person to die!

David shows us a better way. Here, as in other psalms, he vents honestly as he thinks about his enemies and their brazen behavior. But ultimately he lands on a big theological certainty: God is just, and he will one day punish evil. The wicked will not escape. They will have to answer to the Judge of all the earth. When we rest in this truth, we are able to avoid the trap of a bitter heart.

For the next note on *Eternal Perspective*, see Psalm 8:3-5.

[A] **6:2** Or *sick* [B] **7:2** Lit *he*

ripping me apart with no one
to rescue me.

3 LORD my God, if I have done this,
if there is injustice on my hands,
4 if I have done harm to one at peace
with me
or have plundered[A] my adversary
without cause,
5 may an enemy pursue
and overtake me;
may he trample me to the ground
and leave my honor in the dust. *Selah*

6 Rise up, LORD, in your anger;
lift yourself up against the fury
of my adversaries;
awake for me;[B]
you have ordained a judgment.
7 Let the assembly of peoples gather
around you;
take your seat on high over it.
8 The LORD judges the peoples;
vindicate me, LORD,
according to my righteousness
and my integrity.

9 Let the evil of the wicked come to an end,
but establish the righteous.
The one who examines the thoughts
and emotions[C]
is a righteous God.
10 My shield is with God,
who saves the upright in heart.
11 God is a righteous judge
and a God who shows his wrath
every day.

12 If anyone does not repent,
he will sharpen his sword;
he has strung his bow
and made it ready.
13 He has prepared
his deadly weapons;
he tips his arrows with fire.

14 See, the wicked one is pregnant
with evil,
conceives trouble, and gives birth
to deceit.
15 He dug a pit and hollowed it out
but fell into the hole he had made.
16 His trouble comes back
on his own head;
his own violence comes down on top
of his head.

Eternal Perspective | *Personal Value/Worth*

CROWNED WITH GLORY

"When I observe your heavens, the work of your fingers, the moon and the stars, which you set in place, what is a human being that you remember him, a son of man that you look after him? You made him little less than God and crowned him with glory and honor." Psalm 8:3-5

Imagine driving down a pitch-black country road in the middle of nowhere and impulsively pulling your car onto the shoulder. Killing the engine (and your lights), you get out, hop on the trunk, and lean back. As your eyes widen, so does your mouth.

Your pulse quickens. You almost can't catch your breath. Staring up into all that twinkling vastness, you temporarily lose the power of speech, largely because you have no words to describe such beauty. You feel wonder and awe and . . . incredibly insignificant.

David experienced this same wonder. Thankfully, he remembered a vital truth: that we humans—small as we are—are of infinite importance to God.

Maybe today you don't feel what David felt, like you're crowned "with glory and honor." No matter. You are. Take it by faith. Stars or no stars, God's love for you lifts your eyes to him.

For the next note on *Eternal Perspective*, see Psalm 22:1.

[A] **7:4** Or *me and have spared* [B] **7:6** LXX reads *awake, Lord my God* [C] **7:9** Lit *examines hearts and kidneys*

17 I will thank the LORD
for his righteousness;
I will sing about the name of the LORD
Most High.

GOD'S GLORY, HUMAN DIGNITY

8

For the choir director: on the Gittith.
A psalm of David.

1 LORD, our Lord,
how magnificent is your name
throughout the earth!

You have covered the heavens
with your majesty.[A]
2 From the mouths of infants and
nursing babies,
you have established a stronghold[B]
on account of your adversaries
in order to silence the enemy
and the avenger.

3 When I observe your heavens,
the work of your fingers,
the moon and the stars,
which you set in place,
4 what is a human being
that you remember him,
a son of man[C] that you look after him?
5 You made him little less than God[D,E]
and crowned him with glory
and honor.
6 You made him ruler over the works
of your hands;
you put everything under his feet:
7 all the sheep and oxen,
as well as the animals in the wild,
8 the birds of the sky,
and the fish of the sea
that pass through the currents of the seas.

9 LORD, our Lord,
how magnificent is your name
throughout the earth!

CELEBRATION OF GOD'S JUSTICE

9

For the choir director: according to Muth-labben.
A psalm of David.

1 I will thank the LORD with all my heart;
I will declare all
your wondrous works.
2 I will rejoice and boast about you;
I will sing about your name,
Most High.

3 When my enemies retreat,
they stumble and perish before you.
4 For you have upheld my just cause;
you are seated on your throne
as a righteous judge.
5 You have rebuked the nations:
You have destroyed the wicked;
you have erased their name forever
and ever.
6 The enemy has come to eternal ruin.
You have uprooted the cities,
and the very memory of them
has perished.

7 But the LORD sits enthroned forever;
he has established his throne
for judgment.
8 And he judges the world
with righteousness;
he executes judgment on the nations
with fairness.
9 The LORD is a refuge for the persecuted,
a refuge in times of trouble.
10 Those who know your name
trust in you
because you have not abandoned
those who seek you, LORD.

11 Sing to the LORD, who dwells in Zion;
proclaim his deeds
among the nations.
12 For the one who seeks an accounting
for bloodshed remembers them;
he does not forget the cry
of the oppressed.

13 Be gracious to me, LORD;
consider my affliction at the hands
of those who hate me.
Lift me up from the gates of death,
14 so that I may declare all your praises.
I will rejoice in your salvation
within the gates of Daughter Zion.

15 The nations have fallen into the pit
they made;
their foot is caught in the net
they have concealed.
16 The LORD has made himself known;
he has executed justice,
snaring the wicked
by the work of their hands.
Higgaion. Selah

[A] **8:1** Lit *earth, which has set your splendor upon the heavens* [B] **8:2** LXX reads *established praise* [C] **8:4** Or *a mere mortal*
[D] **8:5** LXX reads *angels* [E] **8:5** Or *heavenly beings*; Hb *Elohim*

17 The wicked will return to Sheol —
all the nations that forget God.
18 For the needy will not always
be forgotten;
the hope of the oppressed[A]
will not perish forever.

19 Rise up, LORD! Do not let
mere humans prevail;
let the nations be judged
in your presence.
20 Put terror in them, LORD;
let the nations know they are
only humans. *Selah*

NEED FOR GOD'S JUSTICE

10 LORD,[B,C] why do you stand so far away?
Why do you hide in times of trouble?
2 In arrogance the wicked
relentlessly pursue their victims;
let them be caught in the schemes
they have devised.

3 For the wicked one boasts about
his own cravings;
the one who is greedy curses[D]
and despises the LORD.
4 In all his scheming,
the wicked person arrogantly thinks,[E]
"There's no accountability,
since there's no God."
5 His ways are always secure;[F]
your lofty judgments have no effect
on him;[G]
he scoffs at all his adversaries.
6 He says to himself, "I will never
be moved —
from generation to generation
without calamity."
7 Cursing, deceit, and violence
fill his mouth;
trouble and malice are
under his tongue.
8 He waits in ambush near settlements;
he kills the innocent in secret places.
His eyes are on the lookout
for the helpless;
9 he lurks in secret like a lion in a thicket.
He lurks in order to seize a victim;
he seizes a victim and drags him
in his net.
10 So he is oppressed and beaten down;
helpless people fall because of the
wicked one's strength.
11 He says to himself, "God has forgotten;
he hides his face and will never see."

12 Rise up, LORD God! Lift up your hand.
Do not forget the oppressed.
13 Why has the wicked person
despised God?
He says to himself, "You will not
demand an account."
14 But you yourself have seen trouble
and grief,
observing it in order to take the matter
into your hands.
The helpless one entrusts himself to you;
you are a helper of the fatherless.
15 Break the arm of the wicked,
evil person,
until you look for his wickedness,
but it can't be found.

16 The LORD is King forever and ever;
the nations will perish from his land.
17 LORD, you have heard the desire
of the humble;
you will strengthen their hearts.
You will listen carefully,
18 doing justice for the fatherless
and the oppressed
so that mere humans from the earth
may terrify them no more.

REFUGE IN THE LORD

11 *For the choir director.*
Of David.
1 I have taken refuge in the LORD.
How can you say to me,
"Escape to the mountains[H] like a bird!
2 For look, the wicked string bows;
they put their arrows on bowstrings
to shoot from the shadows
at the upright in heart.
3 When the foundations are destroyed,
what can the righteous do?"

4 The LORD is in his holy temple;
the LORD—his throne is in heaven.
His eyes watch;
his gaze[I] examines everyone.[J]

[A] **9:18** Alt Hb tradition reads *humble* [B] **10:1** Some Hb mss, LXX connect Pss 9–10. [C] **10:1** Together Pss 9–10 form a partial acrostic. [D] **10:3** Or *he blesses the greedy* [E] **10:4** Lit *wicked according to the height of his nose* [F] **10:5** Or *prosperous* [G] **10:5** Lit *judgments are away from in front of him* [H] **11:1** Lit *your mountain* [I] **11:4** Lit *eyelids* [J] **11:4** Or *examines the descendants of Adam*

My Story | Ian

I have been following Jesus for more than half a century. That may read like a long time, but it now seems like no time at all. And "following Jesus" may sound impressive, but it has often been a less than total focus in my life. The benefit of hindsight is seeing not so much the consistency of my faith but the tenacious consistency of God's faithfulness.

While I understand that David probably wrote Psalm 23 early in life, I certainly hope he got to the end of his years with the same thoughts echoing in his heart and mind. The four verbs in verses 2 and 3, "lets, leads, renews, leads" all point to things God does repeatedly and often unexpectedly. That has been my own experience. David only claimed two actions for himself in that song of God's persistent presence: "I fear no danger" and "I will dwell." Everything else is God's doing. Since the second action is a future hope, the only task the psalm writer owns is basing a lack of fear on the reality of God's presence even in the darkest places. I can relate to that acknowledgement of limited capability, but even here I am ashamed to say that on far too many occasions I have feared when I had no need to fear.

The word "renews" in verse 3 has often interrupted wandering times in my life. Each time I have been reminded that I needed some green pastures, quiet waters, or a right path—sometimes all three. These simple pictures have represented so many vivid moments for me. And they have led to a renewed sense that God hadn't altered his view of me or his work in me, no matter where I have found myself at the moment of awareness. Countless times I have discovered what Jeremiah realized about God when he exclaimed, "His mercies never end. They are new every morning" (Lm 3:22-23).

Half a century still comes down to needing God's renewing, merciful work, which is new every morning.

5 The LORD examines the righteous,
but he hates the wicked
and[A] those who love violence.
6 Let him rain burning coals[B] and sulfur
on the wicked;
let a scorching wind be the portion
in their cup.
7 For the LORD is righteous; he loves
righteous deeds.
The upright will see his face.

OPPRESSION BY THE WICKED

12 *For the choir director: according to* Sheminith. *A psalm of David.*

1 Help, LORD, for no faithful one remains;
the loyal have disappeared
from the human race.[C]
2 They lie to one another;
they speak with flattering lips
and deceptive hearts.
3 May the LORD cut off all flattering lips
and the tongue that speaks boastfully.
4 They say, "Through our tongues
we have power;
our lips are our own — who can be
our master?"
5 "Because of the devastation
of the needy
and the groaning of the poor,
I will now rise up," says the LORD.
"I will provide safety for the one
who longs for it."

6 The words of the LORD are pure words,
like silver refined
in an earthen furnace,
purified seven times.

7 You, LORD, will guard us;[D]
you will protect us[E]
from this generation forever.
8 The wicked prowl[F] all around,
and what is worthless is exalted
by the human race.

A PLEA FOR DELIVERANCE

13 *For the choir director. A psalm of David.*

1 How long, LORD? Will you forget me
forever?
How long will you hide your face
from me?

[A] **11:5** Or *righteous and the wicked, and he hates* [B] **11:6** Sym; MT reads *rain snares, fire* [C] **12:1** Or *the descendants of Adam,* also in v. 8 [D] **12:7** Some Hb mss, LXX, Jer; other Hb mss read *them* [E] **12:7** Some Hb mss, LXX; other Hb mss read *him* [F] **12:8** Lit *walk about*

2 How long will I store up
anxious concerns[A] within me,
agony in my mind every day?
How long will my enemy dominate me?

3 Consider me and answer, LORD my God.
Restore brightness to my eyes;
otherwise, I will sleep in death.
4 My enemy will say, "I have triumphed
over him,"
and my foes will rejoice
because I am shaken.

5 But I have trusted in your faithful love;
my heart will rejoice in
your deliverance.
6 I will sing to the LORD
because he has treated
me generously.

A PORTRAIT OF SINNERS

14 *For the choir director. Of David.*
The fool says in his heart,
"There's no God."
They are corrupt; they do vile deeds.
There is no one who does good.
2 The LORD looks down from heaven
on the human race[B]
to see if there is one who is wise,
one who seeks God.

3 All have turned away;
all alike have become corrupt.
There is no one who does good,
not even one.

4 Will evildoers never understand?
They consume my people
as they consume bread;
they do not call on the LORD.

5 Then[C] they will be filled with dread,
for God is with those
who are[D] righteous.
6 You sinners frustrate the plans
of the oppressed,
but the LORD is his refuge.

7 Oh, that Israel's deliverance
would come from Zion!
When the LORD restores the fortunes
of his people,[E]
let Jacob rejoice, let Israel be glad.

A DESCRIPTION OF THE GODLY

15 *A psalm of David.*
LORD, who can dwell in your tent?
Who can live on your holy mountain?

2 The one who lives blamelessly,
practices righteousness,

S Support | *Honest Seeking*

THE ULTIMATE SEEKER

"The LORD looks down from heaven on the human race to see if there is one who is wise, one who seeks God." Psalm 14:2

As hopeful as this verse sounds—that some people might be wise enough to see the truth about God and noble enough to seek after him—the next verse gives the grim "rest of the story." "All have turned away; all alike have become corrupt. There is no one who does good, not even one" (Ps 14:3).

Thankfully, the Bible reveals God to be the ultimate "Seeker." When we run from God, he comes running after us (see Gn 3)! Jesus added in the New Testament that only because the Father first draws us are we able to come to him (Jn 6:44).

This is grace, and this is good news. It means if you find stirrings in your heart to open the Bible, to know God better, to get unstuck spiritually, it's because God is already at work in your soul! Rejoice! Be thankful for God's love. Celebrate! As C. S. Lewis noted, "Unless he wanted you, you would not be wanting him."

For the next note on *Support*, see Psalm 16:7-8.

[A] **13:2** Or *up counsels* [B] **14:2** Or *the descendants of Adam* [C] **14:5** Or *There* [D] **14:5** Lit *with the generation of the* [E] **14:7** Or *restores his captive people*

and acknowledges the truth
in his heart —
3 who does not slander with his tongue,
who does not harm his friend
or discredit his neighbor,
4 who despises the one rejected
by the LORD[A]
but honors those who fear the LORD,
who keeps his word whatever the cost,
5 who does not lend his silver
at interest
or take a bribe against the innocent —
the one who does these things
will never be shaken.

CONFIDENCE IN THE LORD

16 *A Miktam of David.*
Protect me, God, for I take refuge in you.
2 I[B] said to the LORD, "You are my Lord;
I have nothing good besides you."[C]
3 As for the holy people who are
in the land,
they are the noble ones.
All my delight is in them.
4 The sorrows of those who take
another god
for themselves will multiply;
I will not pour out their drink offerings
of blood,
and I will not speak their names
with my lips.

5 LORD, you are my portion[D]
and my cup of blessing;
you hold my future.
6 The boundary lines have fallen for me
in pleasant places;
indeed, I have a beautiful inheritance.

7 I will bless the LORD who counsels me —
even at night when my thoughts
trouble me.[E]
8 I always let the LORD guide me.[F]
Because he is at my right hand,
I will not be shaken.

9 Therefore my heart is glad
and my whole being rejoices;
my body also rests securely.
10 For you will not abandon me to Sheol;
you will not allow your faithful one
to see decay.

S Support | *God's Counsel*

GUIDANCE COUNSELOR

"I will bless the LORD who counsels me — even at night when my thoughts trouble me. I always let the LORD guide me. Because he is at my right hand, I will not be shaken." Psalm 16:7-8

People read horoscopes, consult psychics, hire life coaches, and make appointments with therapists. Why? We know why. People want advice. They want an expert who can provide direction, a guru who will tell them what to do. What about you? Where do you turn when you are confused and uncertain about where to go next?

Here David says, "The LORD . . . counsels me." Then he adds, "I always let [him] guide me."

How does that process work? Some look for divine guidance through mystical experiences: dreams, visions, angelic messengers, prophetic announcements. Others yearn for God's audible voice. Can the Lord direct his people via such channels? Of course! The Bible is filled with examples of such guidance.

But we shouldn't forget that we can also be led as we are filled with God's Spirit (Eph 5:18) and steeped in God's Word (Ps 119:105). The Spirit of God and the Word of God will always be in agreement and will never lead us astray.

For the next note on *Support*, see Psalm 32:8-9.

[A] **15:4** Lit *in his eyes the rejected is despised* [B] **16:2** Some Hb mss, LXX, Syr, Jer; other Hb mss read *You* [C] **16:2** Or *"Lord, my good; there is none besides you."* [D] **16:5** Or *allotted portion* [E] **16:7** Or *at night my heart instructs me* [F] **16:8** Lit *I place the LORD in front of me always*

11 You reveal the path of life to me;
in your presence is abundant joy;
at your right hand are eternal pleasures.

A PRAYER FOR PROTECTION

17 *A prayer of David.*
LORD, hear a just cause;
pay attention to my cry;
listen to my prayer —
from lips free of deceit.
2 Let my vindication come from you,
for you see what is right.
3 You have tested my heart;
you have examined me at night.
You have tried me and found
nothing evil;
I have determined that my mouth
will not sin.[A]
4 Concerning what people do:
by the words from your lips
I have avoided the ways
of the violent.
5 My steps are on your paths;
my feet have not slipped.

6 I call on you, God,
because you will answer me;
listen closely to me;
hear what I say.
7 Display the wonders
of your faithful love,
Savior of all who seek refuge
from those who rebel
against your right hand.[B]
8 Protect me as the pupil of your eye;
hide me in the shadow of your wings
9 from[C] the wicked
who treat me violently,[D]
my deadly enemies
who surround me.

10 They are uncaring;[E]
their mouths speak arrogantly.
11 They advance against me;[F]
now they surround me.
They are determined[G]
to throw me to the ground.
12 They are[H] like a lion eager to tear,
like a young lion lurking in ambush.

13 Rise up, LORD!
Confront him; bring him down.
With your sword, save me
from the wicked.

Other-centeredness | *Loving God*

TO DIE FOR

"I love you, LORD, my strength." Psalm 18:1

A young husband, who honestly doesn't enjoy the theater, takes his new bride to New York to see *three* Broadway shows. Why? An exhausted mom sleeps four nights straight in an uncomfortable chair in a frigid ICU waiting room. Why? A betrayed spouse forgives (and takes back!) an unfaithful partner. Why?

Because love doesn't always make sense. Love takes risks and never says "die." (Why else do people speak of "stubborn love" and being "crazy in love"?) God's love is like that. When we rebelled against him, he sent his Son not to get us, but to *die for us*. Try to wrap your head around such lavish, endless affection!

Have you noticed the way love often creates more love? Knowing we are loved unconditionally frees us to stop being selfish and to start loving. This, of course, is what the Bible says, "We love because he first loved us" (1Jn 4:19).

If you don't feel very loving today—toward God or others—ask the one who *is* love (1Jn 4:8) to fill your heart. Then do loving acts and watch loving feelings follow.

For the next note on *Other-centeredness*, see Psalm 25:21.

[A] **17:3** Or *evil; my mouth will not sin* [B] **17:7** Or *love, you who save with your right hand those seeking refuge from adversaries* [C] **17:9** Lit *from the presence of* [D] **17:9** Or *who plunder me* [E] **17:10** Lit *have closed up their fat* [F] **17:11** Vg; MT reads *Our steps* [G] **17:11** Lit *They set their eyes* [H] **17:12** Lit *He is*

14 With your hand, LORD, save me
from men,
from men of the world
whose portion is in this life:
You fill their bellies with what you have
in store;
their sons are satisfied,
and they leave their surplus
to their children.

15 But I will see your face
in righteousness;
when I awake, I will be satisfied
with your presence.[A]

PRAISE FOR DELIVERANCE

18 *For the choir director. Of the servant of the LORD, David, who spoke the words of this song to the LORD on the day the LORD rescued him from the grasp of all his enemies and from the power of Saul. He said:*

1 I love you, LORD, my strength.
2 The LORD is my rock,
my fortress, and my deliverer,
my God, my rock where I seek refuge,
my shield and the horn of my salvation,
my stronghold.
3 I called to the LORD, who is
worthy of praise,
and I was saved from my enemies.

4 The ropes of death were wrapped
around me;
the torrents of destruction
terrified me.
5 The ropes of Sheol entangled me;
the snares of death confronted me.
6 I called to the LORD in my distress,
and I cried to my God for help.
From his temple he heard my voice,
and my cry to him reached his ears.

7 Then the earth shook and quaked;
the foundations of the mountains
trembled;
they shook because he burned
with anger.
8 Smoke rose from his nostrils,
and consuming fire came
from his mouth;
coals were set ablaze by it.[B]
9 He bent the heavens and came down,
total darkness beneath his feet.
10 He rode on a cherub and flew,
soaring on the wings of the wind.
11 He made darkness his hiding place,
dark storm clouds his canopy
around him.
12 From the radiance of his presence,
his clouds swept onward with hail
and blazing coals.
13 The LORD thundered from[C] heaven;
the Most High made his voice heard.[D]
14 He shot his arrows and scattered them;
he hurled[E] lightning bolts
and routed them.
15 The depths of the sea became visible,
the foundations of the world
were exposed,
at your rebuke, LORD,
at the blast of the breath
of your nostrils.

16 He reached down from on high
and took hold of me;
he pulled me out of deep water.
17 He rescued me
from my powerful enemy
and from those who hated me,
for they were too strong for me.
18 They confronted me in the day
of my calamity,
but the LORD was my support.
19 He brought me out to a spacious place;
he rescued me because he delighted
in me.

20 The LORD rewarded me
according to my righteousness;
he repaid me
according to the cleanness
of my hands.
21 For I have kept the ways of the LORD
and have not turned from my God
to wickedness.
22 Indeed, I let all his ordinances guide me[F]
and have not disregarded his statutes.
23 I was blameless toward him
and kept myself from my iniquity.
24 So the LORD repaid me
according to my righteousness,
according to the cleanness of my hands
in his sight.

25 With the faithful
you prove yourself faithful,

[A] **17:15** Lit *form* [B] **18:8** Or *him* [C] **18:13** Some Hb mss, LXX, Tg, Jer; other Hb mss read *in* [D] **18:13** Some Hb mss read *voice, with hail and blazing coals* [E] **18:14** Or *multiplied* [F] **18:22** Lit *Indeed, all his ordinances have been in front of me*

with the blameless
you prove yourself blameless,
26 with the pure
you prove yourself pure;
but with the crooked
you prove yourself shrewd.
27 For you rescue an oppressed people,
but you humble those
with haughty eyes.
28 LORD, you light my lamp;
my God illuminates my darkness.
29 With you I can attack a barricade,[A]
and with my God
I can leap over a wall.

30 God — his way is perfect;
the word of the LORD is pure.
He is a shield to all who take refuge
in him.
31 For who is God besides the LORD?
And who is a rock? Only our God.
32 God — he clothes me with strength
and makes my way perfect.
33 He makes my feet like the feet
of a deer
and sets me securely on the heights.[B]
34 He trains my hands for war;
my arms can bend a bow of bronze.
35 You have given me the shield
of your salvation;
your right hand upholds me,
and your humility exalts me.
36 You make a spacious place beneath me
for my steps,
and my ankles do not give way.

37 I pursue my enemies
and overtake them;
I do not turn back until they are
wiped out.
38 I crush them, and they cannot get up;
they fall beneath my feet.
39 You have clothed me with strength
for battle;
you subdue my adversaries
beneath me.
40 You have made my enemies retreat
before me;[C]
I annihilate those who hate me.
41 They cry for help, but there is no one
to save them —
they cry to the LORD, but he does not
answer them.
42 I pulverize them like dust
before the wind;
I trample them[D] like mud in the streets.

Rest and Reflection | *Enjoying Creation*

LISTEN UP!

"The heavens declare the glory of God, and the expanse proclaims the work of his hands. Day after day they pour out speech; night after night they communicate knowledge." Psalm 19:1-2

Perhaps on one of those nights he was tending sheep in the Judean countryside, David had an epiphany. Looking into the starry skies, he realized that creation itself testifies loudly and continually to the reality and glory of God.

In other words, for those who are unable to read the written Scriptures, the whole universe is one big Bible! Author A. W. Tozer said that God "is by his nature continuously articulate. He fills the world with his speaking Voice."

So much for the idea that God is silent. On the contrary, he is forever trying to get our attention. The real problem is that we are often tuned to other channels.

Take some time today to listen to creation—if you're near the ocean, or in the mountains, all the better. If you're not, you can still pay attention to the birds, observe people, watch the clouds, feel the wind or the rain. What is God revealing to you about himself?

For the next note on *Rest and Reflection*, see Psalm 27:4.

[A] **18:29** Or *a ridge*, or *raiders* [B] **18:33** Or *on my high places* [C] **18:40** Or *You gave me the necks of my enemies*
[D] **18:42** Some Hb mss, LXX, Syr, Tg; other Hb mss read *I poured them out*

43 You have freed me from the feuds
among the people;
you have appointed me the head
of nations;
a people I had not known serve me.
44 Foreigners submit to me cringing;
as soon as they hear they obey me.
45 Foreigners lose heart
and come trembling
from their fortifications.

46 The LORD lives — blessed be my rock!
The God of my salvation is exalted.
47 God — he grants me vengeance
and subdues peoples under me.
48 He frees me from my enemies.
You exalt me above my adversaries;
you rescue me from violent men.
49 Therefore I will give thanks to you
among the nations, LORD;
I will sing praises about your name.
50 He gives great victories to his king;
he shows loyalty to his anointed,
to David and his descendants forever.

THE WITNESS OF CREATION AND SCRIPTURE

For the choir director. A psalm of David.
The heavens declare the glory of God,
and the expanse proclaims the work
of his hands.
2 Day after day they pour out speech;
night after night
they communicate knowledge.[A]
3 There is no speech; there are
no words;
their voice is not heard.
4 Their message[B] has gone out
to the whole earth,
and their words to the ends
of the world.

In the heavens he has pitched a tent
for the sun.
5 It is like a bridegroom coming from
his home;
it rejoices like an athlete
running a course.
6 It rises from one end of the heavens
and circles to their other end;
nothing is hidden from its heat.

7 The instruction of the LORD is perfect,
renewing one's life;
the testimony of the LORD
is trustworthy,
making the inexperienced wise.
8 The precepts of the LORD are right,
making the heart glad;
the command of the LORD is radiant,
making the eyes light up.

E Exercise of Faith | *Applying God's Word*

READ, CONTEMPLATE, OBEY

"The instruction of the LORD is perfect, renewing one's life; the testimony of the LORD is trustworthy, making the inexperienced wise. The precepts of the LORD are right, making the heart glad; the command of the LORD is radiant, making the eyes light up." Psalm 19:7-8

An infomercial offers a new resource with the potential to do the following: change your life and give you reliable, practical wisdom in situations. Do you think, That sounds too good to be true and change the channel? Or do you grab your cell phone and place an order?

In effect, these are the amazing claims David makes for Holy Scripture. Speaking from his own experience, he calls God's Word perfect, trustworthy, right, and radiant.

So do this: Begin with the earnest prayer of the psalm writer, "Open my eyes so that I may contemplate wondrous things from your instruction" (Ps 119:18).

Then open your Bible and read!

For the next note on *Exercise of Faith*, see Psalm 96:2-4.

[A] **19:2** Or *Day to day pours out speech, and night to night communicates knowledge* [B] **19:4** LXX, Sym, Syr, Vg; MT reads *line*

9 The fear of the LORD is pure,
enduring forever;
the ordinances of the LORD are reliable
and altogether righteous.
10 They are more desirable than gold —
than an abundance of pure gold;
and sweeter than honey
dripping from a honeycomb.
11 In addition, your servant is warned
by them,
and in keeping them there is
an abundant reward.

12 Who perceives his unintentional sins?
Cleanse me from my hidden faults.
13 Moreover, keep your servant
from willful sins;
do not let them rule me.
Then I will be blameless
and cleansed from blatant rebellion.
14 May the words of my mouth
and the meditation of my heart
be acceptable to you,
LORD, my rock and my Redeemer.

DELIVERANCE IN BATTLE

20 *For the choir director. A psalm of David.*
May the LORD answer you in a day
of trouble;
may the name of Jacob's God
protect you.
2 May he send you help
from the sanctuary
and sustain you from Zion.
3 May he remember all your offerings
and accept your burnt offering. *Selah*

4 May he give you what
your heart desires
and fulfill your whole purpose.
5 Let us shout for joy at your victory
and lift the banner in the name
of our God.
May the LORD fulfill all your requests.

6 Now I know that the LORD gives victory
to his anointed;
he will answer him from his holy heaven
with mighty victories
from his right hand.
7 Some take pride in chariots, and others
in horses,
but we take pride in the name of the
LORD our God.
8 They collapse and fall,
but we rise and stand firm.
9 LORD, give victory to the king!
May he[A] answer us on the day that we call.

R Relationships | *Controlling Speech*

TONGUE TROUBLES?

"May the words of my mouth and the meditation of my heart be acceptable to you, LORD, my rock and my Redeemer." Psalm 19:14

A harsh word here. A "little white lie" there. A careless comment that sparks a huge misunderstanding. Oh, the messes we make with our mouths!

Maybe you've got some statements you'd like to take back. Or you wish you could have a do-over of a few entire conversations. Everyone feels that. Of course, we can't unsay words that we've already spoken. We can only seek forgiveness and try, with God's help, to do better in the future.

That's why, for so many, this verse is such a blessing. Memorized and whispered sincerely to God before and during big conversations, this breath prayer has kept many people from saying words they later would regret.

Notice that David focuses not only on his words, but also on the heart behind his words. (When our hearts are right, our words will be good.) Note, also, that God is a "rock and . . . Redeemer." In other words, God steadies the shaky soul who has to say hard things. And he is able to redeem our verbal mess-ups!

For the next note on *Relationships*, see Psalm 26:2.

[A] **20:9** Or *LORD, save. May the king*

THE KING'S VICTORY

21

For the choir director. A psalm of David.

LORD, the king finds joy
in your strength.
How greatly he rejoices in your victory!
2 You have given him his heart's desire
and have not denied the request
of his lips. *Selah*
3 For you meet him with rich blessings;
you place a crown of pure gold
on his head.
4 He asked you for life, and you gave it
to him —
length of days forever and ever.
5 His glory is great through your victory;
you confer majesty and splendor
on him.
6 You give him blessings forever;
you cheer him with joy
in your presence.
7 For the king relies on the LORD;
through the faithful love
of the Most High
he is not shaken.

8 Your hand will capture
all your enemies;
your right hand will seize
those who hate you.
9 You will make them burn
like a fiery furnace when you appear;
the LORD will engulf them in his wrath,
and fire will devour them.
10 You will wipe their progeny
from the earth
and their offspring
from the human race.[A]
11 Though they intend to harm[B] you
and devise a wicked plan,
they will not prevail.
12 Instead, you will put them to flight
when you ready your bowstrings
to shoot at them.

13 Be exalted, LORD, in your strength;
we will sing and praise your might.

FROM SUFFERING TO PRAISE

22

For the choir director: according to "The Deer of the Dawn." A psalm of David.

1 My God, my God, why have you
abandoned me?
Why are you so far
from my deliverance

Eternal Perspective | *God's Character*

REAL LIFE

"My God, my God, why have you abandoned me? Why are you so far from my deliverance and from my words of groaning?" Psalm 22:1

Sometimes we get to enjoy life: Crackling fires. Giggling babies. Sunsets. Old friends. Vacations by the sea. Love so beautiful, it hurts. God's tangible presence.

And sometimes we're forced to endure life: Failures. Good-byes. Break-ups. Pink slips. Crippling fear. Depression. A sense of God's absence.

Enduring life was David's experience. We don't know the specific trouble he faced—only that he'd obviously had better times in life. Notice what he did. First, he *spoke up* to God. He didn't deny the fact that he felt forsaken, ignored, unheard by God. Second, he *looked up* to God. Rather than venting to friends, David took his concerns straight to the Lord. There, while lamenting his situation before God, he began to recall these truths about God—his holiness (22:3), trustworthiness (22:4-5), power (22:20-21), attentiveness (22:24), and the fact that he is in charge (22:28-29).

Something about this simple exercise in remembering God's character changed David's mood. He moved from hopelessness to hopefulness. If you take David's approach, when you have difficulties to endure, you will find joy.

For the next note on *Eternal Perspective*, see Psalm 24:3-4.

[A] **21:10** Or *the descendants of Adam* [B] **21:11** Lit *they stretch out harm against*

and from my words
of groaning?
2 My God, I cry by day, but you
do not answer,
by night, yet I have no rest.
3 But you are holy,
enthroned on the praises of Israel.
4 Our fathers trusted in you;
they trusted, and you rescued them.
5 They cried to you and were set free;
they trusted in you
and were not disgraced.

6 But I am a worm and not a man,
scorned by mankind and despised
by people.
7 Everyone who sees me mocks me;
they sneer[A] and shake their heads:
8 "He relies on[B] the LORD;
let him save him;
let the LORD[C] rescue him,
since he takes pleasure in him."
9 It was you who brought me out
of the womb,
making me secure at my mother's breast.
10 I was given over to you at birth;[D]
you have been my God
from my mother's womb.

11 Don't be far from me, because distress
is near
and there's no one to help.

12 Many bulls surround me;
strong ones of Bashan encircle me.
13 They open their mouths against me —
lions, mauling and roaring.
14 I am poured out like water,
and all my bones are disjointed;
my heart is like wax,
melting within me.
15 My strength is dried up like baked clay;
my tongue sticks to the roof of my mouth.
You put me into the dust of death.
16 For dogs have surrounded me;
a gang of evildoers has closed in on me;
they pierced[E] my hands and my feet.
17 I can count all my bones;
people[F] look and stare at me.
18 They divided my garments
among themselves,
and they cast lots
for my clothing.

19 But you, LORD, don't be far away.
My strength, come quickly to help me.
20 Rescue my life from the sword,
my only life[G] from the power
of these dogs.
21 Save me from the lion's mouth,
from the horns of wild oxen.

You answered me![H]
22 I will proclaim your name
to my brothers and sisters;
I will praise you in the assembly.
23 You who fear the LORD, praise him!
All you descendants of Jacob, honor him!
All you descendants of Israel,
revere him!
24 For he has not despised or abhorred
the torment of the oppressed.
He did not hide his face from him
but listened when he cried to him
for help.

25 I will give praise in the great assembly
because of you;
I will fulfill my vows
before those who fear you.[I]
26 The humble will eat and be satisfied;
those who seek the LORD will praise him.
May your hearts live forever!

27 All the ends of the earth will remember
and turn to the LORD.
All the families of the nations
will bow down before you,
28 for kingship belongs to the LORD;
he rules the nations.
29 All who prosper on earth will eat
and bow down;
all those who go down to the dust
will kneel before him —
even the one who cannot preserve
his life.
30 Their descendants will serve him;
the next generation will be told
about the Lord.
31 They will come and declare
his righteousness;
to a people yet to be born
they will declare what he has done.

[A] **22:7** Lit *separate with the lip* [B] **22:8** Or *Rely on* [C] **22:8** Lit *let him* [D] **22:10** Lit *was cast on you from the womb* [E] **22:16** Some Hb mss, LXX, Syr; other Hb mss read *me; like a lion* [F] **22:17** Lit *they* [G] **22:20** Lit *my only one* [H] **22:21** Or *oxen you rescued me* [I] **22:25** Lit *him*

THE GOOD SHEPHERD

23 *A psalm of David.*
The LORD is my shepherd;
I have what I need.
2 He lets me lie down
in green pastures;
he leads me beside quiet waters.
3 He renews my life;
he leads me along the right paths[A]
for his name's sake.
4 Even when I go
through the darkest valley,[B]
I fear no danger,
for you are with me;
your rod and your staff —
they comfort me.

5 You prepare a table before me
in the presence of my enemies;
you anoint my head with oil;
my cup overflows.
6 Only goodness and faithful love
will pursue me
all the days of my life,
and I will dwell in[C] the house
of the LORD
as long as I live.[D]

THE KING OF GLORY

24 *A psalm of David.*
The earth and everything in it,
the world and its inhabitants,
belong to the LORD;
2 for he laid its foundation on the seas
and established it on the rivers.

3 Who may ascend the mountain
of the LORD?
Who may stand in his holy place?
4 The one who has clean hands
and a pure heart,
who has not appealed
to[E] what is false,
and who has not sworn deceitfully.
5 He will receive blessing from the LORD,
and righteousness[F] from the God
of his salvation.
6 Such is the generation of those
who inquire of him,
who seek the face of the God
of Jacob.[G] *Selah*

7 Lift up your heads, you gates!
Rise up, ancient doors!
Then the King of glory will come in.

Thanksgiving and Contentment | *Comfort*

THE GOOD SHEPHERD

"The LORD is my shepherd; I have what I need. He lets me lie down in green pastures; he leads me beside quiet waters. He renews my life; he leads me along the right paths for his name's sake. Even when I go through the darkest valley, I fear no danger, for you are with me; your rod and your staff—they comfort me." Psalm 23:1-4

The most famous, best-loved psalm? Psalm 23, hands down. How much comfort through the ages these ancient words have given the scared, the sick, the grieving, and the weary!

We can easily see why. If we really are like prone-to-wander sheep, and if God is like an attentive, caring, protective shepherd, then these words are wonderful news.

In the New Testament, Jesus seizes on all these images. He calls himself "the good shepherd" (Jn 10:11, 14). He seats a hungry flock of people in a green pasture and feeds them (Mk 6:39). He quiets stormy waters to comfort the ones he loves (Mk 4:39). He says he is the path, or "the way" (Jn 14:6).

In other words, if you are scared, sick, grieving, or weary today, Jesus is the One you need.

For the next note on *Thanksgiving and Contentment*, see Psalm 32:5.

[A] **23:3** Or *me in paths of righteousness* [B] **23:4** Or *the valley of the shadow of death* [C] **23:6** LXX, Sym, Syr, Tg, Vg, Jer; MT reads *will return to* [D] **23:6** Lit *LORD for length of days*; traditionally *LORD forever* [E] **24:4** Lit *not lifted up his soul to* [F] **24:5** Or *vindication* [G] **24:6** LXX; some Hb mss, Syr read *seek your face, God of Jacob*; some Hb mss read *seek your face, Jacob*

8 Who is this King of glory?
The LORD, strong and mighty,
the LORD, mighty in battle.
9 Lift up your heads, you gates!
Rise up, ancient doors!
Then the King of glory will come in.
10 Who is he, this King of glory?
The LORD of Armies,
he is the King of glory. *Selah*

DEPENDENCE ON THE LORD

25 *Of David.*
LORD, I appeal to you.[A]
2 My God, I trust in you.
Do not let me be disgraced;
do not let my enemies gloat over me.
3 No one who waits for you
will be disgraced;
those who act treacherously
without cause
will be disgraced.

4 Make your ways known to me, LORD;
teach me your paths.
5 Guide me in your truth and teach me,
for you are the God of my salvation;
I wait for you all day long.
6 Remember, LORD, your compassion
and your faithful love,
for they have existed from antiquity.[B]
7 Do not remember the sins of my youth
or my acts of rebellion;
in keeping with your faithful love,
remember me
because of your goodness, LORD.

8 The LORD is good and upright;
therefore he shows sinners the way.
9 He leads the humble in what is right
and teaches them his way.
10 All the LORD's ways show faithful love
and truth
to those who keep his covenant
and decrees.
11 LORD, for the sake of your name,
forgive my iniquity, for it is immense.

12 Who is this person who fears
the LORD?
He will show him the way
he should choose.
13 He will live a good life,
and his descendants will inherit
the land.[C]
14 The secret counsel of the LORD
is for those who fear him,
and he reveals his covenant to them.
15 My eyes are always on the LORD,
for he will pull my feet
out of the net.

E Eternal Perspective | *God's Forgiveness*

PURE-HEARTED PEOPLE

"Who may ascend the mountain of the LORD? Who may stand in his holy place? The one who has clean hands and a pure heart, who has not appealed to what is false, and who has not sworn deceitfully." Psalm 24:3-4

The Bible teaches that God is holy, pure, perfect, and set apart from evil, and that he requires all who would draw close to him to be holy (see Lv 20:26; Heb 12:14).

Logically, this makes perfect sense. Practically, this makes our hearts sink. Who among us is holy? Who lives perfectly for ten minutes, much less all the time? If—to adapt the words of this verse—our hands sometimes do dirty things because our hearts are impure, and if we're *not* always truthful, how can we possibly stand before the Lord?

We can do so through Jesus. He died to pay for our impurities, and he rose to give us his righteousness. This is the gospel or good news. When we put our faith in him, we are forgiven and washed clean. We become new creatures (2Co 5:17), with new, pure hearts. Why is this so important? Because Jesus said, "Blessed are the pure in heart, for they will see God" (Mt 5:8).

For the next note on *Eternal Perspective*, see Psalm 27:14.

[A] **25:1** Or *To you, LORD, I lift up my soul* [B] **25:6** Or *everlasting* [C] **25:13** Or *earth*

16 Turn to me and be gracious to me,
for I am alone and afflicted.
17 The distresses of my heart increase;[A]
bring me out of my sufferings.
18 Consider my affliction and trouble,
and forgive all my sins.
19 Consider my enemies;
they are numerous,
and they hate me violently.
20 Guard me and rescue me;
do not let me be put to shame,
for I take refuge in you.
21 May integrity and what is right
watch over me,
for I wait for you.

22 God, redeem Israel, from all
its distresses.

PRAYER FOR VINDICATION

26 *Of David.*
Vindicate me, LORD,
because I have lived with integrity
and have trusted in the LORD
without wavering.
2 Test me, LORD, and try me;
examine my heart and mind.
3 For your faithful love guides me,[B]
and I live by your truth.
4 I do not sit with the worthless
or associate with hypocrites.
5 I hate a crowd of evildoers,
and I do not sit with the wicked.
6 I wash my hands in innocence
and go around your altar, LORD,
7 raising my voice in thanksgiving
and telling about
your wondrous works.

8 LORD, I love the house where you dwell,
the place where your glory resides.
9 Do not destroy me along with sinners,
or my life along with men
of bloodshed
10 in whose hands are evil schemes
and whose right hands are filled
with bribes.

11 But I live with integrity;
redeem me and be gracious to me.
12 My foot stands on level ground;
I will bless the LORD in the assemblies.

MY STRONGHOLD

27 *Of David.*
The LORD is my light
and my salvation —
whom should I fear?

O Other-centeredness | *Being Honest*

PEOPLE OF INTEGRITY

"May integrity and what is right watch over me, for I wait for you." Psalm 25:21

Integrity is such a good word. It means "wholeness" or "completeness." A bridge with "structural integrity" is complete. It has 100 percent of the girders and bolts it needs—not 89.3 percent. As a result, the bridge is sound and dependable.

More than just a cool word, however, integrity is a vital quality. A person with integrity is morally whole—no glaring gap in his character, no hypocritical disconnect between what he says he believes and the way he behaves. He's not honest in front of the kids and unethical when he's doing a business deal. Integrity is consistency. What you see is what you get.

For these reasons, we can trust people of integrity. They're not perfect, mind you. They fail on a regular basis. But they're quick to admit those failures. They ask forgiveness and seek to do right in the future. In this, they're consistent.

Commit to being a person of integrity.

For the next note on *Other-centeredness*, see Psalm 41:1.

[A] **25:17** Or *Relieve the distresses of my heart* [B] **26:3** Lit *love is in front of my eyes*

The LORD is the stronghold of my life —
whom should I dread?
2 When evildoers came against me
to devour my flesh,
my foes and my enemies stumbled
and fell.
3 Though an army deploys against me,
my heart will not be afraid;
though a war breaks out against me,
I will still be confident.

4 I have asked one thing from the LORD;
it is what I desire:
to dwell in the house of the LORD
all the days of my life,
gazing on the beauty of the LORD
and seeking him in his temple.
5 For he will conceal me in his shelter
in the day of adversity;
he will hide me under the cover
of his tent;
he will set me high on a rock.
6 Then my head will be high
above my enemies around me;
I will offer sacrifices in his tent
with shouts of joy.
I will sing and make music to the LORD.

7 LORD, hear my voice when I call;
be gracious to me and answer me.
8 My heart says this about you:
"Seek[A] his face."
LORD, I will seek your face.
9 Do not hide your face from me;
do not turn your servant away in anger.
You have been my helper;
do not leave me or abandon me,
God of my salvation.
10 Even if my father and mother
abandon me,
the LORD cares for me.

11 Because of my adversaries,
show me your way, LORD,
and lead me on a level path.
12 Do not give me over to the will of my foes,
for false witnesses rise up against me,
breathing violence.

13 I am certain that I will see the
LORD's goodness
in the land of the living.
14 Wait for the LORD;
be strong, and let your heart
be courageous.
Wait for the LORD.

MY STRENGTH

28 *Of David.*
LORD, I call to you;
my rock, do not be deaf to me.
If you remain silent to me,

Relationships | *Taking Personal Inventory*

EXAMINATION

"Test me, LORD, and try me; examine my heart and mind." Psalm 26:2

The esteemed philosopher Socrates said, "The unexamined life is not worth living." But King David, some five hundred years before Socrates, asked God to examine him.

For many, this prospect—looking inward or letting another do so—is terrifying. It needn't be. Submitting to an examination is just plain wise. Think about how often we already do that in other parts of life. That annual physical meant to surface any medical issues. That regular dental checkup designed to help us keep our teeth. Those periodic consultations with our financial advisor so that we stay on track for retirement. A visit to a trainer or coach to correct a flaw in the way we are exercising or swinging.

Admittedly, praying, "Lord, examine me. Show me specifically where I need to change" can be nerve-wracking. (Because deep down, we know we have more blind spots and flaws than politicians have promises!) If we are brave enough to make that request sincerely, however, God will gently show us. Then, if we're humble and teachable, real change can start to happen.

For the next note on *Relationships*, see Psalm 71:18.

[A] **27:8** The command is pl in Hb

I will be like those going down to the Pit.
2 Listen to the sound of my pleading
when I cry to you for help,
when I lift up my hands
toward your holy sanctuary.

3 Do not drag me away with the wicked,
with the evildoers,
who speak in friendly ways
with their neighbors
while malice is in their hearts.
4 Repay them according to what
they have done —
according to the evil of their deeds.
Repay them according to the work
of their hands;
give them back what they deserve.
5 Because they do not consider
what the LORD has done
or the work of his hands,
he will tear them down and not
rebuild them.

6 Blessed be the LORD,
for he has heard the sound
of my pleading.
7 The LORD is my strength and my shield;
my heart trusts in him, and I am helped.
Therefore my heart celebrates,
and I give thanks to him with my song.

8 The LORD is the strength of his people;[A]
he is a stronghold of salvation
for his anointed.
9 Save your people,
bless your possession,
shepherd them, and carry them forever.

THE VOICE OF THE LORD

29 *A psalm of David.*
Ascribe to the LORD,
you heavenly beings,[B]
ascribe to the LORD glory and strength.
2 Ascribe to the LORD the glory due
his name;
worship the LORD
in the splendor of his holiness.[C]

3 The voice of the LORD is
above the waters.
The God of glory thunders —
the LORD, above the vast water,

Rest and Reflection | *Waiting on God*

THE PRESENCE OF GOD

"I have asked one thing from the LORD; it is what I desire: to dwell in the house of the LORD all the days of my life, gazing on the beauty of the LORD and seeking him in his temple." Psalm 27:4

"To dwell in the house of the LORD all the days of my life" is an ancient way of saying, "I want to live 24/7/365 in God's presence."

In one sense we already *do* live in God's presence. This is because God is everywhere. We can't go anywhere where he is not. But in another sense, we *don't* live in God's presence—at least not consciously.

This explains why many Christians engage in the discipline of "practicing God's presence." Their goal is to be deliberately mindful of God's nearness—and then to act accordingly.

Those who do this—who develop the habit of "gazing on the beauty of the LORD"—see their attitudes change. The irritations of life stop overwhelming them. They're more content, peaceful, and joyful (Ps 16:11). This internal shift always affects our external behavior. Because we're enjoying our heart's desire, we're no longer restless, scrambling frantically, chasing after lesser things.

Tell God you want to learn to "practice his presence."

For the next note on *Rest and Reflection*, see Psalm 37:7.

[A] **28:8** Some Hb mss, LXX, Syr; other Hb mss read *strength for them* [B] **29:1** Or *you sons of gods*, or *you sons of mighty ones* [C] **29:2** Or *in holy attire*, or *in holy appearance*

4 the voice of the LORD in power,
the voice of the LORD in splendor.
5 The voice of the LORD
breaks the cedars;
the LORD shatters the cedars
of Lebanon.
6 He makes Lebanon skip like a calf,
and Sirion, like a young wild ox.
7 The voice of the LORD flashes
flames of fire.
8 The voice of the LORD shakes
the wilderness;
the LORD shakes the wilderness
of Kadesh.
9 The voice of the LORD makes the deer
give birth[A]
and strips the woodlands bare.

In his temple all cry, "Glory!"

10 The LORD sits enthroned
over the flood;
the LORD sits enthroned, King forever.
11 The LORD gives his people strength;
the LORD blesses his people with
peace.

JOY IN THE MORNING

30 *A psalm; a dedication song for the house. Of David.*

1 I will exalt you, LORD,
because you have lifted me up
and have not allowed my enemies
to triumph over me.
2 LORD my God,
I cried to you for help, and you
healed me.
3 LORD, you brought me up from Sheol;
you spared me from among those
going down[B] to the Pit.

4 Sing to the LORD, you his faithful ones,
and praise his holy name.
5 For his anger lasts only a moment,
but his favor, a lifetime.
Weeping may stay overnight,
but there is joy in the morning.

6 When I was secure, I said,
"I will never be shaken."
7 LORD, when you showed your favor,
you made me stand
like a strong mountain;

E Eternal Perspective | *Biblical Hope*

WAITING HOPEFULLY

"Wait for the LORD; be strong, and let your heart be courageous. Wait for the LORD." Psalm 27:14

Some people seem to think the word *wait* means to sigh loudly, shake your head, roll your eyes, tap your foot nervously, mutter angrily under your breath, complain bitterly, and give someone a piece of your mind.

Ancient Jews understood the word *wait* to mean, literally, "to hope in or to hope for something." This is why the same Hebrew word is translated "wait" in some passages and "hope" in others. What's more, the Jews defined "hope" not like we do—as wishing for an outcome that is unlikely. Instead, for them it was a "confident expectation."

All this means that when David urges us to "wait for the LORD," he doesn't mean, "Get ready to waste a lot of time—and try not to get frustrated!" On the contrary, he's saying, "Don't quit or lose heart! Instead, get ready for something really good. Expect it, sooner or later!"

Imagine the difference in our moods, relationships, and lives, if we lived and prayed with this kind of biblical hope. No doubt David would agree with our modern saying, "Good things come to those who wait."

For the next note on *Eternal Perspective*, see Psalm 31:7.

[A] **29:9** Or *the oaks shake* [B] **30:3** Some Hb mss, LXX, Theod, Orig, Syr; other Hb mss, Aq, Sym, Tg, Jer read *from going down*

Embracing God's Word | Peace

TROUBLES. DIVISION. WARS INSIDE AND OUT. Surrounded by conflicts and chaos, we long for quiet and calm. Scripture promises peace *with* God and the peace *of* God when we surrender.

I will both lie down and sleep in peace, for you alone, LORD, make me live in safety. –Psalm 4:8

The LORD gives his people strength; the LORD blesses his people with peace. –Psalm 29:11

I will listen to what God will say; surely the LORD will declare peace to his people, his faithful ones, and not let them go back to foolish ways. –Psalm 85:8

Abundant peace belongs to those who love your instruction; nothing makes them stumble. –Psalm 119:165

You will keep the mind that is dependent on you in perfect peace, for it is trusting in you. –Isaiah 26:3

The result of righteousness will be peace; the effect of righteousness will be quiet confidence forever. Then my people will dwell in a peaceful place, in safe and secure dwellings. –Isaiah 32:17-18

I will cut off the chariot from Ephraim and the horse from Jerusalem. The bow of war will be removed, and he will proclaim peace to the nations. –Zechariah 9:10a

[Jesus] got up, rebuked the wind, and said to the sea, "Silence! Be still!" The wind ceased, and there was a great calm. Then he said to them, "Why are you afraid? Do you still have no faith?" –Mark 4:39-40

Peace I leave with you. My peace I give to you. I do not give to you as the world gives. Don't let your heart be troubled or fearful. –John 14:27

I have told you these things so that in me you may have peace. You will have suffering in this world. Be courageous! I have conquered the world. –John 16:33

Therefore, since we have been declared righteous by faith, we have peace with God through our Lord Jesus Christ. –Romans 5:1

Therefore, do not let your good be slandered, for the kingdom of God is not eating and drinking, but righteousness, peace, and joy in the Holy Spirit. –Romans 14:16-17

Grace to you and peace from God our Father and the Lord Jesus Christ. –2 Corinthians 1:2

Don't worry about anything, but in everything, through prayer and petition with thanksgiving, present your requests to God. And the peace of God, which surpasses all understanding, will guard your hearts and minds in Christ Jesus. –Philippians 4:6-7

May the Lord of peace himself give you peace always in every way. –2 Thessalonians 3:16

And the fruit of righteousness is sown in peace by those who cultivate peace. –James 3:18

when you hid your face,
I was terrified.
8 LORD, I called to you;
I sought favor from my Lord:
9 "What gain is there in my death,
if I go down to the Pit?
Will the dust praise you?
Will it proclaim your truth?
10 LORD, listen and be gracious to me;
LORD, be my helper."

11 You turned my lament into dancing;
you removed my sackcloth
and clothed me with gladness,
12 so that I can sing to you and not be silent.
LORD my God, I will praise you forever.

A PLEA FOR PROTECTION

31 *For the choir director. A psalm of David.*
LORD, I seek refuge in you;
let me never be disgraced.
Save me by your righteousness.
2 Listen closely to me; rescue me quickly.
Be a rock of refuge for me,
a mountain fortress to save me.
3 For you are my rock and my fortress;
you lead and guide me
for your name's sake.
4 You will free me from the net
that is secretly set for me,
for you are my refuge.
5 Into your hand I entrust my spirit;
you have redeemed me,[A] LORD,
God of truth.

6 I[B] hate those who are devoted
to worthless idols,
but I trust in the LORD.
7 I will rejoice and be glad
in your faithful love
because you have seen my affliction.
You know the troubles of my soul
8 and have not handed me over
to the enemy.
You have set my feet
in a spacious place.

9 Be gracious to me, LORD,
because I am in distress;
my eyes are worn out
from frustration —
my whole being[C] as well.
10 Indeed, my life is consumed with grief
and my years with groaning;
my strength has failed
because of my iniquity,[D]
and my bones waste away.
11 I am ridiculed by all my adversaries
and even by my neighbors.
I am dreaded by my acquaintances;
those who see me in the street
run from me.

Eternal Perspective | *God's Faithfulness*

GOD'S COVENANT LOVE

"I will rejoice and be glad in your faithful love because you have seen my affliction. You know the troubles of my soul." Psalm 31:7

So many things in this world seem unreliable. People let us down. Appliances stop working. Investments fail. Politicians break promises. If only we had one steady, consistent, sure thing.

According to this psalm, we do: the love of God. Here David used the Hebrew word *chesed*, which means "loyal, covenant love." This love builds—not on anything we have done or might do—but on the dependable character and sure promises of God. God's *chesed* reveals an undying commitment. He never changes or withholds it. God has given his word to pursue his people in love—no matter what. This makes it the surest guarantee in the universe.

Could you use some unfailing kindness and steadfast devotion today? Call out to the God who sees your affliction and knows the troubles of your soul—then rejoice and be glad in his faithful love!

For the next note on *Eternal Perspective*, see Psalm 32:1-2.

[A] **31:5** Or *spirit. Redeem me* [B] **31:6** One Hb ms, LXX, Syr, Vg, Jer read *You* [C] **31:9** Lit *my soul and my belly* [D] **31:10** LXX, Syr, Sym read *affliction*

12 I am forgotten: gone from memory
like a dead person —
like broken pottery.
13 I have heard the gossip of many;
terror is on every side.
When they conspired against me,
they plotted to take my life.

14 But I trust in you, LORD;
I say, "You are my God."
15 The course of my life is
in your power;
rescue me from the power
of my enemies
and from my persecutors.
16 Make your face shine on your servant;
save me by your faithful love.
17 LORD, do not let me be disgraced
when I call on you.
Let the wicked be disgraced;
let them be quiet[A,B] in Sheol.
18 Let lying lips
that arrogantly speak
against the righteous
in proud contempt be silenced.

19 How great is your goodness
that you have stored up for those
who fear you
and accomplished in the sight
of everyone[C]
for those who take refuge in you.
20 You hide them in the protection
of your presence;
you conceal them in a shelter
from human schemes,
from quarrelsome tongues.
21 Blessed be the LORD,
for he has wondrously shown
his faithful love to me
in a city under siege.
22 In my alarm I said,
"I am cut off from your sight."
But you heard the sound of my pleading
when I cried to you for help.

23 Love the LORD, all his faithful ones.
The LORD protects the loyal,
but fully repays the arrogant.
24 Be strong, and let your heart
be courageous,
all you who put your hope in the LORD.

THE JOY OF FORGIVENESS

32 *Of David. A* Maskil.
How joyful is the one
whose transgression is forgiven,
whose sin is covered!

Eternal Perspective | *God's Forgiveness*

THE FREEDOM OF FORGIVENESS

"How joyful is the one whose transgression is forgiven, whose sin is covered! How joyful is a person whom the LORD does not charge with iniquity and in whose spirit is no deceit!" Psalm 32:1-2

Remember how you felt on the last day of school, or when you made that last loan payment, or when someone you'd wronged horribly pulled you close and bear hugged you?

God's forgiveness is something like that. We are set free. A great burden of guilt gets lifted off our shoulders. In the place of shame, we experience honor and joy.

Some think David may have been reflecting here on his affair with Bathsheba (see 2Sm 11). Perhaps so, but that surely wasn't the only time David made a wrong choice in life. He knew what we all need to know: Every failure needs to be acknowledged, and God's forgiveness is enough for them all.

If God brings some wrong attitude or action to your mind, don't let deceit reign in your spirit. Don't deny what's true. Instead, turn to the One who has provided full forgiveness in Jesus Christ. Fall into his merciful arms and experience the joy of a clean heart.

For the next note on *Eternal Perspective*, see Psalm 33:13-15.

[A] **31:17** LXX reads *brought down* [B] **31:17** Or *them wail* [C] **31:19** Or *of the descendants of Adam*

2 How joyful is a person whom
the LORD does not charge
with iniquity
and in whose spirit is no deceit!

3 When I kept silent, my bones
became brittle
from my groaning all day long.
4 For day and night your hand was heavy
on me;
my strength was drained[A]
as in the summer's heat. *Selah*
5 Then I acknowledged my sin to you
and did not conceal my iniquity.
I said, "I will confess my transgressions
to the LORD,"
and you forgave the guilt
of my sin. *Selah*

6 Therefore let everyone who is faithful
pray to you immediately.[B]
When great floodwaters come,
they will not reach him.
7 You are my hiding place;
you protect me from trouble.
You surround me with joyful shouts
of deliverance. *Selah*

8 I will instruct you and show you
the way to go;
with my eye on you,
I will give counsel.
9 Do not be like a horse or mule,
without understanding,
that must be controlled with bit
and bridle
or else it will not come near you.

10 Many pains come to the wicked,
but the one who trusts in the LORD
will have faithful love
surrounding him.
11 Be glad in the LORD and rejoice,
you righteous ones;
shout for joy,
all you upright in heart.

PRAISE TO THE CREATOR

33 Rejoice in the LORD,
you righteous ones;
praise from the upright is beautiful.
2 Praise the LORD with the lyre;
make music to him
with a ten-stringed harp.
3 Sing a new song to him;

Thanksgiving and Contentment | *Confession*

THE TRUTH ABOUT CONFESSION

"Then I acknowledged my sin to you and did not conceal my iniquity. I said, 'I will confess my transgressions to the LORD,' and you forgave the guilt of my sin. Selah." Psalm 32:5

For most people the word *confession* conjures up all sorts of negative images: a person sweating in an "interrogation room" with stony-faced authorities asking trick questions or miserable, life-altering consequences for admitting ugly secrets.

This is *nothing* like Christian confession. Notice how David described his experience: "I acknowledged my sin" (in other words, no rationalizing or excuse-making); "did not conceal my iniquity" (no cover-ups or hiding the truth). And what was the result? Banishment? Eternal doom? Divine disgust? No! "You forgave the guilt of my sin."

When we sin, God wants to restore us, not punish us! He wants us to learn from and move past our failures, not wallow in them. In truth, our admissions of sin aren't for his benefit—he already knows all about our wrong acts! Confession is for our benefit. Only when we confess can we get to taste the limitless mercy and grace of God.

Instead of avoiding the practice of confession, run straight to the One who unfailingly forgives!

For the next note on *Thanksgiving and Contentment*, see Psalm 56:8.

[A] **32:4** Hb obscure [B] **32:6** Lit *you at a time of finding*

play skillfully on the strings,
with a joyful shout.

4 For the word of the LORD is right,
and all his work is trustworthy.
5 He loves righteousness and justice;
the earth is full of the LORD's
unfailing love.

6 The heavens were made by the word
of the LORD,
and all the stars, by the breath
of his mouth.
7 He gathers the water of the sea
into a heap;[A]
he puts the depths into storehouses.
8 Let the whole earth fear the LORD;
let all the inhabitants of the world
stand in awe of him.
9 For he spoke, and it came into being;
he commanded, and it came
into existence.

10 The LORD frustrates the counsel
of the nations;
he thwarts the plans of the peoples.
11 The counsel of the LORD stands forever,
the plans of his heart from generation
to generation.
12 Happy is the nation whose God
is the LORD —
the people he has chosen to be
his own possession!

13 The LORD looks down from heaven;
he observes everyone.
14 He gazes on all the inhabitants
of the earth
from his dwelling place.
15 He forms the hearts of them all;
he considers all their works.
16 A king is not saved by a large army;
a warrior will not be rescued
by great strength.
17 The horse is a false hope for safety;
it provides no escape by
its great power.

18 But look, the LORD keeps his eye on
those who fear him —
those who depend on
his faithful love
19 to rescue them from death
and to keep them alive in famine.

Support | *God's Counsel*

STEER-ABLE

"I will instruct you and show you the way to go; with my eye on you, I will give counsel. Do not be like a horse or mule, without understanding, that must be controlled with bit and bridle or else it will not come near you." Psalm 32:8-9

You may have seen a donkey or nag stubbornly dig in its heels and refuse to budge. The farmer almost needs a backhoe to drag the animal to its destination. We've also seen people ignore sound advice from all sides and go in foolish directions.

The plea in this verse? Don't be like that. Don't be obstinate. Don't drag your feet, spiritually speaking. Be "steer-able."

The promise in this verse? "I will instruct you . . . I will give counsel." We can receive direction and guidance from the One who possesses all wisdom! Think of it: God has given us his Word to show us the way to go, his Spirit to empower us, and his people to encourage us to stay on track and keep going. We are triply blessed.

You have flawless counsel nearby. Ask God for the grace to hear his guiding voice, and the courage to follow it.

For the next note on *Support*, see Psalm 37:5.

[A] **33:7** LXX, Tg, Syr, Vg, Jer read *sea as in a bottle*

20 We wait for the LORD;
he is our help and shield.
21 For our hearts rejoice in him
because we trust in his holy name.
22 May your faithful love rest on us, LORD,
for we put our hope in you.

THE LORD DELIVERS THE RIGHTEOUS

34 *Concerning David, when he pretended to be insane in the presence of Abimelech, who drove him out, and he departed.*

1 I will bless the LORD at all times;
his praise will always be on my lips.
2 I will boast in the LORD;
the humble will hear and be glad.
3 Proclaim the LORD's greatness with me;
let us exalt his name together.

4 I sought the LORD, and he answered me
and rescued me from all my fears.
5 Those who look to him are[A] radiant
with joy;
their faces will never be ashamed.
6 This poor man cried, and the LORD
heard him
and saved him from all his troubles.
7 The angel of the LORD encamps
around those who fear him,
and rescues them.
8 Taste and see that the LORD is good.
How happy is the person who
takes refuge in him!
9 You who are his holy ones,
fear the LORD,
for those who fear him lack nothing.
10 Young lions[B] lack food and go hungry,
but those who seek the LORD
will not lack any good thing.

11 Come, children, listen to me;
I will teach you the fear of the LORD.
12 Who is someone who desires life,
loving a long life to enjoy what is good?
13 Keep your tongue from evil
and your lips from deceitful speech.
14 Turn away from evil and do what is good;
seek peace and pursue it.

15 The eyes of the LORD are
on the righteous,
and his ears are open to their cry
for help.
16 The face of the LORD is set
against those who do what is evil,
to remove[C] all memory of them
from the earth.
17 The righteous[D] cry out,
and the LORD hears,

Eternal Perspective | *God's Knowledge/Omniscience*

HE UNDERSTANDS

"The LORD looks down from heaven; he observes everyone. He gazes on all the inhabitants of the earth from his dwelling place. He forms the hearts of them all; he considers all their works." Psalm 33:13-15

A coworker moans, "Why is my son suddenly acting out?" A loved one laments, "Why do I keep falling into the same old trap?" A friend says, "I don't get why my spouse is so angry."

Who can understand the mysteries and complexities of the human heart? According to this verse, "the LORD" can, that's who. He "looks down from heaven" and "gazes" (this means, he's engaged and attentive, not distracted or busy doing other things). He "observes everyone" (you and all the people in your life). And because he is the One who "forms the hearts" of all of us, he understands exactly what makes us tick.

If you're baffled by powerful feelings or troubling actions in your own heart and life, or if you're weary from trying to figure out the perplexing behavior of someone else, take comfort in these remarkable truths: "God sees" and "God knows." Lean into him, trusting that he gladly gives wisdom to those who ask for it in faith (Jms 1:5).

For the next note on *Eternal Perspective*, see Psalm 40:5.

[A] **34:5** Some Hb mss, LXX, Aq, Syr, Jer read *Look to him and be* [B] **34:10** LXX, Syr, Vg read *The rich* [C] **34:16** Or *cut off* [D] **34:17** Lit *They*

and rescues them from all
their troubles.
18 The LORD is near the brokenhearted;
he saves those crushed in spirit.
19 One who is righteous has
many adversities,
but the LORD rescues him
from them all.
20 He protects all his bones;
not one of them is broken.
21 Evil brings death to the wicked,
and those who hate the righteous
will be punished.
22 The LORD redeems the life of his servants,
and all who take refuge in him will not
be punished.

PRAYER FOR VICTORY

35 *Of David.*
Oppose my opponents, LORD;
fight those who fight me.
2 Take your shields — large and small —
and come to my aid.
3 Draw the spear and javelin
against my pursuers,
and assure me: "I am your deliverance."

4 Let those who intend to take my life
be disgraced and humiliated;
let those who plan to harm me
be turned back and ashamed.
5 Let them be like chaff in the wind,
with the angel of the LORD
driving them away.
6 Let their way be dark and slippery,
with the angel of the LORD
pursuing them.
7 They hid their net for me
without cause;
they dug a pit for me without cause.
8 Let ruin come on him unexpectedly,
and let the net that he hid ensnare him;
let him fall into it — to his ruin.

9 Then I will rejoice in the LORD;
I will delight in his deliverance.
10 All my bones will say,
"LORD, who is like you,
rescuing the poor from one too strong
for him,
the poor or the needy from one
who robs him?"

11 Malicious witnesses come forward;
they question me about things
I do not know.
12 They repay me evil for good,
making me desolate.
13 Yet when they were sick,
my clothing was sackcloth;
I humbled myself with fasting,
and my prayer was genuine.[A]
14 I went about mourning as if
for my friend or brother;
I was bowed down with grief,
like one mourning for a mother.
15 But when I stumbled, they gathered
in glee;
they gathered against me.
Assailants I did not know
tore at me and did not stop.
16 With godless mockery[B]
they gnashed their teeth at me.

17 Lord, how long will you look on?
Rescue me from their ravages;
rescue my precious life
from the young lions.
18 I will praise you in the great assembly;
I will exalt you among many people.
19 Do not let my deceitful enemies rejoice
over me;
do not let those who hate me
without cause
wink at me maliciously.
20 For they do not speak in friendly ways,
but contrive fraudulent schemes[C]
against those who live peacefully
in the land.
21 They open their mouths wide
against me and say,
"Aha, aha! We saw it!"[D]

22 You saw it, LORD; do not be silent.
Lord, do not be far from me.
23 Wake up and rise to my defense,
to my cause, my God and my Lord!
24 Vindicate me, LORD my God,
in keeping with your righteousness,
and do not let them rejoice over me.
25 Do not let them say in their hearts,
"Aha! Just what we wanted."
Do not let them say,
"We have swallowed him up!"
26 Let those who rejoice at my misfortune
be disgraced and humiliated;

[A] **35:13** Lit *prayer returned to my chest* [B] **35:16** Hb obscure [C] **35:20** Lit *but devise fraudulent words* [D] **35:21** Lit *Our eyes saw!*

let those who exalt themselves over me
be clothed with shame and reproach.

27 Let those who want my vindication
shout for joy and be glad;
let them continually say,
"The LORD be exalted.
He takes pleasure in
his servant's well-being."
28 And my tongue will proclaim
your righteousness,
your praise all day long.

HUMAN WICKEDNESS AND GOD'S LOVE

For the choir director.
Of David, the LORD's servant.

1 An oracle within my heart
concerning the transgression of the
wicked person:
Dread of God has no effect on him.[A]
2 For with his flattering opinion
of himself,
he does not discover and hate
his iniquity.
3 The words from his mouth
are malicious and deceptive;
he has stopped acting wisely
and doing good.
4 Even on his bed he makes
malicious plans.
He sets himself on a path
that is not good,
and he does not reject evil.

5 LORD, your faithful love reaches
to heaven,
your faithfulness to the clouds.
6 Your righteousness is
like the highest mountains,
your judgments like the deepest sea.
LORD, you preserve people
and animals.
7 How priceless your faithful love is, God!
People take refuge in the shadow
of your wings.
8 They are filled from the abundance
of your house.
You let them drink from
your refreshing stream.
9 For the wellspring of life is with you.
By means of your light we see light.

10 Spread your faithful love over those
who know you,
and your righteousness
over the upright in heart.
11 Do not let the foot of the arrogant
come near me
or the hand of the wicked
drive me away.

S Support | *Commitment to God*

GIVE IT TO HIM

"Commit your way to the LORD; trust in him, and he will act." Psalm 37:5

How many times does this happen? You come to a fork in the road. You face a decision. You're not certain which way to go or what action to take. What then?

This verse gives us good counsel. The Hebrew word translated "commit" means, literally, "to roll, roll away, roll down." It's actually used elsewhere in the Bible to describe people rolling large boulders over well or cave openings (Gn 29:3; Jos 10:18). Probably, then, when David urges, "Commit your way to the LORD," the idea is that we need to roll our hearts, heavy with hopes and dreams, concerns and questions, over onto the Lord. We give all these weighty matters to him.

Then, with careful, prayerful hearts, we make the best choice we can. As we move forward, we "trust in him"—essentially that "he will act." That he can be counted upon to do what is right. Maybe he'll confirm that we're on the right path. Maybe he'll block our way and turn us around. Maybe he'll open a new door we never imagined. Whatever happens, we can trust that he will act in a way that brings him glory and us good.

For the next note on *Support*, see Psalm 55:17.

[A] **36:1** Lit *There is no dread of God in front of his eyes*

12 There! The evildoers have fallen.
They have been thrown down
and cannot rise.

INSTRUCTION IN WISDOM

37 *Of David.*
Do not be agitated by evildoers;
do not envy those who do wrong.
2 For they wither quickly like grass
and wilt like tender green plants.

3 Trust in the LORD and do what is good;
dwell in the land and live securely.[A]
4 Take delight in the LORD,
and he will give you
your heart's desires.

5 Commit your way to the LORD;
trust in him, and he will act,
6 making your righteousness shine
like the dawn,
your justice like the noonday.

7 Be silent before the LORD and wait
expectantly for him;
do not be agitated by one who prospers
in his way,
by the person who carries out
evil plans.

8 Refrain from anger and give up
your rage;
do not be agitated — it can only
bring harm.
9 For evildoers will be destroyed,
but those who put their hope in the LORD
will inherit the land.

10 A little while, and the wicked person
will be no more;
though you look for him, he will not
be there.
11 But the humble will inherit the land
and will enjoy abundant prosperity.

12 The wicked person schemes
against the righteous
and gnashes his teeth at him.
13 The Lord laughs at him
because he sees that his day is coming.

14 The wicked have drawn the sword
and strung the[B] bow
to bring down the poor and needy
and to slaughter those whose way
is upright.
15 Their swords will enter
their own hearts,
and their bows will be broken.

Rest and Reflection | *Waiting on God*

BE SILENT

"Be silent before the LORD and wait expectantly for him; do not be agitated by one who prospers in his way, by the person who carries out evil plans." Psalm 37:7

The world is busy and noisy. Even so, if we try hard enough (translation, if we wake up early enough or get far enough away from other people), we can usually find a quiet and still place. Then comes the bigger trick—trying to silence all the *internal* noise.

Incessant self-talk, voices from our past, whispers of regret, the angry accusations of the evil one, and the urgent demands of the day that scream for our attention can fill our minds with noise, even when we're surrounded by silence! For frazzled, "agitated" souls like ours, David's counsel is, "Be silent before the LORD."

Quieting our hearts doesn't come naturally; it's a skill we have to develop. Ask God to help you learn this discipline. Start with five minutes. Find a quiet place. Don't focus on doing. Don't read or pray or journal. Just be with God. Breathe deeply. As we learn to quiet our loud, jangly hearts, we will begin to hear the still, small voice of God.

For the next note on *Rest and Reflection*, see Psalm 46:10.

[A] **37:3** Or *and cultivate faithfulness*, or *and befriend faithfulness* [B] **37:14** Lit *their*

16 The little that the righteous person has
is better
than the abundance
of many wicked people.
17 For the arms of the wicked
will be broken,
but the LORD supports the righteous.

18 The LORD watches over the blameless
all their days,
and their inheritance will last forever.
19 They will not be disgraced in times
of adversity;
they will be satisfied in days of hunger.

20 But the wicked will perish;
the LORD's enemies, like the glory
of the pastures,
will fade away —
they will fade away like smoke.

21 The wicked person borrows
and does not repay,
but the righteous one is gracious
and giving.
22 Those who are blessed by the LORD
will inherit the land,
but those cursed by him
will be destroyed.

23 A person's steps are established
by the LORD,
and he takes pleasure in his way.
24 Though he falls, he will not
be overwhelmed,
because the LORD supports him with
his hand.

25 I have been young and now I am old,
yet I have not seen
the righteous abandoned
or his children begging for bread.
26 He is always generous,
always lending,
and his children are a blessing.

27 Turn away from evil, do what is good,
and settle permanently.
28 For the LORD loves justice
and will not abandon his faithful ones.
They are kept safe forever,
but the children of the wicked
will be destroyed.
29 The righteous will inherit the land
and dwell in it permanently.

30 The mouth of the righteous
utters wisdom;
his tongue speaks what is just.
31 The instruction of his God is
in his heart;
his steps do not falter.

32 The wicked one lies in wait
for the righteous
and intends to kill him;
33 the LORD will not leave him
in the power of the wicked one
or allow him to be condemned
when he is judged.

34 Wait for the LORD and keep his way,
and he will exalt you to inherit the land.
You will watch when the wicked
are destroyed.

35 I have seen a wicked, violent person
well-rooted,[A] like
a flourishing native tree.
36 Then I[B] passed by and noticed
he was gone;
I searched for him, but he could not
be found.

37 Watch the blameless and observe
the upright,
for the person of peace will have
a future.[C]
38 But transgressors will all be eliminated;
the future of the wicked
will be destroyed.

39 The salvation of the righteous is
from the LORD,
their refuge in a time of distress.
40 The LORD helps and delivers them;
he will deliver them from the wicked
and will save them
because they take refuge in him.

PRAYER OF A SUFFERING SINNER

38 *A psalm of David for remembrance.*
LORD, do not punish me in your anger
or discipline me in your wrath.
2 For your arrows have sunk into me,
and your hand has pressed down on me.

[A] **37:35** Hb obscure [B] **37:36** LXX, Syr, Vg, Jer; MT reads *he* [C] **37:37** Or *posterity*, also in v. 38

3 There is no soundness in my body
because of your indignation;
there is no health[A] in my bones
because of my sin.
4 For my iniquities have flooded
over my head;
they are a burden too heavy for me
to bear.
5 My wounds are foul and festering
because of my foolishness.
6 I am bent over and brought very low;
all day long I go around in mourning.
7 For my insides are full of burning pain,
and there is no soundness in my body.
8 I am faint and severely crushed;
I groan because of the anguish
of my heart.

9 Lord, my every desire is in front of you;
my sighing is not hidden from you.
10 My heart races, my strength leaves me,
and even the light of my eyes has faded.[B]
11 My loved ones and friends stand back
from my affliction,
and my relatives stand at a distance.
12 Those who intend to kill me set traps,
and those who want to harm me
threaten to destroy me;
they plot treachery all day long.

13 I am like a deaf person; I do not hear.
I am like a speechless person
who does not open his mouth.
14 I am like a man who does not hear
and has no arguments in his mouth.
15 For I put my hope in you, LORD;
you will answer me, my Lord, my God.
16 For I said, "Don't let them rejoice
over me —
those who are arrogant toward me
when I stumble."
17 For I am about to fall,
and my pain is constantly with me.
18 So I confess my iniquity;
I am anxious because of my sin.
19 But my enemies are vigorous
and powerful;[C]
many hate me for no reason.
20 Those who repay evil for good
attack me for pursuing good.

21 LORD, do not abandon me;
my God, do not be far from me.
22 Hurry to help me,
my Lord, my salvation.

THE FLEETING NATURE OF LIFE

39 *For the choir director, for Jeduthun. A psalm of David.*

1 I said, "I will guard my ways
so that I may not sin with my tongue;
I will guard my mouth with a muzzle
as long as the wicked are
in my presence."
2 I was speechless and quiet;
I kept silent, even from speaking good,
and my pain intensified.
3 My heart grew hot within me;
as I mused, a fire burned.
I spoke with my tongue:
4 "LORD, make me aware of my end
and the number of my days
so that I will know how short-lived
I am.
5 In fact, you have made my days just
inches long,
and my life span is as nothing to you.
Yes, every human being stands as
only a vapor. *Selah*
6 Yes, a person goes about
like a mere shadow.
Indeed, they rush around in vain,
gathering possessions
without knowing who will get them.

7 "Now, Lord, what do I wait for?
My hope is in you.
8 Rescue me from all my transgressions;
do not make me the taunt of fools.
9 I am speechless; I do not open
my mouth
because of what you have done.
10 Remove your torment from me.
Because of the force of your hand I am
finished.
11 You discipline a person
with punishment for iniquity,
consuming like a moth
what is precious to him;
yes, every human being is only
a vapor. *Selah*

12 "Hear my prayer, LORD,
and listen to my cry for help;
do not be silent at my tears.
For I am here with you as an alien,

[A] **38:3** Hb *shalom* [B] **38:10** Or *and the light of my eyes — even that is not with me* [C] **38:19** Or *numerous*

a temporary resident like all
my ancestors.
13 Turn your angry gaze from me
so that I may be cheered up
before I die and am gone."

THANKSGIVING AND A CRY FOR HELP

For the choir director. A psalm of David.
I waited patiently for the LORD,
and he turned to me and heard my cry
for help.
2 He brought me up
from a desolate[A] pit,
out of the muddy clay,
and set my feet on a rock,
making my steps secure.
3 He put a new song in my mouth,
a hymn of praise to our God.
Many will see and fear,
and they will trust in the LORD.

4 How happy is anyone
who has put his trust in the LORD
and has not turned to the proud
or to those who run after lies!
5 LORD my God, you have done
many things —
your wondrous works and your plans
for us;
none can compare with you.
If I were to report and speak
of them,
they are more than can be told.

6 You do not delight in sacrifice
and offering;
you open my ears to listen.[B]
You do not ask for
a whole burnt offering
or a sin offering.
7 Then I said, "See, I have come;
in the scroll it is written about me.
8 I delight to do your will, my God,
and your instruction is deep
within me."

9 I proclaim righteousness
in the great assembly;
see, I do not keep
my mouth closed[C] —
as you know, LORD.
10 I did not hide your righteousness
in my heart;
I spoke about your faithfulness
and salvation;
I did not conceal your constant love
and truth
from the great assembly.

E Eternal Perspective | *God's Plans*

OUR ACTIVE GOD

"LORD my God, you have done many things—your wondrous works and your plans for us; none can compare with you. If I were to report and speak of them, they are more than can be told." Psalm 40:5

This passage reminds us that God has "done many . . . wondrous works" in the past. Elsewhere in the Bible, Jesus reveals that our heavenly Father is "still working" (Jn 5:17) up to the present.

What comforting reassurance! Our God is both the CEO and COO of the universe. He doesn't go on vacation or take naps. He's always at work—listening and watching, wooing and rescuing, giving and forgiving, sustaining and supplying, arranging and orchestrating.

Incredible! At this very moment, God is doing a million, zillion things. At this very moment, we can see only a fraction of what he's up to.

If you're discouraged right now, thinking, *Where is God?* remember his track record and rejoice in his past faithfulness. Then rest in the truth that just because you can't see him working doesn't mean he's not. He has great plans for you, just ahead.

For the next note on *Eternal Perspective*, see Psalm 56:3.

[A] **40:2** Or *watery* [B] **40:6** Lit *you hollow out ears for me* [C] **40:9** Lit *not restrain my lips*

11 LORD, you do not[A] withhold
your compassion from me.
Your constant love and truth
will always guard me.
12 For troubles without number
have surrounded me;
my iniquities have overtaken me;
I am unable to see.
They are more than the hairs of my head,
and my courage leaves me.
13 LORD, be pleased to rescue me;
hurry to help me, LORD.

14 Let those who intend to take my life
be disgraced and confounded.
Let those who wish me harm
be turned back and humiliated.
15 Let those who say to me, "Aha, aha!"
be appalled because of their shame.

16 Let all who seek you rejoice and be glad
in you;
let those who love your salvation
continually say,
"The LORD is great!"
17 I am oppressed and needy;
may the Lord think of me.
You are my helper and my deliverer;
my God, do not delay.

VICTORY IN SPITE OF BETRAYAL

41 *For the choir director. A psalm of David.*
Happy is one who is considerate
of the poor;
the LORD will save him in a day
of adversity.
2 The LORD will keep him
and preserve him;
he will be blessed in the land.
You will not give him over to the desire
of his enemies.
3 The LORD will sustain him
on his sickbed;
you will heal him on the bed
where he lies.

4 I said, "LORD, be gracious to me;
heal me, for I have sinned against you."
5 My enemies speak maliciously about me:
"When will he die and be forgotten?"
6 When one of them comes to visit,
he speaks deceitfully;
he stores up evil in his heart;
he goes out and talks.
7 All who hate me whisper together
about me;
they plan to harm me.
8 "Something awful has
overwhelmed him,[B]

Other-centeredness | *Helping People in Need*

GENEROSITY

"Happy is one who is considerate of the poor; the LORD will save him in a day of adversity." Psalm 41:1

Our motivation in giving to others or serving others should never be to get something in return. That's *self*-serving—more about looking out for number one than looking out for others. Yet the reality of giving is that when we are generous with our time, talents, and treasure, we *do* get something in return!

This psalm mentions two specific blessings: first, the happiness or joy that comes from helping those in need. We have experienced this: seeing a grateful look of relief on another's face, experiencing in our own hearts that sense of "this just feels *right*"—how can we not smile in such times?

Second, the verse speaks of how "the LORD will save" (that is, rescue or come to the aid of) generous people when they encounter adversity themselves. It doesn't say how, only that he will.

Ask the Lord to make your heart willing, even eager, to be more generous. When we cooperate with him in helping others, everybody wins.

For the next note on *Other-centeredness*, see Psalm 68:5.

[A] **40:11** Or *LORD, do not* [B] **41:8** Lit *"A thing of worthlessness has been poured into him*

and he won't rise again from where
he lies!"
9 Even my friend[A] in whom I trusted,
one who ate my bread,
has raised his heel against me.

10 But you, LORD, be gracious to me
and raise me up;
then I will repay them.
11 By this I know that you delight in me:
my enemy does not shout in triumph
over me.
12 You supported me because of
my integrity
and set me in your presence forever.

13 Blessed be the LORD God of Israel,
from everlasting to everlasting.
Amen and amen.

BOOK II (Psalms 42–72)

LONGING FOR GOD

42 *For the choir director.*
A Maskil *of the sons of Korah.*
1 As a deer longs for flowing streams,
so I long for you, God.
2 I thirst for God, the living God.
When can I come and appear
before God?
3 My tears have been my food
day and night,
while all day long people say to me,
"Where is your God?"
4 I remember this as I pour out
my heart:
how I walked with many,
leading the festive procession
to the house of God,
with joyful and thankful shouts.

5 Why, my soul, are you so dejected?
Why are you in such turmoil?
Put your hope in God, for I will
still praise him,
my Savior and my God.
6 I[B] am deeply depressed;
therefore I remember you
from the land of Jordan
and the peaks of Hermon,
from Mount Mizar.
7 Deep calls to deep in the roar
of your waterfalls;
all your breakers and your billows
have swept over me.
8 The LORD will send his faithful love
by day;
his song will be with me
in the night —
a prayer to the God of my life.

9 I will say to God, my rock,
"Why have you forgotten me?
Why must I go about in sorrow
because of the enemy's oppression?"
10 My adversaries taunt me,
as if crushing my bones,
while all day long they say to me,
"Where is your God?"
11 Why, my soul, are you so dejected?
Why are you in such turmoil?
Put your hope in God, for I will
still praise him,
my Savior and my God.

43 [C]Vindicate me, God, and champion
my cause
against an unfaithful nation;
rescue me from the deceitful
and unjust person.
2 For you are the God of my refuge.
Why have you rejected me?
Why must I go about in sorrow
because of the enemy's oppression?

3 Send your light and your truth; let them
lead me.
Let them bring me
to your holy mountain,
to your dwelling place.
4 Then I will come to the altar of God,
to God, my greatest joy.
I will praise you with the lyre,
God, my God.

5 Why, my soul, are you so dejected?
Why are you in such turmoil?
Put your hope in God, for I will
still praise him,
my Savior and my God.

ISRAEL'S COMPLAINT

44 *For the choir director.*
A Maskil *of the sons of Korah.*
1 God, we have heard with our ears —
our ancestors have told us —

[A] **41:9** Lit *Even a man of my peace* [B] **42:5-6** Some Hb mss, LXX, Syr; other Hb mss read *him, the salvation of his presence.* [6]*My God, I* [C] **Ps 43** Many Hb mss connect Pss 42 and 43

the work you accomplished in their days,
in days long ago:
2 In order to plant them,
you displaced the nations by your hand;
in order to settle them,
you brought disaster on the peoples.
3 For they did not take the land
by their sword —
their arm did not bring them victory —
but by your right hand, your arm,
and the light of your face,
because you were favorable
toward them.
4 You are my King, my God,
who ordains[A] victories for Jacob.
5 Through you we drive back our foes;
through your name we trample
our enemies.
6 For I do not trust in my bow,
and my sword does not
bring me victory.
7 But you give us victory over our foes
and let those who hate us be disgraced.
8 We boast in God all day long;
we will praise your name forever. *Selah*

9 But you have rejected and humiliated us;
you do not march out with our armies.
10 You make us retreat from the foe,
and those who hate us
have taken plunder for themselves.
11 You hand us over to be eaten
like sheep
and scatter us among the nations.
12 You sell your people for nothing;
you make no profit from selling them.
13 You make us an object of reproach
to our neighbors,
a source of mockery and ridicule
to those around us.
14 You make us a joke among the nations,
a laughingstock[B] among the peoples.
15 My disgrace is before me all day long,
and shame has covered my face,
16 because of the taunts[C] of the scorner
and reviler,
because of the enemy and avenger.

17 All this has happened to us,
but we have not forgotten you
or betrayed your covenant.
18 Our hearts have not turned back;
our steps have not strayed
from your path.
19 But you have crushed us in a haunt
of jackals
and have covered us
with deepest darkness.
20 If we had forgotten the name of our God
and spread out our hands
to a foreign god,
21 wouldn't God have found this out,
since he knows the secrets
of the heart?
22 Because of you we are being put
to death all day long;
we are counted as sheep
to be slaughtered.

23 Wake up, LORD! Why are you sleeping?
Get up! Don't reject us forever!
24 Why do you hide
and forget our affliction
and oppression?
25 For we have sunk down to the dust;
our bodies cling to the ground.
26 Rise up! Help us!
Redeem us because of your faithful love.

A ROYAL WEDDING SONG

45 *For the choir director: according to "The Lilies." A* Maskil *of the sons of Korah. A love song.*

1 My heart is moved by a noble theme
as I recite my verses to the king;
my tongue is the pen of a skillful writer.
2 You are the most handsome of men;[D]
grace flows from your lips.
Therefore God has blessed you forever.

3 Mighty warrior, strap your sword
at your side.
In your majesty and splendor —
4 in your splendor ride triumphantly
in the cause of truth, humility,
and justice.
May your right hand show
your awe-inspiring acts.
5 Your sharpened arrows pierce
the hearts of the king's enemies;
the peoples fall under you.

6 Your throne, God, is[E] forever and ever;
the scepter of your kingdom is
a scepter of justice.

[A] **44:4** LXX, Syr, Aq; MT reads *King, God; ordain* [B] **44:14** Lit *shaking of the head* [C] **44:16** Lit *voice* [D] **45:2** Or *of the descendants of Adam* [E] **45:6** Or *Your divine throne is*, or *Your throne is God's*

7 You love righteousness
and hate wickedness;
therefore God, your God,
has anointed you with the oil of joy
more than your companions.
8 Myrrh, aloes, and cassia perfume
all your garments;
from ivory palaces harps bring you joy.
9 Kings' daughters are
among your honored women;
the queen, adorned with gold
from Ophir,
stands at your right hand.

10 Listen, daughter, pay attention
and consider:
forget your people
and your father's house,
11 and the king will desire your beauty.
Bow down to him, for he is your lord.
12 The daughter of Tyre,
the wealthy people,
will seek your favor with gifts.

13 In her chamber, the royal daughter
is all glorious,
her clothing embroidered with gold.
14 In colorful garments she is led
to the king;
after her, the virgins, her companions,
are brought to you.
15 They are led in with gladness
and rejoicing;
they enter the king's palace.

16 Your sons will succeed
your ancestors;
you will make them princes
throughout the land.
17 I will cause your name
to be remembered
for all generations;
therefore the peoples will praise you
forever and ever.

GOD OUR REFUGE

46 *For the choir director. A song of the sons of Korah. According to* Alamoth.

1 God is our refuge and strength,
a helper who is always found
in times of trouble.
2 Therefore we will not be afraid,
though the earth trembles
and the mountains topple
into the depths of the seas,
3 though its water roars and foams
and the mountains quake
with its turmoil. *Selah*

Rest and Reflection | *Sitting Silent*

THE CURE FOR INSECURITY

"Stop your fighting, and know that I am God, exalted among the nations, exalted on the earth." Psalm 46:10

The question isn't, "Do we ever struggle with insecurity?" Of course we do—some people all the time, and all people some of the time. No, the better question is this: How do we respond in the face of threatening circumstances when we find ourselves feeling insecure? Most people seem to respond in one of three ways.

Some *freeze*. That is, they become paralyzed—incapable of choosing and acting. Others *flee*. When scary situations arise, they turn tail and try to hide. Still others *fight*. They go into attack mode, lashing out, trying to seize control of situations and force outcomes.

But we have a fourth way, a better way. Psalm 46 speaks of a time of great uncertainty in Israel's history. Near the end of the psalm, God commands his people to "stop your fighting," literally to "let go, relax, be still, stop striving." We have no need to panic or flee or be paralyzed by insecurity. Why? Because the Lord is God, the King of the earth.

The more we accept God's control, the less we will feel out of control or that we need to try to take control. Stop fighting and stressing; let him lead.

For the next note on *Rest and Reflection*, see Psalm 51:3-4.

My Story | Marvin

Life was good. My kids, grown and on their own, were flourishing. My wife and I were enjoying the empty nest—no grandkids yet, but plenty to keep us busy, especially at church. Relationships and responsibilities were on track at work. And I felt fine physically. But I suffered from a severe case of the blahs.

As I sat in worship, settling in for the sermon, I heard the pastor read the Bible text on which the message would be based. It was familiar—Psalm 51—so I listened only half paying attention. But when he came to verse 12, "Restore the joy of your salvation to me, and sustain me by giving me a willing spirit," I began to tear up. My reaction was surprising because I don't cry much. But that phrase, "restore the joy of your salvation," got to me. And I realized what was missing—I had lost the joy of my relationship with God. Life was good, but I was going through the motions with my living and faith. So I silently prayed, "O God, please restore the joy. I want to know you, to love you with all that I am, to feel your presence." I'm sure no one sitting nearby had any idea something significant had just happened in me.

The change wasn't dramatic, but I began focusing on God's love and what Jesus had done for me. I also began listening to the Holy Spirit's promptings. Step-by-step, day by day restored.

4 There is a river —
its streams delight the city of God,
the holy dwelling place
of the Most High.
5 God is within her; she will not be toppled.
God will help her
when the morning dawns.
6 Nations rage, kingdoms topple;
the earth melts when he lifts his voice.
7 The LORD of Armies is with us;
the God of Jacob is our stronghold.
Selah

8 Come, see the works of the LORD,
who brings devastation on the earth.
9 He makes wars cease
throughout the earth.
He shatters bows and cuts spears
to pieces;
he sets wagons ablaze.
10 "Stop your fighting, and know that
I am God,
exalted among the nations,
exalted on the earth."
11 The LORD of Armies is with us;
the God of Jacob is our stronghold.
Selah

GOD OUR KING

47 *For the choir director.*
A psalm of the sons of Korah.
1 Clap your hands, all you peoples;
shout to God with a jubilant cry.
2 For the LORD, the Most High,
is awe-inspiring,
a great King over the whole earth.
3 He subdues peoples under us
and nations under our feet.
4 He chooses for us our inheritance —
the pride of Jacob, whom he loves.
Selah

5 God ascends among shouts of joy,
the LORD, with the sound of trumpets.
6 Sing praise to God, sing praise;
sing praise to our King, sing praise!
7 Sing a song of wisdom,[A]
for God is King of the whole earth.

8 God reigns over the nations;
God is seated on his holy throne.
9 The nobles of the peoples
have assembled
with the people of the God of Abraham.
For the leaders[B] of the earth
belong to God;
he is greatly exalted.

ZION EXALTED

48 *A song. A psalm of the sons of Korah.*
The LORD is great and highly praised
in the city of our God.
His holy mountain, 2 rising splendidly,
is the joy of the whole earth.
Mount Zion — the summit of Zaphon —
is the city of the great King.

[A] **47:7** Or *Sing a* maskil [B] **47:9** Lit *shields*

3 God is known as a stronghold
in its citadels.

4 Look! The kings assembled;
they advanced together.
5 They looked and froze with fear;
they fled in terror.
6 Trembling seized them there,
agony like that of a woman in labor,
7 as you wrecked the ships of Tarshish
with the east wind.

8 Just as we heard, so we have seen
in the city of the LORD of Armies,
in the city of our God;
God will establish it forever. *Selah*

9 God, within your temple,
we contemplate your faithful love.
10 Like your name, God, so your praise
reaches to the ends of the earth;
your right hand is filled with justice.
11 Mount Zion is glad.
Judah's villages[A] rejoice
because of your judgments.

12 Go around Zion, encircle it;
count its towers,
13 note its ramparts; tour its citadels
so that you can tell
a future generation:
14 "This God, our God forever and ever —
he will always lead us."[B]

MISPLACED TRUST IN WEALTH

49 *For the choir director.*
A psalm of the sons of Korah.

1 Hear this, all you peoples;
listen, all who inhabit the world,
2 both low and high,
rich and poor together.
3 My mouth speaks wisdom;
my heart's meditation
brings understanding.
4 I turn my ear to a proverb;
I explain my riddle with a lyre.

5 Why should I fear in times of trouble?
The iniquity of my foes surrounds me.
6 They trust in their wealth
and boast of their abundant riches.
7 Yet these cannot redeem a person[C]
or pay his ransom to God —
8 since the price of redeeming him is
too costly,
one should forever stop trying[D] —
9 so that he may live forever
and not see the Pit.

10 For one can see that the wise die;
the foolish and stupid also pass away.
Then they leave their wealth to others.
11 Their graves are
their permanent homes,[E]
their dwellings from generation
to generation,
though they have named estates
after themselves.
12 But despite his assets,[F] mankind
will not last;
he is like the animals that perish.

13 This is the way of those
who are arrogant,
and of their followers,
who approve of their words.[G] *Selah*
14 Like sheep they are headed
for Sheol;
Death will shepherd them.
The upright will rule over them
in the morning,
and their form will waste away in Sheol,[H]
far from their lofty abode.
15 But God will redeem me
from the power of Sheol,
for he will take me. *Selah*

16 Do not be afraid when a person gets rich,
when the wealth[I]
of his house increases.
17 For when he dies, he will take
nothing at all;
his wealth will not follow him down.
18 Though he blesses himself
during his lifetime —
and you are acclaimed when you
do well for yourself —
19 he will go to the generation of his fathers;
they will never see the light.
20 Mankind, with his assets
but without understanding,
is like the animals that perish.

[A] **48:11** Lit *daughters* [B] **48:14** Some Hb mss, LXX; other Hb mss read *over death* [C] **49:7** Or *Certainly he cannot redeem himself*, or *Yet he cannot redeem a brother* [D] **49:8** Or *costly, it will cease forever* [E] **49:11** LXX, Syr, Tg; MT reads *Their inner thought is that their houses are eternal* [F] **49:12** Or *honor* [G] **49:13** Lit *and after them with their mouth they were pleased* [H] **49:14** Hb obscure [I] **49:16** Or *glory*, also in v. 17

GOD AS JUDGE

50 *A psalm of Asaph.*
The Mighty One, God,[A]
the LORD, speaks;
he summons the earth
from the rising of the sun to its setting.
2 From Zion, the perfection of beauty,
God appears in radiance.[B]
3 Our God is coming; he will not be silent!
Devouring fire precedes him,
and a storm rages around him.
4 On high, he summons heaven and earth
in order to judge his people:
5 "Gather my faithful ones to me,
those who made a covenant with me
by sacrifice."
6 The heavens proclaim
his righteousness,
for God is the Judge. *Selah*

7 "Listen, my people, and I will speak;
I will testify against you, Israel.
I am God, your God.
8 I do not rebuke you for your sacrifices
or for your burnt offerings,
which are continually before me.
9 I will not take a bull
from your household
or male goats from your pens,
10 for every animal of the forest is mine,
the cattle on a thousand hills.
11 I know every bird of the mountains,
and the creatures of the field are mine.
12 If I were hungry, I would not tell you,
for the world and everything in it
is mine.
13 Do I eat the flesh of bulls
or drink the blood of goats?
14 Sacrifice a thank offering to God,
and pay your vows to the Most High.
15 Call on me in a day of trouble;
I will rescue you, and you will honor me."

16 But God says to the wicked:
"What right do you have to recite
my statutes
and to take my covenant on your lips?
17 You hate instruction
and fling my words behind you.
18 When you see a thief,
you make friends with him,
and you associate with adulterers.
19 You unleash your mouth for evil
and harness your tongue for deceit.
20 You sit, maligning your brother,
slandering your mother's son.
21 You have done these things,
and I kept silent;

Rest and Reflection | *Honestly Evaluating Yourself*

WHAT TO DO WITH GUILT

"For I am conscious of my rebellion, and my sin is always before me. Against you—you alone—I have sinned and done this evil in your sight. So you are right when you pass sentence; you are blameless when you judge." Psalm 51:3-4

When it comes to guilt, people are all over the map. Some seem to have no conscience whatsoever. They're oblivious (or indifferent) to their faults. They rarely acknowledge, much less take responsibility, for wrongs done. Others are on the opposite end of the spectrum. Morbidly introspective and self-flagellating, you can almost always catch them heaping contempt on their imperfect souls.

We have a third and healthier way. Notice what David does here. He's "conscious" of his rebellion. He owns his wrong choices: "I have sinned and done this evil." Yet for the rest of the psalm, he calls on—and falls on—the astonishing grace of God. This Old Testament picture foreshadows a New Testament truth: Jesus is full of grace and truth (Jn 1:14,17). God's truth declares us guilty, and God's grace says we're loved and forgiven.

Healthy souls hold on tightly to both truths. If we lose either one, we've lost the gospel.

For the next note on *Rest and Reflection*, see Psalm 51:10.

[A] **50:1** Or *The God of gods* [B] **50:2** Or *God shines forth*

you thought I was just like you.
But I will rebuke you
and lay out the case before you.[A]

22 "Understand this, you who forget God,
or I will tear you apart,
and there will be no one to rescue you.
23 Whoever sacrifices a thank offering
honors me,
and whoever orders his conduct,
I will show him the salvation of God."

A PRAYER FOR RESTORATION

51 *For the choir director. A psalm of David, when the prophet Nathan came to him after he had gone to Bathsheba.*

1 Be gracious to me, God,
according to your faithful love;
according to your abundant
compassion,
blot out my rebellion.
2 Completely wash away my guilt
and cleanse me from my sin.
3 For I am conscious of my rebellion,
and my sin is always before me.
4 Against you — you alone —
I have sinned
and done this evil in your sight.
So you are right
when you pass sentence;
you are blameless when you judge.
5 Indeed, I was guilty when I was born;
I was sinful when my mother
conceived me.

6 Surely you desire integrity
in the inner self,
and you teach me wisdom deep within.
7 Purify me with hyssop, and I will be clean;
wash me, and I will be whiter than snow.
8 Let me hear joy and gladness;
let the bones you have crushed rejoice.
9 Turn your face away[B] from my sins
and blot out all my guilt.

10 God, create a clean heart for me
and renew a steadfast[C] spirit within me.
11 Do not banish me from your presence
or take your Holy Spirit from me.
12 Restore the joy of your salvation to me,
and sustain me by giving me
a willing spirit.
13 Then I will teach the rebellious your ways,
and sinners will return to you.

R Rest and Reflection | *Being Willing to Change*

HELP FROM ABOVE

"God, create a clean heart for me and renew a steadfast spirit within me." Psalm 51:10

Most people know their hearts need changing. Why else do we tell ourselves, "I need to do something about my anger," "I shouldn't have such thoughts," "I know I should care more about ______ but I honestly don't!"

Behind such thoughts lies an even bigger question: How can we change?

The change process looks different in each person. But notice where David began when he was trying to rebuild his life after committing adultery and murder (see 2Sm 11). David looked *up*. He called on God to "create a clean heart for me." This is a plea for transformation from the inside out. (And a recognition of exactly what the Lord told his disciples centuries later, "You can do nothing without me," Jn 15:5). A "clean heart" comes from confession and God's forgiveness.

Next, David asked God to "renew a steadfast spirit within me"; in other words, he wanted God to repair his shaky will, to make it firm and reliable. This also is a supernatural work.

Is transformation possible? You bet! Is it quick and painless? Almost never. But if we look to God and cooperate with him, he will gradually mold us into the image of his Son.

For the next note on *Rest and Reflection*, see Psalm 55:6.

[A] **50:21** Lit *lay it out before your eyes* [B] **51:9** Lit *Hide your face* [C] **51:10** Or *right*

14 Save me from the guilt of bloodshed,
God —
God of my salvation —
and my tongue will sing
of your righteousness.
15 Lord, open my lips,
and my mouth will declare your praise.
16 You do not want a sacrifice,
or I would give it;
you are not pleased
with a burnt offering.
17 The sacrifice pleasing to God is[A]
a broken spirit.
You will not despise a broken
and humbled heart, God.

18 In your good pleasure, cause Zion
to prosper;
build the walls of Jerusalem.
19 Then you will delight
in righteous sacrifices,
whole burnt offerings;
then bulls will be offered on your altar.

GOD JUDGES THE PROUD

52 *For the choir director. A* Maskil *of David. When Doeg the Edomite went and reported to Saul, telling him, "David went to Ahimelech's house."*

1 Why boast about evil, you hero!
God's faithful love is constant.
2 Like a sharpened razor,
your tongue devises destruction,
working treachery.
3 You love evil instead of good,
lying instead of
speaking truthfully. *Selah*
4 You love any words that destroy,
you treacherous tongue!

5 This is why God will bring
you down forever.
He will take you, ripping you out of
your tent;
he will uproot you from the land
of the living. *Selah*
6 The righteous will see and fear,
and they will derisively say
about that hero,[B]
7 "Here is the man
who would not make God his refuge,
but trusted in the abundance
of his riches,
taking refuge
in his destructive behavior."
8 But I am like a flourishing olive tree
in the house of God;
I trust in God's faithful love
forever and ever.
9 I will praise you forever for what
you have done.
In the presence of your faithful people,
I will put my hope in your name,
for it is good.

A PORTRAIT OF SINNERS

53 *For the choir director: on* Mahalath. *A* Maskil *of David.*

1 The fool says in his heart,
"There's no God."
They are corrupt, and they do vile deeds.
There is no one who does good.
2 God looks down from heaven
on the human race[C]
to see if there is one who is wise,
one who seeks God.
3 All have turned away;
all alike have become corrupt.
There is no one who does good,
not even one.

4 Will evildoers never understand?
They consume my people
as they consume bread;
they do not call on God.
5 Then they will be filled with dread —
dread like no other —
because God will scatter
the bones of those who besiege you.
You will put them to shame,
for God has rejected them.

6 Oh, that Israel's deliverance
would come from Zion!
When God restores the fortunes
of his people,[D]
let Jacob rejoice, let Israel be glad.

PRAYER FOR DELIVERANCE

54 *For the choir director: with stringed instruments. A* Maskil *of David. When the Ziphites went and said to Saul, "Is David not hiding among us?"*

1 God, save me by your name,
and vindicate me by your might!

[A] **51:17** Lit *The sacrifices of God are* [B] **52:6** Lit *about him* [C] **53:2** Or *the descendants of Adam* [D] **53:6** Or *restores his captive people*

2 God, hear my prayer;
listen to the words from my mouth.
3 For strangers rise up against me,
and violent men intend to kill me.
They do not let God guide them.[A] *Selah*

4 God is my helper;
the Lord is the sustainer of my life.[B]
5 He will repay my adversaries
for their evil.
Because of your faithfulness,
annihilate them.

6 I will sacrifice a freewill offering
to you.
I will praise your name, LORD,
because it is good.
7 For he has rescued me
from every trouble,
and my eye has looked down on
my enemies.

BETRAYAL BY A FRIEND

55 *For the choir director: with stringed instruments. A* Maskil *of David.*

1 God, listen to my prayer
and do not hide from my plea for help.
2 Pay attention to me and answer me.
I am restless and in turmoil
with my complaint,
3 because of the enemy's words,[C]
because of the pressure[D]
of the wicked.
For they bring down disaster on me
and harass me in anger.

4 My heart shudders within me;
terrors of death sweep over me.
5 Fear and trembling grip me;
horror has overwhelmed me.
6 I said, "If only I had wings like a dove!
I would fly away and find rest.
7 How far away I would flee;
I would stay in the wilderness. *Selah*
8 I would hurry to my shelter
from the raging wind and the storm."

9 Lord, confuse[E] and confound
their speech,[F]
for I see violence and strife in the city;
10 day and night they make the rounds
on its walls.
Crime and trouble are within it;
11 destruction is inside it;
oppression and deceit never leave
its marketplace.

Rest and Reflection | *Resting and Recharging*

WANT TO RUN AWAY?

"I said, 'If only I had wings like a dove! I would fly away and find rest.'" *Psalm 55:6*

You hop in the car to grab something at the grocery store. The next thing you know you're thinking, *What if I just kept driving?* Later, while staring blankly at a mountain of dirty clothes on the laundry room floor, you find yourself daydreaming about two weeks at a remote cabin in the Rockies. If this is you—if you are antsy and consumed by thoughts of running away and escaping reality—it's probably a signal you need a break.

David's situation in Psalm 55 was dire. He had been betrayed by a friend and was being hunted. Consequently, he referenced being "in turmoil" (55:2), gripped by "fear and trembling" and being overwhelmed by "horror" (55:5). Weary of running for his life, he wanted to "fly away and find rest" (literally, to settle down in one place).

Whatever the reason(s) for your restlessness, you need to take some time to rest, reflect, and recharge. Since a mountain vacation probably isn't possible, perhaps one day off or a weekend getaway would do the trick.

For the next note on *Rest and Reflection*, see Psalm 62:1.

[A] **54:3** Lit *They do not set God in front of them* [B] **54:4** Or *is with those who sustain my life* [C] **55:3** Lit *voice* [D] **55:3** Or *threat*, or *oppression* [E] **55:9** Or *destroy* [F] **55:9** Lit *and divide their tongue*

12 Now it is not an enemy
who insults me —
otherwise I could bear it;
it is not a foe who rises up against me —
otherwise I could hide from him.
13 But it is you, a man who is my peer,
my companion and good friend!
14 We used to have close fellowship;
we walked with the crowd
into the house of God.

15 Let death take them by surprise;
let them go down to Sheol alive,
because evil is in their homes
and within them.
16 But I call to God,
and the LORD will save me.
17 I complain and groan morning, noon,
and night,
and he hears my voice.
18 Though many are against me,
he will redeem me
from my battle unharmed.
19 God, the one enthroned from long ago,
will hear and will humiliate them *Selah*
because they do not change
and do not fear God.

20 My friend acts violently
against those at peace with him;
he violates his covenant.
21 His buttery words are smooth,
but war is in his heart.
His words are softer than oil,
but they are drawn swords.

22 Cast your burden on the LORD,
and he will sustain you;
he will never allow the righteous
to be shaken.

23 God, you will bring them down
to the Pit of destruction;
men of bloodshed and treachery
will not live out half their days.
But I will trust in you.

A CALL FOR GOD'S PROTECTION

56 *For the choir director: according to "A Silent Dove Far Away." A Miktam of David. When the Philistines seized him in Gath.*

1 Be gracious to me, God, for a man is
trampling me;
he fights and oppresses me all day long.
2 My adversaries trample me all day,
for many arrogantly fight against me.[A]

3 When I am afraid,
I will trust in you.
4 In God, whose word I praise,
in God I trust; I will not be afraid.
What can mere mortals do to me?

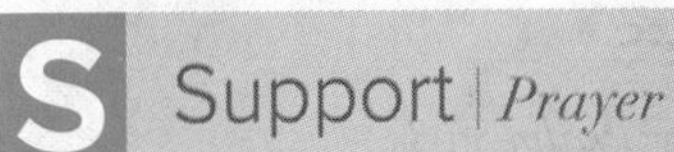

BREAKING THE RULES OF PRAYER

"I complain and groan morning, noon, and night, and he hears my voice." Psalm 55:17

In certain religious circles, the unwritten rules of prayer are as follows: *Always* express deep faith. *Never* mention negative feelings or be overly honest. Use a formal, abnormal voice. Throw in some big, spiritual words. Repeat God's name every third or fourth word to make sure he pays attention.

Contrast this with David's prayer in Psalm 55 (and many other psalms). He probably would not have felt at home (or been welcomed) in those aforementioned prayer groups. Notice how he complains and groans. No façades or fronts—he lays his soul bare. His prayers were unedited and authentic. When he felt hopeless, his prayers sounded like a funeral dirge. When he felt joyous, they resembled a dance party.

Sometimes the book of Psalms is a bit shocking to read—and also quite refreshing. As far as learning how to pray, you will find no better text than this one.

For the next note on *Support*, see Psalm 73:24.

[A] **56:2** Or *many fight against me, O exalted one*, or *many fight against me from the heights*

5 They twist my words all day long;
all their thoughts against me are evil.
6 They stir up strife,[A] they lurk;
they watch my steps
while they wait to take my life.
7 Will they escape in spite of such sin?
God, bring down the nations
in wrath.

8 You yourself have recorded
my wanderings.[B]
Put my tears in your bottle.
Are they not in your book?
9 Then my enemies will retreat
on the day when I call.
This I know: God is for me.

10 In God, whose word I praise,
in the LORD, whose word I praise,
11 in God I trust; I will not be afraid.
What can mere humans do to me?

12 I am obligated by vows[C] to you, God;
I will make my thank offerings to you.
13 For you rescued me from death,
even my feet from stumbling,
to walk before God in the light of life.

PRAISE FOR GOD'S PROTECTION

57 *For the choir director: "Do Not Destroy." A* Miktam *of David. When he fled before Saul into the cave.*

1 Be gracious to me, God, be gracious to me,
for I take refuge in you.
I will seek refuge in the shadow
of your wings
until danger passes.
2 I call to God Most High,
to God who fulfills his purpose for me.[D]
3 He reaches down from heaven
and saves me,
challenging the one who tramples me.
Selah
God sends his faithful love and truth.
4 I am surrounded by lions;
I lie down among devouring lions —
people whose teeth are spears
and arrows,
whose tongues are sharp swords.
5 God, be exalted above the heavens;
let your glory be over the whole earth.
6 They prepared a net for my steps;
I was despondent.
They dug a pit ahead of me,
but they fell into it! *Selah*

Eternal Perspective | *Fear Overcome*

WHEN FEAR STRIKES

"When I am afraid, I will trust in you." Psalm 56:3

Do this experiment. Ask ten people to finish this sentence: "When I am afraid, I . . ."

You'll hear it all: call my mom; eat nervously; stop eating; have a drink—or two or three; try to think about other things; go into hiding; get manic; get catatonic.

Notice David's response, "When I am afraid, I will trust in you" ("you" being, of course, the Lord God Almighty). "Trust" means to be confident in, to rely on, to look to for safety.

To always *feel* confident and trusting would be great, that's not the case. Thus, trust requires us to take action, even when we're shaking in our boots. You pull out your phone, for example, and send the text: "Can we talk?" You show up, nervous, heart racing—all the while leaning on God, counting on him to give you the words, relying on him to help you keep your emotions in check, trusting him to take care of the outcome.

Fear is normal. Believers feel it fully. Yet they walk in faith with God toward the very thing that scares them.

What's scaring you today? What, practically speaking, does trusting God look like in that situation?

For the next note on *Eternal Perspective*, see Psalm 86:15.

[A] **56:6** Or *They attack* [B] **56:8** Or *misery* [C] **56:12** Lit *On me the vows* [D] **57:2** Or *who avenges me*

7 My heart is confident, God, my heart
is confident.
I will sing; I will sing praises.
8 Wake up, my soul!
Wake up, harp and lyre!
I will wake up the dawn.
9 I will praise you, Lord,
among the peoples;
I will sing praises to you
among the nations.
10 For your faithful love is as high as
the heavens;
your faithfulness reaches the clouds.
11 God, be exalted above the heavens;
let your glory be over the whole earth.

A CRY AGAINST INJUSTICE

For the choir director: "Do Not Destroy."
A Miktam *of David.*

1 Do you really speak righteously,
you mighty ones?[A]
Do you judge people fairly?
2 No, you practice injustice
in your hearts;
with your hands
you weigh out violence in the land.

3 The wicked go astray from the womb;
liars wander about from birth.
4 They have venom like the venom
of a snake,
like the deaf cobra that stops up its ears,
5 that does not listen to the sound
of the charmers
who skillfully weave spells.

6 God, knock the teeth out of their mouths;
LORD, tear out the young lions' fangs.
7 May they vanish like water
that flows by;
may they aim their blunted arrows.[B]
8 Like a slug that moves along in slime,
like a woman's miscarried child,
may they not see the sun.

T Thanksgiving and Contentment | *Comfort*

TEARS IN A BOTTLE

"You yourself have recorded my wanderings. Put my tears in your bottle. Are they not in your book?" Psalm 56:8

Saul was so obsessed with and threatened by David's great popularity that he couldn't see his servant's unflinching loyalty. For at least a decade (some scholars think longer), David was on the run. He managed, just barely, to stay a step or two ahead of a paranoid, homicidal king. For David, life was miserable, filled with fear, sleepless nights, adrenaline rushes (and crashes), dark caves, loneliness, and waiting.

Psalm 56 records an incident during these fugitive years when David was seized by the Philistines. In just a few verses, we get a vivid snapshot of the stress David felt even as he tried to cling to God. Midway through this prayer, this exhausted young warrior speaks poignantly of the way God takes notice of his tears.

What a comfort to those who are overcome! According to David, our grief is not insignificant to God. He studies and catalogues our sadness.

At the end of the Bible, we read of a coming day of restoration—when God "will wipe away every tear from their eyes. . . . grief, crying, and pain will be no more" (Rv 21:4). Perhaps in that new heaven and new earth, by an ocean of pure joy, God will pull out the bottles containing our tears, and we will hear him say, "Was it not worth it? For every drop of grief you ever suffered, I now give you twenty thousand leagues of gladness!"

For now, at least know this: God sees your pain. And he doesn't forget your tears. He grieves with those who grieve (see Jn 11).

For the next note on *Thanksgiving and Comfort*, see Psalm 118:24.

[A] **58:1** Or *Can you really speak righteousness in silence?* [B] **58:7** Hb obscure

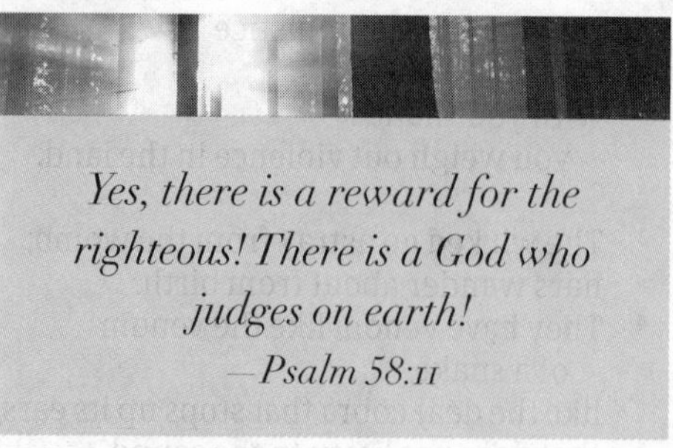

Yes, there is a reward for the righteous! There is a God who judges on earth!
—Psalm 58:11

9 Before your pots can feel the heat of
the thorns —
whether green or burning —
he will sweep them away.[A]
10 The righteous one will rejoice
when he sees the retribution;
he will wash his feet in the blood
of the wicked.
11 Then people will say,
"Yes, there is a reward for the righteous!
There is a God who judges on earth!"

GOD OUR STRONGHOLD

59 *For the choir director: "Do Not Destroy."* A Miktam *of David. When Saul sent agents to watch the house and kill him.*

1 Rescue me from my enemies, my God;
protect me from those who rise up
against me.
2 Rescue me from those
who practice sin,
and save me from men of bloodshed.
3 Because look, LORD, they set an ambush
for me.
Powerful men attack me,
but not because of any sin or rebellion
of mine.
4 For no fault of mine,
they run and take up a position.
Awake to help me, and take notice.
5 LORD God of Armies, you are the
God of Israel.
Rise up to punish all the nations;
do not show favor
to any wicked traitors. *Selah*

6 They return at evening,
snarling like dogs
and prowling around the city.
7 Look, they spew from their mouths —
sharp words from[B] their lips.
"For who," they say, "will hear?"
8 But you laugh at them, LORD;
you ridicule all the nations.
9 I will keep watch for you,
my[C] strength,
because God is my stronghold.
10 My faithful God[D] will come
to meet me;
God will let me look down on
my adversaries.

11 Do not kill them; otherwise, my people
will forget.
By your power, make them
homeless wanderers
and bring them down,
Lord, our shield.
12 For the sin of their mouths and the
words of their lips,
let them be caught in their pride.
They utter curses and lies.
13 Consume them in rage;
consume them until they are gone.
Then people will know
throughout[E] the earth
that God rules over Jacob. *Selah*

14 And they return at evening,
snarling like dogs
and prowling around the city.
15 They scavenge for food;
they growl if they are not satisfied.

16 But I will sing of your strength
and will joyfully proclaim
your faithful love in the morning.
For you have been a stronghold
for me,
a refuge in my day of trouble.
17 To you, my strength, I sing praises,
because God is my stronghold —
my faithful God.

PRAYER IN DIFFICULT TIMES

60 *For the choir director: according to "The Lily of Testimony."* A Miktam *of David for teaching. When he fought with Aram-naharaim and Aram-zobah, and Joab returned and struck Edom in Salt Valley, killing twelve thousand.*

1 God, you have rejected us;
you have broken us down;
you have been angry. Restore us![F]

[A] **58:9** Or *thorns, he will sweep it away, whether raw or cooking* [B] **59:7** Lit *swords are on* [C] **59:9** Some Hb mss, LXX, Vg, Tg; other Hb mss read *his* [D] **59:10** Alt Hb tradition reads *My God in his faithful love* [E] **59:13** Lit *know to the ends of* [F] **60:1** Or *Turn back to us*

2 You have shaken the land
and split it open.
Heal its fissures, for it shudders.
3 You have made your people
suffer hardship;
you have given us wine to drink
that made us stagger.
4 You have given a signal flag to those
who fear you,
so that they can flee
before the archers.[A] *Selah*
5 Save with your right hand,
and answer me,
so that those you love may be rescued.

6 God has spoken in his sanctuary:[B]
"I will celebrate!
I will divide up Shechem.
I will apportion the Valley of Succoth.
7 Gilead is mine, Manasseh is mine,
and Ephraim is my helmet;
Judah is my scepter.
8 Moab is my washbasin.
I throw my sandal on Edom;
I shout in triumph over Philistia."

9 Who will bring me to the fortified city?
Who will lead me to Edom?
10 God, haven't you rejected us?
God, you do not march out
with our armies.
11 Give us aid against the foe,
for human help is worthless.
12 With God we will perform valiantly;
he will trample our foes.

SECURITY IN GOD

61 *For the choir director: on stringed instruments. Of David.*

1 God, hear my cry;
pay attention to my prayer.
2 I call to you from the ends of the earth
when my heart is without strength.
Lead me to a rock that is
high above me,
3 for you have been a refuge for me,
a strong tower in the face of the enemy.
4 I will dwell in your tent forever
and take refuge under the shelter
of your wings. *Selah*

5 God, you have heard my vows;
you have given a heritage
to those who fear your name.
6 Add days to the king's life;
may his years span many generations.
7 May he sit enthroned
before God forever.

Rest and Reflection | *Waiting on God*

SUBSTITUTE SAVIORS

"I am at rest in God alone; my salvation comes from him." Psalm 62:1

We may assume that the word *salvation* always carries spiritual overtones. Not so. *Salvation*, properly defined, simply means "deliverance, help, safety, rescue, prosperity, freedom from danger."

This explains why people set their hope on so many different things: steady job, marriage, social standing, talent or set of abilities, lucrative career, physical strength, good looks or health, smart investments, or political ideology.

None of those are bad in themselves. In truth, they often lead to great blessing. But none are ultimate and enduring. We might enjoy them today, but who's to say we'll have them next year? Some other substitute-saviors *are* bad—like addictive substances and behaviors.

Notice where David's hope was found: "My salvation comes from him." God was David's deliverer, helper, rescuer, and source of blessing. No wonder David found rest "in God alone"!

In what places other than God are you tempted to look for security and satisfaction? "Rest in God alone."

For the next note on *Rest and Reflection*, see Psalm 62:5.

[A] **60:4** Or *can rally before the archers*, or *can rally because of the truth* [B] **60:6** Or *has promised by his holy nature*

Appoint faithful love and truth
to guard him.
8 Then I will continually sing
of your name,
fulfilling my vows day by day.

TRUST IN GOD ALONE

62 *For the choir director: according to Jeduthun. A psalm of David.*

1 I am at rest in God alone;
my salvation comes from him.
2 He alone is my rock and my salvation,
my stronghold; I will never be shaken.

3 How long will you threaten a man?
Will all of you attack[A]
as if he were a leaning wall
or a tottering fence?
4 They only plan to bring him down
from his high position.
They take pleasure in lying;
they bless with their mouths,
but they curse inwardly. *Selah*

5 Rest in God alone, my soul,
for my hope comes from him.
6 He alone is my rock and my salvation,
my stronghold; I will not be shaken.
7 My salvation and glory depend on God,
my strong rock.
My refuge is in God.
8 Trust in him at all times, you people;
pour out your hearts before him.
God is our refuge. *Selah*

9 Common people are only a vapor;
important people, an illusion.
Together on a scale,
they weigh less than[B] a vapor.
10 Place no trust in oppression,
or false hope in robbery.
If wealth increases,
don't set your heart on it.

11 God has spoken once;
I have heard this twice:
strength belongs to God,
12 and faithful love belongs
to you, LORD.
For you repay each according to
his works.

PRAISE GOD WHO SATISFIES

63 *A psalm of David. When he was in the Wilderness of Judah.*

1 God, you are my God; I eagerly seek you.
I thirst for you;
my body faints for you
in a land that is dry, desolate,
and without water.
2 So I gaze on you in the sanctuary
to see your strength and your glory.

R Rest and Reflection | *Remembering God's Truth*

PREACHING TO YOUR OWN SOUL

"Rest in God alone, my soul, for my hope comes from him." Psalm 62:5

Do you talk to yourself? Find yourself muttering under your breath as you go about your day? Do you get embarrassed when you realize you're talking to yourself? Don't feel badly! Scientific research has shown that people who engage in self-talk tend to be smarter and have more efficient brains. (Even the brilliant Albert Einstein did it.) What's more, the practice stimulates memory, brings clarity, and helps with focus.

King David was a self-talker. In an unspecified, but clearly frightening situation, we see him exhorting himself ("my soul") to remember certain truths and to take needed action, specifically to "rest in God alone." After preaching to his own soul like this, David's mood completely flips. He shifts from frantic to peaceful. Other psalms have this same format (see Pss 42; 43; 104; 116; 146).

Try it. Next time you notice that your soul is out of sorts, grab it by the elbow, lead it over to the corner, and whisper God's reassuring truths to it. Be prepared to marvel at the difference this makes.

For the next note on *Rest and Reflection*, see Psalm 68:19.

[A] **62:3** Some Hb mss read *you be struck down* [B] **62:9** Lit *they go up more than*

3 My lips will glorify you
because your faithful love is better
than life.
4 So I will bless you as long as I live;
at your name, I will lift up my hands.
5 You satisfy me as with rich food;[A]
my mouth will praise you
with joyful lips.

6 When I think of you as I lie on my bed,
I meditate on you
during the night watches
7 because you are my helper;
I will rejoice in the shadow of your wings.
8 I follow close to you;
your right hand holds on to me.

9 But those who intend to destroy my life
will go into the depths of the earth.
10 They will be given over to the power
of the sword;
they will become a meal for jackals.
11 But the king will rejoice in God;
all who swear by him will boast,
for the mouths of liars will be shut.

PROTECTION FROM EVILDOERS

64 *For the choir director. A psalm of David.*
God, hear my voice when I am
in anguish.
Protect my life from the terror
of the enemy.
2 Hide me from the scheming
of wicked people,
from the mob of evildoers,
3 who sharpen their tongues like swords
and aim bitter words like arrows,
4 shooting from concealed places
at the blameless.
They shoot at him suddenly
and are not afraid.
5 They adopt[B] an evil plan;
they talk about hiding traps and say,
"Who will see them?"[C]
6 They devise crimes and say,
"We have perfected a secret plan."
The inner man and the heart
are mysterious.

7 But God will shoot them with arrows;
suddenly, they will be wounded.
8 They will be made to stumble;
their own tongues work against them.
All who see them will shake
their heads.
9 Then everyone will fear
and will tell about God's work,
for they will understand
what he has done.

10 The righteous one rejoices in the LORD
and takes refuge in him;
all those who are upright in heart
will offer praise.

GOD'S CARE FOR THE EARTH

65 *For the choir director. A psalm of David.*
A song.
1 Praise is rightfully yours,[D]
God, in Zion;
vows to you will be fulfilled.
2 All humanity will come to you,
the one who hears prayer.
3 Iniquities overwhelm me;
only you can atone for our rebellions.
4 How happy is the one you choose
and bring near to live in your courts!
We will be satisfied with the goodness
of your house,
the holiness of your temple.[E]

5 You answer us in righteousness,
with awe-inspiring works,
God of our salvation,
the hope of all the ends of the earth
and of the distant seas.
6 You establish the mountains
by your power;
you are robed with strength.
7 You silence the roar of the seas,
the roar of their waves,
and the tumult of the nations.
8 Those who live far away are awed
by your signs;
you make east and west shout for joy.

9 You visit the earth
and water it abundantly,
enriching it greatly.
God's stream is filled with water,
for you prepare the earth in this way,
providing people with grain.
10 You soften it with showers and bless
its growth,
soaking its furrows and leveling
its ridges.

[A] **63:5** Lit *with fat and fatness* [B] **64:5** Or *They strengthen themselves with* [C] **64:5** Or *it* [D] **65:1** Or *Praise is silence to you*, or *Praise awaits you* [E] **65:4** Or *house, your holy temple*

11 You crown the year
with your goodness;
your carts overflow with plenty.[A]
12 The wilderness pastures overflow,
and the hills are robed with joy.
13 The pastures are clothed with flocks
and the valleys covered with grain.
They shout in triumph; indeed,
they sing.

PRAISE FOR GOD'S MIGHTY ACTS

66 *For the choir director. A song. A psalm.*
Let the whole earth shout joyfully
to God!
2 Sing about the glory of his name;
make his praise glorious.
3 Say to God, "How awe-inspiring
are your works!
Your enemies will cringe before you
because of your great strength.
4 The whole earth will worship you
and sing praise to you.
They will sing praise to your name."
Selah
5 Come and see the wonders of God;
his acts for humanity[B]
are awe-inspiring.
6 He turned the sea into dry land,
and they crossed the river on foot.
There we rejoiced in him.
7 He rules forever by his might;
he keeps his eye on the nations.
The rebellious should not
exalt themselves. *Selah*
8 Bless our God, you peoples;
let the sound of his praise be heard.
9 He keeps us alive[C]
and does not allow our feet to slip.

10 For you, God, tested us;
you refined us as silver is refined.
11 You lured us into a trap;
you placed burdens on our backs.
12 You let men ride over our heads;
we went through fire and water,
but you brought us out to abundance.[D]

13 I will enter your house
with burnt offerings;
I will pay you my vows
14 that my lips promised
and my mouth spoke during my distress.
15 I will offer you fattened sheep
as burnt offerings,
with the fragrant smoke of rams;
I will sacrifice bulls with goats. *Selah*

16 Come and listen, all who fear God,
and I will tell what he has done for me.
17 I cried out to him with my mouth,
and praise was on my tongue.
18 If I had been aware of malice
in my heart,
the Lord would not have listened.
19 However, God has listened;
he has paid attention to the sound
of my prayer.
20 Blessed be God!
He has not turned away my prayer
or turned his faithful love from me.

ALL WILL PRAISE GOD

67 *For the choir director: with stringed instruments. A psalm. A song.*
1 May God be gracious to us and bless us;
may he make his face shine
upon us *Selah*
2 so that your way may be known
on earth,
your salvation among all nations.

3 Let the peoples praise you, God;
let all the peoples praise you.
4 Let the nations rejoice and shout for joy,
for you judge the peoples with fairness
and lead the nations on earth. *Selah*
5 Let the peoples praise you, God,
let all the peoples praise you.

6 The earth has produced its harvest;
God, our God, blesses us.
7 God will bless us,
and all the ends of the earth
will fear him.

GOD'S MAJESTIC POWER

68 *For the choir director. A psalm of David. A song.*
1 God arises. His enemies scatter,
and those who hate him flee
from his presence.
2 As smoke is blown away,
so you blow them away.
As wax melts before the fire,
so the wicked are destroyed before God.

[A] **65:11** Lit *your paths drip with fat* [B] **66:5** Or *for the descendants of Adam* [C] **66:9** Lit *He sets our soul in life* [D] **66:12** Or *a place of satisfaction*

15 My mouth will tell
about your righteousness
and your salvation all day long,
though I cannot sum them up.
16 I come because of the mighty acts
of the Lord God;
I will proclaim your righteousness,
yours alone.

17 God, you have taught me from my youth,
and I still proclaim your
wondrous works.
18 Even while I am old and gray,
God, do not abandon me,
while I proclaim your power
to another generation,
your strength to all who are to come.
19 Your righteousness reaches
the heights, God,
you who have done great things;
God, who is like you?
20 You caused me to experience
many troubles and misfortunes,
but you will revive me again.
You will bring me up again,
even from the depths of the earth.
21 You will increase my honor
and comfort me once again.
22 Therefore, I will praise you with a harp
for your faithfulness, my God;
I will sing to you with a lyre,
Holy One of Israel.
23 My lips will shout for joy
when I sing praise to you
because you have redeemed me.
24 Therefore, my tongue will proclaim
your righteousness all day long,
for those who intend to harm me
will be disgraced and confounded.

A PRAYER FOR THE KING

72 *Of Solomon.*
God, give your justice to the king
and your righteousness
to the king's son.
2 He will judge your people
with righteousness
and your afflicted ones with justice.
3 May the mountains bring well-being[A]
to the people
and the hills, righteousness.
4 May he vindicate the afflicted
among the people,
help the poor,
and crush the oppressor.

5 May they fear you[B] while the
sun endures
and as long as the moon,
throughout all generations.

Relationships | *Mentoring*

INVESTING IN THE NEXT GENERATION

"Even while I am old and gray, God, do not abandon me, while I proclaim your power to another generation, your strength to all who are to come." Psalm 71:18

On TV, everybody's young and attractive. They ooze confidence and success. Meanwhile, in real life, huge numbers of young adults are floundering. They're disillusioned—realizing that while being fit, fashionable, and financially successful are all great, they're not enough. If you're younger, maybe you feel these frustrations in your own soul. If you're older, perhaps you see them all around you.

Psalm 71 is relevant here. It's the prayer of an old man. Interestingly he's not interested in living out his days golfing or fishing. Rather, because he has spent a lifetime watching God do remarkable things, he wants to proclaim God's "power to another generation." In other words, he wants to be a mentor.

Do you have an older, wiser person in your life like that—who walks with you through the twists and turns of life? Do you play that role in the life of someone younger? Ask God for a mentor, and for the chance to be one.

For the next note on *Relationships*, see Psalm 88:9.

[A] **72:3** Or *peace*, also in v. 7 [B] **72:5** LXX reads *May he continue*

6 May the king be like rain that falls
on the cut grass,
like spring showers that water the earth.
7 May the righteous[A] flourish in his days
and well-being abound
until the moon is no more.

8 May he rule from sea to sea
and from the Euphrates
to the ends of the earth.
9 May desert tribes kneel before him
and his enemies lick the dust.
10 May the kings of Tarshish
and the coasts and islands
bring tribute,
the kings of Sheba and Seba offer gifts.
11 Let all kings bow in homage to him,
all nations serve him.

12 For he will rescue the poor who cry out
and the afflicted who have no helper.
13 He will have pity on the poor and helpless
and save the lives of the poor.
14 He will redeem them from oppression
and violence,
for their lives are[B] precious[C] in his sight.

15 May he live long!
May gold from Sheba be given to him.
May prayer be offered
for him continually,
and may he be blessed all day long.
16 May there be plenty of grain in the land;
may it wave on the tops
of the mountains.
May its crops be like Lebanon.
May people flourish in the cities
like the grass of the field.
17 May his name endure forever;
as long as the sun shines,
may his fame increase.
May all nations be blessed by him
and call him blessed.

18 Blessed be the LORD God, the God
of Israel,
who alone does wonders.
19 Blessed be his glorious name forever;
the whole earth is filled with his glory.
Amen and amen.
20 The prayers of David son of Jesse
are concluded.

BOOK III (Psalms 73–89)

GOD'S WAYS VINDICATED

73 *A psalm of Asaph.*
God is indeed good to Israel,
to the pure in heart.
2 But as for me, my feet almost slipped;
my steps nearly went astray.
3 For I envied the arrogant;
I saw the prosperity of the wicked.

4 They have an easy time until they die,[D]
and their bodies are well fed.[E]
5 They are not in trouble like others;
they are not afflicted like most people.
6 Therefore, pride is their necklace,
and violence covers them
like a garment.
7 Their eyes bulge out from fatness;
the imaginations of their hearts
run wild.
8 They mock, and they speak maliciously;
they arrogantly threaten oppression.
9 They set their mouths against heaven,
and their tongues strut
across the earth.
10 Therefore his people turn to them[F]
and drink in their overflowing words.[G]
11 The wicked say, "How can God know?
Does the Most High know everything?"
12 Look at them — the wicked!
They are always at ease,
and they increase their wealth.

13 Did I purify my heart
and wash my hands in innocence
for nothing?
14 For I am afflicted all day long
and punished every morning.
15 If I had decided to say
these things aloud,
I would have betrayed your people.[H]
16 When I tried to understand all this,
it seemed hopeless[I]
17 until I entered God's sanctuary.
Then I understood their destiny.
18 Indeed, you put them in slippery places;
you make them fall into ruin.
19 How suddenly they become
a desolation!
They come to an end, swept away
by terrors.

[A] **72:7** Some Hb mss, LXX, Syr, Jer read *May righteousness* [B] **72:14** Lit *their blood is* [C] **72:14** Or *valuable* [D] **73:4** Lit *For there are no pangs to their death* [E] **73:4** Lit *fat* [F] **73:10** Lit *turn here* [G] **73:10** Lit *and waters of fullness are drained by them* [H] **73:15** Lit *betrayed the generation of your sons* [I] **73:16** Lit *it was trouble in my eyes*

20 Like one waking from a dream,
Lord, when arising, you will despise
their image.

21 When I became embittered
and my innermost being[A]
was wounded,
22 I was stupid and didn't understand;
I was an unthinking animal
toward you.
23 Yet I am always with you;
you hold my right hand.
24 You guide me with your counsel,
and afterward you will take me up
in glory.[B]
25 Who do I have in heaven but you?
And I desire nothing on earth
but you.
26 My flesh and my heart may fail,
but God is the strength[C] of my heart,
my portion forever.
27 Those far from you
will certainly perish;
you destroy all who are
unfaithful to you.
28 But as for me, God's presence is
my good.
I have made the Lord God my refuge,
so I can tell about all you do.

PRAYER FOR ISRAEL

74 *A Maskil of Asaph.*
Why have you rejected us forever, God?
Why does your anger burn
against the sheep of your pasture?
2 Remember your congregation,
which you purchased long ago
and redeemed as the tribe
for your own possession.
Remember Mount Zion where you dwell.
3 Make your way[D] to the perpetual ruins,
to all that the enemy has destroyed
in the sanctuary.
4 Your adversaries roared
in the meeting place
where you met with us.[E]
They set up their emblems as signs.
5 It was like men in a thicket of trees,
wielding axes,
6 then smashing all the carvings
with hatchets and picks.
7 They set your sanctuary on fire;
they utterly[F] desecrated
the dwelling place of your name.
8 They said in their hearts,
"Let us oppress them relentlessly."
They burned every place
throughout the land
where God met with us.[G]

S Support | *God's Counsel*

GUIDANCE

"You guide me with your counsel, and afterward you will take me up in glory." Psalm 73:24

God is endlessly creative in the way he guides us through life. He gives us plain old common sense. He nudges and pricks our consciences. He sovereignly thwarts some of our plans and orchestrates other unforeseen circumstances. He sends counselors and mentors to speak into our lives. He convinces and comforts us by his Spirit. He prompts friends to remind us of important truths. Best of all, he gives us his Word.

The Bible isn't, as many suppose, a rule book. It's the story of God and his love for the world. It's a record of flesh-and-blood people like us. By showing us their failures and successes, the Bible is both motivational guide and cautionary tale all at once. On every page, we can stop and ask questions like: What does this passage show me about God's character? About human nature? Is there a command here to obey, a promise to claim, or a sin to avoid? What about an example to follow?

Take a few minutes to read all of Psalm 73 that way, asking God, "Guide me with your counsel."

For the next note on *Support*, see Psalm 116:1-2.

[A] **73:21** Lit *my kidneys* [B] **73:24** Or *will receive me with honor* [C] **73:26** Lit *rock* [D] **74:3** Lit *Lift up your steps* [E] **74:4** Lit *in your meeting place* [F] **74:7** Lit *they to the ground* [G] **74:8** Lit *every meeting place of God in the land*

9 There are no signs for us to see.
There is no longer a prophet.
And none of us knows how long
this will last.
10 God, how long will the enemy mock?
Will the foe insult your name forever?
11 Why do you hold back your hand?
Stretch out[A] your right hand
and destroy them!

12 God my King is from ancient times,
performing saving acts on the earth.
13 You divided the sea with your strength;
you smashed the heads
of the sea monsters in the water;
14 you crushed the heads of Leviathan;
you fed him to the creatures
of the desert.
15 You opened up springs and streams;
you dried up ever-flowing rivers.
16 The day is yours, also the night;
you established the moon and the sun.
17 You set all the boundaries of the earth;
you made summer and winter.

18 Remember this: the enemy has mocked
the LORD,
and a foolish people has insulted
your name.
19 Do not give to beasts the life
of your dove;[B]
do not forget the lives
of your poor people forever.
20 Consider the covenant,
for the dark places of the land
are full of violence.
21 Do not let the oppressed turn away
in shame;
let the poor and needy
praise your name.
22 Rise up, God, champion your cause!
Remember the insults
that fools bring against you
all day long.
23 Do not forget the clamor
of your adversaries,
the tumult of your opponents
that goes up constantly.

GOD JUDGES THE WICKED

75 *For the choir director: "Do Not Destroy." A psalm of Asaph. A song.*

1 We give thanks to you, God;
we give thanks to you, for your name
is near.
People tell about
your wondrous works.

2 "When I choose a time,
I will judge fairly.
3 When the earth and all
its inhabitants shake,
I am the one who steadies
its pillars. *Selah*
4 I say to the boastful, 'Do not boast,'
and to the wicked, 'Do not lift up
your horn.
5 Do not lift up your horn
against heaven[C]
or speak arrogantly.' "

6 Exaltation does not come
from the east, the west, or the desert,
7 for God is the Judge:
He brings down one and exalts another.
8 For there is a cup in the LORD's hand,
full of wine blended with spices,
and he pours from it.
All the wicked of the earth will drink,
draining it to the dregs.

9 As for me, I will tell about him forever;
I will sing praise to the God of Jacob.

10 "I will cut off all the horns
of the wicked,
but the horns of the righteous will be
lifted up."

GOD, THE POWERFUL JUDGE

76 *For the choir director: with stringed instruments. A psalm of Asaph. A song.*

1 God is known in Judah;
his name is great in Israel.
2 His tent is in Salem,
his dwelling place in Zion.
3 There he shatters the bow's
flaming arrows,
the shield, the sword, and the weapons
of war. *Selah*

4 You are resplendent and majestic
coming down from the mountains
of prey.
5 The brave-hearted
have been plundered;

[A] **74:11** Lit *From your bosom* [B] **74:19** One Hb ms, LXX, Syr read *life that praises you* [C] **75:5** Lit *horn to the height*

they have slipped into their final sleep.
None of the warriors was able to lift
a hand.
6 At your rebuke, God of Jacob,
both chariot and horse lay still.
7 And you — you are to be feared.[A]
When you are angry,
who can stand before you?
8 From heaven
you pronounced judgment.
The earth feared and grew quiet
9 when God rose up to judge
and to save all the lowly
of the earth. *Selah*
10 Even human wrath will praise you;
you will clothe yourself
with the wrath that remains.[B]

11 Make and keep your vows
to the LORD your God;
let all who are around him
bring tribute
to the awe-inspiring one.[C]
12 He humbles the spirit of leaders;
he is feared by the kings of the earth.

CONFIDENCE IN A TIME OF CRISIS

77 *For the choir director: according to Jeduthun. Of Asaph. A psalm.*

1 I cry aloud to God,
aloud to God, and he will hear me.
2 I sought the Lord in my day of trouble.
My hands were continually lifted up
all night long;
I refused to be comforted.
3 I think of God; I groan;
I meditate; my spirit
becomes weak. *Selah*

4 You have kept me from closing my eyes;
I am troubled and cannot speak.
5 I consider days of old,
years long past.
6 At night I remember my music;
I meditate in my heart,
and my spirit ponders.

7 "Will the Lord reject forever
and never again show favor?
8 Has his faithful love ceased forever?
Is his promise at an end
for all generations?

Rest and Reflection | *Remembering God's Truth*

THE IMPORTANCE OF REMEMBERING

"I will remember the LORD's works; yes, I will remember your ancient wonders." Psalm 77:11

A Bible professor once remarked that the Bible, properly understood, actually contains only about ten big ideas. A student inquired, "Why then is the Bible so long?" The professor smiled and said, "People kept forgetting those truths, so God kept repeating them over and over."

We might quibble over the idea that the Bible has only ten big ideas, but we can't debate that our human tendency is to forget. No wonder the Bible constantly urges us to "remember" and warns "don't forget."

Biblical remembering is more than nostalgia or sentimentality, more than fondly reminiscing about old friends and happy experiences. Biblical remembering impacts the present. When facing uncertainty, we look back in time for reassuring reminders. When we find them, we bring the past into the present—with thoughts like, "God was faithful when I lost my job in 2011, so I know he will be faithful today."

This psalm writer encourages us to do some intentional remembering. Set aside time for the express purpose of recalling what God has done and how he has shown that he loves you. Reading the Bible serves this purpose. Keeping a record of God's actions (for example, a journal) is another way.

What incidents from your spiritual history could, if remembered today, give you renewed faith?

For the next note on *Rest and Reflection*, see Psalm 84:2.

[A] **76:7** Or *are awe-inspiring* [B] **76:10** Hb obscure [C] **76:11** Or *tribute with awe*

9 Has God forgotten to be gracious?
Has he in anger
withheld his compassion?" *Selah*
10 So I say, "I am grieved
that the right hand of the Most High
has changed."[A]
11 I will remember the LORD's works;
yes, I will remember
your ancient wonders.
12 I will reflect on all you have done
and meditate on your actions.

13 God, your way is holy.
What god is great like God?
14 You are the God who works wonders;
you revealed your strength
among the peoples.
15 With power you redeemed your people,
the descendants of Jacob
and Joseph. *Selah*

16 The water saw you, God.
The water saw you; it trembled.
Even the depths shook.
17 The clouds poured down water.
The storm clouds thundered;
your arrows flashed back and forth.
18 The sound of your thunder was
in the whirlwind;
lightning lit up the world.
The earth shook and quaked.
19 Your way went through the sea
and your path through the vast water,
but your footprints were unseen.
20 You led your people like a flock
by the hand of Moses and Aaron.

LESSONS FROM ISRAEL'S PAST

78 *A* Maskil *of Asaph.*
My people, hear my instruction;
listen to the words from my mouth.
2 I will declare wise sayings;
I will speak mysteries from the past —
3 things we have heard and known
and that our fathers have passed down
to us.
4 We will not hide them
from their children,
but will tell a future generation
the praiseworthy acts of the LORD,
his might, and the wondrous works
he has performed.
5 He established a testimony in Jacob
and set up a law in Israel,
which he commanded our fathers
to teach to their children
6 so that a future generation —
children yet to be born — might know.
They were to rise and tell their children
7 so that they might put their confidence
in God
and not forget God's works,
but keep his commands.
8 Then they would not be like their fathers,
a stubborn and rebellious generation,
a generation whose heart was not loyal
and whose spirit was not faithful
to God.

9 The Ephraimite archers turned back
on the day of battle.
10 They did not keep God's covenant
and refused to live by his law.
11 They forgot what he had done,
the wondrous works
he had shown them.
12 He worked wonders in the sight of
their fathers
in the land of Egypt, the territory
of Zoan.
13 He split the sea
and brought them across;
the water stood firm like a wall.
14 He led them with a cloud by day
and with a fiery light
throughout the night.
15 He split rocks in the wilderness
and gave them drink as abundant
as the depths.
16 He brought streams out of the stone
and made water flow down like rivers.

17 But they continued to sin against him,
rebelling in the desert
against the Most High.
18 They deliberately[B] tested God,
demanding the food they craved.
19 They spoke against God, saying,
"Is God able to provide food
in the wilderness?
20 Look! He struck the rock and water
gushed out;
torrents overflowed.
But can he also provide bread
or furnish meat for his people?"

[A] **77:10** Hb obscure [B] **78:18** Lit *in their heart*

My Story | Jill

I sat in the doctor's office as a first-time pregnant mother listening to my doctor explain the images that my husband and I had just seen on the sonogram. We were so excited! We saw our baby girl's little face, fingers, toes, spine, and heart. The doctor began talking I could hear something somber in her tone. I began to feel uneasy. Sure enough, the doctor finally said, "There is an area of concern that we saw on the sonogram." My stomach tightened. She explained that there was an echogenic foci (a bright spot) that showed up on the sonogram in one of the chambers of our daughter's heart that sometimes indicates an abnormality. If it was indeed an actual abnormality, it might also be an indication that our daughter, Tori, could be born with Down syndrome. I don't remember too much more of what the doctor said after that. The doctor asked us to come back in six weeks so that she could get a better look at our baby's heart.

Fear and doubt followed me home from the doctor's office that day, but faith and peace were also present. I knew enough of Scripture to begin to encourage myself, but this was new territory. Regardless of Tori's health, she was ours. We loved her already, whatever the circumstances. However, it's only natural for parents to desire healthy children. Over the next six weeks, I cried and prayed a lot. I tried not to worry, but sometimes I did. A war was raging. My husband's faith was strong, and that strengthened my faith as well. I began to pray longer and harder than I ever had. Multiple times a day, I spoke Psalm 73:26 over Tori—"God is the strength of Tori's heart, and if God is the strength of her heart, she has a very strong heart." As I relied on the Word of God, I began to experience firsthand that God had given me the option of peace, even in the face of fear. We grew in confidence that God would be with us no matter what happened.

The day came for the next sonogram. The technician looked closely at images of Tori's heart. She took her time, making sure she examined every part of Tori's heart. Finally she said, "I don't see anything. She has a beautiful heart."

We brought home a healthy baby girl in November of 2007. She's been one the greatest joys of our lives. To God be the glory for his Word that is our comfort, our peace, our sword, and our strength as we walk through every season of our lives.

21 Therefore, the LORD heard
and became furious;
then fire broke out against Jacob,
and anger flared up against Israel
22 because they did not believe God
or rely on his salvation.
23 He gave a command
to the clouds above
and opened the doors of heaven.
24 He rained manna for them to eat;
he gave them grain from heaven.
25 People[A] ate the bread of angels.[B]
He sent them an abundant supply
of food.
26 He made the east wind blow in the skies
and drove the south wind by his might.
27 He rained meat on them like dust,
and winged birds like the sand
of the seas.
28 He made them fall in the camp,
all around the tents.
29 The people ate and were
completely satisfied,
for he gave them what they craved.
30 Before they had turned from
what they craved,
while the food was still in their mouths,
31 God's anger flared up against them,
and he killed some of their best men.
He struck down Israel's fit young men.

32 Despite all this, they kept sinning
and did not believe
his wondrous works.
33 He made their days end in futility,
their years in sudden disaster.
34 When he killed some of them,
the rest began to seek him;
they repented and searched for God.
35 They remembered that God was
their rock,
the Most High God, their Redeemer.

[A] **78:25** Lit *Man* [B] **78:25** Lit *mighty ones*

36 But they deceived him
with their mouths,
they lied to him with their tongues,
37 their hearts were insincere
toward him,
and they were unfaithful
to his covenant.
38 Yet he was compassionate;
he atoned for their iniquity
and did not destroy them.
He often turned his anger aside
and did not unleash[A] all his wrath.
39 He remembered that they were
only flesh,
a wind that passes and does not return.

40 How often they rebelled against him
in the wilderness
and grieved him in the desert.
41 They constantly tested God
and provoked the Holy One of Israel.
42 They did not remember
his power shown
on the day he redeemed them
from the foe,
43 when he performed
his miraculous signs in Egypt
and his wonders in the territory of Zoan.
44 He turned their rivers into blood,
and they could not drink
from their streams.
45 He sent among them swarms of flies,
which fed on them,
and frogs, which devastated them.
46 He gave their crops to the caterpillar
and the fruit of their labor to the locust.
47 He killed their vines with hail
and their sycamore fig trees
with a flood.
48 He handed over their livestock to hail
and their cattle to lightning bolts.
49 He sent his burning anger
against them:
fury, indignation, and calamity —
a band of deadly messengers.[B]
50 He cleared a path for his anger.
He did not spare them from death
but delivered their lives to the plague.
51 He struck all the firstborn in Egypt,
the first progeny of the tents of Ham.
52 He led his people out like sheep
and guided them like a flock
in the wilderness.
53 He led them safely,
and they were not afraid;
but the sea covered their enemies.
54 He brought them to his holy territory,
to the mountain
his right hand acquired.
55 He drove out nations before them.
He apportioned their inheritance by lot
and settled the tribes of Israel
in their tents.

56 But they rebelliously tested
the Most High God,
for they did not keep his decrees.
57 They treacherously turned away
like their fathers;
they became warped like a faulty bow.
58 They enraged him
with their high places
and provoked his jealousy
with their carved images.
59 God heard and became furious;
he completely rejected Israel.
60 He abandoned the tabernacle at Shiloh,
the tent where he resided
among mankind.
61 He gave up his strength to captivity
and his splendor to the hand of a foe.
62 He surrendered his people
to the sword
because he was enraged
with his heritage.
63 Fire consumed his chosen young men,
and his young women
had no wedding songs.[C]
64 His priests fell by the sword,
and the widows could not lament.

65 The Lord awoke as if from sleep,
like a warrior from the effects of wine.
66 He beat back his foes;
he gave them lasting disgrace.
67 He rejected the tent of Joseph
and did not choose the tribe
of Ephraim.
68 He chose instead the tribe of Judah,
Mount Zion, which he loved.
69 He built his sanctuary like the heights,
like the earth that
he established forever.
70 He chose David his servant
and took him from the sheep pens;
71 he brought him from tending ewes

[A] **78:38** Or *stir up* [B] **78:49** Or *angels* [C] **78:63** Lit *virgins were not praised*

to be shepherd over his people Jacob —
over Israel, his inheritance.
72 He shepherded them with a pure heart
and guided them
with his skillful hands.

FAITH AMID CONFUSION

79 *A psalm of Asaph.*
God, the nations have invaded
your inheritance,
desecrated your holy temple,
and turned Jerusalem into ruins.
2 They gave the corpses of your servants
to the birds of the sky for food,
the flesh of your faithful ones
to the beasts of the earth.
3 They poured out their blood
like water all around Jerusalem,
and there was no one to bury them.
4 We have become an object of reproach
to our neighbors,
a source of mockery and ridicule
to those around us.
5 How long, LORD? Will you
be angry forever?
Will your jealousy keep burning
like fire?
6 Pour out your wrath on the nations
that don't acknowledge you,
on the kingdoms that don't call on
your name,
7 for they have devoured Jacob
and devastated his homeland.
8 Do not hold past iniquities[A] against us;
let your compassion come
to us quickly,
for we have become very weak.

9 God of our salvation, help us —
for the glory of your name.
Rescue us and atone for our sins,
for your name's sake.
10 Why should the nations ask,
"Where is their God?"
Before our eyes,
let vengeance for the shed blood
of your servants
be known among the nations.
11 Let the groans of the prisoners
reach you;
according to your great power,
preserve those condemned to die.
12 Pay back sevenfold to our neighbors
the reproach they have hurled at you,
Lord.
13 Then we, your people, the sheep
of your pasture,
will thank you forever;
we will declare your praise
to generation after generation.

A PRAYER FOR RESTORATION

80 *For the choir director: according to "The Lilies." A testimony of Asaph. A psalm.*
1 Listen, Shepherd of Israel,
who leads Joseph like a flock;
you who sit enthroned
between the cherubim,
shine 2 on Ephraim,
Benjamin, and Manasseh.
Rally your power and come to save us.
3 Restore us, God;
make your face shine on us,
so that we may be saved.
4 LORD God of Armies,
how long will you be angry
with your people's prayers?
5 You fed them the bread of tears
and gave them a full measure[B]
of tears to drink.
6 You put us at odds with our neighbors;
our enemies mock us.
7 Restore us, God of Armies;
make your face shine on us, so that we
may be saved.

8 You dug up a vine from Egypt;
you drove out the nations and planted it.
9 You cleared a place for it;
it took root and filled the land.
10 The mountains were covered
by its shade,
and the mighty cedars[C]
with its branches.
11 It sent out sprouts toward the Sea[D]
and shoots toward the River.[E]
12 Why have you broken down its walls
so that all who pass by pick its fruit?
13 Boars from the forest tear at it
and creatures of the field feed on it.
14 Return, God of Armies.
Look down from heaven and see;
take care of this vine,

[A] **79:8** Or *hold the sins of past generations* [B] **80:5** Lit *a one-third measure* [C] **80:10** Lit *the cedars of God* [D] **80:11** = the Mediterranean [E] **80:11** = the Euphrates

15 the root[A] your right hand planted,
the son[B] that you made strong
for yourself.
16 It was cut down and burned;
they[C] perish at the rebuke
of your countenance.
17 Let your hand be with the man
at your right hand,
with the son of man
you have made strong for yourself.
18 Then we will not turn away from you;
revive us, and we will call
on your name.
19 Restore us, LORD, God of Armies;
make your face shine on us, so
that we may be saved.

A CALL TO OBEDIENCE

81 *For the choir director: on the* Gittith. *Of Asaph.*
1 Sing for joy to God our strength;
shout in triumph to the God of Jacob.
2 Lift up a song — play the tambourine,
the melodious lyre, and the harp.
3 Blow the horn on the day of our feasts[D]
during the new moon
and during the full moon.
4 For this is a statute for Israel,
an ordinance of the God of Jacob.
5 He set it up as a decree for Joseph
when he went throughout[E] the land
of Egypt.

I heard an unfamiliar language:
6 "I relieved his shoulder from the burden;
his hands were freed from carrying
the basket.
7 You called out in distress,
and I rescued you;
I answered you from the thundercloud.
I tested you at the Waters
of Meribah. *Selah*
8 Listen, my people, and I will
admonish you.
Israel, if you would only listen to me!
9 There must not be a strange god
among you;
you must not bow down to a foreign god.
10 I am the LORD your God,
who brought you up from the land
of Egypt.
Open your mouth wide, and I will fill it.

11 "But my people did not listen
to my voice;
Israel did not obey me.
12 So I gave them over
to their stubborn hearts
to follow their own plans.
13 If only my people would listen to me
and Israel would follow my ways,
14 I would quickly subdue their enemies
and turn my hand against their foes."
15 Those who hate the LORD
would cower to him;
their doom would last forever.
16 But he would feed Israel[F]
with the best wheat.
"I would satisfy you with honey
from the rock."

A PLEA FOR RIGHTEOUS JUDGMENT

82 *A psalm of Asaph.*
God stands in the divine assembly;
he pronounces judgment
among the gods:[G]
2 "How long will you judge unjustly
and show partiality to the wicked?
Selah
3 Provide justice for the needy
and the fatherless;
uphold the rights of the oppressed
and the destitute.
4 Rescue the poor and needy;
save them from the power of
the wicked."

5 They do not know or understand;
they wander in darkness.
All the foundations of the earth
are shaken.

6 I said, "You are gods;
you are all sons of the Most High.
7 However, you will die like humans
and fall like any other ruler."

8 Rise up, God, judge the earth,
for all the nations belong to you.

PRAYER AGAINST ENEMIES

83 *A song. A psalm of Asaph.*
God, do not keep silent.
Do not be deaf, God; do not be quiet.
2 See how your enemies make an uproar;

[A] **80:15** Hb obscure [B] **80:15** Or *shoot* [C] **80:16** Or *may they* [D] **81:3** Lit *feast* [E] **81:5** Or *went out against* [F] **81:16** Lit *him*
[G] **82:1** Or *the heavenly beings*, or *the earthly rulers*; Hb *elohim*

those who hate you
have acted arrogantly.[A]
3 They devise clever schemes
against your people;
they conspire against
your treasured ones.
4 They say, "Come, let us wipe them out
as a nation
so that Israel's name will no longer
be remembered."
5 For they have conspired with one mind;
they form an alliance[B] against you —
6 the tents of Edom and the Ishmaelites,
Moab and the Hagrites,
7 Gebal, Ammon, and Amalek,
Philistia with the inhabitants of Tyre.
8 Even Assyria has joined them;
they lend support[C] to the sons
of Lot.[D] *Selah*

9 Deal with them as you did with Midian,
as you did with Sisera
and Jabin at the Kishon River.
10 They were destroyed at En-dor;
they became manure for the ground.
11 Make their nobles like Oreb and Zeeb,
and all their tribal leaders like Zebah
and Zalmunna,
12 who said, "Let us seize God's pastures
for ourselves."
13 Make them like tumbleweed, my God,
like straw before the wind.
14 As fire burns a forest,
as a flame blazes through mountains,
15 so pursue them with your tempest
and terrify them with your storm.
16 Cover their faces with shame
so that they will seek your name, LORD.
17 Let them be put to shame
and terrified forever;
let them perish in disgrace.
18 May they know that you alone —
whose name is the LORD —
are the Most High
over the whole earth.

LONGING FOR GOD'S HOUSE

84 *For the choir director: on the* Gittith.
A psalm of the sons of Korah.
1 How lovely is your dwelling place,
LORD of Armies.
2 I long and yearn
for the courts of the LORD;
my heart and flesh cry out
for[E] the living God.

Rest and Reflection | *Seeking God*

THE LONGINGS OF THE HEART

"I long and yearn for the courts of the LORD; my heart and flesh cry out for the living God." Psalm 84:2

If you could see underneath the expressionless faces of the other commuters, it just might break your heart. The old man by the door has stage four lung cancer and, maybe even worse, crushing regret over the kind of parent he was to his kids. The teenager in headphones is on her way to hook up with a boy she barely knows. The young businesswoman texting furiously is wildly successful—and utterly miserable. She would trade her glamorous career and all its perks in a heartbeat for a faithful soul mate and the chance to start a family.

These assorted longings—for belonging and love, for forgiveness and a world made right—are universal. We see glimpses of them in songs and movies. We sometimes get a taste of them in our own human interactions. The psalmist, however, understood that all these deep yearnings are satisfied ultimately only in the Lord. Saint Augustine put it well, "You have made us for yourself, O God, and our hearts are restless till they rest in you."

When do you sense your earthly longings pointing to something deeper?

For the next note on *Rest and Reflection*, see Psalm 104:24.

[A] **83:2** Lit *have lifted their head* [B] **83:5** Lit *they cut a covenant* [C] **83:8** Lit *they are an arm* [D] **83:8** = Moab and Ammon
[E] **84:2** Or *flesh shout for joy to*

3 Even a sparrow finds a home,
and a swallow, a nest for herself
where she places her young —
near your altars, LORD of Armies,
my King and my God.
4 How happy are those who reside
in your house,
who praise you continually. *Selah*
5 Happy are the people whose strength is
in you,
whose hearts are set on pilgrimage.
6 As they pass through the Valley
of Baca,[A]
they make it a source of spring water;
even the autumn rain will cover it
with blessings.[B]
7 They go from strength to strength;
each appears before God in Zion.

8 LORD God of Armies, hear my prayer;
listen, God of Jacob. *Selah*
9 Consider our shield,[C] God;
look on the face of your anointed one.

10 Better a day in your courts
than a thousand anywhere else.
I would rather stand at the threshold
of the house of my God
than live in the tents of wicked people.
11 For the LORD God is a sun and shield.
The LORD grants favor and honor;
he does not withhold the good
from those who live with integrity.
12 Happy is the person who trusts in you,
LORD of Armies!

RESTORATION OF FAVOR

85 *For the choir director. A psalm of the sons of Korah.*

1 LORD, you showed favor to your land;
you restored the fortunes of Jacob.[D]
2 You forgave your people's guilt;
you covered all their sin. *Selah*
3 You withdrew all your fury;
you turned from your burning anger.

4 Return to us, God of our salvation,
and abandon your displeasure
with us.
5 Will you be angry with us forever?
Will you prolong your anger for all
generations?
6 Will you not revive us again
so that your people may rejoice in you?
7 Show us your faithful love, LORD,
and give us your salvation.

8 I will listen to what God will say;
surely the LORD will declare peace
to his people, his faithful ones,
and not let them go back
to foolish ways.
9 His salvation is very near
those who fear him,
so that glory may dwell in our land.

10 Faithful love and truth
will join together;
righteousness and peace will embrace.
11 Truth will spring up from the earth,
and righteousness will look
down from heaven.
12 Also, the LORD will provide what is good,
and our land will yield its crops.
13 Righteousness will go before him
to prepare the way for his steps.

LAMENT AND PETITION

86 *A prayer of David.*

Listen, LORD, and answer me,
for I am poor and needy.
2 Protect my life, for I am faithful.
You are my God; save your servant
who trusts in you.
3 Be gracious to me, Lord,
for I call to you all day long.
4 Bring joy to your servant's life,
because I appeal to you, Lord.

5 For you, Lord, are kind and ready
to forgive,
abounding in faithful love to all
who call on you.
6 LORD, hear my prayer;
listen to my plea for mercy.
7 I call on you in the day of my distress,
for you will answer me.

8 Lord, there is no one like you
among the gods,
and there are no works like yours.
9 All the nations you have made
will come and bow down
before you, Lord,
and will honor your name.

[A] **84:6** Or *Valley of Tears* [B] **84:6** Or *pools* [C] **84:9** = the king [D] **85:1** Or *restored Jacob from captivity*

10 For you are great
and perform wonders;
you alone are God.
11 Teach me your way, LORD,
and I will live by your truth.
Give me an undivided mind to fear
your name.
12 I will praise you with all my heart,
Lord my God,
and will honor your name forever.
13 For your faithful love for me is great,
and you rescue my life from the depths
of Sheol.

14 God, arrogant people have attacked me;
a gang of ruthless men intends
to kill me.
They do not let you guide them.[A]
15 But you, Lord, are a compassionate
and gracious God,
slow to anger and abounding
in faithful love and truth.
16 Turn to me and be gracious to me.
Give your strength to your servant;
save the son of your female servant.
17 Show me a sign of your goodness;
my enemies will see and be put to shame
because you, LORD, have helped
and comforted me.

ZION, THE CITY OF GOD

87 *A psalm of the sons of Korah. A song.*
The city he founded[B] is
on the holy mountains.
2 The LORD loves Zion's city gates
more than all the dwellings of Jacob.
3 Glorious things are said about you,
city of God. *Selah*

4 "I will make a record of those
who know me:
Rahab, Babylon, Philistia, Tyre,
and Cush —
each one was born there."
5 And it will be said of Zion,
"This one and that one were born in her."
The Most High himself
will establish her.
6 When he registers the peoples,
the LORD will record,
"This one was born there." *Selah*
7 Singers and dancers[C] alike will say,[D]
"My whole source of joy is[E] in you."

A CRY OF DESPERATION

88 *A song. A psalm of the sons of Korah. For the choir director: according to* Mahalath Leannoth. *A* Maskil *of Heman the Ezrahite.*
1 LORD, God of my salvation,
I cry out before you day and night.

Eternal Perspective | *God's Goodness*

COMPASSIONATE AND GRACIOUS

"But you, Lord, are a compassionate and gracious God, slow to anger and abounding in faithful love and truth." Psalm 86:15

Sin entered the world when Adam and Eve questioned God's goodness. It's hard to argue against this point. What person—happily convinced that God wants only his best—does the very thing God forbids?

As the sons and daughters of Adam and Eve, we wrestle with that same question: Is God withholding good things from me? Which is why passages like this one are so helpful.

God is compassionate and gracious. God is slow to anger. God abounds in faithful love and truth to those who follow him.

When you hear the whispered lie, "You can't depend on God for good things," reject it as Satan's ploy to ruin you. Instead, ask God to reveal his compassion, grace, goodness, and love.

For the next note on *Eternal Perspective*, see Psalm 89:1-2.

[A] **86:14** Lit *They do not set you in front of them* [B] **87:1** Lit *His foundation* [C] **87:7** Or *musicians* [D] **87:7** Or *As they dance they will sing* [E] **87:7** Lit *"All my springs, are*

2 May my prayer reach your presence;
listen to my cry.
3 For I have had enough troubles,
and my life is near Sheol.
4 I am counted among those going down
to the Pit.
I am like a man without strength,
5 abandoned[A] among the dead.
I am like the slain lying in the grave,
whom you no longer remember,
and who are cut off from your care.[B]

6 You have put me in the lowest part
of the Pit,
in the darkest places, in the depths.
7 Your wrath weighs heavily on me;
you have overwhelmed me with all
your waves. *Selah*
8 You have distanced my friends
from me;
you have made me repulsive to them.
I am shut in and cannot go out.
9 My eyes are worn out from crying.
LORD, I cry out to you all day long;
I spread out my hands to you.
10 Do you work wonders for the dead?
Do departed spirits rise up
to praise you? *Selah*
11 Will your faithful love be declared
in the grave,
your faithfulness in Abaddon?
12 Will your wonders be known in
the darkness
or your righteousness in the land
of oblivion?

13 But I call to you for help, LORD;
in the morning my prayer meets you.
14 LORD, why do you reject me?
Why do you hide your face from me?
15 From my youth,
I have been suffering and near death.
I suffer your horrors; I am desperate.
16 Your wrath sweeps over me;
your terrors destroy me.
17 They surround me like water
all day long;
they close in on me from every side.
18 You have distanced loved one
and neighbor from me;
darkness is my only friend.[C]

Relationships | *Encouraging Each Other*

THE RELIEF OF "ME, TOO"

"My eyes are worn out from crying. LORD, I cry out to you all day long; I spread out my hands to you." Psalm 88:9

If you have ever had the experience of anxiously confiding in someone else—whether it be your worst failures, greatest frustrations, or deepest doubts—and hearing the other person respond, "Me, too," you know how precious and life-giving those words are.

"Me, too" means you're not alone. Someone else is (or has been) where you are. "Me, too" means you've found a fellow struggler who understands, who gets what you're up against.

"Me, too" may be the reason Psalm 88 is in the Bible. Most scholars agree the song is, hands down, the bleakest and grimmest of the entire collection of 150 psalms. It features a lonely person desperately crying out to God, and hearing only—silence. He finally cries, "LORD, why do you reject me? Why do you hide your face from me?" (88:14). Maybe through sharing his honest anguish and his experience of barely hanging on, the writer wanted to encourage readers down through the ages. Perhaps he reasoned that people at their wit's end could read his words and at least hear one other person saying, "Me, too."

(Note: If, as you read this psalm, you find it hits too close to home, please pick up the phone and call a trusted friend. Don't struggle alone.)

For the next note on *Relationships*, see Psalm 106:3.

[A] **88:5** Or *set free* [B] **88:5** Or *hand* [C] **88:18** Or *from me, my friends. Oh darkness!*

PERPLEXITY ABOUT GOD'S PROMISES

89 *A* Maskil *of Ethan the Ezrahite.*
I will sing about the LORD's
faithful love forever;
I will proclaim your faithfulness to all
generations
with my mouth.
2 For I will declare,
"Faithful love is built up forever;
you establish your faithfulness
in the heavens."

3 The LORD said,
"I have made a covenant
with my chosen one;
I have sworn an oath to David
my servant:
4 'I will establish your offspring forever
and build up your throne
for all generations.'" *Selah*

5 LORD, the heavens praise
your wonders —
your faithfulness also —
in the assembly of the holy ones.
6 For who in the skies can compare
with the LORD?
Who among the heavenly beings[A] is
like the LORD?
7 God is greatly feared in the council
of the holy ones,
more awe-inspiring than[B]
all who surround him.
8 LORD God of Armies,
who is strong like you, LORD?
Your faithfulness surrounds you.
9 You rule the raging sea;
when its waves surge, you still them.
10 You crushed Rahab like one who is slain;
you scattered your enemies
with your powerful arm.
11 The heavens are yours; the earth also
is yours.
The world and everything in it —
you founded them.
12 North and south — you created them.
Tabor and Hermon shout for joy
at your name.
13 You have a mighty arm;
your hand is powerful;
your right hand is lifted high.
14 Righteousness and justice are
the foundation
of your throne;

Eternal Perspective | *God's Faithfulness*

FAITHFUL LOVE

"I will sing about the LORD's faithful love forever; I will proclaim your faithfulness to all generations with my mouth. For I will declare, 'Faithful love is built up forever; you establish your faithfulness in the heavens.'" Psalm 89:1-2

When describing someone as being "faithful," we usually mean that she follows through on promises; we can count on that person to do her job. "Faithfulness" also assumes a level of commitment and loyalty. A faithful friend stands by us in every circumstance. A faithful marriage partner never cheats on his or her spouse.

Knowing we have those who are faithful to us gives a sense of security and contentment. So just imagine the security from realizing that our all-knowing, all-powerful God is faithful to us. He stands by us and always keeps his promises. And more than that, he *loves* us!

No wonder, the writer of this psalm, Ethan, could exclaim that he would "sing about the LORD's faithful love forever."

When we lift our eyes from our conflicts and sorrows and see from God's point of view, we, too, can rejoice in God's faithful love.

For the next note on *Eternal Perspective*, see Psalm 93:4.

[A] **89:6** Or *the angels*, or *the sons of the mighty* [B] **89:7** Or *ones, revered by*

faithful love and truth
go before you.
15 Happy are the people who know
the joyful shout;
LORD, they walk in the light
from your face.
16 They rejoice in your name all day long,
and they are exalted
by your righteousness.
17 For you are their magnificent strength;
by your favor our horn is exalted.
18 Surely our shield[A] belongs to the LORD,
our king to the Holy One of Israel.

19 You once spoke in a vision
to your faithful ones
and said: "I have granted help
to a warrior;
I have exalted one chosen[B]
from the people.
20 I have found David my servant;
I have anointed him with my sacred oil.
21 My hand will always be with him,
and my arm will strengthen him.
22 The enemy will not oppress[C] him;
the wicked will not afflict him.
23 I will crush his foes before him
and strike those who hate him.
24 My faithfulness and love will be
with him,
and through my name
his horn will be exalted.
25 I will extend his power to the sea
and his right hand to the rivers.
26 He will call to me, 'You are my Father,
my God, the rock of my salvation.'
27 I will also make him my firstborn,
greatest of the kings of the earth.
28 I will always preserve my faithful love
for him,
and my covenant with him will endure.
29 I will establish his line forever,
his throne as long as heaven lasts.[D]
30 If his sons abandon my instruction
and do not live by my ordinances,
31 if they dishonor my statutes
and do not keep my commands,
32 then I will call their rebellion
to account with the rod,
their iniquity with blows.
33 But I will not withdraw
my faithful love from him
or betray my faithfulness.
34 I will not violate my covenant
or change what my lips have said.
35 Once and for all
I have sworn an oath by my holiness;
I will not lie to David.
36 His offspring will continue forever,
his throne like the sun before me,
37 like the moon, established forever,
a faithful witness in the sky." *Selah*

38 But you have spurned
and rejected him;
you have become enraged
with your anointed.
39 You have repudiated the covenant
with your servant;
you have completely dishonored
his crown.[E]
40 You have broken down all his walls;
you have reduced his fortified cities
to ruins.
41 All who pass by plunder him;
he has become an object of ridicule
to his neighbors.
42 You have lifted high the right hand
of his foes;
you have made all
his enemies rejoice.
43 You have also turned back
his sharp sword
and have not let him stand in battle.
44 You have made his splendor[F] cease
and have overturned his throne.
45 You have shortened the days
of his youth;
you have covered him
with shame. *Selah*

46 How long, LORD?
Will you hide forever?
Will your anger keep burning
like fire?
47 Remember how short my life is.
Have you created everyone
for nothing?
48 What courageous person can live and
never see death?
Who can save himself from the power
of Sheol? *Selah*
49 Lord, where are the former acts
of your faithful love
that you swore to David
in your faithfulness?

[A] **89:18** = the king [B] **89:19** Or *exalted a young man* [C] **89:22** Or *not exact tribute from* [D] **89:29** Lit *as days of heaven*
[E] **89:39** Lit *have dishonored his crown to the ground* [F] **89:44** Hb obscure

50 Remember, Lord, the ridicule
against your servants —
in my heart I carry abuse from all
the peoples —
51 how your enemies
have ridiculed, LORD,
how they have ridiculed every step
of your anointed.

52 Blessed be the LORD forever.
Amen and amen.

BOOK IV (Psalms 90–106)

ETERNAL GOD AND MORTAL MAN

90 *A prayer of Moses, the man of God.*
Lord, you have been our refuge[A]
in every generation.
2 Before the mountains were born,
before you gave birth to the earth
and the world,
from eternity to eternity, you are God.

3 You return mankind to the dust,
saying, "Return, descendants of Adam."
4 For in your sight a thousand years
are like yesterday that passes by,
like a few hours of the night.
5 You end their lives;[B] they sleep.
They are like grass that grows
in the morning —
6 in the morning it sprouts and grows;
by evening it withers and dries up.

7 For we are consumed by your anger;
we are terrified by your wrath.
8 You have set our iniquities before you,
our secret sins in the light
of your presence.
9 For all our days ebb away
under your wrath;
we end our years like a sigh.
10 Our lives last[C] seventy years
or, if we are strong, eighty years.
Even the best of them are[D] struggle
and sorrow;
indeed, they pass quickly and we
fly away.
11 Who understands the power
of your anger?
Your wrath matches the fear that
is due you.
12 Teach us to number our days carefully
so that we may develop wisdom
in our hearts.[E]

13 LORD — how long?
Turn and have compassion
on your servants.
14 Satisfy us in the morning
with your faithful love
so that we may shout with joy
and be glad all our days.
15 Make us rejoice for as many days
as you have humbled us,
for as many years as
we have seen adversity.
16 Let your work be seen by your servants,
and your splendor by their children.
17 Let the favor of the Lord our God be
on us;
establish for us the work of our hands —
establish the work of our hands!

THE PROTECTION OF THE MOST HIGH

91 The one who lives
under the protection
of the Most High
dwells in the shadow of the Almighty.

2 I will say[F] concerning the LORD, who is
my refuge and my fortress,
my God in whom I trust:
3 He himself will rescue you
from the bird trap,
from the destructive plague.
4 He will cover you with his feathers;
you will take refuge under his wings.
His faithfulness will be
a protective shield.
5 You will not fear the terror of the night,
the arrow that flies by day,
6 the plague that stalks in darkness,
or the pestilence that ravages at noon.
7 Though a thousand fall at your side
and ten thousand at your right hand,
the pestilence will not reach you.
8 You will only see it with your eyes
and witness the punishment
of the wicked.

9 Because you have made the LORD —
my refuge,
the Most High — your dwelling place,

[A] **90:1** Some Hb mss, LXX; other Hb mss read *dwelling place* [B] **90:5** Or *You overwhelm them*; Hb obscure [C] **90:10** Lit *The days of our years in them* [D] **90:10** LXX, Tg, Syr, Vg read *Even their span is*; Hb obscure [E] **90:12** Or *develop a heart of wisdom* [F] **91:1-2** LXX, Syr, Jer read [2]*Almighty, saying*, or [2]*Almighty, he will say*

10 no harm will come to you;
no plague will come near your tent.
11 For he will give his angels orders
concerning you,
to protect you in all your ways.
12 They will support you with their hands
so that you will not strike your foot
against a stone.
13 You will tread on the lion and the cobra;
you will trample the young lion
and the serpent.

14 Because he has his heart set on me,
I will deliver him;
I will protect him because he knows
my name.
15 When he calls out to me,
I will answer him;
I will be with him in trouble.
I will rescue him and give him honor.
16 I will satisfy him with a long life
and show him my salvation.

GOD'S LOVE AND FAITHFULNESS

92 *A psalm. A song for the Sabbath day.*
It is good to give thanks to the LORD,
to sing praise to your name, Most High,
2 to declare your faithful love
in the morning
and your faithfulness at night,
3 with a ten-stringed harp[A]
and the music of a lyre.

4 For you have made me rejoice, LORD,
by what you have done;
I will shout for joy
because of the works of your hands.
5 How magnificent are your works,
LORD,
how profound your thoughts!
6 A stupid person does not know,
a fool does not understand this:
7 though the wicked sprout like grass
and all evildoers flourish,
they will be eternally destroyed.
8 But you, LORD, are exalted forever.
9 For indeed, LORD, your enemies —
indeed, your enemies will perish;
all evildoers will be scattered.
10 You have lifted up my horn
like that of a wild ox;
I have been anointed[B] with
the finest oil.
11 My eyes look at my enemies;

E Eternal Perspective | *God's Majesty*

OUR MAJESTIC GOD

"Greater than the roar of a huge torrent — the mighty breakers of the sea — the LORD on high is majestic." Psalm 93:4

People who witness the Northern Lights are often left speechless. The same is true for those who find themselves for the first time on the rim of the Grand Canyon. Seriously—what words can do justice to such an experience?

And if that's the wonder of finite creation, how much more so of the infinite Creator behind it all.

In Psalm 93, an unnamed songwriter labors to find words to describe the Lord. He writes of God's "majesty" (93:1) or him being "majestic." The Hebrew words convey the idea of splendor or glory or immensity. They suggest one who is exalted, high and lifted up. Excellent. Famous. Awesome. Great. Splendid. Beautiful. Noble. We get the idea—and in truth, we probably don't.

The psalm writer ultimately devotes a good portion of his composition to speaking of "pounding waves" and "mighty breakers." It makes you wonder if he was at the seaside watching a powerful storm come through as he tried to describe his indescribable God.

Whatever the case, here's the encouraging fact: This limitless, majestic God is the One who, in Jesus, said, "Come to me, all of you who are weary and burdened, and I will give you rest" (Mt 11:28).

For the next note on *Eternal Perspective*, see Psalm 100:1-3.

[A] **92:3** Or *ten-stringed instrument and a harp* [B] **92:10** Syr reads *you have anointed me*

when evildoers rise against me,
my ears hear them.

12 The righteous thrive like a palm tree
and grow like a cedar tree in Lebanon.
13 Planted in the house of the LORD,
they thrive in the courts of our God.
14 They will still bear fruit in old age,
healthy and green,
15 to declare: "The LORD is just;
he is my rock,
and there is no unrighteousness in him."

GOD'S ETERNAL REIGN

93 The LORD reigns! He is robed
in majesty;
the LORD is robed,
enveloped in strength.
The world is firmly established;
it cannot be shaken.
2 Your throne has been established
from the beginning;[A]
you are from eternity.
3 The floods have lifted up, LORD,
the floods have lifted up their voice;
the floods lift up their
pounding waves.
4 Greater than the roar of a
huge torrent —
the mighty breakers of the sea —
the LORD on high is majestic.

5 LORD, your testimonies
are completely reliable;
holiness adorns your house
for all the days to come.

THE JUST JUDGE

94 LORD, God of vengeance —
God of vengeance, shine!
2 Rise up, Judge of the earth;
repay the proud what they deserve.
3 LORD, how long will the wicked —
how long will the wicked celebrate?

4 They pour out arrogant words;
all the evildoers boast.
5 LORD, they crush your people;
they oppress your heritage.
6 They kill the widow and
the resident alien
and murder the fatherless.
7 They say, "The LORD doesn't see it.
The God of Jacob
doesn't pay attention."

8 Pay attention, you stupid people!
Fools, when will you be wise?
9 Can the one who shaped the ear
not hear,
the one who formed the eye not see?
10 The one who instructs nations,
the one who teaches
mankind knowledge —
does he not discipline?
11 The LORD knows the thoughts
of mankind;
they are futile.

12 LORD, how happy is anyone
you discipline
and teach from your law
13 to give him relief from
troubled times
until a pit is dug for the wicked.
14 The LORD will not leave his people
or abandon his heritage,
15 for the administration of justice will
again be righteous,
and all the upright in heart
will follow[B] it.

16 Who stands up for me
against the wicked?
Who takes a stand for me
against evildoers?
17 If the LORD had not been my helper,
I would soon rest in the silence
of death.
18 If I say, "My foot is slipping,"
your faithful love
will support me, LORD.
19 When I am filled with cares,
your comfort brings me joy.

20 Can a corrupt throne be your ally,
a throne that makes evil laws?
21 They band together against the life
of the righteous
and condemn the innocent to death.
22 But the LORD is my refuge;
my God is the rock of my protection.
23 He will pay them back for their sins
and destroy them for their evil.
The LORD our God
will destroy them.

[A] **93:2** Lit *from then* [B] **94:15** Or *heart will support*; lit *heart after*

WORSHIP AND WARNING

95 Come, let us shout joyfully
to the LORD,
shout triumphantly to the rock
of our salvation!
2 Let us enter his presence
with thanksgiving;
let us shout triumphantly to him in song.

3 For the LORD is a great God,
a great King above all gods.
4 The depths of the earth are in his hand,
and the mountain peaks are his.
5 The sea is his; he made it.
His hands formed the dry land.

6 Come, let us worship and bow down;
let us kneel before the LORD our Maker.
7 For he is our God,
and we are the people of his pasture,
the sheep under his care.[A]

Today, if you hear his voice:
8 Do not harden your hearts as at Meribah,
as on that day at Massah
in the wilderness
9 where your fathers tested me;
they tried me, though they had seen
what I did.
10 For forty years I was disgusted
with that generation;
I said, "They are a people whose hearts
go astray;
they do not know my ways."
11 So I swore in my anger,
"They will not enter my rest."

KING OF THE EARTH

96 Sing a new song to the LORD;
let the whole earth sing to the LORD.
2 Sing to the LORD, bless his name;
proclaim his salvation from day to day.
3 Declare his glory among the nations,
his wondrous works among all peoples.

4 For the LORD is great and is
highly praised;
he is feared above all gods.

Exercise of Faith | *Sharing Faith/Gospel*

GOOD NEWS IS FOR SHARING

"Sing to the LORD, bless his name; proclaim his salvation from day to day. Declare his glory among the nations, his wondrous works among all peoples. For the LORD is great and is highly praised; he is feared above all gods." Psalm 96:2-4

You land your dream job, get engaged, go on a fabulous vacation, or receive an unexpected windfall. What's the first thing you do? You tell your friends and coworkers—maybe even the clerk at the gas station! Nobody ever has to tell a first-time grandparent, "You should probably think about showing people pictures of your new grandbaby." Sharing good news is the most natural thing in the world.

Yet for some reason, when it comes to our faith, we often get tight-lipped. God has forgiven us in Christ, made us his children, given us new life, promised us a wonderful eternal future—but we're reluctant to say anything.

Apparently this isn't a new phenomenon. In this short song of praise, an anonymous writer called on the Jewish people to "proclaim his salvation" and "declare his glory among the nations, his wondrous works among all peoples."

And this should happen without being obnoxious or preachy. As you learn to let go of worries (or bitterness), cultivate patience and self-control, see relationships restored, and experience joy, you can tell the people in your life about how God is working in you. Who knows what doors this sharing of good news might open?

For the next note on *Exercise of Faith*, see Psalm 103:15-16.

[A] **95:7** Lit *sheep of his hand*

5 For all the gods of the peoples are idols,
but the LORD made the heavens.
6 Splendor and majesty are before him;
strength and beauty are
in his sanctuary.

7 Ascribe to the LORD, you families
of the peoples,
ascribe to the LORD glory and strength.
8 Ascribe to the LORD the glory
of his name;
bring an offering and enter his courts.
9 Worship the LORD in the splendor
of his holiness;
let the whole earth tremble before him.

10 Say among the nations:
"The LORD reigns.
The world is firmly established;
it cannot be shaken.
He judges the peoples fairly."
11 Let the heavens be glad
and the earth rejoice;
let the sea and all that fills it resound.
12 Let the fields and everything
in them celebrate.
Then all the trees of the forest
will shout for joy
13 before the LORD, for he is coming —
for he is coming to judge the earth.
He will judge the world
with righteousness
and the peoples
with his faithfulness.

THE MAJESTIC KING

97 The LORD reigns! Let
the earth rejoice;
let the many coasts and islands
be glad.

2 Clouds and total darkness
surround him;
righteousness and justice are
the foundation of his throne.
3 Fire goes before him
and burns up his foes on every side.
4 His lightning lights up the world;
the earth sees and trembles.
5 The mountains melt like wax
at the presence of the LORD —
at the presence of the Lord
of the whole earth.

6 The heavens proclaim
his righteousness;
all the peoples see his glory.

7 All who serve carved images,
those who boast in idols, will be
put to shame.
All the gods[A] must worship him.

8 Zion hears and is glad,
Judah's villages[B] rejoice
because of your judgments, LORD.
9 For you, LORD,
are the Most High over the whole earth;
you are exalted above all the gods.

10 You who love the LORD, hate evil!
He protects the lives
of his faithful ones;
he rescues them from the power of
the wicked.
11 Light dawns[C,D] for the righteous,
gladness for the upright in heart.
12 Be glad in the LORD,
you righteous ones,
and give thanks to his holy name.[E]

PRAISE THE KING

98 *A psalm.*
Sing a new song to the LORD,
for he has performed wonders;
his right hand and holy arm
have won him victory.
2 The LORD has made his victory known;
he has revealed his righteousness
in the sight of the nations.
3 He has remembered his love
and faithfulness to the house of Israel;
all the ends of the earth
have seen our God's victory.

4 Let the whole earth shout to the LORD;
be jubilant, shout for joy, and sing.
5 Sing to the LORD with the lyre,
with the lyre and melodious song.
6 With trumpets and the blast
of the ram's horn
shout triumphantly
in the presence of the LORD, our King.

7 Let the sea and all that fills it,
the world and those who live in it,
resound.

[A] **97:7** LXX, Syr read *All his angels*; Heb 1:6 [B] **97:8** Lit *daughters* [C] **97:11** One Hb ms, LXX, some ancient versions read *rises to shine*; Ps 112:4 [D] **97:11** Lit *Light is sown* [E] **97:12** Lit *to the memory of his holiness*

8 Let the rivers clap their hands;
let the mountains shout together
for joy
9 before the LORD,
for he is coming to judge the earth.
He will judge the world righteously
and the peoples fairly.

THE KING IS HOLY

99 The LORD reigns! Let
the peoples tremble.
He is enthroned between the cherubim.
Let the earth quake.
2 The LORD is great in Zion;
he is exalted above all the peoples.
3 Let them praise your great
and awe-inspiring name.
He is holy.

4 The mighty King loves justice.
You have established fairness;
you have administered justice
and righteousness in Jacob.
5 Exalt the LORD our God;
bow in worship at his footstool.
He is holy.

6 Moses and Aaron were
among his priests;
Samuel also was among
those calling on his name.
They called to the LORD
and he answered them.
7 He spoke to them in a pillar of cloud;
they kept his decrees and the statutes
he gave them.
8 LORD our God, you answered them.
You were a forgiving God to them,
but an avenger of their sinful actions.

9 Exalt the LORD our God;
bow in worship at his holy mountain,
for the LORD our God is holy.

BE THANKFUL

100 *A psalm of thanksgiving.*
Let the whole earth shout
triumphantly to the LORD!
2 Serve the LORD with gladness;
come before him with joyful songs.
3 Acknowledge that the LORD is God.
He made us, and we are his[A]—
his people, the sheep of his pasture.

Eternal Perspective | *Personal Value/Worth*

HIS

"Let the whole earth shout triumphantly to God! Serve the LORD with gladness; come before him with joyful songs. Acknowledge that the LORD is God. He made us, and we are his— his people, the sheep of his pasture." Psalm 100:1-3

"Don't let anyone else tell you what to do. Take control of your life! Be you. Be free. Do what you like. Pursue your dreams. Blaze your own trail."

Living in a culture that places so much emphasis on personal freedom, we hear mantras like those every day. No wonder we often find ourselves thinking, *My life is mine to live however I choose!*

But then we read the statement here, the Lord "made us, and we are his." And in the New Testament we discover an echo of this same idea from the apostle Paul, "You are not your own, for you were bought at a price" (1Co 6:19-20). According to the Bible, we're doubly God's—by virtue of both creation and salvation. God made us. Then, when we became enslaved to sin, he paid for us—purchasing our freedom.

Far from being confining or limiting, God's ownership brings true liberty. Because he designed us uniquely, he knows exactly what he put us here to do. Because he loves us intensely, he will lead us.

Take a moment to sing this great song of freedom to the One to whom you belong.

For the next note on *Eternal Perspective*, see Psalm 103:7-8.

[A] **100:3** Alt Hb tradition, some Hb mss, LXX, Syr, Vg read *and not we ourselves*

4 Enter his gates with thanksgiving
and his courts with praise.
Give thanks to him and bless his name.
5 For the LORD is good, and his
faithful love endures forever;
his faithfulness,
through all generations.

A VOW OF INTEGRITY

101 *A psalm of David.*
I will sing of faithful love and justice;
I will sing praise to you, LORD.
2 I will pay attention to the way
of integrity.
When will you come to me?
I will live with a heart of integrity
in my house.
3 I will not let anything worthless
guide me.[A]
I hate the practice of transgression;
it will not cling to me.
4 A devious heart will be far from me;
I will not be involved with[B] evil.

5 I will destroy anyone
who secretly slanders his neighbor;
I cannot tolerate anyone
with haughty eyes
or an arrogant heart.
6 My eyes favor the faithful of the land
so that they may sit down with me.
The one who follows the way
of integrity
may serve me.
7 No one who acts deceitfully
will live in my palace;
the one who tells lies
will not be retained here to guide me.[C]
8 Every morning I will destroy
all the wicked of the land,
wiping out all evildoers
from the LORD's city.

AFFLICTION IN LIGHT OF ETERNITY

102 *A prayer of a suffering person who is weak and pours out his lament before the LORD.*
1 LORD, hear my prayer;
let my cry for help come before you.
2 Do not hide your face from me
in my day of trouble.
Listen closely to me;
answer me quickly when I call.
3 For my days vanish like smoke,
and my bones burn like a furnace.
4 My heart is suffering,
withered like grass;
I even forget to eat my food.
5 Because of the sound of my groaning,
my flesh sticks to my bones.
6 I am like an eagle owl,
like a little owl among the ruins.
7 I stay awake;
I am like a solitary bird on a roof.
8 My enemies taunt me all day long;
they ridicule and use my name as a curse.
9 I eat ashes like bread
and mingle my drinks with tears
10 because of your indignation and wrath;
for you have picked me up
and thrown me aside.
11 My days are like a lengthening shadow,
and I wither away like grass.

12 But you, LORD, are enthroned forever;
your fame endures to all generations.
13 You will rise up and have compassion
on Zion,
for it is time to show favor to her —
the appointed time has come.
14 For your servants take delight
in its stones
and favor its dust.

15 Then the nations will fear the name
of the LORD,
and all the kings of the earth your glory,
16 for the LORD will rebuild Zion;
he will appear in his glory.
17 He will pay attention to the prayer
of the destitute
and will not despise their prayer.

18 This will be written
for a later generation,
and a people who have not yet
been created will praise the LORD:
19 He looked down from
his holy heights —
the LORD gazed out from heaven
to earth —
20 to hear a prisoner's groaning,
to set free those condemned to die,[D]
21 so that they might declare
the name of the LORD in Zion
and his praise in Jerusalem,

[A] **101:3** Lit *I will not put a worthless thing in front of my eyes* [B] **101:4** Lit *not know* [C] **101:7** Lit *be established in front of my eyes* [D] **102:20** Lit *free sons of death*

22 when peoples and kingdoms
are assembled
to serve the LORD.

23 He has broken my[A] strength
in midcourse;
he has shortened my days.
24 I say: "My God, do not take me
in the middle of my life![B]
Your years continue
through all generations.
25 Long ago you established the earth,
and the heavens are the work
of your hands.
26 They will perish, but you will endure;
all of them will wear out like clothing.
You will change them like a garment,
and they will pass away.
27 But you are the same,
and your years will never end.
28 Your servants' children will dwell securely,
and their offspring will be established
before you."

THE FORGIVING GOD

103 *Of David.*
My soul, bless the LORD,
and all that is within me, bless
his holy name.
2 My soul, bless the LORD,
and do not forget all his benefits.

3 He forgives all your iniquity;
he heals all your diseases.
4 He redeems your life from the Pit;
he crowns you with faithful love
and compassion.
5 He satisfies you[C] with good things;
your youth is renewed like the eagle.

6 The LORD executes acts of righteousness
and justice for all the oppressed.
7 He revealed his ways to Moses,
his deeds to the people of Israel.
8 The LORD is compassionate
and gracious,
slow to anger and abounding
in faithful love.
9 He will not always accuse us
or be angry forever.
10 He has not dealt with us as
our sins deserve
or repaid us according to our iniquities.

11 For as high as the heavens are above
the earth,
so great is his faithful love
toward those who fear him.

E Eternal Perspective | *God's Compassion*

THE TRUTH ABOUT GOD'S ANGER

"He revealed his ways to Moses, his deeds to the people of Israel. The LORD is compassionate and gracious, slow to anger and abounding in faithful love." Psalm 103:7-8

Did you see it? Tucked away near the end of this wonderful description of God's compassion, grace, and faithful love is a passing reference to divine wrath.

Whoa. For many readers—maybe you—this phrase, "slow to anger," causes serious spiritual heartburn. It stirs questions like: Does this mean if we continue to mess up, we might cause God to blow up? It sounds like God is patient to a point, but then—look out!

Here are some truths to remember about divine anger: First, God's anger is, in reality, God's fierce and holy love directed against anything that threatens to harm the people or things he loves. Second, centuries after this psalm was written, God's righteous anger against sin was poured out and satisfied in the death of Jesus for sin. At the cross, sin was judged so that repentant sinners might find mercy. Those who are in Christ by faith are accepted and adored by God. He will never deal with us except in perfect love.

Hallelujah!

For the next note on *Eternal Perspective*, see Psalm 118:5-6.

[A] **102:23** Some Hb mss, LXX read *his* [B] **102:24** Lit *my days* [C] **103:5** Lit *satisfies your ornament*; Hb obscure

12 As far as the east is from the west,
so far has he removed
our transgressions from us.
13 As a father has compassion
on his children,
so the LORD has compassion on those
who fear him.
14 For he knows what we are made of,
remembering that we are dust.

15 As for man, his days are like grass—
he blooms like a flower of the field;
16 when the wind passes over it,
it vanishes,
and its place is no longer known.[A]
17 But from eternity to eternity
the LORD's faithful love is toward
those who fear him,
and his righteousness
toward the grandchildren
18 of those who keep his covenant,
who remember to observe his precepts.
19 The LORD has established his throne
in heaven,
and his kingdom rules over all.

20 Bless the LORD,
all his angels of great strength,
who do his word,
obedient to his command.
21 Bless the LORD, all his armies,
his servants who do his will.
22 Bless the LORD, all his works
in all the places where he rules.
My soul, bless the LORD!

GOD THE CREATOR

104 My soul, bless the LORD!
LORD my God, you are very great;
you are clothed with majesty
and splendor.
2 He wraps himself in light as if it were
a robe,
spreading out the sky like a canopy,
3 laying the beams of his palace
on the waters above,
making the clouds his chariot,
walking on the wings of the wind,
4 and making the winds his messengers,[B]
flames of fire his servants.

5 He established the earth
on its foundations;
it will never be shaken.
6 You covered it with the deep
as if it were a garment;

Exercise of Faith | *Making the Most of Time on Earth*

LIVING FOR ETERNITY

"As for man, his days are like grass—he blooms like a flower of the field; when the wind passes over it, it vanishes, and its place is no longer known." Psalm 103:15-16

In a Bible full of commentary meant to encourage people who are downcast, why in the world would we highlight a verse about how fleeting life is? *Hey, cheer up everyone—you might not have long to live!*

The point here isn't to make us morbid, so that we obsess over our mortality. On the contrary, the goal is to make us purposeful, so that we live for eternity. We want, in the words of another psalm, "to number our days carefully so that we may develop wisdom in our hearts" (Ps 90:12).

Do this exercise. Count the number of days you've been alive. Then subtract that number from twenty-eight thousand (a rough average of the life expectancy figures mentioned in Ps 90:10). Obviously, we are only speculating. We might have more days than that—or less.

What is God calling you to do for the remainder of your days—however many there are? What's the secret to living wisely and fully?

For the next note on *Exercise of Faith*, see Psalm 119:11.

[A] **103:16** Lit *place no longer knows it* [B] **104:4** Or *angels*

the water stood
above the mountains.
7 At your rebuke the water fled;
at the sound of your thunder
they hurried away —
8 mountains rose and valleys sank[A] —
to the place you established for them.
9 You set a boundary they cannot cross;
they will never cover the earth again.

10 He causes the springs to gush
into the valleys;
they flow between the mountains.
11 They supply water for every wild beast;
the wild donkeys quench their thirst.
12 The birds of the sky live
beside the springs;
they make their voices heard
among the foliage.
13 He waters the mountains
from his palace;
the earth is satisfied by the fruit
of your labor.

14 He causes grass to grow
for the livestock
and provides crops for man to cultivate,
producing food from the earth,
15 wine that makes human hearts glad —
making his face shine with oil —
and bread that sustains human hearts.

16 The trees of the LORD flourish,[B]
the cedars of Lebanon that he planted.
17 There the birds make their nests;
storks make their homes
in the pine trees.
18 The high mountains are
for the wild goats;
the cliffs are a refuge for hyraxes.
19 He made the moon to mark
the[C] festivals;[D]
the sun knows when to set.
20 You bring darkness,
and it becomes night,
when all the forest animals stir.
21 The young lions roar for their prey
and seek their food from God.
22 The sun rises; they go back
and lie down in their dens.
23 Man goes out to his work
and to his labor until evening.

24 How countless are your works, LORD!
In wisdom you have made them all;
the earth is full of your creatures.[E]
25 Here is the sea, vast and wide,

Rest and Reflection | *Enjoying Creation*

OUR CREATIVE GOD

"How countless are your works, LORD! In wisdom you have made them all; the earth is full of your creatures." Psalm 104:24

Why do we gawk at sunrises? Sit mesmerized watching the snow fall? Laugh at toddlers? Post all those adorable animal videos online?

Because something is beautiful and powerful—almost magical—about the created world. Its majesty and mystery point to a Creator who's endlessly imaginative and wonderfully generous. He might have made all birds or flowers, all fish or people the way Henry Ford made Model Ts—one style, one model, and one color only. Instead, he was lavish, almost wasteful, in the way he flooded the world with variety and an infinite number of sights, scents, and sounds.

If you are feeling blah, here's a picker-upper prescription that never fails: Go to a park or garden and soak it all in. Or go to a mall and do a bit of people watching. Visit a dog park. Watch a video of kittens—or river otters. Taste a juicy peach or a ripe strawberry.

In wisdom God made them all.

For the next note on *Rest and Reflection*, see Psalm 119:15-16.

[A] **104:7-8** Or *away. They flowed over the mountains and went down valleys* [B] **104:16** Lit *are satisfied* [C] **104:19** Lit *moon for* [D] **104:19** Or *the appointed times* [E] **104:24** Lit *possessions*

teeming with creatures
beyond number —
living things both large and small.
26 There the ships move about,
and Leviathan, which you formed
to play there.

27 All of them wait for you
to give them their food at the right time.
28 When you give it to them,
they gather it;
when you open your hand,
they are satisfied with good things.
29 When you hide your face,
they are terrified;
when you take away their breath,
they die and return to the dust.
30 When you send your breath,[A]
they are created,
and you renew the surface
of the ground.

31 May the glory of the LORD
endure forever;
may the LORD rejoice in his works.
32 He looks at the earth, and it trembles;
he touches the mountains,
and they pour out smoke.
33 I will sing to the LORD all my life;
I will sing praise to my God while I live.
34 May my meditation be pleasing to him;
I will rejoice in the LORD.
35 May sinners vanish from the earth
and wicked people be no more.
My soul, bless the LORD!
Hallelujah!

GOD'S FAITHFULNESS TO HIS PEOPLE

105 Give thanks to the LORD, call on
his name;
proclaim his deeds among the peoples.
2 Sing to him, sing praise to him;
tell about all his wondrous works!
3 Honor his holy name;
let the hearts of those who seek the
LORD rejoice.
4 Seek the LORD and his strength;
seek his face always.
5 Remember the wondrous works
he has done,
his wonders, and the judgments
he has pronounced,[B]
6 you offspring of Abraham his servant,
Jacob's descendants —
his chosen ones.

7 He is the LORD our God;
his judgments govern the whole earth.
8 He remembers his covenant forever,
the promise he ordained
for a thousand generations —
9 the covenant he made with Abraham,
swore[C] to Isaac,
10 and confirmed to Jacob as a decree
and to Israel as a permanent covenant:
11 "I will give the land of Canaan to you
as your inherited portion."

12 When they were few in number,
very few indeed,
and resident aliens in Canaan,
13 wandering from nation to nation
and from one kingdom to another,
14 he allowed no one to oppress them;
he rebuked kings on their behalf:
15 "Do not touch my anointed ones,
or harm my prophets."

16 He called down famine against the land
and destroyed the entire food supply.
17 He had sent a man ahead of them —
Joseph, who was sold as a slave.
18 They hurt his feet with shackles;
his neck was put in an iron collar.
19 Until the time his prediction came true,
the word of the LORD tested him.
20 The king sent for him and released him;
the ruler of peoples set him free.
21 He made him master of his household,
ruler over all his possessions —
22 binding[D] his officials at will
and instructing his elders.

23 Then Israel went to Egypt;
Jacob lived as an alien in the land
of Ham.[E]
24 The LORD[F] made his people
very fruitful;
he made them more numerous
than their foes,
25 whose hearts he turned to hate
his people
and to deal deceptively
with his servants.
26 He sent Moses his servant,
and Aaron, whom he had chosen.

[A] **104:30** Or *Spirit* [B] **105:5** Lit *judgments of his mouth* [C] **105:9** Lit *and his oath* [D] **105:22** LXX, Syr, Vg read *teaching*
[E] **105:23** = Egypt, also in v. 27 [F] **105:24** Lit *He*

27 They performed his miraculous signs
among them,
and wonders in the land of Ham.
28 He sent darkness,
and it became dark —
for did they not defy his commands?
29 He turned their water into blood
and caused their fish to die.
30 Their land was overrun with frogs,
even in their royal chambers.
31 He spoke, and insects came —
gnats throughout their country.
32 He gave them hail for rain,
and lightning throughout their land.
33 He struck their vines and fig trees
and shattered the trees
of their territory.
34 He spoke, and locusts came —
young locusts without number.
35 They devoured all the vegetation
in their land
and consumed the produce
of their land.
36 He struck all the firstborn in their land,
all their first progeny.
37 Then he brought Israel out with silver
and gold,
and no one among his tribes stumbled.
38 Egypt was glad when they left,
for the dread of Israel[A] had fallen
on them.
39 He spread a cloud as a covering
and gave a fire to light up the night.
40 They asked, and he brought quail
and satisfied them with bread
from heaven.
41 He opened a rock, and water
gushed out;
it flowed like a stream in the desert.
42 For he remembered his holy promise
to Abraham his servant.
43 He brought his people out
with rejoicing,
his chosen ones with shouts of joy.
44 He gave them the lands of the nations,
and they inherited
what other peoples had worked for.

45 All this happened
so that they might keep his statutes
and obey his instructions.
Hallelujah!

ISRAEL'S UNFAITHFULNESS TO GOD

106 Hallelujah!
Give thanks to the LORD,
for he is good;

R Relationships | *Treating Others Fairly*

THAT'S NOT FAIR!

"How happy are those who uphold justice, who practice righteousness at all times." Psalm 106:3

Interestingly, not long after kids learn to speak and start interacting, one of their most repeated sentences is, "That's not fair!" It's as though we have a built-in sense of right and wrong.

Yet for as long as we have been a nation, we've had a whole group of people who do nothing but make new laws. We would think that after all these years, we might finally have enough rules to live by and that we would have learned how to obey all those laws. But, no. People keep circumventing the old rules, and so we keep writing new ones.

Psalm 106 speaks about the blessing we find when we pursue justice and when we "practice righteousness" (do what is right). We don't need a legislature to tell us it's wrong to lie, to cheat or mistreat others, to take advantage of the weak, or to ignore the needs of our neighbor.

What's an injustice you see that you could address? What's a wrong that you have the power to put right?

For the next note on *Relationships*, see Psalm 141:3.

[A] **105:38** Lit *them*

his faithful love
endures forever.
2 Who can declare the LORD's mighty acts
or proclaim all the praise due him?
3 How happy are those
who uphold justice,
who practice righteousness at all times.

4 Remember me, LORD,
when you show favor to your people.
Come to me with your salvation
5 so that I may enjoy the prosperity
of your chosen ones,
rejoice in the joy of your nation,
and boast about your heritage.

6 Both we and our fathers have sinned;
we have done wrong
and have acted wickedly.
7 Our fathers in Egypt did not grasp
the significance of
your wondrous works
or remember your many acts
of faithful love;
instead, they rebelled by the sea —
the Red Sea.
8 Yet he saved them for his name's sake,
to make his power known.
9 He rebuked the Red Sea,
and it dried up;
he led them through the depths
as through a desert.
10 He saved them from the power
of the adversary;
he redeemed them from the power
of the enemy.
11 Water covered their foes;
not one of them remained.
12 Then they believed his promises
and sang his praise.

13 They soon forgot his works
and would not wait for his counsel.
14 They were seized with craving
in the wilderness
and tested God in the desert.
15 He gave them what they asked for,
but sent a wasting disease
among them.

16 In the camp they were envious of Moses
and of Aaron, the LORD's holy one.
17 The earth opened up
and swallowed Dathan;
it covered the assembly of Abiram.
18 Fire blazed throughout their assembly;
flames consumed the wicked.

19 At Horeb they made a calf
and worshiped the cast metal image.
20 They exchanged their glory[A,B]
for the image of a grass-eating ox.
21 They forgot God their Savior,
who did great things in Egypt,
22 wondrous works in the land of Ham,[C]
awe-inspiring acts at the Red Sea.
23 So he said he would have
destroyed them —
if Moses his chosen one
had not stood before him in the breach
to turn his wrath away
from destroying them.

24 They despised the pleasant land
and did not believe his promise.
25 They grumbled in their tents
and did not listen to the LORD.
26 So he raised his hand against them
with an oath
that he would make them fall
in the desert
27 and would disperse their descendants[D]
among the nations,
scattering them throughout the lands.

28 They aligned themselves with Baal
of Peor
and ate sacrifices offered
to lifeless gods.[E]
29 They angered the LORD with their deeds,
and a plague broke out against them.
30 But Phinehas stood up and intervened,
and the plague was stopped.
31 It was credited to him as righteousness
throughout all generations to come.

32 They angered the LORD at the Waters
of Meribah,
and Moses suffered[F] because of them;
33 for they embittered his spirit,[G]
and he spoke rashly with his lips.

34 They did not destroy the peoples
as the LORD had commanded them

[A] **106:20** Alt Hb tradition reads *his glory*, or *my glory* [B] **106:20** = God [C] **106:22** = Egypt [D] **106:27** Syr; MT reads *would make their descendants fall* [E] **106:28** Lit *sacrifices for dead ones* [F] **106:32** Lit *and it was evil for Moses* [G] **106:33** Some Hb mss, LXX, Syr, Jer; other Hb mss read *they rebelled against his Spirit*

35 but mingled with the nations
and adopted their ways.
36 They served their idols,
which became a snare to them.
37 They sacrificed their sons
and daughters to demons.
38 They shed innocent blood —
the blood of their sons and daughters
whom they sacrificed to the idols
of Canaan;
so the land became polluted with blood.
39 They defiled themselves by their actions
and prostituted themselves
by their deeds.

40 Therefore the LORD's anger burned
against his people,
and he abhorred his own inheritance.
41 He handed them over to the nations;
those who hated them ruled over them.
42 Their enemies oppressed them,
and they were subdued
under their power.
43 He rescued them many times,
but they continued to rebel deliberately
and were beaten down by their iniquity.

44 When he heard their cry,
he took note of their distress,
45 remembered his covenant with them,
and relented according to
the abundance
of his faithful love.
46 He caused them to be pitied
before all their captors.

47 Save us, LORD our God,
and gather us from the nations,
so that we may give thanks
to your holy name
and rejoice in your praise.

48 Blessed be the LORD God of Israel,
from everlasting to everlasting.
Let all the people say, "Amen!"
Hallelujah!

BOOK V (Psalms 107–150)

THANKSGIVING FOR GOD'S DELIVERANCE

107 Give thanks to the LORD,
for he is good;
his faithful love endures forever.
2 Let the redeemed of the LORD proclaim
that he has redeemed them
from the power of the foe
3 and has gathered them from the lands —
from the east and the west,
from the north and the south.

4 Some[A] wandered
in the desolate wilderness,
finding no way to a city
where they could live.
5 They were hungry and thirsty;
their spirits failed[B] within them.
6 Then they cried out to the LORD
in their trouble;
he rescued them from their distress.
7 He led them by the right path
to go to a city where they could live.
8 Let them give thanks to the LORD
for his faithful love
and his wondrous works for
all humanity.
9 For he has satisfied the thirsty
and filled the hungry with good things.

10 Others sat in darkness and gloom[C] —
prisoners in cruel chains —
11 because they rebelled
against God's commands
and despised the counsel
of the Most High.
12 He broke their spirits[D] with hard labor;
they stumbled, and there was no one
to help.
13 Then they cried out to the LORD
in their trouble;
he saved them from their distress.
14 He brought them out of darkness
and gloom
and broke their chains apart.
15 Let them give thanks to the LORD
for his faithful love
and his wondrous works for
all humanity.
16 For he has broken down
the bronze gates
and cut through the iron bars.

17 Fools suffered affliction
because of their rebellious ways
and their iniquities.
18 They loathed all food
and came near the gates of death.

[A] **107:4** Lit *They*, also in vv. 10,23 [B] **107:5** Lit *their soul fainted* [C] **107:10** Or *the shadow of death*, also in v. 14 [D] **107:12** Lit *hearts*

19 Then they cried out to the LORD
in their trouble;
he saved them from their distress.
20 He sent his word and healed them;
he rescued them from the Pit.
21 Let them give thanks to the LORD
for his faithful love
and his wondrous works for
all humanity.
22 Let them offer sacrifices
of thanksgiving
and announce his works with shouts
of joy.

23 Others went to sea in ships,
conducting trade on the vast water.
24 They saw the LORD's works,
his wondrous works in the deep.
25 He spoke and raised a stormy wind
that stirred up the waves of the sea.[A]
26 Rising up to the sky, sinking down
to the depths,
their courage[B] melting away in anguish,
27 they reeled and staggered
like a drunkard,
and all their skill was useless.
28 Then they cried out to the LORD
in their trouble,
and he brought them
out of their distress.
29 He stilled the storm to a whisper,
and the waves of the sea[C] were hushed.
30 They rejoiced when the waves[D]
grew quiet.
Then he guided them to the harbor
they longed for.
31 Let them give thanks to the LORD
for his faithful love
and his wondrous works for
all humanity.
32 Let them exalt him in the assembly
of the people
and praise him in the council
of the elders.

33 He turns rivers into desert,
springs into thirsty ground,
34 and fruitful land into salty wasteland,
because of the wickedness
of its inhabitants.
35 He turns a desert into a pool,
dry land into springs.
36 He causes the hungry to settle there,
and they establish a city
where they can live.
37 They sow fields and plant vineyards
that yield a fruitful harvest.
38 He blesses them,
and they multiply greatly;
he does not let their livestock decrease.

39 When they are diminished
and are humbled
by cruel oppression and sorrow,
40 he pours contempt on nobles
and makes them wander
in a trackless wasteland.
41 But he lifts the needy out of
their suffering
and makes their families multiply
like flocks.
42 The upright see it and rejoice,
and all injustice shuts its mouth.

43 Let whoever is wise pay attention
to these things
and consider the LORD's acts
of faithful love.

A PLEA FOR VICTORY

108 *A song. A psalm of David.*
My heart is confident, God;
I will sing; I will sing praises
with the whole of my being.[E]
2 Wake up, harp and lyre!
I will wake up the dawn.
3 I will praise you, LORD,
among the peoples;
I will sing praises to you
among the nations.
4 For your faithful love is higher
than the heavens,
and your faithfulness reaches to
the clouds.
5 God, be exalted above the heavens,
and let your glory be over
the whole earth.
6 Save with your right hand
and answer me
so that those you love may be rescued.

7 God has spoken in his sanctuary:[F]
"I will celebrate!
I will divide up Shechem.
I will apportion the Valley of Succoth.
8 Gilead is mine, Manasseh is mine,

[A] **107:25** Lit *of it* [B] **107:26** Lit *souls* [C] **107:29** Lit *of them* [D] **107:30** Lit *when they* [E] **108:1** Lit *praises, even my glory*
[F] **108:7** Or *has promised by his holy nature*

and Ephraim is my helmet;
Judah is my scepter.
9 Moab is my washbasin;
I throw my sandal on Edom.
I shout in triumph over Philistia."

10 Who will bring me to the fortified city?
Who will lead me to Edom?
11 God, haven't you rejected us?
God, you do not march out
with our armies.
12 Give us aid against the foe,
for human help is worthless.
13 With God we will perform valiantly;
he will trample our foes.

PRAYER AGAINST AN ENEMY

109 *For the choir director. A psalm of David.*
God of my praise, do not be silent.

2 For wicked and deceitful mouths open
against me;
they speak against me
with lying tongues.
3 They surround me with hateful words
and attack me without cause.
4 In return for my love they accuse me,
but I continue to pray.[A]
5 They repay me evil for good,
and hatred for my love.

6 Set a wicked person over him;
let an accuser[B] stand at his right hand.
7 When he is judged, let him
be found guilty,
and let his prayer be counted as sin.
8 Let his days be few;
let another take over his position.
9 Let his children be fatherless
and his wife a widow.
10 Let his children wander as beggars,
searching for food far[C]
from their demolished homes.
11 Let a creditor seize all he has;
let strangers plunder what he has
worked for.
12 Let no one show him kindness,
and let no one be gracious
to his fatherless children.
13 Let the line of his descendants
be cut off;
let their name be blotted out
in the next generation.
14 Let the iniquity of his fathers
be remembered before the LORD,
and do not let his mother's sin
be blotted out.
15 Let their sins[D] always remain
before the LORD,
and let him remove[E] all memory
of them from the earth.

16 For he did not think to show kindness,
but pursued the suffering, needy,
and brokenhearted
in order to put them to death.
17 He loved cursing — let it fall on him;
he took no delight in blessing —
let it be far from him.
18 He wore cursing like his coat —
let it enter his body like water
and go into his bones like oil.
19 Let it be like a robe he wraps
around himself,
like a belt he always wears.
20 Let this be the LORD's payment
to my accusers,
to those who speak evil against me.

21 But you, LORD, my Lord,
deal kindly with me
for your name's sake;
because your faithful love is good,
rescue me.
22 For I am suffering and needy;
my heart is wounded within me.
23 I fade away like a lengthening shadow;
I am shaken off like a locust.
24 My knees are weak from fasting,
and my body is emaciated.[F]
25 I have become an object of ridicule
to my accusers;[G]
when they see me, they shake
their heads in scorn.

26 Help me, LORD my God;
save me according to your faithful love
27 so they may know that this is your hand
and that you, LORD, have done it.
28 Though they curse, you will bless.
When they rise up, they will be
put to shame,
but your servant will rejoice.
29 My accusers will be clothed
with disgrace;
they will wear their shame like a cloak.

[A] **109:4** Lit *but I, prayer* [B] **109:6** Or *adversary* [C] **109:10** LXX reads *beggars, driven far* [D] **109:15** Lit *Let them* [E] **109:15** Or *cut off* [F] **109:24** Lit *denied from fat* [G] **109:25** Lit *to them*

30 I will fervently thank the LORD
with my mouth;
I will praise him in the presence
of many.
31 For he stands at the right hand of
the needy
to save him from those who would
condemn him.

THE PRIESTLY KING

110 *A psalm of David.*
This is the declaration of the LORD
to my Lord:
"Sit at my right hand
until I make your enemies
your footstool."
2 The LORD will extend
your mighty scepter from Zion.
Rule[A] over your surrounding[B] enemies.
3 Your people will volunteer
on your day of battle.[C]
In holy splendor, from the womb
of the dawn,
the dew of your youth belongs to you.[D]
4 The LORD has sworn an oath
and will not take it back:
"You are a priest forever
according to the pattern of Melchizedek."

5 The Lord is at your right hand;
he will crush kings on the day
of his anger.
6 He will judge the nations,
heaping up corpses;
he will crush leaders
over the entire world.
7 He will drink from the brook
by the road;
therefore, he will lift up his head.

PRAISE FOR THE LORD'S WORKS

111 Hallelujah![E]
I will praise the LORD with all
my heart
in the assembly of the upright
and in the congregation.

2 The LORD's works are great,
studied by all who delight in them.
3 All that he does is splendid and majestic;
his righteousness endures forever.
4 He has caused his wondrous works
to be remembered.
The LORD is gracious
and compassionate.
5 He has provided food for those
who fear him;
he remembers his covenant forever.
6 He has shown his people the power
of his works
by giving them the inheritance
of the nations.
7 The works of his hands are truth
and justice;
all his instructions are trustworthy.
8 They are established forever and ever,
enacted in truth and in uprightness.
9 He has sent redemption to his people.
He has ordained his covenant forever.
His name is holy and awe-inspiring.
10 The fear of the LORD is the beginning
of wisdom;
all who follow his instructions[F] have
good insight.
His praise endures forever.

THE TRAITS OF THE RIGHTEOUS

112 Hallelujah![E]
Happy is the person who fears
the LORD,
taking great delight in his commands.

2 His descendants will be powerful
in the land;
the generation of the upright
will be blessed.
3 Wealth and riches are in his house,
and his righteousness endures forever.
4 Light shines in the darkness
for the upright.
He is gracious, compassionate,
and righteous.
5 Good will come to the one
who lends generously
and conducts his business fairly.
6 He will never be shaken.
The righteous one will be
remembered forever.
7 He will not fear bad news;
his heart is confident,
trusting in the LORD.
8 His heart is assured; he will not fear.
In the end he will look in triumph
on his foes.
9 He distributes freely to the poor;

[A] **110:2** One Hb ms, LXX, Tg read *You will rule* [B] **110:2** Lit *Rule in the midst of your* [C] **110:3** Lit *power* [D] **110:3** Hb obscure
[E] **111:1; 112:1** The lines of this poem form an acrostic. [F] **111:10** Lit *follow them*

Embracing God's Word | Provision

RESOURCES DWINDLING, UNKNOWN AND NEGLECTED, we suspect no one knows these feelings and needs. God does. He guides and provides. He cares.

The God of old is your dwelling place, and underneath are the everlasting arms. –Deuteronomy 33:27a

I lie down and sleep; I wake again because the LORD sustains me. –Psalm 3:5

I will both lie down and sleep in peace, for you alone, LORD, make me live in safety. –Psalm 4:8

Display the wonders of your faithful love, Savior of all who seek refuge from those who rebel against your right hand. Protect me as the pupil of your eye; hide me in the shadow of your wings from the wicked who treat me violently, my deadly enemies who surround me. –Psalm 17:7-9

God is our refuge and strength, a helper who is always found in times of trouble. Therefore we will not be afraid, though the earth trembles and the mountains topple into the depths of the seas, though its water roars and foams and the mountains quake with its turmoil. –Psalm 46:1-3

Cast your burden on the LORD, and he will sustain you; he will never allow the righteous to be shaken. –Psalm 55:22

God, hear my cry; pay attention to my prayer. I call to you from the ends of the earth when my heart is without strength. Lead me to a rock that is high above me, for you have been a refuge for me, a strong tower in the face of the enemy. I will live in your tent forever and take refuge under the shelter of your wings. –Psalm 61:1-4

The one who lives under the protection of the Most High dwells in the shadow of the Almighty. –Psalm 91:1

He will not allow your foot to slip; your Protector will not slumber. . . . The LORD will protect your coming and going both now and forever. –Psalm 121:3,8

The name of the LORD is a strong tower; the righteous run to it and are protected. –Proverbs 18:10

The LORD is good, a stronghold in a day of distress; he cares for those who take refuge in him. –Nahum 1:7

Give us today our daily bread. –Matthew 6:11b

If that's how God clothes the grass, which is in the field today and is thrown into the furnace tomorrow, how much more will he do for you—you of little faith? –Luke 12:28

And my God will supply all your needs according to his riches in glory in Christ Jesus. –Philippians 4:19

Humble yourselves, therefore, under the mighty hand of God, so that he may exalt you at the proper time, casting all your cares on him, because he cares about you. –1 Peter 5:6-7

his righteousness endures forever.
His horn will be exalted in honor.

10 The wicked one will see it
and be angry;
he will gnash his teeth in despair.
The desire of the wicked leads to ruin.

PRAISE TO THE MERCIFUL GOD

113 Hallelujah!
Give praise, servants of the LORD;
praise the name of the LORD.
2 Let the name of the LORD be blessed
both now and forever.
3 From the rising of the sun to its setting,
let the name of the LORD be praised.

4 The LORD is exalted above
all the nations,
his glory above the heavens.
5 Who is like the LORD our God —
the one enthroned on high,
6 who stoops down to look
on the heavens and the earth?
7 He raises the poor from the dust
and lifts the needy from the trash heap
8 in order to seat them with nobles —
with the nobles of his people.
9 He gives the childless woman
a household,
making her the joyful mother
of children.
Hallelujah!

GOD'S DELIVERANCE OF ISRAEL

114 When Israel came out of Egypt —
the house of Jacob from a people
who spoke a foreign language —
2 Judah became his sanctuary,
Israel, his dominion.

3 The sea looked and fled;
the Jordan turned back.
4 The mountains skipped like rams,
the hills, like lambs.
5 Why was it, sea, that you fled?
Jordan, that you turned back?
6 Mountains, that you skipped like rams?
Hills, like lambs?

7 Tremble, earth, at the presence
of the Lord,
at the presence of the God of Jacob,
8 who turned the rock into a pool,
the flint into a spring.

GLORY TO GOD ALONE

115 Not to us, LORD, not to us,
but to your name give glory
because of your faithful love,
because of your truth.
2 Why should the nations say,
"Where is their God?"
3 Our God is in heaven
and does whatever he pleases.

4 Their idols are silver and gold,
made by human hands.
5 They have mouths
but cannot speak,
eyes, but cannot see.
6 They have ears but cannot hear,
noses, but cannot smell.
7 They have hands but cannot feel,
feet, but cannot walk.
They cannot make a sound
with their throats.
8 Those who make them are[A] just
like them,
as are all who trust in them.

9 Israel,[B] trust in the LORD!
He is their help and shield.
10 House of Aaron, trust in the LORD!
He is their help and shield.
11 You who fear the LORD,
trust in the LORD!
He is their help and shield.
12 The LORD remembers us
and will bless us.
He will bless the house of Israel;
he will bless the house of Aaron;
13 he will bless those
who fear the LORD —
small and great alike.

14 May the LORD add to your numbers,
both yours and your children's.
15 May you be blessed by the LORD,
the Maker of heaven and earth.
16 The heavens are the LORD's,[C]
but the earth he has given
to the human race.
17 It is not the dead who praise the LORD,
nor any of those descending
into the silence of death.

[A] **115:8** Or *May those who make them become* [B] **115:9** Some Hb mss, LXX, Syr read *House of Israel* [C] **115:16** Lit *the LORD's heavens*

18 But we will bless the LORD,
both now and forever.
Hallelujah!

THANKS TO GOD FOR DELIVERANCE

116 I love the LORD because he has heard
my appeal for mercy.
2 Because he has turned his ear to me,
I will call out to him as long as I live.

3 The ropes of death were wrapped
around me,
and the torments of Sheol overcame me;
I encountered trouble and sorrow.
4 Then I called on the name of the LORD:
"LORD, save me!"
5 The LORD is gracious and righteous;
our God is compassionate.
6 The LORD guards the inexperienced;
I was helpless, and he saved me.
7 Return to your rest, my soul,
for the LORD has been good to you.
8 For you, LORD, rescued me from death,
my eyes from tears,
my feet from stumbling.
9 I will walk before the LORD
in the land of the living.
10 I believed, even when I said,
"I am severely oppressed."
11 In my alarm I said,
"Everyone is a liar."
12 How can I repay the LORD
for all the good he has done
for me?
13 I will take the cup of salvation
and call on the name of the LORD.
14 I will fulfill my vows to the LORD
in the presence of all his people.

15 The death of his faithful ones
is valuable in the LORD's sight.
16 LORD, I am indeed your servant;
I am your servant, the son
of your female servant.
You have loosened my bonds.
17 I will offer you a sacrifice
of thanksgiving
and call on the name of the LORD.
18 I will fulfill my vows to the LORD
in the presence of all his people,
19 in the courts
of the LORD's house —
within you, Jerusalem.
Hallelujah!

UNIVERSAL CALL TO PRAISE

117 Praise the LORD, all nations!
Glorify him, all peoples!
2 For his faithful love to us is great;
the LORD's faithfulness
endures forever.
Hallelujah!

Support | *Prayer*

THE GOD WHO HEARS

"I love the LORD because he has heard my appeal for mercy. Because he has turned his ear to me, I will call out to him as long as I live." Psalm 116:1-2

Listening is a dying art (not that a whole lot of people ever practiced this art to begin with). The reasons aren't hard to find. We are distracted people. To make matters worse, we buy the lie of multitasking. So while we might sometimes glance up from our smartphones in the direction of other talking humans, and though we might notice that their lips are moving, we seldom pay attention to what they are saying.

Contrast this human behavior with the description found here of the Lord. The psalm writer notes how God "turned his ear to me" (this is the picture of someone perking up and leaning in). He adds that God "has heard my appeal" (this verb conveys the idea of listening with interest). In short, the pray-er knows that he has the Almighty's full and undivided attention. And what is the effect of this? "I will call out to him as long as I live."

How do the implications of this verse change your view of prayer?

For the next note on *Support*, see Psalm 143:6-7.

THANKSGIVING FOR VICTORY

118 Give thanks to the LORD,
for he is good;
his faithful love endures forever.
2 Let Israel say,
"His faithful love endures forever."
3 Let the house of Aaron say,
"His faithful love endures forever."
4 Let those who fear the LORD say,
"His faithful love endures forever."

5 I called to the LORD in distress;
the LORD answered me
and put me in a spacious place.[A]
6 The LORD is for me; I will not be afraid.
What can a mere mortal do to me?
7 The LORD is my helper,
Therefore, I will look in triumph
on those who hate me.

8 It is better to take refuge in the LORD
than to trust in humanity.
9 It is better to take refuge in the LORD
than to trust in nobles.

10 All the nations surrounded me;
in the name of the LORD
I destroyed them.
11 They surrounded me, yes,
they surrounded me;
in the name of the LORD
I destroyed them.
12 They surrounded me like bees;
they were extinguished like a fire
among thorns;
in the name of the LORD
I destroyed them.
13 They[B] pushed me hard to make me fall,
but the LORD helped me.
14 The LORD is my strength and my song;
he has become my salvation.

15 There are shouts of joy and victory
in the tents of the righteous:
"The LORD's right hand
performs valiantly!
16 The LORD's right hand is raised.
The LORD's right hand
performs valiantly!"
17 I will not die, but I will live
and proclaim what the LORD has done.
18 The LORD disciplined me severely
but did not give me over to death.

19 Open the gates of righteousness
for me;
I will enter through them
and give thanks to the LORD.
20 This is the LORD's gate;
the righteous will enter through it.

Eternal Perspective | *Fear Overcome*

HE IS FOR YOU

"I called to the LORD in distress; the LORD answered me and put me in a spacious place. The LORD is for me; I will not be afraid. What can a mere mortal do to me?" Psalm 118:5-6

One teaching of the Bible is that the Lord is *with* his people (Ps 23:4; Mt 28:20). Elsewhere we read that the Lord is *in* us (Eph 3:17; Col 1:27). As if those verses weren't encouraging enough, the psalm writer adds here, "The LORD is *for* me."

Psalm 118 is a song that was written for and sung at one of Israel's great festivals (perhaps the Festival of Shelters). It's a thanksgiving psalm, an upbeat hymn of victory. It praises the Lord's faithful love. Through uncertain, scary times, he was *for* his people—always in their corner, always working for their best.

When we're "in distress" (literally, a narrow or confining situation), our view is often obscured by fear. In his kindness, the Lord will lead us to "a spacious place" (literally, an expansive, open meadow) where we can see the truth: We've been safe all along. And why? Because the Lord is *for* us!

For the next note on *Eternal Perspective*, see Psalm 121:5-8.

[A] **118:5** Or *answered me with freedom* [B] **118:13** Lit *You*

21 I will give thanks to you
because you have answered me
and have become my salvation.
22 The stone that the builders rejected
has become the cornerstone.
23 This came from the LORD;
it is wondrous in our sight.
24 This is the day the LORD has made;
let us rejoice and be glad in it.

25 LORD, save us!
LORD, please grant us success!
26 He who comes in the name
of the LORD is blessed.
From the house of the LORD
we bless you.
27 The LORD is God and has given
us light.
Bind the festival sacrifice with cords
to the horns of the altar.
28 You are my God, and I will give
you thanks.
You are my God; I will exalt you.
29 Give thanks to the LORD,
for he is good;
his faithful love endures forever.

DELIGHT IN GOD'S WORD

א Aleph

119 How[A] happy are those whose way
is blameless,
who walk according to the LORD's
instruction!
2 Happy are those who keep his decrees
and seek him with all their heart.
3 They do nothing wrong;
they walk in his ways.
4 You have commanded that your precepts
be diligently kept.
5 If only my ways were committed
to keeping your statutes!
6 Then I would not be ashamed
when I think about all your commands.
7 I will praise you with an upright heart
when I learn your righteous judgments.
8 I will keep your statutes;
never abandon me.

ב Beth

9 How can a young man keep his way
pure?
By keeping your[B] word.
10 I have sought you with all my heart;

Thanksgiving and Contentment | *Thanksgiving*

JOY

"This is the day the LORD has made; let us rejoice and be glad in it." Psalm 118:24

God gave you this once-in-a-lifetime day. In all of history, there has never been a day like today, nor will one like it ever occur again.

Forget yesterday. You can't push a rewind button. You're not going to get a do-over. Stop staring longingly (or with regret) in your rearview mirror.

Forget tomorrow. Sure, you have some hopes (maybe even firm plans) for tonight and the rest of the week, a trip tentatively scheduled in a couple months, but, hey, *nothing* about the future is sure. Don't waste today daydreaming.

What you really have is *this*—right now. This day. What more do you need? What a gift from God! Waking you up and filling your lungs with breath was his way of saying, "C'mon. I have things to show you! I have ways I want to use you!"

So be wise. Come awake. Be fully present in the *now*. Walk in faith and pay attention. See. Gasp. Love. Give. Sing. Laugh. Dance.

Be glad in this day, and thank God for it.

For the next note on *Thanksgiving and Contentment*, see Psalm 136:1.

[A] **119:1** The stanzas of this poem form an acrostic. [B] **119:9** Or *keeping it according to your*

don't let me wander
from your commands.
11 I have treasured your word in my heart
so that I may not sin against you.
12 LORD, may you be blessed;
teach me your statutes.
13 With my lips I proclaim
all the judgments from your mouth.
14 I rejoice in the way revealed by
your decrees
as much as in all riches.
15 I will meditate on your precepts
and think about your ways.
16 I will delight in your statutes;
I will not forget your word.

ג Gimel

17 Deal generously with your servant
so that I might live;
then I will keep your word.
18 Open my eyes so that I may contemplate
wondrous things
from your instruction.
19 I am a resident alien on earth;
do not hide your commands from me.
20 I am continually overcome
with longing for your judgments.
21 You rebuke the arrogant,
the ones under a curse,
who wander from your commands.
22 Take insult and contempt away from me,
for I have kept your decrees.
23 Though princes sit together speaking
against me,
your servant will think
about your statutes;
24 your decrees are my delight
and my counselors.

ד Daleth

25 My life is down in the dust;
give me life through your word.
26 I told you about my life,
and you answered me;
teach me your statutes.
27 Help me understand
the meaning of your precepts
so that I can meditate on your wonders.
28 I am weary[A] from grief;
strengthen me through your word.
29 Keep me from the way of deceit
and graciously give me your instruction.
30 I have chosen the way of truth;
I have set your ordinances before me.
31 I cling to your decrees;
LORD, do not put me to shame.

Exercise of Faith | *Memorizing Scripture*

TUCKING AWAY THE TRUTH

"I have treasured your word in my heart so that I may not sin against you." Psalm 119:11

Some people have a mental block when it comes to memorizing Scripture. "I can't. I've tried. It's too hard. I don't have a mind for that sort of thing."

Granted, some people have a much better memory than others, but consider this: All of us can and do file things away in our minds—all the time. Phone numbers, passwords (at least that really tricky one you always use: QWERTY), song lyrics, movie lines, birthdays and anniversaries (okay, maybe the guys, not so much).

The point is this: Memorizing God's Word isn't easy. It takes intentionality, focus, consistency, and effort. And it's actually tougher and trickier than other kinds of memory work because our great enemy opposes us fiercely in this. He knows that when we're armed with truth, we're dangerous!

Try memorizing one verse this week—Philippians 4:13. Write it on a card. Carry it with you. Pull it out and review it throughout your day. It's worth the work. When the enemy comes against you with lies, you'll have the ammunition you need to fight back.

For the next note on *Exercise of Faith*, see Proverbs 3:5-6.

[A] **119:28** Or *I weep*

32 I pursue the way of your commands,
for you broaden
my understanding.[A]

ה He

33 Teach me, LORD, the meaning[B]
of your statutes,
and I will always keep them.[C]
34 Help me understand your instruction,
and I will obey it
and follow it with all my heart.
35 Help me stay on the path
of your commands,
for I take pleasure in it.
36 Turn my heart to your decrees
and not to dishonest profit.
37 Turn my eyes
from looking at what is worthless;
give me life in your ways.[D]
38 Confirm what you said
to your servant,
for it produces reverence for you.
39 Turn away the disgrace I dread;
indeed, your judgments are good.
40 How I long for your precepts!
Give me life through
your righteousness.

ו Waw

41 Let your faithful love
come to me, LORD,
your salvation, as you promised.
42 Then I can answer the one
who taunts me,
for I trust in your word.
43 Never take the word of truth
from my mouth,
for I hope in your judgments.
44 I will always obey your instruction,
forever and ever.
45 I will walk freely in an open place
because I study your precepts.
46 I will speak of your decrees
before kings
and not be ashamed.
47 I delight in your commands,
which I love.
48 I will lift up my hands
to your commands,
which I love,
and will meditate on your statutes.

ז Zayin

49 Remember your word to your servant;
you have given me hope through it.

Rest and Reflection | *Meditating on God and His Word*

SAVORING SCRIPTURE

"I will meditate on your precepts and think about your ways. I will delight in your statutes; I will not forget your word." Psalm 119:15-16

When Eastern gurus and new age mystics speak of "meditation," they mean an emptying of the mind. When the Bible calls believers to "meditate," it means to fill one's mind with (and then fixate one's thoughts on) God's truth.

This, of course, is exactly what we see in this verse. Notice the object of all the verbs: "meditate on *your precepts* . . . think about *your ways*. . . . delight in *your statutes* . . . [don't] forget *your word*." No emptying of the mind here!

The Hebrew word translated "meditate" conveys the idea of speaking in low tones. Picture someone deep in thought, mumbling silently, obviously wrestling with an idea. That's all Christian meditation is—examining God's Word from every angle, savoring and studying it, rolling it around in your noggin, musing on it, and mulling over how to put it into practice.

Here's the good news: If you're a person who worries, you already know how to meditate! Worry is just meditating on an imagined, negative future. How about if today we meditate on God's truth rather than on devilish lies or man-made hypotheticals?

For the next note on *Rest and Reflection*, see Psalm 127:2.

[A] **119:32** Lit *you enlarge my heart* [B] **119:33** Lit *way* [C] **119:33** Or *will keep it as my reward* [D] **119:37** Some Hb mss, Tg read *word*

50 This is my comfort in my affliction:
Your promise has given me life.
51 The arrogant constantly ridicule me,
but I do not turn away
from your instruction.
52 LORD, I remember your judgments
from long ago
and find comfort.
53 Rage seizes me because of the wicked
who reject your instruction.
54 Your statutes are the theme of my song
during my earthly life.[A]
55 LORD, I remember your name in the night,
and I obey your instruction.
56 This is my practice:
I obey your precepts.

ח Cheth

57 The LORD is my portion;[B]
I have promised to keep your words.
58 I have sought your favor with all
my heart;
be gracious to me according to
your promise.
59 I thought about my ways
and turned my steps back
to your decrees.
60 I hurried, not hesitating
to keep your commands.
61 Though the ropes of the wicked
were wrapped around me,
I did not forget your instruction.
62 I rise at midnight to thank you
for your righteous judgments.
63 I am a friend to all who fear you,
to those who keep your precepts.
64 LORD, the earth is filled with
your faithful love;
teach me your statutes.

ט Teth

65 LORD, you have treated your servant well,
just as you promised.
66 Teach me good judgment
and discernment,
for I rely on your commands.
67 Before I was afflicted I went astray,
but now I keep your word.
68 You are good, and you do what is good;
teach me your statutes.
69 The arrogant have smeared me with lies,
but I obey your precepts with all
my heart.
70 Their hearts are hard and insensitive,
but I delight in your instruction.
71 It was good for me to be afflicted
so that I could learn your statutes.
72 Instruction from your lips is better
for me
than thousands of gold
and silver pieces.

י Yod

73 Your hands made me
and formed me;
give me understanding
so that I can learn your commands.
74 Those who fear you will see me
and rejoice,
for I put my hope in your word.
75 I know, LORD, that your judgments
are just
and that you have afflicted me fairly.
76 May your faithful love comfort me
as you promised your servant.
77 May your compassion come to me
so that I may live,
for your instruction is my delight.
78 Let the arrogant be put to shame
for slandering me with lies;
I will meditate on your precepts.
79 Let those who fear you,
those who know your decrees,
turn to me.
80 May my heart be blameless
regarding your statutes
so that I will not be put to shame.

כ Kaph

81 I long for your salvation;
I put my hope in your word.
82 My eyes grow weary
looking for what you have promised;
I ask, "When will you comfort me?"
83 Though I have become like a wineskin
dried by smoke,
I do not forget your statutes.
84 How many days must
your servant wait?
When will you execute judgment
on my persecutors?
85 The arrogant have dug pits for me;
they violate your instruction.
86 All your commands are true;
people persecute me with lies —
help me!

[A] **119:54** Lit *song in the house of my sojourning* [B] **119:57** Lit *You are my portion, LORD*

87 They almost ended my life on earth,
but I did not abandon your precepts.
88 Give me life in accordance with
your faithful love,
and I will obey the decree
you have spoken.

ל Lamed

89 LORD, your word is forever;
it is firmly fixed in heaven.
90 Your faithfulness is for all generations;
you established the earth,
and it stands firm.
91 Your judgments stand firm today,
for all things are your servants.
92 If your instruction had not been
my delight,
I would have died in my affliction.
93 I will never forget your precepts,
for you have given me life
through them.
94 I am yours; save me,
for I have studied your precepts.
95 The wicked hope to destroy me,
but I contemplate your decrees.
96 I have seen a limit to all perfection,
but your command is without limit.

מ Mem

97 How I love your instruction!
It is my meditation all day long.
98 Your commands make me wiser
than my enemies,
for they are always with me.
99 I have more insight than
all my teachers
because your decrees are my meditation.
100 I understand more than the elders
because I obey your precepts.
101 I have kept my feet from every evil path
to follow your word.
102 I have not turned from
your judgments,
for you yourself have instructed me.
103 How sweet your word is to my taste —
sweeter than honey in my mouth.
104 I gain understanding
from your precepts;
therefore I hate every false way.

נ Nun

105 Your word is a lamp for my feet
and a light on my path.
106 I have solemnly sworn
to keep your righteous judgments.
107 I am severely afflicted;
LORD, give me life according
to your word.
108 LORD, please accept
my freewill offerings of praise,
and teach me your judgments.
109 My life is constantly in danger,[A]
yet I do not forget your instruction.
110 The wicked have set a trap for me,
but I have not wandered
from your precepts.
111 I have your decrees
as a heritage forever;
indeed, they are the joy of my heart.
112 I am resolved to obey your statutes
to the very end.[B]

ס Samek

113 I hate those who are double-minded,
but I love your instruction.
114 You are my shelter and my shield;
I put my hope in your word.
115 Depart from me, you evil ones,
so that I may obey
my God's commands.
116 Sustain me as you promised,
and I will live;
do not let me be ashamed of my hope.
117 Sustain me so that I can be safe
and always be concerned about
your statutes.
118 You reject all who stray
from your statutes,
for their deceit is a lie.
119 You remove all the wicked on earth
as if they were[C] dross from metal;
therefore, I love your decrees.
120 I tremble[D] in awe of you;
I fear your judgments.

ע Ayin

121 I have done what is just and right;
do not leave me to my oppressors.
122 Guarantee your servant's well-being;
do not let the arrogant oppress me.
123 My eyes grow weary looking for
your salvation
and for your righteous promise.
124 Deal with your servant based on
your faithful love;
teach me your statutes.

[A] **119:109** Lit *in my hand* [B] **119:112** Or *statutes; the reward is eternal* [C] **119:119** Some Hb mss, DSS, LXX, Aq, Sym, Jer read *All the wicked of the earth you count as* [D] **119:120** Lit *My flesh shudders*

125 I am your servant;
give me understanding
so that I may know your decrees.
126 It is time for the LORD to act,
for they have violated your instruction.
127 Since I love your commands
more than gold, even the purest gold,
128 I carefully follow all your precepts
and hate every false way.

פ Pe

129 Your decrees are wondrous;
therefore I obey them.
130 The revelation of your words
brings light
and gives understanding
to the inexperienced.
131 I open my mouth and pant
because I long for your commands.
132 Turn to me and be gracious to me,
as is your practice toward those
who love your name.
133 Make my steps steady
through your promise;
don't let any sin dominate me.
134 Redeem me from human oppression,
and I will keep your precepts.
135 Make your face shine
on your servant,
and teach me your statutes.
136 My eyes pour out streams of tears
because people do not follow
your instruction.

צ Tsade

137 You are righteous, LORD,
and your judgments are just.
138 The decrees you issue are righteous
and altogether trustworthy.
139 My anger overwhelms me
because my foes forget your words.
140 Your word is completely pure,
and your servant loves it.
141 I am insignificant and despised,
but I do not forget your precepts.
142 Your righteousness is
an everlasting righteousness,
and your instruction is true.
143 Trouble and distress
have overtaken me,
but your commands are my delight.
144 Your decrees are righteous forever.
Give me understanding, and I will live.

ק Qoph

145 I call with all my heart;
answer me, LORD.
I will obey your statutes.
146 I call to you; save me,
and I will keep your decrees.
147 I rise before dawn and cry out for help;
I put my hope in your word.
148 I am awake through each watch
of the night
to meditate on your promise.
149 In keeping with your faithful love,
hear my voice.
LORD, give me life in keeping with
your justice.
150 Those who pursue evil plans[A] come near;
they are far from your instruction.
151 You are near, LORD,
and all your commands are true.
152 Long ago I learned from your decrees
that you have established them forever.

ר Resh

153 Consider my affliction and rescue me,
for I have not forgotten
your instruction.
154 Champion my cause and redeem me;
give me life as you promised.
155 Salvation is far from the wicked
because they do not study
your statutes.
156 Your compassions are many, LORD;
give me life according to
your judgments.
157 My persecutors and foes are many.
I have not turned from your decrees.
158 I have seen the disloyal and feel disgust
because they do not keep your word.
159 Consider how I love your precepts;
LORD, give me life according to
your faithful love.
160 The entirety of your word is truth,
each of your righteous judgments
endures forever.

ש Sin / ש Shin

161 Princes have persecuted me
without cause,
but my heart fears only your word.
162 I rejoice over your promise
like one who finds vast treasure.
163 I hate and abhor falsehood,
but I love your instruction.

[A] **119:150** Some Hb mss, LXX, Sym, Jer read *who maliciously persecute me*

164 I praise you seven times a day
for your righteous judgments.
165 Abundant peace belongs to those
who love your instruction;
nothing makes them stumble.
166 LORD, I hope for your salvation
and carry out your commands.
167 I obey your decrees
and love them greatly.
168 I obey your precepts and decrees,
for all my ways are before you.

ת Taw

169 Let my cry reach you, LORD;
give me understanding according to
your word.
170 Let my plea reach you;
rescue me according to your promise.
171 My lips pour out praise,
for you teach me your statutes.
172 My tongue sings about your promise,
for all your commands are righteous.
173 May your hand be ready to help me,
for I have chosen your precepts.
174 I long for your salvation, LORD,
and your instruction is my delight.
175 Let me live, and I will praise you;
may your judgments help me.
176 I wander like a lost sheep;
seek your servant,
for I do not forget your commands.

A CRY FOR TRUTH AND PEACE

120 *A song of ascents.*
In my distress I called to the LORD,
and he answered me.
2 "LORD, rescue me
from lying lips
and a deceitful tongue."

3 What will he give you,
and what will he do to you,
you deceitful tongue?
4 A warrior's sharp arrows
with burning charcoal![A]

5 What misery that I have stayed
in Meshech,[B]
that I have lived among the tents
of Kedar![C]
6 I have dwelt too long
with those who hate peace.

E Eternal Perspective | *God's Protection*

NO HARM

"The LORD protects you; the LORD is a shelter right by your side. The sun will not strike you by day or the moon by night. The LORD will protect you from all harm; he will protect your life. The LORD will protect your coming and going both now and forever." Psalm 121:5-8

On the one hand, we read these sweeping assurances—six references to "protection" and the Lord being a "Protector" in this one short psalm.

On the other hand, we have countless examples from real life of faithful believers who have, in fact, experienced great harm in this life. What are we to conclude?

We have to read this psalm the way Jewish pilgrims understood it as they ascended the Mount of Olives in ancient times to worship at the temple. They were anticipating the coming of Messiah (Israel's Savior-King). They were singing longingly of the perfect and ultimate protection he would provide when he would rule in power.

For now, we take comfort in the truth that nothing can harm the soul of a child of God. And we find hope in the promise that when Christ comes again to rule, evil will be vanquished. Harm of every kind will be history.

For the next note on *Eternal Perspective*, see Psalm 139:1-3.

[A] **120:4** Lit *with coals of the broom bush* [B] **120:5** = a people far to the north of Palestine [C] **120:5** = a nomadic people of the desert to the southeast

7 I am for peace; but when I speak,
they are for war.

THE LORD OUR PROTECTOR

121 *A song of ascents.*
I lift my eyes toward the mountains.
Where will my help come from?
2 My help comes from the LORD,
the Maker of heaven and earth.

3 He will not allow your foot to slip;
your Protector will not slumber.
4 Indeed, the Protector of Israel
does not slumber or sleep.

5 The LORD protects you;
the LORD is a shelter right
by your side.[A]
6 The sun will not strike you by day
or the moon by night.

7 The LORD will protect you
from all harm;
he will protect your life.
8 The LORD will protect your coming
and going
both now and forever.

A PRAYER FOR JERUSALEM

122 *A song of ascents. Of David.*
I rejoiced with those who said
to me,
"Let us go to the house of the LORD."
2 Our feet were standing
within your gates, Jerusalem —

3 Jerusalem, built as a city should be,
solidly united,
4 where the tribes, the LORD's tribes, go up
to give thanks to the name of the LORD.
(This is an ordinance for Israel.)
5 There, thrones for judgment are placed,
thrones of the house of David.

6 Pray for the well-being[B] of Jerusalem:
"May those who love you be secure;
7 may there be peace within your walls,
security within your fortresses."
8 Because of my brothers and friends,
I will say, "May peace be in you."[C]
9 Because of the house of the LORD
our God,
I will pursue your prosperity.

LOOKING FOR GOD'S FAVOR

123 *A song of ascents.*
I lift my eyes to you,
the one enthroned in heaven.
2 Like a servant's eyes
on his master's hand,
like a servant girl's eyes
on her mistress's hand,
so our eyes are on the LORD our God
until he shows us favor.

3 Show us favor, LORD, show us favor,
for we've had more than enough
contempt.
4 We've had more than enough
scorn from the arrogant
and contempt from the proud.

THE LORD IS ON OUR SIDE

124 *A song of ascents. Of David.*
If the LORD had not been
on our side —
let Israel say —
2 If the LORD had not been on our side
when people attacked us,
3 then they would have
swallowed us alive
in their burning anger against us.
4 Then the water would have engulfed us;
the torrent would have swept over us;
5 the raging water would have swept
over us.

6 Blessed be the LORD,
who has not let us be ripped apart
by their teeth.
7 We have escaped like a bird
from the hunter's net;
the net is torn, and we have escaped.
8 Our help is in the name of the LORD,
the Maker of heaven and earth.

ISRAEL'S STABILITY

125 *A song of ascents.*
Those who trust in the LORD are
like Mount Zion.
It cannot be shaken; it remains forever.
2 The mountains surround Jerusalem
and the LORD surrounds his people,
both now and forever.

3 The scepter of the wicked
will not remain

[A] **121:5** Lit *is your shelter at your right hand* [B] **122:6** Or *peace* [C] **122:8** = Jerusalem

over the land allotted to the righteous,
so that the righteous will not apply
their hands to injustice.
4 Do what is good, LORD, to the good,
to those whose hearts are upright.
5 But as for those who turn aside
to crooked ways,
the LORD will banish them
with the evildoers.

Peace be with Israel.

ZION'S RESTORATION

126 *A song of ascents.*
When the LORD restored
the fortunes of Zion,[A]
we were like those who dream.
2 Our mouths were filled
with laughter then,
and our tongues with shouts of joy.
Then they said among the nations,
"The LORD has done great things
for them."
3 The LORD had done great things for us;
we were joyful.

4 Restore our fortunes,[B] LORD,
like watercourses in the Negev.
5 Those who sow in tears
will reap with shouts of joy.
6 Though one goes along weeping,
carrying the bag of seed,
he will surely come back with shouts
of joy,
carrying his sheaves.

THE BLESSING OF THE LORD

127 *A song of ascents. Of Solomon.*
Unless the LORD builds a house,
its builders labor over it in vain;
unless the LORD watches over a city,
the watchman stays alert in vain.
2 In vain you get up early
and stay up late,
working hard to have enough food —
yes, he gives sleep to the one he loves.[C]

3 Sons are indeed a heritage from the LORD,
offspring, a reward.
4 Like arrows in the hand of a warrior
are the sons born in one's youth.
5 Happy is the man who has filled
his quiver with them.
They will never be put to shame
when they speak with their enemies
at the city gate.

Rest and Reflection | *Avoiding Burnout*

SWEET SLEEP

"In vain you get up early and stay up late, working hard to have enough food—yes, he gives sleep to the one he loves." Psalm 127:2

Can an entire population be sleep-deprived? The Centers for Disease Control obviously thinks so. In 2011, it declared "insufficient sleep" a public health epidemic—a crisis every bit as deadly as obesity and smoking.

Perhaps you're nodding off to sleep as you read these words. Maybe you're one of the millions who routinely "burns the candle at both ends." The good news is you don't have to stay stuck in this vicious, exhausting cycle.

In this psalm, wise King Solomon reminds us that the Lord is Sovereign. As we lean on the truths that he reigns, sees, and supplies, we find we are able to go off duty. The sky isn't going to fall. The sun will come up tomorrow. In such sweet grace we are able to stop, unplug, relax, and rest.

If you feel pooped all the time, if you're having trouble resting, you might want to ask the giver of all good things to grant you deep sleep. It's amazing how much a good night's rest can restore your perspective and keep you going with joy.

For the next note on *Rest and Reflection*, see Psalm 139:23-24.

[A] **126:1** Or *LORD returned those of Zion who had been captives* [B] **126:4** Or *Return our captives* [C] **127:2** Or *yes, he gives such things to his loved ones while they sleep*

BLESSINGS FOR THOSE WHO FEAR GOD

128 *A song of ascents.*
How happy is everyone who fears
the LORD,
who walks in his ways!
2 You will surely eat
what your hands have worked for.
You will be happy,
and it will go well for you.
3 Your wife will be like a fruitful vine
within your house,
your children, like young olive trees
around your table.
4 In this very way
the man who fears the LORD
will be blessed.

5 May the LORD bless you from Zion,
so that you will see the prosperity
of Jerusalem
all the days of your life
6 and will see your children's children!

Peace be with Israel.

PROTECTION OF THE OPPRESSED

129 *A song of ascents.*
Since my youth they have often
attacked me —
let Israel say —
2 Since my youth they have often
attacked me,
but they have not prevailed against me.
3 Plowmen plowed over my back;
they made their furrows long.
4 The LORD is righteous;
he has cut the ropes of the wicked.

5 Let all who hate Zion
be driven back in disgrace.
6 Let them be like grass on the rooftops,
which withers before it grows up[A]
7 and can't even fill the hands of the reaper
or the arms of the one
who binds sheaves.
8 Then none who pass by will say,
"May the LORD's blessing be on you.
We bless you in the name of the LORD."

AWAITING REDEMPTION

130 *A song of ascents.*
Out of the depths I call
to you, LORD!
2 Lord, listen to my voice;
let your ears be attentive
to my cry for help.

3 LORD, if you kept an account
of iniquities,
Lord, who could stand?
4 But with you there is forgiveness,
so that you may be revered.

I wait for the LORD; I wait and put my hope in his word.
—Psalm 130:5

5 I wait for the LORD; I wait
and put my hope in his word.
6 I wait for the Lord
more than watchmen for the morning —
more than watchmen for the morning.

7 Israel, put your hope in the LORD.
For there is faithful love with the LORD,
and with him is redemption
in abundance.
8 And he will redeem Israel
from all its iniquities.

A CHILDLIKE SPIRIT

131 *A song of ascents. Of David.*
LORD, my heart is not proud;
my eyes are not haughty.
I do not get involved with things
too great or too wondrous for me.
2 Instead, I have calmed and quieted my
soul
like a weaned child with its mother;
my soul is like a weaned child.

3 Israel, put your hope in the LORD,
both now and forever.

DAVID AND ZION CHOSEN

132 *A song of ascents.*
LORD, remember David
and all the hardships he endured,
2 and how he swore
an oath to the LORD,
making a vow to the Mighty One
of Jacob:

[A] **129:6** Or *it can be pulled out*

3 "I will not enter my house
or get into my bed,
4 I will not allow my eyes to sleep
or my eyelids to slumber
5 until I find a place for the LORD,
a dwelling for the Mighty One of Jacob."

6 We heard of the ark in Ephrathah;[A]
we found it in the fields of Jaar.[B]
7 Let us go to his dwelling place;
let us worship at his footstool.
8 Rise up, LORD, come to
your resting place,
you and your powerful ark.
9 May your priests be clothed
with righteousness,
and may your faithful people shout
for joy.
10 For the sake of your servant David,
do not reject your anointed one.[C]

11 The LORD swore an oath to David,
a promise he will not abandon:
"I will set one of your offspring[D]
on your throne.
12 If your sons keep my covenant
and my decrees that I will teach them,
their sons will also sit on
your throne forever."

13 For the LORD has chosen Zion;
he has desired it for his home:
14 "This is my resting place forever;
I will make my home here
because I have desired it.
15 I will abundantly bless its food;
I will satisfy its needy with bread.
16 I will clothe its priests with salvation,
and its faithful people will shout
for joy.
17 There I will make a horn grow
for David;
I have prepared a lamp for
my anointed one.
18 I will clothe his enemies with shame,
but the crown he wears[E]
will be glorious."

LIVING IN HARMONY

133 *A song of ascents. Of David.*
How good and pleasant it is
when brothers live together
in harmony!
2 It is like fine oil on the head,
running down on the beard,
running down Aaron's beard
onto his robes.
3 It is like the dew of Hermon[F]
falling on the mountains of Zion.
For there the LORD has appointed
the blessing —
life forevermore.

CALL TO EVENING WORSHIP

134 *A song of ascents.*
Now bless the LORD,
all you servants of the LORD
who stand in the LORD's house at night!
2 Lift up your hands in the holy place
and bless the LORD!

3 May the LORD,
Maker of heaven and earth,
bless you from Zion.

THE LORD IS GREAT

135 Hallelujah!
Praise the name of the LORD.
Give praise, you servants of the LORD
2 who stand in the house of the LORD,
in the courts of the house of our God.
3 Praise the LORD, for the LORD is good;
sing praise to his name,
for it is delightful.
4 For the LORD has chosen Jacob
for himself,
Israel as his treasured possession.

5 For I know that the LORD is great;
our Lord is greater than all gods.
6 The LORD does whatever he pleases
in heaven and on earth,
in the seas and all the depths.
7 He causes the clouds to rise
from the ends of the earth.
He makes lightning for the rain
and brings the wind
from his storehouses.

8 He struck down the firstborn of Egypt,
both people and animals.
9 He sent signs and wonders
against you, Egypt,
against Pharaoh and all his officials.
10 He struck down many nations
and slaughtered mighty kings:

[A] **132:6** = Bethlehem [B] **132:6** = Kiriath-jearim [C] **132:10** = the king [D] **132:11** Lit *set the fruit of your belly* [E] **132:18** Lit *but on him his crown* [F] **133:3** The tallest mountain in the region, noted for its abundant precipitation

11 Sihon king of the Amorites,
Og king of Bashan,
and all the kings of Canaan.
12 He gave their land as an inheritance,
an inheritance to his people Israel.

13 LORD, your name endures forever,
your reputation, LORD,
through all generations.
14 For the LORD will vindicate his people
and have compassion on his servants.
15 The idols of the nations are of silver
and gold,
made by human hands.
16 They have mouths but cannot speak,
eyes, but cannot see.
17 They have ears but cannot hear;
indeed, there is no breath
in their mouths.
18 Those who make them are just like them,
as are all who trust in them.

19 House of Israel, bless the LORD!
House of Aaron, bless the LORD!
20 House of Levi, bless the LORD!
You who revere the LORD,
bless the LORD!
21 Blessed be the LORD from Zion;
he dwells in Jerusalem.
Hallelujah!

GOD'S LOVE IS ETERNAL

136 Give thanks to the LORD,
for he is good.
His faithful love endures forever.
2 Give thanks to the God of gods.
His faithful love endures forever.
3 Give thanks to the Lord of lords.
His faithful love endures forever.
4 He alone does great wonders.
His faithful love endures forever.
5 He made the heavens skillfully.
His faithful love endures forever.
6 He spread the land on the waters.
His faithful love endures forever.
7 He made the great lights:
His faithful love endures forever.
8 the sun to rule by day,
His faithful love endures forever.
9 the moon and stars to rule by night.
His faithful love endures forever.
10 He struck the firstborn
of the Egyptians
His faithful love endures forever.
11 and brought Israel out from among
them
His faithful love endures forever.

Thanksgiving and Contentment | *Gratitude*

WITH DEEP APPRECIATION

"Give thanks to the LORD, for he is good. His faithful love endures forever." Psalm 136:1

Parents make their children write thank-you notes after Christmas and birthdays, not because Aunt Sue really *needs* a thank-you note (she is, however, probably looking for one). They do it because it's the right thing to do. They also do it because children aren't naturally grateful. They need to learn the attitude of gratitude, and they need to develop the art of expressing that appreciation.

It works like this. Someone was generous when she didn't have to be. Someone gifted you, showed favor to you, or helped you in some way when you were in need. The thankful person pauses and recognizes such kindness. Contemplating these sacrificial acts and generous blessings can be moving, even overwhelming. But thankful people don't stop with mere realizations. They understand that thankfulness needs to culminate in expression.

Spend some time today thinking about the many, many ways God and others have shown kindness and lavished grace on you. Then—either verbally or in writing—speak up. Share from your heart about what those things mean to you. See if, in the process you don't become more thankful and generous, too.

For the next note on *Thanksgiving and Contentment*, see Isaiah 1:18.

12 with a strong hand
and outstretched arm.
His faithful love endures forever.
13 He divided the Red Sea
His faithful love endures forever.
14 and led Israel through,
His faithful love endures forever.
15 but hurled Pharaoh
and his army into the Red Sea.
His faithful love endures forever.
16 He led his people in the wilderness.
His faithful love endures forever.
17 He struck down great kings
His faithful love endures forever.
18 and slaughtered famous kings —
His faithful love endures forever.
19 Sihon king of the Amorites
His faithful love endures forever.
20 and Og king of Bashan —
His faithful love endures forever.
21 and gave their land as an inheritance,
His faithful love endures forever.
22 an inheritance to Israel his servant.
His faithful love endures forever.
23 He remembered us in our humiliation
His faithful love endures forever.
24 and rescued us from our foes.
His faithful love endures forever.
25 He gives food to every creature.
His faithful love endures forever.
26 Give thanks to the God of heaven!
His faithful love endures forever.

LAMENT OF THE EXILES

137 By the rivers of Babylon —
there we sat down and wept
when we remembered Zion.
2 There we hung up our lyres
on the poplar trees,
3 for our captors there asked us for songs,
and our tormentors, for rejoicing:
"Sing us one of the songs of Zion."

4 How can we sing the LORD's song
on foreign soil?
5 If I forget you, Jerusalem,
may my right hand forget its skill.
6 May my tongue stick to the roof
of my mouth
if I do not remember you,
if I do not exalt Jerusalem
as my greatest joy!
7 Remember, LORD,
what the Edomites said
that day[A] at Jerusalem:
"Destroy it! Destroy it
down to its foundations!"
8 Daughter Babylon,
doomed to destruction,
happy is the one
who pays you back
what you have done to us.
9 Happy is he who takes your little ones
and dashes them against the rocks.

A THANKFUL HEART

138 *Of David.*
I will give you thanks
with all my heart;
I will sing your praise
before the heavenly beings.[B]
2 I will bow down
toward your holy temple
and give thanks to your name
for your constant love and truth.
You have exalted your name
and your promise above
everything else.[C]
3 On the day I called,
you answered me;
you increased strength within me.[D]

4 All the kings on earth
will give you thanks, LORD,
when they hear
what you have promised.[E]
5 They will sing of the LORD's ways,
for the LORD's glory is great.
6 Though the LORD is exalted,
he takes note of the humble;
but he knows the haughty
from a distance.

7 If I walk into the thick of danger,
you will preserve my life
from the anger of my enemies.
You will extend your hand;
your right hand will save me.
8 The LORD will fulfill his purpose
for me.
LORD, your faithful love
endures forever;
do not abandon the work
of your hands.

[A] **137:7** The day Jerusalem fell to the Babylonians in 586 BC [B] **138:1** Or *before the gods*, or *before judges*, or *before kings*; Hb *elohim* [C] **138:2** Or *You have exalted your promise above all your name* [D] **138:3** Hb obscure [E] **138:4** Lit *hear the words of your mouth*

THE ALL-KNOWING, EVER-PRESENT GOD

139 *For the choir director. A psalm of David.*
LORD, you have searched me
and known me.
2 You know when I sit down and when
I stand up;
you understand my thoughts
from far away.
3 You observe my travels and my rest;
you are aware of all my ways.
4 Before a word is on my tongue,
you know all about it, LORD.
5 You have encircled me;
you have placed your hand on me.
6 This wondrous knowledge is beyond me.
It is lofty; I am unable to reach it.

7 Where can I go to escape your Spirit?
Where can I flee from your presence?
8 If I go up to heaven, you are there;
if I make my bed in Sheol, you are there.
9 If I live at the eastern horizon
or settle at the western limits,[A]
10 even there your hand will lead me;
your right hand will hold on to me.
11 If I say, "Surely the darkness
will hide me,
and the light around me
will be night" —
12 even the darkness is not dark to you.
The night shines like the day;
darkness and light are alike to you.

13 For it was you who created
my inward parts;[B]
you knit me together
in my mother's womb.
14 I will praise you
because I have been remarkably
and wondrously made.[C,D]
Your works are wondrous,
and I know this very well.
15 My bones were not hidden from you
when I was made in secret,
when I was formed in the depths
of the earth.
16 Your eyes saw me when I was formless;
all my days were written in your book
and planned
before a single one of them began.

17 God, how precious[E] your thoughts are
to me;
how vast their sum is!
18 If I counted them,
they would outnumber the grains
of sand;
when I wake up,[F] I am still with you.

19 God, if only you would kill the wicked —

Eternal Perspective | *God's Knowledge/Omniscience*

HE KNOWS

"LORD, you have searched me and known me. You know when I sit down and when I stand up; you understand my thoughts from far away. You observe my travels and my rest; you are aware of all my ways." Psalm 139:1-3

Be honest with God, we're often exhorted—confess your sins to him, tell him your troubles and struggles, all your concerns and fears, and, of course, let him know exactly what you need.

Why do we do such things when God is all-knowing? We'll never admit something that shocks God. It's not like we've fallen off his radar. He certainly doesn't need updates. As David noted, God is aware of every detail: where you're sitting, what's in your pocket, and who or what is on your mind. He knows the precise temptation you'll face at 10:32 tomorrow morning and what you'll be doing at 10:33.

So many things we don't know: what the future holds, what to say, how to proceed, where the money will come from, why we're stuck. The best news and the truth that can give us hope when we're in such places? God *knows*.

For the next note on *Eternal Perspective*, see Psalm 144:3.

[A] **139:9** Lit *I take up the wings of the dawn; I dwell at the end of the sea* [B] **139:13** Lit *my kidneys* [C] **139:14** DSS, some LXX mss, Syr, Jer read *because you are remarkable and wonderful* [D] **139:14** Hb obscure [E] **139:17** Or *difficult* [F] **139:18** Some Hb mss read *I come to an end*

you bloodthirsty men, stay away
from me —
20 who invoke you deceitfully.
Your enemies swear by you falsely.
21 LORD, don't I hate those who hate you,
and detest those who rebel against you?
22 I hate them with extreme hatred;
I consider them my enemies.

23 Search me, God, and know my heart;
test me and know my concerns.
24 See if there is any offensive[A] way in me;
lead me in the everlasting way.

PRAYER FOR RESCUE

For the choir director. A psalm of David.
Rescue me, LORD, from evil men.
Keep me safe from violent men
2 who plan evil in their hearts.
They stir up wars all day long.
3 They make their tongues
as sharp as a snake's bite;
viper's venom is under their lips. *Selah*

4 Protect me, LORD,
from the power of the wicked.
Keep me safe from violent men
who plan to make me stumble.[B]
5 The proud hide a trap with ropes for me;
they spread a net along the path
and set snares for me. *Selah*

6 I say to the LORD, "You are my God."
Listen, LORD, to my cry for help.
7 LORD, my Lord, my strong Savior,
you shield my head on the day of battle.
8 LORD, do not grant the desires
of the wicked;
do not let them achieve their goals.
Otherwise, they will become proud.
Selah

9 When those who surround me
rise up,[C]
may the trouble their lips cause
overwhelm them.
10 Let hot coals fall on them.
Let them be thrown into the fire,
into the abyss, never again to rise.
11 Do not let a slanderer stay in the land.
Let evil relentlessly[D] hunt down
a violent man.

12 I[E] know that the LORD upholds
the just cause of the poor,
justice for the needy.

R Rest and Reflection | *Identifying the Issue/Difficulty*

GETTING TO THE ROOT ISSUE

"Search me, God, and know my heart; test me and know my concerns. See if there is any offensive way in me; lead me in the everlasting way." Psalm 139:23-24

At the end of Psalm 139, David asks God to "search" him. The idea is that God might put David's heart in his divine MRI and rigorously scan it for *anything* that's unhealthy.

Such an idea would be utterly terrifying—unthinkable, in fact—if not for the rest of the psalm. Before making this request, David has marveled that God: (a) knows him completely (139:1-6); (b) is with him constantly (139:7-12); (c) designed him "wondrously" (139:13-16); and (d) thinks of him continually (139:17-18).

Because of these realities, David isn't terrified by the thought of a divine checkup; in fact he welcomes it! He realizes he is completely safe. He won't be blasted by blunt truth. He is, rather, in the hands of One who is full of "grace and truth" (Jn 1:14,17).

We can welcome God's spotlight on our inner thoughts and desires. This is often the first step to healing and restoration

For the next note on *Rest and Reflection*, see Proverbs 1:5.

[A] **139:24** Or *idolatrous* [B] **140:4** Lit *to trip up my steps* [C] **140:9** Lit *Head of those who surround me* [D] **140:11** Hb obscure
[E] **140:12** Alt Hb tradition reads *You*

13 Surely the righteous will praise
your name;
the upright will live in your presence.

PROTECTION FROM SIN AND SINNERS

141 *A psalm of David.*
LORD, I call on you; hurry to help me.
Listen to my voice when I call on you.
2 May my prayer be set before you
as incense,
the raising of my hands
as the evening offering.

3 LORD, set up a guard for my mouth;
keep watch at the door of my lips.
4 Do not let my heart turn
to any evil thing
or perform wicked acts
with men who commit sin.
Do not let me feast
on their delicacies.
5 Let the righteous one strike me —
it is an act of faithful love;
let him rebuke me —
it is oil for my head;
let me[A] not refuse it.
Even now my prayer is against
the evil acts of the wicked.[B]
6 When their rulers[C] will be thrown off
the sides of a cliff,
the people[D] will listen to my words,
for they are pleasing.

7 As when one plows and breaks up
the soil,
turning up rocks,
so our[E] bones have been scattered
at the mouth of Sheol.

8 But my eyes look to you, LORD, my Lord.
I seek refuge in you; do not let me die.[F]
9 Protect me from the trap they have set
for me,
and from the snares of evildoers.
10 Let the wicked fall into their own nets,
while I pass by safely.

A CRY OF DISTRESS

142 *A* Maskil *of David. When he was in the cave. A prayer.*
1 I cry aloud to the LORD;
I plead aloud to the LORD for mercy.

Relationships | *Controlling Speech*

A FORCE FOR GOOD

"LORD, set up a guard for my mouth; keep watch at the door of my lips." Psalm 141:3

A surgeon can take a scalpel and use it to *save* a life. A convict in a prison hospital can grab that same scalpel and use it to *take* a life.

In a similar way, "death and life are in the power of the tongue" (Pr 18:21). This means we can choose to speak words of truth and encouragement into the souls of others—imparting life and hope. Or we can thoughtlessly and recklessly spew lies and demeaning words—showering death onto all those around us.

Recognizing this grave danger and great opportunity, David prays that God might help him guard his speech. This is comparable to the New Testament idea of offering all the parts of one's self (mouth included) to God as "weapons for righteousness" (Rm 6:13).

How's that for a radical idea? Deliberately choosing in every encounter to use your mouth as a force for good. Deciding in advance not to let a hurtful or negative word pass through your lips out into the world where it can do damage.

Begin doing that today, and watch God restore the souls of those around you.

For the next note on *Relationships*, see Proverbs 9:9.

[A] 141:5 Lit *my head* [B] 141:5 Lit *of them* [C] 141:6 Or *judges* [D] 141:6 Lit *cliff, and they* [E] 141:7 DSS reads *my*; some LXX mss, Syr read *their* [F] 141:8 Or *not pour out my life*

2 I pour out my complaint before him;
I reveal my trouble to him.
3 Although my spirit is weak within me,
you know my way.

Along this path I travel
they have hidden a trap for me.
4 Look to the right and see:[A]
no one stands up for me;
there is no refuge for me;
no one cares about me.

5 I cry to you, LORD;
I say, "You are my shelter,
my portion in the land of the living."
6 Listen to my cry,
for I am very weak.
Rescue me from those
who pursue me,
for they are too strong for me.
7 Free me from prison
so that I can praise your name.
The righteous will gather around me
because you deal generously with me.

A CRY FOR HELP

143 *A psalm of David.*
LORD, hear my prayer.
In your faithfulness listen to my plea,
and in your righteousness answer me.
2 Do not bring your servant into judgment,
for no one alive is righteous in your sight.

3 For the enemy has pursued me,
crushing me to the ground,
making me live in darkness
like those long dead.
4 My spirit is weak within me;
my heart is overcome with dismay.

5 I remember the days of old;
I meditate on all you have done;
I reflect on the work of your hands.
6 I spread out my hands to you;
I am like parched land before you. *Selah*

7 Answer me quickly, LORD;
my spirit fails.
Don't hide your face from me,
or I will be like those
going down to the Pit.
8 Let me experience
your faithful love in the morning,
for I trust in you.
Reveal to me the way I should go
because I appeal to you.
9 Rescue me from my enemies, LORD;
I come to you for protection.[B]
10 Teach me to do your will,
for you are my God.

HOLY DESPERATION

"I spread out my hands to you; I am like parched land before you. Selah. Answer me quickly, LORD; my spirit fails. Don't hide your face from me, or I will be like those going down to the Pit." Psalm 143:6-7

Most of the songs sung and most of the prayers prayed at churches this weekend will be upbeat. They will be full of victorious language.

While focusing on the positive is great, sometimes singing only happy songs to God is inauthentic. What about those times in life when a gritty tragedy, not a feel-good comedy, is playing in the theater of our lives?

The psalms recognize this reality and never depict anyone pretending that life is better than it is. Consider Psalm 143. Here, David feels utterly desperate, and he tells God as much. He doesn't edit his prayer or spin his feelings to make them more suitable to people who might be uncomfortable with messy truths. This is what C. S. Lewis meant when he said, "We must lay before God what is in us, not what ought to be in us."

Whenever we pray, let's make sure we pray honestly.

For the next note on *Support*, see Psalm 145:4.

[A] **142:4** DSS, LXX, Syr, Vg, Tg read *I look to the right and I see* [B] **143:9** One Hb ms, LXX; some Hb mss read *I cover myself to you*

May your gracious Spirit
lead me on level ground.

11 For your name's sake, LORD,
let me live.
In your righteousness deliver me
from trouble,
12 and in your faithful love
destroy my enemies.
Wipe out all those who attack me,
for I am your servant.

A KING'S PRAYER

144 *Of David.*
Blessed be the LORD, my rock
who trains my hands for battle
and my fingers for warfare.
2 He is my faithful love
and my fortress,
my stronghold and my deliverer.
He is my shield,
and I take refuge in him;
he subdues my people[A] under me.

3 LORD, what is a human that you care
for him,
a son of man[B] that you think of him?
4 A human is like a breath;
his days are like a passing shadow.
5 LORD, part your heavens and come down.
Touch the mountains,
and they will smoke.
6 Flash your lightning and scatter the foe;[C]
shoot your arrows and rout them.
7 Reach down[D] from on high;
rescue me from deep water,
and set me free
from the grasp of foreigners
8 whose mouths speak lies,
whose right hands are deceptive.

9 God, I will sing a new song to you;
I will play on a ten-stringed harp
for you —
10 the one who gives victory to kings,
who frees his servant David
from the deadly sword.
11 Set me free and rescue me
from foreigners
whose mouths speak lies,
whose right hands are deceptive.

12 Then our sons will be like plants
nurtured in their youth,
our daughters, like corner pillars
that are carved in the palace style.
13 Our storehouses will be full,
supplying all kinds of produce;

E Eternal Perspective | *God's Knowledge/Omniscience*

DOES GOD SEE?

"LORD, what is a human that you care for him, a son of man that you think of him?" Psalm 144:3

In a big, hectic world filled with big, hairy problems, we can easily feel invisible. Perhaps you feel that way today—as though God doesn't see you, because, well, he has much bigger issues to deal with than your personal struggles.

David was king of Israel. Time and again, he had seen God's amazing acts. He had been empowered by the Lord to kill lions and giants. He had been enabled to outsmart and outlast his other enemies.

As he prepared to lead his troops into battle again, David didn't take God's faithfulness for granted; instead, he was filled with humility and awe as he contemplated God's history of helping. David marveled at how God both *thinks* of and *cares* for him. The word *care* suggests intimate knowledge. This pictures a God who has his people constantly in mind, and who watches us, as it were, from the kitchen window of heaven. He gazes at us, sees our struggles, and knows exactly what we need.

Today, whenever you begin feeling invisible, remember this image.

For the next note on *Eternal Perspective*, see Psalm 145:8-9.

[A] **144:2** Some Hb mss, DSS, Aq, Syr, Tg, Jer read *subdues peoples*; 2Sm 22:48; Ps 18:47 [B] **144:3** Or *a mere mortal* [C] **144:6** Lit *scatter them* [D] **144:7** Lit *down your hands*

our flocks will increase by thousands
and tens of thousands in
our open fields.
14 Our cattle will be well fed.[A]
There will be no breach in the walls,
no going into captivity,[B]
and no cry of lament in
our public squares.
15 Happy are the people with
such blessings.
Happy are the people whose God is
the LORD.

PRAISING GOD'S GREATNESS

145 *A hymn of David.*
I[C] exalt you, my God the King,
and bless your name forever and ever.
2 I will bless you every day;
I will praise your name forever and ever.

3 The LORD is great and is highly praised;
his greatness is unsearchable.
4 One generation will declare your works
to the next
and will proclaim your mighty acts.
5 I[D] will speak of your splendor and
glorious majesty
and[E] your wondrous works.
6 They will proclaim the power
of your awe-inspiring acts,
and I will declare your greatness.[F]
7 They will give a testimony
of your great goodness
and will joyfully sing
of your righteousness.

8 The LORD is gracious
and compassionate,
slow to anger and great in faithful love.
9 The LORD is good to everyone;
his compassion rests on all he has made.
10 All you have made
will thank you, LORD;
the[G] faithful will bless you.
11 They will speak of the glory
of your kingdom
and will declare your might,
12 informing all people
of your mighty acts
and of the glorious splendor
of your[H] kingdom.
13 Your kingdom is
an everlasting kingdom;
your rule is for all generations.
The LORD is faithful in all his words
and gracious in all his actions.[I]

S Support | *Mentors*

PASS IT ON

"One generation will declare your works to the next and will proclaim your mighty acts." Psalm 145:4

Throughout Scripture, we find this teaching for parents and grandparents: By all means, tell your kids and grandkids about God. Pass on the stories and lessons of the Bible. Share your own spiritual experiences. Leave a legacy of faith.

The value of this is inestimable. Not only does this practice point the next generation to ultimate realities, but think about what it does in your own heart. When you relive life-changing moments, recall answered prayers, and rehearse the faithful acts of God, your heart will overflow with gratitude and praise.

Three reminders: (1) The best spiritual instruction happens informally in the home, not formally in the church. Don't offload this responsibility onto others. (2) You can start new traditions with your own family. (3) Notice the contagious power of this habit. David says, "*I* will speak of your splendor and glorious majesty and your wondrous works. *They* will proclaim the power of your awe-inspiring acts, and *I* will declare your greatness" (Ps 145:5-6).

For the next note on *Support*, see Proverbs 11:14.

[A] **144:14** Or *will bear heavy loads*, or *will be pregnant* [B] **144:14** Or *be no plague, no miscarriage* [C] **145:1** The lines of this poem form an acrostic. [D] **145:5** LXX, Syr read *They* [E] **145:5** LXX, Syr read *and they will tell of* [F] **145:6** Alt Hb tradition, Jer read *great deeds* [G] **145:10** Lit *your* [H] **145:12** LXX, Syr, Jer; MT reads *his* [I] **145:13** One Hb ms, DSS, LXX, Syr; some Hb mss omit *The LORD is faithful in all his words and gracious in all his actions.*

14 The LORD helps all who fall;
he raises up all who are oppressed.[A]
15 All eyes look to you,
and you give them their food at the
proper time.
16 You open your hand
and satisfy the desire
of every living thing.

17 The LORD is righteous in all his ways
and faithful in all his acts.
18 The LORD is near all
who call out to him,
all who call out to him with integrity.
19 He fulfills the desires of those
who fear him;
he hears their cry for help and saves them.
20 The LORD guards all those
who love him,
but he destroys all the wicked.
21 My mouth will declare the LORD's praise;
let every living thing
bless his holy name forever and ever.

THE GOD OF COMPASSION

146 Hallelujah!
My soul, praise the LORD.
2 I will praise the LORD all my life;
I will sing to my God as long as I live.
3 Do not trust in nobles,
in a son of man,[B] who cannot save.
4 When his breath[C] leaves him,
he returns to the ground;
on that day his plans die.

5 Happy is the one whose help is the God
of Jacob,
whose hope is in the LORD his God,
6 the Maker of heaven and earth,
the sea and everything in them.
He remains faithful forever,
7 executing justice for the exploited
and giving food to the hungry.
The LORD frees prisoners.
8 The LORD opens the eyes of the blind.
The LORD raises up those
who are oppressed.[A]
The LORD loves the righteous.
9 The LORD protects resident aliens
and helps the fatherless
and the widow,
but he frustrates the ways
of the wicked.

10 The LORD reigns forever;
Zion, your God reigns
for all generations.
Hallelujah!

Eternal Perspective | *God's Compassion*

HIS GREAT LOVE

"The LORD is gracious and compassionate, slow to anger and great in faithful love. The LORD is good to everyone; his compassion rests on all he has made." Psalm 145:8-9

The Hebrew word for "compassion" is identical to the one for "womb." Some scholars speculate that God's compassion reflects the maternal affection and concern a thrilled mother-to-be has for the developing life inside her.

We all know that expectant moms get a major case of "the feels." They weep for joy over sonogram photos and glow with pride as their bellies grow. But maternal compassion is much more than mere emotion. Expectant moms also turn into mama bears. They do whatever it takes to protect and provide for their unborn children. They forego certain activities. They avoid certain environments. They take prenatal vitamins and natural supplements. They change their diets, refusing to ingest any food or drink or medicine that might adversely affect their growing babies.

The next time you see a pregnant woman rubbing her belly, think of how much more God loves each of his children—you included.

For the next note on *Eternal Perspective*, see Proverbs 17:22.

[A] **145:14; 146:8** Lit *bowed down* [B] **146:3** Or *a mere mortal* [C] **146:4** Or *spirit*

GOD RESTORES JERUSALEM

147 Hallelujah!
How good it is to sing to our God,
for praise is pleasant and lovely.

2 The LORD rebuilds Jerusalem;
he gathers Israel's exiled people.
3 He heals the brokenhearted
and bandages their wounds.
4 He counts the number of the stars;
he gives names to all of them.
5 Our Lord is great, vast in power;
his understanding is infinite.[A]
6 The LORD helps the oppressed
but brings the wicked to the ground.

7 Sing to the LORD with thanksgiving;
play the lyre to our God,
8 who covers the sky with clouds,
prepares rain for the earth,
and causes grass to grow on the hills.
9 He provides the animals
with their food,
and the young ravens,
what they cry for.

10 He is not impressed by the strength
of a horse;
he does not value the power
of a warrior.[B]
11 The LORD values those who fear him,
those who put their hope
in his faithful love.

12 Exalt the LORD, Jerusalem;
praise your God, Zion!
13 For he strengthens the bars
of your city gates
and blesses your children within you.
14 He endows your territory
with prosperity;[C]
he satisfies you with the finest wheat.

15 He sends his command
throughout the earth;
his word runs swiftly.
16 He spreads snow like wool;
he scatters frost like ashes;
17 he throws his hailstones like crumbs.
Who can withstand his cold?
18 He sends his word and melts them;
he unleashes his winds,[D]
and the water flows.
19 He declares his word to Jacob,
his statutes and judgments to Israel.
20 He has not done this for every nation;
they do not know his judgments.
Hallelujah!

Hallelujah! Praise the LORD from the heavens; praise him in the heights.
—Psalm 148:1

CREATION'S PRAISE OF THE LORD

148 Hallelujah!
Praise the LORD from the heavens;
praise him in the heights.
2 Praise him, all his angels;
praise him, all his heavenly armies.
3 Praise him, sun and moon;
praise him, all you shining stars.
4 Praise him, highest heavens,
and you waters above the heavens.
5 Let them praise the name of the LORD,
for he commanded,
and they were created.
6 He set them in position
forever and ever;
he gave an order that will never
pass away.

7 Praise the LORD from the earth,
all sea monsters and ocean depths,
8 lightning[E] and hail, snow and cloud,
stormy wind that executes
his command,
9 mountains and all hills,
fruit trees and all cedars,
10 wild animals and all cattle,
creatures that crawl and flying birds,
11 kings of the earth and all peoples,
princes and all judges of the earth,
12 young men as well as young women,
old and young together.
13 Let them praise the name of the LORD,
for his name alone is exalted.
His majesty covers heaven and earth.
14 He has raised up a horn
for his people,

[A] **147:5** Lit *understanding has no number* [B] **147:10** Lit *the legs of the man* [C] **147:14** Or *peace* [D] **147:18** Or *breath*
[E] **148:8** Or *fire*

resulting in praise to all
his faithful ones,
to the Israelites, the people
close to him.
Hallelujah!

PRAISE FOR GOD'S TRIUMPH

149 Hallelujah!
Sing to the LORD a new song,
his praise in the assembly
of the faithful.
2 Let Israel celebrate its Maker;
let the children of Zion rejoice
in their King.
3 Let them praise his name with dancing
and make music to him
with tambourine and lyre.
4 For the LORD takes pleasure
in his people;
he adorns the humble with salvation.
5 Let the faithful celebrate
in triumphal glory;
let them shout for joy on their beds.

6 Let the exaltation of God be
in their mouths[A]
and a double-edged sword
in their hands,
7 inflicting vengeance
on the nations
and punishment on the peoples,
8 binding their kings with chains
and their dignitaries
with iron shackles,
9 carrying out the judgment
decreed against them.
This honor is for all his faithful people.
Hallelujah!

PRAISE THE LORD

150 Hallelujah!
Praise God in his sanctuary.
Praise him in his mighty expanse.
2 Praise him for his powerful acts;
praise him for his abundant greatness.

3 Praise him with trumpet blast;
praise him with harp and lyre.
4 Praise him with tambourine and dance;
praise him with strings and flute.
5 Praise him with resounding cymbals;
praise him with clashing cymbals.

6 Let everything that breathes
praise the LORD.
Hallelujah!

[A] **149:6** Lit *throat*

Proverbs—In the thousand decisions that come at us each day, we want to live well, to do what is right, and enjoy the blessings that come from living God's way. But to know what to do in specific daily circumstances can be difficult, and even more difficult to know how to teach our children how to be wise. Enter Proverbs. Using brief, pithy sayings, it teaches timeless wisdom on a variety of important topics.

The wisdom of Proverbs reminds us to keep our priorities straight and to aspire to be a person of character. The kind of person who makes decisions based on what is right, not on what is attractive or convenient. The kind of person who avoids folly and practices the fear of the Lord, the basis for all wisdom (1:7). Unless we are building our lives on the foundation of a reverent, trusting relationship with God, we will never find true wisdom.

Proverbs is best read in small doses so that the beauty and wisdom of each proverb can shine through. Even so, the collection must be interpreted as a whole, since each proverb presents one nugget of truth. As you read, allow the book of Proverbs along with the rest of Scripture to guide you in interpreting and applying each individual proverb.

PROVERBS

AUTHOR: The bulk of Proverbs was written by Solomon, the wisest man who ever lived (2Ch 1:7-12). The last two chapters are credited to Agur and Lemuel.

DATE WRITTEN: Chapters 1–24 were likely written during the reign of Solomon, 970–931 BC. Chapters 25–29 were Solomon's proverbs that were collected by King Hezekiah, 716–687 BC. Since nothing is known about Agur and Lemuel, we cannot date their proverbs.

ORIGINAL AUDIENCE: The Israelites

SETTING: Solomon's reign was the high point of Israel's peace and prosperity. They were ruled by a wise king, enjoyed great wealth, and were important on the international scene (1Kg 4:20-25). Best of all, they finally possessed the land of promise and had a permanent structure in which God dwelled: the temple.

PURPOSE FOR WRITING: Proverbs are brief, catchy sayings that teach us how to live well. They describe in a memorable phrase what is generally true—the way life tends to work. As with every genre of literature in the Bible, we need to read the book as it was intended to be read. Proverbs are aphorisms or maxims. They are truths based on observation of life from a God-centered worldview. Each one should be savored, meditated on. The images should be enjoyed for their clever comparisons, and the parallel structure appreciated for the way it uses contrasting and complementary thoughts to build on the proverb's meaning.

OUTLINE:

1. A Father's Advice to His Son (1:1–9:18)

   Wisdom and wealth contrasted (1:1–3:20)

   Worthy conduct described (3:21–4:27)

   Lust, idleness, and deceit warned against (5:1–7:27)

   Wisdom personified (8:1–9:18)

2. The Proverbs of Solomon (10:1–29:27)

   Collected proverbs (10:1–22:16)

   Wise sayings (22:17–24:34)

   Hezekiah's collection (25:1–29:27)

3. Other Proverbs (30:1–31:31)

   Words of Agur (30:1-33)

   Words of Lemuel (31:1-9)

   A noble wife (31:10-31)

KEY VERSES:

"Trust in the LORD with all your heart, and do not rely on your own understanding; in all your ways know him, and he will make your paths straight." –Proverbs 3:5-6

RESTORATION THEMES

R	Rest and Reflection	*Listening and Learning—1:5* *Identifying the Issue/Difficulty—20:27*
E	Eternal Perspective	*Biblical Joy—17:22*
S	Support	*Advice/Counsel—11:14* *Humility—15:33* *Accountability—18:1* *Mentors—19:20* *Openness with Others—27:17*
T	Thanksgiving and Contentment	*For the next note, see Isaiah 1:18.*
O	Other-centeredness	*Encouraging—Proverbs 12:25*
R	Relationships	*Mentoring—9:9* *Relating to Coworkers—12:24* *Building Positive Relationships—13:20* *Making Amends—14:9* *Building Healthy Friendships—18:24* *Relating to Children—22:6* *Relating to Friends—27:6* *Admitting Wrongs—28:13*
E	Exercise of Faith	*Trusting God—3:5-6* *Guarding the Heart—4:23*

THE PURPOSE OF PROVERBS

1 The proverbs of Solomon son of David,
king of Israel:
2 For learning wisdom and discipline;
for understanding insightful sayings;
3 for receiving prudent instruction
in righteousness, justice, and integrity;
4 for teaching shrewdness
to the inexperienced,[A]
knowledge and discretion
to a young man —
5 let a wise person listen
and increase learning,
and let a discerning person
obtain guidance —
6 for understanding a proverb
or a parable,[B]
the words of the wise, and their riddles.

7 The fear of the LORD
is the beginning of knowledge;
fools despise wisdom and discipline.

AVOID THE PATH OF THE VIOLENT

8 Listen, my son,
to your father's instruction,
and don't reject
your mother's teaching,
9 for they will be a garland of favor
on your head
and pendants[C] around your neck.
10 My son, if sinners entice you,
don't be persuaded.
11 If they say — "Come with us!
Let's set an ambush and kill someone.[D]
Let's attack some innocent person
just for fun![E]
12 Let's swallow them alive, like Sheol,
whole, like those who go down
to the Pit.
13 We'll find all kinds of valuable property
and fill our houses with plunder.
14 Throw in your lot with us,
and we'll all share the loot"[F] —
15 my son, don't travel that road
with them
or set foot on their path,
16 because their feet run toward evil
and they hurry to shed blood.
17 It is useless to spread a net
where any bird can see it,
18 but they set an ambush
to kill themselves;[G]
they attack their own lives.
19 Such are the paths of all who make
profit dishonestly;

Rest and Reflection | *Listening and Learning*

WE'RE NEVER DONE GROWING

"Let a wise person listen and increase learning, and let a discerning person obtain guidance." Proverbs 1:5

Widely regarded as the wisest man ever to live, King Solomon authored some three thousand pithy maxims about life (1Kg 4:32). At some point, the Holy Spirit guided him to select a few hundred of these insightful sayings and compile them into what we know as the book of Proverbs.

Solomon's primary goal was to teach "shrewdness to the inexperienced" (Pr 1:4). He wanted to help naïve young people avoid the dangers of a foolish life. We see here, however, that he also wanted the wise to "listen and increase learning."

This is a great reminder that we're never done growing. Wisdom isn't like getting a degree (and thinking, *I don't have to learn any more*). It's a lifetime of "continuing ed." We're called to "live" wisdom habitually, not think about it occasionally.

Ask the God of all wisdom to help you cultivate this invaluable character trait. Ask him to help you learn how to take his eternal truth and press it down into the corners and edges of your everyday life.

For the next note on *Rest and Reflection*, see Proverbs 20:27.

[A] **1:4** Or *simple*, or *gullible* [B] **1:6** Or *an enigma* [C] **1:9** Lit *chains* [D] **1:11** Lit *Let's ambush for blood* [E] **1:11** Lit *person for no reason* [F] **1:14** Lit *us; one bag will be for all of us* [G] **1:18** Lit *they ambush for their blood*

it takes the lives of those
who receive it.[A]

WISDOM'S PLEA

20 Wisdom calls out in the street;
she makes her voice heard
in the public squares.
21 She cries out above[B] the commotion;
she speaks at the entrance
of the city gates:
22 "How long, inexperienced ones,
will you love ignorance?
How long will you mockers
enjoy mocking
and you fools hate knowledge?
23 If you respond to my warning,[C]
then I will pour out my spirit on you
and teach you my words.
24 Since I called out and you refused,
extended my hand and no one
paid attention,
25 since you neglected all my counsel
and did not accept my correction,
26 I, in turn, will laugh at your calamity.
I will mock when terror strikes you,
27 when terror strikes you like a storm
and your calamity comes
like a whirlwind,
when trouble and stress overcome you.
28 Then they will call me,
but I won't answer;
they will search for me, but won't
find me.
29 Because they hated knowledge,
didn't choose to fear the LORD,
30 were not interested in my counsel,
and rejected all my correction,
31 they will eat the fruit of their way
and be glutted with their own schemes.
32 For the apostasy of the inexperienced
will kill them,
and the complacency of fools
will destroy them.
33 But whoever listens to me
will live securely
and be undisturbed by the dread
of danger."

WISDOM'S WORTH

2 My son, if you accept my words
and store up my commands within you,
2 listening closely[D] to wisdom
and directing your heart
to understanding;
3 furthermore, if you call out to insight
and lift your voice to understanding,
4 if you seek it like silver
and search for it like hidden treasure,
5 then you will understand the fear
of the LORD
and discover the knowledge of God.
6 For the LORD gives wisdom;
from his mouth come knowledge
and understanding.
7 He stores up success[E] for the upright;
He is a shield for those who live
with integrity
8 so that he may guard the paths
of justice
and protect the way
of his faithful followers.
9 Then you will understand
righteousness, justice,
and integrity — every good path.
10 For wisdom will enter your heart,
and knowledge will delight you.
11 Discretion will watch over you,
and understanding will guard you.
12 It will rescue you from the way
of evil —
from anyone who says perverse things,
13 from those who abandon
the right paths
to walk in ways of darkness,
14 from those who enjoy doing evil
and celebrate perversion,
15 whose paths are crooked,
and whose ways are devious.
16 It will rescue you
from a forbidden woman,
from a wayward woman
with her flattering talk,
17 who abandons the companion
of her youth
and forgets the covenant of her God;
18 for her house sinks down to death
and her ways to the land
of the departed spirits.
19 None return who go to her;
none reach the paths of life.
20 So follow the way of the good,
and keep to the paths of the righteous.
21 For the upright will inhabit the land,
and those of integrity will remain in it;

[A] **1:19** Lit *takes the life of its masters* [B] **1:21** Lit *at the head of* [C] **1:23** Lit *you turn back to my reprimand* [D] **2:2** Lit *you, stretching out your ear* [E] **2:7** Or *resourcefulness*

22 but the wicked will be cut off
from the land,
and the treacherous ripped out of it.

TRUST THE LORD

3 My son, don't forget my teaching,
but let your heart keep my commands;
2 for they will bring you
many days, a full life,[A] and well-being.
3 Never let loyalty and faithfulness
leave you.
Tie them around your neck;
write them on the tablet of your heart.
4 Then you will find favor
and high regard
with God and people.

5 Trust in the LORD with all your heart,
and do not rely on
your own understanding;
6 in all your ways know him,
and he will make your paths straight.
7 Don't be wise in your own eyes;
fear the LORD and turn away
from evil.
8 This will be healing for your body[B]
and strengthening for your bones.
9 Honor the LORD
with your possessions
and with the first produce
of your entire harvest;
10 then your barns will be
completely filled,
and your vats will overflow
with new wine.
11 Do not despise the LORD's instruction,
my son,
and do not loathe his discipline;
12 for the LORD disciplines the one
he loves,
just as a father disciplines the son in
whom he delights.

WISDOM BRINGS HAPPINESS

13 Happy is a man who finds wisdom
and who acquires understanding,
14 for she is more profitable than silver,
and her revenue is better than gold.
15 She is more precious than jewels;
nothing you desire can equal her.
16 Long life[C] is in her right hand;
in her left, riches and honor.
17 Her ways are pleasant,
and all her paths, peaceful.

Exercise of Faith | *Trusting God*

RELIANCE

"Trust in the LORD with all your heart, and do not rely on your own understanding; in all your ways know him, and he will make your paths straight." Proverbs 3:5-6

Susan's husband is unfaithful—and abusive. She fears for her safety but is even more terrified at the thought of taking her two small children and leaving. "Where would I go? What would I do? I don't have any skills—and I have less savings!"

This is situation desperately needs the wisdom of Proverbs 3:5-6. The temptation in scary times is to rely on our own understanding. We inventory our resources and wonder: *What strings can I pull? How much money do I have in the bank? What do others say I should do?*

Those aren't necessarily bad questions to ask. But if we settle for a limited human perspective rather than a limitless, divine one . . . if we look around but never up, we miss out on supernatural possibilities.

This is why most folks trust God with a small part of their hearts, and then supplement that with trust in lots of other things: their charm, wits, creativity, common sense, or connections.

In your current tough situation, don't let God be an afterthought. Make him your consultant and guide. Solicit his wisdom. Then trust and do what he says—even if it's scary and doesn't seem to make sense.

For the next note on *Exercise of Faith*, see Proverbs 4:23.

[A] **3:2** Lit *days, years of life* [B] **3:8** Lit *navel* [C] **3:16** Lit *Length of days*

18 She is a tree of life to those
who embrace her,
and those who hold on to her are happy.

19 The LORD founded the earth by wisdom
and established the heavens
by understanding.
20 By his knowledge the watery depths
broke open,
and the clouds dripped with dew.

21 Maintain sound wisdom
and discretion.
My son, don't lose sight of them.
22 They will be life for you[A]
and adornment[B] for your neck.
23 Then you will go safely on your way;
your foot will not stumble.
24 When you lie[C] down, you will not
be afraid;
you will lie down, and your sleep
will be pleasant.
25 Don't fear sudden danger
or the ruin of the wicked
when it comes,
26 for the LORD will be your confidence[D]
and will keep your foot from a snare.

TREAT OTHERS FAIRLY

27 When it is in your power,[E]
don't withhold good from the one to
whom it belongs.
28 Don't say to your neighbor, "Go away!
Come back later.
I'll give it tomorrow" — when it is there
with you.
29 Don't plan any harm
against your neighbor,
for he trusts you and lives near you.
30 Don't accuse anyone without cause,
when he has done you no harm.
31 Don't envy a violent man
or choose any of his ways;
32 for the devious are detestable
to the LORD,
but he is a friend[F] to the upright.
33 The LORD's curse is on the household
of the wicked,
but he blesses the home
of the righteous;
34 He mocks those who mock,
but gives grace to the humble.
35 The wise will inherit honor,
but he holds up fools
to dishonor.[G]

Exercise of Faith | *Guarding the Heart*

SOUL CARE PRIORITY #1

"Guard your heart above all else, for it is the source of life." Proverbs 4:23

If your goal is a healthier soul, a more vibrant spirituality, what should you focus on? Learning the Bible better? Praying more? Engaging in bolder acts of service?

All these activities are good, but one practice is more important still. "Above all else," Solomon urged, "guard your heart."

He wasn't saying, "Build a wall around your heart to keep others out." He meant, "Diligently monitor your heart and be alert to any changes. Notice when your heart begins to grow cold or when it starts becoming attached to trivial, worldly things.

This is critical, Solomon said, because your heart "is the source of life." For the ancient Jews the heart was more than the blood-pumping organ in our chests. It was the control center of life—the place we feel, think, and choose. Hence the need to keep it healthy! When our hearts are in great shape, our lives will be too.

Make an appointment to get together with an older wiser Christian. Discuss ways to guard your hearts.

For the next note on *Exercise of Faith*, see Isaiah 2:22.

[A] **3:22** Or *be your throat* [B] **3:22** Or *grace* [C] **3:24** LXX reads *sit* [D] **3:26** Or *be at your side* [E] **3:27** Lit *in the power of your hands* [F] **3:32** Or *confidential counsel* [G] **3:35** Or *but haughty fools dishonor*, or *but fools exalt dishonor*

A FATHER'S EXAMPLE

4 Listen, sons, to a father's discipline,
and pay attention so that
you may gain understanding,
2 for I am giving you good instruction.
Don't abandon my teaching.
3 When I was a son with my father,
tender and precious to my mother,
4 he taught me and said:
"Your heart must hold on
to my words.
Keep my commands and live.
5 Get wisdom, get understanding;
don't forget or turn away
from the words from my mouth.
6 Don't abandon wisdom, and she will
watch over you;
love her, and she will guard you.
7 Wisdom is supreme — so get wisdom.
And whatever else you get,
get understanding.
8 Cherish her, and she will exalt you;
if you embrace her, she will honor you.
9 She will place a garland of favor
on your head;
she will give you a crown of beauty."

TWO WAYS OF LIFE

10 Listen, my son. Accept my words,
and you will live many years.
11 I am teaching you the way of wisdom;
I am guiding you on straight paths.
12 When you walk, your steps will not
be hindered;
when you run, you will not stumble.
13 Hold on to instruction; don't let go.
Guard it, for it is your life.
14 Keep off the path of the wicked;
don't proceed on the way of evil ones.
15 Avoid it; don't travel on it.
Turn away from it, and pass it by.
16 For they can't sleep
unless they have done what is evil;
they are robbed of sleep
unless they make someone stumble.
17 They eat the bread of wickedness
and drink the wine of violence.
18 The path of the righteous is
like the light of dawn,
shining brighter and brighter
until midday.
19 But the way of the wicked is
like the darkest gloom;
they don't know what makes
them stumble.

THE STRAIGHT PATH

20 My son, pay attention to my words;
listen closely to my sayings.
21 Don't lose sight of them;
keep them within your heart.
22 For they are life to those
who find them,
and health to one's whole body.
23 Guard your heart above all else,[A]
for it is the source of life.
24 Don't let your mouth speak dishonestly,
and don't let your lips talk deviously.
25 Let your eyes look forward;
fix your gaze[B] straight ahead.
26 Carefully consider the path[C]
for your feet,
and all your ways will be established.
27 Don't turn to the right or to the left;
keep your feet away from evil.

AVOID SEDUCTION

5 My son, pay attention to my wisdom;
listen closely[D] to my understanding
2 so that you may maintain discretion
and your lips safeguard knowledge.
3 Though the lips
of the forbidden woman drip honey
and her words are[E] smoother than oil,
4 in the end she's as bitter as wormwood
and as sharp as a double-edged sword.
5 Her feet go down to death;
her steps head straight for Sheol.
6 She doesn't consider the path of life;
she doesn't know that her ways
are unstable.

7 So now, sons, listen to me,
and don't turn away from the words
from my mouth.
8 Keep your way far from her.
Don't go near the door of her house.
9 Otherwise, you will give up
your vitality to others
and your years to someone cruel;
10 strangers will drain your resources,
and your hard-earned pay will end up
in a foreigner's house.
11 At the end of your life, you will lament
when your physical body
has been consumed,

[A] **4:23** Or *heart with all diligence* [B] **4:25** Lit *eyelids* [C] **4:26** Or *Clear a path* [D] **5:1** Lit *wisdom; stretch out your ear* [E] **5:3** Lit *her palate is*

12 and you will say,
"How I hated discipline,
and how my heart
despised correction.
13 I didn't obey my teachers
or listen closely[A] to my instructors.
14 I am on the verge of complete ruin
before the entire community."

ENJOY MARRIAGE

15 Drink water from your own cistern,
water flowing from your own well.
16 Should your springs flow
in the streets,
streams in the public squares?
17 They should be for you alone
and not for you to share
with strangers.
18 Let your fountain be blessed,
and take pleasure in the wife
of your youth.
19 A loving deer, a graceful doe[B] —
let her breasts always satisfy you;
be lost in her love forever.
20 Why, my son, would you lose yourself
with a forbidden woman
or embrace a wayward woman?
21 For a man's ways are before
the LORD's eyes,
and he considers all his paths.
22 A wicked man's iniquities will
trap him;
he will become tangled in the ropes
of his own sin.
23 He will die because there is
no discipline,
and be lost because of
his great stupidity.

FINANCIAL ENTANGLEMENTS

6 My son, if you have put up security
for your neighbor[C]
or entered into an agreement
with[D] a stranger,
2 you have been snared by the words
of your mouth
trapped by the words
from your mouth.
3 Do this, then, my son, and free yourself,
for you have put yourself
in your neighbor's power:
Go, humble yourself, and plead
with your neighbor.
4 Don't give sleep to your eyes
or slumber to your eyelids.
5 Escape like a gazelle from a hunter,[E]
like a bird from a hunter's trap.[E]

LAZINESS

6 Go to the ant, you slacker!
Observe its ways and become wise.
7 Without leader, administrator, or ruler,
8 it prepares its provisions in summer;
it gathers its food during harvest.
9 How long will you stay in bed,
you slacker?
When will you get up from your sleep?
10 A little sleep, a little slumber,
a little folding of the arms to rest,
11 and your poverty will come like
a robber,
your need, like a bandit.

THE MALICIOUS MAN

12 A worthless person,
a wicked man
goes around speaking dishonestly,
13 winking his eyes, signaling
with his feet,
and gesturing with his fingers.
14 He always plots evil with perversity
in his heart;
he stirs up trouble.
15 Therefore calamity
will strike him suddenly;
he will be shattered instantly,
beyond recovery.

WHAT THE LORD HATES

16 The LORD hates six things;
in fact, seven are detestable to him:
17 arrogant eyes, a lying tongue,
hands that shed innocent blood,
18 a heart that plots wicked schemes,
feet eager to run to evil,
19 a lying witness who gives
false testimony,
and one who stirs up trouble
among brothers.

WARNING AGAINST ADULTERY

20 My son, keep your father's command,
and don't reject
your mother's teaching.
21 Always bind them to your heart;
tie them around your neck.

[A] 5:13 Lit *or turn my ear* [B] 5:19 Or *graceful mountain goat* [C] 6:1 Or *friend* [D] 6:1 Lit *or slapped hands for* [E] 6:5 Lit *hand*

22 When you walk here and there,
they will guide you;
when you lie down, they will
watch over you;
when you wake up, they will talk to you.
23 For a command is a lamp,
teaching is a light,
and corrective discipline is the way
to life.
24 They will protect you
from an evil woman,[A]
from the flattering[B] tongue of
a wayward woman.
25 Don't lust in your heart for her beauty
or let her captivate you
with her eyelashes.
26 For a prostitute's fee is only a loaf
of bread,[C]
but the wife of another man[D] goes after
a precious life.
27 Can a man embrace fire
and his clothes not be burned?
28 Can a man walk on burning coals
without scorching his feet?
29 So it is with the one who sleeps with
another man's wife;
no one who touches her
will go unpunished.
30 People don't despise the thief if he steals
to satisfy himself when he is hungry.
31 Still, if caught, he must pay seven times
as much;
he must give up all the wealth
in his house.
32 The one who commits adultery[E]
lacks sense;
whoever does so destroys himself.
33 He will get a beating[F] and dishonor,
and his disgrace will never be removed.
34 For jealousy enrages a husband,
and he will show no mercy
when he takes revenge.
35 He will not be appeased by anything
or be persuaded by lavish bribes.

7 My son, obey my words,
and treasure my commands.
2 Keep my commands and live,
and guard my instructions
as you would the pupil of your eye.
3 Tie them to your fingers;
write them on the tablet
of your heart.
4 Say to wisdom, "You are my sister,"
and call understanding your relative.
5 She will keep you
from a forbidden woman,
a wayward woman with
her flattering talk.

A STORY OF SEDUCTION

6 At the window of my house
I looked through my lattice.
7 I saw among the inexperienced,[G]
I noticed among the youths,
a young man lacking sense.
8 Crossing the street near her corner,
he strolled down the road to her house
9 at twilight, in the evening,
in the dark of the night.
10 A woman came to meet him
dressed like a prostitute,
having a hidden agenda.[H]
11 She is loud and defiant;
her feet do not stay at home.
12 Now in the street,
now in the squares,
she lurks at every corner.
13 She grabs him and kisses him;
she brazenly says[I] to him,
14 "I've made fellowship offerings;
today I've fulfilled my vows.
15 So I came out to meet you,
to search for you, and I've found you.
16 I've spread coverings on my bed—
richly colored linen from Egypt.
17 I've perfumed my bed
with myrrh, aloes, and cinnamon.
18 Come, let's drink deeply of lovemaking
until morning.
Let's feast on each other's love!
19 My husband isn't home;
he went on a long journey.
20 He took a bag of silver with him
and will come home at the time
of the full moon."
21 She seduces him
with her persistent pleading;
she lures with her flattering[J] talk.
22 He follows her impulsively
like an ox going to the slaughter,
like a deer bounding toward a trap[K]

[A] **6:24** LXX reads *from a married woman* [B] **6:24** Lit *smooth* [C] **6:26** Or *On account of a prostitute, one is left with only a loaf of bread* [D] **6:26** Lit *but a wife of a man* [E] **6:32** Lit *commits adultery with a woman* [F] **6:33** Or *plague* [G] **7:7** Or *simple*, or *gullible*, or *naive* [H] **7:10** Or *prostitute with a guarded heart* [I] **7:13** Lit *she makes her face strong and says* [J] **7:21** Lit *smooth* [K] **7:22** Text emended; MT reads *like a shackle to the discipline of a fool*; Hb obscure

23 until an arrow pierces its[A] liver,
like a bird darting into a snare —
he doesn't know it will cost him his life.

24 Now, sons, listen to me,
and pay attention to the words
from my mouth.
25 Don't let your heart turn aside
to her ways;
don't stray onto her paths.
26 For she has brought many
down to death;
her victims are countless.[B]
27 Her house is the road to Sheol,
descending to the chambers of death.

WISDOM'S APPEAL

8 Doesn't wisdom call out?
Doesn't understanding make her voice
heard?
2 At the heights overlooking the road,
at the crossroads, she takes her stand.
3 Beside the gates leading into the city,
at the main entrance, she cries out:
4 "People, I call out to you;
my cry is to the children of Adam.
5 Learn to be shrewd,
you who are inexperienced;
develop common sense,
you who are foolish.
6 Listen, for I speak of noble things,
and what my lips say is right.
7 For my mouth tells the truth,
and wickedness is detestable to my lips.
8 All the words from my mouth
are righteous;
none of them are deceptive or perverse.
9 All of them are clear to the perceptive,
and right to those
who discover knowledge.
10 Accept my instruction instead of silver,
and knowledge rather than pure gold.
11 For wisdom is better than jewels,
and nothing desirable can equal it.
12 I, wisdom, share a home with shrewdness
and have knowledge and discretion.
13 To fear the LORD is to hate evil.
I hate arrogant pride, evil conduct,
and perverse speech.
14 I possess good advice
and sound wisdom;[C]
I have understanding and strength.

I love those who love me, and those who search for me find me
—Proverbs 8:17

15 It is by me that kings reign
and rulers enact just law;
16 by me, princes lead,
as do nobles
and all righteous judges.[D]
17 I love those who love me,
and those who search for me find me.
18 With me are riches and honor,
lasting wealth and righteousness.
19 My fruit is better than solid gold,
and my harvest than pure silver.
20 I walk in the ways of righteousness,
along the paths of justice,
21 giving wealth as an inheritance
to those who love me,
and filling their treasuries.

22 "The LORD acquired[E] me
at the beginning of his creation,[F]
before his works of long ago.
23 I was formed[G] before ancient times,
from the beginning,
before the earth began.
24 I was born
when there were no watery depths
and no springs filled with water.
25 Before the mountains were established,
prior to the hills, I was given birth —
26 before he made the land, the fields,
or the first soil on earth.
27 I was there when he established
the heavens,
when he laid out the horizon
on the surface of the ocean,
28 when he placed the skies above,
when the fountains of the ocean
gushed out,
29 when he set a limit for the sea
so that the waters would not violate
his command,
when he laid out the foundations
of the earth.
30 I was a skilled craftsman[H] beside him.

[A] 7:23 Or *his* [B] 7:26 Or *and powerful men are all her victims* [C] 8:14 Or *resourcefulness* [D] 8:16 Some Hb mss, LXX read *nobles who judge the earth* [E] 8:22 Or *possessed*, or *made* [F] 8:22 Lit *way* [G] 8:23 Or *consecrated* [H] 8:30 Or *a confidant*, or *a child*, or *was constantly*

I was his[A] delight every day,
always rejoicing before him.
31 I was rejoicing in his inhabited world,
delighting in the children of Adam.

32 "And now, sons, listen to me;
those who keep my ways are happy.
33 Listen to instruction and be wise;
don't ignore it.
34 Anyone who listens to me is happy,
watching at my doors every day,
waiting by the posts of my doorway.
35 For the one who finds me finds life
and obtains favor from the LORD,
36 but the one who misses me[B]
harms himself;
all who hate me love death."

WISDOM VERSUS FOOLISHNESS

9 Wisdom has built her house;
she has carved out her seven pillars.
2 She has prepared her meat;
she has mixed her wine;
she has also set her table.
3 She has sent out her female servants;
she calls out from the highest points
of the city:
4 "Whoever is inexperienced,
enter here!"
To the one who lacks sense,
she says,
5 "Come, eat my bread,
and drink the wine I have mixed.
6 Leave inexperience behind,
and you will live;
pursue the way of understanding.
7 The one who corrects a mocker
will bring abuse on himself;
the one who rebukes the wicked
will get hurt.[C]
8 Don't rebuke a mocker, or he will
hate you;
rebuke the wise, and he will love you.
9 Instruct the wise, and he will be
wiser still;
teach the righteous, and he will
learn more.

10 "The fear of the LORD is the beginning
of wisdom,
and the knowledge of the Holy One
is understanding.
11 For by me your days will be many,
and years will be added to your life.
12 If you are wise, you are wise
for your own benefit;
if you mock, you alone will bear
the consequences."

Relationships | *Mentoring*

THE MARK OF A WISE PERSON

"Instruct the wise, and he will be wiser still; teach the righteous, and he will learn more." Proverbs 9:9

The book of Proverbs offers one surefire test for determining if someone is being wise or foolish. Want to guess what it is?

It's the willingness to accept instruction, counsel, and correction. Over and over, Proverbs says that wise people welcome input. Foolish people, on the other hand, spurn it.

Obviously, you want to grow and be healthy, so pray for a teachable spirit. Let an expert teach you something new each day. And should someone who has been around the block a few more times than you offer a bit of constructive criticism, resist the very natural and powerful urge to argue, give excuses, or tune out. Instead, remember this truth: Wise people are teachable—and my goal is to become wise.

In short, it comes down to the age-old struggle between pride and humility. Fools are resistant. Wise people are receptive. You know the kind of person you want to be.

For the next note on *Relationships*, see Proverbs 12:24.

[A] **8:30** LXX; MT omits *his* [B] **8:36** Or *who sins against me* [C] **9:7** Lit *man: his blemish*

13 Folly is a rowdy woman;
she is gullible and knows nothing.
14 She sits by the doorway of her house,
on a seat at the highest point of the city,
15 calling to those who pass by,
who go straight ahead on their paths:
16 "Whoever is inexperienced, enter here!"
To the one who lacks sense, she says,
17 "Stolen water is sweet,
and bread eaten secretly is tasty!"
18 But he doesn't know
that the departed spirits are there,
that her guests are in the depths
of Sheol.

A COLLECTION OF SOLOMON'S PROVERBS

10 Solomon's proverbs:
A wise son brings joy to his father,
but a foolish son, heartache
to his mother.

2 Ill-gotten gains do not profit anyone,
but righteousness rescues from death.

3 The LORD will not let the righteous
go hungry,
but he denies the wicked
what they crave.

4 Idle hands make one poor,
but diligent hands bring riches.

5 The son who gathers during summer
is prudent;
the son who sleeps during harvest
is disgraceful.

6 Blessings are on the head
of the righteous,
but the mouth of the wicked
conceals violence.

7 The remembrance of the righteous is
a blessing,
but the name of the wicked will rot.

8 A wise heart accepts commands,
but foolish lips will be destroyed.

9 The one who lives with integrity
lives securely,
but whoever perverts his ways will be
found out.

10 A sly wink of the eye causes grief,
and foolish lips will be destroyed.

11 The mouth of the righteous is
a fountain of life,
but the mouth of the wicked
conceals violence.

12 Hatred stirs up conflicts,
but love covers all offenses.

13 Wisdom is found on the lips
of the discerning,
but a rod is for the back of the one
who lacks sense.

14 The wise store up knowledge,
but the mouth of the fool
hastens destruction.

15 The wealth of the rich is
his fortified city;
the poverty of the poor is
their destruction.

16 The reward of the righteous is life;
the wages of the wicked
is punishment.

17 The one who follows instruction is
on the path to life,
but the one who rejects correction
goes astray.

18 The one who conceals hatred has
lying lips,
and whoever spreads slander is a fool.

19 When there are many words,
sin is unavoidable,
but the one who controls his lips
is prudent.

20 The tongue of the righteous is
pure silver;
the heart of the wicked is
of little value.

21 The lips of the righteous feed many,
but fools die for lack of sense.

22 The LORD's blessing enriches,
and he adds no painful effort to it.[A]

[A] **10:22** Or *and painful effort adds nothing to it*

23 As shameful conduct is pleasure
for a fool,
so wisdom is for a person
of understanding.

24 What the wicked dreads will come
to him,
but what the righteous desire
will be given to them.

25 When the whirlwind passes,
the wicked are no more,
but the righteous
are secure forever.

26 Like vinegar to the teeth and smoke
to the eyes,
so the slacker is to the one
who sends him on an errand.

27 The fear of the LORD prolongs life,[A]
but the years of the wicked
are cut short.

28 The hope of the righteous is joy,
but the expectation of the wicked
will perish.

29 The way of the LORD is a stronghold
for the honorable,
but destruction awaits the malicious.

30 The righteous will never be shaken,
but the wicked will not remain
on the earth.

31 The mouth of the righteous
produces wisdom,
but a perverse tongue will be cut out.

32 The lips of the righteous know
what is appropriate,
but the mouth of the wicked,
only what is perverse.

11 Dishonest scales are detestable
to the LORD,
but an accurate weight is his delight.

2 When arrogance comes,
disgrace follows,
but with humility comes wisdom.

3 The integrity of the upright
guides them,

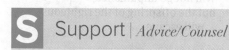

GUIDANCE AND DELIVERANCE

"Without guidance, a people will fall, but with many counselors there is deliverance." Proverbs 11:14

U.S. President Woodrow Wilson famously said, "I not only use all the brains I have, but all I can borrow."

Wise man there. Why move through the world making tough decisions all by your lonesome? Why not take advantage of the discerning people all around you—perhaps a wise grandparent, an astute parent or in-law, a perceptive retiree in the neighborhood, a savvy mentor at work, a godly elder from church?

Some of them are busy, but many would be delighted to share their knowledge, insight, and understanding. Think of it! All those life skills and spiritual gifts, all that life experience and problem-solving ability. You could even form an unofficial "team of life consultants." They wouldn't have to actually meet together with you all at once. But they could serve as a sounding board and offer valuable perspective.

Proverbs reminds us that in the tough situations of life, those kinds of counselors can be the difference between falling on your face and finding deliverance.

For the next note on *Support*, see Proverbs 15:33.

[A] **10:27** Lit *LORD adds to days*

but the perversity of the treacherous
destroys them.

4 Wealth is not profitable on a day
of wrath,
but righteousness rescues from death.

5 The righteousness of the blameless
clears his path,
but the wicked person will fall
because of his wickedness.

6 The righteousness of the upright
rescues them,
but the treacherous are trapped
by their own desires.

7 When the wicked person dies,
his expectation comes to nothing,
and hope placed in wealth[A,B] vanishes.

8 The righteous one is rescued
from trouble;
in his place, the wicked one goes in.

9 With his mouth the ungodly
destroys his neighbor,
but through knowledge the righteous
are rescued.

10 When the righteous thrive,
a city rejoices;
when the wicked die, there is
joyful shouting.

11 A city is built up by the blessing
of the upright,
but it is torn down by the mouth
of the wicked.

12 Whoever shows contempt
for his neighbor lacks sense,
but a person with understanding
keeps silent.

13 A gossip goes around revealing
a secret,
but a trustworthy person keeps
a confidence.

14 Without guidance, a people will fall,
but with many counselors
there is deliverance.

15 If someone puts up security
for a stranger,
he will suffer for it,
but the one who hates such agreements
is protected.

16 A gracious woman gains honor,
but violent[C] people gain only riches.

17 A kind man benefits himself,
but a cruel person brings ruin
on himself.

18 The wicked person earns
an empty wage,
but the one who sows righteousness,
a true reward.

19 Genuine righteousness leads to life,
but pursuing evil leads to death.

20 Those with twisted minds
are detestable to the LORD,
but those with blameless conduct are
his delight.

21 Be assured[D] that a wicked person
will not go unpunished,
but the offspring of the righteous
will escape.

22 A beautiful woman who rejects
good sense
is like a gold ring in a pig's snout.

23 The desire of the righteous
turns out well,
but the hope of the wicked
leads to wrath.

24 One person gives freely,
yet gains more;
another withholds what is right,
only to become poor.

25 A generous person will be enriched,
and the one who gives a drink of water
will receive water.

26 People will curse anyone
who hoards grain,
but a blessing will come to the one
who sells it.

[A] **11:7** LXX reads *hope of the ungodly* [B] **11:7** Or *strength* [C] **11:16** Or *ruthless* [D] **11:21** Lit *Hand to hand*

27 The one who searches for what is good
seeks favor,
but if someone looks for trouble,
it will come to him.

28 Anyone trusting in his riches will fall,
but the righteous will flourish
like foliage.

29 The one who brings ruin
on his household
will inherit the wind,
and a fool will be a slave
to someone whose heart is wise.

30 The fruit of the righteous is a tree
of life,
and a wise person captivates people.

31 If the righteous will be
repaid on earth,
how much more the wicked
and sinful.

12 Whoever loves discipline
loves knowledge,
but one who hates correction is stupid.

2 One who is good obtains favor
from the LORD,
but he condemns a person
who schemes.

3 No one can be made secure
by wickedness,
but the root of the righteous
is immovable.

4 A wife of noble character[A] is
her husband's crown,
but a wife who causes shame
is like rottenness in his bones.

5 The thoughts of the righteous
are just,
but guidance from the wicked
is deceitful.

6 The words of the wicked are
a deadly ambush,
but the speech of the upright
rescues them.

7 The wicked are overthrown
and perish,

R Relationships | *Relating to Coworkers*

WHY DILIGENCE MATTERS

"The diligent hand will rule, but laziness will lead to forced labor." Proverbs 12:24

When we're feeling blah and discouraged, it's as though someone pulled the plug. We have little energy. We just want to veg. Go through the motions. Take the path of least resistance. Do our best Rip Van Winkle impersonation. Often this attitude shows up at work and can harm our relationships with coworkers.

That good-for-nothing feeling is understandable, but here's Solomon's warning: Low motivation can eventually morph into laziness—and that's a terrible trap that leads to a kind of slavery.

Instead, Solomon says, we need a "diligent" hand. The word translated "diligent" here is translated elsewhere as "gold" and "sharp" and "protective trench." Perhaps this is Solomon's way of saying that when we're diligent, we're golden and on point. That is, we're highly valuable to our friends, family, and employers. Also, when we're industrious, we're protected from the grim consequences of laziness.

Having trouble being diligent—at home, on the job? Ask God for new energy—not to run frantically, but just to keep putting one foot in front of the other.

For the next note on *Relationships*, see Proverbs 13:20.

[A] **12:4** Or *A wife of quality*, or *A wife of good character*

but the house of the righteous
will stand.

8 A man is praised for his insight,
but a twisted mind is despised.

9 Better to be disregarded, yet have
a servant,
than to act important
but have no food.

10 The righteous cares about
his animal's health,
but even the merciful acts
of the wicked are cruel.

11 The one who works his land will have
plenty of food,
but whoever chases fantasies
lacks sense.

12 The wicked desire what evil people
have caught,[A]
but the root of the righteous
is productive.

13 By rebellious speech an evil person
is trapped,
but a righteous person escapes
from trouble.

14 A person will be satisfied with good
by the fruit of his mouth,
and the work of a person's hands
will reward him.

15 A fool's way is right in his own eyes,
but whoever listens to counsel
is wise.

16 A fool's displeasure is known
at once,
but whoever ignores an insult
is sensible.

17 Whoever speaks the truth declares
what is right,
but a false witness speaks deceit.

18 There is one who speaks rashly,
like a piercing sword;
but the tongue of the wise
brings healing.

19 Truthful lips endure forever,
but a lying tongue, only a moment.

Other-centeredness | *Encouraging*

A GOOD WORD

"Anxiety in a person's heart weighs it down, but a good word cheers it up." Proverbs 12:25

When a person is weighed down with worry, what does he need most? According to this verse something is even more basic (and often more powerful) than journaling, taking anti-anxiety meds, engaging in an intense workout, or drinking a glass of wine. What's Solomon's ancient prescription for a nervous heart? "A good word."

"A good word" can take a lot of forms. In many cases it can be a simple phrase like "I hear what you're saying" or "I'm so sorry" or "That's really hard and scary" or "I'm praying for you" or "I love you" or "I am here for you."

In other situations "a good word" might be telling your anxious friend a brief, encouraging, personal story of God's faithfulness. It might consist of reminding your friend of ways you've seen God come through similar situations in the past.

If you're the one weighed down with worry, ask God to give you "a good word"—either from his Word, or via a friend.

For the next note on *Other-centeredness*, see Ecclesiastes 3:7.

[A] **12:12** Or *desire a stronghold of evil*

20 Deceit is in the hearts of those
who plot evil,
but those who promote peace have joy.

21 No disaster overcomes the righteous,
but the wicked are full of misery.

22 Lying lips are detestable to the LORD,
but faithful people are his delight.

23 A shrewd person conceals knowledge,
but a foolish heart publicizes stupidity.

24 The diligent hand will rule,
but laziness will lead to forced labor.

25 Anxiety in a person's heart
weighs it down,
but a good word cheers it up.

26 A righteous person is careful in dealing
with his neighbor,[A]
but the ways of the wicked
lead them astray.

27 A lazy hunter doesn't roast his game,
but to a diligent person, his wealth
is precious.

28 There is life in the path
of righteousness,
and in its path there is no death.[B]

13 A wise son responds to his
father's discipline,
but a mocker doesn't listen to rebuke.

2 From the fruit of his mouth,
a person will enjoy good things,
but treacherous people have
an appetite for violence.

3 The one who guards his mouth
protects his life;
the one who opens his lips invites
his own ruin.

4 The slacker craves, yet has nothing,
but the diligent is fully satisfied.

5 The righteous hate lying,
but the wicked bring
disgust and shame.

6 Righteousness guards people
of integrity,[C]
but wickedness undermines the sinner.

7 One person pretends to be rich
but has nothing;
another pretends to be poor but has
abundant wealth.

8 Riches are a ransom for a person's life,
but a poor person hears no threat.

9 The light of the righteous shines brightly,
but the lamp of the wicked is put out.

10 Arrogance leads to nothing but strife,
but wisdom is gained by those
who take advice.

11 Wealth obtained by fraud
will dwindle,
but whoever earns it through labor[D]
will multiply it.

12 Hope delayed makes the heart sick,
but desire fulfilled is a tree of life.

13 The one who has contempt
for instruction will pay the penalty,
but the one who respects a command
will be rewarded.

14 A wise person's instruction is
a fountain of life,
turning people away from the snares
of death.

15 Good sense wins favor,
but the way of the treacherous
never changes.[E]

16 Every sensible person
acts knowledgeably,
but a fool displays his stupidity.

17 A wicked envoy falls into trouble,
but a trustworthy courier
brings healing.

18 Poverty and disgrace come to those
who ignore discipline,
but the one who accepts correction
will be honored.

[A] **12:26** Or *person guides his neighbor* [B] **12:28** Or *righteousness, but the crooked way leads to death* [C] **13:6** Lit *guards integrity of way* [D] **13:11** Lit *whoever gathers upon his hand* [E] **13:15** LXX, Syr, Tg read *treacherous will perish*

19 Desire fulfilled is sweet to the taste,
but to turn from evil is detestable
to fools.

20 The one who walks with the wise
will become wise,
but a companion of fools
will suffer harm.

21 Disaster pursues sinners,
but good rewards the righteous.

22 A good man leaves an inheritance
to his[A] grandchildren,
but the sinner's wealth is stored up
for the righteous.

23 The uncultivated field of the poor
yields abundant food,
but without justice,
it is swept away.

24 The one who will not use the rod hates
his son,
but the one who loves him disciplines
him diligently.

25 A righteous person eats
until he is satisfied,
but the stomach of the wicked
is empty.

14 Every wise woman builds her house,
but a foolish one tears it down
with her own hands.

2 Whoever lives with integrity
fears the LORD,
but the one who is devious in his ways
despises him.

3 The proud speech of a fool brings a rod
of discipline,[B]
but the lips of the wise protect them.

4 Where there are no oxen, the
feeding trough is empty,[C]
but an abundant harvest comes
through the strength of an ox.

5 An honest witness
does not deceive,
but a dishonest witness utters lies.

Relationships | *Building Positive Relationships*

PICKING FRIENDS

"The one who walks with the wise will become wise, but a companion of fools will suffer harm." Proverbs 13:20

We say it different ways . . .

- "Tell me who your friends are, and I'll tell you who *you* are."
- "If you lie down with dogs, you get up with fleas."
- "Bad company corrupts good morals" (1Co 15:33).

But however we say it, the point is the same: Our friendship choices are huge.

As this proverb reminds us, we inevitably become like the people we hang around. This is no new revelation. Think of how teenagers begin using the same catchphrases, or how couples, over time, sometimes even start looking alike.

Perhaps you are struggling or stuck in life because you're surrounded by people who aren't exactly good for you. You had hoped to pull them up; instead, they're dragging you down.

What if you upgraded in the friendship department? What if, starting today, you began cultivating some new relationships with people who are positive, spiritually motivated, and serious about making a difference in the world? Think about the difference that would make in you.

For the next note on *Relationships*, see Proverbs 14:9.

[A] **13:22** Or *inheritance: his* [B] **14:3** Some emend to *In the mouth of a fool is a rod for his back* [C] **14:4** Or *clean*

6 A mocker seeks wisdom
and doesn't find it,
but knowledge comes easily
to the perceptive.

7 Stay away from a foolish person;
you will gain no knowledge
from his speech.

8 The sensible person's wisdom is
to consider his way,
but the stupidity of fools
deceives them.

9 Fools mock at making reparation,[A]
but there is goodwill
among the upright.

10 The heart knows its own bitterness,
and no outsider shares in its joy.

11 The house of the wicked
will be destroyed,
but the tent of the upright will flourish.

12 There is a way that seems right
to a person,
but its end is the way to death.

13 Even in laughter a heart may be sad,
and joy may end in grief.

14 The disloyal one will get
what his conduct deserves,
and a good one, what his deeds deserve.

15 The inexperienced one
believes anything,
but the sensible one watches[B] his steps.

16 A wise person is cautious and turns
from evil,
but a fool is easily angered
and is careless.[C]

17 A quick-tempered person
acts foolishly,
and one who schemes is hated.

18 The inexperienced inherit foolishness,
but the sensible are crowned
with knowledge.

19 The evil bow before those
who are good,
and the wicked, at the gates
of the righteous.

Relationships | *Making Amends*

REPARATIONS

"Fools mock at making reparation, but there is goodwill among the upright." Proverbs 14:9

What is it about human nature that when we make a mistake, we often follow that up by making things worse? For instance, we might give excuses. Or we might act as though what we did wasn't really such a big deal. Or, if we know we were wrong but aren't ready to take full responsibility, we might try an insincere attempt at apologizing.

We can do so much better than that. How about when we make a mess, we confess, we own our actions and make a full, meaningful apology?

Then, what if we go even further? What if we make reparations? That means we repair what we broke, return what we took, calm down what we stirred up. This is the beautiful act of restitution, and it involves action, not mere words. It means restoring or offering recompense. To the extent that we can *do* something, not merely *say* something, to make things right, we expedite the healing.

Reparation isn't magic. It won't undo our mistakes or make things exactly like they were before. But it will make a big difference going forward—which is exactly what we need.

For the next note on *Relationships*, see Proverbs 18:24.

[A] **14:9** Or *at guilt offerings* [B] **14:15** Lit *the prudent understands* [C] **14:16** Or *and falls*

20 A poor person is hated even
by his neighbor,
but there are many
who love the rich.

21 The one who despises
his neighbor sins,
but whoever shows kindness
to the poor will be happy.

22 Don't those who plan evil go astray?
But those who plan good find loyalty
and faithfulness.

23 There is profit in all hard work,
but endless talk[A] leads only to poverty.

24 The crown of the wise is their wealth,
but the foolishness of fools
produces foolishness.

25 A truthful witness rescues lives,
but one who utters lies is deceitful.

26 In the fear of the LORD one has
strong confidence
and his children have a refuge.

27 The fear of the LORD is a fountain of life,
turning people away from the snares
of death.

28 A large population is a king's splendor,
but a shortage of people is
a ruler's devastation.

29 A patient person shows great
understanding,
but a quick-tempered one
promotes foolishness.

30 A tranquil heart is life to the body,
but jealousy is rottenness to the bones.

31 The one who oppresses the poor
person insults his Maker,
but one who is kind to the needy
honors him.

32 The wicked one is thrown down
by his own sin,
but the righteous one has a refuge
in his death.

33 Wisdom resides in the heart
of the discerning;
she is known[B] even among fools.

34 Righteousness exalts a nation,
but sin is a disgrace to any people.

35 A king favors a prudent servant,
but his anger falls on a disgraceful one.

15 A gentle answer turns away anger,
but a harsh word stirs up wrath.

2 The tongue of the wise
makes knowledge attractive,
but the mouth of fools
blurts out foolishness.

3 The eyes of the LORD are everywhere,
observing the wicked and the good.

4 The tongue that heals is a tree of life,
but a devious tongue[C] breaks the spirit.

5 A fool despises his father's discipline,
but a person who accepts correction
is sensible.

6 The house of the righteous
has great wealth,
but trouble accompanies the income
of the wicked.

7 The lips of the wise
broadcast knowledge,
but not so the heart of fools.

8 The sacrifice of the wicked
is detestable to the LORD,
but the prayer of the upright is
his delight.

9 The LORD detests the way of the wicked,
but he loves the one
who pursues righteousness.

10 Discipline is harsh for the one
who leaves the path;
the one who hates correction will die.

11 Sheol and Abaddon lie open
before the LORD —
how much more, human hearts.

[A] **14:23** Lit *but word of lips* [B] **14:33** LXX reads *unknown* [C] **15:4** Lit *but crookedness in it*

12 A mocker doesn't love one
who corrects him;
he will not consult the wise.

13 A joyful heart makes a face cheerful,
but a sad heart produces
a broken spirit.

14 A discerning mind seeks knowledge,
but the mouth of fools feeds
on foolishness.

15 All the days of the oppressed
are miserable,
but a cheerful heart has
a continual feast.

16 Better a little with the fear of the LORD
than great treasure with turmoil.

17 Better a meal of vegetables
where there is love
than a fattened ox with hatred.

18 A hot-tempered person
stirs up conflict,
but one slow to anger calms strife.

19 A slacker's way is like a thorny hedge,
but the path of the upright is a highway.

20 A wise son brings joy to his father,
but a foolish man despises his mother.

21 Foolishness brings joy to one
without sense,
but a person with understanding walks
a straight path.

22 Plans fail when there is no counsel,
but with many advisers they succeed.

23 A person takes joy in giving
an answer;[A]
and a timely word — how good that is!

24 For the prudent the path of life
leads upward,
so that he may avoid going down
to Sheol.

25 The LORD tears apart the house
of the proud,
but he protects the widow's territory.

26 The LORD detests the plans of the one
who is evil,
but pleasant words are pure.

27 The one who profits dishonestly
troubles his household,
but the one who hates bribes will live.

28 The mind of the righteous person
thinks before answering,
but the mouth of the wicked blurts out
evil things.

Support | *Humility*

THE FEAR OF THE LORD

"The fear of the LORD is what wisdom teaches, and humility comes before honor." Proverbs 15:33

Certain people used to be described as "God-fearing." This was a way of saying such a person was devoted *to* God, ever mindful *of* God, and therefore very careful in attitudes, words, and actions.

This is consistent with the way the phrase is used in the Bible. Typically the designation speaks of a kind of reverent awe, a spirit of humility as one lives consciously before the Creator, King, Savior, and Judge of the universe. The fear of God is not usually abject terror or dread unless one becomes aware of sin in his life (see Is 6). It's more an immense respect, a desire to reflect the holy nature of God and to show honor to him out of gratitude and love.

Instead of trying to please everyone, make pleasing God your highest priority.

For the next note on *Support*, see Proverbs 18:1.

[A] **15:23** Lit *in an answer of his mouth*

29 The LORD is far from the wicked,
but he hears the prayer
of the righteous.

30 Bright eyes cheer the heart;
good news strengthens[A] the bones.

31 One who[B] listens to life-giving rebukes
will be at home among the wise.

32 Anyone who ignores discipline
despises himself,
but whoever listens to correction
acquires good sense.[C]

33 The fear of the LORD is what
wisdom teaches,
and humility comes before honor.

16 The reflections of the heart
belong to mankind,
but the answer of the tongue is
from the LORD.

2 All a person's ways seem right to him,
but the LORD weighs motives.[D]

3 Commit your activities to the LORD,
and your plans will be established.

4 The LORD has prepared everything
for his purpose —
even the wicked
for the day of disaster.

5 Everyone with a proud heart is
detestable to the LORD;
be assured,[E] he will not go unpunished.

6 Iniquity is atoned for by loyalty
and faithfulness,
and one turns from evil by the fear
of the LORD.

7 When a person's ways please the LORD,
he makes even his enemies to be
at peace with him.

8 Better a little with righteousness
than great income with injustice.

9 A person's heart plans his way,
but the LORD determines his steps.

10 God's verdict is on the lips of a king;[F]
his mouth should not give
an unfair judgment.

11 Honest balances and scales are
the LORD's;
all the weights in the bag are
his concern.

12 Wicked behavior is detestable to kings,
since a throne is established
through righteousness.

13 Righteous lips are a king's delight,
and he loves one who speaks honestly.

14 A king's fury is a messenger of death,
but a wise person appeases it.

15 When a king's face lights up,
there is life;
his favor is like a cloud
with spring rain.

16 Get wisdom —
how much better it is than gold!
And get understanding —
it is preferable to silver.

17 The highway of the upright avoids evil;
the one who guards his way protects
his life.

18 Pride comes before destruction,
and an arrogant spirit before a fall.

19 Better to be lowly of spirit
with the humble[G]
than to divide plunder
with the proud.

20 The one who understands a matter
finds success,
and the one who trusts in the LORD
will be happy.

21 Anyone with a wise heart
is called discerning,
and pleasant speech[H] increases learning.

22 Insight is a fountain of life
for its possessor,
but the discipline of fools is folly.

[A] 15:30 Lit *makes fat* [B] 15:31 Lit *An ear that* [C] 15:32 Lit *acquires a heart* [D] 16:2 Lit *spirits* [E] 16:5 Lit *hand to hand*
[F] 16:10 Or *A divination is on the lips of a king* [G] 16:19 Alt Hb tradition reads *afflicted* [H] 16:21 Lit *and sweetness of lips*

23 The heart of a wise person instructs
his mouth;
it adds learning to his speech.[A]

24 Pleasant words are a honeycomb:
sweet to the taste[B] and health
to the body.[C]

25 There is a way that seems right
to a person,
but its end is the way to death.

26 A worker's appetite works for him
because his hunger[D] urges him on.

27 A worthless person digs up evil,
and his speech is like a scorching fire.

28 A contrary person spreads conflict,
and a gossip separates close friends.

29 A violent person lures his neighbor,
leading him on a path that is not good.

30 The one who narrows his eyes
is planning deceptions;
the one who compresses his lips
brings about evil.

31 Gray hair is a glorious crown;
it is found in the ways of righteousness.

32 Patience is better than power,
and controlling one's emotions,[E]
than capturing a city.

33 The lot is cast into the lap,
but its every decision is from the LORD.

17 Better a dry crust with peace
than a house full of feasting with strife.

2 A prudent servant will rule over
a disgraceful son
and share an inheritance
among brothers.

3 A crucible for silver, and a smelter
for gold,
and the LORD is the tester of hearts.

4 A wicked person listens to
malicious talk;[F]
a liar pays attention to
a destructive tongue.

5 The one who mocks the poor insults
his Maker,
and one who rejoices over calamity
will not go unpunished.

6 Grandchildren are the crown
of the elderly,
and the pride of children is
their fathers.

7 Eloquent words are not appropriate
on a fool's lips;
how much worse are lies for a ruler.

8 A bribe seems like a magic stone
to its owner;
wherever he turns, he succeeds.

9 Whoever conceals an offense
promotes love,
but whoever gossips about it
separates friends.

10 A rebuke cuts into a perceptive person
more than a hundred lashes into a fool.

11 An evil person desires only rebellion;
a cruel messenger[G] will be sent
against him.

12 Better for a person to meet a bear
robbed of her cubs
than a fool in his foolishness.

13 If anyone returns evil for good,
evil will never depart from his house.

14 To start a conflict is to release a flood;
stop the dispute before it breaks out.

15 Acquitting the guilty and condemning
the just —
both are detestable to the LORD.

16 Why does a fool have money
in his hand
with no intention of buying wisdom?

17 A friend loves at all times,
and a brother is born for a difficult time.

[A] **16:23** Lit *learning upon his lips* [B] **16:24** Lit *throat* [C] **16:24** Lit *bones* [D] **16:26** Lit *mouth* [E] **16:32** Lit *and ruling over one's spirit* [F] **17:4** Lit *to lips of iniquity* [G] **17:11** Or *a merciless angel*

18 One without sense enters
an agreement[A]
and puts up security for his friend.

19 One who loves to offend loves strife;
one who builds a high threshold
invites injury.

20 One with a twisted mind
will not succeed,
and one with deceitful speech
will fall into ruin.

21 A man fathers a fool to his own sorrow;
the father of a fool has no joy.

22 A joyful heart is good medicine,
but a broken spirit
dries up the bones.

23 A wicked person secretly takes a bribe
to subvert the course of justice.

24 Wisdom is the focus of the perceptive,
but a fool's eyes roam to the ends
of the earth.

25 A foolish son is grief to his father
and bitterness to the one
who bore him.

26 It is certainly not good to fine
an innocent person
or to beat a noble for his honesty.[B]

27 The one who has knowledge restrains
his words,
and one who keeps a cool head[C]
is a person of understanding.

28 Even a fool is considered wise
when he keeps silent —
discerning, when he seals his lips.

18 One who isolates himself pursues
selfish desires;
he rebels against all sound wisdom.

2 A fool does not delight
in understanding,
but only wants to show off
his opinions.[D]

3 When a wicked person comes,
contempt also comes,
and along with dishonor, derision.

Eternal Perspective | *Biblical Joy*

ADDRESSING DEPRESSION

"A joyful heart is good medicine, but a broken spirit dries up the bones." Proverbs 17:22

When Solomon speaks of "a broken spirit," he's not referring to a mild case of the blues. The phrase is descriptive of a person who is crushed, beaten down to a state of hopelessness. In Isaiah 16:7, the word is used to describe people who are "completely devastated."

When people find themselves in such a place of despair, the effect transcends emotions. The effects can be physical too (this is the idea behind the phrase "dries up the bones"). If you or someone you love is wrestling with this kind of severe depression, the time has come to seek help. Absolutely no shame—only wisdom—is in that choice. Make an appointment with your primary care doctor. If she suspects the serotonin levels in your brain are low, you may need to see a specialist. The good news is that medication can help with those dark moods.

Solomon refers to another kind of medicine for those who are broken in spirit: "a joyful heart." It doesn't happen instantly, so seek encouraging people who are full of faith and hope, engage in enjoyable activities, serve alongside people who make serving fun, and do things that formerly energized you and made you smile. All of these are ways to treat a broken spirit.

For the next note on *Eternal Perspective*, see Isaiah 6:3.

[A] **17:18** Lit *sense slaps hands* [B] **17:26** Or *noble unfairly* [C] **17:27** Lit *spirit* [D] **18:2** Lit *to uncover his heart*

4 The words of a person's mouth
are deep waters,
a flowing river, a fountain of wisdom.[A]

5 It is not good to show partiality
to the guilty,
denying an innocent
person justice.

6 A fool's lips lead to strife,
and his mouth provokes a beating.

7 A fool's mouth is his devastation,
and his lips are a trap for his life.

8 A gossip's words are like choice food
that goes down
to one's innermost being.[B]

9 The one who is lazy in his work
is brother to a vandal.[C]

10 The name of the LORD is a strong tower;
the righteous run to it
and are protected.[D]

11 The wealth of the rich is
his fortified city;
in his imagination
it is like a high wall.

12 Before his downfall a person's heart
is proud,
but humility comes before honor.

13 The one who gives an answer
before he listens —
this is foolishness and disgrace for him.

14 A person's spirit can endure sickness,
but who can survive a broken spirit?

15 The mind of the discerning
acquires knowledge,
and the ear of the wise seeks it.

16 A person's gift
opens doors[E] for him
and brings him before the great.

17 The first to state his case seems right
until another comes
and cross-examines him.

18 Casting the lot ends quarrels
and separates powerful opponents.

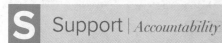

Support | *Accountability*

THE DANGER OF ISOLATION

"One who isolates himself pursues selfish desires; he rebels against all sound wisdom." Proverbs 18:1

Are periodic times of solitude bad for us? Not at all. In fact, time alone, away from the crowd (or from the kids) is actually a healthy discipline that Jesus modeled (Lk 5:16). We would be wise to follow his lead.

But a life of *extreme* isolation is a different matter altogether. One Harvard study found that about a third of the solitary confinement prisoners interviewed were suffering from a wide array of adverse mental conditions—everything from obsessive disorders to panic attacks, to memory loss, paranoia, even psychosis!

No doubt, extreme social isolation isn't good for us. We don't do well all by ourselves. Even if we're on the introverted end of the scale, we need others and they need us. God designed us for relationships; he wants us to congregate. The devil's desire is the precise opposite—to get us to separate and isolate.

Don't isolate yourself.

For the next note on *Support*, see Proverbs 19:20.

[A] **18:4** Or *waters; a fountain of wisdom is a flowing river* [B] **18:8** Lit *to the chambers of the belly* [C] **18:9** Lit *master of destruction* [D] **18:10** Lit *raised high* [E] **18:16** Lit *gift makes room*

19 An offended brother
is harder to reach[A]
than a fortified city,
and quarrels are like the bars
of a fortress.

20 From the fruit of a person's mouth
his stomach is satisfied;
he is filled with the product of his lips.

21 Death and life are in the power
of the tongue,
and those who love it will eat its fruit.

22 A man who finds a wife finds
a good thing
and obtains favor from the LORD.

23 The poor person pleads,
but the rich one answers roughly.

24 One with many friends
may be harmed,[B]
but there is a friend who stays closer
than a brother.

19

Better a poor person who lives
with integrity
than someone who has deceitful lips
and is a fool.

2 Even zeal is not good
without knowledge,
and the one who acts hastily[C] sins.

3 A person's own foolishness leads
him astray,
yet his heart rages against the LORD.

4 Wealth attracts many friends,
but a poor person is separated
from his friend.

5 A false witness
will not go unpunished,
and one who utters lies
will not escape.

6 Many seek a ruler's favor,
and everyone is a friend of one
who gives gifts.

Relationships | *Building Healthy Friendships*

GOING DEEPER

"One with many friends may be harmed, but there is a friend who stays closer than a brother." Proverbs 18:24

What's preferable: having thousands of "friends" and "followers" on social media or a handful of folks who are deeply involved in your life?

"Online community" has some serious built-in weaknesses. Interactions tend to stay on a superficial level. That's not *wrong*, per se, it's just not enough. We're made in the image of the triune God, and so our souls hunger for deeper relationships. Can we really find this in the virtual, disembodied world of cyberspace?

Another temptation online is to project an image that makes us look better than we really are. That inauthenticity doesn't make for true friendships. Then we have the fact that misunderstandings—and hurt feelings—are rampant on social media. Most people aren't great at resolving conflict in person; we might be even worse online. This is why apps give us the option to easily "unfriend" others. Some online relationships don't last fifteen minutes.

Nothing is wrong with reconnecting with old friends and keeping up with acquaintances online. But those relationships can't replace the "friend who stays closer than a brother." Ask God for a couple of deep, real-life friendships. And be that kind of friend yourself.

For the next note on *Relationships*, see Proverbs 22:6.

[A] **18:19** LXX, Syr, Tg, Vg read *is stronger* [B] **18:24** Some LXX mss, Syr, Tg, Vg read *friends must be friendly* [C] **19:2** Lit *who is hasty with feet*

7 All the brothers of a poor person
hate him;
how much more do his friends
keep their distance from him!
He may pursue them with words,
but they are not there.[A]

8 The one who acquires good sense[B]
loves himself;
one who safeguards understanding
finds success.

9 A false witness will not
go unpunished,
and one who utters lies perishes.

10 Luxury is not appropriate for a fool —
how much less for a slave to rule
over princes!

11 A person's insight gives him patience,
and his virtue is to overlook
an offense.

12 A king's rage is like the roaring
of a lion,
but his favor is like dew on the grass.

13 A foolish son is his father's ruin,
and a wife's nagging is
an endless dripping.

14 A house and wealth are inherited
from fathers,
but a prudent wife is from the LORD.

15 Laziness induces deep sleep,
and a lazy person will go hungry.

16 The one who keeps commands
preserves himself;
one who disregards[C] his ways will die.

17 Kindness to the poor is a loan to the LORD,
and he will give a reward to the lender.[D]

18 Discipline your son while there is hope;
don't set your heart on being the cause
of his death.[E]

19 A person with intense anger bears
the penalty;
if you rescue him, you'll have to do
it again.

20 Listen to counsel
and receive instruction
so that you may be wise later in life.[F]

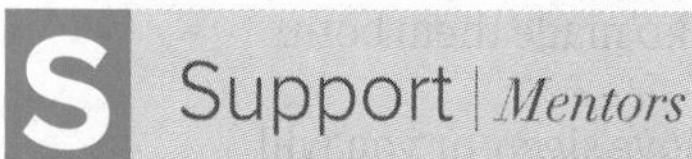

WISE UP

"Listen to counsel and receive instruction so that you may be wise later in life." Proverbs 19:20

Much of what Solomon wrote in Proverbs was directed at youth, specifically, "my son" (see 1:8,10, 15; 2:1; 3:1,21; 4:20; 6:3,20; and many more). That's because young people, even though they have precious little life experience, tend to think they know it all. Remember feeling that way and all those arguments with Mom and Dad?

As we age, however, we discover that older people had a lot of wisdom to impart, and often we think, with regret, *If only I had listened!*

Everyone, young or old, needs to be open to the counsel, advice, and instructions of people with life experience and wisdom. Especially helpful would be those who know God's Word and what it teaches about how to live.

So think carefully about this: What wise person is speaking truth into your life? Find mentors and listen to them.

For the next note on *Support*, see Proverbs 27:17.

[A] **19:7** Hb uncertain [B] **19:8** Lit *acquires a heart* [C] **19:16** Or *despises*, or *treats lightly* [D] **19:17** Lit *to him* [E] **19:18** Lit *don't lift up your soul to his death* [F] **19:20** Lit *in your end*

21 Many plans are in a person's heart,
but the LORD's decree will prevail.

22 What is desirable in a person is
his fidelity;
better to be a poor person than a liar.

23 The fear of the LORD leads to life;
one will sleep at night[A] without danger.

24 The slacker buries his hand in the bowl;
he doesn't even bring it back
to his mouth!

25 Strike a mocker, and the inexperienced
learn a lesson;
rebuke the discerning,
and he gains knowledge.

26 The one who plunders his father
and evicts his mother
is a disgraceful and shameful son.

27 If you stop listening to correction,
my son,
you will stray from the words
of knowledge.

28 A worthless witness mocks justice,
and a wicked mouth
swallows iniquity.

29 Judgments are prepared for mockers,
and beatings for the backs of fools.

20 Wine is a mocker, beer is a brawler;
whoever goes astray[B]
because of them is not wise.

2 A king's terrible wrath is
like the roaring of a lion;
anyone who provokes him
endangers himself.

3 Honor belongs to the person who ends
a dispute,
but any fool can get himself
into a quarrel.

4 The slacker does not plow
during planting season;[C]
at harvest time he looks,[D] and there is
nothing.

5 Counsel in a person's heart is
deep water;
but a person of understanding
draws it out.

6 Many a person proclaims
his own loyalty,
but who can find a trustworthy person?

7 A righteous person acts with integrity;
his children who come after him
will be happy.

8 A king sitting on a throne to judge
separates out all evil with his eyes.

9 Who can say, "I have kept
my heart pure;
I am cleansed from my sin"?

10 Differing weights
and varying measures[E] —
both are detestable to the LORD.

11 Even a young man is known
by his actions —
by whether his behavior is pure
and upright.

12 The hearing ear and the seeing eye —
the LORD made them both.

13 Don't love sleep, or you will
become poor;
open your eyes, and you'll have
enough to eat.

14 "It's worthless, it's worthless!"
the buyer says,
but after he is on his way, he gloats.

15 There is gold and a multitude
of jewels,
but knowledgeable lips are
a rare treasure.

16 Take his garment,
for he has put up security
for a stranger;
get collateral if it is for foreigners.

17 Food gained by fraud is sweet
to a person,

[A] **19:23** Lit *will spend the night satisfied* [B] **20:1** Or *whoever staggers* [C] **20:4** Lit *plow in winter* [D] **20:4** Lit *inquires*
[E] **20:10** Lit *Stone and stone, measure and measure*

but afterward his mouth is full
of gravel.

18 Finalize plans with counsel,
and wage war with sound guidance.

19 The one who reveals secrets is
a constant gossip;
avoid someone with a big mouth.

20 Whoever curses his father or mother —
his lamp will go out
in deep darkness.

21 An inheritance gained prematurely
will not be blessed ultimately.

22 Don't say, "I will avenge this evil!"
Wait on the LORD, and he will
rescue you.

23 Differing weights[A] are detestable
to the LORD,
and dishonest scales are unfair.

24 Even a courageous person's steps
are determined by the LORD,
so how can anyone understand
his own way?

25 It is a trap for anyone to dedicate
something rashly
and later to reconsider his vows.

26 A wise king separates out the wicked
and drives the threshing wheel
over them.

27 The LORD's lamp sheds light on
a person's life,[B]
searching the innermost parts.[C]

28 Loyalty and faithfulness guard
a king;
through loyalty he maintains
his throne.

29 The glory of young men is
their strength,
and the splendor of old men is
gray hair.

30 Lashes and wounds purge away evil,
and beatings cleanse
the innermost parts.[D]

21 A king's heart is like channeled water
in the LORD's hand:
He directs it wherever he chooses.

Rest and Reflection | *Identifying the Issue/Difficulty*

THE LAMP OF GOD'S LOVE

"The LORD's lamp sheds light on a person's life, searching the innermost parts." Proverbs 20:27

Fortunately the time is late, the place is dimly lit, and you forgot your glasses. Because in the bright light of day you'd see just how dirty this diner is and bolt out the door!

Light illuminates. It reveals not-so-pretty realities. That's what Solomon is getting at in this verse. God shines his light of truth on our souls. And we're kidding ourselves if we think we have any secrets from the all-seeing One.

Many find this truth unsettling, uncomfortable, unnerving. They shouldn't. God isn't out to humiliate or embarrass us with his lamp. If Jesus, the One who came to show us what God is like (Jn 1:18), blinds us with truth, it's only so he can then bless us with grace.

God knows us thoroughly, and yet he loves us perfectly. "The LORD's lamp" exposes all our flaws. Then his love forgives and removes them. He is a Revealer, yes, but only so that we will then call on him to be our gracious Redeemer.

For the next note on *Rest and Reflection*, see Ecclesiastes 3:1.

[A] **20:23** Lit *A stone and a stone* [B] **20:27** Lit *breath* [C] **20:27** Lit *the chambers of the belly* [D] **20:30** Lit *beatings the chambers of the belly*

2 All a person's ways seem right to him,
but the LORD weighs hearts.

3 Doing what is righteous and just
is more acceptable to the LORD
than sacrifice.

4 The lamp that guides the wicked —
haughty eyes and an arrogant heart
— is sin.

5 The plans of the diligent certainly lead
to profit,
but anyone who is reckless
certainly becomes poor.

6 Making a fortune through a lying tongue
is a vanishing mist,[A] a pursuit of death.[B,C]

7 The violence of the wicked
sweeps them away
because they refuse to act justly.

8 A guilty one's conduct is crooked,
but the behavior of the innocent
is upright.

9 Better to live on the corner of a roof
than to share a house with a nagging wife.

10 A wicked person desires evil;
he has no consideration[D]
for his neighbor.

11 When a mocker is punished,
the inexperienced become wiser;
when one teaches a wise man,
he acquires knowledge.

12 The Righteous One[E] considers
the house of the wicked;
he brings the wicked to ruin.

13 The one who shuts his ears to the cry
of the poor
will himself also call out
and not be answered.

14 A secret gift soothes anger,
and a covert bribe, fierce rage.

15 Justice executed is a joy
to the righteous
but a terror to those
who practice iniquity.

16 The person who strays from the way
of prudence
will come to rest in the assembly of
the departed spirits.

17 The one who loves pleasure
will become poor;
whoever loves wine and oil will not
get rich.

18 The wicked are a ransom
for the righteous,
and the treacherous, for[F] the upright.

19 Better to live in a wilderness
than with a nagging
and hot-tempered wife.

20 Precious treasure and oil are
in the dwelling of a wise person,
but a fool consumes them.[G]

21 The one who pursues righteousness
and faithful love
will find life, righteousness,
and honor.

22 A wise person went up against a city
of warriors
and brought down its secure fortress.

23 The one who guards his mouth
and tongue
keeps himself out of trouble.

24 The arrogant and proud person,
named "Mocker,"
acts with excessive arrogance.

25 A slacker's craving will kill him
because his hands refuse to work.

26 He is filled with craving[H] all day long,
but the righteous give and don't
hold back.

27 The sacrifice of a wicked person
is detestable —
how much more so
when he brings it
with ulterior motives!

[A] **21:6** Or *a breath blown away* [B] **21:6** Some Hb mss, LXX, Vg read *a snare of death* [C] **21:6** Lit *is vanity, ones seeking death* [D] **21:10** Or *favor* [E] **21:12** Or *righteous one* [F] **21:18** Or *in place of* [G] **21:20** Lit *it* [H] **21:26** Lit *He craves a craving*

28 A lying witness will perish,
but the one who listens
will speak successfully.

29 A wicked person puts on a bold face,
but the upright one considers
his way.

30 No wisdom, no understanding,
and no counsel
will prevail against the LORD.

31 A horse is prepared for the day
of battle,
but victory comes from the LORD.

22 A good name is to be chosen
over great wealth;
favor is better than silver and gold.

2 Rich and poor have this in common:[A]
the LORD makes them all.

3 A sensible person sees danger
and takes cover,
but the inexperienced keep going
and are punished.

4 Humility, the fear of the LORD,
results in wealth, honor, and life.

5 There are thorns and snares
on the way of the crooked;
the one who guards himself stays
far from them.

6 Start a youth out on his way;
even when he grows old he will
not depart from it.

7 The rich rule over the poor,
and the borrower is a slave to the lender.

8 The one who sows injustice
will reap disaster,
and the rod of his fury
will be destroyed.

9 A generous person[B] will be blessed,
for he shares his food with the poor.

10 Drive out a mocker, and conflict
goes too;
then quarreling and dishonor
will cease.

R Relationships | *Relating to Children*

WAYWARD KIDS

"Start a youth out on his way; even when he grows old he will not depart from it." Proverbs 22:6

This is a painful Bible verse for many parents. That's because when their children were small, they latched onto this proverb, thinking it a kind of formula—even a guarantee—for parenting success. They concluded, *If I just immerse my kids in church when they're little, they'll love and serve God all their lives.*

Only it didn't work out that way. When those same "church kids" reached adolescence or young adulthood, they walked or, in some cases, ran away from the faith. And many of them ended up in serious trouble.

If you're one of these parents, here are three important truths and reminders: (1) The proverbs are true observations about the way life generally works—they're not promises. Our hope isn't in "formulas" but in the living God; (2) God loves and knows your kids much deeper and better than you do; and (3) God is infinitely creative and powerful—he can reach your child in ways and places that you never dreamed.

So keep praying, keep trusting, and keep loving. Nothing is too hard for the Lord.

For the next note on *Relationships*, see Proverbs 27:6.

[A] **22:2** Lit *poor meet* [B] **22:9** Lit *Good of eye*

11 The one who loves a pure heart
and gracious lips — the king is
his friend.

12 The LORD's eyes keep watch
over knowledge,
but he overthrows the words
of the treacherous.

13 The slacker says,
"There's a lion outside!
I'll be killed in the public square!"

14 The mouth of the forbidden woman is
a deep pit;
a man cursed by the LORD will fall
into it.

15 Foolishness is bound to the heart
of a youth;
a rod of discipline will separate it
from him.

16 Oppressing the poor to enrich oneself,
and giving to the rich — both lead
only to poverty.

WORDS OF THE WISE

17 Listen closely,[A] pay attention
to the words of the wise,
and apply your mind
to my knowledge.
18 For it is pleasing if you keep them
within you
and if they are[B] constantly
on your lips.
19 I have instructed you today —
even you —
so that your confidence may be
in the LORD.
20 Haven't I written for you thirty sayings[C]
about counsel and knowledge,
21 in order to teach you true
and reliable words,
so that you may give
a dependable report[D]
to those who sent you?

22 Don't rob a poor person
because he is poor,
and don't crush the oppressed at
the city gate,
23 for the LORD will champion their cause
and will plunder those
who plunder them.

24 Don't make friends with an angry person,[E]
and don't be a companion
of a hot-tempered one,
25 or you will learn his ways
and entangle yourself in a snare.

26 Don't be one of those
who enter agreements,[F]
who put up security for loans.
27 If you have nothing with which to pay,
even your bed will be taken
from under you.

28 Don't move an ancient boundary marker
that your fathers set up.

29 Do you see a person skilled in his work?
He will stand in the presence of kings.
He will not stand in the presence
of the unknown.

23 When you sit down to dine
with a ruler,
consider carefully what[G] is before you,
2 and put a knife to your throat
if you have a big[H] appetite;
3 don't desire his choice food,
for that food is deceptive.

4 Don't wear yourself out to get rich;
because you know better, stop!
5 As soon as your eyes fly to it,
it disappears,
for it makes wings for itself
and flies like an eagle to the sky.

6 Don't eat a stingy person's bread,[I]
and don't desire his choice food,
7 for it's like someone calculating
inwardly.[J]
"Eat and drink," he says to you,
but his heart is not with you.
8 You will vomit the little you've eaten
and waste your pleasant words.

[A] **22:17** Lit *Stretch out your ear* [B] **22:18** Or *you; let them be*, or *you, so that they are* [C] **22:20** Text emended; one Hb tradition reads *you previously*; alt Hb tradition reads *you excellent things*; LXX, Syr, Vg read *you three times* [D] **22:21** Lit *give dependable words* [E] **22:24** Lit *with a master of anger* [F] **22:26** Lit *Don't be among hand slappers* [G] **23:1** Or *who* [H] **23:2** Lit *you are the master of an* [I] **23:6** Lit *eat bread of an evil eye* [J] **23:7** LXX reads *it is like someone swallowing a hair in the throat*

My Story | Tim

I can't tell you how many Alcoholics Anonymous meetings I've sat through, by now maybe thousands. I've listened to countless wrenching stories of family abuse, neglect, and all sorts of difficult childhood circumstances that contributed to people seeking relief in a bottle. Those stories sometimes list their excuses for drinking and have not been helpful. But when the hardships are just explanations leading up to their own choices to drink, the stories help. That's because I didn't have any excuses for becoming a drunk. I had loving parents and a great family. My childhood was a wonderful time that included some hard things but was filled with adventure. I have only myself to blame for experimenting wildly with drugs and settling eventually on alcohol as my anesthesia of choice.

I turned my back on everything that part of me knew was right and good. I did it because I could and because another part of me thought I might find something better somewhere out there. By the time I realized nothing better was available, my life was literally out of control. I struggled for a long time. When I staggered into an AA meeting, I was almost dead. Someone had to take me to the hospital. I had nothing left in myself to depend on and was finally ready for help.

My restoration was slow, humiliating, and healthy. I eventually realized the power outside myself that was helping me one day at a time had a name, and he was a familiar person from my past—the same Jesus who had been part of my upbringing. Once I realized that, many things about life became clear.

Sobriety no longer means just not drinking; it means having a life with purpose. And one day at a time is now not so much about staying sober but about following Jesus wherever he leads me. I've come full circle.

9 Don't speak to[A] a fool,
for he will despise the insight
of your words.

10 Don't move an ancient
boundary marker,
and don't encroach on the fields
of the fatherless,
11 for their Redeemer is strong,
and he will champion their cause
against you.

12 Apply yourself to discipline
and listen to words of knowledge.

13 Don't withhold discipline from a youth;
if you punish him with a rod,
he will not die.
14 Punish him with a rod,
and you will rescue his life from Sheol.

15 My son, if your heart is wise,
my heart will indeed rejoice.
16 My innermost being will celebrate
when your lips say what is right.

17 Don't let your heart envy sinners;
instead, always fear the LORD.
18 For then you will have a future,
and your hope will not be dashed.

19 Listen, my son, and be wise;
keep your mind on the right course.
20 Don't associate with those who drink
too much wine
or with those who gorge themselves
on meat.
21 For the drunkard and the glutton
will become poor,
and grogginess will clothe them
in rags.

22 Listen to your father
who gave you life,
and don't despise your mother
when[B] she is old.
23 Buy — and do not sell — truth,
wisdom, instruction,
and understanding.
24 The father of a righteous son
will rejoice greatly,
and one who fathers a wise son
will delight in him.
25 Let your father and mother have joy,
and let her who gave birth to you
rejoice.

[A] **23:9** Lit *in the ears of* [B] **23:22** Or *because*

26 My son, give me your heart,
and let your eyes observe my ways.
27 For a prostitute is a deep pit,
and a wayward woman is
a narrow well;
28 indeed, she sets an ambush
like a robber
and increases the number
of unfaithful people.

29 Who has woe? Who has sorrow?
Who has conflicts?
Who has complaints?
Who has wounds for no reason?
Who has red eyes?
30 Those who linger over wine;
those who go looking for mixed wine.
31 Don't gaze at wine because it is red,
because it gleams in the cup
and goes down smoothly.
32 In the end it bites like a snake
and stings like a viper.
33 Your eyes will see strange things,
and you will say absurd things.[A]
34 You'll be like someone sleeping
out at sea
or lying down on the top
of a ship's mast.
35 "They struck me, but[B] I feel no pain!
They beat me, but I didn't know it!
When will I wake up?
I'll look for another drink."

24 Don't envy the evil
or desire to be with them,
2 for their hearts plan violence,
and their words stir up trouble.

3 A house is built by wisdom,
and it is established
by understanding;
4 by knowledge the rooms are filled
with every precious
and beautiful treasure.

5 A wise warrior is better
than a strong one,[C]
and a man of knowledge than one
of strength;[D]
6 for you should wage war
with sound guidance —
victory comes with many counselors.
7 Wisdom is inaccessible to[E] a fool;
he does not open his mouth
at the city gate.

8 The one who plots evil
will be called a schemer.
9 A foolish scheme is sin,
and a mocker is detestable to people.

10 If you do nothing in a difficult time,
your strength is limited.
11 Rescue those being taken off to death,
and save those stumbling
toward slaughter.
12 If you say, "But we didn't know
about this,"
won't he who weighs hearts
consider it?
Won't he who protects your life know?
Won't he repay a person according to
his work?

13 Eat honey, my son, for it is good,
and the honeycomb is sweet
to your palate;
14 realize that wisdom is the same for you.
If you find it, you will have a future,
and your hope will never fade.

15 Don't set an ambush, you wicked one,
at the camp of the righteous man;
don't destroy his dwelling.
16 Though a righteous person falls
seven times,
he will get up,
but the wicked
will stumble into ruin.

17 Don't gloat when your enemy falls,
and don't let your heart rejoice
when he stumbles,
18 or the LORD will see, be displeased,
and turn his wrath away from him.

19 Don't be agitated by evildoers,
and don't envy the wicked.
20 For the evil have no future;
the lamp of the wicked will be put out.

21 My son, fear the LORD, as well as
the king,
and don't associate with rebels,[F]

[A] **23:33** Or *will speak perversities*, or *inverted things* [B] **23:35** LXX, Syr, Tg, Vg read *me," you will say, "but* [C] **24:5** LXX, Syr; MT reads *is in strength* [D] **24:5** LXX, Syr, Tg; MT reads *knowledge exerts strength* [E] **24:7** Lit *is too high for* [F] **24:21** Or *those given to change*

22 for destruction will come suddenly
from them;
who knows what distress these two
can bring?

23 These sayings also belong to the wise:

It is not good to show partiality
in judgment.
24 Whoever says to the guilty,
"You are innocent" —
peoples will curse him, and nations
will denounce him;
25 but it will go well with those
who convict the guilty,
and a generous blessing will come
to them.

26 He who gives an honest answer
gives a kiss on the lips.

27 Complete your outdoor work,
and prepare your field;
afterward, build your house.

28 Don't testify against your neighbor
without cause.
Don't deceive with your lips.
29 Don't say, "I'll do to him what he did
to me;
I'll repay the man for what he has done."

30 I went by the field of a slacker
and by the vineyard of one lacking sense.
31 Thistles had come up everywhere,
weeds covered the ground,
and the stone wall was ruined.
32 I saw, and took it to heart;
I looked, and received instruction:
33 a little sleep, a little slumber,
a little folding of the arms to rest,
34 and your poverty will come
like a robber,
and your need, like a bandit.

HEZEKIAH'S COLLECTION

25 These too are proverbs of Solomon,
which the men of King Hezekiah
of Judah copied.

2 It is the glory of God to conceal a matter
and the glory of kings to investigate
a matter.
3 As the heavens are high and the earth
is deep,
so the hearts of kings cannot
be investigated.

4 Remove impurities from silver,
and material will be produced[A]
for a silversmith.[B]
5 Remove the wicked
from the king's presence,
and his throne will be established
in righteousness.

6 Don't boast about yourself
before the king,
and don't stand in the place
of the great;
7 for it is better for him to say to you,
"Come up here!"
than to demote you in plain view
of a noble.[C]

8 Don't take a matter to court hastily.
Otherwise, what will
you do afterward
if your opponent[D] humiliates you?
9 Make your case with your opponent
without revealing another's secret;
10 otherwise, the one who hears
will disgrace you,
and you'll never live it down.[E]

A word spoken at the right time is like gold apples in silver settings.
—Proverbs 25:11

11 A word spoken at the right time
is like gold apples in silver settings.
12 A wise correction to a receptive ear
is like a gold ring or an ornament
of gold.

13 To those who send him,
a trustworthy envoy
is like the coolness of snow
on a harvest day;
he refreshes the life of his masters.

[A] **25:4** Lit *will come out*; Ex 32:24 [B] **25:4** Or *and a vessel will be produced by a silversmith* [C] **25:7** Lit *you before a noble whom your eyes see* [D] **25:8** Or *neighbor*, also in v. 9 [E] **25:10** Lit *and your evil report will not turn back*

14 The one who boasts about a gift
that does not exist
is like clouds and wind without rain.
15 A ruler can be persuaded
through patience,
and a gentle tongue can break a bone.
16 If you find honey, eat only
what you need;
otherwise, you'll get sick from it
and vomit.
17 Seldom set foot
in your neighbor's house;
otherwise, he'll get sick of you
and hate you.

18 A person giving false testimony
against his neighbor
is like a club, a sword, or a sharp arrow.
19 Trusting an unreliable person in a
difficult time
is like a rotten tooth
or a faltering foot.

20 Singing songs to a troubled heart
is like taking off clothing
on a cold day
or like pouring vinegar on soda.[A]

21 If your enemy is hungry, give him food
to eat,
and if he is thirsty, give him water
to drink;
22 for you will heap burning coals
on his head,
and the LORD will reward you.

23 The north wind produces rain,
and a backbiting tongue, angry looks.
24 Better to live on the corner of a roof
than to share a house
with a nagging wife.
25 Good news from a distant land
is like cold water to a parched throat.[B]
26 A righteous person who yields
to the wicked
is like a muddied spring
or a polluted well.
27 It is not good to eat too much honey
or to seek glory after glory.[C]
28 A person who does not control
his temper
is like a city whose wall
is broken down.

26 Like snow in summer and rain
at harvest,
honor is inappropriate for a fool.
2 Like a flitting sparrow
or a fluttering swallow,
an undeserved curse goes nowhere.
3 A whip for the horse, a bridle
for the donkey,
and a rod for the backs of fools.
4 Don't answer a fool according to
his foolishness
or you'll be like him yourself.
5 Answer a fool according to
his foolishness
or he'll become wise in his own eyes.
6 The one who sends a message
by a fool's hand
cuts off his own feet
and drinks violence.
7 A proverb in the mouth of a fool
is like lame legs that hang limp.
8 Giving honor to a fool
is like binding a stone in a sling.
9 A proverb in the mouth of a fool
is like a stick with thorns,
brandished by[D] the hand
of a drunkard.
10 The one who hires a fool or who hires
those passing by
is like an archer who wounds everyone.
11 As a dog returns to its vomit,
so also a fool repeats his foolishness.
12 Do you see a person who is wise
in his own eyes?
There is more hope for a fool
than for him.

13 The slacker says, "There's a lion
in the road —
a lion in the public square!"
14 A door turns on its hinges,
and a slacker, on his bed.
15 The slacker buries his hand in the bowl;
he is too weary to bring it
to his mouth!
16 In his own eyes, a slacker is wiser
than seven who can answer sensibly.

17 A person who is passing by and
meddles in a quarrel that's not his
is like one who grabs a dog by the ears.
18 Like a madman who throws
flaming darts and deadly arrows,

[A] **25:20** Lit *natron, or sodium carbonate* [B] **25:25** Or *a weary person* [C] **25:27** Lit *seek their glory, glory* [D] **26:9** Lit *thorn that goes up into*

19 so is the person who deceives
his neighbor
and says, "I was only joking!"

20 Without wood, fire goes out;
without a gossip, conflict dies down.
21 As charcoal for embers and wood
for fire,
so is a quarrelsome person
for kindling strife.
22 A gossip's words are like choice food
that goes down to
one's innermost being.[A]

23 Smooth[B] lips with an evil heart
are like glaze on an earthen vessel.
24 A hateful person disguises himself
with his speech
and harbors deceit within.
25 When he speaks graciously,
don't believe him,
for there are seven detestable things
in his heart.
26 Though his hatred is concealed
by deception,
his evil will be revealed in the assembly.
27 The one who digs a pit will fall into it,
and whoever rolls a stone —
it will come back on him.
28 A lying tongue hates those it crushes,
and a flattering mouth causes ruin.

27 Don't boast about tomorrow,
for you don't know what a day
might bring.

2 Let another praise you, and not
your own mouth —
a stranger, and not your own lips.

3 A stone is heavy and sand, a burden,
but aggravation from a fool
outweighs them both.

4 Fury is cruel, and anger a flood,
but who can withstand jealousy?

5 Better an open reprimand
than concealed love.

6 The wounds of a friend are trustworthy,
but the kisses of an enemy
are excessive.

7 A person who is full tramples
on a honeycomb,
but to a hungry person, any bitter thing
is sweet.

Relationships | *Relating to Friends*

HEALING WOUNDS

"The wounds of a friend are trustworthy, but the kisses of an enemy are excessive." Proverbs 27:6

From getting a shot to getting in shape and from undergoing surgery to undergoing months of grueling rehab, this much is clear: Getting healthy (or staying healthy) almost always involves some pain.

This is a fact of life, and it applies to more than just the physical/medical realm. Every kind of health—relational, emotional, financial, spiritual—requires facing painful realities. Sometimes we can find the courage to look in the mirror ourselves. Most of the time, we need others to hold up a mirror to us.

Here's the problem: When trusted friends summon up the courage to tell us painful truths—"You have a problem. I'm scared for you if you don't get some help"—our instinct is to get defensive. The truth often stings! But Proverbs says that lashing out is the mark of a foolish person, and that the "wounds of a friend" are a precious gift. When confronted in love, we should hug—not try to wring—the other person's neck!

According to Solomon, this willingness to tell the truth is how we know who our true friends are.

For the next note on *Relationships*, see Proverbs 28:13.

[A] **26:22** Lit *to the chambers of the belly* [B] **26:23** LXX; MT reads *Burning*

8 Anyone wandering from his home
is like a bird wandering from its nest.

9 Oil and incense bring joy to the heart,
and the sweetness of a friend is better
than self-counsel.[A]

10 Don't abandon your friend
or your father's friend,
and don't go to your brother's house
in your time of calamity;
better a neighbor nearby
than a brother far away.

11 Be wise, my son, and bring
my heart joy,
so that I can answer anyone
who taunts me.

12 A sensible person sees danger
and takes cover;
the inexperienced keep going
and are punished.

13 Take his garment,
for he has put up security
for a stranger;
get collateral if it is for foreigners.[B]

14 If one blesses his neighbor
with a loud voice early in the morning,
it will be counted as a curse to him.

15 An endless dripping on a rainy day
and a nagging wife are alike;
16 the one who controls her controls
the wind
and grasps oil with his right hand.

17 Iron sharpens iron,
and one person sharpens another.[C]

18 Whoever tends a fig tree will eat
its fruit,
and whoever looks after his master
will be honored.

19 As water reflects the face,
so the heart reflects the person.

20 Sheol and Abaddon are never satisfied,
and people's eyes are never satisfied.

21 A crucible refines silver, a smelter
refines gold,
and a person refines his praise.

22 Though you grind a fool
in a mortar with a pestle
along with grain,

Support | *Openness with Others*

WANT TO BE SHARPER?

"Iron sharpens iron, and one person sharpens another." Proverbs 27:17

They rubbed us the wrong way (or so we thought at the time). The parent who insisted that we respect authority. The coach who pushed us and stretched us further than we ever thought we could go. The teacher who demanded excellence. The boss who fined then fired us when we were chronically late.

By setting high standards, and holding us accountable—through teaching us, encouraging us, and correcting us—these people were actually shaping us, making us better.

Think of how a metal file is used to sharpen a dull axe. It's a process that results in friction and heat, sometimes even sparks! But the end result is a useful tool that enhances life. This is a picture of how mentoring and healthy friendships work.

Beware of people—in fact, *avoid* people—who are grinding you down solely to make themselves feel better. But seek out, and be thankful for, people who will help you smooth away your rough edges. Though it feels like they're rubbing us the wrong way, in truth, it's the right way.

For the next note on *Support*, see Isaiah 30:10-11.

[A] **27:9** LXX reads *heart, but the soul is torn up by affliction* [B] **27:13** Lit *a foreign woman* [C] **27:17** Lit *and a man sharpens his friend's face*

you will not separate his foolishness
from him.

23 Know well the condition of your flock,
and pay attention to your herds,
24 for wealth is not forever;
not even a crown lasts for all time.
25 When hay is removed
and new growth appears
and the grain from the hills
is gathered in,
26 lambs will provide your clothing,
and goats, the price of a field;
27 there will be enough goat's milk
for your food —
food for your household
and nourishment for your
female servants.

28 The wicked flee when no one
is pursuing them,
but the righteous are as bold as a lion.

2 When a land is in rebellion, it has
many rulers,
but with a discerning
and knowledgeable person, it endures.

3 A destitute leader[A] who oppresses
the poor
is like a driving rain that leaves no food.

4 Those who reject the law
praise the wicked,
but those who keep the law pit
themselves against them.

5 The evil do not understand justice,
but those who seek the LORD
understand everything.

6 Better the poor person who lives
with integrity
than the rich one who distorts right
and wrong.[B]

7 A discerning son keeps the law,
but a companion of gluttons humiliates
his father.
8 Whoever increases his wealth
through excessive interest
collects it for one who is kind
to the poor.

9 Anyone who turns his ear
away from hearing the law —
even his prayer is detestable.

10 The one who leads the upright
into an evil way
will fall into his own pit,
but the blameless will inherit
what is good.

11 A rich person is wise in his own eyes,
but a poor one who has discernment
sees through him.

12 When the righteous triumph,
there is great rejoicing,[C]
but when the wicked come to power,
people hide.

13 The one who conceals his sins
will not prosper,
but whoever confesses
and renounces them
will find mercy.

14 Happy is the one who is always
reverent,
but one who hardens his heart falls
into trouble.

15 A wicked ruler over a helpless people
is like a roaring lion
or a charging bear.

16 A leader who lacks understanding
is very oppressive,
but one who hates dishonest profit
prolongs his life.

17 Someone burdened by bloodguilt[D]
will be a fugitive until death.
Let no one help him.

18 The one who lives with integrity
will be helped,
but one who distorts
right and wrong[E]
will suddenly fall.

19 The one who works his land
will have plenty of food,
but whoever chases fantasies
will have his fill of poverty.

[A] **28:3** LXX reads *A wicked man* [B] **28:6** Lit *who twists two ways* [C] **28:12** Lit *glory* [D] **28:17** Lit *the blood of a person*
[E] **28:18** Lit *who is twisted regarding two ways*

20 A faithful person will have
many blessings,
but one in a hurry to get rich
will not go unpunished.

21 It is not good to show partiality—
yet even a courageous person may sin
for a piece of bread.

22 A greedy one[A] is in a hurry for wealth;
he doesn't know that poverty will come
to him.

23 One who rebukes a person
will later find more favor
than one who flatters[B] with his tongue.

24 The one who robs his father or mother
and says, "That's no sin,"
is a companion to a person who destroys.

25 A greedy person stirs up conflict,
but whoever trusts in the LORD
will prosper.

26 The one who trusts in himself[C] is a fool,
but one who walks in wisdom
will be safe.

27 The one who gives to the poor
will not be in need,
but one who turns
his eyes away[D]
will receive many curses.

28 When the wicked come to power,
people hide,
but when they are destroyed,
the righteous flourish.

29 One who becomes stiff-necked,
after many reprimands
will be shattered instantly—
beyond recovery.

2 When the righteous flourish,
the people rejoice,
but when the wicked rule,
people groan.

3 A man who loves wisdom brings joy
to his father,
but one who consorts with prostitutes
destroys his wealth.

4 By justice a king brings stability
to a land,

Relationships | *Admitting Wrongs*

TRUE CONFESSIONS

"The one who conceals his sins will not prosper, but whoever confesses and renounces them will find mercy." Proverbs 28:13

Maybe you can relate to this situation. You do something wrong—really wrong. A trickle of guilt is followed by a wave of shame. Internal voices follow: "How *could* you? You're the *worst!* Only *you* would stoop this low!" Hearing all those accusations, you make a panicked vow, "No one can *ever* know!" Thus begins an exhausting effort of hiding and pretending. It's a miserable, graceless existence.

The good news is that we don't have to settle for that. We can experience mercy!

Admittedly, the process seems counterintuitive. We stop protecting our image. We come out of hiding. We confess our sins to God and—with his help—renounce them. The stunning promise of Scripture is that the Lord forgives *and* cleanses all who are honest about their failures (1Jn 1:9). (Many have found blessing—not cursing—by humbly opening up to a trusted Christian counselor or pastor as well!)

The notion that concealing our sins is the best way to a good life is a devilish lie. Our ugly secrets serve only to imprison us and keep us sick.

For the next note on *Relationships*, see Ecclesiastes 2:18,20.

[A] 28:22 Lit *A man with an evil eye* [B] 28:23 Lit *is smooth* [C] 28:26 Lit *his heart* [D] 28:27 Lit *who shuts his eyes*

but a person who demands
"contributions"[A]
demolishes it.

5 A person who flatters[B] his neighbor
spreads a net for his feet.

6 An evil person is caught by sin,
but the righteous one sings
and rejoices.

7 The righteous person knows the rights[C]
of the poor,
but the wicked one does not
understand these concerns.

8 Mockers inflame a city,
but the wise turn away anger.

9 If a wise person goes to court
with a fool,
there will be ranting and raving
but no resolution.[D]

10 Bloodthirsty men hate
an honest person,
but the upright care about him.[E]

11 A fool gives full vent to his anger,[F]
but a wise person holds it in check.

12 If a ruler listens to lies,
all his officials will be wicked.

13 The poor and the oppressor have this
in common:[G]
the LORD gives light to the eyes of both.

14 A king who judges the poor
with fairness —
his throne will be established forever.

15 A rod of correction imparts wisdom,
but a youth left to himself[H]
is a disgrace to his mother.

16 When the wicked increase,
rebellion increases,
but the righteous will see
their downfall.

17 Discipline your child, and it will bring
you peace of mind
and give you delight.

18 Without revelation[I] people run wild,
but one who follows divine instruction
will be happy.

19 A servant cannot be disciplined
by words;
though he understands,
he doesn't respond.

20 Do you see someone who speaks
too soon?
There is more hope for a fool
than for him.

21 A servant pampered from his youth
will become arrogant[J] later on.

22 An angry person stirs up conflict,
and a hot-tempered one[K]
increases rebellion.

23 A person's pride will humble him,
but a humble spirit will gain honor.

24 To be a thief's partner is to hate oneself;
he hears the curse but will not testify.

25 The fear of mankind is a snare,
but the one who trusts in the LORD
is protected.[L]

26 Many desire a ruler's favor,
but a person receives justice
from the LORD.

27 An unjust person is detestable
to the righteous,
and one whose way is upright
is detestable to the wicked.

THE WORDS OF AGUR

30 The words of Agur son of Jakeh.
The pronouncement.[M]

The man's oration to Ithiel, to Ithiel
and Ucal:[N]

[A] **29:4** The Hb word for *contributions* usually refers to offerings in worship. [B] **29:5** Lit *is smooth on* [C] **29:7** Lit *justice* [D] **29:9** Lit *rest* [E] **29:10** Or *person, and seek the life of the upright* [F] **29:11** Lit *spirit* [G] **29:13** Lit *oppressor meet* [H] **29:15** Lit *youth sent away* [I] **29:18** Lit *vision* [J] **29:21** Hb obscure [K] **29:22** Lit *a master of rage* [L] **29:25** Lit *raised high* [M] **30:1** Or *son of Jakeh from Massa*; Pr 31:1 [N] **30:1** Hb uncertain. Sometimes read with different word division as *oration: I am weary, God, I am weary, God, and I am exhausted*, or *oration: I am not God, I am not God, that I should prevail*. LXX reads *My son, fear my words and when you have received them repent. The man says these things to the believers in God, and I pause.*

2 I am more stupid than
any other person,[A]
and I lack a human's ability
to understand.
3 I have not gained wisdom,
and I have no knowledge
of the Holy One.
4 Who has gone up to heaven
and come down?
Who has gathered the wind
in his hands?
Who has bound up the waters
in a cloak?
Who has established all the ends
of the earth?
What is his name,
and what is the name of his son —
if you know?
5 Every word of God is pure;[B]
he is a shield to those who take refuge
in him.
6 Don't add to his words,
or he will rebuke you, and you will be
proved a liar.

7 Two things I ask of you;
don't deny them to me before I die:
8 Keep falsehood and deceitful words
far from me.
Give me neither poverty nor wealth;
feed me with the food I need.
9 Otherwise, I might have too much
and deny you, saying,
"Who is the LORD?"
or I might have nothing and steal,
profaning[C] the name of my God.

10 Don't slander a servant to his master
or he will curse you, and you will
become guilty.

11 There is a generation that curses
its father
and does not bless its mother.
12 There is a generation that is pure
in its own eyes,
yet is not washed from its filth.
13 There is a generation — how haughty
its eyes
and pretentious its looks.[D]
14 There is a generation whose teeth
are swords,
whose fangs are knives,
devouring the oppressed from the land
and the needy from among mankind.

15 The leech has two daughters:
"Give, Give!"
Three things are never satisfied;
four never say, "Enough!":
16 Sheol; a childless womb;
earth, which is never satisfied
with water;
and fire, which never says, "Enough!"

17 As for the eye that ridicules a father
and despises obedience to a mother,
may ravens of the valley pluck it out
and young vultures eat it.

18 Three things are too wondrous for me;
four I can't understand:
19 the way of an eagle in the sky,
the way of a snake on a rock,
the way of a ship at sea,
and the way of a man
with a young woman.

20 This is the way of an adulteress:
she eats and wipes her mouth
and says, "I've done nothing wrong."

21 The earth trembles under three things;
it cannot bear up under four:
22 a servant when he becomes king,
a fool when he is stuffed with food,
23 an unloved woman when she marries,
and a servant girl when she ousts
her queen.

24 Four things on earth are small,
yet they are extremely wise:
25 ants are not a strong people,
yet they store up their food
in the summer;
26 hyraxes are not a mighty people,
yet they make their homes in the cliffs;
27 locusts have no king,
yet all of them march in ranks;
28 a lizard[E] can be caught in your hands,
yet it lives in kings' palaces.

29 Three things are stately in their stride;
four are stately in their walk:
30 a lion, which is mightiest among beasts
and doesn't retreat before anything;

[A] 30:2 Lit *I am more stupid than a man* [B] 30:5 Lit *refined* [C] 30:9 Lit *grabbing* [D] 30:13 Lit *and its eyelids lifted up*
[E] 30:28 Or *spider*

31 a strutting rooster;[A] a goat;
and a king at the head of his army.[B]

32 If you have been foolish
by exalting yourself
or if you've been scheming,
put your hand over your mouth.
33 For the churning of milk
produces butter,
and twisting a nose draws blood,
and stirring up anger produces strife.

THE WORDS OF LEMUEL

31 The words of King Lemuel,
a pronouncement[C] that his mother
taught him:

2 What should I say, my son?
What, son of my womb?
What, son of my vows?
3 Don't spend your energy on women
or your efforts on those
who destroy kings.
4 It is not for kings, Lemuel,
it is not for kings to drink wine
or for rulers to desire beer.
5 Otherwise, he will drink,
forget what is decreed,
and pervert justice for all
the oppressed.[D]
6 Give beer to one who is dying
and wine to one whose life is bitter.
7 Let him drink so that he can forget
his poverty
and remember his trouble no more.
8 Speak up[E] for those who have no voice,[F]
for the justice of all
who are dispossessed.[G]
9 Speak up, judge righteously,
and defend the cause of the oppressed
and needy.

IN PRAISE OF A WIFE OF NOBLE CHARACTER

10 Who can find a wife of noble character?[H]
She is far more precious than jewels.[I]
11 The heart of her husband trusts in her,
and he will not lack anything good.
12 She rewards him with good, not evil,
all the days of her life.
13 She selects wool and flax
and works with willing hands.
14 She is like the merchant ships,
bringing her food from far away.
15 She rises while it is still night
and provides food for her household
and portions[J] for her female servants.
16 She evaluates a field and buys it;
she plants a vineyard with her earnings.[K]
17 She draws on her strength[L]
and reveals that her arms are strong.
18 She sees that her profits are good,
and her lamp never goes out at night.
19 She extends her hands
to the spinning staff,
and her hands hold the spindle.
20 Her hands reach[M] out to the poor,
and she extends her hands to the needy.
21 She is not afraid for her household
when it snows,
for all in her household
are doubly clothed.[N]
22 She makes her own bed coverings;
her clothing is fine linen and purple.
23 Her husband is known at the city gates,
where he sits among the elders
of the land.
24 She makes and sells linen garments;
she delivers belts[O] to the merchants.
25 Strength and honor are her clothing,
and she can laugh at the time to come.
26 Her mouth speaks wisdom,
and loving instruction[P] is
on her tongue.
27 She watches over the activities
of her household
and is never idle.[Q]
28 Her children rise up
and call her blessed;
her husband also praises her:
29 "Many women[R] have done noble deeds,
but you surpass them all!"
30 Charm is deceptive and beauty
is fleeting,
but a woman who fears the LORD
will be praised.
31 Give her the reward of her labor,[S]
and let her works praise her
at the city gates.

[A] **30:31** Or *a greyhound* [B] **30:31** LXX reads *king addressing his people* [C] **31:1** Or *of Lemuel, king of Massa*, or *of King Lemuel, a burden* [D] **31:5** Lit *sons of affliction* [E] **31:8** Lit *Open your mouth*, also in v. 9 [F] **31:8** Lit *who are mute* [G] **31:8** Lit *all the sons of passing away* [H] **31:10** Or *a wife of quality*, or *a capable wife* [I] **31:10** Vv. 10-31 form an acrostic. [J] **31:15** Or *tasks* [K] **31:16** Or *vineyard by her own labors* [L] **31:17** Lit *She wraps strength around her like a belt* [M] **31:20** Lit *Her hand reaches* [N] **31:21** LXX, Vg; MT reads *are dressed in scarlet* [O] **31:24** Or *sashes* [P] **31:26** Or *and the teaching of kindness* [Q] **31:27** Lit *and does not eat the bread of idleness* [R] **31:29** Lit *daughters* [S] **31:31** Lit *the fruit of her hands*

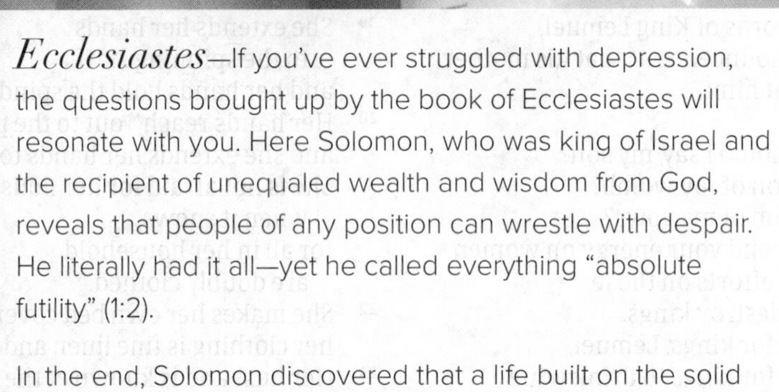

Ecclesiastes—If you've ever struggled with depression, the questions brought up by the book of Ecclesiastes will resonate with you. Here Solomon, who was king of Israel and the recipient of unequaled wealth and wisdom from God, reveals that people of any position can wrestle with despair. He literally had it all—yet he called everything "absolute futility" (1:2).

In the end, Solomon discovered that a life built on the solid foundation of a relationship with God allows even our earthly pleasures to be deeply enjoyed. When we delight in the work and rest he gives, God is also delighted. Every good and perfect gift is meant to be received with gratitude and offered back to God in joyful praise.

You may start reading Ecclesiastes resonating with its tone of despair, but by the end you will find much to be thankful for. The key is to look at the contrast drawn between human life *apart from* God and human life *with* God. With God, we have the assurance of eternal life that brings meaning and joy to the daily tasks of family, work, and relaxation.

ECCLESIASTES

AUTHOR: Solomon

DATE WRITTEN: Toward the end of Solomon's life, no later than 931 BC.

ORIGINAL AUDIENCE: The Israelites

SETTING: Solomon had all the advantages this world has to offer, yet toward the end of his life he wrote this personal wisdom book about his search for meaning.

PURPOSE FOR WRITING: After searching for meaning in the arenas of intellectual pursuit, wealth, political power, and religion, Solomon concluded that our brief time on earth has meaning and joy only if we live a life of reverent faith in God. This book offers an eternal perspective on our temporal existence, and in it we find hope for a purposeful and joyful life. Ecclesiastes shows the emptiness inherent in everything the world offers. Intellectual pursuit, worldly luxury, political power, and even religious zeal ultimately cannot give satisfaction. That is because true satisfaction is only found in relationship with God. Our souls were made for worship of our glorious Creator, the only place we can find deep, lasting joy.

OUTLINE:

1. The Limitations of Earthly Life (1:1–2:26)

   Futility (1:1-11)

   The teacher's quest (1:12-18)

   Emptiness of pleasure, possessions, wisdom, and work (2:1-23)

   God's perspective on pleasure, possessions, wisdom, and work (2:24-26)

2. Time and Eternity (3:1-22)

   Rhythms of life (3:1-8)

   Eternity in time (3:9-15)

   Eternity and death (3:16-22)

3. Injustice, Comfort, and Change in Society (4:1-16)

4. Authentic Religion (5:1-7)

5. Wealth in God's Economy (5:8–6:12)

6. Wise Living (7:1–12:14)

   Proverbs (7:1-14)

   Moderation (7:15-22)

   The limitations of wisdom (7:23-29)

   Community living (8:1-17)

   Enjoyment of life (9:1-10)

   The limitations of wisdom (9:11-18)

   Folly contrasted to wisdom (10:1-20)

   Future investment (11:1-10)

   Final remarks: living well and ending well (12:1-14)

KEY VERSE:

"I know that everything God does will last forever; there is no adding to it or taking from it. God works so that people will be in awe of him." –Ecclesiastes 3:14

RESTORATION THEMES

R	Rest and Reflection	*Avoiding Burnout—3:1*
E	Eternal Perspective	*For the next note, see Isaiah 6:3.*
S	Support	*For the next note, see Isaiah 30:10-11.*
T	Thanksgiving and Contentment	*For the next note, see Isaiah 1:18.*
O	Other-centeredness	*Learning Other People's Stories—Ecclesiastes 3:7*
R	Relationships	*Relating to Coworkers—2:18,20* *Relating to Friends—4:9-10,12*
E	Exercise of Faith	*For the next note, see Isaiah 2:22.*

EVERYTHING IS FUTILE

1 The words of the Teacher,[A] son of David, king in Jerusalem.

2 "Absolute futility," says the Teacher.
"Absolute futility. Everything is futile."
3 What does a person gain for all
his efforts
that he labors at under the sun?
4 A generation goes and a generation
comes,
but the earth remains forever.
5 The sun rises and the sun sets;
panting, it returns to the place
where it rises.
6 Gusting to the south,
turning to the north,
turning, turning, goes the wind,
and the wind returns in its cycles.
7 All the streams flow to the sea,
yet the sea is never full;
to the place where
the streams flow,
there they flow again.
8 All things[B] are wearisome,
more than anyone can say.
The eye is not satisfied by seeing
or the ear filled with hearing.
9 What has been is what will be,
and what has been done is
what will be done;
there is nothing new under the sun.
10 Can one say about anything,
"Look, this is new"?
It has already existed in the ages
before us.
11 There is no remembrance of those
who[C] came before;
and of those who will come after
there will also be no remembrance
by those who follow them.

THE LIMITATIONS OF WISDOM

12 I, the Teacher, have been[D] king over Israel
in Jerusalem. 13 I applied my mind to examine and explore through wisdom all that is
done under heaven. God has given people[E]
this miserable task to keep them occupied.
14 I have seen all the things that are done under the sun and have found everything to be
futile, a pursuit of the wind.[F]

15 What is crooked cannot be straightened;
what is lacking cannot be counted.

16 I said to myself, "See, I have amassed wisdom far beyond all those who were over Jerusalem before me, and my mind has thoroughly
grasped[G] wisdom and knowledge." 17 I applied
my mind to know wisdom and knowledge,
madness and folly; I learned that this too is a
pursuit of the wind.

18 For with much wisdom is much sorrow;
as knowledge increases, grief increases.

THE EMPTINESS OF PLEASURE

2 I said to myself, "Go ahead, I will test you with pleasure; enjoy what is good." But it
turned out to be futile. 2 I said about laughter,
"It is madness," and about pleasure, "What
does this accomplish?" 3 I explored with my
mind the pull of wine on my body — my mind
still guiding me with wisdom — and how to
grasp folly, until I could see what is good for
people to do under heaven[H] during the few
days of their lives.

THE EMPTINESS OF POSSESSIONS

4 I increased my achievements. I built houses
and planted vineyards for myself. 5 I made
gardens and parks for myself and planted
every kind of fruit tree in them. 6 I constructed
reservoirs for myself from which to irrigate a
grove of flourishing trees. 7 I acquired male and
female servants and had slaves who were born
in my house. I also owned livestock — large
herds and flocks — more than all who were
before me in Jerusalem. 8 I also amassed silver
and gold for myself, and the treasure of kings
and provinces. I gathered male and female
singers for myself, and many concubines, the
delights of men.[I,J] 9 So I became great and surpassed all who were before me in Jerusalem;
my wisdom also remained with me. 10 All that
my eyes desired, I did not deny them. I did not
refuse myself any pleasure, for I took pleasure
in all my struggles. This was my reward for
all my struggles. 11 When I considered all that
I had accomplished[K] and what I had labored
to achieve, I found everything to be futile and
a pursuit of the wind.[L] There was nothing to
be gained under the sun.

[A] 1:1 Or *of Qoheleth*, or *of the Leader of the Assembly* [B] 1:8 Or *words* [C] 1:11 Or *of the things that* [D] 1:12 Or *Teacher, was* [E] 1:13 Or *given the descendants of Adam* [F] 1:14 Or *a feeding on wind*, or *an affliction of spirit*; also in v. 17 [G] 1:16 Or *discerned* [H] 2:3 Two Hb mss, LXX, Syr read *the sun* [I] 2:8 LXX, Theod, Syr read *and male cupbearers and female cupbearers*; Aq, Tg, Vg read *a cup and cups*; Hb obscure [J] 2:8 Or *many treasures that people delight in* [K] 2:11 Lit *all my works that my hands had done* [L] 2:11 Or *a feeding on wind*, or *an affliction of spirit*; also in vv. 17,26

THE RELATIVE VALUE OF WISDOM

12 Then I turned to consider wisdom, madness,
and folly, for what will the king's successor[A] be
like? He[B] will do what has already been done.
13 And I realized that there is an advantage to
wisdom over folly, like the advantage of light
over darkness.

14 The wise person has eyes in his head,
but the fool walks in darkness.

Yet I also knew that one fate comes to them
both. 15 So I said to myself, "What happens to
the fool will also happen to me. Why then have
I been overly wise?" And I said to myself that
this is also futile. 16 For, just like the fool, there
is no lasting remembrance of the wise, since in
the days to come both will be forgotten. How
is it that the wise person dies just like the fool?
17 Therefore, I hated life because the work that
was done under the sun was distressing to me.
For everything is futile and a pursuit of the wind.

THE EMPTINESS OF WORK

18 I hated all my work that I labored at under
the sun because I must leave it to the one who
comes after me. 19 And who knows whether he will be wise or a fool? Yet he will take
over all my work that I labored at skillfully
under the sun. This too is futile. 20 So I began
to give myself over[C] to despair concerning
all my work that I had labored at under the
sun. 21 When there is a person whose work
was done with wisdom, knowledge, and skill,
and he must give his portion to a person who
has not worked for it, this too is futile and a
great wrong. 22 For what does a person get
with all his work and all his efforts that he
labors at under the sun? 23 For all his days
are filled with grief, and his occupation is
sorrowful; even at night, his mind does not
rest. This too is futile.

24 There is nothing better for a person than
to eat, drink, and enjoy[D,E] his work. I have seen
that even this is from God's hand, 25 because
who can eat and who can enjoy life[F] apart
from him?[G] 26 For to the person who is pleasing in his sight, he gives wisdom, knowledge,
and joy; but to the sinner he gives the task of
gathering and accumulating in order to give

Relationships | *Relating to Coworkers*

OUR LEAST-FAVORITE FOUR-LETTER WORD

"I hated all my work that I labored at under the sun because I must leave it to the one who comes after me. . . . So I began to give myself over to despair concerning all my work." Ecclesiastes 2:18,20

We won't find many people in this world who truly *love* their jobs, who look forward to waking up and going to work. It's heartbreaking, actually.

For many, work is just a nasty, four-letter word. Granted, to even have a job that pays the bills is a real blessing. But if we're honest, if we're dreaming, we all wish we could find work that: (a) makes a real difference in the world; (b) utilizes our strengths and skills; (c) allows us to come alive, doing things that we really enjoy; and (d) has us working with people we really like.

Maybe you'll get that someday. Maybe you have such a career already. But if work is a daily struggle, don't let Solomon's jaded words here poison your mind. We don't have to hate our jobs. We can, in the words of the New Testament, do them "for the Lord and not for people" (Col 3:23). We can work for an eternal reward, and not just a weekly or bi-weekly paycheck.

If work is currently the grimmest part of your life, taking up a relaxing hobby or engaging in a worthwhile ministry is one way to bring some joy to your days. Or perhaps God is speaking to you through your work misery, encouraging you to pursue something less detrimental to your soul.

For the next note on *Relationships*, see Ecclesiastes 4:9-10,12.

[A] **2:12** Lit *the man who comes after the king* [B] **2:12** Some Hb mss read *They* [C] **2:20** Lit *And I turned to cause my heart* [D] **2:24** Syr, Tg; MT reads *There is no good in a person who eats and drinks and enjoys* [E] **2:24** Lit *and his soul sees good* [F] **2:25** LXX, Theod, Syr read *can drink* [G] **2:25** Some Hb mss, LXX, Syr read *me*

to the one who is pleasing in God's sight. This
too is futile and a pursuit of the wind.

THE MYSTERY OF TIME

3 There is an occasion for everything,
and a time for every activity
under heaven:
2 a time to give birth and a time to die;
a time to plant and a time to uproot;[A]
3 a time to kill and a time to heal;
a time to tear down and a time to build;
4 a time to weep and a time to laugh;
a time to mourn and a time to dance;
5 a time to throw stones and a time
to gather stones;
a time to embrace and a time
to avoid embracing;
6 a time to search and a time to count
as lost;
a time to keep and a time to throw away;
7 a time to tear and a time to sew;
a time to be silent and a time to speak;
8 a time to love and a time to hate;
a time for war and a time for peace.

9 What does the worker gain from his struggles? 10 I have seen the task that God has given
the children of Adam to keep them occupied.
11 He has made everything appropriate[B] in its
time. He has also put eternity in their hearts,[C]
but no one can discover the work God has
done from beginning to end. 12 I know that
there is nothing better for them than to rejoice and enjoy the[D] good life. 13 It is also the
gift of God whenever anyone eats, drinks,
and enjoys all his efforts. 14 I know that everything God does will last forever; there is
no adding to it or taking from it. God works
so that people will be in awe of him. 15 Whatever is, has already been, and whatever will
be, already is. However, God seeks justice for
the persecuted.[E]

THE MYSTERY OF INJUSTICE AND DEATH

16 I also observed under the sun: there is wickedness at the place of judgment and there is
wickedness at the place of righteousness. 17 I
said to myself, "God will judge the righteous
and the wicked, since there is a time for every

Rest and Reflection | *Avoiding Burnout*

PRODUCTIVITY AND CHILLING OUT

"There is an occasion for everything, and a time for every activity under heaven." Ecclesiastes 3:1

Many people in our culture are suffering from burnout. They're out of gas. They move through the world like joyless zombies. The culprit in many cases is the productivity craze. It features a compelling sales pitch for sure. Who doesn't want to be a "peak performer" or "get more done in less time"? (Hey, if some effectiveness is good, more must be better, right?)

Buy in, and soon you're frantically setting goals, filling out planners, and learning to "focus" and "be strategic." Before long, you're multitasking (and getting weary) with the best of them.

While nothing is wrong—and everything right—with trying to be good stewards of our time, we cross a line when we become addicted to *doing* more and more and more. What about simply *being*?

What about agendaless evenings with friends? Leisurely playing with our kids and actually looking into their eyes? Savoring—not rushing through—a good book? What about *not* being a slave to the clock?

Healthy souls trust that God has given them enough time to do what he has called them to do. And if interruptions happen and the to-do list goes undone, the sky won't fall. Life will go on. The unchecked boxes can wait till tomorrow. So what if you didn't read that blog post on how to clean your house in half the time—you had a great conversation with a friend!

For the next note on *Rest and Reflection*, see Isaiah 5:20.

[A] **3:2** Lit *uproot what is planted* [B] **3:11** Or *beautiful* [C] **3:11** Or *has put a sense of past and future into their minds*, or *has placed ignorance in their hearts* [D] **3:12** Lit *his* [E] **3:15** Lit *God seeks what is pursued*

activity and every work." 18 I said to myself,
"This happens so that God may test the children of Adam and they may see for themselves
that they are like animals." 19 For the fate of
the children of Adam and the fate of animals
is the same. As one dies, so dies the other;
they all have the same breath. People have
no advantage over animals since everything
is futile. 20 All are going to the same place; all
come from dust, and all return to dust. 21 Who
knows if the spirits of the children of Adam go
upward and the spirits of animals go downward to the earth? 22 I have seen that there
is nothing better than for a person to enjoy
his activities because that is his reward. For
who can enable him to see what will happen
after he dies?[A]

4 Again, I observed all the acts of oppression being done under the sun. Look at
the tears of those who are oppressed; they
have no one to comfort them. Power is with
those who oppress them; they have no one
to comfort them. 2 So I commended the dead,
who have already died, more than the living,
who are still alive. 3 But better than either of
them is the one who has not yet existed, who
has not seen the evil activity that is done under the sun.

THE LONELINESS OF WEALTH

4 I saw that all labor and all skillful work is due
to one person's jealousy of another. This too
is futile and a pursuit of the wind.[B]

5 The fool folds his arms
and consumes his own flesh.
6 Better one handful with rest
than two handfuls with effort and a
pursuit of the wind.

7 Again, I saw futility under the sun: 8 There
is a person without a companion,[C] without
even a son or brother, and though there is no
end to all his struggles, his eyes are still not
content with riches. "Who am I struggling
for," he asks, "and depriving myself of good
things?" This too is futile and a miserable task.
9 Two are better than one because they have
a good reward for their efforts. 10 For if either
falls, his companion can lift him up; but pity
the one who falls without another to lift him

Other-centeredness | *Learning Other People's Stories*

A TIME TO BE SILENT

"A time to tear and a time to sew; a time to be silent and a time to speak." Ecclesiastes 3:7

Some people are introverted. They're quiet by nature. The Bible's word to them? There's "a time to speak."

Others of us are certified yakkers and need Solomon's reminder about "a time to be silent." When we open our mouths indiscriminately, all kinds of things happen, and many of them aren't good. We break confidences. Create confusion. Start conflicts. Say dumb things and embarrass ourselves. Say hurtful things and wound others. Say inappropriate things (and then, if we keep talking, dig the hole deeper). No wonder Solomon said in another place, "When there are many words, sin is unavoidable, but the one who controls his lips is prudent" (Pr 10:19).

The "time to be silent" is probably more frequent and longer than most of us imagine. When we bite our tongues, we're able to listen to others. We can learn about them—and from them. We can think and pray about our responses (and avoid sticking our big feet in our big mouths).

Someone has said, "I have never regretted my silence." Another has warned, "Nothing is almost always a good thing to say." Today, ask the Spirit of God to control your mouth. Make it your goal to hear others, rather than making yourself heard.

For the next note on *Other-centeredness*, see Isaiah 1:17.

[A] **3:22** Lit *after him* [B] **4:4** Or *a feeding on wind*, or *an affliction of spirit*; also in vv. 6,16 [C] **4:8** Lit *person, but there is not a second,*

up. 11 Also, if two lie down together, they can keep warm; but how can one person alone keep warm? 12 And if someone overpowers one person, two can resist him. A cord of three strands is not easily broken.

13 Better is a poor but wise youth than an old but foolish king who no longer pays attention to warnings. 14 For he came from prison to be king, even though he was born poor in his kingdom. 15 I saw all the living, who move about under the sun, follow[A] a second youth who succeeds him. 16 There is no limit to all the people who were before them, yet those who come later will not rejoice in him. This too is futile and a pursuit of the wind.

CAUTION IN GOD'S PRESENCE

5 Guard your steps when you go to the house of God. Better to approach in obedience than to offer the sacrifice as fools do, for they ignorantly do wrong. 2 Do not be hasty to speak, and do not be impulsive to make a speech before God. God is in heaven and you are on earth, so let your words be few. 3 Just as dreams accompany much labor, so also a fool's voice comes with many words. 4 When you make a vow to God, don't delay fulfilling it, because he does not delight in fools. Fulfill what you vow. 5 Better that you do not vow than that you vow and not fulfill it. 6 Do not let your mouth bring guilt on you, and do not say in the presence of the messenger that it was a mistake. Why should God be angry with your words and destroy the work of your hands? 7 For many dreams bring futility, so do many words. Therefore, fear God.

THE REALITIES OF WEALTH

8 If you see oppression of the poor and perversion of justice and righteousness in the province, don't be astonished at the situation, because one official protects another official, and higher officials protect them. 9 The profit from the land is taken by all; the king is served by the field.[B]

10 The one who loves silver is never satisfied with silver, and whoever loves wealth is never satisfied with income. This too is futile. 11 When good things increase, the ones who consume them multiply; what, then, is the profit to the owner, except to gaze at them with his eyes? 12 The sleep of the worker is sweet, whether he eats little or much, but the abundance of the rich permits him no sleep.

13 There is a sickening tragedy I have seen

Relationships | *Relating to Friends*

SAFETY IN NUMBERS

"Two are better than one because. . . . if either falls, his companion can lift him up; but pity the one who falls without another to lift him up. . . . And if someone overpowers one person, two can resist him. A cord of three strands is not easily broken." Ecclesiastes 4:9-10,12

You may have seen film clips of African lions stalking a herd of wildebeests or zebras. They're not there to make nice; they're hoping for lunch.

In many instances, the herd sticks together, and the lions go home growling and hungry. But for those isolated or sick or slow creatures that get separated from the herd, those are the ones most likely to be picked off. There is great danger in isolation. When we aren't connected to others in healthy relationships, we drift—usually into trouble.

This is why small groups are so vital. We each need the support of a close-knit community. We need others looking out for us. And we need to be there for them, too.

Do you have a handful of Christian friends with whom you're doing life? If not, move that need to the top of your prayer list.

For the next note on *Relationships*, see Song of Songs 2:15.

[A] **4:15** Lit *with* [B] **5:9** Hb obscure

under the sun: wealth kept by its owner to
his harm. 14 That wealth was lost in a bad venture, so when he fathered a son, he was empty-handed. 15 As he came from his mother's
womb, so he will go again, naked as he came;
he will take nothing for his efforts that he can
carry in his hands. 16 This too is a sickening
tragedy: exactly as he comes, so he will go.
What does the one gain who struggles for
the wind? 17 What is more, he eats in darkness
all his days, with much frustration, sickness,
and anger.
18 Here is what I have seen to be good: It is
appropriate to eat, drink, and experience good
in all the labor one does under the sun during
the few days of his life God has given him,
because that is his reward. 19 Furthermore,
everyone to whom God has given riches and
wealth, he has also allowed him to enjoy them,
take his reward, and rejoice in his labor. This
is a gift of God, 20 for he does not often consider the days of his life because God keeps him
occupied with the joy of his heart.

6 Here is a tragedy I have observed under
the sun, and it weighs heavily on humanity:[A] 2 God gives a person riches, wealth, and
honor so that he lacks nothing of all he desires for himself, but God does not allow him
to enjoy them. Instead, a stranger will enjoy
them. This is futile and a sickening tragedy.
3 A man may father a hundred children and
live many years. No matter how long he lives,[B]
if he is not satisfied by good things and does
not even have a proper burial, I say that a
stillborn child is better off than he. 4 For he
comes in futility and he goes in darkness, and
his name is shrouded in darkness. 5 Though
a stillborn child does not see the sun and is
not conscious, it has more rest than he. 6 And
if a person lives a thousand years twice, but
does not experience happiness, do not both
go to the same place?

7 All of a person's labor is
for his stomach,[C]
yet the appetite is never satisfied.

8 What advantage then does the wise person
have over the fool? What advantage is there for
the poor person who knows how to conduct
himself before others? 9 Better what the eyes
see than wandering desire. This too is futile
and a pursuit of the wind.[D]
10 Whatever exists was given its name long
ago,[E] and it is known what mankind is. But he
is not able to contend with the one stronger
than he. 11 For when there are many words,
they increase futility. What is the advantage
for mankind? 12 For who knows what is good
for anyone in life, in the few days of his futile life that he spends like a shadow? Who
can tell anyone what will happen after him
under the sun?

WISE SAYINGS

7 A good name is better than
fine perfume,
and the day of one's death is better
than the day of one's birth.
2 It is better to go to a house of mourning
than to go to a house of feasting,
since that is the end of all mankind,
and the living should take it to heart.
3 Grief is better than laughter,
for when a face is sad, a heart
may be glad.
4 The heart of the wise is in a house
of mourning,
but the heart of fools is in a house
of pleasure.
5 It is better to listen to rebuke
from a wise person
than to listen to the song of fools,
6 for like the crackling of burning thorns
under the pot,
so is the laughter of the fool.
This too is futile.
7 Surely, the practice of extortion turns
a wise person into a fool,
and a bribe corrupts the mind.
8 The end of a matter is better
than its beginning;
a patient spirit is better
than a proud spirit.
9 Don't let your spirit rush to be angry,
for anger abides in the heart of fools.

Wisdom is as good as an inheritance and an advantage to those who see the sun.
—Ecclesiastes 7:11

[A] 6:1 Or *it is common among men* [B] 6:3 Lit *how many years* [C] 6:7 Lit *mouth* [D] 6:9 Or *a feeding on wind*, or *an affliction of spirit* [E] 6:10 Lit *name already*

10 Don't say, "Why were the former days
better than these?"
since it is not wise of you to ask this.
11 Wisdom is as good as an inheritance
and an advantage to those who see
the sun,
12 because wisdom is protection as silver
is protection;
but the advantage of knowledge
is that wisdom preserves the life
of its owner.
13 Consider the work of God,
for who can straighten out
what he has made crooked?

14 In the day of prosperity be joyful, but in
the day of adversity, consider: God has made
the one as well as the other, so that no one can
discover anything that will come after him.

AVOIDING EXTREMES

15 In my futile life[A] I have seen everything:
someone righteous perishes in spite of his
righteousness, and someone wicked lives long
in spite of his evil. 16 Don't be excessively righteous, and don't be overly wise. Why should
you destroy yourself? 17 Don't be excessively
wicked, and don't be foolish. Why should you
die before your time? 18 It is good that you
grasp the one and do not let the other slip
from your hand. For the one who fears God
will end up with both of them.

19 Wisdom makes the wise person
stronger
than ten rulers of a city.
20 There is certainly no one
righteous on the earth
who does good and never sins.

21 Don't pay attention[B] to everything people
say, or you may hear your servant cursing you,
22 for in your heart you know that many times
you yourself have cursed others.

WHAT THE TEACHER FOUND

23 I have tested all this by wisdom. I resolved,
"I will be wise," but it was beyond me. 24 What
exists is beyond reach and very deep. Who can
discover it? 25 I turned my thoughts to know,
explore, and examine wisdom and an explanation for things, and to know that wickedness
is stupidity and folly is madness. 26 And I find
more bitter than death the woman who is a
trap: her heart a net and her hands chains.
The one who pleases God will escape her, but
the sinner will be captured by her. 27 "Look,"
says the Teacher, "I have discovered this by
adding one thing to another to find out the
explanation, 28 which my soul continually
searches for but does not find: I found one
person in a thousand, but none of those was
a woman. 29 Only see this: I have discovered
that God made people upright, but they pursued many schemes."

WISDOM, AUTHORITIES, AND INEQUITIES

8 Who is like the wise person, and who knows
the interpretation of a matter? A person's
wisdom brightens his face, and the sternness
of his face is changed.

2 Keep[C] the king's command because of
your oath made before God. 3 Do not be in a
hurry; leave his presence, and don't persist
in a bad cause, since he will do whatever he
wants. 4 For the king's word is authoritative,
and who can say to him, "What are you doing?" 5 The one who keeps a command will
not experience anything harmful, and a wise
heart knows the right time and procedure.
6 For every activity there is a right time and
procedure, even though a person's troubles
are heavy on him. 7 Yet no one knows what
will happen because who can tell him what
will happen? 8 No one has authority over the
wind[D] to restrain it, and there is no authority
over the day of death; no one is discharged
during battle, and wickedness will not allow
those who practice it to escape. 9 All this I have
seen, applying my mind to all the work that is
done under the sun, at a time when one person has authority over another to his harm.
10 In such circumstances, I saw the wicked
buried. They came and went from the holy place,
and they were praised[E] in the city where they
did those things. This too is futile. 11 Because
the sentence against an evil act is not carried
out quickly, the heart of people is filled with
the desire to commit evil. 12 Although a sinner
does evil a hundred times and prolongs his life,
I also know that it will go well with God-fearing people, for they are reverent before him.
13 However, it will not go well with the wicked,
and they will not lengthen their days like a
shadow, for they are not reverent before God.
14 There is a futility that is done on the earth:
there are righteous people who get what the

[A] **7:15** Lit *days* [B] **7:21** Lit *Don't give your heart* [C] **8:2** Some Hb mss, LXX, Vg, Tg, Syr; other Hb mss read *I, keep* [D] **8:8** Or *life-breath* [E] **8:10** Some Hb mss, LXX, Aq, Theod, Sym; other Hb mss read *forgotten*

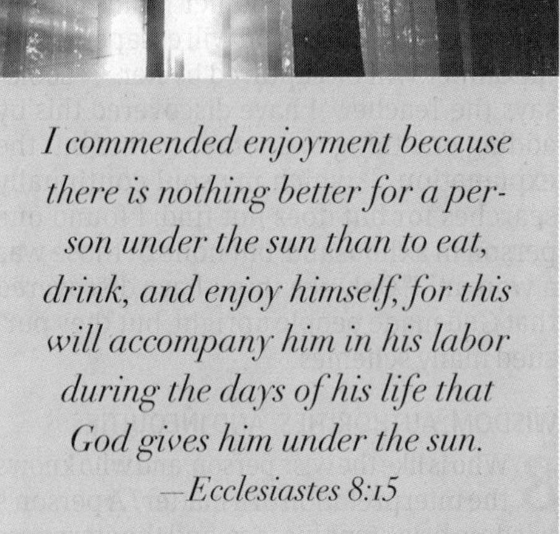
*I commended enjoyment because
there is nothing better for a person under the sun than to eat,
drink, and enjoy himself, for this
will accompany him in his labor
during the days of his life that
God gives him under the sun.*
—*Ecclesiastes 8:15*

actions of the wicked deserve, and there are
wicked people who get what the actions of the
righteous deserve. I say that this too is futile.
15 So I commended enjoyment because there is
nothing better for a person under the sun than
to eat, drink, and enjoy himself, for this will
accompany him in his labor during the days
of his life that God gives him under the sun.
16 When I applied my mind to know wisdom
and to observe the activity that is done on the
earth (even though one's eyes do not close in
sleep day or night), 17 I observed all the work
of God and concluded that a person is unable
to discover the work that is done under the
sun. Even though a person labors hard to explore it, he cannot find it; even if a wise person
claims to know it, he is unable to discover it.

ENJOY LIFE DESPITE DEATH

9 Indeed, I took all this to heart and explained
it all: The righteous, the wise, and their
works are in God's hands. People don't know
whether to expect love or hate. Everything lies
ahead of them. 2 Everything is the same for
everyone: There is one fate for the righteous
and the wicked, for the good and the bad,[A] for
the clean and the unclean, for the one who sacrifices and the one who does not sacrifice. As
it is for the good, so also it is for the sinner; as
it is for the one who takes an oath, so also for
the one who fears an oath. 3 This is an evil in
all that is done under the sun: there is one fate
for everyone. In addition, the hearts of people
are full of evil, and madness is in their hearts
while they live; after that they go to the dead.
4 But there is hope for whoever is joined[B] with
all the living, since a live dog is better than a
dead lion. 5 For the living know that they will
die, but the dead don't know anything. There
is no longer a reward for them because the
memory of them is forgotten. 6 Their love, their
hate, and their envy have already disappeared,
and there is no longer a portion for them in
all that is done under the sun.
7 Go, eat your bread with pleasure, and drink
your wine with a cheerful heart, for God has
already accepted your works. 8 Let your clothes
be white all the time, and never let oil be lacking on your head. 9 Enjoy life with the wife you
love all the days of your fleeting[C] life, which
has been given to you under the sun, all your
fleeting days. For that is your portion in life
and in your struggle under the sun. 10 Whatever your hands find to do, do with all your
strength, because there is no work, planning,
knowledge, or wisdom in Sheol where you
are going.

THE LIMITATIONS OF WISDOM

11 Again I saw under the sun that the race is
not to the swift, or the battle to the strong, or
bread to the wise, or riches to the discerning,
or favor to the skillful; rather, time and chance
happen to all of them. 12 For certainly no one
knows his time: like fish caught in a cruel net or
like birds caught in a trap, so people are trapped
in an evil time as it suddenly falls on them.
13 I have observed that this also is wisdom
under the sun, and it is significant to me:
14 There was a small city with few men in it.
A great king came against it, surrounded it,
and built large siege works against it. 15 Now
a poor wise man was found in the city, and he
delivered the city by his wisdom. Yet no one
remembered that poor man. 16 And I said, "Wisdom is better than strength, but the wisdom
of the poor man is despised, and his words
are not heeded."

17 The calm words of the wise are heeded
more than the shouts of a ruler
over fools.
18 Wisdom is better than weapons of war,
but one sinner can destroy much good.

THE BURDEN OF FOLLY

10 Dead flies make a perfumer's oil
ferment and stink;
so a little folly outweighs wisdom
and honor.

[A] **9:2** LXX, Aq, Syr, Vg; MT omits *and the bad* [B] **9:4** Alt Hb tradition reads *chosen* [C] **9:9** Or *futile*

My Story | Ed

I grew up in the South and had heard my share of religious talk that I ignored well into my teenage years. Numerous people took the time to have a conversation with me about spiritual matters and tell me about Jesus. I wasn't an easy nut to crack. I'll never forget one guy in particular. Two or three of us would often walk to school, and this guy made it a habit to offer us a ride. No sooner would we close the door than he would start talking about how important it was to be saved and to know Christ as our Savior. We often wondered if having to hear his earnest message was worth the energy it saved us by accepting his rides.

I also remember a high school friend who was a Christian but took a somewhat different approach. One day he turned to me and said, "Ed, you know you're going to hell, right?"

At first, I thought he was joking. Then I realized he was serious, but he didn't follow up with anything else. He let me stew in that bit of news. Part of me just knew he had spoken the truth.

A few days later, he handed me a little booklet that looked like a small comic book but told a story of one person's response to the gospel. The message was simple and clear. For some reason, I was finally ready to listen. The last page of the booklet had a challenge to the effect that if I realized the truth of what I had just read, I could pray the prayer below and then sign my name on the line at the bottom of the page.

I prayed the prayer, admitting I was a sinner in need of a Savior and acknowledging that Jesus was that Savior. I was about to sign the page when I remembered the booklet wasn't mine and my friend might want it back.

Then next day at school I looked everywhere for my friend to return his booklet back and tell him what had happened. I couldn't find him. Instead, I realized that I had changed from a guy desperately avoiding God to one who couldn't wait to talk about him. The following day, when I did find my friend, I eagerly told him my experience; and he smiled through my somewhat awkward story. He let me keep the booklet! I remember realizing I had a lot I didn't understand about my new relationship with Jesus, but I did know I was a changed person.

2 A wise person's heart goes
to the[A] right,
but a fool's heart to the left.
3 Even when the fool walks
along the road, his heart lacks sense,
and he shows everyone he is a fool.
4 If the ruler's anger rises against you,
don't leave your post,
for calmness puts great offenses
to rest.

5 There is an evil I have seen under the sun,
an error proceeding from the presence of
the ruler:
6 The fool is appointed to great heights,
but the rich remain in lowly positions.
7 I have seen slaves on horses,
but princes walking on the ground
like slaves.

8 The one who digs a pit may fall into it,
and the one who breaks through a wall
may be bitten by a snake.
9 The one who quarries stones
may be hurt by them;
the one who splits logs
may be endangered by them.
10 If the ax is dull, and one does not
sharpen its edge,
then one must exert more strength;
however, the advantage of wisdom is
that it brings success.
11 If the snake bites before it is charmed,
then there is no advantage
for the charmer.[B]
12 The words from the mouth
of a wise person are gracious,
but the lips of a fool consume him.
13 The beginning of the words
from his mouth is folly,
but the end of his speaking
is evil madness;

[A] **10:2** Lit *his* [B] **10:11** Lit *master of the tongue*

14 yet the fool multiplies words.
No one knows what will happen,
and who can tell anyone
what will happen after him?
15 The struggles of fools weary them,
for they don't know how to go to the city.
16 Woe to you, land, when your king is
a youth
and your princes feast in the morning.
17 Blessed are you, land, when your king
is a son of nobles
and your princes feast
at the proper time —
for strength and not for drunkenness.
18 Because of laziness the roof caves in,
and because of negligent hands
the house leaks.
19 A feast is prepared for laughter,
and wine makes life happy,
and money[A] is the answer
for everything.
20 Do not curse the king
even in your thoughts,
and do not curse a rich person
even in your bedroom,
for a bird of the sky may carry
the message,
and a winged creature may report
the matter.

INVEST IN LIFE

11 Send your bread on the surface
of the water,
for after many days you may find it.
2 Give a portion to seven or even to eight,
for you don't know what disaster
may happen on earth.
3 If the clouds are full, they will pour out
rain on the earth;
whether a tree falls to the south
or the north,
the place where the tree falls,
there it will lie.
4 One who watches the wind
will not sow,
and the one who looks at the clouds
will not reap.
5 Just as you don't know the path
of the wind,
or how bones develop in[B] the womb
of a pregnant woman,
so also you don't know the work of God
who makes everything.
6 In the morning sow your seed,
and at evening do not let your hand rest,
because you don't know
which will succeed,
whether one or the other,
or if both of them
will be equally good.
7 Light is sweet,
and it is pleasing for the eyes to see
the sun.
8 Indeed, if someone lives many years,
let him rejoice in them all,
and let him remember the days
of darkness, since they will be many.
All that comes is futile.
9 Rejoice, young person,
while you are young,
and let your heart be glad in the days
of your youth.
And walk in the ways of your heart
and in the desire of your eyes;
but know that for all of these things
God will bring you to judgment.
10 Remove sorrow from your heart,
and put away pain from your flesh,
because youth and the prime of life
are fleeting.

THE TWILIGHT OF LIFE

12 So remember your Creator in the days
of your youth:
Before the days of adversity come,
and the years approach
when you will say,
"I have no delight in them";
2 before the sun and the light
are darkened,
and the moon and the stars,
and the clouds return
after[C] the rain;
3 on the day when the guardians
of the house tremble,
and the strong men stoop,
the women who grind grain cease
because they are few,
and the ones who watch
through the windows see dimly,
4 the doors at the street are shut
while the sound of the mill fades;
when one rises at the sound
of a bird,
and all the daughters of song
grow faint.

[A] **10:19** Lit *silver* [B] **11:5** Or *know how the life-breath comes to the bones in* [C] **12:2** Or *with*

1 The Song of Songs, which is Solomon's.

Woman

2 Oh, that he would kiss me
with the kisses of his mouth!
For your caresses[A] are more delightful
than wine.
3 The fragrance of your perfume
is intoxicating;
your name is perfume poured out.
No wonder young women[B] adore you.
4 Take me with you — let's hurry.
Oh, that the king would bring[C] me
to his chambers.

Young Women

We will rejoice and be glad in you;
we will celebrate your caresses
more than wine.

Woman

It is only right that they adore you.

5 Daughters of Jerusalem,
I am dark like the tents of Kedar,
yet lovely like the curtains of Solomon.
6 Do not stare at me because I am dark,
for the sun has gazed on me.
My mother's sons were angry with me;
they made me take care of the vineyards.
I have not taken care of
my own vineyard.

7 Tell me, you whom I love:
Where do you pasture your sheep?
Where do you let them rest at noon?
Why should I be like one who veils
herself[D]
beside the flocks of your companions?

Man[E]

8 If you do not know,
most beautiful of women,
follow[F] the tracks of the flock,
and pasture your young goats
near the shepherds' tents.

9 I compare you, my darling,
to a[G] mare among Pharaoh's chariots.
10 Your cheeks are beautiful with jewelry,
your neck with its necklace.
11 We will make gold jewelry for you,
accented with silver.

Woman

12 While the king is on his couch,[H]
my perfume[I] releases its fragrance.
13 The one I love is a sachet of myrrh
to me,
spending the night
between my breasts.
14 The one I love is a cluster
of henna blossoms to me,
in the vineyards of En-gedi.

Man

15 How beautiful you are, my darling.
How very beautiful!
Your eyes are doves.

Woman

16 How handsome you are, my love.
How delightful!
Our bed is verdant;
17 the beams of our house are cedars,
and our rafters are cypresses.[J]
2 I am a wildflower[K] of Sharon,
a lily[L] of the valleys.

Man

2 Like a lily among thorns,
so is my darling
among the young women.

Woman

3 Like an apricot[M] tree among the trees
of the forest,
so is my love among the young men.
I delight to sit in his shade,
and his fruit is sweet to my taste.
4 He brought me to the banquet hall,[N]
and he looked on me with love.[O]
5 Sustain me with raisins;
refresh me with apricots,[P]
for I am lovesick.
6 May his left hand be under my head,
and his right arm embrace me.
7 Young women of Jerusalem, I charge you
by the gazelles and the wild does
of the field,
do not stir up or awaken love
until the appropriate time.[Q]

[A] **1:2** Or *acts of love* [B] **1:3** Or *wonder virgins* [C] **1:4** Or *The king has brought* [D] **1:7** Or *who wanders* [E] **1:8** Some understand the young women to be the speakers in this verse. [F] **1:8** Lit *go out for yourself into* [G] **1:9** Lit *my* [H] **1:12** Or *is at his table* [I] **1:12** Lit *nard* [J] **1:17** Or *firs*, or *pines* [K] **2:1** Traditionally *rose* [L] **2:1** Or *lotus* [M] **2:3** Or *apple* [N] **2:4** Lit *the house of wine* [O] **2:4** Or *and his banner over me is love* [P] **2:5** Or *apples* [Q] **2:7** Lit *until it pleases*

8 Listen! My love is approaching.
Look! Here he comes,
leaping over the mountains,
bounding over the hills.
9 My love is like a gazelle
or a young stag.
See, he is standing
behind our wall,
gazing through the windows,
peering through the lattice.
10 My love calls to me:

Man

Arise, my darling.
Come away, my beautiful one.
11 For now the winter is past;
the rain has ended and gone away.
12 The blossoms appear
in the countryside.
The time of singing[A] has come,
and the turtledove's cooing is heard
in our land.
13 The fig tree ripens its figs;
the blossoming vines give off
their fragrance.
Arise, my darling.
Come away, my beautiful one.

14 My dove, in the clefts of the rock,
in the crevices of the cliff,
let me see your face,[B]
let me hear your voice;
for your voice is sweet,
and your face is lovely.

Woman[C]

15 Catch the foxes for us —
the little foxes that ruin the vineyards —
for our vineyards are in bloom.

Woman

16 My love is mine and I am his;
he feeds among the lilies.
17 Until the day breaks[D]
and the shadows flee,
turn around, my love, and be
like a gazelle
or a young stag
on the divided mountains.[E]

3 In my bed at night[F]
I sought the one I love;
I sought him, but did not find him.[G]
2 I will arise now and go about the city,
through the streets and the plazas.

Relationships | *Relating to Spouse/Marriage*

MARITAL TEAMWORK

"Catch the foxes for us—the little foxes that ruin the vineyards—for our vineyards are in bloom." Song of Songs 2:15

The Song of Songs has been called the most mysterious book in the Bible—and one of the trickiest to interpret. Some see it as allegory of divine love. Others regard it as a passionate tribute to marital love.

While much about the song is hotly debated, this particular passage seems to be clear enough: "catch the foxes . . . that ruin the vineyards . . . in bloom."

Foxes were small, quiet animals, notorious for their tendency to sneak into vineyards and cause havoc. As such, this likely is nothing more than a bride pleading for her husband to be vigilant. It may be a request for the man to take the initiative in heading off potential trouble spots in the relationship.

Wives know that asking such a thing can be tricky. Concern is often misconstrued as nagging. However, husbands need to remember that real needs and real needling are not the same.

If you're a man, and married, reflect on this: Are you proactive or reactive? Do you stop the little foxes before they get into your marriage—or wait until they've created a real problem?

For the next note on *Relationships*, see Jeremiah 15:21.

[A] **2:12** Or *pruning* [B] **2:14** Or *form* [C] **2:15** The speaker could be the woman, the man, or both. [D] **2:17** Lit *breathes* [E] **2:17** Or *the Bether mountains*, or *the mountains of spices*; Hb obscure [F] **3:1** Or *bed night after night* [G] **3:1** LXX adds *I called him, but he did not answer me*

I will seek the one I love.
I sought him, but did not find him.
3 The guards who go about the city
found me.
I asked them, "Have you seen the one
I love?"
4 I had just passed them
when I found the one I love.
I held on to him and would not
let him go
until I brought him
to my mother's house —
to the chamber of the one
who conceived me.
5 Young women of Jerusalem,
I charge you
by the gazelles and the wild does
of the field,
do not stir up or awaken love
until the appropriate time.[A]

Narrator

6 Who is this coming up
from the wilderness
like columns of smoke,
scented with myrrh
and frankincense
from every fragrant powder
of the merchant?

7 Look! Solomon's bed
surrounded by sixty warriors
from the mighty men of Israel.
8 All of them are skilled with swords
and trained in warfare.
Each has his sword at his side
to guard against the terror of the night.

9 King Solomon made a carriage
for himself
with wood from Lebanon.
10 He made its posts of silver,
its back[B] of gold,
and its seat of purple.
Its interior is inlaid with love[C]
by the young women of Jerusalem.
11 Go out, young women of Zion,
and gaze at King Solomon,
wearing the crown his mother placed
on him
on the day of his wedding —
the day of his heart's rejoicing.

Man

4 How beautiful you are, my darling.
How very beautiful!
Behind your veil,
your eyes are doves.
Your hair is like a flock of goats
streaming down Mount Gilead.
2 Your teeth are like a flock
of newly shorn sheep
coming up from washing,
each one bearing twins,
and none has lost its young.[D]
3 Your lips are like a scarlet cord,
and your mouth[E] is lovely.
Behind your veil,
your brow[F] is like a slice
of pomegranate.
4 Your neck is
like the tower of David,
constructed in layers.
A thousand shields are hung on it —
all of them shields of warriors.
5 Your breasts are like two fawns,
twins of a gazelle, that feed
among the lilies.
6 Until the day breaks[G]
and the shadows flee,
I will make my way to the mountain
of myrrh
and the hill of frankincense.
7 You are absolutely beautiful,
my darling;
there is no imperfection in you.

8 Come with me from Lebanon,[H]
my bride;
come with me from Lebanon!
Descend from the peak of Amana,
from the summit of Senir and Hermon,
from the dens of the lions,
from the mountains of the leopards.
9 You have captured my heart, my sister,
my bride.
You have captured my heart
with one glance of your eyes,
with one jewel of your necklace.
10 How delightful your caresses are,
my sister, my bride.
Your caresses are much better
than wine,
and the fragrance of your perfume
than any balsam.

[A] **3:5** Lit *until it pleases* [B] **3:10** Or *base*, or *canopy* [C] **3:10** Or *leather* [D] **4:2** Lit *and no one bereaved among them* [E] **4:3** Or *speech* [F] **4:3** Or *temple*, or *cheek*, or *lips* [G] **4:6** Lit *breathes* [H] **4:8** In Hb, the word for *Lebanon* is similar to "frankincense" in Sg 4:6,14,15.

11 Your lips drip sweetness like
the honeycomb, my bride.
Honey and milk are
under your tongue.
The fragrance of your garments is like
the fragrance of Lebanon.

12 My sister, my bride, you are
a locked garden —
a locked garden[A] and a sealed spring.
13 Your branches are a paradise[B]
of pomegranates
with choicest fruits;
henna with nard,
14 nard and saffron, calamus
and cinnamon,
with all the trees of frankincense,
myrrh and aloes,
with all the best spices.
15 You are a garden spring,
a well of flowing water
streaming from Lebanon.

Woman

16 Awaken, north wind;
come, south wind.
Blow on my garden,
and spread the fragrance of its spices.
Let my love come to his garden
and eat its choicest fruits.

Man

5 I have come to my garden — my sister,
my bride.
I gather[C] my myrrh with my spices.
I eat my honeycomb with my honey.
I drink my wine with my milk.

Narrator

Eat, friends!
Drink, be intoxicated with caresses![D]

Woman

2 I was sleeping, but my heart was awake.
A sound! My love was knocking!

Man

Open to me, my sister, my darling,
my dove, my perfect one.
For my head is drenched with dew,
my hair with droplets of the night.

Woman

3 I have taken off my clothing.
How can I put it back on?
I have washed my feet.
How can I get them dirty?
4 My love thrust his hand
through the opening,
and my feelings were stirred for him.
5 I rose to open for my love.
My hands dripped with myrrh,
my fingers with flowing myrrh
on the handles of the bolt.
6 I opened to my love,
but my love had turned and gone away.
My heart sank[E] because he had left.[F]
I sought him, but did not find him.
I called him, but he did not answer.
7 The guards who go about the city
found me.
They beat and wounded me;
they took my cloak[G] from me —
the guardians of the walls.
8 Young women of Jerusalem, I charge you,
if you find my love,
tell him that I am lovesick.

Young Women

9 What makes the one you love better
than another,
most beautiful of women?
What makes him better than another,
that you would give us this charge?

Woman

10 My love is fit and strong,[H]
notable among ten thousand.
11 His head is purest gold.
His hair is wavy[I]
and black as a raven.
12 His eyes are like doves
beside flowing streams,
washed in milk
and set like jewels.[J]
13 His cheeks are like beds of spice,
mounds of[K] perfume.
His lips are lilies,
dripping with flowing myrrh.
14 His arms[L] are rods of gold
set[M] with beryl.
His body[N] is an ivory panel
covered with lapis lazuli.

[A] **4:12** Some Hb mss read *locked fountain* [B] **4:13** Or *park*, or *orchard* [C] **5:1** Lit *pluck* [D] **5:1** Or *Drink your fill, lovers* [E] **5:6** Lit *My soul went out* [F] **5:6** Or *spoken* [G] **5:7** Or *veil*, or *shawl* [H] **5:10** Or *is radiant and ruddy* [I] **5:11** Or *is like palm leaves*; Hb obscure [J] **5:12** Lit *milk sitting in fullness* [K] **5:13** LXX, Vg read *spice, yielding* [L] **5:14** Lit *hands* [M] **5:14** Lit *filled*; Sg 5:2,12 [N] **5:14** Lit *abdomen*

15 His legs are alabaster pillars
set on pedestals of pure gold.
His presence is like Lebanon,
as majestic as the cedars.
16 His mouth is sweetness.
He is absolutely desirable.
This is my love,
and this is my friend,
young women of Jerusalem.

Young Women

6 Where has your love gone,
most beautiful of women?
Which way has he[A] turned?
We will seek him with you.

Woman

2 My love has gone down to his garden,
to beds of spice,
to feed in the gardens
and gather lilies.
3 I am my love's and my love is mine;
he feeds among the lilies.

Man

4 You are as beautiful as Tirzah,
my darling,
lovely as Jerusalem,
awe-inspiring as an army
with banners.
5 Turn your eyes away from me,
for they captivate me.
Your hair is like a flock of goats
streaming down from Gilead.
6 Your teeth are like a flock of ewes
coming up from washing,
each one having a twin,
and not one missing.[B]
7 Behind your veil,
your brow[C] is like a slice
of pomegranate.
8 There are sixty queens
and eighty concubines
and young women[D] without number.
9 But my dove, my virtuous one,
is unique;
she is the favorite of her mother,
perfect to the one who gave her birth.
Women see her and declare
her fortunate;
queens and concubines also,
and they sing her praises:

10 Who is this who shines like the dawn,
as beautiful as the moon,
bright as the sun,
awe-inspiring as an army
with banners?

Woman

11 I came down to the walnut grove
to see the blossoms of the valley,
to see if the vines were budding
and the pomegranates blooming.
12 I didn't know what was happening
to me.
I felt like I was
in a chariot with a nobleman.[E]

Young Women

13 Come back, come back, Shulammite![F]
Come back, come back, that
we may look at you!

Man

How you gaze at the Shulammite,
as you look at the dance
of the two camps![G]

7 How beautiful are your sandaled feet,
princess![H]
The curves of your thighs are like jewelry,
the handiwork of a master.
2 Your navel is a rounded bowl;
it never lacks mixed wine.
Your belly is a mound of wheat
surrounded by lilies.
3 Your breasts are like two fawns,
twins of a gazelle.
4 Your neck is like a tower of ivory,
your eyes like pools in Heshbon
by Bath-rabbim's gate.
Your nose is like the tower of Lebanon
looking toward Damascus.
5 Your head crowns you[I]
like Mount Carmel,
the hair of your head
like purple cloth —
a king could be held captive
in your tresses.
6 How beautiful you are
and how pleasant,
my love, with such delights!
7 Your stature is like a palm tree;
your breasts are clusters of fruit.

[A] **6:1** Lit *your love* [B] **6:6** Lit *and no one bereaved among them* [C] **6:7** Or *temple*, or *cheek*, or *lips* [D] **6:8** Or *and virgins*; Sg 1:3 [E] **6:12** Hb obscure [F] **6:13** Or *the perfect one*, or *the peaceable one* [G] **6:13** Or *dance of Mahanaim* [H] **7:1** Lit *daughter of a nobleman*, or *prince* [I] **7:5** Lit *head upon you is*

8 I said, "I will climb the palm tree
and take hold of its fruit."
May your breasts be like clusters
of grapes,
and the fragrance of your breath
like apricots.
9 Your mouth[A] is like fine wine —

Woman

flowing smoothly for my love,
gliding past my lips and teeth![B]
10 I am my love's,
and his desire is for me.

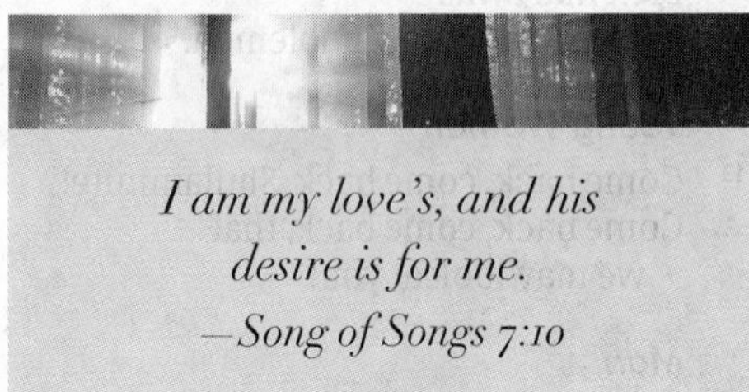

I am my love's, and his desire is for me.

—Song of Songs 7:10

11 Come, my love,
let's go to the field;
let's spend the night
among the henna blossoms.[C]
12 Let's go early to the vineyards;
let's see if the vine has budded,
if the blossom has opened,
if the pomegranates are in bloom.
There I will give you my caresses.
13 The mandrakes give off a fragrance,
and at our doors is every delicacy,
both new and old.
I have treasured them up for you,
my love.

8 If only I could treat you
like my brother,[D]
one who nursed
at my mother's breasts,
I would find you in public
and kiss you,
and no one would scorn me.
2 I would lead you, I would take you,
to the house of my mother
who taught me.[E]
I would give you spiced wine to drink
from the juice of my pomegranate.
3 May his left hand be under my head,
and his right arm embrace me.
4 Young women of Jerusalem, I charge you,
do not stir up or awaken love
until the appropriate time.

Young Women

5 Who is this coming up
from the wilderness,
leaning on the one she loves?

Woman

I awakened you under the apricot tree.
There your mother conceived you;
there she conceived and gave you birth.
6 Set me as a seal on your heart,
as a seal on your arm.
For love is as strong as death;
jealousy is as unrelenting as Sheol.
Love's flames are fiery flames —
an almighty flame![F]
7 A huge torrent cannot extinguish love;
rivers cannot sweep it away.
If a man were to give all his wealth[G]
for love,
it would be utterly scorned.

Brothers

8 Our sister is young;
she has no breasts.
What will we do for our sister
on the day she is spoken for?
9 If she is a wall,
we will build a silver barricade on her.
If she is a door,
we will enclose her with cedar planks.

Woman

10 I am[H] a wall
and my breasts like towers.
So in his eyes I have become
like one who finds[I] peace.[J]

11 Solomon owned a vineyard
in Baal-hamon.
He leased the vineyard to tenants.
Each was to bring for his fruit
one thousand pieces of silver.
12 I have my own vineyard.[K]
The one thousand are for you,
Solomon,
but two hundred for those who take
care of its fruits.

[A] **7:9** Lit *palate* [B] **7:9** LXX, Syr, Vg; MT reads *past lips of sleepers* [C] **7:11** Or *the villages* [D] **8:1** Lit *Would that you were like a brother to me* [E] **8:2** LXX adds *and into the cham ber of the one who bore me* [F] **8:6** Or *the blaze of the LORD* [G] **8:7** Lit *all the wealth of his house* [H] **8:10** Or *was* [I] **8:10** Or *brings* [J] **8:10** In Hb, the word for *peace* sounds similar to Solomon and Shulammite. [K] **8:12** Lit *My vineyard, which is mine, is before me*; Sg 1:6

Man

13 You[A] who dwell in the gardens,
companions are listening
for your voice;
let me hear you!

Woman

14 Run away with me,[B] my love,
and be like a gazelle
or a young stag
on the mountains of spices.

[A] **8:13** In Hb, the word for *You* is feminine. [B] **8:14** Lit *Flee*

The book of *Isaiah* has quite a bit of doom and gloom but also beautiful passages of hope. God promised to send a King, a Suffering Servant who would die to save his people from their sins. He promised restoration and healing from the blight of sin. He promised to bring a remnant of people back to the land of promise and to a relationship of rest and peace. The Judge is also the Prince of Peace, and he will lead his people like a shepherd.

We are fickle and faithless, and apart from God we have no hope. But Isaiah presents the solution: God will save us. He has promised it, and he did it at the cross of Christ. Despite our sin, we can be saved, because our salvation depends not on us but on God who is rich in mercy and unfailing love.

Let the book of Isaiah restore your soul by reminding you that though you are deserving of the judgment described in its pages, you have received by faith the mercy of Christ. The Messiah has freed you from the shackles of sin and ransomed your soul from death. Drink deep of the living water of Christ, and be restored.

ISAIAH

AUTHOR: Isaiah, son of Amoz

DATE WRITTEN: Isaiah's prophetic ministry began in the final year of the reign of Uzziah in Judah (742 BC) and concluded during the reign of Hezekiah (716–686 BC).

ORIGINAL AUDIENCE: The Israelites, specifically Judah

SETTING: Isaiah's call came right after King Uzziah had been stricken with a skin disease for performing a task only the priests were allowed to do and, thus, offending the holiness of God (2Ch 26:16-19). Clearly this was a time when the nation of Judah needed a fresh understanding of God's holiness. Isaiah spent his life prophesying about the destruction that would come if the people failed to live according to the covenantal law that God had established. Sadly, the people failed to heed his warnings.

PURPOSE FOR WRITING: The message of Isaiah is that the holiness of God requires that his people be set apart in obedience. The theme of God's holiness is underscored by the fact that the name used for God throughout the book is the "Holy One of Israel." A holy God demands a holy people, but the people of Isaiah's day—like the people of every age, down to our day—had turned away from him. They needed a reminder of God's holiness and a warning of the threat of future judgment. Rebellion against God leads to judgment, but God in his faithfulness will restore his people through the promised Messiah.

OUTLINE:

1. Rebuke and Promise from the Lord (1:1–6:13)

   Judah on trial (1:1-15)

   Call for cleansing (1:16-31)

   Future hope (2:1–4:6)

   Judgment and exile (5:1-30)

   Isaiah's call (6:1-13)

2. Foretelling of the Messiah (7:1–12:6)

   One rejected by the world (7:1-25)

   Deliverer (8:1–9:7)

   Judge (9:8–10:4)

   Ruler of glorious empire (10:5–12:6)

3. Judgment upon the Nations (13:1–23:18)

4. First Cycle of Judgment and Promise (24:1–27:13)

   Universal judgment for universal sin (24:1-23)

   Praise for deliverance (25:1-12)

   Song of comfort for Judah (26:1-21)

   Promise of preservation (27:1-13)

5. Woes upon Unbelievers of Israel (28:1–33:24)

   Drunkards and scoffers (28:1-29)

   Deceivers and hypocrites (29:1-24)

   Confidence in humans vs. confidence in God (30:1-33)

   Deliverance from God (31:1–32:20)

   Triumph of Christ (33:1-24)

6. Second Cycle of Judgment and Promise (34:1–39:8)

   Destruction of Gentile world powers (34:1-17)

   Bliss of the redeemed (35:1-10)

   Deliverance and healing for King Hezekiah (36:1–39:8)

7. Comfort for God's People (40:1–66:24)

   Purpose of peace (40:1–48:22)

   Prince of Peace (49:1–57:21)

   Program of peace (58:1–66:24)

KEY VERSE:

"'Come, let us settle this,' says the LORD. 'Though your sins are scarlet, they will be as white as snow; though they are crimson red, they will be like wool.'" –Isaiah 1:18

RESTORATION THEMES

R	Rest and Reflection	*Remembering God's Truth—5:20* *Receiving God's Peace—9:6* *Meditating on God and His Word—40:8* *Avoiding Burnout—40:30-31* *Consuming Spiritual Nourishment—55:1-2*
E	Eternal Perspective	*God's Holiness—6:3* *God's Compassion—30:18* *God's Mercy—42:3* *Redemption/Salvation—43:1* *God's Power—46:10* *God's Love—49:15-16* *Personal Limitations—55:8-9* *Biblical Hope—61:1-2*
S	Support	*Openness with Others—30:10-11*
T	Thanksgiving and Contentment	*Confession—1:18* *Repentance—30:15*
O	Other-centeredness	*Helping Widows and Orphans—1:17* *Giving Generously—32:8* *Encouraging—35:3-4*
R	Relationships	*For the next note, see Jeremiah 15:21.*
E	Exercise of Faith	*Trusting God—Isaiah 2:22* *Following God's Lead—6:8* *Praying—37:20*

1 The vision concerning Judah and Jerusalem that Isaiah son of Amoz saw during the reigns[A,B] of Kings Uzziah, Jotham, Ahaz, and Hezekiah of Judah.

JUDAH ON TRIAL

2 Listen, heavens,
and pay attention, earth,
for the LORD has spoken:
"I have raised children[C]
and brought them up,
but they have rebelled against me.
3 The ox knows its owner,
and the donkey its master's
feeding trough,
but Israel does not know;
my people do not understand."

4 Oh sinful nation,
people weighed down with iniquity,
brood of evildoers,
depraved children!
They have abandoned the LORD;
they have despised the Holy One
of Israel;
they have turned their backs on him.

5 Why do you want more beatings?
Why do you keep on rebelling?
The whole head is hurt,
and the whole heart is sick.
6 From the sole of the foot
even to the head,
no spot is uninjured —
wounds, welts, and festering sores
not cleansed, bandaged,
or soothed with oil.

7 Your land is desolate,
your cities burned down;
foreigners devour your fields
right in front of you —
a desolation, like a place demolished
by foreigners.
8 Daughter Zion is abandoned
like a shelter in a vineyard,
like a shack in a cucumber field,
like a besieged city.
9 If the LORD of Armies
had not left us a few survivors,
we would be like Sodom,
we would resemble Gomorrah.

10 Hear the word of the LORD,
you rulers of Sodom!
Listen to the instruction of our God,
you people of Gomorrah!
11 "What are all your sacrifices to me?"

Other-centeredness | *Helping Widows and Orphans*

RELEVANT RELIGION

"Learn to do what is good. Pursue justice. Correct the oppressor. Defend the rights of the fatherless. Plead the widow's cause." Isaiah 1:17

Would you want to trade careers with Isaiah? He was a prophet, meaning his job was to urge spiritually rebellious people to turn back to God. And he did this faithfully for almost six decades—from about 739–681 BC.

As Isaiah ministered in and around Jerusalem, he watched the decadent northern kingdom of Israel fall to the invading Assyrians (722 BC). His message to the southern kingdom of Judah was simple but urgent: Turn back to the One who has chosen and blessed you and promised you a glorious future.

This wasn't an inward call to be more *spiritual* or to engage in more religious activities. It was a call for the people of God to live out their faith in everyday ways that benefited society. "Pursue justice." Fight oppression. Stand up for the weak.

That message can restore us and our culture as well. Do more today than pray and read the Bible. Go visit an elderly neighbor. Help at a homeless shelter. "Learn to do what is good." Then do it.

For the next note on *Other-centeredness*, see Isaiah 32:8.

[A] **1:1** Lit *saw in the days* [B] **1:1** ca 792–686 BC [C] **1:2** Or *sons*, also in v. 4

asks the LORD.
"I have had enough of burnt offerings
and rams
and the fat of well-fed cattle;
I have no desire
for the blood of bulls,
lambs, or male goats.
12 When you come to appear before me,
who requires this from you —
this trampling of my courts?
13 Stop bringing useless offerings.
Your incense is detestable to me.
New Moons and Sabbaths,
and the calling of solemn assemblies —
I cannot stand iniquity
with a festival.
14 I hate your New Moons
and prescribed festivals.
They have become a burden to me;
I am tired of putting up with them.
15 When you spread out your hands
in prayer,
I will refuse to look at you;
even if you offer countless prayers,
I will not listen.
Your hands are covered with blood.

PURIFICATION OF JERUSALEM

16 "Wash yourselves. Cleanse yourselves.
Remove your evil deeds from my sight.
Stop doing evil.
17 Learn to do what is good.
Pursue justice.
Correct the oppressor.[A]
Defend the rights of the fatherless.
Plead the widow's cause.

18 "Come, let us settle this,"
says the LORD.
"Though your sins are scarlet,
they will be as white as snow;
though they are crimson red,
they will be like wool.
19 If you are willing and obedient,
you will eat
the good things of the land.
20 But if you refuse and rebel,
you will be devoured by the sword."
For the mouth of the LORD has spoken.

21 The faithful town —
what an adulteress[B] she has become!
She was once full of justice.

Thanksgiving and Contentment | *Confession*

FORGIVEN!

"'Come, let us settle this,' says the LORD. 'Though your sins are scarlet, they will be as white as snow; though they are crimson red, they will be like wool.'" Isaiah 1:18

Watching some people deal with sin is like watching a lawyered-up billionaire in a high-profile criminal case. You've seen such legal maneuvering: denials; motions to suppress evidence or dismiss charges; requests for continuances; refusing to testify; attempts to impugn the character of the accuser or the fairness of the judge.

What really should be a short process becomes a long, drawn-out affair—and often a circus.

Here through the prophet Isaiah, God says to his sinful people, "Come, let us settle this." In other words, let's not turn this into a time-consuming, emotion-zapping experience.

The idea is simple: If God's people will humbly acknowledge their sinful actions, he will forgive: "They will be as white as snow." God isn't interested in a bunch of religious activity (1:11-15), which is often just a diversionary tactic or sideshow. Nor is he interested in rubbing people's noses in their failure. He simply wants us to admit our sin so he can clean our hearts, and everyone can move on.

Ask God to show you ways in which you drag your feet where sin is involved. Because we are represented by Jesus, confession and repentance never need be long or scary.

For the next note on *Thanksgiving and Confession*, see Isaiah 30:15.

[A] **1:17** Or *Aid the oppressed* [B] **1:21** Or *prostitute*

Righteousness once dwelt in her,
but now, murderers!
22 Your silver has become dross to be
discarded,
your beer[A] is diluted with water.
23 Your rulers are rebels,
friends of thieves.
They all love graft
and chase after bribes.
They do not defend the rights
of the fatherless,
and the widow's case never comes
before them.

24 Therefore the Lord God of Armies,
the Mighty One of Israel, declares:
"Ah, I will get even with my foes;
I will take revenge
against my enemies.
25 I will turn my hand against you
and will burn away
your dross completely;[B]
I will remove all your impurities.
26 I will restore your judges to what they
were at first,[C]
and your advisers to what they were at
the start.[D]
Afterward you will be called
the Righteous City,
a Faithful Town."

27 Zion will be redeemed by justice,
those who repent,
by righteousness.
28 At the same time both rebels
and sinners will be broken,
and those who abandon the Lord
will perish.
29 Indeed, they[E] will be ashamed
of the sacred trees
you desired,
and you will be embarrassed
because of the garden shrines
you have chosen.
30 For you will become like an oak
whose leaves are withered,
and like a garden without water.
31 The strong one will become tinder,
and his work a spark;
both will burn together,
with no one to extinguish
the flames.

THE CITY OF PEACE

2 The vision that Isaiah son of Amoz saw
concerning Judah and Jerusalem:
2 In the last days
the mountain of the Lord's house
will be established
at the top of the mountains
and will be raised above the hills.
All nations will stream to it,
3 and many peoples will come and say,
"Come, let us go up to the mountain
of the Lord,
to the house of the God of Jacob.
He will teach us about his ways
so that we may walk in his paths."
For instruction will go out of Zion
and the word of the Lord
from Jerusalem.
4 He will settle disputes
among the nations
and provide arbitration
for many peoples.
They will beat their swords into plows
and their spears into pruning knives.
Nation will not take up the sword
against nation,
and they will never again train for war.

THE DAY OF THE LORD

5 House of Jacob,
come and let us walk
in the Lord's light.
6 For you have abandoned your people,
the house of Jacob,
because they are full of divination
from the East
and of fortune-tellers like the Philistines.
They are in league[F] with foreigners.
7 Their[G,H] land is full of silver and gold,
and there is no limit to their treasures;
their land is full of horses,
and there is no limit to their chariots.
8 Their land is full of idols;
they worship the work of their hands,
what their fingers have made.
9 So humanity is brought low,
and each person is humbled.
Do not forgive them!
10 Go into the rocks
and hide in the dust
from the terror of the Lord
and from his majestic splendor.

[A] **1:22** Or *wine* [B] **1:25** Lit *dross as with lye* [C] **1:26** Lit *judges as at the first* [D] **1:26** Lit *advisers as at the beginning*
[E] **1:29** Some Hb mss; other Hb mss, Tg read *you* [F] **2:6** Or *They teem*, or *They partner*; Hb obscure [G] **2:7** Lit *Its* [H] **2:7** = the house of Jacob

11 The pride of mankind[A] will be humbled,
and human loftiness
will be brought low;
the LORD alone will be exalted
on that day.

12 For a day belonging to the LORD
of Armies is coming
against all that is proud and lofty,
against all that is lifted up — it will
be humbled —
13 against all the cedars of Lebanon,
lofty and lifted up,
against all the oaks of Bashan,
14 against all the high mountains,
against all the lofty hills,
15 against every high tower,
against every fortified wall,
16 against every ship of Tarshish,
and against every splendid sea vessel.
17 The pride of mankind will be
brought low,
and human loftiness will be humbled;
the LORD alone will be exalted
on that day.
18 The idols will vanish completely.
19 People will go into caves in the rocks
and holes in the ground,
away from the terror of the LORD
and from his majestic splendor,
when he rises to terrify the earth.
20 On that day people will throw
their silver and gold idols,
which they made to worship,
to the moles and the bats.
21 They will go into the caves of the rocks
and the crevices in the cliffs,
away from the terror of the LORD
and from his majestic splendor,
when he rises to terrify the earth.
22 Put no more trust in a mere human,
who has only the breath
in his nostrils.
What is he really worth?

JUDAH'S LEADERS JUDGED

3 Note this: The Lord GOD of Armies
is about to remove from Jerusalem
and from Judah
every kind of security:
the entire supply of bread and water,
2 heroes and warriors,

Exercise of Faith | *Trusting God*

THE PLACE OF PEOPLE

"Put no more trust in a mere human, who has only the breath in his nostrils. What is he really worth?" Isaiah 2:22

Many human relationships get in trouble from the start. This happens when we look to other people to meet our deepest needs. Often we count on friends, a sweetheart, a spouse, or even our own children to complete us, love us unconditionally, understand us perfectly, rescue us, make us happy, give us security, or give us meaning.

To hope that a friend will listen and care is good. But to expect any person to fix us puts a lot of pressure on a mortal, fallible creature.

By the time Isaiah was on the scene, Judah had developed the bad habit of placing their ultimate trust in mere humans: the beguiling words of false prophets, the treaty-making abilities of their own leaders, and the sketchy promises of foreign kings. Through Isaiah, God told them to cut it out. Only he is worthy of such trust.

Let's not set ourselves up for disappointment. People can be used by God, but they're not God. As mortals, the best we can do for one another is to express concern, lend a hand, faithfully pray, and encourage.

In getting help from others, don't over-expect. In coming alongside a hurting friend, don't over-promise.

For the next note on *Exercise of Faith*, see Isaiah 6:8.

[A] **2:11** Lit *Mankind's proud eyes*

judges and prophets,
fortune-tellers and elders,
3 commanders of fifty and dignitaries,
counselors, cunning magicians,[A]
and necromancers.[B]
4 "I will make youths their leaders,
and unstable rulers[C] will govern them."
5 The people will oppress one another,
man against man, neighbor
against neighbor;
the young will act arrogantly
toward the old,
and the worthless
toward the honorable.
6 A man will even seize his brother
in his father's house, saying:
"You have a cloak — you be our leader!
This heap of rubble will be
under your control."
7 On that day he will cry out, saying:
"I'm not a healer.
I don't even have food or clothing
in my house.
Don't make me the leader
of the people!"
8 For Jerusalem has stumbled
and Judah has fallen
because they have spoken and acted
against the LORD,
defying his glorious presence.
9 The look on their faces testifies
against them,
and like Sodom, they flaunt their sin;
they do not conceal it.
Woe to them,
for they have brought disaster
on themselves.
10 Tell the righteous that it will go well
for them,
for they will eat the fruit of their labor.
11 Woe to the wicked — it will go badly
for them,
for what they have done will be done
to them.
12 Youths oppress my people,
and women rule over them.
My people, your leaders mislead you;
they confuse the direction
of your paths.

13 The LORD rises to argue the case
and stands to judge the people.
14 The LORD brings this charge
against the elders and leaders
of his people:
"You have devastated the vineyard.
The plunder from the poor is
in your houses.
15 Why do you crush my people
and grind the faces of the poor?"
This is the declaration
of the Lord GOD of Armies.

JERUSALEM'S WOMEN JUDGED

16 The LORD also says:
Because the daughters of Zion
are haughty,
walking with heads held high
and seductive eyes,
prancing along,
jingling their ankle bracelets,
17 the Lord will put scabs on the heads
of the daughters of Zion,
and the LORD will shave
their foreheads bare.

18 On that day the Lord will strip their finery: ankle bracelets, headbands, crescents,
19 pendants, bracelets, veils, 20 headdresses,
ankle jewelry, sashes, perfume bottles, amu-
lets, 21 signet rings, nose rings, 22 festive robes,
capes, cloaks, purses, 23 garments, linen clothes,
turbans, and shawls.
24 Instead of perfume there will be
a stench;
instead of a belt, a rope;
instead of
beautifully styled hair, baldness;
instead of fine clothes, sackcloth;
instead of beauty, branding.[D]
25 Your men will fall by the sword,
your warriors in battle.
26 Then her gates will lament
and mourn;
deserted, she will sit on the ground.

4 On that day seven women
will seize one man, saying,
"We will eat our own bread
and provide our own clothing.
Just let us bear your name.
Take away our disgrace."

ZION'S FUTURE GLORY

2 On that day the Branch[E] of the LORD will be
beautiful and glorious, and the fruit of the
land will be the pride and glory of Israel's

[A] 3:3 Or *skilled craftsmen* [B] 3:3 Or *mediums* [C] 3:4 Or *mischief-makers* [D] 3:24 DSS read *shame* [E] 4:2 Or *plant*

survivors. 3 Whoever remains in Zion and
whoever is left in Jerusalem will be called
holy — all in Jerusalem written in the book
of life[A] — 4 when the Lord has washed away
the filth of the daughters of Zion and cleansed
the bloodguilt from the heart of Jerusalem by
a spirit of judgment and a spirit of burning.
5 Then the LORD will create a cloud of smoke
by day and a glowing flame of fire by night
over the entire site of Mount Zion and over
its assemblies. For there will be a canopy over
all the glory,[B] 6 and there will be a shelter for
shade from heat by day, and a refuge and shelter from storm and rain.

SONG OF THE VINEYARD

5 I will sing about the one I love,
a song about my loved one's vineyard:
The one I love had a vineyard
on a very fertile hill.
2 He broke up the soil, cleared it
of stones,
and planted it with the finest vines.
He built a tower in the middle of it
and even dug out a winepress there.
He expected it to yield good grapes,
but it yielded worthless grapes.
3 So now, residents of Jerusalem
and men of Judah,
please judge between me
and my vineyard.
4 What more could I have done
for my vineyard
than I did?
Why, when I expected a yield
of good grapes,
did it yield worthless grapes?
5 Now I will tell you
what I am about to do to my vineyard:
I will remove its hedge,
and it will be consumed;
I will tear down its wall,
and it will be trampled.
6 I will make it a wasteland.
It will not be pruned or weeded;
thorns and briers will grow up.
I will also give orders to the clouds
that rain should not fall on it.
7 For the vineyard of the LORD of Armies
is the house of Israel,
and the men[C] of Judah,
the plant he delighted in.
He expected justice
but saw injustice;
he expected righteousness,
but heard cries of despair.

JUDAH'S SINS DENOUNCED

8 Woe to those who add house to house
and join field to field
until there is no more room
and you alone are left in the land.

9 I heard the LORD of Armies say:
Indeed, many houses
will become desolate,
grand and lovely ones
without inhabitants.
10 For a ten-acre[D] vineyard will yield
only six gallons of wine,[E]
and ten bushels[F] of seed will yield
only one bushel of grain.[G]

11 Woe to those who rise early
in the morning
in pursuit of beer,
who linger into the evening,
inflamed by wine.
12 At their feasts they have lyre, harp,
tambourine, flute, and wine.
They do not perceive
the LORD's actions,
and they do not see the work of his hands.

13 Therefore my people will go into exile
because they lack knowledge;
her[H] dignitaries are starving,
and her masses are parched with thirst.
14 Therefore Sheol enlarges its throat
and opens wide its enormous jaws,
and down go Zion's dignitaries,
her masses,
her crowds, and those who celebrate
in her!
15 Humanity is brought low, each
person is humbled,
and haughty eyes are humbled.
16 But the LORD of Armies is exalted
by his justice,
and the holy God shows that he is holy
through his righteousness.
17 Lambs will graze
as if in[I] their own pastures,
and resident aliens[J] will eat
among the ruins of the rich.

[A] 4:3 Lit *Jerusalem recorded for life* [B] 4:5 Or *For glory will be a canopy over all* [C] 5:7 Lit *man* [D] 5:10 Lit *ten-yoke* [E] 5:10 Lit *one bath* [F] 5:10 Lit *one homer* [G] 5:10 Lit *yield an ephah* [H] 5:13 Lit *its* [I] 5:17 Syr reads *graze in* [J] 5:17 LXX reads *sheep*

18 Woe to those who drag iniquity
with cords of deceit
and pull sin along with cart ropes,
19 to those who say:
"Let him hurry up and do
his work quickly
so that we can see it!
Let the plan of the Holy One of Israel
take place
so that we can know it!"
20 Woe to those who call evil good
and good evil,
who substitute darkness for light
and light for darkness,
who substitute bitter for sweet
and sweet for bitter.
21 Woe to those who consider themselves
wise
and judge themselves clever.[A]
22 Woe to those who are heroes
at drinking wine,
who are champions at pouring beer,
23 who acquit the guilty for a bribe
and deprive the innocent of justice.

24 Therefore, as a tongue of fire
consumes straw
and as dry grass shrivels in the flame,
so their roots will become
like something rotten
and their blossoms will blow away
like dust,
for they have rejected
the instruction of the LORD of Armies,
and they have despised
the word of the Holy One of Israel.
25 Therefore the LORD's anger burned
against his people.
He raised his hand against them
and struck them;
the mountains quaked,
and their corpses were like garbage
in the streets.
In all this, his anger has not turned
away,
and his hand is still raised
to strike.

26 He raises a signal flag
for the distant nations
and whistles for them from the ends
of the earth.
Look — how quickly and swiftly
they come!

Rest and Reflection | *Remembering God's Truth*

TOPSY-TURVY TRUTH

"Woe to those who call evil good and good evil, who substitute darkness for light and light for darkness, who substitute bitter for sweet and sweet for bitter." Isaiah 5:20

When people reject divine truth, they don't suddenly believe in "nothing." Rather, they begin to embrace anything and everything. The famous Russian novelist Fyodor Dostoevsky put it this way, "Without God, all things are permitted."

You've seen this phenomenon in your own lifetime. Slipping standards. Redefinitions of right and wrong—actions once considered beyond the pale, not just tolerated, but celebrated.

Isaiah saw this trend in his own day. As his neighbors distanced themselves from God and Judaism's moral absolutes, they lost both the desire and the ability to discern right from wrong. They called evil things good. They labeled good things evil.

The divine word to such people is *woe*. It means "Alas!" or "Oye! Or "Look out!" *Woe*, an expression of lament, is not the sort of thing one says giddily at a party.

Unfortunately, in our desire to be open and accepting, we can drift away from God's truth. Be careful not to blur distinctions in your values and morals.

For the next note on *Rest and Reflection*, see Isaiah 9:6.

[A] **5:21** Lit *and clever before their face*

27 None of them grows weary or stumbles;
no one slumbers or sleeps.
No belt is loose
and no sandal strap broken.
28 Their arrows are sharpened,
and all their bows strung.
Their horses' hooves are like flint;
their chariot wheels are
like a whirlwind.
29 Their roaring is like a lion's;
they roar like young lions;
they growl and seize their prey
and carry it off,
and no one can rescue it.
30 On that day they will roar over it,
like the roaring of the sea.
When one looks at the land,
there will be darkness and distress;
light will be obscured by clouds.[A]

ISAIAH'S CALL AND MISSION

In the year that King Uzziah died, I saw the
Lord seated on a high and lofty throne,
and the hem of his robe filled the temple.
2 Seraphim[B] were standing above him; they
each had six wings: with two they covered
their faces, with two they covered their feet,
and with two they flew. 3 And one called to
another:

Holy, holy, holy is the LORD of Armies;
his glory fills the whole earth.

4 The foundations of the doorways shook at
the sound of their voices, and the temple was
filled with smoke.
5 Then I said:

Woe is me for I am ruined[C]
because I am a man of unclean lips
and live among a people of unclean lips,
and because my eyes have seen the King,
the LORD of Armies.

6 Then one of the seraphim flew to me, and
in his hand was a glowing coal that he had
taken from the altar with tongs. 7 He touched
my mouth with it and said:

Now that this has touched your lips,
your iniquity is removed
and your sin is atoned for.

E Eternal Perspective | *God's Holiness*

SPIRITUAL EXPERIENCES

"And one called to another: Holy, holy, holy is the LORD of Armies; his glory fills the whole earth." Isaiah 6:3

Isaiah was going about his business. The day was like any other—until, suddenly, it wasn't!

Isaiah had a vision in which he "saw the Lord seated on a high and lofty throne" (6:1). He watched heavenly creatures—angels—soar and hover all about the Almighty. As they flew they cried, "Holy, holy, holy is the LORD of Armies" (6:3). This prompted something similar to an earthquake to shake the place violently, filling it with smoke.

We don't know if Isaiah fell on his face and hugged the ground for dear life. We do know he was overwhelmed by a profound sense of sinful unworthiness, until one of the angels assured his forgiveness.

Passages like this prompt the question: Should all believers expect such dramatic, supernatural encounters?

The short answer: That's up to God. We should remember that he deals with each of his children uniquely. Elijah heard a whisper (1Kg 19). The apostle Paul was blinded and bowled over (Ac 9). Peter, James, and John saw Jesus transfigured (Mk 9), but none of the other disciples did.

Our place is not to try to initiate spectacular, spiritual experiences. Authentic ones are God-originated, not human-made. If God speaks to us in unusual ways, our response should be to listen carefully and then obey.

For the next note on *Eternal Perspective*, see Isaiah 30:18.

[A] **5:30** Lit *its clouds* [B] **6:2** = heavenly beings [C] **6:5** Or *I must be silent*

8 Then I heard the voice of the Lord asking:
Who should I send?
Who will go for us?

I said:
Here I am. Send me.

9 And he replied:
Go! Say to these people:
Keep listening, but do not understand;
keep looking, but do not perceive.
10 Make the minds[A] of these people dull;
deafen their ears and blind their eyes;
otherwise they might see
with their eyes
and hear with their ears,
understand with their minds,
turn back, and be healed.

11 Then I said, "Until when, Lord?" And he replied:
Until cities lie in ruins
without inhabitants,
houses are without people,
the land is ruined and desolate,
12 and the LORD drives the people far away,
leaving great emptiness in the land.
13 Though a tenth will remain in the land,
it will be burned again.
Like the terebinth or the oak
that leaves a stump when felled,
the holy seed is the stump.

THE MESSAGE TO AHAZ

7 This took place during the reign of Ahaz,
son of Jotham, son of Uzziah king of Judah:
Aram's King Rezin and Israel's King Pekah son
of Remaliah went to fight against Jerusalem,
but they were not able to conquer it.
2 When it became known to the house of
David that Aram had occupied Ephraim, the
heart of Ahaz[B] and the hearts of his people
trembled like trees of a forest shaking in the
wind.
3 The LORD said to Isaiah, "Go out with your
son Shear-jashub[C] to meet Ahaz at the end
of the conduit of the upper pool, by the road
to the Launderer's Field. 4 Say to him: Calm
down and be quiet. Don't be afraid or cowardly
because of these two smoldering sticks, the
fierce anger of Rezin and Aram, and the son
of Remaliah. 5 For Aram, along with Ephraim
and the son of Remaliah, has plotted harm
against you. They say, 6 'Let us go up against

Exercise of Faith | *Following God's Lead*

AVAILABLE TO SERVE

"Then I heard the voice of the Lord asking: Who should I send? Who will go for us? I said: Here I am. Send me." Isaiah 6:8

Some people have a reputation for being easy. They can't say "no." They're helpful to their own detriment. The word quickly gets around: "If you have a need, if you get in a bind, call _____." At some level, this willingness to help is commendable. Taken to an extreme, it's the expressway to burnout.

What's interesting here is that Isaiah wasn't hearing the voice of some harried temple official. This wasn't the manipulative plea of a weary senior prophet who was running short of volunteers. This wasn't Isaiah's wife guilting him into service or some unhealthy expectation he had heaped on himself. This was "the voice of the Lord."

In this instance, the Lord was "asking" not commanding. Had Isaiah kept his mouth shut, God certainly would have used someone else. But Isaiah volunteered. As a result, he experienced all the exhilaration and exasperation that comes from serving the Lord.

We can't do everything—nor should we try. But we can ask God for the ability to hear his voice above all the rest. And we can ask for the wisdom to do only what will glorify him, bless others, and bring joy to our lives.

For the next note on *Exercise of Faith*, see Isaiah 37:20.

[A] **6:10** Lit *heart* [B] **7:2** Lit *Aram has rested upon Ephraim, his heart* [C] **7:3** = A Remnant Will Return

Judah, terrorize it, and conquer it for ourselves.
Then we can install Tabeel's son as king in it.' "
7 This is what the Lord GOD says:
It will not happen; it will not occur.
8 The[A] chief city of Aram is Damascus,
the chief of Damascus is Rezin
(within sixty-five years
Ephraim will be too shattered to be
a people),
9 the chief city of Ephraim is Samaria,
and the chief of Samaria is the son
of Remaliah.
If you do not stand firm in your faith,
then you will not stand at all.

THE IMMANUEL PROPHECY

10 Then the LORD spoke again to Ahaz: 11 "Ask
for a sign from the LORD your God — it can be
as deep as Sheol or as high as heaven."
12 But Ahaz replied, "I will not ask. I will not
test the LORD."
13 Isaiah said, "Listen, house of David! Is it not
enough for you to try the patience of men? Will
you also try the patience of my God? 14 Therefore, the Lord himself will give you[B] a sign: See,
the virgin will conceive,[C] have a son, and name
him Immanuel.[D] 15 By the time he learns to reject
what is bad and choose what is good, he will be
eating curds[E] and honey. 16 For before the boy
knows to reject what is bad and choose what is
good, the land of the two kings you dread will
be abandoned. 17 The LORD will bring on you,
your people, and your father's house such a
time as has never been since Ephraim separated
from Judah: He will bring the king of Assyria."
18 On that day
the LORD will whistle to flies
at the farthest streams of the Nile
and to bees in the land of Assyria.
19 All of them will come and settle
in the steep ravines, in the clefts
of the rocks,
in all the thornbushes, and in all the
water holes.

20 On that day the Lord will use a razor hired
from beyond the Euphrates River — the king
of Assyria — to shave the hair on your heads,
the hair on your legs, and even your beards.
21 On that day
a man will raise a young cow
and two sheep,
22 and from the abundant milk they give
he will eat curds,
for every survivor in the land
will eat curds and honey.

23 And on that day
every place where there were a
thousand vines,
worth a thousand pieces of silver,
will become thorns and briers.
24 A man will go there with bow
and arrows
because the whole land will be thorns
and briers.
25 You will not go to all the hills
that were once tilled with a hoe,
for fear of the thorns and briers.
Those hills will be places for oxen
to graze
and for sheep to trample.

THE COMING ASSYRIAN INVASION

8 Then the LORD said to me, "Take a large
piece of parchment[F] and write on it with
an ordinary pen:[G] Maher-shalal-hash-baz.[H] 2 I
have appointed[I] trustworthy witnesses — the
priest Uriah and Zechariah son of Jeberechiah."
3 I was then intimate with the prophetess,
and she conceived and gave birth to a son. The
LORD said to me, "Name him Maher-shalal-
hash-baz, 4 for before the boy knows how to
call 'Father,' or 'Mother,' the wealth of Damascus and the spoils of Samaria will be carried
off to the king of Assyria."
5 The LORD spoke to me again:
6 Because these people rejected
the slowly flowing water
of Shiloah
and rejoiced with[J] Rezin
and the son of Remaliah,
7 the Lord will certainly bring
against them
the mighty rushing water
of the Euphrates River —
the king of Assyria and all his glory.
It will overflow its channels
and spill over all its banks.
8 It will pour into Judah,
flood over it, and sweep through,
reaching up to the neck;
and its flooded banks[K]
will fill your entire land, Immanuel!

[A] **7:8** Lit *For the* [B] **7:14** In Hb, the word *you* is pl [C] **7:14** Or *virgin is pregnant, will* [D] **7:14** = God With Us [E] **7:15** Or *sour milk* [F] **8:1** Hb obscure [G] **8:1** Lit *with the pen of a man* [H] **8:1** = Speeding to the Plunder, Hurrying to the Spoil [I] **8:2** Vg; MT, one DSS ms read *I will appoint*; one DSS ms, LXX, Syr, Tg read *Appoint* [J] **8:6** Or *and rejoiced over* [K] **8:8** Lit *its outspread wings*

9 Band together,[A] peoples,
and be broken;
pay attention, all you distant lands;
prepare for war, and be broken;
prepare for war, and be broken.
10 Devise a plan; it will fail.
Make a prediction;
it will not happen.
For God is with us.[B]

THE LORD OF ARMIES, THE ONLY REFUGE

11 For this is what the LORD said to me with
great power, to keep[C] me from going the way
of this people:
12 Do not call everything a conspiracy
these people say is a conspiracy.
Do not fear what they fear;
do not be terrified.
13 You are to regard only the LORD
of Armies as holy.
Only he should be feared;
only he should be held in awe.
14 He will be a sanctuary;
but for the two houses of Israel,
he will be a stone to stumble over
and a rock to trip over,
and a trap and a snare
to the inhabitants of Jerusalem.
15 Many will stumble over these;
they will fall and be broken;
they will be snared and captured.

16 Bind up the testimony.
Seal up the instruction
among my disciples.
17 I will wait for the LORD,
who is hiding his face from the house
of Jacob.
I will wait for him.

18 Here I am with the children the LORD has
given me to be signs and wonders in Israel
from the LORD of Armies who dwells on Mount
Zion. 19 When they say to you, "Inquire of the
mediums and the spiritists who chirp and
mutter," shouldn't a people inquire of their
God?[D] Should they inquire of the dead on behalf of the living? 20 Go to God's instruction
and testimony! If they do not speak according
to this word, there will be no dawn for them.
21 They will wander through the land, dejected and hungry. When they are famished, they
will become enraged, and, looking upward,
will curse their king and their God. 22 They will
look toward the earth and see only distress,
darkness, and the gloom of affliction, and they
will be driven into thick darkness.

BIRTH OF THE PRINCE OF PEACE

9 Nevertheless, the gloom of the distressed
land will not be like that of the former
times when he humbled the land of Zebulun
and the land of Naphtali. But in the future
he will bring honor to the way of the sea, to
the land east of the Jordan, and to Galilee of
the nations.
2 The people walking in darkness
have seen a great light;
a light has dawned
on those living in the land of darkness.
3 You have enlarged the nation
and increased its joy.[E]
The people have rejoiced before you
as they rejoice at harvest time
and as they rejoice
when dividing spoils.
4 For you have shattered
their oppressive yoke
and the rod on their shoulders,
the staff of their oppressor,
just as you did on the day of Midian.
5 For every trampling boot of battle
and the bloodied garments of war
will be burned as fuel for the fire.
6 For a child will be born for us,
a son will be given to us,
and the government will be
on his shoulders.
He will be named
Wonderful Counselor, Mighty God,
Eternal Father, Prince of Peace.
7 The dominion will be vast,
and its prosperity will never end.
He will reign on the throne of David
and over his kingdom,
to establish and sustain it
with justice and righteousness
from now on and forever.
The zeal of the LORD of Armies
will accomplish this.

THE HAND RAISED AGAINST ISRAEL

8 The Lord sent a message
against Jacob;
it came against Israel.
9 All the people —

[A] **8:9** Or *Raise the war cry*, or *Be shattered* [B] **8:10** Hb *Immanuel* [C] **8:11** DSS; MT reads *instruct* [D] **8:19** Or *gods* [E] **9:3** Alt Hb tradition reads *have not increased joy*

Ephraim and the inhabitants
of Samaria — will know it.
They will say with pride and arrogance:
10 "The bricks have fallen,
but we will rebuild with cut stones;
the sycamores have been cut down,
but we will replace them
with cedars."
11 The LORD has raised up
Rezin's adversaries against him
and stirred up his enemies.
12 Aram from the east and Philistia
from the west
have consumed Israel
with open mouths.
In all this, his anger has not turned
away,
and his hand is still raised to strike.

13 The people did not turn to him
who struck them;
they did not seek the LORD of Armies.
14 So the LORD cut off Israel's head
and tail,
palm branch and reed in a single day.
15 The head is the elder, the honored one;
the tail is the prophet, the one teaching
lies.
16 The leaders of the people mislead them,
and those they mislead
are swallowed up.[A]
17 Therefore the Lord does not rejoice
over[B] Israel's young men
and has no compassion
on its fatherless and widows,
for everyone is a godless evildoer,
and every mouth speaks folly.
In all this, his anger has not turned
away,
and his hand is still raised to strike.

18 For wickedness burns like a fire
that consumes thorns and briers
and kindles the forest thickets
so that they go up in a column
of smoke.
19 The land is scorched
by the wrath of the LORD of Armies,
and the people are like fuel for the fire.
No one has compassion on his brother.
20 They carve meat on the right,
but they are still hungry;

Rest and Reflection | *Receiving God's Peace*

PRINCE OF PEACE

"For a child will be born for us, a son will be given to us, and the government will be on his shoulders. He will be named Wonderful Counselor, Mighty God, Eternal Father, Prince of Peace." Isaiah 9:6

Each Christmas, as we celebrate the birth of Christ, we sing, quote, and preach this verse, as much as any other. This is because Christians see Jesus as the ultimate fulfillment of Isaiah's prophecy. He is the long-awaited, much-needed Prince of Peace.

The Hebrew word translated "peace" is the word *shalom*. And what a rich word it is! *Shalom* isn't merely the absence of conflict. *Shalom* is the absence of conflict and the presence of vitality, joy, health, safety, abundance, and prosperity. Consequently, the Jewish greeting, "Shalom!" really means, "I wish you life in all its fullness and goodness. May you experience life the way God meant for it to be!"

When life goes south, we can easily fall into the trap of thinking that God has forgotten us or, even worse, that he has it out for us. Not true. He sent his one and only Son into the world to bring us the life that, deep down, we want. As Jesus put it, "I have come so that they may have life and have it in abundance" (Jn 10:10).

Ask the Prince of Peace to reign in your heart today.

For the next note on *Rest and Reflection*, see Isaiah 40:8.

[A] **9:16** Or *are confused* [B] **9:17** DSS read *not spare*

they have eaten on the left,
but they are still not satisfied.
Each one eats the flesh of his own arm.
21 Manasseh is with Ephraim,
and Ephraim with Manasseh;
together, both are against Judah.
In all this, his anger has not turned
away,
and his hand is still raised to strike.

10 Woe to those enacting
crooked statutes
and writing oppressive laws
2 to keep the poor from getting
a fair trial
and to deprive the needy
among my people of justice,
so that widows can be their spoil
and they can plunder the fatherless.
3 What will you do on the day
of punishment
when devastation comes
from far away?
Who will you run to for help?
Where will you leave your wealth?
4 There will be nothing to do
except crouch among the prisoners
or fall among the slain.
In all this, his anger has not turned
away,
and his hand is still raised to strike.

ASSYRIA, THE INSTRUMENT OF WRATH

5 Woe to Assyria, the rod of my anger —
the staff in their hands is my wrath.
6 I will send him against
a godless nation;
I will command him to go
against a people destined for my rage,
to take spoils, to plunder,
and to trample them down like clay
in the streets.
7 But this is not what he intends;
this is not what he plans.
It is his intent to destroy
and to cut off many nations.
8 For he says,
"Aren't all my commanders kings?
9 Isn't Calno like Carchemish?
Isn't Hamath like Arpad?
Isn't Samaria like Damascus?[A]
10 As my hand seized
the idolatrous kingdoms,
whose idols exceeded
those of Jerusalem and Samaria,
11 and as I did to Samaria
and its worthless images
will I not also do to Jerusalem
and its idols?"

JUDGMENT ON ASSYRIA

12 But when the Lord finishes all his work
against Mount Zion and Jerusalem, he will
say, "I[B] will punish the king of Assyria for his
arrogant acts and the proud look in his eyes."
13 For he said:
I have done this
by my own strength
and wisdom, for I am clever.
I abolished the borders of nations
and plundered their treasures;
like a mighty warrior, I subjugated
the inhabitants.[C]
14 My hand has reached out, as if
into a nest,
to seize the wealth
of the nations.
Like one gathering abandoned eggs,
I gathered the whole earth.
No wing fluttered;
no beak opened or chirped.

15 Does an ax exalt itself
above the one who chops with it?
Does a saw magnify itself
above the one who saws with it?
It would be like a rod waving
the one who lifts[D] it!
It would be like a staff lifting the one
who isn't wood!
16 Therefore the Lord GOD of Armies
will inflict an emaciating disease
on the well-fed of Assyria,
and he will kindle a burning fire
under its glory.
17 Israel's Light will become a fire,
and its Holy One, a flame.
In one day it will burn and consume
Assyria's thorns and thistles.
18 He will completely destroy
the glory of its forests
and orchards
as a sickness consumes a person.
19 The remaining trees of its forest
will be so few in number
that a child could count them.

[A] **10:9** Cities conquered by Assyria [B] **10:12** LXX reads *Jerusalem, he* [C] **10:13** Or *I brought down their kings* [D] **10:15** Some Hb mss, Syr, Vg read *wave he who lifts*

THE REMNANT WILL RETURN

20 On that day the remnant of Israel and the
survivors of the house of Jacob will no longer depend on the one who struck them, but
they will faithfully depend on the LORD, the
Holy One of Israel.

21 The remnant will return, the remnant
of Jacob,
to the Mighty God.
22 Israel, even if your people were
as numerous
as the sand of the sea,
only a remnant of them will return.
Destruction has been decreed;
justice overflows.
23 For throughout the land
the Lord GOD of Armies
is carrying out a destruction
that was decreed.

24 Therefore, the Lord GOD of Armies says
this: "My people who dwell in Zion, do not fear
Assyria, though they strike you with a rod and
raise their staff over you as the Egyptians did.
25 In just a little while my wrath will be spent
and my anger will turn to their destruction."
26 And the LORD of Armies will brandish a whip
against him as he did when he struck Midian
at the rock of Oreb; and he will raise his staff
over the sea as he did in Egypt.

GOD WILL JUDGE ASSYRIA

27 On that day
his burden will fall
from your shoulders,
and his yoke from your neck.
The yoke will be broken
because your neck
will be too large.[A]
28 Assyria has come to Aiath
and has gone through Migron,
storing their equipment at Michmash.
29 They crossed over at the ford, saying,
"We will spend the night at Geba."
The people of Ramah are trembling;
those at Gibeah of Saul have fled.
30 Cry aloud, daughter of Gallim!
Listen, Laishah!
Anathoth is miserable.
31 Madmenah has fled.
The inhabitants of Gebim
have sought refuge.
32 Today the Assyrians will stand at Nob,
shaking their fists at the mountain
of Daughter Zion,
the hill of Jerusalem.
33 Look, the Lord GOD of Armies
will chop off the branches
with terrifying power,
and the tall trees will be cut down,
the high trees felled.
34 He is clearing the thickets of the forest
with an ax,
and Lebanon with its majesty will fall.

REIGN OF THE DAVIDIC KING

11 Then a shoot will grow from the stump
of Jesse,
and a branch from his roots
will bear fruit.
2 The Spirit of the LORD will rest
on him —
a Spirit of wisdom
and understanding,
a Spirit of counsel and strength,
a Spirit of knowledge and of the fear
of the LORD.
3 His delight will be in the fear of the LORD.
He will not judge
by what he sees with his eyes,
he will not execute justice
by what he hears with his ears,
4 but he will judge the poor righteously
and execute justice for the oppressed
of the land.
He will strike the land
with a scepter[B] from his mouth,
and he will kill the wicked
with a command[C] from his lips.
5 Righteousness will be a belt
around his hips;
faithfulness will be a belt
around his waist.
6 The wolf will dwell with the lamb,
and the leopard will lie down
with the goat.
The calf, the young lion,
and the fattened calf will be together,
and a child will lead them.
7 The cow and the bear will graze,
their young ones will lie down together,
and the lion will eat straw like cattle.
8 An infant will play
beside the cobra's pit,
and a toddler will put his hand
into a snake's den.

[A] **10:27** Lit *because of fatness*; Hb obscure [B] **11:4** Lit *the rod* [C] **11:4** Lit *with the breath*

Isaiah | Restoration Profile

2 KINGS 19:2–20:19; ISAIAH

Isaiah spoke for God during the reigns of four kings of Judah, spanning sixty years. His compiled visions formed the longest scroll among the Old Testament prophets, later organized into sixty-six chapters. Although he lived seven hundred years before Christ, he wrote some of the most familiar descriptions of Jesus and his ministry (see Is 9:6-7; 53:1-12). Isaiah's visions and their subsequent fulfillments illustrate a significant characteristic of prophecy: God provided, often in the same vision, a preview of events soon to occur as well as events far into the future. For example, Isaiah's prophecy to King Ahaz about a virgin's conception and the name of her child, Immanuel, was an immediate warning to the king and a wonderful prediction of God's own arrival on earth as Jesus much later.

Perhaps the most significant vision in Isaiah, however, was the one that made all the others possible: the personal vision that restored Isaiah in the year that King Uzziah died (Is 6). Here, God called Isaiah as his servant by displaying his own glory (6:1-4), by letting Isaiah recognize his condition as a human (6:5), by graphically illustrating spiritual restoration (6:6-7), by inviting him to volunteer for duty (6:8), and by giving him a life-message (6:9-13).

When Isaiah saw God's glory, he wasn't just impressed, he was indicted. Isaiah recognized that his sinfulness and unworthiness before a holy God was a death sentence. Yet in the moment of his ruination, God restored him: "Your iniquity is removed and your sin is atoned for" (6:7).

Like Isaiah, if our view of God is not shattering and humbling; it is not a view of God. And if our idea of restoration has us doing it for ourselves, we remain unrestored.

9 They will not harm or destroy each
other
on my entire holy mountain,
for the land will be as full
of the knowledge of the LORD
as the sea is filled with water.

ISRAEL REGATHERED

10 On that day the root of Jesse
will stand as a banner for the peoples.
The nations will look to him for
guidance,
and his resting place will be glorious.

11 On that day the Lord will extend his hand
a second time to recover the remnant of his
people who survive — from Assyria, Egypt,
Pathros, Cush, Elam, Shinar, Hamath, and the
coasts and islands of the west.

12 He will lift up a banner for the nations
and gather the dispersed of Israel;
he will collect the scattered of Judah
from the four corners of the earth.
13 Ephraim's envy will cease;
Judah's harassing will end.
Ephraim will no longer be envious
of Judah,
and Judah will not harass Ephraim.
14 But they will swoop down
on the Philistine flank to the west.
Together they will plunder the people
of the east.
They will extend their power
over Edom and Moab,
and the Ammonites will be
their subjects.
15 The LORD will divide[A,B]
the Gulf of Suez.[C]
He will wave his hand
over the Euphrates
with his mighty wind
and will split it
into seven streams,
letting people walk through on foot.
16 There will be a highway
for the remnant of his people
who will survive from Assyria,
as there was for Israel
when they came up from the land
of Egypt.

[A] **11:15** Text emended; MT reads *destroy* [B] **11:15** Or *dry up* [C] **11:15** Lit *the Sea of Egypt*

Indeed, God is my salvation; I will trust him and not be afraid, for the LORD, the LORD himself, is my strength and my song. He has become my salvation.
—*Isaiah 12:2*

A SONG OF PRAISE

12 On that day you will say:
"I will give thanks to you, LORD,
although you were angry with me.
Your anger has turned away,
and you have comforted me.
2 Indeed, God is my salvation;
I will trust him and not be afraid,
for the LORD, the LORD himself,
is my strength and my song.
He has become my salvation."
3 You will joyfully draw water
from the springs of salvation,
4 and on that day you will say:
"Give thanks to the LORD;
proclaim his name!
Make his works known
among the peoples.
Declare that his name is exalted.
5 Sing to the LORD, for he has done
glorious things.
Let this be known
throughout the earth.
6 Cry out and sing, citizen of Zion,
for the Holy One of Israel is among you
in his greatness."

A PRONOUNCEMENT AGAINST BABYLON

13 A pronouncement concerning Babylon
that Isaiah son of Amoz saw:
2 Lift up a banner on a barren mountain.
Call out to them.
Signal with your hand, and they will go
through the gates of the nobles.
3 I have commanded
my consecrated ones;
yes, I have called my warriors,
who celebrate my triumph,
to execute my wrath.
4 Listen, a commotion on the mountains,
like that of a mighty people!
Listen, an uproar among the kingdoms,
like nations being gathered together!
The LORD of Armies is mobilizing
an army for war.
5 They are coming from a distant land,
from the farthest horizon —
the LORD and the weapons of his wrath —
to destroy the whole country.[A]

6 Wail! For the day of the LORD is near.
It will come as destruction
from the Almighty.
7 Therefore everyone's hands
will become weak,
and every man will lose heart.[B]
8 They will be horrified;
pain and agony will seize them;
they will be in anguish like a woman
in labor.
They will look at each other,
their faces flushed with fear.
9 Look, the day of the LORD is coming —
cruel, with rage and burning anger —
to make the earth a desolation
and to destroy its sinners.
10 Indeed, the stars of the sky
and its constellations[C]
will not give their light.
The sun will be dark when it rises,
and the moon will not shine.
11 I will punish the world for its evil,
and wicked people for their iniquities.
I will put an end to the pride
of the arrogant
and humiliate the insolence of tyrants.
12 I will make a human more scarce
than fine gold,
and mankind more rare than the gold
of Ophir.
13 Therefore I will make
the heavens tremble,
and the earth will shake
from its foundations
at the wrath of the LORD of Armies,
on the day of his burning anger.
14 Like wandering gazelles
and like sheep without a shepherd,
each one will turn to his own people,
each one will flee to his own land.
15 Whoever is found will be stabbed,
and whoever is caught will die
by the sword.

[A] **13:5** Or *earth* [B] **13:7** Lit *every man's heart will melt* [C] **13:10** Or *Orions*

16 Their children will be dashed to pieces
before their eyes;
their houses will be looted,
and their wives raped.
17 Look! I am stirring up the Medes
against them,
who cannot be bought off with[A] silver
and who have no desire for gold.
18 Their bows will cut young men
to pieces.
They will have no compassion
on offspring;
they will not look with pity on children.

19 And Babylon, the jewel of the kingdoms,
the glory of the pride of the Chaldeans,
will be like Sodom and Gomorrah
when God overthrew them.
20 It will never be inhabited
or lived in from generation
to generation;
a nomad will not pitch his tent there,
and shepherds will not let their flocks
rest there.
21 But desert creatures
will lie down there,
and owls will fill the houses.
Ostriches will dwell there,
and wild goats will leap about.
22 Hyenas will howl in the fortresses,
and jackals, in the luxurious palaces.
Babylon's time is almost up;
her days are almost over.

ISRAEL'S RETURN

14 For the LORD will have compassion on
Jacob and will choose Israel again. He
will settle them on their own land. The resident alien will join them and be united with
the house of Jacob. 2 The nations will escort
Israel and bring it to its homeland. Then the
house of Israel will possess them as male and
female slaves in the LORD's land. They will
make captives of their captors and will rule
over their oppressors.

DOWNFALL OF THE KING OF BABYLON

3 When the LORD gives you rest from your pain,
torment, and the hard labor you were forced
to do, 4 you will sing this song of contempt
about the king of Babylon and say:

How the oppressor has quieted down,
and how the raging[B] has become quiet!
5 The LORD has broken the staff
of the wicked,
the scepter of the rulers.
6 It struck the peoples in anger
with unceasing blows.
It subdued the nations in rage
with relentless persecution.
7 The whole earth is calm and at rest;
people shout with a ringing cry.
8 Even the cypresses and the cedars
of Lebanon
rejoice over you:
"Since you have been laid low,
no lumberjack has come against us."

9 Sheol below is eager to greet
your coming,
stirring up the spirits of the departed
for you —
all the rulers[C] of the earth —
making all the kings of the nations
rise from their thrones.
10 They all respond to you, saying,
"You too have become as weak
as we are;
you have become like us!
11 Your splendor has been brought down
to Sheol,
along with the music of your harps.
Maggots are spread out under you,
and worms cover you."

12 Shining morning star,[D]
how you have fallen from the heavens!
You destroyer of nations,
you have been cut down to the ground.
13 You said to yourself,
"I will ascend to the heavens;
I will set up my throne
above the stars of God.
I will sit on the mount
of the gods' assembly,
in the remotest parts of the North.[E]
14 I will ascend above the highest clouds;
I will make myself like the Most High."
15 But you will be brought down to Sheol
into the deepest regions of the Pit.

16 Those who see you will stare at you;
they will look closely at you:
"Is this the man who caused the earth
to tremble,
who shook the kingdoms,

[A] **13:17** Lit *who have no regard for* [B] **14:4** DSS; Hb uncertain [C] **14:9** Lit *rams* [D] **14:12** Or *Day Star, son of the dawn*
[E] **14:13** Or *of Zaphon*

17 who turned the world
into a wilderness,
who destroyed its cities
and would not release the prisoners
to return home?"
18 All the kings of the nations
lie in splendor, each in his own tomb.
19 But you are thrown out without a grave,
like a worthless branch,
covered by those slain with the sword
and dumped into a rocky pit
like a trampled corpse.
20 You will not join them in burial,
because you destroyed your land
and slaughtered your own people.
The offspring of evildoers
will never be mentioned again.
21 Prepare a place of slaughter
for his sons,
because of the iniquity of their fathers.
They will never rise up to possess a land
or fill the surface of the earth
with cities.

22 "I will rise up against them" — this is
the declaration of the LORD of Armies — "and
I will cut off from Babylon her reputation,
remnant, offspring, and posterity" — this is
the LORD's declaration. 23 "I will make her a
swampland and a region for herons,[A] and I
will sweep her away with the broom of destruction."
This is the declaration of the LORD
of Armies.

ASSYRIA WILL BE DESTROYED

24 The LORD of Armies has sworn:
As I have purposed, so it will be;
as I have planned it, so it will happen.
25 I will break Assyria in my land;
I will tread him down on my mountain.
Then his yoke will be taken from them,
and his burden will be removed
from their shoulders.
26 This is the plan prepared
for the whole earth,
and this is the hand stretched out
against all the nations.
27 The LORD of Armies himself
has planned it;
therefore, who can stand in its way?
It is his hand that is outstretched,
so who can turn it back?

A PRONOUNCEMENT AGAINST PHILISTIA

28 In the year that King Ahaz died, this pronouncement came:
29 Don't rejoice, all of you in Philistia,
because the rod of the one
who struck you is broken.
For a viper will come from the root[B]
of a snake,
and from its egg comes a flying serpent.
30 Then the firstborn of the poor will be
well fed,
and the impoverished will lie down
in safety,
but I will kill your root with hunger,
and your remnant will be slain.
31 Wail, you gates! Cry out, city!
Tremble with fear, all Philistia!
For a cloud of dust is coming
from the north,
and there is no one missing from
the invader's ranks.
32 What answer will be given
to the messengers from that nation?
The LORD has founded Zion,
and his oppressed people find refuge
in her.

A PRONOUNCEMENT AGAINST MOAB

15 A pronouncement concerning Moab:
Ar in Moab is devastated,
destroyed in a night.
Kir in Moab is devastated,
destroyed in a night.
2 Dibon went up to its temple
to weep at its high places.
Moab wails on Nebo and at[C] Medeba.
Every head is shaved;
every beard is chopped short.
3 In its streets they wear sackcloth;
on its rooftops and in its public squares
everyone wails,
falling down and weeping.
4 Heshbon and Elealeh cry out;
their voices are heard as far away
as Jahaz.
Therefore the soldiers
of Moab cry out,
and they tremble.[D]
5 My heart cries out over Moab,
whose fugitives flee as far as Zoar,
to Eglath-shelishiyah;
they go up the Ascent
of Luhith weeping;

[A] **14:23** Or *hedgehogs*; Hb obscure [B] **14:29** Or *stock* [C] **15:2** Or *wails over Nebo and over* [D] **15:4** Lit *out, he trembles within himself*

they raise a cry of destruction
on the road to Horonaim.
6 The Waters of Nimrim are desolate;
the grass is withered, the foliage
is gone,
and the vegetation has vanished.
7 So they carry their wealth
and belongings
over the Wadi of the Willows.
8 For their cry echoes
throughout the territory of Moab.
Their wailing reaches Eglaim;
their wailing reaches Beer-elim.
9 The Waters of Dibon[A] are full of blood,
but I will bring on Dibon[A] even more
than this —
a lion for those who escape from Moab,
and for the survivors in the land.

16 Send lambs to the ruler of the land,
from Sela in the desert
to the mountain of Daughter Zion.
2 Like a bird fleeing,
forced from the nest,
the daughters of Moab
will be at the fords of the Arnon.

3 Give us counsel and make a decision.
Shelter us at noonday
with shade that is as dark as night.
Hide the refugees;
do not betray the one who flees.
4 Let my refugees stay with you;
be a refuge for Moab[B]
from the aggressor.

When the oppressor has gone,
destruction has ended,
and marauders have vanished
from the land,
5 a throne will be established in love,
and one will sit on it faithfully[C]
in the tent of David,
judging and pursuing what is right,
quick to execute justice.

6 We have heard of Moab's pride —
how very proud he is —
his haughtiness, his pride,
his arrogance,
and his empty boasting.
7 Therefore let Moab wail;
let every one of them wail for Moab.

A throne will be established in love, and one will sit on it faithfully in the tent of David, judging and pursuing what is right, quick to execute justice.
—Isaiah 16:5

You who are completely devastated,
mourn
for the raisin cakes of Kir-hareseth.
8 For Heshbon's terraced vineyards
and the grapevines of Sibmah
have withered.
The rulers of the nations
have trampled its choice vines
that reached as far as Jazer
and spread to the desert.
Their shoots spread out
and reached the sea.
9 So I join with Jazer
to weep for the vines of Sibmah;
I drench Heshbon and Elealeh
with my tears.
Triumphant shouts have fallen silent[D]
over your summer fruit
and your harvest.
10 Joy and rejoicing have been removed
from the orchard;
no one is singing or shouting for joy
in the vineyards.
No one tramples grapes[E]
in the winepresses.
I have put an end to the shouting.
11 Therefore I moan like the sound of
a lyre for Moab,
as does my innermost being
for Kir-heres.
12 When Moab appears
and tires himself out on the high place
and comes to his sanctuary to pray,
it will do him no good.

13 This is the message that the LORD previously announced about Moab. 14 And now the
LORD says, "In three years, as a hired worker
counts years, Moab's splendor will become

[A] 15:9 DSS, some LXX mss, Vg; MT reads *Dimon* [B] 16:4 Or *you; Moab — be a refuge for him* [C] 16:5 Or *continually* [D] 16:9 Or *Battle cries have fallen* [E] 16:10 Lit *wine*

an object of contempt, in spite of a very large population. And those who are left will be few and weak."

A PRONOUNCEMENT AGAINST DAMASCUS

17 A pronouncement concerning Damascus:
Look, Damascus is no longer a city.
It has become a ruined heap.
2 The cities of Aroer are abandoned;
they will be places for flocks.
They will lie down without fear.
3 The fortress disappears from Ephraim,
and a kingdom from Damascus.
The remnant of Aram will be
like the splendor of the Israelites.
This is the declaration of the LORD
of Armies.

JUDGMENT AGAINST ISRAEL

4 On that day
the splendor of Jacob will fade,
and his healthy body[A]
will become emaciated.
5 It will be as if a reaper had gathered
standing grain —
his arm harvesting the heads
of grain —
and as if one had gleaned heads
of grain
in the Valley of Rephaim.
6 Only gleanings will be left in Israel,
as if an olive tree had been beaten —
two or three olives at the very top
of the tree,
four or five on its fruitful branches.
This is the declaration of the LORD,
the God of Israel.

7 On that day people will look to their Maker and will turn their eyes to the Holy One of
Israel. 8 They will not look to the altars they
made with their hands or to the Asherahs
and shrines[B] they made with their fingers.

9 On that day their strong cities will be
like the abandoned woods
and mountaintops
that were abandoned because of
the Israelites;
there will be desolation.
10 For you have forgotten the God
of your salvation,
and you have failed to remember
the rock of your strength;
therefore you will plant
beautiful plants
and set out cuttings from exotic vines.
11 On the day that you plant,
you will help them to grow,
and in the morning
you will help your seed to sprout,
but the harvest will vanish
on the day of disease
and incurable pain.

JUDGMENT AGAINST THE NATIONS

12 Ah! The roar of many peoples —
they roar like the roaring of the seas.
The raging of the nations —
they rage like the rumble
of rushing water.
13 The nations rage like the rumble of a
huge torrent.
He rebukes them, and they flee
far away,
driven before the wind like chaff
on the hills
and like tumbleweeds before a gale.
14 In the evening — sudden terror!
Before morning — it is gone!
This is the fate of those
who plunder us
and the lot of those who ravage us.

THE LORD'S MESSAGE TO CUSH

18 Woe to the land
of buzzing insect wings[C]
beyond the rivers of Cush,
2 which sends envoys by sea,
in reed vessels over the water.

Go, swift messengers,
to a nation tall and smooth-skinned,
to a people feared far and near,
a powerful nation
with a strange language,[D]
whose land is divided by rivers.
3 All you inhabitants of the world
and you who live on the earth,
when a banner is raised
on the mountains, look!
When a trumpet sounds, listen!

4 For the LORD said to me:
I will quietly look out from my place,
like shimmering heat in sunshine,
like a rain cloud in harvest heat.

[A] 17:4 Lit *and the fat of his flesh* [B] 17:8 Or *incense altars* [C] 18:1 Or *of sailing ships* [D] 18:2 Hb obscure

5 For before the harvest,
when the blossoming is over
and the blossom becomes
a ripening grape,
he will cut off the shoots
with a pruning knife,
and tear away and remove
the branches.
6 They will all be left for the birds of prey
on the hills
and for the wild animals of the land.
The birds of prey will spend
the summer feeding on them,
and all the wild animals the winter.

7 At that time a gift will be brought to
the LORD of Armies from[A] a people tall and
smooth-skinned, a people feared far and near,
a powerful nation with a strange language,
whose land is divided by rivers — to Mount
Zion, the place of the name of the LORD of
Armies.

A PRONOUNCEMENT AGAINST EGYPT

19 A pronouncement concerning Egypt:
Look, the LORD rides on a swift cloud
and is coming to Egypt.
Egypt's idols will tremble before him,
and Egypt will lose heart.[B]
2 I will provoke Egyptians
against Egyptians;
each will fight against his brother
and each against his friend,
city against city,
kingdom against kingdom.
3 Egypt's spirit will be disturbed
within it,
and I will frustrate its plans.
Then they will inquire of idols, ghosts,
and spiritists.
4 I will hand over Egypt
to harsh masters,
and a strong king will rule it.
This is the declaration
of the Lord GOD of Armies.

5 The water of the sea will dry up,
and the river will be parched and dry.
6 The channels will stink;
they will dwindle, and Egypt's canals
will be parched.
Reed and rush will wilt.
7 The reeds by the Nile, by the mouth
of the river,
and all the cultivated areas of the Nile
will wither, blow away, and vanish.
8 Then the fishermen will mourn.
All those who cast hooks into the Nile
will lament,
and those who spread nets
on the water will give up.
9 Those who work with flax
will be dismayed;
those combing it and weaving linen
will turn pale.[C]
10 Egypt's weavers[D] will be dejected;
all her wage earners
will be demoralized.

11 The princes of Zoan are complete fools;
Pharaoh's wisest advisers
give stupid advice!
How can you say to Pharaoh,
"I am one[E] of the wise,
a student of eastern[F] kings"?
12 Where then are your wise men?
Let them tell you and reveal
what the LORD of Armies has planned
against Egypt.
13 The princes of Zoan have been fools;
the princes of Memphis are deceived.
Her tribal chieftains have led
Egypt astray.
14 The LORD has mixed within her a spirit
of confusion.
The leaders have made Egypt stagger
in all she does,
as a drunkard staggers in his vomit.
15 No head or tail, palm or reed,
will be able to do anything for Egypt.

EGYPT WILL KNOW THE LORD

16 On that day Egypt will be like women and will
tremble with fear because of the threatening
hand of the LORD of Armies when he raises it
against them. 17 The land of Judah will terrify
Egypt; whenever Judah is mentioned, Egypt
will tremble because of what the LORD of Armies has planned against it.
18 On that day five cities in the land of Egypt
will speak the language of Canaan and swear
loyalty to the LORD of Armies. One of the cities
will be called the City of the Sun.[G,H]
19 On that day there will be an altar to the LORD

[A] 18:7 DSS, LXX, Vg; MT omits *from* [B] 19:1 Lit *Egypt's heart will melt within it* [C] 19:9 DSS, Tg; MT reads *weavers of white cloth* [D] 19:10 Or *foundations* [E] 19:11 Lit *a son* [F] 19:11 Lit *a son of ancient* [G] 19:18 Some Hb mss, DSS, Sym, Tg, Vg, Arabic; other Hb mss read *of Destruction*; LXX reads *of Righteousness* [H] 19:18 = the ancient Egyptian city Heliopolis

in the center of the land of Egypt and a pillar
to the LORD near her border. 20 It will be a sign
and witness to the LORD of Armies in the land of
Egypt. When they cry out to the LORD because
of their oppressors, he will send them a savior
and leader, and he will rescue them. 21 The LORD
will make himself known to Egypt, and Egypt
will know the LORD on that day. They will offer
sacrifices and offerings; they will make vows
to the LORD and fulfill them. 22 The LORD will
strike Egypt, striking and healing. Then they
will turn to the LORD and he will be receptive
to their prayers and heal them.

23 On that day there will be a highway from
Egypt to Assyria. Assyria will go to Egypt, Egypt
to Assyria, and Egypt will worship with Assyria.

24 On that day Israel will form a triple alliance with Egypt and Assyria — a blessing
within the land. 25 The LORD of Armies will
bless them, saying, "Egypt my people, Assyria my handiwork, and Israel my inheritance
are blessed."

NO HELP FROM CUSH OR EGYPT

20 In the year that the chief commander,
sent by King Sargon of Assyria, came to
Ashdod and attacked and captured it — 2 during that time the LORD had spoken through
Isaiah son of Amoz, saying, "Go, take off your
sackcloth[A] and remove the sandals from your
feet," and he did that, going stripped and barefoot — 3 the LORD said, "As my servant Isaiah
has gone stripped and barefoot three years
as a sign and omen against Egypt and Cush,
4 so the king of Assyria will lead the captives
of Egypt and the exiles of Cush, young and
old alike, stripped and barefoot, with bared
buttocks — to Egypt's shame. 5 Those who
made Cush their hope and Egypt their boast
will be dismayed and ashamed. 6 And the inhabitants of this coastland will say on that
day, 'Look, this is what has happened to those
we relied on and fled to for help to rescue
us from the king of Assyria! Now, how will
we escape?' "

A JUDGMENT ON BABYLON

21 A pronouncement concerning the desert
by the sea:

Like storms that pass over the Negev,
it comes from the desert, from the land
of terror.

2 A troubling vision is declared to me:
"The treacherous one
acts treacherously,
and the destroyer destroys.
Advance, Elam! Lay siege, you Medes!
I will put an end to all the groaning."

3 Therefore I am[B] filled with anguish.
Pain grips me, like the pain of a woman
in labor.
I am too perplexed to hear,
too dismayed to see.
4 My heart staggers;
horror terrifies me.
He has turned my last glimmer of hope[C]
into sheer terror.
5 Prepare a table, and spread out
a carpet!
Eat and drink!
Rise up, you princes, and oil the shields!

6 For the Lord has said to me,
"Go, post a lookout;
let him report what he sees.
7 When he sees riders —
pairs of horsemen,
riders on donkeys,
riders on camels —
he must pay close attention."
8 Then the lookout[D] reported,
"Lord, I stand on the watchtower
all day,
and I stay at my post all night.
9 Look, riders come —
horsemen in pairs."
And he answered, saying,
"Babylon has fallen, has fallen.
All the images of her gods
have been shattered on the ground."

10 My people who have been crushed
on the threshing floor,
I have declared to you
what I have heard from the LORD
of Armies,
the God of Israel.

A PRONOUNCEMENT AGAINST DUMAH

11 A pronouncement concerning Dumah:[E]
One calls to me from Seir,
"Watchman, what is left of the night?
Watchman, what is left of the night?"
12 The watchman said,
"Morning has come, and also night.

[A] 20:2 Lit *off the sackcloth from your waist* [B] 21:3 Lit *my waist is*, or *my insides are* [C] 21:4 Lit *my twilight* [D] 21:8 DSS, Syr; MT reads *Then a lion* [E] 21:11 Some Hb mss, LXX read *Edom*

If you want to ask, ask!
Come back again."

A PRONOUNCEMENT AGAINST ARABIA

13 A pronouncement concerning Arabia:
In the desert[A] brush
you will camp for the night,
you caravans of Dedanites.
14 Bring water for the thirsty.
The inhabitants of the land of Tema
meet[B] the refugees with food.
15 For they have fled from swords,
from the drawn sword,
from the bow that is strung,
and from the stress of battle.

16 For the Lord said this to me: "Within one
year, as a hired worker counts years, all the
glory of Kedar will be gone. 17 The remaining
Kedarite archers will be few in number." For
the LORD, the God of Israel, has spoken.

A PRONOUNCEMENT AGAINST JERUSALEM

22 A pronouncement concerning the Valley of Vision:
What's the matter with you?
Why have all of you gone up
to the rooftops?
2 The noisy city, the jubilant town,
is filled with celebration.
Your dead did not die by the sword;
they were not killed in battle.
3 All your rulers have fled together,
captured without a bow.
All your fugitives
were captured together;
they had fled far away.
4 Therefore I said,
"Look away from me!
Let me weep bitterly!
Do not try to comfort me
about the destruction
of my dear[C] people."
5 For the Lord GOD of Armies
had a day of tumult, trampling,
and confusion
in the Valley of Vision —
people shouting[D] and crying
to the mountains;
6 Elam took up a quiver
with chariots and horsemen,[E]
and Kir uncovered the shield.
7 Your best valleys were full of chariots,
and horsemen were positioned
at the city gates.
8 He removed the defenses of Judah.

On that day you looked to the weapons in
the House of the Forest. 9 You saw that there
were many breaches in the walls of the city
of David. You collected water from the lower
pool. 10 You counted the houses of Jerusalem
so that you could tear them down to fortify the
wall. 11 You made a reservoir between the walls
for the water of the ancient pool, but you did
not look to the one who made it, or consider
the one who created it long ago.

12 On that day the Lord GOD of Armies
called for weeping, for wailing,
for shaven heads,
and for the wearing of sackcloth.
13 But look: joy and gladness,
butchering of cattle,
slaughtering of sheep and goats,
eating of meat, and drinking of wine —
"Let us eat and drink, for tomorrow
we die!"
14 The LORD of Armies has
directly revealed to me:
"This iniquity will not be wiped out for
you people as long as you live."[F]
The Lord GOD of Armies has spoken.

A PRONOUNCEMENT AGAINST SHEBNA

15 The Lord GOD of Armies said: "Go to Shebna,
that steward who is in charge of the palace,
and say to him: 16 What are you doing here?
Who authorized you to carve out a tomb for
yourself here, carving your tomb on the height
and cutting a resting place for yourself out
of rock? 17 Look, you strong man! The LORD
is about to shake you violently. He will take
hold of you, 18 wind you up into a ball, and
sling you into a wide land.[G] There you will
die, and there your glorious chariots will be
— a disgrace to the house of your lord. 19 I
will remove you from your office; you will
be ousted from your position.

20 "On that day I will call for my servant, Eliakim son of Hilkiah. 21 I will clothe him with
your robe and tie your sash around him. I will
hand your authority over to him, and he will
be like a father to the inhabitants of Jerusalem and to the house of Judah. 22 I will place

---

[A] **21:13** LXX, Syr, Tg, Vg read *desert at evening* [B] **21:14** LXX, Syr, Tg, Vg read *meet* as a command [C] **22:4** Lit *of the daughter of my* [D] **22:5** Or *Vision — a tearing down of a wall*, or *Vision — Kir raged*; Hb obscure [E] **22:6** Lit *chariots of man* [F] **22:14** Lit *for you until you die* [G] **22:17-18** Hb obscure

the key of the house of David on his shoulder;
what he opens, no one can close; what he closes, no one can open. 23 I will drive him, like
a peg, into a firm place. He will be a throne
of honor for his father's family. 24 They will
hang on him all the glory of his father's family:
the descendants and the offshoots — all the
small vessels, from bowls to every kind of jar.
25 On that day" — the declaration of the LORD
of Armies — "the peg that was driven into a
firm place will give way, be cut off, and fall,
and the load on it will be destroyed." Indeed,
the LORD has spoken.

A PRONOUNCEMENT AGAINST TYRE

23 A pronouncement concerning Tyre:
Wail, ships of Tarshish,
for your haven has been destroyed.
Word has reached them from the land
of Cyprus.[A]
2 Mourn, inhabitants of the coastland,
you merchants of Sidon;
your agents have crossed the sea[B]
3 over deep water.
Tyre's revenue was the grain
from Shihor —
the harvest of the Nile.
She was the merchant
among the nations.
4 Be ashamed, Sidon, the stronghold
of the sea,
for the sea has spoken:
"I have not been in labor or given birth.
I have not raised young men
or brought up young women."
5 When the news reaches Egypt,
they will be in anguish over the news
about Tyre.
6 Cross over to Tarshish;
wail, inhabitants of the coastland!
7 Is this your jubilant city,
whose origin was in ancient times,
whose feet have taken her
to reside far away?
8 Who planned this against Tyre,
the bestower of crowns,
whose traders are princes,
whose merchants are the honored ones
of the earth?
9 The LORD of Armies planned it,
to desecrate all its glorious beauty,
to disgrace all the honored ones
of the earth.
10 Overflow[C] your land like the Nile,
daughter of Tarshish;
there is no longer anything
to restrain you.[D]
11 He stretched out his hand over the sea;
he made kingdoms tremble.
The LORD has commanded
that the Canaanite fortresses
be destroyed.
12 He said,
"You will not celebrate anymore,
ravished young woman,
daughter of Sidon.
Get up and cross over to Cyprus —
even there you will have no rest!"
13 Look at the land of the Chaldeans —
a people who no longer exist.
Assyria destined it for desert creatures.
They set up their siege towers
and stripped its palaces.
They made it a ruin.
14 Wail, ships of Tarshish,
because your fortress is destroyed!

15 On that day Tyre will be forgotten for seventy years — the life span of one king. At the
end of seventy years, what the song says about
the prostitute will happen to Tyre:

16 Pick up your lyre,
stroll through the city,
you forgotten prostitute.
Play skillfully,
sing many a song
so that you will be remembered.

17 And at the end of the seventy years, the
LORD will restore Tyre and she will go back
into business, prostituting herself with all the
kingdoms of the world throughout the earth.
18 But her profits and wages will be dedicated
to the LORD. They will not be stored or saved,
for her profit will go to those who live in the
LORD's presence, to provide them with ample
food and sacred clothing.

THE EARTH JUDGED

24 Look, the LORD is stripping
the earth bare
and making it desolate.
He will twist its surface and scatter
its inhabitants:
2 people and priest alike,
servant and master,

[A] 23:1 Hb *Kittim* [B] 23:2 DSS; MT reads *Sidon, whom the seafarers have filled* [C] 23:10 DSS, LXX read *Work* [D] 23:10 Or *longer any harbor*

My Story | Casey

Fifteen years had passed since I had crossed the daunting threshold of the room that consumed my youth with false promises of love in the form of images on a screen. Going home was a torrent of mixed emotions. One step through the doorframe of this dungeon flooded my memory with images of a boy running from reality, tears over what was and what was not, and the fear of love never found. I peered at my bunk that represented my hopeless hiding from the world—my nook where most nights I locked myself into a prison cell of immorality, believing the perpetual lies found between my bed sheets with no one but myself and make-believe lovers, aware of the shadow of the divine at the doorway.

Half of my life had passed since first stepping foot in that hellhole that I repeatedly vowed to never return to. Yet there I was, confronted with all the reminders of what I once was and little to encourage what I wanted to be. In those moments of turmoil, I was smitten and overtaken with the grand paradox of my becoming; the shackles of my boyhood, now broken chains in becoming a man. I realize the encounter was necessary to confirm my restoration.

But I can't relate with the affection-starved boy longing for love in the darkest of rooms, though I empathize with him more than I ever could have ever predicted or imagined. I am no longer that boy. Old things have passed away. Those profoundly affirming moments spent contemplating in my childhood prison allowed me to cry the tears of redemption that he couldn't imagine all those years between the sheets.

I realized in those moments that I could once again step into the room that haunted my entire life and not be stained by the memories, guilt, and nightmares that once were. I was finally free. More free than I was before I exited the threshold of this nightmare. This room. I was now able to dream the worthy dreams I had always desired but had been stifled between those sheets as a boy, for that boy was set free to be the man he now is, the silhouette of the divine now clear and welcomed in the room.

female servant and mistress,
buyer and seller,
lender and borrower,
creditor and debtor.
3 The earth will be stripped
completely bare
and will be totally plundered,
for the LORD has spoken this message.

4 The earth mourns and withers;
the world wastes away and withers;
the exalted people of the earth
waste away.
5 The earth is polluted by its inhabitants,
for they have transgressed teachings,
overstepped decrees,
and broken the permanent covenant.
6 Therefore a curse has consumed
the earth,
and its inhabitants have become guilty;
the earth's inhabitants
have been burned,
and only a few survive.
7 The new wine mourns;
the vine withers.
All the carousers now groan.
8 The joyful tambourines have ceased.
The noise of the jubilant has stopped.
The joyful lyre has ceased.
9 They no longer sing and drink wine;
beer is bitter to those who drink it.
10 The city of chaos is shattered;
every house is closed to entry.
11 In the streets they cry[A] for wine.
All joy grows dark;
earth's rejoicing goes into exile.
12 Only desolation remains in the city;
its gate has collapsed in ruins.
13 For this is how it will be on earth
among the nations:
like a harvested olive tree,
like a gleaning after a grape harvest.

14 They raise their voices, they sing out;
they proclaim in the west
the majesty of the LORD.
15 Therefore, in the east honor the LORD!
In the coasts and islands of the west
honor the name of the LORD,
the God of Israel.

[A] **24:11** Lit *streets she cries*

16 From the ends of the earth
we hear songs:
The Splendor of the Righteous One.

But I said, "I waste away! I waste away![A]
Woe is me."
The treacherous act treacherously;
the treacherous deal
very treacherously.

17 Panic, pit, and trap await you
who dwell on the earth.
18 Whoever flees at the sound of panic
will fall into a pit,
and whoever escapes from the pit
will be caught in a trap.
For the windows on high are opened,
and the foundations of the earth
are shaken.
19 The earth is completely devastated;
the earth is split open;
the earth is violently shaken.
20 The earth staggers like a drunkard
and sways like a hut.
Earth's rebellion weighs it down,
and it falls, never to rise again.

21 On that day the LORD will punish
the army of the heights in the heights
and the kings of the ground on the
ground.
22 They will be gathered together
like prisoners in a pit.
They will be confined to a dungeon;
after many days
they will be punished.
23 The moon will be put to shame
and the sun disgraced,
because the LORD of Armies will reign
as king
on Mount Zion in Jerusalem,
and he will display his glory
in the presence of his elders.

SALVATION AND JUDGMENT ON THAT DAY

25 LORD, you are my God;
I will exalt you. I will praise
your name,
for you have accomplished wonders,
plans formed long ago,
with perfect faithfulness.
2 For you have turned the city into a pile
of rocks,
a fortified city, into ruins;
the fortress of barbarians is no longer
a city;
it will never be rebuilt.
3 Therefore, a strong people
will honor you.
The cities of violent nations
will fear you.
4 For you have been a stronghold
for the poor person,
a stronghold for the needy
in his distress,
a refuge from storms and a shade
from heat.
When the breath of the violent
is like a storm against a wall,
5 like heat in a dry land,
you will subdue the uproar
of barbarians.
As the shade of a cloud cools the heat
of the day,
so he will silence the song
of the violent.

6 On this mountain,[B]
the LORD of Armies will prepare for all
the peoples a feast of choice meat,
a feast with aged wine, prime cuts of
choice meat,[C] fine vintage wine.
7 On this mountain
he will destroy the burial shroud,
the shroud over all the peoples,
the sheet covering all the nations;
8 he will destroy death forever.
The Lord GOD will wipe away the tears
from every face
and remove his people's disgrace
from the whole earth,
for the LORD has spoken.

9 On that day it will be said,
"Look, this is our God;
we have waited for him, and he has
saved us.
This is the LORD; we have waited
for him.
Let us rejoice and be glad
in his salvation."
10 For the LORD's power will rest
on this mountain.

But Moab will be trampled in his place[D]
as straw is trampled in a dung pile.

[A] 24:16 Hb obscure [B] 25:6 = Mount Zion [C] 25:6 Lit *wine, fat full of marrow* [D] 25:10 Or *trampled under him*

13 The Lord said:
These people approach me
with their speeches
to honor me with lip-service[A] —
yet their hearts are far from me,
and human rules direct their worship
of me.[B]
14 Therefore, I will again confound
these people
with wonder after wonder.
The wisdom of their wise will vanish,
and the perception of their perceptive
will be hidden.

15 Woe to those who go to great lengths
to hide their plans from the LORD.
They do their works in the dark,
and say, "Who sees us? Who knows us?"
16 You have turned things around,
as if the potter were the same as the clay.
How can what is made say
about its maker,
"He didn't make me"?
How can what is formed
say about the one who formed it,
"He doesn't understand
what he's doing"?

17 Isn't it true that in just a little while
Lebanon will become an orchard,
and the orchard will seem like a forest?
18 On that day the deaf will hear
the words of a document,
and out of a deep darkness
the eyes of the blind will see.
19 The humble will have joy
after joy in the LORD,
and the poor people will rejoice
in the Holy One of Israel.
20 For the ruthless one will vanish,
the scorner will disappear,
and all those who lie in wait
with evil intent
will be killed —
21 those who, with their speech,
accuse a person of wrongdoing,
who set a trap for the one mediating at
the city gate
and without cause deprive
the righteous of justice.

22 Therefore, the LORD who redeemed Abraham says this about the house of Jacob:
Jacob will no longer be ashamed,
and his face will no longer be pale.
23 For when he sees his children,
the work of my hands
within his nation,
they will honor my name,
they will honor the Holy One of Jacob
and stand in awe of the God
of Israel.
24 Those who are confused
will gain understanding,
and those who grumble
will accept instruction.

CONDEMNATION OF THE EGYPTIAN ALLIANCE

30 Woe to the rebellious children!
This is the LORD's declaration.
They carry out a plan, but not mine;
they make an alliance,
but against my will,
piling sin on top of sin.
2 Without asking my advice
they set out to go down to Egypt
in order to seek shelter
under Pharaoh's protection
and take refuge in Egypt's shadow.
3 But Pharaoh's protection will become
your shame,
and refuge in Egypt's shadow
your humiliation.
4 For though his[C] princes are at Zoan
and his messengers reach
as far as Hanes,
5 everyone will be ashamed
because of a people who can't help.
They are of no benefit, they are
no help;
they are good for nothing but shame
and disgrace.

6 A pronouncement concerning the animals
of the Negev:[D]
Through a land of trouble and distress,
of lioness and lion,
of viper and flying serpent,
they carry their wealth on the backs
of donkeys
and their treasures on the humps
of camels,
to a people who will not help them.
7 Egypt's help is completely worthless;
therefore, I call her:
Rahab Who Just Sits.

[A] **29:13** Lit *their mouth and honor me with its lips* [B] **29:13** Lit *their fearing of me is a taught command of men* [C] **30:4** Or *Judah's* [D] **30:6** Or *Southland*

8 Go now, write it on a tablet
in their presence
and inscribe it on a scroll;
it will be for the future,
forever and ever.
9 They are a rebellious people,
deceptive children,
children who do not want to listen to
the LORD's instruction.
10 They say to the seers, "Do not see,"
and to the prophets,
"Do not prophesy the truth to us.
Tell us flattering things.
Prophesy illusions.
11 Get out of the way!
Leave the pathway.
Rid us of the Holy One of Israel."
12 Therefore the Holy One of Israel says:
"Because you have rejected
this message
and have trusted in oppression
and deceit,
and have depended on them,
13 this iniquity of yours will be
like a crumbling gap,
a bulge in a high wall
whose collapse will come in an instant
— suddenly!
14 Its collapse will be like the shattering
of a potter's jar, crushed to pieces,
so that not even a fragment of pottery
will be found among
its shattered remains —
no fragment large enough to take fire
from a hearth
or scoop water from a cistern."
15 For the Lord GOD, the Holy One
of Israel, has said:
"You will be delivered by returning
and resting;
your strength will lie in quiet confidence.
But you are not willing."
16 You say, "No!
We will escape on horses" —
therefore you will escape! —
and, "We will ride on fast horses" —
but those who pursue you
will be faster.
17 One thousand will flee at the threat
of one,

Support | *Openness with Others*

LOVING LIES?

"They say to the seers, 'Do not see,' and to the prophets, 'Do not prophesy the truth to us. Tell us flattering things. Prophesy illusions. Get out of the way! Leave the pathway. Rid us of the Holy One of Israel.'" Isaiah 30:10-11

Ever encounter a situation like one of these?

- A parent urging you to drop that new romantic interest, saying that person is "trouble."
- An academic counselor warning you that if you don't make some changes and soon, you may as well kiss that scholarship goodbye.
- A friend suggesting that the reason the company is offering you such a great salary is because they intend, for all practical purposes, to own you.

If you're like most people, such warnings probably irritate you. Maybe you think, "What do *you* know? I don't need your two cents. It'll be different with me."

This was the situation in Israel when Isaiah was prophesying, except he wasn't just sharing some hunches and opinions. He was delivering the word of the Lord! But rather than hear and heed this divine truth, the people put their hands over their ears and yelled, "Tell us flattering things. Prophesy illusions."

The last thing any of us needs is people telling us only what we want to hear. That's the height of dysfunction. Don't surround yourself with lackeys who will cheer you on to your destruction. And don't be anybody's "yes" man or "yes" woman, either.

For the next note on *Support*, see Jeremiah 20:7,9.

at the threat of five you will flee,
until you remain
like a solitary pole on a mountaintop
or a banner on a hill.

THE LORD'S MERCY TO ISRAEL

18 Therefore the LORD is waiting
to show you mercy,
and is rising up
to show you compassion,
for the LORD is a just God.
All who wait patiently for him
are happy.

19 For people will live on Zion in Jerusalem.
You will never weep again; he will show favor
to you at the sound of your outcry; as soon
as he hears, he will answer you. 20 The Lord
will give you meager bread and water during
oppression, but your Teacher[A] will not hide
any longer. Your eyes will see your Teacher,
21 and whenever you turn to the right or to the
left, your ears will hear this command behind
you: "This is the way. Walk in it." 22 Then you
will defile your silver-plated idols and your
gold-plated images. You will throw them away
like menstrual cloths, and call them filth.
23 Then he will send rain for your seed that
you have sown in the ground, and the food,
the produce of the ground, will be rich and
plentiful. On that day your cattle will graze
in open pastures. 24 The oxen and donkeys
that work the ground will eat salted fodder
scattered with winnowing shovel and fork.
25 Streams flowing with water will be on every high mountain and every raised hill on
the day of great slaughter when the towers
fall. 26 The moonlight will be as bright as the
sunlight, and the sunlight will be seven times
brighter — like the light of seven days — on
the day that the LORD bandages his people's
injuries and heals the wounds he inflicted.

ANNIHILATION OF THE ASSYRIANS

27 Look there! The LORD[B] is coming
from far away,
his anger burning and heavy
with smoke.[C]
His lips are full of fury,
and his tongue is like a consuming fire.

Thanksgiving and Contentment | *Repentance*

THE POWER OF REPENTANCE

"For the Lord GOD, the Holy One of Israel, has said: 'You will be delivered by returning and resting; your strength will lie in quiet confidence. But you are not willing.'" Isaiah 30:15

Human beings are incredibly resourceful creatures—never more so, than when we get into trouble. This isn't always a benefit, however.

Rather than *look* up, we often opt to *ramp* up our efforts. We work every possible angle. If we find that we can't save ourselves, we start working the phones. If our connections don't come through for us, we may turn to our bag of worldly tricks, techniques, and tactics.

When Isaiah's fellow Jews began feeling the effects of their sin, they didn't turn to God. Instead, they foolishly ran to Egypt for help (30:2). The prophet could only shake his head. Their troubles could have been avoided. Deliverance was available through "returning and resting."

"Returning" can also be translated "repenting." Repentance, contrary to popular belief, doesn't mean blubbering over our failures. It means realizing we're going down the wrong road, stopping, turning around, and coming back. Whether or not that involves tears, it definitely involves insight—then humility.

If you're facing trouble in some area of life, before you go into scramble mode, look up. Ask God to show you if you're struggling, at least in part, because you've wandered from what's true and right.

For the next note on *Thanksgiving and Contentment*, see Jeremiah 3:22.

[A] **30:20** Or *teachers* [B] **30:27** Or *Look, the name of the LORD* [C] **30:27** Hb obscure

28 His breath is like an overflowing torrent
that rises to the neck.
He comes to sift the nations in a sieve
of destruction
and to put a bridle on the jaws
of the peoples
to lead them astray.
29 Your singing will be like that
on the night of a holy festival,
and your heart will rejoice
like one who walks to the music
of a flute,
going up to the mountain of the LORD,
to the Rock of Israel.
30 And the LORD will make the splendor
of his voice heard
and reveal his arm striking in
angry wrath
and a flame of consuming fire,
in driving rain, a torrent,
and hailstones.
31 Assyria will be shattered by the voice
of the LORD.
He will strike with a rod.
32 And every stroke
of the appointed[A] staff
that the LORD brings down on him
will be to the sound of tambourines
and lyres;
he will fight against him
with brandished weapons.
33 Indeed! Topheth has been ready
for the king for a long time.
Its funeral pyre is deep and wide,
with plenty of fire and wood.
The breath of the LORD, like a torrent
of burning sulfur,
kindles it.

THE LORD, THE ONLY HELP

31 Woe to those who go down to Egypt
for help
and who depend on horses!
They trust in the abundance of chariots
and in the large number of horsemen.
They do not look to the Holy One
of Israel
and they do not seek the LORD.
2 But he also is wise and brings disaster.
He does not go back on what he says;
he will rise up against the house
of the wicked

Eternal Perspective | *God's Compassion*

THE JUST GOD WHO SAVES

"Therefore the LORD is waiting to show you mercy, and is rising up to show you compassion, for the LORD is a just God. All who wait patiently for him are happy." Isaiah 30:18

A common image of the Old Testament prophets is a stern, grim-faced bunch. In fact, just reading their pointed prophecies is enough to make a person want to duck under the table!

Yet repeatedly, during all their sobering talk of judgment, we find comforting passages like this one: a mention of God's mercy; a reference to his compassion; a reminder that happiness is found in God (and nowhere else).

This helps us keep a proper perspective. God is holy and just. He is also gracious and loving. Though no sin will ever go unpunished, no one who has a personal relationship with Jesus need ever fear punishment!

The book of Isaiah has 66 chapters, much like the Bible has 66 books. And the first 39 chapters of Isaiah—like the Old Testament as a whole—are primarily descriptive of people in great need of salvation. The final 27 chapters—just like the New Testament—focus mostly on God's provision of that salvation.

Isaiah gives as a holistic, picture of God. He is both just *and* merciful!

For the next note on *Eternal Perspective*, see Isaiah 42:3.

[A] **30:32** Some Hb mss read *punishing*

and against the allies of evildoers.
3 Egyptians are men, not God;
their horses are flesh, not spirit.
When the LORD raises his hand
to strike,
the helper will stumble
and the one who is helped will fall;
both will perish together.

4 For this is what the LORD said to me:
As a lion or young lion growls
over its prey
when a band of shepherds is called out
against it,
and is not terrified by their shouting
or subdued by their noise,
so the LORD of Armies will come down
to fight on Mount Zion
and on its hill.

5 Like hovering birds,
so the LORD of Armies
will protect Jerusalem —
by protecting it, he will rescue it,
by sparing it, he will deliver it.

6 Return to the one the Israelites have greatly
rebelled against. 7 For on that day, every one
of you will reject the silver and gold idols that
your own hands have sinfully made.
8 Then Assyria will fall,
but not by human sword;
a sword will devour him,
but not one made by man.
He will flee from the sword;
his young men will be put
to forced labor.
9 His rock[A] will pass away
because of fear,
and his officers will be afraid
because of the signal flag.
This is the LORD's declaration — whose fire
is in Zion and whose furnace is in Jerusalem.

THE RIGHTEOUS KINGDOM ANNOUNCED

32 Indeed, a king will reign righteously,
and rulers will rule justly.
2 Each will be like a shelter
from the wind,
a refuge from the rain,
like flowing streams
in a dry land
and the shade of a massive rock
in an arid land.
3 Then the eyes of those who see will not
be closed,

Other-centeredness | *Giving Generously*

BEING DIFFERENT; MAKING A DIFFERENCE

"But a noble person plans noble things; he stands up for noble causes." Isaiah 32:8

Some people are like thermometers: they simply reflect the environment around them. Some people, however, are like thermostats; they alter and regulate their environment.

This pictures people today, and it accurately pictures the cultural landscape in ancient Israel. The prophet Isaiah points at the foolish person who "lives in a godless way" (32:6) and not only ignores the needy, but "hatches plots to destroy the needy with lies" (32:7). This "scoundrel's" motto seems to be "what can I get away with?" rather than "what is right?"

Then Isaiah speaks of the "noble person" who "plans noble things" and "stands up for noble causes."

What an encouraging thought. We don't have to simply go with the flow. We can swim against cultural currents. The implication seems to be that if we do the opposite of what foolish people do—that is, if we live nobly, if we care deeply for the poor—we incite others toward what's right. We change the temperature of culture.

Don't merely reflect the world around you; take steps to change it.

For the next note on *Other-centeredness*, see Isaiah 35:3-4.

[A] **31:9** Perhaps the Assyrian king

and the ears of those who hear
will listen.
4 The reckless mind will gain knowledge,
and the stammering tongue
will speak clearly and fluently.
5 A fool will no longer be called a noble,
nor a scoundrel said to be important.
6 For a fool speaks foolishness
and his mind plots iniquity.
He lives in a godless way
and speaks falsely about the LORD.
He leaves the hungry empty
and deprives the thirsty of drink.
7 The scoundrel's weapons
are destructive;
he hatches plots to destroy the needy
with lies,
even when the poor person says
what is right.
8 But a noble person plans noble things;
he stands up for noble causes.

9 Stand up, you complacent women;
listen to me.
Pay attention to what I say,
you overconfident daughters.
10 In a little more than a year
you overconfident ones will shudder,
for the grapes will fail
and the harvest will not come.
11 Shudder, you complacent ones;
tremble, you overconfident ones!
Strip yourselves bare
and put sackcloth around your waists.
12 Beat your breasts in mourning
for the delightful fields
and the fruitful vines,
13 for the ground of my people
growing thorns and briers,
indeed, for every joyous house
in the jubilant city.
14 For the palace will be deserted,
the busy city abandoned.
The hill and the watchtower will become
barren places forever,
the joy of wild donkeys,
and a pasture for flocks,
15 until the Spirit[A] from on high
is poured out on us.
Then the desert will become
an orchard,
and the orchard will seem
like a forest.
16 Then justice will inhabit
the wilderness,
and righteousness will dwell
in the orchard.
17 The result of righteousness
will be peace;
the effect of righteousness
will be quiet confidence forever.
18 Then my people will dwell
in a peaceful place,
in safe and secure dwellings.
19 But hail will level the forest,[B]
and the city will sink into the depths.
20 You will be happy as you sow seed
beside abundant water,
and as you let oxen and donkeys
range freely.

THE LORD RISES UP

33 Woe, you destroyer never destroyed,
you traitor never betrayed!
When you have finished destroying,
you will be destroyed.
When you have finished betraying,
they will betray you.

2 LORD, be gracious to us! We wait
for you.
Be our strength every morning
and our salvation in time of trouble.
3 The peoples flee
at the thunderous noise;
the nations scatter when you rise
in your majesty.
4 Your spoil will be gathered as locusts
are gathered;
people will swarm over it
like an infestation of locusts.
5 The LORD is exalted, for he dwells
on high;
he has filled Zion with justice
and righteousness.
6 There will be times of security
for you —
a storehouse of salvation, wisdom,
and knowledge.
The fear of the LORD is Zion's treasure.

7 Listen! Their warriors cry loudly
in the streets;
the messengers of peace weep bitterly.
8 The highways are deserted;
travel has ceased.

[A] **32:15** Or *a wind* [B] **32:19** Hb obscure

An agreement has been broken,
cities[A] despised,
and human life disregarded.
9 The land mourns and withers;
Lebanon is ashamed and wilted.
Sharon is like a desert;
Bashan and Carmel shake off
their leaves.
10 "Now I will rise up," says the LORD.
"Now I will lift myself up.
Now I will be exalted.
11 You will conceive chaff;
you will give birth to stubble.
Your breath is fire that will
consume you.
12 The peoples will be burned to ashes,
like thorns cut down and burned
in a fire.
13 You who are far off, hear what
I have done;
you who are near,
know my strength."

14 The sinners in Zion are afraid;
trembling seizes the ungodly:
"Who among us can dwell
with a consuming fire?
Who among us can dwell
with ever-burning flames?"
15 The one who lives righteously
and speaks rightly,
who refuses profit from extortion,
whose hand never takes a bribe,
who stops his ears from listening
to murderous plots
and shuts his eyes against
evil schemes —
16 he will dwell on the heights;
his refuge will be the rocky fortresses,
his food provided, his water assured.

17 Your eyes will see the King
in his beauty;
you will see a vast land.
18 Your mind will meditate
on the past terror:
"Where is the accountant?[B]
Where is the tribute collector?[C]
Where is the one who spied out
our defenses?"[D]
19 You will no longer see the barbarians,
a people whose speech is difficult
to comprehend —
who stammer in a language that is
not understood.
20 Look at Zion, the city
of our festival times.
Your eyes will see Jerusalem,
a peaceful pasture, a tent
that does not wander;
its tent pegs will not be pulled up
nor will any of its cords be loosened.
21 For the majestic one, our LORD,
will be there,
a place of rivers and broad streams
where ships that are rowed
will not go,
and majestic vessels will not pass.
22 For the LORD is our Judge,
the LORD is our Lawgiver,
the LORD is our King.
He will save us.
23 Your ropes are slack;
they cannot hold the base of the mast
or spread out the flag.
Then abundant spoil will be divided,
the lame will plunder it,
24 and none there will say, "I am sick."
The people who dwell there
will be forgiven their iniquity.

THE JUDGMENT OF THE NATIONS

34 You nations, come here and listen;
you peoples, pay attention!
Let the earth and all that fills it hear,
the world and all that comes from it.
2 The LORD is angry with all the nations,
furious with all their armies.
He will set them apart for destruction,
giving them over to slaughter.
3 Their slain will be thrown out,
and the stench of their corpses will rise;
the mountains will flow[E]
with their blood.
4 All[F] the stars in the sky will dissolve.
The sky will roll up like a scroll,
and its stars will all wither
as leaves wither on the vine,
and foliage on the fig tree.

THE JUDGMENT OF EDOM

5 When my sword has drunk its fill[G]
in the heavens,
it will then come down on Edom
and on the people I have set apart
for destruction.

[A] **33:8** DSS read *witnesses* [B] **33:18** Lit *counter* [C] **33:18** Lit *weigher* [D] **33:18** Lit *who counts towers* [E] **34:3** Or *melt*, or *dissolve* [F] **34:4** DSS read *And the valleys will be split, and all* [G] **34:5** DSS read *sword will appear*

6 The LORD's sword is covered with blood.
It drips with fat,
with the blood of lambs and goats,
with the fat of the kidneys of rams.
For the LORD has a sacrifice in Bozrah,
a great slaughter in the land of Edom.
7 The wild oxen will be struck[A] down
with them,
and young bulls with the mighty bulls.
Their land will be soaked with[B] blood,
and their soil will be saturated with fat.

8 For the LORD has a day of vengeance,
a time of paying back Edom
for its hostility against Zion.
9 Edom's streams will be turned
into pitch,
her soil into sulfur;
her land will become burning pitch.
10 It will never go out — day or night.
Its smoke will go up forever.
It will be desolate, from generation
to generation;
no one will pass through it forever
and ever.
11 Eagle owls[C] and herons[D] will possess it,
and long-eared owls and ravens
will dwell there.
The LORD will stretch out
a measuring line
and a plumb line over her
for her destruction and chaos.
12 No nobles will be left to proclaim
a king,
and all her princes will come
to nothing.
13 Her palaces will be overgrown
with thorns;
her fortified cities, with thistles
and briers.
She will become a dwelling
for jackals,
an abode[E] for ostriches.
14 The desert creatures will meet hyenas,
and one wild goat will call to another.
Indeed, the night birds will stay there
and will find a resting place.
15 Sand partridges[F] will make
their nests there;
they will lay and hatch their eggs
and will gather their broods
under their shadows.
Indeed, the birds of prey
will gather there,
each with its mate.
16 Search and read the scroll of the LORD:
Not one of them will be missing,
none will be lacking its mate,
because he has ordered it
by my[G] mouth,
and he will gather them by his Spirit.
17 He has cast the lot for them;
his hand allotted their portion
with a measuring line.
They will possess it forever;
they will dwell in it from generation
to generation.

THE RANSOMED RETURN TO ZION

35 The wilderness and the dry land
will be glad;
the desert will rejoice and blossom
like a wildflower.[H]
2 It will blossom abundantly
and will also rejoice with joy
and singing.
The glory of Lebanon will be given to it,
the splendor of Carmel and Sharon.
They will see the glory of the LORD,
the splendor of our God.
3 Strengthen the weak hands,
steady the shaking knees!
4 Say to the cowardly:
"Be strong; do not fear!
Here is your God; vengeance is coming.
God's retribution is coming; he will
save you."
5 Then the eyes of the blind
will be opened,
and the ears of the deaf unstopped.
6 Then the lame will leap like a deer,
and the tongue of the mute will sing
for joy,
for water will gush in the wilderness,
and streams in the desert;
7 the parched ground will become a pool,
and the thirsty land springs.
In the haunt of jackals, in their lairs,
there will be grass, reeds, and papyrus.
8 A road will be there and a way;
it will be called the Holy Way.
The unclean will not travel on it,
but it will be for the one who walks
the path.

[A] **34:7** Or *will go* [B] **34:7** Or *will drink its fill of* [C] **34:11** Or *Pelicans* [D] **34:11** Or *hedgehogs* [E] **34:13** DSS, LXX, Syr, Tg; MT reads *jackals, grass* [F] **34:15** Or *Arrow snakes*, or *Owls* [G] **34:16** Some Hb mss; other Hb mss, DSS, Syr, Tg read *his* [H] **35:1** Or *meadow saffron*; traditionally *rose*

Fools will not wander on it.
9 There will be no lion there,
and no vicious beast will go up on it;
they will not be found there.
But the redeemed will walk on it,
10 and the redeemed of the LORD
will return
and come to Zion with singing,
crowned with unending joy.
Joy and gladness will overtake them,
and sorrow and sighing will flee.

SENNACHERIB'S INVASION

36 In the fourteenth year of King Hezekiah,
King Sennacherib of Assyria attacked
all the fortified cities of Judah and captured
them. 2 Then the king of Assyria sent his royal
spokesman, along with a massive army, from
Lachish to King Hezekiah at Jerusalem. The
Assyrian stood near the conduit of the upper
pool, by the road to the Launderer's Field. 3 Eliakim son of Hilkiah, who was in charge of the
palace, Shebna the court secretary, and Joah son
of Asaph, the court historian, came out to him.
4 The royal spokesman said to them, "Tell
Hezekiah:
The great king, the king of Assyria,
says this: What are you relying on?[A]
5 You[B] think mere words are strategy
and strength for war. Who are you now
relying on that you have rebelled against
me? 6 Look, you are relying on Egypt, that
splintered reed of a staff that will pierce
the hand of anyone who grabs it and
leans on it. This is how Pharaoh king of
Egypt is to all who rely on him. 7 Suppose
you say to me, 'We rely on the LORD our
God.' Isn't he the one whose high places
and altars Hezekiah has removed, saying
to Judah and Jerusalem, 'You are to worship at this altar'?

8 "Now make a deal with my master, the
king of Assyria. I'll give you two thousand horses if you're able to supply riders
for them! 9 How then can you drive back
a single officer among the least of my
master's servants? How can you rely on
Egypt for chariots and horsemen? 10 Have
I attacked this land to destroy it without
the LORD's approval? The LORD said to me,
'Attack this land and destroy it.'"

11 Then Eliakim, Shebna, and Joah said to
the royal spokesman, "Please speak to your
servants in Aramaic, since we understand it.

Other-centeredness | *Encouraging*

ENCOURAGED ENCOURAGERS

"Strengthen the weak hands, steady the shaking knees! Say to the cowardly: 'Be strong; do not fear! Here is your God; vengeance is coming. God's retribution is coming; he will save you.'" Isaiah 35:3-4

"What's the use? God has abandoned me. . . . There's no hope. . . . I can't keep going. . . . I'm scared to death!"

Everyone has felt such things and *said* such words. How stunning that a single phone call can bring us to our knees, and one crushing event can wring the hope right out of our souls.

Isaiah's words were written to such weary and worried souls—the Jewish people in Babylonian exile. This message doesn't guarantee an immediate escape from trouble, only the reminder that the Lord reigns in and through life's chaos—in the way that the sun continues to shine, unseen, behind the darkest storm clouds. Suffering and evil will not have the last word. God will come. We will need strong nerves to wait and watch, but God will ultimately make all wrongs right.

This promise gives encouragement to keep going. With such a divine reminder, we also have the opportunity to encourage others, as Isaiah did.

For the next note on *Other-centeredness*, see Jeremiah 9:1.

[A] **36:4** Lit *What is this trust that you trust* [B] **36:5** Many Hb mss, DSS, 2Kg 18:20; MT reads *I*

Don't speak to us in Hebrew[A] within earshot
of the people who are on the wall."
12 But the royal spokesman replied, "Has
my master sent me to speak these words to
your master and to you, and not to the men
who are sitting on the wall, who are destined
with you to eat their own excrement and drink
their own urine?"
13 Then the royal spokesman stood and called
out loudly in Hebrew:

Listen to the words of the great king, the
king of Assyria! 14 This is what the king
says: "Don't let Hezekiah deceive you, for
he cannot rescue you. 15 Don't let Hezekiah persuade you to rely on the LORD,
saying, 'The LORD will certainly rescue us!
This city will not be handed over to the
king of Assyria.'"

16 Don't listen to Hezekiah, for this is what
the king of Assyria says: "Make peace[B]
with me and surrender to me. Then every
one of you may eat from his own vine and
his own fig tree and drink water from
his own cistern 17 until I come and take
you away to a land like your own land
— a land of grain and new wine, a land
of bread and vineyards. 18 Beware that
Hezekiah does not mislead you by saying,
'The LORD will rescue us.' Has any one of
the gods of the nations rescued his land
from the power of the king of Assyria?
19 Where are the gods of Hamath and
Arpad? Where are the gods of Sepharvaim? Have they rescued Samaria from
my power? 20 Who among all the gods of
these lands ever rescued his land from
my power? So will the LORD rescue Jerusalem from my power?"

21 But they kept silent; they didn't say anything, for the king's command was, "Don't
answer him." 22 Then Eliakim son of Hilkiah,
who was in charge of the palace, Shebna the
court secretary, and Joah son of Asaph, the
court historian, came to Hezekiah with their
clothes torn and reported to him the words
of the royal spokesman.

HEZEKIAH SEEKS ISAIAH'S COUNSEL

37 When King Hezekiah heard their report,
he tore his clothes, put on sackcloth, and
went to the LORD's temple. 2 He sent Eliakim,
who was in charge of the palace, Shebna the
court secretary, and the leading priests, who
were wearing sackcloth, to the prophet Isaiah son of Amoz. 3 They said to him, "This is
what Hezekiah says: 'Today is a day of distress,
rebuke, and disgrace. It is as if children have
come to the point of birth, and there is no
strength to deliver them. 4 Perhaps the LORD
your God will hear all the words of the royal spokesman, whom his master the king of
Assyria sent to mock the living God, and will
rebuke him for the words that the LORD your
God has heard. Therefore offer a prayer for
the surviving remnant.'"
5 So the servants of King Hezekiah went to
Isaiah, 6 who said to them, "Tell your master,
'The LORD says this: Don't be afraid because
of the words you have heard, with which the
king of Assyria's attendants have blasphemed
me. 7 I am about to put a spirit in him and he
will hear a rumor and return to his own land,
where I will cause him to fall by the sword.'"

SENNACHERIB'S LETTER

8 When the royal spokesman heard that the
king of Assyria had pulled out of Lachish, he
left and found him fighting against Libnah.
9 The king had heard concerning King Tirhakah
of Cush, "He has set out to fight against you."
So when he heard this, he sent messengers to
Hezekiah, saying, 10 "Say this to King Hezekiah
of Judah: 'Don't let your God, on whom you rely,
deceive you by promising that Jerusalem won't
be handed over to the king of Assyria. 11 Look,
you have heard what the kings of Assyria have
done to all the countries: they completely destroyed them. Will you be rescued? 12 Did the
gods of the nations that my predecessors destroyed rescue them — Gozan, Haran, Rezeph,
and the Edenites in Telassar? 13 Where is the
king of Hamath, the king of Arpad, the king
of the city of[C] Sepharvaim, Hena, or Ivvah?'"

HEZEKIAH'S PRAYER

14 Hezekiah took the letter from the mes-
sengers' hands, read it, then went up to the
LORD's temple and spread it out before the
LORD. 15 Then Hezekiah prayed to the LORD:

16 LORD of Armies, God of Israel, enthroned between the cherubim, you are
God — you alone — of all the kingdoms
of the earth. You made the heavens and
the earth. 17 Listen closely, LORD, and hear;

[A] 36:11 Lit *Judahite*, also in v. 13 [B] 36:16 Lit *a blessing* [C] 37:13 Or *king of Lair*,

open your eyes, LORD, and see. Hear all
the words that Sennacherib has sent to
mock the living God. 18 LORD, it is true that
the kings of Assyria have devastated all
these countries and their lands. 19 They
have thrown their gods into the fire, for
they were not gods but made from wood
and stone by human hands. So they have
destroyed them. 20 Now, LORD our God,
save us from his power so that all the
kingdoms of the earth may know that
you, LORD, are God[A] — you alone.

GOD'S ANSWER THROUGH ISAIAH

21 Then Isaiah son of Amoz sent a message to
Hezekiah: "The LORD, the God of Israel, says,
'Because you prayed to me about King Sen-
nacherib of Assyria, 22 this is the word the
LORD has spoken against him:

Virgin Daughter Zion
despises you and scorns you;
Daughter Jerusalem shakes her head
behind your back.
23 Who is it you have mocked
and blasphemed?
Against whom have you raised
your voice
and lifted your eyes in pride?
Against the Holy One of Israel!
24 You have mocked the Lord
through[B] your servants.
You have said, "With my many chariots
I have gone up to the heights
of the mountains,
to the far recesses of Lebanon.
I cut down its tallest cedars,
its choice cypress trees.
I came to its distant heights,
its densest forest.
25 I dug wells and drank water in foreign
lands.[C]
I dried up all the streams of Egypt
with the soles of my feet."
26 Have you not heard?
I designed it long ago;
I planned it in days gone by.
I have now brought it to pass,
and you have crushed fortified cities
into piles of rubble.
27 Their inhabitants have
become powerless,
dismayed, and ashamed.
They are plants of the field,

Exercise of Faith | *Praying*

GOD-HONORING PRAYER

"Now, LORD our God, save us from his power so that all the kingdoms of the earth may know that you, LORD, are God—you alone." Isaiah 37:20

When Sennacherib, the mighty Assyrian king, invaded Judah, he sent a message to King Hezekiah. Its tone was arrogant, the words intended to create panic. The gist of this threat? "If you think your god is going to deliver you, you're delusional!"

Hezekiah did all the following: He tore his clothes as a sign of mourning; he notified Isaiah the prophet; he took the threatening letter to the temple, spread it out before the Lord, and prayed.

Ultimately, however, his prayer wasn't only a "Save us!" prayer. It was a plea that God would save them, "so that all the kingdoms of the earth may know that you, LORD, are God—you alone."

Is this how we pray when trouble strikes? Is a concern for God's glory the primary catalyst behind our prayers? Is a desire for God's fame the hoped-for outcome of our prayers?

Think about your biggest current trial. Instead of simply praying for it to be over, spread it out before the Lord, and begin praying that he might somehow get great glory from it. Ask him to show up and show off. It could be that he wants to do big things *around* you. Or it might be that he wants to demonstrate his power and goodness by doing great things *in* you.

For the next note on *Exercise of Faith*, see Jeremiah 1:19.

[A] **37:20** *are God* supplied for clarity; see v. 16 [B] **37:24** Lit *by the hand of* [C] **37:25** DSS, 2Kg 19:24; MT omits *in foreign lands*

tender grass,
grass on the rooftops,
blasted by the east wind.[A]

28 But I know your sitting down,
your going out and your coming in,
and your raging against me.
29 Because your raging against me
and your arrogance have reached
my ears,
I will put my hook in your nose
and my bit in your mouth;
I will make you go back
the way you came.

30 " 'This will be the sign for you: This year
you will eat what grows on its own, and in the
second year what grows from that. But in the
third year sow and reap, plant vineyards and
eat their fruit. 31 The surviving remnant of the
house of Judah will again take root downward
and bear fruit upward. 32 For a remnant will
go out from Jerusalem, and survivors from
Mount Zion. The zeal of the LORD of Armies
will accomplish this.'
33 "Therefore, this is what the LORD says
about the king of Assyria:

He will not enter this city,
shoot an arrow here,
come before it with a shield,
or build up a siege ramp against it.
34 He will go back
the way he came,
and he will not enter this city.
This is the LORD's declaration.
35 I will defend this city and rescue it
for my sake
and for the sake of
my servant David."

DEFEAT AND DEATH OF SENNACHERIB

36 Then the angel of the LORD went out and
struck down one hundred eighty-five thousand in the camp of the Assyrians. When the
people got up the next morning — there were
all the dead bodies! 37 So King Sennacherib
of Assyria broke camp and left. He returned
home and lived in Nineveh.
38 One day, while he was worshiping in the
temple of his god Nisroch, his sons Adrammelech and Sharezer struck him down with
the sword and escaped to the land of Ararat.
Then his son Esar-haddon became king in
his place.

HEZEKIAH'S ILLNESS AND RECOVERY

38 In those days Hezekiah became ter-
minally ill. The prophet Isaiah son of
Amoz came and said to him, "This is what
the LORD says: 'Set your house in order, for
you are about to die; you will not recover.' "[B]
2 Then Hezekiah turned his face to the wall
and prayed to the LORD. 3 He said, "Please, LORD,
remember how I have walked before you faithfully and wholeheartedly, and have done what
pleases you."[C] And Hezekiah wept bitterly.
4 Then the word of the LORD came to Isaiah:
5 "Go and tell Hezekiah, 'This is what the LORD
God of your ancestor David says: I have heard
your prayer; I have seen your tears. Look, I am
going to add fifteen years to your life.[D] 6 And
I will rescue you and this city from the grasp
of the king of Assyria; I will defend this city.
7 This is the sign to you from the LORD that he
will do what[E] he has promised:[F] 8 I am going
to make the sun's shadow that goes down on
the stairway of Ahaz go back by ten steps.' "
So the sun's shadow[G] went back the ten steps
it had descended.
9 A poem by King Hezekiah of Judah after
he had been sick and had recovered from his
illness:

10 I said: In the prime[H] of my life
I must go to the gates of Sheol;
I am deprived of the rest of my years.
11 I said: I will never see the LORD,
the LORD in the land of the living;
I will not look on humanity
any longer
with the inhabitants of what is
passing away.[I]
12 My dwelling is plucked up
and removed from me
like a shepherd's tent.
I have rolled up my life like a weaver;
he cuts me off from the loom.
By nightfall[J] you make an end of me.
13 I thought until the morning:
He will break all my bones like a lion.
By nightfall you make an end of me.
14 I chirp like a swallow or a crane;
I moan like a dove.
My eyes grow weak looking upward.
Lord, I am oppressed; support me.

[A] **37:27** DSS; MT reads *rooftops, field before standing grain* [B] **38:1** Lit *live* [C] **38:3** Lit *what is good in your eyes* [D] **38:5** Lit *days*, also in v. 10 [E] **38:7** Lit *this thing* [F] **38:7** Lit *said* [G] **38:8** Lit *And the sun* [H] **38:10** Lit *quiet* [I] **38:11** Some Hb mss, Tg read *of the world* [J] **38:12** Lit *From day until night*, also in v. 13

15 What can I say?
He has spoken to me,
and he himself has done it.
I walk along slowly all my years
because of the bitterness of my soul.
16 Lord, by such things people live,
and in every one of them my spirit
finds life;
you have restored me to health
and let me live.
17 Indeed, it was for my own well-being
that I had such intense bitterness;
but your love has delivered me
from the Pit of destruction,
for you have thrown all my sins
behind your back.
18 For Sheol cannot thank you;
Death cannot praise you.
Those who go down to the Pit
cannot hope for your faithfulness.
19 The living, only the living
can thank you,
as I do today;
a father will make your faithfulness
known to children.
20 The LORD is ready to save me;
we will play stringed instruments
all the days of our lives
at the house of the LORD.

21 Now Isaiah had said, "Let them take a lump
of pressed figs and apply it to his infected skin,
so that he may recover." 22 And Hezekiah had
asked, "What is the sign that I will go up to the
LORD's temple?"

HEZEKIAH'S FOLLY

39 At that time Merodach-baladan son of
Baladan, king of Babylon, sent letters
and a gift to Hezekiah since he heard that he
had been sick and had recovered. 2 Hezekiah
was pleased with the letters, and he showed
the envoys his treasure house — the silver, the
gold, the spices, and the precious oil — and
all his armory, and everything that was found
in his treasuries. There was nothing in his
palace and in all his realm that Hezekiah did
not show them.
3 Then the prophet Isaiah came to King Hezekiah and asked him, "What did these men
say, and where did they come to you from?"
Hezekiah replied, "They came to me from
a distant country, from Babylon."
4 Isaiah asked, "What have they seen in your
palace?"
Hezekiah answered, "They have seen everything in my palace. There isn't anything in my
treasuries that I didn't show them."
5 Then Isaiah said to Hezekiah, "Hear the
word of the LORD of Armies: 6 'Look, the days
are coming when everything in your palace
and all that your fathers have stored up until
today will be carried off to Babylon; nothing will
be left,' says the LORD. 7 'Some of your descendants — who come from you, whom you father
— will be taken away, and they will become
eunuchs in the palace of the king of Babylon.'"
8 Then Hezekiah said to Isaiah, "The word
of the LORD that you have spoken is good," for
he thought: There will be peace and security
during my lifetime.

GOD'S PEOPLE COMFORTED

40 "Comfort, comfort my people,"
says your God.
2 "Speak tenderly to[A] Jerusalem,
and announce to her
that her time of forced labor is over,
her iniquity has been pardoned,
and she has received
from the LORD's hand
double for all her sins."

3 A voice of one crying out:
Prepare the way of the LORD
in the wilderness;
make a straight highway for our God
in the desert.
4 Every valley will be lifted up,
and every mountain and hill
will be leveled;
the uneven ground will become smooth
and the rough places, a plain.
5 And the glory of the LORD will appear,
and all humanity[B] together will see it,
for the mouth of the LORD has spoken.

6 A voice was saying, "Cry out!"
Another said,[C] "What should I cry out?"
"All humanity is grass,
and all its goodness is like the flower
of the field.
7 The grass withers, the flowers fade
when the breath[D] of the LORD blows
on them;[E]
indeed, the people are grass.

[A] **40:2** Lit *Speak to the heart of* [B] **40:5** Lit *flesh* [C] **40:6** DSS, LXX, Vg read *I said* [D] **40:7** Or *wind*, or *Spirit* [E] **40:7** Lit *it*

8 The grass withers, the flowers fade,
but the word of our God
remains forever."

9 Zion, herald of good news,
go up on a high mountain.
Jerusalem, herald of good news,
raise your voice loudly.
Raise it, do not be afraid!
Say to the cities of Judah,
"Here is your God!"
10 See, the Lord God comes with strength,
and his power establishes his rule.
His wages are with him,
and his reward accompanies him.
11 He protects his flock like a shepherd;
he gathers the lambs in his arms
and carries them in the fold
of his garment.
He gently leads those that are nursing.

12 Who has measured the waters
in the hollow of his hand
or marked off the heavens
with the span of his hand?
Who has gathered the dust of the earth
in a measure
or weighed the mountains on a balance
and the hills on the scales?
13 Who has directed[A] the Spirit
of the LORD,
or who gave him counsel?
14 Who did he consult?
Who gave him understanding
and taught him
the paths of justice?
Who taught him knowledge
and showed him the way
of understanding?
15 Look, the nations are like a drop
in a bucket;
they are considered as a speck of dust
on the scales;
he lifts up the islands like fine dust.
16 Lebanon's cedars are not enough
for fuel,
or its animals enough
for a burnt offering.
17 All the nations are as nothing
before him;
they are considered by him
as empty nothingness.

18 With whom will you compare God?
What likeness will you set up for
comparison with him?
19 An idol? — something that
a smelter casts

Rest and Reflection | *Meditating on God and His Word*

GOD'S ENDURING WORD

"The grass withers, the flowers fade, but the word of our God remains forever." Isaiah 40:8

"Obsessed" is the right word for the way contemporary culture views rich and famous, powerful, and beautiful people. Tens of millions follow along on social media, via tabloids and magazines, and by tuning in to so-called reality shows. Every celebrity comment, outfit, romance, and vacation is monitored and discussed.

Even on a smaller, more interpersonal scale, we can easily become absorbed with the lives of those around us. Ever find thoughts like these pinging around in your mind? *If only I had that person's: wit, looks, assets, job, marriage, house, physique, smarts, contacts, talent* (take your pick).

Isaiah puts this obsession with people into perspective. The prophet compares all people, even the great and enviable, to grass that withers and flowers that fade. In contrast, "the word of our God remains forever."

A steady dose of celebrity news will eventually mess with our hearts. Subtly we begin to believe that beauty and money are what matter. Thus, we need God's enduring Word to bring us back to sanity and true reality.

For the next note on *Rest and Reflection*, see Isaiah 40:30-31.

[A] **40:13** Or *measured*, or *comprehended*

and a metalworker plates with gold
and makes silver chains for?
20 A poor person contributes wood for
a pedestal
that will not rot.[A]
He looks for a skilled craftsman
to set up an idol that will not fall over.

21 Do you not know?
Have you not heard?
Has it not been declared to you
from the beginning?
Have you not considered
the foundations of the earth?
22 God is enthroned above the circle
of the earth;
its inhabitants are like grasshoppers.
He stretches out the heavens
like thin cloth
and spreads them out like a tent
to live in.
23 He reduces princes to nothing
and makes judges of the earth like a
wasteland.
24 They are barely planted, barely sown,
their stem hardly takes root
in the ground
when he blows on them
and they wither,
and a whirlwind carries them away
like stubble.

25 "To whom will you compare me,
or who is my equal?"
asks the Holy One.
26 Look up[B] and see!
Who created these?
He brings out the stars by number;
he calls all of them by name.
Because of his great power
and strength,
not one of them is missing.

27 Jacob, why do you say,
and, Israel, why do you assert:
"My way is hidden from the LORD,
and my claim is ignored by my God"?
28 Do you not know?
Have you not heard?
The LORD is the everlasting God,
the Creator of the whole earth.
He never becomes faint or weary;
there is no limit
to his understanding.

Rest and Reflection | *Avoiding Burnout*

RENEWAL

"Youths may become faint and weary, and young men stumble and fall, but those who trust in the LORD will renew their strength; they will soar on wings like eagles; they will run and not become weary; they will walk and not faint." Isaiah 40:30-31

You sit in the coffee shop and listen as a friend reviews the last three years—a painful, unwanted divorce, followed by the loss of a job, then a health scare. Here's how the friend explains having a heart full of peace, even joy: "Looking back, I don't know how I made it through, other than to say, the Lord just carried me. When I was weak, he was strong."

Isaiah's words were intended, most immediately, for an exiled nation—people running short on strength and hope. What a perfect passage for that generation—or for any freaked-out, worn-out person today.

God is able to give strength to the weak day after day. He is able to refill our empty tanks and put a second wind in our sails. The reason is simple: "He never becomes faint or weary" (40:28).

Ask God to give you strength for today's challenges and tomorrow's opportunities.

For the next note on *Rest and Reflection*, see Isaiah 55:1-2.

[A] **40:20** Or *who is too poor for such an offering*, or *who chooses mulberry wood as a votive gift*; Hb obscure [B] **40:26** Lit *Lift up your eyes on high*

29 He gives strength to the faint
and strengthens the powerless.
30 Youths may become faint and weary,
and young men stumble and fall,
31 but those who trust in the LORD
will renew their strength;
they will soar on wings like eagles;
they will run and not become weary,
they will walk and not faint.

THE LORD VERSUS THE NATIONS' GODS

41 "Be silent before me, coasts and
islands!
And let peoples renew their strength.
Let them approach; let them testify;
let's come together for the trial.
2 Who has stirred up someone
from the east?
In righteousness he calls him to
serve.[A,B]
The LORD hands nations over to him,
and he subdues kings.
He makes them like dust
with his sword,
like wind-driven stubble with his bow.
3 He pursues them, going on safely,
hardly touching the path with his feet.
4 Who has performed and done this,
calling the generations
from the beginning?
I am the LORD, the first
and with the last — I am he."

5 The coasts and islands see
and are afraid,
the whole earth trembles.
They approach and arrive.
6 Each one helps the other,
and says to another, "Take courage!"
7 The craftsman encourages
the metalworker;
the one who flattens with the hammer
encourages the one who strikes
the anvil,
saying of the soldering, "It is good."
He fastens it with nails so that
it will not fall over.

8 But you, Israel, my servant,
Jacob, whom I have chosen,
descendant of Abraham, my friend —
9 I brought[C] you from the ends
of the earth
and called you
from its farthest corners.
I said to you: You are my servant;
I have chosen you; I haven't
rejected you.
10 Do not fear, for I am with you;
do not be afraid, for I am your God.
I will strengthen you; I will help you;
I will hold on to you with my righteous
right hand.

11 Be sure that all who are enraged
against you
will be ashamed and disgraced;
those who contend with you
will become as nothing and will perish.
12 You will look for those who contend
with you,
but you will not find them.
Those who war against you
will become absolutely nothing.
13 For I am the LORD your God,
who holds your right hand,
who says to you, 'Do not fear,
I will help you.
14 Do not fear, you worm Jacob,
you men[D] of Israel.
I will help you' —
this is the LORD's declaration.
Your Redeemer is the Holy One
of Israel.
15 See, I will make you
into a sharp threshing board,
new, with many teeth.
You will thresh mountains
and pulverize them
and make hills into chaff.
16 You will winnow them
and a wind will carry them away,
a whirlwind will scatter them.
But you will rejoice in the LORD;
you will boast in the Holy One of Israel.

17 The poor and the needy seek water,
but there is none;
their tongues are parched with thirst.
I will answer them.
I am the LORD, the God of Israel. I
will not abandon them.
18 I will open rivers on the barren heights,
and springs in the middle of the plains.
I will turn the desert into a pool
and dry land into springs.

[A] **41:2** Or *Righteousness calls him to serve* [B] **41:2** Lit *to his foot* [C] **41:9** Or *seized* [D] **41:14** LXX reads *small number*; DSS read *dead ones*

My Story | Christine

I have cancer. Over the past three and a half years, others have supported me, encouraged me, and prayed for me. Also, knowing God's character and the truth of his Word have helped me through this time. I believe what the Bible says is true. God is my reference point; his Word is my authority, and his glory is my purpose.

When the word *cancer* was first mentioned to me, I panicked. Later, I claimed Luke 1:38, Mary's words of surrender to the angel. I apologize for any perceived arrogance here—what Mary said and what I believe is this: God is Sovereign Ruler of all creation. He created me and has ordained all the days of my life (Ps 139:16). He is trustworthy in all he does. I don't have to understand God to submit to his ways. I believe the Holy Spirit is enabling me to follow him even as he asks me to live with cancer.

I've had many fearful thoughts along the way. To a man with serious fears, Jesus said, "Don't be afraid. Only believe" (Mk 5:36). I have serious fears. I decided that these few words of Jesus hold the antidote to my fear as I think about what I believe about God. So, my mantra has become "God is good, he loves me, and his plan for my life is perfect."

God is good (Ps 86:5; 100:5). I find that when I focus on God's goodness, I am calmed and reassured that all will be well—whatever that looks like. He has purpose in what he does even when I don't understand. Part of God's goodness means that he keeps his promises. He is reliable (Nm 23:19; Dt 7:9).

God loves me. His love for me flows out of his goodness (Is 54:10; Jr 31:3). I know he sees my struggle (Lk 12:6-7) and will be *with* me (Dt 31:6) and *before* me (Dt 31:8) and will *carry* me (Dt 33:12). During a recent treatment, this next verse became very personal: [So] do not fear, [Christine,] for I am with you; do not be afraid, for I am your God. I will strengthen you; I will help you; I will hold on to you with my righteous right hand" (Is 41:10). The ultimate proof of God's love for me comes when I look at the cross (Jn 3:16; Rm 5:8). When I think of this, I am delighted and filled with joy—sometimes the feelings surprise me!

God's plan for me is perfect. God's plans for me are inextricably tied up with his goodness, his love for me, and his promises (Ps 18:1-2; 91:5; 119:75-76). Jeremiah 29:11 tells me that no matter what the future on earth holds for me, I have a sure hope waiting for me in heaven. None of the painful things of this world will be there—only what is good, and, most importantly, Jesus will be there. All will be restored.

My favorite passage is Lamentations 3:19-24. These verses speak to the sin and hurt that are sure to enter our lives, which for me includes cancer. These words also bring encouragement and hope—"Because of the LORD's faithful love, we do not perish, for his mercies never end" (Lm 3:22). God is good, he loves me, and his plan for me is perfect.

(Note: shortly after penning these affirming words, Christine entered eternity.)

19 I will plant cedars,
acacias, myrtles, and olive trees
in the wilderness.
I will put juniper trees,
elms, and cypress trees together in the
desert,
20 so that all may see and know,
consider and understand,
that the hand of the LORD has done this,
the Holy One of Israel has created it.

21 "Submit your case," says the LORD.
"Present your arguments,"
says Jacob's King.
22 "Let them come and tell us
what will happen.
Tell us the past events,
so that we may reflect on them
and know the outcome,
or tell us the future.
23 Tell us the coming events,
then we will know that you are gods.
Indeed, do something good or bad,
then we will be in awe[A] when we see it.
24 Look, you are nothing
and your work is worthless.
Anyone who chooses you
is detestable.

[A] **41:23** DSS read *we may hear*

25 "I have stirred up one from the north,
and he has come,
one from the east who invokes
my[A] name.
He will march over rulers as if
they were mud,
like a potter who treads the clay.
26 Who told about this
from the beginning,
so that we might know,
and from times past,
so that we might say, 'He is right'?
No one announced it,
no one told it,
no one heard your words.
27 I was the first to say to Zion,[B]
'Look! Here they are!'
And I gave Jerusalem a herald
with good news.
28 When I look, there is no one;
there is no counselor among them;
when I ask them, they have
nothing to say.
29 Look, all of them are a delusion;[C]
their works are nonexistent;
their images are wind
and emptiness.

THE SERVANT'S MISSION

42 "This is my servant;
I strengthen him,
this is my chosen one; I delight in him.
I have put my Spirit on him;
he will bring justice[D] to the nations.
2 He will not cry out or shout
or make his voice heard in the streets.
3 He will not break a bruised reed,
and he will not put out
a smoldering wick;
he will faithfully bring justice.
4 He will not grow weak
or be discouraged
until he has established justice
on earth.
The coasts and islands will wait
for his instruction."

Eternal Perspective | *God's Mercy*

TENDER MERCY

"He will not break a bruised reed, and he will not put out a smoldering wick; he will faithfully bring justice." Isaiah 42:3

Maybe you've had the experience of feeling as though you are drowning physically, emotionally, relationally, professionally, or financially.

All that kicking and thrashing, and still, your nose is right at the waterline. You're exhausted and scared. Right about the time you desperately need a rope, life comes along and tosses you a bowling ball!

This was the experience for Jews living in Babylonian exile. For them and for struggling souls today, Isaiah had encouraging news. The Lord's "servant" (42:1)—a designation of the Messiah—is gentle and understanding.

Isaiah used the metaphors of a "bruised reed" (think of a crushed water plant) and a "smoldering wick" (picture a flameless lamp that's smoking, not glowing). To snap the former and snuff out the latter would be easy. And that's often what happens in a cold and harsh world where people can be callous and uncaring.

That's not the Lord's way. He sees, cares, and gently helps. He won't ever give us more than we can handle, and he promises to "bring justice"—which is another way of saying, he will always do what is right, and one day he will make all things right.

If you're feeling like a bruised reed or smoldering wick, call on God's tender mercy—then call a friend.

For the next note on *Eternal Perspective*, see Isaiah 43:1.

[A] **41:25** DSS read *his* [B] **41:27** Lit *First to Zion* [C] **41:29** DSS, Syr read *are nothing* [D] **42:1** DSS read *his justice*

5 This is what God, the LORD, says —
who created the heavens and stretched
them out,
who spread out the earth
and what comes from it,
who gives breath to the people on it
and spirit to those who walk on it —
6 "I am the LORD. I have called you
for a righteous purpose,[A]
and I will hold you by your hand.
I will watch over you, and I will appoint
you
to be a covenant for the people
and a light to the nations,
7 in order to open blind eyes,
to bring out prisoners
from the dungeon,
and those sitting in darkness
from the prison house.
8 I am the LORD. That is my name,
and I will not give my glory to another
or my praise to idols.
9 The past events have indeed happened.
Now I declare new events;
I announce them to you
before they occur."

A SONG OF PRAISE

10 Sing a new song to the LORD;
sing his praise from the ends
of the earth,
you who go down to the sea with all
that fills it,
you coasts and islands
with your[B] inhabitants.
11 Let the desert and its cities shout,
the settlements where Kedar dwells
cry aloud.
Let the inhabitants of Sela
sing for joy;
let them cry out
from the mountaintops.
12 Let them give glory to the LORD
and declare his praise in the coasts
and islands.
13 The LORD advances like a warrior;
he stirs up his zeal like a soldier.
He shouts, he roars aloud,
he prevails over his enemies.

14 "I have kept silent from ages past;
I have been quiet
and restrained myself.
But now, I will groan like a woman
in labor,
gasping breathlessly.
15 I will lay waste mountains and hills
and dry up all their vegetation.
I will turn rivers into islands
and dry up marshes.
16 I will lead the blind by a way
they did not know;
I will guide them on paths
they have not known.
I will turn darkness to light in front
of them
and rough places into level ground.
This is what I will do for them,
and I will not abandon them.
17 They will be turned back
and utterly ashamed —
those who trust in an idol
and say to a cast image,
'You are our gods!'

ISRAEL'S BLINDNESS AND DEAFNESS

18 "Listen, you deaf!
Look, you blind, so that you may see.
19 Who is blind but my servant,
or deaf like my messenger
I am sending?
Who is blind like my dedicated one,[C]
or blind like the servant of the LORD?
20 Though seeing many things,[D]
you pay no attention.
Though his ears are open,
he does not listen."

21 Because of his righteousness, the LORD
was pleased
to magnify his instruction
and make it glorious.
22 But this is a people plundered
and looted,
all of them trapped in holes
or imprisoned in dungeons.
They have become plunder
with no one to rescue them
and loot, with no one saying,
"Give it back!"
23 Who among you will hear this?
Let him listen and obey in the future.
24 Who gave Jacob to the robber,[E]
and Israel to the plunderers?
Was it not the LORD?
Have we not sinned against him?

[A] **42:6** Or *you by my righteousness*; lit *you in righteousness* [B] **42:10** Lit *their* [C] **42:19** Hb obscure [D] **42:20** Alt Hb tradition reads *You see many things;* [E] **42:24** Lit *to loot*

They were not willing to walk
in his ways,
and they would not listen
to his instruction.
25 So he poured out his furious anger
and the power of war on Jacob.
It surrounded him with fire,
but he did not know it;
it burned him, but he didn't take it to
heart.

RESTORATION OF ISRAEL

43 Now this is what the LORD says —
the one who created you, Jacob,
and the one who formed you, Israel —
"Do not fear, for I have redeemed you;
I have called you by your name;
you are mine.
2 I will be with you
when you pass through the waters,
and when you pass through the rivers,
they will not overwhelm you.
You will not be scorched
when you walk through the fire,
and the flame will not burn you.
3 For I am the LORD your God,
the Holy One of Israel, and your Savior.
I have given Egypt as a ransom for you,
Cush and Seba in your place.
4 Because you are precious in my sight
and honored, and I love you,
I will give people in exchange for you
and nations instead of your life.
5 Do not fear, for I am with you;
I will bring your descendants
from the east,
and gather you from the west.
6 I will say to the north, 'Give them up!'
and to the south,
'Do not hold them back!'
Bring my sons from far away,
and my daughters from the ends
of the earth —
7 everyone who bears my name
and is created for my glory.
I have formed them;
indeed, I have made them."
8 Bring out a people who are blind,
yet have eyes,
and are deaf, yet have ears.
9 All the nations are gathered together,
and the peoples are assembled.
Who among them can declare this,

E Eternal Perspective | *Redemption/Salvation*

LIVING A GREAT STORY

"Now this is what the LORD says — the one who created you, Jacob, and the one who formed you, Israel — 'Do not fear, for I have redeemed you; I have called you by your name; you are mine.'" Isaiah 43:1

- People who write stories for a living say that good stories depict characters who want something badly—and then go through hard and painful events and challenges to get what they want.
- This basic story formula is the outline for the great story of God. In order to rescue the rebellious humans he loved so much, God formed the nation Israel. In the final part of this book, Isaiah talks about the troubles of that nation (many of them self-caused) and how they never would have made it except that God was committed to them. God was determined to use them to bring forth a Savior for Israel and the world. The New Testament shows that Savior, Jesus, launching a movement called the church. Twenty centuries later, lives are still being changed.
- Our individual stories as believers follow this same outline. When God changes our hearts through faith in Jesus, our desires change, too. We discover new longings to live in ways that honor him and bless others. But for our stories to become truly remarkable, we have to persevere through life's troubles and heartaches. If we keep trusting the Lord through "waters" and "fire" (43:2), if we keep doing right, our stories get read and retold by many others.

For the next note on *Eternal Perspective*, see Isaiah 46:10.

and tell us the former things?
Let them present their witnesses
to vindicate themselves,
so that people may hear and say,
"It is true."
10 "You are my witnesses" —
this is the LORD's declaration —
"and my servant whom I have chosen,
so that you may know and believe me
and understand that I am he.
No god was formed before me,
and there will be none after me.
11 I — I am the LORD.
Besides me, there is no Savior.
12 I alone declared, saved,
and proclaimed —
and not some foreign god[A] among you.
So you are my witnesses" —
this is the LORD's declaration —
"and[B] I am God.
13 Also, from today on I am he alone,
and none can rescue from my power.
I act, and who can reverse it?"

GOD'S DELIVERANCE OF REBELLIOUS ISRAEL

14 This is what the LORD, your Redeemer, the
Holy One of Israel says:
Because of you, I will send an army[C]
to Babylon
and bring all of them as fugitives,[D]
even the Chaldeans in the ships
in which they rejoice.[E]
15 I am the LORD, your Holy One,
the Creator of Israel, your King.

16 This is what the LORD says —
who makes a way in the sea,
and a path through raging water,
17 who brings out the chariot and horse,
the army and the mighty one together
(they lie down, they do not rise again;
they are extinguished, put out
like a wick) —
18 "Do not remember the past events,
pay no attention to things of old.
19 Look, I am about to do something new;
even now it is coming.
Do you not see it?
Indeed, I will make a way
in the wilderness,
rivers[F] in the desert.
20 Wild animals —
jackals and ostriches — will honor me,
because I provide water
in the wilderness,
and rivers in the desert,
to give drink to my chosen people.
21 The people I formed for myself
will declare my praise.

22 "But, Jacob, you have not called on me,
because, Israel, you have
become weary of me.
23 You have not brought me your sheep
for burnt offerings
or honored me with your sacrifices.
I have not burdened you with offerings
or wearied you with incense.[G]
24 You have not bought me aromatic cane
with silver,
or satisfied me with the fat
of your sacrifices.
But you have burdened me
with your sins;
you have wearied me
with your iniquities.

25 "I — I sweep away your transgressions
for my own sake
and remember your sins no more.
26 Remind me. Let's argue
the case together.
Recount the facts, so that you may
be vindicated.
27 Your first father sinned,
and your mediators have rebelled
against me.
28 So I defiled the officers
of the sanctuary,
and set Jacob apart for destruction
and Israel for scorn.

SPIRITUAL BLESSING

44 "And now listen, Jacob my servant,
Israel whom I have chosen.
2 This is the word of the LORD
your Maker, the one who formed you
from the womb:
He will help you.
Do not fear, Jacob my servant,
Jeshurun[H] whom I have chosen.
3 For I will pour water on the thirsty land
and streams on the dry ground;
I will pour out my Spirit
on your descendants
and my blessing on your offspring.

[A] **43:12** Lit *not a foreigner* [B] **43:12** Or *that* [C] **43:14** *an army* supplied for clarity [D] **43:14** Or *will break down all their bars* [E] **43:14** Hb obscure [F] **43:19** DSS read *paths* [G] **43:23** I.e., with demands for offerings and incense [H] **44:2** = Upright One

4 They will sprout among[A] the grass
like poplars by flowing streams.
5 This one will say, 'I am the LORD's';
another will use the name of Jacob;
still another will write on his hand,
'The LORD's,'
and take on the name of Israel."

NO GOD OTHER THAN THE LORD

6 This is what the LORD, the King of Israel and
its Redeemer, the LORD of Armies, says:
I am the first and I am the last.
There is no God but me.
7 Who, like me, can announce the future?
Let him say so and make a case
before me,
since I have established
an ancient people.
Let these gods declare[B]
the coming things,
and what will take place.
8 Do not be startled or afraid.
Have I not told you and declared it
long ago?
You are my witnesses!
Is there any God but me?
There is no other Rock;
I do not know any.

9 All who make idols are nothing,
and what they treasure benefits no one.
Their witnesses do not see
or know anything,
so they will be put to shame.
10 Who makes a god or casts a metal image
that benefits no one?
11 Look, all its worshipers will be
put to shame,
and the craftsmen are humans.
They all will assemble and stand;
they all will be startled
and put to shame.

12 The ironworker labors over the coals,
shapes the idol with hammers,
and works it with his strong arm.
Also he grows hungry
and his strength fails;
he doesn't drink water and is faint.
13 The woodworker stretches out
a measuring line,
he outlines it with a stylus;
he shapes it with chisels
and outlines it with a compass.
He makes it according to
a human form,
like a beautiful person,
to dwell in a temple.
14 He cuts down[C] cedars for his use,
or he takes a cypress or an oak.
He lets it grow strong among the trees
of the forest.
He plants a laurel, and the rain
makes it grow.
15 A person can use it for fuel.
He takes some of it and warms himself;
also he kindles a fire and bakes bread;
he even makes it into a god
and worships it;
he makes an idol from it
and bows down to it.
16 He burns half of it in a fire,
and he roasts meat on that half.
He eats the roast and is satisfied.
He warms himself and says, "Ah!
I am warm, I see the blaze."
17 He makes a god or his idol with the rest
of it.
He bows down to it and worships;
he prays to it, "Save me, for you are
my god."
18 Such people[D] do not comprehend
and cannot understand,
for he has shut their eyes[E]
so they cannot see,
and their minds
so they cannot understand.
19 No one comes to his senses;[F]
no one has the perception or insight
to say,
"I burned half of it in the fire,
I also baked bread on its coals,
I roasted meat and ate.
Should I make something detestable
with the rest of it?
Should I bow down to a block
of wood?"
20 He feeds on[G] ashes.
His deceived mind has led him astray,
and he cannot rescue himself,
or say, "Isn't there a lie
in my right hand?"

21 Remember these things, Jacob,
and Israel, for you are my servant;
I formed you, you are my servant;

[A] **44:4** Some Hb mss, DSS, LXX read *as among* [B] **44:7** Lit *declare them —* [C] **44:14** Lit *To cut down for himself* [D] **44:18** Lit *They* [E] **44:18** Or *for their eyes are shut* [F] **44:19** Lit *No one returns to his heart* [G] **44:20** Or *He shepherds*

Israel, you will never be forgotten
by me.[A]
22 I have swept away your transgressions
like a cloud,
and your sins like a mist.
Return to me,
for I have redeemed you.
23 Rejoice, heavens, for the LORD
has acted;
shout, depths of the earth.
Break out into singing, mountains,
forest, and every tree in it.
For the LORD has redeemed Jacob,
and glorifies himself through Israel.

RESTORATION OF ISRAEL THROUGH CYRUS

24 This is what the LORD, your Redeemer who
formed you from the womb, says:
I am the LORD, who made everything;
who stretched out the heavens
by myself;
who alone spread out the earth;
25 who destroys the omens
of the false prophets
and makes fools of diviners;
who confounds the wise
and makes
their knowledge foolishness;
26 who confirms the message
of his servant
and fulfills the counsel
of his messengers;
who says to Jerusalem, "She will
be inhabited,"
and to the cities of Judah, "They will
be rebuilt,"
and I will restore her ruins;
27 who says to the depths of the sea,
"Be dry,"
and I will dry up your rivers;
28 who says to Cyrus, "My shepherd,
he will fulfill all my pleasure"
and says to Jerusalem, "She will
be rebuilt,"
and of the temple, "Its foundation
will be laid."

45 The LORD says this to Cyrus,
his anointed,
whose right hand I have grasped
to subdue nations before him
and disarm[B] kings,
to open doors before him,
and even city gates will not be shut:
2 "I will go before you
and level the uneven places;[C]
I will shatter the bronze doors
and cut the iron bars in two.
3 I will give you the treasures
of darkness
and riches from secret places,
so that you may know that I am the
LORD.
I am the God of Israel, who calls you
by your name.
4 I call you by your name,
for the sake of my servant Jacob
and Israel my chosen one.
I give a name to you,
though you do not know me.
5 I am the LORD, and there is no other;
there is no God but me.
I will strengthen[D] you,
though you do not know me,
6 so that all may know from the rising
of the sun to its setting
that there is no one but me.
I am the LORD, and there is no other.
7 I form light and create darkness,
I make success and create disaster;
I am the LORD, who does all these things.

8 "Heavens, sprinkle from above,
and let the skies shower righteousness.
Let the earth open up
so that salvation will sprout
and righteousness will spring up
with it.
I, the LORD, have created it.

9 "Woe to the one who argues
with his Maker —
one clay pot among many.[E]
Does clay say to the one forming it,
'What are you making?'
Or does your work say,
'He has no hands'?[F]
10 Woe to the one who says to his father,
'What are you fathering?'
or to his mother,[G]
'What are you giving birth to?'"
11 This is what the LORD,
the Holy One of Israel
and its Maker, says:

[A] **44:21** DSS, LXX, Tg read *Israel, do not forget me* [B] **45:1** Lit *unloosen the waist of* [C] **45:2** DSS, LXX read *the mountains* [D] **45:5** Lit *gird* [E] **45:9** Lit *a clay pot with clay pots of the ground* [F] **45:9** Or *making? Your work has no hands.* [G] **45:10** Lit *to a woman*

"Ask me what is to happen to[A] my sons,
and instruct me about the work
of my hands.
12 I made the earth,
and created humans on it.
It was my hands that stretched out
the heavens,
and I commanded everything in them.
13 I have stirred him up in righteousness,
and will level all roads for him.
He will rebuild my city,
and set my exiles free,
not for a price or a bribe,"
says the LORD of Armies.

GOD ALONE IS THE SAVIOR

14 This is what the LORD says:
"The products of Egypt
and the merchandise of Cush
and the Sabeans, men of stature,
will come over to you
and will be yours;
they will follow you,
they will come over in chains
and bow down to you.
They will confess[B] to you,
'God is indeed with you, and there is
no other;
there is no other God.'"

15 Yes, you are a God who hides,
God of Israel, Savior.
16 All of them are put to shame,
even humiliated;
the makers of idols
go in humiliation together.
17 Israel will be saved by the LORD
with an everlasting salvation;
you will not be put to shame
or humiliated
for all eternity.

18 For this is what the LORD says —
the Creator of the heavens,
the God who formed the earth
and made it,
the one who established it
(he did not create it to be a wasteland,
but formed it to be inhabited) —
he says, "I am the LORD,
and there is no other.
19 I have not spoken in secret,
somewhere in a land of darkness.
I did not say to the descendants
of Jacob:
Seek me in a wasteland.
I am the LORD, who speaks righteously,
who declares what is right.

20 "Come, gather together,
and approach, you fugitives
of the nations.
Those who carry their wooden idols
and pray to a god who cannot save
have no knowledge.
21 Speak up and present your case[C] —
yes, let them consult each other.
Who predicted this long ago?
Who announced it from ancient times?
Was it not I, the LORD?
There is no other God but me,
a righteous God and Savior;
there is no one except me.
22 Turn to me and be saved,
all the ends of the earth.
For I am God,
and there is no other.
23 By myself I have sworn;
truth has gone from my mouth,
a word that will not be revoked:
Every knee will bow to me,
every tongue will swear allegiance.
24 It will be said about me, 'Righteousness
and strength
are found only in the LORD.'"
All who are enraged against him
will come to him and be put to shame.
25 All the descendants of Israel
will be justified and find glory
through the LORD.

THERE IS NO ONE LIKE GOD

46 Bel crouches; Nebo cowers.
Idols depicting them are consigned
to beasts and cattle.
The images you carry are loaded,
as a burden for the weary animal.
2 The gods cower; they crouch together;
they are not able to rescue the burden,
but they themselves go into captivity.

3 "Listen to me, house of Jacob,
all the remnant of the house of Israel,
who have been sustained
from the womb,
carried along since birth.

[A] 45:11 Or *me the coming things about* [B] 45:14 Lit *pray* [C] 45:21 Lit *and approach*

4 I will be the same until your old age,
and I will bear you up when you
turn gray.
I have made you, and I will carry you;
I will bear and rescue you.

5 "Who will you compare me or make me
equal to?
Who will you measure me with,
so that we should be like each other?
6 Those who pour out their bags of gold
and weigh out silver on scales —
they hire a goldsmith and he makes it
into a god.
Then they kneel and bow down to it.
7 They lift it to their shoulder
and bear it along;
they set it in its place, and there
it stands;
it does not budge from its place.
They cry out to it
but it doesn't answer;
it saves no one from his trouble.

8 "Remember this and be brave;[A]
take it to heart, you transgressors!
9 Remember what happened long ago,
for I am God, and there is no other;
I am God, and no one is like me.
10 I declare the end from the beginning,
and from long ago what is not yet done,
saying: my plan will take place,
and I will do all my will.
11 I call a bird of prey[B] from the east,
a man for my purpose
from a far country.
Yes, I have spoken; so I will also
bring it about.
I have planned it; I will also do it.
12 Listen to me, you hardhearted,
far removed from justice:
13 I am bringing my justice near;
it is not far away,
and my salvation will not delay.
I will put salvation in Zion,
my splendor in Israel.

THE FALL OF BABYLON

47 "Go down and sit in the dust,
Virgin Daughter Babylon.
Sit on the ground without a throne,
Daughter Chaldea!
For you will no longer be called
pampered and spoiled.
2 Take millstones and grind flour;
remove your veil,

Eternal Perspective | *God's Power*

THE CAPTAIN AND AUTHOR OF LIFE

"I declare the end from the beginning, and from long ago what is not yet done, saying: my plan will take place, and I will do all my will." Isaiah 46:10

People have tried to explain God's sovereignty (his universal control of everything) in various ways. Here are a couple:

- History is like an ocean liner making its way to a predetermined destination. The vessel will end up there, but the passengers have great freedom while the ship sails.
- Life is like an epic novel, in which the author has planned both the beginning and the end of the story—along with all the major plot twists. But within each individual scene, the characters enjoy agency. That is, they speak and act in ways that enhance the story yet without altering it.

As with all analogies, these fall short or break down. But the truth that God is, as it were, the captain and author of life, is declared all through the Bible. We see it here in the words of Isaiah: "My plan will take place, and I will do all my will."

If you trust the good heart of God, his sovereignty is the best possible news. It means you can sit back and enjoy the cruise. Or you can enjoy being part of the ultimate page-turner!

For the next note on *Eternal Perspective*, see Isaiah 49:15-16.

[A] **46:8** Hb obscure [B] **46:11** = Cyrus

strip off your skirt, bare your thigh,
wade through the streams.
3 Your nakedness will be uncovered,
and your disgrace will be exposed.
I will take vengeance;
I will spare no one."[A]
4 The Holy One of Israel is our Redeemer;
The LORD of Armies is his name.

5 "Daughter Chaldea,
sit in silence and go into darkness.
For you will no longer be called
mistress of kingdoms.
6 I was angry with my people;
I profaned my possession,
and I handed them over to you.
You showed them no mercy;
you made your yoke very heavy
on the elderly.
7 You said, 'I will be the queen forever.'
You did not take these things to heart
or think about their outcome.

8 "So now hear this, lover of luxury,
who sits securely,
who says to herself,
'I am, and there is no one else.
I will never be a widow
or know the loss of children.'
9 These two things will happen to you
suddenly, in one day:
loss of children and widowhood.
They will happen to you
in their entirety,
in spite of your many sorceries
and the potency of your spells.
10 You were secure in your wickedness;
you said, 'No one sees me.'
Your wisdom and knowledge
led you astray.
You said to yourself,
'I am, and there is no one else.'
11 But disaster will happen to you;
you will not know how to avert it.
And it will fall on you,
but you will be unable to ward it off.[B]
Devastation will happen
to you suddenly
and unexpectedly.
12 So take your stand with your spells
and your many sorceries,
which you have wearied yourself with
from your youth.
Perhaps you will be able to succeed;
perhaps you will inspire terror!
13 You are worn out
with your many consultations.
So let the astrologers stand
and save you —
those who observe the stars,
those who predict monthly
what will happen to you.
14 Look, they are like stubble;
fire burns them.
They cannot rescue themselves
from the power[C] of the flame.
This is not a coal
for warming themselves,
or a fire to sit beside!
15 This is what they are to you —
those who have wearied you
and have traded with you
from your youth —
each wanders on his own way;
no one can save you.

ISRAEL MUST LEAVE BABYLON

48 "Listen to this, house of Jacob —
those who are called
by the name Israel
and have descended from[D] Judah,
who swear by the name of the LORD
and declare the God of Israel,
but not in truth or righteousness.
2 For they are named after the Holy City,
and lean on the God of Israel;
his name is the LORD of Armies.
3 I declared the past events long ago;
they came out of my mouth;
I proclaimed them.
Suddenly I acted, and they occurred.
4 Because I know that you are stubborn,
and your neck is iron[E]
and your forehead bronze,
5 therefore I declared to you long ago.
I announced it to you
before it occurred,
so you could not claim, 'My idol
caused them;
my carved image and cast idol
control them.'
6 You have heard it. Observe it all.
Will you not acknowledge it?
From now on I will announce
new things to you,
hidden things that you have not known.

[A] **47:3** Hb obscure [B] **47:11** Or *to atone for it* [C] **47:14** Lit *hand* [D] **48:1** Lit *have come from the waters of* [E] **48:4** Lit *is an iron sinew*

7 They have been created now, and not
long ago;
you have not heard of them
before today,
so you could not claim, 'I already
knew them!'
8 You have never heard; you have
never known;
for a long time your ears have not
been open.
For I knew that you
were very treacherous,
and were known as a rebel from birth.
9 I will delay my anger for the sake
of my name,
and I will restrain myself
for your benefit and for my praise,
so that you will not be destroyed.
10 Look, I have refined you, but not
as silver;
I have tested[A] you in the furnace
of affliction.
11 I will act for my own sake,
indeed, my own,
for how can I[B] be defiled?
I will not give my glory to another.

12 "Listen to me, Jacob,
and Israel, the one called by me:
I am he; I am the first,
I am also the last.
13 My own hand founded the earth,
and my right hand spread out
the heavens;
when I summoned them,
they stood up together.
14 All of you, assemble and listen!
Who among the idols[C] has declared
these things?
The LORD loves him;[D]
he will accomplish his will
against Babylon,
and his arm will be against
the Chaldeans.
15 I — I have spoken;
yes, I have called him;
I have brought him,
and he will succeed in his mission.
16 Approach me and listen to this.
From the beginning I have not spoken
in secret;
from the time anything existed,
I was there."
And now the Lord GOD
has sent me and his Spirit.

17 This is what the LORD, your Redeemer, the
Holy One of Israel says:
I am the LORD your God,
who teaches you for your benefit,
who leads you in the way
you should go.
18 If only you had paid attention
to my commands.
Then your peace would have been
like a river,
and your righteousness like the waves
of the sea.
19 Your descendants would have been
as countless as the sand,
and the offspring of your body
like its grains;
their name would not be cut off
or eliminated from my presence.

20 Leave Babylon,
flee from the Chaldeans!
Declare with a shout of joy,
proclaim this,
let it go out to the end of the earth;
announce,
"The LORD has redeemed
his servant Jacob!"
21 They did not thirst
when he led them through the deserts;
he made water flow from the rock
for them;
he split the rock, and water gushed out.
22 "There is no peace for the wicked,"
says the LORD.

THE SERVANT BRINGS SALVATION

49 Coasts and islands,[E] listen to me;
distant peoples, pay attention.
The LORD called me before I was born.
He named me while I was
in my mother's womb.
2 He made my words like a sharp sword;
he hid me in the shadow of his hand.
He made me like a sharpened arrow;
he hid me in his quiver.
3 He said to me, "You are my servant,
Israel, in whom I will be glorified."
4 But I myself said: I have labored in vain,
I have spent my strength for nothing
and futility;

[A] **48:10** DSS; MT reads *chosen* [B] **48:11** DSS, Syr; MT reads *it* [C] **48:14** Lit *among them* [D] **48:14** = Cyrus [E] **49:1** Or *Islands*

yet my vindication is with the LORD,
and my reward is with my God.
5 And now, says the LORD,
who formed me from the womb to be
his servant,
to bring Jacob back to him
so that Israel might be gathered to him;
for I am honored in the sight
of the LORD,
and my God is my strength —
6 he says,
"It is not enough for you to be
my servant
raising up the tribes of Jacob
and restoring the protected ones
of Israel.
I will also make you a light
for the nations,
to be my salvation to the ends
of the earth."
7 This is what the LORD,
the Redeemer of Israel,
his Holy One, says
to one who is despised,
to one abhorred by people,[A]
to a servant of rulers:
"Kings will see, princes will stand up,
and they[B] will all bow down
because of the LORD,
who is faithful,
the Holy One of Israel —
and he has chosen you."

8 This is what the LORD says:
I will answer you in a time of favor,
and I will help you in the day
of salvation.
I will keep you, and I will appoint you
to be a covenant for the people,
to restore the land,
to make them possess
the desolate inheritances,
9 saying to the prisoners: Come out,
and to those who are in darkness:
Show yourselves.
They will feed along the pathways,
and their pastures will be on all
the barren heights.
10 They will not hunger or thirst,
the scorching heat or sun will not
strike them;
for their compassionate one
will guide them,
and lead them to springs.

Eternal Perspective | *God's Love*

WRITTEN ON HIS PALMS

"Can a woman forget her nursing child, or lack compassion for the child of her womb? Even if these forget, yet I will not forget you. Look, I have inscribed you on the palms of my hands; your walls are continually before me." Isaiah 49:15-16

Tuck this truth away: While our feelings are real, they often do not reflect reality.

Case in point: The exiled Israelites who cried, "The LORD has abandoned me; the Lord has forgotten me!" (49:14).

From their perspective, this *seemed* true. It was not. The Lord talks about having a mother's compassion, about having his people ("Zion" means the people of Jerusalem) "inscribed . . . on the palms of my hands." In other words, in the same way that many contemporary individuals have tattoos of a sweetheart's name or a child's face, the Lord has the names of his beloved children written on his hands! This is God's way of saying to his frightened people, "You feel like I don't see you. I do—of course I do. You are always before me. I not only see, I love you fiercely."

Hold onto this truth today. No matter what you may feel, nothing is more real than God's continual love for you.

For the next note on *Eternal Perspective*, see Isaiah 55:8-9.

[A] **49:7** Or *by the nation* [B] **49:7** Lit *princes and they*

11 I will make all my mountains
into a road,
and my highways will be raised up.
12 See, these will come from far away,
from the north and from the west,[A]
and from the land of Sinim.[B,C]

13 Shout for joy, you heavens!
Earth, rejoice!
Mountains break into joyful shouts!
For the LORD has comforted
his people,
and will have compassion
on his afflicted ones.

ZION REMEMBERED

14 Zion says, "The LORD
has abandoned me;
the Lord has forgotten me!"
15 "Can a woman forget her nursing child,
or lack compassion for the child
of her womb?
Even if these forget,
yet I will not forget you.
16 Look, I have inscribed you on the palms
of my hands;
your walls are continually before me.
17 Your builders[D] hurry;
those who destroy and devastate you
will leave you.
18 Look up, and look around.
They all gather together; they come
to you.
As I live" —
this is the LORD's declaration —
"you will wear all your children[E]
as jewelry,
and put them on as a bride does.
19 For your waste and desolate places
and your land marked by ruins —
will now be indeed too small
for the inhabitants,
and those who swallowed you up
will be far away.
20 Yet as you listen, the children
that you have been deprived of will say,
'This place is too small for me;
make room for me so that I may settle.'
21 Then you will say within yourself,
'Who fathered these for me?
I was deprived of my children
and unable to conceive,
exiled and wandering —
but who brought them up?
See, I was left by myself —
but these, where did they come from?'"[F]

22 This is what the Lord GOD says:
Look, I will lift up my hand
to the nations,
and raise my banner to the peoples.
They will bring your sons in their arms,
and your daughters will be carried
on their shoulders.
23 Kings will be your guardians
and their queens[G]
your nursing mothers.
They will bow down to you
with their faces to the ground
and lick the dust at your feet.
Then you will know that I am the LORD;
those who put their hope in me
will not be put to shame.

24 Can the prey be taken from
a mighty man,
or the captives of a tyrant[H]
be delivered?
25 For this is what the LORD says:
"Even the captives of a mighty man
will be taken,
and the prey of a tyrant will be delivered;
I will contend with the one
who contends with you,
and I will save your children.
26 I will make your oppressors eat
their own flesh,
and they will be drunk
with their own blood
as with sweet wine.
Then all people will know
that I, the LORD, am your Savior,
and your Redeemer, the Mighty One
of Jacob."

50 This is what the LORD says:
Where is your mother's
divorce certificate
that I used to send her away?
Or to which of my creditors
did I sell you?
Look, you were sold for your iniquities,
and your mother was sent away
because of your transgressions.

[A] 49:12 Lit *sea* [B] 49:12 DSS read *of the Syenites* [C] 49:12 Perhaps modern Aswan in southern Egypt [D] 49:17 DSS, Aq, Theod, Vg; MT, Syr, Sym read *sons* [E] 49:18 Lit *all of them* [F] 49:21 Lit *where are they* [G] 49:23 Lit *princesses* [H] 49:24 DSS, Syr, Vg; MT reads *a righteous man*

2 Why was no one there when I came?
Why was there no one to answer
when I called?
Is my arm too weak to redeem?
Or do I have no power to rescue?
Look, I dry up the sea by my rebuke;
I turn the rivers into a wilderness;
their fish rot because of lack of water
and die of thirst.
3 I dress the heavens in black
and make sackcloth their clothing.

THE OBEDIENT SERVANT

4 The Lord God has given me
the tongue of those who are instructed
to know how to sustain the weary
with a word.
He awakens me each morning;
he awakens my ear to listen like those
being instructed.
5 The Lord God has opened my ear,
and I was not rebellious;
I did not turn back.
6 I gave my back to those who beat me,
and my cheeks to those who tore out
my beard.
I did not hide my face from scorn
and spitting.
7 The Lord God will help me;
therefore I have not been humiliated;
therefore I have set my face like flint,
and I know I will not be put to shame.
8 The one who vindicates me is near;
who will contend with me?
Let us confront each other.[A]
Who has a case against me?[B]
Let him come near me!
9 In truth, the Lord God will help me;
who will condemn me?
Indeed, all of them will wear out
like a garment;
a moth will devour them.
10 Who among you fears the LORD
and listens to his servant?
Who among you walks in darkness,
and has no light?
Let him trust in the name of the LORD;
let him lean on his God.
11 Look, all you who kindle a fire,
who encircle yourselves with[C] torches;
walk in the light of your fire
and of the torches you have lit!
This is what you'll get from my hand:
you will lie down
in a place of torment.

SALVATION FOR ZION

51 Listen to me, you
who pursue righteousness,
you who seek the LORD:
Look to the rock from which
you were cut,
and to the quarry from which
you were dug.
2 Look to Abraham your father,
and to Sarah who gave birth to you.
When I called him, he was only one;
I blessed him and made him many.
3 For the LORD will comfort Zion;
he will comfort all her waste places,
and he will make her wilderness
like Eden,
and her desert like the garden
of the LORD.
Joy and gladness will be found in her,
thanksgiving and melodious song.

4 Pay attention to me, my people,
and listen to me, my nation;
for instruction will come from me,
and my justice for a light
to the nations.
I will bring it about quickly.
5 My righteousness is near,
my salvation appears,
and my arms will bring justice
to the nations.
The coasts and islands will put
their hope in me,
and they will look to my strength.[D]
6 Look up to the heavens,
and look at the earth beneath;
for the heavens will vanish
like smoke,
the earth will wear out like a garment,
and its inhabitants will die like gnats.[E]
But my salvation will last forever,
and my righteousness will never
be shattered.

7 Listen to me, you who
know righteousness,
the people in whose heart is
my instruction:
do not fear disgrace by men,
and do not be shattered by their taunts.

[A] **50:8** Lit *us stand* [B] **50:8** Lit *Who is lord of my judgment* [C] **50:11** Syr reads *who set ablaze* [D] **51:5** Lit *arm* [E] **51:6** Or *die in like manner*

8 For moths will devour them
like a garment,
and worms will eat them like wool.
But my righteousness will last forever,
and my salvation for all generations.

9 Wake up, wake up!
Arm of the LORD, clothe yourself with
strength.
Wake up as in days past,
as in generations long ago.
Wasn't it you who hacked Rahab
to pieces,
who pierced the sea monster?
10 Wasn't it you who dried up the sea,
the waters of the great deep,
who made the sea-bed into a road
for the redeemed to pass over?
11 And the redeemed of the LORD will return
and come to Zion with singing,
crowned with unending joy.
Joy and gladness will overtake them,
and sorrow and sighing will flee.

12 I — I am the one who comforts you.
Who are you that you should
fear humans who die,
or a son of man who is given up
like grass?
13 But you have forgotten the LORD,
your Maker,
who stretched out the heavens
and laid the foundations of the earth.
You are in constant dread all day long
because of the fury of the oppressor,
who has set himself to destroy.
But where is the fury of the oppressor?
14 The prisoner[A] is soon to be set free;
he will not die and go to the Pit,
and his food will not be lacking.
15 For I am the LORD your God
who stirs up the sea so that
its waves roar —
his name is the LORD of Armies.
16 I have put my words in your mouth,
and covered you in the shadow
of my hand,
in order to plant[B] the heavens,
to found the earth,
and to say to Zion, "You are my people."

17 Wake yourself, wake yourself up!
Stand up, Jerusalem,
you who have drunk the cup of his fury
from the LORD's hand;
you who have drunk the goblet
to the dregs —
the cup that causes people to stagger.
18 There is no one to guide her
among all the children she has raised;
there is no one to take hold of her hand
among all the offspring
she has brought up.
19 These two things have happened
to you:
devastation and destruction,
famine and sword.
Who will grieve for you?
How can I[C] comfort you?
20 Your children have fainted;
they lie at the head of every street
like an antelope in a net.
They are full of the LORD's fury,
the rebuke of your God.

21 So listen to this, suffering
and drunken one — but not with wine.
22 This is what your Lord says —
the LORD, even your God,
who defends his people —
"Look, I have removed from your hand
the cup that causes staggering;
that goblet, the cup of my fury.
You will never drink it again.
23 I will put it into the hands
of your tormentors,
who said to you:
Lie down, so we can walk over you.
You made your back like the ground,
and like a street for those who walk
on it.

52 "Wake up, wake up;
put on your strength, Zion!
Put on your beautiful garments,
Jerusalem, the Holy City!
For the uncircumcised and the unclean
will no longer enter you.
2 Stand up, shake the dust off yourself!
Take your seat, Jerusalem.
Remove the bonds[D] from your neck,
captive Daughter Zion."
3 For this is what the LORD says:
"You were sold for nothing,
and you will be redeemed
without silver."

[A] **51:14** Hb obscure [B] **51:16** Syr reads *to stretch out* [C] **51:19** DSS, LXX, Syr, Vg read *you? Who can* [D] **52:2** Alt Hb tradition reads *The bonds are removed*

4 For this is what the Lord GOD says:
"At first my people went down to Egypt
to reside there,
then Assyria oppressed them
without cause.[A]
5 So now what have I here" —
this is the LORD's declaration —
"that my people are taken away
for nothing?
Its rulers wail" —
this is the LORD's declaration —
"and my name is continually
blasphemed all day long.
6 Therefore my people will know
my name;
therefore they will know on that day
that I am he who says:
Here I am."

7 How beautiful on the mountains
are the feet of the herald,
who proclaims peace,
who brings news of good things,
who proclaims salvation,
who says to Zion, "Your God reigns!"
8 The voices of your watchmen —
they lift up their voices,
shouting for joy together;
for every eye will see
when the LORD returns to Zion.
9 Be joyful, rejoice together,
you ruins of Jerusalem!
For the LORD has comforted his people;
he has redeemed Jerusalem.
10 The LORD has displayed his holy arm
in the sight of all the nations;
all the ends of the earth will see
the salvation of our God.

11 Leave, leave, go out from there!
Do not touch anything unclean;
go out from her, purify yourselves,
you who carry the vessels of the LORD.
12 For you will not leave in a hurry,
and you will not have to take flight;
because the LORD is going before you,
and the God of Israel is rear guard.

THE SERVANT'S SUFFERING AND EXALTATION

13 See, my servant[B] will be successful;[C]
he will be raised and lifted up
and greatly exalted.
14 Just as many were appalled at you[D] —
his appearance was so disfigured
that he did not look like a man,
and his form did not resemble
a human being —
15 so he will sprinkle many nations.[E]
Kings will shut their mouths
because of him,
for they will see
what had not been told them,
and they will understand
what they had not heard.

53 Who has believed
what we have heard?[F]
And to whom has the arm of the LORD
been revealed?
2 He grew up before him
like a young plant
and like a root out of dry ground.
He didn't have an impressive form
or majesty that we should look at him,
no appearance that we should
desire him.
3 He was despised and rejected by men,
a man of suffering who knew
what sickness was.
He was like someone
people turned away from;[G]
he was despised, and we didn't
value him.

4 Yet he himself bore our sicknesses,
and he carried our pains;
but we in turn regarded him stricken,
struck down by God, and afflicted.
5 But he was pierced because of
our rebellion,
crushed because of our iniquities;
punishment for our peace was on him,
and we are healed by his wounds.
6 We all went astray like sheep;
we all have turned to our own way;
and the LORD has punished him
for[H] the iniquity of us all.

7 He was oppressed and afflicted,
yet he did not open his mouth.
Like a lamb led to the slaughter
and like a sheep silent
before her shearers,
he did not open his mouth.

[A] **52:4** Or *them at last*, or *them for nothing* [B] **52:13** Tg adds *the Messiah* [C] **52:13** Or *will act wisely* [D] **52:14** Some Hb mss, Syr, Tg read *him* [E] **52:15** LXX reads *so many nations will marvel at him* [F] **53:1** Or *believed our report* [G] **53:3** Lit *And like a hiding of faces from him* [H] **53:6** Or *has placed on him*; lit *with*

8 He was taken away because of
oppression and judgment;
and who considered his fate?[A]
For he was cut off from the land
of the living;
he was struck because of
my people's rebellion.
9 He was assigned a grave
with the wicked,
but he was with a rich man at his death,
because he had done no violence
and had not spoken deceitfully.
10 Yet the LORD was pleased to crush him
severely.[B]
When[C] you make him a guilt offering,
he will see his seed, he will prolong
his days,
and by his hand, the LORD's pleasure
will be accomplished.
11 After his anguish,
he will see light[D] and be satisfied.
By his knowledge,
my righteous servant will justify many,
and he will carry their iniquities.
12 Therefore I will give him[E] the many
as a portion,
and he will receive[F] the mighty as spoil,
because he willingly submitted
to death,
and was counted among the rebels;
yet he bore the sin of many
and interceded for the rebels.

FUTURE GLORY FOR ISRAEL

54 "Rejoice, childless one, who did not
give birth;
burst into song and shout,
you who have not been in labor!
For the children of the desolate one
will be more
than the children
of the married woman,"
says the LORD.
2 "Enlarge the site of your tent,
and let your tent curtains
be stretched out;
do not hold back;
lengthen your ropes,
and drive your pegs deep.
3 For you will spread out to the right
and to the left,
and your descendants
will dispossess nations
and inhabit the desolate cities.
4 "Do not be afraid, for you will not
be put to shame;
don't be humiliated, for you will not
be disgraced.
For you will forget the shame
of your youth,
and you will no longer remember
the disgrace of your widowhood.
5 Indeed, your husband is your Maker —
his name is the LORD of Armies —
and the Holy One of Israel is
your Redeemer;
he is called the God of the whole earth.
6 For the LORD has called you,
like a wife deserted and wounded
in spirit,
a wife of one's youth
when she is rejected,"
says your God.
7 "I deserted you for a brief moment,
but I will take you back
with abundant compassion.
8 In a surge of anger
I hid my face from you for a moment,
but I will have compassion on you
with everlasting love,"
says the LORD your Redeemer.
9 "For this is like the days[G] of Noah to me:
when I swore that the water of Noah
would never flood the earth again,
so I have sworn that I will not be angry
with you
or rebuke you.
10 Though the mountains move
and the hills shake,
my love will not be removed from you
and my covenant of peace will not
be shaken,"
says your compassionate LORD.
11 "Poor Jerusalem, storm-tossed,
and not comforted,
I will set your stones in black mortar,[H]
and lay your foundations
in lapis lazuli.
12 I will make your fortifications[I]
out of rubies,
your gates out of sparkling stones,

[A] **53:8** Or *and as for his generation, who considered him?* [B] **53:10** Or *him; he made him sick.* [C] **53:10** Or *If* [D] **53:11** DSS, LXX; MT omits *light* [E] **53:12** Or *him with* [F] **53:12** Or *receive with* [G] **54:9** DSS, Cairo Geniza; MT, LXX read *waters* [H] **54:11** Lit *in antimony* [I] **54:12** Lit *suns*; perhaps *shields*; Ps 84:11

and all your walls out of
precious stones.
13 Then all your children will be taught
by the LORD,
their prosperity will be great,
14 and you will be established
on a foundation of righteousness.
You will be far from oppression,
you will certainly not be afraid;
you will be far from terror,
it will certainly not come near you.
15 If anyone attacks you,
it is not from me;
whoever attacks you
will fall before you.
16 Look, I have created the craftsman
who blows on the charcoal fire
and produces a weapon suitable
for its task;
and I have created the destroyer
to cause havoc.
17 No weapon formed against you
will succeed,
and you will refute any accusation[A]
raised against you in court.
This is the heritage
of the LORD's servants,
and their vindication is from me."
This is the LORD's declaration.

COME TO THE LORD

55 "Come, everyone who is thirsty,
come to the water;
and you without silver,
come, buy, and eat!
Come, buy wine and milk
without silver and without cost!
2 Why do you spend silver on what
is not food,
and your wages on what does not satisfy?
Listen carefully to me, and eat
what is good,
and you will enjoy the choicest
of foods.[B]
3 Pay attention and come to me;
listen, so that you will live.
I will make a permanent covenant
with you
on the basis of the faithful kindnesses
of David.[C]
4 Since I have made him a witness
to the peoples,
a leader and commander
for the peoples,

Rest and Reflection | *Consuming Spiritual Nourishment*

THE BANQUET

"Come, everyone who is thirsty, come to the water; and you without silver, come, buy, and eat! Come, buy wine and milk without silver and without cost! Why do you spend silver on what is not food, and your wages on what does not satisfy? Listen carefully to me, and eat what is good, and you will enjoy the choicest of foods." Isaiah 55:1-2

From the forbidden fruit of Genesis 3 to the marriage supper of the Lamb in Revelation 19, eating is a major focus of the Bible. The calendar of the Jewish people revolved around seven annual festivals (feasts). In the New Testament, one of the Christian church's most meaningful ordinances became a simple meal consisting of bread and wine.

Here, as in many other places, food and drink take on a spiritual meaning. Speaking through the prophet Isaiah, God issues an urgent call for those with thirsty and hungry hearts to "come" (the word occurs four times in verse 1) and enjoy "wine and milk" and the "choicest of foods" (also see 25:6-8).

It's an invitation to the ultimate spiritual banquet—a salvation feast that is "without cost" and where overeating is, frankly, impossible.

Since God offers us the very best of food and drink, why settle for poor substitutes?

For the next note on *Rest and Reflection*, see Jeremiah 2:13.

[A] **54:17** Lit *refute every tongue* [B] **55:2** Lit *enjoy fatness* [C] **55:3** Or *with you, the faithful acts of kindness shown to David*

5 so you will summon a nation
you do not know,
and nations who do not know you
will run to you.
For the LORD your God,
even the Holy One of Israel,
has glorified you."

6 Seek the LORD while he may be found;
call to him while he is near.
7 Let the wicked one abandon his way
and the sinful one his thoughts;
let him return to the LORD,
so he may have compassion on him,
and to our God, for he will
freely forgive.

8 "For my thoughts are not
your thoughts,
and your ways are not my ways."
This is the LORD's declaration.
9 "For as heaven is higher than earth,
so my ways are higher than your ways,
and my thoughts than your thoughts.
10 For just as rain and snow fall
from heaven
and do not return there
without saturating the earth
and making it germinate and sprout,
and providing seed to sow
and food to eat,
11 so my word that comes
from my mouth
will not return to me empty,
but it will accomplish what I please
and will prosper
in what I send it to do."

12 You will indeed go out with joy
and be peacefully guided;
the mountains and the hills will break
into singing before you,
and all the trees of the field will clap
their hands.
13 Instead of the thornbush, a cypress
will come up,
and instead of the brier, a myrtle
will come up;
this will stand as a monument for the
LORD,
an everlasting sign that will not
be destroyed.

Eternal Perspective | *Personal Limitations*

SURRENDERING TO MYSTERY

"'For my thoughts are not your thoughts, and your ways are not my ways.' This is the LORD's declaration. 'For as heaven is higher than earth, so my ways are higher than your ways, and my thoughts than your thoughts.'" Isaiah 55:8-9

If God is wise and good and powerful, how do we explain the existence of evil and suffering in the world? How can one God exist as three distinct persons: Father, Son, and Holy Spirit? How can Jesus be fully God and fully human? How do we reconcile the claim that God is in control of all things with the idea that we are responsible for our choices?

These are only a handful of the great spiritual mysteries and mind-bending questions we face in life. And while theologians sometimes give answers that make logical sense, those explanations don't always satisfy emotionally.

In the end, we must remember the humbling truth that we are finite creatures with limited understanding. So much about God's thoughts and ways we either can't grasp or will never be privy to. Eventually, we have to surrender to the truth that our infinite God is transcendent and awesome and mysterious.

In a real sense, this kind of surrender opens the way to the spiritual life. Learning to be content with some unanswered whys and hows is the path to peace.

For the next note on *Eternal Perspective*, see Isaiah 61:1-2.

A HOUSE OF PRAYER FOR ALL

56 This is what the LORD says:
Preserve justice and do what is right,
for my salvation is coming soon,
and my righteousness will be revealed.
2 Happy is the person who does this,
the son of man who holds it fast,
who keeps the Sabbath
without desecrating it,
and keeps his hand from doing
any evil.

3 No foreigner who has joined himself
to the LORD
should say,
"The LORD will exclude me
from his people,"
and the eunuch should not say,
"Look, I am a dried-up tree."
4 For the LORD says this:
"For the eunuchs who keep
my Sabbaths,
and choose what pleases me,
and hold firmly to my covenant,
5 I will give them, in my house
and within my walls,
a memorial and a name
better than sons and daughters.
I will give each of them
an everlasting name
that will never be cut off.
6 As for the foreigners who join
themselves to the LORD
to minister to him, to
love the name of the LORD,
and to become his servants —
all who keep the Sabbath
without desecrating it
and who hold firmly
to my covenant —
7 I will bring them
to my holy mountain
and let them rejoice in my house
of prayer.
Their burnt offerings and sacrifices
will be acceptable on my altar,
for my house will be called a house
of prayer
for all nations."
8 This is the declaration of the Lord GOD,
who gathers the dispersed of Israel:
"I will gather to them still others
besides those already gathered."

UNRIGHTEOUS LEADERS CONDEMNED

9 All you animals of the field and forest,
come and eat!
10 Israel's[A] watchmen are blind, all of them,
they know nothing;
all of them are mute dogs,
they cannot bark;
they dream, lie down,
and love to sleep.
11 These dogs have fierce appetites;
they never have enough.
And they are shepherds
who have no discernment;
all of them turn to their own way,
every last one for his own profit.
12 "Come, let me get some wine,
let's guzzle some beer;
and tomorrow will be like today,
only far better!"

57 The righteous person perishes,
and no one takes it to heart;
the faithful are taken away,
with no one realizing
that the righteous person is taken away
because of[B] evil.
2 He will enter into peace —
they will rest on their beds[C] —
everyone who lives uprightly.

PAGAN RELIGION DENOUNCED

3 But come here,
you witch's sons,
offspring of an adulterer
and a prostitute![D]
4 Who are you mocking?
Who are you opening your mouth
and sticking out your tongue at?
Isn't it you, you rebellious children,
you offspring of liars,
5 who burn with lust among the oaks,
under every green tree,
who slaughter children in the wadis
below the clefts of the rocks?
6 Your portion is
among the smooth stones of the wadi;
indeed, they are your lot.
You have even poured out
a drink offering to them;
you have offered a grain offering;
should I be satisfied with these?
7 You have placed your bed
on a high and lofty mountain;

[A] **56:10** Or *His*, or *Its* [B] **57:1** Or *taken away from the presence of* [C] **57:2** Either their deathbeds or their graves [D] **57:3** Lit *and she acted as a prostitute*

you also went up there
to offer sacrifice.
8 You have set up your memorial
behind the door and doorpost.
For away from me, you stripped,
went up, and made your bed wide,
and you have made a bargain[A]
for yourself with them.
You have loved their bed;
you have gazed on their genitals.[B,C]
9 You went to the king with oil
and multiplied your perfumes;
you sent your envoys far away
and sent them down even to Sheol.
10 You became weary
on your many journeys,
but you did not say, "It's hopeless!"
You found a renewal of your strength;[D]
therefore you did not grow weak.
11 Who was it you dreaded and feared,
so that you lied and didn't
remember me
or take it to heart?
I have kept silent for a long time,
haven't I?[E]
So you do not fear me.
12 I will announce your righteousness,
and your works — they will not
profit you.
13 When you cry out,
let your collection of idols rescue you!
The wind will carry all of them off,
a breath will take them away.
But whoever takes refuge in me
will inherit the land
and possess my holy mountain.

HEALING AND PEACE

14 He said,
"Build it up, build it up, prepare the way,
remove every obstacle
from my people's way."
15 For the High and Exalted One,
who lives forever, whose name is holy,
says this:
"I live in a high and holy place,
and with the oppressed and lowly
of spirit,
to revive the spirit of the lowly
and revive the heart of the oppressed.
16 For I will not accuse you forever,
and I will not always be angry;
for then the spirit would grow weak
before me,
even the breath, which I have made.
17 Because of his sinful greed I was angry,
so I struck him; I was angry and hid;
but he went on turning back
to the desires of his heart.
18 I have seen his ways,
but I will heal him;
I will lead him and restore comfort
to him and his mourners,
19 creating words of praise."[F]
The LORD says,
"Peace, peace to the one who is far
or near,
and I will heal him.
20 But the wicked are
like the storm-tossed sea,
for it cannot be still,
and its water churns up mire
and muck.
21 There is no peace for the wicked,"
says my God.

TRUE FASTING

58 "Cry out loudly,[G] don't hold back!
Raise your voice like a trumpet.
Tell my people their transgression
and the house of Jacob their sins.
2 They seek me day after day
and delight to know my ways,
like a nation that does what is right
and does not abandon the justice
of their God.
They ask me for righteous judgments;
they delight in the nearness of God."
3 "Why have we fasted,
but you have not seen?
We have denied ourselves,
but you haven't noticed!"[H]
"Look, you do as you please on the day
of your fast,
and oppress all your workers.
4 You fast with contention and strife
to strike viciously with your fist.
You cannot fast as you do today,
hoping to make your voice heard
on high.
5 Will the fast I choose be like this:
A day for a person to deny himself,
to bow his head like a reed,
and to spread out sackcloth and ashes?

[A] **57:8** Lit *you cut* [B] **57:8** Lit *hand* [C] **57:8** In Hb, the word "hand" is probably a euphemism for *genitals*. [D] **57:10** Lit *found life of your hand* [E] **57:11** LXX reads *And I, when I see you, I pass by* [F] **57:19** Lit *creating fruit of the lips* [G] **58:1** Lit *with throat* [H] **58:3** These are Israel's words to God.

The LORD will always lead you,
satisfy you in a parched land,
and strengthen your bones. You
will be like a watered garden
and like a spring whose
water never runs dry.
—Isaiah 58:11

Will you call this a fast
and a day acceptable to the LORD?
6 Isn't this the fast I choose:
To break the chains of wickedness,
to untie the ropes of the yoke,
to set the oppressed free,
and to tear off every yoke?
7 Is it not to share your bread
with the hungry,
to bring the poor and homeless
into your house,
to clothe the naked when you see him,
and not to ignore your own flesh
and blood?[A]
8 Then your light will appear
like the dawn,
and your recovery will come quickly.
Your righteousness will go before you,
and the LORD's glory will be
your rear guard.
9 At that time, when you call, the LORD
will answer;
when you cry out, he will say,
'Here I am.'
If you get rid of the yoke among you,
the finger-pointing
and malicious speaking,
10 and if you offer yourself[B] to the hungry,
and satisfy the afflicted one,
then your light will shine
in the darkness,
and your night will be like noonday.
11 The LORD will always lead you,
satisfy you in a parched land,
and strengthen your bones.
You will be like a watered garden
and like a spring whose water
never runs dry.
12 Some of you will rebuild
the ancient ruins;
you will restore the foundations laid
long ago;
you will be called the repairer
of broken walls,
the restorer of streets
where people live.

13 "If you keep from desecrating[C]
the Sabbath,
from doing whatever you want
on my holy day;
if you call the Sabbath a delight,
and the holy day of the LORD honorable;
if you honor it, not going
your own ways,
seeking your own pleasure,
or talking business;[D,E]
14 then you will delight in the LORD,
and I will make you ride
over the heights of the land,
and let you enjoy the heritage
of your father Jacob."
For the mouth of the LORD has spoken.

SIN AND REDEMPTION

59 Indeed, the LORD's arm is not
too weak to save,
and his ear is not too deaf to hear.
2 But your iniquities are separating you
from your God,
and your sins have hidden his face
from you
so that he does not listen.
3 For your hands are defiled with blood
and your fingers, with iniquity;
your lips have spoken lies,
and your tongues mutter injustice.
4 No one makes claims justly;
no one pleads honestly.
They trust in empty
and worthless words;
they conceive trouble and give birth
to iniquity.
5 They hatch viper's eggs
and weave spider's webs.
Whoever eats their eggs will die;
crack one open,
and a viper is hatched.
6 Their webs cannot become clothing,
and they cannot cover themselves
with their works.

[A] **58:7** Lit *not hide yourself from your flesh* [B] **58:10** Some Hb mss, LXX, Syr read *offer your bread* [C] **58:13** Lit *keep your foot from* [D] **58:13** Or *idly* [E] **58:13** Lit *or speak a word*

Their works are sinful works,
and violent acts are in their hands.
7 Their feet run after evil,
and they rush to shed innocent blood.
Their thoughts are sinful thoughts;
ruin and wretchedness are
in their paths.
8 They have not known the path of peace,
and there is no justice in their ways.
They have made their roads crooked;
no one who walks on them
will know peace.

9 Therefore justice is far from us,
and righteousness does not reach us.
We hope for light, but there is darkness;
for brightness, but we live in the night.
10 We grope along a wall like the blind;
we grope like those without eyes.
We stumble at noon as though
it were twilight;
we are like the dead among those
who are healthy.
11 We all growl like bears
and moan like doves.
We hope for justice, but there is none;
for salvation, but it is far from us.
12 For our transgressions have multiplied
before you,
and our sins testify against us.
For our transgressions are with us,
and we know our iniquities:
13 transgression and deception
against the LORD,
turning away from following our God,
speaking oppression and revolt,
conceiving and uttering lying words
from the heart.
14 Justice is turned back,
and righteousness stands far off.
For truth has stumbled
in the public square,
and honesty cannot enter.
15 Truth is missing,
and whoever turns from evil
is plundered.

The LORD saw that there was no justice,
and he was offended.
16 He saw that there was no man —
he was amazed that there was
no one interceding;
so his own arm brought salvation,
and his own righteousness
supported him.
17 He put on righteousness as body armor,
and a helmet of salvation on his head;
he put on garments of vengeance
for clothing,
and he wrapped himself in zeal
as in a cloak.
18 So he will repay according to
their deeds:
fury to his enemies,
retribution to his foes,
and he will repay the coasts and islands.
19 They will fear the name of the LORD
in the west
and his glory in the east;[A]
for he will come like a rushing stream
driven by the wind of the LORD.
20 "The Redeemer will come to Zion,
and to those in Jacob who turn
from transgression."
This is the LORD's declaration.

21 "As for me, this is my covenant with them,"
says the LORD: "My Spirit who is on you, and my
words that I have put in your mouth, will not
depart from your mouth, or from the mouths
of your children, or from the mouths of your
children's children, from now on and forever,"
says the LORD.

THE LORD'S GLORY IN ZION

60 Arise, shine, for your light has come,
and the glory of the LORD shines
over you.[B]
2 For look, darkness will cover the earth,
and total darkness the peoples;
but the LORD will shine over you,
and his glory will appear over you.
3 Nations will come to your light,
and kings to your shining brightness.
4 Raise your eyes and look around:
they all gather and come to you;
your sons will come from far away,
and your daughters on the hips of
nannies.
5 Then you will see and be radiant,
and your heart will tremble
and rejoice,[C]
because the riches of the sea
will become yours
and the wealth of the nations will come
to you.

[A] 59:19 Lit *sunrise* [B] 60:1 = Jerusalem [C] 60:5 Lit *expand*

6 Caravans of camels will cover
your land[A] —
young camels of Midian and Ephah —
all of them will come from Sheba.
They will carry gold and frankincense
and proclaim the praises of the LORD.
7 All the flocks of Kedar will be gathered
to you;
the rams of Nebaioth will serve you
and go up on my altar
as an acceptable sacrifice.
I will glorify my beautiful house.
8 Who are these who fly like a cloud,
like doves to their shelters?
9 Yes, the coasts and islands will wait
for me
with the ships of Tarshish in the lead,
to bring your children from far away,
their silver and gold with them,
for the honor of the LORD your God,
the Holy One of Israel,
who has glorified you.
10 Foreigners will rebuild your walls,
and their kings will serve you.
Although I struck you in my wrath,
yet I will show mercy to you
with my favor.
11 Your city gates will always be open;
they will never be shut day or night
so that the wealth of the nations
may be brought into you,
with their kings being led
in procession.
12 For the nation and the kingdom
that will not serve you will perish;
those nations will be annihilated.
13 The glory of Lebanon will come
to you —
its pine, elm, and cypress together —
to beautify the place of my sanctuary,
and I will glorify my dwelling place.[B]
14 The sons of your oppressors
will come and bow down to you;
all who reviled you
will fall facedown at your feet.
They will call you the City of the LORD,
Zion of the Holy One of Israel.
15 Instead of your being deserted
and hated,
with no one passing through,
I will make you an object of eternal pride,
a joy from age to age.
16 You will nurse on the milk of nations,
and nurse at the breast of kings;
you will know that I, the LORD,
am your Savior
and Redeemer, the Mighty One
of Jacob.
17 I will bring gold instead of bronze;
I will bring silver instead of iron,
bronze instead of wood,
and iron instead of stones.
I will appoint peace as your government
and righteousness as your overseers.
18 Violence will never again be heard of
in your land;
devastation and destruction
will be gone from your borders.
You will call your walls Salvation
and your city gates Praise.
19 The sun will no longer be your light
by day,
and the brightness of the moon
will not shine on you.
The LORD will be your everlasting light,
and your God will be your splendor.
20 Your sun will no longer set,
and your moon will not fade;
for the LORD will be
your everlasting light,
and the days of your sorrow
will be over.
21 All your people will be righteous;
they will possess the land forever;
they are the branch I planted,
the work of my[C] hands,
so that I may be glorified.
22 The least will become a thousand,
the smallest a mighty nation.
I am the LORD;
I will accomplish it quickly
in its time.

MESSIAH'S JUBILEE

61 The Spirit of the Lord GOD is on me,
because the LORD has anointed me
to bring good news to the poor.
He has sent me to heal[D]
the brokenhearted,
to proclaim liberty to the captives
and freedom to the prisoners;
2 to proclaim the year of the LORD's favor,
and the day of our God's vengeance;
to comfort all who mourn,

[A] **60:6** Lit *cover you* [B] **60:13** Lit *glorify the place of my feet* [C] **60:21** LXX, DSS read *his* [D] **61:1** Lit *bind up*

3 to provide for those who mourn
in Zion;
to give them a crown of beauty
instead of ashes,
festive oil instead of mourning,
and splendid clothes
instead of despair.[A]
And they will be called righteous trees,
planted by the LORD
to glorify him.

4 They will rebuild the ancient ruins;
they will restore
the former devastations;
they will renew the ruined cities,
the devastations
of many generations.
5 Strangers will stand and feed
your flocks,
and foreigners will be your plowmen
and vinedressers.
6 But you will be called
the LORD's priests;
they will speak of you as ministers
of our God;
you will eat the wealth of the nations,
and you will boast in their riches.
7 In place of your shame, you will have
a double portion;
in place of disgrace, they will rejoice
over their share.
So they will possess double
in their land,
and eternal joy will be theirs.

8 For I the LORD love justice;
I hate robbery and injustice;[B]
I will faithfully reward my people
and make a permanent covenant
with them.
9 Their descendants will be known
among the nations,
and their posterity among the peoples.
All who see them will recognize
that they are a people the LORD
has blessed.

10 I rejoice greatly in the LORD,
I exult in my God;
for he has clothed me
with the garments of salvation
and wrapped me in a robe
of righteousness,
as a groom wears a turban

E Eternal Perspective | *Biblical Hope*

THE SAVIOR WE NEED

"The Spirit of the Lord GOD is on me, because the LORD has anointed me to bring good news to the poor. He has sent me to heal the brokenhearted, to proclaim liberty to the captives and freedom to the prisoners; to proclaim the year of the LORD's favor." Isaiah 61:1-2

Skimming the day's headlines can be a bullet train to despair. The world has so much inhumanity and tragedy. Everywhere we look, people are suffering from addiction, disease, and poverty. From war zones to natural disasters to the halls of government, not much news is good.

Which is why this prophetic passage is so marvelous to contemplate. Recorded by Isaiah in about 700 BC, it looks forward to an "anointed" one (the Hebrew word from which we get our English word "Messiah'). Speaking through the prophet, this coming one claims to be guided by "the Spirit of the Lord GOD." He says he is "sent" by the Lord "to bring good news," to heal, and to proclaim liberty.

Jesus did precisely that in his earthly ministry. In fact, he began his public ministry by reading this very passage in his hometown synagogue and declaring it "fulfilled" (Lk 4:16-21).

When the bad news on TV or online gets you down, the good news in the Gospels can restore your hope.

For the next note on *Eternal Perspective*, see Jeremiah 1:5.

[A] **61:3** Lit *a dim spirit* [B] **61:8** Some Hb mss, DSS, LXX, Syr, Tg, Vg; other Hb mss read *robbery with a burnt offering*

and as a bride adorns herself
with her jewels.
11 For as the earth produces its growth,
and as a garden enables what is sown
to spring up,
so the Lord God
will cause righteousness and praise
to spring up before all the nations.

ZION'S RESTORATION

62 I will not keep silent because of Zion,
and I will not keep still
because of Jerusalem,
until her righteousness shines
like a bright light
and her salvation, like a flaming torch.
2 Nations will see your righteousness
and all kings, your glory.
You will be given a new name
that the LORD's mouth will announce.
3 You will be a glorious crown
in the LORD's hand,
and a royal diadem in the palm
of your God's hand.
4 You will no longer be called Deserted,
and your land will not
be called Desolate;
instead, you will be called My Delight
Is in Her,[A]
and your land Married;[B]
for the LORD delights in you,
and your land will be married.
5 For as a young man marries
a young woman,
so your sons will marry you;
and as a groom rejoices over his bride,
so your God will rejoice over you.

6 Jerusalem,
I have appointed watchmen
on your walls;
they will never be silent, day or night.
There is no rest for you,
who remind the LORD.
7 Do not give him rest
until he establishes
and makes Jerusalem
the praise of the earth.

8 The LORD has sworn with his right hand
and his strong arm:
I will no longer give your grain
to your enemies for food,
and foreigners will not drink
the new wine
for which you have labored.
9 For those who gather grain will eat it
and praise the LORD,
and those who harvest the grapes
will drink the wine
in my holy courts.

10 Go out, go out through the city gates;
prepare a way for the people!
Build it up, build up the highway;
clear away the stones!
Raise a banner for the peoples.
11 Look, the LORD has proclaimed
to the ends of the earth,
"Say to Daughter Zion:
Look, your salvation is coming,
his wages are with him,
and his reward accompanies him."
12 And they will be called[C] the Holy People,
the LORD's Redeemed;
and you will be called Cared For,
A City Not Deserted.

THE LORD'S DAY OF VENGEANCE

63 Who is this coming from Edom
in crimson-stained garments
from Bozrah —
this one who is splendid in his apparel,
striding in his formidable[D] might?

It is I, proclaiming vindication,[E]
powerful to save.

2 Why are your clothes red,
and your garments like one who treads
a winepress?

3 I trampled the winepress alone,
and no one from the nations was
with me.
I trampled them in my anger
and ground them underfoot in my fury;
their blood spattered my garments,
and all my clothes were stained.
4 For I planned the day of vengeance,
and the year of my redemption[F] came.
5 I looked, but there was no one to help,
and I was amazed that no one assisted;
so my arm accomplished victory
for me,
and my wrath assisted me.

[A] **62:4** Or *Hephzibah* [B] **62:4** Or *Beulah* [C] **62:12** Lit *will call them* [D] **63:1** Syr, Vg read *apparel, striding forward in* [E] **63:1** Or *righteousness* [F] **63:4** Or *blood retribution*

12 I will destine you for the sword,
and all of you will kneel down
to be slaughtered,
because I called
and you did not answer,
I spoke and you did not hear;
you did what was evil in my sight
and chose what I did not delight in."

13 Therefore, this is what the Lord GOD says:
"My servants will eat,
but you will be hungry;
my servants will drink,
but you will be thirsty;
my servants will rejoice,
but you will be put to shame.
14 My servants will shout for joy
from a glad heart,
but you will cry out
from an anguished heart,
and you will lament out of
a broken spirit.
15 You will leave your name behind
as a curse for my chosen ones,
and the Lord GOD will kill you;
but he will give his servants
another name.
16 Whoever asks for a blessing in the land
will ask for a blessing by the God
of truth,
and whoever swears in the land
will swear by the God of truth.
For the former troubles
will be forgotten
and hidden from my sight.

A NEW CREATION

17 "For I will create a new heaven
and a new earth;
the past events will not be remembered
or come to mind.

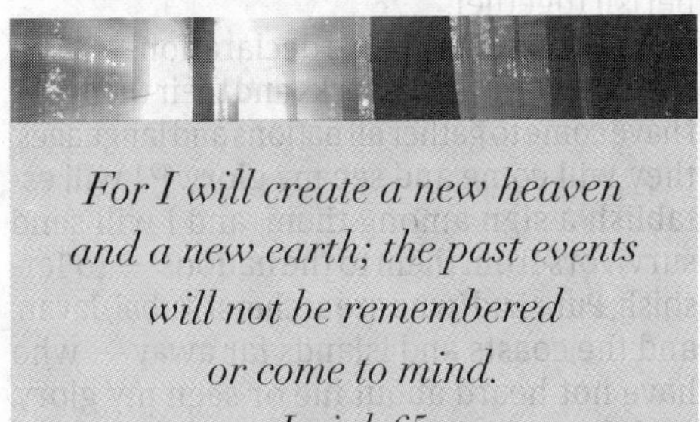

For I will create a new heaven and a new earth; the past events will not be remembered or come to mind.
—Isaiah 65:17

18 Then be glad and rejoice forever
in what I am creating;
for I will create Jerusalem to be a joy
and its people to be a delight.
19 I will rejoice in Jerusalem
and be glad in my people.
The sound of weeping and crying
will no longer be heard in her.
20 In her, a nursing infant will no longer live
only a few days,[A]
or an old man not live out his days.
Indeed, the one who dies at a hundred
years old
will be mourned as a young man,[B]
and the one who misses
a hundred years
will be considered cursed.
21 People will build houses and live
in them;
they will plant vineyards and eat
their fruit.
22 They will not build and others live
in them;
they will not plant and others eat.
For my people's lives will be
like the lifetime of a tree.
My chosen ones will fully enjoy
the work of their hands.
23 They will not labor without success
or bear children destined for disaster,
for they will be a people blessed
by the LORD
along with their descendants.
24 Even before they call, I will answer;
while they are still speaking, I will hear.
25 The wolf and the lamb
will feed together,[C]
and the lion will eat straw like cattle,
but the serpent's food will be dust!
They will not do what is evil or destroy
on my entire holy mountain,"
says the LORD.

FINAL JUDGMENT AND JOYOUS RESTORATION

66 This is what the LORD says:
Heaven is my throne,
and earth is my footstool.
Where could you possibly build a house
for me?
And where would my resting place be?
2 My hand made all these things,
and so they all came into being.
This is the LORD's declaration.

[A] **65:20** Lit *her, no longer infant of days* [B] **65:20** Lit *the youth of a hundred years will die* [C] **65:25** Lit *as one*

I will look favorably on this kind
of person:
one who is humble, submissive[A] in spirit,
and trembles at my word.
3 One person slaughters an ox,
another kills a person;
one person sacrifices a lamb,
another breaks a dog's neck;
one person offers a grain offering,
another offers pig's blood;
one person offers incense,
another praises an idol —
all these have chosen their ways
and delight
in their abhorrent practices.
4 So I will choose their punishment,
and I will bring on them
what they dread
because I called and no one answered;
I spoke and they did not listen;
they did what was evil in my sight
and chose what I did not delight in.

5 You who tremble at his word,
hear the word of the LORD:
"Your brothers who hate
and exclude you
for my name's sake have said,
'Let the LORD be glorified
so that we can see your joy!'
But they will be put to shame."

6 A sound of uproar from the city!
A voice from the temple —
the voice of the LORD,
paying back his enemies
what they deserve!

7 Before Zion was in labor, she gave birth;
before she was in pain, she delivered
a boy.
8 Who has heard of such a thing?
Who has seen such things?
Can a land be born in one day
or a nation be delivered in an instant?
Yet as soon as Zion was in labor,
she gave birth to her sons.
9 "Will I bring a baby to the point of birth
and not deliver it?"
says the LORD;
"or will I who deliver,
close the womb?"
says your God.

10 Be glad for Jerusalem and rejoice
over her,
all who love her.
Rejoice greatly with her,
all who mourn over her —
11 so that you may nurse and be satisfied
from her comforting breast
and drink deeply
and delight yourselves
from her glorious breasts.

12 For this is what the LORD says:
I will make peace flow to her
like a river,
and the wealth[B] of nations
like a flood;
you will nurse and be carried
on her hip
and bounced on her lap.
13 As a mother comforts her son,
so I will comfort you,
and you will be comforted
in Jerusalem.

14 You will see, you will rejoice,
and you[C] will flourish like grass;
then the LORD's power will be revealed
to his servants,
but he will show his wrath
against his enemies.
15 Look, the LORD will come with fire —
his chariots are like the whirlwind —
to execute his anger with fury
and his rebuke with flames of fire.
16 For the LORD will execute judgment
on all people with his fiery sword,
and many will be slain by the LORD.

17 "Those who dedicate and purify themselves
to enter the groves following their leader,[D]
eating meat from pigs, vermin,[E] and rats, will
perish together."
This is the LORD's declaration.
18 "Knowing[F] their works and their thoughts,
I have come to gather all nations and languages;
they will come and see my glory. 19 I will establish a sign among them, and I will send
survivors from them to the nations — to Tarshish, Put,[G] Lud (who are archers), Tubal, Javan,
and the coasts and islands far away — who
have not heard about me or seen my glory.
And they will proclaim my glory among the
nations. 20 They will bring all your brothers

[A] **66:2** Lit *broken* [B] **66:12** Or *glory* [C] **66:14** Lit *your bones* [D] **66:17** Hb obscure [E] **66:17** Lit *abhorrent things* [F] **66:18** LXX, Syr; MT omits *Knowing* [G] **66:19** LXX; MT reads *Pul*

from all the nations as a gift to the LORD on
horses and chariots, in litters, and on mules
and camels, to my holy mountain Jerusalem,"
says the LORD, "just as the Israelites bring an
offering in a clean vessel to the house of the
LORD. 21 I will also take some of them as priests
and Levites," says the LORD.

22 "For just as the new heavens
and the new earth,
which I will make,
will remain before me" —
this is the LORD's declaration —
"so your offspring and your name
will remain.

23 All mankind will come to worship me
from one New Moon to another
and from one Sabbath to another,"
says the LORD.

24 "As they leave, they will see the dead bodies of those who have rebelled against me; for their worm will never die, their fire will never go out, and they will be a horror to all mankind."

Jeremiah—Even the most faithful followers of Christ experience ups and downs in their relationship with him. Throughout the Old Testament God's people also had their ups and downs. They frequently fell into idolatry and neglected the worship of God.

At one of these low points, God called Jeremiah to be his mouthpiece. He gave him messages, visions, and symbolic demonstrations to call the nation of Judah to repentance.

But in the messages of condemnation, we always find hope of restoration. In fact, the book of Jeremiah contains the longest description in the Old Testament of the new covenant (31:31-34). Jesus ushered in this new covenant, and now by the Holy Spirit we have his law in our hearts. We are changed from the inside out, transformed into new creatures by his grace.

If you are struggling to reconcile the judgment and mercy of God, linger in the passages of Jeremiah that describe the restoration God offers to his children. This is a book of hope that shows God tenderly and repeatedly calling his people back to the path of life. Will you respond to his invitation to repent and return to him?

JEREMIAH

AUTHOR: Jeremiah, a priest from the town of Anathoth

DATE WRITTEN: The events in Jeremiah's prophetic ministry described in the book lasted from 640–580 BC.

ORIGINAL AUDIENCE: The Israelites, specifically Judah

SETTING: The kingdom of Israel had already fallen, and it was the last days for the kingdom of Judah before the exile. Following the reforms of King Hezekiah, his son Manasseh turned the nation back to idolatry. During this time, the nation fell so far away from God that they even lost track of the book of the law for a time. Onto this scene came Jeremiah, speaking the Lord's words of judgment against Judah and extending a loving invitation for them to repent and turn back to him.

PURPOSE FOR WRITING: Jeremiah warned the people of Judah to turn back to God before it was too late. God will always take us back, no matter how far we have run away from him. We just need to repent of our sins and turn to him in humble obedience that proves the sincerity of our repentance. Jeremiah reminds us that God lovingly welcomes every repentant sinner into his loving embrace.

OUTLINE:

1. Prologue: Call and Vision (1:1-19)
2. Call for Repentance (2:1–25:38)

   Early messages (2:1–20:18)

   Indictments against Israel's leadership (21:1–24:10)

   Judgment against the nations (25:1-38)
3. Jeremiah's Firm Stand Despite Opposition (26:1–36:32)

   Temple sermon (26:1-24)

   Yoke of Babylon (27:1-22)

   Hananiah, a false prophet (28:1-17)

   Letters to the exiles (29:1-32)

   Book of consolation (30:1–33:26)

   Judgment for Zedekiah (34:1-22)

   Obedience of the Rechabites (35:1-19)

   Writing and rewriting of the scroll (36:1-32)
4. Destruction of Jerusalem (37:1–45:5)

   Jeremiah and King Zedekiah (37:1–38:28)

   Jerusalem's defeat by Babylon; Jeremiah's rescue (39:1-18)

   Judah and Governor Gedaliah (40:1–41:18)

   Jeremiah's advice against going to Egypt (42:1-22)

   The people's rejection of Jeremiah's counsel (43:1–44:30)

   God's word to Baruch (45:1-5)
5. Prophecies against the Nations (46:1–51:64)
6. Epilogue: The Fall of Jerusalem (52:1-34)

KEY VERSE:

"'For I know the plans I have for you'—this is the LORD's declaration—'plans for your well-being, not for disaster, to give you a future and a hope.'" –Jeremiah 29:11

RESTORATION THEMES

R	Rest and Reflection	*Consuming Spiritual Nourishment—2:13*
E	Eternal Perspective	*God's Knowledge/Omniscience—1:5* *Biblical Hope—29:11* *God's Work in Us—31:33* *God's Power—32:26-27*
S	Support	*Prayer—20:7,9*
T	Thanksgiving and Contentment	*Repentance—3:22*
O	Other-centeredness	*Being Compassionate—9:1*
R	Relationships	*Offering Forgiveness—15:21*
E	Exercise of Faith	*Responding to Trials—1:19* *Praying—33:2-3* *Trusting God—38:6* *Rejecting the World's Lies—43:1-2*

1 The words of Jeremiah, the son of Hilkiah,
one of the priests living in Anathoth in the
territory of Benjamin. 2 The word of the LORD
came to him in the thirteenth year of the reign
of Josiah son of Amon, king of Judah. 3 It also
came throughout the days of Jehoiakim son
of Josiah, king of Judah, until the fifth month
of the eleventh year of Zedekiah son of Josiah,
king of Judah, when the people of Jerusalem
went into exile.

THE CALL OF JEREMIAH

4 The word of the LORD came to me:

5 I chose you before I formed you
in the womb;
I set you apart before you were born.
I appointed you a prophet to the nations.

6 But I protested, "Oh no, Lord GOD! Look,
I don't know how to speak since I am only
a youth."
7 Then the LORD said to me:

Do not say, "I am only a youth,"
for you will go to everyone I send you to
and speak whatever I tell you.
8 Do not be afraid of anyone,
for I will be with you to rescue you.
This is the LORD's declaration.

9 Then the LORD reached out his hand,
touched my mouth, and told me:

I have now filled your mouth
with my words.
10 See, I have appointed you today
over nations and kingdoms
to uproot and tear down,
to destroy and demolish,
to build and plant.

TWO VISIONS

11 Then the word of the LORD came to me, asking, "What do you see, Jeremiah?"
I replied, "I see a branch of an almond tree."
12 The LORD said to me, "You have seen correctly, for I watch over[A] my word to accomplish it." 13 Again the word of the LORD came
to me asking, "What do you see?"
And I replied, "I see a boiling pot, its lip tilted
from the north to the south."
14 Then the LORD said to me, "Disaster will be
poured out[B] from the north on all who live in
the land. 15 Indeed, I am about to summon all
the clans and kingdoms of the north."

This is the LORD's declaration.
They will come, and each king
will set up his throne
at the entrance to Jerusalem's gates.

Eternal Perspective | *God's Knowledge/Omniscience*

GOD'S PLAN

"I chose you before I formed you in the womb; I set you apart before you were born. I appointed you a prophet to the nations." Jeremiah 1:5

We were on God's heart before the world even existed. And when the Almighty plotted our lives, he wasn't thinking, *My only desire is that they will believe all the right things and do all the right things.*

Instead, God's purpose for us is found in the phrase in the knowledge that he chose us and formed us even while we were "in the womb." We've been "set apart." Paul explains it this way: "Those he foreknew he also predestined to be conformed to the image of his Son. . . . And those he predestined, he also called; and those he called, he also justified; and those he justified, he also glorified" (Rm 8:29-30).

That is God's ultimate plan for our lives. Not that we pursue a certain career, engage in religious activities, experience health and wealth, get married and have children, or do all the cool stuff on a bucket list. All those things are well and good—so long as they help form Christ within us (Gl 4:19).

Instead of changing your schedule to include some spiritual activities, let Jesus change your character from the inside out.

For the next note on *Eternal Perspective*, see Jeremiah 29:11.

[A] **1:12** In Hb, the word for *almond tree* sounds like the word for *watch over* [B] **1:14** LXX reads *will boil*

They will attack
all her surrounding walls
and all the other cities of Judah.
16 "I will pronounce my judgments against them
for all the evil they did when they abandoned
me to burn incense to other gods and to worship the works of their own hands.
17 "Now, get ready. Stand up and tell them
everything that I command you. Do not be
intimidated by them or I will cause you to
cower before them. 18 Today, I am the one who
has made you a fortified city, an iron pillar, and
bronze walls against the whole land — against
the kings of Judah, its officials, its priests, and
the population. 19 They will fight against you
but never prevail over you, since I am with
you to rescue you."
This is the LORD's declaration.

ISRAEL ACCUSED OF APOSTASY

2 The word of the LORD came to me: 2 "Go
and announce directly to Jerusalem that
this is what the LORD says:

I remember the loyalty of your youth,
your love as a bride —
how you followed me in the wilderness,
in a land not sown.
3 Israel was holy to the LORD,
the firstfruits of his harvest.
All who ate of it found themselves guilty;
disaster came on them."
This is the LORD's declaration.

4 Hear the word of the LORD,
house of Jacob
and all families of the house of Israel.
5 This is what the LORD says:

What fault did your fathers find in me
that they went so far from me,
followed worthless idols,
and became worthless themselves?
6 They stopped asking, "Where is the LORD
who brought us from the land of Egypt,
who led us through the wilderness,
through a land of deserts and ravines,
through a land of drought
and darkness,[A]
a land no one traveled through
and where no one lived?"

Exercise of Faith | *Responding to Trials*

GETTING READY FOR A FIGHT

"'They will fight against you but never prevail over you, since I am with you to rescue you.' This is the LORD's declaration." Jeremiah 1:19

Some people of faith imagine God as the ultimate helicopter parent. More than anything, this God wants to spare his children from physical pain and emotional discomfort. His will is that they should never do without, never face any stress or sickness. This God is all about good feelings and preventing unpleasant or hard situations. This God wants his children to sail through life, hitting every green light, always finding the best parking spaces.

Compare that imagined God with the God we see revealed throughout the Bible. God doesn't promise Jeremiah an easy life. On the contrary, he tells Jeremiah in no uncertain terms that people "will fight against you." Jeremiah is warned that he'll be needing rescue but also promised that God will provide it.

Why mention these uncomfortable realities? Because we need a right perspective and proper expectations, or we will experience deep disappointment. Life comes at us hard in a fallen world. And the people of God are not exempt from trials and tears. Even the beloved Son of God had to drink a bitter cup.

Ultimately God's concern is to make us like Jesus, not make us comfortable. In other words, we should expect some red lights and long parking lot hikes.

For the next note on *Exercise of Faith*, see Jeremiah 33:2-3.

[A] **2:6** Or *shadow of death*

7 I brought you to a fertile land
to eat its fruit and bounty,
but after you entered, you defiled
my land;
you made my inheritance detestable.
8 The priests quit asking, "Where is
the LORD?"
The experts in the law no longer
knew me,
and the rulers rebelled against me.
The prophets prophesied by[A] Baal
and followed useless idols.

9 Therefore, I will bring a case
against you again.
This is the LORD's declaration.
I will bring a case
against your children's children.
10 Cross over to the coasts of Cyprus[B]
and take a look.
Send someone to Kedar
and consider carefully;
see if there has ever been
anything like this:
11 Has a nation ever exchanged its gods?
(But they were not gods!)
Yet my people have exchanged
their[C] Glory
for useless idols.
12 Be appalled at this, heavens;
be shocked and utterly desolated!
This is the LORD's declaration.

13 For my people have committed
a double evil:
They have abandoned me,
the fountain of living water,
and dug cisterns for themselves —
cracked cisterns
that cannot hold water.

CONSEQUENCES OF APOSTASY

14 Is Israel a slave?
Was he born into slavery?[D]
Why else has he become a prey?
15 The young lions have roared at him;
they have roared loudly.
They have laid waste his land.

R Rest and Reflection | *Consuming Spiritual Nourishment*

A DOUBLE EVIL

"For my people have committed a double evil: They have abandoned me, the fountain of living water, and dug cisterns for themselves—cracked cisterns that cannot hold water." Jeremiah 2:13

Even successful and famous people experience setbacks. A man wins the Super Bowl or climbs Mount Everest; a woman wins a Pulitzer or gets to experience a fairy tale wedding. But after an initial surge of euphoria, the nagging question "Now, what?" brings them both—brings us all—crashing to earth.

No matter what earthly prize we chase—and get—business success, public prestige, power and position, cultural fame, or physical pleasure, it's never enough. To be sure, such things can and do result in short-lived satisfaction. They just don't deliver ultimate satisfaction.

God brought his message to his people through the prophet Jeremiah. They had been graciously chosen, miraculously rescued, immeasurably blessed, and showered with promises. But they had repeatedly pushed away the One who is life and ran looking for security and pleasure in other places.

We can call this sin or idolatry. We can call it insanity or stupidity. But whatever we call it, substitutes for God can never fully satisfy. When offered the very best that God has to offer, why pursue and settle for anything less?

Turn away from your "cracked cisterns" and turn back to God's rich resources.

For the next note on *Rest and Reflection*, see Hosea 10:12.

[A] **2:8** = in the name of [B] **2:10** Lit *to the islands of Kittim* [C] **2:11** Alt Hb tradition reads *my* [D] **2:14** Lit *born of a house*

His cities are in ruins,
without inhabitants.
16 The men of Memphis and Tahpanhes
have also broken your skull.
17 Have you not brought this on yourself
by abandoning the LORD your God
while he was leading you along the way?
18 Now what will you gain
by traveling along the way to Egypt
to drink the water of the Nile?[A]
What will you gain
by traveling along the way to Assyria
to drink the water of the Euphrates?
19 Your own evil will discipline you;
your own apostasies
will reprimand you.
Recognize[B] how evil and bitter it is
for you to abandon the LORD your God
and to have no fear of me.
This is the declaration
of the Lord GOD of Armies.

20 For long ago I[C] broke your yoke;
I[C] tore off your chains.
You insisted, "I will not serve!"
On every high hill
and under every green tree
you lay down like a prostitute.

21 I planted you, a choice vine
from the very best seed.
How then could you turn into
a degenerate, foreign vine?

22 Even if you wash with lye
and use a great amount of bleach,[D]
the stain of your iniquity is still
in front of me.
This is the Lord GOD's declaration.
23 How can you protest, "I am not defiled;
I have not followed the Baals"?
Look at your behavior in the valley;
acknowledge what you have done.
You are a swift young camel
twisting and turning on her way,
24 a wild donkey at home[E]
in the wilderness.
She sniffs the wind in the heat
of her desire.
Who can control her passion?
All who look for her will not
become weary;
they will find her
in her mating season.[F]
25 Keep your feet from going bare
and your throat from thirst.
But you say, "It's hopeless;
I love strangers,
and I will continue to follow them."

26 Like the shame of a thief
when he is caught,
so the house of Israel has been
put to shame.
They, their kings, their officials,
their priests, and their prophets
27 say to a tree, "You are my father,"
and to a stone, "You gave birth to me."
For they have turned their back to me
and not their face,
yet in their time of disaster they beg,
"Rise up and save us!"
28 But where are your gods you made
for yourself?
Let them rise up and save you
in your time of disaster if they can,
for your gods are as numerous
as your cities, Judah.

JUDGMENT DESERVED

29 Why do you bring a case against me?
All of you have rebelled against me.
This is the LORD's declaration.
30 I have struck down your children
in vain;
they would not accept discipline.
Your own sword has devoured
your prophets
like a ravaging lion.
31 Evil generation,
pay attention to the word of the LORD!
Have I been a wilderness to Israel
or a land of dense darkness?
Why do my people claim,
"We will go where we want;[G]
we will no longer come to you"?
32 Can a young woman forget her jewelry
or a bride her wedding sash?
Yet my people have forgotten me
for countless days.
33 How skillfully you pursue love;
you also teach evil women your ways.
34 Moreover, your skirts are stained
with the blood of the innocent poor.

[A] **2:18** Lit *of Shihor* [B] **2:19** Lit *Know and see* [C] **2:20** LXX reads *you* [D] **2:22** Lit *cleansing agent* [E] **2:24** Lit *donkey taught* [F] **2:24** Lit *her month* [G] **2:31** Or *"We have taken control*, or *"We can roam*

You did not catch them breaking
and entering.
But in spite of all these things
35 you claim, "I am innocent.
His anger is sure to turn away from me."
But I will certainly judge you
because you have said, "I have
not sinned."
36 How unstable you are,
constantly changing your ways!
You will be put to shame by Egypt
just as you were put to shame
by Assyria.
37 Moreover, you will be
led out from here
with your hands on your head
since the LORD has rejected
those you trust;
you will not succeed even with
their help.[A]

WAGES OF APOSTASY

3 If[B] a man divorces his wife
and she leaves him to marry another,
can he ever return to her?
Wouldn't such a land[C] become
totally defiled?
But you!
You have prostituted yourself
with many partners —
can you return to me?
This is the LORD's declaration.
2 Look to the barren heights and see.
Where have you not been immoral?
You sat waiting for them
beside the highways
like a nomad in the desert.
You have defiled the land
with your prostitution and wickedness.
3 This is why the showers haven't come —
why there has been no spring rain.
You have the brazen look
of a prostitute[D]
and refuse to be ashamed.
4 Haven't you recently called to me,
"My Father.
You were my friend in my youth.
5 Will he bear a grudge forever?
Will he be endlessly infuriated?"
This is what you have said,
but you have done the evil things
you are capable of.

UNFAITHFUL ISRAEL, TREACHEROUS JUDAH

6 In the days of King Josiah the LORD asked
me, "Have you seen what unfaithful Israel
has done? She has ascended every high hill
and gone under every green tree to prostitute herself there. 7 I thought, 'After she has
done all these things, she will return to me.'
But she didn't return, and her treacherous
sister Judah saw it. 8 I[E] observed that it was
because unfaithful Israel had committed adultery that I had sent her away and had given
her a certificate of divorce. Nevertheless, her
treacherous sister Judah was not afraid but
also went and prostituted herself. 9 Indifferent
to[F] her prostitution, she defiled the land and
committed adultery with stones and trees.
10 Yet in spite of all this, her treacherous sister
Judah didn't return to me with all her heart
— only in pretense."
This is the LORD's declaration.
11 The LORD announced to me, "Unfaithful
Israel has shown herself more righteous than
treacherous Judah. 12 Go, proclaim these words
to the north, and say,

'Return, unfaithful Israel.
This is the LORD's declaration.
I will not look on you with anger,[G]
for I am unfailing in my love.
This is the LORD's declaration.
I will not be angry forever.
13 Only acknowledge your guilt —
you have rebelled against the LORD
your God.
You have scattered your favors
to strangers
under every green tree
and have not obeyed me.
This is the LORD's declaration.

14 " 'Return, you faithless children — this
is the LORD's declaration — for I am your
master,[H] and I will take you, one from a city
and two from a family, and I will bring you
to Zion. 15 I will give you shepherds who are
loyal to me,[I] and they will shepherd you with
knowledge and skill. 16 When you multiply and
increase in the land, in those days — this is the
LORD's declaration — no one will say again,
"The ark of the LORD's covenant." It will never
come to mind, and no one will remember or
miss it. Another one will not be made.[J] 17 At
that time Jerusalem will be called The LORD's
Throne, and all the nations will be gathered

[A] **2:37** Lit *with them* [B] **3:1** One Hb ms, LXX, Syr; other Hb mss read *Saying: If* [C] **3:1** LXX reads *woman* [D] **3:3** Lit *have a prostitute's forehead* [E] **3:8** One Hb ms, Syr read *She* [F] **3:9** Lit *From the lightness of* [G] **3:12** Lit *not cause my face to fall on you* [H] **3:14** Or *husband* [I] **3:15** Lit *shepherds according to my heart* [J] **3:16** Or *It will no longer be done*

to it, to the name of the LORD in Jerusalem.
They will cease to follow the stubbornness of
their evil hearts. 18 In those days the house of
Judah will join with the house of Israel, and
they will come together from the land of the
north to the land I have given your ancestors
to inherit.' "

TRUE REPENTANCE

19 I thought, "How I long to make you
my sons
and give you a desirable land,
the most beautiful inheritance of all
the nations."
I thought, "You will call me 'My Father'
and never turn away from me."
20 However, as a woman may betray
her lover,[A]
so you have betrayed me,
house of Israel.
This is the LORD's declaration.

21 A sound is heard on the barren heights:
the children of Israel weeping
and begging for mercy,
for they have perverted their way;
they have forgotten the LORD their God.
22 Return, you faithless children.
I will heal your unfaithfulness.
"Here we are, coming to you,
for you are the LORD our God.
23 Surely, falsehood comes from the hills,
commotion from the mountains,
but the salvation of Israel
is only in the LORD our God.
24 From the time of our youth
the shameful one[B] has consumed
what our fathers have worked for —
their flocks and their herds,
their sons and their daughters.
25 Let us lie down in our shame;
let our disgrace cover us.
We have sinned against the LORD
our God,
both we and our fathers,
from the time of our youth
even to this day.
We have not obeyed the LORD our God."

BLESSING OR CURSE

4 If you return,[C] Israel —
this is the LORD's declaration —
you will return to me,
if you remove your abhorrent idols
from my presence
and do not waver,
2 then you can swear, "As the LORD lives,"
in truth, in justice,
and in righteousness,
then the nations will be blessed[D]
by him
and will pride themselves in him.

T Thanksgiving and Contentment | *Repentance*

COMING HOME

"Return, you faithless children. I will heal your unfaithfulness. 'Here we are, coming to you, for you are the LORD our God.'" Jeremiah 3:22

For many people, the word *repent* (translated here "return") brings to mind all kinds of unpleasant images: angry preachers denouncing "rotten sinners"; being shamed or taken behind the proverbial woodshed; sobbing and groveling for forgiveness from a disgusted God who is reluctant to give it.

How tragic! Biblical repentance is none of that. It is heeding the loving God who is calling us to return, coming home in order to find healing. What did the prodigal son experience when he returned home (Lk 15:11-32)? A tongue-lashing? Scorn? No! A bear hug followed by a party!

Repentance isn't a one-time action; it's a daily discipline in the Christian life. It's the way we begin to walk with God and the way we continue. Today, as you hear the Spirit of God whisper, "Don't go that way. Stop. Turn around. Come back," don't resist. Instead, personalize the words of this verse, "Here I am, coming to you, for you are the Lord my God."

For the next note on *Thanksgiving and Contentment*, see Jonah 3:1.

[A] 3:20 Lit *friend* [B] 3:24 = Baal [C] 4:1 Or *Repent* [D] 4:2 Or *will bless themselves*

3 For this is what the LORD says to the men
of Judah and Jerusalem:
Break up the unplowed ground;
do not sow among the thorns.
4 Circumcise yourselves to the LORD;
remove the foreskin of your hearts,
men of Judah and residents
of Jerusalem.
Otherwise, my wrath will break out
like fire
and burn with no one to extinguish it
because of your evil deeds.

JUDGMENT FROM THE NORTH

5 Declare in Judah, proclaim in Jerusalem,
and say:
Blow the ram's horn
throughout the land.
Cry out loudly and say:
Assemble yourselves,
and let's flee to the fortified cities.
6 Lift up a signal flag toward Zion.
Run for cover! Don't stand still!
For I am bringing disaster
from the north —
a crushing blow.
7 A lion has gone up from his thicket;
a destroyer of nations has set out.
He has left his lair
to make your land a waste.
Your cities will be reduced
to uninhabited ruins.
8 Because of this, put on sackcloth;
mourn and wail,
for the LORD's burning anger
has not turned away from us.

9 "On that day" — this is the LORD's declaration — "the king and the officials will lose
their courage. The priests will tremble in fear,
and the prophets will be scared speechless."
10 I said, "Oh no, Lord GOD, you have certainly deceived this people and Jerusalem,
by announcing, 'You will have peace,' while
a sword is at[A] our throats."
11 "At that time it will be said to this people
and to Jerusalem, 'A searing wind blows from
the barren heights in the wilderness on the
way to my dear[B] people. It comes not to winnow or to sift; 12 a wind too strong for this
comes at my call.[C] Now I will also pronounce
judgments against them.'"
13 Look, he advances like clouds;
his chariots are like a storm.
His horses are swifter than eagles.
Woe to us, for we are ruined!
14 Wash the evil
from your heart, Jerusalem,
so that you will be delivered.
How long will you harbor
malicious thoughts?
15 For a voice announces from Dan,
proclaiming malice
from Mount Ephraim.
16 Warn the nations: Look!
Proclaim to Jerusalem:
Those who besiege are coming
from a distant land;
they raise their voices
against the cities of Judah.
17 They have her surrounded
like those who guard a field,
because she has rebelled against me.
This is the LORD's declaration.
18 Your way and your actions
have brought this on you.
This is your punishment. It is very bitter,
because it has reached your heart!

JEREMIAH'S LAMENT

19 My anguish, my anguish![D] I writhe
in agony!
Oh, the pain in[E] my heart!
My heart pounds;
I cannot be silent.
For you, my soul,
have heard the sound
of the ram's horn —
the shout of battle.
20 Disaster after disaster is reported
because the whole land is destroyed.
Suddenly my tents are destroyed,
my tent curtains, in a moment.
21 How long must I see the signal flag
and hear the sound of the ram's horn?

22 "For my people are fools;
they do not know me.
They are foolish children,
without understanding.
They are skilled in doing what is evil,
but they do not know how to do
what is good."

23 I looked at the earth,
and it was formless and empty.

[A] **4:10** Lit *sword touches* [B] **4:11** Lit *to the daughter of my* [C] **4:12** Lit *comes for me* [D] **4:19** Lit *My inner parts, my inner parts*
[E] **4:19** Lit *the walls of*

I looked to the heavens,
and their light was gone.
24 I looked at the mountains,
and they were quaking;
all the hills shook.
25 I looked, and there was no human
being,
and all the birds of the sky had fled.
26 I looked, and the fertile field was
a wilderness.
All its cities were torn down
because of the LORD
and his burning anger.

27 For this is what the LORD says:
The whole land will be a desolation,
but I will not finish it off.
28 Because of this, the earth will mourn;
the skies above will grow dark.
I have spoken; I have planned,
and I will not relent or turn back from it.

29 Every city flees
at the sound of the horseman
and the archer.
They enter the thickets
and climb among the rocks.
Every city is abandoned;
no inhabitant is left.
30 And you, devastated one, what are
you doing
that you dress yourself in scarlet,
that you adorn yourself
with gold jewelry,
that you enhance your eyes
with makeup?
You beautify yourself for nothing.
Your lovers reject you;
they intend to take your life.
31 I hear a cry like a woman in labor,
a cry of anguish like one bearing
her first child.
The cry of Daughter Zion
gasping for breath,
stretching out her hands:
"Woe is me, for my life is weary
because of the murderers!"

THE DEPRAVITY OF JERUSALEM

5 Roam through the streets of Jerusalem.
Investigate;[A]
search in her squares.
If you find one person,
any who acts justly,
who pursues faithfulness,
then I will forgive her.
2 When they say, "As the LORD lives,"
they are swearing falsely.
3 LORD, don't your eyes
look for faithfulness?
You have struck them, but they felt
no pain.
You finished them off,
but they refused
to accept discipline.
They made their faces harder
than rock,
and they refused to return.

4 Then I thought:
They are just the poor;
they have been foolish.
For they don't understand the way
of the LORD,
the justice of their God.
5 I will go to the powerful
and speak to them.
Surely they know the way of the LORD,
the justice of their God.
However, these also had broken the yoke
and torn off the chains.
6 Therefore, a lion from the forest
will strike them down.
A wolf from arid plains
will ravage them.
A leopard stalks their cities.
Anyone who leaves them will be torn
to pieces
because their rebellious acts are many,
their unfaithful deeds numerous.

7 Why should I forgive you?
Your children have abandoned me
and sworn by those who are not gods.
I satisfied their needs, yet they
committed adultery;
they gashed themselves
at the[B] prostitute's house.
8 They are well-fed,[C] eager[D] stallions,
each neighing after
someone else's wife.
9 Should I not punish them
for these things?
This is the LORD's declaration.
Should I not avenge myself
on such a nation as this?

[A] **5:1** Lit *See and know* [B] **5:7** Or *adultery and trooped to the*, or *adultery and lodged at the*; Hb obscure [C] **5:8** Lit *well-equipped*; Hb obscure [D] **5:8** Lit *early-rising*; Hb obscure

Jeremiah | Restoration Profile

2 CHRONICLES 35–36; JEREMIAH, LAMENTATIONS; DANIEL 9:2; MATTHEW 2:17; 16:14; 27:9

When Jeremiah wrote the words "Because of the LORD's faithful love we do not perish, for his mercies never end. They are new every morning; great is your faithfulness!" (Lm 3:22-23), did he realize he was speaking about restoration? In his contentious relationship with God, how often did he pause to recognize God was faithfully accomplishing good work in him and wouldn't stop? Restoration for Jeremiah was a messy business. How often do we stop to consider that aspect of God's relationship with us?

God's restoration work is always in line with his original design. He doesn't create us and then make us someone else along the way. He is satisfied with his first plan for each of us. Restoration has to do with dealing with the mess we create. God gifted Jeremiah with a deep reservoir of feelings; he cared deeply for those to whom he was called to preach, even as they rejected him. The dark side of Jeremiah's emotional furnace was a tendency toward anger and despair, yet God repeatedly came alongside his prophet with words of comfort and acts of preservation.

One episode vividly pictures Jeremiah's ups and downs alongside God's gracious work. King Zedekiah moved to place the prophet in the hands of his enemies. They promptly dropped him into a well without water but plenty of muck. God tapped an African named Ebed-melech to lead a rescue effort to lift Jeremiah out of the cistern. God always kept the promise he gave Jeremiah at his call: "Then the LORD said to me: Do not say, 'I am only a youth,' for you will go to everyone I send you to and speak whatever I tell you. Do not be afraid of anyone, for I will be with you to rescue you" (Jr 1:7-8).

10 Go up among her vineyard terraces
and destroy them,
but do not finish them off.
Prune away her shoots,
for they do not belong to the LORD.
11 They, the house of Israel and the house
of Judah,
have dealt very treacherously with me.
This is the LORD's declaration.
12 They have contradicted the LORD
and insisted, "It won't happen.[A]
Harm won't come to us;
we won't see sword or famine."
13 The prophets become only wind,
for the LORD's word is not in them.
This will in fact happen to them.

COMING JUDGMENT

14 Therefore, this is what the Lord GOD of Armies says:
Because you have spoken this word,
I am going to make my words
become fire in your mouth.
These people are the wood,
and the fire will consume them.
15 I am about to bring a nation
from far away against you,
house of Israel.
This is the LORD's declaration.
It is an established nation,
an ancient nation,
a nation whose language
you do not know
and whose speech
you do not understand.
16 Their quiver is like an open grave;
they are all warriors.
17 They will consume your harvest
and your food.
They will consume your sons
and your daughters.
They will consume your flocks
and your herds.
They will consume your vines
and your fig trees.
With the sword they will destroy
your fortified cities in which you trust.

18 "But even in those days" — this is the LORD's
declaration — "I will not finish you off. 19 When
people ask, 'For what offense has the LORD
our God done all these things to us?' You will

[A] 5:12 Lit *"He does not exist*

respond to them, 'Just as you abandoned me
and served foreign gods in your land, so will
you serve strangers in a land that is not yours.'
20 "Declare this in the house of Jacob; proclaim it in Judah, saying:
21 Hear this,
you foolish and senseless[A] people.
They have eyes, but they don't see.
They have ears, but they don't hear.
22 Do you not fear me?
This is the LORD's declaration.
Do you not tremble before me,
the one who set the sand
as the boundary of the sea,
an enduring barrier that
it cannot cross?
The waves surge, but they
cannot prevail.
They roar but cannot pass over it.
23 But these people have stubborn
and rebellious hearts.
They have turned aside
and have gone away.
24 They have not said to themselves,
'Let's fear the LORD our God,
who gives the seasonal rains,
both autumn and spring,
who guarantees to us the fixed weeks
of the harvest.'
25 Your guilty acts have diverted
these things from you.
Your sins have withheld my bounty
from you,
26 for wicked men live among my people.
They watch like hunters[B] lying in wait.[C]
They set a trap;
they catch men.
27 Like a cage full of birds,
so their houses are full of deceit.
Therefore they have grown powerful
and rich.
28 They have become fat and sleek.
They have also excelled in evil matters.
They have not taken up cases,
such as the case of the fatherless,
so they might prosper,
and they have not defended the rights
of the needy.
29 Should I not punish them
for these things?
This is the LORD's declaration.
Should I not avenge myself
on such a nation as this?
30 An appalling, horrible thing
has taken place in the land.
31 The prophets prophesy falsely,
and the priests rule
by their own authority.
My people love it like this.
But what will you do at the end of it?

THREATENED SIEGE OF JERUSALEM

6 "Run for cover
out of Jerusalem, Benjaminites.
Sound the ram's horn in Tekoa;
raise a smoke signal
over Beth-haccherem,[D]
for disaster threatens from the north,
even a crushing blow.
2 Though she is beautiful and delicate,
I will destroy[E] Daughter Zion.
3 Shepherds and their flocks will come
against her;
they will pitch their tents all around her.
Each will pasture his own portion.
4 Set them apart for war against her;
rise up, let's attack at noon.
Woe to us, for the day is passing;
the evening shadows grow long.
5 Rise up, let's attack by night.
Let us destroy her fortresses."

6 For this is what the LORD of Armies says:
Cut down the trees;
raise a siege ramp against Jerusalem.
This city must be punished.
There is nothing but oppression
within her.
7 As a well gushes out its water,
so she pours out her evil.[F]
Violence and destruction resound
in her.
Sickness and wounds keep coming
to my attention.
8 Be warned, Jerusalem,
or I will turn away from you;
I will make you a desolation,
a land without inhabitants.

WRATH ON ISRAEL

9 This is what the LORD of Armies says:
Glean the remnant of Israel
as thoroughly as a vine.
Pass your hand once more
like a grape gatherer
over the branches.

[A] **5:21** Lit *without heart* [B] **5:26** Lit *hunters of birds* [C] **5:26** Hb obscure [D] **6:1** = House of the Vineyard [E] **6:2** Or *silence*
[F] **6:7** Or *well keeps its water fresh, so she keeps her evil fresh*

10 Who can I speak to and give
such a warning[A]
that they will listen?
Look, their ear is uncircumcised,[B]
so they cannot pay attention.
See, the word of the LORD
has become contemptible to them —
they find no pleasure in it.
11 But I am full of the LORD's wrath;
I am tired of holding it back.
Pour it out on the children
in the street,
on the gathering of young men as well.
For both husband and wife
will be captured,
the old with the very old.[C]
12 Their houses will be turned over
to others,
their fields and wives as well,
for I will stretch out my hand
against the inhabitants of the land.
This is the LORD's declaration.

13 For from the least to the greatest
of them,
everyone is making profit dishonestly.
From prophet to priest,
everyone deals falsely.
14 They have treated
my people's brokenness superficially,
claiming, "Peace, peace,"
when there is no peace.
15 Were they ashamed when they acted
so detestably?
They weren't at all ashamed.
They can no longer feel humiliation.
Therefore, they will fall among the fallen.
When I punish them, they will collapse,
says the LORD.

Stand by the roadways and look. Ask about the ancient paths, "Which is the way to what is good?" Then take it and find rest for yourselves.
—Jeremiah 6:16

DISASTER BECAUSE OF DISOBEDIENCE

16 This is what the LORD says:
Stand by the roadways and look.
Ask about the ancient paths,
"Which is the way to what is good?"
Then take it
and find rest for yourselves.
But they protested, "We won't!"
17 I appointed watchmen over you
and said, "Listen for the sound
of the ram's horn."
But they protested, "We won't listen!"

18 Therefore listen, you nations
and you witnesses,
learn what the charge is against them.
19 Listen, earth!
I am about to bring disaster
on these people,
the fruit of their own plotting,
for they have paid no attention
to my words.
They have rejected my instruction.
20 What use to me is frankincense
from Sheba
or sweet cane from a distant land?
Your burnt offerings are not acceptable;
your sacrifices do not please me.
21 Therefore, this is what the LORD says:
I am going to place stumbling blocks
before these people;
fathers and sons together will stumble
over them;
friends and neighbors
will also perish.

A CRUEL NATION FROM THE NORTH

22 This is what the LORD says:
Look, an army is coming
from a northern land;
a great nation will be stirred up
from the remote regions of the earth.
23 They grasp bow and javelin.
They are cruel and show no mercy.
Their voice roars like the sea,
and they ride on horses,
lined up like men in battle formation
against you, Daughter Zion.

24 We have heard about it,
and our hands have become weak.
Distress has seized us —
pain, like a woman in labor.

[A] **6:10** Or *and bear witness* [B] **6:10** They are unresponsive to God. [C] **6:11** Lit *with fullness of days*

25 Don't go out to the fields;
don't walk on the road.
For the enemy has a sword;
terror is on every side.

26 My dear[A] people, dress yourselves
in sackcloth
and roll in the dust.
Mourn as you would for an only son,
a bitter lament,
for suddenly the destroyer will come
on us.

JEREMIAH APPOINTED AS AN EXAMINER

27 I have appointed you to be an assayer
among my people —
a refiner[B] —
so you may know and assay their way
of life.
28 All are stubborn rebels
spreading slander.
They are bronze and iron;
all of them are corrupt.
29 The bellows blow,
blasting the lead with fire.
The refining is completely in vain;
the evil ones are not separated out.
30 They are called rejected silver,
for the LORD has rejected them.

FALSE TRUST IN THE TEMPLE

7 This is the word that came to Jeremiah
from the LORD: 2 "Stand in the gate of the
house of the LORD and there call out this word:
'Hear the word of the LORD, all you people
of Judah who enter through these gates to
worship the LORD.
3 " 'This is what the LORD of Armies, the God
of Israel, says: Correct your ways and your actions, and I will allow you to live in this place.
4 Do not trust deceitful words, chanting, "This
is the temple of the LORD, the temple of the
LORD, the temple of the LORD." 5 Instead, if you
really correct your ways and your actions, if
you act justly toward one another,[C] 6 if you
no longer oppress the resident alien, the fatherless, and the widow and no longer shed
innocent blood in this place or follow other
gods, bringing harm on yourselves, 7 I will
allow you to live in this place, the land I gave
to your ancestors long ago and forever. 8 But
look, you keep trusting in deceitful words
that cannot help.
9 " 'Do you steal, murder, commit adultery,
swear falsely, burn incense to Baal, and follow
other gods that you have not known? 10 Then
do you come and stand before me in this house
that bears my name and say, "We are rescued,
so we can continue doing all these detestable
acts"? 11 Has this house, which bears my name,
become a den of robbers in your view? Yes, I
too have seen it.
This is the LORD's declaration.

SHILOH AS A WARNING

12 " 'But return to my place that was at Shiloh,
where I made my name dwell at first. See what I
did to it because of the evil of my people Israel.
13 Now, because you have done all these things
— this is the LORD's declaration — and because
I have spoken to you time and time again[D] but
you wouldn't listen, and I have called to you,
but you wouldn't answer, 14 what I did to Shiloh
I will do to the house that bears my name — the
house in which you trust — the place that I
gave you and your ancestors. 15 I will banish
you from my presence, just as I banished all of
your brothers, all the descendants of Ephraim.'

DO NOT PRAY FOR JUDAH

16 "As for you, do not pray for these people.
Do not offer a cry or a prayer on their behalf,
and do not beg me, for I will not listen to you.
17 Don't you see how they behave in the cities
of Judah and in the streets of Jerusalem? 18 The
sons gather wood, the fathers light the fire, and
the women knead dough to make cakes for
the queen of heaven,[E] and they pour out drink
offerings to other gods so that they provoke
me to anger. 19 But are they really provoking
me?" This is the LORD's declaration. "Isn't it
they themselves being provoked to disgrace?"
20 Therefore, this is what the Lord GOD says:
"Look, my anger — my burning wrath — is
about to be poured out on this place, on people
and animals, on the tree of the field, and on
the produce of the land. My wrath will burn
and not be quenched."

OBEDIENCE OVER SACRIFICE

21 This is what the LORD of Armies, the God of
Israel, says: "Add your burnt offerings to your
other sacrifices, and eat the meat yourselves,
22 for when I brought your ancestors out of
the land of Egypt, I did not speak with them
or command them concerning burnt offering

[A] **6:26** Lit *Daughter of my* [B] **6:27** Text emended; MT reads *fortress* [C] **7:5** Lit *justly between a man and his neighbor*
[D] **7:13** Lit *you rising early and speaking* [E] **7:18** = a pagan goddess

and sacrifice. 23 However, I did give them this
command: 'Obey me, and then I will be your
God, and you will be my people. Follow every
way I command you so that it may go well with
you.' 24 Yet they didn't listen or pay attention but
followed their own advice and their own stubborn, evil heart. They went backward and not
forward. 25 Since the day your ancestors came
out of the land of Egypt until today, I have sent
all my servants the prophets to you time and
time again.[A] 26 However, my people wouldn't
listen to me or pay attention but became obstinate;[B] they did more evil than their ancestors.

A LAMENT FOR DISOBEDIENT JUDAH

27 "When you speak all these things to them,
they will not listen to you. When you call to
them, they will not answer you. 28 Therefore,
declare to them, 'This is the nation that would
not listen to the LORD their God and would not
accept discipline. Truth[C] has perished — it
has disappeared from their mouths. 29 Cut
off the hair of your sacred vow[D] and throw it
away. Raise up a dirge on the barren heights,
for the LORD has rejected and abandoned the
generation under his wrath.'

30 "For the Judeans have done what is evil
in my sight." This is the LORD's declaration.
"They have set up their abhorrent things in the
house that bears my name in order to defile it.
31 They have built the high places of Topheth[E]
in Ben Hinnom Valley[F] in order to burn their
sons and daughters in the fire, a thing I did not
command; I never entertained the thought.[G]

32 "Therefore, look, the days are coming"
— the LORD's declaration — "when this place
will no longer be called Topheth and Ben Hinnom Valley, but the Valley of Slaughter. Topheth
will become a cemetery,[H] because there will be
no other burial place. 33 The corpses of these
people will become food for the birds of the
sky and for the wild animals of the land, with
no one to scare them away. 34 I will remove
from the cities of Judah and the streets of
Jerusalem the sound of joy and gladness and
the voices of the groom and the bride, for the
land will become a desolate waste.

DEATH OVER LIFE

8 "At that time" — this is the LORD's declaration — "the bones of the kings of Judah,
the bones of her officials, the bones of the
priests, the bones of the prophets, and the
bones of the residents of Jerusalem will be
brought out of their graves. 2 They will be exposed to the sun, the moon, and all the stars
in the sky, which they have loved, served,
followed, consulted, and worshiped. Their
bones will not be collected and buried but
will become like manure on the soil's surface.
3 Death will be chosen over life by all the survivors of this evil family, those who remain
wherever I have banished them." This is the
declaration of the LORD of Armies.

4 "You are to say to them: This is what the
LORD says:

Do people fall and not get up again?
If they turn away, do they not return?
5 Why have these people turned away?
Why is Jerusalem always turning away?
They take hold of deceit;
they refuse to return.
6 I have paid careful attention.
They do not speak what is right.
No one regrets his evil,
asking, 'What have I done?'
Everyone has stayed his course
like a horse rushing into battle.
7 Even storks in the sky
know their seasons.
Turtledoves, swallows, and cranes[I]
are aware of their migration,
but my people do not know
the requirements of the LORD.

PUNISHMENT FOR JUDAH'S LEADERS

8 "How can you claim, 'We are wise;
the law of the LORD is with us'?
In fact, the lying pen of scribes
has produced falsehood.
9 The wise will be put to shame;
they will be dismayed and snared.
They have rejected the word of the LORD,
so what wisdom do they really have?
10 Therefore, I will give their wives
to other men,
their fields to new occupants,
for from the least to the greatest,
everyone is making profit dishonestly.
From prophet to priest,
everyone deals falsely.
11 They have treated the brokenness
of my dear[J] people superficially,
claiming, 'Peace, peace,'

[A] **7:25** Lit *you, each day rising early and sending* [B] **7:26** Lit *but stiffened their neck* [C] **7:28** Or *Faithfulness* [D] **7:29** Lit *off your consecration* [E] **7:31** Lit *of the fireplace* [F] **7:31** A valley south of Jerusalem [G] **7:31** Lit *command, and it did not arise on my heart* [H] **7:32** Lit *They will bury in Topheth* [I] **8:7** Hb obscure [J] **8:11** Lit *of the daughter of my*, also in vv. 19,21,22

when there is no peace.
12 Were they ashamed when they acted
so detestably?
They weren't at all ashamed.
They can no longer
feel humiliation.
Therefore, they will fall
among the fallen.
When I punish them, they will collapse,"
says the LORD.

13 I will gather them and bring them
to an end.[A]
This is the LORD's declaration.
There will be no grapes on the vine,
no figs on the fig tree,
and even the leaf will wither.
Whatever I have given them will be lost
to them.

GOD'S PEOPLE UNREPENTANT

14 Why are we just sitting here?
Gather together; let us enter
the fortified cities
and perish there,[B]
for the LORD our God has destroyed[C] us.
He has given us poisoned water to drink,
because we have sinned
against the LORD.
15 We hoped for peace, but there was
nothing good;
for a time of healing, but there was
only terror.

16 From Dan, the snorting
of horses is heard.
At the sound of the neighing
of mighty steeds,
the whole land quakes.
They come to devour the land
and everything in it,
the city and all its residents.
17 Indeed, I am about to send snakes
among you,
poisonous vipers that cannot
be charmed.
They will bite you.
This is the LORD's declaration.

LAMENT OVER JUDAH

18 My joy has flown away;
grief has settled on me.
My heart is sick.
19 Listen — the cry of my dear people
from a faraway land,
"Is the LORD no longer in Zion,
her King not within her?"
Why have they angered me
with their carved images,
with their worthless foreign idols?
20 Harvest has passed,
summer has ended,
but we have not been saved.
21 I am broken by the brokenness
of my dear people.
I mourn; horror has taken hold of me.
22 Is there no balm in Gilead?
Is there no physician there?
So why has the healing of my dear people
not come about?

9 If my head were a flowing spring,
my eyes a fountain of tears,
I would weep day and night
over the slain of my dear[D] people.
2 If only I had a traveler's lodging place
in the wilderness,
I would abandon my people
and depart from them,
for they are all adulterers,
a solemn assembly
of treacherous people.

3 They bent their tongues like their bows;
lies and not faithfulness prevail
in the land,
for they proceed from one evil
to another,
and they do not take me into account.
This is the LORD's declaration.

IMMINENT RUIN AND EXILE

4 Everyone has to be on guard
against his friend.
Don't trust any brother,
for every brother will certainly deceive,
and every friend spread slander.
5 Each one betrays his friend;
no one tells the truth.
They have taught their tongues
to speak lies;
they wear themselves out doing wrong.
6 You live in a world of deception.[E]
In their deception they refuse
to know me.
This is the LORD's declaration.

[A] 8:13 Lit *Gathering I will end them* [B] 8:14 Or *there be silenced* [C] 8:14 Or *silenced* [D] 9:1 Lit *slain among the daughter of my*
[E] 9:6 LXX reads *Oppression on oppression, deceit on deceit*

[7] Therefore, this is what the LORD of Armies says:
I am about to refine them
and test them,
for what else can I do
because of my dear[A] people?[B]
8 Their tongues are deadly arrows —
they speak deception.
With his mouth
one speaks peaceably
with his friend,
but inwardly he sets up an ambush.
9 Should I not punish them
for these things?
This is the LORD's declaration.
Should I not avenge myself
on such a nation as this?
10 I will raise weeping and a lament
over the mountains,
a dirge over the wilderness
grazing land,
for they have been so scorched
that no one passes through.
The sound of cattle is no longer heard.
From the birds of the sky
to the animals,
everything has fled — they have
gone away.
11 I will make Jerusalem a heap of rubble,
a jackals' den.
I will make the cities of Judah
a desolation,
an uninhabited place.

12 Who is the person wise enough to understand this? Who has the LORD spoken to, that
he may explain it? Why is the land destroyed
and scorched like a wilderness, so no one can
pass through?
13 The LORD said, "It is because they abandoned my instruction, which I set before them,
and did not obey my voice or walk according
to it. 14 Instead, they followed the stubbornness
of their hearts and followed the Baals as their
fathers taught them." 15 Therefore, this is what
the LORD of Armies, the God of Israel, says: "I
am about to feed this people wormwood and
give them poisonous water to drink. 16 I will
scatter them among the nations that they and
their fathers have not known. I will send a
sword after them until I have finished them off."

MOURNING OVER JUDAH

17 This is what the LORD of Armies says:
Consider, and summon the women
who mourn;
send for the skillful women.
18 Let them come quickly to raise
a lament over us
so that our eyes may overflow with tears,
our eyelids be soaked with weeping.

Other-centeredness | *Being Compassionate*

A COMPASSIONATE HEART

"If my head were a flowing spring, my eyes a fountain of tears, I would weep day and night over the slain of my dear people." Jeremiah 9:1

Some people view Jeremiah's kind compassion as weird, possibly a sign of instability. We should remember that Jesus wept (Jn 11:35) when he showed up late at a funeral for his good friend Lazarus. And Jesus cried over the lost and rebellious people of Jerusalem (Lk 19:41-42). Compassionate tears are actually a mark of Christian love. In the New Testament, the apostle Paul urged, "Rejoice with those who rejoice; weep with those who weep" (Rm 12:15).

Jeremiah earned the nickname "weeping prophet." No wonder. As he watched the corruption—and subsequent destruction—of his people, he was often a human waterworks!

Ask God to give you a heart like this, a heart that is moved by the misfortunes and pain of others. When people you know face loss or tragedy, the best help you may be able to give is to cry with them.

For the next note on *Other-centeredness*, see Ezekiel 33:11.

[A] **9:7** Lit *of the daughter of my* [B] **9:7** LXX, Tg read *because of their evils*

19 For a sound of lamentation is heard
from Zion:
How devastated we are.
We are greatly ashamed,
for we have abandoned the land;
our dwellings
have been torn down.
20 Now hear the word of the LORD,
you women.
Pay attention to[A] the words
from his mouth.
Teach your daughters
a lament
and one another a dirge,
21 for Death has climbed
through our windows;
it has entered our fortresses,
cutting off children from the streets,
young men from the squares.

22 "Speak as follows: 'This is what the LORD declares: Human corpses will fall like manure on the surface of the field, like newly cut grain after the reaper with no one to gather it.

BOAST IN THE LORD

23 " 'This is what the LORD says:
The wise person should not boast
in his wisdom;
the strong should not boast
in his strength;
the wealthy should not boast
in his wealth.
24 But the one who boasts should boast
in this:
that he understands
and knows me —
that I am the LORD,
showing faithful love,
justice, and righteousness
on the earth,
for I delight in these things.
This is the LORD's declaration.

25 " 'Look, the days are coming — this is the
LORD's declaration — when I will punish all
the circumcised yet uncircumcised: 26 Egypt,
Judah, Edom, the Ammonites, Moab, and all
the inhabitants of the desert who clip the hair
on their temples.[B] All these nations are uncircumcised, and the whole house of Israel
is uncircumcised in heart.' "

FALSE GODS CONTRASTED WITH THE CREATOR

10 Hear the word that the LORD has spoken
to[C] you, house of Israel. 2 This is what
the LORD says:
Do not learn the way of the nations
or be terrified by signs in the heavens,
although the nations are terrified
by them,
3 for the customs of the peoples
are worthless.
Someone cuts down a tree
from the forest;
it is worked by the hands
of a craftsman with a chisel.
4 He decorates it with silver and gold.
It is fastened with hammer and nails,
so it won't totter.
5 Like scarecrows in a cucumber patch,
their idols cannot speak.
They must be carried because
they cannot walk.
Do not fear them for they can do
no harm —
and they cannot do any good.

6 LORD, there is no one like you.
You are great;
your name is great in power.
7 Who should not fear you,
King of the nations?
It is what you deserve.
For among all the wise people
of the nations
and among all their kingdoms,
there is no one like you.
8 They are both stupid and foolish,
instructed by worthless idols
made of wood!
9 Beaten silver is brought from Tarshish
and gold from Uphaz.[D]
The work of a craftsman
and of a goldsmith's hands
is clothed in blue and purple,
all the work of skilled artisans.

The LORD is the true God; he is the living God and eternal King.
—Jeremiah 10:10

[A] 9:20 Lit *Your ears must receive* [B] 9:26 Or *who live in distant places* [C] 10:1 Or *against* [D] 10:9 Or *Ophir*

10 But the LORD is the true God;
he is the living God and eternal King.
The earth quakes at his wrath,
and the nations cannot endure his rage.
11 You are to say this to them: "The gods that
did not make the heavens and the earth will
perish from the earth and from under these
heavens."[A]
12 He made the earth by his power,
established the world by his wisdom,
and spread out the heavens
by his understanding.
13 When he thunders,[B]
the waters in the heavens are in turmoil,
and he causes the clouds to rise
from the ends of the earth.
He makes lightning for the rain
and brings the wind
from his storehouses.

14 Everyone is stupid and ignorant.
Every goldsmith is put to shame
by his carved image,
for his cast images are a lie;
there is no breath in them.
15 They are worthless, a work
to be mocked.
At the time of their punishment
they will be destroyed.
16 Jacob's Portion[C] is not like these
because he is the one who formed
all things.
Israel is the tribe of his inheritance;
the LORD of Armies is his name.

EXILE AFTER THE SIEGE

17 Gather up your belongings[D]
from the ground,
you who live under siege.

18 For this is what the LORD says:
Look, I am flinging away
the land's residents at this time
and bringing them such distress
that they will feel it.

JEREMIAH GRIEVES

19 Woe to me because of
my brokenness —
I am severely wounded!
I exclaimed, "This is
my intense suffering,
but I must bear it."
20 My tent is destroyed;
all my tent cords are snapped.
My sons have departed from me
and are no more.
I have no one to pitch my tent again
or to hang up my curtains.
21 For the shepherds are stupid:
They don't seek the LORD.
Therefore they have not prospered,
and their whole flock is scattered.
22 Listen! A noise — it is coming —
a great commotion from the land
to the north.
The cities of Judah will be
made desolate,
a jackals' den.

23 I know, LORD,
that a person's way of life is not
his own;
no one who walks determines
his own steps.
24 Discipline me, LORD, but with justice —
not in your anger,
or you will reduce me to nothing.
25 Pour out your wrath on the nations
that don't recognize you
and on the families
that don't call on your name,
for they have consumed Jacob;
they have consumed him and finished
him off
and made his homeland desolate.

REMINDER OF THE COVENANT

11 This is the word that came to Jeremiah from the LORD: 2 "Listen to the words
of this covenant and tell them to the men of
Judah and the residents of Jerusalem. 3 Tell
them, 'This is what the LORD, the God of Israel, says: "Let a curse be on the man who does
not obey the words of this covenant, 4 which
I commanded your ancestors when I brought
them out of the land of Egypt, out of the iron
furnace." I declared, "Obey me, and do everything that I command you, and you will be my
people, and I will be your God," 5 in order to
establish the oath I swore to your ancestors,
to give them a land flowing with milk and
honey, as it is today.'"
I answered, "Amen, LORD."
6 The LORD said to me, "Proclaim all these
words in the cities of Judah and in the streets

[A] **10:11** This is the only Aramaic v. in Jr. [B] **10:13** Lit *At his giving of the voice* [C] **10:16** = the LORD [D] **10:17** Lit *bundle*

of Jerusalem: ‘Obey the words of this covenant
and carry them out.’ 7 For I strongly warned
your ancestors when I brought them out of
the land of Egypt until today, warning them
time and time again,[A] ‘Obey me.’ 8 Yet they
would not obey or pay attention; each one
followed the stubbornness of his evil heart.
So I brought on them all the curses of this
covenant, because they had not done what I
commanded them to do.”

9 The LORD said to me, “A conspiracy has been
discovered among the men of Judah and the
residents of Jerusalem. 10 They have returned
to the iniquities of their fathers who refused
to obey my words and have followed other
gods to worship them. The house of Israel
and the house of Judah broke my covenant I
made with their ancestors.

11 “Therefore, this is what the LORD says: I
am about to bring on them disaster that they
cannot escape. They will cry out to me, but I
will not hear them. 12 Then the cities of Judah
and the residents of Jerusalem will go and
cry out to the gods they have been burning
incense to, but they certainly will not save
them in their time of disaster. 13 Your gods are
indeed as numerous as your cities, Judah, and
the altars you have set up to Shame[B] — altars
to burn incense to Baal — as numerous as the
streets of Jerusalem.

14 “As for you, do not pray for these people.
Do not raise up a cry or a prayer on their behalf, for I will not be listening when they call
out to me at the time of their disaster.

15 What right does my beloved have
to be in my house,
having carried out so many
evil schemes?
Can holy meat[C] prevent your disaster[D]
so you can celebrate?
16 The LORD named you
a flourishing olive tree,
beautiful with well-formed fruit.
He has set fire to it,
and its branches are consumed[E]
with the sound of a mighty tumult.

17 “The LORD of Armies who planted you has
decreed disaster against you, because of the
disaster[F] the house of Israel and the house
of Judah brought on themselves when they
angered me by burning incense to Baal.”

18 The LORD informed me, so I knew.
Then you helped me to see their deeds,
19 for I was like a docile[G] lamb led
to slaughter.
I didn't know that they had
devised plots against me:
“Let's destroy the tree with its fruit;[H]
let's cut him off from the land
of the living
so that his name will no longer
be remembered.”
20 But, LORD of Armies,
who judges righteously,
who tests heart[I] and mind,
let me see your vengeance on them,
for I have presented my case to you.

21 Therefore, here is what the LORD says concerning the people of Anathoth who intend to
take your life. They warn, “Do not prophesy
in the name of the LORD, or you will certainly
die at our hand.” 22 Therefore, this is what the
LORD of Armies says: “I am about to punish
them. The young men will die by the sword;
their sons and daughters will die by famine.
23 They will have no remnant, for I will bring
disaster on the people of Anathoth in the year
of their punishment.”

JEREMIAH'S COMPLAINT

12 You will be righteous, LORD,
even if I bring a case against you.
Yet, I wish to contend with you:
Why does the way of the wicked
prosper?
Why do all the treacherous live at ease?
2 You planted them, and they
have taken root.
They have grown and produced fruit.
You are ever on their lips,[J]
but far from their conscience.[I]
3 As for you, LORD, you know me;
you see me.
You test whether my heart is with you.
Drag the wicked away like sheep
to slaughter
and set them apart for the day of killing.
4 How long will the land mourn
and the grass of every field wither?
Because of the evil of its residents,
animals and birds have been
swept away,

[A] 11:7 Lit *today, rising early and warning* [B] 11:13 = Baal [C] 11:15 = sacrificial meat [D] 11:15 LXX; MT reads *meat pass from you* [E] 11:16 Vg; MT reads *broken* [F] 11:17 Or *evil* [G] 11:19 Or *pet* [H] 11:19 Lit *bread* [I] 11:20; 12:2 Lit *kidneys* [J] 12:2 Lit *are near in their mouth*

for the people have said,
"He cannot see what our end will be."[A]

THE LORD'S RESPONSE

5 If you have raced with runners
and they have worn you out,
how can you compete with horses?
If you stumble[B] in a peaceful land,
what will you do in the thickets
of the Jordan?
6 Even your brothers —
your own father's family —
even they were treacherous to you;
even they have cried out loudly
after you.
Do not have confidence in them,
though they speak well of you.

7 I have abandoned my house;
I have deserted my inheritance.
I have handed the love of my life
over to her enemies.
8 My inheritance has behaved toward me
like a lion in the forest.
She has roared against me.
Therefore, I hate her.
9 Is my inheritance like a hyena[C] to me?
Are birds of prey circling her?
Go, gather all the wild animals;
bring them to devour her.
10 Many shepherds have destroyed
my vineyard;
they have trampled my plot of land.
They have turned my desirable plot
into a desolate wasteland.
11 They have made it a desolation.
It mourns, desolate, before me.
All the land is desolate,
but no one takes it to heart.
12 Over all the barren heights
in the wilderness
the destroyers have come,
for the LORD has a sword that devours
from one end of the earth to the other.
No one has peace.
13 They have sown wheat
but harvested thorns.
They have exhausted themselves
but have no profit.
Be put to shame by your harvests
because of the LORD's burning anger.

14 This is what the LORD says: "Concerning
all my evil neighbors who attack the inheritance that I bequeathed to my people, Israel,
I am about to uproot them from their land,
and I will uproot the house of Judah from
them. 15 After I have uprooted them, I will once
again have compassion on them and return
each one to his inheritance and to his land.
16 If they will diligently learn the ways of my
people — to swear by my name, 'As the LORD
lives,' just as they taught my people to swear
by Baal — they will be built up among my
people. 17 However, if they will not obey, then
I will uproot and destroy that nation."
This is the LORD's declaration.

LINEN UNDERWEAR

13 This is what the LORD said to me: "Go
and buy yourself a linen undergarment
and put it on.[D] But do not put it in water." 2 So
I bought underwear as the LORD instructed
me and put it on.
3 Then the word of the LORD came to me a
second time: 4 "Take the underwear that you
bought and are wearing,[E] and go at once to
the Euphrates[F] and hide it in a rocky crevice."
5 So I went and hid it by the Euphrates, as the
LORD commanded me.
6 A long time later the LORD said to me, "Go at
once to the Euphrates and get the underwear
that I commanded you to hide there." 7 So I went
to the Euphrates and dug up the underwear
and got it from the place where I had hidden
it, but it was ruined — of no use at all.
8 Then the word of the LORD came to me:
9 "This is what the LORD says: Just like this I
will ruin the great pride of both Judah and
Jerusalem. 10 These evil people, who refuse to
listen to me, who follow the stubbornness of
their own hearts, and who have followed other
gods to serve and bow in worship — they will
be like this underwear, of no use at all. 11 Just as
underwear clings to one's waist, so I fastened
the whole house of Israel and of Judah to me"
— this is the LORD's declaration — "so that
they might be my people for my fame, praise,
and glory, but they would not obey.

THE WINE JARS

12 "Say this to them: 'This is what the LORD, the
God of Israel, says: Every jar should be filled
with wine.' Then they will respond to you, 'Don't
we know that every jar should be filled with
wine?' 13 And you will say to them, 'This is what

[A] **12:4** LXX reads *see our ways* [B] **12:5** Or *you are secure* [C] **12:9** Hb obscure [D] **13:1** Lit *around your waist* [E] **13:4** Lit *wearing around your waist* [F] **13:4-7** Perhaps a place near Anathoth with the same spelling as the river

the LORD says: I am about to fill all who live in
this land — the kings who reign for David on
his throne, the priests, the prophets, and all the
residents of Jerusalem — with drunkenness.
14 I will smash them against each other, fathers
and sons alike — this is the LORD's declaration.
I will allow no mercy, pity, or compassion to
keep me from destroying them.'"

THE LORD'S WARNING

15 Listen and pay attention.
Do not be proud,
for the LORD has spoken.
16 Give glory to the LORD your God
before he brings darkness,
before your feet stumble
on the mountains at dusk.
You wait for light,
but he brings darkest gloom[A]
and makes total darkness.
17 But if you will not listen,
my innermost being will weep in secret
because of your pride.
My eyes will overflow with tears,
for the LORD's flock has been
taken captive.

18 Say to the king and the queen mother:
Take a humble seat,
for your glorious crowns
have fallen from your heads.
19 The cities of the Negev are under siege;
no one can help them.
All of Judah has been taken into exile,
taken completely into exile.
20 Look up and see
those coming from the north.
Where is the flock entrusted to you,
the sheep that were your pride?

THE DESTINY OF JERUSALEM

21 What will you say when he appoints
close friends as leaders over you,
ones you yourself trained?
Won't labor pains seize you,
as they do a woman in labor?
22 And when you ask yourself,
"Why have these things happened
to me?"
it is because of your great guilt
that your skirts have been stripped off,
your body exposed.[B]
23 Can the Cushite change his skin,
or a leopard his spots?
If so, you might be able to do
what is good,
you who are instructed in evil.
24 I will scatter you[C] like drifting chaff
before the desert wind.
25 This is your lot,
what I have decreed for you —
this is the LORD's declaration —
because you have forgotten me
and trusted in lies.
26 I will pull your skirts up over your face
so that your shame might be seen.
27 Your adulteries and
your lustful neighing,
your depraved prostitution
on the hills, in the fields —
I have seen your abhorrent acts.
Woe to you, Jerusalem!
You are unclean —
for how long yet?

THE DROUGHT

14 This is the word of the LORD that came
to Jeremiah concerning the drought:
2 Judah mourns;
her city gates languish.
Her people are on the ground
in mourning;
Jerusalem's cry rises up.
3 Their nobles send their servants[D]
for water.
They go to the cisterns;
they find no water;
their containers return empty.
They are ashamed and humiliated;
they cover their heads.
4 The ground is cracked
since no rain has fallen on the land.
The farmers are ashamed;
they cover their heads.
5 Even the doe in the field
gives birth and abandons her fawn
since there is no grass.
6 Wild donkeys stand
on the barren heights
panting for air like jackals.
Their eyes fail
because there are no green plants.

7 Though our iniquities testify
against us,
LORD, act for your name's sake.

[A] **13:16** Or *brings a shadow of death* [B] **13:22** Lit *your heels have suffered violence* [C] **13:24** Lit *them* [D] **14:3** Lit *little ones*

Indeed, our rebellions are many;
we have sinned against you.
8 Hope of Israel,
its Savior in time of distress,
why are you like a resident alien
in the land,
like a traveler stopping only for the night?
9 Why are you like a helpless man,
like a warrior unable to save?
Yet you are among us, LORD,
and we bear your name.
Don't leave us!

10 This is what the LORD says concerning
these people:
Truly they love to wander;
they never rest their feet.
So the LORD does not accept them.
Now he will remember their iniquity
and punish their sins.

FALSE PROPHETS TO BE PUNISHED

11 Then the LORD said to me, "Do not pray for
the well-being of these people. 12 If they fast, I
will not hear their cry of despair. If they offer
burnt offering and grain offering, I will not
accept them. Rather, I will finish them off by
sword, famine, and plague."
13 And I replied, "Oh no, Lord GOD! The prophets are telling them, 'You won't see sword or
suffer famine. I will certainly give you lasting
peace in this place.' "
14 But the LORD said to me, "These prophets are prophesying a lie in my name. I did
not send them, nor did I command them or
speak to them. They are prophesying to you
a false vision, worthless divination, the deceit
of their own minds.
15 "Therefore, this is what the LORD says concerning the prophets who prophesy in my
name, though I did not send them, and who
say, 'There will never be sword or famine in
this land.' By sword and famine these prophets will meet their end. 16 The people they are
prophesying to will be thrown into the streets
of Jerusalem because of the famine and the
sword. There will be no one to bury them —
they, their wives, their sons, and their daughters. I will pour out their own evil on them."

JEREMIAH'S REQUEST

17 You are to speak this word to them:
Let my eyes overflow with tears;
day and night may they not stop,
for the virgin daughter of my people
has been destroyed by a crushing blow,
an extremely severe wound.
18 If I go out to the field,
look — those slain by the sword!
If I enter the city,
look — those ill from famine!
For both prophet and priest
travel to a land they do not know.

19 Have you completely rejected Judah?
Do you detest Zion?
Why do you strike us
with no hope of healing for us?
We hoped for peace,
but there was nothing good;
for a time of healing,
but there was only terror.
20 We acknowledge our wickedness, LORD,
the iniquity of our fathers;
indeed, we have sinned against you.
21 For your name's sake, don't despise us.
Don't disdain your glorious throne.
Remember your covenant with us;
do not break it.
22 Can any of the worthless idols
of the nations bring rain?
Or can the skies alone give showers?
Are you not the LORD our God?
We therefore put our hope in you,
for you have done all these things.

THE LORD'S NEGATIVE RESPONSE

15 Then the LORD said to me: "Even if Moses
and Samuel should stand before me, my
compassions would not reach out to these
people. Send them from my presence, and let
them go. 2 If they ask you, 'Where will we go?'
tell them: This is what the LORD says:
Those destined for death, to death;
those destined for the sword, to the sword.
Those destined for famine, to famine;
those destined for captivity, to captivity.

3 "I will ordain four kinds[A] of judgment for
them" — this is the LORD's declaration — "the
sword to kill, the dogs to drag away, and the birds
of the sky and the wild animals of the land to
devour and destroy. 4 I will make them a horror to all the kingdoms of the earth because of
Manasseh son of Hezekiah, the king of Judah,
for what he did in Jerusalem.

[A] 15:3 Lit *families*

5 Who will have pity on you, Jerusalem?
Who will show sympathy toward you?
Who will turn aside
to ask about your well-being?
6 You have left me."
This is the LORD's declaration.
"You have turned your back,
so I have stretched out my hand
against you
and destroyed you.
I am tired of showing compassion.
7 I scattered them with a winnowing fork
at the city gates of the land.
I made them childless; I destroyed
my people.
They would not turn from their ways.
8 I made their widows more numerous
than the sand of the seas.
I brought a destroyer at noon
against the mother of young men.
I suddenly released on her
agitation and terrors.
9 The mother of seven grew faint;
she breathed her last breath.
Her sun set while it was still day;
she was ashamed and humiliated.
The rest of them I will give over
to the sword
in the presence of their enemies."
This is the LORD's declaration.

JEREMIAH'S COMPLAINT

10 Woe is me, my mother,
that you gave birth to me,
a man who incites dispute and conflict
in all the land.
I did not lend or borrow,
yet everyone curses me.

THE LORD'S RESPONSE

11 The LORD said:
Haven't I set you loose for your good?
Haven't I punished you
in a time of trouble,
in a time of distress
with the enemy?[A]

Relationships | *Offering Forgiveness*

A CLEAN SLATE

"I will rescue you from the power of evil people and redeem you from the grasp of the ruthless." Jeremiah 15:21

God promises rescue from evil and ruthless people.

But then what? Jesus would later say, "Forgive us our debts, as we also have forgiven our debtors. . . . If you forgive others their offenses, your heavenly Father will forgive you as well" (Mt 6:12-14). Elsewhere the Bible tells us to forgive because God has forgiven us (Eph 4:32). The idea seems to be: How could we dare hold a grudge against someone else when God doesn't harbor bitterness against us?

And are we really supposed to forgive those evil people?

Jesus challenges us to forgive, not because it's a prerequisite for being forgiven by God (that would make salvation dependent on us), but because doing so enables us to enjoy the rich experience of God's forgiveness.

When people wrong us, we can respond in all sorts of ways. We can keep a record, feel morally superior, get angry, wish them harm, seek vengeance by lashing out, or build a wall. Or, we can remember God's shocking forgiveness and we can choose instead to build a bridge. We can wipe the slate clean.

Ask for the grace to be able to pray like Jesus from the heart, "Father, forgive them, because they do not know what they are doing" (Lk 23:34).

For the next note on *Relationships*, see Micah 5:5.

[A] **15:11** Hb obscure

12 Can anyone smash iron,
iron from the north, or bronze?
13 I will give up your wealth
and your treasures as plunder,
without cost, for all your sins
in all your borders.
14 Then I will make you serve
your enemies[A]
in a land you do not know,
for my anger will kindle a fire
that will burn against you.

JEREMIAH'S PRAYER FOR VENGEANCE

15 You know, LORD;
remember me and take note of me.
Avenge me against my persecutors.
In your patience,[B] don't take me away.
Know that I suffer disgrace
for your honor.
16 Your words were found, and I ate them.
Your words became a delight to me
and the joy of my heart,
for I bear your name,
LORD God of Armies.
17 I never sat with the band of revelers,
and I did not celebrate with them.
Because your hand was on me,
I sat alone,
for you filled me with indignation.
18 Why has my pain become unending,
my wound incurable,
refusing to be healed?
You truly have become like a mirage
to me —
water that is not reliable.

JEREMIAH TOLD TO REPENT

19 Therefore, this is what the LORD says:
If you return, I will take you back;
you will stand in my presence.
And if you speak noble words,
rather than worthless ones,
you will be my spokesman.
It is they who must return to you;
you must not return to them.
20 Then I will make you a fortified wall
of bronze
to this people.
They will fight against you
but will not overcome you,
for I am with you
to save you and rescue you.
This is the LORD's declaration.
21 I will rescue you from the power
of evil people
and redeem you from the grasp
of the ruthless.

NO MARRIAGE FOR JEREMIAH

16 The word of the LORD came to me: 2 "Do
not marry or have sons or daughters
in this place. 3 For this is what the LORD says
concerning sons and daughters born in this
place as well as concerning the mothers who
bear them and the fathers who father them in
this land: 4 They will die from deadly diseases.
They will not be mourned or buried but will
be like manure on the soil's surface. They will
be finished off by sword and famine. Their
corpses will become food for the birds of the
sky and for the wild animals of the land.
5 "For this is what the LORD says: Don't enter a
house where a mourning feast is taking place.[C]
Don't go to lament or sympathize with them,
for I have removed my peace from these people
as well as my faithful love and compassion."
This is the LORD's declaration. 6 "Both great and
small will die in this land without burial. No
lament will be made for them, nor will anyone
cut himself or shave his head for them.[D] 7 Food
won't be provided for the mourner to comfort
him because of the dead. A consoling drink
won't be given him for the loss of his father or
mother. 8 Do not enter the house where feasting is taking place to sit with them to eat and
drink. 9 For this is what the LORD of Armies,
the God of Israel, says: I am about to eliminate
from this place, before your very eyes and in
your time, the sound of joy and gladness, the
voice of the groom and the bride.

ABANDONING THE LORD AND HIS LAW

10 "When you tell these people all these things,
they will say to you, 'Why has the LORD declared
all this terrible disaster against us? What is our
iniquity? What is our sin that we have committed against the LORD our God?' 11 Then you will
answer them, 'Because your fathers abandoned
me — this is the LORD's declaration — and
followed other gods, served them, and bowed
in worship to them. Indeed, they abandoned
me and did not keep my instruction. 12 You did
more evil than your fathers. Look, each one
of you was following the stubbornness of his
evil heart, not obeying me. 13 So I will hurl you
from this land into a land that you and your

[A] **15:14** Some Hb mss, LXX, Syr, Tg; other Hb mss read *you pass through* [B] **15:15** Lit *In the slowness of your anger* [C] **16:5** Lit *house of mourning* [D] **16:6** This custom demonstrated pagan mourning rituals.

fathers are not familiar with. There you will
worship other gods both day and night, for I
will not grant you grace.'[A]
14 "However, look, the days are coming" —
the LORD's declaration — "when it will no longer be said, 'As the LORD lives who brought the
Israelites from the land of Egypt,' 15 but rather,
'As the LORD lives who brought the Israelites
from the land of the north and from all the
other lands where he had banished them.' For
I will return them to their land that I gave to
their ancestors.

PUNISHMENT OF EXILE

16 "I am about to send for many fishermen"
— this is the LORD's declaration — "and they
will fish for them. Then I will send for many
hunters, and they will hunt them down on
every mountain and hill and out of the clefts
of the rocks, 17 for my gaze takes in all their
ways. They are not concealed from me, and
their iniquity is not hidden from my sight. 18 I
will first repay them double for their iniquity
and sin because they have polluted my land.
They have filled my inheritance with the carcasses of their abhorrent and detestable idols."

19 LORD, my strength and my stronghold,
my refuge in a time of distress,
the nations will come to you
from the ends of the earth,
and they will say,
"Our fathers inherited only lies,
worthless idols of no benefit at all."
20 Can one make gods for himself?
But they are not gods.
21 "Therefore, I am about to inform them,
and this time I will make them know
my power and my might;
then they will know that my name
is the LORD."

THE PERSISTENT SIN OF JUDAH

17 The sin of Judah is inscribed
with an iron stylus.
With a diamond point
it is engraved on the tablet of their hearts
and on the horns of their[B] altars,
2 while their children remember
their altars
and their Asherah poles,
by the green trees
on the high hills —
3 my mountains in the countryside.
I will give up your wealth
and all your treasures as plunder
because of the sin of your high places[C]
in all your borders.
4 You will, on your own, relinquish
your inheritance
that I gave you.
I will make you serve your enemies
in a land you do not know,
for you have set my anger on fire;
it will burn forever.

CURSE AND BLESSING

5 This is what the LORD says:
Cursed is the person who trusts
in mankind.
He makes human flesh his strength,
and his heart turns from the LORD.
6 He will be like a juniper in the Arabah;
he cannot see when good comes
but dwells in the parched places
in the wilderness,
in a salt land where no one lives.
7 The person who trusts in the LORD,
whose confidence indeed is the LORD,
is blessed.
8 He will be like a tree planted by water:
it sends its roots out toward a stream,
it doesn't fear when heat comes,
and its foliage remains green.
It will not worry in a year of drought
or cease producing fruit.

THE DECEITFUL HEART

9 The heart is more deceitful
than anything else,
and incurable — who can understand it?
10 I, the LORD, examine the mind,
I test the heart[D]
to give to each according to his way,
according to what his actions deserve.
11 He who makes a fortune unjustly
is like a partridge that hatches eggs
it didn't lay.
In the middle of his life
his riches will abandon him,
so in the end he will be a fool.

12 A glorious throne
on high from the beginning
is the place of our sanctuary.
13 LORD, the hope of Israel,
all who abandon you

[A] **16:13** Or *compassion* [B] **17:1** Some Hb mss, Syr, Vg; other Hb mss read *your* [C] **17:3** Lit *plunder, your high places because of sin*
[D] **17:10** Lit *kidneys*

Heal me, LORD, and I will be healed; save me, and I will be saved, for you are my praise.
—Jeremiah 17:14

will be put to shame.
All who turn away from me
will be written in the dirt,
for they have abandoned
the LORD, the fountain of living water.

JEREMIAH'S PLEA

14 Heal me, LORD, and I will be healed;
save me, and I will be saved,
for you are my praise.
15 Hear how they keep challenging me,
"Where is the word of the LORD?
Let it come!"
16 But I have not run away from being
your shepherd,
and I have not longed for the fatal day.
You know my words were spoken
in your presence.
17 Don't become a terror to me.
You are my refuge in the day of disaster.
18 Let my persecutors be put to shame,
but don't let me be put to shame.
Let them be terrified, but don't let me
be terrified.
Bring on them the day of disaster;
shatter them with total[A] destruction.

OBSERVING THE SABBATH

19 This is what the LORD said to me, "Go and
stand at the People's Gate, through which
the kings of Judah enter and leave, as well
as at all the gates of Jerusalem. 20 Announce
to them, 'Hear the word of the LORD, kings
of Judah, all Judah, and all the residents of
Jerusalem who enter through these gates.
21 This is what the LORD says: Watch yourselves; do not pick up a load and bring it in
through Jerusalem's gates on the Sabbath
day. 22 Do not carry a load out of your houses
on the Sabbath day or do any work, but keep
the Sabbath day holy, just as I commanded
your ancestors. 23 They wouldn't listen or pay
attention but became obstinate, not listening
or accepting discipline.
24 " 'However, if you listen to me — this is
the LORD's declaration — and do not bring
loads through the gates of this city on the
Sabbath day, but keep the Sabbath day holy
and do no work on it, 25 kings and princes will
enter through the gates of this city. They will
sit on the throne of David; they will ride in
chariots and on horses with their officials,
the men of Judah, and the residents of Jerusalem. This city will be inhabited forever.
26 Then people will come from the cities of
Judah and from the area around Jerusalem, from the land of Benjamin and from
the Judean foothills, from the hill country
and from the Negev bringing burnt offerings
and sacrifices, grain offerings and frankincense, and thank offerings to the house of
the LORD. 27 But if you do not listen to me to
keep the Sabbath day holy by not carrying a
load while entering the gates of Jerusalem
on the Sabbath day, I will set fire to its gates,
and it will consume the citadels of Jerusalem
and not be extinguished.' "

PARABLE OF THE POTTER

18 This is the word that came to Jeremiah from the LORD: 2 "Go down at once
to the potter's house; there I will reveal my
words to you." 3 So I went down to the potter's
house, and there he was, working away at the
wheel.[B] 4 But the jar that he was making from
the clay became flawed in the potter's hand,
so he made it into another jar, as it seemed
right for him to do.
5 The word of the LORD came to me: 6 "House
of Israel, can I not treat you as this potter treats
his clay?" — this is the LORD's declaration. "Just
like clay in the potter's hand, so are you in my
hand, house of Israel. 7 At one moment I might
announce concerning a nation or a kingdom
that I will uproot, tear down, and destroy it.
8 However, if that nation about which I have
made the announcement turns from its evil,
I will relent concerning the disaster I had
planned to do to it. 9 At another time I might
announce concerning a nation or a kingdom
that I will build and plant it. 10 However, if it
does what is evil in my sight by not listening
to me, I will relent concerning the good I had
said I would do to it. 11 So now, say to the men of
Judah and to the residents of Jerusalem, 'This

[A] **17:18** Lit *double* [B] **18:3** Lit *pair of stones*

is what the LORD says: Look, I am about to bring
harm to you and make plans against you. Turn
now, each from your evil way, and correct your
ways and your deeds.' 12 But they will say, 'It's
hopeless. We will continue to follow our plans,
and each of us will continue to act according
to the stubbornness of his evil heart.'"

DELUDED ISRAEL

13 Therefore, this is what the LORD says:
Ask among the nations,
who has heard things like these?
Virgin Israel has done
a most horrible thing.
14 Does the snow of Lebanon ever leave
the highland crags?
Or does cold water flowing
from a distance ever fail?
15 Yet my people have forgotten me.
They burn incense to worthless idols
that make them stumble in their ways
on the ancient roads,
and make them walk on new paths,
not the highway.
16 They have made their land a horror,
a perpetual object of scorn;[A]
all who pass by it will be appalled
and shake their heads.
17 I will scatter them before the enemy
like the east wind.
I will show them[B] my back and not
my face
on the day of their calamity.

PLOT AGAINST JEREMIAH

18 Then certain ones said, "Come, let's make
plans against Jeremiah, for instruction will
never be lost from the priest, or counsel from
the wise, or a word from the prophet. Come,
let's denounce him[C] and pay no attention to
all his words."
19 Pay attention to me, LORD.
Hear what my opponents are saying!
20 Should good be repaid with evil?
Yet they have dug a pit for me.
Remember how I stood before you
to speak good on their behalf,
to turn your anger from them.
21 Therefore, hand their children
over to famine,
and give them over to the power of the
sword.
Let their wives become childless
and widowed,
their husbands slain
by deadly disease,[D]
their young men struck down
by the sword in battle.
22 Let a cry be heard from their houses
when you suddenly bring raiders
against them,
for they have dug a pit to capture me
and have hidden snares for my feet.
23 But you, LORD, know
all their deadly plots against me.
Do not wipe out their iniquity;
do not blot out their sin before you.
Let them be forced to stumble
before you;
deal with them in the time of your anger.

THE CLAY JAR

19 This is what the LORD says: "Go, buy a
potter's clay jar. Take[E] some of the elders
of the people and some of the leading priests
2 and go out to Ben Hinnom Valley near the
entrance of the Potsherd Gate. Proclaim there
the words I speak to you. 3 Say, 'Hear the word
of the LORD, kings of Judah and residents of
Jerusalem. This is what the LORD of Armies,
the God of Israel, says: I am going to bring
such disaster on this place that everyone who
hears about it will shudder[F] 4 because they
have abandoned me and made this a foreign
place. They have burned incense in it to other
gods that they, their fathers, and the kings of
Judah have never known. They have filled this
place with the blood of the innocent. 5 They
have built high places to Baal on which to burn
their children in the fire as burnt offerings to
Baal, something I have never commanded or
mentioned; I never entertained the thought.[G]
6 "'Therefore, look, the days are coming —
this is the LORD's declaration — when this
place will no longer be called Topheth and
Ben Hinnom Valley, but Slaughter Valley. 7 I
will spoil the plans of Judah and Jerusalem in
this place. I will make them fall by the sword
before their enemies, by the hand of those
who intend to take their life. I will provide
their corpses as food for the birds of the sky
and for the wild animals of the land. 8 I will
make this city desolate, an object of scorn.
Everyone who passes by it will be appalled

[A] **18:16** Lit *hissing* [B] **18:17** LXX, Lat, Syr, Tg; MT reads *will look at them* [C] **18:18** Lit *let's strike him with the tongue* [D] **18:21** Lit *by death* [E] **19:1** Syr, Tg; MT omits *Take* [F] **19:3** Lit *about it, his ears will tingle*; Hb obscure [G] **19:5** Lit *mentioned, and it did not arise on my heart*

and scoff because of all its wounds. 9 I will
make them eat the flesh of their sons and their
daughters, and they will eat each other's flesh
in the distressing siege inflicted on them by
their enemies who intend to take their life.'
10 "Then you are to shatter the jar in the presence of the people going with you, 11 and you
are to proclaim to them, 'This is what the LORD
of Armies says: I will shatter these people and
this city, like one shatters a potter's jar that
can never again be mended. They will bury
the dead in Topheth because there is no other
place for burials. 12 That is what I will do to this
place — this is the declaration of the LORD
— and to its residents, making this city like
Topheth. 13 The houses of Jerusalem and the
houses of the kings of Judah will become impure like that place Topheth — all the houses
on whose rooftops they have burned incense
to all the stars in the sky and poured out drink
offerings to other gods.' "
14 Jeremiah returned from Topheth, where
the LORD had sent him to prophesy, stood in
the courtyard of the LORD's temple, and proclaimed to all the people, 15 "This is what the
LORD of Armies, the God of Israel, says: 'I am
about to bring on this city — and on all its
cities — every disaster that I spoke against it,
for they have become obstinate, not obeying
my words.' "

JEREMIAH BEATEN BY PASHHUR

20 Pashhur the priest, the son of Immer and
chief official in the temple of the LORD,
heard Jeremiah prophesying these things. 2 So
Pashhur had the prophet Jeremiah beaten and
put him in the stocks at the Upper Benjamin
Gate in the LORD's temple. 3 The next day, when
Pashhur released Jeremiah from the stocks,
Jeremiah said to him, "The LORD does not call
you Pashhur, but Terror Is on Every Side,[A] 4 for
this is what the LORD says, 'I am about to make
you a terror to both yourself and those you
love. They will fall by the sword of their enemies before your very eyes. I will hand Judah
over to the king of Babylon, and he will deport
them to Babylon and put them to the sword.
5 I will give away all the wealth of this city, all
its products and valuables. Indeed, I will hand
all the treasures of the kings of Judah over to

HONEST TO GOD

"You deceived me, LORD, and I was deceived. You seized me and prevailed. I am a laughingstock all the time; everyone ridicules me. . . . I say, 'I won't mention him or speak any longer in his name.' But his message becomes a fire burning in my heart, shut up in my bones. I become tired of holding it in, and I cannot prevail." Jeremiah 20:7,9

Have you ever felt as though God pulled a fast one on you? All you did was try to follow him faithfully—and for that, you got trouble, not blessing?

This was Jeremiah's experience. Here, just carrying out his prophet's duties, he got beat up and put in stocks (20:2)! Upon his release, first he confronted the priest responsible for his pain and humiliation. Then he spoke honestly, from his heart, to God.

Notice his prayer (20:7-18). It's raw, not edited for church. It's not T.C. (theologically correct). In so many words, he says: I feel like you misled me, God! I feel like an idiot for trusting you. Look where it got me—I'm the town punchline and Pashhur's punching bag. I don't want to serve you anymore! It hurts too much. And yet, the minute I contemplate turning in my prophet's badge, I can't sleep, think—do anything. I can't shake this burning calling inside me.

This passage is a model of "honest to God"-type praying. Is this how you pray? Tell God how you feel. He can take it.

For the next note on *Support*, see Lamentations 3:40.

[A] **20:3** = *Magor-missabib*

their enemies. They will plunder them, seize
them, and carry them off to Babylon. 6 As for
you, Pashhur, and all who live in your house,
you will go into captivity. You will go to Babylon. There you will die, and there you will
be buried, you and all your friends to whom
you prophesied lies.'"

JEREMIAH COMPELLED TO PREACH

7 You deceived me, LORD,
and I was deceived.
You seized me and prevailed.
I am a laughingstock all the time;
everyone ridicules me.
8 For whenever I speak, I cry out,
I proclaim, "Violence and destruction!"
so the word of the LORD has become my
constant disgrace and derision.
9 I say, "I won't mention him
or speak any longer in his name."
But his message becomes a fire burning
in my heart,
shut up in my bones.
I become tired of holding it in,
and I cannot prevail.
10 For I have heard the gossip
of many people,
"Terror is on every side!
Report him; let's report him!"
Everyone I trusted[A] watches for my fall.
"Perhaps he will be deceived
so that we might prevail against him
and take our vengeance on him."
11 But the LORD is with me
like a violent warrior.
Therefore, my persecutors will stumble
and not prevail.
Since they have not succeeded,
they will be utterly shamed,
an everlasting humiliation that will
never be forgotten.
12 LORD of Armies, testing the righteous
and seeing the heart[B] and mind,
let me see your vengeance on them,
for I have presented my case to you.
13 Sing to the LORD!
Praise the LORD,
for he rescues the life of the needy
from evil people.

JEREMIAH'S LAMENT

14 May the day I was born
be cursed.
May the day my mother bore me
never be blessed.
15 May the man be cursed
who brought the news
to my father, saying,
"A male child is born to you,"
bringing him great joy.
16 Let that man be like the cities
the LORD demolished
without compassion.
Let him hear an outcry
in the morning
and a war cry at noontime
17 because he didn't kill me in the womb
so that my mother might have been
my grave,
her womb eternally pregnant.
18 Why did I come out of the womb
to see only struggle and sorrow,
to end my life in shame?

ZEDEKIAH'S REQUEST DENIED

21 This is the word that came to Jeremiah from the LORD when King Zedekiah
sent Pashhur son of Malchijah and the priest
Zephaniah son of Maaseiah to Jeremiah, asking, 2 "Inquire of the LORD on our behalf, since
King Nebuchadnezzar[C] of Babylon is making
war against us. Perhaps the LORD will perform
for us something like all his past wondrous
works so that Nebuchadnezzar will withdraw
from us."
3 But Jeremiah answered, "This is what you
are to say to Zedekiah: 4 'This is what the LORD,
the God of Israel, says: I am about to repel the
weapons of war in your hands, those you are
using to fight the king of Babylon and the
Chaldeans[D] who are besieging you outside
the wall, and I will bring them into the center
of this city. 5 I myself will fight against you
with an outstretched hand and a strong arm,
with anger, rage, and intense wrath. 6 I will
strike the residents of this city, both people
and animals. They will die in a severe plague.
7 Afterward — this is the LORD's declaration
— King Zedekiah of Judah, his officers, and
the people — those in this city who survive
the plague, the sword, and the famine — I
will hand over to King Nebuchadnezzar of
Babylon, to their enemies, yes, to those who
intend to take their lives. He will put them to
the sword; he won't spare them or show pity
or compassion.'

[A] 20:10 Lit *Every man of my peace* [B] 20:12 Lit *kidneys* [C] 21:2 Lit *Nebuchadrezzar* [D] 21:4 = Babylonians

A WARNING FOR THE PEOPLE

8 "But tell this people, 'This is what the LORD
says: Look, I am setting before you the way
of life and the way of death. 9 Whoever stays
in this city will die by the sword, famine, and
plague, but whoever goes out and surrenders
to the Chaldeans who are besieging you will
live and will retain his life like the spoils of
war. 10 For I have set my face against this city
to bring disaster and not good — this is the
LORD's declaration. It will be handed over to
the king of Babylon, who will burn it.'
11 "And to the house of the king of Judah say
this: 'Hear the word of the LORD! 12 House of
David, this is what the LORD says:

Administer justice every morning,
and rescue the victim of robbery
from his oppressor,
or my anger will flare up like fire
and burn unquenchably
because of your evil deeds.
13 Beware! I am against you,
you who sit above the valley,
you atop the rocky plateau —
this is the LORD's declaration —
you who say, "Who can come down
against us?
Who can enter our hiding places?"
14 I will punish you according to
what you have done —
this is the LORD's declaration.
I will kindle a fire in your forest
that will consume everything
around it.'"

JUDGMENT AGAINST SINFUL KINGS

22 This is what the LORD says: "Go down
to the palace of the king of Judah and
announce this word there. 2 You are to say,
'Hear the word of the LORD, king of Judah, you
who sit on the throne of David — you, your
officers, and your people who enter these
gates. 3 This is what the LORD says: Administer
justice and righteousness. Rescue the victim
of robbery from his oppressor. Don't exploit or
brutalize the resident alien, the fatherless, or
the widow. Don't shed innocent blood in this
place. 4 For if you conscientiously carry out
this word, then kings sitting on David's throne
will enter through the gates of this palace
riding on chariots and horses — they, their
officers, and their people. 5 But if you do not
obey these words, then I swear by myself —
this is the LORD's declaration — that this house
will become a ruin.'"
6 For this is what the LORD says concerning
the house of the king of Judah:

"You are like Gilead to me,
or the summit of Lebanon,
but I will certainly turn you
into a wilderness,
uninhabited cities.
7 I will set apart destroyers against you,
each with his weapons.
They will cut down the choicest
of your cedars
and throw them into the fire.

8 "Many nations will pass by this city and
ask one another, 'Why did the LORD do such
a thing to this great city?' 9 They will answer,
'Because they abandoned the covenant of the
LORD their God and bowed in worship to other
gods and served them.'"

A MESSAGE CONCERNING SHALLUM

10 Do not weep for the dead;
do not mourn for him.
Weep bitterly for the one
who has gone away,
for he will never return again
and see his native land.

11 For this is what the LORD says concerning
Shallum son of Josiah, king of Judah, who
became king in place of his father Josiah,
and who has left this place: "He will never
return here again, 12 but he will die in the place
where they deported him, never seeing this
land again."

A MESSAGE CONCERNING JEHOIAKIM

13 Woe for the one who builds his palace
through unrighteousness,
his upstairs rooms through injustice,
who makes his neighbor serve
without pay
and will not give him his wages,
14 who says, "I will build myself
a massive palace,
with spacious upstairs rooms."
He will cut windows[A] in it,
and it will be paneled with cedar
and painted bright red.
15 Are you a king because you excel
in cedar?

[A] **22:14** Lit *my windows*

Didn't your father eat and drink
and administer justice
and righteousness?
Then it went well with him.
16 He took up the case of the poor
and needy;
then it went well.
Is this not what it means to know me?
This is the LORD's declaration.
17 But you have eyes and a heart
for nothing
except your own dishonest profit,
shedding innocent blood
and committing extortion
and oppression.

18 Therefore, this is what the LORD says
concerning Jehoiakim son of Josiah, king
of Judah:
They will not mourn for him, saying,
"Woe, my brother!" or "Woe, my sister!"
They will not mourn for him, saying,
"Woe, lord! Woe, his majesty!"
19 He will be buried like a donkey,
dragged off and thrown
outside Jerusalem's gates.
20 Go up to Lebanon and cry out;
raise your voice in Bashan;
cry out from Abarim,
for all your lovers[A] have been crushed.
21 I spoke to you when you were secure.
You said, "I will not listen."
This has been your way since youth;
indeed, you have never listened to me.
22 The wind will take charge of[B] all
your shepherds,
and your lovers will go into captivity.
Then you will be ashamed
and humiliated
because of all your evil.
23 You residents of Lebanon,
nestled among the cedars,
how you will groan[C] when pains
come on you,
agony like a woman in labor.

A MESSAGE CONCERNING CONIAH

24 "As I live" — this is the LORD's declaration
— "though you, Coniah[D] son of Jehoiakim,
the king of Judah, were a signet ring on my
right hand, I would tear you from it. 25 In fact,
I will hand you over to those you dread, who
intend to take your life, to Nebuchadnezzar
king of Babylon and the Chaldeans. 26 I will
hurl you and the mother who gave birth to
you into another land, where neither of you
were born, and there you will both die. 27 They
will never return to the land they long to return to."
28 Is this man Coniah
a despised, shattered pot,
a jar no one wants?
Why are he and his descendants
hurled out
and cast into a land
they have not known?
29 Earth, earth, earth,
hear the word of the LORD!
30 This is what the LORD says:
Record this man as childless,
a man who will not be successful
in his lifetime.
None of his descendants will succeed
in sitting on the throne of David
or ruling again in Judah.

THE LORD AND HIS SHEEP

23 "Woe to the shepherds who destroy
and scatter the sheep of my pasture!"
This is the LORD's declaration. 2 "Therefore,
this is what the LORD, the God of Israel, says
about the shepherds who tend my people:
You have scattered my flock, banished
them, and have not attended to them. I am
about to attend to you because of your evil
acts" — this is the LORD's declaration. 3 "I
will gather the remnant of my flock from
all the lands where I have banished them,
and I will return them to their grazing land.
They will become fruitful and numerous. 4 I
will raise up shepherds over them who will
tend them. They will no longer be afraid or
discouraged, nor will any be missing." This
is the LORD's declaration.

THE RIGHTEOUS BRANCH OF DAVID

5 "Look, the days are coming" — this is
the LORD's declaration —
"when I will raise up a Righteous
Branch for David.
He will reign wisely as king
and administer justice and
righteousness in the land.
6 In his days Judah will be saved,
and Israel will dwell securely.

[A] 22:20 Or *friends*, or *allies*, also in v. 22 [B] 22:22 Lit *will shepherd* [C] 22:23 LXX, Syr, Vg; MT reads *will be pitied*
[D] 22:24 = Jehoiachin

My Story | Jason

I found that before restoration can begin, we must acknowledge that we need to be restored, admitting, first, our sinful ways and how short we fall of God's glory. And accepting Christ is not the end, just the beginning of restoration. We begin a journey of restoration by having a servant's heart and a desire to reflect Jesus himself.

I also found that God uses brokenness to bring restoration. Brokenness in my life has helped restore me and has allowed me to spiritually grow and mature in relationship with him.

I experienced brokenness in several ways. When I lost my job, I was consumed by fear, wondering how I could take care of my family. And I questioned my self-worth.

When my wife died, I lost my best friend, and I watched my friendship with other couples dissolve over time. I experienced dreadful loneliness.

And, more recently, I have struggled with health issues: stage four melanoma, cervical and lumbar spinal fusion, and Cushing's syndrome.

My brokenness helped, and continues to help, me better understand and appreciate God, his boundless love for me, the power of the Spirit to heal, and the infinite grace of his forgiveness. It allows for self-introspection—a better understanding of myself and my deficiencies. And brokenness creates a time to pause and reflect upon God's and my relationship.

I grew up in a Christian home and accepted Christ at camp around the age of twelve. But only around the age of fifty-nine did I understand that it was not the end but the beginning. I realized that I needed to be a *follower* of Christ, exemplifying his life in mine, loving him and others, denying self, and recognizing that my relationship with him would be a restorative process throughout my life. I need him constantly. And how much I need him becomes obvious when I'm faced with great brokenness. How wonderful then, that I can rely on a God who is faithful to me, who is steadfast, patient, loving, forgiving, and, yes, who is teaching me, especially through the most difficult times in my life. He doesn't restore me to be of this world; rather; he restores my soul so that I will be better prepared to be in communion with him in heaven.

What a great God! What a great Dad!

This is the name he will be called:
The LORD Is Our Righteousness.[A]

7 "Look, the days are coming" — the LORD's
declaration — "when it will no longer be said,
'As the LORD lives who brought the Israelites
from the land of Egypt,' 8 but, 'As the LORD
lives, who brought and led the descendants of
the house of Israel from the land of the north
and from all the other countries where I[B] had
banished them.' They will dwell once more in
their own land."

FALSE PROPHETS CONDEMNED

9 Concerning the prophets:
My heart is broken within me,
and all my bones tremble.
I have become like a drunkard,
like a man overcome by wine,
because of the LORD,
because of his holy words.
10 For the land is full of adulterers;
the land mourns because of the curse,
and the grazing lands in the wilderness
have dried up.
Their way of life[C] has become evil,
and their power is not rightly used
11 because both prophet and priest
are ungodly,
even in my house I have found their evil.
This is the LORD's declaration.
12 Therefore, their way will seem
like slippery paths in the gloom.
They will be driven away
and fall down there,
for I will bring disaster on them,
the year of their punishment.
This is the LORD's declaration.

[A] 23:6 = *Yahweh-zidkenu* [B] 23:8 LXX reads *he* [C] 23:10 Lit *Their manner of running*

13 Among the prophets of Samaria
I saw something disgusting:
They prophesied by Baal
and led my people Israel astray.
14 Among the prophets of Jerusalem also
I saw a horrible thing:
They commit adultery and walk in lies.
They strengthen the hands of evildoers,
and none turns his back on evil.
They are all like Sodom to me;
Jerusalem's residents are
like Gomorrah.

15 Therefore, this is what the LORD of Armies
says concerning the prophets:
I am about to feed them wormwood
and give them poisoned water to drink,
for from the prophets of Jerusalem
ungodliness[A] has spread
throughout the land.

16 This is what the LORD of Armies says: "Do
not listen to the words of the prophets who
prophesy to you. They are deluding you. They
speak visions from their own minds, not from
the LORD's mouth. 17 They keep on saying to
those who despise me, 'The LORD has spoken:
You will have peace.' They have said to everyone who follows the stubbornness of his
heart, 'No harm will come to you.'"
18 For who has stood in the council
of the LORD
to see and hear his word?
Who has paid attention to his word
and obeyed?
19 Look, a storm from the LORD!
Wrath has gone out,
a whirling storm.
It will whirl about the heads
of the wicked.
20 The LORD's anger will not turn away
until he has completely fulfilled
the purposes of his heart.
In time to come you will
understand it clearly.

21 I did not send out these prophets,
yet they ran.
I did not speak to them,
yet they prophesied.
22 If they had really stood in my council,
they would have enabled my people
to hear my words
and would have turned them
from their evil ways
and their evil deeds.

23 "Am I a God who is only near" — this is the
LORD's declaration — "and not a God who is
far away? 24 Can a person hide in secret places
where I cannot see him?" — the LORD's declaration. "Do I not fill the heavens and the
earth?" — the LORD's declaration.
25 "I have heard what the prophets who
prophesy a lie in my name have said: 'I had
a dream! I had a dream!' 26 How long will
this continue in the minds of the prophets
prophesying lies, prophets of the deceit of
their own minds? 27 Through their dreams
that they tell one another, they plan to cause
my people to forget my name as their fathers
forgot my name through Baal worship. 28 The
prophet who has only a dream should recount
the dream, but the one who has my word
should speak my word truthfully, for what
is straw compared to grain?" — this is the
LORD's declaration. 29 "Is not my word like fire"
— this is the LORD's declaration — "and like
a hammer that pulverizes rock? 30 Therefore,
take note! I am against the prophets" — the
LORD's declaration — "who steal my words
from each other. 31 I am against the prophets"
— the LORD's declaration — "who use their
own tongues to make a declaration. 32 I am
against those who prophesy false dreams"
— the LORD's declaration — "telling them
and leading my people astray with their
reckless lies. It was not I who sent or commanded them, and they are of no benefit
at all to these people" — this is the LORD's
declaration.

THE BURDEN OF THE LORD

33 "Now when these people or a prophet or a
priest asks you, 'What is the burden[B] of the
LORD?' you will respond to them, 'What is
the burden? I will throw you away! This is
the LORD's declaration.' 34 As for the prophet,
priest, or people who say, 'The burden of the
LORD,' I will punish that man and his household. 35 This is what each man is to say to his
friend and to his brother: 'What has the LORD
answered?' or 'What has the LORD spoken?'
36 But no longer refer to[C] the burden of the
LORD, for each man's word becomes his burden and you pervert the words of the living

[A] **23:15** Or *pollution* [B] **23:33** The Hb word for *burden* (Ex 23:5; 2Sm 15:33) can also mean "oracle" (Is 13:1; Nah 1:10). [C] **23:36** Or *longer remember*

God, the LORD of Armies, our God. 37 Say to the prophet, 'What has the LORD answered you?' or 'What has the LORD spoken?' 38 But if you say, 'The burden of the LORD,' then this is what the LORD says: Because you have said, 'The burden of the LORD,' and I specifically told you not to say, 'The burden of the LORD,' 39 I will surely forget you.[A] I will throw you away from my presence — both you and the city that I gave you and your fathers. 40 I will bring on you everlasting disgrace and humiliation that will never be forgotten."

THE GOOD AND THE BAD FIGS

24 After King Nebuchadnezzar of Babylon had deported Jeconiah[B] son of Jehoiakim king of Judah, the officials of Judah, and the craftsmen and metalsmiths from Jerusalem and had brought them to Babylon, the LORD showed me two baskets of figs placed in front of the temple of the LORD. 2 One basket contained very good figs, like early figs, but the other basket contained very bad figs, so bad they were inedible. 3 The LORD said to me, "What do you see, Jeremiah?"

I said, "Figs! The good figs are very good, but the bad figs are extremely bad, so bad they are inedible."

4 The word of the LORD came to me: 5 "This is what the LORD, the God of Israel, says: Like these good figs, so I regard as good the exiles from Judah I sent away from this place to the land of the Chaldeans. 6 I will keep my eyes on them for their good and will return them to this land. I will build them up and not demolish them; I will plant them and not uproot them. 7 I will give them a heart to know me, that I am the LORD. They will be my people, and I will be their God because they will return to me with all their heart.

8 "But as for the bad figs, so bad they are inedible, this is what the LORD says: In this way I will deal with King Zedekiah of Judah, his officials, and the remnant of Jerusalem — those remaining in this land or living in the land of Egypt. 9 I will make them an object of horror and a disaster to all the kingdoms of the earth, an example for disgrace, scorn, ridicule, and cursing, wherever I have banished them. 10 I will send the sword, famine, and plague against them until they have perished from the land I gave to them and their ancestors."

THE SEVENTY-YEAR EXILE

25 This is the word that came to Jeremiah concerning all the people of Judah in the fourth year of Jehoiakim son of Josiah, king of Judah (which was the first year of King Nebuchadnezzar of Babylon). 2 The prophet Jeremiah spoke concerning all the people of Judah and all the residents of Jerusalem as follows: 3 "From the thirteenth year of Josiah son of Amon, king of Judah, until this very day — twenty-three years — the word of the LORD has come to me, and I have spoken to you time and time again,[C] but you have not obeyed. 4 The LORD sent all his servants the prophets to you time and time again,[D] but you have not obeyed or even paid attention.[E] 5 He announced, 'Turn, each of you, from your evil way of life and from your evil deeds. Live in the land the LORD gave to you and your ancestors long ago and forever. 6 Do not follow other gods to serve them and to bow in worship to them, and do not anger me by the work of your hands. Then I will do you no harm.

7 " 'But you have not obeyed me' — this is the LORD's declaration — 'with the result that you have angered me by the work of your hands and brought disaster on yourselves.'

8 "Therefore, this is what the LORD of Armies says: 'Because you have not obeyed my words, 9 I am going to send for all the families of the north' — this is the LORD's declaration — 'and send for my servant Nebuchadnezzar king of Babylon, and I will bring them against this land, against its residents, and against all these surrounding nations, and I will completely destroy them and make them an example of horror and scorn, and ruins forever. 10 I will eliminate the sound of joy and gladness from them — the voice of the groom and the bride, the sound of the millstones and the light of the lamp. 11 This whole land will become a desolate ruin, and these nations will serve the king of Babylon for seventy years. 12 When the seventy years are completed, I will punish the king of Babylon and that nation' — this is the LORD's declaration — 'the land of the Chaldeans, for their iniquity, and I will make it a ruin forever. 13 I will bring on that land all my words I have spoken against it, all that is written in this book that Jeremiah prophesied against all the nations. 14 For many nations and great kings will enslave them, and I will repay them according to their deeds and the work of their hands.' "

[A] **23:39** Some Hb mss; other Hb mss, LXX, Syr, Vg read *surely lift you up* [B] **24:1** = Jehoiachin [C] **25:3** Lit *you; rising early and speaking* [D] **25:4** Lit *to you, rising early and sending* [E] **25:4** Lit *even inclined your ear to hear*

THE CUP OF GOD'S WRATH

15 This is what the LORD, the God of Israel, said
to me: "Take this cup of the wine of wrath from
my hand and make all the nations to whom
I am sending you drink from it. 16 They will
drink, stagger,[A] and go out of their minds
because of the sword I am sending among
them."
17 So I took the cup from the LORD's hand
and made all the nations to whom the LORD
sent me drink from it.
18 Jerusalem and the other cities of Judah,
its kings and its officials, to make them a
desolate ruin, an example for scorn and
cursing — as it is today;
19 Pharaoh king of Egypt, his officers, his
leaders, all his people,
20 and all the mixed peoples;
all the kings of the land of Uz;
all the kings of the land of the Philistines
— Ashkelon, Gaza, Ekron, and the
remnant of Ashdod;
21 Edom, Moab, and the Ammonites;
22 all the kings of Tyre,
all the kings of Sidon,
and the kings of the coasts and islands;
23 Dedan, Tema, Buz, and all those who
clip the hair on their temples;[B]
24 all the kings of Arabia,
and all the kings of the mixed peoples
who have settled in the desert;
25 all the kings of Zimri,
all the kings of Elam,
and all the kings of Media;
26 all the kings of the north, both near and
far from one another;
that is, all the kingdoms of the world
throughout the earth.
Finally, the king of Sheshach[C] will drink
after them.

27 "Then you are to say to them, 'This is what
the LORD of Armies, the God of Israel, says:
Drink, get drunk, and vomit. Fall down and
never get up again, as a result of the sword I
am sending among you.' 28 If[D] they refuse to
accept the cup from your hand and drink,
you are to say to them, 'This is what the LORD
of Armies says: You must drink! 29 For I am
already bringing disaster on the city that
bears my name, so how could you possibly
go unpunished? You will not go unpunished,
for I am summoning a sword against all the
inhabitants of the earth. This is the declaration of the LORD of Armies.'

JUDGMENT ON THE WHOLE WORLD

30 "As for you, you are to prophesy all these
things to them, and say to them:
The LORD roars from on high;
he makes his voice heard
from his holy dwelling.
He roars loudly over his grazing land;
he calls out with a shout, like those
who tread grapes,
against all the inhabitants of the earth.
31 The tumult reaches to the ends
of the earth
because the LORD brings a case
against the nations.
He enters into judgment with all people.
As for the wicked, he hands them over
to the sword —
this is the LORD's declaration.

32 "This is what the LORD of Armies says:
Pay attention! Disaster spreads
from nation to nation.
A huge storm is stirred up
from the ends of the earth."

33 Those slain by the LORD on that day will
be scattered from one end of the earth to the
other. They will not be mourned, gathered,
or buried. They will be like manure on the
soil's surface.
34 Wail, you shepherds, and cry out.
Roll in the dust, you leaders of the flock.
Because the days of your slaughter
have come,
you will fall and become shattered
like a precious vase.
35 Flight will be impossible
for the shepherds,
and escape, for the leaders of the flock.
36 Hear the sound of the shepherds' cry,
the wail of the leaders of the flock,
for the LORD is destroying
their pasture.
37 Peaceful grazing land
will become lifeless
because of the LORD's burning anger.
38 He has left his den like a lion,
for their land has become a desolation
because of the sword[E] of the oppressor,
because of his burning anger.

[A] 25:16 Or *vomit* [B] 25:23 Or *who live in distant places* [C] 25:26 = Babylon [D] 25:28 Or *When* [E] 25:38 Some Hb mss, LXX, Tg; other Hb mss read *burning*

JEREMIAH'S SPEECH IN THE TEMPLE

26 At the beginning of the reign of Jehoiakim son of Josiah, king of Judah, this word came from the LORD: 2 "This is what the LORD says: Stand in the courtyard of the LORD's temple and speak all the words I have commanded you to speak to all Judah's cities that are coming to worship there. Do not hold back a word. 3 Perhaps they will listen and turn — each from his evil way of life — so that I might relent concerning the disaster that I plan to do to them because of the evil of their deeds. 4 You are to say to them, 'This is what the LORD says: If you do not listen to me by living according to my instruction that I set before you 5 and by listening to the words of my servants the prophets — whom I have been sending to you time and time again,[A] though you did not listen — 6 I will make this temple like Shiloh. I will make this city an example for cursing for all the nations of the earth.' "

JEREMIAH SEIZED

7 The priests, the prophets, and all the people heard Jeremiah speaking these words in the temple of the LORD. 8 When he finished the address the LORD had commanded him to deliver to all the people, immediately the priests, the prophets, and all the people took hold of him, yelling, "You must surely die! 9 How dare you prophesy in the name of the LORD, 'This temple will become like Shiloh and this city will become an uninhabited ruin'!" Then all the people crowded around Jeremiah at the LORD's temple.

10 When the officials of Judah heard about these things, they went from the king's palace to the LORD's temple and sat at the entrance of the New Gate of the LORD's temple.[B] 11 Then the priests and prophets said to the officials and all the people, "This man deserves the death sentence because he has prophesied against this city, as you have heard with your own ears."

JEREMIAH'S DEFENSE

12 Then Jeremiah said to all the officials and all the people, "The LORD sent me to prophesy all the words that you have heard against this temple and city. 13 So now, correct your ways and deeds, and obey the LORD your God so that he might relent concerning the disaster he had pronounced against you. 14 As for me, here I am in your hands; do to me what you think is good and right. 15 But know for certain that if you put me to death, you will bring innocent blood on yourselves, on this city, and on its residents, for it is certain the LORD has sent me to speak all these things directly to you."

JEREMIAH RELEASED

16 Then the officials and all the people told the priests and prophets, "This man doesn't deserve the death sentence, for he has spoken to us in the name of the LORD our God!"

17 Some of the elders of the land stood up and said to all the assembled people, 18 "Micah the Moreshite prophesied in the days of King Hezekiah of Judah and said to all the people of Judah, 'This is what the LORD of Armies says:

Zion will be plowed like a field,
Jerusalem will become ruins,
and the temple's mountain will be
a high thicket.'

19 Did King Hezekiah of Judah and all the people of Judah put him to death? Did not the king fear the LORD and plead for the LORD's favor,[C] and did not the LORD relent concerning the disaster he had pronounced against them? We are about to bring a terrible disaster on ourselves!"

THE PROPHET URIAH

20 Another man was also prophesying in the name of the LORD — Uriah son of Shemaiah from Kiriath-jearim. He prophesied against this city and against this land in words like all those of Jeremiah. 21 King Jehoiakim, all his warriors, and all the officials heard his words, and the king tried to put him to death. When Uriah heard, he fled in fear and went to Egypt. 22 But King Jehoiakim sent men to Egypt: Elnathan son of Achbor and certain other men with him went to Egypt. 23 They brought Uriah out of Egypt and took him to King Jehoiakim, who executed him with the sword and threw his corpse into the burial place of the common people.[D]

24 But Ahikam son of Shaphan supported Jeremiah, so he was not handed over to the people to be put to death.

THE YOKE OF BABYLON

27 At the beginning of the reign of Zedekiah[E] son of Josiah, king of Judah, this word came to Jeremiah from the LORD:[F] 2 This

[A] **26:5** Lit *you, rising early and sending* [B] **26:10** Many Hb mss, Syr, Tg, Vg; other Hb mss read *the New Gate of the LORD*
[C] **26:19** Or *and appease the LORD* [D] **26:23** Lit *the sons of the people* [E] **27:1** Some Hb mss, Syr, Arabic; other Hb mss, DSS read *Jehoiakim* [F] **27:1** LXX omits this v.

is what the LORD said to me: "Make chains and yoke bars for yourself and put them on your neck. 3 Send word to the king of Edom, the king of Moab, the king of the Ammonites, the king of Tyre, and the king of Sidon through messengers who are coming to King Zedekiah of Judah in Jerusalem. 4 Command them to go to their masters, saying, 'This is what the LORD of Armies, the God of Israel, says: Tell this to your masters: 5 "By my great strength and outstretched arm, I made the earth, and the people, and animals on the face of the earth. I give it to anyone I please.[A] 6 So now I have placed all these lands under the authority of my servant Nebuchadnezzar, king of Babylon. I have even given him the wild animals to serve him. 7 All nations will serve him, his son, and his grandson until the time for his own land comes, and then many nations and great kings will enslave him.

8 " ' "As for the nation or kingdom that does not serve King Nebuchadnezzar of Babylon and does not place its neck under the yoke of the king of Babylon, that nation I will punish by sword, famine, and plague — this is the LORD's declaration — until through him I have destroyed it. 9 So you should not listen to your prophets, diviners, dreamers, fortune-tellers, or sorcerers who say to you, 'Don't serve the king of Babylon!' 10 They are prophesying a lie to you so that you will be removed from your land. I will banish you, and you will perish. 11 But as for the nation that will put its neck under the yoke of the king of Babylon and serve him, I will leave it in its own land, and that nation will cultivate[B] it and reside in it. This is the LORD's declaration." ' "

WARNING TO ZEDEKIAH

12 I spoke to King Zedekiah of Judah in the same way: "Put your necks under the yoke of the king of Babylon, serve him and his people, and live! 13 Why should you and your people die by the sword, famine, and plague as the LORD has threatened against any nation that does not serve the king of Babylon? 14 Do not listen to the words of the prophets who are telling you, 'Don't serve the king of Babylon,' for they are prophesying a lie to you. 15 'I have not sent them' — this is the LORD's declaration — 'and they are prophesying falsely in my name; therefore, I will banish you, and you will perish — you and the prophets who are prophesying to you.' "

16 Then I spoke to the priests and all these people, saying, "This is what the LORD says: 'Do not listen to the words of your prophets. They are prophesying to you, claiming, "Look, very soon now the articles of the LORD's temple will be brought back from Babylon." They are prophesying a lie to you. 17 Do not listen to them. Serve the king of Babylon and live! Why should this city become a ruin? 18 If they are indeed prophets and if the word of the LORD is with them, let them intercede with the LORD of Armies not to let the articles that remain in the LORD's temple, in the palace of the king of Judah, and in Jerusalem go to Babylon.' 19 For this is what the LORD of Armies says about the pillars, the basin,[C] the water carts, and the rest of the articles that still remain in this city, 20 those King Nebuchadnezzar of Babylon did not take when he deported Jeconiah[D] son of Jehoiakim, king of Judah, from Jerusalem to Babylon along with all the nobles of Judah and Jerusalem. 21 Yes, this is what the LORD of Armies, the God of Israel, says about the articles that remain in the temple of the LORD, in the palace of the king of Judah, and in Jerusalem: 22 'They will be taken to Babylon and will remain there until I attend to them again.' This is the LORD's declaration. 'Then I will bring them up and restore them to this place.' "

HANANIAH'S FALSE PROPHECY

28 In that same year, at the beginning of the reign of King Zedekiah of Judah, in the fifth month of the fourth year, the prophet Hananiah son of Azzur from Gibeon said to me in the temple of the LORD in the presence of the priests and all the people, 2 "This is what the LORD of Armies, the God of Israel, says: 'I have broken the yoke of the king of Babylon. 3 Within two years I will restore to this place all the articles of the LORD's temple that King Nebuchadnezzar of Babylon took from here and transported to Babylon. 4 And I will restore to this place Jeconiah[D] son of Jehoiakim, king of Judah, and all the exiles from Judah who went to Babylon' — this is the LORD's declaration — 'for I will break the yoke of the king of Babylon.' "

JEREMIAH'S RESPONSE TO HANANIAH

5 The prophet Jeremiah replied to the prophet Hananiah in the presence of the priests and all the people who were standing in the

[A] **27:5** Lit *to whomever is upright in my eyes* [B] **27:11** Lit *work* [C] **27:19** Lit *sea* [D] **27:20; 28:4** = Jehoiachin

temple of the LORD. 6 The prophet Jeremiah said, "Amen! May the LORD do that. May the LORD make the words you have prophesied come true and may he restore the articles of the LORD's temple and all the exiles from Babylon to this place! 7 Only listen to this message I am speaking in your hearing and in the hearing of all the people. 8 The prophets who preceded you and me from ancient times prophesied war, disaster,[A] and plague against many lands and great kingdoms. 9 As for the prophet who prophesies peace — only when the word of the prophet comes true will the prophet be recognized as one the LORD has truly sent."

HANANIAH BREAKS JEREMIAH'S YOKE

10 The prophet Hananiah then took the yoke bar from the neck of the prophet Jeremiah and broke it. 11 In the presence of all the people Hananiah proclaimed, "This is what the LORD says: 'In this way, within two years I will break the yoke of King Nebuchadnezzar of Babylon from the neck of all the nations.' " The prophet Jeremiah then went on his way.

THE LORD'S WORD AGAINST HANANIAH

12 After the prophet Hananiah had broken the yoke bar from the neck of the prophet Jeremiah, the word of the LORD came to Jeremiah: 13 "Go say to Hananiah, 'This is what the LORD says: You broke a wooden yoke bar, but in its place you will make an iron yoke bar. 14 For this is what the LORD of Armies, the God of Israel, says: I have put an iron yoke on the neck of all these nations that they might serve King Nebuchadnezzar of Babylon, and they will serve him. I have even put the wild animals under him.' "

15 The prophet Jeremiah said to the prophet Hananiah, "Listen, Hananiah! The LORD did not send you, but you have led these people to trust in a lie. 16 Therefore, this is what the LORD says: 'I am about to send you off the face of the earth. You will die this year because you have preached rebellion against the LORD.' " 17 And the prophet Hananiah died that year in the seventh month.

JEREMIAH'S LETTER TO THE EXILES

29 This is the text of the letter that the prophet Jeremiah sent from Jerusalem to the remaining exiled elders, the priests, the prophets, and all the people Nebuchadnezzar had deported from Jerusalem to Babylon. 2 This was after King Jeconiah,[B] the queen mother, the court officials, the officials of Judah and Jerusalem, the craftsmen, and the metalsmiths had left Jerusalem. 3 He sent the letter with Elasah son of Shaphan and Gemariah son of Hilkiah, whom Zedekiah king of Judah sent to Babylon to King Nebuchadnezzar of Babylon. The letter stated:

4 This is what the LORD of Armies, the God of Israel, says to all the exiles I deported from Jerusalem to Babylon: 5 "Build houses and live in them. Plant gardens and eat their produce. 6 Find wives for yourselves, and have sons and daughters. Find wives for your sons and give your daughters to men in marriage so that they may bear sons and daughters. Multiply there; do not decrease. 7 Pursue the well-being[C] of the city I have deported you to. Pray to the LORD on its behalf, for when it thrives, you will thrive."

8 For this is what the LORD of Armies, the God of Israel, says: "Don't let your prophets who are among you and your diviners deceive you, and don't listen to the dreams you elicit from them, 9 for they are prophesying falsely to you in my name. I have not sent them." This is the LORD's declaration.

10 For this is what the LORD says: "When seventy years for Babylon are complete, I will attend to you and will confirm my promise concerning you to restore you to this place. 11 For I know the plans I have for you" — this is the LORD's declaration — "plans for your well-being, not for disaster, to give you a future and a hope. 12 You will call to me and come and pray to me, and I will listen to you. 13 You will seek me and find me when you search for me with all your heart. 14 I will be found by you" — this is the LORD's declaration — "and I will restore your fortunes[D] and gather you from all the nations and places where I banished you" — this is the LORD's declaration. "I will restore you to the place from which I deported you."

15 You have said, "The LORD has raised up prophets for us in Babylon!" 16 But this is

[A] **28:8** Some Hb mss, Vg read *famine* [B] **29:2** = Jehoiachin [C] **29:7** Or *peace* [D] **29:14** Or *will end your captivity*

what the LORD says concerning the king
sitting on David's throne and concerning
all the people living in this city — that is,
concerning your brothers who did not
go with you into exile. 17 This is what the
LORD of Armies says: "I am about to send
sword, famine, and plague against them,
and I will make them like rotten figs that
are inedible because they are so bad. 18 I
will pursue them with sword, famine,
and plague. I will make them a horror to
all the kingdoms of the earth — a curse
and a desolation, an object of scorn and
a disgrace among all the nations where
I have banished them. 19 I will do this
because they have not listened to my
words" — this is the LORD's declaration
— "the words that I sent to them with
my servants the prophets time and time
again.[A] And you too have not listened."
This is the LORD's declaration.

20 Hear the word of the LORD, all you
exiles I have sent from Jerusalem to Babylon. 21 This is what the LORD of Armies,
the God of Israel, says about Ahab son
of Kolaiah and concerning Zedekiah son
of Maaseiah, the ones prophesying a lie
to you in my name: "I am about to hand
them over to King Nebuchadnezzar of
Babylon, and he will kill them before
your very eyes. 22 Based on what happens
to them, all the exiles of Judah who are
in Babylon will create a curse that says,
'May the LORD make you like Zedekiah
and Ahab, whom the king of Babylon
roasted in the fire!' 23 because they have
committed an outrage in Israel by committing adultery with their neighbors'
wives and have spoken in my name a lie,
which I did not command them. I am he
who knows, and I am a witness." This is
the LORD's declaration.

24 To Shemaiah the Nehelamite you are to
say, 25 "This is what the LORD of Armies,
the God of Israel, says: You[B] in your own
name have sent out letters to all the people of Jerusalem, to the priest Zephaniah
son of Maaseiah, and to all the priests,
saying, 26 'The LORD has appointed you
priest in place of the priest Jehoiada to
be the chief officer in the temple of the
LORD, responsible for every madman

Eternal Perspective | *Biblical Hope*

GOD'S PLANS

"For I know the plans I have for you' — this is the LORD's declaration — 'plans for your well-being, not for disaster, to give you a future and a hope.'" Jeremiah 29:11

This passage was originally written to ancient Jews captive in Babylon. They were worried that they would always be captives and might never see their homeland again. God told them to settle in — their time of exile would not be over quickly. Only then did he speak this beloved, often-memorized, much quoted verse.

If we are going to be accurate interpreters (and appliers) of God's Word, we modern, Western Christians should not claim this is a specific promise "to us" or "for us." But we can see in this ancient promise important truths about the character and love of our God.

He's faithful, even when his people aren't. He has plans for the ones he loves, though his timetables are different than ours. He's Sovereign over the future. We can trust the revealed character of the One who made it.

Do you believe, in the deepest part of your heart, that God is for you? He wants to give you "a future and a hope." Hang on to that promise.

For the next note on *Eternal Perspective*, see Jeremiah 31:33.

[A] **29:19** Lit *prophets, rising up early and sending* [B] **29:25** Lit *Because you*

who acts like a prophet. You must confine
him in the stocks and an iron collar. 27 So
now, why have you not rebuked Jeremiah
of Anathoth who has been acting like a
prophet among you? 28 For he has sent
word to us in Babylon, claiming, "The exile
will be long. Build houses and settle down.
Plant gardens and eat their produce."'"
29 The priest Zephaniah read this letter in the
hearing of the prophet Jeremiah.

A MESSAGE ABOUT SHEMAIAH

30 Then the word of the LORD came to Jeremiah:
31 "Send a message to all the exiles, saying, 'This
is what the LORD says concerning Shemaiah the
Nehelamite. Because Shemaiah prophesied to
you, though I did not send him, and made you
trust a lie, 32 this is what the LORD says: I am
about to punish Shemaiah the Nehelamite and
his descendants. There will not be even one of
his descendants living among these people, nor
will any ever see the good that I will bring to my
people — this is the LORD's declaration — for
he has preached rebellion against the LORD.'"

RESTORATION FROM CAPTIVITY

30 This is the word that came to Jeremiah
from the LORD. 2 "This is what the LORD,
the God of Israel, says: Write on a scroll all the
words that I have spoken to you, 3 for look, the
days are coming" — this is the LORD's declaration — "when I will restore the fortunes[A] of
my people Israel and Judah," says the LORD.
"I will restore them to the land I gave to their
ancestors and they will possess it."

4 These are the words the LORD spoke to
Israel and Judah. 5 This is what the LORD says:

We have heard a cry of terror,
of dread — there is no peace.
6 Ask and see
whether a male can give birth.
Why then do I see every man
with his hands on his stomach
like a woman in labor
and every face turned pale?
7 How awful that day will be!
There will be no other like it!
It will be a time of trouble for Jacob,
but he will be saved out of it.

8 On that day —
this is the declaration of the LORD
of Armies —
I will break his yoke from your neck
and tear off your chains,
and strangers will never again enslave
him.
9 They will serve the LORD their God
and David their king,
whom I will raise up for them.

10 As for you, my servant Jacob,
do not be afraid —
this is the LORD's declaration —
and do not be discouraged, Israel,
for without fail I will save you out of a
distant place,
your descendants, from the land
of their captivity!
Jacob will return and have calm
and quiet
with no one to frighten him.
11 For I will be with you —
this is the LORD's declaration —
to save you!
I will bring destruction
on all the nations
where I have scattered you;
however, I will not bring destruction
on you.
I will discipline you justly,
and I will by no means
leave you unpunished.

HEALING ZION'S WOUNDS

12 For this is what the LORD says:
Your injury is incurable;
your wound most severe.
13 You have no defender
for your case.
There is no remedy for your sores,
and no healing for you.[B]
14 All your lovers have forgotten you;
they no longer look for you,
for I have struck you
as an enemy would,
with the discipline of someone cruel,
because of your enormous guilt
and your innumerable sins.
15 Why do you cry out about your injury?
Your pain has no cure!
I have done these things to you
because of your enormous guilt
and your innumerable sins.
16 Nevertheless, all who devoured you
will be devoured,

[A] **30:3** Or *will end the captivity* [B] **30:13** Or *No one pleads that your sores should be healed. There is no remedy for you.*

and all your adversaries —
all of them —
will go off into exile.
Those who plunder you
will be plundered,
and all who raid you will be raided.
17 But I will bring you health
and will heal you of your wounds —
this is the LORD's declaration —
for they call you Outcast,
Zion whom no one cares about.

RESTORATION OF THE LAND

18 This is what the LORD says:
I will certainly restore the fortunes[A]
of Jacob's tents
and show compassion
on his dwellings.
Every city will be rebuilt on its mound;
every citadel will stand
on its proper site.
19 Thanksgiving will come out of them,
a sound of rejoicing.
I will multiply them,
and they will not decrease;
I will honor them, and they will not
be insignificant.
20 His children will be as in past days;
his congregation will be established
in my presence.
I will punish all his oppressors.
21 Jacob's leader will be one of them;
his ruler will issue from him.
I will invite him to me, and he will
approach me,
for who would otherwise risk his life
to approach me?
This is the LORD's declaration.
22 You will be my people,
and I will be your God.

THE WRATH OF GOD

23 Look, a storm from the LORD!
Wrath has gone out,
a churning storm.
It will whirl about the heads
of the wicked.
24 The LORD's burning anger will not
turn back
until he has completely fulfilled
the purposes of his heart.
In time to come
you will understand it.

GOD'S RELATIONSHIP WITH HIS PEOPLE

31 "At that time" — this is the LORD's declaration — "I will be the God of all the
families of Israel, and they will be my people."
2 This is what the LORD says:
The people who survived the sword
found favor in the wilderness.
When Israel went to find rest,
3 the LORD appeared to him[B]
from far away.
I have loved you
with an everlasting love;
therefore, I have continued to extend
faithful love to you.
4 Again I will build you so that you will
be rebuilt,
Virgin Israel.
You will take up your tambourines again
and go out in joyful dancing.
5 You will plant vineyards again
on the mountains of Samaria;
the planters will plant and will enjoy
the fruit.
6 For there will be a day when watchmen
will call out
in the hill country of Ephraim,
"Come, let's go up to Zion,
to the LORD our God!"

GOD'S PEOPLE BROUGHT HOME

7 For this is what the LORD says:
Sing with joy for Jacob;
shout for the foremost of the nations!
Proclaim, praise, and say,
"LORD, save your people,
the remnant of Israel!"
8 Watch! I am going to bring them
from the northern land.
I will gather them from remote regions
of the earth —
the blind and the lame will be
with them,
along with those who are pregnant
and those about to give birth.
They will return here
as a great assembly!
9 They will come weeping,
but I will bring them back
with consolation.[C]
I will lead them to wadis filled
with water,
by a smooth way where
they will not stumble,

[A] **30:18** Or *certainly end the captivity* [B] **31:3** LXX; MT reads *me* [C] **31:9** LXX; MT reads *supplications*

for I am Israel's Father,
and Ephraim is my firstborn.
10 Nations, hear the word of the LORD,
and tell it among the far off coasts and
islands!
Say, "The one who scattered Israel
will gather him.
He will watch over him as a shepherd
guards his flock,
11 for the LORD has ransomed Jacob
and redeemed him from the power
of one stronger than he."
12 They will come and shout for joy
on the heights of Zion;
they will be radiant with joy
because of the LORD's goodness,
because of the grain, the new wine,
the fresh oil,
and because of the young of the flocks
and herds.
Their life will be
like an irrigated garden,
and they will no longer grow weak
from hunger.
13 Then the young women will rejoice
with dancing,
while young and old men
rejoice together.
I will turn their mourning
into joy,
give them consolation,
and bring happiness out of grief.
14 I will refresh the priests
with an abundance,[A]
and my people will be satisfied
with my goodness.
This is the LORD's declaration.

LAMENT TURNED TO JOY

15 This is what the LORD says:
A voice was heard in Ramah,
a lament with bitter weeping —
Rachel weeping for her children,
refusing to be comforted
for her children
because they are no more.

16 This is what the LORD says:
Keep your voice from weeping
and your eyes from tears,
for the reward for your work
will come —
this is the LORD's declaration —
and your children will return
from the enemy's land.
17 There is hope for your future —
this is the LORD's declaration —
and your children will return
to their own territory.
18 I have surely heard Ephraim moaning,
"You disciplined me,
and I have been disciplined
like an untrained calf.
Take me back, so that I can return,
for you, LORD, are my God.
19 After my return, I felt regret;
After I was instructed, I struck
my thigh in grief.
I was ashamed and humiliated
because I bore the disgrace
of my youth."
20 Isn't Ephraim a precious son to me,
a delightful child?
Whenever I speak against him,
I certainly still think about him.
Therefore, my inner being yearns
for him;
I will truly have compassion on him.
This is the LORD's declaration.

REPENTANCE AND RESTORATION

21 Set up road markers for yourself;
establish signposts!
Keep the highway in mind,
the way you have traveled.
Return, Virgin Israel!
Return to these cities of yours.
22 How long will you turn here and there,
faithless daughter?
For the LORD creates something new
in the land[B] —
a female[C] will shelter[D] a man.

23 This is what the LORD of Armies, the God
of Israel, says: "When I restore their fortunes,[E]
they will once again speak this word in the land
of Judah and in its cities: 'May the LORD bless
you, righteous settlement, holy mountain.'
24 Judah and all its cities will live in it together
— also farmers and those who move[F] with the
flocks — 25 for I satisfy the thirsty person and
feed all those who are weak."
26 At this I awoke and looked around. My
sleep had been most pleasant to me.
27 "Look, the days are coming" — this is the
LORD's declaration — "when I will sow the

[A] **31:14** Lit *fatness* [B] **31:22** Or *new on earth* [C] **31:22** Or *woman* [D] **31:22** Or *female surrounds*, or *female courts*; Hb obscure
[E] **31:23** Or *I end their captivity* [F] **31:24** Tg, Vg, Aq, Sym; MT reads *and they will move*

house of Israel and the house of Judah with
the seed of people and the seed of animals.
28 Just as I watched over them to uproot and
to tear them down, to demolish and to destroy, and to cause disaster, so will I watch
over them to build and to plant them" — this
is the LORD's declaration. 29 "In those days, it
will never again be said,

'The fathers have eaten sour grapes,
and the children's teeth are set on edge.'

30 Rather, each will die for his own iniquity.
Anyone who eats sour grapes — his own teeth
will be set on edge.

THE NEW COVENANT

31 "Look, the days are coming" — this is the
LORD's declaration — "when I will make a
new covenant with the house of Israel and
with the house of Judah. 32 This one will not
be like the covenant I made with their ancestors on the day I took them by the hand
to lead them out of the land of Egypt — my
covenant that they broke even though I am
their master"[A] — the LORD's declaration. 33 "Instead, this is the covenant I will make with
the house of Israel after those days" — the
LORD's declaration. "I will put my teaching
within them and write it on their hearts. I
will be their God, and they will be my people.
34 No longer will one teach his neighbor or his
brother, saying, 'Know the LORD,' for they will
all know me, from the least to the greatest of
them" — this is the LORD's declaration. "For
I will forgive their iniquity and never again
remember their sin.

35 "This is what the LORD says:

The one who gives the sun for light
by day,
the fixed order of moon and stars
for light by night,
who stirs up the sea and makes
its waves roar —
the LORD of Armies is his name:
36 If this fixed order departs
from before me —
this is the LORD's declaration —
only then will Israel's descendants cease
to be a nation before me forever.

37 "This is what the LORD says:

Eternal Perspective | *God's Work in Us*

CHANGED FROM WITHIN

"'Instead, this is the covenant I will make with the house of Israel after those days'—the LORD's declaration. 'I will put my teaching within them and write it on their hearts. I will be their God, and they will be my people.'" Jeremiah 31:33

Some believers avoid the final seventeen books of the Old Testament, thinking them too gloomy and dark. While the Prophetic Books do emphasize judgment, they also contain numerous hopeful reminders like this one. It's part of a much longer section that reveals the eventual restoration of Israel.

Speaking through Jeremiah, God declares here that because of his "everlasting love" and "faithful love" (31:3), he will bring his people home (31:8). Due to his goodness, they will "be radiant with joy" (31:12). Best of all, he will "make a new covenant" (31:31) with them that will involve him writing his truth "on their hearts" (31:33).

Take note of that. In the time of Moses, God's truth was written on tablets of stone. Obedience was compelled from the outside. Here the Lord was saying that in the future, change would take place from the inside out. The promise (elaborated in Ezk 36) is that the people of God would one day have new hearts that want to obey. This would be done by the Holy Spirit—see 1 John 2:27.

Consider how God's Spirit has written God's Word in your heart, giving you the desire to live for God's glory.

For the next note on *Eternal Perspective*, see Jeremiah 32:26-27.

[A] **31:32** Or *husband*

Only if the heavens above
can be measured
and the foundations
of the earth below explored,
will I reject all of Israel's descendants
because of all they have done —
this is the LORD's declaration.

38 "Look, the days are coming" — the LORD's declaration — "when the city[A] from the Tower of Hananel to the Corner Gate will be rebuilt for the LORD. 39 A measuring line will once again stretch out straight to the hill of Gareb and then turn toward Goah. 40 The whole valley — the corpses, the ashes, and all the fields as far as the Kidron Valley to the corner of the Horse Gate to the east — will be holy to the LORD. It will never be uprooted or demolished again."

JEREMIAH'S LAND PURCHASE

32 This is the word that came to Jeremiah from the LORD in the tenth year of King Zedekiah of Judah, which was the eighteenth year of Nebuchadnezzar. 2 At that time, the army of the king of Babylon was besieging Jerusalem, and the prophet Jeremiah was imprisoned in the guard's courtyard in the palace of the king of Judah. 3 King Zedekiah of Judah had imprisoned him, saying, "Why are you prophesying as you do? You say, 'This is what the LORD says: Look, I am about to hand this city over to Babylon's king, and he will capture it. 4 King Zedekiah of Judah will not escape from the Chaldeans; indeed, he will certainly be handed over to Babylon's king. They will speak face to face[B] and meet eye to eye. 5 He will take Zedekiah to Babylon, where he will stay until I attend to him — this is the LORD's declaration. For you will fight the Chaldeans, but you will not succeed.' "

6 Jeremiah replied, "The word of the LORD came to me: 7 Watch! Hanamel, the son of your uncle Shallum, is coming to you to say, 'Buy my field in Anathoth for yourself, for you own the right of redemption to buy it.'

8 "Then, as the LORD had said, my cousin Hanamel came to the guard's courtyard and urged me, 'Please buy my field in Anathoth in the land of Benjamin, for you own the right of inheritance and redemption. Buy it for yourself.' Then I knew that this was the word of the LORD. 9 So I bought the field in Anathoth from my cousin Hanamel, and I weighed out the silver to him — seventeen shekels[C] of silver. 10 I recorded it on a scroll, sealed it, called in witnesses, and weighed out the silver on the scales. 11 I took the purchase agreement — the sealed copy with its terms and conditions and the open copy — 12 and gave the purchase agreement to Baruch son of Neriah, son of Mahseiah. I did this in the sight of my cousin[D] Hanamel, the witnesses who had signed the purchase agreement, and all the Judeans sitting in the guard's courtyard.

13 "I charged Baruch in their sight, 14 'This is what the LORD of Armies, the God of Israel, says: Take these scrolls — this purchase agreement with the sealed copy and this open copy — and put them in an earthen storage jar so they will last a long time. 15 For this is what the LORD of Armies, the God of Israel, says: Houses, fields, and vineyards will again be bought in this land.'

16 "After I had given the purchase agreement to Baruch, son of Neriah, I prayed to the LORD: 17 Oh, Lord GOD! You yourself made the heavens and earth by your great power and with your outstretched arm. Nothing is too difficult for you! 18 You show faithful love to thousands but lay the fathers' iniquity on their sons' laps after them, great and mighty God whose name is the LORD of Armies, 19 the one great in counsel and powerful in action. Your eyes are on all the ways of the children of men[E] in order to reward each person according to his ways and as the result of his actions. 20 You performed signs and wonders in the land of Egypt and still do today, both in Israel and among all mankind. You made a name for yourself, as is the case today. 21 You brought your people Israel out of Egypt with signs and wonders, with a strong hand and an outstretched arm, and with great terror. 22 You gave them this land you swore to give to their ancestors, a land flowing with milk and honey. 23 They entered and possessed it, but they did not obey you or live according to your instructions. They failed to perform all you commanded them to do, and so you have brought all this disaster on them. 24 Look! Siege ramps have come against the city to capture it, and the city, as a result of the sword, famine, and plague, has been handed over to the Chaldeans who are fighting against it. What you have spoken has happened. Look, you can see it! 25 Yet you, Lord GOD, have said to

---

[A] **31:38** = Jerusalem [B] **32:4** Lit *His mouth will speak with his mouth* [C] **32:9** About seven ounces
[D] **32:12** Some Hb mss, LXX, Syr; other Hb mss read *uncle* [E] **32:19** Or *Adam*

me, 'Purchase the field and call in witnesses'
— even though the city has been handed over
to the Chaldeans!"
[26]The word of the LORD came to Jeremiah:
[27]"Look, I am the LORD, the God over every
creature. Is anything too difficult for me?
[28]Therefore, this is what the LORD says: I am
about to hand this city over to the Chaldeans,
to Babylon's king Nebuchadnezzar, and he will
capture it. [29]The Chaldeans who are fighting
against this city will come and set this city on
fire. They will burn it, including the houses
where incense has been burned to Baal on
their rooftops and where drink offerings have
been poured out to other gods to anger me.
[30]From their youth, the Israelites and Judeans have done nothing but what is evil in my
sight! They have done nothing but anger me by
the work of their hands" — this is the LORD's
declaration — [31]"for this city has caused my
wrath and fury from the day it was built until
now. I will therefore remove it from my presence [32]because of all the evil the Israelites and
Judeans have done to anger me — they, their
kings, their officials, their priests, and their
prophets, the men of Judah, and the residents
of Jerusalem. [33]They have turned their backs to
me and not their faces. Though I taught them
time and time again,[A] they do not listen and
receive discipline. [34]They have placed their
abhorrent things in the house that bears my
name and have defiled it. [35]They have built the
high places of Baal in Ben Hinnom Valley to
sacrifice their sons and daughters in the fire[B]
to Molech — something I had not commanded
them. I had never entertained the thought[C] that
they do this detestable act causing Judah to sin!
[36]"Now therefore, this is what the LORD, the
God of Israel, says to this city about which you
said, 'It has been handed over to Babylon's king
through sword, famine, and plague': [37]I will
certainly gather them from all the lands where
I have banished them in my anger, rage and
intense wrath, and I will return them to this
place and make them live in safety. [38]They will
be my people, and I will be their God. [39]I will
give them integrity of heart and action[D] so that
they will fear me always, for their good and
for the good of their descendants after them.
[40]"I will make a permanent covenant with
them: I will never turn away from doing good
to them, and I will put fear of me in their hearts
so they will never again turn away from me.
[41]I will take delight in them to do what is good

Eternal Perspective | *God's Power*

WHEN THINGS SEEM IMPOSSIBLE

"The word of the LORD came to Jeremiah: 'Look, I am the LORD, the God over every creature. Is anything too difficult for me?'" Jeremiah 32:26-27

The Lord *does* work in mysterious ways.

One day God instructed Jeremiah to buy a plot of land from his cousin. This request had two problems. First, the invading Babylonians under King Nebuchadnezzar already had captured that land. Second, the entire nation of Judah was about to be defeated and carried into exile!

Jeremiah did as he was instructed. Then he prayed a long prayer (32:17-25), which ended in confusion and with an unvoiced question: Why buy property in a country that's on the verge of destruction?

The Lord responded by asking Jeremiah, "Is anything too difficult for me?" After a time of divine discipline, God explained, "I will certainly gather them from all the lands where I have banished them in my anger, rage and intense wrath, and I will return them to this place and make them live in safety. They will be my people, and I will be their God" (32:37-38).

What a good reminder! Just because things seem senseless or impossible now doesn't mean they'll always look and feel that way. Nothing is too difficult for God.

For the next note on *Eternal Perspective*, see Lamentations 3:22-23.

[A] **32:33** Lit *them, rising up early and teaching* [B] **32:35** Lit *to make their sons and daughters pass through the fire* [C] **32:35** Lit *them, and it did not arise on my heart* [D] **32:39** Lit *give them one heart and one way*

for them, and with all my heart and mind I will
faithfully plant them in this land.
42 "For this is what the LORD says: Just as
I have brought all this terrible disaster on
these people, so am I about to bring on them
all the good I am promising them. 43 Fields
will be bought in this land about which you
are saying, 'It's a desolation without people
or animals; it has been handed over to the
Chaldeans!' 44 Fields will be purchased, the
transaction written on a scroll and sealed,
and witnesses will be called on in the land of
Benjamin, in the areas surrounding Jerusalem, and in Judah's cities — the cities of the
hill country, the cities of the Judean foothills,
and the cities of the Negev — because I will
restore their fortunes."[A]

This is the LORD's declaration.

ISRAEL'S RESTORATION

33 While he was still confined in the
guard's courtyard, the word of the LORD
came to Jeremiah a second time: 2 "The LORD
who made the earth,[B] the LORD who forms it
to establish it, the LORD is his name, says this:
3 Call to me and I will answer you and tell you
great and incomprehensible things you do not
know. 4 For this is what the LORD, the God of
Israel, says concerning the houses of this city
and the palaces of Judah's kings, the ones torn
down for defense against the assault ramps
and the sword: 5 The people coming to fight
the Chaldeans will fill the houses with the
corpses of their own men that I strike down
in my wrath and rage. I have hidden my face
from this city because of all their evil. 6 Yet I
will certainly bring health and healing to it
and will indeed heal them. I will let them experience the abundance[C] of true peace. 7 I will
restore the fortunes[D] of Judah and of Israel
and will rebuild them as in former times. 8 I
will purify them from all the iniquity they have
committed against me, and I will forgive all
the iniquities they have committed against
me, rebelling against me. 9 This city will bear
on my behalf a name of joy, praise, and glory
before all the nations of the earth, who will
hear of all the prosperity I will give them. They
will tremble with awe because of all the good
and all the peace I will bring about for them.
10 "This is what the LORD says: In this place,
which you say is a ruin, without people or

Exercise of Faith | *Praying*

GOD'S PHONE NUMBER

"The LORD who made the earth, the LORD who forms it to establish it, the LORD is his name, says this: Call to me and I will answer you and tell you great and incomprehensible things you do not know." Jeremiah 33:2-3

When Jeremiah found himself "confined in the guard's courtyard" (33:1), the word of the Lord came to him suddenly. Exactly how—an audible voice, an internal whisper, or a vision: we're not told. But the means is not nearly as important as the message.

God announced himself to the imprisoned prophet as the great Creator and sustainer of all, the covenant-keeping Lord. Then he commanded Jeremiah, "Call to me." In other words, "Cry out to me, Jeremiah. Summon me. Invite me into your experience." And the promise? "I will answer you and tell you great and incomprehensible things."

In one sense, this was a unique historical experience—God speaking to an ancient prophet. In another sense, however, it shows how God desires to relate to us. He wants to communicate with us. He wants us to know him and his will. He wants our eyes to be on him, not on ourselves. He wants us to rely on him and to partner with him and his people in doing big, wild things.

Some people call Jeremiah 33:3, "God's phone number." Maybe you should give him a call.

For the next note on *Exercise of Faith*, see Jeremiah 38:6.

[A] **32:44** Or *will end their captivity* [B] **33:2** LXX; MT reads *made it* [C] **33:6** Or *fragrance*; Hb obscure [D] **33:7** Or *will end the captivity*, also in v. 11

animals — that is, in Judah's cities and Jerusalem's streets that are a desolation without
people, without inhabitants, and without animals — there will be heard again 11 a sound
of joy and gladness, the voice of the groom
and the bride, and the voice of those saying,

Give thanks to the LORD of Armies,
for the LORD is good;
his faithful love endures forever

as they bring thank offerings to the temple
of the LORD. For I will restore the fortunes of
the land as in former times, says the LORD.

12 "This is what the LORD of Armies says:
In this desolate place — without people or
animals — and in all its cities there will once
more be a grazing land where shepherds may
rest flocks. 13 The flocks will again pass under
the hands of the one who counts them in the
cities of the hill country, the cities of the Judean foothills, the cities of the Negev, the land
of Benjamin — the areas around Jerusalem
and in Judah's cities, says the LORD.

GOD'S COVENANT WITH DAVID

14 "Look, the days are coming" —
this is the LORD's declaration —
"when I will fulfill the good promise
that I have spoken
concerning the house of Israel
and the house of Judah.
15 In those days and at that time
I will cause a Righteous Branch
to sprout up for David,
and he will administer justice
and righteousness in the land.
16 In those days Judah will be saved,
and Jerusalem will dwell securely,
and this is what she will be named:
The LORD Is Our Righteousness.[A]

17 "For this is what the LORD says: David will
never fail to have a man sitting on the throne
of the house of Israel. 18 The Levitical priests
will never fail to have a man always before
me to offer burnt offerings, to burn grain offerings, and to make sacrifices."

19 The word of the LORD came to Jeremiah:
20 "This is what the LORD says: If you can break
my covenant with the day and my covenant with
the night so that day and night cease to come
at their regular time, 21 then also my covenant
with my servant David may be broken. If that
could happen, then he would not have a son
reigning on his throne and the Levitical priests
would not be my ministers. 22 Even as the stars
of heaven cannot be counted, and the sand of
the sea cannot be measured, so too I will make
innumerable the descendants of my servant
David and the Levites who minister to me."

23 The word of the LORD came to Jeremiah:
24 "Have you not noticed what these people
have said? They say, 'The LORD has rejected
the two families he had chosen.' My people
are treated with contempt and no longer regarded as a nation among them. 25 This is what
the LORD says: If I do not keep my covenant
with the day and with the night, and if I fail to
establish the fixed order of heaven and earth,
26 then I might also reject the descendants of
Jacob and of my servant David. That is, I would
not take rulers from his descendants to rule
over the descendants of Abraham, Isaac, and
Jacob. But in fact, I will restore their fortunes[B]
and have compassion on them."

JEREMIAH'S WORD TO KING ZEDEKIAH

34 This is the word that came to Jeremiah from the LORD when King Nebuchadnezzar of Babylon, his whole army, all
the kingdoms of the lands under his control,
and all other peoples were fighting against Jerusalem and all its surrounding cities: 2 "This
is what the LORD, the God of Israel, says: Go,
speak to King Zedekiah of Judah, and tell him,
'This is what the LORD says: I am about to hand
this city over to the king of Babylon, and he
will burn it. 3 As for you, you will not escape
from him but are certain to be captured and
handed over to him. You will meet the king
of Babylon eye to eye and speak face to face;[C]
you will go to Babylon.

4 " 'Yet hear the LORD's word, King Zedekiah
of Judah. This is what the LORD says concerning
you: You will not die by the sword; 5 you will die
peacefully. There will be a burning ceremony
for you just like the burning ceremonies for
your ancestors, the kings of old who came
before you. "Oh, master! " will be the lament
for you, for I have spoken this word. This is
the LORD's declaration.' "

6 So the prophet Jeremiah related all these
words to King Zedekiah of Judah in Jerusalem
7 while the king of Babylon's army was attacking Jerusalem and all of Judah's remaining cities — that is, Lachish and Azekah, for they were
the only ones left of Judah's fortified cities.

[A] **33:16** = *Yahweh-zidkenu* [B] **33:26** Or *I will end their captivity* [C] **34:3** Lit *and his mouth will speak to your mouth*

THE PEOPLE AND THEIR SLAVES

[8] This is the word that came to Jeremiah from the LORD after King Zedekiah made a covenant with all the people who were in Jerusalem to proclaim freedom to them. [9] As a result, each was to let his male and female Hebrew slaves go free, and no one was to enslave his fellow Judean. [10] All the officials and people who entered into covenant to let their male and female slaves go free — in order not to enslave them any longer — obeyed and let them go free. [11] Afterward, however, they changed their minds and took back their male and female slaves they had let go free and forced them to become slaves again.

[12] Then the word of the LORD came to Jeremiah from the LORD: [13] "This is what the LORD, the God of Israel, says: I made a covenant with your ancestors when I brought them out of the land of Egypt, out of the place of slavery, saying, [14] 'At the end of seven years, each of you must let his fellow Hebrew who sold himself[A] to you go. He may serve you six years, but then you must let him go free from your service.' But your ancestors did not obey me or pay any attention. [15] Today you repented and did what pleased me, each of you proclaiming freedom for his neighbor. You made a covenant before me at the house that bears my name. [16] But you have changed your minds and profaned my name. Each has taken back his male and female slaves who had been let go free to go wherever they wanted, and you have again forced them to be your slaves.

[17] "Therefore, this is what the LORD says: You have not obeyed me by proclaiming freedom, each for his fellow Hebrew and for his neighbor. I hereby proclaim freedom for you — this is the LORD's declaration — to the sword, to plague, and to famine! I will make you a horror to all the earth's kingdoms. [18] As for those who disobeyed my covenant, not keeping the terms of the covenant they made before me, I will treat them like the calf they cut in two in order to pass between its pieces. [19] The officials of Judah and Jerusalem, the court officials, the priests, and all the people of the land who passed between the pieces of the calf — [20] all these I will hand over to their enemies, to those who intend to take their life. Their corpses will become food for the birds of the sky and for the wild animals of the land. [21] I will hand King Zedekiah of Judah and his officials over to their enemies, to those who intend to take their lives, to the king of Babylon's army that is withdrawing. [22] I am about to give the command — this is the LORD's declaration — and I will bring them back to this city. They will fight against it, capture it, and burn it. I will make Judah's cities a desolation, without inhabitant."

THE RECHABITES' EXAMPLE

35 This is the word that came to Jeremiah from the LORD in the days of Jehoiakim son of Josiah, king of Judah: [2] "Go to the house of the Rechabites, speak to them, and bring them to one of the chambers of the temple of the LORD to offer them a drink of wine."

[3] So I took Jaazaniah son of Jeremiah, son of Habazziniah, and his brothers and all his sons — the entire house of the Rechabites — [4] and I brought them into the temple of the LORD to a chamber occupied by the sons of Hanan son of Igdaliah, a man of God, who had a chamber near the officials' chamber, which was above the chamber of Maaseiah son of Shallum the doorkeeper. [5] I set jars filled with wine and some cups before the sons of the house of the Rechabites and said to them, "Drink wine!"

[6] But they replied, "We do not drink wine, for Jonadab, son of our ancestor Rechab, commanded: 'You and your descendants must never drink wine. [7] You must not build a house or sow seed or plant a vineyard. Those things are not for you. Rather, you must live in tents your whole life, so you may live a long time on the soil where you stay as a resident alien.' [8] We have obeyed Jonadab, son of our ancestor Rechab, in all he commanded us. So we haven't drunk wine our whole life — we, our wives, our sons, and our daughters. [9] We also have not built houses to live in and do not have vineyard, field, or seed. [10] But we have lived in tents and have obeyed and done everything our ancestor Jonadab commanded us. [11] However, when King Nebuchadnezzar of Babylon marched into the land, we said, 'Come, let's go into Jerusalem to get away from the Chaldean and Aramean armies.' So we have been living in Jerusalem."

[12] Then the word of the LORD came to Jeremiah: [13] "This is what the LORD of Armies, the God of Israel, says: Go, say to the men of Judah and the residents of Jerusalem, 'Will you not accept discipline by listening to my words? —

[A] **34:14** Or *who was sold*

this is the LORD's declaration. 14 The words of
Jonadab, son of Rechab, have been carried
out. He commanded his descendants not to
drink wine, and they have not drunk to this
day because they have obeyed their ancestor's
command. But I have spoken to you time and
time again,[A] and you have not obeyed me!
15 Time and time again[B] I have sent you all my
servants the prophets, proclaiming, "Turn,
each one from his evil way, and correct your
actions. Stop following other gods to serve
them. Live in the land that I gave you and your
ancestors." But you did not pay attention or
obey me. 16 Yes, the sons of Jonadab son of Rechab carried out their ancestor's command he
gave them, but these people have not obeyed
me. 17 Therefore, this is what the LORD, the God
of Armies, the God of Israel, says: I will certainly bring on Judah and on all the residents of
Jerusalem all the disaster I have pronounced
against them because I have spoken to them,
but they have not obeyed, and I have called to
them, but they did not answer.' "

18 But to the house of the Rechabites Jeremiah said, "This is what the LORD of Armies, the
God of Israel, says: 'Because you have obeyed
the command of your ancestor Jonadab and
have kept all his commands and have done
everything he commanded you, 19 this is what
the LORD of Armies, the God of Israel, says:
Jonadab son of Rechab will never fail to have
a man to stand before me always.' "

JEREMIAH DICTATES A SCROLL

36 In the fourth year of Jehoiakim son of
Josiah, king of Judah, this word came to
Jeremiah from the LORD: 2 "Take a scroll, and
write on it all the words I have spoken to you
concerning Israel, Judah, and all the nations
from the time I first spoke to you during Josiah's reign until today. 3 Perhaps when the
house of Judah hears about all the disaster
I am planning to bring on them, each one of
them will turn from his evil way. Then I will
forgive their iniquity and their sin."

4 So Jeremiah summoned Baruch son of Neriah. At Jeremiah's dictation,[C] Baruch wrote on
a scroll all the words the LORD had spoken to
Jeremiah. 5 Then Jeremiah commanded Baruch,
"I am restricted; I cannot enter the temple of the
LORD, 6 so you must go and read from the scroll
— which you wrote at my dictation[D] — the
words of the LORD in the hearing of the people
at the temple of the LORD on a day of fasting.
Read his words in the hearing of all the Judeans who are coming from their cities. 7 Perhaps
their petition will come before the LORD, and
each one will turn from his evil way, for the
anger and fury that the LORD has pronounced
against this people are intense." 8 So Baruch son
of Neriah did everything the prophet Jeremiah
had commanded him. At the LORD's temple he
read the LORD's words from the scroll.

BARUCH READS THE SCROLL

9 In the fifth year of Jehoiakim son of Josiah, king of Judah, in the ninth month, all the
people of Jerusalem and all those coming in
from Judah's cities into Jerusalem proclaimed
a fast before the LORD. 10 Then at the LORD's
temple, in the chamber of Gemariah son of
Shaphan the scribe, in the upper courtyard
at the opening of the New Gate of the LORD's
temple, in the hearing of all the people, Baruch read Jeremiah's words from the scroll.

11 When Micaiah son of Gemariah, son of Shaphan, heard all the words of the LORD from the
scroll, 12 he went down to the scribe's chamber
in the king's palace. All the officials were sitting
there — Elishama the scribe, Delaiah son of
Shemaiah, Elnathan son of Achbor, Gemariah
son of Shaphan, Zedekiah son of Hananiah,
and all the other officials. 13 Micaiah reported to them all the words he had heard when
Baruch read from the scroll in the hearing of
the people. 14 Then all the officials sent word
to Baruch through Jehudi son of Nethaniah,
son of Shelemiah, son of Cushi, saying, "Bring
the scroll that you read in the hearing of the
people, and come." So Baruch son of Neriah
took the scroll and went to them. 15 They said
to him, "Sit down and read it in our hearing."
So Baruch read it in their hearing.

16 When they had heard all the words, they
turned to each other in fear and said to Baruch,
"We must surely tell the king all these things."
17 Then they asked Baruch, "Tell us, how did
you write all these words? At his dictation?"[E]

18 Baruch said to them, "At his dictation. He
recited all these words to me while I was writing on the scroll in ink."

JEHOIAKIM BURNS THE SCROLL

19 The officials said to Baruch, "You and Jeremiah must hide and tell no one where you
are." 20 Then, after depositing the scroll in the

[A] **35:14** Lit *you, rising up early and speaking* [B] **35:15** Lit *Rising up early and sending* [C] **36:4** Lit *From Jeremiah's mouth*
[D] **36:6** Lit *wrote from my mouth* [E] **36:17** Lit *From his mouth*, also in v. 18

My Story | Cord

As a firefighter for many years I witnessed some terrible things and often wondered what God was doing when people were hurting and dying. The problem was I couldn't come up with something or someone better. It took me a long time to realize that in a world where choices matter, terrible things can happen when people make the wrong ones. But I also had a front row seat on some amazing events in which the survival of people, including me, sometimes couldn't be explained any way other than that God intervened.

But the aftermath of a fire finally got my attention as nothing else had. We were called out to a house fire late one night. We soon realized that the fire was located in the den of the house and had consumed most of that room. We were able to quickly extinguish the fire to prevent the rest of the home from going up in flames.

After putting out the fire, we performed a cleanup of all burned materials, making sure there were no hot spots that could flare up again. This is known in fireman's lingo as "salvage" or "overhaul." As I looked around the charred and smoky room, I noticed that the den had a player piano. It had gotten so intensely hot in the den that the keys on the piano had melted into one big lump. Some fires reach a thousand degrees or more.

As I was moving burned debris from a coffee table and sofa, I noticed a large book on the floor. I picked it up and discovered it was a family Bible, covered in ashes. I dusted it off, and it appeared to be in good shape. I carried the Bible out to the lady of the house and offered her my regrets that nothing else in the room had survived. When she opened the book, we realized that the pages were not even singed. The Word of God had gone through the heat undamaged.

I stood amazed as that woman, with tears rolling down her face, told me that nothing in the room was more valuable than the book I had given her. I realized I wasn't giving God much credit for the good things in my life but was quick to blame him for things I didn't like. In an odd way, the survival of that Bible started me on a course that led me to Christ. I still have questions, but I realize now that I don't have to understand everything in order to trust God. And when I decide to trust him, I find I understand things much better.

chamber of Elishama the scribe, the officials
came to the king at the courtyard and reported
everything in the hearing of the king. 21 The
king sent Jehudi to get the scroll, and he took
it from the chamber of Elishama the scribe.
Jehudi then read it in the hearing of the king
and all the officials who were standing by the
king. 22 Since it was the ninth month, the king
was sitting in his winter quarters with a fire
burning in front of him. 23 As soon as Jehudi
would read three or four columns, Jehoiakim
would cut the scroll[A] with a scribe's knife and
throw the columns into the fire in the hearth
until the entire scroll was consumed by the
fire in the hearth. 24 As they heard all these
words, the king and all of his servants did not
become terrified or tear their clothes. 25 Even
though Elnathan, Delaiah, and Gemariah had
urged the king not to burn the scroll, he did not
listen to them. 26 Then the king commanded
Jerahmeel the king's son, Seraiah son of Azriel, and Shelemiah son of Abdeel to seize the
scribe Baruch and the prophet Jeremiah, but
the LORD hid them.

JEREMIAH DICTATES ANOTHER SCROLL

27 After the king had burned the scroll and
the words Baruch had written at Jeremiah's
dictation,[B] the word of the LORD came to Jeremiah: 28 "Take another scroll, and once again
write on it the original words that were on the
original scroll that King Jehoiakim of Judah
burned. 29 You are to proclaim concerning
King Jehoiakim of Judah, 'This is what the
LORD says: You have burned the scroll, asking,
"Why have you written on it that the king of
Babylon will certainly come and destroy this
land and cause it to be without people or animals?" 30 Therefore, this is what the LORD says
concerning King Jehoiakim of Judah: He will

[A] **36:23** Lit *columns, he would tear it* [B] **36:27** Lit *written from Jeremiah's mouth* have no one to sit on David's throne, and his corpse will be thrown out to be exposed to the heat of day and the frost of night. 31 I will punish him, his descendants, and his officers for their iniquity. I will bring on them, on the residents of Jerusalem, and on the people of Judah all the disaster, which I warned them about but they did not listen.'"

32 Then Jeremiah took another scroll and gave it to Baruch son of Neriah, the scribe, and he wrote on it at Jeremiah's dictation[A] all the words of the scroll that Jehoiakim, Judah's king, had burned in the fire. And many other words like them were added.

JERUSALEM'S LAST DAYS

37 Zedekiah son of Josiah reigned as king in the land of Judah in place of Coniah[B] son of Jehoiakim, for King Nebuchadnezzar of Babylon made him king. 2 He and his officers and the people of the land did not obey the words of the LORD that he spoke through the prophet Jeremiah.

3 Nevertheless, King Zedekiah sent Jehucal son of Shelemiah and Zephaniah son of Maaseiah, the priest, to the prophet Jeremiah, requesting, "Please pray to the LORD our God for us!" 4 Jeremiah was going about his daily tasks[C] among the people, for he had not yet been put into the prison. 5 Pharaoh's army had left Egypt, and when the Chaldeans, who were besieging Jerusalem, heard the report, they withdrew from Jerusalem.

6 The word of the LORD came to the prophet Jeremiah: 7 "This is what the LORD, the God of Israel, says: This is what you will say to Judah's king, who is sending you to inquire of me: 'Watch: Pharaoh's army, which has come out to help you, is going to return to its own land of Egypt. 8 The Chaldeans will then return and fight against this city. They will capture it and burn it. 9 This is what the LORD says: Don't deceive yourselves by saying, "The Chaldeans will leave us for good," for they will not leave. 10 Indeed, if you were to strike down the entire Chaldean army that is fighting with you, and there remained among them only the badly wounded[D] men, each in his tent, they would get up and burn this city.'"

JEREMIAH'S IMPRISONMENT

11 When the Chaldean army withdrew from Jerusalem because of Pharaoh's army, 12 Jeremiah started to leave Jerusalem to go to the land of Benjamin to claim his portion there among the people. 13 But when he was at the Benjamin Gate, an officer of the guard was there, whose name was Irijah son of Shelemiah, son of Hananiah, and he apprehended the prophet Jeremiah, saying, "You are defecting to the Chaldeans."

14 "That's a lie," Jeremiah replied. "I am not defecting to the Chaldeans!" Irijah would not listen to him but apprehended Jeremiah and took him to the officials. 15 The officials were angry at Jeremiah and beat him and placed him in jail in the house of Jonathan the scribe, for it had been made into a prison. 16 So Jeremiah went into a cell in the dungeon and stayed there many days.

JEREMIAH SUMMONED BY ZEDEKIAH

17 King Zedekiah later sent for him and received him, and in his house privately asked him, "Is there a word from the LORD?"

"There is," Jeremiah responded. He continued, "You will be handed over to the king of Babylon." 18 Then Jeremiah said to King Zedekiah, "How have I sinned against you or your servants or these people that you have put me in prison? 19 Where are your prophets who prophesied to you, claiming, 'The king of Babylon will not come against you and this land'? 20 So now please listen, my lord the king. May my petition come before you. Don't send me back to the house of Jonathan the scribe, or I will die there."

21 So King Zedekiah gave orders, and Jeremiah was placed in the guard's courtyard. He was given a loaf of bread each day from the bakers' street until all the bread was gone from the city. So Jeremiah remained in the guard's courtyard.

JEREMIAH THROWN INTO A CISTERN

38 Now Shephatiah son of Mattan, Gedaliah son of Pashhur, Jucal[E] son of Shelemiah, and Pashhur son of Malchijah heard the words Jeremiah was speaking to all the people: 2 "This is what the LORD says: 'Whoever stays in this city will die by the sword, famine, and plague, but whoever surrenders to the Chaldeans will live. He will retain his life like the spoils of war and will live.' 3 This is what the LORD says: 'This city will most certainly be handed over to the king of Babylon's army, and he will capture it.'"

[A] **36:32** Lit *it from Jeremiah's mouth* [B] **37:1** = Jehoiachin [C] **37:4** Lit *was coming in and going out* [D] **37:10** Lit *the pierced*
[E] **38:1** = Jehucal in Jr 37:3

4 The officials then said to the king, "This
man ought to die, because he is weakening
the morale[A] of the warriors who remain in
this city and of all the people by speaking
to them in this way. This man is not pursuing
the welfare of this people, but their harm."
5 King Zedekiah said, "Here he is; he's in your
hands since the king can't do anything against
you." 6 So they took Jeremiah and dropped him
into the cistern of Malchiah the king's son,
which was in the guard's courtyard, lowering
Jeremiah with ropes. There was no water in
the cistern, only mud, and Jeremiah sank in
the mud.
7 But Ebed-melech, a Cushite court official
in the king's palace, heard Jeremiah had been
put into the cistern. While the king was sitting at the Benjamin Gate, 8 Ebed-melech went
from the king's palace and spoke to the king:
9 "My lord the king, these men have been evil
in all they have done to the prophet Jeremiah.
They have dropped him into the cistern where
he will die from hunger, because there is no
more bread in the city."
10 So the king commanded Ebed-melech, the
Cushite, "Take from here thirty men under your
authority[B] and pull the prophet Jeremiah up
from the cistern before he dies."
11 So Ebed-melech took the men under his
authority[C] and went to the king's palace to a
place below the storehouse.[D] From there he
took old rags and worn-out clothes and lowered them by ropes to Jeremiah in the cistern.
12 Ebed-melech the Cushite called down to
Jeremiah, "Place these old rags and clothes
between your armpits and the ropes." Jeremiah did this. 13 They pulled him up with the
ropes and lifted him out of the cistern, but he
remained in the guard's courtyard.

ZEDEKIAH'S FINAL MEETING WITH JEREMIAH

14 King Zedekiah sent for the prophet Jeremiah
and received him at the third entrance of the
LORD's temple. The king said to Jeremiah, "I
am going to ask you something; don't hide
anything from me."
15 Jeremiah replied to Zedekiah, "If I tell you,
you will kill me, won't you? Besides, if I give
you advice, you won't listen to me anyway."
16 King Zedekiah swore to Jeremiah in private, "As the LORD lives, who has given us this
life, I will not kill you or hand you over to these
men who intend to take your life."
17 Jeremiah therefore said to Zedekiah, "This
is what the LORD, the God of Armies, the God
of Israel, says: 'If indeed you surrender to the

Exercise of Faith | *Praying*

SERVANTS IN THE MUD

"So they took Jeremiah and dropped him into the cistern of Malchiah the king's son, which was in the guard's courtyard, lowering Jeremiah with ropes. There was no water in the cistern, only mud, and Jeremiah sank in the mud." Jeremiah 38:6

The stories are shocking. And we know so many of them! The ministry volunteer who was wrongly accused of stealing money. The pastor who poured his life into his congregation and then was abruptly fired because he failed to visit a prominent church member in the hospital. The small group leader who was asked to leave the church because his group was growing too big and attracting too many "undesirable" people.

Here's hoping you never experience the dark side of ministry like these folks—or like Jeremiah did. This chapter tells about him ending up in a big muddy pit. And for what? For doing exactly what God asked him to do!

Stories like this have no logic. And we can't spin such experiences so that they don't hurt. But God sees and knows the real situation. And just as he brought Jeremiah out of his mucky pit (see 38:7-28), he will get you through your mess.

For the next note on *Exercise of Faith*, see Jeremiah 43:1-2.

[A] **38:4** Lit *hands* [B] **38:10** Lit *men in your hand* [C] **38:11** Lit *men in his hand* [D] **38:11** Or *treasury*

officials of the king of Babylon, then you will
live, this city will not be burned, and you and
your household will survive. 18 But if you do
not surrender to the officials of the king of
Babylon, then this city will be handed over
to the Chaldeans. They will burn it, and you
yourself will not escape from them.' "
19 But King Zedekiah said to Jeremiah, "I am
worried about the Judeans who have defected
to the Chaldeans. They may hand me over to
the Judeans to abuse me."
20 "They will not hand you over," Jeremiah
replied. "Obey the LORD in what I am telling
you, so it may go well for you and you can live.
21 But if you refuse to surrender, this is the verdict[A] that the LORD has shown me: 22 'All the
women[B] who remain in the palace of Judah's
king will be brought out to the officials of the
king of Babylon and will say to you,[C]

"Your trusted friends[D] misled[E] you
and overcame you.
Your feet sank into the mire,
and they deserted you."

23 All your wives and children will be brought
out to the Chaldeans. You yourself will not
escape from them, for you will be seized by
the king of Babylon and this city will burn.' "
24 Then Zedekiah warned Jeremiah, "Don't
let anyone know about this conversation[F] or
you will die. 25 The officials may hear that I
have spoken with you and come and demand
of you, 'Tell us what you said to the king; don't
hide anything from us and we won't kill you.
Also, what did the king say to you?' 26 If they
do, tell them, 'I was bringing before the king
my petition that he not return me to the house
of Jonathan to die there.' " 27 All the officials
did come to Jeremiah, and they questioned
him. He reported the exact words to them the
king had commanded, and they quit speaking
with him because the conversation[G] had not
been overheard. 28 Jeremiah remained in the
guard's courtyard until the day Jerusalem was
captured, and he was there when it happened.[H]

THE FALL OF JERUSALEM TO BABYLON

39 In the ninth year of King Zedekiah of
Judah, in the tenth month, King Nebuchadnezzar of Babylon advanced against
Jerusalem with his entire army and laid siege
to it. 2 In the fourth month of Zedekiah's eleventh year, on the ninth day of the month, the
city was broken into. 3 All the officials of the
king of Babylon entered and sat at the Middle
Gate: Nergal-sharezer, Samgar, Nebusarse-
chim[I] the chief of staff, Nergal-sharezer the
chief soothsayer, and all the rest of the officials
of Babylon's king.
4 When King Zedekiah of Judah and all the
fighting men saw them, they fled. They left
the city at night by way of the king's garden
through the city gate between the two walls.
They left along the route to the Arabah. 5 However, the Chaldean army pursued them and
overtook Zedekiah in the plains of Jericho.
They arrested him and brought him up to Nebuchadnezzar, Babylon's king, at Riblah in the
land of Hamath. The king passed sentence
on him there.
6 At Riblah the king of Babylon slaughtered Zedekiah's sons before his eyes, and
he also slaughtered all Judah's nobles. 7 Then
he blinded Zedekiah and put him in bronze
chains to take him to Babylon. 8 The Chaldeans next burned down the king's palace and
the people's houses and tore down the walls
of Jerusalem. 9 Nebuzaradan, the captain of
the guards, deported the rest of the people to
Babylon — those who had remained in the
city and those deserters who had defected to
him along with the rest of the people who remained. 10 However, Nebuzaradan, the captain
of the guards, left in the land of Judah some of
the poor people who owned nothing, and he
gave them vineyards and fields at that time.

JEREMIAH FREED BY NEBUCHADNEZZAR

11 Speaking through Nebuzaradan, captain of
the guards, King Nebuchadnezzar of Babylon
gave orders concerning Jeremiah: 12 "Take him
and look after him. Don't do him any harm,
but do for him whatever he says." 13 Nebuzaradan, captain of the guards, Nebushazban
the chief of staff, Nergal-sharezer the chief
soothsayer, and all the captains of Babylon's
king 14 had Jeremiah brought from the guard's
courtyard and turned him over to Gedaliah
son of Ahikam, son of Shaphan, to take him
home. So he settled among his own people.
15 Now the word of the LORD had come to
Jeremiah when he was confined in the guard's
courtyard: 16 "Go tell Ebed-melech the Cushite, 'This is what the LORD of Armies, the God
of Israel, says: I am about to fulfill my words

[A] **38:21** Or *promise*; lit *word* [B] **38:22** Or *wives* [C] **38:22** *to you* supplied for clarity [D] **38:22** Lit *"The men of your peace* [E] **38:22** Or *incited* [F] **38:24** Lit *about these words* [G] **38:27** Lit *word* [H] **38:28** Or *captured. This is what happened when Jerusalem was captured:* [I] **39:3** LXX; MT reads *Samgar-nebu, Sarsechim*

for disaster and not for good against this city. They will take place before your eyes on that day. 17 But I will rescue you on that day — this is the LORD's declaration — and you will not be handed over to the men you dread. 18 Indeed, I will certainly deliver you so that you do not fall by the sword. Because you have trusted in me, you will retain your life like the spoils of war. This is the LORD's declaration.' "

JEREMIAH STAYS IN JUDAH

40 This is the word that came to Jeremiah from the LORD after Nebuzaradan, captain of the guards, released him at Ramah. When he found him, he was bound in chains with all the exiles of Jerusalem and Judah who were being exiled to Babylon. 2 The captain of the guards took Jeremiah and said to him, "The LORD your God decreed this disaster on this place, 3 and the LORD has fulfilled it. He has done just what he decreed. Because you people have sinned against the LORD and have not obeyed him, this thing has happened. 4 Now pay attention: Today I am setting you free from the chains that were on your hands. If it pleases you to come with me to Babylon, come, and I will take care of you. But if it seems wrong to you to come with me to Babylon, go no farther.[A] Look — the whole land is in front of you. Wherever it seems good and right for you to go, go there." 5 When Jeremiah had not yet turned to go, Nebuzaradan said to him,[B] "Return[C] to Gedaliah son of Ahikam, son of Shaphan, whom the king of Babylon has appointed over the cities of Judah, and stay with him among the people or go wherever it seems right for you to go." So the captain of the guards gave him a ration and a gift and released him. 6 Jeremiah therefore went to Gedaliah son of Ahikam at Mizpah, and he stayed with him among the people who remained in the land.

GEDALIAH ADVISES PEACE

7 All the commanders of the armies that were in the countryside — they and their men — heard that the king of Babylon had appointed Gedaliah son of Ahikam over the land. He had been put in charge of the men, women, and children from among the poorest of the land, who had not been deported to Babylon. 8 So they came to Gedaliah at Mizpah. The commanders included Ishmael son of Nethaniah, Johanan and Jonathan the sons of Kareah, Seraiah son of Tanhumeth, the sons of Ephai the Netophathite, and Jezaniah son of the Maacathite — they and their men.

9 Gedaliah son of Ahikam, son of Shaphan, swore an oath to them and their men, assuring them, "Don't be afraid to serve the Chaldeans. Live in the land and serve the king of Babylon, and it will go well for you. 10 As for me, I am going to live in Mizpah to represent you[D] before the Chaldeans who come to us. As for you, gather wine, summer fruit, and oil, place them in your storage jars, and live in the cities you have captured."

11 When all the Judeans in Moab and among the Ammonites and in Edom and in all the other lands also heard that the king of Babylon had left a remnant in Judah and had appointed Gedaliah son of Ahikam, son of Shaphan, over them, 12 they all returned from all the places where they had been banished and came to the land of Judah, to Gedaliah at Mizpah, and harvested a great amount of wine and summer fruit.

13 Meanwhile, Johanan son of Kareah and all the commanders of the armies in the countryside came to Gedaliah at Mizpah 14 and warned him, "Don't you realize that Baalis, king of the Ammonites, has sent Ishmael son of Nethaniah to kill you?" But Gedaliah son of Ahikam would not believe them. 15 Then Johanan son of Kareah suggested to Gedaliah in private at Mizpah, "Let me go kill Ishmael son of Nethaniah. No one will know it. Why should he kill you and allow all of Judah that has gathered around you to scatter and the remnant of Judah to perish?"

16 But Gedaliah son of Ahikam responded to Johanan son of Kareah, "Don't do that! What you're saying about Ishmael is a lie."

GEDALIAH ASSASSINATED BY ISHMAEL

41 In the seventh month, Ishmael son of Nethaniah, son of Elishama, of the royal family and one of the king's chief officers, came with ten men to Gedaliah son of Ahikam at Mizpah. They ate a meal together there in Mizpah, 2 but then Ishmael son of Nethaniah and the ten men who were with him got up and struck down Gedaliah son of Ahikam, son of Shaphan, with the sword; he killed the one the king of Babylon had appointed in the land. 3 Ishmael also struck down all the Judeans who

[A] **40:4** Lit *Babylon, stop* [B] **40:5** *Nebuzaradan said to him* supplied for clarity [C] **40:5** LXX reads *"But if not, run, return*; Hb obscure [D] **40:10** Lit *to stand*

were with Gedaliah at Mizpah, as well as the
Chaldean soldiers who were there.
4 On the day after he had killed Gedaliah,
when no one knew yet, 5 eighty men came
from Shechem, Shiloh, and Samaria who had
shaved their beards, torn their clothes, and
gashed themselves, and who were carrying
grain and incense offerings to bring to the
temple of the LORD. 6 Ishmael son of Nethaniah
came out of Mizpah to meet them, weeping
as he came. When he encountered them, he
said, "Come to Gedaliah son of Ahikam!" 7 But
when they came into the city, Ishmael son of
Nethaniah and the men with him slaughtered
them and threw them into[A] a cistern.
8 However, there were ten men among them
who said to Ishmael, "Don't kill us, for we have
hidden treasure in the field — wheat, barley,
oil, and honey!" So he stopped and did not
kill them along with their companions. 9 Now
the cistern where Ishmael had thrown all the
corpses of the men he had struck down was
a large one[B] that King Asa had made in the
encounter with King Baasha of Israel. Ishmael son of Nethaniah filled it with the slain.
10 Then Ishmael took captive all the rest of
the people of Mizpah including the daughters
of the king — all those who remained in Mizpah over whom Nebuzaradan, captain of the
guards, had appointed Gedaliah son of Ahikam.
Ishmael son of Nethaniah took them captive
and set off to cross over to the Ammonites.

THE CAPTIVES RESCUED BY JOHANAN

11 When Johanan son of Kareah and all the
commanders of the armies with him heard
of all the evil that Ishmael son of Nethaniah
had done, 12 they took all their men and went
to fight with Ishmael son of Nethaniah. They
found him by the great pool in Gibeon. 13 When
all the people held by Ishmael saw Johanan
son of Kareah and all the commanders of the
army with him, they rejoiced. 14 All the people
whom Ishmael had taken captive from Mizpah
turned around and rejoined Johanan son of
Kareah. 15 But Ishmael son of Nethaniah escaped from Johanan with eight men and went
to the Ammonites. 16 Johanan son of Kareah
and all the commanders of the armies with
him then took from Mizpah all the remnant
of the people whom he had recovered from
Ishmael son of Nethaniah after Ishmael had
killed Gedaliah son of Ahikam — men, soldiers,
women, children, and court officials whom
he brought back from Gibeon. 17 They left,
stopping in Geruth Chimham, which is near
Bethlehem, in order to make their way into
Egypt, 18 away from the Chaldeans. For they
feared them because Ishmael son of Nethaniah had struck down Gedaliah son of Ahikam,
whom the king of Babylon had appointed over
the land.

THE PEOPLE SEEK JEREMIAH'S COUNSEL

42 Then all the commanders of the armies,
along with Johanan son of Kareah,
Jezaniah son of Hoshaiah, and all the people
from the least to the greatest, approached 2 the
prophet Jeremiah and said, "May our petition
come before you; pray to the LORD your God
on our behalf, on behalf of this entire remnant
(for few of us remain out of the many, as you
can see with your own eyes), 3 that the LORD
your God may tell us the way we should go
and the thing we should do."
4 So the prophet Jeremiah said to them, "I
have heard. I will now pray to the LORD your
God according to your words, and I will tell
you every word that the LORD answers you; I
won't withhold a word from you."
5 And they said to Jeremiah, "May the LORD
be a true and faithful witness against us if we
don't act according to every word the LORD
your God sends you to tell us. 6 Whether it is
pleasant or unpleasant, we will obey the LORD
our God to whom we are sending you so that
it may go well with us. We will certainly obey
the LORD our God!"

JEREMIAH'S ADVICE TO STAY

7 At the end of ten days, the word of the LORD
came to Jeremiah, 8 and he summoned Johanan son of Kareah, all the commanders of the
armies who were with him, and all the people
from the least to the greatest.
9 He said to them, "This is what the LORD says,
the God of Israel to whom you sent me to bring
your petition before him: 10 'If you will indeed
stay in this land, then I will rebuild and not
demolish you, and I will plant and not uproot
you, because I relent concerning the disaster
that I have brought on you. 11 Don't be afraid
of the king of Babylon whom you now fear;
don't be afraid of him' — this is the LORD's
declaration — 'because I am with you to save
you and rescue you from him. 12 I will grant you

[A] **41:7** Syr; MT reads *slaughtered them in* [B] **41:9** LXX; MT reads *down by the hand of Gedaliah*

compassion, and he[A] will have compassion on
you and allow you to return to your own soil.'
13 "But if you say, 'We will not stay in this
land,' in order to disobey the LORD your God,
14 and if you say, 'No, instead we'll go to the
land of Egypt where we will not see war or
hear the sound of the ram's horn or hunger
for food, and we'll live there,' 15 then hear the
word of the LORD, remnant of Judah! This is
what the LORD of Armies, the God of Israel,
says: 'If you are firmly resolved to go to Egypt
and stay there for a while, 16 then the sword
you fear will overtake you there in the land of
Egypt, and the famine you are worried about
will follow on your heels[B] there to Egypt, and
you will die there. 17 All who resolve to go to
Egypt to stay there for a while will die by the
sword, famine, and plague. They will have no
survivor or fugitive from the disaster I will
bring on them.'
18 "For this is what the LORD of Armies, the
God of Israel, says: 'Just as my anger and fury
were poured out on Jerusalem's residents, so
will my fury pour out on you if you go to Egypt.
You will become an example for cursing, scorn,
execration, and disgrace, and you will never
see this place again.' 19 The LORD has spoken
concerning you, remnant of Judah: 'Don't go
to Egypt.' Know for certain that I have warned
you today! 20 You have gone astray at the cost
of your lives[C] because you are the ones who
sent me to the LORD your God, saying, 'Pray to
the LORD our God on our behalf, and as for all
that the LORD our God says, tell it to us, and we'll
act accordingly.' 21 For I have told you today,
but you have not obeyed the LORD your God in
everything he has sent me to tell you. 22 Now
therefore, know for certain that by the sword,
famine, and plague you will die in the place
where you desired to go to stay for a while."

JEREMIAH'S COUNSEL REJECTED

43 When Jeremiah had finished speaking
to all the people all the words of the
LORD their God — all these words the LORD
their God had sent him to give them — 2 then
Azariah[D] son of Hoshaiah, Johanan son of
Kareah, and all the other arrogant men responded to Jeremiah, "You are speaking a lie!
The LORD our God has not sent you to say, 'You
must not go to Egypt to stay there for a while!'
3 Rather, Baruch son of Neriah is inciting you
against us to hand us over to the Chaldeans
to put us to death or to deport us to Babylon!"

Exercise of Faith | *Rejecting the World's Lies*

WHEN OPPOSITION COMES

"When Jeremiah had finished speaking to all the people . . . all these words the LORD their God had sent him to give them—then Azariah son of Hoshaiah, Johanan son of Kareah, and all the other arrogant men responded to Jeremiah, 'You are speaking a lie! The LORD our God has not sent you . . .'" Jeremiah 43:1-2

Perhaps this has happened to you. You do the God-honoring act. You gently speak the truth. You stand for justice. You oppose evil. And for your trouble? You get treated to a withering assault.

This was Jeremiah's experience. God gave him a message to deliver it, and deliver it he did. Almost immediately the character attacks began. "You're not a faithful prophet of God. You're a lying fraud!"

This kind of bullying hurts and is enough to shut most people down—or to at least make them think long and hard about sticking their necks out in the future. Of course, it didn't silence Jeremiah. He was used to it. What's more he expected it. From the beginning (1:17-19), God had made clear that an unrighteous generation wouldn't want to hear the holy words of heaven.

Jeremiah grasped the truth we all need to take to heart: To be right with God and at odds with the whole world is better than the other way around.

For the next note on *Exercise of Faith*, see Daniel 1:8.

[A] **42:12** LXX reads *I* [B] **42:16** Lit *will cling after you* [C] **42:20** Or *You have led your own selves astray* [D] **43:2** = Jezaniah

4 So Johanan son of Kareah, all the commanders of the armies, and all the people failed to obey the LORD's command to stay in the land of Judah. 5 Instead, Johanan son of Kareah and all the commanders of the armies led away the whole remnant of Judah, those who had returned to stay in the land of Judah from all the nations where they had been banished. 6 They led away the men, women, children, king's daughters, and everyone whom Nebuzaradan, captain of the guards, had allowed to remain with Gedaliah son of Ahikam son of Shaphan. They also led the prophet Jeremiah and Baruch son of Neriah away. 7 They went to the land of Egypt because they did not obey the LORD. They went as far as Tahpanhes.

GOD'S SIGN TO THE PEOPLE IN EGYPT

8 Then the word of the LORD came to Jeremiah at Tahpanhes: 9 "Pick up some large stones and set them in the mortar of the brick pavement that is at the opening of Pharaoh's palace at Tahpanhes. Do this in the sight of the Judean men 10 and tell them, 'This is what the LORD of Armies, the God of Israel, says: I will send for my servant Nebuchadnezzar king of Babylon, and I will place his throne on these stones that I have embedded, and he will pitch his pavilion over them. 11 He will come and strike down the land of Egypt — those destined for death, to death; those destined for captivity, to captivity; and those destined for the sword, to the sword. 12 I[A] will kindle a fire in the temples of Egypt's gods, and he will burn them and take them captive. He will clean the land of Egypt as a shepherd picks lice off[B] his clothes, and he will leave there unscathed. 13 He will smash the sacred pillars of the sun temple[C,D] in the land of Egypt and burn the temples of the Egyptian gods.'"

GOD'S JUDGMENT AGAINST HIS PEOPLE IN EGYPT

44 This is the word that came to Jeremiah for all the Jews living in the land of Egypt — at Migdol, Tahpanhes, Memphis, and in the land of Pathros: 2 "This is what the LORD of Armies, the God of Israel, says: You have seen all the disaster I brought against Jerusalem and all Judah's cities. Look, they are a ruin today without an inhabitant in them 3 because of the evil they committed to anger me, by going and burning incense to serve other gods that they, you, and your fathers did not know. 4 So I sent you all my servants the prophets time and time again,[E] saying, 'Don't commit this detestable action that I hate.' 5 But they did not listen or pay attention; they did not turn from their evil or stop burning incense to other gods. 6 So my fierce wrath poured out and burned in Judah's cities and Jerusalem's streets so that they became the desolate ruin they are today.

7 "So now, this is what the LORD, the God of Armies, the God of Israel, says: Why are you doing such terrible harm to yourselves? You are cutting off man and woman, infant and nursing baby from Judah, leaving yourselves without a remnant. 8 You are angering me by the work of your hands. You are burning incense to other gods in the land of Egypt where you have gone to stay for a while. As a result, you will be cut off and become an example for cursing and insult among all the nations of earth. 9 Have you forgotten the evils of your fathers, the evils of Judah's kings, the evils of their wives, your own evils, and the evils of your wives that were committed in the land of Judah and in the streets of Jerusalem? 10 They have not become humble to this day, and they have not feared or followed my instruction or my statutes that I set before you and your ancestors.

11 "Therefore, this is what the LORD of Armies, the God of Israel, says: I am about to set my face against you to bring disaster, to cut off all Judah. 12 And I will take away the remnant of Judah, those who have set their face to go to the land of Egypt to stay there. All of them will meet their end in the land of Egypt. They will fall by the sword; they will meet their end by famine. From the least to the greatest, they will die by the sword and by famine. Then they will become an example for cursing, scorn, execration, and disgrace. 13 I will punish those living in the land of Egypt just as I punished Jerusalem by sword, famine, and plague. 14 Then the remnant of Judah — those going to live for a while there in the land of Egypt — will have no fugitive or survivor to return to the land of Judah where they are longing[F] to return to stay, for they will not return except for a few fugitives."

THE PEOPLE'S STUBBORN RESPONSE

15 However, all the men who knew that their wives were burning incense to other gods, all

[A] **43:12** LXX, Syr, Vg read *He* [B] **43:12** Or *will wrap himself in the land of Egypt as a shepherd wraps himself in* [C] **43:13** Or *Beth-shemesh* [D] **43:13** = of Heliopolis [E] **44:4** Lit *prophets, rising up early and sending* [F] **44:14** Lit *lifting up their soul*

the women standing by — a great assembly — and all the people who were living in the land of Egypt at Pathros answered Jeremiah, 16 "As for the word you spoke to us in the name of the LORD, we are not going to listen to you! 17 Instead, we will do everything we promised:[A] we will burn incense to the queen of heaven[B] and offer drink offerings to her just as we, our fathers, our kings, and our officials did in Judah's cities and in Jerusalem's streets. Then we had enough food, we were well off, and we saw no disaster, 18 but from the time we ceased to burn incense to the queen of heaven and to offer her drink offerings, we have lacked everything, and through sword and famine we have met our end."

19 And the women said,[C] "When we burned incense to the queen of heaven and poured out drink offerings to her, was it apart from our husbands' knowledge that we made sacrificial cakes in her image and poured out drink offerings to her?"

20 But Jeremiah responded to all the people — the men, women, and all the people who were answering him: 21 "As for the incense you burned in Judah's cities and in Jerusalem's streets — you, your fathers, your kings, your officials, and the people of the land — did the LORD not remember them? He brought this to mind. 22 The LORD can no longer bear your evil deeds and the detestable acts you have committed, so your land has become a waste, a desolation, and an example for cursing, without inhabitant, as you see today. 23 Because you burned incense and sinned against the LORD and didn't obey the LORD and didn't follow his instruction, his statutes, and his testimonies, this disaster has come to you, as you see today."

24 Then Jeremiah said to all the people, including all the women, "Hear the word of the LORD, all you people of Judah who are in the land of Egypt. 25 This is what the LORD of Armies, the God of Israel, says: 'As for you and your wives, you women have spoken with your mouths, and you men fulfilled it by your deeds, saying, "We will keep our vows that we have made to burn incense to the queen of heaven and to pour out drink offerings for her." Go ahead, confirm your vows! Keep your vows!'

26 "Therefore, hear the word of the LORD, all you Judeans who live in the land of Egypt: 'I have sworn by my great name, says the LORD, that my name will never again be invoked by anyone of Judah in all the land of Egypt, saying, "As the Lord GOD lives." 27 I am watching over them for disaster and not for good, and everyone from Judah who is in the land of Egypt will meet his end by sword or famine until they are finished off. 28 Those who escape the sword will return from the land of Egypt to the land of Judah only few in number, and the whole remnant of Judah, the ones going to the land of Egypt to stay there for a while, will know whose word stands, mine or theirs! 29 This will be a sign to you' — this is the LORD's declaration — 'that I will punish you in this place, so you may know that my words of disaster concerning you will certainly come to pass. 30 This is what the LORD says: I am about to hand over Pharaoh Hophra, Egypt's king, to his enemies, to those who intend to take his life, just as I handed over Judah's King Zedekiah to Babylon's King Nebuchadnezzar, who was his enemy, the one who intended to take his life.'"

THE LORD'S MESSAGE TO BARUCH

45 This is the word that the prophet Jeremiah spoke to Baruch son of Neriah when he wrote these words on a scroll at Jeremiah's dictation[D] in the fourth year of Jehoiakim son of Josiah, king of Judah: 2 "This is what the LORD, the God of Israel, says to you, Baruch: 3 'You have said, "Woe is me, because the LORD has added misery to my pain! I am worn out with[E] groaning and have found no rest."'

4 "This is what you are to say to him: 'This is what the LORD says: "What I have built I am about to demolish, and what I have planted I am about to uproot — the whole land! 5 But as for you, do you pursue great things for yourself? Stop pursuing! For I am about to bring disaster on everyone" — this is the LORD's declaration — "but I will grant you your life like the spoils of war wherever you go."'"

PROPHECIES AGAINST THE NATIONS

46 This is the word of the LORD that came to the prophet Jeremiah about the nations:

PROPHECIES AGAINST EGYPT

2 About Egypt and the army of Pharaoh Neco, Egypt's king, which was defeated at Carchemish on the Euphrates River by King

---

[A] 44:17 Lit *do every word that came from our mouth* [B] 44:17 = Ashtoreth, or Astarte [C] 44:19 LXX, Syr; MT omits *And the women said* [D] 45:1 Lit *scroll from Jeremiah's mouth* [E] 45:3 Lit *I labored in my*

Nebuchadnezzar of Babylon in the fourth year
of Judah's King Jehoiakim son of Josiah:

3 Deploy small shields and large;
approach for battle!
4 Harness the horses;
mount the steeds;[A]
take your positions
with helmets on!
Polish the lances;
put on armor!
5 Why have I seen this?
They are terrified,
they are retreating,
their warriors are crushed,
they flee headlong,
they never look back,
terror is on every side!
This is the LORD's declaration.
6 The swift cannot flee,
and the warrior cannot escape!
In the north by the bank
of the Euphrates River,
they stumble and fall.

7 Who is this, rising like the Nile,
with waters that churn like rivers?
8 Egypt rises like the Nile,
and its waters churn like rivers.
He boasts, "I will go up, I will cover
the earth;
I will destroy cities
with their residents."
9 Rise up, you cavalry!
Race furiously, you chariots!
Let the warriors march out —
Cush and Put,
who are able to handle shields,
and the men of Lud,
who are able to handle and string
the bow.
10 That day belongs to the Lord, the GOD
of Armies,
a day of vengeance to avenge himself
against his adversaries.
The sword will devour and be satisfied;
it will drink its fill of their blood,
because it will be a sacrifice
to the Lord, the GOD of Armies,
in the northern land
by the Euphrates River.

11 Go up to Gilead and get balm,
Virgin Daughter Egypt!
You have multiplied remedies in vain;
there is no healing for you.
12 The nations have heard of your dishonor,
and your cries fill the earth,
because warrior stumbles
against warrior
and together both of them have fallen.

13 This is the word the LORD spoke to the
prophet Jeremiah about the coming of King
Nebuchadnezzar of Babylon to defeat the land
of Egypt:

14 Announce it in Egypt, and proclaim it
in Migdol!
Proclaim it in Memphis and in Tahpanhes!
Say, "Take positions! Prepare yourself,
for the sword devours all around you."
15 Why have your strong ones
been swept away?
Each has not stood,
for the LORD has thrust him down.
16 He continues to stumble.
Indeed, each falls over the other.
They say, "Get up! Let's return
to our people
and to our native land,
away from the oppressor's sword."
17 There they will cry out,
"Pharaoh king of Egypt was all noise;
he let the opportune moment pass."
18 As I live —
this is the King's declaration;
the LORD of Armies is his name —
the king of Babylon[B] will come
like Tabor among the mountains
and like Carmel by the sea.
19 Get your bags ready for exile,
inhabitant of Daughter Egypt!
For Memphis will become a desolation,
uninhabited ruins.

20 Egypt is a beautiful young cow,
but a horsefly from the north is coming
against her.[C]
21 Even her mercenaries among her
are like stall-fed calves.
They too will turn back;
together they will flee;
they will not take their stand,
for the day of their calamity is coming
on them,
the time of their punishment.

[A] **46:4** Or *mount up, riders* [B] **46:18** Lit *He* [C] **46:20** Some Hb mss, LXX, Syr; other Hb mss read *is coming, coming*

22 Egypt will hiss like a slithering snake,[A]
for the enemy will come with an army;
with axes they will come against her
like those who cut trees.
23 They will cut down her forest —
this is the LORD's declaration —
though it is dense,
for they are more numerous
than locusts;
they cannot be counted.
24 Daughter Egypt will be put to shame,
handed over to a northern people.

25 The LORD of Armies, the God of Israel, says,
"I am about to punish Amon, god of Thebes,
along with Pharaoh, Egypt, her gods, and her
kings — Pharaoh and those trusting in him.
26 I will hand them over to those who intend to
take their lives — to King Nebuchadnezzar of
Babylon and his officers. But after this, Egypt[B]
will be inhabited again as in ancient times."
This is the LORD's declaration.

REASSURANCE FOR ISRAEL

27 But you, my servant Jacob,
do not be afraid,
and do not be discouraged, Israel,
for without fail I will save you
from far away,
and your descendants from the land
of their captivity!
Jacob will return and have calm
and quiet
with no one to frighten him.
28 And you, my servant Jacob,
do not be afraid —
this is the LORD's declaration —
for I will be with you.
I will bring destruction
on all the nations
where I have banished you,
but I will not bring destruction on you.
I will discipline you with justice,
and I will by no means
leave you unpunished.

PROPHECIES AGAINST THE PHILISTINES

47 This is the word of the LORD that came
to the prophet Jeremiah about the Philistines before Pharaoh defeated Gaza. 2 This
is what the LORD says:
Look, water is rising from the north
and becoming an overflowing wadi.
It will overflow the land and everything
in it,
the cities and their inhabitants.
The people will cry out,
and every inhabitant of the land
will wail.
3 At the sound of the stomping hooves
of his stallions,
the rumbling of his chariots,
and the clatter of their wheels,
fathers will not turn back for their sons.
They will be utterly helpless[C]
4 on account of the day that is coming
to destroy all the Philistines,
to cut off from Tyre and Sidon
every remaining ally.
Indeed, the LORD is about to destroy
the Philistines,
the remnant of the coastland
of Caphtor.[D]
5 Baldness is coming to Gaza;
Ashkelon will become silent.
Remnant of their valley,
how long will you gash yourself?

6 Oh, sword of the LORD!
How long will you be restless?
Go back to your sheath;
be still; be silent!
7 How can it[E] rest
when the LORD has given it
a command?
He has assigned it
against Ashkelon and the shore
of the sea.

PROPHECIES AGAINST MOAB

48 About Moab, this is what the LORD of
Armies, the God of Israel, says:
Woe to Nebo, because it is
about to be destroyed;
Kiriathaim will be put to shame;
it will be taken captive.
The fortress will be put to shame
and dismayed!
2 There is no longer praise for Moab;
they plan harm against her in Heshbon:
Come, let's cut her off
from nationhood.
Also, Madmen, you will be silenced;
the sword will follow you.
3 A voice cries out from Horonaim,
"devastation and a crushing blow!"

[A] 46:22 Lit *Her sound is like a snake as it goes* [B] 46:26 Lit *it* [C] 47:3 Lit *Because of weakened hands* [D] 47:4 Probably Crete
[E] 47:7 LXX, Vg; MT reads *you*

4 Moab will be shattered;
her little ones will cry out.
5 For on the Ascent to Luhith
they will be weeping continually,[A]
and on the descent to Horonaim
will be heard cries of distress
over the destruction:
6 Flee! Save your lives!
Be like a juniper bush[B]
in the wilderness.
7 Because you trust in your works
and treasures,
you will be captured also.
Chemosh will go into exile
with his priests and officials.
8 The destroyer will move
against every town;
not one town will escape.
The valley will perish,
and the plain will be annihilated,
as the LORD has said.
9 Make Moab a salt marsh,[C]
for she will run away;[D]
her towns will become
a desolation,
without inhabitant.

10 The one who does
the LORD's business deceitfully[E]
is cursed,
and the one who withholds
his sword from bloodshed is cursed.

11 Moab has been left quiet
since his youth,
settled like wine on its dregs.
He hasn't been poured
from one container to another
or gone into exile.
So his taste has remained the same,
and his aroma hasn't changed.
12 Therefore look, the days are coming —
this is the LORD's declaration —
when I will send pourers to him,
who will pour him out.
They will empty his containers
and smash his jars.
13 Moab will be put to shame
because of Chemosh,
just as the house of Israel was
put to shame
because of Bethel that they trusted in.

14 How can you say, "We are warriors —
valiant men for battle"?
15 The destroyer of Moab and its towns
has come up,[F]
and the best of its young men
have gone down to slaughter.
This is the King's declaration;
the LORD of Armies is his name.
16 Moab's calamity is near at hand;
his disaster is rushing swiftly.
17 Mourn for him,
all you surrounding nations,
everyone who knows his name.
Say, "How the mighty scepter
is shattered,
the glorious staff!"

18 Come down from glory;
sit on parched ground,
resident of the daughter of Dibon,
for the destroyer of Moab has come
against you;
he has destroyed your fortresses.
19 Stand by the highway and watch,
resident of Aroer!
Ask him who is fleeing or her
who is escaping,
"What happened?"
20 Moab is put to shame,
indeed dismayed.
Wail and cry out!
Declare by the Arnon
that Moab is destroyed.

21 "Judgment has come to the land of the plateau — to Holon, Jahzah, Mephaath, 22 Dibon,
Nebo, Beth-diblathaim, 23 Kiriathaim, Beth-
gamul, Beth-meon, 24 Kerioth, Bozrah, and
all the towns of the land of Moab, those far
and near. 25 Moab's horn is chopped off; his
arm is shattered."
This is the LORD's declaration.
26 "Make him drunk, because he has exalted
himself against the LORD. Moab will wallow in
his own vomit, and he will also become a laughingstock. 27 Wasn't Israel a laughingstock to you?
Was he ever found among thieves? For whenever you speak of him you shake your head."
28 Abandon the towns! Live in the cliffs,
residents of Moab!
Be like a dove
that nests inside the mouth of a cave.

[A] **48:5** Lit *Luhith, weeping goes up with weeping* [B] **48:6** Or *like Aroer*; Is 17:2; Jr 48:19 [C] **48:9** LXX reads *a sign*; Vg reads *a flower*; Syr, Tg read *a crown* [D] **48:9** Hb obscure [E] **48:10** Or *negligently* [F] **48:15** Or *Moab is destroyed; he has come up against its cities*

29 We have heard of Moab's pride,
great pride, indeed —
his insolence, arrogance, pride,
and haughty heart.
30 I know his outburst.
This is the LORD's declaration.
It is empty.
His boast is empty.
31 Therefore, I will wail over Moab.
I will cry out for Moab, all of it;
he will moan for the men of Kir-heres.
32 I will weep for you, vine of Sibmah,
with more than the weeping for Jazer.
Your tendrils have extended to the sea;
they have reached to the sea
and to Jazer.[A]
The destroyer has fallen
on your summer fruit
and grape harvest.
33 Gladness and celebration are taken
from the fertile field
and from the land of Moab.
I have stopped the flow of wine
from the winepresses;
no one will tread with shouts of joy.
The shouting is not a shout of joy.

34 "There is a cry from Heshbon to Elealeh;
they make their voices heard as far as Jahaz
— from Zoar to Horonaim and Eglath-shelishiyah — because even the Waters of Nimrim
have become desolate. 35 In Moab, I will stop"
— this is the LORD's declaration — "the one
who offers sacrifices on the high place and
burns incense to his gods. 36 Therefore, my
heart moans like flutes for Moab, and my heart
moans like flutes for the people of Kir-heres.
And therefore, the wealth he has gained has
perished. 37 Indeed, every head is bald and every beard is chopped short. On every hand is
a gash and sackcloth around the waist. 38 On
all the rooftops of Moab and in her public
squares, everyone is mourning because I have
shattered Moab like a jar no one wants." This
is the LORD's declaration. 39 "How broken it is!
They wail! How Moab has turned his back! He
is ashamed. Moab will become a laughingstock
and a shock to all those around him."

40 For this is what the LORD says:
Look! He will swoop down like an eagle
and spread his wings against Moab.
41 The towns have[B] been captured,
and the strongholds seized.
In that day the heart
of Moab's warriors
will be like the heart of a woman
with contractions.
42 Moab will be destroyed as a people
because he has exalted himself
against the LORD.
43 Panic, pit, and trap
await you, resident of Moab.
This is the LORD's declaration.
44 He who flees from the panic will fall
in the pit,
and he who climbs from the pit
will be captured in the trap,
for I will bring against Moab
the year of their punishment.
This is the LORD's declaration.

45 Those who flee will stand exhausted
in Heshbon's shadow
because fire has come out
from Heshbon
and a flame from within Sihon.
It will devour Moab's forehead
and the skull of the noisemakers.
46 Woe to you, Moab!
The people of Chemosh
have perished
because your sons have been
taken captive
and your daughters have gone
into captivity.
47 Yet, I will restore the fortunes[C] of Moab
in the last days.
This is the LORD's declaration.
The judgment on Moab ends here.

PROPHECIES AGAINST AMMON

49 About the Ammonites, this is what the LORD says:

Does Israel have no sons?
Is he without an heir?
Why then has Milcom[D,E]
dispossessed Gad
and his people settled in their cities?
2 Therefore look, the days are coming —
this is the LORD's declaration —
when I will make the shout
of battle heard
against Rabbah of the Ammonites.
It will become a desolate mound,
and its surrounding villages will be set
on fire.

[A] **48:32** Some Hb mss read *reached as far as Jazer* [B] **48:41** Or *Kerioth has* [C] **48:47** Or *will end the captivity* [D] **49:1** LXX, Syr, Vg; MT reads *Malkam* [E] **49:1** = Molech

Israel will dispossess their dispossessors,
says the LORD.
3 Wail, Heshbon, for Ai is devastated;
cry out, daughters of Rabbah!
Clothe yourselves with sackcloth,
and lament;
run back and forth within your walls,[A]
because Milcom will go into exile
together with his priests and officials.
4 Why do you boast about your valleys,
your flowing valley,[B]
you faithless daughter —
you who trust in your treasures
and say, "Who can attack me?"
5 Look, I am about to bring terror on you —
this is the declaration
of the Lord GOD of Armies —
from all those around you.
You will be banished,
each person headlong,
with no one to gather up the fugitives.
6 But after that, I will restore
the fortunes[C] of the Ammonites.
This is the LORD's declaration.

PROPHECIES AGAINST EDOM

7 About Edom, this is what the LORD of Armies says:
Is there no longer wisdom in Teman?
Has counsel perished
from the prudent?
Has their wisdom rotted away?
8 Run! Turn back! Lie low,
residents of Dedan,
for I will bring Esau's calamity on him
at the time I punish him.
9 If grape harvesters came to you,
wouldn't they leave some gleanings?
Were thieves to come in the night,
they would destroy only
what they wanted.
10 But I will strip Esau bare;
I will uncover his secret places.
He will try to hide, but he will be unable.
His descendants will be destroyed
along with his relatives and neighbors.
He will exist no longer.
11 Abandon your fatherless;
I will preserve them;
let your widows trust in me.

12 For this is what the LORD says: "If those who
do not deserve to drink the cup must drink it,
can you possibly remain unpunished? You will
not remain unpunished, for you must drink it
too. 13 For by myself I have sworn" — this is the
LORD's declaration — "Bozrah[D] will become a
desolation, a disgrace, a ruin, and an example
for cursing, and all its surrounding cities will
become ruins forever."
14 I have heard an envoy
from the LORD;
a messenger has been sent
among the nations:
Assemble yourselves to come against her.
Rise up for war!
15 I will certainly make you insignificant
among the nations,
despised among humanity.
16 As to the terror you cause,[E]
your arrogant heart
has deceived you.
You who live in the clefts of the rock,[F]
you who occupy the mountain summit,
though you elevate your nest
like the eagles,
even from there I will bring you down.
This is the LORD's declaration.

17 "Edom will become a desolation. Everyone
who passes by her will be appalled and scoff
because of all her wounds. 18 As when Sodom
and Gomorrah were overthrown along with
their neighbors," says the LORD, "no one will
live there; no human being will stay in it even
temporarily.
19 "Look, it will be like a lion coming from the
thickets[G] of the Jordan to the watered grazing
land. I will chase Edom away from her land in
a flash. I will appoint whoever is chosen for
her. For who is like me? Who will issue me
a summons? Who is the shepherd who can
stand against me?"
20 Therefore, hear the plans that the LORD has
drawn up against Edom and the strategies he
has devised against the people of Teman: The
flock's little lambs will certainly be dragged
away, and their grazing land will be made desolate because of them. 21 At the sound of their
fall the earth will quake; the sound of her cry
will be heard at the Red Sea. 22 Look! It will be
like an eagle soaring upward, then swooping
down and spreading its wings over Bozrah. In
that day the hearts of Edom's warriors will be
like the heart of a woman with contractions.

[A] 49:3 Or *sheep pens* [B] 49:4 Or *about your strength, your ebbing strength* [C] 49:6 Or *will end the captivity*, also in v. 39
[D] 49:13 = Edom's capital [E] 49:16 Lit *Your horror* [F] 49:16 = Petra [G] 49:19 Lit *pride*

PROPHECIES AGAINST DAMASCUS

23 About Damascus:
Hamath and Arpad are put to shame,
for they have heard a bad report
and are agitated,
like[A] the anxious sea that cannot
be calmed.
24 Damascus has become weak;
she has turned to run;
panic has gripped her.
Distress and labor pains
have seized her
like a woman in labor.
25 How can the city of praise
not be abandoned,
the town that brings me joy?
26 Therefore, her young men will fall
in her public squares;
all the warriors will perish in that day.
This is the declaration of the LORD
of Armies.
27 I will set fire to the wall of Damascus;
it will consume Ben-hadad's citadels.

PROPHECIES AGAINST KEDAR AND HAZOR

28 About Kedar and the kingdoms of Hazor,
which King Nebuchadnezzar of Babylon defeated, this is what the LORD says:
Rise up, attack Kedar,
and destroy the people of the east!
29 They will take their tents and their flocks
along with their tent curtains
and all their equipment.
They will take their camels
for themselves.
They will call out to them,
"Terror is on every side!"
30 Run! Escape quickly! Lie low,
residents of Hazor —
this is the LORD's declaration —
for King Nebuchadnezzar of Babylon
has drawn up a plan against you;
he has devised a strategy against you.

31 Rise up, attack a nation at ease,
one living in security.
This is the LORD's declaration.
They have no doors, not even
a gate bar;
they live alone.
32 Their camels will become plunder,
and their massive herds of cattle will
become spoil.
I will scatter them to the wind
in every direction,
those who clip the hair on
their temples;
I will bring calamity on them
across all their borders.
This is the LORD's declaration.
33 Hazor will become a jackals' den,
a desolation forever.
No one will live there;
no human being will stay in it even
temporarily.

PROPHECIES AGAINST ELAM

34 This is the word of the LORD that came to the
prophet Jeremiah about Elam[B] at the beginning of the reign of King Zedekiah of Judah.
35 This is what the LORD of Armies says:
I am about to shatter Elam's bow,
the source[C] of their might.
36 I will bring the four winds against Elam
from the four corners of the heavens,
and I will scatter them
to all these winds.
There will not be a nation
to which Elam's banished ones
will not go.
37 I will devastate Elam
before their enemies,
before those who intend to take
their lives.
I will bring disaster on them,
my burning anger.
This is the LORD's declaration.
I will send the sword after them
until I finish them off.
38 I will set my throne in Elam,
and I will destroy the king and officials
from there.
This is the LORD's declaration.

39 Yet, in the last days,
I will restore the fortunes of Elam.
This is the LORD's declaration.

PROPHECIES AGAINST BABYLON

50 This is the word the LORD spoke about
Babylon, the land of the Chaldeans,
through the prophet Jeremiah:
2 Announce to the nations;
proclaim and raise up a signal flag;
proclaim, and hide nothing.
Say, "Babylon is captured;

[A] 49:23 Lit *in* [B] 49:34 = modern Iran [C] 49:35 Lit *first*

Bel is put to shame;
Marduk is terrified."
Her idols are put to shame;
her false gods, devastated.
3 For a nation from the north will attack
her;
it will make her land desolate.
No one will be living in it —
both people and animals will escape.[A]
4 In those days and at that time —
this is the LORD's declaration —
the Israelites and Judeans
will come together,
weeping as they come,
and will seek the LORD their God.
5 They will ask about Zion,
turning their faces to this road.
They will come and join themselves[B]
to the LORD
in a permanent covenant that will
never be forgotten.

6 My people were lost sheep;
their shepherds led them astray,
guiding them the wrong way
in the mountains.
They wandered from mountain to hill;
they forgot their resting place.
7 Whoever found them devoured them.
Their adversaries said, "We're not guilty;
instead, they have sinned
against the LORD,
their righteous grazing land,
the hope of their ancestors, the LORD."

8 Escape from Babylon;
depart from the Chaldeans' land.
Be like the rams that lead the flock.
9 For I will soon stir up and bring
against Babylon
an assembly of great nations
from the north country.
They will line up in battle formation
against her;
from there she will be captured.
Their arrows will be
like a skilled[C] warrior
who does not return empty-handed.
10 The Chaldeans will become plunder;
all Babylon's plunderers will be
fully satisfied.
This is the LORD's declaration.
11 Because you rejoice,
because you celebrate —
you who plundered my inheritance —
because you frolic like a young cow
treading grain
and neigh like stallions,
12 your mother will be utterly humiliated;
she who bore you
will be put to shame.
Look! She will lag behind
all[D] the nations —
an arid wilderness, a desert.
13 Because of the LORD's wrath,
she will not be inhabited;
she will become a desolation, every bit
of her.
Everyone who passes through Babylon
will be appalled
and scoff because of all her wounds.
14 Line up in battle formation
around Babylon,
all you archers!
Shoot at her! Do not spare an arrow,
for she has sinned against the LORD.
15 Raise a war cry against her
on every side!
She has thrown up her hands
in surrender;
her defense towers have fallen;
her walls are demolished.
Since this is the LORD's vengeance,
take your vengeance on her;
as she has done, do the same to her.
16 Cut off the sower from Babylon
as well as him who wields the sickle
at harvest time.
Because of the oppressor's sword,
each will turn to his own people,
each will flee to his own land.

THE RETURN OF GOD'S PEOPLE

17 Israel is a stray lamb, chased by lions.
The first who devoured him was
the king of Assyria;
the last who crushed his bones
was King Nebuchadnezzar of Babylon.

18 Therefore, this is what the LORD of Armies, the God of Israel, says: I am about to
punish the king of Babylon and his land just
as I punished the king of Assyria.
19 I will return Israel to his grazing land,
and he will feed on Carmel and Bashan;
he will be satisfied

[A] **50:3** Lit *escape; they will walk* [B] **50:5** LXX; MT reads *Come and join yourselves* [C] **50:9** Some Hb mss, LXX, Syr; other Hb mss read *bereaving* [D] **50:12** Lit *Look! The last of*

in the hill country of Ephraim
and of Gilead.
20 In those days and at that time —
this is the LORD's declaration —
one will search for Israel's iniquity,
but there will be none,
and for Judah's sins,
but they will not be found,
for I will forgive those I leave
as a remnant.

THE INVASION OF BABYLON

21 Attack the land of Merathaim,
and those living in Pekod.
Put them to the sword;
completely destroy them —
this is the LORD's declaration —
do everything I have commanded you.
22 The sound of war is in the land —
a crushing blow!
23 How the hammer of the whole earth
is cut down and smashed!
What a horror Babylon has become
among the nations!
24 Babylon, I laid a trap for you, and you
were caught,
but you did not even know it.
You were found and captured
because you pitted yourself
against the LORD.
25 The LORD opened his armory
and brought out his weapons of wrath,
because it is a task of the Lord GOD
of Armies
in the land of the Chaldeans.
26 Come against her
from the most distant places.[A]
Open her granaries;
pile her up like mounds of grain
and completely destroy her.
Leave her no survivors.
27 Put all her young bulls to the sword;
let them go down to the slaughter.
Woe to them because their day
has come,
the time of their punishment.

THE HUMILIATION OF BABYLON

28 There is a voice of fugitives
and refugees
from the land of Babylon.
The voice announces in Zion
the vengeance of the LORD our God,
the vengeance for his temple.
29 Summon the archers to Babylon,
all who string the bow;
camp all around her; let none escape.
Repay her according to her deeds;
just as she has done, do the same to her,
for she has acted arrogantly
against the LORD,
against the Holy One of Israel.
30 Therefore, her young men will fall
in her public squares;
all the warriors will perish in that day.
This is the LORD's declaration.
31 Look, I am against you,
you arrogant one —
this is the declaration of
the Lord GOD of Armies —
for your day has come,
the time when I will punish you.
32 The arrogant will stumble and fall
with no one to pick him up.
I will set fire to his cities,
and it will consume everything
around him.

THE DESOLATION OF BABYLON

33 This is what the LORD of Armies says:
Israelites and Judeans alike
have been oppressed.
All their captors hold them fast;
they refuse to release them.
34 Their Redeemer is strong;
the LORD of Armies is his name.
He will fervently champion their cause
so that he might bring rest to the earth
but turmoil to those who live
in Babylon.
35 A sword is over the Chaldeans —
this is the LORD's declaration —
against those who live in Babylon,
against her officials, and against
her sages.
36 A sword is against the diviners,
and they will act foolishly.

Their Redeemer is strong; the LORD of Armies is his name.
—Jeremiah 50:34

[A] **50:26** Lit *from the end*

A sword is against her heroic warriors,
and they will be terrified.
37 A sword is against his horses
and chariots
and against all the foreigners
among them,
and they will be like women.
A sword is against her treasuries,
and they will be plundered.
38 A drought will come on her waters,
and they will be dried up.
For it is a land of carved images,
and they go mad because of
terrifying things.[A]

39 Therefore, desert creatures[B] will live
with hyenas,
and ostriches will also live in her.
It will never again be inhabited
or lived in through all generations.
40 Just as God demolished Sodom
and Gomorrah
and their neighboring towns —
this is the LORD's declaration —
so no one will live there;
no human being will stay in it even
temporarily
as a temporary resident.

THE CONQUEST OF BABYLON

41 Look! A people comes from the north.
A great nation and many kings will be
stirred up
from the remote regions of the earth.
42 They grasp bow and javelin.
They are cruel and show no mercy.
Their voice roars like the sea,
and they ride on horses,
lined up like men in battle formation
against you, Daughter Babylon.
43 The king of Babylon has heard
about them;
his hands have become weak.
Distress has seized him —
pain, like a woman in labor.

44 "Look, it will be like a lion coming from the
thickets[C] of the Jordan to the watered grazing
land. I will chase Babylon[D] away from her land
in a flash. I will appoint whoever is chosen
for her. For who is like me? Who will issue
me a summons? Who is the shepherd who
can stand against me?"

45 Therefore, hear the plans that the LORD has
drawn up against Babylon and the strategies
he has devised against the land of the Chaldeans: Certainly the flock's little lambs will
be dragged away; certainly the grazing land
will be made desolate because of them. 46 At
the sound of Babylon's conquest the earth will
quake; a cry will be heard among the nations.

GOD'S JUDGMENT ON BABYLON

51 This is what the LORD says:
I am about to rouse the spirit of a
destroyer[E] against Babylon
and against the population
of Leb-qamai.[F,G]
2 I will send strangers to Babylon
who will scatter her and strip
her land bare,
for they will come against her
from every side in the day of disaster.
3 Don't let the archer string his bow;
don't let him put on[H] his armor.
Don't spare her young men;
completely destroy her entire army!
4 Those who were slain will fall
in the land of the Chaldeans,
those who were pierced through,
in her streets.
5 For Israel and Judah are not
left widowed
by their God, the LORD of Armies,
though their land is full of guilt
against the Holy One of Israel.

6 Leave Babylon;
save your lives, each of you!
Don't perish because of her guilt.
For this is the time
of the LORD's vengeance —
he will pay her what she deserves.
7 Babylon was a gold cup
in the LORD's hand,
making the whole earth drunk.
The nations drank her wine;
therefore, the nations go mad.
8 Suddenly Babylon fell
and was shattered.
Wail for her;
get balm for her wound —
perhaps she can be healed.

9 We tried to heal Babylon,
but she could not be healed.

[A] 50:38 Or *of dreaded gods* [B] 50:39 Or *desert demons* [C] 50:44 Lit *pride* [D] 50:44 Lit *them* [E] 51:1 Or *to stir up a destructive wind* [F] 51:1 Lit *heart of my adversaries* [G] 51:1 = Chaldeans [H] 51:3 Hb obscure

Abandon her!
Let each of us go to his own land,
for her judgment extends to the sky
and reaches as far as the clouds.

10 The LORD has brought about
our vindication;
come, let's tell in Zion
what the LORD our God
has accomplished.

11 Sharpen the arrows!
Fill the quivers![A]
The LORD has roused the spirit
of the kings of the Medes
because his plan is aimed at Babylon
to destroy her,
for it is the LORD's vengeance,
vengeance for his temple.
12 Raise up a signal flag
against the walls of Babylon;
fortify the watch post;
set the watchmen in place;
prepare the ambush.
For the LORD has both planned
and accomplished
what he has threatened
against those who live in Babylon.
13 You who reside by abundant water,
rich in treasures,
your end has come,
your life thread is cut.

14 The LORD of Armies has sworn by himself:
I will fill you up with men
as with locusts,
and they will sing the victory song
over you.

15 He made the earth by his power,
established the world by his wisdom,

He made the earth by his power, established the world by his wisdom, and spread out the heavens by his understanding.
—Jeremiah 51:15

and spread out the heavens
by his understanding.
16 When he thunders,[B]
the waters in the heavens are
tumultuous,
and he causes the clouds
to rise from the ends of the earth.
He makes lightning for the rain
and brings the wind
from his storehouses.

17 Everyone is stupid and ignorant.
Every goldsmith is put to shame
by his carved image,
for his cast images are a lie;
there is no breath in them.
18 They are worthless, a work
to be mocked.
At the time of their punishment
they will be destroyed.
19 Jacob's Portion[C] is not like these
because he is the one who formed
all things.
Israel is the tribe of his inheritance;
the LORD of Armies is his name.

20 You are my war club,
my weapons of war.
With you I will smash nations;
with you I will bring kingdoms to ruin.
21 With you I will smash the horse
and its rider;
with you I will smash the chariot
and its rider.
22 With you I will smash man and woman;
with you I will smash the old man
and the youth;
with you I will smash the young man
and the young woman.
23 With you I will smash the shepherd
and his flock;
with you I will smash the farmer
and his ox-team.[D]
With you I will smash governors
and officials.

24 "Before your very eyes, I will repay Babylon and all the residents of Chaldea for all
their evil they have done in Zion."
This is the LORD's declaration.
25 Look, I am against you,
devastating mountain.
This is the LORD's declaration.

[A] **51:11** Or *Grasp the shields!* [B] **51:16** Lit *At his giving of the voice* [C] **51:19** = The LORD [D] **51:23** Lit *yoke*

You devastate the whole earth.
I will stretch out my hand against you,
roll you down from the cliffs,
and turn you into a charred mountain.
26 No one will be able to retrieve
a cornerstone
or a foundation stone from you,
because you will become
desolate forever.
This is the LORD's declaration.

27 Raise a signal flag in the land;
blow a ram's horn among the nations;
set apart the nations against her.
Summon kingdoms against her —
Ararat, Minni, and Ashkenaz.
Appoint a marshal against her;
bring up horses like a swarm[A] of locusts.
28 Set apart the nations for battle
against her —
the kings of Media,
her governors and all her officials,
and all the lands they rule.
29 The earth quakes and trembles
because the LORD's intentions
against Babylon stand:
to make the land of Babylon
a desolation, without inhabitant.
30 Babylon's warriors have
stopped fighting;
they sit in their strongholds.
Their might is exhausted;
they have become like women.
Babylon's homes have been set ablaze,
her gate bars are shattered.
31 Messenger races to meet messenger,
and herald to meet herald,
to announce to the king of Babylon
that his city has been captured
from end to end.
32 The fords have been seized,
the marshes set on fire,
and the fighting men are terrified.

33 For this is what the LORD of Armies, the
God of Israel, says:
Daughter Babylon is like a threshing floor
at the time it is trampled.
In just a little while her harvest time
will come.

34 "King Nebuchadnezzar of Babylon
has devoured me;
he has crushed me.
He has set me aside like an empty dish;
he has swallowed me
like a sea monster;
he filled his belly with my delicacies;
he has vomited me out.[B]
35 Let the violence done to me
and my family be done to Babylon,"
says the inhabitant of Zion.
"Let my blood be on the inhabitants
of Chaldea,"
says Jerusalem.

36 Therefore, this is what the LORD says:
I am about to champion your cause
and take vengeance on your behalf;
I will dry up her sea
and make her fountain run dry.
37 Babylon will become a heap of rubble,
a jackals' den,
a desolation and an object of scorn,
without inhabitant.
38 They will roar together like young lions;
they will growl like lion cubs.
39 While they are flushed with heat,
I will serve them a feast,
and I will make them drunk so that
they celebrate.[C]
Then they will fall asleep forever
and never wake up.
This is the LORD's declaration.
40 I will bring them down like lambs
to the slaughter,
like rams together with male goats.

41 How Sheshach[D] has been captured,
the praise of the whole earth seized.
What a horror Babylon has become
among the nations!
42 The sea has risen over Babylon;
she is covered
with its tumultuous waves.
43 Her cities have become a desolation,
an arid desert,
a land where no one lives,
where no human being even
passes through.
44 I will punish Bel in Babylon.
I will make him vomit
what he swallowed.
The nations will no longer stream
to him;
even Babylon's wall will fall.

[A] **51:27** Hb obscure [B] **51:34** Lit *has rinsed me off* [C] **51:39** LXX reads *pass out* [D] **51:41** = Babylon

45 Come out from among her, my people!
Save your lives, each of you,
from the LORD's burning anger.
46 May you not become cowardly
and fearful
when the report is proclaimed
in the land,
for the report will come one year,
and then another the next year.
There will be violence in the land
with ruler against ruler.
47 Therefore, look, the days are coming
when I will punish
Babylon's carved images.
Her entire land will suffer shame,
and all her slain will lie fallen within her.
48 Heaven and earth and everything
in them
will shout for joy over Babylon
because the destroyers from the north
will come against her.
This is the LORD's declaration.

49 Babylon must fall because of the slain
of Israel,
even as the slain of the whole earth fell
because of Babylon.
50 You who have escaped the sword,
go and do not stand still!
Remember the LORD from far away,
and let Jerusalem come to your mind.

51 We are ashamed
because we have heard insults.
Humiliation covers our faces
because foreigners have entered
the holy places of the LORD's temple.

52 Therefore, look, the days are coming —
this is the LORD's declaration —
when I will punish her carved images,
and the wounded will groan
throughout her land.
53 Even if Babylon should ascend
to the heavens
and fortify her tall fortresses,
destroyers will come against her
from me.
This is the LORD's declaration.

54 The sound of a cry from Babylon!
The sound of terrible destruction
from the land of the Chaldeans!
55 For the LORD is going
to devastate Babylon;
he will silence her mighty voice.
Their waves roar like a huge torrent;
the tumult of their voice resounds,
56 for a destroyer is coming against her,
against Babylon.
Her warriors will be captured,
their bows shattered,
for the LORD is a God of retribution;
he will certainly repay.
57 I will make her princes and sages drunk,
along with her governors, officials,
and warriors.
Then they will fall asleep forever
and never wake up.
This is the King's declaration;
the LORD of Armies is his name.

58 This is what the LORD of Armies says:
Babylon's thick walls will be
totally demolished,
and her high gates set ablaze.
The peoples will have labored
for nothing;
the nations will weary themselves
only to feed the fire.

59 This is what the prophet Jeremiah commanded Seraiah son of Neriah son of Mahseiah, the quartermaster, when he went to
Babylon with King Zedekiah of Judah in the
fourth year of Zedekiah's reign. 60 Jeremiah
wrote on one scroll about all the disaster that
would come to Babylon; all these words were
written against Babylon.
61 Jeremiah told Seraiah, "When you get to
Babylon, see that you read all these words
aloud. 62 Say, 'LORD, you have threatened to
cut off this place so that no one will live in
it — people or animals. Indeed, it will remain desolate forever.' 63 When you have
finished reading this scroll, tie a stone to it
and throw it into the middle of the Euphrates
River. 64 Then say, 'In the same way, Babylon
will sink and never rise again because of
the disaster I am bringing on her. They will
grow weary.'"
The words of Jeremiah end here.

THE FALL OF JERUSALEM

52 Zedekiah was twenty-one years old
when he became king, and he reigned
eleven years in Jerusalem. His mother's name
was Hamutal daughter of Jeremiah; she was
from Libnah. 2 Zedekiah did what was evil in
the LORD's sight just as Jehoiakim had done.

3 Because of the LORD's anger, it came to the
point in Jerusalem and Judah that he finally
banished them from his presence. Then Zedekiah rebelled against the king of Babylon.

4 In the ninth year of Zedekiah's reign, on
the tenth day of the tenth month, King Nebuchadnezzar of Babylon advanced against
Jerusalem with his entire army. They laid siege
to the city and built a siege wall against it all
around. 5 The city was under siege until King
Zedekiah's eleventh year.

6 By the ninth day of the fourth month the
famine was so severe in the city that the common people had no food. 7 Then the city was
broken into, and all the warriors fled. They
left the city at night by way of the city gate
between the two walls near the king's garden, though the Chaldeans surrounded the
city. They made their way along the route to
the Arabah. 8 The Chaldean army pursued the
king and overtook Zedekiah in the plains of
Jericho. Zedekiah's entire army left him and
scattered. 9 The Chaldeans seized the king
and brought him to the king of Babylon at
Riblah in the land of Hamath, and he passed
sentence on him.

10 At Riblah the king of Babylon slaughtered
Zedekiah's sons before his eyes, and he also
slaughtered the Judean commanders. 11 Then he
blinded Zedekiah and bound him with bronze
chains. The king of Babylon brought Zedekiah
to Babylon, where he kept him in custody[A]
until his dying day.

12 On the tenth day of the fifth month
— which was the nineteenth year of King
Nebuchadnezzar, king of Babylon — Nebuzaradan, the captain of the guards, entered
Jerusalem as the representative of[B] the king
of Babylon. 13 He burned the LORD's temple,
the king's palace, all the houses of Jerusalem;
he burned down all the great houses. 14 The
whole Chaldean army with the captain of the
guards tore down all the walls surrounding
Jerusalem. 15 Nebuzaradan, the captain of
the guards, deported some of the poorest of
the people, as well as the rest of the people
who remained in the city, the deserters who
had defected to the king of Babylon, and the
rest of the craftsmen. 16 But Nebuzaradan,
the captain of the guards, left some of the
poorest of the land to be vinedressers and
farmers.

17 Now the Chaldeans broke into pieces the
bronze pillars for the LORD's temple and the
water carts and the bronze basin[C] that were
in the LORD's temple, and they carried all the
bronze to Babylon. 18 They also took the pots,
shovels, wick trimmers, sprinkling basins,
dishes, and all the bronze articles used in the
temple service. 19 The captain of the guards took
away the bowls, firepans, sprinkling basins,
pots, lampstands, pans, and drink offering
bowls — whatever was gold or silver.

20 As for the two pillars, the one basin, with
the twelve bronze oxen under it, and the water
carts[D] that King Solomon had made for the
LORD's temple, the weight of the bronze of all
these articles was beyond measure. 21 One pillar
was 27 feet[E] tall, had a circumference of 18
feet,[F] was hollow — four fingers thick — 22 and
had a bronze capital on top of it. One capital,
encircled by bronze grating and pomegranates,
stood 7 1/2 feet[G] high. The second pillar was the
same, with pomegranates. 23 Each capital had
ninety-six pomegranates all around it. All the
pomegranates around the grating numbered
one hundred.

24 The captain of the guards also took away
Seraiah the chief priest, Zephaniah the priest
of the second rank, and the three doorkeepers. 25 From the city he took a court official[H]
who had been appointed over the warriors;
seven trusted royal aides[I] found in the city;
the secretary of the commander of the army,
who enlisted the people of the land for military
duty; and sixty men from the common people[J]
who were found within the city. 26 Nebuzaradan, the captain of the guards, took them and
brought them to the king of Babylon at Riblah.
27 The king of Babylon put them to death at
Riblah in the land of Hamath. So Judah went
into exile from its land.

28 These are the people Nebuchadnezzar
deported: in the seventh year, 3,023 Jews; 29 in
his eighteenth year,[K] 832 people from Jerusalem; 30 in Nebuchadnezzar's twenty-third
year, Nebuzaradan, the captain of the guards,
deported 745 Jews. Altogether, 4,600 people
were deported.

JEHOIACHIN PARDONED

31 On the twenty-fifth day of the twelfth month
of the thirty-seventh year of the exile of Judah's King Jehoiachin, King Evil-merodach

---

[A] **52:11** Lit *in a house of guards* [B] **52:12** Lit *Jerusalem; he stood before* [C] **52:17** Lit *sea* [D] **52:20** LXX, Syr; MT reads *oxen under the water carts* [E] **52:21** Lit *18 cubits* [F] **52:21** Lit *12 cubits* [G] **52:22** Lit *five cubits* [H] **52:25** Or *a eunuch* [I] **52:25** Lit *seven men who look on the king's face* [J] **52:25** Lit *the people of the land* [K] **52:29** Some Hb mss, Syr add *he deported*

LAMENT OVER JERUSALEM

א Aleph

1 How[A] she sits alone,
the city once crowded with people!
She who was great among the nations
has become like a widow.
The princess among the provinces
has been put to forced labor.

ב Beth

2 She weeps bitterly during the night,
with tears on her cheeks.
There is no one to offer her comfort,
not one from all her lovers.[B]
All her friends have betrayed her;
they have become her enemies.

ג Gimel

3 Judah has gone into exile
following[C] affliction and harsh slavery;
she lives among the nations
but finds no place to rest.
All her pursuers have overtaken her
in narrow places.

ד Daleth

4 The roads to Zion mourn,
for no one comes
to the appointed festivals.
All her gates are deserted;
her priests groan,
her young women grieve,
and she herself is bitter.

ה He

5 Her adversaries have become her masters;
her enemies are at ease,
for the LORD has made her suffer
because of her many transgressions.
Her children have gone away
as captives before the adversary.

ו Waw

6 All the splendor has vanished
from Daughter Zion.
Her leaders are like stags
that find no pasture;
they stumble away exhausted
before the hunter.

ז Zayin

7 During the days of her affliction
and homelessness
Jerusalem remembers all
her precious belongings
that were hers in days of old.
When her people fell
into the adversary's hand,
she had no one to help.
The adversaries looked at her,
laughing over her downfall.

ח Cheth

8 Jerusalem has sinned grievously;
therefore, she has become an object
of scorn.[D]
All who honored her
now despise her,
for they have seen her nakedness.
She herself groans and turns away.

ט Teth

9 Her uncleanness stains
her skirts.
She never considered her end.
Her downfall was astonishing;
there was no one
to comfort her.
LORD, look on my affliction,
for the enemy boasts.

י Yod

10 The adversary has seized
all her precious belongings.
She has even seen the nations
enter her sanctuary—
those you had forbidden
to enter your assembly.

כ Kaph

11 All her people groan
while they search for bread.
They have traded
their precious belongings for food
in order to stay alive.
LORD, look and see
how I have become despised.

ל Lamed

12 Is this nothing to you, all you
who pass by?
Look and see!
Is there any pain like mine,
which was dealt out to me,
which the LORD made me suffer
on the day of his burning anger?

[A] **1:1** The stanzas in Lm 1–4 form an acrostic. [B] **1:2** = Jerusalem's political allies [C] **1:3** Or *because of* [D] **1:8** Or *become impure*

מ Mem

13 He sent fire from on high into my bones;
he made it descend.[A]
He spread a net for my feet
and turned me back.
He made me desolate,
sick all day long.

נ Nun

14 My transgressions have been formed
into a yoke,[B,C]
fastened together by his hand;
they have been placed on my neck,
and the Lord has broken my strength.
He has handed me over
to those I cannot withstand.

ס Samek

15 The Lord has rejected
all the mighty men within me.
He has summoned an army[D]
against me
to crush my young warriors.
The Lord has trampled
Virgin Daughter Judah
like grapes in a winepress.

ע Ayin

16 I weep because of these things;
my eyes flow[E] with tears.
For there is no one nearby
to comfort me,
no one to keep me alive.
My children are desolate
because the enemy has prevailed.

פ Pe

17 Zion stretches out her hands;
there is no one to comfort her.
The LORD has issued a decree
against Jacob
that his neighbors should be
his adversaries.
Jerusalem has become
something impure among them.

צ Tsade

18 The LORD is just,
for I have rebelled
against his command.
Listen, all you people;
look at my pain.
My young women and young men
have gone into captivity.

ק Qoph

19 I called to my lovers,
but they betrayed me.
My priests and elders
perished in the city
while searching for food
to keep themselves alive.

ר Resh

20 LORD, see how I am in distress.
I am churning within;
my heart is broken,[F]
for I have been very rebellious.
Outside, the sword takes the children;
inside, there is death.

ש Shin

21 People have heard me groaning,
but there is no one to comfort me.
All my enemies have heard
of my misfortune;
they are glad that you have caused it.
Bring on the day you have announced,
so that they may become like me.

ת Taw

22 Let all their wickedness come
before you,
and deal with them
as you have dealt with me
because of all my transgressions.
For my groans are many,
and I am sick at heart.

JUDGMENT ON JERUSALEM

א Aleph

2 How the Lord has overshadowed
Daughter Zion with his anger!
He has thrown down Israel's glory
from heaven to earth.
He did not acknowledge his footstool
in the day of his anger.

ב Beth

2 Without compassion the Lord
has swallowed up
all the dwellings of Jacob.
In his wrath he has demolished
the fortified cities of Daughter Judah.

[A] **1:13** DSS, LXX; MT reads *bones, and it prevailed against them* [B] **1:14** Some Hb mss, LXX read *He kept watch over my transgressions* [C] **1:14** Or *The yoke of my transgressions is bound*; Hb obscure [D] **1:15** Or *has announced an appointed time* [E] **1:16** Lit *my eye, my eye flows* [F] **1:20** Lit *is turned within me*

My Story | Franklyn

Mornings are usually hopeful times for me. The new day stretches ahead, full of possibilities. But sometimes things go downhill, fast. That morning, I was pastor of a thriving city congregation, seemingly doing everything right. I spent part of every day asking God to give me wisdom in leading his church. And I was sure that dependence on him was bearing fruit. I was busy in my work but confident that things at home were in order.

That morning, my wife was quiet at the breakfast table. She looked at me and a tear rolled down her cheek. She quietly said, "I don't want to be married to you anymore." With those soft words, a nightmare of several weeks began. The blows came continuously until I was barely functioning. She had met someone else. She had packed a suitcase the day before that I hadn't even noticed in the corner of the bedroom. Before I could say anything, she got up from the table, retrieved her bag, and walked out the door.

I called the leaders of the church and shared the news, asking for prayer. Several surprised me by promising to pray and then mentioning they had been concerned about me and my marriage for a while. I couldn't bring myself to ask, "Why didn't you say something?"

Predictably, the news spread fast. Later that afternoon, the president of the church board called with news they wanted to meet with me that evening. What I thought would be a time of encouragement and prayer turned into a shattering confrontation during which they fired me. I returned to a suddenly empty house a broken man. I sat in the dark, too numb to pray or imagine that mornings would ever be hopeful again.

God worked miracles in my life and marriage, but they weren't quick and they weren't easy. At first, I was mostly angry at my church. Their almost instantaneous dismissal hurt me deeply, and I wasn't sure I could ever think of church as a safe place again. Ironically, that was the very means God used to bring healing.

One summer Sunday morning a few weeks later I was driving in the country, aimlessly seeking silence and solitude. As I passed through a little town I spotted an old, clapboard-covered church on a corner, surrounded by farm trucks and old cars. Through my rolled-down window I heard familiar music and felt myself drawn to anonymously check them out. As I slipped into the back, a young preacher stood up and began to speak from the Gospel of John, and I felt the Spirit of Jesus fill the space. It wasn't anything he said as much as sensing God showing me this was a safe place. He was there.

For the rest of the summer, that back pew became my weekly place of healing, with no expectations. That young pastor simply affirmed my search for a new start and prayed for me. Every week Jesus met me in the Gospel of John and made himself at home again in my life. Morning gradually regained its hope for me.

He brought them to the ground
and defiled the kingdom and its leaders.

ג Gimel

3 He has cut off every horn of Israel
in his burning anger
and withdrawn his right hand
in the presence of the enemy.
He has blazed against Jacob
like a flaming fire
that consumes everything.

ד Daleth

4 He has strung his bow like an enemy;
his right hand is positioned
like an adversary.
He has killed everyone who was the
delight to the eye,
pouring out his wrath
like fire
on the tent of Daughter Zion.

ה He

5 The Lord is like an enemy;
he has swallowed up Israel.
He swallowed up
all its palaces
and destroyed
its fortified cities.
He has multiplied mourning
and lamentation
within Daughter Judah.

ו Waw

6 He has wrecked his temple[A]
as if it were merely a shack in a field,[B]
destroying his place of meeting.
The LORD has abolished
appointed festivals and Sabbaths in Zion.
He has despised king and priest
in his fierce anger.

ז Zayin

7 The Lord has rejected his altar,
repudiated his sanctuary;
he has handed the walls of her palaces
over to the enemy.
They have raised a shout in the house
of the LORD
as on the day of an appointed festival.

ח Cheth

8 The LORD determined to destroy
the wall of Daughter Zion.
He stretched out a measuring line
and did not restrain himself
from destroying.
He made the ramparts and walls grieve;
together they waste away.

ט Teth

9 Zion's gates have fallen to the ground;
he has destroyed and shattered
the bars on her gates.
Her king and her leaders live
among the nations,
instruction[C] is no more,
and even her prophets receive
no vision from the LORD.

י Yod

10 The elders of Daughter Zion
sit on the ground in silence.
They have thrown dust on their heads
and put on sackcloth.
The young women of Jerusalem
have bowed their heads to the ground.

כ Kaph

11 My eyes are worn out from weeping;
I am churning within.
My heart is poured out in grief[D]
because of the destruction
of my dear people,
because infants and nursing babies faint
in the streets of the city.

ל Lamed

12 They cry out to their mothers,
"Where is the grain and wine?"
as they faint like the wounded
in the streets of the city,
as their life pours out
in the arms of their mothers.

מ Mem

13 What can I say on your behalf?
What can I compare you to,
Daughter Jerusalem?
What can I liken you to,
so that I may console you,
Virgin Daughter Zion?
For your ruin is as vast as the sea.
Who can heal you?

נ Nun

14 Your prophets saw visions for you
that were empty and deceptive;[E]
they did not reveal your iniquity
and so restore your fortunes.
They saw pronouncements for you
that were empty and misleading.

ס Samek

15 All who pass by
scornfully clap their hands at you.
They hiss and shake their heads
at Daughter Jerusalem:
Is this the city that was called
the perfection of beauty,
the joy of the whole earth?

פ Pe

16 All your enemies
open their mouths against you.
They hiss and gnash their teeth,
saying, "We have swallowed her up.
This is the day we have waited for!
We have lived to see it."

ע Ayin

17 The LORD has done
what he planned;
he has accomplished his decree,
which he ordained in days of old.
He has demolished
without compassion,
letting the enemy gloat over you
and exalting the horn
of your adversaries.

[A] **2:6** Lit *booth* [B] **2:6** Lit *it were a garden* [C] **2:9** Or *the law* [D] **2:11** Lit *My liver is poured out on the ground* [E] **2:14** Or *insipid*

צ Tsade

18 The hearts of the people cry out
to the Lord.
Wall of Daughter Zion,
let your tears run down like a river
day and night.
Give yourself no relief
and your[A] eyes no rest.

ק Qoph

19 Arise, cry out in the night
from the first watch of the night.
Pour out your heart like water
before the Lord's presence.
Lift up your hands to him
for the lives of your children
who are fainting from hunger
at the head of every street.

ר Resh

20 LORD, look and consider
to whom you have done this.
Should women eat their own children,
the infants they have nurtured?[B]
Should priests and prophets
be killed in the Lord's sanctuary?

ש Shin

21 Both young and old
are lying on the ground in the streets.
My young women and young men
have fallen by the sword.
You have killed them in the day
of your anger,
slaughtering without compassion.

ת Taw

22 You summon those who terrorize me[C]
on every side,
as if for an appointed festival day;
on the day of the LORD's anger
no one escaped or survived.
My enemy has destroyed
those I nurtured[D] and reared.

HOPE THROUGH GOD'S MERCY

א Aleph

3 I am the man who has seen affliction
under the rod of God's wrath.
2 He has driven me away and forced me
to walk
in darkness instead of light.
3 Yes, he repeatedly turns his hand
against me all day long.

ב Beth

4 He has worn away my flesh and skin;
he has broken my bones.
5 He has laid siege against me,
encircling me with bitterness
and hardship.
6 He has made me dwell in darkness
like those who have been dead for ages.

ג Gimel

7 He has walled me in
so I cannot get out;
he has weighed me down with chains.
8 Even when I cry out and plead for help,
he blocks out my prayer.
9 He has walled in my ways with blocks
of stone;
he has made my paths crooked.

ד Daleth

10 He is[E] a bear waiting in ambush,
a lion in hiding.
11 He forced me off my way and tore me
to pieces;
he left me desolate.
12 He strung his bow
and set me as the target for his arrow.

ה He

13 He pierced my kidneys
with shafts from his quiver.
14 I am a laughingstock
to all my people,[F]
mocked by their songs all day long.
15 He filled me with bitterness,
satiated me with wormwood.

ו Waw

16 He ground my teeth with gravel
and made me cower[G] in the dust.
17 I have been deprived[H] of peace;
I have forgotten what prosperity is.
18 Then I thought, "My future[I] is lost,
as well as my hope from the LORD."

ז Zayin

19 Remember[J] my affliction
and my homelessness,
the wormwood and the poison.

[A] **2:18** Lit *and the daughter of your* [B] **2:20** Or *infants in a healthy condition*; Hb obscure [C] **2:22** Or *terrors* [D] **2:22** Or *I bore healthy*; Hb obscure [E] **3:10** Lit *is to me* [F] **3:14** Some Hb mss, LXX, Vg; other Hb mss, Syr read *all peoples* [G] **3:16** Or *and trampled me* [H] **3:17** Syr, Vg; MT reads *You deprived my soul* [I] **3:18** Or *splendor* [J] **3:19** Or *I remember*

20 I continually remember them
and have become depressed.[A]
21 Yet I call this to mind,
and therefore I have hope:

ח Cheth

22 Because of the LORD's faithful love
we do not perish,[B]
for his mercies never end.
23 They are new every morning;
great is your faithfulness!
24 I say, "The LORD is my portion,
therefore I will put my hope in him."

ט Teth

25 The LORD is good to those who wait
for him,
to the person who seeks him.
26 It is good to wait quietly
for salvation from the LORD.
27 It is good for a man to bear the yoke
while he is still young.

י Yod

28 Let him sit alone and be silent,
for God has disciplined[C] him.
29 Let him put his mouth in the dust —
perhaps there is still hope.
30 Let him offer his cheek
to the one who would strike him;
let him be filled with disgrace.

כ Kaph

31 For the Lord
will not reject us forever.
32 Even if he causes suffering,
he will show compassion
according to the abundance of his
faithful love.
33 For he does not enjoy bringing affliction
or suffering on mankind.

ל Lamed

34 Crushing all the prisoners of the land[D]
beneath one's feet,

Eternal Perspective | *God's Compassion*

GOD'S COMPASSION

"Because of the LORD's faithful love we do not perish, for his mercies never end. They are new every morning; great is your faithfulness!" Lamentations 3:22-23

If you were looking for a pick-me-up, you probably wouldn't go to a funeral service, right? Yet in the book of Lamentations—which is really a series of funeral laments by Jeremiah over the death of Jerusalem—we find one of the most encouraging reminders anyone could ever find anywhere.

The backstory? Because of the shocking rebelliousness of his people, God allowed the Babylonians to lay waste to Judah. The ensuing siege of Jerusalem resulted in gross idolatry—as the people cried out to false gods for help—and ultimately, cannibalism (2:20).

Jeremiah could only watch in horror as he tearfully composed the dirges that make up this book. But then a comforting truth pierced his soul: Though sin's consequences are awful, God will not reject his people forever. His heart is compassionate. His love is faithful. "His mercies . . . are new every morning."

This is the passage that inspired the beloved old hymn, "Great Is Thy Faithfulness." Perhaps the third verse of that song will pick you up today? Why not sing it quietly to God?

> Pardon for sin and a peace that endureth,
> Thine own dear presence to cheer and to guide;
> Strength for today and bright hope for tomorrow,
> Blessings all mine, with ten thousand beside!

For the next note on *Eternal Perspective*, see Ezekiel 37:2-3.

[A] **3:20** Alt Hb tradition reads *and you cause me to collapse* [B] **3:22** One Hb mss, Syr, Tg read *The LORD's faithful love, indeed, does not perish* [C] **3:28** Lit *has laid a burden on* [D] **3:34** Or *earth*

35 denying justice to a man
in the presence of the Most High,
36 or subverting a person in his lawsuit —
the Lord does not approve
of these things.

מ Mem

37 Who is there who speaks and it happens,
unless the Lord has ordained it?
38 Do not both adversity and good
come from the mouth of the Most High?
39 Why should any living
person complain,
any man, because of the punishment
for his sins?

נ Nun

40 Let us examine and probe our ways,
and turn back to the LORD.
41 Let us lift up our hearts and our hands
to God in heaven:
42 "We have sinned and rebelled;
you have not forgiven.

ס Samek

43 "You have covered yourself in anger
and pursued us;
you have killed without compassion.
44 You have covered yourself
with a cloud
so that no prayer can get through.
45 You have made us disgusting filth
among the peoples.

פ Pe

46 "All our enemies
open their mouths against us.
47 We have experienced panic
and pitfall,
devastation and destruction."
48 My eyes flow with streams of tears
because of the destruction
of my dear people.

ע Ayin

49 My eyes overflow unceasingly,
without end,
50 until the LORD looks down
from heaven and sees.
51 My eyes bring me grief
because of the fate of all the women
in my city.

צ Tsade

52 For no reason, my enemies[A]
hunted me like a bird.

Support | *Spiritual and Moral Inventory*

WHEN PAIN IS GOOD

"Let us examine and probe our ways, and turn back to the LORD." Lamentations 3:40

You bend over to pick up a shoe and whoa! Did someone just stick a knife in your back? The stabbing pain is alerting you to a problem and prompting you to get some answers—and soon.

In a sense, this is what we see happening in Lamentations. After stubbornly ignoring a series of prophetic warnings, Jerusalem was being decimated by brutal foreign invaders. (A situation slightly more serious than lower back pain.) Jeremiah used this bitter occasion to say to the people yet again, "Let us examine and probe our ways, and turn back to the LORD."

In the same way that we ask medical doctors to "examine and probe" us when we experience physical pain, we need to "examine and probe" our lives when we encounter relational, emotional, or spiritual pain. To be sure, not every painful experience in life is because we're guilty of wrongdoing. But sometimes there is a connection, and the only way to know is to take a closer look.

Author C. S. Lewis was right: God whispers to us in our pleasures, but shouts to us in our pain. In his severe mercy, God often uses pain to wake us up and get our attention to save us even deeper grief.

For the next note on *Support*, see Habakkuk 1:2-4.

[A] **3:52** Or *Those who were my enemies for no reason*

53 They smothered my life in[A] a pit
and threw stones on me.
54 Water flooded over my head,
and I thought, "I'm going to die!"

ק Qoph

55 I called on your name, LORD,
from the depths of the pit.
56 You heard my plea:
Do not ignore my cry for relief.
57 You came near whenever I called you;
you said, "Do not be afraid."

ר Resh

58 You championed my cause, Lord;
you redeemed my life.
59 LORD, you saw the wrong done to me;
judge my case.
60 You saw all their vengefulness,
all their plots against me.

שׂ Sin / שׁ Shin

61 LORD, you heard their insults,
all their plots against me.
62 The slander[B] and murmuring
of my opponents
attack me all day long.
63 When they sit and when they rise, look,
I am mocked by their songs.

ת Taw

64 You will pay them back
what they deserve, LORD,
according to the work of their hands.
65 You will give them a heart
filled with anguish.[C]
May your curse be on them!
66 You will pursue them in anger
and destroy them
under your heavens.[D]

TERRORS OF THE BESIEGED CITY

א Aleph

4 How the gold has become tarnished,
the fine gold become dull!
The stones of the temple[E] lie scattered
at the head of every street.

ב Beth

2 Zion's precious children —
once worth their weight in pure gold —
how they are regarded as clay jars,
the work of a potter's hands!

ג Gimel

3 Even jackals offer their breasts
to nurse their young,
but my dear people have become cruel
like ostriches in the wilderness.

ד Daleth

4 The nursing baby's tongue
clings to the roof of his mouth
from thirst.
Infants beg for food,
but no one gives them any.

ה He

5 Those who used to eat delicacies
are destitute in the streets;
those who were reared
in purple garments
huddle in trash heaps.

ו Waw

6 The punishment of my dear people
is greater than that of Sodom,
which was overthrown in an instant
without a hand laid on it.

ז Zayin

7 Her dignitaries were brighter
than snow,
whiter than milk;
their bodies[F] were more ruddy
than coral,
their appearance like lapis lazuli.

ח Cheth

8 Now they appear darker than soot;
they are not recognized in the streets.
Their skin has shriveled
on their bones;
it has become dry like wood.

ט Teth

9 Those slain by the sword are better off
than those slain by hunger,
who waste away, pierced with pain
because the fields lack produce.

י Yod

10 The hands of compassionate women
have cooked their own children;
they became their food
during the destruction
of my dear people.

[A] 3:53 Or *They ended my life in*; Hb obscure [B] 3:62 Lit *lips* [C] 3:65 Or *them an obstinate heart*; Hb obscure [D] 3:66 Lit *under the LORD's heavens* [E] 4:1 Or *The sacred gems* [F] 4:7 Lit *bones*

כ Kaph

11 The LORD has exhausted his wrath,
poured out his burning anger;
he has ignited a fire in Zion,
and it has consumed her foundations.

ל Lamed

12 The kings of the earth
and all the world's inhabitants
did not believe
that an enemy or adversary
could enter Jerusalem's gates.

מ Mem

13 Yet it happened because of the sins
of her prophets
and the iniquities of her priests,
who shed the blood of the righteous
within her.

נ Nun

14 Blind, they stumbled in the streets,
defiled by this blood,
so that no one dared
to touch their garments.

ס Samek

15 "Stay away! Unclean!" people shouted
at them.
"Away, away! Don't touch us!"
So they wandered aimlessly.
It was said among the nations,
"They can stay here no longer."

פ Pe

16 The LORD himself has scattered them;
he no longer watches over them.
The priests are not respected;
the elders find no favor.

ע Ayin

17 All the while our eyes were failing
as we looked in vain for help;
we watched from our towers
for a nation that would not save us.

צ Tsade

18 Our steps were closely followed
so that we could not walk
in our streets.
Our end approached;
our time ran out.
Our end had come!

ק Qoph

19 Those who chased us were swifter
than eagles in the sky;
they relentlessly pursued us
over the mountains
and ambushed us in the wilderness.

ר Resh

20 The LORD's anointed, the breath
of our life,[A]
was captured in their traps.
We had said about him,
"We will live under his protection
among the nations."

ש Sin

21 So rejoice and be glad, Daughter Edom,
you resident of the land of Uz!
Yet the cup will pass to you as well;
you will get drunk and expose yourself.

ת Taw

22 Daughter Zion, your punishment
is complete;
he will not lengthen your exile.[B]
But he will punish your iniquity,
Daughter Edom,
and will expose your sins.

PRAYER FOR RESTORATION

5 LORD, remember what has happened
to us.
Look, and see our disgrace!
2 Our inheritance has been turned over
to strangers,
our houses to foreigners.
3 We have become orphans, fatherless;
our mothers are widows.
4 We must pay for the water we drink;
our wood comes at a price.
5 We are closely pursued;
we are tired, and no one offers us rest.
6 We made a treaty with[C] Egypt
and with Assyria, to get enough food.
7 Our fathers sinned; they no longer exist,
but we bear their punishment.
8 Slaves rule over us;
no one rescues us from them.
9 We secure our food at the risk
of our lives
because of the sword in the wilderness.
10 Our skin is as hot[D] as an oven
from the ravages of hunger.

[A] **4:20** Lit *nostrils* [B] **4:22** Or *not deport you again* [C] **5:6** Lit *We gave the hand to* [D] **5:10** Or *black*; Hb obscure

11 Women have been raped in Zion,
virgins in the cities of Judah.
12 Princes have been hung up
by their hands;
elders are shown no respect.
13 Young men labor at millstones;
boys stumble under loads of wood.
14 The elders have left the city gate,
the young men, their music.
15 Joy has left our hearts;
our dancing has turned to mourning.
16 The crown has fallen
from our head.
Woe to us, for we have sinned.
17 Because of this, our heart is sick;
because of these, our eyes grow dim:
18 because of Mount Zion,
which lies desolate
and has jackals prowling in it.
19 You, LORD, are enthroned forever;
your throne endures from generation
to generation.
20 Why do you continually forget us,
abandon us for our entire lives?
21 LORD, bring us back to yourself, so we
may return;
renew our days as in former times,
22 unless you have completely rejected us
and are intensely angry with us.

You, LORD, are enthroned forever; your throne endures from generation to generation.
—Lamentations 5:19

The book of *Ezekiel* effectively communicates that God longs to be with his people. Throughout the book we find a constant refrain of how unlovely and undeserving Israel is, yet how desperately God longs for them. They had defiled themselves with abominations and idol worship, but God would give them a new heart and a new spirit to obey him. He still wanted them, despite their betrayal of the covenant.

One of the most famous passages in the book of Ezekiel describes dry bones that God brings to life (37:1-14). The bones were brittle and old, the flesh long since having decayed to dust; yet through the words of life preached by Ezekiel, God made them live again. This pictures beautifully and powerfully the restoration God would bring to Israel, and the restoration he brings into our lives.

No matter how dead we may feel inside or how dried up our spirit may be, God can bring new life—hearts of flesh to replace our hearts of stone and vibrant joy to replace our despair. The mysterious and unfathomable God of the universe loves us beyond imagining and gives life beyond compare.

EZEKIEL

AUTHOR: Ezekiel, son of Buzi

DATE WRITTEN: 593–570 BC

ORIGINAL AUDIENCE: The Israelite exiles in Babylon

SETTING: Ezekiel's visions took place in the years immediately before and after the destruction of Jerusalem in 586 BC. His first messages were of judgment against the nation's moral depravity and apostasy. After the fall of Jerusalem, his message changed to one of hope in the promise that God would restore what had been destroyed.

PURPOSE FOR WRITING: The primary message of Ezekiel is that God does everything—judgment and restoration—so that the people will know that he is the Lord. Israel's captivity was not vengeful punishment; it was discipline, offered by a loving heavenly Father so the people would return to him.

OUTLINE:

1. Predicting the Fall of Israel (1:1–24:27)

   Ezekiel's call and commission (1:1–3:27)

   First series of symbolic actions (4:1–7:27)

   Vision of Israel's destruction (8:1–11:25)

   Second series of symbolic actions (12:1–14:23)

   Parables of doom (15:1–19:14)

   Indictment against Israel, promise of judgment and restoration (20:1–22:31)

   Parables and last symbolic action (23:1–24:27)

2. Prophecies against the Nations (25:1–32:32)

3. Restoration for Israel (33:1–48:35)

   Call to repentance (33:1-20)

   Jerusalem's fall (33:21-33)

   Promises of restoration (34:1–39:29)

   Vision of restoration (40:1–48:35)

KEY VERSES:

"I will give you a new heart and put a new spirit within you; I will remove your heart of stone and give you a heart of flesh. I will place my Spirit within you and cause you to follow my statutes and carefully observe my ordinances." —Ezekiel 36:26-27

RESTORATION THEMES

R	Rest and Reflection	*For the next note, see Hosea 10:12.*
E	Eternal Perspective	*Biblical Hope—Ezekiel 37:2-3*
S	Support	*For the next note, see Habakkuk 1:2-4.*
T	Thanksgiving and Contentment	*For the next note, see Jonah 3:1.*
O	Other-centeredness	*Praying for Others—Ezekiel 33:11*
R	Relationships	*For the next note, see Micah 5:5.*
E	Exercise of Faith	*For the next note, see Daniel 1:8.*

1 In the thirtieth year, in the fourth month, on the fifth day of the month, while I was among the exiles by the Chebar Canal, the heavens were opened and I saw visions of God. 2 On the fifth day of the month — it was the fifth year of King Jehoiachin's exile — 3 the word of the LORD came directly to the priest Ezekiel son of Buzi, in the land of the Chaldeans by the Chebar Canal. The LORD's hand was on him there.

VISION OF THE LORD'S GLORY

4 I looked, and there was a whirlwind coming from the north, a huge cloud with fire flashing back and forth and brilliant light all around it. In the center of the fire, there was a gleam like amber. 5 The likeness of four living creatures came from it, and this was their appearance: They looked something like a human, 6 but each of them had four faces and four wings. 7 Their legs were straight, and the soles of their feet were like the hooves of a calf, sparkling like the gleam of polished bronze. 8 They had human hands under their wings on their four sides. All four of them had faces and wings. 9 Their wings were touching. The creatures did not turn as they moved; each one went straight ahead. 10 Their faces looked something like the face of a human, and each of the four had the face of a lion on the right, the face of an ox on the left, and the face of an eagle. 11 That is what their faces were like. Their wings were spread upward; each had two wings touching that of another and two wings covering its body. 12 Each creature went straight ahead. Wherever the Spirit[A] wanted to go, they went without turning as they moved.

13 The likeness of the living creatures was like the appearance of blazing coals of fire or like torches. Fire was moving back and forth between the living creatures; it was bright, with lightning coming out of it. 14 The creatures were darting back and forth like flashes of lightning.

15 When I looked at the living creatures, there was one wheel on the ground beside each of the four-faced creatures. 16 The appearance of the wheels and their craftsmanship was like the gleam of beryl, and all four had the same likeness. Their appearance and craftsmanship was like a wheel within a wheel. 17 When they moved, they went in any of the four directions, without turning as they moved. 18 Their rims were tall and awe-inspiring. Each of their four rims were full of eyes all around. 19 When the living creatures moved, the wheels moved beside them, and when the creatures rose from the earth, the wheels also rose. 20 Wherever the Spirit wanted to go, the creatures went in the direction the Spirit was moving. The wheels rose alongside them, for the spirit of the living creatures was in the wheels. 21 When the creatures moved, the wheels moved; when the creatures stopped, the wheels stopped; and when the creatures rose from the earth, the wheels rose alongside them, for the spirit of the living creatures was in the wheels.

22 Over the heads of the living creatures the likeness of an expanse was spread out. It gleamed like awe-inspiring crystal, 23 and under the expanse their wings extended one toward another. They each also had two wings covering their bodies. 24 When they moved, I heard the sound of their wings like the roar of a huge torrent, like the voice of the Almighty, and a sound of tumult like the noise of an army. When they stopped, they lowered their wings.

25 A voice came from above the expanse over their heads; when they stopped, they lowered their wings. 26 Something like a throne with the appearance of lapis lazuli was above the expanse over their heads. On the throne, high above, was someone who looked like a human. 27 From what seemed to be his waist up, I saw a gleam like amber, with what looked like fire enclosing it all around. From what seemed to be his waist down, I also saw what looked like fire. There was a brilliant light all around him. 28 The appearance of the brilliant light all around was like that of a rainbow in a cloud on a rainy day. This was the appearance of the likeness of the LORD's glory. When I saw it, I fell facedown and heard a voice speaking.

MISSION TO REBELLIOUS ISRAEL

2 He said to me, "Son of man, stand up on your feet and I will speak with you." 2 As he spoke to me, the Spirit entered me and set me on my feet, and I listened to the one who was speaking to me. 3 He said to me, "Son of man, I am sending you to the Israelites, to[B] the rebellious pagans who have rebelled against me. The Israelites and their ancestors have

[A] 1:12 Or *spirit*, also in v. 20 [B] 2:3 Or *Israelites and to*

My Story | Jordan

I had worked in this Christian organization for more than two decades, mostly in the field. Over those years, several times I had been offered a position at headquarters. Each time, I had turned down the promotion, however, because I believed that God wanted me in face-to-face ministry, not in an office.

Eventually, I felt that God was leading me to accept because of the opportunities and challenges offered there. So, my family and I moved several hundred miles, and I began my new role as a ministry leader. Between the time of my accepting the job and actually getting to my new office, a new president of the ministry had been elected—so I had a different ultimate boss than I was expecting. I knew this man and thought we would get along, but soon I realized that he didn't like me for whatever reason—we just didn't connect. For a while, I simply kept my head down, worked hard, and tried to be a good soldier.

Eventually, however, I learned that our president was asking others about me—evidently trying to dig up some dirt. And after three years of tension, he fired me. His reason? "Disloyalty."

Besides being a blow to my ego, I was angry. His termination justification made no sense, and my immediate supervisor and coworkers had said I had been performing well.

In the months that followed, I harbored resentment and would speak ill of the ministry president whenever the opportunity arose. And I seethed inside whenever someone, not knowing of my situation, would put him in a positive light. I wanted to set the record straight about his incompetence and malfeasance!

One day I was writing a devotional about "forgiveness," highlighting Jesus's words about loving our enemies (Mt 5:44). And I felt like such a hypocrite. The Holy Spirit was convicting me that I need to let it go, to forgive this man. That wasn't easy—I almost enjoyed holding on to the resentment—but eventually I did. I'd love to be able to say that we became friends; however, he kept his distance. But I was released, free!

transgressed against me to this day. 4 The
descendants are obstinate[A] and hardhearted. I am sending you to them, and you must
say to them, 'This is what the Lord God says.'
5 Whether they listen or refuse to listen — for
they are a rebellious house — they will know
that a prophet has been among them.
6 "But you, son of man, do not be afraid of
them and do not be afraid of their words, even
though briers and thorns are beside you and
you live among scorpions. Don't be afraid of
their words or discouraged by the look on
their faces, for they are a rebellious house.
7 Speak my words to them whether they listen or refuse to listen, for they are rebellious.
8 "And you, son of man, listen to what I tell
you: Do not be rebellious like that rebellious
house. Open your mouth and eat what I am
giving you." 9 So I looked and saw a hand reaching out to me, and there was a written scroll
in it. 10 When he unrolled it before me, it was
written on the front and back; words of lamentation, mourning, and woe were written on it.

3 He said to me: "Son of man, eat what you
find here. Eat this scroll, then go and speak
to the house of Israel." 2 So I opened my mouth,
and he fed me the scroll. 3 "Son of man," he
said to me, "feed your stomach and fill your
belly with this scroll I am giving you." So I ate
it, and it was as sweet as honey in my mouth.
4 Then he said to me: "Son of man, go to
the house of Israel and speak my words to
them. 5 For you are not being sent to a people
of unintelligible speech or a difficult language
but to the house of Israel — 6 not to the many
peoples of unintelligible speech or a difficult
language, whose words you cannot understand. No doubt, if I sent you to them, they
would listen to you. 7 But the house of Israel
will not want to listen to you because they do
not want to listen to me. For the whole house of
Israel is hardheaded and hardhearted. 8 Look,
I have made your face as hard as their faces
and your forehead as hard as their foreheads.
9 I have made your forehead like a diamond,
harder than flint. Don't be afraid of them or

[A] **2:4** Lit *hard of face*

discouraged by the look on their faces, though
they are a rebellious house."
10 Next he said to me: "Son of man, listen
carefully to all my words that I speak to you
and take them to heart. 11 Go to your people,
the exiles, and speak to them. Tell them, 'This
is what the Lord GOD says,' whether they listen
or refuse to listen."
12 The Spirit then lifted me up, and I heard a
loud rumbling sound behind me — bless the
glory of the LORD in his place! — 13 with the[A]
sound of the living creatures' wings brush-
ing against each other and the sound of the
wheels beside them, a loud rumbling sound.
14 The Spirit lifted me up and took me away. I
left in bitterness and in an angry spirit, and
the LORD's hand was on me powerfully. 15 I
came to the exiles at Tel-abib, who were living
by the Chebar Canal, and I sat there among
them stunned for seven days.

EZEKIEL AS A WATCHMAN

16 Now at the end of seven days the word of
the LORD came to me: 17 "Son of man, I have
made you a watchman over the house of Israel. When you hear a word from my mouth,
give them a warning from me. 18 If I say to the
wicked person, 'You will surely die,' but you
do not warn him — you don't speak out to
warn him about his wicked way in order to
save his life — that wicked person will die for
his iniquity. Yet I will hold you responsible for
his blood. 19 But if you warn a wicked person
and he does not turn from his wickedness or
his wicked way, he will die for his iniquity,
but you will have rescued yourself. 20 Now if
a righteous person turns from his righteousness and acts unjustly, and I put a stumbling
block in front of him, he will die. If you did not
warn him, he will die because of his sin, and
the righteous acts he did will not be remembered. Yet I will hold you responsible for his
blood. 21 But if you warn the righteous person
that he should not sin, and he does not sin, he
will indeed live because he listened to your
warning, and you will have rescued yourself."
22 The hand of the LORD was on me there, and
he said to me, "Get up, go out to the plain,
and I will speak with you there." 23 So I got
up and went out to the plain. The LORD's glory
was present there, like the glory I had seen by
the Chebar Canal, and I fell facedown. 24 The
Spirit entered me and set me on my feet. He
spoke with me and said: "Go, shut yourself
inside your house. 25 As for you, son of man,
they will put ropes on you and bind you with
them so you cannot go out among them. 26 I
will make your tongue stick to the roof of your
mouth, and you will be mute and unable to be
a mediator for[B] them, for they are a rebellious
house. 27 But when I speak with you, I will open
your mouth, and you will say to them, 'This is
what the Lord GOD says.' Let the one who listens, listen, and let the one who refuses, refuse
— for they are a rebellious house.

JERUSALEM'S SIEGE DRAMATIZED

4 "Now you, son of man, take a brick, set it
in front of you, and draw the city of Jerusalem on it. 2 Then lay siege against it: Construct a siege wall, build a ramp, pitch military
camps, and place battering rams against it on
all sides. 3 Take an iron plate and set it up as an
iron wall between yourself and the city. Face
it so that it is under siege, and besiege it. This
will be a sign for the house of Israel.
4 "Then lie down on your left side and place
the iniquity[C] of the house of Israel on it. You
will bear their iniquity for the number of days
you lie on your side. 5 For I have assigned you
the years of their iniquity according to the
number of days you lie down, 390 days; so
you will bear the iniquity of the house of Israel. 6 When you have completed these days,
lie down again, but on your right side, and
bear the iniquity of the house of Judah. I have
assigned you forty days, a day for each year.
7 Face the siege of Jerusalem with your arm
bared, and prophesy against it. 8 Be aware
that I will put cords on you so you cannot turn
from side to side until you have finished the
days of your siege.
9 "Also take wheat, barley, beans, lentils, mil-
let, and spelt. Put them in a single container
and make them into bread for yourself. You
are to eat it during the number of days you
lie on your side, 390 days. 10 The food you eat
each day will weigh eight ounces;[D] you will
eat it at set times.[E] 11 You will also drink a ration of water, a sixth of a gallon,[F] which you
will drink at set times. 12 You will eat it as you
would a barley cake and bake it over dried
human excrement in their sight." 13 The LORD
said, "This is how the Israelites will eat their
bread — ceremonially unclean — among the
nations where I will banish them."

[A] **3:12-13** Some emend to *behind me as the glory of the LORD rose from his place: 13the* [B] **3:26** Or *to rebuke* [C] **4:4** Or *punishment* [D] **4:10** Lit *20 shekels* [E] **4:10** Lit *from time to time*, also in v. 11 [F] **4:11** Lit *hin*

14 But I said, "Oh, Lord GOD, I have never been defiled. From my youth until now I have not eaten anything that died naturally or was mauled by wild beasts. And impure meat has never entered my mouth."

15 He replied to me, "Look, I will let you use cow dung instead of human excrement, and you can make your bread over that." 16 He said to me, "Son of man, I am going to cut off the supply of bread in Jerusalem. They will anxiously eat food they have weighed out and in dread drink rationed water 17 for lack of bread and water. Everyone will be devastated and waste away because of their iniquity.

EZEKIEL DRAMATIZES JERUSALEM'S FALL

5 "Now you, son of man, take a sharp sword, use it as you would a barber's razor, and shave your head and beard. Then take a set of scales and divide the hair. 2 You are to burn a third of it in the city when the days of the siege have ended; you are to take a third and slash it with the sword all around the city; and you are to scatter a third to the wind, for I will draw a sword to chase after them. 3 But you are to take a few strands from the hair and secure them in the folds of your robe. 4 Take some more of them, throw them into the fire, and burn them in it. A fire will spread from it to the whole house of Israel.

5 "This is what the Lord GOD says: I have set this Jerusalem in the center of the nations, with countries all around her. 6 She has rebelled against my ordinances with more wickedness than the nations, and against my statutes more than the countries that surround her. For her people have rejected my ordinances and have not walked in my statutes.

7 "Therefore, this is what the Lord GOD says: Because you have been more insubordinate than the nations around you — you have not walked in my statutes or kept my ordinances; you have not even kept the ordinances of the nations around you — 8 therefore, this is what the Lord GOD says: See, I myself am against you, Jerusalem, and I will execute judgments within you in the sight of the nations. 9 Because of all your detestable practices, I will do to you what I have never done before and what I will never do again. 10 As a result, fathers will eat their sons within Jerusalem,[A] and sons will eat their fathers. I will execute judgments against you and scatter all your survivors to every direction of the wind.

11 "Therefore, as I live" — this is the declaration of the Lord GOD — "I will withdraw and show you no pity, because you have defiled my sanctuary with all your abhorrent acts and detestable practices. Yes, I will not spare you. 12 A third of your people will die by plague and be consumed by famine within you; a third will fall by the sword all around you; and I will scatter a third to every direction of the wind, and I will draw a sword to chase after them. 13 When my anger is spent and I have vented my wrath on them, I will be appeased. Then after I have spent my wrath on them, they will know that I, the LORD, have spoken in my jealousy.

14 "I will make you a ruin and a disgrace among the nations around you, in the sight of everyone who passes by. 15 So you[B] will be a disgrace and a taunt, a warning and a horror, to the nations around you when I execute judgments against you in anger, wrath, and furious rebukes. I, the LORD, have spoken. 16 When I shoot deadly arrows of famine at them, arrows for destruction that I will send to destroy you, inhabitants of Jerusalem, I will intensify the famine against you and cut off your supply of bread. 17 I will send famine and dangerous animals against you. They will leave you childless. Plague and bloodshed will sweep through you, and I will bring a sword against you. I, the LORD, have spoken."

PROPHECY AGAINST ISRAEL'S IDOLATRY

6 The word of the LORD came to me: 2 "Son of man, face the mountains of Israel and prophesy against them. 3 You are to say: Mountains of Israel, hear the word of the Lord GOD! This is what the Lord GOD says to the mountains and the hills, to the ravines and the valleys: I am about to bring a sword against you, and I will destroy your high places. 4 Your altars will be desolated and your shrines[C] smashed. I will throw down your slain in front of your idols. 5 I will lay the corpses of the Israelites in front of their idols and scatter your bones around your altars. 6 Wherever you live the cities will be in ruins and the high places will be desolate, so that your altars will lie in ruins and be desecrated,[D] your idols smashed and obliterated, your shrines cut down, and what you have made wiped out. 7 The slain

[A] **5:10** Lit *you* [B] **5:15** DSS, LXX, Syr, Tg, Vg; MT reads *she* [C] **6:4** Or *incense altars*, also in v. 6 [D] **6:6** Hb obscure

will fall among you, and you will know that
I am the LORD.
8 "Yet I will leave a remnant when you are
scattered among the nations, for throughout
the countries there will be some of you who
will escape the sword. 9 Then your survivors
will remember me among the nations where
they are taken captive, how I was crushed by
their promiscuous hearts that turned away
from me and by their eyes that lusted after their
idols. They will loathe themselves because of
the evil things they did, their detestable actions of every kind. 10 And they will know that
I am the LORD; I did not threaten to bring this
disaster on them without a reason.

LAMENT OVER THE FALL OF JERUSALEM

11 "This is what the Lord GOD says: Clap your
hands, stamp your feet, and cry out over
all the evil and detestable practices of the
house of Israel, who will fall by the sword,
famine, and plague. 12 The one who is far off
will die by plague; the one who is near will
fall by the sword; and the one who remains
and is spared[A] will die of famine. In this way
I will exhaust my wrath on them. 13 You will
all know that I am the LORD when their slain
lie among their idols around their altars, on
every high hill, on all the mountaintops, and
under every green tree and every leafy oak
— the places where they offered pleasing
aromas to all their idols. 14 I will stretch out
my hand against them, and wherever they
live I will make the land a desolate waste,
from the wilderness to Diblah.[B] Then they
will know that I am the LORD."

ANNOUNCEMENT OF THE END

7 The word of the LORD came to me: 2 "Son
of man, this is what the Lord GOD says to
the land of Israel:

An end! The end has come
on the four corners of the earth.
3 The end is now upon you;
I will send my anger against you
and judge you according to your ways.
I will punish you for all
your detestable practices.
4 I will not look on you with pity
or spare you,
but I will punish you for your ways
and for your detestable practices
within you.
Then you will know that I am
the LORD."

5 This is what the Lord GOD says:
Look, one disaster after another
is coming!
6 An end has come; the end has come!
It has awakened against you.
Look, it is coming!
7 Doom[C] has come on you,
inhabitants of the land.
The time has come; the day is near.
There will be panic on the mountains
and not celebration.

8 I will pour out my wrath on you
very soon;
I will exhaust my anger against you
and judge you according to your ways.
I will punish you for all your
detestable practices.
9 I will not look on you with pity
or spare you.
I will punish you for your ways
and for your detestable practices
within you.
Then you will know
that it is I, the LORD, who strikes.

10 Here is the day! Here it comes!
Doom is on its way.
The rod has blossomed;
arrogance has bloomed.
11 Violence has grown into a rod
of wickedness.
None of them will remain:
none of that crowd,
none of their wealth,
and none of the eminent[D] among them.

12 The time has come; the day has arrived.
Let the buyer not rejoice
and the seller not mourn,
for wrath is on her whole crowd.
13 The seller will certainly not return
to what was sold
as long as he and the buyer
remain alive.[E]
For the vision concerning
her whole crowd
will not be revoked,
and because of the iniquity of each one,
none will preserve his life.

[A] 6:12 Or *besieged* [B] 6:14 Some Hb mss, some LXX mss read *Riblah*; 2Kg 23:33; Jr 39:5 [C] 7:7 Or *A leash*; Hb obscure, also in v. 10
[D] 7:11 Some Hb mss, Syr, Vg read *and no rest* [E] 7:13 Lit *sold, while still in life is their life*

14 They have blown the trumpet
and prepared everything,
but no one goes to war,
for my wrath is on her whole crowd.
15 The sword is on the outside;
plague and famine are on the inside.
Whoever is in the field will die
by the sword,
and famine and plague will devour
whoever is in the city.

16 The survivors among them will escape
and live on the mountains.
Like doves of the valley,
all of them will moan,
each over his own iniquity.
17 All their hands will become weak,
and all their knees will run with urine.[A]
18 They will put on sackcloth,
and horror will overwhelm them.
Shame will cover all their faces,
and all their heads will be bald.

19 They will throw their silver
into the streets,
and their gold will seem like
something filthy.
Their silver and gold will be unable
to save them
in the day of the LORD's wrath.
They will not satisfy their appetites
or fill their stomachs,
for these were the stumbling blocks
that brought about their iniquity.

20 He appointed his beautiful ornaments
for majesty,
but[B] they made their detestable images
from them,
their abhorrent things.
Therefore, I have made these
into something filthy to them.
21 I will hand these things over
to foreigners as plunder
and to the wicked of the earth as spoil,
and they will profane them.
22 I will turn my face from them
as they profane my treasured place.
Violent men will enter it and profane it.

23 Forge the chain,
for the land is filled with crimes
of bloodshed,
and the city is filled
with violence.
24 So I will bring the most evil of nations
to take possession of their houses.
I will put an end to the pride
of the strong,
and their sacred places
will be profaned.
25 Anguish is coming!
They will look for peace,
but there will be none.
26 Disaster after disaster will come,
and there will be rumor after rumor.
Then they will look for a vision
from a prophet,
but instruction will perish
from the priests
and counsel from the elders.
27 The king will mourn;
the prince will be clothed in grief;
and the hands of the people of the land
will tremble.
I will deal with them according to
their own conduct,
and I will judge them
by their own standards.
Then they will know that I am the LORD.

VISIONARY JOURNEY TO JERUSALEM

8 In the sixth year, in the sixth month, on
the fifth day of the month, I was sitting
in my house and the elders of Judah were
sitting in front of me, and there the hand of
the Lord GOD came down on me. 2 I looked,
and there was someone who looked like a
man.[C] From what seemed to be his waist
down was fire, and from his waist up was
something that looked bright, like the gleam
of amber. 3 He stretched out what appeared
to be a hand and took me by the hair of my
head. Then the Spirit lifted me up between
earth and heaven and carried me in visions
of God to Jerusalem, to the entrance of the
inner gate that faces north, where the offensive statue that provokes jealousy was
located. 4 I saw the glory of the God of Israel
there, like the vision I had seen in the plain.

PAGAN PRACTICES IN THE TEMPLE

5 The LORD said to me, "Son of man, look toward
the north." I looked to the north, and there was
this offensive statue north of the Altar Gate,
at the entrance. 6 He said to me, "Son of man,

[A] **7:17** Lit *knees will go water* [B] **7:20** Or *They turned their beautiful ornaments into objects of pride, and* [C] **8:2** LXX; MT, Vg read *like fire*

do you see what they are doing here — more
detestable acts that the house of Israel is committing — so that I must depart from my sanctuary? You will see even more detestable acts."
7 Then he brought me to the entrance of the
court, and when I looked there was a hole
in the wall. 8 He said to me, "Son of man, dig
through the wall." So I dug through the wall
and discovered a doorway. 9 He said to me, "Go
in and see the detestable, wicked acts they are
committing here."
10 I went in and looked, and there engraved
all around the wall was every kind of abhorrent thing — crawling creatures and beasts
— as well as all the idols of the house of Israel.
11 Seventy elders from the house of Israel were
standing before them, with Jaazaniah son of
Shaphan standing among them. Each had a
firepan in his hand, and a fragrant cloud of
incense was rising up. 12 He said to me, "Son of
man, do you see what the elders of the house
of Israel are doing in the darkness, each at
the shrine of his idol? For they are saying,
'The LORD does not see us. The LORD has abandoned the land.' " 13 Again he said to me, "You
will see even more detestable acts that they
are committing."
14 Then he brought me to the entrance of
the north gate of the LORD's house, and I saw
women sitting there weeping for Tammuz.
15 And he said to me, "Do you see this, son of
man? You will see even more detestable acts
than these."
16 So he brought me to the inner court of the
LORD's house, and there were about twenty-five
men at the entrance of the LORD's temple, between the portico and the altar, with their
backs to the LORD's temple and their faces
turned to the east. They were bowing to the
east in worship of the sun. 17 And he said to me,
"Do you see this, son of man? Is it not enough
for the house of Judah to commit the detestable
acts they are doing here, that they must also fill
the land with violence and repeatedly anger
me, even putting the branch to their nose?[A]
18 Therefore I will respond with wrath. I will
not show pity or spare them. Though they call
loudly in my hearing, I will not listen to them."

VISION OF SLAUGHTER IN JERUSALEM

9 Then he called loudly in my hearing, "Come
near, executioners of the city, each of you
with a destructive weapon in his hand." 2 And
I saw six men coming from the direction of
the Upper Gate, which faces north, each with
a war club in his hand. There was another man
among them, clothed in linen, carrying writing equipment. They came and stood beside
the bronze altar.
3 Then the glory of the God of Israel rose
from above the cherub where it had been,
to the threshold of the temple. He called to
the man clothed in linen and carrying writing equipment. 4 "Pass throughout the city of
Jerusalem," the LORD said to him, "and put a
mark on the foreheads of the men who sigh
and groan over all the detestable practices
committed in it."
5 He spoke to the others in my hearing: "Pass
through the city after him and start killing; do
not show pity or spare them! 6 Slaughter the
old men, the young men and women, as well
as the children and older women, but do not
come near anyone who has the mark. Begin
at my sanctuary." So they began with the elders who were in front of the temple. 7 Then
he said to them, "Defile the temple and fill the
courts with the slain. Go!" So they went out
killing people in the city.
8 While they were killing, I was left alone.
And I fell facedown and cried out, "Oh, Lord
GOD! Are you going to destroy the entire remnant of Israel when you pour out your wrath
on Jerusalem?"
9 He answered me, "The iniquity of the
house of Israel and Judah is extremely great;
the land is full of bloodshed, and the city full
of perversity. For they say, 'The LORD has
abandoned the land; he does not see.' 10 But
as for me, I will not show pity or spare them.
I will bring their conduct down on their own
heads."
11 Then the man clothed in linen and carrying writing equipment reported back, "I have
done all that you commanded me."

GOD'S GLORY LEAVES THE TEMPLE

10 Then I looked, and there above the expanse over the heads of the cherubim
was something like a throne with the appearance of lapis lazuli. 2 The LORD spoke to the
man clothed in linen and said, "Go inside the
wheelwork beneath the cherubim. Fill your
hands with blazing coals from among the
cherubim and scatter them over the city." So
he went in as I watched.

[A] 8:17 Alt Hb tradition reads *my nose*

3 Now the cherubim were standing to the south of the temple when the man went in, and the cloud filled the inner court. 4 Then the glory of the LORD rose from above the cherub to the threshold of the temple. The temple was filled with the cloud, and the court was filled with the brightness of the LORD's glory. 5 The sound of the cherubim's wings could be heard as far as the outer court; it was like the voice of God Almighty when he speaks.

6 After the LORD commanded the man clothed in linen, saying, "Take fire from inside the wheelwork, from among the cherubim," the man went in and stood beside a wheel. 7 Then the cherub reached out his hand to the fire that was among them. He took some and put it into the hands of the man clothed in linen, who took it and went out. 8 The cherubim appeared to have the form of human hands under their wings.

9 I looked, and there were four wheels beside the cherubim, one wheel beside each cherub. The luster of the wheels was like the gleam of beryl. 10 In appearance, all four looked alike, like a wheel within a wheel. 11 When they moved, they would go in any of the four directions, without pivoting as they moved. But wherever the head faced, they would go in that direction, without pivoting as they went. 12 Their entire bodies, including their backs, hands, wings, and the wheels that the four of them had, were full of eyes all around. 13 As I listened the wheels were called "the wheelwork." 14 Each one had four faces: one was the face of a cherub, the second the face of a man, the third the face of a lion, and the fourth the face of an eagle.

15 The cherubim ascended; these were the living creatures I had seen by the Chebar Canal. 16 When the cherubim moved, the wheels moved beside them, and when they lifted their wings to rise from the earth, even then the wheels did not veer away from them. 17 When the cherubim stopped, the wheels stood still, and when they ascended, the wheels ascended with them, for the spirit of the living creatures was in them.

18 Then the glory of the LORD moved away from the threshold of the temple and stopped above the cherubim. 19 The cherubim lifted their wings and ascended from the earth right before my eyes; the wheels were beside them as they went. The glory of the God of Israel was above them, and it stopped at the entrance to the eastern gate of the LORD's house.

20 These were the living creatures I had seen beneath the God of Israel by the Chebar Canal, and I recognized that they were cherubim. 21 Each had four faces and each had four wings, with what looked something like human hands under their wings. 22 Their faces looked like the same faces I had seen by the Chebar Canal. Each creature went straight ahead.

VISION OF ISRAEL'S CORRUPT LEADERS

11 The Spirit then lifted me up and brought me to the eastern gate of the LORD's house, which faces east, and at the gate's entrance were twenty-five men. Among them I saw Jaazaniah son of Azzur, and Pelatiah son of Benaiah, leaders of the people. 2 The LORD[A] said to me, "Son of man, these are the men who plot evil and give wicked advice in this city. 3 They are saying, 'Isn't the time near to build houses?[B] The city is the pot, and we are the meat.' 4 Therefore, prophesy against them. Prophesy, son of man!"

5 Then the Spirit of the LORD came on me, and he told me, "You are to say, 'This is what the LORD says: That is what you are thinking, house of Israel; and I know the thoughts that arise in your mind. 6 You have multiplied your slain in this city, filling its streets with them.

7 " 'Therefore, this is what the Lord GOD says: The slain you have put within it are the meat, and the city is the pot, but I[C] will take you out of it. 8 You fear the sword, so I will bring the sword against you. This is the declaration of the Lord GOD. 9 I will take you out of the city and hand you over to foreigners; I will execute judgments against you. 10 You will fall by the sword, and I will judge you at the border of Israel. Then you will know that I am the LORD. 11 The city will not be a pot for you, and you will not be the meat within it. I will judge you at the border of Israel, 12 so you will know that I am the LORD, whose statutes you have not followed and whose ordinances you have not practiced. Instead, you have acted according to the ordinances of the nations around you.' "

13 Now while I was prophesying, Pelatiah son of Benaiah died. Then I fell facedown and cried out loudly, "Oh, Lord GOD! You are bringing the remnant of Israel to an end!"

PROMISE OF ISRAEL'S RESTORATION

14 The word of the LORD came to me again: 15 "Son of man, your own relatives, those who

---

[A] **11:2** Lit *He* [B] **11:3** Or *"The time is not near to build houses.* [C] **11:7** Some Hb mss, LXX, Syr, Tg, Vg; other Hb mss read *he*

have the right to redeem your property,[A,B] along with the entire house of Israel — all of them — are those to whom the residents of Jerusalem have said, 'You are far from the LORD; this land has been given to us as a possession.'

16 "Therefore say, 'This is what the Lord GOD says: Though I sent them far away among the nations and scattered them among the countries, yet for a little while I have been a sanctuary for them in the countries where they have gone.'

17 "Therefore say, 'This is what the Lord GOD says: I will gather you from the peoples and assemble you from the countries where you have been scattered, and I will give you the land of Israel.'

18 "When they arrive there, they will remove all its abhorrent acts and detestable practices from it. 19 I will give them integrity of[C] heart and put a new spirit within them; I will remove their heart of stone from their bodies[D] and give them a heart of flesh, 20 so that they will follow my statutes, keep my ordinances, and practice them. They will be my people, and I will be their God. 21 But as for those whose hearts pursue their desire for abhorrent acts and detestable practices, I will bring their conduct down on their own heads." This is the declaration of the Lord GOD.

GOD'S GLORY LEAVES JERUSALEM

22 Then the cherubim, with the wheels beside them, lifted their wings, and the glory of the God of Israel was above them. 23 The glory of the LORD rose up from within the city and stopped on the mountain east of the city.[E] 24 The Spirit lifted me up and brought me to Chaldea and to the exiles in a vision from the Spirit of God. After the vision I had seen left me, 25 I spoke to the exiles about all the things the LORD had shown me.

EZEKIEL DRAMATIZES THE EXILE

12 The word of the LORD came to me: 2 "Son of man, you are living among a rebellious house. They have eyes to see but do not see, and ears to hear but do not hear, for they are a rebellious house.

3 "Now you, son of man, get your bags ready for exile and go into exile in their sight during the day. You will go into exile from your place to another place while they watch; perhaps they will understand, though they are a rebellious house. 4 During the day, bring out your bags like an exile's bags while they look on. Then in the evening go out in their sight like those going into exile. 5 As they watch, dig through the wall and take the bags out through it. 6 And while they look on, lift the bags to your shoulder and take them out in the dark; cover your face so that you cannot see the land. For I have made you a sign to the house of Israel."

7 So I did just as I was commanded. In the daytime I brought out my bags like an exile's bags. In the evening I dug through the wall by hand; I took them out in the dark, carrying them on my shoulder in their sight.

8 In the morning the word of the LORD came to me: 9 "Son of man, hasn't the house of Israel, that rebellious house, asked you, 'What are you doing?' 10 Say to them, 'This is what the Lord GOD says: This pronouncement concerns the prince[F] in Jerusalem and the whole house of Israel living there.'[G] 11 You are to say, 'I am a sign for you. Just as I have done, it will be done to them; they will go into exile, into captivity.' 12 The prince who is among them will lift his bags to his shoulder in the dark and go out. They[H] will dig through the wall to bring him out through it. He will cover his face so he cannot see the land with his eyes. 13 But I will spread my net over him, and he will be caught in my snare. I will bring him to Babylon, the land of the Chaldeans, yet he will not see it, and he will die there. 14 I will also scatter all the attendants who surround him and all his troops to every direction of the wind, and I will draw a sword to chase after them. 15 They will know that I am the LORD when I disperse them among the nations and scatter them among the countries. 16 But I will spare a few of them from the sword, famine, and plague, so that among the nations where they go they can tell about all their detestable practices. Then they will know that I am the LORD."

EZEKIEL DRAMATIZES ISRAEL'S ANXIETY

17 The word of the LORD came to me: 18 "Son of man, eat your bread with trembling and drink your water with anxious shaking. 19 Then say to the people of the land, 'This is what the Lord GOD says about the residents of Jerusalem in the land of Israel: They will eat their bread with anxiety and drink their water in dread,

[A] **11:15** LXX, Syr read *your relatives, your fellow exiles* [B] **11:15** Or *own brothers, your relatives* [C] **11:19** Lit *give them one* [D] **11:19** Lit *flesh* [E] **11:23** = the Mount of Olives [F] **12:10** = King Zedekiah [G] **12:10** Lit *Israel among them* [H] **12:12** LXX, Syr read *He*

for their[A,B] land will be stripped of everything
in it because of the violence of all who live
there. 20 The inhabited cities will be destroyed,
and the land will become dreadful. Then you
will know that I am the LORD.'"

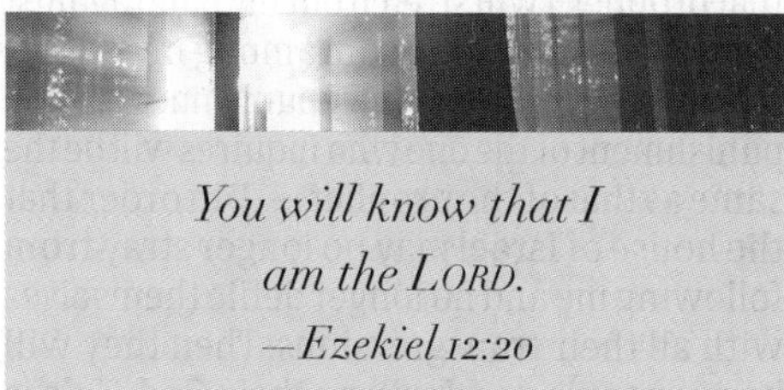
You will know that I
am the LORD.
—Ezekiel 12:20

A DECEPTIVE PROVERB STOPPED

21 Again the word of the LORD came to me:
22 "Son of man, what is this proverb you people
have about the land of Israel, which goes, 'The
days keep passing by, and every vision fails'?
23 Therefore say to them, 'This is what the Lord
GOD says: I will put a stop to this proverb, and
they will not use it again in Israel.' But say
to them, 'The days have arrived, as well as
the fulfillment of every vision. 24 For there
will no longer be any false vision or flattering
divination within the house of Israel. 25 But I,
the LORD, will speak whatever message I will
speak, and it will be done. It will no longer be
delayed. For in your days, rebellious house, I
will speak a message and bring it to pass. This
is the declaration of the Lord GOD.'"

26 The word of the LORD came to me: 27 "Son
of man, notice that the house of Israel is saying, 'The vision that he sees concerns many
years from now; he prophesies about distant
times.' 28 Therefore say to them, 'This is what
the Lord GOD says: None of my words will
be delayed any longer. The message I speak
will be fulfilled. This is the declaration of the
Lord GOD.'"

ISRAEL'S FALSE PROPHETS CONDEMNED

13 The word of the LORD came to me: 2 "Son
of man, prophesy against the prophets
of Israel who are prophesying. Say to those
who prophesy out of their own imagination,
'Hear the word of the LORD! 3 This is what the
Lord GOD says: Woe to the foolish prophets
who follow their own spirit and have seen
nothing. 4 Your prophets, Israel, are like jackals
among ruins. 5 You did not go up to the gaps
or restore the wall around the house of Israel
so that it might stand in battle on the day of
the LORD. 6 They saw false visions and their
divinations were a lie. They claimed, "This is
the LORD's declaration," when the LORD did
not send them, yet they wait for the fulfillment of their message. 7 Didn't you see a false
vision and speak a lying divination when you
proclaimed, "This is the LORD's declaration,"
even though I had not spoken?

8 "'Therefore, this is what the Lord GOD says:
You have spoken falsely and had lying visions;
that's why you discover that I am against you.
This is the declaration of the Lord GOD. 9 My
hand will be against the prophets who see false
visions and speak lying divinations. They will
not be present in the council of my people or
be recorded in the register of the house of Israel, and they will not enter the land of Israel.
Then you will know that I am the Lord GOD.

10 "'Since they have led my people astray by
saying, "Peace," when there is no peace, and
since when a flimsy wall is being built, they
plaster it with whitewash, 11 therefore, tell
those plastering it with whitewash that it will
fall. Torrential rain will come, and I will send
hailstones plunging[C] down, and a whirlwind
will be released. 12 When the wall has fallen,
will you not be asked, "Where's the whitewash
you plastered on it?"

13 "'So this is what the Lord GOD says: I will
release a whirlwind in my wrath. Torrential
rain will come in my anger, and hailstones
will fall in destructive fury. 14 I will demolish
the wall you plastered with whitewash and
knock it to the ground so that its foundation
is exposed. The city will fall, and you will be
destroyed within it. Then you will know that
I am the LORD. 15 After I exhaust my wrath
against the wall and against those who plaster it with whitewash, I will say to you, "The
wall is no more and neither are those who
plastered it — 16 those prophets of Israel who
prophesied to Jerusalem and saw a vision of
peace for her when there was no peace." This
is the declaration of the Lord GOD.'

17 "Now you, son of man, face[D] the wom-
en among your people who prophesy out of
their own imagination, and prophesy against
them. 18 Say, 'This is what the Lord GOD says:
Woe to the women who sew magic bands on
the wrist of every hand and who make veils
for the heads of people of every size in order
to ensnare lives. Will you ensnare the lives

[A] **12:19** Lit *its* [B] **12:19** = Jerusalem's [C] **13:11** One Hb ms, LXX, Vg; other Hb mss read *and you, hailstones, will plunge*
[D] **13:17** Lit *set your face*

of my people but preserve your own? 19 You profane me among my people for handfuls of barley and scraps of bread; you put those to death who should not die and spare those who should not live, when you lie to my people, who listen to lies.

20 " 'Therefore, this is what the Lord GOD says: I am against your magic bands with which you ensnare people like birds, and I will tear them from your arms. I will free the people you have ensnared like birds. 21 I will also tear off your veils and rescue my people from your hands, so that they will no longer be prey in your hands. Then you will know that I am the LORD. 22 Because you have disheartened the righteous person with lies (when I intended no distress), and because you have supported[A] the wicked person so that he does not turn from his evil way to save his life, 23 therefore you will no longer see false visions or practice divination. I will rescue my people from your hands. Then you will know that I am the LORD.' "

IDOLATROUS ELDERS PUNISHED

14 Some of the elders of Israel came to me and sat down in front of me. 2 Then the word of the LORD came to me: 3 "Son of man, these men have set up idols in their hearts and have put their sinful stumbling blocks in front of themselves. Should I actually let them inquire of me?

4 "Therefore, speak to them and tell them, 'This is what the Lord GOD says: When anyone from the house of Israel sets up idols in his heart and puts his sinful stumbling block in front of himself, and then comes to the prophet, I, the LORD, will answer him appropriately.[B] I will answer him according to his many idols, 5 so that I may take hold of the house of Israel by their hearts. They are all estranged from me because of their idols.'

6 "Therefore, say to the house of Israel, 'This is what the Lord GOD says: Repent and turn away from your idols; turn your faces away from all your detestable things. 7 For when anyone from the house of Israel or from the aliens who reside in Israel separates himself from me, setting up idols in his heart and putting his sinful stumbling block in front of himself, and then comes to the prophet to inquire of me, I, the LORD, will answer him myself. 8 I will turn against that one and make him a sign and a proverb; I will cut him off from among my people. Then you will know that I am the LORD.

9 " 'But if the prophet is deceived and speaks a message, it was I, the LORD, who deceived that prophet. I will stretch out my hand against him and destroy him from among my people Israel. 10 They will bear their punishment — the punishment of the one who inquires will be the same as that of the prophet — 11 in order that the house of Israel may no longer stray from following me and no longer defile themselves with all their transgressions. Then they will be my people and I will be their God. This is the declaration of the Lord GOD.' "

FOUR DEVASTATING JUDGMENTS

12 The word of the LORD came to me: 13 "Son of man, suppose a land sins against me by acting faithlessly, and I stretch out my hand against it to cut off its supply of bread, to send famine through it, and to wipe out both man and animal from it. 14 Even if these three men — Noah, Daniel, and Job — were in it, they would rescue only themselves by their righteousness." This is the declaration of the Lord GOD.

15 "Suppose I allow dangerous animals to pass through the land and depopulate it so that it becomes desolate, with no one passing through it for fear of the animals. 16 Even if these three men were in it, as I live" — the declaration of the Lord GOD — "they could not rescue their sons or daughters. They alone would be rescued, but the land would be desolate.

17 "Or suppose I bring a sword against that land and say, 'Let a sword pass through it,' so that I wipe out both man and animal from it. 18 Even if these three men were in it, as I live" — the declaration of the Lord GOD — "they could not rescue their sons or daughters, but they alone would be rescued.

19 "Or suppose I send a plague into that land and pour out my wrath on it with bloodshed to wipe out both man and animal from it. 20 Even if Noah, Daniel, and Job were in it, as I live" — the declaration of the Lord GOD — "they could not rescue their son or daughter. They would rescue only themselves by their righteousness.

21 "For this is what the Lord GOD says: How much worse will it be when I send my four devastating judgments against Jerusalem — sword, famine, dangerous animals, and

[A] **13:22** Lit *strengthened the hand of* [B] **14:4** Alt Hb tradition reads *him who comes*

plague — in order to wipe out both man and animal from it! 22 Even so, there will be survivors left in it, sons and daughters who will be brought out. Indeed, they will come out to you, and you will observe their conduct and actions. Then you will be consoled about the devastation I have brought on Jerusalem, about all I have brought on it. 23 They will bring you consolation when you see their conduct and actions, and you will know that it was not without cause that I have done what I did to it." This is the declaration of the Lord God.

PARABLE OF THE USELESS VINE

15 Then the word of the LORD came to me: 2 "Son of man, how does the wood of the vine, that branch among the trees of the forest, compare to any other wood? 3 Can wood be taken from it to make something useful? Or can anyone make a peg from it to hang things on? 4 In fact, it is put into the fire as fuel. The fire devours both of its ends, and the middle is charred. Can it be useful for anything? 5 Even when it was whole it could not be made into a useful object. How much less can it ever be made into anything useful when the fire has devoured it and it is charred!"

6 Therefore, this is what the Lord God says, "Like the wood of the vine among the trees of the forest, which I have given to the fire as fuel, so I will give up the residents of Jerusalem. 7 I will turn against them. They may have escaped from the fire, but it will still consume them. And you will know that I am the LORD when I turn against them. 8 I will make the land desolate because they have acted unfaithfully." This is the declaration of the Lord God.

PARABLE OF GOD'S ADULTEROUS WIFE

16 The word of the LORD came to me again: 2 "Son of man, confront Jerusalem with her detestable practices. 3 You are to say, 'This is what the Lord God says to Jerusalem: Your origin and your birth were in the land of the Canaanites. Your father was an Amorite and your mother a Hethite. 4 As for your birth, your umbilical cord wasn't cut on the day you were born, and you weren't washed clean[A] with water. You were not rubbed with salt or wrapped in cloths. 5 No one cared enough about you to do even one of these things out of compassion for you. But you were thrown out into the open field because you were despised on the day you were born.

6 " 'I passed by you and saw you thrashing around in your blood, and I said to you as you lay in your blood, "Live!" Yes, I said to you as you lay in your blood, "Live!"[B] 7 I made you thrive[C] like plants of the field. You grew up and matured and became very beautiful.[D] Your breasts were formed and your hair grew, but you were stark naked.

8 " 'Then I passed by you and saw you, and you were indeed at the age for love. So I spread the edge of my garment over you and covered your nakedness. I pledged myself to you, entered into a covenant with you — this is the declaration of the Lord God — and you became mine. 9 I washed you with water, rinsed off your blood, and anointed you with oil. 10 I clothed you in embroidered cloth and provided you with fine leather[A] sandals. I also wrapped you in fine linen and covered you with silk. 11 I adorned you with jewelry, putting bracelets on your wrists and a necklace around your neck. 12 I put a ring in your nose, earrings on your ears, and a beautiful crown on your head. 13 So you were adorned with gold and silver, and your clothing was made of fine linen, silk, and embroidered cloth. You ate fine flour, honey, and oil. You became extremely beautiful and attained royalty. 14 Your fame spread among the nations because of your beauty, for it was perfect through my splendor, which I had bestowed on you. This is the declaration of the Lord God.

15 " 'But you trusted in your beauty and acted like a prostitute because of your fame. You lavished your sexual favors on everyone who passed by. Your beauty became his.[A] 16 You took some of your clothing and made colorful high places for yourself, and you engaged in prostitution on them. These places should not have been built, and this should never have happened![A] 17 You also took your beautiful jewelry made from the gold and silver I had given you, and you made male images so that you could engage in prostitution with them. 18 Then you took your embroidered clothing to cover them and set my oil and incense before them. 19 The food that I gave you — the fine flour, oil, and honey that I fed you — you set it before them as a pleasing aroma. That is what happened. This is the declaration of the Lord God.

[A] **16:4,10,15,16** Hb obscure [B] **16:6** Some Hb mss, LXX, Syr omit *Yes, I said to you as you lay in your blood, "Live!"* [C] **16:7** LXX reads *Thrive; I made you* [D] **16:7** Or *matured and developed the loveliest of ornaments*

20 " 'You even took your sons and daughters you bore to me and sacrificed them to these images as food. Wasn't your prostitution enough? 21 You slaughtered my children and gave them up when you passed them through the fire to the images. 22 In all your detestable practices and acts of prostitution, you did not remember the days of your youth when you were stark naked and thrashing around in your blood.

23 " 'Then after all your evil — Woe, woe to you! — the declaration of the Lord GOD — 24 you built yourself a mound and made yourself an elevated place in every square. 25 You built your elevated place at the head of every street and turned your beauty into a detestable thing. You spread your legs to everyone who passed by and increased your prostitution. 26 You engaged in promiscuous acts with Egyptian men, your well-endowed neighbors, and increased your prostitution to anger me.

27 " 'Therefore, I stretched out my hand against you and reduced your provisions. I gave you over to the desire of those who hate you, the Philistine women, who were embarrassed by your indecent conduct. 28 Then you engaged in prostitution with the Assyrian men because you were not satisfied. Even though you did this with them, you were still not satisfied. 29 So you extended your prostitution to Chaldea, the land of merchants, but you were not even satisfied with this!

30 " 'How your heart was inflamed with lust[A] — the declaration of the Lord GOD — when you did all these things, the acts of a brazen prostitute, 31 building your mound at the head of every street and making your elevated place in every square. But you were unlike a prostitute because you scorned payment. 32 You adulterous wife, who receives strangers instead of her husband! 33 Men give gifts to all prostitutes, but you gave gifts to all your lovers. You bribed them to come to you from all around for your sexual favors. 34 So you were the opposite of other women in your acts of prostitution; no one solicited you. When you paid a fee instead of one being paid to you, you were the opposite.

35 " 'Therefore, you prostitute, hear the word of the LORD! 36 This is what the Lord GOD says: Because your lust was poured out and your nakedness exposed by your acts of prostitution with your lovers, and because of all your detestable idols and the blood of your children that you gave to them, 37 I am therefore going to gather all the lovers you pleased — all those you loved as well as all those you hated. I will gather them against you from all around and expose your nakedness to them so they see you completely naked. 38 I will judge you the way adulteresses and those who shed blood are judged. Then I will bring about the shedding of your blood in jealous wrath. 39 I will hand you over to them, and they will demolish your mounds and tear down your elevated places. They will strip off your clothes, take your beautiful jewelry, and leave you stark naked. 40 They will bring a mob against you to stone you and to cut you to pieces with their swords. 41 They will burn your houses and execute judgments against you in the sight of many women. I will stop you from being a prostitute, and you will never again pay fees for lovers. 42 So I will satisfy my wrath against you, and my jealousy will turn away from you. Then I will be calm and no longer angry. 43 Because you did not remember the days of your youth but enraged me with all these things, I will also bring your conduct down on your own head. This is the declaration of the Lord GOD. Haven't you committed depravity in addition to all your detestable practices?

44 " 'Look, everyone who uses proverbs will quote this proverb about you: "Like mother, like daughter." 45 You are the daughter of your mother, who despised her husband and children. You are the sister of your sisters, who despised their husbands and children. Your mother was a Hethite and your father an Amorite. 46 Your older sister was Samaria, who lived with her daughters to the north of you, and your younger sister was Sodom, who lived with her daughters to the south of you. 47 Didn't you walk in their ways and do their detestable practices? It was only a short time before all your ways were more corrupt than theirs.

48 " 'As I live — the declaration of the Lord GOD — your sister Sodom and her daughters have not behaved as you and your daughters have. 49 Now this was the iniquity of your sister Sodom: She and her daughters had pride, plenty of food, and comfortable security, but didn't support[B] the poor and needy. 50 They were haughty and did detestable acts before me, so I removed them when I saw this.[C] 51 But

[A] **16:30** Or *was sick* [B] **16:49** Lit *strengthen the hand of* [C] **16:50** Or *them as you have seen*

Samaria did not commit even half your sins. You have multiplied your detestable practices beyond theirs and made your sisters appear righteous by all the detestable acts you have committed. 52 You must also bear your disgrace, since you have helped your sisters out.[A] For they appear more righteous than you because of your sins, which you committed more detestably than they did. So you also, be ashamed and bear your disgrace, since you have made your sisters appear righteous.

53 " 'I will restore their fortunes, the fortunes of Sodom and her daughters and those of Samaria and her daughters. I will also restore[B] your fortunes among them, 54 so you will bear your disgrace and be ashamed of all you did when you comforted them. 55 As for your sisters, Sodom and her daughters and Samaria and her daughters will return to their former state. You and your daughters will also return to your former state. 56 Didn't you treat your sister Sodom as an object of scorn when you were proud, 57 before your wickedness was exposed? It was like the time you were scorned by the daughters of Aram[C] and all those around her, and by the daughters of the Philistines — those who treated you with contempt from every side. 58 You yourself must bear the consequences of your depravity and detestable practices — this is the LORD's declaration.

59 " 'For this is what the Lord GOD says: I will deal with you according to what you have done, since you have despised the oath by breaking the covenant. 60 But I will remember the covenant I made with you in the days of your youth, and I will establish a permanent covenant with you. 61 Then you will remember your ways and be ashamed when you[D] receive your older and younger sisters. I will give them to you as daughters, but not because of your covenant. 62 I will establish my covenant with you, and you will know that I am the LORD, 63 so that when I make atonement for all you have done, you will remember and be ashamed, and never open your mouth again because of your disgrace. This is the declaration of the Lord GOD.' "

PARABLE OF THE EAGLES

17 The word of the LORD came to me: 2 "Son of man, pose a riddle and speak a parable to the house of Israel. 3 You are to say, 'This is what the Lord GOD says: A huge eagle with powerful wings, long feathers, and full plumage of many colors came to Lebanon and took the top of the cedar. 4 He plucked off its topmost shoot, brought it to the land of merchants, and set it in a city of traders. 5 Then he took some of the land's seed and put it in a fertile field; he set it like a willow, a plant[E] by abundant water. 6 It sprouted and became a spreading vine, low in height with its branches turned toward him, yet its roots stayed under it. So it became a vine, produced branches, and sent out shoots.

7 " 'But there was another huge eagle with powerful wings and thick plumage. And this vine bent its roots toward him! It stretched out its branches to him from the plot where it was planted, so that he might water it. 8 It had been planted in a good field by abundant water in order to produce branches, bear fruit, and become a splendid vine.'

9 "You are to say, 'This is what the Lord GOD says: Will it flourish? Will he not tear out its roots and strip off its fruit so that it shrivels? All its fresh leaves will wither! Great strength and many people will not be needed to pull it from its roots. 10 Even though it is planted, will it flourish? Won't it wither completely when the east wind strikes it? It will wither on the plot where it sprouted.' "

11 The word of the LORD came to me: 12 "Now say to that rebellious house, 'Don't you know what these things mean?' Tell them, 'The king of Babylon came to Jerusalem, took its king and officials, and brought them back with him to Babylon. 13 He took one of the royal family and made a covenant with him, putting him under oath. Then he took away the leading men of the land, 14 so that the kingdom would be humble and not exalt itself but would keep his covenant in order to endure. 15 However, this king revolted against him by sending his ambassadors to Egypt so they might give him horses and a large army. Will he flourish? Will the one who does such things escape? Can he break a covenant and still escape?

16 " 'As I live — this is the declaration of the Lord GOD — he will die in Babylon, in the land of the king who put him on the throne, whose oath he despised and whose covenant he broke. 17 Pharaoh with his mighty army and vast company will not help him in battle, when ramps are built and siege walls constructed to destroy many lives. 18 He despised the oath by

[A] **16:52** Lit *you have been the advocate for your sisters* [B] **16:53** LXX, Vg; MT reads *Samaria and her daughters and the fortunes of* [C] **16:57** Some Hb mss, Syr read *Edom* [D] **16:61** Some LXX mss, Syr read *I* [E] **17:5** Hb obscure

breaking the covenant. He did all these things even though he gave his hand in pledge. He will not escape!
[19] " 'Therefore, this is what the Lord GOD says: As I live, I will bring down on his head my oath that he despised and my covenant that he broke. [20] I will spread my net over him, and he will be caught in my snare. I will bring him to Babylon and execute judgment on him there for the treachery he committed against me.
[21] All the fugitives[A] among his troops will fall by the sword, and those who survive will be scattered to every direction of the wind. Then you will know that I, the LORD, have spoken.
[22] " 'This is what the Lord GOD says:

I will take a sprig
from the lofty top of the cedar
and plant it.
I will pluck a tender sprig
from its topmost shoots,
and I will plant it
on a high towering mountain.
23 I will plant it on Israel's
high mountain
so that it may bear branches,
produce fruit,
and become a majestic cedar.
Birds of every kind will nest under it,
taking shelter in the shade
of its branches.
24 Then all the trees of the field will know
that I am the LORD.
I bring down the tall tree,
and make the low tree tall.
I cause the green tree to wither
and make the withered tree thrive.
I, the LORD, have spoken
and I will do it.' "

PERSONAL RESPONSIBILITY FOR SIN

18 The word of the LORD came to me: [2] "What do you mean by using this proverb concerning the land of Israel:

'The fathers eat sour grapes,
and the children's teeth are set on edge'?

[3] As I live" — this is the declaration of the Lord GOD — "you will no longer use this proverb in Israel. [4] Look, every life belongs to me. The life of the father is like the life of the son — both belong to me. The person who sins is the one who will die.
[5] "Suppose a man is righteous and does what is just and right: [6] He does not eat at the mountain shrines[B] or look to the idols of the house of Israel. He does not defile his neighbor's wife or approach a woman during her menstrual impurity. [7] He doesn't oppress anyone but returns his collateral to the debtor. He does not commit robbery, but gives his bread to the hungry and covers the naked with clothing. [8] He doesn't lend at interest or for profit but keeps his hand from injustice and carries out true justice between men. [9] He follows my statutes and keeps my ordinances, acting faithfully. Such a person is righteous; he will certainly live." This is the declaration of the Lord GOD.
[10] "But suppose the man has a violent son, who sheds blood and does any of these things,
[11] though the father has done none of them. Indeed, when the son eats at the mountain shrines and defiles his neighbor's wife, [12] and when he oppresses the poor and needy, commits robbery, and does not return collateral, and when he looks to the idols, commits detestable acts, [13] and lends at interest or for profit, will he live? He will not live! Since he has committed all these detestable acts, he will certainly die. His death will be his own fault.[C]
[14] "Now suppose he has a son who sees all the sins his father has committed, and though he sees them, he does not do likewise. [15] He does not eat at the mountain shrines or look to the idols of the house of Israel. He does not defile his neighbor's wife. [16] He doesn't oppress anyone, hold collateral, or commit robbery. He gives his bread to the hungry and covers the naked with clothing. [17] He keeps his hand from harming the poor, not taking interest or profit on a loan. He practices my ordinances and follows my statutes. Such a person will not die for his father's iniquity. He will certainly live.
[18] "As for his father, he will die for his own iniquity because he practiced fraud, robbed his brother, and did among his people what was not good. [19] But you may ask, 'Why doesn't the son suffer punishment for the father's iniquity?' Since the son has done what is just and right, carefully observing all my statutes, he will certainly live. [20] The person who sins is the one who will die. A son won't suffer punishment for the father's iniquity, and a father won't suffer punishment for the son's iniquity. The righteousness of the righteous

[A] **17:21** Some Hb mss, LXX, Syr, Tg read *choice men* [B] **18:6** Lit *the mountains*, also in vv. 11,15 [C] **18:13** Lit *His blood will be on him*

My Story | Sherry

Growing up in the 50s, I would have to say that my childhood self-identity was "a good girl." I was naïve, protected, and careful not to step out of line. I couldn't imagine doing anything that would hurt my mother's feelings. Now I realize that part of my home life was shaped by the painful fact that my older sister had died shortly after I was born and that I had a younger brother who also had died not long after birth. Both my siblings were born with health problems they could not overcome. I instinctively tried hard not to bring any added pain into our home. Later, a little sister arrived, and we grew up together.

Around the time that I was ten, my parents, who had been driven to seek God's help during their grief, found that the church they were attending was increasingly disconnected from what they felt was a genuine faith in God. The Bible was devalued, and Jesus was demoted to some sort of wise teacher who probably lived but certainly didn't actually rise from the dead. Hope of the resurrection was one of the things that had gotten my parents through their devastating loses. They began to search for a new church.

My uncle introduced them to an amazing lady who had a ministry sharing the gospel while she did chalk drawings that illustrated her message. She visited our home to meet with my parents and suggested that I listen to the conversation. We sat around the kitchen table as she answered my parents' questions and very simply told the gospel story. At one point she turned to me and said, "Sherry, would you like to be forgiven of your sins and know you are going to heaven after this life?"

In my little mind, I remember thinking, "Who wouldn't want to go to heaven?" Saying yes was easy. My mother was already a believer, but my father and I trusted Jesus as our Savior that night.

I know I have had a lot to learn, but the experience I had when I went to bed later was unforgettable. A weight was lifted from my soul. I seemed to have a glow of contentment and peace even in my dark room. I understood that I no longer had to worry about being good enough; I sensed I was forgiven.

Years later, when I'm confused or tired of life, God steers my mind back to that evening and renews me with the reality of his presence that has never left me since he entered my life with light.

person will be on him, and the wickedness of
the wicked person will be on him.
21 "But if the wicked person turns from all
the sins he has committed, keeps all my statutes, and does what is just and right, he will
certainly live; he will not die. 22 None of the
transgressions he has committed will be held
against him. He will live because of the righteousness he has practiced. 23 Do I take any
pleasure in the death of the wicked?" This
is the declaration of the Lord God. "Instead,
don't I take pleasure when he turns from his
ways and lives? 24 But when a righteous person
turns from his righteousness and acts unjustly,
committing the same detestable acts that the
wicked do, will he live? None of the righteous
acts he did will be remembered. He will die
because of the treachery he has engaged in
and the sin he has committed.
25 "But you say, 'The Lord's way isn't fair.'
Now listen, house of Israel: Is it my way that
is unfair? Instead, isn't it your ways that are
unfair? 26 When a righteous person turns from
his righteousness and acts unjustly, he will die
for this. He will die because of the injustice
he has committed. 27 But if a wicked person
turns from the wickedness he has committed
and does what is just and right, he will preserve his life. 28 He will certainly live because
he thought it over and turned from all the
transgressions he had committed; he will not
die. 29 But the house of Israel says, 'The Lord's
way isn't fair.' Is it my ways that are unfair,
house of Israel? Instead, isn't it your ways
that are unfair?
30 "Therefore, house of Israel, I will judge
each one of you according to his ways." This is
the declaration of the Lord God. "Repent and
turn from all your rebellious acts, so they will
not become a sinful stumbling block to you.
31 Throw off all the transgressions you have
committed, and get yourselves a new heart
and a new spirit. Why should you die, house
of Israel? 32 For I take no pleasure in anyone's
death." This is the declaration of the Lord God.
"So repent and live!

A LAMENT FOR ISRAEL'S PRINCES

19 "As for you, take up a lament for the princes of Israel, 2 and say:
What was your mother? A lioness!
She lay down among the lions;
she reared her cubs
among the young lions.
3 She brought up one of her cubs,
and he became a young lion.
After he learned to tear prey,
he devoured people.
4 When the nations heard about him,
he was caught in their pit.
Then they led him away with hooks
to the land of Egypt.

5 When she saw that she waited in vain,
that her hope was lost,
she took another of her cubs
and made him a young lion.
6 He prowled among the lions,
and he became a young lion.
After he learned to tear prey,
he devoured people.
7 He devastated their strongholds[A]
and destroyed their cities.
The land and everything in it shuddered
at the sound of his roaring.
8 Then the nations from
the surrounding provinces
set out against him.
They spread their net over him;
he was caught in their pit.
9 They put a wooden yoke on him[B]
with hooks
and led him away to the king
of Babylon.
They brought him into the fortresses
so his roar could no longer be heard
on the mountains of Israel.

10 Your mother was like a vine
in your vineyard,[C]
planted by the water;
it was fruitful and full of branches
because of abundant water.
11 It had strong branches, fit for
the scepters of rulers;
its height towered among the clouds.[D]
So it was conspicuous for its height
as well as its many branches.
12 But it was uprooted in fury,
thrown to the ground,
and the east wind dried up its fruit.
Its strong branches were torn off
and dried up;
fire consumed them.
13 Now it is planted in the wilderness,
in a dry and thirsty land.
14 Fire has gone out from its main branch[E]
and has devoured its fruit,
so that it no longer has a strong branch,
a scepter for ruling.

This is a lament and should be used as a lament."

ISRAEL'S REBELLION

20 In the seventh year, in the fifth month,
on the tenth day of the month, some
of Israel's elders came to inquire of the LORD,
and they sat down in front of me. 2 Then the
word of the LORD came to me: 3 "Son of man,
speak with the elders of Israel and tell them,
'This is what the Lord GOD says: Are you coming to inquire of me? As I live, I will not let
you inquire of me. This is the declaration of
the Lord GOD.'
4 "Will you pass judgment against them, will
you pass judgment, son of man? Explain the
detestable practices of their fathers to them.
5 Say to them, 'This is what the Lord GOD says:
On the day I chose Israel, I swore an oath[F] to
the descendants of Jacob's house and made
myself known to them in the land of Egypt.
I swore to them, saying, "I am the LORD your
God." 6 On that day I swore[G] to them that I would
bring them out of the land of Egypt into a land
I had searched out for them, a land flowing
with milk and honey, the most beautiful of all
lands. 7 I also said to them, "Throw away, each
of you, the abhorrent things that you prize,[H]
and do not defile yourselves with the idols of
Egypt. I am the LORD your God."
8 "'But they rebelled against me and were
unwilling to listen to me. None of them threw
away the abhorrent things that they prized,[I]
and they did not abandon the idols of Egypt.
So I considered pouring out my wrath on them,
exhausting my anger against them within the
land of Egypt. 9 But I acted for the sake of my
name, so that it would not be profaned in the
eyes of the nations they were living among,
in whose sight I had made myself known to
Israel by bringing them out of Egypt.

[A] **19:7** Tg, Aq; MT reads *knew their widows* [B] **19:9** Or *put him in a cage* [C] **19:10** Some Hb mss; other Hb mss read *blood* [D] **19:11** Or *thick foliage* [E] **19:14** Lit *from the branch of its parts* [F] **20:5** Lit *I lifted my hand* [G] **20:6** Lit *lifted my hand*, also in vv. 15,23,28,42 [H] **20:7** Lit *things of your eyes* [I] **20:8** Lit *things of their eyes*

10 " 'So I brought them out of the land of Egypt
and led them into the wilderness. 11 Then I gave
them my statutes and explained my ordinances
to them — the person who does them will
live by them. 12 I also gave them my Sabbaths
to serve as a sign between me and them, so
that they would know that I am the LORD who
consecrates them.
13 " 'But the house of Israel rebelled against
me in the wilderness. They did not follow my
statutes and they rejected my ordinances —
the person who does them will live by them.
They also completely profaned my Sabbaths.
So I considered pouring out my wrath on them
in the wilderness to put an end to them. 14 But I
acted for the sake of my name, so that it would
not be profaned in the eyes of the nations in
whose sight I had brought them out. 15 However,
I swore to them in the wilderness that I would
not bring them into the land I had given them
— the most beautiful of all lands, flowing with
milk and honey — 16 because they rejected
my ordinances, profaned my Sabbaths, and
did not follow my statutes. For their hearts
went after their idols. 17 Yet I spared them from
destruction and did not bring them to an end
in the wilderness.
18 " 'Then I said to their children in the wilderness, "Don't follow the statutes of your
fathers, defile yourselves with their idols, or
keep their ordinances. 19 I am the LORD your
God. Follow my statutes, keep my ordinances,
and practice them. 20 Keep my Sabbaths holy,
and they will be a sign between me and you, so
you may know that I am the LORD your God."
21 " 'But the children rebelled against me.
They did not follow my statutes or carefully
keep my ordinances — the person who does
them will live by them. They also profaned my
Sabbaths. So I considered pouring out my wrath
on them and exhausting my anger against
them in the wilderness. 22 But I withheld my
hand and acted for the sake of my name, so
that it would not be profaned in the eyes of
the nations in whose sight I brought them out.
23 However, I swore to them in the wilderness
that I would disperse them among the nations
and scatter them among the countries. 24 For
they did not practice my ordinances but rejected my statutes and profaned my Sabbaths,
and their eyes were fixed on their fathers'
idols. 25 I also gave them statutes that were
not good and ordinances they could not live
by. 26 When they sacrificed every firstborn in
the fire,[A] I defiled them through their gifts in
order to devastate them so they would know
that I am the LORD.'
27 "Therefore, son of man, speak to the house
of Israel, and tell them, 'This is what the Lord
GOD says: In this way also your fathers blasphemed me by committing treachery against
me: 28 When I brought them into the land that
I swore to give them and they saw any high
hill or leafy tree, they offered their sacrifices
and presented their offensive offerings there.
They also sent up their pleasing aromas and
poured out their drink offerings there. 29 So I
asked them, "What is this high place you are
going to?" And it is still called Bamah[B] today.'
30 "Therefore say to the house of Israel, 'This
is what the Lord GOD says: Are you defiling
yourselves the way your fathers did, and prostituting yourselves with their abhorrent things?
31 When you offer your gifts, sacrificing your
children in the fire,[C] you still continue to defile
yourselves with all your idols today. So should
I let you inquire of me, house of Israel? As I
live — this is the declaration of the Lord GOD
— I will not let you inquire of me!

ISRAEL'S RESTORATION

32 " 'When you say, "Let us be like the nations,
like the clans of other countries, serving wood
and stone," what you have in mind will never
happen. 33 As I live — the declaration of the
Lord GOD — I will reign over you with a strong
hand, an outstretched arm, and outpoured
wrath. 34 I will bring you from the peoples
and gather you from the countries where you
were scattered, with a strong hand, an outstretched arm, and outpoured wrath. 35 I will
lead you into the wilderness of the peoples
and enter into judgment with you there face
to face. 36 Just as I entered into judgment with
your fathers in the wilderness of the land of
Egypt, so I will enter into judgment with you.
This is the declaration of the Lord GOD. 37 I will
make you pass under the rod and will bring
you into the bond of the covenant. 38 I will
purge you of those who rebel and transgress
against me. I will bring them out of the land
where they live as foreign residents, but they
will not enter the land of Israel. Then you will
know that I am the LORD.
39 " 'As for you, house of Israel, this is what
the Lord GOD says: Go and serve your idols,

[A] **20:26** Lit *they made every firstborn pass through the fire* [B] **20:29** = High Place [C] **20:31** Lit *gifts, making your children pass through the fire*

each of you. But afterward you will surely
listen to me, and you will no longer defile my
holy name with your gifts and idols. 40 For on
my holy mountain, Israel's high mountain —
the declaration of the Lord GOD — there the
entire house of Israel, all of them, will serve
me in the land. There I will accept them and
will require your contributions and choicest
gifts, all your holy offerings. 41 When I bring
you from the peoples and gather you from
the countries where you have been scattered,
I will accept you as a pleasing aroma. And I
will demonstrate my holiness through you
in the sight of the nations. 42 When I lead you
into the land of Israel, the land I swore to give
your fathers, you will know that I am the LORD.
43 There you will remember your ways and all
your deeds by which you have defiled yourself,
and you will loathe yourselves for all the evil
things you have done. 44 You will know that
I am the LORD, house of Israel, when I have
dealt with you for the sake of my name rather
than according to your evil ways and corrupt
acts. This is the declaration of the Lord GOD.' "

FIRE IN THE SOUTH

45 The word of the LORD came to me: 46 "Son
of man, face the south and preach against it.
Prophesy against the forest land in the Negev,
47 and say to the forest there, 'Hear the word of
the LORD! This is what the Lord GOD says: I am
about to ignite a fire in you, and it will devour
every green tree and every dry tree in you.
The blazing flame will not be extinguished,
and every face from the south to the north
will be scorched by it. 48 Then all people will
see that I, the LORD, have kindled it. It will not
be extinguished.' "

49 Then I said, "Oh, Lord GOD, they are saying
of me, 'Isn't he just composing parables?' "

GOD'S SWORD OF JUDGMENT

21 The word of the LORD came to me again:
2 "Son of man, face Jerusalem and preach
against the sanctuaries. Prophesy against the
land of Israel, 3 and say to it, 'This is what the
LORD says: I am against you. I will draw my
sword from its sheath and cut off from you
both the righteous and the wicked. 4 Since I
will cut off[A] both the righteous and the wicked, my sword will therefore come out of its
sheath against all people from the south to
the north. 5 So all people will know that I, the
LORD, have taken my sword from its sheath
— it will not be sheathed again.'

6 "But you, son of man, groan! Groan bitterly with a broken heart[B] right before their
eyes. 7 And when they ask you, 'Why are you
groaning?' then say, 'Because of the news that
is coming. Every heart will melt, and every
hand will become weak. Every spirit will be
discouraged, and all knees will run with urine.[C]
Yes, it is coming and it will happen. This is the
declaration of the Lord GOD.' "

8 The word of the LORD came to me: 9 "Son of
man, prophesy, 'This is what the Lord says!'
You are to proclaim,

'A sword! A sword is sharpened
and also polished.
10 It is sharpened for slaughter,
polished to flash like lightning!
Should we rejoice?
The scepter of my son,
the sword despises every tree.[D]
11 The sword is given to be polished,
to be grasped in the hand.
It is sharpened, and it is polished,
to be put in the hand of the slayer.'

12 "Cry out and wail, son of man, for it is against
my people. It is against all the princes of Israel!
They are given over to the sword with my people.
Therefore strike your thigh in grief. 13 Surely it
will be a trial! And what if the sword despises
even the scepter? The scepter will not continue."[D] This is the declaration of the Lord GOD.

14 "So you, son of man, prophesy and clap
your hands together:

Let the sword strike two times,
even three.
It is a sword for massacre,
a sword for great massacre —
it surrounds[E] them!
15 I have appointed a sword for slaughter[D]
at all their gates,
so that their hearts may melt
and many may stumble.
Yes! It is ready to flash like lightning;
it is drawn[D] for slaughter.
16 Slash to the right;
turn to the left —
wherever your blade is directed.

17 I also will clap my hands together, and I will
satisfy my wrath. I, the LORD, have spoken."

18 The word of the LORD came to me: 19 "Now
you, son of man, mark out two roads that the

[A] 21:4 Lit *off from you* [B] 21:6 Lit *insides*, or *waist* [C] 21:7 Lit *knees will go water* [D] 21:10,13,15 Hb obscure [E] 21:14 Or *penetrates*

sword of Babylon's king can take. Both of them
should originate from the same land. And make
a signpost at the fork in the road to each city.
20 Mark out a road that the sword can take to
Rabbah of the Ammonites and to Judah into
fortified Jerusalem. 21 For the king of Babylon
stands at the split in the road, at the fork of the
two roads, to practice divination: he shakes
the arrows, consults the idols, and observes
the liver. 22 The answer marked[A] Jerusalem
appears in his right hand, indicating that he
should set up battering rams, give the order
to[B] slaughter, raise a battle cry, set battering
rams against the gates, build a ramp, and construct a siege wall. 23 It will seem like false
divination to those who have sworn an oath
to the Babylonians,[C] but it will draw attention
to their guilt so that they will be captured.
24 "Therefore, this is what the Lord GOD says:
Because you have drawn attention to your guilt,
exposing your transgressions, so that your sins
are revealed in all your actions — since you
have done this, you will be captured by them.
25 And you, profane and wicked prince of Israel,[D] the day has come for your punishment.[E]
26 "This is what the Lord GOD says:

Remove the turban, and take off
the crown.
Things will not remain as they are;[F]
exalt the lowly and bring down
the exalted.
27 A ruin, a ruin,
I will make it a ruin!
Yet this will not happen
until he comes;
I have given the judgment to him.[G]

28 "Now you, son of man, prophesy, and say,
'This is what the Lord GOD says concerning
the Ammonites and their contempt.' You are
to proclaim,

'A sword! A sword
is drawn for slaughter,
polished to consume, to flash
like lightning.
29 While they offer false visions
and lying divinations about you,
the time has come to put you
to the necks of the profane wicked ones;
the day has come
for final punishment.
30 " 'Return it to its sheath!

" 'I will judge you[H]
in the place where you were created,
in the land of your origin.
31 I will pour out my indignation on you;
I will blow the fire of my fury on you.
I will hand you over to brutal men,
skilled at destruction.
32 You will be fuel for the fire.
Your blood will be spilled
within the land.
You will not be remembered,
for I, the LORD, have spoken.' "

INDICTMENT OF SINFUL JERUSALEM

22 The word of the LORD came to me: 2 "As
for you, son of man, will you pass judgment? Will you pass judgment against the
city of blood? Then explain all her detestable
practices to her. 3 You are to say, 'This is what
the Lord GOD says: A city that sheds blood
within her walls so that her time of judgment
has come and who makes idols for herself so
that she is defiled! 4 You are guilty of the blood
you have shed, and you are defiled from the
idols you have made. You have brought your
judgment[I] days near and have come to your
years of punishment.[J] Therefore, I have made
you a disgrace to the nations and a mockery to
all the lands. 5 Those who are near and those
far away from you will mock you, you infa-
mous one full of turmoil.
6 " 'Look, every prince of Israel within you
has used his strength to shed blood. 7 Father
and mother are treated with contempt, and
the resident alien is exploited within you.
The fatherless and widow are oppressed in
you. 8 You despise my holy things and profane my Sabbaths. 9 There are men within you
who slander in order to shed blood. People
who live in you eat at the mountain shrines;[K]
they commit depraved acts within you. 10 Men
within you have sexual intercourse with their
father's wife and violate women during their
menstrual impurity. 11 One man within you
commits a detestable act with his neighbor's
wife; another defiles his daughter-in-law with
depravity; and yet another violates his sister,
his father's daughter. 12 People who live in you
accept bribes in order to shed blood. You take

[A] **21:22** Lit *The divination for* [B] **21:22** Lit *rams, open the mouth in* [C] **21:23** Lit *them* [D] **21:25** = King Zedekiah [E] **21:25** Lit *come in the time of the punishment of the end*, also in v. 29 [F] **21:26** Lit *This not this* [G] **21:27** Or *comes to whom it rightfully belongs, and I will give it to him* [H] **21:30** = the Ammonites [I] **22:4** *judgment* supplied for clarity [J] **22:4** *punishment* supplied for clarity [K] **22:9** Lit *the mountains*

interest and profit on a loan and brutally extort your neighbors. You have forgotten me. This is the declaration of the Lord GOD.

13 "'Now look, I clap my hands together against the dishonest profit you have made and against the blood shed among you. 14 Will your courage endure or your hands be strong in the days when I deal with you? I, the LORD, have spoken, and I will act. 15 I will disperse you among the nations and scatter you among the countries; I will purge your uncleanness. 16 You[A] will be profaned in the sight of the nations. Then you will know that I am the LORD.'"

JERUSALEM AS GOD'S FURNACE

17 The word of the LORD came to me: 18 "Son of man, the house of Israel has become merely dross to me. All of them are copper, tin, iron, and lead inside the furnace; they are just dross from silver. 19 Therefore, this is what the Lord GOD says: Because all of you have become dross, I am about to gather you into Jerusalem. 20 Just as one gathers silver, copper, iron, lead, and tin into the furnace to blow fire on them and melt them, so I will gather you in my anger and wrath, put you inside, and melt you. 21 Yes, I will gather you together and blow on you with the fire of my fury, and you will be melted within the city. 22 As silver is melted inside a furnace, so you will be melted inside the city. Then you will know that I, the LORD, have poured out my wrath on you."

INDICTMENT OF A SINFUL LAND

23 The word of the LORD came to me: 24 "Son of man, say to her, 'You are a land that has not been cleansed, that has not received rain in the day of indignation.' 25 The conspiracy of her prophets within her is[B] like a roaring lion tearing its prey: they devour people, seize wealth and valuables, and multiply the widows within her. 26 Her priests do violence to my instruction and profane my holy things. They make no distinction between the holy and the common, and they do not explain the difference between the clean and the unclean. They close their eyes to my Sabbaths, and I am profaned among them.

27 "Her officials within her are like wolves tearing their prey, shedding blood, and destroying lives in order to make profit dishonestly. 28 Her prophets plaster for them with whitewash by seeing false visions and lying divinations, saying, 'This is what the Lord GOD says,' when the LORD has not spoken. 29 The people of the land have practiced extortion and committed robbery. They have oppressed the poor and needy and unlawfully exploited the resident alien. 30 I searched for a man among them who would repair the wall and stand in the gap before me on behalf of the land so that I might not destroy it, but I found no one. 31 So I have poured out my indignation on them and consumed them with the fire of my fury. I have brought their conduct down on their own heads." This is the declaration of the Lord GOD.

THE TWO IMMORAL SISTERS

23 The word of the LORD came to me again: 2 "Son of man, there were two women, daughters of the same mother, 3 who acted like prostitutes in Egypt, behaving promiscuously in their youth. Their breasts were fondled there, and their virgin nipples caressed. 4 The older one was named Oholah,[C] and her sister was Oholibah.[D] They became mine and gave birth to sons and daughters. As for their names, Oholah represents Samaria and Oholibah represents Jerusalem.

5 "Oholah acted like a prostitute even though she was mine. She lusted after her lovers, the Assyrians: warriors 6 dressed in blue, governors and prefects, all of them desirable young men, horsemen riding on steeds. 7 She offered her sexual favors to them; all of them were the elite of Assyria. She defiled herself with all those she lusted after and with all their idols. 8 She didn't give up her promiscuity that began in Egypt, when men slept with her in her youth, caressed her virgin nipples, and poured out their lust on her. 9 Therefore, I handed her over to her lovers, the Assyrians she lusted for. 10 They exposed her nakedness, seized her sons and daughters, and killed her with the sword. Since they executed judgment against her, she became notorious among women.

11 "Now her sister Oholibah saw this, but she was even more depraved in her lust than Oholah, and made her promiscuous acts worse than those of her sister. 12 She lusted after the Assyrians: governors and prefects, warriors splendidly dressed, horsemen riding on steeds, all of them desirable young men. 13 And I saw that she had defiled herself; both of them had taken the same path. 14 But she increased her

[A] **22:16** One Hb ms, LXX, Syr, Vg read *I* [B] **22:24-25** LXX reads *indignation,* [25]*whose princes within her are* [C] **23:4** = Her Tent [D] **23:4** = My Tent Is in Her

promiscuity when she saw male figures carved
on the wall, images of the Chaldeans, engraved
in bright red, 15 wearing belts on their waists
and flowing turbans on their heads; all of them
looked like officers, a depiction of the Babylonians in Chaldea, their native land. 16 At the
sight of them[A] she lusted after them and sent
messengers to them in Chaldea. 17 Then the
Babylonians came to her, to the bed of love,
and defiled her with their lust. But after she
was defiled by them, she turned away from
them in disgust. 18 When she flaunted her promiscuity and exposed her nakedness, I turned
away from her in disgust just as I turned away
from her sister. 19 Yet she multiplied her acts
of promiscuity, remembering the days of her
youth when she acted like a prostitute in the
land of Egypt 20 and lusted after their lovers,
whose sexual members[B] were like those of
donkeys and whose emission was like that
of stallions. 21 So you revisited the depravity
of your youth, when the Egyptians caressed
your nipples to enjoy your youthful breasts.

22 "Therefore, Oholibah, this is what the
Lord God says: I am going to incite your
lovers against you, those you turned away
from in disgust. I will bring them against you
from every side: 23 the Babylonians and all
the Chaldeans; Pekod, Shoa, and Koa; and all
the Assyrians with them — desirable young
men, all of them governors and prefects, officers and administrators, all of them riding on
steeds. 24 They will come against you with an
assembly of peoples and with weapons, chariots, and[C] wagons. They will set themselves
against you on every side with large and small
shields and helmets. I will delegate judgment
to them, and they will judge you by their own
standards. 25 When I vent my jealous rage on
you, they will deal with you in wrath. They
will cut off your nose and ears, and the rest
of you[D] will fall by the sword. They will seize
your sons and daughters, and the rest of you
will be consumed by fire. 26 They will strip off
your clothes and take your beautiful jewelry.
27 So I will put an end to your depravity and
sexual immorality, which began in the land
of Egypt, and you will not look longingly at
them or remember Egypt anymore.

28 "For this is what the Lord God says: I am
going to hand you over to those you hate, to
those you turned away from in disgust. 29 They
will treat you with hatred, take all you have
worked for, and leave you stark naked, so that
the shame of your debauchery will be exposed,
both your depravity and promiscuity. 30 These
things will be done to you because you acted like a prostitute with the nations, defiling
yourself with their idols. 31 You have followed
the path of your sister, so I will put her cup
in your hand."

32 This is what the Lord God says:

"You will drink your sister's cup,
which is deep and wide.
You will be an object of[E] ridicule
  and scorn,
for it holds so much.
33 You will be filled with drunkenness
  and grief,
with a cup of devastation
  and desolation,
the cup of your sister Samaria.
34 You will drink it and drain it;
then you will gnaw its broken pieces,
and tear your breasts.
For I have spoken."
  This is the declaration
  of the Lord God.

35 Therefore, this is what the Lord God says:
"Because you have forgotten me and cast me
behind your back, you must bear the consequences of your indecency and promiscuity."
36 Then the Lord said to me: "Son of man, will
you pass judgment against Oholah and Oholibah? Then declare their detestable practices to
them. 37 For they have committed adultery, and
blood is on their hands; they have committed
adultery with their idols. And the children they
bore to me they have sacrificed in the fire[F] as
food for the idols. 38 They also did this to me:
they defiled my sanctuary on that same day
and profaned my Sabbaths. 39 On the same
day they slaughtered their children for their
idols, they entered my sanctuary to profane
it. Yes, that is what they did inside my house.

40 "In addition, they sent for men who came
from far away when a messenger was dispatched to them. And look how they came!
You bathed, painted your eyes, and adorned
yourself with jewelry for them. 41 You sat on
a luxurious couch with a table spread before
it, on which you had set my incense and oil.
42 The sound of a carefree crowd was there.
Drunkards[G] from the desert were brought in,
along with common men. They put bracelets

[A] 23:16 Lit *of her eyes* [B] 23:20 Lit *whose flesh* [C] 23:24 LXX reads *peoples, from the north, chariots and*; Hb obscure
[D] 23:25 Or *and your descendants* [E] 23:32 Or *It will bring* [F] 23:37 Lit *have made pass through the fire* [G] 23:42 Or *Sabeans*

on the women's hands and beautiful tiaras
on their heads. 43 Then I said concerning this
woman worn out by adultery: Will they[A] now
have illicit sex with her, even her? 44 Yet they
had sex with her as one does with a prostitute.
This is how they had sex with Oholah and Oholibah, those depraved women. 45 But righteous
men will judge them the way adulteresses and
those who shed blood are judged, for they
are adulteresses and blood is on their hands.
46 "This is what the Lord GOD says: Summon[B]
an assembly against them and consign them to
terror and plunder. 47 The assembly will stone
them and cut them down with their swords.
They will kill their sons and daughters and
burn their houses. 48 So I will put an end to
depravity in the land, and all the women will
be admonished not to imitate your depraved
behavior. 49 They will punish you for your depravity, and you will bear the consequences
for your sins of idolatry. Then you will know
that I am the Lord GOD."

PARABLE OF THE BOILING POT

24 The word of the LORD came to me in
the ninth year, in the tenth month, on
the tenth day of the month: 2 "Son of man,
write down today's date, this very day. The
king of Babylon has laid siege to Jerusalem
this very day. 3 Now speak a parable to the
rebellious house. Tell them, 'This is what the
Lord GOD says:

Put the pot on the fire —
put it on,
and then pour water into it!
4 Place the pieces of meat in it,
every good piece —
thigh and shoulder.
Fill it with choice bones.
5 Take the choicest of the flock
and also pile up the fuel[C] under it.
Bring it to a boil
and cook the bones in it.

6 " 'Therefore, this is what the Lord GOD says:
Woe to the city of bloodshed,
the pot that has corrosion inside it,
and its corrosion has not come out of it!
Empty it piece by piece;
lots should not be cast for its contents.
7 For the blood she shed[D] is still within her.
She put it out on the bare rock;
she didn't pour it on the ground
to cover it with dust.
8 In order to stir up wrath
and take vengeance,
I have put her blood on the bare rock,
so that it would not be covered.

9 " 'Therefore, this is what the Lord GOD says:
Woe to the city of bloodshed!
I myself will make the pile
of kindling large.
10 Pile on the logs and kindle the fire!
Cook the meat well
and mix in the spices![E,F]
Let the bones be burned!
11 Set the empty pot on its coals
so that it becomes hot
and its copper glows.
Then its impurity will melt inside it;
its corrosion will be consumed.
12 It has frustrated every effort;[G]
its thick corrosion will not come off.
Into the fire with its corrosion!
13 Because of the depravity
of your uncleanness
since I tried to purify you,
but you would not be purified
from your uncleanness —
you will not be pure again
until I have satisfied
my wrath on you.
14 I, the LORD, have spoken.
It is coming, and I will do it!
I will not refrain, I will not show pity,
and I will not relent.
I[H] will judge you
according to your ways and deeds.
This is the declaration
of the Lord GOD.' "

THE DEATH OF EZEKIEL'S WIFE: A SIGN

15 Then the word of the LORD came to me: 16 "Son
of man, I am about to take the delight of your
eyes away from you with a fatal blow. But you
must not lament or weep or let your tears flow.
17 Groan quietly; do not observe mourning
rites for the dead. Put on your turban and
strap your sandals on your feet; do not cover
your mustache or eat the bread of mourners."[I]
18 I spoke to the people in the morning, and
my wife died in the evening. The next morning I did just as I was commanded. 19 Then the

[A] **23:43** Or *They will* [B] **23:46** Or *I will summon* [C] **24:5** Lit *bones* [D] **24:7** Lit *For her blood* [E] **24:10** Some Hb mss read *well; remove the broth*; LXX reads *fire so that the meat may be cooked and the broth may be reduced* [F] **24:10** Or *and stir the broth* [G] **24:12** Hb obscure [H] **24:14** Some Hb mss, LXX, Syr, Tg, Vg; other Hb mss read *They* [I] **24:17** Lit *men*, also in v. 22

people asked me, "Won't you tell us what these
things you are doing mean for us?"
20 So I answered them: "The word of the LORD
came to me: 21 Say to the house of Israel, 'This
is what the Lord GOD says: I am about to desecrate my sanctuary, the pride of your power, the delight of your eyes, and the desire of
your heart. Also, the sons and daughters you
left behind will fall by the sword. 22 Then you
will do just as I have done: You will not cover
your mustache or eat the bread of mourners.
23 Your turbans will remain on your heads and
your sandals on your feet. You will not lament
or weep but will waste away because of your
iniquities and will groan to one another. 24 Now
Ezekiel will be a sign for you. You will do everything that he has done. When this happens,
you will know that I am the Lord GOD.'
25 "As for you, son of man, know that on that
day I will take from them their stronghold
— their pride and joy, the delight of their eyes,
and the longing of their hearts — as well as
their sons and daughters. 26 On that day a fugitive will come to you and report the news.
27 On that day your mouth will be opened to
talk with him; you will speak and no longer
be mute. So you will be a sign for them, and
they will know that I am the LORD."

PROPHECIES AGAINST THE NATIONS

JUDGMENT AGAINST AMMON

25 Then the word of the LORD came to me:
2 "Son of man, face the Ammonites and
prophesy against them. 3 Say to the Ammonites,
'Hear the word of the Lord GOD: This is what
the Lord GOD says: Because you said, "Aha!"
about my sanctuary when it was desecrated, about the land of Israel when it was laid
waste, and about the house of Judah when
they went into exile, 4 therefore I am about
to give you to the people of the east as a possession. They will set up their encampments
and pitch their tents among you. They will eat
your fruit and drink your milk. 5 I will make
Rabbah a pasture for camels and Ammon a
resting place for sheep. Then you will know
that I am the LORD.
6 " 'For this is what the Lord GOD says: Because you clapped your hands, stamped your
feet, and rejoiced over the land of Israel with
wholehearted contempt, 7 therefore I am about
to stretch out my hand against you and give
you as plunder to the nations. I will cut you
off from the peoples and eliminate you from
the countries. I will destroy you, and you will
know that I am the LORD.

JUDGMENT AGAINST MOAB

8 " 'This is what the Lord GOD says: Because
Moab and Seir said, "Look, the house of Judah
is like all the other nations." 9 Therefore I am
about to expose Moab's flank beginning with
its[A] frontier cities, the splendor of the land:
Beth-jeshimoth, Baal-meon, and Kiriathaim.
10 I will give it along with Ammon to the people
of the east as a possession, so that Ammon will
not be remembered among the nations. 11 So
I will execute judgments against Moab, and
they will know that I am the LORD.

JUDGMENT AGAINST EDOM

12 " 'This is what the Lord GOD says: Because
Edom acted vengefully against the house of
Judah and incurred grievous guilt by taking
revenge on them, 13 therefore this is what
the Lord GOD says: I will stretch out my hand
against Edom and cut off both man and animal from it. I will make it a wasteland; they
will fall by the sword from Teman to Dedan.
14 I will take my vengeance on Edom through
my people Israel, and they will deal with Edom
according to my anger and wrath. So they will
know my vengeance. This is the declaration
of the Lord GOD.

JUDGMENT AGAINST PHILISTIA

15 " 'This is what the Lord GOD says: Because
the Philistines acted in vengeance and took
revenge with deep contempt, destroying because of their perpetual hatred, 16 therefore
this is what the Lord GOD says: I am about to
stretch out my hand against the Philistines,
cutting off the Cherethites and wiping out
what remains of the coastal peoples.[B] 17 I will
execute severe vengeance against them with
furious rebukes. They will know that I am the
LORD when I take my vengeance on them.' "

THE DOWNFALL OF TYRE

26 In the eleventh year, on the first day of
the month, the word of the LORD came
to me: 2 "Son of man, because Tyre said about
Jerusalem, 'Aha! The gateway to the peoples
is shattered. She has been turned over to
me.[C] I will be filled now that she lies in ruins,'

[A] 25:9 Lit *with the cities, with its* [B] 25:16 Lit *the seacoast* [C] 26:2 Or *It has swung open for me*

3 therefore this is what the Lord GOD says: See,
I am against you, Tyre! I will raise up many
nations against you, just as the sea raises its
waves. 4 They will destroy the walls of Tyre
and demolish her towers. I will scrape the soil
from her and turn her into a bare rock. 5 She
will become a place in the sea to spread nets,
for I have spoken." This is the declaration of
the Lord GOD. "She will become plunder for
the nations, 6 and her villages on the mainland
will be slaughtered by the sword. Then they
will know that I am the LORD."
7 For this is what the Lord GOD says: "See,
I am about to bring King Nebuchadnezzar[A]
of Babylon, king of kings, against Tyre from
the north with horses, chariots, cavalry, and
a huge assembly of troops. 8 He will slaughter your villages on the mainland with the
sword. He will set up siege works, build a ramp,
and raise a wall of shields against you. 9 He
will direct the blows of his battering rams
against your walls and tear down your towers
with his iron tools. 10 His horses will be so numerous that their dust will cover you. When
he enters your gates as an army entering a
breached city, your walls will shake from the
noise of cavalry, wagons, and chariots. 11 He
will trample all your streets with the hooves
of his horses. He will slaughter your people
with the sword, and your mighty pillars will
fall to the ground. 12 They will take your wealth
as spoil and plunder your merchandise. They
will also demolish your walls and tear down
your beautiful homes. Then they will throw
your stones, timber, and soil into the water.
13 I will put an end to the noise of your songs,
and the sound of your lyres will no longer be
heard. 14 I will turn you into a bare rock, and
you will be a place to spread nets. You will
never be rebuilt, for I, the LORD, have spoken."
This is the declaration of the Lord GOD.
15 This is what the Lord GOD says to Tyre:
"Won't the coasts and islands quake at the
sound of your downfall, when the wounded groan and slaughter occurs within you?
16 All the princes of the sea will descend from
their thrones, remove their robes, and strip
off their embroidered garments. They will
clothe themselves with trembling; they will
sit on the ground, tremble continually, and
be appalled at you. 17 Then they will lament
for you and say of you,

'How you have perished, city of renown,
you who were populated
from the seas![B]
She who was powerful on the sea,
she and all of her inhabitants
inflicted their terror.[C]
18 Now the coastlands tremble
on the day of your downfall;
the islands in the sea
are alarmed by your demise.' "

19 For this is what the Lord GOD says: "When
I make you a ruined city like other deserted
cities, when I raise up the deep against you
so that the mighty waters cover you, 20 then
I will bring you down to be with those who
descend to the Pit, to the people of antiquity. I
will make you dwell in the underworld[D] like[E]
the ancient ruins, with those who descend to
the Pit, so that you will no longer be inhabited or display your splendor[F] in the land of
the living. 21 I will make you an object of horror, and you will no longer exist. You will be
sought but will never be found again." This is
the declaration of the Lord GOD.

THE SINKING OF TYRE

27 The word of the LORD came to me:
2 "Now, son of man, lament for Tyre.
3 Say to Tyre, who is located at the entrance
of the sea, merchant of the peoples to many
coasts and islands, 'This is what the Lord GOD
says:

Tyre, you declared,
"I am perfect in beauty."
4 Your realm was in the heart of the sea;
your builders perfected your beauty.
5 They constructed all your planking
with pine trees from Senir.
They took a cedar from Lebanon
to make a mast for you.
6 They made your oars of oaks
from Bashan.
They made your deck of cypress wood
from the coasts of Cyprus,
inlaid with ivory.
7 Your sail was made of
fine embroidered linen from Egypt,
and served as your banner.
Your awning was of blue
and purple fabric
from the coasts of Elishah.

[A] **26:7** Lit *Nebuchadrezzar* [B] **26:17** Some LXX mss read *'How you were destroyed from the seas, city of renown!* [C] **26:17** Lit *and all her inhabitants who put their terror on all her inhabitants*; Hb obscure [D] **26:20** Lit *the lower parts of the earth* [E] **26:20** Some Hb mss, LXX; other Hb mss, Syr read *in* [F] **26:20** LXX reads *or appear*

8 The inhabitants of Sidon and Arvad
were your rowers.
Your wise men were within you, Tyre;
they were your captains.
9 The elders of Gebal and its wise men
were within you, repairing your leaks.

" 'All the ships of the sea
and their sailors
came to you to barter for your goods.
10 Men of Persia, Lud, and Put
were in your army, serving
as your warriors.
They hung shields and helmets in you;
they gave you splendor.
11 Men of Arvad and Helech
were stationed on your walls
all around,
and Gammadites were in your towers.
They hung their shields[A] all around
your walls;
they perfected your beauty.

12 " 'Tarshish was your trading partner because of your abundant wealth of every kind.
They exchanged silver, iron, tin, and lead for
your merchandise. 13 Javan, Tubal, and Meshech were your merchants. They exchanged
slaves[B] and bronze utensils for your goods.
14 Those from Beth-togarmah exchanged
horses, war horses, and mules for your merchandise. 15 Men of Dedan[C] were also your
merchants; many coasts and islands were
your regular markets. They brought back ivory
tusks and ebony as your payment. 16 Aram[D]
was your trading partner because of your numerous products. They exchanged turquoise,[E]
purple and embroidered cloth, fine linen, coral,[E] and rubies[E] for your merchandise. 17 Judah
and the land of Israel were your merchants.
They exchanged wheat from Minnith, meal,[F]
honey, oil, and balm, for your goods. 18 Damascus was also your trading partner because of
your numerous products and your abundant
wealth of every kind, trading in wine from
Helbon and white wool.[G] 19 Vedan[H] and Javan from Uzal[E] dealt in your merchandise;
wrought iron, cassia, and aromatic cane were
exchanged for your goods. 20 Dedan was your
merchant in saddlecloths for riding. 21 Arabia and all the princes of Kedar were your
business partners, trading with you in lambs,
rams, and goats. 22 The merchants of Sheba
and Raamah traded with you. For your merchandise they exchanged the best of all spices
and all kinds of precious stones as well as
gold. 23 Haran, Canneh, Eden, the merchants
of Sheba, Asshur, and Chilmad traded with
you. 24 They were your merchants in choice
garments, cloaks of blue and embroidered
materials, and multicolored carpets,[E] which
were bound and secured with cords in your
marketplace. 25 Ships of Tarshish were the
carriers for your goods.

" 'So you became full
and heavily loaded[I]
in the heart of the sea.
26 Your rowers have brought you
onto the high seas,
but the east wind has wrecked you
in the heart of the sea.
27 Your wealth, merchandise, and goods,
your sailors and captains,
those who repair your leaks,
those who barter for your goods,
and all the warriors on board,
with all the other people within you,
sink into the heart of the sea
on the day of your downfall.

28 " 'The countryside shakes
at the sound of your sailors' cries.
29 All the oarsmen
disembark from their ships.
The sailors and all the captains
of the sea
stand on the shore.
30 Because of you, they raise their voices
and cry out bitterly.
They throw dust on their heads;
they roll in ashes.
31 They shave their heads because of you
and wrap themselves in sackcloth.
They weep over you
with deep anguish
and bitter mourning.

32 " 'In their wailing they lament for you,
mourning over you:
"Who was like Tyre,
silenced[E] in the middle of the sea?
33 When your merchandise was unloaded
from the seas,
you satisfied many peoples.

[A] **27:11** Or *quivers*; Hb obscure [B] **27:13** Lit *souls of men* [C] **27:15** LXX reads *Rhodes* [D] **27:16** Some Hb mss, Aq, Syr read *Edom* [E] **27:16,19,24,32** Hb obscure [F] **27:17** Or *resin*; Hb obscure [G] **27:18** Or *and wool from Zahar* [H] **27:19** Or *Dan* [I] **27:25** Or *and very glorious*

You enriched the kings of the earth
with your abundant wealth and goods.
34 Now you are wrecked by the sea
in the depths of the waters;
your goods and the people within you
have gone down.
35 All the inhabitants of the coasts
and islands
are appalled at you.
Their kings shudder with fear;
their faces are contorted.
36 Those who trade among the peoples
scoff[A] at you;
you have become an object of horror
and will never exist again.'"

THE FALL OF TYRE'S RULER

28 The word of the LORD came to me:
2 "Son of man, say to the ruler of Tyre,
'This is what the Lord GOD says: Your[B] heart
is proud, and you have said, "I am a god; I sit
in the seat of gods in the heart of the sea."
Yet you are a man and not a god, though you
have regarded your heart as that of a god.
3 Yes, you are wiser than Daniel; no secret
is hidden from you! 4 By your wisdom and
understanding you have acquired wealth
for yourself. You have acquired gold and silver for your treasuries. 5 By your great skill
in trading you have increased your wealth,
but your heart has become proud because
of your wealth.

6 "'Therefore, this is what the Lord GOD says:
Because you regard your heart as that
of a god,
7 I am about to bring strangers
against you,
ruthless men from the nations.
They will draw their swords
against your magnificent wisdom
and will pierce your splendor.
8 They will bring you down to the Pit,
and you will die a violent death
in the heart of the sea.
9 Will you still say, "I am a god,"
in the presence of those
who slay[C] you?
Yet you will be only a man, not a god,
in the hands of those who kill you.
10 You will die the death
of the uncircumcised
at the hands of strangers.
For I have spoken.
This is the declaration
of the Lord GOD.'"

A LAMENT FOR TYRE'S KING

11 The word of the LORD came to me: 12 "Son of
man, lament for the king of Tyre and say to
him, 'This is what the Lord GOD says:
You were the seal[D] of perfection,[E]
full of wisdom and perfect in beauty.
13 You were in Eden, the garden of God.
Every kind of precious stone
covered you:
carnelian, topaz, and diamond,[E]
beryl, onyx, and jasper,
lapis lazuli, turquoise[F] and emerald.[G]
Your mountings and settings
were crafted in gold;
they were prepared on the day
you were created.
14 You were an anointed guardian cherub,
for[H] I had appointed you.
You were on the holy mountain of God;
you walked among the fiery stones.
15 From the day you were created
you were blameless in your ways
until wickedness was found in you.
16 Through the abundance of your trade,
you were filled with violence,
and you sinned.
So I expelled you in disgrace
from the mountain of God,
and banished you, guardian cherub,[I]
from among the fiery stones.
17 Your heart became proud because of
your beauty;
For the sake of your splendor
you corrupted your wisdom.
So I threw you down to the ground;[J]
I made you a spectacle before kings.
18 You profaned your sanctuaries
by the magnitude of your iniquities
in your dishonest trade.
So I made fire come from within you,
and it consumed you.
I reduced you to ashes on the ground
in the sight of everyone watching you.
19 All those who know you
among the peoples
are appalled at you.
You have become an object of horror
and will never exist again.'"

[A] 27:36 Lit *hiss* [B] 28:2 Lit *Because your* [C] 28:9 Some Hb mss, LXX, Syr, Vg; other Hb mss read *of the one who kills* [D] 28:12 Or *sealer* [E] 28:12,13 Hb obscure [F] 28:13 Or *malachite*, or *garnet* [G] 28:13 Or *beryl* [H] 28:14 Or *With an anointed guardian cherub* [I] 28:16 Or *and the guardian cherub banished you* [J] 28:17 Or *earth*

A PROPHECY AGAINST SIDON

20 The word of the LORD came to me: **21** "Son of
man, face Sidon and prophesy against it. **22** You
are to say, 'This is what the Lord GOD says:

Look! I am against you, Sidon,
and I will display my glory within you.
They will know that I am the LORD
when I execute judgments against her
and demonstrate my holiness
through her.

23 I will send a plague against her
and bloodshed in her streets;
the slain will fall within her,
while the sword is against her[A]
on every side.
Then they will know that I am the LORD.

24 " 'The house of Israel will no longer be hurt
by[B] prickly briers or painful thorns from all
their neighbors who treat them with contempt.
Then they will know that I am the Lord GOD.
25 " 'This is what the Lord GOD says: When I
gather the house of Israel from the peoples
where they are scattered, I will demonstrate
my holiness through them in the sight of the
nations, and they will live in their own land,
which I gave to my servant Jacob. **26** They will
live there securely, build houses, and plant
vineyards. They will live securely when I execute judgments against all their neighbors
who treat them with contempt. Then they will
know that I am the LORD their God.' "

A PROPHECY OF EGYPT'S RUIN

29 In the tenth year, in the tenth month on
the twelfth day of the month, the word
of the LORD came to me: **2** "Son of man, face
Pharaoh king of Egypt and prophesy against
him and against all of Egypt. **3** Speak to him
and say, 'This is what the Lord GOD says:

Look, I am against you, Pharaoh
king of Egypt,
the great monster[C] lying in the middle
of his Nile,
who says, "My Nile is my own;
I made it for myself."

4 I will put hooks in your jaws
and make the fish of your streams
cling to your scales.
I will haul you up
from the middle of your Nile,
and all the fish of your streams
will cling to your scales.

5 I will leave you in the desert,
you and all the fish of your streams.
You will fall on the open ground
and will not be taken away
or gathered for burial.
I have given you
to the wild creatures of the earth
and the birds of the sky as food.

6 " 'Then all the inhabitants of Egypt
will know that I am the LORD,
for they[D] have been a staff made of reed
to the house of Israel.

7 When Israel grasped you by the hand,
you splintered, tearing all
their shoulders;
when they leaned on you,
you shattered and made all
their hips unsteady.[E]

8 " 'Therefore, this is what the Lord GOD says:
I am going to bring a sword against you and
cut off both man and animal from you. **9** The
land of Egypt will be a desolate ruin. Then they
will know that I am the LORD. Because you[F]
said, "The Nile is my own; I made it," **10** therefore, I am against you and your Nile. I will turn
the land of Egypt into ruins, a desolate waste
from Migdol to Syene, as far as the border of
Cush. **11** No human foot will pass through it,
and no animal foot will pass through it. It will
be uninhabited for forty years. **12** I will make
the land of Egypt a desolation among[G] desolate lands, and its cities will be a desolation
among[H] ruined cities for forty years. I will
disperse the Egyptians among the nations
and scatter them throughout the lands.
13 " 'For this is what the Lord GOD says: At the
end of forty years I will gather the Egyptians
from the peoples where they were dispersed.
14 I will restore the fortunes of Egypt and bring
them back to the land of Pathros, the land of
their origin. There they will be a lowly kingdom. **15** Egypt will be the lowliest of kingdoms
and will never again exalt itself over the nations. I will make them so small they cannot
rule over the nations. **16** It will never again
be an object of trust for the house of Israel,
drawing attention to their iniquity of turning
to the Egyptians. Then they will know that I
am the Lord GOD.' "

[A] **28:23** Or *within her by the sword* [B] **28:24** Lit *longer have* [C] **29:3** Or *crocodile* [D] **29:6** LXX, Syr, Vg read *you* [E] **29:7** LXX, Syr, Vg; MT reads *and you caused their hips to stand* [F] **29:9** LXX, Syr, Vg; MT reads *he* [G] **29:12** Or *Egypt the most desolate of* [H] **29:12** Or *be the most desolate of*

BABYLON RECEIVES EGYPT AS COMPENSATION

17 In the twenty-seventh year, in the first month,
on the first day of the month, the word of the
LORD came to me: 18 "Son of man, King Nebuchadnezzar of Babylon made his army labor
strenuously against Tyre. Every head was made
bald and every shoulder chafed, but he and his
army received no compensation from Tyre for
the labor he expended against it. 19 Therefore,
this is what the Lord GOD says: I am going to give
the land of Egypt to King Nebuchadnezzar of
Babylon, and he will carry off its wealth, seizing
its spoil and taking its plunder. This will be his
army's compensation. 20 I have given him the
land of Egypt as the pay he labored for, since
they worked for me." This is the declaration of
the Lord GOD. 21 "In that day I will cause a horn
to sprout for the house of Israel, and I will enable you to speak out among them. Then they
will know that I am the LORD."

EGYPT'S DOOM

30 The word of the LORD came to me: 2 "Son of man, prophesy and say, 'This is what the Lord GOD says:

Wail, "Woe because of that day!"
3 For a day is near;
a day belonging to the LORD is near.
It will be a day of clouds,
a time of doom[A] for the nations.
4 A sword will come against Egypt,
and there will be anguish in Cush
when the slain fall in Egypt,
and its wealth is taken away,
and its foundations are demolished.
5 Cush, Put, and Lud,
and all the various foreign troops,[B]
plus Libya[C] and the men
of the covenant land
will fall by the sword along with them.
6 This is what the LORD says:
Those who support Egypt will fall,
and its proud strength will collapse.
From Migdol to Syene
they will fall within it by the sword.
This is the declaration
of the Lord GOD.
7 They will be desolate
among[D] desolate lands,
and their cities will lie
among ruined[E] cities.
8 They will know that I am the LORD
when I set fire to Egypt
and all its allies are shattered.

9 On that day, messengers will go out from me
in ships to terrify confident Cush. Anguish
will come over them on the day of Egypt's
doom.[F] For indeed it is coming.

10 " 'This is what the Lord GOD says:
I will put an end to the hordes[G] of Egypt
by the hand of King Nebuchadnezzar
of Babylon.
11 He along with his people,
ruthless men from the nations,
will be brought in to destroy the land.
They will draw their swords
against Egypt
and fill the land with the slain.
12 I will make the streams dry
and sell the land to evil men.
I will bring desolation
on the land and everything in it
by the hands of foreigners.
I, the LORD, have spoken.

13 " 'This is what the Lord GOD says:
I will destroy the idols and put an end
to the false gods in Memphis.
There will no longer be
a prince from the land of Egypt.
And I will instill fear in that land.
14 I will make Pathros desolate,
set fire to Zoan,
and execute judgments on Thebes.
15 I will pour out my wrath on Pelusium,
the stronghold of Egypt,
and will wipe out the hordes of Thebes.
16 I will set fire to Egypt;
Pelusium will writhe in anguish,
Thebes will be breached,
and Memphis will face foes
in broad daylight.[H]
17 The young men of On[I] and Pi-beseth
will fall by the sword,
and those cities[J] will go into captivity.
18 The day will be dark[K] in Tehaphnehes,
when I break the yoke
of Egypt there
and its proud strength
comes to an end in the city.
A cloud will cover Tehaphnehes,[L]

[A] **30:3** *of doom* supplied for clarity [B] **30:5** Or *all Arabia* [C] **30:5** Lit *Cub*; Hb obscure [D] **30:7** Or *be the most desolate of* [E] **30:7** Or *will be the most ruined of* [F] **30:9** Lit *of Egypt* [G] **30:10** Or *pomp*, or *wealth*, also in v. 15 [H] **30:16** Or *foes daily* [I] **30:17** LXX, Vg; MT reads *iniquity* [J] **30:17** Or *and the women*; lit *and they* [K] **30:18** Some Hb mss, LXX, Syr, Tg, Vg; other Hb mss read *will withhold* [L] **30:18** Or *Egypt*

18 "Son of man, wail over the hordes of Egypt
and bring Egypt and the daughters of mighty
nations down to the underworld,[A] to be with
those who descend to the Pit:
19 Who do you surpass in loveliness?
Go down and be laid to rest
with the uncircumcised!
20 They will fall among those slain
by the sword.
A sword is appointed!
They drag her and all her hordes away.
21 Warrior leaders will speak
from the middle of Sheol
about him[B] and his allies:
'They have come down;
the uncircumcised lie
slain by the sword.'

22 "Assyria is there with
her whole assembly;
her graves are all around her.
All of them are slain, fallen
by the sword.
23 Her graves are set
in the deepest regions of the Pit,
and her assembly is all around
her burial place.
All of them are slain, fallen
by the sword —
those who once spread terror
in the land of the living.

24 "Elam is there
with all her hordes around her grave.
All of them are slain, fallen
by the sword —
those who went down
to the underworld uncircumcised,
who once spread their terror
in the land of the living.
They bear their disgrace
with those who descend to the Pit.
25 Among the slain
they prepare a bed for Elam
with all her hordes.
Her graves are all around her.
All of them are uncircumcised,
slain by the sword,
although their terror was once spread
in the land of the living.
They bear their disgrace
with those who descend to the Pit.
They are placed among the slain.

26 "Meshech and Tubal[C] are there,
with all their hordes.
Their graves are all around them.
All of them are uncircumcised,
slain by the sword,
although their terror was once spread
in the land of the living.
27 They do not lie down
with the fallen warriors
of the uncircumcised,[D]
who went down to Sheol
with their weapons of war,
whose swords were placed
under their heads[E]
and their shields[F]
rested on their bones,
although the terror of these warriors
was once in the land of the living.
28 But you will be shattered
and will lie down
among the uncircumcised,
with those slain by the sword.

29 "Edom is there, her kings and all
her princes,
who, despite their strength,
have been placed
among those slain by the sword.
They lie down with the uncircumcised,
with those who descend to the Pit.
30 All the leaders of the north
and all the Sidonians are there.
They went down in shame
with the slain,
despite the terror
their strength inspired.
They lie down uncircumcised
with those slain by the sword.
They bear their disgrace
with those who descend to the Pit.

31 "Pharaoh will see them
and be comforted over all his hordes —
Pharaoh and his whole army,
slain by the sword."
This is the declaration
of the Lord God.
32 "For I will spread my[G] terror
in the land of the living,
so Pharaoh and all his hordes

[A] **32:18** Lit *the lower parts of the earth*, also in v. 24 [B] **32:21** Either Pharaoh or Egypt [C] **32:26** Lit *Meshech-tubal* [D] **32:27** LXX reads *of antiquity* [E] **32:27** Or *Do they not . . . heads?* [F] **32:27** Emended; MT reads *iniquities* [G] **32:32** Alt Hb tradition, LXX, Syr read *his*

will be laid to rest
among the uncircumcised,
with those slain by the sword."
This is the declaration
of the Lord GOD.

EZEKIEL AS ISRAEL'S WATCHMAN

33 The word of the LORD came to me: 2 "Son
of man, speak to your people and tell
them, 'Suppose I bring the sword against
a land, and the people of that land select a
man from among them, appointing him as
their watchman. 3 And suppose he sees the
sword coming against the land and blows his
trumpet to warn the people. 4 Then, if anyone
hears the sound of the trumpet but ignores the
warning, and the sword comes and takes him
away, his death will be his own fault.[A] 5 Since
he heard the sound of the trumpet but ignored
the warning, his death is his own fault.[B] If
he had taken warning, he would have saved
his life. 6 However, suppose the watchman
sees the sword coming but doesn't blow the
trumpet, so that the people aren't warned, and
the sword comes and takes away their lives.
Then they have been taken away because of
their iniquity, but I will hold the watchman
accountable for their blood.'
7 "As for you, son of man, I have made you
a watchman for the house of Israel. When
you hear a word from my mouth, give them
a warning from me. 8 If I say to the wicked,
'Wicked one, you will surely die,' but you do
not speak out to warn him about his way, that
wicked person will die for his iniquity, yet I
will hold you responsible for his blood. 9 But
if you warn a wicked person to turn from his
way and he doesn't turn from it, he will die for
his iniquity, but you will have rescued yourself.
10 "Now as for you, son of man, say to the
house of Israel, 'You have said this: "Our transgressions and our sins are heavy on us, and
we are wasting away because of them! How
then can we survive?"' 11 Tell them, 'As I live
— this is the declaration of the Lord GOD — I
take no pleasure in the death of the wicked,
but rather that the wicked person should turn
from his way and live. Repent, repent of your
evil ways! Why will you die, house of Israel?'
12 "Now, son of man, say to your people, 'The
righteousness of the righteous person will
not save him on the day of his transgression;

Other-centeredness | *Praying for Others*

GOD'S HEART FOR THE LOST

"Tell them, 'As I live—this is the declaration of the Lord GOD—I take no pleasure in the death of the wicked, but rather that the wicked person should turn from his way and live. Repent, repent of your evil ways! Why will you die, house of Israel?'" Ezekiel 33:11

Go on almost any news website. Find a story with a religious angle. Scan the comments following the article. In almost every instance, you'll find some angry skeptics, and—hurling insults right back—some equally hostile believers. Using Bible verses like punches, they almost seem gleeful telling unbelievers they're lost without Christ. Sadly, some people of faith are far more condemning than compassionate.

Surely this breaks God's heart. In Ezekiel, the Lord makes clear that he takes "no pleasure in the death of the wicked." On the contrary, he wants those who are far from God to turn around and find life.

This is consistent with the New Testament that declares, "God our Savior . . . wants everyone to be saved and to come to the knowledge of the truth" (1Tm 2:3-4; see also 2Pt 3:9).

When you engage with unbelievers, do you get angry? Do you take their jabs personally? Don't pick or participate in spiritual fights! Pray compassionately for God to open the eyes of those who have been blinded by "the god of this age" (2Co 4:4).

For the next note on *Other-centeredness*, see Amos 5:24.

[A] **33:4** Lit *his blood will be on his head* [B] **33:5** Lit *his blood will be on him*

neither will the wickedness of the wicked person cause him to stumble on the day he turns
from his wickedness. The righteous person
won't be able to survive by his righteousness
on the day he sins. 13 When I tell the righteous
person that he will surely live, but he trusts
in his righteousness and acts unjustly, then
none of his righteousness will be remembered,
and he will die because of the injustice he has
committed.

14 " 'So when I tell the wicked person, "You
will surely die," but he repents of his sin and
does what is just and right — 15 he returns
collateral, makes restitution for what he has
stolen, and walks in the statutes of life without
committing injustice — he will certainly live;
he will not die. 16 None of the sins he committed
will be held[A] against him. He has done what
is just and right; he will certainly live.

17 " 'But your people say, "The Lord's way isn't
fair," even though it is their own way that isn't
fair. 18 When a righteous person turns from
his righteousness and commits injustice, he
will die for it. 19 But if a wicked person turns
from his wickedness and does what is just and
right, he will live because of it. 20 Yet you say,
"The Lord's way isn't fair." I will judge each of
you according to his ways, house of Israel.' "

THE NEWS OF JERUSALEM'S FALL

21 In the twelfth year of our exile, in the tenth
month, on the fifth day of the month, a fugitive from Jerusalem came to me and reported,
"The city has been taken!" 22 Now the hand of
the LORD had been on me the evening before
the fugitive arrived, and he opened my mouth
before the man came to me in the morning.
So my mouth was opened and I was no longer mute.

ISRAEL'S CONTINUED REBELLION

23 Then the word of the LORD came to me:
24 "Son of man, those who live in the[B] ruins
in the land of Israel are saying, 'Abraham was
only one person, yet he received possession
of the land. But we are many; surely the land
has been given to us as a possession.' 25 Therefore say to them, 'This is what the Lord GOD
says: You eat meat with blood in it, look to
your idols, and shed blood. Should you then
receive possession of the land? 26 You have
relied on your swords, you have committed
detestable acts, and each of you has defiled
his neighbor's wife. Should you then receive
possession of the land?'

27 "Tell them this: 'This is what the Lord
GOD says: As surely as I live, those who are
in the ruins will fall by the sword, those in the
open field I have given to wild animals to be
devoured, and those in the strongholds and
caves will die by plague. 28 I will make the land
a desolate waste, and its proud strength will
come to an end. The mountains of Israel will
become desolate, with no one passing through.
29 They will know that I am the LORD when I
make the land a desolate waste because of
all the detestable acts they have committed.'

30 "As for you, son of man, your people are
talking about you near the city walls and in
the doorways of their houses. One person
speaks to another, each saying to his brother, 'Come and hear what the message is that
comes from the LORD!' 31 So my people come
to you in crowds,[C] sit in front of you, and hear
your words, but they don't obey them. Their
mouths go on passionately, but their hearts
pursue dishonest profit. 32 Yes, to them you
are like a singer of passionate songs who has
a beautiful voice and plays skillfully on an
instrument. They hear your words, but they
don't obey them. 33 Yet when all this comes
true — and it definitely will — then they will
know that a prophet has been among them."

THE SHEPHERDS AND GOD'S FLOCK

34 The word of the LORD came to me:
2 "Son of man, prophesy against the
shepherds of Israel. Prophesy, and say to
them, 'This is what the Lord GOD says to the
shepherds: Woe to the shepherds of Israel,
who have been feeding themselves! Shouldn't
the shepherds feed their flock? 3 You eat the
fat, wear the wool, and butcher the fattened
animals, but you do not tend the flock. 4 You
have not strengthened the weak, healed the
sick, bandaged the injured, brought back the
strays, or sought the lost. Instead, you have
ruled them with violence and cruelty. 5 They
were scattered for lack of a shepherd; they
became food for all the wild animals when
they were scattered. 6 My flock went astray
on all the mountains and every high hill. My
flock was scattered over the whole face of
the earth, and there was no one searching
or seeking for them.

7 " 'Therefore, you shepherds, hear the word

[A] **33:16** Lit *remembered* [B] **33:24** Lit *these* [C] **33:31** Lit *you like the coming of a people*

of the LORD. 8 As I live — this is the declaration
of the Lord GOD — because my flock, lacking
a shepherd, has become prey and food for every wild animal, and because my shepherds
do not search for my flock, and because the
shepherds feed themselves rather than my
flock, 9 therefore, you shepherds, hear the
word of the LORD!

10 " 'This is what the Lord GOD says: Look,
I am against the shepherds. I will demand
my flock from them[A] and prevent them from
shepherding the flock. The shepherds will no
longer feed themselves, for I will rescue my
flock from their mouths so that they will not
be food for them.

11 " 'For this is what the Lord GOD says: See,
I myself will search for my flock and look for
them. 12 As a shepherd looks for his sheep on
the day he is among his scattered flock, so I
will look for my flock. I will rescue them from
all the places where they have been scattered
on a day of clouds and total darkness. 13 I will
bring them out from the peoples, gather them
from the countries, and bring them to their own
soil. I will shepherd them on the mountains of
Israel, in the ravines, and in all the inhabited
places of the land. 14 I will tend them in good
pasture, and their grazing place will be on
Israel's lofty mountains. There they will lie
down in a good grazing place; they will feed
in rich pasture on the mountains of Israel. 15 I
will tend my flock and let them lie down. This
is the declaration of the Lord GOD. 16 I will seek
the lost, bring back the strays, bandage the
injured, and strengthen the weak, but I will
destroy[B] the fat and the strong. I will shepherd
them with justice.

17 " 'As for you, my flock, the Lord GOD says
this: Look, I am going to judge between one
sheep and another, between the rams and
goats. 18 Isn't it enough for you to feed on the
good pasture? Must you also trample the rest
of the pasture with your feet? Or isn't it enough
that you drink the clear water? Must you also
muddy the rest with your feet? 19 Yet my flock
has to feed on what your feet have trampled,
and drink what your feet have muddied.

20 " 'Therefore, this is what the Lord GOD says
to them: See, I myself will judge between the
fat sheep and the lean sheep. 21 Since you have
pushed with flank and shoulder and butted all
the weak ones with your horns until you scattered them all over, 22 I will save my flock. They
will no longer be prey, and I will judge between
one sheep and another. 23 I will establish over
them one shepherd, my servant David, and he
will shepherd them. He will tend them himself
and will be their shepherd. 24 I, the LORD, will
be their God, and my servant David will be a
prince among them. I, the LORD, have spoken.

25 " 'I will make a covenant of peace with them
and eliminate dangerous creatures from the

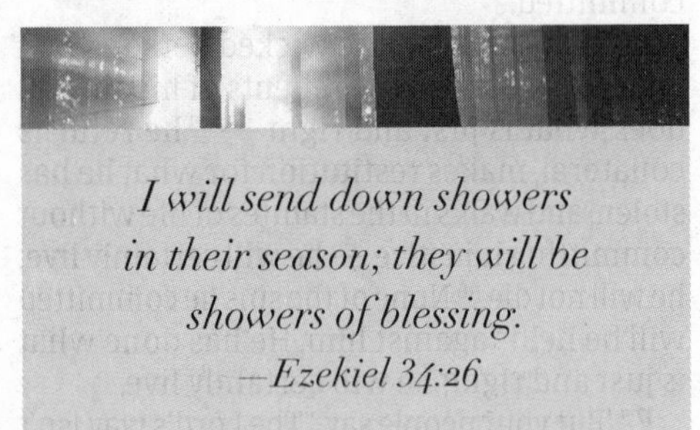
*I will send down showers
in their season; they will be
showers of blessing.*
— Ezekiel 34:26

land, so that they may live securely in the wilderness and sleep in the forest. 26 I will make
them and the area around my hill a blessing: I
will send down showers in their season; they
will be showers of blessing. 27 The trees of the
field will yield their fruit, and the land will yield
its produce; my flock will be secure in their
land. They will know that I am the LORD when
I break the bars of their yoke and rescue them
from the power of those who enslave them.
28 They will no longer be prey for the nations,
and the wild creatures of the earth will not
consume them. They will live securely, and no
one will frighten them. 29 I will establish for
them a place renowned for its agriculture,[C] and
they will no longer be victims of famine in the
land. They will no longer endure the insults of
the nations. 30 Then they will know that I, the
LORD their God, am with them, and that they,
the house of Israel, are my people. This is the
declaration of the Lord GOD. 31 You are my flock,
the human flock of my pasture, and I am your
God. This is the declaration of the Lord GOD.' "

A PROPHECY AGAINST EDOM

35 The word of the LORD came to me: 2 "Son
of man, face Mount Seir and prophe-
sy against it. 3 Say to it, 'This is what the Lord
GOD says:

Look! I am against you, Mount Seir.
I will stretch out my hand against you
and make you a desolate waste.

[A] 34:10 Lit *their hand* [B] 34:16 Some Hb mss, LXX, Syr, Vg read *watch over* [C] 34:29 LXX, Syr read *a plant of peace*

4 I will turn your cities into ruins,
and you will become a desolation.
Then you will know that I am the LORD.

5 " 'Because you maintained a perpetual hatred and gave the Israelites over to the power
of the sword in the time of their disaster, the
time of final punishment, 6 therefore, as I live
— this is the declaration of the Lord GOD — I
will destine you for bloodshed, and it will pursue you. Since you did not hate bloodshed, it
will pursue you. 7 I will make Mount Seir a
desolate waste and will cut off from it those
who come and go. 8 I will fill its mountains
with the slain; those slain by the sword will
fall on your hills, in your valleys, and in all
your ravines. 9 I will make you a perpetual
desolation; your cities will not be inhabited.
Then you will know that I am the LORD.
10 " 'Because you said, "These two nations
and two lands will be mine, and we will possess them" — though the LORD was there —
11 therefore, as I live — this is the declaration
of the Lord GOD — I will treat you according
to the anger and jealousy you showed in your
hatred of them. I will make myself known
among them[A] when I judge you. 12 Then you
will know that I, the LORD, have heard all the
blasphemies you uttered against the mountains of Israel, saying, "They are desolate. They
have been given to us to devour!" 13 You boasted
against me with your mouth, and spoke many
words against me. I heard it myself!
14 " 'This is what the Lord GOD says: While
the whole world rejoices, I will make you a
desolation. 15 Just as you rejoiced over the
inheritance of the house of Israel because it
became a desolation, I will deal the same way
with you: you will become a desolation, Mount
Seir, and so will all Edom in its entirety. Then
they will know that I am the LORD.'

RESTORATION OF ISRAEL'S MOUNTAINS

36 "Son of man, prophesy to the mountains
of Israel and say, 'Mountains of Israel,
hear the word of the LORD. 2 This is what the Lord
GOD says: Because the enemy has said about
you, "Aha! The ancient heights have become
our possession," ' 3 therefore, prophesy and
say: 'This is what the Lord GOD says: Because
they have made you desolate and have trampled you from every side, so that you became
a possession for the rest of the nations and an
object of people's gossip and slander, 4 therefore, mountains of Israel, hear the word of the
Lord GOD. This is what the Lord GOD says to the
mountains and hills, to the ravines and valleys,
to the desolate ruins and abandoned cities,
which have become plunder and a mockery
to the rest of the nations all around.
5 " 'This is what the Lord GOD says: Certainly
in my burning zeal I speak against the rest of
the nations and all of Edom, who took[B] my land
as their own possession with wholehearted
rejoicing and utter contempt so that its pastureland became[C] plunder. 6 Therefore, prophesy
concerning the land of Israel and say to the
mountains and hills, to the ravines and valleys:
This is what the Lord GOD says: Look, I speak in
my burning zeal because you have endured the
insults of the nations. 7 Therefore, this is what
the Lord GOD says: I swear[D] that the nations
all around you will endure their own insults.
8 " 'You, mountains of Israel, will produce
your branches and bear your fruit for my people Israel, since their arrival is near. 9 Look! I
am on your side; I will turn toward you, and
you will be tilled and sown. 10 I will fill you
with people, with the whole house of Israel
in its entirety. The cities will be inhabited and
the ruins rebuilt. 11 I will fill you with people
and animals, and they will increase and be
fruitful. I will make you inhabited as you once
were and make you better off than you were
before. Then you will know that I am the LORD.
12 I will cause people, my people Israel, to walk
on you; they will possess you, and you will be
their inheritance. You will no longer deprive
them of their children.
13 " 'This is what the Lord GOD says: Because
some are saying to you, "You devour people
and deprive your nation of children," 14 therefore, you will no longer devour people and
deprive your nation of children.[E] This is the
declaration of the Lord GOD. 15 I will no longer
allow the insults of the nations to be heard
against you, and you will not have to endure
the reproach of the peoples anymore; you will
no longer cause your nation to stumble.[F] This
is the declaration of the Lord GOD.' "

RESTORATION OF ISRAEL'S PEOPLE

16 The word of the LORD came to me: 17 "Son of
man, while the house of Israel lived in their

[A] **35:11** LXX reads *you* [B] **36:5** Lit *gave* [C] **36:5** Or *contempt, to empty it of*; Hb obscure [D] **36:7** Lit *lift up my hand*
[E] **36:14** Alt Hb tradition reads *and cause your nation to stumble* [F] **36:15** Some Hb mss, Tg read *no longer bereave your nation of children*

land, they defiled it with their conduct and actions. Their behavior before me was like menstrual impurity. 18 So I poured out my wrath on them because of the blood they had shed on the land, and because they had defiled it with their idols. 19 I dispersed them among the nations, and they were scattered among the countries. I judged them according to their conduct and actions. 20 When they came to the nations where they went, they profaned my holy name, because it was said about them, 'These are the people of the LORD, yet they had to leave his land in exile.' 21 Then I had concern for my holy name, which the house of Israel profaned among the nations where they went.

22 "Therefore, say to the house of Israel, 'This is what the Lord GOD says: It is not for your sake that I will act, house of Israel, but for my holy name, which you profaned among the nations where you went. 23 I will honor the holiness of my great name, which has been profaned among the nations — the name you have profaned among them. The nations will know that I am the LORD — this is the declaration of the Lord GOD — when I demonstrate my holiness through you in their sight.

24 " 'For I will take you from the nations and gather you from all the countries, and will bring you into your own land. 25 I will also sprinkle clean water on you, and you will be clean. I will cleanse you from all your impurities and all your idols. 26 I will give you a new heart and put a new spirit within you; I will remove your heart of stone[A] and give you a heart of flesh. 27 I will place my Spirit within you and cause you to follow my statutes and carefully observe my ordinances. 28 You will live in the land that I gave your fathers; you will be my people, and I will be your God. 29 I will save you from all your uncleanness. I will summon the grain and make it plentiful, and I will not bring famine on you. 30 I will also make the fruit of the trees and the produce of the field plentiful, so that you will no longer experience reproach among the nations on account of famine.

31 " 'You will remember your evil ways and your deeds that were not good, and you will loathe yourselves for your iniquities and detestable practices. 32 It is not for your sake that I will act — this is the declaration of the Lord GOD — let this be known to you. Be ashamed and humiliated because of your ways, house of Israel!

33 " 'This is what the Lord GOD says: On the day I cleanse you from all your iniquities, I will cause the cities to be inhabited, and the ruins will be rebuilt. 34 The desolate land will be cultivated instead of lying desolate in the sight of everyone who passes by. 35 They will say, "This land that was desolate has become like the garden of Eden. The cities that were once ruined, desolate, and demolished are now fortified and inhabited." 36 Then the nations that remain around you will know that I, the LORD, have rebuilt what was demolished and have replanted what was desolate. I, the LORD, have spoken and I will do it.

37 " 'This is what the Lord GOD says: I will respond to the house of Israel and do this for them: I will multiply them in number like a flock.[B] 38 So the ruined cities will be filled with a flock of people, just as Jerusalem is filled with a flock of sheep for sacrifice[C] during its appointed festivals. Then they will know that I am the LORD.' "

I will give you a new heart and put a new spirit within you; I will remove your heart of stone and give you a heart of flesh.
—Ezekiel 36:26

THE VALLEY OF DRY BONES

37 The hand of the LORD was on me, and he brought me out by his Spirit and set me down in the middle of the valley; it was full of bones. 2 He led me all around them. There were a great many of them on the surface of the valley, and they were very dry. 3 Then he said to me, "Son of man, can these bones live?"

I replied, "Lord GOD, only you know."

4 He said to me, "Prophesy concerning these bones and say to them: Dry bones, hear the word of the LORD! 5 This is what the Lord GOD says to these bones: I will cause breath to enter you, and you will live. 6 I will put tendons on you, make flesh grow on you, and cover you with skin. I will put breath in you so that

[A] **36:26** Lit *stone from your flesh* [B] **36:37** Lit *flock of people* [C] **36:38** Lit *as the consecrated flock, as the flock of Jerusalem*

you come to life. Then you will know that I
am the LORD."
7 So I prophesied as I had been commanded.
While I was prophesying, there was a noise, a
rattling sound, and the bones came together,
bone to bone. 8 As I looked, tendons appeared
on them, flesh grew, and skin covered them,
but there was no breath in them. 9 He said to
me, "Prophesy to the breath,[A] prophesy, son
of man. Say to it: This is what the Lord GOD
says: Breath, come from the four winds and
breathe into these slain so that they may live!"
10 So I prophesied as he commanded me; the
breath entered them, and they came to life
and stood on their feet, a vast army.
11 Then he said to me, "Son of man, these
bones are the whole house of Israel. Look
how they say, 'Our bones are dried up, and
our hope has perished; we are cut off.' 12 Therefore, prophesy and say to them: 'This is what
the Lord GOD says: I am going to open your
graves and bring you up from them, my people,
and lead you into the land of Israel. 13 You will
know that I am the LORD, my people, when I
open your graves and bring you up from them.
14 I will put my Spirit in you, and you will live,
and I will settle you in your own land. Then
you will know that I am the LORD. I have spoken, and I will do it. This is the declaration of
the LORD.'"

THE REUNIFICATION OF ISRAEL

15 The word of the LORD came to me: 16 "Son
of man, take a single stick and write on it:
Belonging to Judah and the Israelites associated with him. Then take another stick and
write on it: Belonging to Joseph — the stick
of Ephraim — and all the house of Israel associated with him. 17 Then join them together
into a single stick so that they become one
in your hand. 18 When your people ask you,
'Won't you explain to us what you mean by
these things?' — 19 tell them, 'This is what the
Lord GOD says: I am going to take the stick of
Joseph, which is in the hand of Ephraim, and
the tribes of Israel associated with him, and
put them together with the stick of Judah. I
will make them into a single stick so that they
become one in my hand.'
20 "When the sticks you have written on are
in your hand and in full view of the people,
21 tell them, 'This is what the Lord GOD says:
I am going to take the Israelites out of the
nations where they have gone. I will gather
them from all around and bring them into
their own land. 22 I will make them one nation
in the land, on the mountains of Israel, and
one king will rule over all of them. They will
no longer be two nations and will no longer
be divided into two kingdoms. 23 They will not
defile themselves anymore with their idols,

Eternal Perspective | *Biblical Hope*

DRY BONES

"He led me all around them. There were a great many of them on the surface of the valley, and they were very dry. Then he said to me, 'Son of man, can these bones live?' I replied, 'Lord GOD, only you know.'" Ezekiel 37:2-3

The friendship appears broken beyond repair. The dream seems to have gone up in smoke. The marriage, in everyone's opinion, was over years ago. Is there any hope at all?

In this beloved Old Testament passage, we read about the prophet's most famous vision. The Lord takes him to a dusty valley filled with human bones and commands him to prophesy to the bones. Ezekiel is then dumbstruck with amazement as God assembles the bones into skeletons, puts flesh on them, and brings them back to life! This was, of course, a message to despondent Jewish exiles, assuring the eventual restoration of Israel. But it reminds us that we serve a God who can make dead things live. And we have no better picture of that than the resurrection of Jesus!

What are the situations in your life that look hopeless? Where do you need to see the power and life-giving goodness of God?

For the next note on *Eternal Perspective*, see Joel 2:12-13.

[A] **37:9** Or *wind*, or *spirit*, also in v. 10

their abhorrent things, and all their transgressions. I will save them from all their apostasies by which[A] they sinned, and I will cleanse them. Then they will be my people, and I will be their God. 24 My servant David will be king over them, and there will be one shepherd for all of them. They will follow my ordinances, and keep my statutes and obey them.

25 " 'They will live in the land that I gave to my servant Jacob, where your fathers lived. They will live in it forever with their children and grandchildren, and my servant David will be their prince forever. 26 I will make a covenant of peace with them; it will be a permanent covenant with them. I will establish and multiply them and will set my sanctuary among them forever. 27 My dwelling place will be with them; I will be their God, and they will be my people. 28 When my sanctuary is among them forever, the nations will know that I, the LORD, sanctify Israel.' "

THE DEFEAT OF GOG

38 The word of the LORD came to me: 2 "Son of man, face Gog, of the land of Magog, the chief prince of[B] Meshech and Tubal. Prophesy against him 3 and say, 'This is what the Lord GOD says: Look, I am against you, Gog, chief prince of Meshech and Tubal. 4 I will turn you around, put hooks in your jaws, and bring you out with all your army, including horses and riders, who are all splendidly dressed, a huge assembly armed with large and small shields, all of them brandishing swords. 5 Persia, Cush, and Put are with them, all of them with shields and helmets; 6 Gomer with all its troops; and Beth-togarmah from the remotest parts of the north along with all its troops — many peoples are with you.

7 " 'Be prepared and get yourself ready, you and your whole assembly that has been mobilized around you; you will be their guard. 8 After a long time you will be summoned. In the last years you will enter a land that has been restored from war[C] and regathered from many peoples to the mountains of Israel, which had long been a ruin. They were brought out from the peoples, and all of them now live securely. 9 You, all of your troops, and many peoples with you will advance, coming like a thunderstorm; you will be like a cloud covering the land.

10 " 'This is what the Lord GOD says: On that day, thoughts will arise in your mind, and you will devise an evil plan. 11 You will say, "I will advance against a land of open villages; I will come against a tranquil people who are living securely, all of them living without walls and without bars or gates" — 12 in order to seize spoil and carry off plunder, to turn your hand against ruins now inhabited and against a people gathered from the nations, who have been acquiring cattle and possessions and who live at the center of the world. 13 Sheba and Dedan and the merchants of Tarshish with all its rulers[D] will ask you, "Have you come to seize spoil? Have you mobilized your assembly to carry off plunder, to make off with silver and gold, to take cattle and possessions, to seize plenty of spoil?" '

14 "Therefore prophesy, son of man, and say to Gog, 'This is what the Lord GOD says: On that day when my people Israel are dwelling securely, will you not know this 15 and come from your place in the remotest parts of the north — you and many peoples with you, who are all riding horses — a huge assembly, a powerful army? 16 You will advance against my people Israel like a cloud covering the land. It will happen in the last days, Gog, that I will bring you against my land so that the nations may know me, when I show myself holy through you in their sight.

17 " 'This is what the Lord GOD says: Are you the one I spoke about in former times through my servants, the prophets of Israel, who for years prophesied in those times that I would bring you against them? 18 Now on that day, the day when Gog comes against the land of Israel — this is the declaration of the Lord GOD — my wrath will flare up.[E] 19 I swear in my zeal and fiery rage: On that day there will be a great earthquake in the land of Israel. 20 The fish of the sea, the birds of the sky, the animals of the field, every creature that crawls on the ground, and every human being on the face of the earth will tremble before me. The mountains will be demolished, the cliffs will collapse, and every wall will fall to the ground. 21 I will call for a sword against him on all my mountains — this is the declaration of the Lord GOD — and every man's sword will be against his brother. 22 I will execute judgment on him with plague and bloodshed. I will pour out torrential rain, hailstones, fire, and burning sulfur on him, as well as his troops and the many peoples who

[A] **37:23** Some Hb mss, LXX, Sym; other Hb mss read *their settlements where* [B] **38:2** Or *the prince of Rosh,* [C] **38:8** Lit *from the sword* [D] **38:13** Lit *young lions*, or *villages* [E] **38:18** Lit *up in my anger*

are with him. 23 I will display my greatness and holiness, and will reveal myself in the sight of many nations. Then they will know that I am the LORD.'

THE DISPOSAL OF GOG

39 "As for you, son of man, prophesy against Gog and say, 'This is what the Lord GOD says: Look, I am against you, Gog, chief prince of[A] Meshech and Tubal. 2 I will turn you around, drive you on, and lead you up from the remotest parts of the north. I will bring you against the mountains of Israel. 3 Then I will knock your bow from your left hand and make your arrows drop from your right hand. 4 You, all your troops, and the peoples who are with you will fall on the mountains of Israel. I will give you as food to every kind of predatory bird and to the wild animals. 5 You will fall on the open field, for I have spoken. This is the declaration of the Lord GOD.

6 " 'I will send fire against Magog and those who live securely on the coasts and islands. Then they will know that I am the LORD. 7 So I will make my holy name known among my people Israel and will no longer allow it to be profaned. Then the nations will know that I am the LORD, the Holy One in Israel. 8 Yes, it is coming, and it will happen. This is the declaration of the Lord GOD. This is the day I have spoken about.

9 " 'Then the inhabitants of Israel's cities will go out, kindle fires, and burn the weapons — the small and large shields, the bows and arrows, the clubs and spears. For seven years they will use them to make fires. 10 They will not gather wood from the countryside or cut it down from the forests, for they will use the weapons to make fires. They will take the loot from those who looted them and plunder those who plundered them. This is the declaration of the Lord GOD.

11 " 'Now on that day I will give Gog a burial place there in Israel — the Travelers' Valley[B] east of the Sea. It will block those who travel through, for Gog and all his hordes will be buried there. So it will be called Hordes of Gog[C] Valley. 12 The house of Israel will spend seven months burying them in order to cleanse the land. 13 All the people of the land will bury them and their fame will spread on the day I display my glory. This is the declaration of the Lord GOD.

14 " 'They will appoint men on a full-time basis to pass through the land and bury the invaders[D] who remain on the surface of the ground, in order to cleanse it. They will make their search at the end of the seven months. 15 When they pass through the land and one of them sees a human bone, he will set up a marker next to it until the buriers have buried it in Hordes of Gog Valley. 16 There will even be a city named Hamonah[E] there. So they will cleanse the land.'

17 "Son of man, this is what the Lord GOD says: Tell every kind of bird and all the wild animals, 'Assemble and come! Gather from all around to my sacrificial feast that I am slaughtering for you, a great feast on the mountains of Israel; you will eat flesh and drink blood. 18 You will eat the flesh of mighty men and drink the blood of the earth's princes: rams, lambs, male goats, and all the fattened bulls of Bashan. 19 You will eat fat until you are satisfied and drink blood until you are drunk, at my sacrificial feast that I have prepared for you. 20 At my table you will eat your fill of horses and riders, of mighty men and all the warriors. This is the declaration of the Lord GOD.'

ISRAEL'S RESTORATION TO GOD

21 "I will display my glory among the nations, and all the nations will see the judgment I have executed and the hand I have laid on them. 22 From that day forward the house of Israel will know that I am the LORD their God. 23 And the nations will know that the house of Israel went into exile on account of their iniquity, because they dealt unfaithfully with me. Therefore, I hid my face from them and handed them over to their enemies, so that they all fell by the sword. 24 I dealt with them according to their uncleanness and transgressions, and I hid my face from them.

25 "So this is what the Lord GOD says: Now I will restore the fortunes of Jacob and have compassion on the whole house of Israel, and I will be jealous for my holy name. 26 They will feel remorse for[F,G] their disgrace and all the unfaithfulness they committed against me, when they live securely in their land with no one to frighten them. 27 When I bring them

[A] **39:1** Or *Gog, prince of Rosh,* [B] **39:11** Hb obscure [C] **39:11** = Hamon-gog, also in v. 15 [D] **39:14** Or *basis, some to pass through the land, and with them some to bury those* [E] **39:16** In Hb, *Hamonah* is related to the word "horde." [F] **39:26** Some emend to *will forget* [G] **39:26** Lit *will bear*

back from the peoples and gather them from the countries of their enemies, I will demonstrate my holiness through them in the sight of many nations. 28 They will know that I am the LORD their God when I regather them to their own land after having exiled them among the nations. I will leave none of them behind.[A] 29 I will no longer hide my face from them, for I will pour out my Spirit on the house of Israel." This is the declaration of the Lord GOD.

THE NEW TEMPLE

40 In the twenty-fifth year of our exile, at the beginning of the year, on the tenth day of the month in the fourteenth year after Jerusalem had been captured, on that very day the LORD's hand was on me, and he brought me there. 2 In visions of God he took me to the land of Israel and set me down on a very high mountain. On its southern slope was a structure resembling a city. 3 He brought me there, and I saw a man whose appearance was like bronze, with a linen cord and a measuring rod in his hand. He was standing by the city gate. 4 He spoke to me: "Son of man, look with your eyes, listen with your ears, and pay attention to everything I am going to show you, for you have been brought here so that I might show it to you. Report everything you see to the house of Israel."

THE WALL AND OUTER GATES

5 Now there was a wall surrounding the outside of the temple. The measuring rod in the man's hand was six units of twenty-one inches;[B] each unit was the standard length plus three inches.[C] He measured the thickness of the wall structure; it was 10 ½ feet,[D] and its height was the same. 6 Then he came to the gate that faced east and climbed its steps. He measured the threshold of the gate; it was 10 ½ feet deep — one threshold was 10 ½ feet deep. 7 Each recess was 10 ½ feet long and 10 ½ feet deep, and there was a space of 8 ¾ feet[E] between the recesses. The inner threshold of the gate on the temple side next to the gate's portico was 10 ½ feet. 8 Next he measured the gate's portico; 9 it[F] was 14 feet,[G] and its jambs were 3 ½ feet.[H] The gate's portico was on the temple side.

10 There were three recesses on each side of the east gate, each with the same measurements, and the jambs on either side also had the same measurements. 11 Then he measured the width of the gate's entrance; it was 17 ½ feet,[I] while the width[J] of the gate was 22 ¾ feet.[K] 12 There was a barrier of 21 inches[L] in front of the recesses on both sides, and the recesses on each side were 10 ½ feet[M] square. 13 Then he measured the gate from the roof of one recess to the roof of the opposite one; the distance was 43 ¾ feet.[N] The openings of the recesses faced each other. 14 Next, he measured the porch — 105 feet.[O,P] 15 The distance from the front of the gate at the entrance to the front of the gate's portico on the inside was 87 ½ feet.[Q] 16 The recesses and their jambs had beveled windows all around the inside of the gate. The porticoes also had windows all around on the inside. Each jamb was decorated with palm trees.

17 Then he brought me into the outer court, and there were chambers and a paved surface laid out all around the court. Thirty chambers faced the pavement, 18 which flanked the courtyard's gates and corresponded to the length of the gates; this was the lower pavement. 19 Then he measured the distance from the front of the lower gate to the exterior front of the inner court; it was 175 feet.[R] This was the east; next the north is described.

20 He measured the gate of the outer court facing north, both its length and width. 21 Its three recesses on each side, its jambs, and its portico had the same measurements as the first gate: 87 ½ feet long and 43 ¾ feet wide. 22 Its windows, portico, and palm trees had the same measurements as those of the gate that faced east. Seven steps led up to the gate, and its portico was ahead of them. 23 The inner court had a gate facing the north gate, like the one on the east. He measured the distance from gate to gate; it was 175 feet.

24 He brought me to the south side, and there was also a gate on the south. He measured its jambs and portico; they had the same measurements as the others. 25 Both the gate and its portico had windows all around, like the other windows. It was 87 ½ feet long and 43 ¾ feet wide. 26 Its stairway had seven steps, and

[A] **39:28** Lit *behind there any longer* [B] **40:5** = a long cubit [C] **40:5** Lit *six cubits by the cubit and a handbreadth* [D] **40:5** Lit *was one rod*, also in v. 7 [E] **40:7** Lit *five cubits*, also in v. 30 [F] **40:8-9** Some Hb mss, Syr, Vg; other Hb mss read *gate facing the temple side; it was one rod. 9Then he measured the gate's portico; it* [G] **40:9** Lit *eight cubits* [H] **40:9** Lit *two cubits* [I] **40:11** Lit *10 cubits* [J] **40:11** Lit *length* [K] **40:11** Lit *13 cubits* [L] **40:12** Lit *one cubit*, also in v. 42 [M] **40:12** Lit *six cubits* [N] **40:13** Lit *25 cubits*, also in vv. 21,25,29,33,36 [O] **40:14** MT adds *To the jamb of the court, the gate was all around*; Hb obscure [P] **40:14** Lit *60 cubits* [Q] **40:15** Lit *50 cubits*, also in vv. 21,25,29,33,36 [R] **40:19** Lit *100 cubits*, also in vv. 23,27,47

its portico was ahead of them. It had palm trees on its jambs, one on each side. 27 The inner court had a gate on the south. He measured from gate to gate on the south; it was 175 feet.

THE INNER GATES

28 Then he brought me to the inner court through the south gate. When he measured the south gate, it had the same measurements as the others. 29 Its recesses, jambs, and portico had the same measurements as the others. Both it and its portico had windows all around. It was 87 ½ feet long and 43 ¾ feet wide. 30 (There were porticoes all around, 43 ¾ feet long and 8 ¾ feet wide.[A]) 31 Its portico faced the outer court, and its jambs were decorated with palm trees. Its stairway had eight steps.

32 Then he brought me to the inner court on the east side. When he measured the gate, it had the same measurements as the others. 33 Its recesses, jambs, and portico had the same measurements as the others. Both it and its portico had windows all around. It was 87 ½ feet long and 43 ¾ feet wide. 34 Its portico faced the outer court, and its jambs were decorated with palm trees on each side. Its stairway had eight steps.

35 Then he brought me to the north gate. When he measured it, it had the same measurements as the others, 36 as did its recesses, jambs, and portico. It also had windows all around. It was 87 ½ feet long and 43 ¾ feet wide. 37 Its portico[B] faced the outer court, and its jambs were decorated with palm trees on each side. Its stairway had eight steps.

ROOMS FOR PREPARING SACRIFICES

38 There was a chamber whose door opened into the gate's portico.[C] The burnt offering was to be washed there. 39 Inside the gate's portico there were two tables on each side, on which to slaughter the burnt offering, sin offering, and guilt offering. 40 Outside, as one approaches the entrance of the north gate, there were two tables on one side and two more tables on the other side of the gate's portico. 41 So there were four tables inside the gate and four outside, eight tables in all on which the slaughtering was to be done. 42 There were also four tables of cut stone for the burnt offering, each 31 ½ inches[D] long, 31 ½ inches wide, and 21 inches high. The utensils used to slaughter the burnt offerings and other sacrifices were placed on them. 43 There were three-inch[E] hooks[F] fastened all around the inside of the room, and the flesh of the offering was to be laid on the tables.

ROOMS FOR SINGERS AND PRIESTS

44 Outside the inner gate, within the inner court, there were chambers for the singers:[G] one[H] beside the north gate, facing south, and another beside the south[I] gate, facing north. 45 Then the man said to me: "This chamber that faces south is for the priests who keep charge of the temple. 46 The chamber that faces north is for the priests who keep charge of the altar. These are the sons of Zadok, the ones from the sons of Levi who may approach the LORD to serve him." 47 Next he measured the court. It was square, 175 feet long and 175 feet wide. The altar was in front of the temple.

48 Then he brought me to the portico of the temple and measured the jambs of the portico; they were 8 ¾ feet thick on each side. The width of the gate was 24 ½ feet,[J] and the side walls of the gate were[K] 5 ¼ feet[L] wide on each side. 49 The portico was 35 feet[M] across and 21[N] feet[O] deep, and 10 steps led[P] up to it. There were pillars by the jambs, one on each side.

INSIDE THE TEMPLE

41 Next he brought me into the great hall and measured the jambs; on each side the width of the jamb was 10 ½ feet.[Q,R] 2 The width of the entrance was 17 ½ feet,[S] and the side walls of the entrance were 8 ¾ feet[T] wide on each side. He also measured the length of the great hall, 70 feet,[U] and the width, 35 feet.[V] 3 He went inside the next room and measured the jambs at the entrance; they were 3 ½ feet[W] wide. The entrance was 10 ½ feet wide, and the width of the entrance's side walls on each side[X] was 12 ¼ feet.[Y] 4 He then measured the length of the room adjacent to the great hall,

---

[A] **40:30** Some Hb mss, LXX omit v. 30 [B] **40:37** LXX; MT reads *jambs* [C] **40:38** Text emended; MT reads *door was by the jambs, at the gates* [D] **40:42** Lit *one and a half cubits* [E] **40:43** Lit *one handbreadth* [F] **40:43** Or *ledges* [G] **40:44** LXX reads *were two chambers* [H] **40:44** LXX; MT reads *singers, which was* [I] **40:44** LXX; MT reads *east* [J] **40:48** Lit *14 cubits* [K] **40:48** LXX; MT omits *24 ½ feet, and the side walls of the gate were* [L] **40:48** Lit *three cubits* [M] **40:49** Lit *20 cubits* [N] **40:49** LXX; MT reads *19 ¼* [O] **40:49** Lit *12 cubits* [P] **40:49** MT reads *and it was on steps that they would go* [Q] **41:1** LXX; MT reads *jambs; they were 10 ½ feet wide on each side — the width of the tabernacle* [R] **41:1** Lit *six cubits*, also in vv. 3,5 [S] **41:2** Lit *10 cubits* [T] **41:2** Lit *five cubits*, also in vv. 9,11,12 [U] **41:2** Lit *40 cubits* [V] **41:2** Lit *20 cubits*, also in vv. 4,10 [W] **41:3** Lit *two cubits*, also in v. 22 [X] **41:3** LXX; MT reads *width of the entrance* [Y] **41:3** Lit *seven cubits*

35 feet, and the width, 35 feet. And he said to me, "This is the most holy place."

OUTSIDE THE TEMPLE

5 Then he measured the wall of the temple; it was 10 ½ feet thick. The width of the side rooms all around the temple was 7 feet.[A] 6 The side rooms were arranged one above another in three stories of thirty rooms each.[B] There were ledges on the wall of the temple all around to serve as supports for the side rooms, so that the supports would not be in the temple wall itself. 7 The side rooms surrounding the temple widened at each successive story, for the structure surrounding the temple went up by stages. This was the reason for the temple's broadness as it rose. And so, one would go up from the lowest story to the highest by means of the middle one.[C]

8 I saw that the temple had a raised platform surrounding it; this foundation for the side rooms was 10 ½ feet high.[D] 9 The thickness of the outer wall of the side rooms was 8 ¾ feet. The free space between the side rooms of the temple 10 and the outer chambers was 35 feet wide all around the temple. 11 The side rooms opened into the free space, one entrance toward the north and another to the south. The area of free space was 8 ¾ feet wide all around.

12 Now the building that faced the temple yard toward the west was 122 ½ feet[E] wide. The wall of the building was 8 ¾ feet thick on all sides, and the building's length was 157 ½ feet.[F]

13 Then the man measured the temple; it was 175 feet[G] long. In addition, the temple yard and the building, including its walls, were 175 feet long. 14 The width of the front of the temple along with the temple yard to the east was 175 feet. 15 Next he measured the length of the building facing the temple yard to the west, with its galleries[H] on each side; it was 175 feet.

INTERIOR WOODEN STRUCTURES

The interior of the great hall and the porticoes of the court — 16 the thresholds, the beveled windows, and the balconies all around with their three levels opposite the threshold — were overlaid with wood on all sides. They were paneled from the ground to the windows (but the windows were covered), 17 reaching to the top of the entrance, and as far as the inner temple and on the outside. On every wall all around, on the inside and outside, was a pattern 18 carved with cherubim and palm trees. There was a palm tree between each pair of cherubim. Each cherub had two faces: 19 a human face turned toward the palm tree on one side, and a lion's face turned toward it on the other. They were carved throughout the temple on all sides. 20 Cherubim and palm trees were carved from the ground to the top of the entrance and on the wall of the great hall.

21 The doorposts of the great hall were square, and the front of the sanctuary had the same appearance. 22 The altar was[I] made of wood, 5 ¼ feet[J] high and 3 ½ feet long.[K] It had corners, and its length[L] and sides were of wood. The man told me, "This is the table that stands before the LORD."

23 The great hall and the sanctuary each had a double door, 24 and each of the doors had two swinging panels. There were two panels for one door and two for the other. 25 Cherubim and palm trees were carved on the doors of the great hall like those carved on the walls. There was a wooden canopy[C] outside, in front of the portico. 26 There were beveled windows and palm trees on both sides, on the side walls of the portico, the side rooms of the temple, and the canopies.[C]

THE PRIESTS' CHAMBERS

42 Then the man led me out by way of the north gate into the outer court. He brought me to the group of chambers opposite the temple yard and opposite the building to the north. 2 Along the length of the chambers, which was 175 feet,[M] there was an entrance on the north; the width was 87 ½ feet.[N] 3 Opposite the 35 foot space[O] belonging to the inner court and opposite the paved surface belonging to the outer court, the structure rose gallery by gallery in three tiers. 4 In front of the chambers was a walkway toward the inside, 17 ½ feet[P] wide and 175 feet long,[Q] and their entrances were on the north. 5 The upper chambers were narrower because the galleries took away

[A] **41:5** Lit *four cubits* [B] **41:6** Lit *another three and thirty times* [C] **41:7,25,26** Hb obscure [D] **41:8** Lit *a full rod of six cubits of a joint*; Hb obscure [E] **41:12** Lit *70 cubits* [F] **41:12** Lit *90 cubits* [G] **41:13** Lit *100 cubits* [H] **41:15** Or *ledges* [I] **41:21-22** Or *and in front of the sanctuary was something that looked like* [22] *an altar* [J] **41:22** Lit *three cubits* [K] **41:22** LXX reads *long and 3 ½ feet wide* [L] **41:22** LXX reads *base* [M] **42:2** Lit *100 cubits*, also in vv. 4,8 [N] **42:2** Lit *50 cubits*, also in v. 7 [O] **42:3** Lit *20 cubits* [P] **42:4** Lit *10 cubits* [Q] **42:4** LXX, Syr; MT reads *wide, a way of one cubit*

more space from them than from the lower
and middle stories of the building. 6 For they
were arranged in three stories and had no
pillars like the pillars of the courts; therefore
the upper chambers were set back from the
ground more than the lower and middle stories. 7 A wall on the outside ran in front of the
chambers, parallel to them, toward the outer
court; it was 87 ½ feet long. 8 For the chambers
on the outer court were 87 ½ feet long, while
those facing the great hall were 175 feet long.
9 At the base of these chambers there was an
entryway on the east side as one enters them
from the outer court.
10 In the thickness of the wall of the court
toward the south,[A] there were chambers facing the temple yard and the western building,
11 with a passageway in front of them, just like
the chambers that faced north. Their length and
width, as well as all their exits, measurements,
and entrances, were identical. 12 The entrance
at the beginning of the passageway, the way in
front of the corresponding[B] wall as one enters
on the east side, was similar to the entrances
of the chambers that were on the south side.
13 Then the man said to me, "The northern
and southern chambers that face the courtyard
are the holy chambers where the priests who
approach the LORD will eat the most holy offerings. There they will deposit the most holy offerings — the grain offerings, sin offerings, and
guilt offerings — for the place is holy. 14 Once
the priests have entered, they are not to go
out from the holy area to the outer court until
they have removed the clothes they minister
in, for these are holy. They are to put on other
clothes before they approach the public area."

OUTSIDE DIMENSIONS OF THE TEMPLE COMPLEX

15 When he finished measuring inside the temple complex, he led me out by way of the gate
that faced east and measured all around the
complex.
16 He measured the east side with a
measuring rod;
it was 875 feet[C] by the measuring rod.[D]
17 He[E] measured the north side;
it was 875 feet by the measuring rod.
18 He[F] measured the south side;
it was 875 feet by the measuring rod.
19 Then he turned to the west side
and measured 875 feet by the measuring
rod.
20 He measured the temple complex on all four
sides. It had a wall all around it, 875 feet long
and 875 feet wide, to separate the holy from
the common.

RETURN OF THE LORD'S GLORY

43 He led me to the gate, the one that faces
east, 2 and I saw the glory of the God of
Israel coming from the east. His voice sounded
like the roar of a huge torrent, and the earth
shone with his glory. 3 The vision I saw was
like the one I had seen when he[G] came to destroy the city, and like the ones I had seen by
the Chebar Canal. I fell facedown. 4 The glory
of the LORD entered the temple by way of the
gate that faced east. 5 Then the Spirit lifted me
up and brought me to the inner court, and the
glory of the LORD filled the temple.
6 While the man was standing beside me, I
heard someone speaking to me from the temple. 7 He said to me: "Son of man, this is the place
of my throne and the place for the soles of my
feet, where I will dwell among the Israelites
forever. The house of Israel and their kings
will no longer defile my holy name by their
religious prostitution and by the corpses[H] of
their kings at their high places.[I] 8 Whenever
they placed their threshold next to my threshold and their doorposts beside my doorposts,
with only a wall between me and them, they
were defiling my holy name by the detestable
acts they committed. So I destroyed them in
my anger. 9 Now let them remove their prostitution and the corpses of their kings far from
me, and I will dwell among them forever.
10 "As for you, son of man, describe the temple to the house of Israel, so that they may be
ashamed of their iniquities. Let them measure
its pattern, 11 and they will be ashamed of all
that they have done. Reveal[J] the design of the
temple to them — its layout with its exits and
entrances — its complete design along with
all its statutes, design specifications, and laws.
Write it down in their sight so that they may
observe its complete design and all its statutes
and may carry them out. 12 This is the law of
the temple: All its surrounding territory on
top of the mountain will be especially holy.
Yes, this is the law of the temple.

[A] **42:10** LXX; MT reads *east* [B] **42:12** Or *protective*; Hb obscure [C] **42:16** Lit *500 in rods*, also in vv. 17,18,19 [D] **42:16** Lit *rod all around*, also in vv. 17,18,19 [E] **42:17** LXX reads *Then he turned to the north and* [F] **42:18** LXX reads *Then he turned to the south and* [G] **43:3** Some Hb mss, Theod, Vg; other Hb mss, LXX, Syr read *I* [H] **43:7** Or *monuments*, also in v. 9 [I] **43:7** Some Hb mss, Theod, Tg read *their death* [J] **43:10-11** LXX, Vg; MT reads *pattern.* [11]*And if they are ashamed . . . done, reveal*

THE ALTAR

13 “These are the measurements of the altar in units of length (each unit being the standard length plus three inches):[A] The gutter is 21 inches[B] deep and 21 inches wide, with a rim of nine inches[C] around its edge. This is the base[D] of the altar. 14 The distance from the gutter on the ground to the lower ledge is 3 ½ feet,[E] and the width of the ledge is 21 inches. There are 7 feet[F] from the small ledge to the large ledge, whose width is also 21 inches. 15 The altar hearth[G] is 7 feet high, and four horns project upward from the hearth. 16 The hearth is square, 21 feet[H] long by 21 feet wide. 17 The ledge is 24 ½ feet[I] long by 24 ½ feet wide, with four equal sides. The rim all around it is 10 ½ inches,[J] and its gutter is 21 inches all around it. The altar's steps face east.”

18 Then he said to me: “Son of man, this is what the Lord God says: These are the statutes for the altar on the day it is constructed, so that burnt offerings may be sacrificed on it and blood may be splattered on it: 19 You are to give a bull from the herd as a sin offering to the Levitical priests who are from the offspring of Zadok, who approach me in order to serve me.” This is the declaration of the Lord God. 20 “You are to take some of its blood and apply it to the four horns of the altar, the four corners of the ledge, and all around the rim. In this way you will purify the altar and make atonement for it. 21 Then you are to take away the bull for the sin offering, and it must be burned outside the sanctuary in the place appointed for the temple.

22 “On the second day you are to present an unblemished male goat as a sin offering. They will purify the altar just as they did with the bull. 23 When you have finished the purification, you are to present a young, unblemished bull and an unblemished ram from the flock. 24 You are to present them before the Lord; the priests will throw salt on them and sacrifice them as a burnt offering to the Lord. 25 You will offer a goat for a sin offering each day for seven days. A young bull and a ram from the flock, both unblemished, are also to be offered. 26 For seven days the priests are to make atonement for the altar and cleanse it. In this way they will consecrate it[K] 27 and complete the days of purification. Then on the eighth day and afterward, the priests will offer your burnt offerings and fellowship offerings on the altar, and I will accept you.” This is the declaration of the Lord God.

THE PRINCE'S PRIVILEGE

44 The man then brought me back toward the sanctuary's outer gate that faced east, and it was closed. 2 The Lord said to me: “This gate will remain closed. It will not be opened, and no one will enter through it, because the Lord, the God of Israel, has entered through it. Therefore it will remain closed. 3 The prince himself will sit in the gate to eat a meal before the Lord. He is to enter by way of the portico of the gate and go out the same way.”

4 Then the man brought me by way of the north gate to the front of the temple. I looked, and the glory of the Lord filled his temple. And I fell facedown. 5 The Lord said to me: “Son of man, pay attention; look with your eyes and listen with your ears to everything I tell you about all the statutes and laws of the Lord's temple. Take careful note of the entrance of the temple along with all the exits of the sanctuary.

THE LEVITES' DUTIES AND PRIVILEGES

6 “Say to the rebellious people, the house of Israel, ‘This is what the Lord God says: I have had enough of all your detestable practices, house of Israel. 7 When you brought in foreigners, uncircumcised in both heart and flesh, to occupy my sanctuary, you defiled my temple while you offered my food — the fat and the blood. You[L] broke my covenant by all your detestable practices. 8 You have not kept charge of my holy things but have appointed others to keep charge of my sanctuary for you.’

9 “This is what the Lord God says: No foreigner, uncircumcised in heart and flesh, may enter my sanctuary, not even a foreigner who is among the Israelites. 10 Surely the Levites who wandered away from me when Israel went astray, and who strayed from me after their idols, will bear the consequences of their iniquity. 11 Yet they will occupy my sanctuary, serving as guards at the temple gates and ministering at the temple. They will slaughter the burnt offerings and other sacrifices for the people and will stand before them to serve them. 12 Because they ministered to the house

[A] **43:13** Lit *in cubits (a cubit being a cubit plus a handbreadth)* [B] **43:13** Lit *one cubit*, also in vv. 14,17 [C] **43:13** Lit *one span* [D] **43:13** LXX reads *height* [E] **43:14** Lit *two cubits* [F] **43:14** Lit *four cubits*, also in v. 15 [G] **43:15** Hb obscure [H] **43:16** Lit *12 cubits* [I] **43:17** Lit *14 cubits* [J] **43:17** Lit *one-half cubit* [K] **43:26** Lit *will fill its hands* [L] **44:7** LXX, Syr, Vg; MT reads *They*

of Israel before their idols and became a sinful stumbling block to them, therefore I swore an oath[A] against them" — this is the declaration of the Lord God — "that they would bear the consequences of their iniquity. 13 They must not approach me to serve me as priests or come near any of my holy things or the most holy things. They will bear their disgrace and the consequences of the detestable acts they committed. 14 Yet I will make them responsible for the duties of the temple — for all its work and everything done in it.

THE PRIESTS' DUTIES AND PRIVILEGES

15 "But the Levitical priests descended from Zadok, who kept charge of my sanctuary when the Israelites went astray from me, will approach me to serve me. They will stand before me to offer me fat and blood." This is the declaration of the Lord God. 16 "They are the ones who may enter my sanctuary and approach my table to serve me. They will keep my mandate. 17 When they enter the gates of the inner court they are to wear linen garments; they must not have on them anything made of wool when they minister at the gates of the inner court and within it. 18 They are to wear linen turbans on their heads and linen undergarments around their waists. They are not to put on anything that makes them sweat. 19 Before they go out to the outer court,[B] to the people, they must take off the clothes they have been ministering in, leave them in the holy chambers, and dress in other clothes so that they do not transmit holiness to the people through their clothes.

20 "They may not shave their heads or let their hair grow long, but are to carefully trim their hair. 21 No priest may drink wine before he enters the inner court. 22 He is not to marry a widow or a divorced woman, but may marry only a virgin from the offspring of the house of Israel, or a widow who is the widow of a priest. 23 They are to teach my people the difference between the holy and the common, and explain to them the difference between the clean and the unclean.

24 "In a dispute, they will officiate as judges and decide the case according to my ordinances. They are to observe my laws and statutes regarding all my appointed festivals, and keep my Sabbaths holy. 25 A priest may not come near a dead person so that he becomes defiled. However, he may defile himself for a father, a mother, a son, a daughter, a brother, or an unmarried sister. 26 After he is cleansed, he is to count off seven days for himself. 27 On the day he goes into the sanctuary, into the inner court to minister in the sanctuary, he is to present his sin offering." This is the declaration of the Lord God.

28 "This will be their inheritance: I am their inheritance. You are to give them no possession in Israel: I am their possession. 29 They will eat the grain offering, the sin offering, and the guilt offering. Everything in Israel that is permanently dedicated to the LORD will belong to them. 30 The best of all the firstfruits of every kind and contribution of every kind from all your gifts will belong to the priests. You are to give your first batch of dough to the priest so that a blessing may rest on your homes. 31 The priests may not eat any bird or animal that died naturally or was mauled by wild beasts.

THE SACRED PORTION OF THE LAND

45 "When you divide the land by lot as an inheritance, set aside a donation to the LORD, a holy portion of the land, 8 1/3 miles[C] long and 6 2/3 miles[D] wide. This entire region will be holy. 2 In this area there will be a square section[E] for the sanctuary, 875 by 875 feet,[F] with 87 1/2 feet[G] of open space all around it. 3 From this holy portion,[H] you will measure off an area 8 1/3 miles long and 3 1/3 miles[I] wide, in which the sanctuary, the most holy place, will stand.[J] 4 It will be a holy area of the land to be used by the priests who minister in the sanctuary, who approach to serve the LORD. It will be a place for their houses, as well as a holy area for the sanctuary. 5 There will be another area 8 1/3 miles long and 3 1/3 miles wide for the Levites who minister in the temple; it will be their possession for towns to live in.[K]

6 "As the property of the city, set aside an area 1 2/3 miles[L] wide and 8 1/3 miles long, adjacent to the holy donation of land. It will be for the whole house of Israel. 7 And the prince will have the area on each side of the holy donation of land and the city's property, adjacent to the holy donation and the city's property, stretching to the west on the west side and to the east on the east side. Its length will correspond

[A] **44:12** Lit *I lifted my hand* [B] **44:19** Some Hb mss, LXX, Syr, Vg; other Hb mss read *court, to the outer court* [C] **45:1** Lit *25,000 cubits*, also in vv. 3,5,6 [D] **45:1** LXX reads *20,000 cubits*; MT reads *10,000 cubits* [E] **45:2** Lit *square all around* [F] **45:2** Lit *500 by 500 cubits* [G] **45:2** Lit *50 cubits* [H] **45:3** Lit *this measured portion* [I] **45:3** Lit *10,000 cubits*, also in v. 5 [J] **45:3** Lit *be* [K] **45:5** LXX; MT, Syr, Tg, Vg read *possession — 20 chambers* [L] **45:6** Lit *5,000 cubits*

to one of the tribal portions from the western boundary to the eastern boundary. 8 This
will be his land as a possession in Israel. My
princes will no longer oppress my people but
give the rest of the land to the house of Israel
according to their tribes.
9 "This is what the Lord GOD says: You have
gone too far,[A] princes of Israel! Put away violence and oppression and do what is just
and right. Put an end to your evictions of my
people." This is the declaration of the Lord GOD.
10 "You are to have honest scales, an honest dry
measure,[B] and an honest liquid measure.[C] 11 The
dry measure[D] and the liquid measure[E] will be
uniform, with the liquid measure containing
5 ½ gallons[F] and the dry measure holding half
a bushel.[F] Their measurement will be a tenth of
the standard larger capacity measure.[G] 12 The
shekel[H] will weigh twenty gerahs. Your mina
will equal sixty shekels.

THE PEOPLE'S CONTRIBUTION TO THE SACRIFICES

13 "This is the contribution you are to offer:
Three quarts[I] from five bushels[J] of wheat
and[K] three quarts from five bushels of barley. 14 The quota of oil in liquid measures[L]
will be one percent of every[M] cor. The cor
equals ten liquid measures or one standard
larger capacity measure,[N] since ten liquid
measures equal one standard larger capacity
measure. 15 And the quota from the flock is
one animal out of every two hundred from
the well-watered pastures of Israel. These
are for the grain offerings, burnt offerings,
and fellowship offerings, to make atonement
for the people." This is the declaration of the
Lord GOD. 16 "All the people of the land must
take part in this contribution for the prince
in Israel. 17 Then the burnt offerings, grain
offerings, and drink offerings for the festivals, New Moons, and Sabbaths — for all the
appointed times of the house of Israel — will
be the prince's responsibility. He will provide the sin offerings, grain offerings, burnt
offerings, and fellowship offerings to make
atonement on behalf of the house of Israel.
18 "This is what the Lord GOD says: In the
first month, on the first day of the month,
you are to take a young, unblemished bull
and purify the sanctuary. 19 The priest is to
take some of the blood from the sin offering
and apply it to the temple doorposts, the four
corners of the altar's ledge, and the doorposts
of the gate of the inner court. 20 You are to
do the same thing on the seventh day of the
month for everyone who sins unintentionally or through ignorance. In this way you will
make atonement for the temple.
21 "In the first month, on the fourteenth day
of the month, you are to celebrate the Passover, a festival of seven days during which
unleavened bread will be eaten. 22 On that day
the prince will provide a bull as a sin offering
on behalf of himself and all the people of the
land. 23 During the seven days of the festival,
he will provide seven bulls and seven rams
without blemish as a burnt offering to the
LORD on each of the seven days, along with a
male goat each day for a sin offering. 24 He will
also provide a grain offering of half a bushel[O]
per bull and half a bushel per ram, along with
a gallon[P] of oil for every half bushel. 25 At the
festival that begins on the fifteenth day of the
seventh month,[Q] he will provide the same
things for seven days — the same sin offerings, burnt offerings, grain offerings, and oil.

SACRIFICES AT APPOINTED TIMES

46 "This is what the Lord GOD says: The gate
of the inner court that faces east is to be
closed during the six days of work, but it will
be opened on the Sabbath day and opened on
the day of the New Moon. 2 The prince should
enter from the outside by way of the gate's
portico and stand at the gate's doorpost while
the priests sacrifice his burnt offerings and
fellowship offerings. He will bow in worship
at the gate's threshold and then depart, but
the gate is not to be closed until evening. 3 The
people of the land will also bow in worship
before the LORD at the entrance of that gate
on the Sabbaths and New Moons.
4 "The burnt offering that the prince presents to the LORD on the Sabbath day is to be
six unblemished lambs and an unblemished
ram. 5 The grain offering will be half a bushel[R]
with the ram, and the grain offering with the
lambs will be whatever he wants to give, as
well as a gallon[S] of oil for every half bushel.

[A] 45:9 Lit *Enough of you* [B] 45:10 Lit *an honest ephah* [C] 45:10 Lit *and an honest bath* [D] 45:11 Lit *The ephah* [E] 45:11 Lit *the bath* [F] 45:11 Lit *one-tenth of a homer* [G] 45:11 Lit *be based on the homer* [H] 45:12 A shekel is about two-fifths of an ounce of silver [I] 45:13 Lit *One-sixth of an ephah* [J] 45:13 Lit *a homer* [K] 45:13 LXX, Vg; MT reads *and you are to give* [L] 45:14 Lit *oil, the bath, the oil* [M] 45:14 Lit *be a tenth of the bath from the* [N] 45:14 Lit *10 baths, a homer* [O] 45:24 Lit *an ephah* [P] 45:24 Lit *a hin* [Q] 45:25 = the Festival of Shelters [R] 46:5 Lit *an ephah*, also in vv. 7,11 [S] 46:5 Lit *a hin*, also in vv. 7,11

6 On the day of the New Moon, the burnt offering is to be a young, unblemished bull, as well
as six lambs and a ram without blemish. 7 He
will provide a grain offering of half a bushel
with the bull, half a bushel with the ram, and
whatever he can afford with the lambs, together with a gallon of oil for every half bushel.
8 When the prince enters, he is to go in by way
of the gate's portico and go out the same way.
9 "When the people of the land come before
the LORD at the appointed times,[A] whoever
enters by way of the north gate to worship is
to go out by way of the south gate, and whoever enters by way of the south gate is to go
out by way of the north gate. No one may return through the gate by which he entered,
but is to go out by the opposite gate. 10 When
the people enter, the prince will enter with
them, and when they leave, he will leave.
11 At the festivals and appointed times, the
grain offering will be half a bushel with the
bull, half a bushel with the ram, and whatever
he wants to give with the lambs, along with a
gallon of oil for every half bushel.
12 "When the prince makes a freewill offering, whether a burnt offering or a fellowship
offering as a freewill offering to the LORD, the
gate that faces east is to be opened for him.
He is to offer his burnt offering or fellowship
offering just as he does on the Sabbath day.
Then he will go out, and the gate is to be closed
after he leaves.
13 "You are to offer an unblemished year-old
male lamb as a daily burnt offering to the LORD;
you will offer it every morning. 14 You are also
to prepare a grain offering every morning
along with it: three quarts,[B] with one-third of
a gallon[C] of oil to moisten the fine flour — a
grain offering to the LORD. This is a permanent
statute to be observed regularly. 15 They will
offer the lamb, the grain offering, and the oil
every morning as a regular burnt offering.

TRANSFER OF ROYAL LANDS

16 "This is what the Lord GOD says: If the prince
gives a gift to each of his sons as their inheritance, it will belong to his sons. It will become
their property by inheritance. 17 But if he gives a
gift from his inheritance to one of his servants,
it will belong to that servant until the year of
freedom, when it will revert to the prince. His
inheritance belongs only to his sons; it is theirs.
18 The prince must not take any of the people's
inheritance, evicting them from their property. He is to provide an inheritance for his sons
from his own property, so that none of my people will be displaced from his own property."

THE TEMPLE KITCHENS

19 Then he brought me through the entrance
that was at the side of the gate, into the priests'
holy chambers, which faced north. I saw a
place there at the far western end. 20 He said
to me, "This is the place where the priests will
boil the guilt offering and the sin offering,
and where they will bake the grain offering,
so that they do not bring them into the outer
court and transmit holiness to the people."
21 Next he brought me into the outer court
and led me past its four corners. There was a
separate court in each of its corners. 22 In the
four corners of the outer court there were
enclosed[D] courts, 70 feet[E] long by 52 ½ feet[F]
wide. All four corner areas had the same dimensions. 23 There was a stone wall[G] around
the inside of them, around the four of them,
with ovens built at the base of the walls on all
sides. 24 He said to me: "These are the kitchens
where those who minister at the temple will
cook the people's sacrifices."

THE LIFE-GIVING RIVER

47 Then he brought me back to the entrance of the temple and there was
water flowing from under the threshold of
the temple toward the east, for the temple
faced east. The water was coming down from
under the south side of the threshold of the
temple, south of the altar. 2 Next he brought
me out by way of the north gate and led me
around the outside to the outer gate that faced
east; there the water was trickling from the
south side. 3 As the man went out east with a
measuring line in his hand, he measured off a
third of a mile[H] and led me through the water.
It came up to my ankles. 4 Then he measured
off a third of a mile and led me through the
water. It came up to my knees. He measured
off another third of a mile and led me through
the water. It came up to my waist. 5 Again he
measured off a third of a mile, and it was a
river that I could not cross on foot. For the
water had risen; it was deep enough to swim
in, a river that could not be crossed on foot.
6 He asked me, "Do you see this, son of man?"
Then he led me back to the bank of the river.

[A] **46:9** Or *the festivals* [B] **46:14** Lit *one-sixth of an ephah* [C] **46:14** Lit *one-third of a hin* [D] **46:22** Hb obscure [E] **46:22** Lit *40 cubits* [F] **46:22** Lit *30 cubits* [G] **46:23** Or *a row* [H] **47:3** Lit *1,000 cubits*, also in vv. 4,5

7 When I had returned, I saw a very large number of trees along both sides of the riverbank.
8 He said to me, "This water flows out to the
eastern region and goes down to the Arabah.
When it enters the sea, the sea of foul water,[A,B]
the water of the sea becomes fresh. 9 Every
kind of living creature that swarms will live
wherever the river flows,[C] and there will be a
huge number of fish because this water goes
there. Since the water will become fresh, there
will be life everywhere the river goes. 10 Fishermen will stand beside it from En-gedi to
En-eglaim.[D] These will become places where
nets are spread out to dry. Their fish will consist of many different kinds, like the fish of
the Mediterranean Sea. 11 Yet its swamps and
marshes will not be healed; they will be left
for salt. 12 All kinds of trees providing food
will grow along both banks of the river. Their
leaves will not wither, and their fruit will not
fail. Each month they will bear fresh fruit because the water comes from the sanctuary.
Their fruit will be used for food and their leaves
for medicine."

THE BORDERS OF THE LAND

13 This is what the Lord God says: "This is[E] the
border you will use to divide the land as an
inheritance for the twelve tribes of Israel. Joseph will receive two shares. 14 You will inherit
it in equal portions, since I swore[F] to give it
to your ancestors. So this land will fall to you
as an inheritance.

15 This is to be the border of the land:
On the north side it will extend from the
Mediterranean Sea by way of Hethlon
and Lebo-hamath to Zedad,[G] 16 Berothah,
and Sibraim (which is between the border
of Damascus and the border of Hamath),
as far as Hazer-hatticon, which is on the
border of Hauran. 17 So the border will
run from the sea to Hazar-enon at the
border of Damascus, with the territory
of Hamath to the north. This will be the
northern side.

18 On the east side it will run between
Hauran and Damascus, along the Jordan
between Gilead and the land of Israel; you
will measure from the northern border to
the eastern sea.[B] This will be the eastern
side.

19 On the south side it will run from Tamar
to the Waters of Meribath-kadesh,[H]
and on to the Brook of Egypt as far as
the Mediterranean Sea. This will be the
southern side.

20 On the west side the Mediterranean Sea
will be the border, from the southern border up to a point opposite Lebo-hamath.
This will be the western side.

21 "You are to divide this land among yourselves according to the tribes of Israel. 22 You
will allot it as an inheritance for yourselves
and for the aliens residing among you, who
have fathered children among you. You will
treat them[I] like native-born Israelites; along
with you, they will be allotted an inheritance
among the tribes of Israel. 23 In whatever tribe
the alien resides, you will assign his inheritance there." This is the declaration of the
Lord God.

THE TRIBAL ALLOTMENTS

48 "Now these are the names of the tribes:
From the northern end, along the
road of Hethlon, to Lebo-hamath as far
as Hazar-enon, at the northern border
of Damascus, alongside Hamath and
extending from the eastern side to the
sea, will be Dan — one portion.
2 Next to the territory of Dan, from the
east side to the west, will be Asher — one
portion.
3 Next to the territory of Asher, from the
east side to the west, will be Naphtali —
one portion.
4 Next to the territory of Naphtali,
from the east side to the west, will be
Manasseh — one portion.
5 Next to the territory of Manasseh, from
the east side to the west, will be Ephraim
— one portion.
6 Next to the territory of Ephraim, from
the east side to the west, will be Reuben
— one portion.
7 Next to the territory of Reuben, from the
east side to the west, will be Judah — one
portion.

8 "Next to the territory of Judah, from the
east side to the west, will be the portion you

[A] **47:8** Or *enters the sea, being brought out to the sea*; Hb obscure [B] **47:8,18** = the Dead Sea [C] **47:9** LXX, Vg; MT reads *the two rivers flow* [D] **47:10** Two springs near the Dead Sea [E] **47:13** Tg, Vg; Syr reads *The valley of* [F] **47:14** Lit *lifted my hand* [G] **47:15** LXX; MT reads *and Lebo to Zedad, Hamath*; Ezk 48:1 [H] **47:19** = Kadesh-barnea [I] **47:22** Lit *They will be to you*

donate to the LORD, 8 ⅓ miles[A] wide, and as
long as one of the tribal portions from the
east side to the west. The sanctuary will be
in the middle of it.
9 "The special portion you donate to the
LORD will be 8 ⅓ miles long and 3 ⅓ miles[B]
wide. 10 This holy donation will be set apart
for the priests alone. It will be 8 ⅓ miles long
on the northern side, 3 ⅓ miles wide on the
western side, 3 ⅓ miles wide on the eastern
side, and 8 ⅓ miles long on the southern side.
The LORD's sanctuary will be in the middle of
it. 11 It is for the consecrated priests, the sons
of Zadok, who kept my charge and did not go
astray as the Levites did when the Israelites
went astray. 12 It will be a special donation for
them out of the holy donation of the land, a
most holy place adjacent to the territory of
the Levites.
13 "Next to the territory of the priests, the
Levites will have an area 8 ⅓ miles long and
3 ⅓ miles wide. The total length will be 8 ⅓
miles and the width 3 ⅓ miles. 14 They must
not sell or exchange any of it, and they must
not transfer this choice part of the land, for
it is holy to the LORD.
15 "The remaining area, 1 ⅔ miles[C] wide and
8 ⅓ miles long, will be for common use by
the city, for both residential and open space.
The city will be in the middle of it. 16 These
are the city's measurements:

1 ½ miles[D] on the north side;
1 ½ miles on the south side;
1 ½ miles on the east side;
and 1 ½ miles on the west side.

17 The city's open space will extend:

425 feet[E] to the north,
425 feet to the south,
425 feet to the east,
and 425 feet to the west.

18 "The remainder of the length alongside
the holy donation will be 3 ⅓ miles to the east
and 3 ⅓ miles to the west. It will run alongside the holy donation. Its produce will be
food for the workers of the city. 19 The city's
workers from all the tribes of Israel will cultivate it. 20 The entire donation will be 8 ⅓
miles by 8 ⅓ miles; you are to set apart the
holy donation along with the city property
as a square area.
21 "The remaining area on both sides of
the holy donation and the city property will
belong to the prince. He will own the land
adjacent to the tribal portions, next to the
8 ⅓ miles of the donation as far as the eastern border and[F] next to the 8 ⅓ miles of the
donation as far as the western border. The
holy donation and the sanctuary of the temple will be in the middle of it. 22 Except for
the Levitical property and the city property
in the middle of the area belonging to the
prince, the area between the territory of
Judah and that of Benjamin will belong to
the prince.

23 "As for the rest of the tribes:
From the east side to the west, will be
Benjamin — one portion.
24 Next to the territory of Benjamin, from
the east side to the west, will be Simeon
— one portion.
25 Next to the territory of Simeon, from
the east side to the west, will be Issachar
— one portion.
26 Next to the territory of Issachar, from
the east side to the west, will be Zebulun
— one portion.
27 Next to the territory of Zebulun, from
the east side to the west, will be Gad —
one portion.

28 Next to the territory of Gad toward the south
side, the border will run from Tamar to the
Waters of Meribath-kadesh, to the Brook of
Egypt, and out to the Mediterranean Sea.
29 This is the land you are to allot as an inheritance to Israel's tribes, and these will be
their portions." This is the declaration of the
Lord GOD.

THE NEW CITY

30 "These are the exits of the city:
On the north side, which measures 1 ½
miles, 31 there will be three gates facing
north, the gates of the city being named
for the tribes of Israel: one, the gate of
Reuben; one, the gate of Judah; and one,
the gate of Levi.
32 On the east side, which is 1 ½ miles,
there will be three gates: one, the gate of
Joseph; one, the gate of Benjamin; and
one, the gate of Dan.
33 On the south side, which measures 1 ½
miles, there will be three gates: one, the
gate of Simeon; one, the gate of Issachar;
and one, the gate of Zebulun.
34 On the west side, which is 1 ½ miles,

[A] **48:8** Lit *25,000 cubits*, also in vv. 9,10,13,15,20,21 [B] **48:9** Lit *10,000 cubits*, also in vv. 10,13,18 [C] **48:15** Lit *5,000 cubits* [D] **48:16** Lit *4,500 cubits*, also in vv. 30,32,33,34 [E] **48:17** Lit *250 cubits* [F] **48:21** Lit *border, and to the west,*

there will be three gates: one, the gate of
Gad; one, the gate of Asher; and one, the
gate of Naphtali.
35 The perimeter of the city will be six miles,[A]
and the name of the city from that day on will
be, The LORD Is There."

[A] 48:35 Lit *18,000 cubits*

The name of the city from that day on will be, The LORD Is There.
—Ezekiel 48:35

over the entire province of Babylon and chief
governor over all the wise men of Babylon.
49 At Daniel's request, the king appointed Shadrach, Meshach, and Abednego to manage the
province of Babylon. But Daniel remained at
the king's court.

NEBUCHADNEZZAR'S GOLD STATUE

3 King Nebuchadnezzar made a gold statue,
ninety feet high and nine feet wide.[A] He
set it up on the plain of Dura in the province
of Babylon. 2 King Nebuchadnezzar sent word
to assemble the satraps, prefects, governors,
advisers, treasurers, judges, magistrates, and
all the rulers of the provinces to attend the
dedication of the statue King Nebuchadnezzar
had set up. 3 So the satraps, prefects, governors,
advisers, treasurers, judges, magistrates, and
all the rulers of the provinces assembled for
the dedication of the statue the king had set
up. Then they stood before the statue Nebuchadnezzar had set up.
4 A herald loudly proclaimed, "People of every nation and language, you are commanded:
5 When you hear the sound of the horn, flute,
zither,[B] lyre,[C] harp, drum,[D] and every kind of
music, you are to fall facedown and worship
the gold statue that King Nebuchadnezzar has
set up. 6 But whoever does not fall down and
worship will immediately be thrown into a
furnace of blazing fire."
7 Therefore, when all the people heard the
sound of the horn, flute, zither, lyre, harp, and
every kind of music, people of every nation
and language fell down and worshiped the
gold statue that King Nebuchadnezzar had
set up.

THE FURNACE OF BLAZING FIRE

8 Some Chaldeans took this occasion to come
forward and maliciously accuse[E] the Jews.
9 They said to King Nebuchadnezzar, "May the
king live forever. 10 You as king have issued a
decree that everyone who hears the sound of
the horn, flute, zither, lyre, harp, drum, and every kind of music must fall down and worship
the gold statue. 11 Whoever does not fall down
and worship will be thrown into a furnace of
blazing fire. 12 There are some Jews you have
appointed to manage the province of Babylon:
Shadrach, Meshach, and Abednego. These
men have ignored you, the king; they do not
serve your gods or worship the gold statue
you have set up."
13 Then in a furious rage Nebuchadnezzar
gave orders to bring in Shadrach, Meshach,
and Abednego. So these men were brought before the king. 14 Nebuchadnezzar asked them,
"Shadrach, Meshach, and Abednego, is it true
that you don't serve my gods or worship the
gold statue I have set up? 15 Now if you're ready,
when you hear the sound of the horn, flute,
zither, lyre, harp, drum, and every kind of music, fall down and worship the statue I made.
But if you don't worship it, you will immediately be thrown into a furnace of blazing fire
— and who is the god who can rescue you
from my power?"
16 Shadrach, Meshach, and Abednego replied to the king, "Nebuchadnezzar, we don't
need to give you an answer to this question.
17 If the God we serve exists, then he can rescue us from the furnace of blazing fire, and
he can[F] rescue us from the power of you, the
king. 18 But even if he does not rescue us,[G] we
want you as king to know that we will not
serve your gods or worship the gold statue
you set up."

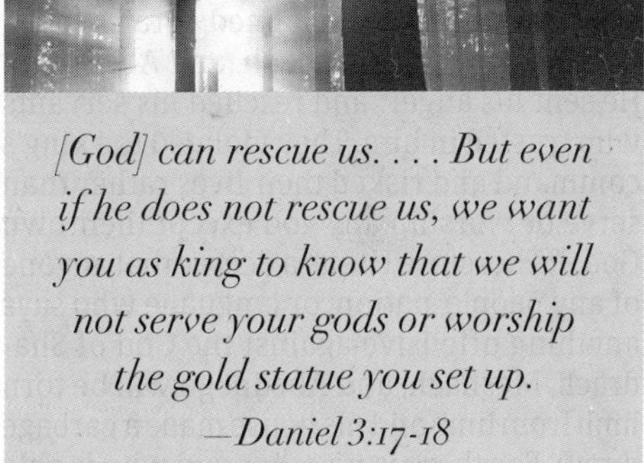
[God] can rescue us. . . . But even
if he does not rescue us, we want
you as king to know that we will
not serve your gods or worship
the gold statue you set up.
—Daniel 3:17-18

19 Then Nebuchadnezzar was filled with
rage, and the expression on his face changed
toward Shadrach, Meshach, and Abednego. He
gave orders to heat the furnace seven times
more than was customary, 20 and he commanded some of the best soldiers in his army to tie
up Shadrach, Meshach, and Abednego and
throw them into the furnace of blazing fire.
21 So these men, in their trousers, robes, head
coverings,[H] and other clothes, were tied up
and thrown into the furnace of blazing fire.
22 Since the king's command was so urgent[I]

[A] **3:1** Lit *statue, its height sixty cubits, its width six cubits* [B] **3:5** Or *lyre* [C] **3:5** Or *sambuke* [D] **3:5** Or *pipe* [E] **3:8** Lit *and eat the pieces of* [F] **3:17** Or *If the God whom we serve is willing to save us from the furnace of blazing fire, then he will* [G] **3:18** Lit *But if not* [H] **3:21** The identity of these articles of clothing is uncertain. [I] **3:22** Or *harsh*

and the furnace extremely hot, the raging
flames[A] killed those men who carried Shadrach, Meshach, and Abednego up. 23 And
these three men, Shadrach, Meshach, and
Abednego fell, bound, into the furnace of
blazing fire.

DELIVERED FROM THE FIRE

24 Then King Nebuchadnezzar jumped up in
alarm. He said to his advisers, "Didn't we throw
three men, bound, into the fire?"
"Yes, of course, Your Majesty," they replied
to the king.
25 He exclaimed, "Look! I see four men, not
tied, walking around in the fire unharmed;
and the fourth looks like a son of the gods."[B]
26 Nebuchadnezzar then approached the
door of the furnace of blazing fire and called:
"Shadrach, Meshach, and Abednego, you servants of the Most High God — come out!"
So Shadrach, Meshach, and Abednego came
out of the fire. 27 When the satraps, prefects,
governors, and the king's advisers gathered
around, they saw that the fire had no effect
on[C] the bodies of these men: not a hair of their
heads was singed, their robes were unaffected, and there was no smell of fire on them.
28 Nebuchadnezzar exclaimed, "Praise to the
God of Shadrach, Meshach, and Abednego!
He sent his angel[D] and rescued his servants
who trusted in him. They violated the king's
command and risked their lives rather than
serve or worship any god except their own
God. 29 Therefore I issue a decree that anyone
of any people, nation, or language who says
anything offensive against the God of Shadrach, Meshach, and Abednego will be torn
limb from limb and his house made a garbage
dump. For there is no other god who is able
to deliver like this." 30 Then the king rewarded Shadrach, Meshach, and Abednego in the
province of Babylon.

NEBUCHADNEZZAR'S PROCLAMATION

4 King Nebuchadnezzar,

To those of every people, nation, and language, who live on the whole earth:

May your prosperity increase. 2 I am
pleased to tell you about the miracles
and wonders the Most High God has
done for me.

3 How great are his miracles,
and how mighty his wonders!
His kingdom is an eternal kingdom,
and his dominion is from generation
to generation.

THE DREAM

4 I, Nebuchadnezzar, was at ease in my house
and flourishing in my palace. 5 I had a dream,
and it frightened me; while in my bed, the
images and visions in my mind alarmed me.
6 So I issued a decree to bring all the wise men
of Babylon to me in order that they might
make the dream's interpretation known to me.
7 When the magicians, mediums, Chaldeans,
and diviners came in, I told them the dream,
but they could not make its interpretation
known to me.
8 Finally Daniel, named Belteshazzar after
the name of my god — and a spirit of the holy
gods is in him — came before me. I told him the
dream: 9 "Belteshazzar, head of the magicians,
because I know that you have the spirit of the
holy gods and that no mystery puzzles you,
explain to me the visions of my dream that I
saw, and its interpretation. 10 In the visions
of my mind as I was lying in bed, I saw this:

There was a tree in the middle
of the earth,
and it was very tall.
11 The tree grew large and strong;
its top reached to the sky,
and it was visible to the ends
of the[E] earth.
12 Its leaves were beautiful, its fruit
was abundant,
and on it was food for all.
Wild animals found shelter under it,
the birds of the sky lived in its branches,
and every creature was fed from it.

13 "As I was lying in my bed, I also saw in the
visions of my mind a watcher, a holy one,[F] coming down from heaven. 14 He called out loudly:

Cut down the tree and chop off
its branches;
strip off its leaves and scatter its fruit.
Let the animals flee from under it,
and the birds from its branches.
15 But leave the stump with its roots
in the ground
and with a band of iron and bronze
around it

[A] 3:22 Lit *the flame of the fire* [B] 3:25 Or *of a divine being* [C] 3:27 Lit *fire had not overcome* [D] 3:28 Or *messenger* [E] 4:11 Lit *of all the* [F] 4:13 = an angel

in the tender grass of the field.
Let him be drenched with dew
from the sky
and share the plants of the earth
with the animals.
16 Let his mind be changed from that
of a human,
and let him be given the mind
of an animal
for seven periods of time.[A,B]
17 This word is by decree of the watchers,
and the decision is by command
from the holy ones.
This is so that the living will know
that the Most High is ruler
over human kingdoms.
He gives them to anyone he wants
and sets the lowliest of people over them.
18 This is the dream that I, King Nebuchadnezzar, had. Now, Belteshazzar, tell me the
interpretation, because none of the wise men
of my kingdom can make the interpretation
known to me. But you can, because you have
a spirit of the holy gods."

THE DREAM INTERPRETED

19 Then Daniel, whose name is Belteshazzar,
was stunned for a moment, and his thoughts
alarmed him. The king said, "Belteshazzar, don't
let the dream or its interpretation alarm you."
Belteshazzar answered, "My lord, may the
dream apply to those who hate you, and its
interpretation to your enemies! 20 The tree you
saw, which grew large and strong, whose top
reached to the sky and was visible to the whole
earth, 21 and whose leaves were beautiful and
its fruit abundant — and on it was food for
all, under it the wild animals lived, and in its
branches the birds of the sky lived — 22 that
tree is you, Your Majesty. For you have become
great and strong: your greatness has grown
and even reaches the sky, and your dominion
extends to the ends of the earth.
23 "The king saw a watcher, a holy one, coming
down from heaven and saying, 'Cut down the
tree and destroy it, but leave the stump with
its roots in the ground and with a band of iron
and bronze around it in the tender grass of the
field. Let him be drenched with dew from the
sky and share food with the wild animals for
seven periods of time.' 24 This is the interpretation, Your Majesty, and this is the decree of
the Most High that has been issued against
my lord the king: 25 You will be driven away
from people to live with the wild animals. You
will feed on grass like cattle and be drenched
with dew from the sky for seven periods of
time, until you acknowledge that the Most
High is ruler over human kingdoms, and he
gives them to anyone he wants. 26 As for the
command to leave the tree's stump with its
roots, your kingdom will be restored[C] to you as
soon as you acknowledge that Heaven[D] rules.
27 Therefore, may my advice seem good to you
my king. Separate yourself from your sins by
doing what is right, and from your injustices
by showing mercy to the needy. Perhaps there
will be an extension of your prosperity."

THE SENTENCE EXECUTED

28 All this happened to King Nebuchadnezzar.
29 At the end of twelve months, as he was walking on the roof of the royal palace in Babylon,
30 the king exclaimed, "Is this not Babylon the
Great that I have built to be a royal residence
by my vast power and for my majestic glory?"
31 While the words were still in the king's
mouth, a voice came from heaven: "King Nebuchadnezzar, to you it is declared that the kingdom has departed from you. 32 You will be driven
away from people to live with the wild animals,
and you will feed on grass like cattle for seven
periods of time, until you acknowledge that the
Most High is ruler over human kingdoms, and
he gives them to anyone he wants."
33 At that moment the message against Nebuchadnezzar was fulfilled. He was driven away
from people. He ate grass like cattle, and his
body was drenched with dew from the sky,
until his hair grew like eagles' feathers and
his nails like birds' claws.

NEBUCHADNEZZAR'S PRAISE

34 But at the end of those days, I, Nebuchadnezzar, looked up to heaven, and my sanity returned to me. Then I praised the Most High and
honored and glorified him who lives forever:
For his dominion is
an everlasting dominion,
and his kingdom is from generation
to generation.
35 All the inhabitants of the earth
are counted as nothing,
and he does what he wants
with the army of heaven
and the inhabitants of the earth.

[A] **4:16** Lit *animal as seven times pass over him* [B] **4:16** Perhaps seven years [C] **4:26** Lit *enduring* [D] **4:26** = God

There is no one who can block his hand
or say to him, "What have you done?"

36 At that time my sanity returned to me, and my majesty and splendor returned to me for the glory of my kingdom. My advisers and my nobles sought me out, I was reestablished over my kingdom, and even more greatness came to me. 37 Now I, Nebuchadnezzar, praise, exalt, and glorify the King of the heavens, because all his works are true and his ways are just. He is able to humble those who walk in pride.

BELSHAZZAR'S FEAST

5 King Belshazzar held a great feast for a thousand of his nobles and drank wine in their presence. 2 Under the influence of[A] the wine, Belshazzar gave orders to bring in the gold and silver vessels that his predecessor[B] Nebuchadnezzar had taken from the temple in Jerusalem, so that the king and his nobles, wives, and concubines could drink from them. 3 So they brought in the gold[C] vessels that had been taken from the temple, the house of God in Jerusalem, and the king and his nobles, wives, and concubines drank from them. 4 They drank the wine and praised their gods made of gold and silver, bronze, iron, wood, and stone.

THE HANDWRITING ON THE WALL

5 At that moment the fingers of a man's hand appeared and began writing on the plaster of the king's palace wall next to the lampstand. As the king watched the hand[D] that was writing, 6 his face turned pale,[E] and his thoughts so terrified him that he soiled himself[F] and his knees knocked together. 7 The king shouted to bring in the mediums, Chaldeans, and diviners. He said to these wise men of Babylon, "Whoever reads this inscription and gives me its interpretation will be clothed in purple, have a gold chain around his neck, and have the third highest position in the kingdom." 8 So all the king's wise men came in, but none could read the inscription or make its interpretation known to him. 9 Then King Belshazzar became even more terrified, his face turned pale,[G] and his nobles were bewildered.

10 Because of the outcry of the king and his nobles, the queen[H] came to the banquet hall. "May the king live forever," she said. "Don't let your thoughts terrify you or your face be pale.[I] 11 There is a man in your kingdom who has a spirit of the holy gods in him. In the days of your predecessor he was found to have insight, intelligence, and wisdom like the wisdom of the gods. Your predecessor, King Nebuchadnezzar, appointed him chief of the magicians, mediums, Chaldeans, and diviners. Your own predecessor, the king, 12 did this because Daniel, the one the king named Belteshazzar, was found to have an extraordinary spirit, knowledge and intelligence, and the ability to interpret dreams, explain riddles, and solve problems. Therefore, summon Daniel, and he will give the interpretation."

DANIEL BEFORE THE KING

13 Then Daniel was brought before the king. The king said to him, "Are you Daniel, one of the Judean exiles that my predecessor the king brought from Judah? 14 I've heard that you have a spirit of the gods in you, and that insight, intelligence, and extraordinary wisdom are found in you. 15 Now the wise men and mediums were brought before me to read this inscription and make its interpretation known to me, but they could not give its interpretation. 16 However, I have heard about you that you can give interpretations and solve problems. Therefore, if you can read this inscription and give me its interpretation, you will be clothed in purple, have a gold chain around your neck, and have the third highest position in the kingdom."

17 Then Daniel answered the king, "You may keep your gifts and give your rewards to someone else; however, I will read the inscription for the king and make the interpretation known to him. 18 Your Majesty, the Most High God gave sovereignty, greatness, glory, and majesty to your predecessor Nebuchadnezzar. 19 Because of the greatness he gave him, all peoples, nations, and languages were terrified and fearful of him. He killed anyone he wanted and kept alive anyone he wanted; he exalted anyone he wanted and humbled anyone he wanted. 20 But when his heart was exalted and his spirit became arrogant, he was deposed from his royal throne and his glory was taken from him. 21 He was driven away from people, his mind was like an animal's, he lived with the wild donkeys, he was fed grass like cattle, and his body was drenched with dew from the sky until he acknowledged that the Most High God is ruler over human kingdoms and sets anyone he wants over them.

[A] **5:2** Or *When he tasted* [B] **5:2** Or *father*, or *grandfather* [C] **5:3** Theod, Vg add *and silver* [D] **5:5** Lit *part of the hand* [E] **5:5-6** Lit *writing, ⁶the king's brightness changed* [F] **5:6** Lit *that the knots of his loins were loosed* [G] **5:9** Lit *his brightness changed on him* [H] **5:10** Perhaps the queen mother [I] **5:10** Lit *your brightness change*

My Story | Rita

When folks talked about living through a "fiery furnace" experience or being thrown into the "lions' den" in their lives, I nodded sympathetically. I felt sorry for the troubles they had faced but truly had little empathy. My life had been too good. I could say with David, "The boundary lines have fallen for me in pleasant places; indeed, I have a beautiful inheritance" (Ps 16:6).

That is, until I married and discovered that my husband had a penchant for having a secret life. Early on in our marriage, it stayed pretty much under wraps, but when the internet arrived with its vast ability to see those "greener pastures" with many other women on numerous dating sites, our marriage began to implode.

It has been a long difficult road, and often the old demons come back to haunt us. We've had our ups and downs, even as we've tried to rediscover God and each other through this.

While my husband works through counseling to deal with his addiction, I've had my own trust issues to deal with—not just the trust broken with him, but also trust broken with God. I couldn't understand why years of prayers went unanswered, why we would constantly move one step forward and two steps back, and why God seemed to want me to stay in this toxic situation.

But through it all, God has shown me himself. He is with me as the fire burns around me and the lions roar. When I've felt most alone, God has been most present. I know that part of my purpose is to help my husband through his own fire and den of lions. So, we're in it together, one day at a time.

22 "But you his successor, Belshazzar, have not
humbled your heart, even though you knew
all this. 23 Instead, you have exalted yourself
against the Lord of the heavens. The vessels
from his house were brought to you, and as
you and your nobles, wives, and concubines
drank wine from them, you praised the gods
made of silver and gold, bronze, iron, wood, and
stone, which do not see or hear or understand.
But you have not glorified the God who holds
your life-breath in his hand and who controls
the whole course of your life.[A] 24 Therefore, he
sent the hand, and this writing was inscribed.

THE INSCRIPTION'S INTERPRETATION

25 "This is the writing that was inscribed: MENE,
MENE, TEKEL, and PARSIN. 26 This is the interpretation of the message:

'Mene'[B] means that God has numbered[C]
the days of your kingdom and brought it
to an end.
27 'Tekel'[D] means that you have been
weighed[E] on the balance and found
deficient.
28 'Peres'[F,G] means that your kingdom has
been divided and given to the Medes and
Persians."[H]

29 Then Belshazzar gave an order, and they
clothed Daniel in purple, placed a gold chain
around his neck, and issued a proclamation
concerning him that he should be the third
ruler in the kingdom.
30 That very night Belshazzar the king of
the Chaldeans was killed, 31 and Darius the
Mede received the kingdom at the age of
sixty-two.

THE PLOT AGAINST DANIEL

6 Darius decided[I] to appoint 120 satraps
over the kingdom, stationed throughout
the realm, 2 and over them three administrators, including Daniel. These satraps would be
accountable to them so that the king would
not be defrauded. 3 Daniel[J] distinguished himself above the administrators and satraps because he had an extraordinary spirit, so the
king planned to set him over the whole realm.
4 The administrators and satraps, therefore,
kept trying to find a charge against Daniel regarding the kingdom. But they could find no
charge or corruption, for he was trustworthy,
and no negligence or corruption was found
in him. 5 Then these men said, "We will never
find any charge against this Daniel unless we

[A] 5:23 Lit *and all your ways belong to him* [B] 5:26 Or *a mina* [C] 5:26 The Aramaic word for *numbered* sounds like *mene*. [D] 5:27 Or *a shekel* [E] 5:27 The Aramaic word for *weighed* sounds like *tekel*. [F] 5:28 Or *half a shekel* [G] 5:28 In Aramaic, the word *peres* is the sg form of "parsin" in v. 25. [H] 5:28 The Aramaic word for *divided* and *Persians* sounds like *peres*. [I] 6:1 Lit *It was pleasing before Darius* [J] 6:3 Lit *Now this Daniel*

find something against him concerning the
law of his God."
6 So the administrators and satraps went together to the king and said to him, "May King
Darius live forever. 7 All the administrators of
the kingdom, the prefects, satraps, advisers,
and governors have agreed that the king should
establish an ordinance and enforce an edict
that for thirty days, anyone who petitions any
god or man except you, the king, will be thrown
into the lions' den. 8 Therefore, Your Majesty,
establish the edict and sign the document so
that, as a law of the Medes and Persians, it is
irrevocable and cannot be changed." 9 So King
Darius signed the written edict.

DANIEL IN THE LIONS' DEN

10 When Daniel learned that the document
had been signed, he went into his house. The
windows in its upstairs room opened toward
Jerusalem, and three times a day he got down
on his knees, prayed, and gave thanks to his
God, just as he had done before. 11 Then these
men went as a group and found Daniel peti-
tioning and imploring his God. 12 So they approached the king and asked about his edict:
"Didn't you sign an edict that for thirty days
any person who petitions any god or man
except you, the king, will be thrown into the
lions' den?"
The king answered, "As a law of the Medes
and Persians, the order stands[A] and is irrevocable."
13 Then they replied to the king, "Daniel, one
of the Judean exiles, has ignored you, the king,
and the edict you signed, for he prays three
times a day." 14 As soon as the king heard this,
he was very displeased; he set his mind on
rescuing Daniel and made every effort until
sundown to deliver him.
15 Then these men went together to the king
and said to him, "You know, Your Majesty, that
it is a law of the Medes and Persians that no
edict or ordinance the king establishes can
be changed."
16 So the king gave the order, and they
brought Daniel and threw him into the lions'
den. The king said to Daniel, "May your God,
whom you continually serve, rescue you!" 17 A
stone was brought and placed over the mouth
of the den. The king sealed it with his own signet ring and with the signet rings of his nobles,
so that nothing in regard to Daniel could be
changed. 18 Then the king went to his palace
and spent the night fasting. No diversions[B]
were brought to him, and he could not sleep.

DANIEL RELEASED

19 At the first light of dawn the king got up and
hurried to the lions' den. 20 When he reached
the den, he cried out in anguish to Daniel.
"Daniel, servant of the living God," the king
said,[C] "has your God, whom you continually
serve, been able to rescue you from the lions?"
21 Then Daniel spoke with the king: "May
the king live forever. 22 My God sent his angel
and shut the lions' mouths; and they haven't
harmed me, for I was found innocent before
him. And also before you, Your Majesty, I have
not done harm."
23 The king was overjoyed and gave orders
to take Daniel out of the den. When Daniel was
brought up from the den, he was found to be
unharmed, for he trusted in his God. 24 The
king then gave the command, and those men
who had maliciously accused Daniel[D] were
brought and thrown into the lions' den — they,
their children, and their wives. They had not
reached the bottom of the den before the lions
overpowered them and crushed all their bones.

DARIUS HONORS GOD

25 Then King Darius wrote to those of every
people, nation, and language who live on the
whole earth: "May your prosperity abound.
26 I issue a decree that in all my royal dominion, people must tremble in fear before the
God of Daniel:

For he is the living God,
and he endures forever;
his kingdom will never be destroyed,
and his dominion has no end.
27 He rescues and delivers;
he performs signs and wonders
in the heavens and on the earth,
for he has rescued Daniel
from the power of the lions."

28 So Daniel prospered during the reign of
Darius and[E] the reign of Cyrus the Persian.

DANIEL'S VISION OF THE FOUR BEASTS

7 In the first year of King Belshazzar of Babylon, Daniel had a dream with visions in
his mind as he was lying in his bed. He wrote
down the dream, and here is the summary[F] of

[A] **6:12** Lit *the word is certain* [B] **6:18** Aramaic obscure [C] **6:20** Lit *said to Daniel* [D] **6:24** Lit *had eaten his pieces* [E] **6:28** Or *Darius, even* [F] **7:1** Lit *beginning*

his account. 2 Daniel said, "In my vision at night
I was watching, and suddenly the four winds
of heaven stirred up the great sea. 3 Four huge
beasts came up from the sea, each different
from the other.
4 "The first was like a lion but had eagle's
wings. I continued watching until its wings
were torn off. It was lifted up from the ground,
set on its feet like a man, and given a human
mind.
5 "Suddenly, another beast appeared, a second one, that looked like a bear. It was raised
up on one side, with three ribs in its mouth
between its teeth. It was told, 'Get up! Gorge
yourself on flesh.'
6 "After this, while I was watching, suddenly
another beast appeared. It was like a leopard
with four wings of a bird on its back. It had
four heads, and it was given dominion.
7 "After this, while I was watching in the night
visions, suddenly a fourth beast appeared,
frightening and dreadful, and incredibly
strong, with large iron teeth. It devoured and
crushed, and it trampled with its feet whatever
was left. It was different from all the beasts
before it, and it had ten horns.
8 "While I was considering the horns, suddenly another horn, a little one, came up among
them, and three of the first horns were uprooted before it. And suddenly in this horn
there were eyes like the eyes of a human and
a mouth that was speaking arrogantly.

THE ANCIENT OF DAYS AND THE SON OF MAN

9 "As I kept watching,
thrones were set in place,
and the Ancient of Days took his seat.
His clothing was white like snow,
and the hair of his head
like whitest wool.
His throne was flaming fire;
its wheels were blazing fire.
10 A river of fire was flowing,
coming out from his presence.
Thousands upon thousands served him;
ten thousand times ten thousand
stood before him.
The court was convened,
and the books were opened.

11 "I watched, then, because of the sound of
the arrogant words the horn was speaking.
As I continued watching, the beast was killed
and its body destroyed and given over to the
burning fire. 12 As for the rest of the beasts,
their dominion was removed, but an extension of life was granted to them for a certain
period of time. 13 I continued watching in the
night visions,
and suddenly one like a son of man
was coming with the clouds of heaven.
He approached the Ancient of Days
and was escorted before him.
14 He was given dominion,
and glory, and a kingdom;
so that those of every people,
nation, and language
should serve him.
His dominion is an everlasting dominion
that will not pass away,
and his kingdom is one
that will not be destroyed.

INTERPRETATION OF THE VISION

15 "As for me, Daniel, my spirit was deeply distressed within me,[A] and the visions in my mind
terrified me. 16 I approached one of those who
were standing by and asked him to clarify
all this. So he let me know the interpretation
of these things: 17 'These huge beasts, four in
number, are four kings who will rise from the
earth. 18 But the holy ones of the Most High will
receive the kingdom and possess it forever,
yes, forever and ever.'
19 "Then I wanted to be clear about the
fourth beast, the one different from all the
others, extremely terrifying, with iron teeth
and bronze claws, devouring, crushing, and
trampling with its feet whatever was left. 20 I
also wanted to know about the ten horns on
its head and about the other horn that came
up, before which three fell — the horn that
had eyes, and a mouth that spoke arrogantly,
and that looked bigger than the others. 21 As I
was watching, this horn waged war against
the holy ones and was prevailing over them
22 until the Ancient of Days arrived and a judgment was given in favor of the holy ones of
the Most High, for the time had come, and the
holy ones took possession of the kingdom.
23 "This is what he said: 'The fourth beast will
be a fourth kingdom on the earth, different
from all the other kingdoms. It will devour
the whole earth, trample it down, and crush
it. 24 The ten horns are ten kings who will rise
from this kingdom. Another king, different

[A] **7:15** Lit *was distressed in the middle of its sheath*

from the previous ones, will rise after them and subdue three kings. 25 He will speak words against the Most High and oppress[A] the holy ones of the Most High. He will intend to change religious festivals[B] and laws, and the holy ones will be handed over to him for a time, times, and half a time.[C] 26 But the court will convene, and his dominion will be taken away, to be completely destroyed forever. 27 The kingdom, dominion, and greatness of the kingdoms under all of heaven will be given to the people, the holy ones of the Most High. His kingdom will be an everlasting kingdom, and all rulers will serve and obey him.'

28 "This is the end of the account. As for me, Daniel, my thoughts terrified me greatly, and my face turned pale,[D] but I kept the matter to myself."

THE VISION OF A RAM AND A GOAT

8 In the third year of King Belshazzar's reign, a vision appeared to me, Daniel, after the one that had appeared to me earlier. 2 I saw the vision, and as I watched, I was in the fortress city of Susa, in the province of Elam. I saw in the vision that I was beside the Ulai Canal. 3 I looked up,[E] and there was a ram standing beside the canal. He had two horns. The two horns were long, but one was longer than the other, and the longer one came up last. 4 I saw the ram charging to the west, the north, and the south. No animal could stand against him, and there was no rescue from his power. He did whatever he wanted and became great.

5 As I was observing, a male goat appeared, coming from the west across the surface of the entire earth without touching the ground. The goat had a conspicuous horn[F] between his eyes. 6 He came toward the two-horned ram I had seen standing beside the canal and rushed at him with savage fury. 7 I saw him approaching the ram, and infuriated with him, he struck the ram, breaking his two horns, and the ram was not strong enough to stand against him. The goat threw him to the ground and trampled him, and there was no one to rescue the ram from his power. 8 Then the male goat acted even more arrogantly, but when he became powerful, the large horn was broken. Four conspicuous horns came up in its place, pointing toward the four winds of heaven.

THE LITTLE HORN

9 From one of them a little horn emerged and grew extensively toward the south and the east and toward the beautiful land.[G] 10 It grew as high as the heavenly army, made some of the army and some of the stars[H] fall to the earth, and trampled them. 11 It acted arrogantly even against the Prince of the heavenly army; it revoked his regular sacrifice and overthrew the place of his sanctuary. 12 In the rebellion, the army was given up, together with the regular sacrifice. The horn threw truth to the ground and was successful in what it did.

13 Then I heard a holy one speaking, and another holy one said to the speaker, "How long will the events of this vision last — the regular sacrifice, the rebellion that makes desolate, and the giving over of the sanctuary and of the army to be trampled?"

14 He said to me,[I] "For 2,300 evenings and mornings; then the sanctuary will be restored."

INTERPRETATION OF THE VISION

15 While I, Daniel, was watching the vision and trying to understand it, there stood before me someone who appeared to be a man. 16 I heard a human voice calling from the middle of the Ulai: "Gabriel, explain the vision to this man."

17 So he approached where I was standing; when he came near, I was terrified and fell facedown. "Son of man," he said to me, "understand that the vision refers to the time of the end." 18 While he was speaking to me, I fell into a deep sleep, with my face to the ground. Then he touched me, made me stand up, 19 and said, "I am here to tell you what will happen at the conclusion of the time of wrath, because it refers to the appointed time of the end. 20 The two-horned ram that you saw represents the kings of Media and Persia. 21 The shaggy goat represents the king of Greece, and the large horn between his eyes represents the first king.[J] 22 The four horns that took the place of the broken horn represent four kingdoms. They will rise from that nation, but without its power.

23 Near the end of their kingdoms,
when the rebels have reached
the full measure of their sin,[K]
a ruthless[L] king, skilled in intrigue,[M]
will come to the throne.

[A] 7:25 Lit *wear out* [B] 7:25 Lit *change times* [C] 7:25 Or *for three and a half years* [D] 7:28 Lit *my brightness changed on me* [E] 8:3 Lit *I lifted my eyes and looked* [F] 8:5 Lit *a horn of a vision* [G] 8:9 = Israel [H] 8:10 Or *some of the army, that is, some of the stars* [I] 8:14 LXX, Theod, Syr, Vg read *him* [J] 8:21 = Alexander the Great [K] 8:23 Lit *have become complete* [L] 8:23 Lit *strong of face* [M] 8:23 Lit *king, and understanding riddles*

24 His power will be great,
but it will not be his own.
He will cause outrageous destruction
and succeed in whatever he does.
He will destroy the powerful
along with the holy people.
25 He will cause deceit to prosper
through his cunning
and by his influence,
and in his own mind he will
exalt himself.
He will destroy many in a time of peace;
he will even stand against the Prince
of princes.
Yet he will be broken — not by
human hands.
26 The vision of the evenings
and the mornings
that has been told is true.
Now you are to seal up the vision
because it refers to many days
in the future."

27 I, Daniel, was overcome and lay sick for
days. Then I got up and went about the king's
business. I was greatly disturbed by the vision
and could not understand it.

DANIEL'S PRAYER

9 In the first year of Darius, the son of Ahasuerus, a Mede by birth, who was made king
over the Chaldean kingdom — 2 in the first
year of his reign, I, Daniel, understood from
the books according to the word of the LORD
to the prophet Jeremiah that the number of
years for the desolation of Jerusalem would
be seventy. 3 So I turned my attention to the
Lord God to seek him by prayer and petitions,
with fasting, sackcloth, and ashes.
4 I prayed to the LORD my God and confessed:
Ah, Lord — the great and awe-inspiring
God who keeps his gracious covenant
with those who love him and keep his
commands — 5 we have sinned, done
wrong, acted wickedly, rebelled, and
turned away from your commands and
ordinances. 6 We have not listened to
your servants the prophets, who spoke in
your name to our kings, leaders, fathers,
and all the people of the land.

7 Lord, righteousness belongs to you, but
this day public shame belongs to us: the
men of Judah, the residents of Jerusalem,
and all Israel — those who are near and
those who are far, in all the countries
where you have banished them because
of the disloyalty they have shown toward
you. 8 LORD, public shame belongs to us,
our kings, our leaders, and our fathers,
because we have sinned against you.
9 Compassion and forgiveness belong
to the Lord our God, though we have
rebelled against him 10 and have not
obeyed the LORD our God by following his
instructions that he set before us through
his servants the prophets.

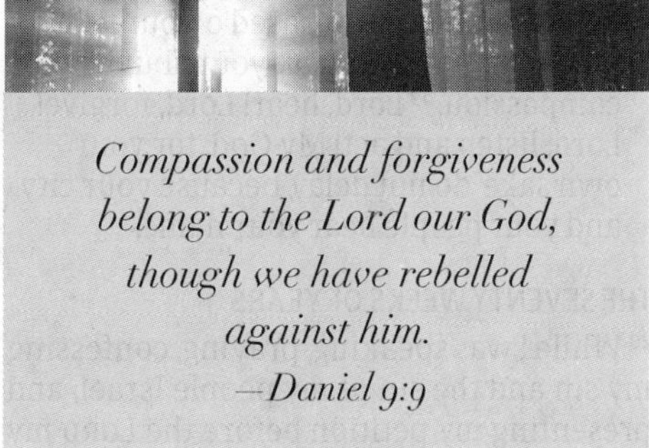
Compassion and forgiveness belong to the Lord our God, though we have rebelled against him.
—*Daniel 9:9*

11 All Israel has broken your law and
turned away, refusing to obey you. The
promised curse[A] written in the law of
Moses, the servant of God, has been
poured out on us because we have
sinned against him. 12 He has carried out
his words that he spoke against us and
against our rulers[B] by bringing on us a
disaster that is so great that nothing like
what has been done to Jerusalem has
ever been done under all of heaven. 13 Just
as it is written in the law of Moses, all this
disaster has come on us, yet we have not
sought the favor of the LORD our God by
turning from our iniquities and paying
attention to your truth. 14 So the LORD
kept the disaster in mind and brought
it on us, for the LORD our God is righteous in all he has done. But we have not
obeyed him.

15 Now, Lord our God, who brought your
people out of the land of Egypt with a
strong hand and made your name renowned as it is this day, we have sinned,
we have acted wickedly. 16 Lord, in

[A] **9:11** Lit *The curse and the oath* [B] **9:12** Lit *against rulers who ruled us*

keeping with all your righteous acts, may
your anger and wrath turn away from
your city Jerusalem, your holy mountain;
for because of our sins and the iniquities
of our fathers, Jerusalem and your people
have become an object of ridicule to all
those around us.

17 Therefore, our God, hear the prayer and
the petitions of your servant. Make your
face shine on your desolate sanctuary
for the Lord's sake. 18 Listen closely,[A] my
God, and hear. Open your eyes and see
our desolations and the city that bears
your name. For we are not presenting our
petitions before you based on our righteous acts, but based on your abundant
compassion. 19 Lord, hear! Lord, forgive!
Lord, listen and act! My God, for your
own sake, do not delay, because your city
and your people bear your name.

THE SEVENTY WEEKS OF YEARS

20 While I was speaking, praying, confessing
my sin and the sin of my people Israel, and
presenting my petition before the LORD my
God concerning the holy mountain of my
God — 21 while I was praying, Gabriel, the
man I had seen in the first vision, reached me
in my extreme weariness, about the time of
the evening offering. 22 He gave me this explanation: "Daniel, I've come now to give you
understanding. 23 At the beginning of your
petitions an answer went out, and I have come
to give it, for you are treasured by God.[B] So
consider the message and understand the
vision:

24 Seventy weeks are decreed
about your people
and your holy city —
to bring the rebellion to an end,
to put a stop to sin,
to atone for iniquity,
to bring in everlasting righteousness,
to seal up vision and prophecy,
and to anoint the most holy place.
25 Know and understand this:
From the issuing of the decree
to restore and rebuild Jerusalem
until an Anointed One, the ruler,[C]
will be seven weeks
and sixty-two weeks.
It will be rebuilt with a plaza
and a moat,
but in difficult times.
26 After those sixty-two weeks
the Anointed One will be cut off
and will have nothing.
The people of the coming ruler
will destroy the city and the sanctuary.[D]
The[E] end will come with a flood,
and until the end there will be[F] war;
desolations are decreed.
27 He will make a firm covenant[G]
with many for one week,
but in the middle of the week
he will put a stop to sacrifice
and offering.
And the abomination of desolation
will be on a wing of the temple[H,I]
until the decreed destruction
is poured out on the desolator."

VISION OF A GLORIOUS ONE

10 In the third year of King Cyrus of Persia, a message was revealed to Daniel,
who was named Belteshazzar. The message
was true and was about a great conflict. He
understood the message and had understanding of the vision.

2 In those days I, Daniel, was mourning for
three full weeks. 3 I didn't eat any rich food, no
meat or wine entered my mouth, and I didn't
put any oil on my body until the three weeks
were over. 4 On the twenty-fourth day of the
first month,[J] as I was standing on the bank
of the great river, the Tigris, 5 I looked up, and
there was a man dressed in linen, with a belt
of gold from Uphaz[K] around his waist. 6 His
body was like beryl,[L] his face like the brilliance
of lightning, his eyes like flaming torches,
his arms and feet like the gleam of polished
bronze, and the sound of his words like the
sound of a multitude.

7 Only I, Daniel, saw the vision. The men who
were with me did not see it, but a great terror
fell on them, and they ran and hid. 8 I was left
alone, looking at this great vision. No strength
was left in me; my face grew deathly pale,[M]
and I was powerless. 9 I heard the words he

[A] **9:18** Lit *Stretch out your ear* [B] **9:23** *by God* added for clarity [C] **9:25** Or *until an anointed one, a prince* [D] **9:26** MT; Theod, some mss read *The city and the sanctuary will be destroyed when the ruler comes.* [E] **9:26** Lit *Its*, or *His* [F] **9:26** Or *end of a* [G] **9:27** Or *will enforce a covenant* [H] **9:27** LXX; MT reads *of abominations* [I] **9:27** Or *And the desolator will be on the wing of abominations*, or *And the desolator will come on the wings of monsters* (or *of horror*); Hb obscure [J] **10:4** = Nisan (March–April) [K] **10:5** Some Hb mss read *Ophir* [L] **10:6** The identity of this stone is uncertain. [M] **10:8** Lit *my splendor was turned on me to ruin*

said, and when I heard them I fell into a deep
sleep,[A] with my face to the ground.

ANGELIC CONFLICT

10 Suddenly, a hand touched me and set me
shaking on my hands and knees. 11 He said to
me, "Daniel, you are a man treasured by God.[B]
Understand the words that I'm saying to you.
Stand on your feet, for I have now been sent to
you." After he said this to me, I stood trembling.
12 "Don't be afraid, Daniel," he said to me, "for
from the first day that you purposed to understand and to humble yourself before your God,
your prayers were heard. I have come because
of your prayers. 13 But the prince of the kingdom
of Persia opposed me for twenty-one days. Then
Michael, one of the chief princes, came to help
me after I had been left there with the kings of
Persia. 14 Now I have come to help you understand what will happen to your people in the
last days, for the vision refers to those days."
15 While he was saying these words to me,
I turned my face toward the ground and was
speechless. 16 Suddenly one with human likeness touched my lips. I opened my mouth and
said to the one standing in front of me, "My
lord, because of the vision, anguish overwhelms me and I am powerless. 17 How can
someone like me, your servant,[C] speak with
someone like you, my lord? Now I have no
strength, and there is no breath in me."
18 Then the one with a human appearance
touched me again and strengthened me. 19 He
said, "Don't be afraid, you who are[D] treasured
by God. Peace to you; be very strong!"
As he spoke to me, I was strengthened and
said, "Let my lord speak, for you have strengthened me."
20 He said, "Do you know why I've come to
you? I must return at once to fight against the
prince of Persia, and when I leave, the prince
of Greece will come. 21 However, I will tell you
what is recorded in the book of truth. (No one
has the courage to support me against those
11 princes except Michael, your prince. 1 In
the first year of Darius the Mede, I stood
up to strengthen and protect him.) 2 Now I will
tell you the truth.

PROPHECIES ABOUT PERSIA AND GREECE

"Three more kings will arise in Persia, and the
fourth will be far richer than the others. By the
power he gains through his riches, he will stir
up everyone against the kingdom of Greece.
3 Then a warrior king will arise; he will rule
a vast realm and do whatever he wants. 4 But
as soon as he is established, his kingdom will
be broken up and divided to the four winds of
heaven, but not to his descendants; it will not
be the same kingdom that he ruled, because
his kingdom will be uprooted and will go to
others besides them.

KINGS OF THE SOUTH AND THE NORTH

5 "The king of the South will grow powerful,
but one of his commanders will grow more
powerful and will rule a kingdom greater
than his. 6 After some years they will form
an alliance, and the daughter of the king of
the South will go to the king of the North to
seal the agreement. She will not retain power,
and his strength will not endure. She will be
given up, together with her entourage, her
father,[E] and the one who supported her during those times. 7 In the place of the king of
the South, one from her family[F] will rise up,
come against the army, and enter the fortress
of the king of the North. He will take action
against them and triumph. 8 He will take even
their gods captive to Egypt, with their metal
images and their precious articles of silver
and gold. For some years he will stay away
from the king of the North, 9 who will enter
the kingdom of the king of the South and then
return to his own land.
10 "His sons will mobilize for war and assemble a large number of armed forces. They
will advance, sweeping through like a flood,[G]
and will again wage war as far as his fortress.
11 Infuriated, the king of the South will march
out to fight with the king of the North, who
will raise a large army, but they will be handed
over to his enemy. 12 When the army is carried
off, he will become arrogant and cause tens
of thousands to fall, but he will not triumph.
13 The king of the North will again raise a multitude larger than the first. After some years[H]
he will advance with a great army and many
supplies.
14 "In those times many will rise up against
the king of the South. Violent ones among your
own people will assert themselves to fulfill a
vision, but they will fail. 15 Then the king of the
North will come, build up a siege ramp, and

[A] **10:9** Lit *a sleep on my face* [B] **10:11** *by God* added for clarity, also in v. 19 [C] **10:17** Lit *Can I, a servant of my lord* [D] **10:19** Lit *afraid, man* [E] **11:6** Some Hb mss, Theod read *the child*; Syr, Vg read *her children* [F] **11:7** Lit *from the shoot of her roots* [G] **11:10** Lit *advance and overflow and pass through* [H] **11:13** Lit *At the end of the times*

capture a well-fortified city. The forces of the South will not stand; even their select troops will not be able to resist. 16 The king of the North who comes against him will do whatever he wants, and no one can oppose him. He will establish himself in the beautiful land[A] with total destruction in his hand. 17 He will resolve to come with the force of his whole kingdom and will reach an agreement with him.[B] He will give him a daughter in marriage[C] to destroy it,[D] but she will not stand with him or support him. 18 Then he will turn his attention to the coasts and islands[E] and capture many. But a commander will put an end to his taunting; instead, he will turn his taunts against him. 19 He will turn his attention back to the fortresses of his own land, but he will stumble, fall, and be no more.

20 "In his place one will arise who will send out a tax collector for the glory of the kingdom; but within a few days he will be broken, though not in anger[F] or in battle.

21 "In his place a despised person will arise; royal honors will not be given to him, but he will come during a time of peace[G] and seize the kingdom by intrigue. 22 A flood of forces will be swept away before him; they will be broken, as well as the covenant prince. 23 After an alliance is made with him, he will act deceitfully. He will rise to power with a small nation.[H] 24 During a time of peace,[I] he will come into the richest parts of the province and do what his fathers and predecessors never did. He will lavish plunder, loot, and wealth on his followers, and he will make plans against fortified cities, but only for a time.

25 "With a large army he will stir up his power and his courage against the king of the South. The king of the South will prepare for battle with an extremely large and powerful army, but he will not succeed, because plots will be made against him. 26 Those who eat his provisions will destroy him; his army will be swept away, and many will fall slain. 27 The two kings, whose hearts are bent on evil, will speak lies at the same table but to no avail, for still the end will come at the appointed time. 28 The king of the North will return to his land with great wealth, but his heart will be set against the holy covenant;[J] he will take action, then return to his own land.

29 "At the appointed time he will come again to the South, but this time[K] will not be like the first. 30 Ships of Kittim[L] will come against him, and being intimidated, he will withdraw. Then he will rage against the holy covenant and take action. On his return, he will favor those who abandon the holy covenant. 31 His forces will rise up and desecrate the temple fortress. They will abolish the regular sacrifice and set up the abomination of desolation. 32 With flattery he will corrupt those who act wickedly toward the covenant, but the people who know their God will be strong and take action. 33 Those who have insight among the people will give understanding to many, yet they will fall by the sword and flame, and be captured and plundered for a time. 34 When they fall, they will be helped by some, but many others will join them insincerely. 35 Some of those who have insight will fall so that they may be refined, purified, and cleansed until the time of the end, for it will still come at the appointed time.

36 "Then the king will do whatever he wants. He will exalt and magnify himself above every god, and he will say outrageous things against the God of gods. He will be successful until the time of wrath is completed, because what has been decreed will be accomplished. 37 He will not show regard for the gods[M] of his fathers, the god desired by women, or for any other god, because he will magnify himself above all. 38 Instead, he will honor a god of fortresses — a god his fathers did not know — with gold, silver, precious stones, and riches. 39 He will deal with the strongest fortresses with the help of a foreign god. He will greatly honor those who acknowledge him,[N] making them rulers over many and distributing land as a reward.

40 "At the time of the end, the king of the South will engage him in battle, but the king of the North will storm against him with chariots, horsemen, and many ships. He will invade countries and sweep through them like a flood. 41 He will also invade the beautiful land, and many will fall. But these will escape from his power: Edom, Moab, and the prominent people[O] of the Ammonites. 42 He will extend his power against the countries, and not even the land of Egypt will escape. 43 He will get control over the hidden treasures of gold and silver

---

[A] **11:16** = Israel [B] **11:17** = the king of the South [C] **11:17** Lit *him the daughter of women* [D] **11:17** Perhaps the kingdom [E] **11:18** of the Mediterranean [F] **11:20** Or *not openly* [G] **11:21** Or *come without warning* [H] **11:23** Or *a few people* [I] **11:24** Or *Without warning* [J] **11:28** Or *the Jewish people and religion* [K] **11:29** Lit *but the last* [L] **11:30** = the Romans [M] **11:37** Or *God* [N] **11:39** Or *those he acknowledges* [O] **11:41** Lit *the first*

and over all the riches of Egypt. The Libyans
and Cushites will also be in submission.[A] 44 But
reports from the east and the north will terrify him, and he will go out with great fury to
annihilate and completely destroy many. 45 He
will pitch his royal tents between the sea and[B]
the beautiful holy mountain, but he will meet
his end with no one to help him.

12 At that time
Michael, the great prince
who stands watch over your people,
will rise up.
There will be a time of distress
such as never has occurred
since nations came into being
until that time.
But at that time all your people
who are found written in the book
will escape.
2 Many who sleep in the dust
of the earth will awake,
some to eternal life,
and some to disgrace
and eternal contempt.
3 Those who have insight will shine
like the bright expanse of the heavens,
and those who lead many
to righteousness,
like the stars forever and ever.

4 "But you, Daniel, keep these words secret
and seal the book until the time of the end.
Many will roam about, and knowledge will
increase."[C]
5 Then I, Daniel, looked, and two others were
standing there, one on this bank of the river
and one on the other. 6 One of them said to
the man dressed in linen, who was above the

Those who have insight will shine like the bright expanse of the heavens, and those who lead many to righteousness, like the stars forever and ever.
—Daniel 12:3

water of the river, "How long until the end of
these wondrous things?" 7 Then I heard the
man dressed in linen, who was above the
water of the river. He raised both his hands[D]
toward heaven and swore by him who lives
eternally that it would be for a time, times,
and half a time. When the power of the holy
people is shattered, all these things will be
completed.
8 I heard but did not understand. So I asked,
"My lord, what will be the outcome of these
things?"
9 He said, "Go on your way, Daniel, for the
words are secret and sealed until the time of
the end. 10 Many will be purified, cleansed,
and refined, but the wicked will act wickedly;
none of the wicked will understand, but those
who have insight will understand. 11 From the
time the daily sacrifice is abolished and the
abomination of desolation is set up, there will
be 1,290 days. 12 Happy is the one who waits
for and reaches 1,335 days. 13 But as for you,
go on your way to the end;[E] you will rest, and
then you will stand to receive your allotted
inheritance at the end of the days."

[A] **11:43** Lit *Cushites at his steps* [B] **11:45** Or *the seas at* [C] **12:4** LXX reads *and the earth will be filled with unrighteousness* [D] **12:7** Lit *raised his right and his left* [E] **12:13** LXX omits *to the end*

Hosea—No doubt Hosea's friends felt sorry for him, though perhaps they thought he had gotten what he deserved for marrying a prostitute. Hosea's tragic circumstance, however, was at God's direction, and he used Hosea's personal pain to speak an important message about his love for his people.

Just as Hosea and Gomer shared a covenant relationship that should have been exclusive, so God loves his people with a covenant love and wants them for himself. And just as Gomer was unfaithful to Hosea, so also God's people were unfaithful to him. They were violating their covenant requirements, rejecting God, engaging in idolatry, and trusting in earthly powers instead of God. This sounds similar to today, where even many Christians are halfhearted in their commitment to God.

In the same way that Hosea was persistent in his love and pursuit of Gomer, God continues to woo his people back. The tender voice of love and longing woven throughout the book of Hosea also speaks to us.

We are loved by God in the same way, drawn by his "ropes of love" (11:4), and we, too, can return to God and live in the "shade" of his blessing (14:7).

HOSEA

AUTHOR: Hosea

DATE WRITTEN: Hosea's ministry spanned at least forty years, beginning during the reign of Jeroboam II (793–782 BC) and ending during the reign of Hezekiah (716–686 BC).

ORIGINAL AUDIENCE: The Israelites, especially the northern kingdom

SETTING: The beginning of Hosea's story occurred when the northern kingdom of Israel was in a strong position and the future looked rosy. Social unrest ensued after Jeroboam's death in 753 BC, and Israel had a quick succession of kings, most of whom were assassinated. Israel was crumbling.

PURPOSE FOR WRITING: Hosea's message—couched in the details of his own personal tragedies—is that although Israel had been faithless, God is faithful. The details of Hosea's marriage to a prostitute, her continued unfaithfulness, and his seeking of his wayward bride mirror God's covenant love for his people.

OUTLINE:

1. The Pain and Persistence of God's Love (1:1–3:5)

   God speaking through Hosea's family (1:1–2:23)

   Waiting for restoration (3:1-5)

2. Accusation and Call to Repent (4:1–7:16)

   Indictment and warning (4:1–5:15)

   Call to repent (6:1–7:16)

3. Lament over Israel's Betrayal (8:1–14:9)

   Failure of false hopes (8:1–10:15)

   Punishment for rebellion (11:1–13:16)

   Final plea to repent (14:1-9)

KEY VERSE:

"Let whoever is wise understand these things, and whoever is insightful recognize them. For the ways of the LORD are right, and the righteous walk in them." —Hosea 14:9

RESTORATION THEMES

R	Rest and Reflection	*Being Willing to Change—10:12*
E	Eternal Perspective	*For the next note, see Joel 2:12-13.*
S	Support	*For the next note, see Habakkuk 1:2-4.*
T	Thanksgiving and Contentment	*For the next note, see Jonah 3:1.*
O	Other-centeredness	*For the next note, see Amos 5:24.*
R	Relationships	*For the next note, see Micah 5:5.*
E	Exercise of Faith	*Applying God's Word—Hosea 4:6* *Staying Close to Christ—6:6*

1 The word of the LORD that came to Hosea son of Beeri during the reigns of Uzziah, Jotham, Ahaz, and Hezekiah, kings of Judah, and of Jeroboam son of Jehoash, king of Israel.

HOSEA'S MARRIAGE AND CHILDREN

2 When the LORD first spoke to Hosea, he said this to him:

Go and marry a woman
of promiscuity,
and have children of promiscuity,
for the land is committing
blatant acts of promiscuity
by abandoning the LORD.

3 So he went and married Gomer daughter
of Diblaim, and she conceived and bore him
a son. 4 Then the LORD said to him:

Name him Jezreel,[A] for in a little while
I will bring the bloodshed of Jezreel
on the house of Jehu
and put an end to the kingdom
of the house of Israel.
5 On that day I will break
the bow of Israel
in the Valley of Jezreel.

6 She conceived again and gave birth to a
daughter, and the LORD said to him:

Name her Lo-ruhamah,[B]
for I will no longer have compassion
on the house of Israel.
I will certainly take them away.
7 But I will have compassion
on the house of Judah,
and I will deliver them by
the LORD their God.
I will not deliver them by bow, sword,
or war,
or by horses and cavalry.

8 After Gomer had weaned Lo-ruhamah,
she conceived and gave birth to a son. 9 Then
the LORD said:

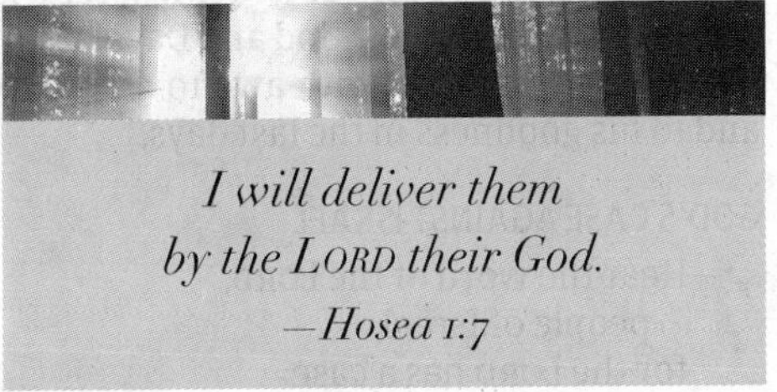
I will deliver them
by the LORD their God.
—Hosea 1:7

Name him Lo-ammi,[C]
for you are not my people,
and I will not be your God.[D]
10 Yet the number of the Israelites
will be like the sand of the sea,
which cannot be measured or counted.
And in the place where they were told:
You are not my people,
they will be called:
Sons of the living God.
11 And the Judeans and the Israelites
will be gathered together.
They will appoint for themselves
a single ruler
and go up from[E] the land.
For the day of Jezreel will be great.

2 Call[F] your brothers: My People
and your sisters: Compassion.

ISRAEL'S ADULTERY REBUKED

2 Rebuke your mother; rebuke her.
For she is not my wife and I am not
her husband.
Let her remove the promiscuous look
from her face
and her adultery
from between her breasts.
3 Otherwise, I will strip her naked
and expose her as she was on the day
of her birth.
I will make her like a desert
and like a parched land,
and I will let her die of thirst.
4 I will have no compassion
on her children
because they are the children
of promiscuity.
5 Yes, their mother is promiscuous;
she conceived them
and acted shamefully.
For she thought, "I will follow
my lovers,
the men who give me my food
and water,
my wool and flax, my oil and drink."
6 Therefore, this is what I will do:
I will block her[G] way with thorns;
I will enclose her with a wall,
so that she cannot find her paths.
7 She will pursue her lovers
but not catch them;
she will look for them but not find them.
Then she will think,

[A] **1:4** = God Sows [B] **1:6** = No Compassion [C] **1:9** = Not My People [D] **1:9** Lit *not be yours* [E] **1:11** Or *and flourish in*; Hb obscure [F] **2:1** Lit *Say to* [G] **2:6** LXX, Syr; MT reads *your*

"I will go back to my former husband,
for then it was better for me than now."
8 She does not recognize
that it is I who gave her the grain,
the new wine, and the fresh oil.
I lavished silver and gold on her,
which they used for Baal.
9 Therefore, I will take back my grain
in its time
and my new wine in its season;
I will take away my wool and linen,
which were to cover her nakedness.
10 Now I will expose her shame
in the sight of her lovers,
and no one will rescue her
from my power.
11 I will put an end to all her celebrations:
her feasts, New Moons, and Sabbaths —
all her festivals.
12 I will devastate her vines and fig trees.
She thinks that these are her wages
that her lovers have given her.
I will turn them into a thicket,
and the wild animals will eat them.
13 And I will punish her for the days
of the Baals,
to which she burned incense.
She put on her rings and her jewelry
and followed her lovers,
but she forgot me.
This is the LORD's declaration.

ISRAEL'S ADULTERY FORGIVEN

14 Therefore, I am going to persuade her,
lead her to the wilderness,
and speak tenderly to her.[A]
15 There I will give her vineyards
back to her
and make the Valley of Achor[B]
into a gateway of hope.
There she will respond as she did
in the days of her youth,
as in the day she came out of the land
of Egypt.
16 In that day —
this is the LORD's declaration —
you will call me, "My husband,"
and no longer call me, "My Baal."[C]
17 For I will remove the names
of the Baals
from her mouth;
they will no longer be remembered
by their names.
18 On that day I will make a covenant
for them
with the wild animals, the birds of the sky,
and the creatures that crawl
on the ground.
I will shatter bow, sword,
and weapons of war in the land[D]
and will enable the people
to rest securely.
19 I will take you to be my wife forever.
I will take you to be my wife
in righteousness,
justice, love, and compassion.
20 I will take you to be my wife
in faithfulness,
and you will know the LORD.
21 On that day I will respond —
this is the LORD's declaration.
I will respond to the sky,
and it will respond to the earth.
22 The earth will respond to the grain,
the new wine, and the fresh oil,
and they will respond to Jezreel.
23 I will sow her[E] in the land for myself,
and I will have compassion
on Lo-ruhamah;
I will say to Lo-ammi:
You are my people,
and he will say, "You are my God."

WAITING FOR RESTORATION

3 Then the LORD said to me, "Go again; show
love to a woman who is loved by another
man and is an adulteress, just as the LORD loves
the Israelites though they turn to other gods
and love raisin cakes."
2 So I bought her for fifteen shekels of silver
and five bushels of barley.[F,G] 3 I said to her, "You
are to live with me many days. You must not
be promiscuous or belong to any man, and I
will act the same way toward you."
4 For the Israelites must live many days without king or prince, without sacrifice or sacred
pillar, and without ephod or household idols.
5 Afterward, the people of Israel will return
and seek the LORD their God and David their
king. They will come with awe to the LORD
and to his goodness in the last days.

GOD'S CASE AGAINST ISRAEL

4 Hear the word of the LORD,
people of Israel,
for the LORD has a case

[A] 2:14 Lit *speak to her heart* [B] 2:15 = Trouble [C] 2:16 Or *My Master* [D] 2:18 Or *war on the earth* [E] 2:23 = Israel [F] 3:2 LXX reads *barley and a measure of wine* [G] 3:2 Lit *silver, a homer of barley, and a lethek of barley*

against the inhabitants of the land:
There is no truth, no faithful love,
and no knowledge of God in the land!
2 Cursing, lying, murder, stealing,
and adultery are rampant;
one act of bloodshed follows another.
3 For this reason the land mourns,
and everyone who lives
in it languishes,
along with the wild animals
and the birds of the sky;
even the fish of the sea disappear.
4 But let no one dispute;
let no one argue,
for my case is against you priests.[A,B]
5 You will stumble by day;
the prophet will also stumble with you
by night.
And I will destroy your mother.
6 My people are destroyed for lack
of knowledge.
Because you have rejected knowledge,
I will reject you from serving
as my priest.
Since you have forgotten the law
of your God,
I will also forget your sons.
7 The more they multiplied,
the more they sinned against me.
I[C] will change their[D] honor
into disgrace.
8 They feed on the sin[E] of my people;
they have an appetite for their iniquity.
9 The same judgment will happen
to both people and priests.
I will punish them for their ways
and repay them for their deeds.
10 They will eat but not be satisfied;
they will be promiscuous
but not multiply.
For they have abandoned
their devotion to the LORD.
11 Promiscuity, wine, and new wine
take away one's understanding.

12 My people consult
their wooden idols,
and their divining rods inform them.
For a spirit of promiscuity
leads them astray;
they act promiscuously
in disobedience to[F] their God.
13 They sacrifice on the mountaintops,
and they burn offerings on the hills,

Exercise of Faith | *Applying God's Word*

OUR NEED TO KNOW

"My people are destroyed for lack of knowledge." Hosea 4:6

As of mid-2017 there were reportedly some 4.5 billion webpages on the Internet. This means if sheer information were enough to save humanity, we'd be living in paradise!

Since we're *not* experiencing heaven on earth, we obviously need more than mere facts and data. According to the Lord—speaking here through the prophet Hosea—what is needed is *knowledge*. "There is no truth, no faithful love, and no knowledge of God in the land!" (4:1). Because the priests had failed to adequately teach God's truth to the people (4:4), the ancient Israelites were spiritually ignorant, and they were being destroyed.

Knowledge means "understanding, insight, discernment, or wisdom." A knowledge of God's Word, then, means more than just being able to win a Bible trivia game; it means being able to skillfully apply God's eternal Word to everyday life. More specifically, *knowledge of God* means more than learning a few theological facts about God; it means having a close, personal relationship with the Almighty.

Given all this, how solid are you when it comes to the knowledge of God, and knowledge of his Word?

For the next note on *Exercise of Faith*, see Hosea 6:6.

[A] 4:4 Text emended; MT reads *argue, and your people are like those contending with a priest* [B] 4:4 Hb obscure [C] 4:7 Alt Hb tradition, Syr, Tg read *They* [D] 4:7 Alt Hb tradition reads *my* [E] 4:8 Or *sin offerings* [F] 4:12 Lit *promiscuously from under*

and under oaks, poplars, and terebinths,
because their shade is pleasant.
And so your daughters
act promiscuously
and your daughters-in-law
commit adultery.
14 I will not punish your daughters
when they act promiscuously
or your daughters-in-law
when they commit adultery,
for the men themselves go off
with prostitutes
and make sacrifices
with cult prostitutes.
People without discernment
are doomed.

WARNINGS FOR ISRAEL AND JUDAH

15 Israel, if you act promiscuously,
don't let Judah become guilty!
Do not go to Gilgal
or make a pilgrimage to Beth-aven,[A]
and do not swear an oath:
As the LORD lives!
16 For Israel is as obstinate
as a stubborn cow.
Can the LORD now shepherd them
like a lamb in an open meadow?
17 Ephraim is attached to idols;
leave him alone!
18 When their drinking is over,
they turn to promiscuity.
Israel's leaders[B] fervently
love disgrace.[C]
19 A wind with its wings will
carry them off,[D]
and they will be ashamed
of their sacrifices.

5 Hear this, priests!
Pay attention, house of Israel!
Listen, royal house!
For the judgment applies to you
because you have been a snare at Mizpah
and a net spread out on Tabor.
2 Rebels are deeply involved in slaughter;
I will be a punishment for all of them.[C]
3 I know Ephraim,
and Israel is not hidden from me.
For now, Ephraim,
you have acted promiscuously;
Israel is defiled.
4 Their actions do not allow them
to return to their God,
for a spirit of promiscuity
is among them,
and they do not know the LORD.
5 Israel's arrogance testifies
against them.[E]
Both Israel and Ephraim stumble
because of their iniquity;
even Judah will stumble with them.
6 They go with their flocks and herds
to seek the LORD
but do not find him;
he has withdrawn from them.
7 They betrayed the LORD;
indeed, they gave birth
to illegitimate children.
Now the New Moon will devour them
along with their fields.

8 Blow the horn in Gibeah,
the trumpet in Ramah;
raise the war cry in Beth-aven:
Look behind you,[F] Benjamin!
9 Ephraim will become a desolation
on the day of punishment;
I announce what is certain
among the tribes of Israel.
10 The princes of Judah are like those
who move boundary markers;
I will pour out my fury on them
like water.
11 Ephraim is oppressed,
crushed in judgment,
for he is determined to follow
what is worthless.[G]
12 So I am like rot to Ephraim
and like decay to the house of Judah.
13 When Ephraim saw his sickness
and Judah his wound,
Ephraim went to Assyria
and sent a delegation
to the great king.[H]
But he cannot cure you or heal
your wound.
14 For I am like a lion to Ephraim
and like a young lion to the house
of Judah.
Yes, I will tear them to pieces
and depart.
I will carry them off,
and no one can rescue them.

[A] **4:15** = House of Wickedness [B] **4:18** Lit *Her shields*; Ps 47:9; 89:18 [C] **4:18; 5:2** Hb obscure [D] **4:19** Lit *wind will bind it in its wings* [E] **5:5** Lit *against his face* [F] **5:8** Or *We will follow you* [G] **5:11** Or *follow a command*; Hb obscure [H] **5:13** Or *to King Yareb*

15 I will depart and return to my place
until they recognize their guilt
and seek my face;
they will search for me in their distress.

A CALL TO REPENTANCE

6 Come, let us return to the LORD.
For he has torn us,
and he will heal us;
he has wounded us,
and he will bind up our wounds.
2 He will revive us after two days,
and on the third day he will raise us up
so we can live in his presence.
3 Let us strive to know the LORD.
His appearance is as sure as the dawn.
He will come to us like the rain,
like the spring showers that water
the land.

THE LORD'S FIRST LAMENT

4 What am I going to do
with you, Ephraim?
What am I going to do with you, Judah?
Your love is like the morning mist
and like the early dew that vanishes.
5 This is why I have used the prophets
to cut them down;[A]
I have killed them with the words
from my mouth.
My judgment strikes like lightning.[B]
6 For I desire faithful love
and not sacrifice,
the knowledge of God rather than
burnt offerings.
7 But they, like Adam,[C] have violated
the covenant;
there they have betrayed me.
8 Gilead is a city of evildoers,
tracked with bloody footprints.
9 Like raiders who wait in ambush
for someone,
a band of priests murders on the road
to Shechem.
They commit atrocities.
10 I have seen something horrible
in the house of Israel:
Ephraim's promiscuity is there;
Israel is defiled.

E Exercise of Faith | *Staying Close to Christ*

INTIMACY NOT ACTIVITY

"For I desire faithful love and not sacrifice, the knowledge of God rather than burnt offerings." Hosea 6:6

A guilt-ridden person gives a big sum of money to charity. An absent father tries to compensate for his workaholic ways by taking his daughter car shopping. After a drunken rage, a husband sends his wife three dozen roses.

The urge to make things right is common, even in the spiritual life. In ancient Israel, the people of God often tried to compensate for their failures via religious ritual; that is, they offered elaborate sacrifices and costly burnt offerings, but their hearts weren't in it. Through the prophet Hosea, God told his wayward people that what he really wanted was their "faithful love." He wanted a relationship with them ("the knowledge of God").

New cars and pretty flowers are nice, but they're not what a daughter or wife wants most. In the same way, nothing is wrong with religious activity—unless it comes as a substitute for whole-hearted affection.

God wants *us*. Giving him time, money, and effort but withholding our love amounts to nothing.

Tell God how much you love him and for the desire and strength to know him even deeper. Each day lift your heart and mind to him.

For the next note on *Exercise of Faith*, see Micah 5:13.

[A] **6:5** Or *have cut down the prophets* [B] **6:5** LXX, Syr, Tg; MT reads *Your judgments go out as light* [C] **6:7** Or *they, as at Adam,* or *they, like men,*

11 A harvest is also appointed
for you, Judah.

When I[A] return my people from captivity,
7 1 when I heal Israel,
the iniquity of Ephraim and the crimes
of Samaria
will be exposed.
For they practice fraud;
a thief breaks in;
a raiding party pillages outside.
2 But they never consider
that I remember all their evil.
Now their actions are all around them;
they are right in front of my face.

ISRAEL'S CORRUPTION

3 They please the king with their evil,
the princes with their lies.
4 All of them commit adultery;
they are like an oven heated
by a baker
who stops stirring the fire
from the kneading of the dough
until it is leavened.
5 On the day of our king,
the princes are sick with the heat
of wine —
there is a conspiracy with traitors.[B]
6 For they — their hearts like an oven —
draw him into their oven.
Their anger smolders all night;
in the morning it blazes
like a flaming fire.
7 All of them are as hot as an oven,
and they consume their rulers.
All their kings fall;
not one of them calls on me.[C]

8 Ephraim has allowed himself
to get mixed up with the nations.
Ephraim is unturned bread
baked on a griddle.
9 Foreigners consume his strength,
but he does not notice.
Even his hair is streaked with gray,
but he does not notice.
10 Israel's arrogance testifies
against them,[D]
yet they do not return to the LORD
their God,
and for all this, they do not seek him.
11 So Ephraim has become like a silly,
senseless dove;
they call to Egypt, and they go
to Assyria.
12 As they are going, I will spread my net
over them;
I will bring them down like birds
of the sky.
I will discipline them in accordance
with the news that reaches[E]
their assembly.

THE LORD'S SECOND LAMENT

13 Woe to them, for they fled from me;
destruction to them, for they rebelled
against me!
Though I want to redeem them,
they speak lies against me.
14 They do not cry to me from their hearts;
rather, they wail on their beds.
They slash themselves[F] for grain
and new wine;
they turn away from me.
15 I trained and strengthened their arms,
but they plot evil against me.
16 They turn, but not to what is above;[G]
they are like a faulty bow.
Their leaders will fall by the sword
because of their insolent tongue.
They will be ridiculed for this
in the land of Egypt.

ISRAEL'S FALSE HOPES

8 Put the horn to your mouth!
One like an eagle comes
against the house of the LORD,
because they transgress my covenant
and rebel against my law.
2 Israel cries out to me,
"My God, we know you!"
3 Israel has rejected what is good;
an enemy will pursue him.

4 They have installed kings,
but not through me.
They have appointed leaders,
but without my approval.
They make their silver and gold
into idols for themselves
for their own destruction.[H]
5 Your calf-idol[I] is rejected, Samaria.
My anger burns against them.

[A] **6:11** Or *you. Judah, when I* [B] **7:5** Lit *wine — he stretches out his hand to scorners*; Hb obscure [C] **7:3-7** These vv. may refer to a king's assassination; Hb obscure. [D] **7:10** Lit *against his face* [E] **7:12** Lit *news to* [F] **7:14** Some Hb mss, LXX; other Hb mss read *They stay* [G] **7:16** Some emend to *turn to what is useless* [H] **8:4** Lit *themselves that it might be cut off* [I] **8:5** Lit *calf*

How long will they be incapable
of innocence?
6 For this thing is from Israel —
a craftsman made it, and it is not God.
The calf of Samaria will be smashed
to bits!

7 Indeed, they sow the wind
and reap the whirlwind.
There is no standing grain;
what sprouts fails to yield flour.
Even if they did,
foreigners would swallow it up.
8 Israel is swallowed up!
Now they are among the nations
like discarded pottery.
9 For they have gone up to Assyria
like a wild donkey going off
on its own.
Ephraim has paid for love.
10 Even though they hire lovers
among the nations,
I will now round them up,
and they will begin to decrease
in number
under the burden of the king
and leaders.

11 When Ephraim multiplied his altars
for sin,
they became his altars for sinning.
12 Though I were to write out for him
ten thousand points of my instruction,
they would be[A] regarded
as something strange.
13 Though they offer sacrificial gifts[B]
and eat the flesh,
the LORD does not accept them.
Now he will remember their guilt
and punish their sins;
they will return to Egypt.
14 Israel has forgotten his Maker
and built palaces;
Judah has also multiplied
fortified cities.
I will send fire on their cities,
and it will consume their citadels.

THE COMING EXILE

9 Israel, do not rejoice jubilantly
as the nations do,
for you have acted promiscuously,
leaving your God.
You love the wages of a prostitute
on every grain-threshing floor.
2 Threshing floor and wine vat will not
sustain them,
and the new wine will fail them.
3 They will not stay in the land of the LORD.
Instead, Ephraim will return to Egypt,
and they will eat unclean food in Assyria.

4 They will not pour out
their wine offerings to the LORD,
and their sacrifices will not please him.
Their food will be like the bread
of mourners;
all who eat it become defiled.
For their bread will be
for their appetites alone;
it will not enter the house of the LORD.
5 What will you do on a festival day,
on the day of the LORD's feast?
6 For even if they flee from devastation,
Egypt will gather them, and Memphis
will bury them.
Thistles will take possession
of their precious silver;
thorns will invade their tents.

7 The days of punishment have come;
the days of retribution have come.
Let Israel recognize it!
The prophet is a fool,
and the inspired man is insane,
because of the magnitude
of your iniquity and hostility.
8 Ephraim's watchman is with my God.
Yet the prophet encounters a bird trap
on all his pathways.
Hostility is in the house of his God!
9 They have deeply corrupted themselves
as in the days of Gibeah.
He will remember their iniquity;
he will punish their sins.

EPHRAIM BEREAVED OF OFFSPRING

10 I discovered Israel
like grapes in the wilderness.
I saw your fathers
like the first fruit of the fig tree
in its first season.
But they went to Baal-peor,
consecrated themselves to Shame,[C]
and became abhorrent,
like the thing they loved.

[A] **8:12** Or *Though I wrote out . . . instruction, they are* [B] **8:13** Hb obscure [C] **9:10** = Baal

11 Ephraim's glory will fly away like a bird:
no birth, no pregnancy, no conception.
12 Even if they raise children,
I will bereave them of each one.
Yes, woe to them when I depart
from them!
13 I have seen Ephraim like Tyre,
planted in a meadow,
so Ephraim will bring out his children
to the executioner.
14 Give them, LORD —
What should you give?
Give them a womb that miscarries
and breasts that are dry!

15 All their evil appears at Gilgal,
for there I began to hate them.
I will drive them from my house
because of their evil, wicked actions.
I will no longer love them;
all their leaders are rebellious.
16 Ephraim is struck down;
their roots are withered;
they cannot bear fruit.
Even if they bear children,
I will kill the precious offspring
of their wombs.
17 My God will reject them
because they have not listened to him;
they will become wanderers
among the nations.

THE VINE AND THE CALF

10 Israel is a lush[A] vine;
it yields fruit for itself.
The more his fruit increased,
the more he increased the altars.
The better his land produced,
the better they made
the sacred pillars.
2 Their hearts are devious;[B]
now they must bear their guilt.
The LORD will break down their altars
and demolish their sacred pillars.
3 In fact, they are now saying,
"We have no king!
For we do not fear the LORD.
What can a king do for us?"
4 They speak mere words,
taking false oaths
while making covenants.
So lawsuits break out
like poisonous weeds in the furrows
of a field.

Rest and Reflection | *Being Willing to Change*

A HARVEST OF RIGHTEOUSNESS

"Sow righteousness for yourselves and reap faithful love; break up your unplowed ground. It is time to seek the LORD until he comes and sends righteousness on you like the rain." Hosea 10:12

If you've ever gardened, you can appreciate all the agricultural imagery in this verse, used to highlight certain spiritual realities. "Break up your unplowed ground" is a command to soften our hearts so that we can receive God's truth. Instead of being resistant or hard-hearted toward God and his Word, we repent. We open ourselves to his transforming presence, and we listen.

"Sow" refers to planting or scattering seed. In this case, we are to plant "righteousness," or live the right way, as God commanded. If we do this we will "reap faithful love." That is, we will get to enjoy God's loyal, covenant love springing to life in and through us. In Galatians 5:22-23, the apostle Paul describes such spiritual fruit: "love, joy, peace, patience, kindness, goodness, faithfulness, gentleness, and self-control."

Bringing in a bumper crop requires more than sporadic flurries of activity. Gardening is hard, vigilant work over a long period. In the same way, spiritual fruit requires that we "seek the LORD until he comes," by daily inviting the Holy Spirit to lead, correct, and strengthen us so our hearts can be fruitful soil.

For the next note on *Rest and Reflection*, see Zechariah 4:6.

[A] **10:1** Or *ravaged* [B] **10:2** Or *divided*

5 The residents of Samaria
will have anxiety
over the calf of Beth-aven.
Indeed, its idolatrous priests rejoiced
over it;
the people will mourn over it,
over its glory.
It will certainly go into exile.
6 The calf itself will be taken to Assyria
as an offering to the great king.[A]
Ephraim will experience shame;
Israel will be ashamed of its counsel.
7 Samaria's king will disappear[B]
like foam[C] on the surface of the water.
8 The high places of Aven,
the sin of Israel,
will be destroyed;
thorns and thistles will grow
over their altars.
They will say to the mountains,
"Cover us!"
and to the hills, "Fall on us!"

ISRAEL'S DEFEAT BECAUSE OF SIN

9 Israel, you have sinned
since the days of Gibeah;
they have taken their stand there.
Will not war against the unjust
overtake them in Gibeah?
10 I will discipline them at my discretion;
nations will be gathered against them
to put them in bondage[D]
for their double iniquity.

11 Ephraim is a well-trained calf
that loves to thresh,
but I will place a yoke on[E] her fine neck.
I will harness Ephraim;
Judah will plow;
Jacob will do the final plowing.
12 Sow righteousness for yourselves
and reap faithful love;
break up your unplowed ground.
It is time to seek the LORD
until he comes
and sends righteousness
on you like the rain.

13 You have plowed wickedness
and reaped injustice;
you have eaten the fruit of lies.
Because you have trusted
in your own way[F]
and in your large number of soldiers,
14 the roar of battle will rise
against your people,
and all your fortifications
will be demolished
in a day of war,
like Shalman's destruction
of Beth-arbel.
Mothers will be dashed to pieces
along with their children.
15 So it will be done to you, Bethel,
because of your extreme evil.
At dawn the king of Israel will be
totally destroyed.

THE LORD'S LOVE FOR ISRAEL

11 When Israel was a child, I loved him,
and out of Egypt I called my son.
2 Israel called to the Egyptians
even as Israel was leaving them.[G]
They kept sacrificing to the Baals
and burning offerings to idols.
3 It was I who taught Ephraim to walk,
taking them[H] by the hand,[I]
but they never knew
that I healed them.
4 I led them with human cords,
with ropes of love.
To them I was like one
who eases the yoke from their jaws;
I bent down to give them food.
5 Israel will not return to the land
of Egypt
and Assyria will be his king,
because they refused to repent.
6 A sword will whirl through his cities;
it will destroy and devour the bars
of his gates,[J]
because of their schemes.
7 My people are bent on turning from me.
Though they call to him on high,
he will not exalt them at all.

8 How can I give you up, Ephraim?
How can I surrender you, Israel?
How can I make you like Admah?
How can I treat you like Zeboiim?
I have had a change of heart;
my compassion is stirred!

[A] **10:6** Or *to King Yareb* [B] **10:7** Or *will be cut off* [C] **10:7** Or *a stick* [D] **10:10** LXX, Syr, Vg read *against them when they are disciplined* [E] **10:11** Lit *will pass over* [F] **10:13** LXX reads *your chariots* [G] **11:2** Lit *They called to them; thus they went from before them* [H] **11:3** LXX, Syr, Vg; MT reads *him* [I] **11:3** Lit *them on his arms* [J] **11:6** Or *devour his empty talkers*, or *devour his limbs*; Hb obscure

9 I will not vent the full fury of my anger;
I will not turn back to destroy Ephraim.
For I am God and not man,
the Holy One among you;
I will not come in rage.[A]
10 They will follow the LORD;
he will roar like a lion.
When he roars,
his children will come trembling
from the west.
11 They will be roused like birds from Egypt
and like doves from the land of Assyria.
Then I will settle them in their homes.
This is the LORD's declaration.
12 Ephraim surrounds me with lies,
the house of Israel, with deceit.
Judah still wanders with God
and is faithful to the holy ones.[B]

GOD'S CASE AGAINST JACOB'S HEIRS

12 Ephraim chases[C] the wind
and pursues the east wind.
He continually multiplies lies and violence.
He makes a covenant with Assyria,
and olive oil is carried to Egypt.

2 The LORD also has a dispute with Judah.
He is about to punish Jacob
according to his conduct;
he will repay him based on his actions.
3 In the womb he grasped
his brother's heel,
and as an adult he wrestled with God.
4 Jacob struggled with the angel
and prevailed;
he wept and sought his favor.
He found him at Bethel,
and there he spoke with him.[D]
5 The LORD is the God of Armies;
the LORD is his name.
6 But you must return to your God.
Maintain love and justice,
and always put your hope in God.

7 A merchant loves to extort
with dishonest scales in his hands.
8 But Ephraim thinks,
"How rich I have become;
I made it all myself.
In all my earnings,
no one can find any iniquity in me
that I can be punished for!"[E]

JUDGMENT ON APOSTATE ISRAEL

9 I have been the LORD your God
ever since[F] the land of Egypt.
I will make you live in tents again,
as in the festival days.
10 I will speak through the prophets
and grant many visions;
I will give parables through the prophets.
11 Since Gilead is full of evil,
they will certainly come to nothing.
They sacrifice bulls in Gilgal;
even their altars will be
like piles of rocks
on the furrows of a field.

FURTHER INDICTMENT OF JACOB'S HEIRS

12 Jacob fled to the territory of Aram.
Israel worked to earn a wife;
he tended flocks for a wife.
13 The LORD brought Israel from Egypt
by a prophet,
and Israel was tended by a prophet.

14 Ephraim has provoked bitter anger,
so his Lord will leave his bloodguilt
on him
and repay him for his contempt.

13 When Ephraim spoke,
there was trembling;
he was exalted in Israel.
But he incurred guilt through Baal
and died.

2 Now they continue to sin
and make themselves a cast image,
idols skillfully made from their silver,
all of them the work of craftsmen.
People say about them,
"Let the men who sacrifice[G] kiss
the calves."
3 Therefore, they will be
like the morning mist,
like the early dew that vanishes,
like chaff blown from a threshing floor,
or like smoke from a window.

DEATH AND RESURRECTION

4 I have been the LORD your God
ever since[H] the land of Egypt;
you know no God but me,
and no Savior exists besides me.

[A] **11:9** Or *come into any city*; Hb obscure [B] **11:12** Hb obscure [C] **12:1** Or *grazes on*, or *tends* [D] **12:4** LXX, Syr; MT reads *us*
[E] **12:8** Lit *iniquity which is sin* [F] **12:9** LXX reads *God who brought you out of* [G] **13:2** Or *"Those who make human sacrifices*
[H] **13:4** DSS, LXX read *God who brought you out of*

RESTORATION THEMES

R	Rest and Reflection	*For the next note, see Zechariah 4:6.*
E	Eternal Perspective	*God's Grace/Kindness—Joel 2:12-13*
S	Support	*For the next note, see Habakkuk 1:2-4.*
T	Thanksgiving and Contentment	*For the next note, see Jonah 3:1.*
O	Other-centeredness	*For the next note, see Amos 5:24.*
R	Relationships	*For the next note, see Micah 5:5.*
E	Exercise of Faith	*For the next note, see Micah 5:13.*

1 The word of the LORD that came to Joel son of Pethuel:

A PLAGUE OF LOCUSTS

2 Hear this, you elders;
listen, all you inhabitants of the land.
Has anything like this ever happened
in your days
or in the days of your ancestors?
3 Tell your children about it,
and let your children tell their children,
and their children the next generation.
4 What the devouring locust has left,
the swarming locust has eaten;
what the swarming locust has left,
the young locust has eaten;
and what the young locust has left,
the destroying locust has eaten.

5 Wake up, you drunkards, and weep;
wail, all you wine drinkers,
because of the sweet wine,
for it has been taken from your mouth.
6 For a nation has invaded my land,
powerful and without number;
its teeth are the teeth of a lion,
and it has the fangs of a lioness.
7 It has devastated my grapevine
and splintered my fig tree.
It has stripped off its bark
and thrown it away;
its branches have turned white.
8 Grieve like a young woman dressed
in sackcloth,
mourning for the husband
of her youth.
9 Grain and drink offerings have been
cut off
from the house of the LORD;
the priests, who are ministers
of the LORD, mourn.
10 The fields are destroyed;
the land grieves;
indeed, the grain is destroyed;
the new wine is dried up;
and the fresh oil fails.
11 Be ashamed, you farmers,
wail, you vinedressers,[A]
over the wheat and the barley,
because the harvest of the field
has perished.
12 The grapevine is dried up,
and the fig tree is withered;
the pomegranate, the date palm,
and the apple —
all the trees of the orchard —
have withered.
Indeed, human joy has dried up.

13 Dress in sackcloth and lament,
you priests;
wail, you ministers of the altar.
Come and spend the night in sackcloth,
you ministers of my God,
because grain and drink offerings
are withheld from the house of your God.
14 Announce a sacred fast;
proclaim an assembly!
Gather the elders
and all the residents of the land
at the house of the LORD your God,
and cry out to the LORD.

THE DAY OF THE LORD

15 Woe because of that day!
For the day of the LORD is near
and will come as devastation
from the Almighty.
16 Hasn't the food been cut off
before our eyes,
joy and gladness
from the house of our God?
17 The seeds lie shriveled in their casings.[B]
The storehouses are in ruin,
and the granaries are broken down,
because the grain has withered away.
18 How the animals groan!
The herds of cattle wander in confusion
since they have no pasture.
Even the flocks of sheep and goats
suffer punishment.
19 I call to you, LORD,
for fire has consumed
the pastures of the wilderness,
and flames have devoured
all the trees of the orchard.
20 Even the wild animals cry out to[C] you,
for the river beds are dried up,
and fire has consumed
the pastures of the wilderness.

2 Blow the horn in Zion;
sound the alarm on my holy mountain!
Let all the residents of the land tremble,
for the day of the LORD is coming;
in fact, it is near —

[A] 1:11 Or *The farmers are dismayed, the vinedressers wail* [B] 1:17 Or *clods*; Hb obscure [C] 1:20 Or *animals pant for*; Hb obscure

2 a day of darkness and gloom,
a day of clouds and total darkness,
like the dawn spreading
over the mountains;
a great and strong people appears,
such as never existed in ages past
and never will again
in all the generations to come.

3 A fire devours in front of them,
and behind them a flame blazes.
The land in front of them
is like the garden of Eden,
but behind them,
it is like a desert wasteland;
there is no escape from them.
4 Their appearance is
like that of horses,
and they gallop like war horses.
5 They bound on the tops
of the mountains.
Their sound is like the sound
of chariots,
like the sound of fiery flames
consuming stubble,
like a mighty army deployed for war.
6 Nations writhe
in horror before them;
all faces turn pale.
7 They attack as warriors attack;
they scale walls as men of war do.
Each goes on his own path,
and they do not change their course.
8 They do not push each other;
each proceeds on his own path.
They dodge the arrows,
never stopping.
9 They storm the city;
they run on the wall;
they climb into the houses;
they enter through the windows
like thieves.

10 The earth quakes before them;
the sky shakes.
The sun and moon grow dark,
and the stars cease their shining.
11 The LORD makes his voice heard
in the presence of his army.
His camp is very large;
those who carry out his command
are powerful.

Eternal Perspective | *God's Grace/Kindness*

SO MUCH JUDGMENT!

"Even now—this is the LORD's declaration—turn to me with all your heart, with fasting, weeping, and mourning. Tear your hearts, not just your clothes, and return to the LORD your God. For he is gracious and compassionate, slow to anger, abounding in faithful love, and he relents from sending disaster." Joel 2:12-13

Those who read through the Bible are sometimes shell-shocked midway through the Prophetical Books. "Why so much judgment?" they ask.

Take the book of Joel for example. It starts with the threat of a devastating locust invasion and drought. Then it repeatedly mentions the great and terrible "day of the LORD."

Here's why: Sin is destabilizing, like a brazen, violent coup against a government. It's demoralizing, challenging the very notion of justice. It's deadly, like cancer. Unacknowledged and unchecked, it metastasizes and spreads its malignancy everywhere. It ruins lives and families.

For these reasons, a holy God must judge sin—severely and thoroughly. He doesn't let things slide any more than a surgeon is okay with a germ-infested operating room. Would you want to live in a society where crime was never punished?

As this verse shows, God judges sin because he is "abounding in faithful love." Nowhere is this truth better demonstrated than at the cross of Jesus. The worst sinner who turns to him finds grace.

For the next note on *Eternal Perspective*, see Jonah 4:6-8.

Indeed, the day of the LORD is terrible
and dreadful —
who can endure it?

GOD'S CALL FOR REPENTANCE

12 Even now —
this is the LORD's declaration —
turn to me with all your heart,
with fasting, weeping, and mourning.
13 Tear your hearts,
not just your clothes,
and return to the LORD your God.
For he is gracious and compassionate,
slow to anger, abounding in faithful love,
and he relents from sending disaster.
14 Who knows? He may turn and relent
and leave a blessing behind him,
so you can offer grain and wine
to the LORD your God.

15 Blow the horn in Zion!
Announce a sacred fast;
proclaim an assembly.
16 Gather the people;
sanctify the congregation;
assemble the aged;[A]
gather the infants,
even babies nursing at the breast.
Let the groom leave his bedroom,
and the bride her honeymoon chamber.
17 Let the priests, the LORD's ministers,
weep between the portico and the altar.
Let them say:
"Have pity on your people, LORD,
and do not make your inheritance
a disgrace,
an object of scorn among the nations.
Why should it be said among the peoples,
'Where is their God?'"

GOD'S RESPONSE TO HIS PEOPLE

18 Then the LORD became jealous for his land
and spared his people. 19 The LORD answered
his people:
Look, I am about to send you
grain, new wine, and fresh oil.
You will be satiated with them,
and I will no longer make you
a disgrace among the nations.

20 I will drive the northerner far from you
and banish him to a dry
and desolate land,
his front ranks into the Dead Sea,
and his rear guard
into the Mediterranean Sea.
His stench will rise;
yes, his rotten smell will rise,
for he has done astonishing things.

21 Don't be afraid, land;
rejoice and be glad,
for the LORD has done
astonishing things.
22 Don't be afraid, wild animals,
for the wilderness pastures
have turned green,
the trees bear their fruit,
and the fig tree and grapevine yield
their riches.
23 Children of Zion, rejoice and be glad
in the LORD your God,
because he gives you the autumn rain
for your vindication.[B]
He sends showers for you,
both autumn and spring rain as before.
24 The threshing floors will be full of grain,
and the vats will overflow
with new wine and fresh oil.

25 I will repay you for the years
that the swarming locust ate,
the young locust, the destroying locust,
and the devouring locust —
my great army that I sent against you.
26 You will have plenty to eat
and be satisfied.
You will praise the name of the
LORD your God,
who has dealt wondrously with you.
My people will never again be put
to shame.
27 You will know that I am present
in Israel
and that I am the LORD your God,
and there is no other.
My people will never again be put
to shame.

GOD'S PROMISE OF HIS SPIRIT

28 After this
I will pour out my Spirit on all humanity;
then your sons and your daughters
will prophesy,
your old men will have dreams,
and your young men will see visions.

[A] 2:16 Or *elders* [B] 2:23 Or *righteousness*

29 I will even pour out my Spirit
on the male and female slaves
in those days.
30 I will display wonders
in the heavens and on the earth:
blood, fire, and columns of smoke.
31 The sun will be turned to darkness
and the moon to blood
before the great and terrible day
of the LORD comes.
32 Then everyone who calls
on the name of the LORD will be saved,
for there will be an escape
for those on Mount Zion
and in Jerusalem,
as the LORD promised,
among the survivors the LORD calls.

Then everyone who calls on the name of the LORD will be saved.
—Joel 2:32

JUDGMENT OF THE NATIONS

3 Yes, in those days and at that time,
when I restore the fortunes of Judah
and Jerusalem,
2 I will gather all the nations
and take them to the Valley
of Jehoshaphat.[A]
I will enter into judgment
with them there
because of my people,
my inheritance Israel.
The nations have scattered the Israelites
in foreign countries
and divided up my land.
3 They cast lots for my people;
they bartered a boy for a prostitute
and sold a girl for wine to drink.

4 And also: Tyre, Sidon, and all the territories
of Philistia — what are you to me? Are you
paying me back or trying to get even with
me? I will quickly bring retribution on your
heads. 5 For you took my silver and gold and
carried my finest treasures to your temples.
6 You sold the people of Judah and Jerusalem
to the Greeks to remove them far from their
own territory. 7 Look, I am about to rouse them
up from the place where you sold them; I will
bring retribution on your heads. 8 I will sell
your sons and daughters to the people of Judah, and they will sell them to the Sabeans,[B]
to a distant nation, for the LORD has spoken.

9 Proclaim this among the nations:
Prepare for holy war;
rouse the warriors;
let all the men of war advance
and attack!
10 Beat your plows into swords
and your pruning knives into spears.
Let even the weakling say, "I am
a warrior."
11 Come quickly,[C] all
you surrounding nations;
gather yourselves.
Bring down your warriors there, LORD.

12 Let the nations be roused
and come to the Valley of Jehoshaphat,
for there I will sit down
to judge all the surrounding nations.
13 Swing the sickle
because the harvest is ripe.
Come and trample the grapes
because the winepress is full;
the wine vats overflow
because the wickedness of the nations
is extreme.

14 Multitudes, multitudes
in the valley of decision!
For the day of the LORD is near
in the valley of decision.
15 The sun and moon will grow dark,
and the stars will cease their shining.
16 The LORD will roar from Zion
and make his voice heard
from Jerusalem;
heaven and earth will shake.
But the LORD will be a refuge
for his people,
a stronghold for the Israelites.

ISRAEL BLESSED

17 Then you will know
that I am the LORD your God,
who dwells in Zion, my holy mountain.
Jerusalem will be holy,
and foreigners will never
overrun it again.

[A] **3:2** = The LORD Will Judge [B] **3:8** Probably the south Arabian kingdom of Sheba (modern Yemen) [C] **3:11** LXX, Syr, Tg read *Gather yourselves and come*; Hb obscure

18 In that day
the mountains will drip
with sweet wine,
and the hills will flow with milk.
All the streams of Judah will flow
with water,
and a spring will issue
from the LORD's house,
watering the Valley of Acacias.[A]
19 Egypt will become desolate,
and Edom a desert wasteland,
because of the violence done
to the people of Judah
in whose land they shed
innocent blood.
20 But Judah will be
inhabited forever,
and Jerusalem from generation
to generation.
21 I will pardon their bloodguilt,[B]
which I have not pardoned,
for the LORD dwells in Zion.

[A] **3:18** Or *Shittim* [B] **3:21** LXX, Syr read *I will avenge their blood*

Amos—With money in the bank and food in the pantry, we can feel self-sufficient and forget that everything comes from God. In Amos's day, God's people were prosperous, but they were starting to forget God. Arrogantly, they believed they didn't need God and that their religious acts were almost a favor to him. They had no fear of God's judgment because they were his chosen people.

So, God sent Amos to remind the people that God is Sovereign and they were helpless and hopeless apart from him. Amos warned the Israelites that because of their pride and religious hypocrisy, God's judgment was imminent.

As with most Prophetic Books, Amos ends on a high note. God promises to restore the fortunes of his people (9:11-15). One day he would return them to their land, and they would never be uprooted again. They would be fruitful and enjoy his blessings.

This is how God deals with his people. When we become proud and forget to give him the glory he deserves, he calls us to repentance. When we repent, he restores us to sweet relationship with him, offering the peace of reconciliation and salvation.

AMOS

AUTHOR: Amos, a shepherd from Tekoa

DATE WRITTEN: This summary of Amos's prophecies was written after he returned to Judah following his prophecy in Samaria and Israel, which took place around 760 BC.

ORIGINAL AUDIENCE: The Israelites, especially those who were wealthy and powerful

SETTING: Amos prophesied during the reigns of Uzziah in Judah (792–740 BC) and Jeroboam II in Israel (793–753 BC). Both kingdoms enjoyed prosperity and military strength; Samaria, the capital city of Israel, was especially luxurious.

PURPOSE FOR WRITING: Amos speaks out against hypocrisy. The Israelites were going through the motions of religious devotion, but their hearts were far from God. Amos taught that God would judge all nations fairly, and that he particularly despises pride and injustice toward the poor. The people's religious acts would not save them; only true repentance and redemption through God's anointed one could bring salvation.

OUTLINE:

1. Prophecies against the Nations (1:1–2:16)

   Indictment against neighboring nations (1:1–2:3)

   Indictment of Judah (2:4-5)

   Indictment of Israel (2:6-16)

2. Discourses against Israel (3:1–6:14)

   Declaration of judgment (3:1-15)

   Description of Israel's depravity (4:1-13)

   Lament for Israel (5:1–6:14)

3. Visions of Israel's Condition (7:1–9:10)

   Devouring locusts (7:1-3)

   Flaming fire (7:4-6)

   Plumb line (7:7-17)

   Basket of ripe fruit (8:1-14)

   The Lord at the altar (9:1-10)

4. Promises of Restoration (9:11-15)

KEY VERSE:

"Hate evil and love good; establish justice in the city gate." —Amos 5:15

RESTORATION THEMES

R	Rest and Reflection	*For the next note, see Zechariah 4:6.*
E	Eternal Perspective	*For the next note, see Jonah 4:6-8.*
S	Support	*For the next note, see Habakkuk 1:2-4.*
T	Thanksgiving and Contentment	*For the next note, see Jonah 3:1.*
O	Other-centeredness	*Helping People in Need—Amos 5:24*
R	Relationships	*For the next note, see Micah 5:5.*
E	Exercise of Faith	*For the next note, see Micah 5:13.*

1 The words of Amos, who was one of the
sheep breeders[A] from Tekoa — what he
saw regarding Israel in the days of King Uzziah
of Judah and Jeroboam son of Jehoash, king
of Israel, two years before the earthquake.
2 He said:
The LORD roars from Zion
and makes his voice heard
from Jerusalem;
the pastures of the shepherds mourn,[B]
and the summit of Carmel withers.

JUDGMENT ON ISRAEL'S NEIGHBORS

3 The LORD says:
I will not relent
from punishing Damascus
for three crimes, even four,
because they threshed Gilead
with iron sledges.
4 Therefore, I will send fire
against Hazael's palace,
and it will consume Ben-hadad's citadels.
5 I will break down the gates[C]
of Damascus.
I will cut off the ruler
from the Valley of Aven,
and the one who wields the scepter
from Beth-eden.
The people of Aram will be exiled to Kir.
The LORD has spoken.

6 The LORD says:
I will not relent from punishing Gaza
for three crimes, even four,
because they exiled a whole community,
handing them over to Edom.
7 Therefore, I will send fire
against the walls of Gaza,
and it will consume its citadels.
8 I will cut off the ruler from Ashdod,
and the one who wields the scepter
from Ashkelon.
I will also turn my hand against Ekron,
and the remainder of the Philistines
will perish.
The Lord GOD has spoken.

9 The LORD says:
I will not relent from punishing Tyre
for three crimes, even four,
because they handed over
a whole community of exiles to Edom
and broke[D] a treaty of brotherhood.
10 Therefore, I will send fire
against the walls of Tyre,
and it will consume its citadels.

11 The LORD says:
I will not relent from punishing Edom
for three crimes, even four,
because he pursued his brother
with the sword.
He stifled his compassion,
his anger tore at him continually,
and he harbored his rage incessantly.
12 Therefore, I will send fire against Teman,
and it will consume the citadels
of Bozrah.

13 The LORD says:
I will not relent from punishing
the Ammonites
for three crimes, even four,
because they ripped open
the pregnant women of Gilead
in order to enlarge their territory.
14 Therefore, I will set fire to the walls
of Rabbah,
and it will consume its citadels.
There will be shouting on the day
of battle
and a violent wind on the day
of the storm.
15 Their king and his princes
will go into exile together.
The LORD has spoken.

2 The LORD says:
I will not relent from punishing Moab
for three crimes, even four,
because he burned the bones
of the king of Edom to lime.
2 Therefore, I will send fire against Moab,
and it will consume the citadels
of Kerioth.
Moab will die with a tumult,
with shouting and the sound
of the ram's horn.
3 I will cut off the judge from the land
and kill all its officials with him.
The LORD has spoken.

JUDGMENT ON JUDAH

4 The LORD says:
I will not relent from punishing Judah
for three crimes, even four,

[A] **1:1** Or *the shepherds* [B] **1:2** Or *dry up* [C] **1:5** Lit *gate bars* [D] **1:9** Lit *and did not remember*

because they have rejected
the instruction of the LORD
and have not kept his statutes.
The lies that their ancestors followed
have led them astray.
5 Therefore, I will send fire against Judah,
and it will consume the citadels
of Jerusalem.

JUDGMENT ON ISRAEL

6 The LORD says:
I will not relent from punishing Israel
for three crimes, even four,
because they sell a righteous person
for silver
and a needy person for a pair
of sandals.
7 They trample the heads of the poor
on the dust of the ground
and obstruct the path of the needy.
A man and his father
have sexual relations
with the same girl,
profaning my holy name.
8 They stretch out beside every altar
on garments taken as collateral,
and in the house of their God
they drink wine obtained
through fines.

9 Yet I destroyed the Amorite
as Israel advanced;
his height was like the cedars,
and he was as sturdy as the oaks;
I destroyed his fruit above
and his roots beneath.
10 And I brought you from the land
of Egypt
and led you forty years
in the wilderness
in order to possess the land
of the Amorite.
11 I raised up some of your sons
as prophets
and some of your young men
as Nazirites.
Is this not the case, Israelites?
This is the LORD's declaration.
12 But you made the Nazirites drink wine
and commanded the prophets,
"Do not prophesy."
13 Look, I am about to crush[A] you
in your place
as a wagon crushes when
full of grain.
14 Escape will fail the swift,
the strong one will not
maintain his strength,
and the warrior will not save his life.
15 The archer will not stand his ground,
the one who is swift of foot
will not save himself,
and the one riding a horse will not save
his life.
16 Even the most courageous
of the warriors
will flee naked on that day —
this is the LORD's declaration.

GOD'S REASONS FOR PUNISHING ISRAEL

3 Listen to this message that the LORD has
spoken against you, Israelites, against
the entire clan that I brought from the land
of Egypt:
2 I have known only you
out of all the clans of the earth;
therefore, I will punish you for all
your iniquities.
3 Can two walk together
without agreeing to meet?
4 Does a lion roar in the forest
when it has no prey?
Does a young lion growl from its lair
unless it has captured something?
5 Does a bird land in a trap on the ground
if there is no bait for it?
Does a trap spring from the ground
when it has caught nothing?
6 If a ram's horn is blown in a city,
aren't people afraid?
If a disaster occurs in a city,
hasn't the LORD done it?
7 Indeed, the Lord GOD does nothing
without revealing his counsel
to his servants the prophets.
8 A lion has roared;
who will not fear?

Can two walk together without agreeing to meet?
—Amos 3:3

[A] **2:13** Or *hinder*; Hb obscure

The Lord God has spoken;
who will not prophesy?

9 Proclaim on the citadels in Ashdod
and on the citadels in the land of Egypt:
Assemble on the mountains of Samaria,
and see the great turmoil in the city
and the acts of oppression within it.
10 The people are incapable
of doing right —
this is the Lord's declaration —
those who store up violence
and destruction
in their citadels.
11 Therefore, the Lord God says:
An enemy will surround the land;
he will destroy your strongholds
and plunder your citadels.

12 The Lord says:
As the shepherd snatches two legs
or a piece of an ear
from the lion's mouth,
so the Israelites who live in Samaria
will be rescued
with only the corner of a bed
or the[A] cushion[B] of a couch.[C]

13 Listen and testify against the house
of Jacob —
this is the declaration
of the Lord God,
the God of Armies.
14 I will punish the altars of Bethel
on the day I punish Israel for its crimes;
the horns of the altar will be cut off
and fall to the ground.
15 I will demolish the winter house
and the summer house;
the houses inlaid with ivory
will be destroyed,
and the great houses will come
to an end.
This is the Lord's declaration.

SOCIAL AND SPIRITUAL CORRUPTION

4 Listen to this message, you cows
of Bashan
who are on the hill of Samaria,
women who oppress the poor
and crush the needy,
who say to their husbands,
"Bring us something to drink."
2 The Lord God has sworn by his holiness:
Look, the days are coming[D]
when you will be taken away
with hooks,
every last one of you with fishhooks.
3 You will go through breaches
in the wall,
each woman straight ahead,
and you will be driven along
toward Harmon.
This is the Lord's declaration.

4 Come to Bethel and rebel;
rebel even more at Gilgal!
Bring your sacrifices
every morning,
your tenths every three days.
5 Offer leavened bread as
a thank offering,
and loudly proclaim
your freewill offerings,
for that is what you Israelites
love to do!
This is the declaration
of the Lord God.

GOD'S DISCIPLINE AND ISRAEL'S APOSTASY

6 I gave you absolutely nothing to eat[E]
in all your cities,
a shortage of food in all
your communities,
yet you did not return to me.
This is the Lord's declaration.

7 I also withheld the rain from you
while there were still three months
until harvest.
I sent rain on one city
but no rain on another.
One field received rain
while a field with no rain withered.
8 Two or three cities staggered
to another city to drink water
but were not satisfied,
yet you did not return to me.
This is the Lord's declaration.

9 I struck you with blight and mildew;
the locust devoured
your many gardens and vineyards,
your fig trees and olive trees,
yet you did not return to me.
This is the Lord's declaration.

[A] **3:12** Or *Israelites will be rescued, those who sit in Samaria on a corner of a bed or a* [B] **3:12** Hb obscure [C] **3:12** LXX, Aq, Sym, Theod, Syr, Tg, Vg read *or in Damascus* [D] **4:2** Lit *coming on you* [E] **4:6** Lit *you cleanness of teeth*

10 I sent plagues like those of Egypt;
I killed your young men
with the sword,
along with your captured horses.
I caused the stench of your camp
to fill your nostrils,
yet you did not return to me.
This is the LORD's declaration.

11 I overthrew some of you
as I[A] overthrew Sodom and Gomorrah,
and you were like a burning stick
snatched from a fire,
yet you did not return to me —
This is the LORD's declaration.

12 Therefore, Israel, that is what I will do
to you,
and since I will do that to you,
Israel, prepare to meet your God!
13 He is here:
the one who forms the mountains,
creates the wind,
and reveals his thoughts to man,
the one who makes the dawn
out of darkness
and strides on the heights of the earth.
The LORD, the God of Armies,
is his name.

LAMENTATION FOR ISRAEL

5 Listen to this message that I am singing
for you, a lament, house of Israel:
2 She has fallen;
Virgin Israel will never rise again.
She lies abandoned on her land
with no one to raise her up.
3 For the Lord GOD says:
The city that marches out
a thousand strong
will have only a hundred left,
and the one that marches out
a hundred strong
will have only ten left in the house
of Israel.

SEEK GOD AND LIVE

4 For the LORD says to the house of Israel:
Seek me and live!
5 Do not seek Bethel
or go to Gilgal
or journey to Beer-sheba,
for Gilgal will certainly go into exile,
and Bethel will come to nothing.
6 Seek the LORD and live,
or he will spread like fire
throughout the house of Joseph;
it will consume everything
with no one at Bethel to extinguish it.
7 Those who turn justice into wormwood
also throw righteousness
to the ground.

8 The one who made the Pleiades
and Orion,
who turns darkness[B] into dawn
and darkens day into night,
who summons the water of the sea
and pours it out over the surface
of the earth —
the LORD is his name.
9 He brings destruction[C] on the strong,[D]
and it falls on the fortress.

10 They hate the one who convicts
the guilty
at the city gate,
and they despise the one who speaks
with integrity.
11 Therefore, because you trample on
the poor
and exact a grain tax from him,
you will never live in the houses
of cut stone
you have built;
you will never drink the wine
from the lush vineyards
you have planted.
12 For I know your crimes are many
and your sins innumerable.
They oppress the righteous,
take a bribe,
and deprive the poor of justice
at the city gates.
13 Therefore, those who have insight
will keep silent[E]
at such a time,
for the days are evil.

14 Pursue good and not evil
so that you may live,
and the LORD, the God of Armies,
will be with you
as you have claimed.
15 Hate evil and love good;
establish justice in the city gate.

[A] **4:11** Lit *God* [B] **5:8** Or *turns the shadow of death* [C] **5:9** Hb obscure [D] **5:9** Or *stronghold* [E] **5:13** Or *who are prudent will perish*

Perhaps the LORD, the God of Armies,
will be gracious
to the remnant of Joseph.

16 Therefore the LORD, the God of Armies,
the Lord, says:
There will be wailing in all
the public squares;
they will cry out in anguish[A] in all
the streets.
The farmer will be called on to mourn,
and professional mourners[B] to wail.
17 There will be wailing in all
the vineyards,
for I will pass among you.
The LORD has spoken.

THE DAY OF THE LORD

18 Woe to you who long for the day
of the LORD!
What will the day of the LORD
be for you?
It will be darkness and not light.
19 It will be like a man who flees
from a lion
only to have a bear confront him.
He goes home and rests his hand
against the wall
only to have a snake bite him.
20 Won't the day of the LORD
be darkness rather than light,
even gloom without any brightness in it?
21 I hate, I despise, your feasts!
I can't stand the stench
of your solemn assemblies.
22 Even if you offer me
your burnt offerings
and grain offerings,
I will not accept them;
I will have no regard
for your fellowship offerings
of fattened cattle.
23 Take away from me the noise
of your songs!
I will not listen to the music
of your harps.
24 But let justice flow like water,
and righteousness,
like an unfailing stream.

25 "House of Israel, was it sacrifices and grain
offerings that you presented to me during the

Other-centeredness | *Helping People in Need*

RIVERS OF LIVING WATER

"But let justice flow like water, and righteousness, like an unfailing stream." Amos 5:24

Many Bible readers regard Amos as the most fascinating prophet, and we can to see why. First, he wasn't a religious professional; he was a rancher. He ran a giant fig farm and had large flocks of sheep. Second, with his gruff manner and take-no-prisoners style, he was the anti-Jeremiah.

Amos ministered during a time when the economy was humming in the northern kingdom of Israel. A good thing? Not really. All that material prosperity was taking a heavy spiritual toll. Never one to soften his words, Amos bluntly warned of the dangers of greed and apathy. He even called a group of rich, high-society women "cows of Bashan" (4:1—the cattle from that region were exceedingly plump and well fed).

Mostly, Amos blasted Jewish society as a whole for ignoring, even abusing, the poor. In words later made famous by Dr. Martin Luther King, Jr., this part-time prophet called on his countrymen to let justice and righteousness flow "like an unfailing stream."

The straight-shooting Amos reminds us that it's possible to be rich in all the wrong ways and poor in the one way that really counts. His haunting question: Do our lives flow with righteousness and a desire for justice?

For the next note on *Other-centeredness*, see Obadiah 3-4.

[A] **5:16** Lit *will say, "Alas! Alas!"* [B] **5:16** Lit *and those skilled in lamentation*

forty years in the wilderness? 26 But you have
taken up[A] Sakkuth your king and Kaiwan your
star god,[B] images you have made for yourselves. 27 So I will send you into exile beyond
Damascus." The LORD, the God of Armies, is
his name. He has spoken.

WOE TO THE COMPLACENT

6 Woe to those who are at ease in Zion
and to those who feel secure on the hill
of Samaria —
the notable people in this first
of the nations,
those the house of Israel comes to.
2 Cross over to Calneh and see;
go from there to great Hamath;
then go down to Gath of the Philistines.
Are you better than these kingdoms?
Is their territory larger than yours?
3 You dismiss any thought of the evil day
and bring in a reign of violence.

4 They lie on beds inlaid with ivory,
sprawled out on their couches,
and dine on lambs from the flock
and calves from the stall.
5 They improvise songs[C] to the sound
of the harp
and invent[D] their own
musical instruments like David.
6 They drink wine by the bowlful
and anoint themselves
with the finest oils
but do not grieve over the ruin
of Joseph.
7 Therefore, they will now go into exile
as the first of the captives,
and the feasting of those who sprawl out
will come to an end.

ISRAEL'S PRIDE JUDGED

8 The Lord GOD has sworn by himself — this is
the declaration of the LORD, the God of Armies:
I loathe Jacob's pride
and hate his citadels,
so I will hand over the city
and everything in it.

9 And if there are ten men left in one house,
they will die. 10 A close relative[E] and burner[F]
will remove his corpse[G] from the house. He
will call to someone in the inner recesses of
the house, "Any more with you?"
That person will reply, "None."
Then he will say, "Silence, because the LORD's
name must not be invoked."
11 For the LORD commands:
The large house will be smashed
to pieces,
and the small house to rubble.

12 Do horses gallop on the cliffs?
Does anyone plow there with oxen?[H]
Yet you have turned justice into poison
and the fruit of righteousness
into wormwood —
13 you who rejoice over Lo-debar
and say, "Didn't we capture Karnaim
for ourselves by our own strength?"
14 But look, I am raising up a nation
against you, house of Israel —
this is the declaration of the Lord,
the GOD of Armies —
and they will oppress you
from the entrance of Hamath[I]
to the Brook of the Arabah.[J]

FIRST VISION: LOCUSTS

7 The Lord GOD showed me this: He was forming a swarm of locusts at the time the spring
crop first began to sprout — after the cutting
of the king's hay. 2 When the locusts finished
eating the vegetation of the land, I said, "Lord
GOD, please forgive! How will Jacob survive
since he is so small?"
3 The LORD relented concerning this. "It will
not happen," he said.

SECOND VISION: FIRE

4 The Lord GOD showed me this: The Lord GOD
was calling for a judgment by fire. It consumed
the great deep and devoured the land. 5 Then
I said, "Lord GOD, please stop! How will Jacob
survive since he is so small?"
6 The LORD relented concerning this. "This
will not happen either," said the Lord GOD.

THIRD VISION: A PLUMB LINE

7 He showed me this: The Lord was standing
there by a vertical wall with a plumb line in
his hand. 8 The LORD asked me, "What do you
see, Amos?"

[A] **5:26** Or *you will lift up* [B] **5:26** LXX reads *taken up the tent of Molech and the star of your god Rephan*; Ac 7:43 [C] **6:5** Hb obscure [D] **6:5** Or *compose on* [E] **6:10** Lit *His uncle* [F] **6:10** A burner of incense, a memorial fire, or a body; Hb obscure [G] **6:10** Lit *remove bones* [H] **6:12** Some emend to *plow the sea* [I] **6:14** Or *from Lebo-hamath* [J] **6:14** Probably the Valley of Zared at the southeast end of the Dead Sea

I replied, "A plumb line."
Then the Lord said, "I am setting a plumb
line among my people Israel; I will no longer
spare them:

9 Isaac's high places will be deserted,
and Israel's sanctuaries
will be in ruins;
I will rise up
against the house of Jeroboam
with a sword."

AMAZIAH'S OPPOSITION

10 Amaziah the priest of Bethel sent word to
King Jeroboam of Israel, saying, "Amos has
conspired against you right here in the house
of Israel. The land cannot endure all his words,
11 for Amos has said this: 'Jeroboam will die
by the sword, and Israel will certainly go into
exile from its homeland.'"
12 Then Amaziah said to Amos, "Go away,
you seer! Flee to the land of Judah. Earn your
living[A] and give your prophecies there, 13 but
don't ever prophesy at Bethel again, for it is
the king's sanctuary and a royal temple."
14 So Amos answered Amaziah, "I was[B] not
a prophet or the son of a prophet;[C] rather, I
was[B] a herdsman, and I took care of sycamore
figs. 15 But the LORD took me from following
the flock and said to me, 'Go, prophesy to my
people Israel.'"
16 Now hear the word of the LORD. You say:
Do not prophesy against Israel;
do not preach against the house
of Isaac.

17 Therefore, this is what the LORD says:
Your wife will be a prostitute in the city,
your sons and daughters will fall
by the sword,
and your land will be divided up
with a measuring line.
You yourself will die on pagan[D] soil,
and Israel will certainly go into exile
from its homeland.

FOURTH VISION: A BASKET OF SUMMER FRUIT

8 The Lord GOD showed me this: a basket
of summer fruit. 2 He asked me, "What do
you see, Amos?"
I replied, "A basket of summer fruit."[E]
The LORD said to me, "The end has come for
my people Israel; I will no longer spare them.
3 In that day the temple[F] songs will become
wailing" — this is the Lord GOD's declaration.
"Many dead bodies, thrown everywhere! Silence!"

4 Hear this, you who trample
on the needy
and do away with the poor of the land,
5 asking, "When will the New Moon
be over
so we may sell grain,
and the Sabbath,
so we may market wheat?
We can reduce the measure
while increasing the price[G]
and cheat with dishonest scales.
6 We can buy the poor with silver
and the needy for a pair of sandals
and even sell the chaff!"

7 The LORD has sworn by the Pride of Jacob:[H]
I will never forget all their deeds.
8 Because of this, won't the land quake
and all who dwell in it mourn?
All of it will rise like the Nile;
it will surge and then subside
like the Nile in Egypt.

9 And in that day —
this is the declaration
of the Lord GOD —
I will make the sun go down at noon;
I will darken the land in the daytime.
10 I will turn your feasts into mourning
and all your songs into lamentation;
I will cause everyone[I] to wear sackcloth
and every head to be shaved.
I will make that grief
like mourning for an only son
and its outcome like a bitter day.

11 Look, the days are coming —
this is the declaration
of the Lord GOD —
when I will send a famine
through the land:
not a famine of bread or a thirst
for water,
but of hearing the words of the LORD.
12 People will stagger from sea to sea
and roam from north to east
seeking the word of the LORD,
but they will not find it.

[A] **7:12** Lit *Eat bread* [B] **7:14** Or *am* [C] **7:14** = a prophet's disciple or a member of a prophetic guild [D] **7:17** Lit *unclean* [E] **8:2** In Hb the word for *summer fruit* sounds like the word for *end*. [F] **8:3** Or *palace* [G] **8:5** Lit *reduce the ephah and make the shekel great* [H] **8:7** = the LORD or the promised land [I] **8:10** Lit *every waist*

13 In that day the beautiful young women,
the young men also, will faint
from thirst.
14 Those who swear by the guilt
of Samaria
and say, "As your god lives, Dan,"
or, "As the way[A,B] of Beer-sheba lives" —
they will fall, never to rise again.

FIFTH VISION: THE LORD BESIDE THE ALTAR

9 I saw the Lord standing beside the altar,
and he said:
Strike the capitals of the pillars
so that the thresholds shake;
knock them down on the heads of all
the people.
Then I will kill the rest of them
with the sword.
None of those who flee will get away;
none of the fugitives will escape.
2 If they dig down to Sheol,
from there my hand will take them;
if they climb up to heaven,
from there I will bring them down.
3 If they hide
on the top of Carmel,
from there I will track them down
and seize them;
if they conceal themselves
from my sight on the sea floor,
from there I will command
the sea serpent to bite them.
4 And if they are driven
by their enemies into captivity,
from there I will command
the sword to kill them.
I will keep my eye on them
for harm and not for good.

5 The Lord, the GOD of Armies —
he touches the earth;
it melts, and all who dwell
in it mourn;
all of it rises like the Nile
and subsides like the Nile of Egypt.
6 He builds his upper chambers
in the heavens
and lays the foundation of his vault
on the earth.
He summons the water of the sea
and pours it out over the surface
of the earth.
The LORD is his name.

ANNOUNCEMENT OF JUDGMENT

7 Israelites, are you not like the Cushites
to me?
This is the LORD's declaration.
Didn't I bring Israel from the land
of Egypt,
the Philistines from Caphtor,[C]
and the Arameans from Kir?
8 Look, the eyes of the Lord GOD
are on the sinful kingdom,
and I will obliterate it
from the face of the earth.
However, I will not totally destroy
the house of Jacob —
this is the LORD's declaration —
9 for I am about to give the command,
and I will shake the house of Israel
among all the nations,
as one shakes a sieve,
but not a pebble will fall to the ground.
10 All the sinners among my people
who say: "Disaster will never overtake[D]
or confront us,"
will die by the sword.

ANNOUNCEMENT OF RESTORATION

11 In that day
I will restore the fallen shelter
of David:
I will repair its gaps,
restore its ruins,
and rebuild it as in the days of old,
12 so that they may possess
the remnant of Edom
and all the nations
that bear my name[E] —
this is the declaration of the LORD;
he will do this.

I will restore the fortunes of my people Israel. They will rebuild and occupy ruined cities, plant vineyards and drink their wine, make gardens and eat their produce.

—Amos 9:14

[A] **8:14** LXX reads *god* [B] **8:14** Or *power* [C] **9:7** Probably Crete [D] **9:10** Or *"You will not let disaster come near* [E] **9:12** LXX reads *so that the remnant of man and all the nations . . . may seek me*; Ac 15:17

13 Look, the days are coming —
this is the LORD's declaration —
when the plowman will overtake
the reaper
and the one who treads grapes,
the sower of seed.
The mountains will drip
with sweet wine,
and all the hills
will flow with it.
14 I will restore the fortunes
of my people Israel.[A]
They will rebuild and occupy
ruined cities,
plant vineyards and drink their wine,
make gardens and eat their produce.
15 I will plant them on their land,
and they will never again be uprooted
from the land I have given them.
The LORD your God has spoken.

[A] **9:14** Or *restore my people Israel from captivity*

Obadiah—When confronted with injustice, the human heart longs for resolution. We want right to win over wrong and evil to be punished. The book of Obadiah gives us the satisfaction of seeing God judge evil and care for his own. Unlike other Prophetic Books, it says nothing about Israel's sin, only that of Edom. God would defend his people against their enemies, proving his sovereign care for his own.

The words of Obadiah to Edom serve as both warning and comfort. They are a warning not to fall into the sin of arrogance and to care for those who are in need. We are to love our neighbors as ourselves and to do good to our enemies, as Jesus taught. But when we are mistreated, we can look forward with hope to the justice God will bring at the end of time. Evil will be punished—Jesus has already defeated sin and death. And we who love the Lord will be fully restored in a place with no sorrow, sin, sickness, or death.

OBADIAH

AUTHOR: Obadiah ("servant of the Lord")

DATE WRITTEN: Likely around 586 BC, shortly after the final destruction of Jerusalem by the Babylonians

ORIGINAL AUDIENCE: Edom

SETTING: The Edomites were descendants of Jacob's brother, Esau. Over its history, Edom (also known as Seir) was an enemy of Israel despite the fact that they were kin who should have been at least cordial, if not an ally. They opposed Israel during the exodus from Egypt (Nm 20:14-21; 21:4) and rejoiced at Israel's fall to Babylon.

PURPOSE FOR WRITING: Obadiah speaks out against Edom's arrogance. They trusted in their geographical location (1:3-5), diplomacy (1:7), and wise men (1:8) rather than God. Even worse, they participated in and celebrated the downfall of their brother Jacob (1:10-14). For these reasons, God promised to wipe them out—and he did, for by AD 70 they had completely disappeared.

OUTLINE:

1. Oracle against Edom (1-9)
2. Esau's Sin against Jacob (10-14)
3. The Day of the Lord (15-18)
4. Israel's Restoration (19-21)

KEY VERSE:

"But there will be a deliverance on Mount Zion, and it will be holy." —Obadiah 17

RESTORATION THEMES

R	Rest and Reflection	*For the next note, see Zechariah 4:6.*
E	Eternal Perspective	*For the next note, see Jonah 4:6-8.*
S	Support	*For the next note, see Habakkuk 1:2-4.*
T	Thanksgiving and Contentment	*For the next note, see Jonah 3:1.*
O	Other-centeredness	*Being Humble—Obadiah 3-4*
R	Relationships	*For the next note, see Micah 5:5.*
E	Exercise of Faith	*For the next note, see Micah 5:13.*

The vision of Obadiah.

EDOM'S CERTAIN JUDGMENT

This is what the Lord God has said about Edom:
We have heard a message
from the LORD;
an envoy has been sent
among the nations:
"Rise up, and let us go to war
against her."[A]
2 Look, I will make you insignificant
among the nations;
you will be deeply despised.
3 Your arrogant heart
has deceived you,
you who live in clefts of the rock[B,C]
in your home on the heights,
who say to yourself,
"Who can bring me down
to the ground?"
4 Though you seem to soar[D]
like an eagle
and make your nest among the stars,
even from there I will bring you down.
This is the LORD's declaration.
5 If thieves came to you,
if marauders by night —
how ravaged you would be! —
wouldn't they steal only
what they wanted?
If grape pickers came to you,
wouldn't they leave some grapes?
6 How Esau will be pillaged,
his hidden treasures searched out!
7 Everyone who has a treaty with you
will drive you to the border;
everyone at peace with you
will deceive and conquer you.
Those who eat your bread
will set[E] a trap for you.
He will be unaware of it.
8 In that day —
this is the LORD's declaration —
will I not eliminate the wise ones
of Edom
and those who understand
from the hill country of Esau?
9 Teman,[F] your warriors will be terrified
so that everyone
from the hill country of Esau
will be destroyed by slaughter.

Other-centeredness | *Being Humble*

THE RESULTS OF PRIDE

"Your arrogant heart has deceived you, you who live in clefts of the rock in your home on the heights, who say to yourself, 'Who can bring me down to the ground?' Though you seem to soar like an eagle and make your nest among the stars, even from there I will bring you down. This is the LORD's declaration." Obadiah 3-4

When the big-headed, smack-talking athlete endures a humiliating defeat, grins are hard to suppress. This is because cocky people are annoying. We enjoy seeing them, as the old saying goes, "get brought down to earth."

In Obadiah we read where God tells the prideful people of Edom, "Assume the crash position because you are going down!"

The Edomites were descendants of Esau, so they were related to the Israelites (descendants of Jacob). Yet on multiple occasions, Edom had sided with Israel's enemies. When the Babylonians conquered Jerusalem (Ps 137:7), the Edomites haughtily cheered.

Events transpired just as God said. The Edomites faded from history. But they live on as a cautionary tale. Their legacy? "Pride comes before destruction, and an arrogant spirit before a fall" (Pr 16:18).

For the next note on *Other-centeredness*, see Matthew 7:1.

[A] **1** = Edom [B] **3** Or *in Sela*; probably = Petra [C] **3** Probably Petra [D] **4** Or *to build high* [E] **7** Some LXX mss, Sym, Tg, Vg; MT reads *They will set your bread as* [F] **9** = a region or city in Edom

EDOM'S SINS AGAINST JUDAH

10 You will be covered with shame
and destroyed forever
because of violence done
to your brother Jacob.
11 On the day you stood aloof,
on the day strangers captured
his wealth,[A]
while foreigners entered his city gate
and cast lots for Jerusalem,
you were just like one of them.
12 Do not[B] gloat over your brother
in the day of his calamity;
do not rejoice over the people
of Judah
in the day of their destruction;
do not boastfully mock[C]
in the day of distress.
13 Do not enter my people's city gate
in the day of their disaster,
Yes, you — do not gloat
over their misery
in the day of their disaster,
and do not appropriate
their possessions
in the day of their disaster.
14 Do not stand at the crossroads[D]
to cut off their fugitives,
and do not hand over their survivors
in the day of distress.

JUDGMENT OF THE NATIONS

15 For the day of the LORD is near,
against all the nations.
As you have done, it will be done
to you;
what you deserve will return
on your own head.
16 As you have drunk
on my holy mountain,
so all the nations will
drink continually.
They will drink and gulp down
and be as though
they had never been.
17 But there will be a deliverance
on Mount Zion,
and it will be holy;
the house of Jacob will dispossess
those who dispossessed them.[E]
18 Then the house of Jacob will be
a blazing fire,
and the house of Joseph,
a burning flame,
but the house of Esau will be stubble;
Jacob[F] will set them on fire
and consume Edom.[G]
Therefore no survivor will remain
of the house of Esau,
for the LORD has spoken.

FUTURE BLESSING FOR ISRAEL

19 People from the Negev will possess
the hill country of Esau;
those from the Judean foothills
will possess
the land of the Philistines.
They[H] will possess
the territories of Ephraim and Samaria,
while Benjamin will possess Gilead.
20 The exiles of the Israelites who are
in Halah[I]
and who are among the Canaanites
as far as Zarephath
as well as the exiles of Jerusalem
who are in Sepharad
will possess the cities of the Negev.
21 Saviors[J] will ascend Mount Zion
to rule over the hill country of Esau,
but the kingdom will be the LORD's.

[A] **11** Or *forces* [B] **12-14** Or *You should not* throughout vv. 12-14 [C] **12** Lit *not make your mouth big* [D] **14** Hb obscure [E] **17** DSS, LXX, Syr, Vg, Tg; MT reads *Jacob will possess its inheritance* [F] **18** Lit *they* [G] **18** Lit *them* [H] **19** = The house of Jacob [I] **20** Or *of this host of the Israelites*; Hb obscure [J] **21** Or *Those who have been delivered*

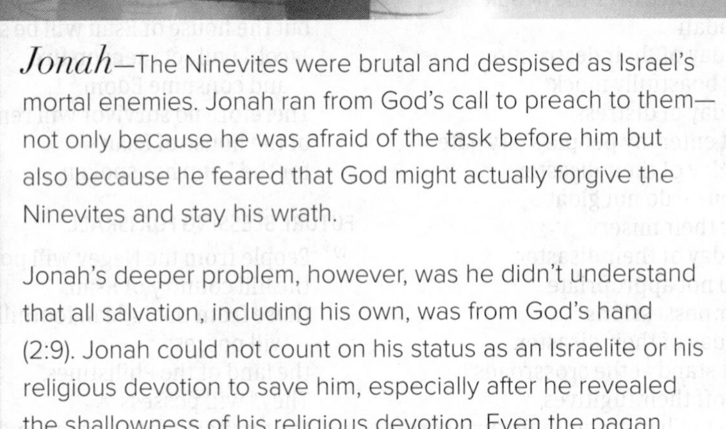

Jonah—The Ninevites were brutal and despised as Israel's mortal enemies. Jonah ran from God's call to preach to them—not only because he was afraid of the task before him but also because he feared that God might actually forgive the Ninevites and stay his wrath.

Jonah's deeper problem, however, was he didn't understand that all salvation, including his own, was from God's hand (2:9). Jonah could not count on his status as an Israelite or his religious devotion to save him, especially after he revealed the shallowness of his religious devotion. Even the pagan sailors had more faith in God than Jonah!

God is Sovereign over nature, able to direct storms and big fish, and he is also over the hearts of humankind. He shows mercy to whomever he wills, and to question his judgments is not our place. This is a warning and a source of great hope. No one is outside of God's mercy, not our enemies, our loved ones, or even you when you attempt to run from him.

JONAH

AUTHOR: Anonymous

DATE WRITTEN: From 2 Kings 14:25, we know that Jonah was a prophet from the territory of Zebulun in northern Israel. He prophesied in the first half of the eighth century BC and predicted the restoration that occurred during the reign of Jeroboam II (793–753 BC). The actual composition of the book could have occurred soon after the events described or as late as the end of the Old Testament period.

ORIGINAL AUDIENCE: The Israelites

SETTING: Jonah's prophecy was directed at Nineveh, an Assyrian city known for its cruelty. They were longtime enemies of Israel and used barbaric practices of warfare.

PURPOSE FOR WRITING: The remarkable events of Jonah demonstrate that God is willing and able to save even the most wicked. His grace and compassion extend beyond the Israelites to the Gentiles, even the most unexpected and undeserving ones. Other themes include God's sovereignty over nature, his ability to perform miracles, and the utter futility of trying to run away from God.

OUTLINE:

1. Jonah Flees from God (1:1-17)

   God calls; Jonah rebels (1:1-3)

   God sends a storm (1:4-6)

   The sailors intervene (1:7-16)

   God sends a big fish (1:17)

2. Jonah Prays (2:1-9)

3. Jonah Preaches in Nineveh (3:1-10)

   Jonah obeys God's call (3:1-4)

   Ninevites repent (3:5-9)

   The Lord shows mercy (3:10)

4. Jonah Is Angry at God's Mercy (4:1-11)

   Jonah is displeased with God (4:1-5)

   God is displeased with Jonah (4:6-10)

   The Lord shows mercy (4:11)

KEY VERSE:

"I called to the LORD in my distress, and he answered me. I cried out for help from deep inside Sheol; you heard my voice."
—Jonah 2:2

RESTORATION THEMES

R	Rest and Reflection	*For the next note, see Zechariah 4:6.*
E	Eternal Perspective	*God's Purposes—Jonah 4:6-8*
S	Support	*For the next note, see Habakkuk 1:2-4.*
T	Thanksgiving and Contentment	*Grace Received—Jonah 3:1*
O	Other-centeredness	*For the next note, see Matthew 7:1.*
R	Relationships	*For the next note, see Micah 5:5.*
E	Exercise of Faith	*For the next note, see Micah 5:13.*

Jonah | Restoration Profile

2 KINGS 14:25; JONAH; MATTHEW 12:39-41; 16:4

Some people fight God's restoring work. When God came to Jonah and told him to "Get up! Go to the great city of Nineveh and preach against it" (Jnh 1:2), Jonah immediately got up and ran in the opposite direction. Whether from hatred or fear, Jonah's attitude against Nineveh was what God wanted to repair. And God was working on this even as he accomplished the much larger task of restoring a large city filled with desperately wicked and spiritually ignorant people.

Jonah didn't want to preach against Nineveh. He eventually explains why he had fled to Tarshish: "I knew that you are a gracious and compassionate God, slow to anger, abounding in faithful love, and one who relents from sending disaster" (Jnh 4:2). Jonah didn't want Nineveh warned; he wanted them wiped out. He even refused to answer God's question about his anger.

So, God gave Jonah a personal and painful lesson about his own spiritual blindness. He provided the prophet a shade plant to shield him from the sun. Then, just as Jonah was grudgingly grateful for the relief, God killed the plant. That loss brought a second death wish from Jonah and a resentful admission that he had a right to be angry at God for causing his discomfort. That was Jonah's teachable moment. In essence, God asked, "You claimed the right to care about that plant that wasn't even yours; can't I care about the hundred and twenty thousand lost people in this city?"

We are left with Jonah's unfinished restoration. God's question left unanswered rests with us. Until we care about what God cares about, we cannot be completely restored in our relationship with him.

JONAH'S FLIGHT

1 The word of the LORD came to Jonah son
of Amittai: 2 "Get up! Go to the great city of
Nineveh and preach against it because their
evil has come up before me." 3 Jonah got up to
flee to Tarshish from the LORD's presence. He
went down to Joppa and found a ship going
to Tarshish. He paid the fare and went down
into it to go with them to Tarshish from the
LORD's presence.
4 But the LORD threw a great wind onto the
sea, and such a great storm arose on the sea
that the ship threatened to break apart. 5 The
sailors were afraid, and each cried out to his
god. They threw the ship's cargo into the sea to
lighten the load. Meanwhile, Jonah had gone
down to the lowest part of the vessel and had
stretched out and fallen into a deep sleep.
6 The captain approached him and said,
"What are you doing sound asleep? Get up!
Call to your god.[A] Maybe this god will consider us, and we won't perish."
7 "Come on!" the sailors said to each other. "Let's cast lots. Then we'll know who is to
blame for this trouble we're in." So they cast
lots, and the lot singled out Jonah. 8 Then they
said to him, "Tell us who is to blame for this
trouble we're in. What is your business, and
where are you from? What is your country,
and what people are you from?"
9 He answered them, "I'm a Hebrew. I worship[B] the LORD, the God of the heavens, who
made the sea and the dry land."
10 Then the men were seized by a great fear
and said to him, "What is this you've done?"
The men knew he was fleeing from the LORD's
presence because he had told them. 11 So they
said to him, "What should we do to you so that
the sea will calm down for us?" For the sea
was getting worse and worse.
12 He answered them, "Pick me up and throw
me into the sea so that it will calm down for
you, for I know that I'm to blame for this great
storm that is against you." 13 Nevertheless,
the men rowed hard to get back to dry land,
but they couldn't because the sea was raging
against them more and more.
14 So they called out to the LORD: "Please,
LORD, don't let us perish because of this man's
life, and don't charge us with innocent blood!
For you, LORD, have done just as you pleased."
15 Then they picked up Jonah and threw him
into the sea, and the sea stopped its raging.
16 The men were seized by great fear of the

[A] **1:6** Or *God* [B] **1:9** Or *fear*

LORD, and they offered a sacrifice to the LORD and made vows.
17 The LORD appointed a great fish to swallow Jonah, and Jonah was in the belly of the fish three days and three nights.

As my life was fading away,
I remembered the LORD, and
my prayer came to you,
to your holy temple.
—Jonah 2:7

JONAH'S PRAYER

2 Jonah prayed to the LORD his God from the belly of the fish:

2 I called to the LORD in my distress,
and he answered me.
I cried out for help
from deep inside[A] Sheol;
you heard my voice.
3 You threw me into the depths,
into the heart of the seas,
and the current[B] overcame me.
All your breakers and your billows
swept over me.
4 But I said, "I have been banished
from your sight,
yet I will look once more[C]
toward your holy temple.
5 The water engulfed me up to the neck;[D]
the watery depths overcame me;
seaweed was wrapped
around my head.
6 I sank to the foundations
of the mountains,
the earth's gates shut
behind me forever!
Then you raised my life from the Pit,
LORD my God!
7 As my life was fading away,
I remembered the LORD,
and my prayer came to you,
to your holy temple.
8 Those who cherish worthless idols
abandon their faithful love,
9 but as for me, I will sacrifice to you
with a voice of thanksgiving.
I will fulfill what I have vowed.
Salvation[E] belongs to the LORD."

10 Then the LORD commanded the fish, and it vomited Jonah onto dry land.

Thanksgiving and Contentment | *Grace Received*

SECOND CHANCES

"The word of the LORD came to Jonah a second time." Jonah 3:1

When God said, "Get up! Go to the great city of Nineveh and preach against it" (1:2), Jonah's non-verbal response was to board a ship headed the opposite direction. Interesting that a prophet, of all people, didn't stop to realize, *This decision probably will not go well for me.*

It did *not* go well. In his vain attempt to flee from God and God's calling, Jonah sailed straight into a ferocious storm. Tossed overboard, he was promptly swallowed by a great fish. After three dark days and three lonely nights in the depths of the Mediterranean, Jonah was vomited onto dry land. Then, "the word of the LORD came to Jonah *a second time.*"

The Bible is full of beautiful phrases. Not many can top this one. "A second time" means another chance. It signifies that even those who have sinned brazenly can find forgiveness and still be used by God. In truth, most of the characters of Scripture have a story like this. The Bible tells us those stories, not to make light of sin but to make much of God's grace.

Are you running away? What second chance is God offering you today?

For the next note on *Thanksgiving and Contentment*, see Habakkuk 3:17-19.

[A] **2:2** Lit *from the stomach of* [B] **2:3** Lit *river* [C] **2:4** LXX reads *said, "Indeed, will I look . . . ?* [D] **2:5** Or *me, threatening my life* [E] **2:9** Or *Deliverance*

JONAH'S PREACHING

3 The word of the LORD came to Jonah a
second time: 2 "Get up! Go to the great city
of Nineveh and preach the message that I tell
you." 3 Jonah got up and went to Nineveh according to the LORD's command.
Now Nineveh was an extremely great city,[A]
a three-day walk. 4 Jonah set out on the first
day of his walk in the city and proclaimed,
"In forty days Nineveh will be demolished!"
5 Then the people of Nineveh believed God.
They proclaimed a fast and dressed in sackcloth — from the greatest of them to the
least.
6 When word reached the king of Nineveh,
he got up from his throne, took off his royal
robe, put on sackcloth, and sat in ashes. 7 Then
he issued a decree in Nineveh:

> By order of the king and his nobles: No
> person or animal, herd or flock, is to
> taste anything at all. They must not eat or
> drink water. 8 Furthermore, both peo-
> ple and animals must be covered with
> sackcloth, and everyone must call out
> earnestly to God. Each must turn from
> his evil ways and from his wrongdoing.[B]
> 9 Who knows? God may turn and relent;
> he may turn from his burning anger so
> that we will not perish.

10 God saw their actions — that they had
turned from their evil ways — so God relented from the disaster he had threatened them
with. And he did not do it.

JONAH'S ANGER

4 Jonah was greatly displeased and became
furious. 2 He prayed to the LORD: "Please,
LORD, isn't this what I thought while I was still
in my own country? That's why I fled toward
Tarshish in the first place. I knew that you
are a gracious and compassionate God, slow
to anger, abounding in faithful love, and one
who relents from sending disaster. 3 And now,
LORD, take my life from me, for it is better for
me to die than to live."
4 The LORD asked, "Is it right for you to be
angry?"
5 Jonah left the city and found a place east of
it. He made himself a shelter there and sat in
its shade to see what would happen to the city.
6 Then the LORD God appointed a plant, and it
grew over Jonah to provide shade for his head
to rescue him from his trouble.[C] Jonah was

Eternal Perspective | *God's Purposes*

THE DIRECTOR

"Then the LORD God appointed a plant. . . . The next day, God appointed a worm that attacked the plant, and it withered. As the sun was rising, God appointed a scorching east wind." Jonah 4:6-8

Life can sometimes feel very random. Events happen to us, and all around us, but they often don't make sense. We can't always connect the dots.

The story of Jonah helps by giving us a behind-the-scenes peek at a gracious God with an obvious love for people. In Jonah, we watch in awe as God orchestrated all kinds of events to accomplish his purposes.

In Jonah, God is constantly *appointing* created things—storms, fish, plant, worms—to do his bidding. Interestingly, the only creature who tried, in vain, to resist God's direction was Jonah himself!

God had engineered a host of wild circumstances to reveal himself to people. Some rough-around-the-edges sailors got to witness his power. The pagan city of Nineveh experienced his mercy. A sullen, disobedient prophet received a short course in divine compassion.

Let this story encourage you today with the truth that God is in the business of orchestrating and directing. In other words, nothing—not one thing—about your life is random.

For the next note on *Eternal Perspective*, see Micah 5:2.

[A] **3:3** Or *was a great city to God* [B] **3:8** Or *injustice*, or *violence* [C] **4:6** Or *disaster*, or *evil*

greatly pleased with the plant. 7 When dawn
came the next day, God appointed a worm that
attacked the plant, and it withered.

8 As the sun was rising, God appointed a
scorching east wind. The sun beat down on
Jonah's head so much that he almost fainted,
and he wanted to die. He said, "It's better for
me to die than to live."

9 Then God asked Jonah, "Is it right for you
to be angry about the plant?"

"Yes, it's right!" he replied. "I'm angry enough
to die!"

10 So the LORD said, "You cared about the
plant, which you did not labor over and did
not grow. It appeared in a night and perished
in a night. 11 But may I not care about the great
city of Nineveh, which has more than a hundred and twenty thousand people who cannot
distinguish between their right and their left,
as well as many animals?"

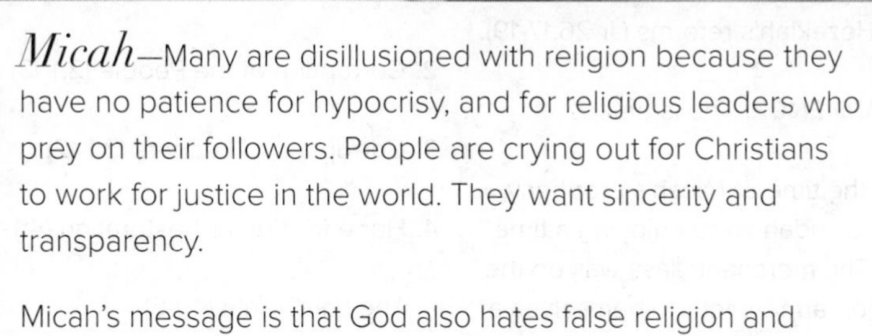

Micah—Many are disillusioned with religion because they have no patience for hypocrisy, and for religious leaders who prey on their followers. People are crying out for Christians to work for justice in the world. They want sincerity and transparency.

Micah's message is that God also hates false religion and hypocrisy. At the heart of Micah's message is the truth that a holy God demands true spiritual devotion, not half-hearted religion where people merely go through spiritual motions. True religion is wholehearted love for God that results in godly living.

Micah's message of restoration is that God will not allow his people to remain in their sin. He uses the rod of correction and even judgment to bring his people back to him, to an understanding of who he is and the obedience that brings blessing.

This a powerful reminder that in order to be close to God, we must submit to his loving, fatherly discipline that calls us back to repentance and life.

MICAH

AUTHOR: Micah ("Who is like Yahweh?")

DATE WRITTEN: Micah prophesied late in Jotham's reign, through the reign of Ahaz, and early in Hezekiah's reign, placing his ministry between approximately 730 and 690 BC. His ministry overlapped with Isaiah's, and he was remembered during Jeremiah's as an instigator of Hezekiah's reforms (Jr 26:17-19).

ORIGINAL AUDIENCE: The Israelites

SETTING: At the time of Micah's prophecy, both Israel and Judah were enjoying a time of affluence. The merchant class was on the rise, while poor farmers found themselves at the receiving end of corruption and oppression. The secular and unjust culture went against God's covenant regulations.

PURPOSE FOR WRITING: In an increasingly secular culture, where the rich amassed their wealth at the expense of the poor and the people were blatantly disregarding God's laws, Micah proclaimed the message that God would punish his people for their sin. Unless they repented, they would face exile (1:10-16), silence from God (3:6-7), and frustration (6:13-16). But this litany of coming judgment has a slender vein of hope: God would save a remnant of his people and restore them.

OUTLINE:

1. Prediction of Defeat and Destruction (1:1-16)

   God's condemnation (1:1-7)

   Micah's lament (1:8-16)

2. Corruption of the People (2:1-13)
3. Corruption of Leaders (3:1-12)
4. Hope for Future Restoration (4:1–5:15)

   The Lord's rule (4:1-5)

   The remnant (4:6-10)

   God's plan (4:11–5:1)

   God's ruler (5:2-9)

   God's rule over the nations (5:10-15)

5. Corruption of the City and Its Leaders (6:1-16)
6. Corruption of the People (7:1-7)
7. Future Reversal of Destruction (7:8-20)

KEY VERSE:

"Mankind, he has told each of you what is good and what it is the LORD requires of you: to act justly, to love faithfulness, and to walk humbly with your God." —Micah 6:8

RESTORATION THEMES

R	Rest and Reflection	*For the next note, see Zechariah 4:6.*
E	Eternal Perspective	*God's Plans—Micah 5:2* *God's Mercy—7:8*
S	Support	*For the next note, see Habakkuk 1:2-4.*
T	Thanksgiving and Contentment	*For the next note, see Habakkuk 1:17-19.*
O	Other-centeredness	*For the next note, see Matthew 7:1.*
R	Relationships	*Making Peace—Micah 5:5*
E	Exercise of Faith	*Rejecting Idols—5:13* *Showing Mercy—6:8*

1 The word of the LORD that came to Micah the Moreshite — what he saw regarding Samaria and Jerusalem in the days of Jotham, Ahaz, and Hezekiah, kings of Judah.

COMING JUDGMENT ON ISRAEL

2 Listen, all you peoples;
pay attention, earth[A] and everyone in it!
The Lord GOD will be a witness
against you,
the Lord, from his holy temple.
3 Look, the LORD is leaving his place
and coming down to trample
the heights[B] of the earth.
4 The mountains will melt beneath him,
and the valleys will split apart,
like wax near a fire,
like water cascading down
a mountainside.
5 All this will happen because of
Jacob's rebellion
and the sins of the house of Israel.
What is the rebellion of Jacob?
Isn't it Samaria?
And what is the high place of Judah?
Isn't it Jerusalem?
6 Therefore, I will make Samaria
a heap of ruins in the countryside,
a planting area for a vineyard.
I will roll her stones into the valley
and expose her foundations.
7 All her carved images will be smashed
to pieces;
all her wages will be burned in the fire,
and I will destroy all her idols.
Since she collected the wages
of a prostitute,
they will be used again for a prostitute.

MICAH'S LAMENT

8 Because of this I will lament and wail;
I will walk barefoot and naked.
I will howl like the jackals
and mourn like ostriches.[C]
9 For her wound is incurable
and has reached even Judah;
it has approached my people's city gate,
as far as Jerusalem.

10 Don't announce it in Gath,
don't weep at all.
Roll in the dust in Beth-leaphrah.
11 Depart in shameful nakedness,
you residents of Shaphir;
the residents of Zaanan will not
come out.
Beth-ezel is lamenting;
its support[D] is taken from you.
12 Though the residents of Maroth
anxiously wait for something good,
disaster has come from the LORD
to the gate of Jerusalem.
13 Harness the horses to the chariot,
you residents of Lachish.
This was the beginning of sin
for Daughter Zion
because Israel's acts of rebellion
can be traced to you.
14 Therefore, send farewell gifts
to Moresheth-gath;
the houses of Achzib are a deception
to the kings of Israel.
15 I will again bring a conqueror
against you who live in Mareshah.
The nobility[E] of Israel will come
to Adullam.
16 Shave yourselves bald and cut off
your hair
in sorrow for your precious children;
make yourselves as bald as an eagle,
for they have been taken from you
into exile.

OPPRESSORS JUDGED

2 Woe to those who dream
up wickedness
and prepare evil plans on their beds!
At morning light they accomplish it
because the power is in their hands.
2 They covet fields and seize them;
they also take houses.
They deprive a man of his home,
a person of his inheritance.

3 Therefore, the LORD says:
I am now planning a disaster
against this nation;
you cannot free your necks from it.
Then you will not walk so proudly
because it will be an evil time.
4 In that day one will take up a taunt
against you
and lament mournfully, saying,
"We are totally ruined!
He measures out the allotted land
of my people.

[A] 1:2 Or *land* [B] 1:3 Or *high places* [C] 1:8 Or *eagle owls*; lit *daughters of the desert* [D] 1:11 Lit *its standing place*; Hb obscure
[E] 1:15 Lit *glory*

My Story | Mandy

Over spring break one year, I was part of a small team that led fifteen college students on a service trip to Corpus Christi, Texas, to serve with a relief ministry doing cleanup and rebuilding work in the aftermath of Hurricane Harvey. Our group included students we knew well and some we had never met before. None of the students had ever been involved in that kind of hands-on project with hurting people, and I was eager to see what God would do while we were on the road.

A mission trip can be an eye-opening, life-changing experience. Traveling, eating, living, and serving together for a week is not something you do very often or with very many people. The extended time together in somewhat stressful and sometimes uncomfortable situations tends to bring out the best and the worst in people. The conversations, experiences, growth, and memories you share build a unique bond.

That was certainly the case on this trip. Just one of the many stories from the trip is of a student whom I was meeting with one-on-one each week and who attended our weekly large group meetings and many of our special events. I knew he felt stuck between two worlds—the life of following Christ and the mess of letting the world shape his life. Like many college students, he was struggling with smoking and binge drinking when he was on campus.

But for that week away he was not able to do either. Stepping out of the distractions for a time allowed him to see them in a new light. He remarked both on the trip and after how close to God and energized he felt. He has exhibited a deeper commitment to Christ and greater spiritual maturity since we returned.

And for me, how refreshing to see him have a taste of God's grace and power! I find my own confidence in God strengthened as I watched him work in others' lives.

How he removes it from me!
He allots our fields to traitors."
5 Therefore, there will be no one
in the assembly of the LORD
to divide the land by casting lots.[A]

GOD'S WORD REJECTED

6 "Quit your preaching," they[B] preach.
"They should not preach these things;
shame will not overtake us."[C]
7 House of Jacob, should it be asked,
"Is the Spirit of the LORD impatient?
Are these the things he does?"
Don't my words bring good
to the one who walks uprightly?
8 But recently my people have risen up
like an enemy:
You strip off the splendid robe
from those who are
passing through confidently,
like those returning from war.
9 You force the women of my people
out of their comfortable homes,
and you take my blessing[D]
from their children forever.
10 Get up and leave,
for this is not your place of rest
because defilement
brings destruction —
a grievous destruction!
11 If a man comes
and utters empty lies —
"I will preach to you about wine
and beer" —
he would be just the preacher
for this people!

THE REMNANT REGATHERED

12 I will indeed gather all of you, Jacob;
I will collect the remnant of Israel.
I will bring them together like sheep
in a pen,
like a flock in the middle of its pasture.
It will be noisy with people.
13 One who breaks open the way
will advance before them;
they will break out, pass
through the city gate,
and leave by it.
Their King will pass through
before them,
the LORD as their leader.

[A] **2:5** Lit *LORD stretching the measuring line by lot* [B] **2:6** = the prophets [C] **2:6** Text emended; MT reads *things. Shame will not depart* [D] **2:9** Perhaps the land

UNJUST LEADERS JUDGED

3 Then I said, "Now listen,
leaders of Jacob,
you rulers of the house of Israel.
Aren't you supposed to know
what is just?
2 You hate good and love evil.
You tear off people's skin
and strip their flesh from their bones.
3 You eat the flesh of my people
after you strip their skin from them
and break their bones.
You chop them up
like flesh for the cooking pot,
like meat in a cauldron."
4 Then they will cry out to the LORD,
but he will not answer them.
He will hide his face from them
at that time
because of the crimes
they have committed.

FALSE PROPHETS JUDGED

5 This is what the LORD says
concerning the prophets
who lead my people astray,
who proclaim peace
when they have food to sink
their teeth into
but declare war against the one
who puts nothing in their mouths.
6 Therefore, it will be night for you —
without visions;
it will grow dark for you —
without divination.
The sun will set on these prophets,
and the daylight will turn black
over them.
7 Then the seers will be ashamed
and the diviners disappointed.
They will all cover their mouths[A]
because there will be no answer
from God.

8 As for me, however, I am filled with power
by the Spirit of the LORD,
with justice and courage,
to proclaim to Jacob his rebellion
and to Israel his sin.

ZION'S DESTRUCTION

9 Listen to this, leaders of the house
of Jacob,
you rulers of the house of Israel,
who abhor justice
and pervert everything that is right,
10 who build Zion with bloodshed
and Jerusalem with injustice.
11 Her leaders issue rulings for a bribe,
her priests teach for payment,
and her prophets practice divination
for silver.
Yet they lean on the LORD, saying,
"Isn't the LORD among us?
No disaster will overtake us."
12 Therefore, because of you,
Zion will be plowed like a field,
Jerusalem will become ruins,
and the temple's mountain
will be a high thicket.

THE LORD'S RULE FROM RESTORED ZION

4 In the last days
the mountain of the LORD's house
will be established
at the top of the mountains
and will be raised above the hills.
Peoples will stream to it,
2 and many nations will come and say,
"Come, let us go up to the mountain
of the LORD,
to the house of the God of Jacob.
He will teach us about his ways
so we may walk in his paths."
For instruction will go out of Zion
and the word of the LORD
from Jerusalem.
3 He will settle disputes
among many peoples
and provide arbitration
for strong nations
that are far away.
They will beat their swords into plows
and their spears into pruning knives.
Nation will not take up the sword
against nation,
and they will never again train
for war.
4 But each person will sit
under his grapevine
and under his fig tree
with no one to frighten him.
For the mouth of the LORD of Armies
has spoken.
5 Though all the peoples each walk
in the name of their gods,

[A] 3:7 Lit *mustache*

We will walk in the name of the LORD our God forever and ever.
—Micah 4:5

we will walk in the name of the
LORD our God
forever and ever.

6 On that day —
this is the LORD's declaration —
I will assemble the lame
and gather the scattered,
those I have injured.
7 I will make the lame into a remnant,
those far removed
into a strong nation.
Then the LORD will reign over them
in Mount Zion
from this time on and forever.
8 And you, watchtower for the flock,
fortified hill[A] of Daughter Zion,
the former rule will come to you;
sovereignty will come
to Daughter Jerusalem.

FROM EXILE TO VICTORY

9 Now, why are you shouting loudly?
Is there no king with you?
Has your counselor perished
so that anguish grips you like a woman
in labor?
10 Writhe and cry out,[B] Daughter Zion,
like a woman in labor,
for now you will leave the city
and camp in the open fields.
You will go to Babylon;
there you will be rescued;
there the LORD will redeem you
from the grasp of your enemies!
11 Many nations have now assembled
against you;
they say, "Let her be defiled,
and let us feast our eyes on Zion."
12 But they do not know
the LORD's intentions
or understand his plan,
that he has gathered them
like sheaves to the threshing floor.
13 Rise and thresh, Daughter Zion,
for I will make your horns iron
and your hooves bronze
so you can crush many peoples.
Then you[C] will set apart their plunder
for the LORD,

Eternal Perspective | *God's Plans*

SMALL AND MIGHTY

"Bethlehem Ephrathah, you are small among the clans of Judah; one will come from you to be ruler over Israel for me. His origin is from antiquity, from ancient times." Micah 5:2

A recurring theme of the Bible is that God uses little things in big ways.

He chose a tiny nation (the descendants of Abraham) to bless the whole world. He used a small shepherd boy to take down a mighty giant. Through the prophet Micah, God decreed that the little town of Bethlehem is where the King of kings would make his appearance. When that ruler arrived, he was a helpless baby (Lk 2:1-7). When the child grew up, he fed the masses with a little boy's small lunch (Jn 6:1-14), and to his miniscule band of followers he spoke of tiny mustard seeds and the power of leaven particles (Lk 13:18-21).

If you are feeling insignificant today—because your gifts, abilities, or resources are few, or because your influence and opportunities seem small—remember the teaching of this passage. If salvation can come from a tiny, nothing town like Bethlehem, just imagine what big and good results could God bring from your small life!

For the next note on *Eternal Perspective*, see Micah 7:8.

[A] **4:8** Or *flock, Ophel* [B] **4:10** Hb obscure [C] **4:13** LXX, Syr, Tg; MT reads *I*

their wealth for the Lord of the
whole earth.

FROM DEFEATED RULER TO CONQUERING KING

5 Now, daughter who is under attack,
you slash yourself in grief;
a siege is set against us!
They are striking the judge of Israel
on the cheek with a rod.
2 Bethlehem Ephrathah,
you are small among the clans
of Judah;
one will come from you
to be ruler over Israel for me.
His origin[A] is from antiquity,
from ancient times.
3 Therefore, Israel will be abandoned
until the time
when she who is in labor
has given birth;
then the rest of the ruler's brothers
will return
to the people of Israel.
4 He will stand and shepherd them
in the strength of the LORD,
in the majestic name of the LORD
his God.
They will live securely,
for then his greatness will extend
to the ends of the earth.
5 He will be their peace.
When Assyria invades our land,
when it marches against our fortresses,
we will raise against it
seven shepherds,
even eight leaders of men.
6 They will shepherd the land of Assyria
with the sword,
the land of Nimrod
with a drawn blade.[B]
So he will rescue us from Assyria
when it invades our land,
when it marches against our territory.

THE GLORIOUS AND PURIFIED REMNANT

7 Then the remnant of Jacob
will be among many peoples
like dew from the LORD,
like showers on the grass,
which do not wait for anyone
or linger for mankind.
8 Then the remnant of Jacob
will be among the nations,
among many peoples,
like a lion among animals of the forest,
like a young lion among flocks of sheep,
which tramples and tears
as it passes through,

Relationships | *Making Peace*

TEARING DOWN WALLS

"He will be their peace." Micah 5:5

The Robert Frost poem "Mending Wall" describes the annual ritual of two neighbors meeting to repair the old stone wall that separates their properties. The wall keeps crumbling. The neighbors keep rebuilding it. The punchline of the poem? "Something there is that doesn't love a wall, that wants it down."

God is in the wall-busting business. And he does that through Jesus, who came to build bridges, not walls. Because he is the Prince of Peace, he came to bring peace: peace between humanity and God, peace in individual hearts, peace among people.

Certainly our world is more divided than ever. Mistrust, suspicion, and paranoia are rampant. But we don't have to be part of the divisiveness. We can be part of the solution. We can be like Jesus, fostering restoration by pursuing peace.

What one specific and practical step could you take today to begin bringing peace in a situation that separates you and a neighbor, a family member, a coworker, a fellow church member?

For the next note on *Relationships*, see Matthew 18:2,5.

[A] **5:2** Lit *His going out* [B] **5:6** Aq, Vg; MT, Sym read *Nimrod at its gateways*

and there is no one to rescue them.
9 Your hand will be lifted up
against your adversaries,
and all your enemies will be destroyed.

10 In that day —
this is the LORD's declaration —
I will remove your horses from you
and wreck your chariots.
11 I will remove the cities of your land
and tear down all your fortresses.
12 I will remove sorceries
from your hands,
and you will not have
any more fortune-tellers.
13 I will remove your carved images
and sacred pillars from you
so that you will no longer worship
the work of your hands.
14 I will pull up the Asherah poles
from among you
and demolish your cities.[A]
15 I will take vengeance in anger
and wrath
against the nations that have not
obeyed me.

GOD'S LAWSUIT AGAINST JUDAH

6 Now listen to what the LORD is saying:
Rise, plead your case
before the mountains,
and let the hills hear your complaint.[B]
2 Listen to the LORD's lawsuit,
you mountains
and enduring foundations
of the earth,
because the LORD has a case
against his people,
and he will argue it against Israel.
3 My people, what have I done to you,
or how have I wearied you?
Testify against me!
4 Indeed, I brought you up from the land
of Egypt
and redeemed you from that place
of slavery.
I sent Moses, Aaron, and Miriam
ahead of you.
5 My people,
remember what King
Balak of Moab proposed,
what Balaam son of Beor
answered him,

Exercise of Faith | *Rejecting Idols*

NO OTHER GODS

"I will remove your carved images and sacred pillars from you so that you will no longer worship the work of your hands." Micah 5:13

When we hear or read the word *idolatry*, we tend to have two thoughts: That's where primitive peoples bow before a totem pole or a statue as though it's God; and I never do that.

Idolatry, however, is much broader. It's looking to something or someone other than the one true God to save or satisfy us, or give us significance, meaning, or purpose.

In Micah's day, idolatry looked like this: Israel's neighbors worshiped an array of gods and goddesses, thought to possess various powers. Depending on one's need or desire—having children, rain for a good harvest, safe passage at sea, and so forth—people would pray or make sacrifices to homemade images of these gods. Despite numerous warnings, Israel repeatedly fell into this trap, which both angered and grieved God.

Modern-day idolatry is more sophisticated. Instead of sacrificing animals, we sacrifice our time and energy. Or we pour money into certain things, hoping we will find satisfaction and life, blessing and joy.

When you think about idolatry from this perspective, can you honestly say, "I never do that"? If you can't, ask God to forgive you and free your heart from devotion to anything other than him.

For the next note on *Exercise of Faith*, see Micah 6:8.

[A] **5:14** Or *shrines* [B] **6:1** Lit *voice*

and what happened from
the Acacia Grove[A] to Gilgal
so that you may acknowledge
the LORD's righteous acts.

6 What should I bring before the LORD
when I come to bow before God
on high?
Should I come before him
with burnt offerings,
with year-old calves?
7 Would the LORD be pleased
with thousands of rams
or with ten thousand streams of oil?
Should I give my firstborn
for my transgression,
the offspring of my body for my own sin?
8 Mankind, he has told each of you
what is good
and what it is the LORD requires of you:
to act justly,
to love faithfulness,
and to walk humbly with your God.

VERDICT OF JUDGMENT

9 The voice of the LORD calls out
to the city[B]
(and it is wise to fear your name):
"Pay attention to the rod
and the one who ordained it.[C]
10 Are there still[D] the treasures
of wickedness
and the accursed short measure
in the house of the wicked?
11 Can I excuse wicked scales
or bags of deceptive weights?
12 For the wealthy of the city are full
of violence,
and its residents speak lies;
the tongues in their mouths are deceitful.

13 "As a result, I have begun to strike
you severely,[E]
bringing desolation because of
your sins.
14 You will eat but not be satisfied,
for there will be hunger within you.
What you acquire, you cannot save,

Exercise of Faith | *Showing Mercy*

STANDARD EQUIPMENT

"Mankind, he has told each of you what is good and what it is the LORD requires of you: to act justly, to love faithfulness, and to walk humbly with your God." Micah 6:8

What does God *really* want from his people? That we go to church faithfully and give 10 percent of our money back to him? That we boycott businesses that promote immoral products? That we avoid watching raunchy movies and steer clear of neighbors who say bad words? That we vote for a specific candidate?

Micah's point here is that the spiritual life doesn't consist of religious rituals we only practice on certain days and at sacred places with a few like-minded souls. Nor is it a moral code of sins to avoid, or just an internal, private thing.

God wants his people "to act justly." This means moving out into a world of injustice and dealing fairly with others. He requires that we "love faithfulness" (or love mercy), meaning we are consistently merciful toward others. He wants us to "walk humbly" with him. In other words, we renounce pride and serve with a glad heart.

If we engage in a lot of external religious activity but neglect these basic things, we've completely missed the point. That's like buying a new car with all kinds of cool options and add-ons, but without the standard equipment of an engine and four tires!

For the next note on *Exercise of Faith*, see Zephaniah 1:12.

[A] **6:5** Or *from Shittim* [B] **6:9** = Jerusalem [C] **6:9** Or *attention, you tribe. Who has ordained it?*; Hb obscure [D] **6:10** Hb obscure
[E] **6:13** LXX, Aq, Theod, Syr, Vg; MT reads *I have made you sick by striking you down*

and what you do save,
I will give to the sword.[A]
15 You will sow but not reap;
you will press olives
but not anoint yourself with oil;
and you will tread grapes
but not drink the wine.
16 The statutes of Omri
and all the practices of Ahab's house
have been observed;
you have followed their policies.
Therefore, I will make you
a desolate place
and the city's[B] residents an object
of contempt;[C]
you will bear the scorn of my people."[D]

ISRAEL'S MORAL DECLINE

7 How sad for me!
For I am like one who —
when the summer fruit
has been gathered
after the gleaning of the grape harvest —
finds no grape cluster to eat,
no early fig, which I crave.
2 Faithful people have vanished
from the land;
there is no one upright
among the people.
All of them wait in ambush
to shed blood;
they hunt each other with a net.
3 Both hands are good
at accomplishing evil:
the official and the judge demand
a bribe;
when the powerful man communicates
his evil desire,
they plot it together.
4 The best of them is like a brier;
the most upright is worse than a hedge
of thorns.
The day of your watchmen,
the day of your punishment, is coming;
at this time their panic is here.
5 Do not rely on a friend;
don't trust in a close companion.
Seal your mouth
from the woman who lies in your arms.
6 Surely a son considers his father a fool,
a daughter opposes her mother,
and a daughter-in-law is
against her mother-in-law;
a man's enemies are the men
of his own household.
7 But I will look to the LORD;
I will wait for the God of my salvation.
My God will hear me.

E Eternal Perspective | *God's Mercy*

HIS LIGHT

"Do not rejoice over me, my enemy! Though I have fallen, I will stand up; though I sit in darkness, the LORD will be my light." Micah 7:8

Failing is bad enough, but then to have others celebrate your missteps and gloat over your misery? This was Israel's plight during the ministry of the prophet Micah.

Speaking on behalf of demoralized nation, Micah announced, "Though I sit in darkness, the LORD will be my light." Then he added that one day the roles would be reversed, "Then my enemy will see, and she will be covered with shame, the one who said to me, 'Where is the LORD your God?'" (7:10).

Let's hope you don't have flesh-and-blood enemies who taunt you when you screw up. But even if you don't have human opponents, you have temptations and attacks from Satan. Paul wrote about Christians needing to arm ourselves against "the devil" and "cosmic powers" and "spiritual forces" (Eph 6:11-12).

Next time you hear some sinister voice mocking you for some failure, quote Romans 16:20 out loud: "The God of peace will soon crush Satan under your feet. The grace of our Lord Jesus be with you."

For the next note on *Eternal Perspective*, see Nahum 1:7.

[A] **6:14** Hb obscure [B] **6:16** Lit *and its* [C] **6:16** Lit *residents a hissing* [D] **6:16** LXX reads *of the peoples*

ZION'S VINDICATION

8 Do not rejoice over me, my enemy!
Though I have fallen, I will stand up;
though I sit in darkness,
the LORD will be my light.
9 Because I have sinned against him,
I must endure the LORD's rage
until he champions my cause
and establishes justice for me.
He will bring me into the light;
I will see his salvation.[A]
10 Then my enemy will see,
and she will be covered with shame,
the one who said to me,
"Where is the LORD your God?"
My eyes will look at her in triumph;
at that time she will be trampled
like mud in the streets.

11 A day will come for rebuilding
your walls;
on that day your boundary
will be extended.
12 On that day people will come to you
from Assyria and the cities of Egypt,
even from Egypt
to the Euphrates River
and from sea to sea
and mountain to mountain.
13 Then the earth will become
a wasteland
because of its inhabitants
and as a result of their actions.

MICAH'S PRAYER ANSWERED

14 Shepherd your people with your staff,
the flock that is your possession.
They live alone in a woodland
surrounded by pastures.
Let them graze in Bashan and Gilead
as in ancient times.

15 I will perform miracles for them[B]
as in the days of your exodus
from the land of Egypt.
16 Nations will see and be ashamed
of[C] all their power.
They will put their hands
over their mouths,
and their ears will become deaf.
17 They will lick the dust like a snake;
they will come trembling out of
their hiding places
like reptiles slithering on the ground.
They will tremble in the presence of the
LORD our God;
they will stand in awe of you.

18 Who is a God like you,
forgiving iniquity and passing
over rebellion
for the remnant of his inheritance?
He does not hold on
to his anger forever
because he delights in faithful love.
19 He will again have compassion
on us;
he will vanquish our iniquities.
You will cast all our[D] sins
into the depths of the sea.
20 You will show loyalty to Jacob
and faithful love to Abraham,
as you swore to our fathers
from days long ago.

[A] 7:9 Or *righteousness* [B] 7:15 = Israel [C] 7:16 Or *ashamed in spite of* [D] 7:19 Some Hb mss, LXX, Syr, Vg; other Hb mss read *their*

Nahum—Judah was in danger of being taken over by the evil Assyrian Empire, whose capital city was Nineveh. Could God save them? Nahum assured the people that God's sovereign control extends to all human empires and that he judges the nations fairly. At his command, the mighty city of Nineveh would fall. Though the future looked bleak, God's people had nothing to fear.

In Nahum's prophecy God reveals that he is patient (1:3) and good (1:7). He will work his purposes, namely to build the faith of his people (2:2). And one day his people will live in peace and joy.

The original hearers of Nahum's prophecy experienced that in microcosm when Nineveh fell, but all believers will experience it at the end of time when God establishes his rule over the new heavens and the new earth. Just as the judgment of Nineveh was good news for God's people, so also the final day of judgment will be a day of hope and final restoration for those who love God.

NAHUM

AUTHOR: Nahum

DATE WRITTEN: Shortly after the fall of Thebes in 663 BC and before the destruction of Nineveh in 612 BC

ORIGINAL AUDIENCE: The Israelites, particularly Judah, which was being oppressed by Nineveh

SETTING: Nahum preached to the Ninevites a century after Jonah. During Jonah's time they had repented, but a generation or so later they had again become a wicked and godless nation.

PURPOSE FOR WRITING: Nahum describes the impending judgment of Nineveh and the deliverance that would bring to Judah. In the same way Nineveh had brutally mistreated their enemies, now God would brutally mistreat them. The wrath of God poured out on Nineveh was an expression of his jealous love for his people and his anger against sin; the same day would bring judgment against God's enemies and deliverance for his people.

OUTLINE:

1. Introduction (1:1-10)

2. Nineveh's Destruction at the Hand of God (1:11–3:19)

   Deliverance of Judah and judgment of Assyria (1:11-15)

   Complete destruction of Nineveh (2:1-13)

   Reason for Nineveh's destruction (3:1-19)

KEY VERSE:

"The LORD is good, a stronghold in a day of distress; he cares for those who take refuge in him." —Nahum 1:7

RESTORATION THEMES

R	Rest and Reflection	*For the next note, see Zechariah 4:6.*
E	Eternal Perspective	*God's Goodness—Nahum 1:7*
S	Support	*For the next note, see Habakkuk 1:2-4.*
T	Thanksgiving and Contentment	*For the next note, see Habakkuk 3:17-19.*
O	Other-centeredness	*For the next note, see Matthew 7:1.*
R	Relationships	*For the next note, see Matthew 18:2,5.*
E	Exercise of Faith	*For the next note, see Zephaniah 1:12.*

1 The pronouncement concerning Nineveh. The book of the vision of Nahum the Elkoshite.

GOD'S VENGEANCE

2 The LORD is a jealous and avenging God;
the LORD takes vengeance
and is fierce in[A] wrath.
The LORD takes vengeance
against his foes;
he is furious with his enemies.
3 The LORD is slow to anger but great
in power;
the LORD will never leave
the guilty unpunished.
His path is in the whirlwind and storm,
and clouds are the dust beneath his feet.
4 He rebukes the sea and dries it up,
and he makes all the rivers run dry.
Bashan and Carmel wither;
even the flower of Lebanon withers.
5 The mountains quake before him,
and the hills melt;
the earth trembles[B,C] at his presence —
the world and all who live in it.
6 Who can withstand his indignation?
Who can endure his burning anger?
His wrath is poured out like fire;
even rocks are shattered before him.

DESTRUCTION OF NINEVEH

7 The LORD is good,
a stronghold in a day of distress;
he cares for those who take refuge
in him.
8 But he will completely
destroy Nineveh[D]
with an overwhelming flood,
and he will chase his enemies
into darkness.

9 Whatever you[E] plot against the LORD,
he will bring it to complete destruction;
oppression will not rise up
a second time.
10 For they will be consumed
like entangled thorns,
like the drink of a drunkard
and like straw that is fully dry.[F]
11 One has gone out from you,[G]
who plots evil against the LORD,
and is a wicked counselor.

PROMISE OF JUDAH'S DELIVERANCE

12 This is what the LORD says:
Though they are strong[H]
and numerous,
they will still be mowed down,
and he[I] will pass away.

Eternal Perspective | *God's Goodness*

THE LORD IS GOOD

"The LORD is good, a stronghold in a day of distress; he cares for those who take refuge in him." Nahum 1:7

You're having a bad hair day. And underneath all that, you also have a bad headache. The morning commute is bad, thanks to bad weather and a bad wreck on the expressway. In a meeting, you have to put up with one coworker's bad mood and another's bad jokes. At lunch, while eating a bad sandwich, the mechanic calls. Bad news. Your other car's transmission is in bad shape. In the afternoon, you learn that a big client has bad-mouthed you to your boss.

What else can be said except, "In a world that's broken, a lot of bad happens." Thankfully, however, even when our situations and circumstances aren't good, God always is. This was the reminder from the prophet Nahum. Goodness is God's essential nature, meaning he is the moral opposite of evil. All his purposes and plans, all his thoughts and actions toward us? Only good, all the time.

The challenge is clinging to the truth that God is good—when life all around you feels anything but good. Ask the Lord to help you trust that. And take time to thank and praise God for his goodness.

For the next note on *Eternal Perspective*, see Zephaniah 3:15.

[A] **1:2** Lit *is a master of* [B] **1:5** Some emend to *earth is laid waste* [C] **1:5** Lit *lifts* [D] **1:8** Lit *her place* [E] **1:9** = Nineveh [F] **1:10** Hb obscure [G] **1:11** Possibly Nineveh [H] **1:12** Lit *intact* [I] **1:12** Either the king of Assyria or his army

Though I have punished you,[A]
I will punish you no longer.
13 For I will now break off his yoke from you
and tear off your shackles.

THE ASSYRIAN KING'S DEMISE

14 The LORD has issued an order concerning
you:
There will be no offspring
to carry on your name.[B]
I will eliminate the carved idol
and cast image
from the house of your gods;
I will prepare your grave,
for you are contemptible.

15 Look to the mountains —
the feet of the herald,
who proclaims peace.
Celebrate your festivals, Judah;
fulfill your vows.
For the wicked one will never again
march through you;
he will be entirely wiped out.

ATTACK AGAINST NINEVEH

2 One who scatters is coming up
against you.
Man the fortifications!
Watch the road!
Brace[C] yourself!
Summon all your strength!

2 For the LORD will restore the majesty
of Jacob,
yes,[D] the majesty of Israel,
though ravagers have ravaged them
and ruined their vine branches.

3 The shields of his[E] warriors
are dyed red;
the valiant men are dressed in scarlet.
The fittings of the chariot flash like fire
on the day of its battle preparations,
and the spears are brandished.
4 The chariots dash madly
through the streets;
they rush around in the plazas.
They look like torches;
they dart back and forth like lightning.
5 He gives orders to his officers;
they stumble as they advance.
They race to its wall;
the protective shield is set in place.
6 The river gates are opened,
and the palace erodes away.

7 Beauty[F] is stripped;[G]
she is carried away;
her ladies-in-waiting moan
like the sound of doves
and beat their breasts.
8 Nineveh has been like a pool of water
from her first days,[G]
but they are fleeing.
"Stop! Stop!" they cry,
but no one turns back.
9 "Plunder the silver! Plunder the gold!"
There is no end to the treasure,
an abundance of every precious thing.
10 Desolation, decimation, devastation!
Hearts melt,
knees tremble,
insides churn,
every face grows pale!

11 Where is the lions' lair,
or the feeding ground of the young lions,
where the lion and lioness prowled,
and the lion's cub,
with nothing to frighten them away?
12 The lion mauled whatever
its cubs needed
and strangled prey for its lionesses.
It filled up its dens with the kill,
and its lairs with mauled prey.
13 Beware, I am against you.
This is the declaration of the LORD
of Armies.
I will make your chariots go up
in smoke,[H]
and the sword will devour
your young lions.
I will cut off your prey from the earth,
and the sound of your messengers
will never be heard again.

NINEVEH'S DOWNFALL

3 Woe to the city of blood,
totally deceitful,
full of plunder,
never without prey.
2 The crack of the whip
and rumble of the wheel,

[A] **1:12** = Judah [B] **1:14** Lit *It will not be sown from your name any longer* [C] **2:1** Lit *Strengthen* [D] **2:2** Or *like* [E] **2:3** = the army commander attacking Nineveh [F] **2:7** Text emended; MT reads *Huzzab* [G] **2:7,8** Hb obscure [H] **2:13** Lit *will burn her chariots in smoke*

galloping horse
and jolting chariot!
3 Charging horseman,
flashing sword,
shining spear;
heaps of slain,
mounds of corpses,
dead bodies without end —
they stumble over their dead.
4 Because of the continual prostitution
of the prostitute,
the attractive mistress of sorcery,
who treats nations
and clans like merchandise
by her prostitution and sorcery,
5 I am against you.
This is the declaration of the LORD
of Armies.
I will lift your skirts over your face
and display your nakedness to nations,
your shame to kingdoms.
6 I will throw filth on you
and treat you with contempt;
I will make a spectacle of you.
7 Then all who see you will recoil
from you, saying,
"Nineveh is devastated;
who will show sympathy to her?"
Where can I find anyone
to comfort you?

8 Are you better than Thebes[A]
that sat along the Nile
with water surrounding her,
whose rampart was the sea,
the river[B,C] her wall?
9 Cush and Egypt were
her endless source of strength;
Put and Libya were among her[D] allies.
10 Yet she became an exile;
she went into captivity.
Her children were also dashed
to pieces
at the head of every street.
They cast lots for her dignitaries,
and all her nobles were bound
in chains.
11 You[E] also will become drunk;
you will hide.[F]
You also will seek refuge
from the enemy.
12 All your fortresses are fig trees
with figs that ripened first;
when shaken, they fall —
right into the mouth of the eater!

13 Look, your troops are like women
among you;
your land's city gates
are wide open to your enemies.
Fire will devour the bars
of your gates.

14 Draw water for the siege;
strengthen your fortresses.
Step into the clay and tread the mortar;
take hold of the brick-mold!
15 The fire will devour you there;
the sword will cut you down.
It will devour you like the young locust.
Multiply yourselves
like the young locust;
multiply like the swarming locust!
16 You have made your merchants
more numerous than the stars
of the sky.
The young locust strips[G] the land
and flies away.
17 Your court officials are
like the swarming locust,
and your scribes like clouds of locusts,
which settle on the walls on a cold day;
when the sun rises, they take off,
and no one knows where they are.

18 King of Assyria,
your shepherds slumber;
your officers sleep.
Your people are scattered
across the mountains
with no one to gather them together.
19 There is no remedy for your injury;
your wound is severe.
All who hear the news about you
will clap their hands because of you,
for who has not experienced
your constant cruelty?

[A] 3:8 Hb *No-amon* [B] 3:8 LXX, Syr, Vg read *water* [C] 3:8 Lit *sea from sea* [D] 3:9 Lit *your* [E] 3:11 = Nineveh [F] 3:11 Or *will be overcome* [G] 3:16 Or *sheds its skin*

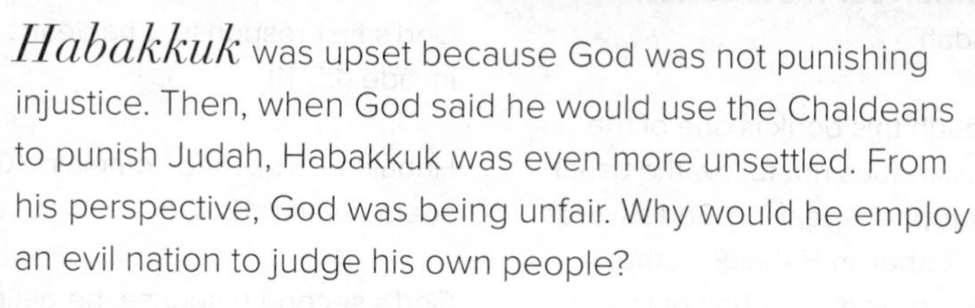

Habakkuk was upset because God was not punishing injustice. Then, when God said he would use the Chaldeans to punish Judah, Habakkuk was even more unsettled. From his perspective, God was being unfair. Why would he employ an evil nation to judge his own people?

We also may wonder why wicked people prosper, why the godly suffer, and why we struggle when we've spent a lifetime trying to do what pleases God. The basic question is whether we can trust God or not. Is he really in control, and does he care about us? God's ways often don't line up with what we think is just and right—and that can be tough to take.

God gives us the same response he gave Habakkuk: trust my character and be patient; the story isn't over. Habakkuk wanted explanations; instead, God revealed his power and glory, and that was enough.

God is all-powerful and perfectly good. We need to trust that he will do what is right and that eventually his promise for eternal life will be fulfilled. Restoration now comes from trusting in and praising God while we wait with hopeful anticipation for the final restoration of all things at the end of time.

HABAKKUK

AUTHOR: Habakkuk

DATE WRITTEN: During the reign of Jehoiakim, probably before the Babylonian invasion of Judah, around 609–605 BC

ORIGINAL AUDIENCE: The Israelites, particularly Judah

SETTING: Though this book is one of the Minor Prophets, it does not follow the usual format of the prophet speaking God's words to the people. Rather, in Habakkuk, the prophet speaks to God on behalf of the people. He wrote these words during a time of trouble for Judah after the reign of Josiah.

PURPOSE FOR WRITING: As in Job, Habakkuk wrestles with questions related to suffering: Why does God allow injustice? How long will God allow evil to continue? Habakkuk's conclusion is that God is worthy of praise even though he could not understand God's ways or see the answers to his prayers.

OUTLINE:

1. Dialogue between God and Habakkuk (1:1–2:20)

   Habakkuk's first complaint: injustice (1:1-4)

   God's first response: Chaldeans would invade (1:5-11)

   Habakkuk's second complaint: God's ways seem unfair (1:12–2:1)

   God's second response: be patient; justice will prevail (2:2-20)

2. Habakkuk's Psalm (3:1-19)

   Habakkuk's fear (3:1)

   God's appearance (3:2-15)

   Habakkuk's faith (3:16-19)

KEY VERSE:

"The LORD my Lord is my strength; he makes my feet like those of a deer and enables me to walk on mountain heights!"
—Habakkuk 3:19

RESTORATION THEMES

R	Rest and Reflection	*For the next note, see Zechariah 4:6.*
E	Eternal Perspective	*For the next note, see Zephaniah 3:15.*
S	Support	*Prayer—Habakkuk 1:2-4*
T	Thanksgiving and Contentment	*Praise—3:17-19*
O	Other-centeredness	*For the next note, see Matthew 7:1.*
R	Relationships	*For the next note, see Matthew 18:2,5.*
E	Exercise of Faith	*For the next note, see Zephaniah 1:12.*

1 The pronouncement that the prophet Habakkuk saw.

HABAKKUK'S FIRST PRAYER

2 How long, LORD, must I call for help
and you do not listen
or cry out to you about violence
and you do not save?
3 Why do you force me to look
at injustice?
Why do you tolerate[A] wrongdoing?
Oppression and violence are right
in front of me.
Strife is ongoing, and conflict escalates.
4 This is why the law is ineffective
and justice never emerges.
For the wicked restrict the righteous;
therefore, justice comes out perverted.

GOD'S FIRST ANSWER

5 Look at the nations[B] and observe —
be utterly astounded!
For I am doing something in your days
that you will not believe
when you hear about it.
6 Look! I am raising up the Chaldeans,[C]
that bitter, impetuous nation
that marches across
the earth's open spaces
to seize territories not its own.
7 They are fierce and terrifying;
their views of justice and sovereignty
stem from themselves.
8 Their horses are swifter than leopards
and more fierce[D] than wolves
of the night.
Their horsemen charge ahead;
their horsemen come
from distant lands.
They fly like eagles,
swooping to devour.
9 All of them come to do violence;
their faces are set in determination.[E]
They gather prisoners like sand.
10 They mock kings,
and rulers are a joke to them.
They laugh at every fortress
and build siege ramps to capture it.
11 Then they sweep by like the wind
and pass through.

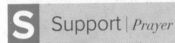

Support | *Prayer*

DO SOMETHING, LORD!

"How long, LORD, must I call for help and you do not listen or cry out to you about violence and you do not save? Why do you force me to look at injustice? Why do you tolerate wrongdoing? Oppression and violence are right in front of me. Strife is ongoing, and conflict escalates. This is why the law is ineffective and justice never emerges. For the wicked restrict the righteous; therefore, justice comes out perverted." Habakkuk 1:2-4

Christian theology says that God is in control of all things—that he rules over the world. The day's headlines portray a much different story—Violence! Injustice! Wrongdoing! Oppression! Strife! This discrepancy between what the Bible claims and what news outlets say prompts many people to wonder if the faith they proclaim is perhaps closer to wishful thinking.

The prophet Habakkuk had a similar experience. When he surveyed his nation he thought: *Lord, if you're really in control, why don't you act? Why do you stand by and allow such wickedness?*

And instead of just sitting in his frustrations and doubts, he voiced them to God. Shocking, right? Especially if your prayers take a much milder form. Note that God doesn't zap Habakkuk or even criticize him for his questions. This shows that we can talk with God about anything and everything.

Deepen your prayers—tell God how you really feel. He can take it!

For the next note on *Support*, see Matthew 7:9-11.

[A] **1:3** Lit *observe*, also in v. 13 [B] **1:5** DSS, LXX, Syr read *Look, you treacherous people* [C] **1:6** = the Babylonians [D] **1:8** Or *and quicker* [E] **1:9** Hb obscure

They are guilty;[A] their strength
is their god.

HABAKKUK'S SECOND PRAYER

12 Are you not from eternity,
LORD my God?
My Holy One, you[B] will not die.
LORD, you appointed them
to execute judgment;
my Rock, you destined them
to punish us.
13 Your eyes are too pure to look on evil,
and you cannot tolerate wrongdoing.
So why do you tolerate those
who are treacherous?
Why are you silent
while one[C] who is wicked swallows up
one[D] who is more righteous
than himself?
14 You have made mankind
like the fish of the sea,
like marine creatures that have
no ruler.
15 The Chaldeans pull them all up
with a hook,
catch them in their dragnet,
and gather them in their fishing net;
that is why they are glad and rejoice.
16 That is why they sacrifice
to their dragnet
and burn incense to their fishing net,
for by these things their portion
is rich
and their food plentiful.
17 Will they therefore empty their net
and continually slaughter nations
without mercy?

HABAKKUK WAITS FOR GOD'S RESPONSE

2 I will stand at my guard post
and station myself
on the lookout tower.
I will watch to see what he will say
to me
and what I should[E] reply
about my complaint.

GOD'S SECOND ANSWER

2 The LORD answered me:
Write down this vision;
clearly inscribe it on tablets
so one may easily read it.[F]
3 For the vision is yet
for the appointed time;
it testifies about the end
and will not lie.
Though it delays, wait for it,
since it will certainly come and not
be late.
4 Look, his ego is inflated;[G]
he is without integrity.
But the righteous one will live
by his faith.[H]
5 Moreover, wine[I] betrays;
an arrogant man is never at rest.[J]
He enlarges his appetite like Sheol,
and like Death he is never satisfied.
He gathers all the nations to himself;
he collects all the peoples for himself.

THE FIVE WOE ORACLES

6 Won't all of these take up a taunt
against him,
with mockery and riddles about him?
They will say:

Woe to him who amasses
what is not his —
how much longer? —
and loads himself with goods
taken in pledge.
7 Won't your creditors suddenly arise,
and those who disturb you wake up?
Then you will become spoil for them.
8 Since you have plundered
many nations,
all the peoples who remain
will plunder you —
because of human bloodshed
and violence against lands, cities,
and all who live in them.

9 Woe to him who dishonestly makes
wealth for his house[K]
to place his nest on high,
to escape the grasp of disaster!
10 You have planned shame
for your house
by wiping out many peoples
and sinning against your own self.
11 For the stones will cry out
from the wall,
and the rafters will answer them
from the woodwork.

[A] **1:11** Or *wind, and transgress and incur guilt* [B] **1:12** Alt Hb tradition reads *we* [C] **1:13** = Babylon [D] **1:13** = Judah [E] **2:1** Syr reads *what he will* [F] **2:2** Lit *one who reads in it may run* [G] **2:4** Hb obscure [H] **2:4** Or *faithfulness* [I] **2:5** DSS read *wealth* [J] **2:5** Or *man does not endure*; Hb obscure [K] **2:9** Or *dynasty*

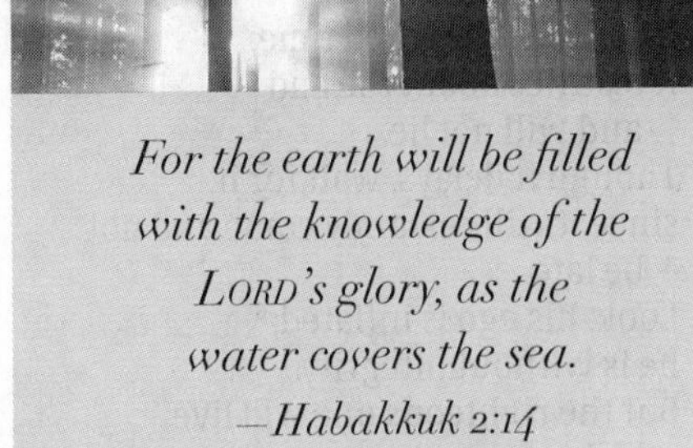

For the earth will be filled with the knowledge of the LORD's glory, as the water covers the sea.
—Habakkuk 2:14

12 Woe to him who builds a city
with bloodshed
and founds a town with injustice!
13 Is it not from the LORD of Armies
that the peoples labor only to fuel
the fire
and countries exhaust themselves
for nothing?
14 For the earth will be filled
with the knowledge of the LORD's glory,
as the water covers the sea.

15 Woe to him who gives
his neighbors drink,
pouring out your wrath[A]
and even making them drunk,
in order to look at their nakedness!
16 You will be filled with disgrace
instead of glory.
You also — drink,
and expose your uncircumcision![B]
The cup in the LORD's right hand
will come around to you,
and utter disgrace will cover
your glory.
17 For your violence against Lebanon
will overwhelm you;
the destruction of animals
will terrify you[C]
because of your human bloodshed
and violence
against lands, cities, and all who live
in them.

18 What use is a carved idol
after its craftsman carves it?
It is only a cast image, a teacher of lies.
For the one who crafts its shape
trusts in it
and makes idols that cannot speak.
19 Woe to him who says to wood: Wake up!
or to mute stone: Come alive!
Can it teach?
Look! It may be plated with gold
and silver,
yet there is no breath in it at all.

20 But the LORD is in his holy temple;
let the whole earth
be silent in his presence.

HABAKKUK'S THIRD PRAYER

3 A prayer of the prophet Habakkuk. According to *Shigionoth*.[D]
2 LORD, I have heard the report about you;
LORD, I stand in awe of your deeds.
Revive your work in these years;
make it known in these years.
In your wrath remember mercy!

3 God comes from Teman,
the Holy One from Mount Paran. *Selah*
His splendor covers the heavens,
and the earth is full of his praise.
4 His brilliance is like light;
rays are flashing from his hand.
This is where his power is hidden.
5 Plague goes before him,
and pestilence follows in his steps.
6 He stands and shakes[E] the earth;
he looks and startles the nations.
The age-old mountains break apart;
the ancient hills sink down.
His pathways are ancient.
7 I see the tents of Cushan[F] in distress;
the tent curtains of the land
of Midian tremble.
8 Are you angry at the rivers, LORD?
Is your wrath against the rivers?
Or is your rage against the sea
when you ride on your horses,
your victorious chariot?
9 You took the sheath from your bow;
the arrows are ready[G] to be used
with an oath.[H] *Selah*
You split the earth with rivers.
10 The mountains see you and shudder;
a downpour of water sweeps by.
The deep roars with its voice
and lifts its waves[I] high.
11 Sun and moon stand still
in their lofty residence,

[A] **2:15** Or *venom* [B] **2:16** DSS, LXX, Aq, Syr, Vg read *and stagger* [C] **2:17** DSS, LXX, Aq, Syr, Tg, Vg; MT reads *them* [D] **3:1** Perhaps a passionate song with rapid changes of rhythm, or a dirge [E] **3:6** Or *surveys* [F] **3:7** = Midian [G] **3:9** Or *set* [H] **3:9** Hb obscure [I] **3:10** Lit *hands*

at the flash of your flying arrows,
at the brightness of your shining spear.
12 You march across the earth
with indignation;
you trample down the nations in wrath.
13 You come out to save your people,
to save your anointed.[A]
You crush the leader of the house
of the wicked
and strip him from foot[B] to neck. *Selah*
14 You pierce his head
with his own spears;
his warriors storm out to scatter us,
gloating as if ready to secretly devour
the weak.
15 You tread the sea with your horses,
stirring up the vast water.

HABAKKUK'S CONFIDENCE IN GOD EXPRESSED

16 I heard, and I trembled within;
my lips quivered at the sound.
Rottenness entered my bones;
I trembled where I stood.
Now I must quietly wait for the day
of distress
to come against the people
invading us.
17 Though the fig tree does not bud
and there is no fruit on the vines,
though the olive crop fails
and the fields produce no food,
though the flocks disappear
from the pen
and there are no herds in the stalls,
18 yet I will celebrate in the LORD;
I will rejoice in the God
of my salvation!
19 The LORD my Lord is my strength;
he makes my feet like those of a deer
and enables me to walk
on mountain heights!

For the choir director: on[C] stringed instruments.

Thanksgiving and Contentment | *Praise*

FROM PROTEST TO PRAISE

"Though the fig tree does not bud and there is no fruit on the vines, though the olive crop fails and the fields produce no food, though the flocks disappear from the pen and there are no herds in the stalls, yet I will celebrate in the LORD; I will rejoice in the God of my salvation! The LORD my Lord is my strength; he makes my feet like those of a deer and enables me to walk on mountain heights!" Habakkuk 3:17-19

Habakkuk was *bothered* by God's seeming indifference to the evil all around him (1:1-4). But when he learned that God was planning to clean house by using the barbaric Chaldeans (1:5-11), he was *horrified*.

Habakkuk told God what he thought, then waited for God's reply (2:1). He didn't have to wait long. And what he heard was epic. God led with the life-changing statement that the righteous person "will live by his faith" (2:4). He concluded with the truth that "the LORD is in his holy temple; let the whole earth be silent in his presence" (2:20).

These reminders filled Habakkuk with awe (3:2). And though the coming judgment caused him to tremble (3:16), the greater truth expressed here—God's strength and faithfulness in dark times—brought him to a place of celebration.

Ask God to give you this kind of confidence in his providence.

For the next note on *Thanksgiving and Contentment*, see Malachi 3:7.

[A] **3:13** The Davidic king or the nation of Israel [B] **3:13** Lit *foundation* [C] **3:19** Lit *on my*

Zephaniah gives a harsh description of judgment, revealing God as the Lord of Armies, the One who leads earthly and heavenly forces into battle. Unlike long sieges, common in ancient warfare, God's judgment would be swift and absolute. The Israelites could choose: Would they align themselves with God or fight against him? Those who resist God always lose, but the great warrior King defends those who repent and live in covenant relationship with him. God judges his enemies and saves his people.

Like other prophetic utterances, this book offers hope. God will stay true to his covenant promises and faithfully preserve a remnant of his people, including, even, foreigners (3:9). Beyond that immediate hope, God's people have eternal hope.

When Christ returns to earth in the final day of the Lord, his people will experience complete and final deliverance from the grip of sin and death. For believers, this is a day of hope and joy rather than judgment.

As we await that day, Zephaniah encourages us to sing of the Lord our God who lives among us, a warrior who saves us and rejoices over us with gladness. Let him make you whole.

ZEPHANIAH

AUTHOR: Zephaniah, a prophet whose genealogy suggests that he was of royal descent and had some Cushite blood

DATE WRITTEN: During Josiah's reign (640–609 BC), most likely early in his rule (635–622 BC), prior to the discovery of the book of the law

ORIGINAL AUDIENCE: The Israelites, particularly Judah

SETTING: Judah had endured several wicked kings in a row before Josiah took the throne. Josiah was a good king, and he attempted to do away with the pagan and syncretistic practices that had taken over the land. In 621 BC, the book of the law was recovered and read publicly. This discovery resulted in a series of religious reforms, including the tearing down of altars and dismissing false priests.

PURPOSE FOR WRITING: Zephaniah wrote to warn the people of impending judgment. The day of the Lord was at hand; unless the people repented of their sin and sought God alone, they would be wiped out in a single day by God's mighty army.

OUTLINE:

1. Prophecy of Judgment (1:1–2:3)

2. Judgment against the Nations (2:4-15)

3. Judgment against Jerusalem (3:1-8)

4. Promise of Restoration (3:9-20)

KEY VERSE:

"The LORD your God is among you, a warrior who saves. He will rejoice over you with gladness. He will be quiet in his love. He will delight in you with singing." —Zephaniah 3:17

RESTORATION THEMES

R	Rest and Reflection	*For the next note, see Zechariah 4:6.*
E	Eternal Perspective	*God's Forgiveness—Zephaniah 3:15* *God's Love—3:17*
S	Support	*For the next note, see Matthew 7:9-11.*
T	Thanksgiving and Contentment	*For the next note, see Malachi 3:7.*
O	Other-centeredness	*For the next note, see Matthew 7:1.*
R	Relationships	*For the next note, see Matthew 18:2,5.*
E	Exercise of Faith	*Guarding the Heart—Zephaniah 1:12*

1 The word of the LORD that came to Zephaniah son of Cushi, son of Gedaliah, son of Amariah, son of Hezekiah, in the days of Josiah son of Amon, king of Judah.

THE GREAT DAY OF THE LORD

2 I will completely
sweep away everything
from the face of the earth —
this is the LORD's declaration.
3 I will sweep away people and animals;
I will sweep away the birds of the sky
and the fish of the sea,
and the ruins[A] along with the wicked.
I will cut off mankind
from the face of the earth.
This is the LORD's declaration.

4 I will stretch out my hand against Judah
and against all the residents
of Jerusalem.
I will cut off every vestige of Baal
from this place,
the names of the pagan priests
along with the priests;
5 those who bow in worship
on the rooftops
to the stars in the sky;
those who bow and pledge loyalty
to the LORD
but also pledge loyalty to Milcom;[B]
6 and those who turn back
from following the LORD,
who do not seek the LORD or inquire
of him.
7 Be silent in the presence
of the Lord GOD,
for the day of the LORD is near.
Indeed, the LORD has prepared
a sacrifice;
he has consecrated his guests.

8 On the day of the LORD's sacrifice
I will punish the officials,
the king's sons,
and all who are dressed
in foreign clothing.
9 On that day I will punish
all who skip over the threshold,[C]
who fill their master's house
with violence and deceit.

10 On that day —
this is the LORD's declaration —

Exercise of Faith | *Guarding the Heart*

COMPLACENCY KILLS

"And at that time I will search Jerusalem with lamps and punish those who settle down comfortably, who say to themselves: The LORD will not do good or evil." Zephaniah 1:12

The southern kingdom of Judah watched Assyria decimate the northern kingdom of Israel (2Kg 17). When Hezekiah was king, only a gracious, eye-popping miracle of God kept them from the same fate (2Kg 19).

We would think all this would prompt the people of Judah to return to worshiping and obeying God. It did not. Hezekiah's son Manasseh was more evil than all the rest. Then Manasseh's son Amon (one of the sons he didn't sacrifice in fire to a false god) followed in his footsteps. Through all this, the people of Judah didn't much bat an eye.

When Josiah became king, the prophet Zephaniah stepped forward with a word from the Lord. It was for the complacent, all the people who had concluded God was too busy or preoccupied to notice their sins. It was directed at the ones who thought "the LORD will not do good or evil."

Life's troubles and struggles may leave you passive, numb, and complacent. God sees you. He knows your problems and how big they are. Ask God to keep your heart soft and your mind open to him.

For the next note on *Exercise of Faith*, see Haggai 1:5.

[A] **1:3** Perhaps objects connected with idolatry [B] **1:5** Some LXX mss, Syr, Vg; MT, other LXX mss read *their king* [C] **1:9** Hb obscure

there will be an outcry
from the Fish Gate,
a wailing from the Second District,
and a loud crashing from the hills.
11 Wail, you residents of the Hollow,[A]
for all the merchants[B] will be silenced;
all those loaded with silver will be
cut off.

12 And at that time I will search Jerusalem
with lamps
and punish
those who settle down comfortably,[C]
who say to themselves:
The LORD will not do good or evil.
13 Their wealth will become plunder
and their houses a ruin.
They will build houses but never live
in them,
plant vineyards but never drink
their wine.

14 The great day of the LORD is near,
near and rapidly approaching.
Listen, the day of the LORD —
then the warrior's cry is bitter.
15 That day is a day of wrath,
a day of trouble and distress,
a day of destruction and desolation,
a day of darkness and gloom,
a day of clouds and total darkness,
16 a day of trumpet blast and battle cry
against the fortified cities,
and against the high corner towers.
17 I will bring distress on mankind,
and they will walk like the blind
because they have sinned
against the LORD.
Their blood will be poured out like dust
and their flesh like dung.
18 Their silver and their gold
will be unable to rescue them
on the day of the LORD's wrath.
The whole earth will be consumed
by the fire of his jealousy,
for he will make a complete,
yes, a horrifying end
of all the inhabitants of the earth.

A CALL TO REPENTANCE

2 Gather yourselves together;
gather together, undesirable[D] nation,
2 before the decree takes effect

Seek the LORD, all you humble of the earth, who carry out what he commands. Seek righteousness, seek humility.
—Zephaniah 2:3

and the day passes like chaff,
before the burning of the LORD's anger
overtakes you,
before the day of the LORD's anger
overtakes you.
3 Seek the LORD, all you humble
of the earth,
who carry out what he commands.
Seek righteousness, seek humility;
perhaps you will be concealed
on the day of the LORD's anger.

JUDGMENT AGAINST THE NATIONS

4 For Gaza will be abandoned,
and Ashkelon will become a ruin.
Ashdod will be driven out at noon,
and Ekron will be uprooted.
5 Woe, inhabitants of the seacoast,
nation of the Cherethites![E]
The word of the LORD is against you,
Canaan, land of the Philistines:
I will destroy you until there is
no one left.
6 The seacoast will
become pasturelands
with caves for shepherds and pens
for sheep.
7 The coastland will belong
to the remnant
of the house of Judah;
they will find pasture there.
They will lie down in the evening
among the houses of Ashkelon,
for the LORD their God will return
to them
and restore their fortunes.

8 I have heard the taunting of Moab
and the insults of the Ammonites,
who have taunted my people
and threatened their territory.

[A] **1:11** Or *the market district* [B] **1:11** Or *Canaanites* [C] **1:12** Lit *who thicken on their dregs* [D] **2:1** Or *shameless* [E] **2:5** = Sea Peoples

9 Therefore, as I live —
this is the declaration of the LORD
of Armies,
the God of Israel —
Moab will be like Sodom
and the Ammonites like Gomorrah:
a place overgrown with weeds,
a salt pit, and
a perpetual wasteland.
The remnant of my people
will plunder them;
the remainder of my nation
will dispossess them.
10 This is what they get for their pride,
because they have taunted
and acted arrogantly
against the people of the LORD
of Armies.
11 The LORD will be terrifying to them
when he starves all the gods
of the earth.
Then all the distant coasts and islands
of the nations
will bow in worship to him,
each in its own place.

12 You Cushites will also be slain
by my sword.

13 He will also stretch out his hand
against the north
and destroy Assyria;
he will make Nineveh a desolate ruin,
dry as the desert.
14 Herds will lie down in the middle of it,
every kind of wild animal.[A]
Both eagle owls[B] and herons[C]
will roost in the capitals
of its pillars.
Their calls will sound[D]
from the window,
but devastation[E] will be
on the threshold,
for he will expose the cedar work.[F]
15 This is the jubilant city
that lives in security,
that thinks to herself:
I exist, and there is no one else.
What a desolation she has become,
a place for wild animals to lie down!
Everyone who passes by her
scoffs[G] and shakes his fist.

WOE TO OPPRESSIVE JERUSALEM

3 Woe to the city that is rebellious[H]
and defiled,
the oppressive city!
2 She has not obeyed;
she has not accepted discipline.
She has not trusted in the LORD;
she has not drawn near to her God.
3 The[I] princes within her are
roaring lions;
her judges are wolves of the night,
which leave nothing for[J] the morning.
4 Her prophets are reckless —
treacherous men.
Her priests profane the sanctuary;
they do violence to instruction.
5 The righteous LORD is in her;
he does no wrong.
He applies his justice morning
by morning;
he does not fail at dawn,
yet the one who does wrong
knows no shame.

6 I have cut off nations;
their corner towers are destroyed.
I have laid waste their streets,
with no one to pass through.
Their cities lie devastated,
without a person,
without an inhabitant.
7 I thought: You will certainly fear me
and accept correction.
Then her dwelling place[K]
would not be cut off
based on all that I had allocated to her.
However, they became more corrupt
in all their actions.
8 Therefore, wait for me —
this is the LORD's declaration —
until the day I rise up for plunder.[L]
For my decision is to gather nations,
to assemble kingdoms,
in order to pour out my indignation
on them,
all my burning anger;
for the whole earth will be consumed
by the fire of my jealousy.

FINAL RESTORATION PROMISED

9 For I will then restore
pure speech to the peoples

[A] **2:14** Lit *every wild animal of a nation* [B] **2:14** Or *the pelicans* [C] **2:14** Or *the hedgehogs* [D] **2:14** Lit *sing* [E] **2:14** LXX, Vg read *ravens* [F] **2:14** Hb obscure [G] **2:15** Or *hisses* [H] **3:1** Or *filthy* [I] **3:3** Lit *Her* [J] **3:3** Or *that had nothing to gnaw in* [K] **3:7** LXX, Syr read *her eyes* [L] **3:8** LXX, Syr read *for a witness*; Vg reads *up forever*

so that all of them may call
on the name of the LORD
and serve him
with a single purpose.[A]
10 From beyond the rivers of Cush
my supplicants, my dispersed people,
will bring an offering to me.
11 On that day you[B] will not be put
to shame
because of everything you have done
in rebelling against me.
For then I will remove
from among you your jubilant,
arrogant people,
and you will never again be haughty
on my holy mountain.
12 I will leave
a meek and humble people among you,
and they will take refuge in the name
of the LORD.
13 The remnant of Israel will no longer
do wrong or tell lies;
a deceitful tongue will not be found
in their mouths.
They will pasture and lie down,
with nothing to make them afraid.
14 Sing for joy, Daughter Zion;
shout loudly, Israel!
Be glad and celebrate with all
your heart,
Daughter Jerusalem!
15 The LORD has removed
your punishment;
he has turned back your enemy.
The King of Israel, the LORD,
is among you;
you need no longer fear harm.
16 On that day it will be said to Jerusalem:
"Do not fear;
Zion, do not let your hands
grow weak.
17 The LORD your God is among you,
a warrior who saves.
He will rejoice over you
with gladness.
He will be quiet[C] in his love.
He will delight in you with singing."

Eternal Perspective | *God's Forgiveness*

THAT'S NOT GOD'S VOICE

"The LORD has removed your punishment; he has turned back your enemy. The King of Israel, the LORD, is among you; you need no longer fear harm." Zephaniah 3:15

Some people are new believers in Jesus for only thirty minutes before they start hearing "the voice." You've surely heard it yourself. You did something selfish. Privately or publicly—it doesn't matter. And the truth is, you knew better but plowed ahead anyway. As soon as the dust settled, there it was there. That mocking voice. Condescending. Disgusted. Accusatory with an extra helping of scorn: How can God forgive you? You'll never learn. Might as well give up this whole Christian thing. You'll never be good enough.

God's people probably thought the same thing. How could God possibly forgive? One glimpse at their history (going all the way back to before they exited Egypt) shows a people constantly turning away from God,

Here's what you need to understand. That voice you hear is not God's voice. His voice is found here in this passage penned by Zephaniah: "The LORD has removed your punishment." Paul wrote something similar: "There is now no condemnation for those in Christ Jesus" (Rm 8:1).

No condemnation. None whatsoever. The next time you fail, don't spend two seconds listening to the accuser. The moment he starts in on you, quote these true and hope-filled words of that other "Voice" to him. Then tell him to hit the road.

For the next note on *Eternal Perspective*, see Zephaniah 3:17.

[A] **3:9** Lit *with one shoulder* [B] **3:11** = Israel [C] **3:17** LXX, Syr read *He will renew you*

18 I will gather those
who have been driven
from the appointed festivals;
they will be a tribute from you[A]
and a reproach on her.[B]
19 Yes, at that time
I will deal with all who oppress you.
I will save the lame and gather
the outcasts;
I will make those who were disgraced
throughout the earth
receive praise and fame.
20 At that time I will bring you[C] back,
yes, at the time I will gather you.
I will give you fame and praise
among all the peoples
of the earth,
when I restore your fortunes
before your eyes.
The LORD has spoken.

Eternal Perspective | *God's Love*

THE GOD WHO SINGS

"The LORD your God is among you, a warrior who saves. He will rejoice over you with gladness. He will be quiet in his love. He will delight in you with singing." Zephaniah 3:17

Ask ten random people on the street what God is like, and you'll get all kinds of responses. Some, of course, will deny the existence of God. But others will describe an impersonal force, a Creator/King who rules the world in power, a Savior who rescues those in trouble, or a Judge who smites (punishes) wrongdoers. Ask what God's personality is like, and many will choose words like aloof, stern, serious, or angry.

Compare these common ideas to this verse penned by the prophet Zephaniah. And note especially the final sentence, "He will delight in you with singing." Wait—what? Who knew that? This description sounds like a father rocking and comforting his beloved infant in the middle of the night, smiling broadly, eyes full of love, singing lullabies or silly songs.

In your life, have you ever thought of God in such terms—as delighting in you? Or *singing* softly over you in love? What does it do to your heart to contemplate such reality?

For the next note on *Eternal Perspective*, see Haggai 2:9.

[A] **3:18** = Jerusalem [B] **3:18** Hb obscure [C] **3:20** = people of Israel

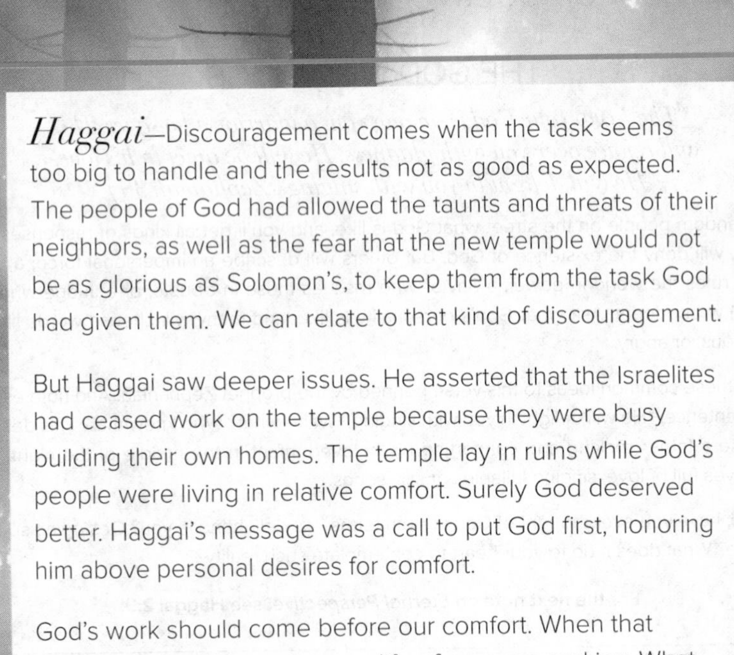

Haggai—Discouragement comes when the task seems too big to handle and the results not as good as expected. The people of God had allowed the taunts and threats of their neighbors, as well as the fear that the new temple would not be as glorious as Solomon's, to keep them from the task God had given them. We can relate to that kind of discouragement.

But Haggai saw deeper issues. He asserted that the Israelites had ceased work on the temple because they were busy building their own homes. The temple lay in ruins while God's people were living in relative comfort. Surely God deserved better. Haggai's message was a call to put God first, honoring him above personal desires for comfort.

God's work should come before our comfort. When that happens, we will experience a life of purpose and joy. What has God called you to do?

HAGGAI

AUTHOR: Not explicitly stated, but the words were spoken to the prophet Haggai

DATE WRITTEN: 520 BC

ORIGINAL AUDIENCE: The Israelites in Jerusalem following the exile

SETTING: King Cyrus of Persia had permitted the Israelites to return to Jerusalem to rebuild the temple (Ezr 1:1-11). Now, nearly twenty years later, the temple still lay in ruins. The people of God had allowed obstacles and threats to cause them to abandon the work.

PURPOSE FOR WRITING: Haggai urged the Israelites to resume the work of rebuilding the temple and to renew their commitment to the covenant.

OUTLINE:

1. Reprimand and Call to Rebuild God's House (1:1-15)
2. Reminder of God's Presence and the Glory of the Temple (2:1-9)
3. Descriptions of Holiness and Uncleanness (2:10-19)
4. Promise of Restoration (2:20-23)

KEY VERSE:

"Even so, be strong, Zerubbabel—this is the LORD's declaration. Be strong, Joshua son of Jehozadak, high priest. Be strong, all you people of the land—this is the LORD's declaration. Work! For I am with you—the declaration of the LORD of Armies."
—Haggai 2:4

RESTORATION THEMES

R	Rest and Reflection	*For the next note, see Zechariah 4:6.*
E	Eternal Perspective	*Forward Look—Haggai 2:9*
S	Support	*For the next note, see Matthew 7:9-11.*
T	Thanksgiving and Contentment	*For the next note, see Malachi 3:7.*
O	Other-centeredness	*For the next note, see Matthew 7:1.*
R	Relationships	*For the next note, see Matthew 18:2,5.*
E	Exercise of Faith	*Making the Most of Time on Earth—Haggai 1:5*

COMMAND TO REBUILD THE TEMPLE

1 In the second year of King Darius,[A] on the
first day of the sixth month, the word of
the LORD came through the prophet Haggai
to Zerubbabel son of Shealtiel, the governor
of Judah, and to Joshua son of Jehozadak, the
high priest:
2 "The LORD of Armies says this: These people say: The time has not come for the house
of the LORD to be rebuilt."
3 The word of the LORD came through the
prophet Haggai: 4 "Is it a time for you yourselves to live in your paneled houses, while
this house[B] lies in ruins?" 5 Now, the LORD
of Armies says this: "Think carefully about[C]
your ways:

6 You have planted much
but harvested little.
You eat
but never have enough to be satisfied.
You drink
but never have enough to be happy.
You put on clothes
but never have enough to get warm.
The wage earner puts his wages
into a bag with a hole in it."

7 The LORD of Armies says this: "Think carefully about your ways. 8 Go up into the hills,
bring down lumber, and build the house; and
I will be pleased with it and be glorified," says
the LORD. 9 "You expected much, but then it
amounted to little. When you brought the harvest to your house, I ruined[D] it. Why?" This is
the declaration of the LORD of Armies. "Because
my house still lies in ruins, while each of you
is busy with his own house.

10 So on your account,[E]
the skies have withheld the dew
and the land its crops.
11 I have summoned a drought
on the fields and the hills,
on the grain, new wine, fresh oil,
and whatever the ground yields,
on man and animal,
and on all that
your hands produce."

THE PEOPLE'S RESPONSE

12 Then Zerubbabel son of Shealtiel, the high
priest Joshua son of Jehozadak, and the entire
remnant of the people obeyed the LORD their
God and the words of the prophet Haggai,

Exercise of Faith | *Making the Most of Time on Earth*

TRAJECTORIES

"Now the LORD of Armies says this: 'Think carefully about your ways.'" Haggai 1:5

This prophecy was meant to motivate the people of Israel to finish the task of rebuilding the temple. Speaking through Haggai, twice the Lord said, "Think carefully about your ways."

In other words, consider the direction of your life. Think long and hard about where you are headed. Here's why: The path you are on leads to a specific place; therefore, if you stay on the path, you will eventually come to that place! If it's a place worth going to, terrific! But if it's *not*, now is the time to pick a better path.

This is simple, but brilliant, wisdom. It gets to the age-old idea that our lives have a certain trajectory. Every person is headed in a certain direction. This is what people mean when they say, if you keep doing what you've been doing, you'll keep getting what you've been getting. It's what Pulitzer Prize-winning author Annie Dillard meant when she said, "How we spend our days is, of course, how we spend our lives."

What's your life trajectory? What way are you headed? Ask yourself: If I keep going the way I'm going for ten more years, will I be where I want to be? If not, what changes should you make?

For the next note on *Exercise of Faith*, see Malachi 3:8,10.

[A] **1:1** King of Persia reigned 522–486 BC [B] **1:4** = the temple [C] **1:5** Lit *Place your heart on*, also in v. 7 [D] **1:9** Lit *blew on* [E] **1:10** Or *So above you*

because the LORD their God had sent him. So
the people feared the LORD.
13 Then Haggai, the LORD's messenger, delivered the LORD's message to the people: "I
am with you — this is the LORD's declaration."
14 The LORD roused the spirit of Zerubbabel
son of Shealtiel, governor of Judah, the spirit
of the high priest Joshua son of Jehozadak,
and the spirit of all the remnant of the people.
They began work on the house of the LORD
of Armies, their God, 15 on the twenty-fourth
day of the sixth month, in the second year of
King Darius.

ENCOURAGEMENT AND PROMISE

2 On the twenty-first day of the seventh
month, the word of the LORD came through
the prophet Haggai: 2 "Speak to Zerubbabel
son of Shealtiel, governor of Judah, to the high
priest Joshua son of Jehozadak, and to the
remnant of the people: 3 'Who is left among
you who saw this house in its former glory?
How does it look to you now? Doesn't it seem
to you like nothing by comparison? 4 Even so,
be strong, Zerubbabel — this is the LORD's
declaration. Be strong, Joshua son of Jehozadak, high priest. Be strong, all you people
of the land — this is the LORD's declaration.
Work! For I am with you — the declaration
of the LORD of Armies. 5 This is the promise
I made to you when you came out of Egypt,
and my Spirit is present among you; don't
be afraid.'"
6 For the LORD of Armies says this: "Once
more, in a little while, I am going to shake the
heavens and the earth, the sea and the dry
land. 7 I will shake all the nations so that the
treasures of all the nations will come, and I
will fill this house with glory," says the LORD
of Armies. 8 "The silver and gold belong to
me" — this is the declaration of the LORD of
Armies. 9 "The final glory of this house[A] will
be greater than the first," says the LORD of
Armies. "I will provide peace in this place"
— this is the declaration of the LORD of Armies.

FROM DEPRIVATION TO BLESSING

10 On the twenty-fourth day of the ninth month,
in the second year of Darius, the word of the
LORD came to the prophet Haggai: 11 "This is
what the LORD of Armies says: Ask the priests
for a ruling. 12 If a man is carrying consecrated
meat in the fold of his garment, and it touches
bread, stew, wine, oil, or any other food, does
it become holy?"
The priests answered, "No."

Eternal Perspective | *Forward Look*

NOSTALGIA IS OVERRATED

"'The final glory of this house will be greater than the first,' says the LORD of Armies. 'I will provide peace in this place' — this is the declaration of the LORD of Armies." Haggai 2:9

Old-timers like to say, "They don't make 'em like they used to." Something in us longs for the good old days. We like to reminisce about how, "back in the day," *everything* was better and cheaper, and life was more wholesome.

In Haggai's day, the temple in Jerusalem was being rebuilt following the exile. Nostalgia was rampant, causing discouragement in the present. Haggai called out some of the older Jews who were fondly remembering the glory of Solomon's temple: "Who is left among you who saw this house in its former glory? How does it look to you now? Doesn't it seem to you like nothing by comparison?" (2:3).

Zerubbabel's efforts might not have been as showy as Solomon's temple, but the Lord went on to say through Haggai that this newer temple would be even more glorious. Why? Because the Messiah would bless it with his presence.

God has, indeed, done amazing work in the past. But let's not fixate there. Amazing things are still to come.

For the next note on *Eternal Perspective*, see Zechariah 12:8.

[A] 2:9 Or *The glory of this latter house*

PLEA FOR REPENTANCE

1 In the eighth month, in the second year of
Darius, the word of the LORD came to the
prophet Zechariah son of Berechiah, son of
Iddo: 2 "The LORD was extremely angry with
your ancestors. 3 So tell the people, 'This is
what the LORD of Armies says: Return to me
— this is the declaration of the LORD of Armies
— and I will return to you, says the LORD of
Armies. 4 Do not be like your ancestors; the
earlier prophets proclaimed to them: This
is what the LORD of Armies says: Turn from
your evil ways and your evil deeds. But they
did not listen or pay attention to me — this
is the LORD's declaration. 5 Where are your
ancestors now? And do the prophets live forever? 6 But didn't my words and my statutes
that I commanded my servants the prophets
overtake your ancestors?'"
So the people repented and said, "As the
LORD of Armies decided to deal with us for our
ways and our deeds, so he has dealt with us."

THE NIGHT VISIONS

7 On the twenty-fourth day of the eleventh
month, which is the month of Shebat, in the
second year of Darius, the word of the LORD
came to the prophet Zechariah son of Berechiah, son of Iddo:

FIRST VISION: HORSEMEN

8 I looked out in the night and saw a man riding
on a chestnut[A] horse. He was standing among
the myrtle trees in the valley.[B] Behind him
were chestnut, brown, and white horses. 9 I
asked, "What are these, my lord?"
The angel who was talking to me replied,
"I will show you what they are."
10 Then the man standing among the myrtle
trees explained, "They are the ones the LORD
has sent to patrol the earth."
11 They reported to the angel of the LORD
standing among the myrtle trees, "We have
patrolled the earth, and right now the whole
earth is calm and quiet."
12 Then the angel of the LORD responded,
"How long, LORD of Armies, will you withhold mercy from Jerusalem and the cities of
Judah that you have been angry with these
seventy years?" 13 The LORD replied with kind
and comforting words to the angel who was
speaking with me.
14 So the angel who was speaking with me
said, "Proclaim: The LORD of Armies says: I am
extremely jealous for Jerusalem and Zion. 15 I
am fiercely angry with the nations that are at
ease, for I was a little angry, but they made the
destruction worse.[C] 16 Therefore, this is what
the LORD says: In mercy, I have returned to
Jerusalem; my house will be rebuilt within it
— this is the declaration of the LORD of Armies
— and a measuring line will be stretched out
over Jerusalem.
17 "Proclaim further: This is what the LORD of
Armies says: My cities will again overflow with
prosperity; the LORD will once more comfort
Zion and again choose Jerusalem."

SECOND VISION: FOUR HORNS AND CRAFTSMEN

18 Then I looked up and saw four horns. 19 So I
asked the angel who was speaking with me,
"What are these?"
And he said to me, "These are the horns
that scattered Judah, Israel, and Jerusalem."
20 Then the LORD showed me four craftsmen. 21 I asked, "What are they coming to do?"
He replied, "These are the horns that scattered Judah so no one could raise his head.
These craftsmen have come to terrify them,
to cut off[D] the horns of the nations that raised
a horn against the land of Judah to scatter it."

THIRD VISION: SURVEYOR

2 I looked up and saw a man with a measuring line in his hand. 2 I asked, "Where
are you going?"
He answered me, "To measure Jerusalem
to determine its width and length."
3 Then the angel who was speaking with
me went out, and another angel went out to
meet him. 4 He said to him, "Run and tell this
young man: Jerusalem will be inhabited without walls because of the number of people and
livestock in it." 5 The declaration of the LORD:
"I myself will be a wall of fire around it, and
I will be the glory within it."
6 "Listen! Listen! Flee from the land of the
north" — this is the LORD's declaration — "for
I have scattered you like the four winds of heav-
en" — this is the LORD's declaration. 7 "Listen,
Zion! Escape, you who are living with Daughter
Babylon." 8 For the LORD of Armies says this:
"In pursuit of his glory, he sent me against the
nations plundering you, for whoever touches

[A] 1:8 Lit *red* [B] 1:8 Lit *depths* [C] 1:15 Lit *they helped for evil* [D] 1:21 Lit *throw down*

you touches the pupil[A] of my[B] eye. 9 For look, I
am raising my hand against them, and they will
become plunder for their own servants. Then you
will know that the LORD of Armies has sent me.
10 "Daughter Zion, shout for joy and be glad,
for I am coming to dwell among you" — this
is the LORD's declaration. 11 "Many nations will
join themselves to the LORD on that day and
become my[C] people. I will dwell among you,
and you will know that the LORD of Armies has
sent me to you. 12 The LORD will take possession
of Judah as his portion in the Holy Land, and
he will once again choose Jerusalem. 13 Let all
people be silent before the LORD, for from his
holy dwelling he has roused himself."

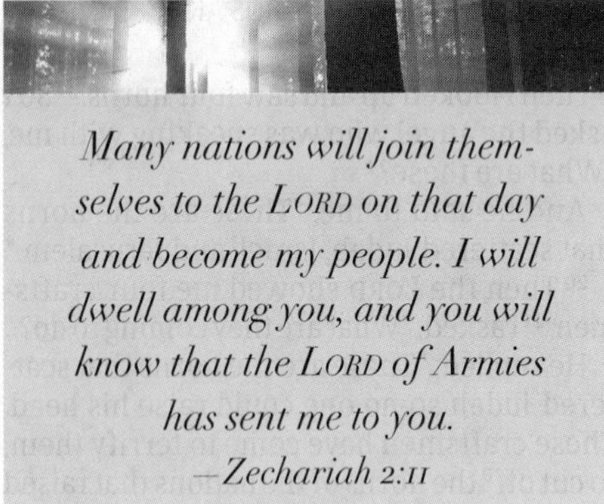
Many nations will join themselves to the LORD on that day and become my people. I will dwell among you, and you will know that the LORD of Armies has sent me to you.
—*Zechariah 2:11*

FOURTH VISION: HIGH PRIEST AND BRANCH

3 Then he showed me the high priest Joshua
standing before the angel of the LORD, with
Satan[D] standing at his right side to accuse him.
2 The LORD[E] said to Satan: "The LORD rebuke
you, Satan! May the LORD who has chosen Jerusalem rebuke you! Isn't this man a burning
stick snatched from the fire?"
3 Now Joshua was dressed with filthy[F]
clothes as he stood before the angel. 4 So the
angel of the LORD[G] spoke to those[H] standing
before him, "Take off his filthy clothes!" Then
he said to him, "See, I have removed your iniquity from you, and I will clothe you with
festive robes."
5 Then I said, "Let them put a clean turban on
his head." So a clean turban was placed on his
head, and they clothed him in garments while
the angel of the LORD was standing nearby.
6 Then the angel of the LORD charged Joshua: 7 "This is what the LORD of Armies says: If
you walk in my ways and keep my mandates,
you will both rule my house and take care of
my courts; I will also grant you access among
these who are standing here.
8 "Listen, High Priest Joshua, you and your
colleagues sitting before you; indeed, these
men are a sign that I am about to bring my
servant, the Branch. 9 Notice the stone I have
set before Joshua; on that one stone are sev-
en eyes. I will engrave an inscription on it"
— this is the declaration of the LORD of Armies — "and I will take away the iniquity of
this land in a single day. 10 On that day, each
of you will invite his neighbor to sit under
his vine and fig tree." This is the declaration
of the LORD of Armies.

FIFTH VISION: GOLD LAMPSTAND

4 The angel who was speaking with me then
returned and roused me as one awakened
out of sleep. 2 He asked me, "What do you see?"
I replied, "I see a solid gold lampstand with a
bowl at the top. The lampstand also has seven
lamps at the top with seven spouts for each
of[I] the lamps. 3 There are also two olive trees
beside it, one on the right of the bowl and the
other on its left."
4 Then I asked the angel who was speaking
with me, "What are these, my lord?"
5 "Don't you know what they are?" replied
the angel who was speaking with me.
I said, "No, my lord."
6 So he answered me, "This is the word of
the LORD to Zerubbabel: 'Not by strength or
by might, but by my Spirit,' says the LORD of
Armies. 7 'What are you, great mountain? Before Zerubbabel you will become a plain. And
he will bring out the capstone accompanied
by shouts of: Grace, grace to it!'"
8 Then the word of the LORD came to me:
9 "Zerubbabel's hands have laid the foundation
of this house, and his hands will complete it.
Then you will know that the LORD of Armies
has sent me to you. 10 For who despises the day
of small things? These seven eyes of the LORD,
which scan throughout the whole earth, will
rejoice when they see the ceremonial stone[J]
in Zerubbabel's hand."
11 I asked him, "What are the two olive trees
on the right and left of the lampstand?" 12 And
I questioned him further, "What are the two
streams[K] of the olive trees, from which the

[A] 2:8 Or *apple* [B] 2:8 Alt Hb tradition; MT reads *his* [C] 2:11 LXX, Syr read *his* [D] 3:1 Or *the accuser* [E] 3:2 Syr reads *The Angel of the LORD* [F] 3:3 Probably stained with human excrement [G] 3:4 Lit *he* [H] 3:4 = the angels [I] 4:2 Or *seven lips to* [J] 4:10 Lit *the tin stone* [K] 4:12 Or *branches*

golden oil is pouring through the two golden
conduits?"
¹³ Then he inquired of me, "Don't you know
what these are?"
"No, my lord," I replied.
¹⁴ "These are the two anointed ones,"[A] he
said, "who stand by the Lord of the whole
earth."

SIXTH VISION: FLYING SCROLL

5 I looked up again and saw a flying scroll.
² "What do you see?" he asked me.
"I see a flying scroll," I replied, "thirty feet[B]
long and fifteen feet[C] wide."
³ Then he said to me, "This is the curse that
is going out over the whole land, for everyone
who is a thief, contrary to what is written on
one side, has gone unpunished,[D] and everyone
who swears falsely, contrary to what is written on the other side, has gone unpunished.
⁴ I will send it out," — this is the declaration
of the LORD of Armies — "and it will enter the
house of the thief and the house of the one
who swears falsely by my name. It will stay
inside his house and destroy it along with its
timbers and stones."

SEVENTH VISION: WOMAN IN THE BASKET

⁵ Then the angel who was speaking with me
came forward and told me, "Look up and see
what this is that is approaching."
⁶ So I asked, "What is it?"
He responded, "It's a measuring basket[E] that
is approaching." And he continued, "This is
their iniquity[F] in all the land." ⁷ Then a lead
cover was lifted, and there was a woman sitting inside the basket. ⁸ "This is Wickedness,"
he said. He shoved her down into the basket
and pushed the lead weight over its opening.
⁹ Then I looked up and saw two women approaching with the wind in their wings. Their
wings were like those of a stork, and they
lifted up the basket between earth and sky.
¹⁰ So I asked the angel who was speaking
with me, "Where are they taking the basket?"
¹¹ "To build a shrine for it in the land of Shinar," he told me. "When that is ready, the basket
will be placed there on its pedestal."

EIGHTH VISION: FOUR CHARIOTS

6 Then I looked up again and saw four chariots coming from between two mountains.
The mountains were made of bronze. ² The

Rest and Reflection | *Surrendering/Submitting to God*

POWER FROM ON HIGH

"So he answered me, 'This is the word of the LORD to Zerubbabel: "Not by strength or by might, but by my Spirit," says the LORD of Armies.'" Zechariah 4:6

Some people are like hummingbirds, whirling dervishes, or that bunny that advertises batteries on TV. They never stop. They have an endless supply of energy. They get more done by nine o'clock in the morning than most people do all day long.

Then we have the rest of us. We often feel worn out and depleted. Some of it is probably physical (age, a bad mattress, a poor diet, a lack of exercise or sleep), but our fatigue can also have spiritual or emotional roots.

Zechariah saw this phenomenon up close and personal. He ministered after the exile when the Jews were back in their land, but life was hard and much work was to be done. The big project to rebuild the temple (under Zerubbabel) began in earnest and with lots of buzz. But then it languished. Here the Lord gave Zechariah a good reminder that physical exertion was not enough. They needed spiritual strength, too.

Where do you need spiritual strength today? Parenting? Taking care of aging parents? Dealing with a difficult person? If you're out of gas, ask God to fill you back up. Rely on his Spirit to make you equal to the task.

For the next note on *Rest and Reflection*, see Matthew 6:10.

[A] **4:14** = Joshua and Zerubbabel [B] **5:2** Lit *20 cubits* [C] **5:2** Lit *10 cubits* [D] **5:3** Or *side, will be removed* [E] **5:6** Lit *It's an ephah* [F] **5:6** One Hb ms, LXX, Syr; other Hb mss read *eye*

first chariot had chestnut[A] horses, the second chariot black horses, 3 the third chariot
white horses, and the fourth chariot dappled
horses — all strong horses. 4 So I inquired of
the angel who was speaking with me, "What
are these, my lord?"
5 The angel told me, "These are the four
spirits[B] of heaven going out after presenting themselves to the Lord of the whole earth.
6 The one with the black horses is going to
the land of the north, the white horses are
going after them, but the dappled horses are
going to the land of the south." 7 As the strong
horses went out, they wanted to go patrol
the earth, and the LORD said, "Go, patrol the
earth." So they patrolled the earth. 8 Then he
summoned me saying, "See, those going to
the land of the north have pacified my Spirit
in the northern land."

CROWNING OF THE BRANCH

9 The word of the LORD came to me: 10 "Take
an offering from the exiles, from Heldai, Tobijah, and Jedaiah, who have arrived from
Babylon, and go that same day to the house
of Josiah son of Zephaniah. 11 Take silver and
gold, make a crown,[C] and place it on the head
of Joshua son of Jehozadak, the high priest.
12 You are to tell him: This is what the LORD
of Armies says: Here is a man whose name
is Branch; he will branch out from his place
and build the LORD's temple. 13 Yes, he will
build the LORD's temple; he will be clothed
in splendor and will sit on his throne and
rule. There will also be a priest on his throne,
and there will be peaceful counsel between
the two of them. 14 The crown will reside in
the LORD's temple as a memorial to Heldai,
Tobijah, Jedaiah, and Hen[D] son of Zephaniah. 15 People who are far off will come and
build the LORD's temple, and you will know
that the LORD of Armies has sent me to you.
This will happen when you fully obey the
LORD your God."

DISOBEDIENCE AND FASTING

7 In the fourth year of King Darius, the word
of the LORD came to Zechariah on the fourth
day of the ninth month, which is Chislev. 2 Now
the people of Bethel had sent Sharezer, Regem-
melech, and their men to plead for the LORD's
favor 3 by asking the priests who were at the
house of the LORD of Armies as well as the

Make fair decisions. Show faithful love and compassion to one another. Do not oppress the widow or the fatherless, the resident alien or the poor, and do not plot evil in your hearts against one another.
—Zechariah 7:9-10

prophets, "Should we mourn and fast in the
fifth month as we have done these many years?"
4 Then the word of the LORD of Armies came
to me: 5 "Ask all the people of the land and
the priests: When you fasted and lamented
in the fifth and in the seventh months for
these seventy years, did you really fast for
me? 6 When you eat and drink, don't you eat
and drink simply for yourselves? 7 Aren't
these the words that the LORD proclaimed
through the earlier prophets when Jerusalem was inhabited and secure,[E] along with
its surrounding cities, and when the southern region and the Judean foothills were
inhabited?"
8 The word of the LORD came to Zechariah:
9 "The LORD of Armies says this: 'Make fair
decisions. Show faithful love and compassion to one another. 10 Do not oppress the
widow or the fatherless, the resident alien or
the poor, and do not plot evil in your hearts
against one another.' 11 But they refused to
pay attention and turned a stubborn shoulder; they closed their ears so they could not
hear. 12 They made their hearts like a rock
so as not to obey the law or the words that
the LORD of Armies had sent by his Spirit
through the earlier prophets. Therefore intense anger came from the LORD of Armies.
13 Just as he had called, and they would not
listen, so when they called, I would not listen,
says the LORD of Armies. 14 I scattered them
with a windstorm over all the nations that
had not known them, and the land was left
desolate behind them, with no one coming
or going. They turned a pleasant land into
a desolation."

[A] 6:2 Lit *red* [B] 6:5 Or *winds* [C] 6:11 Lit *crowns* [D] 6:14 Probably Josiah [E] 7:7 Or *prosperous*

OBEDIENCE AND FEASTING

8 The word of the LORD of Armies came:
2 The LORD of Armies says this: "I am extremely jealous for Zion; I am jealous for her
with great wrath." 3 The LORD says this: "I will
return to Zion and live in Jerusalem. Then
Jerusalem will be called the Faithful City; the
mountain of the LORD of Armies will be called
the Holy Mountain." 4 The LORD of Armies says
this: "Old men and women will again sit along
the streets of Jerusalem, each with a staff in
hand because of advanced age. 5 The streets
of the city will be filled with boys and girls
playing in them." 6 The LORD of Armies says
this: "Though it may seem impossible to the
remnant of this people in those days, should
it also seem impossible to me?" — this is the
declaration of the LORD of Armies. 7 The LORD
of Armies says this: "I will save my people
from the land of the east and the land of the
west.[A] 8 I will bring them back to live in Jerusalem. They will be my people, and I will be
their faithful and righteous God."

9 The LORD of Armies says this: "Let your
hands be strong, you who now hear these
words that the prophets spoke when the foundations were laid for the rebuilding of the
temple, the house of the LORD of Armies. 10 For
prior to those days neither man nor animal had
wages. There was no safety from the enemy
for anyone who came or went, for I turned everyone against his neighbor. 11 But now, I will
not treat the remnant of this people as in the
former days" — this is the declaration of the
LORD of Armies. 12 "For they will sow in peace:
the vine will yield its fruit, the land will yield
its produce, and the skies will yield their dew.
I will give the remnant of this people all these
things as an inheritance. 13 As you have been a
curse among the nations, house of Judah and
house of Israel, so I will save you, and you will
be a blessing. Don't be afraid; let your hands
be strong." 14 For the LORD of Armies says this:
"As I resolved to treat you badly when your

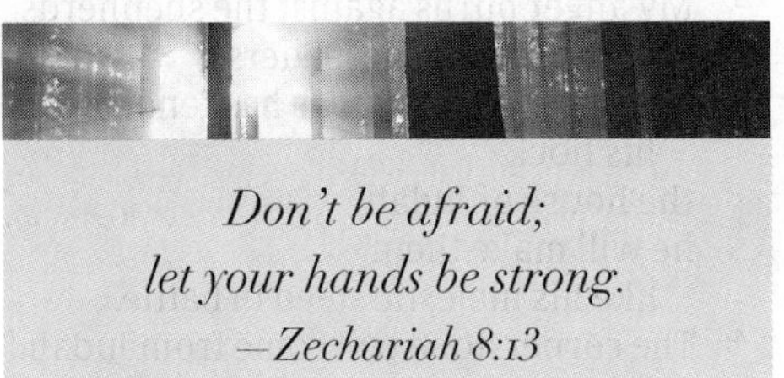
Don't be afraid;
let your hands be strong.
—Zechariah 8:13

fathers provoked me to anger, and I did not
relent," says the LORD of Armies, 15 "so I have
resolved again in these days to do what is
good to Jerusalem and the house of Judah.
Don't be afraid. 16 These are the things you
must do: Speak truth to one another; make
true and sound decisions within your city
gates. 17 Do not plot evil in your hearts against
your neighbor, and do not love perjury, for I
hate all this" — this is the LORD's declaration.

18 Then the word of the LORD of Armies
came to me: 19 The LORD of Armies says this:
"The fast of the fourth month, the fast of the
fifth, the fast of the seventh, and the fast of
the tenth will become times of joy, gladness,
and cheerful festivals for the house of Judah.
Therefore, love truth and peace." 20 The LORD
of Armies says this: "Peoples will yet come,
the residents of many cities; 21 the residents
of one city will go to another, saying: Let's
go at once to plead for the LORD's favor and
to seek the LORD of Armies. I am also going.
22 Many peoples and strong nations will come
to seek the LORD of Armies in Jerusalem and
to plead for the LORD's favor." 23 The LORD of
Armies says this: "In those days, ten men from
nations of every language will grab the robe
of a Jewish man tightly, urging: Let us go with
you, for we have heard that God is with you."

JUDGMENT OF ZION'S ENEMIES

9 A pronouncement:
The word of the LORD
is against the land of Hadrach,
and Damascus is its resting place —
for the eyes of humanity
and all the tribes of Israel
are on the LORD[B] —
2 and also against Hamath,
which borders it,
as well as Tyre and Sidon,
though they are very shrewd.
3 Tyre has built herself a fortress;
she has heaped up silver like dust
and gold like the dirt of the streets.
4 Listen! The Lord will impoverish her
and cast her wealth into the sea;
she herself will be consumed by fire.
5 Ashkelon will see it and be afraid;
Gaza too, and will writhe in great pain,
as will Ekron, for her hope will fail.
There will cease to be a king in Gaza,
and Ashkelon will become uninhabited.

[A] **8:7** Lit *sunset* [B] **9:1** Or *eyes of the LORD are on mankind* —

6 A mongrel people will live in Ashdod,
and I will destroy the pride
of the Philistines.
7 I will remove the blood
from their mouths
and the abhorrent things
from between their teeth.
Then they too will become a remnant
for our God;
they will become like a clan in Judah
and Ekron like the Jebusites.
8 I will encamp at my house as a guard,
against those who march
back and forth,
and no oppressor will march
against them again,
for now I have seen with my own eyes.

THE COMING OF ZION'S KING

9 Rejoice greatly, Daughter Zion!
Shout in triumph,
Daughter Jerusalem!
Look, your King is coming to you;
he is righteous and victorious,[A]
humble and riding on a donkey,
on a colt, the foal of a donkey.
10 I will cut off the chariot from Ephraim
and the horse from Jerusalem.
The bow of war will be removed,
and he will proclaim peace
to the nations.
His dominion will extend from sea
to sea,
from the Euphrates River
to the ends of the earth.
11 As for you,
because of the blood of your covenant,
I will release your prisoners
from the waterless cistern.

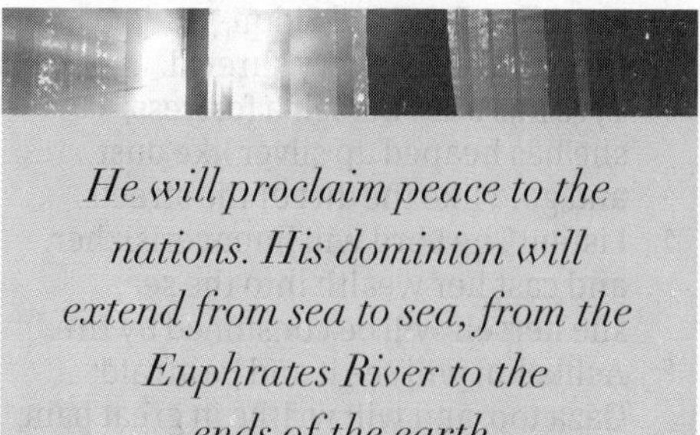

He will proclaim peace to the nations. His dominion will extend from sea to sea, from the Euphrates River to the ends of the earth.
—Zechariah 9:10

12 Return to a stronghold,
you prisoners who have hope;
today I declare that I will restore
double to you.
13 For I will bend Judah as my bow;
I will fill that bow with Ephraim.
I will rouse your sons, Zion,
against your sons, Greece.[B]
I will make you like a warrior's sword.
14 Then the LORD will appear over them,
and his arrow will fly like lightning.
The Lord GOD will sound the trumpet
and advance with the southern storms.
15 The LORD of Armies will defend them.
They will consume and conquer
with slingstones;
they will drink and be rowdy as if
with wine.
They will be as full as
the sprinkling basin,
like those at the corners of the altar.
16 The LORD their God will save them
on that day
as the flock of his people;
for they are like jewels in a crown,
sparkling over his land.
17 How lovely and beautiful!
Grain will make
the young men flourish,
and new wine, the young women.

THE LORD RESTORES HIS PEOPLE

10 Ask the LORD for rain
in the season of spring rain.
The LORD makes the rain clouds,
and he will give them showers of rain
and crops in the field for everyone.
2 For the idols speak falsehood,
and the diviners see illusions;
they relate empty dreams
and offer empty comfort.
Therefore the people wander like sheep;
they suffer affliction because there is
no shepherd.
3 My anger burns against the shepherds,
so I will punish the leaders.[C]
For the LORD of Armies has tended
his flock,
the house of Judah;
he will make them
like his majestic steed in battle.
4 The cornerstone will come from Judah.[D]
The tent peg will come from them

[A] 9:9 Or *and has salvation* [B] 9:13 Lit *Javan* [C] 10:3 Lit *male goats* [D] 10:4 Lit *him*

and also the battle bow and every[A] ruler.
Together [5] they will be like warriors
in battle
trampling down the mud of the streets.
They will fight because the LORD is
with them,
and they will put horsemen to shame.
6 I will strengthen the house of Judah
and deliver the house of Joseph.[B]
I will restore[C] them
because I have compassion on them,
and they will be
as though I had never rejected them.
For I am the LORD their God,
and I will answer them.
7 Ephraim will be like a warrior,
and their hearts will be glad as if
with wine.
Their children will see it and be glad;
their hearts will rejoice in the LORD.

8 I will whistle and gather them
because I have redeemed them;
they will be as numerous as
they once were.
9 Though I sow them among the nations,
they will remember me
in the distant lands;
they and their children will live
and return.
10 I will bring them back from the land
of Egypt
and gather them from Assyria.
I will bring them to the land of Gilead
and to Lebanon,
but it will not be enough for them.
11 The LORD[D] will pass through the sea
of distress
and strike the waves of the sea;
all the depths of the Nile will dry up.
The pride of Assyria will be
brought down,
and the scepter of Egypt will come
to an end.
12 I will strengthen them in the LORD,
and they will march in his name —
this is the LORD's declaration.

ISRAEL'S SHEPHERDS: GOOD AND BAD

11 Open your gates, Lebanon,
and fire will consume your cedars.
2 Wail, cypress, for the cedar has fallen;
the glorious trees are destroyed!
Wail, oaks of Bashan,
for the stately forest has fallen!
3 Listen to the wail
of the shepherds,
for their glory is destroyed.
Listen to the roar of young lions,
for the thickets of the Jordan
are[E] destroyed.

4 The LORD my God says this: "Shepherd the
flock intended for slaughter. 5 Those who buy
them slaughter them but are not punished.
Those who sell them say: Blessed be the LORD
because I have become rich! Even their own
shepherds have no compassion for them.
6 Indeed, I will no longer have compassion
on the inhabitants of the land" — this is the
LORD's declaration. "Instead, I will turn everyone over to his neighbor and his king. They
will devastate the land, and I will not rescue
it from their hand."
7 So I shepherded the flock intended for
slaughter, the oppressed of the flock.[F] I took
two staffs, calling one Favor and the other
Union, and I shepherded the flock. 8 In one
month I got rid of three shepherds. I became
impatient with them, and they also detested
me. 9 Then I said, "I will no longer shepherd
you. Let what is dying die, and let what is perishing perish; let the rest devour each other's
flesh." 10 Next I took my staff called Favor and
cut it in two, annulling the covenant I had
made with all the peoples. 11 It was annulled
on that day, and so the oppressed of the flock[G]
who were watching me knew that it was the
word of the LORD. 12 Then I said to them, "If it
seems right to you, give me my wages; but if
not, keep them." So they weighed my wages,
thirty pieces of silver.
13 "Throw it to the potter,"[H] the LORD said
to me — this magnificent price I was valued
by them. So I took the thirty pieces of silver
and threw it into the house of the LORD, to the
potter.[I] 14 Then I cut in two my second staff,
Union, annulling the brotherhood between
Judah and Israel.
15 The LORD also said to me: "Take the equipment of a foolish shepherd. 16 I am about to
raise up a shepherd in the land who will not
care for those who are perishing, and he will
not seek the lost[J] or heal the broken. He will

[A] **10:4** Lit *also from him the . . . , from him every* [B] **10:6** = the northern kingdom [C] **10:6** Other Hb mss, LXX read *settle*
[D] **10:11** Lit *He* [E] **11:3** Lit *for the majesty of the Jordan is* [F] **11:7** LXX reads *slaughter that belonged to the sheep merchants*
[G] **11:11** LXX reads *and the sheep merchants* [H] **11:13** Syr reads *treasury* [I] **11:13** One Hb ms, Syr read *treasury* [J] **11:16** Or *young*

not sustain the healthy,[A] but he will devour the
flesh of the fat sheep and tear off their hooves.

17 Woe to the worthless shepherd
who deserts the flock!
May a sword strike[B] his arm
and his right eye!
May his arm wither away
and his right eye go completely blind!"

JUDAH'S SECURITY

12 A pronouncement:
The word of the LORD
concerning Israel.
A declaration of the LORD,
who stretched out the heavens,
laid the foundation of the earth,
and formed the spirit of man within him.

2 "Look, I will make Jerusalem a cup that
causes staggering for the peoples who surround the city. The siege against Jerusalem will
also involve Judah. 3 On that day I will make
Jerusalem a heavy stone for all the peoples;
all who try to lift it will injure themselves severely when all the nations of the earth gather
against her. 4 On that day" — this is the LORD's
declaration — "I will strike every horse with
panic and its rider with madness. I will keep a
watchful eye on the house of Judah but strike
all the horses of the nations with blindness.
5 Then each of the leaders of Judah will think
to himself: The residents of Jerusalem are my
strength through the LORD of Armies, their
God. 6 On that day I will make the leaders of
Judah like a firepot in a woodpile, like a flaming
torch among sheaves; they will consume all the
peoples around them on the right and the left,
while Jerusalem continues to be inhabited on
its site, in Jerusalem. 7 The LORD will save the
tents of Judah first, so that the glory of David's
house and the glory of Jerusalem's residents
may not be greater than that of Judah. 8 On
that day the LORD will defend the inhabitants
of Jerusalem, so that on that day the one who
is weakest among them will be like David on
that day, and the house of David will be like
God, like the angel of the LORD, before them.
9 On that day I will set out to destroy all the
nations that come against Jerusalem.

MOURNING FOR THE PIERCED ONE

10 "Then I will pour out a spirit[C] of grace and
prayer on the house of David and the residents
of Jerusalem, and they will look at[D] me whom

Eternal Perspective | *God's Goodness*

ON THAT DAY

"On that day the LORD will defend the inhabitants of Jerusalem, so that on that day the one who is weakest among them will be like David on that day." Zechariah 12:8

Most people are waiting and wondering—and no doubt, worrying—about future events and possible outcomes: What will the lab results say? What will happen to my child? Where are we going to get that money? What if we *don't* get that money? What if . . . ?

Fretting over the future is human nature. Which is why Zechariah 12–14 is such a good passage for us. In these chapters, the ancient Jewish prophet was seeing and describing Israel's future, and eighteen times he used the phrase "on that day."

At first glance, this may not seem like a powerful phrase, but what it signifies is breathtaking. Our God not only sees and knows the future, he controls everything that will take place. If we accept that our God is powerful and Sovereign over all things, then it follows that nothing can happen apart from his will. And everything is always subject to his good heart.

Are you waiting and wondering—and perhaps worrying—today about something yet in the future? Zechariah would say "on *this* day" go ahead and skip the worrying part.

For the next note on *Eternal Perspective,* see Malachi 3:6.

[A] **11:16** Or *exhausted* [B] **11:17** Lit *be against* [C] **12:10** Or *out the Spirit* [D] **12:10** Or *to*

they pierced. They will mourn for him as one
mourns for an only child and weep bitterly for
him as one weeps for a firstborn. 11 On that day
the mourning in Jerusalem will be as great as
the mourning of Hadad-rimmon in the plain of
Megiddo. 12 The land will mourn, every family
by itself: the family of David's house by itself
and their women by themselves; the family
of Nathan's[A] house by itself and their women
by themselves; 13 the family of Levi's house
by itself and their women by themselves; the
family of Shimei[B] by itself and their women by
themselves; 14 all the remaining families, every
family by itself, and their women by themselves.

GOD'S PEOPLE CLEANSED

13 "On that day a fountain will be opened for
the house of David and for the residents
of Jerusalem, to wash away sin and impurity.
2 On that day" — this is the declaration of the
LORD of Armies — "I will remove the names of
the idols from the land, and they will no longer
be remembered. I will banish the prophets[C]
and the unclean spirit from the land. 3 If a man
still prophesies, his father and his mother who
bore him will say to him: You cannot remain
alive because you have spoken a lie in the name
of the LORD. When he prophesies, his father
and his mother who bore him will pierce him
through. 4 On that day every prophet will be
ashamed of his vision when he prophesies;
they will not put on a hairy cloak in order
to deceive. 5 He will say: I am not a prophet;
I work the land, for a man purchased[D] me as
a servant since my youth. 6 If someone asks
him: What are these wounds on your chest?[E]
— then he will answer: I received the wounds
in the house of my friends.

7 Sword, awake against my shepherd,
against the man who is my associate —
this is the declaration of the LORD
of Armies.
Strike the shepherd, and the sheep
will be scattered;
I will turn my hand
against the little ones.
8 In the whole land —
this is the LORD's declaration —
two-thirds[F] will be cut off and die,
but a third will be left in it.
9 I will put this third through the fire;
I will refine them as silver is refined
and test them as gold is tested.
They will call on my name,
and I will answer them.
I will say: They are my people,
and they will say: The LORD is our God."

THE LORD'S TRIUMPH AND REIGN

14 Look, a day belonging to the LORD is
coming when the plunder taken from
you will be divided in your presence. 2 I will
gather all the nations against Jerusalem for
battle. The city will be captured, the houses
looted, and the women raped. Half the city
will go into exile, but the rest of the people
will not be removed from the city.
3 Then the LORD will go out to fight against
those nations as he fights on a day of battle.
4 On that day his feet will stand on the Mount
of Olives, which faces Jerusalem on the east.
The Mount of Olives will be split in half from
east to west, forming a huge valley, so that half
the mountain will move to the north and half
to the south. 5 You will flee by my mountain
valley,[G] for the valley of the mountains will
extend to Azal. You will flee as you fled[H] from
the earthquake in the days of King Uzziah of
Judah. Then the LORD my God will come and
all the holy ones with him.[I]
6 On that day there will be no light; the sunlight and moonlight will diminish.[J,K] 7 It will be
a unique day known only to the LORD, without
day or night, but there will be light at evening.
8 On that day living water will flow out from
Jerusalem, half of it toward the eastern sea[L]
and the other half toward the western sea,[M]
in summer and winter alike. 9 On that day
the LORD will become King over the whole
earth — the LORD alone, and his name alone.
10 All the land from Geba to Rimmon south
of Jerusalem will be changed into a plain.
But Jerusalem will be raised up and will remain[N] on its site from the Benjamin Gate
to the place of the First Gate,[O] to the Corner Gate, and from the Tower of Hananel
to the royal winepresses. 11 People will live
there, and never again will there be a curse
of complete destruction. So Jerusalem will
dwell in security.

[A] **12:12** = a son of David [B] **12:13** = a descendant of Levi [C] **13:2** = false prophets [D] **13:5** Or *sold* [E] **13:6** Lit *wounds between your hands* [F] **13:8** Lit *two-thirds in it* [G] **14:5** Some Hb mss, LXX, Sym, Tg read *The valley of my mountains will be blocked* [H] **14:5** LXX reads *It will be blocked as it was blocked* [I] **14:5** Some Hb mss, LXX, Vg, Tg, Syr; other Hb mss read *you* [J] **14:6** LXX, Sym, Syr, Tg, Vg read *no light or cold or ice* [K] **14:6** Lit *no light; the precious ones will congeal* [L] **14:8** = the Dead Sea [M] **14:8** = the Mediterranean Sea [N] **14:10** Or *will be inhabited* [O] **14:10** Or *the former gate*

12 This will be the plague with which the
LORD strikes all the people who have warred
against Jerusalem: their flesh will rot while
they stand on their feet, their eyes will rot
in their sockets, and their tongues will rot
in their mouths. 13 On that day a great panic
from the LORD will be among them, so that
each will seize the hand of another, and the
hand of one will rise against the other. 14 Judah
will also fight at Jerusalem, and the wealth of
all the surrounding nations will be collected:
gold, silver, and clothing in great abundance.
15 The same plague as the previous one will
strike[A] the horses, mules, camels, donkeys,
and all the animals that are in those camps.
16 Then all the survivors from the nations
that came against Jerusalem will go up year
after year to worship the King, the LORD of Armies, and to celebrate the Festival of Shelters.
17 Should any of the families of the earth not go
up to Jerusalem to worship the King, the LORD
of Armies, rain will not fall on them. 18 And if
the people[B] of Egypt will not go up and enter,
then rain will not fall on them; this will be the
plague the LORD inflicts on the nations who do
not go up to celebrate the Festival of Shelters.
19 This will be the punishment of Egypt and all
the nations that do not go up to celebrate the
Festival of Shelters.
20 On that day, the words HOLY TO THE LORD
will be on the bells of the horses. The pots in
the house of the LORD will be like the sprinkling basins before the altar. 21 Every pot in
Jerusalem and in Judah will be holy to the
LORD of Armies. All who sacrifice will come
and use the pots to cook in. And on that day
there will no longer be a Canaanite[C] in the
house of the LORD of Armies.

[A] **14:15** Lit *be on* [B] **14:18** Lit *family* [C] **14:21** Or *merchant*

RESTORATION THEMES

R	Rest and Reflection	*For the next note, see Matthew 6:10.*
E	Eternal Perspective	*God Never Changing—Malachi 3:6*
S	Support	*For the next note, see Matthew 7:9-11.*
T	Thanksgiving and Contentment	*Repentance—Malachi 3:7*
O	Other-centeredness	*For the next note, see Matthew 7:1.*
R	Relationships	*For the next note, see Matthew 18:2,5.*
E	Exercise of Faith	*Tithing—Malachi 3:8,10*

THE LORD'S LOVE FOR ISRAEL

1 A pronouncement:
The word of the LORD to Israel through
Malachi.[A]
2 "I have loved you," says the LORD.
Yet you ask, "How have you loved us?"
"Wasn't Esau Jacob's brother?" This is the
LORD's declaration. "Even so, I loved Jacob,
3 but I hated Esau. I turned his mountains into
a wasteland, and gave his inheritance to the
desert jackals."
4 Though Edom says: "We have been devastated, but we will rebuild[B] the ruins," the
LORD of Armies says this: "They may build,
but I will demolish. They will be called a
wicked country and the people the LORD
has cursed[C] forever. 5 Your own eyes will see
this, and you yourselves will say, 'The LORD
is great, even beyond[D] the borders of Israel.'

DISOBEDIENCE OF THE PRIESTS

6 "A son honors his father, and a servant his
master. But if I am a father, where is my hon-
or? And if I am a master, where is your fear of
me? says the LORD of Armies to you priests,
who despise my name."
Yet you ask: "How have we despised your
name?"
7 "By presenting defiled food on my altar."
"How have we defiled you?" you ask.
When you say: "The LORD's table is contemptible."
8 "When you present a blind animal for sacrifice, is it not wrong? And when you present
a lame or sick animal, is it not wrong? Bring it
to your governor! Would he be pleased with
you or show you favor?" asks the LORD of Armies. 9 "And now plead for God's favor. Will he
be gracious to us? Since this has come from
your hands, will he show any of you favor?"
asks the LORD of Armies. 10 "I wish one of you
would shut the temple doors, so that you would
no longer kindle a useless fire on my altar! I
am not pleased with you," says the LORD of
Armies, "and I will accept no offering from
your hands.
11 "My name will be great among the nations, from the rising of the sun to its setting.
Incense[E] and pure offerings will be presented
in my name in every place because my name
will be great among the nations,"[F] says the
LORD of Armies.

Eternal Perspective | *God Never Changing*

OUR UNCHANGING GOD

"Because I, the LORD, have not changed, you descendants of Jacob have not been destroyed." Malachi 3:6

Think about how often life is stressful and uncertain because the people in our lives are all over the map. They're moody, inconsistent, and unpredictable. Daily we shake our heads at how others vacillate, flip-flop, or reinvent themselves. Every person is guilty of this: We routinely lose interest and change opinions or direction.

At best, all this change keeps us on our toes; at worst, it keeps us up at night! Thankfully, Malachi's prophecy contains a divine truth that can restore our peace of mind: *the Lord doesn't change*. He "is the same yesterday, today, and forever" (Heb 13:8). Theologians refer to this divine quality as *immutability*.

Practically speaking, immutability means we don't have to worry about divine mood swings. No need to walk on eggshells when you pray or hold your breath when you attend worship. God's love isn't contingent on your behavior. His memory doesn't fade, nor does his strength ebb and flow. Life includes all sorts of changing people and evolving situations. But the Author of life is unchanging.

Spend some time thanking God for being eternally steady.

For the next note on *Eternal Perspective*, see Matthew 6:33.

[A] **1:1** = My Messenger [B] **1:4** Or *will return and build* [C] **1:4** Or *LORD is angry with* [D] **1:5** Or *great over* [E] **1:11** Or *Burnt offerings* [F] **1:11** Or *is great . . . are presented . . . is great*

12 “But you are profaning it when you say: ‘The
Lord’s table is defiled, and its product, its food,
is contemptible.’ 13 You also say: ‘Look, what a
nuisance!’ And you scorn[A] it,”[B] says the LORD
of Armies. “You bring stolen,[C] lame, or sick
animals. You bring this as an offering! Am I to
accept that from your hands?” asks the LORD.
14 “The deceiver is cursed who has an acceptable male in his flock and makes a vow but
sacrifices a defective animal to the Lord. For I
am a great King,” says the LORD of Armies, “and
my name will be feared among the nations.

WARNING TO THE PRIESTS

2 “Therefore, this decree is for you priests:
2 If you don’t listen, and if you don’t take
it to heart to honor my name,” says the LORD
of Armies, “I will send a curse among you,
and I will curse your blessings. In fact, I have
already begun to curse them because you are
not taking it to heart.
3 “Look, I am going to rebuke your descendants, and I will spread animal waste[D] over
your faces, the waste from your festival sacrifices, and you will be taken away with it. 4 Then
you will know that I sent you this decree, so
that my covenant with Levi may continue,”
says the LORD of Armies. 5 “My covenant with
him was one of life and peace, and I gave
these to him; it called for reverence, and he
revered me and stood in awe of my name.
6 True instruction was in his mouth, and nothing wrong was found on his lips. He walked
with me in peace and integrity and turned
many from iniquity. 7 For the lips of a priest
should guard knowledge, and people should
desire instruction from his mouth, because
he is the messenger of the LORD of Armies.
8 “You, on the other hand, have turned from
the way. You have caused many to stumble
by your instruction. You have violated[E] the
covenant of Levi,” says the LORD of Armies.
9 “So I in turn have made you despised and
humiliated before all the people because you
are not keeping my ways but are showing
partiality in your instruction.”

JUDAH’S MARITAL UNFAITHFULNESS

10 Don’t all of us have one Father? Didn’t one God
create us? Why then do we act treacherously

Thanksgiving and Contentment | *Repentance*

BEING DEFENSIVE

“‘Since the days of your fathers, you have turned from my statutes; you have not kept them. Return to me, and I will return to you,’ says the LORD of Armies. Yet you ask, ‘How can we return?’” Malachi 3:7

When confronted, people often rely on a few standard defense mechanisms: mock confusion (“What exactly do you mean?”); feigned shock or outrage (“How could you even think such a thing!”); denial/dismissal (“You have it all wrong!”); attempts to minimize (“It’s not a big deal”); rationalization (“Everybody does it!”). If none of these works, we resort to other tricks, including playing the victim card, blame-shifting, or even counter-attacking.

This was the case when God, through the prophet Malachi, confronted the Israelites who were living back in the promised land after the exile. After the excitement of building a new temple and repairing Jerusalem’s walls had faded, the people once again slipped into apathy and spiritual hard-heartedness. With each pointed question of the Lord (see 1:2,6-7; 2:17; 3:7-8,13), the people pretended to be befuddled. “We don’t understand. How so? What are you suggesting?” It was all a sly ploy to avoid doing what they needed to do.

Why are defense mechanisms so counterproductive to those who want to be healthy? Of all the defense mechanisms listed here, to which ones do you find yourself resorting when confronted? Instead, be honest with yourself and God, admit your wrong attitude or action, and do what you know is right.

For the next note on *Thanksgiving and Contentment*, see Matthew 5:8.

[A] 1:13 Lit *blow at* [B] 1:13 Alt Hb tradition reads *me* [C] 1:13 Or *injured* [D] 2:3 Dung or entrails [E] 2:8 Lit *corrupted*

against one another, profaning the covenant of
our fathers? 11 Judah has acted treacherously,
and a detestable act has been done in Israel
and in Jerusalem. For Judah has profaned
the LORD's sanctuary,[A] which he loves, and
has married the daughter of a foreign god.[B]
12 May the LORD cut off from the tents of Jacob
the man who does this, whoever he may be,[C]
even if he presents an offering to the LORD
of Armies.

13 This is another thing you do. You are covering the LORD's altar with tears, with weeping
and groaning, because he no longer respects
your offerings or receives them gladly from
your hands.

14 And you ask, "Why?" Because even though
the LORD has been a witness between you and
the wife of your youth, you have acted treacherously against her. She was your marriage
partner and your wife by covenant. 15 Didn't
God make them one and give them a portion
of spirit? What is the one seeking?[C] Godly offspring. So watch yourselves carefully,[D] so that
no one acts treacherously against the wife
of his[E] youth.

16 "If he hates and divorces his wife," says
the LORD God of Israel, "he[F] covers his garment with injustice," says the LORD of Armies.
Therefore, watch yourselves carefully,[G] and
do not act treacherously.

JUDGMENT AT THE LORD'S COMING

17 You have wearied the LORD with your
words.

Yet you ask, "How have we wearied him?"

When you say, "Everyone who does what
is evil is good in the LORD's sight, and he is
delighted with them, or else where is the God
of justice?"

3 "See, I am going to send my messenger,
and he will clear the way before me. Then
the Lord you seek will suddenly come to his
temple, the Messenger of the covenant you
delight in — see, he is coming," says the LORD
of Armies. 2 But who can endure the day of
his coming? And who will be able to stand

Exercise of Faith | *Tithing*

CONDUIT

"'Will a man rob God? Yet you are robbing me!' 'How do we rob you?' you ask. 'By not making the payments of the tenth and the contributions. . . . Bring the full tenth into the storehouse so that there may be food in my house. Test me in this way,' says the LORD of Armies. 'See if I will not open the floodgates of heaven and pour out a blessing for you without measure.'" Malachi 3:8,10

When the issue is money, the options are three: spend it, save/invest it, or give it away.

We have the spending part down, so much so, that collectively we have spent trillions of dollars we haven't even earned yet! We're not so consistent when it comes to saving and giving. The latest statistics say the average person gives away only around 2 to 3 percent of her income.

This isn't a new problem. In Malachi's day, the Israelites were failing to give the tithe (10 percent of one's earnings) prescribed by the law of Moses.

They had a trust issue—just as we do. Those mired in scarcity thinking ("This is all I have, and I might not get more; therefore, I have to keep what I've got for me and mine") become hoarders. They give reluctantly and sparingly, if at all. Those who trust ("God is good, and his supplies are infinite!") become conduits of his generosity. They learn to share the joy of sharing in God's work and others' needs.

Determine to be a conduit, not a hoarder.

For the next note on *Exercise of Faith*, see Matthew 7:7.

[A] **2:11** Or *profaned what is holy to the LORD* [B] **2:11** = a woman who worshiped a foreign god [C] **2:12,15** Hb obscure [D] **2:15** Lit *So guard yourselves in your spirit* [E] **2:15** Lit *your* [F] **2:16** Or *The LORD God of Israel says that he hates divorce and the one who* [G] **2:16** Lit *Therefore, guard yourselves in your spirit*

when he appears? For he will be like a refiner's fire and like launderer's bleach.[A] 3 He
will be like a refiner and purifier of silver;
he will purify the sons of Levi and refine
them like gold and silver. Then they will present offerings to the LORD in righteousness.
4 And the offerings of Judah and Jerusalem
will please the LORD as in days of old and
years gone by.
5 "I will come to you in judgment, and I will
be ready to witness against sorcerers and
adulterers; against those who swear falsely;
against those who oppress the hired worker,
the widow, and the fatherless; and against
those who deny justice to the resident alien.
They do not fear me," says the LORD of Armies. 6 "Because I, the LORD, have not changed,
you descendants of Jacob have not been destroyed.[B]

ROBBING GOD

7 "Since the days of your fathers, you have
turned from my statutes; you have not kept
them. Return to me, and I will return to you,"
says the LORD of Armies.
Yet you ask, "How can we return?"
8 "Will a man rob God? Yet you are robbing
me!"
"How do we rob you?" you ask.
"By not making the payments of the tenth
and the contributions. 9 You are suffering
under a curse, yet[C] you — the whole nation
— are still robbing me. 10 Bring the full tenth
into the storehouse so that there may be food
in my house. Test me in this way," says the
LORD of Armies. "See if I will not open the
floodgates of heaven and pour out a blessing
for you without measure. 11 I will rebuke the
devourer[D] for you, so that it will not ruin the
produce of your land and your vine in your
field will not fail to produce fruit," says the
LORD of Armies. 12 "Then all the nations will
consider you fortunate, for you will be a delightful land," says the LORD of Armies.

THE RIGHTEOUS AND THE WICKED

13 "Your words against me are harsh," says
the LORD.
Yet you ask, "What have we spoken against
you?"
14 You have said: "It is useless to serve God.
What have we gained by keeping his requirements and walking mournfully before the
LORD of Armies? 15 So now we consider the
arrogant to be fortunate. Not only do those
who commit wickedness prosper, they even
test God and escape."
16 At that time those who feared the LORD
spoke to one another. The LORD took notice
and listened. So a book of remembrance was
written before him for those who feared
the LORD and had high regard for his name.
17 "They will be mine," says the LORD of Armies, "my own possession on the day I am
preparing. I will have compassion on them
as a man has compassion on his son who
serves him. 18 So you will again see the difference between the righteous and the wicked,
between one who serves God and one who
does not serve him.

THE DAY OF THE LORD

4 "For look, the day is coming, burning
like a furnace, when all the arrogant
and everyone who commits wickedness will
become stubble. The coming day will consume them," says the LORD of Armies, "not
leaving them root or branches. 2 But for you
who fear my name, the sun of righteousness
will rise with healing in its wings, and you
will go out and playfully jump like calves
from the stall.[E] 3 You will trample the wicked, for they will be ashes under the soles of
your feet on the day I am preparing," says
the LORD of Armies.

A FINAL WARNING

4 "Remember the instruction of Moses my
servant, the statutes and ordinances I commanded him at Horeb for all Israel. 5 Look, I am
going to send you the prophet Elijah before
the great and terrible day of the LORD comes.
6 And he will turn the hearts of fathers to their
children and the hearts of children to their
fathers. Otherwise, I will come and strike the
land[F] with a curse."

[A] **3:2** Lit *cleansing agent* [B] **3:6** Or *Because I, the LORD, do not change, you descendants of Jacob are not destroyed* [C] **3:9** Or *because* [D] **3:11** Perhaps locusts [E] **4:2** Or *like stall-fed calves* [F] **4:6** Or *earth*

The New Testament

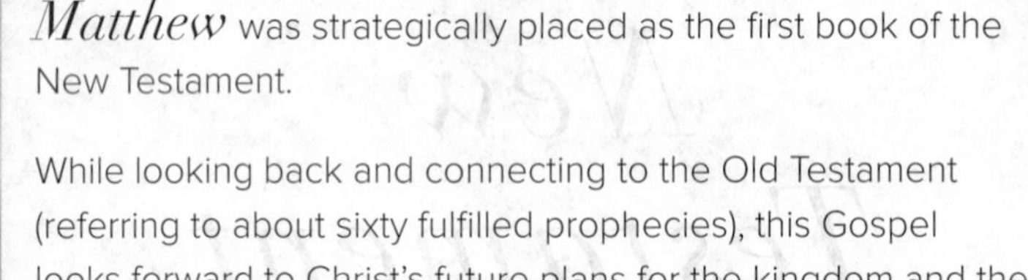

Matthew was strategically placed as the first book of the New Testament.

While looking back and connecting to the Old Testament (referring to about sixty fulfilled prophecies), this Gospel looks forward to Christ's future plans for the kingdom and the spread of the gospel throughout the earth.

Matthew, therefore, is an essential link between the Old and New Testaments. Without this book, neither Testament can be fully understood.

Matthew's Gospel tells the story of Jesus, from genealogy to Great Commission, and reveals his profound promises of soul restoration for all who follow him: outcasts, marginalized, deformed, hurting, tax collectors . . . and you.

MATTHEW

AUTHOR: Matthew (Levi), a Jewish tax collector and one of Jesus's original twelve disciples

DATE WRITTEN: Around AD 60–65

ORIGINAL AUDIENCE: Greek-speaking Jews who believed in Jesus as the Messiah.

SETTING: Probably written from Antioch (in Syria) because many of the original disciples had migrated there (Ac 11:19-27).

None of the Gospels refer to any specific incident or occasion that motivated Matthew to write his account of Jesus's life.

PURPOSE FOR WRITING: To prove that Jesus was and is the promised Messiah-King (sacrificial Son of Abraham and sovereign Son of David).

Until the conversion of Cornelius (Ac 10) and Paul's missionary journeys (Ac 13–28), nearly all the earlier followers of Jesus were Jews. These new believers needed to be reassured that Jesus had fulfilled all the Old Testament prophecies and was, in fact, the Messiah. This book gave those believers confirmation and helped them refute those who would say otherwise. Note: the events recorded do not appear in exact chronological order but were arranged to bolster Matthew's purpose.

We know little about Matthew—background, family, friends—except he was a tax collector who became a disciple of Jesus, he hosted a dinner to introduce Jesus to his friends, and he wrote this book to tell the story of Jesus.

Matthew probably enjoyed prosperity and privilege, but Jews who collected taxes for the Romans were despised and reviled by their countrymen. So what might Matthew have been feeling when he met Jesus? Again, we don't know. But we know what Jesus said to him and how he responded: "[Jesus] saw a man named Matthew sitting at the toll booth, and he said to him, 'Follow me,' and he got up and followed him" (9:9). Two words spoken with compassion and authority: "Follow me." Matthew heard something in that simple command—hope, love, healing, purpose, divine calling—and he "got up and followed." Matthew's life was transformed.

Jesus continues to walk by and speak. Imagine him coming by your place of work or your home, looking you in the eye, and simply stating, "Follow me." How would you respond?

OUTLINE:

1. Jesus's Ancestry, Birth, and Preparation (1:1–2:23)
2. Jesus's Public Ministry (3:1–4:25)
3. Jesus's Teaching about the Kingdom of God (5:1–7:29)
4. Jesus's Miraculous Works (8:1–10:42)
5. Jesus's Rejection by the Jews (11:1–25:46)
6. Jesus's Death, Glorious Resurrection, and Commissioning of His Followers (26:1–28:20)

KEY VERSE:

"Come to me, all of you who are weary and burdened, and I will give you rest."
–Matthew 11:28

RESTORATION THEMES

R	Rest and Reflection	*Surrendering/Submitting to God—6:10* *Not Worrying—6:34* *Resting in Christ—11:28* *Being Alone with God—14:13*
E	Eternal Perspective	*God's Plans—6:33* *Personal Value/Worth—10:29-31* *God's Power—19:25-26* *Stewardship—25:21*
S	Support	*Prayer—7:9-11* *Humility/Pride Overcome—18:4*
T	Thanksgiving and Contentment	*Purity—5:8*
O	Other-centeredness	*Not Being Judgmental—7:1* *Being Compassionate—9:35-36* *Helping People in Need—25:40*
R	Relationships	*Relating to Children—18:2,5* *Relating to Spouse—19:4-6* *Loving Our Neighbors—22:39-40*
E	Exercise of Faith	*Praying—7:7* *Sharing the Gospel—10:32* *Making Right Choices—16:25-26* *Serving—20:28* *Working with Missions—28:18-20*

THE GENEALOGY OF JESUS CHRIST

1 An account of the genealogy of Jesus Christ, the Son of David, the Son of Abraham:

FROM ABRAHAM TO DAVID

2 Abraham fathered[A] Isaac,
Isaac fathered Jacob,
Jacob fathered Judah and his brothers,
3 Judah fathered Perez and Zerah by Tamar,
Perez fathered Hezron,
Hezron fathered Aram,
4 Aram fathered Amminadab,
Amminadab fathered Nahshon,
Nahshon fathered Salmon,
5 Salmon fathered Boaz by Rahab,
Boaz fathered Obed by Ruth,
Obed fathered Jesse,
6 and Jesse fathered King David.

FROM DAVID TO THE BABYLONIAN EXILE

David fathered Solomon[B] by Uriah's wife,
7 Solomon fathered Rehoboam,
Rehoboam fathered Abijah,
Abijah fathered Asa,[C]
8 Asa[C] fathered Jehoshaphat,
Jehoshaphat fathered Joram,[D]
Joram fathered Uzziah,
9 Uzziah fathered Jotham,
Jotham fathered Ahaz,
Ahaz fathered Hezekiah,
10 Hezekiah fathered Manasseh,
Manasseh fathered Amon,[E]
Amon fathered Josiah,
11 and Josiah fathered Jeconiah
and his brothers
at the time of the exile to Babylon.

FROM THE EXILE TO THE CHRIST

12 After the exile to Babylon
Jeconiah fathered Shealtiel,
Shealtiel fathered Zerubbabel,
13 Zerubbabel fathered Abiud,
Abiud fathered Eliakim,
Eliakim fathered Azor,
14 Azor fathered Zadok,
Zadok fathered Achim,
Achim fathered Eliud,
15 Eliud fathered Eleazar,
Eleazar fathered Matthan,
Matthan fathered Jacob,
16 and Jacob fathered Joseph the husband
of Mary,
who gave birth to Jesus who is called
the Christ.

17 So all the generations from Abraham to
David were fourteen generations; and from
David until the exile to Babylon, fourteen generations; and from the exile to Babylon until
the Christ, fourteen generations.

THE NATIVITY OF THE CHRIST

18 The birth of Jesus Christ came about this
way: After his mother Mary had been engaged[F] to Joseph, it was discovered before
they came together that she was pregnant
from the Holy Spirit. 19 So her husband Joseph, being a righteous man, and not wanting
to disgrace her publicly, decided to divorce
her secretly.
20 But after he had considered these things,
an angel of the Lord appeared to him in a
dream, saying, "Joseph, son of David, don't
be afraid to take Mary as your wife, because
what has been conceived in her is from the
Holy Spirit. 21 She will give birth to a son, and
you are to name him Jesus, because he will
save his people from their sins."
22 Now all this took place to fulfill what was
spoken by the Lord through the prophet:
23 **See, the virgin will become pregnant**
and give birth to a son,
and they will name him Immanuel,[G]
which is translated "God is with us."
24 When Joseph woke up, he did as the Lord's
angel had commanded him. He married her
25 but did not have sexual relations with her
until she gave birth to a son.[H] And he named
him Jesus.

WISE MEN VISIT THE KING

2 After Jesus was born in Bethlehem of Judea in the days of King Herod, wise men
from the east arrived in Jerusalem, 2 saying,
"Where is he who has been born king of the
Jews? For we saw his star at its rising and
have come to worship him."[I]
3 When King Herod heard this, he was deeply
disturbed, and all Jerusalem with him. 4 So he
assembled all the chief priests and scribes of
the people and asked them where the Christ
would be born.
5 "In Bethlehem of Judea," they told him, "because this is what was written by the prophet:

[A] **1:2** In vv. 2-16 either a son, as here, or a later descendant, as in v. 8 [B] **1:6** Other mss add *King* [C] **1:7,8** Other mss read *Asaph*
[D] **1:8** = Jehoram [E] **1:10** Other mss read *Amos* [F] **1:18** Or *betrothed* [G] **1:23** Is 7:14 [H] **1:25** Other mss read *to her firstborn son*
[I] **2:2** Or *to pay him homage*

6 **And you, Bethlehem, in the land**
of Judah,
are by no means least
among the rulers of Judah:
Because out of you will come a ruler
who will shepherd my people
Israel."[A]

7 Then Herod secretly summoned the wise
men and asked them the exact time the star
appeared. 8 He sent them to Bethlehem and
said, "Go and search carefully for the child.
When you find him, report back to me so that
I too can go and worship him."[B]
9 After hearing the king, they went on their
way. And there it was — the star they had
seen at its rising. It led them until it came and
stopped above the place where the child was.
10 When they saw the star, they were overwhelmed with joy. 11 Entering the house, they
saw the child with Mary his mother, and falling to their knees, they worshiped him.[C] Then
they opened their treasures and presented
him with gifts: gold, frankincense, and myrrh.
12 And being warned in a dream not to go back
to Herod, they returned to their own country
by another route.

THE FLIGHT INTO EGYPT

13 After they were gone, an angel of the Lord
appeared to Joseph in a dream, saying, "Get
up! Take the child and his mother, flee to
Egypt, and stay there until I tell you. For Herod
is about to search for the child to kill him."
14 So he got up, took the child and his mother during the night, and escaped to Egypt.
15 He stayed there until Herod's death, so that
what was spoken by the Lord through the
prophet might be fulfilled: **Out of Egypt I
called my Son.**[D]

THE MASSACRE OF THE INNOCENTS

16 Then Herod, when he realized that he had
been outwitted by the wise men, flew into a
rage. He gave orders to massacre all the boys
in and around Bethlehem who were two years
old and under, in keeping with the time he
had learned from the wise men. 17 Then what
was spoken through Jeremiah the prophet
was fulfilled:

18 **A voice was heard in Ramah,**
weeping,[E] **and great mourning,**
Rachel weeping for her children;
and she refused to be consoled,
because they are no more.[F]

THE RETURN TO NAZARETH

19 After Herod died, an angel of the Lord appeared in a dream to Joseph in Egypt, 20 saying,
"Get up, take the child and his mother, and go to
the land of Israel, because those who intended
to kill the child are dead." 21 So he got up, took
the child and his mother, and entered the land of
Israel. 22 But when he heard that Archelaus was
ruling over Judea in place of his father Herod,
he was afraid to go there. And being warned in
a dream, he withdrew to the region of Galilee.
23 Then he went and settled in a town called
Nazareth to fulfill what was spoken through the
prophets, that he would be called a Nazarene.

THE HERALD OF THE CHRIST

3 In those days John the Baptist came,
preaching in the wilderness of Judea 2 and
saying, "Repent, because the kingdom of heav-
en has come near!" 3 For he is the one spoken
of through the prophet Isaiah, who said:

A voice of one crying out
in the wilderness:
Prepare the way for the Lord;
make his paths straight![G]

4 Now John had a camel-hair garment with
a leather belt around his waist, and his food
was locusts and wild honey. 5 Then people
from Jerusalem, all Judea, and all the vicinity of the Jordan were going out to him, 6 and
they were baptized by him in the Jordan River,
confessing their sins.

7 When he saw many of the Pharisees and
Sadducees coming to his baptism, he said
to them, "Brood of vipers! Who warned you
to flee from the coming wrath? 8 Therefore
produce fruit consistent with[H] repentance.
9 And don't presume to say to yourselves, 'We
have Abraham as our father.' For I tell you that
God is able to raise up children for Abraham
from these stones. 10 The ax is already at the
root of the trees. Therefore, every tree that
doesn't produce good fruit will be cut down
and thrown into the fire.

11 "I baptize you with[I] water for repentance,
but the one who is coming after me is more
powerful than I. I am not worthy to remove[J] his
sandals. He himself will baptize you with the
Holy Spirit and fire. 12 His winnowing shovel

[A] 2:6 Mc 5:2 [B] 2:8 Or *and pay him homage* [C] 2:11 Or *they paid him homage* [D] 2:15 Hs 11:1 [E] 2:18 Other mss read *Ramah, lamentation, and weeping,* [F] 2:18 Jr 31:15 [G] 3:3 Is 40:3 [H] 3:8 Lit *fruit worthy of* [I] 3:11 Or *in* [J] 3:11 Or *to carry*

John the Baptist | Restoration Profile

MATTHEW 3:1-17; 11:1-15; 14:1-12; MARK 1:2-11;
6:14-29; LUKE 1:5-25,39-80; 7:18-35; 9:7-9

After telling about Jesus's unique background and birth, Matthew introduced John the Baptist into his Gospel full-grown and thundering repentance. Mark actually began his Gospel with John the Baptist's ministry as the messenger of the Messiah. Luke took the time to tell us about John's miraculous birth to aged parents and his eagerness, even in the womb, to announce the coming Savior. The purpose of John's life also set him on a collision course with religious and political powers unwilling to accept his announcement.

Luke summarized John's adolescence in a phrase: "The child grew up and became spiritually strong, and he was in the wilderness until the day of his public appearance to Israel" (Lk 1:80). Few of us understand God's call on our lives as John did, and yet he shared the same need for restoration and assurance we all have. Two moments of uncertainty stand out in his life: Jesus's baptism and his own arrest. Jesus's request for baptism jolted John's worldview. Why would the Lamb of God submit to a symbol of repentance unless he who was sinless was identifying with sinners he came to save? And from prison John wondered why Jesus wasn't fulfilling the expected political role that had been shaped for the Messiah? Jesus's word of restoration to John pointed the baptizer to think again about what God's Word really said about the Savior (Mt 11:4-6). The Messiah John had announced was doing exactly what God had promised.

The heart of restoration is found in God's Son and God's Word. Discouragement and doubt dissipate if we continue to seek first the life God has given us. Sometimes we have to be reminded to get back on track.

is in his hand, and he will clear his threshing floor and gather his wheat into the barn. But the chaff he will burn with fire that never goes out."

THE BAPTISM OF JESUS

13 Then Jesus came from Galilee to John at the
Jordan, to be baptized by him. 14 But John tried
to stop him, saying, "I need to be baptized by you, and yet you come to me?"
15 Jesus answered him, "Allow it for now, because this is the way for us to fulfill all righteousness." Then John allowed him to be baptized.
16 When Jesus was baptized, he went up immediately from the water. The heavens suddenly opened for him,[A] and he saw the Spirit of God descending like a dove and coming down on him.
17 And a voice from heaven said: "This is my beloved Son, with whom I am well-pleased."

THE TEMPTATION OF JESUS

4 Then Jesus was led up by the Spirit into the wilderness to be tempted by the devil.
2 After he had fasted forty days and forty nights, he was hungry.
3 Then the tempter approached him and said, "If you are the Son of God, tell these stones to become bread."
4 He answered, "It is written: **Man must not live on bread alone but on every word that comes from the mouth of God.**"[B]
5 Then the devil took him to the holy city, had him stand on the pinnacle of the temple,
6 and said to him, "If you are the Son of God, throw yourself down. For it is written:

He will give his angels orders
concerning you,
and they will support you
with their hands
so that you will not strike
your foot against a stone."[C]

7 Jesus told him, "It is also written: **Do not test the Lord your God.**"[D]
8 Again, the devil took him to a very high mountain and showed him all the kingdoms of the world and their splendor.
9 And he said to him, "I will give you all these things if you will fall down and worship me."[E]
10 Then Jesus told him, "Go away,[F] Satan! For

[A] **3:16** Other mss omit *for him* [B] **4:4** Dt 8:3 [C] **4:6** Ps 91:11-12 [D] **4:7** Dt 6:16 [E] **4:9** Or *and pay me homage* [F] **4:10** Other mss read *"Get behind me*

it is written: **Worship the Lord your God, and**
serve only him."[A]
11 Then the devil left him, and angels came
and began to serve him.

MINISTRY IN GALILEE

12 When he heard that John had been arrested,
he withdrew into Galilee. 13 He left Nazareth
and went to live in Capernaum by the sea, in
the region of Zebulun and Naphtali. 14 This was
to fulfill what was spoken through the prophet Isaiah:

15 **Land of Zebulun and land of Naphtali,**
along the road by the sea,
beyond the Jordan,
Galilee of the Gentiles.
16 **The people who live in darkness**
have seen a great light,
and for those living in the land of the
shadow of death,
a light has dawned.[B,C]

17 From then on Jesus began to preach, "Repent, because the kingdom of heaven has
come near."

THE FIRST DISCIPLES

18 As he was walking along the Sea of Galilee, he
saw two brothers, Simon (who is called Peter),
and his brother Andrew. They were casting a
net into the sea — for they were fishermen.
19 "Follow me," he told them, "and I will make
you fish for[D] people." 20 Immediately they left
their nets and followed him.
21 Going on from there, he saw two other
brothers, James the son of Zebedee, and his
brother John. They were in a boat with Zebedee their father, preparing their nets, and he
called them. 22 Immediately they left the boat
and their father and followed him.

TEACHING, PREACHING, AND HEALING

23 Now Jesus began to go all over Galilee, teaching
in their synagogues, preaching the good news
of the kingdom, and healing every[E] disease and
sickness[F] among the people. 24 Then the news
about him spread throughout Syria. So they
brought to him all those who were afflicted,
those suffering from various diseases and intense pains, the demon-possessed, the epileptics,
and the paralytics. And he healed them. 25 Large
crowds followed him from Galilee, the Decapolis, Jerusalem, Judea, and beyond the Jordan.

THE SERMON ON THE MOUNT

5 When he saw the crowds, he went up on
the mountain, and after he sat down, his
disciples came to him. 2 Then[G] he began to
teach them, saying:

THE BEATITUDES

3 "Blessed are the poor in spirit,
for the kingdom of heaven is theirs.
4 Blessed are those who mourn,
for they will be comforted.
5 Blessed are the humble,
for they will inherit the earth.
6 Blessed are those who hunger and
thirst for righteousness,
for they will be filled.
7 Blessed are the merciful,
for they will be shown mercy.
8 Blessed are the pure in heart,
for they will see God.
9 Blessed are the peacemakers,
for they will be called sons of God.
10 Blessed are those who are persecuted
because of righteousness,
for the kingdom of heaven is theirs.

11 "You are blessed when they insult you and
persecute you and falsely say every kind of
evil against you because of me. 12 Be glad and
rejoice, because your reward is great in heaven.
For that is how they persecuted the prophets
who were before you.

BELIEVERS ARE SALT AND LIGHT

13 "You are the salt of the earth. But if the salt
should lose its taste, how can it be made salty?[H]
It's no longer good for anything but to be
thrown out and trampled under people's feet.
14 "You are the light of the world. A city situat-
ed on a hill cannot be hidden. 15 No one lights a
lamp and puts it under a basket, but rather on a
lampstand, and it gives light for all who are in
the house. 16 In the same way, let your light shine
before others, so that they may see your good
works and give glory to your Father in heaven.

CHRIST FULFILLS THE LAW

17 "Don't think that I came to abolish the Law
or the Prophets. I did not come to abolish but
to fulfill. 18 For truly I tell you, until heaven
and earth pass away, not the smallest letter[I]

[A] **4:10** Dt 6:13 [B] **4:16** Lit *dawned on them* [C] **4:15-16** Is 9:1-2 [D] **4:19** Or *you fishers of* [E] **4:23** Or *every kind of* [F] **4:23** Or *physical ailment* [G] **5:2** Lit *Then opening his mouth* [H] **5:13** Or *how can the earth be salted?* [I] **5:18** Or *not one iota* ; *iota* is the smallest letter of the Gk alphabet.

or one stroke of a letter will pass away from
the law until all things are accomplished.
19 Therefore, whoever breaks one of the least
of these commands and teaches others to do
the same will be called least in the kingdom of
heaven. But whoever does and teaches these
commands will be called great in the kingdom of heaven. 20 For I tell you, unless your
righteousness surpasses that of the scribes
and Pharisees, you will never get into the
kingdom of heaven.

MURDER BEGINS IN THE HEART

21 "You have heard that it was said to our ancestors, **Do not murder**,[A] and whoever murders
will be subject to judgment. 22 But I tell you,
everyone who is angry with his brother or
sister[B] will be subject to judgment. Whoever
insults[C] his brother or sister, will be subject
to the court.[D] Whoever says, 'You fool!' will
be subject to hellfire.[E] 23 So if you are offering
your gift on the altar, and there you remember that your brother or sister has something
against you, 24 leave your gift there in front of
the altar. First go and be reconciled with your
brother or sister, and then come and offer
your gift. 25 Reach a settlement quickly with
your adversary while you're on the way with
him to the court, or your adversary will hand
you over to the judge, and the judge to[F] the
officer, and you will be thrown into prison.
26 Truly I tell you, you will never get out of there
until you have paid the last penny.[G]

ADULTERY BEGINS IN THE HEART

27 "You have heard that it was said, **Do not
commit adultery.**[H] 28 But I tell you, everyone
who looks at a woman lustfully has already
committed adultery with her in his heart. 29 If
your right eye causes you to sin, gouge it out
and throw it away. For it is better that you lose
one of the parts of your body than for your
whole body to be thrown into hell. 30 And if
your right hand causes you to sin, cut it off
and throw it away. For it is better that you lose
one of the parts of your body than for your
whole body to go into hell.

DIVORCE PRACTICES CENSURED

31 "It was also said, **Whoever divorces his
wife must give her a written notice of divorce.**[I] 32 But I tell you, everyone who divorces his wife, except in a case of sexual
immorality, causes her to commit adultery.
And whoever marries a divorced woman
commits adultery.

Thanksgiving and Contentment | *Purity*

CLEAN!

"Blessed are the pure in heart, for they will see God." Matthew 5:8

Anyone who has ever been really dirty or sweaty knows how fantastic a hot shower or bath feels. Few things are as wonderful as getting and being clean.

In the same way, everyone who has ever wallowed in moral or spiritual guilt knows how amazing it is to be cleansed from sin. When we come humbly to God, admitting our need for his grace and trusting in his no-strings-attached provision of forgiveness through Jesus, the chilly storm clouds of shame and remorse lift and fade. All that's left is the warm sunshine of God's amazing grace. Only in Christ, and only because of his sacrifice, are we able to find such acceptance. Those who put their trust in Jesus become "God's chosen ones, holy and dearly loved" (Col 3:12).

This is salvation! This is the spiritual bath Jesus referred to in John 13:10. In God's eyes, this makes us "clean." Following that, as we walk with God, we confess our frequent shortcomings and failures, not in order to earn God's favor, but so that we might fully experience the spiritual blessings of intimacy with him.

For the next note on *Thanksgiving and Contentment*, see Luke 12:34.

[A] **5:21** Ex 20:13; Dt 5:17 [B] **5:22** Other mss add *without a cause* [C] **5:22** Lit *Whoever says 'Raca'*; an Aramaic term of abuse that puts someone down, insulting one's intelligence [D] **5:22** Lit *Sanhedrin* [E] **5:22** Lit *the gehenna of fire* [F] **5:25** Other mss read *judge will hand you over to* [G] **5:26** Lit *quadrans*, the smallest and least valuable Roman coin, worth 1/64 of a daily wage [H] **5:27** Ex 20:14; Dt 5:18 [I] **5:31** Dt 24:1

TELL THE TRUTH

33 "Again, you have heard that it was said to our
ancestors, **You must not break your oath,
but you must keep your oaths to the Lord.**[A]
34 But I tell you, don't take an oath at all: either
by heaven, because it is God's throne; 35 or by
the earth, because it is his footstool; or by Jerusalem, because it is the city of the great King.
36 Do not swear by your head, because you cannot make a single hair white or black. 37 But let
your 'yes' mean 'yes,' and your 'no' mean 'no.'
Anything more than this is from the evil one.

GO THE SECOND MILE

38 "You have heard that it was said, **An eye for
an eye and a tooth for a tooth.**[B] 39 But I tell
you, don't resist[C] an evildoer. On the contrary, if
anyone slaps you on your right cheek, turn the
other to him also. 40 As for the one who wants
to sue you and take away your shirt, let him
have your coat as well. 41 And if anyone forces
you to go one mile, go with him two. 42 Give
to the one who asks you, and don't turn away
from the one who wants to borrow from you.

LOVE YOUR ENEMIES

43 "You have heard that it was said, **Love your
neighbor**[D] and hate your enemy. 44 But I tell
you, love your enemies[E] and pray for those
who[F] persecute you, 45 so that you may be[G]
children of your Father in heaven. For he
causes his sun to rise on the evil and the
good, and sends rain on the righteous and
the unrighteous. 46 For if you love those who
love you, what reward will you have? Don't
even the tax collectors do the same? 47 And
if you greet only your brothers and sisters,
what are you doing out of the ordinary?[H]
Don't even the Gentiles[I] do the same? 48 Be
perfect, therefore, as your heavenly Father
is perfect.

HOW TO GIVE

6 "Be careful not to practice your righteousness[J] in front of others to be seen
by them. Otherwise, you have no reward
with your Father in heaven. 2 So whenever
you give to the poor, don't sound a trumpet
before you, as the hypocrites do in the synagogues and on the streets, to be applauded
by people. Truly I tell you, they have their
reward. 3 But when you give to the poor, don't
let your left hand know what your right hand
is doing, 4 so that your giving may be in secret. And your Father who sees in secret
will reward you.[K]

Rest and Reflection | *Surrendering/Submitting to God*

WHOSE KINGDOM?

"Your kingdom come. Your will be done." Matthew 6:10

The famous "Lord's Prayer" isn't a spiritual incantation that Christians are called to repeat mindlessly. It's a model for God-honoring prayer. First and foremost, we approach God trusting that he is our good and perfect "Father in heaven." Next, we align all our requests with the goal that his "name be honored." This results in prayers that enhance God's reputation, that both celebrate and further his glory and not our own. Healthy followers of Jesus lay aside self-centered ambitions. They submit "my will" and "my agenda" to God's eternal plan. They remember that God has veto power over their prayers today because of better plans tomorrow. And they cling to the biblical claim that he knows and pursues what is best.

The first humans got in trouble by disregarding God's will. We find rescue and peace when we stop trying to run the universe, and when we daily bow to the Lord. Is it difficult to continually crown Jesus King over every facet of our lives? Yes. But we must trust his heart.

For the next note on *Rest and Reflection*, see Matthew 6:34.

[A] **5:33** Lv 19:12; Nm 30:2; Dt 23:21 [B] **5:38** Ex 21:24; Lv 24:20; Dt 19:21 [C] **5:39** Or *don't set yourself against*, or *don't retaliate against* [D] **5:43** Lv 19:18 [E] **5:44** Other mss add *bless those who curse you, do good to those who hate you,* [F] **5:44** Other mss add *mistreat you and* [G] **5:45** Or *may become*, or *may show yourselves to be* [H] **5:47** Or *doing that is superior*; lit *doing more* [I] **5:47** Other mss read *tax collectors* [J] **6:1** Other mss read *charitable giving* [K] **6:4** Other mss read *will himself reward you openly*

HOW TO PRAY

5 "Whenever you pray, you must not be like
the hypocrites, because they love to pray
standing in the synagogues and on the street
corners to be seen by people. Truly I tell you,
they have their reward. 6 But when you pray,
go into your private room, shut your door,
and pray to your Father who is in secret. And
your Father who sees in secret will reward
you.[A] 7 When you pray, don't babble like the
Gentiles, since they imagine they'll be heard
for their many words. 8 Don't be like them,
because your Father knows the things you
need before you ask him.

THE LORD'S PRAYER

9 "Therefore, you should pray like this:
Our Father in heaven,
your name be honored as holy.
10 Your kingdom come.
Your will be done
on earth as it is in heaven.
11 Give us today our daily bread.[B]
12 And forgive us our debts,
as we also have forgiven our debtors.
13 And do not bring us
into[C] temptation,
but deliver us from the evil one.[D]

14 "For if you forgive others their offenses,
your heavenly Father will forgive you as well.
15 But if you don't forgive others,[E] your Father
will not forgive your offenses.

HOW TO FAST

16 "Whenever you fast, don't be gloomy like
the hypocrites. For they make their faces un-
attractive[F] so that their fasting is obvious to
people. Truly I tell you, they have their reward.
17 But when you fast, put oil on your head and
wash your face, 18 so that your fasting isn't
obvious to others but to your Father who is
in secret. And your Father who sees in secret
will reward you.[A]

GOD AND POSSESSIONS

19 "Don't store up for yourselves treasures[G]
on earth, where moth and rust destroy and
where thieves break in and steal. 20 But
store up for yourselves treasures in heav-
en, where neither moth nor rust destroys,
and where thieves don't break in and steal.
21 For where your treasure is, there your heart
will be also.
22 "The eye is the lamp of the body. If your
eye is healthy, your whole body will be full
of light. 23 But if your eye is bad, your whole

E Eternal Perspective | *God's Plans*

ETERNAL MATTERS

"But seek first the kingdom of God and his righteousness, and all these things will be provided for you." Matthew 6:33

The way of Jesus is consistently counterintuitive: Lead by serving. Lose your life in order to find your life.

And, of course, we have this enigmatic verse: Your basic needs will be met as you forget all about your needs and focus intensely on serving in God's kingdom.

How do we find the faith to pull this off? Jesus suggests the key is to focus on the character of God. He is—in the words of the popular praise chorus—"a good, good Father"—meaning we can concentrate on carrying out his plans and purposes because we can trust him to take care of the details of our lives. Or, as the Bible promises in another place, "And my God will supply all your needs according to his riches in glory in Christ Jesus" (Php 4:19).

When we trust that our God will tend to our temporal needs—and we don't have to scramble and fret to do so—we are freed up to focus on eternal matters. And that is freedom indeed!

For the next note on *Eternal Perspective*, see Matthew 10:29-31.

[A] **6:6,18** Other mss add *openly* [B] **6:11** Or *our necessary bread*, or *our bread for tomorrow* [C] **6:13** Or *do not cause us to come into* [D] **6:13** Or *from evil*; some later mss add *For yours is the kingdom and the power and the glory forever. Amen.* [E] **6:15** Other mss add *their wrongdoing* [F] **6:16** Or *unrecognizable*, or *disfigured* [G] **6:19** Or *valuables*

body will be full of darkness. So if the light within you is darkness, how deep is that darkness!

24 "No one can serve two masters, since either he will hate one and love the other, or he will be devoted to one and despise the other. You cannot serve both God and money.

THE CURE FOR ANXIETY

25 "Therefore I tell you: Don't worry about your life, what you will eat or what you will drink; or about your body, what you will wear. Isn't life more than food and the body more than clothing? 26 Consider the birds of the sky: They don't sow or reap or gather into barns, yet your heavenly Father feeds them. Aren't you worth more than they? 27 Can any of you add one moment to his life span[A] by worrying? 28 And why do you worry about clothes? Observe how the wildflowers of the field grow: They don't labor or spin thread. 29 Yet I tell you that not even Solomon in all his splendor was adorned like one of these. 30 If that's how God clothes the grass of the field, which is here today and thrown into the furnace tomorrow, won't he do much more for you—you of little faith? 31 So don't worry, saying, 'What will we eat?' or 'What will we drink?' or 'What will we wear?' 32 For the Gentiles eagerly seek all these things, and your heavenly Father knows that you need them. 33 But seek first the kingdom of God[B] and his righteousness, and all these things will be provided for you. 34 Therefore don't worry about tomorrow, because tomorrow will worry about itself. Each day has enough trouble of its own.

DO NOT JUDGE

7 "Do not judge, so that you won't be judged. 2 For you will be judged by the same standard with which you judge others, and you will be measured by the same measure you use. 3 Why do you look at the splinter in your brother's eye but don't notice the beam of wood in your own eye? 4 Or how can you say to your brother, 'Let me take the splinter out of your eye,' and look, there's a beam of wood in your own eye? 5 Hypocrite! First take the beam of wood out of your eye, and then you will see clearly to take the splinter out of your brother's eye. 6 Don't give what is holy to dogs or toss your pearls before pigs, or they will trample them under their feet, turn, and tear you to pieces.

ASK, SEARCH, KNOCK

7 "Ask, and it will be given to you. Seek, and you will find. Knock, and the door[C] will be opened to you. 8 For everyone who asks receives, and the one who seeks finds, and to the one who knocks, the door will be opened. 9 Who among

Rest and Reflection | *Not Worrying*

THE WASTE OF WORRY

"Therefore don't worry about tomorrow, because tomorrow will worry about itself. Each day has enough trouble of its own." Matthew 6:34

Someone has quipped that "95 percent of all Christians admit to struggles with worry—and obviously, the other 5 percent struggle with lying." Worry is a real and pervasive problem. If we're not anxious over friends or family members, we're fretting about money or politics or health issues.

Jesus talked extensively about worry. He noted our human tendency to peer into the future and fear the worst. That's all worry is: the mental habit of making negative assumptions about things to come. This habit is not only silly (only God knows the future), it's detrimental. As Jesus pointed out (Mt 6:27), worrying doesn't add anything to our lives (except stress). Worrying doesn't help tomorrow, but it ruins today.

Memorize three or four Bible promises. Then ask the Spirit of God to help you cultivate a new mental discipline: Each time your heart begins racing over potential dire outcomes, substitute solid reminders of what *is* for those vague (and probably groundless) fears of what *might* be.

For the next note on *Rest and Reflection*, see Matthew 11:28.

[A] **6:27** Or *add a single cubit to his height* [B] **6:33** Other mss omit *of God* [C] **7:7** Lit *and it*

you, if his son asks him for bread, will give
him a stone? 10 Or if he asks for a fish, will give
him a snake? 11 If you then, who are evil, know
how to give good gifts to your children, how
much more will your Father in heaven give
good things to those who ask him. 12 Therefore, whatever you want others to do for you,
do also the same for them, for this is the Law
and the Prophets.

ENTERING THE KINGDOM

13 "Enter through the narrow gate. For the gate
is wide and the road broad that leads to destruction, and there are many who go through
it. 14 How narrow is the gate and difficult the
road that leads to life, and few find it.
15 "Be on your guard against false prophets who come to you in sheep's clothing but
inwardly are ravaging wolves. 16 You'll recognize them by their fruit. Are grapes gathered
from thornbushes or figs from thistles? 17 In
the same way, every good tree produces good
fruit, but a bad tree produces bad fruit. 18 A
good tree can't produce bad fruit; neither can
a bad tree produce good fruit. 19 Every tree
that doesn't produce good fruit is cut down
and thrown into the fire. 20 So you'll recognize
them by their fruit.
21 "Not everyone who says to me, 'Lord, Lord,'
will enter the kingdom of heaven, but only the
one who does the will of my Father in heav-
en. 22 On that day many will say to me, 'Lord,
Lord, didn't we prophesy in your name, drive
out demons in your name, and do many miracles in your name?' 23 Then I will announce
to them, 'I never knew you. **Depart from me,
you lawbreakers!**'[A,B]

THE TWO FOUNDATIONS

24 "Therefore, everyone who hears these words
of mine and acts on them will be like a wise
man who built his house on the rock. 25 The
rain fell, the rivers rose, and the winds blew
and pounded that house. Yet it didn't collapse,
because its foundation was on the rock. 26 But
everyone who hears these words of mine and
doesn't act on them will be like a foolish man
who built his house on the sand. 27 The rain fell,
the rivers rose, the winds blew and pounded
that house, and it collapsed. It collapsed with
a great crash."
28 When Jesus had finished saying these
things, the crowds were astonished at his
teaching, 29 because he was teaching them
like one who had authority, and not like their
scribes.

Other-centeredness | *Not Being Judgmental*

CRITICAL REVIEW

"Do not judge, so that you won't be judged." Matthew 7:1

This famous statement by Jesus—perhaps the one and only Bible verse that unbelievers love to quote—doesn't mean that we are never to form opinions, have convictions, make distinctions between right and wrong, or conclude that certain things are foolish or evil.

Like many of Jesus's remarks in the Sermon on the Mount, this statement called to mind Israel's proud, condescending religious leaders who liked to trumpet their religious résumés and who were experts in criticizing and condemning others.

Don't be like them, Jesus was saying. Instead of obsessing over what others are doing (or not doing), focus on your own relationship with God. Forget the splinter in your brother's eye. Focus instead on "the beam of wood in your own eye" (Mt 7:3). The apostle Paul attacked this ugly tendency to judge with a question, "Who are you to judge another's household servant? Before his own Lord he stands or falls" (Rm 14:4).

Since guarding our own hearts and lives is a full-time job (Pr 4:23), we can resign our posts as self-appointed moral policeman. Ask God to give you the grace to live this day without judging others.

For the next note on *Other-centeredness*, see Matthew 9:35-36.

[A] **7:23** Lit *you who work lawlessness* [B] **7:23** Ps 6:8

A MAN CLEANSED

8 When he came down from the mountain,
large crowds followed him. 2 Right away a
man with leprosy[A] came up and knelt before
him, saying, "Lord, if you are willing, you can
make me clean."
3 Reaching out his hand, Jesus touched him,
saying, "I am willing; be made clean." Immediately his leprosy was cleansed. 4 Then Jesus told
him, "See that you don't tell anyone; but go, show
yourself to the priest, and offer the gift that
Moses commanded, as a testimony to them."

A CENTURION'S FAITH

5 When he entered Capernaum, a centurion
came to him, pleading with him, 6 "Lord, my
servant is lying at home paralyzed, in terrible agony."
7 He said to him, "Am I to come and heal him?"[B]
8 "Lord," the centurion replied, "I am not worthy to have you come under my roof. But just
say the word, and my servant will be healed.
9 For I too am a man under authority, having
soldiers under my command.[C] I say to this
one, 'Go,' and he goes; and to another, 'Come,'
and he comes; and to my servant, 'Do this!'
and he does it."
10 Hearing this, Jesus was amazed and said
to those following him, "Truly I tell you, I have
not found anyone in Israel with so great a faith.
11 I tell you that many will come from east and
west to share the banquet[D] with Abraham,
Isaac, and Jacob in the kingdom of heaven.
12 But the sons of the kingdom will be thrown
into the outer darkness where there will be
weeping and gnashing of teeth." 13 Then Jesus
told the centurion, "Go. As you have believed,
let it be done for you." And his servant was
healed that very moment.[E]

HEALINGS AT CAPERNAUM

14 Jesus went into Peter's house and saw his
mother-in-law lying in bed with a fever. 15 So he
touched her hand, and the fever left her. Then
she got up and began to serve him. 16 When
evening came, they brought to him many who
were demon-possessed. He drove out the spirits with a word and healed all who were sick,
17 so that what was spoken through the prophet
Isaiah might be fulfilled:

> **He himself took our weaknesses**
> **and carried our diseases.**[F]

THE COST OF FOLLOWING JESUS

18 When Jesus saw a large crowd[G] around him,
he gave the order to go to the other side of
the sea. 19 A scribe approached him and said,
"Teacher, I will follow you wherever you go."

Exercise of Faith | *Praying*

DRAWING NEAR TO GOD

"Ask, and it will be given to you. Seek, and you will find. Knock, and the door will be opened to you." Matthew 7:7

In the famous "Sermon on the Mount," Jesus taught extensively on the subject of prayer. After giving a rough outline for the kind of praying that pleases God (Mt 6:9-13), Jesus here encouraged prayer that is persistent. "Ask," "seek," and "knock" are present tense commands. They can be translated, "Keep on asking, seeking, and knocking." In other words, pray continuously.

This is important because prayer, when stripped to its essence, is the most basic expression of faith. In prayer, we draw near to God, believing "that he exists and that he rewards those who seek him" (Heb 11:6). In prayer, we attempt to connect with the Almighty. It's an expression of need, desire, longing. If we pray only to get blessings from God, we will often be frustrated. But when we see prayer as a way of simply being *with* God, we can never be disappointed.

What if you viewed prayer less as a grocery list for God and more as a way to both experience the love of God and express love for God?

For the next note on *Exercise of Faith*, see Matthew 10:32.

[A] **8:2** Gk *lepros*; a term for various skin diseases, also in v. 3; see Lv 13–14 [B] **8:7** Or *"I will come and heal him."* [C] **8:9** Lit *under me* [D] **8:11** Lit *recline at the table* [E] **8:13** Or *that hour*; lit *very hour* [F] **8:17** Is 53:4 [G] **8:18** Other mss read *saw large crowds*

20 Jesus told him, "Foxes have dens, and birds
of the sky have nests, but the Son of Man has
no place to lay his head."
21 "Lord," another of his disciples said, "first
let me go bury my father."
22 But Jesus told him, "Follow me, and let
the dead bury their own dead."

WIND AND WAVES OBEY JESUS

23 As he got into the boat, his disciples followed
him. 24 Suddenly, a violent storm arose on the
sea, so that the boat was being swamped by
the waves — but Jesus kept sleeping. 25 So the
disciples came and woke him up, saying, "Lord,
save us! We're going to die!"
26 He said to them, "Why are you afraid, you
of little faith?" Then he got up and rebuked the
winds and the sea, and there was a great calm.
27 The men were amazed and asked, "What
kind of man is this? Even the winds and the
sea obey him!"

DEMONS DRIVEN OUT BY JESUS

28 When he had come to the other side, to the region of the Gadarenes,[A] two demon-possessed
men met him as they came out of the tombs.
They were so violent that no one could pass
that way. 29 Suddenly they shouted, "What do
you have to do with us,[B] Son of God? Have you
come here to torment us before the time?"
30 A long way off from them, a large herd
of pigs was feeding. 31 "If you drive us out,"
the demons begged him, "send us into the
herd of pigs."
32 "Go!" he told them. So when they had come
out, they entered the pigs, and the whole herd
rushed down the steep bank into the sea and
perished in the water. 33 Then the men who
tended them fled. They went into the city and
reported everything, especially what had happened to those who were demon-possessed.
34 At that, the whole town went out to meet
Jesus. When they saw him, they begged him
to leave their region.

THE SON OF MAN FORGIVES AND HEALS

9 So he got into a boat, crossed over, and came
to his own town. 2 Just then some men[C]
brought to him a paralytic lying on a stretcher. Seeing their faith, Jesus told the paralytic,
"Have courage, son, your sins are forgiven."
3 At this, some of the scribes said to themselves, "He's blaspheming!"
4 Perceiving their thoughts, Jesus said, "Why
are you thinking evil things in your hearts?[D]
5 For which is easier: to say, 'Your sins are forgiven,' or to say, 'Get up and walk'? 6 But so that
you may know that the Son of Man has authority on earth to forgive sins" — then he told the
paralytic, "Get up, take your stretcher, and go
home." 7 So he got up and went home. 8 When
the crowds saw this, they were awestruck[E,F]

Support | *Prayer*

GOD'S GOOD GIFTS

"Who among you, if his son asks him for bread, will give him a stone? Or if he asks for a fish, will give him a snake? If you then, who are evil, know how to give good gifts to your children, how much more will your Father in heaven give good things to those who ask him." Matthew 7:9-11

Simple, earnest prayer is the ultimate example of the biblical "ask-for-help" principle. This kind of petition says, "God, I am not independent, much less self-sufficient. I am not, in the proud words of the famous poem, 'master of my fate . . . captain of my soul.' I absolutely need you. I cannot save or sustain myself. I am looking to you and counting on you."

Jesus noted the powerful, universal desire of earthly parents to provide for the needs of their children. Seizing on this, he spoke of our Father in heaven who runs toward us when we humbly ask him to meet our needs. A life of hope and great joy is rooted in this knowledge—that, as children of God, we can look heavenward and trust that we have a Father who loves to "give good things."

For the next note on *Support*, see Matthew 18:4.

[A] **8:28** Other mss read *Gergesenes* [B] **8:29** Other mss add *Jesus* [C] **9:2** Lit *then they* [D] **9:4** Or *minds* [E] **9:8** Other mss read *amazed* [F] **9:8** Lit *afraid*

and gave glory to God, who had given such
authority to men.

THE CALL OF MATTHEW

9 As Jesus went on from there, he saw a man
named Matthew sitting at the toll booth, and
he said to him, "Follow me," and he got up and
followed him.
10 While he was reclining at the table in the
house, many tax collectors and sinners came
to eat with Jesus and his disciples. 11 When the
Pharisees saw this, they asked his disciples,
"Why does your teacher eat with tax collectors and sinners?"
12 Now when he heard this, he said, "It is
not those who are well who need a doctor,
but those who are sick. 13 Go and learn what
this means: **I desire mercy and not sacrifice.**[A] For I didn't come to call the righteous,
but sinners."[B]

A QUESTION ABOUT FASTING

14 Then John's disciples came to him, saying,
"Why do we and the Pharisees fast often, but
your disciples do not fast?"
15 Jesus said to them, "Can the wedding
guests[C] be sad while the groom is with them?
The time[D] will come when the groom will be
taken away from them, and then they will
fast. 16 No one patches an old garment with
unshrunk cloth, because the patch pulls away
from the garment and makes the tear worse.
17 And no one puts[E] new wine into old wineskins. Otherwise, the skins burst, the wine
spills out, and the skins are ruined. No, they
put new wine into fresh wineskins, and both
are preserved."

A GIRL RESTORED AND A WOMAN HEALED

18 As he was telling them these things, suddenly one of the leaders came and knelt down
before him, saying, "My daughter just died,[F]
but come and lay your hand on her, and she
will live." 19 So Jesus and his disciples got up
and followed him.
20 Just then, a woman who had suffered from
bleeding for twelve years approached from
behind and touched the end of his robe, 21 for
she said to herself, "If I can just touch his robe,
I'll be made well."[G]
22 Jesus turned and saw her. "Have courage, daughter," he said. "Your faith has saved
you."[H] And the woman was made well from
that moment.[I]

Other-centeredness | *Being Compassionate*

AFFECTION IN ACTION

"Jesus continued going around to all the towns and villages, teaching in their synagogues, preaching the good news of the kingdom, and healing every disease and every sickness. When he saw the crowds, he felt compassion for them, because they were distressed and dejected, like sheep without a shepherd." Matthew 9:35-36

Looking at the needy masses that thronged around him, Jesus "felt compassion." The Greek word used by Matthew here is a word that originally meant "intestines." The idea is that Jesus was deeply moved—his heart went out to all those in need around him. Seeing their pain and misery was like a punch in the gut to Christ.

Of course, Jesus didn't merely become emotional. Compassion is much more than a feeling. He healed the sick, gave sight to the blind, fed the hungry, taught the confused. Compassion is tender affection that culminates in action.

Compassion is one of the marks of a person who is spiritually and emotionally healthy. Do you feel moved when you see people who are hurting? Are you able to put yourself in their shoes? Do you make it a priority to find concrete ways to alleviate their suffering?

For the next note on *Other-centeredness*, see Matthew 25:40.

[A] **9:13** Hs 6:6 [B] **9:13** Other mss add *to repentance* [C] **9:15** Lit *the sons of the bridal chamber* [D] **9:15** Lit *days* [E] **9:17** Lit *And they do not put* [F] **9:18** Lit *daughter has now come to the end* [G] **9:21** Or *be saved* [H] **9:22** Or *has made you well* [I] **9:22** Lit *hour*

teacher and a slave like his master. If they
called the head of the house 'Beelzebul,' how
much more the members of his household!

FEAR GOD

26 "Therefore, don't be afraid of them, since
there is nothing covered that won't be uncovered and nothing hidden that won't be made
known. 27 What I tell you in the dark, speak in
the light. What you hear in a whisper,[A] proclaim on the housetops. 28 Don't fear those who
kill the body but are not able to kill the soul;
rather, fear him who is able to destroy both
soul and body in hell. 29 Aren't two sparrows
sold for a penny?[B] Yet not one of them falls to
the ground without your Father's consent.[C]
30 But even the hairs of your head have all
been counted. 31 So don't be afraid; you are
worth more than many sparrows.

ACKNOWLEDGING CHRIST

32 "Therefore, everyone who will acknowledge
me before others, I will also acknowledge him
before my Father in heaven. 33 But whoever
denies me before others, I will also deny him
before my Father in heaven. 34 Don't assume
that I came to bring peace on the earth. I did
not come to bring peace, but a sword. 35 For
I came to turn

a man against his father,
a daughter against her mother,
a daughter-in-law against
her mother-in-law;
36 **and a man's enemies will be**
the members of his household.[D]

37 The one who loves a father or mother more
than me is not worthy of me; the one who loves
a son or daughter more than me is not worthy
of me. 38 And whoever doesn't take up his cross
and follow me is not worthy of me. 39 Anyone
who finds his life will lose it, and anyone who
loses his life because of me will find it.

A CUP OF COLD WATER

40 "The one who welcomes you welcomes me,
and the one who welcomes me welcomes
him who sent me. 41 Anyone who welcomes a
prophet because he is a prophet[E] will receive a
prophet's reward. And anyone who welcomes
a righteous person because he's righteous[F] will
receive a righteous person's reward. 42 And
whoever gives even a cup of cold water to one
of these little ones because he is a disciple,[G]
truly I tell you, he will never lose his reward."

Exercise of Faith | *Sharing the Gospel*

REPRESENTING CHRIST TO THE WORLD

"Therefore, everyone who will acknowledge me before others, I will also acknowledge him before my Father in heaven." Matthew 10:32

Some loud, preachy Christians wield their faith like a sledgehammer. They patrol the world (and the Internet) like self-appointed moral referees, eager to invoke judgment on rule-breakers.

At the same time, some mousy, tight-lipped believers downplay their devotion to Christ. They keep a low profile and look for the nearest exit at the first sign of trouble.

By his words and his example, Jesus made clear that both extremes are wrong. Neither is healthy. Neither life results in joy and blessing. We should remember that Jesus was (and is) full of "grace and truth" (Jn 1:14,17). Meaning, if he lives in us as Lord, we should increasingly take on this same character. We should have compassion and grace for the broken. We should also gently but firmly stand for truth.

Are you pushy—or even obnoxious—with the gospel? Do you find you're afraid to acknowledge your faith in front of unbelievers? Sit down with an older believer and talk through this struggle. Ask God for more wisdom, discernment, and courage.

For the next note on *Exercise of Faith*, see Matthew 16:25-26.

[A] **10:27** Lit *in the ear* [B] **10:29** Gk *assarion*, a small copper coin [C] **10:29** Lit *ground apart from your Father* [D] **10:35-36** Mc 7:6 [E] **10:41** Lit *prophet in the name of a prophet* [F] **10:41** Lit *person in the name of a righteous person* [G] **10:42** Lit *little ones in the name of a disciple*

JOHN THE BAPTIST DOUBTS

11 When Jesus had finished giving instructions to his twelve disciples, he moved on
from there to teach and preach in their towns.
2 Now when John heard in prison what the
Christ was doing, he sent a message through
his disciples 3 and asked him, "Are you the one
who is to come, or should we expect someone else?"
4 Jesus replied to them, "Go and report to
John what you hear and see: 5 The blind receive
their sight, the lame walk, those with leprosy[A]
are cleansed, the deaf hear, the dead are raised,
and the poor are told the good news, 6 and
blessed is the one who isn't offended by me."
7 As these men were leaving, Jesus began
to speak to the crowds about John: "What did
you go out into the wilderness to see? A reed
swaying in the wind? 8 What then did you go
out to see? A man dressed in soft clothes?
See, those who wear soft clothes are in royal
palaces. 9 What then did you go out to see? A
prophet? Yes, I tell you, and more than a prophet. 10 This is the one about whom it is written:

See, I am sending my messenger
ahead of you;
he will prepare your way
before you.[B]

11 "Truly I tell you, among those born of wom-
en no one greater than John the Baptist has
appeared,[C] but the least in the kingdom of
heaven is greater than he. 12 From the days
of John the Baptist until now, the kingdom
of heaven has been suffering violence,[D] and
the violent have been seizing it by force. 13 For
all the prophets and the law prophesied until
John. 14 And if you're willing to accept it, he is
the Elijah who is to come. 15 Let anyone who
has ears[E] listen.

AN UNRESPONSIVE GENERATION

16 "To what should I compare this generation?
It's like children sitting in the marketplaces
who call out to other children:

17 We played the flute for you,
but you didn't dance;
we sang a lament,
but you didn't mourn![F]

18 For John came neither eating nor drinking,
and they say, 'He has a demon!' 19 The Son of
Man came eating and drinking, and they say,
'Look, a glutton and a drunkard, a friend of

Rest and Reflection | *Resting in Christ*

COME TO ME . . . AND . . . REST

"Come to me, all of you who are weary and burdened,
and I will give you rest." Matthew 11:28

During the American Civil War, President Abraham Lincoln reportedly said, "I am the tiredest man on earth." We hear that frank admission and nod knowingly. Life—even when we're not tasked with leading a war-torn nation—has a way of sapping us. What's more, weariness comes in a myriad of forms. We know of physical fatigue and relational exhaustion. But perhaps you are experiencing emotional burnout and spiritual depletion.

If so, Jesus's offer might seem too good to be true. We can stop carrying the weight of the world all by ourselves. We can actually feel "light" instead of "heavy" all the time. Really?

Yes, but only if we drag our exhausted selves to Christ, and take up his yoke (Mt 11:29-30). When we link ourselves to the Lord of the universe (who is also the Shepherd of our hearts), we find a lighter load and rest along the way.

What's burdening you? What situations or relationships are wearing you out? A vacation might be nice. Amusements might distract. But only spending time with Jesus can give you rest in the depths of your soul.

For the next note on *Rest and Reflection*, see Matthew 14:13.

[A] **11:5** Gk *lepros*; a term for various skin diseases; see Lv 13–14 [B] **11:10** Mal 3:1 [C] **11:11** Lit *arisen* [D] **11:12** Or *has been forcefully advancing* [E] **11:15** Other mss add *to hear* [F] **11:17** Or *beat your chests in grief*

tax collectors and sinners!' Yet wisdom is vindicated[A] by her deeds."[B]
20 Then he proceeded to denounce the towns
where most of his miracles were done, because they did not repent: 21 "Woe to you,
Chorazin! Woe to you, Bethsaida! For if the
miracles that were done in you had been done
in Tyre and Sidon, they would have repented
in sackcloth and ashes long ago. 22 But I tell
you, it will be more tolerable for Tyre and
Sidon on the day of judgment than for you.
23 And you, Capernaum, will you be exalted
to heaven? No, you will go down to Hades.
For if the miracles that were done in you had
been done in Sodom, it would have remained
until today. 24 But I tell you, it will be more
tolerable for the land of Sodom on the day
of judgment than for you."

THE SON GIVES KNOWLEDGE AND REST

25 At that time Jesus said, "I praise you, Father,
Lord of heaven and earth, because you have
hidden these things from the wise and intelligent and revealed them to infants. 26 Yes,
Father, because this was your good pleasure.[C]
27 All things have been entrusted to me by my
Father. No one knows the Son except the Father, and no one knows the Father except the
Son and anyone to whom the Son desires[D] to
reveal him.
28 "Come to me, all of you who are weary
and burdened, and I will give you rest. 29 Take
up my yoke and learn from me, because I am
lowly and humble in heart, and you will find
rest for your souls. 30 For my yoke is easy and
my burden is light."

LORD OF THE SABBATH

12 At that time Jesus passed through the
grainfields on the Sabbath. His disciples were hungry and began to pick and eat
some heads of grain. 2 When the Pharisees
saw this, they said to him, "See, your disciples are doing what is not lawful to do on
the Sabbath."
3 He said to them, "Haven't you read what
David did when he and those who were with
him were hungry: 4 how he entered the house
of God, and they ate[E] the bread of the Presence
— which is not lawful for him or for those
with him to eat, but only for the priests? 5 Or
haven't you read in the law that on Sabbath
days the priests in the temple violate the Sabbath and are innocent? 6 I tell you that something greater than the temple is here. 7 If you
had known what this means, **I desire mercy
and not sacrifice**,[F] you would not have condemned the innocent. 8 For the Son of Man is
Lord of the Sabbath."

THE MAN WITH THE SHRIVELED HAND

9 Moving on from there, he entered their
synagogue. 10 There he saw a man who had
a shriveled hand, and in order to accuse him
they asked him, "Is it lawful to heal on the
Sabbath?"
11 He replied to them, "Who among you, if
he had a sheep that fell into a pit on the Sabbath, wouldn't take hold of it and lift it out?
12 A person is worth far more than a sheep; so
it is lawful to do what is good on the Sabbath."
13 Then he told the man, "Stretch out your
hand." So he stretched it out, and it was restored, as good as the other. 14 But the Pharisees
went out and plotted against him, how they
might kill him.

THE SERVANT OF THE LORD

15 Jesus was aware of this and withdrew. Large
crowds[G] followed him, and he healed them all.
16 He warned them not to make him known,
17 so that what was spoken through the prophet
Isaiah might be fulfilled:

18 **Here is my servant**
whom I have chosen,
my beloved in whom I delight;
I will put my Spirit on him,
and he will proclaim justice
to the nations.
19 **He will not argue or shout,**
and no one will hear his voice
in the streets.
20 **He will not break a bruised reed,**
and he will not put out
a smoldering wick,
until he has led justice to victory.[H]
21 **The nations will put their hope**
in his name.[I]

A HOUSE DIVIDED

22 Then a demon-possessed man who was
blind and unable to speak was brought to
him. He healed him, so that the man[J] could
both speak and see. 23 All the crowds were

[A] **11:19** Or *declared right* [B] **11:19** Other mss read *children* [C] **11:26** Lit *was well-pleasing in your sight* [D] **11:27** Or *wills*, or *chooses* [E] **12:4** Other mss read *he ate* [F] **12:7** Hs 6:6 [G] **12:15** Other mss read *Many* [H] **12:20** Or *until he has successfully put forth justice* [I] **12:18-21** Is 42:1-4 [J] **12:22** Lit *mute*

astounded and said, "Could this be the Son
of David?"
24 When the Pharisees heard this, they said,
"This man drives out demons only by Beelzebul, the ruler of the demons."
25 Knowing their thoughts, he told them:
"Every kingdom divided against itself is headed for destruction, and no city or house divided against itself will stand. 26 If Satan drives
out Satan, he is divided against himself. How
then will his kingdom stand? 27 And if I drive
out demons by Beelzebul, by whom do your
sons drive them out? For this reason they
will be your judges. 28 If I drive out demons
by the Spirit of God, then the kingdom of
God has come upon you. 29 How can someone enter a strong man's house and steal
his possessions unless he first ties up the
strong man? Then he can plunder his house.
30 Anyone who is not with me is against me,
and anyone who does not gather with me
scatters. 31 Therefore, I tell you, people will
be forgiven every sin and blasphemy, but
the blasphemy against[A] the Spirit will not be
forgiven.[B] 32 Whoever speaks a word against
the Son of Man, it will be forgiven him; but
whoever speaks against the Holy Spirit, it
will not be forgiven him, either in this age
or in the one to come.

A TREE AND ITS FRUIT

33 "Either make the tree good and its fruit will
be good, or make the tree bad[C] and its fruit will
be bad; for a tree is known by its fruit. 34 Brood
of vipers! How can you speak good things when
you are evil? For the mouth speaks from the
overflow of the heart. 35 A good person produces good things from his storeroom of good,
and an evil person produces evil things from
his storeroom of evil. 36 I tell you that on the
day of judgment people will have to account
for every careless[D] word they speak.[E] 37 For
by your words you will be acquitted, and by
your words you will be condemned."

THE SIGN OF JONAH

38 Then some of the scribes and Pharisees
said to him, "Teacher, we want to see a sign
from you."
39 He answered them, "An evil and adulterous
generation demands a sign, but no sign will be
given to it except the sign of the prophet Jonah.
40 For as Jonah was in the belly of the huge fish[F]
three days and three nights, so the Son of Man
will be in the heart of the earth three days and
three nights. 41 The men of Nineveh will stand
up at the judgment with this generation and
condemn it, because they repented at Jonah's
preaching; and look — something greater than
Jonah is here. 42 The queen of the south will rise
up at the judgment with this generation and
condemn it, because she came from the ends of
the earth to hear the wisdom of Solomon; and
look — something greater than Solomon is here.

AN UNCLEAN SPIRIT'S RETURN

43 "When an unclean spirit comes out of a
person, it roams through waterless places
looking for rest but doesn't find any. 44 Then
it says, 'I'll go back to my house that I came
from.' Returning, it finds the house vacant,
swept, and put in order. 45 Then it goes and
brings with it seven other spirits more evil
than itself, and they enter and settle down
there. As a result, that person's last condition
is worse than the first. That's how it will also
be with this evil generation."

TRUE RELATIONSHIPS

46 While he was still speaking with the crowds,
his mother and brothers were standing outside wanting to speak to him. 47 Someone told
him, "Look, your mother and your brothers
are standing outside, wanting to speak to
you."[G]
48 He replied to the one who was speaking
to him, "Who is my mother and who are my
brothers?" 49 Stretching out his hand toward
his disciples, he said, "Here are my mother and
my brothers! 50 For whoever does the will of
my Father in heaven is my brother and sister
and mother."

THE PARABLE OF THE SOWER

13 On that day Jesus went out of the house
and was sitting by the sea. 2 Such large
crowds gathered around him that he got into
a boat and sat down, while the whole crowd
stood on the shore.
3 Then he told them many things in parables,
saying: "Consider the sower who went out to
sow. 4 As he sowed, some seed fell along the
path, and the birds came and devoured them.
5 Other seed fell on rocky ground where it
didn't have much soil, and it grew up quickly
since the soil wasn't deep. 6 But when the sun

[A] **12:31** Or *of* [B] **12:31** Other mss add *people* [C] **12:33** Or *decayed*; lit *rotten* [D] **12:36** Lit *worthless* [E] **12:36** Lit *will speak*
[F] **12:40** Or *sea creature*; Jnh 1:17 [G] **12:47** Other mss omit this v.

came up, it was scorched, and since it had no
root, it withered away. 7 Other seed fell among
thorns, and the thorns came up and choked
it. 8 Still other seed fell on good ground and
produced fruit: some a hundred, some sixty,
and some thirty times what was sown. 9 Let
anyone who has ears[A] listen."

WHY JESUS USED PARABLES

10 Then the disciples came up and asked him,
"Why are you speaking to them in parables?"
11 He answered, "Because the secrets of the
kingdom of heaven have been given for you to
know, but it has not been given to them. 12 For
whoever has, more will be given to him, and
he will have more than enough; but whoever does not have, even what he has will be
taken away from him. 13 That is why I speak
to them in parables, because looking they
do not see, and hearing they do not listen or
understand. 14 Isaiah's prophecy is fulfilled
in them, which says:

You will listen and listen,
but never understand;
you will look and look,
but never perceive.
15 **For this people's heart**
has grown callous;
their ears are hard of hearing,
and they have shut their eyes;
otherwise they might see
with their eyes,
and hear with their ears, and
understand with their hearts,
and turn back —
and I would heal them.[B]

16 "Blessed are your eyes because they do see,
and your ears because they do hear. 17 For truly I tell you, many prophets and righteous
people longed to see the things you see but
didn't see them, to hear the things you hear
but didn't hear them.

THE PARABLE OF THE SOWER EXPLAINED

18 "So listen to the parable of the sower: 19 When
anyone hears the word about the kingdom and
doesn't understand it, the evil one comes and
snatches away what was sown in his heart. This
is the one sown along the path. 20 And the one
sown on rocky ground — this is one who hears
the word and immediately receives it with joy.
21 But he has no root and is short-lived. When
distress or persecution comes because of the
word, immediately he falls away. 22 Now the
one sown among the thorns — this is one who
hears the word, but the worries of this age and
the deceitfulness[C] of wealth choke the word,
and it becomes unfruitful. 23 But the one sown
on the good ground — this is one who hears
and understands the word, who does produce
fruit and yields: some a hundred, some sixty,
some thirty times what was sown."

THE PARABLE OF THE WHEAT AND THE WEEDS

24 He presented another parable to them: "The
kingdom of heaven may be compared to a man
who sowed good seed in his field. 25 But while
people were sleeping, his enemy came, sowed
weeds among the wheat, and left. 26 When
the plants sprouted and produced grain, then
the weeds also appeared. 27 The landowner's
servants came to him and said, 'Master, didn't
you sow good seed in your field? Then where
did the weeds come from?'
28 " 'An enemy did this,' he told them.
" 'So, do you want us to go and pull them
up?' the servants asked him.
29 " 'No,' he said. 'When you pull up the weeds,
you might also uproot the wheat with them.
30 Let both grow together until the harvest. At
harvest time I'll tell the reapers: Gather the
weeds first and tie them in bundles to burn
them, but collect the wheat in my barn.' "

THE PARABLES OF THE MUSTARD SEED AND OF THE LEAVEN

31 He presented another parable to them: "The
kingdom of heaven is like a mustard seed that
a man took and sowed in his field. 32 It's the
smallest of all the seeds, but when grown, it's
taller than the garden plants and becomes
a tree, so that the birds of the sky come and
nest in its branches."
33 He told them another parable: "The kingdom of heaven is like leaven[D] that a woman
took and mixed into fifty pounds[E] of flour
until all of it was leavened."

USING PARABLES FULFILLS PROPHECY

34 Jesus told the crowds all these things in
parables, and he did not tell them anything
without a parable, 35 so that what was spoken
through the prophet might be fulfilled:

I will open my mouth in parables;
I will declare things kept secret
from the foundation of the world.[F,G]

[A] **13:9** Other mss add *to hear* [B] **13:14-15** Is 6:9-10 [C] **13:22** Or *pleasure* [D] **13:33** Or *yeast* [E] **13:33** Lit *three sata*; about 40 liters [F] **13:35** Some mss omit *of the world* [G] **13:35** Ps 78:2

JESUS INTERPRETS THE PARABLE OF THE WHEAT AND THE WEEDS

36 Then he left the crowds and went into the house. His disciples approached him and said, "Explain to us the parable of the weeds in the field."

37 He replied: "The one who sows the good seed is the Son of Man; 38 the field is the world; and the good seed — these are the children of the kingdom. The weeds are the children of the evil one, 39 and the enemy who sowed them is the devil. The harvest is the end of the age, and the harvesters are angels. 40 Therefore, just as the weeds are gathered and burned in the fire, so it will be at the end of the age. 41 The Son of Man will send out his angels, and they will gather from his kingdom all who cause sin[A] and those guilty of lawlessness.[B] 42 They will throw them into the blazing furnace where there will be weeping and gnashing of teeth. 43 Then the righteous will shine like the sun in their Father's kingdom. Let anyone who has ears[C] listen.

THE PARABLES OF THE HIDDEN TREASURE AND OF THE PRICELESS PEARL

44 "The kingdom of heaven is like treasure, buried in a field, that a man found and reburied. Then in his joy he goes and sells everything he has and buys that field.

45 "Again, the kingdom of heaven is like a merchant in search of fine pearls. 46 When he found one priceless[D] pearl, he went and sold everything he had and bought it.

THE PARABLE OF THE NET

47 "Again, the kingdom of heaven is like a large net thrown into the sea. It collected every kind of fish, 48 and when it was full, they dragged it ashore, sat down, and gathered the good fish into containers, but threw out the worthless ones. 49 So it will be at the end of the age. The angels will go out, separate the evil people from the righteous, 50 and throw them into the blazing furnace, where there will be weeping and gnashing of teeth.

THE STOREHOUSE OF TRUTH

51 "Have you understood all these things?"[E]

They answered him, "Yes."

52 "Therefore," he said to them, "every teacher of the law[F] who has become a disciple in the kingdom of heaven is like the owner of a house who brings out of his storeroom treasures new and old."

REJECTION AT NAZARETH

53 When Jesus had finished these parables, he left there. 54 He went to his hometown and began to teach them in their synagogue, so that they were astonished and said, "Where did this man get this wisdom and these miraculous powers? 55 Isn't this the carpenter's son? Isn't his mother called Mary, and his brothers James, Joseph,[G] Simon, and Judas? 56 And his sisters, aren't they all with us? So where does he get all these things?" 57 And they were offended by him.

Jesus said to them, "A prophet is not without honor except in his hometown and in his household." 58 And he did not do many miracles there because of their unbelief.

JOHN THE BAPTIST BEHEADED

14 At that time Herod the tetrarch heard the report about Jesus. 2 "This is John the Baptist," he told his servants. "He has been raised from the dead, and that's why miraculous powers are at work in him."

3 For Herod had arrested John, chained[H] him, and put him in prison on account of Herodias, his brother Philip's wife, 4 since John had been telling him, "It's not lawful for you to have her." 5 Though Herod wanted to kill John, he feared the crowd since they regarded John as a prophet.

6 When Herod's birthday celebration came, Herodias's daughter danced before them[I] and pleased Herod. 7 So he promised with an oath to give her whatever she asked. 8 Prompted by her mother, she answered, "Give me John the Baptist's head here on a platter." 9 Although the king regretted it, he commanded that it be granted because of his oaths and his guests. 10 So he sent orders and had John beheaded in the prison. 11 His head was brought on a platter and given to the girl, who carried it to her mother. 12 Then his disciples came, removed the corpse,[J] buried it, and went and reported to Jesus.

FEEDING OF THE FIVE THOUSAND

13 When Jesus heard about it, he withdrew from there by boat to a remote place to be

[A] 13:41 Or *stumbling* [B] 13:41 Or *those who do lawlessness* [C] 13:43 Other mss add *to hear* [D] 13:46 Or *very precious* [E] 13:51 Other mss add *Jesus asked them* [F] 13:52 Or *every scribe* [G] 13:55 Other mss read *Joses*; Mk 6:3 [H] 14:3 Or *bound* [I] 14:6 Lit *danced in the middle* [J] 14:12 Other mss read *body*

alone. When the crowds heard this, they followed him on foot from the towns. 14 When
he went ashore,[A] he saw a large crowd, had
compassion on them, and healed their sick.
15 When evening came, the disciples approached him and said, "This place is deserted,
and it is already late.[B] Send the crowds away
so that they can go into the villages and buy
food for themselves."
16 "They don't need to go away," Jesus told
them. "You give them something to eat."
17 "But we only have five loaves and two fish
here," they said to him.
18 "Bring them here to me," he said. 19 Then
he commanded the crowds to sit down on
the grass. He took the five loaves and the two
fish, and looking up to heaven, he blessed
them. He broke the loaves and gave them
to the disciples, and the disciples gave them
to the crowds. 20 Everyone ate and was satisfied. They picked up twelve baskets full of
leftover pieces. 21 Now those who ate were
about five thousand men, besides women
and children.

WALKING ON THE WATER

22 Immediately he[C] made the disciples get
into the boat and go ahead of him to the
other side, while he dismissed the crowds.
23 After dismissing the crowds, he went up
on the mountain by himself to pray. Well
into the night, he was there alone. 24 Meanwhile, the boat was already some distance[D]
from land,[E] battered by the waves, because
the wind was against them. 25 Jesus came
toward them walking on the sea very early
in the morning.[F] 26 When the disciples saw
him walking on the sea, they were terrified.
"It's a ghost!" they said, and they cried out
in fear.
27 Immediately Jesus spoke to them. "Have
courage! It is I. Don't be afraid."
28 "Lord, if it's you," Peter answered him,
"command me to come to you on the water."
29 He said, "Come."
And climbing out of the boat, Peter started
walking on the water and came toward Jesus.
30 But when he saw the strength of the wind,[G]
he was afraid, and beginning to sink he cried
out, "Lord, save me!"
31 Immediately Jesus reached out his hand,
caught hold of him, and said to him, "You of
little faith, why did you doubt?"
32 When they got into the boat, the wind
ceased. 33 Then those in the boat worshiped
him and said, "Truly you are the Son of God."

Rest and Reflection | *Being Alone with God*

THE POWER OF SOLITUDE

"When Jesus heard about it, he withdrew from there by boat to a remote place to be alone. When the crowds heard this, they followed him on foot from the towns." Matthew 14:13

When Jesus got word that John the Baptist had been executed by Herod, his immediate response was to suspend what he was doing and seek out a place of solitude, ostensibly to commune with God.

This is a far cry from the way most people typically react to bad news. Some rant (embarrassingly so) on social media. Others go have drinks. Still others take on extra projects at work or home so they won't have time to think about unpleasant matters. While these actions may seem to do the trick at the time, they don't address the deeper, longer-term heart issues that need to be resolved.

Rather than broadcasting, temporarily numbing, or burying our pain and confusion, the wiser and healthier course is to do what Jesus did. Be intentional. Step out of your normal routine. Then prayerfully and carefully contemplate your situation, keeping in mind everything you know to be eternally true. Many have also found the practice of journaling to be a helpful exercise in such times.

For the next note on *Rest and Reflection*, see Mark 6:31.

[A] **14:14** Lit *Coming out* (of the boat) [B] **14:15** Lit *and the time* (for the evening meal) *has already passed* [C] **14:22** Other mss read *Jesus* [D] **14:24** Lit *already many stadia*; one *stadion* = 600 feet [E] **14:24** Other mss read *already in the middle of the sea* [F] **14:25** Lit *fourth watch of the night* = 3 to 6 a.m. [G] **14:30** Other mss read *saw the wind*

MIRACULOUS HEALINGS

34 When they had crossed over, they came to
shore at Gennesaret. 35 When the men of that
place recognized him, they alerted the whole
vicinity and brought to him all who were sick.
36 They begged him that they might only touch
the end of his robe, and as many as touched
it were healed.

THE TRADITION OF THE ELDERS

15 Then Jesus was approached by Pharisees
and scribes from Jerusalem, who asked,
2 "Why do your disciples break the tradition
of the elders? For they don't wash their hands
when they eat."[A]
3 He answered them, "Why do you break
God's commandment because of your tradition? 4 For God said:[B] **Honor your father and**
your mother;[C] and, **Whoever speaks evil of**
father or mother must be put to death.[D] 5 But
you say, 'Whoever tells his father or mother,
"Whatever benefit you might have received
from me is a gift committed to the temple,"
6 he does not have to honor his father.'[E] In this
way, you have nullified the word of God[F] because of your tradition. 7 Hypocrites! Isaiah
prophesied correctly about you when he said:

8 **This people[G] honors me**
with their lips,
but their heart is far from me.
9 **They worship me in vain,**
teaching as doctrines
human commands."[H]

DEFILEMENT IS FROM WITHIN

10 Summoning the crowd, he told them, "Listen
and understand: 11 It's not what goes into the
mouth that defiles a person, but what comes
out of the mouth — this defiles a person."
12 Then the disciples came up and told him,
"Do you know that the Pharisees took offense
when they heard what you said?"
13 He replied, "Every plant that my heavenly
Father didn't plant will be uprooted. 14 Leave
them alone! They are blind guides.[I] And if the
blind guide the blind, both will fall into a pit."
15 Then Peter said, "Explain this parable to us."
16 "Do you still lack understanding?" he[J]
asked. 17 "Don't you realize[K] that whatever goes
into the mouth passes into the stomach and is
eliminated?[L] 18 But what comes out of the mouth
comes from the heart, and this defiles a person. 19 For from the heart come evil thoughts,
murders, adulteries, sexual immoralities, thefts,
false testimonies, slander. 20 These are the things
that defile a person; but eating with unwashed
hands does not defile a person."

A GENTILE MOTHER'S FAITH

21 When Jesus left there, he withdrew to the
area of Tyre and Sidon. 22 Just then a Canaanite woman from that region came and kept
crying out,[M] "Have mercy on me, Lord, Son
of David! My daughter is severely tormented
by a demon."
23 Jesus did not say a word to her. His disciples approached him and urged him, "Send
her away because she's crying out after us."
24 He replied, "I was sent only to the lost
sheep of the house of Israel."
25 But she came, knelt before him, and said,
"Lord, help me!"
26 He answered, "It isn't right to take the
children's bread and throw it to the dogs."
27 "Yes, Lord," she said, "yet even the dogs eat
the crumbs that fall from their masters' table."
28 Then Jesus replied to her, "Woman, your
faith is great. Let it be done for you as you
want." And from that moment[N] her daughter
was healed.

HEALING MANY PEOPLE

29 Moving on from there, Jesus passed along
the Sea of Galilee. He went up on a mountain
and sat there, 30 and large crowds came to him,
including the lame, the blind, the crippled,
those unable to speak, and many others. They
put them at his feet, and he healed them. 31 So
the crowd was amazed when they saw those
unable to speak talking, the crippled restored,
the lame walking, and the blind seeing, and
they gave glory to the God of Israel.

FEEDING OF THE FOUR THOUSAND

32 Jesus called his disciples and said, "I have compassion on the crowd, because they've already
stayed with me three days and have nothing
to eat. I don't want to send them away hungry,
otherwise they might collapse on the way."
33 The disciples said to him, "Where could

[A] **15:2** Lit *eat bread* = eat a meal [B] **15:4** Other mss read *commanded, saying* [C] **15:4** Ex 20:12; Dt 5:16 [D] **15:4** Ex 21:17; Lv 20:9
[E] **15:6** Other mss read *then he does not have to honor his father or mother* [F] **15:6** Other mss read *commandment*
[G] **15:8** Other mss add *draw near to me with their mouths, and* [H] **15:8-9** Is 29:13 LXX [I] **15:14** Other mss add *for the blind*
[J] **15:16** Other mss read *Jesus* [K] **15:17** Other mss add *yet* [L] **15:17** Lit *and goes out into the toilet* [M] **15:22** Other mss read *and cried out to him* [N] **15:28** Lit *hour*

My Story | Morris

In 1999 I was diagnosed with a thyroid disease. At the time, I didn't know what the function of a thyroid gland was, much less anything about hypothyroidism or Grave's disease. The disease caused me to lose weight rapidly, I was hungry all the time, my hair thinned, I couldn't sleep at night, I had a constantly rapid heartbeat, and I always felt exhausted. During the years of thyroid treatment under the supervision of my endocrinologist, several nodules were detected inside of my thyroid three times and the doctor performed a biopsy each time to make sure the cells were not malignant. Thankfully, the nodules were not cancerous!

It became clear that a lot of my health problems were a result of chronic stress, dehydration, and insufficient exercise. I spent most of my life internalizing emotional stress stemming from unfavorable childhood experiences. Through Christian counseling, the Lord revealed some areas in my life that I had not completely surrendered to him. After the six years of treatment and the third biopsy, I made the choice to forgive and let go of my baggage, to choose not to worry about things I could not control, and to exercise and run as a way to release stress. Changing my whole lifestyle made a huge difference, and I thank God for my good health today!

we get enough bread in this desolate place to
feed such a crowd?"
34 "How many loaves do you have?" Jesus
asked them.
"Seven," they said, "and a few small fish."
35 After commanding the crowd to sit down
on the ground, 36 he took the seven loaves and
the fish, gave thanks, broke them, and gave
them to the disciples, and the disciples gave
them to the crowds. 37 They all ate and were
satisfied. They collected the leftover pieces
— seven large baskets full. 38 Now there were
four thousand men who had eaten, besides
women and children. 39 After dismissing the
crowds, he got into the boat and went to the
region of Magadan.[A]

THE LEAVEN OF THE PHARISEES AND THE SADDUCEES

16 The Pharisees and Sadducees approached, and tested him, asking him
to show them a sign from heaven. 2 He replied,
"When evening comes you say, 'It will be good
weather because the sky is red.' 3 And in the
morning, 'Today will be stormy because the
sky is red and threatening.' You[B] know how
to read the appearance of the sky, but you
can't read the signs of the times.[C] 4 An evil
and adulterous generation demands a sign,
but no sign will be given to it except the sign
of[D] Jonah." Then he left them and went away.
5 The disciples reached the other shore,[E]
and they had forgotten to take bread. 6 Then
Jesus told them, "Watch out and beware of
the leaven[F] of the Pharisees and Sadducees."
7 They were discussing among themselves,
"We didn't bring any bread."
8 Aware of this, Jesus said, "You of little faith,
why are you discussing among yourselves that
you do not have bread? 9 Don't you understand
yet? Don't you remember the five loaves for
the five thousand and how many baskets you
collected? 10 Or the seven loaves for the four
thousand and how many large baskets you
collected? 11 Why is it you don't understand
that when I told you, 'Beware of the leaven of
the Pharisees and Sadducees,' it wasn't about
bread?" 12 Then they understood that he had not
told them to beware of the leaven in bread, but
of the teaching of the Pharisees and Sadducees.

PETER'S CONFESSION OF THE MESSIAH

13 When Jesus came to the region of Caesarea
Philippi,[G] he asked his disciples, "Who do people say that the Son of Man is?"[H]
14 They replied, "Some say John the Baptist;
others, Elijah; still others, Jeremiah or one of
the prophets."
15 "But you," he asked them, "who do you
say that I am?"
16 Simon Peter answered, "You are the Messiah, the Son of the living God."
17 Jesus responded, "Blessed are you, Simon
son of Jonah,[I] because flesh and blood did not

[A] **15:39** Other mss read *Magdala* [B] **16:3** Other mss read *Hypocrites! You* [C] **16:2-3** Other mss omit *When* (v. 2) through end of v. 3 [D] **16:4** Other mss add *the prophet* [E] **16:5** Lit *disciples went to the other side* [F] **16:6** Or *yeast*, also in vv. 11,12 [G] **16:13** A town north of Galilee at the base of Mount Hermon [H] **16:13** Other mss read *that I, the Son of Man, am* [I] **16:17** Or *son of John*

reveal this to you, but my Father in heaven.
18 And I also say to you that you are Peter, and
on this rock I will build my church, and the
gates of Hades will not overpower it. 19 I will
give you the keys of the kingdom of heaven,
and whatever you bind on earth will have been
bound[A] in heaven, and whatever you loose
on earth will have been loosed[B] in heaven."
20 Then he gave the disciples orders to tell no
one that he was[C] the Messiah.

HIS DEATH AND RESURRECTION PREDICTED

21 From then on Jesus began to point out to
his disciples that it was necessary for him to
go to Jerusalem and suffer many things from
the elders, chief priests, and scribes, be killed,
and be raised the third day. 22 Peter took him
aside and began to rebuke him, "Oh no,[D] Lord!
This will never happen to you!"

23 Jesus turned and told Peter, "Get behind
me, Satan! You are a hindrance to me because
you're not thinking about God's concerns[E] but
human concerns."

TAKE UP YOUR CROSS

24 Then Jesus said to his disciples, "If anyone
wants to follow after me, let him deny himself,
take up his cross, and follow me. 25 For whoever
wants to save his life will lose it, but whoever
loses his life because of me will find it. 26 For
what will it benefit someone if he gains the
whole world yet loses his life? Or what will
anyone give in exchange for his life? 27 For the
Son of Man is going to come with his angels in
the glory of his Father, and then he will reward
each according to what he has done. 28 Truly
I tell you, there are some standing here who
will not taste death until they see the Son of
Man coming in his kingdom."

THE TRANSFIGURATION

17 After six days Jesus took Peter, James,
and his brother John and led them up
on a high mountain by themselves. 2 He was
transfigured in front of them, and his face
shone like the sun; his clothes became as
white as the light. 3 Suddenly, Moses and
Elijah appeared to them, talking with him.
4 Then Peter said to Jesus, "Lord, it's good
for us to be here. I will set up[F] three shelters here: one for you, one for Moses, and
one for Elijah."

5 While he was still speaking, suddenly a
bright cloud covered[G] them, and a voice from

Exercise of Faith | *Making Right Choices*

TAKING RISKS

"For whoever wants to save his life will lose it, but whoever loses his life because of me will find it. For what will it benefit someone if he gains the whole world yet loses his life? Or what will anyone give in exchange for his life?" Matthew 16:25-26

Most people are risk-averse. They will never ride a snowboard off a mountain cliff or invest their life savings in a business venture that has only a 30 percent probability of success. Swing for the fence? No thanks. Most people live with low-grade fear (that often flares up into abject panic). We like safety, guarantees, sure things. We want life to be manageable and predictable.

Then Jesus comes along urging us to go all in. If you want to follow me, he essentially says, you can't hedge your bets. You have to throw caution to the wind. If you do risk everything, however, you'll gain everything—and then some.

Are you trying to line your life with safeguards? Scrambling to protect yourself against any and all difficulty? Healthy faith means entrusting yourself and your future—and all outcomes—to the one we call the Good Shepherd.

For the next note on *Exercise of Faith*, see Matthew 20:28.

[A] **16:19** Or *earth will be bound* [B] **16:19** Or *earth will be loosed* [C] **16:20** Other mss add *Jesus* [D] **16:22** Lit *"Mercy to you = "May God have mercy on you* [E] **16:23** Lit *about the things of God* [F] **17:4** Other mss read *Let's make* [G] **17:5** Or *enveloped*; Ex 40:34-35

the cloud said: "This is my beloved Son, with whom I am well-pleased. Listen to him!" 6 When the disciples heard this, they fell face-down and were terrified.

7 Jesus came up, touched them, and said, "Get up; don't be afraid." 8 When they looked up they saw no one except Jesus alone.

9 As they were coming down the mountain, Jesus commanded them, "Don't tell anyone about the vision until the Son of Man is raised[A] from the dead."

10 So the disciples asked him, "Why then do the scribes say that Elijah must come first?"

11 "Elijah is coming[B] and will restore everything," he replied.[C] 12 "But I tell you: Elijah has already come, and they didn't recognize him. On the contrary, they did whatever they pleased to him. In the same way the Son of Man is going to suffer at their hands." 13 Then the disciples understood that he had spoken to them about John the Baptist.

THE POWER OF JESUS OVER A DEMON

14 When they reached the crowd, a man approached and knelt down before him. 15 "Lord," he said, "have mercy on my son, because he has seizures[D] and suffers terribly. He often falls into the fire and often into the water. 16 I brought him to your disciples, but they couldn't heal him."

17 Jesus replied, "You unbelieving and perverse generation, how long will I be with you? How long must I put up with you? Bring him here to me." 18 Then Jesus rebuked the demon,[E] and it[F] came out of him, and from that moment[G] the boy was healed.

19 Then the disciples approached Jesus privately and said, "Why couldn't we drive it out?"

20 "Because of your little faith," he[H] told them. "For truly I tell you, if you have faith the size of[I] a mustard seed, you will tell this mountain, 'Move from here to there,' and it will move. Nothing will be impossible for you."[J]

THE SECOND PREDICTION OF HIS DEATH

22 As they were gathering together[K] in Galilee, Jesus told them, "The Son of Man is about to be betrayed into the hands of men. 23 They will kill him, and on the third day he will be raised up." And they were deeply distressed.

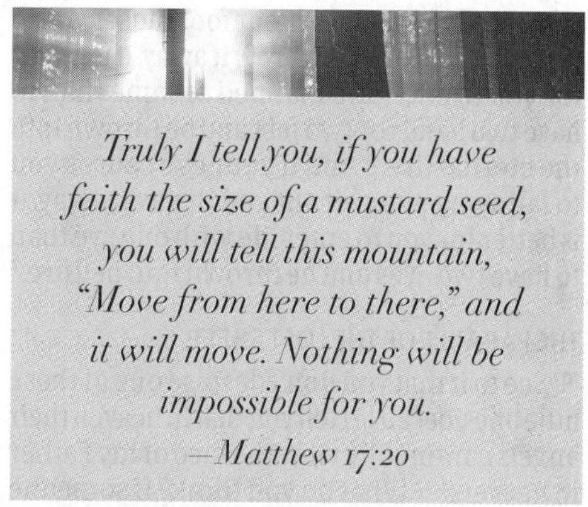
Truly I tell you, if you have faith the size of a mustard seed, you will tell this mountain, "Move from here to there," and it will move. Nothing will be impossible for you.
—Matthew 17:20

PAYING THE TEMPLE TAX

24 When they came to Capernaum, those who collected the temple tax approached Peter and said, "Doesn't your teacher pay the temple tax?"

25 "Yes," he said.

When he went into the house, Jesus spoke to him first,[L] "What do you think, Simon? From whom do earthly kings collect tariffs or taxes? From their sons or from strangers?"[M]

26 "From strangers," he said.[N]

"Then the sons are free," Jesus told him. 27 "But, so we won't offend them, go to the sea, cast in a fishhook, and take the first fish that you catch. When you open its mouth you'll find a coin.[O] Take it and give it to them for me and you."

WHO IS THE GREATEST?

18 At that time[G] the disciples came to Jesus and asked, "So who is greatest in the kingdom of heaven?" 2 He called a child and had him stand among them. 3 "Truly I tell you," he said, "unless you turn and become like children, you will never enter the kingdom of heaven. 4 Therefore, whoever humbles himself like this child — this one is the greatest in the kingdom of heaven. 5 And whoever welcomes[P] one child like this in my name welcomes me.

6 "But whoever causes one of these little ones who believe in me to fall away — it would be better for him if a heavy millstone were hung around his neck and he were drowned in the depths of the sea. 7 Woe to the world because of offenses. For offenses will inevitably come, but woe to that person by whom the offense

[A] **17:9** Other mss read *Man has risen* [B] **17:11** Other mss add *first* [C] **17:11** Other mss read *Jesus said to them* [D] **17:15** Lit *he is moonstruck*; thought to be a form of epilepsy [E] **17:18** Lit *rebuked him*, or *it* [F] **17:18** Lit *the demon* [G] **17:18; 18:1** Lit *hour* [H] **17:20** Other mss read *your unbelief, Jesus* [I] **17:20** Lit *faith like* [J] **17:20** Some mss include v. 21: *"However, this kind does not come out except by prayer and fasting."* [K] **17:22** Other mss read *were staying* [L] **17:25** Lit *Jesus anticipated him by saying* [M] **17:25** Or *foreigners* [N] **17:26** Other mss read *Peter said to him* [O] **17:27** Gk *stater*, worth 2 double-drachmas [P] **18:5** Or *receives*

comes. 8 If your hand or your foot causes you to
fall away, cut it off and throw it away. It is better
for you to enter life maimed or lame than to
have two hands or two feet and be thrown into
the eternal fire. 9 And if your eye causes you
to fall away, gouge it out and throw it away. It
is better for you to enter life with one eye than
to have two eyes and be thrown into hellfire.[A]

THE PARABLE OF THE LOST SHEEP

10 "See to it that you don't despise one of these
little ones, because I tell you that in heaven their
angels continually view the face of my Father
in heaven.[B] 12 What do you think? If someone
has a hundred sheep, and one of them goes
astray, won't he leave the ninety-nine on the
hillside and go and search for the stray? 13 And
if he finds it, truly I tell you, he rejoices over
that sheep[C] more than over the ninety-nine
that did not go astray. 14 In the same way, it is
not the will of your Father in heaven that one
of these little ones perish.

RESTORING A BROTHER

15 "If your brother sins against you,[D] go and
rebuke him in private.[E] If he listens to you, you
have won your brother. 16 But if he won't listen,
take one or two others with you, so that **by the
testimony[F] of two or three witnesses every
fact may be established.**[G] 17 If he doesn't pay
attention to them, tell the church.[H] If he doesn't
pay attention even to the church, let him be like
a Gentile and a tax collector to you. 18 Truly I tell
you, whatever you bind on earth will have been
bound[I] in heaven, and whatever you loose on
earth will have been loosed[J] in heaven. 19 Again,
truly I tell you, if two of you on earth agree
about any matter that you[K] pray for, it will be
done for you[L] by my Father in heaven. 20 For
where two or three are gathered together in
my name, I am there among them."

THE PARABLE OF THE UNFORGIVING SERVANT

21 Then Peter approached him and asked, "Lord,
how many times shall I forgive my brother
or sister who sins against me? As many as
seven times?"

22 "I tell you, not as many as seven," Jesus
replied, "but seventy times seven.[M]

23 "For this reason, the kingdom of heaven
can be compared to a king who wanted to
settle accounts with his servants. 24 When he

Relationships | *Relating to Children*

WELCOMING JESUS

"He called a child and had him stand among them. . . . And whoever welcomes one child like this in my name welcomes me." Matthew 18:2,5

Ancient cultures (some would no doubt argue most modern cultures as well) were male-dominated. Men called the shots and enjoyed all privilege and power. Women were seen as subservient, less valuable, second-class citizens (if they got to be citizens at all). And children? They were even lower on the proverbial totem pole, perhaps "seen" on occasion, but surely never "heard." Leave it to Jesus to teach and model a different view.

In response to the question, "Who is greatest in the kingdom of heaven?" Jesus plucked from the crowd not a powerful and prominent religious leader but a small, nameless boy. His point was that childlike humility is what grants us status in God's kingdom. And he went on to suggest that the very people culture regards as insignificant (and often treats with contempt) should be afforded the utmost respect and acceptance. In so many words, Jesus was saying, "Treat them as you would me."

When we treat others with dignity, it just "feels right"—no doubt because it is right. Try it today, and watch your own soul swell with joy.

For the next note on *Relationships*, see Matthew 19:4-6.

[A] **18:9** Lit *gehenna of fire* [B] **18:10** Some mss include v. 11: *For the Son of Man has come to save the lost.* [C] **18:13** Lit *over it* [D] **18:15** Other mss omit *against you* [E] **18:15** Lit *him between you and him alone* [F] **18:16** Lit *mouth* [G] **18:16** Dt 19:15 [H] **18:17** Or *congregation* [I] **18:18** Or *earth will be bound* [J] **18:18** Or *earth will be loosed* [K] **18:19** Lit *they* [L] **18:19** Lit *for them* [M] **18:22** Or *but seventy-seven times*

began to settle accounts, one who owed ten
thousand talents[A] was brought before him.
25 Since he did not have the money to pay it
back, his master commanded that he, his wife,
his children, and everything he had be sold to
pay the debt.
26 "At this, the servant fell facedown before
him and said, 'Be patient with me, and I will
pay you everything.' 27 Then the master of that
servant had compassion, released him, and
forgave him the loan.
28 "That servant went out and found one of
his fellow servants who owed him a hundred
denarii.[B] He grabbed him, started choking
him, and said, 'Pay what you owe!'
29 "At this, his fellow servant fell down[C] and
began begging him, 'Be patient with me, and
I will pay you back.' 30 But he wasn't willing.
Instead, he went and threw him into prison
until he could pay what was owed. 31 When
the other servants saw what had taken place,
they were deeply distressed and went and
reported to their master everything that had
happened. 32 Then, after he had summoned
him, his master said to him, 'You wicked servant! I forgave you all that debt because you
begged me. 33 Shouldn't you also have had
mercy on your fellow servant, as I had mercy on you?' 34 And because he was angry, his
master handed him over to the jailers to be
tortured until he could pay everything that
was owed. 35 So also my heavenly Father will
do to you unless every one of you forgives his
brother or sister[D] from your[E] heart."

THE QUESTION OF DIVORCE

19 When Jesus had finished saying these
things, he departed from Galilee and
went to the region of Judea across the Jordan.
2 Large crowds followed him, and he healed
them there. 3 Some Pharisees approached him
to test him. They asked, "Is it lawful for a man
to divorce his wife on any grounds?"
4 "Haven't you read," he replied, "that he
who created[F] them in the beginning **made
them male and female**,[G] 5 and he also said,
'**For this reason a man will leave his father
and mother and be joined to his wife, and
the two will become one flesh**'?[H] 6 So they are
no longer two, but one flesh. Therefore, what
God has joined together, let no one separate."
7 "Why then," they asked him, "did Moses
command us to give divorce papers and to
send her away?"

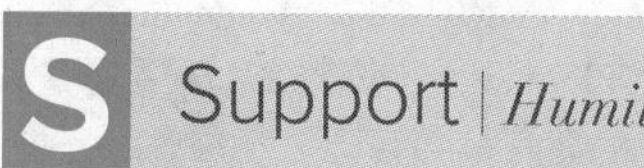

THE BLESSING OF HUMILITY

"Therefore, whoever humbles himself like this child—this one is the greatest in the kingdom of heaven." Matthew 18:4

Children—at least until they reach a certain age—have zero inhibitions about admitting their inabilities and asking for help. They call out. They reach up their hands. By these outward gestures (and others), they express an inward reality: "I can't. I need you. Please help me!" This is the childlike humility that Jesus praised. This kind of holy helplessness pleases God—and makes miracles possible. When we admit our weakness and dependence, the Almighty rushes in with desperately needed help.

Perhaps you view neediness as pathetic and embarrassing. If so, realize this: Jesus sees this kind of humble vulnerability as a prerequisite for rescue and healing. In fact, he noted that only those who know they're sick ever realize their need for a doctor (implying that only they find healing, see Mt 9:12). What does the Bible say elsewhere? "God resists the proud but gives grace to the humble" (1Pt 5:5).

Want God to flood your life with grace? Humble yourself. Acknowledge your inadequacies, so that you can experience his infinite supply of favor.

For the next note on *Support*, see Mark 9:23-24.

[A] **18:24** A talent is worth about 6,000 denarii, or twenty years' wages for a laborer [B] **18:28** A denarius = one day's wage [C] **18:29** Other mss add *at his feet* [D] **18:35** Other mss add *their trespasses* [E] **18:35** Lit *his* [F] **19:4** Other mss read *made* [G] **19:4** Gn 1:27; 5:2 [H] **19:5** Gn 2:24

8 He told them, "Moses permitted you to
divorce your wives because of the hardness
of your hearts, but it was not like that from
the beginning. 9 I tell you, whoever divorces
his wife, except for sexual immorality, and
marries another commits adultery."[A]
10 His disciples said to him, "If the relationship of a man with his wife is like this, it's
better not to marry."
11 He responded, "Not everyone can accept
this saying, but only those to whom it has
been given. 12 For there are eunuchs who
were born that way from their mother's
womb, there are eunuchs who were made
by men, and there are eunuchs who have
made themselves that way because of the
kingdom of heaven. The one who is able to
accept it should accept it."

BLESSING THE CHILDREN

13 Then children were brought to Jesus for
him to place his hands on them and pray,
but the disciples rebuked them. 14 Jesus said,
"Leave the children alone, and don't try to
keep them from coming to me, because the
kingdom of heaven belongs to such as these."[B]
15 After placing his hands on them, he went
on from there.

THE RICH YOUNG RULER

16 Just then someone came up and asked him,
"Teacher, what good must I do to have eternal life?"
17 "Why do you ask me about what is good?"[C]
he said to him. "There is only one who is good.[D]
If you want to enter into life, keep the commandments."
18 "Which ones?" he asked him.
Jesus answered: **Do not murder; do not
commit adultery; do not steal; do not bear
false witness;** 19 **honor your father and your
mother; and love your neighbor as yourself.**[E]
20 "I have kept all these,"[F] the young man
told him. "What do I still lack?"
21 "If you want to be perfect,"[G] Jesus said to
him, "go, sell your belongings and give to the
poor, and you will have treasure in heaven.
Then come, follow me."
22 When the young man heard that, he went
away grieving, because he had many possessions.

POSSESSIONS AND THE KINGDOM

23 Jesus said to his disciples, "Truly I tell you,
it will be hard for a rich person to enter the
kingdom of heaven. 24 Again I tell you, it is
easier for a camel to go through the eye of

Relationships | *Relating to Spouse*

MARRIAGE MATTERS

"'Haven't you read,' he replied, 'that he who created them in the beginning made them male and female,' and he also said, 'For this reason a man will leave his father and mother and be joined to his wife, and the two will become one flesh? So they are no longer two, but one flesh. Therefore, what God has joined together, let no one separate.'" Matthew 19:4-6

Marriage is a big deal because it was designed by God to picture the intimate union Christ has with his church (Eph 5:21-33). When husbands love sacrificially and unconditionally, when wives respond with faithful affection, when both give and forgive lavishly, a marriage is eye-catching and breathtaking. It's like a living billboard for the beauty and mystery of the gospel.

A thriving, healthy marriage honors God, blesses the world, and brings joy to a man and his wife. But what if your marriage is struggling and a source of frequent grief?

Call it what it is. Ask God and others for help. Then be humble—willing to admit your contribution to the situation. All that is required is that you do your part.

For the next note on *Relationships*, see Matthew 22:39-40.

[A] **19:9** Other mss add *Also whoever marries a divorced woman commits adultery*; Mt 5:32 [B] **19:14** Lit *heaven is of such ones* [C] **19:17** Other mss read *"Why do you call me good?"* [D] **19:17** Other mss read *"No one is good but one — God* [E] **19:18-19** Ex 20:12-16; Lv 19:18; Dt 5:16-20 [F] **19:20** Other mss add *from my youth* [G] **19:21** Or *complete*

a needle than for a rich person to enter the
kingdom of God."
25 When the disciples heard this, they were
utterly astonished and asked, "Then who can
be saved?"
26 Jesus looked at them and said, "With man
this is impossible, but with God all things are
possible."
27 Then Peter responded to him, "See, we have
left everything and followed you. So what will
there be for us?"
28 Jesus said to them, "Truly I tell you, in the
renewal of all things, when the Son of Man sits
on his glorious throne, you who have followed
me will also sit on twelve thrones, judging the
twelve tribes of Israel. 29 And everyone who
has left houses or brothers or sisters or father
or mother[A] or children or fields because of my
name will receive a hundred times more and
will inherit eternal life. 30 But many who are
first will be last, and the last first.

THE PARABLE OF THE VINEYARD WORKERS

20 "For the kingdom of heaven is like a
landowner who went out early in the
morning to hire workers for his vineyard. 2 After
agreeing with the workers on one denarius,[B] he
sent them into his vineyard for the day. 3 When
he went out about nine in the morning,[C] he
saw others standing in the marketplace doing
nothing. 4 He said to them, 'You also go into my
vineyard, and I'll give you whatever is right.' So
off they went. 5 About noon and about three,[D] he
went out again and did the same thing. 6 Then
about five[E] he went and found others standing
around[F] and said to them, 'Why have you been
standing here all day doing nothing?'
7 "'Because no one hired us,' they said to him.
"'You also go into my vineyard,' he told
them.[G] 8 When evening came, the owner of
the vineyard told his foreman, 'Call the workers and give them their pay, starting with the
last and ending with the first.'
9 "When those who were hired about five
came, they each received one denarius. 10 So
when the first ones came, they assumed they
would get more, but they also received a denarius each. 11 When they received it, they
began to complain to the landowner: 12 'These
last men put in one hour, and you made them
equal to us who bore the burden of the day's
work and the burning heat.'

Eternal Perspective | *God's Power*

LIMITLESS STRENGTH

"When the disciples heard this, they were utterly astonished and asked, 'Then who can be saved?' Jesus looked at them and said, 'With man this is impossible, but with God all things are possible.'" Matthew 19:25-26

The world is full of naysayers who revel in speaking of impossibilities. We are surrounded by pessimists who delight in telling us all the reasons our dreams are dumb, our plans our stupid, our prayers are futile.

However, we are also loved, cared for, and called by One who asks rhetorically, "Is anything impossible for the LORD?" (Gn 18:14). In another place, Job tells God, "I know that you can do anything and no plan of yours can be thwarted" (Jb 42:2).

The question becomes, "Which perspective will we embrace?" Clearly, the Bible's declarations ought to give us great confidence—especially when we face dire circumstances or situations that, humanly speaking, look hopeless. Nothing—absolutely nothing—is too hard for the One we call the Almighty! He is more than able. He is stronger and bigger than all else. This isn't "positive thinking," it's "truth trusting"! Will you let the truth of God's omnipotence overshadow every gloomy and "doomy" situation in your life?

For the next note on *Eternal Perspective*, see Matthew 25:21.

[A] **19:29** Other mss add *or wife* [B] **20:2** A denarius = one day's wage, also in vv. 9,10,13 [C] **20:3** Lit *about the third hour* [D] **20:5** Lit *about the sixth hour and the ninth hour* [E] **20:6** Lit *about the eleventh hour*, also in v. 9 [F] **20:6** Other mss add *doing nothing* [G] **20:7** Other mss add *'and you'll get whatever is right.'*

13 "He replied to one of them, 'Friend, I'm
doing you no wrong. Didn't you agree with
me on a denarius? 14 Take what's yours and
go. I want to give this last man the same as I
gave you. 15 Don't I have the right to do what
I want with what is mine? Are you jealous[A]
because I'm generous?'[B]
16 "So the last will be first, and the first last."[C]

THE THIRD PREDICTION OF HIS DEATH

17 While going up to Jerusalem, Jesus took the
twelve disciples aside privately and said to them
on the way, 18 "See, we are going up to Jerusalem. The Son of Man will be handed over to the
chief priests and scribes, and they will condemn
him to death. 19 They will hand him over to the
Gentiles to be mocked, flogged,[D] and crucified,
and on the third day he will be raised."[E]

SUFFERING AND SERVICE

20 Then the mother of Zebedee's sons approached him with her sons. She knelt down
to ask him for something. 21 "What do you
want?" he asked her.
"Promise,"[F] she said to him, "that these two
sons of mine may sit, one on your right and
the other on your left, in your kingdom."
22 Jesus answered, "You don't know what
you're asking. Are you able to drink the cup
that I am about to drink?"[G]
"We are able," they said to him.
23 He told them, "You will indeed drink my
cup,[H] but to sit at my right and left is not mine
to give; instead, it is for those for whom it has
been prepared by my Father."
24 When the ten disciples heard this, they became indignant with the two brothers. 25 Jesus
called them over and said, "You know that the
rulers of the Gentiles lord it over them, and
those in high positions act as tyrants over
them. 26 It must not be like that among you.
On the contrary, whoever wants to become
great among you must be your servant, 27 and
whoever wants to be first among you must
be your slave; 28 just as the Son of Man did
not come to be served, but to serve, and to
give his life as a ransom for many."

TWO BLIND MEN HEALED

29 As they were leaving Jericho, a large crowd
followed him. 30 There were two blind men sitting by the road. When they heard that Jesus was
passing by, they cried out, "Lord, have mercy
on us, Son of David!" 31 The crowd demanded
that they keep quiet, but they cried out all the
more, "Lord, have mercy on us, Son of David!"

Exercise of Faith | *Serving*

GIVING OUR LIVES AWAY

"Just as the Son of Man did not come to be served, but to serve, and to give his life as a ransom for many." Matthew 20:28

Many people assume the cure for a bout with the blues is a visit to a good therapist and perhaps a new antidepressant. But years ago, when someone put this question to acclaimed psychiatrist Dr. Karl Menninger, he responded, "Lock up your house, go across the railroad tracks, find someone in need, and help that person."

This was the ministry of Jesus. This is the message of the gospel. We were created by the God who "is love" (1Jn 4:8) to be objects and agents of love, to be other-centered. This means self-absorption is not only sinful, it's dysfunctional and detrimental. Hope, happiness, and healing are found only in serving others. When we lay down our lives for the sake of family and friends, neighbors and—yes—enemies, we not only bless them, we get to experience the blessing and rewards of obedience.

Who has God put in your path for you to serve today? What one act of service will you commit to do? Lock up your house and go!

For the next note on *Exercise of Faith*, see Matthew 28:18-20.

[A] **20:15** Lit *Is your eye evil*; an idiom for jealousy or stinginess [B] **20:15** Lit *good* [C] **20:16** Other mss add *"For many are called, but few are chosen."* [D] **20:19** Or *scourged* [E] **20:19** Other mss read *will rise again* [F] **20:21** Lit *Say* [G] **20:22** Other mss add *and (or) to be baptized with the baptism which I am baptized?"* [H] **20:23** Other mss add *and be baptized with the baptism with which I am baptized.*

32 Jesus stopped, called them, and said, "What
do you want me to do for you?"
33 "Lord," they said to him, "open our eyes."
34 Moved with compassion, Jesus touched their
eyes. Immediately they could see, and they
followed him.

THE TRIUMPHAL ENTRY

21 When they approached Jerusalem and
came to Bethphage at the Mount of
Olives, Jesus then sent two disciples, 2 telling them, "Go into the village ahead of you.
At once you will find a donkey tied there
with her foal. Untie them and bring them
to me. 3 If anyone says anything to you, say
that the Lord needs them, and he will send
them at once."
4 This took place so that what was spoken
through the prophet might be fulfilled:

5 **Tell Daughter Zion,**
"See, your King is coming to you,
gentle, and mounted on a donkey,
and on a colt,
the foal of a donkey."[A]

6 The disciples went and did just as Jesus
directed them. 7 They brought the donkey and
its foal; then they laid their clothes on them,
and he sat on them. 8 A very large crowd spread
their clothes on the road; others were cutting
branches from the trees and spreading them
on the road. 9 Then the crowds who went ahead
of him and those who followed shouted:

Hosanna **to the Son of David!**
Blessed is he who comes in the name
of the Lord![B]
Hosanna **in the highest heaven!**

10 When he entered Jerusalem, the whole city
was in an uproar, saying, "Who is this?" 11 The
crowds were saying, "This is the prophet Jesus
from Nazareth in Galilee."

CLEANSING THE TEMPLE

12 Jesus went into the temple[C] and threw out
all those buying and selling. He overturned the
tables of the money changers and the chairs of
those selling doves. 13 He said to them, "It is written, **my house will be called a house of prayer,**[D]
but you are making it **a den of thieves!**"[E]

CHILDREN PRAISE JESUS

14 The blind and the lame came to him in the
temple, and he healed them. 15 When the chief
priests and the scribes saw the wonders that
he did and the children shouting in the temple,
"*Hosanna* to the Son of David!" they were indignant 16 and said to him, "Do you hear what
these children are saying?"
Jesus replied, "Yes, have you never read:

You have prepared[F] **praise**
from the mouths of infants
and nursing babies?"[G]

17 Then he left them, went out of the city to
Bethany, and spent the night there.

THE BARREN FIG TREE

18 Early in the morning, as he was returning to
the city, he was hungry. 19 Seeing a lone fig tree
by the road, he went up to it and found nothing
on it except leaves. And he said to it, "May no
fruit ever come from you again!" At once the
fig tree withered.
20 When the disciples saw it, they were
amazed and said, "How did the fig tree wither so quickly?"
21 Jesus answered them, "Truly I tell you, if you
have faith and do not doubt, you will not only
do what was done to the fig tree, but even if you
tell this mountain, 'Be lifted up and thrown into
the sea,' it will be done. 22 And if you believe, you
will receive whatever you ask for in prayer."

THE AUTHORITY OF JESUS CHALLENGED

23 When he entered the temple, the chief priests
and the elders of the people came to him as
he was teaching and said, "By what authority
are you doing these things? Who gave you this
authority?"
24 Jesus answered them, "I will also ask you
one question, and if you answer it for me, then I
will tell you by what authority I do these things.
25 Did John's baptism come from heaven, or
was it of human origin?"
They discussed it among themselves, "If we
say, 'From heaven,' he will say to us, 'Then why
didn't you believe him?' 26 But if we say, 'Of human origin,' we're afraid of the crowd, because
everyone considers John to be a prophet."
27 So they answered Jesus, "We don't know."
And he said to them, "Neither will I tell you
by what authority I do these things.

THE PARABLE OF THE TWO SONS

28 "What do you think? A man had two sons.
He went to the first and said, 'My son, go work
in the vineyard today.'

[A] **21:5** Is 62:11; Zch 9:9 [B] **21:9** Ps 118:25-26 [C] **21:12** Other mss add *of God* [D] **21:13** Is 56:7 [E] **21:13** Jr 7:11 [F] **21:16** Or *restored*
[G] **21:16** Ps 8:2

29 "He answered, 'I don't want to,' but later he
changed his mind and went. 30 Then the man
went to the other and said the same thing. 'I
will, sir,' he answered, but he didn't go. 31 Which
of the two did his father's will?"

They said, "The first."

Jesus said to them, "Truly I tell you, tax collectors and prostitutes are entering the kingdom
of God before you. 32 For John came to you in
the way of righteousness, and you didn't believe him. Tax collectors and prostitutes did
believe him; but you, when you saw it, didn't
even change your minds then and believe him.

THE PARABLE OF THE VINEYARD OWNER

33 "Listen to another parable: There was a landowner, who planted a vineyard, put a fence
around it, dug a winepress in it, and built a
watchtower. He leased it to tenant farmers
and went away. 34 When the time came to harvest fruit, he sent his servants to the farmers
to collect his fruit. 35 The farmers took his servants, beat one, killed another, and stoned a
third. 36 Again, he sent other servants, more
than the first group, and they did the same to
them. 37 Finally, he sent his son to them. 'They
will respect my son,' he said.

38 "But when the tenant farmers saw the
son, they said to each other, 'This is the heir.
Come, let's kill him and take his inheritance.'
39 So they seized him, threw him out of the
vineyard, and killed him. 40 Therefore, when
the owner of the vineyard comes, what will
he do to those farmers?"

41 "He will completely destroy those terrible
men," they told him, "and lease his vineyard
to other farmers who will give him his fruit
at the harvest."

42 Jesus said to them, "Have you never read
in the Scriptures:

> **The stone that the builders rejected**
> **has become the cornerstone.**[A]
> **This is what the Lord has done**
> **and it is wonderful in our eyes?**[B]

43 Therefore I tell you, the kingdom of God
will be taken away from you and given to a
people producing its fruit. 44 Whoever falls
on this stone will be broken to pieces; but on
whomever it falls, it will shatter him."[C]

45 When the chief priests and the Pharisees
heard his parables, they knew he was speaking
about them. 46 Although they were looking for
a way to arrest him, they feared the crowds,
because the people regarded him as a prophet.

THE PARABLE OF THE WEDDING BANQUET

22 Once more Jesus spoke to them in parables: 2 "The kingdom of heaven is like
a king who gave a wedding banquet for his
son. 3 He sent his servants to summon those
invited to the banquet, but they didn't want
to come. 4 Again, he sent out other servants
and said, 'Tell those who are invited: See, I've
prepared my dinner; my oxen and fattened
cattle have been slaughtered, and everything
is ready. Come to the wedding banquet.'

5 "But they paid no attention and went away,
one to his own farm, another to his business,
6 while the rest seized his servants, mistreated
them, and killed them. 7 The king[D] was enraged,
and he sent out his troops, killed those murderers, and burned down their city.

8 "Then he told his servants, 'The banquet is
ready, but those who were invited were not
worthy. 9 Go then to where the roads exit the
city and invite everyone you find to the banquet.' 10 So those servants went out on the roads
and gathered everyone they found, both evil
and good. The wedding banquet[E] was filled
with guests.[F] 11 When the king came in to see
the guests, he saw a man there who was not
dressed for a wedding. 12 So he said to him,
'Friend, how did you get in here without wedding clothes?' The man was speechless.

13 "Then the king told the attendants, 'Tie
him up hand and foot,[G] and throw him into the
outer darkness, where there will be weeping
and gnashing of teeth.'

14 "For many are invited, but few are chosen."

GOD AND CAESAR

15 Then the Pharisees went and plotted how to
trap him by what he said.[H] 16 So they sent their
disciples to him, along with the Herodians.
"Teacher," they said, "we know that you are
truthful and teach truthfully the way of God.
You don't care what anyone thinks nor do you
show partiality.[I] 17 Tell us, then, what you think.
Is it lawful to pay taxes to Caesar or not?"

18 Perceiving their malicious intent, Jesus
said, "Why are you testing me, hypocrites?
19 Show me the coin used for the tax." They
brought him a denarius.[J] 20 "Whose image and
inscription is this?" he asked them.

[A] **21:42** Lit *the head of the corner* [B] **21:42** Ps 118:22-23 [C] **21:44** Some mss omit this verse [D] **22:7** Other mss read *But when the (that) king heard about it he* [E] **22:10** Other mss read *wedding hall* [F] **22:10** Lit *those reclining* (to eat) [G] **22:13** Other mss add *take him away* [H] **22:15** Lit *trap him in a word* [I] **22:16** Lit *don't look on the face of men* [J] **22:19** A denarius = one day's wage

21 "Caesar's," they said to him.
Then he said to them, "Give, then, to Caesar the things that are Caesar's, and to God
the things that are God's." 22 When they heard
this, they were amazed. So they left him and
went away.

THE SADDUCEES AND THE RESURRECTION

23 That same day some Sadducees, who say
there is no resurrection, came up to him and
questioned him: 24 "Teacher, Moses said, **if a
man dies, having no children, his brother
is to marry his wife and raise up offspring
for his brother.**[A] 25 Now there were seven
brothers among us. The first got married
and died. Having no offspring, he left his
wife to his brother. 26 The same thing happened to the second also, and the third, and
so on to all seven. 27 Last of all, the woman
died. 28 In the resurrection, then, whose wife
will she be of the seven? For they all had
married her."[B]
29 Jesus answered them, "You are mistaken,
because you don't know the Scriptures or the
power of God. 30 For in the resurrection they
neither marry nor are given in marriage but
are like[C] angels in heaven. 31 Now concerning
the resurrection of the dead, haven't you read
what was spoken to you by God: 32 **I am the
God of Abraham and the God of Isaac and
the God of Jacob?**[D] He[E] is not the God of the
dead, but of the living."
33 And when the crowds heard this, they
were astonished at his teaching.

THE PRIMARY COMMANDS

34 When the Pharisees heard that he had silenced the Sadducees, they came together.
35 And one of them, an expert in the law, asked
a question to test him: 36 "Teacher, which command in the law is the greatest?"
37 He said to him, "**Love the Lord your God
with all your heart, with all your soul, and
with all your mind.**[F] 38 This is the greatest and
most important[G] command. 39 The second is
like it: **Love your neighbor as yourself.**[H] 40 All
the Law and the Prophets depend[I] on these
two commands."

THE QUESTION ABOUT THE CHRIST

41 While the Pharisees were together, Jesus
questioned them, 42 "What do you think about
the Messiah? Whose son is he?"
They replied, "David's."
43 He asked them, "How is it then that David,
inspired by the Spirit,[J] calls him 'Lord':
44 **The Lord declared to my Lord,
'Sit at my right hand**

Relationships | *Loving Our Neighbors*

LOVING GOD AND LOVING OTHERS

"The second is like it: Love your neighbor as yourself. All the Law and the Prophets depend on these two commands." Matthew 22:39-40

In stating the famous "Great Commandment," Jesus was essentially summarizing the Ten Commandments. He boiled them down, in effect making the spiritual life an inseparable package deal of loving God and loving others. It's a both-and, not an either-or. The rest of the Bible makes clear that we cannot truly love others apart from God's love (because he's the ultimate source of love). What's more, to say we love God if we are busy being hateful to the people he's put in our path is hypocritical (see 1Jn 4:7-20).

So, what does "love your neighbor as yourself" mean? Since biblical love is always action-oriented, it must mean more than just thinking warm thoughts about others. At the very least it must mean we are to seek their best and take steps to meet their needs.

Pray that you might become a more faithful conduit of God's love. Then commit to one concrete action you will take today to "love your neighbor as yourself."

For the next note on *Relationships*, see Luke 4:28-29.

[A] **22:24** Dt 25:5 [B] **22:28** Lit *all had her* [C] **22:30** Other mss add *God's* [D] **22:32** Ex 3:6,15-16 [E] **22:32** Other mss read *God*
[F] **22:37** Dt 6:5 [G] **22:38** Lit *and first* [H] **22:39** Lv 19:18 [I] **22:40** Or *hang* [J] **22:43** Lit *David in Spirit*

until I put your enemies
under your feet'?[A,B]
45 "If David calls him 'Lord,' how then can he be
his son?" 46 No one was able to answer him at
all,[C] and from that day no one dared to question him anymore.

RELIGIOUS HYPOCRITES DENOUNCED

23 Then Jesus spoke to the crowds and to
his disciples: 2 "The scribes and the Pharisees are seated in the chair of Moses. 3 Therefore do whatever they tell you, and observe it.
But don't do what they do, because they don't
practice what they teach. 4 They tie up heavy
loads that are hard to carry[D] and put them on
people's shoulders, but they themselves aren't
willing to lift a finger to move them. 5 They do
everything[E] to be seen by others: They enlarge
their phylacteries and lengthen their tassels.[F]
6 They love the place of honor at banquets, the
front seats in the synagogues, 7 greetings in the
marketplaces, and to be called 'Rabbi' by people.
8 "But you are not to be called 'Rabbi,' because you have one Teacher,[G] and you are all
brothers and sisters. 9 Do not call anyone on
earth your father, because you have one Father, who is in heaven. 10 You are not to be
called instructors either, because you have
one Instructor, the Messiah. 11 The greatest
among you will be your servant. 12 Whoever
exalts himself will be humbled, and whoever
humbles himself will be exalted.
13 "Woe to you, scribes and Pharisees, hypocrites! You shut the door of the kingdom of
heaven in people's faces. For you don't go in,
and you don't allow those entering to go in.[H]
15 "Woe to you, scribes and Pharisees, hypocrites! You travel over land and sea to make
one convert, and when he becomes one, you
make him twice as fit for hell[I] as you are!
16 "Woe to you, blind guides, who say, 'Whoever takes an oath by the temple, it means
nothing. But whoever takes an oath by the gold
of the temple is bound by his oath.'[J] 17 Blind
fools! For which is greater, the gold or the temple that sanctified the gold? 18 Also, 'Whoever
takes an oath by the altar, it means nothing;
but whoever takes an oath by the gift that is
on it is bound by his oath.' 19 Blind people![K]
For which is greater, the gift or the altar that
sanctifies the gift? 20 Therefore, the one who
takes an oath by the altar takes an oath by it
and by everything on it. 21 The one who takes
an oath by the temple takes an oath by it and
by him who dwells in it. 22 And the one who
takes an oath by heaven takes an oath by God's
throne and by him who sits on it.
23 "Woe to you, scribes and Pharisees, hypocrites! You pay a tenth of[L] mint, dill, and cumin,
and yet you have neglected the more important matters of the law — justice, mercy, and
faithfulness.[M] These things should have been
done without neglecting the others. 24 Blind
guides! You strain out a gnat, but gulp down
a camel!
25 "Woe to you, scribes and Pharisees, hypocrites! You clean the outside of the cup and
dish, but inside they are full of greed[N] and
self-indulgence. 26 Blind Pharisee! First clean
the inside of the cup,[O] so that the outside of
it[P] may also become clean.
27 "Woe to you, scribes and Pharisees, hypocrites! You are like whitewashed tombs, which
appear beautiful on the outside, but inside are
full of the bones of the dead and every kind
of impurity. 28 In the same way, on the outside
you seem righteous to people, but inside you
are full of hypocrisy and lawlessness.
29 "Woe to you, scribes and Pharisees, hypocrites! You build the tombs of the prophets and decorate the graves of the righteous,
30 and you say, 'If we had lived in the days of
our ancestors, we wouldn't have taken part
with them in shedding the prophets' blood.'
31 So you testify against yourselves that you
are descendants of those who murdered the
prophets. 32 Fill up, then, the measure of your
ancestors' sins!
33 "Snakes! Brood of vipers! How can you
escape being condemned to hell?[Q] 34 This is
why I am sending you prophets, sages, and
scribes. Some of them you will kill and crucify, and some of them you will flog in your
synagogues and pursue from town to town.
35 So all the righteous blood shed on the earth
will be charged to you,[R] from the blood of
righteous Abel to the blood of Zechariah, son
of Berechiah, whom you murdered between

[A] **22:44** Other mss read *until I make your enemies your footstool'* [B] **22:44** Ps 110:1 [C] **22:46** Lit *answer him a word* [D] **23:4** Other mss omit *that are hard to carry* [E] **23:5** Lit *do all their works* [F] **23:5** Other mss add *on their robes* [G] **23:8** Other mss add *the Christ* [H] **23:13** Some mss include v. 14: *"Woe to you, scribes and Pharisees, hypocrites! You devour widows' houses and make long prayers just for show. This is why you will receive a harsher punishment.* [I] **23:15** Lit *twice the son of gehenna* [J] **23:16** Lit *is obligated*, also in v. 18 [K] **23:19** Other mss read *Fools and blind* [L] **23:23** Or *You tithe* [M] **23:23** Or *faith* [N] **23:25** Or *full of violence* [O] **23:26** Other mss add *and dish* [P] **23:26** Other mss read *of them* [Q] **23:33** Lit *escape from the judgment of gehenna* [R] **23:35** Lit *will come on you*

the sanctuary and the altar. 36 Truly I tell you, all these things will come on this generation.

JESUS'S LAMENTING OVER JERUSALEM

37 "Jerusalem, Jerusalem, who kills the prophets and stones those who are sent to her. How often I wanted to gather your children together, as a hen gathers her chicks[A] under her wings, but you were not willing! 38 See, your house is left to you desolate. 39 For I tell you, you will not see me again until you say, **'Blessed is he who comes in the name of the Lord'**!"[B]

DESTRUCTION OF THE TEMPLE PREDICTED

24 As Jesus left and was going out of the temple, his disciples came up and called his attention to its buildings. 2 He replied to them, "Do you see all these things? Truly I tell you, not one stone will be left here on another that will not be thrown down."

SIGNS OF THE END OF THE AGE

3 While he was sitting on the Mount of Olives, the disciples approached him privately and said, "Tell us, when will these things happen? And what is the sign of your coming and of the end of the age?"

4 Jesus replied to them: "Watch out that no one deceives you. 5 For many will come in my name, saying, 'I am the Messiah,' and they will deceive many. 6 You are going to hear of wars and rumors of wars. See that you are not alarmed, because these things must take place, but the end is not yet. 7 For nation will rise up against nation, and kingdom against kingdom. There will be famines[C] and earthquakes in various places. 8 All these events are the beginning of labor pains.

PERSECUTIONS PREDICTED

9 "Then they will hand you over to be persecuted, and they will kill you. You will be hated by all nations because of my name. 10 Then many will fall away, betray one another, and hate one another. 11 Many false prophets will rise up and deceive many. 12 Because lawlessness will multiply, the love of many will grow cold. 13 But the one who endures to the end will be saved. 14 This good news of the kingdom will be proclaimed in all the world[D] as a testimony to all nations, and then the end will come.

THE GREAT TRIBULATION

15 "So when you see **the abomination of desolation**,[E] spoken of by the prophet Daniel, standing in the holy place" (let the reader understand), 16 "then those in Judea must flee to the mountains. 17 A man on the housetop[F] must not come down to get things out of his house, 18 and a man in the field must not go back to get his coat. 19 Woe to pregnant women and nursing mothers in those days! 20 Pray that your escape may not be in winter or on a Sabbath. 21 For at that time there will be great distress,[G] the kind that hasn't taken place from the beginning of the world until now and never will again. 22 Unless those days were cut short, no one would[H] be saved. But those days will be cut short because of the elect.

23 "If anyone tells you then, 'See, here is the Messiah!' or, 'Over here!' do not believe it. 24 For false messiahs and false prophets will arise and perform great signs and wonders to lead astray, if possible, even the elect. 25 Take note: I have told you in advance. 26 So if they tell you, 'See, he's in the wilderness!' don't go out; or, 'See, he's in the storerooms!' do not believe it. 27 For as the lightning comes from the east and flashes as far as the west, so will be the coming of the Son of Man. 28 Wherever the carcass is, there the vultures[I] will gather.

THE COMING OF THE SON OF MAN

29 "Immediately after the distress of those days, the sun will be darkened, and the moon will not shed its light; the stars will fall from the sky, and the powers of the heavens will be shaken. 30 Then the sign of the Son of Man will appear in the sky, and then all the peoples of the earth[J] will mourn;[K] and they will see the Son of Man coming on the clouds of heaven with power and great glory. 31 He will send out his angels with a loud trumpet, and they will gather his elect from the four winds, from one end of the sky to the other.

THE PARABLE OF THE FIG TREE

32 "Learn this lesson from the fig tree: As soon as its branch becomes tender and sprouts leaves, you know that summer is near. 33 In the same way, when you see all these things, recognize[L] that he[M] is near — at the door. 34 Truly I tell you, this generation will certainly not

---

[A] **23:37** Or *as a mother bird gathers her young* [B] **23:39** Ps 118:26 [C] **24:7** Other mss add *epidemics* [D] **24:14** Or *in all the inhabited earth* [E] **24:15** Dn 9:27 [F] **24:17** Or *roof* [G] **24:21** Or *tribulation*, also in v. 29 [H] **24:22** Lit *short, all flesh would not* [I] **24:28** Or *eagles* [J] **24:30** Or *all the tribes of the land* [K] **24:30** Lit *will beat*; that is, beat their chests [L] **24:33** Or *things, you know* [M] **24:33** Or *it*; that is, summer

pass away until all these things take place.
35 Heaven and earth will pass away, but my
words will never pass away.

NO ONE KNOWS THE DAY OR HOUR

36 "Now concerning that day and hour no one
knows — neither the angels of heaven nor
the Son[A] — except the Father alone. 37 As the
days of Noah were, so the coming of the Son
of Man will be. 38 For in those days before the
flood they were eating and drinking, marrying and giving in marriage, until the day Noah
boarded the ark. 39 They didn't know until the
flood came and swept them all away. This is
the way the coming of the Son of Man will be.
40 Then two men will be in the field; one will
be taken and one left. 41 Two women will be
grinding grain with a hand mill; one will be
taken and one left. 42 Therefore be alert, since
you don't know what day[B] your Lord is coming. 43 But know this: If the homeowner had
known what time[C] the thief was coming, he
would have stayed alert and not let his house
be broken into. 44 This is why you are also to
be ready, because the Son of Man is coming at
an hour you do not expect.

FAITHFUL SERVICE TO CHRIST

45 "Who then is a faithful and wise servant,
whom his master has put in charge of his
household, to give them food at the proper
time? 46 Blessed is that servant whom the
master finds doing his job when he comes.
47 Truly I tell you, he will put him in charge of
all his possessions. 48 But if that wicked servant says in his heart, 'My master is delayed,'
49 and starts to beat his fellow servants, and
eats and drinks with drunkards, 50 that servant's master will come on a day he does not
expect him and at an hour he does not know.
51 He will cut him to pieces and assign him a
place with the hypocrites, where there will
be weeping and gnashing of teeth.

THE PARABLE OF THE TEN VIRGINS

25 "At that time the kingdom of heaven
will be like ten virgins[D] who took their
lamps[E] and went out to meet the groom. 2 Five
of them were foolish and five were wise. 3 When
the foolish took their lamps, they didn't take oil
with them; 4 but the wise ones took oil in their
flasks with their lamps. 5 When the groom was
delayed, they all became drowsy and fell asleep.

Eternal Perspective | *Stewardship*

WELL DONE!

"His master said to him, 'Well done, good and faithful servant! You were faithful over a few things; I will put you in charge of many things. Share your master's joy.'" Matthew 25:21

In ancient times, a steward was a reliable servant entrusted with the high privilege of overseeing some or all of his master's estate. Implicit in this arrangement was the idea that the servant was accountable to the master for how well he managed the resources of the master.

Jesus used this relationship to picture the "stewardship" to which all Christians are called. The Lord is our Master, and we are his servants or stewards. He has entrusted so much to us: the truth of the gospel, various spiritual gifts and blessings, natural abilities, untold service opportunities, material resources, and more.

The question is: How faithfully are we stewarding all these things? Are we misusing what God has placed in our care? Hiding these things? Ignoring our calling? Or are we using all we've been given to honor God and bless those around us?

As we act in the Master's best interests, we have the joy of knowing that one day we'll hear those glorious words, "Well done, good and faithful servant!"

For the next note on *Eternal Perspective*, see Mark 7:32-33.

[A] **24:36** Other mss omit *nor the Son* [B] **24:42** Other mss read *hour*; = time [C] **24:43** Lit *watch*; a division of the night in ancient times [D] **25:1** Or *bridesmaids* [E] **25:1** Or *torches*, also in vv. 3,4,7,8

6 "In the middle of the night there was a shout: 'Here's the groom! Come out to meet him.'

7 "Then all the virgins got up and trimmed their lamps. 8 The foolish ones said to the wise ones, 'Give us some of your oil, because our lamps are going out.'

9 "The wise ones answered, 'No, there won't be enough for us and for you. Go instead to those who sell oil, and buy some for yourselves.'

10 "When they had gone to buy some, the groom arrived, and those who were ready went in with him to the wedding banquet, and the door was shut. 11 Later the rest of the virgins also came and said, 'Master, master, open up for us!'

12 "He replied, 'Truly I tell you, I don't know you!'

13 "Therefore be alert, because you don't know either the day or the hour.[A]

THE PARABLE OF THE TALENTS

14 "For it is just like a man about to go on a journey. He called his own servants and entrusted his possessions to them. 15 To one he gave five talents,[B] to another two talents, and to another one talent, depending on each one's ability. Then he went on a journey. Immediately 16 the man who had received five talents went, put them to work, and earned five more. 17 In the same way the man with two earned two more. 18 But the man who had received one talent went off, dug a hole in the ground, and hid his master's money.

19 "After a long time the master of those servants came and settled accounts with them. 20 The man who had received five talents approached, presented five more talents, and said, 'Master, you gave me five talents. See, I've earned five more talents.'

21 "His master said to him, 'Well done, good and faithful servant! You were faithful over a few things; I will put you in charge of many things. Share your master's joy.'

22 "The man with two talents also approached. He said, 'Master, you gave me two talents. See, I've earned two more talents.'

23 "His master said to him, 'Well done, good and faithful servant! You were faithful over a few things; I will put you in charge of many things. Share your master's joy.'

24 "The man who had received one talent also approached and said, 'Master, I know you. You're a harsh man, reaping where you haven't sown and gathering where you haven't scattered seed. 25 So I was afraid and went off and hid your talent in the ground. See, you have what is yours.'

26 "His master replied to him, 'You evil, lazy

Other-centeredness | *Helping People in Need*

FOR THE LEAST OF THESE

"And the King will answer them, 'Truly I tell you, whatever you did for one of the least of these brothers and sisters of mine, you did for me.'" Matthew 25:40

In a passage that many call the parable of "The Sheep and the Goats," Jesus speaks of an impending time of judgment. On this coming day of accountability, the Lord will assess each person's life. Believers or "sheep" (that is, members of his flock) will be called forward and commended. And how about this shocker: Jesus will count every instance of pure-hearted ministry to the hungry, the thirsty, the lonely, the naked, the sick, and the imprisoned, as ministry to him!

This verse helps those who are weary of caring for others or cynical about the endless cycle of need all about them. It's probably the inspiration behind Paul's later command to "serve with a good attitude, as to the Lord and not to people, knowing that whatever good each one does, slave or free, he will receive this back from the Lord" (Eph 6:7-8).

Doing that—seeing our ministry as "to the Lord" and not to ungrateful people—has a way of renewing our joy.

For the next note on *Other-centeredness*, see Mark 2:17.

[A] **25:13** Other mss add *in which the Son of Man is coming.* [B] **25:15** A talent is worth about 6,000 denarii, or twenty years' wages for a laborer

servant! If you knew that I reap where I haven't
sown and gather where I haven't scattered,
27 then[A] you should have deposited my money
with the bankers, and I would have received my
money[B] back with interest when I returned.
28 " 'So take the talent from him and give it to
the one who has ten talents. 29 For to everyone
who has, more will be given, and he will have
more than enough. But from the one who does
not have, even what he has will be taken away
from him. 30 And throw this good-for-nothing
servant into the outer darkness, where there
will be weeping and gnashing of teeth.'

THE SHEEP AND THE GOATS

31 "When the Son of Man comes in his glory,
and all the angels[C] with him, then he will sit
on his glorious throne. 32 All the nations[D] will
be gathered before him, and he will separate
them one from another, just as a shepherd
separates the sheep from the goats. 33 He will
put the sheep on his right and the goats on
the left. 34 Then the King will say to those on
his right, 'Come, you who are blessed by my
Father; inherit the kingdom prepared for you
from the foundation of the world.
35 " 'For I was hungry and you gave me something to eat; I was thirsty and you gave me
something to drink; I was a stranger and you
took me in; 36 I was naked and you clothed me;
I was sick and you took care of me; I was in
prison and you visited me.'
37 "Then the righteous will answer him, 'Lord,
when did we see you hungry and feed you,
or thirsty and give you something to drink?
38 When did we see you a stranger and take
you in, or without clothes and clothe you?
39 When did we see you sick, or in prison, and
visit you?'
40 "And the King will answer them, 'Truly I
tell you, whatever you did for one of the least
of these brothers and sisters of mine, you did
for me.'
41 "Then he will also say to those on the left,
'Depart from me, you who are cursed, into
the eternal fire prepared for the devil and his
angels! 42 For I was hungry and you gave me
nothing to eat; I was thirsty and you gave me
nothing to drink; 43 I was a stranger and you
didn't take me in; I was naked and you didn't
clothe me, sick and in prison and you didn't
take care of me.'
44 "Then they too will answer, 'Lord, when
did we see you hungry, or thirsty, or a stranger,
or without clothes, or sick, or in prison, and
not help you?'
45 "Then he will answer them, 'Truly I tell
you, whatever you did not do for one of the
least of these, you did not do for me.'
46 "And they will go away into eternal punishment, but the righteous into eternal life."

THE PLOT TO KILL JESUS

26 When Jesus had finished saying all
these things, he told his disciples, 2 "You
know[E] that the Passover takes place after two
days, and the Son of Man will be handed over
to be crucified."
3 Then the chief priests[F] and the elders of
the people assembled in the courtyard of the
high priest, who was named Caiaphas, 4 and
they conspired to arrest Jesus in a treacherous
way and kill him. 5 "Not during the festival,"
they said, "so there won't be rioting among
the people."

THE ANOINTING AT BETHANY

6 While Jesus was in Bethany at the house of
Simon the leper,[G] 7 a woman approached him
with an alabaster jar of very expensive perfume. She poured it on his head as he was
reclining at the table. 8 When the disciples
saw it, they were indignant. "Why this waste?"
they asked. 9 "This might have been sold for a
great deal and given to the poor."
10 Aware of this, Jesus said to them, "Why
are you bothering this woman? She has done
a noble thing for me. 11 You always have the
poor with you, but you do not always have me.
12 By pouring this perfume on my body, she has
prepared me for burial. 13 Truly I tell you, wherever this gospel is proclaimed in the whole
world, what she has done will also be told in
memory of her."
14 Then one of the Twelve, the man called Judas Iscariot, went to the chief priests 15 and said,
"What are you willing to give me if I hand him
over to you?" So they weighed out thirty pieces
of silver for him. 16 And from that time he started
looking for a good opportunity to betray him.

BETRAYAL AT THE PASSOVER

17 On the first day of Unleavened Bread the
disciples came to Jesus and asked, "Where do

[A] 25:26-27 Or *So you knew . . . scattered? Then* (as a question) [B] 25:27 Lit *received what is mine* [C] 25:31 Other mss read *holy angels* [D] 25:32 Or *the Gentiles* [E] 26:2 Or *"Know* (as a command) [F] 26:3 Other mss add *and the scribes* [G] 26:6 Gk *lepros*; a term for various skin diseases; see Lv 13–14

Mary, Martha, and Lazarus | Restoration Profile

MATTHEW 26:6-13; MARK 14:3-9; LUKE 10:38-42; JOHN 11:11-45; 12:1-11

Jesus restores individuals and he also restores relationships. His insistence that the greatest directive over human life can be expressed in the dual command to love God and neighbor (Mt 22:37-40) indicates that restoration ultimately must deeply affect both those categories of relationship. This is true even when our neighbor is part of our family.

Sibling relationships are the context for many Bible stories. Cain and Abel are simply the first in a long line of brothers and or sisters whose treatment of one another was destructive, yet God often intervened with restoration. Mary, Martha, and Lazarus lived in Bethany and frequently hosted Jesus and his disciples on their trips to Jerusalem. In the course of their times with the Lord, each member of this family was beautifully and uniquely restored. Lazarus, who got sick and died, was restored to life (Jn 11:43-44). Martha, who was a servant-hostess by nature, learned to carry out her tasks without demanding attention or expecting others to be like her (Lk 10:38-42). And Mary, the passive disciple, learned she could not only sit at Jesus's feet but also anoint them with costly oil as a sacrifice of gratitude (Jn 12:2-3).

Jesus's restoring work was never rushed. The changes were deep and lasting because he practiced a Master's timing in the words and touches that brought about change. He could confront, console, or call a dead man back from the grave. He always knew what actually needed to be done, even if those under his care couldn't grasp his methods or predict the outcome. Ultimately, what they had to do was surrender to his work in them. So must we today.

you want us to make preparations for you to
eat the Passover?"
18 "Go into the city to a certain man," he said,
"and tell him, 'The Teacher says: My time is near;
I am celebrating the Passover at your place[A] with
my disciples.'" 19 So the disciples did as Jesus
had directed them and prepared the Passover.
20 When evening came, he was reclining at the table with the Twelve. 21 While they were eating, he
said, "Truly I tell you, one of you will betray me."
22 Deeply distressed, each one began to say
to him, "Surely not I, Lord?"
23 He replied, "The one who dipped his hand
with me in the bowl — he will betray me. 24 The
Son of Man will go just as it is written about
him, but woe to that man by whom the Son
of Man is betrayed! It would have been better
for him if he had not been born."
25 Judas, his betrayer, replied, "Surely not
I, Rabbi?"
"You have said it," he told him.

THE FIRST LORD'S SUPPER

26 As they were eating, Jesus took bread, blessed
and broke it, gave it to the disciples, and said,
"Take and eat it; this is my body." 27 Then he
took a cup, and after giving thanks, he gave
it to them and said, "Drink from it, all of you.
28 For this is my blood of the covenant,[B] which
is poured out for many for the forgiveness of
sins. 29 But I tell you, I will not drink from this
fruit of the vine from now on until that day
when I drink it new with you in my Father's
kingdom." 30 After singing a hymn, they went
out to the Mount of Olives.

PETER'S DENIAL PREDICTED

31 Then Jesus said to them, "Tonight all of you
will fall away because of me, for it is written:

I will strike the shepherd,
and the sheep of the flock
will be scattered.[C]

32 But after I have risen, I will go ahead of you
to Galilee."
33 Peter told him, "Even if everyone falls
away because of you, I will never fall away."
34 "Truly I tell you," Jesus said to him, "tonight, before the rooster crows, you will deny
me three times."
35 "Even if I have to die with you," Peter told
him, "I will never deny you," and all the disciples said the same thing.

[A] **26:18** Lit *Passover with you* [B] **26:28** Other mss read *new covenant* [C] **26:31** Zch 13:7

THE PRAYER IN THE GARDEN

36 Then Jesus came with them to a place called
Gethsemane, and he told the disciples, "Sit
here while I go over there and pray." 37 Taking
along Peter and the two sons of Zebedee, he
began to be sorrowful and troubled. 38 He said
to them, "I am deeply grieved[A] to the point
of death. Remain here and stay awake with
me." 39 Going a little farther,[B] he fell facedown
and prayed, "My Father, if it is possible, let
this cup pass from me. Yet not as I will, but
as you will."

40 Then he came to the disciples and found
them sleeping. He asked Peter, "So, couldn't
you stay awake with me one hour? 41 Stay
awake and pray, so that you won't enter into
temptation. The spirit is willing, but the flesh
is weak."

42 Again, a second time, he went away and
prayed, "My Father, if this[C] cannot pass[D] unless
I drink it, your will be done." 43 And he came
again and found them sleeping, because they
could not keep their eyes open.

44 After leaving them, he went away again
and prayed a third time, saying the same thing
once more. 45 Then he came to the disciples
and said to them, "Are you still sleeping and
resting? See, the time is near. The Son of Man
is betrayed into the hands of sinners. 46 Get
up; let's go. See, my betrayer is near."

JUDAS'S BETRAYAL OF JESUS

47 While he was still speaking, Judas, one of
the Twelve, suddenly arrived. A large mob
with swords and clubs was with him from the
chief priests and elders of the people. 48 His
betrayer had given them a sign: "The one I kiss,
he's the one; arrest him." 49 So immediately he
went up to Jesus and said, "Greetings, Rabbi!"
and kissed him.

50 "Friend," Jesus asked him, "why have you
come?"[E]

Then they came up, took hold of Jesus, and
arrested him. 51 At that moment one of those
with Jesus reached out his hand and drew
his sword. He struck the high priest's servant
and cut off his ear.

52 Then Jesus told him, "Put your sword back
in its place because all who take up the sword
will perish by the sword. 53 Or do you think that
I cannot call on my Father, and he will provide
me here and now with more than twelve legions
of angels? 54 How, then, would the Scriptures
be fulfilled that say it must happen this way?"

55 At that time Jesus said to the crowds, "Have
you come out with swords and clubs, as if I
were a criminal,[F] to capture me? Every day I
used to sit, teaching in the temple, and you
didn't arrest me. 56 But all this has happened
so that the writings of the prophets would
be fulfilled." Then all the disciples deserted
him and ran away.

JESUS FACES THE SANHEDRIN

57 Those who had arrested Jesus led him away
to Caiaphas the high priest, where the scribes
and the elders had convened. 58 Peter was following him at a distance right to the high
priest's courtyard. He went in and was sitting
with the servants to see the outcome.

59 The chief priests and the whole Sanhedrin were looking for false testimony against
Jesus so that they could put him to death, 60 but
they could not find any, even though many
false witnesses came forward.[G] Finally, two[H]
who came forward 61 stated, "This man said,
'I can destroy the temple of God and rebuild
it in three days.'"

62 The high priest stood up and said to him,
"Don't you have an answer to what these men
are testifying against you?" 63 But Jesus kept
silent. The high priest said to him, "I charge
you under oath by the living God: Tell us if you
are the Messiah, the Son of God."

64 "You have said it," Jesus told him. "But I
tell you, in the future[I] you will see **the Son of
Man seated at the right hand** of Power and
coming on the clouds of heaven."[J]

65 Then the high priest tore his robes and
said, "He has blasphemed! Why do we still
need witnesses? See, now you've heard the
blasphemy. 66 What is your decision?"

They answered, "He deserves death!"
67 Then they spat in his face and beat him;
others slapped him 68 and said, "Prophesy to
us, Messiah! Who was it that hit you?"

PETER DENIES HIS LORD

69 Now Peter was sitting outside in the courtyard. A servant girl approached him and said,
"You were with Jesus the Galilean too."

70 But he denied it in front of everyone: "I
don't know what you're talking about."

71 When he had gone out to the gateway,

[A] **26:38** Lit *"My soul is swallowed up in sorrow* [B] **26:39** Other mss read *Drawing nearer* [C] **26:42** Other mss add *cup* [D] **26:42** Other mss add *from me* [E] **26:50** Or *Jesus told him, "do what you have come for."* [F] **26:55** Lit *as against a criminal* [G] **26:60** Other mss add *they found none* [H] **26:60** Other mss add *false witnesses* [I] **26:64** Lit *you, from now* [J] **26:64** Ps 110:1; Dn 7:13

another woman saw him and told those who
were there, "This man was with Jesus the Nazarene!"
72 And again he denied it with an oath: "I
don't know the man!"
73 After a little while those standing there
approached and said to Peter, "You really are
one of them, since even your accent[A] gives
you away."
74 Then he started to curse and to swear with
an oath, "I don't know the man!" Immediately
a rooster crowed, 75 and Peter remembered the
words Jesus had spoken, "Before the rooster
crows, you will deny me three times." And he
went outside and wept bitterly.

JESUS HANDED OVER TO PILATE

27 When daybreak came, all the chief
priests and the elders of the people plotted against Jesus to put him to death. 2 After
tying him up, they led him away and handed
him over to Pilate,[B] the governor.

JUDAS HANGS HIMSELF

3 Then Judas, his betrayer, seeing that Jesus
had been condemned, was full of remorse
and returned the thirty pieces of silver to the
chief priests and elders. 4 "I have sinned by
betraying innocent blood," he said.
"What's that to us?" they said. "See to it yourself!" 5 So he threw the silver into the temple and departed. Then he went and hanged
himself.
6 The chief priests took the silver and said,
"It's not permitted to put it into the temple
treasury, since it is blood money." 7 They conferred together and bought the potter's field
with it as a burial place for foreigners. 8 Therefore that field has been called "Blood Field" to
this day. 9 Then what was spoken through the
prophet Jeremiah was fulfilled: **They took**[C]
the thirty pieces of silver, the price of him
whose price was set by the Israelites, 10 and
they gave[D] **them for the potter's field, as**
the Lord directed me.[E]

JESUS FACES THE GOVERNOR

11 Now Jesus stood before the governor. "Are you
the King of the Jews?" the governor asked him.
Jesus answered, "You say so." 12 While he
was being accused by the chief priests and
elders, he didn't answer.
13 Then Pilate said to him, "Don't you hear
how much they are testifying against you?"
14 But he didn't answer him on even one charge,
so that the governor was quite amazed.

JESUS OR BARABBAS

15 At the festival the governor's custom was to
release to the crowd a prisoner they wanted.
16 At that time they had a notorious prisoner
called Barabbas.[F] 17 So when they had gathered together, Pilate said to them, "Who is it
you want me to release for you — Barabbas,
or Jesus who is called Christ?" 18 For he knew
it was because of envy that they had handed
him over.
19 While he was sitting on the judge's bench,
his wife sent word to him, "Have nothing to
do with that righteous man, for today I've
suffered terribly in a dream because of him."
20 The chief priests and the elders, however,
persuaded the crowds to ask for Barabbas
and to execute Jesus. 21 The governor asked
them, "Which of the two do you want me to
release for you?"
"Barabbas!" they answered.
22 Pilate asked them, "What should I do then
with Jesus, who is called Christ?"
They all answered, "Crucify him!"
23 Then he said, "Why? What has he done
wrong?"
But they kept shouting all the more, "Crucify him!"
24 When Pilate saw that he was getting nowhere, but that a riot was starting instead, he
took some water, washed his hands in front
of the crowd, and said, "I am innocent of this
man's blood.[G] See to it yourselves!"
25 All the people answered, "His blood be on
us and on our children!" 26 Then he released
Barabbas to them and, after having Jesus
flogged, handed him over to be crucified.

MOCKED BY THE MILITARY

27 Then the governor's soldiers took Jesus into
the governor's residence and gathered the
whole company[H] around him. 28 They stripped
him and dressed him in a scarlet robe. 29 They
twisted together a crown of thorns, put it on
his head, and placed a staff in his right hand.
And they knelt down before him and mocked
him: "Hail, King of the Jews!" 30 Then they spat
on him, took the staff, and kept hitting him on

[A] **26:73** Or *speech* [B] **27:2** Other mss read *Pontius Pilate* [C] **27:9** Or *I took* [D] **27:10** Some mss read *I gave* [E] **27:9-10** Jr 32:6-9; Zch 11:12-13 [F] **27:16** Other mss read *Jesus Barabbas*, also in v. 17 [G] **27:24** Other mss read *this righteous man's blood* [H] **27:27** Lit *cohort*

the head. 31 After they had mocked him, they stripped him of the robe, put his own clothes on him, and led him away to crucify him.

CRUCIFIED BETWEEN TWO CRIMINALS

32 As they were going out, they found a Cyrenian man named Simon. They forced him to carry his cross. 33 When they came to a place called *Golgotha* (which means Place of the Skull), 34 they gave him wine[A] mixed with gall to drink. But when he tasted it, he refused to drink it. 35 After crucifying him, they divided his clothes by casting lots.[B] 36 Then they sat down and were guarding him there. 37 Above his head they put up the charge against him in writing: THIS IS JESUS, THE KING OF THE JEWS.

38 Then two criminals[C] were crucified with him, one on the right and one on the left. 39 Those who passed by were yelling insults at[D] him, shaking their heads 40 and saying, "You who would destroy the temple and rebuild it in three days, save yourself! If you are the Son of God, come down from the cross!" 41 In the same way the chief priests, with the scribes and elders,[E] mocked him and said, 42 "He saved others, but he cannot save himself! He is the King of Israel! Let him[F] come down now from the cross, and we will believe in him. 43 He trusts in God; let God rescue him now — if he takes pleasure in him![G] For he said, 'I am the Son of God.' " 44 In the same way even the criminals who were crucified with him taunted him.

THE DEATH OF JESUS

45 From noon until three in the afternoon[H] darkness came over the whole land.[I] 46 About three in the afternoon Jesus cried out with a loud voice, *"Elí, Elí, lemá*[J] *sabachtháni?"* that is, "**My God, my God, why have you abandoned me?**"[K]

47 When some of those standing there heard this, they said, "He's calling for Elijah."

48 Immediately one of them ran and got a sponge, filled it with sour wine, put it on a stick, and offered him a drink. 49 But the rest said, "Let's see if Elijah comes to save him."

50 But Jesus cried out again with a loud voice and gave up his spirit. 51 Suddenly, the curtain of the sanctuary was torn in two from top to bottom, the earth quaked, and the rocks were split. 52 The tombs were also opened and many bodies of the saints who had fallen asleep were raised. 53 And they came out of the tombs after his resurrection, entered the holy city, and appeared to many.

54 When the centurion and those with him, who were keeping watch over Jesus, saw the earthquake and the things that had happened, they were terrified and said, "Truly this man was the Son of God!"

55 Many women who had followed Jesus from Galilee and looked after him were there, watching from a distance. 56 Among them were Mary Magdalene, Mary the mother of James and Joseph, and the mother of Zebedee's sons.

THE BURIAL OF JESUS

57 When it was evening, a rich man from Arimathea named Joseph came, who himself had also become a disciple of Jesus. 58 He approached Pilate and asked for Jesus's body. Then Pilate ordered that it[L] be released. 59 So Joseph took the body, wrapped it in clean, fine linen, 60 and placed it in his new tomb, which he had cut into the rock. He left after rolling a great stone against the entrance of the tomb. 61 Mary Magdalene and the other Mary were seated there, facing the tomb.

THE CLOSELY GUARDED TOMB

62 The next day, which followed the preparation day, the chief priests and the Pharisees gathered before Pilate 63 and said, "Sir, we remember that while this deceiver was still alive he said, 'After three days I will rise again.' 64 So give orders that the tomb be made secure until the third day. Otherwise, his disciples may come, steal him, and tell the people, 'He has been raised from the dead,' and the last deception will be worse than the first."

65 "You have[M] a guard of soldiers," Pilate told them. "Go and make it as secure as you know how." 66 They went and secured the tomb by setting a seal on the stone and placing the guard.

RESURRECTION MORNING

28 After the Sabbath, as the first day of the week was dawning, Mary Magdalene and the other Mary went to view the tomb. 2 There was a violent earthquake, because

---

[A] **27:34** Other mss read *sour wine* [B] **27:35** Other mss add *that what was spoken by the prophet might be fulfilled: "They divided my clothes among them, and for my clothing they cast lots."* [C] **27:38** Or *revolutionaries* [D] **27:39** Lit *passed by blasphemed*, or *were blaspheming* [E] **27:41** Other mss add *and Pharisees* [F] **27:42** Other mss read *If he . . . Israel, let him* [G] **27:43** Or *if he wants him* [H] **27:45** Lit *From the sixth hour to the ninth hour* [I] **27:45** Or *whole earth* [J] **27:46** Some mss read *lama*; other mss read *lima* [K] **27:46** Ps 22:1 [L] **27:58** Other mss read *that the body* [M] **27:65** Or *"Take*

RESTORATION THEMES

R	Rest and Reflection	*Resting and Recharging—6:31*
E	Eternal Perspective	*God's Work in Us—7:32-33; 8:24-25* *God's Children—14:36*
S	Support	*Openness with God—9:23-24; 10:47-48* *Openness with Others—14:33-34*
T	Thanksgiving and Contentment	*For the next note, see Luke 12:34.*
O	Other-centeredness	*Not Being Judgmental—Mark 2:17* *Identifying Those We Have Wronged—11:25*
R	Relationships	*For the next note, see Luke 4:28-29.*
E	Exercise of Faith	*Sharing Faith/Gospel—Mark 1:28* *Serving—9:35*

THE MESSIAH'S HERALD

1 The beginning of the gospel of Jesus Christ,
the Son of God.[A] 2 As it is written in Isaiah
the prophet:[B]

See, I am sending my messenger
ahead of you;
he will prepare your way.[C,D]
3 **A voice of one crying out**
in the wilderness:
Prepare the way
for the Lord;
make his paths straight![E]

4 John came baptizing[F] in the wilderness and
proclaiming a baptism of repentance for the
forgiveness of sins. 5 The whole Judean countryside and all the people of Jerusalem were
going out to him, and they were baptized by
him in the Jordan River, confessing their sins.
6 John wore a camel-hair garment with a leather belt around his waist and ate locusts and
wild honey.

7 He proclaimed, "One who is more powerful than I am is coming after me. I am not
worthy to stoop down and untie the strap of
his sandals. 8 I baptize you with[G] water, but he
will baptize you with the Holy Spirit."

THE BAPTISM OF JESUS

9 In those days Jesus came from Nazareth in
Galilee and was baptized in the Jordan by John.
10 As soon as he came up out of the water, he
saw the heavens being torn open and the Spirit
descending on him like a dove. 11 And a voice
came from heaven: "You are my beloved Son;
with you I am well-pleased."

THE TEMPTATION OF JESUS

12 Immediately the Spirit drove him into the
wilderness. 13 He was in the wilderness forty
days, being tempted by Satan. He was with
the wild animals, and the angels were serving him.

MINISTRY IN GALILEE

14 After John was arrested, Jesus went to Galilee, proclaiming the good news[H,I] of God: 15 "The
time is fulfilled, and the kingdom of God has
come near. Repent and believe the good news!"

Exercise of Faith | *Sharing Faith/Gospel*

GOING VIRAL

"At once the news about him spread throughout the entire vicinity of Galilee." Mark 1:28

Witnessing. Evangelism. Sharing the gospel.

Many Christians feel uneasy when it comes to speaking to others about their faith. The reasons are varied: We've seen some of our more zealous brethren come on too strong. We've been part of organized evangelism efforts in the past that felt mechanical and forced. We've watched fellow believers get ostracized for talking openly about spiritual matters. The result? Tight lips. Reluctance.

Notice the opposite phenomenon here in Mark's Gospel: "The news about [Jesus] spread throughout the entire vicinity of Galilee." Everybody was talking to everybody! We would call this "going viral."

Amazing! In a culture and era with no television, radio, newspapers, Internet, or social media, everybody heard the news about Jesus. This happened without organized witnessing campaigns and evangelism training seminars. Just wide-eyed people telling friends and neighbors, "Did you hear what Jesus did the other day?"

As long as we see our faith as a product that we have to try to convince outsiders to buy, we'll remain quiet. But the more we think of the gospel as good news about Jesus—"He delivered me from lifelong guilt" or "He healed my friend's marriage" or "He is helping me forgive my abuser"—we'll be more likely to speak up in ways that cause others to perk up.

For the next note on *Exercise of Faith*, see Mark 9:35.

[A] **1:1** Some mss omit *the Son of God* [B] **1:2** Other mss read *in the prophets* [C] **1:2** Other mss add *before you* [D] **1:2** Mal 3:1
[E] **1:3** Is 40:3 [F] **1:4** Or *John the Baptist came* [G] **1:8** Or *in* [H] **1:14** Other mss add *of the kingdom* [I] **1:14** Or *gospel*

THE FIRST DISCIPLES

16 As he passed alongside the Sea of Galilee,
he saw Simon and Andrew, Simon's brother,
casting a net into the sea — for they were fishermen. 17 "Follow me," Jesus told them, "and I
will make you fish for[A] people." 18 Immediately
they left their nets and followed him. 19 Going
on a little farther, he saw James the son of Zebedee and his brother John in a boat putting
their nets in order. 20 Immediately he called
them, and they left their father Zebedee in the
boat with the hired men and followed him.

DRIVING OUT AN UNCLEAN SPIRIT

21 They went into Capernaum, and right away
he entered the synagogue on the Sabbath and
began to teach. 22 They were astonished at
his teaching because he was teaching them
as one who had authority, and not like the
scribes.

23 Just then a man with an unclean spirit
was in their synagogue. He cried out, 24 "What
do you have to do with us, Jesus of Nazareth?
Have you come to destroy us? I know who you
are — the Holy One of God!"

25 Jesus rebuked him saying, "Be silent, and
come out of him!" 26 And the unclean spirit
threw him into convulsions, shouted with a
loud voice, and came out of him.

27 They were all amazed, and so they began
to ask each other: "What is this? A new teaching with authority![B] He commands even the
unclean spirits, and they obey him." 28 At once
the news about him spread throughout the
entire vicinity of Galilee.

HEALINGS AT CAPERNAUM

29 As soon as they left the synagogue, they
went into Simon and Andrew's house with
James and John. 30 Simon's mother-in-law
was lying in bed with a fever, and they told
him about her at once. 31 So he went to her,
took her by the hand, and raised her up. The
fever left her,[C] and she began to serve them.

32 When evening came, after the sun had
set, they brought to him all those who were
sick and demon-possessed. 33 The whole town
was assembled at the door, 34 and he healed
many who were sick with various diseases
and drove out many demons. And he would
not permit the demons to speak, because they
knew him.

PREACHING IN GALILEE

35 Very early in the morning, while it was still
dark, he got up, went out, and made his way
to a deserted place; and there he was praying.
36 Simon and his companions searched for
him, 37 and when they found him they said,
"Everyone is looking for you."

38 And he said to them, "Let's go on to the
neighboring villages so that I may preach there
too. This is why I have come."

A MAN CLEANSED

39 He went into all of Galilee, preaching in their
synagogues and driving out demons. 40 Then
a man with leprosy[D] came to him and, on his
knees,[E] begged him: "If you are willing, you can
make me clean." 41 Moved with compassion,[F]
Jesus reached out his hand and touched him.
"I am willing," he told him. "Be made clean."
42 Immediately the leprosy left him, and he
was made clean. 43 Then he sternly warned
him and sent him away at once, 44 telling him,
"See that you say nothing to anyone; but go
and show yourself to the priest, and offer what
Moses commanded for your cleansing, as a
testimony to them."[G] 45 Yet he went out and
began to proclaim it widely and to spread
the news, with the result that Jesus could no
longer enter a town openly. But he was out in
deserted places, and they came to him from
everywhere.

THE SON OF MAN FORGIVES AND HEALS

2 When he entered Capernaum again after
some days, it was reported that he was at
home. 2 So many people gathered together
that there was no more room, not even in the
doorway, and he was speaking the word to
them. 3 They came to him bringing a paralytic, carried by four of them. 4 Since they were
not able to bring him to[H] Jesus because of the
crowd, they removed the roof above him, and
after digging through it, they lowered the mat
on which the paralytic was lying. 5 Seeing their
faith, Jesus told the paralytic, "Son, your sins
are forgiven."

6 But some of the scribes were sitting there,
questioning in their hearts: 7 "Why does he
speak like this? He's blaspheming! Who can
forgive sins but God alone?"

8 Right away Jesus perceived in his spirit that
they were thinking like this within themselves

[A] **1:17** Or *you to become fishers of* [B] **1:27** Other mss read *"What is this? What is this new teaching? For with authority* [C] **1:31** Other mss add *at once* [D] **1:40** Gk *lepros*; a term for various skin diseases, also in v. 42; see Lv 13–14 [E] **1:40** Other mss omit *on his knees* [F] **1:41** Other mss *Moved with indignation* [G] **1:44** Or *against them* [H] **2:4** Other mss read *able to get near*

and said to them, "Why are you thinking these
things in your hearts? 9 Which is easier: to say
to the paralytic, 'Your sins are forgiven,' or to
say, 'Get up, take your mat, and walk'? 10 But
so that you may know that the Son of Man
has authority on earth to forgive sins" — he
told the paralytic — 11 "I tell you: get up, take
your mat, and go home."
12 Immediately he got up, took the mat, and
went out in front of everyone. As a result, they
were all astounded and gave glory to God, saying, "We have never seen anything like this!"

THE CALL OF LEVI

13 Jesus went out again beside the sea. The
whole crowd was coming to him, and he was
teaching them. 14 Then, passing by, he saw Levi
the son of Alphaeus sitting at the toll booth,
and he said to him, "Follow me," and he got
up and followed him.
15 While he was reclining at the table in Levi's
house, many tax collectors and sinners were
eating[A] with Jesus and his disciples, for there
were many who were following him. 16 When
the scribes who were Pharisees[B] saw that he
was eating with sinners and tax collectors,
they asked his disciples, "Why does he eat[C]
with tax collectors and sinners?"
17 When Jesus heard this, he told them, "It
is not those who are well who need a doctor,
but those who are sick. I didn't come to call
the righteous, but sinners."

A QUESTION ABOUT FASTING

18 Now John's disciples and the Pharisees[D] were
fasting. People came and asked him, "Why do
John's disciples and the Pharisees' disciples
fast, but your disciples do not fast?"
19 Jesus said to them, "The wedding guests
cannot fast while the groom is with them,
can they? As long as they have the groom
with them, they cannot fast. 20 But the time[E]
will come when the groom will be taken away
from them, and then they will fast on that day.
21 No one sews a patch of unshrunk cloth on
an old garment. Otherwise, the new patch
pulls away from the old cloth, and a worse
tear is made. 22 And no one puts new wine
into old wineskins. Otherwise, the wine will
burst the skins, and the wine is lost as well

Other-centeredness | *Not Being Judgmental*

ONLY THE BROKEN NEED APPLY

"When Jesus heard this, he told them, 'It is not those who are well who need a doctor, but those who are sick. I didn't come to call the righteous, but sinners.'" Mark 2:17

If we had a time machine and could go back to first-century Palestine, what are the odds we'd see a Jewish scribe (a teacher of the law) or a prominent Pharisee having lunch with an irreligious person? That's easy. Zero. No chance whatsoever. These pious moralists weren't about to leave their holy huddle to mingle with "sinners."

So, we can probably guess their reaction when Jesus came on the scene and started going to dinner parties with tax collectors and showing kindness to prostitutes. The scribes and Pharisees were appalled.

Jesus told them: "I didn't come to call the righteous, but sinners." Translation: If you think you're not spiritually sick and sinful, then I can't help you. My gospel is good news only to those who know they are broken and need help.

Here are two good lessons. First, if you feel like you're screwed up—don't despair! You're exactly the one Jesus wants to rescue! Second, if you're looking down your nose at certain people, thinking you're better or more holy, stop it! Pray for the grace to see as Jesus sees.

For the next note on *Other-centeredness*, see Mark 11:25.

[A] **2:15** Lit *reclining together* [B] **2:16** Other mss read *scribes and Pharisees* [C] **2:16** Other mss add *and drink* [D] **2:18** Other mss read *The disciples of John and of the Pharisees* [E] **2:20** Or *the days*

The Paralyzed Man | Restoration Profile

MATTHEW 9:1-8; MARK 2:1-12; LUKE 5:17-26

Paralysis comes in many forms, some of which have little to do with the inability to move physically. Three of the Gospel writers include the story of an unnamed paralyzed man Jesus healed; but several clues in the accounts reveal that his physical healing was not what captured the attention of those who were watching Jesus's every move. The man's physical healing was incidental to a more significant restoration and a glimpse of Jesus practicing his role as the Son of Man. Plus, in Mark's account, we see the important place others can sometimes have in making restoration possible.

Mark locates the action in a house where Jesus was preaching, surrounded by interested people, healed followers, and the ever-present critics. Each Gospel writer notes that the paralyzed man was delivered by friends, but Mark briefly depicts their unique method of presenting him to Jesus, lowering him through the roof of a packed house when they couldn't get in the door. Jesus saw this as an act of faith. And his response was, in part, because of that faith. Bringing a friend to Jesus means we get the joy of participating in restoration (see Jms 5:19-20).

Dangling in obvious helplessness before Jesus, the last thing the paralyzed man or anyone else expected to hear was the statement, "Son, your sins are forgiven" (Mk 2:5). Jesus saw what everyone else saw, but he recognized more. This man needed a restored spirit even more than he needed to get up and walk. So Jesus forgave the man, just as God would. And when some of those around were offended as well as confused, he demonstrated why he could actually forgive by restoring the man to physical health.

Jesus always knows exactly what restoration we need.

as the skins. No, new wine is put into fresh
wineskins."

LORD OF THE SABBATH

23 On the Sabbath he was going through the
grainfields, and his disciples began to make
their way, picking some heads of grain. 24 The
Pharisees said to him, "Look, why are they
doing what is not lawful on the Sabbath?"
25 He said to them, "Have you never read
what David and those who were with him did
when he was in need and hungry — 26 how he
entered the house of God in the time of Abiathar the high priest and ate the bread of the
Presence — which is not lawful for anyone to
eat except the priests — and also gave some to
his companions?" 27 Then he told them, "The
Sabbath was made for[A] man and not man for
the Sabbath. 28 So then, the Son of Man is Lord
even of the Sabbath."

3 Jesus entered the synagogue again, and a
man was there who had a shriveled hand.
2 In order to accuse him, they were watching
him closely to see whether he would heal him
on the Sabbath. 3 He told the man with the
shriveled hand, "Stand before us." 4 Then he
said to them, "Is it lawful to do good on the
Sabbath or to do evil, to save life or to kill?"
But they were silent. 5 After looking around
at them with anger, he was grieved at the
hardness of their hearts and told the man,
"Stretch out your hand." So he stretched it
out, and his hand was restored. 6 Immediately
the Pharisees went out and started plotting
with the Herodians against him, how they
might kill him.

MINISTERING TO THE MULTITUDE

7 Jesus departed with his disciples to the sea,
and a large crowd followed from Galilee, and
a large crowd followed from Judea, 8 Jerusalem, Idumea, beyond the Jordan, and around
Tyre and Sidon. The large crowd came to him
because they heard about everything he was
doing. 9 Then he told his disciples to have a
small boat ready for him, so that the crowd
wouldn't crush him. 10 Since he had healed
many, all who had diseases were pressing
toward him to touch him. 11 Whenever the
unclean spirits saw him, they fell down before

[A] **2:27** Or *because of*

him and cried out, "You are the Son of God!" 12 And he would strongly warn them not to make him known.

THE TWELVE APOSTLES

13 Jesus went up the mountain and summoned those he wanted, and they came to him. 14 He appointed twelve, whom he also named apostles,[A] to be with him, to send them out to preach, 15 and to have authority to[B] drive out demons. 16 He appointed the Twelve:[C] To Simon, he gave the name Peter; 17 and to James the son of Zebedee, and to his brother John, he gave the name "Boanerges" (that is, "Sons of Thunder"); 18 Andrew; Philip and Bartholomew; Matthew and Thomas; James the son of Alphaeus, and Thaddaeus; Simon the Zealot, 19 and Judas Iscariot, who also betrayed him.

A HOUSE DIVIDED

20 Jesus entered a house, and the crowd gathered again so that they were not even able to eat.[D] 21 When his family heard this, they set out to restrain him, because they said, "He's out of his mind."

22 The scribes who had come down from Jerusalem said, "He is possessed by Beelzebul," and, "He drives out demons by the ruler of the demons."

23 So he summoned them and spoke to them in parables: "How can Satan drive out Satan? 24 If a kingdom is divided against itself, that kingdom cannot stand. 25 If a house is divided against itself, that house cannot stand. 26 And if Satan opposes himself and is divided, he cannot stand but is finished. 27 But no one can enter a strong man's house and plunder his possessions unless he first ties up the strong man. Then he can plunder his house.

28 "Truly I tell you, people will be forgiven for all sins and whatever blasphemies they utter. 29 But whoever blasphemes against the Holy Spirit never has forgiveness, but is guilty of an eternal sin"[E] — 30 because they were saying, "He has an unclean spirit."

TRUE RELATIONSHIPS

31 His mother and his brothers came, and standing outside, they sent word to him and called him. 32 A crowd was sitting around him and told him, "Look, your mother, your brothers, and your sisters[F] are outside asking for you."

33 He replied to them, "Who are my mother and my brothers?" 34 Looking at those sitting in a circle around him, he said, "Here are my mother and my brothers! 35 Whoever does the will of God is my brother and sister and mother."

THE PARABLE OF THE SOWER

4 Again he began to teach by the sea, and a very large crowd gathered around him. So he got into a boat on the sea and sat down, while the whole crowd was by the sea on the shore. 2 He taught them many things in parables, and in his teaching he said to them: 3 "Listen! Consider the sower who went out to sow. 4 As he sowed, some seed fell along the path, and the birds came and devoured it. 5 Other seed fell on rocky ground where it didn't have much soil, and it grew up quickly, since the soil wasn't deep. 6 When the sun came up, it was scorched, and since it had no root, it withered away. 7 Other seed fell among thorns, and the thorns came up and choked it, and it didn't produce fruit. 8 Still other seed fell on good ground and it grew up, producing fruit that increased thirty, sixty, and a hundred times." 9 Then he said, "Let anyone who has ears to hear listen."

WHY JESUS USED PARABLES

10 When he was alone, those around him with the Twelve, asked him about the parables. 11 He answered them, "The secret of the kingdom of God has been given to you, but to those outside, everything comes in parables 12 so that

they may indeed look,
and yet not perceive;
they may indeed listen,
and yet not understand;
otherwise, they might turn back
and be forgiven."[G,H]

THE PARABLE OF THE SOWER EXPLAINED

13 Then he said to them: "Don't you understand this parable? How then will you understand all of the parables? 14 The sower sows the word. 15 Some are like the word sown on the path. When they hear, immediately Satan comes and takes away the word sown in them.[I] 16 And

[A] **3:14** Other mss omit *he also named them apostles* [B] **3:15** Other mss add *heal diseases, and to* [C] **3:16** Other mss omit *He appointed the Twelve* [D] **3:20** Or *eat a meal*; lit *eat bread* [E] **3:29** Other mss read *is subject to eternal judgment* [F] **3:32** Other mss omit *and your sisters* [G] **4:12** Other mss read *and their sins be forgiven them* [H] **4:12** Is 6:9-10 [I] **4:15** Other mss read *in their hearts*

others are like seed sown on rocky ground.
When they hear the word, immediately they
receive it with joy. 17 But they have no root;
they are short-lived. When distress or persecution comes because of the word, they
immediately fall away. 18 Others are like seed
sown among thorns; these are the ones who
hear the word, 19 but the worries of this age,
the deceitfulness[A] of wealth, and the desires
for other things enter in and choke the word,
and it becomes unfruitful. 20 And those like
seed sown on good ground hear the word,
welcome it, and produce fruit thirty, sixty, and
a hundred times what was sown."

USING YOUR LIGHT

21 He also said to them, "Is a lamp brought in
to be put under a basket or under a bed? Isn't
it to be put on a lampstand? 22 For there is
nothing hidden that will not be revealed, and
nothing concealed that will not be brought
to light. 23 If anyone has ears to hear, let him
listen." 24 And he said to them, "Pay attention
to what you hear. By the measure you use, it
will be measured to you — and more will be
added to you. 25 For whoever has, more will
be given to him, and whoever does not have,
even what he has will be taken away from him."

THE PARABLE OF THE GROWING SEED

26 "The kingdom of God is like this," he said. "A
man scatters seed on the ground. 27 He sleeps
and rises night and day; the seed sprouts and
grows, although he doesn't know how. 28 The
soil produces a crop by itself — first the blade,
then the head, and then the full grain on the
head. 29 As soon as the crop is ready, he sends
for the sickle, because the harvest has come."

THE PARABLE OF THE MUSTARD SEED

30 And he said, "With what can we compare
the kingdom of God, or what parable can we
use to describe it? 31 It's like a mustard seed
that, when sown upon the soil, is the smallest
of all the seeds on the ground. 32 And when
sown, it comes up and grows taller than all the
garden plants, and produces large branches, so
that the birds of the sky can nest in its shade."

USING PARABLES

33 He was speaking the word to them with
many parables like these, as they were able
to understand. 34 He did not speak to them
without a parable. Privately, however, he explained everything to his own disciples.

WIND AND WAVES OBEY JESUS

35 On that day, when evening had come, he
told them, "Let's cross over to the other side
of the sea." 36 So they left the crowd and took
him along since he was in the boat. And other
boats were with him. 37 A great windstorm
arose, and the waves were breaking over
the boat, so that the boat was already being
swamped. 38 He was in the stern, sleeping on
the cushion. So they woke him up and said
to him, "Teacher! Don't you care that we're
going to die?"

39 He got up, rebuked the wind, and said to
the sea, "Silence! Be still!" The wind ceased,
and there was a great calm. 40 Then he said
to them, "Why are you afraid? Do you still
have no faith?"

41 And they were terrified[B] and asked one
another, "Who then is this? Even the wind and
the sea obey him!"

DEMONS DRIVEN OUT BY JESUS

5 They came to the other side of the sea, to
the region of the Gerasenes.[C] 2 As soon as
he got out of the boat, a man with an unclean
spirit came out of the tombs and met him.
3 He lived in the tombs, and no one was able
to restrain him anymore — not even with a
chain — 4 because he often had been bound
with shackles and chains, but had torn the
chains apart and smashed the shackles. No
one was strong enough to subdue him. 5 Night
and day among the tombs and on the mountains, he was always crying out and cutting
himself with stones.

6 When he saw Jesus from a distance, he ran
and knelt down before him. 7 And he cried out
with a loud voice, "What do you have to do
with me, Jesus, Son of the Most High God? I
beg you before God, don't torment me!" 8 For
he had told him, "Come out of the man, you
unclean spirit!"

9 "What is your name?" he asked him.

"My name is Legion," he answered him, "because we are many." 10 And he begged him
earnestly not to send them out of the region.

11 A large herd of pigs was there, feeding on
the hillside. 12 The demons[D] begged him, "Send
us to the pigs, so that we may enter them." 13 So
he gave them permission, and the unclean

[A] **4:19** Or *seduction* [B] **4:41** Or *were filled with awe* [C] **5:1** Some mss read *Gadarenes*; other mss read *Gergesenes* [D] **5:12** Other mss read *All the demons*

spirits came out and entered the pigs. The herd of about two thousand rushed down the steep bank into the sea and drowned there.

14 The men who tended them[A] ran off and reported it in the town and the countryside, and people went to see what had happened. 15 They came to Jesus and saw the man who had been demon-possessed, sitting there, dressed and in his right mind; and they were afraid. 16 Those who had seen it described to them what had happened to the demon-possessed man and told about the pigs. 17 Then they began to beg him to leave their region.

18 As he was getting into the boat, the man who had been demon-possessed begged him earnestly that he might remain with him. 19 Jesus did not let him but told him, "Go home to your own people, and report to them how much the Lord has done for you and how he has had mercy on you." 20 So he went out and began to proclaim in the Decapolis how much Jesus had done for him, and they were all amazed.

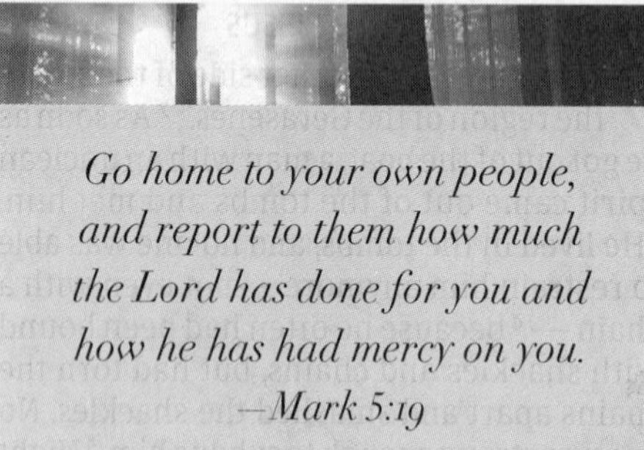
Go home to your own people,
and report to them how much
the Lord has done for you and
how he has had mercy on you.
—Mark 5:19

A GIRL RESTORED AND A WOMAN HEALED

21 When Jesus had crossed over again by boat[B] to the other side, a large crowd gathered around him while he was by the sea. 22 One of the synagogue leaders, named Jairus, came, and when he saw Jesus, he fell at his feet 23 and begged him earnestly, "My little daughter is dying. Come and lay your hands on her so that she can get well[C] and live." 24 So Jesus went with him, and a large crowd was following and pressing against him.

25 Now a woman suffering from bleeding for twelve years 26 had endured much under many doctors. She had spent everything she had and was not helped at all. On the contrary, she became worse. 27 Having heard about Jesus, she came up behind him in the crowd and touched his clothing. 28 For she said, "If I just touch his clothes, I'll be made well." 29 Instantly her flow of blood ceased, and she sensed in her body that she was healed of her affliction.

30 At once Jesus realized in himself that power had gone out from him. He turned around in the crowd and said, "Who touched my clothes?"

31 His disciples said to him, "You see the crowd pressing against you, and yet you say, 'Who touched me?'"

32 But he was looking around to see who had done this. 33 The woman, with fear and trembling, knowing what had happened to her, came and fell down before him, and told him the whole truth. 34 "Daughter," he said to her, "your faith has saved you. Go in peace and be healed from your affliction."

35 While he was still speaking, people came from the synagogue leader's house and said, "Your daughter is dead. Why bother the teacher anymore?"

36 When Jesus overheard[D] what was said, he told the synagogue leader, "Don't be afraid. Only believe." 37 He did not let anyone accompany him except Peter, James, and John, James's brother. 38 They came to the leader's house, and he saw a commotion — people weeping and wailing loudly. 39 He went in and said to them, "Why are you making a commotion and weeping? The child is not dead but asleep." 40 They laughed at him, but he put them all outside. He took the child's father, mother, and those who were with him, and entered the place where the child was. 41 Then he took the child by the hand and said to her, "*Talitha koum*"[E] (which is translated, "Little girl, I say to you, get up"). 42 Immediately the girl got up and began to walk. (She was twelve years old.) At this they were utterly astounded. 43 Then he gave them strict orders that no one should know about this and told them to give her something to eat.

REJECTION AT NAZARETH

6 He left there and came to his hometown, and his disciples followed him. 2 When the Sabbath came, he began to teach in the synagogue, and many who heard him were astonished. "Where did this man get these things?" they said. "What is this wisdom that has been given to him, and how are these miracles performed by his hands? 3 Isn't this the carpenter, the son of Mary, and the brother

---

[A] **5:14** Other mss read *tended the pigs* [B] **5:21** Other mss omit *by boat* [C] **5:23** Or *she might be saved* [D] **5:36** Or *ignored*
[E] **5:41** An Aramaic expression

of James, Joses, Judas, and Simon? And aren't
his sisters here with us?" So they were offended by him.
4 Jesus said to them, "A prophet is not without honor except in his hometown, among
his relatives, and in his household." 5 He was
not able to do a miracle there, except that he
laid his hands on a few sick people and healed
them. 6 And he was amazed at their unbelief.
He was going around the villages teaching.

COMMISSIONING THE TWELVE

7 He summoned the Twelve and began to send
them out in pairs and gave them authority
over unclean spirits. 8 He instructed them to
take nothing for the road except a staff — no
bread, no traveling bag, no money in their
belts, 9 but to wear sandals and not put on an
extra shirt. 10 He said to them, "Whenever you
enter a house, stay there until you leave that
place. 11 If any place does not welcome you
or listen to you, when you leave there, shake
the dust off your feet as a testimony against
them."[A] 12 So they went out and preached that
people should repent. 13 They drove out many
demons, anointed many sick people with oil
and healed them.

JOHN THE BAPTIST BEHEADED

14 King Herod heard about it, because Jesus's
name had become well known. Some[B] said,
"John the Baptist has been raised from the
dead, and that's why miraculous powers are at
work in him." 15 But others said, "He's Elijah."
Still others said, "He's a prophet, like one of
the prophets from long ago."
16 When Herod heard of it, he said, "John,
the one I beheaded, has been raised!"
17 For Herod himself had given orders to arrest John and to chain him in prison on account
of Herodias, his brother Philip's wife, because
he had married her. 18 John had been telling
Herod, "It is not lawful for you to have your
brother's wife." 19 So Herodias held a grudge
against him and wanted to kill him. But she
could not, 20 because Herod feared John and
protected him, knowing he was a righteous
and holy man. When Herod heard him he
would be very perplexed,[C] and yet he liked
to listen to him.

Rest and Reflection | *Resting and Recharging*

RETREAT

"He said to them, 'Come away by yourselves to a remote place and rest for a while.' For many people were coming and going, and they did not even have time to eat." Mark 6:31

The twelve disciples had just returned from a busy, productive mission trip (Mk 6:7-13). After debriefing together with Jesus (6:30), he proposed the idea of a retreat.

"Come ye yourselves apart . . . and rest a while" is the way the old King James Bible expresses Jesus's words, leading to the tongue-in-cheek observation that "followers of Jesus who refuse to come apart and rest will eventually just come apart."

Corny, but true. We are not machines. We can only do so much. Unlike our Creator who never tires (Is 40:28) and never slumbers or sleeps (Ps 121:4), we creatures were designed to go dormant for about one-third of each day.

God further decreed that his people suspend their normal activities and rest one day in seven. On top of that, he gave them a national calendar punctuated by seven festivals that gave them routine breaks from working and doing.

Are you overworked and under-rested? According to Jesus, to stop and take a break is not just okay, it's necessary. Get some rest!

For the next note on *Rest and Reflection*, see Luke 2:52.

[A] **6:11** Other mss add *Truly I tell you, it will be more tolerable for Sodom or Gomorrah on judgment day than for that town.*
[B] **6:14** Other mss read *He* [C] **6:20** Other mss read *When he heard him, he did many things*

21 An opportune time came on his birthday, when Herod gave a banquet for his nobles, military commanders, and the leading men of Galilee. 22 When Herodias's own daughter[A] came in and danced, she pleased Herod and his guests. The king said to the girl, "Ask me whatever you want, and I'll give it to you." 23 He promised her with an oath: "Whatever you ask me I will give you, up to half my kingdom."

24 She went out and said to her mother, "What should I ask for?"

"John the Baptist's head," she said.

25 At once she hurried to the king and said, "I want you to give me John the Baptist's head on a platter immediately." 26 Although the king was deeply distressed, because of his oaths and the guests[B] he did not want to refuse her. 27 The king immediately sent for an executioner and commanded him to bring John's head. So he went and beheaded him in prison, 28 brought his head on a platter, and gave it to the girl. Then the girl gave it to her mother. 29 When John's disciples heard about it, they came and removed his corpse and placed it in a tomb.

FEEDING OF THE FIVE THOUSAND

30 The apostles gathered around Jesus and reported to him all that they had done and taught. 31 He said to them, "Come away by yourselves to a remote place and rest for a while." For many people were coming and going, and they did not even have time to eat.

32 So they went away in the boat by themselves to a remote place, 33 but many saw them leaving and recognized them, and they ran on foot from all the towns and arrived ahead of them.[C]

34 When he went ashore, he saw a large crowd and had compassion on them, because they were like sheep without a shepherd. Then he began to teach them many things.

35 When it grew late, his disciples approached him and said, "This place is deserted, and it is already late. 36 Send them away so that they can go into the surrounding countryside and villages to buy themselves something to eat."

37 "You give them something to eat," he responded.

They said to him, "Should we go and buy two hundred denarii[D] worth of bread and give them something to eat?"

38 He asked them, "How many loaves do you have? Go and see."

When they found out they said, "Five, and two fish." 39 Then he instructed them to have all the people sit down in groups on the green grass. 40 So they sat down in groups of hundreds and fifties. 41 He took the five loaves and the two fish, and looking up to heaven, he blessed and broke the loaves. He kept giving them to his disciples to set before the people. He also divided the two fish among them all. 42 Everyone ate and was satisfied. 43 They picked up twelve baskets full of pieces of bread and fish. 44 Now those who had eaten the loaves were five thousand men.

WALKING ON THE WATER

45 Immediately he made his disciples get into the boat and go ahead of him to the other side, to Bethsaida, while he dismissed the crowd. 46 After he said good-bye to them, he went away to the mountain to pray. 47 Well into the night, the boat was in the middle of the sea, and he was alone on the land. 48 He saw them straining at the oars,[E] because the wind was against them. Very early in the morning[F] he came toward them walking on the sea and wanted to pass by them. 49 When they saw him walking on the sea, they thought it was a ghost and cried out, 50 because they all saw him and were terrified. Immediately he spoke with them and said, "Have courage! It is I. Don't be afraid." 51 Then he got into the boat with them, and the wind ceased. They were completely astounded, 52 because they had not understood about the loaves. Instead, their hearts were hardened.

MIRACULOUS HEALINGS

53 When they had crossed over, they came to shore at Gennesaret and anchored there.

54 As they got out of the boat, people immediately recognized him. 55 They hurried throughout that region and began to carry the sick on mats to wherever they heard he was. 56 Wherever he went, into villages, towns, or the country, they laid the sick in the marketplaces and begged him that they might touch just the end of his robe. And everyone who touched it was healed.

THE TRADITIONS OF THE ELDERS

7 The Pharisees and some of the scribes who had come from Jerusalem gathered around him. 2 They observed that some of his disciples

[A] **6:22** Other mss read *When his daughter Herodias* [B] **6:26** Lit *and those reclining at the table* [C] **6:33** Other mss add *and gathered around him* [D] **6:37** A denarius = one day's wage [E] **6:48** Or *them being battered as they rowed* [F] **6:48** Lit *Around the fourth watch of the night* = 3 to 6 a.m.

were eating bread with unclean — that is,
unwashed — hands. 3 (For the Pharisees and
all the Jews do not eat unless they give their
hands a ceremonial washing, keeping the tradition of the elders. 4 When they come from the
marketplace, they do not eat unless they have
washed. And there are many other customs
they have received and keep, like the washing
of cups, pitchers, kettles, and dining couches.[A])
5 So the Pharisees and the scribes asked him,
"Why don't your disciples live according to
the tradition of the elders, instead of eating
bread with ceremonially unclean[B] hands?"
6 He answered them, "Isaiah prophesied
correctly about you hypocrites, as it is written:

This people honors me
with their lips,
but their heart is far from me.
7 **They worship me in vain,**
teaching as doctrines
human commands.[C]

8 Abandoning the command of God, you hold
on to human tradition."[D] 9 He also said to them,
"You have a fine way of invalidating God's
command in order to set up[E] your tradition!
10 For Moses said: **Honor your father and
your mother**;[F] and **Whoever speaks evil of
father or mother must be put to death.**[G] 11 But
you say, 'If anyone tells his father or mother:
Whatever benefit you might have received
from me is *corban*'" (that is, an offering devoted to God), 12 "you no longer let him do
anything for his father or mother. 13 You nullify
the word of God by your tradition that you
have handed down. And you do many other
similar things."
14 Summoning the crowd again, he told
them, "Listen to me, all of you, and understand: 15 Nothing that goes into a person from
outside can defile him but the things that come
out of a person are what defile him."[H]
17 When he went into the house away from
the crowd, his disciples asked him about the
parable. 18 He said to them, "Are you also as
lacking in understanding? Don't you realize
that nothing going into a person from the

Eternal Perspective | *God's Work in Us*

OUR UNPREDICTABLE LORD

"They brought to him a deaf man who had difficulty speaking and begged Jesus to lay his hand on him. So he took him away from the crowd in private. After putting his fingers in the man's ears and spitting, he touched his tongue." Mark 7:32-33

Hang around people long enough, and you can start to predict exactly how they will respond to certain situations.

Not so with Jesus. Reading through the Gospels, we're stunned at how he almost never does the same thing twice. Here he heals a deaf mute "in private" by touching his ears and tongue and spitting. In another place, he spits and makes mud, which he rubs, publicly, on a blind man's eyes (Jn 9:6). On other occasions, he heals by merely speaking a word—sometimes even from long distance.

We see the same creativity in the way Jesus explains spiritual truths. To a Jewish religious leader, he talks about being "born again" (Jn 3:3). To a big group of people, he talks about seeds and soil (Mk 4:1-20). To a Samaritan woman, he talks about spiritual thirst (Jn 4). In short, Jesus deals with people on an individual basis. Each one has a different experience.

All this means we shouldn't compare our encounters with Jesus. How he works in someone else's life is not our business (see Jn 21:21-22). What counts is trusting him to work in your life in unexpected ways.

For the next note on *Eternal Perspective*, see Mark 8:24-25.

[A] **7:4** Other mss omit *and dining couches* [B] **7:5** Other mss read *with unwashed* [C] **7:6-7** Is 29:13 [D] **7:8** Other mss add *The washing of jugs, and cups, and many other similar things you practice.* [E] **7:9** Or *to maintain* [F] **7:10** Ex 20:12; Dt 5:16 [G] **7:10** Ex 21:17; Lv 20:9 [H] **7:15** Some mss include v. 16: *"If anyone has ears to hear, let him listen."*

outside can defile him? 19 For it doesn't go into his heart but into the stomach and is eliminated" (thus he declared all foods clean[A]). 20 And he said, "What comes out of a person is what defiles him. 21 For from within, out of people's hearts, come evil thoughts, sexual immoralities, thefts, murders, 22 adulteries, greed, evil actions, deceit, self-indulgence, envy,[B] slander, pride, and foolishness. 23 All these evil things come from within and defile a person."

A GENTILE MOTHER'S FAITH

24 He got up and departed from there to the region of Tyre.[C] He entered a house and did not want anyone to know it, but he could not escape notice. 25 Instead, immediately after hearing about him, a woman whose little daughter had an unclean spirit came and fell at his feet. 26 The woman was a Gentile,[D] a Syrophoenician by birth, and she was asking him to cast the demon out of her daughter. 27 He said to her, "Let the children be fed first, because it isn't right to take the children's bread and throw it to the dogs."

28 But she replied to him, "Lord, even the dogs under the table eat the children's crumbs."

29 Then he told her, "Because of this reply, you may go. The demon has left your daughter." 30 When she went back to her home, she found her child lying on the bed, and the demon was gone.

JESUS DOES EVERYTHING WELL

31 Again, leaving the region of Tyre, he went by way of Sidon to the Sea of Galilee, through[E] the region of the Decapolis. 32 They brought to him a deaf man who had difficulty speaking and begged Jesus to lay his hand on him. 33 So he took him away from the crowd in private. After putting his fingers in the man's ears and spitting, he touched his tongue. 34 Looking up to heaven, he sighed deeply and said to him, "*Ephphatha!*"[F] (that is, "Be opened!"). 35 Immediately his ears were opened, his tongue was loosened, and he began to speak clearly. 36 He ordered them to tell no one, but the more he ordered them, the more they proclaimed it.

37 They were extremely astonished and said, "He has done everything well. He even makes the deaf hear and the mute speak."

FEEDING FOUR THOUSAND

8 In those days there was again a large crowd, and they had nothing to eat. He called the disciples and said to them, 2 "I have compassion on the crowd, because they've already stayed with me three days and have nothing to eat. 3 If I send them home hungry, they will collapse on the way, and some of them have come a long distance."

4 His disciples answered him, "Where can anyone get enough bread here in this desolate place to feed these people?"

5 "How many loaves do you have?" he asked them.

"Seven," they said. 6 He commanded the crowd to sit down on the ground. Taking the seven loaves, he gave thanks, broke them, and gave them to his disciples to set before the people. So they served them to the crowd. 7 They also had a few small fish, and after he had blessed them, he said these were to be served as well. 8 They ate and were satisfied. Then they collected seven large baskets of leftover pieces. 9 About four thousand were there. He dismissed them. 10 And he immediately got into the boat with his disciples and went to the district of Dalmanutha.

THE LEAVEN OF THE PHARISEES AND HEROD

11 The Pharisees came and began to argue with him, demanding of him a sign from heaven to test him. 12 Sighing deeply in his spirit, he said, "Why does this generation demand a sign? Truly I tell you, no sign will be given to this generation." 13 Then he left them, got back into the boat, and went to the other side.

14 The disciples had forgotten to take bread and had only one loaf with them in the boat. 15 Then he gave them strict orders: "Watch out! Beware of the leaven[G] of the Pharisees and the leaven of Herod." 16 They were discussing among themselves that they did not have any bread. 17 Aware of this, he said to them, "Why are you discussing the fact you have no bread? Don't you understand or comprehend? Do you have hardened hearts? 18 **Do you have eyes and not see; do you have ears and not hear?**[H] And do you not remember? 19 When I broke the five loaves for the five thousand, how many baskets full of leftovers did you collect?"

"Twelve," they told him.

20 "When I broke the seven loaves for the

[A] **7:19** Other mss read *is eliminated, making all foods clean"* [B] **7:22** Or *evil eye* [C] **7:24** Many early mss add *and Sidon* [D] **7:26** Or *a Greek (speaker)* [E] **7:31** Or *into* [F] **7:34** An Aramaic expression [G] **8:15** Or *yeast* [H] **8:18** Jr 5:21; Ezk 12:2

four thousand, how many baskets full of pieces
did you collect?"
"Seven," they said.
21 And he said to them, "Don't you understand yet?"

HEALING A BLIND MAN

22 They came to Bethsaida. They brought a
blind man to him and begged him to touch
him. 23 He took the blind man by the hand
and brought him out of the village. Spitting
on his eyes and laying his hands on him, he
asked him, "Do you see anything?"
24 He looked up and said, "I see people — they
look like trees walking."
25 Again Jesus placed his hands on the man's
eyes. The man looked intently and his sight
was restored and he saw everything clearly.
26 Then he sent him home, saying, "Don't even
go into the village."[A]

PETER'S CONFESSION OF THE MESSIAH

27 Jesus went out with his disciples to the villages of Caesarea Philippi. And on the road
he asked his disciples, "Who do people say
that I am?"
28 They answered him, "John the Baptist;
others, Elijah; still others, one of the prophets."
29 "But you," he asked them, "who do you
say that I am?"
Peter answered him, "You are the Messiah."
30 And he strictly warned them to tell no one
about him.

HIS DEATH AND RESURRECTION PREDICTED

31 Then he began to teach them that it was
necessary for the Son of Man to suffer many
things and be rejected by the elders, chief
priests, and scribes, be killed, and rise after
three days. 32 He spoke openly about this. Peter took him aside and began to rebuke him.
33 But turning around and looking at his disciples, he rebuked Peter and said, "Get behind
me, Satan! You are not thinking about God's
concerns[B] but human concerns."

TAKE UP YOUR CROSS

34 Calling the crowd along with his disciples,
he said to them, "If anyone wants to follow
after me, let him deny himself, take up his
cross, and follow me. 35 For whoever wants
to save his life will lose it, but whoever loses

Eternal Perspective | *God's Work in Us*

ALL AT ONCE OR GRADUAL?

"He looked up and said, 'I see people—they look like trees walking.' Again, Jesus placed his hands on the man's eyes. The man looked intently and his sight was restored and he saw everything clearly." Mark 8:24-25

Many Christians want instant transformation. Michael is a good example. He's battling envy and lust. A friend has offered to meet with him weekly to pray and work through an in-depth, thirteen-week Bible study. Michael is willing to do that, but, honestly, he'd much rather experience freedom through one intense prayer time or during a single exciting church service.

Is that how it works? Can God bring instant healing or immediate deliverance? Of course he can! But many are discouraged because God doesn't always choose to work like that. Sometimes, as in this passage, the Lord works gradually, in stages.

Paul may have been hinting at this reality when he encouraged the believers at Philippi to "work out your own salvation with fear and trembling. For it is God who is working in you" (Php 2:12-13). Often growth, life change, or the work of God comes as the result of an arduous process, not an easy point in time.

Are you waiting for change (and wishing it would hurry up and happen)? Ask God for the grace to enjoy the process and not just fixate on the result.

For the next note on *Eternal Perspective*, see Mark 14:36.

[A] **8:26** Other mss add *or tell anyone in the village* [B] **8:33** Or *about the things of God*

his life because of me and the gospel will save
it. 36 For what does it benefit someone to gain
the whole world and yet lose his life? 37 What
can anyone give in exchange for his life? 38 For
whoever is ashamed of me and my words in
this adulterous and sinful generation, the Son
of Man will also be ashamed of him when
he comes in the glory of his Father with the
holy angels."

9 Then he said to them, "Truly I tell you,
there are some standing here who will
not taste death until they see the kingdom
of God come in power."

THE TRANSFIGURATION

2 After six days Jesus took Peter, James, and
John and led them up a high mountain by
themselves to be alone. He was transfigured
in front of them, 3 and his clothes became dazzling — extremely white as no launderer on
earth could whiten them. 4 Elijah appeared to
them with Moses, and they were talking with
Jesus. 5 Peter said to Jesus, "Rabbi, it's good for
us to be here. Let us set up three shelters: one
for you, one for Moses, and one for Elijah" —
6 because he did not know what to say, since
they were terrified.

7 A cloud appeared, overshadowing them,
and a voice came from the cloud: "This is my
beloved Son; listen to him! "

8 Suddenly, looking around, they no longer
saw anyone with them except Jesus.

9 As they were coming down the mountain,
he ordered them to tell no one what they had
seen until the Son of Man had risen from the
dead. 10 They kept this word to themselves,
questioning what "rising from the dead" meant.

11 Then they asked him, "Why do the scribes
say that Elijah must come first? "

12 "Elijah does come first and restores all
things," he replied. "Why then is it written that
the Son of Man must suffer many things and
be treated with contempt? 13 But I tell you that
Elijah has come, and they did whatever they
pleased to him, just as it is written about him."

THE POWER OF FAITH OVER A DEMON

14 When they came to the disciples, they saw
a large crowd around them and scribes dis-
puting with them. 15 When the whole crowd
saw him, they were amazed and ran to greet
him. 16 He asked them, "What are you arguing
with them about? "

17 Someone from the crowd answered him,
"Teacher, I brought my son to you. He has a
spirit that makes him unable to speak. 18 Whenever it seizes him, it throws him down, and
he foams at the mouth, grinds his teeth, and
becomes rigid. I asked your disciples to drive
it out, but they couldn't."

Support | *Openness with God*

FAITH AND DOUBT

"Jesus said to him, 'If you can'? Everything is possible for the one who believes.' Immediately the father of the boy cried out, 'I do believe; help my unbelief!'" Mark 9:23-24

On the one hand, we see the boy, haunted and hounded by a destructive demon. This means every moment of every day he faces danger. He has been this way for years. Nobody and nothing has ever been able to help. Can you see why the father might feel hopeless?

On the other hand, we see Jesus. Word on the street is that he is a powerful healer with a great heart of compassion. Can you see why the man might feel a faint glimmer of hope?

"I do believe; help my unbelief!" is surely one of the best prayers of the Bible. It's honest. It's heartfelt. It's human. It's a great confession and a petition at all once. It's a reminder of Jesus's statement that we can do nothing—not even believe—without his help (Jn 15:5).

If you're having a hard time believing today, realize this: Even if what you're bringing to Jesus is mostly doubts, just by coming to him, you're demonstrating faith.

For the next note on *Support*, see Mark 10:47-48.

19 He replied to them, "You unbelieving generation, how long will I be with you? How long
must I put up with you? Bring him to me."
20 So they brought the boy to him. When the
spirit saw him, it immediately threw the boy
into convulsions. He fell to the ground and
rolled around, foaming at the mouth. 21 "How
long has this been happening to him?" Jesus
asked his father.
"From childhood," he said. 22 "And many
times it has thrown him into fire or water to
destroy him. But if you can do anything, have
compassion on us and help us."
23 Jesus said to him, "'If you can'?[A] Everything is possible for the one who believes."
24 Immediately the father of the boy cried
out, "I do believe; help my unbelief!"
25 When Jesus saw that a crowd was quickly gathering, he rebuked the unclean spirit,
saying to it, "You mute and deaf spirit, I command you: Come out of him and never enter
him again."
26 Then it came out, shrieking and throwing
him[B] into terrible convulsions. The boy became
like a corpse, so that many said, "He's dead."
27 But Jesus, taking him by the hand, raised
him, and he stood up.
28 After he had gone into the house, his disciples asked him privately, "Why couldn't we
drive it out?"
29 And he told them, "This kind can come
out by nothing but prayer."[C]

THE SECOND PREDICTION OF HIS DEATH

30 Then they left that place and made their way
through Galilee, but he did not want anyone
to know it. 31 For he was teaching his disciples
and telling them, "The Son of Man is going to
be betrayed[D] into the hands of men. They will
kill him, and after he is killed, he will rise three
days later." 32 But they did not understand this
statement, and they were afraid to ask him.

WHO IS THE GREATEST?

33 They came to Capernaum. When he was
in the house, he asked them, "What were
you arguing about on the way?" 34 But they
were silent, because on the way they had
been arguing with one another about who
was the greatest. 35 Sitting down, he called the

Exercise of Faith | *Serving*

TRUE GREATNESS

"Sitting down, he called the Twelve and said to them, 'If anyone wants to be first, he must be last and servant of all.'" Mark 9:35

We may cringe that Jesus's disciples—bless their clumsy hearts—"had been arguing with one another about who was the greatest" (Mk 9:34). They weren't kidding around. They were serious. Question: How insecure or how arrogant do you have to be to engage in a heated debate like this?

We moderns are far more sophisticated. We get that nobody but a narcissist would ever blurt out in a group, "I'm superior to the rest of you!" So, we don't say such things, but we are tempted, daily, to show we're better in a thousand and one ways. We measure ourselves against others in our hearts, using all sorts of yardsticks: careers, income levels, vacations, homes, kids' schools and accomplishments.

Jesus knew all about this inane discussion because he had been within earshot when it happened. When they arrived at Capernaum, he asked pointedly, "What were you arguing about on the way?" (9:33).

Embarrassment. Silence. Sensing a teachable moment, Jesus explained that true greatness means being the "servant of all."

Ponder that. Absolutely refuse to keep score today. Instead of measuring how you stack up against others, focus on serving them.

For the next note on *Exercise of Faith*, see Luke 7:9.

[A] **9:23** Other mss add *believe* [B] **9:26** Other mss omit *him* [C] **9:29** Other mss add *and fasting* [D] **9:31** Or *handed over*

Twelve and said to them, "If anyone wants to be first, he must be last and servant of all." 36 He took a child, had him stand among them, and taking him in his arms, he said to them, 37 "Whoever welcomes[A] one little child such as this in my name welcomes me. And whoever welcomes me does not welcome me, but him who sent me."

IN HIS NAME

38 John said to him, "Teacher, we saw someone[B] driving out demons in your name, and we tried to stop him because he wasn't following us."

39 "Don't stop him," said Jesus, "because there is no one who will perform a miracle in my name who can soon afterward speak evil of me. 40 For whoever is not against us is for us. 41 And whoever gives you a cup of water to drink in my name, because you belong to Christ — truly I tell you, he will never lose his reward.

WARNINGS FROM JESUS

42 "But whoever causes one of these little ones who believe in me to fall away — it would be better for him if a heavy millstone were hung around his neck and he were thrown into the sea.

43 "And if your hand causes you to fall away, cut it off. It is better for you to enter life maimed than to have two hands and go to hell, the unquenchable fire.[C] 45 And if your foot causes you to fall away, cut it off. It is better for you to enter life lame than to have two feet and be thrown into hell.[D] 47 And if your eye causes you to fall away, gouge it out. It is better for you to enter the kingdom of God with one eye than to have two eyes and be thrown into hell, 48 where **their worm does not die, and the fire is not quenched.**[E] 49 For everyone will be salted with fire.[F,G] 50 Salt is good, but if the salt should lose its flavor, how can you season it? Have salt among yourselves, and be at peace with one another."

THE QUESTION OF DIVORCE

10 He set out from there and went to the region of Judea and across the Jordan. Then crowds converged on him again, and as was his custom he taught them again.

2 Some Pharisees came to test him, asking, "Is it lawful for a man to divorce his wife?"

3 He replied to them, "What did Moses command you?"

4 They said, "Moses permitted us to write divorce papers and send her away."

5 But Jesus told them, "He wrote this command for you because of the hardness of your hearts. 6 But from the beginning of creation God[H] **made them male and female.**[I] 7 **For this reason a man will leave his father and mother**[J] 8 **and the two will become one flesh.**[K] So they are no longer two, but one flesh. 9 Therefore what God has joined together, let no one separate."

10 When they were in the house again, the disciples questioned him about this matter. 11 He said to them, "Whoever divorces his wife and marries another commits adultery against her. 12 Also, if she divorces her husband and marries another, she commits adultery."

BLESSING THE CHILDREN

13 People were bringing little children to him in order that he might touch them, but the disciples rebuked them. 14 When Jesus saw it, he was indignant and said to them, "Let the little children come to me. Don't stop them, because the kingdom of God belongs to such as these. 15 Truly I tell you, whoever does not receive[L] the kingdom of God like a little child will never enter it." 16 After taking them in his arms, he laid his hands on them and blessed them.

THE RICH YOUNG RULER

17 As he was setting out on a journey, a man ran up, knelt down before him, and asked him, "Good teacher, what must I do to inherit eternal life?"

18 "Why do you call me good?" Jesus asked him. "No one is good except God alone. 19 You know the commandments: **Do not murder; do not commit adultery; do not steal; do not bear false witness; do not defraud; honor your father and mother.**"[M]

20 He said to him, "Teacher, I have kept all these from my youth."

21 Looking at him, Jesus loved him and said to him, "You lack one thing: Go, sell all you have and give to the poor, and you will have treasure in

---

[A] **9:37** Or *"Whoever receives* [B] **9:38** Other mss add *who didn't go along with us* [C] **9:43** Some mss include v. 44: *Where their worm does not die, and the fire is not quenched.* [D] **9:45** Some mss include v. 46: *Where their worm does not die, and the fire is not quenched.* [E] **9:48** Is 66:24 [F] **9:49** Other mss add *and every sacrifice will be salted with salt* [G] **9:49** Lv 2:13; Ezk 43:24 [H] **10:6** Other mss omit *God* [I] **10:6** Gn 1:27; 5:2 [J] **10:7** Some mss add *and be joined to his wife* [K] **10:7-8** Gn 2:24 [L] **10:15** Or *not welcome* [M] **10:19** Ex 20:12-16; Dt 5:16-20

heaven. Then come,[A] follow me." 22 But he was
dismayed by this demand, and he went away
grieving, because he had many possessions.

POSSESSIONS AND THE KINGDOM

23 Jesus looked around and said to his disciples,
"How hard it is for those who have wealth to
enter the kingdom of God!"
24 The disciples were astonished at his words.
Again Jesus said to them, "Children, how hard it
is[B] to enter the kingdom of God! 25 It is easier for
a camel to go through the eye of a needle than
for a rich person to enter the kingdom of God."
26 They were even more astonished, saying
to one another, "Then who can be saved?"
27 Looking at them, Jesus said, "With man it
is impossible, but not with God, because all
things are possible with God."
28 Peter began to tell him, "Look, we have
left everything and followed you."
29 "Truly I tell you," Jesus said, "there is no
one who has left house or brothers or sisters
or mother or father[C] or children or fields for my
sake and for the sake of the gospel, 30 who will
not receive a hundred times more, now at this
time — houses, brothers and sisters, mothers
and children, and fields, with persecutions —
and eternal life in the age to come. 31 But many
who are first will be last, and the last first."

THE THIRD PREDICTION OF HIS DEATH

32 They were on the road, going up to Jerusalem, and Jesus was walking ahead of them.
The disciples were astonished, but those who
followed him were afraid. Taking the Twelve
aside again, he began to tell them the things
that would happen to him. 33 "See, we are going
up to Jerusalem. The Son of Man will be handed
over to the chief priests and the scribes, and
they will condemn him to death. Then they
will hand him over to the Gentiles, 34 and they
will mock him, spit on him, flog[D] him, and kill
him, and he will rise after three days."

SUFFERING AND SERVICE

35 James and John, the sons of Zebedee, approached him and said, "Teacher, we want
you to do whatever we ask you."
36 "What do you want me to do for you?"
he asked them.

Support | *Openness with God*

WHAT DO YOU WANT?

"When he heard that it was Jesus of Nazareth, he began to cry out, 'Jesus, Son of David, have mercy on me!' Many warned him to keep quiet, but he was crying out all the more, 'Have mercy on me, Son of David!'" Mark 10:47-48

He was blind. That meant he couldn't get a job, so he had to beg.

Though his eyes didn't work, nothing was wrong with his ears. He heard the crowd approaching, and when someone told him Jesus was passing by, his heart began to race. He'd heard the stories. He believed they were true. This was his chance of a lifetime.

The man began to holler, "Jesus, Son of David, have mercy on me!" When some in the crowd told him to hush, he got louder and more insistent. Repeatedly he used the messianic title "Son of David."

Jesus heard Bartimaeus. He called for him and said, "What do you want me to do for you?" (Mk 10:51). It was less a question than a wild invitation.

"I want to see," the blind man blurted out. And so it was.

If you have a need, Jesus is the One you're looking for. Don't let anyone discourage you from asking Jesus to rescue you. Keep crying out to him. Tell him exactly what you want him to do for you.

For the next note on *Support*, see Mark 14:33-34.

[A] **10:21** Other mss add *taking up the cross, and* [B] **10:24** Other mss add *for those trusting in wealth* [C] **10:29** Other mss add *or wife* [D] **10:34** Or *scourge*

37 They answered him, "Allow us to sit at your
right and at your left in your glory."
38 Jesus said to them, "You don't know what
you're asking. Are you able to drink the cup I
drink or to be baptized with the baptism I am
baptized with?"
39 "We are able," they told him.
Jesus said to them, "You will drink the cup I
drink, and you will be baptized with the baptism I am baptized with. 40 But to sit at my
right or left is not mine to give; instead, it is
for those for whom it has been prepared."
41 When the ten disciples heard this, they
began to be indignant with James and John.
42 Jesus called them over and said to them, "You
know that those who are regarded as rulers
of the Gentiles lord it over them, and those
in high positions act as tyrants over them.
43 But it is not so among you. On the contrary,
whoever wants to become great among you
will be your servant, 44 and whoever wants
to be first among you will be a slave to all.
45 For even the Son of Man did not come to
be served, but to serve, and to give his life as
a ransom for many."[A]

A BLIND MAN HEALED

46 They came to Jericho. And as he was leaving
Jericho with his disciples and a large crowd,
Bartimaeus (the son of Timaeus), a blind beggar, was sitting by the road. 47 When he heard
that it was Jesus of Nazareth, he began to cry
out, "Jesus, Son of David, have mercy on me!"
48 Many warned him to keep quiet, but he was
crying out all the more, "Have mercy on me,
Son of David!"
49 Jesus stopped and said, "Call him."
So they called the blind man and said to
him, "Have courage! Get up; he's calling for
you." 50 He threw off his coat, jumped up, and
came to Jesus.
51 Then Jesus answered him, "What do you
want me to do for you?"
"*Rabboni*,"[B] the blind man said to him, "I
want to see."
52 Jesus said to him, "Go, your faith has saved
you." Immediately he could see and began to
follow Jesus on the road.

THE TRIUMPHAL ENTRY

11 When they approached Jerusalem, at
Bethphage and Bethany near the Mount
of Olives, he sent two of his disciples 2 and told
them, "Go into the village ahead of you. As
soon as you enter it, you will find a colt tied
there, on which no one has ever sat. Untie it
and bring it. 3 If anyone says to you, 'Why are
you doing this?' say, 'The Lord needs it and
will send it back here right away.'"
4 So they went and found a colt outside in the
street, tied by a door. They untied it, 5 and some
of those standing there said to them, "What are
you doing, untying the colt?" 6 They answered
them just as Jesus had said; so they let them go.
7 They brought the donkey to Jesus and threw
their clothes on it, and he sat on it. 8 Many
people spread their clothes on the road, and
others spread leafy branches cut from the
fields.[C] 9 Those who went ahead and those
who followed shouted:

Hosanna!
Blessed is he who comes
in the name of the Lord![D]
10 **Blessed is the coming kingdom**
of our father David!
Hosanna **in the highest heaven!**

11 He went into Jerusalem and into the temple.
After looking around at everything, since it
was already late, he went out to Bethany with
the Twelve.

THE BARREN FIG TREE IS CURSED

12 The next day when they went out from Bethany, he was hungry. 13 Seeing in the distance a
fig tree with leaves, he went to find out if there
was anything on it. When he came to it, he found
nothing but leaves; for it was not the season for
figs. 14 He said to it, "May no one ever eat fruit
from you again!" And his disciples heard it.

CLEANSING THE TEMPLE

15 They came to Jerusalem, and he went into
the temple and began to throw out those buying and selling. He overturned the tables of
the money changers and the chairs of those
selling doves, 16 and would not permit anyone
to carry goods through the temple. 17 He was
teaching them: "Is it not written, **My house will**
be called a house of prayer for all nations?[E]
But you have made it **a den of thieves**!"[F]
18 The chief priests and the scribes heard it
and started looking for a way to kill him. For
they were afraid of him, because the whole
crowd was astonished by his teaching.
19 Whenever evening came, they would go
out of the city.

[A] **10:45** Or *in the place of many*; Is 53:10-12 [B] **10:51** Hb word for *my lord* [C] **11:8** Other mss read *others were cutting leafy branches from the trees and spreading them on the road* [D] **11:9** Ps 118:26 [E] **11:17** Is 56:7 [F] **11:17** Jr 7:11

THE BARREN FIG TREE IS WITHERED

20 Early in the morning, as they were passing by, they saw the fig tree withered from
the roots up. 21 Then Peter remembered and
said to him, "Rabbi, look! The fig tree that you
cursed has withered."
22 Jesus replied to them, "Have faith in God.
23 Truly I tell you, if anyone says to this mountain, 'Be lifted up and thrown into the sea,' and
does not doubt in his heart, but believes that
what he says will happen, it will be done for
him. 24 Therefore I tell you, everything you pray
and ask for — believe that you have received[A] it
and it will be yours. 25 And whenever you stand
praying, if you have anything against anyone,
forgive him, so that your Father in heaven will
also forgive you your wrongdoing."[B]

THE AUTHORITY OF JESUS CHALLENGED

27 They came again to Jerusalem. As he was
walking in the temple, the chief priests, the
scribes, and the elders came 28 and asked him,
"By what authority are you doing these things?
Who gave you this authority to do these things?"
29 Jesus said to them, "I will ask you one
question; then answer me, and I will tell you
by what authority I do these things. 30 Was
John's baptism from heaven or of human origin? Answer me."
31 They discussed it among themselves: "If
we say, 'From heaven,' he will say, 'Then why
didn't you believe him?' 32 But if we say, 'Of
human origin'" — they were afraid of the
crowd, because everyone thought that John
was truly a prophet. 33 So they answered Jesus,
"We don't know."
And Jesus said to them, "Neither will I tell
you by what authority I do these things."

THE PARABLE OF THE VINEYARD OWNER

12 He began to speak to them in parables:
"A man planted a vineyard, put a fence
around it, dug out a pit for a winepress, and
built a watchtower. Then he leased it to tenant
farmers and went away. 2 At harvest time he
sent a servant to the farmers to collect some
of the fruit of the vineyard from them. 3 But
they took him, beat him, and sent him away
empty-handed. 4 Again he sent another servant to them, and they[C] hit him on the head
and treated him shamefully.[D] 5 Then he sent
another, and they killed that one. He also sent
many others; some they beat, and others they
killed. 6 He still had one to send, a beloved son.

Other-centeredness | *Identifying Those We Have Wronged*

RECONCILIATION

"Whenever you stand praying, if you have anything against anyone, forgive him, so that your Father in heaven will also forgive you your wrongdoing." Mark 11:25

Healthy, gospel-centered people are self-aware even as they remain other-focused. They don't blindly bulldoze their way through life, oblivious to how they interact with others. They are *we*-centered, not *me*-centered. They're sensitive. They make preserving and protecting relationships a priority. They carefully consider how their words and actions impact the people around them.

Consequently, Jesus says that when his followers become aware of a hurtful action, some specific offense against another person, they should acknowledge it. They should drop everything to make it right. They should be agents of reconciliation.

Is this how you operate? Are you humble enough (and secure enough in God's unconditional love) to admit your shortcomings and failures? Do you take the initiative to make amends? Seeking out a person you've wronged is scary, but it's also a holy act. "I was wrong. Will you please forgive me?" are perhaps the eight most healing words a person can ever say.

For the next note on *Other-centeredness*, see Luke 6:8-9.

[A] **11:24** Some mss read *you receive*; other mss read *you will receive* [B] **11:25** Some mss include v. 26: *"But if you don't forgive, neither will your Father in heaven forgive your wrongdoing."* [C] **12:4** Other mss add *threw stones and* [D] **12:4** Other mss add *and sent him off*

Finally he sent him to them, saying, 'They will
respect my son.' 7 But those tenant farmers
said to one another, 'This is the heir. Come,
let's kill him, and the inheritance will be ours.'
8 So they seized him, killed him, and threw him
out of the vineyard. 9 What then will the owner[A] of the vineyard do? He will come and kill
the farmers and give the vineyard to others.
10 Haven't you read this Scripture:

The stone that the builders rejected
has become the cornerstone.
11 **This came about from the Lord**
and is wonderful in our eyes?"[B]

12 They were looking for a way to arrest him
but feared the crowd because they knew he
had spoken this parable against them. So they
left him and went away.

GOD AND CAESAR

13 Then they sent some of the Pharisees and the Herodians to Jesus to trap him in his words. 14 When
they came, they said to him, "Teacher, we know you
are truthful and don't care what anyone thinks,
nor do you show partiality but teach the way of
God truthfully. Is it lawful to pay taxes to Caesar
or not? Should we pay or shouldn't we?"
15 But knowing their hypocrisy, he said to them,
"Why are you testing me? Bring me a denarius[C] to look at." 16 They brought a coin. "Whose
image and inscription is this?" he asked them.
"Caesar's," they replied.
17 Jesus told them, "Give to Caesar the things
that are Caesar's, and to God the things that are
God's." And they were utterly amazed at him.

THE SADDUCEES AND THE RESURRECTION

18 Sadducees, who say there is no resurrection,
came to him and questioned him: 19 "Teacher,
Moses wrote for us that **if a man's brother**
dies, leaving a wife behind but **no child, that**
man should take the wife and raise up off-
spring for his brother.[D] 20 There were seven
brothers. The first married a woman, and dying, left no offspring. 21 The second also took
her, and he died, leaving no offspring. And
the third likewise. 22 None of the seven[E] left
offspring. Last of all, the woman died too. 23 In
the resurrection, when they rise,[F] whose wife
will she be, since the seven had married her?"
24 Jesus spoke to them, "Isn't this the reason
why you're mistaken: you don't know the Scriptures or the power of God? 25 For when they rise
from the dead, they neither marry nor are given
in marriage but are like angels in heaven. 26 And
as for the dead being raised — haven't you read
in the book of Moses, in the passage about the
burning bush, how God said to him: **I am the**
God of Abraham and the God of Isaac and
the God of Jacob?[G] 27 He is not the God of the
dead but of the living. You are badly mistaken."

THE PRIMARY COMMANDS

28 One of the scribes approached. When he
heard them debating and saw that Jesus answered them well, he asked him, "Which command is the most important of all?"
29 Jesus answered, "The most important[H] is
Listen, O Israel! The Lord our God, the Lord
is one.[I] 30 **Love the Lord your God with all**
your heart, with all your soul, with all your
mind, and with all your strength.[J,K] 31 The
second is, **Love your neighbor as yourself.**[L]
There is no other command greater than these."
32 Then the scribe said to him, "You are right,
teacher. You have correctly said that he is one,
and there is no one else except him. 33 And to
love him with all your heart, with all your understanding,[M] and with all your strength, and to
love your neighbor as yourself, is far more important than all the burnt offerings and sacrifices."
34 When Jesus saw that he answered wisely,
he said to him, "You are not far from the kingdom of God." And no one dared to question
him any longer.

THE QUESTION ABOUT THE CHRIST

35 While Jesus was teaching in the temple, he
asked, "How can the scribes say that the Messiah is the son of David? 36 David himself says
by the Holy Spirit:

The Lord declared to my Lord,
'Sit at my right hand
until I put your enemies
under your feet.'[N]

37 David himself calls him 'Lord'; how then
can he be his son?" And the large crowd was
listening to him with delight.

WARNING AGAINST THE SCRIBES

38 He also said in his teaching, "Beware of the
scribes, who want to go around in long robes

[A] **12:9** Or *lord* [B] **12:10-11** Ps 118:22-23 [C] **12:15** A denarius = one day's wage [D] **12:19** Gn 38:8; Dt 25:5 [E] **12:22** Other mss add *had taken her and* [F] **12:23** Other mss omit *when they rise* [G] **12:26** Ex 3:6,15-16 [H] **12:29** Other mss add *of all the commands* [I] **12:29** Or *the Lord our God is Lord alone.* [J] **12:30** Other mss add *This is the first commandment.* [K] **12:30** Dt 6:4-5; Jos 22:5 [L] **12:31** Lv 19:18 [M] **12:33** Other mss add *with all your soul* [N] **12:36** Ps 110:1

John Mark | Restoration Profile

MARK 14:51-52; ACTS 12:12–13:13; 15:36-40; COLOSSIANS 4:10-11; 2 TIMOTHY 4:11; PHILEMON 24; 1 PETER 5:13

As one of the early followers of Jesus, John Mark had a significant problem with discouragement and fear that had to be overcome. His actions damaged his relationship with the apostle Paul and affected other people in such a way that his restoration was necessary. If it hadn't happened, much of our New Testament and the ministry of Paul would have been affected dramatically.

Though John Mark was around during Jesus's final days, he wasn't identified as a participant in the early church until Luke mentioned him (Ac 12:12). Shortly thereafter he became a traveling companion of Paul and Barnabas. He embarked with them on their first missionary journey. At their second stop, John Mark left them to return to Jerusalem. This later became a problem when Paul and Barnabas planned another journey. Barnabas wanted to take John Mark again, but Paul vehemently disagreed. So, the two of them parted company. We have no idea how John Mark felt, but we can see that Barnabas was a master of restoration. He had done it with an impossible candidate, Paul himself. Now, he would do it with John Mark.

Ten years passed. The next time Mark is mentioned, Paul is commending him and sending him as a representative (Col 4:10-11). Possibly by this time Mark has been involved with Peter in writing the Gospel that bears his name. Later, when he wrote 2 Timothy, Paul specifically requested Mark to join him because "he is useful to me in the ministry" (2Tm 4:11). Mark had been restored.

Much as the apostle John signed his Gospel with the repeated phrase "the disciple Jesus loved," John Mark may have inserted a signature of sorts in his Gospel, noting the somewhat humorous incident at the arrest of Jesus during which a young man ran off in such terror that he left his clothes behind (Mk 14:51-52).

and who want greetings in the marketplaces,
39 the best seats in the synagogues, and the
places of honor at banquets. 40 They devour
widows' houses and say long prayers just for
show. These will receive harsher judgment."

THE WIDOW'S GIFT

41 Sitting across from the temple treasury, he
watched how the crowd dropped money into
the treasury. Many rich people were putting
in large sums. 42 Then a poor widow came
and dropped in two tiny coins worth very
little. 43 Summoning his disciples, he said to
them, "Truly I tell you, this poor widow has
put more into the treasury than all the others.
44 For they all gave out of their surplus, but
she out of her poverty has put in everything
she had — all she had to live on."

DESTRUCTION OF THE TEMPLE PREDICTED

13 As he was going out of the temple, one of his disciples said to him, "Teacher, look! What massive stones! What impressive buildings!"
2 Jesus said to him, "Do you see these great
buildings? Not one stone will be left upon
another — all will be thrown down."

SIGNS OF THE END OF THE AGE

3 While he was sitting on the Mount of Olives
across from the temple, Peter, James, John, and
Andrew asked him privately, 4 "Tell us, when
will these things happen? And what will be
the sign when all these things are about to be
accomplished?"
5 Jesus told them, "Watch out that no one
deceives you. 6 Many will come in my name,
saying, 'I am he,' and they will deceive many.
7 When you hear of wars and rumors of wars,
don't be alarmed; these things must take place,
but it is not yet the end. 8 For nation will rise up
against nation, and kingdom against kingdom.
There will be earthquakes in various places, and
famines.[A] These are the beginning of birth pains.

PERSECUTIONS PREDICTED

9 "But you, be on your guard! They will hand
you over to local courts,[B] and you will be
flogged in the synagogues. You will stand

[A] **13:8** Other mss add *and disturbances* [B] **13:9** Or *sanhedrins* before governors and kings because of me, as a witness to them. 10 And it is necessary that the gospel be preached to all nations. 11 So when they arrest you and hand you over, don't worry beforehand what you will say, but say whatever is given to you at that time, for it isn't you speaking, but the Holy Spirit.

12 "Brother will betray brother to death, and a father his child. Children will rise up against parents and have them put to death. 13 You will be hated by everyone because of my name, but the one who endures to the end will be saved.

THE GREAT TRIBULATION

14 "When you see **the abomination of desolation**[A] standing where it should not be" (let the reader understand), "then those in Judea must flee to the mountains. 15 A man on the housetop must not come down or go in to get anything out of his house, 16 and a man in the field must not go back to get his coat. 17 Woe to pregnant women and nursing mothers in those days!

18 "Pray it[B] won't happen in winter. 19 For those will be days of tribulation, the kind that hasn't been from the beginning of creation until now and never will be again. 20 If the Lord had not cut those days short, no one would be saved. But he cut those days short for the sake of the elect, whom he chose.

21 "Then if anyone tells you, 'See, here is the Messiah! See, there!' do not believe it. 22 For false messiahs and false prophets will arise and will perform signs and wonders to lead astray, if possible, the elect. 23 And you must watch! I have told you everything in advance.

THE COMING OF THE SON OF MAN

24 "But in those days, after that tribulation: The sun will be darkened, and the moon will not shed its light; 25 the stars will be falling from the sky, and the powers in the heavens will be shaken. 26 Then they will see the Son of Man coming in clouds with great power and glory. 27 He will send out the angels and gather his elect from the four winds, from the ends of the earth to the ends of heaven.

THE PARABLE OF THE FIG TREE

28 "Learn this lesson from the fig tree: As soon as its branch becomes tender and sprouts leaves, you know that summer is near. 29 In the same way, when you see these things happening, recognize[C] that he[D] is near — at the door.

30 "Truly I tell you, this generation will certainly not pass away until all these things take place. 31 Heaven and earth will pass away, but my words will never pass away.

NO ONE KNOWS THE DAY OR HOUR

32 "Now concerning that day or hour no one knows — neither the angels in heaven nor the Son — but only the Father.

33 "Watch! Be alert![E] For you don't know when the time is coming.

34 "It is like a man on a journey, who left his house, gave authority to his servants, gave each one his work, and commanded the doorkeeper to be alert. 35 Therefore be alert, since you don't know when the master of the house is coming — whether in the evening or at midnight or at the crowing of the rooster or early in the morning. 36 Otherwise, when he comes suddenly he might find you sleeping. 37 And what I say to you, I say to everyone: Be alert!"

THE PLOT TO KILL JESUS

14 It was two days before the Passover and the Festival of Unleavened Bread. The chief priests and the scribes were looking for a cunning way to arrest Jesus and kill him. 2 "Not during the festival," they said, "so that there won't be a riot among the people."

THE ANOINTING AT BETHANY

3 While he was in Bethany at the house of Simon the leper,[F] as he was reclining at the table, a woman came with an alabaster jar of very expensive perfume of pure nard. She broke the jar and poured it on his head. 4 But some were expressing indignation to one another: "Why has this perfume been wasted? 5 For this perfume might have been sold for more than three hundred denarii[G] and given to the poor." And they began to scold her.

6 Jesus replied, "Leave her alone. Why are you bothering her? She has done a noble thing for me. 7 You always have the poor with you, and you can do what is good for them whenever you want, but you do not always have me. 8 She has done what she could; she has anointed my body in advance for burial. 9 Truly I tell you, wherever the gospel is proclaimed in the whole world, what she has done will also be told in memory of her."

[A] **13:14** Dn 9:27 [B] **13:18** Other mss read *"Pray that your escape and pray* [C] **13:29** Or *you know* [D] **13:29** Or *it* [E] **13:33** Other mss add *and pray* [F] **14:3** Gk *lepros*; a term for various skin diseases; see Lv 13–14 [G] **14:5** A denarius = one day's wage

10 Then Judas Iscariot, one of the Twelve,
went to the chief priests to betray Jesus to
them. 11 And when they heard this, they were
glad and promised to give him money. So he
started looking for a good opportunity to betray him.

PREPARATION FOR PASSOVER

12 On the first day of Unleavened Bread, when
they sacrifice the Passover lamb, his disciples
asked him, "Where do you want us to go and
prepare the Passover so that you may eat it?"
13 So he sent two of his disciples and told
them, "Go into the city, and a man carrying
a jar of water will meet you. Follow him.
14 Wherever he enters, tell the owner of
the house, 'The Teacher says, "Where is my
guest room where I may eat the Passover
with my disciples?"' 15 He will show you a
large room upstairs, furnished and ready.
Make the preparations for us there." 16 So
the disciples went out, entered the city, and
found it just as he had told them, and they
prepared the Passover.

BETRAYAL AT THE PASSOVER

17 When evening came, he arrived with the
Twelve. 18 While they were reclining and eating,
Jesus said, "Truly I tell you, one of you will betray me — one who is eating with me."
19 They began to be distressed and to say to
him one by one, "Surely not I?"
20 He said to them, "It is one of the Twelve
— the one who is dipping bread in the bowl
with me. 21 For the Son of Man will go just
as it is written about him, but woe to that
man by whom the Son of Man is betrayed!
It would have been better for him if he had
not been born."

THE FIRST LORD'S SUPPER

22 As they were eating, he took bread, blessed
and broke it, gave it to them, and said, "Take it;
this is my body." 23 Then he took a cup, and after
giving thanks, he gave it to them, and they all
drank from it. 24 He said to them, "This is my
blood of the covenant,[A] which is poured out
for many. 25 Truly I tell you, I will no longer
drink of the fruit of the vine until that day
when I drink it new[B] in the kingdom of God."
26 After singing a hymn, they went out to
the Mount of Olives.

PETER'S DENIAL PREDICTED

27 Then Jesus said to them, "All of you will fall
away,[C] because it is written:

Support | *Openness with Others*

JESUS'S STRUGGLE

"He took Peter, James, and John with him, and he began to be deeply distressed and troubled. He said to them, 'I am deeply grieved to the point of death. Remain here and stay awake.'" Mark 14:33-34

The night he was arrested, Jesus was, humanly speaking, an emotional wreck. Mark, who most scholars agree relied on Peter for such details in writing his Gospel, describes Jesus in Gethsemane as "deeply distressed and troubled." With this phrase, something is lost in the translation. The Greek words are stronger, suggesting great fear, even terror. They signify extreme suffering to the point of darkest, bleakest anguish.

Mark further records Jesus as saying, "I am deeply grieved to the point of death."

All this is enough to make us want to look away. But we can find comfort in this account of Christ's passion. Because Jesus has been in the deepest valley, he understands our great emotional struggles and woes. When we're scared and depressed, Jesus knows all too well what we're feeling.

If that's you today, do what Jesus did. Call upon your closest friends to pray with you. Level with them.

For the next note on *Support*, see Luke 11:9.

[A] **14:24** Other mss read *the new covenant* [B] **14:25** Or *drink new wine*; lit *drink it new* [C] **14:27** Other mss add *because of me this night*

I will strike the shepherd,
and the sheep will be scattered.[A]
28 But after I have risen, I will go ahead of you
to Galilee."
29 Peter told him, "Even if everyone falls
away, I will not."
30 "Truly I tell you," Jesus said to him, "today,
this very night, before the rooster crows twice,
you will deny me three times."
31 But he kept insisting, "If I have to die with
you, I will never deny you." And they all said
the same thing.

THE PRAYER IN THE GARDEN

32 Then they came to a place named Gethsemane, and he told his disciples, "Sit here
while I pray." 33 He took Peter, James, and
John with him, and he began to be deeply
distressed and troubled. 34 He said to them,
"I am deeply grieved[B] to the point of death.
Remain here and stay awake." 35 He went a
little farther, fell to the ground, and prayed
that if it were possible, the hour might pass
from him. 36 And he said, "*Abba*,[C] Father! All
things are possible for you. Take this cup away
from me. Nevertheless, not what I will, but
what you will." 37 Then he came and found
them sleeping. He said to Peter, "Simon, are
you sleeping? Couldn't you stay awake one
hour? 38 Stay awake and pray so that you
won't enter into temptation.[D] The spirit is
willing, but the flesh is weak." 39 Once again
he went away and prayed, saying the same
thing. 40 And again he came and found them
sleeping, because they could not keep their
eyes open. They did not know what to say to
him. 41 Then he came a third time and said
to them, "Are you still sleeping and resting?
Enough! The time has come. See, the Son of
Man is betrayed into the hands of sinners.
42 Get up; let's go. See, my betrayer is near."

JUDAS'S BETRAYAL OF JESUS

43 While he was still speaking, Judas, one of the
Twelve, suddenly arrived. With him was a mob,
with swords and clubs, from the chief priests,
the scribes, and the elders. 44 His betrayer had
given them a signal. "The one I kiss," he said,
"he's the one; arrest him and take him away
under guard." 45 So when he came, immediately he went up to Jesus and said, "Rabbi!"
and kissed him. 46 They took hold of him and
arrested him. 47 One of those who stood by
drew his sword, struck the high priest's servant, and cut off his ear.
48 Jesus said to them, "Have you come out
with swords and clubs, as if I were a criminal,[E]
to capture me? 49 Every day I was among you,

Eternal Perspective | *God's Children*

DADDY!

"He said, 'Abba, Father! All things are possible for you.'" Mark 14:36

According to the apostle John, Jesus came to show the world what God is like (Jn 1:18). And according to Jesus, God is like a Father (Mt 6:9). Here and elsewhere, God is not like a remote and divine parent; he's called "Abba." The best English renderings of this beautiful Hebrew word are the intimate titles "Daddy" and "Papa." Jesus here called God his Abba Father. And Paul wrote to the believers in Rome, "You did not receive a spirit of slavery to fall back into fear. Instead, you received the Spirit of adoption, by whom we cry out, 'Abba, Father!'" (Rm 8:15).

For many people, all this talk of God as a Father-Abba figure is a tough sell. Many never had any sort of paternal presence, much less a loving, doting "Papa." Or if a man was around, he was distant or violent, abusive or cold.

The Spirit wants all believers to see that God is nothing like that. He adopted you because he wanted you in his family. You don't have to fear. His heart is good. He's a divine Daddy.

Ask God to open your eyes to the truth that he is your loving Abba.

For the next note on *Eternal Perspective*, see Luke 1:37.

[A] **14:27** Zch 13:7 [B] **14:34** Or *"My soul is swallowed up in sorrow* [C] **14:36** Aramaic for *father* [D] **14:38** Or *won't be put to the test* [E] **14:48** Or *insurrectionist*

Mary Magdalene | Restoration Profile

MATTHEW 27–28; MARK 15–16; LUKE 8:1-3; JOHN 19–20

The Bible is very matter-of-fact about demonic possession. Evil in people wasn't just a nebulous influence but often controlling and personal. Demons had names. This naturally flies in the face of a lot of modern sensibilities but might force us to think about the source of that sensitivity. Do we reject evil and its demonic demonstrationism or are we simply uncomfortable and afraid of forces and reality beyond what is available to our senses? Faced with frequent biblical cases like the restoration of Mary Magdalene, we can wonder if we aren't denying or downplaying too much the very personal and evil side of the spiritual world. In Jesus's eyes, Mary was worth restoring. There is hope for us.

Mary Magdalene was a central figure in the closing events of Jesus's time here on earth. She was the first to see the risen Lord and first to share the joyous news that he was alive. Only in Luke 8 do we find a significant clue about her background and extended time with the other disciples who followed Jesus, "and also some women who had been healed of evil spirits and sicknesses: Mary, called Magdalene (seven demons had come out of her)" (Lk 8:2).

When dealing with hurting people, Jesus always included the spiritual aspects of their needs in his diagnosis. The effects of sin and the resident influence of sin had to be addressed, just as much as the visible and reported need for restoration. And when it comes to healing of any kind, what ails us isn't as significant as the fact that Jesus has authority over any and all of it to restore.

teaching in the temple, and you didn't arrest
me. But the Scriptures must be fulfilled."
[50] Then they all deserted him and ran away.
[51] Now a certain young man, wearing nothing
but a linen cloth, was following him. They
caught hold of him, [52] but he left the linen
cloth behind and ran away naked.

JESUS FACES THE SANHEDRIN

[53] They led Jesus away to the high priest, and
all the chief priests, the elders, and the scribes
assembled. [54] Peter followed him at a distance,
right into the high priest's courtyard. He was
sitting with the servants,[A] warming himself
by the fire.
[55] The chief priests and the whole Sanhedrin were looking for testimony against Jesus
to put him to death, but they could not find
any. [56] For many were giving false testimony
against him, and the testimonies did not agree.
[57] Some stood up and gave false testimony
against him, stating, [58] "We heard him say, 'I
will destroy this temple made with human
hands, and in three days I will build another
not made by hands.' " [59] Yet their testimony
did not agree even on this.
[60] Then the high priest stood up before
them all and questioned Jesus, "Don't you
have an answer to what these men are testifying against you?" [61] But he kept silent and
did not answer. Again the high priest questioned him, "Are you the Messiah, the Son of
the Blessed One?"
[62] "I am," said Jesus, "and you will see **the
Son of Man seated at the right hand** of Power
and **coming with the clouds of heaven**."[B]
[63] Then the high priest tore his robes and
said, "Why do we still need witnesses? [64] You
have heard the blasphemy. What is your decision?" They all condemned him as deserving
death.
[65] Then some began to spit on him, to blind-
fold him, and to beat him, saying, "Prophesy!" The temple servants also took him and
slapped him.

PETER DENIES HIS LORD

[66] While Peter was in the courtyard below,
one of the high priest's maidservants came.
[67] When she saw Peter warming himself, she
looked at him and said, "You also were with
Jesus, the man from Nazareth."
[68] But he denied it: "I don't know or understand what you're talking about." Then he went
out to the entryway,[C] and a rooster crowed.[D]
[69] When the maidservant saw him again,

[A] **14:54** Or *temple police*, or *officers*, also in v. 65 [B] **14:62** Ps 110:1; Dn 7:13 [C] **14:68** Or *forecourt* [D] **14:68** Other mss omit *and a rooster crowed*

she began to tell those standing nearby, "This man is one of them."

70 But again he denied it. After a little while those standing there said to Peter again, "You certainly are one of them, since you're also a Galilean."[A]

71 Then he started to curse and swear, "I don't know this man you're talking about!"

72 Immediately a rooster crowed a second time, and Peter remembered when Jesus had spoken the word to him, "Before the rooster crows twice, you will deny me three times." And he broke down and wept.

JESUS FACES PILATE

15 As soon as it was morning, having held a meeting with the elders, scribes, and the whole Sanhedrin, the chief priests tied Jesus up, led him away, and handed him over to Pilate.

2 So Pilate asked him, "Are you the King of the Jews?"

He answered him, "You say so."

3 And the chief priests accused him of many things. 4 Pilate questioned him again, "Aren't you going to answer? Look how many things they are accusing you of!" 5 But Jesus still did not answer, and so Pilate was amazed.

JESUS OR BARABBAS

6 At the festival Pilate used to release for the people a prisoner whom they requested. 7 There was one named Barabbas, who was in prison with rebels who had committed murder during the rebellion. 8 The crowd came up and began to ask Pilate to do for them as was his custom. 9 Pilate answered them, "Do you want me to release the King of the Jews for you?" 10 For he knew it was because of envy that the chief priests had handed him over. 11 But the chief priests stirred up the crowd so that he would release Barabbas to them instead. 12 Pilate asked them again, "Then what do you want me to do with the one you call the King of the Jews?"

13 Again they shouted, "Crucify him!"

14 Pilate said to them, "Why? What has he done wrong?"

But they shouted all the more, "Crucify him!"

15 Wanting to satisfy the crowd, Pilate released Barabbas to them; and after having Jesus flogged, he handed him over to be crucified.

MOCKED BY THE MILITARY

16 The soldiers led him away into the palace (that is, the governor's residence) and called the whole company together. 17 They dressed him in a purple robe, twisted together a crown of thorns, and put it on him. 18 And they began to salute him, "Hail, King of the Jews!" 19 They were hitting him on the head with a stick and spitting on him. Getting down on their knees, they were paying him homage. 20 After they had mocked him, they stripped him of the purple robe and put his clothes on him.

CRUCIFIED BETWEEN TWO CRIMINALS

They led him out to crucify him. 21 They forced a man coming in from the country, who was passing by, to carry Jesus's cross. He was Simon of Cyrene, the father of Alexander and Rufus.

22 They brought Jesus to the place called *Golgotha* (which means Place of the Skull). 23 They tried to give him wine mixed with myrrh, but he did not take it.

24 Then they crucified him and divided his clothes, casting lots for them to decide what each would get. 25 Now it was nine in the morning[B] when they crucified him. 26 The inscription of the charge written against him was: THE KING OF THE JEWS. 27 They crucified two criminals[C] with him, one on his right and one on his left.[D]

29 Those who passed by were yelling insults at[E] him, shaking their heads, and saying, "Ha! The one who would destroy the temple and rebuild it in three days, 30 save yourself by coming down from the cross!" 31 In the same way, the chief priests with the scribes were mocking him among themselves and saying, "He saved others, but he cannot save himself! 32 Let the Messiah, the King of Israel, come down now from the cross, so that we may see and believe." Even those who were crucified with him taunted him.

THE DEATH OF JESUS

33 When it was noon,[F] darkness came over the whole land until three in the afternoon.[G] 34 And at three Jesus cried out with a loud voice, *"Eloi, Eloi, lemá sabachtháni?"* which is translated, **"My God, my God, why have you abandoned me?"**[H]

35 When some of those standing there heard this, they said, "See, he's calling for Elijah."

[A] **14:70** Other mss add *and your speech shows it* [B] **15:25** Lit *was the third hour* [C] **15:27** Or *revolutionaries* [D] **15:27** Some mss include v. 28: *So the Scripture was fulfilled that says: And he was counted among criminals.* [E] **15:29** Or *passed by blasphemed* [F] **15:33** Lit *the sixth hour* [G] **15:33** Lit *the ninth hour*, also in v. 34 [H] **15:34** Ps 22:1

36 Someone ran and filled a sponge with sour wine, fixed it on a stick, offered him a drink, and said, "Let's see if Elijah comes to take him down."

37 Jesus let out a loud cry and breathed his last. 38 Then the curtain of the temple was torn in two from top to bottom. 39 When the centurion, who was standing opposite him, saw the way he[A] breathed his last, he said, "Truly this man was the Son of God!"[B]

40 There were also women watching from a distance. Among them were Mary Magdalene, Mary the mother of James the younger and of Joses, and Salome. 41 In Galilee these women followed him and took care of him. Many other women had come up with him to Jerusalem.

THE BURIAL OF JESUS

42 When it was already evening, because it was the day of preparation (that is, the day before the Sabbath), 43 Joseph of Arimathea, a prominent member of the Sanhedrin who was himself looking forward to the kingdom of God, came and boldly went to Pilate and asked for Jesus's body. 44 Pilate was surprised that he was already dead. Summoning the centurion, he asked him whether he had already died. 45 When he found out from the centurion, he gave the corpse to Joseph. 46 After he bought some linen cloth, Joseph took him down and wrapped him in the linen. Then he laid him in a tomb cut out of the rock and rolled a stone against the entrance to the tomb. 47 Mary Magdalene and Mary the mother of Joses were watching where he was laid.

RESURRECTION MORNING

16 When the Sabbath was over, Mary Magdalene, Mary the mother of James, and Salome bought spices, so that they could go and anoint him. 2 Very early in the morning, on the first day of the week, they went to the tomb at sunrise. 3 They were saying to one another, "Who will roll away the stone from the entrance to the tomb for us?" 4 Looking up, they noticed that the stone — which was very large — had been rolled away.

5 When they entered the tomb, they saw a young man dressed in a white robe sitting on the right side; they were alarmed. 6 "Don't be

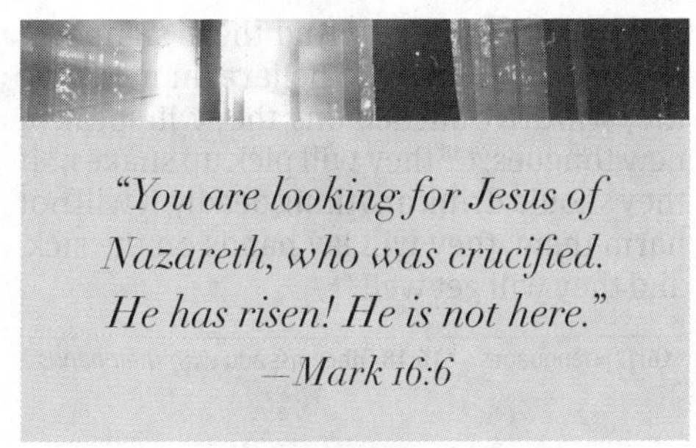
"You are looking for Jesus of
Nazareth, who was crucified.
He has risen! He is not here."
—Mark 16:6

alarmed," he told them. "You are looking for Jesus of Nazareth, who was crucified. He has risen! He is not here. See the place where they put him. 7 But go, tell his disciples and Peter, 'He is going ahead of you to Galilee; you will see him there just as he told you.'"

8 They went out and ran from the tomb, because trembling and astonishment overwhelmed them. And they said nothing to anyone, since they were afraid.

[Some of the earliest mss conclude with 16:8.][C]

THE LONGER ENDING OF MARK: APPEARANCES OF THE RISEN LORD

[9 Early on the first day of the week, after he had risen, he appeared first to Mary Magdalene, out of whom he had driven seven demons. 10 She went and reported to those who had been with him, as they were mourning and weeping. 11 Yet, when they heard that he was alive and had been seen by her, they did not believe it.

12 After this, he appeared in a different form to two of them walking on their way into the country. 13 And they went and reported it to the rest, who did not believe them either.

THE GREAT COMMISSION

14 Later he appeared to the Eleven themselves as they were reclining at the table. He rebuked their unbelief and hardness of heart, because they did not believe those who saw him after he had risen. 15 Then he said to them, "Go into all the world and preach the gospel to all creation. 16 Whoever believes and is baptized will be saved, but whoever does not believe

---

[A] **15:39** Other mss read *saw that he cried out like this and* [B] **15:39** Or *a son of God* [C] **16:8** Other mss include vv. 9-20 as a longer ending. The following shorter ending is found in some mss between v. 8 and v. 9 and in one ms after v. 8 (each of which omits vv. 9-20): *And all that had been commanded to them they quickly reported to those around Peter. After these things, Jesus himself sent out through them from east to west, the holy and imperishable proclamation of eternal salvation. Amen.*

will be condemned. 17 And these signs will
accompany those who believe: In my name
they will drive out demons; they will speak in
new tongues;[A] 18 they will pick up snakes;[B] if
they should drink anything deadly, it will not
harm them; they will lay hands on the sick,
and they will get well."

THE ASCENSION

19 So the Lord Jesus, after speaking to them,
was taken up into heaven and sat down at
the right hand of God. 20 And they went out
and preached everywhere, while the Lord
worked with them and confirmed the word
by the accompanying signs.]

[A] 16:17 = languages [B] 16:18 Other mss add *with their hands*

Luke's orderly and formal style appeals to the researcher in everyone. His attention to detail leaves no doubt that he is presenting a true, historical account of the life of Jesus of Nazareth, the most important figure to ever walk the earth. We discover Jesus, the Rabbi, who uses parables and object lessons to communicate God's love to the outcast, the sinner, and the impoverished. Luke's Gospel teaches that the Messiah came to seek and save those who are lost.

The central theme of Luke is that Jesus presents a great reversal of expected outcomes. The poor and humble are exalted, while the rich and proud are brought low. The religious insiders are far from the kingdom of God, but the desperate sinners are welcomed in. Ethnic outsiders and despised tax collectors who repent find family and forgiveness, and even women are given a position of dignity. To his original Gentile audience, this was encouraging news—the kingdom of God is for all people.

That is Luke's message to us as well. Regardless of background, external circumstances, or internal struggles, the kingdom of God is here, and the gates are wide open for any who wish to enter by repenting and following Christ. In him is hope and restoration for all who believe.

LUKE

AUTHOR: Luke, a Gentile doctor and coworker of Paul (Col 4:14; Phm 24)

DATE WRITTEN: The book of Luke was most likely written after Matthew and Mark, likely in the AD 70s or 80s.

ORIGINAL AUDIENCE: The immediate audience was Theophilus, a person of high standing who was curious about the Christian faith. In a larger sense, however, the audience was Gentile Christians who needed assurance that Jesus was the Messiah despite the fact that many Jews rejected him.

SETTING: In the late first century AD, a rift was developing between the Christian church and the Jewish synagogue. Christians considered themselves the fulfillment of Judaism, but the Jews rejected Jesus and continued to await the Messiah. Luke wrote to prove that the true people of God are those who believe that Jesus is the promised Messiah.

PURPOSE FOR WRITING: Luke's account is the longest of the Gospels and the most detailed. He used his scientific curiosity to write an orderly account, and more than half of his material is unique to his book. Luke sought to record an organized narrative of the life of Christ so that his readers would grow in their faith.

OUTLINE:

1. Preparation for Ministry (1:1–4:13)
2. Jesus's Ministry in Galilee (4:14–9:50)
3. Jesus's Ministry in Judea and Perea (9:51–19:10)
4. Jesus's Ministry in Jerusalem (19:11–24:53)

KEY VERSE:

"For the Son of Man has come to seek and to save the lost." —Luke 19:10

RESTORATION THEMES

R	Rest and Reflection	*Finding Balance—2:52* *Being Alone with God—5:16* *Surrendering/Submitting to God—22:42*
E	Eternal Perspective	*God's Power—1:37* *God's Mercy—1:49-50* *Personal Value/Worth—2:25-26* *God's Compassion—15:20* *God's Inside View—16:14-15*
S	Support	*Honest Seeking—11:9* *Spiritual and Moral Inventory—16:13*
T	Thanksgiving and Contentment	*Giving Back—12:34*
O	Other-centeredness	*Dealing with Difficult People—6:8* *Not Being Judgmental—6:37* *Being Humble—14:11*
R	Relationships	*Relating to Family—4:28-29* *Telling the Truth—6:26-27* *Confronting in Love—17:4*
E	Exercise of Faith	*Increasing Faith—7:9; 17:5* *Sharing Story—8:39* *Making Right Choices/Priorities/Values—10:41-42; 12:31; 18:22*

THE DEDICATION TO THEOPHILUS

1 Many have undertaken to compile a narrative about the events that have been fulfilled[A] among us, 2 just as the original eyewitnesses and servants of the word handed them down to us. 3 It also seemed good to me, since I have carefully investigated everything from the very first, to write to you in an orderly sequence, most honorable Theophilus, 4 so that you may know the certainty of the things about which you have been instructed.[B]

GABRIEL PREDICTS JOHN'S BIRTH

5 In the days of King Herod of Judea, there was a priest of Abijah's division named Zechariah. His wife was from the daughters of Aaron, and her name was Elizabeth. 6 Both were righteous in God's sight, living without blame according to all the commands and requirements of the Lord. 7 But they had no children because Elizabeth could not conceive, and both of them were well along in years.

8 When his division was on duty and he was serving as priest before God, 9 it happened that he was chosen by lot, according to the custom of the priesthood, to enter the sanctuary of the Lord and burn incense. 10 At the hour of incense the whole assembly of the people was praying outside. 11 An angel of the Lord appeared to him, standing to the right of the altar of incense. 12 When Zechariah saw him, he was terrified and overcome with fear. 13 But the angel said to him: "Do not be afraid, Zechariah, because your prayer has been heard. Your wife Elizabeth will bear you a son, and you will name him John. 14 There will be joy and delight for you, and many will rejoice at his birth. 15 For he will be great in the sight of the Lord and will never drink wine or beer. He will be filled with the Holy Spirit while still in his mother's womb. 16 He will turn many of the children of Israel to the Lord their God. 17 And he will go before him in the spirit and power of Elijah, to turn the hearts of fathers to their children, and the disobedient to the understanding of the righteous, to make ready for the Lord a prepared people."

18 "How can I know this?" Zechariah asked the angel. "For I am an old man, and my wife is well along in years."

19 The angel answered him, "I am Gabriel, who stands in the presence of God, and I was sent to speak to you and tell you this good news. 20 Now listen. You will become silent and unable to speak until the day these things take place, because you did not believe my words, which will be fulfilled in their proper time."

21 Meanwhile, the people were waiting for Zechariah, amazed that he stayed so long in the sanctuary. 22 When he did come out, he could not speak to them. Then they realized that he had seen a vision in the sanctuary. He was making signs to them and remained speechless. 23 When the days of his ministry were completed, he went back home.

24 After these days his wife Elizabeth conceived and kept herself in seclusion for five months. She said, 25 "The Lord has done this for me. He has looked with favor in these days to take away my disgrace among the people."

GABRIEL PREDICTS JESUS'S BIRTH

26 In the sixth month, the angel Gabriel was sent by God to a town in Galilee called Nazareth, 27 to a virgin engaged[C] to a man named Joseph, of the house of David. The virgin's name was Mary. 28 And the angel came to her and said, "Greetings, favored woman! The Lord is with you."[D] 29 But she was deeply troubled by this statement, wondering what kind of greeting this could be. 30 Then the angel told her: "Do not be afraid, Mary, for you have found favor with God. 31 Now listen: You will conceive and give birth to a son, and you will name him Jesus. 32 He will be great and will be called the Son of the Most High, and the Lord God will give him the throne of his father David. 33 He will reign over the house of Jacob forever, and his kingdom will have no end."

34 Mary asked the angel, "How can this be, since I have not had sexual relations with a man?"[E]

35 The angel replied to her: "The Holy Spirit will come upon you, and the power of the Most High will overshadow you. Therefore, the holy one to be born will be called the Son of God. 36 And consider your relative Elizabeth — even she has conceived a son in her old age, and this is the sixth month for her who was called childless. 37 For nothing will be impossible with God."

38 "I am the Lord's servant," said Mary. "May it be done to me according to your word." Then the angel left her.

[A] **1:1** Or *events that have been accomplished*, or *events most surely believed* [B] **1:4** Or *informed* [C] **1:27** Lit *betrothed*
[D] **1:28** Other mss add *Blessed are you among women.* [E] **1:34** Lit *since I do not know a man*

MARY'S VISIT TO ELIZABETH

39 In those days Mary set out and hurried to a
town in the hill country of Judah 40 where she
entered Zechariah's house and greeted Elizabeth. 41 When Elizabeth heard Mary's greeting,
the baby leaped inside her, and Elizabeth was
filled with the Holy Spirit. 42 Then she exclaimed
with a loud cry: "Blessed are you among women,
and your child will be blessed![A] 43 How could
this happen to me, that the mother of my Lord
should come to me? 44 For you see, when the
sound of your greeting reached my ears, the
baby leaped for joy inside me. 45 Blessed is she
who has believed that the Lord would fulfill
what he has spoken to her!"

MARY'S PRAISE

46 And Mary said:
My soul praises the greatness
of[B] the Lord,
47 and my spirit rejoices in God my Savior,
48 because he has looked with favor
on the humble condition of his servant.
Surely, from now on all generations
will call me blessed,
49 because the Mighty One
has done great things for me,
and his name is holy.
50 His mercy is from generation
to generation
on those who fear him.
51 He has done a mighty deed with his arm;
he has scattered the proud
because of the thoughts of their hearts;
52 he has toppled the mighty
from their thrones
and exalted the lowly.
53 He has satisfied the hungry
with good things
and sent the rich away empty.
54 He has helped his servant Israel,
remembering his mercy
55 to Abraham and his
descendants[C] forever,
just as he spoke to our ancestors.

56 And Mary stayed with her about three
months; then she returned to her home.

THE BIRTH AND NAMING OF JOHN

57 Now the time had come for Elizabeth to give
birth, and she had a son. 58 Then her neighbors

Eternal Perspective | *God's Power*

IMPOSSIBILITIES?

"For nothing will be impossible with God." Luke 1:37

"Will my child ever turn back to God?" "How will I recover from this crushing divorce?" "Where am I going to find a job in this economy? How will we pay our bills?" We live in a world where lots of things seem improbable, if not impossible.

So did the people of Israel at the beginning of the first century. For much of the previous six centuries, they had suffered under foreign domination: the Babylonians, the Greeks, then the Romans. "Will God ever save us? Will the Messiah ever come?"

Then an angel paid a visit to the priest Zechariah, with the message that his aging barren wife would become pregnant with the forerunner of the Messiah. Next the angel visited a girl named Mary and declared that she would be the mother of the Messiah. "How can this be," the startled teenager asked, "since I have not had sexual relations with a man?" (Lk 1:34). The angel gave her a short answer that was more divine than biological. Maybe the puzzled look on her face caused him to add, "For nothing will be impossible with God."

We should take to heart the angel's words. When things look bleak, remember God's power. God will not do exactly what we want, when and how we want. Instead, his "possible" may exceed anything we could ask or imagine.

For the next note on *Eternal Perspective*, see Luke 1:49-50.

[A] **1:42** Lit *and the fruit of your abdomen* (or *womb*) *is blessed* [B] **1:46** Or *soul magnifies* [C] **1:55** Or *offspring*; lit *seed*

and relatives heard that the Lord had shown
her his great mercy, and they rejoiced with her.
59 When they came to circumcise the child on
the eighth day, they were going to name him
Zechariah, after his father. 60 But his mother
responded, "No. He will be called John."
61 Then they said to her, "None of your relatives has that name." 62 So they motioned to
his father to find out what he wanted him to
be called. 63 He asked for a writing tablet and
wrote: "His name is John." And they were all
amazed. 64 Immediately his mouth was opened
and his tongue set free, and he began to speak,
praising God. 65 Fear came on all those who lived
around them, and all these things were being
talked about throughout the hill country of Judea. 66 All who heard about him took it to heart,
saying, "What then will this child become?" For,
indeed, the Lord's hand was with him.

ZECHARIAH'S PROPHECY

67 Then his father Zechariah was filled with
the Holy Spirit and prophesied:

68 Blessed is the Lord, the God of Israel,
because he has visited
and provided redemption for his people.
69 He has raised up a horn of salvation
for us
in the house of his servant David,
70 just as he spoke by the mouth
of his holy prophets in ancient times;
71 salvation from our enemies
and from the hand of those
who hate us.
72 He has dealt mercifully
with our fathers
and remembered his holy covenant —
73 the oath that he swore to our father
Abraham.
He has given us the privilege,
74 since we have been rescued
from the hand of our enemies,
to serve him without fear
75 in holiness and righteousness
in his presence all our days.
76 And you, child, will be called
a prophet of the Most High,
for you will go before the Lord
to prepare his ways,
77 to give his people knowledge
of salvation
through the forgiveness of their sins.
78 Because of our God's merciful
compassion,
the dawn from on high will visit us
79 to shine on those who live in darkness
and the shadow of death,
to guide our feet into the way of peace.

80 The child grew up and became spiritually
strong, and he was in the wilderness until the
day of his public appearance to Israel.

Eternal Perspective | *God's Mercy*

MERCY ME!

"The Mighty One has done great things for me, and his name is holy. His mercy is from generation to generation on those who fear him." Luke 1:49-50

The Bible has almost 17,000 words. Surely the word *mercy* ranks as one of the most beautiful.

Throughout the Bible, *mercy* describes the way God forgives and faithfully keeps his promises to his chosen people despite their rebelliousness. It means pity, goodness, compassion, and kindness.

As Mary pondered the staggering fact that she was carrying the Savior King of Israel and the world in her teenaged womb, she burst into praise. She felt so . . . unworthy! How could a poor young girl like her be the vehicle for so much blessing? She was stunned. Overcome. Awed by the truth that God would choose a lowly nobody like her for such a glorious task.

The only explanation? God is merciful!

Perhaps, like Mary, your soul would burst with praise today by simply remembering God's faithfulness to you even during all those times you weren't so faithful. Give it a try.

For the next note on *Eternal Perspective*, see Luke 2:25-26.

THE BIRTH OF JESUS

2 In those days a decree went out from Caesar
Augustus that the whole empire[A] should
be registered. 2 This first registration took
place while[B] Quirinius was governing Syria.
3 So everyone went to be registered, each to
his own town.

4 Joseph also went up from the town of Nazareth in Galilee, to Judea, to the city of David,
which is called Bethlehem, because he was of the
house and family line of David, 5 to be registered
along with Mary, who was engaged to him[C] and
was pregnant. 6 While they were there, the time
came for her to give birth. 7 Then she gave birth
to her firstborn son, and she wrapped him tightly in cloth and laid him in a manger,[D] because
there was no guest room available for them.

THE SHEPHERDS AND THE ANGELS

8 In the same region, shepherds were staying
out in the fields and keeping watch at night
over their flock. 9 Then an angel of the Lord
stood before them, and the glory of the Lord
shone around them, and they were terrified.[E]
10 But the angel said to them, "Don't be afraid,
for look, I proclaim to you good news of great
joy that will be for all the people:[F] 11 Today in
the city of David a Savior was born for you,
who is the Messiah, the Lord. 12 This will be
the sign for you: You will find a baby wrapped
tightly in cloth and lying in a manger."
13 Suddenly there was a multitude of the
heavenly host[G] with the angel, praising God
and saying:

14 Glory to God in the highest heaven,
and peace on earth to people he favors![H,I]

15 When the angels had left them and returned to heaven, the shepherds said to one
another, "Let's go straight to Bethlehem and
see what has happened, which the Lord has
made known to us."

16 They hurried off and found both Mary
and Joseph, and the baby who was lying in the
manger. 17 After seeing them, they reported
the message they were told about this child,
18 and all who heard it were amazed at what
the shepherds said to them. 19 But Mary was
treasuring up all these things in her heart
and meditating on them. 20 The shepherds
returned, glorifying and praising God for all
the things they had seen and heard, which
were just as they had been told.

THE CIRCUMCISION AND PRESENTATION OF JESUS

21 When the eight days were completed for his
circumcision, he was named Jesus — the name

Eternal Perspective | *Personal Value/Worth*

ALL THE LITTLE PEOPLE

"There was a man in Jerusalem whose name was Simeon. This man was righteous and devout, looking forward to Israel's consolation, and the Holy Spirit was on him. It had been revealed to him by the Holy Spirit that he would not see death before he saw the Lord's Messiah." Luke 2:25-26

At big cultural happenings—championship sporting events, big political gatherings, entertainment extravaganzas—the rich and beautiful, the famous and outrageous are always prominent. In the kingdom of God, the poor and wretched, the forgotten and humble are the special guests.

Take the birth of Jesus, for example. The powerful political leaders, cultural icons, or leading religious scholars weren't blessed to be present. No, the people with a ringside seat to the incarnation were a few socially marginalized shepherds (Lk 2:8-15), some foreign visitors (Mt 2:1-11), and, as we see here, an elderly man at the temple in Jerusalem.

This is the enormous difference between the world's value system and God's. In God's eyes, right faith, hope in him, and the presence of the Holy Spirit are the credentials that matter.

For the next note on *Eternal Perspective*, see Luke 15:20.

[A] **2:1** Or *the whole inhabited world* [B] **2:2** Or *This registration was the first while*, or *This registration was before* [C] **2:5** Lit *betrothed* [D] **2:7** Or *feeding trough*, also in vv. 12,16 [E] **2:9** Lit *they feared a great fear* [F] **2:10** Or *the whole nation* [G] **2:13** Lit *heavenly army* [H] **2:14** Other mss read *earth good will to people* [I] **2:14** Or *earth to men of good will*

given by the angel before he was conceived.
[22] And when the days of their purification according to the law of Moses were finished,
they brought him up to Jerusalem to present
him to the Lord [23] (just as it is written in the
law of the Lord, **Every firstborn male will
be dedicated**[A] **to the Lord**[B]) [24] and to offer a
sacrifice (according to what is stated in the
law of the Lord, **a pair of turtledoves or two
young pigeons**[C]).

SIMEON'S PROPHETIC PRAISE

[25] There was a man in Jerusalem whose name
was Simeon. This man was righteous and devout, looking forward to Israel's consolation,
and the Holy Spirit was on him. [26] It had been
revealed to him by the Holy Spirit that he would
not see death before he saw the Lord's Messiah.
[27] Guided by the Spirit, he entered the temple.
When the parents brought in the child Jesus to
perform for him what was customary under
the law, [28] Simeon took him up in his arms,
praised God, and said,

29 Now, Master,
you can dismiss your servant in peace,
as you promised.
30 For my eyes have seen your salvation.
31 You have prepared it
in the presence of all peoples —
32 a light for revelation to the Gentiles[D]
and glory to your people Israel.

[33] His father and mother[E] were amazed at
what was being said about him. [34] Then Simeon blessed them and told his mother Mary:
"Indeed, this child is destined to cause the fall
and rise of many in Israel and to be a sign that
will be opposed[F] — [35] and a sword will pierce
your own soul — that the thoughts[G] of many
hearts may be revealed."

ANNA'S TESTIMONY

[36] There was also a prophetess, Anna, a daughter of Phanuel, of the tribe of Asher. She was
well along in years, having lived with her husband seven years after her marriage,[H] [37] and
was a widow for eighty-four years.[I] She did
not leave the temple, serving God night and
day with fasting and prayers. [38] At that very
moment,[J] she came up and began to thank God

Rest and Reflection | *Finding Balance*

A BALANCED LIFE

"Jesus increased in wisdom and stature, and in favor with God and with people." Luke 2:52

Your exercise bike has become a dusty clothes rack. The last thought-provoking book you read was back in college. New neighbors moved in two doors down several *months* ago and all you've done is wave hello. It's tough to keep life in balance, isn't it?

That's why, for many busy and scattered people, this verse has become a helpful life assessment tool. Luke probably included it in his Gospel because he was writing primarily to a Greek audience, and Greek culture was obsessed with the idea of a perfect man. This was Luke's way of saying, "Jesus is the One you Greeks need to be obsessing over."

We can see four areas of life represented here: physical, mental, social, and spiritual. So, here are four questions to ask: (1) How am I doing mentally/intellectually; that is, am I learning, gaining knowledge, growing wise? (2) What's my physical condition—am I taking steps to healthier living? (3) Am I healthy socially—engaging in God-honoring relationships with family, friends, neighbors, and coworkers? (4) How's my relationship with God—am I drawing near to him daily?

To periodically ask those questions is to imitate Jesus. Don't let your honest answers discourage you. Let them encourage you to take steps toward balance and health.

For the next note on *Rest and Reflection*, see Luke 5:16.

[A] **2:23** Lit *be called holy* [B] **2:23** Ex 13:2,12 [C] **2:24** Lv 5:11; 12:8 [D] **2:32** Or *the nations* [E] **2:33** Other mss read *But Joseph and his mother* [F] **2:34** Or *spoken against* [G] **2:35** Or *schemes* [H] **2:36** Lit *years from her virginity* [I] **2:37** Or *she was a widow until the age of eighty-four* [J] **2:38** Lit *very hour*

and to speak about him to all who were looking forward to the redemption of Jerusalem.[A]

THE FAMILY'S RETURN TO NAZARETH

39 When they had completed everything according to the law of the Lord, they returned to
Galilee, to their own town of Nazareth. 40 The
boy grew up and became strong, filled with
wisdom, and God's grace was on him.

IN HIS FATHER'S HOUSE

41 Every year his parents traveled to Jerusalem
for the Passover Festival. 42 When he was twelve
years old, they went up according to the custom
of the festival. 43 After those days were over, as
they were returning, the boy Jesus stayed behind
in Jerusalem, but his parents[B] did not know it.
44 Assuming he was in the traveling party, they
went a day's journey. Then they began looking for him among their relatives and friends.
45 When they did not find him, they returned to
Jerusalem to search for him. 46 After three days,
they found him in the temple sitting among the
teachers, listening to them and asking them
questions. 47 And all those who heard him were
astounded at his understanding and his answers. 48 When his parents saw him, they were
astonished, and his mother said to him, "Son,
why have you treated us like this? Your father
and I have been anxiously searching for you."
49 "Why were you searching for me?" he
asked them. "Didn't you know that it was necessary for me to be in my Father's house?"[C]
50 But they did not understand what he said
to them.

IN FAVOR WITH GOD AND WITH PEOPLE

51 Then he went down with them and came to
Nazareth and was obedient to them. His mother
kept all these things in her heart. 52 And Jesus
increased in wisdom and stature, and in favor
with God and with people.

THE MESSIAH'S HERALD

3 In the fifteenth year of the reign of Tiberius
Caesar, while Pontius Pilate was governor
of Judea, Herod was tetrarch[D] of Galilee, his
brother Philip tetrarch of the region of Iturea
and Trachonitis, and Lysanias tetrarch of Abilene, 2 during the high priesthood of Annas
and Caiaphas, God's word came to John the
son of Zechariah in the wilderness. 3 He went
into all the vicinity of the Jordan, proclaiming
a baptism of repentance for the forgiveness of
sins, 4 as it is written in the book of the words
of the prophet Isaiah:

A voice of one crying out
in the wilderness:
Prepare the way for the Lord;
make his paths straight!
5 **Every valley will be filled,**
and every mountain and hill will be
made low;[E]
the crooked will become straight,
the rough ways smooth,
6 **and everyone will see the salvation**
of God.[F]

7 He then said to the crowds who came out
to be baptized by him, "Brood of vipers! Who
warned you to flee from the coming wrath?
8 Therefore produce fruit consistent with repentance. And don't start saying to yourselves,
'We have Abraham as our father,' for I tell you
that God is able to raise up children for Abraham from these stones. 9 The ax is already at
the root of the trees. Therefore, every tree that
doesn't produce good fruit will be cut down
and thrown into the fire."
10 "What then should we do?" the crowds
were asking him.
11 He replied to them, "The one who has two
shirts must share with someone who has none,
and the one who has food must do the same."
12 Tax collectors also came to be baptized,
and they asked him, "Teacher, what should
we do?"
13 He told them, "Don't collect any more than
what you have been authorized."
14 Some soldiers also questioned him, "What
should we do?"
He said to them, "Don't take money from
anyone by force or false accusation, and be
satisfied with your wages."
15 Now the people were waiting expectantly, and all of them were questioning in their
hearts whether John might be the Messiah.
16 John answered them all, "I baptize you with
water, but one who is more powerful than I am
is coming. I am not worthy to untie the strap
of his sandals. He will baptize you with[G] the
Holy Spirit and fire. 17 His winnowing shovel
is in his hand to clear his threshing floor and
gather the wheat into his barn, but the chaff
he will burn with fire that never goes out."
18 Then, along with many other exhortations,

[A] **2:38** Other mss read *in Jerusalem* [B] **2:43** Other mss read *but Joseph and his mother* [C] **2:49** Or *be involved in my Father's interests* (or *things*), or *be among my Father's people* [D] **3:1** Or *ruler* [E] **3:5** Lit *be humbled* [F] **3:4-6** Is 40:3-5 [G] **3:16** Or *in*

he proclaimed good news to the people. 19 But
when John rebuked Herod the tetrarch because
of Herodias, his brother's wife, and all the evil
things he had done, 20 Herod added this to everything else — he locked up John in prison.

THE BAPTISM OF JESUS

21 When all the people were baptized, Jesus
also was baptized. As he was praying, heav-
en opened, 22 and the Holy Spirit descended
on him in a physical appearance like a dove.
And a voice came from heaven: "You are my
beloved Son; with you I am well-pleased."

THE GENEALOGY OF JESUS CHRIST

23 As he began his ministry, Jesus was about
thirty years old and was thought to be the
son of Joseph, son of Heli,
24 son of Matthat, son of Levi,
son of Melchi, son of Jannai,
son of Joseph, 25 son of Mattathias,
son of Amos, son of Nahum,
son of Esli, son of Naggai,
26 son of Maath, son of Mattathias,
son of Semein, son of Josech,
son of Joda, 27 son of Joanan,
son of Rhesa, son of Zerubbabel,
son of Shealtiel, son of Neri,
28 son of Melchi, son of Addi,
son of Cosam, son of Elmadam,
son of Er, 29 son of Joshua,
son of Eliezer, son of Jorim,
son of Matthat, son of Levi,
30 son of Simeon, son of Judah,
son of Joseph, son of Jonam,
son of Eliakim, 31 son of Melea,
son of Menna, son of Mattatha,
son of Nathan, son of David,
32 son of Jesse, son of Obed,
son of Boaz, son of Salmon,[A]
son of Nahshon, 33 son of Amminadab,
son of Ram,[B] son of Hezron,
son of Perez, son of Judah,
34 son of Jacob, son of Isaac,
son of Abraham, son of Terah,
son of Nahor, 35 son of Serug,
son of Reu, son of Peleg,
son of Eber, son of Shelah,
36 son of Cainan, son of Arphaxad,
son of Shem, son of Noah,
son of Lamech, 37 son of Methuselah,
son of Enoch, son of Jared,
son of Mahalalel, son of Cainan,
38 son of Enos, son of Seth,
son of Adam, son of God.

THE TEMPTATION OF JESUS

4 Then Jesus left the Jordan, full of the Holy
Spirit, and was led by the Spirit in the wilderness 2 for forty days to be tempted by the
devil. He ate nothing during those days, and
when they were over, he was hungry. 3 The
devil said to him, "If you are the Son of God,
tell this stone to become bread."
4 But Jesus answered him, "It is written: **Man
must not live on bread alone.**"[C,D]
5 So he took him up[E] and showed him all
the kingdoms of the world in a moment of
time. 6 The devil said to him, "I will give you
their splendor and all this authority, because
it has been given over to me, and I can give it
to anyone I want. 7 If you, then, will worship
me,[F] all will be yours."
8 And Jesus answered him,[G] "It is written:
**Worship the Lord your God, and serve him
only.**"[H]
9 So he took him to Jerusalem, had him stand
on the pinnacle of the temple, and said to him,
"If you are the Son of God, throw yourself
down from here. 10 For it is written:

He will give his angels orders
concerning you,
to protect you,[I] 11 **and**
they will support you
with their hands,
so that you will not strike
your foot against a stone."[J]

12 And Jesus answered him, "It is said: **Do
not test the Lord your God.**"[K]
13 After the devil had finished every temptation, he departed from him for a time.

MINISTRY IN GALILEE

14 Then Jesus returned to Galilee in the power of
the Spirit, and news about him spread throughout the entire vicinity. 15 He was teaching in
their synagogues, being praised[L] by everyone.

REJECTION AT NAZARETH

16 He came to Nazareth, where he had been
brought up. As usual, he entered the synagogue

[A] **3:32** Other mss read *Sala* [B] **3:33** Other mss read *Amminadab, son of Aram, son of Joram* ; other mss read *Amminadab, son of Admin, son of Arni* [C] **4:4** Other mss add *but on every word of God* [D] **4:4** Dt 8:3 [E] **4:5** Other mss read *So the devil took him up on a high mountain* [F] **4:7** Lit *will fall down before me* [G] **4:8** Other mss add *"Get behind me, Satan!* [H] **4:8** Dt 6:13 [I] **4:10** Ps 91:11 [J] **4:11** Ps 91:12 [K] **4:12** Dt 6:16 [L] **4:15** Or *glorified*

on the Sabbath day and stood up to read. [17] The
scroll of the prophet Isaiah was given to him,
and unrolling the scroll, he found the place
where it was written:

18 **The Spirit of the Lord is on me,**
because he has anointed me
to preach good news to the poor.
He has sent me[A]
to proclaim release[B] **to the captives**
and recovery of sight to the blind,
to set free the oppressed,
19 **to proclaim the year**
of the Lord's favor.[C]

20 He then rolled up the scroll, gave it back
to the attendant, and sat down. And the eyes
of everyone in the synagogue were fixed on
him. 21 He began by saying to them, "Today as
you listen, this Scripture has been fulfilled."
22 They were all speaking well of him[D] and
were amazed by the gracious words that came
from his mouth; yet they said, "Isn't this Joseph's son?"
23 Then he said to them, "No doubt you will
quote this proverb[E] to me: 'Doctor, heal yourself. What we've heard that took place in Capernaum, do here in your hometown also.'"
24 He also said, "Truly I tell you, no prophet is
accepted in his hometown. 25 But I say to you,
there were certainly many widows in Israel
in Elijah's days, when the sky was shut up
for three years and six months while a great
famine came over all the land. 26 Yet Elijah
was not sent to any of them except a widow
at Zarephath in Sidon. 27 And in the prophet
Elisha's time, there were many in Israel who
had leprosy,[F] and yet not one of them was
cleansed except Naaman the Syrian."
28 When they heard this, everyone in the
synagogue was enraged. 29 They got up, drove
him out of town, and brought him to the edge
of the hill that their town was built on, intending to hurl him over the cliff. 30 But he
passed right through the crowd and went
on his way.

DRIVING OUT AN UNCLEAN SPIRIT

31 Then he went down to Capernaum, a town
in Galilee, and was teaching them on the Sabbath. 32 They were astonished at his teaching
because his message had authority. 33 In the
synagogue there was a man with an unclean
demonic spirit who cried out with a loud voice,

Relationships | *Relating to Family*

TROUBLE AT HOME

"When they heard this, everyone in the synagogue was enraged. They got up, drove him out of town, and brought him to the edge of the hill that their town was built on, intending to hurl him over the cliff." Luke 4:28-29

How many people have had a life-changing encounter with Jesus, have gone home eagerly to tell their family and friends, and have run headlong into a storm of disapproval?

More than we can count. Maybe you're one of them. If so, you know how painful this experience is. You're joyful, excited—and the people who know you best and whom you love the most greet you with rejection and scorn.

"No prophet is accepted in his hometown," Jesus warned long ago (Lk 4:24). He should know. He lived this experience. Luke records the time he went to his hometown synagogue and claimed to be the Messiah predicted in Isaiah 61. A few minutes later his neighbors were trying to "hurl him over the cliff" on the outskirts of Nazareth!

If you have friends and family who aren't exactly thrilled about your faith, remember two things: Jesus knows what you're up against, and your job is to live a life of truth and grace. You can't make anyone believe the things you believe. Only God can soften a hard heart.

For the next note on *Relationships*, see Luke 6:26-27.

[A] **4:18** Other mss add *to heal the brokenhearted,* [B] **4:18** Or *freedom*, or *forgiveness* [C] **4:18-19** Is 61:1-2 [D] **4:22** Or *They were testifying against him* [E] **4:23** Or *parable* [F] **4:27** Gk *lepros*; a term for various skin diseases; see Lv 13–14

34 "Leave us alone! What do you have to do with us, Jesus of Nazareth? Have you come to destroy us? I know who you are — the Holy One of God!"

35 But Jesus rebuked him and said, "Be silent and come out of him!" And throwing him down before them, the demon came out of him without hurting him at all.

36 Amazement came over them all, and they were saying to one another, "What is this message? For he commands the unclean spirits with authority and power, and they come out!" 37 And news about him began to go out to every place in the vicinity.

HEALINGS AT CAPERNAUM

38 After he left the synagogue, he entered Simon's house. Simon's mother-in-law was suffering from a high fever, and they asked him about her. 39 So he stood over her and rebuked the fever, and it left her. She got up immediately and began to serve them.

40 When the sun was setting, all those who had anyone sick with various diseases brought them to him. As he laid his hands on each one of them, he healed them. 41 Also, demons were coming out of many, shouting and saying, "You are the Son of God!" But he rebuked them and would not allow them to speak, because they knew he was the Christ.

42 When it was day, he went out and made his way to a deserted place. But the crowds were searching for him. They came to him and tried to keep him from leaving them. 43 But he said to them, "It is necessary for me to proclaim the good news about the kingdom of God to the other towns also, because I was sent for this purpose." 44 And he was preaching in the synagogues of Judea.[A]

THE FIRST DISCIPLES

5 As the crowd was pressing in on Jesus to hear God's word, he was standing by Lake Gennesaret. 2 He saw two boats at the edge of the lake; the fishermen had left them and were washing their nets. 3 He got into one of the boats, which belonged to Simon, and asked him to put out a little from the land. Then he sat down and was teaching the crowds from the boat.

4 When he had finished speaking, he said to Simon, "Put out into deep water and let down your nets for a catch."

5 "Master," Simon replied, "we've worked hard all night long and caught nothing. But if you say so, I'll let down the nets."[B]

6 When they did this, they caught a great number of fish, and their nets[B] began to tear. 7 So they signaled to their partners in the other boat to come and help them; they came and filled both boats so full that they began to sink.

8 When Simon Peter saw this, he fell at Jesus's knees and said, "Go away from me, because I'm a sinful man, Lord!" 9 For he and all those with him were amazed at the catch of fish they had taken, 10 and so were James and John, Zebedee's sons, who were Simon's partners.

"Don't be afraid," Jesus told Simon. "From now on you will be catching people." 11 Then they brought the boats to land, left everything, and followed him.

A MAN CLEANSED

12 While he was in one of the towns, a man was there who had leprosy[C] all over him. He saw Jesus, fell facedown, and begged him: "Lord, if you are willing, you can make me clean."

13 Reaching out his hand, Jesus touched him, saying, "I am willing; be made clean," and immediately the leprosy left him. 14 Then he ordered him to tell no one: "But go and show yourself to the priest, and offer what Moses commanded for your cleansing as a testimony to them."

15 But the news[D] about him spread even more, and large crowds would come together to hear him and to be healed of their sicknesses. 16 Yet he often withdrew to deserted places and prayed.

THE SON OF MAN FORGIVES AND HEALS

17 On one of those days while he was teaching, Pharisees and teachers of the law were sitting there who had come from every village of Galilee and Judea, and also from Jerusalem. And the Lord's power to heal was in him. 18 Just then some men came, carrying on a stretcher a man who was paralyzed. They tried to bring him in and set him down before him. 19 Since they could not find a way to bring him in because of the crowd, they went up on the roof and lowered him on the stretcher through the roof tiles into the middle of the crowd before Jesus.

20 Seeing their faith he said, "Friend,[E] your sins are forgiven."

[A] **4:44** Other mss read *Galilee* [B] **5:5,6** Other mss read *net* (Gk sg) [C] **5:12** Gk *lepros*; a term for various skin diseases, also in v. 13; see Lv 13–14 [D] **5:15** Lit *the word* [E] **5:20** Lit *"Man*

21 Then the scribes and the Pharisees began
to think to themselves: "Who is this man who
speaks blasphemies? Who can forgive sins
but God alone?"
22 But perceiving their thoughts, Jesus replied to them, "Why are you thinking this in
your hearts?[A] 23 Which is easier: to say, 'Your
sins are forgiven,' or to say, 'Get up and walk'?
24 But so that you may know that the Son of
Man has authority on earth to forgive sins"
— he told the paralyzed man, "I tell you: Get
up, take your stretcher, and go home."
25 Immediately he got up before them, picked
up what he had been lying on, and went home
glorifying God. 26 Then everyone was astounded, and they were giving glory to God. And
they were filled with awe and said, "We have
seen incredible things today."

THE CALL OF LEVI

27 After this, Jesus went out and saw a tax
collector named Levi sitting at the tax office,
and he said to him, "Follow me." 28 So, leaving
everything behind, he got up and began to
follow him.
29 Then Levi hosted a grand banquet for him
at his house. Now there was a large crowd of
tax collectors and others who were guests[B]
with them. 30 But the Pharisees and their
scribes were complaining to his disciples,
"Why do you eat and drink with tax collectors
and sinners?"
31 Jesus replied to them, "It is not those who
are healthy who need a doctor, but those who
are sick. 32 I have not come to call the righteous,
but sinners to repentance."

A QUESTION ABOUT FASTING

33 Then they said to him, "John's disciples fast
often and say prayers, and those of the Pharisees do the same, but yours eat and drink."[C]
34 Jesus said to them, "You can't make the
wedding guests fast while the groom is with
them, can you? 35 But the time[D] will come
when the groom will be taken away from
them — then they will fast in those days."
36 He also told them a parable: "No one tears
a patch from a new garment and puts it on
an old garment. Otherwise, not only will he
tear the new, but also the piece from the new
garment will not match the old. 37 And no one
puts new wine into old wineskins. Otherwise,
the new wine will burst the skins, it will spill,
and the skins will be ruined. 38 No, new wine

Rest and Reflection | *Being Alone with God*

THE DISCIPLINE OF SOLITUDE

"Yet he often withdrew to deserted places and prayed." Luke 5:16

Some people hear the phrase "spiritual disciplines" and immediately think, *Nope! That's not for people like me.* "Disciplines" sounds like something religious professionals do—monks at remote monasteries, nuns on retreats, that sort of thing.

Not so! A spiritual discipline is any practice we do intentionally and habitually to be with God and open our hearts to him. That means going to church, reading the Bible, praying regularly with a friend, memorizing Scripture, serving the poor, attending worship—all these are spiritual disciplines.

Here we see Jesus engaging in the spiritual disciple of solitude. Notice he "often withdrew" from his loud, busy, people-packed life and sought out "deserted places" where he "prayed." Jesus was isolating himself in order to talk to his heavenly Father.

The beauty of solitude is that when we're alone with God, we have no one to try to impress. God knows us through and through—all our compulsions, inconsistencies, and insecurities. Yet he loves us exactly as we are. Solitude is very freeing and healing.

Try spending fifteen minutes alone with God today. Sit in a quiet place or walk to the nearest park. Feel no pressure to do anything. Just be with him. Be attentive. Listen for his voice.

For the next note on *Rest and Reflection*, see Luke 22:42.

[A] **5:22** Or *minds* [B] **5:29** Lit *were reclining* [C] **5:33** Other mss read *"Why do John's . . . drink?"* (as a question) [D] **5:35** Lit *days*

is put into fresh wineskins.[A] 39 And no one,
after drinking old wine, wants new, because
he says, 'The old is better.' "[B]

LORD OF THE SABBATH

6 On a Sabbath, he passed through the grainfields. His disciples were picking heads
of grain, rubbing them in their hands, and
eating them. 2 But some of the Pharisees said,
"Why are you doing what is not lawful on the
Sabbath?"
3 Jesus answered them, "Haven't you read
what David and those who were with him did
when he was hungry — 4 how he entered the
house of God and took and ate the bread of
the Presence, which is not lawful for any but
the priests to eat? He even gave some to those
who were with him." 5 Then he told them, "The
Son of Man is Lord of the Sabbath."
6 On another Sabbath he entered the synagogue and was teaching. A man was there
whose right hand was shriveled. 7 The scribes
and Pharisees were watching him closely, to
see if he would heal on the Sabbath, so that
they could find a charge against him. 8 But he
knew their thoughts and told the man with
the shriveled hand, "Get up and stand here."[C]
So he got up and stood there. 9 Then Jesus said
to them, "I ask you: Is it lawful to do good on
the Sabbath or to do evil, to save life or to destroy it?" 10 After looking around at them all,
he told him, "Stretch out your hand." He did,
and his hand was restored.[D] 11 They, however,
were filled with rage and started discussing
with one another what they might do to Jesus.

THE TWELVE APOSTLES

12 During those days he went out to the mountain to pray and spent all night in prayer to
God. 13 When daylight came, he summoned his
disciples, and he chose twelve of them, whom
he also named apostles: 14 Simon, whom he
also named Peter, and Andrew his brother;
James and John; Philip and Bartholomew;
15 Matthew and Thomas; James the son of Alphaeus, and Simon called the Zealot; 16 Judas
the son of James, and Judas Iscariot, who became a traitor.

TEACHING AND HEALING

17 After coming down with them, he stood
on a level place with a large crowd of his

Other-centeredness | *Dealing with Difficult People*

RESPONSE-ABILITY

"But he knew their thoughts and told the man with the shriveled hand, 'Get up and stand here.' So he got up and stood there. Then Jesus said to [the scribes and Pharisees], 'I ask you: Is it lawful to do good on the Sabbath or to do evil, to save life or to destroy it?'" Luke 6:8-9

The unreasonable boss. The impossible-to-please parent. The critical spouse. How do we deal with demanding and unfair people?

The world tells us to fight fire with fire. The world counsels us to power up, to give as well as we take. Jesus tells us to take a radically different course of action. Rather than responding in kind, Jesus calls us to counter injustice by creatively exposing it. Turn the other cheek, go the extra mile, give your shirt as well as your coat—even just show your faith through your actions, as Jesus did here. The idea in these commands isn't to be a doormat but to jar your opponent and to shock a watching world. Suddenly a bully's ugly actions and petty, vindictive demands are seen vividly against the glaring light of what is good, fair, and reasonable—and life-changing.

Of course, the only way one can do this successfully is to trust that God sees and that one day he will make every wrong thing right. As we believe this, we are freed from the temptation to succumb to bitterness and the insatiable need to seek revenge.

For the next note on *Other-centeredness*, see Luke 6:37.

[A] **5:38** Other mss add *And so both are preserved.* [B] **5:39** Other mss read *is good* [C] **6:8** Lit *stand in the middle* [D] **6:10** Other mss add *as sound as the other*

disciples and a great number of people from
all Judea and Jerusalem and from the seacoast
of Tyre and Sidon. 18 They came to hear him
and to be healed of their diseases; and those
tormented by unclean spirits were made
well. 19 The whole crowd was trying to touch
him, because power was coming out from
him and healing them all.

THE BEATITUDES

20 Then looking up at his disciples, he said:
Blessed are you who are poor,
because the kingdom of God is yours.
21 Blessed are you who are now hungry,
because you will be filled.
Blessed are you who weep now,
because you will laugh.
22 Blessed are you when people
hate you,
when they exclude you, insult you,
and slander your name as evil
because of the Son of Man.

23 "Rejoice in that day and leap for joy. Take
note — your reward is great in heaven, for
this is the way their ancestors used to treat
the prophets.

WOE TO THE SELF-SATISFIED

24 But woe to you who are rich,
for you have received your comfort.
25 Woe to you who are now full,
for you will be hungry.
Woe to you[A] who are now laughing,
for you will mourn and weep.
26 Woe to you[A]
when all people speak well of you,
for this is the way their ancestors
used to treat the false prophets.

LOVE YOUR ENEMIES

27 "But I say to you who listen: Love your enemies, do what is good to those who hate you,
28 bless those who curse you, pray for those
who mistreat you. 29 If anyone hits you on the
cheek, offer the other also. And if anyone takes
away your coat, don't hold back your shirt
either. 30 Give to everyone who asks you, and
from someone who takes your things, don't
ask for them back. 31 Just as you want others
to do for you, do the same for them. 32 If you
love those who love you, what credit is that to
you? Even sinners love those who love them.
33 If you do what is good to those who are good

Relationships | *Telling the Truth*

THE PEOPLE-PLEASING TRAP

"Woe to you when all people speak well of you, for this is the way their ancestors used to treat the false prophets. But I say to you who listen: Love your enemies, do what is good to those who hate you." Luke 6:26-27

A people-pleaser is someone like Craig who wants everyone to like him, or Deborah who wants everyone to speak well of her. People-pleasers are always agreeable and nice. They don't rock the boat. They never voice an opinion. They don't question anyone. If backed into a corner, they struggle telling others the truth—especially when that truth might rub someone the wrong way.

In this passage, Jesus was warning his followers not to be people-pleasers—like the false prophets of ancient Israel. Instead of being honest and delivering bad news when necessary, they lied, saying only the kinds of things that others wanted to hear. In short, they craved the approval of people more than the approval of God.

This is a terrible way to live. It's dishonest. It doesn't honor God, nor does it do anyone any good. People-pleasers live in fear, not freedom. They're always at the mercy of what others think (or might think).

Ask God for the courage to be truthful. It might cost you some friends and make you some enemies—but the Lord will give you the grace to love them too!

For the next note on *Relationships*, see Luke 17:4.

[A] **6:25,26** Other mss omit *to you*

to you, what credit is that to you? Even sinners do that. 34 And if you lend to those from whom you expect to receive, what credit is that to you? Even sinners lend to sinners to be repaid in full. 35 But love your enemies, do what is good, and lend, expecting nothing in return. Then your reward will be great, and you will be children of the Most High. For he is gracious to the ungrateful and evil. 36 Be merciful, just as your Father also is merciful.

DO NOT JUDGE

37 "Do not judge, and you will not be judged. Do not condemn, and you will not be condemned. Forgive, and you will be forgiven. 38 Give, and it will be given to you; a good measure — pressed down, shaken together, and running over — will be poured into your lap. For with the measure you use, it will be measured back to you."

39 He also told them a parable: "Can the blind guide the blind? Won't they both fall into a pit? 40 A disciple is not above his teacher, but everyone who is fully trained will be like his teacher.

41 "Why do you look at the splinter in your brother's eye, but don't notice the beam of wood in your own eye? 42 Or how can you say to your brother, 'Brother, let me take out the splinter that is in your eye,' when you yourself don't see the beam of wood in your eye? Hypocrite! First take the beam of wood out of your eye, and then you will see clearly to take out the splinter in your brother's eye.

A TREE AND ITS FRUIT

43 "A good tree doesn't produce bad fruit; on the other hand, a bad tree doesn't produce good fruit.[A] 44 For each tree is known by its own fruit. Figs aren't gathered from thornbushes, or grapes picked from a bramble bush. 45 A good person produces good out of the good stored up in his heart. An evil person produces evil out of the evil stored up in his heart, for his mouth speaks from the overflow of the heart.

THE TWO FOUNDATIONS

46 "Why do you call me 'Lord, Lord,' and don't do the things I say? 47 I will show you what someone is like who comes to me, hears my words, and acts on them: 48 He is like a man building a house, who dug deep and laid the foundation on the rock. When the flood came, the river crashed against that house and couldn't shake it, because it was well built. 49 But the one who hears and does not act is like a man who built a house on the ground without a foundation. The river crashed against it, and immediately it collapsed. And the destruction of that house was great."

Other-centeredness | *Not Being Judgmental*

CRITICS ANONYMOUS

"Do not judge, and you will not be judged. Do not condemn, and you will not be condemned. Forgive, and you will be forgiven." Luke 6:37

Some hop on social media and go from 0–60 cpm (criticisms per minute) in four seconds flat: *I can't believe he posted that! Someone should tell her that's NOT a flattering picture. If I have to see one more picture of what they ate for lunch. . . . There he goes again, off on his daily rant!* We act like real-life referees, moving across the Web and through the world, calling fouls and pointing out infractions.

Question: Who appointed *us* the arbiters of what is acceptable and unacceptable, proper and improper? Answer: Nobody.

The Lord is the "Judge of the earth" (Ps 94:2). That is why the apostle Paul asked, "Who are you to judge another's household servant?" (Rm 14:4). Instead of worrying about what others are doing or not doing, we should focus on our own upcoming one-on-one appointment with the Lord (Rm 14:12; 2Co 5:10).

For the next note on *Other-centeredness*, see Luke 14:11.

[A] **6:43** Lit *on the other hand, again, a bad tree doesn't produce good fruit*

A CENTURION'S FAITH

7 When he had concluded saying all this to
the people who were listening, he entered
Capernaum. 2 A centurion's servant, who was
highly valued by him, was sick and about to
die. 3 When the centurion heard about Jesus,
he sent some Jewish elders to him, requesting
him to come and save the life of his servant.
4 When they reached Jesus, they pleaded with
him earnestly, saying, "He is worthy for you to
grant this, 5 because he loves our nation and
has built us a synagogue."
6 Jesus went with them, and when he was not
far from the house, the centurion sent friends
to tell him, "Lord, don't trouble yourself, since
I am not worthy to have you come under my
roof. 7 That is why I didn't even consider myself worthy to come to you. But say the word,
and my servant will be healed.[A] 8 For I too am
a man placed under authority, having soldiers
under my command. I say to this one, 'Go,' and
he goes; and to another, 'Come,' and he comes;
and to my servant, 'Do this,' and he does it."
9 Jesus heard this and was amazed at him,
and turning to the crowd following him, he
said, "I tell you, I have not found so great a
faith even in Israel." 10 When those who had
been sent returned to the house, they found
the servant in good health.

A WIDOW'S SON RAISED TO LIFE

11 Afterward he was on his way to a town
called Nain. His disciples and a large crowd
were traveling with him. 12 Just as he neared
the gate of the town, a dead man was being
carried out. He was his mother's only son,
and she was a widow. A large crowd from
the city was also with her. 13 When the Lord
saw her, he had compassion on her and said,
"Don't weep." 14 Then he came up and touched
the open coffin, and the pallbearers stopped.
And he said, "Young man, I tell you, get up!"
15 The dead man sat up and began to speak,
and Jesus gave him to his mother. 16 Then fear[B]
came over everyone, and they glorified God,
saying, "A great prophet has risen among us,"
and "God has visited[C] his people." 17 This report about him went throughout Judea and
all the vicinity.

IN PRAISE OF JOHN THE BAPTIST

18 Then John's disciples told him about all these
things. So John summoned two of his disciples
19 and sent them to the Lord, asking, "Are you

Exercise of Faith | *Increasing Faith*

AMAZING JESUS

"Jesus heard this and was amazed at him, and turning to the crowd following him, he said, 'I tell you, I have not found so great a faith even in Israel.'" Luke 7:9

The Gospels contain many instances in which Jesus made statements or took actions that people found amazing. Yet only two times is Jesus himself described as being "amazed": once, at the shocking unbelief of the people in his hometown (Mk 6:6), and here at the unusual faith expressed by a Roman centurion.

The centurion's beloved servant was gravely ill. He sent for Jesus but then thought better of it as Jesus approached his house. He sent some friends to say, "Lord, don't trouble yourself, since I am not worthy to have you come under my roof. . . . But say the word, and my servant will be healed" (Lk 7:6-7).

Jesus was stunned, wowed, flabbergasted by this non-Jew's matter-of-fact confidence. So much so, that he turned to the crowd and said, in so many words, "Can you believe how strongly this guy believes? I've never seen anything like it!"

Whatever goals you have in life, this might be a good one to add to your list: "To develop a faith that causes even Jesus to be amazed."

For the next note on *Exercise of Faith*, see Luke 8:39.

[A] **7:7** Other mss read *and let my servant be healed* [B] **7:16** Or *awe* [C] **7:16** Or *come to help*

the one who is to come, or should we expect someone else?"

20 When the men reached him, they said, "John the Baptist sent us to ask you, 'Are you the one who is to come, or should we expect someone else?'"

21 At that time Jesus healed many people of diseases, afflictions, and evil spirits, and he granted sight to many blind people. 22 He replied to them, "Go and report to John what you have seen and heard: The blind receive their sight, the lame walk, those with leprosy[A] are cleansed, the deaf hear, the dead are raised, and the poor are told the good news, 23 and blessed is the one who isn't offended by me."

24 After John's messengers left, he began to speak to the crowds about John: "What did you go out into the wilderness to see? A reed swaying in the wind? 25 What then did you go out to see? A man dressed in soft clothes? See, those who are splendidly dressed and live in luxury are in royal palaces. 26 What then did you go out to see? A prophet? Yes, I tell you, and more than a prophet. 27 This is the one about whom it is written:

> **See, I am sending my messenger**
> **ahead of you;**
> **he will prepare your way**
> **before you.**[B]

28 I tell you, among those born of women no one is greater than John,[C] but the least in the kingdom of God is greater than he."

29 (And when all the people, including the tax collectors, heard this, they acknowledged God's way of righteousness, because they had been baptized with John's baptism. 30 But since the Pharisees and experts in the law had not been baptized by him, they rejected the plan of God for themselves.)

AN UNRESPONSIVE GENERATION

31 "To what then should I compare the people of this generation, and what are they like? 32 They are like children sitting in the marketplace and calling to each other:

> We played the flute for you,
> but you didn't dance;
> we sang a lament,
> but you didn't weep!

33 For John the Baptist did not come eating bread or drinking wine, and you say, 'He has a demon!' 34 The Son of Man has come eating and drinking, and you say, 'Look, a glutton and a drunkard, a friend of tax collectors and sinners!' 35 Yet wisdom is vindicated by all her children."

MUCH FORGIVENESS, MUCH LOVE

36 Then one of the Pharisees invited him to eat with him. He entered the Pharisee's house and reclined at the table. 37 And a woman in the town who was a sinner found out that Jesus was reclining at the table in the Pharisee's house. She brought an alabaster jar of perfume 38 and stood behind him at his feet, weeping, and began to wash his feet with her tears. She wiped his feet with her hair, kissing them and anointing them with the perfume.

39 When the Pharisee who had invited him saw this, he said to himself, "This man, if he were a prophet, would know who and what kind of woman this is who is touching him—she's a sinner!"

40 Jesus replied to him, "Simon, I have something to say to you."

He said, "Say it, teacher."

41 "A creditor had two debtors. One owed five hundred denarii,[D] and the other fifty. 42 Since they could not pay it back, he graciously forgave them both. So, which of them will love him more?"

43 Simon answered, "I suppose the one he forgave more."

"You have judged correctly," he told him. 44 Turning to the woman, he said to Simon, "Do you see this woman? I entered your house; you gave me no water for my feet, but she, with her tears, has washed my feet and wiped them with her hair. 45 You gave me no kiss, but she hasn't stopped kissing my feet since I came in. 46 You didn't anoint my head with olive oil, but she has anointed my feet with perfume. 47 Therefore I tell you, her many sins have been forgiven; that's why she loved much. But the one who is forgiven little, loves little." 48 Then he said to her, "Your sins are forgiven."

49 Those who were at the table with him began to say among themselves, "Who is this man who even forgives sins?"

50 And he said to the woman, "Your faith has saved you. Go in peace."

MANY WOMEN SUPPORT CHRIST'S WORK

8 Afterward he was traveling from one town and village to another, preaching and telling the good news of the kingdom of

[A] **7:22** Gk *lepros*; a term for various skin diseases; see Lv 13–14 [B] **7:27** Mal 3:1 [C] **7:28** Other mss read *women is not a greater prophet than John the Baptist* [D] **7:41** A denarius = one day's wage

God. The Twelve were with him, 2 and also some women who had been healed of evil spirits and sicknesses: Mary, called Magdalene (seven demons had come out of her); 3 Joanna the wife of Chuza, Herod's steward; Susanna; and many others who were supporting them from their possessions.

THE PARABLE OF THE SOWER

4 As a large crowd was gathering, and people were coming to Jesus from every town, he said in a parable: 5 "A sower went out to sow his seed. As he sowed, some seed fell along the path; it was trampled on, and the birds of the sky devoured it. 6 Other seed fell on the rock; when it grew up, it withered away, since it lacked moisture. 7 Other seed fell among thorns; the thorns grew up with it and choked it. 8 Still other seed fell on good ground; when it grew up, it produced fruit: a hundred times what was sown." As he said this, he called out, "Let anyone who has ears to hear listen."

WHY JESUS USED PARABLES

9 Then his disciples asked him, "What does this parable mean?" 10 So he said, "The secrets of the kingdom of God have been given for you to know, but to the rest it is in parables, so that

> **Looking they may not see,**
> **and hearing they may**
> **not understand.**[A]

THE PARABLE OF THE SOWER EXPLAINED

11 "This is the meaning of the parable: The seed is the word of God. 12 The seed along the path are those who have heard and then the devil comes and takes away the word from their hearts, so that they may not believe and be saved. 13 And the seed on the rock are those who, when they hear, receive the word with joy. Having no root, these believe for a while and fall away in a time of testing. 14 As for the seed that fell among thorns, these are the ones who, when they have heard, go on their way and are choked with worries, riches, and pleasures of life, and produce no mature fruit. 15 But the seed in the good ground—these are the ones who, having heard the word with an honest and good heart, hold on to it and by enduring, produce fruit.

USING YOUR LIGHT

16 "No one, after lighting a lamp, covers it with a basket or puts it under a bed, but puts it on a lampstand so that those who come in may see its light. 17 For nothing is concealed that won't be revealed, and nothing hidden that won't be made known and brought to light. 18 Therefore take care how you listen. For whoever has, more will be given to him; and whoever does not have, even what he thinks he has will be taken away from him."

TRUE RELATIONSHIPS

19 Then his mother and brothers came to him, but they could not meet with him because of the crowd. 20 He was told, "Your mother and your brothers are standing outside, wanting to see you."

21 But he replied to them, "My mother and my brothers are those who hear and do the word of God."

WIND AND WAVES OBEY JESUS

22 One day he and his disciples got into a boat, and he told them, "Let's cross over to the other side of the lake." So they set out, 23 and as they were sailing he fell asleep. Then a fierce windstorm came down on the lake; they were being swamped and were in danger. 24 They came and woke him up, saying, "Master, Master, we're going to die!"

Then he got up and rebuked the wind and the raging waves. So they ceased, and there was a calm. 25 He said to them, "Where is your faith?"

They were fearful and amazed, asking one another, "Who then is this? He commands even the winds and the waves, and they obey him!"

DEMONS DRIVEN OUT BY JESUS

26 Then they sailed to the region of the Gerasenes,[B] which is opposite Galilee. 27 When he got out on land, a demon-possessed man from the town met him. For a long time he had worn no clothes and did not stay in a house but in the tombs. 28 When he saw Jesus, he cried out, fell down before him, and said in a loud voice, "What do you have to do with me, Jesus, Son of the Most High God? I beg you, don't torment me!" 29 For he had commanded the unclean spirit to come out of the man. Many times it had seized him, and though he was guarded, bound by chains and shackles, he would snap the restraints and be driven by the demon into deserted places.

30 "What is your name?" Jesus asked him.

"Legion," he said, because many demons

[A] **8:10** Is 6:9 [B] **8:26** Other mss read *the Gadarenes*

had entered him. 31 And they begged him not
to banish them to the abyss.
32 A large herd of pigs was there, feeding
on the hillside. The demons begged him to
permit them to enter the pigs, and he gave
them permission. 33 The demons came out of
the man and entered the pigs, and the herd
rushed down the steep bank into the lake and
drowned.
34 When the men who tended them saw what
had happened, they ran off and reported it
in the town and in the countryside. 35 Then
people went out to see what had happened.
They came to Jesus and found the man the
demons had departed from, sitting at Jesus's
feet, dressed and in his right mind. And they
were afraid. 36 Meanwhile, the eyewitnesses
reported to them how the demon-possessed
man was delivered. 37 Then all the people of
the Gerasene region[A] asked him to leave them,
because they were gripped by great fear. So
getting into the boat, he returned.
38 The man from whom the demons had
departed begged him earnestly to be with
him. But he sent him away and said, 39 "Go
back to your home, and tell all that God has
done for you." And off he went, proclaiming
throughout the town how much Jesus had
done for him.

A GIRL RESTORED AND A WOMAN HEALED

40 When Jesus returned, the crowd welcomed
him, for they were all expecting him. 41 Just
then, a man named Jairus came. He was a leader
of the synagogue. He fell down at Jesus's feet
and pleaded with him to come to his house,
42 because he had an only daughter about
twelve years old, and she was dying.
While he was going, the crowds were nearly crushing him. 43 A woman suffering from
bleeding for twelve years, who had spent all she
had on doctors[B] and yet could not be healed by
any, 44 approached from behind and touched
the end of his robe. Instantly her bleeding
stopped.
45 "Who touched me?" Jesus asked.
When they all denied it, Peter[C] said, "Master,
the crowds are hemming you in and pressing
against you."[D]
46 "Someone did touch me," said Jesus. "I
know that power has gone out from me."
47 When the woman saw that she was discovered, she came trembling and fell down
before him. In the presence of all the people,

Exercise of Faith | *Sharing Story*

SHARING YOUR STORY

"'Go back to your home, and tell all that God has done for you.' And off he went, proclaiming throughout the town how much Jesus had done for him." Luke 8:39

We've seen enough courtroom dramas on TV to know what a witness does: she shares from personal experience. "Here's what I saw." "I heard these things." "This is what happened to me."

Here, after healing a demon-possessed man, Jesus told him to go back to his home and talk about his experience. In other words, go be a witness.

No divinity school degree required. No need to argue theology. No pressure to make anyone think a certain way. Just tell your story. If you are a credible witness, if your words ring true, that will be enough to convince those who are listening—the jury, as it were.

Think about that. What *is* your experience of Jesus? Maybe you were suicidal, and he loved you back to life. Or confused and he gave you meaning and purpose. Or guilt-ridden and his forgiveness set you free. Or hung up on money—and he delivered you from greed and worry. Whatever your experience, whenever the opportunity arises, simply talk about what Jesus has done for you.

For the next note on *Exercise of Faith*, see Luke 10:41-42.

[A] **8:37** Other mss read *the Gadarenes* [B] **8:43** Other mss omit *who had spent all she had on doctors* [C] **8:45** Other mss add *and those with him* [D] **8:45** Other mss add *and you say, 'Who touched me?'*

she declared the reason she had touched him
and how she was instantly healed. 48 "Daughter," he said to her, "your faith has saved you.[A]
Go in peace."
49 While he was still speaking, someone came
from the synagogue leader's house and said,
"Your daughter is dead. Don't bother the teacher anymore."
50 When Jesus heard it, he answered him,
"Don't be afraid. Only believe, and she will be
saved."[B] 51 After he came to the house, he let no
one enter with him except Peter, John, James,
and the child's father and mother. 52 Everyone
was crying and mourning for her. But he said,
"Stop crying, because she is not dead but asleep."
53 They laughed at him, because they knew
she was dead. 54 So he[C] took her by the hand
and called out, "Child, get up!" 55 Her spirit
returned, and she got up at once. Then he gave
orders that she be given something to eat. 56 Her
parents were astounded, but he instructed
them to tell no one what had happened.

COMMISSIONING THE TWELVE

9 Summoning the Twelve, he gave them power and authority over all the demons and
to heal diseases. 2 Then he sent them to proclaim the kingdom of God and to heal the sick.
3 "Take nothing for the road," he told them,
"no staff, no traveling bag, no bread, no money; and don't take an extra shirt. 4 Whatever
house you enter, stay there and leave from
there. 5 If they do not welcome you, when
you leave that town, shake off the dust from
your feet as a testimony against them." 6 So
they went out and traveled from village to
village, proclaiming the good news and healing everywhere.

HEROD'S DESIRE TO SEE JESUS

7 Herod the tetrarch heard about everything
that was going on. He was perplexed, because
some said that John had been raised from the
dead, 8 some that Elijah had appeared, and
others that one of the ancient prophets had
risen. 9 "I beheaded John," Herod said, "but
who is this I hear such things about?" And
he wanted to see him.

FEEDING OF THE FIVE THOUSAND

10 When the apostles returned, they reported
to Jesus all that they had done. He took them
along and withdrew privately to a[D] town called
Bethsaida. 11 When the crowds found out, they
followed him. He welcomed them, spoke to
them about the kingdom of God, and healed
those who needed healing.
12 Late in the day, the Twelve approached
and said to him, "Send the crowd away, so that
they can go into the surrounding villages and
countryside to find food and lodging, because
we are in a deserted place here."
13 "You give them something to eat," he told
them.

"We have no more than five loaves and two
fish," they said, "unless we go and buy food for
all these people." 14 (For about five thousand
men were there.)

Then he told his disciples, "Have them sit
down[E] in groups of about fifty each." 15 They
did what he said, and had them all sit down.
16 Then he took the five loaves and the two
fish, and looking up to heaven, he blessed
and broke them. He kept giving them to the
disciples to set before the crowd. 17 Everyone
ate and was filled. They picked up twelve baskets of leftover pieces.

PETER'S CONFESSION OF THE MESSIAH

18 While he was praying in private and his disciples were with him, he asked them, "Who
do the crowds say that I am?"
19 They answered, "John the Baptist; others, Elijah; still others, that one of the ancient
prophets has come back."[F]
20 "But you," he asked them, "who do you
say that I am?"

Peter answered, "God's Messiah."

HIS DEATH AND RESURRECTION PREDICTED

21 But he strictly warned and instructed them
to tell this to no one, 22 saying, "It is necessary
that the Son of Man suffer many things and
be rejected by the elders, chief priests, and
scribes, be killed, and be raised the third day."

TAKE UP YOUR CROSS

23 Then he said to them all, "If anyone wants
to follow after[G] me, let him deny himself,
take up his cross daily,[H] and follow me. 24 For
whoever wants to save his life will lose it,
but whoever loses his life because of me will
save it. 25 For what does it benefit someone
if he gains the whole world, and yet loses or

[A] **8:48** Or *has made you well* [B] **8:50** Or *she will be made well* [C] **8:54** Other mss add *having put them all outside* [D] **9:10** Other mss add *deserted place near a* [E] **9:14** Lit *them recline* [F] **9:19** Lit *has risen* [G] **9:23** Lit *come after* [H] **9:23** Other mss omit *daily*

forfeits himself? [26] For whoever is ashamed of me and my words, the Son of Man will be ashamed of him when he comes in his glory and that of the Father and the holy angels. [27] Truly I tell you, there are some standing here who will not taste death until they see the kingdom of God."

THE TRANSFIGURATION

[28] About eight days after this conversation, he took along Peter, John, and James and went up on the mountain to pray. [29] As he was praying, the appearance of his face changed, and his clothes became dazzling white. [30] Suddenly, two men were talking with him — Moses and Elijah. [31] They appeared in glory and were speaking of his departure, which he was about to accomplish in Jerusalem.

[32] Peter and those with him were in a deep sleep,[A] and when they became fully awake, they saw his glory and the two men who were standing with him. [33] As the two men were departing from him, Peter said to Jesus, "Master, it's good for us to be here. Let us set up three shelters: one for you, one for Moses, and one for Elijah" — not knowing what he was saying.

[34] While he was saying this, a cloud appeared and overshadowed them. They became afraid as they entered the cloud. [35] Then a voice came from the cloud, saying: "This is my Son, the Chosen One;[B] listen to him!"

[36] After the voice had spoken, Jesus was found alone. They kept silent, and at that time told no one what they had seen.

THE POWER OF JESUS OVER A DEMON

[37] The next day, when they came down from the mountain, a large crowd met him. [38] Just then a man from the crowd cried out, "Teacher, I beg you to look at my son, because he's my only child. [39] A spirit seizes him; suddenly he shrieks, and it throws him into convulsions until he foams at the mouth; severely bruising him, it scarcely ever leaves him. [40] I begged your disciples to drive it out, but they couldn't."

[41] Jesus replied, "You unbelieving and perverse[C] generation, how long will I be with you and put up with you? Bring your son here."

[42] As the boy was still approaching, the demon knocked him down and threw him into severe convulsions. But Jesus rebuked the unclean spirit, healed the boy, and gave him back to his father. [43] And they were all astonished at the greatness of God.

THE SECOND PREDICTION OF HIS DEATH

While everyone was amazed at all the things he was doing, he told his disciples, [44] "Let these words sink in:[D] The Son of Man is about to be betrayed into the hands of men."

[45] But they did not understand this statement; it was concealed from them so that they could not grasp it, and they were afraid to ask him about it.

WHO IS THE GREATEST?

[46] An argument started among them about who was the greatest of them. [47] But Jesus, knowing their inner thoughts,[E] took a little child and had him stand next to him. [48] He told them, "Whoever welcomes[F] this little child in my name welcomes me. And whoever welcomes me welcomes him who sent me. For whoever is least among you — this one is great."

IN HIS NAME

[49] John responded, "Master, we saw someone driving out demons in your name, and we tried to stop him because he does not follow us."

[50] "Don't stop him," Jesus told him, "because whoever is not against you is for you."[G]

THE JOURNEY TO JERUSALEM

[51] When the days were coming to a close for him to be taken up, he determined[H] to journey to Jerusalem. [52] He sent messengers ahead of himself, and on the way they entered a village of the Samaritans to make preparations for him. [53] But they did not welcome him, because he determined to journey to Jerusalem. [54] When the disciples James and John saw this, they said, "Lord, do you want us to call down fire from heaven to consume them?"[I]

[55] But he turned and rebuked them,[J] [56] and they went to another village.

FOLLOWING JESUS

[57] As they were traveling on the road someone said to him, "I will follow you wherever you go."

[A] **9:32** Lit *were weighed down with sleep* [B] **9:35** Other mss read *the Beloved* [C] **9:41** Or *corrupt*, or *perverted*, or *twisted*; Dt 32:5 [D] **9:44** Lit *"Put these words in your ears* [E] **9:47** Lit *the thoughts of their hearts* [F] **9:48** Or *receives*, throughout the verse [G] **9:50** Other mss read *against us is for us* [H] **9:51** Lit *he stiffened his face to go*; Is 50:7 [I] **9:54** Other mss add *as Elijah also did* [J] **9:55-56** Other mss add *and said, "You don't know what kind of spirit you belong to.* [56]*For the Son of Man did not come to destroy people's lives but to save them,"*

3 Give us each day our daily bread.[A]
4 And forgive us our sins,
for we ourselves also forgive everyone
in debt to us.[B]
And do not bring us into temptation."[C]

ASK, SEARCH, KNOCK

5 He also said to them: "Suppose one of you[D]
has a friend and goes to him at midnight and
says to him, 'Friend, lend me three loaves of
bread, 6 because a friend of mine on a journey
has come to me, and I don't have anything to
offer him.' 7 Then he will answer from inside
and say, 'Don't bother me! The door is already
locked, and my children and I have gone to
bed. I can't get up to give you anything.' 8 I
tell you, even though he won't get up and
give him anything because he is his friend,
yet because of his friend's shameless boldness,[E] he will get up and give him as much
as he needs.
9 "So I say to you, ask, and it will be given to
you. Seek, and you will find. Knock, and the
door will be opened to you. 10 For everyone who
asks receives, and the one who seeks finds,
and to the one who knocks, the door will be
opened. 11 What father among you, if his son[F]
asks for a fish, will give him a snake instead of
a fish? 12 Or if he asks for an egg, will give him
a scorpion? 13 If you then, who are evil, know
how to give good gifts to your children, how
much more will the heavenly Father give the
Holy Spirit to those who ask him?"

A HOUSE DIVIDED

14 Now he was driving out a demon that was
mute. When the demon came out, the man
who had been mute spoke, and the crowds
were amazed. 15 But some of them said, "He
drives out demons by Beelzebul, the ruler of
the demons." 16 And others, as a test, were demanding of him a sign from heaven.
17 Knowing their thoughts, he told them, "Every kingdom divided against itself is headed
for destruction, and a house divided against
itself falls. 18 If Satan also is divided against
himself, how will his kingdom stand? For you
say I drive out demons by Beelzebul. 19 And if
I drive out demons by Beelzebul, by whom
do your sons drive them out? For this reason
they will be your judges. 20 If I drive out demons by the finger of God, then the kingdom
of God has come upon you. 21 When a strong
man, fully armed, guards his estate, his possessions are secure. 22 But when one stronger
than he attacks and overpowers him, he takes

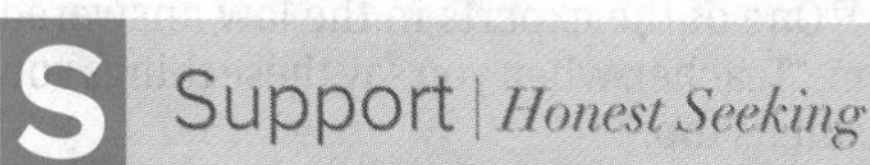

A LESSON IN PRAYER

"So I say to you, ask, and it will be given to you. Seek, and you will find. Knock, and the door will be opened to you." Luke 11:9

If God *knows* all things and if he *controls* all things, then doesn't prayer seem sort of unnecessary?

That's a mystery theologians and believers have been wrestling with for millennia. But here's what we know for sure. In multiple places in the Bible, people of faith are commanded to pray.

Jesus tells a story here about a man who pestered his neighbor at midnight for three loaves of bread (to feed a late-arriving guest). The man keeps banging at his friend's door with "shameless boldness" (Lk 11:8) until he gets what he came for. Jesus also gives the illustration of a boy asking his dad for a fish or an egg to eat. What father, Jesus asks, would respond to such a request by giving his child a snake or a scorpion?

His point was that God wants us to ask, seek, and knock. We may never understand exactly how prayer fits with the sovereign plan of God, but when we come to the Lord in bold faith, when we pray stubbornly and trust his good heart, we will see him supply our needs.

For the next note on *Support*, see Luke 16:13.

[A] **11:3** Or *our bread for tomorrow* [B] **11:4** Or *everyone who wrongs us* [C] **11:4** Other mss add *But deliver us from the evil one*
[D] **11:5** Lit *Who of you* [E] **11:8** Or *persistence* [F] **11:11** Other mss read *son asks for bread, would give him a stone? Or if he*

from him all his weapons[A] he trusted in, and divides up his plunder. 23 Anyone who is not with me is against me, and anyone who does not gather with me scatters.

AN UNCLEAN SPIRIT'S RETURN

24 "When an unclean spirit comes out of a person, it roams through waterless places looking for rest, and not finding rest, it then[B] says, 'I'll go back to my house that I came from.' 25 Returning, it finds the house swept and put in order. 26 Then it goes and brings seven other spirits more evil than itself, and they enter and settle down there. As a result, that person's last condition is worse than the first."

TRUE BLESSEDNESS

27 As he was saying these things, a woman from the crowd raised her voice and said to him, "Blessed is the womb that bore you and the one who nursed you!"

28 He said, "Rather, blessed are those who hear the word of God and keep it."

THE SIGN OF JONAH

29 As the crowds were increasing, he began saying: "This generation is an evil generation. It demands a sign, but no sign will be given to it except the sign of Jonah.[C] 30 For just as Jonah became a sign to the people of Nineveh, so also the Son of Man will be to this generation. 31 The queen of the south will rise up at the judgment with the men of this generation and condemn them, because she came from the ends of the earth to hear the wisdom of Solomon, and look — something greater than Solomon is here. 32 The men of Nineveh will stand up at the judgment with this generation and condemn it, because they repented at Jonah's preaching, and look — something greater than Jonah is here.

THE LAMP OF THE BODY

33 "No one lights a lamp and puts it in the cellar or under a basket,[D] but on a lampstand, so that those who come in may see its light. 34 Your eye is the lamp of the body. When your eye is healthy, your whole body is also full of light. But when it is bad, your body is also full of darkness. 35 Take care, then, that the light in you is not darkness. 36 If, therefore, your whole body is full of light, with no part of it in darkness, it will be entirely illuminated, as when a lamp shines its light on you."

RELIGIOUS HYPOCRISY DENOUNCED

37 As he was speaking, a Pharisee asked him to dine with him. So he went in and reclined at the table. 38 When the Pharisee saw this, he was amazed that he did not first perform the ritual washing[E] before dinner. 39 But the Lord said to him, "Now you Pharisees clean the outside of the cup and dish, but inside you are full of greed and evil. 40 Fools! Didn't he who made the outside make the inside too? 41 But give from what is within to the poor,[F] and then everything is clean for you.

42 "But woe to you Pharisees! You give a tenth[G] of mint, rue, and every kind of herb, and you bypass[H] justice and love for God.[I] These things you should have done without neglecting the others.

43 "Woe to you Pharisees! You love the front seat in the synagogues and greetings in the marketplaces.

44 "Woe to you![J] You are like unmarked graves; the people who walk over them don't know it."

45 One of the experts in the law answered him, "Teacher, when you say these things you insult us too."

46 Then he said: "Woe also to you experts in the law! You load people with burdens that are hard to carry, and yet you yourselves don't touch these burdens with one of your fingers.

47 "Woe to you! You build tombs[K] for the prophets, and your fathers killed them. 48 Therefore, you are witnesses that you approve[L] the deeds of your fathers, for they killed them, and you build their monuments.[M] 49 Because of this, the wisdom of God said, 'I will send them prophets and apostles, and some of them they will kill and persecute,' 50 so that this generation may be held responsible for the blood of all the prophets shed since the foundation of the world[N] — 51 from the blood of Abel to the blood of Zechariah, who perished between the altar and the sanctuary.

[A] **11:22** Gk *panoplia*, the armor and weapons of a foot soldier; Eph 6:11,13 [B] **11:24** Other mss omit *then* [C] **11:29** Other mss add *the prophet* [D] **11:33** Other mss omit *or under a basket* [E] **11:38** Lit *he did not first wash* [F] **11:41** Or *But donate from the heart as charity* [G] **11:42** Or *a tithe* [H] **11:42** Or *neglect* [I] **11:42** Lit *the justice and the love of God* [J] **11:44** Other mss add *scribes and Pharisees, hypocrites!* [K] **11:47** Or *graves* [L] **11:48** Lit *witnesses and approve* [M] **11:48** Other mss omit *their monuments* [N] **11:50** Lit *so that the blood of all . . . world may be required of this generation,*

"Yes, I tell you, this generation will be held
responsible.[A]
52 "Woe to you experts in the law! You have
taken away the key to knowledge. You didn't
go in yourselves, and you hindered those who
were trying to go in."
53 When he left there,[B] the scribes and the
Pharisees began to oppose him fiercely and
to cross-examine him about many things;
54 they were lying in wait for him to trap him
in something he said.[C]

BEWARE OF RELIGIOUS HYPOCRISY

12 Meanwhile, a crowd of many thousands
came together, so that they were trampling on one another. He began to say to his
disciples first, "Be on your guard against the
leaven[D] of the Pharisees, which is hypocrisy.
2 There is nothing covered that won't be uncovered, nothing hidden that won't be made
known. 3 Therefore, whatever you have said
in the dark will be heard in the light, and what
you have whispered in an ear in private rooms
will be proclaimed on the housetops.

FEAR GOD

4 "I say to you, my friends, don't fear those who
kill the body, and after that can do nothing
more. 5 But I will show you the one to fear:
Fear him who has authority to throw people
into hell after death. Yes, I say to you, this is
the one to fear! 6 Aren't five sparrows sold for
two pennies?[E] Yet not one of them is forgotten in God's sight. 7 Indeed, the hairs of your
head are all counted. Don't be afraid; you are
worth more than many sparrows.

ACKNOWLEDGING CHRIST

8 "And I say to you, anyone who acknowledges
me before others, the Son of Man will also
acknowledge him before the angels of God,
9 but whoever denies me before others will
be denied before the angels of God. 10 Anyone
who speaks a word against the Son of Man
will be forgiven, but the one who blasphemes
against the Holy Spirit will not be forgiven.
11 Whenever they bring you before synagogues
and rulers and authorities, don't worry about
how you should defend yourselves or what
you should say. 12 For the Holy Spirit will teach
you at that very hour what must be said."

THE PARABLE OF THE RICH FOOL

13 Someone from the crowd said to him, "Teacher, tell my brother to divide the inheritance
with me."

Exercise of Faith | *Making Right Choices/Priorities/Values*

THE ANTIDOTE FOR ANXIETY

"But seek his kingdom, and these things will be provided for you." Luke 12:31

A video of these moments would be interesting. Maybe Andrew was pacing nervously. Perhaps Thomas had a flare-up of restless leg syndrome. Whatever the truth, Jesus could tell his followers were anxious.

Can we really blame them? They had walked away from solid jobs or family businesses in order to follow Jesus all over the countryside. The experience was jaw-dropping and nerve-wracking all at once. They didn't know from day to day if they'd be rubbing shoulders with lepers or bumping into demons. They never knew where they'd be staying or what they'd be eating. For stretches of time, they were clueless as to how their families were doing back home. They hadn't packed extra clothes—and the outfits they had were looking bad. Winter was coming. How would they pay the bills? What were their neighbors thinking and saying?

Jesus could tell that they were fretful, so he addressed their concerns, assuring them of God's faithful provision. Focus on God's will, and he will supply your needs.

Whether we say, "Seek his kingdom," or "Put his desires first," it's a good reminder. Are your values focused on earth or on God's kingdom? Perhaps it's time for a reorientation.

For the next note on *Exercise of Faith*, see Luke 17:5.

[A] **11:51** Lit *you, it will be required of this generation* [B] **11:53** Other mss read *And as he was saying these things to them* [C] **11:54** Other mss add *so that they might bring charges against him* [D] **12:1** Or *yeast* [E] **12:6** Lit *two assaria*; a small copper coin

14 "Friend,"[A] he said to him, "who appointed me a judge or arbitrator over you?" 15 He
then told them, "Watch out and be on guard
against all greed, because one's life is not in
the abundance of his possessions."
16 Then he told them a parable: "A rich man's
land was very productive. 17 He thought to
himself, 'What should I do, since I don't have
anywhere to store my crops? 18 I will do this,'
he said. 'I'll tear down my barns and build
bigger ones and store all my grain and my
goods there. 19 Then I'll say to myself, "You
have many goods stored up for many years.
Take it easy; eat, drink, and enjoy yourself."'
20 "But God said to him, 'You fool! This very
night your life is demanded of you. And the
things you have prepared — whose will they
be?'
21 "That's how it is with the one who stores
up treasure for himself and is not rich toward
God."

THE CURE FOR ANXIETY

22 Then he said to his disciples: "Therefore
I tell you, don't worry about your life, what
you will eat; or about the body, what you will
wear. 23 For life is more than food and the
body more than clothing. 24 Consider the
ravens: They don't sow or reap; they don't
have a storeroom or a barn; yet God feeds
them. Aren't you worth much more than the
birds? 25 Can any of you add one moment to
his life span[B] by worrying? 26 If then you're
not able to do even a little thing, why worry
about the rest?
27 "Consider how the wildflowers grow: They
don't labor or spin thread. Yet I tell you, not
even Solomon in all his splendor was adorned
like one of these. 28 If that's how God clothes
the grass, which is in the field today and is
thrown into the furnace tomorrow, how much
more will he do for you — you of little faith?
29 Don't strive for what you should eat and
what you should drink, and don't be anxious. 30 For the Gentile world eagerly seeks
all these things, and your Father knows that
you need them.
31 "But seek his kingdom, and these things
will be provided for you. 32 Don't be afraid, little
flock, because your Father delights to give you
the kingdom. 33 Sell your possessions and give
to the poor. Make money-bags for yourselves
that won't grow old, an inexhaustible treasure
in heaven, where no thief comes near and no
moth destroys. 34 For where your treasure is,
there your heart will be also.

Thanksgiving and Contentment | *Giving Back*

TREASURE

"For where your treasure is, there your heart will be also." Luke 12:34

Long before psychologists talked about "addiction," Jesus referenced the way the human heart inevitably attaches to whatever it loves, whatever it deems most precious. For example, we watch the person who craves financial security above all else spend his best waking moments laser-focused on amassing more wealth. He wakes thinking about his portfolio or what money can buy. He falls asleep scheming and dreaming about how to make and stockpile and invest more money (for even bigger returns).

In time, the goal—to never be without, to never have to rely on another—becomes all-consuming. The quest becomes addictive. To paraphrase Jesus, because this person treasures the acquisition of money above all else, his heart will eventually be captured by money. It's unavoidable. Our hearts attach to whatever we treasure.

One way to combat money's seductive lure is simple: Give it away. When we loosen our grip on money, it is less able to grip us. Another way to avoid treasuring money is to ask the Lord to show us how to give our hearts more completely to him. By design, our hearts have room for only one master (Mt 6:24).

For the next note on *Thanksgiving and Contentment*, see John 10:27-29.

[A] **12:14** Lit *Man* [B] **12:25** Or *add a cubit to his height*

READY FOR THE MASTER'S RETURN

35 "Be ready for service[A] and have your lamps lit. 36 You are to be like people waiting for their master to return from the wedding banquet so that when he comes and knocks, they can open the door for him at once. 37 Blessed will be those servants the master finds alert when he comes. Truly I tell you, he will get ready,[B] have them recline at the table, then come and serve them. 38 If he comes in the middle of the night, or even near dawn,[C] and finds them alert, blessed are those servants. 39 But know this: If the homeowner had known at what hour the thief was coming, he would not have let his house be broken into. 40 You also be ready, because the Son of Man is coming at an hour you do not expect."

REWARDS AND PUNISHMENT

41 "Lord," Peter asked, "are you telling this parable to us or to everyone?"

42 The Lord said: "Who then is the faithful and sensible manager his master will put in charge of his household servants to give them their allotted food at the proper time? 43 Blessed is that servant whom the master finds doing his job when he comes. 44 Truly I tell you, he will put him in charge of all his possessions. 45 But if that servant says in his heart, 'My master is delaying his coming,' and starts to beat the male and female servants, and to eat and drink and get drunk, 46 that servant's master will come on a day he does not expect him and at an hour he does not know. He will cut him to pieces[D] and assign him a place with the unfaithful.[E] 47 And that servant who knew his master's will and didn't prepare himself or do it[F] will be severely beaten. 48 But the one who did not know and did what deserved punishment will receive a light beating. From everyone who has been given much, much will be required; and from the one who has been entrusted with much, even more will be expected.[G]

NOT PEACE BUT DIVISION

49 "I came to bring fire on the earth, and how I wish it were already set ablaze! 50 But I have a baptism to undergo, and how it consumes me until it is finished! 51 Do you think that I came here to bring peace on the earth? No, I tell you, but rather division. 52 From now on, five in one household will be divided: three against two, and two against three.

53 **They will be divided, father**
against son,
son against father,
mother against daughter,
daughter against mother,
mother-in-law against
her daughter-in-law,
and daughter-in-law
against mother-in-law."[H]

INTERPRETING THE TIME

54 He also said to the crowds: "When you see a cloud rising in the west, right away you say, 'A storm is coming,' and so it does. 55 And when the south wind is blowing, you say, 'It's going to be hot,' and it is. 56 Hypocrites! You know how to interpret the appearance of the earth and the sky, but why don't you know how to interpret this present time?

SETTLING ACCOUNTS

57 "Why don't you judge for yourselves what is right? 58 As you are going with your adversary to the ruler, make an effort to settle with him on the way. Then he won't drag you before the judge, the judge hand you over to the bailiff, and the bailiff throw you into prison. 59 I tell you, you will never get out of there until you have paid the last cent."[I]

REPENT OR PERISH

13 At that time, some people came and reported to him about the Galileans whose blood Pilate had mixed with their sacrifices. 2 And he[J] responded to them, "Do you think that these Galileans were more sinful than all the other Galileans because they suffered these things? 3 No, I tell you; but unless you repent, you will all perish as well. 4 Or those eighteen that the tower in Siloam fell on and killed — do you think they were more sinful than all the other people who live in Jerusalem? 5 No, I tell you; but unless you repent, you will all perish as well."

THE PARABLE OF THE BARREN FIG TREE

6 And he told this parable: "A man had a fig tree that was planted in his vineyard. He came looking for fruit on it and found none. 7 He

[A] **12:35** Lit *"Let your loins be girded*; an idiom for tying up loose outer clothing in preparation for action; Ex 12:11 [B] **12:37** Lit *will gird himself* [C] **12:38** Lit *even in the second or third watch* [D] **12:46** Lit *him in two* [E] **12:46** Or *unbelievers* [F] **12:47** Lit *or do toward his will,* [G] **12:48** Or *much* [H] **12:53** Mc 7:6 [I] **12:59** Gk *lepton*, the smallest and least valuable copper coin in use
[J] **13:2** Other mss read *Jesus*

told the vineyard worker, 'Listen, for three years I have come looking for fruit on this fig tree and haven't found any. Cut it down! Why should it even waste the soil?'

8 "But he replied to him, 'Sir,[A] leave it this year also, until I dig around it and fertilize it. 9 Perhaps it will produce fruit next year, but if not, you can cut it down.' "

HEALING A DAUGHTER OF ABRAHAM

10 As he was teaching in one of the synagogues on the Sabbath, 11 a woman was there who had been disabled by a spirit[B] for over eighteen years. She was bent over and could not straighten up at all.[C] 12 When Jesus saw her, he called out to her,[D] "Woman, you are free of your disability." 13 Then he laid his hands on her, and instantly she was restored and began to glorify God.

14 But the leader of the synagogue, indignant because Jesus had healed on the Sabbath, responded by telling the crowd, "There are six days when work should be done; therefore come on those days and be healed and not on the Sabbath day."

15 But the Lord answered him and said, "Hypocrites! Doesn't each one of you untie his ox or donkey from the feeding trough on the Sabbath and lead it to water? 16 Satan has bound this woman, a daughter of Abraham, for eighteen years — shouldn't she be untied from this bondage[E] on the Sabbath day?"

17 When he had said these things, all his adversaries were humiliated, but the whole crowd was rejoicing over all the glorious things he was doing.

THE PARABLES OF THE MUSTARD SEED AND OF THE LEAVEN

18 He said, therefore, "What is the kingdom of God like, and what can I compare it to? 19 It's like a mustard seed that a man took and sowed in his garden. It grew and became a tree, and the birds of the sky nested in its branches."

20 Again he said, "What can I compare the kingdom of God to? 21 It's like leaven[F] that a woman took and mixed into fifty pounds[G] of flour until all of it was leavened."

THE NARROW WAY

22 He went through one town and village after another, teaching and making his way to Jerusalem. 23 "Lord," someone asked him, "are only a few people going to be saved?"

He said to them, 24 "Make every effort to enter through the narrow door, because I tell you, many will try to enter and won't be able 25 once the homeowner gets up and shuts the door. Then you will stand outside and knock on the door, saying, 'Lord, open up for us!' He will answer you, 'I don't know you or where you're from.' 26 Then you will say, 'We ate and drank in your presence, and you taught in our streets.' 27 But he will say, 'I tell you, I don't know you or where you're from. Get away from me, all you evildoers!' 28 There will be weeping and gnashing of teeth in that place, when you see Abraham, Isaac, Jacob, and all the prophets in the kingdom of God, but yourselves thrown out. 29 They will come from east and west, from north and south, to share the banquet[H] in the kingdom of God. 30 Note this: Some who are last will be first, and some who are first will be last."

JESUS AND HEROD ANTIPAS

31 At that time some Pharisees came and told him, "Go, get out of here. Herod wants to kill you."

32 He said to them, "Go tell that fox, 'Look, I'm driving out demons and performing healings today and tomorrow, and on the third day I will complete my work.'[I] 33 Yet it is necessary that I travel today, tomorrow, and the next day, because it is not possible for a prophet to perish outside of Jerusalem.

JESUS'S LAMENTATION OVER JERUSALEM

34 "Jerusalem, Jerusalem, who kills the prophets and stones those who are sent to her. How often I wanted to gather your children together, as a hen gathers her chicks under her wings, but you were not willing! 35 See, your house is abandoned to you. I tell you, you will not see me until the time comes when[J] you say, '**Blessed is he who comes in the name of the Lord**'!"[K]

A SABBATH CONTROVERSY

14 One Sabbath, when he went in to eat[L] at the house of one of the leading Pharisees, they were watching him closely. 2 There in front of him was a man whose body was swollen with fluid. 3 In response, Jesus asked

[A] **13:8** Or *Lord* [B] **13:11** Lit *had a spirit of disability* [C] **13:11** Or *straighten up completely* [D] **13:12** Or *he summoned her*
[E] **13:16** Or *isn't it necessary that she be untied from this bondage* [F] **13:21** Or *yeast* [G] **13:21** Lit *three sata*; about forty liters
[H] **13:29** Lit *recline at the table* [I] **13:32** Lit *I will be finished* [J] **13:35** Other mss omit *the time comes when* [K] **13:35** Ps 118:26
[L] **14:1** Lit *eat bread*

the law experts and the Pharisees, "Is it lawful to heal on the Sabbath or not?" 4 But they
kept silent. He took the man, healed him,
and sent him away. 5 And to them, he said,
"Which of you whose son or ox falls into a
well, will not immediately pull him out on the
Sabbath day?" 6 They could find no answer
to these things.

TEACHINGS ON HUMILITY

7 He told a parable to those who were invited,
when he noticed how they would choose the
best places for themselves: 8 "When you are
invited by someone to a wedding banquet,
don't recline at the best place, because a more
distinguished person than you may have been
invited by your host. 9 The one who invited
both of you may come and say to you, 'Give
your place to this man,' and then in humiliation, you will proceed to take the lowest place.
10 "But when you are invited, go and recline
in the lowest place, so that when the one who
invited you comes, he will say to you, 'Friend,
move up higher.' You will then be honored
in the presence of all the other guests. 11 For
everyone who exalts himself will be humbled, and the one who humbles himself will
be exalted."
12 He also said to the one who had invited
him, "When you give a lunch or a dinner, don't
invite your friends, your brothers or sisters,
your relatives, or your rich neighbors, because
they might invite you back, and you would be
repaid. 13 On the contrary, when you host a
banquet, invite those who are poor, maimed,
lame, or blind. 14 And you will be blessed, because they cannot repay you; for you will be
repaid at the resurrection of the righteous."

THE PARABLE OF THE LARGE BANQUET

15 When one of those who reclined at the table
with him heard these things, he said to him,
"Blessed is the one who will eat bread in the
kingdom of God!"
16 Then he told him: "A man was giving a
large banquet and invited many. 17 At the time
of the banquet, he sent his servant to tell those
who were invited, 'Come, because everything
is now ready.'
18 "But without exception[A] they all began
to make excuses. The first one said to him, 'I
have bought a field, and I must go out and see
it. I ask you to excuse me.'
19 "Another said, 'I have bought five yoke of
oxen, and I'm going to try them out. I ask you
to excuse me.'

Other-centeredness | *Being Humble*

HUMILITY IS THE WAY TO GO

"For everyone who exalts himself will be humbled, and the one who humbles himself will be exalted." Luke 14:11

Someone has called this "the presentation generation." Anyone with a smartphone and a few apps can "present" his or her life to the world, 24/7. Consequently, millions do: Check out where I went. Look at what I ate. Listen to what I think. Look at who I know. And while you're here, give me a "follow." Also, here's a new "selfie"—in case you don't remember how I looked yesterday. Is this innocent connecting—or something else?

At a dinner party, Jesus watched the invited guests scramble and jockey for the best seats—you know, the prominent seats, up front, at the tables where the bigwigs sit. The unwritten rule: *Get seen with the movers and shakers, and you're golden! That's how you make a name for yourself.*

Jesus warned against exalting ourselves. Instead of vaunting or hyping ourselves, Jesus was saying it is far better to let God exalt you (in his own way and his time).

This is not to suggest Christians shouldn't be on social media, only that we should be humble there, just like we ought to be humble everywhere.

For the next note on *Other-centeredness*, see John 15:12-13.

[A] **14:18** Lit *"And from one* (voice)

20 "And another said, 'I just got married, and
therefore I'm unable to come.'
21 "So the servant came back and reported
these things to his master. Then in anger, the
master of the house told his servant, 'Go out
quickly into the streets and alleys of the city,
and bring in here the poor, maimed, blind,
and lame.'
22 "'Master,' the servant said, 'what you ordered has been done, and there's still room.'
23 "Then the master told the servant, 'Go out
into the highways and hedges and make them
come in, so that my house may be filled. 24 For
I tell you, not one of those people who were
invited will enjoy my banquet.'"

THE COST OF FOLLOWING JESUS

25 Now great crowds were traveling with him.
So he turned and said to them: 26 "If anyone
comes to me and does not hate his own father
and mother, wife and children, brothers and
sisters — yes, and even his own life — he cannot be my disciple. 27 Whoever does not bear
his own cross and come after me cannot be
my disciple.
28 "For which of you, wanting to build a tower,
doesn't first sit down and calculate the cost
to see if he has enough to complete it? 29 Otherwise, after he has laid the foundation and
cannot finish it, all the onlookers will begin
to ridicule him, 30 saying, 'This man started
to build and wasn't able to finish.'
31 "Or what king, going to war against another king, will not first sit down and decide
if he is able with ten thousand to oppose the
one who comes against him with twenty thousand? 32 If not, while the other is still far off,
he sends a delegation and asks for terms of
peace. 33 In the same way, therefore, every
one of you who does not renounce[A] all his
possessions cannot be my disciple.
34 "Now, salt is good, but if salt should lose
its taste, how will it be made salty? 35 It isn't
fit for the soil or for the manure pile; they
throw it out. Let anyone who has ears to hear
listen."

THE PARABLE OF THE LOST SHEEP

15 All the tax collectors and sinners were
approaching to listen to him. 2 And the
Pharisees and scribes were complaining, "This
man welcomes sinners and eats with them."
3 So he told them this parable: 4 "What man
among you, who has a hundred sheep and loses
one of them, does not leave the ninety-nine in
the open field[B] and go after the lost one until
he finds it? 5 When he has found it, he joyfully
puts it on his shoulders, 6 and coming home,
he calls his friends and neighbors together,
saying to them, 'Rejoice with me, because I
have found my lost sheep!' 7 I tell you, in the
same way, there will be more joy in heaven over
one sinner who repents than over ninety-nine
righteous people who don't need repentance.

THE PARABLE OF THE LOST COIN

8 "Or what woman who has ten silver coins,[C,D]
if she loses one coin, does not light a lamp,
sweep the house, and search carefully until
she finds it? 9 When she finds it, she calls her
friends and neighbors together, saying, 'Rejoice with me, because I have found the silver
coin I lost!' 10 I tell you, in the same way, there
is joy in the presence of God's angels over one
sinner who repents."

THE PARABLE OF THE LOST SON

11 He also said: "A man had two sons. 12 The
younger of them said to his father, 'Father,
give me the share of the estate I have coming to me.' So he distributed the assets[E] to
them. 13 Not many days later, the younger son
gathered together all he had and traveled to
a distant country, where he squandered his
estate in foolish living. 14 After he had spent
everything, a severe famine struck that country, and he had nothing.[F] 15 Then he went to
work for one of the citizens of that country,
who sent him into his fields to feed pigs. 16 He
longed to eat his fill from[G] the pods that the
pigs were eating, but no one would give him
anything. 17 When he came to his senses,[H] he
said, 'How many of my father's hired workers
have more than enough food, and here I am
dying of hunger![I] 18 I'll get up, go to my father,
and say to him, "Father, I have sinned against
heaven and in your sight. 19 I'm no longer worthy to be called your son. Make me like one of
your hired workers."' 20 So he got up and went
to his father. But while the son was still a long
way off, his father saw him and was filled with
compassion. He ran, threw his arms around
his neck, and kissed him. 21 The son said to
him, 'Father, I have sinned against heaven

[A] **14:33** Or *leave* [B] **15:4** Or *the wilderness* [C] **15:8** Gk *ten drachmas* [D] **15:8** A Gk drachma was equivalent to a Roman denarius = one day's wage [E] **15:12** Or *life*, or *livelihood*, also in v. 30 [F] **15:14** Lit *and he began to be in need* [G] **15:16** Other mss read *to fill his stomach with* [H] **15:17** Lit *to himself* [I] **15:17** Or *dying in the famine*; v. 14

My Story | Colin

When I read the parable of the Prodigal Son, I find many of the details eerily similar to my experience with some important differences. I am a younger brother, and I had not only a loving father but also a loving mother. And I grew up learning all about my loving heavenly Father. At moments, I understood God did love me, but I also lived with a restless spirit. Beyond my family there were hurts, betrayals, and bullying that left me angry.

By the time I finished high school, I was ready to leave home. I chose a college far from my family, packed my belongings, and embarked on my adventure. I didn't ask my father for my share of the inheritance—it wasn't an option. I did carry a rich legacy of family values with me that I didn't consider worth much at the time. But I departed with my parents' blessing to attend a school that promised to encourage my faith and train me for a productive life. Unfortunately, I was less interested in either of those pursuits than I was in the lack of restraints and my apparent newfound freedom.

I quickly developed friendships beyond my Christian campus community that ushered me into a lifestyle that was at first intoxicating and then completely controlling. I dropped out of college and quickly discovered the limited work options open to me. I was living with my girlfriend in what I can now see was a mutually dependent, extremely unhealthy relationship. Menial work got me into a job in a trucking company that put my natural engineering skills to work. But gradually I felt I was settling for a life without purpose or direction. I was aware that I was stuck in a destructive relationship with no hope of improvement. Several times I phoned home and expressed a desire to return, which was met with eager encouragement. But I couldn't break away. God had to intervene, and he did.

Restoration began on my radio at work. I started listening to a wise woman giving practical, hard-nosed responses to questions about life. She frequently credited the Bible as the source of her wisdom. She sounded like home. She pointed to a life that was familiar to me but no longer my life. I now realized I was going to have to go back in order to move forward. Meanwhile, the gradual changes in me provoked resistance from my girlfriend and friends. They instinctively resented my expressions of almost-forgotten values. They didn't like the new me. I knew I couldn't stay.

One day I gave my work notice, packed a small rental truck with two years of accumulated stuff, and headed home. My surprise return was prevented when the truck broke down and I had to phone for help. My father's warm response and encouragement helped solve the mechanical issue but also assured me of a welcome waiting. I pulled in the driveway, sat in the vehicle, and wept. Before Mom and Dad noticed and rushed out tearfully to embrace me, I had a moment to sense that God had allowed me a fresh start I didn't want to squander.

I quietly murmured, "Thanks, Lord, for bringing me home."

and in your sight. I'm no longer worthy to be
called your son.'
22 "But the father told his servants, 'Quick!
Bring out the best robe and put it on him; put
a ring on his finger and sandals on his feet.
23 Then bring the fattened calf and slaughter
it, and let's celebrate with a feast, 24 because
this son of mine was dead and is alive again;
he was lost and is found!' So they began to
celebrate.
25 "Now his older son was in the field; as he
came near the house, he heard music and dancing. 26 So he summoned one of the servants,
questioning what these things meant. 27 'Your
brother is here,' he told him, 'and your father
has slaughtered the fattened calf because he
has him back safe and sound.'[A]
28 "Then he became angry and didn't want
to go in. So his father came out and pleaded
with him. 29 But he replied to his father, 'Look,
I have been slaving many years for you, and
I have never disobeyed your orders, yet you
never gave me a goat so that I could celebrate
with my friends. 30 But when this son of yours
came, who has devoured your assets[B] with
prostitutes, you slaughtered the fattened calf
for him.'
31 " 'Son,'[C] he said to him, 'you are always

[A] **15:27** Lit *him back healthy* [B] **15:30** Or *life*, or *livelihood* [C] **15:31** Lit *Child*

with me, and everything I have is yours. 32 But
we had to celebrate and rejoice, because this
brother of yours was dead and is alive again;
he was lost and is found.'"

THE PARABLE OF THE DISHONEST MANAGER

16 Now he said to the disciples: "There was
a rich man who received an accusation
that his manager was squandering his possessions. 2 So he called the manager in and
asked, 'What is this I hear about you? Give an
account of your management, because you
can no longer be my manager.'
3 "Then the manager said to himself, 'What
will I do since my master is taking the management away from me? I'm not strong enough to
dig; I'm ashamed to beg. 4 I know what I'll do
so that when I'm removed from management,
people will welcome me into their homes.'
5 "So he summoned each one of his master's
debtors. 'How much do you owe my master?'
he asked the first one.
6 "'A hundred measures of olive oil,' he said.
"'Take your invoice,' he told him, 'sit down
quickly, and write fifty.'
7 "Next he asked another, 'How much do
you owe?'
"'A hundred measures of wheat,' he said.
"'Take your invoice,' he told him, 'and write
eighty.'
8 "The master praised the unrighteous manager because he had acted shrewdly. For the
children of this age are more shrewd than
the children of light in dealing with their
own people.[A] 9 And I tell you, make friends
for yourselves by means of worldly wealth[B]
so that when it fails,[C] they may welcome you
into eternal dwellings. 10 Whoever is faithful in very little is also faithful in much, and
whoever is unrighteous in very little is also
unrighteous in much. 11 So if you have not
been faithful with worldly wealth, who will
trust you with what is genuine? 12 And if you
have not been faithful with what belongs to
someone else, who will give you what is your
own? 13 No servant can serve two masters,

Eternal Perspective | *God's Compassion*

A PICTURE OF GOD

"So he got up and went to his father. But while the son was still a long way off, his father saw him and was filled with compassion. He ran, threw his arms around his neck, and kissed him." Luke 15:20

Most people consider it the best story Jesus ever told.

A restless young man asks for his inheritance early so he can go live it up, see the world, and find himself. The father complies.

After a wild blur of doing every wild and crazy thing he can think of, the son finds himself broke and far from home. He gets a job on a pig farm that pays next to nothing. In time, even the slop he's serving the swine starts making him salivate!

The young man has an epiphany. He hits on a plan. He will return home, humbly admit his stupidity to his father, and then plead for a job. At least working on his father's estate, he won't starve to death.

All the way home, the son rehearses his speech. But when he gets within view of the house, he's shocked to see his father running frantically down the road toward him. The man smothers his son in a hug so hard it almost knocks him over! After he catches his breath, the boy starts his speech. The father cuts him off. It's a time for celebration, not negotiation.

Jesus wants us to see in this story a picture of what God is like. Whatever other image you may have, this one needs to replace it.

For the next note on *Eternal Perspective*, see Luke 16:14-15.

[A] **16:8** Lit *own generation* [B] **16:9** Lit *unrighteous money*, also in v. 11 [C] **16:9** Other mss read *when you fail*, or *pass away*

since either he will hate one and love the other, or he will be devoted to one and despise the other. You cannot serve both God and money."

KINGDOM VALUES

14 The Pharisees, who were lovers of money, were listening to all these things and scoffing at him. 15 And he told them, "You are the ones who justify yourselves in the sight of others, but God knows your hearts. For what is highly admired by people is revolting in God's sight.

16 "The Law and the Prophets were until John; since then, the good news of the kingdom of God has been proclaimed, and everyone is urgently invited to enter it.[A] 17 But it is easier for heaven and earth to pass away than for one stroke of a letter in the law to drop out.

18 "Everyone who divorces his wife and marries another woman commits adultery, and everyone who marries a woman divorced from her husband commits adultery.

THE RICH MAN AND LAZARUS

19 "There was a rich man who would dress in purple and fine linen, feasting lavishly every day. 20 But a poor man named Lazarus, covered with sores, was lying at his gate. 21 He longed to be filled with what fell from the rich man's table, but instead the dogs would come and lick his sores. 22 One day the poor man died and was carried away by the angels to Abraham's side.[B] The rich man also died and was buried. 23 And being in torment in Hades, he looked up and saw Abraham a long way off, with Lazarus at his side. 24 'Father Abraham!' he called out, 'Have mercy on me and send Lazarus to dip the tip of his finger in water and cool my tongue, because I am in agony in this flame!'

25 "'Son,'[C] Abraham said, 'remember that during your life you received your good things, just as Lazarus received bad things, but now he is comforted here, while you are in agony. 26 Besides all this, a great chasm has been fixed between us and you, so that those who want to pass over from here to you cannot; neither can those from there cross over to us.'

27 "'Father,' he said, 'then I beg you to send him to my father's house — 28 because I have five brothers — to warn them, so they won't also come to this place of torment.'

29 "But Abraham said, 'They have Moses and the prophets; they should listen to them.'

30 "'No, father Abraham,' he said. 'But if

Support | *Spiritual and Moral Inventory*

WHAT CAPTURES YOUR HEART?

"No servant can serve two masters, since either he will hate one and love the other, or he will be devoted to one and despise the other. You cannot serve both God and money." Luke 16:13

In the strictest sense, *worship* (from the old English word *worthship*) is less a religious term and more a statement about what we consider worthy of our attention, our allegiance, our affection. Because every human indeed values someone or something (over other things), the question isn't "Will we worship?" but "What will we worship?"

Here Jesus warns his followers about the danger of becoming obsessed with earthly stuff—specifically money. If we're not careful, we can fall into the universal trap of treating good things (gifts from God like a career, wealth, sex, a hobby, marriage, food, etc.) like ultimate things. When that happens—when we become more enamored with God's blessings than we are with God himself—we are guilty of idolatry, serving and valuing what has been created more than we serve and value the Creator.

What about you? Is your heart "torn between two lovers"? Are you trying to serve God even as you treasure something else as much or more than you value God?

For the next note on *Support*, see John 16:13.

[A] **16:16** Or *everyone is forcing his way into it* [B] **16:22** Or *to Abraham's bosom*; lit *to the fold of Abraham's robe*; Jn 13:23
[C] **16:25** Lit *Child*

someone from the dead goes to them, they
will repent.'
31 "But he told him, 'If they don't listen to
Moses and the prophets, they will not be persuaded if someone rises from the dead.' "

WARNINGS FROM JESUS

17 He said to his disciples, "Offenses
will certainly come,[A] but woe to the
one through whom they come! 2 It would
be better for him if a millstone were hung
around his neck and he were thrown into
the sea than for him to cause one of these
little ones to stumble. 3 Be on your guard.
If your brother sins,[B] rebuke him, and if he
repents, forgive him. 4 And if he sins against
you seven times in a day, and comes back
to you seven times, saying, 'I repent,' you
must forgive him."

FAITH AND DUTY

5 The apostles said to the Lord, "Increase our
faith."
6 "If you have faith the size of[C] a mustard
seed," the Lord said, "you can say to this
mulberry tree, 'Be uprooted and planted in
the sea,' and it will obey you.
7 "Which one of you having a servant tending sheep or plowing will say to him when he
comes in from the field, 'Come at once and sit
down to eat'? 8 Instead, will he not tell him,
'Prepare something for me to eat, get ready,
and serve me while I eat and drink; later you
can eat and drink'? 9 Does he thank that servant because he did what was commanded?[D]
10 In the same way, when you have done all
that you were commanded, you should say,
'We are worthless servants; we've only done
our duty.' "

TEN MEN HEALED

11 While traveling to Jerusalem, he passed between[E] Samaria and Galilee. 12 As he entered a
village, ten men with leprosy[F] met him. They
stood at a distance 13 and raised their voices,
saying, "Jesus, Master, have mercy on us!"
14 When he saw them, he told them, "Go and
show yourselves to the priests." And while
they were going, they were cleansed.
15 But one of them, seeing that he was healed,

Eternal Perspective | *God's Inside View*

MONEY, MONEY, MONEY, MONEY

"The Pharisees, who were lovers of money, were listening to all these things and scoffing at him. And he told them, 'You are the ones who justify yourselves in the sight of others, but God knows your hearts. For what is highly admired by people is revolting in God's sight.'" Luke 16:14-15

Why did Jesus talk repeatedly about money? Because money, like few other things on earth, has the power to capture our hearts.

Here he told an eyebrow-raising story about a desperate but shrewd manager who cooked the books to provide for his future. He was actually making the point that we should use money for eternal purposes. The listening Pharisees scoffed at this, because they were "lovers of money." Give it away? How naïve! No thanks. They wanted to hoard it, stockpile it. And why not? Isn't that what most normal people do?

Jesus rebuked this mindset. What others do or say or think doesn't matter. God sees our hearts. He knows our true motives. And besides, many of the values and habits of worldly people are "revolting in God's sight."

Are you a user of money—or a lover of it? Ask Jesus for the wisdom and grace to embrace his views of money. He sees your heart.

For the next note on *Eternal Perspective*, see John 2:2-3.

[A] 17:1 Lit *"It is impossible for offenses not to come* [B] 17:3 Other mss add *against you* [C] 17:6 Lit *faith like* [D] 17:9 Other mss add *I don't think so* [E] 17:11 Other mss read *through the middle of* [F] 17:12 Gk *lepros*; a term for various skin diseases; see Lv 13–14

returned and, with a loud voice, gave glory to
God. 16 He fell facedown at his feet, thanking
him. And he was a Samaritan.
17 Then Jesus said, "Were not ten cleansed?
Where are the nine? 18 Didn't any return to give
glory to God except this foreigner?" 19 And he
told him, "Get up and go on your way. Your
faith has saved you."[A]

THE COMING OF THE KINGDOM

20 Being asked by the Pharisees when the
kingdom of God would come, he answered
them, "The kingdom of God is not coming with
something observable; 21 no one will say,[B] 'See
here!' or 'There!' For you see, the kingdom of
God is in your midst."[C]
22 Then he told the disciples: "The days are
coming when you will long to see one of the
days of the Son of Man, but you won't see it.
23 They will say to you, 'See there!' or 'See here!'
Don't follow or run after them. 24 For as the
lightning flashes from horizon to horizon and
lights up the sky, so the Son of Man will be in
his day. 25 But first it is necessary that he suffer
many things and be rejected by this generation.
26 "Just as it was in the days of Noah, so it
will be in the days of the Son of Man: 27 People
went on eating, drinking, marrying and giving
in marriage until the day Noah boarded the
ark, and the flood came and destroyed them
all. 28 It will be the same as it was in the days of
Lot: People went on eating, drinking, buying,
selling, planting, building. 29 But on the day
Lot left Sodom, fire and sulfur rained from
heaven and destroyed them all. 30 It will be
like that on the day the Son of Man is revealed.
31 On that day, a man on the housetop, whose
belongings are in the house, must not come
down to get them. Likewise the man who is
in the field must not turn back. 32 Remember
Lot's wife! 33 Whoever tries to make his life
secure[D,E] will lose it, and whoever loses his
life will preserve it. 34 I tell you, on that night
two will be in one bed; one will be taken and
the other will be left. 35 Two women will be
grinding grain together; one will be taken
and the other left."[F]
37 "Where, Lord?" they asked him.
He said to them, "Where the corpse is, there
also the vultures will be gathered."

Relationships | *Confronting in Love*

LEANING IN

"If he sins against you seven times in a day, and comes back to you seven times, saying, 'I repent,' you must forgive him." Luke 17:4

The vast majority of people nearly come unglued at the thought of addressing an offense. "Confront the person who wronged me? Bring up a difficult subject? Why would I want to start World War III? No thanks! It's not worth it."

But if we eat it, if we stuff our "stuff," we get bitter, maybe even depressed. We become wary. We withdraw from relationships.

The problem is a misunderstanding of confrontation. Yes we forgive, as this verse says. But somewhere along the way a conversation is needed. The word *confrontation* literally means to "turn your face toward." In other words, instead of looking away, we focus and lean in. We don't ignore the "elephant in the room." We address it. And we refuse to do so with theatrics and fireworks. We pray for humility. Then we speak with grace, because the goal is reconciliation. Our desire is to win back a treasured friend, not win a dumb argument.

Become a person who confronts in a healthy fashion. Overlook small slights, but on bigger matters, refuse to look the other way. Don't pretend the weirdness didn't happen. Engage. Speak the truth in love.

For the next note on *Relationships*, see John 13:34-35.

[A] **17:19** Or *faith has made you well* [B] **17:21** Lit *they will not say* [C] **17:21** Or *within you* [D] **17:33** Other mss read *to save his life* [E] **17:33** Or *tries to retain his life* [F] **17:35** Some mss include v. 36: *"Two will be in a field: One will be taken, and the other will be left."*

THE PARABLE OF THE PERSISTENT WIDOW

18 Now he told them a parable on the need for them to pray always and not give up. 2 "There was a judge in a certain town who didn't fear God or respect people. 3 And a widow in that town kept coming to him, saying, 'Give me justice against my adversary.'

4 "For a while he was unwilling, but later he said to himself, 'Even though I don't fear God or respect people, 5 yet because this widow keeps pestering me,[A] I will give her justice, so that she doesn't wear me out[B] by her persistent coming.' "

6 Then the Lord said, "Listen to what the unjust judge says. 7 Will not God grant justice to his elect who cry out to him day and night? Will he delay helping them?[C] 8 I tell you that he will swiftly grant them justice. Nevertheless, when the Son of Man comes, will he find faith on earth?"

THE PARABLE OF THE PHARISEE AND THE TAX COLLECTOR

9 He also told this parable to some who trusted in themselves that they were righteous and looked down on everyone else: 10 "Two men went up to the temple to pray, one a Pharisee and the other a tax collector. 11 The Pharisee was standing and praying like this about himself:[D] 'God, I thank you that I'm not like other people — greedy, unrighteous, adulterers, or even like this tax collector. 12 I fast twice a week; I give a tenth[E] of everything I get.'

13 "But the tax collector, standing far off, would not even raise his eyes to heaven but kept striking his chest and saying, 'God, have mercy on me,[F] a sinner!' 14 I tell you, this one went down to his house justified rather than the other; because everyone who exalts himself will be humbled, but the one who humbles himself will be exalted."

BLESSING THE CHILDREN

15 People were bringing infants to him so he might touch them, but when the disciples saw it, they rebuked them. 16 Jesus, however, invited them: "Let the little children come to me, and don't stop them, because the kingdom of God belongs to such as these. 17 Truly I tell you, whoever does not receive the kingdom of God like a little child will never enter it."

THE RICH YOUNG RULER

18 A ruler asked him, "Good teacher, what must I do to inherit eternal life?"

19 "Why do you call me good?" Jesus asked

Exercise of Faith | *Increasing Faith*

MORE FAITH, PLEASE?

"The apostles said to the Lord, 'Increase our faith.'" Luke 17:5

Faith is a major emphasis in the Bible.

Through faith we are saved (Eph 2:8-9). By faith we are called to live (Gl 2:20). The eleventh chapter of Hebrews—sometimes called "God's Hall of Faith"—says that without faith, we can't please God; however, with it we can live extraordinary lives.

Given all that, we have to believe this request by the disciples made Jesus smile. After all, this was the same stumbling, bumbling bunch whom he once asked, "Where is your faith?" (Lk 8:25).

Jesus told his followers they didn't need a ton of faith: even a tiny bit ("the size of a mustard seed," Lk 17:6) is enough to uproot a mulberry tree. Anyone who has tried to dig up one of these deeply rooted trees can truly appreciate this reference.

Maybe we could adapt the apostles' prayer to something like this: "Lord, rather than a dump truckload of vague, pseudo, half-hearted faith, just give me a few granules of the real deal—genuine faith in you."

For the next note on *Exercise of Faith*, see Luke 18:22.

[A] **18:5** Lit *widow causes me trouble* [B] **18:5** Or *doesn't ruin my reputation* [C] **18:7** Or *Will he put up with them?* [D] **18:11** Or *by himself* [E] **18:12** Or *give tithes* [F] **18:13** Or *God, turn your wrath from me*

Bartimaeus | Restoration Profile

MATTHEW 20:29-34; MARK 10:46-52; LUKE 18:35-43

Bartimaeus was a fixture on the road between Jericho and Jerusalem, spending his days in blindness as he begged from the passing traffic. Mark tells us his name, Luke notes his awareness, and Matthew mentions he wasn't alone. Misfortune often brings company, if not encouragement. In the ancient world, blindness was a disability that invited societal disapproval. The disciples recognized a blind man and asked Jesus, "Who sinned, this man or his parents?" (Jn 9:2), assuming sin was the cause.

One day, Bartimaeus sensed an unusual commotion. When he heard Jesus was passing, he and his companion did their best to get Jesus's attention. They called him "Son of David," asking for mercy (Mk 10:47). This was a seldom-used title that identified Jesus as the Messiah. Told to be quiet, the blind men redoubled their efforts until Jesus asked what they wanted him to do. They asked for their sight to be restored. Matthew tells us the Lord was moved with compassion, touched their eyes, and they were healed. They also began to follow Jesus up the road (Mt 20:34).

Both Mark and Luke record what Jesus said as he healed them: "Your faith has saved you" (Mk 10:52; cp. Lk 18:42). Jesus's point was that in calling him Son of David, they were expressing faith in him as the Savior. Their trust in him began their restoration; Jesus's touch completed it.

Faith that brings about restoration must have an object—faith in someone. Only faith in Christ brings about eternal restoration.

him. "No one is good except God alone. 20 You
know the commandments: **Do not commit
adultery; do not murder; do not steal; do
not bear false witness; honor your father
and mother.**"[A]
21 "I have kept all these from my youth," he
said.
22 When Jesus heard this, he told him, "You
still lack one thing: Sell all you have and distribute it to the poor, and you will have treasure in heaven. Then come, follow me."
23 After he heard this, he became extremely
sad, because he was very rich.

POSSESSIONS AND THE KINGDOM

24 Seeing that he became sad,[B] Jesus said,
"How hard it is for those who have wealth
to enter the kingdom of God! 25 For it is eas-
ier for a camel to go through the eye of a needle than for a rich person to enter the kingdom of God."
26 Those who heard this asked, "Then who
can be saved?"
27 He replied, "What is impossible with man
is possible with God."
28 Then Peter said, "Look, we have left what
we had and followed you."
29 So he said to them, "Truly I tell you, there
is no one who has left a house, wife or brothers or sisters, parents or children because of
the kingdom of God, 30 who will not receive
many times more at this time, and eternal life in the age to come."

THE THIRD PREDICTION OF HIS DEATH

31 Then he took the Twelve aside and told them,
"See, we are going up to Jerusalem. Everything that is written through the prophets about
the Son of Man will be accomplished. 32 For
he will be handed over to the Gentiles, and he
will be mocked, insulted, spit on; 33 and after
they flog him, they will kill him, and he will rise on the third day."
34 They understood none of these things.
The meaning of the saying[C] was hidden from them, and they did not grasp what was said.

A BLIND MAN RECEIVES HIS SIGHT

35 As he approached Jericho, a blind man
was sitting by the road begging. 36 Hearing
a crowd passing by, he inquired what was happening. 37 "Jesus of Nazareth is passing
by," they told him.
38 So he called out, "Jesus, Son of David, have

[A] **18:20** Ex 20:12-16; Dt 5:16-20 [B] **18:24** Other mss omit *he became sad* [C] **18:34** Lit *This saying*

mercy on me!" 39 Then those in front told him
to keep quiet,[A] but he kept crying out all the
more, "Son of David, have mercy on me!"
40 Jesus stopped and commanded that he be
brought to him. When he came closer, he asked
him, 41 "What do you want me to do for you?"
"Lord," he said, "I want to see."
42 "Receive your sight." Jesus told him. "Your
faith has saved you." 43 Instantly he could see,
and he began to follow him, glorifying God.
All the people, when they saw it, gave praise
to God.

JESUS VISITS ZACCHAEUS

19 He entered Jericho and was passing
through. 2 There was a man named Zacchaeus who was a chief tax collector, and he was
rich. 3 He was trying to see who Jesus was, but
he was not able because of the crowd, since he
was a short man. 4 So running ahead, he climbed
up a sycamore tree to see Jesus, since he was
about to pass that way. 5 When Jesus came to
the place, he looked up and said to him, "Zacchaeus, hurry and come down because today
it is necessary for me to stay at your house."
6 So he quickly came down and welcomed
him joyfully. 7 All who saw it began to complain, "He's gone to stay with a sinful man."
8 But Zacchaeus stood there and said to the
Lord, "Look, I'll give half of my possessions to
the poor, Lord. And if I have extorted anything
from anyone, I'll pay back four times as much."
9 "Today salvation has come to this house,"
Jesus told him, "because he too is a son of
Abraham. 10 For the Son of Man has come to
seek and to save the lost."

THE PARABLE OF THE TEN MINAS

11 As they were listening to this, he went on to
tell a parable because he was near Jerusalem,
and they thought the kingdom of God was
going to appear right away.
12 Therefore he said: "A nobleman traveled
to a far country to receive for himself authority to be king[B] and then to return. 13 He called
ten of his servants, gave them ten minas,[C]
and told them, 'Engage in business until I
come back.'
14 "But his subjects hated him and sent a
delegation after him, saying, 'We don't want
this man to rule over us.'
15 "At his return, having received the authority

Exercise of Faith | *Making Right Choices/Priorities/Values*

A CONVERSATION ABOUT SALVATION

"When Jesus heard this, he told him, 'You still lack one thing: Sell all you have and distribute it to the poor, and you will have treasure in heaven. Then come, follow me.'" Luke 18:22

This discussion began with a young man's question about what he needed to "do to inherit eternal life" (Lk 18:18). It ended with Jesus telling the man to liquidate his assets, give everything to the poor, and "come, follow me." Lots of people read this and scratch their heads. *Does salvation require great acts of philanthropy? Taking a vow of poverty?*

Some clarification is helpful. This young man was under the false impression that salvation is something we can earn—by doing assorted good deeds. Jesus played along, essentially saying, "Okay, if you're into good deeds, here's a *really* good deed—go do this!" He knew that his questioner was "very rich" (18:23) and that he loved his stuff.

Jesus was showing the man that no one is perfect when it comes to doing good deeds, and as long as money was his ultimate security, God could never be his true Savior. We find salvation in Jesus alone. Only he can satisfy the deep needs of your soul by trusting solely in him.

Ask God for the grace to see that only Jesus can save, and the faith to follow him without reservation.

For the next note on *Exercise of Faith*, see John 1:35-37.

[A] **18:39** Or *those in front rebuked him* [B] **19:12** Lit *to receive for himself a kingdom*, or *sovereignty*, also in v. 15 [C] **19:13** = Gk coin worth a hundred drachmas or about a hundred days' wages

Zacchaeus | Restoration Profile

LUKE 19:1-10

Curiosity often paves the way for restoration. As he encountered Jesus on the road through Jericho, Zacchaeus had four significant handicaps: he was a despised tax collector, he was rich, he was short, and he was late. But twice Luke mentions that Zacchaeus wanted to "see" Jesus (Lk 19:3-4), to observe him. Each of his handicaps made it difficult for Zacchaeus to accomplish his goal. The crowd already lining the road resented his presence and had no interest in letting him through so he could see. His wealth, role, height, and timing seemed to cut him off from Jesus.

Zacchaeus's solution was an attempt to overcome his height disadvantage. He climbed a tree overhanging the route. Jesus noticed him, named him, called him, and invited himself to Zacchaeus's home. Each of those actions on Jesus's part had a restoring effect on the little, hated, rich, tax collector. But the crowd didn't change its mind about him and, in fact, immediately resented Jesus's interest in Zacchaeus, who proceeded to joyfully take Jesus home.

We're not told what actually transpired during Jesus's visit or the subject of their conversation. But the results were astonishing. By the time Jesus left his house, Zacchaeus was a changed person, and his restoration led to radical decisions. His previous god—money—suddenly became a disposable resource to bless others. He committed himself to generosity and restitution. But Jesus's declaration was the seal on Zacchaeus's transformation, "'Today salvation has come to this house,' Jesus told him, 'because he too is a son of Abraham. For the Son of Man has come to seek and to save the lost'" (Lk 19:9-10). Curiosity brought this lost man to a precarious perch on a tree branch, where Jesus found and restored him.

to be king, he summoned those servants he had
given the money to, so that he could find out
how much they had made in business. 16 The
first came forward and said, 'Master, your
mina has earned ten more minas.'
17 " 'Well done, good[A] servant!' he told him.
'Because you have been faithful in a very small
matter, have authority over ten towns.'
18 "The second came and said, 'Master, your
mina has made five minas.'
19 "So he said to him, 'You will be over five
towns.'
20 "And another came and said, 'Master, here
is your mina. I have kept it safe in a cloth 21 because I was afraid of you since you're a harsh
man: you collect what you didn't deposit and
reap what you didn't sow.'
22 "He told him, 'I will condemn you by what
you have said, you evil servant! If you knew
I was a harsh man, collecting what I didn't
deposit and reaping what I didn't sow, 23 why,
then, didn't you put my money in the bank?
And when I returned, I would have collected
it with interest.' 24 So he said to those standing
there, 'Take the mina away from him and give
it to the one who has ten minas.'
25 "But they said to him, 'Master, he has ten
minas.'
26 " 'I tell you, that to everyone who has, more
will be given; and from the one who does not
have, even what he does have will be taken
away. 27 But bring here these enemies of mine,
who did not want me to rule over them, and
slaughter[B] them in my presence.' "

THE TRIUMPHAL ENTRY

28 When he had said these things, he went
on ahead, going up to Jerusalem. 29 As he
approached Bethphage and Bethany, at the
place called the Mount of Olives, he sent two
of the disciples 30 and said, "Go into the village
ahead of you. As you enter it, you will find a
young donkey tied there, on which no one
has ever sat. Untie it and bring it. 31 If anyone
asks you, 'Why are you untying it?' say this:
'The Lord needs it.' "
32 So those who were sent left and found
it just as he had told them. 33 As they were
untying the young donkey, its owners said
to them, "Why are you untying the donkey?"
34 "The Lord needs it," they said. 35 Then they
brought it to Jesus, and after throwing their

[A] **19:17** Or *capable* [B] **19:27** Or *execute*

clothes on the donkey, they helped Jesus get on
it. 36 As he was going along, they were spreading their clothes on the road. 37 Now he came
near the path down the Mount of Olives, and
the whole crowd of the disciples began to
praise God joyfully with a loud voice for all
the miracles they had seen:

38 **Blessed is the King who comes**
in the name of the Lord.[A]
Peace in heaven
and glory in the highest heaven!

39 Some of the Pharisees from the crowd
told him, "Teacher, rebuke your disciples."
40 He answered, "I tell you, if they were to
keep silent, the stones would cry out."

JESUS'S LOVE FOR JERUSALEM

41 As he approached and saw the city, he wept
for it, 42 saying, "If you knew this day what
would bring peace — but now it is hidden
from your eyes. 43 For the days will come on
you when your enemies will build a barricade
around you, surround you, and hem you in on
every side. 44 They will crush you and your
children among you to the ground, and they
will not leave one stone on another in your
midst, because you did not recognize the time
when God visited you."

CLEANSING THE TEMPLE

45 He went into the temple and began to throw
out those who were selling,[B] 46 and he said, "It is
written, **my house will be a house of prayer**,
but you have made it **a den of thieves**!"[C]
47 Every day he was teaching in the temple.
The chief priests, the scribes, and the leaders
of the people were looking for a way to kill
him, 48 but they could not find a way to do
it, because all the people were captivated by
what they heard.

THE AUTHORITY OF JESUS CHALLENGED

20 One day as he was teaching the people
in the temple and proclaiming the good
news, the chief priests and the scribes, with
the elders, came 2 and said to him: "Tell us, by
what authority are you doing these things?
Who is it who gave you this authority?"
3 He answered them, "I will also ask you a
question. Tell me, 4 was the baptism of John
from heaven or of human origin?"
5 They discussed it among themselves: "If we
say, 'From heaven,' he will say, 'Why didn't you
believe him?' 6 But if we say, 'Of human origin,'
all the people will stone us, because they are
convinced that John was a prophet." 7 So they
answered that they did not know its origin.
8 And Jesus said to them, "Neither will I tell
you by what authority I do these things."

THE PARABLE OF THE VINEYARD OWNER

9 Now he began to tell the people this parable:
"A man planted a vineyard, leased it to tenant
farmers, and went away for a long time. 10 At
harvest time he sent a servant to the farmers
so that they might give him some fruit from
the vineyard. But the farmers beat him and
sent him away empty-handed. 11 He sent yet
another servant, but they beat that one too,
treated him shamefully, and sent him away
empty-handed. 12 And he sent yet a third, but
they wounded this one too and threw him out.
13 "Then the owner of the vineyard said, 'What
should I do? I will send my beloved son. Perhaps[D] they will respect him.'
14 "But when the tenant farmers saw him,
they discussed it among themselves and said,
'This is the heir. Let's kill him, so that the inheritance will be ours.' 15 So they threw him
out of the vineyard and killed him.
"What then will the owner of the vineyard do
to them? 16 He will come and kill those farmers
and give the vineyard to others."
But when they heard this they said, "That
must never happen!"
17 But he looked at them and said, "Then what
is the meaning of this Scripture:[E]

The stone that the builders rejected
has become the cornerstone?[F]

18 Everyone who falls on that stone will be
broken to pieces, but on whomever it falls, it
will shatter him."
19 Then the scribes and the chief priests
looked for a way to get their hands on him
that very hour, because they knew he had
told this parable against them, but they feared
the people.

GOD AND CAESAR

20 They watched closely and sent spies who
pretended to be righteous,[G] so that they could
catch him in what he said, to hand him over
to the governor's rule and authority. 21 They
questioned him, "Teacher, we know that you
speak and teach correctly, and you don't show

[A] **19:38** Ps 118:26 [B] **19:45** Other mss add *and buying in it* [C] **19:46** Is 56:7; Jr 7:11 [D] **20:13** Other mss add *when they see him*
[E] **20:17** Lit *"What then is this that is written* [F] **20:17** Ps 118:22 [G] **20:20** Or *upright*

partiality[A] but teach truthfully the way of God.
22 Is it lawful for us to pay taxes to Caesar or
not?"

23 But detecting their craftiness, he said to
them,[B] 24 "Show me a denarius.[C] Whose image
and inscription does it have?"

"Caesar's," they said.

25 "Well then," he told them, "give to Caesar
the things that are Caesar's, and to God the
things that are God's."

26 They were not able to catch him in what
he said in public, and being amazed at his answer, they became silent.

THE SADDUCEES AND THE RESURRECTION

27 Some of the Sadducees, who say there is no
resurrection, came up and questioned him:
28 "Teacher, Moses wrote for us that **if a man's
brother** has a wife, and **dies childless, his
brother should take the wife and produce
offspring for his brother.**[D] 29 Now there were
seven brothers. The first took a wife and died
without children. 30 Also the second[E] 31 and
the third took her. In the same way, all seven
died and left no children. 32 Finally, the woman died too. 33 In the resurrection, therefore,
whose wife will the woman be? For all seven
had married her."

34 Jesus told them, "The children of this age
marry and are given in marriage. 35 But those
who are counted worthy to take part in that age
and in the resurrection from the dead neither
marry nor are given in marriage. 36 For they can
no longer die, because they are like angels and
are children of God, since they are children of
the resurrection. 37 Moses even indicated in the
passage about the burning bush that the dead
are raised, where he calls the Lord **the God of
Abraham and the God of Isaac and the God
of Jacob.**[F] 38 He is not the God of the dead but
of the living, because all are living to[G] him."

39 Some of the scribes answered, "Teacher,
you have spoken well." 40 And they no longer
dared to ask him anything.

THE QUESTION ABOUT THE CHRIST

41 Then he said to them, "How can they say
that the Christ is the son of David? 42 For David
himself says in the Book of Psalms:

The Lord declared to my Lord,
'Sit at my right hand
43 **until I make your enemies**
your footstool.'[H]

44 David calls him 'Lord'; how then can the
Christ be his son?"

WARNING AGAINST THE SCRIBES

45 While all the people were listening, he said
to his disciples, 46 "Beware of the scribes, who
want to go around in long robes and who love
greetings in the marketplaces, the best seats
in the synagogues, and the places of honor
at banquets. 47 They devour widows' houses
and say long prayers just for show. These will
receive harsher judgment."[I]

THE WIDOW'S GIFT

21 He looked up and saw the rich dropping
their offerings into the temple treasury.
2 He also saw a poor widow dropping in two
tiny coins.[J] 3 "Truly I tell you," he said, "this
poor widow has put in more than all of them.
4 For all these people have put in gifts out of
their surplus, but she out of her poverty has
put in all she had to live on."

DESTRUCTION OF THE TEMPLE PREDICTED

5 As some were talking about the temple, how
it was adorned with beautiful stones and gifts
dedicated to God, he said, 6 "These things that
you see—the days will come when not one
stone will be left on another that will not be
thrown down."

SIGNS OF THE END OF THE AGE

7 "Teacher," they asked him, "so when will these
things happen? And what will be the sign when
these things are about to take place?"

8 Then he said, "Watch out that you are not
deceived. For many will come in my name,
saying, 'I am he,' and, 'The time is near.' Don't
follow them. 9 When you hear of wars and
rebellions,[K] don't be alarmed. Indeed, it is necessary that these things take place first, but
the end won't come right away."

10 Then he told them: "Nation will be raised
up against nation, and kingdom against kingdom. 11 There will be violent earthquakes,
and famines and plagues in various places,
and there will be terrifying sights and great
signs from heaven. 12 But before all these
things, they will lay their hands on you and

[A] **20:21** Lit *you don't receive a face* [B] **20:23** Other mss add *"Why are you testing me?* [C] **20:24** A denarius = one day's wage
[D] **20:28** Dt 25:5 [E] **20:30** Other mss add *took her as wife, and he died without children* [F] **20:37** Ex 3:6,15 [G] **20:38** Or *with*
[H] **20:42-43** Ps 110:1 [I] **20:47** Or *judgment* [J] **21:2** Lit *two lepta*; the *lepton* was the smallest and least valuable Gk coin in use.
[K] **21:9** Or *insurrections*, or *revolutions*, or *chaos*

persecute you. They will hand you over to
the synagogues and prisons, and you will
be brought before kings and governors because of my name. 13 This will give you an
opportunity to bear witness. 14 Therefore
make up your minds[A] not to prepare your
defense ahead of time, 15 for I will give you
such words and a wisdom that none of your
adversaries will be able to resist or contradict. 16 You will even be betrayed by parents,
brothers, relatives, and friends. They will kill
some of you. 17 You will be hated by everyone because of my name, 18 but not a hair of
your head will be lost. 19 By your endurance,
gain[B] your lives.

THE DESTRUCTION OF JERUSALEM

20 "When you see Jerusalem surrounded by
armies, then recognize that its desolation
has come near. 21 Then those in Judea must
flee to the mountains. Those inside the city
must leave it, and those who are in the country must not enter it, 22 because these are
days of vengeance to fulfill all the things
that are written. 23 Woe to pregnant women
and nursing mothers in those days, for there
will be great distress in the land[C] and wrath
against this people. 24 They will be killed by
the sword[D] and be led captive into all the
nations, and Jerusalem will be trampled by
the Gentiles[E] until the times of the Gentiles
are fulfilled.

THE COMING OF THE SON OF MAN

25 "Then there will be signs in the sun, moon,
and stars; and there will be anguish on the
earth among nations bewildered by the roaring
of the sea and the waves. 26 People will faint
from fear and expectation of the things that
are coming on the world, because the powers
of the heavens will be shaken. 27 Then they
will see the Son of Man coming in a cloud
with power and great glory. 28 But when these
things begin to take place, stand up and lift up
your heads, because your redemption is near."

THE PARABLE OF THE FIG TREE

29 Then he told them a parable: "Look at the
fig tree, and all the trees. 30 As soon as they
put out leaves you can see for yourselves
and recognize that summer is already near.
31 In the same way, when you see these things
happening, recognize[F] that the kingdom of God
is near. 32 Truly I tell you, this generation will
certainly not pass away until all things take
place. 33 Heaven and earth will pass away, but
my words will never pass away.

THE NEED FOR WATCHFULNESS

34 "Be on your guard, so that your minds are
not dulled[G] from carousing,[H] drunkenness,
and worries of life, or that day will come on
you unexpectedly 35 like a trap. For it will come
on all who live on the face of the whole earth.
36 But be alert at all times, praying that you may
have strength[I] to escape all these things that
are going to take place and to stand before
the Son of Man."
37 During the day, he was teaching in the
temple, but in the evening he would go out
and spend the night on what is called the
Mount of Olives. 38 Then all the people would
come early in the morning to hear him in
the temple.

THE PLOT TO KILL JESUS

22 The Festival of Unleavened Bread, which
is called Passover, was approaching.
2 The chief priests and the scribes were looking
for a way to put him to death, because they
were afraid of the people.
3 Then Satan entered Judas, called Iscariot, who was numbered among the Twelve.
4 He went away and discussed with the chief
priests and temple police how he could hand
him over to them. 5 They were glad and agreed
to give him silver.[J] 6 So he accepted the offer
and started looking for a good opportunity
to betray him to them when the crowd was
not present.

PREPARATION FOR PASSOVER

7 Then the Day of Unleavened Bread came when
the Passover lamb had to be sacrificed. 8 Jesus
sent Peter and John, saying, "Go and make
preparations for us to eat the Passover."
9 "Where do you want us to prepare it?"
they asked him.
10 "Listen," he said to them, "when you've entered the city, a man carrying a water jug will
meet you. Follow him into the house he enters.
11 Tell the owner of the house, 'The Teacher
asks you, "Where is the guest room where
I can eat the Passover with my disciples?"'

[A] 21:14 Lit *Therefore place* (determine) *in your hearts* [B] 21:19 Other mss read *endurance, you will gain* [C] 21:23 Or *the earth* [D] 21:24 Lit *will fall by the edge of the sword* [E] 21:24 Or *nations* [F] 21:31 Or *you know* [G] 21:34 Lit *your hearts are not weighed down* [H] 21:34 Or *hangovers* [I] 21:36 Other mss read *you may be counted worthy* [J] 22:5 Or *money*

12 Then he will show you a large, furnished
room upstairs. Make the preparations there."
13 So they went and found it just as he had
told them, and they prepared the Passover.

THE FIRST LORD'S SUPPER

14 When the hour came, he reclined at the table, and the apostles with him. 15 Then he said
to them, "I have fervently desired to eat this
Passover with you before I suffer. 16 For I tell
you, I will not eat it again[A] until it is fulfilled
in the kingdom of God." 17 Then he took a cup,
and after giving thanks, he said, "Take this
and share it among yourselves. 18 For I tell
you, from now on I will not drink of the fruit
of the vine until the kingdom of God comes."
19 And he took bread, gave thanks, broke
it, gave it to them, and said, "This is my body,
which is given for you. Do this in remembrance of me."
20 In the same way he also took the cup
after supper and said, "This cup is the new
covenant in my blood, which is poured out
for you.[B] 21 But look, the hand of the one betraying me is at the table with me. 22 For the
Son of Man will go away as it has been determined, but woe to that man by whom he
is betrayed!"
23 So they began to argue among themselves
which of them it could be who was going to do it.

THE DISPUTE OVER GREATNESS

24 Then a dispute also arose among them about
who should be considered the greatest. 25 But
he said to them, "The kings of the Gentiles lord
it over them, and those who have authority
over them have themselves called[C] 'Bene-
factors.' 26 It is not to be like that among you.
On the contrary, whoever is greatest among
you should become like the youngest, and
whoever leads, like the one serving. 27 For
who is greater, the one at the table or the
one serving? Isn't it the one at the table? But
I am among you as the one who serves. 28 You
are those who stood by me in my trials. 29 I
bestow on you a kingdom, just as my Father
bestowed one on me, 30 so that you may eat
and drink at my table in my kingdom. And
you will sit on thrones judging the twelve
tribes of Israel.

Rest and Reflection | *Surrendering/Submitting to God*

YOUR WILL BE DONE

"Father, if you are willing, take this cup away from me—nevertheless, not my will, but yours, be done." Luke 22:42

No one can ever accuse Jesus of not practicing what he preached.

In showing his followers how to pray, he had instructed them to say, "Your will be done" (Mt 6:10). Here, in the garden of Gethsemane, on the eve of the day he would be savagely beaten, hung on a cross, take the sins of the world upon himself, and be abandoned by God, he prayed the very same prayer.

Jesus wrestled with God. He cried out in agony, the tiny veins under his skin bursting from sheer stress, causing him to look like he was sweating blood (Lk 22:44). Don't make me do this, he essentially pleaded, before adding, "Nevertheless, not my will, but yours, be done."

This is the picture of what a servant of God looks like. This is the prayer that pleases God: Honest—expressing desires and fears—but then submitting all of that to the will of the One who is perfectly wise and good.

Is this how you pray? "Lord, I really want . . ." to be married one day, to have children, to get a better job, to enjoy this vacation, to fulfill this dream, to not be sick, to avoid this trial or crisis . . . *"nevertheless, not my will, but yours, be done"*?

For the next note on *Rest and Reflection*, see John 4:14.

[A] **22:16** Other mss omit *again* [B] **22:19-20** Other mss omit *which is given for you* (v. 19) through the end of v. 20 [C] **22:25** Or *them call themselves*

PETER'S DENIAL PREDICTED

31 "Simon, Simon,[A] look out. Satan has asked to
sift you like wheat. 32 But I have prayed for you
that your faith may not fail. And you, when you
have turned back, strengthen your brothers."
33 "Lord," he told him, "I'm ready to go with
you both to prison and to death."
34 "I tell you, Peter," he said, "the rooster will
not crow today until[B] you deny three times
that you know me."

BE READY FOR TROUBLE

35 He also said to them, "When I sent you out
without money-bag, traveling bag, or sandals,
did you lack anything?"
"Not a thing," they said.
36 Then he said to them, "But now, whoever
has a money-bag should take it, and also
a traveling bag. And whoever doesn't have a
sword should sell his robe and buy one. 37 For
I tell you, what is written must be fulfilled in
me:[C] **And he was counted among the lawless.**[D] Yes, what is written about me is coming
to its fulfillment."
38 "Lord," they said, "look, here are two
swords."
"That is enough!" he told them.

THE PRAYER IN THE GARDEN

39 He went out and made his way as usual to
the Mount of Olives, and the disciples followed him. 40 When he reached the place, he
told them, "Pray that you may not fall into
temptation." 41 Then he withdrew from them
about a stone's throw, knelt down, and began
to pray, 42 "Father, if you are willing, take this
cup away from me — nevertheless, not my
will, but yours, be done."
43 Then an angel from heaven appeared to
him, strengthening him. 44 Being in anguish,
he prayed more fervently, and his sweat became like drops of blood falling to the ground.[E]
45 When he got up from prayer and came to the
disciples, he found them sleeping, exhausted
from their grief. 46 "Why are you sleeping?"
he asked them. "Get up and pray, so that you
won't fall into temptation."

JUDAS'S BETRAYAL OF JESUS

47 While he was still speaking, suddenly a mob
came, and one of the Twelve named Judas
was leading them. He came near Jesus to kiss
him, 48 but Jesus said to him, "Judas, are you
betraying the Son of Man with a kiss?"
49 When those around him saw what was
going to happen, they asked, "Lord, should we
strike with the sword?" 50 Then one of them
struck the high priest's servant and cut off
his right ear.
51 But Jesus responded, "No more of this!" And
touching his ear, he healed him. 52 Then Jesus
said to the chief priests, temple police, and the
elders who had come for him, "Have you come
out with swords and clubs as if I were a criminal?[F] 53 Every day while I was with you in the
temple, you never laid a hand on me. But this is
your hour — and the dominion of darkness."

PETER DENIES HIS LORD

54 They seized him, led him away, and brought
him into the high priest's house. Meanwhile
Peter was following at a distance. 55 They lit
a fire in the middle of the courtyard and sat
down together, and Peter sat among them.
56 When a servant saw him sitting in the light,
and looked closely at him, she said, "This man
was with him too."
57 But he denied it: "Woman, I don't know
him."
58 After a little while, someone else saw him
and said, "You're one of them too."
"Man, I am not!" Peter said.
59 About an hour later, another kept insisting, "This man was certainly with him, since
he's also a Galilean."
60 But Peter said, "Man, I don't know what
you're talking about!" Immediately, while he
was still speaking, a rooster crowed. 61 Then
the Lord turned and looked at Peter. So Peter
remembered the word of the Lord, how he
had said to him, "Before the rooster crows
today, you will deny me three times." 62 And
he went outside and wept bitterly.

JESUS MOCKED AND BEATEN

63 The men who were holding Jesus started
mocking and beating him. 64 After blindfolding
him, they kept[G] asking, "Prophesy! Who was it
that hit you?" 65 And they were saying many
other blasphemous things to him.

JESUS FACES THE SANHEDRIN

66 When daylight came, the elders[H] of the
people, both the chief priests and the scribes,

[A] **22:31** Other mss read *Then the Lord said, "Simon, Simon* [B] **22:34** Other mss read *before* [C] **22:37** Or *it is necessary that what is written be fulfilled in me* [D] **22:37** Is 53:12 [E] **22:43-44** Other mss omit vv. 43-44 [F] **22:52** Lit *as against a thief*, or *a bandit* [G] **22:64** Other mss add *striking him on the face and* [H] **22:66** Or *council of elders*

My Story | Marcus

In college, I was an easygoing agnostic with atheistic tendencies. I discovered that admitting I wasn't sure if God existed gave me a lot of freedom to do whatever I wanted. Part of me actually thought that if God was that easy to manipulate, he couldn't possibly exist. Looking back, I realize I was playing a dangerous game with my life. Fortunately for me, God was a better player than I was.

Since my school was fairly small and located in a rural town, students had a lot of interaction with the community. Those of us who were not able to travel home for holidays were often hosted by local families. Those home-cooked meals were memorable.

For Easter one year, I joined a family for the day, which included an early church service and then a community brunch involving many students and host families. Hearing the somewhat familiar story of the resurrection of Jesus got my attention in a way it hadn't before. I remember having the unexpected thought that if Jesus had really risen from the dead, I might have to reevaluate my stance on God. It unsettled me.

After church, my adopted family and I joined others for a wonderful luncheon and several hours of relaxed conversation. After the meal, as the topics around our table flowed from school experiences to future plans, someone at the table asked students about their hopes and dreams. That led to some funny comments. Then the young mom in my host family turned to me and said, "I noticed you looked puzzled several times during the sermon this morning. What does it mean to you when the preacher says, 'God loves you'?"

The most honest answer I could come up with was that while I did not believe in God, I also knew I could learn some things from Christianity. She didn't seem at all offended by my reply. In fact, she smiled and said, "While you're figuring that out, Marcus, I want you to know that our family loves you. I hope you can learn to see our love as an extension of God's love for you."

At that moment, I still felt far from the faith that seemed so real in her life, yet I also sensed something real was being offered to me. I was drawn to that family's unconditional love. They accepted me even though I was reluctant to share their faith. But their love gradually demolished my defenses and disarmed my excuses for keeping God at a distance.

I now chuckle when I tell others that I finally admitted God existed when someone convinced me they would keep loving me as long as it took me to realize God loved me.

convened and brought him before their Sanhedrin. 67 They said, "If you are the Messiah,
tell us."
But he said to them, "If I do tell you, you
will not believe. 68 And if I ask you, you will
not answer. 69 But from now on, the Son of
Man will be seated at the right hand of the
power of God."
70 They all asked, "Are you, then, the Son of
God?"
And he said to them, "You say that I am."
71 "Why do we need any more testimony,"
they said, "since we've heard it ourselves from
his mouth?"

JESUS FACES PILATE

23 Then their whole assembly rose up and
brought him before Pilate. 2 They began
to accuse him, saying, "We found this man
misleading our nation, opposing payment of
taxes to Caesar, and saying that he himself is
the Messiah, a king."
3 So Pilate asked him, "Are you the king of
the Jews?"
He answered him, "You say so."[A]
4 Pilate then told the chief priests and the
crowds, "I find no grounds for charging this
man."
5 But they kept insisting, "He stirs up the
people, teaching throughout all Judea, from
Galilee where he started even to here."

JESUS FACES HEROD ANTIPAS

6 When Pilate heard this,[B] he asked if the man
was a Galilean. 7 Finding that he was under
Herod's jurisdiction, he sent him to Herod,
who was also in Jerusalem during those days.
8 Herod was very glad to see Jesus; for a long

[A] **23:3** Or *"That is true."* [B] **23:6** Other mss read *heard "Galilee"*

time he had wanted to see him because he had heard about him and was hoping to see some miracle[A] performed by him. 9 So he kept asking him questions, but Jesus did not answer him. 10 The chief priests and the scribes stood by, vehemently accusing him. 11 Then Herod, with his soldiers, treated him with contempt, mocked him, dressed him in bright clothing, and sent him back to Pilate. 12 That very day Herod and Pilate became friends.[B] Previously, they had been enemies.

JESUS OR BARABBAS

13 Pilate called together the chief priests, the leaders, and the people, 14 and said to them, "You have brought me this man as one who misleads the people. But in fact, after examining him in your presence, I have found no grounds to charge this man with those things you accuse him of. 15 Neither has Herod, because he sent him back to us. Clearly, he has done nothing to deserve death. 16 Therefore, I will have him whipped[C] and then release him."[D]

18 Then they all cried out together, "Take this man away! Release Barabbas to us!" 19 (He had been thrown into prison for a rebellion that had taken place in the city, and for murder.)

20 Wanting to release Jesus, Pilate addressed them again, 21 but they kept shouting, "Crucify! Crucify him!"

22 A third time he said to them, "Why? What has this man done wrong? I have found in him no grounds for the death penalty. Therefore, I will have him whipped and then release him."

23 But they kept up the pressure, demanding with loud voices that he be crucified, and their voices[E] won out. 24 So Pilate decided to grant their demand 25 and released the one they were asking for, who had been thrown into prison for rebellion and murder. But he handed Jesus over to their will.

THE WAY TO THE CROSS

26 As they led him away, they seized Simon, a Cyrenian, who was coming in from the country, and laid the cross on him to carry behind Jesus. 27 A large crowd of people followed him, including women who were mourning and lamenting him. 28 But turning to them, Jesus said, "Daughters of Jerusalem, do not weep for me, but weep for yourselves and your children. 29 Look, the days are coming when they will say, 'Blessed are the women without children, the wombs that never bore, and the breasts that never nursed!' 30 Then they will begin **to say to the mountains, 'Fall on us!' and to the hills, 'Cover us!'**[F] 31 For if they do these things when the wood is green, what will happen when it is dry?"

CRUCIFIED BETWEEN TWO CRIMINALS

32 Two others — criminals — were also led away to be executed with him. 33 When they arrived at the place called The Skull, they crucified him there, along with the criminals, one on the right and one on the left. 34 Then Jesus said, "Father, forgive them, because they do not know what they are doing."[G] And they divided his clothes and cast lots.

35 The people stood watching, and even the leaders were scoffing: "He saved others; let him save himself if this is God's Messiah, the Chosen One!" 36 The soldiers also mocked him. They came offering him sour wine 37 and said, "If you are the King of the Jews, save yourself!"

38 An inscription was above him:[H] THIS IS THE KING OF THE JEWS.

39 Then one of the criminals hanging there began to yell insults at[I] him: "Aren't you the Messiah? Save yourself and us!"

40 But the other answered, rebuking him: "Don't you even fear God, since you are undergoing the same punishment? 41 We are punished justly, because we're getting back what we deserve for the things we did, but this man has done nothing wrong." 42 Then he said, "Jesus, remember me[J] when you come into your kingdom."

43 And he said to him, "Truly I tell you, today you will be with me in paradise."

THE DEATH OF JESUS

44 It was now about noon,[K] and darkness came over the whole land[L] until three,[M] 45 because the sun's light failed.[N] The curtain of the sanctuary was split down the middle. 46 And Jesus called out with a loud voice, "Father, **into your hands I entrust my spirit**."[O] Saying this, he breathed his last.

47 When the centurion saw what happened,

[A] 23:8 Or *sign* [B] 23:12 Lit *friends with one another* [C] 23:16 Gk *paideuo*; to discipline or "teach a lesson" [D] 23:16 Some mss include v. 17: *For according to the festival he had to release someone to them.* [E] 23:23 Other mss add *and those of the chief priests* [F] 23:30 Hs 10:8 [G] 23:34 Other mss omit *Then Jesus said, "Father, forgive them, because they do not know what they are doing."* [H] 23:38 Other mss add *written in Greek, Latin, and Hebrew letters* [I] 23:39 Or *began to blaspheme* [J] 23:42 Other mss add *Lord* [K] 23:44 Lit *about the sixth hour* [L] 23:44 Or *whole earth* [M] 23:44 Lit *the ninth hour* [N] 23:45 Other mss read *three, and the sun was darkened* [O] 23:46 Ps 31:5

RESTORATION THEMES

R	Rest and Reflection	*Consuming Spiritual Nourishment—4:14* *Honestly Evaluating Yourself—8:32* *Resting in Christ—15:4-5*
E	Eternal Perspective	*Biblical Joy—2:2-3* *God's Love—3:16* *Death's Defeat/Resurrection—11:35* *Heaven and Hell—14:1-3* *Biblical Peace—16:33* *God's Work in Us—17:3*
S	Support	*Holy Spirit's Counsel—16:13*
T	Thanksgiving and Contentment	*Praise for God's Security—10:27-29* *Praise for Salvation—14:6* *Comparisons—21:22*
O	Other-centeredness	*Being Unselfish—15:12-13*
R	Relationships	*Relating to Church Family—13:34-35* *Working for Unity in the Church—17:23*
E	Exercise of Faith	*Sharing Faith/Gospel—1:35-37* *Staying Close to Christ—6:66-68* *Enduring Suffering—9:1-2* *Trusting God—12:37*

PROLOGUE

1 In the beginning was the Word, and the Word
was with God, and the Word was God. 2 He
was with God in the beginning. 3 All things were
created through him, and apart from him not
one thing was created that has been created.
4 In him was life,[A] and that life was the light of
men. 5 That light shines in the darkness, and
yet the darkness did not overcome[B] it.

6 There was a man sent from God whose name
was John. 7 He came as a witness to testify about
the light, so that all might believe through him.[C]
8 He was not the light, but he came to testify
about the light. 9 The true light that gives light
to everyone, was coming into the world.[D]

10 He was in the world, and the world was
created through him, and yet the world did
not recognize him. 11 He came to his own, and
his own people did not receive him. 12 But to all
who did receive him, he gave them the right
to be[E] children of God, to those who believe
in his name, 13 who were born, not of natural
descent,[F] or of the will of the flesh, or of the
will of man,[G] but of God.

14 The Word became flesh and dwelt[H] among
us. We observed his glory, the glory as the
one and only Son[I] from the Father, full of
grace and truth. 15 (John testified concerning him and exclaimed, "This was the one
of whom I said, 'The one coming after me
ranks ahead of me, because he existed before
me.' ") 16 Indeed, we have all received grace
upon[J] grace from his fullness, 17 for the law
was given through Moses; grace and truth
came through Jesus Christ. 18 No one has
ever seen God. The one and only Son, who is
himself God and is at the Father's side[K] —he
has revealed him.

JOHN THE BAPTIST'S TESTIMONY

19 This was John's testimony when the Jews
from Jerusalem sent priests and Levites to
ask him, "Who are you?"

20 He didn't deny it but confessed: "I am not
the Messiah."

21 "What then?" they asked him. "Are you
Elijah?"

"I am not," he said.

E Exercise of Faith | *Sharing Faith/Gospel*

POINTING OTHERS TO CHRIST

"The next day, John was standing with two of his disciples. When he saw Jesus passing by, he said, 'Look, the Lamb of God!' The two disciples heard him say this and followed Jesus." John 1:35-37

When John the Baptist burst on the scene, people showed up in droves to listen to this strange, bug-eating preacher dressed in animal skins. Despite John's blunt, sin-denouncing sermons, the crowds kept growing. Israel's religious leaders make the trek out into the desert too. Like everyone else, they wanted to know: Who *is* this wild man?

John was quick to discourage anyone who tried to make a big deal about him, saying, I'm just "a voice . . . crying out in the wilderness" (Jn 1:23).

When Jesus joined the festivities, John made clear, "*He's* the One I came to talk about. *He's* the One you should be making a fuss over." After baptizing Christ reluctantly—John said he didn't feel worthy for such a task—he started encouraging his loyal followers to follow Jesus instead.

With all the political battles of right versus left and with people so disappointed in the church and fellow Christians, we must keep centered on Jesus as the focus of our faith.

For the next note on *Exercise of Faith*, see John 6:66-68.

[A] **1:3-4** Other punctuation is possible: . . . *not one thing was created. What was created in him was life* [B] **1:5** Or *grasp*, or *comprehend*, or *overtake*; Jn 12:35 [C] **1:7** Or *it (the light)* [D] **1:9** Or *The true light who comes into the world gives light to everyone*, or *The true light enlightens everyone coming into the world.* [E] **1:12** Or *become* [F] **1:13** Lit *blood* [G] **1:13** Or *not of human lineage, or of human capacity, or of human volition* [H] **1:14** Or *and dwelt in a tent*; lit *and tabernacled* [I] **1:14** *Son* is implied from the reference to the Father and from Gk usage. [J] **1:16** Or *in place of* [K] **1:18** Other mss read *The one and only Son, who is at the Father's side*

"Are you the Prophet?"

"No," he answered.

22 "Who are you, then?" they asked. "We need to give an answer to those who sent us. What can you tell us about yourself?"

23 He said, "I am a **voice of one crying out in the wilderness: Make straight the way of the Lord**[A] — just as Isaiah the prophet said."

24 Now they had been sent from the Pharisees. 25 So they asked him, "Why then do you baptize if you aren't the Messiah, or Elijah, or the Prophet?"

26 "I baptize with[B] water," John answered them. "Someone stands among you, but you don't know him. 27 He is the one coming after me,[C] whose sandal strap I'm not worthy to untie." 28 All this happened in Bethany[D] across the Jordan, where John was baptizing.

THE LAMB OF GOD

29 The next day John saw Jesus coming toward him and said, "Here is the Lamb of God, who takes away the sin of the world! 30 This is the one I told you about: 'After me comes a man who ranks ahead of me, because he existed before me.' 31 I didn't know him, but I came baptizing with water so he might be revealed to Israel." 32 And John testified, "I saw the Spirit descending from heaven like a dove, and he rested on him. 33 I didn't know him, but he who sent me to baptize with water told me, 'The one you see the Spirit descending and resting on — he is the one who baptizes with the Holy Spirit.' 34 I have seen and testified that this is the Son of God."[E]

35 The next day, John was standing with two of his disciples. 36 When he saw Jesus passing by, he said, "Look, the Lamb of God!"

37 The two disciples heard him say this and followed Jesus. 38 When Jesus turned and noticed them following him, he asked them, "What are you looking for?"

They said to him, "Rabbi" (which means "Teacher"), "where are you staying?"

39 "Come and you'll see," he replied. So they went and saw where he was staying, and they stayed with him that day. It was about four in the afternoon.[F]

40 Andrew, Simon Peter's brother, was one of the two who heard John and followed him. 41 He first found his own brother Simon and told him, "We have found the Messiah"[G] (which is translated "the Christ"), 42 and he brought Simon to Jesus.

When Jesus saw him, he said, "You are Simon, son of John.[H] You will be called Cephas" (which is translated "Peter"[I]).

PHILIP AND NATHANAEL

43 The next day Jesus[J] decided to leave for Galilee. He found Philip and told him, "Follow me."

44 Now Philip was from Bethsaida, the hometown of Andrew and Peter. 45 Philip found Nathanael and told him, "We have found the one Moses wrote about in the law (and so did the prophets): Jesus the son of Joseph, from Nazareth."

46 "Can anything good come out of Nazareth?" Nathanael asked him.

"Come and see," Philip answered.

47 Then Jesus saw Nathanael coming toward him and said about him, "Here truly is an Israelite in whom there is no deceit."

48 "How do you know me?" Nathanael asked.

"Before Philip called you, when you were under the fig tree, I saw you," Jesus answered.

49 "Rabbi," Nathanael replied, "You are the Son of God; you are the King of Israel!"

50 Jesus responded to him, "Do you believe because I told you I saw you under the fig tree? You will see greater things than this." 51 Then he said, "Truly I tell you, you will see heaven opened and the angels of God ascending and descending on the Son of Man."

THE FIRST SIGN: TURNING WATER INTO WINE

2 On the third day a wedding took place in Cana of Galilee. Jesus's mother was there, and 2 Jesus and his disciples were invited to the wedding as well. 3 When the wine ran out, Jesus's mother told him, "They don't have any wine."

4 "What does that have to do with you and me,[K] woman?" Jesus asked. "My hour has not yet come."

5 "Do whatever he tells you," his mother told the servants.

6 Now six stone water jars had been set there for Jewish purification. Each contained twenty or thirty gallons.[L]

[A] **1:23** Is 40:3 [B] **1:26** Or *in*, also in vv. 31,33 [C] **1:27** Other mss add *who came before me* [D] **1:28** Other mss read *in Bethabara* [E] **1:34** Other mss read *is the Chosen One of God* [F] **1:39** Lit *about the tenth hour* [G] **1:41** Both Hb *Messiah* and Gk *Christos* mean "anointed one" [H] **1:42** Other mss read *"Simon, son of Jonah* [I] **1:42** Both Aramaic *Cephas* and Gk *Petros* mean "rock" [J] **1:43** Lit *he* [K] **2:4** Or *"You and I see things differently*; lit *"What to me and to you*; Mt 8:29; Mk 1:24; 5:7; Lk 8:28 [L] **2:6** Lit *two or three measures*

[7] "Fill the jars with water," Jesus told them.
So they filled them to the brim. [8] Then he said
to them, "Now draw some out and take it to
the headwaiter."[A] And they did.
[9] When the headwaiter tasted the water
(after it had become wine), he did not know
where it came from — though the servants
who had drawn the water knew. He called the
groom [10] and told him, "Everyone sets out the
fine wine first, then, after people are drunk,
the inferior. But you have kept the fine wine
until now."
[11] Jesus did this, the first of his signs, in Cana
of Galilee. He revealed his glory, and his disciples believed in him.
[12] After this, he went down to Capernaum,
together with his mother, his brothers, and his
disciples, and they stayed there only a few days.

CLEANSING THE TEMPLE

[13] The Jewish Passover was near, and so Jesus
went up to Jerusalem. [14] In the temple he found
people selling oxen, sheep, and doves, and he
also found the money changers sitting there.
[15] After making a whip out of cords, he drove
everyone out of the temple with their sheep
and oxen. He also poured out the money changers' coins and overturned the tables. [16] He told
those who were selling doves, "Get these things
out of here! Stop turning my Father's house
into a marketplace!"[B]
[17] And his disciples remembered that it is written: **Zeal for your house will consume me.**[C]
[18] So the Jews replied to him, "What sign will
you show us for doing these things?"
[19] Jesus answered, "Destroy this temple,[D]
and I will raise it up in three days."
[20] Therefore the Jews said, "This temple took
forty-six years to build,[E] and will you raise it
up in three days?"
[21] But he was speaking about the temple of
his body. [22] So when he was raised from the
dead, his disciples remembered that he had
said this, and they believed the Scripture and
the statement Jesus had made.
[23] While he was in Jerusalem during the
Passover Festival, many believed in his name
when they saw the signs he was doing. [24] Jesus,
however, would not entrust himself to them,
since he knew them all [25] and because he did

Eternal Perspective | *Biblical Joy*

WEDDING JOY

"Jesus and his disciples were invited to the wedding as well. When the wine ran out, Jesus's mother told him, 'They don't have any wine.'" John 2:2-3

Every wedding seems to have a snafu—a groomsman locks his knees and passes out, the three-year-old ring bearer refuses to go down the aisle, or the chocolate fountain stops flowing.

At this Jewish wedding in Cana of Galilee, someone under-ordered on the wine or underestimated the crowd. Either way, in a culture where hospitality was everything and weddings were a bigger production than they are even in our time, this was a certified disaster.

In brief, Mary informed Jesus. He then performed his very first miracle (John calls them "signs"). He turned six giant stone jars full of water (for ceremonial washing) into 120–180 gallons of the most exquisite wine anyone had ever tasted.

The water jars were requirements for ceremonial purity under Moses's law. And in the Bible, wine is symbolic of joy. Even as Jesus graciously rescued this wedding, he seemed to be sending a larger message: "In the place of the old law with its exacting, taxing rituals, I'm ushering in a new day where joy overflows!"

If your relationship with Jesus has become tired, worn, or burdensome, rediscover the joy that he wants to bring.

For the next note on *Eternal Perspective*, see John 3:16.

[A] **2:8** Lit *ruler of the table* [B] **2:16** Lit *a house of business* [C] **2:17** Ps 69:9 [D] **2:19** Or *sanctuary*, also in vv. 20,21 [E] **2:20** Or *was built forty-six years ago*

My Story | Mickey

A decade ago, I was suffering from a terrible depression that led me to start thinking about suicide. During that time, I went online to talk with others about my problems. Although most of the advice didn't help much, one of those people told me a little bit about Jesus. People encouraged me to pray, but I wondered who to pray to. It was hard to imagine talking out loud to God. But one of the things I had discovered about Jesus is that he told his followers to pray in his name. I finally realized why most prayers I had heard others pray ended with "In Jesus's name." My own first prayers started, "So, God, whoever you are . . ." and ended with "In Jesus's name." And since I really didn't know how to pray, I just told God what was on my mind. It was more like a conversation, with some long times of silence when I felt not so much that God was talking to me but that he was moving close to me.

Eventually, I began to realize that even the person who had told me some about Jesus couldn't really help me. It seemed as though the only one who could help me was the Lord himself. I felt like I couldn't trust people, so I turned to him. I started reading the stories of Jesus's life in the Bible and gradually felt he was someone who would understand me. My praying became talking to Jesus every day, asking him to help me and change me. When I got to John 3:16 and read it for myself the first time, I suddenly knew it told me what I needed to do—believe in Jesus. So I did.

It was so simple I laughed. And then I cried from the relief. I knew I had been looking all along for someone who would love me as a mixed-up, angry, and even suicidal person. But as soon as I realized Jesus really loved me, I didn't want to be any of those things anymore.

Now I'm doing a lot better, and I'm no longer suicidal. I trust people more, and the Lord has changed me so much! Thanks to Jesus, I no longer want to die! Now I've got eternal life to look forward to and lots more to learn about Jesus in this life, just like John 3:16 says.

not need anyone to testify about man; for he
himself knew what was in man.

JESUS AND NICODEMUS

3 There was a man from the Pharisees named
Nicodemus, a ruler of the Jews. 2 This man
came to him at night and said, "Rabbi, we know
that you are a teacher who has come from
God, for no one could perform these signs
you do unless God were with him."
3 Jesus replied, "Truly I tell you, unless someone is born again,[A] he cannot see the kingdom
of God."
4 "How can anyone be born when he is old?"
Nicodemus asked him. "Can he enter his mother's womb a second time and be born?"
5 Jesus answered, "Truly I tell you, unless
someone is born of water and the Spirit, he
cannot enter the kingdom of God. 6 Whatever
is born of the flesh is flesh, and whatever is
born of the Spirit is spirit. 7 Do not be amazed
that I told you that you must be born again.
8 The wind blows where it pleases, and you
hear its sound, but you don't know where it
comes from or where it is going. So it is with
everyone born of the Spirit."
9 "How can these things be?" asked Nicodemus.
10 "Are you a teacher[B] of Israel and don't
know these things?" Jesus replied. 11 "Truly
I tell you, we speak what we know and we
testify to what we have seen, but you do not
accept our testimony. 12 If I have told you about
earthly things and you don't believe, how will
you believe if I tell you about heavenly things?
13 No one has ascended into heaven except
the one who descended from heaven — the
Son of Man.[C]
14 "Just as Moses lifted up the snake in the
wilderness, so the Son of Man must be lifted up,
15 so that everyone who believes in him may[D]
have eternal life. 16 For God loved the world in
this way:[E] He gave[F] his one and only Son, so that 
everyone who believes in him will not perish
but have eternal life. 17 For God did not send
his Son into the world to condemn the world,
but to save the world through him. 18 Anyone
who believes in him is not condemned, but

[A] **3:3** Or *from above*, also in v. 7 [B] **3:10** Or *the teacher* [C] **3:13** Other mss add *who is in heaven* [D] **3:15** Other mss add *not perish, but* [E] **3:16** Or *this much* [F] **3:16** Or *For in this way God loved the world, and so he gave*, or *For God so loved the world that he gave*

anyone who does not believe is already condemned, because he has not believed in the
name of the one and only Son of God. 19 This
is the judgment: The light has come into the
world, and people loved darkness rather than
the light because their deeds were evil. 20 For
everyone who does evil hates the light and
avoids it,[A] so that his deeds may not be exposed. 21 But anyone who lives by[B] the truth
comes to the light, so that his works may be
shown to be accomplished by God."

JESUS AND JOHN THE BAPTIST

22 After this, Jesus and his disciples went to
the Judean countryside, where he spent time
with them and baptized.
23 John also was baptizing in Aenon near
Salim, because there was plenty of water
there. People were coming and being baptized, 24 since John had not yet been thrown
into prison.
25 Then a dispute arose between John's disciples and a Jew[C] about purification. 26 So they
came to John and told him, "Rabbi, the one you
testified about, and who was with you across
the Jordan, is baptizing — and everyone is
going to him."
27 John responded, "No one can receive
anything unless it has been given to him
from heaven. 28 You yourselves can testify
that I said, 'I am not the Messiah, but I've
been sent ahead of him.' 29 He who has the
bride is the groom. But the groom's friend,
who stands by and listens for him, rejoices
greatly[D] at the groom's voice. So this joy of
mine is complete. 30 He must increase, but I
must decrease." *

THE ONE FROM HEAVEN

31 The one who comes from above is above
all. The one who is from the earth is earthly
and speaks in earthly terms.[E] The one who
comes from heaven is above all. 32 He testifies to what he has seen and heard, and yet
no one accepts his testimony. 33 The one who
has accepted his testimony has affirmed
that God is true. 34 For the one whom God
sent speaks God's words, since he[F] gives
the Spirit without measure. 35 The Father
loves the Son and has given all things into
his hands. 36 The one who believes in the Son
has eternal life, but the one who rejects the
Son[G] will not see life; instead, the wrath of
God remains on him.

Eternal Perspective | *God's Love*

THE GIFT

"For God loved the world in this way: He gave his one and only Son, so that everyone who believes in him will not perish but have eternal life." John 3:16

This has to be the most famous Bible verse. We surely can't think of a Scripture more breathtaking.

The love of God for the world. Not divine sentimentality that sits back and feels pity from afar. No, God's love culminated in him doing the unthinkable: "He gave his one and only Son." He sent Jesus into the world he loves.

This eternal Word (Jn 1:1) stepped out of eternity into time (1:14). He came to reveal God—that is, to show us what the Almighty is like (1:18). The Son's mission was to keep us from perishing, to give us "eternal life."

Understand, eternal life isn't some abstract, future life—*after* death. It begins *now*. It's a relationship with God *now* (17:3). It's a life full of "abundance" *now* (10:10).

"Everyone" is encouraged to believe this announcement. Bank on it. Put your trust in the One who said it. If you haven't given yourself completely to Jesus, accept his gift of eternal life. If you already have this life from God who is in love with this lost world, fall on your face in gratitude and wonder.

For the next note on *Eternal Perspective*, see John 11:35.

[A] **3:20** Lit *and does not come to the light* [B] **3:21** Lit *who does* [C] **3:25** Other mss read *and the Jews* [D] **3:29** Lit *with joy rejoices* [E] **3:31** Or *of earthly things* [F] **3:34** Other mss read *since God* [G] **3:36** Or *refuses to believe in the Son*, or *disobeys the Son*

JESUS AND THE SAMARITAN WOMAN

4 When Jesus[A] learned that the Pharisees
had heard he was making and baptizing
more disciples than John [2] (though Jesus himself was not baptizing, but his disciples were),
[3] he left Judea and went again to Galilee. [4] He
had to travel through Samaria; [5] so he came
to a town of Samaria called Sychar near the
property[B] that Jacob had given his son Joseph.
[6] Jacob's well was there, and Jesus, worn out
from his journey, sat down at the well. It was
about noon.[C]

[7] A woman of Samaria came to draw water.
"Give me a drink," Jesus said to her, [8] because
his disciples had gone into town to buy food.
[9] "How is it that you, a Jew, ask for a drink
from me, a Samaritan woman?" she asked him.
For Jews do not associate with[D] Samaritans.[E]
[10] Jesus answered, "If you knew the gift
of God, and who is saying to you, 'Give me a
drink,' you would ask him, and he would give
you living water."
[11] "Sir," said the woman, "you don't even have
a bucket, and the well is deep. So where do you
get this 'living water'? [12] You aren't greater
than our father Jacob, are you? He gave us
the well and drank from it himself, as did his
sons and livestock."
[13] Jesus said, "Everyone who drinks from
this water will get thirsty again. [14] But whoever drinks from the water that I will give him
will never get thirsty again. In fact, the water
I will give him will become a well[F] of water
springing up in him for eternal life."
[15] "Sir," the woman said to him, "give me this
water so that I won't get thirsty and come here
to draw water."
[16] "Go call your husband," he told her, "and
come back here."
[17] "I don't have a husband," she answered.
"You have correctly said, 'I don't have a
husband,'" Jesus said. [18] "For you've had five
husbands, and the man you now have is not
your husband. What you have said is true."
[19] "Sir," the woman replied, "I see that you
are a prophet. [20] Our fathers worshiped on this
mountain, but you Jews say that the place to
worship is in Jerusalem."
[21] Jesus told her, "Believe me, woman, an
hour is coming when you will worship the

Rest and Reflection | *Consuming Spiritual Nourishment*

THIRSTY PEOPLE

"But whoever drinks from the water that I will give him will never get thirsty again. In fact, the water I will give him will become a well of water springing up in him for eternal life." John 4:14

For those who live in Western, first-world nations, *thirst* is not an everyday problem. If we want to sip some clean water, it's right there. Hot or cold? Just turn the knob. Or grab a water bottle. Or stick your glass under the dispenser on the refrigerator door and press the button. Would you like some ice with that? Cubes or crushed?

Contrast this with most of the world throughout history. Water has been a serious issue. And in many places still, getting a drink takes a lot of effort. You'll probably have to hike to a well, river, or spring. Then, you'll need to boil the water you've fetched. You'll work up a serious thirst just trying to quench your thirst!

So when Jesus talked about thirst to this Samaritan woman at Jacob's well near Sychar, his words resonated. And when he made the conversation about *spiritual* thirst and how he could quench the aching dryness in her soul, everything clicked.

Jesus makes a remarkable claim here. He wants to satisfy us internally and eternally. The outlandish promise? Take a drink—become a well.

For the next note on *Rest and Reflection*, see John 8:32.

[A] **4:1** Other mss read *the Lord* [B] **4:5** Lit *piece of land* [C] **4:6** Lit *about the sixth hour* [D] **4:9** Or *do not share vessels with*
[E] **4:9** Other mss omit *For Jews do not associate with Samaritans.* [F] **4:14** Or *spring*

Father neither on this mountain nor in Jerusalem. 22 You Samaritans worship what you do not know. We worship what we do know, because salvation is from the Jews. 23 But an hour is coming, and is now here, when the true worshipers will worship the Father in Spirit and in truth.[A] Yes, the Father wants such people to worship him. 24 God is spirit, and those who worship him must worship in Spirit and in truth."

25 The woman said to him, "I know that the Messiah is coming" (who is called Christ). "When he comes, he will explain everything to us."

26 Jesus told her, "I, the one speaking to you, am he."

THE RIPENED HARVEST

27 Just then his disciples arrived, and they were amazed that he was talking with a woman. Yet no one said, "What do you want?" or "Why are you talking with her?"

28 Then the woman left her water jar, went into town, and told the people, 29 "Come, see a man who told me everything I ever did. Could this be the Messiah?" 30 They left the town and made their way to him.

31 In the meantime the disciples kept urging him, "Rabbi, eat something."

32 But he said, "I have food to eat that you don't know about."

33 The disciples said to one another, "Could someone have brought him something to eat?"

34 "My food is to do the will of him who sent me and to finish his work," Jesus told them. 35 "Don't you say, 'There are still four more months, and then comes the harvest'? Listen to what I'm telling you: Open[B] your eyes and look at the fields, because they are ready[C] for harvest. 36 The reaper is already receiving pay and gathering fruit for eternal life, so that the sower and reaper can rejoice together. 37 For in this case the saying is true: 'One sows and another reaps.' 38 I sent you to reap what you didn't labor for; others have labored, and you have benefited from[D] their labor."

THE SAVIOR OF THE WORLD

39 Now many Samaritans from that town believed in him because of what the woman said[E] when she testified, "He told me everything I ever did." 40 So when the Samaritans came to him, they asked him to stay with them, and he stayed there two days. 41 Many more believed because of what he said.[F] 42 And they told the woman, "We no longer believe because of what you said, since we have heard for ourselves and know that this really is the Savior of the world."[G]

A GALILEAN WELCOME

43 After two days he left there for Galilee. 44 (Jesus himself had testified that a prophet has no honor in his own country.) 45 When they entered Galilee, the Galileans welcomed him because they had seen everything he did in Jerusalem during the festival. For they also had gone to the festival.

THE SECOND SIGN: HEALING AN OFFICIAL'S SON

46 He went again to Cana of Galilee, where he had turned the water into wine. There was a certain royal official whose son was ill at Capernaum. 47 When this man heard that Jesus had come from Judea into Galilee, he went to him and pleaded with him to come down and heal his son, since he was about to die.

48 Jesus told him, "Unless you people see signs and wonders, you will not believe."

49 "Sir," the official said to him, "come down before my boy dies."

50 "Go," Jesus told him, "your son will live." The man believed what[H] Jesus said to him and departed.

51 While he was still going down, his servants met him saying that his boy was alive. 52 He asked them at what time he got better. "Yesterday at one in the afternoon[I] the fever left him," they answered. 53 The father realized this was the very hour at which Jesus had told him, "Your son will live." So he himself believed, along with his whole household.

54 Now this was also the second sign Jesus performed after he came from Judea to Galilee.

THE THIRD SIGN: HEALING THE SICK

5 After this, a Jewish festival took place, and Jesus went up to Jerusalem. 2 By the Sheep Gate in Jerusalem there is a pool, called Bethesda[J] in Aramaic, which has five colonnades. 3 Within these lay a large number of the disabled — blind, lame, and paralyzed.[K]

[A] **4:23** Or *in spirit and truth*, also in v. 24 [B] **4:35** Lit *Raise* [C] **4:35** Lit *white* [D] **4:38** Lit *you have entered into* [E] **4:39** Lit *because of the woman's word* [F] **4:41** Lit *because of his word* [G] **4:42** Other mss add *, the Messiah* [H] **4:50** Lit *the word* [I] **4:52** Lit *at the seventh hour* [J] **5:2** Some mss read *Bethzatha*; other mss read *Bethsaida* [K] **5:3** Some mss include vv. 3b-4: *— waiting for the moving of the water, 4because an angel would go down into the pool from time to time and stir up the water. Then the first one who got in after the water was stirred up recovered from whatever ailment he had.*

Woman at the Well | Restoration Profile

JOHN 4:1-43

She came to fill her water jug and probably avoid seeing anyone but left with her life brimming with living water and anxious to tell others. Her story represents the deeply personal and shockingly persistent nature of God's restoring work. As an aside, Jesus used the occasion of their conversation to teach some profound lessons on the nature of worship. His words led to transformation in her life, throughout her village, and countless lives and villages ever since.

Jesus immediately affirmed this Samaritan woman's dignity by ignoring her gender, race, and questionable moral status and addressing her with a simple request. "Give me a drink" (Jn 4:7) may sound abrupt to modern ears, but the text includes no indication of tone. So stunned was the woman that Jesus acknowledged her in any way that she was drawn into conversation, curious about his offer of "living water" (4:10).

In the exchange that followed, the woman did her best to avoid admitting why she was so thirsty for living water, but Jesus was relentless. When she questioned his qualification to offer better water than "our father Jacob" (4:12), Jesus simply reasserted that his water led to eternal life.

When she asked for the water, his response led to her answering with a half-truth about her marital status, which Jesus gently unmasked. The woman deflected that shameful truth by shifting the conversation to popular religious arguments. Again, Jesus responded to her tactic by explaining that God would soon forever move beyond being one nation's God or limited to a certain geographical location. He was seeking worshipers ready to approach him in spirit and truth, no matter their racial background or country.

That woman's restoration left her transparent. She ran and told the rest of Sychar, "Come, see a man who told me everything I ever did. Could this be the Messiah?" (4:29).

And her heartfelt invitation was amazingly effective.

5 One man was there who had been disabled
for thirty-eight years. 6 When Jesus saw him
lying there and realized he had already been
there a long time, he said to him, "Do you want
to get well?"
7 "Sir," the disabled man answered, "I have
no one to put me into the pool when the water
is stirred up, but while I'm coming, someone
goes down ahead of me."
8 "Get up," Jesus told him, "pick up your mat
and walk." 9 Instantly the man got well, picked
up his mat, and started to walk.
Now that day was the Sabbath, 10 and so the
Jews said to the man who had been healed,
"This is the Sabbath. The law prohibits you
from picking up your mat."
11 He replied, "The man who made me well
told me, 'Pick up your mat and walk.'"
12 "Who is this man who told you, 'Pick up
your mat and walk'?" they asked. 13 But the
man who was healed did not know who it
was, because Jesus had slipped away into the
crowd that was there.[A]
14 After this, Jesus found him in the temple
and said to him, "See, you are well. Do not sin
anymore, so that something worse doesn't
happen to you." 15 The man went and reported
to the Jews that it was Jesus who had made
him well. 16 Therefore, the Jews began persecuting Jesus[B] because he was doing these
things on the Sabbath.

HONORING THE FATHER AND THE SON

17 Jesus responded to them, "My Father is still
working, and I am working also." 18 This is why
the Jews began trying all the more to kill him:
Not only was he breaking the Sabbath, but he
was even calling God his own Father, making
himself equal to God.
19 Jesus replied, "Truly I tell you, the Son is
not able to do anything on his own, but only
what he sees the Father doing. For whatever

[A] **5:13** Lit *slipped away, there being a crowd in that place* [B] **5:16** Other mss add *and trying to kill him*

the Father[A] does, the Son likewise does these
things. 20 For the Father loves the Son and
shows him everything he is doing, and he will
show him greater works than these so that
you will be amazed. 21 And just as the Father
raises the dead and gives them life, so the
Son also gives life to whom he wants. 22 The
Father, in fact, judges no one but has given all
judgment to the Son, 23 so that all people may
honor the Son just as they honor the Father.
Anyone who does not honor the Son does not
honor the Father who sent him.

LIFE AND JUDGMENT

24 "Truly I tell you, anyone who hears my word
and believes him who sent me has eternal life
and will not come under judgment but has
passed from death to life.

25 "Truly I tell you, an hour is coming, and is
now here, when the dead will hear the voice of
the Son of God, and those who hear will live.
26 For just as the Father has life in himself, so
also he has granted to the Son to have life in
himself. 27 And he has granted him the right to
pass judgment, because he is the Son of Man.
28 Do not be amazed at this, because a time is
coming when all who are in the graves will
hear his voice 29 and come out — those who
have done good things, to the resurrection of
life, but those who have done wicked things,
to the resurrection of condemnation.

30 "I can do nothing on my own. I judge only
as I hear, and my judgment is just, because I
do not seek my own will, but the will of him
who sent me.

WITNESSES TO JESUS

31 "If I testify about myself, my testimony is not
true. 32 There is another who testifies about me,
and I know that the testimony he gives about
me is true. 33 You sent messengers to John, and
he testified to the truth. 34 I don't receive human testimony, but I say these things so that
you may be saved. 35 John[B] was a burning and
shining lamp, and you were willing to rejoice
for a while in his light.

36 "But I have a greater testimony than
John's because of the works that the Father
has given me to accomplish. These very works
I am doing testify about me that the Father
has sent me. 37 The Father who sent me has
himself testified about me. You have not heard
his voice at any time, and you haven't seen
his form. 38 You don't have his word residing in you, because you don't believe the
one he sent. 39 You pore over the Scriptures
because you think you have eternal life in
them, and yet they testify about me. 40 But
you are not willing to come to me so that
you may have life.

41 "I do not accept glory from people, 42 but
I know you — that you have no love for God
within you. 43 I have come in my Father's name,
and yet you don't accept me. If someone else
comes in his own name, you will accept him.
44 How can you believe, since you accept glory
from one another but don't seek the glory that
comes from the only God? 45 Do not think that
I will accuse you to the Father. Your accuser
is Moses, on whom you have set your hope.
46 For if you believed Moses, you would believe me, because he wrote about me. 47 But
if you don't believe what he wrote, how will
you believe my words?"

THE FOURTH SIGN: FEEDING OF THE FIVE THOUSAND

6 After this, Jesus crossed the Sea of Galilee
(or Tiberias). 2 A huge crowd was following
him because they saw the signs that he was
performing by healing the sick. 3 Jesus went
up a mountain and sat down there with his
disciples.

4 Now the Passover, a Jewish festival, was
near. 5 So when Jesus looked up and noticed
a huge crowd coming toward him, he asked
Philip, "Where will we buy bread so that these
people can eat?" 6 He asked this to test him,
for he himself knew what he was going to do.

7 Philip answered him, "Two hundred denarii[C] worth of bread wouldn't be enough
for each of them to have a little."

8 One of his disciples, Andrew, Simon Peter's
brother, said to him, 9 "There's a boy here who
has five barley loaves and two fish — but what
are they for so many?"

10 Jesus said, "Have the people sit down."

There was plenty of grass in that place; so
they sat down. The men numbered about five
thousand. 11 Then Jesus took the loaves, and
after giving thanks he distributed them to
those who were seated — so also with the
fish, as much as they wanted.

12 When they were full, he told his disciples,
"Collect the leftovers so that nothing is wasted." 13 So they collected them and filled twelve

---

[A] **5:19** Lit *whatever that one* [B] **5:35** Lit *That man* [C] **6:7** A denarius = one day's wage

baskets with the pieces from the five barley
loaves that were left over by those who had
eaten.

14 When the people saw the sign[A] he had
done, they said, "This truly is the Prophet who
is to come into the world."

15 Therefore, when Jesus realized that they
were about to come and take him by force
to make him king, he withdrew again to the
mountain by himself.

THE FIFTH SIGN: WALKING ON WATER

16 When evening came, his disciples went down
to the sea, 17 got into a boat, and started across
the sea to Capernaum. Darkness had already
set in, but Jesus had not yet come to them. 18 A
high wind arose, and the sea began to churn.
19 After they had rowed about three or four
miles,[B] they saw Jesus walking on the sea.
He was coming near the boat, and they were
afraid. 20 But he said to them, "It is I.[C] Don't
be afraid." 21 Then they were willing to take
him on board, and at once the boat was at the
shore where they were heading.

THE BREAD OF LIFE

22 The next day, the crowd that had stayed on
the other side of the sea saw there had been
only one boat.[D] They also saw that Jesus had
not boarded the boat with his disciples, but
that his disciples had gone off alone. 23 Some
boats from Tiberias came near the place where
they had eaten the bread after the Lord had
given thanks. 24 When the crowd saw that neither Jesus nor his disciples were there, they
got into the boats and went to Capernaum
looking for Jesus. 25 When they found him
on the other side of the sea, they said to him,
"Rabbi, when did you get here?"

26 Jesus answered, "Truly I tell you, you are
looking for me, not because you saw[E] the signs,
but because you ate the loaves and were filled.
27 Don't work for the food that perishes but
for the food that lasts for eternal life, which
the Son of Man will give you, because God the
Father has set his seal of approval on him."

28 "What can we do to perform the works
of God?" they asked.

29 Jesus replied, "This is the work of God
— that you believe in the one he has sent."

30 "What sign, then, are you going to do so
we may see and believe you?" they asked.
"What are you going to perform? 31 Our ancestors ate the manna in the wilderness, just
as it is written: **He gave them bread from
heaven to eat.**"[F]

32 Jesus said to them, "Truly I tell you, Moses
didn't give you the bread from heaven, but my
Father gives you the true bread from heaven.
33 For the bread of God is the one who comes
down from heaven and gives life to the world."

34 Then they said, "Sir, give us this bread
always."

35 "I am the bread of life," Jesus told them.
"No one who comes to me will ever be hungry,
and no one who believes in me will ever be
thirsty again. 36 But as I told you, you've seen
me,[G] and yet you do not believe. 37 Everyone
the Father gives me will come to me, and the
one who comes to me I will never cast out.
38 For I have come down from heaven, not
to do my own will, but the will of him who
sent me. 39 This is the will of him who sent
me: that I should lose none of those he has
given me but should raise them up on the
last day. 40 For this is the will of my Father:
that everyone who sees the Son and believes
in him will have eternal life, and I will raise
him up on the last day."

41 Therefore the Jews started complaining
about him because he said, "I am the bread
that came down from heaven." 42 They were
saying, "Isn't this Jesus the son of Joseph, whose
father and mother we know? How can he now
say, 'I have come down from heaven'?"

43 Jesus answered them, "Stop complaining
among yourselves. 44 No one can come to me
unless the Father who sent me draws[H] him,
and I will raise him up on the last day. 45 It is
written in the Prophets: **And they will all
be taught by God.**[I] Everyone who has listened to and learned from the Father comes
to me — 46 not that anyone has seen the Father except the one who is from God. He has
seen the Father.

47 "Truly I tell you, anyone who believes[J] has
eternal life. 48 I am the bread of life. 49 Your
ancestors ate the manna in the wilderness,
and they died. 50 This is the bread that comes
down from heaven so that anyone may eat
of it and not die. 51 I am the living bread that
came down from heaven. If anyone eats of
this bread he will live forever. The bread that
I will give for the life of the world is my flesh."

[A] **6:14** Other mss read *signs* [B] **6:19** Lit *twenty-five or thirty stadia*; one *stadion* = 600 feet [C] **6:20** Lit "*I am* [D] **6:22** Other mss add *into which his disciples had entered* [E] **6:26** Or *perceived* [F] **6:31** Ex 16:4; Ps 78:24 [G] **6:36** Other mss omit *me* [H] **6:44** Or *brings*, or *leads* [I] **6:45** Is 54:13 [J] **6:47** Other mss add *in me*

52 At that, the Jews argued among themselves, "How can this man give us his flesh
to eat?"
53 So Jesus said to them, "Truly I tell you,
unless you eat the flesh of the Son of Man
and drink his blood, you do not have life in
yourselves. 54 The one who eats my flesh and
drinks my blood has eternal life, and I will
raise him up on the last day, 55 because my
flesh is true food and my blood is true drink.
56 The one who eats my flesh and drinks my
blood remains in me, and I in him. 57 Just as the
living Father sent me and I live because of the
Father, so the one who feeds on me will live
because of me. 58 This is the bread that came
down from heaven; it is not like the manna[A]
your ancestors ate — and they died. The one
who eats this bread will live forever."
59 He said these things while teaching in the
synagogue in Capernaum.

MANY DISCIPLES DESERT JESUS

60 Therefore, when many of his disciples heard
this, they said, "This teaching is hard. Who
can accept[B] it?"
61 Jesus, knowing in himself that his
disciples were complaining about this, asked
them, "Does this offend you? 62 Then what if
you were to observe the Son of Man ascending to where he was before? 63 The Spirit is
the one who gives life. The flesh doesn't help
at all. The words that I have spoken to you
are spirit and are life. 64 But there are some
among you who don't believe." (For Jesus
knew from the beginning those who did not[C]
believe and the one who would betray him.)
65 He said, "This is why I told you that no one
can come to me unless it is granted to him
by the Father."
66 From that moment[D] many of his disciples
turned back and no longer accompanied him.
67 So Jesus said to the Twelve, "You don't want
to go away too, do you?"
68 Simon Peter answered, "Lord, to whom
will we go? You have the words of eternal life.
69 We have come to believe and know that you
are the Holy One of God."[E]
70 Jesus replied to them, "Didn't I choose
you, the Twelve? Yet one of you is a devil."
71 He was referring to Judas, Simon Iscariot's
son,[F] one of the Twelve, because he was going
to betray him.

Exercise of Faith | *Staying Close to Christ*

NO TURNING BACK

"From that moment many of his disciples turned back and no longer accompanied him. So Jesus said to the Twelve, 'You don't want to go away too, do you?' Simon Peter answered, 'Lord, to whom will we go? You have the words of eternal life.'" John 6:66-68

Deny yourself? Serve others? Love your enemies? Forgive the people who wrong you? Be generous? Turn away from sin? Stand against the culture?

No wonder Christians are tempted at times to say, "I can't do this. Forget it!" Jesus's teachings are tough and confusing.

Such feelings aren't new. It has been like this from the beginning. Jesus said metaphorically, "I am the bread of life" (Jn 6:48). He then went on to say that his disciples needed to "eat the flesh of the Son of Man and drink his blood" (6:53). It didn't go over well. "This teaching is hard. Who can accept it?" the crowd responded (6:60). Many of them stopped following.

This passage reminds us that walking *with* Jesus may be hard, but walking *away from* him is death. In everything we learn about the Christian faith, we must consistently come to Jesus. No matter our troubles, fears, or problems, we won't find real life anywhere else.

For the next note on *Exercise of Faith*, see John 9:1-2.

[A] **6:58** Other mss omit *the manna* [B] **6:60** Lit *hear* [C] **6:64** Other mss omit *not* [D] **6:66** Or *Because of this* [E] **6:69** Other mss read *you are the Messiah, the Son of the Living God* [F] **6:71** Or *Judas Iscariot, Simon's son*

THE UNBELIEF OF JESUS'S BROTHERS

7 After this, Jesus traveled in Galilee, since
he did not want to travel in Judea because
the Jews were trying to kill him. 2 The Jewish
Festival of Shelters[A] was near. 3 So his brothers said to him, "Leave here and go to Judea
so your disciples can see your works that you
are doing. 4 For no one does anything in secret
while he's seeking public recognition. If you
do these things, show yourself to the world."
5 (For not even his brothers believed in him.)
6 Jesus told them, "My time has not yet arrived, but your time is always at hand. 7 The
world cannot hate you, but it does hate me
because I testify about it — that its works are
evil. 8 Go up to the festival yourselves. I'm not
going up to this festival,[B] because my time has
not yet fully come." 9 After he had said these
things, he stayed in Galilee.

JESUS AT THE FESTIVAL OF SHELTERS

10 After his brothers had gone up to the festival, then he also went up, not openly but
secretly. 11 The Jews were looking for him
at the festival and saying, "Where is he?"
12 And there was a lot of murmuring about
him among the crowds. Some were saying,
"He's a good man." Others were saying, "No,
on the contrary, he's deceiving the people."
13 Still, nobody was talking publicly about
him for fear of the Jews.
14 When the festival was already half over,
Jesus went up into the temple and began to
teach. 15 Then the Jews were amazed and said,
"How is this man so learned, since he hasn't
been trained?"
16 Jesus answered them, "My teaching isn't
mine but is from the one who sent me. 17 If
anyone wants to do his will, he will know
whether the teaching is from God or whether I am speaking on my own. 18 The one who
speaks on his own seeks his own glory; but
he who seeks the glory of the one who sent
him is true, and there is no unrighteousness
in him. 19 Didn't Moses give you the law? Yet
none of you keeps the law. Why are you trying to kill me?"
20 "You have a demon!" the crowd responded. "Who is trying to kill you?"
21 "I performed one work, and you are all
amazed," Jesus answered. 22 "This is why Moses
has given you circumcision — not that it comes
from Moses but from the fathers — and you
circumcise a man on the Sabbath. 23 If a man
receives circumcision on the Sabbath so that
the law of Moses won't be broken, are you angry at me because I made a man entirely well
on the Sabbath? 24 Stop judging according to
outward appearances; rather judge according
to righteous judgment."

THE IDENTITY OF THE MESSIAH

25 Some of the people of Jerusalem were saying, "Isn't this the man they are trying to kill?
26 Yet, look, he's speaking publicly and they're
saying nothing to him. Can it be true that the
authorities know he is the Messiah? 27 But
we know where this man is from. When the
Messiah comes, nobody will know where he
is from."
28 As he was teaching in the temple, Jesus
cried out, "You know me and you know where
I am from. Yet I have not come on my own, but
the one who sent me is true. You don't know
him; 29 I know him because I am from him,
and he sent me."
30 Then they tried to seize him. Yet no one
laid a hand on him because his hour had not
yet come. 31 However, many from the crowd
believed in him and said, "When the Messiah
comes, he won't perform more signs than this
man has done, will he?" 32 The Pharisees heard
the crowd murmuring these things about him,
and so the chief priests and the Pharisees sent
servants[C] to arrest him.
33 Then Jesus said, "I am only with you for a
short time. Then I'm going to the one who sent
me. 34 You will look for me, but you will not
find me; and where I am, you cannot come."
35 Then the Jews said to one another, "Where
does he intend to go so we won't find him?
He doesn't intend to go to the Jewish people
dispersed[D] among the Greeks and teach the
Greeks, does he? 36 What is this remark he
made: 'You will look for me, and you will not
find me; and where I am, you cannot come'?"

THE PROMISE OF THE SPIRIT

37 On the last and most important day of the
festival, Jesus stood up and cried out, "If anyone is thirsty, let him come to me[E] and drink.
38 The one who believes in me, as the Scripture
has said, will have streams of living water
flow from deep within him." 39 He said this
about the Spirit. Those who believed in Jesus
were going to receive the Spirit, for the Spirit[F]

[A] 7:2 Or *Tabernacles*, or *Booths* [B] 7:8 Other mss add *yet* [C] 7:32 Or *temple police*, or *officers*, also in vv. 45,46 [D] 7:35 Gk *diaspora*; Jewish people scattered throughout Gentile lands [E] 7:37 Other mss omit *to me* [F] 7:39 Other mss read *Holy Spirit*

had not yet been given[A] because Jesus had
not yet been glorified.

THE PEOPLE ARE DIVIDED OVER JESUS

40 When some from the crowd heard these
words, they said, "This truly is the Prophet."
41 Others said, "This is the Messiah." But some
said, "Surely the Messiah doesn't come from
Galilee, does he? 42 Doesn't the Scripture say
that the Messiah comes from David's offspring[B]
and from the town of Bethlehem, where David
lived?" 43 So the crowd was divided because
of him. 44 Some of them wanted to seize him,
but no one laid hands on him.

DEBATE OVER JESUS'S CLAIMS

45 Then the servants came to the chief priests
and Pharisees, who asked them, "Why didn't
you bring him?"
46 The servants answered, "No man ever
spoke like this!"[C]
47 Then the Pharisees responded to them:
"Are you fooled too? 48 Have any of the rulers
or Pharisees believed in him? 49 But this crowd,
which doesn't know the law, is accursed."
50 Nicodemus — the one who came to him
previously and who was one of them — said
to them, 51 "Our law doesn't judge a man before it hears from him and knows what he's
doing, does it?"
52 "You aren't from Galilee too, are you?"
they replied. "Investigate and you will see that
no prophet arises from Galilee."

[The earliest mss do not include 7:53–8:11.][D]

8 [53 Then each one went to his house. 1 But
Jesus went to the Mount of Olives.

AN ADULTERESS FORGIVEN

2 At dawn he went to the temple again, and all
the people were coming to him. He sat down
and began to teach them.
3 Then the scribes and the Pharisees brought
a woman caught in adultery, making her stand
in the center. 4 "Teacher," they said to him, "this
woman was caught in the act of committing
adultery. 5 In the law Moses commanded us
to stone such women. So what do you say?"
6 They asked this to trap him, in order that they
might have evidence to accuse him.
Jesus stooped down and started writing on
the ground with his finger. 7 When they persisted in questioning him, he stood up and said to
them, "The one without sin among you should
be the first to throw a stone at her." 8 Then he
stooped down again and continued writing
on the ground. 9 When they heard this, they
left one by one, starting with the older men.
Only he was left, with the woman in the center.
10 When Jesus stood up, he said to her, "Woman,
where are they? Has no one condemned you?"
11 "No one, Lord,"[E] she answered.
"Neither do I condemn you," said Jesus. "Go,
and from now on do not sin anymore."]

THE LIGHT OF THE WORLD

12 Jesus spoke to them again: "I am the light
of the world. Anyone who follows me will
never walk in the darkness but will have the
light of life."
13 So the Pharisees said to him, "You are
testifying about yourself. Your testimony is
not valid."
14 "Even if I testify about myself," Jesus replied,
"My testimony is true, because I know where I
came from and where I'm going. But you don't
know where I come from or where I'm going.
15 You judge by human standards.[F] I judge no
one. 16 And if I do judge, my judgment is true,
because it is not I alone who judge, but I and
the Father who sent me. 17 Even in your law it is
written that the testimony of two witnesses is
true. 18 I am the one who testifies about myself,
and the Father who sent me testifies about me."
19 Then they asked him, "Where is your Father?"
"You know neither me nor my Father," Jesus
answered. "If you knew me, you would also
know my Father." 20 He spoke these words by
the treasury, while teaching in the temple.
But no one seized him, because his hour had
not yet come.

JESUS PREDICTS HIS DEPARTURE

21 Then he said to them again, "I'm going away;
you will look for me, and you will die in your
sin. Where I'm going, you cannot come."
22 So the Jews said again, "He won't kill himself, will he, since he says, 'Where I'm going,
you cannot come'?"
23 "You are from below," he told them, "I am

[A] **7:39** Lit *the Spirit was not yet* [B] **7:42** Lit *seed* [C] **7:46** Other mss read *like this man* [D] **7:53–8:11** Other mss include all or some of the passage after Jn 7:36,44,52; 21:25; or Lk 21:38. [E] **8:11** Or *Sir*; Jn 4:15,49; 5:7; 6:34; 9:36 [F] **8:15** Lit *You judge according to the flesh*

Woman Caught in Adultery | Restoration Profile

JOHN 8:2-11

Sinful people fail to see the obvious evil intention in words and actions that, on the surface, proclaim righteousness. Those who brought the woman "caught in the act of committing adultery" (Jn 8:4) saw no irony, humor, or blatant deceit in the impossibility of someone being caught *alone* in the act of adultery. Their willingness to ignore the other guilty party and treat someone as a pawn in a religious argument revealed their real intention. Jesus managed to avoid their trap while at the same time restoring a person others were willing to destroy.

The Bible is abundantly clear that "all have sinned and fall short of the glory of God" (Rm 3:23). This does not mean we can't see or even confront others' sins; it does mean, however, that we should keep our own sinfulness in mind in dealing with the sins of others. Readiness to condemn is frequently accompanied by resistance to repent, which the woman's accusers revealed by their retreat. In the mirror of their own guilt, the accusers dropped their rocks and walked away.

Jesus gave love and forgiveness without condoning the woman's past behavior. His final statement to her, "Neither do I condemn you. . . . Go, and from now on do not sin anymore" (Jn 8:11), was not an expectation of perfection but an encouragement to live in new freedom.

Jesus wasn't sending this woman out to try harder. She had just met someone who had treated her as no one else had ever done. She called him Lord, and he implied that he could have condemned her but chose to release her. The reality of her restoration would depend on her ongoing relationship with the Lord, not her ability to avoid sin.

The ongoing effectiveness of our restoration lies in our dependence on the One who has restored us.

from above. You are of this world; I am not of
this world. 24 Therefore I told you that you will
die in your sins. For if you do not believe that
I am he, you will die in your sins."
25 "Who are you?" they questioned.
"Exactly what I've been telling you from the
very beginning," Jesus told them. 26 "I have
many things to say and to judge about you,
but the one who sent me is true, and what
I have heard from him — these things I tell
the world."
27 They did not know he was speaking to
them about the Father. 28 So Jesus said to them,
"When you lift up the Son of Man, then you
will know that I am he, and that I do nothing
on my own. But just as the Father taught me,
I say these things. 29 The one who sent me is
with me. He has not left me alone, because I
always do what pleases him."

TRUTH AND FREEDOM

30 As he was saying these things, many believed in him.
31 Then Jesus said to the Jews who had believed him, "If you continue in my word,[A] you
really are my disciples. 32 You will know the
truth, and the truth will set you free."
33 "We are descendants[B] of Abraham," they
answered him, "and we have never been enslaved to anyone. How can you say, 'You will
become free'?"
34 Jesus responded, "Truly I tell you, everyone
who commits sin is a slave of sin. 35 A slave
does not remain in the household forever, but
a son does remain forever. 36 So if the Son sets
you free, you really will be free. 37 I know you
are descendants of Abraham, but you are trying to kill me because my word has no place
among you. 38 I speak what I have seen in the
presence of the Father;[C] so then, you do what
you have heard from your father."
39 "Our father is Abraham," they replied.
"If you were Abraham's children," Jesus
told them, "you would do what Abraham did.
40 But now you are trying to kill me, a man
who has told you the truth that I heard from
God. Abraham did not do this. 41 You're doing
what your father does."
"We weren't born of sexual immorality," they
said. "We have one Father — God."

[A] **8:31** Or *my teaching*, or *my message*, also in v. 37 [B] **8:33** Or *offspring*; lit *seed*, also in v. 37; Jn 7:42 [C] **8:38** Other mss read *of my Father*

42 Jesus said to them, "If God were your Father, you would love me, because I came from God and I am here. For I didn't come on my own, but he sent me. 43 Why don't you understand what I say? Because you cannot listen to[A] my word. 44 You are of your father the devil, and you want to carry out your father's desires. He was a murderer from the beginning and does not stand in the truth, because there is no truth in him. When he tells a lie, he speaks from his own nature,[B] because he is a liar and the father of lies. 45 Yet because I tell the truth, you do not believe me. 46 Who among you can convict me of sin? If I am telling the truth, why don't you believe me? 47 The one who is from God listens to God's words. This is why you don't listen, because you are not from God."

JESUS AND ABRAHAM

48 The Jews responded to him, "Aren't we right in saying that you're a Samaritan and have a demon?"

49 "I do not have a demon," Jesus answered. "On the contrary, I honor my Father and you dishonor me. 50 I do not seek my own glory; there is one who seeks it and judges. 51 Truly I tell you, if anyone keeps my word, he will never see death."

52 Then the Jews said, "Now we know you have a demon. Abraham died and so did the prophets. You say, 'If anyone keeps my word, he will never taste death.' 53 Are you greater than our father Abraham who died? And the prophets died. Who do you claim to be?"

54 "If I glorify myself," Jesus answered, "my glory is nothing. My Father — about whom you say, 'He is our God' — he is the one who glorifies me. 55 You do not know him, but I know him. If I were to say I don't know him, I would be a liar like you. But I do know him, and I keep his word. 56 Your father Abraham rejoiced to see my day; he saw it and was glad."

57 The Jews replied, "You aren't fifty years old yet, and you've seen Abraham?"[C]

58 Jesus said to them, "Truly I tell you, before Abraham was, I am."

59 So they picked up stones to throw at him. But Jesus was hidden[D] and went out of the temple.[E]

THE SIXTH SIGN: HEALING A MAN BORN BLIND

9 As he was passing by, he saw a man blind from birth. 2 His disciples asked him: "Rabbi, who sinned, this man or his parents, that he was born blind?"

Rest and Reflection | *Honestly Evaluating Yourself*

TRUE FREEDOM

"Then Jesus said to the Jews who had believed him, 'If you continue in my word, you really are my disciples. You will know the truth, and the truth will set you free.'" John 8:31-32

Political freedom. Personal freedom. Sexual freedom. Everyone wants complete autonomy, freedom.

Perhaps then, we should give Jesus a listen. In this famous discourse with a group of Jews who had "believed in him" (Jn 8:30), he talked about what freedom really means and looks like.

He claimed that his words are "*the* truth" (not "one of many truths"). And he added that they have the power to set people free. He taught that those who ignore his words and live however they please are the opposite of free. Such people are, in fact, slaves of sin.

The good news? No one has to remain in that condition! Elsewhere Jesus said he was sent by God "to proclaim release to the captives . . . to set free the oppressed" (Lk 4:18). He offers ultimate freedom, saying "if the Son sets you free, you really will be free" (Jn 8:36).

What's the path to personal freedom? We must read, engage, absorb, and follow his Word.

For the next note on *Rest and Reflection*, see John 15:4-5.

[A] **8:43** Or *cannot hear* [B] **8:44** Lit *from his own things* [C] **8:57** Other mss read *and Abraham has seen you?* [D] **8:59** Or *Jesus hid himself* [E] **8:59** Other mss add *and having gone through their midst, he passed by*

3 "Neither this man nor his parents sinned,"
Jesus answered. "This came about so that God's
works might be displayed in him. 4 We[A] must
do the works of him who sent me[B] while it is
day. Night is coming when no one can work.
5 As long as I am in the world, I am the light
of the world."
6 After he said these things he spit on the
ground, made some mud from the saliva, and
spread the mud on his eyes. 7 "Go," he told him,
"wash in the pool of Siloam" (which means
"Sent"). So he left, washed, and came back
seeing.
8 His neighbors and those who had seen
him before as a beggar said, "Isn't this the
one who used to sit begging?" 9 Some said,
"He's the one." Others were saying, "No, but
he looks like him."
He kept saying, "I'm the one."
10 So they asked him, "Then how were your
eyes opened?"
11 He answered, "The man called Jesus made
mud, spread it on my eyes, and told me, 'Go to
Siloam and wash.' So when I went and washed
I received my sight."
12 "Where is he?" they asked.
"I don't know," he said.

THE HEALED MAN'S TESTIMONY

13 They brought the man who used to be blind
to the Pharisees. 14 The day that Jesus made
the mud and opened his eyes was a Sabbath.
15 Then the Pharisees asked him again how
he received his sight.
"He put mud on my eyes," he told them. "I
washed and I can see."
16 Some of the Pharisees said, "This man is
not from God, because he doesn't keep the
Sabbath." But others were saying, "How can
a sinful man perform such signs?" And there
was a division among them.
17 Again they asked the blind man, "What
do you say about him, since he opened your
eyes?"
"He's a prophet," he said.
18 The Jews did not believe this about him
— that he was blind and received sight — until
they summoned the parents of the one who
had received his sight.
19 They asked them, "Is this your son, the
one you say was born blind? How then does
he now see?"
20 "We know this is our son and that he was
born blind," his parents answered. 21 "But we
don't know how he now sees, and we don't

Exercise of Faith | *Enduring Suffering*

SUFFERING AND GLORY

"As he was passing by, he saw a man blind from birth. His disciples asked him: 'Rabbi, who sinned, this man or his parents, that he was born blind?'" John 9:1-2

The ancients believed that misfortune befell a person because she had done something to offend the gods—or, in religions like Judaism, the one true God. Suffering? You must have sinned. Now you are being punished as a result. Jesus's disciples demonstrated such thinking in this passage.

Jesus responded by saying that this man's blindness wasn't due to divine retribution. Rather, "This came about so that God's works might be displayed in him" (Jn 9:3).

Here is a hard but consistent teaching of the Bible: God chooses broken and weak people and through them showcases his glory (2Co 12:9-11). In this instance, the man's sight was restored. But sometimes an illness or trial doesn't go away. Even then, because God gives grace, others are able to see the power of God in the way a suffering person perseveres, clings to hope, continues to love and trust, or finds joy in the midst of sorrow.

What's your struggle? Be sure of this: God wants to glorify himself in and through your situation. How God will do that is up to him. How you respond is up to you.

For the next note on *Exercise of Faith*, see John 12:37.

[A] **9:4** Other mss read *I* / [B] **9:4** Other mss read *us*

know who opened his eyes. Ask him; he's of
age. He will speak for himself." 22 His parents
said these things because they were afraid of
the Jews, since the Jews had already agreed
that if anyone confessed him as the Messiah,
he would be banned from the synagogue.
23 This is why his parents said, "He's of age;
ask him."
24 So a second time they summoned the man
who had been blind and told him, "Give glory
to God. We know that this man is a sinner."
25 He answered, "Whether or not he's a sinner, I don't know. One thing I do know: I was
blind, and now I can see!"
26 Then they asked him, "What did he do to
you? How did he open your eyes?"
27 "I already told you," he said, "and you didn't
listen. Why do you want to hear it again? You
don't want to become his disciples too, do you?"
28 They ridiculed him: "You're that man's disciple, but we're Moses's disciples. 29 We know
that God has spoken to Moses. But this man
— we don't know where he's from."
30 "This is an amazing thing!" the man told
them. "You don't know where he is from,
and yet he opened my eyes. 31 We know that
God doesn't listen to sinners, but if anyone
is God-fearing and does his will, he listens to
him. 32 Throughout history[A] no one has ever
heard of someone opening the eyes of a person
born blind. 33 If this man were not from God,
he wouldn't be able to do anything."
34 "You were born entirely in sin," they replied, "and are you trying to teach us?" Then
they threw him out.

SPIRITUAL BLINDNESS

35 Jesus heard that they had thrown the man
out, and when he found him, he asked, "Do
you believe in the Son of Man?"[B]
36 "Who is he, Sir, that I may believe in him?"
he asked.
37 Jesus answered, "You have seen him; in
fact, he is the one speaking with you."
38 "I believe, Lord!" he said, and he worshiped him.
39 Jesus said, "I came into this world for judgment, in order that those who do not see will
see and those who do see will become blind."
40 Some of the Pharisees who were with
him heard these things and asked him, "We
aren't blind too, are we?"
41 "If you were blind," Jesus told them, "you
wouldn't have sin. But now that you say, 'We
see,' your sin remains.

THE GOOD SHEPHERD

10 "Truly I tell you, anyone who doesn't enter
the sheep pen by the gate but climbs in
some other way is a thief and a robber. 2 The
one who enters by the gate is the shepherd
of the sheep. 3 The gatekeeper opens it for
him, and the sheep hear his voice. He calls
his own sheep by name and leads them out.
4 When he has brought all his own outside,
he goes ahead of them. The sheep follow him
because they know his voice. 5 They will never
follow a stranger; instead they will run away
from him, because they don't know the voice
of strangers." 6 Jesus gave them this figure of
speech, but they did not understand what he
was telling them.
7 Jesus said again, "Truly I tell you, I am
the gate for the sheep. 8 All who came before
me[C] are thieves and robbers, but the sheep
didn't listen to them. 9 I am the gate. If anyone enters by me, he will be saved and will
come in and go out and find pasture. 10 A
thief comes only to steal and kill and destroy.
I have come so that they may have life and
have it in abundance.
11 "I am the good shepherd. The good shepherd lays down his life for the sheep. 12 The
hired hand, since he is not the shepherd and
doesn't own the sheep, leaves them[D] and runs
away when he sees a wolf coming. The wolf
then snatches and scatters them. 13 This happens because he is a hired hand and doesn't
care about the sheep.
14 "I am the good shepherd. I know my own,
and my own know me, 15 just as the Father
knows me, and I know the Father. I lay down
my life for the sheep. 16 But I have other sheep
that are not from this sheep pen; I must bring
them also, and they will listen to my voice.
Then there will be one flock, one shepherd.
17 This is why the Father loves me, because
I lay down my life so that I may take it up
again. 18 No one takes it from me, but I lay
it down on my own. I have the right to lay
it down, and I have the right to take it up
again. I have received this command from
my Father."
19 Again the Jews were divided because of
these words. 20 Many of them were saying, "He
has a demon and he's crazy. Why do you listen

[A] **9:32** Lit *From the age* [B] **9:35** Other mss read *the Son of God* [C] **10:8** Other mss omit *before me* [D] **10:12** Lit *leaves the sheep*

to him?" [21] Others were saying, "These aren't the
words of someone who is demon-possessed.
Can a demon open the eyes of the blind?"

JESUS AT THE FESTIVAL OF DEDICATION

[22] Then the Festival of Dedication took place
in Jerusalem, and it was winter. [23] Jesus was
walking in the temple in Solomon's Colonnade.
[24] The Jews surrounded him and asked, "How
long are you going to keep us in suspense?[A] If
you are the Messiah, tell us plainly."[B]
[25] "I did tell you and you don't believe," Jesus
answered them. "The works that I do in my Father's name testify about me. [26] But you don't
believe because you are not of my sheep.[C] [27] My
sheep hear my voice, I know them, and they
follow me. [28] I give them eternal life, and they
will never perish. No one will snatch them
out of my hand. [29] My Father, who has given
them to me, is greater than all. No one is able
to snatch them out of the Father's hand. [30] I
and the Father are one."

RENEWED EFFORTS TO STONE JESUS

[31] Again the Jews picked up rocks to stone him.
[32] Jesus replied, "I have shown you many
good works from the Father. For which of
these works are you stoning me?"
[33] "We aren't stoning you for a good work,"
the Jews answered, "but for blasphemy, because you — being a man — make yourself
God."
[34] Jesus answered them, "Isn't it written
in your law,[D] **I said, you are gods**?[E] [35] If he
called those whom the word of God came to
'gods' — and the Scripture cannot be broken — [36] do you say, 'You are blaspheming'
to the one the Father set apart and sent into
the world, because I said: I am the Son of God?
[37] If I am not doing my Father's works, don't
believe me. [38] But if I am doing them and you
don't believe me, believe the works. This way
you will know and understand[F] that the Father is in me and I in the Father." [39] Then they
were trying again to seize him, but he eluded
their grasp.

MANY BEYOND THE JORDAN BELIEVE IN JESUS

[40] So he departed again across the Jordan to the
place where John had been baptizing earlier,
and he remained there. [41] Many came to him
and said, "John never did a sign, but everything

Thanksgiving and Contentment | *Praise for God's Security*

UNSNATCHABLE

"My sheep hear my voice, I know them, and they follow me. I give them eternal life, and they will never perish. No one will snatch them out of my hand. My Father, who has given them to me, is greater than all. No one is able to snatch them out of the Father's hand." John 10:27-29

Sometimes the thoughts are paralyzing: *I did it again! Why do I keep screwing up! What if I went too far? What if God finally gets fed up with me and says, "I'm done with you"?*

In his famous "good shepherd" message, Jesus addressed these common concerns of believers. Notice his promise: "I give them eternal life." In other words, salvation is a gift.

"They will never perish." In other words, believers are safe. Then, just in case minds were wandering, he mentioned us being in his hand, and, beyond that, also in the Father's hand. Does anyone really think God Almighty suffers from a weak grip? No power can pry us out of the hand of the King of kings and Lord of lords.

The point? Believers are safe. We are kept. Eternal life is a free gift—not a merit-based reward, subject to revocation. Paul said it like this, "If we are faithless, he remains faithful, for he cannot deny himself" (2Tm 2:13). You are secure in him.

For the next note on *Thanksgiving and Contentment*, see John 14:6.

[A] **10:24** Lit *"How long are you taking away our life?* [B] **10:24** Or *openly*, or *publicly* [C] **10:26** Other mss add *just as I told you*
[D] **10:34** Other mss read *in the scripture* [E] **10:34** Ps 82:6 [F] **10:38** Other mss read *know and believe*

John said about this man was true." 42 And
many believed in him there.

LAZARUS DIES AT BETHANY

11 Now a man was sick, Lazarus from Bethany, the village of Mary and her sister
Martha. 2 Mary was the one who anointed the
Lord with perfume and wiped his feet with
her hair, and it was her brother Lazarus who
was sick. 3 So the sisters sent a message to him:
"Lord, the one you love is sick."

4 When Jesus heard it, he said, "This sickness
will not end in death but is for the glory of
God, so that the Son of God may be glorified
through it." 5 Now Jesus loved Martha, her
sister, and Lazarus. 6 So when he heard that he
was sick, he stayed two more days in the place
where he was. 7 Then after that, he said to the
disciples, "Let's go to Judea again."

8 "Rabbi," the disciples told him, "just now
the Jews tried to stone you, and you're going
there again?"

9 "Aren't there twelve hours in a day?" Jesus
answered. "If anyone walks during the day, he
doesn't stumble, because he sees the light of this
world. 10 But if anyone walks during the night,
he does stumble, because the light is not in him."

11 He said this, and then he told them, "Our
friend Lazarus has fallen asleep, but I'm on
my way to wake him up."

12 Then the disciples said to him, "Lord, if he
has fallen asleep, he will get well."

13 Jesus, however, was speaking about his
death, but they thought he was speaking about
natural sleep. 14 So Jesus then told them plainly, "Lazarus has died. 15 I'm glad for you that
I wasn't there so that you may believe. But
let's go to him."

16 Then Thomas (called "Twin"[A]) said to his
fellow disciples, "Let's go too so that we may
die with him."

THE RESURRECTION AND THE LIFE

17 When Jesus arrived, he found that Lazarus had already been in the tomb four days.
18 Bethany was near Jerusalem (less than two
miles[B] away). 19 Many of the Jews had come
to Martha and Mary to comfort them about
their brother.

20 As soon as Martha heard that Jesus was
coming, she went to meet him, but Mary remained seated in the house. 21 Then Martha
said to Jesus, "Lord, if you had been here, my
brother wouldn't have died. 22 Yet even now
I know that whatever you ask from God, God
will give you."

23 "Your brother will rise again," Jesus told
her.

24 Martha said to him, "I know that he will
rise again in the resurrection at the last day."

25 Jesus said to her, "I am the resurrection and
the life. The one who believes in me, even if he
dies, will live. 26 Everyone who lives and believes
in me will never die. Do you believe this?"

27 "Yes, Lord," she told him, "I believe you
are the Messiah, the Son of God, who comes
into the world."

JESUS SHARES THE SORROW OF DEATH

28 Having said this, she went back and called
her sister Mary, saying in private, "The Teacher
is here and is calling for you."

29 As soon as Mary heard this, she got up
quickly and went to him. 30 Jesus had not yet
come into the village but was still in the place
where Martha had met him. 31 The Jews who
were with her in the house consoling her saw
that Mary got up quickly and went out. They
followed her, supposing that she was going
to the tomb to cry there.

32 As soon as Mary came to where Jesus was
and saw him, she fell at his feet and told him,
"Lord, if you had been here, my brother would
not have died!"

33 When Jesus saw her crying, and the Jews
who had come with her crying, he was deeply
moved[C] in his spirit and troubled. 34 "Where
have you put him?" he asked.

"Lord," they told him, "come and see."

35 Jesus wept.

36 So the Jews said, "See how he loved him!"
37 But some of them said, "Couldn't he who
opened the blind man's eyes also have kept
this man from dying?"

THE SEVENTH SIGN: RAISING LAZARUS FROM THE DEAD

38 Then Jesus, deeply moved again, came to
the tomb. It was a cave, and a stone was lying
against it. 39 "Remove the stone," Jesus said.

Martha, the dead man's sister, told him,
"Lord, there is already a stench because he
has been dead four days."

40 Jesus said to her, "Didn't I tell you that if
you believed you would see the glory of God?"

41 So they removed the stone. Then Jesus

[A] **11:16** Gk *Didymus* [B] **11:18** Lit *fifteen stadia*; one *stadion* = 600 feet [C] **11:33** Or *angry*, also in v. 38

raised his eyes and said, "Father, I thank you
that you heard me. 42 I know that you always
hear me, but because of the crowd standing
here I said this, so that they may believe you
sent me." 43 After he said this, he shouted with
a loud voice, "Lazarus, come out!" 44 The dead
man came out bound hand and foot with linen
strips and with his face wrapped in a cloth. Jesus
said to them, "Unwrap him and let him go."

THE PLOT TO KILL JESUS

45 Therefore, many of the Jews who came to
Mary and saw what he did believed in him.
46 But some of them went to the Pharisees and
told them what Jesus had done.
47 So the chief priests and the Pharisees convened the Sanhedrin and were saying, "What
are we going to do since this man is doing
many signs? 48 If we let him go on like this,
everyone will believe in him, and the Romans
will come and take away both our place and
our nation."
49 One of them, Caiaphas, who was high
priest that year, said to them, "You know
nothing at all! 50 You're not considering that
it is to your[A] advantage that one man should
die for the people rather than the whole nation
perish." 51 He did not say this on his own, but
being high priest that year he prophesied that
Jesus was going to die for the nation, 52 and
not for the nation only, but also to unite the
scattered children of God. 53 So from that day
on they plotted to kill him.
54 Jesus therefore no longer walked openly among the Jews but departed from there
to the countryside near the wilderness, to
a town called Ephraim, and he stayed there
with the disciples.
55 Now the Jewish Passover was near, and
many went up to Jerusalem from the country to purify themselves before the Passover.
56 They were looking for Jesus and asking one
another as they stood in the temple: "What
do you think? He won't come to the festival,
will he?" 57 The chief priests and the Pharisees
had given orders that if anyone knew where
he was, he should report it so that they could
arrest him.

Eternal Perspective | *Death's Defeat/Resurrection*

THE TEARS OF GOD

"Jesus wept." John 11:35

When Jesus heard his good friend Lazarus was ill, he appeared nonchalant. "This sickness will not end in death," he said, matter-of-factly, "but is for the glory of God" (Jn 11:4).

Knowing the outcome, Jesus seemed to take his sweet time traveling to Bethany. ("Dawdling" is probably a better word.) By the time he got there, "Lazarus had already been in the tomb four days" (11:17).

Mary and Mary, Lazarus's sisters, were distraught—and more than a little miffed at Jesus. Separately they chided him, "If you had been here" (translation: If you hadn't dillydallied like you did), "my brother wouldn't have died" (11:21).

Because he knew that Lazarus's sickness would not end in death, Jesus had to know what he was about to do—that unbridled joy was moments away. Yet, when he saw Mary's tears, and the other mourners, and when he approached Lazarus's tomb, John tells us that "Jesus wept."

His tears were, in part, tears of compassion. He wept because his friends were sad (11:33). But perhaps he also wept over a broken world that was never meant to know death or have places like cemeteries and funeral homes.

The anticlimactic ending of the story—the resurrection of Lazarus—reminds us of this: Because Jesus is Lord over death, even our most bitter tears are just a prelude to deep joy.

For the next note on *Eternal Perspective*, see John 14:1-3.

[A] **11:50** Other mss read *to our*

THE ANOINTING AT BETHANY

12 Six days before the Passover, Jesus came
to Bethany where Lazarus[A] was, the one
Jesus had raised from the dead. 2 So they gave
a dinner for him there; Martha was serving
them, and Lazarus was one of those reclining at the table with him. 3 Then Mary took a
pound of perfume, pure and expensive nard,
anointed Jesus's feet, and wiped his feet with
her hair. So the house was filled with the fragrance of the perfume.
4 Then one of his disciples, Judas Iscariot (who
was about to betray him), said, 5 "Why wasn't this
perfume sold for three hundred denarii[B] and
given to the poor?" 6 He didn't say this because
he cared about the poor but because he was a
thief. He was in charge of the money-bag and
would steal part of what was put in it.
7 Jesus answered, "Leave her alone; she has
kept it for the day of my burial. 8 For you always have the poor with you, but you do not
always have me."

THE DECISION TO KILL LAZARUS

9 Then a large crowd of the Jews learned he
was there. They came not only because of Jesus
but also to see Lazarus, the one he had raised
from the dead. 10 But the chief priests had decided to kill Lazarus also, 11 because he was
the reason many of the Jews were deserting
them[C] and believing in Jesus.

THE TRIUMPHAL ENTRY

12 The next day, when the large crowd that had
come to the festival heard that Jesus was coming to Jerusalem, 13 they took palm branches
and went out to meet him. They kept shouting:

"***Hosanna!***
Blessed is he who comes in the name
of the Lord[D] **— the King of Israel!**"

14 Jesus found a young donkey and sat on it,
just as it is written:

15 **Do not be afraid,**
Daughter Zion. Look, your King
is coming,
sitting on a donkey's colt.[E]

16 His disciples did not understand these things
at first. However, when Jesus was glorified,
then they remembered that these things had
been written about him and that they had
done these things to him.
17 Meanwhile, the crowd, which had been
with him when he called Lazarus out of the
tomb and raised him from the dead, continued to testify.[F] 18 This is also why the crowd
met him, because they heard he had done this
sign. 19 Then the Pharisees said to one another,
"You see? You've accomplished nothing. Look,
the world has gone after him!"

JESUS PREDICTS HIS CRUCIFIXION

20 Now some Greeks were among those who
went up to worship at the festival. 21 So they
came to Philip, who was from Bethsaida in
Galilee, and requested of him, "Sir, we want
to see Jesus." 22 Philip went and told Andrew;
then Andrew and Philip went and told Jesus.
23 Jesus replied to them, "The hour has come
for the Son of Man to be glorified. 24 Truly I tell
you, unless a grain of wheat falls to the ground
and dies, it remains by itself. But if it dies, it
produces much fruit. 25 The one who loves his
life will lose it, and the one who hates his life
in this world will keep it for eternal life. 26 If
anyone serves me, he must follow me. Where
I am, there my servant also will be. If anyone
serves me, the Father will honor him.
27 "Now my soul is troubled. What should
I say — Father, save me from this hour? But
that is why I came to this hour. 28 Father, glorify your name."[G]
Then a voice came from heaven: "I have glorified it, and I will glorify it again."
29 The crowd standing there heard it and
said it was thunder. Others said, "An angel
has spoken to him."
30 Jesus responded, "This voice came, not for
me, but for you. 31 Now is the judgment of this
world. Now the ruler of this world will be cast
out. 32 As for me, if I am lifted up[H] from the earth
I will draw all people to myself." 33 He said this to
indicate what kind of death he was about to die.
34 Then the crowd replied to him, "We have
heard from the law that the Messiah will remain
forever. So how can you say, 'The Son of Man
must be lifted up'? Who is this Son of Man?"
35 Jesus answered, "The light will be with you
only a little longer. Walk while you have the
light so that darkness doesn't overtake you.
The one who walks in darkness doesn't know
where he's going. 36 While you have the light,
believe in the light so that you may become
children of light." Jesus said this, then went
away and hid from them.

[A] **12:1** Other mss read *Lazarus who died* [B] **12:5** A denarius = one day's wage [C] **12:11** Lit *going away* [D] **12:13** Ps 118:25-26 [E] **12:15** Zch 9:9 [F] **12:17** Other mss read *Meanwhile the crowd, which had been with him, continued to testify that he had called Lazarus out of the tomb and raised him from the dead.* [G] **12:28** Other mss read *your Son* [H] **12:32** Or *exalted*, also in v. 34

ISAIAH'S PROPHECIES FULFILLED

37 Even though he had performed so many
signs in their presence, they did not believe
in him. 38 This was to fulfill the word of Isaiah
the prophet, who said:[A]

Lord, who has believed
our message?
And to whom has the arm
of the Lord been revealed?[B]

39 This is why they were unable to believe,
because Isaiah also said:

40 **He has blinded their eyes**
and hardened their hearts,
so that they would not see
with their eyes
or understand with their hearts,
and turn,
and I would heal them.[C]

41 Isaiah said these things because[D] he saw
his glory and spoke about him.
42 Nevertheless, many did believe in him
even among the rulers, but because of the
Pharisees they did not confess him, so that
they would not be banned from the synagogue.
43 For they loved human praise more than
praise from God.

A SUMMARY OF JESUS'S MISSION

44 Jesus cried out, "The one who believes in me
believes not in me, but in him who sent me. 45 And
the one who sees me sees him who sent me. 46 I
have come as light into the world, so that everyone who believes in me would not remain
in darkness. 47 If anyone hears my words and
doesn't keep them, I do not judge him; for I did
not come to judge the world but to save the world.
48 The one who rejects me and doesn't receive my
sayings has this as his judge:[E] The word I have
spoken will judge him on the last day. 49 For I have
not spoken on my own, but the Father himself
who sent me has given me a command to say
everything I have said. 50 I know that his command is eternal life. So the things that I speak, I
speak just as the Father has told me."

JESUS WASHES HIS DISCIPLES' FEET

13 Before the Passover Festival, Jesus knew
that his hour had come to depart from
this world to the Father. Having loved his own
who were in the world, he loved them to the end.
2 Now when it was time for supper, the devil had already put it into the heart of Judas,
Simon Iscariot's son,[F] to betray him. 3 Jesus
knew that the Father had given everything

Exercise of Faith | *Trusting God*

FOLLOW THE SIGNS

"Even though he had performed so many signs in their presence, they did not believe in him." John 12:37

John refers to the miracles of Jesus as "signs."

Think for a moment about the purpose of a sign. On a remote highway you don't see people stopping to "ooh" and "ahh" over a billboard that advertises, "LAST GAS for the next 150 miles—next exit." No, you see those motorists exiting the highway and filling their tanks. A sign is only a directional signal. It isn't the attraction; it's merely a pointer to the attraction.

The miracles of Jesus were not then nor are they now intended to wow people or merely to help people, though many of them did and do alleviate suffering. The signs of Jesus are to point people to this truth: *I am the One I claim to be, the Son of God, the Savior of the world.* In the end, the signs are meant to prompt one specific action—belief.

John, who was an eyewitness to all these spectacular signs, says that, tragically, many of his fellow Jews who also saw the signs "did not believe" in Jesus. Some totally rejected Jesus; some continued to follow at a distance; many trusted him with their hearts and minds. We have the same choice today. Let us wholeheartedly follow him.

For the next note on *Exercise of Faith*, see Acts 1:8.

[A] **12:38** Lit *which he said* [B] **12:38** Is 53:1 [C] **12:40** Is 6:10 [D] **12:41** Other mss read *when* [E] **12:48** Lit *has the one judging him* [F] **13:2** Or *Judas Iscariot, Simon's son*

into his hands, that he had come from God,
and that he was going back to God. 4 So he got
up from supper, laid aside his outer clothing,
took a towel, and tied it around himself. 5 Next,
he poured water into a basin and began to
wash his disciples' feet and to dry them with
the towel tied around him.
6 He came to Simon Peter, who asked him,
"Lord, are you going to wash my feet?"
7 Jesus answered him, "What I'm doing you
don't realize now, but afterward you will understand."
8 "You will never wash my feet," Peter said.
Jesus replied, "If I don't wash you, you have
no part with me."
9 Simon Peter said to him, "Lord, not only my
feet, but also my hands and my head."
10 "One who has bathed," Jesus told him,
"doesn't need to wash anything except his
feet, but he is completely clean. You are clean,
but not all of you." 11 For he knew who would
betray him. This is why he said, "Not all of
you are clean."

THE MEANING OF FOOT WASHING

12 When Jesus had washed their feet and put
on his outer clothing, he reclined again and
said to them, "Do you know what I have done
for you? 13 You call me Teacher and Lord — and
you are speaking rightly, since that is what I am.
14 So if I, your Lord and Teacher, have washed
your feet, you also ought to wash one another's
feet. 15 For I have given you an example, that
you also should do just as I have done for you.
16 "Truly I tell you, a servant is not greater
than his master,[A] and a messenger is not greater than the one who sent him. 17 If you know
these things, you are blessed if you do them.
18 "I'm not speaking about all of you; I know
those I have chosen. But the Scripture must be
fulfilled: **The one who eats my bread[B] has
raised his heel against me.**[C] 19 I am telling
you now before it happens, so that when it
does happen you will believe that I am he.
20 Truly I tell you, whoever receives anyone I
send receives me, and the one who receives
me receives him who sent me."

JUDAS'S BETRAYAL PREDICTED

21 When Jesus had said this, he was troubled
in his spirit and testified, "Truly I tell you, one
of you will betray me."
22 The disciples started looking at one another — uncertain which one he was speaking

Relationships | *Relating to Church Family*

WHAT'S OUR BRAND?

"I give you a new command: Love one another. Just as I have loved you, you are also to love one another. By this everyone will know that you are my disciples, if you love one another." John 13:34-35

Today we hear much talk about "branding." This is a marketing term that refers to a person or organization's unique identity or reputation. A best-selling novelist is known for cranking out legal thrillers. A restaurant chain is known for inexpensive sandwiches made to order. A computer company has a worldwide reputation for technological innovation, imagination, and design.

As Jesus gathered with his disciples one final time, he gave them, as it were, their brand. They—and all who joined his movement—were to be known for how well they loved one another. Love was to be their calling card.

Churches and individual believers can easily fall into the trap of thinking that we should focus on other matters: theological knowledge, close-knit families, defending the faith, exuberant worship, Christian education, and more. While all of these are commendable, they are not—according to Jesus—the primary way we are to distinguish ourselves in the world. Our great distinctive, our brand, should be love—especially in how we relate to others in the Christian family.

How do people know you? Let love for your brothers and sisters in Christ be your "brand."

For the next note on *Relationships*, see John 17:23.

[A] **13:16** Or *lord* [B] **13:18** Other mss read *eats bread with me* [C] **13:18** Ps 41:9

about. [23] One of his disciples, the one Jesus
loved, was reclining close beside Jesus.[A] [24] Simon Peter motioned to him to find out who it
was he was talking about. [25] So he leaned back
against Jesus and asked him, "Lord, who is it?"
[26] Jesus replied, "He's the one I give the piece
of bread to after I have dipped it." When he had
dipped the bread, he gave it to Judas, Simon
Iscariot's son.[B] [27] After Judas ate the piece of
bread, Satan entered him. So Jesus told him,
"What you're doing, do quickly."
[28] None of those reclining at the table knew
why he said this to him. [29] Since Judas kept
the money-bag, some thought that Jesus was
telling him, "Buy what we need for the festival," or that he should give something to the
poor. [30] After receiving the piece of bread, he
immediately left. And it was night.

THE NEW COMMAND

[31] When he had left, Jesus said, "Now the Son
of Man is glorified, and God is glorified in
him. [32] If God is glorified in him,[C] God will also
glorify him in himself and will glorify him at
once. [33] Children, I am with you a little while
longer. You will look for me, and just as I told
the Jews, so now I tell you: 'Where I am going,
you cannot come.'
[34] "I give you a new command: Love one
another. Just as I have loved you, you are also
to love one another. [35] By this everyone will
know that you are my disciples, if you love
one another."

PETER'S DENIALS PREDICTED

[36] "Lord," Simon Peter said to him, "where are
you going?"
Jesus answered, "Where I am going you cannot follow me now, but you will follow later."
[37] "Lord," Peter asked, "why can't I follow you
now? I will lay down my life for you."
[38] Jesus replied, "Will you lay down your
life for me? Truly I tell you, a rooster will not
crow until you have denied me three times.

THE WAY TO THE FATHER

14 "Don't let your heart be troubled. Believe[D]
in God; believe also in me. [2] In my Father's
house are many rooms; if not, I would have
told you. I am going away to prepare a place

Eternal Perspective | *Heaven and Hell*

A REAL PLACE

"Don't let your heart be troubled. Believe in God; believe also in me. In my Father's house are many rooms; if not, I would have told you. I am going away to prepare a place for you. If I go away and prepare a place for you, I will come again and take you to myself, so that where I am you may be also." John 14:1-3

The disciples were confused and concerned. What was Jesus up to? Why this cryptic talk about leaving (Jn 13:33)? Why these overt comments about "going up to Jerusalem . . . to be mocked, flogged, and crucified" (Mt 20:18-19)? Where was he, where was all this, going?

The consummate shepherd, Jesus could tell his little flock was skittish, so he attempted to calm them. In a real room full of real people filled with real fear, Jesus spoke about a real place. He mentioned his "Father's house," and said, "I am going away to prepare a place for you." He also promised to "come again" and take them to that place.

If heaven's not real, then we're left with two bad choices: Jesus was either horribly misguided or cruelly dishonest. If it were not true, a loving leader would have warned them. Since everything here on earth has come to pass exactly as he said it would, however, why would we doubt his promises about heaven?

Whenever doubts or fears about the future assail us, we can remember Jesus's words and trust him.

For the next note on *Eternal Perspective*, see John 16:33.

[A] **13:23** Lit *reclining at Jesus's breast*; that is, on his right; Jn 1:18 [B] **13:26** Or *Judas Iscariot, Simon's son* [C] **13:32** Other mss omit *If God is glorified in him* [D] **14:1** Or *You believe*

for you. 3 If I go away and prepare a place for
you, I will come again and take you to myself,
so that where I am you may be also. 4 You know
the way to where I am going."[A]
5 "Lord," Thomas said, "we don't know where
you're going. How can we know the way?"
6 Jesus told him, "I am the way, the truth,
and the life. No one comes to the Father except through me. 7 If you know me, you will
also know[B] my Father. From now on you do
know him and have seen him."

JESUS REVEALS THE FATHER

8 "Lord," said Philip, "show us the Father, and
that's enough for us."
9 Jesus said to him, "Have I been among
you all this time and you do not know me,
Philip? The one who has seen me has seen
the Father. How can you say, 'Show us the
Father'? 10 Don't you believe that I am in the
Father and the Father is in me? The words I
speak to you I do not speak on my own. The
Father who lives in me does his works. 11 Believe me that I am in the Father and the Father
is in me. Otherwise, believe[C] because of the
works themselves.

PRAYING IN JESUS'S NAME

12 "Truly I tell you, the one who believes in me
will also do the works that I do. And he will
do even greater works than these, because I
am going to the Father. 13 Whatever you ask in
my name, I will do it so that the Father may be
glorified in the Son. 14 If you ask me[D] anything
in my name, I will do it.[E]

ANOTHER COUNSELOR PROMISED

15 "If you love me, you will keep[F] my commands.
16 And I will ask the Father, and he will give you
another Counselor[G] to be with you forever.
17 He is the Spirit of truth. The world is unable
to receive him because it doesn't see him or
know him. But you do know him, because he
remains with you and will be[H] in you.

Thanksgiving and Contentment | *Praise for Salvation*

THE WAY

"I am the way, the truth, and the life. No one comes to the Father except through me." John 14:6

More and more we hear the charge: "You are so intolerant! How bigoted and narrow-minded to say that only you Christians are going to heaven!"

Forget about what Christians claim. Examine the words of Christ himself. Here John quotes him saying, "I am the way" and "the truth." (Notice it's not "*a* way" and "*a* truth.") And lest anyone miss the exclusive nature of his claim, Jesus adds, "No one comes to the Father except through me."

That's pretty clear. And, yes, it's surely "intolerant" of competing claims about God or alternative ways to God. But exclusionary? Not at all. Here's why: Multiple times, Jesus made clear that *everyone* is welcome in his kingdom and *anyone* who believes will have eternal life (Jn 5:24; 6:47, 51; 7:37; 8:51; 10:9).

Imagine driving late at night down a lonely highway. You're ravenous, about to eat some two-year-old fast food ketchup packets from your glove compartment, when suddenly you come upon a bustling little diner. It's the only restaurant around. You have a choice: You can rant about no other options being available, or you can pull in and eat. And, unless you stopped, how would you ever know that the owner there is a world-class chef?

Thank God that he has made a way to eternal life (the only way) through Christ.

For the next note on *Thanksgiving and Contentment*, see John 21:22.

[A] **14:4** Other mss read this verse: *And you know where I am going, and you know the way* [B] **14:7** Other mss read *If you had known me, you would have known* [C] **14:11** Other mss read *believe me* [D] **14:14** Other mss omit *me* [E] **14:14** Other mss omit all of v. 14 [F] **14:15** Other mss read *"If you love me, keep* (as a command) [G] **14:16** Or *advocate*, or *comforter*, also in v. 26 [H] **14:17** Other mss read *and is*

THE FATHER, THE SON, AND THE HOLY SPIRIT

18 "I will not leave you as orphans; I am coming to you. 19 In a little while the world will no
longer see me, but you will see me. Because I
live, you will live too. 20 On that day you will
know that I am in my Father, you are in me,
and I am in you. 21 The one who has my commands and keeps them is the one who loves
me. And the one who loves me will be loved
by my Father. I also will love him and will reveal myself to him."
22 Judas (not Iscariot) said to him, "Lord, how
is it you're going to reveal yourself to us and
not to the world?"
23 Jesus answered, "If anyone loves me, he
will keep my word. My Father will love him,
and we will come to him and make our home
with him. 24 The one who doesn't love me will
not keep my words. The word that you hear is
not mine but is from the Father who sent me.
25 "I have spoken these things to you while
I remain with you. 26 But the Counselor, the
Holy Spirit, whom the Father will send in my
name, will teach you all things and remind
you of everything I have told you.

JESUS'S GIFT OF PEACE

27 "Peace I leave with you. My peace I give to
you. I do not give to you as the world gives.
Don't let your heart be troubled or fearful.
28 You have heard me tell you, 'I am going away
and I am coming to you.' If you loved me, you
would rejoice that I am going to the Father,
because the Father is greater than I. 29 I have
told you now before it happens so that when
it does happen you may believe. 30 I will not
talk with you much longer, because the ruler
of the world is coming. He has no power over
me.[A] 31 On the contrary, so that the world may
know that I love the Father, I do as the Father
commanded me.
"Get up; let's leave this place.

THE VINE AND THE BRANCHES

15 "I am the true vine, and my Father is the
gardener. 2 Every branch in me that does
not produce fruit he removes, and he prunes
every branch that produces fruit so that it will
produce more fruit. 3 You are already clean
because of the word I have spoken to you.
4 Remain in me, and I in you. Just as a branch
is unable to produce fruit by itself unless it
remains on the vine, neither can you unless
you remain in me. 5 I am the vine; you are the
branches. The one who remains in me and I
in him produces much fruit, because you can
do nothing without me. 6 If anyone does not
remain in me, he is thrown aside like a branch
and he withers. They gather them, throw them
into the fire, and they are burned. 7 If you remain in me and my words remain in you, ask
whatever you want and it will be done for you.
8 My Father is glorified by this: that you produce much fruit and prove to be[B] my disciples.

Rest and Reflection | *Resting in Christ*

STAYING CLOSE

"Remain in me, and I in you. Just as a branch is unable to produce fruit by itself unless it remains on the vine, neither can you unless you remain in me. I am the vine; you are the branches. The one who remains in me and I in him produces much fruit, because you can do nothing without me." John 15:4-5

The idea of the Greek word translated *remain* (and found four times in these two verses) is "stay" or "live" or "make yourself at home" in him.

Jesus doesn't want us making ourselves strangers, stopping by to see him briefly on Sunday mornings. We are to draw our strength from Jesus and live out his love and care for others *in* him.

When we do this, Jesus says, we've become like the fruitful branch of a grapevine. When we're connected to Jesus and remain in him, our lives become a blessing and delight to those around us. Remain close to the nurturing vine.

For the next note on *Rest and Reflection*, see Acts 26:18.

[A] **14:30** Lit *He has nothing in me* [B] **15:8** Or *and become*

CHRISTLIKE LOVE

9 "As the Father has loved me, I have also loved
you. Remain in my love. 10 If you keep my commands you will remain in my love, just as I
have kept my Father's commands and remain
in his love.
11 "I have told you these things so that my joy
may be in you and your joy may be complete.
12 "This is my command: Love one another
as I have loved you. 13 No one has greater love
than this: to lay down his life for his friends.
14 You are my friends if you do what I command
you. 15 I do not call you servants anymore, because a servant doesn't know what his master[A]
is doing. I have called you friends, because I
have made known to you everything I have
heard from my Father. 16 You did not choose
me, but I chose you. I appointed you to go
and produce fruit and that your fruit should
remain, so that whatever you ask the Father
in my name, he will give you.
17 "This is what I command you: Love one
another.

PERSECUTIONS PREDICTED

18 "If the world hates you, understand that it
hated me before it hated you. 19 If you were of
the world, the world would love you as its own.
However, because you are not of the world,
but I have chosen you out of it, the world hates
you. 20 Remember the word I spoke to you: 'A
servant is not greater than his master.' If they
persecuted me, they will also persecute you. If
they kept my word, they will also keep yours.
21 But they will do all these things to you on
account of my name, because they don't know
the one who sent me. 22 If I had not come and
spoken to them, they would not be guilty of sin.
Now they have no excuse for their sin. 23 The
one who hates me also hates my Father. 24 If I
had not done the works among them that no
one else has done, they would not have sin.
Now they have seen and hated both me and
my Father. 25 But this happened so that the
statement written in their law might be fulfilled: **They hated me for no reason.**[B]

THE COUNSELOR'S MINISTRY

26 "When the Counselor comes, the one I will
send to you from the Father—the Spirit of
truth who proceeds from the Father—he will
testify about me. 27 You also will testify, because
you have been with me from the beginning.
16 "I have told you these things to keep you
from stumbling. 2 They will ban you from
the synagogues. In fact, a time is coming when

Other-centeredness | *Being Unselfish*

LOVE LIKE JESUS

"This is my command: Love one another as I have loved you. No one has greater love than this: to lay down his life for his friends." John 15:12-13

The meal was unforgettable. It began with Jesus taking on the role of a lowly servant and washing the dirty feet of his followers. An awkward confusion and uncertainty hung in the air. Something felt so different—so final.

The men ate the Passover lamb and unleavened bread. Jesus then began talking. Because he was the consummate Teacher, he always had a lot of good things to say, but on this night the words fell from his lips like a waterfall, on a variety of topics. Chilling statements mixed with amazing promises.

Then he dropped this bombshell, "Love one another as I have loved you."

If you close your eyes, you can almost see these nervous men clearing their throats and looking away—over at the platter holding the lamb carcass or down at their clean feet.

Lay down our lives for others? This would be an impossible command, except for one provision. The One who gave it (and modeled it) promised to live inside the ones he gave it to. What will this look like for you?

For the next note on *Other-centeredness*, see Acts 4:32.

[A] **15:15** Or *lord* [B] **15:25** Ps 69:4

anyone who kills you will think he is offering service to God. [3] They will do these things because they haven't known the Father or me. [4] But I have told you these things so that when their time[A] comes you will remember I told them to you. I didn't tell you these things from the beginning, because I was with you. [5] But now I am going away to him who sent me, and not one of you asks me, 'Where are you going?' [6] Yet, because I have spoken these things to you, sorrow has filled your heart. [7] Nevertheless, I am telling you the truth. It is for your benefit that I go away, because if I don't go away the Counselor will not come to you. If I go, I will send him to you. [8] When he comes, he will convict the world about sin, righteousness, and judgment: [9] About sin, because they do not believe in me; [10] about righteousness, because I am going to the Father and you will no longer see me; [11] and about judgment, because the ruler of this world has been judged.

[12] "I still have many things to tell you, but you can't bear them now. [13] When the Spirit of truth comes, he will guide you into all the truth. For he will not speak on his own, but he will speak whatever he hears. He will also declare to you what is to come. [14] He will glorify me, because he will take from what is mine and declare it to you. [15] Everything the Father has is mine. This is why I told you that he takes from what is mine and will declare it to you.

SORROW TURNED TO JOY

[16] "A little while and you will no longer see me; again a little while and you will see me."[B]

[17] Then some of his disciples said to one another, "What is this he's telling us: 'A little while and you will not see me; again a little while and you will see me' and, 'because I am going to the Father'?" [18] They said, "What is this he is saying,[C] 'A little while'? We don't know what he's talking about."

[19] Jesus knew they wanted to ask him, and so he said to them, "Are you asking one another about what I said, 'A little while and you will not see me; again a little while and you will see me'? [20] Truly I tell you, you will weep and mourn, but the world will rejoice. You will become sorrowful, but your sorrow will turn to joy. [21] When a woman is in labor, she has pain because her time has come. But when she has given birth to a child, she no longer remembers the suffering because of

Support | *Holy Spirit's Counsel*

THE SPIRIT OF TRUTH

"When the Spirit of truth comes, he will guide you into all the truth. For he will not speak on his own, but he will speak whatever he hears. He will also declare to you what is to come." John 16:13

To know what to believe can be difficult. We're inundated by urban legends, conspiracy theories, and propaganda. People labeled "experts" flatly contradict one another. Spiritually speaking, the Bible says the enemy of our souls is a "liar and the father of lies" (Jn 8:44) "who deceives the whole world" (Rv 12:9). What are we to think? What are we to do?

Thankfully, Jesus, on the eve of the crucifixion, told his followers that he was giving them "another Counselor to be with you forever" (Jn 14:16). Jesus called him "the Spirit of truth" and said that "he remains with you and will be in you" (14:17).

Here, Jesus mentions this indwelling Counselor again, saying, "He will guide you into all the truth." For those living in an era of spin and fake news, this is a comfort indeed.

Ask the Holy Spirit, this Counselor who lives in you, to help you identify any false ideas or bogus beliefs you've embraced. Ask the Spirit of truth to make you a person of truth.

For the next note on *Support*, see Acts 6:4.

[A] **16:4** Other mss read *when the time* [B] **16:16** Other mss add *because I am going to the Father* [C] **16:18** Other mss omit *he is saying*

the joy that a person has been born into the
world. 22 So you also have sorrow[A] now. But
I will see you again. Your hearts will rejoice,
and no one will take away your joy from you.
23 "In that day you will not ask me anything.
Truly I tell you, anything you ask the Father
in my name, he will give you. 24 Until now
you have asked for nothing in my name. Ask
and you will receive, so that your joy may be
complete.

JESUS THE VICTOR

25 "I have spoken these things to you in figures
of speech. A time is coming when I will no longer speak to you in figures, but I will tell you
plainly about the Father. 26 On that day you will
ask in my name, and I am not telling you that
I will ask the Father on your behalf. 27 For the
Father himself loves you, because you have
loved me and have believed that I came from
God.[B] 28 I came from the Father and have come
into the world. Again, I am leaving the world
and going to the Father."
29 His disciples said, "Look, now you're
speaking plainly and not using any figurative
language. 30 Now we know that you know everything and don't need anyone to question
you. By this we believe that you came from
God."
31 Jesus responded to them, "Do you now
believe? 32 Indeed, an hour is coming, and has
come, when each of you will be scattered to
his own home, and you will leave me alone.
Yet I am not alone, because the Father is with
me. 33 I have told you these things so that in
me you may have peace. You will have suffering in this world. Be courageous! I have
conquered the world."

JESUS PRAYS FOR HIMSELF

17 Jesus spoke these things, looked up to
heaven, and said: "Father, the hour has
come. Glorify your Son so that the Son may
glorify you, 2 since you gave him authority
over all flesh,[C] so that he may give eternal
life to everyone you have given him. 3 This is
eternal life: that they may know you, the only
true God, and the one you have sent — Jesus
Christ. 4 I have glorified you on the earth by
completing the work you gave me to do. 5 Now,

Eternal Perspective | *Biblical Peace*

PEACE THROUGH THE TURMOIL

"I have told you these things so that in me you may have peace. You will have suffering in this world. Be courageous! I have conquered the world." John 16:33

During his final meal with his closest followers, Jesus brought up a number of disturbing realities: One of the Twelve would betray him (Jn 13:21). He was going to a place they couldn't go (13:33). The world would hate them, and they would be persecuted (15:19-20) and ostracized by their fellow Jews (16:2). They were about to endure a time of weeping and grieving (16:20-22), during which they would be scattered and alone (16:32).

Then he added, "I have told you these things so that in me you may have peace."

How is any of this news peace-inducing?

It's not. But some other statements by Jesus are. He promised blessing if they would follow his example (13:17). He assured them of a place in heaven (14:1-3). He vowed to answer their prayers (14:13) and to send a Counselor, also known as the Spirit of truth (14:15-17,25; 16:7), to be in them. He pledged to return (14:28), and to make them fruitful (15:1-16). In the end, he prayed for them.

Notice where Jesus said his followers would find peace in this scary, godless world.

"In me." Know Jesus, know peace—in every circumstance.

For the next note on *Eternal Perspective*, see John 17:3.

[A] **16:22** Other mss read *will have sorrow* [B] **16:27** Other mss read *from the Father* [C] **17:2** Or *people*

Father, glorify me in your presence with that
glory I had with you before the world existed.

JESUS PRAYS FOR HIS DISCIPLES

6 "I have revealed your name to the people you
gave me from the world. They were yours,
you gave them to me, and they have kept your
word. 7 Now they know that everything you
have given me is from you, 8 because I have
given them the words you gave me. They have
received them and have known for certain
that I came from you. They have believed that
you sent me.
9 "I pray[A] for them. I am not praying for the
world but for those you have given me, because
they are yours. 10 Everything I have is yours, and
everything you have is mine, and I am glorified
in them. 11 I am no longer in the world, but they
are in the world, and I am coming to you. Holy
Father, protect[B] them by your name that you
have given me, so that they may be one as we are
one. 12 While I was with them, I was protecting
them by your name that you have given me. I
guarded them and not one of them is lost, except
the son of destruction,[C] so that the Scripture
may be fulfilled. 13 Now I am coming to you, and
I speak these things in the world so that they
may have my joy completed in them. 14 I have
given them your word. The world hated them
because they are not of the world, just as I am
not of the world. 15 I am not praying that you
take them out of the world but that you protect
them from the evil one. 16 They are not of the
world, just as I am not of the world. 17 Sanctify
them by the truth; your word is truth. 18 As you
sent me into the world, I also have sent them
into the world. 19 I sanctify myself for them, so
that they also may be sanctified by the truth.

JESUS PRAYS FOR ALL BELIEVERS

20 "I pray not only for these, but also for those
who believe in me through their word. 21 May
they all be one, as you, Father, are in me and
I am in you. May they also be[D] in us, so that
the world may believe you sent me. 22 I have
given them the glory you have given me, so
that they may be one as we are one. 23 I am
in them and you are in me, so that they may
be made completely one, that the world may
know you have sent me and have loved them
as you have loved me.
24 "Father, I want those you have given me
to be with me where I am, so that they will see
my glory, which you have given me because
you loved me before the world's foundation.
25 Righteous Father, the world has not known

Eternal Perspective | *God's Work in Us*

THE TRUTH ABOUT ETERNAL LIFE

"This is eternal life: that they may know you, the only true God, and the one you have sent—Jesus Christ." John 17:3

Some Christians explain salvation in terms like these: "Eternal life is a hard-to-explain 'holy status' one gets as a result of trusting in Christ. It's sort of like a promissory note, or a 'get-out-of-jail-free' card. It exempts you from hell and qualifies you for heaven. It functions like an insurance policy. It pays off after you die."

Eternal life isn't all that hard to explain, and it isn't something that starts in the future. According to this verse, eternal life is knowing God and his Son Jesus. In other words, eternal life is a relationship. And it begins the moment a person believes in Christ. Remember what Jesus said in another place? "Truly I tell you, anyone who hears my word and believes him who sent me has eternal life" (Jn 5:24). Jesus's prayer says a believer "*has* eternal life," not "*will get* eternal life one day."

This only makes sense. If God, who is the very essence of life, moves suddenly into a cold, dead heart, that's a lot more than the promise of life in the future, don't you think? You have real life, eternal life, now.

For the next note on *Eternal Perspective*, see Acts 15:11.

[A] **17:9** Lit *ask* (throughout this passage) [B] **17:11** Lit *keep* (throughout this passage) [C] **17:12** The one destined for destruction, loss, or perdition [D] **17:21** Other mss add *one*

you. However, I have known you, and they
have known that you sent me. 26 I made your
name known to them and will continue to
make it known, so that the love you have
loved me with may be in them and I may be
in them."

JESUS BETRAYED

18 After Jesus had said these things, he
went out with his disciples across the
Kidron Valley, where there was a garden, and
he and his disciples went into it. 2 Judas, who
betrayed him, also knew the place, because
Jesus often met there with his disciples. 3 So
Judas took a company of soldiers and some
officials[A] from the chief priests and the Pharisees and came there with lanterns, torches,
and weapons.

4 Then Jesus, knowing everything that was
about to happen to him, went out and said to
them, "Who is it that you're seeking?"

5 "Jesus of Nazareth," they answered.

"I am he," Jesus told them.

Judas, who betrayed him, was also standing with them. 6 When Jesus told them, "I am
he," they stepped back and fell to the ground.
7 Then he asked them again, "Who is it that
you're seeking?"

"Jesus of Nazareth," they said.

8 "I told you I am he," Jesus replied. "So if
you're looking for me, let these men go." 9 This
was to fulfill the words he had said: "I have not
lost one of those you have given me."

10 Then Simon Peter, who had a sword, drew
it, struck the high priest's servant, and cut off
his right ear. (The servant's name was Malchus.)
11 At that, Jesus said to Peter, "Put your sword
away! Am I not to drink the cup the Father
has given me?"

JESUS ARRESTED AND TAKEN TO ANNAS

12 Then the company of soldiers, the commander, and the Jewish officials arrested Jesus and
tied him up. 13 First they led him to Annas, since
he was the father-in-law of Caiaphas, who
was high priest that year. 14 Caiaphas was the
one who had advised the Jews that it would
be better for one man to die for the people.

PETER DENIES JESUS

15 Simon Peter was following Jesus, as was
another disciple. That disciple was an

Relationships | *Working for Unity in the Church*

THE POWER OF UNITY

"I am in them and you are in me, so that they may be made completely one, that the world may know you have sent me and have loved them as you have loved me." John 17:23

On the night before Jesus went to the cross, he prayed that his followers might be made "completely one." This was not some spontaneous, off-the-cuff request. This is the thrust of the entire Bible.

When sin entered the world in the garden of Eden, it brought disunity. Humanity became separated from God. People and nations became estranged from one another. The result was a world full of tension, suspicion, animosity, and conflict. So God launched a plan, described by the apostle Paul, "to bring everything together in Christ" (Eph 1:10).

Reconciliation with God resulting in unity among men and women—this is the essence of the gospel. And that's why discord among believers is so devastating. When we bicker and divide, the world says, "If this is what belief in Jesus produces, no thanks. I already know how to do disunity."

When we are one, however, the world sees that Jesus is, indeed, the Son of God. What's more, it marvels at his unfathomable, life-changing love.

What interpersonal conflict in your life, if resolved, would show the world the powerful reality of Christ?

For the next note on *Relationships*, see Acts 10:34-35.

[A] **18:3** Or *temple police*, or *officers*, also in vv. 12,18,22

acquaintance of the high priest; so he went
with Jesus into the high priest's courtyard.
16 But Peter remained standing outside by the
door. So the other disciple, the one known
to the high priest, went out and spoke to the
girl who was the doorkeeper and brought
Peter in.
17 Then the servant girl who was the doorkeeper said to Peter, "You aren't one of this
man's disciples too, are you?"
"I am not," he said. 18 Now the servants and
the officials had made a charcoal fire, because
it was cold. They were standing there warming themselves, and Peter was standing with
them, warming himself.

JESUS BEFORE ANNAS

19 The high priest questioned Jesus about his
disciples and about his teaching.
20 "I have spoken openly to the world," Jesus
answered him. "I have always taught in the
synagogue and in the temple, where all the
Jews congregate, and I haven't spoken anything in secret. 21 Why do you question me?
Question those who heard what I told them.
Look, they know what I said."
22 When he had said these things, one of the
officials standing by slapped Jesus, saying,
"Is this the way you answer the high priest?"
23 "If I have spoken wrongly," Jesus answered
him, "give evidence[A] about the wrong; but if
rightly, why do you hit me?" 24 Then Annas
sent him bound to Caiaphas the high priest.

PETER DENIES JESUS TWICE MORE

25 Now Simon Peter was standing and warming himself. They said to him, "You aren't one
of his disciples too, are you?"
He denied it and said, "I am not."
26 One of the high priest's servants, a relative of the man whose ear Peter had cut off,
said, "Didn't I see you with him in the garden?" 27 Peter denied it again. Immediately a
rooster crowed.

JESUS BEFORE PILATE

28 Then they led Jesus from Caiaphas to the
governor's headquarters. It was early morning.
They did not enter the headquarters themselves; otherwise they would be defiled and
unable to eat the Passover.
29 So Pilate came out to them and said, "What
charge do you bring against this man?"
30 They answered him, "If this man weren't
a criminal,[B] we wouldn't have handed him
over to you."
31 Pilate told them, "You take him and judge
him according to your law."
"It's not legal for us to put anyone to death,"
the Jews declared. 32 They said this so that
Jesus's words might be fulfilled indicating
what kind of death he was going to die.
33 Then Pilate went back into the headquarters, summoned Jesus, and said to him, "Are
you the King of the Jews?"
34 Jesus answered, "Are you asking this on
your own, or have others told you about me?"
35 "I'm not a Jew, am I?" Pilate replied. "Your
own nation and the chief priests handed you
over to me. What have you done?"
36 "My kingdom is not of this world," said
Jesus. "If my kingdom were of this world, my
servants would fight, so that I wouldn't be
handed over to the Jews. But as it is,[C] my kingdom is not from here."
37 "You are a king then?" Pilate asked.
"You say that I'm a king," Jesus replied. "I was
born for this, and I have come into the world
for this: to testify to the truth. Everyone who
is of the truth listens to my voice."
38 "What is truth?" said Pilate.

JESUS OR BARABBAS

After he had said this, he went out to the Jews
again and told them, "I find no grounds for
charging him. 39 You have a custom that I release one prisoner to you at the Passover. So,
do you want me to release to you the King of
the Jews?"
40 They shouted back, "Not this man, but
Barabbas!" Now Barabbas was a revolutionary.[D]

JESUS FLOGGED AND MOCKED

19 Then Pilate took Jesus and had him
flogged. 2 The soldiers also twisted together a crown of thorns, put it on his head,
and clothed him in a purple robe. 3 And they
kept coming up to him and saying, "Hail, King
of the Jews!" and were slapping his face.
4 Pilate went outside again and said to them,
"Look, I'm bringing him out to you to let you
know I find no grounds for charging him."
5 Then Jesus came out wearing the crown of
thorns and the purple robe. Pilate said to them,
"Here is the man!"

[A] **18:23** Or *him, "testify* [B] **18:30** Lit *an evil doer* [C] **18:36** Or *But now* [D] **18:40** Or *robber*; see Jn 10:1,8 for the same Gk word used here

PILATE SENTENCES JESUS TO DEATH

6 When the chief priests and the temple servants[A] saw him, they shouted, "Crucify! Crucify!"

Pilate responded, "Take him and crucify him yourselves, since I find no grounds for charging him."

7 "We have a law," the Jews replied to him, "and according to that law he ought to die, because he made himself the Son of God."

8 When Pilate heard this statement, he was more afraid than ever. 9 He went back into the headquarters and asked Jesus, "Where are you from?" But Jesus did not give him an answer. 10 So Pilate said to him, "Do you refuse to speak to me? Don't you know that I have the authority to release you and the authority to crucify you?"

11 "You would have no authority over me at all," Jesus answered him, "if it hadn't been given you from above. This is why the one who handed me over to you has the greater sin."

12 From that moment Pilate kept trying[B] to release him. But the Jews shouted, "If you release this man, you are not Caesar's friend. Anyone who makes himself a king opposes Caesar!"

13 When Pilate heard these words, he brought Jesus outside. He sat down on the judge's seat in a place called the Stone Pavement (but in Aramaic,[C] *Gabbatha*). 14 It was the preparation day for the Passover, and it was about noon.[D] Then he told the Jews, "Here is your king!"

15 They shouted, "Take him away! Take him away! Crucify him!"

Pilate said to them, "Should I crucify your king?"

"We have no king but Caesar!" the chief priests answered.

16 Then he handed him over to be crucified.

THE CRUCIFIXION

Then they took Jesus away.[E] 17 Carrying the cross by himself, he went out to what is called Place of the Skull, which in Aramaic is called *Golgotha*. 18 There they crucified him and two others with him, one on either side, with Jesus in the middle. 19 Pilate also had a sign made and put on the cross. It said: JESUS OF NAZARETH, THE KING OF THE JEWS. 20 Many of the Jews read this sign, because the place where Jesus was crucified was near the city, and it was written in Aramaic, Latin, and Greek. 21 So the chief priests of the Jews said to Pilate, "Don't write, 'The King of the Jews,' but that he said, 'I am the King of the Jews.'"

22 Pilate replied, "What I have written, I have written."

23 When the soldiers crucified Jesus, they took his clothes and divided them into four parts, a part for each soldier. They also took the tunic, which was seamless, woven in one piece from the top. 24 So they said to one another, "Let's not tear it, but cast lots for it, to see who gets it." This happened that the Scripture might be fulfilled that says: **They divided my clothes among themselves, and they cast lots for my clothing.**[F] This is what the soldiers did.

JESUS'S PROVISION FOR HIS MOTHER

25 Standing by the cross of Jesus were his mother, his mother's sister, Mary the wife of Clopas, and Mary Magdalene. 26 When Jesus saw his mother and the disciple he loved standing there, he said to his mother, "Woman, here is your son." 27 Then he said to the disciple, "Here is your mother." And from that hour the disciple took her into his home.

THE FINISHED WORK OF JESUS

28 After this, when Jesus knew that everything was now finished that the Scripture might be fulfilled, he said, "I'm thirsty." 29 A jar full of sour wine was sitting there; so they fixed a sponge full of sour wine on a hyssop branch and held it up to his mouth.

30 When Jesus had received the sour wine, he said, "It is finished." Then bowing his head, he gave up his spirit.

JESUS'S SIDE PIERCED

31 Since it was the preparation day, the Jews did not want the bodies to remain on the cross on the Sabbath (for that Sabbath was a special[G] day). They requested that Pilate have the men's legs broken and that their bodies be taken away. 32 So the soldiers came and broke the legs of the first man and of the other one who had been crucified with him. 33 When they came to Jesus, they did not break his legs since they saw that he was already dead. 34 But one of the soldiers pierced his side with a spear, and at once blood and water came out. 35 He who saw this has testified so that you also may believe. His testimony is true,

---

[A] **19:6** Or *temple police*, or *officers* [B] **19:12** Lit *Pilate was trying* [C] **19:13** Or *Hebrew*, also in vv. 17,20 [D] **19:14** Lit *about the sixth hour* [E] **19:16** Other mss add *and led him out* [F] **19:24** Ps 22:18 [G] **19:31** Lit *great*

Nicodemus | Restoration Profile

JOHN 3:1-21; 7:50-51; 19:39-42

When Jesus met Nicodemus for the first time, one of his lasting lessons for the Pharisee was a description of the Holy Spirit's restoring work. "The wind blows where it pleases, and you hear its sound, but you don't know where it comes from or where it is going. So it is with everyone born of the Spirit" (Jn 3:8). In the years that followed, Nicodemus became a living case study of Jesus's description. We are never told exactly how the Spirit moved in his life, but we have several examples of the wind blowing through him.

John next recorded Nicodemus speaking up in a gathering of Pharisees who were adamantly rejecting Jesus. On that occasion, he simply confronted his peers with their obvious bias and injustice. He was ridiculed for even bringing up the possible validity of Jesus's claims. Speaking with courage doesn't necessarily mean we will be heard. But a bold awareness of the truth is a mark of restoration.

Later, after the crucifixion, when the primary disciples of Jesus were nowhere to be found, Nicodemus joined Joseph of Arimathea to remove Jesus's body from the cross and entomb it in Joseph's rock-hewn grave. This is the last time Nicodemus is mentioned by name in the New Testament. Perhaps he was one of those described by Luke in Acts 6:7, "So the word of God spread, the disciples in Jerusalem increased greatly in number, and a large group of priests became obedient to the faith."

and he knows he is telling the truth. 36 For
these things happened so that the Scripture
would be fulfilled: **Not one of his bones will
be broken.**[A] 37 Also, another Scripture says:
They will look at the one they pierced.[B]

JESUS'S BURIAL

38 After this, Joseph of Arimathea, who was
a disciple of Jesus — but secretly because of
his fear of the Jews — asked Pilate that he
might remove Jesus's body. Pilate gave him
permission; so he came and took his body away.
39 Nicodemus (who had previously come to
him at night) also came, bringing a mixture of
about seventy-five pounds[C] of myrrh and aloes.
40 They took Jesus's body and wrapped it in
linen cloths with the fragrant spices, according
to the burial custom of the Jews. 41 There was
a garden in the place where he was crucified.
A new tomb was in the garden; no one had yet
been placed in it. 42 They placed Jesus there
because of the Jewish day of preparation and
since the tomb was nearby.

THE EMPTY TOMB

20 On the first day of the week Mary Magdalene came to the tomb early, while
it was still dark. She saw that the stone had
been removed from the tomb. 2 So she went
running to Simon Peter and to the other disciple, the one Jesus loved, and said to them,
"They've taken the Lord out of the tomb, and
we don't know where they've put him!"
3 At that, Peter and the other disciple went
out, heading for the tomb. 4 The two were running together, but the other disciple outran
Peter and got to the tomb first. 5 Stooping
down, he saw the linen cloths lying there,
but he did not go in. 6 Then, following him,
Simon Peter also came. He entered the tomb
and saw the linen cloths lying there. 7 The
wrapping that had been on his head was not
lying with the linen cloths but was folded
up in a separate place by itself. 8 The other
disciple, who had reached the tomb first,
then also went in, saw, and believed. 9 For
they did not yet understand the Scripture
that he must rise from the dead. 10 Then the
disciples returned to the place where they
were staying.

MARY MAGDALENE SEES THE RISEN LORD

11 But Mary stood outside the tomb, crying. As
she was crying, she stooped to look into the
tomb. 12 She saw two angels in white sitting
where Jesus's body had been lying, one at the

[A] **19:36** Ex 12:46; Nm 9:12; Ps 34:20 [B] **19:37** Zch 12:10 [C] **19:39** Lit *a hundred litrai*; a Roman *litrai* = 12 ounces

head and the other at the feet. 13 They said to
her, "Woman, why are you crying?"
"Because they've taken away my Lord," she told
them, "and I don't know where they've put him."
14 Having said this, she turned around and
saw Jesus standing there, but she did not know
it was Jesus. 15 "Woman," Jesus said to her, "why
are you crying? Who is it that you're seeking?"
Supposing he was the gardener, she replied,
"Sir, if you've carried him away, tell me where
you've put him, and I will take him away."
16 Jesus said to her, "Mary."
Turning around, she said to him in Aramaic,[A] "*Rabboni!*" — which means "Teacher."
17 "Don't cling to me," Jesus told her, "since I
have not yet ascended to the Father. But go to
my brothers and tell them that I am ascending to my Father and your Father, to my God
and your God."
18 Mary Magdalene went and announced to
the disciples, "I have seen the Lord!" And she
told them what[B] he had said to her.

THE DISCIPLES COMMISSIONED

19 When it was evening of that first day of the
week, the disciples were gathered together
with the doors locked because they feared
the Jews. Jesus came, stood among them, and
said to them, "Peace be with you."
20 Having said this, he showed them his hands
and his side. So the disciples rejoiced when
they saw the Lord.
21 Jesus said to them again, "Peace to you.
As the Father has sent me, I also send you."
22 After saying this, he breathed on them and
said,[C] "Receive the Holy Spirit. 23 If you forgive
the sins of any, they are forgiven them; if you
retain the sins of any, they are retained."

THOMAS SEES AND BELIEVES

24 But Thomas (called "Twin"[D]), one of the
Twelve, was not with them when Jesus came.
25 So the other disciples were telling him, "We've
seen the Lord!"
But he said to them, "If I don't see the mark
of the nails in his hands, put my finger into
the mark of the nails, and put my hand into
his side, I will never believe."
26 A week later his disciples were indoors
again, and Thomas was with them. Even though
the doors were locked, Jesus came and stood
among them and said, "Peace be with you."
27 Then he said to Thomas, "Put your finger
here and look at my hands. Reach out your
hand and put it into my side. Don't be faithless, but believe."
28 Thomas responded to him, "My Lord and
my God!"
29 Jesus said, "Because you have seen me,
you have believed.[E] Blessed are those who
have not seen and yet believe."

THE PURPOSE OF THIS GOSPEL

30 Jesus performed many other signs in the
presence of his disciples that are not written
in this book. 31 But these are written so that
you may believe that Jesus is the Messiah, the
Son of God,[F] and that by believing you may
have life in his name.

JESUS'S THIRD APPEARANCE TO THE DISCIPLES

21 After this, Jesus revealed himself again
to his disciples by the Sea of Tiberias.
He revealed himself in this way:
2 Simon Peter, Thomas (called "Twin"[D]), Nathanael from Cana of Galilee, Zebedee's sons,
and two others of his disciples were together.
3 "I'm going fishing," Simon Peter said to them.
"We're coming with you," they told him.
They went out and got into the boat, but that
night they caught nothing.
4 When daybreak came, Jesus stood on the
shore, but the disciples did not know it was
Jesus. 5 "Friends,"[G] Jesus called to them, "you
don't have any fish, do you?"
"No," they answered.
6 "Cast the net on the right side of the boat,"
he told them, "and you'll find some." So they
did,[H] and they were unable to haul it in because
of the large number of fish. 7 The disciple, the
one Jesus loved, said to Peter, "It is the Lord!"
When Simon Peter heard that it was the
Lord, he tied his outer clothing around him
(for he had taken it off) and plunged into the
sea. 8 Since they were not far from land (about
a hundred yards[I] away), the other disciples
came in the boat, dragging the net full of fish.
9 When they got out on land, they saw a charcoal fire there, with fish lying on it, and bread.
10 "Bring some of the fish you've just caught,"
Jesus told them. 11 So Simon Peter climbed up
and hauled the net ashore, full of large fish
— 153 of them. Even though there were so
many, the net was not torn.

[A] **20:16** Or *Hebrew* [B] **20:18** Lit *these things* [C] **20:22** Lit *he breathed and said to them* [D] **20:24; 21:2** Gk *Didymus* [E] **20:29** Or *have you believed?* [F] **20:31** Or *that the Messiah, the Son of God, is Jesus* [G] **21:5** Lit *"Children"* [H] **21:6** Lit *they cast* [I] **21:8** Lit *about two hundred cubits*

Thomas | Restoration Profile

MATTHEW, MARK, LUKE, JOHN, ACTS 1:13

The apostle Thomas may have invited "becoming" synonymous with "doubting," but his life is a wider story of restoration. Underlying his tendency to impulsively view life from a jaundiced perspective beat a heart of genuine belief. When Thomas voiced doubts, he wasn't expressing an unbelieving attitude but a willingness to act in faith.

Thomas's reputation rests on three statements he made in the closing weeks of Jesus's ministry on earth. In the episode leading to the resurrection of Lazarus, despite the very real dangers posed to Jesus by journeying to Bethany, Thomas spurred his fellow reluctant disciples into motion by his somewhat negative statement, "Let's go too so that we may die with him" (Jn 11:16). During the Last Supper, after Jesus addressed the disciples' troubled hearts with his promise of many rooms in his Father's house, Thomas expressed their shared confusion. "'Lord,' Thomas said, 'we don't know where you're going. How can we know the way?'" (14:5). This set up one of Jesus's classic "I am" statements that indicated his unique role as Savior (14:6).

Then, after the resurrection, when Jesus first appeared to the gathered disciples, Thomas was absent. Rather than immediately believe his fellow followers' testimony, he rather insistently expressed his own need to see the risen Lord (20:25). Jesus met his request, not so much to satisfy Thomas as to make the point that he expected his followers to believe even when they couldn't see.

Thomas experienced the same ebb and flow of doubts, fears, and confusion that we share. Unlike many, he was transparent with his weaknesses and, as a result, became an example of the continued, one-day-at-a-time restoration God is willing to work out in our lives.

12 "Come and have breakfast," Jesus told
them. None of the disciples dared ask him,
"Who are you?" because they knew it was the
Lord. 13 Jesus came, took the bread, and gave it
to them. He did the same with the fish. 14 This
was now the third time Jesus appeared[A] to the
disciples after he was raised from the dead.

JESUS'S THREEFOLD RESTORATION OF PETER

15 When they had eaten breakfast, Jesus asked
Simon Peter, "Simon, son of John,[B] do you love
me more than these?"
"Yes, Lord," he said to him, "you know that
I love you."
"Feed my lambs," he told him. 16 A second
time he asked him, "Simon, son of John, do
you love me?"
"Yes, Lord," he said to him, "you know that
I love you."
"Shepherd my sheep," he told him.
17 He asked him the third time, "Simon, son
of John, do you love me?"
Peter was grieved that he asked him the third
time, "Do you love me?" He said, "Lord, you
know everything; you know that I love you."
"Feed my sheep," Jesus said. 18 "Truly I tell
you, when you were younger, you would tie
your belt and walk wherever you wanted. But
when you grow old, you will stretch out your
hands and someone else will tie you and carry you where you don't want to go." 19 He said
this to indicate by what kind of death Peter
would glorify God. After saying this, he told
him, "Follow me."

CORRECTING A FALSE REPORT

20 So Peter turned around and saw the disciple
Jesus loved following them, the one who had
leaned back against Jesus at the supper and
asked, "Lord, who is the one that's going to
betray you?" 21 When Peter saw him, he said
to Jesus, "Lord, what about him?"
22 "If I want him to remain until I come,"
Jesus answered, "what is that to you? As for
you, follow me."
23 So this rumor[C] spread to the brothers
and sisters that this disciple would not die.
Yet Jesus did not tell him that he would not
die, but, "If I want him to remain until I come,
what is that to you?"

[A] **21:14** Lit *was revealed* (v. 1) [B] **21:15-17** Other mss read *"Simon, son of Jonah*; Mt 16:17; Jn 1:42 [C] **21:23** Lit *this word*

EPILOGUE

24 This is the disciple who testifies to these things and who wrote them down. We know that his testimony is true.

25 And there are also many other things that Jesus did, which, if every one of them were written down, I suppose not even the world itself could contain the books[A] that would be written.

Thanksgiving and Contentment | *Comparisons*

LIVING YOUR STORY

"'If I want him to remain until I come,' Jesus answered, 'what is that to you? As for you, follow me.'" John 21:22

Social media is great when it reminds us of birthdays or informs us of big news (good or bad) in the lives of friends and acquaintances. But what about when we become so absorbed in the lives of others that we stop living our own lives?

If you find that a big part of what *you* do each day is scrolling through your social media focusing on what *others* are doing or not doing, Jesus has a word for you.

Following the resurrection, Jesus was eating breakfast on the beach with his followers. He gave Peter a peek into his future, at which point Peter turned and looked over at John. "Lord," Peter asked, "what about him?" (Jn 21:21).

"What is that to you?" Jesus responded. It was his polite way of saying, "That's not your business, Peter. What I have planned for John is between him and me. Quit wondering about him and stop worrying about others. Instead, focus on one thing: following me."

If social media helps you follow Jesus, great! If it's turning you into a spectator of life rather than a participant in life, maybe you should take a break.

For the next note on *Thanksgiving and Contentment*, see Romans 3:23-24.

A **21:25** Lit *scroll*

RESTORATION THEMES

R	Rest and Reflection	*Resting and Recharging—26:17-18*
E	Eternal Perspective	*God's Grace/Kindness—15:11* *God's Plans—16:6-7*
S	Support	*Prayer—6:4*
T	Thanksgiving and Contentment	*For the next note, see Roman 3:23-24.*
O	Other-centeredness	*Giving Generously—Acts 4:32* *Praying for Others—9:3-4* *Encouraging—9:26-27*
R	Relationships	*Being Impartial—10:34-35* *Resolving Arguments/Disagreements/Conflicts—15:37-39*
E	Exercise of Faith	*Sharing Faith/Gospel—1:8; 4:19-20; 16:14* *Being Involved in Church—2:42* *Reflecting Christ—4:13* *Setting a Good Example—7:59-60* *Rejecting False Teaching—20:30* *Sharing Story—22:3*

PROLOGUE

1 I wrote the first narrative, Theophilus, about
all that Jesus began to do and teach 2 until
the day he was taken up, after he had given
instructions through the Holy Spirit to the
apostles he had chosen. 3 After he had suffered,
he also presented himself alive to them by
many convincing proofs, appearing to them
over a period of forty days and speaking about
the kingdom of God.

THE HOLY SPIRIT PROMISED

4 While he was[A] with them, he commanded
them not to leave Jerusalem, but to wait for
the Father's promise. "Which," he said, "you
have heard me speak about; 5 for John baptized
with water, but you will be baptized with the
Holy Spirit in a few days."

6 So when they had come together, they asked
him, "Lord, are you restoring the kingdom to
Israel at this time?"

7 He said to them, "It is not for you to know
times or periods that the Father has set by his
own authority. 8 But you will receive power
when the Holy Spirit has come on you, and
you will be my witnesses in Jerusalem, in all
Judea and Samaria, and to the end of the earth."

THE ASCENSION

9 After he had said this, he was taken up as they
were watching, and a cloud took him out of
their sight. 10 While he was going, they were
gazing into heaven, and suddenly two men in
white clothes stood by them. 11 They said, "Men
of Galilee, why do you stand looking up into
heaven? This same Jesus, who has been taken
from you into heaven, will come in the same
way that you have seen him going into heaven."

UNITED IN PRAYER

12 Then they returned to Jerusalem from the
Mount of Olives, which is near Jerusalem
— a Sabbath day's journey away. 13 When
they arrived, they went to the room upstairs
where they were staying: Peter, John, James,
Andrew, Philip, Thomas, Bartholomew, Matthew, James the son of Alphaeus, Simon the
Zealot, and Judas the son of James. 14 They
all were continually united in prayer,[B] along
with the women, including Mary the mother
of Jesus, and his brothers.

MATTHIAS CHOSEN

15 In those days Peter stood up among the brothers and sisters[C] — the number of people who

Exercise of Faith | *Sharing Faith/Gospel*

POWER TO WITNESS

"But you will receive power when the Holy Spirit has come on you, and you will be my witnesses in Jerusalem, in all Judea and Samaria, and to the end of the earth." Acts 1:8

From Spiderman to Ironman to Wonder Woman, contemporary culture is fascinated by superheroes with super powers. So, if you could have any power, what power would you want to have?

Just before returning to heaven, Jesus promised to give his followers a supernatural power. This divine strengthening wouldn't give anyone the ability to leap tall buildings in a single bound. But it would enable believers to be Christ's witnesses—all over the world. The source of this spiritual strength would be the Holy Spirit of God, whom Jesus promised would shortly come upon believers.

They didn't have to wait long. At Pentecost in Jerusalem, God filled the assembled Jewish believers with his Spirit (2:1-4). Afterward, Peter preached a short message (2:14-36) to the massive crowd gathered at the temple. As a result, many "were pierced to the heart" (2:37), and more than three thousand put their faith in Jesus (2:41)!

Why not request that "super power"—the power to be a potent spokesman for the gospel? Ask God to fill you with his Spirit and to give you opportunities to talk about what Jesus has done for you.

For the next note on *Exercise of Faith*, see Acts 2:42.

[A] **1:4** Or *he was eating*, or *he was lodging* [B] **1:14** Other mss add *and petition* [C] **1:15** Other mss read *disciples*

were together was about a hundred and twenty — and said: 16 "Brothers and sisters, it was
necessary that the Scripture be fulfilled that
the Holy Spirit through the mouth of David
foretold about Judas, who became a guide to
those who arrested Jesus. 17 For he was one of
our number and shared in this ministry." 18 Now
this man acquired a field with his unrighteous
wages. He fell headfirst, his body burst open
and his intestines spilled out. 19 This became
known to all the residents of Jerusalem, so
that in their own language that field is called
Hakeldama (that is, Field of Blood). 20 "For it
is written in the Book of Psalms:

Let his dwelling become desolate;
let no one live in it;[A] **and**
Let someone else take his position.[B]

21 "Therefore, from among the men who have
accompanied us during the whole time the
Lord Jesus went in and out among us — 22 beginning from the baptism of John until the
day he was taken up from us — from among
these, it is necessary that one become a witness with us of his resurrection."
23 So they proposed two: Joseph, called Barsabbas, who was also known as Justus, and Matthias.
24 Then they prayed, "You, Lord, know everyone's
hearts; show which of these two you have chosen
25 to take the place[C] in this apostolic ministry
that Judas left to go where he belongs." 26 Then
they cast lots for them, and the lot fell to Matthias and he was added to the eleven apostles.

PENTECOST

2 When the day of Pentecost had arrived,
they were all together in one place. 2 Suddenly a sound like that of a violent rushing
wind came from heaven, and it filled the whole
house where they were staying. 3 They saw
tongues like flames of fire that separated
and rested on each one of them. 4 Then they
were all filled with the Holy Spirit and began
to speak in different tongues,[D] as the Spirit
enabled them.
5 Now there were Jews staying in Jerusalem,
devout people from every nation under heav-
en. 6 When this sound occurred, a crowd came
together and was confused because each one
heard them speaking in his own language.
7 They were astounded and amazed, saying,[E]
"Look, aren't all these who are speaking Galileans? 8 How is it that each of us can hear
them in our own native language? 9 Parthians,
Medes, Elamites; those who live in Mesopotamia, in Judea and Cappadocia, Pontus and
Asia, 10 Phrygia and Pamphylia, Egypt and
the parts of Libya near Cyrene; visitors from
Rome (both Jews and converts), 11 Cretans and
Arabs — we hear them declaring the magnificent acts of God in our own tongues." 12 They
were all astounded and perplexed, saying to
one another, "What does this mean?" 13 But
some sneered and said, "They're drunk on
new wine."

PETER'S SERMON

14 Peter stood up with the Eleven, raised his
voice, and proclaimed to them: "Fellow Jews
and all you residents of Jerusalem, let me
explain this to you and pay attention to my
words. 15 For these people are not drunk, as you
suppose, since it's only nine in the morning.[F]
16 On the contrary, this is what was spoken
through the prophet Joel:

17 **And it will be** in the last days,
says God,
that I will pour out my Spirit
on all people;
then your sons and your daughters
will prophesy,
your young men will see visions,
and your old men will
dream dreams.
18 **I will even pour out my Spirit**
on my servants in those days, both
men and women
and they will prophesy.
19 **I will display wonders**
in the heaven above
and signs on the earth below:
blood and fire and a cloud of smoke.
20 **The sun will be turned to darkness**
and the moon to blood
before the great and glorious day of
the Lord comes.
21 **Then everyone who calls**
on the name of the Lord
will be saved.[G]

22 "Fellow Israelites, listen to these words:
This Jesus of Nazareth was a man attested to
you by God with miracles, wonders, and signs
that God did among you through him, just as
you yourselves know. 23 Though he was delivered up according to God's determined plan

[A] **1:20** Ps 69:25 [B] **1:20** Ps 109:8 [C] **1:25** Other mss read *to share* [D] **2:4** languages, also in v. 11 [E] **2:7** Other mss add *to one another* [F] **2:15** Lit *it's the third hour of the day* [G] **2:17-21** Jl 2:28-32

and foreknowledge, you used[A] lawless people
to nail him to a cross and kill him. 24 God raised
him up, ending the pains of death, because it
was not possible for him to be held by death.
25 For David says of him:

I saw the Lord ever before me;
because he is at my right hand,
I will not be shaken.
26 **Therefore my heart is glad**
and my tongue rejoices.
Moreover, my flesh will rest
in hope,
27 **because you will not abandon me**
in Hades
or allow your holy one to see decay.
28 **You have revealed the paths of life**
to me;
you will fill me with gladness
in your presence.[B]

29 "Brothers and sisters, I can confidently
speak to you about the patriarch David: He
is both dead and buried, and his tomb is with
us to this day. 30 Since he was a prophet, he
knew that God had sworn an oath to him to
seat one of his descendants[C] on his throne.
31 Seeing what was to come, he spoke concerning the resurrection of the Messiah: He[D]
was not abandoned in Hades, and his flesh
did not experience decay.[E]

32 "God has raised this Jesus; we are all witnesses of this. 33 Therefore, since he has been
exalted to the right hand of God and has received from the Father the promised Holy
Spirit, he has poured out what you both see
and hear. 34 For it was not David who ascended
into the heavens, but he himself says:

The Lord declared to my Lord,
'Sit at my right hand
35 **until I make your enemies**
your footstool.'[F]

36 "Therefore let all the house of Israel know
with certainty that God has made this Jesus,
whom you crucified, both Lord and Messiah."

CALL TO REPENTANCE

37 When they heard this, they were pierced
to the heart and said to Peter and the rest of
the apostles: "Brothers, what should we do?"
38 Peter replied, "Repent and be baptized,
each of you, in the name of Jesus Christ for the

Exercise of Faith | *Being Involved in Church*

WHAT'S A CHURCH TO DO?

"They devoted themselves to the apostles' teaching, to the fellowship, to the breaking of bread, and to prayer." Acts 2:42

Most Christians see the coming of the Spirit upon believers in Jesus at Pentecost (Ac 2) as the birthday of the "church." Since that word has so much meaning (good and bad) to so many people, and since so many different variations of "church" are on the horizon, let's look at the earliest version.

First, church is "they." The church is people—not a building—all the people who have put their faith in Christ.

These early Christians were "devoted." This conveys a strong commitment. It's means to "remain by" or "stay with." And to what activities were they devoted? "The apostles' teaching" (the truth of God fully revealed in and through Jesus) and "the fellowship" (the common life and calling believers have in Christ). This fellowship included "the breaking of bread," most likely the Lord's Supper shared, and "prayer." This the earliest order of service in the New Testament.

Churches typically offer all sorts of activities. Seek a church built on these essentials: a high commitment to the authority of God's Word, deep relationships, regular celebration of the Lord's Supper, and devotion to prayer.

For the next note on *Exercise of Faith*, see Acts 4:13.

[A] **2:23** Other mss read *you have taken* [B] **2:25-28** Ps 16:8-11 [C] **2:30** Other mss add *according to the flesh to raise up the Messiah* [D] **2:31** Other mss read *His soul* [E] **2:31** Ps 16:10 [F] **2:34-35** Ps 110:1

forgiveness of your sins, and you will receive
the gift of the Holy Spirit. 39 For the promise is
for you and for your children, and for all who
are far off, as many as the Lord our God will
call." 40 With many other words he testified
and strongly urged them, saying, "Be saved
from this corrupt[A] generation!" 41 So those
who accepted his message were baptized, and
that day about three thousand people were
added to them.

A GENEROUS AND GROWING CHURCH

42 They devoted themselves to the apostles'
teaching, to the fellowship, to the breaking
of bread, and to prayer.
43 Everyone was filled with awe, and many
wonders and signs were being performed
through the apostles. 44 Now all the believers
were together and held all things in common.
45 They sold their possessions and property
and distributed the proceeds to all, as any had
need. 46 Every day they devoted themselves
to meeting together in the temple, and broke
bread from house to house. They ate their food
with joyful and sincere hearts, 47 praising God
and enjoying the favor of all the people. Every
day the Lord added to their number[B] those
who were being saved.

HEALING OF A LAME MAN

3 Now Peter and John were going up to the
temple for the time of prayer at three in
the afternoon.[C] 2 A man who was lame from
birth was being carried there. He was placed
each day at the temple gate called Beautiful,
so that he could beg from those entering the
temple. 3 When he saw Peter and John about to
enter the temple, he asked for money. 4 Peter,
along with John, looked straight at him and
said, "Look at us." 5 So he turned to them, expecting to get something from them. 6 But Peter
said, "I don't have silver or gold, but what I do
have, I give you: In the name of Jesus Christ
of Nazareth, get up and walk!" 7 Then, taking
him by the right hand he raised him up, and
at once his feet and ankles became strong.
8 So he jumped up and started to walk, and
he entered the temple with them — walking,
leaping, and praising God. 9 All the people saw
him walking and praising God, 10 and they recognized that he was the one who used to sit
and beg at the Beautiful Gate of the temple. So
they were filled with awe and astonishment
at what had happened to him.

PREACHING IN SOLOMON'S COLONNADE

11 While he[D] was holding on to Peter and John,
all the people, utterly astonished, ran toward
them in what is called Solomon's Colonnade.
12 When Peter saw this, he addressed the people: "Fellow Israelites, why are you amazed at
this? Why do you stare at us, as though we had
made him walk by our own power or godliness?
13 The God of Abraham, Isaac, and Jacob, the
God of our ancestors, has glorified his servant
Jesus, whom you handed over and denied before Pilate, though he had decided to release
him. 14 You denied the Holy and Righteous
One and asked to have a murderer released
to you. 15 You killed the source[E] of life, whom
God raised from the dead; we are witnesses of
this. 16 By faith in his name, his name has made
this man strong, whom you see and know. So
the faith that comes through Jesus has given
him this perfect health in front of all of you.
17 "And now, brothers and sisters, I know that
you acted in ignorance, just as your leaders
also did. 18 In this way God fulfilled what he
had predicted through all the prophets — that
his Messiah would suffer. 19 Therefore repent
and turn back, so that your sins may be wiped
out, 20 that seasons of refreshing may come
from the presence of the Lord, and that he
may send Jesus, who has been appointed for
you as the Messiah. 21 Heaven must receive
him until the time of the restoration of all
things, which God spoke about through his
holy prophets from the beginning. 22 Moses
said:[F] **The Lord your God will raise up for
you a prophet like me from among your
brothers and sisters. You must listen to
everything he tells you.** 23 **And everyone
who does not listen to that prophet will
be completely cut off from the people.**[G]
24 "In addition, all the prophets who have
spoken, from Samuel and those after him,
have also foretold these days. 25 You are the
sons[H] of the prophets and of the covenant
that God made with your ancestors, saying to
Abraham, **And all the families of the earth
will be blessed through your offspring.**[I]
26 God raised up his servant[J] and sent him
first to you to bless you by turning each of
you from your evil ways."

[A] **2:40** Or *crooked*, or *twisted* [B] **2:47** Other mss read *to the church* [C] **3:1** Lit *at the ninth hour* [D] **3:11** Other mss read *the lame man who was healed* [E] **3:15** Or *the Prince*, or *the Ruler* [F] **3:22** Other mss add *to the fathers* [G] **3:22-23** Dt 18:15-19 [H] **3:25** = heirs [I] **3:25** Gn 12:3; 18:18; 22:18; 26:4 [J] **3:26** Other mss add *Jesus*

PETER AND JOHN ARRESTED

4 While they were speaking to the people,
the priests, the captain of the temple police,
and the Sadducees confronted them, 2 because
they were annoyed that they were teaching
the people and proclaiming in Jesus the resurrection of the dead. 3 So they seized them
and took them into custody until the next day
since it was already evening. 4 But many of
those who heard the message believed, and
the number of the men[A] came to about five
thousand.

PETER AND JOHN FACE THE JEWISH LEADERSHIP

5 The next day, their rulers, elders, and scribes
assembled in Jerusalem 6 with Annas the high
priest, Caiaphas, John, Alexander, and all the
members of the high-priestly family. 7 After
they had Peter and John stand before them,
they began to question them: "By what power
or in what name have you done this?"
8 Then Peter was filled with the Holy Spirit
and said to them, "Rulers of the people and
elders:[B] 9 If we are being examined today about
a good deed done to a disabled man, by what
means he was healed, 10 let it be known to all
of you and to all the people of Israel, that by
the name of Jesus Christ of Nazareth, whom
you crucified and whom God raised from the
dead — by him this man is standing here before you healthy. 11 This Jesus is

the stone rejected by you builders,
which has become the cornerstone.[C]

12 There is salvation in no one else, for there is
no other name under heaven given to people
by which we must be saved."

THE BOLDNESS OF THE DISCIPLES

13 When they observed the boldness of Peter
and John and realized that they were uneducated and untrained men, they were amazed
and recognized that they had been with Jesus.
14 And since they saw the man who had been
healed standing with them, they had nothing
to say in opposition. 15 After they ordered
them to leave the Sanhedrin, they conferred
among themselves, 16 saying, "What should we
do with these men? For an obvious sign has
been done through them, clear to everyone
living in Jerusalem, and we cannot deny it.
17 But so that this does not spread any further
among the people, let's threaten them against
speaking to anyone in this name again." 18 So

Exercise of Faith | *Reflecting Christ*

LIKE JESUS

"When they observed the boldness of Peter and John and realized that they were uneducated and untrained men, they were amazed and recognized that they had been with Jesus." Acts 4:13

"Your mother taught you well—this tastes every bit as good as her apple pie!" "I can tell you studied under Dr. Walker—you have so many of his mannerisms."

This is what happens when we train under someone, formally or informally. Our teachers and mentors mark us. Their influence shows in a variety of ways. We tend to borrow their lingo, co-opt their ideas, and even mimic their behaviors. Thus, we must wisely choose our teachers.

When the apostles were summoned to appear before the Jewish Sanhedrin (the same ruling council that had met and schemed only weeks before to get Jesus condemned), Luke says the authorities "were amazed." And they "recognized that [Peter and John] had been with Jesus." In other words, after spending three years walking and talking with Jesus and learning from him, Peter and John were like him. They may have lacked formal, rabbinical training (Jesus did too), but they were bold.

Here's a good question to ask ourselves: When people observe us, can they tell that we've "been with Jesus"?

For the next note on *Exercise of Faith*, see Acts 4:19-20.

[A] **4:4** Or *people* [B] **4:8** Other mss add *of Israel* [C] **4:11** Ps 118:22

IN AND OUT OF PRISON

17 Then the high priest rose up. He and all who were with him, who belonged to the party of the Sadducees, were filled with jealousy. 18 So they arrested the apostles and put them in the public jail. 19 But an angel of the Lord opened the doors of the jail during the night, brought them out, and said, 20 "Go and stand in the temple, and tell the people all about this life." 21 Hearing this, they entered the temple at daybreak and began to teach.

THE APOSTLES ON TRIAL AGAIN

When the high priest and those who were with him arrived, they convened the Sanhedrin — the full council of the Israelites — and sent orders to the jail to have them brought. 22 But when the servants[A] got there, they did not find them in the jail, so they returned and reported, 23 "We found the jail securely locked, with the guards standing in front of the doors, but when we opened them, we found no one inside." 24 As[B] the captain of the temple police and the chief priests heard these things, they were baffled about them, wondering what would come of this.

25 Someone came and reported to them, "Look! The men you put in jail are standing in the temple and teaching the people." 26 Then the commander went with the servants and brought them in without force, because they were afraid the people might stone them. 27 After they brought them in, they had them stand before the Sanhedrin, and the high priest asked, 28 "Didn't we strictly order you not to teach in this name? Look, you have filled Jerusalem with your teaching and are determined to make us guilty of this man's blood."

29 Peter and the apostles replied, "We must obey God rather than people. 30 The God of our ancestors raised up Jesus, whom you had murdered by hanging him on a tree. 31 God exalted this man to his right hand as ruler and Savior, to give repentance to Israel and forgiveness of sins. 32 We are witnesses of these things, and so is the Holy Spirit whom God has given to those who obey him."

GAMALIEL'S ADVICE

33 When they heard this, they were enraged and wanted to kill them. 34 But a Pharisee named Gamaliel, a teacher of the law who was respected by all the people, stood up in the Sanhedrin and ordered the men[C] to be taken outside for a little while. 35 He said to them, "Men of Israel, be careful about what you're about to do to these men. 36 Some time ago Theudas rose up, claiming to be somebody, and a group of about four hundred men rallied to him. He was killed, and all his followers were dispersed and came to nothing. 37 After this man, Judas the Galilean rose up in the days of the census and attracted a following. He also perished, and all his followers were scattered. 38 So in the present case, I tell you, stay away from these men and leave them alone. For if this plan or this work is of human origin, it will fail; 39 but if it is of God, you will not be able to overthrow them. You may even be found fighting against God." They were persuaded by him. 40 After they called in the apostles and had them flogged, they ordered them not to speak in the name of Jesus and released them. 41 Then they went out from the presence of the Sanhedrin, rejoicing that they were counted worthy to be treated shamefully on behalf of the Name.[D] 42 Every day in the temple, and in various homes, they continued teaching and proclaiming the good news that Jesus is the Messiah.

SEVEN CHOSEN TO SERVE

6 In those days, as the disciples were increasing in number, there arose a complaint by the Hellenistic Jews against the Hebraic Jews that their widows were being overlooked in the daily distribution. 2 The Twelve summoned the whole company of the disciples and said, "It would not be right for us to give up preaching the word of God to wait on tables. 3 Brothers and sisters, select from among you seven men of good reputation, full of the Spirit and wisdom, whom we can appoint to this duty. 4 But we will devote ourselves to prayer and to the ministry of the word." 5 This proposal pleased the whole company. So they chose Stephen, a man full of faith and the Holy Spirit, and Philip, Prochorus, Nicanor, Timon, Parmenas, and Nicolaus, a convert from Antioch. 6 They had them stand before the apostles, who prayed and laid their hands on them.

7 So the word of God spread, the disciples in Jerusalem increased greatly in number, and a large group of priests became obedient to the faith.

[A] **5:22** Or *temple police*, or *officers*, also in v. 26 [B] **5:24** Other mss add *the high priest and* [C] **5:34** Other mss read *apostles*
[D] **5:41** Other mss add *of Jesus*, or *of Christ*

STEPHEN ACCUSED OF BLASPHEMY

8 Now Stephen, full of grace and power, was
performing great wonders and signs among
the people. 9 Opposition arose, however, from
some members of the Freedmen's Synagogue,
composed of both Cyrenians and Alexandri-
ans, and some from Cilicia and Asia, and they
began to argue with Stephen. 10 But they were
unable to stand up against his wisdom and
the Spirit by whom he was speaking.
11 Then they secretly persuaded some men
to say, "We heard him speaking blasphemous
words against Moses and God." 12 They stirred
up the people, the elders, and the scribes; so
they came, seized him, and took him to the
Sanhedrin. 13 They also presented false witnesses who said, "This man never stops speaking
against this holy place and the law. 14 For we
heard him say that this Jesus of Nazareth will
destroy this place and change the customs
that Moses handed down to us." 15 And all who
were sitting in the Sanhedrin looked intently
at him and saw that his face was like the face
of an angel.

STEPHEN'S SERMON

7 "Are these things true?" the high priest asked.
2 "Brothers and fathers," he replied, "listen: The God of glory appeared to our father
Abraham when he was in Mesopotamia, before
he settled in Haran, 3 and said to him: **Leave
your country and relatives, and come to
the land that I will show you.**[A]
4 "Then he left the land of the Chaldeans
and settled in Haran. From there, after his
father died, God had him move to this land
in which you are now living. 5 He didn't give
him an inheritance in it — not even a foot of
ground — but he promised to give it to him
as a possession, and to his descendants after him, even though he was childless. 6 God
spoke in this way: His **descendants** would
be strangers in a foreign country, and they
would **enslave and oppress them for four
hundred years. 7 I will judge the nation that
they will serve as slaves**, God said. **After this,
they will come out and worship me in this
place.**[B] 8 And so he gave Abraham the covenant
of circumcision. After this, he fathered Isaac
and circumcised him on the eighth day. Isaac
became the father of Jacob, and Jacob became
the father of the twelve patriarchs.

THE PATRIARCHS IN EGYPT

9 "The patriarchs became jealous of Joseph and
sold him into Egypt, but God was with him 10 and
rescued him out of all his troubles. He gave him
favor and wisdom in the sight of Pharaoh, king

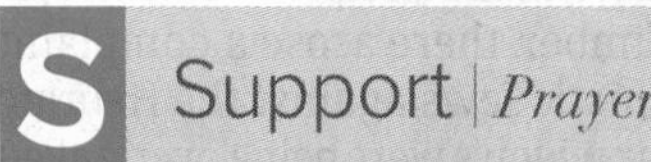

THE PRIORITY OF PRAYER

"But we will devote ourselves to prayer and to the ministry of the word." Acts 6:4

People sometimes complain that the local church seems too "institutional." Once you get beyond a few people gathered informally under a tree or in someone's living room, you inevitably have to start thinking about all kinds of things: formal events requiring lots of prep and cleanup, buildings, staff, meetings, parking, and more. When this happens, church can start to feel less like a living organism and more like a big, complicated organization.

This was a problem even in the early church. The church was already big. Then the believers sponsored a feeding program (6:1). It was wildly successful, attracting many poor people—including a number of widows. Before long the spiritual leaders of the church, the apostles, were spending the bulk of their time waiting tables!

To their credit, these men wisely returned to their God-given calling: praying for the flock and teaching people God's Word. If you're involved in a church, take some time to pray for your leaders. Ministry is a hard and lonely calling. Even ministers get weary and burned out. Lift them up to the Father.

For the next note on *Support*, see Romans 8:27.

[A] **7:3** Gn 12:1 [B] **7:6-7** Gn 15:13-14

of Egypt, who appointed him ruler over Egypt
and over his whole household. 11 Now a famine
and great suffering came over all of Egypt and
Canaan, and our ancestors could find no food.
12 When Jacob heard there was grain in Egypt,
he sent our ancestors there the first time. 13 The
second time, Joseph revealed himself to his
brothers, and Joseph's family became known
to Pharaoh. 14 Joseph invited his father Jacob
and all his relatives, seventy-five people in all,
15 and Jacob went down to Egypt. He and our
ancestors died there, 16 were carried back to
Shechem, and were placed in the tomb that
Abraham had bought for a sum of silver from
the sons of Hamor in Shechem.

MOSES, A REJECTED SAVIOR

17 "As the time was approaching to fulfill the
promise that God had made to Abraham, the
people flourished and multiplied in Egypt
18 until a different king who did not know Joseph ruled over Egypt.[A] 19 He dealt deceitfully
with our race and oppressed our ancestors by
making them abandon their infants outside
so that they wouldn't survive. 20 At this time
Moses was born, and he was beautiful in God's
sight. He was cared for in his father's home
for three months. 21 When he was put outside,
Pharaoh's daughter adopted and raised him
as her own son. 22 So Moses was educated in
all the wisdom of the Egyptians and was powerful in his speech and actions.

23 "When he was forty years old, he decided
to visit his own people, the Israelites. 24 When
he saw one of them being mistreated, he came
to his rescue and avenged the oppressed
man by striking down the Egyptian. 25 He
assumed his people would understand that
God would give them deliverance through
him, but they did not understand. 26 The next
day he showed up while they were fighting
and tried to reconcile them peacefully, saying,
'Men, you are brothers. Why are you mistreating each other?'

27 "But the one who was mistreating his
neighbor pushed Moses aside, saying: **Who
appointed you a ruler and a judge over us?
28 Do you want to kill me, the same way you
killed the Egyptian yesterday?**[B]

29 "When he heard this, Moses fled and became an exile in the land of Midian, where
he became the father of two sons. 30 After
forty years had passed, an angel[C] appeared
to him in the wilderness of Mount Sinai, in
the flame of a burning bush. 31 When Moses
saw it, he was amazed at the sight. As he was
approaching to look at it, the voice of the
Lord came: **32 I am the God of your ancestors — the God of Abraham, of Isaac, and
of Jacob.**[D] Moses began to tremble and did
not dare to look.

33 "The Lord said to him: **Take off the sandals
from your feet, because the place where
you are standing is holy ground. 34 I have
certainly seen the oppression of my people
in Egypt; I have heard their groaning and
have come down to set them free. And now,
come, I will send you to Egypt.**[E]

35 "This Moses, whom they rejected when
they said, **Who appointed you a ruler and
a judge?**[B] — this one God sent as a ruler and
a deliverer through the angel who appeared
to him in the bush. 36 This man led them out
and performed wonders and signs in the land
of Egypt, at the Red Sea, and in the wilderness
for forty years.

ISRAEL'S REBELLION AGAINST GOD

37 "This is the Moses who said to the Israelites: **God**[F] **will raise up for you a prophet
like me from among your brothers and
sisters.**[G] 38 He is the one who was in the assembly in the wilderness, with the angel who
spoke to him on Mount Sinai, and with our
ancestors. He received living oracles to give
to us. 39 Our ancestors were unwilling to obey
him. Instead, they pushed him aside, and in
their hearts turned back to Egypt. 40 They told
Aaron: **Make us gods who will go before
us. As for this Moses who brought us out
of the land of Egypt, we don't know what's
happened to him.**[H] 41 They even made a calf
in those days, offered sacrifice to the idol,
and were celebrating what their hands had
made. 42 God turned away and gave them up
to worship the stars of heaven, as it is written
in the book of the prophets:

House of Israel, did you bring me
offerings and sacrifices
for forty years in the wilderness?
43 **You took up the tent of Moloch**
and the star of your god Rephan,
the images that you made
to worship.
So I will send you into exile
beyond Babylon.[I]

[A] **7:18** Other mss omit *over Egypt* [B] **7:27-28,35** Ex 2:14 [C] **7:30** Other mss add *of the Lord* [D] **7:32** Ex 3:6,15 [E] **7:33-34** Ex 3:5,7-8,10 [F] **7:37** Other mss read *The Lord your God* [G] **7:37** Dt 18:15 [H] **7:40** Ex 32:1,23 [I] **7:42-43** Am 5:25-27

GOD'S REAL TABERNACLE

44 "Our ancestors had the tabernacle of the
testimony in the wilderness, just as he who
spoke to Moses commanded him to make it
according to the pattern he had seen. 45 Our
ancestors in turn received it and with Joshua
brought it in when they dispossessed the nations that God drove out before them, until the
days of David. 46 He found favor in God's sight
and asked that he might provide a dwelling
place for the God[A] of Jacob. 47 It was Solomon,
rather, who built him a house, 48 but the Most
High does not dwell in sanctuaries made with
hands, as the prophet says:

49 Heaven is my throne,
and the earth my footstool.
What sort of house will you build
for me?
says the Lord,
or what will be
my resting place?
50 Did not my hand make all
these things?[B]

RESISTING THE HOLY SPIRIT

51 "You stiff-necked people with uncircumcised hearts and ears! You are always resisting
the Holy Spirit. As your ancestors did, you
do also. 52 Which of the prophets did your
ancestors not persecute? They even killed
those who foretold the coming of the Righteous One, whose betrayers and murderers
you have now become. 53 You received the
law under the direction of angels and yet
have not kept it."

THE FIRST CHRISTIAN MARTYR

54 When they heard these things, they were
enraged[C] and gnashed their teeth at him.
55 Stephen, full of the Holy Spirit, gazed into
heaven. He saw the glory of God, and Jesus
standing at the right hand of God. 56 He said,
"Look, I see the heavens opened and the Son
of Man standing at the right hand of God!"
57 They yelled at the top of their voices, covered their ears, and together rushed against
him. 58 They dragged him out of the city and
began to stone him. And the witnesses laid
their garments at the feet of a young man
named Saul. 59 While they were stoning Stephen, he called out: "Lord Jesus, receive my
spirit!" 60 He knelt down and cried out with a
loud voice, "Lord, do not hold this sin against
them!" And after saying this, he died.[D]

Exercise of Faith | *Setting a Good Example*

A LIFE OF IMPACT

"While they were stoning Stephen, he called out: 'Lord Jesus, receive my spirit!' He knelt down and cried out with a loud voice, 'Lord, do not hold this sin against them!' And after saying this, he died." Acts 7:59-60

The real measure of a life is *how* we live; that matters far more than *how long* we live.

Stephen is evidence of this truth. Though brief, his life had major impact. He was the church's first martyr, killed for proclaiming the truth about Jesus. With his last breath, he prayed that his attackers might be forgiven.

Were they forgiven? At least one was. A short time later, we read about the conversion of the young man who had watched the coats of the men who stoned Stephen to death—Saul, who became the apostle Paul (Ac 7:58; 9:1-16).

Preaching one sermon that incites a crowd to kill you may not seem like a successful ministry. But when the fruit of your life, your dying prayer, is for someone known as "the apostle Paul," you've left quite a legacy.

You may not ever experience opposition such as Stephen faced, but people are watching how you react to hardships, opposition, set-backs, and hurts. You are making an impact—hopefully for Christ.

For the next note on *Exercise of Faith*, see Acts 16:14.

[A] **7:46** Other mss read *house* [B] **7:49-50** Is 66:1-2 [C] **7:54** Or *were cut to the quick* [D] **7:60** Lit *he fell asleep*

SAUL THE PERSECUTOR

8 Saul agreed with putting him to death.
On that day a severe persecution broke
out against the church in Jerusalem, and all
except the apostles were scattered throughout
the land of Judea and Samaria. 2 Devout men
buried Stephen and mourned deeply over him.
3 Saul, however, was ravaging the church. He
would enter house after house, drag off men
and women, and put them in prison.

PHILIP IN SAMARIA

4 So those who were scattered went on their
way preaching the word. 5 Philip went down to
a[A] city in Samaria and proclaimed the Messiah
to them. 6 The crowds were all paying attention
to what Philip said, as they listened and saw
the signs he was performing. 7 For unclean
spirits, crying out with a loud voice, came
out of many who were possessed, and many
who were paralyzed and lame were healed.
8 So there was great joy in that city.

THE RESPONSE OF SIMON

9 A man named Simon had previously practiced
sorcery in that city and amazed the Samaritan
people, while claiming to be somebody great.
10 They all paid attention to him, from the least
of them to the greatest, and they said, "This
man is called the Great Power of God."[B] 11 They
were attentive to him because he had amazed
them with his sorceries for a long time. 12 But
when they believed Philip, as he proclaimed
the good news about the kingdom of God and
the name of Jesus Christ, both men and women
were baptized. 13 Even Simon himself believed.
And after he was baptized, he followed Philip
everywhere and was amazed as he observed
the signs and great miracles that were being
performed.

SIMON'S SIN

14 When the apostles who were at Jerusalem
heard that Samaria had received the word of
God, they sent Peter and John to them. 15 After
they went down there, they prayed for them so
the Samaritans might receive the Holy Spirit
because he had not yet come down on any of
them. 16 (They had only been baptized in the
name of the Lord Jesus.) 17 Then Peter and John
laid their hands on them, and they received
the Holy Spirit.
18 When Simon saw that the Spirit[C] was given
through the laying on of the apostles' hands,
he offered them money, 19 saying, "Give me this
power also so that anyone I lay hands on may
receive the Holy Spirit."
20 But Peter told him, "May your silver be
destroyed with you, because you thought you
could obtain the gift of God with money! 21 You
have no part or share in this matter, because
your heart is not right before God. 22 Therefore
repent of this wickedness of yours, and pray
to the Lord that, if possible, your heart's intent
may be forgiven. 23 For I see you are poisoned
by bitterness and bound by wickedness."
24 "Pray to the Lord for me," Simon replied,
"so that nothing you have said may happen
to me."
25 So, after they had testified and spoken the
word of the Lord, they traveled back to Jerusalem, preaching the gospel in many villages
of the Samaritans.

THE CONVERSION OF THE ETHIOPIAN OFFICIAL

26 An angel of the Lord spoke to Philip: "Get
up and go south to the road that goes down
from Jerusalem to Gaza." (This is the desert
road.[D]) 27 So he got up and went. There was an
Ethiopian man, a eunuch and high official of
Candace, queen of the Ethiopians, who was
in charge of her entire treasury. He had come
to worship in Jerusalem 28 and was sitting
in his chariot on his way home, reading the
prophet Isaiah aloud.
29 The Spirit told Philip, "Go and join that
chariot."
30 When Philip ran up to it, he heard him
reading the prophet Isaiah, and said, "Do you
understand what you're reading?"
31 "How can I," he said, "unless someone
guides me?" So he invited Philip to come up
and sit with him. 32 Now the Scripture passage
he was reading was this:

He was led like a sheep
to the slaughter,
and as a lamb is silent
before its shearer,
so he does not open his mouth.
33 **In his humiliation justice**
was denied him.
Who will describe his generation?
For his life is taken from the earth.[E]

34 The eunuch said to Philip, "I ask you, who
is the prophet saying this about — himself

[A] **8:5** Other mss read *the* [B] **8:10** Or *"This is the power of God called Great* [C] **8:18** Other mss add *Holy* [D] **8:26** Or *is a desert place* [E] **8:32-33** Is 53:7-8

or someone else?" 35 Philip proceeded to tell
him the good news about Jesus, beginning
with that Scripture.
36 As they were traveling down the road, they
came to some water. The eunuch said, "Look,
there's water. What would keep me from being
baptized?"[A] 38 So he ordered the chariot to stop,
and both Philip and the eunuch went down
into the water, and he baptized him. 39 When
they came up out of the water, the Spirit of the
Lord carried Philip away, and the eunuch did
not see him any longer but went on his way
rejoicing. 40 Philip appeared in[B] Azotus,[C] and
he was traveling and preaching the gospel in
all the towns until he came to Caesarea.

THE DAMASCUS ROAD

9 Now Saul was still breathing threats and
murder against the disciples of the Lord.
He went to the high priest 2 and requested letters from him to the synagogues in Damascus,
so that if he found any men or women who
belonged to the Way, he might bring them as
prisoners to Jerusalem. 3 As he traveled and
was nearing Damascus, a light from heaven
suddenly flashed around him. 4 Falling to the
ground, he heard a voice saying to him, "Saul,
Saul, why are you persecuting me?"
5 "Who are you, Lord?" Saul said.
"I am Jesus, the one you are persecuting," he
replied. 6 "But get up and go into the city, and
you will be told what you must do."
7 The men who were traveling with him stood
speechless, hearing the sound but seeing no
one. 8 Saul got up from the ground, and though
his eyes were open, he could see nothing. So
they took him by the hand and led him into
Damascus. 9 He was unable to see for three
days and did not eat or drink.

SAUL'S BAPTISM

10 There was a disciple in Damascus named
Ananias, and the Lord said to him in a vision,
"Ananias."
"Here I am, Lord," he replied.
11 "Get up and go to the street called Straight,"
the Lord said to him, "to the house of Judas,
and ask for a man from Tarsus named Saul,
since he is praying there. 12 In a vision[D] he
has seen a man named Ananias coming in
and placing his hands on him so that he may
regain his sight."

Other-centeredness | *Praying for Others*

AMAZING GRACE

"As he traveled and was nearing Damascus, a light from heaven suddenly flashed around him. Falling to the ground, he heard a voice saying to him, 'Saul, Saul, why are you persecuting me?'" Acts 9:3-4

Saul wasn't on a search for spiritual answers. As a devout Jew, he was convinced he already had the truth. Saul wasn't interested in "following Jesus." On the contrary, he was hoping to rid the earth of all Jesus followers.

This means Saul's life-changing encounter with the risen Christ on the Damascus Road was completely the Lord's doing. It was all grace. Think of it—Jesus came crashing into the life of the least likely candidate for the gospel, perhaps in history. When Saul departed for Damascus, he was the church's fiercest opponent. By the time he arrived, he was its biggest proponent.

For those who have loved ones or friends who do not yet believe, this is comforting news. We do not have to worry about the fact that they are not seeking God. Saul's story shows us that God is the ultimate Seeker!

Grace isn't merely God's response to an open heart. God's grace is what opens hearts in the first place. Your best prayer for those you love is for the grace of God to enfold them.

For the next note on *Other-centeredness*, see Acts 9:26-27.

[A] **8:36** Some mss include v. 37: *Philip said, "If you believe with all your heart you may." And he replied, "I believe that Jesus Christ is the Son of God."* [B] **8:40** Or *Philip was found at*, or *Philip found himself in* [C] **8:40** Or *Ashdod* [D] **9:12** Other mss omit *In a vision*

13 "Lord," Ananias answered, "I have heard
from many people about this man, how much
harm he has done to your saints in Jerusalem.
14 And he has authority here from the chief
priests to arrest all who call on your name."
15 But the Lord said to him, "Go, for this man
is my chosen instrument to take my name to
Gentiles, kings, and Israelites. 16 I will show
him how much he must suffer for my name."
17 Ananias went and entered the house. He
placed his hands on him and said, "Brother
Saul, the Lord Jesus, who appeared to you on
the road you were traveling, has sent me so
that you may regain your sight and be filled
with the Holy Spirit."
18 At once something like scales fell from
his eyes, and he regained his sight. Then he
got up and was baptized. 19 And after taking
some food, he regained his strength.

SAUL PROCLAIMING THE MESSIAH

Saul was with the disciples in Damascus for
some time. 20 Immediately he began proclaiming Jesus in the synagogues: "He is the Son
of God."
21 All who heard him were astounded and
said, "Isn't this the man in Jerusalem who
was causing havoc for those who called on
this name and came here for the purpose of
taking them as prisoners to the chief priests?"
22 But Saul grew stronger and kept confound-
ing the Jews who lived in Damascus by proving
that Jesus is the Messiah.
23 After many days had passed, the Jews
conspired to kill him, 24 but Saul learned of
their plot. So they were watching the gates
day and night intending to kill him, 25 but his
disciples took him by night and lowered him in
a large basket through an opening in the wall.

SAUL IN JERUSALEM

26 When he arrived in Jerusalem, he tried to
join the disciples, but they were all afraid
of him, since they did not believe he was a
disciple. 27 Barnabas, however, took him and
brought him to the apostles and explained
to them how Saul had seen the Lord on the
road and that the Lord had talked to him, and
how in Damascus he had spoken boldly in the
name of Jesus. 28 Saul was coming and going
with them in Jerusalem, speaking boldly in
the name of the Lord. 29 He conversed and

Other-centeredness | *Encouraging*

EVERYONE NEEDS A BARNABAS

"When he arrived in Jerusalem, he tried to join the disciples, but they were all afraid of him, since they did not believe he was a disciple. Barnabas, however, took him and brought him to the apostles and explained to them how Saul had seen the Lord on the road and that the Lord had talked to him, and how in Damascus he had spoken boldly in the name of Jesus." Acts 9:26-27

Saul was a gospel-hating church destroyer until an unexpected encounter with the resurrected Jesus gave him a new heart and a new calling as gospel-preaching church planter.

The problem was no one believed him. Converted in a blinding light on the Damascus Road? Nice try, Saul! They believed this was a ruse to get inside the church so he could get the names and addresses of more Christians to arrest. It wasn't until the respected Barnabas came along and vouched for Saul that people finally lowered their guards. *Barnabas* means "son of encouragement," and the name fit him perfectly. In fact, largely because of Barnabas and his encouraging friendship, Saul's ministry took off.

Everyone needs a Barnabas. We need someone who believes in us and stands by us—when few others will.

You can be a "Barnabas." Think of who you might encourage today.

For the next note on *Other-centeredness*, see Romans 2:1.

debated with the Hellenistic Jews, but they
tried to kill him. 30 When the brothers found
out, they took him down to Caesarea and sent
him off to Tarsus.

THE CHURCH'S GROWTH

31 So the church throughout all Judea, Galilee,
and Samaria had peace and was strengthened. Living in the fear of the Lord and encouraged by the Holy Spirit, it increased in
numbers.

THE HEALING OF AENEAS

32 As Peter was traveling from place to place,
he also came down to the saints who lived in
Lydda. 33 There he found a man named Aeneas,
who was paralyzed and had been bedridden
for eight years. 34 Peter said to him, "Aeneas, Jesus Christ heals you. Get up and make
your bed,"[A] and immediately he got up. 35 So
all who lived in Lydda and Sharon saw him
and turned to the Lord.

DORCAS RESTORED TO LIFE

36 In Joppa there was a disciple named Tabitha (which is translated Dorcas). She was
always doing good works and acts of charity. 37 About that time she became sick and
died. After washing her, they placed her in a
room upstairs. 38 Since Lydda was near Joppa,
the disciples heard that Peter was there and
sent two men to him who urged him, "Don't
delay in coming with us." 39 Peter got up and
went with them. When he arrived, they led
him to the room upstairs. And all the widows
approached him, weeping and showing him
the robes and clothes that Dorcas had made
while she was with them. 40 Peter sent them
all out of the room. He knelt down, prayed,
and turning toward the body said, "Tabitha,
get up." She opened her eyes, saw Peter, and
sat up. 41 He gave her his hand and helped her
stand up. He called the saints and widows and
presented her alive. 42 This became known
throughout Joppa, and many believed in the
Lord. 43 Peter stayed for some time in Joppa
with Simon, a leather tanner.

CORNELIUS'S VISION

10 There was a man in Caesarea named Cornelius, a centurion of what was called the
Italian Regiment. 2 He was a devout man and
feared God along with his whole household.
He did many charitable deeds for the Jewish
people and always prayed to God. 3 About three
in the afternoon[B] he distinctly saw in a vision
an angel of God who came in and said to him,
"Cornelius."

4 Staring at him in awe, he said, "What is
it, Lord?"

The angel told him, "Your prayers and your
acts of charity have ascended as a memorial
offering before God. 5 Now send men to Joppa
and call for Simon, who is also named Peter.
6 He is lodging with Simon, a tanner, whose
house is by the sea."

7 When the angel who spoke to him had gone,
he called two of his household servants and
a devout soldier, who was one of those who
attended him. 8 After explaining everything
to them, he sent them to Joppa.

PETER'S VISION

9 The next day, as they were traveling and
nearing the city, Peter went up to pray on the
roof about noon.[C] 10 He became hungry and
wanted to eat, but while they were preparing something, he fell into a trance. 11 He saw
heaven opened and an object that resembled
a large sheet coming down, being lowered by
its four corners to the earth. 12 In it were all
the four-footed animals and reptiles of the
earth, and the birds of the sky. 13 A voice said
to him, "Get up, Peter; kill and eat."

14 "No, Lord!" Peter said. "For I have never
eaten anything impure and ritually unclean."

15 Again, a second time, the voice said to
him, "What God has made clean, do not call
impure." 16 This happened three times, and
suddenly the object was taken up into heaven.

PETER VISITS CORNELIUS

17 While Peter was deeply perplexed about what
the vision he had seen might mean, right away
the men who had been sent by Cornelius, having asked directions to Simon's house, stood
at the gate. 18 They called out, asking if Simon,
who was also named Peter, was lodging there.

19 While Peter was thinking about the vision, the Spirit told him, "Three men are here
looking for you. 20 Get up, go downstairs, and
go with them with no doubts at all, because I
have sent them."

21 Then Peter went down to the men and
said, "Here I am, the one you're looking for.
What is the reason you're here?"

[A] **9:34** Or *and get ready to eat* [B] **10:3** Lit *About the ninth hour* [C] **10:9** Lit *about the sixth hour*

[22] They said, "Cornelius, a centurion, an upright and God-fearing man, who has a good
reputation with the whole Jewish nation, was
divinely directed by a holy angel to call you to
his house and to hear a message from you."
[23] Peter then invited them in and gave them
lodging.

The next day he got up and set out with them,
and some of the brothers from Joppa went with
him. [24] The following day he entered Caesarea.
Now Cornelius was expecting them and had
called together his relatives and close friends.
[25] When Peter entered, Cornelius met him, fell
at his feet, and worshiped him.

[26] But Peter lifted him up and said, "Stand up.
I myself am also a man." [27] While talking with
him, he went in and found a large gathering
of people. [28] Peter said to them, "You know
it's forbidden for a Jewish man to associate
with or visit a foreigner, but God has shown
me that I must not call any person impure
or unclean. [29] That's why I came without any
objection when I was sent for. So may I ask
why you sent for me?"

[30] Cornelius replied, "Four days ago at this
hour, at three in the afternoon,[A] I was[B] praying in my house. Just then a man in dazzling
clothing stood before me [31] and said, 'Cornelius,
your prayer has been heard, and your acts of
charity have been remembered in God's sight.
[32] Therefore send someone to Joppa and invite Simon here, who is also named Peter. He
is lodging in Simon the tanner's house by the
sea.'[C] [33] So I immediately sent for you, and it
was good of you to come. So now we are all in
the presence of God to hear everything you
have been commanded by the Lord."

GOOD NEWS FOR GENTILES

[34] Peter began to speak: "Now I truly understand that God doesn't show favoritism, [35] but
in every nation the person who fears him and
does what is right is acceptable to him. [36] He
sent the message to the Israelites, proclaiming the good news of peace through Jesus
Christ — he is Lord of all. [37] You know the
events that took place throughout all Judea,
beginning from Galilee after the baptism that
John preached: [38] how God anointed Jesus of
Nazareth with the Holy Spirit and with power, and how he went about doing good and
healing all who were under the tyranny of
the devil, because God was with him. [39] We
ourselves are witnesses of everything he did
in both the Judean country and in Jerusalem,
and yet they killed him by hanging him on a

Relationships | *Being Impartial*

PLAYING FAVORITES?

"Peter began to speak: 'Now I truly understand that God doesn't show favoritism, but in every nation the person who fears him and does what is right is acceptable to him.'" Acts 10:34-35

Favoritism is the way of the world. It is as natural as breathing. Teachers are partial to their pets. Coaches give preferential treatment to their stars, and employers have their golden boys and rising-star girls. If you are rich or famous, you can probably arrange a meeting with any politician anywhere. Even some parents are guilty of this, gravitating toward one child over another—to the detriment of the whole family. People of faith as well can begin to prefer one group and shun another.

After centuries of what can only be called religious elitism, snobbery, or even discrimination, God gave Peter a vision in which he made clear that all people (not just the Jews) are objects of his love and part of his eternal plan. In fact, because "God doesn't show favoritism." James—the half brother of our Lord—commanded Christians: "Do not show favoritism" (Jms 2:1).

Showing favoritism and bias is natural. Living without it is supernatural. Ask God to help you root every form of prejudice from your heart.

For the next note on *Relationships*, see Acts 15:37-39.

[A] **10:30** Lit *at the ninth hour* [B] **10:30** Other mss add *fasting and* [C] **10:32** Other mss add *When he arrives, he will speak to you.*

tree. 40 God raised up this man on the third day and caused him to be seen, 41 not by all the people, but by us whom God appointed as witnesses, who ate and drank with him after he rose from the dead. 42 He commanded us to preach to the people and to testify that he is the one appointed by God to be the judge of the living and the dead. 43 All the prophets testify about him that through his name everyone who believes in him receives forgiveness of sins."

GENTILE CONVERSION AND BAPTISM

44 While Peter was still speaking these words, the Holy Spirit came down on all those who heard the message. 45 The circumcised believers who had come with Peter were amazed because the gift of the Holy Spirit had been poured out even on the Gentiles. 46 For they heard them speaking in other tongues[A] and declaring the greatness of God.

Then Peter responded, 47 "Can anyone withhold water and prevent these people from being baptized, who have received the Holy Spirit just as we have?" 48 He commanded them to be baptized in the name of Jesus Christ. Then they asked him to stay for a few days.

GENTILE SALVATION DEFENDED

11 The apostles and the brothers and sisters who were throughout Judea heard that the Gentiles had also received the word of God. 2 When Peter went up to Jerusalem, the circumcision party criticized him, 3 saying, "You went to uncircumcised men and ate with them."

4 Peter began to explain to them step by step: 5 "I was in the town of Joppa praying, and I saw, in a trance, an object that resembled a large sheet coming down, being lowered by its four corners from heaven, and it came to me. 6 When I looked closely and considered it, I saw the four-footed animals of the earth, the wild beasts, the reptiles, and the birds of the sky. 7 I also heard a voice telling me, 'Get up, Peter; kill and eat.'

8 " 'No, Lord!' I said. 'For nothing impure or ritually unclean has ever entered my mouth.' 9 But a voice answered from heaven a second time, 'What God has made clean, you must not call impure.'

10 "Now this happened three times, and everything was drawn up again into heaven. 11 At that very moment, three men who had been sent to me from Caesarea arrived at the house where we were. 12 The Spirit told me to accompany them with no doubts at all. These six brothers also accompanied me, and we went into the man's house. 13 He reported to us how he had seen the angel standing in his house and saying, 'Send[B] to Joppa, and call for Simon, who is also named Peter. 14 He will speak a message to you by which you and all your household will be saved.'

15 "As I began to speak, the Holy Spirit came down on them, just as on us at the beginning. 16 I remembered the word of the Lord, how he said, 'John baptized with water, but you will be baptized with the Holy Spirit.' 17 If, then, God gave them the same gift that he also gave to us when we believed in the Lord Jesus Christ, how could I possibly hinder God?"

18 When they heard this they became silent. And they glorified God, saying, "So then, God has given repentance resulting in life even to the Gentiles."

THE CHURCH IN ANTIOCH

19 Now those who had been scattered as a result of the persecution that started because of Stephen made their way as far as Phoenicia, Cyprus, and Antioch, speaking the word to no one except Jews. 20 But there were some of them, men from Cyprus and Cyrene, who came to Antioch and began speaking to the Greeks[C] also, proclaiming the good news about the Lord Jesus. 21 The Lord's hand was with them, and a large number who believed turned to the Lord. 22 News about them reached[D] the church in Jerusalem, and they sent out Barnabas to travel[E] as far as Antioch. 23 When he arrived and saw the grace of God, he was glad and encouraged all of them to remain true to the Lord with devoted hearts, 24 for he was a good man, full of the Holy Spirit and of faith. And large numbers of people were added to the Lord.

25 Then he[F] went to Tarsus to search for Saul, 26 and when he found him he brought him to Antioch. For a whole year they met with the church and taught large numbers. The disciples were first called Christians at Antioch.

FAMINE RELIEF

27 In those days some prophets came down from Jerusalem to Antioch. 28 One of them, named Agabus, stood up and predicted by

[A] **10:46** languages [B] **11:13** Other mss add *men* [C] **11:20** Lit *Hellenists* [D] **11:22** Lit *reached the ears of* [E] **11:22** Other mss omit *to travel* [F] **11:25** Other mss read *Barnabas*

Peter | Restoration Profile

MATTHEW; MARK; LUKE; JOHN; ACTS; 1 PETER; 2 PETER

The apostle Peter's life shows us, perhaps like no other, the spiritual dynamics at play in restoration. At the center of his relationship with Jesus are these stunning words: "Simon, Simon, look out. Satan has asked to sift you like wheat. But I have prayed for you that your faith may not fail. And you, when you have turned back, strengthen your brothers" (Lk 22:31-32). Jesus didn't pray that Peter wouldn't fail; he prayed that Peter's *faith* wouldn't fail. Jesus knew his disciple would fall flat on his face. The reality of Peter's faith would not be his personal failure under pressure but the fact that he would "turn back" and be able to strengthen others. Our miserable failures hide the wisdom that allows us to accept restoration and then help in the restoration of others.

Peter failed spectacularly and repeatedly. He jumped out of the boat to walk on water with Jesus when his eleven peers cowered behind, then proceeded to sink like the stone he was (Mt 14:28-31). He boldly declared the identity of Jesus as the saving Son of God, then chastised Jesus for describing that salvation would require his death (Mt 16:16-23). He insisted he would never deny Jesus, then thrice and with vehemence denied him (Mt 26:33-34). His restoration required a lot of sifting.

Jesus's restoration of Peter, recorded in John 21:15-22, gives some important clues about the tone of his restoring work in us. Jesus's affirmation of Peter went beyond the disciple to the assignment Jesus had for him. Restoration wasn't meant to make Peter feel better about himself but to focus his attention of the task of helping others. Restoration didn't mean an easier life for Peter. It also meant a plan for him unlike anyone else's.

God keeps those same priorities in mind in our restoration.

the Spirit that there would be a severe famine
throughout the Roman world.[A] This took place
during the reign of Claudius. 29 Each of the
disciples, according to his ability, determined
to send relief to the brothers and sisters who
lived in Judea. 30 They did this, sending it to
the elders by means of Barnabas and Saul.

JAMES MARTYRED AND PETER JAILED

12 About that time King Herod violently attacked some who belonged to the church,
2 and he executed James, John's brother, with
the sword. 3 When he saw that it pleased the
Jews, he proceeded to arrest Peter too, during the Festival of Unleavened Bread. 4 After
the arrest, he put him in prison and assigned
four squads of four soldiers each to guard
him, intending to bring him out to the people after the Passover. 5 So Peter was kept in
prison, but the church was praying fervently
to God for him.

PETER RESCUED

6 When Herod was about to bring him out
for trial, that very night Peter, bound with
two chains, was sleeping between two soldiers, while the sentries in front of the door
guarded the prison. 7 Suddenly an angel of the
Lord appeared, and a light shone in the cell.
Striking Peter on the side, he woke him up
and said, "Quick, get up!" And the chains fell
off his wrists. 8 "Get dressed," the angel told
him, "and put on your sandals." And he did.
"Wrap your cloak around you," he told him,
"and follow me." 9 So he went out and followed,
and he did not know that what the angel did
was really happening, but he thought he was
seeing a vision. 10 After they passed the first
and second guards, they came to the iron gate
that leads into the city, which opened to them
by itself. They went outside and passed one
street, and suddenly the angel left him.

11 When Peter came to himself, he said, "Now
I know for certain that the Lord has sent his
angel and rescued me from Herod's grasp
and from all that the Jewish people expected." 12 As soon as he realized this, he went to
the house of Mary, the mother of John Mark,[B]
where many had assembled and were praying.
13 He knocked at the door of the outer gate,

[A] **11:28** Or *the whole world* [B] **12:12** Lit *John who was called Mark*

and a servant named Rhoda came to answer.
14 She recognized Peter's voice, and because
of her joy, she did not open the gate but ran
in and announced that Peter was standing at
the outer gate.

15 "You're out of your mind!" they told her.
But she kept insisting that it was true, and they
said, "It's his angel." 16 Peter, however, kept on
knocking, and when they opened the door
and saw him, they were amazed.

17 Motioning to them with his hand to be
silent, he described to them how the Lord had
brought him out of the prison. "Tell these things
to James and the brothers," he said, and he
left and went to another place.

18 At daylight, there was a great commotion among the soldiers as to what had become of Peter. 19 After Herod had searched
and did not find him, he interrogated the
guards and ordered their execution. Then
Herod went down from Judea to Caesarea
and stayed there.

HEROD'S DEATH

20 Herod had been very angry with the people of
Tyre and Sidon. Together they presented themselves before him. After winning over Blastus,
who was in charge of the king's bedroom, they
asked for peace, because their country was
supplied with food from the king's country.
21 On an appointed day, dressed in royal robes
and seated on the throne, Herod delivered a
speech to them. 22 The assembled people began
to shout, "It's the voice of a god and not of a
man!" 23 At once an angel of the Lord struck
him because he did not give the glory to God,
and he was eaten by worms and died.

24 But the word of God flourished and multiplied. 25 After they had completed their relief mission, Barnabas and Saul returned to[A]
Jerusalem, taking along John who was called
Mark.

PREPARING FOR THE MISSION FIELD

13 Now in the church at Antioch there were
prophets and teachers: Barnabas, Simeon who was called Niger, Lucius of Cyrene,
Manaen, a close friend of Herod the tetrarch,
and Saul.

2 As they were worshiping[B] the Lord and
fasting, the Holy Spirit said, "Set apart for me
Barnabas and Saul for the work to which I
have called them." 3 Then after they had fasted,
prayed, and laid hands on them, they sent
them off.

THE MISSION TO CYPRUS

4 So being sent out by the Holy Spirit, they went
down to Seleucia, and from there they sailed to
Cyprus. 5 Arriving in Salamis, they proclaimed
the word of God in the Jewish synagogues.
They also had John as their assistant. 6 When
they had traveled the whole island as far as
Paphos, they came across a sorcerer, a Jewish
false prophet named Bar-Jesus. 7 He was with
the proconsul, Sergius Paulus, an intelligent
man. This man summoned Barnabas and Saul
and wanted to hear the word of God. 8 But
Elymas the sorcerer (that is the meaning of
his name) opposed them and tried to turn the
proconsul away from the faith.

9 But Saul — also called Paul — filled with
the Holy Spirit, stared straight at Elymas 10 and
said, "You are full of all kinds of deceit and
trickery, you son of the devil and enemy of all
that is right. Won't you ever stop perverting
the straight paths of the Lord? 11 Now, look, the
Lord's hand is against you. You are going to
be blind, and will not see the sun for a time."
Immediately a mist and darkness fell on him,
and he went around seeking someone to lead
him by the hand.

12 Then, when he saw what happened, the
proconsul believed, because he was astonished at the teaching of the Lord.

PAUL'S SERMON IN ANTIOCH OF PISIDIA

13 Paul and his companions set sail from Paphos and came to Perga in Pamphylia, but
John left them and went back to Jerusalem.
14 They continued their journey from Perga
and reached Pisidian Antioch. On the Sabbath day they went into the synagogue and sat
down. 15 After the reading of the Law and the
Prophets, the leaders of the synagogue sent
word to them, saying, "Brothers, if you have
any word of encouragement for the people,
you can speak."

16 Paul stood up and motioned with his hand
and said: "Fellow Israelites, and you who fear
God, listen! 17 The God of this people Israel
chose our ancestors, made the people prosper during their stay in the land of Egypt, and
led them out of it with a mighty[C] arm. 18 And
for about forty years he put up with them[D] in
the wilderness; 19 and after destroying seven

[A] **12:25** Other mss read *from* [B] **13:2** Or *were ministering to* [C] **13:17** Lit *with an uplifted* [D] **13:18** Other mss read *he cared for them*

nations in the land of Canaan, he gave them
their land as an inheritance. 20 This all took
about 450 years. After this, he gave them judges
until Samuel the prophet. 21 Then they asked
for a king, and God gave them Saul the son of
Kish, a man of the tribe of Benjamin, for forty years. 22 After removing him, he raised up
David as their king and testified about him:
'**I have found David** the son of Jesse to be **a
man after my own heart,**[A] who will carry
out all my will.'

23 "From this man's descendants, as he promised, God brought to Israel the Savior, Jesus.[B]
24 Before his coming to public attention, John
had previously proclaimed a baptism of repentance to all the people of Israel. 25 Now
as John was completing his mission, he said,
'Who do you think I am? I am not the one. But
one is coming after me, and I am not worthy
to untie the sandals on his feet.'

26 "Brothers and sisters, children of Abraham's race, and those among you who fear
God, it is to us that the word of this salvation
has been sent. 27 Since the residents of Jerusalem and their rulers did not recognize him
or the sayings of the prophets that are read
every Sabbath, they have fulfilled their words
by condemning him. 28 Though they found no
grounds for the death sentence, they asked
Pilate to have him killed. 29 When they had
carried out all that had been written about
him, they took him down from the tree and
put him in a tomb. 30 But God raised him from
the dead, 31 and he appeared for many days to
those who came up with him from Galilee to
Jerusalem, who are now his witnesses to the
people. 32 And we ourselves proclaim to you
the good news of the promise that was made
to our ancestors. 33 God has fulfilled this for
us, their children, by raising up Jesus, as it is
written in the second Psalm:

You are my Son;
today I have become your Father.[C,D]

34 As to his raising him from the dead, never
to return to decay, he has spoken in this way,
**I will give you the holy and sure promises
of David.**[E] 35 Therefore he also says in another
passage, **You will not let your Holy One see
decay.**[F] 36 For David, after serving God's purpose in his own generation, fell asleep, was
buried with his fathers, and decayed, 37 but the
one God raised up did not decay. 38 Therefore,

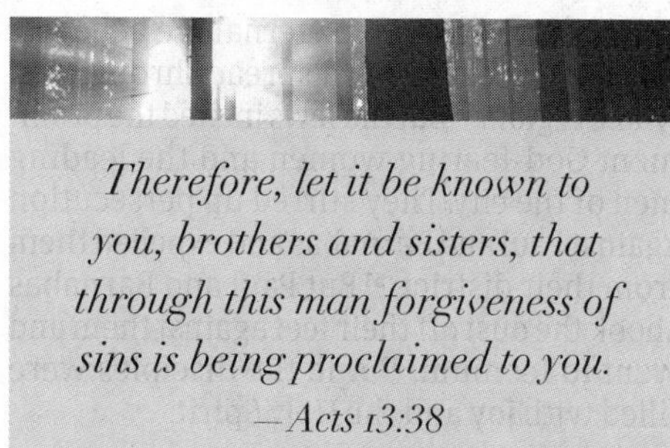
*Therefore, let it be known to
you, brothers and sisters, that
through this man forgiveness of
sins is being proclaimed to you.*
—Acts 13:38

let it be known to you, brothers and sisters, that
through this man forgiveness of sins is being
proclaimed to you. 39 Everyone who believes
is justified[G] through him from everything that
you could not be justified from through the
law of Moses. 40 So beware that what is said in
the prophets does not happen to you:

41 **Look, you scoffers,**
marvel and vanish away,
because I am doing a work
in your days,
a work that you will never believe,
even if someone were to explain it
to you."[H]

PAUL AND BARNABAS IN ANTIOCH

42 As they were leaving, the people[I] urged them
to speak about these matters the following
Sabbath. 43 After the synagogue had been dismissed, many of the Jews and devout converts
to Judaism followed Paul and Barnabas, who
were speaking with them and urging them to
continue in the grace of God.

44 The following Sabbath almost the whole
town assembled to hear the word of the Lord.[J]
45 But when the Jews saw the crowds, they were
filled with jealousy and began to contradict
what Paul was saying, insulting him.

46 Paul and Barnabas boldly replied, "It was
necessary that the word of God be spoken to
you first. Since you reject it and judge yourselves unworthy of eternal life, we are turning
to the Gentiles. 47 For this is what the Lord has
commanded us:

I have made you
a light for the Gentiles
to bring salvation
to the end of the earth."[K]

48 When the Gentiles heard this, they rejoiced
and honored the word of the Lord, and all who

[A] **13:22** 1Sm 13:14; Ps 89:20 [B] **13:23** Other mss read *brought salvation* [C] **13:33** Or *I have begotten you* [D] **13:33** Ps 2:7
[E] **13:34** Is 55:3 [F] **13:35** Ps 16:10 [G] **13:39** Or *freed*, also later in verse [H] **13:41** Hab 1:5 [I] **13:42** Other mss read *they were leaving the synagogue of the Jews, the Gentiles* [J] **13:44** Other mss read *of God* [K] **13:47** Is 49:6

had been appointed to eternal life believed.
49 The word of the Lord spread through the
whole region. 50 But the Jews incited the prominent God-fearing women and the leading
men of the city. They stirred up persecution
against Paul and Barnabas and expelled them
from their district. 51 But Paul and Barnabas
shook the dust off their feet against them and
went to Iconium. 52 And the disciples were
filled with joy and the Holy Spirit.

GROWTH AND PERSECUTION IN ICONIUM

14 In Iconium they entered the Jewish synagogue, as usual, and spoke in such a way
that a great number of both Jews and Greeks
believed. 2 But the unbelieving Jews stirred up
the Gentiles and poisoned their minds against
the brothers. 3 So they stayed there a long time
and spoke boldly for the Lord, who testified
to the message of his grace by enabling them
to do signs and wonders. 4 But the people of
the city were divided, some siding with the
Jews and others with the apostles. 5 When an
attempt was made by both the Gentiles and
Jews, with their rulers, to mistreat and stone
them, 6 they found out about it and fled to
the Lycaonian towns of Lystra and Derbe and
to the surrounding countryside. 7 There they
continued preaching the gospel.

MISTAKEN FOR GODS IN LYSTRA

8 In Lystra a man was sitting who was without
strength in his feet, had never walked, and
had been lame from birth. 9 He listened as
Paul spoke. After looking directly at him and
seeing that he had faith to be healed, 10 Paul
said in a loud voice, "Stand up on your feet!"
And he jumped up and began to walk around.

11 When the crowds saw what Paul had done,
they shouted, saying in the Lycaonian language, "The gods have come down to us in
human form!" 12 Barnabas they called Zeus,
and Paul, Hermes, because he was the chief
speaker. 13 The priest of Zeus, whose temple
was just outside the town, brought bulls and
wreaths to the gates because he intended,
with the crowds, to offer sacrifice.

14 The apostles Barnabas and Paul tore their
robes when they heard this and rushed into
the crowd, shouting: 15 "People! Why are you
doing these things? We are people also, just
like you, and we are proclaiming good news to
you, that you turn from these worthless things
to the living God, **who made the heaven, the
earth, the sea, and everything in them.**[A] 16 In
past generations he allowed all the nations to
go their own way, 17 although he did not leave
himself without a witness, since he did what
is good by giving you rain from heaven and
fruitful seasons and filling you with food and
your[B] hearts with joy." 18 Even though they said
these things, they barely stopped the crowds
from sacrificing to them.

19 Some Jews came from Antioch and Iconium, and when they won over the crowds,
they stoned Paul and dragged him out of the
city, thinking he was dead. 20 After the disciples gathered around him, he got up and
went into the town. The next day he left with
Barnabas for Derbe.

CHURCH PLANTING

21 After they had preached the gospel in that
town and made many disciples, they returned to
Lystra, to Iconium, and to Antioch, 22 strengthening the[C] disciples by encouraging them to
continue in the faith and by telling them, "It
is necessary to go through many hardships to
enter the kingdom of God." 23 When they had
appointed elders for them in every church and
prayed with fasting, they committed them to
the Lord in whom they had believed.

24 They passed through Pisidia and came to
Pamphylia. 25 After they had spoken the word
in Perga, they went down to Attalia. 26 From
there they sailed back to Antioch where they
had been commended to the grace of God for
the work they had now completed. 27 After they
arrived and gathered the church together, they
reported everything God had done with them
and that he had opened the door of faith to
the Gentiles. 28 And they spent a considerable
time with the disciples.

DISPUTE IN ANTIOCH

15 Some men came down from Judea and
began to teach the brothers: "Unless you
are circumcised according to the custom prescribed by Moses, you cannot be saved." 2 After
Paul and Barnabas had engaged them in serious argument and debate, Paul and Barnabas
and some others were appointed to go up to
the apostles and elders in Jerusalem about
this issue. 3 When they had been sent on their
way by the church, they passed through both
Phoenicia and Samaria, describing in detail the

[A] **14:15** Ex 20:11; Ps 146:6 [B] **14:17** Other mss read *our* [C] **14:22** Lit *the souls of the*

conversion of the Gentiles, and they brought
great joy to all the brothers and sisters.
4 When they arrived at Jerusalem, they were
welcomed by the church, the apostles, and
the elders, and they reported all that God had
done with them. 5 But some of the believers
who belonged to the party of the Pharisees
stood up and said, "It is necessary to circumcise them and to command them to keep the
law of Moses."

THE JERUSALEM COUNCIL

6 The apostles and the elders gathered to
consider this matter. 7 After there had been
much debate, Peter stood up and said to them:
"Brothers and sisters, you are aware that in
the early days God made a choice among
you,[A] that by my mouth the Gentiles would
hear the gospel message and believe. 8 And
God, who knows the heart, bore witness to
them by giving them the Holy Spirit, just as
he also did to us. 9 He made no distinction
between us and them, cleansing their hearts
by faith. 10 Now then, why are you testing God
by putting a yoke on the disciples' necks that
neither our ancestors nor we have been able
to bear? 11 On the contrary, we believe that we
are saved through the grace of the Lord Jesus
in the same way they are."
12 The whole assembly became silent and
listened to Barnabas and Paul describe all the
signs and wonders God had done through
them among the Gentiles. 13 After they stopped
speaking, James responded: "Brothers and
sisters, listen to me. 14 Simeon[B] has reported how God first intervened to take from
the Gentiles a people for his name. 15 And
the words of the prophets agree with this,
as it is written:

16 **After these things I will return**
and rebuild David's fallen tent.
I will rebuild its ruins
and set it up again,
17 **so the rest of humanity**
may seek the Lord —
even all the Gentiles
who are called by my name —
declares the Lord

Eternal Perspective | *God's Grace/Kindness*

SAVED BY GRACE

"On the contrary, we believe that we are saved through the grace of the Lord Jesus in the same way they are." Acts 15:11

Every religion wrestles with the question, How can a person be acceptable to God? And, of course, each one offers a different answer to this question.

Until about AD 30, Judaism answered this question by urging non-Jews to become Jewish proselytes—to get circumcised, baptized, and busy following the Mosaic law.

Then Jesus showed up, claiming to be the long-awaited Jewish Messiah and the only way to know God (Jn 14:6). After his death and resurrection, his followers—almost exclusively Jewish—began teaching that the way to be right with God was *not* by observing Jewish religious rituals or keeping the Mosaic law but by trusting in Jesus alone.

This created enormous conflict with the Jewish establishment and much confusion among Gentile followers of Jesus. Did Jewish followers of Jesus still need to keep the law? Did Gentile believers in Jesus have to start living like Jews? The leaders of the church discussed these ideas at a big council in Jerusalem. Their conclusion? Salvation—becoming a child of God (Jn 1:12) and having eternal life (3:16)—is the result of "the grace of the Lord Jesus," not human effort. It's a gift, not a reward.

Your salvation rests on Jesus's work, not yours. You could never be good enough to deserve or earn eternal life. You are forgiven, freed, and bound for heaven by grace alone. Rejoice, revel in God's love, and share this great news.

For the next note on *Eternal Perspective*, see Acts 16:6-7.

[A] **15:7** Other mss read *us* [B] **15:14** Simon (Peter)

who makes these things 18 known
from long ago.[A,B]
19 Therefore, in my judgment, we should not
cause difficulties for those among the Gentiles
who turn to God, 20 but instead we should write
to them to abstain from things polluted by idols,
from sexual immorality, from eating anything
that has been strangled, and from blood. 21 For
since ancient times, Moses has had those who
proclaim him in every city, and every Sabbath
day he is read aloud in the synagogues."

THE LETTER TO THE GENTILE BELIEVERS

22 Then the apostles and the elders, with the
whole church, decided to select men who were
among them and to send them to Antioch with
Paul and Barnabas: Judas, called Barsabbas,
and Silas, both leading men among the brothers. 23 They wrote:

"From the apostles and the elders, your brothers,
To the brothers and sisters among the Gentiles in Antioch, Syria, and Cilicia:
Greetings.

24 Since we have heard that some without
our authorization went out from us
and troubled you with their words and
unsettled your hearts,[C] 25 we have unanimously decided to select men and send
them to you along with our dearly loved
Barnabas and Paul, 26 who have risked
their lives for the name of our Lord Jesus
Christ. 27 Therefore we have sent Judas and
Silas, who will personally report the same
things by word of mouth. 28 For it was the
Holy Spirit's decision — and ours — not to
place further burdens on you beyond these
requirements: 29 that you abstain from
food offered to idols, from blood, from eating anything that has been strangled, and
from sexual immorality. You will do well
if you keep yourselves from these things.
Farewell."

THE OUTCOME OF THE JERUSALEM LETTER

30 So they were sent off and went down to
Antioch, and after gathering the assembly,
they delivered the letter. 31 When they read
it, they rejoiced because of its encouragement. 32 Both Judas and Silas, who were also

Relationships | *Resolving Arguments/Disagreements/Conflicts*

CONFLICT

"Barnabas wanted to take along John Mark. But Paul insisted that they should not take along this man. . . . They had such a sharp disagreement that they parted company." Acts 15:37-39

If you've been around church world for long, you have seen Christians disagree, maybe even in heated ways. That can be disillusioning. We think, "Wait, don't we all love Jesus here? We're called to unity, and we have the Holy Spirit! Why can't we get along?"

Sadly, conflict is a fact of life in a fallen world—and in an imperfect church. Here, as Paul and Barnabas prepared for a second missionary trip, they argued about including John Mark (the young man who had left their first mission abruptly, mid-trip—see 13:13). The phrase "sharp disagreement" indicates the two men were worked up. Think red faces, raised voices, and fireworks.

Paul wasn't interested in a helper who might not be reliable. Barnabas wanted to give his young cousin (Col 4:10) a second chance. The Bible doesn't suggest that either man was wrong in his thinking. When neither would budge, Paul partnered with Silas, and Barnabas took John Mark. Suddenly the church had two missionary teams. Maybe that's one of the lessons here: Not even our disagreements can thwart the plan of God.

When facing conflict with a Christian brother or sister, ask God to give you the proper response and to bring glory to his name through the situation.

For the next note on *Relationships*, see Romans 1:16.

[A] **15:17-18** Other mss read *says the Lord who does all these things. Known to God from long ago are all his works.*
[B] **15:16-18** Am 9:11-12; Is 45:21 [C] **15:24** Other mss add *by saying, 'Be circumcised and keep the law,'*

prophets themselves, encouraged the brothers and sisters and strengthened them with
a long message. 33 After spending some time
there, they were sent back in peace by the
brothers and sisters to those who had sent
them.[A,B] 35 But Paul and Barnabas, along with
many others, remained in Antioch, teaching
and proclaiming the word of the Lord.

PAUL AND BARNABAS PART COMPANY

36 After some time had passed, Paul said to
Barnabas, "Let's go back and visit the brothers and sisters in every town where we have
preached the word of the Lord and see how
they're doing." 37 Barnabas wanted to take
along John Mark.[C] 38 But Paul insisted that
they should not take along this man who had
deserted them in Pamphylia and had not gone
on with them to the work. 39 They had such
a sharp disagreement that they parted company, and Barnabas took Mark with him and
sailed off to Cyprus. 40 But Paul chose Silas
and departed, after being commended by
the brothers and sisters to the grace of the
Lord. 41 He traveled through Syria and Cilicia,
strengthening the churches.

PAUL SELECTS TIMOTHY

16 Paul went on to Derbe and Lystra, where
there was a disciple named Timothy, the
son of a believing Jewish woman, but his father was a Greek. 2 The brothers and sisters
at Lystra and Iconium spoke highly of him.
3 Paul wanted Timothy to go with him; so he
took him and circumcised him because of the
Jews who were in those places, since they all
knew that his father was a Greek. 4 As they
traveled through the towns, they delivered the
decisions reached by the apostles and elders
at Jerusalem for the people to observe. 5 So the
churches were strengthened in the faith and
grew daily in numbers.

EVANGELIZATION OF EUROPE

6 They went through the region of Phrygia
and Galatia; they had been forbidden by the
Holy Spirit to speak the word in Asia. 7 When
they came to Mysia, they tried to go into

Eternal Perspective | *God's Plans*

THWARTED!

"They went through the region of Phrygia and Galatia; they had been forbidden by the Holy Spirit to speak the word in Asia. When they came to Mysia, they tried to go into Bithynia, but the Spirit of Jesus did not allow them." Acts 16:6-7

Have you ever attempted something really good only to run into obstacles and meet with failure? Perhaps you went back to the drawing board, tweaked your plans, and came at your goal from a different angle, only to be thwarted again! What gives? You're trying to honor God, but he won't grant you success. Why?

Many explanations are possible, but how about this one? Maybe God doesn't want you doing that—at least not right now? Maybe he's trying to steer you in a different direction?

This was Paul's experience. On his second missionary journey, he had an ambitious plan to take the gospel to Asia. But God blocked Paul's team—not once but twice.

Paul was only human. This turn of events must have been mystifying, perhaps even frustrating, until he had a vision during which he received the famous "Macedonian call." The reason Asia was a no-go? God wanted Paul and his team in Europe.

If you are being thwarted in some way right now, don't despair. God may simply be trying to get you in a different place where he has a better plan waiting.

For the next note on *Eternal Perspective*, see Romans 5:6.

[A] **15:33** Other mss read *the brothers to the apostles* [B] **15:33** Other mss add v. 34: *But Silas decided to stay there.*
[C] **15:37** Lit *John who was called Mark*

Bithynia, but the Spirit of Jesus did not allow
them. 8 Passing by Mysia they went down to
Troas. 9 During the night Paul had a vision in
which a Macedonian man was standing and
pleading with him, "Cross over to Macedonia
and help us!" 10 After he had seen the vision,
we immediately made efforts to set out for
Macedonia, concluding that God had called
us to preach the gospel to them.

LYDIA'S CONVERSION

11 From Troas we put out to sea and sailed
straight for Samothrace, the next day to Neapolis, 12 and from there to Philippi, a Roman
colony and a leading city of the district of
Macedonia. We stayed in that city for several
days. 13 On the Sabbath day we went outside
the city gate by the river, where we expected to
find a place of prayer. We sat down and spoke
to the women gathered there. 14 A God-fearing
woman named Lydia, a dealer in purple cloth
from the city of Thyatira, was listening. The
Lord opened her heart to respond to what Paul
was saying. 15 After she and her household
were baptized, she urged us, "If you consider
me a believer in the Lord, come and stay at my
house." And she persuaded us.

PAUL AND SILAS IN PRISON

16 Once, as we were on our way to prayer, a
slave girl met us who had a spirit by which
she predicted the future. She made a large
profit for her owners by fortune-telling. 17 As
she followed Paul and us she cried out, "These
men, who are proclaiming to you[A] the way of
salvation, are the servants of the Most High
God." 18 She did this for many days.

Paul was greatly annoyed. Turning to the
spirit, he said, "I command you in the name
of Jesus Christ to come out of her!" And it
came out right away.

19 When her owners realized that their hope
of profit was gone, they seized Paul and Silas
and dragged them into the marketplace to
the authorities. 20 Bringing them before the
chief magistrates, they said, "These men are
seriously disturbing our city. They are Jews
21 and are promoting customs that are not

Exercise of Faith | *Sharing Faith/Gospel*

HEART-OPENING, NOT ARM-TWISTING

"A God-fearing woman named Lydia, a dealer in purple cloth from the city of Thyatira, was listening. The Lord opened her heart to respond to what Paul was saying." Acts 16:14

What can and should we do with friends and loved ones who are uninterested in spiritual things? Hit them with a bunch of Bible verses? Hand them books to read? Drag them to church? Question their lifestyles to make them feel guilty?

Notice how Luke described this conversation between the apostle Paul and a group of women on a river bank in Philippi one Saturday morning. Writing of one specific businesswoman named Lydia, Luke reports, "The Lord opened her heart to respond."

This is a great reminder that salvation is the work of God. He can and does use people and our words (as he did here with Paul). But unless and until he opens a person's heart, no life change is going happen.

Remember the words of Jesus: "No one can come to me unless the Father who sent me draws him" (Jn 6:44). Only as God stirs hearts and takes off the blinders at just the right moment can a person believe. Until then no amount of arm-twisting will do any good.

Pray continually. Be sensitive and available to the Spirit. And talk about your faith boldly. But let God be in charge of the outcomes.

For the next note on *Exercise of Faith*, see Acts 20:30.

[A] **16:17** Other mss read *us*

legal for us as Romans to adopt or practice."
22 The crowd joined in the attack against them,
and the chief magistrates stripped off their
clothes and ordered them to be beaten with
rods. 23 After they had severely flogged them,
they threw them in jail, ordering the jailer to
guard them carefully. 24 Receiving such an
order, he put them into the inner prison and
secured their feet in the stocks.

A MIDNIGHT DELIVERANCE

25 About midnight Paul and Silas were praying
and singing hymns to God, and the prisoners
were listening to them. 26 Suddenly there was
such a violent earthquake that the foundations of the jail were shaken, and immediately
all the doors were opened, and everyone's
chains came loose. 27 When the jailer woke
up and saw the doors of the prison standing
open, he drew his sword and was going to
kill himself, since he thought the prisoners
had escaped.

28 But Paul called out in a loud voice, "Don't
harm yourself, because we're all here!"

29 The jailer called for lights, rushed in, and
fell down trembling before Paul and Silas. 30 He
escorted them out and said, "Sirs, what must
I do to be saved?"

31 They said, "Believe in the Lord Jesus, and
you will be saved — you and your household."
32 And they spoke the word of the Lord to him
along with everyone in his house. 33 He took
them the same hour of the night and washed
their wounds. Right away he and all his family were baptized. 34 He brought them into his
house, set a meal before them, and rejoiced
because he had come to believe in God with
his entire household.

AN OFFICIAL APOLOGY

35 When daylight came, the chief magistrates
sent the police to say, "Release those men."

36 The jailer reported these words to Paul:
"The magistrates have sent orders for you to
be released. So come out now and go in peace."

37 But Paul said to them, "They beat us in
public without a trial, although we are Roman
citizens, and threw us in jail. And now are they
going to send us away secretly? Certainly not!
On the contrary, let them come themselves
and escort us out."

38 The police reported these words to the
magistrates. They were afraid when they heard
that Paul and Silas were Roman citizens. 39 So
they came to appease them, and escorting them
from prison, they urged them to leave town.
40 After leaving the jail, they came to Lydia's
house, where they saw and encouraged the
brothers and sisters, and departed.

A SHORT MINISTRY IN THESSALONICA

17 After they passed through Amphipolis
and Apollonia, they came to Thessalonica, where there was a Jewish synagogue. 2 As
usual, Paul went into the synagogue, and on
three Sabbath days reasoned with them from
the Scriptures, 3 explaining and proving that it
was necessary for the Messiah to suffer and
rise from the dead: "This Jesus I am proclaiming
to you is the Messiah." 4 Some of them were
persuaded and joined Paul and Silas, including
a large number of God-fearing Greeks, as well
as a number of the leading women.

RIOT IN THE CITY

5 But the Jews became jealous, and they brought
together some wicked men from the marketplace, formed a mob, and started a riot in the
city. Attacking Jason's house, they searched for
them to bring them out to the public assembly.
6 When they did not find them, they dragged
Jason and some of the brothers before the
city officials, shouting, "These men who have
turned the world upside down have come here
too, 7 and Jason has welcomed them. They are
all acting contrary to Caesar's decrees, saying
that there is another king — Jesus." 8 The crowd
and city officials who heard these things were
upset. 9 After taking a security bond from Jason
and the others, they released them.

THE BEREANS SEARCH THE SCRIPTURES

10 As soon as it was night, the brothers and
sisters sent Paul and Silas away to Berea. Upon
arrival, they went into the synagogue of the
Jews. 11 The people here were of more noble
character than those in Thessalonica, since
they received the word with eagerness and
examined the Scriptures daily to see if these
things were so. 12 Consequently, many of them
believed, including a number of the prominent
Greek women as well as men. 13 But when the
Jews from Thessalonica found out that the
word of God had been proclaimed by Paul
at Berea, they came there too, agitating and
upsetting[A] the crowds. 14 Then the brothers

[A] **17:13** Other mss omit *and upsetting*

and sisters immediately sent Paul away to go to the coast, but Silas and Timothy stayed on there. 15 Those who escorted Paul brought him as far as Athens, and after receiving instructions for Silas and Timothy to come to him as quickly as possible, they departed.

PAUL IN ATHENS

16 While Paul was waiting for them in Athens, he was deeply distressed when he saw that the city was full of idols. 17 So he reasoned in the synagogue with the Jews and with those who worshiped God, as well as in the marketplace every day with those who happened to be there. 18 Some of the Epicurean and Stoic philosophers also debated with him. Some said, "What is this ignorant show-off[A] trying to say?"

Others replied, "He seems to be a preacher of foreign deities" — because he was telling the good news about Jesus and the resurrection.

19 They took him and brought him to the Areopagus,[B] and said, "May we learn about this new teaching you are presenting? 20 Because what you say sounds strange to us, and we want to know what these things mean." 21 Now all the Athenians and the foreigners residing there spent their time on nothing else but telling or hearing something new.

THE AREOPAGUS ADDRESS

22 Paul stood in the middle of the Areopagus and said: "People of Athens! I see that you are extremely religious in every respect. 23 For as I was passing through and observing the objects of your worship, I even found an altar on which was inscribed: 'To an Unknown God.' Therefore, what you worship in ignorance, this I proclaim to you. 24 The God who made the world and everything in it — he is Lord of heaven and earth — does not live in shrines made by hands. 25 Neither is he served by human hands, as though he needed anything, since he himself gives everyone life and breath and all things. 26 From one man[C] he has made every nationality to live over the whole earth and has determined their appointed times and the boundaries of where they live. 27 He did this so that they might seek God, and perhaps they might reach out and find him, though he is not far from each one of us. 28 For in him we live and move and have our being, as even some of your own poets have said, 'For we are also his offspring.' 29 Since we are God's offspring then, we shouldn't think that the divine nature is like gold or silver or stone, an image fashioned by human art and imagination.

30 "Therefore, having overlooked the times of ignorance, God now commands all people everywhere to repent, 31 because he has set a day when he is going to judge the world in righteousness by the man he has appointed. He has provided proof of this to everyone by raising him from the dead."

32 When they heard about the resurrection of the dead, some began to ridicule him, but others said, "We'd like to hear from you again about this." 33 So Paul left their presence. 34 However, some people joined him and believed, including Dionysius the Areopagite, a woman named Damaris, and others with them.

FOUNDING THE CORINTHIAN CHURCH

18 After this, he[D] left Athens and went to Corinth, 2 where he found a Jew named Aquila, a native of Pontus, who had recently come from Italy with his wife Priscilla because Claudius had ordered all the Jews to leave Rome. Paul came to them, 3 and since they were of the same occupation, tentmakers by trade, he stayed with them and worked. 4 He reasoned in the synagogue every Sabbath and tried to persuade both Jews and Greeks.

5 When Silas and Timothy arrived from Macedonia, Paul devoted himself to preaching the word[E] and testified to the Jews that Jesus is the Messiah. 6 When they resisted and blasphemed, he shook out his clothes and told them, "Your blood is on your own heads! I am innocent.[F] From now on I will go to the Gentiles." 7 So he left there and went to the house of a man named Titius Justus, a worshiper of God, whose house was next door to the synagogue. 8 Crispus, the leader of the synagogue, believed in the Lord, along with his whole household. Many of the Corinthians, when they heard, believed and were baptized.

9 The Lord said to Paul in a night vision, "Don't be afraid, but keep on speaking and don't be silent. 10 For I am with you, and no one will lay a hand on you to hurt you, because I have many people in this city." 11 He stayed there a year and a half, teaching the word of God among them.

12 While Gallio was proconsul of Achaia, the

[A] **17:18** Lit *this seed picker* [B] **17:19** Or *Mars Hill* [C] **17:26** Other mss read *blood* [D] **18:1** Other mss read *Paul* [E] **18:5** Other mss read *was urged by the Spirit* [F] **18:6** Lit *clean*

Jews made a united attack against Paul and brought him to the tribunal. 13 "This man," they said, " is persuading people to worship God in ways contrary to the law."

14 As Paul was about to open his mouth, Gallio said to the Jews, "If it were a matter of wrongdoing or of a serious crime, it would be reasonable for me to put up with you Jews. 15 But if these are questions about words, names, and your own law, see to it yourselves. I refuse to be a judge of such things." 16 So he drove them from the tribunal. 17 And they all[A] seized Sosthenes, the leader of the synagogue, and beat him in front of the tribunal, but none of these things mattered to Gallio.

THE RETURN TRIP TO ANTIOCH

18 After staying for some time, Paul said farewell to the brothers and sisters and sailed away to Syria, accompanied by Priscilla and Aquila. He shaved his head at Cenchreae because of a vow he had taken. 19 When they reached Ephesus he left them there, but he himself entered the synagogue and debated with the Jews. 20 When they asked him to stay for a longer time, he declined, 21 but he said farewell and added,[B] "I'll come back to you again, if God wills." Then he set sail from Ephesus.

22 On landing at Caesarea, he went up to Jerusalem and greeted the church, then went down to Antioch.

23 After spending some time there, he set out, traveling through one place after another in the region of Galatia and Phrygia, strengthening all the disciples.

THE ELOQUENT APOLLOS

24 Now a Jew named Apollos, a native Alexandrian, an eloquent man who was competent in the use of the Scriptures, arrived in Ephesus. 25 He had been instructed in the way of the Lord; and being fervent in spirit,[C] he was speaking and teaching accurately about Jesus, although he knew only John's baptism. 26 He began to speak boldly in the synagogue. After Priscilla and Aquila heard him, they took him aside[D] and explained the way of God to him more accurately. 27 When he wanted to cross over to Achaia, the brothers and sisters wrote to the disciples to welcome him. After he arrived, he was a great help to those who by grace had believed. 28 For he vigorously refuted the Jews in public, demonstrating through the Scriptures that Jesus is the Messiah.

TWELVE DISCIPLES OF JOHN THE BAPTIST

19 While Apollos was in Corinth, Paul traveled through the interior regions and came to Ephesus. He found some disciples 2 and asked them, "Did you receive the Holy Spirit when you believed?"

"No," they told him, "we haven't even heard that there is a Holy Spirit."

3 "Into what then were you baptized?" he asked them.

"Into John's baptism," they replied.

4 Paul said, "John baptized with a baptism of repentance, telling the people that they should believe in the one who would come after him, that is, in Jesus."

5 When they heard this, they were baptized into the name of the Lord Jesus. 6 And when Paul had laid his hands on them, the Holy Spirit came on them, and they began to speak in other tongues[E] and to prophesy. 7 Now there were about twelve men in all.

IN THE LECTURE HALL OF TYRANNUS

8 Paul entered the synagogue and spoke boldly over a period of three months, arguing and persuading them about the kingdom of God. 9 But when some became hardened and would not believe, slandering the Way in front of the crowd, he withdrew from them, taking the disciples, and conducted discussions every day in the lecture hall of Tyrannus. 10 This went on for two years, so that all the residents of Asia, both Jews and Greeks, heard the word of the Lord.

DEMONISM DEFEATED AT EPHESUS

11 God was performing extraordinary miracles by Paul's hands, 12 so that even facecloths or aprons[F] that had touched his skin were brought to the sick, and the diseases left them, and the evil spirits came out of them.

13 Now some of the itinerant Jewish exorcists also attempted to pronounce the name of the Lord Jesus over those who had evil spirits, saying, "I command you by the Jesus that Paul preaches!" 14 Seven sons of Sceva, a Jewish high priest, were doing this. 15 The evil spirit answered them, "I know Jesus, and I recognize Paul — but who are you?" 16 Then the man who had the evil spirit jumped on them,

---

[A] **18:17** Other mss read *Then all the Greeks* [B] **18:21** Other mss add *"By all means it is necessary to keep the coming festival in Jerusalem. But* [C] **18:25** Or *in the Spirit* [D] **18:26** Lit *they received him* [E] **19:6** languages [F] **19:12** Or *sweat cloths*

overpowered them all, and prevailed against
them, so that they ran out of that house naked
and wounded. 17 When this became known to
everyone who lived in Ephesus, both Jews and
Greeks, they became afraid, and the name of
the Lord Jesus was held in high esteem.
18 And many who had become believers
came confessing and disclosing their practices, 19 while many of those who had practiced
magic collected their books and burned them
in front of everyone. So they calculated their
value and found it to be fifty thousand pieces
of silver. 20 In this way the word of the Lord
flourished and prevailed.

THE RIOT IN EPHESUS

21 After these events, Paul resolved by the Spirit[A]
to pass through Macedonia and Achaia and go
to Jerusalem. "After I've been there," he said,
"It is necessary for me to see Rome as well."
22 After sending to Macedonia two of those
who assisted him, Timothy and Erastus, he
himself stayed in Asia for a while.
23 About that time there was a major disturbance about the Way. 24 For a person named
Demetrius, a silversmith who made silver
shrines of Artemis, provided a great deal of
business for the craftsmen. 25 When he had
assembled them, as well as the workers engaged in this type of business, he said: "Men,
you know that our prosperity is derived from
this business. 26 You see and hear that not only
in Ephesus, but in almost all of Asia, this man
Paul has persuaded and misled a considerable
number of people by saying that gods made by
hand are not gods. 27 Not only do we run a risk
that our business may be discredited, but also
that the temple of the great goddess Artemis
may be despised and her magnificence come
to the verge of ruin — the very one all of Asia
and the world worship."
28 When they had heard this, they were filled
with rage and began to cry out, "Great is Artemis of the Ephesians!" 29 So the city was filled
with confusion, and they rushed all together
into the amphitheater, dragging along Gaius and Aristarchus, Macedonians who were
Paul's traveling companions. 30 Although Paul
wanted to go in before the people, the disciples
did not let him. 31 Even some of the provincial
officials of Asia, who were his friends, sent
word to him, pleading with him not to venture[B]
into the amphitheater. 32 Some were shouting
one thing and some another, because the assembly was in confusion, and most of them
did not know why they had come together.
33 Some Jews in the crowd gave instructions
to Alexander[C] after they pushed him to the
front. Motioning with his hand, Alexander
wanted to make his defense to the people.
34 But when they recognized that he was a
Jew, they all shouted in unison for about two
hours: "Great is Artemis of the Ephesians!"
35 When the city clerk had calmed the crowd
down, he said, "People of Ephesus! What person
is there who doesn't know that the city of the
Ephesians is the temple guardian of the great[D]
Artemis, and of the image that fell from heaven?
36 Therefore, since these things are undeniable,
you must keep calm and not do anything rash.
37 For you have brought these men here who are
not temple robbers or blasphemers of our[E] goddess. 38 So if Demetrius and the craftsmen who
are with him have a case against anyone, the
courts are in session, and there are proconsuls.
Let them bring charges against one another.
39 But if you seek anything further, it must be
decided in a legal assembly. 40 In fact, we run a
risk of being charged with rioting for what happened today, since there is no justification that
we can give as a reason for this disturbance."
41 After saying this, he dismissed the assembly.

PAUL IN MACEDONIA

20 After the uproar was over, Paul sent for
the disciples, encouraged them, and
after saying farewell, departed to go to Macedonia. 2 And when he had passed through
those areas and offered them many words of
encouragement, he came to Greece 3 and stayed
three months. The Jews plotted against him
when he was about to set sail for Syria, and
so he decided to go back through Macedonia.
4 He was accompanied[F] by Sopater son of Pyrrhus[G] from Berea, Aristarchus and Secundus
from Thessalonica, Gaius from Derbe, Timothy,
and Tychicus and Trophimus from the province of Asia. 5 These men went on ahead and
waited for us in Troas, 6 but we sailed away
from Philippi after the Festival of Unleavened
Bread. In five days we reached them at Troas,
where we spent seven days.

EUTYCHUS REVIVED AT TROAS

7 On the first day of the week, we[H] assembled to break bread. Paul spoke to them, and

[A] **19:21** Or *in his spirit* [B] **19:31** Lit *not to give himself* [C] **19:33** Or *thought it was about Alexander* [D] **19:35** Other mss add *goddess* [E] **19:37** Other mss read *your* [F] **20:4** Other mss add *to Asia* [G] **20:4** Other mss omit *son of Pyrrhus* [H] **20:7** Other mss read *the disciples*

since he was about to depart the next day, he kept on talking until midnight. 8 There were many lamps in the room upstairs where we were assembled, 9 and a young man named Eutychus was sitting on a window sill and sank into a deep sleep as Paul kept on talking. When he was overcome by sleep, he fell down from the third story and was picked up dead. 10 But Paul went down, bent over him, embraced him, and said, "Don't be alarmed, because he's alive." 11 After going upstairs, breaking the bread, and eating, Paul talked a long time until dawn. Then he left. 12 They brought the boy home alive and were greatly comforted.

FROM TROAS TO MILETUS

13 We went on ahead to the ship and sailed for Assos, where we were going to take Paul on board, because these were his instructions, since he himself was going by land. 14 When he met us at Assos, we took him on board and went on to Mitylene. 15 Sailing from there, the next day we arrived off Chios. The following day we crossed over to Samos, and[A] the day after, we came to Miletus. 16 For Paul had decided to sail past Ephesus to avoid spending time in the province of Asia, because he was hurrying to be in Jerusalem, if possible, for the day of Pentecost.

FAREWELL ADDRESS TO THE EPHESIAN ELDERS

17 Now from Miletus, he sent to Ephesus and summoned the elders of the church. 18 When they came to him, he said to them: "You know, from the first day I set foot in Asia, how I was with you the whole time, 19 serving the Lord with all humility, with tears, and during the trials that came to me through the plots of the Jews. 20 You know that I did not avoid proclaiming to you anything that was profitable or from teaching you publicly and from house to house. 21 I testified to both Jews and Greeks about repentance toward God and faith in our Lord Jesus.

22 "And now I am on my way to Jerusalem, compelled by the Spirit,[B] not knowing what I will encounter there, 23 except that in every town the Holy Spirit warns me that chains and afflictions are waiting for me. 24 But I consider my life of no value to myself; my purpose is to finish my course[C] and the ministry I received from the Lord Jesus, to testify to the gospel of God's grace.

25 "And now I know that none of you, among whom I went about preaching the kingdom,

Exercise of Faith | *Rejecting False Teaching*

BE ON GUARD!

"Men will rise up even from your own number and distort the truth to lure the disciples into following them." Acts 20:30

Just as ancient Israel had false prophets, so did the early church. Paul alerted the Ephesian elders to this sobering reality. "Be on guard," he urged. "Savage wolves will come in among you, not sparing the flock" (Ac 20:28-29). Indeed, many of the New Testament letters focus on these people who "distort the truth" and try "to lure the disciples into following them."

Sadly, almost twenty centuries later, nothing has changed. Certain men and women, within the church and outside it, take God's Word and distort it. They twist it to suit their own purposes—to enrich themselves, to gain a following, to promote their own strange ideas.

This means "be on guard" is still good counsel. And it means the Berean believers mentioned in Acts 17:11 are a good model to follow. After listening to Paul and Silas teach, do you remember what they did? They "examined the Scriptures daily to see if these things were so."

It's just a fact: The better we know God's Word, the less likely we are to fall prey to those who distort the truth.

For the next note on *Exercise of Faith*, see Acts 22:3.

[A] **20:15** Other mss add *after staying at Trogyllium* [B] **20:22** Or *in my spirit* [C] **20:24** Other mss add *with joy*

will ever see me again. 26 Therefore I declare to
you this day that I am innocent[A] of the blood of
all of you, 27 because I did not avoid declaring
to you the whole plan of God. 28 Be on guard
for yourselves and for all the flock of which
the Holy Spirit has appointed you as overseers,
to shepherd the church of God,[B] which he purchased with his own blood. 29 I know that after my departure savage wolves will come in
among you, not sparing the flock. 30 Men will
rise up even from your own number and distort
the truth to lure the disciples into following
them. 31 Therefore be on the alert, remembering that night and day for three years I never
stopped warning each one of you with tears.

32 "And now[C] I commit you to God and to the
word of his grace, which is able to build you up
and to give you an inheritance among all who
are sanctified. 33 I have not coveted anyone's
silver or gold or clothing. 34 You yourselves
know that I worked with my own hands to
support myself and those who are with me.
35 In every way I've shown you that it is necessary to help the weak by laboring like this
and to remember the words of the Lord Jesus,
because he said, 'It is more blessed to give
than to receive.'"

36 After he said this, he knelt down and
prayed with all of them. 37 There were many
tears shed by everyone. They embraced Paul
and kissed him, 38 grieving most of all over his
statement that they would never see his face
again. And they accompanied him to the ship.

WARNINGS ON THE JOURNEY TO JERUSALEM

21 After we tore ourselves away from
them, we set sail straight for Cos, the
next day to Rhodes, and from there to Patara.
2 Finding a ship crossing over to Phoenicia,
we boarded and set sail. 3 After we sighted
Cyprus, passing to the south of it,[D] we sailed
on to Syria and arrived at Tyre, since the ship
was to unload its cargo there. 4 We sought out
the disciples and stayed there seven days.
Through the Spirit they told Paul not to go to
Jerusalem. 5 When our time had come to an
end, we left to continue our journey, while
all of them, with their wives and children,
accompanied us out of the city. After kneeling
down on the beach to pray, 6 we said farewell
to one another and boarded the ship, and
they returned home.

7 When we completed our voyage[E] from Tyre,
we reached Ptolemais, where we greeted the
brothers and sisters and stayed with them for
a day. 8 The next day we left and came to Caesarea, where we entered the house of Philip
the evangelist, who was one of the Seven, and
stayed with him. 9 This man had four virgin
daughters who prophesied.

10 After we had been there for several days,
a prophet named Agabus came down from
Judea. 11 He came to us, took Paul's belt, tied
his own feet and hands, and said, "This is what
the Holy Spirit says: 'In this way the Jews in
Jerusalem will bind the man who owns this belt
and deliver him over to the Gentiles.'" 12 When
we heard this, both we and the local people
pleaded with him not to go up to Jerusalem.

13 Then Paul replied, "What are you doing,
weeping and breaking my heart? For I am
ready not only to be bound but also to die in
Jerusalem for the name of the Lord Jesus."

14 Since he would not be persuaded, we said
no more except, "The Lord's will be done."

CONFLICT OVER THE GENTILE MISSION

15 After this we got ready and went up to Jerusalem. 16 Some of the disciples from Caesarea
also went with us and brought us to Mnason
of Cyprus, an early disciple, with whom we
were to stay.

17 When we reached Jerusalem, the brothers and sisters welcomed us warmly. 18 The
following day Paul went in with us to James,
and all the elders were present. 19 After greeting them, he reported in detail what God
had done among the Gentiles through his
ministry.

20 When they heard it, they glorified God
and said, "You see, brother, how many thousands of Jews there are who have believed,
and they are all zealous for the law. 21 But they
have been informed about you — that you
are teaching all the Jews who are among the
Gentiles to abandon Moses, telling them not
to circumcise their children or to live according to our customs. 22 So what is to be done?[F]
They will certainly hear that you've come.
23 Therefore do what we tell you: We have four
men who have made a vow. 24 Take these men,
purify yourself along with them, and pay for
them to get their heads shaved. Then everyone
will know that what they were told about you

[A] **20:26** Lit *clean* [B] **20:28** Some mss read *church of the Lord*; other mss read *church of the Lord and God* [C] **20:32** Other mss add *brothers and sisters* [D] **21:3** Lit *leaving it on the left* [E] **21:7** Or *As we continued our voyage* [F] **21:22** Other mss add *A multitude has to come together, since*

amounts to nothing, but that you yourself are
also careful about observing the law. 25 With
regard to the Gentiles who have believed, we
have written a letter containing our decision
that[A] they should keep themselves from food
sacrificed to idols, from blood, from what is
strangled, and from sexual immorality."

THE RIOT IN THE TEMPLE

26 So the next day, Paul took the men, having
purified himself along with them, and entered
the temple, announcing the completion of the
purification days when the offering would be
made for each of them. 27 When the seven days
were nearly over, some Jews from the province of Asia saw him in the temple, stirred up
the whole crowd, and seized him, 28 shouting,
"Fellow Israelites, help! This is the man who
teaches everyone everywhere against our
people, our law, and this place. What's more,
he also brought Greeks into the temple and
has defiled this holy place." 29 For they had
previously seen Trophimus the Ephesian in
the city with him, and they supposed that Paul
had brought him into the temple.

30 The whole city was stirred up, and the
people rushed together. They seized Paul,
dragged him out of the temple, and at once
the gates were shut.

31 As they were trying to kill him, word went
up to the commander of the regiment that
all Jerusalem was in chaos. 32 Taking along
soldiers and centurions, he immediately ran
down to them. Seeing the commander and the
soldiers, they stopped beating Paul. 33 Then
the commander approached, took him into
custody, and ordered him to be bound with
two chains. He asked who he was and what he
had done. 34 Some in the crowd were shouting
one thing and some another. Since he was not
able to get reliable information because of
the uproar, he ordered him to be taken into
the barracks. 35 When Paul got to the steps,
he had to be carried by the soldiers because
of the violence of the crowd, 36 for the mass
of people followed, yelling, "Get rid of him!"

PAUL'S DEFENSE BEFORE THE JERUSALEM MOB

37 As he was about to be brought into the barracks, Paul said to the commander, "Am I allowed to say something to you?"

He replied, "You know how to speak Greek?
38 Aren't you the Egyptian who started a revolt
some time ago and led four thousand men of
the Assassins into the wilderness?"

39 Paul said, "I am a Jewish man from Tarsus
of Cilicia, a citizen of an important city. Now I
ask you, let me speak to the people."

40 After he had given permission, Paul stood
on the steps and motioned with his hand to
the people. When there was a great hush, he
addressed them in Aramaic:[B]
22 1 "Broth-
ers and fathers, listen now to my defense before you." 2 When they heard that
he was addressing them in Aramaic,[B] they
became even quieter. 3 He continued, "I am
a Jew, born in Tarsus of Cilicia but brought
up in this city, educated at the feet of Gamaliel according to the law of our ancestors.
I was zealous for God, just as all of you are
today. 4 I persecuted this Way to the death,
arresting and putting both men and women
in jail, 5 as both the high priest and the whole
council of elders can testify about me. After
I received letters from them to the brothers,
I traveled to Damascus to arrest those who
were there and bring them to Jerusalem to
be punished.

PAUL'S TESTIMONY

6 "As I was traveling and approaching Damascus, about noon an intense light from heav-
en suddenly flashed around me. 7 I fell to the
ground and heard a voice saying to me, 'Saul,
Saul, why are you persecuting me?'

8 "I answered, 'Who are you, Lord?'

"He said to me, 'I am Jesus of Nazareth, the
one you are persecuting.' 9 Now those who
were with me saw the light,[C] but they did not
hear the voice of the one who was speaking
to me.

10 "I said, 'What should I do, Lord?'

"The Lord told me, 'Get up and go into Damascus, and there you will be told everything
that you have been assigned to do.'

11 "Since I couldn't see because of the brightness of the light,[D] I was led by the hand by those
who were with me, and went into Damascus.
12 Someone named Ananias, a devout man
according to the law, who had a good reputation with all the Jews living there, 13 came
and stood by me and said, 'Brother Saul, regain
your sight.' And in that very hour I looked up
and saw him. 14 And he said, 'The God of our
ancestors has appointed you to know his will,
to see the Righteous One, and to hear the words

[A] **21:25** Other mss add *they should observe no such thing, except that* [B] **21:40; 22:2** Or *Hebrew* [C] **22:9** Other mss add *and were afraid* [D] **22:11** Lit *the glory of that light*

from his mouth, 15 since you will be a witness
for him to all people of what you have seen
and heard. 16 And now, why are you delaying?
Get up and be baptized, and wash away your
sins, calling on his name.'
17 "After I returned to Jerusalem and was
praying in the temple, I fell into a trance 18 and
saw him telling me, 'Hurry and get out of Jerusalem quickly, because they will not accept
your testimony about me.'
19 "But I said, 'Lord, they know that in synagogue after synagogue I had those who believed in you imprisoned and beaten. 20 And
when the blood of your witness Stephen was
being shed, I stood there giving approval[A] and
guarding the clothes of those who killed him.'
21 "He said to me, 'Go, because I will send
you far away to the Gentiles.' "

PAUL'S ROMAN PROTECTION

22 They listened to him up to this point. Then
they raised their voices, shouting, "Wipe this
man off the face of the earth! He should not
be allowed to live!"
23 As they were yelling and flinging aside
their garments and throwing dust into the air,
24 the commander ordered him to be brought
into the barracks, directing that he be interrogated with the scourge to discover the reason
they were shouting against him like this. 25 As
they stretched him out for the lash, Paul said
to the centurion standing by, "Is it legal for you
to scourge a man who is a Roman citizen and
is uncondemned?"
26 When the centurion heard this, he went
and reported to the commander, saying, "What
are you going to do? For this man is a Roman
citizen."
27 The commander came and said to him,
"Tell me, are you a Roman citizen?"
"Yes," he said.
28 The commander replied, "I bought this
citizenship for a large amount of money."
"But I was born a citizen," Paul said.
29 So those who were about to examine
him withdrew from him immediately. The
commander too was alarmed when he realized Paul was a Roman citizen and he had
bound him.

PAUL BEFORE THE SANHEDRIN

30 The next day, since he wanted to find out
exactly why Paul was being accused by the
Jews, he released him[B] and instructed the chief

Exercise of Faith | *Sharing Story*

WHAT'S YOUR STORY?

"He continued, 'I am a Jew, born in Tarsus of Cilicia but brought up in this city, educated at the feet of Gamaliel according to the law of our ancestors. I was zealous for God, just as all of you are today.'" Acts 22:3

On more than one occasion, Luke records the apostle Paul sharing his spiritual story. Paul recounts his life before he had put his faith in Jesus, the circumstances surrounding his dramatic encounter with Christ on the road to Damascus, and then, how meeting and following Jesus completely transformed his heart and life.

That's all a "testimony" is. It's not a sermon, a rant about some social issue, or a statement about one's moral beliefs. A testimony is a person's unique spiritual biography. In a clear, concise, and compelling way, you just tell the truth about how you met Jesus and how entering a relationship with him has altered your existence.

Think about the best stories you know. All great novels and movies feature a character who wants something desperately and then overcomes obstacles in trying to get or find that object of desire. What is it you wanted that led you to Jesus—love, acceptance, meaning, significance, freedom, forgiveness? See if you can take the true facts of your spiritual journey and put them in an intriguing sixty-second testimony.

For the next note on *Exercise of Faith*, see Romans 5:3-4.

[A] **22:20** Other mss add *of his murder* [B] **22:30** Other mss add *from his chains*

priests and all the Sanhedrin to convene. He
brought Paul down and placed him before

23 them. 1 Paul looked straight at the Sanhedrin and said, "Brothers, I have lived
my life before God in all good conscience to this
day." 2 The high priest Ananias ordered those
who were standing next to him to strike him
on the mouth. 3 Then Paul said to him, "God
is going to strike you, you whitewashed wall!
You are sitting there judging me according to
the law, and yet in violation of the law are you
ordering me to be struck?"

4 Those standing nearby said, "Do you dare
revile God's high priest?"

5 "I did not know, brothers, that he was the
high priest," replied Paul. "For it is written,
**You must not speak evil of a ruler of your
people.**"[A] 6 When Paul realized that one part
of them were Sadducees and the other part
were Pharisees, he cried out in the Sanhedrin,
"Brothers, I am a Pharisee, a son of Pharisees.
I am being judged because of the hope of the
resurrection of the dead!" 7 When he said this,
a dispute broke out between the Pharisees
and the Sadducees, and the assembly was
divided. 8 For the Sadducees say there is no
resurrection, and neither angel nor spirit,
but the Pharisees affirm them all.

9 The shouting grew loud, and some of the
scribes of the Pharisees' party got up and argued vehemently: "We find nothing evil in this
man. What if a spirit or an angel has spoken
to him?"[B]

10 When the dispute became violent, the commander feared that Paul might be torn apart
by them and ordered the troops to go down,
take him away from them, and bring him into
the barracks. 11 The following night, the Lord
stood by him and said, "Have courage! For
as you have testified about me in Jerusalem,
so it is necessary for you to testify in Rome."

THE PLOT AGAINST PAUL

12 When it was morning, the Jews formed a
conspiracy and bound themselves under a
curse not to eat or drink until they had killed
Paul. 13 There were more than forty who had
formed this plot. 14 These men went to the
chief priests and elders and said, "We have
bound ourselves under a solemn curse that
we won't eat anything until we have killed
Paul. 15 So now you, along with the Sanhedrin,
make a request to the commander that he
bring him down to you[C] as if you were going
to investigate his case more thoroughly. But,
before he gets near, we are ready to kill him."

16 But the son of Paul's sister, hearing about
their ambush, came and entered the barracks
and reported it to Paul. 17 Paul called one of the
centurions and said, "Take this young man to
the commander, because he has something
to report to him."

18 So he took him, brought him to the commander, and said, "The prisoner Paul called
me and asked me to bring this young man to
you, because he has something to tell you."

19 The commander took him by the hand,
led him aside, and inquired privately, "What
is it you have to report to me?"

20 "The Jews," he said, "have agreed to ask
you to bring Paul down to the Sanhedrin tomorrow, as though they are going to hold a
somewhat more careful inquiry about him.
21 Don't let them persuade you, because there
are more than forty of them lying in ambush
— men who have bound themselves under
a curse not to eat or drink until they have
killed him. Now they are ready, waiting for
your consent."

22 So the commander dismissed the young
man and instructed him, "Don't tell anyone
that you have informed me about this."

TO CAESAREA BY NIGHT

23 He summoned two of his centurions and
said, "Get two hundred soldiers ready with
seventy cavalry and two hundred spearmen
to go to Caesarea at nine tonight.[D] 24 Also provide mounts for Paul to ride and bring him
safely to Felix the governor."

25 He wrote the following letter:[E]

26 Claudius Lysias,
To the most excellent governor Felix:
Greetings.

27 When this man had been seized by the
Jews and was about to be killed by them,
I arrived with my troops and rescued
him because I learned that he is a Roman
citizen. 28 Wanting to know the charge
they were accusing him of, I brought him
down before their Sanhedrin. 29 I found
out that the accusations were concerning
questions of their law, and that there was
no charge that merited death or imprisonment. 30 When I was informed that
there was a plot against the man,[F] I sent

[A] 23:5 Ex 22:28 [B] 23:9 Other mss add *Let us not fight God.* [C] 23:15 Other mss add *tomorrow* [D] 23:23 Lit *at the third hour tonight* [E] 23:25 Or *He wrote a letter to this effect:* [F] 23:30 Other mss add *by the Jews*

him to you right away. I also ordered his accusers to state their case against him in your presence.[A]

31 So the soldiers took Paul during the night and brought him to Antipatris as they were ordered. 32 The next day, they returned to the barracks, allowing the cavalry to go on with him. 33 When these men entered Caesarea and delivered the letter to the governor, they also presented Paul to him. 34 After he[B] read it, he asked what province he was from. When he learned he was from Cilicia, 35 he said, "I will give you a hearing whenever your accusers also get here." He ordered that he be kept under guard in Herod's palace.[C]

THE ACCUSATION AGAINST PAUL

24 Five days later Ananias the high priest came down with some elders and a lawyer named Tertullus. These men presented their case against Paul to the governor. 2 When Paul was called in, Tertullus began to accuse him and said: "We enjoy great peace because of you, and reforms are taking place for the benefit of this nation because of your foresight. 3 We acknowledge this in every way and everywhere, most excellent Felix, with utmost gratitude. 4 But, so that I will not burden you any further, I request that you would be kind enough to give us a brief hearing. 5 For we have found this man to be a plague, an agitator among all the Jews throughout the Roman world, and a ringleader of the sect of the Nazarenes. 6 He even tried to desecrate the temple, and so we apprehended him.[D] By examining him yourself you will be able to discern the truth about these charges we are bringing against him." 9 The Jews also joined in the attack, alleging that these things were true.

PAUL'S DEFENSE BEFORE FELIX

10 When the governor motioned for him to speak, Paul replied: "Because I know you have been a judge of this nation for many years, I am glad to offer my defense in what concerns me. 11 You can verify for yourself that it is no more than twelve days since I went up to worship in Jerusalem. 12 They didn't find me arguing with anyone or causing a disturbance among the crowd, either in the temple or in the synagogues or anywhere in the city. 13 Neither can they prove the charges they are now making against me. 14 But I admit this to you: I worship the God of my ancestors according to the Way, which they call a sect, believing everything that is in accordance with the law and written in the prophets. 15 I have a hope in God, which these men themselves also accept, that there will be a resurrection,[E] both of the righteous and the unrighteous. 16 I always strive to have a clear conscience toward God and men. 17 After many years, I came to bring charitable gifts and offerings to my people. 18 While I was doing this, some Jews from Asia found me ritually purified in the temple, without a crowd and without any uproar. 19 It is they who ought to be here before you to bring charges, if they have anything against me. 20 Or let these men here state what wrongdoing they found in me when I stood before the Sanhedrin, 21 other than this one statement I shouted while standing among them, 'Today I am on trial before you concerning the resurrection of the dead.'"

THE VERDICT POSTPONED

22 Since Felix was well informed about the Way, he adjourned the hearing, saying, "When Lysias the commander comes down, I will decide your case." 23 He ordered that the centurion keep Paul under guard, though he could have some freedom, and that he should not prevent any of his friends from meeting[F] his needs.

24 Several days later, when Felix came with his wife Drusilla, who was Jewish, he sent for Paul and listened to him on the subject of faith in Christ Jesus. 25 Now as he spoke about righteousness, self-control, and the judgment to come, Felix became afraid and replied, "Leave for now, but when I have an opportunity I'll call for you." 26 At the same time he was also hoping that Paul would offer him money.[G] So he sent for him quite often and conversed with him.

27 After two years had passed, Porcius Festus succeeded Felix, and because Felix wanted to do the Jews a favor, he left Paul in prison.

APPEAL TO CAESAR

25 Three days after Festus arrived in the province, he went up to Jerusalem from Caesarea. 2 The chief priests and the leaders

[A] **23:30** Other mss add *Farewell* [B] **23:34** Other mss read *the governor* [C] **23:35** Or *headquarters* [D] **24:6** Some mss include vv. 6b-8a: *and wanted to judge him according to our law. 7But Lysias the commander came and took him from our hands with great force, 8commanding his accusers to come to you.* [E] **24:15** Other mss add *of the dead* [F] **24:23** Other mss add *or visiting* [G] **24:26** Other mss add *so that he might release him*

Paul | Restoration Profile

ACTS; 13 LETTERS; 2 PETER 3:15

Restoration doesn't always mean wholeness. And what we often sincerely believe will alleviate our feelings of pain, brokenness, or incompleteness is not necessarily what God desires for us. What we see as handicaps to be repaired or weaknesses to be replaced with strength God sees differently. Faced with the apostle Paul's repeated pleading for a certain restoration, God said to him, "My grace is sufficient for you, for my power is perfected in weakness" (2Co 12:9).

The apostle Paul was no stranger to restoration. Anyone who could consider himself to have been a candidate for "worst" of sinners (1Tm 1:15) also had a special understanding of God's grace.

Paul is one of the best examples in history of the truth that religious zealots are some of the people most in need of God's restoring work. He grew up under the finest in Jewish education of his time yet was blind to his own spiritual condition and violent in his rejection of the gospel. He was well on his way to a career in wreaking havoc among early Christians when Jesus himself confronted Saul on the road to Damascus (Ac 9:1-9). That encounter left Saul physically blind but with wide-eyed spiritual vision. God restored his sight and allowed him to suddenly see the truth in all that he had learned in his training. He had *his* Emmaus road experience on the way to Damascus.

Despite Paul awareness and achievements, and perhaps because of them, he also carried what he called "a thorn in the flesh" (2Co 12:7), some kind of physical malady that plagued him. And though he asked the Lord for relief through restoration, God instead helped him endure the weakness and thereby display God's strength. Complete wholeness could wait until heaven.

of the Jews presented their case against Paul
to him; and they appealed, 3 asking for a favor against Paul, that Festus summon him to
Jerusalem. They were, in fact, preparing an
ambush along the road to kill him. 4 Festus,
however, answered that Paul should be kept at
Caesarea, and that he himself was about to go
there shortly. 5 "Therefore," he said, "let those of
you who have authority go down with me and
accuse him, if he has done anything wrong."
6 When he had spent not more than eight or
ten days among them, he went down to Caesarea. The next day, seated at the tribunal, he
commanded Paul to be brought in. 7 When he
arrived, the Jews who had come down from
Jerusalem stood around him and brought many
serious charges that they were not able to
prove. 8 Then Paul made his defense: "Neither
against the Jewish law, nor against the temple,
nor against Caesar have I sinned in any way."
9 But Festus, wanting to do the Jews a favor, replied to Paul, "Are you willing to go up
to Jerusalem to be tried before me there on
these charges?"
10 Paul replied: "I am standing at Caesar's
tribunal, where I ought to be tried. I have done
no wrong to the Jews, as even you yourself
know very well. 11 If then I did anything wrong
and am deserving of death, I am not trying to
escape death; but if there is nothing to what
these men accuse me of, no one can give me
up to them. I appeal to Caesar!"
12 Then after Festus conferred with his council, he replied, "You have appealed to Caesar;
to Caesar you will go."

KING AGRIPPA AND BERNICE VISIT FESTUS

13 Several days later, King Agrippa and Bernice arrived in Caesarea and paid a courtesy
call on Festus. 14 Since they were staying there
several days, Festus presented Paul's case to
the king, saying, "There's a man who was left
as a prisoner by Felix. 15 When I was in Jerusalem, the chief priests and the elders of the
Jews presented their case and asked that he
be condemned. 16 I answered them that it is
not the Roman custom to give someone up[A]
before the accused faces the accusers and has
an opportunity for a defense against the charges. 17 So when they had assembled here, I did
not delay. The next day I took my seat at the
tribunal and ordered the man to be brought

[A] **25:16** Other mss add *to destruction*

in. 18 The accusers stood up but brought no
charge against him of the evils I was expecting. 19 Instead they had some disagreements
with him about their own religion and about
a certain Jesus, a dead man Paul claimed to be
alive. 20 Since I was at a loss in a dispute over
such things, I asked him if he wanted to go to
Jerusalem and be tried there regarding these
matters. 21 But when Paul appealed to be held
for trial by the Emperor,[A] I ordered him to be
kept in custody until I could send him to Caesar."
22 Agrippa said to Festus, "I would like to
hear the man myself."

"Tomorrow you will hear him," he replied.

PAUL BEFORE AGRIPPA

23 So the next day, Agrippa and Bernice came
with great pomp and entered the auditorium
with the military commanders and prominent men of the city. When Festus gave the
command, Paul was brought in. 24 Then Festus said: "King Agrippa and all men present
with us, you see this man. The whole Jewish
community has appealed to me concerning
him, both in Jerusalem and here, shouting
that he should not live any longer. 25 I found
that he had not done anything deserving of
death, but when he himself appealed to the
Emperor, I decided to send him. 26 I have nothing definite to write to my lord about him.
Therefore, I have brought him before all of
you, and especially before you, King Agrippa,
so that after this examination is over, I may
have something to write. 27 For it seems unreasonable to me to send a prisoner without
indicating the charges against him."

PAUL'S DEFENSE BEFORE AGRIPPA

26 Agrippa said to Paul, "You have permission to speak for yourself."

Then Paul stretched out his hand and began
his defense: 2 "I consider myself fortunate,
that it is before you, King Agrippa, I am to
make my defense today against all the accusations of the Jews, 3 especially since you
are very knowledgeable about all the Jewish
customs and controversies. Therefore I beg
you to listen to me patiently.

4 "All the Jews know my way of life from
my youth, which was spent from the beginning among my own people and in Jerusalem.
5 They have known me for a long time, if they
are willing to testify, that according to the
strictest sect of our religion I lived as a Pharisee. 6 And now I stand on trial because of the
hope in what God promised to our ancestors,
7 the promise our twelve tribes hope to reach
as they earnestly serve him night and day.
King Agrippa, I am being accused by the Jews
because of this hope. 8 Why do any of you consider it incredible that God raises the dead?
9 In fact, I myself was convinced that it was
necessary to do many things in opposition
to the name of Jesus of Nazareth. 10 I actually
did this in Jerusalem, and I locked up many of
the saints in prison, since I had received authority for that from the chief priests. When
they were put to death, I was in agreement
against them. 11 In all the synagogues I often
punished them and tried to make them blaspheme. Since I was terribly enraged at them, I
pursued them even to foreign cities.

PAUL'S ACCOUNT OF HIS CONVERSION AND COMMISSION

12 "I was traveling to Damascus under these
circumstances with authority and a commission from the chief priests. 13 King Agrippa,
while on the road at midday, I saw a light from
heaven brighter than the sun, shining around
me and those traveling with me. 14 We all fell
to the ground, and I heard a voice speaking to
me in Aramaic,[B] 'Saul, Saul, why are you persecuting me? It is hard for you to kick against
the goads.'

15 "I asked, 'Who are you, Lord?'

"And the Lord replied: 'I am Jesus, the one
you are persecuting. 16 But get up and stand
on your feet. For I have appeared to you for
this purpose, to appoint you as a servant and
a witness of what you have seen and will see
of me. 17 I will rescue you from your people
and from the Gentiles. I am sending you to
them 18 to open their eyes so that they may
turn[C] from darkness to light and from the
power of Satan to God, that they may receive
forgiveness of sins and a share among those
who are sanctified by faith in me.'

19 "So then, King Agrippa, I was not disobedient to the heavenly vision. 20 Instead, I preached
to those in Damascus first, and to those in
Jerusalem and in all the region of Judea, and
to the Gentiles, that they should repent and
turn to God, and do works worthy of repentance. 21 For this reason the Jews seized me
in the temple and were trying to kill me. 22 To

[A] **25:21** Lit *his majesty*, also in v. 25 [B] **26:14** Or *Hebrew* [C] **26:18** Or *to turn them*

this very day, I have had help from God, and I stand and testify to both small and great, saying nothing other than what the prophets and Moses said would take place — [23] that the Messiah must suffer, and that, as the first to rise from the dead, he would proclaim light to our people and to the Gentiles."

AGRIPPA NOT QUITE PERSUADED

[24] As he was saying these things in his defense, Festus exclaimed in a loud voice, "You're out of your mind, Paul! Too much study is driving you mad."

[25] But Paul replied, "I'm not out of my mind, most excellent Festus. On the contrary, I'm speaking words of truth and good judgment. [26] For the king knows about these matters, and I can speak boldly to him. For I am convinced that none of these things has escaped his notice, since this was not done in a corner. [27] King Agrippa, do you believe the prophets? I know you believe."

[28] Agrippa said to Paul, "Are you going to persuade me to become a Christian so easily?"[A]

[29] "I wish before God," replied Paul, "that whether easily or with difficulty,[B] not only you but all who listen to me today might become as I am — except for these chains."

[30] The king, the governor, Bernice, and those sitting with them got up, [31] and when they had left they talked with each other and said, "This man is not doing anything to deserve death or imprisonment."

[32] Agrippa said to Festus, "This man could have been released if he had not appealed to Caesar."

SAILING FOR ROME

27 When it was decided that we were to sail to Italy, they handed over Paul and some other prisoners to a centurion named Julius, of the Imperial Regiment.[C] [2] When we had boarded a ship of Adramyttium, we put to sea, intending to sail to ports along the coast of Asia. Aristarchus, a Macedonian of Thessalonica, was with us. [3] The next day we put in at Sidon, and Julius treated Paul kindly and allowed him to go to his friends to receive their care. [4] When we had put out to sea from there, we sailed along the northern coast[D] of Cyprus because the winds were against us. [5] After sailing through the open sea off Cilicia and Pamphylia, we reached Myra in Lycia. [6] There the centurion found an Alexandrian ship sailing for Italy and put us on board.

Rest and Reflection | *Resting and Recharging*

POWER FOR LIVING

"I will rescue you from your people and from the Gentiles. I am sending you to them to open their eyes so that they may turn from darkness to light and from the power of Satan to God, that they may receive forgiveness of sins and a share among those who are sanctified by faith in me." Acts 26:17-18

Maybe we should stop asking each other, "Are you tired?" and start asking, "*How* are you tired?" Lord knows we can be worn out in a variety of ways. If we're not spiritually weary and physically spent, we might be emotionally exhausted and relationally drained.

Paul was on trial, telling again the story of Jesus's call on his life. Was Paul tired? Tired of telling the story? Tired of being beaten up for telling it? Perhaps. But in any case, he didn't stop. Before this king, he gave an eloquent account of what God had called him to do—open people's eyes, help them turn from darkness to light (from the power of Satan to the power of God), so that they might receive forgiveness, and then share that faith with others.

A tall order. An exhausting order. Yet God had clearly said "I" am doing this. And with that great call came great help to do the task. Ask God to open your eyes to his incomparable power. Ask him to fill you with his limitless strength so that you can do all the things he's set before you today.

For the next note on *Rest and Reflection*, see Romans 7:18-19.

[A] **26:28** Or *so quickly* [B] **26:29** Or *whether a short time or long* [C] **27:1** Or *Augustan Cohort* [D] **27:4** Lit *sailed under the lee,* also in v. 7

7 Sailing slowly for many days, with difficulty we arrived off Cnidus. Since the wind did not allow us to approach it, we sailed along the south side of Crete off Salmone. 8 With still more difficulty we sailed along the coast and came to a place called Fair Havens near the city of Lasea.

PAUL'S ADVICE IGNORED

9 By now much time had passed, and the voyage was already dangerous. Since the Day of Atonement[A] was already over, Paul gave his advice 10 and told them, "Men, I can see that this voyage is headed toward disaster and heavy loss, not only of the cargo and the ship but also of our lives." 11 But the centurion paid attention to the captain and the owner of the ship rather than to what Paul said. 12 Since the harbor was unsuitable to winter in, the majority decided to set sail from there, hoping somehow to reach Phoenix, a harbor on Crete facing the southwest and northwest, and to winter there.

STORM-TOSSED SHIP

13 When a gentle south wind sprang up, they thought they had achieved their purpose. They weighed anchor and sailed along the shore of Crete. 14 But before long, a fierce wind called the "northeaster" rushed down from the island. 15 Since the ship was caught and unable to head into the wind, we gave way to it and were driven along. 16 After running under the shelter of a little island called Cauda,[B] we were barely able to get control of the skiff. 17 After hoisting it up, they used ropes and tackle and girded the ship. Fearing they would run aground on the Syrtis, they lowered the drift-anchor, and in this way they were driven along. 18 Because we were being severely battered by the storm, they began to jettison the cargo the next day. 19 On the third day, they threw the ship's tackle overboard with their own hands. 20 For many days neither sun nor stars appeared, and the severe storm kept raging. Finally all hope was fading that we would be saved.

21 Since they had been without food for a long time, Paul then stood up among them and said, "You men should have followed my advice not to sail from Crete and sustain this damage and loss. 22 Now I urge you to take courage, because there will be no loss of any of your lives, but only of the ship. 23 For last night an angel of the God I belong to and serve stood by me 24 and said, 'Don't be afraid, Paul. It is necessary for you to appear before Caesar. And indeed, God has graciously given you all those who are sailing with you.' 25 So take courage, men, because I believe God that it will be just the way it was told to me. 26 But we have to run aground on some island."

27 When the fourteenth night came, we were drifting in the Adriatic Sea, and about midnight the sailors thought they were approaching land. 28 They took soundings and found it to be a hundred and twenty feet[C] deep; when they had sailed a little farther and sounded again, they found it to be ninety feet[D] deep. 29 Then, fearing we might run aground on the rocks, they dropped four anchors from the stern and prayed for daylight to come. 30 Some sailors tried to escape from the ship; they had let down the skiff into the sea, pretending that they were going to put out anchors from the bow. 31 Paul said to the centurion and the soldiers, "Unless these men stay in the ship, you cannot be saved." 32 Then the soldiers cut the ropes holding the skiff and let it drop away.

33 When it was about daylight, Paul urged them all to take food, saying, "Today is the fourteenth day that you have been waiting and going without food, having eaten nothing. 34 So I urge you to take some food. For this is for your survival, since none of you will lose a hair from your head." 35 After he said these things and had taken some bread, he gave thanks to God in the presence of all of them, and after he broke it, he began to eat. 36 They all were encouraged and took food themselves. 37 In all there were 276 of us on the ship. 38 When they had eaten enough, they began to lighten the ship by throwing the grain overboard into the sea.

SHIPWRECK

39 When daylight came, they did not recognize the land but sighted a bay with a beach. They planned to run the ship ashore if they could. 40 After cutting loose the anchors, they left them in the sea, at the same time loosening the ropes that held the rudders. Then they hoisted the foresail to the wind and headed for the beach. 41 But they struck a sandbar and ran the ship aground. The bow jammed fast and remained immovable, while the stern began

[A] **27:9** Lit *the Fast* [B] **27:16** Or *Clauda* [C] **27:28** Lit *twenty fathoms* [D] **27:28** Lit *fifteen fathoms*

RESTORATION THEMES

R	Rest and Reflection	*Admitting Powerlessness—7:18-19*
E	Eternal Perspective	*God's Timing—5:6* *God's Love—5:8; 8:38-39* *God's View of Sin—6:23* *Biblical Hope—15:13* *God's Family—16:14*
S	Support	*Openness with God—8:27* *Truthfulness with Self—12:3*
T	Thanksgiving and Contentment	*Grace Received—3:23-24* *Confession—6:13* *Perspective—8:28*
O	Other-centeredness	*Not Being Judgmental—2:1*
R	Relationships	*Relating to Church Family—1:16; 12:15-18*
E	Exercise of Faith	*Responding to Trials—5:3-4* *Sharing Faith/Gospel—10:13-14* *Guarding the Heart—13:14*

THE GOSPEL OF GOD FOR ROME

1 Paul, a servant of Christ Jesus, called as
an apostle[A] and set apart for the gospel
of God — 2 which he promised beforehand
through his prophets in the Holy Scriptures —
3 concerning his Son, Jesus Christ our Lord, who
was a descendant of David[B] according to the
flesh 4 and was appointed to be the powerful
Son of God according to the Spirit of holiness[C]
by the resurrection of the dead. 5 Through him
we have received grace and apostleship to bring
about[D] the obedience of faith for the sake of
his name among all the Gentiles,[E] 6 including
you who are also called by Jesus Christ.

7 To all who are in Rome, loved by God, called
as saints.

Grace to you and peace from God our Father
and the Lord Jesus Christ.

PAUL'S DESIRE TO VISIT ROME

8 First, I thank my God through Jesus Christ
for all of you because the news of your faith[F]
is being reported in all the world. 9 God is
my witness, whom I serve with my spirit in
telling the good news about his Son — that
I constantly mention you, 10 always asking
in my prayers that if it is somehow in God's
will, I may now at last succeed in coming to
you. 11 For I want very much to see you, so
that I may impart to you some spiritual gift
to strengthen you, 12 that is, to be mutually
encouraged by each other's faith, both yours
and mine.

13 Now I don't want you to be unaware, brothers and sisters, that I often planned to come
to you (but was prevented until now) in order
that I might have a fruitful ministry[G] among
you, just as I have had among the rest of the
Gentiles. 14 I am obligated both to Greeks and
barbarians,[H] both to the wise and the foolish.
15 So I am eager to preach the gospel to you
also who are in Rome.

THE RIGHTEOUS WILL LIVE BY FAITH

16 For I am not ashamed of the gospel,[I] because
it is the power of God for salvation to everyone
who believes, first to the Jew, and also to the
Greek. 17 For in it the righteousness of God

Relationships | *Relating to Church Family*

NOT ASHAMED

"For I am not ashamed of the gospel, because it is the power of God for salvation to everyone who believes, first to the Jew, and also to the Greek." Romans 1:16

Andre can't sleep. Earlier in the evening he lashed out at his daughter, reducing her to tears. Meanwhile, Sofia is tossing and turning, too. She can't believe the ungracious way some of her church friends are reacting on social media to a divisive cultural issue.

What Andre and Sofia are feeling, of course, is shame. Embarrassment. Andre, because of something he did; Sofia, because of what others in her camp are doing. *What if my irreligious friends lump me in with my religious friends?*

Paul suggests the gospel of Jesus is the antidote for shame. It's the only truly good news for sinners and screw-ups worldwide. It says we are loved by God, warts and all. God's provision of forgiveness in Christ alone has the power to deliver us from sin, guilt, and shame.

As far as the embarrassing words and actions of Christian brothers and sisters, we have to remember that though the gospel of Jesus is unfailingly beautiful and perfect, the followers of Jesus are not and we can't fix the flaws of others. All we can do is to seek personally to live in ways that bring honor to God and praise to the gospel.

For the next note on *Relationships*, see Romans 12:15-18.

[A] **1:1** Or *Jesus, a called apostle* [B] **1:3** Lit *was of the seed of David* [C] **1:4** Or *the spirit of holiness*, or *the Holy Spirit* [D] **1:5** Or *him for*; lit *him into* [E] **1:5** Or *nations*, also in v. 13 [F] **1:8** Or *because your faith* [G] **1:13** Lit *have some fruit* [H] **1:14** Or *non-Greeks* [I] **1:16** Other mss add *of Christ*

is revealed from faith to faith,[A] just as it is written: **The righteous will live by faith.**[B,C]

THE GUILT OF THE GENTILE WORLD

18 For God's wrath is revealed from heaven against all godlessness and unrighteousness of people who by their unrighteousness suppress the truth, 19 since what can be known[D] about God is evident among them, because God has shown it to them. 20 For his invisible attributes, that is, his eternal power and divine nature, have been clearly seen since the creation of the world, being understood through what he has made. As a result, people are without excuse. 21 For though they knew God, they did not glorify him as God or show gratitude. Instead, their thinking became worthless, and their senseless hearts were darkened. 22 Claiming to be wise, they became fools 23 and exchanged the glory of the immortal God for images resembling mortal man, birds, four-footed animals, and reptiles.

24 Therefore God delivered them over in the desires of their hearts to sexual impurity, so that their bodies were degraded among themselves. 25 They exchanged the truth of God for a lie, and worshiped and served what has been created instead of the Creator, who is praised forever. Amen.

FROM IDOLATRY TO DEPRAVITY

26 For this reason God delivered them over to disgraceful passions. Their women[E] exchanged natural sexual relations[F] for unnatural ones. 27 The men[G] in the same way also left natural relations with women and were inflamed in their lust for one another. Men committed shameless acts with men and received in their own persons[H] the appropriate penalty of their error.

28 And because they did not think it worthwhile to acknowledge God, God delivered them over to a corrupt mind so that they do what is not right. 29 They are filled with all unrighteousness,[I] evil, greed, and wickedness. They are full of envy, murder, quarrels, deceit, and malice. They are gossips, 30 slanderers, God-haters, arrogant, proud, boastful, inventors of evil, disobedient to parents, 31 senseless, untrustworthy, unloving,[J] and unmerciful. 32 Although they know God's just sentence — that those who practice such things deserve to die[K] — they not only do them, but even applaud[L] others who practice them.

GOD'S RIGHTEOUS JUDGMENT

2 Therefore, every one of you[M] who judges is without excuse. For when you judge another, you condemn yourself, since you, the judge, do the same things. 2 We know that God's judgment on those who do such things is based on the truth. 3 Do you really think — anyone of you who judges those who do such things yet do the same — that you will escape God's judgment? 4 Or do you despise the riches of his kindness, restraint, and patience, not recognizing[N] that God's kindness is intended to lead you to repentance? 5 Because of your hardened and unrepentant heart you are storing up wrath for yourself in the day of wrath, when God's righteous judgment is revealed. 6 **He will repay each one according to his works**:[O] 7 eternal life to those who by persistence in doing good seek glory, honor, and immortality; 8 but wrath and anger to those who are self-seeking and disobey the truth while obeying unrighteousness. 9 There will be affliction and distress for every human being who does evil, first to the Jew, and also to the Greek; 10 but glory, honor, and peace for everyone who does what is good, first to the Jew, and also to the Greek. 11 For there is no favoritism with God.

12 All who sin without the law will also perish without the law, and all who sin under[P] the law will be judged by the law. 13 For the hearers of the law are not righteous before God, but the doers of the law will be justified.[Q] 14 So, when Gentiles, who do not by nature have the law, do[R] what the law demands, they are a law to themselves even though they do not have the law. 15 They show that the work of the law[S] is written on their hearts. Their consciences confirm this. Their competing thoughts either accuse or even excuse them[T] 16 on the day when God judges what people have kept secret, according to my gospel through Christ Jesus.

[A] **1:17** Or *revealed out of faith into faith* [B] **1:17** Or *The one who is righteous by faith will live* [C] **1:17** Hab 2:4 [D] **1:19** Or *what is known* [E] **1:26** Lit *females*, also in v. 27 [F] **1:26** Lit *natural use*, also in v. 27 [G] **1:27** Lit *males*, also later in v. [H] **1:27** Or *in themselves* [I] **1:29** Other mss add *sexual immorality* [J] **1:31** Other mss add *unforgiving* [K] **1:32** Lit *things are worthy of death* [L] **1:32** Lit *even take pleasure in* [M] **2:1** Lit *Therefore, O man, every one* [N] **2:4** Or *patience, because you do not recognize* [O] **2:6** Ps 62:12; Pr 24:12 [P] **2:12** Lit *in* [Q] **2:13** Or *acquitted* [R] **2:14** Or *who do not have the law, instinctively do* [S] **2:15** The code of conduct required by the law [T] **2:15** Internal debate, either in a person or among the pagan moralists

JEWISH VIOLATION OF THE LAW

17 Now if[A] you call yourself a Jew, and rely on
the law, and boast in God, 18 and know his will,
and approve the things that are superior, being instructed from the law, 19 and if you are
convinced that you are a guide for the blind,
a light to those in darkness, 20 an instructor of
the ignorant, a teacher of the immature, having
the embodiment of knowledge and truth in the
law — 21 you then, who teach another, don't
you teach yourself? You who preach, "You must
not steal" — do you steal? 22 You who say, "You
must not commit adultery" — do you commit
adultery? You who detest idols, do you rob their
temples? 23 You who boast in the law, do you
dishonor God by breaking the law? 24 For, as it
is written: **The name of God is blasphemed
among the Gentiles because of you.**[B]

CIRCUMCISION OF THE HEART

25 Circumcision benefits you if you observe
the law, but if you are a lawbreaker, your
circumcision has become uncircumcision.
26 So if an uncircumcised man keeps the law's
requirements, will not his uncircumcision
be counted as circumcision? 27 A man who is
physically uncircumcised, but who keeps the
law, will judge you who are a lawbreaker in
spite of having the letter of the law and circumcision. 28 For a person is not a Jew who
is one outwardly, and true circumcision is
not something visible in the flesh. 29 On the
contrary, a person is a Jew who is one inwardly, and circumcision is of the heart — by the
Spirit, not the letter.[C] That person's praise is
not from people but from God.

PAUL ANSWERS AN OBJECTION

3 So what advantage does the Jew have?
Or what is the benefit of circumcision?
2 Considerable in every way. First, they were
entrusted with the very words of God. 3 What
then? If some were unfaithful, will their unfaithfulness nullify God's faithfulness? 4 Absolutely not! Let God be true, even though
everyone is a liar, as it is written:

That you may be justified
in your words
and triumph when you judge.[D]

5 But if our unrighteousness highlights[E] God's

Other-centeredness | *Not Being Judgmental*

NO ROOM TO JUDGE

"Therefore, every one of you who judges is without excuse. For when you judge another, you condemn yourself, since you, the judge, do the same things." Romans 2:1

Something about religiosity breeds pride. Clustering with the pious is easy, looking outward at our irreligious neighbors and coworkers and beginning to feel smug, superior. *Aren't you glad we're not like them?* Give in to this mindset, even momentarily, and we can unconsciously morph into a self-proclaimed "Chief Justice." Suddenly, we're moving through the world banging our gavel at all the wrong behavior of all the messed-up people around us. What's worse, we can become so busy railing against sins in others that we don't notice the ugly stuff in our own souls. When this happens, the ungodly cluster and shake their heads. *Can you believe how hypocritical those religious wackos are?*

Paul's point is that all of us stand guilty before a holy God. Every human heart is rebellious, from the scowling death row inmate to the smiling TV preacher. We all need Jesus. We all need his forgiveness. And we all need to heed his call to focus on the beam in our own eye, not the splinter in our neighbor's (Mt 7:3).

Instead of casting judging glances and thoughts at others, look inward with an honest and Spirit-led evaluation and bring *your* sins and shortcomings to the cross.

For the next note on *Other-centeredness*, see 1 Corinthians 13:6-7.

[A] **2:17** Other mss read *Look —* [B] **2:24** Is 52:5 [C] **2:29** Or *heart — spiritually, not literally* [D] **3:4** Ps 51:4 [E] **3:5** Or *shows*, or *demonstrates*

righteousness, what are we to say? I am using a human argument:[A] Is God unrighteous
to inflict wrath? 6 Absolutely not! Otherwise,
how will God judge the world? 7 But if by my
lie God's truth abounds to his glory, why am I
also still being judged as a sinner? 8 And why
not say, just as some people slanderously claim
we say, "Let us do what is evil so that good
may come"? Their condemnation is deserved!

THE WHOLE WORLD GUILTY BEFORE GOD

9 What then? Are we any better off?[B] Not at
all! For we have already charged that both
Jews and Gentiles[C] are all under sin,[D] 10 as it
is written:

There is no one righteous,
not even one.
11 **There is no one who understands;**
there is no one who seeks God.
12 **All have turned away;**
all alike have become worthless.
There is no one who does what is good,
not even one.[E]
13 **Their throat is an open grave;**
they deceive with their tongues.[F]
Vipers' venom is under their lips.[G]
14 **Their mouth is full of cursing**
and bitterness.[H]
15 **Their feet are swift to shed blood;**
16 **ruin and wretchedness are**
in their paths,
17 **and the path of peace**
they have not known.[I]
18 **There is no fear of God before their eyes.**[J]

19 Now we know that whatever the law says,
it speaks to those who are subject to the law,[K]
so that every mouth may be shut and the whole
world may become subject to God's judgment.[L]
20 For no one will be justified[M] in his sight by
the works of the law, because the knowledge
of sin comes through the law.

THE RIGHTEOUSNESS OF GOD THROUGH FAITH

21 But now, apart from the law, the righteousness of God has been revealed, attested by the
Law and the Prophets.[N] 22 The righteousness
of God is through faith in Jesus Christ[O] to all

Thanksgiving and Contentment | *Grace Received*

JUSTIFIED FREELY

"For all have sinned and fall short of the glory of God. They are justified freely by his grace through the redemption that is in Christ Jesus." Romans 3:23-24

F-R-E-E is one of our favorite four-letter words. It means without cost or charge, something for nothing. Paul says the good news of Jesus is like this.

Adam and Eve, our oldest ancestors, were created to reflect the glory of God (Gn 1–2). Instead, they doubted his goodness, rejected his authority, and went looking for life apart from the One who is life (Gn 3). This shocking rebelliousness altered everything. It permeated humanity's DNA, meaning we're infected, too. Paul therefore declares, "All have sinned and fall short of the glory of God." That's the bad news before the good news.

The good news announces joyfully that Jesus provided redemption. That is, he willingly paid the steep price—death—that sin against a holy God demanded. Because he died in our place, sin's debt is fully paid. Now Jesus can offer sinners the promise of justification (right standing with God). The promise of this passage? Those who believe are "justified freely."

This means forgiveness comes at no cost to us. It's *gratis* (Latin for "grace").

Have you believed this promise? Do you live like you believe it?

For the next note on *Thanksgiving and Contentment*, see Romans 6:13.

[A] **3:5** Lit *I speak as a man* [B] **3:9** Are we Jews any better than the Gentiles? [C] **3:9** Lit *Greeks* [D] **3:9** Under sin's power or dominion [E] **3:10-12** Ps 14:1-3; 53:1-3; Ec 7:20 [F] **3:13** Ps 5:9 [G] **3:13** Ps 140:3 [H] **3:14** Ps 10:7 [I] **3:15-17** Is 59:7-8 [J] **3:18** Ps 36:1 [K] **3:19** Lit *those in the law* [L] **3:19** Or *become guilty before God*, or *may be accountable to God* [M] **3:20** Or *will be declared righteous*, or *will be acquitted* [N] **3:21** When capitalized, *the Law and the Prophets* = OT [O] **3:22** Or *through the faithfulness of Jesus Christ*

who believe, since there is no distinction. 23 For
all have sinned and fall short of the[A] glory of
God. 24 They are justified freely by his grace
through the redemption that is in Christ Jesus.
25 God presented him as an atoning sacrifice[B]
in his blood, received through faith, to demonstrate his righteousness, because in his
restraint God passed over the sins previously
committed. 26 God presented him to demonstrate his righteousness at the present time,
so that he would be righteous and declare
righteous[C] the one who has faith in Jesus.

BOASTING EXCLUDED

27 Where, then, is boasting? It is excluded. By
what kind of law?[D] By one of works? No, on the
contrary, by a law[E] of faith. 28 For we conclude
that a person is justified by faith apart from
the works of the law. 29 Or is God the God of
Jews only? Is he not the God of Gentiles too?
Yes, of Gentiles too, 30 since there is one God
who will justify the circumcised by faith and
the uncircumcised through faith. 31 Do we then
nullify the law through faith? Absolutely not!
On the contrary, we uphold the law.

ABRAHAM JUSTIFIED BY FAITH

4 What then will we say that Abraham, our
forefather according to the flesh, has
found?[F] 2 If Abraham was justified[G] by works,
he has something to boast about — but not
before God. 3 For what does the Scripture say?
**Abraham believed God, and it was credited
to him for righteousness.**[H] 4 Now to the one
who works, pay is not credited as a gift, but as
something owed. 5 But to the one who does not
work, but believes on him who declares the
ungodly to be righteous, his faith is credited
for righteousness.

DAVID CELEBRATING THE SAME TRUTH

6 Just as David also speaks of the blessing of
the person to whom God credits righteousness apart from works:

7 **Blessed are those whose lawless acts**
are forgiven
and whose sins
are covered.
8 **Blessed is the person**
the Lord will never charge
with sin.[I]

Exercise of Faith | *Responding to Trials*

AFFLICTIONS APLENTY

"And not only that, but we also rejoice in our afflictions, because we know that affliction produces endurance, endurance produces proven character, and proven character produces hope." Romans 5:3-4

Think about most of the believers you know and then complete this sentence: "When trouble comes, we ______." What word or words did you supply? *Fall apart and give up? Cuss a blue streak? Grumble at God and question his goodness? Run away?* What?

Notice how Paul filled in the blank, "We . . . *rejoice* in our afflictions." Rejoice? Is this a joke? How in the world could anyone respond like this?

Here's how: Paul saw trouble and hardship as a fact of life in a fallen world. Moreover, he embraced the not-so-popular biblical teaching that God turns suffering on its head. He uses it—much more than blessings—to shape us and make us like Christ. Rather than resist this process, Paul welcomed it. Elsewhere he said that we come to know Jesus intimately through suffering (Php 3). He also claimed that when we're weak and hurting, God is able to do his best work in and through us (2Co 12).

God can use your current trials to shape your character. It begins by cooperating with him, one step at a time.

For the next note on *Exercise of Faith*, see Romans 10:13-14.

[A] **3:23** Or *and lack the* [B] **3:25** Or *a propitiation*, or *a place of atonement* [C] **3:26** Or *and justify*, or *and acquit* [D] **3:27** Or *what principle?* [E] **3:27** Or *a principle* [F] **4:1** Or *What then shall we say? Have we found Abraham to be our forefather according to the flesh?* or *What, then, shall we say that Abraham our forefather found according to the flesh?* [G] **4:2** Or *was declared righteous*, or *was acquitted* [H] **4:3** Gn 15:6 [I] **4:7-8** Ps 32:1-2

ABRAHAM JUSTIFIED BEFORE CIRCUMCISION

9 Is this blessing only for the circumcised,
then? Or is it also for the uncircumcised?
For we say, **Faith was credited to Abraham**
for righteousness.[A] 10 In what way then was
it credited — while he was circumcised, or
uncircumcised? It was not while he was circumcised, but uncircumcised. 11 And he received the sign of circumcision as a seal of
the righteousness that he had by faith[B] while
still uncircumcised. This was to make him the
father of all who believe but are not circumcised, so that righteousness may be credited
to them also. 12 And he became the father of
the circumcised, who are not only circumcised but who also follow in the footsteps of
the faith our father Abraham had while he
was still uncircumcised.

THE PROMISE GRANTED THROUGH FAITH

13 For the promise to Abraham or to his descendants that he would inherit the world
was not through the law, but through the righteousness that comes by faith. 14 If those who
are of the law are heirs, faith is made empty
and the promise nullified, 15 because the law
produces wrath. And where there is no law,
there is no transgression.

16 This is why the promise is by faith, so that
it may be according to grace, to guarantee it to
all the descendants — not only to those who
are of the law[C] but also to those who are of
Abraham's faith. He is the father of us all. 17 As
it is written: **I have made you the father of**
many nations.[D] He is our father in God's sight, in
whom Abraham believed — the God who gives
life to the dead and calls things into existence
that do not exist. 18 He believed, hoping against
hope, so that he became **the father of many**
nations[D] according to what had been spoken:
So will your descendants be.[E] 19 He did not
weaken in faith when he considered[F] his own
body to be already dead (since he was about a
hundred years old) and also the deadness of
Sarah's womb. 20 He did not waver in unbelief
at God's promise but was strengthened in his
faith and gave glory to God, 21 because he was
fully convinced that what God had promised,
he was also able to do. 22 Therefore, **it was cred-**
ited to him for righteousness.[A] 23 Now **it was**
credited to him[A] was not written for Abraham
alone, 24 but also for us. It will be credited to us

Eternal Perspective | *God's Timing*

TIMING IS EVERYTHING

"For while we were still helpless, at the right time,
Christ died for the ungodly." Romans 5:6

A comedian pauses ever so briefly and then delivers the punch line. The audience howls with laughter. A stock trader watches and waits, watches and waits, and then suddenly pulls the trigger on buying twenty thousand shares of a certain stock. Overnight he makes a cool $100,000. Timing, as they say, is everything.

Nobody has better timing than God. The Bible declares that God sent Jesus "when the time came to completion" (Gl 4:4). Here Paul says Christ died "at the right time."

We need to realize that God's perfect timing doesn't just apply to big moves by God. Whether it shows up in unanswered prayer, meeting a financial need, a person bumping into the future spouse, receiving a hoped-for job offer, or getting pregnant, God's timing is always right. God may make us wait, but he'll never be too late.

You may feel frustrated by God's timetable. You may wish he'd hurry some things up. Ask him for the grace to say from your heart, "Not my will and schedule, but yours be done." The more we trust his love for us, the more we will rest in his timing.

For the next note on *Eternal Perspective*, see Romans 5:8.

[A] **4:9,22,23** Gn 15:6 [B] **4:11** Lit *righteousness of faith*, also in v. 13 [C] **4:16** Or *not to those who are of the law only* [D] **4:17,18** Gn 17:5 [E] **4:18** Gn 15:5 [F] **4:19** Other mss read *He did not consider*

who believe in him who raised Jesus our Lord
from the dead. 25 He was delivered up for[A] our
trespasses and raised for our justification.

FAITH TRIUMPHS

5 Therefore, since we have been declared
righteous by faith, we have peace[B] with
God through our Lord Jesus Christ. 2 We have
also obtained access through him by faith[C] into
this grace in which we stand, and we rejoice[D] in
the hope of the glory of God. 3 And not only that,
but we also rejoice in our afflictions, because
we know that affliction produces endurance,
4 endurance produces proven character, and
proven character produces hope. 5 This hope
will not disappoint us, because God's love has
been poured out in our hearts through the
Holy Spirit who was given to us.

THOSE DECLARED RIGHTEOUS ARE RECONCILED

6 For while we were still helpless, at the right
time, Christ died for the ungodly. 7 For rarely
will someone die for a just person — though
for a good person perhaps someone might
even dare to die. 8 But God proves his own
love for us in that while we were still sinners,
Christ died for us. 9 How much more then,
since we have now been declared righteous by
his blood, will we be saved through him from
wrath. 10 For if, while we were enemies, we
were reconciled to God through the death of
his Son, then how much more, having been reconciled, will we be saved by his life. 11 And not
only that, but we also rejoice in God through
our Lord Jesus Christ, through whom we have
now received this reconciliation.

DEATH THROUGH ADAM AND LIFE THROUGH CHRIST

12 Therefore, just as sin entered the world
through one man, and death through sin,
in this way death spread to all people, because all sinned.[E] 13 In fact, sin was in the
world before the law, but sin is not charged

Eternal Perspective | *God's Love*

PROOF

"But God proves his own love for us in that while we were still sinners, Christ died for us." Romans 5:8

You want proof that God loves the world? Here it is, Paul says: "While we were still sinners, Christ died for us."

Pay close attention to what happened on Jesus's last day. Take note of the disciples who ran away from him as quick as their freshly washed feet would go. See the bored, burly soldiers who took turns punching him and spitting in his innocent face. The crowds who called for his death. The religious leaders who made jokes. The dying thief who insulted him. All of them real people—and representative of us. God alone knows what we might have done had we been in Jerusalem on that fateful Friday.

Looking down on them all from his bloody perch and through his swollen eyes, what did Jesus say? "Father, forgive them, because they do not know what they are doing" (Lk 23:34).

We like to say that "Talk is cheap" and "Actions speak louder than words." We mean, of course, that what people do, not just what they say, is what really matters.

In God's case, he didn't merely dispatch a few prophets to declare his love. And he didn't settle for some apostles writing letters about divine compassion. He sent his Son to die in our place. He surely has more than enough love to get you through your tough times.

God loves you!

For the next note on *Eternal Perspective*, see Romans 6:23.

[A] **4:25** Or *because of* [B] **5:1** Other mss read *faith, let us have peace*, which can also be translated *faith, let us grasp the fact that we have peace* [C] **5:2** Other mss omit *by faith* [D] **5:2** Lit *boast*, also in vv. 3,11 [E] **5:12** Or *have sinned*

to a person's account when there is no law.
14 Nevertheless, death reigned from Adam
to Moses, even over those who did not sin
in the likeness of Adam's transgression. He
is a type of the Coming One.
15 But the gift is not like the trespass. For
if by the one man's trespass the many died,
how much more have the grace of God and
the gift which comes through the grace of
the one man Jesus Christ overflowed to the
many. 16 And the gift is not like the one man's
sin, because from one sin came the judgment,
resulting in condemnation, but from many
trespasses came the gift, resulting in justification.[A] 17 Since by the one man's trespass,
death reigned through that one man, how
much more will those who receive the overflow of grace and the gift of righteousness
reign in life through the one man, Jesus Christ.
18 So then, as through one trespass there is
condemnation for everyone, so also through
one righteous act there is justification leading
to life for everyone. 19 For just as through one
man's disobedience the many were made sinners, so also through the one man's obedience
the many will be made righteous. 20 The law
came along to multiply the trespass. But where
sin multiplied, grace multiplied even more 21 so
that, just as sin reigned in death, so also grace
will reign through righteousness, resulting
in eternal life through Jesus Christ our Lord.

THE NEW LIFE IN CHRIST

6 What should we say then? Should we continue in sin so that grace may multiply?
2 Absolutely not! How can we who died to sin
still live in it? 3 Or are you unaware that all of
us who were baptized into Christ Jesus were
baptized into his death? 4 Therefore we were
buried with him by baptism into death, in
order that, just as Christ was raised from the
dead by the glory of the Father, so we too may
walk in newness[B] of life. 5 For if we have been
united with him in the likeness of his death,
we will certainly also be[C] in the likeness of
his resurrection. 6 For we know that our old
self[D] was crucified with him so that the body
ruled by sin[E] might be rendered powerless
so that we may no longer be enslaved to sin,
7 since a person who has died is freed[F] from
sin. 8 Now if we died with Christ, we believe
that we will also live with him, 9 because we
know that Christ, having been raised from
the dead, will not die again. Death no longer
rules over him. 10 For the death he died, he
died to sin once for all time; but the life he

Thanksgiving and Contentment | *Confession*

A DAILY OFFERING

"But as those who are alive from the dead, offer yourselves to God, and all the parts of yourselves to God as weapons for righteousness." Romans 6:13

After making the argument that sin no longer has real power over those who live in close union with Christ (Rm 6:1-11), Paul suggests a practical way for believers to live out this truth, "Offer yourselves . . . all the parts of yourselves to God."

Many have found victory over sin by literally praying a kind of head-to-toe prayer each morning. Something like this:

"Lord, I give you my mind today. Grant that I might think only pure and noble thoughts. I offer you my ears and eyes. Give me the desire and the strength to look at and listen only to those things that will build me up and bring you honor. Take my mouth, and use it as a force for good—to speak words of encouragement and life. Lord, move my hands and feet this day, as the old hymn says, 'at the impulse of your love.' Grant that I might go for you and serve, touch, and bless others. In each moment, Jesus, live through me. I want every part of me to be a weapon for righteousness. In Jesus's name. Amen."

For the next note on *Thanksgiving and Contentment*, see Romans 8:23.

[A] **5:16** Or *acquittal* [B] **6:4** Or *a new way* [C] **6:5** Be joined with him [D] **6:6** Lit *man* [E] **6:6** Lit *that the body of sin* [F] **6:7** Or *justified*; lit *acquitted*

lives, he lives to God. 11 So, you too consider yourselves dead to sin and alive to God in Christ Jesus.[A]

12 Therefore do not let sin reign in your mortal body, so that you obey[B] its desires. 13 And do not offer any parts[C] of it to sin as weapons for unrighteousness. But as those who are alive from the dead, offer yourselves to God, and all the parts of yourselves to God as weapons for righteousness. 14 For sin will not rule over you, because you are not under the law but under grace.

FROM SLAVES OF SIN TO SLAVES OF GOD

15 What then? Should we sin because we are not under the law but under grace? Absolutely not! 16 Don't you know that if you offer yourselves to someone[D] as obedient slaves, you are slaves of that one you obey — either of sin leading to death or of obedience leading to righteousness? 17 But thank God that, although you used to be slaves of sin, you obeyed from the heart that pattern of teaching to which you were handed[E] over, 18 and having been set free from sin, you became enslaved to righteousness. 19 I am using a human analogy because of the weakness of your flesh.[F] For just as you offered the parts of yourselves as slaves to impurity, and to greater and greater lawlessness, so now offer them as slaves to righteousness, which results in sanctification. 20 For when you were slaves of sin, you were free with regard to righteousness.[G] 21 So what fruit was produced[H] then from the things you are now ashamed of? The outcome of those things is death. 22 But now, since you have been set free from sin and have become enslaved to God, you have your fruit, which results in sanctification — and the outcome is eternal life! 23 For the wages of sin is death, but the gift of God is eternal life in Christ Jesus our Lord.

AN ILLUSTRATION FROM MARRIAGE

7 Since I am speaking to those who know the law, brothers and sisters, don't you know that the law rules over someone as long as he lives? 2 For example, a married woman is legally bound to her husband while he lives. But if her husband dies, she is released from the law regarding the husband. 3 So then, if she is married to another man while her husband is living, she will be called an adulteress. But

Eternal Perspective | *God's View of Sin*

WAGE VS. GIFT

"For the wages of sin is death, but the gift of God is eternal life in Christ Jesus our Lord." Romans 6:23

If you have a job, you know what wages are. They're payment. Remuneration. Compensation. Wages are—in theory at least—what we deserve for what we have done.

Notice Paul says, "The wages of sin is death." In other words, the payment we humans deserve for not loving the Lord with all our hearts, not honoring and obeying him as King is *death*. Nobody should expect a reward for ignoring him.

On the other hand, everyone knows what a gift is. It's an undeserved present, not a deserved payment. Gifts are born out of delight, not duty. In truth they say as much about the giver as they do about the recipient. So what is "the gift of God" that Paul writes about?

"Eternal life in Christ Jesus our Lord." Seriously? Eternal life is a *gift?* Free? No strings attached? You read it right. And no matter if you read the verse ten thousand times, it's still amazing. We deserve death. What we've *earned* is death. But God, in grace and love, offers us instead the gift of life.

As they say in west Texas, if that doesn't ring your bell, your clapper's broke.

For the next note on *Eternal Perspective*, see Romans 8:38-39.

[A] **6:11** Other mss add *our Lord* [B] **6:12** Other mss add *sin* (lit *it*) *in* [C] **6:13** Or *members*, also in v. 19 [D] **6:16** Lit *that to whom you offer yourselves* [E] **6:17** Or *entrusted* [F] **6:19** Or *your human nature* [G] **6:20** Lit *free to righteousness* [H] **6:21** Lit *what fruit do you have*

if her husband dies, she is free from that law.
Then, if she is married to another man, she is
not an adulteress.
4 Therefore, my brothers and sisters, you
also were put to death in relation to the law
through the body of Christ so that you may
belong to another. You belong to him who was
raised from the dead in order that we may
bear fruit for God. 5 For when we were in the
flesh, the sinful passions aroused through
the law were working in us[A] to bear fruit for
death. 6 But now we have been released from
the law, since we have died to what held us, so
that we may serve in the newness of the Spirit
and not in the old letter of the law.

SIN'S USE OF THE LAW

7 What should we say then? Is the law sin?
Absolutely not! On the contrary, I would not
have known sin if it were not for the law. For
example, I would not have known what it is to
covet if the law had not said, **Do not covet.**[B]
8 And sin, seizing an opportunity through the
commandment, produced in me coveting of
every kind. For apart from the law sin is dead.
9 Once I was alive apart from the law, but when
the commandment came, sin sprang to life
again 10 and I died. The commandment that
was meant for life resulted in death for me.
11 For sin, seizing an opportunity through the
commandment, deceived me, and through it
killed me. 12 So then, the law is holy, and the
commandment is holy and just and good.
13 Therefore, did what is good become death
to me? Absolutely not! On the contrary, sin,
in order to be recognized as sin, was producing death in me through what is good, so that
through the commandment, sin might become
sinful beyond measure.

THE PROBLEM OF SIN IN US

14 For we know that the law is spiritual, but I
am of the flesh,[C] sold as a slave to sin.[D] 15 For I
do not understand what I am doing, because
I do not practice what I want to do, but I do
what I hate. 16 Now if I do what I do not want
to do, I agree with the law that it is good. 17 So
now I am no longer the one doing it, but it is
sin living in me. 18 For I know that nothing
good lives in me, that is, in my flesh. For the
desire to do what is good is with me, but there
is no ability to do it. 19 For I do not do the good
that I want to do, but I practice the evil that I
do not want to do. 20 Now if I do what I do not

Rest and Reflection | *Admitting Powerlessness*

DESIRES AND STRUGGLES

"For I know that nothing good lives in me, that is, in my flesh. For the desire to do what is good is with me, but there is no ability to do it. For I do not do the good that I want to do, but I practice the evil that I do not want to do." Romans 7:18-19

Faith in Jesus solves our biggest spiritual problem—the need for forgiveness and new life. But that new life comes with new struggles. Just because we are under new management doesn't mean we've yet learned new habits. Even though we have God's indwelling Spirit prompting us to live in new ways, our minds are not yet fully renewed (see Rm 12:2).

The result is what Paul describes here—a fierce internal tug-of-war. Our old unredeemed human nature violently resists the new life of the Spirit. One moment we are reading the Bible and loving it; the next moment we are feeling a strong pull to engage in sinful thoughts or behavior.

At such times, we should pause and reflect, asking, *What is it I most deeply want—the momentary pleasure of a selfish action guaranteed to leave me feeling empty, guilty, and full of regret, or a life that's pleasing to God?* After admitting that we can't do this on our own, the next step is to submit God, asking him to give us the desire and power to do life his way.

For the next note on *Rest and Reflection*, see 1 Corinthians 4:3-4.

[A] **7:5** Lit *in our members* [B] **7:7** Ex 20:17 [C] **7:14** Or *unspiritual* [D] **7:14** Lit *under sin*

want, I am no longer the one that does it, but it is the sin that lives in me. 21 So I discover this law:[A] When I want to do what is good,[B] evil is present with me. 22 For in my inner self[C] I delight in God's law, 23 but I see a different law in the parts of my body,[D] waging war against the law of my mind and taking me prisoner to the law of sin in the parts of my body. 24 What a wretched man I am! Who will rescue me from this body of death? 25 Thanks be to God through Jesus Christ our Lord! So then, with my mind I myself am serving the law of God, but with my flesh, the law of sin.

THE LIFE-GIVING SPIRIT

8 Therefore, there is now no condemnation for those in Christ Jesus,[E] 2 because the law of the Spirit of life in Christ Jesus has set you[F] free from the law of sin and death. 3 What the law could not do since it was weakened by the flesh, God did. He condemned sin in the flesh by sending his own Son in the likeness of sinful flesh as a sin offering,[G] 4 in order that the law's requirement would be fulfilled in us who do not walk according to the flesh but according to the Spirit. 5 For those who live according to the flesh have their minds set on the things of the flesh, but those who live according to the Spirit have their minds set on the things of the Spirit. 6 Now the mind-set of the flesh is death, but the mind-set of the Spirit is life and peace. 7 The mind-set of the flesh is hostile to God because it does not submit to God's law. Indeed, it is unable to do so. 8 Those who are in the flesh cannot please God. 9 You, however, are not in the flesh, but in the Spirit, if indeed the Spirit of God lives in you. If anyone does not have the Spirit of Christ, he does not belong to him. 10 Now if Christ is in you, the body is dead because of sin, but the Spirit[H] gives life[I] because of righteousness. 11 And if the Spirit of him who raised Jesus from the dead lives in you, then he who raised Christ from the dead will also bring your mortal bodies to life through[J] his Spirit who lives in you.

THE HOLY SPIRIT'S MINISTRIES

12 So then, brothers and sisters, we are not obligated to the flesh to live according to the

S Support | *Openness with God*

NOTHING HIDDEN

"And he who searches our hearts knows the mind of the Spirit, because he intercedes for the saints according to the will of God." Romans 8:27

Romans 8 is one of the most beloved chapters of the Bible for good reason. Like a brilliant lawyer, Paul has been building an airtight case that we are made right with God by grace alone, through faith alone in Christ alone. The more he writes, the more glorious the message becomes. By this chapter—a kind of summation—the blessings Paul rattles off are like waves at the shore, washing over our dry hearts, one right after another.

He speaks of the gracious way the Spirit prays for us in our troubles and says that God "searches our hearts."

Maybe that chills rather than soothes you. Perhaps such a thought reminds you of creepy stalkers or nefarious hackers invading your privacy.

It shouldn't. Paul is reminding us that God sees and knows all. Nothing in us surprises him. Nothing we do or fail to do alters his love. And when he searches us, he doesn't just see what's wrong, he also sees what is good—what we can become, what we were made to be.

Open your heart to him. He only wants to save your life.

For the next note on *Support*, see Romans 12:3.

[A] **7:21** Or *principle* [B] **7:21** Or *I find with respect to the law that when I want to do good* [C] **7:22** Lit *inner man* [D] **7:23** Lit *my members* [E] **8:1** Other mss add *who do not walk according to the flesh but according to the Spirit* [F] **8:2** Other mss read *me* [G] **8:3** Or *for sin* [H] **8:10** Or *spirit* [I] **8:10** Or *your spirit is alive* [J] **8:11** Other mss read *because of*

that they have zeal for God, but not according
to knowledge. 3 Since they are ignorant of the
righteousness of God and attempted to establish their own righteousness, they have not
submitted to God's righteousness. 4 For Christ
is the end[A] of the law for righteousness to
everyone who believes, 5 since Moses writes
about the righteousness that is from the law:
The one who does these things will live by
them.[B] 6 But the righteousness that comes
from faith speaks like this: **Do not say in your**
heart, "Who will go up to heaven?"[C] that is,
to bring Christ down 7 or, **"Who will go down**
into the abyss?"[D] that is, to bring Christ up
from the dead. 8 On the contrary, what does it
say? **The message is near you, in your mouth**
and in your heart.[E] This is the message of faith
that we proclaim: 9 If you confess with your
mouth, "Jesus is Lord," and believe in your
heart that God raised him from the dead, you
will be saved. 10 One believes with the heart,
resulting in righteousness, and one confesses
with the mouth, resulting in salvation. 11 For
the Scripture says, **Everyone who believes**
on him will not be put to shame,[F] 12 since
there is no distinction between Jew and Greek,
because the same Lord of all richly blesses all
who call on him. 13 For **everyone who calls on**
the name of the Lord will be saved.[G]

ISRAEL'S REJECTION OF THE MESSAGE

14 How, then, can they call on him they have
not believed in? And how can they believe
without hearing about him? And how can
they hear without a preacher? 15 And how
can they preach unless they are sent? As it
is written: **How beautiful**[H] **are the feet of**
those who bring good news.[I] 16 But not all
obeyed the gospel. For Isaiah says, **Lord, who**
has believed our message?[J] 17 So faith comes
from what is heard, and what is heard comes
through the message about Christ.[K] 18 But I ask,
"Did they not hear?" Yes, they did:

Their voice has gone out to
the whole earth,
and their words to the ends
of the world.[L]

19 But I ask, "Did Israel not understand?" First,
Moses said,

I will make you jealous
of those who are not a nation;
I will make you angry by a nation
that lacks understanding.[M]

20 And Isaiah says boldly,

I was found
by those who were not looking
for me;
I revealed myself
to those who were not asking
for me.[N]

21 But to Israel he says, **All day long I have**
held out my hands to a disobedient and
defiant people.[O]

ISRAEL'S REJECTION NOT TOTAL

11 I ask, then, has God rejected his people?
Absolutely not! For I too am an Israelite,
a descendant of Abraham, from the tribe of
Benjamin. 2 God has not rejected his people
whom he foreknew. Or don't you know what
the Scripture says in the passage about Elijah
—how he pleads with God against Israel?
3 **Lord, they have killed your prophets and**
torn down your altars. I am the only one
left, and they are trying to take my life![P]
4 But what was God's answer to him? **I have**
left seven thousand for myself who have
not bowed down to Baal.[Q] 5 In the same way,
then, there is also at the present time a remnant chosen by grace. 6 Now if by grace, then
it is not by works; otherwise grace ceases to
be grace.[R]

7 What then? Israel did not find what it was
looking for, but the elect did find it. The rest
were hardened, 8 as it is written,

God gave them a spirit of stupor,
eyes that cannot see
and ears that cannot hear,
to this day.[S]

9 And David says,

Let their table become a snare
and a trap,
a pitfall and a retribution to them.
10 **Let their eyes be darkened**
so that they cannot see,
and their backs be bent continually.[T]

ISRAEL'S REJECTION NOT FINAL

11 I ask, then, have they stumbled so as to
fall? Absolutely not! On the contrary, by
their transgression, salvation has come to
the Gentiles to make Israel jealous. 12 Now if

[A] **10:4** Or *goal* [B] **10:5** Lv 18:5 [C] **10:6** Dt 9:4; 30:12 [D] **10:7** Dt 30:13 [E] **10:8** Dt 30:14 [F] **10:11** Is 28:16 [G] **10:13** Jl 2:32 [H] **10:15** Or *welcome*, or *timely* [I] **10:15** Is 52:7; Nah 1:15 [J] **10:16** Is 53:1 [K] **10:17** Other mss read *God* [L] **10:18** Ps 19:4 [M] **10:19** Dt 32:21 [N] **10:20** Is 65:1 [O] **10:21** Is 65:2 [P] **11:3** 1Kg 19:10,14 [Q] **11:4** 1Kg 19:18 [R] **11:6** Other mss add *But if of works it is no longer grace; otherwise work is no longer work.* [S] **11:8** Dt 29:4; Is 29:10 [T] **11:9-10** Ps 69:22-23

their transgression brings riches for the world,
and their failure riches for the Gentiles, how
much more will their fullness bring!
13 Now I am speaking to you Gentiles. Insofar
as I am an apostle to the Gentiles, I magnify
my ministry, 14 if I might somehow make my
own people[A] jealous and save some of them.
15 For if their rejection brings reconciliation
to the world, what will their acceptance mean
but life from the dead? 16 Now if the firstfruits
are holy, so is the whole batch. And if the root
is holy, so are the branches.
17 Now if some of the branches were broken off, and you, though a wild olive branch,
were grafted in among them and have come
to share in the rich root[B] of the cultivated
olive tree, 18 do not boast that you are better than those branches. But if you do boast
— you do not sustain the root, but the root
sustains you. 19 Then you will say, "Branches
were broken off so that I might be grafted in."
20 True enough; they were broken off because
of unbelief, but you stand by faith. Do not be
arrogant, but beware,[C] 21 because if God did
not spare the natural branches, he will not
spare you either. 22 Therefore, consider God's
kindness and severity: severity toward those
who have fallen but God's kindness toward
you — if you remain in his kindness. Otherwise you too will be cut off. 23 And even they, if
they do not remain in unbelief, will be grafted
in, because God has the power to graft them
in again. 24 For if you were cut off from your
native wild olive tree and against nature were
grafted into a cultivated olive tree, how much
more will these — the natural branches — be
grafted into their own olive tree?
25 I don't want you to be ignorant of this mystery, brothers and sisters, so that you will not
be conceited: A partial hardening has come
upon Israel until the fullness of the Gentiles
has come in. 26 And in this way all[D] Israel will
be saved, as it is written,

The Deliverer will come from Zion;
he will turn godlessness away
from Jacob.
27 **And this will be my covenant**
with them[E]
when I take away their sins.[F]

28 Regarding the gospel, they are enemies for
your advantage, but regarding election, they
are loved because of the patriarchs, 29 since
God's gracious gifts and calling are irrevocable.[G] 30 As you once disobeyed God but now
have received mercy through their disobedience, 31 so they too have now disobeyed,

Support | *Truthfulness with Self*

SENSIBLE THINKING

"For by the grace given to me, I tell everyone among you not to think of himself more highly than he should think. Instead, think sensibly, as God has distributed a measure of faith to each one." Romans 12:3

Comparing ourselves with others is natural and unhealthy: looks, intellect, career status, financial resources, lifestyle, and even spirituality. When we see those who are less or lower than we are, we can get an inflated view of ourselves. Conversely, when confronted by those who are better or who have more, we can feel envious and discouraged about our resources and status.

Of all people, Christians should be the last to engage in this practice because we know that God has created us, Jesus died for us, and the Holy Spirit lives in us and empowers us. We are sinners deserving a terrible punishment for our sins, but in God's grace we are saved.

Practically speaking, this means that we should rest in who we are as God has made us and use our gifts as he leads us. It also means celebrating others' successes and accolades, even if what we do for the Lord seems to go unnoticed. And to those who are struggling and seem to have less, we should encourage and support. God has given each of us our own "measure of faith."

For the next note on *Support*, see 1 Corinthians 2:3.

[A] **11:14** Lit *flesh* [B] **11:17** Other mss read *the root and the richness* [C] **11:20** Lit *fear* [D] **11:26** Or *And then all* [E] **11:26-27** Is 59:20-21 [F] **11:27** Jr 31:31-34 [G] **11:29** Or *are not taken back*

resulting in mercy to you, so that they also
may now[A] receive mercy. 32 For God has imprisoned all in disobedience so that he may
have mercy on all.

A HYMN OF PRAISE

33 Oh, the depth of the riches
both of the wisdom
and of the knowledge of God!
How unsearchable
his judgments
and untraceable his ways!
34 **For who has known the mind
of the Lord?
Or who has been his counselor?**
35 **And who has ever given to God,
that he should be repaid?**[B]
36 For from him and through him
and to him are all things.
To him be the glory forever. Amen.

A LIVING SACRIFICE

12 Therefore, brothers and sisters, in view
of the mercies of God, I urge you to present your bodies as a living sacrifice, holy and
pleasing to God; this is your true worship.[C] 2 Do
not be conformed to this age, but be transformed by the renewing of your mind, so that
you may discern what is the good, pleasing,
and perfect will of God.

MANY GIFTS BUT ONE BODY

3 For by the grace given to me, I tell everyone among you not to think of himself more
highly than he should think. Instead, think
sensibly, as God has distributed a measure
of faith to each one. 4 Now as we have many
parts in one body, and all the parts do not
have the same function, 5 in the same way
we who are many are one body in Christ
and individually members of one another.
6 According to the grace given to us, we have
different gifts: If prophecy, use it according
to the proportion of one's[D] faith; 7 if service,
use it in service; if teaching, in teaching; 8 if
exhorting, in exhortation; giving, with generosity; leading, with diligence; showing mercy,
with cheerfulness.

CHRISTIAN ETHICS

9 Let love be without hypocrisy. Detest evil;
cling to what is good. 10 Love one another deeply

Relationships | *Relating to Church Family*

RADICAL COMMUNITY

"Rejoice with those who rejoice; weep with those who weep. Live in harmony with one another. Do not be proud; instead, associate with the humble. Do not be wise in your own estimation. Do not repay anyone evil for evil. Give careful thought to do what is honorable in everyone's eyes. If possible, as far as it depends on you, live at peace with everyone." Romans 12:15-18

Imagine a community where good news results in high fives, maybe even a spontaneous party and where bad news is confronted with tight hugs, tears, and sympathetic ears. Imagine a community with a fierce commitment to harmony and peace—where the members agree that in times of tension, they will talk truthfully and tenderly till they work it out. Imagine a community that says, "We will not retaliate. We reject the notion of 'getting even.' We will forgive, as God, in Christ, has forgiven us." Imagine a community where humility reigns, where people don't think they are "better" than others, but where each treats all the rest with honor.

This is the community Jesus imagined for his followers. And it's the community that we can have when we give ourselves fully to God (Rm 12:1). But we can't, or we shouldn't, wait for someone else to get the ball rolling. Radical relationships start with each person. You can initiate these risky moves for harmony today.

For the next note on *Relationships*, see 1 Corinthians 3:5-6.

[A] **11:31** Other mss omit *now* [B] **11:34-35** Jb 41:11; Is 40:13; Jr 23:18 [C] **12:1** Or *your reasonable service* [D] **12:6** Or *the*, also in v. 19

as brothers and sisters. Outdo one another
in showing honor. 11 Do not lack diligence in
zeal; be fervent in the Spirit;[A] serve the Lord.
12 Rejoice in hope; be patient in affliction; be
persistent in prayer. 13 Share with the saints in
their needs; pursue hospitality. 14 Bless those
who persecute you; bless and do not curse.
15 Rejoice with those who rejoice; weep with
those who weep. 16 Live in harmony with one
another. Do not be proud; instead, associate
with the humble. Do not be wise in your own
estimation. 17 Do not repay anyone evil for evil.
Give careful thought to do what is honorable
in everyone's eyes. 18 If possible, as far as it
depends on you, live at peace with everyone.
19 Friends, do not avenge yourselves; instead,
leave room for God's wrath, because it is written, **Vengeance belongs to me; I will repay,**[B]
says the Lord. 20 But

If your enemy is hungry, feed him.
If he is thirsty, give him something
to drink.
For in so doing
you will be heaping fiery coals
on his head.[C]

21 Do not be conquered by evil, but conquer
evil with good.

A CHRISTIAN'S DUTIES TO THE STATE

13 Let everyone submit to the governing
authorities, since there is no authority
except from God, and the authorities that exist
are instituted by God. 2 So then, the one who resists the authority is opposing God's command,
and those who oppose it will bring judgment
on themselves. 3 For rulers are not a terror to
good conduct, but to bad. Do you want to be
unafraid of the authority? Do what is good,
and you will have its approval. 4 For it is God's
servant for your good. But if you do wrong, be
afraid, because it does not carry the sword for
no reason. For it is God's servant, an avenger
that brings wrath on the one who does wrong.
5 Therefore, you must submit, not only because
of wrath but also because of your conscience.
6 And for this reason you pay taxes, since the
authorities are God's servants, continually attending to these tasks.[D] 7 Pay your obligations
to everyone: taxes to those you owe taxes, tolls
to those you owe tolls, respect to those you owe
respect, and honor to those you owe honor.

LOVE, OUR PRIMARY DUTY

8 Do not owe anyone anything, except to love
one another, for the one who loves another

Exercise of Faith | *Guarding the Heart*

POOR PLANNING

"But put on the Lord Jesus Christ, and don't make plans to gratify the desires of the flesh." Romans 13:14

At the end of his deeply theological letter to Christians in first-century Rome, Paul got intensely practical. In a world full of "carousing and drunkenness . . . sexual impurity and promiscuity. . . quarreling and jealousy" (Rm 13:13), he talked about how to live in ways that honor God.

Two practices should become daily habits. First, Paul said, "Put on the Lord Jesus Christ." This is a clothing metaphor. We should cover or adorn ourselves in Jesus. Think of athletes or soldiers putting on uniforms and/or protective gear (13:12). They represent something bigger. Much is at stake.

Second, "don't make plans to gratify the desires of the flesh." In other words, don't knowingly plan ahead to do things that will subject you to certain temptation. Don't install that app on your phone that will give you access to the very website you don't need to be browsing. Don't schedule that meeting with your cute colleague in a quiet, solitary place. Don't browse in that store that always makes you discontented and wanting things you can't afford.

Plan ahead each morning by doing two things. Dress—in Christ—for success. Determine to pursue what's good and to avoid what's detrimental.

For the next note on *Exercise of Faith*, see 1 Corinthians 5:6.

[A] **12:11** Or *in spirit* [B] **12:19** Dt 32:35 [C] **12:20** Pr 25:21-22 [D] **13:6** Lit *to this very thing*

has fulfilled the law. 9 The commandments, **Do not commit adultery; do not murder; do not steal;**[A] **do not covet;**[B] and any other commandment, are summed up by this commandment: **Love your neighbor as yourself.**[C] 10 Love does no wrong to a neighbor. Love, therefore, is the fulfillment of the law.

PUT ON CHRIST

11 Besides this, since you know the time, it is already the hour for you[D] to wake up from sleep, because now our salvation is nearer than when we first believed. 12 The night is nearly over, and the day is near; so let us discard the deeds of darkness and put on the armor of light. 13 Let us walk with decency, as in the daytime: not in carousing and drunkenness; not in sexual impurity and promiscuity; not in quarreling and jealousy. 14 But put on the Lord Jesus Christ, and don't make plans to gratify the desires of the flesh.

THE LAW OF LIBERTY

14 Accept anyone who is weak in faith, but don't argue about disputed matters. 2 One person believes he may eat anything, while one who is weak eats only vegetables. 3 One who eats must not look down on one who does not eat, and one who does not eat must not judge one who does, because God has accepted him. 4 Who are you to judge another's household servant? Before his own Lord he stands or falls. And he will stand, because the Lord is able[E] to make him stand.

5 One person judges one day to be more important than another day. Someone else judges every day to be the same. Let each one be fully convinced in his own mind. 6 Whoever observes the day, observes it for the honor of the Lord.[F] Whoever eats, eats for the Lord, since he gives thanks to God; and whoever does not eat, it is for the Lord that he does not eat it, and he gives thanks to God. 7 For none of us lives for himself, and no one dies for himself. 8 If we live, we live for the Lord; and if we die, we die for the Lord. Therefore, whether we live or die, we belong to the Lord. 9 Christ died and returned to life for this: that he might be Lord over both the dead and the living. 10 But you, why do you judge your brother or sister? Or you, why do you despise your brother or sister? For we will all stand before the judgment seat of God.[G] 11 For it is written,

As I live, says the Lord,
every knee will bow to me,
and every tongue will give praise
to God.[H]

12 So then, each of us will give an account of himself to God.

THE LAW OF LOVE

13 Therefore, let us no longer judge one another. Instead decide never to put a stumbling block or pitfall in the way of your brother or sister. 14 I know and am persuaded in the Lord Jesus that nothing is unclean in itself. Still, to someone who considers a thing to be unclean, to that one it is unclean. 15 For if your brother or sister is hurt by what you eat, you are no longer walking according to love. Do not destroy, by what you eat, someone for whom Christ died. 16 Therefore, do not let your good be slandered, 17 for the kingdom of God is not eating and drinking, but righteousness, peace, and joy in the Holy Spirit. 18 Whoever serves Christ in this way is acceptable to God and receives human approval.

19 So then, let us pursue what promotes peace and what builds up one another. 20 Do not tear down God's work because of food. Everything is clean, but it is wrong to make someone fall by what he eats. 21 It is a good thing not to eat meat, or drink wine, or do anything that makes your brother or sister stumble.[I] 22 Whatever you believe about these things, keep between yourself and God. Blessed is the one who does not condemn himself by what he approves. 23 But whoever doubts stands condemned if he eats, because his eating is not from faith,[J] and everything that is not from faith is sin.

PLEASING OTHERS, NOT OURSELVES

15 Now we who are strong have an obligation to bear the weaknesses of those without strength, and not to please ourselves. 2 Each one of us is to please his neighbor for his good, to build him up. 3 For even Christ did not please himself. On the contrary, as it is written, **The insults of those who insult you have fallen on me.**[K] 4 For whatever was written in the past was written for our instruction, so that we may have hope through endurance

[A] **13:9** Other mss add *do not bear false witness* [B] **13:9** Ex 20:13-17; Dt 5:17-21 [C] **13:9** Lv 19:18 [D] **13:11** Other mss read *for us* [E] **14:4** Other mss read *For God has the power* [F] **14:6** Other mss add *but whoever does not observe the day, it is to the Lord that he does not observe it* [G] **14:10** Other mss read *of Christ* [H] **14:11** Is 45:23; 49:18 [I] **14:21** Other mss add *or offended or weakened* [J] **14:23** Or *conviction* [K] **15:3** Ps 69:9

and through the encouragement from the
Scriptures. 5 Now may the God who gives[A]
endurance and encouragement grant you to
live in harmony with one another, according
to Christ Jesus, 6 so that you may glorify the
God and Father of our Lord Jesus Christ with
one mind and one voice.

GLORIFYING GOD TOGETHER

7 Therefore accept one another, just as Christ
also accepted you, to the glory of God. 8 For I
say that Christ became a servant of the circumcised[B] on behalf of God's truth, to confirm the
promises to the fathers, 9 and so that Gentiles
may glorify God for his mercy. As it is written,

Therefore I will praise you
among the Gentiles,
and I will sing praise to your name.[C]

10 Again it says, **Rejoice, you Gentiles, with
his people!**[D] 11 And again,

Praise the Lord, all you Gentiles;
let all the peoples praise him![E]

12 And again, Isaiah says,

The root of Jesse will appear,
the one who rises to rule the Gentiles;
the Gentiles will hope in him.[F]

13 Now may the God of hope fill you with all joy
and peace as you believe so that you may overflow with hope by the power of the Holy Spirit.

FROM JERUSALEM TO ILLYRICUM

14 My brothers and sisters, I myself am convinced about you that you also are full of
goodness, filled with all knowledge, and
able to instruct one another. 15 Nevertheless,
I have written to remind you more boldly
on some points[G] because of the grace giv-
en me by God 16 to be a minister of Christ
Jesus to the Gentiles, serving as a priest of
the gospel of God. My purpose is that the
Gentiles may be an acceptable offering,
sanctified by the Holy Spirit. 17 Therefore I
have reason to boast in Christ Jesus regarding what pertains to God. 18 For I would not
dare say anything except what Christ has
accomplished through me by word and deed
for the obedience of the Gentiles, 19 by the
power of miraculous signs and wonders,
and by the power of God's Spirit. As a result, I have fully proclaimed the gospel of
Christ from Jerusalem all the way around to
Illyricum.[H] 20 My aim is to preach the gospel
where Christ has not been named, so that I
will not build on someone else's foundation,
21 but, as it is written,

Those who were not told about him
will see,
and those who have not heard
will understand.[I]

Eternal Perspective | *Biblical Hope*

HOPE OVERFLOWING

"Now may the God of hope fill you with all joy and peace as you believe so that you may overflow with hope by the power of the Holy Spirit." Romans 15:13

Things always go wrong. My spouse will never change. I will never find a decent job. For those who can't shake such hopeless feelings, this verse is a great comfort.

Notice the phrase, "the God of hope." If we will "believe," he will fill us with joy and peace to the point that we will "overflow with hope." In other words, we won't just find a sip or two of hope to get us through the day, but hope will spill out of our hearts and lives onto those around us. We will be springs of hope. This is the power of the Spirit of God who indwells every believer.

If you are running low on hope today, spend a few minutes putting your name into this benediction. "O God of hope, fill me with all joy and peace as I believe. Cause me to overflow with hope by the power of your Holy Spirit." Pray earnestly. Pray from your heart. Pray this every day—all during the day. God hears and will answer. Watch what he will do.

For the next note on *Eternal Perspective*, see Romans 16:14.

[A] **15:5** Lit *God of* [B] **15:8** The Jews [C] **15:9** 2Sm 22:50; Ps 18:49 [D] **15:10** Dt 32:43 [E] **15:11** Ps 117:1 [F] **15:12** Is 11:10 [G] **15:15** Other mss add *brothers* [H] **15:19** A Roman province northwest of Greece on the eastern shore of the Adriatic Sea [I] **15:21** Is 52:15

Embracing God's Word | Hope

NO EXIT. NO ANSWER. NO PROGRESS. NO HELP. Alone with dashed dreams, tarnished expectation, and bleak prospects, we can feel helpless and lose heart. But God's promises pierce the gloom, his light showing the way forward, giving us hope.

But I know that my Redeemer lives, and at the end he will stand on the dust. Even after my skin has been destroyed, yet I will see God in my flesh. I will see him myself; my eyes will look at him, and not as a stranger. My heart longs within me. –Job 19:25-27

For the needy will not always be forgotten; the hope of the oppressed will not perish forever. Psalm 9:18

The L*ORD will send his faithful love by day; his song will be with me in the night—a prayer to the God of my life. . . . Why, my soul, are you so dejected? Why are you in such turmoil? Put your hope in God, for I will still praise him, my Savior and my God.* –Psalm 42:8,11

Rest in God alone, my soul, for my hope comes from him. He alone is my rock and my salvation, my stronghold; I will not be shaken. –Psalm 62:5-6

"For I know the plans I have for you"—this is the L*ORD's declaration—"plans for your well-being, not for disaster, to give you a future and a hope."* –Jeremiah 29:11

For the creation was subjected to futility—not willingly, but because of him who subjected it—in the hope that the creation itself will also be set free from the bondage to decay into the glorious freedom of God's children. For we know that the whole creation has been groaning together with labor pains until now. –Romans 8:20-22

Now may the God of hope fill you with all joy and peace as you believe so that you may overflow with hope by the power of the Holy Spirit. –Romans 15:13

I pray that the eyes of your heart may be enlightened so that you may know what is the hope of his calling, what is the wealth of his glorious inheritance in the saints. –Ephesians 1:18

. . . while we wait for the blessed hope, the appearing of the glory of our great God and Savior, Jesus Christ. –Titus 2:13

. . . so that through two unchangeable things, in which it is impossible for God to lie, we who have fled for refuge might have strong encouragement to seize the hope set before us. We have this hope as an anchor for the soul, firm and secure. –Hebrews 6:18-19

Let us hold on to the confession of our hope without wavering, since he who promised is faithful. –Hebrews 10:23

He was foreknown before the foundation of the world but was revealed in these last times for you. Through him you believe in God, who raised him from the dead and gave him glory, so that your faith and hope are in God. –1 Peter 1:20-21

PAUL'S TRAVEL PLANS

22 That is why I have been prevented many
times from coming to you. 23 But now I no
longer have any work to do in these regions,[A]
and I have strongly desired for many years to
come to you 24 whenever I travel to Spain.[B] For
I hope to see you when I pass through and to
be assisted by you for my journey there, once
I have first enjoyed your company for a while.
25 Right now I am traveling to Jerusalem to
serve the saints, 26 because Macedonia and
Achaia were pleased to make a contribution for
the poor among the saints in Jerusalem. 27 Yes,
they were pleased, and indeed are indebted to
them. For if the Gentiles have shared in their
spiritual benefits, then they are obligated to
minister to them in material needs. 28 So when
I have finished this and safely delivered the
funds[C] to them,[D] I will visit you on the way to
Spain. 29 I know that when I come to you, I will
come in the fullness of the blessing[E] of Christ.
30 Now I appeal to you, brothers and sisters,
through our Lord Jesus Christ and through the
love of the Spirit, to strive together with me in
fervent prayers to God on my behalf. 31 Pray
that I may be rescued from the unbelievers in
Judea, that my ministry to[F] Jerusalem may be
acceptable to the saints, 32 and that, by God's
will, I may come to you with joy and be refreshed together with you.
33 May the God of peace be with all of you.
Amen.

PAUL'S COMMENDATION OF PHOEBE

16 I commend to you our sister Phoebe, who
is a servant[G] of the church in Cenchreae.
2 So you should welcome her in the Lord in a
manner worthy of the saints and assist her in
whatever matter she may require your help.
For indeed she has been a benefactor of many
— and of me also.

GREETING TO ROMAN CHRISTIANS

3 Give my greetings to Prisca[H] and Aquila, my
coworkers in Christ Jesus, 4 who risked their
own necks for my life. Not only do I thank them,

Eternal Perspective | *God's Family*

THE PEOPLE OF GOD

"Greet Asyncritus, Phlegon, Hermes, Patrobas, Hermas, and the brothers and sisters who are with them." Romans 16:14

After all the previous deep theological promises and pronouncements, chapter 16 might feel like an unimportant postscript, a laundry list of names. But if we rush past these personal notes from Paul to get to the "spiritual meat" of 1 Corinthians 1, we will miss a blessing.

The twenty-six souls named here are our forefathers and foremothers in the faith. This was a wide range of people who quietly and faithfully served Christ in the capital of the Roman Empire during the first century. We don't know much, if anything, about most of them. We don't know how Paul knew most of these folks, only that he felt an obvious and genuine affection for them. Before sending his letter, he wanted to send his love.

Read through the list, and you'll find men and women, singles and couples, no doubt freemen and slaves, rich and poor, Romans and Greeks—and surely some Jews, too. This is the church Jesus promised to build: the wild hodgepodge of souls who comprise one body under a single head, Christ.

Looking at a biblical list like this, we see that God keeps records. He sees and remembers. He knows each person by name.

Rejoice in the fact that you belong to a family of faithful believers that stretches back through human history and that God knows and loves you. And remember that if you are faithful today, years from now others will reap the benefits.

For the next note on *Eternal Perspective*, see 2 Corinthians 4:17-18.

[A] **15:23** Lit *now, having no longer a place in these parts* [B] **15:24** Other mss add *I will come to you.* [C] **15:28** Lit *delivered this fruit* [D] **15:28** Or *and placed my seal of approval on this fruit for them* [E] **15:29** Other mss add *of the gospel* [F] **15:31** Lit *that my service for* [G] **16:1** Others interpret this term in a technical sense: *deacon*, or *deaconess*, or *minister*, or *courier* [H] **16:3** Traditionally, *Priscilla*, as in Ac 18:2,18,26

GREETING

1 Paul, called as an apostle of Christ Jesus
by God's will, and Sosthenes our brother:
2 To the church of God at Corinth, to those
sanctified in Christ Jesus, called as saints,
with all those in every place who call on the
name of Jesus Christ our Lord — both their
Lord and ours.
3 Grace to you and peace from God our Father and the Lord Jesus Christ.

THANKSGIVING

4 I always thank my God for you because of
the grace of God given to you in Christ Jesus,
5 that you were enriched in him in every way, in
all speech and all knowledge. 6 In this way, the
testimony about Christ was confirmed among
you, 7 so that you do not lack any spiritual gift
as you eagerly wait for the revelation of our
Lord Jesus Christ. 8 He will also strengthen you
to the end, so that you will be blameless in the
day of our Lord Jesus Christ. 9 God is faithful;
you were called by him into fellowship with
his Son, Jesus Christ our Lord.

DIVISIONS AT CORINTH

10 Now I urge you, brothers and sisters, in the
name of our Lord Jesus Christ, that all of you
agree in what you say, that there be no divisions
among you, and that you be united with the
same understanding and the same conviction.
11 For it has been reported to me about you, my
brothers and sisters, by members of Chloe's
people, that there is rivalry among you. 12 What
I am saying is this: One of you says, "I belong
to Paul," or "I belong to Apollos," or "I belong
to Cephas," or "I belong to Christ." 13 Is Christ
divided? Was Paul crucified for you? Or were
you baptized in Paul's name? 14 I thank God[A,B]
that I baptized none of you except Crispus and
Gaius, 15 so that no one can say you were baptized in my name. 16 I did, in fact, baptize the
household of Stephanas; beyond that, I don't
recall if I baptized anyone else. 17 For Christ did
not send me to baptize, but to preach the gospel — not with eloquent wisdom, so that the
cross of Christ will not be emptied of its effect.

CHRIST THE POWER AND WISDOM OF GOD

18 For the word of the cross is foolishness to
those who are perishing, but it is the power
of God to us who are being saved. 19 For it is
written,

> **I will destroy the wisdom of the wise,**
> **and I will set aside the intelligence**
> **of the intelligent.**[C]

Thanksgiving and Contentment | *Grace Received*

GRACE FROM FIRST TO LAST

"Grace to you and peace from God our Father and the Lord Jesus Christ." 1 Corinthians 1:3

In each of his New Testament letters, Paul routinely says "Grace to you."

Grace. Paul never ceased to be amazed that God actually pours out his favor on undeserving people. And we can hardly blame him. Paul was, after all, exhibit A of grace. He didn't choose Christ, but Christ chose him. Paul had been a hater of Jesus when he left for Damascus that fateful day. Before he reached the city limits, he found himself knocked on his backside by the fierce love of Christ (see Ac 9). How odd that he needed a blinding light to open his eyes. But he—and the world—would never be the same. Paul always wished grace on people because grace was far and away the best gift he had ever received.

Soak in God's grace today. Grace means you are loved and accepted, forgiven and rescued, period. End of story. No strings. No steps. No conditions. No fine print.

Because grace is what saves and sustains us, nobody should ever get cocky and prideful. A full heart, yes. A big head? No way.

For the next note on *Thanksgiving and Contentment*, see 2 Corinthians 1:3-4.

[A] **1:14** Other mss omit *God* [B] **1:14** Or *I am thankful* [C] **1:19** Is 29:14

20 Where is the one who is wise? Where is the
teacher of the law?[A] Where is the debater of
this age? Hasn't God made the world's wisdom
foolish? 21 For since, in God's wisdom, the world
did not know God through wisdom, God was
pleased to save those who believe through
the foolishness of what is preached. 22 For
the Jews ask for signs and the Greeks seek
wisdom, 23 but we preach Christ crucified,
a stumbling block to the Jews and foolishness to the Gentiles.[B] 24 Yet to those who are
called, both Jews and Greeks, Christ is the
power of God and the wisdom of God, 25 because God's foolishness is wiser than human
wisdom, and God's weakness is stronger than
human strength.

BOASTING ONLY IN THE LORD

26 Brothers and sisters, consider your calling:
Not many were wise from a human perspective,[C] not many powerful, not many of noble
birth. 27 Instead, God has chosen what is foolish
in the world to shame the wise, and God has
chosen what is weak in the world to shame the
strong. 28 God has chosen what is insignificant
and despised in the world — what is viewed as
nothing — to bring to nothing what is viewed
as something, 29 so that no one[D] may boast in
his presence. 30 It is from him that you are in
Christ Jesus, who became wisdom from God
for us — our righteousness, sanctification, and
redemption, 31 in order that, as it is written:
Let the one who boasts, boast in the Lord.[E]

PAUL'S PROCLAMATION

2 When I came to you, brothers and sisters,
announcing the mystery[F] of God to you,
I did not come with brilliance of speech or
wisdom. 2 I decided to know nothing among
you except Jesus Christ and him crucified. 3 I
came to you in weakness, in fear, and in much
trembling. 4 My speech and my preaching were
not with persuasive words of wisdom[G] but
with a demonstration of the Spirit's power, 5 so
that your faith might not be based on human
wisdom but on God's power.

SPIRITUAL WISDOM

6 We do, however, speak a wisdom among
the mature, but not a wisdom of this age, or
of the rulers of this age, who are coming to
nothing. 7 On the contrary, we speak God's
hidden wisdom in a mystery, a wisdom God
predestined before the ages for our glory.
8 None of the rulers of this age knew this wisdom, because if they had known it, they would

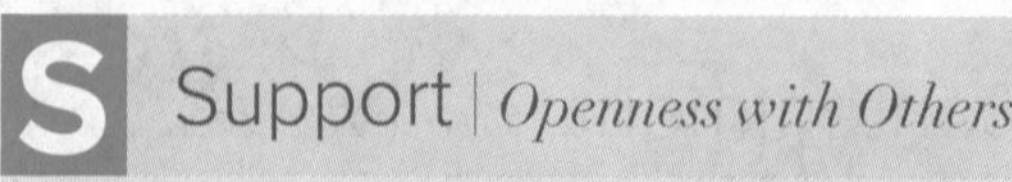

AUTHENTICITY

"I came to you in weakness, in fear, and in much trembling." 1 Corinthians 2:3

So much about our modern world encourages phoniness, putting on a front—especially in leadership circles. "Don't show weakness!" we're told. "Never admit ignorance. Even if you don't have a clue what you're doing, act like you do. Always project an air of confidence. Never let 'em see you sweat."

Contrast this with Paul's interactions with the church at Corinth. Notice how candid he is: He writes of weakness, fear, and trembling. He's the very definition of transparent, even vulnerable. In so many words, *I was scared to death. I felt completely inadequate. But I trusted in God's power* (see 1Co 2:5).

Those of us who are leaders (whether parents, coaches, teachers, pastors, business owners, etc.) don't need to divulge *every* dark feeling we have to everyone we meet. But something is both attractive and encouraging when people in authority are less image-conscious and more humble, human, and real. This posture makes us relatable and approachable. Most of all, it makes us like Jesus. Remember his raw honesty when he was agonizing in the garden of Gethsemane? Pray to become a more authentic person.

For the next note on *Support*, see Galatians 1:10.

[A] **1:20** Or *scholar* [B] **1:23** Other mss read *Greeks* [C] **1:26** Lit *wise according to the flesh* [D] **1:29** Lit *that not all flesh* [E] **1:31** Jr 9:24 [F] **2:1** Other mss read *testimony* [G] **2:4** Other mss read *human wisdom*

not have crucified the Lord of glory. 9 But as
it is written,

What no eye has seen, no ear
has heard,
and no human heart
has conceived —
God has prepared these things
for those who love him.[A]

10 Now God has revealed these things to us by
the Spirit, since the Spirit searches everything,
even the depths of God. 11 For who knows a person's thoughts[B] except his spirit within him?
In the same way, no one knows the thoughts of
God except the Spirit of God. 12 Now we have
not received the spirit of the world, but the
Spirit who comes from God, so that we may
understand what has been freely given to us
by God. 13 We also speak these things, not in
words taught by human wisdom, but in those
taught by the Spirit, explaining spiritual things
to spiritual people.[C] 14 But the person without the Spirit[D] does not receive what comes
from God's Spirit, because it is foolishness to
him; he is not able to understand it since it is
evaluated[E] spiritually. 15 The spiritual person,
however, can evaluate[F] everything, and yet he
himself cannot be evaluated by anyone. 16 For

who has known the Lord's mind,
that he may instruct him?[G]

But we have the mind of Christ.

THE PROBLEM OF IMMATURITY

3 For my part, brothers and sisters, I was
not able to speak to you as spiritual people but as people of the flesh, as babies in
Christ. 2 I gave you milk to drink, not solid
food, since you were not yet ready for it. In
fact, you are still not ready, 3 because you
are still worldly. For since there is envy and
strife[H] among you, are you not worldly and
behaving like mere humans? 4 For whenever
someone says, "I belong to Paul," and another,
"I belong to Apollos," are you not acting like
mere humans?

THE ROLE OF GOD'S SERVANTS

5 What then is Apollos? What is Paul? They are
servants through whom you believed, and each
has the role the Lord has given. 6 I planted, Apollos watered, but God gave the growth. 7 So then
neither the one who plants nor the one who
waters is anything, but only God who gives the
growth. 8 Now he who plants and he who waters
are one,[I] and each will receive his own reward

Relationships | *Relating to Spiritual Leaders*

NO CELEBRITY

"What then is Apollos? What is Paul? They are servants through whom you believed, and each has the role the Lord has given. I planted, Apollos watered, but God gave the growth." 1 Corinthians 3:5-6

The church in ancient Corinth was a lot like the church of modern times. It featured a celebrity culture. Some people couldn't stop talking about Apollos (because he was really smart and an extremely gifted communicator). Others were devotees of Paul. Even the apostle Peter had a loyal following (1Co 3:22) in Corinth.

Paul thought the whole thing silly, even dangerous, and he said as much. "*We're* not the point, We're just 'servants through whom you believed.' God gave us each a role to play and we played it, but God is the One who opens eyes, and changes hearts. He 'gave the growth.'"

This is a timeless warning. Go ahead and listen to your favorite leader's sermons and podcasts. Follow her on social media. But realize all the gifts that person possesses came from God. Remember that the work of God is much bigger than any one person. And run for the hills if your favorite leader stops acting like a humble servant or stops giving the glory to God.

For the next note on *Relationships*, see 1 Corinthians 6:1.

[A] **2:9** Is 52:15; 64:4 [B] **2:11** Or *things* [C] **2:13** Or *things with spiritual words* [D] **2:14** Lit *natural person* [E] **2:14** Or *judged*, or *discerned*, also in v. 15 [F] **2:15** Or *judge*, or *discern* [G] **2:16** Is 40:13 [H] **3:3** Other mss add *and divisions* [I] **3:8** Or *of equal status*, or *united in purpose*

according to his own labor. 9 For we are God's
coworkers.[A] You are God's field, God's building.
10 According to God's grace that was given
to me, I have laid a foundation as a skilled
master builder,[B] and another builds on it. But
each one is to be careful how he builds on it.
11 For no one can lay any other foundation than
what has been laid down. That foundation is
Jesus Christ. 12 If anyone builds on the foundation with gold, silver, costly stones, wood,
hay, or straw, 13 each one's work will become
obvious. For the day will disclose it, because
it will be revealed by fire; the fire will test
the quality of each one's work. 14 If anyone's
work that he has built survives, he will receive
a reward. 15 If anyone's work is burned up,
he will experience[C] loss, but he himself will
be saved — but only as through fire.
16 Don't you yourselves know that you are
God's temple and that the Spirit of God lives
in you? 17 If anyone destroys God's temple, God
will destroy him; for God's temple is holy, and
that is what you are.

THE FOLLY OF HUMAN WISDOM

18 Let no one deceive himself. If anyone among
you thinks he is wise in this age, let him become
a fool so that he can become wise. 19 For the
wisdom of this world is foolishness with
God, since it is written, **He catches the wise
in their craftiness**;[D] 20 and again, **The Lord
knows that the reasonings of the wise are
futile.**[E] 21 So let no one boast in human leaders,
for everything is yours — 22 whether Paul or
Apollos or Cephas or the world or life or death
or things present or things to come — everything is yours, 23 and you belong to Christ, and
Christ belongs to God.

THE FAITHFUL MANAGER

4 A person should think of us in this way:
as servants of Christ and managers of the
mysteries of God. 2 In this regard, it is required
that managers be found faithful. 3 It is of little
importance to me that I should be judged by
you or by any human court.[F] In fact, I don't
even judge myself. 4 For I am not conscious of
anything against myself, but I am not justified
by this. It is the Lord who judges me. 5 So don't
judge anything prematurely, before the Lord
comes, who will both bring to light what is
hidden in darkness and reveal the intentions
of the hearts. And then praise will come to
each one from God.

Rest and Reflection | *Surrendering/Submitting to God*

AUDIENCE OF ONE

"It is of little importance to me that I should be judged by you or by any human court. In fact, I don't even judge myself. For I am not conscious of anything against myself, but I am not justified by this. It is the Lord who judges me." 1 Corinthians 4:3-4

Some people torture themselves by always wondering, *What do others think about me?* Consequently, they move through the world doing a continual "relational calculus": *I can't wear that . . . express that . . . admit I like that . . . question that. What would everyone say?* This is a paralyzing, enslaving way to live because the opinions of others are always fickle and contradictory, and usually they're wrong.

Paul embraced a different mind-set. He reasoned, "I'm not even competent to judge my own motives and actions. So why would I willingly give that power to another fallible person? God is my Judge. He's the One to whom I have to give an account."

To live with Christ as our only focus—an audience of one—frees us tremendously, especially when we remember that in him we are unconditionally accepted, forgiven, and adored. When you love, trust, and obey God, you don't have to worry about anyone else.

For the next note on *Rest and Reflection*, see 1 Corinthians 6:19-20.

[A] **3:9** Or *are coworkers belonging to God* [B] **3:10** Or *wise master builder* [C] **3:15** Or *suffer* [D] **3:19** Jb 5:13 [E] **3:20** Ps 94:11
[F] **4:3** Lit *a human day*

THE APOSTLES' EXAMPLE OF HUMILITY

6 Now, brothers and sisters, I have applied
these things to myself and Apollos for your
benefit, so that you may learn from us the
meaning of the saying: "Nothing beyond what
is written." The purpose is that none of you
will be arrogant, favoring one person over
another. 7 For who makes you so superior?
What do you have that you didn't receive? If,
in fact, you did receive it, why do you boast
as if you hadn't received it? 8 You are already
full! You are already rich! You have begun to
reign as kings without us — and I wish you
did reign, so that we could also reign with
you! 9 For I think God has displayed us, the
apostles, in last place, like men condemned
to die: We have become a spectacle to the
world, both to angels and to people. 10 We are
fools for Christ, but you are wise in Christ!
We are weak, but you are strong! You are distinguished, but we are dishonored! 11 Up to
the present hour we are both hungry and
thirsty; we are poorly clothed, roughly treated,
homeless; 12 we labor, working with our own
hands. When we are reviled, we bless; when
we are persecuted, we endure it; 13 when we
are slandered, we respond graciously. Even
now, we are like the scum of the earth, like
everyone's garbage.

PAUL'S FATHERLY CARE

14 I'm not writing this to shame you, but to warn
you as my dear children. 15 For you may have
countless instructors in Christ, but you don't
have many fathers. For I became your father in
Christ Jesus through the gospel. 16 Therefore
I urge you to imitate me. 17 This is why I have
sent Timothy to you. He is my dearly loved and
faithful child in the Lord. He will remind you
about my ways in Christ Jesus, just as I teach
everywhere in every church.

18 Now some are arrogant, as though I were
not coming to you. 19 But I will come to you
soon, if the Lord wills, and I will find out not
the talk, but the power of those who are arrogant. 20 For the kingdom of God is not a matter
of talk but of power. 21 What do you want?
Should I come to you with a rod, or in love
and a spirit of gentleness?

IMMORAL CHURCH MEMBERS

5 It is actually reported that there is sexual
immorality among you, and the kind of
sexual immorality that is not even tolerated[A]

Exercise of Faith | *Standing Firm*

A TOLERANCE FAIL

"Your boasting is not good. Don't you know that a little leaven leavens the whole batch of dough?" 1 Corinthians 5:6

A man was carrying on a very public affair with his stepmother. Scandalous, right? Not to the Christian community in first century Corinth. No one stepped forward and said, "That's wrong. You can't do that." On the contrary, folks seem to have been bragging about how tolerant they were with this adulterous couple.

Paul labeled the church's response "not good." Then he used the illustration of how a tiny bit of leaven ends up spreading through a whole batch of dough. His point was that sin, if it isn't checked, spreads like cancer metastasizing throughout a body.

Remember this about "tolerance." First, not all tolerance is good. Do you want to schedule your surgery in a hospital that is tolerant of germs? Or use an airline that hires and tolerates shoddy mechanics? Second, *everyone* is intolerant about something. Everybody draws lines—the only question is where. Third, when people accuse you of being intolerant, what they're really saying is, "I don't like where you have drawn your lines; you should be forced to abide by my intolerant lines."

Pray for a heart that tolerates what God tolerates and refuses to tolerate the things he says are wrong.

For the next note on *Exercise of Faith*, see 1 Corinthians 9:24-25.

[A] **5:1** Other mss read *named*

among the Gentiles — a man is sleeping with
his father's wife. 2 And you are arrogant!
Shouldn't you be filled with grief and remove
from your congregation the one who did this?
3 Even though I am absent in the body, I am
present in spirit. As one who is present with
you in this way, I have already pronounced
judgment on the one who has been doing such
a thing. 4 When you are assembled in the name
of our Lord Jesus, and I am with you in spirit,
with the power of our Lord Jesus, 5 hand that
one over to Satan for the destruction of the
flesh, so that his spirit may be saved in the
day of the Lord.
6 Your boasting is not good. Don't you know
that a little leaven[A] leavens the whole batch of
dough? 7 Clean out the old leaven so that you
may be a new unleavened batch, as indeed you
are. For Christ our Passover lamb has been
sacrificed.[B] 8 Therefore, let us observe the
feast, not with old leaven or with the leaven
of malice and evil, but with the unleavened
bread of sincerity and truth.

CHURCH DISCIPLINE

9 I wrote to you in a letter not to associate with
sexually immoral people. 10 I did not mean the
immoral people of this world or the greedy and
swindlers or idolaters; otherwise you would
have to leave the world. 11 But actually, I wrote[C]
you not to associate with anyone who claims
to be a brother or sister and is sexually immoral or greedy, an idolater or verbally abusive, a drunkard or a swindler. Do not even eat
with such a person. 12 For what business is it
of mine to judge outsiders? Don't you judge
those who are inside? 13 God judges outsiders.
Remove the evil person from among you.[D]

LAWSUITS AMONG BELIEVERS

6 If any of you has a dispute against another, how dare you take it to court before
the unrighteous,[E] and not before the saints?
2 Or don't you know that the saints will judge
the world? And if the world is judged by you,
are you unworthy to judge the trivial cases?
3 Don't you know that we will judge angels
— how much more matters of this life? 4 So
if you have such matters, do you appoint as
your judges those who have no standing in
the church? 5 I say this to your shame! Can it
be that there is not one wise person among
you who is able to arbitrate between fellow
believers? 6 Instead, brother goes to court
against brother, and that before unbelievers!
7 As it is, to have legal disputes against one
another is already a defeat for you. Why not
rather be wronged? Why not rather be cheated?

Relationships | *Relating to Church Family*

WHEN CHRISTIANS FIGHT

"If any of you has a dispute against another, how dare you take it to court before the unrighteous, and not before the saints?" 1 Corinthians 6:1

When Paul heard that some of the Corinthian believers were filing lawsuits against one another, he responded in shocked disbelief, "How dare you."

Such relational squabbles, Paul argued forcefully, should be settled in-house (in the church) for several reasons. First, since at the end of time the people of God "will judge the world" (1Co 6:2), shouldn't we learn to resolve our petty differences now? Second, why would we outsource our search for interpersonal justice to unbelievers? Do we not think God has given wisdom to anyone within the family of God? Third, what does feuding publicly say about the power of the gospel to bring peace? How is friction a good advertisement for the faith?

If you're at odds with a fellow Christian and nothing you've tried has yet resolved the issue, consult an older, wiser believer. See if that person can help mediate your dispute. Taking such a step is what it looks like to be a peacemaker. And when we get good at peacemaking, people will be reminded of the Son of God and realize that we're his children, too (Mt 5:9).

For the next note on *Relationships*, see 1 Corinthians 8:13.

[A] **5:6** Or *yeast*, also in vv. 7,8 [B] **5:7** Other mss add *for us* [C] **5:11** Or *But now I am writing* [D] **5:13** Dt 17:7 [E] **6:1** Unbelievers; v. 6

8 Instead, you yourselves do wrong and cheat — and you do this to brothers and sisters! 9 Don't you know that the unrighteous will not inherit God's kingdom? Do not be deceived: No sexually immoral people, idolaters, adulterers, or males who have sex with males,[A] 10 no thieves, greedy people, drunkards, verbally abusive people, or swindlers will inherit God's kingdom. 11 And some of you used to be like this. But you were washed, you were sanctified, you were justified in the name of the Lord Jesus Christ and by the Spirit of our God.

GLORIFYING GOD IN BODY AND SPIRIT

12 "Everything is permissible for me," but not everything is beneficial. "Everything is permissible for me," but I will not be mastered by anything. 13 "Food is for the stomach and the stomach for food," and God will do away with both of them. However, the body is not for sexual immorality but for the Lord, and the Lord for the body. 14 God raised up the Lord and will also raise us up by his power. 15 Don't you know that your bodies are a part of Christ's body? So should I take a part of Christ's body and make it part of a prostitute? Absolutely not! 16 Don't you know that anyone joined to a prostitute is one body with her? For Scripture says, **The two will become one flesh.**[B] 17 But anyone joined to the Lord is one spirit with him.

18 Flee sexual immorality! Every other sin[C] a person commits is outside the body, but the person who is sexually immoral sins against his own body. 19 Don't you know that your body is a temple of the Holy Spirit who is in you, whom you have from God? You are not your own, 20 for you were bought at a price. So glorify God with your body.[D]

PRINCIPLES OF MARRIAGE

7 Now in response to the matters you wrote[E] about: "It is good for a man not to use[F] a woman for sex." 2 But because sexual immorality is so common,[G] each man should have sexual relations with his own wife, and each woman should have sexual relations with her own husband. 3 A husband should fulfill his marital duty to his wife, and likewise a wife to her husband. 4 A wife does not have the right over her own body, but her husband does. In

Rest and Reflection | *Watching Health*

THE ONLY BODY YOU HAVE

"Don't you know that your body is a temple of the Holy Spirit who is in you, whom you have from God? You are not your own, for you were bought at a price. So glorify God with your body." 1 Corinthians 6:19-20

When it comes to health and fitness, you probably have friends on both ends of the spectrum. Some work out obsessively and eat things you didn't even know were food, and others will eat anything that doesn't eat them first and haven't exercised since the Reagan administration.

Let's skip the question of "Who's right?" and just make a couple observations. First, we each get one body, one earth suit, in this life. Doesn't it make sense to take care of it? Second, Paul reminds us that the Spirit of Almighty God lives in us. And he's not just a houseguest; he's the owner of the house. We are the ones who are tenants, so that's another reason we need to do regular upkeep.

Paul's conclusion? "Glorify God with your body." How do we do that? Eating right, exercising regularly, resting adequately, and not ingesting substances that can hurt us are all ways to bring God honor. We do those things not to look good and impress others but so we can serve the God who made us by loving the people all around us.

How's your "temple"? Take care to watch your health so you can live more fully and effectively for Christ.

For the next note on *Rest and Reflection*, see Ephesians 1:1.

[A] **6:9** Both passive and active participants in homosexual acts [B] **6:16** Gn 2:24 [C] **6:18** Lit *Every sin* [D] **6:20** Other mss add *and in your spirit, which belong to God.* [E] **7:1** Other mss add *to me* [F] **7:1** Lit *"It is good for a man not to touch a woman* [G] **7:2** Lit *because of immoralities*

the same way, a husband does not have the right over his own body, but his wife does. 5 Do not deprive one another — except when you agree for a time, to devote yourselves to[A] prayer. Then come together again; otherwise, Satan may tempt you because of your lack of self-control. 6 I say this as a concession, not as a command. 7 I wish that all people were as I am. But each has his own gift from God, one person has this gift, another has that.

A WORD TO THE UNMARRIED

8 I say to the unmarried[B] and to widows: It is good for them if they remain as I am. 9 But if they do not have self-control, they should marry, since it is better to marry than to burn with desire.

ABOUT MARRIED PEOPLE

10 To the married I give this command — not I, but the Lord — a wife is not to leave[C] her husband. 11 But if she does leave, she must remain unmarried or be reconciled to her husband — and a husband is not to divorce his wife. 12 But I (not the Lord) say to the rest: If any brother has an unbelieving wife and she is willing to live with him, he must not divorce her. 13 Also, if any woman has an unbelieving husband and he is willing to live with her, she must not divorce her husband. 14 For the unbelieving husband is made holy by the wife, and the unbelieving wife is made holy by the husband.[D] Otherwise your children would be unclean, but as it is they are holy. 15 But if the unbeliever leaves, let him leave. A brother or a sister is not bound in such cases. God has called you[E] to live in peace. 16 Wife, for all you know, you might save your husband. Husband, for all you know, you might save your wife.[F]

VARIOUS SITUATIONS OF LIFE

17 Let each one live his life in the situation the Lord assigned when God called him.[G] This is what I command in all the churches. 18 Was anyone already circumcised when he was called? He should not undo his circumcision. Was anyone called while uncircumcised? He should not get circumcised. 19 Circumcision does not matter and uncircumcision does not matter. Keeping God's commands is what matters. 20 Let each of you remain in the situation[H] in which he was called. 21 Were you called while a slave? Don't let it concern you. But if you can become free, by all means take the opportunity.[I] 22 For he who is called by the Lord as a slave is the Lord's freedman. Likewise he who is called as a free man is Christ's slave. 23 You were bought at a price; do not become slaves of people. 24 Brothers and sisters, each person is to remain with God in the situation in which he was called.

ABOUT THE UNMARRIED AND WIDOWS

25 Now about virgins:[J] I have no command from the Lord, but I do give an opinion as one who by the Lord's mercy is faithful. 26 Because of the present distress, I think that it is good for a man to remain as he is. 27 Are you bound to a wife? Do not seek to be released. Are you released from a wife? Do not seek a wife. 28 However, if you do get married, you have not sinned, and if a virgin[K] marries, she has not sinned. But such people will have trouble in this life,[L] and I am trying to spare you.

29 This is what I mean, brothers and sisters: The time is limited, so from now on those who have wives should be as though they had none, 30 those who weep as though they did not weep, those who rejoice as though they did not rejoice, those who buy as though they didn't own anything, 31 and those who use the world as though they did not make full use of it. For this world in its current form is passing away.

32 I want you to be without concerns. The unmarried man is concerned about the things of the Lord — how he may please the Lord. 33 But the married man is concerned about the things of the world — how he may please his wife — 34 and his interests are divided. The unmarried woman or virgin is concerned about the things of the Lord, so that she may be holy both in body and in spirit. But the married woman is concerned about the things of the world — how she may please her husband. 35 I am saying this for your own benefit, not to put a restraint on you, but to promote what is proper and so that you may be devoted to the Lord without distraction.

36 If any man thinks he is acting improperly toward the virgin he is engaged to,[M] if she is

---

[A] **7:5** Other mss add *fasting and to* [B] **7:8** Or *widowers* [C] **7:10** Or *separate from*, or *divorce* [D] **7:14** Lit *the brother* [E] **7:15** Other mss read *us* [F] **7:16** Or *Wife, how do you know that you will save your husband? Husband, how do you know that you will save your wife?* [G] **7:17** Lit *called each* [H] **7:20** Lit *in the calling* [I] **7:21** Or *But even though you can become free, make the most of your position as a slave* [J] **7:25** Or *betrothed*, or *those not yet married* [K] **7:28** Or *betrothed woman* [L] **7:28** Lit *in the flesh* [M] **7:36** Or *toward his virgin daughter*

getting beyond the usual age for marriage,
and he feels he should marry — he can do
what he wants. He is not sinning; they can
get married. 37 But he who stands firm in his
heart (who is under no compulsion, but has
control over his own will) and has decided in
his heart to keep her as his fiancée, will do
well. 38 So then he who marries[A] his fiancée
does well, but he who does not marry[B] will
do better.

39 A wife is bound[C] as long as her husband
is living. But if her husband dies, she is free
to be married to anyone she wants — only in
the Lord. 40 But she is happier if she remains
as she is, in my opinion. And I think that I also
have the Spirit of God.

FOOD OFFERED TO IDOLS

8 Now about food sacrificed to idols: We
know that "we all have knowledge." Knowledge puffs up, but love builds up. 2 If anyone
thinks he knows anything, he does not yet
know it as he ought to know it. 3 But if anyone
loves God, he is known by him.

4 About eating food sacrificed to idols, then,
we know that "an idol is nothing in the world,"[D]
and that "there is no God but one." 5 For even
if there are so-called gods, whether in heaven
or on earth — as there are many "gods" and
many "lords" — 6 yet for us there is one God,
the Father. All things are from him, and we
exist for him. And there is one Lord, Jesus
Christ. All things are through him, and we
exist through him.

7 However, not everyone has this knowledge.
Some have been so used to idolatry up until
now that when they eat food sacrificed to an
idol, their conscience, being weak, is defiled.
8 Food will not bring us close to God.[E] We are
not worse off if we don't eat, and we are not
better if we do eat. 9 But be careful that this
right of yours in no way becomes a stumbling
block to the weak. 10 For if someone sees you,
the one who has knowledge, dining in an idol's
temple, won't his weak conscience be encouraged[F] to eat food offered to idols? 11 So the weak
person, the brother or sister for whom Christ
died, is ruined[G] by your knowledge. 12 Now
when you sin like this against brothers and
sisters and wound their weak conscience,
you are sinning against Christ. 13 Therefore, if
food causes my brother or sister to fall, I will
never again eat meat, so that I won't cause my
brother or sister to fall.

Relationships | *Helping Weaker Believers*

GIVING UP RIGHTS

"Therefore, if food causes my brother or sister to fall, I will never again eat meat, so that I won't cause my brother or sister to fall." 1 Corinthians 8:13

The church in Corinth was like the church in every place and every era—a collection of people from assorted backgrounds and with varied spiritual convictions.

Some didn't want anything to do with the meat sold in the Corinthian marketplace—out of fear that it had might have been part of pagan sacrifices. Others had no such qualms. In certain settings, these different convictions resulted in a flurry of (often unstated) suspicions and accusations: *How could he be so uptight about such a silly thing?* or *Why is she so cavalier about such a serious matter?*

Paul's solution was to call for loving sensitivity. Do we have full freedom in Christ in areas where the Scripture doesn't specifically forbid an action? Yes. Should we use our freedom in situations where others might be tempted to violate their own consciences? Never. Love for God and for others is always our highest calling. It trumps every other rule.

What actions or freedoms would you be willing to forego in order to keep from causing a "brother or sister to fall"?

For the next note on *Relationships*, see 1 Corinthians 15:33.

[A] **7:38** Or *marries off* [B] **7:38** Or *marry her off* [C] **7:39** Other mss add *by law* [D] **8:4** Or *an idol has no real existence* [E] **8:8** Or *bring us before* (the judgment seat of) *God* [F] **8:10** Or *built up* [G] **8:11** Or *destroyed*

PAUL'S EXAMPLE AS AN APOSTLE

9 Am I not free? Am I not an apostle? Have
I not seen Jesus our Lord? Are you not my
work in the Lord? 2 If I am not an apostle to
others, at least I am to you, because you are
the seal of my apostleship in the Lord.
3 My defense to those who examine me is
this: 4 Don't we have the right to eat and drink?
5 Don't we have the right to be accompanied
by a believing wife[A] like the other apostles,
the Lord's brothers, and Cephas? 6 Or do only
Barnabas and I have no right to refrain from
working? 7 Who serves as a soldier at his own
expense? Who plants a vineyard and does
not eat its fruit? Or who shepherds a flock
and does not drink the milk from the flock?
8 Am I saying this from a human perspective? Doesn't the law also say the same thing?
9 For it is written in the law of Moses, **Do not
muzzle an ox while it treads out grain.**[B]
Is God really concerned about oxen? 10 Isn't
he really saying it for our sake? Yes, this is
written for our sake, because he who plows
ought to plow in hope, and he who threshes
should thresh in hope of sharing the crop. 11 If
we have sown spiritual things for you, is it too
much if we reap material benefits from you?
12 If others have this right to receive benefits
from you, don't we even more? Nevertheless,
we have not made use of this right; instead, we
endure everything so that we will not hinder
the gospel of Christ.
13 Don't you know that those who perform
the temple services eat the food from the temple, and those who serve at the altar share
in the offerings of the altar? 14 In the same
way, the Lord has commanded that those who
preach the gospel should earn their living by
the gospel.
15 For my part I have used none of these
rights, nor have I written these things that
they may be applied in my case. For it would
be better for me to die than for anyone to deprive me of my boast! 16 For if I preach the
gospel, I have no reason to boast, because I
am compelled to preach[C] — and woe to me
if I do not preach the gospel! 17 For if I do this
willingly, I have a reward, but if unwillingly,
I am entrusted with a commission. 18 What
then is my reward? To preach the gospel and
offer it free of charge and not make full use
of my rights in the gospel.
19 Although I am free from all and not anyone's slave, I have made myself a slave to

Exercise of Faith | *Finishing Strong*

THE RACE OF FAITH

"Don't you know that the runners in a stadium all race, but only one receives the prize? Run in such a way to win the prize. Now everyone who competes exercises self-control in everything. They do it to receive a perishable crown, but we an imperishable crown." 1 Corinthians 9:24-25

Writing to Greeks who were familiar with the biannual Isthmian Games, Paul used the analogy of a fiercely competitive race to illustrate what's required to "win" in a life of faith and ministry to others.

From watching the Olympic Games, we get Paul's point. We know what's involved in taking home the gold: wholehearted dedication, unwavering commitment, day after day and year after year of hard work. Talk to any Olympic champion: that strict diet; all those lonely hours of training; saying no to worldly pleasures; saying yes to grueling exercise. "You pushed yourself beyond all reasonable limits. You kept going when you wanted to quit. Tell us, was it worth it?"

Glancing down at the medal and remembering the national anthem, the athlete nods and breaks into a broad grin. "Of course. Totally!"

If people will do all that for an earthly award that's destined to tarnish and fade, how serious should believers be in running the greatest race of all? Think about the prize you're pursuing.

For the next note on *Exercise of Faith*, see 1 Corinthians 10:13.

[A] **9:5** Lit *a sister as a wife* [B] **9:9** Dt 25:4 [C] **9:16** Lit *because necessity is laid upon me*

everyone, in order to win more people. 20 To the Jews I became like a Jew, to win Jews; to those under the law, like one under the law — though I myself am not under the law[A] — to win those under the law. 21 To those who are without the law, like one without the law — though I am not without God's law but under the law of Christ — to win those without the law. 22 To the weak I became weak, in order to win the weak. I have become all things to all people, so that I may by every possible means save some. 23 Now I do all this because of the gospel, so that I may share in the blessings.

24 Don't you know that the runners in a stadium all race, but only one receives the prize? Run in such a way to win the prize. 25 Now everyone who competes exercises self-control in everything. They do it to receive a perishable crown, but we an imperishable crown. 26 So I do not run like one who runs aimlessly or box like one beating the air. 27 Instead, I discipline my body and bring it under strict control, so that after preaching to others, I myself will not be disqualified.

WARNINGS FROM ISRAEL'S PAST

10 Now I do not want you to be unaware, brothers and sisters, that our ancestors were all under the cloud, all passed through the sea, 2 and all were baptized into Moses in the cloud and in the sea. 3 They all ate the same spiritual food, 4 and all drank the same spiritual drink. For they drank from the spiritual rock that followed them, and that rock was Christ. 5 Nevertheless God was not pleased with most of them, since they were struck down in the wilderness.

6 Now these things took place as examples for us, so that we will not desire evil things as they did.[B] 7 Don't become idolaters as some of them were; as it is written, **The people sat down to eat and drink, and got up to party.**[C,D] 8 Let us not commit sexual immorality as some of them did,[E] and in a single day twenty-three thousand people died. 9 Let us not test Christ as some of them did[F] and were destroyed by snakes. 10 And don't complain as some of them did,[G] and were killed by the destroyer.[H] 11 These things happened to them as examples, and they were written for our

Exercise of Faith | *Resisting Temptation*

NOT IRRESISTIBLE

"No temptation has come upon you except what is common to humanity. But God is faithful; he will not allow you to be tempted beyond what you are able, but with the temptation he will also provide a way out so that you may be able to bear it." 1 Corinthians 10:13

When certain temptations rear their alluring heads at certain moments, we feel almost powerless, as though we're enchanted, under a spell. Succumbing feels unavoidable.

It isn't. Not according to this promise-packed verse. First, your temptation isn't new or unusual. It's "common to humanity." That means countless people have faced your same struggle. Second, "God is faithful." He's not about to ignore your plight. Third, he won't let the temptation reach the point of being irresistible. To be sure, giving in might *feel* inevitable, but it never is for the child of God. Because of the indwelling Spirit of God, we always have the power to choose righteousness. Fourth, God pledges to "provide a way out." Your escape may be as normal as hurrying from the room, putting away your phone, or using it to call a friend who can urge you to say no to sin and yes to God.

Don't buy the lies that "I couldn't help it" or "The pressure was just too strong." According to the Bible, such things are never true. When tempted, say, "Thank you, God, for trusting me that much. Now what do you want me to do?" Then look for and take his "way out."

For the next note on *Exercise of Faith*, see 1 Corinthians 10:31.

[A] **9:20** Other mss omit *though I myself am not under the law* [B] **10:6** Lit *they desired* [C] **10:7** Or *to dance* [D] **10:7** Ex 32:6 [E] **10:8** Lit *them committed sexual immorality* [F] **10:9** Lit *them tested* [G] **10:10** Lit *them complained* [H] **10:10** Or *the destroying angel*

instruction, on whom the ends of the ages[A]
have come. 12 So, whoever thinks he stands
must be careful not to fall. 13 No temptation
has come upon you except what is common to
humanity. But God is faithful; he will not allow
you to be tempted beyond what you are able,
but with the temptation he will also provide
a way out so that you may be able to bear it.

WARNING AGAINST IDOLATRY

14 So then, my dear friends, flee from idolatry.
15 I am speaking as to sensible people. Judge
for yourselves what I am saying. 16 The cup of
blessing that we bless, is it not a sharing in the
blood of Christ? The bread that we break, is
it not a sharing in the body of Christ? 17 Because there is one bread, we who are many
are one body, since all of us share the one
bread. 18 Consider the people of Israel.[B] Do
not those who eat the sacrifices participate
in the altar? 19 What am I saying then? That
food sacrificed to idols is anything, or that an
idol is anything? 20 No, but I do say that what
they[C] sacrifice, they sacrifice to demons and
not to God. I do not want you to be participants with demons! 21 You cannot drink the
cup of the Lord and the cup of demons. You
cannot share in the Lord's table and the table
of demons. 22 Or are we provoking the Lord to
jealousy? Are we stronger than he?

CHRISTIAN LIBERTY

23 "Everything is permissible,"[D] but not everything is beneficial. "Everything is permissible,"[D] but not everything builds up. 24 No one
is to seek his own good, but the good of the
other person.
25 Eat everything that is sold in the meat
market, without raising questions for the
sake of conscience, 26 since **the earth is the
Lord's, and all that is in it.**[E] 27 If any of the unbelievers invites you over and you want to go,
eat everything that is set before you, without
raising questions for the sake of conscience.
28 But if someone says to you, "This is food
from a sacrifice," do not eat it, out of consideration for the one who told you, and for the
sake of conscience.[F] 29 I do not mean your own
conscience, but the other person's. For why
is my freedom judged by another person's
conscience? 30 If I partake with thanksgiving,
why am I criticized because of something for
which I give thanks?
31 So, whether you eat or drink, or whatever

Exercise of Faith | *Honoring/Glorifying God*

REASON FOR BEING

"So, whether you eat or drink, or whatever you do, do everything for the glory of God." 1 Corinthians 10:31

Do you sometimes think, *Why am I here? What's my reason for being?* Good news! Here, in just a few words, Paul summarizes believers' mission in life. We exist "for the glory of God." In other words, we are to wake up each morning with this laser-focused mission, "I want to honor God today. I want my life to make him smile."

"Whatever you do" means in every imaginable situation and includes all times, places, and activities. Doing "everything for the glory of God" consists of work life, home life, social life, and sex life. We are called to make much of God while cooking, studying, exercising, shopping, commuting, conversing with a neighbor, working through a conflict with a colleague, making a budget, and surfing the Internet.

By developing the habit of asking and answering the question, "How can I honor God in this moment?" we are on our way to a life of greater purpose, purity, and power. A warning is warranted. As you do this sincerely, you will find that some activities are no longer possible for you.

For the next note on *Exercise of Faith*, see 1 Corinthians 11:1.

[A] **10:11** Or *goals of the ages*, or *culmination of the ages* [B] **10:18** Lit *Look at Israel according to the flesh* [C] **10:20** Other mss read *Gentiles* [D] **10:23** Other mss add *for me* [E] **10:26** Ps 24:1 [F] **10:28** Other mss add *"For the earth is the Lord's and all that is in it."*

Embracing God's Word | Love

NEWLYWED EMBRACE; CRADLED NEWBORN; family reunion; golden anniversary—wanted, chosen, belonging, cherished. We need love. Left out and alone, we shrivel and shiver in the cold. Beyond human relationship, God's love is real, deep, and eternal. Know him; know love.

But you, Lord, are a compassionate and gracious God, slow to anger and abounding in faithful love and truth. –Psalm 86:15

Give thanks to the LORD, for he is good. His faithful love endures forever. Give thanks to the God of gods. His faithful love endures forever. Give thanks to the Lord of lords. His faithful love endures forever. –Psalm 136:1-3

I love those who love me, and those who search for me find me. –Proverbs 8:17

For God loved the world in this way: He gave his one and only Son, so that everyone who believes in him will not perish but have eternal life. –John 3:16

I give you a new command: Love one another. Just as I have loved you, you are also to love one another. By this everyone will know that you are my disciples, if you love one another. –John 13:34-35

For I am persuaded that neither death nor life, nor angels nor rulers, nor things present nor things to come, nor powers, nor height nor depth, nor any other created thing will be able to separate us from the love of God that is in Christ Jesus our Lord. –Romans 8:38-39

If I speak human or angelic tongues but do not have love, I am a noisy gong or a clanging cymbal. . . . Now these three remain: faith, hope, and love—but the greatest of these is love. –1 Corinthians 13:1,13

I pray that you, being rooted and firmly established in love, may be able to comprehend with all the saints what is the length and width, height and depth of God's love, and to know Christ's love that surpasses knowledge, so you may be filled with all the fullness of God. –Ephesians 3:17-19

Above all, maintain constant love for one another, since love covers a multitude of sins. –1 Peter 4:8

See what great a love the Father has given us that we should be called God's children—and we are! . . . This is how we have come to know love: He laid down his life for us. We should also lay down our lives for our brothers and sisters. –1 John 3:1,16

Dear friends, let us love one another, because love is from God, and everyone who loves has been born of God and knows God. The one who does not love does not know God, because God is love. God's love was revealed among us in this way: God sent his one and only Son into the world so that we might live through him. Love consists in this: not that we loved God, but that he loved us and sent his Son to be the atoning sacrifice for our sins. Dear friends, if God loved us in this way, we also must love one another. No one has ever seen God. If we love one another, God remains in us and his love is made complete in us. –1 John 4:7-12

and adult in your thinking. 21 It is written in
the law,

I will speak to this people
by people of other tongues
and by the lips of foreigners,
and even then, they will not listen
to me,[A]

says the Lord. 22 Speaking in other tongues,
then, is intended as a sign, not for believers
but for unbelievers, while prophecy is not for
unbelievers but for believers. 23 If, therefore,
the whole church assembles together and all
are speaking in other tongues and people who
are outsiders or unbelievers come in, will they
not say that you are out of your minds? 24 But
if all are prophesying and some unbeliever or
outsider comes in, he is convicted by all and
is called to account by all. 25 The secrets of his
heart will be revealed, and as a result he will
fall facedown and worship God, proclaiming,
"God is really among you."

ORDER IN CHURCH MEETINGS

26 What then, brothers and sisters? Whenever
you come together, each one[B] has a hymn, a
teaching, a revelation, another tongue, or an
interpretation. Everything is to be done for
building up. 27 If anyone speaks in another
tongue, there are to be only two, or at the most
three, each in turn, and let someone interpret.
28 But if there is no interpreter, that person is
to keep silent in the church and speak to himself and God. 29 Two or three prophets should
speak, and the others should evaluate. 30 But
if something has been revealed to another
person sitting there, the first prophet should
be silent. 31 For you can all prophesy one by
one, so that everyone may learn and everyone
may be encouraged. 32 And the prophets' spirits are subject to the prophets, 33 since God is
not a God of disorder but of peace.

As in all the churches of the saints, 34 the
women[C] should be silent in the churches, for
they are not permitted to speak, but are to
submit themselves, as the law also says. 35 If
they want to learn something, let them ask
their own husbands at home, since it is disgraceful for a woman to speak in the church.
36 Or did the word of God originate from you,
or did it come to you only?

37 If anyone thinks he is a prophet or spiritual, he should recognize that what I write
to you is the Lord's command. 38 If anyone
ignores this, he will be ignored.[D] 39 So then,
my brothers and sisters, be eager to prophesy,
and do not forbid speaking in other tongues.

Exercise of Faith | *Using Gifts*

RESTORATION THROUGH SERVING

"Since you are zealous for spiritual gifts, seek to excel in building up the church." 1 Corinthians 14:12

Someone once asked the world-renowned psychiatrist Karl Menninger what counsel he would give someone feeling on the verge of a nervous breakdown. The wise old man thought for a few minutes, then responded, "Lock up your house, go across the railroad tracks, find someone in need, and do something for them."

Paul would no doubt give Christians a similar prescription, "Take the spiritual gift God has imparted to you, and go. Find people in need. Do something tangible to encourage them. Build up the church."

That's how the body of Christ is supposed to work. We serve one another, using all the abilities that God has imparted—leading, giving, teaching, shepherding, encouraging, showing mercy, and more. As we are focused on others, we won't have time to obsess over our own troubles. And, ironically, as we pour ourselves out, we find that our own souls are replenished. As we live and serve in community, others bless us while we are ministering to them. We find hope and joy. Imagine that—the more we give, the more we receive.

For the next note on *Exercise of Faith*, see 1 Corinthians 15:6.

[A] **14:21** Is 28:11-12 [B] **14:26** Other mss add *of you* [C] **14:34** Other mss read *your women* [D] **14:38** Other mss read *he should be ignored*

40 But everything is to be done decently and
in order.

RESURRECTION ESSENTIAL TO THE GOSPEL

15 Now I want to make clear for you, brothers and sisters, the gospel I preached to
you, which you received, on which you have
taken your stand 2 and by which you are being
saved, if you hold to the message I preached
to you — unless you believed in vain. 3 For I
passed on to you as most important what I also
received: that Christ died for our sins according
to the Scriptures, 4 that he was buried, that he
was raised on the third day according to the
Scriptures, 5 and that he appeared to Cephas,
then to the Twelve. 6 Then he appeared to over
five hundred brothers and sisters at one time;
most of them are still alive, but some have fall-
en asleep. 7 Then he appeared to James, then
to all the apostles. 8 Last of all, as to one born
at the wrong time,[A] he also appeared to me.
9 For I am the least of the apostles, not worthy
to be called an apostle, because I persecuted
the church of God. 10 But by the grace of God
I am what I am, and his grace toward me was
not in vain. On the contrary, I worked harder
than any of them, yet not I, but the grace of
God that was with me. 11 Whether, then, it is I or
they, so we proclaim and so you have believed.

RESURRECTION ESSENTIAL TO THE FAITH

12 Now if Christ is proclaimed as raised from
the dead, how can some of you say, "There is
no resurrection of the dead"? 13 If there is no
resurrection of the dead, then not even Christ
has been raised; 14 and if Christ has not been
raised, then our proclamation is in vain, and
so is your faith.[B] 15 Moreover, we are found to
be false witnesses about God, because we have
testified wrongly about God that he raised up
Christ — whom he did not raise up, if in fact
the dead are not raised. 16 For if the dead are

Exercise of Faith | *Dealing with Doubt*

A RELIABLE FAITH

"Then he appeared to over five hundred brothers and sisters at one time; most of them are still alive, but some have fallen asleep." 1 Corinthians 15:6

Ever have troubling thoughts and nagging questions like this: *I've never seen Jesus or heard him speak audibly. And if I'm honest, much of the time he seems more like a vague idea or an imaginary friend than a living presence in my life. How can I know that my Christian faith is credible?*

Paul cites one piece of helpful evidence for doubters here: Jesus rose from the dead. And the witnesses weren't limited to those lucky few who witnessed this miracle. A large crowd, "over five hundred" people saw him. Paul adds, "Most of them are still alive." The implication? "If you don't want to take my word for it, feel free to talk to one of them."

Among those eyewitnesses were the original apostles. Remember the night Jesus was arrested? Peter denied knowing him. The others ran. To a man, they were devastated by his death.

But then something happened. Something big enough to transform these scared disciples into a team of world-changers, something that made them choose martyrdom rather than renounce their faith. What? The best explanation is what Paul said, that, "[Jesus] was raised on the third day according to the Scriptures, and . . . he appeared . . ." (1Co 15:4-5).

In truth, the only reason you're reading this right now is because those first followers of Jesus were permanently changed by the fact of the resurrection.

When doubt begins to nibble at the edges of your spirit, remember Jesus's resurrection and the eyewitnesses.

For the next note on *Exercise of Faith*, see 2 Corinthians 5:7.

[A] **15:8** Or *one whose birth was unusual* [B] **15:14** Or *proclamation is useless, and your faith also is useless*, or *proclamation is empty, and your faith also is empty*

not raised, not even Christ has been raised.
17 And if Christ has not been raised, your faith
is worthless; you are still in your sins. 18 Those,
then, who have fallen asleep in Christ have
also perished. 19 If we have put our hope in
Christ for this life only, we should be pitied
more than anyone.

CHRIST'S RESURRECTION GUARANTEES OURS

20 But as it is, Christ has been raised from the
dead, the firstfruits of those who have fall-
en asleep. 21 For since death came through a
man, the resurrection of the dead also comes
through a man. 22 For just as in Adam all die,
so also in Christ all will be made alive.
23 But each in his own order: Christ, the firstfruits; afterward, at his coming, those who
belong to Christ. 24 Then comes the end, when
he hands over the kingdom to God the Father,
when he abolishes all rule and all authority
and power. 25 For he must reign until he puts
all his enemies under his feet. 26 The last enemy to be abolished is death. 27 For **God has
put everything under his feet.**[A] Now when
it says "everything" is put under him, it is obvious that he who puts everything under him
is the exception. 28 When everything is subject
to Christ, then the Son himself will also be
subject to the one who subjected everything
to him, so that God may be all in all.

RESURRECTION SUPPORTED BY CHRISTIAN EXPERIENCE

29 Otherwise what will they do who are being
baptized for the dead?[B] If the dead are not raised
at all, then why are people baptized for them?[C]
30 Why are we in danger every hour? 31 I face
death every day, as surely as I may boast about
you, brothers and sisters, in Christ Jesus our
Lord. 32 If I fought wild beasts in Ephesus as a
mere man, what good did that do me? If the
dead are not raised, **Let us eat and drink, for
tomorrow we die.**[D] 33 Do not be deceived: "Bad
company corrupts good morals." 34 Come to
your senses[E] and stop sinning; for some people
are ignorant about God. I say this to your shame.

THE NATURE OF THE RESURRECTION BODY

35 But someone will ask, "How are the dead
raised? What kind of body will they have when
they come?" 36 You fool! What you sow does not
come to life unless it dies. 37 And as for what
you sow — you are not sowing the body that
will be, but only a seed, perhaps of wheat or
another grain. 38 But God gives it a body as he
wants, and to each of the seeds its own body.
39 Not all flesh is the same flesh; there is one
flesh for humans, another for animals, another
for birds, and another for fish. 40 There are heavenly bodies and earthly bodies, but the splendor
of the heavenly bodies is different from that

Relationships | *Building Healthy Friendships*

HEALTHY FRIENDSHIPS

"Do not be deceived: 'Bad company corrupts good morals.'" 1 Corinthians 15:33

In this letter Paul discusses a myriad of concerns, but the issue he brings up repeatedly is relational influence. He argues that false teachers will lead believers astray if we are open to them. If we tolerate sin in the church, before long it will be in our own hearts.

Near the end of his letter in a discussion about the resurrection—and how some in Corinth were denying this doctrine—Paul returns to this theme. He actually quotes the famous Roman poet, Menander, "Bad company corrupts good morals." Apparently the lessons our elders tried to teach us are true after all. One bad apple *can* spoil the whole bunch. If we lie down with dogs, we *will* get up with fleas.

How about your close relationships—do they push you in good directions or entice you to think, act, and speak in ways that dishonor God? If you have people in your life who consistently discourage you from pursuing Christ, you need to steer a wide berth.

For the next note on *Relationships*, see 2 Corinthians 2:14.

[A] **15:27** Ps 8:6 [B] **15:29** Or *baptized on account of the dead* [C] **15:29** Other mss read *for the dead* [D] **15:32** Is 22:13 [E] **15:34** Lit *Sober up*

My Story | Josh

My wife and I met on the school bus at a very young age. We were both raised in a Christian home, but during our teenage years we rebelled together against God, our parents, and our family. We engaged in premarital sex among other worldly things and had our first and second child while we were both still teenagers. This forced us to "grow up" very quickly as we took on the adult responsibilities of work, paying bills, and raising our children. We married shortly after the birth of our second child, but by our mid-twenties we were separated and heading full-steam towards divorce.

During our separation, God convicted me of the rebellion and sin I had engaged in for so many years. I began reading my Bible again and attending church regularly. This led to a desire to reconcile with my wife and become the man, husband, and father God had called me to be (1Co 16:13–14). God gave me strength to trust him with my marriage and family and to love my wife as "Christ loved the church and gave himself up for her" (Eph 5:25).

After many months, my wife started to see real change in me brought about by the power of Christ and the Holy Spirit living in me (Php 4:13). She started to see that my word and my actions aligned. In a miracle buzzer beater that I fully believe was orchestrated by God in his perfect timing, we reconciled the night before our divorce was to be final.

Many years later, I cannot say that life and marriage has been a bed of roses without difficulty and hardship, but we are now both committed to face the difficulty and hardship together with Christ at the center of our marriage. We offer each other "grace upon grace" (Jn 1:16) daily in the same way Christ loves and does for all of us.

of the earthly ones. 41 There is a splendor of
the sun, another of the moon, and another of
the stars; in fact, one star differs from another
star in splendor. 42 So it is with the resurrection of the dead: Sown in corruption, raised
in incorruption; 43 sown in dishonor, raised
in glory; sown in weakness, raised in power;
44 sown a natural body, raised a spiritual body. If
there is a natural body, there is also a spiritual
body. 45 So it is written, **The first man Adam
became a living being**;[A] the last Adam became
a life-giving spirit. 46 However, the spiritual is
not first, but the natural, then the spiritual.

47 The first man was from the earth, a man of
dust; the second man is[B] from heaven. 48 Like
the man of dust, so are those who are of the
dust; like the man of heaven, so are those who
are of heaven. 49 And just as we have borne the
image of the man of dust, we will also bear
the image of the man of heaven.

VICTORIOUS RESURRECTION

50 What I am saying, brothers and sisters, is this:
Flesh and blood cannot inherit the kingdom of
God, nor can corruption inherit incorruption.
51 Listen, I am telling you a mystery: We will
not all fall asleep, but we will all be changed,
52 in a moment, in the twinkling of an eye, at
the last trumpet. For the trumpet will sound,
and the dead will be raised incorruptible, and
we will be changed. 53 For this corruptible
body must be clothed with incorruptibility,
and this mortal body must be clothed with
immortality. 54 When this corruptible body is
clothed with incorruptibility, and this mortal
body is clothed with immortality, then the
saying that is written will take place:

Death has been swallowed up in
victory.[C]
55 **Where, death, is your victory?**
Where, death, is your sting?[D]

56 The sting of death is sin, and the power of sin
is the law. 57 But thanks be to God, who gives
us the victory through our Lord Jesus Christ!

58 Therefore, my dear brothers and sisters,
be steadfast, immovable, always excelling in
the Lord's work, because you know that your
labor in the Lord is not in vain.

COLLECTION FOR THE JERUSALEM CHURCH

16 Now about the collection for the saints:
Do the same as I instructed the Galatian
churches. 2 On the first day of the week, each
of you is to set something aside and save in
keeping with how he is prospering, so that
no collections will need to be made when I

[A] **15:45** Gn 2:7 [B] **15:47** Other mss add *the Lord* [C] **15:54** Is 25:8 [D] **15:55** Hs 13:14

come. [3] When I arrive, I will send with letters
those you recommend to carry your gift to
Jerusalem. [4] If it is suitable for me to go as
well, they will travel with me.

PAUL'S TRAVEL PLANS

[5] I will come to you after I pass through Macedonia — for I will be traveling through Macedonia — [6] and perhaps I will remain with you
or even spend the winter, so that you may send
me on my way wherever I go. [7] I don't want to
see you now just in passing, since I hope to
spend some time with you, if the Lord allows.
[8] But I will stay in Ephesus until Pentecost,
[9] because a wide door for effective ministry
has opened for me[A] — yet many oppose me.
[10] If Timothy comes, see that he has nothing
to fear while with you, because he is doing
the Lord's work, just as I am. [11] So let no one
look down on him. Send him on his way in
peace so that he can come to me, because I
am expecting him with the brothers.

[12] Now about our brother Apollos: I strongly
urged him to come to you with the brothers, but
he was not at all willing to come now. However, he will come when he has an opportunity.

FINAL EXHORTATION

[13] Be alert, stand firm in the faith, be courageous,[B] be strong. [14] Do everything in love.

[15] Brothers and sisters, you know the household of Stephanas: They are the firstfruits of
Achaia and have devoted themselves to serving the saints. I urge you [16] also to submit to
such people, and to everyone who works and
labors with them. [17] I am delighted to have
Stephanas, Fortunatus, and Achaicus present,
because these men have made up for your
absence. [18] For they have refreshed my spirit
and yours. Therefore recognize such people.

CONCLUSION

[19] The churches of Asia send you greetings. Aquila and Priscilla send you greetings warmly
in the Lord, along with the church that meets
in their home. [20] All the brothers and sisters
send you greetings. Greet one another with
a holy kiss.

[21] This greeting is in my own hand — Paul.
[22] If anyone does not love the Lord, a curse be
on him. Our Lord, come![C] [23] The grace of the
Lord Jesus be with you. [24] My love be with all
of you in Christ Jesus.

[A] **16:9** Lit *door has opened to me, great and effective* [B] **16:13** Lit *act like men* [C] **16:22** Aramaic *Marana tha*

2 Corinthians — At the heart of Paul's second letter to the Corinthians is a verse that is a favorite of many: "My grace is sufficient for you, for my power is perfected in weakness" (12:9). In proving his apostolic authority, Paul rested not in his credentials or his powers of persuasion, but in his weakness. Paul's awareness of his own inability is what enabled him to rely on God's power. God uses weak vessels, those who know that their only boast is in him.

A secondary theme in 2 Corinthians is reconciliation. Christ's death on the cross enables us to be restored to right relationship with God, and we are then to devote ourselves to helping others be reconciled to him (5:19-21). In a world where many are isolated and abandoned, the Christian message offers the hope of peace and belonging.

The themes of power perfected in weakness and the reconciliation made possible through the cross of Christ make 2 Corinthians a book of hope for those who feel beat up by life. Whether our struggle is emotional or physical, we are not overwhelmed, for our troubles are only light and momentary in comparison with the eternal weight of glory that awaits us (4:8-18).

2 CORINTHIANS

AUTHOR: The apostle Paul

DATE WRITTEN: Shortly after 1 Corinthians, in AD 56

ORIGINAL AUDIENCE: Paul ministered in Corinth for eighteen months, visiting there in response to a vision he had while on his second missionary journey (Ac 16:9; 18:1-18). His first letter to them was lost; then he wrote 1 Corinthians to address the factions that had arisen within the church. When that was not well received by the church, Paul visited them in person (2Co 2:1; 13:2). False apostles stirred up the church against him, and he wrote another now lost letter of rebuke (2:3-4,9). The church then repented and accepted Paul's authority (7:5-7), and in response he wrote this letter to them and promised another visit (12:14; 13:1; Ac 20:2-3).

SETTING: Paul had a stormy relationship with the Corinthian church, and this letter is one of joy and reconciliation.

PURPOSE FOR WRITING: In this letter, Paul reaffirms his apostolic authority and calls on the Corinthian church as coworkers to take up an offering for the saints in Jerusalem.

OUTLINE:

1. Greetings and Thanksgiving (1:1-11)

2. Paul's Apostolic Ministry (1:12–7:16)

3. Collection for Jerusalem (8:1–9:15)

4. The Case against False Apostles (10:1–13:10)

5. Final Greetings (13:11-14)

KEY VERSE:

"My grace is sufficient for you, for my power is perfected in weakness."
—2 Corinthians 12:9

RESTORATION THEMES

R	Rest and Reflection	*For the next note, see Ephesians 1:1.*
E	Eternal Perspective	*Forward Look—2 Corinthians 4:17-18* *Christ Focus—11:3*
S	Support	*For the next note, see Galatians 1:10.*
T	Thanksgiving and Contentment	*Comfort—2 Corinthians 1:3-4; 7:6* *Blessings—3:5* *Shortcomings/Weaknesses—5:21; 12:9* *Repentance—7:9-10* *Comparisons—10:12*
O	Other-centeredness	*Giving Generously—9:7* *Dealing with Difficult People—10:3*
R	Relationships	*Resolving Arguments/Disagreements/Conflicts—2:14* *Avoiding Harmful Relationships—6:14*
E	Exercise of Faith	*Living by Faith—5:7* *Experiencing New Life in Christ—5:17*

GREETING

1 Paul, an apostle of Christ Jesus by God's
will, and Timothy our[A] brother:
To the church of God at Corinth, with all the
saints who are throughout Achaia.
2 Grace to you and peace from God our Father and the Lord Jesus Christ.

THE GOD OF COMFORT

3 Blessed be the God and Father of our Lord
Jesus Christ, the Father of mercies and the
God of all comfort. 4 He comforts us in all our
affliction,[B] so that we may be able to comfort those who are in any kind of affliction,
through the comfort we ourselves receive
from God. 5 For just as the sufferings of Christ
overflow to us, so also through Christ our
comfort overflows. 6 If we are afflicted, it
is for your comfort and salvation. If we are
comforted, it is for your comfort, which produces in you patient endurance of the same
sufferings that we suffer. 7 And our hope for
you is firm, because we know that as you
share in the sufferings, so you will also share
in the comfort.
8 We don't want you to be unaware, brothers
and sisters, of our affliction that took place
in Asia. We were completely overwhelmed —
beyond our strength — so that we even de-
spaired of life itself. 9 Indeed, we felt that we
had received the sentence of death, so that we
would not trust in ourselves but in God who
raises the dead. 10 He has delivered us from
such a terrible death, and he will deliver us.
We have put our hope in him that he will deliver us again 11 while you join in helping us
by your prayers. Then many will give thanks
on our[C] behalf for the gift that came to us
through the prayers of many.

A CLEAR CONSCIENCE

12 Indeed, this is our boast: The testimony of
our conscience is that we have conducted
ourselves in the world, and especially toward
you, with godly sincerity and purity, not by
human wisdom but by God's grace. 13 For we
are writing nothing to you other than what
you can read and also understand. I hope you
will understand completely — 14 just as you
have partially understood us — that we are
your reason for pride, just as you also are ours
in the day of our[D] Lord Jesus.

A VISIT POSTPONED

15 Because of this confidence, I planned to
come to you first, so that you could have a

Thanksgiving and Contentment | *Comfort*

AFFLICTION

"Blessed be the God and Father of our Lord Jesus Christ, the Father of mercies and the God of all comfort. He comforts us in all our affliction, so that we may be able to comfort those who are in any kind of affliction, through the comfort we ourselves receive from God." 2 Corinthians 1:3-4

We may not use the word *affliction* much in daily conversation, but we sure do encounter it every day of our lives. In the Bible, the word means "hardship, pressure, or distress." For most people, the question isn't "Do you have difficulty in your life today?" but rather, "What kind of trouble are you facing?"

In a fallen world, affliction is a given—like death and taxes. Thankfully for believers, so is "comfort." God's Word tells strugglers that the God and Father of Jesus is "the Father of mercies and the God of all comfort." In other words, God has all the help and mercy we'll ever need. He comes alongside us and generously doles out encouragement and reassurance—enough for us to turn around and share with others!

God comforts us by the indwelling presence of the Holy Spirit. Remember that Jesus called him the "Counselor," or Comforter (Jn 14:16-17; 16:7).

Whatever your affliction, trust in God and his unfailing love for you and find comfort.

For the next note on *Thanksgiving and Contentment*, see 2 Corinthians 3:5.

[A] **1:1** Lit *the* [B] **1:4** Or *trouble*, or *tribulation*, or *trials*, or *oppression* [C] **1:11** Other mss read *your* [D] **1:14** Other mss omit *our*

Embracing God's Word | Victory

PRESSURED, SURROUNDED, TRAPPED, frantically struggling with bonds and battles, we cry for help. God hears our despair and desperation and responds with love and power. He has promised to save, and we are victorious with him. Take him at his word.

He will rescue you from six calamities; no harm will touch you in seven. –Job 5:19

Turn, LORD! Rescue me; save me because of your faithful love. –Psalm 6:4

He reached down from on high and took hold of me; he pulled me out of deep water. He rescued me from my powerful enemy and from those who hated me, for they were too strong for me. They confronted me in the day of my calamity, but the LORD was my support. He brought me out to a spacious place; he rescued me because he delighted in me. –Psalm 18:16-19

The righteous cry out, and the LORD hears, and rescues them from all their troubles. –Psalm 34:17

I waited patiently for the LORD, and he turned to me and heard my cry for help. He brought me up from a desolate pit, out of the muddy clay, and set my feet on a rock, making my steps secure. –Psalm 40:1-2

But I call to God, and the LORD will save me. –Psalm 55:16

The LORD is near all who call out to him, all who call out to him with integrity. He fulfills the desires of those who fear him; he hears their cry for help and saves them. –Psalm 145:18-19

I will be with you when you pass through the waters, and when you pass through the rivers, they will not overwhelm you. You will not be scorched when you walk through the fire, and the flame will not burn you. –Isaiah 43:2

Shadrach, Meshach, and Abednego replied to the king, "Nebuchadnezzar, we don't need to give you an answer to this question. If the God we serve exists, then he can rescue us from the furnace of blazing fire, and he can rescue us from the power of you, the king. But even if he does not rescue us, we want you as king to know that we will not serve your gods or worship the gold statue you set up." –Daniel 3:16-18

In all these things we are more than conquerors through him who loved us. –Romans 8:37

No temptation has come upon you except what is common to humanity. But God is faithful; he will not allow you to be tempted beyond what you are able, but with the temptation he will also provide a way out so that you are able to bear it. –1 Corinthians 10:13

Indeed, we felt that we had received the sentence of death, so that we would not trust in ourselves but in God who raises the dead. He has delivered us from such a terrible death, and he will deliver us. We have put our hope in him that he will deliver us again. –2 Corinthians 1:9-10

You are from God, little children, and you have conquered them, because the one who is in you is greater than the one who is in the world. –1 John 4:4

second benefit,[A] 16 and to visit you on my way
to Macedonia, and then come to you again
from Macedonia and be helped by you on
my journey to Judea. 17 Now when I planned
this, was I of two minds? Or what I plan, do I
plan in a purely human[B] way so that I say "Yes,
yes" and "No, no" at the same time? 18 As God
is faithful, our message to you is not "Yes and
no." 19 For the Son of God, Jesus Christ, whom
we proclaimed among you — Silvanus,[C] Timothy, and I — did not become "Yes and no." On
the contrary, in him it is always "Yes." 20 For
every one of God's promises is "Yes" in him.
Therefore, through him we also say "Amen" to
the glory of God. 21 Now it is God who strengthens us together with you in Christ, and who
has anointed us. 22 He has also put his seal on
us and given us the Spirit in our hearts as a
down payment.

23 I call on God as a witness, on my life, that
it was to spare you that I did not come to
Corinth. 24 I do not mean that we lord it over
your faith, but we are workers with you for
your joy, because you stand firm in your faith.

1 In fact, I made up my mind about this:
I would not come to you on another painful visit.[D] 2 For if I cause you pain, then who
will cheer me other than the one being hurt
by me?[E] 3 I wrote this very thing so that when
I came I wouldn't have pain from those who
ought to give me joy, because I am confident
about all of you that my joy will also be yours.
4 For I wrote to you with many tears out of
an extremely troubled and anguished heart
— not to cause you pain, but that you should
know the abundant love I have for you.

A SINNER FORGIVEN

5 If anyone has caused pain, he has caused
pain not so much to me but to some degree
— not to exaggerate — to all of you. 6 This
punishment by the majority is sufficient
for that person. 7 As a result, you should instead forgive and comfort him. Otherwise,
he may be overwhelmed by excessive grief.
8 Therefore I urge you to reaffirm your love
to him. 9 I wrote for this purpose: to test
your character to see if you are obedient in
everything. 10 Anyone you forgive, I do too.
For what I have forgiven — if I have forgiv-
en anything — it is for your benefit in the
presence of Christ, 11 so that we may not be
taken advantage of by Satan. For we are not
ignorant of his schemes.

R Relationships | *Resolving Arguments/Disagreements/Conflicts*

FRAGRANCE . . . OR STENCH?

"But thanks be to God, who always leads us in Christ's triumphal procession and through us spreads the aroma of the knowledge of him in every place." 2 Corinthians 2:14

In ancient times, conquering Roman generals would typically return from battle at the head of a victory parade, with their prisoners walking behind them. Along the way, incense was burned to commemorate the leader's great triumph.

Paul relates this historical practice to spiritual realities. Believers are like Christ's "conquered" prisoners, in the sense that we follow after him. And we leave behind an "aroma" in the world—"the fragrance of Christ" (2Co 2:15). To those who are indifferent or hostile to the gospel, our new life in Christ produces a stench or bad odor. But to all those who belong to Jesus, our lives are an "aroma of life leading to life" (2:16).

Paul's thankful expression here is an important reminder that we will never please everyone. If we commit ourselves fully to Jesus (see Rm 12:1-2), our lives will be like ancient sacrifices that are "pleasing" to the Lord (Gn 8:21; Lv 26:31; Nm 28:6). But we won't necessarily smell so delightful to lots of other people.

For the next note on *Relationships*, see 2 Corinthians 6:14.

[A] **1:15** Other mss read *a second joy* [B] **1:17** Or *a worldly*, or *a fleshly*, or *a selfish* [C] **1:19** Or *Silas*; Ac 15:22-32; 16:19-40; 17:1-16
[D] **2:1** Lit *not again in sorrow to come to you* [E] **2:2** Lit *the one pained*

A TRIP TO MACEDONIA

12 When I came to Troas to preach the gospel
of Christ, even though the Lord opened a door
for me, 13 I had no rest in my spirit because I
did not find my brother Titus. Instead, I said
good-bye to them and left for Macedonia.

A MINISTRY OF LIFE OR DEATH

14 But thanks be to God, who always leads us
in Christ's triumphal procession and through
us spreads the aroma of the knowledge of
him in every place. 15 For to God we are the
fragrance of Christ among those who are
being saved and among those who are perishing. 16 To some we are an aroma of death
leading to death, but to others, an aroma of
life leading to life. Who is adequate for these
things? 17 For we do not market the word of
God for profit like so many.[A] On the contrary,
we speak with sincerity in Christ, as from God
and before God.

LIVING LETTERS

3 Are we beginning to commend ourselves
again? Or do we need, like some, letters of
recommendation to you or from you? 2 You
yourselves are our letter, written on our hearts,
known and read by everyone. 3 You show that
you are Christ's letter, delivered[B] by us, not
written with ink but with the Spirit of the
living God — not on tablets of stone but on
tablets of human hearts.[C]

PAUL'S COMPETENCE

4 Such is the confidence we have through Christ
before God. 5 It is not that we are competent in[D]
ourselves to claim anything as coming from
ourselves, but our adequacy is from God. 6 He
has made us competent to be ministers of a
new covenant, not of the letter, but of the Spirit. For the letter kills, but the Spirit gives life.

NEW COVENANT MINISTRY

7 Now if the ministry that brought death, chis-
eled in letters on stones, came with glory, so
that the Israelites were not able to gaze steadily
at Moses's face because of its glory, which was
set aside, 8 how will the ministry of the Spirit
not be more glorious? 9 For if the ministry that
brought condemnation had glory, the ministry
that brings righteousness overflows with even
more glory. 10 In fact, what had been glorious
is not glorious now by comparison because of
the glory that surpasses it. 11 For if what was
set aside was glorious, what endures will be
even more glorious.
12 Since, then, we have such a hope, we act
with great boldness. 13 We are not like Moses,
who used to put a veil over his face to prevent
the Israelites from gazing steadily until the

T Thanksgiving and Contentment | *Blessings*

ADEQUATE IN HIM

"It is not that we are competent in ourselves to claim anything as coming from ourselves, but our adequacy is from God." 2 Corinthians 3:5

In a declaration of independence, the toddler cries fiercely, "I do it myself!" Of course, we know how this story usually ends—with tearful pleas for help.

This portrays our condition. We detest being dependent, and yet that's the spiritual life in a nutshell. Here the apostle Paul freely admits his weakness and inability. To the extent that his life displays any competency or success, Paul is quick to credit God as being the source. In a prior letter to the Corinthian Christians, he had asked rhetorically, "What do you have that you didn't receive?" (1Co 4:7).

This humbles us. Everything good in life—our spiritual blessings, material resources, intellectual gifts, physical abilities, career opportunities, and life accomplishments—comes "from God."

Take a few minutes today to take inventory of your life. Thank God for all his tangible generosity. Instead of saying, "I do it myself!" invite the Lord to work in and through you.

For the next note on *Thanksgiving and Contentment*, see 2 Corinthians 5:21.

[A] **2:17** Other mss read *like the rest* [B] **3:3** Lit *ministered to* [C] **3:3** Lit *fleshly hearts* [D] **3:5** Lit *from*

end[A] of the glory of what was being set aside,
14 but their minds were hardened. For to this
day, at the reading of the old covenant, the
same veil remains; it is not lifted, because
it is set aside only in Christ. 15 Yet still today,
whenever Moses is read, a veil lies over their
hearts, 16 but whenever a person turns to the
Lord, the veil is removed. 17 Now the Lord is
the Spirit, and where the Spirit of the Lord is,
there is freedom. 18 We all, with unveiled faces, are looking as in a mirror at[B] the glory of
the Lord and are being transformed into the
same image from glory to glory; this is from
the Lord who is the Spirit.[C]

THE LIGHT OF THE GOSPEL

4 Therefore, since we have this ministry
because we were shown mercy, we do not
give up. 2 Instead, we have renounced secret
and shameful things, not acting deceitfully or
distorting the word of God, but commending
ourselves before God to everyone's conscience
by an open display of the truth. 3 But if our
gospel is veiled, it is veiled to those who are
perishing. 4 In their case, the god of this age
has blinded the minds of the unbelievers to
keep them from seeing the light of the gospel
of the glory of Christ,[D] who is the image of
God. 5 For we are not proclaiming ourselves
but Jesus Christ as Lord, and ourselves as your
servants for Jesus's sake. 6 For God who said,
"Let light shine out of darkness," has shone in
our hearts to give the light of the knowledge
of God's glory in the face of Jesus Christ.

TREASURE IN CLAY JARS

7 Now we have this treasure in clay jars, so that
this extraordinary power may be from God
and not from us. 8 We are afflicted in every
way but not crushed; we are perplexed but
not in despair; 9 we are persecuted but not
abandoned; we are struck down but not destroyed. 10 We always carry the death of Jesus
in our body, so that the life of Jesus may also
be displayed in our body. 11 For we who live are
always being given over to death for Jesus's
sake, so that Jesus's life may also be displayed
in our mortal flesh. 12 So then, death is at work
in us, but life in you. 13 And since we have the
same spirit of faith in keeping with what is
written, **I believed, therefore I spoke,**[E] we also
believe, and therefore speak. 14 For we know
that the one who raised the Lord Jesus will
also raise us with Jesus and present us with
you. 15 Indeed, everything is for your benefit
so that, as grace extends through more and

E Eternal Perspective | *Forward Look*

TEMPORARY TROUBLES

"For our momentary light affliction is producing for us an absolutely incomparable eternal weight of glory. So we do not focus on what is seen, but on what is unseen. For what is seen is temporary, but what is unseen is eternal." 2 Corinthians 4:17-18

When we need help, we seek out people who have been there. We want those with real-life experience. So, regarding suffering, who better to listen to than Paul? This man had been "afflicted in every way . . . perplexed . . . persecuted . . . struck down" (2Co 4:8-9). Twice more in this same letter, he rattles off a long list of painful and scary experiences (6:4-10; 11:23-28).

Yet this veteran of trouble shockingly calls them "momentary," "light," and "temporary." How can he say such things? Because he is comparing his earthly afflictions to the "eternal weight of glory" that awaits believers in the life to come.

Paul knows that life's tragedies hurt. But our losses here can't outweigh the gains we'll enjoy there. Heaven is real. Its infinite pleasures will more than cancel out the deepest pains we experience on earth.

For the next note on *Eternal Perspective*, see 2 Corinthians 11:3.

[A] **3:13** Or *at the outcome* [B] **3:18** Or *are reflecting* [C] **3:18** Or *from the Spirit of the Lord*, or *from the Lord, the Spirit* [D] **4:4** Or *the gospel of the glorious Christ*, or *the glorious gospel of Christ* [E] **4:13** Ps 116:10 LXX

more people, it may cause thanksgiving to
increase to the glory of God.
16 Therefore we do not give up. Even though
our outer person is being destroyed, our inner person is being renewed day by day. 17 For
our momentary light affliction is producing
for us an absolutely incomparable eternal
weight of glory. 18 So we do not focus on what
is seen, but on what is unseen. For what is seen
is temporary, but what is unseen is eternal.

OUR FUTURE AFTER DEATH

5 For we know that if our earthly tent we live
in is destroyed, we have a building from
God, an eternal dwelling in the heavens, not
made with hands. 2 Indeed, we groan in this
tent, desiring to put on our heavenly dwelling,
3 since, when we have taken it off,[A] we will not
be found naked. 4 Indeed, we groan while we
are in this tent, burdened as we are, because
we do not want to be unclothed but clothed,
so that mortality may be swallowed up by
life. 5 Now the one who prepared us for this
very purpose is God, who gave us the Spirit
as a down payment.
6 So we are always confident and know that
while we are at home in the body we are away
from the Lord. 7 For we walk by faith, not by
sight. 8 In fact, we are confident, and we would
prefer to be away from the body and at home
with the Lord. 9 Therefore, whether we are at
home or away, we make it our aim to be pleasing to him. 10 For we must all appear before
the judgment seat of Christ, so that each may
be repaid for what he has done in the body,
whether good or evil.
11 Therefore, since we know the fear of the
Lord, we try to persuade people. What we are is
plain to God, and I hope it is also plain to your
consciences. 12 We are not commending ourselves to you again, but giving you an opportunity to be proud of us, so that you may have
a reply for those who take pride in outward
appearance rather than in the heart. 13 For if
we are out of our mind, it is for God; if we are
in our right mind, it is for you. 14 For the love
of Christ compels us, since we have reached
this conclusion: If one died for all, then all
died. 15 And he died for all so that those who
live should no longer live for themselves, but
for the one who died for them and was raised.

THE MINISTRY OF RECONCILIATION

16 From now on, then, we do not know anyone
from a worldly perspective.[B] Even if we have
known Christ from a worldly perspective,[C]
yet now we no longer know him in this way.
17 Therefore, if anyone is in Christ, he is a new

Exercise of Faith | *Living by Faith*

THE WAY THINGS REALLY ARE

"For we walk by faith, not by sight." 2 Corinthians 5:7

Every moment of every day we are faced with the same choice: Am I going to base my thoughts, moods, and choices on what *seems* true or on what God *says* is true?

This is the spiritual life. First, faith is a "walk" we undertake, not an idea we bat around in our minds. Second, faith is taking God at his word and acting accordingly. It's trusting and obeying him, even when everyone else is recommending or doing otherwise. To "walk by faith," we stop putting our confidence on what we can see or what the majority thinks or what our gut tells us. If those things line up with what God has revealed, fine. But if not, we have to discount all the loud voices for God's quiet voice.

Faith, therefore, is uncomfortable, unnerving, unpredictable. When Jesus says to follow him, he doesn't give us a detailed itinerary for the next five days, much less for the next five years. It isn't like driving down an interstate highway where we can see all the way to the horizon. No, it's more like climbing up a twisting, turning mountain trail that often disappears for stretches. What's ahead? Only God knows.

Ask the Lord for the grace to trust him more deeply. Tell him you want to walk by faith, not by sight.

For the next note on *Exercise of Faith*, see 2 Corinthians 5:17.

[A] **5:3** Other mss read *when we have put on* [B] **5:16** Lit *anyone according to the flesh* [C] **5:16** Lit *Christ according to the flesh*

creation; the old has passed away, and see, the
new has[A] come! 18 Everything is from God, who
has reconciled us to himself through Christ
and has given us the ministry of reconciliation. 19 That is, in Christ, God was reconciling
the world to himself, not counting their trespasses against them, and he has committed
the message of reconciliation to us.
20 Therefore, we are ambassadors for Christ,
since God is making his appeal through us.
We plead on Christ's behalf: "Be reconciled to
God." 21 He made the one who did not know
sin to be sin[B] for us, so that in him we might
become the righteousness of God.

6 Working together with him, we also appeal
to you, "Don't receive the grace of God in
vain." 2 For he says:

> **At an acceptable time I listened to you,**
> **and in the day of salvation I helped**
> **you.**[C]

See, now is the acceptable time; now is the
day of salvation!

THE CHARACTER OF PAUL'S MINISTRY

3 We are not giving anyone an occasion for offense, so that the ministry will not be blamed.
4 Instead, as God's ministers, we commend
ourselves in everything: by great endurance,
by afflictions, by hardships, by difficulties,
5 by beatings, by imprisonments, by riots, by
labors, by sleepless nights, by times of hunger, 6 by purity, by knowledge, by patience,
by kindness, by the Holy Spirit, by sincere
love, 7 by the word of truth,[D] by the power
of God; through weapons of righteousness
for the right hand and the left, 8 through glory and dishonor, through slander and good
report; regarded as deceivers, yet true; 9 as
unknown, yet recognized; as dying, yet see
— we live; as being disciplined, yet not killed;
10 as grieving, yet always rejoicing; as poor,
yet enriching many; as having nothing, yet
possessing everything. 11 We have spoken
openly to you, Corinthians; our heart has been
opened wide. 12 We are not withholding our
affection from you, but you are withholding
yours from us. 13 I speak as to my children;
as a proper response, open your heart to us.

SEPARATION TO GOD

14 Don't become partners with those who do
not believe. For what partnership is there
between righteousness and lawlessness? Or
what fellowship does light have with darkness? 15 What agreement does Christ have
with Belial?[E] Or what does a believer have

Exercise of Faith | *Experiencing New Life in Christ*

THE NEW HAS COME

"Therefore, if anyone is in Christ, he is a new creation; the old has passed away, and see, the new has come!" 2 Corinthians 5:17

The trendy, just-opened coffee shop on the corner. That smell of fresh paint and new carpet in the remodeled guest room. The must-have smartphone that can do everything but tie your shoes.

We humans have a love affair with all things "new," which is why Paul's declaration ought to make us perk up and smile. The person who is in union or in relationship with Christ by faith "is a new creation." It means our old lives, our old nature "has passed away," died off. We're no longer the people we used be; therefore, we have no business living the way we used to live.

In Christ, we have a new standing with God (righteous), a new identity (child of God), a new nature, new desires (to please God), new capacities (thanks to the indwelling Spirit), a new mission (being a disciple who makes disciples) and destiny (heaven).

Let your old way of living before Christ die off. Put those desires and habits away like worn-out clothes. Let Jesus help you see people in a new way, opportunities you never had, and strength you never thought possible.

For the next note on *Exercise of Faith*, see Galatians 2:20.

[A] **5:17** Other mss read *look, all new things have* [B] **5:21** Or *be a sin offering* [C] **6:2** Is 49:8 [D] **6:7** Or *by truthful speech*
[E] **6:15** Or *Beliar*

in common with an unbeliever? 16 And what
agreement does the temple of God have with
idols? For we[A] are the temple of the living
God, as God said:

I will dwell
and walk among them,
and I will be their God,
and they will be my people.[B]

Thanksgiving and Contentment | *Shortcomings/Weaknesses*

SYMPATHETIC TO SHORTCOMINGS

"He made the one who did not know sin to be sin for us, so that in him we might become the righteousness of God." 2 Corinthians 5:21

The old, corny joke says that Adam and Eve, after sinning in Eden, "raised Cain." The more accurate and not-so-funny truth is that the rebellious couple heard God coming, ran from him, dove into the bushes, and hid.

Sin turns us into shamed-faced fugitives, doesn't it? We can't bring ourselves to face the One we've defied. In such moments, what we need most is to confess our sin. What we want to do least is make confession.

This gospel truth liberates: Our great high priest, Jesus, can sympathize with us. Not because he knows what it's like to sin; in fact, he "did not know sin." Yet he can sympathize because, in his earthly life, he experienced the powerful pull of sin's assorted temptations. Then, he even became "sin for us" when he endured the shame of the cross (Heb 12:2). In so doing, he opened the way for us to the Father, so that we might be able to experience righteousness.

If you are feeling ashamed Jesus is the One you need to talk to. He completely understands.

For the next note on *Thanksgiving and Contentment*, see 2 Corinthians 7:6.

Relationships | *Avoiding Harmful Relationships*

PARTNERSHIPS

"Don't become partners with those who do not believe. For what partnership is there between righteousness and lawlessness? Or what fellowship does light have with darkness?" 2 Corinthians 6:14

Paul urges the Corinthian believers to avoid intimate associations with unbelievers. The phrase "don't become partners" is rendered in some Bible translations as "don't be unequally yoked." It conveys the picture of two very different animals—a donkey and an ox, let's say—being paired up to pull a wagon or a plow. Those who know farming agree this sort of partnership would not go well.

When followers of Jesus enter into serious, binding agreements—dating relationships, marriage, business partnerships, for example—with those who have vastly different values and perspectives, the result is generally headaches and heartache.

We still can have relationships with unbelievers and should show love to those with whom we disagree. But we will be affected when we link up with others in deep ways.

Reserve your deepest commitments to those with whom you are like-minded in the essentials of life.

For the next note on *Relationships*, see Galatians 3:28.

[A] **6:16** Other mss read *you* [B] **6:16** Lv 26:12; Jr 31:33; 32:38; Ezk 37:26

17 **Therefore, come out**
from among them
and be separate, says the Lord;
do not touch any unclean thing,
and I will welcome you.[A]
18 **And I will be a Father to you,**
and you will be sons and daughters
to me,
says the Lord Almighty.[B]

7 So then, dear friends, since we have these
promises, let us cleanse ourselves from every impurity of the flesh and spirit, bringing
holiness to completion[C] in the fear of God.

JOY AND REPENTANCE

2 Make room for us in your hearts. We have
wronged no one, corrupted no one, taken advantage of no one. 3 I don't say this to condemn
you, since I have already said that you are in
our hearts, to die together and to live together.
4 I am very frank with you; I have great pride
in you. I am filled with encouragement; I am
overflowing with joy in all our afflictions.
5 In fact, when we came into Macedonia,
we[D] had no rest. Instead, we were troubled
in every way: conflicts on the outside, fears
within. 6 But God, who comforts the downcast,
comforted us by the arrival of Titus, 7 and not
only by his arrival but also by the comfort
he received from you. He told us about your
deep longing, your sorrow, and your zeal for
me, so that I rejoiced even more. 8 For even
if I grieved you with my letter, I don't regret
it. And if I regretted it — since I saw that the
letter grieved you, yet only for a while — 9 I
now rejoice, not because you were grieved,
but because your grief led to repentance. For
you were grieved as God willed, so that you
didn't experience any loss from us. 10 For godly grief produces a repentance that leads to
salvation without regret, but worldly grief
produces death. 11 For consider how much diligence this very thing — this grieving as God
wills — has produced in you: what a desire to
clear yourselves, what indignation, what fear,
what deep longing, what zeal, what justice! In
every way you showed yourselves to be pure
in this matter. 12 So even though I wrote to you,
it was not because of the one who did wrong,

Thanksgiving and Contentment | *Comfort*

WHEN YOU'RE LOW

"But God, who comforts the downcast, comforted us by the arrival of Titus." 2 Corinthians 7:6

You know the feeling. You're down. Low. Blah. Blue.

Many situations and events can trigger such a mood—but probably nothing more than relational troubles. Life isn't fun when we have drama, misunderstandings, and tension swirling about with people we love.

This was Paul's situation with the Corinthian church. As a pastor, he loved these new Christians fiercely, but they were such a fickle bunch. He was "downcast," but notice what happened. God comforted him and his colleagues "by the arrival of Titus."

The Lord uses people to touch his downcast people. This is exactly what Paul wrote in 1 Corinthians 12: We are the body of Christ. We're his hands and feet, appointed to be bringers of comfort.

Notice something else: Comfort has a ripple effect. Paul goes on to say, "We rejoiced even more over the joy Titus had, because his spirit was refreshed by all of you" (2Co 7:13). In other words, the Corinthians comforted Titus. Titus comforted Paul. Paul—writing almost two thousand years ago—is comforting us today with these reminders.

Need some comfort? Find a Christian friend. Then be that for another downcast soul.

For the next note on *Relationships*, see 2 Corinthians 7:9-10.

[A] **6:17** Is 52:11 [B] **6:18** 2Sm 7:14; Is 43:6; 49:22; 60:4; Hs 1:10 [C] **7:1** Or *spirit, perfecting holiness* [D] **7:5** Lit *our flesh*

My Story | Rhonda

Like a lot of people, my spiritual life really took off during college. I was away from home, making a lot of decisions on my own for the first time, and figuring out if the faith I had grown up with was the faith I wanted to live. Jesus became real to me during those years when I didn't have all the immediate reinforcements around me like my family and friends from church.

My friendships at college were all across the board, from Christians who set an example for me to people who had very little interest in Jesus. One of the test areas for my faith was this assortment of relationships including my boyfriends. When it came to close relationships with the opposite sex, I had a difficult past. And frankly, I wasn't quick to consider faith as a significant component in deciding to go out with guys. But the more I got to know about Jesus, the more I felt growing discomfort with some of my relationships.

I was talking with a Christian friend about my struggles with my boyfriend when she asked the "duh" question: "Is he a Christian?" I admit that my shrugged response was a mixture of "I don't know" and even, "Why should I care?" that revealed a lot of immaturity. She had me read, out loud, 2 Corinthians 6:14-16. After I was finished reading, she asked, "So what do you think God wants you to do?"

The answer came out of my mouth like a revelation: "I need to break up with my boyfriend." Along with the answer came a little panic that told me I was having to make a relationship choice between Jesus and my boyfriend. As I looked at the choice, I made two crucial discoveries. The good parts of my relationship with my boyfriend did not outweigh the negative aspects of pressures to compromise my spiritual and moral standards. It wasn't his fault. Agreeing to that level of relationship with him created certain expectations I suddenly knew I couldn't fulfill without devaluing my relationship with Jesus.

Breaking up with him wasn't easy or painless. But as soon as I did, I experienced a clarity in my relationship with God that I really needed. It was one thing to consider making sacrifices for what I believed in; it was another thing to make a sacrifice. I had to face my fears of being alone by practicing my trust in Christ, which had been hard to do when I was using a human substitute. In the times of dreaded loneliness, I found God's presence real in ways I couldn't have known until I ventured out in trust.

or because of the one who was wronged, but
in order that your devotion to us might be
made plain to you in the sight of God. 13 For
this reason we have been comforted.

In addition to our own comfort, we rejoiced
even more over the joy Titus had, because his
spirit was refreshed by all of you. 14 For if I have
made any boast to him about you, I have not
been disappointed; but as I have spoken everything to you in truth, so our boasting to Titus
has also turned out to be the truth. 15 And his
affection toward you is even greater as he remembers the obedience of all of you, and how
you received him with fear and trembling. 16 I
rejoice that I have complete confidence in you.

APPEAL TO COMPLETE THE COLLECTION

8 We want you to know, brothers and sisters, about the grace of God that was giv-
en to the churches of Macedonia: 2 During a
severe trial brought about by affliction, their
abundant joy and their extreme poverty overflowed in a wealth of generosity on their part.
3 I can testify that, according to their ability
and even beyond their ability, of their own
accord, 4 they begged us earnestly for the privilege of sharing in the ministry to the saints,
5 and not just as we had hoped. Instead, they
gave themselves first to the Lord and then to
us by God's will. 6 So we urged Titus that just
as he had begun, so he should also complete
among you this act of grace.

7 Now as you excel in everything — in faith,
speech, knowledge, and in all diligence, and
in your love for us[A] — excel also in this act of
grace. 8 I am not saying this as a command.
Rather, by means of the diligence of others, I
am testing the genuineness of your love. 9 For
you know the grace of our Lord Jesus Christ:
Though he was rich, for your sake he became
poor, so that by his poverty you might become
rich. 10 And in this matter I am giving advice

[A] **8:7** Other mss read *in our love for you*

because it is profitable for you, who began
last year not only to do something but also
to want to do it. 11 Now also finish the task, so
that just as there was an eager desire, there
may also be a completion, according to what
you have. 12 For if the eagerness is there, the
gift is acceptable according to what a person
has, not according to what he does not have.
13 It is not that there should be relief for others
and hardship for you, but it is a question of
equality.[A] 14 At the present time your surplus
is available for their need, so that their abundance may in turn meet your need, in order
that there may be equality. 15 As it is written:
The person who had much did not have
too much, and the person who had little
did not have too little.[B]

ADMINISTRATION OF THE COLLECTION

16 Thanks be to God, who put the same concern for you into the heart of Titus. 17 For he
welcomed our appeal and, being very diligent, went out to you by his own choice.
18 We have sent with him the brother who
is praised among all the churches for his
gospel ministry.[C] 19 And not only that, but
he was also appointed by the churches to
accompany us with this gracious gift that
we are administering for the glory of the
Lord himself and to show our eagerness to
help. 20 We are taking this precaution so that
no one will criticize us about this large sum
that we are administering. 21 Indeed, we are
giving careful thought to do what is right,
not only before the Lord but also before
people. 22 We have also sent with them our
brother. We have often tested him in many
circumstances and found him to be diligent
— and now even more diligent because of
his great confidence in you. 23 As for Titus,
he is my partner and coworker for you; as
for our brothers, they are the messengers of
the churches, the glory of Christ. 24 Therefore, show them proof before the churches
of your love and of our boasting about you.

MOTIVATIONS FOR GIVING

9 Now concerning the ministry to the saints,
it is unnecessary for me to write to you.
2 For I know your eagerness, and I boast about
you to the Macedonians: "Achaia has been
ready since last year," and your zeal has stirred
up most of them. 3 But I am sending the brothers so that our boasting about you in this matter would not prove empty, and so that you
would be ready just as I said. 4 Otherwise, if

Thanksgiving and Contentment | *Repentance*

GODLY GRIEF

"I now rejoice, not because you were grieved, but because your grief led to repentance. For you were grieved as God willed, so that you didn't experience any loss from us. For godly grief produces a repentance that leads to salvation without regret, but worldly grief produces death." 2 Corinthians 7:9-10

Paul speaks of two kinds of grief. One he labels a "worldly grief." This is where an offender's main regret is *I got caught! I'm so mortified! I can never show my face in public again*. The primary focus of "worldly grief" is me, me, me, with little sorrow for the fact that one has sinned against God and hurt others. The person's anguish is tied to losing public face rather than having a rebellious heart.

Paul calls the other grief "godly grief." It leads to much more than embarrassment. It brings a person to "repentance." Biblical repentance means a change of mind that results in a change of direction.

When we blow it, we must come clean before the gospel can ever make us clean. Don't settle for superficial, self-centered sorrow. Let your failure and shame bring you to Jesus. He forgives and transforms. His grace lifts our heads and makes us new.

For the next note on *Thanksgiving and Contentment*, see 2 Corinthians 10:12.

[A] **8:13** Lit *but from equality* [B] **8:15** Ex 16:18 [C] **8:18** Lit *churches, in the gospel*

any Macedonians come with me and find you
unprepared, we, not to mention you, would be
put to shame in that situation.[A] 5 Therefore I
considered it necessary to urge the brothers
to go on ahead to you and arrange in advance
the generous gift you promised, so that it will
be ready as a gift and not as an extortion.
6 The point is this:[B] The person who sows
sparingly will also reap sparingly, and the
person who sows generously will also reap
generously. 7 Each person should do as he has
decided in his heart — not reluctantly or out of
compulsion, since God loves a cheerful giver.
8 And God is able to make every grace overflow
to you, so that in every way, always having
everything you need, you may excel in every
good work. 9 As it is written:

He distributed freely;
he gave to the poor;
his righteousness endures forever.[C]

10 Now the one who provides seed for the sower and bread for food will also provide and
multiply your seed and increase the harvest of
your righteousness. 11 You will be enriched in
every way for all generosity, which produces
thanksgiving to God through us. 12 For the ministry of this service is not only supplying the
needs of the saints but is also overflowing in
many expressions of thanks to God. 13 Because
of the proof provided by this ministry, they
will glorify God for your obedient confession
of the gospel of Christ, and for your generosity in sharing with them and with everyone.
14 And as they pray on your behalf, they will
have deep affection for you because of the
surpassing grace of God in you. 15 Thanks be
to God for his indescribable gift!

PAUL'S APOSTOLIC AUTHORITY

10 Now I Paul, myself, appeal to you by the
meekness and gentleness of Christ — I
who am humble among you in person but bold
toward you when absent. 2 I beg you that when
I am present I will not need to be bold with
the confidence by which I plan to challenge
certain people who think we are behaving
according to the flesh. 3 For although we live
in the flesh, we do not wage war according to
the flesh, 4 since the weapons of our warfare
are not of the flesh, but are powerful through
God for the demolition of strongholds. We
demolish arguments 5 and every proud thing
that is raised up against the knowledge of God,
and we take every thought captive to obey
Christ. 6 And we are ready to punish any disobedience, once your obedience is complete.

Other-centeredness | *Giving Generously*

GIVING IN GRACE

"Each person should do as he has decided in his heart—not reluctantly or out of compulsion, since God loves a cheerful giver." 2 Corinthians 9:7

Chapters 8 and 9 constitute the most extensive teaching on giving in the entire Bible. But don't stop reading—the message is not what you might expect. Paul employs no guilt or wheedling, no slick appeals or tugging on heart strings.

As with everything else, Paul approaches the subject with grace. Don't give "reluctantly or out of compulsion" he says. In other words, don't turn giving into a duty. Do that, Paul suggests, and you'll end up sour and resentful. God doesn't want that. He's looking for "cheerful" givers.

Two things are worth noting. First, God doesn't *need* us to give our money; *we* need to give our money. God is only interested in freeing us from a love of money that will ruin our lives. Second, the Greek word for "cheerful" here is the word from which we get our English word "hilarious." Try to wrap your mind around that. What would "hilarious" giving even look like?

Give what you want—but if you find yourself wanting to give very little, ask yourself, "Why is generosity difficult for me?"

For the next note on *Other-centeredness*, see 2 Corinthians 10:3.

[A] **9:4** Or *in this confidence* [B] **9:6** Lit *And this* [C] **9:9** Ps 112:9

7 Look at what is obvious.[A] If anyone is confident that he belongs to Christ, let him remind
himself of this: Just as he belongs to Christ, so
do we. 8 For if I boast a little too much about
our authority, which the Lord gave for building
you up and not for tearing you down, I will
not be put to shame. 9 I don't want to seem as
though I am trying to terrify you with my letters. 10 For it is said, "His letters are weighty and
powerful, but his physical presence is weak
and his public speaking amounts to nothing."
11 Let such a person consider this: What we are
in our letters, when we are absent, we will
also be in our actions when we are present.
12 For we don't dare classify or compare ourselves with some who commend themselves.
But in measuring themselves by themselves
and comparing themselves to themselves, they
lack understanding. 13 We, however, will not
boast beyond measure but according to the
measure of the area of ministry that God has
assigned to us, which reaches even to you.
14 For we are not overextending ourselves, as
if we had not reached you, since we have come
to you with the gospel of Christ. 15 We are not
boasting beyond measure about other people's
labors. On the contrary, we have the hope that
as your faith increases, our area of ministry will
be greatly enlarged, 16 so that we may preach
the gospel to the regions beyond you without
boasting about what has already been done in
someone else's area of ministry. 17 So **let the
one who boasts, boast in the Lord.**[B] 18 For it
is not the one commending himself who is
approved, but the one the Lord commends.

PAUL AND THE FALSE APOSTLES

11 I wish you would put up with a little foolishness from me. Yes, do put up with me![C]
2 For I am jealous for you with a godly jealousy,
because I have promised you in marriage to one
husband — to present a pure virgin to Christ.
3 But I fear that, as the serpent deceived Eve
by his cunning, your minds may be seduced
from a sincere and pure[D] devotion to Christ.
4 For if a person comes and preaches another
Jesus, whom we did not preach, or you receive
a different spirit, which you had not received,
or a different gospel, which you had not accepted, you put up with it splendidly!
5 Now I consider myself in no way inferior to
those "super-apostles." 6 Even if I am untrained

Other-centeredness | *Dealing with Difficult People*

MINISTERING IN A HOSTILE WORLD

"For although we live in the flesh, we do not wage war according to the flesh." 2 Corinthians 10:3

Ever find yourself in a spiritual war of wits with someone espousing a different viewpoint? Maybe they trash your beliefs or call into question your sincerity or sanity.

All sorts of reactions are possible. Some Christians power up, raise their voices, trot out all their best arguments. Others get quiet. Still others get downright hostile. They mock and belittle. And many, when feeling vulnerable, twist the truth or resort to character assassination.

Paul rejects those common behaviors. Though we live in the world and are surrounded by worldly people, we're not to utilize worldly tactics when engaging with others. We have powerful spiritual weapons (the Bible, prayer, the indwelling Spirit of God, and the communion of saints) that are able to dismantle others' biases and wrong presuppositions.

Nobody can argue anyone into the kingdom of God. And all the shame-inducing rants and lectures in the world will never change a single heart. Kindness and listening are the best weapons we have. Love is what overcomes evil and liberates evil's captives.

Instead of debating, try praying and listening.

For the next note on *Other-centeredness*, see Philippians 2:3-4.

[A] **10:7** Or *You are looking at things outwardly* [B] **10:17** Jr 9:24 [C] **11:1** Or *Yes, you are putting up with me* [D] **11:3** Other mss omit *and pure*

in public speaking, I am certainly not untrained in knowledge. Indeed, we have in every way made that clear to you in everything. [7] Or did I commit a sin by humbling myself so that you might be exalted, because I preached the gospel of God to you free of charge? [8] I robbed other churches by taking pay from them to minister to you. [9] When I was present with you and in need, I did not burden anyone, since the brothers who came from Macedonia supplied my needs. I have kept myself, and will keep myself, from burdening you in any way. [10] As the truth of Christ is in me, this boasting of mine will not be stopped[A] in the regions of Achaia. [11] Why? Because I don't love you? God knows I do!

[12] But I will continue to do what I am doing, in order to deny[B] an opportunity to those who want to be regarded as our equals in what they boast about. [13] For such people are false apostles, deceitful workers, disguising themselves as apostles of Christ. [14] And no wonder! For Satan disguises himself as an angel of light. [15] So it is no great surprise if his servants also disguise themselves as servants of righteousness. Their end will be according to their works.

PAUL'S SUFFERINGS FOR CHRIST

[16] I repeat: Let no one consider me a fool. But if you do, at least accept me as a fool so that I can also boast a little. [17] What I am saying in this matter[C] of boasting, I don't speak as the Lord would, but as it were, foolishly. [18] Since many boast according to the flesh, I will also boast. [19] For you, being so wise, gladly put up with fools! [20] In fact, you put up with it if someone enslaves you, if someone exploits you, if someone takes advantage of you, if someone is arrogant toward you, if someone slaps you in the face. [21] I say this to our shame: We have been too weak for that!

But in whatever anyone dares to boast — I am talking foolishly — I also dare: [22] Are they Hebrews? So am I. Are they Israelites? So am I. Are they the descendants of Abraham? So am I. [23] Are they servants of Christ? I'm talking like a madman — I'm a better one: with far more labors, many more imprisonments, far worse beatings, many times near death.

[24] Five times I received the forty lashes minus one from the Jews. [25] Three times I was beaten with rods. Once I received a stoning. Three times I was shipwrecked. I have spent a night and a day in the open sea. [26] On frequent journeys, I

Thanksgiving and Contentment | *Comparisons*

THE TRAP

"For we don't dare classify or compare ourselves with some who commend themselves. But in measuring themselves by themselves and comparing themselves to themselves, they lack understanding." 2 Corinthians 10:12

As small children, we could win a contest or championship and think quite highly of ourselves. We may even have declared to anyone who would listen that we were "the best—world champs!" In reality, the world was much larger than our school, playground, neighborhood, and community. Without a broader perspective and with limited comparisons, we had an inflated view of our abilities and accomplishments.

Comparisons can be a deadly trap because we can use them to justify ungodly values and harmful actions. If everyone seems to be "doing it" or cultural winds are blowing in a certain direction, we can go along and feel okay about ourselves.

Paul warns of this tendency. Instead, we should ask how we are measuring up to God's standards and his calling on our lives.

Don't be trapped. Instead of worrying how you're doing according to what everyone else seems to be saying is right and good, focus on Christ-honoring values and goals.

For the next note on *Thanksgiving and Contentment*, see 2 Corinthians 12:9.

[A] **11:10** Or *silenced* [B] **11:12** Lit *cut off* [C] **11:17** Or *business*, or *confidence*

faced dangers from rivers, dangers from robbers, dangers from my own people, dangers
from Gentiles, dangers in the city, dangers in
the wilderness, dangers at sea, and dangers
among false brothers; 27 toil and hardship, many
sleepless nights, hunger and thirst, often without food, cold, and without clothing. 28 Not to
mention[A] other things, there is the daily pressure
on me: my concern for all the churches. 29 Who
is weak, and I am not weak? Who is made to
stumble, and I do not burn with indignation?

30 If boasting is necessary, I will boast about
my weaknesses. 31 The God and Father of the
Lord Jesus, who is blessed forever, knows I
am not lying. 32 In Damascus, a ruler[B] under
King Aretas guarded the city of Damascus
in order to arrest me. 33 So I was let down in
a basket through a window in the wall and
escaped from his hands.

SUFFICIENT GRACE

Boasting is necessary. It is not profit-
able, but I will move on to visions and
revelations of the Lord. 2 I know a man in
Christ who was caught up to the third heaven
fourteen years ago. Whether he was in the
body or out of the body, I don't know; God
knows. 3 I know that this man — whether in
the body or out of the body I don't know; God
knows — 4 was caught up into paradise and
heard inexpressible words, which a human
being is not allowed to speak. 5 I will boast
about this person, but not about myself, except of my weaknesses.

6 For if I want to boast, I wouldn't be a fool,
because I would be telling the truth. But I will
spare you, so that no one can credit me with
something beyond what he sees in me or hears
from me, 7 especially because of the extraordinary revelations. Therefore, so that I would
not exalt myself, a thorn in the flesh was given
to me, a messenger of Satan to torment me so
that I would not exalt myself. 8 Concerning
this, I pleaded with the Lord three times that
it would leave me. 9 But he said to me, "My
grace is sufficient for you, for my power is
perfected in weakness."

Therefore, I will most gladly boast all the
more about my weaknesses, so that Christ's
power may reside in me. 10 So I take pleasure in

E Eternal Perspective | *Christ Focus*

PURE DEVOTION

"But I fear that, as the serpent deceived Eve by his cunning, your minds may be seduced from a sincere and pure devotion to Christ." 2 Corinthians 11:3

Ancient Corinth was a decadent, cosmopolitan city, teeming with all sorts of pagan ideas and an endless parade of experts peddling assorted philosophical ideas. Sounds like most major cities today. We should not be surprised, therefore, to learn that the baby Christians in Corinth struggled as much as or more than any other church that Paul had helped launch.

When some religious charlatans showed up and began attacking Paul and his ministry, many of these brand-new believers foolishly believed the allegations. Before long they were also embracing ideas that were against the gospel of Jesus.

Paul compared this turn of events to the sly way Eve had been tricked by the serpent in the garden of Eden. He called it a seduction.

Perhaps you've been bamboozled like that, burned in the past by some smooth-talking, convincing religious leader? Maybe with a trusting heart, you were taken advantage of and still feel the sting of disappointment.

This is why Paul holds up "sincere and pure devotion to Christ" as the standard. Don't pledge absolute loyalty to any fallible human leader. Instead, give your heart fully to the trustworthy Jesus. He will never let you down.

For the next note on *Eternal Perspective*, see Galatians 4:4-5.

[A] **11:28** Lit *Apart from* [B] **11:32** Gk *ethnarches*; a leader of an ethnic community

RESTORATION THEMES

R	Rest and Reflection	*For the next note, see Ephesians 1:1.*
E	Eternal Perspective	*God's Children—Galatians 4:4-5*
S	Support	*Motives—1:10*
T	Thanksgiving and Contentment	*For the next note, see Philippians 4:12-13.*
O	Other-centeredness	*For the next note, see Philippians 2:3-4.*
R	Relationships	*Being Impartial—Galatians 3:28*
E	Exercise of Faith	*Living by Faith—2:20* *Following God's Lead—5:25* *Discipling Others—6:1* *Continuing to Do Good—6:9*

GREETING

1 Paul, an apostle — not from men or by man,
but by Jesus Christ and God the Father who
raised him from the dead — 2 and all the brothers who are with me:
To the churches of Galatia.
3 Grace to you and peace from God the Father and our Lord[A] Jesus Christ, 4 who gave
himself for our sins to rescue us from this
present evil age, according to the will of our
God and Father. 5 To him be the glory forever
and ever. Amen.

NO OTHER GOSPEL

6 I am amazed that you are so quickly turning
away from him who called you by the grace of
Christ and are turning to a different gospel —
7 not that there is another gospel, but there are
some who are troubling you and want to distort
the gospel of Christ. 8 But even if we or an angel
from heaven should preach to you a gospel contrary to what we have preached to you, a curse
be on him![B] 9 As we have said before, I now say
again: If anyone is preaching to you a gospel
contrary to what you received, a curse be on him!
10 For am I now trying to persuade people,[C]
or God? Or am I striving to please people? If I
were still trying to please people, I would not
be a servant of Christ.

PAUL DEFENDS HIS APOSTLESHIP

11 For I want you to know, brothers and sisters,
that the gospel preached by me is not of human origin. 12 For I did not receive it from a
human source and I was not taught it, but it
came by a revelation of Jesus Christ.
13 For you have heard about my former way
of life in Judaism: I intensely persecuted God's
church and tried to destroy it. 14 I advanced in
Judaism beyond many contemporaries among
my people, because I was extremely zealous
for the traditions of my ancestors. 15 But when
God, who from my mother's womb set me apart
and called me by his grace, was pleased 16 to
reveal his Son in me, so that I could preach
him among the Gentiles, I did not immediately consult with anyone.[D] 17 I did not go up to
Jerusalem to those who had become apostles
before me; instead I went to Arabia and came
back to Damascus.
18 Then after three years I did go up to Jerusalem to get to know Cephas,[E] and I stayed
with him fifteen days. 19 But I didn't see any
of the other apostles except James, the Lord's

Support | *Motives*

WHAT'S YOUR MOTIVE?

"For am I now trying to persuade people, or God? Or am I striving to please people? If I were still trying to please people, I would not be a servant of Christ." Galatians 1:10

When Paul traveled through Asia preaching the message that people are made right with God through faith in Jesus and not by following religious rules, some Jews became furious. They accused Paul of saying such things only to please his irreligious listeners. Paul scoffed at this charge, insisting that his sole motivation in life was to please God by serving Christ. For that reason, he preached the gospel of God's amazing grace through Christ.

This reminds us that everyone is motivated by something. Depending on the situation, the motive might be a desire to please people, to gain fame, to be comfortable, or to be in control. At any given moment, a person—even a follower of Jesus—can be motivated by insecurity, fear, pride, anger, shame, lust, and the list goes on.

This is why stopping and taking stock is always a good idea. Get in the habit of asking yourself, *Why—really—am I doing this?* If the honest answer isn't "a loving desire to bring honor to God and blessing to others," our "good" efforts may need to stop or be redirected.

For the next note on *Support*, see Hebrews 3:13.

[A] **1:3** Other mss read *God our Father and the Lord* [B] **1:8** Or *you, let him be condemned*, or *you, let him be condemned to hell*; Gk *anathema* [C] **1:10** Or *win the approval of people* [D] **1:16** Lit *flesh and blood* [E] **1:18** Other mss read *Peter*

brother. 20 I declare in the sight of God: I am
not lying in what I write to you.
21 Afterward, I went to the regions of Syria and Cilicia. 22 I remained personally unknown to the Judean churches that are in
Christ. 23 They simply kept hearing: "He who
formerly persecuted us now preaches the faith
he once tried to destroy." 24 And they glorified
God because of me.[A]

PAUL DEFENDS HIS GOSPEL AT JERUSALEM

2 Then after fourteen years I went up again
to Jerusalem with Barnabas, taking Titus
along also. 2 I went up according to a revelation
and presented to them the gospel I preach
among the Gentiles, but privately to those
recognized as leaders. I wanted to be sure I
was not running, and had not been running,
in vain. 3 But not even Titus, who was with
me, was compelled to be circumcised, even
though he was a Greek. 4 This matter arose
because some false brothers had infiltrated
our ranks to spy on the freedom we have in
Christ Jesus in order to enslave us. 5 But we
did not give up and submit to these people
for even a moment, so that the truth of the
gospel would be preserved for you.
6 Now from those recognized as important
(what they[B] once were makes no difference
to me; God does not show favoritism[C]) — they
added nothing to me. 7 On the contrary, they
saw that I had been entrusted with the gospel for the uncircumcised, just as Peter was
for the circumcised, 8 since the one at work
in Peter for an apostleship to the circumcised
was also at work in me for the Gentiles. 9 When
James, Cephas,[D] and John — those recognized
as pillars — acknowledged the grace that had
been given to me, they gave the right hand of
fellowship to me and Barnabas, agreeing that
we should go to the Gentiles and they to the
circumcised. 10 They asked only that we would
remember the poor, which I had made every
effort to do.

FREEDOM FROM THE LAW

11 But when Cephas[D] came to Antioch, I opposed
him to his face because he stood condemned.[E]
12 For he regularly ate with the Gentiles before
certain men came from James. However, when
they came, he withdrew and separated himself,
because he feared those from the circumcision party. 13 Then the rest of the Jews joined
his hypocrisy, so that even Barnabas was led
astray by their hypocrisy. 14 But when I saw
that they were deviating from the truth of the
gospel, I told Cephas[D] in front of everyone,
"If you, who are a Jew, live like a Gentile and

Exercise of Faith | *Living by Faith*

DAILY TRUST

"I have been crucified with Christ, and I no longer live, but Christ lives in me. The life I now live in the body, I live by faith in the Son of God, who loved me and gave himself for me." Galatians 2:20

While stating that no one obeys God's law perfectly, Paul gives this memorable testimony. He declares three truths about our relationship with Christ.

First, we were crucified with him. In a mysterious but real way, faith unites us so closely with Jesus that we were with him in his death. Because of that, our old selfish, human nature has been killed. Yet while it is technically dead, it doesn't always act dead. Second, Christ makes his home in our hearts (Eph 3:17). He's not just near or with us. He's *in* us! Our old values and beliefs are no longer driving us—his new ones are. Third, he showed his love by giving his life for us.

A Savior who would do all this for you is surely willing and able to help you live each day as God wants. Today, let the One who died for you also lead you. Ask him to govern your attitudes and thoughts. Remember that he loves you, and let him guide your actions and words.

For the next note on *Exercise of Faith*, see Galatians 5:25.

[A] **1:24** Or *in me* [B] **2:6** Lit *the recognized ones* [C] **2:6** Or *God is not a respecter of persons*; lit *God does not receive the face of man* [D] **2:9,11,14** Other mss read *Peter* [E] **2:11** Or *he was in the wrong*

not like a Jew, how can you compel Gentiles
to live like Jews?"[A]
15 We are Jews by birth and not "Gentile
sinners," 16 and yet because we know that a
person is not justified by the works of the law
but by faith in Jesus Christ,[B] even we ourselves
have believed in Christ Jesus. This was so that
we might be justified by faith in Christ[C] and
not by the works of the law, because by the
works of the law no human being will[D] be
justified. 17 But if we ourselves are also found
to be "sinners" while seeking to be justified
by Christ, is Christ then a promoter[E] of sin?
Absolutely not! 18 If I rebuild those things that
I tore down, I show myself to be a lawbreaker.
19 For through the law I died to the law, so that
I might live for God. 20 I have been crucified
with Christ, and I no longer live, but Christ
lives in me. The life I now live in the body,[F] I
live by faith in the Son of God, who loved me
and gave himself for me. 21 I do not set aside
the grace of God, for if righteousness comes
through the law, then Christ died for nothing.

JUSTIFICATION THROUGH FAITH

3 You foolish Galatians! Who has cast a spell
on you,[G] before whose eyes Jesus Christ
was publicly portrayed[H] as crucified? 2 I only
want to learn this from you: Did you receive the
Spirit by the works of the law or by believing
what you heard?[I] 3 Are you so foolish? After
beginning by the Spirit, are you now finishing
by the flesh? 4 Did you experience[J] so much
for nothing — if in fact it was for nothing?
5 So then, does God give you the Spirit and
work miracles among you by your doing the
works of the law? Or is it by believing what
you heard — 6 just like Abraham who **believed God, and it was credited to him for
righteousness**?[K]
7 You know, then, that those who have faith,
these are Abraham's sons. 8 Now the Scripture
saw in advance that God would justify the
Gentiles by faith and proclaimed the gospel
ahead of time to Abraham, saying, **All the
nations[L] will be blessed through you.**[M] 9 Consequently those who have faith are blessed
with Abraham, who had faith.[N]

LAW AND PROMISE

10 For all who rely on the works of the law are
under a curse, because it is written, **Everyone
who does not do everything written in the
book of the law is cursed.**[O] 11 Now it is clear
that no one is justified before God by the law,
because **the righteous will live by faith.**[P]

Relationships | *Being Impartial*

THE PROBLEM WITH PREJUDICE

"There is no Jew or Greek, slave or free, male and female; since you are all one in Christ Jesus." Galatians 3:28

We say opposites attract, but in truth our human nature pulls us toward those who look, think, and act just like we do. And our sinful nature looks with suspicion at and avoids anyone who seems different. Soon we are dividing the world into "us" and "them." Before long, our differences become division, division breeds distrust, and distrust leads to disgust.

The good news of the gospel declares a resounding "No!" to all of this. We are made by the same God, and we come from common stock. Regardless of our skin color, zip code, native language, net worth, gender, or favorite musical genre, we all have the same problem (sin), the same need (salvation), and the same Savior (Jesus). The gospel of Jesus breaks down walls and unites people. The Bible doesn't condone hostility, and heaven won't be segregated (Rv 7:9), so why should we tolerate divisions here and now?

Ask God to help you see Jesus in everyone you meet.

For the next note on *Relationships*, see Ephesians 4:31.

[A] **2:14** Some translations continue the quotation through v. 16 or v. 21. [B] **2:16** Or *by the faithfulness of Jesus Christ* [C] **2:16** Or *by the faithfulness of Christ* [D] **2:16** Lit *law all flesh will not* [E] **2:17** Or *servant* [F] **2:20** Lit *flesh* [G] **3:1** Other mss add *not to obey the truth* [H] **3:1** Other mss add *among you* [I] **3:2** Lit *hearing with faith*, also in v. 5 [J] **3:4** Or *suffer* [K] **3:6** Gn 15:6 [L] **3:8** Or *Gentiles* [M] **3:8** Gn 12:3; 18:18 [N] **3:9** Or *with believing Abraham* [O] **3:10** Dt 27:26 [P] **3:11** Hab 2:4

12 But the law is not based on faith; instead,
the one who does these things will live by
them.[A] 13 Christ redeemed us from the curse of
the law by becoming a curse for us, because it
is written, **Cursed is everyone who is hung**
on a tree.[B] 14 The purpose was that the blessing of Abraham would come to the Gentiles
by Christ Jesus, so that we could receive the
promised Spirit through faith.

15 Brothers and sisters, I'm using a human
illustration. No one sets aside or makes addi-
tions to a validated human will.[C] 16 Now the
promises were spoken to Abraham and to his
seed. He does not say "and to seeds," as though
referring to many, but referring to one, **and to**
your seed,[D] who is Christ. 17 My point is this:
The law, which came 430 years later, does not
invalidate a covenant previously established by
God[E] and thus cancel the promise. 18 For if the
inheritance is based on the law, it is no longer
based on the promise; but God has graciously given it to Abraham through the promise.

THE PURPOSE OF THE LAW

19 Why then was the law given? It was added
for the sake of transgressions[F] until the Seed
to whom the promise was made would come.
The law was put into effect through angels
by means of a mediator. 20 Now a mediator
is not just for one person alone, but God is
one. 21 Is the law therefore contrary to God's
promises? Absolutely not! For if the law had
been granted with the ability to give life, then
righteousness would certainly be on the basis of the law. 22 But the Scripture imprisoned
everything under sin's power,[G] so that the
promise might be given on the basis of faith
in Jesus Christ to those who believe. 23 Before
this faith came, we were confined under the
law, imprisoned until the coming faith was
revealed. 24 The law, then, was our guardian
until Christ, so that we could be justified by
faith. 25 But since that faith has come, we are
no longer under a guardian, 26 for through
faith you are all sons of God in Christ Jesus.

SONS AND HEIRS

27 For those of you who were baptized into Christ
have been clothed with Christ. 28 There is no
Jew or Greek, slave or free, male and female;
since you are all one in Christ Jesus. 29 And if
you belong to Christ, then you are Abraham's

4 seed, heirs according to the promise. 1 Now
I say that as long as the heir is a child, he
differs in no way from a slave, though he is
the owner of everything. 2 Instead, he is under
guardians and trustees until the time set by his
father. 3 In the same way we also, when we were

E Eternal Perspective | *God's Children*

GOD'S CHILDREN

"God sent his Son, born of a woman, born under the law, to redeem those under the law, so that we might receive adoption as sons." Galatians 4:4-5

Because growing numbers of people are adopting, more eyes are being opened to the beauty of this practice. What a profound picture of love and acceptance! In this case, a passionate couple doesn't suddenly discover that they're going to *have* a baby. No, the purposeful couple willfully decides they're going to *get* a child. Pregnancy is often a surprise, but adoption is always a choice.

Can you imagine what this experience is like for a child in an orphanage? To have smiling, kind strangers come along and say with sincerity, "We want you in our family. We choose you." You haven't done anything to warrant such acceptance, but you can see the love in their eyes.

This is what the Bible says God has done for us. In Christ, he comes to where we are, and says, "I choose you. I want you to be part of my big forever family." It sounds too good to be true. But it *is* true. And we need to let that truth—and not the pain and rejection we've experienced—govern how we see ourselves today.

For the next note on *Eternal Perspective*, see Ephesians 1:7.

[A] **3:12** Lv 18:5 [B] **3:13** Dt 21:23 [C] **3:15** Or *a human covenant that has been ratified* [D] **3:16** Gn 12:7; 13:15; 17:8; 24:7 [E] **3:17** Other mss add *in Christ* [F] **3:19** Or *because of transgressions* [G] **3:22** Lit *under sin*

children, were in slavery under the elements[A]
of the world. 4 When the time came to completion, God sent his Son, born of a woman, born
under the law, 5 to redeem those under the law,
so that we might receive adoption as sons. 6 And
because you are sons, God sent the Spirit of his
Son into our[B] hearts, crying, "*Abba*,[C] Father!"
7 So you are no longer a slave but a son, and if
a son, then God has made you an heir.

PAUL'S CONCERN FOR THE GALATIANS

8 But in the past, since you didn't know God,
you were enslaved to things[D] that by nature
are not gods. 9 But now, since you know God, or
rather have become known by God, how can
you turn back again to the weak and worthless elements? Do you want to be enslaved
to them all over again? 10 You are observing
special days, months, seasons, and years. 11 I
am fearful for you, that perhaps my labor for
you has been wasted.

12 I beg you, brothers and sisters: Become
like me, for I also became like you. You have
not wronged me; 13 you know[E] that previously I preached the gospel to you because of a
weakness of the flesh. 14 You did not despise or
reject me though my physical condition was
a trial for you.[F] On the contrary, you received
me as an angel of God, as Christ Jesus himself.

15 Where, then, is your blessing? For I testify
to you that, if possible, you would have torn
out your eyes and given them to me. 16 So then,
have I become your enemy because I told you
the truth? 17 They court you eagerly, but not for
good. They want to exclude you from me, so
that you would pursue them. 18 But it is always
good to be pursued[G] in a good manner — and
not just when I am with you. 19 My children, I
am again suffering labor pains for you until
Christ is formed in you. 20 I would like to be with
you right now and change my tone of voice,
because I don't know what to do about you.

SARAH AND HAGAR: TWO COVENANTS

21 Tell me, you who want to be under the law,
don't you hear the law? 22 For it is written that
Abraham had two sons, one by a slave and
the other by a free woman. 23 But the one by
the slave was born as a result of the flesh,
while the one by the free woman was born
through promise. 24 These things are being
taken figuratively, for the women represent
two covenants. One is from Mount Sinai and
bears children into slavery — this is Hagar.

Exercise of Faith | *Following God's Lead*

THE SPIRIT OF GOD

"If we live by the Spirit, let us also keep in step with the Spirit." Galatians 5:25

Paul says, "We live by the Spirit." In other words, no spiritual life—much less spiritual growth or health—happens apart from the gracious presence, leading, and power of the Holy Spirit of God.

The Spirit brings about spiritual birth (Jn 3). When that miracle happens, the Spirit not only makes us alive to God, he also takes up residence in our lives (Rm 8:9). From within, the Spirit then leads us into truth (Jn 16:13), pours out God's love in our hearts (Rm 5:5), empowers us to tell others about our faith (Ac 1:8), assures us that we belong to God (1Co 3:23), makes us holy (1Pt 1:2), and produces Christlike qualities in us (Gl 5:22-23).

And from within, the Spirit guides us. He wants us to join him in the work he is doing in the world. But in order for him to guide us, of course, we have to be guidable. That's like putting on the headset and listening to the tour guide.

In what situations do you sense the Spirit nudging you to take a certain action or to avoid doing something else? Follow his lead and watch what he does!

For the next note on *Exercise of Faith*, see Galatians 6:1.

[A] **4:3** Or *spirits*, or *principles* [B] **4:6** Other mss read *your* [C] **4:6** Aramaic for *father* [D] **4:8** Or *beings* [E] **4:12-13** Or [12] *Become like I am, because I — inasmuch as you are brothers and sisters — am not requesting anything of you. You wronged me.* [13] *You know* [F] **4:14** Other mss read *me* [G] **4:18** Lit *zealously courted*

are the ones who would compel you to be circumcised — but only to avoid being persecuted for the cross of Christ. [13] For even the circumcised don't keep the law themselves, and yet they want you to be circumcised in order to boast about your flesh. [14] But as for me, I will never boast about anything except the cross of our Lord Jesus Christ. The world has been crucified to me through the cross, and I to the world. [15] For[A] both circumcision and uncircumcision mean nothing; what matters instead is a new creation. [16] May peace come to all those who follow this standard, and mercy even to the Israel of God![B]

[17] From now on, let no one cause me trouble, because I bear on my body the marks of Jesus. [18] Brothers and sisters, the grace of our Lord Jesus Christ be with your spirit. Amen.

[A] **6:15** Other mss add *in Christ Jesus* [B] **6:16** Or *And for those who follow this standard, may peace and mercy be upon them, even upon the Israel of God*, or *And as many who will follow this standard, peace be upon them and mercy even upon the Israel of God.*

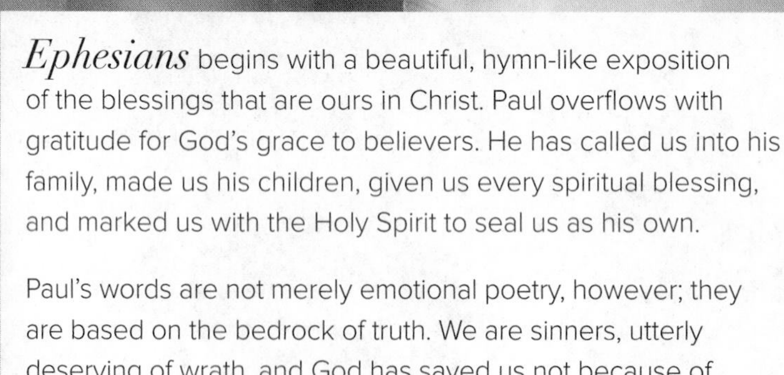

Ephesians begins with a beautiful, hymn-like exposition of the blessings that are ours in Christ. Paul overflows with gratitude for God's grace to believers. He has called us into his family, made us his children, given us every spiritual blessing, and marked us with the Holy Spirit to seal us as his own.

Paul's words are not merely emotional poetry, however; they are based on the bedrock of truth. We are sinners, utterly deserving of wrath, and God has saved us not because of anything we have done but because of his mercy. That is true for every believer. No matter what we have done or who we are, we are saved by God's grace and on equal footing with every other Christian, whether the world views us as better or worse. It is a message of hope and rest that brings soul-healing.

When we realize that we are sinners saved by grace, we will welcome others in humility and love, regardless of the external differences that may divide us. When we conduct ourselves in this way, our relationships will be restored. If you are experiencing conflict in your relationships or defeat in your spiritual life, let the book of Ephesians renew you as you focus on the reality of who you are in Christ.

GREETING

1 Paul, an apostle of Christ Jesus by God's will:
To the faithful saints in Christ Jesus[A] at
Ephesus.[B]
2 Grace to you and peace from God our Father and the Lord Jesus Christ.

GOD'S RICH BLESSINGS

3 Blessed is the God and Father of our Lord
Jesus Christ, who has blessed us with every
spiritual blessing in the heavens in Christ.
4 For he chose us in him, before the foundation of the world, to be holy and blameless
in love before him.[C] 5 He predestined us to
be adopted as sons through Jesus Christ for
himself, according to the good pleasure of
his will, 6 to the praise of his glorious grace
that he lavished on us in the Beloved One.
7 In him we have redemption through his
blood, the forgiveness of our trespasses, according to the riches of his grace 8 that he richly
poured out on us with all wisdom and understanding.[D] 9 He made known to us the mystery of
his will, according to his good pleasure that he
purposed in Christ 10 as a plan for the right time[E]
— to bring everything together in Christ, both
things in heaven and things on earth in him.
11 In him we have also received an inheritance,[F] because we were predestined according
to the plan of the one who works out everything in agreement with the purpose of his
will, 12 so that we who had already put our
hope in Christ might bring praise to his glory.
13 In him you also were sealed with the
promised Holy Spirit when you heard the
word of truth, the gospel of your salvation,
and when you believed. 14 The Holy Spirit is
the down payment of our inheritance, until the redemption of the possession, to the
praise of his glory.

PRAYER FOR SPIRITUAL INSIGHT

15 This is why, since I heard about your faith in
the Lord Jesus and your love for all the saints,
16 I never stop giving thanks for you as I remember you in my prayers. 17 I pray that the
God of our Lord Jesus Christ, the glorious Father,[G] would give you the Spirit[H] of wisdom
and revelation in the knowledge of him. 18 I
pray that the eyes of your heart may be enlightened so that you may know what is the
hope of his calling, what is the wealth of his
glorious inheritance in the saints, 19 and what
is the immeasurable greatness of his power

Rest and Reflection | *Resting in Christ*

YOU'RE IN!

"Paul, an apostle of Christ Jesus by God's will: To the faithful saints in Christ Jesus at Ephesus." Ephesians 1:1

To be "in" something means to be immersed in and completely affected by it. Think of the beaming freshman who just got an invitation to be in a certain sorority. Within twenty-four hours, she'll have Greek letters painted, glued, or embroidered on everything she owns! Or think of the person in love. Suddenly, the whole world is wonderful and beautiful. Being "in" anything—trouble, training, the witness protection program—means one's whole perspective and lifestyle will be impacted by that reality.

Fourteen times in the short letter of Ephesians, Paul talks about believers being "in Christ" or "in Christ Jesus." And the phrase "in him" appears nine times!

The implications are clear: All that Jesus is and all that he has done for us are ours. We may be in the world, but far deeper than that, we are "in Christ." Paul's great declaration is that "God . . . has blessed us with every spiritual blessing in the heavens *in Christ*" (Eph 1:3).

Today you might be *in* a bad mood or *in* rush-hour traffic or *in* trouble at work. Ask God to help you remember the bigger and better truth: You are "in Christ Jesus."

For the next note on *Rest and Reflection*, see 1 Timothy 1:15.

[A] **1:1** Or *to the saints, the believers in Christ Jesus* [B] **1:1** Other mss omit *at Ephesus* [C] **1:4** Or *in his sight. In love* [D] **1:8** Or *on us. With all wisdom and understanding* [E] **1:10** Or *the fulfillment of times* [F] **1:11** Or *In him we are also an inheritance,* [G] **1:17** Or *the Father of glory* [H] **1:17** Or *a spirit*

toward us who believe, according to the mighty working of his strength.

GOD'S POWER IN CHRIST

20 He exercised this power in Christ by raising him from the dead and seating him at his right hand in the heavens — 21 far above every ruler and authority, power and dominion, and every title given,[A] not only in this age but also in the one to come. 22 And **he subjected everything under his feet**[B] and appointed him[C] as head over everything for the church, 23 which is his body, the fullness of the one who fills all things in every way.

FROM DEATH TO LIFE

2 And you were dead in your trespasses and sins 2 in which you previously lived according to the ways of this world, according to the ruler of the power of the air, the spirit now working in the disobedient.[D] 3 We too all previously lived among them in our fleshly desires, carrying out the inclinations of our flesh and thoughts, and we were by nature children under wrath as the others were also. 4 But God, who is rich in mercy, because of his great love that he had for us,[E] 5 made us alive with Christ even though we were dead in trespasses. You are saved by grace! 6 He also raised us up with him and seated us with him in the heavens in Christ Jesus, 7 so that in the coming ages he might display the immeasurable riches of his grace through his kindness to us in Christ Jesus. 8 For you are saved by grace through faith, and this is not from yourselves; it is God's gift — 9 not from works, so that no one can boast. 10 For we are his workmanship, created in Christ Jesus for good works, which God prepared ahead of time for us to do.

UNITY IN CHRIST

11 So then, remember that at one time you were Gentiles in the flesh — called "the uncircumcised" by those called "the circumcised," which is done in the flesh by human hands. 12 At that time you were without Christ, excluded from the citizenship of Israel, and foreigners to the covenants of promise, without hope and without God in

Eternal Perspective | *Redemption/Salvation*

ALL IS FORGIVEN

"In him we have redemption through his blood, the forgiveness of our trespasses, according to the riches of his grace." Ephesians 1:7

Many people have something in their past they can't quite shake. Not a thoughtless, accidental mistake, but a deliberate, foolish choice. Like a ghost, the memory haunts them. Always, they feel huge regret. And with the memory comes the nagging question, "Could God really forgive and forget *that*?"

In the opening to this letter, Paul lists our blessings in Christ. He seems almost breathless, as though he can't get the words out fast enough. Halfway through his list, he speaks of "the forgiveness of our trespasses."

Notice it's not "our *minor* trespasses" or "some of our less-grievous offenses." It's trespasses, period. In other words, all of them. The meanest, most selfish, ugliest thing you ever did is forgiven by Jesus.

How? "Through his blood." Why? Because of "the riches of his grace."

Our problem is that we think our sins are vast like the ocean. In truth, God's grace is the ocean, and our sins, even our worst ones, are mere grains of sand in comparison.

Dare to believe this today, "In him, I have the forgiveness of *all* my trespasses."

For the next note on *Eternal Perspective*, see Ephesians 2:4-5.

[A] **1:21** Lit *every name named* [B] **1:22** Ps 8:6 [C] **1:22** Lit *gave him* [D] **2:2** Lit *sons of disobedience* [E] **2:4** Lit *love with which he loved us*

the world. 13 But now in Christ Jesus, you
who were far away have been brought near
by the blood of Christ. 14 For he is our peace,
who made both groups one and tore down
the dividing wall of hostility. In his flesh,
15 he made of no effect the law consisting
of commands and expressed in regulations,
so that he might create in himself one new
man from the two, resulting in peace. 16 He
did this so that he might reconcile both to
God in one body through the cross by which
he put the hostility to death.[A] 17 He came and

Eternal Perspective | *God's Mercy*

THANKFUL!

"But God, who is rich in mercy, because of his great love that he had for us, made us alive with Christ even though we were dead in trespasses. You are saved by grace!" Ephesians 2:4-5

The next time you're down in the dumps, remember these words. Try to read them without smiling. You can't. It's the ultimate pick-me-up. Look carefully at what it says about God. He's "rich in mercy." He has "great love . . . for us."

How great is this divine love? Well, it came to us "even though we were dead in trespasses." Despite the fact that humanity turned away from the One who is life itself and ran headlong into sin and death, God "made us alive with Christ." In other words, when we were helpless and hopeless, God resurrected us! Paul, who must have been thinking about his own encounter with Jesus on the Damascus Road, puts it this way, "You are saved by grace!"

Our salvation is hard to fathom. But don't just ponder it, praise God for it. A sagging spirit can be revived by showing gratitude. The more we express our appreciation to God for rescuing us, the more thankful, and less despondent, we'll feel.

For the next note on *Eternal Perspective*, see Ephesians 2:10.

Eternal Perspective | *Personal Value/Worth*

GOD'S MASTERPIECE

"For we are his workmanship, created in Christ Jesus for good works, which God prepared ahead of time for us to do." Ephesians 2:10

You may not feel very special, but according to this verse, you—along with all believers—are God's "workmanship." The Greek word Paul uses here is the word from which we get our English word "poem." In other words, you are the product of the ultimate artist. You are God's one-of-a-kind masterpiece. Imagine that: the Mona Lisa, Shakespeare's sonnets, the Sistine Chapel, and . . . you!

The good news gets better. God created you "in Christ Jesus for good works." You're not only the handiwork of a perfect God, but God has something good and important for you to do.

So, enough of those negative thoughts of being worthless. (Is Michelangelo's "David" worthless?) And enough of feeling like your life is an accident. God made you purposefully. He made you to make a real difference.

Visualize yourself as God's workmanship. Then pray for the wisdom and strength to carry out the good works "which God prepared ahead of time" for you to do.

For the next note on *Eternal Perspective*, see Ephesians 3:1.

[A] **2:16** Or *death in himself*

proclaimed the good news of peace to you
who were far away and peace to those who
were near. 18 For through him we both have
access in one spirit to the Father. 19 So then
you are no longer foreigners and strangers, but fellow citizens with the saints, and
members of God's household, 20 built on the
foundation of the apostles and prophets, with
Christ Jesus himself as the cornerstone. 21 In
him the whole building, being put together,
grows into a holy temple in the Lord. 22 In him
you are also being built together for God's
dwelling in the Spirit.

PAUL'S MINISTRY TO THE GENTILES

3 For this reason, I, Paul, the prisoner of
Christ Jesus on behalf of you Gentiles —
2 you have heard, haven't you, about the administration of God's grace that he gave to
me for you? 3 The mystery was made known
to me by revelation, as I have briefly written above. 4 By reading this you are able to
understand my insight into the mystery of
Christ. 5 This was not made known to people[A]
in other generations as it is now revealed to
his holy apostles and prophets by the Spirit:
6 The Gentiles are coheirs, members of the
same body, and partners in the promise in
Christ Jesus through the gospel. 7 I was made
a servant of this gospel by the gift of God's
grace that was given to me by the working
of his power.

8 This grace was given to me — the least of
all the saints — to proclaim to the Gentiles
the incalculable riches of Christ, 9 and to shed
light for all about the administration of the
mystery hidden for ages in God who created
all things. 10 This is so that God's multi-faceted
wisdom may now be made known through
the church to the rulers and authorities in
the heavens. 11 This is according to his eternal purpose accomplished in Christ Jesus
our Lord. 12 In him we have boldness and
confident access through faith in him.[B] 13 So
then I ask you not to be discouraged over
my afflictions on your behalf, for they are
your glory.

PRAYER FOR SPIRITUAL POWER

14 For this reason I kneel before the Father[C]
15 from whom every family in heaven and on
earth is named. 16 I pray that he may grant
you, according to the riches of his glory, to
be strengthened with power in your inner
being through his Spirit, 17 and that Christ may
dwell in your hearts through faith. I pray that
you, being rooted and firmly established in
love, 18 may be able to comprehend with all the
saints what is the length and width, height and
depth of God's love, 19 and to know Christ's love

Eternal Perspective | *God's Purposes*

LIFE ROLES

"For this reason, I, Paul, the prisoner of Christ Jesus on behalf of you Gentiles . . ." Ephesians 3:1

When Paul wrote this letter, he was imprisoned in Rome—the globe-trotting apostle, incarcerated. But Paul never viewed himself as a victim of a vast Jewish conspiracy or at the mercy of his Roman captors. He described himself as "the prisoner of Christ Jesus." With this phrase, Paul was essentially saying, "Jesus is Lord, and I'm in jail; therefore, he must want me serving him right here in my current role of 'prisoner.'"

This perspective helps us navigate our own difficult seasons and assorted roles in life. Instead of merely seeing yourself as a parent, employee, boss, coach, volunteer, citizen, or student, you begin to see yourself in these roles *for Christ's sake*. So you're not just a neighbor you're a neighbor "of [belonging to] Christ." Or you're a cancer patient "for Christ."

No matter what our situation or place in life, this sort or mind-set can restore a sense of sanity and dignity. It reminds us that the Lord has us exactly where he wants us.

For the next note on *Eternal Perspective*, see Ephesians 3:17-19.

[A] **3:5** Lit *to the sons of men* [B] **3:12** Or *through his faithfulness* [C] **3:14** Other mss add *of our Lord Jesus Christ*

that surpasses knowledge, so that you may be
filled with all the fullness of God.
20 Now to him who is able to do above and
beyond all that we ask or think according to
the power that works in us — 21 to him be
glory in the church and in Christ Jesus to all
generations, forever and ever. Amen.

UNITY AND DIVERSITY IN THE BODY OF CHRIST

4 Therefore I, the prisoner in the Lord, urge
you to live worthy of the calling you have
received, 2 with all humility and gentleness,
with patience, bearing with one another in
love, 3 making every effort to keep the unity of
the Spirit through the bond of peace. 4 There
is one body and one Spirit — just as you were
called to one hope[A] at your calling — 5 one
Lord, one faith, one baptism, 6 one God and
Father of all, who is above all and through
all and in all.
7 Now grace was given to each one of us according to the measure of Christ's gift. 8 For
it says:

When he ascended on high,
he took the captives captive;
he gave gifts to people.[B]

9 But what does "he ascended" mean except
that he[C] also descended to the lower parts
of the earth?[D] 10 The one who descended is
also the one who ascended far above all the
heavens, to fill all things. 11 And he himself
gave some to be apostles, some prophets,
some evangelists, some pastors and teachers,
12 equipping the saints for the work of ministry,
to build up the body of Christ, 13 until we all
reach unity in the faith and in the knowledge
of God's Son, growing into maturity with a
stature measured by Christ's fullness. 14 Then
we will no longer be little children, tossed by
the waves and blown around by every wind of
teaching, by human cunning with cleverness
in the techniques of deceit. 15 But speaking the
truth in love, let us grow in every way into
him who is the head — Christ. 16 From him the
whole body, fitted and knit together by every
supporting ligament, promotes the growth
of the body for building up itself in love by
the proper working of each individual part.

LIVING THE NEW LIFE

17 Therefore, I say this and testify in the Lord:
You should no longer live as the Gentiles live,
in the futility of their thoughts. 18 They are
darkened in their understanding, excluded
from the life of God, because of the ignorance
that is in them and because[E] of the hardness

Eternal Perspective | *God's Love*

THE PHYSICS OF DIVINE LOVE

"I pray that you, being rooted and firmly established in love, may be able to comprehend with all the saints what is the length and width, height and depth of God's love, and to know Christ's love that surpasses knowledge, so that you may be filled with all the fullness of God." Ephesians 3:17-19

"My goal this semester," the professor smiles, "is to help you understand all these wonderful new discoveries, that, quite honestly, even the world's top physicists don't understand." The class laughs.

In a sense, this is the kind of paradoxical request Paul prays for his readers: that they might "know Christ's love that surpasses knowledge." As prayers go, can you think of a more exciting or worthwhile one? Suppose God said yes. Imagine being rooted and grounded deeply in the miraculous love of God. Imagine receiving ever-more-glorious glimpses—and experiences—of the infinite love of God. It's divine affection that fills the universe. In truth, it's higher and deeper than the cosmos itself.

Want to see your soul and your relationships restored? Make this most paradoxical of prayers your own. Ask the One who is love itself (1Jn 4:8) to help you comprehend the incomprehensible.

For the next note on *Eternal Perspective*, see Ephesians 4:1.

[A] **4:4** Lit *called in one hope* [B] **4:8** Ps 68:18 [C] **4:9** Other mss add *first* [D] **4:9** Or *the lower parts, namely, the earth* [E] **4:18** Or *in them because*

of their hearts. 19 They became callous and
gave themselves over to promiscuity for the
practice of every kind of impurity with a desire for more and more.[A]
20 But that is not how you came to know
Christ, 21 assuming you heard about him and
were taught by him, as the truth is in Jesus,
22 to take off[B] your former way of life, the old
self that is corrupted by deceitful desires, 23 to
be renewed[C] in the spirit of your minds, 24 and
to put on[D] the new self, the one created according to God's likeness in righteousness
and purity of the truth.
25 Therefore, putting away lying, **speak the
truth, each one to his neighbor,**[E] because we
are members of one another. 26 **Be angry and
do not sin.**[F] Don't let the sun go down on your
anger, 27 and don't give the devil an opportunity. 28 Let the thief no longer steal. Instead,
he is to do honest work with his own hands,
so that he has something to share with anyone in need. 29 No foul language should come
from your mouth, but only what is good for
building up someone in need,[G] so that it gives
grace to those who hear. 30 And don't grieve
God's Holy Spirit. You were sealed by him[H]
for the day of redemption. 31 Let all bitterness,
anger and wrath, shouting and slander be removed from you, along with all malice. 32 And
be kind and compassionate to one another,
forgiving one another, just as God also forgave
you[I] in Christ.

5 Therefore, be imitators of God, as dearly loved children, 2 and walk in love, as
Christ also loved us and gave himself for us, a
sacrificial and fragrant offering to God. 3 But
sexual immorality and any impurity or greed
should not even be heard of[J] among you, as
is proper for saints. 4 Obscene and foolish
talking or crude joking are not suitable, but
rather giving thanks. 5 For know and recognize this: Every sexually immoral or impure
or greedy person, who is an idolater, does
not have an inheritance in the kingdom of
Christ and of God.

LIGHT VERSUS DARKNESS

6 Let no one deceive you with empty arguments,
for God's wrath is coming on the disobedient[K]
because of these things. 7 Therefore, do not
become their partners. 8 For you were once
darkness, but now you are light in the Lord.
Live as children of light — 9 for the fruit of the
light[L] consists of all goodness, righteousness,

Eternal Perspective | *Identity in Christ*

BRAND NEW

"Therefore I, the prisoner in the Lord, urge you to live worthy of the calling you have received." Ephesians 4:1

In the first half of his letter to the Ephesians, Paul asks the "What?" question: *What has God done for believers in Christ?* We see, among many other spiritual riches and blessings, that we are chosen and loved by God (Eph 1:4; 2:4), adopted into God's own household (1:5; 2:19), forgiven (1:7), indwelt by the Spirit (1:13), made alive spiritually (2:5), saved by grace through faith (2:8), brought near to God (2:13), and granted unfathomable power (3:20).

The incarcerated apostle then uses the final three chapters of his letter to ask and answer the "So what?" question: *In light of all that God has done for us, how should we live?*

In short, Paul's answer is this verse: "live worthy of the calling you have received." You're new people! Why would you go on living in old ways? Live out your new identity!

You will have no quicker way to lose heart than to forget who you are in Christ. But you'll have no quicker way to a restored perspective than to remember that God has made you brand new.

For the next note on *Eternal Perspective*, see Philippians 1:6.

[A] **4:19** Lit *with greediness* [B] **4:21-22** Or *Jesus. This means: take off* (as a command) [C] **4:22-23** Or *desires; renew* (as a command) [D] **4:23-24** Or *minds; and put on* (as a command) [E] **4:25** Zch 8:16 [F] **4:26** Ps 4:4 [G] **4:29** Lit *for the building up of the need* [H] **4:30** Or *Spirit, by whom you were sealed* [I] **4:32** Other mss read *us* [J] **5:3** Or *be named* [K] **5:6** Lit *sons of disobedience* [L] **5:9** Other mss read *fruit of the Spirit*

and truth — [10] testing what is pleasing to the
Lord. [11] Don't participate in the fruitless works
of darkness, but instead expose them. [12] For
it is shameful even to mention what is done
by them in secret. [13] Everything exposed by
the light is made visible, [14] for what makes
everything visible is light. Therefore it is said:

Get up, sleeper, and rise up
from the dead,
and Christ will shine on you.

CONSISTENCY IN THE CHRISTIAN LIFE

[15] Pay careful attention, then, to how you live —
not as unwise people but as wise — [16] making

Relationships | *Building Positive Relationships*

DRESSING FOR RELATIONAL SUCCESS

"Let all bitterness, anger and wrath, shouting and slander be removed from you, along with all malice." Ephesians 4:31

Sometimes we talk about the first-century church in glowing, unrealistic terms. We remember all the great miracles but forget all the fierce struggles. The result is that our recollections are more an exercise in revisionist history and spiritual nostalgia than they are in truth.

So, what is the truth about the early church? Well, notice what Paul tells the Ephesian believers here: Stop being so bitter and angry at each other! Quit all your fighting and lying!

This reminds us that in every generation—even after they've been redeemed—are still capable of some very ungodly reactions. In other words, we're not the first generation of Christians to struggle relationally.

How can we experience renewed, restored relationships? Back up a few verses: "take off your former way of life" (Eph 4:22), "be renewed in the spirit of your minds" (4:23), "put on the new self" (4:24).

Ask God to help you dress for relational success by changing your mind and attitude and living his way.

For the next note on *Relationships*, see Ephesians 5:21.

Exercise of Faith | *Making Right Choices/Priorities/Values*

PAYING ATTENTION?

"Pay careful attention, then, to how you live—not as unwise people but as wise." Ephesians 5:15

Everyone is paying careful attention to something—the size of the lottery jackpot, the powerful hurricane brewing off the coast, the mysterious rash on a child, the saber-rattling between two nuclear superpowers. Maybe you choose to focus on manicuring your yard. Or you continue to look at the reflection you see staring back at you in the health club mirror. Or you monitor your finances the way an early bird watches an early worm.

Paul's instruction here is to "pay careful attention . . . to how you live." He means lifestyle choices, our interactions with others, our words, and behind all that, the motives that drive us. He adds that this is what wise people do.

Good looks or a good living—nothing is wrong with such things. But that's just it, they're *things*. The best things in life aren't things at all. What is *best* in life? Life itself, a wise, good, God-honoring life. Pay attention to yours!

For the next note on *Exercise of Faith*, see Philippians 1:29.

the most of the time,[A] because the days are evil. 17 So don't be foolish, but understand what the Lord's will is. 18 And don't get drunk with wine, which leads to reckless living, but be filled by the Spirit: 19 speaking to one another in psalms, hymns, and spiritual songs, singing and making music with your heart to the Lord, 20 giving thanks always for everything to God the Father in the name of our Lord Jesus Christ, 21 submitting to one another in the fear of Christ.

WIVES AND HUSBANDS

22 Wives, submit[B] to your husbands as to the Lord, 23 because the husband is the head of the wife as Christ is the head of the church. He is the Savior of the body. 24 Now as the church submits to Christ, so also wives are to submit to their husbands in everything. 25 Husbands, love your wives, just as Christ loved the church and gave himself for her 26 to make her holy, cleansing[C] her with the washing of water by the word. 27 He did this to present the church to himself in splendor, without spot or wrinkle or anything like that, but holy and blameless. 28 In the same way, husbands are to love their wives as their own bodies. He who loves his wife loves himself. 29 For no one ever hates his own flesh but provides and cares for it, just as Christ does for the church, 30 since we are members of his body.[D] 31 **For this reason a man will leave his father and mother and be joined to his wife, and the two will become one flesh.**[E] 32 This mystery is profound, but I am talking about Christ and the church. 33 To sum up, each one of you is to love his wife as himself, and the wife is to respect her husband.

CHILDREN AND PARENTS

6 Children, obey your parents in the Lord, because this is right. 2 **Honor your father and mother**, which is the first commandment with a promise, 3 **so that it may go well with you and that you may have a long life in the land.**[F,G] 4 Fathers, don't stir up anger in your children, but bring them up in the training and instruction of the Lord.

SLAVES AND MASTERS

5 Slaves, obey your human[H] masters with fear and trembling, in the sincerity of your heart, as you would Christ. 6 Don't work only while being watched, as people-pleasers, but as slaves of Christ, do God's will from your heart. 7 Serve with a good attitude, as to the Lord and not to people, 8 knowing that whatever good each one does, slave or free, he will receive

Relationships | *Submitting to Others*

THE S-WORD

"Submitting to one another in the fear of Christ." Ephesians 5:21

Christians are to engage in a lifestyle of "submitting to one another." For most, the immediate reaction is a cold shiver and the thought, *Uh, thanks, but I think I'll pass.*

Submission is a word that needs an image makeover. For most, it calls to mind tyrannical bosses and the mousy people they bulldoze. Or we think of that grade school bully twisting our arm on the playground until we cried. Submit? Be somebody's doormat or punching bag? We'd rather get a root canal!

This isn't the *submission* Paul is calling for. Biblical submission is voluntarily putting ourselves under someone else. It's what Jesus did—taking on a servant mind-set and setting aside his privileges and "rights." It's humbly treating others as more important than us (Php 2:3). Instead of "looking out for number one," the submissive person looks out for the interests of others (2:4).

The way of the world is to think, "How can I get the upper hand and make these people do my bidding?" The way of the restored soul is to think, "How can I subordinate my agenda to the needs of those around me and serve them well?"

For the next note on *Relationships*, see Ephesians 5:33.

[A] **5:16** Lit *buying back the time* [B] **5:22** Other mss omit *submit* [C] **5:26** Or *having cleansed* [D] **5:30** Other mss add *and of his flesh and of his bones* [E] **5:31** Gn 2:24 [F] **6:3** Or *life on the earth* [G] **6:2-3** Ex 20:12 [H] **6:5** Lit *according to the flesh*

this back from the Lord. 9 And masters, treat your slaves the same way, without threatening them, because you know that both their Master and yours is in heaven, and there is no favoritism with him.

CHRISTIAN WARFARE

10 Finally, be strengthened by the Lord and by his vast strength. 11 Put on the full armor of God so that you can stand against the schemes of the devil. 12 For our struggle is not against

Relationships | *Relating to Spouse/Marriage*

HEALTHIER, HAPPIER MARRIAGES

"To sum up, each one of you is to love his wife as himself, and the wife is to respect her husband." Ephesians 5:33

Marriage may not be easy, but at least it's not complicated. Here in one short verse, Paul sums up our marital job descriptions: husbands, love; wives, respect.

Love and respect. If that's all marriage involves, why do so many find it so tough?

Because the passage has no asterisks, fine print, or loopholes. The commands aren't "Guys, love your wives *so long as* they remain lovable. Or "New bride, respect your husband *until* the day he does something amazingly stupid and irresponsible." No, the commands are unconditional. Love . . . respect, period. The end. *This* is why it's difficult. A secret must be there, right?

Yes, and it's not a "secret." Back up a few verses to Ephesians 5:18. Do you see the command that comes before the commands to "love" and "respect"? It's "be filled by the Spirit."

In other words, only as we allow the Spirit of the living God to control and empower us are husbands and wives able to interact in healthy and happy ways. In truth, all relationships can be improved by a Spirit-filled heart.

Ask God to give you the desire and power to love and respect.

For the next note on *Relationships*, see Ephesians 6:4.

Relationships | *Relating to Children*

RESTORING PARENT-CHILD RELATIONSHIPS

"Fathers, don't stir up anger in your children, but bring them up in the training and instruction of the Lord." Ephesians 6:4

Mike is fighting back tears. "My son is convinced I hate him. When he stormed out of the house last night he screamed at me, 'You don't approve of anything I've ever done!' He's *so* angry with me. And honestly, I can't blame him. I *have been* too demanding. I've been worse than a drill sergeant."

Maybe you're one of the millions of dads or moms with a less-than-great relationship with an older child.

Though you can't get a do-over and alter the past, you can do right today and going forward. Did you crush your kids' spirits? Did you nitpick them to death? Humble yourself. Ask forgiveness for the times you exasperated them. If you were overly critical or guilty of favoritism, if you created a million hoops for them to jump through and then communicated conditional love, the first step to a restored relationship is to acknowledge your failings. Take responsibility. The ten most powerful words you can say are: "I was wrong. I'm *so* sorry. Will you forgive me?"

And if you doubt God's power to heal and restore a damaged relationship, reread Ephesians 3:20.

For the next note on *Relationships*, see Ephesians 6:19.

flesh and blood, but against the rulers, against
the authorities, against the cosmic powers
of this darkness, against evil, spiritual forces in the heavens. 13 For this reason take up
the full armor of God, so that you may be
able to resist in the evil day, and having prepared everything, to take your stand. 14 Stand,
therefore, with truth like a belt around your
waist, righteousness like armor on your chest,
15 and your feet sandaled with readiness for
the gospel of peace. 16 In every situation take
up the shield of faith with which you can
extinguish all the flaming arrows of the evil
one. 17 Take the helmet of salvation and the
sword of the Spirit — which is the word of
God. 18 Pray at all times in the Spirit with every prayer and request, and stay alert with
all perseverance and intercession for all the
saints. 19 Pray also for me, that the message
may be given to me when I open my mouth
to make known with boldness the mystery
of the gospel. 20 For this I am an ambassador
in chains. Pray that I might be bold enough
to speak about it as I should.

PAUL'S FAREWELL

21 Tychicus, our dearly loved brother and faithful servant[A] in the Lord, will tell you all the
news about me so that you may be informed.
22 I am sending him to you for this very reason,
to let you know how we are and to encourage
your hearts.

23 Peace to the brothers and sisters, and love
with faith, from God the Father and the Lord
Jesus Christ. 24 Grace be with all who have
undying love for our Lord Jesus Christ.[B,C]

Relationships | *Admitting Weakness*

PRAY FOR ME

"Pray also for me." Ephesians 6:19

We can look at people who seem to have life all figured out and think, *Am I the only person in the world who is barely keeping my head above the water?*

Entertain such thoughts for long and we begin to feel sheepish. *I'm not about to admit my struggles to anyone!* So we hide our weaknesses and cover up our needs. *Ask someone to pray for me? No way!* When someone asks how we're doing, we smile and lie, "Great! I'm just great!"

Paul wasn't about to fall into this trap. After encouraging the church at Ephesus to be mighty in prayer, he added, "Pray also for me." Granted, he was asking for prayer that he might be a bold witness for Christ in his imprisonment. But even this noble request was an admission of weakness. It was a plea for help by a renowned Christian leader: "I'm not as strong as you might think. I'd appreciate it if you would lift me up."

What a great example for us! Paul shows that there's no shame—in fact, there's great wisdom—in admitting, "I'm feeling shaky. I need strength. I need your prayers."

Whom could you ask to pray for you today?

For the next note on *Relationships*, see Colossians 4:5-6.

[A] **6:21** Or *deacon* [B] **6:24** Other mss add *Amen.* [C] **6:24** Lit *all who love our Lord Jesus Christ in incorruption*

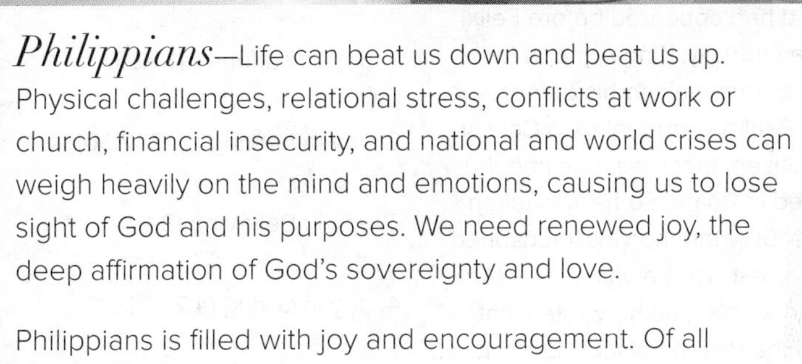

Philippians—Life can beat us down and beat us up. Physical challenges, relational stress, conflicts at work or church, financial insecurity, and national and world crises can weigh heavily on the mind and emotions, causing us to lose sight of God and his purposes. We need renewed joy, the deep affirmation of God's sovereignty and love.

Philippians is filled with joy and encouragement. Of all people, Paul could have been filled with despair, considering his Roman confinement and path to get there. Called to spread the good news, Paul had endured unrelenting hardships and persecutions in a malicious and hostile culture. Yet he tells the first-century recipients of this letter—the believers at Philippi—to rejoice with him, even if he were to be killed for his faith in Christ (2:17-18). And regardless of their circumstances, they should "Rejoice in the Lord always. I will say it again: Rejoice!" (4:4).

As you read this small and powerful letter, hear Paul's words and be encouraged; hear God's message and be filled with joy.

PHILIPPIANS

AUTHOR: The apostle Paul

DATE WRITTEN: Around AD 60

ORIGINAL AUDIENCE: Believers in Philippi

SETTING: Written in Rome, while Paul was imprisoned. Paul had been arrested in Jerusalem and had appeared before Felix, Festus, and, eventually, King Agrippa (Ac 26:1-32). Just before making his defense before Agrippa, Paul had appealed to Caesar. As a Roman citizen, that meant he had the right to be tried in Rome. So he was taken to Rome (26:1-16) where he was imprisoned under house arrest while awaiting trial (Ac 28:30-31). During this time he wrote what are known as the Prison Epistles: Ephesians, Philippians, Colossians, and Philemon.

PURPOSE FOR WRITING: To encourage and strengthen the Philippian believers and thank them for their gift. Paul and Silas had planted the church in Philippi during the second missionary journey in AD 51 (Ac 16:9-40). Paul felt very close to this church, and they enjoyed a strong relationship, so much so that they had taken up a collection and had sent it to him in Rome.

OUTLINE:

1. Joy in Suffering (1:1-26)

2. Joy in Serving (1:27–2:30)

3. Joy in Believing (3:1–4:1)

4. Joy in Giving (4:2-23)

KEY VERSE:

"I am sure of this, that he who started a good work in you will carry it on to completion until the day of Christ Jesus." —Philippians 1:6

RESTORATION THEMES

R	Rest and Reflection	*For the next note, see 1 Timothy 1:15.*
E	Eternal Perspective	*God's Purposes—Philippians 1:6* *God's Work in Us—2:12-13* *Positive Focus—2:14* *Forward Look—3:13-14* *Biblical Joy—4:4*
S	Support	*For the next note, see Hebrews 3:13.*
T	Thanksgiving and Contentment	*Contentment— Philippians 4:12-13*
O	Other-centeredness	*Being Unselfish—2:3-4*
R	Relationships	*For the next note, see Colossians 4:6.*
E	Exercise of Faith	*Enduring Suffering— Philippians 1:29* *Knowing Christ—3:7-8* *Praying—4:6-7*

GREETING

1 Paul and Timothy, servants of Christ Jesus:
To all the saints in Christ Jesus who are in
Philippi, including the overseers and deacons.
2 Grace to you and peace from God our Father and the Lord Jesus Christ.

THANKSGIVING AND PRAYER

3 I give thanks to my God for every remembrance of you,[A] 4 always praying with joy for
all of you in my every prayer, 5 because of your
partnership in the gospel from the first day
until now. 6 I am sure of this, that he who started
a good work in you[B] will carry it on to completion until the day of Christ Jesus. 7 Indeed,
it is right for me to think this way about all of
you, because I have you in my heart,[C] and you
are all partners with me in grace, both in my
imprisonment and in the defense and confirmation of the gospel. 8 For God is my witness,
how deeply I miss all of you with the affection
of Christ Jesus. 9 And I pray this: that your love
will keep on growing in knowledge and every
kind of discernment, 10 so that you may approve
the things that are superior and may be pure
and blameless in the day of Christ, 11 filled with
the fruit of righteousness that comes through
Jesus Christ to the glory and praise of God.

ADVANCE OF THE GOSPEL

12 Now I want you to know, brothers and
sisters, that what has happened to me has
actually advanced the gospel, 13 so that it
has become known throughout the whole
imperial guard, and to everyone else, that
my imprisonment is because I am in Christ.
14 Most of the brothers have gained confidence in the Lord from my imprisonment
and dare even more to speak the word[D] fear-
lessly. 15 To be sure, some preach Christ out of
envy and rivalry, but others out of good will.
16 These preach out of love, knowing that I
am appointed for the defense of the gospel;
17 the others proclaim Christ out of selfish
ambition, not sincerely, thinking that they
will cause me trouble in my imprisonment.
18 What does it matter? Only that in every way,
whether from false motives or true, Christ
is proclaimed, and in this I rejoice. Yes, and
I will continue to rejoice 19 because I know
this will lead to my salvation[E] through your
prayers and help from the Spirit of Jesus
Christ. 20 My eager expectation and hope is
that I will not be ashamed about anything, but
that now as always, with all courage, Christ
will be highly honored in my body, whether
by life or by death.

Eternal Perspective | *God's Purposes*

PARDON OUR PROGRESS

"I am sure of this, that he who started a good work in you will carry it on to completion until the day of Christ Jesus." *Philippians 1:6*

Did you think you'd be further along in the faith by now? More peaceful. Less susceptible to envy. More joyful? More patient? Perhaps you find yourself wondering: *Why do I find loving certain people so difficult?* Or, *Why do I struggle with forgiving people who have wronged me?*

Here's some encouragement: You're under construction! You're in process! The Almighty who "started a good work in you will carry it on to completion." If you're searching for a promise to cling to, that's as good a guarantee as you'll ever find! God's not done with you! In fact, you're right on schedule!

Instead of focusing today on how far you still have to go, look back and see how far God has already brought you. Think of the changes God has made in your thoughts and desires, attitudes and actions over the last year or (perhaps) decade.

God always finishes what he starts. Always. And you should expect some mess while you're under construction.

For the next note on *Eternal Perspective*, see Philippians 2:12-13.

[A] **1:3** Or *for your every remembrance of me* [B] **1:6** Or *work among you* [C] **1:7** Or *because you have me in your heart*
[D] **1:14** Other mss add *of God* [E] **1:19** Or *vindication*

My Story | Cara

I am twenty-nine years old, and life is good. It hasn't always been that way, though. At age sixteen I was an avid drug user and drinker. I didn't know anything about the Lord, although when I was a child, my mother had me on the church bus every Sunday to get me out of her hair for a couple of hours. Not until I was about twenty and walking home one evening from one of the bars I frequented, that a bus full of Christians asked if I needed a ride. I agreed, and they led me to the Lord.

For years after that, I didn't go to church or build any relationship with God. I still did drugs and drank. One day, I felt I had hit rock bottom and needed help. I remembered how I had felt on that bus when those people had introduced me to Christ. To convince me that I needed help as a sinner hadn't taken much. What I didn't realize at the time was that when I invited Jesus into my life, he actually came in. Even though I felt like I was starting over, I cried out to the Lord, and he was there for me. Eventually, he freed me from all drugs. I have been clean for six years, praise God. I know I couldn't have quit on my own, but God took it all away.

Now I have three beautiful children who know the Lord, and a husband who is learning. I still have a struggle with alcohol, but God is doing a work in me. He has saved me so many times from the grip of hell. I know he will continue to watch over me. Philippians 1:6 means everything in my life: "I am sure of this, that he who started a good work in you will carry it on to completion until the day of Christ Jesus."

I'm living proof that Jesus persists in his restoring work.

LIVING IS CHRIST

21 For me, to live is Christ and to die is gain. 22 Now
if I live on in the flesh, this means fruitful work
for me; and I don't know which one I should
choose. 23 I am torn between the two. I long
to depart and be with Christ — which is far
better — 24 but to remain in the flesh is more
necessary for your sake. 25 Since I am persuaded
of this, I know that I will remain and continue
with all of you for your progress and joy in the
faith, 26 so that, because of my coming to you
again, your boasting in Christ Jesus may abound.
27 Just one thing: As citizens of heaven, live
your life worthy of the gospel of Christ. Then,
whether I come and see you or am absent, I
will hear about you that you are standing firm
in one spirit, in one accord,[A] contending together for the faith of the gospel, 28 not being
frightened in any way by your opponents. This
is a sign of destruction for them, but of your
salvation — and this is from God. 29 For it has
been granted to you on Christ's behalf not only
to believe in him, but also to suffer for him,
30 since you are engaged in the same struggle
that you saw I had and now hear that I have.

CHRISTIAN HUMILITY

2 If then there is any encouragement in Christ, if any consolation of love, if any fellowship with the Spirit, if any affection and
mercy, 2 make my joy complete by thinking
the same way, having the same love, united
in spirit, intent on one purpose. 3 Do nothing out of selfish ambition or conceit, but in
humility consider others as more important
than yourselves. 4 Everyone should look out
not only for his own interests, but also for the
interests of others.

CHRIST'S HUMILITY AND EXALTATION

5 Adopt the same attitude as that of Christ Jesus,
6 who, existing in the form of God,
did not consider equality with God
as something to be exploited.[B]
7 Instead he emptied himself
by assuming the form of a servant,
taking on the likeness of humanity.
And when he had come as a man,
8 he humbled himself
by becoming obedient
to the point of death —
even to death on a cross.
9 For this reason God highly exalted him
and gave him the name
that is above every name,
10 so that at the name of Jesus
every knee will bow —
in heaven and on earth
and under the earth —

[A] **1:27** Lit *soul* [B] **2:6** Or *to be grasped*, or *to be held on to*

11 and every tongue will confess
that Jesus Christ is Lord,
to the glory of God the Father.

LIGHTS IN THE WORLD

12 Therefore, my dear friends, just as you have
always obeyed, so now, not only in my presence
but even more in my absence, work out your
own salvation with fear and trembling. 13 For
it is God who is working in you both to will
and to work according to his good purpose.
14 Do everything without grumbling and arguing, 15 so that you may be blameless and pure,
children of God who are faultless in a crooked
and perverted generation, among whom you
shine like stars in the world, 16 by holding firm
to the word of life. Then I can boast in the day
of Christ that I didn't run or labor for nothing.
17 But even if I am poured out as a drink offering
on the sacrificial service of your faith, I am glad
and rejoice with all of you. 18 In the same way
you should also be glad and rejoice with me.

TIMOTHY AND EPAPHRODITUS

19 Now I hope in the Lord Jesus to send Timothy
to you soon so that I too may be encouraged
by news about you. 20 For I have no one else
like-minded who will genuinely care about
your interests; 21 all seek their own interests,
not those of Jesus Christ. 22 But you know
his proven character, because he has served
with me in the gospel ministry like a son with
a father. 23 Therefore, I hope to send him as
soon as I see how things go with me. 24 I am
confident in the Lord that I myself will also
come soon.
25 But I considered it necessary to send you
Epaphroditus — my brother, coworker, and
fellow soldier, as well as your messenger and
minister to my need — 26 since he has been
longing for all of you and was distressed because you heard that he was sick. 27 Indeed, he
was so sick that he nearly died. However, God
had mercy on him, and not only on him but
also on me, so that I would not have sorrow
upon sorrow. 28 For this reason, I am very eager to send him so that you may rejoice again
when you see him and I may be less anxious.
29 Therefore, welcome him in the Lord with
great joy and hold people like him in honor,
30 because he came close to death for the work
of Christ, risking his life to make up what was
lacking in your ministry to me.

KNOWING CHRIST

3 In addition, my brothers and sisters, rejoice
in the Lord. To write to you again about this
is no trouble for me and is a safeguard for you.

Exercise of Faith | *Enduring Suffering*

UNREALISTIC EXPECTATIONS?

"For it has been granted to you on Christ's behalf not only to believe in him, but also to suffer for him." Philippians 1:29

Our need for restoration can take many forms. We have a weary soul or a wounded heart. We may have embraced wrong expectations.

Writing from a Roman prison, the apostle Paul reminded his Christian readers of an unpleasant truth: "It has been granted to you on Christ's behalf . . . to suffer for him."

Can't you just hear all the marketing gurus groaning? "Gee whiz, Paul! 'Expect suffering'? If *that* is your message, you'll *never* go viral!"

Can't you just hear Paul saying, "I'm more interested in truth than tweets"?

Paul was only repeating what Jesus promised (Jn 16:33). Believers shouldn't expect a pass when it comes to suffering. As much as we might wish it were so, God doesn't exempt his children from trouble. But we *can* avoid the self-induced heartburn we bring on ourselves by embracing the unrealistic expectation that we will be spared from suffering.

Are you shocked when suffering comes your way? Ask God to help you see that through it you are becoming more like Jesus.

For the next note on *Exercise of Faith*, see Philippians 3:7-8.

[2] Watch out for the dogs, watch out for the
evil workers, watch out for those who mutilate
the flesh. [3] For we are the circumcision, the
ones who worship by the Spirit of God, boast
in Christ Jesus, and do not put confidence
in the flesh — [4] although I have reasons for
confidence in the flesh. If anyone else thinks
he has grounds for confidence in the flesh, I
have more: [5] circumcised the eighth day; of
the nation of Israel, of the tribe of Benjamin,
a Hebrew born of Hebrews; regarding the law,
a Pharisee; [6] regarding zeal, persecuting the

Other-centeredness | *Being Unselfish*

SELFLESS

"Do nothing out of selfish ambition or conceit, but in humility consider others as more important than yourselves. Everyone should look out not only for his own interests, but also for the interests of others." Philippians 2:3-4

Paul is asking if we would like the recipe for a happier life and healthier relationships—because it isn't complicated. Be selfless. That's it. Put others first. Stop thinking solely about your needs and desires and focus instead on helping, encouraging, and affirming others. Rather than wonder why people aren't catering to your every whim, put on an apron and get busy serving.

This seems counterintuitive. We think, *If I don't look out for me, who will?* God says, "I promise to look out for you, which means you are now free to focus on looking out for others."

Millions can testify to the genius of this divine truth. God meets all our needs as we hurl ourselves into the lifelong mission of serving him by serving others.

Selflessness is the way to a fulfilling life.

For the next note on *Other-centeredness*, see Colossians 1:9-11.

Eternal Perspective | *God's Work in Us*

THE MYSTERY OF GROWTH

"Work out your own salvation with fear and trembling. For it is God who is working in you both to will and to work according to his good purpose." Philippians 2:12-13

When thinking about Christian growth, lots of people embrace either-or thinking. *Either* they assume spiritual maturity is entirely up to God—that it happens effortlessly, often in a flash, as the result of some kind of "divine zap." *Or* they suppose their progress in the faith is all their responsibility and frequently feel discouraged.

This is not an either-or arrangement; it's a both-and proposition. "Work out your own salvation," we're told. This doesn't mean we work to *earn* salvation from God (see Ti 3:5). It does mean we exert effort to live out the new life that God has so graciously given us in Christ. And while we do that work—engaging in spiritual disciplines like prayer, study, service, witness, and more—we rest in the wonderful truth that God is simultaneously at work in us "to will and to work according to his good purpose."

The deal is both-and. God plays the primary role. He's the ultimate change agent in our lives. But we have a role to play, too. We submit and follow him as he guides, grows, shapes, and trains us.

Trust—and obey.

For the next note on *Eternal Perspective*, see Philippians 2:14.

church; regarding the righteousness that is
in the law, blameless.
7 But everything that was a gain to me, I have
considered to be a loss because of Christ. 8 More
than that, I also consider everything to be a
loss in view of the surpassing value of knowing
Christ Jesus my Lord. Because of him I have
suffered the loss of all things and consider
them as dung, so that I may gain Christ 9 and
be found in him, not having a righteousness of
my own from the law, but one that is through
faith in Christ[A] — the righteousness from God
based on faith. 10 My goal is to know him and
the power of his resurrection and the fellowship of his sufferings, being conformed to his
death, 11 assuming that I will somehow reach
the resurrection from among the dead.

REACHING FORWARD TO GOD'S GOAL

12 Not that I have already reached the goal or
am already perfect, but I make every effort to
take hold of it because I also have been taken
hold of by Christ Jesus. 13 Brothers and sisters,
I do not[B] consider myself to have taken hold
of it. But one thing I do: Forgetting what is behind and reaching forward to what is ahead,
14 I pursue as my goal the prize promised by
God's heavenly[C] call in Christ Jesus. 15 Therefore, let all of us who are mature think this
way. And if you think differently about anything, God will reveal this also to you. 16 In any
case, we should live up to whatever truth we
have attained. 17 Join in imitating me, brothers
and sisters, and pay careful attention to those
who live according to the example you have
in us. 18 For I have often told you, and now say
again with tears, that many live as enemies
of the cross of Christ. 19 Their end is destruction; their god is their stomach; their glory is
in their shame. They are focused on earthly
things, 20 but our citizenship is in heaven, and
we eagerly wait for a Savior from there, the
Lord Jesus Christ. 21 He will transform the body
of our humble condition into the likeness of
his glorious body, by the power that enables
him to subject everything to himself.

4 So then, my dearly loved and longed for
brothers and sisters, my joy and crown,
in this manner stand firm in the Lord, dear
friends.

PRACTICAL COUNSEL

2 I urge Euodia and I urge Syntyche to agree
in the Lord. 3 Yes, I also ask you, true partner,[D]
to help these women who have contended
for the gospel at my side, along with Clement
and the rest of my coworkers whose names
are in the book of life. 4 Rejoice in the Lord

Eternal Perspective | *Positive Focus*

COMPLAINERS

"Do everything without grumbling and arguing." Philippians 2:14

The news reports are totally negative: crime stories followed by disaster and then rumblings of war, a few celebrity scandals, and reports of incessant political strife. Then most "news" shows are followed by panels of people who rant and yell at one another!

We don't need a PhD in human psychology to realize that even a few days on such a toxic diet is enough to turn anyone into a sour, dour person. If we're not careful, we can morph into pessimistic, glass-half-full people, who move through the world looking for a fight.

Paul urged the Philippian believers to say no to "grumbling and arguing." All of it. "Do everything without" complaining and bickering. Can you imagine a marriage, a household, or a workplace without constant harping on all that's wrong and messed up. Imagine relationships where tensions and differences are calmly discussed instead of pridefully and angrily debated.

You want to restore some sanity to your life? Be grateful and agreeable instead of grumbly and argumentative. Turn off all the negativity. And when others enter into that stuff, look for the nearest exit.

For the next note on *Eternal Perspective*, see Philippians 3:13-14.

[A] **3:9** Or *through the faithfulness of Christ* [B] **3:13** Other mss read *not yet* [C] **3:14** Or *upward* [D] **4:3** Or *true Syzygus*, possibly a person's name

always. I will say it again: Rejoice! 5 Let your
graciousness[A] be known to everyone. The Lord
is near. 6 Don't worry about anything, but in
everything, through prayer and petition with
thanksgiving, present your requests to God.
7 And the peace of God, which surpasses all
understanding, will guard your hearts and
minds in Christ Jesus.

Exercise of Faith | *Knowing Christ*

SURPASSING VALUE

"But everything that was a gain to me, I have considered to be a loss because of Christ. More than that, I also consider everything to be a loss in view of the surpassing value of knowing Christ Jesus my Lord. Because of him I have suffered the loss of all things and consider them as dung, so that I may gain Christ." Philippians 3:7-8

At one time in Paul's life, he took enormous pride in his pious accomplishments (Php 3:4-6). Nobody had the kind of religious résumé he had. Nobody ever kept the rules like he did.

But then Paul met the resurrected Jesus (see Ac 9). In a flash—literally—everything changed. His description here reads like the journal of someone madly in love, doesn't it? Nothing else matters but "knowing Christ Jesus my Lord." The things that used to matter so much are now like "dung." And yes, that word means exactly what you think it means.

Paul sounds like the man in Jesus's short parable who finds a treasure in a field and joyfully sells everything he owns to buy that field (Mt 13:44). Only in Paul's case, it's a person he must have at all costs.

Ask the Lord to kindle that kind of desire for him in your heart.

For the next note on *Exercise of Faith*, see Philippians 4:6-7.

Eternal Perspective | *Forward Look*

AHEAD

"Brothers and sisters, I do not consider myself to have taken hold of it. But one thing I do: Forgetting what is behind and reaching forward to what is ahead, I pursue as my goal the prize promised by God's heavenly call in Christ Jesus." Philippians 3:13-14

We drive to work by peering through our windshields, not staring into our rearview mirrors. So why do so many of us move through life constantly looking back over our shoulders?

Many are stuck in the past because of regret: the futile wish for a do-over. For others, the problem is plain old nostalgia—a longing for the "good old days." Paul would have none of that. Life's too short, and besides, we can't turn back the clock. Since Paul didn't want a longing for a previous experience of God to cause him to miss the next encounter, he embraced this motto: "Forgetting what is behind and reaching forward to what is ahead."

This is similar to the Christian woman whose favorite part of every meal was dessert. When she died, she asked that everybody at her funeral be given a dessert fork. It was her humorous way of reminding her friends and loved ones that "the best is yet to come."

Consider how you can develop a more forward-looking perspective.

For the next note on *Eternal Perspective*, see Philippians 4:4.

[A] **4:5** Or *gentleness*

8 Finally[A] brothers and sisters, whatever is
true, whatever is honorable, whatever is just,
whatever is pure, whatever is lovely, whatever
is commendable — if there is any moral excellence and if there is anything praiseworthy
— dwell on these things. 9 Do what you have
learned and received and heard from me, and
seen in me, and the God of peace will be with you.

APPRECIATION OF SUPPORT

10 I rejoiced in the Lord greatly because once
again you renewed your care for me. You were,
in fact, concerned about me but lacked the opportunity to show it. 11 I don't say this out of need,
for I have learned to be content in whatever
circumstances I find myself. 12 I know both how
to make do with little, and I know how to make
do with a lot. In any and all circumstances I have
learned the secret of being content — whether
well fed or hungry, whether in abundance or
in need. 13 I am able to do all things through
him[B] who strengthens me. 14 Still, you did well
by partnering with me in my hardship.
15 And you Philippians know that in the early days of the gospel, when I left Macedonia,
no church shared with me in the matter of
giving and receiving except you alone. 16 For
even in Thessalonica you sent gifts for my
need several times. 17 Not that I seek the gift,
but I seek the profit[C] that is increasing to your
account. 18 But I have received everything in
full, and I have an abundance. I am fully supplied,[D] having received from Epaphroditus
what you provided — a fragrant offering, an
acceptable sacrifice, pleasing to God. 19 And
my God will supply all your needs according
to his riches in glory in Christ Jesus. 20 Now
to our God and Father be glory forever and
ever. Amen.

FINAL GREETINGS

21 Greet every saint in Christ Jesus. The brothers who are with me send you greetings. 22 All
the saints send you greetings, especially those
who belong to Caesar's household. 23 The grace
of the Lord Jesus Christ be with your spirit.[E]

Eternal Perspective | *Biblical Joy*

REJOICE

"Rejoice in the Lord always. I will say it again: Rejoice!" Philippians 4:4

We can think that rejoicing is a reaction, a response, assuming it is something we do *after* we start feeling joyful. That may be the case, but Paul hints here at another important truth for people who seek a restored heart.

Paul was imprisoned in Rome—not vacationing on the Riviera—when he wrote these words. Yet look at his exhortation: "Rejoice in the Lord always." In other words, rejoice even when you're in jail, and maybe not feeling so "up."

Rejoicing is a deliberate action that often leads to a sense of joy. We rejoice, not just *because* we feel joyful, but also *in order to* experience joy. The choice to rejoice—expressing gratitude and gladness to God—can literally alter a person's mood.

This is so important. We don't have to wait around for "positive" circumstances to make us happy. In every circumstance, we can give thanks for the good things in life and celebrate the forever goodness of the Lord. And millions of saints through the ages would testify: When we do this, we find joy!

Today, don't think of rejoicing merely as a response to positive and pleasurable events. See it also as a path to a good and right perspective.

For the next note on *Eternal Perspective*, see Colossians 1:15-17.

[A] **4:8** Or *In addition* [B] **4:13** Other mss read *Christ* [C] **4:17** Lit *fruit* [D] **4:18** Or *Here, then, is my receipt for everything, I have an abundance, for I am fully supplied* [E] **4:23** Other mss add *Amen.*

RESTORATION THEMES

R	Rest and Reflection	*For the next note, see 1 Timothy 1:15.*
E	Eternal Perspective	*Supremacy of Christ—Colossians 1:15-17*
S	Support	*For the next note, see Hebrews 3:13.*
T	Thanksgiving and Contentment	*Perspective—Colossians 3:2*
O	Other-centeredness	*Praying for Others—1:9-11; 4:12*
R	Relationships	*Controlling Speech—4:5-6*
E	Exercise of Faith	*Living by Faith—2:6* *Representing Christ—3:17*

GREETING

1 Paul, an apostle of Christ Jesus by God's
will, and Timothy our brother:
²To the saints in Christ at Colossae, who
are faithful brothers and sisters.
Grace to you and peace from God our Father.[A]

THANKSGIVING

³We always thank God, the Father of our Lord
Jesus Christ, when we pray for you, ⁴for we
have heard of your faith in Christ Jesus and of
the love you have for all the saints ⁵because
of the hope reserved for you in heaven. You
have already heard about this hope in the
word of truth, the gospel ⁶that has come to
you. It is bearing fruit and growing all over
the world, just as it has among you since the
day you heard it and came to truly appreciate
God's grace.[B] ⁷You learned this from Epaphras,
our dearly loved fellow servant. He is a faithful minister of Christ on your[C] behalf, ⁸and
he has told us about your love in the Spirit.

PRAYER FOR SPIRITUAL GROWTH

⁹For this reason also, since the day we heard
this, we haven't stopped praying for you. We are
asking that you may be filled with the knowledge of his will in all wisdom and spiritual
understanding,[D] ¹⁰so that you may walk worthy of the Lord, fully pleasing to him: bearing
fruit in every good work and growing in the
knowledge of God, ¹¹being strengthened with
all power, according to his glorious might, so
that you may have great endurance and patience, joyfully ¹²giving thanks to the Father,
who has enabled you[E] to share in the saints'
inheritance in the light. ¹³He has rescued us
from the domain of darkness and transferred
us into the kingdom of the Son he loves. ¹⁴In
him we have redemption,[F] the forgiveness
of sins.

THE CENTRALITY OF CHRIST

15 He is the image of the invisible God,
the firstborn over all creation.
16 For everything was created by him,
in heaven and on earth,
the visible and the invisible,
whether thrones or dominions
or rulers or authorities —
all things have been created
through him and for him.
17 He is before all things,
and by him all things hold together.
18 He is also the head of the body,
the church;

Other-centeredness | *Praying for Others*

PRAYING FOR MORE

"We are asking that you may be filled with the knowledge of his will in all wisdom and spiritual understanding, so that you may walk worthy of the Lord, fully pleasing to him: bearing fruit in every good work and growing in the knowledge of God, being strengthened with all power, according to his glorious might, so that you may have great endurance and patience." Colossians 1:9-11

We're instructed to pray about everything, so praying like this isn't wrong: "Lord, please help Jack find a job." But notice the requests Paul made for his friends: "the knowledge of [God's] will," a worthy walk, good works that lead to fruit, a deeper knowledge of God, spiritual strength.

Perhaps we could modify our prayers in this way: "Lord, I pray that as Jack seeks work, he'd understand that you are with him. I pray that in this trying time he'd come to know you in a deeper way. Give him wisdom to know where to apply. Strengthen him, and give him endurance in a tough job market. May he represent you well in his interviews."

More than asking for better circumstances, we can pray that hearts and souls will be transformed.

For the next note on *Other-centeredness*, see Colossians 4:12.

[A] **1:2** Other mss add *and the Lord Jesus Christ* [B] **1:6** Or *and truly recognized God's grace* [C] **1:7** Other mss read *our* [D] **1:9** Or *all spiritual wisdom and understanding* [E] **1:12** Other mss read *us* [F] **1:14** Other mss add *through his blood*

he is the beginning,
the firstborn from the dead,
so that he might come to have
first place in everything.
19 For God was pleased to have
all his fullness dwell in him,
20 and through him to reconcile
everything to himself,
whether things on earth or things
in heaven,
by making peace
through his blood, shed on the cross.[A]

21 Once you were alienated and hostile in
your minds expressed in your evil actions.
22 But now he has reconciled you by his physical
body through his death, to present you holy,
faultless, and blameless before him — 23 if
indeed you remain grounded and steadfast
in the faith and are not shifted away from the
hope of the gospel that you heard. This gospel
has been proclaimed in all creation under
heaven, and I, Paul, have become a servant of it.

PAUL'S MINISTRY

24 Now I rejoice in my sufferings for you, and
I am completing in my flesh what is lacking
in Christ's afflictions for his body, that is, the
church. 25 I have become its servant, according
to God's commission that was given to me for
you, to make the word of God fully known,
26 the mystery hidden for ages and generations but now revealed to his saints. 27 God
wanted to make known among the Gentiles
the glorious wealth of this mystery, which is
Christ in you, the hope of glory. 28 We proclaim
him, warning and teaching everyone with all
wisdom, so that we may present everyone
mature in Christ. 29 I labor for this, striving
with his strength that works powerfully in me.

2 For I want you to know how greatly I am
struggling for you, for those in Laodicea,
and for all who have not seen me in person. 2 I
want their hearts to be encouraged and joined
together in love, so that they may have all the
riches of complete understanding and have
the knowledge of God's mystery — Christ.[B] 3 In
him are hidden all the treasures of wisdom
and knowledge.

CHRIST VERSUS THE COLOSSIAN HERESY

4 I am saying this so that no one will deceive
you with arguments that sound reasonable.
5 For I may be absent in body, but I am with you
in spirit, rejoicing to see how well ordered you
are and the strength of your faith in Christ.

Eternal Perspective | *Supremacy of Christ*

JESUS

"He is the image of the invisible God, the firstborn over all creation. For everything was created by him, in heaven and on earth, the visible and the invisible, whether thrones or dominions or rulers or authorities—all things have been created through him and for him. He is before all things, and by him all things hold together." Colossians 1:15-17

The false teachers in Colossae were teaching something worse than telling people not to believe in Jesus. They were essentially treating Jesus as though he was one more spiritual option among many other equally valid options.

Paul issued an emphatic "No!" to all such talk. Jesus "is the *image* of the invisible God." In other words, he bears God's likeness (Jn 14:9; Heb 1:3). When you see him, Paul argued, you're looking at an exact representation, a living presentation of the God you can't otherwise see.

Jesus was more than a mere man. "Everything was created by him . . . and by him all things hold together." Jesus is Creator and sustainer of life. He's the cosmic glue of the universe. *And* he's the One who lives in your heart. So rely on him to hold you together.

For the next note on *Eternal Perspective*, see 2 Thessalonians 3:16.

[A] **1:20** Other mss add *through him* [B] **2:2** Other mss read *mystery of God, both of the Father and of Christ*; other ms variations exist on this v.

6 So then, just as you have received Christ Jesus as Lord, continue to live in him, 7 being rooted and built up in him and established in the faith, just as you were taught, and overflowing with gratitude.

8 Be careful that no one takes you captive through philosophy and empty deceit based on human tradition, based on the elements of the world, rather than Christ. 9 For the entire fullness of God's nature dwells bodily[A] in Christ, 10 and you have been filled by him, who is the head over every ruler and authority. 11 You were also circumcised in him with a circumcision not done with hands, by putting off the body of flesh, in the circumcision of Christ, 12 when you were buried with him in baptism, in which you were also raised with him through faith in the working of God, who raised him from the dead. 13 And when you were dead in trespasses and in the uncircumcision of your flesh, he made you alive with him and forgave us all our trespasses. 14 He erased the certificate of debt, with its obligations, that was against us and opposed to us, and has taken it away by nailing it to the cross. 15 He disarmed the rulers and authorities and disgraced them publicly; he triumphed over them in him.[B]

16 Therefore, don't let anyone judge you in regard to food and drink or in the matter of a festival or a new moon or a Sabbath day.[C] 17 These are a shadow of what was to come; the substance is[D] Christ. 18 Let no one condemn[E] you by delighting in ascetic practices and the worship of angels, claiming access to a visionary realm. Such people are inflated by empty notions of their unspiritual[F] mind. 19 He doesn't hold on to the head, from whom the whole body, nourished and held together by its ligaments and tendons, grows with growth from God.

20 If you died with Christ to the elements of this world, why do you live as if you still belonged to the world? Why do you submit to regulations: 21 "Don't handle, don't taste, don't touch"? 22 All these regulations refer to what is destined to perish by being used up; they are human commands and doctrines. 23 Although these have a reputation for wisdom by promoting self-made religion, false humility, and severe treatment of the body, they are not of any value in curbing self-indulgence.[G]

THE LIFE OF THE NEW MAN

3 So if you have been raised with Christ, seek the things above, where Christ is, seated at the right hand of God. 2 Set your minds on things above, not on earthly things. 3 For you died, and your life is hidden with Christ in

Exercise of Faith | *Living by Faith*

A LIFE OF TRUST

"So then, just as you have received Christ Jesus as Lord, continue to live in him." Colossians 2:6

Contrary to what some think, receiving Jesus (Jn 1:12) isn't the end of the spiritual journey; it's the beginning. This should come as no surprise. Jesus claimed he was both the "gate" (or doorway—see Jn 10:9) and the "way" (or path—see Jn 14:6).

We are called initially to repent and believe the good news (Mk 1:15). Then, we are commanded, "As you have received Christ Jesus as Lord, continue to live in him."

This means that turning to the Lord and trusting him doesn't happen just once. We're called to a whole lifetime of repenting—seeing the error of our ways as Christ reveals it to us and changing our course accordingly. And we're called to a lifestyle of continual trust.

Today, what exactly does continuing in the faith look like for you? From what wrong ways of thinking, speaking, or acting do you need to turn away? How can you live *by* faith and live *out* your faith?

For the next note on *Exercise of Faith*, see Colossians 3:17.

[A] **2:9** Or *nature lives in a human body* [B] **2:15** Or *them through it* [C] **2:16** Or *or sabbaths* [D] **2:17** Or *substance belongs to* [E] **2:18** Or *disqualify* [F] **2:18** Lit *fleshly* [G] **2:23** Lit *value against indulgence of the flesh*

My Story | Cliff

I had just stepped away from many fruitful years of ministry in churches, rescue missions, and youth camps. Just weeks after leaving the spotlight of senior leadership and sitting behind the wheel of a school bus, symptoms appeared that spoke to my not handling the change very well.

This was the first tap on the shoulder to alert me that I had been drawing critical amounts of my identity, significance, and purpose from something other than the finished work of Jesus Christ in me. I was going through a kind of withdrawal that men often experience when they retire from their profession. I became short-fused, restless, and unproductive at necessary tasks. I experienced a kind of directionless, inward drifting. Those days, I would pull into a parking lot and sit for an hour, blankly stare off, feeling lost, directionless.

The second tap (more like a *whop*) came when my wife announced she was leaving—after more than a decade of her emotional needs being neglected, after begging me all that time to leave the ministry role I had been in (*What? Give up the spotlight?*). Now, with my retirement at hand, she did not want to face more daily time at home with the man I had become.

The third *whop* came weeks later when one of my adult children called me from the county jail. A ten-year-old alcohol addiction (news to me!) had led to a second DWI arrest (double news to me!). The tap, *whop! whop!* happened within twelve weeks.

I was an utter failure on all fronts. I wondered what people who knew me from a past ministry would think. They would know I was a fraud. The accuser had a heyday.

Catch the order my thoughts followed just now—employment first, marriage second, parenting third. What about the health of my spiritual life, my walk with the Savior? My reflection on the latter finally came. When it did, by the Spirit's grace, his recovery work in me began to move forward.

God first planted Colossians 3:1-4 in my head and on my heart. I had set my heart on all the wrong things. Then, I resisted the devil's call to avoid the body of Christ and became part of a wonderful congregation. A Christian therapist, an associate pastor with a degree in family counseling, a senior pastor who preached the Scriptures, and loving elders were all used by the Holy Spirit to bring peace back into my heart.

After first identifying myself by all the wrong earthly markers, then equally wrong by all my failures, the Holy Spirit used a moment in a sermon, eight months into my broken state, to set my identity back in Christ. The topic was not grace, but the pastor made one clear declaration of the mercies and grace of God through his Son, Jesus Christ, and said, "That is what identifies us as Christ's, not our sin."

I left worship that day securely on the road to recovery.

God. 4 When Christ, who is your[A] life, appears,
then you also will appear with him in glory.
5 Therefore, put to death what belongs to
your earthly nature: sexual immorality, impurity, lust, evil desire, and greed, which is
idolatry. 6 Because of these, God's wrath is
coming upon the disobedient,[B] 7 and you once
walked in these things when you were living
in them. 8 But now, put away all the following:
anger, wrath, malice, slander, and filthy language from your mouth. 9 Do not lie to one
another, since you have put off the old self with
its practices 10 and have put on the new self.
You are being renewed in knowledge according to the image of your[C] Creator. 11 In Christ
there is not Greek and Jew, circumcision and
uncircumcision, barbarian, Scythian, slave
and free; but Christ is all and in all.

THE CHRISTIAN LIFE

12 Therefore, as God's chosen ones, holy and
dearly loved, put on compassion, kindness,
humility, gentleness, and patience, 13 bearing
with one another and forgiving one another if
anyone has a grievance against another. Just
as the Lord has forgiven you, so you are also

[A] **3:4** Other mss read *our* [B] **3:6** Other mss omit *upon the disobedient* [C] **3:10** Lit *his*

to forgive. 14 Above all, put on love, which is
the perfect bond of unity. 15 And let the peace
of Christ, to which you were also called in one
body, rule your hearts. And be thankful. 16 Let
the word of Christ dwell richly among you, in
all wisdom teaching and admonishing one
another through psalms, hymns, and spiritual songs,[A] singing to God with gratitude in
your hearts. 17 And whatever you do, in word
or in deed, do everything in the name of the
Lord Jesus, giving thanks to God the Father
through him.

CHRIST IN YOUR HOME

18 Wives, submit yourselves to your husbands,
as is fitting in the Lord. 19 Husbands, love your
wives and don't be bitter toward them. 20 Children, obey your parents in everything, for this
pleases the Lord. 21 Fathers, do not exasperate
your children, so that they won't become discouraged. 22 Slaves, obey your human masters
in everything. Don't work only while being
watched, as people-pleasers, but work wholeheartedly, fearing the Lord. 23 Whatever you
do, do it from the heart, as something done for
the Lord and not for people, 24 knowing that
you will receive the reward of an inheritance
from the Lord. You serve the Lord Christ. 25 For
the wrongdoer will be paid back for whatever
wrong he has done, and there is no favoritism.

4 Masters, deal with your slaves justly and
fairly, since you know that you too have
a Master in heaven.

SPEAKING TO GOD AND OTHERS

2 Devote yourselves to prayer; stay alert in it
with thanksgiving. 3 At the same time, pray
also for us that God may open a door to us for
the word, to speak the mystery of Christ, for
which I am in chains, 4 so that I may make it
known as I should. 5 Act wisely toward outsiders, making the most of the time. 6 Let your
speech always be gracious, seasoned with
salt, so that you may know how you should
answer each person.

FINAL GREETINGS

7 Tychicus, our dearly loved brother, faithful
minister, and fellow servant in the Lord, will
tell you all the news about me. 8 I have sent
him to you for this very purpose, so that you
may know how we are[B] and so that he may
encourage your hearts. 9 He is coming with
Onesimus, a faithful and dearly loved brother, who is one of you. They will tell you about
everything here.

Thanksgiving and Contentment | *Perspective*

THE RIGHT MIND-SET

"Set your minds on things above, not on earthly things." Colossians 3:2

Some people have been criticized for being "so heavenly-minded, they're no earthly good." Focused on the life to come, they quit living fully here and now. The ultimate example of this is the tiny Christian sect that gives away all its possessions and gathers on a rooftop to wait for the return of Christ.

None of that describes Paul. He didn't live that way, and surely that is not what he means here. The tireless apostle moved through the world, seeing and meeting needs. But always he looked at life through the lens of an eternal perspective.

An alien and stranger, he realized this world was not his home. His citizenship was in heaven. He understood that the things that God has prepared for his people far exceed anything we might ever find in this unrestored world.

It was this mind-set that gave Paul such power and freedom. Everything was a gift. He was able to enjoy earthly blessings without letting them capture his affections.

That's the mind-set we want: developing a heart for the world, even as we guard against having the world capture ours.

For the next note on *Thanksgiving and Contentment*, see 1 Thessalonians 5:18.

[A] **3:16** Or *and songs prompted by the Spirit* [B] **4:8** Other mss read *that he may know how you are*

10 Aristarchus, my fellow prisoner, sends you
greetings, as does Mark, Barnabas's cousin (concerning whom you have received instructions:
if he comes to you, welcome him), 11 and so does
Jesus who is called Justus. These alone of the
circumcised are my coworkers for the kingdom of God, and they have been a comfort to
me. 12 Epaphras, who is one of you, a servant of

Exercise of Faith | *Representing Christ*

IN HIS NAME

"And whatever you do, in word or in deed, do everything in the name of the Lord Jesus, giving thanks to God the Father through him." Colossians 3:17

"In Jesus's name" isn't a magical formula—the Christian version of "abracadabra." It's much more than a phrase we tack onto the ends of our prayers. In ancient times, a person's name represented that person's essential nature. Thus, to do things "in the name of Caesar," for example, meant to do what he would approve of, in ways that would enhance, not tarnish, his reputation.

This has huge significance for Christians. "Whatever" we do, Paul writes, we are to do "in the name of the Lord Jesus." The command is all-encompassing. It covers "word" and "deed." "Everything" is included in this mandate.

With thankful hearts, we get to exercise, date, parent children, and post on social media "in the name of the Lord Jesus." Studying, eating, competing, investing, and building relationships with neighbors and coworkers—none of it is for our names and reputations. All of it is for his.

When we live out this truth—that we exist for God's glory, and not the other way around—our souls will find true rest and joy.

For the next note on *Exercise of Faith*, see 1 Thessalonians 1:3.

Relationships | *Controlling Speech*

WINSOME WITNESSES

"Act wisely toward outsiders, making the most of the time. Let your speech always be gracious, seasoned with salt, so that you may know how you should answer each person." Colossians 4:5-6

How should Christian "insiders" interact with "outsiders"—those who don't share their spiritual beliefs? Paul had a few words of counsel. "Act wisely" and make "the most of the time." In other words, be strategic and intentional. Seize on God-given opportunities to speak naturally about your hope.

"Let your speech always be gracious," Paul says. To understand what that means, consider the nature of grace. It is surprising and delightful, warm and inviting. It is always other-centered. It never ceases to bless. "Have conversations marked by those qualities," Paul is essentially saying.

What does he mean to let one's speech be "seasoned with salt"? Since salt was used in Paul's day to preserve and to add flavor, probably the phrase means to speak in in a wholesome and winsome way. Be engaging, interesting, and tactful.

Form the habit of praying this verse: "May the words of my mouth and the meditation of my heart be acceptable to you, LORD, my rock and my Redeemer" (Ps 19:14).

For the next note on *Relationships*, see 2 Timothy 2:16.

Christ Jesus, sends you greetings. He is always
wrestling for you in his prayers, so that you
can stand mature and fully assured[A] in everything God wills. 13 For I testify about him that
he works hard[B] for you, for those in Laodicea,
and for those in Hierapolis. 14 Luke, the dearly
loved physician, and Demas send you greetings.
15 Give my greetings to the brothers and sisters
in Laodicea, and to Nympha and the church in
her home. 16 After this letter has been read at
your gathering, have it read also in the church
of the Laodiceans; and see that you also read the
letter from Laodicea. 17 And tell Archippus, "Pay
attention to the ministry you have received in
the Lord, so that you can accomplish it."

18 I, Paul, am writing this greeting with my
own hand. Remember my chains. Grace be
with you.[C]

Other-centeredness | *Praying for Others*

WRESTLING IN PRAYER

"Epaphras, who is one of you, a servant of Christ Jesus, sends you greetings. He is always wrestling for you in his prayers, so that you can stand mature and fully assured in everything God wills." Colossians 4:12

Perhaps you've heard Christians speak of someone being a "prayer warrior." Epaphras was a "prayer wrestler." When it came to praying for his Colossian friends, he was willing to go to the mat for them.

The word Paul chose to describe Epaphras's prayer habits—"always wrestling"—is the word from which we get our English words *agony* and *agonize*. (The Greeks actually called the arena where contests were held or the stadium where gladiators fought the *agon*.) The intended picture is of someone forcefully struggling, exerting maximum effort in fierce conflict.

So prayer is not a quiet, orderly, proper exercise. For Epaphras it was a wild, no-holds-barred, all-out war.

At the very least, the example of Epaphras raises the question, *Who are you lifting up before God on a regular basis?* And it challenges us to pray as if hearts and lives depend on it. Because, in truth, they do.

For the next note on *Other-centeredness*, see 1 Timothy 2:1-2.

[A] **4:12** Other mss read *and complete* [B] **4:13** Other mss read *he has a great zeal* [C] **4:18** Other mss add *Amen.*

1 Thessalonians—When recent converts to the faith experience hardship, we often wait with apprehension to see if their faith will be enough to carry them through. Paul had this anxiety for the church in Thessalonica. They lacked depth and longevity, and the founders of their church had been forced to leave due to extreme persecution. He nervously awaited word on how they had fared. Paul was overjoyed to hear that the sincerity of their belief was enough—even though they lacked the knowledge and deep understanding that we view as the mark of a mature Christian.

The Thessalonians' story, and their faith, offers hope to those who feel like babies in the faith, or who look on helplessly as loved ones who are new to the faith go through times of difficulty. The scope of our knowledge will not help us stand firm in the faith but the faithful love of the One who holds us fast will (5:23-24). When we root ourselves in his Word, God promises to keep us in his love until he returns and takes us to live with him forever. That is the message of hope that enables us to be always joyful and thankful in every situation (5:16-18).

1 THESSALONIANS

AUTHOR: The apostle Paul

DATE WRITTEN: AD 50–51, making this Paul's earliest letter, except for perhaps Galatians

ORIGINAL AUDIENCE: Thessalonica was a port city on the Aegean Sea, located in what we know today as Greece. The city was known for worship of Greek and Roman gods as well as the emperor. Paul taught in the Jewish synagogue here (Ac 17:3), persuading some Jews and some devout Greeks who founded a church there.

SETTING: Paul and Silas encountered opposition in Thessalonica and were dragged before the city authorities. That night they fled to Berea and then on to Athens (Ac 17:1-9). This letter was written from Corinth after Paul had received an encouraging report about the Thessalonian church from Timothy (1Th 3:6).

PURPOSE FOR WRITING: The Thessalonian church was holding fast to the faith in the midst of persecution, and Paul wrote to encourage them in their faithful labors and patient hope. He focuses on four themes: (1) his own ministry as an example to them; (2) standing firm in suffering; (3) sanctification in the life of a believer; and (4) the second coming of Christ.

OUTLINE:

1. Greeting (1:1)
2. Commendation for the Thessalonians (1:2-10)
3. Conduct in Ministry (2:1-16)

   Paul's example (2:1-12)

   Varied responses (2:13-16)
4. Concern for the Thessalonians (2:17–3:13)
5. Call to Sanctification (4:1-12)

   Sexual ethics (4:1-8)

   Brotherly love (4:9-12)
6. Christ's Second Coming (4:13–5:11)

   Comfort for the saved (4:13-18)

   Warning for the unsaved (5:1-11)
7. Concluding Exhortations and Blessings (5:12-28)

KEY VERSES:

"Rejoice always, pray constantly, give thanks in everything; for this is God's will for you in Christ Jesus." —1 Thessalonians 5:16-18

RESTORATION THEMES

R	Rest and Reflection	*For the next note, see 1 Timothy 1:15.*
E	Eternal Perspective	*For the next note, see 2 Thessalonians 3:16.*
S	Support	*For the next note, see Hebrews 3:13.*
T	Thanksgiving and Contentment	*Thanksgiving—1 Thessalonians 5:18*
O	Other-centeredness	*For the next note, see 1 Timothy 2:1-2.*
R	Relationships	*For the next note, see 2 Timothy 2:16.*
E	Exercise of Faith	*Persevering—1 Thessalonians 1:3* *Making the Most of Time on Earth—5:6* *Praying—5:17*

GREETING

1 Paul, Silvanus,[A] and Timothy:
To the church of the Thessalonians in God
the Father and the Lord Jesus Christ.
Grace to you and peace.[B]

THANKSGIVING

2 We always thank God for all of you, making
mention of you constantly in our prayers. 3 We
recall, in the presence of our God and Father,
your work produced by faith, your labor motivated by love, and your endurance inspired by
hope in our Lord Jesus Christ. 4 For we know,
brothers and sisters loved by God, that he has
chosen you, 5 because our gospel did not come
to you in word only, but also in power, in the
Holy Spirit, and with full assurance. You know
how we lived among you for your benefit,
6 and you yourselves became imitators of us
and of the Lord when, in spite of severe persecution, you welcomed the message with joy
from the Holy Spirit. 7 As a result, you became
an example to all the believers in Macedonia
and Achaia. 8 For the word of the Lord rang out
from you, not only in Macedonia and Achaia,
but in every place that your faith[C] in God has
gone out. Therefore, we don't need to say anything, 9 for they themselves report[D] what kind
of reception we had from you: how you turned
to God from idols to serve the living and true
God 10 and to wait for his Son from heaven,
whom he raised from the dead — Jesus, who
rescues us from the coming wrath.

PAUL'S CONDUCT

2 For you yourselves know, brothers and
sisters, that our visit with you was not
without result. 2 On the contrary, after we had
previously suffered and were treated out-
rageously in Philippi, as you know, we were
emboldened by our God to speak the gospel
of God to you in spite of great opposition.
3 For our exhortation didn't come from error
or impurity or an intent to deceive. 4 Instead,
just as we have been approved by God to be
entrusted with the gospel, so we speak, not
to please people, but rather God, who examines our hearts. 5 For we never used flattering
speech, as you know, or had greedy motives
— God is our witness — 6 and we didn't seek

Exercise of Faith | *Persevering*

FAITH, HOPE, AND LOVE

"We recall, in the presence of our God and Father, your work produced by faith, your labor motivated by love, and your endurance inspired by hope in our Lord Jesus Christ." 1 Thessalonians 1:3

"Faith, hope, and love" is more than a good church slogan. And taken individually, these things are more than mere concepts or fickle feelings.

Paul praises the Thessalonians for their "work produced by faith," their "labor motivated by love," and their "endurance inspired by hope" in Jesus.

This is a snapshot of the spiritual life as God intended. True faith is active and vigorous. Because it's more verb than noun, faith puts on its hard hat and gets busy. James says a faith that doesn't work like this is dead (Jms 2:14-26). Faith always involves action.

In the same way, Christian love transcends emotions and sentimental talk. The love God gives rolls up its sleeves and labors side by side with faith to make an eternal difference. And hope? Hope is there when faith and love are weary, whispering, "Endure. Don't give up. Keep going. The good things ahead will be worth infinitely more than all this work and pain."

Ask God for the necessary faith, hope, and love to restore your own heart—and the hearts of those around you.

For the next note on *Exercise of Faith*, see 1 Thessalonians 5:6.

[A] **1:1** Or *Silas*; Ac 15:22-32; 16:19-40; 17:1-16 [B] **1:1** Other mss add *from God our Father and the Lord Jesus Christ* [C] **1:8** Or *in every place news of your faith* [D] **1:9** Lit *report about us*

glory from people, either from you or from others. 7 Although we could have been a burden as Christ's apostles, instead we were gentle[A] among you, as a nurse[B] nurtures her own children. 8 We cared so much for you that we were pleased to share with you not only the gospel of God but also our own lives, because you had become dear to us. 9 For you remember our labor and hardship, brothers and sisters. Working night and day so that we would not burden any of you, we preached God's gospel to you. 10 You are witnesses, and so is God, of how devoutly, righteously, and blamelessly we conducted ourselves with you believers. 11 As you know, like a father with his own children, 12 we encouraged, comforted, and implored each one of you to live worthy of God, who calls you into his own kingdom and glory.

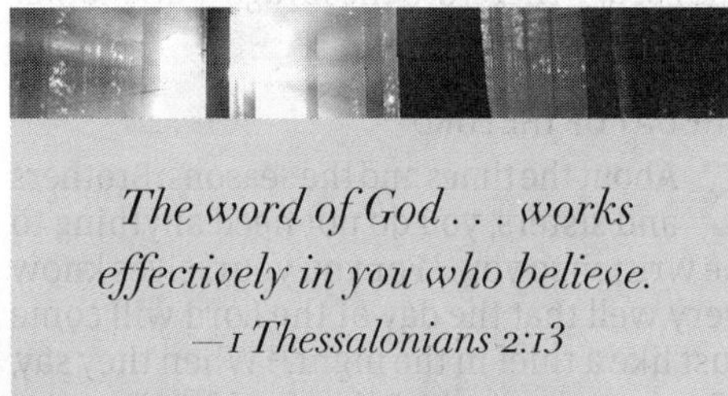
The word of God . . . works effectively in you who believe.
—1 Thessalonians 2:13

RECEPTION AND OPPOSITION TO THE MESSAGE

13 This is why we constantly thank God, because when you received the word of God that you heard from us, you welcomed it not as a human message, but as it truly is, the word of God, which also works effectively in you who believe. 14 For you, brothers and sisters, became imitators of God's churches in Christ Jesus that are in Judea, since you have also suffered the same things from people of your own country, just as they did from the Jews 15 who killed the Lord Jesus and the prophets and persecuted us. They displease God and are hostile to everyone, 16 by keeping us from speaking to the Gentiles so that they may be saved. As a result, they are constantly filling up their sins to the limit, and wrath has overtaken them at last.[C]

PAUL'S DESIRE TO SEE THEM

17 But as for us, brothers and sisters, after we were forced to leave you[D] for a short time (in person, not in heart), we greatly desired and made every effort to return and see you face to face. 18 So we wanted to come to you — even I, Paul, time and again — but Satan hindered us. 19 For who is our hope or joy or crown of boasting in the presence of our Lord Jesus at his coming? Is it not you? 20 Indeed you are our glory and joy!

ANXIETY IN ATHENS

3 Therefore, when we could no longer stand it, we thought it was better to be left alone in Athens. 2 And we sent Timothy, our brother and God's coworker[E] in the gospel of Christ, to strengthen and encourage you concerning your faith, 3 so that no one will be shaken by these afflictions. For you yourselves know that we are appointed to this. 4 In fact, when we were with you, we told you in advance that we were going to experience affliction, and as you know, it happened. 5 For this reason, when I could no longer stand it, I also sent him to find out about your faith, fearing that the tempter had tempted you and that our labor might be for nothing.

ENCOURAGED BY TIMOTHY

6 But now Timothy has come to us from you and brought us good news about your faith and love. He reported that you always have good memories of us and that you long to see us, as we also long to see you. 7 Therefore, brothers and sisters, in all our distress and affliction, we were encouraged about you through your faith. 8 For now we live, if you stand firm in the Lord. 9 How can we thank God for you in return for all the joy we experience before our God because of you, 10 as we pray very earnestly night and day to see you face to face and to complete what is lacking in your faith?

PRAYER FOR THE CHURCH

11 Now may our God and Father himself, and our Lord Jesus, direct our way to you. 12 And may the Lord cause you to increase and overflow with love for one another and for everyone, just as we do for you. 13 May he make your hearts blameless in holiness before our God and Father at the coming of our Lord Jesus with all his saints. Amen.[F]

THE CALL TO SANCTIFICATION

4 Additionally then, brothers and sisters, we ask and encourage you in the Lord Jesus, that as you have received instruction from us

---

[A] **2:7** Many mss read *infants* [B] **2:7** Or *nursing mother* [C] **2:16** Or *to the end* [D] **2:17** Lit *orphaned from you* [E] **3:2** Other mss read *servant* [F] **3:13** Other mss omit *Amen.*

on how you should live and please God — as
you are doing[A] — do this even more. 2 For you
know what commands we gave you through
the Lord Jesus.
3 For this is God's will, your sanctification:
that you keep away from sexual immorality,
4 that each of you knows how to control his
own body[B] in holiness and honor, 5 not with
lustful passions, like the Gentiles, who don't
know God. 6 This means one must not transgress against and take advantage of a brother
or sister in this manner, because the Lord is
an avenger of all these offenses, as we also
previously told and warned you. 7 For God
has not called us to impurity but to live in
holiness. 8 Consequently, anyone who rejects
this does not reject man, but God, who gives
you his Holy Spirit.

LOVING AND WORKING

9 About brotherly love: You don't need me to
write you because you yourselves are taught
by God to love one another. 10 In fact, you are
doing this toward all the brothers and sisters
in the entire region of Macedonia. But we encourage you, brothers and sisters, to do this
even more, 11 to seek to lead a quiet life, to mind
your own business,[C] and to work with your
own hands, as we commanded you, 12 so that
you may behave properly in the presence of
outsiders and not be dependent on anyone.[D]

THE COMFORT OF CHRIST'S COMING

13 We do not want you to be uninformed, brothers and sisters, concerning those who are
asleep, so that you will not grieve like the
rest, who have no hope. 14 For if we believe
that Jesus died and rose again, in the same
way, through Jesus, God will bring with him
those who have fallen asleep. 15 For we say this
to you by a word from the Lord: We who are
still alive at the Lord's coming will certainly
not precede those who have fallen asleep.
16 For the Lord himself will descend from
heaven with a shout,[E] with the archangel's
voice, and with the trumpet of God, and the
dead in Christ will rise first. 17 Then we who
are still alive, who are left, will be caught up
together with them in the clouds to meet the
Lord in the air, and so we will always be with
the Lord. 18 Therefore encourage[F] one another
with these words.

THE DAY OF THE LORD

5 About the times and the seasons: Brothers
and sisters, you do not need anything to
be written to you. 2 For you yourselves know
very well that the day of the Lord will come
just like a thief in the night. 3 When they say,
"Peace and security," then sudden destruction will come upon them, like labor pains
on a pregnant woman, and they will not escape. 4 But you, brothers and sisters, are not

Exercise of Faith | *Making the Most of Time on Earth*

WAKE UP!

"So then, let us not sleep, like the rest, but let us stay awake and be self-controlled." 1 Thessalonians 5:6

The Centers for Disease Control now lists insufficient sleep as a serious public health crisis. But here, at the end of this letter to Thessalonian believers, Paul warns against *too much sleep*. What gives?

Paul is speaking spiritually and metaphorically. While discussing the return of Christ, he notes a kind of spiritual drowsiness that overtakes people. This stupor renders them unconscious, and therefore oblivious, to spiritual realities. No amount of shaking, poking, or yelling can bring them out of their deep slumber. Apart from the gracious intervention of God, they will sleepwalk their way through this life—never waking up to the great truth of the gospel.

Apparently even believers can fall victim to this narcolepsy of the soul. So Paul urges his readers (including us) to "Stay awake."

For the next note on *Exercise of Faith*, see 1 Thessalonians 5:17.

[A] **4:1** Lit *walking* [B] **4:4** Or *to acquire his own wife*; lit *to possess his own vessel* [C] **4:11** Lit *to practice one's own things*
[D] **4:12** Or *not need anything*, or *not be in need* [E] **4:16** Or *command* [F] **4:18** Or *comfort*

in the dark, for this day to surprise you like
a thief. 5 For you are all children of light and
children of the day. We do not belong to the
night or the darkness. 6 So then, let us not
sleep, like the rest, but let us stay awake and
be self-controlled. 7 For those who sleep, sleep
at night, and those who get drunk, get drunk
at night. 8 But since we belong to the day, let
us be self-controlled and put on the armor
of faith and love, and a helmet of the hope
of salvation. 9 For God did not appoint us to
wrath, but to obtain salvation through our
Lord Jesus Christ, 10 who died for us, so that
whether we are awake or asleep, we may live
together with him. 11 Therefore encourage
one another and build each other up as you
are already doing.

EXHORTATIONS AND BLESSINGS

12 Now we ask you, brothers and sisters, to
give recognition to those who labor among
you and lead you[A] in the Lord and admonish
you, 13 and to regard them very highly in love
because of their work. Be at peace among
yourselves. 14 And we exhort you, brothers and
sisters: warn those who are idle,[B] comfort the
discouraged, help the weak, be patient with
everyone. 15 See to it that no one repays evil
for evil to anyone, but always pursue what
is good for one another and for all. 16 Rejoice
always, 17 pray constantly, 18 give thanks in
everything; for this is God's will for you in
Christ Jesus. 19 Don't stifle the Spirit. 20 Don't
despise prophecies, 21 but test all things. Hold
on to what is good. 22 Stay away from every
kind of evil.

23 Now may the God of peace himself sanctify
you completely. And may your whole spirit,
soul, and body be kept sound and blameless
at the coming of our Lord Jesus Christ. 24 He
who calls you is faithful; he will do it. 25 Brothers and sisters, pray for us also. 26 Greet all
the brothers and sisters with a holy kiss. 27 I
charge you by the Lord that this letter be read
to all the brothers and sisters. 28 The grace of
our Lord Jesus Christ be with you.

Exercise of Faith | *Praying*

CONSTANTLY

"Pray constantly." 1 Thessalonians 5:17

"I thought I was doing okay to pray a few minutes each morning, bow my head before meals, and say a quick prayer at bedtime. Now, Paul's telling me I have to pray *all the time*?"

A few clarifications are in order. First, you *are* doing okay. Second, prayer isn't an obligation; it's a privilege. Third, Paul is suggesting here that prayer is less about time slots and more about communion with God. It's engaging in a running conversation with the Father.

Brother Lawrence exemplified this kind of life. A seventeenth-century French monk, this humble man realized that he could "practice the presence of God" at all times—even when he was immersed in common activities like peeling onions and washing dishes. Over time, God became his dearest companion and most trusted confidant.

You can develop such intimacy with God by paying attention to what's happening in and around you, then simply mention all that to the One who will never leave you: "God, calm my daughter who's nervous about school." "Lord, fill me with your Spirit so that I might say only what is needed in this conversation." "Father, comfort my coworker who's grieving."

Constant praying is as much an attitude as an action. Even our God-directed thoughts are a kind of praying.

For the next note on *Exercise of Faith*, see 2 Thessalonians 1:3.

[A] **5:12** Or *care for you* [B] **5:14** Or *who are disorderly*, or *who are undisciplined*

T Thanksgiving and Contentment | *Thanksgiving*

IN EVERYTHING

"Give thanks in everything; for this is God's will for you in Christ Jesus." 1 Thessalonians 5:18

Just preceding this statement, Paul wrote, "Rejoice always" (1Th 5:16). Putting the two together, we might think that we should be grateful and joyful about everything that happens in the world generally and in our lives, with no time for sadness or sorrow.

We understand rejoicing and thanksgiving in good times. In fact, we thank him, as we should, for our family, friends, good health, food, clothing, and enjoyable experiences. But thanking God for pain and suffering is another matter. How can we possibly thank God for terrorism, natural disasters, job loss, terrible illness, or the death of a loved one?

But notice that Paul doesn't say to give thanks *for* everything but *in* everything. Big difference. We live in a fallen world; we are sinners surrounded by other sinners. We will experience the results of sin and the reality of our mortality. But we also know that God has not left us to deal with pain and suffering on our own. He is with us every step of the way and is working out his perfect plan, regardless of what is happening (Rm 8:28).

So when faced with struggles or hardships of any kind, we should be thankful *in* those painful circumstances, know that God is with us, that he loves us, and that he is working in and through us. We can rejoice that this life is not all there is and that one day full restoration will come.

For the next note on *Thanksgiving and Contentment*, see Titus 3:4-5.

2 Thessalonians—When life is a struggle and the situation seems to go from bad to worse, we can be encouraged by the message of 2 Thessalonians—God is still in control. In the time after Paul's first letter, the situation had worsened in Thessalonica. In addition, some believers were becoming lazy in their Christian life. Paul wrote this letter to respond to specific needs in the church. It offers us a glimpse into Paul's pastoral heart and a model for responding to misunderstandings in the church.

Paul wrote first of the greatness of God and his calling, showing the Thessalonians that the motivation to stand firm in the faith is the magnificence of Christ and the privilege of sharing in his suffering. Paul then reminded them of their great hope—Christ would return to overthrow evil and they would be saved. Finally, Paul warned them of the dangers of lazy spirituality. In light of Christ's return, believers must work to fulfill their calling.

This short book offers hope in our struggles. One day everything will be made right, for the Lord Jesus will return to bring justice to the earth. Until then, our time is valuable. God has given us work and joy in this world as we await Christ's certain return.

2 THESSALONIANS

AUTHOR: The apostle Paul

DATE WRITTEN: AD 50–51, shortly after 1 Thessalonians

ORIGINAL AUDIENCE: Thessalonica was a port city on the Aegean Sea, located in what we know today as Greece. The city was known for worship of Greek and Roman gods as well as the emperor. In Thessalonica, Paul had taught in the Jewish synagogue (Ac 17:3), persuading some Jews and some devout Greeks who founded a church there.

SETTING: After the encouraging report Paul had initially received, the persecution increased and some Thessalonian believers had become lazy. Paul writes with a word of rebuke to remind them of their calling.

PURPOSE FOR WRITING: Due to the extreme persecution they were experiencing, some Thessalonian believers thought that the day of the Lord (2:2) had arrived. Paul assured them that this was not yet the end times (2:6-7), and that they needed to continue to work hard for the Lord (3:10-11).

OUTLINE:

1. Introduction (1:1-12)

   Greeting (1:1-2)

   Thanksgiving (1:3-10)

   Prayer (1:11-12)

2. Instruction for the Thessalonians (2:1-17)

   Misconceptions about the day of the Lord (2:1-2)

   Man of lawlessness (2:3-10)

   Judgment of unbelievers (2:11-12)

   Thanksgiving and prayer (2:13-17)

3. Injunctions to the Thessalonians (3:1-16)

   Call to prayer (3:1-5)

   Warning against laziness (3:6-15)

   Concluding prayer (3:16)

4. Conclusion (3:17-18)

KEY VERSES:

"May our Lord Jesus Christ himself and God our Father, who has loved us and given us eternal encouragement and good hope by grace, encourage your hearts and strengthen you in every good work and word."
—2 Thessalonians 2:16-17

RESTORATION THEMES

R	Rest and Reflection	*For the next note, see 1 Timothy 1:15.*
E	Eternal Perspective	*Biblical Peace—2 Thessalonians 3:16*
S	Support	*For the next note, see Hebrews 3:13.*
T	Thanksgiving and Contentment	*For the next note, see Titus 3:4-5.*
O	Other-centeredness	*For the next note, see 1 Timothy 2:1-2.*
R	Relationships	*For the next note, see 2 Timothy 2:16.*
E	Exercise of Faith	*Living by Faith—2 Thessalonians 1:3*

GREETING

1 Paul, Silvanus,[A] and Timothy:
To the church of the Thessalonians in God
our Father and the Lord Jesus Christ.
2 Grace to you and peace from God our Father and the Lord Jesus Christ.

GOD'S JUDGMENT AND GLORY

3 We ought to thank God always for you, brothers and sisters, and rightly so, since your faith
is flourishing and the love each one of you
has for one another is increasing. 4 Therefore,
we ourselves boast about you among God's
churches — about your perseverance and
faith in all the persecutions and afflictions
that you are enduring. 5 It is clear evidence
of God's righteous judgment that you will be
counted worthy of God's kingdom, for which
you also are suffering, 6 since it is just for God
to repay with affliction those who afflict you
7 and to give relief to you who are afflicted,
along with us. This will take place at the revelation of the Lord Jesus from heaven with his
powerful angels, 8 when he takes vengeance
with flaming fire on those who don't know
God and on those who don't obey the gospel
of our Lord Jesus. 9 They will pay the penalty of
eternal destruction from the Lord's presence
and from his glorious strength 10 on that day
when he comes to be glorified by his saints
and to be marveled at by all those who have
believed, because our testimony among you
was believed. 11 In view of this, we always pray
for you that our God will make you worthy of
his calling, and by his power fulfill your every
desire to do good[B] and your work produced
by faith, 12 so that the name of our Lord Jesus
will be glorified by you, and you by him, according to the grace of our God and the Lord
Jesus Christ.

THE MAN OF LAWLESSNESS

2 Now concerning the coming of our Lord
Jesus Christ and our being gathered to him:
We ask you, brothers and sisters, 2 not to be
easily upset or troubled, either by a prophecy[C]
or by a message or by a letter supposedly from
us, alleging that the day of the Lord[D] has come.
3 Don't let anyone deceive you in any way. For
that day will not come unless the apostasy[E]
comes first and the man of lawlessness[F] is
revealed, the man doomed to destruction.
4 He opposes and exalts himself above every
so-called god or object of worship, so that
he sits[G] in God's temple, proclaiming that he
himself is God.

Exercise of Faith | *Living by Faith*

GETTING BIGGER

"We ought to thank God always for you, brothers and sisters, and rightly so, since your faith is flourishing and the love each one of you has for one another is increasing." 2 Thessalonians 1:3

A child was asked what he wanted to be when he grew up. He thought for a second and replied, "Big." Meanwhile the hope of many adults is to be smaller, right?

Paul wrote about big matters in 2 Thessalonians. Notice how his letter begins. "Your faith is flourishing," the apostle points out. Literally, this means their faith was growing to an extreme limit. In other places, this same word is used to suggest fruitfulness.

And not just their faith was being enlarged. Notice what else Paul says: "The love each one of you has for one another is increasing." This word translated "increasing" describes an overflowing sea or someone with excessive amounts of money. The idea is a "super abundance."

Gigantic faith, massive amounts of love—this is what God wants for us. In these two areas, bigger is definitely better. If your faith and love currently seem puny, ask God to increase them.

For the next note on *Exercise of Faith*, see 1 Timothy 4:7.

[A] **1:1** Or *Silas*; Ac 15:22-32; 16:19-40; 17:1-16 [B] **1:11** Or *power bring to fruition your desire to do good* [C] **2:2** Or *spiritual utterance* [D] **2:2** Other mss read *Christ* [E] **2:3** Or *rebellion* [F] **2:3** Other mss read *man of sin* [G] **2:4** Other mss add *as God*

5 Don't you remember that when I was still
with you I used to tell you about this? 6 And
you know what currently restrains him, so
that he will be revealed in his time. 7 For the
mystery of lawlessness is already at work,
but the one now restraining will do so until
he is out of the way, 8 and then the lawless one
will be revealed. The Lord Jesus will destroy
him with the breath of his mouth and will
bring him to nothing at the appearance of
his coming. 9 The coming of the lawless one
is based on Satan's working, with all kinds
of false miracles, signs, and wonders, 10 and
with every wicked deception among those
who are perishing. They perish because they
did not accept the love of the truth and so be
saved. 11 For this reason God sends them a
strong delusion so that they will believe the
lie, 12 so that all will be condemned — those
who did not believe the truth but delighted
in unrighteousness.

STAND FIRM

13 But we ought to thank God always for you,
brothers and sisters loved by the Lord, because
from the beginning[A] God has chosen you for
salvation through sanctification by the Spirit
and through belief in the truth. 14 He called you
to this through our gospel, so that you might
obtain the glory of our Lord Jesus Christ. 15 So
then, brothers and sisters, stand firm and hold
to the traditions you were taught, whether by
what we said or what we wrote.
16 May our Lord Jesus Christ himself and
God our Father, who has loved us and given
us eternal encouragement and good hope by
grace, 17 encourage your hearts and strengthen
you in every good work and word.

God has chosen you for salvation through sanctification by the Spirit and through belief in the truth.

—2 Thessalonians 2:13

PRAY FOR US

3 In addition, brothers and sisters, pray for
us that the word of the Lord may spread
rapidly and be honored, just as it was with you,
2 and that we may be delivered from wicked

Eternal Perspective | *Biblical Peace*

SERENITY

"May the Lord of peace himself give you peace always in every way. The Lord be with all of you." 2 Thessalonians 3:16

For many, peace is an idea on a par with Sasquatch. Mythical, not actual. More like an unproven rumor—and, at times, a bad joke. Real life all too often involves deep angst over finances, unease about health issues, or fretfulness over relationships. For many people, this inner restlessness almost never subsides.

Which is why, of all the blessings in the Bible, this is one of the sweetest: "Peace always in every way." Hard to see how Paul could have covered any more ground than that. "Peace always" necessarily means peace in every situation—even unexpected and unpleasant circumstances.

Does this notion of pervading, uninterrupted serenity sound impossible or at least far-fetched to you? It isn't. Paul gives this beautiful blessing: Our God is "the Lord of peace."

The One who is with us and in us is the Prince of Peace. He has the power to make storms hush (Mk 4:39). He brings unearthly calm even to those with raging spirits (5:15). If you are troubled, ask the Lord to step into your anxious life and give you peace "in every way."

For the next note on *Eternal Perspective*, see 2 Timothy 1:7.

[A] **2:13** Other mss read *because as a firstfruit*

and evil people, for not all have faith.[A] 3 But the
Lord is faithful; he will strengthen and guard
you from the evil one. 4 We have confidence
in the Lord about you, that you are doing and
will continue to do what we command. 5 May
the Lord direct your hearts to God's love and
Christ's endurance.

WARNING AGAINST IRRESPONSIBLE BEHAVIOR

6 Now we command you, brothers and sisters,
in the name of our Lord Jesus Christ, to keep
away from every brother or sister who is idle
and does not live according to the tradition
received from us. 7 For you yourselves know
how you should imitate us: We were not idle
among you; 8 we did not eat anyone's food
free of charge; instead, we labored and toiled,
working night and day, so that we would not
be a burden to any of you. 9 It is not that we
don't have the right to support, but we did it
to make ourselves an example to you so that
you would imitate us. 10 In fact, when we were
with you, this is what we commanded you:
"If anyone isn't willing to work, he should
not eat." 11 For we hear that there are some
among you who are idle. They are not busy
but busybodies. 12 Now we command and
exhort such people by the Lord Jesus Christ
to work quietly and provide for themselves.[B]
13 But as for you, brothers and sisters, do not
grow weary in doing good.
14 If anyone does not obey our instruction
in this letter, take note of that person; don't
associate with him, so that he may be ashamed.
15 Yet don't consider him as an enemy, but warn
him as a brother.

FINAL GREETINGS

16 May the Lord of peace himself give you peace
always in every way. The Lord be with all of
you. 17 I, Paul, am writing this greeting with my
own hand, which is an authenticating mark in
every letter; this is how I write. 18 The grace of
our Lord Jesus Christ be with you all.

[A] **3:2** Or *for the faith is not in everyone* [B] **3:12** Lit *they may eat their own bread*

1 Timothy—In Paul's view, the church is more of a family than an institution. The household of faith in Ephesus was in peril, and his fatherly heart toward his young protégé, Timothy, as well as the body of believers, shines through in this highly personal letter. Timothy was not just a student to Paul but like a son (1:2,18). Paul's stern warnings against false teachers sound like a shepherd defending his flock against ravenous wolves in sheep's clothing.

Paul's words to the ancient Ephesian church are highly applicable to our own day when false teachers lie in wait to entice young believers and use them to accumulate wealth for themselves. His instructions for church governance, pastoral priorities, and care for the needy can be easily applied to our church policy books and ministry initiatives. This is sound advice for the church in every age.

We must not forget to treat our own local body of believers as family, and Paul's words to Timothy help us to do that. We need to guard what God has entrusted to us (6:20), to pursue righteousness, to be rich in good works, and to be generous to those in need (6:11,18). When we and our church leaders do these things, we will be able to hold tightly to the eternal life to which God has called us (6:12).

1 TIMOTHY

AUTHOR: The apostle Paul

DATE WRITTEN: AD 63, after the events recorded in Acts

ORIGINAL AUDIENCE: Paul wrote a personal letter to his coworker Timothy, who had been Paul's traveling partner (Ac 19:22) but was now charged with the task of managing difficulties in the church at Ephesus. This is the first of Paul's Pastoral Letters (which include Titus).

SETTING: The well-established church in Ephesus was in crisis. Church leaders had begun teaching false doctrines, and many believers were being led astray. Paul sent Timothy to restore order, and he sent this letter to encourage and advise Timothy in that task.

PURPOSE FOR WRITING: In addition to offering personal encouragement, Paul tackles areas that false teachers were targeting: prayer, women's teaching, and leadership. He also offers guidance on how to deal with the false teachers (6:2-21).

OUTLINE:

1. Greetings (1:1-2)

2. Introduction (1:3-20)

   The problems at Ephesus (1:3-17)

   Charge to Timothy (1:18-20)

3. Worship in the Church (2:1-15)

4. Qualifications for Church Leaders (3:1-13)

   Overseers (3:1-7)

   Deacons (3:8-13)

5. Ministry during Difficult Times (3:14–4:16)

6. Conduct toward Others (5:1–6:2)

   Care for widows (5:1-16)

   Honor for elders (5:17-25)

   Submission to masters (6:1-2)

7. Conclusion (6:3-21)

KEY VERSES:

"Pursue righteousness, godliness, faith, love, endurance, and gentleness. Fight the good fight of the faith. Take hold of eternal life to which you were called and about which you have made a good confession."
—1 Timothy 6:11-12

Timothy | Restoration Profile

ACTS 16:1-5; 17:14-15; 18:5; 19:22; 20:4; IS MENTIONED IN ROMANS, 1 CORINTHIANS, 2 CORINTHIANS, PHILIPPIANS, COLOSSIANS, 1 THESSALONIANS, 2 THESSALONIANS, PHILEMON, HEBREWS; IS THE ADDRESSEE IN TWO OF PAUL'S LETTERS

Restoration doesn't always involve radical transformation. For many, the healing changes may seem small, yet no less impossible to accomplish on our own. In the process of restoration, God does the real work; thus, the scope of the work, which may or may not seem impressive, is equally and effectively performed by our heavenly Father. Timothy is a great example of common restoration.

Timothy seems to have had a personality that tended toward timidity or even fear. But rather than berate his spiritual offspring, Paul repeatedly encouraged Timothy and entrusted him with responsibilities designed to bring out the best in him, even if they were difficult to perform. On several occasions, Timothy traveled to distant churches as Paul's appointed representative.

Paul instructed Timothy in restoration maintenance, giving the younger disciple the disciplines he would need to carry out his duties and to preserve his relationship with Christ under the pressures of daily living. Rather than telling Timothy he could do anything he set his mind to, Paul told him to fill his mind with God's Word (2Tm 2:15) and seek to live out the specific spiritual gifts he had been given (2Tm 1:6). Timothy didn't have to go looking for these things; other believers had laid hands on and spoken into the young man's life, letting him know what God had shown them about his restoration and equipping for service.

Timothy is a helpful example of why we need to give other believers permission to tell us what they see in us by way of spiritual gifting. And we need to let God speak into our lives by giving diligent attention to his Word. It will restore us to completeness and prepare us for what God wants us to do (2Tm 3:17).

7 But have nothing to do with pointless and
silly myths. Rather, train yourself in godliness. 8 For the training of the body has limited
benefit, but godliness is beneficial in every
way, since it holds promise for the present
life and also for the life to come. 9 This saying
is trustworthy and deserves full acceptance.
10 For this reason we labor and strive,[A] because
we have put our hope in the living God, who
is the Savior of all people, especially of those
who believe.

INSTRUCTIONS FOR MINISTRY

11 Command and teach these things. 12 Don't let
anyone despise your youth, but set an example
for the believers in speech, in conduct, in love,[B]
in faith, and in purity. 13 Until I come, give your
attention to public reading, exhortation, and
teaching. 14 Don't neglect the gift that is in you;
it was given to you through prophecy, with the
laying on of hands by the council of elders.
15 Practice these things; be committed to them,
so that your progress may be evident to all. 16 Pay
close attention to your life and your teaching;
persevere in these things, for in doing this you
will save both yourself and your hearers.

5 Don't rebuke an older man, but exhort
him as a father, younger men as brothers,
2 older women as mothers, and the younger
women as sisters with all purity.

THE SUPPORT OF WIDOWS

3 Support[C] widows who are genuinely in need.
4 But if any widow has children or grandchildren, let them learn to practice godliness
toward their own family first and to repay
their parents, for this pleases God. 5 The widow
who is truly in need and left all alone has put
her hope in God and continues night and day
in her petitions and prayers; 6 however, she
who is self-indulgent is dead even while she
lives. 7 Command this also, so that they will
be above reproach. 8 But if anyone does not
provide for his own family, especially for his
own household, he has denied the faith and
is worse than an unbeliever.

[A] **4:10** Other mss read *and suffer reproach* [B] **4:12** Other mss add *in spirit,* [C] **5:3** Lit *Honor*

9 No widow is to be enrolled on the list for
support unless she is at least sixty years old,
has been the wife of one husband, 10 and is
well known for good works — that is, if she
has brought up children, shown hospitality,
washed the saints' feet, helped the afflicted,
and devoted herself to every good work. 11 But
refuse to enroll younger widows, for when they
are drawn away from Christ by desire, they
want to marry 12 and will therefore receive
condemnation because they have renounced
their original pledge. 13 At the same time, they
also learn to be idle, going from house to house;
they are not only idle, but are also gossips and
busybodies, saying things they shouldn't say.
14 Therefore, I want younger women to marry,
have children, manage their households, and
give the adversary no opportunity to accuse
us. 15 For some have already turned away to
follow Satan. 16 If any[A] believing woman has
widows in her family, let her help them. Let
the church not be burdened, so that it can
help widows in genuine need.

HONORING THE ELDERS

17 The elders who are good leaders are to be
considered worthy of double honor,[B] especially
those who work hard at preaching and teaching. 18 For the Scripture says: **Do not muzzle
an ox while it is treading out the grain,**[C] and
the worker is worthy of his wages.
19 Don't accept an accusation against an
elder unless it is supported by two or three
witnesses. 20 Publicly rebuke those who sin,
so that the rest will be afraid. 21 I solemnly charge you before God and Christ Jesus
and the elect angels to observe these things
without prejudice, doing nothing out of favoritism. 22 Don't be too quick to appoint[D]
anyone as an elder, and don't share in the
sins of others. Keep yourself pure. 23 Don't
continue drinking only water, but use a little wine because of your stomach and your
frequent illnesses. 24 Some people's sins are
obvious, preceding them to judgment, but
the sins of others surface[E] later. 25 Likewise,
good works are obvious, and those that are
not obvious cannot remain hidden.

HONORING MASTERS

6 All who are under the yoke as slaves should
regard their own masters[F] as worthy of
all respect, so that God's name and his teaching will not be blasphemed. 2 Let those who

Exercise of Faith | *Setting a Good Example*

EXEMPLARY

"Don't let anyone despise your youth, but set an example for the believers in speech, in conduct, in love, in faith, and in purity." 1 Timothy 4:12

First, somebody is watching you. We're not talking about God here, or "big brother." We're talking about a neighbor or coworker who knows that you profess faith in Christ. Or perhaps a child who, for this reason or that, looks up to you. Maybe it's someone who follows you on social media.

Second, you *are* setting an example, whether you realize it or not. That example is either positive or negative, good or bad.

Paul urges young Timothy to live in such a way that people forget how young he is. It's Paul's way of saying, "Don't be immature—don't do foolish, childish things." On the contrary, "set an example"—and obviously Paul means a *good* example. He clarifies. Be a shining example "in speech, in conduct, in love, in faith, and in purity."

What kind of example are you setting in the way you talk and act, in how you show compassion to others and live out your faith? Is there impurity in your life? If so, confess it and forsake it. Little eyes—and big ones—are watching.

For the next note on *Exercise of Faith*, see 1 Timothy 6:9-10.

[A] **5:16** Other mss add *believing man or* [B] **5:17** Or *of respect and remuneration* [C] **5:18** Dt 25:4 [D] **5:22** Lit *to lay hands on*
[E] **5:24** Lit *follow* [F] **6:1** Or *owners*

have believing masters not be disrespectful to them because they are brothers, but serve them even better, since those who benefit from their service are believers and dearly loved.[A]

FALSE DOCTRINE AND HUMAN GREED

Teach and encourage these things. 3 If anyone teaches false doctrine and does not agree with the sound teaching of our Lord Jesus Christ and with the teaching that promotes godliness, 4 he is conceited and understands nothing, but has an unhealthy interest in disputes and arguments over words. From these come envy, quarreling, slander, evil suspicions, 5 and constant disagreement among people whose minds are depraved and deprived of the truth, who imagine that godliness is a way to material gain.[B] 6 But godliness with contentment is great gain. 7 For we brought nothing into the world, and[C] we can take nothing out. 8 If we have food and clothing,[D] we will be content with these. 9 But those who want to be rich fall into temptation, a trap, and many foolish and harmful desires, which plunge people into ruin and destruction. 10 For the love of money is a root[E] of all kinds of evil, and by craving it, some have wandered away from the faith and pierced themselves with many griefs.

FIGHT THE GOOD FIGHT

11 But you, man of God, flee from these things, and pursue righteousness, godliness, faith, love, endurance, and gentleness. 12 Fight the good fight of the faith. Take hold of eternal life to which you were called and about which you have made a good confession in the presence of many witnesses. 13 In the presence of God, who gives life to all, and of Christ Jesus, who gave a good confession before Pontius Pilate, I charge you 14 to keep this command without fault or failure until the appearing of our Lord Jesus Christ. 15 God will bring this about in his own time. He is the blessed and only Sovereign, the King of kings, and the Lord of lords, 16 who alone is immortal and who lives in unapproachable light, whom no one has seen or can see, to him be honor and eternal power. Amen.

INSTRUCTIONS TO THE RICH

17 Instruct those who are rich in the present age not to be arrogant or to set their hope on the uncertainty of wealth, but on God,[F]

Exercise of Faith | *Managing Money*

THE MONEY TRAP

"But those who want to be rich fall into temptation, a trap, and many foolish and harmful desires, which plunge people into ruin and destruction. For the love of money is a root of all kinds of evil, and by craving it, some have wandered away from the faith and pierced themselves with many griefs." 1 Timothy 6:9-10

Having a lot of money and nice things is *not* sinful. Many Bible characters—Abraham, Jacob, Job, David, Solomon, Lydia, Joseph of Arimathea, and others are depicted as having been very well-off.

Paul isn't cautioning about *having* wealth; he's warning against *loving* and *craving* and *hoarding* wealth. That's the danger—when we begin to dream and scheme about getting more and more. That's when our hearts get wrapped up in earthly stuff. And that's when we're at risk of falling "into temptation, a trap, and many foolish and harmful desires."

If you find yourself wanting to stockpile riches more than you want to share them, it's a red flag. Probably that's when you could benefit most from the discipline of giving. Generosity is one good way to mend a greedy heart.

For the next note on *Exercise of Faith*, see 1 Timothy 6:12.

[A] **6:2** Or *because, as believers who are dearly loved, they are devoted to others' welfare* [B] **6:5** Other mss add *From such people withdraw yourself.* [C] **6:7** Other mss add *it is clear that* [D] **6:8** Or *food and shelter* [E] **6:10** Or *is the root* [F] **6:17** Other mss read *on the living God*

who richly provides us with all things to
enjoy. [18] Instruct them to do what is good,
to be rich in good works, to be generous
and willing to share, [19] storing up treasure
for themselves as a good foundation for the
coming age, so that they may take hold of
what is truly life.

GUARD THE HERITAGE

[20] Timothy, guard what has been entrusted to
you, avoiding irreverent and empty speech
and contradictions from what is falsely called
knowledge. [21] By professing it, some people
have departed from the faith.

Grace be with you all.

Exercise of Faith | *Persevering*

THE FIGHT OF FAITH

"Fight the good fight of the faith. Take hold of eternal life to which you were called and about which you have made a good confession in the presence of many witnesses." 1 Timothy 6:12

Everything about faith is a fight. It's a fight to overcome pride and admit you're in a mess. It's a struggle to humble yourself and ask for rescue. Trusting the promises of Scripture in times of crisis is no walk in the park—more like an all-night, double-time march. Trying to help others grow spiritually can be like being caught in a withering cross-fire. Follow Jesus when it feels like the whole world is going the other direction? We sometimes want to go AWOL. Resist strong temptation? An all-out war!

For all these reasons and more, when we read Paul's words to Timothy, "Fight the good fight of the faith," we nod instinctively. We get it. The military metaphor resonates. It just rings true.

Paul, however, says it's a "good fight." In other words, it's well worth it.

Today, if you feel like waving the white flag, hang on. Help is on the way. Don't surrender. The fight of faith is a fight worth pursuing.

For the next note on *Exercise of Faith*, see 2 Timothy 3:16-17.

2 Timothy—More than truth to believe, the gospel is something to live. Paul's life is the prime example of that, for he had boldly proclaimed it and suffered for it. As he wrote these words to Timothy, he was preparing to die for it. Paul understood the meaning of taking up one's cross for the sake of Christ. So, when he urges Timothy to do that, his words carry weight.

In 2 Timothy we see an elder pastor who has finished his race well and has endured to the end. Now he is passing to Timothy the secret for perseverance in the faith: sound doctrine, which he calls a "pattern of sound teaching" and a "good deposit" (1:13-14). Paul urges Timothy to continue this process, passing the faith to the next generation (2:2). Far from being empty or cold facts, the Scriptures are what make us complete and "equipped for every good work" (3:17).

In the pursuit of restoration and wholeness, our greatest tool is the Word of God—the key to fighting the good fight to the end (4:7). If you are feeling discouraged, read the Bible. If you are confused or unsure of a decision, read the Bible. If you need hope or encouragement—read the Bible. These are supernaturally charged words of life and light, but to benefit from them we must read, study, meditate on, and apply them.

2 TIMOTHY

AUTHOR: The apostle Paul

DATE WRITTEN: This letter was written during Paul's final imprisonment in Rome, around AD 64–65.

ORIGINAL AUDIENCE: Timothy, Paul's coworker in the work of the gospel

SETTING: Not much is known about the circumstances of Paul's final imprisonment or the occasion of this letter. We probably should think of it as the last words of a pastor to the younger minister he has trained and for whom he has a deep personal affection.

PURPOSE FOR WRITING: The immediate purpose of Paul's letter is to urge Timothy to come visit him (4:9,21). Beyond that, these words offer perspective on the difficulties of ministry. Though he will face persecution and suffering, Timothy can stand firm to the end in the power of God, faithfully discharging the call of the gospel.

OUTLINE:

1. Greetings and Thanksgiving (1:1-7)
2. Exhortation to Service (1:8–2:26)
    - Courageous testimony (1:8-12)
    - Loyal witness (1:13–2:2)
    - Endurance in suffering (2:3-13)
    - Diligent service (2:14-26)
3. Exhortation to Sound Doctrine (3:1–4:8)
    - Hard times in the last days (3:1-9)
    - God's Word stands firm (3:10-17)
    - Charge to Timothy (4:1-8)
4. Final Instructions (4:9-18)
5. Benediction (4:19-22)

KEY VERSES:

"I have fought the good fight, I have finished the race, I have kept the faith. There is reserved for me the crown of righteousness, which the Lord, the righteous Judge, will give me on that day, and not only to me, but to all those who have loved his appearing."
—2 Timothy 4:7-8

RESTORATION THEMES

R	Rest and Reflection	*For the next note, see Hebrews 4:1.*
E	Eternal Perspective	*Fear Overcome—2 Timothy 1:7*
S	Support	*For the next note, see Hebrews 3:13.*
T	Thanksgiving and Contentment	*For the next note, see Titus 3:4-5.*
O	Other-centeredness	*Being Patient—2 Timothy 2:24-25*
R	Relationships	*Controlling Speech—2:16* *Dealing with Persecution—3:12*
E	Exercise of Faith	*Applying God's Word—3:16-17* *Finishing Strong—4:7-8*

GREETING

1 Paul, an apostle of Christ Jesus by God's
will, for the sake of the promise of life in
Christ Jesus:
2 To Timothy, my dearly loved son.
Grace, mercy, and peace from God the Father and Christ Jesus our Lord.

THANKSGIVING

3 I thank God, whom I serve with a clear conscience as my ancestors did, when I constantly
remember you in my prayers night and day.
4 Remembering your tears, I long to see you
so that I may be filled with joy. 5 I recall your
sincere faith that first lived in your grandmother Lois and in your mother Eunice and
now, I am convinced, is in you also.
6 Therefore, I remind you to rekindle the
gift of God that is in you through the laying
on of my hands. 7 For God has not given us
a spirit of fear, but one of power,[A] love, and
sound judgment.

NOT ASHAMED OF THE GOSPEL

8 So don't be ashamed of the testimony about
our Lord, or of me his prisoner. Instead, share
in suffering for the gospel, relying on the power
of God. 9 He has saved us and called us with
a holy calling, not according to our works,
but according to his own purpose and grace,
which was given to us in Christ Jesus before
time began. 10 This has now been made evident through the appearing of our Savior
Christ Jesus, who has abolished death and has
brought life and immortality to light through
the gospel. 11 For this gospel I was appointed a
herald, apostle, and teacher,[B] 12 and that is why
I suffer these things. But I am not ashamed,
because I know whom I have believed and am
persuaded that he is able to guard what has
been entrusted to me[C] until that day.

BE LOYAL TO THE FAITH

13 Hold on to the pattern of sound teaching
that you have heard from me, in the faith and
love that are in Christ Jesus. 14 Guard the good
deposit through the Holy Spirit who lives in
us. 15 You know that all those in the province
of Asia have deserted me, including Phygelus
and Hermogenes. 16 May the Lord grant mercy
to the household of Onesiphorus, because he
often refreshed me and was not ashamed of

Eternal Perspective | *Fear Overcome*

NO FEAR

"For God has not given us a spirit of fear, but one of power, love, and sound judgment." 2 Timothy 1:7

People are terrified of countless things—but three of humanity's biggest fears get voiced like this: (1) "What if I don't have what it takes to do what's been asked of me?" (2) "What if I move toward others and they reject me?" and (3) "What if I make a wrong decision?"

If you are asking these questions, you're not alone. Apparently, Timothy felt these three common fears, so much so that he seems to be shrinking from his duties as a young pastor in the big city of Ephesus. The apostle Paul wrote these words of encouragement to him.

"You don't have to be afraid," Paul essentially argued. "You *do* have what it takes—God has given you 'a spirit . . . of power.' He has also given you the capacity to love others regardless of how they respond. What's more, God has given you wisdom, 'a spirit of . . . sound judgment.' Stop doubting yourself all the time."

This is similar to what the great wizard Gandalf told Bilbo Baggins in J. R. R. Tolkien's classic book *The Hobbit*: "There is more to you than you know." Or maybe we should adapt that to "There is more to the God who dwells in us than we know." Ask the Holy Spirit to drive out your fear.

For the next note on *Eternal Perspective*, see Titus 2:13.

[A] **1:7** Or *For the Spirit God gave us does not make us fearful, but gives us power* [B] **1:11** Other mss add *of the Gentiles*
[C] **1:12** Or *guard what I have entrusted to him*, or *guard my deposit*

my chains. 17 On the contrary, when he was in
Rome, he diligently searched for me and found
me. 18 May the Lord grant that he obtain mercy
from him on that day. You know very well how
much he ministered at Ephesus.

BE STRONG IN GRACE

2 You, therefore, my son, be strong in the
grace that is in Christ Jesus. 2 What you
have heard from me in the presence of many
witnesses, commit to faithful men[A] who will
be able to teach others also.
3 Share in suffering as a good soldier of Christ
Jesus. 4 No one serving as a soldier gets entangled in the concerns of civilian life; he seeks to
please the commanding officer. 5 Also, if anyone competes as an athlete, he is not crowned
unless he competes according to the rules.
6 The hardworking farmer ought to be the first
to get a share of the crops. 7 Consider what I
say, for the Lord will give you understanding
in everything.
8 Remember Jesus Christ, risen from the
dead and descended from David, according
to my gospel, 9 for which I suffer to the point
of being bound like a criminal. But the word
of God is not bound. 10 This is why I endure
all things for the elect: so that they also may
obtain salvation, which is in Christ Jesus, with
eternal glory. 11 This saying is trustworthy:

For if we died with him,
we will also live with him;
12 if we endure, we will also reign
with him;
if we deny him, he will also deny us;
13 if we are faithless, he remains faithful,
for he cannot deny himself.

AN APPROVED WORKER

14 Remind them of these things, and charge
them before God[B] not to fight about words. This
is useless and leads to the ruin of those who
listen. 15 Be diligent to present yourself to God
as one approved, a worker who doesn't need
to be ashamed, correctly teaching the word of
truth. 16 Avoid irreverent and empty speech,
since those who engage in it will produce even
more godlessness, 17 and their teaching will
spread like gangrene. Hymenaeus and Philetus
are among them. 18 They have departed from
the truth, saying that the resurrection has already taken place, and are ruining the faith of
some. 19 Nevertheless, God's solid foundation
stands firm, bearing this inscription: **The Lord
knows those who are his**,[C] and let everyone
who calls on the name of[D] the Lord turn away
from wickedness.
20 Now in a large house there are not only
gold and silver vessels, but also those of wood
and clay; some for honorable[E] use and some

Relationships | *Controlling Speech*

TALK

"Avoid irreverent and empty speech, since those who engage in it will produce even more godlessness." 2 Timothy 2:16

Paul was writing to a professional "talker" (Timothy was a pastor/preacher by calling). So, for the wise, old apostle to bring up the subject of *speech* only makes sense. After all, if you speak for a living, you're likely to say words you shouldn't say.

"Avoid irreverent and empty speech," Paul urges Timothy—for the second time (see 1Tm 6:20). *Irreverent* conveys the idea of profane or unholy. It means "not of God." *Empty* means "vain or useless, worthless chatter." That kind of talk leads to nothing good.

Paul is not suggesting that every utterance needs to include a Bible verse or some over-the-top religious sentiment. He is reminding us that we should daily dedicate our mouths and lips to God's service (Rm 6:12-13). We should determine to honor God and encourage and affirm others with the words we utter.

For the next note on *Relationships*, see 2 Timothy 3:12.

[A] **2:2** Or *faithful people* [B] **2:14** Other mss read *before the Lord* [C] **2:19** Nm 16:5 [D] **2:19** Lit *everyone who names the name of*
[E] **2:20** Or *special*

for dishonorable.[A] 21 So if anyone purifies himself from anything dishonorable,[B] he will be
a special[C] instrument, set apart, useful to the
Master, prepared for every good work.
22 Flee from youthful passions, and pursue righteousness, faith, love, and peace,
along with those who call on the Lord from
a pure heart. 23 But reject foolish and ignorant disputes, because you know that they
breed quarrels. 24 The Lord's servant must
not quarrel, but must be gentle to everyone,
able to teach,[D] and patient, 25 instructing his
opponents with gentleness. Perhaps God will
grant them repentance leading them to the
knowledge of the truth. 26 Then they may
come to their senses and escape the trap
of the devil, who has taken them captive to
do his will.

DIFFICULT TIMES AHEAD

3 But know this: Hard times will come in
the last days. 2 For people will be lovers
of self, lovers of money, boastful, proud, demeaning, disobedient to parents, ungrateful,
unholy, 3 unloving, irreconcilable, slanderers,
without self-control, brutal, without love for
what is good, 4 traitors, reckless, conceited,
lovers of pleasure rather than lovers of God,
5 holding to the form of godliness but denying
its power. Avoid these people.
6 For among them are those who worm their
way into households and deceive gullible wom-
en overwhelmed by sins and led astray by a
variety of passions, 7 always learning and never able to come to a knowledge of the truth.
8 Just as Jannes and Jambres resisted Moses,
so these also resist the truth. They are men
who are corrupt in mind and worthless in
regard to the faith. 9 But they will not make
further progress, for their foolishness will be
clear to all, as was the foolishness of Jannes
and Jambres.

STRUGGLES IN THE CHRISTIAN LIFE

10 But you have followed my teaching, conduct, purpose, faith, patience, love, and endurance, 11 along with the persecutions and
sufferings that came to me in Antioch, Iconium, and Lystra. What persecutions I endured
— and yet the Lord rescued me from them
all. 12 In fact, all who want to live a godly
life in Christ Jesus will be persecuted. 13 Evil

Other-centeredness | *Being Patient*

PRODUCTIVE CONVERSATIONS

"The Lord's servant must not quarrel, but must be gentle to everyone, able to teach, and patient, instructing his opponents with gentleness. Perhaps God will grant them repentance leading them to the knowledge of the truth." 2 Timothy 2:24-25

- Thanks to social media, we now have a whole world of people who are skilled at ranting, name-calling, and bickering. Maybe we should call it *antisocial media*. If we are ever going to see civility restored, we desperately need a generation of thoughtful and gentle people.
- Paul urges Timothy in particular and all believers in general to resist the temptation to engage in fruitless quarrels with those who hold differing viewpoints. "The Lord's servant . . . must be gentle to everyone, able to teach, and patient."
- In speaking of being "able to teach" and "instructing his opponents," Paul is saying, "You need to know your stuff." Read. Listen. Become informed about your faith and about other belief systems.
- But we're not to use that information like a club. Engaging in shouting matches is never productive. Have cordial conversations. Be respectful. If we are patient and gentle with those far from Christ, "perhaps God will grant . . . repentance."
- Be patient with people, even those who strongly oppose you. Focus on winning people to Christ, not on winning arguments.

For the next note on *Other-centeredness*, see Philemon 4-5.

[A] **2:20** Or *ordinary* [B] **2:21** Lit *from these* [C] **2:21** Or *an honorable* [D] **2:24** Or *everyone, skillful in teaching*

people and impostors will become worse, deceiving and being deceived. [14] But as for you, continue in what you have learned and firmly believed. You know those who taught you, [15] and you know that from infancy you have known the sacred Scriptures, which

Relationships | *Dealing with Persecution*

UNPOPULAR MINORITY

"In fact, all who want to live a godly life in Christ Jesus will be persecuted." 2 Timothy 3:12

This is not the sort of Bible promise that gets turned into a plaque on the wall. This is one of those verses that makes us wince. We avert our gaze and rush past.

Here's why Western Christians have so much trouble connecting with these words. We live in nations that have historically tolerated—if not celebrated—Judeo-Christian values. Believers, especially in America, have always had influence, a seat at the table. In many locales and eras, Christian ideals have permeated culture for centuries.

A number of signs suggest, however, that those longtime realities may be changing. Instead of being a dominant majority, followers of Jesus may soon find themselves an unpopular minority. Could overt persecution follow? If so, we shouldn't be shocked. Our Christian brothers and sisters in many parts of the world have been experiencing persecution for almost twenty centuries.

Don't fear the prospect of suffering. God will care for us just as he cared for Paul and Timothy. Instead, we should fixate on the phrase "live a godly life." That's one thing we can control.

For the next note on *Relationships*, see Hebrews 6:10.

Exercise of Faith | *Applying God's Word*

GOD'S WONDERFUL WORD

"All Scripture is inspired by God and is profitable for teaching, for rebuking, for correcting, for training in righteousness, so that the man of God may be complete, equipped for every good work." 2 Timothy 3:16-17

For people who are interested in restoration—spiritual renewal, getting a second wind in life, relational and emotional healing—this verse is good news indeed. God has "breathed out" (that's the idea behind the word *inspired*) a book! This book—variously called the Word of God, the Bible, or Scripture—claims to be the revelation of God given through human authors to the human race.

No wonder the Bible is valuable—it shows us the way to live ("teaching"), points out our errors ("rebuking"), helps us get back on track ("correcting"), and helps us mature spiritually ("training").

The result is that we are "complete, equipped for every good work." The picture is of a ship that's headed out on a long voyage and has been fully stocked and furnished with everything the crew will need to arrive safely.

This can't be emphasized enough: Our attempts at spiritual restoration require biblical input in the same way our bodies require oxygen. Without it, we're doomed.

Make reading, studying, and applying Scripture your regular routine.

For the next note on *Exercise of Faith*, see 2 Timothy 4:7-8.

are able to give you wisdom for salvation
through faith in Christ Jesus. 16 All Scripture is inspired by God[A] and is profitable
for teaching, for rebuking, for correcting,
for training in righteousness, 17 so that the
man of God may be complete, equipped for
every good work.

FULFILL YOUR MINISTRY

4 I solemnly charge you before God and
Christ Jesus, who is going to judge the
living and the dead, and because of his appearing and his kingdom: 2 Preach the word;
be ready in season and out of season; rebuke,
correct, and encourage with great patience
and teaching. 3 For the time will come when
people will not tolerate sound doctrine, but
according to their own desires, will multiply teachers for themselves because they
have an itch to hear what they want to hear.
4 They will turn away from hearing the truth
and will turn aside to myths. 5 But as for you,
exercise self-control in everything, endure
hardship, do the work of an evangelist, fulfill
your ministry.
6 For I am already being poured out as a
drink offering, and the time for my departure
is close. 7 I have fought the good fight, I have
finished the race, I have kept the faith. 8 There
is reserved for me the crown of righteousness,
which the Lord, the righteous Judge, will give
me on that day, and not only to me, but to all
those who have loved his appearing.[B]

FINAL INSTRUCTIONS

9 Make every effort to come to me soon, 10 because Demas has deserted me, since he loved
this present world, and has gone to Thessalonica. Crescens has gone to Galatia, Titus to
Dalmatia. 11 Only Luke is with me. Bring Mark
with you, for he is useful to me in the ministry.
12 I have sent Tychicus to Ephesus. 13 When
you come, bring the cloak I left in Troas with
Carpus, as well as the scrolls, especially the
parchments. 14 Alexander the coppersmith
did great harm to me. The Lord will repay
him according to his works. 15 Watch out for
him yourself because he strongly opposed
our words.
16 At my first defense, no one stood by me, but

Exercise of Faith | *Finishing Strong*

FAMOUS LAST WORDS

"I have fought the good fight, I have finished the race, I have kept the faith. There is reserved for me the crown of righteousness, which the Lord, the righteous Judge, will give me on that day, and not only to me, but to all those who have loved his appearing." 2 Timothy 4:7-8

Most scholars agree these are Paul's last words. Some even think he was taken out onto the Appian Way outside Rome and executed shortly after writing this letter.

Whether the end came one hour or one month later, Paul sensed his time was running out. Yet the old saint had not a smidgen of sadness. No resignation. No fear whatsoever.

Quite the contrary—Paul's words ring with satisfaction and accomplishment. Why so upbeat? Because the great battle, the long marathon of life, presents ample opportunities to lose one's faith. Or abandon it. Paul did neither. He could declare joyfully, "I have kept the faith."

How can a person hang on like that old bulldog Paul, all the way to the end—perhaps even a bitter end? It takes grace. The infinite grace of a good God.

It also takes grit. The human determination to keep holding on, and keep putting one foot in front of another.

Ask God for both, so that one day you can echo Paul's words.

For the next note on *Exercise of Faith*, see 1 John 2:15.

[A] **3:16** Lit *breathed out by God* [B] **4:8** Or *have longed for his appearing*

everyone deserted me. May it not be counted
against them. 17 But the Lord stood with me
and strengthened me, so that I might fully
preach the word and all the Gentiles might
hear it. So I was rescued from the lion's mouth.
18 The Lord will rescue me from every evil
work and will bring me safely into his heavenly kingdom. To him be the glory forever
and ever! Amen.

BENEDICTION

19 Greet Prisca and Aquila, and the household
of Onesiphorus. 20 Erastus has remained at Corinth; I left Trophimus sick at Miletus. 21 Make
every effort to come before winter. Eubulus
greets you, as do Pudens, Linus, Claudia, and
all the brothers and sisters.

22 The Lord be with your spirit. Grace be
with you all.

Titus—Wherever productive ministry for the kingdom of God exists, we can be certain that Satan is also at work. That was the situation in Crete, where Titus had been left in charge. Though the church was young, false teachers had already arisen. Paul wrote to advise Titus in how to deal with their arguments head on, how to establish church leadership, and how to teach Christian living in light of the threat of false teachers.

The church in Crete lacked the leadership and experience to withstand the attacks that had arisen against the faith. Paul's instructions to Titus, then, were to establish the basic structures of church governance and conduct. The themes developed here of responsible leadership, sound doctrine, and Christian living are the issues that should be addressed at the most basic level of church organization.

Titus can help us individually and corporately as we strive to counteract false teaching in today's churches. The simplicity of Paul's words to Titus remind us that the Christian life need not be complicated or difficult to understand. Trusting responsiveness to God's Word and common-sense application of the truth are within our grasp. When we devote ourselves to obeying God, we will have confidence in our eternal standing before him.

TITUS

AUTHOR: The apostle Paul

DATE WRITTEN: AD 63, around the same time as Paul's other Pastoral Letters, 1 and 2 Timothy

ORIGINAL AUDIENCE: Titus, a Greek believer who was a close friend and confidante of Paul. He is mentioned thirteen times in Paul's letters and appears to have worked with Paul in Ephesus during his third missionary journey.

SETTING: Paul had begun the church in Crete during his first missionary journey (1:5; 3:15). He had not been able to stay long enough to establish church leadership, so he delegated that responsibility to Titus.

PURPOSE FOR WRITING: The church in Crete was young and inexperienced. The culture around them was negatively influencing them, and false teachers were stirring up trouble in the community. This businesslike letter set out to instruct Titus in establishing strong church leadership that would position the church to withstand the pressures of a pagan culture.

OUTLINE:

1. Greeting (1:1-4)
2. Instructions Concerning Elders (1:5-9)
3. Warnings against False Teachers (1:10-16)
4. Instructions on Sound Teaching for the Christian Life (2:1–3:11)

    Moral responsibilities (2:1-10)

    Grace and good works (2:11-15)

    Relating to those outside the faith (3:1-11)

5. Final Instructions (3:12-15)

KEY VERSE:

"He saved us—not by works of righteousness that we had done, but according to his mercy—through the washing of regeneration and renewal by the Holy Spirit." —Titus 3:5

RESTORATION THEMES

R	Rest and Reflection	*For the next note, see Hebrews 4:1.*
E	Eternal Perspective	*Biblical Hope—Titus 2:13*
S	Support	*For the next note, see Hebrews 3:13.*
T	Thanksgiving and Contentment	*Goodness and Mercy—Titus 3:4-5*
O	Other-centeredness	*For the next note, see Philemon 4-5.*
R	Relationships	*For the next note, see Hebrews 6:10.*
E	Exercise of Faith	*For the next note, see 1 John 2:15.*

GREETING

1 Paul, a servant of God and an apostle of
Jesus Christ, for[A] the faith of God's elect
and their knowledge of the truth that leads[B]
to godliness, 2 in the hope of eternal life that
God, who cannot lie, promised before time
began. 3 In his own time he has revealed his
word in the preaching with which I was entrusted by the command of God our Savior:
4 To Titus, my true son in our common faith.
Grace and peace from God the Father and
Christ Jesus our Savior.

TITUS'S MINISTRY IN CRETE

5 The reason I left you in Crete was to set right
what was left undone and, as I directed you,
to appoint elders in every town. 6 An elder
must be blameless: the husband of one wife,
with faithful[C] children who are not accused
of wildness or rebellion. 7 As an overseer of
God's household, he must be blameless: not
arrogant, not hot-tempered, not an excessive
drinker, not a bully, not greedy for money,
8 but hospitable, loving what is good, sensible,
righteous, holy, self-controlled, 9 holding to the
faithful message as taught, so that he will be
able both to encourage with sound teaching
and to refute those who contradict it.
10 For there are many rebellious people,
full of empty talk and deception, especially
those from the circumcision party. 11 It is necessary to silence them; they are ruining entire
households by teaching what they shouldn't
in order to get money dishonestly. 12 One of
their very own prophets said, "Cretans are
always liars, evil beasts, lazy gluttons." 13 This
testimony is true. For this reason, rebuke
them sharply, so that they may be sound in
the faith 14 and may not pay attention to Jewish myths and the commands of people who
reject the truth.
15 To the pure, everything is pure, but to those
who are defiled and unbelieving nothing is
pure; in fact, both their mind and conscience
are defiled. 16 They claim to know God, but they
deny him by their works. They are detestable,
disobedient, and unfit for any good work.

SOUND TEACHING AND CHRISTIAN LIVING

2 But you are to proclaim things consistent
with sound teaching. 2 Older men are to
be self-controlled, worthy of respect, sensible,
and sound in faith, love, and endurance. 3 In
the same way, older women are to be reverent in behavior, not slanderers, not slaves to
excessive drinking. They are to teach what is

Eternal Perspective | *Biblical Hope*

BLESSED HOPE

"We wait for the blessed hope, the appearing of the glory of our great God and Savior, Jesus Christ." Titus 2:13

"If I go away . . . I will come again," Jesus had assured his followers (Jn 14:3). Following his death, burial, and resurrection, he carried out the first part of that promise. Before a group of wide-eyed disciples, he ascended bodily into heaven. The two angelic messengers who were there asked, "Men of Galilee, why do you stand looking up into heaven? This same Jesus, who has been taken from you into heaven, will come in the same way that you have seen him going into heaven" (Ac 1:11).

That future reality has been the "blessed hope" of Christians worldwide for almost two thousand years. While global events keep us guessing, we never have to wonder or worry over how it will all end. History really is *his* story.

To be sure, an intense, long-running debate has been waged among believers about the timing of Christ's return, the signs that will precede his coming again, the sequence of end-time events, and so forth, but we know he is coming back—no argument there.

We have his word on it. Live as though Christ could return at any moment.

For the next note on *Eternal Perspective*, see Revelation 21:1.

[A] **1:1** Or *according to* [B] **1:1** Or *corresponds* [C] **1:6** Or *believing*

good, [4] so that they may encourage the young
women to love their husbands and to love
their children, [5] to be self-controlled, pure,
workers at home, kind, and in submission to
their husbands, so that God's word will not
be slandered.
[6] In the same way, encourage the young men
to be self-controlled [7] in everything. Make yourself an example of good works with integrity
and dignity[A] in your teaching. [8] Your message
is to be sound beyond reproach, so that any
opponent will be ashamed, because he doesn't
have anything bad to say about us.
[9] Slaves are to submit to their masters in everything, and to be well-pleasing, not talking
back [10] or stealing, but demonstrating utter
faithfulness, so that they may adorn the teaching of God our Savior in everything.
[11] For the grace of God has appeared, bringing salvation[B] for all people, [12] instructing us to
deny godlessness and worldly lusts and to live
in a sensible, righteous, and godly way in the
present age, [13] while we wait for the blessed
hope, the appearing of the glory of our great
God and Savior, Jesus Christ. [14] He gave himself
for us to redeem us from all lawlessness and
to cleanse for himself a people for his own
possession, eager to do good works.
[15] Proclaim these things; encourage and
rebuke with all authority. Let no one disregard[C] you.

CHRISTIAN LIVING AMONG OUTSIDERS

3 Remind them to submit to rulers and authorities, to obey, to be ready for every good
work, [2] to slander no one, to avoid fighting,
and to be kind, always showing gentleness
to all people. [3] For we too were once foolish,
disobedient, deceived, enslaved by various
passions and pleasures, living in malice and
envy, hateful, detesting one another.
[4] But when the kindness of God our Savior and his love for mankind appeared, [5] he
saved us — not by works of righteousness
that we had done, but according to his mercy
— through the washing of regeneration and
renewal by the Holy Spirit. [6] He poured out his
Spirit on us abundantly through Jesus Christ
our Savior [7] so that, having been justified by
his grace, we may become heirs with the hope
of eternal life. [8] This saying is trustworthy. I
want you to insist on these things, so that
those who have believed God might be careful
to devote themselves to good works. These
are good and profitable for everyone. [9] But
avoid foolish debates, genealogies, quarrels,
and disputes about the law, because they are
unprofitable and worthless. [10] Reject a divisive

Thanksgiving and Contentment | *Goodness and Mercy*

GOOD GOD

"But when the kindness of God our Savior and his love for mankind appeared, he saved us—not by works of righteousness that we had done, but according to his mercy—through the washing of regeneration and renewal by the Holy Spirit." Titus 3:4-5

If this passage were the only one we had to tell us about God, we'd have enough truth for a lifetime. Play Bible detective for a few moments. Look closely at all the divine clues that these two short verses reveal.

God is marked by "kindness." God is a "Savior." God has a "love for mankind." God's love for mankind "appeared" (a not-so-veiled reference to the coming of Jesus). God "saved us"—not because of anything we did, Paul explains, but "according to his mercy" (therefore, God is merciful). Our salvation included "washing" (or cleansing, a reference to forgiveness). It resulted in our "regeneration" (our being brought to life) and in "renewal by the Holy Spirit."

Put all these facts together and the only conclusion is that our God is unimaginably good, and we are unbelievably blessed. We are made new and alive by the Holy Spirit.

For the next note on *Thanksgiving and Contentment*, see Hebrews 7:23-25.

[A] **2:7** Other mss add *and incorruptibility* [B] **2:11** Or *appeared with saving power* [C] **2:15** Or *despise*

person after a first and second warning. 11 For
you know that such a person has gone astray
and is sinning; he is self-condemned.

FINAL INSTRUCTIONS AND CLOSING

12 When I send Artemas or Tychicus to you,
make every effort to come to me in Nicopolis,
because I have decided to spend the winter
there. 13 Diligently help Zenas the lawyer and
Apollos on their journey, so that they will lack
nothing.

14 Let our people learn to devote themselves
to good works for pressing needs, so that they
will not be unfruitful. 15 All those who are with
me send you greetings. Greet those who love
us in the faith. Grace be with all of you.

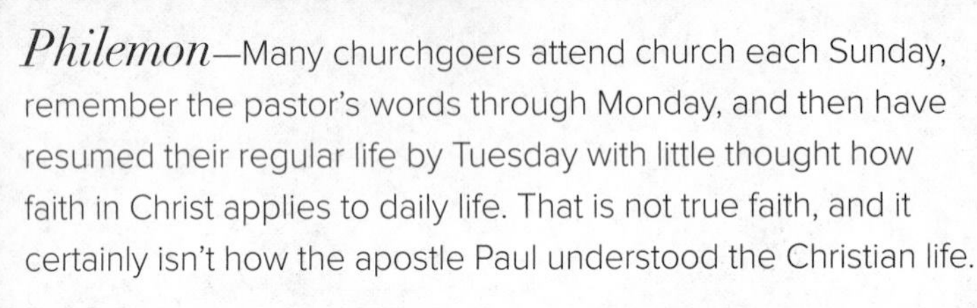

Philemon—Many churchgoers attend church each Sunday, remember the pastor's words through Monday, and then have resumed their regular life by Tuesday with little thought how faith in Christ applies to daily life. That is not true faith, and it certainly isn't how the apostle Paul understood the Christian life.

The brief letter of Philemon is a case study in how faith in Christ transforms a person's life, attitudes, and relationships. Onesimus was a slave who had robbed his master, Philemon, and then escaped to Rome. There he met the apostle Paul, heard the gospel, and was transformed. Now he planned to return to his master, so Paul wrote to ensure that Philemon would receive him as a brother in Christ rather than a fugitive deserving of death.

Onesimus the slave became a brother on equal standing before God and deserving of liberty. As such, he is a picture of all of us—once slaves to sin, now free in Christ with all the rights and responsibilities of children of God. In addition, all people have dignity and worth as God's image-bearers; therefore, any social institution that treats one group as inferior to another is antithetical to God's Word and the natural order he created.

PHILEMON

AUTHOR: The apostle Paul

DATE WRITTEN: Sometime between AD 60–61, while Paul was imprisoned in Rome

ORIGINAL AUDIENCE: Philemon, a prosperous businessman and slave owner from Colossae who was a brother in the faith (Col 4:9)

SETTING: Philemon's slave Onesimus had run away, taking some of his master's money with him, and taken refuge in Rome. There he had met Paul, been converted to the faith, and was now ready to face the consequences of his actions.

PURPOSE FOR WRITING: Paul wrote to ensure a loving reception for Onesimus with his master. Though according to the law Onesimus deserved the death penalty, Paul hoped that Philemon would receive him as a brother and free him to a life of service.

OUTLINE:

1. Greetings (1-3)
2. Thanksgiving for Philemon's Faith and Love (4-7)
3. Appeal for Onesimus (8-20)
4. Personal Greetings (21-25)

KEY VERSE:

"I pray that your participation in the faith may become effective through knowing every good thing that is in us for the glory of Christ." —Philemon 6

RESTORATION THEMES

R	Rest and Reflection	*For the next note, see Hebrews 4:1.*
E	Eternal Perspective	*For the next note, see Revelation 21:1.*
S	Support	*For the next note, see Hebrews 3:13.*
T	Thanksgiving and Contentment	*For the next note, see Hebrews 7:23-25.*
O	Other-centeredness	*Loving Others—Philemon 1:4-5*
R	Relationships	*For the next note, see Hebrews 6:10.*
E	Exercise of Faith	*For the next note, see 1 John 2:15.*

GREETING

Paul, a prisoner of Christ Jesus, and Timothy our brother:

To Philemon our dear friend and coworker, ²to Apphia our sister,[A] to Archippus our fellow soldier, and to the church that meets in your home.

³Grace to you and peace from God our Father and the Lord Jesus Christ.

PHILEMON'S LOVE AND FAITH

⁴I always thank my God when I mention you in my prayers, ⁵because I hear of your love for all the saints and the faith that you have in the Lord Jesus. ⁶I pray that your participation in the faith may become effective through knowing every good thing that is in us[B] for the glory of Christ. ⁷For I have great joy and encouragement from your love, because the hearts of the saints have been refreshed through you, brother.

AN APPEAL FOR ONESIMUS

⁸For this reason, although I have great boldness in Christ to command you to do what is right, ⁹I appeal to you, instead, on the basis of love. I, Paul, as an elderly man[C] and now also as a prisoner of Christ Jesus, ¹⁰appeal to you for my son, Onesimus.[D] I became his father while I was in chains. ¹¹Once he was useless to you, but now he is useful both to you and to me. ¹²I am sending him back to you — I am sending my very own heart.[E,F] ¹³I wanted to keep him with me, so that in my imprisonment for the gospel he might serve me in your place. ¹⁴But I didn't want to do anything without your consent, so that your good deed might not be out of obligation, but of your own free will. ¹⁵For perhaps this is why he was separated from you for a brief time, so that you might get him back permanently, ¹⁶no longer as a slave, but more than a slave — as a dearly loved brother. He is especially so to me, but how much more to you, both in the flesh and in the Lord.

¹⁷So if you consider me a partner, welcome him as you would me. ¹⁸And if he has wronged you in any way, or owes you anything, charge that to my account. ¹⁹I, Paul, write this with my own hand: I will repay it — not to mention to you that you owe me even your very

Other-centeredness | *Loving Others*

REFRESHER OF HEARTS

"I always thank my God when I mention you in my prayers, because I hear of your love for all the saints and the faith that you have in the Lord Jesus." Philemon 4-5

Philemon was the kind of guy you'd want as a neighbor, son-in-law, or business partner. If he were in your church, you'd nominate him for a leadership position.

Paul describes him as "our dear friend and coworker" (1). He then gushes about Philemon's "love for all the saints," his "faith . . . in the Lord Jesus," and the faithful way he has refreshed "the hearts of the saints" (5,7). By the end of this short letter—not much more than a postcard, actually—Paul is inviting himself for a future stay at Philemon's house (22).

But a phrase near the beginning of this note really stands out. Paul admits, "I always thank my God when I mention you in my prayers." How about that? Just the thought of Philemon sparks an outburst of gratitude in the apostle.

Wouldn't it be something if the mention of your name prompted others to smile and say a silent prayer of thanks? It can happen—if your life is all about loving people and trusting God.

Ask God to make this a reality in your experience. Pray that you'll learn to become a refresher of hearts.

For the next note on *Other-centeredness*, see Hebrews 12:14.

[A] **2** Other mss read *our beloved* [B] **6** Other mss read *in you* [C] **9** Or *an ambassador* [D] **10** In Gk, *Onesimus* means "useful"
[E] **12** Other mss read *him back. Receive him, my own heart.* [F] **12** Lit *you — that is, my own heart*

self. 20 Yes, brother, may I benefit from you in
the Lord; refresh my heart in Christ. 21 Since I
am confident of your obedience, I am writing
to you, knowing that you will do even more
than I say. 22 Meanwhile, also prepare a guest
room for me, since I hope that through your
prayers I will be restored to you.

FINAL GREETINGS

23 Epaphras, my fellow prisoner in Christ Jesus,
sends you greetings, and so do 24 Mark, Aristarchus, Demas, and Luke, my coworkers.
25 The grace of the Lord[A] Jesus Christ be
with your spirit.

Onesimus | Restoration Profile

COLOSSIANS 4:9; PHILEMON

In the world of the New Testament, slavery was a fact of life. Throughout the Roman Empire, slaves far outnumbered citizens. Many early Christians were slaves. The gospel had a radical social effect as an equalizing message that gave all people the same standing before God as sinners capable of experiencing his saving and restoring work. Given those conditions, not surprisingly Paul, in one of his most compelling descriptions of Jesus Christ, reminds us that the Son of God chose to take on the role of a servant (Php 2:7) in order to be our Savior.

Onesimus was a slave from Colossae, and his master was a Christian named Philemon, a church leader. We have no evidence that Paul was ever in Colossae, so he may have met Philemon and even Onesimus in Laodicea during a missionary journey. At some point, Onesimus had run away and made his way to Rome, where he had met Paul, who was in prison. Through Paul, Onesimus also met Christ. Eventually, Paul sent the runaway slave home to Philemon with a cover letter.

Paul's purpose was to ease Onesimus's return by reminding Philemon of the relationship all three men now shared with Christ. He didn't deny Philemon's possible anger with his wayward slave but reminded him that God had made use of Onesimus's wandering to bring him to a place of restoration. If restitution was necessary, Paul accepted the responsibility. Rather than argue against the reality of slavery in his time, Paul planted the seeds of human dignity accomplished on the cross that eventually demolished the acceptance of slavery. Onesimus's restoration was a matter far bigger than his social status. Master and slave were now brothers. What people call impossible, God calls restoration.

[A] 25 Other mss read *our Lord*

Hebrews—We have experienced times of stagnation in our faith, those times when our prayers don't seem to go anywhere. At these times, we need deep soul restoration to renew our hope and our zeal for the gospel. Hebrews breaks us out of our complacency, urging us to mature in our faith as we consider the glorious person and work of Jesus Christ.

Hebrews first encourages us to consider Jesus Christ in comparison to the Old Testament. In every way, he fulfills the requirements of the law and the symbols of the faith, but he does so in a way that reveals the old covenant to be a mere shadow of the ultimate reality. The promises Jesus offers are far better than we could ever think. Our eternal destiny is sure and will be superior in every way to all that we imagine.

In light of this hope, the author of Hebrews exhorts us to live for Christ. Our exaltation of Christ calls for a response—a life of worship and devotion to the Creator and sustainer of the universe who has saved us by his blood. Jesus, the One who is superior to the angels, to Moses, and to the Levitical priesthood, deserves our utmost love and wholehearted devotion.

HEBREWS

AUTHOR: Unknown

DATE WRITTEN: Also unknown, perhaps the early AD 60s during the persecution under Nero, but internal evidence suggests it was written prior to the fall of Jerusalem (AD 70).

ORIGINAL AUDIENCE: Early Jewish believers who had a good knowledge of the Old Testament, perhaps a group of house churches in Rome

SETTING: The book of Hebrews is more sermon than letter. It has no personal greetings or specifics of a situation to which the author was responding. Rather, it contains a complex and sustained theological description of God's redemption through Christ. Hebrews is for all believers as we strive to understand the glorious beauty of Christ and the faith to which we are called.

PURPOSE FOR WRITING: The writer has one overarching purpose: to exalt Jesus Christ. This complex book is tied together through the repeated use of the word "better." In comparison to everything else, Jesus Christ is better.

OUTLINE:

1. The Superiority of the Son of God (1:1–2:18)
2. The Superiority of the Son's Faithfulness (3:1–4:16)
3. The Superiority of the Son's Work (5:1–6:20)
4. The Superiority of the Son's Priesthood (7:1–10:39)
5. The Superiority of the Christian Faith (11:1–12:2)
6. The Superiority of the Father's Way (12:3-29)
7. The Superiority of the Christian Life (13:1-25)

KEY VERSE:

"Therefore, let us approach the throne of grace with boldness, so that we may receive mercy and find grace to help us in time of need." —Hebrews 4:16

RESTORATION THEMES

R	Rest and Reflection	*Observing Sabbath—4:1* *Being Alone with God—4:9-11*
E	Eternal Perspective	*For the next note, see Revelation 21:1.*
S	Support	*Small Groups—Hebrews 3:13* *Prayer—4:16*
T	Thanksgiving and Contentment	*Praise for Jesus and His Work—7:23-25* *Forgiveness—8:12*
O	Other-centeredness	*Living Peacefully—12:14* *Caring—13:1* *Being Unselfish—13:16*
R	Relationships	*Relating to Church Family—6:10* *Building Positive Relationships—10:24* *Relating to Spiritual Leaders—13:17*
E	Exercise of Faith	*For the next note, see 1 John 2:15.*

THE NATURE OF THE SON

1 Long ago God spoke to the fathers by the
prophets at different times and in different
ways. 2 In these last days, he has spoken to us
by his Son. God has appointed him heir of all
things and made the universe[A] through him.
3 The Son is the radiance[B] of God's glory and
the exact expression[C] of his nature, sustaining
all things by his powerful word. After making
purification for sins,[D] he sat down at the right
hand of the Majesty on high.[E] 4 So he became
superior to the angels, just as the name he
inherited is more excellent than theirs.

THE SON SUPERIOR TO ANGELS

5 For to which of the angels did he ever say,
You are my Son;
today I have become your Father,[F,G]
or again,
I will be his Father,
and he will be my Son?[H]
6 Again, when he[I] brings his firstborn into
the world, he says,
And let all God's angels worship
him.[J]
7 And about the angels he says:
He makes his angels winds,[K]
and his servants[L] **a fiery flame,**[M]
8 but to[N] the Son:
Your throne, O God,
is forever and ever,
and the scepter of your kingdom
is a scepter of justice.
9 **You have loved righteousness**
and hated lawlessness;
this is why God, your God,
has anointed you
with the oil of joy
beyond your companions.[O,P]
10 And:
In the beginning, Lord,
you established the earth,
and the heavens are the works
of your hands;
11 **they will perish, but you remain.**
They will all wear out like clothing;
12 **you will roll them up like a cloak,**[Q]
and they will be changed
like clothing.
But you are the same,
and your years will never end.[R]
13 Now to which of the angels has he ever said:
Sit at my right hand
until I make your enemies
your footstool?[S]
14 Are they not all ministering spirits sent out to
serve those who are going to inherit salvation?

WARNING AGAINST NEGLECT

2 For this reason, we must pay attention all
the more to what we have heard, so that
we will not drift away. 2 For if the message
spoken through angels was legally binding[T]
and every transgression and disobedience
received a just punishment, 3 how will we escape if we neglect such a great salvation? This
salvation had its beginning when it was spoken
of by the Lord, and it was confirmed to us by
those who heard him. 4 At the same time, God
also testified by signs and wonders, various
miracles, and distributions of gifts from the
Holy Spirit according to his will.

JESUS AND HUMANITY

5 For he has not subjected to angels the world
to come that we are talking about. 6 But someone somewhere has testified:
What is man that you remember him,
or the son of man that you care
for him?
7 **You made him lower than the angels**
for a short time;
you crowned him with glory
and honor[U]
8 **and subjected everything**
under his feet.[V]
For in **subjecting everything** to him, he left
nothing that is not subject to him. As it is, we
do not yet see **everything subjected** to him.
9 But we do see Jesus — **made lower than**
the angels for a short time so that by God's
grace he might taste death for everyone —
crowned with glory and honor because he
suffered death.
10 For in bringing many sons and daughters
to glory, it was entirely appropriate that God
— for whom and through whom all things
exist — should make the source[W] of their

[A] **1:2** Lit *ages* [B] **1:3** Or *reflection* [C] **1:3** Or *representation*, or *copy*, or *reproduction* [D] **1:3** Other mss read *for our sins by himself* [E] **1:3** Or *he sat down on high at the right hand of the Majesty* [F] **1:5** Or *have begotten you* [G] **1:5** Ps 2:7 [H] **1:5** 2Sm 7:14; 1Ch 17:13 [I] **1:6** Or *When he again* [J] **1:6** Dt 32:43 LXX; Ps 97:7 [K] **1:7** Or *spirits* [L] **1:7** Or *ministers* [M] **1:7** Ps 104:4 [N] **1:8** Or *about* [O] **1:9** Or *associates* [P] **1:8-9** Ps 45:6-7 [Q] **1:12** Other mss omit *like a cloak* [R] **1:10-12** Ps 102:25-27 [S] **1:13** Ps 110:1 [T] **2:2** Or *valid*, or *reliable* [U] **2:7** Other mss add *and set him over the works of your hands* [V] **2:6-8** Ps 8:5-7 LXX [W] **2:10** Or *pioneer*, or *leader*

salvation perfect through sufferings. 11 For
the one who sanctifies and those who are
sanctified all have one Father.[A] That is why
Jesus is not ashamed to call them brothers
and sisters, 12 saying:

I will proclaim your name
to my brothers and sisters;
I will sing hymns to you
in the congregation.[B]

13 Again, **I will trust in him.**[C] And again, **Here**
I am with the children God gave me.[D]
14 Now since the children have flesh and
blood in common, Jesus also shared in these,
so that through his death he might destroy
the one holding the power of death — that
is, the devil — 15 and free those who were
held in slavery all their lives by the fear of
death. 16 For it is clear that he does not reach
out to help angels, but to help Abraham's
offspring. 17 Therefore, he had to be like his
brothers and sisters in every way, so that he
could become a merciful and faithful high
priest in matters[E] pertaining to God, to make
atonement[F] for the sins of the people. 18 For
since he himself has suffered when he was
tempted, he is able to help those who are
tempted.

For since he himself has suffered when he was tempted, he is able to help those who are tempted.
—Hebrews 2:18

OUR APOSTLE AND HIGH PRIEST

3 Therefore, holy brothers and sisters, who
share in a heavenly calling, consider Jesus,
the apostle and high priest of our confession.
2 He was faithful to the one who appointed
him, just as Moses was in all God's household.
3 For Jesus is considered worthy of more glory
than Moses, just as the builder has more honor
than the house. 4 Now every house is built by
someone, but the one who built everything is
God. 5 Moses was faithful as a servant in all
God's household, as a testimony to what would
be said in the future. 6 But Christ was faithful
as a Son over his household. And we are that
household if we hold on to our confidence
and the hope in which we boast.[G]

Support | *Small Groups*

EACH OTHER

"But encourage each other daily, while it is still called today, so that none of you is hardened by sin's deception." Hebrews 3:13

The biblical verb *encourage* has a range of meanings. The most familiar one is "to comfort or console another, especially one who is upset or grieving." Think of a mom patting a tearful child's hand and say, "There, there. Everything will be okay. Have a cookie." Or picture a friend wrapping a hurting companion in a tight bear hug.

The word *encourage* can also convey the stronger action of calling out, exhorting, challenging, or urging. Think of a coach rallying his dejected team at halftime: "Guys, you see this big mirror on the wall here? Look into it! See that guy staring back at you? That guy is *better* than what he just showed out there in the first half. You know it, and he knows it. Now look at me. Forget the score. Let's go out there and play this second half like you know you can! One play at a time! Now bring it in."

In the spiritual life, we need—and we need to give—both kinds of encouragement. Gentle pats on the back, and firm but loving kicks a little further south on the backside. This can happen one-on-one and in small groups.

Where do you encourage and get encouraged?

For the next note on *Support*, see Hebrews 4:16.

[A] **2:11** Or *father*, or *origin*; lit *all are of one* [B] **2:12** Ps 22:22 [C] **2:13** 2Sm 22:3 LXX; Is 8:17 LXX; 12:2 LXX [D] **2:13** Is 8:18 LXX [E] **2:17** Lit *things* [F] **2:17** Or *propitiation* [G] **3:6** Other mss add *firm to the end*

WARNING AGAINST UNBELIEF

[7] Therefore, as the Holy Spirit says:
Today, if you hear his voice,
8 **do not harden your hearts**
as in the rebellion,
on the day of testing
in the wilderness,
9 **where your fathers tested me,**
tried me,
and saw my works [10] for forty years.
Therefore I was provoked to anger
with that generation
and said, "They always go astray
in their hearts,
and they have not known
my ways."
11 **So I swore in my anger,**
"They will not enter my rest."[A]
[12] Watch out, brothers and sisters, so that there
won't be in any of you an evil, unbelieving
heart that turns away from the living God.
[13] But encourage each other daily, while it is
still called **today**, so that none of you is hardened by sin's deception. [14] For we have become
participants in Christ if we hold firmly until
the end the reality[B] that we had at the start.
[15] As it is said:
Today, if you hear his voice,
do not harden your hearts
as in the rebellion.[C]
[16] For who heard and rebelled? Wasn't it all
who came out of Egypt under Moses? [17] With
whom was God angry for forty years? Wasn't
it with those who sinned, whose bodies fell
in the wilderness? [18] And to whom did he
swear that they would not enter his rest,
if not to those who disobeyed? [19] So we see
that they were unable to enter because of
unbelief.

THE PROMISED REST

4 Therefore, since the promise to enter his
rest remains, let us beware[D] that none of
you be found to have fallen short.[E] [2] For we also
have received the good news just as they did.
But the message they heard did not benefit
them, since they were not united with those
who heard it in faith.[F] [3] For we who have believed enter the rest, in keeping with what[G]
he has said,

Rest and Reflection | *Observing Sabbath*

A TIME TO REST

"Therefore, since the promise to enter his rest remains, let us beware that none of you be found to have fallen short." Hebrews 4:1

Liberated from slavery in Egypt, and fresh off the experience of entering a covenant with God at Mount Sinai, the Israelites found themselves on the edge of the promised land. It was exactly as advertised: a good land, "flowing with milk and honey" (Ex 3:8,17; 33:3). Here, God had promised to give his people a new life of joy, peace, and rest.

Except the Israelites balked. The people of the land intimidated them, so they refused to accept the rest offered by God. The consequence? A restless forty-year time-out in the Judean wilderness.

Now, through faith in Christ, God offers his new covenant people a new life of joy, peace, and rest. And one of the ways we experience this life is by keeping the Sabbath, a day of rest that God instituted at the time of creation (Gn 2:2).

Sabbath means stopping. Going off duty. Ceasing our mad scramble to accomplish and achieve. Anyone who's tried it will tell you that practicing Sabbath in a culture that worships productivity takes every bit as much faith and determination as the ancient people of God needed to enter Canaan.

Taking one day a week to simply *be* and not *do* feels irresponsible. It's not. It's a healing step of great faith. Entering Sabbath is how our souls find restoration and replenishment.

For the next note on *Rest and Reflection*, see Hebrews 4:9-11.

[A] **3:7-11** Ps 95:7-11 [B] **3:14** Or *confidence* [C] **3:15** Ps 95:7-8 [D] **4:1** Lit *fear* [E] **4:1** Or *that any of you might seem to have missed it* [F] **4:2** Other mss read *since it was not united by faith in those who heard* [G] **4:3** Or *rest, just as*

So I swore in my anger,
"They will not enter my rest,"[A]
even though his works have been finished
since the foundation of the world. 4 For somewhere he has spoken about the seventh day
in this way: **And on the seventh day God**
rested from all his works.[B] 5 Again, in that
passage he says, **They will never enter my**
rest.[C] 6 Therefore, since it remains for some
to enter it, and those who formerly received
the good news did not enter because of disobedience, 7 he again specifies a certain day
— **today**. He specified this speaking through
David after such a long time:

Today, if you hear his voice,
do not harden your hearts.[D]

8 For if Joshua had given them rest, God
would not have spoken later about another
day. 9 Therefore, a Sabbath rest remains for
God's people. 10 For the person who has entered his rest has rested from his own works,
just as God did from his. 11 Let us then make
every effort to enter that rest, so that no one
will fall into the same pattern of disobedience.
12 For the word of God is living and effective
and sharper than any double-edged sword,
penetrating as far as the separation of soul
and spirit, joints and marrow. It is able to judge
the thoughts and intentions of the heart. 13 No
creature is hidden from him, but all things
are naked and exposed to the eyes of him to
whom we must give an account.

OUR GREAT HIGH PRIEST

14 Therefore, since we have a great high priest
who has passed through the heavens — Jesus
the Son of God — let us hold fast to our confession. 15 For we do not have a high priest who
is unable to sympathize with our weaknesses,
but one who has been tempted in every way
as we are, yet without sin. 16 Therefore, let us
approach the throne of grace with boldness,
so that we may receive mercy and find grace
to help us in time of need.

CHRIST, A HIGH PRIEST

5 For every high priest taken from among
men is appointed in matters pertaining
to God for the people, to offer both gifts and
sacrifices for sins. 2 He is able to deal gently
with those who are ignorant and are going
astray, since he is also clothed with weakness.
3 Because of this, he must make an offering
for his own sins as well as for the people. 4 No

Rest and Reflection | *Being Alone with God*

WHAT TO DO ON THE SABBATH?

"Therefore, a Sabbath rest remains for God's people. For the person who has entered his rest has rested from his own works, just as God did from his. Let us then make every effort to enter that rest, so that no one will fall into the same pattern of disobedience." Hebrews 4:9-11

The Bible says much about *rest*: God resting after his work of creation (Gn 2:2); the Israelites resting after subduing and settling Canaan (Jos 21:44); the tantalizing rest offered by Jesus (Mt 11:28-30); eternal rest in the life to come (Rv 21:1-5).

And then we have the Sabbath—God telling his people that on one day each week they should stop and just *be*. Keeping the Sabbath restores our souls. It reminds our proud hearts that we aren't God—the world doesn't stop spinning when we briefly cease our frenetic activity. The Sabbath gives us time and space to catch our breath. It offers us a chance to reflect, review, and reorder our lives. When we stop and reflect, we can't help but thank the One who has given us so much.

Try it one day this week. It doesn't have to be Sunday or, as Jews observe it, sundown Friday to sundown Saturday. Just take twenty-four hours completely off. Forget your to-do list. Forget the urgent. Focus instead on the important. Spend time with God and with those you love, just enjoying their company.

For the next note on *Rest and Reflection*, see James 1:2.

[A] **4:3** Ps 95:11 [B] **4:4** Gn 2:2 [C] **4:5** Ps 95:11 [D] **4:7** Ps 95:7-8

one takes this honor on himself; instead, a
person is called by God, just as Aaron was.
5 In the same way, Christ did not exalt himself to become a high priest, but God who
said to him,

You are my Son;
today I have become your Father,[A,B]

6 also says in another place,

You are a priest forever
according to the order
of Melchizedek.[C]

7 During his earthly life,[D] he offered prayers
and appeals with loud cries and tears to the
one who was able to save him from death,
and he was heard because of his reverence.
8 Although he was the Son, he learned obedience from what he suffered. 9 After he was
perfected, he became the source of eternal
salvation for all who obey him, 10 and he was
declared by God a high priest according to
the order of Melchizedek.

THE PROBLEM OF IMMATURITY

11 We have a great deal to say about this, and
it is difficult to explain, since you have become too lazy to understand. 12 Although by
this time you ought to be teachers, you need
someone to teach you the basic principles
of God's revelation again. You need milk, not
solid food. 13 Now everyone who lives on milk
is inexperienced with the message about righteousness, because he is an infant. 14 But solid
food is for the mature — for those whose senses have been trained to distinguish between
good and evil.

WARNING AGAINST FALLING AWAY

6 Therefore, let us leave the elementary
teaching about Christ and go on to maturity, not laying again a foundation of repentance
from dead works, faith in God, 2 teaching about
ritual washings,[E] laying on of hands, the resurrection of the dead, and eternal judgment.
3 And we will do this if God permits.
4 For it is impossible to renew to repentance
those who were once enlightened, who tasted
the heavenly gift, who shared in the Holy Spirit,
5 who tasted God's good word and the powers
of the coming age, 6 and who have fallen away.
This is because,[F] to their own harm, they are
recrucifying the Son of God and holding him
up to contempt. 7 For the ground that drinks the
rain that often falls on it and that produces vegetation useful to those for whom it is cultivated
receives a blessing from God. 8 But if it produces
thorns and thistles, it is worthless and about to
be cursed, and at the end will be burned.

HOLY BOLDNESS

"Therefore, let us approach the throne of grace with boldness, so that we may receive mercy and find grace to help us in time of need." Hebrews 4:16

One of the more curious aspects of the blockbuster movie *Castaway* is the fact that the main character (played by Tom Hanks) never once looked up into the heavens and cried out for help, even when he was stranded on a remote island. (Even if we think that he must have been an agnostic, surveys have shown that a good percentage of skeptics *do* resort to prayer in emergencies.)

Prayer requires humility. It admits inadequacy. It requests help.

Only *you* really know what you're facing today, but chances are good that in some area of life you are in over your head. Don't try to muscle through life in your own strength. Don't be too proud to say, "This is too big to tackle by myself."

God has a "throne of grace." The One who sits on that throne offers "mercy" and "help . . . in time of need." Going boldly—not sheepishly—to him for assistance isn't weak. It's wise.

For the next note on *Support*, see James 4:2.

[A] **5:5** Lit *I have begotten you* [B] **5:5** Ps 2:7 [C] **5:6** Gn 14:18-20; Ps 110:4 [D] **5:7** Lit *In the days of his flesh* [E] **6:2** Or *about baptisms* [F] **6:6** Or *while*

Embracing God's Word | Renewal

TRUDGING, WILDERNESS MEANDER—lambs lost, exhausted, and famished. Thoroughly drained, we need divine nourishment, rest, renewal. But our loving Shepherd is near—hallelujah.

And [God] replied, "My presence will go with you, and I will give you rest." –Exodus 33:14

The LORD gave them rest on every side according to all he had sworn to their fathers. None of their enemies were able to stand against them, for the LORD handed over all their enemies to them. –Joshua 21:44

The LORD is my shepherd; I have what I need. He lets me lie down in green pastures; he leads me beside quiet waters. He renews my life. –Psalm 23:1-3

Restore the joy of your salvation to me, and sustain me my giving me a willing spirit. –Psalm 51:12

I said, "If only I had wings like a dove! I would fly away and find rest." –Psalm 55:6

Return to your rest, my soul, for the LORD has been good to you. –Psalm 116:7

For the Lord GOD, the Holy One of Israel, has said: "You will be delivered by returning and resting; your strength will lie in quiet confidence." –Isaiah 30:15

For the High and Exalted One, who lives forever, whose name is holy, says this: "I live in a high and holy place, and with the oppressed and lowly of spirit, to revive the spirit of the lowly and revive the heart of the oppressed." –Isaiah 57:15

LORD, bring us back to yourself, so we may return; renew our days as in former times. –Lamentations 5:21

The LORD your God is among you, a warrior who saves. He will rejoice over you with gladness. He will be quiet in his love. He will delight in you with singing. –Zephaniah 3:17

Come to me, all of you who are weary and burdened, and I will give you rest. Take up my yoke and learn from me, because I am lowly and humble in heart, and you will find rest for your souls. For my yoke is easy and my burden is light. –Matthew 11:28-30

Therefore we do not give up. Even though our outer person is being destroyed, our inner person is being renewed day by day. –2 Corinthians 4:16

Since it is just for God to repay with affliction those who afflict you and to give relief to you who are afflicted, along with us. –2 Thessalonians 1:6-7

Therefore, a Sabbath rest remains for God's people. For the person who has entered his rest has rested from his own works, just as God did from his. Let us then make every effort to enter that rest, so that no one will fall into the same pattern of disobedience. –Hebrews 4:9-11

The God of all grace, who called you to his eternal glory in Christ, will himself restore, establish, strengthen, and support you after you have suffered a little while. –1 Peter 5:10

9 Even though we are speaking this way,
dearly loved friends, in your case we are confident of things that are better and that per-
tain to salvation. 10 For God is not unjust; he
will not forget your work and the love[A] you
demonstrated for his name by serving the
saints — and by continuing to serve them.
11 Now we desire each of you to demonstrate
the same diligence for the full assurance of
your hope until the end, 12 so that you won't
become lazy but will be imitators of those
who inherit the promises through faith and
perseverance.

INHERITING THE PROMISE

13 For when God made a promise to Abraham,
since he had no one greater to swear by, he
swore by himself: 14 **I will indeed bless you,
and I will greatly multiply you.**[B] 15 And so,
after waiting patiently, Abraham obtained the
promise. 16 For people swear by something
greater than themselves, and for them a con-
firming oath ends every dispute. 17 Because God
wanted to show his unchangeable purpose
even more clearly to the heirs of the promise, he guaranteed it with an oath, 18 so that
through two unchangeable things, in which it
is impossible for God to lie, we who have fled
for refuge might have strong encouragement
to seize the hope set before us. 19 We have this
hope as an anchor for the soul, firm and secure. It enters the inner sanctuary behind the
curtain. 20 Jesus has entered there on our behalf as a forerunner, because he has become
a high priest forever according to the order
of Melchizedek.

THE GREATNESS OF MELCHIZEDEK

7 For this Melchizedek, king of Salem, priest
of God Most High, met Abraham and
blessed him as he returned from defeating
the kings, 2 and Abraham gave him a tenth
of everything. First, his name means king of
righteousness, then also, king of Salem, meaning king of peace. 3 Without father, mother, or
genealogy, having neither beginning of days
nor end of life, but resembling the Son of God,
he remains a priest forever.

4 Now consider how great this man was:
even Abraham the patriarch gave a tenth of
the plunder to him. 5 The sons of Levi who
receive the priestly office have a command
according to the law to collect a tenth from
the people — that is, from their brothers and

Relationships | *Relating to Church Family*

THE DARK SIDE—AND UPSIDE—OF SERVING

"For God is not unjust; he will not forget your work and the love you demonstrated for his name by serving the saints— and by continuing to serve them." Hebrews 6:10

A big reason we often resist serving? We don't like being treated like servants. You knock yourself out for others, and what do you get in return? Often people don't even acknowledge your efforts. Or worse, they find fault with what you've done. As someone has said, "No good deed goes unpunished!"

Yes, serving others is often a thankless task. But another, bigger truth is in play, too. "God . . . will not forget your work." The Almighty sees your sacrificial service, even if no one else does. The Lord takes note of the love you pour out on others.

Instead of focusing on the dark side of service—that people are ungrateful—remember the upside. God is faithful. As long as we serve to get thanks from people, we will continually be disappointed. When we desire simply to demonstrate love for God, we can never lose heart.

Are you weary today? Sick and tired of people taking you for granted? Keep demonstrating your love "for his name by serving the saints."

For the next note on *Relationships*, see Hebrews 10:24.

[A] **6:10** Other mss read *labor of love* [B] **6:14** Gn 22:17

sisters — though they have also descended
from Abraham. 6 But one without this[A] lineage
collected a tenth from Abraham and blessed
the one who had the promises. 7 Without a
doubt, the inferior is blessed by the superior.
8 In the one case, men who will die receive a
tenth, but in the other case, Scripture testifies
that he lives. 9 And in a sense Levi himself, who
receives a tenth, has paid a tenth through
Abraham, 10 for he was still within his ancestor[B] when Melchizedek met him.

A SUPERIOR PRIESTHOOD

11 Now if perfection came through the Levitical priesthood (for on the basis of it the people received the law), what further need was
there for another priest to appear, said to be
according to the order of Melchizedek and
not according to the order of Aaron? 12 For
when there is a change of the priesthood, there
must be a change of law as well. 13 For the one
these things are spoken about belonged to a
different tribe. No one from it has served at
the altar. 14 Now it is evident that our Lord
came from Judah, and Moses said nothing
about that tribe concerning priests.
15 And this becomes clearer if another priest
like Melchizedek appears, 16 who did not become a priest based on a legal regulation
about physical[C] descent but based on the
power of an indestructible life. 17 For it has
been testified:

You are a priest forever
according to the order
of Melchizedek.[D]

18 So the previous command is annulled because it was weak and unprofitable 19 (for the
law perfected nothing), but a better hope is introduced, through which we draw near to God.
20 None of this happened without an oath.
For others became priests without an oath,
21 but he became a priest with an oath made
by the one who said to him:

The Lord has sworn
and will not change his mind,
"You are a priest forever."[E]

22 Because of this oath, Jesus has also become
the guarantee of a better covenant.
23 Now many have become Levitical priests,
since they are prevented by death from remaining in office. 24 But because he remains
forever, he holds his priesthood permanently.

Thanksgiving and Contentment | *Praise for Jesus and His Work*

WHAT A PRIEST!

"Now many have become Levitical priests, since they are prevented by death from remaining in office. But because he remains forever, he holds his priesthood permanently. Therefore, he is able to save completely those who come to God through him, since he always lives to intercede for them." Hebrews 7:23-25

A priest is, strictly put, a mediator between God and human beings. He speaks and acts on behalf of God to people, and he speaks and acts on behalf of people to God. Mediating a weighty calling, but a priest can't really *save* anybody—he can only point people to the One who does save.

Hebrews teaches that Jesus is the ultimate priest (or high priest) of all who believe. Unlike the old priest at a church across town who passed away last spring after forty-five years of ministry, Jesus "remains forever." His priesthood is permanent.

This fact should make us delirious with gratitude. It means when you need to confess some sin or receive a bit of counsel, or when you need someone to listen to you and pray for you, or when you want someone who will see that you make it safely to your heavenly home—you're in great shape. In Jesus, you find everything you'd ever need.

Contemplate this promise: "He is able to save completely those who come to God through him."

For the next note on *Thanksgiving and Contentment*, see Hebrews 8:12.

[A] **7:6** Lit *their* [B] **7:10** Lit *still in his father's loins* [C] **7:16** Or *fleshly* [D] **7:17** Ps 110:4 [E] **7:21** Ps 110:4

25 Therefore, he is able to save completely those
who come to God through him, since he always lives to intercede for them.
26 For this is the kind of high priest we need:
holy, innocent, undefiled, separated from sinners, and exalted above the heavens. 27 He
doesn't need to offer sacrifices every day, as
high priests do — first for their own sins, then
for those of the people. He did this once for
all time when he offered himself. 28 For the
law appoints as high priests men who are
weak, but the promise of the oath, which came
after the law, appoints a Son, who has been
perfected forever.

A HEAVENLY PRIESTHOOD

8 Now the main point of what is being said
is this: We have this kind of high priest,
who sat down at the right hand of the throne
of the Majesty in the heavens, 2 a minister of
the sanctuary and the true tabernacle that
was set up by the Lord and not man. 3 For every high priest is appointed to offer gifts and
sacrifices; therefore, it was necessary for this
priest also to have something to offer. 4 Now if
he were on earth, he wouldn't be a priest, since
there are those[A] offering the gifts prescribed
by the law. 5 These serve as a copy and shadow
of the heavenly things, as Moses was warned
when he was about to complete the tabernacle. For God said, **Be careful that you make
everything according to the pattern that
was shown to you on the mountain.**[B] 6 But
Jesus has now obtained a superior ministry,
and to that degree he is the mediator of a better covenant, which has been established on
better promises.

A SUPERIOR COVENANT

7 For if that first covenant had been faultless,
there would have been no occasion for a second one. 8 But finding fault with his people,[C]
he says:[D]

See, the days are coming,
says the Lord,
when I will make a new covenant
with the house of Israel
and with the house of Judah —
9 **not like the covenant**
that I made with their ancestors
on the day I took them
by the hand
to lead them out of the land
of Egypt.

Thanksgiving and Contentment | *Forgiveness*

GOODBYE TO GUILT

"For I will forgive their wrongdoing, and I will never again remember their sins." Hebrews 8:12

Guilt is a large, ugly buzzard, slowly circling one's soul, steadily coming closer. It is the grim reaper with wings, a morbid preview of the end—at least the end of life as you've come to know it.

Perhaps that's the issue you're battling just now: guilt. You did something you can't undo. Or you failed to do some important things you should have done—and now it's too late. The guilt hovers over you, pecking at you, consuming you.

If so, ask yourselves these questions:

- Have I sincerely asked forgiveness for wrong things done and good things left undone? Have I done this with God and with those I hurt?
- What does God pledge to do when his children confess their sins (1Jn 1:9)?
- Why would I keep listening to the accusations of the enemy (Rv 12:10) when the lover of my soul says I am not guilty?
- How can I express my appreciation to God for his willingness to forgive my sins and remember them no more?

For the next note on *Thanksgiving and Contentment*, see 1 Peter 1:3-4.

[A] **8:4** Other mss read *priests* [B] **8:5** Ex 25:40 [C] **8:8** Lit *with them* [D] **8:8** Other mss read *finding fault, he says to them*

I showed no concern for them,
says the Lord,
because they did not continue
in my covenant.
10 For this is the covenant
that I will make with the house
of Israel
after those days, says the Lord:
I will put my laws into their minds
and write them on their hearts.
I will be their God,
and they will be my people.
11 And each person will not teach
his fellow citizen,[A]
and each his brother or sister, saying,
"Know the Lord,"
because they will all know me,
from the least to the greatest
of them.
12 For I will forgive their wrongdoing,
and I will never again remember
their sins.[B,C]

13 By saying **a new covenant**, he has declared
that the first is obsolete. And what is obsolete
and growing old is about to pass away.

OLD COVENANT MINISTRY

9 Now the first covenant also had regulations for ministry and an earthly sanctuary. 2 For a tabernacle was set up, and in
the first room, which is called the holy place,
were the lampstand, the table, and the presentation loaves. 3 Behind the second curtain
was a tent called the most holy place. 4 It had
the gold altar of incense and the ark of the
covenant, covered with gold on all sides, in
which was a gold jar containing the manna,
Aaron's staff that budded, and the tablets of
the covenant. 5 The cherubim of glory were
above the ark overshadowing the mercy seat.
It is not possible to speak about these things
in detail right now.

6 With these things prepared like this, the
priests enter the first room repeatedly, performing their ministry. 7 But the high priest
alone enters the second room, and he does
that only once a year, and never without blood,
which he offers for himself and for the sins the
people had committed in ignorance. 8 The Holy
Spirit was making it clear that the way into
the most holy place had not yet been disclosed
while the first tabernacle was still standing.
9 This is a symbol for the present time, during
which gifts and sacrifices are offered that cannot perfect the worshiper's conscience. 10 They
are physical regulations and only deal with
food, drink, and various washings imposed
until the time of the new order.

NEW COVENANT MINISTRY

11 But Christ has appeared as a high priest of
the good things that have come.[D] In the greater
and more perfect tabernacle not made with
hands (that is, not of this creation), 12 he entered
the most holy place once for all time, not by
the blood of goats and calves, but by his own
blood, having obtained eternal redemption.
13 For if the blood of goats and bulls and the
ashes of a young cow, sprinkling those who
are defiled, sanctify for the purification of
the flesh, 14 how much more will the blood of
Christ, who through the eternal Spirit offered
himself without blemish to God, cleanse our[E]
consciences from dead works so that we can
serve the living God?

15 Therefore, he is the mediator of a new covenant,[F] so that those who are called might receive the promise of the eternal inheritance,
because a death has taken place for redemption
from the transgressions committed under the
first covenant. 16 Where a will exists, the death
of the one who made it must be established.
17 For a will is valid only when people die, since
it is never in effect while the one who made it
is living. 18 That is why even the first covenant
was inaugurated with blood. 19 For when every
command had been proclaimed by Moses to
all the people according to the law, he took the
blood of calves and goats,[G] along with water,
scarlet wool, and hyssop, and sprinkled the
scroll itself and all the people, 20 saying, **This
is the blood of the covenant that God has ordained for you.**[H] 21 In the same way, he sprinkled
the tabernacle and all the articles of worship
with blood. 22 According to the law almost everything is purified with blood, and without
the shedding of blood there is no forgiveness.

23 Therefore, it was necessary for the cop-
ies of the things in the heavens to be purified
with these sacrifices, but the heavenly things
themselves to be purified with better sacrifices than these. 24 For Christ did not enter a
sanctuary made with hands (only a model[I] of
the true one) but into heaven itself, so that he

[A] **8:11** Other mss read *neighbor* [B] **8:12** Other mss add *and their lawless deeds* [C] **8:8-12** Jr 31:31-34 [D] **9:11** Other mss read *that are to come* [E] **9:14** Other mss read *your* [F] **9:15** The Gk word used here can be translated covenant, will, or testament, also in vv. 16,17,18. [G] **9:19** Some mss omit *and goats* [H] **9:20** Ex 24:8 [I] **9:24** Or *antitype*, or *figure*

might now appear in the presence of God for
us. 25 He did not do this to offer himself many
times, as the high priest enters the sanctuary
yearly with the blood of another. 26 Otherwise,
he would have had to suffer many times since
the foundation of the world. But now he has
appeared one time, at the end of the ages, for
the removal of sin by the sacrifice of himself.
27 And just as it is appointed for people to die
once — and after this, judgment — 28 so also
Christ, having been offered once to bear the
sins of many, will appear a second time, not
to bear sin, but[A] to bring salvation to those
who are waiting for him.

THE PERFECT SACRIFICE

10 Since the law has only a shadow of the
good things to come, and not the reality itself of those things, it can never perfect
the worshipers by the same sacrifices they
continually offer year after year. 2 Otherwise,
wouldn't they have stopped being offered,
since the worshipers, purified once and for
all, would no longer have any consciousness
of sins? 3 But in the sacrifices there is a reminder of sins year after year. 4 For it is impossible for the blood of bulls and goats to
take away sins.
5 Therefore, as he was coming into the world,
he said:

You did not desire sacrifice
and offering,
but you prepared a body for me.
6 **You did not delight**
in whole burnt offerings
and sin offerings.
7 **Then I said, "See —**
it is written about me
in the scroll —
I have come to do your will,
O God."[B]

8 After he says above, **You did not desire or**
delight in sacrifices and offerings, whole
burnt offerings and sin offerings (which are
offered according to the law), 9 he then says, **See,**
I have come to do your will.[C] He takes away
the first to establish the second. 10 By this will,
we have been sanctified through the offering
of the body of Jesus Christ once for all time.
11 Every priest stands day after day ministering and offering the same sacrifices time
after time, which can never take away sins.
12 But this man, after offering one sacrifice
for sins forever, sat down at the right hand of
God.[D] 13 He is now waiting until his enemies
are made his footstool. 14 For by one offering he has perfected forever those who are
sanctified. 15 The Holy Spirit also testifies to
us about this. For after he says:

16 **This is the covenant I will make**
with them
after those days,
the Lord says,
I will put my laws on their hearts
and write them on their minds,
17 and **I will never again remember**
their sins and their lawless acts.[E]

18 Now where there is forgiveness of these,
there is no longer an offering for sin.

EXHORTATIONS TO GODLINESS

19 Therefore, brothers and sisters, since we
have boldness to enter the sanctuary through
the blood of Jesus — 20 he has inaugurated[F]
for us a new and living way through the curtain (that is, through his flesh) — 21 and since
we have a great high priest over the house
of God, 22 let us draw near with a true heart
in full assurance of faith, with our hearts
sprinkled clean from an evil conscience
and our bodies washed in pure water. 23 Let
us hold on to the confession of our hope
without wavering, since he who promised
is faithful. 24 And let us watch out for one
another to provoke love and good works,
25 not neglecting to gather together, as some
are in the habit of doing, but encouraging
each other, and all the more as you see the
day approaching.

WARNING AGAINST DELIBERATE SIN

26 For if we deliberately go on sinning after
receiving the knowledge of the truth, there
no longer remains a sacrifice for sins, 27 but
a terrifying expectation of judgment and the
fury of a fire about to consume the adversaries. 28 Anyone who disregarded the law
of Moses died without mercy, based on the
testimony of two or three witnesses. 29 How
much worse punishment do you think one
will deserve who has trampled on the Son of
God, who has regarded as profane[G] the blood
of the covenant by which he was sanctified,
and who has insulted the Spirit of grace? 30 For
we know the one who has said,

[A] **9:28** Lit *time, apart from sin,* [B] **10:5-7** Ps 40:6-8 [C] **10:9** Other mss add *God* [D] **10:12** Or *offering one sacrifice for sins, sat down forever at the right hand of God* [E] **10:16-17** Jr 31:33-34 [F] **10:20** Or *opened* [G] **10:29** Or *ordinary*

Vengeance belongs to me;
I will repay,[A,B]
and again,
The Lord will judge his people.[C]
31 It is a terrifying thing to fall into the hands
of the living God.
32 Remember the earlier days when, after
you had been enlightened, you endured a hard
struggle with sufferings. 33 Sometimes you
were publicly exposed to taunts and afflictions,
and at other times you were companions of
those who were treated that way. 34 For you
sympathized with the prisoners[D] and accepted
with joy the confiscation of your possessions,
because you know that you yourselves have
a better and enduring possession.[E] 35 So don't
throw away your confidence, which has a
great reward. 36 For you need endurance, so
that after you have done God's will, you may
receive what was promised.
37 For yet in a **very little while,**
the Coming One will come
and not delay.
38 **But my righteous one**[F] **will live**
by faith;
and if he draws back,
I have no pleasure[G] **in him.**[H]
39 But we are not those who draw back and
are destroyed, but those who have faith and
are saved.

LIVING BY FAITH

11 Now faith is the reality[I] of what is hoped
for, the proof[J] of what is not seen. 2 For by
it our ancestors won God's approval.
3 By faith we understand that the universe
was[K] created by the word of God, so that what
is seen was made from things that are not
visible.[L]
4 By faith Abel offered to God a better sacrifice than Cain did. By faith he was approved
as a righteous man, because God approved
his gifts, and even though he is dead, he still
speaks through his faith.
5 By faith Enoch was taken away, and so he
did not experience death. **He was not to be**
found because God took him away.[M] For
before he was taken away, he was approved
as one who pleased God. 6 Now without faith
it is impossible to please God, since the one
who draws near to him must believe that he
exists and that he rewards those who seek him.

Relationships | *Building Positive Relationships*

WATCH OUT!

"And let us watch out for one another to provoke love and good works." Hebrews 10:24

In the early years of television, the popular sitcom *Bewitched* featured a memorable character named Gladys Kravitz. Gladys was the prototypical nosey neighbor, constantly peeking out her front window, always monitoring the activities of others and giving her long-suffering husband a blow-by-blow commentary. All by herself, Gladys embodied the phrase "Neighborhood Watch."

In one sense at least, Christians are called to emulate crazy, quirky Gladys. Notice that the writer of Hebrews says, "Let us watch out for one another." This is not in order that we might critique or gossip. Rather, we are to "watch out for one another," so we can "provoke love and good works."

In other words, we keep watch. We observe. We pay attention. And when we see someone hurting emotionally or dragging spiritually, we swing into action. An encouraging word here. A helpful hand there. An invite to lunch. An offer to assist with a project. Sometimes a simple five-minute gesture can make a huge difference.

Open your eyes today. Who around you is struggling?

For the next note on *Relationships*, see Hebrews 13:17.

[A] **10:30** Other mss add *says the Lord* [B] **10:30** Dt 32:35 [C] **10:30** Dt 32:36 [D] **10:34** Other mss read *sympathized with my imprisonment* [E] **10:34** Other mss add *in heaven* [F] **10:38** Other mss read *the righteous one* [G] **10:38** Lit *my soul has no pleasure* [H] **10:37-38** Is 26:20 LXX; Hab 2:3-4 [I] **11:1** Or *assurance* [J] **11:1** Or *conviction* [K] **11:3** Or *the worlds were*, or *the ages were* [L] **11:3** Or *so that what is seen was made out of what was not visible* [M] **11:5** Gn 5:21-24

7 By faith Noah, after he was warned about
what was not yet seen and motivated by godly
fear, built an ark to deliver his family. By faith
he condemned the world and became an heir
of the righteousness that comes by faith.

8 By faith Abraham, when he was called,
obeyed and set out for a place that he was
going to receive as an inheritance. He went
out, even though he did not know where he
was going. 9 By faith he stayed as a foreigner
in the land of promise, living in tents as did
Isaac and Jacob, coheirs of the same promise. 10 For he was looking forward to the city
that has foundations, whose architect and
builder is God.

11 By faith even Sarah herself, when she was
unable to have children, received power to
conceive offspring, even though she was past
the age, since she[A] considered that the one who
had promised was faithful. 12 Therefore, from
one man — in fact, from one as good as dead
— came offspring as numerous as the stars
of the sky and as innumerable as the grains
of sand along the seashore.

13 These all died in faith, although they had
not received the things that were promised.
But they saw them from a distance, greeted
them, and confessed that they were foreigners
and temporary residents on the earth. 14 Now
those who say such things make it clear that
they are seeking a homeland. 15 If they were
thinking about where they came from, they
would have had an opportunity to return. 16 But
they now desire a better place — a heavenly
one. Therefore, God is not ashamed to be called
their God, for he has prepared a city for them.

17 By faith Abraham, when he was tested,
offered up Isaac. He received the promises
and yet he was offering his one and only son,
18 the one to whom it had been said, **Your offspring**[B] **will be traced through Isaac.**[C] 19 He
considered God to be able even to raise someone from the dead; therefore, he received him
back, figuratively speaking.[D]

20 By faith Isaac blessed Jacob and Esau
concerning things to come. 21 By faith Jacob,
when he was dying, blessed each of the sons
of Joseph, and **he worshiped, leaning on the
top of his staff.**[E] 22 By faith Joseph, as he was
nearing the end of his life, mentioned[F] the
exodus of the Israelites and gave instructions
concerning his bones.

23 By faith Moses, after he was born, was hidden by his parents for three months, because
they saw that the child was beautiful, and they
didn't fear the king's edict. 24 By faith Moses,

Other-centeredness | *Living Peacefully*

PURSUING PEACE

"Pursue peace with everyone, and holiness — without it no one will see the Lord." Hebrews 12:14

How much of the turmoil in our souls can be traced to turmoil in our relationships? Probably more than we think. And perhaps this is why Hebrews challenges us to "pursue peace with everyone."

A couple of observations are in order. Notice the verse says we are to "pursue" peace, not "forge" peace. In other words, the burden of reconciliation isn't solely on our shoulders. Peace requires two willing participants. We can't *make* other people talk or let go of grudges or bury the hatchet. Those decisions are between them and God. All we can do is make overtures and good faith efforts to resolve conflict. We can pray for humility and for the healing of broken relationships, and we can take the initiative to extend an olive branch to someone who is upset. But then, the matter is in God's hands. He determines the outcome.

Notice one other thing: We are called to do this with "everyone." This means the people who infuriate and intimidate us. Often the relationship we least want to fix causes most of our angst.

For the next note on *Other-centeredness*, see Hebrews 13:1.

[A] **11:11** Or *By faith Abraham, even though he was past age — and Sarah herself was barren — received the ability to procreate since he* [B] **11:18** Lit *seed* [C] **11:18** Gn 21:12 [D] **11:19** Or *back, as a foreshadowing,* or *as a type*
[E] **11:21** Gn 47:31 [F] **11:22** Or *remembered*

when he had grown up, refused to be called the son of Pharaoh's daughter 25 and chose to suffer with the people of God rather than to enjoy the fleeting pleasure of sin. 26 For he considered reproach for the sake of Christ to be greater wealth than the treasures of Egypt, since he was looking ahead to the reward.

27 By faith he left Egypt behind, not being afraid of the king's anger, for Moses persevered as one who sees him who is invisible. 28 By faith he instituted the Passover and the sprinkling of the blood, so that the destroyer of the firstborn might not touch the Israelites. 29 By faith they crossed the Red Sea as though they were on dry land. When the Egyptians attempted to do this, they were drowned.

30 By faith the walls of Jericho fell down after being marched around by the Israelites for seven days. 31 By faith Rahab the prostitute welcomed the spies in peace and didn't perish with those who disobeyed.

32 And what more can I say? Time is too short for me to tell about Gideon, Barak, Samson, Jephthah, David, Samuel, and the prophets, 33 who by faith conquered kingdoms, administered justice, obtained promises, shut the mouths of lions, 34 quenched the raging of fire, escaped the edge of the sword, gained strength in weakness, became mighty in battle, and put foreign armies to flight. 35 Women received their dead, raised to life again. Other people were tortured, not accepting release, so that they might gain a better resurrection. 36 Others experienced mockings and scourgings, as well as bonds and imprisonment. 37 They were stoned,[A] they were sawed in two, they died by the sword, they wandered about in sheepskins, in goatskins, destitute, afflicted, and mistreated. 38 The world was not worthy of them. They wandered in deserts and on mountains, hiding in caves and holes in the ground.

39 All these were approved through their faith, but they did not receive what was promised, 40 since God had provided something better for us, so that they would not be made perfect without us.

THE CALL TO ENDURANCE

12 Therefore, since we also have such a large cloud of witnesses surrounding us, let us lay aside every hindrance and the sin that so easily ensnares us. Let us run with endurance the race that lies before us, 2 keeping our eyes on Jesus,[B] the source and perfecter[C] of our faith. For the joy that lay before him,[D] he

Other-centeredness | *Caring*

COMPASSIONATE ACTION

"Let brotherly love continue." Hebrews 13:1

If you had a brother growing up, or if you are raising two sons, you may shake your head at the phrase "brotherly love." Perhaps your experience has been (or is) more like "brotherly dislike" or "brotherly war."

Christians are called to something different, something better. The Greek word here is *philadelphia*. It refers to a genuine love between those who share deep bonds (in this case, those who by faith are part of the body of Christ, the church). This "brotherly love" is not just a warm feeling, it produces kindness—it prompts kind words and leads to kind actions.

God knows that in a harsh world where criticism is rampant and callous actions are the norm, we can all use this kind of caring affection.

Do this experiment. Determine to keep your eyes open today for those who have been either beaten down or beaten up (neither is good). When you do encounter someone who's discouraged—and it won't take long—think, *What tangible action can I take to show kindness and care?* Don't settle for words alone—wrap any encouraging remarks in compassionate action.

For the next note on *Other-centeredness*, see Hebrews 13:16.

[A] **11:37** Other mss add *they were tempted,* [B] **12:2** Or *us, looking to Jesus* [C] **12:2** Or *the founder and completer,* or *pioneer and perfecter* [D] **12:2** Or *who instead of the joy lying before him*

endured the cross, despising the shame, and
sat down at the right hand of the throne of God.

FATHERLY DISCIPLINE

3 For consider him who endured such hostility from sinners against himself, so that you
won't grow weary and give up. 4 In struggling
against sin, you have not yet resisted to the
point of shedding your blood. 5 And you have
forgotten the exhortation that addresses you
as sons:

My son, do not take the Lord's
discipline lightly
or lose heart when you are
reproved by him,
6 **for the Lord disciplines the one**
he loves
and punishes every son he receives.[A]

7 Endure suffering as discipline: God is dealing with you as sons. For what son is there
that a father does not discipline? 8 But if you
are without discipline — which all receive[B]
— then you are illegitimate children and not
sons. 9 Furthermore, we had human fathers
discipline us, and we respected them. Shouldn't
we submit even more to the Father of spirits
and live? 10 For they disciplined us for a short
time based on what seemed good to them, but
he does it for our benefit, so that we can share
his holiness. 11 No discipline seems enjoyable
at the time, but painful. Later on, however, it
yields the peaceful fruit of righteousness to
those who have been trained by it.

12 Therefore, strengthen your tired hands
and weakened knees, 13 and make straight
paths for your feet, so that what is lame may
not be dislocated[C] but healed instead.

WARNING AGAINST REJECTING GOD'S GRACE

14 Pursue peace with everyone, and holiness
— without it no one will see the Lord. 15 Make
sure that no one falls short of the grace of
God and that no root of bitterness springs
up, causing trouble and defiling many. 16 And
make sure that there isn't any immoral[D] or
irreverent person like Esau, who sold his birthright in exchange for a single meal. 17 For you
know that later, when he wanted to inherit
the blessing, he was rejected, even though
he sought it with tears, because he didn't find
any opportunity for repentance.

18 For you have not come to what could be

Other-centeredness | *Being Unselfish*

TAKE THE EXIT

"Don't neglect to do what is good and to share, for God is pleased with such sacrifices." Hebrews 13:16

That pain in your lower back. That impossible-to-please boss who is making your life miserable. That restless longing for joy. Strange that our personal situations and private aspirations seem to conspire to consume all our attention. Without trying to be selfish, we can easily fall into a lifestyle of thinking primarily about ourselves and our problems.

Here's the irony: Giving in to this kind of self-absorption never leads to a happy life. In truth, focusing primarily on self leads to a dead end. Or, to use an even better traffic analogy, it's like going around in a traffic circle and never exiting, where we just keep looping around and around our own issues and never arriving at any place good.

Try this. Exit this cyclical, self-centered existence. Look for someone in need. Then "do what is good." Not only will God be "pleased with such sacrifices," but you will find a more meaningful and satisfying life.

Looking outward and acting in loving ways doesn't minimize our own troubles, but it does put them in perspective. And it definitely makes life better for others.

For the next note on *Other-centeredness*, see James 3:15-16.

[A] **12:6** Pr 3:11-12 [B] **12:8** Lit *discipline, of which all have become participants* [C] **12:13** Or *so that the lame will not be turned aside* [D] **12:16** Or *sexually immoral*

touched, to a blazing fire, to darkness, gloom,
and storm, 19 to the blast of a trumpet, and the
sound of words. Those who heard it begged
that not another word be spoken to them, 20 for
they could not bear what was commanded: **If
even an animal touches the mountain, it
must be stoned.**[A] 21 The appearance was so
terrifying that Moses said, **I am trembling
with fear.**[B] 22 Instead, you have come to Mount
Zion, to the city of the living God (the heavenly Jerusalem), to myriads of angels, a festive
gathering, 23 to the assembly of the firstborn
whose names have been written[C] in heaven,
to a Judge, who is God of all, to the spirits of
righteous people made perfect, 24 and to Jesus,
the mediator of a new covenant, and to the
sprinkled blood, which says better things than
the blood of Abel.

25 See to it that you do not reject the one who
speaks. For if they did not escape when they
rejected him who warned them on earth, even
less will we if we turn away from him who
warns us from heaven. 26 His voice shook the
earth at that time, but now he has promised,
**Yet once more I will shake not only the
earth but also the heavens.**[D] 27 This expression, "Yet once more," indicates the removal of
what can be shaken — that is, created things
— so that what is not shaken might remain.
28 Therefore, since we are receiving a kingdom
that cannot be shaken, let us be thankful. By it,
we may serve God acceptably, with reverence
and awe, 29 for our God is a consuming fire.

FINAL EXHORTATIONS

13 Let brotherly love continue. 2 Don't neglect to show hospitality, for by doing this
some have welcomed angels as guests without
knowing it. 3 Remember those in prison, as
though you were in prison with them, and the
mistreated,[E] as though you yourselves were
suffering bodily.[F] 4 Marriage is to be honored
by all and the marriage bed kept undefiled,
because God will judge the sexually immoral and adulterers. 5 Keep your life free from
the love of money. Be satisfied with what you
have, for he himself has said, **I will never
leave you or abandon you.**[G] 6 Therefore, we
may boldly say,

> **The Lord is my helper;**
> **I will not be afraid.**
> **What can man do to me?**[H]

7 Remember your leaders who have spoken
God's word to you. As you carefully observe
the outcome of their lives, imitate their faith.
8 Jesus Christ is the same yesterday, today,
and forever. 9 Don't be led astray by various

Relationships | *Relating to Spiritual Leaders*

SUBMIT?

"Obey your leaders and submit to them, since they keep watch over your souls as those who will give an account, so that they can do this with joy and not with grief, for that would be unprofitable for you." Hebrews 13:17

Sadly, a lot of people in the world have church horror stories or, more specifically, horror stories involving unhealthy spiritual leaders who were manipulative at best or abusive at worst. Given that ugly reality, no wonder the command to "obey your leaders and submit to them" causes heartburn for so many people of faith.

But notice what the text says: "those [leaders] . . . will give an account." That is, those leaders are answerable to God. He knows the ones who have pure motives and the ones who don't. Of this we can be sure. Eventually the former will receive commendation, and the latter condemnation.

Until that day, be careful about the spiritual leaders you choose. No perfect ones exist, of course, but plenty of good ones are available. When you find one you trust, be supportive. Be a follower who makes the leader's life joyful, not grievous.

For the next note on *Relationships*, see James 1:19-20.

[A] **12:20** Ex 19:12 [B] **12:21** Dt 9:19 [C] **12:23** Or *registered* [D] **12:26** Hg 2:6 [E] **13:3** Or *tortured* [F] **13:3** Or *mistreated, since you are also in a body* [G] **13:5** Dt 31:6 [H] **13:6** Ps 118:6

kinds of strange teachings; for it is good for the heart to be established by grace and not by food regulations, since those who observe them have not benefited. 10 We have an altar from which those who worship at the tabernacle do not have a right to eat. 11 For the bodies of those animals whose blood is brought into the most holy place by the high priest as a sin offering are burned outside the camp. 12 Therefore, Jesus also suffered outside the gate, so that he might sanctify[A] the people by his own blood. 13 Let us then go to him outside the camp, bearing his disgrace. 14 For we do not have an enduring city here; instead, we seek the one to come. 15 Therefore, through him let us continually offer up to God a sacrifice of praise, that is, the fruit of lips that confess his name. 16 Don't neglect to do what is good and to share, for God is pleased with such sacrifices. 17 Obey your leaders[B] and submit to them, since they keep watch over your souls as those who will give an account, so that they can do this with joy and not with grief, for that would be unprofitable for you. 18 Pray for us, for we are convinced that we have a clear conscience, wanting to conduct ourselves honorably in everything. 19 And I urge you all the more to pray[C] that I may be restored to you very soon.

BENEDICTION AND FAREWELL

20 Now may the God of peace, who brought up from the dead our Lord Jesus — the great Shepherd of the sheep — through the blood of the everlasting covenant, 21 equip[D] you with everything good to do his will, working in us what is pleasing in his sight, through Jesus Christ, to whom be glory forever and ever.[E] Amen.

22 Brothers and sisters, I urge you to receive this message of exhortation, for I have written to you briefly. 23 Be aware that our brother Timothy has been released. If he comes soon enough, he will be with me when I see you. 24 Greet all your leaders and all the saints. Those who are from Italy send you greetings. 25 Grace be with you all.

[A] **13:12** Or *set apart*, or *consecrate* [B] **13:17** Or *rulers* [C] **13:19** Lit *to do this* [D] **13:21** Or *perfect* [E] **13:21** Other mss omit *and ever*

James—Soon after Jesus's death and resurrection, persecution forced Christians to flee Jerusalem. God used this to spread the gospel to "the end of the earth" (Ac 1:8), but this dispersion caused isolation and confusion. God's will can be like that—our trials bring him glory, but while we are struggling, we can't see it.

James urged these believers to change their attitude toward trials (Jms 1:2). Not only would their suffering work God's purposes, but it would produce in them endurance and mature faith (1:3-4). James is a practical book, encouraging us to obey God's wisdom rather than our own, to seek the humble life rather than earthly recognition, and to rein in the tongue. James urges us to live out what we profess to believe. He has no patience for hypocrisy.

James has been criticized for his emphasis on works, but his approach perfectly aligns with Jesus's words in the Sermon on the Mount. Good works do not save us, but they prove the genuineness of our faith. James does not encourage external obedience to a set of regulations but a living faith that expresses itself in good works.

Today James would tell us: Live out what you profess to believe!

JAMES

AUTHOR: James, the brother of Jesus, who was a leader in the Jerusalem church (Ac 15:13-21)

DATE WRITTEN: AD 48–52

ORIGINAL AUDIENCE: Jewish Christians who had been scattered by persecution

SETTING: Following the stoning of Stephen, Jewish believers had fled to various locations to avoid persecution (Ac 8:1; 11:19). These scattered believers faced isolation and hardship, not quite fitting in with either the secular culture or the Jewish faith.

PURPOSE FOR WRITING: James is mainly concerned with the conduct of Christians. For believers living in a hostile culture, undivided loyalty to God is essential. Moral behavior is what proves that our faith is genuine.

OUTLINE:

1. Greeting (1:1)
2. Perseverance in Trials (1:2-18)

   Joy in trials (1:2-12)

   Temptation in the Christian life (1:13-15)

   God's good gifts (1:16-18)
3. True Religion (1:19–2:26)

   Hearing and doing the Word (1:19-27)

   The sin of favoritism (2:1-13)

   Faith and works (2:14-26)
4. Wise Teachers (3:1-18)

   Control of the tongue (3:1-12)

   Wisdom from above (3:13-18)
5. Peace with God and Others (4:1-17)

   Pride and humility (4:1-12)

   Submission to God's will (4:13-17)
6. Discipline in the Christian Life (5:1-20)

   The dangers of wealth (5:1-6)

   Patience (5:7-11)

   Effective prayer (5:12-18)

   Ministry to those in error (5:19-20)

KEY VERSES:

"Consider it a great joy, my brothers and sisters, whenever you experience various trials, because you know that the testing of your faith produces endurance. And let endurance have its full effect, so that you may be mature and complete, lacking nothing."
—James 1:2-4

RESTORATION THEMES

R	Rest and Reflection	*Reflecting—1:2* *Asking for Wisdom—1:5* *Waiting on God—4:8* *Taking Personal Responsibility—4:17*
E	Eternal Perspective	*For the next note, see Revelation 21:1.*
S	Support	*Advice/Counsel—James 4:2*
T	Thanksgiving and Contentment	*For the next note, see 1 Peter 1:3-4.*
O	Other-centeredness	*Avoiding Jealousy/Coveting—James 3:15-16* *Being Honest—5:12*
R	Relationships	*Dealing with Anger and Hatred—1:19-20* *Being Impartial—2:1* *Admitting Wrongs—5:16*
E	Exercise of Faith	*For the next note, see 1 John 2:15.*

GREETING

1 James, a servant of God and of the Lord
Jesus Christ:
To the twelve tribes dispersed abroad.[A]
Greetings.

TRIALS AND MATURITY

2 Consider it a great joy, my brothers and sisters, whenever you experience various trials,
3 because you know that the testing of your
faith produces endurance. 4 And let endurance
have its full effect, so that you may be mature
and complete, lacking nothing.
5 Now if any of you lacks wisdom, he should
ask God — who gives to all generously and
ungrudgingly — and it will be given to him.
6 But let him ask in faith without doubting.[B] For
the doubter is like the surging sea, driven and
tossed by the wind. 7 That person should not
expect to receive anything from the Lord, 8 being
double-minded and unstable in all his ways.[C]
9 Let the brother of humble circumstances boast in his exaltation, 10 but let the rich
boast in his humiliation because he will pass
away like a flower of the field. 11 For the sun
rises and, together with the scorching wind,
dries up the grass; its flower falls off, and its
beautiful appearance perishes. In the same
way, the rich person will wither away while
pursuing his activities.
12 Blessed is the one who endures trials, because when he has stood the test he will receive
the crown of life that God[D] has promised to
those who love him.
13 No one undergoing a trial should say, "I am
being tempted by God," since God is not tempted
by evil, and he himself doesn't tempt anyone.
14 But each person is tempted when he is drawn
away and enticed by his own evil desire. 15 Then
after desire has conceived, it gives birth to sin,
and when sin is fully grown, it gives birth to death.
16 Don't be deceived, my dear brothers and
sisters. 17 Every good and perfect gift is from
above, coming down from the Father of lights,
who does not change like shifting shadows.
18 By his own choice, he gave us birth by the
word of truth so that we would be a kind of
firstfruits of his creatures.

HEARING AND DOING THE WORD

19 My dear brothers and sisters, understand
this: Everyone should be quick to listen, slow

Rest and Reflection | *Reflecting*

UNLIKELY JOY

"Consider it a great joy, my brothers and sisters, whenever you experience various trials." James 1:2

Most folks consider trials a great inconvenience, a great pain in the neck, a great disaster. Anything but a "great joy." What was James thinking? Why would he say such a thing?

James was writing to believers who were being persecuted for their faith. And he was echoing the words of his half brother Jesus, "When they insult you and persecute you. . . . Be glad and rejoice, because your reward is great in heaven" (Mt 5:11-12).

Still, the question is, "How?" How do we get to the place where we can think about trials—and respond to them—in such a counterintuitive way? Can we really experience joy in the midst of suffering?

Spending time daily in quiet contemplation has great value. By prayerful reflection, meditating on the verses that follow this one, we can find reasons for joy.

James reminds us that though our trials may seem random, they're not. God uses them to shape us, making us like his Son. If we endure, we develop character and strength.

The process is not fun, however; it's like giving birth—very painful. But after all the agony? Ecstasy!

For the next note on *Rest and Reflection*, see James 1:5.

[A] **1:1** Gk *diaspora*; Jewish people scattered throughout Gentile lands [B] **1:6** Or *without divided loyalties* [C] **1:8** Or *in all his conduct* [D] **1:12** Other mss read *that the Lord*

Rest and Reflection | *Asking for Wisdom*

A GENEROUS GIFT

"Now if any of you lacks wisdom, he should ask God—who gives to all generously and ungrudgingly—and it will be given to him." James 1:5

When trials come—and by the way, they *will* come (notice James says "when" [Jms 1:2] not "if")—we often have scores of questions: Why is this happening to me? How can I get out of this mess? Where should I turn? Whom can I call for help? What should I do first? How will I survive this?

No wonder in tough times some people become immobilized, and others react without thinking, often making the situation even worse.

James suggests a better way: "Ask God" for wisdom.

"Wisdom? Seriously? If I'm asking God for something, can't I just ask him to make my trials go away?"

That desire, while understandable, is unrealistic. God knows that growth without trials is impossible. Struggles are an integral part of the journey to maturity. The good news, James explains, is that God is generous, not stingy, when doling out wisdom. He's glad to give us the insights we need to navigate our trials sensibly and safely. But we have to ask, and we have to believe that he will answer (1:6-8).

For the next note on *Rest and Reflection*, see James 4:8.

Relationships | *Dealing with Anger and Hatred*

SHHHHH

"My dear brothers and sisters, understand this: Everyone should be quick to listen, slow to speak, and slow to anger, for human anger does not accomplish God's righteousness." James 1:19-20

Here are three truths about modern culture: (1) Few people feel listened to. (2) More and more people feel the freedom to blurt out whatever comes to their mind. (3) A scary number of people feel angry all the time.

Are these connected? James sure seems to think so.

"Be quick to listen," he urges. In other words, respect others. Put down your smartphone or book and be fully present. Ask questions and pay close attention. As you do these things, you'll probably find yourself clamoring to respond. So . . .

"[Be] slow to speak," James warns. In other words, you don't have to react to everything. Bite your tongue, and learn to nod. In the wise words of Will Rogers, "Never miss a good chance to shut up."

What about conflict situations, when you feel the anger rising in you? Call time out. Take some time to pray and cool off. Ambrose Bierce said it best, "Speak when you are angry, and you will make the best speech you will ever regret."

These simple acts—if turned into habits—will revolutionize your relationships.

For the next note on *Relationships*, see James 2:1.

to speak, and slow to anger, 20 for human anger does not accomplish God's righteousness.
21 Therefore, ridding yourselves of all moral
filth and the evil that is so prevalent,[A] humbly
receive the implanted word, which is able to
save your souls.
22 But be doers of the word and not hearers
only, deceiving yourselves. 23 Because if anyone is a hearer of the word and not a doer, he
is like someone looking at his own face[B] in a
mirror. 24 For he looks at himself, goes away,
and immediately forgets what kind of person
he was. 25 But the one who looks intently into
the perfect law of freedom and perseveres
in it, and is not a forgetful hearer but a doer
who works — this person will be blessed in
what he does.
26 If anyone[C] thinks he is religious without
controlling his tongue, his religion is useless
and he deceives himself. 27 Pure and undefiled
religion before God the Father is this: to look
after orphans and widows in their distress
and to keep oneself unstained from the world.

THE SIN OF FAVORITISM

2 My brothers and sisters, do not show favoritism as you hold on to the faith in our
glorious Lord Jesus Christ. 2 For if someone
comes into your meeting wearing a gold ring
and dressed in fine clothes, and a poor person dressed in filthy clothes also comes in,
3 if you look with favor on the one wearing
the fine clothes and say, "Sit here in a good
place," and yet you say to the poor person,
"Stand over there," or "Sit here on the floor by
my footstool," 4 haven't you made distinctions
among yourselves and become judges with
evil thoughts?
5 Listen, my dear brothers and sisters: Didn't
God choose the poor in this world to be rich
in faith and heirs of the kingdom that he has
promised to those who love him? 6 Yet you have
dishonored the poor. Don't the rich oppress you
and drag you into court? 7 Don't they blaspheme
the good name that was invoked over you?
8 Indeed, if you fulfill the royal law prescribed in the Scripture, **Love your neighbor
as yourself**,[D] you are doing well. 9 If, however,
you show favoritism, you commit sin and are
convicted by the law as transgressors. 10 For
whoever keeps the entire law, and yet stumbles at one point, is guilty of breaking it all.
11 For he who said, **Do not commit adultery**,[E]
also said, **Do not murder**.[F] So if you do not
commit adultery, but you murder, you are a
lawbreaker.

Relationships | *Being Impartial*

CHOOSING FAVORITES?

"My brothers and sisters, do not show favoritism as you hold on to the faith in our glorious Lord Jesus Christ." James 2:1

One of the questions James raises to help believers gauge how healthy their faith is this: How do you treat different types of people? In his example, the poor are shunned while the rich are given preferential treatment.

Whatever we call this—bias, prejudice, segregation or discrimination—the practice is reprehensible. This tendency to size people up (almost always in a superficial way), then label and assign a value to them so we can either dismiss them or fawn over them is what James calls becoming "judges with evil thoughts" (2:4). And lest we think this isn't a big deal, he continues. "If . . . you show favoritism, you commit sin and are convicted by the law as transgressors" (2:9). It gets worse. If that were our only sin, James argues, we'd be as bad off as a person who committed every sin in the book!

Do you struggle with accepting certain groups of people? Do you discriminate against those who are different racially? Socioeconomically? Educationally? Culturally? Just remember that Jesus died for all these different people. And if he can accept you, then you can accept them.

For the next note on *Relationships*, see James 5:16.

[A] **1:21** Or *the abundance of evil* [B] **1:23** Or *at his natural face* [C] **1:26** Other mss add *among you* [D] **2:8** Lv 19:18 [E] **2:11** Ex 20:14; Dt 5:18 [F] **2:11** Ex 20:13; Dt 5:17

12 Speak and act as those who are to be judged
by the law of freedom. 13 For judgment is without mercy to the one who has not shown mercy.
Mercy triumphs over judgment.

FAITH AND WORKS

14 What good is it, my brothers and sisters, if
someone claims to have faith but does not
have works? Can such faith save him?
15 If a brother or sister is without clothes
and lacks daily food 16 and one of you says to
them, "Go in peace, stay warm, and be well fed,"
but you don't give them what the body needs,
what good is it? 17 In the same way faith, if it
doesn't have works, is dead by itself.
18 But someone will say, "You have faith, and
I have works."[A] Show me your faith without
works, and I will show you faith by my works.
19 You believe that God is one. Good! Even the
demons believe — and they shudder.
20 Senseless person! Are you willing to
learn that faith without works is useless?
21 Wasn't Abraham our father justified by
works in offering Isaac his son on the altar?
22 You see that faith was active together with
his works, and by works, faith was made
complete, 23 and the Scripture was fulfilled
that says, **Abraham believed God, and it**
was credited to him as righteousness,[B]
and he was called God's friend. 24 You see
that a person is justified by works and not
by faith alone. 25 In the same way, wasn't Rahab the prostitute also justified by works
in receiving the messengers and sending
them out by a different route? 26 For just as
the body without the spirit is dead, so also
faith without works is dead.

CONTROLLING THE TONGUE

3 Not many should become teachers, my
brothers,[C] because you know that we
will receive a stricter judgment. 2 For we all
stumble in many ways. If anyone does not
stumble in what he says, he is mature, able
also to control the whole body. 3 Now if we
put bits into the mouths of horses so that
they obey us, we direct their whole bodies.
4 And consider ships: Though very large and
driven by fierce winds, they are guided by a
very small rudder wherever the will of the
pilot directs. 5 So too, though the tongue is a
small part of the body, it boasts great things.
Consider how a small fire sets ablaze a large
forest. 6 And the tongue is a fire. The tongue, a
world of unrighteousness, is placed[D] among
our members. It stains the whole body, sets the
course of life on fire, and is itself set on fire
by hell. 7 Every kind of animal, bird, reptile,

Other-centeredness | *Avoiding Jealousy/Coveting*

SELF*LESS* AMBITION

"Such wisdom does not come down from above but is earthly, unspiritual, demonic. For where there is envy and selfish ambition, there is disorder and every evil practice." James 3:15-16

In his blunt, take-no-prisoners style, James spells out what biblical faith looks like. Genuine faith, he says, endures trials (1:1-27) and refuses to show favoritism (2:1-13). Real, robust faith also manifests itself in good deeds (2:14-26), alters the way we speak (3:1-12), and affects the way we engage with others (3:13–4:12).

In this area of relationships, James cites the common problem of "envy and selfish ambition." Imagine what he might have said if social media had existed in his day! His point: While we should expect such things in worldly settings, we should never tolerate them among the people of God.

Examine your own heart. If you find yourself longing for someone else's life or experience or of ways to get noticed or get ahead of others, confess these attitudes that lead to "disorder and every evil practice." Then go and do something for someone else—to take your mind off yourself.

For the next note on *Other-centeredness*, see James 5:12.

[A] **2:18** The quotation may end here or after v. 18b or v. 19. [B] **2:23** Gn 15:6 [C] **3:1** Or *brothers and sisters* [D] **3:6** Or *places itself*, or *appoints itself*

and fish is tamed and has been tamed by humankind, 8 but no one can tame the tongue. It
is a restless evil, full of deadly poison. 9 With
the tongue we bless our Lord and Father, and
with it we curse people who are made in God's
likeness. 10 Blessing and cursing come out of
the same mouth. My brothers and sisters,
these things should not be this way. 11 Does a
spring pour out sweet and bitter water from
the same opening? 12 Can a fig tree produce
olives, my brothers and sisters, or a grapevine
produce figs? Neither can a saltwater spring
yield fresh water.

THE WISDOM FROM ABOVE

13 Who among you is wise and understanding?
By his good conduct he should show that his
works are done in the gentleness that comes
from wisdom. 14 But if you have bitter envy and
selfish ambition in your heart, don't boast and
deny the truth. 15 Such wisdom does not come
down from above but is earthly, unspiritual,
demonic. 16 For where there is envy and selfish ambition, there is disorder and every evil
practice. 17 But the wisdom from above is first
pure, then peace-loving, gentle, compliant, full
of mercy and good fruits, unwavering, without
pretense. 18 And the fruit of righteousness is
sown in peace by those who cultivate peace.

PROUD OR HUMBLE

4 What is the source of wars and fights
among you? Don't they come from your
passions that wage war within you?[A] 2 You
desire and do not have. You murder and covet
and cannot obtain. You fight and wage war.[B]
You do not have because you do not ask. 3 You
ask and don't receive because you ask with
wrong motives, so that you may spend it on
your pleasures.

4 You adulterous people![C] Don't you know
that friendship with the world is hostility toward God? So whoever wants to be the friend
of the world becomes the enemy of God. 5 Or
do you think it's without reason that the Scripture says: The spirit he made to dwell in us
envies intensely?[D]

6 But he gives greater grace. Therefore he
says:

> **God resists the proud,**
> **but gives grace to the humble.**[E]

7 Therefore, submit to God. Resist the devil,
and he will flee from you. 8 Draw near to God,

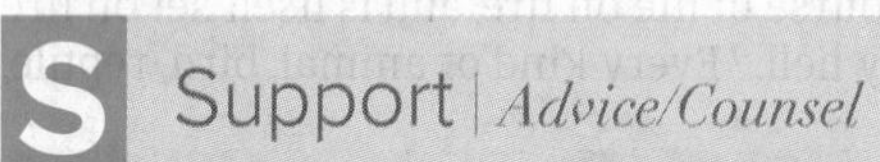

JUST ASK

"You desire and do not have. You murder and covet and cannot obtain. You fight and wage war. You do not have because you do not ask." James 4:2

After a humiliating experience a few years ago, Pam has become something of a recluse. Most days she watches TV for hours, adding her own gloomy commentary to whatever is on the screen. Then she scrolls through Facebook, frowning at all the pictures of smiling people in beautiful places. Sometimes she mumbles withering criticisms or imagines conversations in which she tells this person or that one a thing or two.

Pam is lonely. She doesn't have the one thing she desperately wants and deeply needs—people in her life. She desires companionship for the same reason we all do—because we were made to connect with others. But she's also deeply afraid to trust anybody.

Pam could begin to resolve her issue by asking—asking God how to get out of her hole. Then taking the risk to ask others to drink coffee or go eat lunch. Asking them what they need or how she can pray for them.

James says it clearly, "You do not have because you do not ask."

For the next note on *Support*, see 1 Peter 4:19.

[A] **4:1** Or *war in your members* [B] **4:2** Or *You desire and do not have, so you murder. You covet and cannot obtain, so you fight and wage war.* [C] **4:4** Lit *Adulteresses* [D] **4:5** Or *Scripture says: He jealously yearns for the spirit he made to live in us?*, or *Scripture says: The Spirit he made to dwell in us longs jealously?* [E] **4:6** Pr 3:34

and he will draw near to you. Cleanse your
hands, sinners, and purify your hearts, you
double-minded. 9 Be miserable and mourn and
weep. Let your laughter be turned to mourning
and your joy to gloom. 10 Humble yourselves
before the Lord, and he will exalt you.
11 Don't criticize one another, brothers and
sisters. Anyone who defames or judges a fellow

Rest and Reflection | *Waiting on God*

DRAWING NEAR

"Draw near to God, and he will draw near to you. Cleanse your hands, sinners, and purify your hearts, you double-minded." James 4:8

Augustine of Hippo (AD 354–430) famously said, "You have made us for yourself, O God, and our hearts are restless until they rest in you."

James, recognizing this same truth three to four centuries earlier, urged his readers, "Draw near to God, and he will draw near to you." This, in brief, is the only way to find what our hearts need most. We were created *by* God and *for* God. Apart from him, we can have no true satisfaction.

In language reminiscent of Psalm 24, however, James adds that to draw near to God we must have clean hands and a pure heart. We cannot rest deeply in God and engage stubbornly in sin at the same time. The cleansing James speaks of involves *repentance* (seeing the foolishness of our sin and turning from it) and *confession* (taking responsibility for our wrong thoughts and actions and then taking them to Jesus).

When we draw near to God in this way, we experience this breathtaking promise: "He will draw near to you."

For the next note on *Rest and Reflection*, see James 4:17.

Rest and Reflection | *Taking Personal Responsibility*

SINS OF OMISSION

"So it is sin to know the good and yet not do it." James 4:17

Most think of "sinning" as breaking one of The Ten Commandments or doing other wrong things, such as making a catty comment about someone, fudging the numbers on tax returns, or leaving work a few minutes early when the supervisor isn't around. In each case, we know you shouldn't, but we do it anyway. Those are sins of *commission*.

Here James speaks of a second category of sin: sins of *omission*. This involves *not* doing right things. A neighbor, for example, is going through an illness and you think, *I should reach out*. But then you remember how she was rude to your daughter last month. You know what you should do, but you don't do it.

For this reason, we urgently need time for reflection—to be honest with ourselves and take personal responsibility. Find a quiet place. Solicit the Spirit's help. Search your life for specific instances where you've had opportunities to bless others and yet have avoided doing those things. Confess these failures to God, claim the forgiveness available in Christ, and determine today to follow the Spirit's lead in doing what is right and good.

Knowing what's right isn't enough, James says. We have to *do* it.

For the next note on *Rest and Reflection*, see 1 Peter 1:24-25.

believer[A] defames and judges the law. If you
judge the law, you are not a doer of the law
but a judge. 12 There is one lawgiver and judge[B]
who is able to save and to destroy. But who
are you to judge your neighbor?

OUR WILL AND GOD'S WILL

13 Come now, you who say, "Today or tomorrow we will travel to such and such a city and
spend a year there and do business and make a
profit." 14 Yet you do not know what tomorrow
will bring — what your life will be! For you
are like vapor that appears for a little while,
then vanishes.

15 Instead, you should say, "If the Lord wills,
we will live and do this or that." 16 But as it is,
you boast in your arrogance. All such boasting is evil. 17 So it is sin to know the good and
yet not do it.

WARNING TO THE RICH

Come now, you rich people, weep and wail
over the miseries that are coming on you.
2 Your wealth has rotted and your clothes are
moth-eaten. 3 Your gold and silver are cor-
roded, and their corrosion will be a witness
against you and will eat your flesh like fire.
You have stored up treasure in the last days.
4 Look! The pay that you withheld from the
workers who mowed your fields cries out,
and the outcry of the harvesters has reached
the ears of the Lord of Hosts.[C] 5 You have lived
luxuriously on the earth and have indulged
yourselves. You have fattened your hearts in
a day of slaughter. 6 You have condemned,
you have murdered the righteous, who does
not resist you.

WAITING FOR THE LORD

7 Therefore, brothers and sisters, be patient
until the Lord's coming. See how the farmer
waits for the precious fruit of the earth and
is patient with it until it receives the early
and the late rains. 8 You also must be patient.
Strengthen your hearts, because the Lord's
coming is near.

9 Brothers and sisters, do not complain about
one another, so that you will not be judged.
Look, the judge stands at the door!

10 Brothers and sisters, take the prophets
who spoke in the Lord's name as an example
of suffering and patience. 11 See, we count as
blessed those who have endured.[D] You have
heard of Job's endurance and have seen the
outcome that the Lord brought about — the
Lord is compassionate and merciful.

O Other-centeredness | *Being Honest*

BEING HONEST/INTEGRITY

"Above all, my brothers and sisters, do not swear, either by heaven or by earth or with any other oath. But let your 'yes' mean 'yes,' and your 'no' mean 'no,' so that you won't fall under judgment." James 5:12

Not long ago, people sealed deals with a verbal agreement and a handshake. Today, we seem to need a couple of law firms and an acre of timber (for the mountain of paper those attorneys will generate). Finalizing the deal then requires more autographs than a sports superstar signs in an entire season! Depositions? Oaths? Having to sign a second document that says you signed the first document? James must be rolling over in his grave!

Though we can't navigate modern society without occasionally jumping through these sorts of legal hoops, we can and should do something else. "Let your 'yes' mean 'yes,' and your 'no' mean 'no,'" James urges. In other words, be a person of integrity. Be known by others as someone who always does exactly what you say you are going to do.

Go ahead and sign the paper if you must. But make it your focus to live in such a way that others never have to look at the contract again.

For the next note on *Other-centeredness*, see 2 Peter 3:9.

[A] **4:11** Or *his brother or sister* [B] **4:12** Other mss omit *and judge* [C] **5:4** Gk *Sabaoth*; or *the Lord of Armies* [D] **5:11** Or *persevered*

TRUTHFUL SPEECH

[12] Above all, my brothers and sisters, do not
swear, either by heaven or by earth or with
any other oath. But let your "yes" mean "yes,"
and your "no" mean "no," so that you won't
fall under judgment.[A]

EFFECTIVE PRAYER

[13] Is anyone among you suffering? He should
pray. Is anyone cheerful? He should sing praises. [14] Is anyone among you sick? He should
call for the elders of the church, and they are
to pray over him, anointing him with oil in
the name of the Lord. [15] The prayer of faith
will save the sick person, and the Lord will
raise him up; if he has committed sins, he
will be forgiven. [16] Therefore, confess your
sins to one another and pray for one another,
so that you may be healed. The prayer of a
righteous person is very powerful in its effect. [17] Elijah was a human being as we are,
and he prayed earnestly that it would not
rain, and for three years and six months it
did not rain on the land. [18] Then he prayed
again, and the sky gave rain and the land
produced its fruit.

[19] My brothers and sisters, if any among you
strays from the truth, and someone turns him
back, [20] let that person know that whoever
turns a sinner from the error of his way will
save his soul from death and cover a multitude of sins.

Relationships | *Admitting Wrongs*

NO SECRETS

"Therefore, confess your sins to one another and pray for one another, so that you may be healed. The prayer of a righteous person is very powerful in its effect." James 5:16

Any book on the subject of "spiritual disciplines" will probably have a chapter on confession.

The mere suggestion sends our hearts into arrhythmia. *Share my failures with another person? Talk openly about the very things I want to keep secret? Have you lost your mind!*

James states unequivocally, "Confess your sins to one another." This obviously means that we confess wrongdoing to anyone we've wronged. For example, "Hey, I need to tell you something. I wasn't completely honest with you in our conversation yesterday. I'm sorry. Please forgive me."

But this is also a call to let others into our lives—to come clean about sins that don't necessarily involve them. We need to admit our failures, because keeping secrets is a toxic way to live. In the dark, they haunt and control us. In the light, they lose their power.

If you're struggling—and mostly losing the battle—with a certain sin, ask God for courage. Approach a trusted friend who's walking with God, someone who can keep a confidence. Tell the person what is really going on. James says this kind of courageous humility will spark what you need most—powerful prayer that leads to healing.

For the next note on *Relationships*, see 1 Peter 3:8-9.

[A] **5:12** Other mss read *fall into hypocrisy*

1 Peter—The people to whom Peter wrote were being persecuted for their faith on a level that we cannot imagine and very few will ever experience; therefore, the hope that Peter assures them of is surely enough for any difficulty we may face.

Peter declares that believers can stand firm in any difficulty if they remember that they are made for a better place—eternity with God himself. This life is temporary, and believers will never quite fit in here. We should therefore not be surprised when life is hard but rather rest in the hope of our future inheritance, the eternal blessings of heaven where we will be forever at home.

Your struggle, your pain, can either cause you to despair or to cling to your hope in Christ. The choice is yours. Let the words of 1 Peter lift your gaze to what is unseen and remind you that God is good (2:3). The glory he has called you to is eternal, and he will restore, establish, strengthen, and support you (5:10). This is a promise that can carry you through any tribulation and bring you safely to heaven, your true home.

1 PETER

AUTHOR: The apostle Peter

DATE WRITTEN: AD 62–64, during the persecution of Christians under Nero

ORIGINAL AUDIENCE: Peter identifies his audience as "exiles dispersed abroad in Pontus, Galatia, Cappadocia, Asia, and Bithynia" (1:1). These were Roman provinces in modern-day Turkey, and the residents to whom he wrote were Gentile Christians. They had once been idolaters (4:3) but were now God's people (2:9-10).

SETTING: Nero was the last emperor of Rome, and he was known as a corrupt and cruel leader who viciously put Christians to death for his own entertainment. Christians were indeed suffering a "fiery ordeal" (4:12).

PURPOSE FOR WRITING: Peter's message to the exiles was to stand firm in the midst of trials. If they placed their hope in their eternal destination, they could endure the difficulties of this temporary existence with patience and perspective.

OUTLINE:

1. Opening (1:1-2)

2. Living as Exiles (1:3–2:10)

   A living hope (1:3-12)

   Future inheritance (1:13-21)

   Living as God's people (1:22–2:10)

3. Living as Strangers in a Hostile World (2:11–4:11)

   Holiness (2:11-12)

   A Christian's social responsibility (2:13–3:12)

   Response to suffering (3:13–4:11)

4. Perseverance in Suffering (4:12–5:11)

   Sharing in the sufferings of Christ (4:12-19)

   Exhortations to elders and others (5:1-11)

5. Conclusion (5:12-14)

KEY VERSES:

"You rejoice in this, even though now for a short time, if necessary, you suffer grief in various trials so that the proven character of your faith—more valuable than gold which, though perishable, is refined by fire—may result in praise, glory, and honor at the revelation of Jesus Christ." —1 Peter 1:6-7

RESTORATION THEMES

R	Rest and Reflection	*Meditating on God and His Word—1:24-25*
E	Eternal Perspective	*For the next note, see Revelation 21:1.*
S	Support	*Commitment to God—1 Peter 4:19* *Mentors—5:5* *Prayer—5:7*
T	Thanksgiving and Contentment	*Praise for Salvation—1:3-4* *Goodness and Mercy—2:9-10*
O	Other-centeredness	*For the next note, see 2 Peter 3:9.*
R	Relationships	*Restoring Damaged Relationships—1 Peter 3:8-9* *Relating to Church Family—4:8*
E	Exercise of Faith	*For the next note, see 1 John 2:15.*

GREETING

1 Peter, an apostle of Jesus Christ:
To those chosen, living as exiles dispersed
abroad[A] in Pontus, Galatia, Cappadocia, Asia,
and Bithynia, chosen 2 according to the foreknowledge of God the Father, through the sanc-
tifying work of the Spirit, to be obedient and
to be sprinkled with the blood of Jesus Christ.
May grace and peace be multiplied to you.

A LIVING HOPE

3 Blessed be the God and Father of our Lord
Jesus Christ. Because of his great mercy he has
given us new birth into a living hope through
the resurrection of Jesus Christ from the dead
4 and into an inheritance that is imperishable,
undefiled, and unfading, kept in heaven for
you. 5 You are being guarded by God's power
through faith for a salvation that is ready to be
revealed in the last time. 6 You rejoice in this,[B]
even though now for a short time, if necessary,
you suffer grief in various trials 7 so that the
proven character of your faith — more valuable than gold which, though perishable, is
refined by fire — may result in praise, glory,
and honor at the revelation of Jesus Christ.
8 Though you have not seen him, you love him;
though not seeing him now, you believe in
him, and you rejoice with inexpressible and
glorious joy, 9 because you are receiving the
goal of your faith, the salvation of your souls.
10 Concerning this salvation, the prophets, who prophesied about the grace that
would come to you, searched and carefully
investigated. 11 They inquired into what time
or what circumstances the Spirit of Christ
within them was indicating when he testified in advance to the sufferings of Christ
and the glories that would follow.[C] 12 It was
revealed to them that they were not serving
themselves but you. These things have now
been announced to you through those who
preached the gospel to you by the Holy Spirit
sent from heaven — angels long to catch a
glimpse of these things.

A CALL TO HOLY LIVING

13 Therefore, with your minds ready for action,
be sober-minded and set your hope completely
on the grace to be brought to you at the revelation of Jesus Christ. 14 As obedient children,
do not be conformed to the desires of your
former ignorance. 15 But as the one who called
you is holy, you also are to be holy in all your
conduct; 16 for it is written, **Be holy, because
I am holy.**[D] 17 If you appeal to the Father who

Thanksgiving and Contentment | *Praise for Salvation*

SOME INHERITANCE!

"Blessed be the God and Father of our Lord Jesus Christ. Because of his great mercy he has given us new birth into a living hope through the resurrection of Jesus Christ from the dead and into an inheritance that is imperishable, undefiled, and unfading, kept in heaven for you." *1 Peter 1:3-4*

On the excitement scale, watching someone write a letter ranks with watching paint dry or grass grow—except maybe here. Reading the opening words of this letter, we get the sense that Peter was beside himself with joy. The fisherman-turned-apostle oozed adjectives as he thought about the "great mercy" of God. If we had a video, what would we see? Was he smiling? Did he push back his chair and shake his head in wonder? Did tears of joy drip down onto the parchment?

Peter then writes of the gift of "new birth into a living hope." In other words, our God, in Christ, gives believers a brand new life full of purpose. We have an unfathomably good future. And in that life to come? "An inheritance" that is sure, perfect, and eternal.

Spend some time prayerfully pondering Peter's words. See if your own heart swells with joy and gratitude.

For the next note on *Thanksgiving and Contentment*, see 1 Peter 2:9-10.

[A] **1:1** Gk *diaspora*; Jewish people scattered throughout Gentile lands [B] **1:6** Or *In this fact rejoice* [C] **1:11** Or *the glories after that*
[D] **1:16** Lv 11:44-45; 19:2; 20:7

judges impartially according to each one's
work, you are to conduct yourselves in reverence during your time living as strangers.
18 For you know that you were redeemed from
your empty way of life inherited from your
fathers, not with perishable things like silver
or gold, 19 but with the precious blood of Christ,
like that of an unblemished and spotless lamb.
20 He was foreknown before the foundation of
the world but was revealed in these last times
for you. 21 Through him you believe in God,
who raised him from the dead and gave him
glory, so that your faith and hope are in God.
22 Since you have purified yourselves by your
obedience to the truth,[A] so that you show sincere brotherly love for each other, from a pure[B]
heart love one another constantly,[C] 23 because
you have been born again — not of perishable
seed but of imperishable — through the living
and enduring word of God. 24 For

All flesh is like grass,
and all its glory like a flower
of the grass.
The grass withers,
and the flower falls,
25 **but the word of the Lord**
endures forever.[D]

And this word is the gospel that was proclaimed to you.

THE LIVING STONE AND A HOLY PEOPLE

2 Therefore, rid yourselves of all malice, all
deceit, hypocrisy, envy, and all slander.
2 Like newborn infants, desire the pure milk
of the word,[E] so that you may grow up into
your salvation,[F] 3 if **you have tasted that the**
Lord is good.[G] 4 As you come to him, a living
stone — rejected by people but chosen and
honored by[H] God — 5 you yourselves, as living
stones, a spiritual house, are being built to be
a holy priesthood[I] to offer spiritual sacrifices
acceptable to God through Jesus Christ. 6 For
it stands in Scripture:

See, I lay a stone in Zion,
a chosen and honored[J] cornerstone,
and the one who believes in him
will never be put to shame.[K]

7 So honor will come to you who believe; but
for the unbelieving,

The stone that the builders rejected —

Rest and Reflection | *Meditating on God and His Word*

GOD'S ENDURING WORD

"For 'All flesh is like grass, and all its glory like a flower of the grass. The grass withers, and the flower falls, but the word of the Lord endures forever.' And this word is the gospel that was proclaimed to you." 1 Peter 1:24-25

The politician's power, the movie star's beauty, the athlete's prowess—all are fleeting. That hot new fad, those to-die-for fashions—better enjoy them today. Tomorrow something else will be taking their place.

This constant changing is the way of the world and the reason people of the world are so often restless. Of course we are twitchy! When we set our hearts on the temporal and unstable, how can we expect to find deep and lasting peace?

Peter points believers to "the word of the Lord" that "endures forever." In a world of ethereal fluff, Scripture is substantive and weighty. It keeps us grounded. It anchors us when strong, shifting cultural winds are blowing away yesterday's silly illusions.

Realize that just *having* God's truth is not enough. A strong and enduring faith is forged through regular times of reading and reflection.

Take time to consistently mull over God's Word.

For the next note on *Rest and Reflection*, see 2 Peter 1:12.

[A] 1:22 Other mss add *through the Spirit* [B] 1:22 Other mss omit *pure* [C] 1:22 Or *fervently* [D] 1:24-25 Is 40:6-8 [E] 2:2 Or *desire pure spiritual milk* [F] 2:2 Other mss omit *for your salvation* [G] 2:3 Ps 34:8 [H] 2:4 Or *precious to* [I] 2:5 Or *you yourselves, as living stones, are being built into a spiritual house for a holy priesthood* [J] 2:6 Or *precious* [K] 2:6 Is 28:16 LXX

My Story | Neil

I didn't know my grandfather that well, but I loved him. He had infectious laughter that seems to have passed in our DNA in the form of speech patterns in our family that often end sentences with a chuckle. Other stuff got passed on, too.

Grandpa outlived my grandmother and was fortunate to have had two long-suffering women to share his life. He wasn't abusive, but he was abrupt in an unnecessary way. He wasn't patient with those closest to him. Innocent and curiosity-driven questions were often cut off with a slightly raised and forceful answer that shut down further discussion. When I read the phrase in 1 Peter 3:7, "Live with your wives in an understanding way," I think that my grandpa, as great as he was, fell short at that point.

I grew up watching and hearing this same pattern in my parents' relationship. It took me a while to recognize this in my dad. In fact, it didn't really bother me until several years into my own marriage, and I realized I treated my wife abruptly and with little understanding. Breaking this rooted pattern has been a painful, ongoing aspect of my relationship with God. His Spirit has had to continually interrupt my recurring practice of this same attitude. I, too, have had a loving wife who has patiently encouraged my restoration. I have had to recognize over time how painful it is to be cut off and answered disrespectfully. God has had to show me how much I despise being treated that way and how little right I have to treat someone I love that way.

Things would look less hopeful if I didn't have a God and wife who are committed to bringing the best out of me. I've been encouraged to see much less of this pattern in my children's marriages. I know God has been at work.

this one has become
the cornerstone,[A]
8 and
A stone to stumble over,
and a rock to trip over.[B]
They stumble because they disobey the word;
they were destined for this.
9 But you are **a chosen race,**[C,D] **a royal priest-**
hood,[E] **a holy nation,**[F] **a people for his posses-**
sion,[G] **so that you may proclaim the praises**[H,I]
of the one who called you out of darkness into his
marvelous light. 10 Once you were not a people,
but now you are God's people; you had not received mercy, but now you have received mercy.

A CALL TO GOOD WORKS

11 Dear friends, I urge you as strangers and
exiles to abstain from sinful desires that wage
war against the soul. 12 Conduct yourselves
honorably among the Gentiles,[J] so that when
they slander you as evildoers, they will observe your good works and will glorify God
on the day he visits.
13 Submit to every human authority because
of the Lord, whether to the emperor[K] as the
supreme authority 14 or to governors as those
sent out by him to punish those who do what
is evil and to praise those who do what is good.
15 For it is God's will that you silence the ignorance of foolish people by doing good. 16 Submit
as free people, not using your freedom as a
cover-up for evil, but as God's slaves. 17 Honor
everyone. Love the brothers and sisters. Fear
God. Honor the emperor.

SUBMISSION OF SLAVES TO MASTERS

18 Household slaves, submit to your masters
with all reverence not only to the good and
gentle ones but also to the cruel. 19 For it brings
favor if, because of a consciousness of God,
someone endures grief from suffering unjustly. 20 For what credit is there if when you
do wrong and are beaten, you endure it? But
when you do what is good and suffer, if you
endure it, this brings favor with God.
21 For you were called to this, because Christ
also suffered for you, leaving you an example,
that you should follow in his steps. 22 He did
not commit sin, **and no deceit was found in**
his mouth;[L] 23 when he was insulted, he did

[A] **2:7** Ps 118:22 [B] **2:8** Is 8:14 [C] **2:9** Or *generation*, or *nation* [D] **2:9** Dt 7:6; 10:15; Is 43:20 LXX [E] **2:9** Ex 19:6; 23:22 LXX; Is 61:6 [F] **2:9** Ex 19:6; 23:22 LXX [G] **2:9** Ex 19:5; 23:22 LXX; Dt 4:20; 7:6; Is 43:21 LXX [H] **2:9** Or *the mighty deeds* [I] **2:9** Is 42:12; 43:21 [J] **2:12** Or *among the nations*, or *among the pagans* [K] **2:13** Or *king* [L] **2:22** Is 53:9

not insult in return; when he suffered, he did
not threaten but entrusted himself to the one
who judges justly. 24 He himself bore our sins
in his body on the tree; so that, having died to
sins, we might live for righteousness. **By his
wounds**[A] **you have been healed.** 25 For you
were like sheep going astray,[B] but you have
now returned to the Shepherd and Overseer[C]
of your souls.

WIVES AND HUSBANDS

3 In the same way, wives, submit yourselves to your own husbands so that,
even if some disobey the word, they may be
won over without a word by the way their
wives live 2 when they observe your pure,
reverent lives. 3 Don't let your beauty consist
of outward things like elaborate hairstyles
and wearing gold jewelry or fine clothes,
4 but rather what is inside the heart[D] — the
imperishable quality of a gentle and quiet
spirit, which is of great worth in God's sight.
5 For in the past, the holy women who put
their hope in God also adorned themselves in
this way, submitting to their own husbands,
6 just as Sarah obeyed Abraham, calling him
lord. You have become her children when
you do what is good and do not fear any
intimidation.

7 Husbands, in the same way, live with your
wives in an understanding way, as with a weaker partner, showing them honor as coheirs
of the grace of life, so that your prayers will
not be hindered.

DO NO EVIL

8 Finally, all of you be like-minded and sympathetic, love one another, and be compassionate
and humble,[E] 9 not paying back evil for evil or
insult for insult but, on the contrary, giving
a blessing, since you were called for this, so
that you may inherit a blessing.

10 For **the one who wants to love life**
and to see good days,
let him keep his tongue
from evil
and his lips
from speaking deceit,
11 **and let him turn away from evil**
and do what is good.

Thanksgiving and Contentment | *Goodness and Mercy*

INSTEAD

"But you are a chosen race, a royal priesthood, a holy nation,
a people for his possession, so that you may proclaim the praises
of the one who called you out of darkness into his marvelous light.
Once you were not a people, but now you are God's people;
you had not received mercy, but now you have received mercy."
1 Peter 2:9-10

At the dog park, a yappy Yorkie decides—unprovoked—to lunge at and bite a German Shepherd. In a nanosecond, the large dog has the little dog pinned, its massive mouth around that tiny neck. The laws of nature would say the offended dog has every right to clamp its jaws and dispatch its attacker. But suddenly, the Shepherd releases its grip, turns and walks away.

It's a picture of mercy, of course; instead of justice, kindness.

The gospel says that for our treasonous acts against the high King of the universe, we deserve death. But Jesus took the punishment we deserved and gave us mercy instead (Rm 5:10). Because of Christ, God's enemies are able become "God's people."

If you haven't thanked God in a while for his mercy, confess that ingratitude. Then thank him for not giving you what you deserve.

For the next note on *Thanksgiving and Contentment*, see 2 Peter 1:3.

[A] **2:24** Is 53:5 [B] **2:25** Is 53:6 [C] **2:25** Or *Guardian* [D] **3:4** Or *rather, the hidden person of the heart* [E] **3:8** Other mss read *courteous*

Let him seek peace and pursue it,
12 because the eyes of the Lord are
on the righteous
and his ears are open to their prayer.
But the face of the Lord is against
those who do what is evil.[A]

Relationships | *Restoring Damaged Relationships*

"GOTCHA LAST"

"Finally, all of you be like-minded and sympathetic, love one another, and be compassionate and humble, not paying back evil for evil or insult for insult but, on the contrary, giving a blessing, since you were called for this, so that you may inherit a blessing." 1 Peter 3:8-9

Remember the game we played as children in which a sibling or friend would poke you (or someone else) and say the phrase, "Gotcha last!" This would spark laughter, then retaliation, then a slow escalation. Soon it wasn't a game anymore. Almost every time, what began as gentle pushes morphed into hard punches.

The sad truth: Kids aren't the only ones who play this game. Adults do a sophisticated version of it, too. Nations engage in a deadly version.

If we want better relationships, Peter says we can't play this game. We can't go around "paying back evil for evil or insult for insult." Instead of being people who get (even), we need to be people who give (blessings).

"Gotcha last" never leads anywhere good. It is always a silly competition between two childish people and only ends when one of the parties decides to be the grown-up. Let that be you today. Choose loving, compassionate, and humble actions, not a "get-even" lifestyle.

For the next note on *Relationships*, see 1 Peter 4:8.

Relationships | *Relating to Church Family*

THE STRONG LOVE THAT PROTECTS

"Above all, maintain constant love for one another, since love covers a multitude of sins." 1 Peter 4:8

For some strange reason, many are under the impression that Christian love equals maudlin music and sappy Hallmark® cards. Nothing could be further from the truth.

When Peter says, "maintain constant love for one another," he's calling for believers to exert themselves in fervent, strenuous action. The word he uses suggests intensity. It means "to strain or stretch," much like an athlete would do in lunging for the goal line or finish line. Wimpy? Sentimental? Not at all! The love among God's people is to be vigorous and brave. It risks and goes the extra mile.

It also does something else. Notice that this love "covers a multitude of sins." In other words, it mercifully refuses to divulge matters that don't need to be made public (Pr 10:12). Don't misunderstand—love isn't blind. It doesn't turn away from issues that need to be addressed, but it is always discrete and gracious. Love is incompatible with gossip and with most of what happens on social media most days.

Do you love others like that? With a strong yet protective love? Ask God to enable you to love in such a way today.

For the next note on *Relationships*, see 2 Peter 3:18.

[A] **3:10-12** Ps 34:12-16

UNDESERVED SUFFERING

13 Who then will harm you if you are devoted to what is good? 14 But even if you should
suffer for righteousness, you are blessed. **Do
not fear what they fear[A] or be intimidated,**[B]
15 but in your hearts regard[C] Christ[D] the Lord
as holy, ready at any time to give a defense
to anyone who asks you for a reason for the
hope that is in you. 16 Yet do this with gentleness and respect, keeping a clear conscience,
so that when you are accused,[E] those who
disparage your good conduct in Christ will
be put to shame. 17 For it is better to suffer for
doing good, if that should be God's will, than
for doing evil.
18 For Christ also suffered for sins once for
all, the righteous for the unrighteous, that he
might bring you to God. He was put to death
in the flesh[F] but made alive by the Spirit,[G]
19 in which[H] he also went and made proclamation to the spirits in prison 20 who in the
past were disobedient, when God patiently
waited in the days of Noah while the ark was
being prepared. In it a few — that is, eight people[I] — were saved through water. 21 Baptism,
which corresponds to this, now saves you (not
as the removal of dirt from the body, but the
pledge[J] of a good conscience toward God)
through the resurrection of Jesus Christ, 22 who
has gone into heaven and is at the right hand
of God with angels, authorities, and powers
subject to him.

FOLLOWING CHRIST

4 Therefore, since Christ suffered[K] in the
flesh, arm yourselves also with the same
understanding[L] — because the one who suffers in the flesh is finished with sin[M] — 2 in
order to live the remaining time in the flesh
no longer for human desires, but for God's
will. 3 For there has already been enough time
spent in doing what the Gentiles choose to
do: carrying on in unrestrained behavior, evil
desires, drunkenness, orgies, carousing, and
lawless idolatry. 4 They are surprised that you
don't join them in the same flood of wild living — and they slander[N] you. 5 They will give
an account to the one who stands ready to
judge the living and the dead. 6 For this reason
the gospel was also preached to those who
are now dead,[O] so that, although they might
be judged in the flesh according to human

Support | *Commitment to God*

ENTRUSTING

"So then, let those who suffer according to God's will entrust themselves to a faithful Creator while doing what is good." 1 Peter 4:19

When you find yourself among "those who suffer," how do you typically respond? Do you cry? Chase after temporary relief? Complain on social media? Curse? Curl up in the fetal position?

Probably, depending on how long the trial lasts, you do several of those reactions—maybe even in the same day! But notice what Peter urges: "Let those who suffer . . . entrust themselves to a faithful Creator while doing what is good."

Entrusting ourselves to God means presenting our lives and our situations to him. It is an act of surrender, a way of saying, "If this is my lot in life, at least for now, then so be it. I trust that you are faithful. I look to you for help."

One other point: When we are hurting and confused, we long for reassurance—if only God would wrap us in his arms. Well, according to the Bible (1Co 12), other believers are his arms, hands, and feet. In their support, we find God's support and love—and the strength to keep "doing what is good." Entrust yourself to God as he works through your Christian brothers and sisters.

For the next note on *Support*, see 1 Peter 5:5.

[A] **3:14** Or *Do not fear them* [B] **3:14** Is 8:12 [C] **3:15** Or *sanctify*, or *set apart* [D] **3:15** Other mss read *set God* [E] **3:16** Other mss read *when they speak against you as evildoers* [F] **3:18** Or *by the flesh*, or *in the fleshly realm* [G] **3:18** Or *in the spirit*, or *in the Spirit*, or *in the spiritual realm* [H] **3:19** Or *by whom*, or *in whom*, or *at that time* [I] **3:20** Or *souls* [J] **3:21** Or *the appeal* [K] **4:1** Other mss read *suffered for us* [L] **4:1** Or *perspective*, or *attitude* [M] **4:1** Or *the one who suffered in the flesh has finished with sin* [N] **4:4** Or *blaspheme* [O] **4:6** Or *those who are dead*

standards, they might live in the spirit according to God's standards.

END-TIME ETHICS

7 The end of all things is near; therefore, be alert and sober-minded for prayer. 8 Above all, maintain constant love for one another, since **love covers a multitude of sins.**[A] 9 Be hospitable to one another without complaining. 10 Just as each one has received a gift, use it to serve others, as good stewards of the varied grace of God. 11 If anyone speaks, let it be as one who speaks God's words; if anyone serves, let it be from the strength God provides, so that God may be glorified through Jesus Christ in everything. To him be the glory and the power forever and ever. Amen.

CHRISTIAN SUFFERING

12 Dear friends, don't be surprised when the fiery ordeal comes among you to test you as if something unusual were happening to you. 13 Instead, rejoice as you share in the sufferings of Christ, so that you may also rejoice with great joy when his glory is revealed. 14 If you are ridiculed for the name of Christ, you are blessed, because the Spirit of glory and of God[B] rests on you. 15 Let none of you suffer as a murderer, a thief, an evildoer, or a meddler.[C] 16 But if anyone suffers as a Christian, let him not be ashamed but let him glorify God in having that name.[D] 17 For the time has come for judgment to begin with God's household, and if it begins with us, what will the outcome be for those who disobey the gospel of God?

18 And **if a righteous person is saved**
with difficulty,
what will become of the ungodly
and the sinner?[E]

19 So then, let those who suffer according to God's will entrust themselves to a faithful Creator while doing what is good.

ABOUT THE ELDERS

5 I exhort the elders among you as a fellow elder and witness to the sufferings of Christ, as well as one who shares in the glory about to be revealed: 2 Shepherd God's flock among you, not overseeing[F] out of compulsion but willingly, as God would have you;[G] not out of greed for money but eagerly; 3 not

Support | *Mentors*

ELDERLY WISDOM

"In the same way, you who are younger, be subject to the elders. All of you clothe yourselves with humility toward one another, because God resists the proud but gives grace to the humble." 1 Peter 5:5

Some cultures revere the elderly. People seek them out for their wisdom. In other cultures, senior citizens, told they have nothing left to offer, congregate in retirement villages to play bocce ball and make quilts. Or worse, they are shuttled off to nursing homes to watch TV.

What a tragedy! What a waste!

Peter urges a different mind-set and practice. "Be subject to the elders," he says. This means respecting and valuing the older generation, paying attention to them, eagerly soliciting their counsel and advice.

Do you do this? Do you have an older person in your life on speed dial? Having someone available to share life lessons and time-tested perspectives isn't desperate or needy. It shows incredible wisdom.

Only the proud person barrels ahead foolishly, thinking the lessons of the past don't apply to today's situations. As Solomon warned, "When arrogance comes, disgrace follows, but with humility comes wisdom" (Pr 11:2).

For the next note on *Support*, see 1 Peter 5:7.

[A] **4:8** Pr 10:12 [B] **4:14** Or *God's glorious Spirit* [C] **4:15** Or *as one who defrauds others* [D] **4:16** Other mss read *in that case* [E] **4:18** Pr 11:31 LXX [F] **5:2** Other mss omit *overseeing* [G] **5:2** Other mss omit *as God would have you*

lording it over those entrusted to you, but
being examples to the flock. 4 And when the
chief Shepherd appears, you will receive the
unfading crown of glory. 5 In the same way,
you who are younger, be subject to the elders.
All of you clothe yourselves with[A] humility
toward one another, because

God resists the proud
but gives grace to the humble.[B]

CONCLUSION

6 Humble yourselves, therefore, under the
mighty hand of God, so that he may exalt you at
the proper time, 7 casting all your cares on him,
because he cares about you. 8 Be sober-minded,
be alert. Your adversary the devil is prowling
around like a roaring lion, looking for anyone
he can devour. 9 Resist him, firm in the faith,
knowing that the same kind of sufferings are
being experienced by your fellow believers
throughout the world.

10 The God of all grace, who called you to his
eternal glory in Christ,[C] will himself restore,
establish, strengthen, and support you after
you have suffered a little while.[D] 11 To him be
dominion[E] forever.[F] Amen.

12 Through Silvanus,[G] a faithful brother (as
I consider him), I have written to you briefly
in order to encourage you and to testify that
this is the true grace of God. Stand firm in it!
13 She who is in Babylon, chosen together with
you, sends you greetings, as does Mark, my
son. 14 Greet one another with a kiss of love.
Peace to all of you who are in Christ.[H]

CARE CASTING

"Casting all your cares on him, because he cares about you." 1 Peter 5:7

A child in trouble. A medical emergency. A financial crisis.

When these sorts of situations come our way, our natural tendency is to take them to heart and cling tightly to them. Throughout the day, we focus on them, obsessing over what they mean and where they might lead. Soon we are fretting and freaking out.

Notice, however, what Peter says about our "cares," our anxious concerns. We are to *cast* them on God. This word typically means "to throw with great force; to hurl."

Casting your cares on God just makes sense. First, most problems in life are far too complex for you to solve. Second, the Almighty "cares about you."

Peter is saying, "Toss your cares to the One who cares." Novelist Victor Hugo put it this way, "Have courage for the great sorrows of life and patience for the small ones; and when you have laboriously accomplished your daily task, go to sleep in peace. God is awake."

For the next note on *Support*, see 2 Peter 2:1.

[A] **5:5** Or *you tie around yourselves* [B] **5:5** Pr 3:34 LXX [C] **5:10** Other mss read *in Christ Jesus* [D] **5:10** Or *to a small extent*
[E] **5:11** Some mss read *dominion and glory*; other mss read *glory and dominion* [F] **5:11** Other mss read *forever and ever*
[G] **5:12** Or *Silas*; Ac 15:22-32; 16:19-40; 17:1-16 [H] **5:14** Other mss read *Christ Jesus. Amen.*

2 Peter—gives a number of haunting images of false teachers, including that they are "springs without water" (2:17). Their teaching has no substance, for they are enslaved to corruption (2:19). Thus, they cannot offer true hope. Only by rejecting them and their teaching can we find the peace we long for (3:14).

One of the primary ways to discern false teachers from teachers of the truth is their lifestyles. Do their habits and behaviors line up with the Bible, or are they out for personal gain and illicit pleasure? Second Peter offers us a list of tests for church leaders, showing how both their teaching and behavior need to align with Scripture.

We must be discerning about the teachers we hear and what we read. Scripture is the final authority for all matters of faith and godliness; thus, we need to be diligent students of the truth so we can recognize truth from error. If you find yourself confused, discouraged, or hopeless, turn for answers in God's Word. That is where your teachers and leaders should be pointing you. If not, then you need to find new voices who will speak to you words of truth and life.

2 PETER

AUTHOR: The apostle Peter

DATE WRITTEN: Peter mentions his death as near (1:14), which places this letter close to AD 67.

ORIGINAL AUDIENCE: No audience is listed, but Peter calls this a "second letter" (3:1). If his first letter was 1 Peter, then the recipients are the same as that letter: "exiles dispersed abroad in Pontus, Galatia, Cappadocia, Asia, and Bithynia" (1Pt 1:1).

SETTING: At the writing of this letter, the church was facing an even greater threat than persecution from the government: false teaching from within. Some leaders were denying Christ's return and leading people astray.

PURPOSE FOR WRITING: Peter writes in a pastoral tone to warn his readers against false teachers. He responds to specific arguments that false teachers were making against the Christian faith.

OUTLINE:

1. Greeting (1:1-2)
2. Growth in the Faith (1:3-11)
3. Peter's Testimony (1:12-21)
4. Warning against False Teachers (2:1-22)
5. The Day of the Lord (3:1-9)
6. Life in Light of Christ's Return (3:10-18)

KEY VERSE:

"His divine power has given us everything required for life and godliness through the knowledge of him who called us by his own glory and goodness." —2 Peter 1:3

RESTORATION THEMES

R	Rest and Reflection	*Remembering God's Truth—1:12*
E	Eternal Perspective	*For the next note, see Revelation 21:1.*
S	Support	*Small Groups—2 Peter 2:1*
T	Thanksgiving and Contentment	*Praise for God's Equipping—1:3*
O	Other-centeredness	*Loving the Unlovable—3:9*
R	Relationships	*Encouraging Each Other—3:18*
E	Exercise of Faith	*For the next note, see 1 John 2:15.*

GREETING

1 Simeon[A] Peter, a servant and an apostle of Jesus Christ:

To those who have received a faith equal to ours through the righteousness of our God and Savior Jesus Christ.

2 May grace and peace be multiplied to you through the knowledge of God and of Jesus our Lord.

GROWTH IN THE FAITH

3 His[B] divine power has given us everything required for life and godliness through the knowledge of him who called us by[C] his own glory and goodness. 4 By these he has given us very great and precious promises, so that through them you may share in the divine nature, escaping the corruption that is in the world because of evil desire. 5 For this very reason, make every effort to supplement your faith with goodness, goodness with knowledge, 6 knowledge with self-control, self-control with endurance, endurance with godliness, 7 godliness with brotherly affection, and brotherly affection with love. 8 For if you possess these qualities in increasing measure, they will keep you from being useless or unfruitful in the knowledge of our Lord Jesus Christ. 9 The person who lacks these things is blind and shortsighted and has forgotten the cleansing from his past sins. 10 Therefore, brothers and sisters, make every effort to confirm your calling and election, because if you do these things you will never stumble. 11 For in this way, entry into the eternal kingdom of our Lord and Savior Jesus Christ will be richly provided for you.

12 Therefore I will always remind you about these things, even though you know them and are established in the truth you now have. 13 I think it is right, as long as I am in this bodily tent, to wake you up with a reminder, 14 since I know that I will soon lay aside my tent, as our Lord Jesus Christ has indeed made clear to me. 15 And I will also make every effort so that you are able to recall these things at any time after my departure.[D]

THE TRUSTWORTHY PROPHETIC WORD

16 For we did not follow cleverly contrived myths when we made known to you the power and coming of our Lord Jesus Christ; instead, we were eyewitnesses of his majesty. 17 For he received honor and glory from God the

Thanksgiving and Contentment | *Praise for God's Equipping*

EVERYTHING REQUIRED

"His divine power has given us everything required for life and godliness through the knowledge of him who called us by his own glory and goodness." 2 Peter 1:3

The enemy whispers this unspoken sentence to our hearts a hundred times a day: "You don't have what it takes to _______."

The words in the blank change constantly, don't they? "Do this job . . . parent this child . . . resist this temptation . . . overcome this habit . . . develop this skill."

Of course, all these suggestions are falsehoods—straight from the father of lies (Jn 8:44). Peter tells us God has "given us everything required for life and godliness." In Christ, we are complete (Col 2:10). We are sufficiently equipped (2Tm 3:17). We can do whatever God sets before us (Php 4:13). In other words, we do have what it takes to live godly lives in an ungodly world.

Spend a few minutes today thanking God for this stunning truth. Ask him to show you anything in your life that is keeping you from tapping into his infinite provisions. (And for extra protection, memorize Philippians 4:13 and let it be your go-to response to the devilish statement "You don't have what it takes.")

For the next note on *Thanksgiving and Contentment*, see 1 John 1:9.

[A] **1:1** Other mss read *Simon* [B] **1:3** Lit *As his* [C] **1:3** Or *to* [D] **1:15** Or *death*

Father when the voice came to him from the
Majestic Glory, saying "This is my beloved
Son,[A] with whom I am well-pleased! " 18 We
ourselves heard this voice when it came from
heaven while we were with him on the holy
mountain. 19 We also have the prophetic word
strongly confirmed, and you will do well to pay
attention to it, as to a lamp shining in a dark
place, until the day dawns and the morning
star rises in your hearts. 20 Above all, you know
this: No prophecy of Scripture comes from
the prophet's own interpretation, 21 because
no prophecy ever came by the will of man;
instead, men spoke from God as they were
carried along by the Holy Spirit.

THE JUDGMENT OF FALSE TEACHERS

2 There were indeed false prophets among
the people, just as there will be false teachers among you. They will bring in destructive
heresies, even denying the Master who bought
them, and will bring swift destruction on themselves. 2 Many will follow their depraved ways,
and the way of truth will be maligned because
of them. 3 They will exploit you in their greed
with made-up stories. Their condemnation,
pronounced long ago, is not idle, and their
destruction does not sleep.
4 For if God didn't spare the angels who
sinned but cast them into hell[B] and delivered
them in chains[C] of utter darkness to be kept
for judgment; 5 and if he didn't spare the ancient world, but protected Noah, a preacher
of righteousness, and seven others,[D] when he
brought the flood on the world of the ungodly; 6 and if he reduced the cities of Sodom and
Gomorrah to ashes and condemned them to
extinction,[E] making them an example of what
is coming to the ungodly;[F] 7 and if he rescued
righteous Lot, distressed by the depraved behavior of the immoral 8 (for as that righteous
man lived among them day by day, his righteous soul was tormented by the lawless deeds
he saw and heard) — 9 then the Lord knows
how to rescue the godly from trials and to
keep the unrighteous under punishment for
the day of judgment, 10 especially those who
follow the polluting desires of the flesh and
despise authority.

Bold, arrogant people! They are not afraid
to slander the glorious ones; 11 however, angels, who are greater in might and power, do

Rest and Reflection | *Remembering God's Truth*

THE IMPORTANCE OF REMINDERS

"Therefore I will always remind you about these things, even though you know them and are established in the truth you now have." 2 Peter 1:12

Thanks to verbal reminders last night and this morning, a text message mid-afternoon, and a yellow Post-It® note on your dashboard, you actually *remembered* to pick up the dry cleaning on your way home from work! It's a minor miracle!

Why are we so forgetful? Senility? Try overload. We live in a culture of busyness and distraction. Think about it: At any given moment, you're multitasking mentally and physically, trying to manage innumerable thoughts and feelings, people and projects, responsibilities and desires. Most people can't juggle three balls—who can keep thirty or three hundred in the air?

This is a reality in the spiritual realm, too. Often the problem is not that we don't know what God has said about a certain issue, it's that in the fog of war (daily life), we forget it. This is probably why Peter mentioned the need for reminders three times in his short letter.

A daily quiet time or devotional time can serve this purpose—helping you recall and reflect regularly on eternal truths.

For the next note on *Rest and Reflection*, see Revelation 2:3-4.

[A] **1:17** Other mss read *my Son, my beloved* [B] **2:4** Gk *Tartarus* [C] **2:4** Other mss read *in pits* [D] **2:5** Lit *Noah, the eighth, a preacher of righteousness* [E] **2:6** Other mss omit *to extinction* [F] **2:6** Other mss read *an example of what is going to happen to the ungodly*

not bring a slanderous charge against them
before the Lord.[A] 12 But these people, like irra-
tional animals — creatures of instinct born
to be caught and destroyed — slander what
they do not understand, and in their destruction they too will be destroyed. 13 They will
be paid back with harm for the harm they
have done. They consider it a pleasure to ca-
rouse in broad daylight. They are spots and
blemishes, delighting in their deceptions[B]
while they feast with you. 14 They have eyes
full of adultery that never stop looking for
sin. They seduce unstable people and have
hearts trained in greed. Children under a
curse! 15 They have gone astray by abandoning
the straight path and have followed the path
of Balaam, the son of Bosor,[C] who loved the
wages of wickedness 16 but received a rebuke for his lawlessness: A speechless donkey
spoke with a human voice and restrained the
prophet's madness.

17 These people are springs without water,
mists driven by a storm. The gloom of darkness has been reserved for them. 18 For by
uttering boastful, empty words, they seduce,
with fleshly desires and debauchery, people
who have barely escaped[D] from those who
live in error. 19 They promise them freedom,
but they themselves are slaves of corruption,
since people are enslaved to whatever defeats
them. 20 For if, having escaped the world's impurity through the knowledge of the Lord[E] and
Savior Jesus Christ, they are again entangled
in these things and defeated, the last state is
worse for them than the first. 21 For it would
have been better for them not to have known
the way of righteousness than, after knowing it, to turn back from the holy command
delivered to them. 22 It has happened to them
according to the true proverb: **A dog returns
to its own vomit**,[F] and, "a washed sow returns
to wallowing in the mud."

THE DAY OF THE LORD

3 Dear friends, this is now the second letter I have written to you; in both letters,
I want to stir up your sincere understanding
by way of reminder, 2 so that you recall the

Support | *Small Groups*

BECOMING DISCERNING

"There were indeed false prophets among the people, just as there will be false teachers among you. They will bring in destructive heresies, even denying the Master who bought them, and will bring swift destruction on themselves." 2 Peter 2:1

We live in an era of unprecedented social upheaval. Long-accepted standards of right and wrong—the tectonic plates upon which culture has stood for centuries—are shifting dramatically. Even in religious circles, fierce debates rage about the nature of God, the meaning of spirituality, heaven and hell, marriage and sexuality. The kind of changes (in public attitudes and opinions) that used to take place slowly over generations now happen in a blink.

Perhaps the Internet is responsible? It does, after all, give every viewpoint a platform. Thankfully, the online cranks and kooks are generally easy to spot and dismiss. But many other voices make intriguing claims. And some are compelling and persuasive. Are they speaking truth or spouting lies?

We also need people in our lives who are committed to biblical authority because healthy small group community can help us learn to discern between God's truth and the "destructive heresies" of "false teachers."

Off of whom do you bounce ideas? Where do you go for a second opinion when you hear a slick new idea?

For the next note on *Support*, see 1 John 1:8.

[A] **2:11** Other mss read *them from the Lord* [B] **2:13** Other mss read *delighting in the love feasts* [C] **2:15** Other mss read *Beor*
[D] **2:18** Or *people who are actually escaping* [E] **2:20** Other mss read *our Lord* [F] **2:22** Pr 26:11

words previously spoken by the holy prophets and the command of our Lord and Savior
given through your apostles. 3 Above all, be
aware of this: Scoffers will come in the last
days scoffing and following their own evil
desires, 4 saying, "Where is his 'coming' that
he promised? Ever since our ancestors fell
asleep, all things continue as they have been
since the beginning of creation." 5 They deliberately overlook this: By the word of God
the heavens came into being long ago and
the earth was brought about from water and
through water. 6 Through these the world of
that time perished when it was flooded. 7 By
the same word, the present heavens and earth
are stored up for fire, being kept for the day
of judgment and destruction of the ungodly.
8 Dear friends, don't overlook this one
fact: With the Lord one day is like a thousand years, and a thousand years like one
day. 9 The Lord does not delay his promise, as
some understand delay, but is patient with
you, not wanting any to perish but all to come
to repentance.
10 But the day of the Lord will come like a
thief;[A] on that day the heavens will pass away
with a loud noise, the elements will burn and
be dissolved, and the earth and the works on
it will be disclosed.[B,C] 11 Since all these things
are to be dissolved in this way, it is clear what
sort of people you should be in holy conduct
and godliness 12 as you wait for the day of God
and hasten its coming.[D] Because of that day,
the heavens will be dissolved with fire and the
elements will melt with heat. 13 But based on
his promise, we wait for new heavens and a
new earth, where righteousness dwells.

CONCLUSION

14 Therefore, dear friends, while you wait for
these things, make every effort to be found
without spot or blemish in his sight, at peace.
15 Also, regard the patience of our Lord as
salvation, just as our dear brother Paul has
written to you according to the wisdom giv-
en to him. 16 He speaks about these things in
all his letters. There are some matters that
are hard to understand. The untaught and
unstable will twist them to their own destruction, as they also do with the rest of
the Scriptures.
17 Therefore, dear friends, since you know

Other-centeredness | *Loving the Unlovable*

SEEING OTHERS AS GOD SEES

"The Lord does not delay his promise, as some understand delay, but is patient with you, not wanting any to perish but all to come to repentance." 2 Peter 3:9

Atheists and spiritual cynics have always been around. But in recent years, unbelievers have become more outspoken (and more vitriolic) in their opposition to faith. Unfortunately, some Christians have taken these insults personally and responded with hateful name-calling and gleeful threats of divine judgment.

In this short letter that describes scoffing unbelievers in the last days, Peter reminds us of some important divine realities: God is *not* eager to bring judgment on the earth. He is being "patient" with the world. And why? Because he doesn't want "any to perish but all to come to repentance."

In other words, God loves that foul-mouthed atheist who mocks Christ, and he gives that smug skeptic time to turn humbly from his unbelief and seek forgiveness.

If God feels this way about those who are far from him, should we feel any different?

What matters ultimately is not how savagely unbelievers insult the people of God, but how faithfully the people of God demonstrate love to those unbelievers.

For the next note on *Other-centeredness*, see 1 John 3:17.

[A] **3:10** Other mss add *in the night* [B] **3:10** Other mss read *will be burned up* [C] **3:10** Some Syriac and Coptic mss read *will not be found* [D] **3:12** Or *and speed the coming*

this in advance, be on your guard, so that you are not led away by the error of lawless people and fall from your own stable position. 18 But grow in the grace and knowledge of our Lord and Savior Jesus Christ. To him be the glory both now and to the day of eternity.[A]

Relationships | *Encouraging Each Other*

GROWING TOGETHER

"But grow in the grace and knowledge of our Lord and Savior Jesus Christ. To him be the glory both now and to the day of eternity." 2 Peter 3:18

Often, when we modern Christians read the Bible, we do so with an individualistic mind-set. We do this, especially in Western cultures, because we tend to view the spiritual life as a private rather than a corporate pursuit.

Our first-century forefathers in the faith didn't think (or function) this way. Whereas we value *autonomy* above all, they prized *community*. The writers of Scripture went out of their way to emphasize the idea that faith is a "we" thing, not a "me" thing.

Take this closing challenge from Peter, for example. In Greek (the original language of the New Testament writings), verb endings are either singular or plural. Because Peter wrote this particular verse to a group of Christians, the verb *grow* is plural. It means that growing "in the grace and knowledge of our Lord and Savior Jesus Christ" is a project believers need to do *together*. It clearly implies that we can't do this all by ourselves (and we shouldn't try).

What group of people helps you grow in your relationship with Jesus?

For the next note on *Relationships*, see 1 John 2:10-11.

[A] **3:18** Other mss add *Amen.*

RESTORATION THEMES

R	Rest and Reflection	*For the next note, see Revelation 2:3-4.*
E	Eternal Perspective	*For the next note, see Revelation 21:1.*
S	Support	*Truthfulness with Self—1 John 1:8* *Prayer—5:14-15*
T	Thanksgiving and Contentment	*Confession—1:9* *Praise for God's Love—4:9* *Repentance—5:18*
O	Other-centeredness	*Helping People in Need—3:17* *Loving Others—3:18*
R	Relationships	*Dealing with Anger and Hatred—2:10-11*
E	Exercise of Faith	*Making Right Choices/Priorities/Values—2:15*

PROLOGUE: OUR DECLARATION

1 What was from the beginning, what we have
heard, what we have seen with our eyes, what
we have observed and have touched with our
hands, concerning the word of life — 2 that life
was revealed, and we have seen it and we testify
and declare to you the eternal life that was with
the Father and was revealed to us — 3 what we
have seen and heard we also declare to you,
so that you may also have fellowship with us;
and indeed our fellowship is with the Father
and with his Son Jesus Christ. 4 We are writing
these things[A] so that our[B] joy may be complete.

FELLOWSHIP WITH GOD

5 This is the message we have heard from him
and declare to you: God is light, and there is
absolutely no darkness in him. 6 If we say, "We
have fellowship with him," and yet we walk in
darkness, we are lying and are not practicing
the truth. 7 If we walk in the light as he himself is in the light, we have fellowship with
one another, and the blood of Jesus his Son
cleanses us from all sin. 8 If we say, "We have
no sin," we are deceiving ourselves, and the
truth is not in us. 9 If we confess our sins, he
is faithful and righteous to forgive us our sins
and to cleanse us from all unrighteousness.
10 If we say, "We have not sinned," we make
him a liar, and his word is not in us.

2 My little children, I am writing you these
things so that you may not sin. But if anyone
does sin, we have an advocate with the Father
— Jesus Christ the righteous one. 2 He himself is
the atoning sacrifice[C] for our sins, and not only
for ours, but also for those of the whole world.

GOD'S COMMANDS

3 This is how we know that we know him: if
we keep his commands. 4 The one who says, "I
have come to know him," and yet doesn't keep
his commands, is a liar, and the truth is not in
him. 5 But whoever keeps his word, truly in him
the love of God is made complete. This is how
we know we are in him: 6 The one who says he
remains in him should walk just as he walked.
7 Dear friends, I am not writing you a new
command but an old command that you have
had from the beginning. The old command is
the word you have heard. 8 Yet I am writing you

Support | *Truthfulness with Self*

SELF-DECEIT AND SELF-AWARENESS

"If we say, 'We have no sin,' we are deceiving ourselves, and the truth is not in us." 1 John 1:8

We can never be healthy as long as we are self-absorbed or self-focused. We will never be healthy until we are self-aware.

To be self-aware means to have an accurate sense of how and where we are weak and what our hang-ups are. Self-awareness is hard to come by because we often can't see ourselves accurately. We have blind spots, and even more, our foolish pride typically doesn't want us to see ugly truths about us (only truths flattering to us).

Here's an example: Let's say you get into an animated discussion with a friend. The whole time you think you're being calm and unemotional. But later a third friend (who witnessed the whole interaction) informs you that, actually, you raised your voice significantly and got extremely defensive. We need other people to hold up a mirror to us.

Consequently, healthy souls do at least these two wise things: (1) they enter into community; and (2) they give someone in that community permission to help them see the things about themselves that they can't see but need to see.

All this has to take place in relationships of trust, of course. But when it does take place, the results are remarkable. Do you have such relationships in your life?

For the next note on *Support*, see 1 John 5:14-15.

[A] **1:4** Other mss add *to you* [B] **1:4** Other mss read *your* [C] **2:2** Or *the propitiation*

REMAINING WITH GOD

24 What you have heard from the beginning is to
remain in you. If what you have heard from the
beginning remains in you, then you will remain
in the Son and in the Father. 25 And this is the
promise that he himself made to us: eternal life.
26 I have written these things to you concerning those who are trying to deceive you. 27 As
for you, the anointing you received from him
remains in you, and you don't need anyone
to teach you. Instead, his anointing teaches
you about all things and is true and is not a
lie; just as it has taught you,[A] remain in him.

GOD'S CHILDREN

28 So now, little children, remain in him so that
when he appears we may have confidence and
not be ashamed before him at his coming. 29 If
you know that he is righteous, you know this
as well: Everyone who does what is right has

been born of him. 1 See what great love[B]
the Father has given us that we should
be called God's children — and we are! The
reason the world does not know us is that it
didn't know him. 2 Dear friends, we are God's
children now, and what we will be has not yet
been revealed. We know that when he appears,[C]
we will be like him because we will see him
as he is. 3 And everyone who has this hope in
him purifies himself just as he is pure.
4 Everyone who commits sin practices lawlessness; and sin is lawlessness. 5 You know that
he was revealed so that he might take away
sins,[D] and there is no sin in him. 6 Everyone
who remains in him does not sin;[E] everyone
who sins[F] has not seen him or known him.
7 Children, let no one deceive you. The one
who does what is right is righteous, just as
he is righteous. 8 The one who commits[G] sin
is of the devil, for the devil has sinned from
the beginning. The Son of God was revealed
for this purpose: to destroy the devil's works.
9 Everyone who has been born of God does
not sin,[H] because his seed remains in him;
he is not able to sin,[I] because he has been
born of God. 10 This is how God's children
and the devil's children become obvious.
Whoever does not do what is right is not of
God, especially the one who does not love
his brother or sister.

O Other-centeredness | *Helping People in Need*

SEE AND ACT

"If anyone has this world's goods and sees a fellow believer in need but withholds compassion from him — how does God's love reside in him?" 1 John 3:17

Not long after Jesus met John, he tagged him (and his brother James) with the not-so-flattering nickname "Sons of Thunder" (Mk 3:17). Perhaps this related to the time the residents of an unnamed Samaritan village had been inhospitable to Jesus, and the brothers had asked if they could "call down fire from heaven to consume them" (Lk 9:54).

That wasn't their best moment. Thankfully, following Jesus has a way of changing a person over time. And that's what happened to John. The love of Jesus radically transformed his heart.

By the time John wrote his Gospel, he was describing himself as "the one Jesus loved" (Jn 13:23; 20:2; 21:7,20). And in John's first letter, we find almost *fifty* references to love!

Here's what we need to see: The love John calls believers to isn't mushy. It's something we *do*, not a sentiment we feel. In truth, John saw Jesus demonstrate this kind of love day after day, all the way up to the day we remember as Good Friday. This love sees people in need and acts with compassion.

Who around you has a material need? How—practically and specifically—will you respond?

For the first note on *Other-centeredness*, see 1 John 3:18.

[A] **2:27** Or *as he has taught you* [B] **3:1** Or *what sort of love* [C] **3:2** Or *when it appears* [D] **3:5** Other mss read *our sins* [E] **3:6** Or *not keep on sinning* [F] **3:6** Or *who keeps on sinning* [G] **3:8** Or *practices* [H] **3:9** Or *not practice sin* [I] **3:9** Or *to keep on sinning*

LOVE IN ACTION

[11] For this is the message you have heard from
the beginning: We should love one another,
[12] unlike Cain, who was of the evil one and
murdered his brother. And why did he murder him? Because his deeds were evil, and his
brother's were righteous.
[13] Do not be surprised, brothers and sisters,
if the world hates you. [14] We know that we have
passed from death to life because we love our
brothers and sisters. The one who does not
love remains in death. [15] Everyone who hates
his brother or sister is a murderer, and you
know that no murderer has eternal life residing
in him. [16] This is how we have come to know
love: He laid down his life for us. We should
also lay down our lives for our brothers and
sisters. [17] If anyone has this world's goods and
sees a fellow believer[A] in need but withholds
compassion from him — how does God's love
reside in him? [18] Little children, let us not love
in word or speech, but in action and in truth.
[19] This is how we will know that we belong
to the truth and will reassure our hearts before him [20] whenever our hearts condemn
us; for God is greater than our hearts, and he
knows all things.
[21] Dear friends, if our hearts don't condemn
us, we have confidence before God [22] and receive whatever we ask from him because we
keep his commands and do what is pleasing
in his sight. [23] Now this is his command: that
we believe in the name of his Son Jesus Christ,
and love one another as he commanded us.
[24] The one who keeps his commands remains
in him, and he in him. And the way we know
that he remains in us is from the Spirit he
has given us.

THE SPIRIT OF TRUTH AND THE SPIRIT OF ERROR

4 Dear friends, do not believe every spirit,
but test the spirits to see if they are from
God, because many false prophets have gone
out into the world.
[2] This is how you know the Spirit of God:
Every spirit that confesses that Jesus Christ
has come in the flesh is from God, [3] but every spirit that does not confess Jesus[B] is not
from God. This is the spirit of the antichrist,
which you have heard is coming; even now
it is already in the world.
[4] You are from God, little children, and you
have conquered them, because the one who
is in you is greater than the one who is in the
world. [5] They are from the world. Therefore
what they say is from the world, and the world

Other-centeredness | *Loving Others*

WHEN PRAYER IS NOT ENOUGH

"Little children, let us not love in word or speech, but in action and in truth." 1 John 3:18

A neighbor loses everything in a fire. Many believers respond by immediately posting a message on social media or sending a text that says something like, "I'm so sorry. Please know you are in my prayers. Let me know how I can help."

The problem is, most people in crisis or tragedy are too stunned to think coherently. They are unlikely to get back to you anytime soon with a list of ways you can help.

Try something different. Go ahead and send the sweet message, but change that last line to something more specific and practical. Say something like: "We have two empty bedrooms. Do you need temporary housing?" or "Can we take you to lunch or have you over for supper this week?" Or, "Can I bring you a couple of gift cards?" Or "Can I run errands for you, or would you like me to watch your kids while you meet with insurance people?"

According to John, thoughtful words mean a lot, but they mean even more when coupled with thoughtful and loving actions.

For the first note on *Other-centeredness*, see 3 John 10.

[A] **3:17** Lit *sees his brother or sister* [B] **4:3** Other mss read *confess that Jesus has come in the flesh*

listens to them. 6 We are from God. Anyone
who knows God listens to us; anyone who
is not from God does not listen to us. This is
how we know the Spirit of truth and the spirit
of deception.

KNOWING GOD THROUGH LOVE

7 Dear friends, let us love one another, because love is from God, and everyone who
loves has been born of God and knows God.
8 The one who does not love does not know
God, because God is love. 9 God's love was
revealed among us[A] in this way: God sent
his one and only Son into the world so that
we might live through him. 10 Love consists
in this: not that we loved God, but that he
loved us and sent his Son to be the atoning
sacrifice[B] for our sins. 11 Dear friends, if God
loved us in this way, we also must love one
another. 12 No one has ever seen God. If we
love one another, God remains in[C] us and his
love is made complete in us. 13 This is how
we know that we remain in him and he in
us: He has given us of his Spirit. 14 And we
have seen and we testify that the Father has
sent his Son as the world's Savior. 15 Whoever
confesses that Jesus is the Son of God — God
remains in him and he in God. 16 And we have
come to know and to believe the love that
God has for us.

God is love, and the one who remains in
love remains in God, and God remains in
him. 17 In this, love is made complete with
us so that we may have confidence in the
day of judgment, because as he is, so also
are we in this world. 18 There is no fear in
love; instead, perfect love drives out fear,
because fear involves punishment.[D] So the
one who fears is not complete in love. 19 We
love[E] because he first loved us. 20 If anyone
says, "I love God," and yet hates his brother or sister, he is a liar. For the person who
does not love his brother or sister whom he
has seen cannot love God whom he has not
seen.[F] 21 And we have this command from
him: The one who loves God must also love
his brother and sister.

5 Everyone who believes that Jesus is the
Christ has been born of God, and everyone who loves the Father[G] also loves the one
born of him. 2 This is how we know that we
love God's children: when we love God and
obey[H] his commands. 3 For this is what love
for God is: to keep his commands. And his
commands are not a burden, 4 because everyone who has been born of God conquers the

Thanksgiving and Contentment | *Praise for God's Love*

MADE ALIVE TO LOVE

"God's love was revealed among us in this way: God sent his one and only Son into the world so that we might live through him." 1 John 4:9

Have you ever noticed how people seem to come alive when they fall in love? Your wallflower co-worker, for example, meets a special someone, and blossoms overnight into someone who's chatty and charming. Or the focused, driven young professional who lives next door suddenly has a faraway look in his eyes and a new, goofy grin.

Lovers talk about their hearts singing or going pitter-patter or doing somersaults. No wonder: Love always does a number on the human heart. It wrecks us in all kinds of good ways: piercing the hard-hearted, healing the brokenhearted, resurrecting those whose hearts are all but dead.

This, John says, pictures the way God loved us. He "sent his one and only Son into the world so that we *might live* through him." In other words, as wonderful as the love of people is, the love of God really makes us come alive.

Take a few moments now to thank the Lord for such love. Ask that it might animate you today.

For the first note on *Thanksgiving and Contentment*, see 1 John 5:18.

[A] **4:9** Or *in us* [B] **4:10** Or *the propitiation* [C] **4:12** Or *remains among* [D] **4:18** Or *fear has its own punishment* or *torment* [E] **4:19** Other mss add *him* [F] **4:20** Other mss read *has seen, how is he able to love . . . seen?* (as a question) [G] **5:1** Or *loves the one who has given birth* [H] **5:2** Other mss read *keep*

world. This is the victory that has conquered
the world: our faith.

THE CERTAINTY OF GOD'S TESTIMONY

5 Who is the one who conquers the world but
the one who believes that Jesus is the Son
of God? 6 Jesus Christ — he is the one who
came by water and blood, not by water only,
but by water and by blood. And the Spirit is
the one who testifies, because the Spirit is
the truth. 7 For there are three that testify:[A]
8 the Spirit, the water, and the blood — and
these three are in agreement. 9 If we accept
human testimony, God's testimony is greater, because it is God's testimony that he has
given about his Son. 10 The one who believes
in the Son of God has this testimony within
himself. The one who does not believe God
has made him a liar, because he has not believed in the testimony God has given about
his Son. 11 And this is the testimony: God has
given us eternal life, and this life is in his
Son. 12 The one who has the Son has life. The
one who does not have the Son of God does
not have life. 13 I have written these things
to you who believe in the name of the Son
of God so that you may know that you have
eternal life.

EFFECTIVE PRAYER

14 This is the confidence we have before him: If
we ask anything according to his will, he hears
us. 15 And if we know that he hears whatever
we ask, we know that we have what we have
asked of him.
16 If anyone sees a fellow believer[B] committing a sin that doesn't lead to death, he
should ask, and God will give life to him — to
those who commit sin that doesn't lead to
death. There is sin[C] that leads to death. I am
not saying he should pray about that. 17 All
unrighteousness is sin, and there is sin that
doesn't lead to death.

CONCLUSION

18 We know that everyone who has been
born of God does not sin, but the one who
is born of God keeps him,[D] and the evil one
does not touch him. 19 We know that we are
of God, and the whole world is under the

Support | *Prayer*

CONFIDENT PRAYERS

"This is the confidence we have before him: If we ask anything according to his will, he hears us. And if we know that he hears whatever we ask, we know that we have what we have asked of him." 1 John 5:14-15

The Bible makes clear that God won't answer certain prayers; for example, prayers that aren't offered in faith (Mk 11:24) and prayers that are rooted in wrong motivations (Jms 4:3).

Here, however, we see the kind of prayer that God promises to answer *every single time:* requests that are "according to his will."

This assurance gives us "confidence." How could it not? In fact, God clearly spells out his will for us in the Bible. For example, we are called to love, forgive, share, help, encourage, trust, serve, grow, and be holy and spiritually healthy. Imagine how pleased God would be—and how different your life would be—if you prayed for such things yourself and if you got others to pray for you along these lines!

Look at the promise again: "he hears" requests that are "according to his will." And if God hears us, "we know that we have what we have asked of him."

Pray in confidence.

For the first note on *Support*, see Revelation 3:20.

[A] **5:7-8** A few late Gk mss and some late Vg mss add *testify in heaven: the Father, the Word, and the Holy Spirit, and these three are one.* [8]*And there are three who bear witness on earth:* [B] **5:16** Lit *sees his brother or sister* [C] **5:16** Or *is a sin* [D] **5:18** Other mss read *himself*

GREETING

The elder:
To the elect lady and her children, whom I
love in the truth — and not only I, but also all
who know the truth — 2 because of the truth
that remains in us and will be with us forever.
3 Grace, mercy, and peace will be with us
from God the Father and from Jesus Christ,
the Son of the Father, in truth and love.

TRUTH AND DECEPTION

4 I was very glad to find some of your children
walking in truth, in keeping with a command
we have received from the Father. 5 So now I
ask you, dear lady — not as if I were writing
you a new command, but one we have had
from the beginning — that we love one another. 6 This is love: that we walk according
to his commands. This is the command as
you have heard it from the beginning: that
you walk in love.[A]
7 Many deceivers have gone out into the
world; they do not confess the coming of Jesus
Christ in the flesh. This is the deceiver and the
antichrist. 8 Watch yourselves so you don't lose
what we[B] have worked for, but that you may
receive a full reward. 9 Anyone who does not
remain in Christ's teaching but goes beyond
it does not have God. The one who remains in
that teaching, this one has both the Father and
the Son. 10 If anyone comes to you and does
not bring this teaching, do not receive him
into your home, and don't greet him; 11 for the
one who greets him shares in his evil works.

FAREWELL

12 Though I have many things to write to you,
I don't want to use paper and ink. Instead, I
hope to come to you and talk face to face so
that our joy may be complete.
13 The children of your elect sister send you
greetings.

Relationships | *Communicating*

FACE-TO-FACE

"Though I have many things to write to you, I don't want to use paper and ink. Instead, I hope to come to you and talk face to face so that our joy may be complete." 2 John 12

Let's say you need to discuss a situation with somebody. Why would you go through the monumental hassle of dropping by the person's house (or office or cubicle) for a personal visit, when you could just pull out your smartphone and call? And come to think of it, why would you bother calling, when you could just shoot a quick text?

Welcome to the new world of human interaction. We live in a culture where people—sometimes sitting in the very same room—communicate primarily via texting, email, and social media.

Some twenty centuries ago, the apostle John saw the power and value of looking others in the eyes. "I don't want to use paper and ink," he said. "I hope to come to you and talk face to face." Letters are fine, he was saying, but talking in person is best.

Try this. At least a few times today, resist the urge to text. Call instead. Then, at least once, pay a personal visit. Walk down the hall or across the street. Face-to-face beats phone to phone (or computer to computer) almost every time.

For the next note on *Relationships*, see Revelation 5:9.

[A] **6** Or *in it* [B] **8** Other mss read *you*

3 John—No matter how much we love our local church and the people in it, personality conflicts will always arise and have to be worked out. This was true in the early church as well, and 3 John gives us a glimpse into how John the elder dealt with such matters.

John minced no words in denouncing Diotrephes, who was rejecting apostolic authority and stirring up trouble by telling untruths about the apostles. In addition, he was refusing to welcome people into the church. Slander and elitism have no place in the body of Christ and must be firmly dealt with.

In contrast, Gaius and Demetrius were supporting the work of ministry by practical service in welcoming people into the body of believers and upholding the truth. Their example is one we should emulate, and honoring people who serve in this way is a healthy way to build the church. This short book provides a good reminder to stand for truth, welcome strangers, and honor those who serve the body of Christ.

RESTORATION THEMES

R	Rest and Reflection	*Reflecting—2:3-4; 22:12*
E	Eternal Perspective	*God's Purposes—21:1* *God's Plans—21:4-5*
S	Support	*Openness with God—3:20*
T	Thanksgiving and Contentment	*Praise—7:11-12* *Praise for God's Greatness—19:6*
O	Other-centeredness	*For the first note, see Exodus 20:17.*
R	Relationships	*Celebrating Diversity—Revelation 5:9*
E	Exercise of Faith	*For the first note, see Genesis 15:6.*

PROLOGUE

1 The revelation of[A] Jesus Christ that God gave
him to show his servants what must soon
take place. He made it known by sending his
angel to his servant John, 2 who testified to the
word of God and to the testimony[B] of Jesus
Christ, whatever he saw.[C] 3 Blessed is the one
who reads aloud the words of this prophecy,
and blessed are those who hear the words of
this prophecy and keep[D] what is written in it,
because the time is near.

4 John: To the seven churches in Asia. Grace
and peace to you from[E] the one who is, who
was, and who is to come, and from the seven
spirits[F] before his throne, 5 and from Jesus
Christ, the faithful witness, the firstborn from
the dead and the ruler of the kings of the earth.

To him who loves us and has set us free[G]
from our sins by his blood, 6 and made us a
kingdom,[H] priests[I] to his God and Father — to
him be glory and dominion forever and ever.
Amen.

7 **Look, he is coming with the clouds,**
and every eye will see him,
even those who pierced him.
And all the tribes[J] of the earth[K]
will mourn over him.[L,M]
So it is to be. Amen.

8 "I am the Alpha and the Omega," says the
Lord God, "the one who is, who was, and who
is to come, the Almighty."

JOHN'S VISION OF THE RISEN LORD

9 I, John, your brother and partner in the affliction, kingdom, and endurance that are in
Jesus, was on the island called Patmos because
of the word of God and the testimony of Jesus.
10 I was in the Spirit[N] on the Lord's day, and I
heard a loud voice behind me like a trumpet
11 saying, "Write on a scroll[O] what you see and
send it to the seven churches: Ephesus, Smyr-
na, Pergamum, Thyatira, Sardis, Philadelphia,
and Laodicea."

12 Then I turned to see whose voice it was
that spoke to me. When I turned I saw seven
golden lampstands, 13 and among the lampstands was one like the Son of Man,[P] dressed in
a robe and with a golden sash wrapped around
his chest. 14 The hair of his head was white as
wool — white as snow — and his eyes like a
fiery flame. 15 His feet were like fine bronze as

Rest and Reflection | *Reflecting*

WHERE IS THE LOVE?

"I know that you have persevered and endured hardships for the sake of my name, and have not grown weary. But I have this against you: You have abandoned the love you had at first." Revelation 2:3-4

The scientific law of entropy says that everything moves toward disorder. The new paint eventually peels. The hairline recedes. The waistline expands. The sidewalk cracks. The garden gets weedy.

A similar kind of spiritual entropy is also at work in our souls. When we're not vigilant, our relationship with Christ begins to show signs of deterioration.

This is precisely what happened to believers in the church at Ephesus toward the end of the first century. They were good, solid folks, faithfully hanging in there for Jesus. You would want such people for neighbors. But the passionate love they "had at first" for Jesus was nowhere to be seen. Perhaps they just got weary? Hardships are, after all, hard.

The example of the Ephesian believers provides a good warning. Do you take time on a regular basis to watch over your heart (Pr 4:23) and assess how you're doing? Mini-retreats and times of reflection can help us see where entropy is undermining our faith.

For the next note on *Rest and Reflection*, see Revelation 22:12.

[A] **1:1** Or *Revelation of*, or *A revelation of* [B] **1:2** Or *witness* [C] **1:2** Or *as many as he saw* [D] **1:3** Or *follow*, or *obey* [E] **1:4** Other mss add *God* [F] **1:4** Or *the sevenfold Spirit* [G] **1:5** Other mss read *has washed us* [H] **1:6** Other mss read *kings and* [I] **1:6** Or *made us into* (or *to be*) *a kingdom of priests*; Ex 19:6 [J] **1:7** Or *peoples* [K] **1:7** Gn 12:3; 28:14; Zch 14:17 [L] **1:7** Or *will wail because of him* [M] **1:7** Dn 7:13; Zch 12:10 [N] **1:10** Or *in spirit*; lit *I became in the Spirit* [O] **1:11** Or *book* [P] **1:13** Or *like a son of man*

John | Restoration Profile

MATTHEW, MARK, LUKE, JOHN, ACTS, 1 JOHN, 2 JOHN, 3 JOHN, REVELATION

The apostle John had an amazing life, and think how far he traveled from his humble start as a fisherman along the Sea of Galilee. And this all happened because one day Jesus walked by and said, "Follow me" (Mk 1:16-20).

John discovered the amazing restorative power of being loved. In his Gospel, rather than name himself, he simply refers to himself as "the disciple Jesus loved." By this expression, John did not mean, "The disciple Jesus loved more than the rest." Instead, he seems to be saying, "the disciple who could never get over the wonder that Jesus loved even him."

Love had some hard ground to till in John's life. Not only did he share with the other disciples some cultural and religious topsoil that had to be plowed under, he also had a bedrock of character that Jesus had to expose and restore. Jesus called John and his brother James "Sons of Thunder" (Mk 3:17). Grasping for position of power in Jesus's kingdom (Mk 10:35-37), struggling with a volatile temper (Lk 9:54), and fears (Lk 5:10) crowded John's life and made following Jesus a challenge. By the time he wrote 1 John, the old apostle could say from personal experience that "perfect love drives out fear" (1Jn 4:18). And his awareness of his place had been radically transformed: "This is how we have come to know love: He laid down his life for us. We should also lay down our lives for our brothers and sisters" (1Jn 3:16).

In his restoration, John never forgot that the security he experienced in God's love was never an excuse to turn away from loving others. God's love requires a response Godward and toward our neighbor—always.

it is fired in a furnace, and his voice like the
sound of cascading[A] waters. 16 He had seven
stars in his right hand; a sharp double-edged
sword came from his mouth, and his face was
shining like the sun at full strength.
17 When I saw him, I fell at his feet like a dead
man. He laid his right hand on me and said,
"Don't be afraid. I am the First and the Last,
18 and the Living One. I was dead, but look — I
am alive forever and ever, and I hold the keys
of death and Hades. 19 Therefore write what
you have seen, what is, and what will take
place after this. 20 The mystery of the seven
stars you saw in my right hand and of the seven golden lampstands is this: The seven stars
are the angels[B] of the seven churches, and the
seven lampstands[C] are the seven churches.

THE LETTERS TO THE SEVEN CHURCHES

THE LETTER TO EPHESUS

2 "Write to the angel[D] of the church in Ephesus: Thus says the one who holds the
seven stars in his right hand and who walks
among the seven golden lampstands: 2 I know
your works, your labor, and your endurance,
and that you cannot tolerate evil people. You
have tested those who call themselves apostles and are not, and you have found them to
be liars. 3 I know that you have persevered
and endured hardships for the sake of my
name, and have not grown weary. 4 But I have
this against you: You have abandoned the
love you had at first. 5 Remember then how
far you have fallen; repent, and do the works
you did at first. Otherwise, I will come to you[E]
and remove your lampstand from its place,
unless you repent. 6 Yet you do have this: You
hate the practices of the Nicolaitans, which
I also hate.
7 "Let anyone who has ears to hear listen
to what the Spirit says to the churches. To
the one who conquers, I will give the right
to eat from the tree of life, which is in[F] the
paradise of God.

THE LETTER TO SMYRNA

8 "Write to the angel of the church in Smyr-
na: Thus says the First and the Last, the one
who was dead and came to life: 9 I know your[G]

[A] **1:15** Lit *many* [B] **1:20** Or *messengers* [C] **1:20** Other mss add *that you saw* [D] **2:1** Or *messenger*, also in vv. 8,12,18 [E] **2:5** Other mss add *quickly* [F] **2:7** Other mss read *in the midst of* [G] **2:9** Other mss add *works and*

affliction and poverty, but you are rich. I know
the slander of those who say they are Jews
and are not, but are a synagogue of Satan.
10 Don't be afraid of what you are about to
suffer. Look, the devil is about to throw some
of you into prison to test you, and you will
experience affliction for ten days. Be faithful
to the point of death, and I will give you the
crown[A] of life.

11 "Let anyone who has ears to hear listen
to what the Spirit says to the churches. The
one who conquers will never be harmed by
the second death.

THE LETTER TO PERGAMUM

12 "Write to the angel of the church in Pergamum: Thus says the one who has the sharp,
double-edged sword: 13 I know[B] where you
live — where Satan's throne is. Yet you are
holding on to my name and did not deny
your faith in me,[C] even in the days of Antipas,
my faithful witness who was put to death
among you, where Satan lives. 14 But I have a
few things against you. You have some there
who hold to the teaching of Balaam, who
taught Balak to place a stumbling block[D] in
front of the Israelites: to eat meat sacrificed
to idols and to commit sexual immorality.
15 In the same way, you also have those who
hold to the teaching of the Nicolaitans.[E] 16 So
repent! Otherwise, I will come to you quickly and fight against them with the sword of
my mouth.

17 "Let anyone who has ears to hear listen
to what the Spirit says to the churches. To
the one who conquers, I will give some of the
hidden manna.[F] I will also give him a white
stone, and on the stone a new name is inscribed that no one knows except the one
who receives it.

THE LETTER TO THYATIRA

18 "Write to the angel of the church in Thyatira: Thus says the Son of God, the one whose
eyes are like a fiery flame and whose feet are
like fine bronze: 19 I know your works — your
love, faithfulness,[G] service, and endurance. I
know that your last works are greater than
the first. 20 But I have this against you: You tolerate the woman Jezebel, who calls herself a
prophetess and teaches and deceives my servants to commit sexual immorality and to eat
meat sacrificed to idols. 21 I gave her time to
repent, but she does not want to repent of her
sexual immorality. 22 Look, I will throw her into
a sickbed and those who commit adultery with
her into great affliction. Unless they repent of
her[H] works, 23 I will strike her children dead.[I]
Then all the churches will know that I am the
one who examines minds and hearts, and I will
give to each of you according to your works.
24 I say to the rest of you in Thyatira, who do
not hold this teaching, who haven't known
"the so-called secrets[J] of Satan" — as they say
— I am not putting any other burden on you.
25 Only hold on to what you have until I come.
26 The one who conquers and who keeps my
works to the end: I will give him authority over
the nations —

27 **and he will rule[K] them**
with an iron scepter;
he will shatter them like pottery[L] —

28 just as I have received this from my Father.
I will also give him the morning star.

29 "Let anyone who has ears to hear listen to
what the Spirit says to the churches.

THE LETTER TO SARDIS

3 "Write to the angel[M] of the church in Sardis: Thus says the one who has the seven
spirits of God and the seven stars: I know your
works; you have a reputation[N] for being alive,
but you are dead. 2 Be alert and strengthen[O]
what remains, which is about to die,[P] for I
have not found your works complete before
my God. 3 Remember, then, what you have
received and heard; keep it, and repent. If
you are not alert, I will come[Q] like a thief, and
you have no idea at what hour I will come
upon you. 4 But you have a few people[R] in
Sardis who have not defiled[S] their clothes,
and they will walk with me in white, because
they are worthy.

5 "In the same way, the one who conquers
will be dressed in white clothes, and I will
never erase his name from the book of life
but will acknowledge his name before my
Father and before his angels.

6 "Let anyone who has ears to hear listen to
what the Spirit says to the churches.

[A] **2:10** Or *wreath* [B] **2:13** Other mss add *your works and* [C] **2:13** Or *deny my faith* [D] **2:14** Or *to place a trap* [E] **2:15** Other mss add *which I hate* [F] **2:17** Other mss add *to eat* [G] **2:19** Or *faith* [H] **2:22** Other mss read *their* [I] **2:23** Or *with a plague* [J] **2:24** Or *the secret things* [K] **2:27** Or *shepherd* [L] **2:27** Ps 2:9 [M] **3:1** Or *messenger*, also in vv. 7,14 [N] **3:1** Or *have a name* [O] **3:2** Other mss read *guard* [P] **3:2** Or *strengthen who remain, who are about to die* [Q] **3:3** Other mss add *upon you* [R] **3:4** Lit *few names* [S] **3:4** Or *soiled*

THE LETTER TO PHILADELPHIA

7 "Write to the angel of the church in Philadelphia: Thus says the Holy One, the true one, the one who has the key of David, who opens and no one will close, and who closes and no one opens: 8 I know your works. Look, I have placed before you an open door that no one can close because you have but little power; yet you have kept my word and have not denied my name. 9 Note this: I will make those from the synagogue of Satan, who claim to be Jews and are not, but are lying — I will make them come and bow down at your feet, and they will know that I have loved you. 10 Because you have kept my command to endure, I will also keep you from the hour of testing that is going to come on the whole world to test those who live on the earth. 11 I am coming soon. Hold on to what you have, so that no one takes your crown.

12 "The one who conquers I will make a pillar in the temple of my God, and he will never go out again. I will write on him the name of my God and the name of the city of my God — the new Jerusalem, which comes down out of heaven from my God — and my new name.

13 "Let anyone who has ears to hear listen to what the Spirit says to the churches.

THE LETTER TO LAODICEA

14 "Write to the angel of the church in Laodicea: Thus says the Amen, the faithful and true witness, the originator[A] of God's creation: 15 I know your works, that you are neither cold nor hot. I wish that you were cold or hot. 16 So, because you are lukewarm, and neither hot nor cold, I am going to vomit[B] you out of my mouth. 17 For you say, 'I'm rich; I have become wealthy and need nothing,' and you don't realize that you are wretched, pitiful, poor, blind, and naked. 18 I advise you to buy from me gold refined in the fire so that you may be rich, white clothes so that you may be dressed and your shameful nakedness not be exposed, and ointment to spread on your eyes so that you may see. 19 As many as I love, I rebuke and discipline. So be zealous and repent. 20 See! I stand at the door and knock. If anyone hears my voice and opens the door, I will come in to him and eat with him, and he with me.

21 "To the one who conquers I will give the right to sit with me on my throne, just as I also conquered and sat down with my Father on his throne.

22 "Let anyone who has ears to hear listen to what the Spirit says to the churches."

Support | *Openness with God*

WHEN THE LORD KNOCKS

"See! I stand at the door and knock. If anyone hears my voice and opens the door, I will come in to him and eat with him, and he with me." Revelation 3:20

This familiar verse, quoted so often in evangelistic tracts and gospel presentations, presents a shocking image—poor Jesus knocking on the door of an unbeliever's heart, begging for admission.

The truth, however, is something very different. In this passage, Jesus speaks to half-hearted *believers*, not unbelievers. These Laodicean Christians were "lukewarm" (Rv 3:16) toward God and self-sufficient in life. Intimacy with Jesus? More like indifference. They were spiritually impoverished—and too blind to see it. Imagine a church supper where Jesus isn't allowed inside, where he's forced to stand in the parking lot.

This disturbing passage gives a bracing challenge, reminding us of a key truth, and it raises a pointed question. Here's the truth: We're not as strong or as independent as we think we are. Spiritually healthy believers know they need Jesus the same way they need air. As a result, their desire mirrors Christ's words: to be "with him" and have him "with me." Here's the question: Are you treating Jesus like a beloved family member or like a stranger? Have you shut him out?

Open your heart's door.

For the first note on *Thanksgiving and Contentment*, see Exodus 15:2.

[A] **3:14** Or *beginning of God's creation*, or *ruler of God's creation* [B] **3:16** Or *spit*

THE THRONE ROOM OF HEAVEN

4 After this I looked, and there in heaven
was an open door. The first voice that I
had heard speaking to me like a trumpet said,
"Come up here, and I will show you what must
take place after this."
2 Immediately I was in the Spirit, and there
was a throne in heaven and someone was
seated on it. 3 The one seated[A] there had the
appearance of jasper and carnelian stone. A
rainbow that had the appearance of an emerald surrounded the throne.
4 Around the throne were twenty-four
thrones, and on the thrones sat twenty-four
elders dressed in white clothes, with golden
crowns on their heads.
5 Flashes of lightning and rumblings and
peals of thunder came from the throne. Seven
fiery torches were burning before the throne,
which are the seven spirits of God. 6 Something
like a sea of glass, similar to crystal, was also
before the throne.
Four living creatures covered with eyes in
front and in back were around the throne on
each side. 7 The first living creature was like
a lion; the second living creature was like an
ox; the third living creature had a face like a
man; and the fourth living creature was like
a flying eagle. 8 Each of the four living creatures had six wings; they were covered with
eyes around and inside. Day and night they
never stop,[B] saying,

Holy, holy, holy,
Lord God, the Almighty,
who was, who is, and who is to come.

9 Whenever the living creatures give glory,
honor, and thanks to the one seated on the
throne, the one who lives forever and ever,
10 the twenty-four elders fall down before the
one seated on the throne and worship the one
who lives forever and ever. They cast their
crowns before the throne and say,

11 Our Lord and God,[C]
you are worthy to receive
glory and honor and power,
because you have created all things,
and by your will
they exist and were created.

THE LAMB TAKES THE SCROLL

5 Then I saw in the right hand of the one
seated on the throne a scroll with writing
on both sides, sealed with seven seals. 2 I also
saw a mighty angel proclaiming with a loud
voice, "Who is worthy to open the scroll and
break its seals?" 3 But no one in heaven or on
earth or under the earth was able to open the
scroll or even to look in it. 4 I wept and wept
because no one was found worthy to open[D]
the scroll or even to look in it. 5 Then one of
the elders said to me, "Do not weep. Look, the
Lion from the tribe of Judah, the Root of David,
has conquered so that he is able to open the
scroll and[E] its seven seals."
6 Then I saw one like a slaughtered lamb
standing in the midst of the throne and the
four living creatures and among the elders.
He had seven horns and seven eyes, which
are the seven spirits of God sent into all the
earth. 7 He went and took the scroll out of the
right hand of the one seated on the throne.

THE LAMB IS WORTHY

8 When he took the scroll, the four living creatures and the twenty-four elders fell down before the Lamb. Each one had a harp and golden
bowls filled with incense, which are the prayers
of the saints. 9 And they sang a new song:

You are worthy to take the scroll
and to open its seals,
because you were slaughtered,
and you purchased[F] people[G]
for God by your blood
from every tribe and language
and people and nation.
10 You made them a kingdom[H]
and priests to our God,
and they will reign on the earth.

11 Then I looked and heard the voice of many
angels around the throne, and also of the living creatures and of the elders. Their number
was countless thousands, plus thousands of
thousands. 12 They said with a loud voice,

Worthy is the Lamb who was
slaughtered
to receive power and riches
and wisdom and strength
and honor and glory
and blessing!

13 I heard every creature in heaven, on earth,
under the earth, on the sea, and everything
in them say,

Blessing and honor and glory
and power
be to the one seated on the throne,

[A] **4:3** Other mss omit *The one seated* [B] **4:8** Or *rest* [C] **4:11** Some mss add *the Holy One*; other mss read *Lord* [D] **5:4** Other mss add *and read* [E] **5:5** Other mss add *loose* [F] **5:9** Or *redeemed* [G] **5:9** Other mss read *us* [H] **5:10** Other mss read *them kings*

and to the Lamb, forever and ever!
14 The four living creatures said, "Amen," and
the elders fell down and worshiped.

THE FIRST SEAL ON THE SCROLL

6 Then I saw the Lamb open one of the sev-
en[A] seals, and I heard one of the four living creatures say with a voice like thunder,
"Come!" 2 I looked, and there was a white
horse. Its rider held a bow; a crown was giv-
en to him, and he went out as a conqueror in
order to conquer.[B]

THE SECOND SEAL

3 When he opened the second seal, I heard the
second living creature say, "Come!" 4 Then
another horse went out, a fiery red one, and
its rider was allowed to take peace from the
earth, so that people would slaughter one another. And a large sword was given to him.

THE THIRD SEAL

5 When he opened the third seal, I heard the
third living creature say, "Come!" And I looked,
and there was a black horse. Its rider held a set
of scales in his hand. 6 Then I heard something
like a voice among the four living creatures
say, "A quart of wheat for a denarius,[C] and
three quarts of barley for a denarius, but do
not harm the oil and the wine."

THE FOURTH SEAL

7 When he opened the fourth seal, I heard the
voice of the fourth living creature say, "Come!"
8 And I looked, and there was a pale green[D]
horse. Its rider was named Death, and Hades
was following after him. They were[E] given
authority over a fourth of the earth, to kill by
the sword, by famine, by plague, and by the
wild animals of the earth.

THE FIFTH SEAL

9 When he opened the fifth seal, I saw under
the altar the souls of those who had been
slaughtered because of the word of God and
the testimony they had given.[F] 10 They cried out
with a loud voice: "Lord,[G] the one who is holy
and true, how long until you judge those who
live on the earth and avenge our blood?" 11 So
they were each given a white robe, and they
were told to rest a little while longer until the
number would be completed of their fellow
servants and their brothers and sisters, who
were going to be killed just as they had been.

Relationships | *Celebrating Diversity*

ALL UNITED

"And they sang a new song: You are worthy to take the scroll and to open its seals, because you were slaughtered, and you purchased people for God by your blood from every tribe and language and people and nation." Revelation 5:9

When Jesus gave John a peek into the future and a glimpse into heaven itself, one of the scenes the old apostle tried to describe was this one. A vision of angelic beings and other, strange, unearthly creatures, countless thousands clustered about the throne of God, uniting their voices in thunderous song.

Tucked in all these staggering sights is a statement we can easily miss but too important not to ponder: Heaven will consist of people "from every tribe and language and people and nation."

That one sentence provides all the proof anyone would ever need to show the demonic nature of racism and prejudice. If God doesn't practice segregation, discrimination, or favoritism, what makes humans think we have that right?

God is color-blind. He's an equal-opportunity Savior. He's concerned about our hearts not our skin color. What about you? Are your relationships governed by superficial labels?

For the first note on *Exercise of Faith*, see Genesis 15:6.

[A] **6:1** Other mss omit *seven* [B] **6:2** Or *went out conquering and in order to conquer* [C] **6:6** A denarius = one day's wage
[D] **6:8** Or *a greenish gray* [E] **6:8** Other mss read *He was* [F] **6:9** Other mss add *about the Lamb* [G] **6:10** Or *"Master*

THE SIXTH SEAL

12 Then I saw him open[A] the sixth seal. A violent
earthquake occurred; the sun turned black
like sackcloth made of hair; the entire moon[B]
became like blood; 13 the stars[C] of heaven fell
to the earth as a fig tree drops its unripe figs
when shaken by a high wind; 14 the sky was
split apart like a scroll being rolled up; and
every mountain and island was moved from
its place.
15 Then the kings of the earth, the nobles, the
generals, the rich, the powerful, and every slave
and free person hid in the caves and among
the rocks of the mountains. 16 And they said
to the mountains and to the rocks, "Fall on us
and hide us from the face of the one seated on
the throne and from the wrath of the Lamb,
17 because the great day of their[D] wrath has
come! And who is able to stand?"

THE SEALED OF ISRAEL

After this I saw four angels standing at
the four corners of the earth, restraining
the four winds of the earth so that no wind
could blow on the earth or on the sea or on
any tree. 2 Then I saw another angel rising up
from the east, who had the seal of the living
God. He cried out in a loud voice to the four
angels who were allowed to harm the earth
and the sea: 3 "Don't harm the earth or the
sea or the trees until we seal the servants of
our God on their foreheads." 4 And I heard the
number of the sealed:

144,000 sealed from every tribe
of the Israelites:
5 12,000 sealed from the tribe of Judah,
12,000[E] from the tribe of Reuben,
12,000 from the tribe of Gad,
6 12,000 from the tribe of Asher,
12,000 from the tribe of Naphtali,
12,000 from the tribe of Manasseh,
7 12,000 from the tribe of Simeon,
12,000 from the tribe of Levi,
12,000 from the tribe of Issachar,
8 12,000 from the tribe of Zebulun,
12,000 from the tribe of Joseph,
12,000 sealed from the tribe
of Benjamin.

A MULTITUDE FROM THE GREAT TRIBULATION

9 After this I looked, and there was a vast multitude from every nation, tribe, people, and

T Thanksgiving and Contentment | *Praise*

THE POWER OF PRAISE

"All the angels stood around the throne, and along with the elders and the four living creatures they fell facedown before the throne and worshiped God, saying, Amen! Blessing and glory and wisdom and thanksgiving and honor and power and strength be to our God forever and ever. Amen." Revelation 7:11-12

Imagine being there when your team finally wins the championship. Then imagine being forbidden to react. No clapping, cheering, or high-fiving allowed. No discussing the game later with fellow fans. Talk about a buzz-kill! Half the enjoyment is getting to express our joy, right? The victory is wonderful in itself, but the celebration of that victory puts the experience over the top.

This is the genius of worship. When we encounter God's glory, we are moved to respond. Like the angels in Revelation, we feel compelled to bow to him, brag on him, and shout his praises. When we do this, a couple things happen. First, God is honored. But second, our satisfaction goes through the roof.

The next time you're in a corporate worship service, forget everyone and everything else. Focus on the God who has given you so much. Then worship. Let yourself feel (and express!) all that God is and everything he has done.

For the next note on *Thanksgiving and Contentment*, see Revelation 19:6.

[A] **6:12** Or *I saw when he opened* [B] **6:12** Or *the full moon* [C] **6:13** Perhaps meteors [D] **6:17** Other mss read *his* [E] **7:5-8** Other mss add *sealed* after each number

language, which no one could number, standing before the throne and before the Lamb.
They were clothed in white robes with palm
branches in their hands. 10 And they cried out
in a loud voice:

Salvation belongs to our God,
who is seated on the throne,
and to the Lamb!

11 All the angels stood around the throne, and
along with the elders and the four living creatures they fell facedown before the throne
and worshiped God, 12 saying,

Amen! Blessing and glory and wisdom
and thanksgiving and honor
and power and strength
be to our God forever and ever. Amen.

13 Then one of the elders asked me, "Who
are these people in white robes, and where
did they come from?"
14 I said to him, "Sir,[A] you know."
Then he told me: These are the ones coming out of the great tribulation. They washed
their robes and made them white in the blood
of the Lamb.

15 For this reason they are
before the throne of God,
and they serve him day and night
in his temple.
The one seated on the throne
will shelter[B] them:
16 They will no longer hunger;
they will no longer thirst;
the sun will no longer strike them,
nor will any scorching heat.
17 For the Lamb who is at the center
of the throne
will shepherd them;
he will guide them to springs of the
waters of life,
and God will wipe away every tear
from their eyes.

THE SEVENTH SEAL

8 When he opened the seventh seal, there
was silence in heaven for about half an
hour. 2 Then I saw the seven angels who stand
in the presence of God; seven trumpets were
given to them. 3 Another angel, with a golden
incense burner, came and stood at the altar. He
was given a large amount of incense to offer
with the prayers of all the saints on the golden
altar in front of the throne. 4 The smoke of the
incense, with the prayers of the saints, went up
in the presence of God from the angel's hand.
5 The angel took the incense burner, filled it
with fire from the altar, and hurled it to the
earth; there were peals of thunder, rumblings,
flashes of lightning, and an earthquake.

THE SEVEN TRUMPETS

6 And the seven angels who had the seven
trumpets prepared to blow them.

THE FIRST TRUMPET

7 The first angel blew his trumpet, and hail
and fire, mixed with blood, were hurled to
the earth. So a third of the earth was burned
up, a third of the trees were burned up, and
all the green grass was burned up.

THE SECOND TRUMPET

8 The second angel blew his trumpet, and something like a great mountain ablaze with fire was
hurled into the sea. So a third of the sea became
blood, 9 a third of the living creatures in the sea
died, and a third of the ships were destroyed.

THE THIRD TRUMPET

10 The third angel blew his trumpet, and a great
star, blazing like a torch, fell from heaven.
It fell on a third of the rivers and springs of
water. 11 The name of the star is Wormwood,
and a third of the waters became wormwood.
So, many of the people died from the waters,
because they had been made bitter.

THE FOURTH TRUMPET

12 The fourth angel blew his trumpet, and a
third of the sun was struck, a third of the moon,
and a third of the stars, so that a third of them
were darkened. A third of the day was without
light and also a third of the night.
13 I looked and heard an eagle[C] flying high
overhead, crying out in a loud voice, "Woe!
Woe! Woe to those who live on the earth, because of the remaining trumpet blasts that
the three angels are about to sound!"

THE FIFTH TRUMPET

9 The fifth angel blew his trumpet, and I
saw a star that had fallen from heaven
to earth. The key for the shaft to the abyss
was given to him. 2 He opened the shaft to the
abyss, and smoke came up out of the shaft
like smoke from a great[D] furnace so that the

[A] **7:14** Or *"My lord* [B] **7:15** Or *will spread his tent over* [C] **8:13** Other mss read *angel* [D] **9:2** Other mss omit *great*

sun and the air were darkened by the smoke
from the shaft. 3 Then locusts came out of the
smoke on to the earth, and power[A] was given
to them like the power that scorpions have on
the earth. 4 They were told not to harm the
grass of the earth, or any green plant, or any
tree, but only those people who do not have
God's seal on their foreheads. 5 They were not
permitted to kill them but were to torment
them for five months; their torment is like
the torment caused by a scorpion when it
stings someone. 6 In those days people will
seek death and will not find it; they will long
to die, but death will flee from them.

7 The appearance of the locusts was like horses prepared for battle. Something like golden
crowns was on their heads; their faces were
like human faces; 8 they had hair like women's
hair; their teeth were like lions' teeth; 9 they had
chests like iron breastplates; the sound of their
wings was like the sound of many chariots with
horses rushing into battle; 10 and they had tails
with stingers like scorpions, so that with their
tails they had the power to harm people for five
months. 11 They had as their king[B] the angel of
the abyss; his name in Hebrew is Abaddon,[C] and
in Greek he has the name Apollyon.[D]

12 The first woe has passed. There are still
two more woes to come after this.

THE SIXTH TRUMPET

13 The sixth angel blew his trumpet. From the
four[E] horns of the golden altar that is before
God, I heard a voice 14 say to the sixth angel
who had the trumpet, "Release the four angels
bound at the great river Euphrates." 15 So the
four angels who were prepared for the hour,
day, month, and year were released to kill
a third of the human race. 16 The number of
mounted troops was two hundred million;[F]
I heard their number. 17 This is how I saw the
horses and their riders in the vision: They had
breastplates that were fiery red, hyacinth blue,
and sulfur yellow. The heads of the horses were
like the heads of lions, and from their mouths
came fire, smoke, and sulfur. 18 A third of the
human race was killed by these three plagues
—by the fire, the smoke, and the sulfur that
came from their mouths. 19 For the power of
the horses is in their mouths and in their tails,
because their tails, which resemble snakes,
have heads that inflict injury.

20 The rest of the people, who were not killed
by these plagues, did not repent of the works
of their hands to stop worshiping demons and
idols of gold, silver, bronze, stone, and wood,
which cannot see, hear, or walk. 21 And they
did not repent of their murders, their sorceries, their sexual immorality, or their thefts.

THE MIGHTY ANGEL AND THE SMALL SCROLL

10 Then I saw another mighty angel coming
down from heaven, wrapped in a cloud,
with a rainbow over his head.[G] His face was
like the sun, his legs[H] were like pillars of fire,
2 and he held a little scroll opened in his hand.
He put his right foot on the sea, his left on the
land, 3 and he called out with a loud voice like
a roaring lion. When he cried out, the seven
thunders raised their voices. 4 And when the
seven thunders spoke, I was about to write,
but I heard a voice from heaven, saying, "Seal
up what the seven thunders said, and do not
write it down!"

5 Then the angel that I had seen standing on
the sea and on the land raised his right hand
to heaven. 6 He swore by the one who lives
forever and ever, who created heaven and
what is in it, the earth and what is in it, and
the sea and what is in it: "There will no longer
be a delay, 7 but in the days when the seventh
angel will blow his trumpet, then the mystery
of God will be completed, as he announced to
his servants the prophets."

8 Then the voice that I heard from heaven
spoke to me again and said, "Go, take the scroll
that lies open in the hand of the angel who is
standing on the sea and on the land."

9 So I went to the angel and asked him to
give me the little scroll. He said to me, "Take
and eat it; it will be bitter in your stomach, but
it will be as sweet as honey in your mouth."

10 Then I took the little scroll from the angel's hand and ate it. It was as sweet as honey
in my mouth, but when I ate it, my stomach
became bitter. 11 And they said to me, "You
must prophesy again about[I] many peoples,
nations, languages, and kings."

THE TWO WITNESSES

11 Then I was given a measuring reed like a
rod,[J] with these words: "Go[K] and measure
the temple of God and the altar, and count
those who worship there. 2 But exclude the

[A] **9:3** Or *authority*, also in v. 10 [B] **9:11** Or *as king over them* [C] **9:11** Or *Destruction* [D] **9:11** Or *Destroyer* [E] **9:13** Other mss omit *four* [F] **9:16** Other mss read *a hundred million* [G] **10:1** Or *a halo on his head* [H] **10:1** Or *feet* [I] **10:11** Or *prophesy again against* [J] **11:1** Other mss add *and the angel stood up* [K] **11:1** Lit *"Arise*

Embracing God's Word | Comfort

EXCRUCIATING LOSS, OVERWHELMING SADNESS, STREAMING TEARS. Whatever the cause—failure, broken relationship, devastation, or death—the grief is real and unrelenting. We need the Father's comfort. God is with us. He understands.

Even when I go through the darkest valley, I fear no danger, for you are with me; your rod and your staff—they comfort me. –Psalm 23:4

The LORD is near the brokenhearted; he saves those crushed in spirit. –Psalm 34:18

When I am filled with cares, your comfort brings me joy. –Psalm 94:19

The LORD is compassionate and gracious, slow to anger and abounding in faithful love. . . . As a father has compassion on his children, so the LORD has compassion on those who fear him. –Psalm 103:8,13

May your faithful love comfort me as you promised your servant. –Psalm 119:76

The LORD is gracious and compassionate, slow to anger and great in faithful love. The LORD is good to everyone; his compassion rests on all he has made. –Psalm 145:8-9

He heals the brokenhearted and bandages their wounds. –Psalm 147:3

"Comfort, comfort my people," says your God. –Isaiah 40:1

Shout for joy, you heavens! Earth, rejoice! Mountains break into joyful shouts! For the LORD has comforted his people, and will have compassion on his afflicted ones. –Isaiah 49:13

Who is a God like you, forgiving iniquity and passing over rebellion for the remnant of his inheritance? He does not hold on to his anger forever because he delights in faithful love. He will again have compassion on us; he will vanquish our iniquities. You will cast all our sins into the depths of the sea. –Micah 7:18-19

Blessed are those who mourn, for they will be comforted. –Matthew 5:4

Blessed be the God and Father of our Lord Jesus Christ, the Father of mercies and the God of all comfort. He comforts us in all our affliction, so that we may be able to comfort those who are in any kind of affliction, through the comfort we ourselves receive from God. For just as the sufferings of Christ overflow to us, so also through Christ our comfort overflows. If we are afflicted, it is for your comfort and salvation. If we are comforted, it is for your comfort, which produces in you patient endurance of the same sufferings that we suffer. And our hope for you is firm, because we know that as you share in the sufferings, so you will also share in the comfort. –2 Corinthians 1:3-7

May our Lord Jesus Christ himself and God our Father, who has loved us and given us eternal encouragement and good hope by grace, encourage your hearts and strengthen you in every good work and word. –2 Thessalonians 2:16-17

He will wipe away every tear from their eyes. Death will be no more; grief, crying, and pain will be no more, because the previous things have passed away. –Revelation 21:4

courtyard outside the temple. Don't measure
it, because it is given to the nations,[A] and they
will trample the holy city for forty-two months.
3 I will grant[B] my two witnesses authority to
prophesy for 1,260 days, dressed in sackcloth."
4 These are the two olive trees and the two
lampstands that stand before the Lord[C] of
the earth. 5 If anyone wants to harm them,
fire comes from their mouths and consumes
their enemies; if anyone wants to harm them,
he must be killed in this way. 6 They have authority to close up the sky so that it does not
rain during the days of their prophecy. They
also have power over the waters to turn them
into blood and to strike the earth with every
plague whenever they want.

THE WITNESSES MARTYRED

7 When they finish their testimony, the beast
that comes up out of the abyss will make war
on them, conquer them, and kill them. 8 Their
dead bodies[D] will lie in the main street[E] of the
great city, which figuratively[F] is called Sodom
and Egypt, where also their Lord was crucified.
9 And some of[G] the peoples, tribes, languages,
and nations will view their bodies for three
and a half days and not permit their bodies
to be put into a tomb. 10 Those who live on
the earth will gloat over them and celebrate
and send gifts to one another because these
two prophets had tormented those who live
on the earth.

THE WITNESSES RESURRECTED

11 But after three and a half days, the breath[H]
of life from God entered them, and they stood
on their feet. Great fear fell on those who saw
them. 12 Then they heard[I] a loud voice from
heaven saying to them, "Come up here." They
went up to heaven in a cloud, while their enemies watched them. 13 At that moment a violent
earthquake took place, a tenth of the city fell,
and seven thousand people were killed in the
earthquake. The survivors were terrified and
gave glory to the God of heaven.

14 The second woe has passed. Take note:
The third woe is coming soon!

THE SEVENTH TRUMPET

15 The seventh angel blew his trumpet, and
there were loud voices in heaven saying,

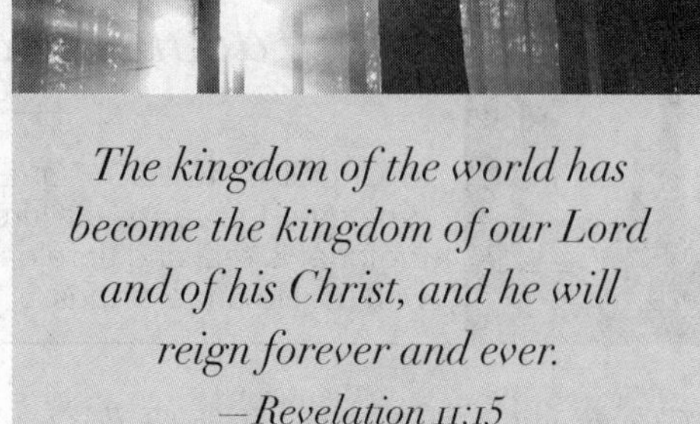
The kingdom of the world has
become the kingdom of our Lord
and of his Christ, and he will
reign forever and ever.
—Revelation 11:15

The kingdom of the world has become
 the kingdom
of our Lord and of his Christ,
and he will reign forever and ever.

16 The twenty-four elders, who were seated
before God on their thrones, fell facedown
and worshiped God, 17 saying,

We give you thanks, Lord God,
 the Almighty,
who is and who was,[J]
because you have taken
 your great power
and have begun to reign.
18 The nations were angry,
but your wrath has come.
The time has come
for the dead to be judged
and to give the reward
to your servants the prophets,
to the saints, and to those who fear
 your name,
both small and great,
and the time has come to destroy
those who destroy the earth.

19 Then the temple of God in heaven was
opened, and the ark of his covenant[K] appeared
in his temple. There were flashes of lightning,
rumblings and peals of thunder, an earthquake,[L] and severe hail.

THE WOMAN, THE CHILD, AND THE DRAGON

12 A great sign[M] appeared in heaven: a
woman clothed with the sun, with the
moon under her feet and a crown of twelve
stars on her head. 2 She was pregnant and
cried out in labor and agony as she was about
to give birth. 3 Then another sign[N] appeared
in heaven: There was a great fiery red dragon

[A] **11:2** Or *Gentiles* [B] **11:3** Or *I will give to* [C] **11:4** Other mss read *God* [D] **11:8** Or *Their corpse* [E] **11:8** Or *lie on the broad street* [F] **11:8** Or *spiritually* [G] **11:9** Lit *And from* [H] **11:11** Or *spirit* [I] **11:12** Other mss read *Then I heard* [J] **11:17** Other mss add *and who is to come* [K] **11:19** Other mss read *ark of the covenant of the Lord* [L] **11:19** Other mss omit *an earthquake* [M] **12:1** Or *great symbolic display*; see Rv 12:3 [N] **12:3** Or *another symbolic display*

having seven heads and ten horns, and on
its heads were seven crowns.[A] 4 Its tail swept
away a third of the stars in heaven and hurled
them to the earth. And the dragon stood in
front of the woman who was about to give
birth, so that when she did give birth it might
devour her child. 5 She gave birth to a Son, a
male who is going to rule[B] all nations with
an iron rod. Her child was caught up to God
and to his throne. 6 The woman fled into the
wilderness, where she had a place prepared
by God, to be nourished there[C] for 1,260 days.

THE DRAGON THROWN OUT OF HEAVEN

7 Then war broke out in heaven: Michael and
his angels fought against the dragon. The dragon and his angels also fought, 8 but he could
not prevail, and there was no place for them
in heaven any longer. 9 So the great dragon
was thrown out — the ancient serpent, who
is called the devil and Satan, the one who deceives the whole world. He was thrown to
earth, and his angels with him. 10 Then I heard
a loud voice in heaven say,

The salvation and the power
and the kingdom of our God
and the authority of his Christ
have now come,
because the accuser of our brothers
and sisters,
who accuses them
before our God day and night,
has been thrown down.
11 They conquered him
by the blood of the Lamb
and by the word of their testimony;
for they did not love their lives
to the point of death.
12 Therefore rejoice, you heavens,
and you who dwell in them!
Woe to the earth and the sea,
because the devil has come down to you
with great fury,
because he knows his time is short.

THE WOMAN PERSECUTED

13 When the dragon saw that he had been
thrown down to the earth, he persecuted[D]
the woman who had given birth to the male
child. 14 The woman was given two wings of
a great eagle, so that she could fly from the
serpent's presence to her place in the wilderness, where she was nourished for a time,
times, and half a time. 15 From his mouth the
serpent spewed water like a river flowing after
the woman, to sweep her away with a flood.
16 But the earth helped the woman. The earth
opened its mouth and swallowed up the
river that the dragon had spewed from his
mouth. 17 So the dragon was furious with the
woman and went off to wage war against
the rest of her offspring[E] — those who keep
the commands of God and hold firmly to the
testimony about Jesus.

THE BEAST FROM THE SEA

18 The dragon[F] stood on the sand of the sea.[G]
13 And I saw a beast coming up out of the
sea. It had ten horns and seven heads. On
its horns were ten crowns,[A] and on its heads
were blasphemous names.[H] 2 The beast I saw
was like a leopard, its feet were like a bear's,
and its mouth was like a lion's mouth. The
dragon gave the beast his power, his throne,
and great authority. 3 One of its heads appeared
to be fatally wounded, but its fatal wound was
healed.

The whole earth was amazed and followed
the beast. 4 They worshiped the dragon because he gave authority to the beast. And they
worshiped the beast, saying, "Who is like the
beast? Who is able to wage war against it?"

5 The beast was given a mouth to utter boasts
and blasphemies. It was allowed to exercise
authority[I,J] for forty-two months. 6 It began to
speak[K] blasphemies against God: to blaspheme
his name and his dwelling — those who dwell
in heaven. 7 And it was permitted to wage war
against the saints and to conquer them. It was
also given authority over every tribe, people,
language, and nation. 8 All those who live on
the earth will worship it, everyone whose
name was not written from the foundation
of the world in the book[L] of life of the Lamb
who was slaughtered.[M]

9 If anyone has ears to hear, let him listen.
10 If anyone is to be taken captive,
into captivity he goes.
If anyone is to be killed[N] with a sword,
with a sword he will be killed.

[A] **12:3; 13:1** Or *diadems* [B] **12:5** Or *shepherd* [C] **12:6** Or *God, that they might feed her there* [D] **12:13** Or *pursued* [E] **12:17** Or *seed* [F] **12:18** Or *he*; other mss read *I* [G] **12:18** Some translations put Rv 12:18 either in Rv 12:17 or Rv 13:1 [H] **13:1** Other mss read *heads was a blasphemous name* [I] **13:5** Other mss read *to wage war* [J] **13:5** Or *to rule* [K] **13:6** Or *He opened his mouth in* [L] **13:8** Or *scroll* [M] **13:8** Or *written in the book of life of the Lamb who was slaughtered from the foundation of the world* [N] **13:10** Other mss read *anyone kills*

This calls for endurance[A] and faithfulness
from the saints.

THE BEAST FROM THE EARTH

11 Then I saw another beast coming up out of
the earth; it had two horns like a lamb,[B] but
it spoke like a dragon. 12 It exercises all the
authority of the first beast on its behalf and
compels the earth and those who live on it to
worship the first beast, whose fatal wound
was healed. 13 It also performs great signs,
even causing fire to come down from heaven
to earth in front of people. 14 It deceives those
who live on the earth because of the signs that
it is permitted to perform in the presence of
the beast, telling those who live on the earth to
make an image[C] of the beast who was wounded
by the sword and yet lived. 15 It was permitted
to give breath[D] to the image of the beast, so
that the image of the beast could both speak
and cause whoever would not worship the
image of the beast to be killed. 16 And it makes
everyone — small and great, rich and poor,
free and slave — to receive a mark on his right
hand or on his forehead, 17 so that no one can
buy or sell unless he has the mark: the beast's
name or the number of its name.
18 This calls for wisdom:[E] Let the one who
has understanding calculate[F] the number of
the beast, because it is the number of a person. Its number is 666.[G]

THE LAMB AND THE 144,000

14 Then I looked, and there was the Lamb,
standing on Mount Zion, and with him
were 144,000 who had his name and his Father's name written on their foreheads. 2 I
heard a sound[H] from heaven like the sound
of cascading waters and like the rumbling
of loud thunder. The sound I heard was like
harpists playing on their harps. 3 They sang[I]
a new song before the throne and before the
four living creatures and the elders, but no one
could learn the song except the 144,000 who
had been redeemed from the earth. 4 These are
the ones who have not defiled themselves with
women, since they remained virgins. These
are the ones who follow the Lamb wherever
he goes. They were redeemed[J] from humanity as the firstfruits for God and the Lamb.
5 No lie was found in their mouths; they are
blameless.

THE PROCLAMATION OF THREE ANGELS

6 Then I saw another angel flying high overhead, with the eternal gospel to announce to
the inhabitants of the earth — to every nation,
tribe, language, and people. 7 He spoke with
a loud voice: "Fear God and give him glory,
because the hour of his judgment has come.
Worship the one who made heaven and earth,
the sea and the springs of water."
8 And another, a second angel, followed, saying, "It has fallen, Babylon the Great has fallen.[K]
She made all the nations drink the wine of
her sexual immorality,[L] which brings wrath."
9 And another, a third angel, followed them
and spoke with a loud voice: "If anyone worships the beast and its image and receives a
mark on his forehead or on his hand, 10 he will
also drink the wine of God's wrath, which is
poured full strength into the cup of his anger.
He will be tormented with fire and sulfur in
the sight of the holy angels and in the sight of
the Lamb, 11 and the smoke of their torment
will go up forever and ever. There is no rest[M]
day or night for those who worship the beast
and its image, or anyone who receives the
mark of its name. 12 This calls for endurance
from the saints, who keep God's commands
and their faith in Jesus."[N]
13 Then I heard a voice from heaven saying,
"Write: Blessed are the dead who die in the
Lord from now on."
"Yes," says the Spirit, "so they will rest from
their labors, since their works follow them."

REAPING THE EARTH'S HARVEST

14 Then I looked, and there was a white cloud,
and one like the Son of Man[O] was seated on the
cloud, with a golden crown on his head and a
sharp sickle in his hand. 15 Another angel came
out of the temple, crying out in a loud voice
to the one who was seated on the cloud, "Use
your sickle and reap, for the time to reap has
come, since the harvest of the earth is ripe." 16 So
the one seated on the cloud swung his sickle
over the earth, and the earth was harvested.
17 Then another angel who also had a sharp
sickle came out of the temple in heaven. 18 Yet

[A] **13:10** Or *Here is the perseverance* [B] **13:11** Or *ram* [C] **13:14** Or *a statue*, or *a likeness* [D] **13:15** Or *a spirit*, or *life* [E] **13:18** Or *Here is wisdom* [F] **13:18** Or *count*, or *figure out* [G] **13:18** Other Gk mss read *616* [H] **14:2** Or *voice* [I] **14:3** Other mss add *as it were* [J] **14:4** Other mss add *by Jesus* [K] **14:8** Other mss omit the second *has fallen* [L] **14:8** Or *wine of her passionate immorality* [M] **14:11** Or *They have no rest* [N] **14:12** Or *and the faith of Jesus*, or *and faithfulness to Jesus* [O] **14:14** Or *like a son of man*

another angel, who had authority over fire, came from the altar, and he called with a loud voice to the one who had the sharp sickle, "Use your sharp sickle and gather the clusters of grapes from the vineyard of the earth, because its grapes have ripened." 19 So the angel swung his sickle at the earth and gathered the grapes from the vineyard of the earth, and he threw them into the great winepress of God's wrath. 20 Then the press was trampled outside the city, and blood flowed out of the press up to the horses' bridles for about 180 miles.[A]

PREPARATION FOR THE BOWL JUDGMENTS

15 Then I saw another great and awe-inspiring sign[B] in heaven: seven angels with the seven last plagues; for with them God's wrath will be completed. 2 I also saw something like a sea of glass mixed with fire, and those who had won the victory over the beast, its image,[C] and the number of its name, were standing on the sea of glass with harps from God. 3 They sang the song of God's servant Moses and the song of the Lamb:

Great and awe-inspiring are your works,
Lord God, the Almighty;
just and true are your ways,
King of the nations.[D]
4 Lord, who will not fear
and glorify your name?
For you alone are holy.
All the nations will come
and worship before you
because your righteous acts
have been revealed.

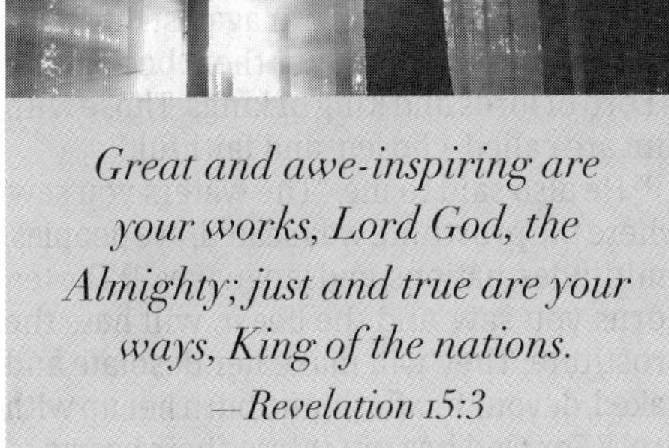
Great and awe-inspiring are your works, Lord God, the Almighty; just and true are your ways, King of the nations.
—*Revelation 15:3*

5 After this I looked, and the heavenly temple — the tabernacle of testimony — was opened. 6 Out of the temple came the seven angels with the seven plagues, dressed in pure, bright linen, with golden sashes wrapped around their chests. 7 One of the four living creatures gave the seven angels seven golden bowls filled with the wrath of God who lives forever and ever. 8 Then the temple was filled with smoke from the glory of God and from his power, and no one could enter the temple until the seven plagues of the seven angels were completed.

THE FIRST BOWL

16 Then I heard a loud voice from the temple saying to the seven angels, "Go and pour out the seven[E] bowls of God's wrath on the earth." 2 The first went and poured out his bowl on the earth, and severely painful sores broke out on the people who had the mark of the beast and who worshiped its image.

THE SECOND BOWL

3 The second[F] poured out his bowl into the sea. It turned to blood like that of a dead person, and all life in the sea died.

THE THIRD BOWL

4 The third[F] poured out his bowl into the rivers and the springs of water, and they became blood. 5 I heard the angel of the waters say,

You are just,
the Holy One, who is and who was,
because you have passed judgment
on these things.
6 Because they poured out
the blood of the saints and the prophets,
you have given them blood to drink;
they deserve it!

7 I heard the altar say,

Yes, Lord God, the Almighty,
true and just are your judgments.

THE FOURTH BOWL

8 The fourth[F] poured out his bowl on the sun. It was allowed to scorch people with fire, 9 and people were scorched by the intense heat. So they blasphemed the name of God, who has the power[G] over these plagues, and they did not repent and give him glory.

THE FIFTH BOWL

10 The fifth[F] poured out his bowl on the throne of the beast, and its kingdom was plunged into darkness. People[H] gnawed their tongues because of their pain 11 and blasphemed the God of heaven because of their pains and their sores, but they did not repent of their works.

[A] **14:20** Lit *1,600 stadia* [B] **15:1** Or *and awesome symbolic display* [C] **15:2** Other mss add *his mark* [D] **15:3** Other mss read *ages* [E] **16:1** Other mss omit *seven* [F] **16:3,4,8,10** Other mss add *angel* [G] **16:9** Or *authority* [H] **16:10** Lit *They*

THE SIXTH BOWL

12 The sixth[A] poured out his bowl on the great river Euphrates, and its water was dried up to prepare the way for the kings from the east. 13 Then I saw three unclean spirits like frogs coming from the dragon's mouth, from the beast's mouth, and from the mouth of the false prophet. 14 For they are demonic spirits performing signs, who travel to the kings of the whole world to assemble them for the battle on the great day of God, the Almighty. 15 "Look, I am coming like a thief. Blessed is the one who is alert and remains clothed[B] so that he may not go around naked and people see his shame." 16 So they assembled the kings at the place called in Hebrew, Armageddon.[C]

THE SEVENTH BOWL

17 Then the seventh[A] poured out his bowl into the air,[D] and a loud voice came out of the temple[E] from the throne, saying, "It is done!" 18 There were flashes of lightning, rumblings, and peals of thunder. And a severe earthquake occurred like no other since people have been on the earth, so great was the quake. 19 The great city split into three parts, and the cities of the nations[F] fell. Babylon the Great was remembered in God's presence; he gave her the cup filled with the wine of his fierce anger. 20 Every island fled, and the mountains disappeared. 21 Enormous hailstones, each weighing about a hundred pounds,[G] fell from the sky on people, and they blasphemed God for the plague of hail because that plague was extremely severe.

THE WOMAN AND THE SCARLET BEAST

17 Then one of the seven angels who had the seven bowls came and spoke with me: "Come, I will show you the judgment of the notorious prostitute[H] who is seated on many[I] waters. 2 The kings of the earth committed sexual immorality with her, and those who live on the earth became drunk on the wine of her sexual immorality." 3 Then he carried me away in the Spirit[J] to a wilderness.

I saw a woman sitting on a scarlet beast that was covered[K] with blasphemous names and had seven heads and ten horns. 4 The woman was dressed in purple and scarlet, adorned with gold, jewels, and pearls. She had a golden cup in her hand filled with everything detestable and with the impurities of her[L] prostitution. 5 On her forehead was written a name, a mystery: BABYLON THE GREAT, THE MOTHER OF PROSTITUTES AND OF THE DETESTABLE THINGS OF THE EARTH. 6 Then I saw that the woman was drunk with the blood of the saints and with the blood of the witnesses to Jesus. When I saw her, I was greatly astonished.

THE MEANING OF THE WOMAN AND OF THE BEAST

7 Then the angel said to me, "Why are you astonished? I will explain to you the mystery of the woman and of the beast, with the seven heads and the ten horns, that carries her. 8 The beast that you saw was, and is not, and is about to come up from the abyss and go to destruction. Those who live on the earth whose names have not been written in the book of life from the foundation of the world will be astonished when they see the beast that was, and is not, and is to come. 9 This calls for a mind that has wisdom.[M]

"The seven heads are seven mountains on which the woman is seated. They are also seven kings: 10 Five have fallen, one is, the other has not yet come, and when he comes, he must remain for only a little while. 11 The beast that was and is not, is itself an eighth king, but it belongs to the seven and is going to destruction. 12 The ten horns you saw are ten kings who have not yet received a kingdom, but they will receive authority as kings with the beast for one hour. 13 These have one purpose, and they give their power and authority to the beast. 14 These will make war against the Lamb, but the Lamb will conquer them because he is Lord of lords and King of kings. Those with him are called, chosen, and faithful."

15 He also said to me, "The waters you saw, where the prostitute was seated, are peoples, multitudes, nations, and languages. 16 The ten horns you saw, and the beast, will hate the prostitute. They will make her desolate and naked, devour her flesh, and burn her up with fire. 17 For God has put it into their hearts to carry out his plan by having one purpose and to give their kingdom[N] to the beast until the words of God are fulfilled. 18 And the woman

[A] **16:12,17** Other mss add *angel* [B] **16:15** Or *and guards his clothes* [C] **16:16** Some mss read *Armagedon*; other mss read *Harmegedon*; other mss read *Mageddon*; other mss read *Magedon* [D] **16:17** Or *bowl on the air* [E] **16:17** Other mss add *of heaven* [F] **16:19** Or *the Gentile cities* [G] **16:21** Lit *about a talent*; talents varied in weight upwards from 75 pounds
[H] **17:1** Traditionally translated *the great whore* [I] **17:1** Or *by many* [J] **17:3** Or *in spirit* [K] **17:3** Or *was filled* [L] **17:4** Other mss read *earth's* [M] **17:9** Or *Here is the mind of wisdom* [N] **17:17** Or *sovereignty*

you saw is the great city that has royal power
over the kings of the earth."

THE FALL OF BABYLON THE GREAT

18 After this I saw another angel with great
authority coming down from heaven,
and the earth was illuminated by his splendor.
2 He called out in a mighty voice:
It has fallen,[A]
Babylon the Great has fallen!
She has become a home for demons,
a haunt for every unclean spirit,
a haunt for every unclean bird,
and a haunt[B] for every unclean
and despicable beast.[C]
3 For all the nations have drunk[D]
the wine of her sexual immorality,
which brings wrath.
The kings of the earth
have committed sexual immorality
with her,
and the merchants of the earth
have grown wealthy
from her sensuality and excess.
4 Then I heard another voice from heaven:
Come out of her, my people,
so that you will not share in her sins
or receive any of her plagues.
5 For her sins are piled up[E] to heaven,
and God has remembered her crimes.
6 Pay her back the way she also paid,
and double it according to her works.
In the cup in which she mixed,
mix a double portion for her.
7 As much as she glorified herself
and indulged her sensual and
excessive ways,
give her that much torment and grief.
For she says in her heart,
"I sit as a queen;
I am not a widow,
and I will never see grief."
8 For this reason her plagues will come
in just one day —
death and grief and famine.
She will be burned up with fire,
because the Lord God who judges her
is mighty.

THE WORLD MOURNS BABYLON'S FALL

9 The kings of the earth who have committed
sexual immorality and shared her sensual and
excessive ways will weep and mourn over her
when they see the smoke from her burning.
10 They will stand far off in fear of her torment, saying,
Woe, woe, the great city,
Babylon, the mighty city!
For in a single hour
your judgment has come.

11 The merchants of the earth will weep and
mourn over her, because no one buys their
cargo any longer — 12 cargo of gold, silver,
jewels, and pearls; fine linen, purple, silk, and
scarlet; all kinds of fragrant wood products;
objects of ivory; objects of expensive wood,
brass,[F] iron, and marble; 13 cinnamon, spice,[G]
incense, myrrh,[H] and frankincense; wine, olive
oil, fine flour, and grain; cattle and sheep; horses and carriages; and slaves — human lives.
14 The fruit you craved has left you.
All your splendid and glamorous things
are gone;
they will never find them again.

15 The merchants of these things, who became rich from her, will stand far off in fear of
her torment, weeping and mourning, 16 saying,
Woe, woe, the great city,
dressed in fine linen, purple, and scarlet,
adorned with gold, jewels, and pearls;
17 for in a single hour
such fabulous wealth was destroyed!

And every shipmaster, seafarer, the sailors,
and all who do business by sea, stood far off
18 as they watched the smoke from her burning and kept crying out: "Who was like the
great city?" 19 They threw dust on their heads
and kept crying out, weeping, and mourning,
Woe, woe, the great city,
where all those who have ships
on the sea
became rich from her wealth;
for in a single hour she was destroyed.
20 Rejoice over her, heaven,
and you saints, apostles, and prophets,
because God has pronounced on her
the judgment she passed on you!

THE FINALITY OF BABYLON'S FALL

21 Then a mighty angel picked up a stone like a
large millstone and threw it into the sea, saying,

[A] **18:2** Other mss omit *It has fallen* [B] **18:2** Or *prison* [C] **18:2** Other mss omit the words *and a haunt for every unclean beast.* The words *and despicable* then refer to the *bird* of the previous line. [D] **18:3** Some mss read *collapsed*; other mss read *fallen* [E] **18:5** Or *sins have reached up* [F] **18:12** Or *bronze*, or *copper* [G] **18:13** Other mss omit *spice* [H] **18:13** Or *perfume*

In this way, Babylon the great city
will be thrown down violently
and never be found again.
22 The sound of harpists, musicians,
flutists, and trumpeters
will never be heard in you again;
no craftsman of any trade
will ever be found in you again;
the sound of a mill
will never be heard in you again;
23 the light of a lamp
will never shine in you again;
and the voice of a groom and bride
will never be heard in you again.
All this will happen
because your merchants
were the nobility of the earth,
because all the nations were deceived
by your sorcery.
24 In her was found the blood of prophets
and saints,
and of all those slaughtered
on the earth.

CELEBRATION IN HEAVEN

19 After this I heard something like the loud voice of a vast multitude in heaven, saying,
Hallelujah!
Salvation, glory, and power belong
to our God,
2 because his judgments are true[A]
and righteous,
because he has judged
the notorious prostitute
who corrupted the earth
with her sexual immorality;
and he has avenged the blood
of his servants
that was on her hands.
3 A second time they said,
Hallelujah!
Her smoke ascends forever and ever!
4 Then the twenty-four elders and the four
living creatures fell down and worshiped God,
who is seated on the throne, saying,
Amen! Hallelujah!
5 A voice came from the throne, saying,
Praise our God,
all his servants, and the ones
who fear him,
both small and great!
6 Then I heard something like the voice of a vast
multitude, like the sound of cascading waters,
and like the rumbling of loud thunder, saying,
Hallelujah, because our Lord God,
the Almighty,
reigns!

Thanksgiving and Contentment | *Praise for God's Greatness*

LARGE AND IN CHARGE

"Then I heard something like the voice of a vast multitude, like the sound of cascading waters, and like the rumbling of loud thunder, saying, Hallelujah, because our Lord God, the Almighty, reigns!" Revelation 19:6

In Christian circles, we often hear references to God's "sovereignty." That's a fancy way of saying that God is in charge or in control of all things. He rules the universe. Or as John puts it here, "Our Lord God, the Almighty, reigns!"

This truth ought to provoke at least two responses in us. First, it should prompt us to confess our ongoing propensity to be control freaks. In varying degrees, everyone tries to manipulate people, situations, and outcomes. This is not only wrong (God never asked us to take charge of such things), it's silly (as if we have any real power to make the world work in all the ways we think it should).

Second, God's sovereignty should drive us to our knees in gratitude. No matter how things may seem, the world is not spinning out of control, and our individual futures aren't up in the air. God's got us. He will see us home.

No wonder John observed the creatures with the clearest view of ultimate reality saying, "Hallelujah!"

For the first note on *Other-centeredness*, see Exodus 20:17.

[A] **19:2** Valid; Jn 8:16; 19:35

7 Let us be glad, rejoice,
and give him glory,
because the marriage of the Lamb
has come,
and his bride has prepared herself.
8 She was given fine linen to wear, bright
and pure.
For the fine linen represents the righteous
acts of the saints.
9 Then he[A] said to me, "Write: Blessed are
those invited to the marriage feast of the
Lamb!" He also said to me, "These words of
God are true." 10 Then I fell at his feet to worship
him, but he said to me, "Don't do that! I am a
fellow servant with you and your brothers
and sisters who hold firmly to the testimony
of Jesus. Worship God, because the testimony
of Jesus is the spirit[B] of prophecy."

THE RIDER ON A WHITE HORSE

11 Then I saw heaven opened, and there was
a white horse. Its rider is called Faithful and
True, and he judges and makes war with justice. 12 His eyes were like a fiery flame, and
many crowns[C] were on his head. He had a
name written that no one knows except himself. 13 He wore a robe dipped in blood, and
his name is called the Word of God. 14 The
armies that were in heaven followed him on
white horses, wearing pure white linen. 15 A
sharp[D] sword came from his mouth, so that he
might strike the nations with it. He will rule[E]
them with an iron rod. He will also trample
the winepress of the fierce anger of God, the
Almighty. 16 And he has a name written on
his robe and on his thigh: KING OF KINGS AND
LORD OF LORDS.

THE BEAST AND ITS ARMIES DEFEATED

17 Then I saw an angel standing in the sun,
and he called out in a loud voice, saying to
all the birds flying high overhead, "Come,
gather together for the great supper of God,
18 so that you may eat the flesh of kings, the
flesh of military commanders, the flesh of
the mighty, the flesh of horses and of their
riders, and the flesh of everyone, both free
and slave, small and great."
19 Then I saw the beast, the kings of the
earth, and their armies gathered together
to wage war against the rider on the horse
and against his army. 20 But the beast was
taken prisoner, and along with it the false
prophet, who had performed the signs in its
presence. He deceived those who accepted the
mark of the beast and those who worshiped
its image with these signs. Both of them were
thrown alive into the lake of fire that burns
with sulfur. 21 The rest were killed with the
sword that came from the mouth of the rider
on the horse, and all the birds ate their fill of
their flesh.

SATAN BOUND

20 Then I saw an angel coming down from
heaven holding the key to the abyss
and a great chain in his hand. 2 He seized the
dragon, that ancient serpent who is the devil and Satan,[F] and bound him for a thousand
years. 3 He threw him into the abyss, closed
it, and put a seal on it so that he would no
longer deceive the nations until the thousand
years were completed. After that, he must be
released for a short time.

THE SAINTS REIGN WITH CHRIST

4 Then I saw thrones, and people seated on
them who were given authority to judge. I
also saw the souls of those who had been beheaded because of their testimony about Jesus
and because of the word of God, who had not
worshiped the beast or his image, and who
had not accepted the mark on their foreheads
or their hands. They came to life and reigned
with Christ for a thousand years. 5 The rest of
the dead did not come to life until the thousand years were completed.
This is the first resurrection. 6 Blessed and
holy is the one who shares in the first resurrection! The second death has no power[G]
over them, but they will be priests of God and
of Christ, and they will reign with him for a
thousand years.

SATANIC REBELLION CRUSHED

7 When the thousand years are completed,
Satan will be released from his prison 8 and
will go out to deceive the nations at the four
corners of the earth, Gog and Magog, to gather
them for battle. Their number is like the sand
of the sea. 9 They came up across the breadth of
the earth and surrounded the encampment
of the saints, the beloved city. Then fire came
down from heaven[H] and consumed them. 10 The
devil who deceived them was thrown into
the lake of fire and sulfur where the beast

[A] **19:9** Probably an angel; Rv 17:1; 22:8-9 [B] **19:10** Or *the Spirit* [C] **19:12** Or *diadems* [D] **19:15** Other mss add *double-edged* [E] **19:15** Or *shepherd* [F] **20:2** Other mss add *who deceives the whole world* [G] **20:6** Or *authority* [H] **20:9** Other mss add *from God*

and the false prophet are, and they will be tormented day and night forever and ever.

THE GREAT WHITE THRONE JUDGMENT

11 Then I saw a great white throne and one seated on it. Earth and heaven fled from his presence, and no place was found for them. 12 I also saw the dead, the great and the small, standing before the throne, and books were opened. Another book was opened, which is the book of life, and the dead were judged according to their works by what was written in the books. 13 Then the sea gave up the dead that were in it, and death and Hades gave up the dead that were in them; each one was judged according to their works. 14 Death and Hades were thrown into the lake of fire. This is the second death, the lake of fire.[A] 15 And anyone whose name was not found written in the book of life was thrown into the lake of fire.

THE NEW CREATION

21 Then I saw a new heaven and a new earth; for the first heaven and the first earth had passed away, and the sea was no more. 2 I also saw the holy city, the new Jerusalem, coming down out of heaven from God, prepared like a bride adorned for her husband.

3 Then I heard a loud voice from the throne:[B] Look, God's dwelling[C] is with humanity, and he will live with them. They will be his peoples,[D] and God himself will be with them and will be their God.[E] 4 He will wipe away every tear from their eyes. Death will be no more; grief, crying, and pain will be no more, because the previous things[F] have passed away.

5 Then the one seated on the throne said, "Look, I am making everything new." He also said, "Write, because these words[G] are faithful and true." 6 Then he said to me, "It is done! I am the Alpha and the Omega, the beginning and the end. I will freely give to the thirsty from the spring of the water of life. 7 The one who conquers will inherit these things, and I will be his God, and he will be my son. 8 But the cowards, faithless,[H] detestable, murderers, sexually immoral, sorcerers, idolaters, and all liars — their share will be in the lake that burns with fire and sulfur, which is the second death."

Eternal Perspective | *God's Purposes*

A BROKEN WORLD

"Then I saw a new heaven and a new earth; for the first heaven and the first earth had passed away, and the sea was no more." Revelation 21:1

When Adam and Eve sinned against God in Eden, the consequences were catastrophic and comprehensive. The book of Genesis reveals that this wayward couple—and their offspring—experienced alienation from God, the emotional devastation of guilt, fear, and shame, interpersonal difficulties, and physical disintegration leading to death. The Bible further suggests that their act of rebellion resulted in the whole universe being placed under a curse (Gn 3:17-19).

Can this really be? Are hurricanes, droughts, earthquakes, and epidemics the tangible evidence that our world is broken? Are dying stars in heaven and climate change on earth the signs of a cosmos that is groaning and yearning for restoration?

So much is a mystery. For now, what we can say for sure is that the Bible speaks of a coming age in which the redeemed of God will experience life in "a new heaven and a new earth." And in case anyone missed that mind-blowing promise, John quotes Jesus just four verses later saying, "Look, I am making everything new" (21:5).

When you, along with creation, are groaning under burden of a fallen world, remember that this is not the end of the story. Thank God for his eternal purposes and find your hope and joy in him.

For the next note on *Eternal Perspective*, see Revelation 21:4-5.

[A] **20:14** Other mss omit *the lake of fire* [B] **21:3** Other mss read *from heaven* [C] **21:3** Or *tent*, or *tabernacle* [D] **21:3** Other mss read *people* [E] **21:3** Other mss omit *and will be their God* [F] **21:4** Or *the first things* [G] **21:5** Other mss add *of God* [H] **21:8** Other mss add *the sinful,*

THE NEW JERUSALEM

[9] Then one of the seven angels, who had held
the seven bowls filled with the seven last
plagues, came and spoke with me: "Come, I
will show you the bride, the wife of the Lamb."
[10] He then carried me away in the Spirit[A] to a
great, high mountain and showed me the holy
city, Jerusalem, coming down out of heaven
from God, [11] arrayed with God's glory. Her radiance was like a precious jewel, like a jasper
stone, clear as crystal. [12] The city had a massive
high wall, with twelve gates. Twelve angels
were at the gates; the names of the twelve
tribes of Israel's sons were inscribed on the
gates. [13] There were three gates on the east,
three gates on the north, three gates on the
south, and three gates on the west. [14] The city
wall had twelve foundations, and the twelve
names of the twelve apostles of the Lamb were
on the foundations.

[15] The one who spoke with me had a gold-
en measuring rod to measure the city, its
gates, and its wall. [16] The city is laid out in a
square; its length and width are the same.
He measured the city with the rod at 12,000
stadia.[B] Its length, width, and height are
equal. [17] Then he measured its wall, 144 cubits
according to human measurement, which
the angel used. [18] The building material of its
wall was jasper, and the city was pure gold
clear as glass. [19] The foundations of the city
wall were adorned with every kind of jewel: the first foundation is jasper, the second
sapphire, the third chalcedony, the fourth
emerald, [20] the fifth sardonyx, the sixth carnelian, the seventh chrysolite, the eighth
beryl, the ninth topaz, the tenth chrysoprase,
the eleventh jacinth, the twelfth amethyst.
[21] The twelve gates are twelve pearls; each
individual gate was made of a single pearl.
The main street[C] of the city was pure gold,
transparent as glass.

[22] I did not see a temple in it, because the
Lord God the Almighty and the Lamb are its
temple. [23] The city does not need the sun or
the moon to shine on it, because the glory of
God illuminates it, and its lamp is the Lamb.
[24] The nations[D] will walk by its light, and the
kings of the earth will bring their glory into
it.[E] [25] Its gates will never close by day because

Eternal Perspective | *God's Plans*

EVERYTHING NEW

"He will wipe away every tear from their eyes. Death will be no more; grief, crying, and pain will be no more, because the previous things have passed away. Then the one seated on the throne said, 'Look, I am making everything new.'" Revelation 21:4-5

Consider that even as you read this sentence . . .

- Scientists in labs all over the world are trying to eliminate bad DNA from the human genome.
- Medical researchers are testing new wonder drugs in the fight against killer diseases.
- Environmentalists are working to reduce various forms of pollution.
- Farmers are seeking more efficient, less expensive ways to produce natural, healthy foods.

All these—mostly well-meaning—efforts stem from humanity's restless desire to forestall death. But according to John, only the Lord can and will bring an end to what Paul called "the last enemy" (1Co 15:26).

If you are restless today because you live in a world full of "death . . . grief, crying, and pain," remember that you can find rest in the One who will one day eliminate "every tear" from our eyes.

Indeed, his promise here is worth reflecting upon, "Look, I am making everything new." All creation, including you, will be restored.

For the first note on *Support*, see Numbers 14:9.

[A] **21:10** Or *in spirit* [B] **21:16** A *stadion* (sg) = about 600 feet; 12,000 *stadia* = 1,400 miles. [C] **21:21** Or *The public square*
[D] **21:24** Other mss add *of those who are saved* [E] **21:24** Other mss read *will bring to him the nations' glory and honor*

it will never be night there. [26] They will bring
the glory and honor of the nations into it.[A]
[27] Nothing unclean will ever enter it, nor anyone who does what is detestable or false, but
only those written in the Lamb's book of life.

THE SOURCE OF LIFE

22 Then he showed me the river[B] of the
water of life, clear as crystal, flowing
from the throne of God and of the Lamb [2] down
the middle of the city's main street. The tree
of life was on each side of the river, bearing
twelve kinds of fruit, producing its fruit every
month. The leaves of the tree are for healing
the nations, [3] and there will no longer be any
curse. The throne of God and of the Lamb will
be in the city, and his servants will worship
him. [4] They will see his face, and his name will
be on their foreheads. [5] Night will be no more;
people will not need the light of a lamp or the
light of the sun, because the Lord God will give
them light, and they will reign forever and ever.

THE TIME IS NEAR

[6] Then he said to me, "These words are faithful[C]
and true. The Lord, the God of the spirits of
the prophets,[D] has sent his angel to show his
servants what must soon take place."

[7] "Look, I am coming soon! Blessed is the
one who keeps the words of the prophecy
of this book."

[8] I, John, am the one who heard and saw
these things. When I heard and saw them, I
fell down to worship at the feet of the angel
who had shown them to me. [9] But he said to
me, "Don't do that! I am a fellow servant with
you, your brothers the prophets, and those
who keep the words of this book. Worship
God!"

[10] Then he said to me, "Don't seal up the
words of the prophecy of this book, because
the time is near. [11] Let the unrighteous go on
in unrighteousness; let the filthy still be filthy;
let the righteous go on in righteousness; let
the holy still be holy."

[12] "Look, I am coming soon, and my reward
is with me to repay each person according to
his work. [13] I am the Alpha and the Omega, the
first and the last, the beginning and the end.

[14] "Blessed are those who wash their robes,[E]
so that they may have the right to the tree of
life and may enter the city by the gates. [15] Outside are the dogs, the sorcerers, the sexually
immoral, the murderers, the idolaters, and
everyone who loves and practices falsehood.

[16] "I, Jesus, have sent my angel to attest these

Rest and Reflection | *Reflecting*

ONE EYE ON THE FUTURE

"Look, I am coming soon, and my reward is with me to repay each person according to his work." Revelation 22:12

Socrates famously said, "The unexamined life is not worth living."

Anyone who has been around a while has experienced this truth. Life has a way of sucking us in and turning us into hamsters on a wheel. Soon we are running furiously, but we have no idea why. Some people spend an entire lifetime never asking important questions such as, *Where am I going? Why am I doing what I'm doing? Am I spending my life in ways that matter?*

Thus the value of an examined life! Of regularly calling time out. Of routinely unplugging from all the trivial froth and bubble of life. Of rigorously reflecting on what's true—like this promise of the Lord.

Do you see it? Jesus will return! And when he does, John says we will each have a face-to-face audience with him. It will be like an annual job review—only this one will encompass our entire lives!

Because this great eternal reality is true, we must take time to examine and reflect. Healthy souls do this—they live fully and wisely in the present, but always with one eye on this great day still to come.

For the first note on *Eternal Perspective*, see Genesis 1:1.

[A] **21:26** Other mss add *in order that they might go in* [B] **22:1** Other mss read *pure river* [C] **22:6** Or *trustworthy* [D] **22:6** Other mss read *God of the holy prophets* [E] **22:14** Other mss read *who keep his commands*

things to you for the churches. I am the root
and descendant of David, the bright morning star."
17 Both the Spirit and the bride say, "Come!"
Let anyone who hears, say, "Come!" Let the one
who is thirsty come. Let the one who desires
take the water of life freely.
18 I testify to everyone who hears the words
of the prophecy of this book: If anyone adds
to them, God will add to him the plagues that
are written in this book.
19 And if anyone takes
away from the words of the book of this prophecy, God will take away his share of the tree
of life and the holy city, which are written
about in this book.
20 He who testifies about these things says,
"Yes, I am coming soon."

Amen! Come, Lord Jesus!
21 The grace of the Lord Jesus[A] be with everyone.[B] Amen.[C]

[A] **22:21** Other mss add *Christ* [B] **22:21** Other mss read *with all the saints* [C] **22:21** Other mss omit *Amen.*

Notes

Topical Index

When you need:

Acceptance

RESTORE Notes: Hosea 6:6; Ephesians 1:1

You may not be accepted by the world, but God has accepted you. (John 17:9-14)

You have been accepted and face no condemnation because of Christ. (Romans 8:1)

Christ made you acceptable to God. (1 Corinthians 1:30)

By faith, you belong in God's family. (Ephesians 1:3-6)

Assurance

RESTORE Notes: Job 23:12; Psalm 116:1-2; John 14:6; Hebrews 7:23-25; 1 Peter 1:3-4; 1:24-25; 4:19; Jude 24-25; Revelation 5:9; 19:6

Restoration Profiles: John the Baptist (Matthew 3)

My Story Notes: Christine (Isaiah 41)

Embracing God's Word Chart: Victory (2 Corinthians 1)

You can be sure that you will live again. (Isaiah 26:19)

You can be sure that even small faith can accomplish much. (Matthew 17:20)

Jesus assured you of your salvation. (John 5:24)

Christ in you is your assurance of eternal glory. (Colossians 1:27)

You can know for sure that you are saved. (1 John 5:13)

Blessings

RESTORE Notes: Isaiah 55:1-2; 2 Corinthians 3:5

The path of blessing is serving others. (John 13:12-17)

You have God's greatest blessings because of your faith. (Galatians 3:9-14)

Because you belong to Christ, you have every spiritual blessing. (Ephesians 1:3)

Comfort

RESTORE Notes: Psalm 23:1-4; 2 Corinthians 1:3-4; 7:6

My Story Notes: Bonnie (Genesis 30); Mia (Job 9); Jason (Jeremiah 23)

Embracing God's Word Chart: Comfort (Revelation 9)

God listens to your cries and will comfort you. (Psalm 10:17)

God can bring you comfort even in your doubts. (Psalm 94:19)

God comforts the brokenhearted. (Isaiah 61:1)

God will be with you wherever you go. (Haggai 1:13)

As God comforts you, you will be able to comfort others. (2 Corinthians 1:4-7)

Compassion

RESTORE Notes: Job 29:12-13; Psalm 41:1; 68:5; 103:7-8; 145:8-9; Isaiah 1:17; 30:18; 32:8; Jeremiah 9:1; Lamentations 3:22-23; Ezekiel 33:11; Amos 5:24; Matthew 9:35-36; 20:28; 22:39-40; 25:40; 28:18-20; Mark 9:35; Luke 15:20; 2 Corinthians 9:7; Hebrews 13:1; 13:16; 1 John 3:17; 3:18

My Story Notes: Mandy (Micah 2)

Because of God's compassion, he wipes away your sin. (Psalm 51:1)

Come to the Lord and receive compassion. (Isaiah 30:18)

God has compassion on his people. (Isaiah 49:13)

Jesus has compassion for those in need. (Mark 6:34)

Confidence

RESTORE Notes: Deuteronomy 31:6; Habakkuk 3:17-19; Matthew 19:25-26; Galatians 6:1; Philippians 2:14; 1 John 5:14-15

Better to trust God than put confidence in people. (Psalm 118:8-9)

You are blessed by putting your confidence in the Lord. (Jeremiah 17:7)

Be confident of your salvation. (1 Thessalonians 5:8)

You can hold God's promises with confidence. (Hebrews 6:18)

Be confident that God hears your prayers. (1 John 5:14)

Contentment

RESTORE Notes: Isaiah 55:8-9; Jeremiah 2:13; Philippians 4:12-13

Satan tries to make you discontent. (Genesis 3:1-10)

Not found in money or material things. (Psalm 17:13-15)

You can learn contentment in every situation. (Philippians 4:10-14)

Your faith plus contentment equals great wealth. (1 Timothy 6:6)

Courage

RESTORE Notes: Joshua 1:9; Matthew 16:25-26; Mark 1:28; Luke 4:28-29; 6:26-27; 17:4; Hebrews 4:16; James 5:16

Restoration Profiles: Nicodemus (John 19); Timothy (1 Timothy 3)

Embracing God's Word Chart: Courage (1 Chronicles 28)

You can have courage because God is with you. (Joshua 1:9)

Be brave and courageous and wait for the Lord. (Psalm 27:14)

Take new courage as you trust Christ. (Hebrews 6:18)

Stay close to Christ and he will give you courage. (1 John 2:28)

Endurance/Perseverance

RESTORE Notes: Joshua 23:11; 1 Samuel 12:23; Psalm 22:1; 143:6-7; Proverbs 12:24; Ecclesiastes 2:18,20; Galatians 6:9; Colossians 4:12; 1 Thessalonians 1:3; 1 Timothy 6:12; 2 Timothy 4:7-8

Restoration Profiles: Joseph (Genesis 37)

My Story Notes: Tim (Proverbs 23); Rita (Daniel 6)

Those who endure to the end will be saved. (Matthew 10:22)

Endurance develops your character. (Romans 5:3-4)

You may have to endure many troubles. (2 Corinthians 6:4)

Endure and receive a crown. (James 1:12)

Faith

RESTORE Notes: Deuteronomy 4:29; 6:4-5; Job 19:25-27; Psalm 96:2-4; Isaiah 43:1; 46:10; Jeremiah 33:2-3; Micah 5:13; Matthew 6:10; 6:33; 7:7; Mark 9:23-24; 10:47-48; Luke 7:9; 17:5; John 6:66-68; 12:37; 1 Corinthians 9:24-25; 15:6; 2 Corinthians 5:7; Galatians 2:20; Colossians 2:6; 2 Thessalonians 1:3; 1 Peter 1:24-25

Restoration Profiles: Rahab (Joshua 6); Hannah (1 Samuel 1); Bartimaeus (Luke 18)

My Story Notes: Ed (Ecclesiastes 12); Sherry (Ezekiel 18); Javier (Hosea 11); Marcus (Luke 23); Sabrina (Romans 9)

You have been made right with God through faith, not obedience. (Romans 3:27-31)

God gives you a shield called "faith" to help you stand strong. (Ephesians 6:16)

Christ will give you the faith you need. (Hebrews 12:1-2)

Trials may test your faith, but hang on to it! (1 Peter 1:7)

Forgiveness

RESTORE Notes: Leviticus 25:17; Numbers 5:6-7; Psalm 24:3-4; 32:1-2; 32:5; Isaiah 1:18; Jeremiah 3:22; Zephaniah 3:15; Ephesians 1:7; 6:4; Hebrews 8:12; James 4:17; 1 John 1:9; 5:18

Restoration Profiles: Paralyzed Man (Mark 2)

My Story Notes: Joey (2 Samuel 12); Colin (Luke 15)

Embracing God's Word Chart: Forgiveness (Matthew 27)

God's forgiveness makes you white as snow. (Isaiah 1:18)

God cleanses you from sin. (Ezekiel 36:25)

Trust in Christ for forgiveness. (Acts 13:38-39)

Jesus died so you could be forgiven. (Hebrews 9:22)

Recognize sin and ask God to forgive you. (1 John 1:8-9)

God's Presence

RESTORE Notes: 2 Samuel 22:2-4; Psalm 5:3; 27:4; Matthew 14:13; Mark 14:36; Luke 5:16; Philippians 3:7-8; Hebrews 4:9-11; James 4:8; 2 Peter 1:12; Revelation 3:20

God is always with you. (Psalm 16:8)

God promises to be with you. (Isaiah 41:10)

Jesus is with you until the end of the age. (Matthew 28:20)

Jesus is with you—in you—through the Holy Spirit. (John 14:16-21)

God's Will

RESTORE Notes: 1 Chronicles 16:11; Luke 10:41-42; 22:42; Acts 16:6-7; Romans 5:6; 8:27; Galatians 5:25; Colossians 3:17; 1 Thessalonians 5:17; 2 Timothy 3:16-17; Revelation 21:1; 21:4-5

You can ask God to show you his will. (Psalm 143:10)

When you ask for God's will, be willing to do it. (Mark 14:36)

Understand that patient endurance is sometimes needed. (Hebrews 10:36)

God's will is for you to live a good life. (1 Peter 2:15)

Grace

RESTORE Notes: Exodus 20:12; Psalm 86:15; Proverbs 20:27; Joel 2:12-13; Jonah 3:1; Acts 9:3-4; 15:11; Romans 3:23-24; 6:23; 1 Corinthians 1:3; 2 Corinthians 7:6

Restoration Profiles: Zacchaeus (Luke 19); Woman at the Well (John 4)

You have been set free by God's grace. (Romans 6:14)

By God's grace, you can come to him. (2 Corinthians 4:15)

Come to God's throne and receive grace. (Hebrews 4:16)

God's grace is always with you. (1 Peter 5:12)

Guidance

RESTORE Notes: Joshua 24:15; 1 Chronicles 16:11; Psalm 16:7-8; 32:8-9; 73:24; Proverbs 3:5-6; 11:14; Luke 10:41-42; Galatians 5:25; James 4:2

God promises to guide his people. (Exodus 15:13)

You can ask God to show you the path to walk. (Psalm 25:4-21)

You can ask for God to guide you with his light and truth. (Psalm 43:3)

Guidance may come through the advice of trusted people. (Proverbs 13:13)

Healing/Recovery

RESTORE Notes: 1 Samuel 2:26; Job 6:24; Hosea 10:12; Mark 8:24-25; John 4:14

Restoration Profiles: Elijah (1 Kings 17); Naaman (2 Kings 5); Paralyzed Man (Mark 2); Mary Magdalene (Mark 15)

My Story Notes: Dawn (Judges 16); Lucy (1 Kings 15); Shayleen (1 Chronicles 4); Franklyn (Lamentations 2); Josh (1 Corinthians 16); Cara (Philippians 1)

God may use physicians and medicines to bring healing. (2 Kings 20:1-7)

Do not be afraid to ask for healing. (Psalm 6)

Jesus may heal you as part of a demonstration of his power and authority. (Matthew 9:6)

Sometimes God says no because he has a higher purpose. (2 Corinthians 12:7-10)

Hope

RESTORE Notes: Esther 4:13-14; Psalm 22:1; 27:14; 55:17; 62:1; 62:5; 88:9; Proverbs 22:6; Isaiah 61:1-2; Jeremiah 29:11; Ezekiel 37:2-3; Luke 1:37; Acts 9:3-4; Romans 15:13; Philippians 3:13-14; 1 Timothy 2:1-2; Titus 2:13

Restoration Profiles: Naomi (Ruth 3); Hannah (1 Samuel 1)

My Story Notes: Lucy (1 Kings 15); Shayleen (1 Chronicles 4); Mickey (John 3)

Embracing God's Word Chart: Hope (Romans 14)

Strengthen your hope by reading the promises in God's Word. (Psalm 130:5)

You have hope because of Christ. (2 Thessalonians 2:16-17)

In the Bible, hope is not wishful thinking—it is assurance. (Hebrews 10:23)

Your hope for the end of time is the certainty of Jesus's return. (Revelation 22:18-21)

Humility

RESTORE Notes: 2 Samuel 22:28; 2 Chronicles 7:14; 34:27; Job 42:2; 42:6; Psalm 26:2; 51:10;

Proverbs 15:33; Obadiah 3-4; Malachi 3:7; Matthew 18:4; Mark 2:17; 9:35; 11:25; Luke 14:11; Ephesians 5:21; Philippians 2:3-4; Hebrews 6:10; 10:24; 1 Peter 3:8-9; 5:5

My Story Notes: Neil (1 Peter 3)

Thinking of others first will help you learn humility. (Philippians 2:3-10)

A refusal to gossip or quarrel will help you become humble. (Titus 3:2)

Service to others will help you learn humility. (1 Peter 5:5)

God's mighty power will help you become humble. (1 Peter 5:6)

Integrity

RESTORE Notes: Psalm 25:21; 1 Corinthians 2:3; 5:6; 11:1; James 5:12

Ask God to help you live a blameless life, even at home, in order to show integrity. (Psalm 101:2)

Following the Lord will help you learn integrity. (Psalm 119:1)

God will give you integrity like a shield for your life. (Proverbs 2:7)

Let your life reflect what you believe. (Titus 2:7)

Joy

RESTORE Notes: Exodus 15:13; Nehemiah 8:10; Psalm 118:24; John 2:2-3; Philippians 3:7-8; 4:4; James 1:2; Revelation 7:11-12

My Story Notes: Steve (2 Kings 11); Marvin (Psalm 48)

Embracing God's Word Chart: Joy (Philippians 3)

You can find joy in God's presence. (Psalm 16:11)

You can find joy in God's commands. (Psalm 19:8)

You can find joy by trusting God even through the tough times. (Psalm 30:5)

Jesus promised to give his followers abundant joy. (John 16:20-24)

Given as a fruit of the Spirit. (Galatians 5:22-23)

Love

RESTORE Notes: Psalm 18:1; 31:7; 86:15; 89:1-2; Isaiah 49:15-16; Zephaniah 3:17; John 3:16; 13:34-35; 15:12-13; Romans 5:8; 8:38-39; 1 Corinthians 13:6-7; Ephesians 3:17-19; 1 Timothy 1:15; 1 Peter 4:8; 1 John 4:9; Revelation 2:3-4

Restoration Profiles: John (Revelation 1)

My Story Notes: Marcus (Luke 23)

Embracing God's Word Chart: Love (1 Corinthians 13)

God loved you so much that he sent his Son to die for you. (John 3:16)

You can love others because Jesus first loved you. (John 13:34)

Nothing can separate you from God's love. (Romans 8:35-39)

How to love your neighbor as yourself. (Romans 13:8-10)

Real love is more than feelings. (1 Corinthians 13:4-14)

Given as a fruit of the Spirit. (Galatians 5:22-23)

God is love. Be assured of his love for you. (1 John 4:16-21)

Mercy

RESTORE Notes: Proverbs 28:13; Isaiah 30:18; 42:3; Micah 6:8; 7:8; Luke 1:49-50; Ephesians 2:4-5; Titus 3:4-5; 1 Peter 2:9-10; Jude 22

Restoration Profiles: Woman Caught in Adultery (John 8)

God gives mercy to even the worst sinners. (1 Timothy 1:16)

Come directly to God's throne and receive his mercy. (Hebrews 4:16)

Accept the mercy God has given so that you may be saved. (1 Peter 1:3)

You can show mercy because of the mercy God has shown you. (Jude 22-23)

Patience

RESTORE Notes: Numbers 23:19; Acts 16:14; 2 Corinthians 10:3; 2 Timothy 2:24-25; James 4:8

My Story Notes: Rita (Daniel 6)

God will give you patience. (Romans 15:5)

Given as a fruit of the Spirit. (Galatians 5:22-23)

Patience means allowing for others' faults out of love. (Ephesians 4:2)

You can learn patience from the examples of prophets in the Bible. (James 5:10-11)

Peace

RESTORE Notes: Psalm 19:1-2; 37:5; 37:7; 68:19; Isaiah 9:6; Micah 5:5; John 16:33; 1 Corinthians 6:1; Philippians 4:6-7; 2 Thessalonians 3:16; Hebrews 12:14; 1 Peter 5:7

My Story Notes: Rhonda (2 Corinthians 6)

Embracing God's Word Chart: Peace (Psalm 29)

Jesus has given you peace of heart and mind. (John 14:27)

You have peace with God because of Christ. (Romans 5:1)

Given as a fruit of the Spirit. (Galatians 5:22-23)

Tell God all your needs, and he will give you his peace in return. (Philippians 4:6-9)

Perspective

RESTORE Notes: Deuteronomy 7:13; 2 Kings 6:16-17; Psalm 93:4; 103:15-16; Isaiah 37:20; Jeremiah 1:19; 32:26-27; Haggai 1:5; 2:9; Matthew 7:1; 18:2,5;

Luke 10:41-42; 16:14-15; John 1:35-37; 17:3; Acts 10:34-35; Romans 2:1; 8:28; 1 Corinthians 3:5-6; 2 Corinthians 6:14; Galatians 3:28; Ephesians 1:1; Colossians 1:9-11; 3:2; 1 Timothy 6:9-10; Revelation 5:9

My Story Notes: Mandy (Micah 2); Neil (1 Peter 3)

Even the bad things that happen can have great good. (Genesis 50:20)

Understand that all sin is ultimately against God. (Psalm 51:4)

What seems impossible for you is possible with God. (Luke 18:27)

God can cause everything to work together for good. (Romans 8:28)

Nothing can separate you from God's love. (Romans 8:35-39)

Priorities

RESTORE Notes: Leviticus 19:10; 27:30; Deuteronomy 12:5-6; Joshua 24:15; Luke 2:52; 12:34; 16:13; 16:14-15; 18:22; Acts 6:4; 1 Corinthians 8:13; 1 John 2:15

My Story Notes: Mandy (Micah 2); Cliff (Colossians 2)

Right priorities begin with God. (Proverbs 3:1-6)

Getting wisdom is a high priority, and it comes from God. (Proverbs 4:7)

Your primary concern should be God and the growth of his kingdom. (Matthew 6:33)

Your priority in life should be to love God and love others. (Mark 12:29-31)

Protection

RESTORE Notes: Exodus 15:2; Numbers 6:24-26; Psalm 121:5-8; Romans 6:13; 2 Timothy 3:12; Jude 24-25

Restoration Profiles: Jeremiah (Jeremiah 5)

God can be your hiding place when you need protection. (Psalm 32:7)

God's faithful promises are your protection. (Psalm 91)

Fear and trust God; let him protect you. (Proverbs 19:23)

Protection may not always be physical, but you can still trust God. (Daniel 3:16-18)

God promises to protect you and give you his promises. (1 Peter 1:5)

Provision

RESTORE Notes: 2 Samuel 23:5; Luke 11:9; 2 Peter 1:3

Embracing God's Word Chart: Provision (Psalm 111)

God will care for those in need. (Deuteronomy 10:18)

God promises to care for your needs. (Matthew 6:25-34)

Pray to God for the daily food you need. (Luke 11:3)

Trust God, yet work hard as you are able. (2 Thessalonians 3:10-12)

Purpose

RESTORE Notes: Psalm 71:18; 145:4; Jeremiah 1:5; Jonah 4:6-8; Matthew 25:21; 28:18-20; Romans 12:15-18; 1 Corinthians 6:19-20; 10:31; 12:7; 14:12; Ephesians 3:1; Revelation 22:12

My Story Notes: Colin (Luke 15); Cliff (Colossians 2)

God has a purpose for your life. (Psalm 57:2)

Make your plans, but hold them loosely as you trust God with them. (Proverbs 19:21)

Because God called you, he will work out his purpose in your life. (Romans 8:28)

God wants to use you to build his kingdom, but you need to obey him. (2 Timothy 2:21)

Restoration

RESTORE Notes: Ezra 3:10-11; Psalm 84:2; 139:23-24; John 17:23; Romans 7:18-19; 2 Corinthians 5:17; Revelation 21:4-5

Restoration Profiles: Jacob (Genesis 26); David (2 Samuel 2); Hezekiah (2 Chronicles 29); Matthew (Matthew 9); Mary, Martha, and Lazarus (Matthew 26); Peter (Acts 11)

Embracing God's Word Chart: Renewal (Hebrews 5)

You can pray to God to restore you. (Psalm 6)

God can restore your joy. (Psalm 51:12)

God's commandments can restore you. (Psalm 119:93)

God can restore you to a firm foundation. (1 Peter 5:10)

Self-control

RESTORE Notes: Judges 8:22-23; Psalm 1:1-3; 19:14; 141:3; Ecclesiastes 3:7; Colossians 4:5-6; 1 Timothy 4:12; 6:9-10; 2 Timothy 2:16

Restoration Profiles: Samson (Judges 13)

Given as a fruit of the Spirit. (Galatians 5:22-23)

Pray for self-control in order to live for God in the world. (Titus 2:12)

Knowing God leads to self-control. (2 Peter 1:6)

Self-esteem/Self-worth

RESTORE Notes: Genesis 1:1; 1:27; 1 Samuel 16:7; Nehemiah 9:6; Psalm 5:4; 8:3-5; 100:1-3; 139:1-3; Jeremiah 1:5; Matthew 10:29-31; Luke 2:25-26; Romans 16:14; Galatians 4:4-5; Ephesians 2:10; 4:1

Restoration Profiles: Isaiah (Isaiah 11)

My Story Notes: Cliff (Colossians 2)

You are made just a bit lower than the angels. (Psalm 8:3-5)

God knows everything you do and think. (Psalm 139)

God knows everything about you. (Luke 12:7)

God loved you so much he sent his Son to die for you. (John 3:16)

Strength

RESTORE Notes: 2 Samuel 7:22; 22:47; Micah 7:8; Zechariah 4:6; John 15:4-5; Acts 1:8; 26:17-18; 2 Corinthians 2:14; 10:3; Ephesians 5:33; 2 Timothy 4:7-8; 2 Peter 1:3

Restoration Profiles: Paul (Acts 24)

The Lord promises to be your strength. (Exodus 15:2)

Obedience in the small things gives the strength to do God's will in the big things. (Deuteronomy 11:8)

Wait on the Lord and he will renew your strength. (Isaiah 40:1)

God gives strength. (2 Thessalonians 2:16-17)

God supplies the strength to use your gifts for him. (1 Peter 4:11)

Truth

RESTORE Notes: Exodus 23:1; 1 Chronicles 29:17; Psalm 62:5; 77:11; 119:11; Proverbs 27:6; 27:17; Isaiah 5:20; John 16:13; 2 Peter 1:12; 2:1; 1 John 1:8

Jesus is the truth; follow him. (John 14:6)

You find the truth by reading God's Word. (John 17:17)

The gospel you received is the final truth. (Colossians 1:5-23)

You can trust God's truth to stand forever. (2 Timothy 2:19)

Wisdom

RESTORE Notes: Joshua 9:14; 1 Kings 3:9-10; Psalm 19:7-8; 33:13-15; Proverbs 1:5; 9:9; 13:20; 19:20; Song of Songs 2:15; Isaiah 6:8; 30:10-11; Hosea 4:6; Matthew 10:32; 1 Corinthians 6:1; 15:33; Galatians 1:10; Ephesians 5:15; Colossians 4:5-6; Hebrews 13:17; James 1:5; 2:1; 1 Peter 5:5; 2 Peter 2:1; 3:9; 3 John 10

The Lord grants wisdom. (Proverbs 2:6-22)

Fear of the Lord is the beginning of wisdom. (Proverbs 9:10)

In Christ are all the treasures of wisdom and knowledge. (Colossians 2:2-3)

God will give you wisdom if you ask. (James 1:5)

When you feel:

Afraid

RESTORE Notes: Exodus 14:13-14; Psalm 56:3; 118:5-6; Mark 14:33-34; 2 Timothy 1:7

Restoration Profiles: John Mark (Mark 13); Timothy (1 Timothy 3); Onesimus (Philemon)

My Story Notes: Jill (Psalm 79); Christine (Isaiah 41)

Stay close to God. (Psalm 23)

God will be with you in the battle. (2 Chronicles 20:15)

Let God be your light in the darkness. (Psalm 27:1-3)

Remember that God will keep his promises. (Revelation 2:10)

Angry

RESTORE Notes: Psalm 106:3; Jeremiah 15:21; Luke 6:8-9; Ephesians 4:31; James 1:19-20; 1 John 2:10-11

My Story Notes: Jordan (Ezekiel 3)

Control it; don't have a hasty temper. (Proverbs 14:29)

Respond with a gentle answer. (Proverbs 15:1)

Don't let it get the better of you. (Matthew 5:22)

Don't sin in your anger. (Ephesians 4:26-27)

Ashamed

RESTORE Notes: Isaiah 1:18; Jeremiah 3:22; Matthew 5:8; Mark 2:17; John 10:27-29; Romans 1:16; 7:18-19; 2 Corinthians 5:21; Ephesians 6:4

Restoration Profiles: Rahab (Joshua 6)

Let shame over sin cause you to repent. (Psalm 51)

Don't be ashamed to share your faith. (Psalm 119:46)

Don't be ashamed to acknowledge that you are a believer. (Matthew 10:32-33)

Don't be ashamed of the gospel—for it has brought you salvation. (Romans 1:16-17)

Bitter

RESTORE Notes: Psalm 5:6; Jeremiah 15:21; Luke 6:8-9; Ephesians 4:31; James 1:19-20; 1 John 2:10-11

My Story Notes: Jordan (Ezekiel 3)

Bitterness can be removed by forgiveness. (Luke 15:11-32)

Ask God to help you love others. (Ephesians 4:31-32)

Deal with the root cause before it affects others. (Hebrews 12:14-17)

Bored

RESTORE Notes: Psalm 103:15-16; 104:24; 1 Thessalonians 5:6; Revelation 2:3-4

My Story Notes: Marvin (Psalm 48)

You can praise. (Psalm 34:1)

You can serve someone. (Galatians 5:13)

You can pray. (1 Thessalonians 5:17)

Burned Out

RESTORE Notes: Genesis 2:2-3; Exodus 20:8-10; 1 Kings 19:11-12; Psalm 55:6; 127:2; Ecclesiastes 3:1; Isaiah 40:30-31; Mark 6:31; Acts 26:17-18; Hebrews 4:1

My Story Notes: Cathy (Leviticus 23)

Delegate some of your responsibilities. (Exodus 18:13-26)

Wait on the Lord and let him renew your strength. (Isaiah 40:31)

Give your burdens to the Lord. (Matthew 11:28-30)

Get some rest. (Mark 6:31-32)

Criticized

RESTORE Notes: Numbers 32:23; Acts 4:19-20; 7:59-60; 2 Timothy 3:12

My Story Notes: Franklyn (Lamentations 2)

Be willing to accept it if it might be true and helpful. (Proverbs 13:18)

Listening to valid criticism can make you wise. (Proverbs 15:31-32)

Criticism from a wise person can be profitable. (Ecclesiastes 7:5)

Teach the truth and don't set yourself up for criticism. (Titus 2:8)

Ignore unjust criticism. (James 4:11)

Depressed

RESTORE Notes: Proverbs 17:22; Mark 14:33-34

Restoration Profiles: Elijah (1 Kings 17)

My Story Notes: Mickey (John 3)

Realize that depression can follow great success. (1 Kings 19:1-9)

Place your hope in God. (Psalm 42:5-11)

Put your hope in God and his Word. (Psalm 130)

Remind yourself that your feelings are not permanent. (Isaiah 61:3)

Disappointed

RESTORE Notes: Deuteronomy 7:9; Isaiah 2:22; Jeremiah 20:7,9; 2 Corinthians 11:3

Remember that your hope in God will not be disappointed. (Proverbs 23:18)

While others may disappoint you, God will not. (Romans 5:5)

Your faith in Christ will never disappoint you. (1 Peter 2:6)

Discouraged

RESTORE Notes: Deuteronomy 10:12; 20:3-4; Psalm 40:5; Proverbs 12:24; Isaiah 35:3-4; Nahum 1:7; Philippians 1:6; 2:14; 1 Timothy 2:1-2; Hebrews 3:13

Restoration Profiles: John Mark (Mark 13)

Remember that the Lord is with you. (Deuteronomy 31:8)

Ask God to encourage you. (2 Corinthians 7:6)

Remind yourself that you will reap a great harvest of blessing. (Galatians 6:9)

If God is disciplining you, know that he loves you. (Hebrews 12:5-6)

Doubtful

RESTORE Notes: Genesis 15:6; Job 19:25-27; Isaiah 6:3; Jeremiah 31:33; 32:26-27; Habakkuk 1:2-4; Mark 7:32-33; 9:23-24; John 8:31-32; 14:1-3; Acts 20:30; 1 Corinthians 15:6; 1 Peter 4:19; Jude 22

Restoration Profiles: Moses (Exodus 2); Thomas (John 20)

My Story Notes: Jill (Psalm 79); Cord (Jeremiah 36); Sabrina (Romans 9)

Allow doubts to help you grow in your faith. (Matthew 17:14-23)

Bring your doubts to the One who can answer them. (Luke 7:18-23)

Jesus is willing to answer your concerns. (John 20:24-29)

Be careful that doubt doesn't shipwreck your faith. (James 1:5-8)

Grief/Sorrow

RESTORE Notes: Ruth 1:20-21; Psalm 56:8; John 9:1-2; 11:35; Acts 7:59-60; Romans 5:3-4; 2 Corinthians 1:3-4; 4:17-18; 7:6; Philippians 1:29; James 1:2

Restoration Profiles: Naomi (Ruth 3); Job (Job 2)

My Story Notes: Mia (Job 9)

Express your grief, but do it in healthy ways. (2 Samuel 1:1-16)

You can overcome grief by prayer and action. (Nehemiah 1:1-11)

Know that Jesus understands your grief firsthand. (John 11:33)

Take heart; Jesus has overcome the world. (John 16:33)

Guilty

RESTORE Notes: Judges 3:7-9; Ezra 10:1; Psalm 32:5; 51:3-4; Proverbs 14:9; Isaiah 30:15; Zephaniah 3:15; Matthew 5:8; Ephesians 1:7; Hebrews 8:12

My Story Notes: Casey (Isaiah 24)

Know that your guilt can be removed by Christ. (Romans 3:21-31)

Accept that you have been freed

from condemnation for your sins. (Romans 8:1-17)

Christ can relieve your guilty conscience. (1 John 3:11-24)

Hurt

RESTORE Notes: Leviticus 6:2-5; 19:17; 19:18; Jeremiah 38:6; Lamentations 3:40; Matthew 19:4-6; Acts 15:37,39; 2 Corinthians 11:3; 1 Peter 3:8-9

My Story Notes: Jordan (Ezekiel 3)

One day God will remove all hurt. (Isaiah 11:9)

Pray for those who hurt you. (Luke 6:28)

God can use the hurt to help you grow. (1 Thessalonians 3:1-8)

Insecure

RESTORE Notes: Daniel 1:8; Micah 5:2; Malachi 3:6; 3:8,10; Acts 4:13; 9:26-27; Romans 8:27; 1 Corinthians 4:3-4; Philippians 2:12-13

If God gives you a task, he will enable you to do it. (Exodus 3:7–4:17)

With God on your side, you can do anything. (Numbers 13:25-30)

God gives you the gifts you have, so use them to his glory! (1 Peter 4:11)

Jealous

RESTORE Notes: Exodus 20:17; Isaiah 40:8; John 21:22; 2 Corinthians 10:12; James 3:15-16

Pray for God's love, for that has no room for jealousy. (1 Corinthians 13:4)

Pray for wisdom that can help overcome jealousy. (James 3:13-18)

Ask God to rid your life of jealousy. (1 Peter 2:1)

Lonely

RESTORE Notes: Leviticus 26:45; 1 Samuel 18:1-3; 25:24; Psalm 88:9; 144:3; Proverbs 18:1; 18:24; Ecclesiastes 4:9-10,12; Isaiah 49:15-16; Acts 2:42; 2 Peter 3:18; 2 John 12

Beware of self-pity; realize that others may feel the same. (1 Kings 19:1-18)

Remember that you have the family of God. (Psalm 68:6)

You can never be completely alone because the Holy Spirit is with you. (John 16:1-16)

Don't neglect going to church. (Hebrews 10:25)

Rebellious

RESTORE Notes: Psalm 14:2; Luke 6:37; Romans 13:14; 1 Corinthians 8:13

Restoration Profiles: Jonah (Jonah 1)

Consider that God judges rebellion against him as a sin. (1 Samuel 15:23)

Consider the consequences before you act. (Proverbs 27:12)

God warns against rebellious people. (Titus 1:10)

Rejected

RESTORE Notes: Numbers 14:9; Psalm 22:1; Jeremiah 38:6; 43:1-2

The Lord will never reject his own. (Psalm 27:9-10)

Think about all that God has promised you. (Psalm 77:1-12)

God will not reject you. (Jeremiah 33:25)

Jesus understands how you feel. (Mark 6:1-13)

Sad

RESTORE Notes: 1 Chronicles 16:8

Pour out your heart to the Lord and then leave the problem with him. (1 Samuel 1:15-18)

Ask for the Lord to give you his joy. (Nehemiah 8:10-12)

Put your hope in God. (Psalm 42:5-11)

If others are sad, share their sorrow. (Romans 12:15)

Stressed

RESTORE Notes: Psalm 46:10; Isaiah 40:30-31; Matthew 11:28; Mark 6:31

My Story Notes: Morris (Matthew 15)

Delegate some of your responsibilities. (Exodus 18:13-26)

Pray for God to release your stress. (Psalm 62:1-8)

Give your burdens to the Lord. (Matthew 11:28-30)

Get some rest. (Mark 6:31-32)

Tempted

RESTORE Notes: Genesis 2:24; 1 Kings 11:4; Job 31:7-8; Proverbs 4:23; Daniel 1:8; Romans 13:14; 1 Corinthians 10:13

Temptation is not a sin; giving in is a sin. (Matthew 4:1-11)

Keep alert and pray. Watch out for temptation. (Mark 14:38)

Remember that God never allows a temptation that you cannot handle. He will show a way of escape. (1 Corinthians 10:13)

Jesus understand temptation and is there to help. (Hebrews 2:18)

Thankful

RESTORE Notes: 1 Chronicles 16:25; Ezra 3:10-11; Nehemiah 9:5; Psalm 136:1; Luke 8:39; Acts 4:32;

22:3; Romans 10:13-14;
1 Thessalonians 5:18; Philemon 4-5

My Story Notes: Ian (Psalm 11)

Tell others what God has done for you. (1 Chronicles 16:8)

Let God know how thankful you are. (Colossians 3:15-17)

Receive God's gifts gladly. (1 Timothy 4:4)

Sing praises to the Lord. (James 5:13)

Weak

RESTORE Notes: Joshua 1:5; Micah 5:2; Matthew 7:9-11; Romans 12:3; 2 Corinthians 12:9; Ephesians 6:19; Colossians 1:15-17; 1 Timothy 4:7

Restoration Profiles: Moses (Exodus 2)

You may feel weak, but God will be the strength of your heart. (Psalm 73:26)

God can use your weakness for his glory. (2 Corinthians 12:1-10)

Though you feel weak, you have access to God's power within you. (2 Corinthians 13:3-4)

One day God will give you a new body full of strength and power. (Philippians 3:21)

Worried

RESTORE Notes: Psalm 118:5-6; 119:15-16; Proverbs 12:25; 22:6; Zephaniah 1:12; Zechariah 12:8; Matthew 6:34; Luke 12:31; Acts 6:4; 1 Peter 5:7

My Story Notes: Judith (Joshua 20)

Worry has no value for your life. (Matthew 6:25-34)

Don't worry; worship. (Luke 10:38-42)

Don't worry; pray. (Philippians 4:6-9)

Give all your worries and cares to God. (1 Peter 5:7)

If you wonder what the Bible says about:

Abortion

All people are made in God's image. (Genesis 1:26)

God knows each person before birth. (Psalm 139)

God has plans for each person, while still in the womb. (Jeremiah 1:5)

Children are to be welcomed as Christ welcomed them. (Mark 9:36-37)

Adultery

One of the Ten Commandments. (Exodus 20:14)

It was seen as so serious, that it called for the death penalty. (Leviticus 20:10)

Adultery can lead to other sins. (2 Samuel 11)

Be faithful to your spouse; adultery leads to hurt and ruin. (Proverbs 5:15-23)

Adultery has no place in the lives of believers. (Romans 13:9)

God will judge adultery. (Hebrews 13:4)

Aging

We should show respect for the aged. (Leviticus 19:32)

God can use the aged to serve him. (Psalm 92:12-15)

Gray hair is a crown of glory. (Proverbs 16:31)

The gray hair of experience is the splendor of age. (Proverbs 20:29)

Older men and women should be training the younger. (Titus 2:1-8)

Appearance

God looks at the heart. (1 Samuel 16:7)

Seek to be attractive on the inside. (Proverbs 19:22)

True beauty comes from attitude and good deeds. (1 Timothy 2:9-10)

Inward beauty is most important (1 Peter 3:1-7)

Astrology

Do not worship the stars. (Deuteronomy 4:19)

God made the stars and their constellations. (Job 9:9)

God controls the movements of the stars. (Isaiah 45:12)

Do not try to read the future in the stars. (Jeremiah 10:2)

Authority

God gave Jesus authority. (Matthew 11:27)

Jesus is our authority. (Acts 4:2-12)

We should obey the government if it does not demand that we go against Christ. (Romans 13:1-7)

We have been given authority in our service to Christ. (2 Corinthians 2:17)

Belief

You are blessed because even though you have not seen, you believe. (John 20:25-29)

If you believe in Christ, God will consider you to be righteous. (Romans 4:16-24)

If you believe, you will be saved. (Romans 10:9-10)

It's not enough to just believe God exists; belief should lead to action. (James 2:14-24)

Character

Your character is developed through challenges. (Psalm 105:16-22)

Christ is the model for what your character should look like. (Matthew 5:43-48)

Your character is developed through difficulties. (Romans 5:1-11)

Strong character makes you ready for anything. (James 1:2-4)

Church

God has built the church and he will strengthen and protect it. (Matthew 16:18)

The church is more than a building; it is the whole body of believers. (Ephesians 2:21)

The church has the responsibility to spread the gospel. (Ephesians 4:11-12)

Don't neglect regular church attendance. (Hebrews 10:25)

Confession

God hears when you confess your sins. (Psalm 66:16-20)

Confession helps believers have real fellowship. (James 5:13-20)

God forgives when you confess your sins. (1 John 1:8-10)

Conscience

Your conscience can move you to repent or to resist. (Proverbs 28:13-18)

Your conscience and the Holy Spirit will guide you. (Romans 9:1)

Clinging tightly to faith can help you keep a clear conscience. (1 Timothy 1:19)

Your conscience can be evil and defiled, but Christ can make it clean. (Hebrews 10:22)

Consequences

God will allow you to suffer the consequences of your sin. (Genesis 3:1-24)

It is wise to consider the consequences of an action before moving ahead. (Proverbs 27:12)

If you live to satisfy only yourself, you will face the consequences. (Galatians 6:8)

Cults

The cults twist the truths of the Bible. (2 Corinthians 11:3-4)

Some distortions sound like the truth. (Ephesians 4:9-16)

The cults deny the truths in the Bible. (1 Timothy 6:3-5)

God has harsh words for anyone who distorts the message of the gospel. (2 Peter 2:1)

Death

God promises to walk with you through death. (Psalm 23:4)

People die because sin brought death into the world. (Romans 5:15)

Death is only a doorway into eternal life for the believer. (1 Corinthians 15:50-58)

Death is unavoidable, so you need to be prepared. (Hebrews 9:27-28)

Devil

The devil can disguise himself and look good and harmless. (2 Corinthians 11:14)

The devil and his demons are always trying to trip you up. (Ephesians 6:11)

When you stand strong in your faith, he will flee from you. (1 Peter 5:8-9)

The devil is a defeated enemy. (Revelation 12:10-12)

Divorce

God's plan from the beginning was that spouses stay together. (Genesis 2:21-24)

God hates divorce. (Malachi 2:13-16)

Jesus would have you try to restore your marriage instead of ending it. (Matthew 19:3-11)

If it's not an unsafe situation, Paul advises you to stick it out—and pray! (1 Corinthians 7:10-16)

Eternal Life

Eternal life is for those who believe; eternal punishment is for those who refuse. (Matthew 25:46)

Eternal life is promised to those who believe in Christ as Savior. (John 3:16)

Eternal life will be radically different from this life. (2 Corinthians 5:1-10)

We cannot earn eternal life; we have it only because of Christ. (1 John 5:1-12)

Evolution

God created the earth, all living things, and all people. (Genesis 1:1-31)

When God created people, he made them in his likeness right away—not to evolve and change over time. (Genesis 5:1-2)

Some things about the beginnings we may never understand completely. (Job 38:4)

God created humans just a little lower than himself. (Psalm 8:3-9)

God is in complete control. (Psalm 33:4-11)

Family

Families can build unity by sharing their stories of faith. (Exodus 10:2)

Family members should talk together about their faith. (Deuteronomy 6:6-7)

Family members should honor one another. (Ephesians 5:22–6:4)

Family responsibilities should be a priority for all believers. (1 Timothy 3:5)

Friendship

Real friendship does not involve gossip. (Proverbs 16:28)

Real friendship involves loyalty. (Proverbs 17:17)

Real friendship involves honesty. (Proverbs 27:6,9)

Jesus promises to be a true friend. (John 15:15)

God's Acceptance

God's acceptance comes not because of good deeds, but because of faith. (Romans 3:27-30)

God's acceptance is a free gift given to you. (Romans 5:12-16)

Because God accepted you, you should accept others. (Romans 15:7)

God's acceptance of you in love means that at times he will discipline you. (Hebrews 12:6)

Greed

Greed will rob you of life. (Proverbs 1:15-19)

Greed has no place in a believer's life. (Ephesians 5:3-5)

Greed is really idolatry. (Colossians 3:5)

Heaven

Believers will be in heaven with God forever. (Daniel 7:27)

Heaven is God's throne, where God lives. (Isaiah 66:1)

Jesus is preparing places in heaven for his followers. (John 14:2-3)

God created heaven and earth, and he will make a new heaven and earth at the end of time. (Revelation 21:1)

Hell

Hell is the place of eternal punishment for those who refuse salvation in Christ. (Matthew 25:41-46)

The punishment of hell is just. (Romans 1:18)

There are no second chances in hell. (Revelation 20:14)

Homosexuality

Homosexuality is called a detestable sin. (Leviticus 18:22)

The Bible condemns homosexual behavior. (Romans 1:26-27)

Those who indulge in this sin cannot share in God's kingdom. (1 Corinthians 6:9)

Hospitality

Hospitality is a way to serve those who serve you. (Luke 10:7)

God desires that his people show hospitality. (Romans 12:13)

By being hospitable, you might entertain angels and not know it! (Hebrews 13:2)

Hypocrisy

Hypocrites practice religion for attention, not out of devotion to God. (Matthew 6:2-16)

Hypocrisy is claiming faith, but not living it. (Matthew 23:1-39)

Hypocrisy has no place in the life of a true believer. (1 Peter 2:1)

Judgmentalism

Judge others by God's standards of fairness. (Isaiah 11:3-5)

You ought not judge others with wrong motives. (Matthew 7:1-6)

Judgment is appropriate when confronting sin. ((1 Corinthians 5:12)

God is the great and final Judge. (James 5:9)

Justice

God requires that his people deal justly with others. (Deuteronomy 16:19-20)

God will bring justice on the wicked. (Psalm 75:2)

God is just. (Daniel 9:14)

God's justice demands that he punish sin. (Romans 2:1-4)

Leadership

Leaders need to recognize that they need to trust in God. (1 Chronicles 12:18)

Wise leaders can change the course of a nation. (Proverbs 28:2)

Effective leaders know how to serve. (Luke 22:25)

If you have been given the responsibility to lead, take it seriously. (Romans 12:8)

Legalism

Legalism makes rules more important than God. (Mark 7:6-9)

Legalism takes away joy and enslaves you to rules. (Galatians 4:8-12)

Legalism can do nothing to change a person's heart. (Colossians 2:17-23)

Marriage

Marriage is a commitment between a man and a woman. (Genesis 2:23-24)

Marriage is meant to be a commitment for life. (Matthew 19:4-8)

Marriage works best when spouses submit to and serve each other. (Ephesians 5:21-26)

God wants married couples to be faithful and honor each other. (Hebrews 13:4)

Materialism

God can help you turn your eyes away from useless things and toward him. (Psalm 119:37)

God has given you all that you have, so be willing to share as you can. (Matthew 10:21)

The desire for things can crowd out the message of salvation. (Mark 4:19)

The desire for everything you see is a temptation of this evil world. (1 John 2:16)

Money

Money can take the place of God in a person's life. (Matthew 6:19-24)

Money can be a barrier between people and God. (Mark 10:23)

Love of money is at the root of all kinds of evil. (1 Timothy 6:10)

Money should be used for good. (1 Timothy 6:17-18)

Occult

God forbids involvement in the occult and witchcraft. (Deuteronomy 18:10-14)

Involvement in the occult leads to evil. (2 Chronicles 33:6)

Occult powers are no match for God. (Isaiah 47:9)

Those who consult demonic powers will face the same punishment as Satan. (Revelation 21:8)

Parenting

Parents should train their children in the Scriptures. (Deuteronomy 6:6-7)

Parents are to be good role models for their children. (Proverbs 1:8)

Parents should teach the children the right paths in life. (Proverbs 22:6)

Parents need to discipline with love and fairness. (Ephesians 6:4)

Prayer

Prayer is communicating with God. (Psalm 5:1-2)

God answers prayer. (Psalm 138:3)

Believers' lives should be characterized by prayer. (Colossians 4:2)

Prayer is a great privilege. (Hebrews 4:14-16)

Prejudice

Longstanding prejudices are overcome by Christ's love. (Luke 10:25-37)

Christ makes peace between people. (Ephesians 2:14)

In God's kingdom, there are no barriers between people. (Colossians 3:11)

Both rich and poor should be treated with equal respect. (James 2:1-9)

Pride

God hates pride. (Proverbs 16:5)

Pride goes before destruction. (Proverbs 16:18)

Pride is a sin that comes from within. (Mark 7:20-23)

Pride can cut you off from God and others. (Luke 18:14)

Purity

You can stay pure by obeying God's Word. (Psalm 119:9)

You are made pure because of Christ. (1 Corinthians 1:30)

When you remain pure, God can greatly use you. (2 Timothy 2:21-22)

Trusting in Christ will help you to remain pure. (1 John 3:2-3)

Repentance

Repentance means sorrow for sin and a desire to change. (2 Kings 22:19)

Without repentance of your sin, you will perish. (Luke 13:5)

Being sorry but refusing to repent accomplishes nothing. (2 Corinthians 7:10)

God desires that people repent and come to him. (2 Peter 3:9)

Rest

Rest is given to you by God. (Exodus 20:8-10)

Jesus offers to give you rest if you come to him. (Matthew 11:28-29)

Sometimes you may need to get away and rest. (Mark 6:31)

Rest is a part of God's ultimate plan for his people. (Hebrews 4:9-11)

Revenge

Revenge should be set aside in favor of love. (Leviticus 19:18)

God will one day have ultimate revenge on all the wicked. (Nahum 1:2)

Revenge should be left in God's hands. (Romans 12:19)

Salvation

Salvation is offered to all people. (Acts 2:21)

Salvation is through Christ alone. (Acts 4:12)

Salvation is simple, yet powerful. (Romans 10:8-10)

Salvation is a gift from God; it cannot be earned. (Ephesians 2:8-9)

Satan (see Devil)

Second Coming

No one will know the day or hour of Christ's return. (Matthew 25:13)

Jesus's second coming will include all believers from all time. (1 Thessalonians 4:13-14)

When Christ returns, we will go with him and be with him forever. (1 Thessalonians 4:17)

While there will be signs of his coming, it will happen unexpectedly. (1 Thessalonians 5:2-6)

Sex

God created sex for union between husband and wife. (Genesis 2:24)

Sexual sin begins in the mind. (Matthew 5:28)

Sexual sin is destructive. (1 Corinthians 6:18)

Sex is meant for enjoyment in marriage and for procreation. (1 Thessalonians 4:3-5)

Sin

Sin is disobeying God. (Genesis 3:17)

Sin separates all humanity from a holy God. (Romans 3:23)

The only way to be set free of the power and punishment of sin is to believe in Jesus Christ as Lord. (Romans 6:23)

Sin is not just things you do, but also right things you don't do. (James 4:17)

If you confess your sin, God promises to forgive. (1 John 1:9)

Singleness

The Bible recognizes that some will marry and some will remain single. (Matthew 19:12)

Both marriage and singleness are gifts from God. (1 Corinthians 7:6-7)

A good reason to remain single is to use the time and freedom to serve God in ways you might not be able to if married. (1 Corinthians 7:27-34)

Submission

Mutual submission is a key to harmonious relationships. (1 Corinthians 11:11-12)

Mutual submission in marriage is vitally important. (Ephesians 5:21-33)

All believers must submit to the Lord. (Hebrews 12:9)

Success

Commit your work to the Lord if you want it to succeed. (Proverbs 16:3)

God's view of success may be very different from the world's. (Mark 9:33-37)

Success comes from God. (2 Corinthians 3:5)

Suffering

Jesus said that this life will include suffering. (Luke 21:17-19)

Suffering is not always a result of sin. (John 9:2-3)

Jesus understands your suffering and will help you through it. (Hebrews 2:18)

Suffering can be used by God to help you grow. (James 1:2-3)

Even though suffering occurs, one day it will end. (1 Peter 4:12-16)

Suicide

The choice to end one's life reflects an unwillingness to trust God. (1 Chronicles 10:1-7)

Wait patiently for the Lord; he will pull you through. (Psalm 40:1-3)

God has great plans for you. (Jeremiah 29:11)

With God on your side, you can overcome any difficulty. (Ephesians 1:15-21)

Worship

Worship is an encounter with the living God. (Psalm 24:6)

Worship is only as real as your involvement and your desire to follow Christ. (Mark 7:7)

Worship should be in spirit and in truth; it should come from the heart. (John 4:21-24)

Worship focuses on Christ and what he has done. (Philippians 3:3)

Bible Reading Plans

Introduction

The *CSB Restoration Bible* offers two plans for reading through the Bible. The first plan developed by Heather Collins-Grattan Floyd is structured to take a person through the Bible in three years. This plan may appeal to busy persons who have a limited amount of time each day to read the Scriptures. Reading a smaller portion each day may enable the person to spend more time reading, studying, and meditating on the passage for the day.

The second plan was developed by the late Robert Murray M'Cheyne. This plan takes the reader to four portions of Scripture each day from various parts of the Bible. Following this plan, a person will read through the Old Testament once and the New Testament twice within a year.

Approaching the Bible

In reading and studying the Bible, we draw on the same knowledge, skills, and competencies we use in reading other documents. However, with the Bible there is an added dimension. The Bible was written by human beings but the ultimate Author who worked through a variety of human authors is God himself. In what may have been his last written words to Timothy, Paul reminded his protégé that all Scripture is inspired by God. For this reason, John Wesley said that Scripture can only be understood with the help of the Spirit who inspired these sixty-six books. Therefore, as believers come to read and study Scripture, they need to remember the Author of Scripture and ask for the Spirit's help in understanding what they read.

Come to the Bible expecting to grow. It is like both milk (1Pt 2:2) and solid food (Heb 5:14) providing nourishment for both the young and those more mature.

Come to the Bible for understanding and direction. It is like a counselor (Ps 119:24) and provides light for your journey (Ps 119:105,130).

Come to the Bible for correction and purification. It is like:

- a mirror in which the believer sees himself and the changes that God requires,
- fire and a hammer (Jr 23:29),
- a scalpel by which God performs spiritual surgery on the heart (Heb 4:12),
- water that washes and purifies (Eph 5:26).

Come to the Bible for pleasure. God's Word is like honey (Ps 19:9; 119:103).

Come daily to the Bible with these attitudes and expectations, and you will be changed. This is God's multifaceted instrument for conforming you to the image of his Son.

Three-Year Bible Reading Plan

Edited by Heather Collins-Grattan Floyd

YEAR ONE

JANUARY

Genesis 1:1-26 1st
Genesis 1:27–2:25 2nd
Genesis 3:1-24 3rd
Genesis 4:1-26 4th
Genesis 5:1-32 5th
Genesis 6:1–7:10 6th
Genesis 7:11–8:22 7th
Genesis 9:1-29 8th
Genesis 10:1-32 9th
Genesis 11:1–12:9 10th
Genesis 12:10–13:18 11th
Genesis 14:1-24 12th
Genesis 15:1–16:16 13th
Genesis 17:1-27 14th
Genesis 18:1-15 15th
Genesis 18:16-33 16th
Genesis 19:1-29 17th
Genesis 19:30–20:18 18th
Genesis 21:1-34 19th
Genesis 22:1-24 20th
Genesis 23:1–24:14 21st
Genesis 24:15-44 22nd
Genesis 24:45-67 23rd
Genesis 25:1-18 24th
Genesis 25:19-34 25th
Genesis 26:1-25 26th
Genesis 26:26–27:20 27th
Genesis 27:21-46 28th
Genesis 28:1–29:12 29th
Genesis 29:13–30:11 30th
Genesis 30:12-43 31st

FEBRUARY

Genesis 31:1-35 1st
Genesis 31:36-55 2nd
Genesis 32:1-32 3rd
Genesis 33:1-20 4th
Genesis 34:1-31 5th
Genesis 35:1–36:8 6th
Genesis 36:9-43 7th
Genesis 37:1-36 8th
Genesis 38:1-30 9th
Genesis 39:1-23 10th
Genesis 40:1–41:14 11th
Genesis 41:15-49 12th
Genesis 41:50–42:26 13th
Genesis 42:27–43:14 14th
Genesis 43:15-34 15th
Genesis 44:1-34 16th
Genesis 45:1-28 17th
Genesis 46:1-34 18th
Genesis 47:1-31 19th
Genesis 48:1-22 20th
Genesis 49:1-28 21st
Genesis 49:29–50:26 22nd
Exodus 1:1-22 23rd
Exodus 2:1-25 24th
Exodus 3:1-22 25th
Exodus 4:1-31 26th
Exodus 5:1–6:13 27th
Exodus 6:14–7:13 28th

MARCH

Exodus 7:14–8:19 1st
Exodus 8:20–9:12 2nd
Exodus 9:13-35 3rd
Exodus 10:1-20 4th
Exodus 10:21–11:10 5th
Exodus 12:1-28 6th
Exodus 12:29–13:16 7th
Exodus 13:17–14:31 8th
Exodus 15:1-27 9th
Exodus 16:1-36 10th
Exodus 17:1-16 11th
Exodus 18:1-27 12th
Exodus 19:1-25 13th
Exodus 20:1-26 14th
Exodus 21:1-36 15th
Exodus 22:1-31 16th
Exodus 23:1-33 17th
Exodus 24:1–25:9 18th
Exodus 25:10-40 19th
Exodus 26:1-37 20th
Exodus 27:1–28:14 21st
Exodus 28:15-43 22nd
Exodus 29:1-34 23rd
Exodus 29:35–30:21 24th
Exodus 30:22–31:18 25th
Exodus 32:1-35 26th
Exodus 33:1–34:9 27th
Exodus 34:10-35 28th
Exodus 35:1–36:1 29th
Exodus 36:2-38 30th
Exodus 37:1-24 31st

APRIL

Exodus 37:25–38:20 1st
Exodus 38:21–39:7 2nd
Exodus 39:8-43 3rd
Exodus 40:1-38 4th
Leviticus 1:1–2:16 5th
Leviticus 3:1–4:12 6th
Leviticus 4:13-35 7th
Leviticus 5:1–6:7 8th
Leviticus 6:8–7:10 9th
Leviticus 7:11-38 10th
Leviticus 8:1-36 11th
Leviticus 9:1-24 12th
Leviticus 10:1–11:8 13th
Leviticus 11:9-40 14th
Leviticus 11:41–13:8 15th
Leviticus 13:9-39 16th
Leviticus 13:40-59 17th
Leviticus 14:1-32 18th
Leviticus 14:33-57 19th
Leviticus 15:1-33 20th
Leviticus 16:1-34 21st
Leviticus 17:1-16 22nd
Leviticus 18:1-30 23rd
Leviticus 19:1-37 24th
Leviticus 20:1-27 25th
Leviticus 21:1–22:16 26th
Leviticus 22:17–23:8 27th
Leviticus 23:9-32 28th
Leviticus 23:33–24:23 29th
Leviticus 25:1-17 30th

MAY

Leviticus 25:18-46 1st
Leviticus 25:47–26:13 2nd
Leviticus 26:14-46 3rd
Leviticus 27:1-34 4th
Numbers 1:1-31 5th
Numbers 1:32-54 6th
Numbers 2:1-34 7th
Numbers 3:1-39 8th
Numbers 3:40–4:20 9th
Numbers 4:21-49 10th
Numbers 5:1-31 11th
Numbers 6:1-27 12th
Numbers 7:1-35 13th
Numbers 7:36-65 14th
Numbers 7:66–8:4 15th
Numbers 8:5-26 16th
Numbers 9:1-23 17th
Numbers 10:1-36 18th
Numbers 11:1-30 19th
Numbers 11:31–13:16 20th
Numbers 13:17–14:10 21st
Numbers 14:11-38 22nd
Numbers 14:39–15:21 23rd
Numbers 15:22-41 24th
Numbers 16:1-24 25th
Numbers 16:25-50 26th
Numbers 17:1–18:7 27th
Numbers 18:8-32 28th
Numbers 19:1-22 29th
Numbers 20:1-29 30th
Numbers 21:1-20 31st

JUNE

Numbers 21:21-35 1st
Numbers 22:1-21 2nd
Numbers 22:22–23:12 3rd
Numbers 23:13–24:14 4th
Numbers 24:15–25:18 5th
Numbers 26:1-37 6th
Numbers 26:38-65 7th
Numbers 27:1–28:8 8th
Numbers 28:9–29:6 9th
Numbers 29:7-40 10th
Numbers 30:1–31:24 11th
Numbers 31:25-54 12th
Numbers 32:1-42 13th
Numbers 33:1-49 14th
Numbers 33:50–34:29 15th
Numbers 35:1-34 16th
Numbers 36:1-13 17th
Deuteronomy 1:1-25 18th
Deuteronomy 1:26-46 19th
Deuteronomy 2:1-23 20th
Deuteronomy 2:24–3:20 21st

Deuteronomy 3:21–4:14 22nd
Deuteronomy 4:15-49 23rd
Deuteronomy 5:1-33 24th
Deuteronomy 6:1-25 25th
Deuteronomy 7:1-26 26th
Deuteronomy 8:1–9:6 27th
Deuteronomy 9:7–10:11 28th
Deuteronomy 10:12–11:7 29th
Deuteronomy 11:8-32 30th

JULY

Deuteronomy 12:1-32 1st
Deuteronomy 13:1–14:21 2nd
Deuteronomy 14:22–15:23 3rd
Deuteronomy 16:1–17:7 4th
Deuteronomy 17:8–18:22 5th
Deuteronomy 19:1-21 6th
Deuteronomy 20:1–21:14 7th
Deuteronomy 21:15–22:21 8th
Deuteronomy 22:22–23:25 9th
Deuteronomy 24:1–25:4 10th
Deuteronomy 25:5–26:15 11th
Deuteronomy 26:16–27:26 12th
Deuteronomy 28:1-35 13th
Deuteronomy 28:36-68 14th
Deuteronomy 29:1-29 15th
Deuteronomy 30:1–31:8 16th
Deuteronomy 31:9-29 17th
Deuteronomy 31:30–32:25 18th
Deuteronomy 32:26-52 19th
Deuteronomy 33:1-19 20th
Deuteronomy 33:20–34:12 21st
Joshua 1:1-18 22nd
Joshua 2:1-24 23rd
Joshua 3:1-17 24th
Joshua 4:1-5:9 25th
Joshua 5:10–6:21 26th
Joshua 6:22–7:15 27th
Joshua 7:16–8:23 28th
Joshua 8:24–9:15 29th
Joshua 9:16–10:15 30th
Joshua 10:16-43 31st

AUGUST

Joshua 11:1-23 1st
Joshua 12:1–13:7 2nd
Joshua 13:8–14:5 3rd
Joshua 14:6–15:19 4th
Joshua 15:20–16:4 5th
Joshua 16:5–17:18 6th
Joshua 18:1-28 7th
Joshua 19:1-39 8th
Joshua 19:40–21:8 9th
Joshua 21:9-42 10th
Joshua 21:43–22:20 11th
Joshua 22:21–23:16 12th
Joshua 24:1-33 13th
Judges 1:1-36 14th
Judges 2:1-23 15th
Judges 3:1-31 16th
Judges 4:1–5:5 17th
Judges 5:6-31 18th
Judges 6:1-24 19th
Judges 6:25-40 20th
Judges 7:1-25 21st
Judges 8:1-35 22nd
Judges 9:1-21 23rd
Judges 9:22-57 24th
Judges 10:1–11:11 25th
Judges 11:12-40 26th
Judges 12:1-15 27th
Judges 13:1-25 28th
Judges 14:1-20 29th
Judges 15:1-20 30th
Judges 16:1-22 31st

SEPTEMBER

Judges 16:23–17:13 1st
Judges 18:1-31 2nd
Judges 19:1-30 3rd
Judges 20:1-18 4th
Judges 20:19-48 5th
Judges 21:1-25 6th
Ruth 1:1-22 7th
Ruth 2:1-23 8th
Ruth 3:1-18 9th
Ruth 4:1-22 10th
1 Samuel 1:1-28 11th
1 Samuel 2:1-26 12th
1 Samuel 2:27–3:18 13th
1 Samuel 3:19–5:5 14th
1 Samuel 5:6–6:18 15th
1 Samuel 6:19–8:9 16th
1 Samuel 8:10–9:17 17th
1 Samuel 9:18–10:16 18th
1 Samuel 10:17–11:15 19th
1 Samuel 12:1-25 20th
1 Samuel 13:1-22 21st
1 Samuel 13:23–14:30 22nd
1 Samuel 14:31-52 23rd
1 Samuel 15:1-35 24th
1 Samuel 16:1-23 25th
1 Samuel 17:1-37 26th
1 Samuel 17:38-58 27th
1 Samuel 18:1-30 28th
1 Samuel 19:1-24 29th
1 Samuel 20:1-34 30th

OCTOBER

1 Samuel 20:35–22:5 1st
1 Samuel 22:6–23:6 2nd
1 Samuel 23:7-29 3rd
1 Samuel 24:1–25:13 4th
1 Samuel 25:14-44 5th
1 Samuel 26:1–27:4 6th
1 Samuel 27:5–28:25 7th
1 Samuel 29:1–30:20 8th
1 Samuel 30:21–31:13 9th
2 Samuel 1:1-27 10th
2 Samuel 2:1–3:5 11th
2 Samuel 3:6-39 12th
2 Samuel 4:1–5:16 13th
2 Samuel 5:17–6:23 14th
2 Samuel 7:1-29 15th
2 Samuel 8:1–9:13 16th
2 Samuel 10:1-19 17th
2 Samuel 11:1-27 18th
2 Samuel 12:1-31 19th
2 Samuel 13:1-27 20th
2 Samuel 13:28–14:17 21st
2 Samuel 14:18–15:12 22nd
2 Samuel 15:13–16:4 23rd
2 Samuel 16:5-22 24th
2 Samuel 16:23–17:29 25th
2 Samuel 18:1-27 26th
2 Samuel 18:28–19:23 27th
2 Samuel 19:24–20:10 28th
2 Samuel 20:11–21:14 29th
2 Samuel 21:15–22:24 30th
2 Samuel 22:25–23:7 31st

NOVEMBER

2 Samuel 23:8-39 1st
2 Samuel 24:1-25 2nd
1 Kings 1:1-31 3rd
1 Kings 1:32–2:12 4th
1 Kings 2:13-38 5th
1 Kings 2:39–3:28 6th
1 Kings 4:1-34 7th
1 Kings 5:1-18 8th
1 Kings 6:1-38 9th
1 Kings 7:1-26 10th
1 Kings 7:27-51 11th
1 Kings 8:1-26 12th
1 Kings 8:27-43 13th
1 Kings 8:44-66 14th
1 Kings 9:1-28 15th
1 Kings 10:1-29 16th
1 Kings 11:1-25 17th
1 Kings 11:26–12:11 18th
1 Kings 12:12-33 19th
1 Kings 13:1-34 20th
1 Kings 14:1-31 21st
1 Kings 15:1-32 22nd
1 Kings 15:33–16:28 23rd
1 Kings 16:29–17:24 24th
1 Kings 18:1-35 25th
1 Kings 18:36–19:18 26th
1 Kings 19:19–20:28 27th
1 Kings 20:29–21:10 28th
1 Kings 21:11-29 29th
1 Kings 22:1-28 30th

DECEMBER

1 Kings 22:29-53 1st
2 Kings 1:1-18 2nd
2 Kings 2:1-25 3rd
2 Kings 3:1–4:7 4th
2 Kings 4:8-44 5th
2 Kings 5:1-27 6th
2 Kings 6:1-33 7th
2 Kings 7:1-20 8th
2 Kings 8:1-29 9th
2 Kings 9:1-29 10th
2 Kings 9:30–10:17 11th
2 Kings 10:18-36 12th
2 Kings 11:1-20 13th
2 Kings 11:21–12:21 14th
2 Kings 13:1-25 15th
2 Kings 14:1-29 16th
2 Kings 15:1-31 17th
2 Kings 15:32–17:6 18th
2 Kings 17:7-33 19th
2 Kings 17:34–18:18 20th
2 Kings 18:19-37 21st
2 Kings 19:1-28 22nd
2 Kings 19:29–20:21 23rd
2 Kings 21:1-26 24th
2 Kings 22:1–23:3 25th
2 Kings 23:4-27 26th
2 Kings 23:28–24:20 27th
2 Kings 25:1-30 28th
1 Chronicles 1:1-31 29th
1 Chronicles 1:32–2:9 30th
1 Chronicles 2:10-41 31st

YEAR TWO

JANUARY

1 Chronicles 2:42–3:16 1st
1 Chronicles 3:17–4:23 2nd
1 Chronicles 4:24–5:10 3rd
1 Chronicles 5:11–6:15 4th
1 Chronicles 6:16-53 5th
1 Chronicles 6:54-81 6th
1 Chronicles 7:1-29 7th
1 Chronicles 7:30–8:40 8th
1 Chronicles 9:1-34 9th
1 Chronicles 9:35–11:9 10th
1 Chronicles 11:10-47 11th
1 Chronicles 12:1-37 12th
1 Chronicles 12:38–14:17 13th
1 Chronicles 15:1–16:6 14th
1 Chronicles 16:7-43 15th
1 Chronicles 17:1-27 16th
1 Chronicles 18:1-17 17th
1 Chronicles 19:1–20:8 18th
1 Chronicles 21:1–22:1 19th
1 Chronicles 22:2–23:14 20th
1 Chronicles 23:15–24:19 21st
1 Chronicles 24:20–25:31 22nd
1 Chronicles 26:1-32 23rd
1 Chronicles 27:1-34 24th
1 Chronicles 28:1-21 25th
1 Chronicles 29:1-30 26th
2 Chronicles 1:1–2:10 27th
2 Chronicles 2:11–3:17 28th
2 Chronicles 4:1–5:1 29th
2 Chronicles 5:2–6:11 30th
2 Chronicles 6:12-31 31st

FEBRUARY

2 Chronicles 6:32–7:11 1st
2 Chronicles 7:12–8:18 2nd
2 Chronicles 9:1-31 3rd
2 Chronicles 10:1–11:4 4th
2 Chronicles 11:5–12:16 5th
2 Chronicles 13:1–14:1 6th
2 Chronicles 14:2–15:19 7th
2 Chronicles 16:1–17:19 8th
2 Chronicles 18:1-27 9th
2 Chronicles 18:28–19:11 10th
2 Chronicles 20:1-30 11th
2 Chronicles 20:31–21:20 12th
2 Chronicles 22:1–23:15 13th
2 Chronicles 23:16–24:22 14th
2 Chronicles 24:23–25:16 15th
2 Chronicles 25:17–26:10 16th
2 Chronicles 26:11–28:8 17th
2 Chronicles 28:9–29:11 18th
2 Chronicles 29:12-36 19th
2 Chronicles 30:1–31:1 20th
2 Chronicles 31:2-21 21st
2 Chronicles 32:1-31 22nd
2 Chronicles 32:32–33:25 23rd
2 Chronicles 34:1-28 24th
2 Chronicles 34:29–35:19 25th
2 Chronicles 35:20–36:8 26th
2 Chronicles 36:9-23 27th
Ezra 1:1-2:42 28th

MARCH

Ezra 2:43–3:7 1st
Ezra 3:8–4:16 2nd
Ezra 4:17–5:17 3rd
Ezra 6:1-22 4th
Ezra 7:1-28 5th
Ezra 8:1-30 6th
Ezra 8:31–9:15 7th
Ezra 10:1-17 8th
Ezra 10:18-44 9th
Nehemiah 1:1–2:10 10th
Nehemiah 2:11–3:19 11th
Nehemiah 3:20–4:14 12th
Nehemiah 4:15–5:19 13th
Nehemiah 6:1-7:3 14th
Nehemiah 7:4-60 15th
Nehemiah 7:61–8:12 16th
Nehemiah 8:13–9:18 17th
Nehemiah 9:19-37 18th
Nehemiah 9:38–10:39 19th
Nehemiah 11:1-36 20th
Nehemiah 12:1-26 21st
Nehemiah 12:27–13:5 22nd
Nehemiah 13:6-31 23rd
Esther 1:1-22 24th
Esther 2:1-23 25th
Esther 3:1–4:17 26th
Esther 5:1–6:14 27th
Esther 7:1–8:17 28th
Esther 9:1-17 29th
Esther 9:18–10:3 30th
Job 1:1–2:10 31st

APRIL

Job 2:11–4:11 1st
Job 4:12–5:27 2nd
Job 6:1-30 3rd
Job 7:1-21 4th
Job 8:1-22 5th
Job 9:1-35 6th
Job 10:1-22 7th
Job 11:1-20 8th
Job 12:1–13:19 9th
Job 13:20–14:22 10th
Job 15:1-35 11th
Job 16:1–17:16 12th
Job 18:1–19:20 13th
Job 19:21–20:29 14th
Job 21:1-34 15th
Job 22:1-30 16th
Job 23:1-17 17th
Job 24:1–25:6 18th
Job 26:1–27:23 19th
Job 28:1-28 20th
Job 29:1-25 21st
Job 30:1-31 22nd
Job 31:1-40 23rd
Job 32:1-22 24th
Job 33:1-33 25th
Job 34:1-37 26th
Job 35:1-16 27th
Job 36:1-33 28th
Job 37:1-24 29th
Job 38:1-41 30th

MAY

Job 39:1-30 1st
Job 40:1-24 2nd
Job 41:1-34 3rd
Job 42:1-17 4th
Psalms 1:1–3:8 5th
Psalms 4:1–6:10 6th
Psalms 7:1–8:9 7th
Psalm 9:1-20 8th
Psalm 10:1-18 9th
Psalms 11:1–13:6 10th
Psalms 14:1–16:11 11th
Psalms 17:1–18:15 12th
Psalm 18:16-50 13th
Psalms 19:1–21:7 14th
Psalms 21:8–22:26 15th
Psalms 22:27–24:10 16th
Psalm 25:1-22 17th
Psalms 26:1–27:14 18th
Psalms 28:1–30:12 19th
Psalm 31:1-24 20th
Psalms 32:1–33:22 21st
Psalm 34:1-22 22nd
Psalm 35:1-28 23rd
Psalms 36:1–37:20 24th
Psalms 37:21–38:12 25th
Psalms 38:13–40:10 26th
Psalms 40:11–42:4 27th
Psalms 42:5–44:16 28th
Psalms 44:17–46:3 29th
Psalms 46:4–48:14 30th
Psalm 49:1-20 31st

JUNE

Psalm 50:1-23 1st
Psalm 51:1-19 2nd
Psalms 52:1–54:7 3rd
Psalms 55:1–56:13 4th
Psalms 57:1–58:11 5th
Psalms 59:1–60:12 6th
Psalms 61:1–63:11 7th
Psalms 64:1–65:13 8th
Psalms 66:1–67:7 9th
Psalm 68:1-27 10th
Psalms 68:28–69:21 11th
Psalms 69:22–71:16 12th
Psalms 71:17–72:20 13th
Psalm 73:1-28 14th
Psalms 74:1–75:10 15th
Psalms 76:1–77:20 16th
Psalm 78:1-39 17th
Psalm 78:40-72 18th
Psalms 79:1–80:19 19th
Psalms 81:1–82:8 20th
Psalms 83:1–84:12 21st
Psalms 85:1–86:17 22nd
Psalms 87:1–88:18 23rd
Psalm 89:1-18 24th
Psalm 89:19-52 25th
Psalms 90:1–91:16 26th
Psalms 92:1–94:23 27th
Psalms 95:1–97:12 28th
Psalms 98:1–99:9 29th
Psalms 100:1–102:17 30th

JULY

Psalms 102:18–103:22 1st
Psalm 104:1-35 2nd
Psalm 105:1-45 3rd
Psalm 106:1-39 4th
Psalms 106:40–107:22 5th
Psalms 107:23–108:13 6th
Psalm 109:1-31 7th
Psalms 110:1–112:10 8th
Psalms 113:1–115:18 9th
Psalms 116:1–117:2 10th
Psalm 118:1-29 11th
Psalm 119:1-48 12th
Psalm 119:49-88 13th
Psalm 119:89-136 14th
Psalms 119:137–120:7 15th
Psalms 121:1–124:8 16th
Psalms 125:1–129:8 17th
Psalms 130:1–134:3 18th
Psalms 135:1–136:26 19th
Psalms 137:1–138:8 20th
Psalm 139:1-24 21st
Psalms 140:1–141:10 22nd
Psalms 142:1–143:12 23rd
Psalm 144:1-15 24th
Psalm 145:1-21 25th
Psalms 146:1–147:20 26th
Psalms 148:1–150:6 27th
Proverbs 1:1-33 28th
Proverbs 2:1-22 29th
Proverbs 3:1-35 30th
Proverbs 4:1-27 31st

AUGUST

Proverbs 5:1–6:19 1st
Proverbs 6:20–7:27 2nd
Proverbs 8:1-36 3rd
Proverbs 9:1-18 4th
Proverbs 10:1-32 5th
Proverbs 11:1-31 6th
Proverbs 12:1-28 7th
Proverbs 13:1-25 8th
Proverbs 14:1-35 9th
Proverbs 15:1-33 10th
Proverbs 16:1-33 11th
Proverbs 17:1-28 12th
Proverbs 18:1-24 13th
Proverbs 19:1-29 14th
Proverbs 20:1-30 15th
Proverbs 21:1-31 16th
Proverbs 22:1-29 17th
Proverbs 23:1-35 18th
Proverbs 24:1-34 19th
Proverbs 25:1-28 20th
Proverbs 26:1-28 21st
Proverbs 27:1-27 22nd
Proverbs 28:1-28 23rd
Proverbs 29:1-27 24th
Proverbs 30:1-33 25th
Proverbs 31:1-31 26th
Ecclesiastes 1:1-18 27th
Ecclesiastes 2:1-26 28th
Ecclesiastes 3:1-22 29th
Ecclesiastes 4:1-16 30th
Ecclesiastes 5:1–6:12 31st

SEPTEMBER

Ecclesiastes 7:1-29 1st
Ecclesiastes 8:1–9:10 2nd
Ecclesiastes 9:11–10:20 3rd
Ecclesiastes 11:1–12:14 4th
Song of Songs 1:1–2:7 5th
Song of Songs 2:8–3:11 6th
Song of Songs 4:1–5:2 7th
Song of Songs 5:3–6:13 8th
Song of Songs 7:1–8:14 9th
Isaiah 1:1-20 10th
Isaiah 1:21–2:11 11th
Isaiah 2:12–3:15 12th
Isaiah 3:16–5:7 13th
Isaiah 5:8-30 14th
Isaiah 6:1–7:9 15th
Isaiah 7:10–8:10 16th
Isaiah 8:11–9:7 17th
Isaiah 9:8–10:4 18th
Isaiah 10:5-26 19th
Isaiah 10:27–11:16 20th
Isaiah 12:1–13:22 21st
Isaiah 14:1-27 22nd
Isaiah 14:28–15:9 23rd
Isaiah 16:1-14 24th
Isaiah 17:1–18:7 25th
Isaiah 19:1–20:6 26th
Isaiah 21:1-17 27th
Isaiah 22:1-25 28th
Isaiah 23:1-18 29th
Isaiah 24:1-23 30th

OCTOBER

Isaiah 25:1-12 1st
Isaiah 26:1-21 2nd
Isaiah 27:1-13 3rd
Isaiah 28:1-22 4th
Isaiah 28:23–29:12 5th
Isaiah 29:13-30:7 6th
Isaiah 30:8-33 7th
Isaiah 31:1–32:20 8th
Isaiah 33:1-24 9th
Isaiah 34:1–35:3 10th
Isaiah 35:4–36:22 11th
Isaiah 37:1-20 12th
Isaiah 37:21-38 13th
Isaiah 38:1–39:8 14th
Isaiah 40:1-26 15th
Isaiah 40:27–41:16 16th
Isaiah 41:17–42:9 17th
Isaiah 42:10–43:7 18th
Isaiah 43:8–44:5 19th
Isaiah 44:6-23 20th
Isaiah 44:24–45:17 21st
Isaiah 45:18–46:13 22nd
Isaiah 47:1-15 23rd
Isaiah 48:1-22 24th
Isaiah 49:1-21 25th
Isaiah 49:22–51:3 26th
Isaiah 51:4-23 27th
Isaiah 52:1-15 28th
Isaiah 53:1-12 29th
Isaiah 54:1–55:5 30th
Isaiah 55:6–56:12 31st

NOVEMBER

Isaiah 57:1-21 1st
Isaiah 58:1-14 2nd
Isaiah 59:1-21 3rd
Isaiah 60:1-22 4th
Isaiah 61:1–62:12 5th
Isaiah 63:1-19 6th
Isaiah 64:1–65:7 7th
Isaiah 65:8–66:4 8th
Isaiah 66:5-24 9th
Jeremiah 1:1–2:3 10th
Jeremiah 2:4-25 11th
Jeremiah 2:26–3:13 12th
Jeremiah 3:14-4:4 13th
Jeremiah 4:5-31 14th
Jeremiah 5:1-19 15th
Jeremiah 5:20–6:12 16th
Jeremiah 6:13-30 17th
Jeremiah 7:1-34 18th
Jeremiah 8:1-22 19th
Jeremiah 9:1-22 20th
Jeremiah 9:23–10:18 21st
Jeremiah 10:19–11:23 22nd
Jeremiah 12:1-17 23rd
Jeremiah 13:1-27 24th
Jeremiah 14:1-22 25th
Jeremiah 15:1-21 26th
Jeremiah 16:1-21 27th
Jeremiah 17:1-27 28th
Jeremiah 18:1-23 29th
Jeremiah 19:1–20:6 30th

DECEMBER

Jeremiah 20:7–21:14 1st
Jeremiah 22:1-23 2nd
Jeremiah 22:24–23:17 3rd
Jeremiah 23:18–24:10 4th
Jeremiah 25:1-31 5th
Jeremiah 25:32–26:24 6th
Jeremiah 27:1-22 7th
Jeremiah 28:1-17 8th
Jeremiah 29:1-32 9th
Jeremiah 30:1-24 10th
Jeremiah 31:1-22 11th
Jeremiah 31:23-40 12th
Jeremiah 32:1-25 13th
Jeremiah 32:26–33:9 14th
Jeremiah 33:10–34:7 15th
Jeremiah 34:8–35:19 16th
Jeremiah 36:1-32 17th
Jeremiah 37:1–38:13 18th
Jeremiah 38:14–39:18 19th
Jeremiah 40:1–41:10 20th
Jeremiah 41:11–42:22 21st
Jeremiah 43:1–44:6 22nd
Jeremiah 44:7-30 23rd
Jeremiah 45:1–46:19 24th
Jeremiah 46:20–47:7 25th
Jeremiah 48:1-25 26th
Jeremiah 48:26-47 27th
Jeremiah 49:1-22 28th
Jeremiah 49:23-39 29th
Jeremiah 50:1-16 30th
Jeremiah 50:17-32 31st

YEAR THREE

JANUARY

Jeremiah 50:33–51:10	1st
Jeremiah 51:11-32	2nd
Jeremiah 51:33-48	3rd
Jeremiah 51:49-64	4th
Jeremiah 52:1-34	5th
Lamentations 1:1-15	6th
Lamentations 1:16–2:9	7th
Lamentations 2:10–3:9	8th
Lamentations 3:10-57	9th
Lamentations 3:58–4:15	10th
Lamentations 4:16–5:22	11th
Ezekiel 1:1-28	12th
Ezekiel 2:1–3:27	13th
Ezekiel 4:1–5:17	14th
Ezekiel 6:1–7:9	15th
Ezekiel 7:10-27	16th
Ezekiel 8:1–9:11	17th
Ezekiel 10:1–11:15	18th
Ezekiel 11:16–12:28	19th
Ezekiel 13:1–14:11	20th
Ezekiel 14:12–16:14	21st
Ezekiel 16:15-43	22nd
Ezekiel 16:44-63	23rd
Ezekiel 17:1-24	24th
Ezekiel 18:1-32	25th
Ezekiel 19:1-14	26th
Ezekiel 20:1-31	27th
Ezekiel 20:32–21:13	28th
Ezekiel 21:14-32	29th
Ezekiel 22:1-31	30th
Ezekiel 23:1-34	31st

FEBRUARY

Ezekiel 23:35–24:14	1st
Ezekiel 24:15–25:17	2nd
Ezekiel 26:1-21	3rd
Ezekiel 27:1-27	4th
Ezekiel 27:28–28:10	5th
Ezekiel 28:11-26	6th
Ezekiel 29:1-21	7th
Ezekiel 30:1-26	8th
Ezekiel 31:1–32:6	9th
Ezekiel 32:7-28	10th
Ezekiel 32:29–33:20	11th
Ezekiel 33:21–34:19	12th
Ezekiel 34:20–35:15	13th
Ezekiel 36:1-32	14th
Ezekiel 36:33–37:28	15th
Ezekiel 38:1-23	16th
Ezekiel 39:1–40:4	17th
Ezekiel 40:5-37	18th
Ezekiel 40:38–41:12	19th
Ezekiel 41:13–42:20	20th
Ezekiel 43:1-27	21st
Ezekiel 44:1-31	22nd
Ezekiel 45:1-25	23rd
Ezekiel 46:1-24	24th
Ezekiel 47:1-23	25th
Ezekiel 48:1-35	26th
Daniel 1:1–2:16	27th
Daniel 2:17-49	28th

MARCH

Daniel 3:1-30	1st
Daniel 4:1-27	2nd
Daniel 4:28–5:16	3rd
Daniel 5:17–6:18	4th
Daniel 6:19–7:14	5th
Daniel 7:15–8:22	6th
Daniel 8:23–9:19	7th
Daniel 9:20–11:4	8th
Daniel 11:5-35	9th
Daniel 11:36–12:13	10th
Hosea 1:1–2:13	11th
Hosea 2:14–4:11	12th
Hosea 4:12–5:15	13th
Hosea 6:1–7:16	14th
Hosea 8:1–9:9	15th
Hosea 9:10–10:15	16th
Hosea 11:1–12:14	17th
Hosea 13:1–14:9	18th
Joel 1:1-20	19th
Joel 2:1-17	20th
Joel 2:18-32	21st
Joel 3:1-21	22nd
Amos 1:1–2:5	23rd
Amos 2:6–3:15	24th
Amos 4:1-13	25th
Amos 5:1-27	26th
Amos 6:1–7:9	27th
Amos 7:10–8:14	28th
Amos 9:1-15	29th
Obadiah	30th
Jonah 1:1–2:10	31st

APRIL

Jonah 3:1–4:11	1st
Micah 1:1–2:5	2nd
Micah 2:6–4:2	3rd
Micah 4:3–5:9	4th
Micah 5:10–6:16	5th
Micah 7:1-20	6th
Nahum 1:1–2:10	7th
Micah 2:11–3:19	8th
Habakkuk 1:1-17	9th
Habakkuk 2:1-20	10th
Habakkuk 3:1-19	11th
Zephaniah 1:1-18	12th
Zephaniah 2:1-15	13th
Zephaniah 3:1-20	14th
Haggai 1:1-15	15th
Haggai 2:1-23	16th
Zechariah 1:1–2:13	17th
Zechariah 3:1–5:11	18th
Zechariah 6:1–7:14	19th
Zechariah 8:1–9:8	20th
Zechariah 9:9–10:12	21st
Zechariah 11:1–12:14	22nd
Zechariah 13:1–14:21	23rd
Malachi 1:1-14	24th
Malachi 2:1–3:6	25th
Malachi 3:7–4:6	26th
Matthew 1:1–2:6	27th
Matthew 2:7–3:17	28th
Matthew 4:1–5:12	29th
Matthew 5:13–6:4	30th

MAY

Matthew 6:5–7:12	1st
Matthew 7:13–8:27	2nd
Matthew 8:28–9:34	3rd
Matthew 9:35–10:31	4th
Matthew 10:32–11:30	5th
Matthew 12:1-37	6th
Matthew 12:38–13:23	7th
Matthew 13:24-58	8th
Matthew 14:1-36	9th
Matthew 15:1-39	10th
Matthew 16:1–17:13	11th
Matthew 17:14–18:20	12th
Matthew 18:21–19:15	13th
Matthew 19:16–20:19	14th
Matthew 20:20–21:22	15th
Matthew 21:23-46	16th
Matthew 22:1-46	17th
Matthew 23:1-39	18th
Matthew 24:1-35	19th
Matthew 24:36–25:30	20th
Matthew 25:31–26:25	21st
Matthew 26:26-68	22nd
Matthew 26:69–27:26	23rd
Matthew 27:27-56	24th
Matthew 27:57–28:20	25th
Mark 1:1-39	26th
Mark 1:40–2:22	27th
Mark 2:23–3:35	28th
Mark 4:1-41	29th
Mark 5:1-43	30th
Mark 6:1-29	31st

JUNE

Mark 6:30-56	1st
Mark 7:1-37	2nd
Mark 8:1–9:1	3rd
Mark 9:2-37	4th
Mark 9:38–10:22	5th
Mark 10:23–11:11	6th
Mark 11:12–12:17	7th
Mark 12:18-44	8th
Mark 13:1-37	9th
Mark 14:1-31	10th
Mark 14:32-72	11th
Mark 15:1-41	12th
Mark 15:42–16:20	13th
Luke 1:1-38	14th
Luke 1:39-80	15th
Luke 2:1-40	16th
Luke 2:41–3:20	17th
Luke 3:21–4:13	18th
Luke 4:14-44	19th
Luke 5:1-39	20th
Luke 6:1-36	21st
Luke 6:37–7:17	22nd
Luke 7:18-50	23rd
Luke 8:1-25	24th
Luke 8:26-56	25th
Luke 9:1-36	26th
Luke 9:37-62	27th
Luke 10:1-37	28th
Luke 10:38–11:28	29th
Luke 11:29-54	30th

JULY

Luke 12:1-34	1st
Luke 12:35-59	2nd
Luke 13:1-30	3rd
Luke 13:31–14:24	4th
Luke 14:25–15:32	5th
Luke 16:1-31	6th
Luke 17:1-37	7th
Luke 18:1-34	8th
Luke 18:35–19:27	9th
Luke 19:28-48	10th
Luke 20:1-26	11th
Luke 20:27–21:4	12th
Luke 21:5-38	13th
Luke 22:1-38	14th
Luke 22:39-65	15th
Luke 22:66–23:25	16th
Luke 23:26–24:12	17th
Luke 24:13-53	18th
John 1:1-34	19th
John 1:35–2:12	20th
John 2:13–3:21	21st
John 3:22–4:26	22nd
John 4:27-54	23rd
John 5:1-30	24th
John 5:31–6:24	25th
John 6:25-71	26th
John 7:1-44	27th
John 7:45–8:29	28th
John 8:30-59	29th
John 9:1-41	30th
John 10:1-42	31st

AUGUST

John 11:1-44	1st
John 11:45–12:19	2nd
John 12:20-50	3rd
John 13:1-38	4th
John 14:1-31	5th
John 15:1–16:4	6th
John 16:5-33	7th
John 17:1-26	8th
John 18:1-24	9th
John 18:25-40	10th
John 19:1-27	11th
John 19:28–20:18	12th
John 20:19–21:14	13th
John 21:15-25	14th
Acts 1:1–2:13	15th
Acts 2:14-40	16th
Acts 2:41–3:26	17th
Acts 4:1-31	18th
Acts 4:32–5:16	19th
Acts 5:17–6:7	20th
Acts 6:8–7:22	21st
Acts 7:23-53	22nd
Acts 7:54–8:25	23rd
Acts 8:26–9:9	24th
Acts 9:10-43	25th
Acts 10:1-43	26th
Acts 10:44–11:30	27th
Acts 12:1–13:3	28th
Acts 13:4-41	29th
Acts 13:42–14:7	30th
Acts 14:8-28	31st

SEPTEMBER

Acts 15:1-35	1st
Acts 15:36–16:15	2nd
Acts 16:16-40	3rd
Acts 17:1-34	4th
Acts 18:1–19:7	5th
Acts 19:8-41	6th
Acts 20:1-38	7th
Acts 21:1-36	8th
Acts 21:37–22:21	9th
Acts 22:22–23:10	10th
Acts 23:11-35	11th
Acts 24:1-27	12th
Acts 25:1-27	13th
Acts 26:1-32	14th
Acts 27:1-26	15th
Acts 27:27–28:10	16th
Acts 28:11-31	17th
Romans 1:1-32	18th
Romans 2:1-29	19th
Romans 3:1-31	20th
Romans 4:1-25	21st
Romans 5:1–6:14	22nd
Romans 6:15–7:25	23rd
Romans 8:1-39	24th
Romans 9:1-33	25th
Romans 10:1–11:10	26th
Romans 11:11-36	27th
Romans 12:1–13:14	28th
Romans 14:1–15:13	29th
Romans 15:14-33	30th

OCTOBER

Romans 16:1-27	1st
1 Corinthians 1:1–2:5	2nd
1 Corinthians 2:6–3:23	3rd
1 Corinthians 4:1–5:13	4th
1 Corinthians 6:1-20	5th
1 Corinthians 7:1-40	6th
1 Corinthians 8:1–9:27	7th
1 Corinthians 10:1–11:1	8th
1 Corinthians 11:2-34	9th
1 Corinthians 12:1–13:13	10th
1 Corinthians 14:1-40	11th
1 Corinthians 15:1-34	12th
1 Corinthians 15:35-58	13th
1 Corinthians 16:1-24	14th
2 Corinthians 1:1-2:4	15th
2 Corinthians 2:5–3:18	16th
2 Corinthians 4:1–5:15	17th
2 Corinthians 5:16–7:1	18th
2 Corinthians 7:2–8:15	19th
2 Corinthians 8:16–9:15	20th
2 Corinthians 10:1–11:15	21st
2 Corinthians 11:16–12:10	22nd
2 Corinthians 12:11–13:13	23rd
Galatians 1:1–2:10	24th
Galatians 2:11–3:26	25th
Galatians 3:27–4:31	26th
Galatians 5:1–6:18	27th
Ephesians 1:1–2:10	28th
Ephesians 2:11–3:21	29th
Ephesians 4:1–5:14	30th
Ephesians 5:15–6:24	31st

NOVEMBER

Philippians 1:1–2:11	1st
Philippians 2:12–3:11	2nd
Philippians 3:12–4:23	3rd
Colossians 1:1–2:3	4th
Colossians 2:4–3:17	5th
Colossians 3:18–4:18	6th
1 Thessalonians 1:1–2:16	7th
1 Thessalonians 2:17–4:12	8th
1 Thessalonians 4:13–5:28	9th
2 Thessalonians 1:1–2:12	10th
2 Thessalonians 2:13–3:18	11th
1 Timothy 1:1–2:15	12th
1 Timothy 3:1–5:2	13th
1 Timothy 5:3-25	14th
1 Timothy 6:1-21	15th
2 Timothy 1:1–2:13	16th
2 Timothy 2:14–3:9	17th
2 Timothy 3:10–4:22	18th
Titus 1:1–2:15	19th
Titus 3:1-15	20th
Philemon	21st
Hebrews 1:1–2:4	22nd
Hebrews 2:5–3:19	23rd
Hebrews 4:1–5:10	24th
Hebrews 5:11–7:10	25th
Hebrews 7:11–8:13	26th
Hebrews 9:1-28	27th
Hebrews 10:1-39	28th
Hebrews 11:1-40	29th
Hebrews 12:1-29	30th

DECEMBER

Hebrews 13:1-25	1st
James 1:1–2:13	2nd
James 2:14–3:18	3rd
James 4:1–5:20	4th
1 Peter 1:1-25	5th
1 Peter 2:1–3:7	6th
1 Peter 3:8–4:11	7th
1 Peter 4:12–5:14	8th
2 Peter 1:1-21	9th
2 Peter 2:1-22	10th
2 Peter 3:1-18	11th
1 John 1:1–2:17	12th
1 John 2:18–3:24	13th
1 John 4:1–5:21	14th
2 John–3 John	15th
Jude	16th
Revelation 1:1-2:7	17th
Revelation 2:8–3:6	18th
Revelation 3:7–4:11	19th
Revelation 5:1–6:11	20th
Revelation 6:12–8:6	21st
Revelation 8:7–9:21	22nd
Revelation 10:1–11:19	23rd
Revelation 12:1–13:10	24th
Revelation 13:11–14:20	25th
Revelation 15:1–16:16	26th
Revelation 16:17–17:18	27th
Revelation 18:1-24	28th
Revelation 19:1–20:6	29th
Revelation 20:7–21:27	30th
Revelation 22:1-21	31st

One-Year Bible Reading Plan

Compiled by the late Rev. Robert Murray M'Cheyne, M.A.

JANUARY

This is my beloved Son, with whom I am well-pleased. Listen to him (Mt 17:5)!

Genesis 1	Matthew 1	1st	Ezra 1	Acts 1
Genesis 2	Matthew 2	2nd	Ezra 2	Acts 2
Genesis 3	Matthew 3	3rd	Ezra 3	Acts 3
Genesis 4	Matthew 4	4th	Ezra 4	Acts 4
Genesis 5	Matthew 5	5th	Ezra 5	Acts 5
Genesis 6	Matthew 6	6th	Ezra 6	Acts 6
Genesis 7	Matthew 7	7th	Ezra 7	Acts 7
Genesis 8	Matthew 8	8th	Ezra 8	Acts 8
Genesis 9–10	Matthew 9	9th	Ezra 9	Acts 9
Genesis 11	Matthew 10	10th	Ezra 10	Acts 10
Genesis 12	Matthew 11	11th	Nehemiah 1	Acts 11
Genesis 13	Matthew 12	12th	Nehemiah 2	Acts 12
Genesis 14	Matthew 13	13th	Nehemiah 3	Acts 13
Genesis 15	Matthew 14	14th	Nehemiah 4	Acts 14
Genesis 16	Matthew 15	15th	Nehemiah 5	Acts 15
Genesis 17	Matthew 16	16th	Nehemiah 6	Acts 16
Genesis 18	Matthew 17	17th	Nehemiah 7	Acts 17
Genesis 19	Matthew 18	18th	Nehemiah 8	Acts 18
Genesis 20	Matthew 19	19th	Nehemiah 9	Acts 19
Genesis 21	Matthew 20	20th	Nehemiah 10	Acts 20
Genesis 22	Matthew 21	21st	Nehemiah 11	Acts 21
Genesis 23	Matthew 22	22nd	Nehemiah 12	Acts 22
Genesis 24	Matthew 23	23rd	Nehemiah 13	Acts 23
Genesis 25	Matthew 24	24th	Esther 1	Acts 24
Genesis 26	Matthew 25	25th	Esther 2	Acts 25
Genesis 27	Matthew 26	26th	Esther 3	Acts 26
Genesis 28	Matthew 27	27th	Esther 4	Acts 27
Genesis 29	Matthew 28	28th	Esther 5	Acts 28
Genesis 30	Mark 1	29th	Esther 6	Romans 1
Genesis 31	Mark 2	30th	Esther 7	Romans 2
Genesis 32	Mark 3	31st	Esther 8	Romans 3

FEBRUARY

I have treasured the words from his mouth more than my daily food (Jb 23:12).

Genesis 33	Mark 4	1st	Esther 9–10	Romans 4
Genesis 34	Mark 5	2nd	Job 1	Romans 5
Genesis 35–36	Mark 6	3rd	Job 2	Romans 6
Genesis 37	Mark 7	4th	Job 3	Romans 7
Genesis 38	Mark 8	5th	Job 4	Romans 8
Genesis 39	Mark 9	6th	Job 5	Romans 9
Genesis 40	Mark 10	7th	Job 6	Romans 10
Genesis 41	Mark 11	8th	Job 7	Romans 11
Genesis 42	Mark 12	9th	Job 8	Romans 12
Genesis 43	Mark 13	10th	Job 9	Romans 13
Genesis 44	Mark 14	11th	Job 10	Romans 14
Genesis 45	Mark 15	12th	Job 11	Romans 15
Genesis 46	Mark 16	13th	Job 12	Romans 16
Genesis 47	Luke 1:1-38	14th	Job 13	1 Corinthians 1
Genesis 48	Luke 1:39-80	15th	Job 14	1 Corinthians 2
Genesis 49	Luke 2	16th	Job 15	1 Corinthians 3
Genesis 50	Luke 3	17th	Job 16–17	1 Corinthians 4
Exodus 1	Luke 4	18th	Job 18	1 Corinthians 5
Exodus 2	Luke 5	19th	Job 19	1 Corinthians 6
Exodus 3	Luke 6	20th	Job 20	1 Corinthians 7
Exodus 4	Luke 7	21st	Job 21	1 Corinthians 8
Exodus 5	Luke 8	22nd	Job 22	1 Corinthians 9
Exodus 6	Luke 9	23rd	Job 23	1 Corinthians 10
Exodus 7	Luke 10	24th	Job 24	1 Corinthians 11

Exodus 8	Luke 11	25th	Job 25–26	1 Corinthians 12
Exodus 9	Luke 12	26th	Job 27	1 Corinthians 13
Exodus 10	Luke 13	27th	Job 28	1 Corinthians 14
Exodus 11–12:21	Luke 14	28th	Job 29	1 Corinthians 15

MARCH

But Mary was treasuring up all these things in her heart and meditating on them (Lk 2:19).

Exodus 12:22ff.	Luke 15	1st	Job 30	1 Corinthians 16
Exodus 13	Luke 16	2nd	Job 31	2 Corinthians 1
Exodus 14	Luke 17	3rd	Job 32	2 Corinthians 2
Exodus 15	Luke 18	4th	Job 33	2 Corinthians 3
Exodus 16	Luke 19	5th	Job 34	2 Corinthians 4
Exodus 17	Luke 20	6th	Job 35	2 Corinthians 5
Exodus 18	Luke 21	7th	Job 36	2 Corinthians 6
Exodus 19	Luke 22	8th	Job 37	2 Corinthians 7
Exodus 20	Luke 23	9th	Job 38	2 Corinthians 8
Exodus 21	Luke 24	10th	Job 39	2 Corinthians 9
Exodus 22	John 1	11th	Job 40	2 Corinthians 10
Exodus 23	John 2	12th	Job 41	2 Corinthians 11
Exodus 24	John 3	13th	Job 42	2 Corinthians 12
Exodus 25	John 4	14th	Proverbs 1	2 Corinthians 13
Exodus 26	John 5	15th	Proverbs 2	Galatians 1
Exodus 27	John 6	16th	Proverbs 3	Galatians 2
Exodus 28	John 7	17th	Proverbs 4	Galatians 3
Exodus 29	John 8	18th	Proverbs 5	Galatians 4
Exodus 30	John 9	19th	Proverbs 6	Galatians 5
Exodus 31	John 10	20th	Proverbs 7	Galatians 6
Exodus 32	John 11	21st	Proverbs 8	Ephesians 1
Exodus 33	John 12	22nd	Proverbs 9	Ephesians 2
Exodus 34	John 13	23rd	Proverbs 10	Ephesians 3
Exodus 35	John 14	24th	Proverbs 11	Ephesians 4
Exodus 36	John 15	25th	Proverbs 12	Ephesians 5
Exodus 37	John 16	26th	Proverbs 13	Ephesians 6
Exodus 38	John 17	27th	Proverbs 14	Philippians 1
Exodus 39	John 18	28th	Proverbs 15	Philippians 2
Exodus 40	John 19	29th	Proverbs 16	Philippians 3
Leviticus 1	John 20	30th	Proverbs 17	Philippians 4
Leviticus 2–3	John 21	31st	Proverbs 18	Colossians 1

APRIL

Send your light and your truth; let them lead me (Ps 43:3).

Leviticus 4	Psalms 1–2	1st	Proverbs 19	Colossians 2
Leviticus 5	Psalms 3–4	2nd	Proverbs 20	Colossians 3
Leviticus 6	Psalms 5–6	3rd	Proverbs 21	Colossians 4
Leviticus 7	Psalms 7–8	4th	Proverbs 22	1 Thessalonians 1
Leviticus 8	Psalm 9	5th	Proverbs 23	1 Thessalonians 2
Leviticus 9	Psalm 10	6th	Proverbs 24	1 Thessalonians 3
Leviticus 10	Psalms 11–12	7th	Proverbs 25	1 Thessalonians 4
Leviticus 11–12	Psalms 13–14	8th	Proverbs 26	1 Thessalonians 5
Leviticus 13	Psalms 15–16	9th	Proverbs 27	2 Thessalonians 1
Leviticus 14	Psalm 17	10th	Proverbs 28	2 Thessalonians 2
Leviticus 15	Psalm 18	11th	Proverbs 29	2 Thessalonians 3
Leviticus 16	Psalm 19	12th	Proverbs 30	1 Timothy 1
Leviticus 17	Psalms 20–21	13th	Proverbs 31	1 Timothy 2
Leviticus 18	Psalm 22	14th	Ecclesiastes 1	1 Timothy 3
Leviticus 19	Psalms 23–24	15th	Ecclesiastes 2	1 Timothy 4
Leviticus 20	Psalm 25	16th	Ecclesiastes 3	1 Timothy 5
Leviticus 21	Psalms 26–27	17th	Ecclesiastes 4	1 Timothy 6
Leviticus 22	Psalms 28–29	18th	Ecclesiastes 5	2 Timothy 1
Leviticus 23	Psalm 30	19th	Ecclesiastes 6	2 Timothy 2
Leviticus 24	Psalm 31	20th	Ecclesiastes 7	2 Timothy 3
Leviticus 25	Psalm 32	21st	Ecclesiastes 8	2 Timothy 4
Leviticus 26	Psalm 33	22nd	Ecclesiastes 9	Titus 1
Leviticus 27	Psalm 4	23rd	Ecclesiastes 10	Titus 2
Numbers 1	Psalm 35	24th	Ecclesiastes 11	Titus 3
Numbers 2	Psalm 36	25th	Ecclesiastes 12	Philemon

Numbers 3	Psalm 37	26th	Song of Songs 1	Hebrews 1
Numbers 4	Psalm 38	27th	Song of Songs 2	Hebrews 2
Numbers 5	Psalm 39	28th	Song of Songs 3	Hebrews 3
Numbers 6	Psalms 40–41	29th	Song of Songs 4	Hebrews 4
Numbers 7	Psalms 42–43	30th	Song of Songs 5	Hebrews 5

MAY

From infancy you have known the sacred Scriptures (2Tm 3:15).

Numbers 8	Psalm 44	1st	Song of Songs 6	Hebrews 6
Numbers 9	Psalm 45	2nd	Song of Songs 7	Hebrews 7
Numbers 10	Psalms 46–47	3rd	Song of Songs 8	Hebrews 8
Numbers 11	Psalm 48	4th	Isaiah 1	Hebrews 9
Numbers 12-13	Psalm 49	5th	Isaiah 2	Hebrews 10
Numbers 14	Psalm 50	6th	Isaiah 3–4	Hebrews 11
Numbers 15	Psalm 51	7th	Isaiah 5	Hebrews 12
Numbers 16	Psalms 52–54	8th	Isaiah 6	Hebrews 13
Numbers 17–18	Psalm 55	9th	Isaiah 7	James 1
Numbers 19	Psalms 56–57	10th	Isaiah 8–9:7	James 2
Numbers 20	Psalms 58–59	11th	Isaiah 9:8–10:4	James 3
Numbers 21	Psalms 60–61	12th	Isaiah 10:5ff.	James 4
Numbers 22	Psalms 62–63	13th	Isaiah 11–12	James 5
Numbers 23	Psalms 64–65	14th	Isaiah 13	1 Peter 1
Numbers 24	Psalms 66–67	15th	Isaiah 14	1 Peter 2
Numbers 25	Psalm 68	16th	Isaiah 15	1 Peter 3
Numbers 26	Psalm 69	17th	Isaiah 16	1 Peter 4
Numbers 27	Psalms 70–71	18th	Isaiah 17–18	1 Peter 5
Numbers 28	Psalm 72	19th	Isaiah 19–20	2 Peter 1
Numbers 29	Psalm 73	20th	Isaiah 21	2 Peter 2
Numbers 30	Psalm 74	21st	Isaiah 22	2 Peter 3
Numbers 31	Psalms 75–76	22nd	Isaiah 23	1 John 1
Numbers 32	Psalm 77	23rd	Isaiah 24	1 John 2
Numbers 33	Psalm 78:1-37	24th	Isaiah 25	1 John 3
Numbers 34	Psalm 78:38ff.	25th	Isaiah 26	1 John 4
Numbers 35	Psalm 79	26th	Isaiah 27	1 John 5
Numbers 36	Psalm 80	27th	Isaiah 28	2 John
Deuteronomy 1	Psalms 81–82	28th	Isaiah 29	3 John
Deuteronomy 2	Psalms 83–84	29th	Isaiah 30	Jude
Deuteronomy 3	Psalm 85	30th	Isaiah 31	Revelation 1
Deuteronomy 4	Psalms 86–87	31st	Isaiah 32	Revelation 2

JUNE

Blessed is the one who reads aloud the words of this prophecy, and blessed are those who hear the words of this prophecy and keep what is written in it (Rv 1:3).

Deuteronomy 5	Psalm 88	1st	Isaiah 33	Revelation 3
Deuteronomy 6	Psalm 89	2nd	Isaiah 34	Revelation 4
Deuteronomy 7	Psalm 90	3rd	Isaiah 35	Revelation 5
Deuteronomy 8	Psalm 91	4th	Isaiah 36	Revelation 6
Deuteronomy 9	Psalms 92–93	5th	Isaiah 37	Revelation 7
Deuteronomy 10	Psalm 94	6th	Isaiah 38	Revelation 8
Deuteronomy 11	Psalms 95–96	7th	Isaiah 39	Revelation 9
Deuteronomy 12	Psalms 97–98	8th	Isaiah 40	Revelation 10
Deuteronomy 13–14	Psalms 99–101	9th	Isaiah 41	Revelation 11
Deuteronomy 15	Psalm 102	10th	Isaiah 42	Revelation 12
Deuteronomy 16	Psalm 103	11th	Isaiah 43	Revelation 13
Deuteronomy 17	Psalm 104	12th	Isaiah 44	Revelation 14
Deuteronomy 18	Psalm 105	13th	Isaiah 45	Revelation 15
Deuteronomy 19	Psalm 106	14th	Isaiah 46	Revelation 16
Deuteronomy 20	Psalm 107	15th	Isaiah 47	Revelation 17
Deuteronomy 21	Psalms 108–109	16th	Isaiah 48	Revelation 18
Deuteronomy 22	Psalms 110–111	17th	Isaiah 49	Revelation 19
Deuteronomy 23	Psalms 112–113	18th	Isaiah 50	Revelation 20
Deuteronomy 24	Psalms 114–115	19th	Isaiah 51	Revelation 21
Deuteronomy 25	Psalm 116	20th	Isaiah 52	Revelation 22
Deuteronomy 26	Psalms 117–118	21st	Isaiah 53	Matthew 1
Deuteronomy 27–28:19	Psalm 119:1-24	22nd	Isaiah 54	Matthew 2
Deuteronomy 28:20ff.	Psalm 119:25-48	23rd	Isaiah 55	Matthew 3

Deuteronomy 29	Psalm 119:49-72	24th	Isaiah 56	Matthew 4
Deuteronomy 30	Psalm 119:73-96	25th	Isaiah 57	Matthew 5
Deuteronomy 31	Psalm 119:97-120	26th	Isaiah 58	Matthew 6
Deuteronomy 32	Psalm 119:121-144	27th	Isaiah 59	Matthew 7
Deuteronomy 33–34	Psalm 119:145-176	28th	Isaiah 60	Matthew 8
Joshua 1	Psalms 120–122	29th	Isaiah 61	Matthew 9
Joshua 2	Psalms 123–125	30th	Isaiah 62	Matthew 10

JULY

They received the word with eagerness and examined the Scriptures daily to see if these things were so (Ac 17:11).

Joshua 3	Psalms 126–128	1st	Isaiah 63	Matthew 11
Joshua 4	Psalms 129–131	2nd	Isaiah 64	Matthew 12
Joshua 5–6:5	Psalms 132–134	3rd	Isaiah 65	Matthew 13
Joshua 6:6ff.	Psalms 135–136	4th	Isaiah 66	Matthew 14
Joshua 7	Psalms 137–138	5th	Jeremiah 1	Matthew 15
Joshua 8	Psalm 139	6th	Jeremiah 2	Matthew 16
Joshua 9	Psalms 140–141	7th	Jeremiah 3	Matthew 17
Joshua 10	Psalms 142–143	8th	Jeremiah 4	Matthew 18
Joshua 11	Psalm 144	9th	Jeremiah 5	Matthew 19
Joshua 12–13	Psalm 145	10th	Jeremiah 6	Matthew 20
Joshua 14–15	Psalms 146–147	11th	Jeremiah 7	Matthew 21
Joshua 16–17	Psalm 148	12th	Jeremiah 8	Matthew 22
Joshua 18–19	Psalms 149–150	13th	Jeremiah 9	Matthew 23
Joshua 20–21	Acts 1	14th	Jeremiah 10	Matthew 24
Joshua 22	Acts 2	15th	Jeremiah 11	Matthew 25
Joshua 23	Acts 3	16th	Jeremiah 12	Matthew 26
Joshua 24	Acts 4	17th	Jeremiah 13	Matthew 27
Judges 1	Acts 5	18th	Jeremiah 14	Matthew 28
Judges 2	Acts 6	19th	Jeremiah 15	Mark 1
Judges 3	Acts 7	20th	Jeremiah 16	Mark 2
Judges 4	Acts 8	21st	Jeremiah 17	Mark 3
Judges 5	Acts 9	22nd	Jeremiah 18	Mark 4
Judges 6	Acts 10	23rd	Jeremiah 19	Mark 5
Judges 7	Acts 11	24th	Jeremiah 20	Mark 6
Judges 8	Acts 12	25th	Jeremiah 21	Mark 7
Judges 9	Acts 13	26th	Jeremiah 22	Mark 8
Judges 10–11:11	Acts 14	27th	Jeremiah 23	Mark 9
Judges 11:12ff.	Acts 15	28th	Jeremiah 24	Mark 10
Judges 12	Acts 16	29th	Jeremiah 25	Mark 11
Judges 13	Acts 17	30th	Jeremiah 26	Mark 12
Judges 14	Acts 18	31st	Jeremiah 27	Mark 13

AUGUST

"Speak LORD, for your servant is listening" (1Sm 3:10).

Judges 15	Acts 19	1st	Jeremiah 28	Mark 14
Judges 16	Acts 20	2nd	Jeremiah 29	Mark 15
Judges 17	Acts 21	3rd	Jeremiah 30–31	Mark 16
Judges 18	Acts 22	4th	Jeremiah 32	Psalms 1–2
Judges 19	Acts 23	5th	Jeremiah 33	Psalms 3–4
Judges 20	Acts 24	6th	Jeremiah 34	Psalms 5–6
Judges 21	Acts 25	7th	Jeremiah 35	Psalms 7–8
Ruth 1	Acts 26	8th	Jeremiah 36	Psalm 9
Ruth 2	Acts 27	9th	Jeremiah 37	Psalm 10
Ruth 3–4	Acts 28	10th	Jeremiah 38	Psalms 11–12
1 Samuel 1	Romans 1	11th	Jeremiah 39	Psalms 13–14
1 Samuel 2	Romans 2	12th	Jeremiah 40	Psalms 15–16
1 Samuel 3	Romans 3	13th	Jeremiah 41	Psalm 17
1 Samuel 4	Romans 4	14th	Jeremiah 42	Psalm 18
1 Samuel 5–6	Romans 5	15th	Jeremiah 43	Psalm 19
1 Samuel 7–8	Romans 6	16th	Jeremiah 44	Psalms 20–21
1 Samuel 9	Romans 7	17th	Jeremiah 46	Psalm 22
1 Samuel 10	Romans 8	18th	Jeremiah 47	Psalms 23–24
1 Samuel 11	Romans 9	19th	Jeremiah 48	Psalm 25
1 Samuel 12	Romans 10	20th	Jeremiah 49	Psalms 26–27
1 Samuel 13	Romans 11	21st	Jeremiah 50	Psalms 28–29
1 Samuel 14	Romans 12	22nd	Jeremiah 51	Psalm 30

1 Samuel 15	Romans 13	23rd	Jeremiah 52	Psalm 31
1 Samuel 16	Romans 14	24th	Lamentations 1	Psalm 32
1 Samuel 17	Romans 15	25th	Lamentations 2	Psalm 33
1 Samuel 18	Romans 16	26th	Lamentations 3	Psalm 34
1 Samuel 19	1 Corinthians 1	27th	Lamentations 4	Psalm 35
1 Samuel 20	1 Corinthians 2	28th	Lamentations 5	Psalm 36
1 Samuel 21–22	1 Corinthians 3	29th	Ezekiel 1	Psalm 37
1 Samuel 23	1 Corinthians 4	30th	Ezekiel 2	Psalm 38
1 Samuel 24	1 Corinthians 5	31st	Ezekiel 3	Psalm 39

SEPTEMBER

The instruction of the LORD is perfect, renewing one's life (Ps 19:7).

1 Samuel 25	1 Corinthians 6	1st	Ezekiel 4	Psalms 40–41
1 Samuel 26	1 Corinthians 7	2nd	Ezekiel 5	Psalms 42–43
1 Samuel 27	1 Corinthians 8	3rd	Ezekiel 6	Psalm 44
1 Samuel 28	1 Corinthians 9	4th	Ezekiel 7	Psalm 45
1 Samuel 29–30	1 Corinthians 10	5th	Ezekiel 8	Psalms 46–47
1 Samuel 31	1 Corinthians 11	6th	Ezekiel 9	Psalm 48
2 Samuel 1	1 Corinthians 12	7th	Ezekiel 10	Psalm 49
2 Samuel 2	1 Corinthians 13	8th	Ezekiel 11	Psalm 50
2 Samuel 3	1 Corinthians 14	9th	Ezekiel 12	Psalm 51
2 Samuel 4–5	1 Corinthians 15	10th	Ezekiel 13	Psalms 52–54
2 Samuel 6	1 Corinthians 16	11th	Ezekiel 14	Psalm 55
2 Samuel 7	2 Corinthians 1	12th	Ezekiel 15	Psalms 56–57
2 Samuel 8–9	2 Corinthians 2	13th	Ezekiel 16	Psalms 58–59
2 Samuel 10	2 Corinthians 3	14th	Ezekiel 17	Psalms 60–61
2 Samuel 11	2 Corinthians 4	15th	Ezekiel 18	Psalms 62–63
2 Samuel 12	2 Corinthians 5	16th	Ezekiel 19	Psalms 64–65
2 Samuel 13	2 Corinthians 6	17th	Ezekiel 20	Psalms 66–67
2 Samuel 14	2 Corinthians 7	18th	Ezekiel 21	Psalm 68
2 Samuel 15	2 Corinthians 8	19th	Ezekiel 22	Psalm 69
2 Samuel 16	2 Corinthians 9	20th	Ezekiel 23	Psalms 70–71
2 Samuel 17	2 Corinthians 10	21st	Ezekiel 24	Psalm 72
2 Samuel 18	2 Corinthians 11	22nd	Ezekiel 25	Psalm 73
2 Samuel 19	2 Corinthians 12	23rd	Ezekiel 26	Psalm 74
2 Samuel 20	2 Corinthians 13	24th	Ezekiel 27	Psalms 75–76
2 Samuel 21	Galatians 1	25th	Ezekiel 28	Psalm 77
2 Samuel 22	Galatians 2	26th	Ezekiel 29	Psalm 78:1-37
2 Samuel 23	Galatians 3	27th	Ezekiel 30	Psalm 78:38ff.
2 Samuel 24	Galatians 4	28th	Ezekiel 31	Psalm 79
1 Kings 1	Galatians 5	29th	Ezekiel 32	Psalm 80
1 Kings 2	Galatians 6	30th	Ezekiel 33	Psalms 81–82

OCTOBER

How I love your instruction! It is my meditation all day long (Ps 119:97).

1 Kings 3	Ephesians 1	1st	Ezekiel 34	Psalms 83–84
1 Kings 4–5	Ephesians 2	2nd	Ezekiel 35	Psalm 85
1 Kings 6	Ephesians 3	3rd	Ezekiel 36	Psalm 86
1 Kings 7	Ephesians 4	4th	Ezekiel 37	Psalms 87–88
1 Kings 8	Ephesians 5	5th	Ezekiel 38	Psalm 89
1 Kings 9	Ephesians 6	6th	Ezekiel 39	Psalm 90
1 Kings 10	Philippians 1	7th	Ezekiel 40	Psalm 91
1 Kings 11	Philippians 2	8th	Ezekiel 41	Psalms 92–93
1 Kings 12	Philippians 3	9th	Ezekiel 42	Psalm 94
1 Kings 13	Philippians 4	10th	Ezekiel 43	Psalms 95–96
1 Kings 14	Colossians 1	11th	Ezekiel 44	Psalms 97–98
1 Kings 15	Colossians 2	12th	Ezekiel 45	Psalms 99–101
1 Kings 16	Colossians 3	13th	Ezekiel 46	Psalm 102
1 Kings 17	Colossians 4	14th	Ezekiel 47	Psalm 103
1 Kings 18	1 Thessalonians 1	15th	Ezekiel 48	Psalm 104
1 Kings 19	1 Thessalonians 2	16th	Daniel 1	Psalm 105
1 Kings 20	1 Thessalonians 3	17th	Daniel 2	Psalm 106
1 Kings 21	1 Thessalonians 4	18th	Daniel 3	Psalm 107
1 Kings 22	1 Thessalonians 5	19th	Daniel 4	Psalms 108–109
2 Kings 1	2 Thessalonians 1	20th	Daniel 5	Psalms 110–111
2 Kings 2	2 Thessalonians 2	21st	Daniel 6	Psalms 112–113

2 Kings 3	2 Thessalonians 3	22nd	Daniel 7	Psalms 114–115
2 Kings 4	1 Timothy 1	23rd	Daniel 8	Psalm 116
2 Kings 5	1 Timothy 2	24th	Daniel 9	Psalms 117–118
2 Kings 6	1 Timothy 3	25th	Daniel 10	Psalm 119:1-24
2 Kings 7	1 Timothy 4	26th	Daniel 11	Psalm 119:25-48
2 Kings 8	1 Timothy 5	27th	Daniel 12	Psalm 119:49-72
2 Kings 9	1 Timothy 6	28th	Hosea 1	Psalm 119:73-96
2 Kings 10	2 Timothy 1	29th	Hosea 2	Psalm 119:97-120
2 Kings 11–12	2 Timothy 2	30th	Hosea 3–4	Psalm 119:121-144
2 Kings 13	2 Timothy 3	31st	Hosea 5–6	Psalm 119:145-176

NOVEMBER

Like newborn infants, desire the pure milk of the word, so that you may grow up into your salvation (1Pt 2:2).

2 Kings 14	2 Timothy 4	1st	Hosea 7	Psalms 120–122
2 Kings 15	Titus 1	2nd	Hosea 8	Psalms 123–125
2 Kings 16	Titus 2	3rd	Hosea 9	Psalms 126–128
2 Kings 17	Titus 3	4th	Hosea 10	Psalms 129–131
2 Kings 18	Philemon 1	5th	Hosea 11	Psalms 132–134
2 Kings 19	Hebrews 1	6th	Hosea 12	Psalms 135–136
2 Kings 20	Hebrews 2	7th	Hosea 13	Psalms 137–138
2 Kings 21	Hebrews 3	8th	Hosea 14	Psalm 139
2 Kings 22	Hebrews 4	9th	Joel 1	Psalms 140–141
2 Kings 23	Hebrews 5	10th	Joel 2	Psalm 142
2 Kings 24	Hebrews 6	11th	Joel 3	Psalm 143
2 Kings 25	Hebrews 7	12th	Amos 1	Psalm 144
1 Chronicles 1–2	Hebrews 8	13th	Amos 2	Psalm 145
1 Chronicles 3–4	Hebrews 9	14th	Amos 3	Psalms 146–147
1 Chronicles 5–6	Hebrews 10	15th	Amos 4	Psalms 148–150
1 Chronicles 7–8	Hebrews 11	16th	Amos 5	Luke 1:1-38
1 Chronicles 9–10	Hebrews 12	17th	Amos 6	Luke 1:39ff.
1 Chronicles 11–12	Hebrews 13	18th	Amos 7	Luke 2
1 Chronicles 13–14	James 1	19th	Amos 8	Luke 3
1 Chronicles 15	James 2	20th	Amos 9	Luke 4
1 Chronicles 16	James 3	21st	Obadiah	Luke 5
1 Chronicles 17	James 4	22nd	Jonah 1	Luke 6
1 Chronicles 18	James 5	23rd	Jonah 2	Luke 7
1 Chronicles 19–20	1 Peter 1	24th	Jonah 3	Luke 8
1 Chronicles 21	1 Peter 2	25th	Jonah 4	Luke 9
1 Chronicles 22	1 Peter 3	26th	Micah 1	Luke 10
1 Chronicles 23	1 Peter 4	27th	Micah 2	Luke 11
1 Chronicles 24–25	1 Peter 5	28th	Micah 3	Luke 12
1 Chronicles 26–27	2 Peter 1	29th	Micah 4	Luke 13
1 Chronicles 28	2 Peter 2	30th	Micah 5	Luke 14

DECEMBER

The instruction of his God is in his heart; his steps do not falter (Ps 37:31).

1 Chronicles 29	2 Peter 3	1st	Micah 6	Luke 15
2 Chronicles 1	1 John 1	2nd	Micah 7	Luke 16
2 Chronicles 2	1 John 2	3rd	Nahum 1	Luke 17
2 Chronicles 3–4	1 John 3	4th	Nahum 2	Luke 18
2 Chronicles 5–6:11	1 John 4	5th	Nahum 3	Luke 19
2 Chronicles 6:12ff.	1 John 5	6th	Habakkuk 1	Luke 20
2 Chronicles 7	2 John	7th	Habakkuk 2	Luke 21
2 Chronicles 8	3 John	8th	Habakkuk 3	Luke 22
2 Chronicles 9	Jude	9th	Zephaniah 1	Luke 23
2 Chronicles 10	Revelation 1	10th	Zephaniah 2	Luke 24
2 Chronicles 11–12	Revelation 2	11th	Zephaniah 3	John 1
2 Chronicles 13	Revelation 3	12th	Haggai 1	John 2
2 Chronicles 14–15	Revelation 4	13th	Haggai 2	John 3
2 Chronicles 16	Revelation 5	14th	Zechariah 1	John 4
2 Chronicles 17	Revelation 6	15th	Zechariah 2	John 5
2 Chronicles 18	Revelation 7	16th	Zechariah 3	John 6
2 Chronicles 19–20	Revelation 8	17th	Zechariah 4	John 7
2 Chronicles 21	Revelation 9	18th	Zechariah 5	John 8
2 Chronicles 22–23	Revelation 10	19th	Zechariah 6	John 9
2 Chronicles 24	Revelation 11	20th	Zechariah 7	John 10

2 Chronicles 25	Revelation 12	21st	Zechariah 8	John 11
2 Chronicles 26	Revelation 13	22nd	Zechariah 9	John 12
2 Chronicles 27–28	Revelation 14	23rd	Zechariah 10	John 13
2 Chronicles 29	Revelation 15	24th	Zechariah 11	John 14
2 Chronicles 30	Revelation 16	25th	Zechariah 12–13:1	John 15
2 Chronicles 31	Revelation 17	26th	Zechariah 13:2ff.	John 16
2 Chronicles 32	Revelation 18	27th	Zechariah 14	John 17
2 Chronicles 33	Revelation 19	28th	Malachi 1	John 18
2 Chronicles 34	Revelation 20	29th	Malachi 2	John 19
2 Chronicles 35	Revelation 21	30th	Malachi 3	John 20
2 Chronicles 36	Revelation 22	31st	Malachi 4	John 21

52-Week Scripture Memory Plan

If you were walking down an old country road at night would you prefer to be carrying a penlight, a flashlight, or a floodlight?

Most of us would choose the floodlight. We want to see the most we can with the hope of avoiding danger. The more light we have, the better off we will be on that dark road. The same is true of God's Word. As we navigate the dark roads of life, we can carry a penlight (ten or so Bible verses), a flashlight (one hundred or so Bible verses) or a floodlight (one thousand Bible verses). Each verse we memorize will add to the strength of the light we have to guide our steps in this world. We need those words.

Human beings live on words. Words are the fuel that sustains and shapes us as creatures made in God's image. The words we ingest and live by have great consequences in our life on earth and beyond. That's why that cunning serpent in the garden of Eden focused on God's words to Adam and Eve when he talked with Eve.

"Did God really say, 'You can't eat from any tree in the garden'?", asked the serpent. Up until that moment God's clear word governed the first couple's choices and behavior. The serpent's question had the effect of neutralizing God's word to Adam and Eve. We know the consequences.

Fast forward. Jesus had just been baptized and was about to begin his public ministry. The tempter who came to Eden approached Jesus in the wilderness of Judea with three attractive temptations. With each temptation, Jesus responded with sacred words that had he had memorized and that shaped his thoughts, his affections, and his decision making. We know and are eternally grateful for the consequences.

Dallas Willard, who has written extensively on spiritual disciplines, says that "Bible memorization is absolutely fundamental to spiritual formation. If I had to choose between all the disciplines of the spiritual life, I would choose Bible memorization, because it is a fundamental way of filling our mind with what it needs."

Here is a fifty-two-week plan of Bible memorization. Two Scriptures on the same topic are suggested for each week. The plan begins with some major theological truths. It then takes the participant on a chronological journey ranging from Abraham through the Hebrew prophets. The plan then moves back into a more topical orientation designed to set forth God's way of reconciling human beings to himself, creating his body (the church), and then guiding believers into an ever-growing likeness of God's Son, Jesus Christ. Each week's passage set is also identified by a Biblical Concept. These fifteen Biblical Concepts serve as a tool for categorizing the major truths presented in the Bible. All ongoing Bible study curriculum developed by LifeWay Christian Resources addresses these fifteen Biblical Concepts over time. If you are using LifeWay Bible study resources, this fifty-two-week memory plan will strengthen your understanding of the fifteen Biblical Concepts.

	Topic	Basic	Challenge	Biblical Concept
1.	God the Creator	Genesis 1:1	John 1:1-5	God
2.	Human Beings	Genesis 1:26-28	Psalm 8	Humanity/Self
3.	Sin	Genesis 3:6-7	James 1:12-15	Rebellion and Sin
4.	Sin's Consequences	Romans 6:23	John 8:34-35	Rebellion and Sin
5.	Jesus Christ	John 14:6	Matthew 1:21-23	Jesus
6.	The Scriptures	2 Timothy 3:16-17	Romans 15:4	Revelation and Authority/Bible

	Topic	Basic	Challenge	Biblical Concept
7.	God's Revelation: Creation	Romans 1:20	Psalm 19:1-6	Creation, Sovereignty, and Providence
8.	God's Revelation: Law	Psalm 119:13-16	Psalm 19:7-14	Revelation and Authority/Bible
9.	Scripture: Jesus's View	Matthew 5:17-20	Luke 24:44-45	Revelation and Authority/Bible
10.	Abraham: Father of a Multitude	Genesis 12:1-3	Genesis 15:1	Creation, Sovereignty, and Providence
11.	God's Grace to Jacob/ Israel	Genesis 28:14-15	Genesis 48:16	Creation, Sovereignty, and Providence
12.	Joseph: Man of Character	Genesis 50:19-21	Hebrews 11:22	Creation, Sovereignty, and Providence
13.	Moses: Servant of the LORD	Exodus 3:14-15	Hebrews 11:22-26	God
14.	Moses: Remember	Deuteronomy 6:4-9	Deuteronomy 8:2-3	Discipleship and the Christian Life
15.	Joshua's Charge	Joshua 1:6-9	Joshua 24:14-15	Discipleship and the Christian Life
16.	Retreat to Idolatry	Judges 1:11-13	Judges 21:25	Rebellion and Sin
17.	Faithfulness: Human and Divine	Ruth 1:16-17	Ruth 4:14-16	Family
18.	Samuel: Israel's Intercessor	1 Samuel 3:10	1 Samuel 12:23-25	Discipleship and the Christian Life
19.	David's Reign and Dynasty	2 Samuel 5:4-5	2 Samuel 7:12-13	Creation, Sovereignty, and Providence
20.	Psalms of David	Psalm 23	Psalm 32:1-2	Salvation
21.	Solomon's Prayer/God's Answer	1 Kings 3:7-9	1 Kings 3:10-14	Reason and Faith
22.	Wisdom's Source	Proverbs 1:7	Proverbs 3:1-12	Reason and Faith
23.	Hollow Worship	Isaiah 29:13-14	Isaiah 29:15-16	Rebellion and Sin
24.	Eternal God	Isaiah 40:6-8	Isaiah 40:27-31	God
25.	Judgment	John 3:19-21	Luke 16:15	Rebellion and Sin
26.	A New Heart	Ezekiel 36:26-27	Ezekiel 37:14	Salvation
27.	God's Gift	Romans 3:23-26	1 Peter 3:18	Salvation
28.	Jesus Christ: Our Substitute	Isaiah 53:4-6	Hebrews 9:11-14	Jesus
29.	New Birth	John 3:5-8	John 3:14-17	Salvation
30.	Peace	Romans 5:1-5	Hebrews 13:20-21	Discipleship and the Christian Life
31.	Repent	Mark 1:15	Acts 17:30	Salvation
32.	Baptism	Acts 2:38-40	Romans 6:4-5	Discipleship and the Christian Life
33.	The Comforter	John 14:16	John 16:8-11	Holy Spirit
34.	The Body of Christ	Acts 2:41-43	Ephesians 4:15-16	Church and Kingdom

	Topic	Basic	Challenge	Biblical Concept
35.	Serving Others	James 2:15-17	Matthew 25:37-40	Church and Kingdom
36.	Prayer	Matthew 6:5-8	Romans 8:26-27	Discipleship and the Christian Life
37.	Building Well	Ecclesiastes 12:13-14	Matthew 7:24-27	Discipleship and the Christian Life
38.	Anger	Matthew 5:21-22	Proverbs 22:24	Ethics and Morality
39.	Lust	Matthew 5:27-30	Proverbs 5:18	Ethics and Morality
40.	Enemies	Matthew 5:43-48	Ephesians 6:10-18	Discipleship and the Christian Life
41.	Jealousy	Ecclesiastes 4:4	James 3:13-18	Reason and Faith
42.	Sloth	Proverbs 18:9	2 Thessalonians 3:10	Ethics and Morality
43.	Greed	Hebrews 13:5	Malachi 3:8-12	Discipleship and the Christian Life
44.	Pride	Ezekiel 16:49	Jeremiah 13:15-17	Rebellion and Sin
45.	Depression	Psalm 42:5	Isaiah 26:3	Discipleship and the Christian Life
46.	Priorities	Philippians 3:13-14	Matthew 6:33-34	Discipleship and the Christian Life
47.	Influence	Matthew 5:13-16	Matthew 18:6	Community and World
48.	Witness	Matthew 28:18-20	1 Peter 3:14-16	Discipleship and the Christian Life
49.	Marriage: God's Design	Genesis 2:22-24	Song of Songs 8:6-7	Family
50.	Husbands/Wives	Ephesians 5:25-26	Ephesians 5:22-24	Family
51.	Resurrection	1 Corinthians 15:3-8	1 Corinthians 15:20-22	Time and Eternity
52.	Glory	Revelation 21:1-4	Revelation 22:17-21	Time and Eternity

Notes

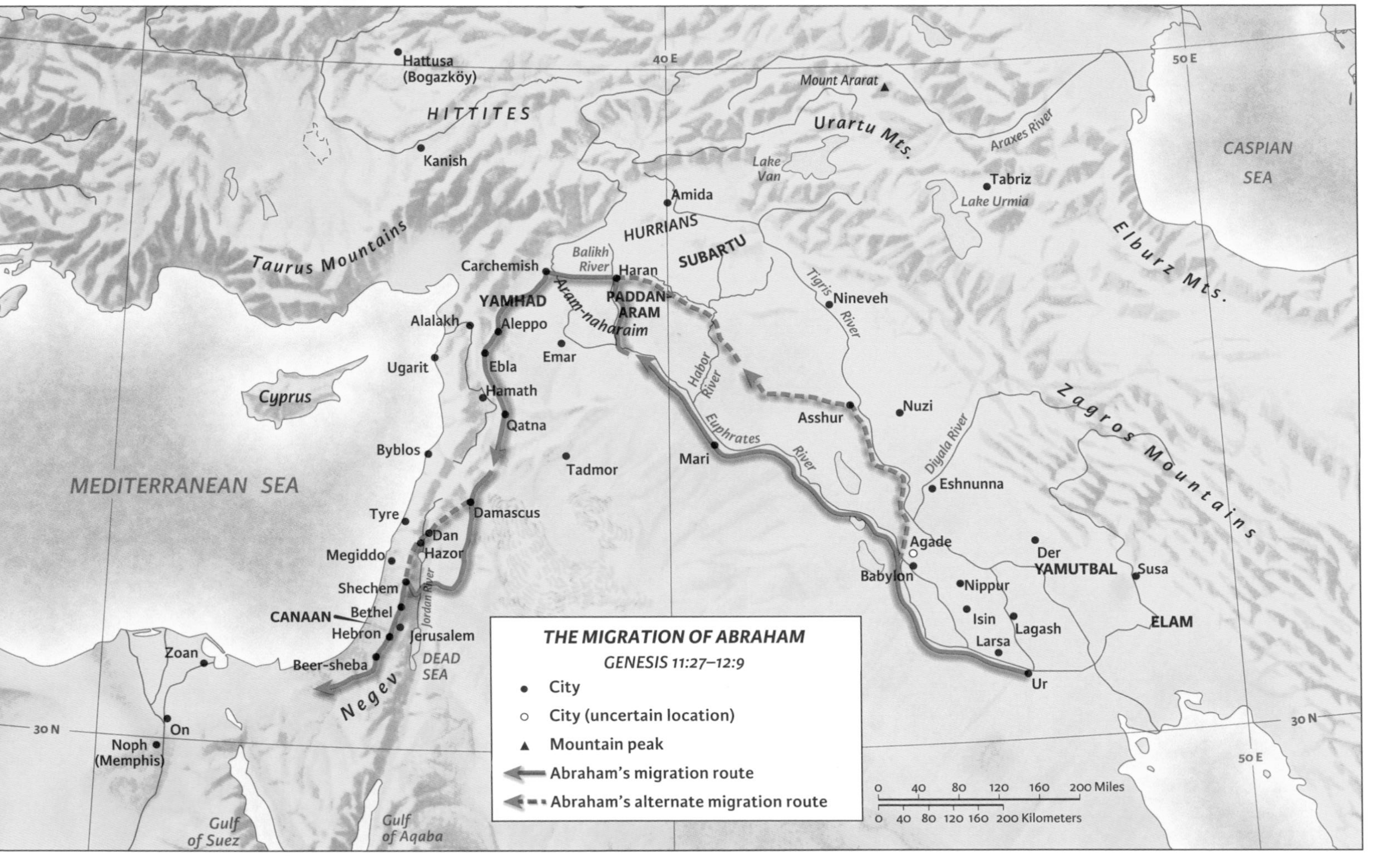

THE MIGRATION OF ABRAHAM
GENESIS 11:27–12:9
City
City (uncertain location)
Mountain peak
Abraham's migration route
Abraham's alternate migration route
0 40 80 120 160 200 Miles
0 40 80 120 160 200 Kilometers
Hattusa (Bogazköy)
HITTITES
Kanish
Taurus Mountains
Mount Ararat
Urartu Mts.
Araxes River
CASPIAN SEA
Lake Van
Tabriz
Lake Urmia
Amida
HURRIANS
SUBARTU
Elburz Mts.
Carchemish
Balikh River
Haran
PADDAN-ARAM
Aram-naharaim
YAMHAD
Alalakh
Aleppo
Ebla
Emar
Ugarit
Cyprus
Hamath
Qatna
Byblos
Tadmor
MEDITERRANEAN SEA
Damascus
Tyre
Dan
Hazor
Megiddo
Shechem
Jordan River
CANAAN
Bethel
Hebron
Jerusalem
Beer-sheba
DEAD SEA
Negev
Zoan
On
Noph (Memphis)
Gulf of Suez
Gulf of Aqaba
Nineveh
Tigris River
Habor River
Euphrates River
Mari
Asshur
Nuzi
Zagros Mountains
Diyala River
Eshnunna
Agade
Babylon
Der
YAMUTBAL
Susa
Nippur
Isin
Lagash
Larsa
Ur
ELAM
40 E
50 E
30 N

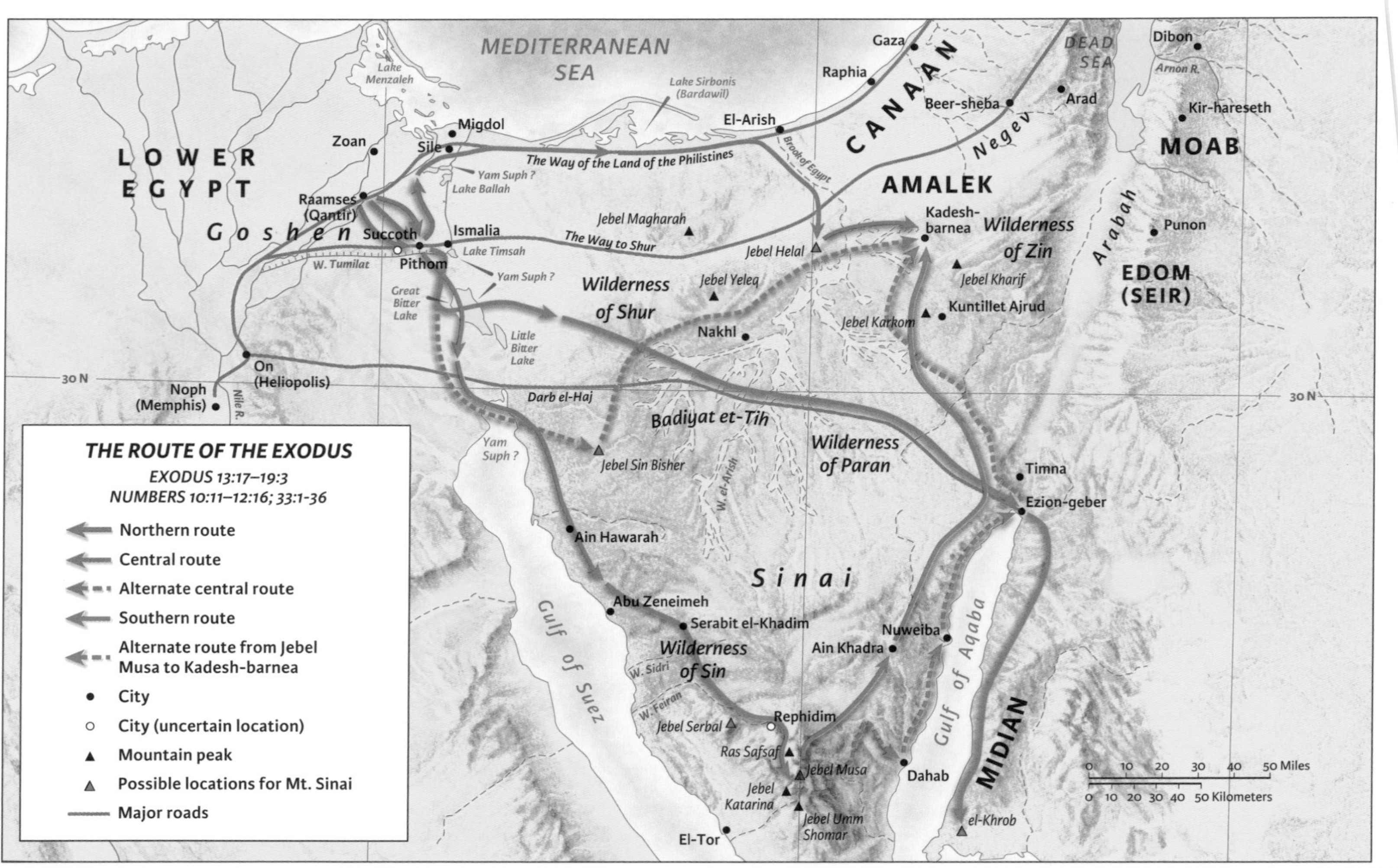
THE ROUTE OF THE EXODUS
EXODUS 13:17–19:3
NUMBERS 10:11–12:16; 33:1-36
Northern route
Central route
Alternate central route
Southern route
Alternate route from Jebel Musa to Kadesh-barnea
City
City (uncertain location)
Mountain peak
Possible locations for Mt. Sinai
Major roads
MEDITERRANEAN SEA
LOWER EGYPT
Goshen
CANAAN
AMALEK
MOAB
EDOM (SEIR)
MIDIAN
Sinai
Lake Menzaleh
Lake Sirbonis (Bardawil)
Zoan
Migdol
Sile
Raamses (Qantir)
Succoth
Pithom
Ismalia
Lake Timsah
Lake Ballah
Yam Suph ?
W. Tumilat
Great Bitter Lake
Little Bitter Lake
On (Heliopolis)
Noph (Memphis)
Nile R.
30 N
The Way of the Land of the Philistines
The Way to Shur
Darb el-Haj
El-Arish
Brook of Egypt
Raphia
Gaza
Beer-sheba
Arad
Negev
DEAD SEA
Dibon
Arnon R.
Kir-hareseth
Punon
Arabah
Kadesh-barnea
Wilderness of Zin
Jebel Kharif
Kuntillet Ajrud
Jebel Karkom
Jebel Helal
Jebel Magharah
Jebel Yeleq
Wilderness of Shur
Nakhl
Badiyat et-Tih
Jebel Sin Bisher
Wilderness of Paran
W. el-Arish
Timna
Ezion-geber
Yam Suph ?
Ain Hawarah
Abu Zeneimeh
Serabit el-Khadim
Wilderness of Sin
W. Sidri
W. Feiran
Jebel Serbal
Rephidim
Ras Safsaf
Jebel Musa
Jebel Katarina
Jebel Umm Shomar
El-Tor
Ain Khadra
Nuweiba
Dahab
Gulf of Suez
Gulf of Aqaba
el-Khrob
0 10 20 30 40 50 Miles
0 10 20 30 40 50 Kilometers

THE TRIBAL ALLOTMENTS OF ISRAEL
JOSHUA 13:8–19:49
City
City (uncertain location)
Mountain peak
TYRE
ARAM
ASHER
NAPHTALI
EAST MANASSEH
ZEBULUN
ISSACHAR
WEST MANASSEH
EPHRAIM
DAN
BENJAMIN
GAD
AMMON
REUBEN
JUDAH
SIMEON
MOAB
EDOM
MEDITERRANEAN SEA
DEAD SEA
Sea of Galilee
Lake Huleh
Sidon
Damascus
Mt. Hermon
Pharpar River
Litani River
Ijon
Tyre
Dan
Beth-anath
Kedesh
Yiron
Hazor
Merom
Acco
Cabul
Capernaum
Aphek
Mishal
Nahalal
Hannathon
Rimmon
Rakkath
Golan
Ashtaroth
Achshaph
Hammath
Mt. Carmel
Kishon River
Chesulloth
Helkath
Daberath
Jabneel
Yarmuk River
Sarid
Tabor
Mt. Tabor
En-haddah
Yokneam
Lo-debar
En-dor
Edrei
Megiddo
Shunem
Jarmuth
Dor
Jezreel
Taanach
Ramoth-gilead
Beth-shan
En-gannim
Dothan
Ibleam
Jabesh-gilead
Socoh
Jordan River
Tirzah
Gerasa
Zaphon
Mt. Ebal
Penuel
Mahanaim
Shechem
Succoth
Jabbok River
Pirathon
Mt. Gerizim
Janoah
Yarkon River
Aphek
Tappuah
Gath-rimmon
Shiloh
Joppa
Jazer
Ophrah
Jehud
Bethel
Amman
Lod
Upper Beth-horon
Gittaim
Mizpah
Naaran
Gilgal
Beth-nimrah
Shaalbim
Gibeon
Jabneel
Gezer
Chephirah
Ramah
Jericho
Abel-shittim
Heshbon
Baalath
Gibbethon
Aijalon
Chesalon
Kiriath-jearim
Adummim
Jerusalem
Beth-hoglah
Bezer
Ashdod
Ekron
Zorah
Eshtaol
Mt. Nebo
Timnah
Beth-shemesh
Medeba
Bethlehem
Gath
Tekoa
Kedemoth
Ashkelon
Beth-zur
Mareshah
Lachish
Hebron
Jahaz
Eglon
Dibon
Aroer
Gaza
Juttah
En-gedi
N. Besor
Arnon River
Eshtemoa
Gerar
Ziklag
Jattir
Bethul
Ashan
Arad
Sharuhen
Kabzeel
Beer-sheba
Hormah
Kir-hareseth
Hazar-shual
Baalah
Eltolad
Ezem
Zered River
Tamar
Arabah
35 E
36 E
0 10 20 30 40 Miles
0 10 20 30 40 Kilometers

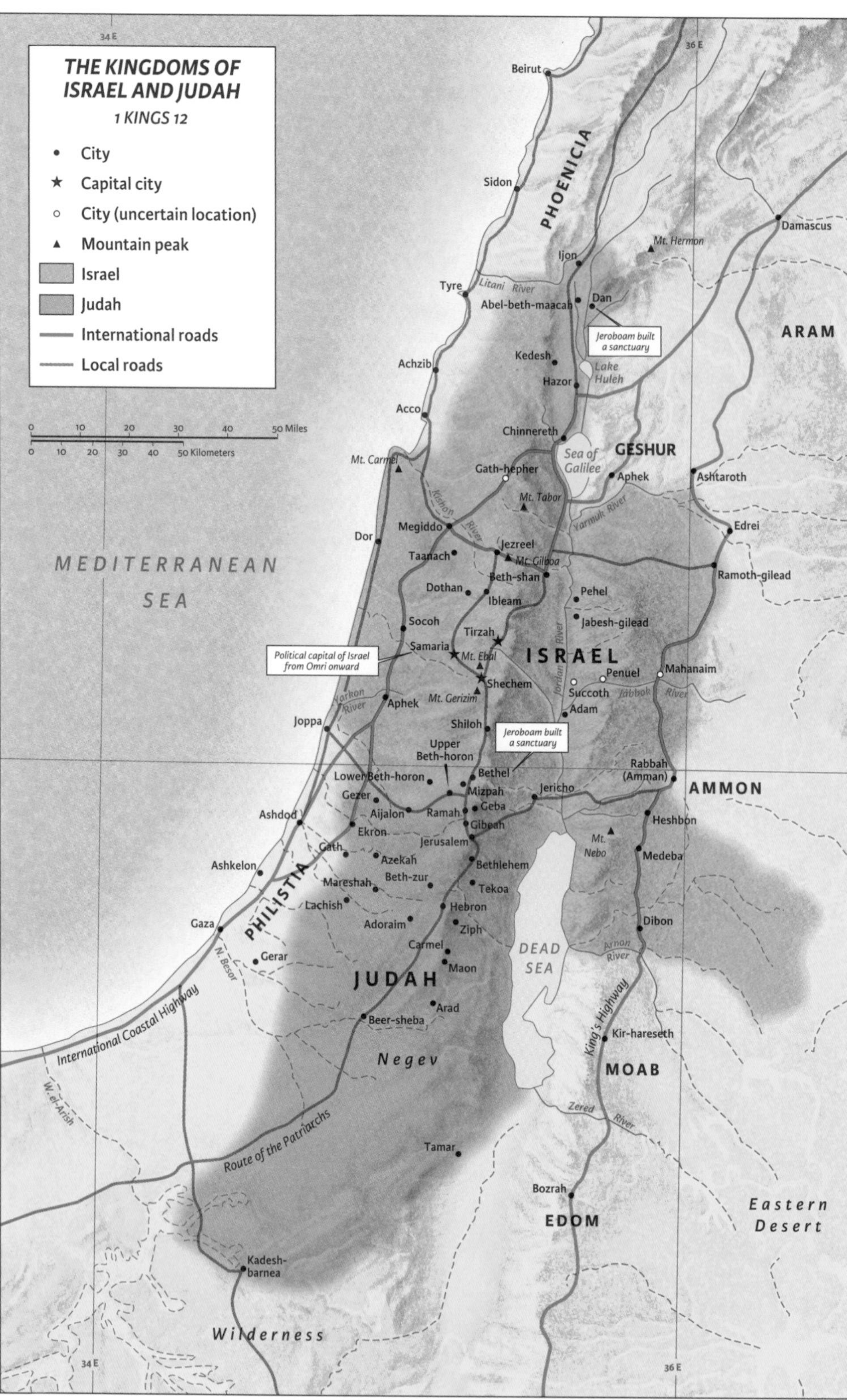

THE KINGDOMS OF ISRAEL AND JUDAH
1 KINGS 12
City
Capital city
City (uncertain location)
Mountain peak
Israel
Judah
International roads
Local roads
0 10 20 30 40 50 Miles
0 10 20 30 40 50 Kilometers
34 E
36 E
MEDITERRANEAN SEA
PHOENICIA
ARAM
GESHUR
ISRAEL
AMMON
PHILISTIA
JUDAH
MOAB
EDOM
Negev
Wilderness
Eastern Desert
Beirut
Sidon
Damascus
Mt. Hermon
Ijon
Tyre
Litani River
Abel-beth-maacah
Dan
Jeroboam built a sanctuary
Kedesh
Achzib
Lake Huleh
Hazor
Acco
Chinnereth
Sea of Galilee
Mt. Carmel
Gath-hepher
Aphek
Ashtaroth
Mt. Tabor
Kishon River
Yarmuk River
Edrei
Dor
Megiddo
Jezreel
Taanach
Mt. Gilboa
Ramoth-gilead
Beth-shan
Dothan
Pehel
Ibleam
Jabesh-gilead
Socoh
Tirzah
Samaria
Political capital of Israel from Omri onward
Mt. Ebal
Jordan River
Mahanaim
Penuel
Shechem
Succoth
Jabbok River
Yarkon River
Aphek
Mt. Gerizim
Adam
Joppa
Shiloh
Jeroboam built a sanctuary
Upper Beth-horon
Rabbah (Amman)
Lower Beth-horon
Bethel
Gezer
Mizpah
Jericho
Aijalon
Ramah
Geba
Ashdod
Heshbon
Ekron
Gibeah
Jerusalem
Mt. Nebo
Gath
Azekah
Bethlehem
Medeba
Ashkelon
Beth-zur
Mareshah
Tekoa
Lachish
Hebron
Gaza
Adoraim
Ziph
Dibon
Carmel
DEAD SEA
Arnon River
Gerar
N. Besor
Maon
International Coastal Highway
Arad
King's Highway
Beer-sheba
Kir-hareseth
W. el-Arish
Zered River
Route of the Patriarchs
Tamar
Bozrah
Kadesh-barnea

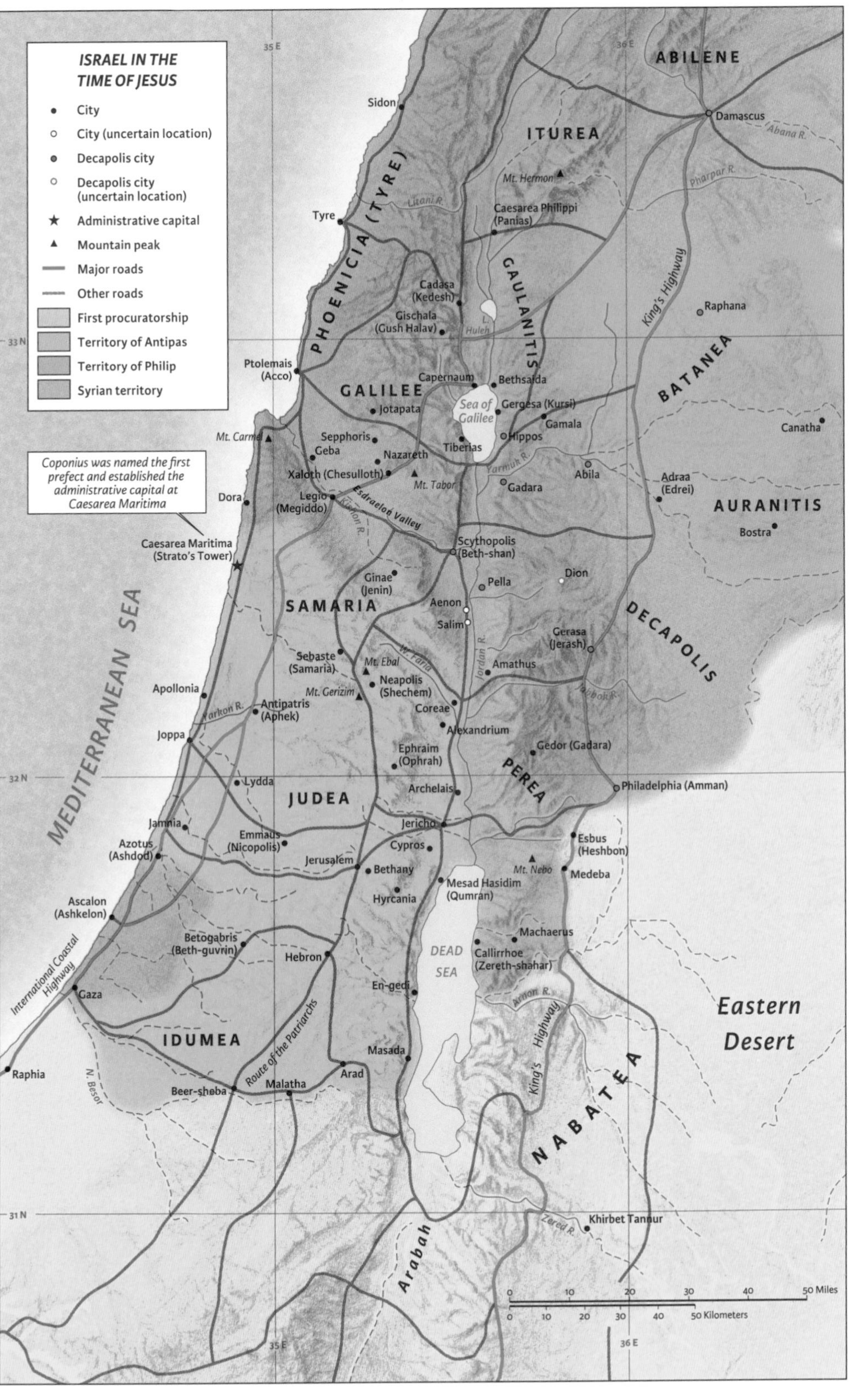

ISRAEL IN THE TIME OF JESUS
City
City (uncertain location)
Decapolis city
Decapolis city (uncertain location)
Administrative capital
Mountain peak
Major roads
Other roads
First procuratorship
Territory of Antipas
Territory of Philip
Syrian territory
Coponius was named the first prefect and established the administrative capital at Caesarea Maritima
ABILENE
ITUREA
PHOENICIA (TYRE)
GAULANITIS
GALILEE
BATANEA
AURANITIS
SAMARIA
DECAPOLIS
JUDEA
PEREA
IDUMEA
NABATEA
MEDITERRANEAN SEA
Eastern Desert
Sidon
Damascus
Abana R.
Pharpar R.
Mt. Hermon
Litani R.
Tyre
Caesarea Philippi (Panias)
King's Highway
Cadasa (Kedesh)
Gischala (Gush Halav)
L. Huleh
Raphana
Ptolemais (Acco)
Capernaum
Bethsaida
Sea of Galilee
Gergesa (Kursi)
Gamala
Jotapata
Canatha
Mt. Carmel
Sepphoris
Tiberias
Hippos
Geba
Nazareth
Yarmuk R.
Abila
Xaloth (Chesulloth)
Mt. Tabor
Gadara
Adraa (Edrei)
Dora
Legio (Megiddo)
Esdraelon Valley
Kishon R.
Bostra
Caesarea Maritima (Strato's Tower)
Scythopolis (Beth-shan)
Ginae (Jenin)
Pella
Dion
Aenon
Salim
Gerasa (Jerash)
Sebaste (Samaria)
W. Faria
Mt. Ebal
Jordan R.
Amathus
Neapolis (Shechem)
Mt. Gerizim
Apollonia
Yarkon R.
Antipatris (Aphek)
Jabbok R.
Coreae
Joppa
Alexandrium
Ephraim (Ophrah)
Gedor (Gadara)
Lydda
Archelais
Philadelphia (Amman)
Jamnia
Jericho
Emmaus (Nicopolis)
Esbus (Heshbon)
Azotus (Ashdod)
Cypros
Jerusalem
Mt. Nebo
Bethany
Medeba
Mesad Hasidim (Qumran)
Hyrcania
Ascalon (Ashkelon)
Machaerus
Betogabris (Beth-guvrin)
DEAD SEA
Hebron
Callirrhoe (Zereth-shahar)
International Coastal Highway
Gaza
En-gedi
Arnon R.
Route of the Patriarchs
Masada
Raphia
Arad
N. Besor
Beer-sheba
Malatha
Khirbet Tannur
Zered R.
Arabah
35 E
36 E
33 N
32 N
31 N
0 10 20 30 40 50 Miles
0 10 20 30 40 50 Kilometers

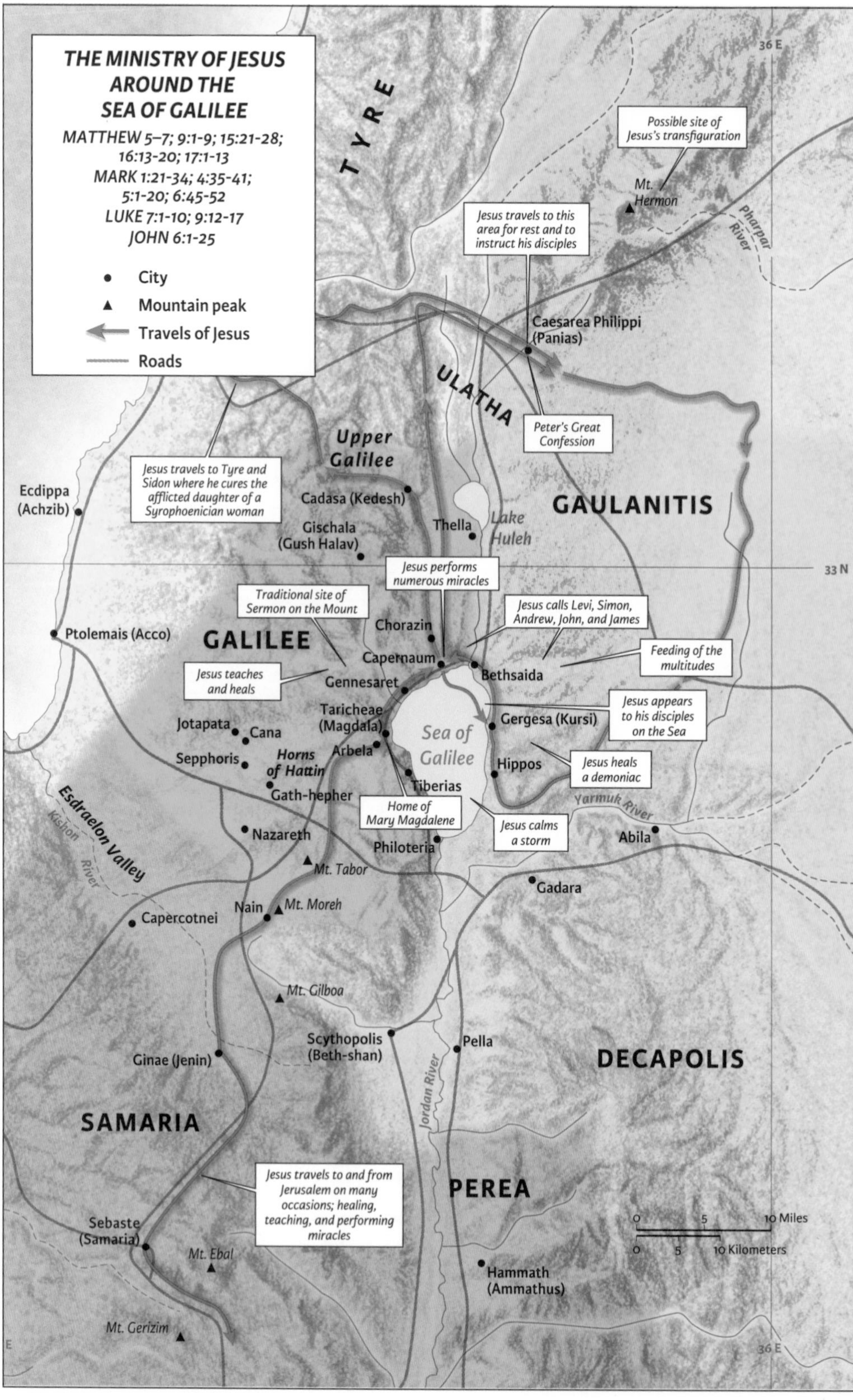
THE MINISTRY OF JESUS AROUND THE SEA OF GALILEE
MATTHEW 5–7; 9:1-9; 15:21-28; 16:13-20; 17:1-13
MARK 1:21-34; 4:35-41; 5:1-20; 6:45-52
LUKE 7:1-10; 9:12-17
JOHN 6:1-25
City
Mountain peak
Travels of Jesus
Roads
TYRE
Possible site of Jesus's transfiguration
Mt. Hermon
Pharpar River
Jesus travels to this area for rest and to instruct his disciples
Caesarea Philippi (Panias)
ULATHA
Peter's Great Confession
Upper Galilee
Jesus travels to Tyre and Sidon where he cures the afflicted daughter of a Syrophoenician woman
Ecdippa (Achzib)
Cadasa (Kedesh)
GAULANITIS
Gischala (Gush Halav)
Thella
Lake Huleh
Jesus performs numerous miracles
33 N
Traditional site of Sermon on the Mount
Jesus calls Levi, Simon, Andrew, John, and James
Ptolemais (Acco)
GALILEE
Chorazin
Capernaum
Feeding of the multitudes
Bethsaida
Jesus teaches and heals
Gennesaret
Taricheae (Magdala)
Jesus appears to his disciples on the Sea
Gergesa (Kursi)
Jotapata
Cana
Sea of Galilee
Sepphoris
Horns of Hattin
Arbela
Hippos
Jesus heals a demoniac
Tiberias
Gath-hepher
Esdraelon Valley
Kishon River
Home of Mary Magdalene
Jesus calms a storm
Yarmuk River
Abila
Nazareth
Philoteria
Mt. Tabor
Gadara
Nain
Mt. Moreh
Capercotnei
Mt. Gilboa
Scythopolis (Beth-shan)
Pella
Ginae (Jenin)
Jordan River
DECAPOLIS
SAMARIA
Jesus travels to and from Jerusalem on many occasions; healing, teaching, and performing miracles
PEREA
Sebaste (Samaria)
Mt. Ebal
0 5 10 Miles
0 5 10 Kilometers
Hammath (Ammathus)
Mt. Gerizim
36 E

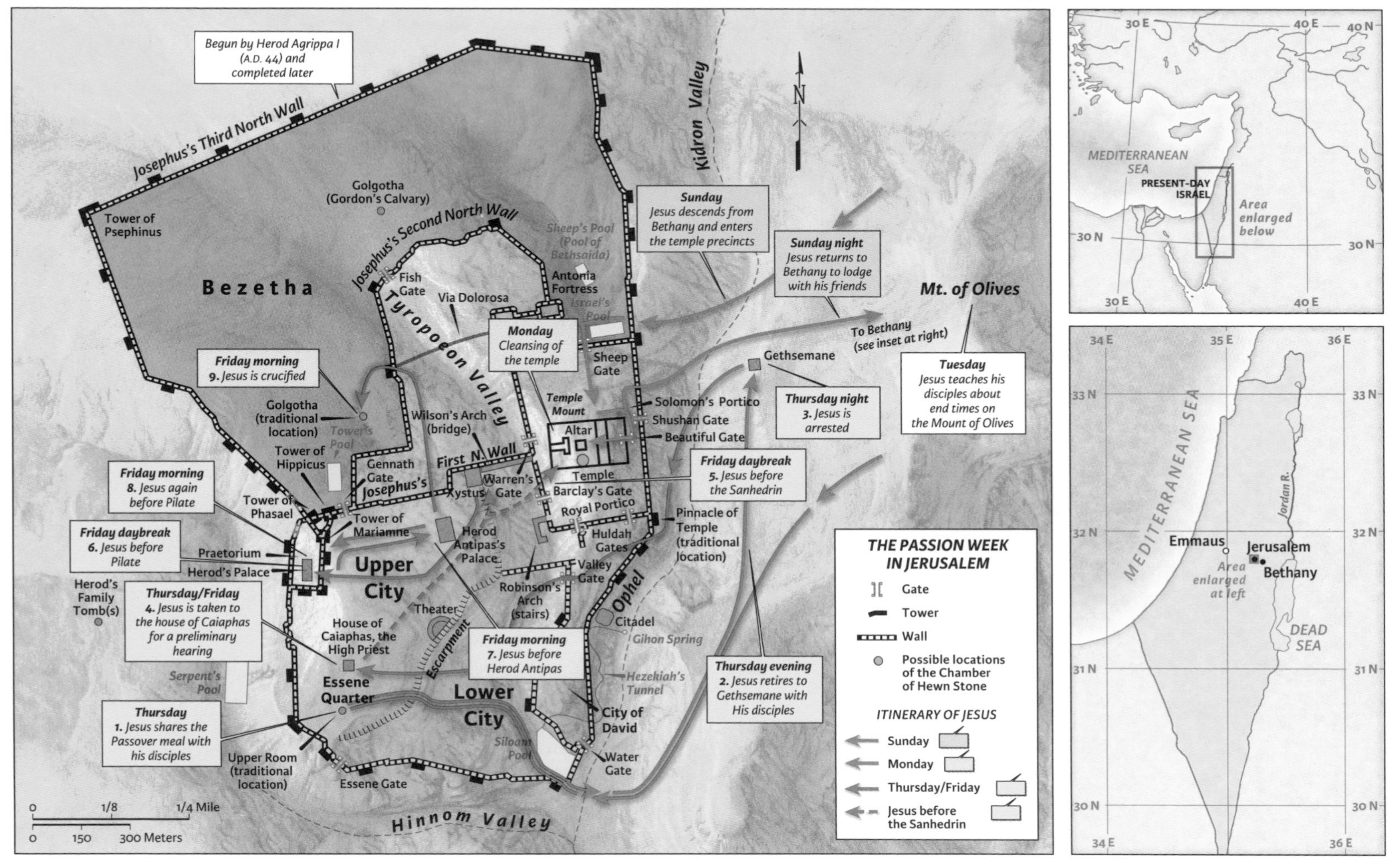
THE PASSION WEEK IN JERUSALEM
Gate
Tower
Wall
Possible locations of the Chamber of Hewn Stone
ITINERARY OF JESUS
Sunday
Monday
Thursday/Friday
Jesus before the Sanhedrin
Sunday
Jesus descends from Bethany and enters the temple precincts
Sunday night
Jesus returns to Bethany to lodge with his friends
Monday
Cleansing of the temple
Tuesday
Jesus teaches his disciples about end times on the Mount of Olives
Thursday
1. Jesus shares the Passover meal with his disciples
Thursday evening
2. Jesus retires to Gethsemane with His disciples
Thursday night
3. Jesus is arrested
Thursday/Friday
4. Jesus is taken to the house of Caiaphas for a preliminary hearing
Friday daybreak
5. Jesus before the Sanhedrin
Friday daybreak
6. Jesus before Pilate
Friday morning
7. Jesus before Herod Antipas
Friday morning
8. Jesus again before Pilate
Friday morning
9. Jesus is crucified
Begun by Herod Agrippa I (A.D. 44) and completed later
Josephus's Third North Wall
Josephus's Second North Wall
Josephus's First N. Wall
Tower of Psephinus
Bezetha
Golgotha (Gordon's Calvary)
Golgotha (traditional location)
Sheep's Pool (Pool of Bethsaida)
Antonia Fortress
Israel's Pool
Fish Gate
Via Dolorosa
Tyropoeon Valley
Sheep Gate
Temple Mount
Altar
Temple
Solomon's Portico
Shushan Gate
Beautiful Gate
Wilson's Arch (bridge)
Tower's Pool
Tower of Hippicus
Gennath Gate
Xystus
Warren's Gate
Barclay's Gate
Royal Portico
Pinnacle of Temple (traditional location)
Huldah Gates
Tower of Phasael
Tower of Mariamne
Herod Antipas's Palace
Praetorium
Herod's Palace
Upper City
Valley Gate
Robinson's Arch (stairs)
Herod's Family Tomb(s)
Theater
Escarpment
Ophel
Citadel
Gihon Spring
House of Caiaphas, the High Priest
Serpent's Pool
Essene Quarter
Lower City
Hezekiah's Tunnel
City of David
Siloam Pool
Water Gate
Upper Room (traditional location)
Essene Gate
Hinnom Valley
Kidron Valley
Gethsemane
Mt. of Olives
To Bethany (see inset at right)
N
0 1/8 1/4 Mile
0 150 300 Meters
MEDITERRANEAN SEA
PRESENT-DAY ISRAEL
Area enlarged below
30 E
40 E
40 N
30 N
34 E
35 E
36 E
33 N
32 N
31 N
30 N
MEDITERRANEAN SEA
Jordan R.
Emmaus
Jerusalem
Bethany
Area enlarged at left
DEAD SEA

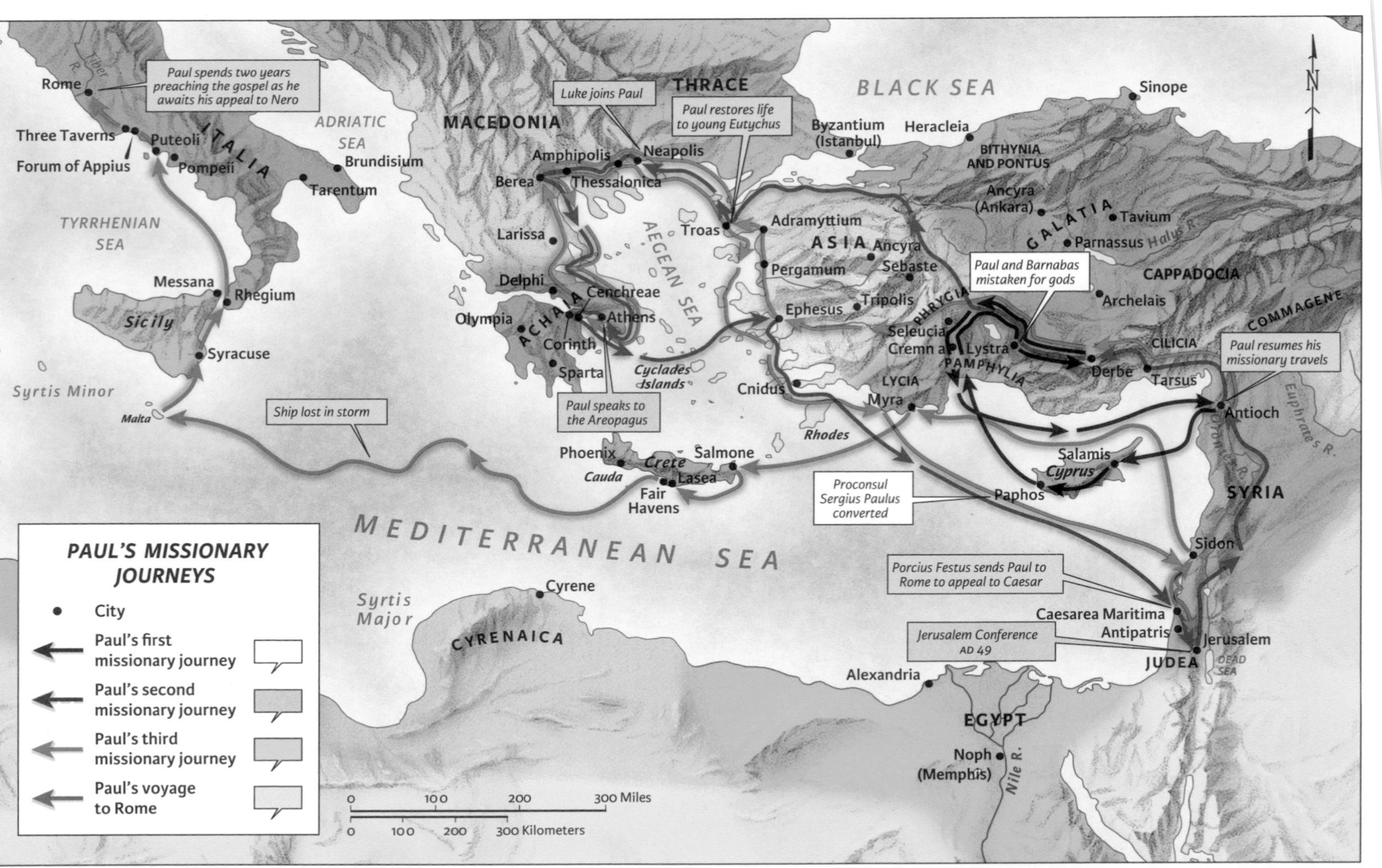
PAUL'S MISSIONARY JOURNEYS
City
Paul's first missionary journey
Paul's second missionary journey
Paul's third missionary journey
Paul's voyage to Rome
Paul spends two years preaching the gospel as he awaits his appeal to Nero
Luke joins Paul
Paul restores life to young Eutychus
Paul and Barnabas mistaken for gods
Paul resumes his missionary travels
Paul speaks to the Areopagus
Ship lost in storm
Proconsul Sergius Paulus converted
Porcius Festus sends Paul to Rome to appeal to Caesar
Jerusalem Conference AD 49
BLACK SEA
ADRIATIC SEA
TYRRHENIAN SEA
AEGEAN SEA
MEDITERRANEAN SEA
Syrtis Minor
Syrtis Major
MACEDONIA
THRACE
ITALIA
ACHAIA
ASIA
PHRYGIA
PAMPHYLIA
LYCIA
GALATIA
BITHYNIA AND PONTUS
CAPPADOCIA
CILICIA
COMMAGENE
SYRIA
JUDEA
EGYPT
CYRENAICA
Rome
Three Taverns
Forum of Appius
Puteoli
Pompeii
Brundisium
Tarentum
Messana
Rhegium
Sicily
Syracuse
Malta
Berea
Amphipolis
Thessalonica
Neapolis
Larissa
Delphi
Olympia
Corinth
Cenchreae
Athens
Sparta
Cyclades Islands
Troas
Byzantium (Istanbul)
Heracleia
Sinope
Adramyttium
Pergamum
Ephesus
Ancyra
Sebaste
Tripolis
Seleucia
Cremn a
Lystra
Derbe
Tarsus
Antioch
Ancyra (Ankara)
Tavium
Parnassus
Halys R.
Archelais
Euphrates R.
Orontes R.
Cnidus
Myra
Rhodes
Salamis
Cyprus
Paphos
Phoenix
Crete
Salmone
Cauda
Lasea
Fair Havens
Sidon
Caesarea Maritima
Antipatris
Jerusalem
DEAD SEA
Alexandria
Noph (Memphis)
Nile R.
Cyrene
Tiber R.
0 100 200 300 Miles
0 100 200 300 Kilometers
N